The Bill James Handbook 2023

Sports Info Solutions

www.sportsinfosolutions.com

Published by ACTA Sports

A Division of ACTA Publications

ACTA SPORTS

Front Cover Photos by Joe Robbins and Rick Ulreich, Icon Sportswire
Back Cover Photo by Larry Radloff, Icon Sportswire

First Edition: November 2022

Published by:
ACTA Sports, a division of ACTA Publications
4848 North Clark Street
Chicago, IL 60640
(800) 397-2282
www.actasports.com www.actapublications.com

Perfect Bound ISBN: 978-0-87946-721-0 Spiral Bound ISBN: 978-0-87946-722-7
ISSN: 1940-8668

Printed in the United States of America by Total Printing Systems

Dedication

First, this book is dedicated to my sisters and parents for their continued support, and always pushing me to follow my dreams.

Second, I'd like to dedicate the book to my friends for always being there for me, and for keeping my sanity in check (particularly these past few years).

Finally, this book is dedicated to all my fellow SIS employees, both past and present, for making this company such a great place to work. I'd like to especially thank John Dewan; I wouldn't be where I'm at without the opportunities you've given me over the years.

Will Creager
Sports Info Solutions Senior ISO Analyst

Table of Contents

Introduction

Play Ball!

A statement that many of us wondered would be enunciated this season after the collective bargaining agreement expired, canceling Winter Meetings along with delaying Spring Training and Opening Day.

How lucky we were, dear fellow fans and readers, that the 2022 season existed.

Honestly, I was concerned that the fiery passion that burns inside of me for the sport may have dwindled over the years as it seems the evolution in play style and rules has moved the game beyond my childhood memories.

My concern was unmerited. In fact, quite the opposite. I'd like to share with all of you the letter that I wrote to my father this past weekend on the 10th anniversary of his death …

Dad,

You're missing some great baseball, and your Phillies are back in the playoffs after an 11-season hiatus. The new playoff system expanded the number of postseason teams to 12, allowing the Phils to slide in with the last NL slot. A lot more teams qualify now than when grandpop and you used to watch.

This is going to be hard to believe, but there is now the designated hitter in the National League.

It is also the last season of the unregulated shift and next year will bring the pitch clock to the majors. I think that shift changes will still evolve as we just have some arbitrary lines drawn on a playing field going forward, but the pitch clock seems like a wise permanent fixture to help pace of play.

It was very exciting following Yankees' slugger Aaron Judge as he passed Roger Maris with his 62nd home run on October 4th.

Out in Anaheim, Shohei Ohtani continues to dazzle as a true two-way player in the majors. He is such a skilled batter that he DH's for himself.

The Field of Dreams game, held in Dyersville, Iowa, turned out to be quite the event. There was a part where Ken Griffey and Ken Griffey Jr. walked out of the corn and played catch. It reminded me ... how much I miss you, Dad.

And more importantly, how our national pastime transcends generations. Grandpop taught you how to throw and hit. You did the same for me. The game might play a bit different than the past, but the core fundamentals remain unchanged.

Sincerely, your son.

History will determine whether the adjustments are for the better or worse. However, passion and love of the game are unlikely to waiver for those who remember what it was like to have someone first show you how to grip a bat or how to properly condition your leather glove.

I wish all our readers an exciting journey through the pages of our latest Handbook edition. Perhaps it's worthy to reflect upon how you came to this destination.

Rob Dougherty

Danielsville, PA

October 17, 2022

The Young Superstar Stage

Bill James

If I were to say that there are more young superstars than true superstars, would you understand what I meant by that? "Young superstar" is not a career destination, nor is it a departure point. It's a stage, early in the career of a few special players, at which great possibilities have been seen, and reality has not yet bit you in the ass. A newborn baby can be anything; he can be President, or he can be an NFL quarterback, or he can be a movie star. By the time he gets to be ten years old, you can rule out, like, "OK, maybe he's not going to be an NFL quarterback."

A baseball player's career is kind of the same; when he starts out, he can be anything. You can look at an 18-year-old Anthony Rizzo taking batting practice—which I did; we were both with the Red Sox at the time—but you can look at an 18-year-old Anthony Rizzo taking batting practice, and you can see Lou Gehrig. Then he gets cancer, and he gets traded, and some other things happen, and it turns out he's not Lou Gehrig; he's really good, but he's not Lou Gehrig.

When I was a kid, there was a "next Willie Mays" every three or four years. The first next Willie Mays was Vada Pinson, and then there was José Cardenal; Cardenal hit 35 home runs and stole 64 bases his first season in the minors, when he was 17, and then he had 36 and 35 when he was 19, hitting over .300 both times, so he was the next Willie Mays. Then Tommie Agee was the next Willie Mays, 1966 and 1969, and then Bobby Bonds was, and then César Cedeño, and then Andre Dawson, and then Eric Davis, and then eventually people kind of stopped looking for the next Willie Mays and started looking for the next Rickey Henderson or somebody.

The point is that there is a difference between being the next Willie Mays and being the real Willie Mays, but César Cedeño and Andre Dawson were really good, too. "Young Superstar" is a transition stage in which a player who appears to have unlimited potential has not yet stuck his hand into a cactus or jumped out of a moving vehicle in an argument with his wife or lost a fight with a water cooler or fallen off of a bicycle, and I don't even want to talk about what happened to César Cedeño. In 2019 Ronald Acuña Jr., 21 years old at the time, hit 41 homers and stole 37 bases, the very definition of the next Willie Mays, if we were still doing that. Since then, he hasn't been able to play at that level—whereas Willie Mays got to that level and then went on doing it for 15 years.

Sometimes it will seem that the fields are just blooming with young superstars, and sometimes it will seem to you that the Atlanta Braves have them all and your team, whoever you root for, doesn't ever get them. There are two questions that are driving us here, which are:

    1) How many of these young superstars are there?

    2) How many young superstars mature into TRUE superstars?

In 2016 to 2018 Francisco Lindor looked like he might be perhaps the greatest shortstop in the history of the game, and then a few things happened, reality bites you in the ass, and he's back to being really good now, but he's probably not the greatest shortstop in the history of the game. But what are the odds, that's what I am trying to get to? I favor the death penalty for anybody who uses the phrase "The Face of Baseball." A little off topic there, but Lindor was the face of baseball for a time, before Shohei was.

Before we can move on to the two questions we want to address, however, we first have to wrestle with the technical question, ***How do we identify a "young superstar."*** This is the process that I came up with.

First of all, subtract the player's AGE in that season (age as of June 30).. ..subtract that from 40. Then multiply the result times the player's Win Shares in the season. Add 50 points if the player is a pitcher. We'll call that the Qualifying Score. If the Qualifying Score is 340 or more, that is called a Qualifying Season. To be tagged a young superstar in this study, however, a player must have a Qualifying Season and a Confirming Season; that is, he must have TWO seasons in which his Qualifying Score is 340 or more.

For example, Shohei Ohtani in 2018 was 23 years old, and he had 20 Win Shares. 40 minus 23 is 17, 17 times 20 is 340, so that's a Qualifying Season. Ohtani did not have a score of 340 in either the 2019 or 2020 season, however, so he did not make the lists of Young Superstars until 2021. In 2021 he was 26 years old; 40 minus 26 is 14. Ohtani had 38 Win Shares, 14 times 38 is 532, so that's a confirming season, so Ohtani makes the list of Young Superstars, and we enter him as 2018, since 2018 was his first qualifying season. There is an additional rule to my system that no player can be listed as a Young Superstar if his first qualifying season is after the age of 26. The additional rule only eliminates 10 players who would otherwise be listed.

It's not a perfect system, but these are the players who have been listed as Young Superstars since 2015:

Mookie	Betts	2015
Nolan	Arenado	2015
Kris	Bryant	2015
Xander	Bogaerts	2015
Carlos	Correa	2015
Jose	Ramirez	2016
Francisco	Lindor	2016
Corey	Seager	2016
Alex	Bregman	2017
Aaron	Judge	2017
Cody	Bellinger	2017
Andrew	Benintendi	2017
Ozzie	Albies	2018
Matt	Chapman	2018
Ronald	Acuña Jr.	2018
Shohei	Ohtani	2018
Gleyber	Torres	2018
Juan	Soto	2019
Rafael	Devers	2019
Fernando	Tatis Jr.	2019

This article was written in mid-season, 2022. I'm not sure who will be added to the list after the 2022 season. . . certainly Austin Riley and Vladimir Guerrero Jr., possibly Ty France, maybe somebody else, I don't know.

Anyway, it is not a perfect system, a perfect set of rules, but I'm happy with it. I think you have to admit: that's a pretty good list of the most exciting young players to emerge since 2015, isn't it? It looks at two things: youth, and the quality of the season.

The system doesn't ALWAYS work. I ran the system back to 1920, identifying all of the Young Superstars to emerge in the last 100 years. When I originally ran the list, I had set the standard for a Qualifying Season at 350, but there were players who I thought should be on the list who did not qualify. When I dropped the standard to 340, I picked up almost all of those players, but I also picked up some guys I didn't really want on the list—for example, Terry Puhl. Terry Puhl when he was 21 years old had a really fine season, hitting .289, scoring 87 runs, stealing 32 bases. At age 22 he had basically the same season. OK, those are fine seasons for a 21, 22 year old player, but should he really be listed as a "young superstar"? Probably not, but the seasons clear the Qualifying Mark, so we're stuck with him.

Since 1920 there have been 417 players who are listed as Young Superstars. That's a few too many. I would be happier if the number was 350, rather than 417, but I really don't see any way to kick the Andrew Benintendis and Terry Puhls and Ron Fairlys OFF the list without eliminating as many players who deserve to be there. When doing quasi-scientific research, one is not allowed to arbitrarily eliminate people from the study. There are 3 to 5 players per season who enter the Young Superstar Stage.

As a player ages, it becomes more and more impossible for him to have a Qualifying Season, thus it becomes more and more difficult for him to be certified as a Young Superstar. At age 20, a player has a Qualifying Season if he has 17 or more Win Shares. At age 23, he needs 20 Win Shares; at age 26, he needs 25 Win Shares. At age 29, he needs 31 Win Shares; at age 32 he needs 43 Win Shares. The only player in baseball history to have a Qualifying Season OLDER than age 32 was Honus Wagner in 1909. Since 1920, the only two players to have Qualifying Seasons AT age 32 are Babe Ruth in 1927 and Dolf Luque in 1923. Of course, it didn't matter in the case of Ruth or Wagner, because they had had two Qualifying seasons many years earlier, and in the case of Dolf Luque, it didn't matter because he never had a second Qualifying Season.

Here are a few notes from the study, before I get to questions I listed earlier, that are driving the research.

1) As I just mentioned, as a player ages it becomes almost impossible for him to have a Qualifying Season. The most Qualifying Seasons in a career since 1920 is 11, by Mel Ott, then two players—Mays and Mantle—had 10 each. Then there are 11 players who had nine qualifying seasons before Father Time started to catch up with them: A-Rod, Aaron, Barry Bonds, Miguel Cabrera, Jimmie Foxx, Lou Gehrig, Eddie Mathews, Joe Morgan, Stan Musial, Albert Pujols and Frank Robinson.

2) 417 players are listed as going through the Young Superstar Stage, but 463 were eliminated because they had only one Qualifying Season.

In almost all of those 463 cases, it is obvious that the player should NOT be listed as having been a Young Superstar. They're guys like Elvis Andrus, Ewell Blackwell, Cecil Fielder, Norm Cash and Von Hayes who had a lot of ability and did have a terrific season somewhere along the line, but just never followed through on it, enough that it would be reasonable to say that they were a Young Superstar at some point. Odubel Herrera and Oddibe McDowell. It is really hard to see that there is ANYBODY on that list that I wish had been included in the study.

3) The most common age for a young superstar to have his first qualifying season is 23. There are 96 players whose first qualifying season was at age 23. The full spectrum: 5 players at age 19, 34 at 20, 60 at 21, 75 at 22, 96 at 23, 69 at 24, 50 at 25, 28 at 26.

4) Since 1920 there have been three seasons in which NO Young Superstar was added to the list: 1920, 1994, and 2020.

5) The year in which the MOST Young Superstars emerged was 1962, when there were 12 (!).

1961-1962 were, of course, expansion seasons, so there is a tendency to assume that expansion artificially inflated the count for the 1962 season, That doesn't really seem to be true. Of the 12 Young Superstars registered for the 1962 season, three are in the Hall of Fame (Yastrzemski, Jim Kaat and Juan Marichal), a fourth probably should be (Curt Flood.) Most of the others had good or very good careers—ie, Frank Howard, Tommy Davis, Willie Davis, Johnny Callison, Dean Chance. Chance was the only one of the 12 who could reasonably be described as an expansion player, and he was a completely legitimate guy.

There were 11 Young Superstars who emerged in 1975, six of whom are now in the Hall of Fame—Dennis Eckersley, George Brett, Jim Rice, Dave Winfield, Goose Gossage and Gary Carter. Early in the 1976 season *Baseball Digest* wrote an article on the best young players in baseball, but somehow left George Brett off the list; he probably should have been the #1 man. I fired off an angry letter to the editor under a pseudonym because they sometimes published my articles, and they did publish the letter and put Brett on the cover of that issue, acknowledging that they were doing so because they realized he should have been included. Which you have to respect that; thank you, John Kuenstler. The other five Young Superstars from 1975 included three players who COULD reasonably be in the Hall of Fame—Fred Lynn, Dave Parker and Bill Madlock.

Now we come to the questions with which I began this research:

1) How many Young Superstars are there, over time?
2) Is that number going up or down? And
3) What happens to them? Do they mostly go on to be Hall of Famers, or do half of them wipe out, or what?

I am, of course, trying to anticipate the future by studying the past. You look at guys like Vladimir Guerrero Jr. and Austin Riley; does their brilliant beginning usually presage a brilliant career, or are there a lot of young guys like that who just disappear into the mists of time, like Jeff Burroughs, Pete Ward and Jim Ray Hart? Repeating those three questions:

1) *How many Young Superstars are there, over time?*
An average of essentially four per season, over time.

2) *Is that number going up or down?*

It is quite clearly going down. In the 1920s there were 38 Young Superstars, but with 16 teams each year, that is .24 Young Superstars per team per season. In the 2010s there were 37 Young Superstars, but with 30 teams each year, that is .12 Young Superstars per team per season.

Per decade, the numbers go 39-36-26-30 for the 1920s, the 1930s, the 1940s and the 1950s, or 131 in 40 years. Then in the 1960s there were 69 players who earned the "Young Superstar" label.

Expansion clearly was a major cause of that change. There were 16 major league teams at the start of the decade, 24 at the end of the decade, and the expansions clearly created opportunities for more players with less minor league experience. As more players got an opportunity at a very young age, more players had big seasons at a very young age, thus were counted in our study as Young Superstars. 21 of the 69 Young Superstars went on to Hall of Fame careers, a historically normal percentage.

But after 69 Young Superstars emerging in the 1960s, there were only 57 in the 1970s, 44 in the 1980s, 36 in the 1990s, 44 in the 2000s, and 37 in the last completed decade. 69 in the 1960s is .32 per team. 37 in the 2010s is .12 per team. We just do not see as many young superstars emerging now as we did in earlier decades.

Why? Two reasons, I think. With more players going to college and more players playing well in their thirties, there just are not as many players getting an opportunity at a young age as there used to be. And second, the game gets harder to dominate over time. With fewer young players and less dominance by the stars, you have fewer Young Superstars, using a constant definition of what is a Young Superstar.

3) What happens to Young Superstars? Do they mostly go on to be Hall of Famers, or do half of them wipe out, or what?

They mostly do very well. Of the 417 young superstars, 81 have emerged since 2000, so we can't reach any conclusion about their careers. Some of them are obvious Hall of Famers, like Pujols and Trout, and others, we'll just have to wait and see how it goes.

So that leaves us with 336 Young Superstars who emerged in the years 1920 to 1999. Of those 336 players, 123 are now in the Hall of Fame. That's 37%. However, of the other 213 Young Superstars, 28 retired with 300 or more career Win Shares, 58 retired with 250 or more, 116 retired with 200 or more, and 161 retired with 150 or more. Only 52 retired with less than 150 Win Shares.

Naming names.

Retired with less than 150 Win Shares. A player with less than 150 Career Win Shares has no chance of making the Hall of Fame as a player. Over half of the Young Superstars who retired with no real chance of Hall of Fame selection are pitchers.

In the study as a whole, 88 of the 336 Young Superstars who emerged before 2000 were pitchers, or 26%. Among players who pulled up short of 150 Win Shares, almost always because of injury, 52% were pitchers, or 27 out of 52. This group includes Johnny Antonelli (1954), Herb Score (1955), Dean Chance (1962), Jim Maloney (1963), Denny McLain (1965), Steve Busby (1974), Randy Jones (1975), Steve Avery (1991), and 19 others.

Position players who had spectacular starts but weren't able to stay around include Pete Reiser (1941), Jim Ray Hart (1964),Tony Conigliaro (1965), Tommie Agee (1966), Bobby Tolan (1969), Dickie Thon (1982), Vince Coleman (1985), and Kal Daniels (1987).

Retired with 150 to 199 Win Shares. A player who retires with 150 to 199 Career Win Shares does not normally wind up in the Hall of Fame, but it does happen occasionally. Sandy Koufax, Bruce Sutter and Dizzy Dean were Young Superstars who are in this group, and did make the Hall of Fame.

Of the non-Hall of Famers in this group, again, over half are pitchers, 23 of 45 or 52%. Those include Don Newcombe (1949), Sam McDowell (1965), Fernando Valenzuela (1981), Dwight Gooden (1984), Bret Saberhagen (1985) and 18 others. Newcombe, Valenzuela, Gooden and Saberhagen, at least, would still have some chance of being selected to the Hall of Fame.

Non-pitchers in this group include Al Rosen (1950), Jeff Burroughs (1973), Alvin Davis (1984) and Carlos Baerga (1992). I don't see any non-pitchers in this group who would have a realistic chance of Hall of Fame selection.

Retired with 200 to 249 Win Shares. I think about 15% of players who retire with 200 to 249 career Win Shares eventually make the Hall of Fame, which means that about 85% do not or at least haven't yet. There are 70 Young Superstars in our study who retired with 200 to 249 Win Shares, and 12 of those are in the Hall of Fame, which is 17%. That list includes Catfish Hunter, Goose Gossage, Hack Wilson, Phil Rizzuto, Ralph Kiner, Tony Oliva and six others.

Of the 58 players in this group who are NOT in the Hall of Fame, 15 (or 26%) were pitchers. That list includes Curt Simmons, Billy Pierce, Mickey Lolich, Jerry Koosman, Vida Blue, Frank Tanana, Dave Stieb and eight others.

That means there are 43 players who:

(a) Were Young Superstars,
(b) Emerged before the year 2000,
(c) Were not pitchers,

(d) Were Not Hall of Famers, and

(e) Retired with 200 to 249 Career Win Shares, a record that will sometimes get you elected to Cooperstown.

That list includes Roger Maris, Curt Flood, Johnny Callison, Thurman Munson, Bill Madlock, Pedro Guerrero, Eric Davis, Juan Gonzalez, Albert Belle, Nomar Garciaparra and 33 others.

Retired with 250 to 299 Career Win Shares. Players who retire with 250 to 299 Career Win Shares generally have a 30 to 40% chance to make the Hall of Fame.

In this study there are 52 players who were Young Superstars before 2000, and retired in this range. 22 of those 52 are currently in the Hall of Fame. Interestingly enough, there have been seven pitchers who were Young Superstars, and who retired with 250 to 299 Win Shares. All seven of them are in the Hall of Fame. There are no pitchers in this group who have not been elected to the Hall of Fame. The pitchers include Pedro Martinez, Bob Feller, Juan Marichal, Don Drysdale and three others.

For the non-pitchers, 15 of 45 in this range have been selected to the Hall of Fame—and more will be, later. There are well-qualified candidates in there. The Hall of Famers in the group include Minnie Miñoso (yay!), Hank Greenberg, Larry Doby, Jim Rice and Kirby Puckett. The non-Hall of Famers include Amos Otis (1970), César Cedeño (1972), Steve Garvey (1974), Fred Lynn (1975), Dale Murphy (1980), Darryl Strawberry (1983), Don Mattingly (1984), José Canseco (1986), Kenny Lofton (1992) and Andruw Jones (1998).

Young Superstars who Retired with 300 or more Win Shares. Generally speaking, players who retire with 300 or more Win Shares will eventually make the Hall of Fame unless they were touched by scandal. More than "touched"; they'll generally make the Hall of Fame unless they are buried in scandal. In this study, there have been 112 players who were Young Superstars, and who retired with 300 or more Win Shares. Of those 112 players, 84 are now in the Hall of Fame, which is exactly 75%.

The only pitcher who

(a) Was a Young Superstar,
(b) Before 2000,
(c) Retired with 300 Win Shares, and
(d) Is not in the Hall of Fame

The only one is Roger Clemens. Non-pitchers who fit the same description include Vada Pinson (1959), Pete Rose (1963), Dick Allen (1964), Jimmy Wynn (1965), Reggie Smith (1967), Bobby Grich (1963), Dave Parker (1975), Keith Hernandez (1977), Willie Randolph (1977), Lou Whitaker (1979), Mark McGwire (1987), Barry Bonds (1987), Fred McGriff (1988), Gary Sheffield (1990), Manny Ramirez (1995), Alex Rodriguez (1996), Scott Rolen (1997) and Bobby Abreu (1998).

And finally, there are some players who make the baseball Hall of Fame, but who never made the Young Superstars list, mostly because their careers were late getting started. Most Hall of Famers WERE young superstars, but, for example, Warren Spahn and Jackie Robinson were not, because their careers were late getting started, and Hoyt Wilhelm was not (same reason). Craig Biggio was never a Young Superstar, and Harold Baines was not. Carlton Fisk and Whitey Ford were not, and Randy Johnson was not; it took too long for him to find his control. Nellie Fox was not, and Bob Gibson was not. But most of them were.

Thank you all for reading.

Aaron Judge's Wonderful Season

Joe Posnanski

Through the years, home run records have inflicted quite a bit of pain on any number of players. It's an odd thing. You would expect home run chases to be boundless baseball celebrations. I mean, we all love home runs, right? We all love records being broken. You would think a home run chase would be like a good party.

And yet … going back even to the days of Jimmie Foxx and Hank Greenberg, home run chases have come at a devastating cost. Roger Maris was so distraught in the final weeks of his pursuit of 61 homers in 1961 that he began losing his hair. For decades, Henry Aaron refused to even talk about the racist horrors he dealt with as he closed in on his 715th home run. The joyful Mark McGwire and Sammy Sosa home run race of 1998 turned very dark once baseball reluctantly began to deal with its steroid issues.

And Barry Bonds … well, we'll get back to Barry Bonds.

In 2022, Aaron Judge had one of the most wonderful seasons in baseball history. Judge himself is such a wonderful absurdity – he has to be the biggest player in the history of baseball. He's listed at 6-foot-7, 282 pounds. He looks taller and heavier than that. For fun, here is just a small list of people he is both taller and heavier than:

-- Charles Barkley

-- Rob Gronkowski

-- Stone Cold Steve Austin

-- Lennox Lewis

-- Anthony Muñoz

Now, take a player that size and give him all the baseball tools. All of them. Judge is a good fielder with a powerful arm and pretty good speed. In addition to everything else he did this year, he stole 16 of 19 bases, and he hit .311, and he played a whole bunch of center field because the Yankees needed him out there.

None of those things are supposed to be possible for a Hulk-Hogan-sized baseball player. There simply hasn't been anyone like him in the history of the game – it's like he was sent from the future to either save or destroy mankind, depending on how you feel about the Yankees.

But instead of marveling at this once-in-a-generation season, we as a baseball society mostly fell back on doing what we know how to do: Count home runs. Judge started the season off sluggishly, hitting just one homer in his first 13 games. It felt like nobody was hitting home runs in those early days of the 2022 season; MLB had taken some of the life out of the baseballs and there was still some winter in the air.

But on April 22, Judge hit two home runs against Cleveland and he was off and running. He hit 26 home runs in his next 54 games, the Yankees won 42 of them, and a home run chase was most definitely on.

Then the question is: Which record was he chasing? Certainly, Barry Bonds' record of 73 home runs was out of his reach. But Bonds, among many other things, played in the National League. So did Mark McGwire (who hit 70 home runs) and Sammy Sosa (who hit 66). That meant that Roger Maris' American League record – and within that, the New York Yankees record – of 61 home runs still stood 61 years after he set it.

And so, we settled in to see if Aaron Judge could hit 62 home runs.

It was thrilling, no question about it. In late July, Judge hit 13 homers in 16 games. Then he cooled a little bit, and the Yankees went into a slide and watched their gigantic lead in the American League East dwindle. Judge picked it up, smacked nine homers in 14 games as New York righted the ship, and once again took command in the division.

That meant the last month or so of the season was dedicated to Aaron Judge and whether or not he could get to 62. But since Judge already had 55 home runs on September 7 – it seemed all but certain he would get to 62 – so, in many ways, the bigger conversation was: *What would it mean when he hit his 62nd home run?*

People had opinions.

"He should be revered for being the actual single-season home run champ," said Roger Maris Jr. "That's really who he is if he hits 62."

Ah. OK, well, that's one opinion – that Bonds' record is null and void because it was later determined that he must have used steroids*.

We can never be entirely certain that he used steroids in 2001 because baseball did not have any testing and did not make any efforts whatsoever to prevent players from using PEDs – a fact that is too often overlooked -- but the preponderance of evidence suggests Bonds certainly used them.

It was definitely a popular opinion. But there were counterarguments – one of those coming from a guy named Aaron Judge. He grew up in the Bay Area, and he idolized Barry Bonds, saying on numerous occasions that Bonds was the player who inspired him most. He repeatedly and without hesitation stated that there was one home run record, and only one home run record, and it belonged to Barry Bonds.

"I watched (Bonds) do it," Judge said. "I stayed up late watching him do it. That's the record. No one can take that from him."

But here's the thing that has always been true about home run chases: The person doing the chasing does not get to set the agenda. People may have enjoyed watching Aaron Judge hit home runs; but they would decide exactly what it meant.

"Bonds is the official home run champion," *Sports Illustrated*'s Tom Verducci wrote. "Judge is the authentic champion."

"Bonds is not the single-season home run king," Chris Russo said on ESPN.

"Aaron Judge Ties the Real Home Run Record," was the headline in *Rolling Stone*, with the just-in-case-you-missed-the-point subtitle of "No, those steroid-fueled home run hitters don't count."

Judge got to 60 home runs on September 20, which left him two weeks to hit his 61st and 62nd home run. That seemed like more than enough time; in fact, there were those who wondered if he might not go on one of his home run booms and make an actual run at Bonds' 73.

But then the home runs dried up. Was he feeling the pressure? Maybe. Probably. But the truth is that home runs, even for Jolly Green Giants like Aaron Judge, are mysterious and fantastic collisions of power and timing and weather and luck. For one thing, you need a good pitch to hit, and pitchers didn't see much plus-side in pitching to him; they walked him 12 times in his next seven games. For another thing, you need a Zen-like approach that isn't easy to employ, particularly when the whole world is watching.

Sometimes, most of the time, the home run comes when you do not go for it.

"You know something?" George Brett once told me. "In my entire career, I never once hit a home run when I was trying to hit a home run. Not even one time." Brett, admittedly, was not a pure home run hitter, but he still hit 317 of them, and he says they were all happy accidents. Aaron Judge was not in a position to wait for a happy accident. The pressure to hit a home run was on him every single pitch.

Finally, on September 28, Judge hit home run No. 61 in Toronto off Blue Jays reliever Tim Mayza. That's when *Rolling Stone* took the opportunity to delete Barry Bonds. Judge was more cheerful. "I'm playing a kid's game," he said. "I love this. I love these moments."

He still had No. 62 to hit, and he could not manage to do it in three home games against Baltimore. That left only a final series in Texas. In the second game of a Tuesday doubleheader on baseball's penultimate day, he finally got No. 62, a home run off a Rangers pitcher named Jesus Tinoco.

"I challenged him, and he hit it," Tinoco said afterward. "That's my job. All I can say is congratulations to him."

Yes, congratulations to Aaron Judge. He had a simply incredible season, one of the most remarkable I've seen in my lifetime. Does he have the real home run record? In my view: No. Of course not. Barry Bonds hit 73 home runs. Mark McGwire hit 70. Sammy Sosa hit 66. I don't see any value whatsoever in trying to rewrite history.

More, though, I see negative value in straining to believe that there was ever a period of time when baseball was pure and the records set were entirely authentic. This is a game that did not include Black players for a half-century. A game where amphetamines were kept in jars in the clubhouse, like they were M&Ms. A game where the most famous home run ever hit – Bobby Thomson's Shot Heard Round the World – probably came on a pitch he knew was coming thanks to the Giants illegal sign-stealing system. A game where Babe Ruth and Pete Rose probably corked their bats, where numerous pitchers in the Hall of Fame spit on and scuffed baseballs, where cheating had not only been tolerated but cherished.

Barry Bonds is the home run record holder. You don't have to admire how he got there, and you don't have to accept his legitimacy. That's a wonderful thing about baseball: You can be a fan of the game any way you like. But, for me, absolutely, Barry Bonds is the all-time record holder for home runs, and I don't think anyone is going to approach his record for a while.

That doesn't take one thing away from Judge's season, though.

The Corners Are Covered:
Goldschmidt & Arenado Thrived in 2022

Mark Simon

If we're going to talk about the best corner combos in major league history, we can begin by producing a list of instances in which a team's usual first and third basemen each posted 5 WAR (per Baseball-Reference) in a season.

Doing so nets us 43 sets of combos in baseball's modern era (since 1900) with some pairs showing up twice (Kris Bryant and Anthony Rizzo for the younger folks; Ken Boyer and Bill White for our older readers; Home Run Baker and Stuffy McInnis for the SABR crowd).

If we raise the bar to each recording a 6-WAR season, the list thins to only seven pairs, each of whom made it once.

Among them, White Sox teammates Frank Thomas and Robin Ventura circa 1992, who were the first to do so in 47 years, when Phil Cavarretta and Stan Hack had memorable seasons on the other side of Chicago for the World Series–bound Cubs in 1945.

Bump it to 7 WAR and we're in rare pair air.

There are only three such corner combos, and our Handbook cover subjects Nolan Arenado and Paul Goldschmidt are one of them.

The others are first baseman Frank Chance and third baseman Harry Steinfeldt of the 1906 Cubs and the standard-setter, Albert Pujols and Scott Rolen for the 2004 Cardinals.

So it's worth appreciating just how great the Goldschmidt/Arenado combo was.

The amazing thing about the two of them is how closely aligned in overall value they are.

	Arenado	Goldschmidt
Baseball-Reference WAR	7.9	7.8
FanGraphs WAR	7.3	7.1
Total Runs	140	138

--

You've watched baseball long enough that you know what makes both of them great.

But what made them so special in 2022?

For both Goldschmidt and Arenado, 2022 was the greatest offensive season of their careers when considering how they did relative to the rest of MLB.

	Goldschmidt	Arenado
OPS	.981	.891
OPS+	180*	154*
HR	35	30
RBI	115	103

* Career-high

In 2022 MLB hitters had a .706 OPS, down 22 points from 2021 (despite the DH becoming permanent in the NL) and 52 points from 2019.

Goldschmidt's OPS jumped by 102 points from 2021 to 2022. Heck, Goldschmidt's OPS with two strikes was .785, 79 points better than the MLB *overall* OPS.

If you've ever regularly watched Goldschmidt during a full season (I did in 2018), you'd know that he goes through periods of time in which the baseball looks like a beach ball.

In 2022, that covered 51 games from May 7 to July 2, in which he hit .383 with a .455 on-base percentage and a .755 slugging percentage, with 17 home runs and 54 RBI.

It had taken him a little while to get going. His first homer of the season didn't come until April 29 when he hit one on the 12th pitch of an at-bat versus Madison Bumgarner.

In that hot streak, Goldschmidt thrashed mistake pitches.

If you threw him something within the middle-third of the strike zone (as opposed to inside or outside) and he contacted it, you were in trouble.

When an at-bat ended on a pitch there, he hit .477 (31-for-65) with 8 home runs.

Arenado's OPS increased by 84 points from 2021 to 2022. Let's remember too that he's more than proved that he can hit outside of Coors Field. He also cut his strikeout rate to 11.6%, the lowest for any full season in his 10-year career.

Arenado finished with 30 home runs and 72 strikeouts. There were 23 players with 30 home runs in 2022. The only other one with fewer than 100 strikeouts was Kyle Tucker with 95.

Peak Arenado showed up twice. In the first 20 games of the season, he hit .368 with a 1.133 OPS.

Then, over the nearly two-and-a-half months from June 17 to August 29, he hit .345 with a 1.065 OPS and 16 home runs in 58 games. Arenado's numbers against that middle-third location in that time resembled Goldschmidt's in his hot streak.

In AB Ending With Middle-Third Pitches During Hot Streak

	Goldschmidt (May 7–July 2)	Arenado (June 17–Aug 29)
BA	.477	.452
Hits	31	28
Home Runs	8	8

>> MLB BA vs midde-third pitches in 2022: .278

--

Left unsaid to this point are the aesthetics. Goldschmidt does everything well. He's not just a hitter. Did you know he's got a streak going of 23 consecutive successful stolen base attempts? Our VP of Baseball, Bobby Scales, has told me many times how Goldschmidt is one of the best baserunners in baseball.

Goldschmidt may not have played Fielding Bible Award–worthy defense this season, but the Cardinals did lead MLB in how often they turned groundballs and bunts into outs, so he deserves some credit for that. And he has won the Fielding Bible Award four times in the past. He turned 35 in September but he doesn't play like a 35-year-old. At least not yet.

Arenado similarly just plays the game *well*. He'll turn 32 not long after Opening Day in 2023. But he still plays defense like he's in his prime.

A scout said this about him in 2017 and it still holds true:

"He makes all the plays because his instincts off the bat enable his quick feet and body control," the scout said of Arenado. "He has a great backhand with an easy, strong arm. He's solid on slow rollers and bunt plays. His arm is accurate and strong from all angles.

"He's amazing. He's a vacuum cleaner."

By the time most of you read this article, the MVP will have been awarded to one of them, or they'll have split the vote and come up a little bit short.

Regardless, the joint value that the two of them provided this season was virtually unprecedented and is something that likely won't be seen again for quite some time.

Unless they reunite to do it next season, of course.

The Cardinal Not On The Cover

For the last seven weeks of the 2022 season, Albert Pujols turned the clock back to the earliest version of himself. He hit .310 with a 1.108 OPS and 16 home runs and 42 RBI in 44 games.

You may have seen some variation of this already. It's pretty cool.

	First 44 Games, 2001	Last 44 Games, 2022
OPS	1.121	1.108
Home Runs	14	16
RBI	44	42
Age	21	42

That late burst boosted him to fourth all-time in home runs (703), second all-time in RBI (2,218), and third all-time in extra-base hits (1,405).

Let's not forget his defense, particularly in his prime. Pujols' 138 Defensive Runs Saved are the most of any first baseman since SIS began tracking the stat in 2003.

Pujols' welcome to the game and departure from it were both equally surprising and remarkably impressive. In between, we marveled at his excellence, which puts him in an iconic place in baseball history.

The Longevity of Wainwright and Molina

Rob Neyer

Maybe it snuck up on you, as it did on me. On September 14 in St. Louis, 41-year-old pitcher Adam Wainwright and 40-year-old catcher Yadier Molina broke a longstanding MLB record when they started their 325th game together.

I don't know precisely why this delighted me so much. Perhaps because Wainwright and Molina are both (like me!) middle-aged. Perhaps because I didn't know it was happening until it actually happened (which meant a nice surprise!). Or perhaps it was because, not so long ago, most people probably figured the old record—like most (non-strikeout) records—was largely safe.

Okay, the correct answer is (d) all of the above.

Honestly, in this era of starting pitchers not starting as often and catchers getting more time off and players getting traded ($$) and signing free-agent deals (ditto) this way and that way, did *you* think, a few years ago, that in 2022 you might see a pitcher and catcher set the ALL-TIME RECORD for appearances as a starting battery? Because I sure didn't. Sure, I could be in somewhat better touch with current events but this wasn't on my radar screen. At all.

So how did this happen? And how unlikely was it, really?

Adam Wainwright's MLB Story began in 2005, when he made a couple of brief relief appearances as a September call-up. That's when the Wainwright-Molina Story began, too; in Wainwright's second outing (a flawless one-inning stint in Milwaukee), Molina was behind the plate.

(By the way, here's a trivia question for your Cardinal friends: Who was Adam Wainwright's *first* catcher in the majors? The answer is Mike Mahoney, who joined Wainwright as a ninth-inning replacement against the Mets and was behind the dish for a single, a walk, two stolen bases, two lineouts, a three-run homer, and finally, mercifully, an inning-ending pop fly. Mahoney, then nearly 33 years old, would get into a couple more games that month before bowing out of the Show with a .180 batting average. I wonder how well Adam Wainwright remembers his very first catcher.)

In 2006, Wainwright pitched impressively out of the bullpen, especially during the Cardinals' championship run, striking out both the final out of the LCS and World Series. It wasn't until 2007 that Wainwright earned a spot in the St. Louis rotation, and since then he's made only four regular-season relief outings.

In all the years since, 2007 through '22, Wainwright has pitched in 394 regular-season games, and started 390 of them. And Molina, like Wainwright a Forever Cardinal, also started the great majority of those 390.

While Molina is nearly a year older than Wainwright, he established himself in the majors quite a bit earlier; just as he was turning 21 in 2004, Molina became veteran Mike Matheny's understudy in St. Louis, and by the next spring—when Wainwright was still mastering Triple-A—Molina was the Cardinals' No. 1 catcher. Once they got going, though, they just kept going. Sure, there were some bumps: Wainwright's injuries, mostly, but last summer Molina missed some time and wasn't completely committed to coming back. Ultimately, though, both played big parts in the Cardinals' eighth division title and 12th postseason appearance since they became teammates.

With Molina retiring after the 2022 season, their start on October 2 was their 328th and final outing together (as starters; of course Molina caught Wainwright many times during his fine rookie season). Of the *next* 22 batteries on the all-time list, *none* began their résumés in the 21st century. Shoot, of those next 22, only one pitched *at all* in this century: Tom Glavine and Javy López, with 248 starts from 1994 through 2002.

And compared to Wainlina's 328 … well, 248 doesn't seem like a lot, does it?

In fact, only three other combos have reached even 300: Red Faber and Ray Schalk with 306; Warren Spahn and Del Crandall with 316; and Mickey Lolich and Bill Freehan, with 324 the champion battery for nearly half a century.

At this point, can we reasonably *imagine* another battery getting *close* to Wainwright and Molina?

I'm not sure about reasonably. But considering they've literally just finished their run, we should at least entertain the possibility, just as we should entertain the possibility that someone will break Aaron Judge's American League record for home runs, or that some team will break the Seattle Mariners' record for wins in one season.

Here's the thing, though: What really distinguishes Wainwright and Molina isn't how many games they started together (Lolich and Freehan were close) or how many years they've played in the majors (Spahn pitched forever, and guys like Carlton Fisk and Rick Dempsey caught forever). No, what truly sets Wainwright and Molina apart is how long they *stayed* together.

Faber and Schalk: 13 years
Spahn and Crandall: 15 years
Lolich and Freehan: 13 years
Wainwright and Molina: 16 years!

Okay, so they've got just one year, technically speaking, on Spahn and Crandall. Which does include Crandall's two years (1951 and '52) in the army, along with Wainwright's three injury-plagued seasons (2011, '15, and '18), but does *not* include his cup of coffee in 2005 or his '06 bullpen season. But we all recognize, don't we, that today's players are more peripatetic than those of Spahn's and Crandall's era?

But, wait. There is more.

Aaron Judge's record might not stand forever, or even for long, because the game is trending *toward* (or at least with) home runs: optimized swings, bigger hitters, smaller ballparks. The Mariners' record might not stand forever, or even for long, because the game is trending toward even larger differences between the best teams and the worst teams.

What is the game trending *away* from? Players spending 15-20 years with one team, and pitchers starting more than 33 games in a season.

Sixteen years ago, St. Louis finished its World Series run with a 4-2 victory over the Tigers in Game 5. Molina collected three of the Cardinals' eight hits, and scored twice. In the ninth, Wainwright—despite having recorded only three saves during the regular season—entered to close the game, and made his ninth straight scoreless postseason outing while earning his fourth postseason save. The Series ended when Brandon Inge struck out swinging, and seconds later Wainwright and Molina were both in mid-air, embracing.

But nobody in their right mind could have guessed that Wainwright would become a Hall of Fame-quality starting pitcher, that both he and Molina would remain teammates into their early 40s, and the tandem would set a record for durability during an era in which durability has come to seem an outdated attribute.

There was a great deal of talk in 2022 about all the *intangibles* floating around in St. Louis, what with franchise legends in their 40s spreading all their geriatric wisdom and love. But let's not ignore the tangibles? All three of those quadragenarians were key contributors as the Cardinals ultimately cruised to another N.L. Central title.

Career-wise, Wainwright has posted a 3.25 ERA with Molina behind the plate … and a relatively whopping 4.06 ERA with his other 17 catchers (Tony Cruz, Andrew Knizner, and Gary Bennett are the only three who've caught more than 31 of Wainwright's innings, although that of course will change if he pitches much after 2022).

Granted, Wainwright threw so few innings with other catchers that we can't say Molina *made* Wainwright the pitcher he was; most of the credit goes to Wainwright himself, of course, along with pitching coaches, teammates, and his brother, who Wainwright says taught him the curveball. But it's clear from their comments that Wainwright and Molina have fed off each other for many years, and that being teammates and friends helped push them to greatness, and perhaps helped keep them in St. Louis.

Cardinals fans have a great deal for which to be thankful during this century. But just as it's difficult to imagine anyone breaking Wainwright's and Molina's record—the now-active leaders are Kyle Hendricks and Willson Contreras, with 105 starts together and poor prospects for more—it's difficult to imagine a greater gift for St. Louis baseball fans than what these two lifetime Cardinals have given them.

Hall of Fame Monitor

Alex Vigderman

The last ten years or so have featured an evolution in how we think about aging and the notion of "prime years." The early development of superstars like Mike Trout, Bryce Harper, Juan Soto, and Ronald Acuña Jr. has put a spotlight on players in their early 20's who can dominate.

This year, the pendulum swung back towards the 90's kids. MVP ballots will be full of stars who may have had a Beanie Baby or two, like Mookie Betts, Manny Machado, Aaron Judge, Nolan Arenado, Jose Altuve, and Freddie Freeman.

Of that group, Arenado and Altuve already have careers that suggest they'll be Hall of Famers, with Monitor scores of 112 and 123, respectively. Betts and Freeman will help each other take their credentials over the top during their time in Los Angeles, as each of them is just short of a plaque-worthy career so far.

The least-qualified player of that group is Judge, who just posted a league-leading OPS while playing a competent center field half the time. Oh, and he hit a home run or two.

I did leave off one older name from the MVP list above. Last year in this space, Mark Simon wrote, "You know who has a tough Hall of Fame case? St. Louis Cardinals first baseman Paul Goldschmidt." Not so tough now!

The Hall of Fame Monitor is meant as an estimate for what Hall of Fame voters will do when a player comes onto the ballot, not a measure of their deservedness (a further explanation is in the glossary). A score of 100 or more suggests a likely Hall of Famer, but as with all predictors of this sort, there's some wiggle room around that number for snubs and surprises. Because we produce the book just after the regular season ends, this year's awards aren't included in the numbers that follow.

Hall of Fame Monitor

Player	Age	2022	Career
Juan Soto	**23**	**2**	**24**
Bo Bichette	23	5	15
Ronald Acuna Jr.	**24**	**1**	**22**
Yordan Alvarez	24	8	19
Rafael Devers	**25**	**5**	**32**
Julio Urias	25	10	28
Ozzie Albies	25	0	24
Austin Riley	25	6	16
Kyle Tucker	25	6	13
Cody Bellinger	**26**	**1**	**41**
Sandy Alcantara	26	9	19
Bryan Reynolds	26	2	15
Dylan Cease	26	4	12
Pete Alonso	**27**	**13**	**33**
Carlos Correa	27	2	27
Andrew Benintendi	27	3	16
German Marquez	27	1	15
Lucas Giolito	27	1	12
Shohei Ohtani	27	4	10
Jose Alvarado	27	1	10
Francisco Lindor	**28**	**4**	**48**
Edwin Diaz	28	10	43
Alex Bregman	28	3	35
Corey Seager	28	2	30
Matt Olson	28	7	24
Josh Hader	28	3	21
Jose Berrios	28	2	19
Jorge Polanco	28	0	18
Ketel Marte	28	2	17
Joey Gallo	28	0	14
Framber Valdez	28	9	13
Lou Trivino	28	2	13
Max Fried	28	3	12
Rougned Odor	28	0	12
Lance McCullers Jr.	28	0	11
A.J. Minter	28	3	10
Diego Castillo	28	1	10
Mookie Betts	**29**	**9**	**91**
Bryce Harper	29	0	78
Manny Machado	29	9	60
Jose Ramirez	29	8	54
Xander Bogaerts	29	5	54
Trea Turner	29	7	38
Javier Baez	29	1	38
Blake Snell	29	0	28
Aaron Nola	29	4	27
Trevor Story	29	0	27
Kyle Schwarber	29	10	20
Josh Bell	29	1	18
Matt Chapman	29	1	18
Joe Musgrove	29	2	17
Tim Anderson	29	0	16
Kyle Freeland	29	1	15
Gary Sanchez	29	0	15
Scott Barlow	29	4	14
Jordan Romano	29	5	13
Eduardo Rodriguez	29	0	13
Zach Davies	29	1	12
Archie Bradley	29	0	12
Noah Syndergaard	29	0	12
Carlos Rodon	29	4	11
Teoscar Hernandez	29	2	11
Luis Castillo	29	1	11
Jorge Lopez	29	4	10
Brandon Woodruff	29	2	10
Taijuan Walker	29	2	10

Player	Age	2022	Career
Carlos Estevez	29	1	10
Michael Fulmer	29	1	10
Mike Trout	**30**	**5**	**137**
Aaron Judge	30	21	51
Christian Yelich	30	1	51
Kris Bryant	30	0	44
Nick Castellanos	30	1	32
Robbie Ray	30	3	30
Eugenio Suarez	30	2	25
Jonathan Schoop	30	1	17
Willson Contreras	30	0	16
Jorge Soler	30	0	15
Marco Gonzales	30	1	14
Corey Knebel	30	0	14
Eddie Rosario	30	0	14
Joc Pederson	30	0	14
Michael Wacha	30	0	14
Jeff McNeil	30	6	12
Sean Manaea	30	1	12
Trey Mancini	30	1	12
Carl Edwards Jr.	30	1	11
Alex Claudio	30	0	11
Giovanny Gallegos	30	1	10
Nolan Arenado	**31**	**8**	**112**
Gerrit Cole	31	11	68
Marcus Semien	31	2	30
Marcell Ozuna	31	1	30
J.T. Realmuto	31	3	23
Alex Wood	31	1	22
Ken Giles	31	0	21
Max Muncy	31	1	20
Taylor Rogers	31	4	17
Hansel Robles	31	0	17
Kevin Gausman	31	3	16
Chris Devenski	31	0	16
Ender Inciarte	31	0	14
Jonathan Villar	31	0	14
Mike Clevinger	31	0	14
Martin Perez	31	3	12
Dylan Floro	31	1	12
Tyler Rogers	31	1	12
Adam Cimber	31	3	11
Jordan Lyles	31	2	11
Emilio Pagan	31	1	11
Marcus Stroman	31	1	11
Avisail Garcia	31	0	11
Chris Taylor	31	0	11
Mitch Haniger	31	0	11
Wil Myers	31	0	11
Jake Lamb	31	0	10
Jose Altuve	**32**	**8**	**123**
Freddie Freeman	32	13	85
Madison Bumgarner	32	1	74
Giancarlo Stanton	32	1	69
Salvador Perez	32	0	67
Anthony Rizzo	32	3	61
Anthony Rendon	32	0	44
Jeurys Familia	32	0	41
Eric Hosmer	32	0	37
George Springer	32	2	34
Brad Hand	32	1	29
Jean Segura	32	0	29
Raisel Iglesias	32	3	27
Will Smith	32	2	22
Patrick Corbin	32	1	22
Kyle Hendricks	32	0	22
Zack Wheeler	32	2	21
Andrelton Simmons	32	0	18
Jason Heyward	32	0	18

Player	Age	2022	Career
Sonny Gray	32	0	18
Matt Barnes	32	0	17
Andrew Chafin	32	2	15
Jackie Bradley Jr.	32	0	14
Mychal Givens	32	1	12
Nathan Eovaldi	32	0	12
Paul Sewald	32	4	11
Cesar Hernandez	32	1	11
Jake Odorizzi	32	0	11
Travis Shaw	32	0	11
C.J. Cron	32	3	10
DJ LeMahieu	**33**	**1**	**56**
Chris Sale	33	0	52
Stephen Strasburg	33	0	39
Whit Merrifield	33	1	36
Liam Hendriks	33	3	35
Elvis Andrus	33	1	31
Alex Colome	33	1	30
Starling Marte	33	2	27
Jose Quintana	33	2	25
Mike Moustakas	33	0	20
Chris Archer	33	1	19
Hector Neris	33	1	19
Miles Mikolas	33	4	17
Ryan Pressly	33	3	17
Shane Greene	33	0	16
Hunter Strickland	33	2	15
Eduardo Escobar	33	1	15
Corey Dickerson	33	0	15
Adam Duvall	33	0	13
Justin Grimm	33	0	13
Merrill Kelly	33	5	12
Jose Alvarez	33	0	12
Yasmani Grandal	33	0	12
Matt Moore	33	4	11
Marwin Gonzalez	33	0	11
Drew Smyly	33	0	10
Michael Pineda	33	0	10
Clayton Kershaw	**34**	**1**	**150**
Craig Kimbrel	34	3	110
Paul Goldschmidt	34	12	94
Kenley Jansen	34	9	91
J.D. Martinez	34	2	71
Aroldis Chapman	34	0	60
Jacob deGrom	34	0	53
Dallas Keuchel	34	0	41
Justin Upton	34	0	39
Zack Britton	34	0	39
Dee Strange-Gordon	34	0	36
Blake Treinen	34	0	28
Bryan Shaw	34	1	24
Brad Boxberger	34	2	22
Mike Minor	34	0	21
Joe Kelly	34	0	17
Brandon Belt	34	0	16
Aaron Loup	34	1	15
Kyle Gibson	34	1	15
David Peralta	34	0	15
Pedro Baez	34	0	14
Tommy Pham	34	1	13
Garrett Richards	34	0	13
Jhoulys Chacin	34	0	13
A.J. Pollock	34	1	12
Justin Wilson	34	0	11
Alex Cobb	34	1	10
Ryan Tepera	34	1	10
Chase Anderson	34	0	10
Jose Abreu	**35**	**6**	**66**
Andrew McCutchen	35	1	58
Charlie Blackmon	35	1	58
Lance Lynn	35	0	41

Player	Age	2022	Career
Michael Brantley	35	0	41
Brandon Crawford	35	0	36
Yu Darvish	35	3	33
Carlos Carrasco	35	2	27
Kirby Yates	35	0	23
Alcides Escobar	35	0	22
Jake McGee	35	0	21
Wade Miley	35	0	21
Hyun-Jin Ryu	35	0	18
Daniel Hudson	35	0	17
Sean Doolittle	35	0	16
Tommy Hunter	35	0	15
Jake Diekman	35	1	12
Collin McHugh	35	1	11
Luis Garcia	35	1	10
David Price	**36**	**0**	**89**
Corey Kluber	36	1	84
Josh Donaldson	36	1	56
Johnny Cueto	36	0	51
Evan Longoria	36	0	50
Greg Holland	36	0	50
Carlos Santana	36	1	37
Matt Carpenter	36	0	34
Steve Cishek	36	1	28
Lorenzo Cain	36	0	28
Adam Ottavino	36	2	18
Max Scherzer	**37**	**0**	**141**
Mark Melancon	37	2	62
Ian Kennedy	37	1	41
David Robertson	37	2	31
Tyler Clippard	37	0	29
Justin Turner	37	1	24
Daniel Bard	37	5	16
Zack Greinke	**38**	**1**	**96**
Joey Votto	38	0	94
Charlie Morton	38	2	27
Yuli Gurriel	38	2	26
Anibal Sanchez	38	0	23
Joe Smith	38	0	20
Jesse Chavez	38	1	14
Jed Lowrie	38	0	14
Kurt Suzuki	38	0	13
Craig Stammen	38	0	11
Miguel Cabrera	**39**	**0**	**198**
Justin Verlander	39	16	186
Robinson Cano	39	0	132
Yadier Molina	39	0	84
Sergio Romo	39	0	44
Darren O'Day	39	0	25
Adam Wainwright	**40**	**1**	**85**
Oliver Perez	40	0	20
Nelson Cruz	**41**	**1**	**86**
Albert Pujols	**42**	**0**	**243**
Rich Hill	42	1	14

Hall of Fame Value

Brian Reiff

How do you measure a year? A question asked in the 1996 musical *Rent*, and one that despite its existential complexities proved easier to answer than the one presented in this section: How do you measure a Hall of Fame candidate?

This is the second of two approaches this book takes to attempt to answer the question (the first being the Hall of Fame Monitor). The Hall of Fame Value Standard was created by Bill James for the *2019 Bill James Handbook*, and rather than compare players against what he called "magic numbers", it instead attempts to evaluate a player's candidacy using a combination of some of the best analytical tools we have at our disposal—Wins Above Replacement (WAR) and Win Shares.

In his study of 987 actual and potential Hall of Famers, James found that for a player with a score above 500, there were more Hall of Famers with a lower score than there were non–Hall of Famers with a higher score, thus making it a good target for players hoping to be elected in. (The Hall of Fame Value score is equal to Win Shares + 4 * Baseball-Reference WAR.)

There are nine players likely to be on next year's ballot who have a Hall of Fame Value over 500. Eight of them are returning, with the sole newcomer being Carlos Beltrán with a score of 649.4. The three players above him (Alex Rodriguez, Manny Ramírez and Gary Sheffield) would all be locks on paper, but their involvement in various PED scandals has put their induction into question. Among the players on this year's ballot, Scott Rolen had the most support last year at 63.2 percent. His score of 584.4 would suggest he is deserving of crossing the 75 percent threshold this time around in his sixth year on the ballot.

Among the players on the edge of 500 is Max Scherzer (508.3), who crossed the threshold in 2022 in his age-37 season. Just below him are Andrew McCutchen (499.2) and Freddie Freeman (499.9), both rounding errors away from 500 and poised to reach the mark next season.

Hall of Fame Values by Age Group

Player	Age	2022 Season			Career		
		Win Shares	WAR	HoF Value	Win Shares	WAR	HoF Value
Franco, Wander	21	13	2.6	23.4	28	6.1	52.4
Soto, Juan	23	24	5.6	46.4	108	23.1	200.6
Guerrero Jr., Vladimir	23	21	4.0	37.1	65	13.5	118.9
Gimenez, Andres	23	29	7.2	57.6	38	9.0	74.0
Kirk, Alejandro	23	22	3.9	37.6	28	5.0	57.8
Carlson, Dylan	23	11	2.0	18.8	33	5.3	54.1
Acuna Jr., Ronald	24	16	2.8	27.1	86	17.6	156.5
Bichette, Bo	24	21	3.6	35.3	57	12.8	108.4
Robert, Luis	24	12	2.1	20.3	32	7.4	61.8
Manoah, Alek	24	18	5.9	41.7	27	8.7	61.6
Clase, Emmanuel	24	17	2.8	28.3	35	6.6	61.3
Lux, Gavin	24	14	2.5	24.1	30	5.4	51.4
Devers, Rafael	25	25	4.4	42.8	96	15.2	156.8
Albies, Ozzie	25	7	0.9	10.5	92	15.3	153.2
Torres, Gleyber	25	15	4.1	31.4	79	11.5	124.9
Alvarez, Yordan	25	25	6.8	52.0	57	13.6	111.5
Tucker, Kyle	25	24	5.2	44.6	59	12.7	110.0
Riley, Austin	25	27	6.5	52.9	60	12.0	108.0
Urias, Julio	25	17	4.9	36.6	51	13.0	102.9
Arraez, Luis	25	23	4.4	40.7	59	10.4	100.5
Grisham, Trent	25	12	2.4	21.6	36	8.8	71.0
Urias, Luis	25	11	3.1	23.3	37	7.1	65.4
Hayes, Ke'Bryan	25	14	4.3	31.2	30	8.5	64.0
Webb, Logan	25	15	4.8	34.1	29	8.4	62.4
Hoerner, Nico	25	20	4.5	37.9	33	6.6	59.3
Jimenez, Eloy	25	12	1.7	19.0	37	5.3	58.0
Varsho, Daulton	25	18	4.9	37.6	26	6.6	55.7
Robles, Victor	25	4	1.8	11.3	29	6.4	54.7
Bellinger, Cody	26	12	1.2	16.6	97	17.8	168.3
Adames, Willy	26	22	4.4	39.7	76	15.5	138.1
Rosario, Amed	26	20	4.1	36.3	76	9.6	114.4
Alcantara, Sandy	26	22	8.1	54.2	50	15.9	113.5
Gallen, Zac	26	16	5.1	36.2	34	12.4	83.6
Verdugo, Alex	26	14	1.2	18.9	47	8.5	81.0
Cease, Dylan	26	19	6.4	44.6	35	9.5	72.9
Lowe, Nathaniel	26	24	3.3	37.3	47	6.5	72.8
Flaherty, Jack	26	1	-0.1	0.6	35	8.7	70.0
Keller, Brad	26	3	0.2	3.6	33	8.3	66.0
Suarez, Ranger	26	9	2.4	18.7	31	8.6	65.3
Lopez, Pablo	26	11	3.0	23.0	27	8.3	60.2
Hays, Austin	26	14	2.3	23.0	33	6.4	58.7
Kim, Ha-seong	26	22	4.9	41.7	27	7.0	55.0
Reyes, Franmil	26	4	-0.9	0.4	42	2.9	53.4
Correa, Carlos	27	24	5.4	45.8	148	39.5	306.2
Ohtani, Shohei	27	38	9.6	76.3	109	24.6	207.4
Benintendi, Andrew	27	19	3.2	31.6	97	15.7	159.8
Marquez, German	27	10	1.4	15.6	70	18.2	142.8
Alonso, Pete	27	29	4.4	46.7	78	14.2	134.8
Moncada, Yoan	27	9	0.9	12.8	79	13.5	133.1
Reynolds, Bryan	27	20	3.0	32.1	70	13.6	124.4
Bieber, Shane	27	15	3.5	29.2	60	15.0	120.2
Edman, Tommy	27	22	6.3	47.2	59	15.1	119.5
Happ, Ian	27	19	4.3	36.2	75	10.8	118.4
Smith, Will	27	20	4.1	36.4	55	10.7	117.3
Lowe, Brandon	27	8	0.9	11.8	69	11.8	116.1
Crawford, J.P.	27	16	2.8	27.1	67	10.7	109.8
Margot, Manuel	27	10	1.5	16.1	60	11.5	106.1
Buehler, Walker	27	4	0.4	5.7	47	12.9	98.4
France, Ty	27	21	3.0	33.2	61	8.1	93.2
Laureano, Ramon	27	7	0.8	10.3	51	10.4	92.6
Giolito, Lucas	27	6	0.4	7.8	44	11.4	89.4
Murphy, Sean	27	21	3.5	34.9	42	7.9	88.3
Mullins II, Cedric	27	23	3.8	38.0	51	9.2	87.7
Burnes, Corbin	27	15	4.1	31.2	43	10.4	84.4
Kiner-Falefa, Isiah	27	13	2.9	24.8	41	10.1	83.7
O'Neill, Tyler	27	10	1.3	15.0	44	9.8	83.3
Meadows, Austin	27	4	0.7	6.9	56	6.7	82.9

Hall of Fame Values by Age Group

Player	Age	2022 Season			Career		
		Win Shares	WAR	HoF Value	Win Shares	WAR	HoF Value
McMahon, Ryan	27	11	3.0	23.0	44	9.5	82.0
Arozarena, Randy	27	19	2.8	30.1	45	8.0	77.2
Jansen, Danny	27	13	2.9	24.6	34	6.5	71.8
Mazara, Nomar	27	6	0.2	6.6	64	1.2	68.7
Arcia, Orlando	27	8	0.8	11.3	54	2.9	65.7
Mahle, Tyler	27	7	2.2	15.6	30	8.4	63.6
Biggio, Cavan	27	8	0.9	11.6	37	6.3	62.0
Senzatela, Antonio	27	4	0.5	5.8	35	6.7	61.9
Straw, Myles	27	11	2.7	21.7	34	6.6	60.6
Quantrill, Cal	27	12	2.0	19.8	30	6.9	57.5
Santander, Anthony	27	18	2.1	26.3	37	4.7	56.0
Kelly, Carson	27	7	0.8	10.3	30	3.5	52.6
Lopez, Nicky	27	4	-0.2	3.1	34	4.1	50.5
Lindor, Francisco	**28**	**31**	**5.4**	**52.7**	**168**	**36.6**	**314.2**
Bregman, Alex	28	26	4.5	44.0	143	30.6	265.4
Seager, Corey	28	20	4.1	36.5	140	25.4	241.8
Olson, Matt	28	22	3.4	35.8	105	21.6	191.3
Marte, Ketel	28	12	1.5	18.0	98	19.5	175.9
Polanco, Jorge	28	15	2.8	26.2	111	15.3	172.4
Swanson, Dansby	28	30	5.7	52.6	101	14.5	158.9
Buxton, Byron	28	11	4.0	27.0	63	20.2	143.9
Gallo, Joey	28	7	0.2	7.9	74	14.6	132.6
Odor, Rougned	28	11	-0.4	9.4	102	6.4	127.6
Fried, Max	28	17	5.9	40.7	52	17.9	123.6
DeJong, Paul	28	4	0.2	5.0	68	13.1	120.6
Diaz, Edwin	28	15	3.2	27.8	68	10.7	110.9
Severino, Luis	28	7	1.6	13.3	47	13.5	100.9
Bader, Harrison	28	10	1.2	14.8	53	11.8	100.1
Cronenworth, Jake	28	28	4.1	44.6	57	10.6	99.5
Hader, Josh	28	5	-1.0	0.9	61	9.4	98.6
Berrios, Jose	28	4	-0.5	1.9	56	10.2	97.0
Fletcher, David	28	5	1.1	9.4	55	10.5	97.0
McCullers Jr., Lance	28	5	1.4	10.8	46	11.4	91.6
Candelario, Jeimer	28	9	0.5	11.1	59	7.4	88.4
Gurriel Jr., Lourdes	28	12	2.2	20.7	54	8.0	85.8
Winker, Jesse	28	13	-0.3	12.0	59	5.1	79.4
Valdez, Framber	28	16	3.7	30.8	35	7.7	66.0
Gonsolin, Tony	28	14	4.6	32.5	26	8.0	58.2
Eflin, Zach	28	4	0.9	7.6	27	7.2	55.6
Lopez, Reynaldo	28	7	1.5	12.9	30	5.7	52.7
Leclerc, Jose	28	4	0.9	7.7	29	5.9	52.6
Machado, Manny	**29**	**32**	**6.8**	**59.4**	**229**	**52.0**	**437.1**
Betts, Mookie	29	27	6.4	52.7	205	56.4	430.6
Harper, Bryce	29	15	2.5	24.9	234	42.6	404.4
Ramirez, Jose	29	34	6.0	57.9	182	40.2	343.0
Bogaerts, Xander	29	28	5.7	50.7	176	34.8	315.3
Turner, Trea	29	27	4.9	46.6	144	29.7	262.7
Story, Trevor	29	13	2.5	23.0	110	29.2	227.0
Baez, Javier	29	18	2.6	28.2	116	26.0	220.0
Chapman, Matt	29	20	3.5	34.1	100	26.7	206.7
Nola, Aaron	29	15	6.0	38.8	82	30.3	203.1
Anderson, Tim	29	11	1.3	16.0	90	18.2	162.9
Nimmo, Brandon	29	28	5.0	47.9	87	17.1	155.4
Sanchez, Gary	29	10	0.9	13.6	73	12.6	147.9
Kepler, Max	29	7	2.1	15.3	76	16.9	143.6
Schwarber, Kyle	29	20	2.2	28.7	98	11.1	143.6
Hoskins, Rhys	29	19	3.0	31.2	88	11.3	133.2
Castillo, Luis	29	11	4.1	27.3	56	18.0	128.2
Syndergaard, Noah	29	7	1.8	14.0	56	17.6	126.4
Freeland, Kyle	29	11	2.4	20.6	56	17.2	124.6
Bell, Josh	29	16	3.0	28.0	88	9.0	124.0
Rodon, Carlos	29	15	5.4	36.7	56	17.0	123.9
Rodriguez, Eduardo	29	4	0.1	4.5	58	15.3	119.4
Hernandez, Teoscar	29	16	2.7	27.0	73	10.8	116.0
Snell, Blake	29	8	2.0	16.2	57	14.6	115.4
Woodruff, Brandon	29	12	2.7	22.8	49	14.9	108.8
Sano, Miguel	29	0	-0.8	-3.1	75	7.6	105.5
Anderson, Brian	29	5	0.3	6.4	67	9.4	104.6
Profar, Jurickson	29	19	3.1	31.5	68	6.3	93.1
Musgrove, Joe	29	13	3.2	25.9	46	11.3	91.2
Fulmer, Michael	29	5	0.8	8.1	42	11.5	87.9
Walker, Taijuan	29	10	2.6	20.4	46	10.1	86.4
Davies, Zach	29	5	0.7	7.7	48	9.5	85.8

Hall of Fame Values by Age Group

Player	Age	2022 Season			Career		
		Win Shares	WAR	HoF Value	Win Shares	WAR	HoF Value
Sanchez, Aaron	29	0	-1.0	-3.9	38	8.6	72.5
Franco, Maikel	29	3	-1.1	-1.4	69	0.6	71.5
Bundy, Dylan	29	3	-0.3	1.7	36	8.3	69.1
Bradley, Archie	29	1	-0.4	-0.7	44	5.5	66.0
Montgomery, Jordan	29	11	1.6	17.4	32	8.4	65.5
Alfaro, Jorge	29	6	0.7	8.9	42	3.0	63.9
Barlow, Scott	29	13	2.8	24.2	35	7.0	63.0
Means, John	29	0	0.2	0.8	22	9.8	61.2
Garcia, Adolis	29	19	3.6	33.4	32	7.0	60.1
Montas, Frankie	29	6	1.1	10.4	30	6.6	56.4
Romano, Jordan	29	12	2.9	23.5	29	5.8	52.2
Drury, Brandon	29	17	2.6	27.3	44	2.0	52.0
Slater, Austin	29	10	1.2	14.8	36	3.9	51.5
Pivetta, Nick	29	8	2.6	18.4	26	6.3	51.4
Trout, Mike	**30**	**22**	**6.3**	**47.1**	**341**	**82.4**	**670.4**
Yelich, Christian	30	19	2.7	29.7	194	36.1	338.4
Judge, Aaron	30	45	10.6	87.4	144	37.0	291.8
Bryant, Kris	30	2	0.4	3.6	150	29.1	266.5
Contreras, Willson	30	18	3.9	33.7	94	20.8	210.0
Suarez, Eugenio	30	25	4.0	41.1	132	18.1	204.3
Schoop, Jonathan	30	5	0.2	5.9	106	20.2	187.0
Castellanos, Nick	30	11	-0.1	10.6	135	12.2	183.9
Pederson, Joc	30	20	1.3	25.1	103	11.5	148.9
McNeil, Jeff	30	30	5.7	52.7	77	16.9	144.5
Hernandez, Kike	30	8	0.8	11.2	79	16.2	143.9
Ray, Robbie	30	10	2.1	18.4	73	17.1	141.4
Herrera, Odubel	30	3	0.2	3.8	81	13.4	134.6
Rosario, Eddie	30	2	-1.6	-4.4	86	11.3	131.4
Frazier, Adam	30	12	0.7	15.0	81	12.2	130.0
Grichuk, Randal	30	11	0.3	12.2	83	11.2	127.9
Flores, Wilmer	30	18	0.6	20.5	96	6.9	123.6
Renfroe, Hunter	30	17	2.7	27.7	68	10.7	110.8
Mancini, Trey	30	14	1.3	19.0	67	9.3	104.3
Narvaez, Omar	30	6	0.2	7.0	59	7.0	104.2
Gray, Jon	30	5	1.4	10.5	53	12.3	102.1
Wacha, Michael	30	10	3.3	23.3	57	10.2	98.0
Urshela, Gio	30	16	3.1	28.5	62	8.3	95.4
Taillon, Jameson	30	10	1.2	14.8	45	11.7	91.9
Diaz, Yandy	30	23	3.5	37.0	58	8.2	90.9
Manaea, Sean	30	3	-0.8	-0.4	44	11.3	89.2
Gonzales, Marco	30	6	-0.1	5.7	44	9.8	83.2
Sanchez, Yolmer	30	1	-0.6	-1.6	57	6.3	82.2
Soler, Jorge	30	5	0.4	6.7	64	4.0	79.9
Kemp, Tony	30	15	1.2	19.6	52	4.6	70.4
Lorenzen, Michael	30	5	1.0	9.1	42	7.0	70.2
Knebel, Corey	30	5	0.6	7.2	40	5.6	62.4
Williams, Trevor	30	6	1.5	11.8	34	6.7	60.8
Gamel, Ben	30	12	0.0	11.8	52	1.2	56.9
Owings, Chris	30	1	-0.5	-1.0	46	2.2	54.9
Claudio, Alex	30	0	0.1	0.4	30	6.0	54.0
Pinder, Chad	30	6	-0.8	2.7	37	3.5	50.8
Gallegos, Giovanny	30	8	0.6	10.5	34	4.0	50.1
Arenado, Nolan	**31**	**26**	**7.9**	**57.5**	**202**	**52.1**	**410.5**
Realmuto, J.T.	31	27	6.5	52.8	151	29.8	321.1
Semien, Marcus	31	23	5.7	45.7	163	34.4	300.6
Cole, Gerrit	31	12	2.4	21.5	121	34.1	257.3
Wong, Kolten	31	15	3.2	27.9	129	22.9	220.8
Ozuna, Marcell	31	5	-0.8	1.9	136	20.1	216.4
Myers, Wil	31	8	1.1	12.3	118	13.4	171.7
Muncy, Max	31	16	2.7	26.9	94	17.3	163.2
Taylor, Chris	31	9	0.5	11.0	98	15.6	160.4
Inciarte, Ender	31	0	0.0	-0.1	88	17.9	159.5
Stroman, Marcus	31	7	2.5	17.1	73	21.0	157.0
Gausman, Kevin	31	11	3.0	23.1	74	19.8	153.2
Haniger, Mitch	31	8	1.4	13.7	85	15.4	146.8
Villar, Jonathan	31	4	-1.2	-0.8	96	12.2	144.6
Garcia, Avisail	31	2	-1.1	-2.3	94	9.8	133.2
Zunino, Mike	31	2	-0.8	-1.3	70	9.8	131.1
Barnhart, Tucker	31	5	0.0	5.0	70	7.1	117.5
Wood, Alex	31	3	0.3	4.0	59	13.0	111.2
Perez, Martin	31	13	5.0	33.1	60	12.2	109.0
Clevinger, Mike	31	5	0.7	7.6	53	13.9	108.4
Vazquez, Christian	31	12	2.1	20.3	63	7.0	108.2

Hall of Fame Values by Age Group

Player	Age	2022 Season			Career		
		Win Shares	WAR	HoF Value	Win Shares	WAR	HoF Value
Piscotty, Stephen	31	3	-0.8	-0.1	79	6.4	104.8
Duffy, Matt	31	5	-0.4	3.4	65	8.9	100.8
Taylor, Michael A.	31	9	3.2	21.8	57	9.3	94.1
Hamilton, Billy	31	0	-0.1	-0.5	54	10.0	93.8
Diaz, Aledmys	31	8	1.0	11.9	58	8.5	92.1
Yastrzemski, Mike	31	12	2.0	19.9	52	9.6	90.6
Marisnick, Jake	31	1	0.2	2.0	43	11.6	89.3
Garver, Mitch	31	3	0.4	4.6	43	7.7	87.7
Lamb, Jake	31	0	-0.2	-0.8	56	7.2	84.7
Giles, Ken	31	1	0.2	1.7	53	7.8	84.3
Walker, Christian	31	19	5.1	39.4	47	8.8	82.1
Voit, Luke	31	10	0.8	13.3	53	5.7	75.6
Matz, Steven	31	1	-0.3	-0.4	37	9.0	73.1
Choi, Ji-Man	31	16	1.1	20.4	52	5.1	72.6
Graveman, Kendall	31	7	1.0	10.9	39	8.3	72.2
Green, Chad	31	1	0.1	1.2	39	8.1	71.3
Rogers, Taylor	31	6	-0.7	3.3	45	5.5	66.8
Boyd, Matthew	31	2	0.4	3.8	33	8.1	65.6
Miller, Shelby	31	0	-0.2	-0.8	35	7.4	64.4
Garcia, Leury	31	3	-1.0	-0.9	48	4.0	63.9
Naquin, Tyler	31	6	-0.1	5.7	46	3.4	59.6
Spangenberg, Cory	31	0	0.0	0.0	37	4.7	55.7
Heaney, Andrew	31	4	0.7	6.7	31	6.0	55.0
Cooper, Garrett	31	12	1.0	16.1	37	4.3	54.2
Diaz, Elias	31	6	0.4	7.5	32	3.0	52.7
Plawecki, Kevin	31	3	-1.2	-1.8	35	2.3	52.7
Freeman, Freddie	**32**	**34**	**5.9**	**57.6**	**304**	**49.0**	**499.9**
Altuve, Jose	32	29	5.1	49.6	254	46.5	440.1
Stanton, Giancarlo	32	12	0.7	14.8	207	44.7	386.0
Rizzo, Anthony	32	15	2.3	24.2	222	39.1	378.6
Perez, Salvador	32	18	2.7	28.8	175	32.3	364.5
Heyward, Jason	32	1	-0.6	-1.6	183	38.7	337.8
Rendon, Anthony	32	5	1.0	9.1	167	33.2	299.8
Springer, George	32	20	4.0	36.1	155	34.2	291.8
Bumgarner, Madison	32	3	-0.8	-0.1	132	37.3	281.3
Simmons, Andrelton	32	1	-0.2	0.1	130	37.1	278.4
Segura, Jean	32	10	1.8	17.1	164	28.1	276.4
Hosmer, Eric	32	9	1.1	13.2	185	19.2	261.6
Kiermaier, Kevin	32	7	1.1	11.4	95	31.8	222.2
Gregorius, Didi	32	5	-0.4	3.2	121	17.8	192.4
Gray, Sonny	32	9	2.3	18.3	89	24.7	187.9
Hernandez, Cesar	32	11	0.7	13.7	131	13.1	183.4
Wheeler, Zack	32	13	5.0	33.2	74	26.2	178.8
Hendricks, Kyle	32	2	0.5	4.1	84	22.8	175.1
Bradley Jr., Jackie	32	4	-0.5	2.1	89	17.3	158.1
Iglesias, Jose	32	11	1.2	15.6	106	11.7	152.8
Cron, C.J.	32	16	2.1	24.4	101	12.9	152.6
Grossman, Robbie	32	11	0.3	12.0	101	9.7	139.8
Hicks, Aaron	32	9	1.8	16.1	80	14.0	136.2
Corbin, Patrick	32	0	-2.5	-9.9	72	14.8	131.0
Iglesias, Raisel	32	10	1.6	16.3	76	13.0	127.8
Eovaldi, Nathan	32	6	1.5	12.1	58	16.1	122.4
Odorizzi, Jake	32	4	-0.1	3.6	65	12.8	116.2
McCann, James	32	4	-0.1	3.5	69	6.8	115.4
Miller, Brad	32	4	-1.6	-2.4	88	6.4	113.4
Wendle, Joey	32	10	2.5	20.1	58	13.8	113.4
Ahmed, Nick	32	1	-0.1	0.8	62	12.4	111.5
Shaw, Travis	32	0	-0.7	-2.6	72	8.3	105.4
Hand, Brad	32	5	0.9	8.6	69	7.6	99.4
Anderson, Tyler	32	15	4.3	32.1	46	12.4	95.5
Familia, Jeurys	32	0	-0.7	-2.8	58	6.8	85.0
Aguilar, Jesus	32	8	-1.1	3.8	67	4.0	83.1
Smith, Will	32	2	-0.6	-0.3	57	5.9	80.4
Givens, Mychal	32	4	0.8	7.4	43	9.2	79.8
Lugo, Seth	32	5	0.8	8.0	40	9.2	77.0
DeSclafani, Anthony	32	0	-0.8	-3.1	39	9.4	76.5
Stripling, Ross	32	10	2.7	20.9	37	7.6	67.3
Peterson, Jace	32	8	2.3	17.4	52	3.6	66.4
Chafin, Andrew	32	5	0.3	6.2	37	6.8	64.2
Stallings, Jacob	32	8	-0.7	5.1	32	5.3	63.6
Barnes, Matt	32	3	0.2	3.8	42	4.8	61.2
Nola, Austin	32	9	1.9	16.6	32	5.5	61.2
Barnes, Austin	32	4	0.8	7.0	32	5.0	61.0
Beckham, Tim	32	0	-0.5	-2.2	45	3.2	57.9

Hall of Fame Values by Age Group

| Player | Age | 2022 Season | | | Career | | |
		Win Shares	WAR	HoF Value	Win Shares	WAR	HoF Value
Ramirez, Erasmo	32	5	1.5	10.9	33	5.0	52.8
Suter, Brent	32	4	0.3	5.0	30	5.2	51.0
Andrus, Elvis	**33**	**18**	**3.0**	**30.2**	**230**	**33.5**	**363.9**
Sale, Chris	33	0	0.0	0.1	148	46.5	333.8
Marte, Starling	33	17	3.8	32.0	175	38.6	329.4
LeMahieu, DJ	33	14	3.8	29.4	177	30.4	298.5
Grandal, Yasmani	33	4	-1.5	-2.0	141	20.2	262.3
Strasburg, Stephen	33	0	-0.3	-1.2	108	32.9	239.7
Quintana, Jose	33	13	3.5	26.8	103	27.1	211.3
Merrifield, Whit	33	12	0.0	12.1	114	17.2	182.6
Escobar, Eduardo	33	12	1.2	16.6	125	13.0	177.1
Moustakas, Mike	33	3	-1.0	-1.0	117	12.9	168.4
Dickerson, Corey	33	7	0.1	7.6	95	13.9	150.4
Pillar, Kevin	33	0	-0.2	-0.6	81	16.3	146.3
Canha, Mark	33	19	2.4	28.4	94	12.3	143.1
Gonzalez, Marwin	33	1	0.8	4.3	85	14.3	142.2
Rojas, Miguel	33	13	2.5	23.1	78	12.9	129.5
d'Arnaud, Travis	33	16	2.8	27.4	74	7.2	122.7
Archer, Chris	33	2	0.0	2.0	65	13.1	117.4
Duvall, Adam	33	7	-0.1	6.5	69	10.3	110.4
Pineda, Michael	33	0	-0.6	-2.4	54	12.0	102.1
Bassitt, Chris	33	12	3.2	25.0	49	13.2	101.9
Hendriks, Liam	33	11	1.7	17.9	64	9.2	100.8
Smyly, Drew	33	6	1.9	13.4	52	12.0	99.9
Perez, Roberto	33	2	0.6	4.2	50	8.1	98.8
Pressly, Ryan	33	10	0.9	13.6	60	9.7	98.8
Lagares, Juan	33	0	-0.9	-3.6	48	11.2	93.0
Colome, Alex	33	2	-0.9	-1.6	66	6.0	89.9
Neris, Hector	33	6	0.5	8.0	56	8.0	88.0
Casali, Curt	33	5	1.5	10.8	34	6.6	71.8
Moore, Matt	33	8	2.4	17.7	44	6.7	70.8
Mikolas, Miles	33	12	2.4	21.7	40	7.6	70.4
Souza Jr., Steven	33	0	-0.3	-1.2	41	5.1	61.5
La Stella, Tommy	33	2	-0.7	-0.9	47	3.6	61.4
Kelly, Merrill	33	14	3.5	28.1	30	7.4	59.8
Peralta, Wily	33	4	0.7	6.7	42	4.0	58.2
Strickland, Hunter	33	4	0.1	4.3	35	4.8	54.2
Leon, Sandy	33	1	-0.4	-0.8	39	1.1	52.1
Alvarez, Jose	33	1	-0.1	0.7	32	4.5	50.2
Kershaw, Clayton	**34**	**12**	**3.8**	**27.0**	**227**	**75.7**	**529.6**
Goldschmidt, Paul	34	34	7.8	65.2	285	58.5	518.9
Upton, Justin	34	0	-0.3	-1.4	211	32.3	340.4
Martinez, J.D.	34	10	1.1	14.4	183	27.9	294.7
deGrom, Jacob	34	5	1.4	10.8	113	44.9	292.8
Belt, Brandon	34	4	0.3	5.4	164	27.6	274.3
Kimbrel, Craig	34	7	0.2	7.8	143	22.1	231.3
Jansen, Kenley	34	11	0.9	14.6	151	19.5	228.9
Pollock, A.J.	34	8	0.6	10.2	123	23.3	216.2
Chapman, Aroldis	34	3	-0.2	2.2	126	19.0	202.0
Gomes, Yan	34	4	0.8	7.1	87	17.7	188.0
Harrison, Josh	34	9	1.4	14.5	114	17.5	184.1
Calhoun, Kole	34	5	-1.5	-1.1	120	14.0	176.2
Peralta, David	34	15	0.7	17.7	113	15.0	172.9
Keuchel, Dallas	34	0	-2.6	-10.4	89	19.5	166.9
Strange-Gordon, Dee	34	1	-0.4	-0.4	106	12.6	156.5
Chacin, Jhoulys	34	0	-1.4	-5.7	78	19.1	154.5
Pham, Tommy	34	9	0.4	10.5	86	16.4	151.6
Minor, Mike	34	1	-0.6	-1.4	73	18.1	145.2
Britton, Zack	34	0	-0.1	-0.3	85	14.0	140.9
Cobb, Alex	34	8	2.6	18.5	67	16.9	134.5
Gibson, Kyle	34	5	0.6	7.4	69	13.5	123.1
Treinen, Blake	34	1	0.2	1.6	60	10.4	101.6
Richards, Garrett	34	1	-0.4	-0.6	52	8.2	84.6
Solano, Donovan	34	7	0.8	10.4	63	4.8	82.3
Wilson, Justin	34	0	0.1	0.5	46	7.5	75.8
Anderson, Chase	34	0	-0.2	-0.8	46	7.3	75.2
Shaw, Bryan	34	1	-0.9	-2.7	55	4.9	74.5
Kelly, Joe	34	0	-0.6	-2.4	48	5.9	71.7
Loup, Aaron	34	2	-0.9	-1.6	38	6.8	65.0
Boxberger, Brad	34	6	1.1	10.2	45	4.2	61.7
Tepera, Ryan	34	6	0.6	8.5	33	5.5	55.0
McCutchen, Andrew	**35**	**12**	**1.1**	**16.4**	**311**	**47.1**	**499.2**

Hall of Fame Values by Age Group

Player	Age	2022 Season			Career		
		Win Shares	WAR	HoF Value	Win Shares	WAR	HoF Value
Brantley, Michael	35	10	1.3	15.2	190	34.2	326.8
Abreu, Jose	35	21	4.2	37.7	187	31.9	314.6
Crawford, Brandon	35	11	0.6	13.3	184	30.7	306.8
Blackmon, Charlie	35	12	-0.2	11.2	181	19.3	258.1
Lynn, Lance	35	6	0.8	9.1	111	30.1	231.5
Darvish, Yu	35	15	4.5	32.9	102	30.9	225.8
Carrasco, Carlos	35	8	1.3	13.1	96	21.7	183.0
Escobar, Alcides	35	3	-0.5	0.9	128	10.0	168.0
Castro, Jason	35	1	-0.6	-1.5	86	12.4	162.6
Miley, Wade	35	2	0.0	2.2	83	16.5	149.0
Ryu, Hyun-Jin	35	1	-0.3	-0.2	70	19.2	146.8
Maldonado, Martin	35	8	0.2	8.7	76	7.5	126.5
McHugh, Collin	35	7	2.0	14.9	66	12.8	117.0
Hunter, Tommy	35	2	0.3	3.3	71	11.4	116.7
Doolittle, Sean	35	1	0.4	2.5	66	10.3	107.0
McGee, Jake	35	0	-1.1	-4.5	65	7.2	93.7
Hudson, Daniel	35	4	0.6	6.4	60	7.2	88.9
Phelps, David	35	5	1.1	9.6	45	7.4	74.4
Pina, Manny	35	0	-0.1	-0.4	36	6.3	73.6
Diekman, Jake	35	3	-0.3	1.7	40	3.6	54.5
Milone, Tommy	35	0	-0.2	-0.6	37	4.3	54.4
Yates, Kirby	35	0	-0.1	-0.2	33	4.4	50.8
Longoria, Evan	**36**	**9**	**0.6**	**11.6**	**251**	**58.0**	**483.1**
Donaldson, Josh	36	12	2.4	21.4	216	46.7	403.6
Santana, Carlos	36	12	1.2	16.8	216	32.8	362.4
Price, David	36	4	0.7	7.0	152	41.0	316.1
Carpenter, Matt	36	11	2.4	20.4	199	29.2	315.8
Cain, Lorenzo	36	1	-0.2	0.1	155	38.4	308.8
Cueto, Johnny	36	11	3.5	24.8	144	36.4	289.5
Kluber, Corey	36	5	0.6	7.5	119	34.3	256.0
Cishek, Steve	36	3	0.3	4.2	88	13.6	142.4
Holland, Greg	36	0	-0.3	-1.2	90	12.4	139.5
Ottavino, Adam	36	9	2.3	18.0	70	13.8	125.2
Scherzer, Max	**37**	**14**	**5.3**	**35.1**	**219**	**72.3**	**508.3**
Turner, Justin	37	19	1.9	26.5	194	34.6	332.2
Robertson, David	37	10	2.6	20.5	106	18.3	179.2
Kennedy, Ian	37	1	-1.1	-3.5	100	17.0	167.8
Clippard, Tyler	37	0	-0.1	-0.2	97	16.1	161.4
Melancon, Mark	37	3	-0.9	-0.4	108	13.1	160.4
Vogt, Stephen	37	2	-0.6	-0.6	62	7.0	104.7
Bard, Daniel	37	16	3.8	31.0	50	8.4	83.7
Votto, Joey	**38**	**7**	**-0.3**	**6.0**	**340**	**64.3**	**597.4**
Greinke, Zack	38	6	2.5	15.8	242	75.6	544.2
Suzuki, Kurt	38	1	-0.4	-0.7	143	19.5	265.2
Sanchez, Anibal	38	3	0.8	6.4	103	27.8	214.1
Lowrie, Jed	38	0	-1.2	-4.9	147	15.8	210.1
Gurriel, Yuli	38	9	-0.3	7.7	89	13.5	142.9
Morton, Charlie	38	7	1.6	13.4	88	13.4	141.8
Chirinos, Robinson	38	5	0.0	4.9	64	12.6	137.1
Smith, Joe	38	0	-0.6	-2.4	78	13.0	129.9
Stammen, Craig	38	1	-0.1	0.5	64	9.7	102.9
Chavez, Jesse	38	5	0.4	6.6	52	4.7	70.8
Cabrera, Miguel	**39**	**8**	**-1.0**	**4.0**	**428**	**67.7**	**699.0**
Cano, Robinson	39	0	-1.5	-5.9	349	68.1	621.4
Verlander, Justin	39	20	5.9	43.8	258	77.7	568.8
Molina, Yadier	39	4	0.0	4.1	301	42.1	561.3
O'Day, Darren	39	1	0.1	1.3	75	17.5	144.8
Romo, Sergio	39	0	-0.7	-2.8	90	9.7	128.9
Wainwright, Adam	**40**	**10**	**1.8**	**17.4**	**182**	**46.5**	**367.8**
Perez, Oliver	40	0	-0.7	-2.7	72	10.6	114.5
Cruz, Nelson	**41**	**7**	**0.2**	**7.6**	**266**	**42.6**	**436.3**
Pujols, Albert	**42**	**13**	**2.0**	**21.2**	**507**	**101.6**	**913.4**
Hill, Rich	42	6	0.9	9.4	80	16.5	146.0

Potential Players on 2023 Hall of Fame Ballot

Player	Win Shares	WAR	HOF Value	HOF Monitor
Rodriguez, Alex	491	117.5	961.1	283
Ramirez, Manny	408	69.3	685.2	169
Sheffield, Gary	430	60.5	672.2	103
Beltran, Carlos	369	70.1	649.4	110
Abreu, Bobby	356	60.2	596.7	76
Rolen, Scott	304	70.1	584.4	82
Helton, Todd	318	61.8	565.0	128
Kent, Jeff	339	55.4	560.8	94
Jones, Andruw	276	62.7	526.8	57
Rollins, Jimmy	303	47.6	493.4	89
Hunter, Torii	277	50.6	479.6	42
Pettitte, Andy	224	60.2	464.9	104
Vizquel, Omar	282	45.6	464.3	72
Buehrle, Mark	220	59.1	456.2	76
Peralta, Jhonny	212	30.4	333.6	27
Werth, Jayson	207	29.2	323.8	25
Lackey, John	170	37.3	319.0	61
Wagner, Billy	182	27.7	292.8	81
Ellsbury, Jacoby	164	31.2	288.6	42
Weaver, Jered	145	34.6	283.5	54
Hardy, J.J.	166	28.1	278.2	26
Napoli, Mike	141	26.3	268.0	30
Ruiz, Carlos	133	22.5	267.5	13
Rodriguez, Francisco	168	24.1	264.4	89
Ethier, Andre	172	21.5	258.0	23
Hill, Aaron	159	24.4	256.4	28
Aybar, Erick	145	22.8	236.1	13
Cain, Matt	114	29.1	230.4	39
Arroyo, Bronson	127	23.4	220.7	40
Dickey, R.A.	109	23.7	203.6	43
Drew, Stephen	131	15.9	194.7	16
Street, Huston	125	14.5	182.8	42
Lind, Adam	132	12.7	182.8	17
Jimenez, Ubaldo	94	20.4	175.6	27
Benoit, Joaquin	103	17.9	174.5	22
Blanton, Joe	83	11.9	130.4	26
Broxton, Jonathan	79	8.7	113.8	25
Perkins, Glen	61	8.9	96.4	21
Qualls, Chad	73	5.8	96.0	21
Grilli, Jason	53	4.6	71.5	15

In Memoriam – Vin Scully

Mark Simon

One of the assignments in my high school forensics class was to do a comprehensive analysis of any voices that intrigued you. You could focus on the sound of their voice, the way they spoke, the words they chose, or anything else that struck you.

I remember writing two such analyses. One was on James Earl Jones. The other was on Vin Scully.

I don't remember exactly what I wrote but I'm trying to recreate it here.

Scully's voice is calm. If you were going to the dentist, it would be a voice that relaxed you. He could just as easily be a pastor delivering sermons as a baseball announcer providing descriptions. It rises with the moment. There's no accent. It's like he's reading poetry. When people call the Dodgers offices and get put on hold there's no music. It's just Vin Scully doing highlights. His voice is beloved internationally. The top baseball broadcasters in Japan and Venezuela have done their calls in Scully's style.

One of Scully's lesser-known broadcasts (he has so many well-known ones!) was Game 7 of the 1991 World Series between the Braves and Twins for CBS Radio. Just before the last pitch of the game, which was struck for a walk-off single, he noted "You can almost taste the pressure …"

Taste the pressure.

Who tastes pressure? You feel pressure. You don't taste it.

But it sounds so perfect coming from Scully's voice. Of course, we taste pressure. Because Vin Scully says we do.

There were so many famous calls.

Hank Aaron's record-breaking home run

"A Black man is getting a standing ovation in the deep south for breaking the record of an all-time baseball idol."

Kirk Gibson's dramatic home run in 1988

"She is gone!"

Sometimes the best choice was no words at all. After the ball rolled through Bill Buckner's legs to end the Mets amazing comeback in Game 6 of the 1986 World Series, Scully made his call:

"Here comes Knight and the Mets win it!"

This time Scully went silent for 3 minutes and 23 seconds. He then returned to say:

"If one picture is worth a thousand words, you have seen about a million words. But more than that, you have seen an absolutely bizarre finish to Game 6 of the 1986 World Series. The Mets are not only alive, they are well, and they will play the Red Sox in Game 7 tomorrow."

We were treated to an alive and well Vin Scully for nearly 95 years and 67 seasons in the broadcast booth. He said well more than a million words. And he was flawless.

Can you ever recall Vin Scully saying "um?"

And his voice never changed. You can go on YouTube and find clips of Scully calling games in every decade of his career. The consistency is remarkable. The lasting legacy of Scully is in his voice and his words. He shall be forever remembered for both.

Vin Scully died on August 2, 2022 at age 94.

In Memoriam – Bruce Sutter

In the days before every reliever threw 99 MPH, a pitcher closing games without such a pitch needed some trickery in order to be effective.

For Bruce Sutter, that meant putting the split-fingered fastball to use.

That pitch made Sutter baseball's premier closer for the eight seasons spanning 1977 to 1984. In that time, Sutter led the NL in saves five times in six years, twice for the Cubs and three times for the Cardinals, including their World Series-winning 1982 season. He finished within the top eight in the NL MVP voting five times and won a Cy Young Award in 1979.

Sutter developed the splitter in the Cubs organization, then refined it under pitching coach Mike Roarke, who worked for both the Cubs and Cardinals.

Sutter used it in an era in which closing usually meant pitching more than one inning. He threw 100 innings in relief five times (in fact, he never started a game).

Sutter ranks tied for 30th all time with 300 career saves. But his 188 saves of more than one inning trail only his fellow Hall of Famers Rollie Fingers (201) and Rich Gossage (193).

His legacy is that of a great, trendsetting pitcher. Sutter has an off-the-field legacy too.

He set himself and his family up, and inspired future generations of MLB contracts, with his free agent deal with the Atlanta Braves, one that included 30 years of deferred payments of more than $1 million per year. It concluded in 2022.

Bruce Sutter died on October 13, 2022 at age 69.

In Memoriam

Other notable people who passed away since the publication of last year's Handbook include:

Julio Cruz, who stole 343 bases in a 10-year career with the Mariners and White Sox. **Tommy Davis**, a two-time batting champion who totaled 2,121 hits in an 18-year MLB career. **Pedro Feliciano**, who earned the nickname "Perpetual Pedro" for his frequent appearances. **Jeremy Giambi**, an outfielder/DH on two A's playoff teams in the early 2000s and the brother of slugger Jason Giambi. **Joe Horlen** who pitched a no-hitter for the White Sox in 1967, when he also led the AL in ERA. **LaMarr Hoyt**, who won a Cy Young Award with the White Sox in 1983. **Doug Jones**, who used a nasty changeup to record 303 saves in 16 seasons. **Mark Littell**, a top reliever from 1976 to 1979 who was on two AL West-winning Royals teams and is best remembered for allowing a pennant-winning homer to Chris Chambliss. **Julio Lugo**, the starting shortstop for the 2007 World Series winning Red Sox. **Leo Posada**, a star Cuban athlete who played three seasons in MLB and then managed in the minor leagues. His nephew, Jorge Posada, became a star with the Yankees. **Jerry Remy**, a beloved Red Sox second baseman and longtime broadcaster. **Dick Schofield**, who played 19 MLB seasons and had a son of the same name who became a longtime major leaguer. **Ralph Terry**, who pitched the 1962 Yankees to a 1-0 win in Game 7 of the World Series against the Giants, two years after giving up a Series-ending walk-off home run to Bill Mazeroski. **Lee Thomas,** who won a pennant as GM of the 1993 Phillies. **Anthony Varvaro**, who retired after a six-year MLB career to become a police officer. **Bill Virdon**, who won a World Series with the 1960 Pirates and later managed the Pirates and Astros to division titles. Five time All-Star shortstop **Maury Wills**, who set a then-MLB record with 104 stolen bases for the 1962 Dodgers, and led the NL in steals for six straight seasons. Well-liked former Yankees outfielder **Gerald Williams**, who also had a key hit and scored the NL pennant-winning run for the 1999 Braves. **John Wockenfuss**, a 12-year major leaguer, who sported an unusual batting stance in which he stood as far back in the batter's box as he could.

Run Participation and Run Creation

Bill James

This article, and the research supporting it, grew out of a Twitter discussion before the trade deadline, when I was periodically deriding the notion that Andrew Benintendi would be a valuable addition to a contending team. At the time he was traded from the Royals to the Yankees, KC had played 98 games; Benintendi had scored 40 runs and driven in 39. He was on pace to score 66 runs by season's end and drive in 64. Those are not good numbers. He had a .320 batting average, yes, but with a secondary average of .202. Secondary average is a summation of power, walks and stolen bases. Benintendi's then-teammate M. J. Melendez at that time was hitting .228, but with a secondary average over .300. He was driving in and scoring runs at a more rapid pace than Benintendi was, with the same team. A Twitterspat developed in which others were arguing that Benintendi was only driving in and scoring two runs a week because he was playing on a weak offensive team, and I was arguing that he was only driving in and scoring two runs a week because his .320 batting average was an empty shell.

I was being hoisted here upon my own petard. It would help me out if I actually knew what a petard was, or is. Do you have any petards in your house? How about a hoist? The expression "hoisted on your own petard", which may be archaic, means that you have become the victim of your own argument, or your own weapon. Decades ago, I was the one telling people to stop paying attention to Runs Scored and RBI, but to focus instead on what the batter himself has done. At one time I was virtually the ONLY person in the baseball writing universe who would make that argument. Now, that position is SO dominant that if you cite runs scored and RBI—even appropriately—somebody will ridicule you for it.

In the midst of this twitterspat, someone—actually a very nice person who was simply trying to have a fair discussion—wrote to me "but isn't it true that Runs Scored and RBI are mostly a creation of the players hitting around you?" I responded instinctively, "Well, no, that's not remotely true." But then it occurred to me: I don't really know, do I?

I had spotted a gap in my understanding of the game. This is what I live for. My life's work has been to spot gaps in my understanding of the game or my understanding of something else, and figure out how to fix those gaps, how to plaster some actual knowledge into that gap. That's what I do, that's who I am, that's why you know who I am. I have never actually studied the relationship between a player's runs scored/RBI and his run creation. As far as I know, no one has ever studied it. It's a gopher hole in our putting green, a pot hole on our highway, a rip in our underwear. Somebody needs to fix it.

For the rest of this article I will often refer to Runs + RBI as "Run Participation".

My first effort to study the issue was to do a matched-set comparison. Essentially, I was trying to identify sets of players who hit the same number of singles, the same number of doubles, triples, homers, drew the same number of walks and stole the same number of bases, but one of whom played for a good team and the other of whom played for some bunch of losers. I love doing matched-set studies, because it is just fun to see who turns up matched with who. It has probably never occurred to you, I am guessing, to pair up Ken McMullen, 1969, with Hector Lopez in 1956, but McMullen in 1969 was 153-for-562, and Lopez in 1956 was 153-for-561. McMullen had 25 doubles, 2 triples and 19 homers, whereas Lopez had 27-3-18, which is pretty much the same. McMullen had 239 total bases, Lopez had 240. There's a small difference in walks (70-63), but both players stole 4 bases and were caught stealing 5 times. They're a match.

After working on this problem for two or three days, I had identified 300 matches like this—Patsy Tebeau in 1894 with Homer Smoot in 1904, for example. Tommy Harper in 1971 and Jason Kipnis in 2012. My assumption was that if you took two players who had almost exactly the same numbers of singles, doubles, triples and everything, then you could identify those who played for strong offensive teams and those who played for the Wimps and the Weenies, and you could measure the extent to which playing for a good team increases a player's run participation rate.

That was what I was trying to do, but I didn't know exactly HOW I was going to do it. I was in "I'll cross that bridge when I come to it" mode, but when I actually came to that point. . . no bridge. I couldn't figure out a good way to complete the study. I had just wasted two or three days, although, you know, when you meet Homer Smoot in your research, it is never truly a wasted day.

Then it occurred to me that there was a better way to study it. One of the implicated issues here is the effect of batting third, let's say, as opposed to the effect of batting leadoff, or batting eighth. What I did next, then, was to go to Retrosheet and copy out teams' "splits" for hitters who hit first, second, third, fourth. . . .ninth, etc. I did that for every major league team in the years 2010 to 2021, a total of 330 teams, or 2,970 batting lines. (11 seasons, 30 teams per season, 9 batting lines per team, 11 X 30 X 9 = 2970.)

We're no longer dealing with individual players now, we're now dealing with batting lines compiled somewhat by a mix of players, but that's actually slightly better for what we are studying. We're studying what the effects of the OTHER players are on the focus player's runs and RBI. Any peculiarities of the individual player, such as for example if he is an exceptionally good or exceptionally bad baserunner.. ..anything like that is a screen obscuring what we are really trying to measure. Using mixes of players, rather than individual players, gives a slightly cleaner look at the issue—plus, each line of the study now represents 162 complete games, rather than sometimes 155 games and sometimes 109, which is also better for the study.

Then I figured the Runs Created by the batting stats at each position. For example, the leadoff men for the Houston Astros in 2019 hit .276, but with 50 homers, 89 walks, 134 Runs Scored, 122 RBI. 133 Runs Created. I think that was mostly George Springer. The key numbers there are 133 Runs Created, 134 Runs Scored, 122 RBI.

The first thing we have to establish here is the normal relationship of Runs Participated In to Runs Created. For every 100 Runs Created there are 100 Runs Scored and 95 RBI, so the overall ratio is 1.95 to 1.

This ratio, however, is not the same for cleanup hitters as it is for 8th place hitters, for example. Well, actually it pretty much is.

The ratio of Runs Created to Run Participation is essentially the same for the 2nd through the 8th spots in the batting order. The ratio of Runs/RBI to Runs Created for cleanup hitters is 1.98 to 1. For 8th place hitters, it is 1.98 to 1. Third-place hitters have a 4% disadvantage in terms of run participation, a little bit less than 4%; second-place hitters are at a 3% disadvantage. No other position, 4 through 8, has an advantage or disadvantage as large as 2%.

Leadoff hitters, however, are at a small but meaningful disadvantage. The 330 leadoff "hitters"—actually the leadoff positions for the 330 teams. Anyway, the leadoff men created an average of 93 runs, based on their individual batting stats. They scored an average of 102 runs but, for reasons you can figure out yourself unless you are secretly Dan Shaughnessy, they drove in an average of only 65. That's a ratio of 1.80 Runs Participated in for each Run Created, which is 8% below the norm of 1.95. Leadoff hitters are at an 8% disadvantage in the RBI/Runs Scored categories, all of which is in the RBI portion, of course.

Batting Order Position	Runs	RBI	RC	Ratio
Leadoff	102	65	93	1.80
Second Place	96	74	90	1.89
Third Place	93	95	100	1.88
Cleanup	86	99	94	1.98
Fifth Place	80	87	84	1.99
Sixth Place	72	77	76	1.95
Seventh Place	66	70	69	1.96
Eighth Place	63	62	63	1.98
Ninth Place	54	49	43	2.41
9--American	64	56	55	2.16
9--National	46	44	33	2.77

And ninth place hitters have a 24% advantage in Run Participation, actually 11% in the American League and 42% in the National League.

Very weak hitters have somewhat non-representative runs scored and RBI, because it IS a shared activity. A hard worker and a lazy man go into business together and split the income, the lazy man will be overpaid and the hard worker will be underpaid. Same thing. When a good hitter and a bad hitter combine to create runs, the bad hitter gets more than his share of Run Participation. I will refer to that as the good hitter/weak hitter effect.

OK, we're creeping toward a better understanding of this, but what we are trying to get to is discrepancy vs. expectation. A player, by his own production, creates an *expectation* for how many runs he should participate in. That expectation is 1.95 times his runs created. But, because of his circumstances, his teammates and his batting order position and other things, he won't exactly meet expectation. That's the *discrepancy*. **What we are asking here is, to what extent are the player's run participation totals created by expectation, and to what extent are they created by the discrepancy?** You can call it expectation and discrepancy, or you can call it production and context; in this discussion it means broadly the same thing. Did Andrew Benintendi not participate in very many runs mostly because of expectation (his production), or because of discrepancy (context)? If it is 70/30 discrepancy, then we should barely glance at runs scored and RBI totals as we are on the way to the hotdog stand. But if it is 20/80 toward expectation, then the people who say we shouldn't pay any attention to Runs and RBI are missing out on valuable information.

I'll give you a temporary, first-hit answer to that question. Of the variance in run participation between different hitters, 65% is created by the variance in productivity (that is, created by expectation) and 35% is created by all other factors. How do we know that?

Well, the 2,970 "players" created an average of 79 runs, and the variation between expected runs and actual run participation (discrepancy) is an average of 16 runs, so that would suggest that the answer is 83% expectation, 17% discrepancy. That, however, is the wrong way to look at the data. What we need to look at is not how many of the runs are created this way or that way, but how much of the difference between one hitter and another hitter is explained in this way (expectation or performance) or that way (discrepancy or context.) What we need to look at is not the average of runs, but the standard deviation.

The average is 79 runs created (per batting order slot), but with a standard deviation of 23.65. The average discrepancy from expected run participation is 20.49, but that has been "stretched out" by the fact that we have multiplied runs created by 1.95 in order to create that figure, so it's no longer on the same scale as runs created. Adjusting for that problem, the standard deviation of the discrepancy is 12.79. . . .I don't know if this is making any sense to you any more, but if you read it three or four times it should. So the relevant figures are:

Standard deviation of expectation (productivity):   23.65

Standard deviation of discrepancy (context):   12.79

So our estimate, at this point, is the split is 65/35. We would currently estimate that 65% of a player's run production is based on his own productivity, and 35% is based on other factors. But we're not to the end of the road yet. As a parenthetical aside, the discrepancy does not INCREASE the standard deviation of Runs Participated In; it decreases it. It decreases it because of the good hitter/ weak hitter effect. A great hitter will have a lower ratio of RPI to runs created than a weak hitter, which pushes everybody toward the center, which decreases the standard deviation of runs participated in.

But as I said, we're not at the end of the road yet. What we have here is the discrepancy—in other words, the difference between the number of runs we would expect the player to participate in vs. the number he actually participated in. But there are many different things that contribute to that discrepancy. There are really three categories of things that can cause a player to participate in more runs than expected or fewer runs than expected:

1) Special characteristics of the player, such as baserunning or perfor- mance with runners in scoring position,
2) Luck, or
3) Playing for a good hitting or weak hitting team.

We are only interested in Category 3. Did Andrew Benintendi not participate in very many runs with Kansas City because the KC offense was poor, or was it something else?

Here's how we can study that. Suppose that we divide the candidates into a 7 by 6 matrix—seven layers of hitters, and six layers of teams. Group 1A is the best hitters (that is, the strongest batting slots) who created the most runs by their own actions, and who play for the teams that score the most runs. Group 1B is the best hitters, who play for good-hitting teams but not THE BEST hitting teams. Group 1F is really good hitters playing for really weak-hitting teams, while Group 6A is very weak hitters playing for good hitting teams. These are the charts that were used:

Hitters Group	Runs Created
1	104 or more
2	93 to 103
3	85 to 92
4	77 to 84
5	69 to 76
6	57 to 68
7	Up to 56

Team Group	Runs Scored
A	785 or more
B	739 to 784
C	712 to 738
D	677 to 711
E	635 to 676
F	up to 634

So a hitter in Study Group 3A would be a "hitter" (actually a batting order position) who created 85 to 92 runs, playing on a team that scored 785 or more runs, whereas a hitter in group 3F would be a hitter who created 85 to 92 runs, but playing on a team that scored 634 or fewer runs. The question is, what is the effect on the player's Run Participation of playing on a good-hitting team, as opposed to a weak-hitting team?

Since we are talking 3A and 3F. . . .3A is somewhat above-average hitter who plays for a team that scores lots of runs, and 3F is a somewhat above-average hitter who plays for a team which scores very few runs. There are 66 players in the study in group 3A, and 59 players in group 3F. This chart gives the number of players (positional batting lines) represented in each of the 42 cadres of the study:

1A	1B	1C	1D	1E	1F
158	104	70	37	36	12

2A	2B	2C	2D	2E	2F
86	86	85	70	54	32

3A	3B	3C	3D	3E	3F
66	76	65	72	74	59

4A	4B	4C	4D	4E	4F
40	84	77	80	78	79

5A	5B	5C	5D	5E	5F
57	49	61	67	70	90

6A	6B	6C	6D	6E	6F
47	59	66	84	99	115

7A	7B	7C	7D	7E	7F
31	56	71	67	84	117

That will show you that there are more good hitters on teams that score more runs, but you probably could have figured that out on your own.

The real work here is to compare the Run Participation Numbers for players of essentially the same offensive quality. We'll start with 3A and 3F:

Group	RC	RPI
3A	88.5	178.6
3F	88.4	157.2

The 66 players in Group 3A created an average of 88.5 runs, and participated in an average of 178.6 runs, which we could say would be 92 runs scored and 87 RBI. The 59 players in Group 3F created an average of 88.4 runs, and participated in an average of 157 runs, which we could say was 80 and 77.

So that's what playing for a great hitting team as opposed to a weak-hitting team means; you get 92 runs scored and 87 RBI, as opposed to 80 and 77. An extra 12 runs and 10 RBI.

This little slice of the data—that is, the data for players in the "3" group—would suggest that a player playing on a very weak offensive team is working at a 7% disadvantage in terms of Run Participation (7% compared to the average), and a hitter playing for a really good hitting team has a 6% advantage, compared to the average. This chart summarizes the data for all 42 player groups in the data, and for all seven levels of hitters:

1A	117.6	218.5	103	5A	72.5	152.8	106
1B	115.1	207.4		5B	72.7	146.3	
1C	113.8	201.7		5C	72.6	144.7	
1D	112.4	195.7		5D	73.1	145.1	
1E	112.7	187.0		5E	72.4	142.3	
1F	108.8	182.2	93	5F	72.7	137.3	95
1 A-F	115.2	207.1		5 A-F	72.7	144.0	
2A	97.6	191.8	106	6A	63.1	142.2	110
2B	97.5	182.4		6B	63.7	133.3	
2C	97.9	182.6		6C	63.8	132.4	
2D	97.5	176.4		6D	63.4	130.0	
2E	97.9	171.6		6E	63.1	126.3	
2F	98.7	165.7	91	6F	62.4	123.5	97
2 A-F	97.8	180.7		6 A-F	63.2	129.6	

3A	88.5	178.6	106		7A	40.4	114.7	111
3B	88.8	171.5			7B	40.6	106.4	
3C	88.4	170.2			7C	40.6	104.6	
3D	87.9	169.3			7D	39.9	103.7	
3E	88.1	162.2			7E	38.3	98.5	
3F	88.4	157.2	93		7F	39.2	95.0	95
3 A-F	88.4	168.3			7 A-F	39.6	101.6	
4A	81.2	164.7	105					
4B	80.6	160.9						
4C	80.6	158.1						
4D	80.1	156.7						
4E	80.1	149.2						
4F	80.2	147.4	95					
4 A-F	80.4	155.5						

Combining the data from all seven groups, we reach the conclusion that a hitter playing in a very strong offensive lineup (785 runs scored or more) has a 7% advantage in Runs Scored and RBI, as opposed to a player on an average team. A player on a very weak offensive team (634 runs scored or less) has a 6% disadvantage in terms of runs scored and RBI, as opposed to a player on an average team. A player on a very strong team has a 14% advantage in terms of runs scored and RBI, as opposed to a player on a weak offensive team.

I think the data shows that I was basically right about Benintendi, but there's no gloating in science; just take it for what it is. The split between expectation and discrepancy is 65-35, but a relatively small portion of the discrepancy is actually attributable to team context. Therefore, it is unwise to ignore run participation in evaluating a player, because the team context issue is only about a 14% distraction in the extreme case.

There is another issue that came up in the course of the Twitter discussion. One guy, joining in the discussion, wrote that. . . .well, it's Twitter, so I had a little bit of trouble understanding EXACTLY what he was saying. But I think what he was saying was that, comparing two players who create the same number of runs, but one of whom hits more home runs than the other, then the player who hits more home runs will drive in/score more runs, because, of course, the Home Run is guaranteed to be attached to at least one run scored and one RBI.

I did not comment on that thread of the discussion, because I did not know at that time whether what the man was saying was or was not true. Having now studied the issue (as a part of this research), I can confirm that the gentleman's claim is quite certainly true.

That part of the study was done by creating matched sets of players—that is, players who "created" exactly the same number of runs, but one of whom hit significantly more home runs than the other. For example, the second place hitters for the 2017 Milwaukee Brewers and the leadoff hitters for the 2011 New York Mets are each credited with creating 124 runs. However, the second place hitters for the 2017 Brewers (mostly Eric Thames and Domingo Santana) hit 40 home runs; they hit .271 with 2 triples and 11 stolen bases, but they did hit 40 home runs. The leadoff hitters for the 2011 New York Mets (mostly Jose Reyes) hit .318 with 16 triples and 49 stolen bases, but only 11 home runs. The 2011 Mets had 228 hits from their leadoff men, as Jose Reyes won the batting championship; the 2017 Brewers had 168 hits from their #2 hitters, although they did walk a lot.

A second example, to illustrate the point with less productive hitters, the 8th place hitters for the 2021 Texas Rangers and the 8th place hitters for the 2012 San Francisco Giants are each credited with creating 50 runs in 162 games, which is a very low number. But the 8th place hitters for the 2021 Rangers hit just .216, but with 16 homers. The 8th place hitters for the 2012 Giants hit for a little bit better average (.232), hit more singles (101-75), hit more triples, drew more walks, and grounded into half as many double plays (9 vs. 18), but hit only 3 home runs. The 26 singles and 9 double plays, etc., offset the 13 home runs, so they created just as many runs.

There were 442 players in each part of the study; it is really easy to find matched sets of players when you are only matching them on two parameters, actually matching them on one parameter (runs created) and dividing them on the other (home runs). But in that study, the home run hitters hit an average of 28 home runs. The non-home run hitters, although they were better at almost everything else, hit an average of only 10 home runs.

The singles hitters scored an average of 80 runs; the power hitters scored an average of 79. But the singles hitters drove in an average of only 61 runs; the home run hitters drove in an average of 85. The 18 extra homers of the power-hitting group led to an increase of 23 extra Runs Participated In.

That number was exaggerated somewhat because the singles-hitting group had far, far more leadoff men than the power-hitting group, and (as demonstrated earlier in the article) leadoff men are at a competitive disadvantage when it comes to driving in and scoring runs. Of the 442 power-hitting positions in the study, less than 10% were leadoff men or #2 hitters. Of the 442 singles hitters, just barely short of half were leadoff men or #2 hitters. That emphasized the run participation advantage of the power hitters, but certainly did not create it.

Thank you all for reading.

RBI Percentages

Brian Reiff

Bill James, the guy whose name is on the front of the book you're reading, has imparted innumerable bits of knowledge to the sabermetrics community. One of my personal favorites is his adage that a good metric should pass the eye test four out of five times and surprise you one out of five. A metric with all surprises is probably wrong; a metric with no surprises is probably useless.

RBI percentage, at least this year, certainly fits that criteria.

On the next page's leaderboard, you'll find four of the best players in baseball—Aaron Judge, Paul Goldschmidt, Mike Trout and José Ramírez—ranked second, third, fourth and fifth, respectively, in RBI percentage for 2022 among players with at least 150 at-bats. And at the top of the leaderboard…Jazz Chisholm Jr., who drove in 45 runs through 60 games before injuries cut his season short.

Now, no disrespect to Chisholm—he's still only 24 and just posted a 139 OPS+. But to see him included in a group with those other four is…surprising.

How exactly did he end up atop the leaderboard? To answer that, we need to explain what RBI opportunities are. There's a more detailed explanation in the glossary, but essentially, players accumulate RBI opportunities by either A) driving in runs, or B) making an out when they could have driven in a run. Each RBI is worth one RBI opportunity. Missed RBI opportunities are weighted by how many runs could have been expected to score.

Despite driving in only 45 runs, Chisholm did so with 92.4 RBI Opportunities, good for a .487 RBI percentage. The player behind him, Judge, drove in 131 runs with 272.8 opportunities—nearly three times as many as Chisholm—for a .480 percentage. Basically, Chisholm had many fewer chances to drive in runs, but he made the most of the chances he got.

RBI Percentages by Batter

Player	AB	RBI	RBI Opps	Pct
Chisholm Jr., Jazz	213	45	92.4	.487
Judge, Aaron	570	131	272.8	.480
Goldschmidt, Paul	561	115	244.8	.470
Trout, Mike	438	80	174.6	.458
Ramirez, Jose	601	126	282.7	.446
Ohtani, Shohei	586	95	220.8	.430
Jansen, Danny	215	44	102.9	.428
Jimenez, Eloy	292	54	126.4	.427
Pujols, Albert	307	68	159.6	.426
Alonso, Pete	597	131	308.1	.425
Pederson, Joc	380	70	165.0	.424
Freeman, Freddie	612	100	239.9	.417
Drury, Brandon	518	87	210.9	.413
Alvarez, Yordan	470	97	236.2	.411
Cruz, Oneil	331	54	131.5	.411
Perez, Salvador	445	76	184.9	.411
Harris II, Michael	414	64	157.4	.407
Stephenson, Tyler	166	35	86.3	.406
Tucker, Kyle	544	107	266.5	.402
Harper, Bryce	370	65	162.2	.401
Fraley, Jake	216	28	70.4	.398
Machado, Manny	578	102	258.4	.395
Realmuto, J.T.	504	84	213.7	.393
Vaughn, Andrew	510	76	193.6	.393
Rodriguez, Julio	511	75	193.0	.389
Schwarber, Kyle	577	94	243.6	.386
Arenado, Nolan	557	103	267.2	.385
Buxton, Byron	340	51	132.5	.385
d'Arnaud, Travis	396	60	155.9	.385
Devers, Rafael	555	88	228.3	.385
Swanson, Dansby	640	96	249.6	.385
Adames, Willy	563	98	255.2	.384
Blackmon, Charlie	530	78	203.1	.384
Garcia, Adolis	605	101	263.2	.384
Naylor, Josh	449	79	206.5	.383
Turner, Justin	468	81	212.4	.381
Varsho, Daulton	531	74	194.9	.380
Springer, George	513	76	200.5	.379
Stanton, Giancarlo	398	78	207.5	.376
Betts, Mookie	572	82	219.7	.373
Cronenworth, Jake	587	88	236.2	.373
Marte, Starling	466	63	168.7	.373
McCarthy, Jake	321	43	115.3	.373
Lindor, Francisco	630	107	287.8	.372
Haniger, Mitch	224	34	91.6	.371
Thompson, Trayce	219	41	110.4	.371
Cron, C.J.	575	102	275.8	.370
Tellez, Rowdy	529	89	241.4	.369
Turner, Trea	652	100	270.9	.369
Guerrero Jr., Vladimir	638	97	263.6	.368
Altuve, Jose	527	57	155.9	.366
Bregman, Alex	548	93	253.9	.366
Seager, Corey	593	83	226.9	.366
O'Neill, Tyler	334	58	158.8	.365
Olson, Matt	616	103	283.1	.364
Story, Trevor	357	66	181.1	.364
Flores, Wilmer	525	71	195.7	.363
Albies, Ozzie	247	35	96.8	.362
Grichuk, Randal	506	73	201.7	.362
Smith, Will	508	87	240.5	.362
Brown, Seth	500	73	202.2	.361
Ramirez, Harold	403	58	160.7	.361
Donovan, Brendan	391	45	125.5	.359
France, Ty	551	83	231.3	.359
Robert, Luis	380	56	155.8	.359
Farmer, Kyle	526	78	217.8	.358
Suarez, Eugenio	543	87	242.7	.358
Raleigh, Cal	370	63	176.5	.357
Riley, Austin	615	93	260.8	.357

Player	AB	RBI	RBI Opps	Pct
Mountcastle, Ryan	555	85	238.8	.356
Alfaro, Jorge	256	40	112.6	.355
Pena, Jeremy	521	63	177.5	.355
Walker, Christian	583	94	265.1	.355
Nimmo, Brandon	580	64	181.0	.354
Semien, Marcus	657	83	234.6	.354
Hoskins, Rhys	589	79	223.6	.353
Lowe, Nathaniel	593	76	215.2	.353
Renfroe, Hunter	474	72	204.1	.353
Gimenez, Andres	491	69	196.2	.352
Longoria, Evan	266	42	119.2	.352
Margot, Manuel	336	47	133.6	.352
Naquin, Tyler	310	46	130.5	.352
Polanco, Jorge	375	56	159.0	.352
Kirk, Alejandro	470	63	179.6	.351
Hernandez, Teoscar	499	77	219.7	.350
Diaz, Yandy	473	57	163.4	.349
Ward, Taylor	495	65	186.1	.349
Witt Jr., Bobby	591	80	229.0	.349
Higgins, P.J.	201	30	86.1	.348
Nootbaar, Lars	290	40	114.9	.348
Rojas, Josh	443	56	161.5	.347
Choi, Ji-Man	356	52	150.5	.346
Gamel, Ben	371	46	133.6	.344
Kiermaier, Kevin	206	22	63.9	.344
Arozarena, Randy	586	89	259.8	.343
Taylor, Tyrone	373	51	148.8	.343
Bichette, Bo	652	93	272.2	.342
Contreras, William	334	45	131.6	.342
Brantley, Michael	243	26	76.2	.341
Haase, Eric	323	44	129.0	.341
Refsnyder, Rob	153	21	61.6	.341
Hoerner, Nico	481	55	161.9	.340
McCormick, Chas	359	44	129.5	.340
Santander, Anthony	574	89	262.1	.340
Rizzo, Anthony	465	75	221.4	.339
Diaz, Aledmys	305	38	112.5	.338
Melendez, MJ	460	62	183.7	.338
Muncy, Max	464	69	204.4	.338
Santana, Carlos	431	60	177.4	.338
McCutchen, Andrew	515	69	205.0	.337
Miller, Brad	222	32	95.0	.337
Villar, David	156	24	71.2	.337
Vogelbach, Daniel	386	59	175.0	.337
Trevino, Jose	335	43	127.9	.336
Acuna Jr., Ronald	467	50	150.0	.333
Moncada, Yoan	397	51	153.1	.333
Garver, Mitch	188	24	72.2	.332
Arcia, Orlando	209	30	90.5	.331
Duvall, Adam	287	36	108.8	.331
India, Jonathan	386	41	123.8	.331
Cruz, Nelson	448	64	194.2	.330
Murphy, Sean	537	66	200.3	.330
Andrus, Elvis	535	58	176.5	.329
Cabrera, Oswaldo	154	19	57.8	.329
Estrada, Thairo	488	62	188.5	.329
Marsh, Brandon	424	52	158.0	.329
Rendon, Anthony	166	24	72.9	.329
Sanchez, Gary	419	61	185.5	.329
Gurriel Jr., Lourdes	453	52	158.6	.328
Myers, Wil	261	41	125.1	.328
Peralta, David	439	59	179.7	.328
Canha, Mark	462	61	186.6	.327
Correa, Carlos	522	64	196.5	.326
Burger, Jake	168	26	79.9	.325
Cooper, Garrett	414	50	153.8	.325
Pratto, Nick	158	20	61.6	.325
Contreras, Willson	416	55	169.7	.324
Mazara, Nomar	159	18	55.5	.324

Player	AB	RBI	RBI Opps	Pct
Vogt, Stephen	168	23	71.0	.324
Baez, Javier	555	67	208.8	.321
Castro, Harold	420	47	146.6	.321
Dickerson, Corey	281	36	112.0	.321
Iglesias, Jose	439	47	146.2	.321
Reynolds, Bryan	542	62	192.9	.321
Smith, Pavin	245	33	102.8	.321
Wong, Kolten	430	47	146.5	.321
Meneses, Joey	222	34	106.2	.320
Merrifield, Whit	504	58	181.4	.320
Sheets, Gavin	377	53	165.8	.320
Gordon, Nick	405	50	156.8	.319
Vazquez, Christian	398	52	163.1	.319
Abreu, Jose	601	75	236.0	.318
Friedl, T.J.	225	25	78.7	.318
Garcia, Luis	360	45	141.7	.318
Soto, Juan	524	62	194.9	.318
Tapia, Raimel	411	52	163.3	.318
Bogaerts, Xander	557	73	230.0	.317
Kim, Ha-seong	517	59	186.0	.317
Miranda, Jose	444	66	208.1	.317
Reyes, Victor	315	34	107.1	.317
Urias, Ramon	403	51	161.1	.317
Arraez, Luis	547	49	155.3	.316
Chapman, Matt	538	76	240.6	.316
Diaz, Elias	351	51	161.3	.316
Velazquez, Nelson	185	26	82.2	.316
Bohm, Alec	586	72	228.4	.315
Suzuki, Seiya	397	46	145.9	.315
Wade Jr., LaMonte	217	26	82.5	.315
Ruf, Darin	334	45	143.1	.314
Barnes, Austin	179	26	83.0	.313
Cordero, Franchy	242	29	92.7	.313
Gonzalez, Luis	311	36	115.2	.313
Votto, Joey	322	41	131.0	.313
Candelario, Jeimer	429	50	160.1	.312
Voit, Luke	500	69	221.0	.312
Benintendi, Andrew	461	51	164.1	.311
Duran, Ezequiel	208	25	80.4	.311
McMahon, Ryan	529	67	215.7	.311
Donaldson, Josh	478	62	199.9	.310
Edman, Tommy	577	57	184.1	.310
Higashioka, Kyle	229	31	100.1	.310
Kemp, Tony	497	46	148.4	.310
Slater, Austin	277	34	109.8	.310
Almora Jr., Albert	215	29	94.0	.309
Hernandez, Yadiel	305	41	132.6	.309
Hiura, Keston	234	32	103.6	.309
Jeffers, Ryan	212	27	87.4	.309
Mancini, Trey	519	63	204.1	.309
Castellanos, Nick	524	62	201.3	.308
De La Cruz, Bryan	329	43	139.8	.308
LeMahieu, DJ	467	46	149.2	.308
Montero, Elehuris	176	20	64.9	.308
Paredes, Isaac	331	45	145.9	.308
Yelich, Christian	575	57	185.0	.308
Verdugo, Alex	593	74	240.7	.307
Castillo, Diego	262	29	94.9	.306
Gonzalez, Oscar	362	43	140.4	.306
Morel, Christopher	379	47	153.6	.306
Calhoun, Kole	388	49	161.7	.303
Greene, Riley	376	42	138.6	.303
Happ, Ian	573	72	238.0	.303
Meyers, Jake	150	15	49.5	.303
Nola, Austin	347	40	132.2	.303
Torres, Gleyber	526	76	250.7	.303
Bellinger, Cody	504	68	224.8	.302
Hernandez, Kike	361	45	149.1	.302
Rivera, Emmanuel	330	40	132.6	.302
Rosario, Amed	637	71	234.8	.302

Player	AB	RBI	RBI Opps	Pct
Rutschman, Adley	398	42	139.0	.302
Mullins II, Cedric	608	64	212.3	.301
Pinder, Chad	361	42	139.4	.301
Chirinos, Robinson	195	22	73.3	.300
Urshela, Gio	501	64	213.4	.300
Wendle, Joey	347	32	106.8	.300
Wisdom, Patrick	469	66	220.0	.300
Odor, Rougned	426	53	177.3	.299
Soler, Jorge	270	34	113.6	.299
Cabrera, Miguel	397	43	144.3	.298
DeJong, Paul	210	25	83.8	.298
Grossman, Robbie	411	45	150.9	.298
McNeil, Jeff	533	62	207.8	.298
Winker, Jesse	456	53	178.7	.297
Castro, Rodolfo	253	27	91.2	.296
Grisham, Trent	451	53	178.9	.296
Haggerty, Sam	176	23	77.8	.296
Arroyo, Christian	280	36	122.0	.295
Chavis, Michael	401	49	166.1	.295
Rodgers, Brendan	527	63	213.7	.295
Bader, Harrison	292	30	102.0	.294
Daza, Yonathan	372	34	115.8	.294
Hays, Austin	535	60	204.4	.294
Hosmer, Eric	380	44	150.3	.293
Miller, Owen	424	51	174.2	.293
Neuse, Sheldon	271	26	88.7	.293
Larnach, Trevor	160	18	61.6	.292
Maldonado, Martin	344	45	154.2	.292
Pollock, A.J.	489	56	191.9	.292
Bell, Josh	552	71	243.6	.291
Escobar, Eduardo	495	69	237.5	.291
Lowe, Brandon	235	25	85.9	.291
Pham, Tommy	554	63	216.6	.291
Schwindel, Frank	271	36	123.6	.291
Alcantara, Sergio	205	29	100.0	.290
Cave, Jake	164	20	69.0	.290
Kiner-Falefa, Isiah	483	48	165.3	.290
Bethancourt, Christian	318	34	117.6	.289
Rosario, Eddie	250	24	83.1	.289
Caratini, Victor	272	34	117.9	.288
Yepez, Juan	253	30	104.3	.288
Aguilar, Jesus	464	51	177.9	.287
Franco, Wander	314	33	115.2	.286
Gallo, Joey	350	47	164.1	.286
Gorman, Nolan	283	35	122.8	.285
Heim, Jonah	406	48	168.4	.285
Olivares, Edward	161	15	52.6	.285
Profar, Jurickson	575	58	203.2	.285
Espinal, Santiago	449	51	179.8	.284
Suwinski, Jack	326	38	134.0	.284
Peterson, Jace	288	34	120.3	.283
Urias, Luis	406	47	165.9	.283
Vargas, Ildemaro	209	23	81.2	.283
Rengifo, Luis	489	52	184.2	.282
Stott, Bryson	427	49	173.5	.282
Taveras, Leody	314	34	120.5	.282
Yastrzemski, Mike	485	57	202.2	.282
Luplow, Jordan	205	28	99.7	.281
Ozuna, Marcell	470	56	199.4	.281
Aquino, Aristides	259	30	107.0	.280
Kwan, Steven	563	52	185.6	.280
Toro, Abraham	324	35	125.3	.279
Wynns, Austin	162	21	75.3	.279
Davis, J.D.	318	35	125.9	.278
Marte, Ketel	492	52	187.1	.278
Mejia, Francisco	289	31	111.4	.278
Crawford, Brandon	407	52	187.4	.277
Zavala, Seby	178	21	75.7	.277
Garlick, Kyle	150	18	65.3	.276
Laureano, Ramon	346	34	123.2	.276

Player	AB	RBI	RBI Opps	Pct
Sosa, Edmundo	176	21	76.1	.276
Bradley Jr., Jackie	344	38	138.5	.274
Pasquantino, Vinnie	258	26	94.8	.274
Sanchez, Jesus	313	36	132.1	.273
Thomas, Alek	381	39	143.1	.273
Duran, Jarren	204	17	62.4	.272
Herrera, Odubel	185	21	77.3	.272
Taylor, Michael A.	414	43	158.0	.272
Newman, Kevin	288	24	88.4	.271
Rivas, Alfonso	251	25	92.3	.271
Molina, Yadier	262	24	88.8	.270
Thomas, Lane	498	52	192.9	.270
Walsh, Jared	423	44	163.7	.269
Dalbec, Bobby	317	39	146.2	.267
Hummel, Cooper	176	17	63.7	.267
Villar, Jonathan	202	18	67.5	.267
Perdomo, Geraldo	431	40	150.3	.266
Kepler, Max	388	43	162.1	.265
Reyes, Franmil	438	47	177.8	.264
Ortega, Rafael	316	35	133.1	.263
Camargo, Johan	152	15	57.3	.262
Fortes, Nick	217	24	91.5	.262
Massey, Michael	173	17	65.0	.262
Moustakas, Mike	252	25	95.3	.262
Martinez, J.D.	533	62	237.1	.261
Segura, Jean	354	33	127.0	.260
Fletcher, David	216	17	65.6	.259
Nevin, Tyler	157	16	61.7	.259
Isbel, Kyle	256	28	109.0	.257
Castro, Willi	365	31	121.2	.256
Gomes, Yan	277	31	121.2	.256
Solano, Donovan	278	24	93.6	.256
Kelly, Carson	317	35	137.3	.255
Mateo, Jorge	494	50	197.2	.254
Moore, Dylan	205	24	95.2	.252
Anderson, Tim	332	25	99.6	.251
Taylor, Chris	402	43	171.3	.251
Berti, Jon	358	28	112.2	.250
Franco, Maikel	371	39	155.7	.250
Gurriel, Yuli	545	53	211.7	.250
Carlson, Dylan	432	42	169.2	.248
Hicks, Aaron	384	40	161.0	.248
McCann, James	174	18	72.6	.248
Reynolds, Matt	244	23	93.1	.247
Robles, Victor	366	33	133.6	.247
Rojas, Miguel	471	36	145.7	.247
Velazquez, Andrew	322	28	113.5	.247
Lux, Gavin	421	42	170.8	.246
Anderson, Brian	338	28	114.5	.245
Lowrie, Jed	167	16	65.4	.245
Torrens, Luis	151	15	61.3	.245
Tsutsugo, Yoshi	170	19	77.5	.245
Bart, Joey	261	25	102.4	.244
Vierling, Matt	325	32	130.9	.244
Garcia, Avisail	357	35	143.9	.243
Hayes, Ke'Bryan	505	41	168.5	.243
Dubon, Mauricio	243	24	99.0	.242
Marcano, Tucupita	160	13	53.8	.242
Adell, Jo	268	27	112.2	.241
Kelenic, Jarred	163	17	70.5	.241
McKinstry, Zach	166	14	58.7	.239
Stallings, Jacob	346	34	142.0	.239
Stassi, Max	333	30	126.2	.238
Chang, Yu	168	15	63.3	.237
Smith, Josh	213	16	67.6	.237
VanMeter, Josh	171	14	59.0	.237
Narvaez, Omar	262	23	97.6	.236
Crawford, J.P.	518	42	178.7	.235
Gregorius, Didi	214	19	81.0	.235
Hedges, Austin	294	30	127.8	.235

Player	AB	RBI	RBI Opps	Pct
Duffy, Matt	228	16	68.7	.233
Lowe, Josh	181	13	55.9	.233
Alberto, Hanser	156	15	64.9	.231
Nido, Tomas	284	28	121.0	.231
Knizner, Andrew	260	25	108.7	.230
Maile, Luke	181	17	74.3	.229
Walls, Taylor	407	33	143.8	.229
Abrams, CJ	284	21	92.6	.227
Delay, Jason	155	11	48.5	.227
McGuire, Reese	249	22	97.5	.226
Pache, Cristian	241	18	79.9	.225
Biggio, Cavan	257	24	107.2	.224
Mitchell, Calvin	212	17	75.9	.224
Phillips, Brett	201	15	67.2	.223
Ruiz, Keibert	394	36	161.1	.223
Frazier, Adam	541	42	190.0	.221
Leblanc, Charles	156	11	50.3	.219
Senzel, Nick	373	25	114.8	.218
Siri, Jose	301	24	110.3	.218
Belt, Brandon	254	23	106.5	.216
Dozier, Hunter	462	41	190.5	.215
Bryant, Kris	160	14	65.4	.214
Diaz, Lewin	160	11	51.4	.214
Schoop, Jonathan	481	38	179.0	.212
Grandal, Yasmani	327	27	128.8	.210
Plawecki, Kevin	168	13	61.8	.210
Hernandez, Cesar	560	34	162.7	.209
La Stella, Tommy	180	14	67.0	.209
Celestino, Gilberto	311	24	116.5	.206
Joe, Connor	404	28	136.2	.206
Engel, Adam	245	17	83.0	.205
Garcia, Leury	300	20	97.7	.205
Bleday, J.J.	204	16	78.6	.204
McKenna, Ryan	156	11	54.0	.204
Gonzalez, Marwin	184	18	88.7	.203
Hampson, Garrett	199	15	74.0	.203
Machin, Vimael	223	13	64.0	.203
Serven, Brian	187	16	78.9	.203
Torkelson, Spencer	360	28	139.4	.201
Harrison, Josh	386	27	135.5	.199
Allen, Nick	299	19	97.0	.196
Hilliard, Sam	174	14	71.8	.195
Straw, Myles	535	32	167.0	.192
Thompson, Bubba	170	9	49.9	.180
Barnhart, Tucker	281	16	93.7	.171
Heineman, Tyler	157	9	53.5	.168
Guillorme, Luis	297	17	110.0	.155
Baddoo, Akil	201	9	60.8	.148
Barrero, Jose	165	10	68.0	.147
Azocar, Jose	202	10	69.0	.145
Lopez, Nicky	436	20	148.9	.134
Madrigal, Nick	209	7	55.8	.125
Bride, Jonah	162	6	54.9	.109
Clement, Ernie	163	6	55.9	.107

The World's Best Hitter

Mark Simon

In last year's Handbook, Bill James introduced a formula to ascertain the World's Best Hitter. This was intended to be a companion to the World's No. 1 Starting Pitcher formula that Bill produced for his website several years ago.

World's Best Hitter, like its pitcher counterpart, uses a single-game Game Score formula as its primary source. You can find more about that in the Glossary under Runs Created (Single Game).

If you can, scan the QR code here to read last year's article.

Simply put, you want your hitter getting on base and doing as much damage as possible with some night-to-night consistency. Most recent performance is most important. Players build up an accumulation of value over time.

As you'd expect, Aaron Judge currently ranks as the World's Best Hitter. The gap between him and No. 2 Paul Goldschmidt is substantial. Goldschmidt actually had the lead on Judge at the All-Star Break and was close enough to Judge entering September that he could have caught him.

But then this happened.

Judge and Goldschmidt since September 1

	BA	OPS	HR
Aaron Judge	.380	1.323	11
Paul Goldschmidt	.245	.716	2

If you've seen those pictures of Aaron Judge next to an average-sized player and marveled at how large Aaron Judge is, the gap between him and Goldschmidt for World's Best Hitter is now about that large. It's about the same as the gap between the No. 10 hitter, José Ramirez, and the No. 57 hitter, Jorge Polanco.

Here's the current Top 10:

Player
1. Aaron Judge
2. Paul Goldschmidt
3. Mike Trout
4. Freddie Freeman
5. Yordan Alvarez
6. Mookie Betts
7. Pete Alonso
8. Jose Altuve
9. Manny Machado
10. José Ramírez

I ran an experiment, albeit one with a sample size of one. I had one of our product managers, Noah Gatsik, rank the top 20 batters in baseball using whatever criteria he wanted. Noah's sharp. He helps lead our Scout School. He's previously worked for the Reds and Rays. He follows the game avidly, and though he's not familiar with World's Best Hitter, he's reasonably statistically minded. He's the right person for the task.

Full disclosure: He had FanGraphs at his fingertips when he was making his list. But Noah and World's Best Hitter each interpreted the stats in their own way.

Here's that same Best Hitter Top 10 compared to what Noah had on his list.

World's Best Hitter	Noah's Best Hitter
1. Aaron Judge	1. Aaron Judge
2. Paul Goldschmidt	2. Mike Trout
3. Mike Trout	3. Freddie Freeman
4. Freddie Freeman	4. Yordan Alvarez
5. Yordan Alvarez	5. Manny Machado
6. Mookie Betts	6. Nolan Arenado
7. Pete Alonso	7. Mookie Betts
8. Jose Altuve	8. Paul Goldschmidt
9. Manny Machado	9. José Ramírez
10. José Ramírez	10. Jose Altuve

Noah and the system agreed on 9 of the 10 players in the Top 10, with Noah having Nolan Arenado in his Top 10 in place of Pete Alonso. There isn't perfect agreement here (Goldschmidt's season-end cratering clearly dipped him in Noah's eyes) but it's pretty close.

Here are the players they ranked 11 to 20. With Noah's rankings, the number in parentheses represents where World's Best Hitter ranked them if they weren't in the Top 20.

World's Best Hitter	Noah's Best Hitter
11. George Springer	11. Juan Soto
12. Bryce Harper	12. Austin Riley (33)
13. Trea Turner	13. Shohei Ohtani (27)
14. Juan Soto	14. Jeff McNeil (51)
15. Fernando Tatis Jr.	15. Rafael Devers (22)
16. Francisco Lindor	16. Pete Alonso
17. Nolan Arenado	17. Trea Turner
18. Marcus Semien	18. Julio Rodríguez
19. Julio Rodríguez	19. Bryce Harper
20. Kyle Schwarber	20. Vladimir Guerrero Jr. (21)

For anyone wondering, Fernando Tatis Jr. is on the list because a player does not lose value for dealing with injuries and/or suspensions.

In all, 17 of the players in Noah's Top 20 were in the Top 22 in the World's Best Hitter Rankings, missing by more than a couple spots on only Austin Riley, Shohei Ohtani, and Jeff McNeil (who were in place of George Springer, Tatis, and Francisco Lindor).

Riley is a head-scratcher to us given that he led the NL in Total Bases and ranked 5th in OPS. He was 19th in World's Best Hitter at the All-Star Break and 19th entering September.

What happened is that Riley didn't have enough games befitting a Top 20 hitter in August and September (he hit .223 with a .724 OPS from Aug. 4 on), and enough of the players who were clumped near him in the rankings were able to pass him.

World's Best Hitter has been a little lower on Ohtani than public perception. He ranked 42nd in 2021 and 27th in 2022. Ohtani dug himself a little bit of a hole relative to Top 20 hitters by hitting .229 in a 385 at-bats spanning from August 1, 2021 to June 3, 2022. He was AWESOME from that point on and got very close to Top 20 status, but didn't quite reach it.

McNeil is a product of bias on Noah's part. He admitted to putting a premium on McNeil's .326 batting average and low strikeout rate that he didn't necessarily apply to others. World's Best Hitter applies the same rules to everyone.

Though McNeil had a high batting average, his lack of power and thus lack of high-impact Runs Created games dampened his potential for Top 20 inclusion (as did his unimpressive 2021 numbers, which weighed his ranking down).

Lindor has more of a long-term track record than Riley and McNeil do, which would explain why he's viewed favorably in World's Best Hitter. Springer's presence so high was a bit of a surprise, but don't underestimate the .536 slugging percentage since 2019. Only three players with at least 1,500 plate appearances have a higher one in that time.

In the end, this little experiment played out exactly as it should. A reasonable-minded person with basic statistical knowledge and a reasonable-minded system built on the wisdom of more than 40 years experience put their heads together, producing a strong consensus, with a few disagreements varying in scale.

Hitter Rankings

Player	April 7 Score	April 7 Rank	May 1 Rank	June 1 Rank	July 1 Rank	Aug 1 Rank	Sept 1 Rank	Oct 5 Score	Oct 5 Rank
Judge, Aaron	529.6	15	7	5	3	1	1	628.3	1
Goldschmidt, Paul	538.7	8	12	2	1	2	2	587.6	2
Trout, Mike	563.2	1	1	3	2	6	6	584.6	3
Freeman, Freddie	543.2	4	5	7	8	3	4	582.3	4
Alvarez, Yordan	519.3	22	16	16	6	4	7	570.1	5
Betts, Mookie	538.0	9	8	1	5	7	3	569.6	6
Alonso, Pete	517.5	24	21	11	9	8	11	566.3	7
Altuve, Jose	536.5	10	15	12	14	14	12	560.5	8
Machado, Manny	512.7	30	13	15	12	18	9	557.2	9
Ramirez, Jose	529.8	14	3	6	7	10	8	553.6	10
Springer, George	541.4	5	6	8	11	16	15	551.8	11
Harper, Bryce	547.4	3	4	4	4	5	5	551.2	12
Turner, Trea	523.6	20	20	17	17	12	14	542.6	13
Soto, Juan	560.1	2	2	9	13	11	10	542.2	14
Tatis Jr., Fernando	540.1	7	9	13	16	17	19	540.1	15
Lindor, Francisco	497.4	55	37	20	31	23	25	538.4	16
Arenado, Nolan	495.8	57	23	33	32	34	13	537.3	17
Semien, Marcus	531.7	13	26	40	27	27	26	536.8	18
Rodriguez, Julio			274	157	73	45	38	536.7	19
Schwarber, Kyle	506.8	41	36	48	19	28	31	536.1	20
Guerrero Jr., Vladimir	532.7	11	11	22	15	15	16	535.7	21
Devers, Rafael	527.9	16	17	10	10	9	24	535.3	22
Bregman, Alex	511.1	33	40	45	46	40	17	534.9	23
Olson, Matt	531.9	12	14	21	24	19	21	533.1	24
Marte, Starling	510.8	34	34	19	26	21	22	533.1	25
Nimmo, Brandon	486.8	72	62	56	64	46	55	532.8	26
Ohtani, Shohei	504.9	46	41	29	23	33	23	532.6	27
Bichette, Bo	514.3	27	49	34	40	49	71	532.3	28
Hernandez, Teoscar	523.6	19	18	35	30	26	32	529.9	29
Arozarena, Randy	508.4	40	57	42	54	58	29	529.4	30
Tucker, Kyle	516.2	26	30	32	21	38	28	528.4	31
Seager, Corey	525.2	17	19	24	39	20	20	528.0	32
Riley, Austin	512.9	29	28	30	38	13	18	527.4	33
Abreu, Jose	521.9	21	29	28	20	22	27	526.8	34
Correa, Carlos	514.0	28	38	37	28	42	57	526.2	35
Suarez, Eugenio	466.8	127	102	91	93	99	44	523.1	36
Realmuto, J.T.	478.9	104	106	104	120	64	40	523.0	37
Acuna Jr., Ronald	540.3	6	10	14	18	35	30	522.4	38
Turner, Justin	491.9	67	98	67	92	56	53	521.4	39
Haniger, Mitch	516.7	25	31	31	43	44	37	521.3	40
Adames, Willy	482.4	88	63	53	47	48	43	520.5	41
Rizzo, Anthony	479.1	103	24	44	33	24	33	520.5	42
Buxton, Byron	493.2	63	33	46	29	36	36	519.7	43
Stanton, Giancarlo	509.5	37	45	25	22	32	42	518.9	44
Smith, Will	494.3	62	56	54	59	51	39	518.7	45
Muncy, Max	525.1	18	25	38	56	68	60	518.5	46
Lowe, Nathaniel	469.2	122	111	132	86	72	34	517.1	47
Diaz, Yandy	465.6	129	108	128	134	70	41	516.8	48
Torres, Gleyber	451.9	157	168	122	110	83	129	515.6	49
Garcia, Adolis	452.6	151	113	98	55	50	47	515.1	50
McNeil, Jeff	448.0	165	93	81	85	113	85	514.6	51
Hoskins, Rhys	505.7	43	59	51	34	41	35	514.2	52
O'Neill, Tyler	511.4	32	54	70	53	62	51	514.0	53
France, Ty	496.8	56	22	18	25	29	45	513.9	54
Swanson, Dansby	474.6	115	120	84	44	47	49	513.4	55
Reynolds, Bryan	502.8	50	64	76	50	69	66	513.3	56
Polanco, Jorge	508.8	39	48	49	49	37	54	513.1	57
Lowe, Brandon	518.7	23	32	27	35	31	46	511.8	58
Perez, Salvador	510.7	35	44	82	66	54	58	510.9	59
Cronenworth, Jake	482.1	90	72	109	45	55	65	510.8	60
Canha, Mark	489.5	69	75	50	72	82	52	510.8	61
Bogaerts, Xander	502.4	51	43	41	48	52	50	510.2	62
Walker, Christian	450.2	161	161	115	102	117	63	509.7	63
Kwan, Steven	377.5	415	271	284	238	162	119	509.3	64
Jimenez, Eloy	468.0	125	132	156	166	152	104	509.3	65
Renfroe, Hunter	480.7	95	79	71	96	59	56	508.1	66
Ward, Taylor	445.4	171	67	36	63	98	109	507.4	67
Franco, Wander	483.9	84	42	57	82	79	83	507.0	68
Chisholm Jr., Jazz	456.1	141	100	74	61	63	72	505.8	69
Escobar, Eduardo	480.3	97	73	97	101	125	182	505.8	70
Santander, Anthony	459.8	136	115	112	131	81	67	505.1	71

69

Hitter Rankings

Player	April 7 Score	April 7 Rank	May 1 Rank	June 1 Rank	July 1 Rank	Aug 1 Rank	Sept 1 Rank	Oct 5 Score	Oct 5 Rank
Rosario, Amed	468.1	124	150	179	119	87	94	505.0	72
Arraez, Luis	442.2	187	187	105	68	66	62	505.0	73
Pujols, Albert	389.8	354	295	247	380	272	141	504.9	74
Anderson, Tim	511.8	31	27	26	41	53	74	504.9	75
Harris II, Michael				473	214	194	91	504.9	76
Contreras, Willson	460.4	135	124	64	42	75	70	504.4	77
Murphy, Sean	445.2	174	117	159	147	105	64	503.7	78
Drury, Brandon	387.9	365	345	225	114	91	80	503.4	79
Albies, Ozzie	498.3	53	55	60	74	73	79	503.3	80
Robert, Luis	495.4	58	65	55	52	30	48	503.3	81
Story, Trevor	470.2	121	133	62	78	77	78	503.0	82
Yelich, Christian	486.0	76	71	77	69	67	73	503.0	83
Chapman, Matt	483.2	86	89	134	95	39	69	500.8	84
LeMahieu, DJ	484.4	82	66	80	57	25	61	500.7	85
Verdugo, Alex	477.6	110	118	135	89	135	88	500.0	86
Happ, Ian	484.7	80	74	79	58	80	68	499.9	87
Andrus, Elvis	443.7	177	178	164	205	156	173	499.2	88
Rendon, Anthony	505.4	45	51	47	77	78	82	499.0	89
Carpenter, Matt	375.0	436	503	403	247	71	86	498.9	90
Edman, Tommy	474.0	117	80	61	67	116	96	498.9	91
Martinez, J.D.	508.9	38	35	23	37	57	90	498.8	92
Gimenez, Andres	392.2	346	224	168	142	109	89	496.2	93
Bell, Josh	486.6	74	53	66	36	43	59	495.2	94
McCutchen, Andrew	484.0	83	107	142	81	65	84	495.1	95
Brown, Seth	439.1	202	184	183	161	142	197	494.6	96
Voit, Luke	471.9	120	134	113	97	76	81	494.0	97
Brantley, Michael	480.0	99	87	107	91	95	97	492.8	98
Gonzalez, Oscar				426	291	308	269	492.5	99
Pederson, Joc	433.3	230	126	68	80	150	123	491.9	100
Gurriel Jr., Lourdes	488.5	71	70	126	70	60	93	491.7	101
d'Arnaud, Travis	429.9	244	155	199	104	151	114	491.6	102
Rutschman, Adley				513	304	175	139	491.5	103
Mullins II, Cedric	482.5	87	86	117	106	90	95	491.3	104
Meneses, Joey							148	491.2	105
Jansen, Danny	447.5	166	135	121	153	160	144	490.3	106
Bohm, Alec	422.5	267	177	228	186	96	75	490.2	107
Bryant, Kris	485.1	79	92	110	143	103	100	490.0	108
Benintendi, Andrew	478.3	108	84	94	135	115	102	489.7	109
Baez, Javier	494.4	61	52	153	144	132	170	489.5	110
Ramirez, Harold	431.6	237	188	175	150	106	77	488.7	111
Winker, Jesse	503.1	49	58	92	75	101	87	488.6	112
Mountcastle, Ryan	486.6	75	90	87	65	93	107	488.5	113
Naylor, Josh	410.8	299	220	108	117	92	146	488.1	114
Vaughn, Andrew	429.3	245	146	124	107	84	76	488.1	115
Urshela, Gio	436.6	212	244	158	173	138	140	487.0	116
Conforto, Michael	486.7	73	81	86	105	111	106	486.7	117
Donovan, Brendan			502	252	128	169	147	486.2	118
Seager, Kyle	485.7	77	83	88	108	112	112	485.7	119
Kemp, Tony	452.4	152	167	201	235	228	183	485.6	120
Cruz, Oneil	375.0	436	503	543	369	314	275	485.1	121
Donaldson, Josh	485.7	78	88	83	133	163	124	483.6	122
Merrifield, Whit	476.2	113	166	120	146	114	152	483.4	123
Kirk, Alejandro	418.4	274	353	152	60	74	98	483.2	124
Profar, Jurickson	376.9	423	266	186	99	85	110	483.1	125

OPS and Runs Scored

Bill James

I have some 40-year-old egg on my face. The mixing of metaphors there suggests that I may not have washed my face in the last 40 years, which I promise you I have, three or four times. Before I was going to appear on television.

OPS was sold to the public as a stand-in for offensive productivity about 40 years ago. There were a few guys in my field who had some access to high-level media, and they were passing around a document saying essentially that "we all agree to use OPS as a standard measure of a hitter's effectiveness." I refused to sign the document. . . .well, I declined. I declined to sign the document, but the sales pitch worked without my help. OPS was gradually accepted as a standard summation of a batter's production. I don't think any of those guys made any money by doing that, by the way; they just wanted to do it.

In the process of trying to convince me to sign on, I was told that one advantage of OPS is that it bore a **straight-line** relationship to runs scored. Let me repeat for more emphasis: a straight-line relationship. I don't know if you understand this or not, but the normal relationship of run elements to runs scored is a relationship of squares. If you compare a .275 hitter to a .250 hitter, other things being equal, the .275 hitter isn't creating 10% more runs than the .250 hitter; he is creating 21% more runs than the .250 hitter. 1.10 squared is 1.21. Run elements means singles, doubles, triples, homers, walks, stolen bases, etc. A 1% increase in run elements will lead to a 2% increase in runs. This happens because runs are formed by COMBINATIONS of run elements.

Generalizing a little bit, arithmetic combinations form straight-line relationships, whereas geometric combinations often form lines that curve rapidly upward. 40 years ago, I was told that one advantage of OPS is that, because of the way it is formed, it has an arithmetic relationship to runs scored. If a team's OPS goes up 10%, they score 10% more runs. To my shame and regret, I never checked that out for myself. I am now very, very ashamed to admit. . . insert several more very's in there. Because I respected the people involved, or perhaps this is not what they told me at all, I just misunderstood it, but in any case I am now very embarrassed to discover that this isn't true, at all. It isn't 1% true. It is totally, absolutely, completely untrue. The relationship of OPS to Runs Scored by a team is exactly and precisely the same as the relationship of run elements to runs scored. It isn't loosely a relationship of squares; it is precisely a relationship of squares. If one team has an OPS 10% higher than another team, they will not score 10% more runs; they will score 21% more runs. EXACTLY 21% more, on average.

And if a hitter has an OPS+ of 110, he is not creating 10% more runs than an average hitter, he is creating 21% more runs than an average hitter. Having never checked this out for myself, I parroted what I was told 40 years ago, and thus spread misinformation on this subject. I am very embarrassed to discover that I have done so.

However, I should add that OPS actually DOES correlate closely with runs scored. OPS raw is a terrible predictor of runs scored, useless, but OPS SQUARED is an excellent predictor of runs scored. It is stunningly accurate, used correctly, used appropriately. Not knocking OPS; just beating myself up for my own failures, and apologizing to you for them.

Lessons Learned From Talking To Baseball Players

Mark Simon

Rays and Orioles outfielder Brett Phillips remembers the first time he ever made a great defensive play.

"We're in the championship (of his Little League). A ball gets hit to left center and I remember, for the first time in my career, making a diving catch to my left. We won the game, we won the championship and that was the deciding factor, which is really cool.

"From that moment on, I loved playing the outfield. I always craved playing the outfield. That's a testament to who I am as a defender today because of all the reps I got as a kid when everyone else thought playing the outfield was boring."

Phillips was one of 11 current players we interviewed this season on *The Sports Info Solutions Baseball Podcast*. He's someone who loves defensive excellence, which is the topic we most enjoy talking to players about. In his case, practice, and lots of it, made perfect.

And as we went through the season, we wanted to know:

How do players like Phillips do what they do and do it so well?

Here are some excerpts of what our guests had to say.

Steven Kwan

Steven Kwan led all left fielders in Defensive Runs Saved this season. One thing that was challenging was learning ballparks in which he was playing for the first time.

"I take BP super seriously. It's the best time to get reps. We have a lot of righties who launch the ball so it gives me a chance to see some line drives and balls off the wall.

"It was interesting tackling (Fenway Park) the first day. I had some people recommending on hard line drives (off the Green Monster) that you want to be able to catch it before it hits the ground, so you can have a chance to throw the hitter out at second.

"I was playing balls too aggressively and got burned the first day. I went back and tested angles in BP the next day. That made it a little better."

Christian Walker

Christian Walker made great strides on defense this season, so much so that he led all first basemen in Defensive Runs Saved by a wide margin. He had 17. No one else had more than 6.

"What's changed most recently is just learning how to practice defense.

"In the last 3 or 4 years, working with (Diamondbacks coach) Tony Perezchica, and some of the great defenders that I've crossed paths with here, Nick Ahmed and Paul Goldschmidt, seeing how seriously they take their practice.

"It's not about necessarily taking 100 ground balls every day, but the 10 or 20 I take, I treat them like game speed. I'm going to act like there's a runner on the bases. I'm going to make sure a throwing lane is open. I'm going to entertain different scenarios. I'm gonna take ground balls from a shifted position, shading the line.

"For me, how I developed as a defender came from practicing fast, practicing hard and taking every rep very seriously."

Isiah Kiner-Falefa

Kiner-Falefa, who won a Gold Glove at third base with the Rangers in 2020, was part of the Yankees makeover that led to them posting 129 Runs Saved, the most in a season since Runs Saved was first tracked in 2003.

Kiner-Falefa traces his success back to his early baseball days growing up in Hawaii, where an infield drill taught him how to make the really hard play.

"If I'm playing shortstop, I'll play behind second base, get a jogging start, and then I'll start sprinting. And I'll have the fungo hitter hit it deep in the hole. That way I'm out of control, I can't control my body.

"That makes me slow down, control my body and try to make the play. You do those enough, you get used to game speed balls and you're able to finish the play.

"Then you go to third base, go to the backhand side, start sprinting and have the coach hit it behind second base. Then you can go to left field, get a sprinting start and have the left fielder hit a slow roller, and you've got to figure out how to make a barehand play. That drill allows you to build out your own style."

Gunnar Henderson

For MLB Pipeline's No. 1 midseason prospect, he needed to learn how to best use his long, 6-foot-4 frame. The family favorite at third base is Manny Machado and Henderson thinks his arm can someday match Machado's.

"I'm a taller guy so I need to stay low. Stay low to catch the ball and then whenever I throw I can get up a little taller and let my arm action work. I have a strong arm, so I just let it do its thing. Last year we worked on getting a higher throwing motion to clean up some throwing mistakes. I feel like we got that cleaned up."

Adonys Guzman

Adonys Guzman is headed to Boston College on a baseball scholarship to be a catcher. Guzman was one of the more highly-regarded high school catching prospects in the country, particularly for his defense and his strong throwing arm. Guzman, whose family is Dominican, borrows something from that country's baseball culture to make himself better.

"The one thing I do that's a little bit unique in the United States is that I toss with softballs a lot. Just so that when I get a grip on the baseball that it's a little lighter and I have more control of it.

"When I was younger, going to different places and being around people who did it a lot in the Dominican Republic, I picked it up."

Eric Brown

Eric Brown was the Brewers' first-round pick out of Coastal Carolina after excelling there as a shortstop. Brown was considered one of the top defensive infielders in 2022's draft class. As a kid, he did a lot of film study on major leaguers to see if what they did might work for him.

"I watched José Iglesias on YouTube. Just seeing how he made plays look. It looked effortless and so smooth. He has all these different arm angles that he can throw from. I've added that to my game, a lower arm slot, because of him."

--

Check out *The Sports Info Solutions Baseball Podcast* wherever you get your podcasts.

Team Statistics

Jackson Lewis

In comparison to the two decades worth of data collected by Sports Info Solutions, the 2022 season was noteworthy in many aspects. Here are a few ways in which teams this season topped the rest:

- The Mets appeared to be in control of the NL East at multiple points this season, building leads of 10½ and 7 games in June and August, respectively. However, they managed to squander both in remarkable fashion. In the SIS era, 10½ games clocks in as the largest divisional collapse at any point in the season, while their 7 game August-or-later slip is topped only by one team… the 2007 Mets. Additionally, their 176 days leading or sharing the lead of the East is the most by any non-division winner.

- On the brighter side, the Yankees impressed on defense by racking up 129 Defensive Runs Saved, the most since SIS began tracking the stat in 2003. Furthermore, their combined Pitcher/Catcher clip ties the 2018 Reds as the highest for a single season battery.

- The Dodgers and Nationals bookended this year's pitching season. The Dodgers starting pitchers notched the second-highest winning percentage (73%) over the past 20 years, behind only the 2020 version of themselves. In fact, if we include their 2021 season, their rotation has the top three marks, and it's not particularly close. They also recorded the lowest team and starting pitcher ERA over the course of this season.

  On the opposite end of the spectrum, the National's rotation recorded the sixth-lowest winning percentage we've seen, winning in merely 26% of starts. Their starting pitchers' 5.97 ERA also comes in as our fifth-lowest single season mark.

2022 American League Standings

Overall

Team	W-L	Pct	GB	D1	LD1	LLd	Team	W-L	Pct	GB	D1	LD1	LLd	Team	W-L	Pct	GB	D1	LD1	LLd
EAST							**CENTRAL**							**WEST**						
New York Yankees	99-63	.611	0.0	169	10/5	15.5	Cleveland Guardians	92-70	.568	0.0	67	10/5	11.0	Houston Astros	106-56	.654	0.0	158	10/5	18.0
Toronto Blue Jays	92-70	.568	7.0	17	4/26	1.0	Chicago White Sox	81-81	.500	11.0	11	4/20	2.0	Seattle Mariners	90-72	.556	16.0	6	4/26	1.0
Tampa Bay Rays	86-76	.531	13.0	7	4/14	1.0	Minnesota Twins	78-84	.481	14.0	105	9/4	5.5	Los Angeles Angels	73-89	.451	33.0	19	5/10	2.5
Baltimore Orioles	83-79	.512	16.0	0	-	0.0	Detroit Tigers	66-96	.407	26.0	1	4/8	0.0	Texas Rangers	68-94	.420	38.0	0	-	0.0
Boston Red Sox	78-84	.481	21.0	1	4/19	0.0	Kansas City Royals	65-97	.401	27.0	4	4/10	1.0	Oakland Athletics	60-102	.370	46.0	1	4/19	0.0

Wild Card Clinch Dates: Toronto 9/29, Seattle 9/30, Tampa Bay 9/30. Division Clinch Dates: Houston 9/19, Cleveland 9/25, New York 9/27.

D1 = Number of days a team had at least a share of first place of their division; LD1 = Last date the team had at least a share of first place; LLd = The largest number of games that a team led their division by.

East Division

Tm	AT		VERSUS						CONDITIONS				GAME			MONTHLY						ALL-STAR	
	Home	Road	East	Cent	West	NL	LHS	RHS	Day	Night	Grass	Turf	1-Rn	5+Rn	Xinn	April	May	June	July	Aug	Sept	Pre	Post
NYY	57-24	42-39	47-29	25-8	17-16	10-10	26-15	73-48	32-18	67-45	86-53	13-10	31-27	32-6	10-8	15-6	19-9	22-6	13-13	10-18	20-11	64-28	35-35
Tor	47-34	45-36	43-33	19-15	17-15	13-7	12-20	80-50	34-27	58-43	39-30	53-40	30-20	26-18	8-7	14-8	14-12	15-13	14-12	13-14	22-11	50-43	42-27
TB	51-30	35-46	40-36	15-17	19-15	12-8	22-16	64-60	34-27	52-49	26-39	60-37	27-27	24-17	11-10	12-9	16-12	12-14	14-13	18-9	14-19	51-41	35-35
Bal	45-36	38-43	34-42	16-17	21-12	12-8	27-23	56-56	24-34	59-45	73-67	10-12	23-24	18-19	8-5	7-14	14-16	14-12	16-9	17-10	15-18	46-46	37-33
Bos	43-38	35-46	26-50	18-15	25-8	9-11	23-13	55-71	24-26	54-58	73-66	5-18	24-26	22-28	7-11	9-13	14-14	20-6	8-19	12-16	15-16	48-45	30-39

Central Division

Tm	AT		VERSUS						CONDITIONS				GAME			MONTHLY						ALL-STAR	
	Home	Road	East	Cent	West	NL	LHS	RHS	Day	Night	Grass	Turf	1-Rn	5+Rn	Xinn	April	May	June	July	Aug	Sept	Pre	Post
Cle	46-35	46-35	15-17	47-29	18-16	12-8	28-17	64-53	37-29	55-41	85-68	7-2	28-17	19-18	13-6	9-12	12-12	18-10	13-15	16-11	24-10	46-44	46-26
CWS	37-44	44-37	15-17	37-39	18-16	11-9	17-20	64-61	37-31	44-50	77-75	4-6	27-16	20-21	6-9	8-12	15-12	12-15	16-11	13-16	17-15	46-46	35-35
Min	46-35	32-49	18-16	39-37	13-19	8-12	27-22	51-62	32-33	46-51	72-78	6-6	20-28	27-27	5-10	12-9	18-12	13-15	10-12	14-14	11-22	50-44	28-40
Det	36-46	30-50	11-21	34-42	12-19	11-9	20-24	46-72	31-42	35-54	60-89	6-7	22-20	15-29	3-7	7-13	12-17	10-15	12-17	9-18	16-16	37-55	29-41
KC	39-42	26-55	13-22	33-43	12-19	7-13	20-21	45-76	29-38	36-59	62-87	3-10	16-20	12-30	5-5	7-12	9-20	11-13	13-15	13-16	12-19	36-56	29-41

West Division

Tm	AT		VERSUS						CONDITIONS				GAME			MONTHLY						ALL-STAR	
	Home	Road	East	Cent	West	NL	LHS	RHS	Day	Night	Grass	Turf	1-Rn	5+Rn	Xinn	April	May	June	July	Aug	Sept	Pre	Post
Hou	55-26	51-30	17-15	26-8	51-25	12-8	42-12	64-44	42-13	64-43	94-51	12-5	28-16	35-13	5-6	11-10	21-8	16-9	19-9	17-11	22-9	59-32	47-24
Sea	46-35	44-37	16-17	21-12	41-35	12-8	22-20	68-52	36-27	54-45	80-63	10-9	34-22	21-14	11-5	11-10	10-18	16-13	18-7	17-10	18-14	51-42	39-30
LAA	40-41	33-48	11-23	18-14	37-39	7-13	23-26	50-63	21-28	52-61	65-78	8-11	18-28	21-26	7-8	14-8	13-15	10-18	6-18	14-15	16-15	39-53	34-36
Tex	34-47	34-47	9-24	17-16	31-45	11-9	27-28	41-66	23-34	45-60	30-42	38-52	15-35	19-18	6-9	7-14	17-10	12-14	10-17	12-16	10-23	41-49	27-45
Oak	29-51	31-51	13-20	12-21	30-46	5-15	16-27	44-75	28-43	32-59	52-94	8-8	17-25	10-29	6-4	10-11	10-21	5-21	14-12	10-17	11-20	32-61	28-41

Team vs. Team Breakdown

Team	EAST					CENTRAL					WEST				
	NYY	Tor	TB	Bal	Bos	Cle	CWS	Min	Det	KC	Hou	Sea	LAA	Tex	Oak
New York Yankees	-	11	11	12	13	5	4	5	6	2	2	4	4	5	
Toronto Blue Jays	8	-	9	10	16	2	4	3	5	5	4	2	4	4	3
Tampa Bay Rays	8	10	-	10	12	2	2	2	5	4	1	5	5	4	4
Baltimore Orioles	7	9	9	-	9	3	5	3	1	4	4	2	6	6	3
Boston Red Sox	6	3	7	10	-	5	2	3	5	3	4	6	4	6	5
Cleveland Guardians	1	5	4	3	2	-	12	13	10	12	3	1	3	5	6
Chicago White Sox	3	2	4	2	4	7	-	9	12	9	3	4	3	3	5
Minnesota Twins	2	4	4	4	4	6	10	-	11	12	0	4	2	2	5
Detroit Tigers	1	2	2	5	1	9	7	8	-	10	0	1	3	4	2
Kansas City Royals	1	2	3	3	4	7	10	7	9	-	2	2	3	2	3
Houston Astros	5	2	5	3	2	4	4	6	7	5	-	12	13	14	12
Seattle Mariners	4	5	2	4	1	6	2	3	6	4	7	-	9	14	11
Los Angeles Angels	2	3	2	1	3	4	4	4	3	3	6	10	-	9	12
Texas Rangers	3	2	3	0	1	1	4	5	3	4	5	5	10	-	11
Oakland Athletics	2	3	3	4	1	1	2	1	5	3	7	8	7	8	-

2022 National League Standings

Overall

EAST							CENTRAL							WEST						
Team	W-L	Pct	GB	D1	LD1	LLd	Team	W-L	Pct	GB	D1	LD1	LLd	Team	W-L	Pct	GB	D1	LD1	LLd
Atlanta Braves	101-61	.623	0.0	9	10/5	2.0	St Louis Cardinals	93-69	.574	0.0	96	10/5	9.5	Los Angeles Dodgers	111-51	.685	0.0	170	10/5	23.0
New York Mets	101-61	.623	0.0	176	10/5	10.5	Milwaukee Brewers	86-76	.531	7.0	92	8/5	4.5	San Diego Padres	89-73	.549	22.0	5	6/17	0.5
Philadelphia Phillies	87-75	.537	14.0	1	4/11	0.5	Chicago Cubs	74-88	.457	19.0	7	4/14	0.5	San Francisco Giants	81-81	.500	30.0	9	4/30	0.5
Miami Marlins	69-93	.426	32.0	0	-	0.0	Pittsburgh Pirates	62-100	.383	31.0	0	-	0.0	Arizona Diamondbacks	74-88	.457	37.0	1	4/7	1.0
Washington Nationals	55-107	.340	46.0	0	-	0.0	Cincinnati Reds	62-100	.383	31.0	1	4/7	0.0	Colorado Rockies	68-94	.420	43.0	6	4/19	0.5

Wild Card Clinch Dates: New York 9/19, San Diego 10/2, Philadelphia 10/4. Division Clinch Dates: Los Angeles 9/13, St Louis 9/27, Atlanta 10/4.

D1 = Number of days a team had at least a share of first place of their division; LD1 = Last date the team had at least a share of first place; LLd = The largest number of games that a team led their division

East Division

Tm	AT		VERSUS						CONDITIONS				GAME			MONTHLY						ALL-STAR	
	Home	Road	East	Cent	West	AL	LHS	RHS	Day	Night	Grass	Turf	1-Rn	5+Rn	Xinn	April	May	June	July	Aug	Sept	Pre	Post
Atl	55-26	46-35	48-28	21-12	19-14	13-7	37-17	64-44	24-26	77-35	92-54	9-7	26-18	26-8	6-7	10-12	13-15	21-6	18-8	18-10	21-10	56-38	45-23
NYM	54-27	47-34	50-26	23-10	19-14	9-11	32-23	69-38	37-18	64-43	92-58	9-3	21-15	31-19	10-2	15-7	19-10	13-12	17-8	19-11	18-13	58-35	43-26
Phi	47-34	40-41	41-35	20-13	17-16	9-11	28-18	59-57	25-28	62-47	80-65	7-10	22-25	26-22	8-6	11-11	10-18	19-8	15-10	18-11	14-17	49-43	38-32
Mia	34-47	35-46	34-42	15-18	12-21	8-12	18-20	51-73	25-34	44-59	34-42	35-51	24-40	11-24	4-9	12-8	7-19	15-13	13-15	8-20	14-18	43-48	26-45
Was	26-55	29-52	17-59	15-18	15-18	8-12	16-40	39-67	25-37	30-70	50-97	5-10	17-22	19-39	3-7	7-16	11-17	11-16	6-19	9-18	11-21	31-63	24-44

Central Division

Tm	AT		VERSUS						CONDITIONS				GAME			MONTHLY						ALL-STAR	
	Home	Road	East	Cent	West	AL	LHS	RHS	Day	Night	Grass	Turf	1-Rn	5+Rn	Xinn	April	May	June	July	Aug	Sept	Pre	Post
StL	53-28	40-41	16-18	48-28	19-13	10-10	24-11	69-58	30-27	63-42	87-64	6-5	26-17	29-19	8-4	11-9	17-12	15-14	11-13	22-7	17-14	50-44	43-25
Mil	46-35	40-41	13-18	42-34	16-19	15-5	27-25	59-51	33-31	53-45	81-72	5-4	28-23	17-19	9-9	15-7	17-12	12-15	13-11	12-15	17-16	50-43	36-33
ChC	37-44	37-44	21-10	37-39	10-25	6-14	19-24	55-64	34-32	40-56	69-84	5-4	26-27	19-26	7-12	8-13	12-16	10-17	11-14	15-15	18-13	35-57	39-31
Pit	34-47	28-53	9-26	35-41	14-17	4-16	22-33	40-67	27-35	35-65	59-92	3-8	21-27	16-30	4-9	9-12	12-15	10-18	9-17	9-19	13-19	39-54	23-46
Cin	33-48	29-52	12-22	28-48	10-22	12-8	17-29	45-71	24-37	38-63	57-96	5-4	21-23	15-32	6-5	3-18	14-13	9-18	14-12	11-17	11-22	34-57	28-43

West Division

Tm	AT		VERSUS						CONDITIONS				GAME			MONTHLY						ALL-STAR	
	Home	Road	East	Cent	West	AL	LHS	RHS	Day	Night	Grass	Turf	1-Rn	5+Rn	Xinn	April	May	June	July	Aug	Sept	Pre	Post
LAD	57-24	54-27	19-14	23-10	54-22	15-5	32-16	79-35	32-14	79-37	110-47	10-4	16-15	42-8	6-9	13-7	20-9	14-12	21-5	22-6	21-12	60-30	51-21
SD	44-37	45-36	19-15	21-11	41-35	8-12	31-23	58-50	28-30	61-43	81-68	8-5	30-17	26-22	12-5	14-8	16-11	16-13	11-14	16-13	16-14	52-42	37-31
SF	44-37	37-44	19-14	19-14	33-43	10-10	29-26	52-55	36-33	45-48	76-73	5-8	22-27	21-19	7-7	14-7	13-14	13-13	11-17	10-17	20-13	48-43	33-38
Ari	40-41	34-47	16-15	17-18	29-47	12-8	23-25	51-63	29-30	45-58	31-47	43-41	17-29	23-22	5-7	10-12	15-14	9-16	11-14	16-12	13-20	40-52	34-36
Col	41-40	27-54	10-24	16-16	33-43	9-11	29-32	39-62	25-36	43-58	61-86	7-8	23-24	10-30	6-8	12-9	10-17	11-17	13-14	10-18	12-19	43-50	25-44

Team vs. Team Breakdown

	EAST					CENTRAL					WEST				
	Atl	NYM	Phi	Mia	Was	StL	Mil	ChC	Pit	Cin	LAD	SD	SF	Ari	Col
Atlanta Braves	-	10	11	13	14	4	3	3	7	4	2	3	4	4	6
New York Mets	9	-	14	13	14	5	4	3	6	5	4	2	4	4	5
Philadelphia Phillies	8	5	-	12	16	4	4	0	6	6	4	4	1	3	5
Miami Marlins	6	6	7	-	15	2	4	2	4	3	1	3	3	1	4
Washington Nationals	5	5	3	4	-	3	3	2	3	4	3	3	2	3	4
St Louis Cardinals	3	2	3	4	4	-	10	13	13	12	2	4	4	5	4
Milwaukee Brewers	3	2	2	3	3	9	-	9	11	13	3	3	3	3	4
Chicago Cubs	3	4	6	4	4	6	10	-	10	11	0	2	2	3	3
Pittsburgh Pirates	0	1	1	3	4	6	8	9	-	12	5	2	1	3	3
Cincinnati Reds	3	1	4	1	4	7	6	8	7	-	0	0	4	4	2
Los Angeles Dodgers	4	3	3	6	3	4	4	7	1	7	-	14	15	14	11
San Diego Padres	4	4	3	4	4	2	4	5	4	6	5	-	13	14	9
San Francisco Giants	3	3	5	4	4	3	4	5	5	2	4	6	-	9	14
Arizona Diamondbacks	2	2	3	5	4	2	4	4	4	3	5	5	10	-	9
Colorado Rockies	1	2	2	2	3	2	3	4	3	4	8	10	5	10	-

American League Batting

Tm	G	AB	H	2B	3B	HR	(Hm	Rd)	TB	R	RBI	TBB	IBB	SO	HBP	SH	SF	ShO	SB	CS	SB%	GDP	LOB	Avg	OBP	Slg
																			BASERUNNING					PERCENTAGES		
NYY	162	5422	1308	225	8	254	(136	118)	2311	807	764	620	36	1391	70	14	41	12	102	33	.76	121	1632	.241	.325	.426
Tor	162	5555	1464	307	12	200	(102	98)	2395	775	756	500	13	1242	55	8	33	8	67	35	.66	136	1667	.264	.329	.431
Hou	162	5409	1341	284	13	214	(116	98)	2293	737	715	528	18	1179	60	9	42	11	83	22	.79	118	1615	.248	.319	.424
Bos	162	5539	1427	352	12	155	(86	69)	2268	735	704	478	23	1373	63	12	50	4	52	20	.72	131	1666	.258	.321	.409
Tex	162	5478	1308	224	20	198	(101	97)	2166	707	670	456	12	1446	47	10	38	4	128	41	.76	82	1532	.239	.301	.395
Cle	162	5558	1410	273	31	127	(50	77)	2126	698	662	450	36	1122	81	22	52	12	119	27	.82	115	1780	.254	.316	.383
Min	162	5476	1356	269	18	178	(89	89)	2195	696	668	518	11	1353	62	10	46	13	38	17	.69	133	1687	.248	.317	.401
Sea	162	5375	1236	229	19	197	(97	100)	2094	690	663	596	17	1397	89	9	45	12	83	27	.75	120	1679	.230	.315	.390
CWS	162	5611	1435	272	9	149	(77	72)	2172	686	654	388	9	1269	73	16	35	6	58	10	.85	127	1651	.256	.310	.387
Bal	162	5429	1281	275	25	171	(79	92)	2119	674	639	476	10	1390	83	12	43	11	95	31	.75	95	1606	.236	.305	.390
TB	162	5412	1294	296	17	139	(71	68)	2041	666	634	500	13	1395	57	7	31	10	95	37	.72	93	1613	.239	.309	.377
KC	162	5437	1327	247	38	138	(65	73)	2064	640	613	460	7	1287	48	20	44	16	104	34	.75	101	1641	.244	.306	.380
LAA	162	5423	1265	219	31	190	(106	84)	2116	623	600	449	28	1539	54	25	25	12	77	27	.74	95	1578	.233	.297	.390
Oak	162	5314	1147	249	15	137	(53	84)	1837	568	537	433	7	1389	59	22	33	14	78	23	.77	109	1457	.216	.281	.346
Det	162	5378	1240	235	27	110	(52	58)	1859	557	530	380	8	1413	58	10	44	22	47	24	.66	108	1542	.231	.286	.346
AL	1215	81816	19839	3956	295	2557	(1280	1277)	32056	10259	9809	7232	248	20185	959	206	602	171	1226	408	.75	1684	24346	.242	.309	.392

American League Pitching

Tm	G	CG	Rel	IP	BFP	H	R	ER	HR	SH	SF	HB	TBB	IBB	SO	WP	Bk	W	L	Pct.	ShO	Sv-Op	Hld	OAvg	OOBP	OSlg	ERA
	HOW MUCH THEY PITCHED					WHAT THEY GAVE UP												THE RESULTS									
Hou	162	3	480	1445.1	5856	1121	518	465	134	13	30	60	458	6	1524	56	6	106	56	.654	18	53-69	102	.212	.281	.332	2.90
NYY	162	1	507	1451.2	5938	1177	567	532	157	13	27	65	444	10	1459	40	5	99	63	.611	16	47-68	80	.219	.285	.355	3.30
TB	162	0	572	1435.2	5930	1260	614	544	172	15	34	66	384	15	1384	54	4	86	76	.531	10	44-77	106	.232	.289	.379	3.41
Sea	162	0	536	1447.0	5986	1277	623	577	186	18	35	56	447	24	1391	45	0	90	72	.556	10	40-55	91	.235	.298	.389	3.59
Cle	162	1	507	1456.0	5989	1252	634	560	172	14	36	57	435	14	1390	49	2	92	70	.568	8	51-68	61	.230	.292	.373	3.46
LAA	162	2	490	1435.2	6038	1241	668	601	168	17	33	60	540	23	1383	64	3	73	89	.451	17	38-66	78	.230	.306	.379	3.77
Tor	162	0	584	1441.1	6053	1356	679	620	180	14	42	76	424	15	1390	29	5	92	70	.568	10	46-69	91	.247	.308	.399	3.87
Min	162	0	548	1437.0	6042	1320	684	636	184	10	39	66	468	19	1336	50	4	78	84	.481	17	28-54	100	.242	.307	.400	3.98
Bal	162	2	541	1433.1	6058	1406	688	632	171	8	47	64	443	8	1214	47	4	83	79	.512	15	46-77	56	.247	.317	.407	3.97
Det	162	0	580	1419.2	6047	1336	713	637	167	17	56	57	511	9	1195	59	2	66	96	.407	8	38-55	90	.247	.316	.393	4.04
CWS	162	2	549	1447.2	6145	1330	717	631	166	14	47	51	533	15	1450	64	6	81	81	.500	14	48-70	102	.242	.312	.387	3.92
Tex	162	1	532	1435.0	6167	1345	743	673	169	16	44	71	581	16	1314	66	7	79	94	.420	10	37-65	85	.247	.325	.397	4.22
Oak	162	0	530	1426.1	6121	1394	770	717	195	15	38	72	503	37	1203	62	5	60	102	.370	7	34-59	105	.254	.323	.428	4.52
Bos	162	5	576	1431.0	6167	1411	787	721	185	7	45	72	526	17	1346	60	8	78	84	.481	10	39-66	87	.256	.326	.419	4.53
KC	162	0	560	1416.0	6249	1493	810	740	173	19	65	71	589	15	1191	88	6	65	97	.401	9	33-54	80	.271	.346	.425	4.70
AL	1215	17	8092	21558.2	90786	19719	10215	9286	2579	210	618	964	7286	243	20170	833	67	1217	1213	.501	179	622-952	1337	.241	.309	.391	3.88

American League Fielding

Team	G	Inn	PO	Ast	OFAst	E	(Throw	Field)	TC	DP	GDP	SB	CS	SB%	CPkof	PPkof	PB	UER	UERA	FPct
Seattle	162	1447.0	4341	1317	24	69	36	33	5727	114	100	89	35	.72	0	3	4	46	0.29	.988
New York	162	1451.2	4355	1473	27	74	31	43	5902	103	90	49	28	.64	4	6	8	35	0.22	.987
Houston	162	1445.1	4336	1290	22	72	36	36	5698	122	110	76	23	.77	2	2	12	53	0.33	.987
Kansas City	162	1416.0	4248	1499	22	82	38	44	5829	153	135	58	25	.70	1	5	8	70	0.44	.986
Toronto	162	1441.1	4324	1347	31	82	44	38	5753	120	97	83	33	.72	5	4	2	59	0.37	.986
Tampa Bay	162	1435.2	4307	1386	17	84	37	47	5777	110	98	76	26	.75	1	2	9	70	0.44	.985
Los Angeles	162	1435.2	4307	1382	20	84	41	43	5773	134	121	99	23	.81	0	2	10	67	0.42	.985
Minnesota	162	1437.0	4311	1308	30	83	48	35	5702	119	107	92	23	.80	0	4	12	48	0.30	.985
Boston	162	1431.0	4293	1447	22	85	48	37	5825	134	116	102	28	.78	1	4	6	66	0.42	.985
Baltimore	162	1433.1	4300	1530	29	91	47	44	5921	151	134	52	24	.68	0	2	5	56	0.35	.985
Oakland	162	1426.1	4279	1465	17	92	45	47	5836	139	118	77	29	.73	3	4	3	53	0.33	.984
Texas	162	1435.0	4305	1529	28	96	48	48	5930	141	123	104	27	.79	0	3	11	70	0.44	.984
Detroit	162	1419.2	4259	1403	16	94	45	49	5756	137	122	79	33	.71	0	3	9	76	0.48	.984
Cleveland	162	1456.0	4368	1444	31	97	54	43	5909	127	107	94	29	.76	2	3	2	74	0.46	.984
Chicago	162	1447.2	4343	1293	16	102	43	59	5738	120	101	96	26	.79	0	5	15	86	0.53	.982
American League	1215	21558.2	64676	21113	352	1287	641	646	87076	1926	1679	1226	412	.75	19	52	116	929	0.39	.985

National League Batting

Tm	G	AB	H	2B	3B	HR	(Hm	Rd)	TB	R	RBI	TBB	IBB	SO	HBP	SH	SF	ShO	SB	CS	SB%	GDP	LOB	Avg	OBP	Slg
LAD	162	5526	1418	325	31	212	(106	106)	2441	847	812	607	22	1374	56	3	53	7	98	18	.84	85	1695	.257	.333	.442
Atl	162	5509	1394	298	11	243	(125	118)	2443	789	753	470	13	1498	66	1	36	5	87	31	.74	103	1544	.253	.317	.443
NYM	162	5489	1422	272	27	171	(81	90)	2261	772	735	510	25	1217	112	20	44	8	62	22	.74	122	1747	.259	.332	.412
StL	162	5496	1386	290	21	197	(98	99)	2309	772	739	537	11	1226	80	5	45	16	95	25	.79	112	1717	.252	.325	.420
Phi	162	5496	1392	255	29	205	(107	98)	2320	747	719	478	15	1363	52	6	44	14	105	28	.79	116	1637	.253	.317	.422
Mil	162	5417	1271	251	17	219	(110	109)	2213	725	703	577	25	1464	80	11	37	11	96	30	.76	117	1655	.235	.315	.409
SF	162	5392	1261	255	18	183	(86	97)	2101	716	683	571	14	1462	95	6	53	9	64	16	.80	109	1622	.234	.315	.390
SD	162	5468	1317	275	18	153	(77	76)	2087	705	682	574	24	1327	65	17	46	11	49	22	.69	95	1728	.241	.318	.382
Ari	162	5351	1232	262	24	173	(71	102)	2061	702	658	531	14	1341	60	31	50	15	104	29	.78	97	1576	.230	.304	.385
Col	162	5540	1408	280	34	149	(98	51)	2203	698	669	453	10	1330	61	10	40	12	45	20	.69	139	1665	.254	.315	.398
ChC	162	5425	1293	265	31	159	(73	86)	2097	657	620	507	16	1448	84	19	36	12	111	37	.75	130	1662	.238	.311	.387
Cin	162	5380	1264	235	18	156	(89	67)	2003	648	618	452	6	1430	92	12	33	9	58	33	.64	127	1556	.235	.304	.372
Was	162	5434	1351	252	20	136	(76	60)	2051	603	583	442	12	1221	60	20	37	12	75	31	.71	140	1668	.249	.310	.377
Pit	162	5331	1186	221	29	158	(74	84)	1939	591	555	476	14	1497	54	19	32	15	89	32	.74	96	1512	.222	.291	.364
Mia	162	5395	1241	248	20	144	(71	73)	1961	586	554	436	6	1429	70	4	36	14	122	29	.81	120	1558	.230	.294	.363
NL	1215	81649	19836	3984	348	2658	(1342	1316)	32490	10558	10079	7621	227	20627	1087	184	622	170	1260	403	.76	1708	24542	.243	.314	.398

National League Pitching

Tm	G	CG	Rel	IP	BFP	H	R	ER	HR	SH	SF	HB	TBB	IBB	SO	WP	Bk	W	L	Pct.	ShO	Sv-Op	Hld	OAvg	OOBP	OSlg	ERA
LAD	162	1	563	1451.1	5865	1114	513	451	152	15	32	75	407	13	1465	38	3	111	51	.685	15	43-61	90	.209	.273	.344	2.80
NYM	162	0	483	1438.2	5950	1274	606	570	169	12	27	71	428	13	1565	35	2	101	61	.623	19	41-56	76	.236	.299	.377	3.57
Atl	162	1	518	1448.0	6031	1224	609	556	148	9	46	62	500	21	1554	55	4	101	61	.623	9	55-83	114	.226	.297	.354	3.46
StL	162	3	466	1435.2	6014	1335	637	605	146	14	39	60	489	11	1177	43	3	93	69	.574	17	37-53	65	.247	.314	.382	3.79
SD	162	0	487	1443.1	6047	1263	660	611	173	8	48	88	468	6	1451	54	5	89	73	.549	15	48-70	70	.232	.301	.377	3.81
Mia	162	6	532	1437.1	6056	1311	676	618	173	14	32	76	511	19	1437	54	3	69	93	.426	10	41-70	73	.242	.314	.406	3.87
Phi	162	3	516	1428.1	6006	1330	685	630	150	10	35	68	463	16	1423	47	3	87	75	.537	15	42-60	87	.245	.310	.391	3.97
Mil	162	0	548	1446.0	6057	1238	688	615	190	13	44	67	521	12	1530	47	4	86	76	.531	11	52-81	103	.229	.302	.388	3.83
SF	162	1	576	1433.0	6070	1397	697	613	132	18	37	52	441	16	1370	53	2	81	81	.500	8	39-59	74	.253	.313	.390	3.85
ChC	162	0	528	1443.2	6162	1342	731	642	207	5	35	73	540	19	1383	53	8	74	88	.457	11	44-74	57	.244	.318	.414	4.00
Ari	162	0	546	1430.0	6065	1345	740	676	191	13	40	59	504	18	1216	51	3	74	88	.457	10	33-60	76	.247	.315	.414	4.25
Cin	162	1	574	1423.1	6220	1366	815	768	213	11	47	110	612	21	1414	58	5	62	100	.383	6	31-52	99	.251	.336	.429	4.86
Pit	162	0	504	1421.0	6263	1432	817	735	164	13	34	87	586	23	1250	62	5	62	100	.383	6	33-60	67	.259	.337	.411	4.66
Was	162	2	588	1411.2	6220	1469	855	785	244	13	51	75	558	12	1220	59	2	55	107	.340	4	28-44	59	.266	.339	.452	5.00
Col	162	1	497	1425.1	6240	1516	873	802	184	12	59	59	539	12	1187	65	3	68	94	.420	6	43-64	65	.272	.340	.446	5.06
NL	1215	19	7926	21516.2	91266	19956	10602	9677	2636	180	606	1082	7567	232	20642	774	55	1213	1217	.499	162	610-947	1135	.244	.314	.399	4.05

National League Fielding

Team	G	Inn	PO	Ast	OFAst	E	(Throw	Field)	TC	DP	GDP	SB	CS	SB%	CPkof	PPkof	PB	UER	UERA	FPct
St Louis	162	1435.2	4307	1701	28	66	34	32	6074	181	157	49	20	.71	0	0	5	32	0.20	.989
New York	162	1438.2	4316	1358	20	67	35	32	5741	128	116	86	28	.75	2	13	5	36	0.23	.988
Miami	162	1437.1	4312	1460	25	69	40	29	5841	143	124	92	27	.77	1	6	2	58	0.36	.988
Philadelphia	162	1428.1	4285	1416	22	69	41	28	5770	129	106	56	37	.60	2	6	5	55	0.35	.988
San Diego	162	1443.1	4330	1362	18	76	38	38	5768	116	105	89	13	.87	1	1	13	49	0.31	.987
Atlanta	162	1448.0	4344	1382	14	77	31	46	5803	110	99	82	22	.79	0	4	7	53	0.33	.987
Los Angeles	162	1451.1	4354	1351	16	83	46	37	5788	120	101	68	19	.78	0	1	6	62	0.38	.986
Cincinnati	162	1423.1	4270	1296	35	81	47	34	5647	115	98	122	31	.68	2	0	9	47	0.30	.986
Arizona	162	1430.0	4290	1370	30	86	39	47	5746	134	107	84	32	.72	2	8	13	64	0.40	.985
Milwaukee	162	1446.0	4338	1419	22	91	49	42	5848	122	101	79	28	.74	0	7	12	73	0.45	.984
Chicago	162	1443.2	4331	1453	23	96	51	45	5880	139	119	77	32	.71	2	0	12	89	0.55	.984
Colorado	162	1425.1	4276	1592	26	100	53	47	5968	154	134	101	28	.78	5	3	5	71	0.45	.983
San Francisco	162	1433.0	4299	1546	23	100	52	48	5945	130	112	86	22	.80	1	2	7	84	0.53	.983
Washington	162	1411.2	4235	1410	24	104	66	38	5749	125	106	97	28	.78	4	1	7	70	0.45	.982
Pittsburgh	162	1421.0	4263	1507	16	121	49	72	5891	152	128	92	32	.74	3	1	7	82	0.52	.979
National League	1215	21516.2	64550	21623	342	1286	671	615	87459	1998	1713	1260	399	.76	25	53	115	925	0.39	.985

Team Pitching Staff Summary

Team	Starters				Bullpen					
	IP	ERA	ERA Rank	W-L	IP	ERA	ERA Rank	W-L	Sv-Opp	Sv Pct
Arizona Diamondbacks	872.0	4.05	19	44-47	558.0	4.58	25	30-41	33-60	55%
Atlanta Braves	890.1	3.72	9	70-40	557.2	3.03	4	31-21	55-83	66%
Baltimore Orioles	802.1	4.35	21	41-50	631.0	3.49	9	42-29	46-57	81%
Boston Red Sox	807.2	4.49	22	45-51	623.1	4.59	26	33-33	39-66	59%
Chicago Cubs	786.2	3.95	17	37-52	657.0	4.12	21	37-36	44-74	59%
Chicago White Sox	865.1	3.89	15	52-59	582.1	4.00	19	29-22	48-70	69%
Cincinnati Reds	809.2	4.97	28	33-73	613.2	4.72	28	29-27	31-52	60%
Cleveland Guardians	907.0	3.73	10	49-51	549.0	3.05	5	43-19	51-68	75%
Colorado Rockies	859.2	5.22	29	39-66	565.2	4.85	30	29-28	43-64	67%
Detroit Tigers	802.2	4.51	23	35-63	617.0	3.43	8	31-33	38-55	69%
Houston Astros	950.0	2.95	2	84-39	495.1	2.80	1	22-17	53-69	77%
Kansas City Royals	832.2	4.76	27	32-70	583.1	4.66	27	33-27	33-54	61%
Los Angeles Angels	843.1	3.67	6	52-59	592.1	3.95	18	21-30	38-66	58%
Los Angeles Dodgers	870.1	2.75	1	73-27	581.0	2.87	2	38-24	43-61	70%
Miami Marlins	881.2	3.70	8	44-61	555.2	4.15	22	25-32	41-70	59%
Milwaukee Brewers	849.2	3.75	11	50-44	596.1	3.94	17	36-32	52-81	64%
Minnesota Twins	782.2	4.11	20	44-49	654.1	3.84	15	34-35	28-54	52%
New York Mets	878.0	3.61	5	70-42	560.2	3.55	10	31-19	41-56	73%
New York Yankees	894.1	3.51	4	54-33	557.1	2.97	3	45-30	47-68	69%
Oakland Athletics	850.1	4.69	26	40-74	576.0	4.31	24	20-28	34-59	58%
Philadelphia Phillies	896.2	3.80	13	59-47	531.2	4.27	23	28-28	42-60	70%
Pittsburgh Pirates	767.1	4.61	24	21-62	653.2	4.72	28	41-38	33-60	55%
San Diego Padres	901.0	3.80	13	55-49	542.1	3.83	14	34-24	48-70	69%
San Francisco Giants	783.0	3.68	7	47-47	650.0	4.08	20	34-34	39-59	66%
Seattle Mariners	903.0	3.75	11	56-52	544.0	3.33	6	34-20	40-55	73%
St Louis Cardinals	864.1	3.92	16	52-53	571.1	3.61	11	41-16	37-53	70%
Tampa Bay Rays	753.0	3.45	3	43-42	682.2	3.36	7	43-34	44-77	57%
Texas Rangers	793.1	4.63	25	37-53	641.2	3.72	12	31-41	37-65	57%
Toronto Blue Jays	827.2	3.98	18	55-43	613.2	3.77	13	37-27	46-69	67%
Washington Nationals	773.2	5.97	30	30-86	638.0	3.84	15	25-21	28-44	64%

Team Defense
Defensive Runs Saved by Position and Team

Team	P	C	1B	2B	3B	SS	LF	CF	RF	Shifts	Total
New York Yankees	21	24	1	9	19	12	10	-5	13	17	129
Los Angeles Dodgers	2	10	-1	5	7	-1	-2	0	16	38	86
Cleveland Guardians	-1	6	1	12	-1	7	21	12	0	9	79
Houston Astros	-6	-3	-1	-9	-4	15	7	10	14	35	67
St Louis Cardinals	8	-2	2	7	27	14	-3	6	-3	18	67
Arizona Diamondbacks	6	-10	17	-6	-4	-9	1	13	15	30	56
Milwaukee Brewers	3	4	-7	-1	7	7	4	8	1	22	53
Toronto Blue Jays	-2	15	6	2	1	-15	4	-5	-5	16	44
Seattle Mariners	-5	10	4	0	-4	-9	-9	3	14	26	36
Baltimore Orioles	1	8	4	-9	8	12	-5	5	6	3	36
Atlanta Braves	2	2	6	-5	5	9	-15	8	-4	28	31
Minnesota Twins	-8	5	-5	-4	3	1	7	10	10	23	27
Detroit Tigers	-1	-17	-2	8	-5	-4	21	1	-2	25	25
Tampa Bay Rays	-10	2	-7	5	-4	11	-3	-1	9	11	15
New York Mets	12	12	-5	1	-14	-3	-4	-2	1	12	13
Miami Marlins	-5	-6	-2	13	-12	21	2	-3	0	22	11
Los Angeles Angels	-8	-9	-3	3	-6	12	6	-4	-7	20	10
Colorado Rockies	-1	-12	10	17	12	-12	15	-16	-15	11	9
San Diego Padres	-14	-11	-7	2	-1	10	1	8	7	20	8
Texas Rangers	-7	5	-8	10	0	-5	-4	3	-2	20	5
Chicago Cubs	-1	-2	6	-4	-6	11	11	-19	-9	16	4
Pittsburgh Pirates	-1	7	-1	-8	22	-3	3	-16	-20	18	2
Boston Red Sox	-10	-2	-16	10	-8	5	-1	-13	-6	26	-4
Oakland Athletics	-3	0	1	-1	-4	-2	-5	-8	-3	10	-29
Philadelphia Phillies	17	8	3	-1	-15	-13	-14	-6	-9	10	-33
Chicago White Sox	-12	-2	-2	-1	0	-10	-6	-3	-13	12	-35
Cincinnati Reds	-12	-5	1	-23	-10	2	11	-13	12	13	-35
Kansas City Royals	3	-23	-1	-10	-9	-18	6	16	-6	13	-40
Washington Nationals	-5	-12	-1	-6	-2	-34	-7	15	-8	16	-47
San Francisco Giants	3	-4	0	-21	-10	-6	-27	-9	-8	23	-53

Batting By Position

Pos	AB	H	2B	3B	HR	(Hm	Rd)	TB	R	RBI	TBB	IBB	SO	HBP	SH	SF	SB	CS	SB%	GDP	LOB	Avg	OBP	Slg
P	123	30	4	1	3	(2	1)	45	11	18	16	0	28	1	0	0	2	0	1.00	1	34	.244	.336	.366
C	16729	3812	762	28	511	(271	240)	6163	1867	1995	1429	16	4247	217	90	127	81	27	.75	396	5395	.228	.295	.368
1B	18212	4570	939	38	701	(338	363)	7688	2247	2447	1776	85	4400	245	7	144	116	42	.73	453	5553	.251	.323	.422
2B	17952	4458	901	87	457	(229	228)	6904	2327	1955	1532	34	3829	258	54	146	356	112	.76	348	5323	.248	.314	.385
3B	17931	4424	915	71	619	(290	329)	7338	2276	2319	1676	59	4327	213	38	143	214	70	.75	402	5328	.247	.316	.409
SS	18230	4556	859	94	481	(251	230)	7046	2290	2126	1330	34	4055	196	63	126	437	125	.78	380	5151	.250	.306	.387
LF	17838	4456	877	85	562	(282	280)	7189	2300	2148	1750	39	4589	213	36	130	298	113	.73	305	5104	.250	.322	.403
CF	17648	4190	796	108	531	(268	263)	6795	2375	1942	1494	39	4791	212	60	116	425	122	.78	291	5073	.237	.303	.385
RF	18086	4350	906	74	639	(323	316)	7321	2335	2237	1638	42	4637	203	22	119	303	109	.74	376	5385	.241	.309	.405
DH	17932	4235	864	52	645	(304	341)	7138	2212	2297	1840	100	4950	239	10	147	144	62	.70	378	5316	.236	.313	.398
PH	2778	594	117	5	66	(36	30)	919	293	404	371	27	955	48	10	26	26	8	.76	62	1218	.214	.314	.331
PR	2	0	0	0	0	(0	0)	0	284	0	1	0	0	1	0	0	84	21	.80	0	8	.000	.500	.000

Fielding By Position

Pos	Inn	PO	Ast	E	(Throw	Field)	TC	DP	GDP	FPct
P	43075.1	2343	3630	309	238	71	6282	274	192	.951
C	43075.1	41404	1819	301	191	93	43524	204	6	.993
1B	43075.1	37379	2709	235	57	165	40323	3609	211	.994
2B	43075.1	8002	11813	344	159	184	20159	2837	889	.983
3B	43075.1	3580	9350	481	269	211	13411	1037	782	.964
SS	43075.1	5932	12721	526	284	242	19179	2497	1310	.973
LF	43075.1	8747	240	126	32	92	9113	40	2	.986
CF	43075.1	11919	173	110	28	82	12202	40		.991
RF	43075.1	9920	281	141	54	86	10342	61		.986

A Runs Created Method for the Manfred Era

Bill James

The reasons why you cannot un-think some previous thought are more profound than the reasons that you cannot un-see what you have seen or un-hear what you have heard. New understandings are built upon the assumptions inherent in old ideas. What you have seen lingers on your eyeballs for a few seconds or for a few minutes, stays in your memory for an hour or decades, highly variable. What you have assumed to be true will be with you until you die, and you will build upon it and pass it on to those who follow you.

The cornerstone of sabermetrics is the realization that there is a largely predictable relationship between the team's won-lost record and the statistics of an individual player. Runs and Runs Scored predict Wins and Losses. Home Runs, Batting Average and all other batting stats predict Runs Scored. There are still many people around us who don't understand that or don't understand the implications of that, but the baseball world itself does. That's why they hire people like me; that's why they hire analysts, and rely upon them to a certain extent. People who came to baseball once that realization was established have great difficulty conceiving of what the baseball world was like before then. Sportscasters and sportswriters could make absolutely inane generalizations about baseball statistics and about why teams win and lose, because they had no mental map that showed the pathways that led through the wilderness of numbers toward the goal of victory.

Runs Created formulas are one of those pathways. Runs Created formulas put together all of the other hitting stats into one number, which is the important number. You don't win because you have a higher batting average than another team, or because you have a higher slugging percentage or a higher OPS; you win because you have more runs created. Well. . .runs scored, but if you have more runs created, you're going to have more runs scored a very high percentage of the time. It would be great if there was a universal Runs Created formula that works in every era, and there is, sort of. There is a basic or universal runs created formula, but there are also changes that take place in baseball over time. Baseball teams 100 years ago committed what seem today like phenomenal numbers of errors, which increased the number of runs resulting from a given collection of hits, walks, and other stuff. The frequency of double plays changes, and the frequency of bunts and stolen base attempts and home runs. How runs are scored changes. Since we started figuring "Manufactured Runs" about 15 years ago, Manufactured Runs have dropped by about 25%, being replaced by home runs and strikeouts.

Because the game changes, we tinker with our Runs Created formulas to make them work best in their own time. Baseball has changed tremendously in the last ten or fifteen years, probably more than it has changed in any equivalent time period since maybe 1908 to 1923. That's my impression, not the result of a study; maybe I should study the issue. Anyway, baseball offenses (and baseball itself) have changed tremendously in recent years, and this has had some impact on the accuracy of the Runs Created formula that we have been using.

In looking at the 2022 edition of this book—last year's book—we realized that 29 out of 30 teams had scored more runs than we had credited them with creating. That would be what you could call an unacceptable level of predictive accuracy. We began then a process to review the formula and to. . .well, to get the license plate of the truck that ran over us. It took me an embarrassingly long time to realize that the problem was blindingly obvious. It's the ghost runners in extra innings. Teams score an average of 11 runs a year by way of runners who, as far as the batting statistics are aware, were never on base to begin with. That explained about half of the difference between runs scored and created.

By the time I realized that, however, I had spent a good many hours trying to re-tool the runs created formula, and I had come up with some adjustments that helped. So we have a new runs created formula.

Runs Created formulas take the general form of (A * B) / C = Runs Created, where A is times on base, B is runner advancement, and C is opportunity or plate appearances. In THIS new version of the formula, A is

Hits plus Walks plus Hit Batsmen plus CI minus Caught Stealing

All of that times .9

Minus GIDP (Grounded into Double Play)

CI is a term used for "Reached Base on Catcher's Interference." It very rarely happens and hasn't been included in previous runs created formulas, but what the hey.

The New York Yankees in 2022 had 1,308 hits, drew 620 walks, had 70 Batters Hit by Pitches, five guys who reached base on Catcher's Interference and 33 runners caught stealing. You add all of that together, you've got 1,970 runners on base (after the caught stealing). Multiply that by .90, it is 1,773. They grounded into 121 double plays; take those out and you've got an "A" factor of 1,652.

The "B" factor (or advancement factor) in the new formula is

Total Bases, plus

.4 times the sum of Stolen Bases, Sacrifice Hits, and Sacrifice Flies, plus

.25 times walks minus intentional walks, plus

1.71 times Home Runs

In essence, we are treating a home run as if was 5.71 total bases, rather than 4. The Yankees had 2,311 total bases, 102 stolen bases, 41 Sacrifice Flies, 14 Sacrifice Hits, 620 walks, of which 36 were intentional, and they hit 254 homers. In the formula, that becomes:

$$2311 + .4 * (102 + 41 + 14) + .25 * (620 - 36) + 1.71 * 254$$

Which is 2954.14.

The C Factor is just Plate Appearances minus Sacrifice Hits. For the Yankees, that is just 6,172 minus 14, or 6,158. So the Yankees runs created is 1,652 * 2,954.14 divided by 6158. That works out to 792.5 Runs Created. The Yankees had 31 Ghost Runners, of whom we could expect, 17.41 to score. Add that to the 792.5, and we could expect the Yankees to score 809.9 runs. They actually scored 807 runs, so the formula is off by a little less than three runs.

What, you didn't think I was going to outline the data for a team that didn't work out right, did you? A bad example would be like the Oakland A's, who should have scored 522 runs but actually scored 568. That was the worst in the majors last year, an error of 46 runs.

Formulas are not perfect. We COULD round up other pieces of information and put them into the formulas, but the goal is not to make the formulas perfect; it is to gain understanding of what has happened, to gain understanding of what teams win and why they lose. Thank you for reading.

Team Efficiency

Bill James

As mentioned in the introduction to the new Runs Created Method, the cornerstone of sabermetrics is the understanding that there is a ***predictable*** relationship between individual player stats and team wins. Predictable does not mean perfect. Predictable means that if we say that here is a group of teams that, based on the individual stats of the players, should win 90 games each on average, that they will win 90 games each on average. What it does NOT mean is that every team will win exactly 90 games. It means that most of the teams will be very close to 90 wins, and the average will be 90, but we know that occasionally, one time in 100, one of them will be 78 games and one of them will win 102.

"Team Efficiency" is, in essence, a way of taking note of what our formulas are not otherwise catching. If a team should win 65 games based on their stats but actually wins 75—which does not happen very often, but it does happen—if it happens, we say that that team was efficient. I don't know what else you would call it.

Three elements of efficiency:

1) Scoring more or fewer runs than expected based on your hitting stats,
2) Allowing fewer or more runs than expected based on your pitching stats, and
3) Winning more games or fewer games than expected based on your runs scored and runs allowed.

Calling it "efficient" does not explain why it happens or how it happens. It merely notes that it HAS happened. There are many different reasons why a team which should score 700 runs gets all efficient on us and scores 725 instead. It could be because they hit very well, as a team, with runners in scoring position. It could be because their opponents have committed an unusual number of errors.

It could be because they hit home runs more often when there were men on base than when there were not. It could be because they did an exceptionally good job of going from first to third on a single. Perhaps they just did it to annoy us.

Elements of team wins are combined into actual team wins. Sometimes they are added up efficiently, and sometimes not. These few pages take note of that.

2022 American League Team Efficiency Summary

	RC	Runs	Hit Eff	Exp RA	RA	Pit Eff	Exp Wins	Wins	Runs Eff	Eff Wins	Wins	Overall Eff
Oakland Athletics	522	568	109	781	770	101	57	60	105	50	60	120
Detroit Tigers	520	557	107	722	713	101	61	66	107	55	66	119
Baltimore Orioles	671	674	100	740	688	108	79	83	105	73	83	114
Kansas City Royals	637	640	100	861	810	106	62	65	104	57	65	113
Chicago White Sox	674	686	102	720	717	100	77	81	105	76	81	107
Cleveland Guardians	678	698	103	637	634	101	89	92	104	86	92	107
Boston Red Sox	724	735	101	787	787	100	75	78	103	74	78	105
Seattle Mariners	697	690	99	655	623	105	89	90	101	86	90	105
Tampa Bay Rays	646	666	103	626	614	102	88	86	98	84	86	103
Toronto Blue Jays	792	775	98	700	679	103	92	92	100	91	92	101
Houston Astros	762	737	97	536	518	103	108	106	98	108	106	98
Minnesota Twins	710	696	98	703	684	103	82	78	95	82	78	95
Texas Rangers	686	707	103	759	743	102	77	68	88	73	68	93
Los Angeles Angels	655	623	95	667	668	100	75	73	97	80	73	92
New York Yankees	810	807	100	576	567	102	108	99	91	108	99	92

2022 National League Team Efficiency Summary

	RC	Runs	Hit Eff	Exp RA	RA	Pit Eff	Exp Wins	Wins	Runs Eff	Eff Wins	Wins	Overall Eff
Pittsburgh Pirates	581	591	102	827	817	101	56	62	111	54	62	116
Cincinnati Reds	610	648	106	833	815	102	63	62	99	57	62	110
Colorado Rockies	682	698	102	865	873	99	63	68	108	62	68	109
Chicago Cubs	664	657	99	773	731	106	72	74	102	69	74	107
Washington Nationals	622	603	97	913	855	107	54	55	102	51	55	107
New York Mets	759	772	102	638	606	105	100	101	101	95	101	106
San Diego Padres	688	705	102	662	660	100	86	89	103	84	89	106
Arizona Diamondbacks	659	702	107	740	740	100	77	74	96	72	74	103
Miami Marlins	585	586	100	700	676	103	70	69	99	67	69	103
St Louis Cardinals	778	772	99	675	637	106	96	93	96	92	93	101
San Francisco Giants	695	716	103	694	697	100	83	81	97	81	81	100
Atlanta Braves	810	789	97	615	609	101	102	101	99	103	101	98
Milwaukee Brewers	738	725	98	679	688	99	85	86	101	88	86	98
Philadelphia Phillies	755	747	99	670	685	98	88	87	99	91	87	96
Los Angeles Dodgers	864	847	98	531	513	103	119	111	94	118	111	94

Pitchers' Repertoires

Brandon Tew

In 2022, baseball has embraced the shift in how pitchers attack hitters. With so much data and numbers, pitchers can gameplan against lineups each and every game.

This year the league embraced breaking balls and offspeed pitches. In the most pivotal moments in a game, pitchers threw non-fastballs to get hitters out. Pitchers such as Corbin Burnes and Emannuel Clase throw hard pitches with cutting action that are almost impossible to hit.

Sandy Alcantara is the ultimate pitch-mix wizard. With arguably the best pitching season this year, he has become a balanced force of power and movement coupled with excellent command and three pitches he can throw in any count. Sandy's pitch mix is masterful. He threw 28% changeup, 25% two-seam FB, 25% four-seam FB, and 22% slider. He sprinkled in seven curveballs and scrapped that pitch because why not throw your three most dominant pitches as much as you can?

The two-seam moves violently at 100 mph. Pair this with the movement and deception of his changeup that baffles hitters at around 92 mph as it dives to the plate. A hitter can't sit on just one pitch, and it's what makes him so special!

Next, look at the pitch that is returning as the go-to pitch for many pitchers, the slider. With the advances in technology and analytics, players can fine-tune their arsenals and look at pitch grips with high-speed cameras and tinker with specific grips or arm actions to create a certain type of movement profile.

A perfect example of this is Dylan Cease, who started throwing a slider with sharp vertical action this year. He threw the pitch 43% of the time, while only throwing his fastball 41% of the time. Cease identified a breaking pitch that worked for him and began to tunnel it off of his fastball as much as he could. The slider plays in and out of the zone as Cease racks up swings and misses.

Cease ranked 10th in put-away rate, throwing 472 sliders with two-strike counts and striking out 131 hitters for a 27.8% strikeout rate. The pitch has become a nightmare for hitters. Even when they know it's coming, it's very difficult to pick up. Only Cease and Robbie Ray threw at least 400 sliders in two-strike counts this year.

Now, what happens when you throw your best pitches to one specific spot in the zone? Well, you get Edwin Díaz's usage of slider and fastball. Not only does he have one of the best if not the best closer entrance in baseball—cue the trumpets—he also features a devastating two-pitch arsenal that he relentlessly throws glove side to hitters. Diaz led the league in putaway rate among pitchers who threw at least 150 sliders (38.4%). With his menacing slider that breaks glove-side with incredible late movement, batters rarely put good at-bats together against the Mets shutdown man. Sure, at times he would miss and spray the ball, but his goal was to throw glove side as much as possible. When you throw triple digits and have a slider in the low 90s you can torment hitters, even when they know what pitch is coming and where it's being located.

The harder slider is not the only pitch that became more popular this year. The league saw a shift towards more sweepers being thrown than ever before. The movement profile of this pitch type is hard to pin down sometimes and can't just be classified into one pitch, although it is mostly thought of as a slider with more horizontal break because of the spin profile. The rise in slider usage can be attributed to the growing amount of sweepers being thrown throughout the league.

Then there are two players such as Shohei Ohtani and Yu Darvish who could teach a master class on how to vary arm angles and pitch location along with an advanced pitch repertoire. The two Japanese pitchers dazzle and amaze with how they are able to manipulate and spin the baseball.

Ohtani added a couple of new pitches down the stretch this season with a ridiculous two-seamer that reached 100 mph at times and new variations on his slider that move with depth or sweep depending on how he throws it. Dropping his arm angle at times, he also mixes pitches based on feel for that particular day in terms of his cutter, splitter, and curveball.

What about Darvish? Well, he throws 11 different pitches and has many different types of one particular pitch, some of which are hard to classify and chart. There's his slow cutter which he uses to set up the rest of his repertoire tunneling-wise. There's also the harder cutter he throws up in the zone. With two types of sliders, including a spiked slider grip that he can modify, Darvish keeps hitters off of his cutters.

Darvish also has two distinct curveballs to mix in with a sharper harder one in the 80s, and a slow cartoonish looping one that he throws in the low 70s. He even threw a curve at 64 mph this year and will routinely try to freeze hitters or have them out in front on these rainbow curves. His four-seam and two-seam fastballs are thrown more to right-handed batters than left. Both still get plenty of game action, but in the end, he wants to spin the baseball. Add in a splitter and rare changeup that he pulls out every once and a while to left-handed hitters and you have an array of pitches to choose from. I didn't even mention a couple of other pitches he throws that are truly hard to classify. Darvish has fully embraced his outstanding ability to spin the baseball and throw more breaking pitches.

Pitchers' repertoires can be unique and yet similar, like Ohtani and Darvish. If you love pitching as much as I do, you might find some interesting quirks and even some trends in this vast collection of data. Look for pitchers with a high Pitch Mix Index (PMI).

Player	Tommy John SX	Fastball Velocity	Fastball	Slider	Change	Cutter	Curve	Splitter	Other	PMI
Abbott, Cory	-	91.4	51%	-	-	27%	22%	-		2.90
Abreu, Albert	-	98.4	61%	29%	10%	-	-	-		2.68
Abreu, Bryan	-	97.2	45%	37%	<1%	-	18%	-		3.04
Acevedo, Domingo	-	93.0	43%	35%	22%	-	-	-		2.95
Adam, Jason	-	94.8	32%	36%	32%	-	-	-		3.00
Adon, Joan	-	95.0	69%	<1%	7%	-	23%	-		2.73
Akin, Keegan	-	93.6	52%	29%	18%	-	<1%	-		3.07
Alcantara, Sandy	-	97.9	50%	22%	28%	-	<1%	-		3.06
Alexander, Jason	-	92.5	61%	23%	16%	-	-	-		2.75
Alexander, Tyler	-	90.1	43%	11%	18%	28%	-	-		3.77
Almonte, Yency	-	95.8	45%	48%	7%	-	-	-		2.64
Alvarado, Jose	-	99.6	56%	43%	-	-	1%	-		2.29
Anderson, Chase	-	92.1	38%	8%	28%	18%	8%	-		4.55
Anderson, Ian	-	94.0	48%	-	33%	-	19%	-		2.90
Anderson, Tyler	-	90.5	45%	-	32%	22%	1%	-		3.29
Arano, Victor	-	94.1	53%	47%	-	-	-	-		2.00
Archer, Chris	-	93.1	36%	44%	15%	-	5%	-		3.52
Arihara, Kohei	-	90.8	28%	14%	19%	26%	<1%	13%		5.11
Armstrong, Shawn	-	95.5	64%	-	-	29%	7%	-		2.55
Ashby, Aaron	-	95.7	37%	29%	21%	-	13%	-		3.86
Ashcraft, Graham	-	97.2	21%	27%	<1%	51%	-	-		3.16
Assad, Javier	-	92.6	52%	9%	7%	27%	4%	-		4.08
Baker, Bryan	-	96.3	56%	26%	17%	-	-	-		2.83
Banda, Anthony	June `18	94.4	53%	-	37%	-	10%	-		2.73
Banks, Tanner	-	92.9	45%	30%	20%	-	5%	-		3.59
Banuelos, Manny	Oct `12	93.6	41%	26%	10%	-	23%	-		3.78
Bard, Daniel	-	98.0	55%	43%	2%	-	-	-		2.40
Barlow, Joe	-	94.6	31%	60%	-	-	9%	-		2.66
Barlow, Scott	June `12	93.7	24%	44%	-	-	31%	-		2.95
Barnes, Jacob	-	95.3	48%	10%	-	42%	-	-		2.74
Barnes, Matt	-	95.0	46%	<1%	7%	-	47%	-		2.83
Barria, Jaime	-	91.9	39%	47%	14%	-	-	-		2.83
Bass, Anthony	-	95.3	40%	56%	-	-	-	4%		2.50
Bassitt, Chris	May `16	92.9	47%	15%	6%	18%	14%	-		4.48
Baumann, Mike	-	95.8	48%	28%	4%	-	19%	-		3.51
Bautista, Felix	-	99.2	61%	12%	-	-	-	26%		2.71
Baz, Shane	Sept `22	96.0	40%	37%	8%	-	14%	-		3.65
Bednar, David	-	96.5	54%	-	-	-	29%	17%		2.84
Beede, Tyler	Mar `20	95.7	47%	15%	26%	-	11%	-		3.72
Beeks, Jalen	Sept `20	95.1	48%	-	49%	1%	1%	-		2.62
Bellatti, Andrew	Feb `18	94.4	40%	52%	7%	-	-	-		2.65
Bello, Brayan	-	96.6	54%	22%	24%	-	<1%	-		3.07
Berrios, Jose	-	94.0	54%	-	15%	-	31%	-		2.83
Bickford, Phil	-	94.2	68%	32%	-	-	-	-		1.93
Bieber, Shane	-	91.3	35%	28%	2%	17%	18%	-		4.45
Bird, Jake	-	95.1	58%	-	2%	25%	15%	-		3.21
Blach, Ty	July `20	91.1	55%	17%	20%	-	8%	-		3.56
Blackburn, Paul	-	91.7	46%	5%	12%	20%	18%	-		4.44
Bleier, Richard	-	89.9	54%	16%	7%	23%	-	-		3.53
Borucki, Ryan	Mar `13	95.1	50%	-	11%	39%	-	-		2.77
Boxberger, Brad	-	92.8	55%	22%	23%	-	-	-		2.86
Bradish, Kyle	-	94.7	49%	30%	9%	-	13%	-		3.59
Brash, Matt	-	96.9	36%	45%	<1%	-	19%	-		3.21
Brasier, Ryan	June `14	96.0	56%	43%	1%	-	-	-		2.30
Brazoban, Huascar	-	97.2	33%	42%	25%	-	-	-		2.97
Brebbia, John	June `20	94.4	46%	54%	-	-	-	-		2.00
Brieske, Beau	-	94.3	53%	21%	22%	-	4%	-		3.43
Brigham, Jeff	July `12	94.5	42%	58%	-	-	-	-		1.99
Brogdon, Connor	-	95.2	32%	-	43%	25%	-	-		2.96
Brubaker, JT	-	93.1	48%	31%	5%	-	16%	-		3.51
Bubic, Kris	-	91.9	51%	-	28%	-	22%	-		2.90

Player	Tommy John SX	Fastball Velocity	Fastball	Slider	Change	Cutter	Curve	Splitter	Other	PMI
Buehler, Walker	Aug `22 Aug `15	95.2	39%	11%	8%	25%	17%	-		4.63
Bumgarner, Madison	-	91.2	33%	36%	11%	-	19%	-		3.81
Bummer, Aaron	Aug `15	94.5	64%	27%	<1%	8%	-	-		2.85
Bundy, Dylan	June `13	89.2	47%	24%	19%	-	11%	-		3.73
Burke, Brock	-	95.0	67%	20%	13%	-	-	-		2.64
Burnes, Corbin	-	96.3	7%	9%	10%	55%	19%	-		4.23
Bush, Matt	July `19 Aug `07	97.3	49%	15%	-	-	35%	-		2.85
Cabrera, Edward	-	96.0	32%	15%	32%	-	21%	-		3.91
Cabrera, Genesis	-	96.1	52%	<1%	18%	-	30%	-		3.18
Cano, Yennier	-	95.4	43%	27%	30%	-	-	-		2.97
Carrasco, Carlos	Sept `11	92.9	47%	23%	24%	-	6%	-		3.60
Castano, Daniel	-	91.1	18%	28%	13%	41%	-	-		3.82
Castellanos, Humberto	Aug `22	90.2	43%	21%	10%	26%	-	-		3.78
Castillo, Diego	-	95.3	37%	63%	-	-	-	-		1.96
Castillo, Luis	-	97.1	57%	21%	22%	-	-	-		2.83
Castillo, Max	-	93.0	48%	19%	33%	-	-	-		2.90
Castro, Miguel	-	97.9	36%	45%	19%	-	-	-		2.91
Cease, Dylan	July `14	96.8	41%	43%	2%	-	14%	-		3.32
Cessa, Luis	-	93.5	42%	39%	19%	-	-	-		2.92
Chacin, Jhoulys	-	92.9	45%	25%	2%	28%	-	<1%		3.61
Chafin, Andrew	June `09	91.6	68%	32%	<1%	-	-	-		2.09
Chapman, Aroldis	-	97.7	61%	25%	-	-	-	15%		2.75
Chavez, Jesse	-	91.1	30%	-	13%	56%	2%	-		3.17
Cimber, Adam	-	86.5	65%	35%	-	-	-	-		1.96
Cishek, Steve	-	89.6	62%	37%	<1%	-	-	-		2.15
Cisnero, Jose	May `14	95.4	68%	26%	6%	-	-	-		2.50
Civale, Aaron	-	91.2	31%	4%	-	34%	28%	4%		4.21
Clarke, Taylor	Jan `13	95.7	42%	36%	21%	-	-	-		2.94
Clase, Emmanuel	-	99.6	62%	38%	-	-	-	-		1.97
Clevinger, Mike	Nov `20 Aug `12	93.5	52%	21%	9%	15%	3%	-		4.19
Cobb, Alex	May `15	94.8	42%	-	42%	-	15%	-		2.87
Cole, Gerrit	-	97.8	52%	23%	8%	6%	11%	-		4.26
Coleman, Dylan	-	97.6	58%	42%	-	-	-	-		1.99
Colome, Alex	-	94.5	16%	-	-	84%	-	-		1.73
Contreras, Roansy	-	95.6	49%	34%	3%	-	14%	-		3.35
Corbin, Patrick	Mar `14	92.7	62%	29%	8%	-	-	-		2.62
Cortes, Nestor	-	91.8	47%	19%	4%	30%	<1%	-		3.66
Cotton, Jharel	Mar `18	92.8	45%	11%	40%	-	4%	-		3.38
Crawford, Kutter	Oct `19	94.6	39%	6%	7%	31%	17%	-		4.45
Crismatt, Nabil	-	90.4	29%	<1%	50%	-	20%	-		3.10
Crowe, Wil	Apr `15	94.7	38%	31%	28%	-	3%	-		3.52
Cuas, Jose	-	93.1	62%	37%	2%	-	-	-		2.30
Cueto, Johnny	Aug `18	91.4	43%	16%	20%	20%	1%	-		4.21
Danish, Tyler	-	91.0	44%	41%	8%	<1%	-	7%		3.70
Darvish, Yu	Mar `15	95.0	34%	16%	<1%	35%	7%	6%		4.84
Davidson, Tucker	-	93.2	43%	44%	4%	-	8%	-		3.32
Davies, Zach	-	89.6	54%	1%	33%	6%	6%	-		3.61
Davis, Austin	-	94.1	46%	38%	16%	-	-	-		2.87
De Jong, Chase	-	92.9	47%	29%	1%	-	23%	-		3.26
De Los Santos, Enyel	-	95.3	60%	28%	11%	-	-	-		2.70
De Los Santos, Yerry	Jan `15	95.3	60%	40%	-	-	-	-		1.98
deGrom, Jacob	Oct `10	98.9	47%	39%	8%	-	5%	-		3.34
Detmers, Reid	-	93.2	45%	26%	11%	-	18%	-		3.76
Detwiler, Ross	-	92.2	50%	44%	3%	-	3%	-		2.96
Diaz, Alexis	May `16	95.7	65%	35%	-	-	-	-		1.96
Diaz, Edwin	-	99.1	42%	58%	-	-	-	-		1.99
Diekman, Jake	-	95.6	64%	35%	1%	-	-	-		2.25
Dominguez, Seranthony	July `20	98.0	70%	26%	5%	-	-	-		2.43
Doval, Camilo	-	99.0	56%	44%	-	-	-	-		1.99

Player	Tommy John SX	Fastball Velocity	Fastball	Slider	Change	Cutter	Curve	Splitter	Other	PMI
Duffey, Tyler	-	92.4	51%	-	4%	-	44%	-		2.54
Dunn, Justin	-	92.2	49%	24%	5%	<1%	21%	-		3.78
Dunning, Dane	Mar `19	89.5	40%	28%	20%	12%		-		3.82
Duran, Jhoan	-	100.9	49%	3%	-	-	31%	16%		3.40
Edwards Jr., Carl	-	94.7	68%	-	10%	-	23%	-		2.59
Effross, Scott	-	90.5	45%	40%	15%	-	-	-		2.85
Eflin, Zach	-	92.8	56%	4%	6%	14%	20%	-		4.06
Elder, Bryce	-	90.8	48%	27%	12%	13%	-	-		3.69
Eovaldi, Nathan	Aug `16 May `07	95.8	38%	12%	-	10%	19%	21%		4.72
Espino, Paolo	-	88.6	48%	21%	5%	-	26%	-		3.54
Espinoza, Anderson	Apr `19 July `17	93.9	77%	18%	2%	-	4%	-		2.63
Estevez, Carlos	-	97.6	71%	15%	15%	-	-	-		2.58
Faedo, Alex	Dec `20	92.8	52%	35%	13%	-	-	-		2.80
Fairbanks, Pete	Aug `17 Jan `11	99.0	61%	38%	<1%	-	-	-		2.18
Falter, Bailey	-	91.2	64%	-	4%	15%	17%	-		3.25
Familia, Jeurys	-	95.3	71%	15%	-	-	-	15%		2.58
Farmer, Buck	-	94.7	44%	-	24%	-	32%	-		2.95
Faucher, Calvin	-	95.4	41%	45%	-	-	14%	-		2.84
Fedde, Erick	June `14	92.6	40%	29%	4%	27%	-	-		3.54
Feltner, Ryan	-	94.2	55%	29%	6%	-	10%	-		3.39
Ferguson, Caleb	Sept `20 May `14	94.9	67%	-	-	-	33%	-		1.94
Festa, Matthew	Mar `20	92.6	43%	57%	-	-	-	-		1.99
Finnegan, Kyle	-	97.1	79%	12%	-	-	-	9%		2.36
Flaherty, Jack	-	93.1	54%	29%	<1%	-	16%	-		3.11
Fleming, Josh	-	91.3	55%	-	19%	15%	11%	-		3.60
Flexen, Chris	July `14	91.7	40%	8%	16%	32%	4%	-		4.32
Floro, Dylan	-	92.6	63%	-	15%	22%	-	-		2.72
Foley, Jason	July `17	96.3	70%	24%	7%	-	-	-		2.50
Foster, Matt	-	93.8	52%	30%	10%	<1%	7%	-		3.74
Freeland, Kyle	-	90.0	45%	23%	14%	-	18%	-		3.79
Frias, Luis	-	97.0	62%	3%	5%	-	30%	-		2.96
Fried, Max	Aug `14	93.9	46%	18%	14%	-	22%	-		3.79
Fulmer, Michael	Mar `19	94.4	28%	63%	6%	-	2%	-		2.96
Gallegos, Giovanny	Jan `11	94.4	48%	47%	5%	-	-	-		2.56
Gallen, Zac	-	94.2	48%	6%	14%	9%	22%	-		4.40
Garcia, Jarlin	-	93.9	43%	28%	29%	-	-	-		2.97
Garcia, Luis	-	98.7	55%	32%	-	-	-	13%		2.78
Garcia, Luis	-	94.0	42%	9%	9%	29%	10%	-		4.47
Garcia, Rony	-	92.8	58%	32%	10%	-	-	-		2.70
Garcia, Yimi	Oct `16	94.7	59%	17%	7%	17%	-	-		3.46
Garrett, Amir	-	94.2	44%	56%	-	-	-	-		1.99
Garrett, Braxton	June `17	91.2	48%	32%	10%	-	10%	-		3.58
Garza, Ralph	-	88.7	49%	23%	18%	8%	2%	-		4.15
Gausman, Kevin	-	95.0	49%	14%	<1%	-	-	36%		3.14
German, Domingo	Mar `15	92.7	40%	-	23%	-	37%	-		2.96
Gibaut, Ian	-	95.9	44%	22%	11%	22%	-	-		3.78
Gibson, Kyle	Sept `11	91.8	40%	21%	11%	21%	7%	-		4.58
Gilbert, Logan	-	96.2	55%	24%	8%	-	13%	-		3.50
Gilbert, Tyler	-	89.6	41%	-	-	35%	11%	13%		3.71
Gilbreath, Lucas	-	93.9	73%	25%	-	-	-	2%		2.23
Ginkel, Kevin	-	96.4	62%	38%	<1%	-	-	-		2.10
Giolito, Lucas	Aug `12	92.6	48%	24%	25%	-	3%	-		3.46
Givens, Mychal	-	93.5	51%	30%	19%	-	-	-		2.88
Gomber, Austin	-	91.0	41%	25%	18%	-	17%	-		3.87
Gonsolin, Tony	-	93.2	39%	21%	-	-	12%	28%		3.83
Gonzales, Marco	Apr `16	88.5	37%	-	30%	19%	13%	-		3.86
Gonzalez, Chi Chi	July `17	92.5	51%	32%	15%	2%	-	-		3.31
Gore, MacKenzie	-	94.7	61%	15%	6%	-	18%	-		3.37

Player	Tommy John SX	Fastball Velocity	Fastball	Slider	Change	Cutter	Curve	Splitter	Other	PMI
Gose, Anthony	Sept `22	97.0	65%	35%	-	-	-	-		1.95
Gott, Trevor	-	95.1	55%	-	<1%	33%	10%	-		3.03
Goudeau, Ashton	-	92.4	55%	-	17%	-	28%	-		2.83
Graterol, Brusdar	Aug `15	99.7	53%	18%	-	29%	-	-		2.86
Graveman, Kendall	July `18	96.5	55%	27%	14%	-	4%	-		3.36
Gray, Jon	-	96.0	51%	36%	9%	-	4%	-		3.31
Gray, Josiah	-	94.5	43%	29%	3%	-	25%	-		3.48
Gray, Sonny	-	92.1	54%	10%	1%	9%	25%	-		3.87
Greene, Hunter	Apr `19	99.0	54%	41%	5%	-	-	-		2.57
Greinke, Zack	-	89.2	41%	12%	16%	10%	20%	-		4.66
Grove, Michael	May `17	94.4	51%	20%	-	-	29%	-		2.89
Gustave, Jandel	June `17	96.0	64%	36%	-	-	-	-		1.96
Gutierrez, Vladimir	July `22	92.9	50%	22%	15%	-	13%	-		3.71
Hader, Josh	-	97.5	69%	28%	2%	-	-	-		2.29
Hand, Brad	-	92.6	48%	52%	-	-	-	-		2.00
Harvey, Hunter	July `16	98.3	78%	<1%	-	-	7%	15%		2.54
Head, Louis	-	93.7	40%	55%	5%	-	-	-		2.53
Heaney, Andrew	July `16	93.0	63%	32%	5%	-	-	-		2.51
Hearn, Taylor	-	94.6	63%	25%	9%	3%	-	-		3.14
Heasley, Jon	-	93.4	49%	13%	21%	-	17%	-		3.72
Helsley, Ryan	-	99.7	57%	-	<1%	32%	10%	-		2.97
Hembree, Heath	-	94.2	52%	45%	-	-	3%	-		2.45
Hendricks, Kyle	-	86.7	57%	-	31%	-	12%	-		2.74
Hendriks, Liam	-	97.6	61%	29%	-	-	10%	-		2.69
Henry, Tommy	-	91.6	56%	20%	10%	-	15%	-		3.56
Hentges, Sam	July `16	95.8	63%	16%	-	-	21%	-		2.73
Herget, Jimmy	-	90.6	31%	34%	7%	-	27%	-		3.74
Hernandez, Carlos	-	96.8	50%	17%	-	-	23%	10%		3.67
Hernandez, Elieser	-	91.7	50%	36%	14%	-	-	-		2.82
Hernandez, Jonathan	Apr `21	98.0	43%	36%	21%	-	-	-		2.93
Hicks, Jordan	June `19	99.4	66%	32%	-	-	-	3%		2.36
Hill, Garrett	Jan `16	91.9	59%	19%	12%	-	11%	-		3.48
Hill, Rich	June `11	88.3	38%	11%	-	13%	36%	2%		4.23
Hill, Tim	-	90.2	85%	9%	-	6%	-	-		2.15
Hjelle, Sean	-	93.8	55%	38%	7%	-	-	-		2.62
Hoffman, Jeff	May `14	94.3	52%	24%	24%	-	-	-		2.89
Holderman, Colin	Apr `18	96.2	50%	43%	1%	-	6%	-		2.93
Holmes, Clay	Mar `14	97.1	80%	20%	-	-	-	-		1.80
Houck, Tanner	-	94.9	53%	41%	-	-	-	6%		2.60
Houser, Adrian	July `16	94.0	65%	13%	9%	-	12%	-		3.33
Howard, Spencer	-	94.4	50%	36%	3%	-	11%	-		3.30
Hudson, Dakota	Sept `20	91.8	55%	27%	4%	-	14%	-		3.37
Hudson, Daniel	June `13 July `12	97.0	55%	42%	3%	-	-	-		2.47
Hughes, Brandon	-	93.2	53%	46%	1%	-	-	-		2.28
Hutchison, Drew	Aug `12	92.5	53%	37%	10%	-	-	-		2.74
Iglesias, Raisel	-	95.0	50%	26%	24%	-	-	-		2.91
Irvin, Cole	Feb `14	90.6	59%	11%	18%	2%	10%	-		3.92
Jackson, Zach	-	94.5	54%	45%	1%	-	-	-		2.27
Jameson, Drey	-	95.3	62%	25%	8%	-	4%	-		3.19
Jansen, Kenley	-	93.7	23%	13%	-	64%	-	-		2.69
Javier, Cristian	-	93.9	60%	28%	4%	-	8%	-		3.21
Jax, Griffin	-	95.5	34%	48%	14%	-	4%	-		3.43
Jefferies, Daulton	Sept `22 Apr `17	92.5	48%	14%	20%	19%	-	-		3.76
Jimenez, Dany	-	94.0	38%	-	<1%	-	61%	-		2.14
Jimenez, Joe	-	95.8	64%	31%	5%	-	-	-		2.52
Junis, Jakob	-	91.9	33%	51%	16%	-	-	-		2.85
Kaprielian, James	Apr `17	94.1	54%	23%	10%	-	13%	-		3.56
Karinchak, James	-	95.2	60%	-	-	-	40%	-		1.98
Keller, Brad	-	94.1	58%	36%	5%	-	-	-		2.56
Keller, Mitch	-	95.1	56%	23%	7%	-	15%	-		3.49

Player	Tommy John SX	Fastball Velocity	Fastball	Slider	Change	Cutter	Curve	Splitter	Other	PMI
Kelley, Trevor	-	90.0	64%	25%	6%	4%	-	-		3.10
Kelly, Joe	-	97.9	40%	-	9%	-	52%	-		2.69
Kelly, Merrill	-	92.7	46%	<1%	21%	19%	13%	-		3.95
Kennedy, Ian	-	93.4	81%	-	<1%	2%	6%	10%		2.86
Kershaw, Clayton	-	90.8	40%	43%	<1%	-	16%	-		3.13
Keuchel, Dallas	-	87.3	51%	8%	26%	15%	-	-		3.59
Kikuchi, Yusei	-	95.0	51%	30%	-	6%	-	14%		3.51
Kimbrel, Craig	-	95.8	69%	-	-	-	31%	-		1.93
King, John	Jan `17	92.4	52%	14%	25%	9%	-	-		3.59
King, Michael	-	95.9	60%	-	10%	-	31%	-		2.68
Kinley, Tyler	-	95.4	47%	53%	<1%	-	-	-		2.20
Kirby, George	-	95.2	58%	21%	8%	-	13%	-		3.48
Kluber, Corey	-	88.9	28%	-	10%	35%	27%	-		3.83
Knebel, Corey	Apr `19	95.7	70%	3%	-	-	27%	-		2.34
Koenig, Jared	-	89.3	50%	15%	13%	-	22%	-		3.71
Kopech, Michael	Sept `18	94.9	62%	26%	1%	-	11%	-		3.03
Krehbiel, Joey	-	94.5	34%	29%	33%	-	3%	-		3.56
Kremer, Dean	-	93.2	41%	-	15%	31%	12%	-		3.77
Kuhl, Chad	Sept `18	92.8	45%	37%	7%	-	12%	-		3.52
Kuhnel, Joel	-	96.1	55%	30%	15%	-	-	-		2.82
Lambert, Jimmy	June `19	94.4	45%	33%	14%	-	8%	-		3.63
Lamet, Dinelson	Apr `18	95.4	46%	54%	-	-	-	-		2.00
Lange, Alex	-	96.2	32%	-	20%	-	49%	-		2.90
Lauer, Eric	-	93.4	43%	18%	3%	19%	16%	-		4.42
Law, Derek	June `14	95.2	22%	12%	5%	49%	13%	-		4.33
Lawrence, Justin	-	95.2	55%	45%	-	-	-	-		1.99
Leclerc, Jose	Mar `21	96.5	37%	7%	22%	-	<1%	34%		3.93
Lee, Dylan	-	92.2	45%	48%	6%	-	-	-		2.63
Leiter Jr., Mark	Mar `19	91.0	46%	5%	-	9%	17%	23%		4.39
Leone, Dominic	-	95.6	37%	36%	-	27%	-	-		2.99
Liberatore, Matthew	-	93.4	55%	11%	11%	-	23%	-		3.56
Littell, Zack	-	94.5	51%	-	-	37%	-	12%		2.79
Loaisiga, Jonathan	May `16	98.1	65%	20%	15%	-	-	-		2.70
Lodolo, Nick	-	94.2	59%	31%	11%	<1%	-	-		2.78
Logue, Zach	-	90.2	50%	16%	14%	21%	-	-		3.72
Long, Sammy	-	94.7	44%	-	29%	-	27%	-		2.96
Lopez, Jorge	-	97.7	55%	10%	16%	-	19%	-		3.59
Lopez, Pablo	Nov `13	93.6	47%	-	35%	10%	8%	-		3.53
Lopez, Reynaldo	-	97.1	55%	32%	5%	-	8%	-		3.27
Lorenzen, Michael	-	94.3	44%	20%	22%	11%	2%	-		4.27
Loup, Aaron	-	91.2	49%	3%	13%	36%	-	-		3.31
Luetge, Lucas	June `17	87.6	-	31%	-	55%	14%	-		2.80
Lugo, Seth	-	94.5	51%	13%	2%	-	34%	-		3.21
Luzardo, Jesus	Mar `16	96.1	47%	30%	23%	-	-	-		2.93
Lyles, Jordan	-	91.5	49%	24%	11%	3%	13%	-		4.19
Lynch, Daniel	-	94.0	46%	30%	18%	-	5%	-		3.55
Lynn, Lance	Nov `15	92.7	59%	-	4%	28%	9%	-		3.22
Machado, Andres	Jan `15	95.4	64%	20%	16%	-	-	-		2.70
Mahle, Tyler	-	93.3	52%	12%	-	12%	-	24%		3.63
Manaea, Sean	-	91.2	62%	15%	24%	-	-	-		2.74
Manning, Matt	-	93.2	59%	23%	7%	-	11%	-		3.40
Manoah, Alek	-	93.6	62%	27%	11%	-	-	-		2.68
Mantiply, Joe	Mar `18	90.5	44%	30%	26%	-	-	-		2.96
Marinaccio, Ron	-	94.7	44%	18%	38%	-	-	-		2.90
Marquez, German	-	95.4	54%	20%	3%	-	23%	-		3.35
Marte, Yunior	-	97.3	62%	38%	-	-	-	-		1.97
Martin, Brett	-	93.6	45%	18%	-	-	37%	-		2.90
Martin, Chris	-	95.2	51%	8%	-	32%	-	9%		3.47
Martin, Corbin	July `19	94.1	55%	11%	17%	-	17%	-		3.61
Martin, Davis	-	94.1	46%	32%	11%	-	11%	-		3.62
Martinez, Adrian	Feb `16	93.9	50%	22%	28%	-	-	-		2.91
Martinez, Nick	-	93.4	41%	-	26%	18%	16%	-		3.86

Player	Tommy John SX	Fastball Velocity	Fastball	Slider	Change	Cutter	Curve	Splitter	Other	PMI
Martinez, Seth	-	91.6	53%	30%	12%	4%	-	-		3.37
Maton, Phil	-	90.9	50%	19%	-	-	31%	-		2.89
Matz, Steven	May `10	94.6	49%	3%	29%	-	20%	-		3.39
Matzek, Tyler	-	94.1	77%	23%	-	-	<1%	-		2.01
May, Dustin	May `21	97.7	52%	-	6%	21%	21%	-		3.53
May, Trevor	Mar `17	96.1	52%	26%	21%	-	-	-		2.88
Mayers, Mike	-	93.6	47%	35%	8%	8%	2%	-		3.97
Mayza, Tim	Sept `19	93.7	83%	17%	-	-	-	-		1.76
McCarty, Kirk	-	92.6	39%	-	8%	42%	11%	-		3.56
McClanahan, Shane	Oct `15	96.8	36%	15%	-	-	24%	25%		3.92
McCullers Jr., Lance	Nov `18	93.1	25%	26%	17%	7%	25%	-		4.79
McFarland, T.J.	-	88.8	63%	15%	22%	-	-	-		2.73
McGee, Jake	July `08	94.4	83%	17%	-	-	-	-		1.75
McHugh, Collin	-	89.0	<1%	48%	-	48%	3%	-		2.75
McKenzie, Triston	-	92.5	56%	22%	-	-	22%	-		2.84
Medina, Adonis	-	93.4	47%	24%	17%	-	11%	-		3.72
Megill, Trevor	May `13	98.1	55%	14%	-	-	31%	-		2.79
Megill, Tylor	-	95.8	57%	19%	18%	<1%	5%	-		3.55
Melancon, Mark	Oct `06	91.2	7%	2%	2%	59%	30%	-		3.47
Merryweather, Julian	Mar `18	97.3	52%	34%	10%	-	5%	-		3.35
Mikolas, Miles	-	93.3	50%	25%	4%	-	21%	-	Knuckleball 0%	3.55
Miley, Wade	-	89.0	17%	7%	31%	43%	3%	-		4.17
Mills, Wyatt	-	91.7	62%	38%	-	-	-	-		1.97
Milner, Hoby	-	89.0	47%	33%	20%	-	-	-		2.92
Minor, Mike	-	90.4	42%	25%	23%	-	10%	-		3.79
Minter, A.J.	Mar `15	96.7	50%	32%	18%	-	-	-		2.88
Misiewicz, Anthony	-	93.3	31%	-	-	35%	34%	-		3.00
Moll, Sam	-	93.4	45%	55%	-	-	-	-		1.99
Montas, Frankie	-	95.9	51%	24%	-	-	-	25%		2.91
Montero, Rafael	Mar `18	96.3	69%	12%	19%	-	-	-		2.61
Montgomery, Jordan	June `18	93.1	52%	-	22%	4%	22%	-		3.45
Moore, Matt	Apr `14	94.0	45%	-	17%	-	38%	-		2.89
Moran, Jovani	-	93.4	51%	4%	45%	-	-	-		2.49
Morejon, Adrian	Apr `21	96.9	69%	14%	-	-	13%	4%		3.12
Moreta, Dauri	-	96.0	55%	24%	21%	-	-	-		2.85
Morgan, Eli	-	92.2	55%	16%	28%	-	1%	-		3.14
Moronta, Reyes	Jan `13	95.3	53%	37%	10%	-	-	-		2.72
Morris, Cody	June `15	94.7	45%	-	17%	31%	7%	-		3.63
Morton, Charlie	June `12	94.9	44%	-	9%	9%	38%	-		3.53
Munoz, Andres	Mar `20	100.2	35%	65%	-	-	-	-		1.96
Murfee, Penn	-	89.0	49%	51%	-	-	-	-		2.00
Musgrove, Joe	-	92.9	31%	24%	6%	19%	19%	-		4.74
Nance, Tommy	Jan `13	94.1	42%	18%	-	-	39%	-		2.91
Nardi, Andrew	-	94.5	62%	32%	6%	-	-	-		2.55
Naughton, Packy	Jan `13	92.8	54%	21%	25%	-	-	-		2.87
Nelson, Kyle	-	91.9	36%	64%	-	-	<1%	-		2.08
Nelson, Nick	-	96.3	43%	24%	29%	-	4%	-		3.52
Neris, Hector	-	94.4	63%	7%	-	-	-	31%		2.57
Newcomb, Sean	-	94.3	56%	33%	<1%	-	11%	-		3.03
Nogosek, Stephen	-	95.1	41%	16%	9%	31%	2%	-		4.20
Nola, Aaron	-	92.6	52%	-	15%	7%	27%	-		3.52
Norris, Daniel	-	91.2	42%	29%	28%	-	1%	-		3.36
Norwood, James	-	96.6	50%	9%	-	-	-	41%		2.73
O'Day, Darren	-	86.0	52%	48%	-	-	-	-		2.00
Ober, Bailey	Mar `15	91.6	49%	23%	16%	-	12%	-		3.70
Odorizzi, Jake	-	92.1	51%	8%	17%	21%	4%	-		4.20
Ohtani, Shohei	Oct `18	97.3	31%	39%	-	9%	9%	12%		4.51
Okert, Steven	-	93.7	32%	68%	-	-	-	-		1.93
Oller, Adam	-	93.4	43%	20%	12%	25%	-	-		3.81
Ort, Kaleb	-	96.3	60%	33%	7%	-	-	-		2.60
Ortega, Oliver	-	95.9	61%	-	-	-	39%	-		1.98
Ottavino, Adam	May `15	94.4	45%	43%	-	5%	-	7%		3.31

Player	Tommy John SX	Fastball Velocity	Fastball	Slider	Change	Cutter	Curve	Splitter	Other	PMI
Otto, Glenn	-	92.2	50%	28%	7%	-	15%	-		3.58
Overton, Connor	Mar `17	90.9	49%	20%	19%	-	13%	-		3.73
Oviedo, Johan	-	96.1	43%	40%	6%	-	11%	-		3.45
Paddack, Chris	May `22 Aug `16	93.0	51%	4%	26%	<1%	18%	-		3.70
Pagan, Emilio	-	95.7	52%	21%	-	-	2%	25%		3.36
Pallante, Andre	-	95.2	64%	20%	<1%	-	17%	-		2.80
Patino, Luis	-	94.5	57%	30%	13%	-	-	-		2.76
Payamps, Joel	-	94.7	50%	36%	14%	-	-	-		2.82
Pepiot, Ryan	-	94.0	56%	18%	26%	-	-	-		2.83
Peralta, Freddy	-	92.7	55%	18%	10%	-	16%	-		3.60
Peralta, Wandy	-	95.5	42%	16%	42%	-	-	-		2.87
Peralta, Wily	Jan `07	95.5	49%	30%	-	-	-	21%		2.91
Perez, Cionel	-	96.9	61%	39%	-	-	<1%	-		2.14
Perez, Martin	May `14	92.7	43%	1%	28%	24%	3%	-		3.91
Peters, Dillon	July `14	92.7	50%	11%	24%	-	14%	-		3.66
Peterson, David	-	93.6	50%	29%	16%	-	5%	-		3.50
Phelps, David	Mar `18	93.2	42%	-	7%	25%	26%	-		3.71
Phillips, Evan	-	96.1	28%	44%	-	28%	-	-		2.96
Pilkington, Konnor	-	92.2	64%	8%	21%	-	7%	-		3.27
Pineda, Michael	July `17	89.9	59%	21%	19%	-	-	-		2.80
Pivetta, Nick	-	93.5	51%	20%	2%	-	27%	-		3.34
Plesac, Zach	Apr `16	92.0	43%	24%	22%	-	10%	-		3.78
Poche, Colin	July `20 June `14	93.3	78%	22%	-	-	-	-		1.83
Pop, Zach	May `19	96.5	77%	23%	<1%	-	-	-		1.96
Poppen, Sean	-	94.6	62%	34%	3%	-	-	-		2.43
Poteet, Cody	Aug `22	94.7	37%	22%	38%	-	3%	-		3.46
Pressly, Ryan	-	94.5	33%	37%	4%	-	27%	-		3.55
Price, David	-	92.3	68%	-	11%	18%	4%	-		3.14
Pruitt, Austin	-	91.5	34%	-	5%	41%	19%	-		3.61
Puk, A.J.	Apr `18	96.6	62%	38%	<1%	-	-	-		2.09
Quantrill, Cal	Mar `15	93.6	48%	36%	12%	-	4%	-		3.39
Quijada, Jose	-	94.6	85%	4%	11%	-	-	-		2.12
Quintana, Jose	-	91.3	52%	6%	19%	-	22%	-		3.53
Ragans, Cole	May `19 Mar `18	92.1	44%	-	33%	16%	6%	-		3.59
Rainey, Tanner	Aug `22	97.0	70%	29%	<1%	-	-	-		2.17
Raley, Brooks	-	90.7	23%	38%	20%	19%	-	-		3.91
Ramirez, Erasmo	-	93.3	44%	7%	3%	46%	-	-		3.19
Ramirez, Noe	-	89.8	37%	31%	31%	-	-	-		2.99
Ramirez, Yohan	-	95.4	68%	32%	-	-	-	-		1.93
Rasmussen, Drew	Aug `17 Mar `16	95.5	39%	24%	-	33%	4%	-		3.59
Ray, Robbie	-	93.4	60%	37%	<1%	-	2%	-		2.58
Richards, Garrett	July `18	94.4	25%	38%	35%	-	2%	-		3.45
Richards, Trevor	-	93.5	44%	18%	38%	-	-	-		2.91
Robertson, David	Aug `19	93.1	-	23%	-	51%	27%	-		2.90
Robles, Hansel	-	96.0	50%	33%	-	-	-	17%		2.86
Rodon, Carlos	May `19	95.6	61%	31%	2%	-	6%	-		2.96
Rodriguez, Eduardo	-	91.8	56%	4%	16%	24%	-	-		3.39
Rodriguez, Elvin	-	93.1	54%	22%	13%	-	11%	-		3.59
Rodriguez, Joely	-	92.8	55%	6%	39%	-	-	-		2.59
Rogers, Josh	July `19 Apr `13	90.3	55%	35%	10%	-	-	-		2.71
Rogers, Taylor	-	94.3	43%	57%	-	-	-	-		1.99
Rogers, Trevor	-	94.6	53%	18%	29%	-	-	-		2.86
Rogers, Tyler	-	83.3	54%	46%	-	-	-	-		2.00
Romano, Jordan	Mar `15	96.9	48%	52%	-	-	-	-		2.00
Rucker, Michael	-	94.7	44%	18%	9%	11%	18%	-		4.58
Ruiz, Jose	-	96.9	48%	-	23%	-	29%	-		2.93
Ruiz, Norge	-	93.1	44%	38%	17%	-	-	-		2.90

Player	Tommy John SX	Fastball Velocity	Fastball	Slider	Change	Cutter	Curve	Splitter	Other	PMI
Ryan, Joe	-	92.1	60%	21%	12%	-	7%	-		3.40
Ryu, Hyun-Jin	June `22 Jan `04	89.3	42%	4%	24%	10%	21%	-		4.39
Sampson, Adrian	July `09	92.2	65%	21%	14%	-	-	-		2.67
Sanchez, Aaron	-	92.2	62%	-	10%	-	28%	-		2.67
Sanchez, Anibal	Jan `03	89.5	34%	5%	26%	31%	5%	-		4.37
Sanchez, Cristopher	-	93.0	61%	19%	20%	-	-	-		2.77
Sandlin, Nick	-	93.6	48%	45%	-	-	-	8%		2.67
Sandoval, Patrick	-	93.2	37%	29%	25%	-	10%	-		3.80
Sands, Cole	-	91.7	50%	7%	2%	-	23%	17%		4.11
Sanmartin, Reiver	-	90.7	41%	27%	32%	-	-	-		2.98
Santana, Dennis	-	96.9	46%	40%	13%	-	-	-		2.83
Santillan, Tony	-	96.2	50%	50%	-	-	-	-		2.00
Sawamura, Hirokazu	-	96.0	49%	14%	-	-	-	37%		2.83
Sborz, Josh	-	97.0	52%	25%	-	-	24%	-		2.90
Scherzer, Max	-	94.1	45%	23%	13%	9%	9%	-		4.51
Schmidt, Clarke	May `17	94.9	39%	38%	5%	-	18%	-		3.57
Schreiber, John	-	94.0	55%	38%	7%	-	-	-		2.65
Scott, Tanner	-	96.9	38%	62%	-	-	-	-		1.97
Seabold, Connor	-	92.2	53%	22%	21%	-	4%	-		3.44
Sears, JP	-	93.2	57%	26%	18%	-	-	-		2.82
Senzatela, Antonio	-	94.2	59%	27%	7%	-	6%	-		3.29
Severino, Luis	Feb `20	96.3	49%	20%	22%	9%	-	-		3.66
Sewald, Paul	-	92.6	51%	49%	-	-	-	-		2.00
Shaw, Bryan	-	93.2	6%	6%	3%	77%	8%	<1%		3.60
Shreve, Chasen	-	90.6	45%	18%	-	-	-	37%		2.91
Silseth, Chase	-	95.3	46%	21%	-	-	5%	27%		3.58
Singer, Brady	-	93.8	54%	38%	8%	-	-	-		2.66
Skubal, Tarik	Apr `16	94.4	48%	31%	15%	-	6%	-		3.56
Smeltzer, Devin	-	89.5	40%	7%	25%	10%	18%	-		4.54
Smith, Caleb	-	92.0	46%	29%	22%	-	3%	-		3.47
Smith, Drew	Mar `19	95.8	53%	36%	6%	-	6%	-		3.27
Smith, Joe	-	84.7	73%	27%	-	-	-	-		1.89
Smith, Will	Mar `17	92.2	42%	48%	<1%	-	9%	-		3.02
Smyly, Drew	July `17	92.6	36%	-	<1%	20%	43%	-		3.09
Snead, Kirby	-	93.4	56%	37%	7%	-	-	-		2.63
Snell, Blake	-	95.9	56%	24%	5%	-	15%	-		3.43
Snider, Collin	-	96.0	49%	49%	2%	-	-	-		2.37
Soto, Gregory	-	98.4	77%	22%	<1%	-	-	-		2.09
Sousa, Bennett	-	94.1	43%	57%	-	-	-	-		1.99
Springs, Jeffrey	-	91.5	41%	25%	35%	-	-	-		2.97
Stammen, Craig	-	91.5	55%	13%	2%	22%	7%	-		4.01
Stanek, Ryne	-	98.4	58%	18%	-	-	-	23%		2.80
Staumont, Josh	-	96.4	65%	-	-	-	35%	-		1.95
Steele, Justin	Aug `17	92.1	64%	29%	2%	-	5%	-		2.89
Stephan, Trevor	-	96.6	47%	25%	-	-	-	28%		2.94
Stephens, Jackson	-	94.2	58%	3%	10%	-	29%	-		3.23
Stephenson, Robert	-	96.9	48%	51%	<1%	-	1%	-		2.50
Stout, Eric	-	92.1	35%	47%	12%	-	6%	-		3.47
Strahm, Matt	July `13	94.2	53%	21%	9%	-	17%	-		3.61
Stratton, Chris	-	92.9	45%	19%	7%	-	29%	-		3.65
Strickland, Hunter	May `13	95.0	57%	39%	-	-	-	4%		2.47
Strider, Spencer	Feb `19	98.2	67%	28%	5%	-	-	-		2.46
Stripling, Ross	Apr `14	91.6	41%	22%	27%	-	10%	-		3.77
Stroman, Marcus	-	92.1	48%	26%	12%	11%	3%	-		4.24
Strzelecki, Peter	Sept `15	93.5	53%	33%	14%	-	-	-		2.80
Suarez, Jose	-	92.5	43%	20%	24%	-	13%	-		3.82
Suarez, Ranger	-	92.8	58%	4%	21%	9%	8%	-		4.02
Suarez, Robert	Apr `17	97.7	65%	2%	21%	8%	4%	-		3.57
Sulser, Beau	-	92.9	37%	-	32%	23%	8%	-		3.76
Sulser, Cole	Jan `15 Apr `11	91.9	50%	10%	39%	-	1%	-		3.11

101

Player	Tommy John SX	Fastball Velocity	Pitch Repertoire							PMI
			Fastball	Slider	Change	Cutter	Curve	Splitter	Other	
Suter, Brent	July '18	86.6	70%	5%	25%	-	-	-		2.41
Swanson, Erik	-	93.7	55%	20%	-	-	-	25%		2.85
Swarmer, Matt	-	90.6	39%	59%	2%	-	-	-		2.34
Syndergaard, Noah	Mar '20	93.8	47%	22%	19%	-	11%	-		3.73
Taillon, Jameson	Aug '19 Apr '14	94.2	47%	19%	8%	11%	15%	-		4.52
Tapia, Domingo	May '15	97.6	68%	15%	16%	-	-	-		2.63
Tate, Dillon	-	94.0	52%	25%	24%	-	-	-		2.90
Tepera, Ryan	-	92.7	48%	6%	-	37%	-	9%		3.40
Tetreault, Jackson	-	94.6	58%	32%	3%	-	8%	-		3.13
Thielbar, Caleb	-	92.9	49%	25%	1%	-	25%	-		3.25
Thompson, Keegan	June '15	93.5	52%	4%	5%	21%	17%	-		4.10
Thompson, Mason	Mar '15	95.9	75%	24%	1%	-	-	-		2.16
Thompson, Ryan	Jan '18	90.3	59%	39%	1%	<1%	-	-		2.50
Thompson, Zach	-	92.3	37%	-	9%	33%	21%	-		3.75
Thompson, Zack	-	94.8	54%	-	8%	6%	31%	-		3.36
Thornburg, Tyler	Sept '20	93.6	58%	7%	14%	-	22%	-		3.44
Thornton, Trent	-	93.8	46%	39%	-	<1%	15%	-		2.99
Tinoco, Jesus	-	96.1	48%	44%	<1%	-	7%	-		2.96
Toussaint, Touki	-	92.1	47%	-	-	-	33%	20%		2.92
Trivino, Lou	-	95.7	48%	24%	11%	16%	2%	-		4.22
Uelmen, Erich	-	93.6	62%	29%	9%	-	-	-		2.65
Underwood Jr., Duane	-	95.5	37%	-	22%	28%	13%	-		3.87
Urena, Jose	-	95.7	59%	25%	16%	-	-	-		2.78
Urias, Julio	-	93.1	49%	-	17%	-	33%	-		2.88
Urquidy, Jose	Jan '17	93.6	53%	14%	15%	5%	14%	-		4.31
Valdez, Framber	-	94.0	53%	-	9%	11%	28%	-		3.52
Varland, Louie	-	93.9	48%	19%	15%	18%	-	-		3.77
Velasquez, Vince	Sept '10	93.0	52%	22%	9%	-	17%	-		3.61
VerHagen, Drew	June '08	94.8	47%	22%	16%	3%	13%	-		4.29
Verlander, Justin	Sept '20	95.1	50%	28%	2%	-	19%	-		3.36
Vesia, Alex	-	94.2	63%	32%	5%	-	-	-		2.48
Vespi, Nick	-	88.6	47%	37%	-	-	16%	-		2.87
Vest, Will	Jan '16	95.2	56%	33%	11%	-	-	-		2.73
Voth, Austin	-	93.5	41%	5%	<1%	22%	31%	-		3.90
Wacha, Michael	-	93.0	46%	-	30%	17%	7%	-		3.64
Wainwright, Adam	Feb '11	88.5	37%	-	6%	25%	32%	-		3.68
Waldichuk, Ken	-	94.1	56%	21%	15%	-	8%	-		3.51
Walker, Taijuan	Apr '18	93.5	41%	18%	-	5%	9%	27%		4.45
Wantz, Andrew	-	93.8	49%	29%	6%	16%	-	-		3.53
Warren, Art	Jan '14	93.5	42%	58%	-	-	-	-		1.99
Watkins, Spenser	-	91.4	40%	18%	4%	28%	10%	-		4.44
Weaver, Luke	-	94.9	60%	-	26%	4%	9%	-		3.25
Webb, Logan	June '16	91.9	36%	33%	31%	-	-	-		3.00
Weems, Jordan	-	96.9	64%	24%	-	-	3%	9%		3.11
Wells, Tyler	May '19	93.6	42%	7%	18%	27%	7%	-		4.43
Wendelken, J.B.	Oct '16	94.9	60%	23%	16%	-	1%	-		3.08
Wentz, Joey	Mar '20	92.4	56%	-	14%	21%	9%	-		3.54
Wesneski, Hayden	-	92.7	48%	32%	8%	12%	-	-		3.57
Wheeler, Zack	Mar '15	95.8	60%	14%	-	13%	12%	2%		3.92
White, Mitch	Nov '13	93.8	52%	27%	4%	-	17%	-		3.43
Whitlock, Garrett	July '19	95.3	62%	18%	20%	-	-	-		2.75
Wick, Rowan	-	94.9	60%	5%	-	13%	22%	<1%		3.45
Williams, Devin	Mar '17	94.0	38%	-	58%	4%	-	-		2.50
Williams, Trevor	-	90.9	65%	16%	13%	-	5%	-		3.26
Wilson, Bryse	-	92.4	57%	16%	15%	-	13%	-		3.58
Wilson, Steven	Jan '17	95.1	52%	42%	6%	-	-	-		2.59
Winckowski, Josh	-	94.0	52%	28%	9%	10%	-	-		3.55
Winder, Josh	-	94.1	40%	33%	14%	-	12%	-		3.75
Wisler, Matt	-	89.8	9%	91%	-	-	-	-		1.56
Wittgren, Nick	-	91.3	44%	11%	23%	22%	-	-		3.77
Wood, Alex	Jan '09	92.4	46%	36%	19%	-	-	-		2.91

Player	Tommy John SX	Fastball Velocity	Pitch Repertoire							PMI
			Fastball	Slider	Change	Cutter	Curve	Splitter	Other	
Woodford, Jake	-	92.1	60%	28%	4%	-	8%	-		3.19
Woodruff, Brandon	-	96.2	60%	11%	16%	-	13%	-		3.49
Wright, Kyle	-	94.7	43%	7%	15%	-	34%	-		3.62
Yajure, Miguel	Nov `16	93.0	37%	10%	19%	7%	26%	-		4.63
Yarbrough, Ryan	-	86.8	19%	27%	24%	30%	-	-		3.97
Young, Alex	-	90.9	27%	-	33%	26%	15%	-		3.92
Zimmermann, Bruce	-	90.6	39%	19%	29%	-	13%	-		3.83

The World's #1 Starting Pitcher

Alex Vigderman

Thank <insert deity of your choosing> for Sandy Alcantara.

The Marlins ace finished the season with three straight starts of eight or more innings and one earned run allowed, claiming the crown of World's No. 1 Starting Pitcher from Max Scherzer.

First off, I'm glad to see some new blood at the top of these rankings. Since the start of 2019, one of Gerrit Cole or Scherzer has held that spot more than 80 percent of the time.

But more importantly, Alcantara is a counterweight to the general decline of the workhorse in a world that's changing how it views starting pitching.

Back in 2010, Félix Hernández won the AL Cy Young Award with a league-leading 2.27 ERA and 249.2 innings pitched. That result reflected a change in the way we view pitching excellence, because his 13-12 record paled in comparison to his closest competitors.

(He finished that regular season as the World's No. 1 Starting Pitcher but lost the crown to Roy Halladay in the playoffs. Halladay no-hit the Reds in his first playoff outing, a game which I was fortunate enough to attend.)

Last year, Corbin Burnes' selection as the NL Cy Young winner might be indicative of another shift in the mindset of award voters. Almost all modern Cy Young winners have thrown 200 innings, but Burnes took home the hardware with just 167 innings. If he had missed one more start—he made 28—he wouldn't have qualified for the ERA title.

Burnes wasn't the World's No. 1 Starting Pitcher at any point in that season, because he was not elite prior and didn't pile up enough elite innings to make a quick ascent. He did claim the title for a stretch this summer when he didn't allow more than three earned runs for a month.

Alcantara blends the old world and the new world. He throws as fast a fastball as anyone, and he also doubled the next-most complete games by a starter this year. (You can find both of those facts in the Leaderboards section of this book!)

All right, enough about the top guy; let's find a transition to other topics.

Speaking of new things and fastballs…the highest-ranked player who is new to the list is Atlanta's Spencer Strider, who didn't even start a game until May 30th. Last year's best debut was Alek Manoah, whose All-Star campaign in 2022 got him into the top ten by the end of the year.

In terms of quality pitching staffs, it's no surprise that playoff teams dominate this list. The Astros, Dodgers, Braves, and Cardinals each have at least four pitchers in the top 60, and the Brewers just barely missed the postseason with the same qualification.

On the flip side, six teams didn't have any starters in the top 60. The odd team out in that group is the Orioles, who had a winning record and won 17 more games than any of the others without a top-60 starter. The Nationals didn't have a starter in the top 100 (if only barely), with Josiah Gray ranking 101st.

World's No. 1 Reliever

The World's No. 1 Reliever, at least for 2022 was Mets closer Edwin Díaz.

Diaz finished the year with a 1.31 ERA and 0.90 FIP and got better as the season went.

From May 27 on, he was 22-for-22 in save opportunities with 84 strikeouts in 43⅓ innings pitched.

His ERA in that span was 0.62. His FIP was 0.00.

Starting Pitcher Rankings

Player	April 7 Score	April 7 Rank	May 1 Rank	June 1 Rank	July 1 Rank	Aug 1 Rank	Sept 1 Rank	Oct 5 Score	Oct 5 Rank
Alcantara, Sandy	404.9	15	14	4	2	3	2	493.0	1
Scherzer, Max	456.1	1	1	1	5	1	1	492.1	2
Urias, Julio	410.2	13	10	13	10	9	4	483.0	3
Cole, Gerrit	432.4	3	4	3	3	4	3	482.4	4
Burnes, Corbin	424.6	7	2	2	1	2	6	482.2	5
Fried, Max	419.6	8	6	6	4	5	5	480.9	6
Cease, Dylan	379.2	35	29	25	21	8	7	480.8	7
Gallen, Zac	365.6	50	42	34	38	30	12	480.2	8
Ohtani, Shohei	385.5	31	28	23	15	13	15	479.3	9
Manoah, Alek	371.6	44	25	20	17	16	20	477.1	10
Darvish, Yu	394.6	22	26	26	20	14	16	476.7	11
Nola, Aaron	390.5	25	21	14	7	7	13	476.0	12
Woodruff, Brandon	419.1	9	11	18	27	18	24	475.3	13
Rodon, Carlos	386.2	29	17	24	13	11	14	472.6	14
Wheeler, Zack	431.5	4	8	5	6	6	9	467.8	15
Bieber, Shane	383.7	33	24	31	26	27	18	466.0	16
Verlander, Justin	325.0	108	70	45	31	22	19	464.6	17
McKenzie, Triston	346.2	72	61	49	55	31	28	460.1	18
Kershaw, Clayton	393.6	23	18	22	33	26	33	453.6	19
Valdez, Framber	372.4	40	43	28	25	21	17	452.8	20
Ray, Robbie	425.0	6	7	10	8	17	8	451.8	21
Gausman, Kevin	410.9	11	5	7	14	23	23	450.4	22
Morton, Charlie	433.6	2	9	17	12	12	11	449.2	23
Musgrove, Joe	389.1	26	16	11	9	15	25	449.1	24
Webb, Logan	398.3	18	23	19	16	19	27	448.8	25
McClanahan, Shane	361.8	56	31	21	11	10	10	448.7	26
Cortes, Nestor	338.1	84	69	43	46	38	36	446.7	27
Castillo, Luis	397.5	19	47	47	35	24	26	445.6	28
Anderson, Tyler	342.8	80	82	57	52	36	32	443.4	29
Kelly, Merrill	346.2	73	45	61	45	25	24	441.2	30
Javier, Cristian	325.0	108	165	111	66	72	49	441.0	31
Bassitt, Chris	389.0	27	22	27	30	32	29	438.6	32
Garcia, Luis	372.2	41	32	35	32	35	46	429.3	33
Gonsolin, Tony	325.0	108	99	58	29	37	30	427.1	34
Strider, Spencer				186	114	77	39	426.4	35
Stroman, Marcus	373.9	39	40	42	74	61	66	426.2	36
Mikolas, Miles	325.0	108	72	71	48	42	54	425.5	37
Perez, Martin	325.0	108	103	46	49	41	41	425.1	38
Quantrill, Cal	362.1	55	56	53	54	67	37	424.4	39
Wright, Kyle	325.0	108	68	55	51	46	34	423.9	40
Montgomery, Jordan	358.3	61	55	48	41	50	35	423.8	41
Gilbert, Logan	340.4	82	54	44	39	39	60	423.5	42
Snell, Blake	374.3	38	87	128	120	98	73	422.4	43
Quintana, Jose	325.0	108	115	80	81	73	74	422.2	44
Marquez, German	383.9	32	36	59	57	52	42	421.6	45
Lauer, Eric	358.5	60	41	41	59	53	48	420.9	46
Singer, Brady	326.5	103	184	116	115	76	59	420.5	47
Wainwright, Adam	413.0	10	19	12	19	20	21	420.3	48
Giolito, Lucas	410.9	12	13	15	37	47	61	419.8	49
Gray, Sonny	371.8	43	51	37	36	54	38	419.5	50
Taillon, Jameson	355.0	63	65	50	53	56	57	419.1	51
Peralta, Freddy	391.5	24	27	29	44	65	47	418.9	52
Mahle, Tyler	387.9	28	38	38	28	29	31	418.2	53
Rasmussen, Drew	325.3	105	107	84	110	91	56	416.1	54
Lopez, Pablo	347.6	71	44	36	42	48	55	415.1	55
Urquidy, Jose	345.6	74	92	100	82	58	43	414.6	56
Pivetta, Nick	369.4	47	60	33	22	44	40	414.6	57
Ryan, Joe	325.0	108	67	70	79	90	78	412.1	58
Eovaldi, Nathan	400.2	17	12	16	24	40	52	411.3	59
Walker, Taijuan	343.7	76	89	87	63	51	69	411.0	60
Springs, Jeffrey			167	106	93	108	87	411.0	61
Sandoval, Patrick	325.0	108	93	85	80	95	67	410.2	62
Stripling, Ross	325.0	108	119	159	102	87	75	408.7	63
Montas, Frankie	397.0	20	20	9	18	28	44	408.7	64
Greene, Hunter			140	107	86	70	96	408.2	65
Suarez, Ranger	350.8	70	78	82	77	66	62	405.5	66
Buehler, Walker	431.4	5	3	8	23	33	45	405.4	67
Gray, Jon	353.6	66	80	65	47	45	65	404.8	68
Berrios, Jose	410.2	14	15	32	40	34	51	404.4	69
Lodolo, Nick			137	197	220	142	116	403.9	70
Freeland, Kyle	352.1	69	63	73	61	62	83	403.6	71

Starting Pitcher Rankings

	April 7		May 1	June 1	July 1	Aug 1	Sept 1	Oct 5	
Player	Score	Rank	Rank	Rank	Rank	Rank	Rank	Score	Rank
Steele, Justin	325.0	108	147	110	92	82	53	401.2	72
Cobb, Alex	331.6	97	163	134	124	94	80	400.2	73
Keller, Mitch	325.0	108	124	154	136	93	104	399.6	74
Wacha, Michael	333.1	94	74	69	65	86	68	398.9	75
Hill, Rich	364.6	52	59	67	62	81	86	398.5	76
Lynn, Lance	401.3	16	35	140	157	154	98	397.4	77
Cueto, Johnny	325.0	108	184	144	98	74	63	397.3	78
Gonzales, Marco	375.1	37	46	52	43	68	76	395.2	79
Detmers, Reid	325.0	108	121	92	105	71	71	395.1	80
Skubal, Tarik	354.0	65	64	30	50	43	64	394.6	81
Severino, Luis			108	83	58	75	100	393.7	82
Luzardo, Jesus	325.0	108	95	121	150	162	120	393.6	83
Lyles, Jordan	345.5	75	91	88	109	88	89	393.5	84
Kirby, George				133	123	104	81	393.5	85
deGrom, Jacob	372.1	42	94	214	220	227	102	393.2	86
Kremer, Dean	325.0	108	184	214	125	137	103	392.3	87
Irvin, Cole	335.1	87	79	91	90	57	58	392.0	88
Manaea, Sean	364.9	51	34	40	34	55	84	391.7	89
Kopech, Michael	325.0	108	88	66	64	64	70	391.3	90
Greinke, Zack	376.6	36	33	63	69	79	88	391.1	91
Smyly, Drew	325.0	108	109	102	135	138	90	389.0	92
Sampson, Adrian	325.0	108	184	214	194	144	142	387.8	93
Gibson, Kyle	362.7	54	37	51	60	63	50	387.6	94
Kluber, Corey	325.0	108	111	104	89	83	85	387.0	95
Wood, Alex	366.3	49	49	60	67	49	72	386.5	96
Carrasco, Carlos	325.0	108	118	90	117	80	94	385.8	97
Davies, Zach	325.0	108	123	122	78	111	91	385.7	98
Kaprielian, James	331.6	96	184	151	132	103	121	384.1	99
Suarez, Jose	329.8	99	143	199	154	148	110	384.0	100
Gray, Josiah	325.0	108	84	103	73	78	82	383.8	101
Otto, Glenn	325.0	108	139	127	163	141	107	383.5	102
Anderson, Ian	386.0	30	30	39	56	60	77	382.8	103
Syndergaard, Noah	325.0	108	105	108	95	96	99	382.7	104
Dunning, Dane	325.0	108	102	99	84	102	92	380.9	105
Flexen, Chris	360.2	57	53	62	71	59	79	380.8	106
Bradish, Kyle			176	188	220	188	126	379.0	107
Rodriguez, Eduardo	369.8	46	52	56	87	115	123	378.4	108
Clevinger, Mike	325.0	108	184	164	130	92	101	377.7	109
Cabrera, Edward	325.0	108	184	153	166	199	129	377.1	110
Voth, Austin	325.0	108	184	214	171	140	109	376.5	111
Brubaker, JT	325.0	108	134	94	94	100	97	374.2	112
Civale, Aaron	334.4	89	178	173	181	151	134	374.0	113
Bumgarner, Madison	353.2	68	50	54	68	69	114	373.9	114
Plesac, Zach	342.8	81	85	101	70	84	93	373.8	115
Garrett, Braxton	325.0	108	184	214	188	120	115	372.8	116
German, Domingo	325.0	108	184	214	220	193	131	371.9	117
Rogers, Trevor	364.0	53	58	75	88	106	118	371.9	118
Peterson, David	325.0	108	110	135	108	97	95	371.6	119
Contreras, Roansy	325.0	108	184	163	147	147	136	370.9	120
Sanchez, Anibal	325.0	108	184	214	220	202	149	370.8	121
Heaney, Andrew	325.0	108	113	172	177	166	140	369.8	122
Falter, Bailey	325.0	108	184	210	200	170	146	368.8	123
Bundy, Dylan	325.0	108	96	136	121	122	105	368.3	124
Wells, Tyler			144	98	75	85	108	368.0	125

Relief Pitching

Jackson Lewis

The showmanship surrounding pitching changes has gotten plenty of media attention this year. And while the expectation is probably for me to spend these next few paragraphs talking about Edwin Díaz's phenomenal season, I'm going to pause the trumpets and take a closer look at some of the less popular, but equally as notable, bullpen stories of 2022.

I'll start by giving the Orioles' relievers props for producing in virtually any scenario. Leading the league in tough save opportunities and inherited runners doesn't exactly make life easy, but nonetheless they delivered, turning in league-leading conversion rates for tough saves (72%!) and overall saves (81%).

Naturally, most of the credit will be divvied up between closers Félix Bautista and now-departed Jorge López, but it's difficult to understate the brilliance of set-up man Cionel Pérez, who led the team in clean outings despite shouldering the most inherited runners. Pérez also boasted 24 holds on the season, good for seventh among all relievers and most without recording a blown save.

Kansas City's Amir Garrett tied Twins reliever Caleb Thielbar for the most stranded inherited runners this season with 35. Garrett's season was a peculiar one, as he was quite effective when inheriting runners, allowing eight runs (seven of them earned) in a little over 19 innings pitched, good for a 3.26 ERA. However, when working with a clean slate, his ERA skyrocketed to 6.23 in 26 innings. While some of this discrepancy can be attributed to luck (his FIP between the two scenarios is different by only 0.40), there's still at least a sliver of deviation there to explore.

Moving on, this year's save leader, Guardians' closer Emmanuel Clase, also led the league in consecutive days, appearing in back-to-back games 26 times this season. He was exceptional in those appearances, converting 17-of-18 save opportunities while only allowing a single earned run. Furthermore, his blown save came in extra innings, where the tying run started on 2nd base, so his performance is even more impressive than the stat line suggests.

Now it's time to discuss one of the more surprising trade-deadline moves of the season involving former Brewers closer Josh Hader. To start the season Hader had been lights out, recording 24 saves in 25 opportunities and allowing only 10 hits and 3 runs in 24 innings of work. However, Hader's July was disastrous. In only 9 innings, Hader allowed 16 hits and 13 runs. After being traded to the Padres, Hader didn't exactly regain his early season form. In 19 appearances he posted a 7.31 ERA while converting 7-of-9 save opportunities. Hader did rebound near the end of the season and in the postseason.

Moving off one of the best closers of the game while sitting atop your division isn't a typical move, regardless of how much he's struggled in the prior month. Maybe it was the contract, or perhaps Milwaukee wanted to make room for emerging star Devin Williams, the true reason we'll never know. Taylor Rogers' struggles have continued despite the change in scenery, and Dinelson Lamet is no longer with the organization.

Whatever the Brewers' plan is, they'll need to shore things up quickly, as outside of Hader and Williams they had 23 blown saves and recorded a 77% save/hold percentage.

Arizona Diamondbacks

Pitcher	Pos	T	Usage					Inherited Runners			Saves			Relief Results						
			Rel G	Early Entry	Cons Days	Long	Lev Ind	#	Scrd	Pct	Easy	Reg	Tough	Clean	BS Win	BS	Holds	Sv/Hld Pct	Opp OPS	Rel ERA
Mantiply, Joe	SU	L	69	10	21	2	1.5	35	16	.46	1-3	1-1	0-4	49	0	6	22	.80	.640	2.85
Kennedy, Ian	SU	R	57	3	12	3	1.7	7	1	.14	5-5	5-11	0-0	37	1	6	10	.77	.849	5.36
Holton, Tyler	LT	L	10	3	0	1	0.4	3	1	.33	0-0	0-0	0-0	7	0	0	0		.615	3.00
Smith, Caleb	LM	L	43	20	6	23	0.6	15	3	.20	0-0	0-0	0-0	25	0	0	4	1.00	.723	3.65
Nelson, Kyle	LM	L	42	22	7	1	1.1	21	8	.38	0-0	0-0	0-0	31	0	0	11	1.00	.587	2.25
Melancon, Mark	UR	R	62	0	16	2	1.7	3	1	.33	11-11	7-10	0-0	39	0	3	1	.86	.738	4.66
Ramirez, Noe	UR	R	55	9	11	4	1.1	24	6	.25	0-1	0-2	0-1	38	1	4	10	.71	.797	5.22
Ginkel, Kevin	UR	R	30	11	7	1	1.1	14	5	.36	1-2	0-0	0-1	22	0	2	4	.71	.648	3.38
Poppen, Sean	UR	R	29	8	4	1	1.0	13	1	.08	0-0	0-1	0-0	18	0	1	4	.80	.826	4.40
Wendelken, J.B.	UR	R	29	12	4	3	0.7	12	4	.33	0-0	0-0	0-0	19	0	1	1	1.00	.702	5.28
Middleton, Keynan	UR	R	18	7	3	2	0.9	11	2	.18	0-0	0-0	0-2	11	0	2	1	.33	.841	5.29
Moronta, Reyes	UR	R	17	2	3	0	1.6	9	5	.56	2-2	0-1	0-1	9	0	2	4	.75	.648	4.50
Frias, Luis	UR	R	15	3	1	7	0.7	7	0	.00	0-0	0-0	0-0	9	0	0	3	1.00	.914	10.59
Widener, Taylor	UR	R	14	8	0	5	0.7	7	4	.57	0-0	0-1	0-0	7	0	1	1	.50	.798	3.63
Weaver, Luke	UR	R	11	5	1	3	0.6	0	0	.00	0-0	0-0	0-0	7	0	0	0		.641	3.55
Devenski, Chris	UR	R	10	3	0	0	1.0	0	0	.00	0-0	0-0	0-0	5	0	0	0		.992	7.59
Uceta, Edwin	UR	R	10	3	1	4	0.2	8	4	.50	0-0	0-0	0-0	4	0	0	0		.671	5.82

Atlanta Braves

Pitcher	Pos	T	Usage					Inherited Runners			Saves			Relief Results						
			Rel G	Early Entry	Cons Days	Long	Lev Ind	#	Scrd	Pct	Easy	Reg	Tough	Clean	BS Win	BS	Holds	Sv/Hld Pct	Opp OPS	Rel ERA
Jansen, Kenley	CL	R	65	0	16	4	1.9	4	3	.75	34-35	7-13	0-0	46	1	7	0	.85	.612	3.38
Minter, A.J.	SU	L	75	8	18	1	1.4	23	6	.26	4-4	1-5	0-0	57	2	4	34	.91	.556	2.06
McHugh, Collin	SU	R	58	31	4	10	1.0	38	10	.26	0-1	0-1	0-3	40	0	5	17	.77	.556	2.60
Smith, Will	SU	L	41	0	10	4	1.4	13	6	.46	5-6	0-1	0-1	21	0	3	10	.83	.764	4.38
Iglesias, Raisel	SU	R	28	0	9	0	1.4	4	1	.25	1-1	0-1	0-0	25	0	1	15	.94	.450	0.34
Lee, Dylan	LT	L	46	20	8	7	1.0	31	11	.35	0-0	0-1	0-2	34	1	3	9	.75	.572	2.13
Matzek, Tyler	LT	L	42	12	1	3	0.9	20	2	.10	1-1	0-0	0-0	29	0	0	8	1.00	.590	3.50
Chavez, Jesse	LM	R	45	16	3	8	0.8	27	9	.33	0-0	0-1	0-1	32	0	2	10	.83	.663	2.42
Stephens, Jackson	UR	R	38	5	1	9	0.7	6	2	.33	0-0	2-3	0-0	22	0	1	2	.80	.633	3.38
O'Day, Darren	UR	R	28	7	3	0	0.9	8	2	.25	0-0	0-1	0-0	19	0	1	5	.83	.757	4.15
Strider, Spencer	UR	R	11	5	0	6	0.9	3	0	.00	0-0	0-1	0-0	8	0	1	2	.67	.477	2.22

Baltimore Orioles

Pitcher	Pos	T	Usage					Inherited Runners			Saves			Relief Results						
			Rel G	Early Entry	Cons Days	Long	Lev Ind	#	Scrd	Pct	Easy	Reg	Tough	Clean	BS Win	BS	Holds	Sv/Hld Pct	Opp OPS	Rel ERA
Bautista, Felix	CL	R	65	9	16	2	1.6	36	7	.19	4-4	6-7	5-6	49	0	2	13	.93	.536	2.19
Lopez, Jorge	CL	R	44	0	13	6	1.9	16	2	.13	10-10	4-6	5-7	33	0	4	0	.83	.529	1.68
Tate, Dillon	SU	R	67	15	10	9	1.3	23	2	.09	3-3	0-0	2-3	42	0	1	16	.95	.615	3.05
Perez, Cionel	SU	L	66	13	12	1	1.4	40	13	.33	1-1	0-0	0-0	52	0	0	24	1.00	.568	1.40
Fry, Paul	LT	L	12	3	1	2	0.5	16	5	.31	0-0	0-0	0-0	7	0	0	1	1.00	.688	6.00
Hall, DL	LT	L	10	6	0	2	0.9	8	6	.75	0-0	0-1	0-0	7	0	0	0	1.00	.643	3.60
Baker, Bryan	LM	R	64	30	6	8	1.0	29	9	.31	0-0	1-2	0-1	40	0	2	9	.83	.611	3.27
Krehbiel, Joey	LM	R	56	28	6	8	1.0	37	13	.35	0-0	0-0	1-1	35	0	0	10	1.00	.737	3.90
Akin, Keegan	LM	L	44	24	4	24	0.7	27	10	.37	0-0	2-2	0-0	27	0	0	3	1.00	.647	3.06
Vespi, Nick	LM	L	25	12	4	4	0.8	17	5	.29	1-1	0-1	0-0	17	0	1	1	.67	.849	4.10
Gillaspie, Logan	UR	R	17	6	1	2	0.6	9	3	.33	0-0	0-1	0-0	13	0	1	0	.00	.750	3.12

Boston Red Sox

Pitcher	Pos	T	Usage					Inherited Runners			Saves			Relief Results						
			Rel G	Early Entry	Cons Days	Long	Lev Ind	#	Scrd	Pct	Easy	Reg	Tough	Clean	BS Win	BS	Holds	Sv/Hld Pct	Opp OPS	Rel ERA
Schreiber, John	SU	R	64	13	16	5	1.6	45	14	.31	1-1	5-6	2-3	47	0	2	22	.94	.577	2.22
Strahm, Matt	SU	L	50	13	11	4	1.5	26	7	.27	0-0	4-7	0-2	30	0	5	12	.76	.664	3.83
Diekman, Jake	SU	L	44	15	10	7	1.5	24	9	.38	0-1	1-1	0-2	26	0	3	12	.81	.744	4.23
Robles, Hansel	SU	R	26	2	8	1	1.8	7	2	.29	1-3	0-2	1-3	14	0	6	7	.60	.831	5.84
Davis, Austin	LM	L	47	20	8	11	0.5	24	10	.42	0-0	0-1	0-0	31	0	1	3	.75	.799	6.19
Danish, Tyler	LM	R	32	11	3	10	0.6	7	3	.43	0-0	0-0	0-0	20	0	0	3	1.00	.763	5.13
Ort, Kaleb	LM	R	25	12	7	11	0.7	7	4	.57	1-1	0-0	0-1	13	0	1	1	.67	.845	6.35
Whitlock, Garrett	LM	R	22	5	1	10	1.1	1	0	.00	1-1	5-7	0-0	14	0	2	4	.83	.547	2.75
Brasier, Ryan	UR	R	68	26	12	6	1.0	23	12	.52	0-0	1-3	0-1	39	0	3	13	.82	.793	5.78
Sawamura, Hirokazu	UR	R	49	21	8	10	0.6	33	16	.48	0-0	0-0	0-0	31	0	0	3	1.00	.664	3.73
Barnes, Matt	UR	R	44	6	7	5	1.3	3	0	.00	3-3	4-6	1-1	31	0	2	4	.86	.676	4.31
Houck, Tanner	UR	R	28	6	6	8	1.4	7	2	.29	5-5	2-3	1-1	20	1	1	1	.90	.587	2.70
Valdez, Phillips	UR	R	13	5	2	4	0.4	3	1	.33	0-0	0-0	0-0	9	0	0	0		.589	4.41
Kelly, Zack	UR	R	13	6	2	3	0.9	4	3	.75	0-0	0-0	0-0	8	0	0	1	1.00	.731	3.95
Bazardo, Eduard	UR	R	12	6	1	3	0.3	3	3	1.00	0-0	0-0	0-0	8	0	0	0		.718	2.76
Familia, Jeurys	UR	R	10	5	1	2	1.0	3	0	.00	0-0	0-1	0-0	5	0	1	1	.50	.812	6.10

Chicago Cubs

Pitcher	Pos	T	Usage					Inherited Runners			Saves			Relief Results						
			Rel G	Early Entry	Cons Days	Long	Lev Ind	#	Scrd	Pct	Easy	Reg	Tough	Clean	BS Win	BS	Holds	Sv/Hld Pct	Opp OPS	Rel ERA
Robertson, David	CL	R	36	0	9	7	2.5	9	1	.11	4-4	9-14	1-1	28	0	5	0	.74	.554	2.23
Hughes, Brandon	SU	L	57	13	15	7	1.3	29	5	.17	2-2	4-8	2-2	36	1	4	8	.80	.684	3.12
Effross, Scott	SU	R	46	20	12	2	1.4	28	4	.14	0-1	1-2	0-0	36	0	2	13	.88	.559	2.74
Newcomb, Sean	LT	L	16	5	2	7	0.8	7	0	.00	0-0	0-0	0-0	10	0	0	2	1.00	.891	9.61
Rucker, Michael	LM	R	41	19	8	13	0.7	23	5	.22	0-0	0-0	0-0	25	0	0	4	1.00	.702	3.95
Martin, Chris	LM	R	34	14	5	2	1.0	12	4	.33	0-0	0-0	0-0	22	0	1	6	.86	.816	4.31
Leiter Jr., Mark	LM	R	31	14	1	11	1.1	14	5	.36	2-2	0-2	1-1	18	0	2	4	.78	.577	2.87
Norris, Daniel	LM	L	26	12	4	6	0.7	12	4	.33	0-0	0-0	0-0	12	0	0	2	1.00	.834	6.28
Uelmen, Erich	LM	R	25	11	5	5	1.1	16	5	.31	0-0	1-1	0-1	14	1	1	3	.80	.739	4.67
Thompson, Keegan	LM	R	12	8	0	12	1.0	13	4	.31	0-0	1-1	0-1	7	0	1	0	.50	.480	1.47
Wick, Rowan	UR	R	64	12	14	9	1.4	17	5	.29	5-5	3-5	1-4	43	0	5	4	.72	.847	4.22
Givens, Mychal	UR	R	40	3	6	3	1.4	9	3	.33	2-4	0-0	0-1	31	1	3	6	.73	.652	2.66
Rodriguez, Manuel	UR	R	14	1	2	0	1.9	6	1	.17	1-1	2-4	1-1	8	1	2	2	.75	.688	3.29

Chicago White Sox

Pitcher	Pos	T	Usage					Inherited Runners			Saves			Relief Results						
			Rel G	Early Entry	Cons Days	Long	Lev Ind	#	Scrd	Pct	Easy	Reg	Tough	Clean	BS Win	BS	Holds	Sv/Hld Pct	Opp OPS	Rel ERA
Hendriks, Liam	CL	R	58	0	16	8	2.1	8	4	.50	24-25	13-14	0-2	43	1	4	0	.90	.620	2.81
Graveman, Kendall	SU	R	65	2	13	2	1.8	8	2	.25	4-5	2-6	0-1	45	2	6	27	.85	.693	3.18
Kelly, Joe	SU	R	42	5	6	5	1.3	9	4	.44	1-1	0-0	0-0	28	0	0	15	1.00	.704	5.75
Bummer, Aaron	SU	L	32	6	5	2	1.7	19	8	.42	2-3	0-1	0-2	20	1	4	10	.75	.734	2.36
Diekman, Jake	LT	L	26	6	4	1	0.8	9	3	.33	0-0	0-0	0-0	13	0	0	4	1.00	.880	6.52
Banks, Tanner	LM	L	35	13	4	15	0.4	9	5	.56	0-0	0-0	0-0	24	0	0	1	1.00	.596	3.06
Sousa, Bennett	LM	L	25	13	4	2	0.8	19	6	.32	0-0	0-0	1-2	13	1	1	5	.86	.833	8.41
Velasquez, Vince	LM	R	18	5	1	12	0.6	6	4	.67	0-0	0-0	0-0	9	0	0	1	1.00	.640	4.25
Crick, Kyle	LM	R	14	10	1	5	0.7	6	2	.33	0-0	0-0	0-0	8	0	0	3	1.00	.575	4.02
Ruiz, Jose	UR	R	63	10	14	12	0.6	28	11	.39	0-0	0-0	0-0	39	0	0	11	1.00	.735	4.60
Lopez, Reynaldo	UR	R	60	24	10	6	1.2	27	8	.30	0-0	0-3	0-2	43	1	5	9	.64	.572	2.84
Foster, Matt	UR	R	48	15	12	6	0.7	19	9	.47	0-0	1-1	0-0	32	0	0	5	1.00	.703	4.40
Lambert, Jimmy	UR	R	40	14	5	4	0.9	25	10	.40	0-0	0-0	0-1	25	0	1	10	.91	.651	2.90

Cincinnati Reds

Pitcher	Pos	T	Usage					Inherited Runners			Saves			Relief Results						
			Rel G	Early Entry	Cons Days	Long	Lev Ind	#	Scrd	Pct	Easy	Reg	Tough	Clean	BS Win	BS	Holds	Sv/Hld Pct	Opp OPS	Rel ERA
Diaz, Alexis	SU	R	59	10	8	10	1.7	27	4	.15	4 - 4	4 - 6	2 - 4	41	1	4	13	.85	.476	1.84
Santillan, Tony	SU	R	21	7	1	5	2.0	16	5	.31	2 - 3	0 - 1	2 - 3	12	0	3	6	.77	.839	5.49
Detwiler, Ross	LT	L	30	10	8	2	0.6	14	5	.36	1 - 1	0 - 0	0 - 0	18	0	0	1	1.00	.851	4.44
Sanmartin, Reiver	LM	L	41	17	6	10	0.8	26	9	.35	0 - 0	0 - 0	0 - 0	27	0	0	7	1.00	.694	2.96
Cessa, Luis	LM	R	36	17	3	2	0.9	19	8	.42	0 - 1	0 - 0	0 - 0	21	1	1	5	.83	.757	4.91
Hoffman, Jeff	LM	R	34	15	0	14	0.5	16	8	.50	0 - 1	0 - 0	0 - 0	19	0	1	1	.50	.745	3.98
Gibaut, Ian	LM	R	33	12	4	9	0.9	12	3	.25	0 - 0	1 - 3	0 - 0	20	0	2	3	.67	.812	4.67
Strickland, Hunter	UR	R	66	4	14	8	1.0	14	4	.29	6 - 7	1 - 4	0 - 0	44	2	4	4	.73	.791	4.91
Kuhnel, Joel	UR	R	53	13	6	9	0.7	17	6	.35	1 - 1	0 - 1	0 - 1	32	0	2	5	.75	.805	6.36
Farmer, Buck	UR	R	44	13	8	10	0.8	25	9	.36	1 - 1	0 - 0	0 - 1	30	0	1	5	.88	.611	3.83
Warren, Art	UR	R	39	8	5	4	1.0	20	10	.50	1 - 2	2 - 3	0 - 1	20	1	3	4	.70	.813	6.50
Moreta, Dauri	UR	R	34	8	6	7	0.4	8	2	.25	0 - 0	0 - 0	1 - 1	23	0	0	1	1.00	.763	4.97
Law, Derek	UR	R	15	7	2	2	1.0	8	3	.38	0 - 0	0 - 0	0 - 0	11	0	0	3	1.00	.775	4.08
Cruz, Fernando	UR	R	12	7	1	1	1.0	11	5	.45	0 - 0	0 - 0	0 - 0	6	0	0	1	1.00	.658	1.59

Cleveland Guardians

Pitcher	Pos	T	Usage					Inherited Runners			Saves			Relief Results						
			Rel G	Early Entry	Cons Days	Long	Lev Ind	#	Scrd	Pct	Easy	Reg	Tough	Clean	BS Win	BS	Holds	Sv/Hld Pct	Opp OPS	Rel ERA
Clase, Emmanuel	CL	R	77	0	26	0	1.8	5	2	.40	25 - 26	17 - 20	0 - 0	61	2	4	0	.91	.425	1.36
Stephan, Trevor	SU	R	66	7	12	8	1.6	20	5	.25	1 - 2	2 - 2	0 - 1	50	1	2	19	.92	.628	2.69
Karinchak, James	SU	R	38	2	8	9	1.2	6	3	.50	3 - 3	0 - 1	0 - 0	31	0	1	8	.92	.516	2.08
Hentges, Sam	LT	L	57	19	11	8	0.8	23	5	.22	0 - 0	1 - 1	0 - 0	40	0	0	8	1.00	.516	2.32
Gose, Anthony	LT	L	22	7	1	3	0.6	8	2	.25	0 - 0	0 - 1	0 - 0	15	0	1	0	.00	.760	4.71
McCarty, Kirk	LM	L	11	6	0	10	0.9	1	0	.00	0 - 0	0 - 0	0 - 0	4	0	0	0		.746	3.45
Shaw, Bryan	UR	R	58	11	12	8	0.9	19	5	.26	0 - 0	1 - 1	0 - 0	41	0	0	5	1.00	.738	5.17
De Los Santos, Enyel	UR	R	50	14	2	4	0.8	33	9	.27	0 - 0	0 - 0	1 - 2	33	1	1	3	.80	.603	3.04
Morgan, Eli	UR	R	49	16	4	10	1.0	25	6	.24	0 - 1	0 - 2	0 - 1	32	0	4	10	.71	.618	3.25
Sandlin, Nick	UR	R	46	16	7	8	1.5	30	10	.33	0 - 0	0 - 1	0 - 2	31	0	3	7	.70	.548	2.25
Castro, Anthony	UR	R	12	4	1	3	0.4	7	2	.29	0 - 0	0 - 1	0 - 0	4	0	1	0	.00	1.101	7.43

Colorado Rockies

Pitcher	Pos	T	Usage					Inherited Runners			Saves			Relief Results						
			Rel G	Early Entry	Cons Days	Long	Lev Ind	#	Scrd	Pct	Easy	Reg	Tough	Clean	BS Win	BS	Holds	Sv/Hld Pct	Opp OPS	Rel ERA
Bard, Daniel	CL	R	57	0	12	7	2.2	2	0	.00	19 - 19	14 - 17	1 - 1	44	1	3	0	.92	.503	1.79
Estevez, Carlos	SU	R	62	4	11	6	1.1	23	6	.26	2 - 4	0 - 1	0 - 1	43	0	4	13	.79	.663	3.47
Gilbreath, Lucas	SU	L	47	10	15	5	1.1	30	16	.53	0 - 0	0 - 0	0 - 2	28	0	2	12	.86	.680	4.19
Kinley, Tyler	SU	R	25	2	8	3	1.3	8	3	.38	0 - 0	0 - 0	0 - 0	21	0	0	10	1.00	.560	0.75
Stephenson, Robert	LM	R	45	7	7	5	0.7	18	4	.22	0 - 0	0 - 1	0 - 0	25	0	2	6	.75	.862	6.04
Lawrence, Justin	LM	R	38	17	6	8	0.9	28	7	.25	0 - 1	1 - 1	0 - 1	20	0	2	7	.80	.736	5.70
Chacin, Jhoulys	LM	R	35	20	3	13	0.6	34	8	.24	0 - 0	0 - 0	0 - 2	14	0	0	2	1.00	.848	7.61
Blach, Ty	LM	L	23	12	1	11	0.5	14	4	.29	0 - 0	1 - 2	0 - 0	11	0	1	0	.50	.785	5.88
Gomber, Austin	LM	L	16	13	0	12	0.8	17	10	.59	0 - 0	0 - 0	0 - 0	3	0	0	0		.754	5.11
Colome, Alex	UR	R	53	1	10	2	1.5	0	0	.00	4 - 4	0 - 3	0 - 0	33	0	3	7	.79	.853	5.74
Bird, Jake	UR	R	38	11	5	11	0.8	16	6	.38	0 - 0	0 - 0	0 - 1	18	0	1	5	.83	.763	4.91
Lamet, Dinelson	UR	R	19	0	3	4	0.9	1	1	1.00	0 - 0	0 - 2	0 - 0	12	0	2	3	.60	.635	4.05
Smith, Chad	UR	R	15	7	2	6	0.7	14	9	.64	0 - 0	0 - 0	0 - 1	7	0	1	0	.00	.791	7.50
Goudeau, Ashton	UR	R	12	7	0	7	0.7	11	4	.36	1 - 1	0 - 0	0 - 0	3	0	0	0	1.00	.836	7.08

Detroit Tigers

Pitcher	Pos	T	Usage					Inherited Runners			Saves			Relief Results						
			Rel G	Early Entry	Cons Days	Long	Lev Ind	#	Scrd	Pct	Easy	Reg	Tough	Clean	BS Win	BS	Holds	Sv/Hld Pct	Opp OPS	Rel ERA
Soto, Gregory	CL	L	64	0	14	8	2.0	10	2	.20	18 - 18	11 - 14	1 - 1	45	0	3	2	.91	.660	3.28
Lange, Alex	SU	R	71	20	14	6	1.4	22	7	.32	0 - 1	0 - 2	0 - 1	51	0	4	21	.84	.620	3.41
Chafin, Andrew	SU	L	64	14	13	3	1.3	36	5	.14	0 - 0	2 - 3	1 - 1	45	0	1	19	.96	.619	2.83
Fulmer, Michael	SU	R	41	0	7	1	1.7	12	1	.08	1 - 2	1 - 3	0 - 1	30	1	4	18	.83	.580	3.20
Norris, Daniel	LT	L	12	6	1	4	0.6	2	0	.00	0 - 0	0 - 0	0 - 0	7	0	0	0		.687	4.74
Peralta, Wily	LM	R	27	14	2	12	0.7	5	2	.40	0 - 0	0 - 0	0 - 0	17	0	0	2	1.00	.679	2.72
Barnes, Jacob	LM	R	22	12	0	0	0.6	6	2	.33	0 - 0	0 - 0	0 - 1	14	0	1	2	.67	.827	6.10
Jimenez, Joe	UR	R	62	8	10	0	0.9	8	2	.25	1 - 2	0 - 1	1 - 1	46	0	2	11	.87	.609	3.49
Foley, Jason	UR	R	60	23	9	5	0.5	28	14	.50	0 - 0	0 - 0	0 - 1	43	0	1	4	.80	.697	3.88
Vest, Will	UR	R	57	25	7	9	0.7	29	9	.31	0 - 0	0 - 0	1 - 1	38	0	0	4	1.00	.662	3.82
Cisnero, Jose	UR	R	28	7	2	2	1.0	9	2	.22	0 - 0	0 - 0	0 - 0	22	0	0	5	1.00	.545	1.08
Alexander, Tyler	UR	L	10	7	0	6	0.8	13	6	.46	0 - 0	0 - 0	0 - 0	5	0	0	1	1.00	.565	1.29
Hutchison, Drew	UR	R	10	5	0	6	1.0	1	0	.00	0 - 0	0 - 0	0 - 0	6	0	0	0		.683	4.60

Houston Astros

Pitcher	Pos	T	Usage					Inherited Runners			Saves			Relief Results						
			Rel G	Early Entry	Cons Days	Long	Lev Ind	#	Scrd	Pct	Easy	Reg	Tough	Clean	BS Win	BS	Holds	Sv/Hld Pct	Opp OPS	Rel ERA
Pressly, Ryan	CL	R	50	0	11	2	2.0	7	2	.29	21 - 23	12 - 14	0 - 0	38	1	4	0	.89	.516	2.98
Montero, Rafael	SU	R	71	2	13	4	1.4	21	5	.24	11 - 11	2 - 3	1 - 2	56	0	2	23	.95	.535	2.37
Neris, Hector	SU	R	70	0	14	3	1.4	7	1	.14	3 - 4	0 - 3	0 - 0	52	2	4	25	.88	.580	3.72
Stanek, Ryne	SU	R	59	8	5	3	1.4	22	9	.41	1 - 2	0 - 2	0 - 1	45	0	4	17	.82	.556	1.15
Smith, Will	LT	L	24	2	5	1	0.6	4	3	.75	0 - 0	0 - 0	0 - 0	16	0	0	6	1.00	.759	3.27
Taylor, Blake	LT	L	19	5	2	2	0.7	9	3	.33	0 - 0	0 - 0	0 - 0	14	0	0	4	1.00	.659	3.94
Martinez, Seth	LM	R	29	10	1	8	0.5	15	1	.07	0 - 0	0 - 0	0 - 0	23	0	0	2	1.00	.532	2.09
Maton, Phil	UR	R	67	19	9	10	0.9	25	5	.20	0 - 1	0 - 1	0 - 0	44	0	2	14	.88	.730	3.84
Abreu, Bryan	UR	R	55	17	5	9	0.8	27	10	.37	1 - 1	0 - 0	1 - 1	41	0	0	8	1.00	.570	1.94

Kansas City Royals

Pitcher	Pos	T	Usage					Inherited Runners			Saves			Relief Results						
			Rel G	Early Entry	Cons Days	Long	Lev Ind	#	Scrd	Pct	Easy	Reg	Tough	Clean	BS Win	BS	Holds	Sv/Hld Pct	Opp OPS	Rel ERA
Barlow, Scott	CL	R	69	0	16	10	1.7	37	13	.35	11 - 13	9 - 9	4 - 6	51	0	4	6	.88	.590	2.18
Clarke, Taylor	SU	R	47	10	10	8	1.1	22	10	.45	3 - 3	0 - 4	0 - 1	32	1	5	10	.72	.718	4.04
Speier, Gabe	LT	L	16	7	3	2	0.7	11	5	.45	0 - 0	0 - 0	0 - 1	10	0	1	2	.67	.680	2.60
Misiewicz, Anthony	LT	L	15	3	3	2	0.8	4	2	.50	0 - 0	0 - 0	0 - 0	8	0	0	1	1.00	.684	4.11
Garrett, Amir	LM	L	60	33	15	1	1.0	42	7	.17	0 - 0	0 - 0	0 - 1	44	0	1	10	.91	.572	4.96
Cuas, Jose	LM	R	47	27	13	4	1.3	38	8	.21	0 - 0	0 - 0	1 - 1	31	0	0	11	1.00	.757	3.58
Snider, Collin	LM	R	42	26	12	2	1.2	31	6	.19	0 - 1	0 - 0	0 - 1	27	0	2	7	.78	.824	6.55
Payamps, Joel	LM	R	29	10	5	15	0.6	20	6	.30	0 - 1	0 - 1	0 - 0	14	0	2	0	.00	.771	3.16
Hernandez, Carlos	LM	R	20	8	3	6	0.9	9	1	.11	0 - 0	0 - 0	0 - 0	10	0	0	1	1.00	.756	5.47
Mills, Wyatt	LM	R	19	8	3	7	0.7	9	2	.22	0 - 0	0 - 0	0 - 0	12	0	0	4	1.00	.745	4.79
Coleman, Dylan	UR	R	68	11	16	6	1.3	26	9	.35	0 - 1	0 - 0	0 - 2	50	0	3	16	.84	.617	2.78
Staumont, Josh	UR	R	42	2	10	4	1.2	7	2	.29	1 - 1	2 - 4	0 - 1	26	0	3	5	.73	.805	6.45
Weaver, Luke	UR	R	14	1	0	6	0.1	14	8	.57	0 - 0	0 - 0	0 - 0	5	0	0	0		.863	5.59
Keller, Brad	UR	R	13	5	1	6	0.9	0	0	.00	1 - 1	0 - 0	0 - 0	6	0	0	1	1.00	.854	6.23

Los Angeles Angels

Pitcher	Pos	T	Usage					Inherited Runners			Saves			Relief Results						
			Rel G	Early Entry	Cons Days	Long	Lev Ind	#	Scrd	Pct	Easy	Reg	Tough	Clean	BS Win	BS	Holds	Sv/Hld Pct	Opp OPS	Rel ERA
Iglesias, Raisel	CL	R	39	0	7	4	1.4	14	8	.57	15 - 17	1 - 2	0 - 0	27	0	3	0	.84	.656	4.04
Loup, Aaron	SU	L	65	21	12	3	1.3	37	10	.27	0 - 0	1 - 2	0 - 4	37	0	5	18	.79	.671	3.84
Tepera, Ryan	SU	R	59	1	4	3	1.6	21	9	.43	2 - 2	3 - 6	1 - 3	39	0	5	17	.82	.618	3.61
Herget, Jimmy	SU	R	48	15	3	11	1.2	26	9	.35	3 - 3	5 - 5	1 - 4	31	0	3	6	.83	.575	2.45
Quijada, Jose	SU	L	42	8	7	4	1.6	28	4	.14	3 - 3	0 - 1	0 - 1	29	0	2	12	.88	.636	3.98
Wantz, Andrew	LM	R	41	21	2	9	0.9	17	3	.18	0 - 0	0 - 1	0 - 0	28	0	1	7	.88	.668	3.28
Barria, Jaime	LM	R	34	13	0	22	0.7	19	8	.42	0 - 0	0 - 3	0 - 0	15	1	3	5	.63	.660	2.53
Ortega, Oliver	LM	R	27	14	0	8	1.1	10	4	.40	0 - 0	1 - 1	0 - 0	15	0	0	5	1.00	.745	3.71
Mayers, Mike	LM	R	21	9	1	9	0.7	16	6	.38	0 - 1	0 - 0	0 - 0	9	0	1	1	.50	.881	6.25
Bradley, Archie	UR	R	21	8	3	2	1.2	16	5	.31	1 - 1	0 - 0	1 - 3	11	0	2	4	.75	.632	4.82
Warren, Austin	UR	R	14	8	1	3	0.7	9	8	.89	0 - 0	0 - 1	0 - 0	6	0	1	0	.00	.896	5.63
Peguero, Elvis	UR	R	13	6	0	7	0.3	14	4	.29	0 - 0	0 - 0	0 - 0	6	0	0	0		.933	6.75
Weiss, Zack	UR	R	12	4	1	3	0.5	6	4	.67	0 - 0	0 - 0	0 - 0	7	0	0	1	1.00	.577	3.38
Chavez, Jesse	UR	R	11	1	2	3	0.8	6	3	.50	0 - 1	0 - 0	0 - 1	7	1	2	0	.00	.967	7.59
Marte, Jose	UR	R	11	4	0	6	0.3	6	2	.33	0 - 0	0 - 0	0 - 0	6	0	0	0		.848	7.36

Los Angeles Dodgers

Pitcher	Pos	T	Usage					Inherited Runners			Saves			Relief Results						
			Rel G	Early Entry	Cons Days	Long	Lev Ind	#	Scrd	Pct	Easy	Reg	Tough	Clean	BS Win	BS	Holds	Sv/Hld Pct	Opp OPS	Rel ERA
Kimbrel, Craig	CL	R	63	4	15	10	1.5	3	1	.33	21 - 21	1 - 6	0 - 0	41	1	5	2	.83	.675	3.75
Phillips, Evan	SU	R	64	15	14	2	1.4	22	5	.23	0 - 0	2 - 3	0 - 1	56	0	2	19	.91	.430	1.14
Vesia, Alex	SU	L	63	17	12	2	1.2	27	7	.26	0 - 1	0 - 1	1 - 1	49	0	2	16	.89	.527	2.15
Graterol, Brusdar	SU	R	45	11	7	2	1.2	24	8	.33	3 - 3	0 - 0	1 - 2	30	0	1	10	.93	.571	2.96
Almonte, Yency	SU	R	33	10	5	4	1.1	7	2	.29	0 - 0	1 - 1	0 - 1	28	0	1	8	.90	.470	1.02
Hudson, Daniel	SU	R	25	2	5	1	1.5	6	1	.17	3 - 3	2 - 2	0 - 1	20	0	1	9	.93	.511	2.22
Price, David	LT	L	40	11	4	2	0.7	12	4	.33	2 - 2	0 - 2	0 - 0	29	1	2	4	.75	.704	2.45
Ferguson, Caleb	LT	L	36	12	0	1	0.8	3	0	.00	0 - 0	0 - 2	0 - 0	30	0	1	7	1.00	.585	1.87
Bruihl, Justin	LT	L	24	8	5	2	0.8	5	0	.00	0 - 0	0 - 1	1 - 1	15	0	1	3	.80	.756	3.80
Bickford, Phil	UR	R	60	16	14	6	0.6	12	5	.42	0 - 0	0 - 1	0 - 0	40	0	1	6	.86	.729	4.72
Martin, Chris	UR	R	26	10	4	1	1.1	15	1	.07	0 - 0	1 - 2	1 - 1	22	0	1	3	.83	.343	1.46
Moronta, Reyes	UR	R	22	2	4	4	0.2	4	1	.25	0 - 0	0 - 0	0 - 0	13	0	0	0		.703	4.18
Kahnle, Tommy	UR	R	13	3	1	0	1.1	0	0	.00	0 - 0	1 - 1	0 - 0	11	0	0	1	1.00	.521	2.84
Alberto, Hanser	ER	R	10	0	2	1	0.0	0	0	.00	0 - 0	0 - 0	0 - 0	6	0	0	0		.726	4.09

Miami Marlins

Pitcher	Pos	T	Usage					Inherited Runners			Saves			Relief Results						
			Rel G	Early Entry	Cons Days	Long	Lev Ind	#	Scrd	Pct	Easy	Reg	Tough	Clean	BS Win	BS	Holds	Sv/Hld Pct	Opp OPS	Rel ERA
Scott, Tanner	CL	L	67	7	17	12	1.7	8	5	.63	15 - 16	5 - 11	0 - 0	45	1	7	4	.77	.711	4.31
Okert, Steven	SU	L	60	10	15	5	1.5	19	5	.26	0 - 1	0 - 1	0 - 2	41	0	4	19	.83	.648	2.98
Floro, Dylan	SU	R	56	17	16	1	1.3	12	4	.33	9 - 9	0 - 2	1 - 3	41	0	4	5	.79	.625	3.02
Bass, Anthony	SU	R	45	0	12	2	1.4	16	3	.19	0 - 1	0 - 0	0 - 2	35	1	3	16	.84	.514	1.41
Bleier, Richard	LT	L	54	14	12	2	0.9	27	14	.52	0 - 0	0 - 1	0 - 0	31	0	2	7	.80	.797	3.44
Nance, Tommy	LM	R	33	13	5	9	0.8	15	9	.60	0 - 0	0 - 1	0 - 1	17	0	2	2	.50	.788	4.66
Brazoban, Huascar	LM	R	27	13	7	8	1.0	15	6	.40	0 - 0	0 - 0	0 - 1	17	0	1	4	.80	.700	3.09
Head, Louis	LM	R	23	9	3	4	0.5	8	4	.50	0 - 0	1 - 1	0 - 0	16	0	0	1	1.00	.890	7.23
Pop, Zach	LM	R	18	10	2	4	0.9	12	1	.08	0 - 0	0 - 0	0 - 0	13	0	0	1	1.00	.688	3.60
Brigham, Jeff	LM	R	16	8	1	8	0.9	13	1	.08	1 - 1	0 - 0	0 - 0	9	0	0	2	1.00	.731	3.38
Nardi, Andrew	LM	L	13	6	1	9	0.5	5	5	1.00	0 - 0	0 - 0	0 - 0	5	0	0	1	1.00	1.151	9.82
Sulser, Cole	UR	R	39	4	5	2	1.0	17	3	.18	1 - 2	0 - 2	1 - 1	25	0	3	5	.70	.864	5.29
Bender, Anthony	UR	R	22	3	7	0	1.8	12	3	.25	3 - 3	2 - 4	1 - 1	15	0	2	3	.82	.716	3.26
Hernandez, Elieser	UR	R	10	3	2	4	0.8	3	3	1.00	0 - 0	0 - 0	0 - 1	6	1	1	0	.00	1.003	7.47
Poteet, Cody	UR	R	10	5	0	7	0.4	5	4	.80	0 - 0	0 - 0	0 - 0	6	0	0	1	1.00	.722	3.10

Milwaukee Brewers

Pitcher	Pos	T	Usage					Inherited Runners			Saves			Relief Results						
			Rel G	Early Entry	Cons Days	Long	Lev Ind	#	Scrd	Pct	Easy	Reg	Tough	Clean	BS Win	BS	Holds	Sv/Hld Pct	Opp OPS	Rel ERA
Hader, Josh	CL	L	37	0	8	2	2.4	4	0	.00	20 - 21	9 - 10	0 - 0	29	0	2	0	.94	.698	4.24
Boxberger, Brad	SU	R	70	9	18	8	1.8	26	11	.42	0 - 0	1 - 4	0 - 4	49	1	7	29	.81	.649	2.95
Williams, Devin	SU	R	65	0	18	7	2.4	13	2	.15	7 - 7	7 - 9	1 - 1	55	0	2	26	.95	.472	1.93
Gott, Trevor	SU	R	45	22	11	3	1.1	21	3	.14	0 - 0	0 - 3	0 - 1	31	0	4	11	.73	.661	4.14
Bush, Matt	SU	R	24	1	6	0	1.4	5	0	.00	2 - 2	0 - 4	0 - 0	14	0	4	9	.73	.688	3.57
Milner, Hoby	LT	L	67	30	16	8	0.9	37	5	.14	0 - 0	0 - 1	0 - 0	48	0	1	9	.90	.686	3.76
Suter, Brent	LT	L	54	17	8	14	0.7	18	11	.61	0 - 0	0 - 0	0 - 0	30	0	0	1	1.00	.713	3.78
Rogers, Taylor	LT	L	24	1	6	1	1.7	6	2	.33	3 - 3	0 - 3	0 - 0	16	1	3	4	.70	.845	5.48
Strzelecki, Peter	LM	R	30	11	3	7	0.9	9	3	.33	1 - 1	0 - 2	0 - 0	19	0	2	4	.71	.632	2.83
Kelley, Trevor	LM	R	18	6	3	8	0.4	8	0	.00	0 - 1	0 - 0	0 - 0	11	0	1	2	.67	.868	6.08
Gustave, Jandel	UR	R	27	11	7	3	0.7	10	4	.40	0 - 0	0 - 0	0 - 0	15	0	0	2	1.00	.675	3.86
Perdomo, Luis	UR	R	14	7	2	5	0.7	7	2	.29	0 - 0	0 - 0	0 - 0	9	0	0	1	1.00	.716	3.80
Sanchez, Miguel	UR	R	12	5	3	2	1.1	6	2	.33	0 - 0	0 - 0	0 - 0	7	0	0	2	1.00	.855	4.05
Cousins, Jake	UR	R	12	4	3	5	0.9	5	2	.40	0 - 0	0 - 0	0 - 1	8	1	1	1	.50	.706	2.70

Minnesota Twins

Pitcher	Pos	T	Usage					Inherited Runners			Saves			Relief Results						
			Rel G	Early Entry	Cons Days	Long	Lev Ind	#	Scrd	Pct	Easy	Reg	Tough	Clean	BS Win	BS	Holds	Sv/Hld Pct	Opp OPS	Rel ERA
Thielbar, Caleb	SU	L	67	35	14	4	1.3	43	8	.19	0 - 0	1 - 2	0 - 0	47	0	1	18	.95	.613	3.49
Jax, Griffin	SU	R	65	25	11	10	1.1	19	8	.42	0 - 0	1 - 6	0 - 1	44	0	6	18	.76	.607	3.36
Pagan, Emilio	SU	R	59	13	9	12	1.3	13	5	.38	3 - 4	6 - 10	0 - 2	37	0	7	7	.70	.776	4.43
Duran, Jhoan	SU	R	57	4	5	10	1.6	9	2	.22	3 - 3	5 - 5	0 - 0	45	0	0	18	1.00	.571	1.86
Smith, Joe	SU	R	34	8	7	2	1.4	14	0	.00	0 - 1	0 - 1	0 - 0	24	0	2	14	.88	.893	4.61
Fulmer, Michael	SU	R	26	7	6	1	1.6	5	1	.20	0 - 0	0 - 0	1 - 1	18	0	0	7	1.00	.874	3.70
Coulombe, Danny	LT	L	10	6	0	5	0.6	3	1	.33	0 - 0	0 - 0	0 - 0	7	0	0	0		.511	1.46
Moran, Jovani	LM	L	31	8	2	11	0.4	9	3	.33	0 - 0	1 - 1	0 - 0	22	0	0	2	1.00	.490	2.21
Cotton, Jharel	LM	R	25	9	1	9	0.7	8	6	.75	0 - 1	0 - 0	0 - 1	15	0	2	2	.50	.680	2.83
Duffey, Tyler	UR	R	40	10	2	9	0.9	9	4	.44	1 - 2	1 - 3	0 - 0	28	0	3	9	.79	.800	4.91
Megill, Trevor	UR	R	40	14	3	12	0.8	16	4	.25	0 - 1	0 - 1	0 - 0	21	0	2	3	.60	.748	4.80
Lopez, Jorge	UR	R	23	0	6	3	1.6	1	0	.00	3 - 4	1 - 2	0 - 0	17	0	2	1	.71	.757	4.37
Stashak, Cody	UR	R	11	5	0	2	0.4	7	6	.86	0 - 0	0 - 0	0 - 0	6	0	0	1	1.00	.621	3.86
Cano, Yennier	UR	R	10	6	1	5	0.4	3	0	.00	0 - 0	0 - 0	0 - 0	4	0	0	0		.968	9.22

New York Mets

Pitcher	Pos	T	Usage					Inherited Runners			Saves			Relief Results						
			Rel G	Early Entry	Cons Days	Long	Lev Ind	#	Scrd	Pct	Easy	Reg	Tough	Clean	BS Win	BS	Holds	Sv/Hld Pct	Opp OPS	Rel ERA
Diaz, Edwin	CL	R	61	0	12	3	1.8	10	2	.20	18 - 18	14 - 17	0 - 0	51	1	3	4	.92	.446	1.31
Ottavino, Adam	SU	R	66	9	11	7	1.1	38	14	.37	3 - 3	0 - 1	0 - 2	50	0	3	18	.88	.591	2.06
Lugo, Seth	SU	R	62	13	9	8	1.0	24	11	.46	2 - 3	1 - 2	0 - 1	42	1	3	16	.86	.668	3.60
Smith, Drew	SU	R	44	6	3	7	1.2	14	8	.57	0 - 1	0 - 1	0 - 0	30	0	2	14	.88	.687	3.33
Rodriguez, Joely	LT	L	55	9	7	2	0.8	17	3	.18	0 - 0	0 - 0	0 - 0	35	0	0	9	1.00	.634	4.47
Shreve, Chasen	LM	L	25	15	1	4	0.6	17	9	.53	0 - 0	0 - 1	0 - 0	14	0	1	4	.80	.781	6.49
Williams, Trevor	LM	R	21	14	0	13	0.5	13	9	.69	0 - 0	1 - 1	0 - 1	9	0	1	1	.67	.682	2.47
Hunter, Tommy	LM	R	18	7	1	3	0.7	8	2	.25	0 - 0	0 - 0	0 - 0	11	0	0	1	1.00	.727	2.42
May, Trevor	UR	R	26	4	1	6	0.8	6	0	.00	1 - 1	0 - 0	0 - 0	17	0	0	6	1.00	.756	5.04
Givens, Mychal	UR	R	18	4	2	3	0.7	7	3	.43	0 - 0	0 - 0	0 - 1	12	0	1	1	.50	.889	5.03
Holderman, Colin	UR	R	15	5	1	1	0.6	8	0	.00	0 - 0	0 - 0	0 - 0	11	0	0	1	1.00	.489	2.04
Medina, Adonis	UR	R	14	7	0	8	0.7	6	3	.50	0 - 0	1 - 1	0 - 0	9	0	0	0	1.00	.809	6.08
Nogosek, Stephen	UR	R	12	7	1	7	0.2	7	2	.29	0 - 0	0 - 0	0 - 0	8	0	0	0		.697	2.45

New York Yankees

Pitcher	Pos	T	Usage Rel G	Early Entry	Cons Days	Long	Lev Ind	Inherited Runners #	Scrd	Pct	Saves Easy	Reg	Tough	Relief Results Clean	BS Win	BS	Holds	Sv/Hld Pct	Opp OPS	Rel ERA
Holmes, Clay	CL	R	62	2	14	3	1.9	23	7	.30	12-12	8-12	0-1	45	0	5	7	.84	.547	2.54
Peralta, Wandy	SU	L	56	10	10	5	1.4	28	6	.21	1-2	2-3	1-4	40	0	5	9	.72	.534	2.72
King, Michael	SU	R	34	10	5	12	1.6	21	3	.14	0-0	0-1	1-2	22	0	2	16	.89	.547	2.29
Luetge, Lucas	LT	L	50	20	6	12	0.8	32	13	.41	0-0	2-2	0-1	32	1	1	6	.89	.721	2.67
Chapman, Aroldis	LT	L	43	3	10	2	1.3	5	2	.40	8-8	1-1	0-0	30	0	0	1	1.00	.654	4.46
Schmidt, Clarke	LM	R	26	10	1	12	1.1	12	3	.25	0-1	2-2	0-0	15	0	1	4	.86	.639	2.74
Abreu, Albert	LM	R	22	6	1	5	0.7	10	6	.60	0-0	0-0	0-1	10	0	1	1	.50	.656	3.16
Loaisiga, Jonathan	UR	R	50	7	11	5	1.7	25	5	.20	0-1	2-2	0-0	36	1	1	10	.92	.599	4.13
Marinaccio, Ron	UR	R	40	12	5	9	1.0	27	7	.26	0-0	0-0	0-0	29	0	0	6	1.00	.525	2.05
Castro, Miguel	UR	R	34	12	6	2	1.1	15	5	.33	0-0	0-0	0-1	26	0	1	9	.90	.741	4.03
Trivino, Lou	UR	R	25	10	6	1	1.4	28	7	.25	0-0	1-1	0-1	17	0	1	2	.75	.607	1.66
Green, Chad	UR	R	14	5	3	1	1.5	6	3	.50	0-1	1-2	0-1	9	1	3	3	.57	.647	3.00
Effross, Scott	UR	R	13	2	1	0	2.1	5	0	.00	2-2	1-1	0-0	11	0	0	3	1.00	.557	2.13
Weissert, Greg	UR	R	12	6	2	3	0.7	8	2	.25	0-0	0-0	0-0	8	0	0	1	1.00	.515	5.56

Oakland Athletics

Pitcher	Pos	T	Usage Rel G	Early Entry	Cons Days	Long	Lev Ind	Inherited Runners #	Scrd	Pct	Saves Easy	Reg	Tough	Relief Results Clean	BS Win	BS	Holds	Sv/Hld Pct	Opp OPS	Rel ERA
Jimenez, Dany	CL	R	34	2	5	3	1.8	13	2	.15	8-9	2-3	1-2	24	1	3	4	.83	.537	3.41
Acevedo, Domingo	SU	R	70	20	11	0	1.2	30	10	.33	2-3	1-4	1-1	50	0	4	20	.86	.636	3.33
Puk, A.J.	SU	L	62	16	9	10	1.4	22	7	.32	2-3	0-1	2-5	42	0	5	20	.83	.667	3.12
Jackson, Zach	SU	R	54	6	12	6	1.7	16	3	.19	2-2	0-2	1-2	37	0	3	26	.91	.547	3.00
Moll, Sam	SU	L	53	22	10	1	1.3	42	14	.33	0-0	0-0	0-2	37	0	2	16	.89	.646	2.91
Snead, Kirby	LT	L	46	11	8	10	0.7	25	6	.24	0-1	1-1	0-1	30	0	2	5	.75	.861	5.84
Selman, Sam	LT	L	16	5	2	2	0.3	11	5	.45	0-0	0-0	0-1	11	0	1	0	.00	.757	4.91
Kolarek, Adam	LT	L	15	3	3	6	0.2	7	0	.00	0-0	0-0	0-0	10	0	0	0		.804	4.58
Trivino, Lou	UR	R	39	5	9	4	1.5	20	2	.10	7-8	2-3	1-1	25	0	2	2	.86	.906	6.47
Pruitt, Austin	UR	R	38	12	5	10	0.5	12	5	.42	0-2	1-1	0-0	20	0	2	2	.60	.757	4.65
Grimm, Justin	UR	R	15	8	1	3	0.5	9	2	.22	0-0	0-0	0-0	8	0	0	3	1.00	.807	4.11
Ruiz, Norge	UR	R	14	5	2	6	0.4	8	2	.25	0-1	0-0	0-0	6	0	1	1	.50	.981	7.11
Payamps, Joel	UR	R	12	4	1	2	1.0	6	2	.33	0-0	0-0	0-0	8	0	0	0	1.00	.687	3.46
Tapia, Domingo	UR	R	11	4	1	9	0.1	5	3	.60	0-0	0-0	0-0	4	0	0	0		.971	8.47
Cyr, Tyler	UR	R	11	2	1	1	0.5	3	1	.33	0-0	0-0	0-0	9	0	0	1	1.00	.571	2.08

Philadelphia Phillies

Pitcher	Pos	T	Usage Rel G	Early Entry	Cons Days	Long	Lev Ind	Inherited Runners #	Scrd	Pct	Saves Easy	Reg	Tough	Relief Results Clean	BS Win	BS	Holds	Sv/Hld Pct	Opp OPS	Rel ERA
Alvarado, Jose	SU	L	59	6	12	4	1.5	25	7	.28	1-1	0-1	1-2	44	1	2	22	.92	.585	3.18
Hand, Brad	SU	L	55	7	9	2	1.4	17	8	.47	4-4	1-3	0-0	38	2	2	13	.90	.654	2.80
Dominguez, Seranthony	SU	R	54	7	11	4	1.6	20	7	.35	4-4	5-7	0-0	40	0	2	15	.92	.596	3.00
Nelson, Nick	LM	R	45	21	2	21	0.6	23	6	.26	0-0	0-0	1-1	26	0	0	3	1.00	.692	4.73
Sanchez, Cristopher	LM	L	12	8	0	9	0.7	11	6	.55	0-0	1-1	0-0	3	0	0	1	1.00	.755	6.75
Bellatti, Andrew	UR	R	58	19	12	4	0.9	31	9	.29	2-2	0-0	0-1	35	0	1	9	.92	.687	3.04
Brogdon, Connor	UR	R	47	14	5	2	1.0	28	9	.32	2-3	0-0	0-1	29	0	2	6	.80	.713	3.27
Knebel, Corey	UR	R	46	5	7	6	1.7	14	5	.36	6-7	6-9	0-0	33	0	4	2	.78	.662	3.43
Familia, Jeurys	UR	R	38	5	8	4	0.9	13	5	.38	0-1	0-0	0-1	22	1	2	6	.75	.933	6.09
Robertson, David	UR	R	22	0	2	3	1.7	0	0	.00	3-3	3-6	0-0	17	0	3	3	.75	.649	2.70
Norwood, James	UR	R	20	5	3	4	0.4	4	0	.00	0-0	0-0	0-0	12	0	0	1	1.00	.822	8.31
Coonrod, Sam	UR	R	12	2	1	3	0.3	1	0	.00	0-0	0-0	0-0	7	0	0	3	1.00	.802	7.82

Pittsburgh Pirates

Pitcher	Pos	T	Usage					Inherited Runners			Saves			Relief Results						
			Rel G	Early Entry	Cons Days	Long	Lev Ind	#	Scrd	Pct	Easy	Reg	Tough	Clean	BS Win	BS	Holds	Sv/Hld Pct	Opp OPS	Rel ERA
Bednar, David	CL	R	45	1	8	7	1.9	8	1	.13	9 - 10	9 - 12	1 - 1	34	2	4	4	.85	.618	2.61
Crowe, Wil	SU	R	59	15	6	19	1.5	19	6	.32	2 - 2	2 - 7	0 - 1	38	0	6	16	.77	.682	4.38
Stratton, Chris	SU	R	39	4	9	6	1.4	17	8	.47	1 - 2	1 - 3	0 - 2	21	0	5	8	.67	.830	5.17
De Jong, Chase	LM	R	42	17	0	26	0.8	22	5	.23	0 - 2	1 - 2	0 - 0	24	0	3	3	.57	.679	2.64
Banuelos, Manny	LM	L	31	14	2	6	1.1	22	7	.32	0 - 0	0 - 0	0 - 1	18	0	1	5	.83	.656	4.96
Banda, Anthony	LM	L	23	14	3	3	0.9	18	8	.44	0 - 0	0 - 0	0 - 0	13	0	0	2	1.00	.969	6.41
Beede, Tyler	LM	R	20	10	0	11	0.8	8	2	.25	0 - 0	0 - 0	0 - 0	10	0	0	3	1.00	.721	3.44
Peters, Dillon	LM	L	18	14	0	9	0.9	9	5	.56	0 - 0	0 - 0	0 - 0	10	0	0	3	1.00	.763	4.45
Stout, Eric	LM	L	18	10	3	5	0.7	13	7	.54	0 - 0	1 - 1	0 - 1	9	0	1	1	.67	.850	5.79
Underwood Jr., Duane	UR	R	50	15	9	11	1.3	20	6	.30	0 - 0	1 - 4	0 - 0	27	0	3	10	.79	.651	4.31
De Los Santos, Yerry	UR	R	26	4	7	6	1.2	11	5	.45	0 - 1	2 - 2	1 - 2	14	0	2	2	.71	.676	4.91
Ramirez, Yohan	UR	R	22	1	3	8	0.8	9	2	.22	1 - 1	0 - 0	0 - 0	14	0	0	2	1.00	.629	3.67
Hembree, Heath	UR	R	20	8	5	1	0.8	13	7	.54	0 - 0	0 - 0	0 - 1	10	0	1	2	.67	1.010	7.16
Stephenson, Robert	UR	R	13	2	1	0	1.0	4	0	.00	0 - 0	0 - 1	0 - 0	9	0	1	2	.67	.649	3.38
Yajure, Miguel	UR	R	11	5	0	9	0.6	3	1	.33	0 - 0	1 - 1	0 - 0	3	0	0	0	1.00	.939	10.62

San Diego Padres

Pitcher	Pos	T	Usage					Inherited Runners			Saves			Relief Results						
			Rel G	Early Entry	Cons Days	Long	Lev Ind	#	Scrd	Pct	Easy	Reg	Tough	Clean	BS Win	BS	Holds	Sv/Hld Pct	Opp OPS	Rel ERA
Rogers, Taylor	CL	L	42	0	11	6	2.2	11	3	.27	18 - 19	9 - 13	1 - 3	27	1	7	0	.80	.659	4.35
Hader, Josh	CL	L	19	0	3	2	2.0	6	2	.33	4 - 5	3 - 4	0 - 0	13	0	2	0	.78	.737	7.31
Garcia, Luis	SU	R	64	3	12	5	1.5	21	8	.38	0 - 1	3 - 3	0 - 0	43	1	1	19	.96	.617	3.39
Suarez, Robert	SU	R	45	8	4	7	1.5	17	5	.29	1 - 1	0 - 0	0 - 3	33	0	3	11	.80	.569	2.27
Martinez, Nick	SU	R	37	10	6	11	1.0	19	8	.42	2 - 2	6 - 6	0 - 1	23	0	1	8	.94	.599	2.67
Johnson, Pierce	SU	R	15	3	1	3	1.6	1	0	.00	0 - 0	0 - 1	0 - 0	11	0	1	6	.86	.683	5.02
Hill, Tim	LT	L	55	6	11	3	0.8	29	8	.28	0 - 0	0 - 0	0 - 0	42	0	0	7	1.00	.629	3.56
Morejon, Adrian	LT	L	26	8	3	7	0.9	9	0	.00	0 - 0	0 - 0	0 - 0	16	0	0	5	1.00	.652	4.24
Stammen, Craig	LM	R	32	11	4	10	0.6	18	12	.67	0 - 0	0 - 0	0 - 1	17	0	1	2	.67	.763	3.58
Crismatt, Nabil	UR	R	49	17	7	16	0.9	12	7	.58	0 - 3	0 - 1	0 - 0	31	0	4	5	.56	.654	3.08
Wilson, Steven	UR	R	49	19	10	8	0.9	24	13	.54	0 - 1	1 - 2	0 - 0	29	1	2	5	.75	.632	3.12
Lamet, Dinelson	UR	R	13	3	1	4	0.3	13	7	.54	0 - 0	0 - 0	0 - 0	3	0	0	1	1.00	.979	9.49

San Francisco Giants

Pitcher	Pos	T	Usage					Inherited Runners			Saves			Relief Results						
			Rel G	Early Entry	Cons Days	Long	Lev Ind	#	Scrd	Pct	Easy	Reg	Tough	Clean	BS Win	BS	Holds	Sv/Hld Pct	Opp OPS	Rel ERA
Doval, Camilo	CL	R	68	2	21	4	1.9	19	5	.26	18 - 19	6 - 7	3 - 4	48	0	3	1	.90	.624	2.53
Brebbia, John	SU	R	65	25	11	2	1.3	24	7	.29	0 - 2	0 - 2	0 - 0	47	0	4	18	.82	.758	3.63
Leone, Dominic	SU	R	55	12	15	3	1.5	14	8	.57	1 - 1	2 - 6	0 - 0	34	1	4	11	.78	.822	4.01
Alexander, Scott	SU	L	13	3	4	0	1.2	8	0	.00	1 - 1	0 - 0	1 - 1	11	0	0	5	1.00	.506	1.38
Garcia, Jarlin	LT	L	58	22	12	10	0.7	29	10	.34	0 - 2	1 - 1	0 - 0	41	0	2	4	.71	.710	3.74
McGee, Jake	LT	L	24	2	7	2	1.1	8	2	.25	3 - 4	0 - 1	0 - 1	13	1	3	4	.70	.838	7.17
Alvarez, Jose	LT	L	21	6	3	2	1.1	13	6	.46	1 - 1	0 - 0	0 - 2	11	0	2	1	.50	.870	5.28
Szapucki, Thomas	LT	L	10	6	1	3	0.7	8	4	.50	0 - 0	0 - 0	0 - 0	5	0	0	1	1.00	.756	1.98
Marte, Yunior	LM	R	39	14	7	14	0.4	10	5	.50	0 - 0	0 - 0	0 - 0	22	0	0	2	1.00	.742	5.44
Littell, Zack	LM	R	39	23	6	9	0.8	15	5	.33	0 - 0	1 - 1	0 - 0	25	0	0	5	1.00	.809	5.08
Young, Alex	LM	L	23	10	5	3	1.1	19	5	.26	0 - 1	0 - 0	0 - 0	16	0	1	5	.83	.710	2.10
Long, Sammy	LM	L	22	7	2	9	0.6	16	5	.31	0 - 0	0 - 0	1 - 1	12	0	0	0	1.00	.788	3.90
Rogers, Tyler	UR	R	68	18	16	8	1.2	11	6	.55	0 - 1	0 - 0	0 - 0	50	0	1	15	.94	.682	3.57
Llovera, Mauricio	UR	R	16	3	4	3	0.5	5	0	.00	0 - 0	0 - 0	0 - 0	12	0	0	1	1.00	.696	4.70

Seattle Mariners

Pitcher	Pos	T	Rel G	Early Entry	Cons Days	Long	Lev Ind	#	Scrd	Pct	Easy	Reg	Tough	Clean	BS Win	BS	Holds	Sv/Hld Pct	Opp OPS	Rel ERA
			Usage					Inherited Runners			Saves			Relief Results						
Sewald, Paul	CL	R	65	4	16	4	1.5	13	5	.38	10 - 11	10 - 12	0 - 2	47	1	5	8	.85	.521	2.67
Munoz, Andres	SU	R	64	8	14	2	1.5	25	4	.16	2 - 3	1 - 3	1 - 2	49	1	4	22	.87	.523	2.49
Swanson, Erik	SU	R	56	9	16	3	1.1	12	4	.33	1 - 1	1 - 2	1 - 2	46	0	2	14	.89	.552	1.74
Borucki, Ryan	LT	L	21	2	3	1	0.9	8	4	.50	0 - 0	0 - 0	0 - 0	11	0	0	4	1.00	.744	4.26
Misiewicz, Anthony	LT	L	17	5	4	1	0.8	11	5	.45	0 - 0	0 - 0	0 - 0	11	0	0	3	1.00	.782	4.61
Boyd, Matthew	LT	L	10	3	0	2	1.0	0	0	.00	0 - 0	0 - 0	0 - 0	9	0	0	1	1.00	.386	1.35
Murfee, Penn	UR	R	63	28	11	4	0.6	27	4	.15	0 - 0	0 - 0	0 - 0	46	0	0	7	1.00	.571	3.07
Castillo, Diego	UR	R	59	1	11	2	1.4	12	3	.25	3 - 3	3 - 3	1 - 1	43	0	0	9	1.00	.588	3.64
Festa, Matthew	UR	R	53	17	11	7	0.8	12	7	.58	1 - 1	1 - 2	0 - 0	36	0	1	6	.89	.717	4.17
Brash, Matt	UR	R	34	12	7	2	1.1	20	3	.15	0 - 0	0 - 0	0 - 0	29	0	0	9	1.00	.548	2.35
Romo, Sergio	UR	R	17	5	5	4	1.0	9	3	.33	0 - 0	0 - 0	0 - 0	10	0	0	4	1.00	1.005	8.16
Steckenrider, Drew	UR	R	16	3	0	2	1.3	0	0	.00	0 - 0	2 - 4	0 - 0	10	0	2	4	.75	.922	5.65
Flexen, Chris	UR	R	11	1	1	5	0.8	0	0	.00	1 - 1	1 - 1	0 - 0	7	0	0	0	1.00	.525	1.62

St Louis Cardinals

Pitcher	Pos	T	Rel G	Early Entry	Cons Days	Long	Lev Ind	#	Scrd	Pct	Easy	Reg	Tough	Clean	BS Win	BS	Holds	Sv/Hld Pct	Opp OPS	Rel ERA
			Usage					Inherited Runners			Saves			Relief Results						
Gallegos, Giovanny	CL	R	57	3	11	9	1.7	11	5	.45	6 - 8	7 - 11	1 - 1	42	0	6	12	.81	.594	3.05
Helsley, Ryan	CL	R	54	2	8	9	1.6	21	3	.14	10 - 10	8 - 10	1 - 3	43	2	4	7	.87	.438	1.25
Cabrera, Genesis	SU	L	39	8	5	8	1.3	16	8	.50	0 - 0	1 - 1	0 - 1	23	0	1	13	.93	.745	4.63
Hicks, Jordan	SU	R	27	16	3	7	1.3	17	4	.24	0 - 0	0 - 1	0 - 0	18	1	1	8	.89	.590	4.37
McFarland, T.J.	LT	L	28	10	6	5	0.3	25	11	.44	0 - 0	0 - 0	0 - 0	15	0	0	1	1.00	.874	6.61
Romero, JoJo	LT	L	15	3	3	1	0.8	8	1	.13	0 - 0	0 - 0	0 - 0	10	0	0	0		.683	3.77
Pallante, Andre	LM	R	37	19	2	14	1.1	23	9	.39	0 - 0	0 - 1	0 - 0	22	0	1	9	.90	.691	2.35
Naughton, Packy	LM	L	23	12	3	5	0.8	17	5	.29	0 - 0	1 - 1	0 - 1	16	0	1	3	.80	.681	3.24
Thompson, Zack	LM	L	21	9	2	7	0.5	5	3	.60	0 - 0	0 - 1	0 - 0	15	0	0	0	1.00	.413	0.91
VerHagen, Drew	LM	R	19	9	2	7	1.0	10	1	.10	0 - 0	0 - 1	0 - 0	9	0	1	2	.67	.907	6.65
Wittgren, Nick	UR	R	29	11	8	5	0.6	24	6	.25	0 - 0	0 - 0	1 - 1	15	0	0	4	1.00	.787	5.90
Woodford, Jake	UR	R	26	8	2	10	0.3	13	3	.23	0 - 0	0 - 0	0 - 0	18	0	0	0		.620	2.30
Stratton, Chris	UR	R	20	7	0	4	1.0	16	5	.31	0 - 0	0 - 0	0 - 0	13	0	0	0		.655	2.78
Whitley, Kodi	UR	R	14	2	2	5	0.4	5	2	.40	0 - 0	0 - 0	0 - 0	8	0	0	1	1.00	.777	5.68
Oviedo, Johan	UR	R	13	7	0	6	0.8	12	6	.50	0 - 0	0 - 0	0 - 0	6	0	0	0		.704	2.66
Fernandez, Junior	UR	R	13	6	3	3	1.0	10	7	.70	0 - 0	0 - 0	0 - 1	8	0	1	3	.75	.843	2.93

Tampa Bay Rays

Pitcher	Pos	T	Rel G	Early Entry	Cons Days	Long	Lev Ind	#	Scrd	Pct	Easy	Reg	Tough	Clean	BS Win	BS	Holds	Sv/Hld Pct	Opp OPS	Rel ERA
			Usage					Inherited Runners			Saves			Relief Results						
Fairbanks, Pete	CL	R	24	1	4	1	1.6	4	1	.25	4 - 4	4 - 4	0 - 0	21	0	0	6	1.00	.393	1.13
Adam, Jason	SU	R	67	18	22	1	1.5	31	3	.10	4 - 4	4 - 7	0 - 1	56	0	4	21	.88	.471	1.56
Poche, Colin	SU	L	65	8	18	3	1.6	14	4	.29	5 - 5	1 - 6	1 - 2	44	2	6	23	.83	.690	3.99
Raley, Brooks	SU	L	60	16	14	2	1.4	21	6	.29	2 - 2	3 - 6	1 - 1	47	0	3	22	.90	.542	2.68
Thompson, Ryan	SU	R	47	19	14	3	1.4	20	7	.35	2 - 3	0 - 4	1 - 1	30	0	5	10	.72	.648	3.80
Feyereisen, J.P.	SU	R	20	3	5	1	1.2	10	1	.10	1 - 1	0 - 0	0 - 1	18	0	1	7	.89	.264	0.00
Armstrong, Shawn	LM	R	40	12	7	11	0.7	18	8	.44	0 - 0	2 - 3	0 - 0	22	0	1	2	.80	.742	3.99
Beeks, Jalen	LM	L	35	17	2	12	1.2	9	3	.33	1 - 2	1 - 2	0 - 2	23	0	4	4	.60	.640	2.79
Garza, Ralph	LM	R	19	5	4	12	0.6	4	3	.75	0 - 0	0 - 2	0 - 0	8	0	2	0	.00	.794	3.34
Chargois, JT	LM	R	18	9	4	1	0.8	7	0	.00	0 - 0	0 - 0	0 - 0	14	0	0	3	1.00	.583	1.47
Cleavinger, Garrett	LM	L	13	10	1	2	0.7	3	0	.00	0 - 0	0 - 0	0 - 0	10	0	0	0		.395	2.41
Yarbrough, Ryan	LM	L	11	11	0	11	1.0	0	0	.00	0 - 0	0 - 0	0 - 0	3	0	0	0		.848	4.54
Wisler, Matt	UR	R	34	15	5	5	1.2	7	2	.29	0 - 1	1 - 2	0 - 1	23	0	3	5	.67	.636	2.23
Faucher, Calvin	UR	R	22	4	5	5	0.8	6	2	.33	1 - 1	0 - 1	0 - 0	12	0	1	1	.67	.811	5.48
Guerra, Javy	UR	R	17	6	4	2	1.1	4	0	.00	0 - 0	0 - 0	0 - 0	13	0	0	2	1.00	.702	3.38
Kittredge, Andrew	UR	R	17	1	4	0	1.6	3	0	.00	3 - 4	2 - 4	0 - 0	11	0	3	0	.63	.638	3.15

Texas Rangers

Pitcher	Pos	T	Usage					Inherited Runners			Saves			Relief Results						
			Rel G	Early Entry	Cons Days	Long	Lev Ind	#	Scrd	Pct	Easy	Reg	Tough	Clean	BS Win	BS	Holds	Sv/Hld Pct	Opp OPS	Rel ERA
Barlow, Joe	CL	R	35	1	8	2	1.2	2	0	.00	12 - 13	1 - 4	0 - 0	24	1	4	0	.76	.679	3.86
Moore, Matt	SU	L	63	12	9	16	1.1	21	7	.33	3 - 3	2 - 3	0 - 0	47	0	1	14	.95	.564	1.95
Santana, Dennis	SU	R	62	20	12	6	1.2	41	9	.22	1 - 1	0 - 1	0 - 1	40	0	2	19	.91	.637	5.24
King, John	SU	L	39	14	2	7	1.0	13	6	.46	0 - 1	0 - 4	0 - 0	22	0	5	8	.62	.754	4.03
Bush, Matt	SU	R	35	2	4	3	1.3	11	0	.00	1 - 3	0 - 0	0 - 1	25	0	3	9	.77	.587	3.13
Martin, Brett	LT	L	54	17	12	3	1.1	33	13	.39	2 - 2	1 - 3	0 - 1	30	0	3	7	.77	.712	4.22
Allard, Kolby	LT	L	10	5	1	5	0.6	6	3	.50	1 - 1	0 - 0	0 - 0	4	0	0	0	1.00	.972	7.29
Burke, Brock	LM	L	52	27	1	26	1.1	11	2	.18	0 - 2	0 - 2	0 - 1	36	0	5	9	.64	.630	1.97
Hearn, Taylor	LM	L	18	13	0	15	0.9	4	1	.25	0 - 0	1 - 2	0 - 0	10	0	1	2	.75	.595	3.51
Tinoco, Jesus	LM	R	15	9	3	4	1.0	10	3	.30	0 - 0	0 - 0	0 - 0	12	0	0	4	1.00	.490	2.04
Leclerc, Jose	UR	R	39	6	5	9	1.2	18	8	.44	4 - 4	3 - 5	0 - 0	26	0	2	4	.85	.625	2.83
Richards, Garrett	UR	R	30	12	2	8	0.4	4	0	.00	0 - 0	1 - 1	0 - 0	17	0	0	3	1.00	.700	5.22
Hernandez, Jonathan	UR	R	29	0	4	5	1.4	2	1	.50	2 - 3	2 - 2	0 - 1	21	0	2	3	.78	.669	2.97
Sborz, Josh	UR	R	18	4	2	4	0.5	7	5	.71	0 - 0	0 - 0	0 - 0	10	0	0	1	1.00	.865	6.75

Toronto Blue Jays

Pitcher	Pos	T	Usage					Inherited Runners			Saves			Relief Results						
			Rel G	Early Entry	Cons Days	Long	Lev Ind	#	Scrd	Pct	Easy	Reg	Tough	Clean	BS Win	BS	Holds	Sv/Hld Pct	Opp OPS	Rel ERA
Romano, Jordan	CL	R	63	1	16	2	2.4	15	3	.20	14 - 16	18 - 21	4 - 5	50	1	6	2	.86	.531	2.11
Cimber, Adam	SU	R	77	15	20	2	1.3	31	9	.29	3 - 3	1 - 3	0 - 2	52	2	4	19	.85	.669	2.80
Mayza, Tim	SU	L	63	15	19	0	1.4	36	8	.22	1 - 1	1 - 4	0 - 1	45	1	4	16	.82	.688	3.14
Garcia, Yimi	SU	R	61	6	11	3	1.6	16	2	.13	1 - 2	0 - 3	0 - 0	46	0	4	22	.85	.621	3.10
Borucki, Ryan	LT	L	11	3	2	1	1.1	6	4	.67	0 - 0	0 - 0	0 - 0	7	0	0	2	1.00	.945	9.95
Gage, Matt	LT	L	11	3	2	1	0.7	7	0	.00	0 - 0	0 - 1	0 - 0	8	0	1	0	.00	.509	1.38
Thornton, Trent	LM	R	32	16	3	8	0.5	17	1	.06	0 - 1	0 - 0	0 - 0	21	0	1	3	.75	.703	4.11
Pop, Zach	LM	R	18	10	3	0	0.6	9	3	.33	0 - 0	0 - 0	0 - 0	11	0	0	2	1.00	.608	1.89
Phelps, David	UR	R	64	22	10	8	0.8	27	6	.22	0 - 0	1 - 2	0 - 0	44	0	1	9	.91	.619	2.87
Richards, Trevor	UR	R	58	25	11	12	0.7	28	8	.29	0 - 0	0 - 1	0 - 0	36	0	1	8	.89	.734	5.58
Bass, Anthony	UR	R	28	6	9	0	1.0	15	4	.27	0 - 0	0 - 0	0 - 0	21	0	0	7	1.00	.665	1.75
Merryweather, Julian	UR	R	25	9	3	2	0.7	9	6	.67	0 - 0	0 - 1	0 - 0	13	0	1	1	.50	.834	6.66
Kikuchi, Yusei	UR	L	12	6	0	6	1.0	7	0	.00	0 - 0	1 - 1	0 - 0	6	0	0	0	1.00	.837	4.91

Washington Nationals

Pitcher	Pos	T	Usage					Inherited Runners			Saves			Relief Results						
			Rel G	Early Entry	Cons Days	Long	Lev Ind	#	Scrd	Pct	Easy	Reg	Tough	Clean	BS Win	BS	Holds	Sv/Hld Pct	Opp OPS	Rel ERA
Rainey, Tanner	CL	R	29	0	5	1	2.1	3	0	.00	7 - 8	4 - 7	1 - 1	20	1	4	1	.76	.691	3.30
Finnegan, Kyle	SU	R	66	4	17	3	1.5	23	10	.43	4 - 5	5 - 6	2 - 4	46	1	4	14	.86	.665	3.51
Edwards Jr., Carl	SU	R	57	13	13	9	1.3	18	4	.22	0 - 1	1 - 3	1 - 1	41	0	3	13	.83	.652	2.76
Rogers, Josh	LT	L	13	7	3	2	0.7	8	5	.63	0 - 0	0 - 0	0 - 0	7	0	0	1	1.00	.742	5.11
McGee, Jake	LT	L	12	3	2	0	0.6	2	2	1.00	0 - 0	0 - 0	0 - 0	8	0	0	0		.682	6.30
Perez, Francisco	LT	L	10	3	3	4	0.1	1	1	1.00	0 - 0	0 - 0	0 - 0	6	0	0	0		.997	7.27
Ramirez, Erasmo	LM	R	58	30	9	14	0.5	33	9	.27	0 - 0	0 - 0	0 - 0	39	0	0	5	1.00	.649	2.46
Machado, Andres	LM	R	51	26	9	13	0.6	24	4	.17	0 - 0	0 - 0	0 - 0	31	0	0	3	1.00	.722	3.34
Weems, Jordan	LM	R	32	23	6	10	0.4	18	6	.33	0 - 0	0 - 0	0 - 0	18	0	0	0		.726	5.22
Voth, Austin	LM	R	19	10	3	4	0.4	10	0	.00	0 - 0	0 - 0	0 - 0	11	0	0	1	1.00	.994	10.13
Cishek, Steve	UR	R	69	29	12	9	0.8	31	14	.45	0 - 0	1 - 2	0 - 1	45	0	2	6	.78	.709	4.21
Arano, Victor	UR	R	43	17	6	6	0.9	25	12	.48	0 - 0	1 - 2	0 - 0	26	1	1	7	.89	.747	4.50
Harvey, Hunter	UR	R	38	15	8	5	1.0	14	5	.36	0 - 0	0 - 1	0 - 0	27	0	1	6	.86	.620	2.52
Thompson, Mason	UR	R	24	5	6	2	0.4	9	0	.00	0 - 0	1 - 2	0 - 0	20	0	1	0	.50	.612	2.92
Espino, Paolo	UR	R	23	3	1	5	0.7	9	2	.22	0 - 0	0 - 0	0 - 0	17	0	0	0		.611	2.12

Christian Walker
Brendan Rodgers
Nolan Arenado
Jorge Mateo

Tommy Edman

Steven Kwan
Myles Straw
Mookie Betts

Jose Trevino
Ranger Suárez

THE FIELDING BIBLE AWARDS 2022

The Fielding Bible Awards 2022

Mark Simon

Lots of new faces at the Fielding Bible Awards party this year, as this is the first time there are eight first-time winners since the second year of the awards, 2007.

Say hello to **Ranger Suárez** (Phillies, pitcher), **Jose Trevino** (Yankees, catcher), **Christian Walker** (Diamondbacks, first base), **Brendan Rodgers** (Rockies, second base), **Jorge Mateo** (Orioles, shortstop), **Steven Kwan** (Guardians, left field), **Myles Straw** (Guardians, center field), and **Tommy Edman** (Cardinals, multi-position).

The only two award winners this year who had won the award previously are a pair of players nearing the lead for most Awards won: **Nolan Arenado** (Cardinals, third base) and **Mookie Betts** (Dodgers, right field), who each won their fifth Fielding Bible Award, one shy of Andrelton Simmons and Yadier Molina, whose six are the gold standard.

This year's Fielding Bible Awards were determined by a 15-person expert voting panel. The panel awards 10 winners each year, one at each position plus an additional award that goes to the best defensive multi-position player.

The criteria for the multi-position award changed in 2021 to prioritize players who had a high degree of positional versatility and value; players who usually play many positions in a season, might move from position to position within a game, and have demonstrated the ability to handle high leverage positions when the team needs them to.

Voters selected their Top 10 from a list of 15 players that required the highest Defensive Versatility Score, a formula created by Bill James.

Our panel voted on 10 players at each position on a scale from 1 to 10. A first-place vote gets 10 points, second place nine points, third place eight points, etc. We total up the points for each player, and the player with the most points wins the award at that position. A perfect score is 150 points.

Close races were a theme this year, with four positional awards decided by 11 or fewer points in the voting. The closest was at third base, where Arenado nosed out Ke'Bryan Hayes by two points, and shortstop, where Mateo topped Miguel Rojas by a similar margin. Straw beat Michael A. Taylor by eight points in center field. Betts won by an 11-point margin over Kyle Tucker.

Also of note: In seven of the 10 wins, it marked the first time a player from that team won at that position.

Lots of newness this year.

First Base – Christian Walker, Arizona Diamondbacks

Walker was the runaway leader in Defensive Runs Saved at first base with 17. No other first baseman had more than 6. Walker's 17 Runs Saved were the most by a first baseman since Joey Votto had 18 in 2017.

Walker dominated defensively because his range was outstanding, particularly to his right. He was the only first baseman to convert more than 50% of opportunities on those balls into outs (opportunities = balls with a >0% out probability).

Walker joined Paul Goldschmidt as the only Diamondbacks to win the award at first base. Goldschmidt won it with the Diamondbacks in 2013, 2015, and 2017.

Previous Winners:

2021	Paul Goldschmidt	2015	Paul Goldschmidt	2009	Albert Pujols
2020	Matt Olson	2014	Adrián González	2008	Albert Pujols
2019	Matt Olson	2013	Paul Goldschmidt	2007	Albert Pujols
2018	Matt Olson	2012	Mark Teixeira	2006	Albert Pujols
2017	Paul Goldschmidt	2011	Albert Pujols		
2016	Anthony Rizzo	2010	Daric Barton		

Second Base – Brendan Rodgers, Colorado Rockies

Rodgers made quite the climb, going from -5 Runs Saved and one 10th-place vote for his play at second base in 2021 to leading all second basemen in Defensive Runs Saved with 22 and winning the award in 2022.

Rodgers, a converted shortstop, won with an aggressive style. He led all second basemen in diving plays with 19, using them to extend his range and make near-impossible plays possible.

Rodgers is the second Rockies second baseman to win the award, joining DJ LeMahieu.

Previous Winners:

2021	Whit Merrifield	2015	Ian Kinsler	2009	Aaron Hill
2020	Kolten Wong	2014	Dustin Pedroia	2008	Brandon Phillips
2019	Kolten Wong	2013	Dustin Pedroia	2007	Aaron Hill
2018	Kolten Wong	2012	Darwin Barney	2006	Orlando Hudson
2017	DJ LeMahieu	2011	Dustin Pedroia		
2016	Dustin Pedroia	2010	Chase Utley		

Third Base – Nolan Arenado, St. Louis Cardinals

Arenado returned to the top spot at third base in an extremely close vote, edging out last year's winner Ke'Bryan Hayes by two points. Arenado's 19 Runs Saved were a 13-run improvement from 2021, when he finished third in the voting. He got back to what he did best in previous seasons, making plays on balls hit to his left.

Arenado's five Fielding Bible Awards are the most by a third baseman. He's one shy of Andrelton Simmons and Yadier Molina for the most Awards won overall. He's also the first Cardinals player to win the award at third base.

Previous Winners:

2021	Ke'Bryan Hayes	2015	Nolan Arenado	2009	Ryan Zimmerman
2020	Nolan Arenado	2014	Josh Donaldson	2008	Adrián Beltré
2019	Matt Chapman	2013	Manny Machado	2007	Pedro Feliz
2018	Matt Chapman	2012	Adrián Beltré	2006	Adrián Beltré
2017	Nolan Arenado	2011	Adrián Beltré		
2016	Nolan Arenado	2010	Evan Longoria		

Shortstop – Jorge Mateo, Baltimore Orioles

Mateo won in a crowded field, as six different shortstops received a first-place vote. Mateo was instrumental to the Orioles resurgence, finishing a close third among shortstops with 14 Defensive Runs Saved and tied for second in Good Fielding Plays with 28. Mateo was the No. 1 shortstop in double play conversion rate, turning two on 72% of opportunities.

He's the first Oriole shortstop to win the award.

Previous Winners:

2021	Carlos Correa	2015	Andrelton Simmons	2009	Jack Wilson
2020	Javier Báez	2014	Andrelton Simmons	2008	Jimmy Rollins
2019	Nick Ahmed	2013	Andrelton Simmons	2007	Troy Tulowitzki
2018	Andrelton Simmons	2012	Brendan Ryan	2006	Adam Everett
2017	Andrelton Simmons	2011	Troy Tulowitzki		
2016	Andrelton Simmons	2010	Troy Tulowitzki		

Left Field – Steven Kwan, Cleveland Guardians

Kwan was the only unanimous winner of a Fielding Bible Award this year. He easily led all left fielders with 21 Runs Saved and his 20 Good Fielding Plays tied for the left field lead.

Kwan was above average in making plays on balls hit to all parts of left field, be they shallow, medium, or deep. His 19 Range Runs Saved in left field were more than any outfielder had at any one position.

Kwan is the first Guardians player to win the award for left field.

Previous Winners:

2021	Tyler O'Neill	2015	Starling Marte	2009	Carl Crawford
2020	Tyler O'Neill	2014	Alex Gordon	2008	Carl Crawford
2019	David Peralta	2013	Alex Gordon	2007	Eric Byrnes
2018	Alex Gordon	2012	Alex Gordon	2006	Carl Crawford
2017	Brett Gardner	2011	Brett Gardner		
2016	Starling Marte	2010	Brett Gardner		

Center Field – Myles Straw, Cleveland Guardians

Straw edged last year's winner, Michael A. Taylor, in a close vote. Straw finished a close second to Taylor with 17 Defensive Runs Saved but led all center fielders in Good Fielding Plays (24) and Outfield Arm Runs Saved (7).

Straw is the first Guardians player to win the award in center field. In fact, Straw and Kwan are the first Guardians outfielders to win a Fielding Bible Award since Franklin Gutierrez won as a right fielder in 2008.

Previous Winners:

2021	Michael A. Taylor	2015	Kevin Kiermaier	2009	Franklin Gutierrez
2020	Kevin Kiermaier	2014	Juan Lagares	2008	Carlos Beltrán
2019	Lorenzo Cain	2013	Carlos Gómez	2007	Andruw Jones
2018	Lorenzo Cain	2012	Mike Trout	2006	Carlos Beltrán
2017	Byron Buxton	2011	Austin Jackson		
2016	Kevin Pillar	2010	Michael Bourn		

Right Field – Mookie Betts, Los Angeles Dodgers

Betts finished second to Aristides Aquino in Defensive Runs Saved in right field but led right fielders in the range component of that stat. His 15 Runs Saved in right field were an 11-run jump from 2021.

Betts won his fifth Fielding Bible Award, one shy of Andrelton Simmons and Yadier Molina for most overall. A Dodgers player has won three of the last four Fielding Bible Awards in right field, with Betts winning two of those and Cody Bellinger winning one.

Previous Winners:

2021	Aaron Judge	2015	Jason Heyward	2009	Ichiro Suzuki
2020	Mookie Betts	2014	Jason Heyward	2008	Franklin Gutierrez
2019	Cody Bellinger	2013	Gerardo Parra	2007	Álex Ríos
2018	Mookie Betts	2012	Jason Heyward	2006	Ichiro Suzuki
2017	Mookie Betts	2011	Justin Upton		
2016	Mookie Betts	2010	Ichiro Suzuki		

Catcher – Jose Trevino, New York Yankees

Trevino, who was acquired in a trade by the Yankees just before the season started, led all catchers with 21 Defensive Runs Saved. He was the premier catcher in our pitch framing stat, Strike Zone Runs Saved, and rated above-average in both pitch blocking and limiting stolen bases.

Trevino is the first Yankees catcher to win a Fielding Bible Award.

Previous Winners:

2021	Jacob Stallings	2015	Buster Posey	2009	Yadier Molina
2020	Roberto Pérez	2014	Jonathan Lucroy	2008	Yadier Molina
2019	Roberto Pérez	2013	Yadier Molina	2007	Yadier Molina
2018	Jeff Mathis	2012	Yadier Molina	2006	Iván Rodríguez
2017	Martin Maldonado	2011	Matt Wieters		
2016	Buster Posey	2010	Yadier Molina		

Pitcher – Ranger Suárez, Philadelphia Phillies

Suárez led all pitchers with 9 Defensive Runs Saved. Not only was Suárez good at coming off the mound to make plays, he didn't allow a stolen base all season (in fact, there were only two attempts!).

Suárez finished second on the Phillies in Runs Saved, trailing only batterymate J.T. Realmuto with 11. Suárez is the first Phillies pitcher to win a Fielding Bible Award.

Previous Winners:

2021	Dallas Keuchel	2015	Dallas Keuchel	2009	Mark Buehrle
2020	Max Fried	2014	Dallas Keuchel	2008	Kenny Rogers
2019	Zack Greinke	2013	R.A. Dickey	2007	Johan Santana
2018	Zack Greinke	2012	Mark Buehrle	2006	Greg Maddux
2017	Dallas Keuchel	2011	Mark Buehrle		
2016	Dallas Keuchel	2010	Mark Buehrle		

Multi-Position – Tommy Edman, St. Louis Cardinals

Edman played a near identical number of innings at second base and shortstop and was fundamentally sound at both spots. He ranked third with 12 Defensive Runs Saved at second base, while playing far fewer innings than the players who ranked No. 1, 2, and 4. On a per-inning basis, he had the second-fewest misplays at second base and the fewest at shortstop.

He's the first Cardinals player to win the multi-position award, which was first awarded in 2014.

Previous Winners:

2021	Kiké Hernández	2018	Javier Báez	2015	Ender Inciarte
2020	Kiké Hernández	2017	Javier Báez	2014	Lorenzo Cain
2019	Cody Bellinger	2016	Javier Báez		

Background of the Fielding Bible Awards

While the five volumes of *The Fielding Bible* put a lot of emphasis on the numbers, especially Defensive Runs Saved and the PART system (formerly the Range and Positioning System, and before that, the Plus-Minus System), we feel that visual observation and subjective judgment are still very important parts of determining the best defensive players. Also, we believe people have a right to know who is voting and all the players they are voting for. Therefore, in setting up the Fielding Bible Awards, we took the following steps:

1. ***We appointed a panel of experts to vote***. We have a panel of 15 experts (See below.)

2. ***We rate everybody in one group.*** The Gold Glove vote is divided into National League and American League. We make ours different by putting everybody together. Besides, is playing shortstop in the American League one thing and playing shortstop in the National League a different thing, or are they really very much the same thing?

In the early years of the awards, we had a great example of the benefits of this decision. Without the Fielding Bible Award, Jack Wilson wins nada, because he switched leagues in mid-year. According to our panelists (and unlike the Gold Glove voters), Jack was the best fielding shortstop in baseball in 2009. Period. He deserved to be recognized.

3. ***We use a ten-man ballot and a ten-point scale***. We use a ten-man ballot. We give ten points for first place, nine points for second place, etc, down to one point for tenth place. We feel strongly that a ten-man ballot with weighted positions leads to more accurate outcomes.

4. ***We defined the list of candidates***. Only players who actually were regulars at the position are candidates. This eliminates the possibility of a vote going to somebody who wasn't really playing the position.

5. ***We are publishing the balloting***. We summarize the voting at each position, clearly identifying whom everybody voted for. Publishing the actual vote totals encourages the voters to take their votes more seriously. Also, we feel the public will have more respect for the voting if they have more insight into the process.

A perfect score is 150 points. If all 15 voters place one player first on their ballot, he scores 150. Steven Kwan was our only unanimous pick in 2022.

We have modified our tiebreaker rules. They are applied one at a time until we have a winner:

1. Most first-place votes wins.
2. Most second-place votes wins, if still tied then most third-place votes etc.
3. Award goes to player with the higher defensive runs saved.

Ballots were due a week after the end of the regular season.

Here is this year's panel:

Emma Baccellieri is a staff writer at *Sports Illustrated*, where she primarily, though not exclusively, covers baseball. She previously wrote for *Baseball Prospectus* and *Deadspin*.

Dan Casey started at SIS in 2007 and is the Lead Analyst, Baseball Operations. Before coming to SIS, Dan worked for the Yankees in several departments.

For over 25 years, SIS co-founder **John Dewan** has analyzed and published in-depth baseball statistics and analysis. He has focused his baseball analytics work on defense and has authored or co-authored five volumes of *The Fielding Bible*.

Chris Dial has been studying defensive statistics since 1996, and developed Runs Effectively Defended (RED). RED was featured in Popular Science in 2008 as an example of the future of defensive assessments. He has written predominantly at Baseball Think Factory and currently at Mets360.com. He is a member of SABR's SDI Committee, which plays a large role in the voting for the Gold Glove awards.

Alyson Footer is the executive editor of national content for MLB.com. She began her career in media relations with the Astros before joining MLB.com in 2001 to cover the Astros as a beat reporter. She served as the Astros' social media director from 2009-12 and then rejoined MLB.com as a national correspondent.

Peter Gammons is a senior writer for *The Athletic*, who regularly appears on MLB Network. He is the 56th recipient of the J. G. Taylor Spink Award for outstanding baseball writing given by the BBWAA.

Bill James is the lead author of this book, which is not to be taken to suggest that he actually does a lot of the work. He has been inventing ways to measure things about baseball professionally for almost a half of a century, and studies fielding as intensely as he studies anything else. He no longer has any association with the Boston Red Sox, but then a lot of people say that after a season like they just had.

Moses Massena has been with MLB Network since 2009 working as a Researcher, Associate Producer, Segment Producer and as a Producer since 2019. Moses has also done stats for FOX Baseball Telecasts from 2010-2017 and ESPN *Sunday Night Baseball* from 2018 to 2021.

Eduardo Pérez played 13 seasons in the major leagues with 6 teams and was a hitting coach with the Marlins and bench coach with the Astros. He is currently an analyst on ESPN's telecasts of *Sunday Night Baseball* and also works on the Little League World Series and College World Series, and has broadcast MLB's World Series on ESPN Radio. His father, Tony Pérez, is a Baseball Hall of Famer.

The man who created Strat-O-Matic Baseball, **Hal Richman**, continues to lead his company's annual in-depth analysis of each player's season. Hal cautions SOM players that his voting on this ballot may or may not reflect the eventual fielding ratings for players in his game. Ballots were due prior to the completion of his annual research effort to evaluate player defense.

Travis Sawchik is a sportswriter for *The Score*. He is the author of the New York Times best-selling book *Big Data Baseball: Math, Miracles, and the End of a 20-Year Losing Streak* and co-author of *The MVP Machine: How Baseball's New Nonconformists Are Using Data to Build Better Players*. He previously covered the Pittsburgh Pirates for the *Pittsburgh Tribune-Review*.

Bobby Scales began working at Sports Info Solutions as its VP of Baseball in 2022. He played pro baseball from 1999 to 2012, including two seasons with the Chicago Cubs. After his playing career, he served as the Director of Player Development and later, Special Assistant to the General Manager for the Angels. Most recently, he served as the Minor League Field Coordinator and Coordinator of Strategic Initiatives for Player Development for the Pirates.

Joe Sheehan publishes the *Joe Sheehan Baseball Newsletter*, one of the first subscription baseball newsletters, now in its 13th season. He was a founding member of *Baseball Prospectus* and has contributed to ESPN, *Sports Illustrated, Baseball America, The Wall Street Journal, The Washington Post*, and *The New York Times* in a 25-year career.

Mark Simon helps oversee SIS' public-facing content. He writes regularly for our website and hosts *The Sports Info Solutions Baseball Podcast*. He previously worked at ESPN for nearly 16 years, including 8 years on *Baseball Tonight*. He is the author of the book *The Yankees Index*.

The **SIS Video Scouts** study every game of the season multiple times, charting a huge list of valuable game details.

Fielding Bible Awards Voting

Below we show the final point tally for The Fielding Bible Awards in the 2022 season. We asked a panel of experts to complete a 10-man ballot ranking players from 1 to 10 based on their defensive abilities. We show the ranks in the tables below. We then awarded 10 points for a first place vote, 9 for second, etc., down to 1 point for 10th place. We cover all nine positions, looking at only their fielding work for the 2022 season. Position players are eligible if they played at least 600 innings while catchers require a minimum of 500 innings. Either can qualify with 10 Runs Saved, as well. Pitchers require a minimum of 120 innings pitched or 5 Runs Saved.

In 2014, we introduced a Multi-Position Award for fielders who are excellent defensive players but do not call any one position their home. Eligible players include those who exhibit a high degree of positional versatility and value; players who usually play many positions over the course of the season, might move from position to position within a game, and have demonstrated the ability to handle high leverage positions when the team needs him to.

First Basemen

First Basemen	Alyson	Bill	Bobby	Chris	Dan	Eduardo	Emma	Hal	Joe	John	Mark	Moses	Peter	SIS Video Scouts	Travis	Total Points
Christian Walker	2	1	1	1	1	1	1	4	1	2	1	1	1	1	1	145
Matt Olson	1	6	2		2	2	2	2	2	1	2	4	2	2	2	122
Paul Goldschmidt	4	2	5	4	5	4		1	6	4	3	3	4			87
Freddie Freeman	3	9	4		7	3	7	3	3	8	4	5	6	7	7	78
Luis Arraez	5		3		3	9	3		7	3	6	8	7	3	3	72
C.J. Cron			6			8	5	6	5	5	7	9	3	4	4	59
Vladimir Guerrero Jr.		5	9	6		5	6	10	4		9		9	8	9	41
Alfonso Rivas			7	9			4			7	5		5	6	8	37
Carlos Santana	8		8	8	8		8			6				5	10	27
Ty France				5				7	9	10	8	6	10			22

Others receiving points: Anthony Rizzo 21, Ryan Mountcastle 18, Seth Brown 16, Yuli Gurriel 16, Rowdy Tellez 14, Michael Chavis 11, Rhys Hoskins 8, Ji-Man Choi 8, Eric Hosmer 7, Jose Abreu 4, Bobby Dalbec 4, Josh Bell 3, Jared Walsh 3, Owen Miller 1, Pete Alonso 1

Second Basemen

Second Basemen	Alyson	Bill	Bobby	Chris	Dan	Eduardo	Emma	Hal	Joe	John	Mark	Moses	Peter	SIS Video Scouts	Travis	Total Points
Brendan Rodgers	3	1	1	5	1	1	1	3	1	1	1	4	1	3	2	136
Andres Gimenez	7	5	3	2	4	8	3	1	3	4	2	1	3	2	1	116
Jonathan Schoop	2	2	4	1	3	4	4	4	4	3	3	5	5	1	5	115
Marcus Semien	1	3	2	6	2	3	2	6	2	2	4		2	4	3	112
Trevor Story	9	7	6	3	8		6	2	5	6	6	7	4	6	6	73
Gleyber Torres	8	6	5	4	7	5	5	10	10	8	5		9	7	4	61
Jake Cronenworth	6		7	7	6		7	8	7	7		6	6	8	9	48
Kolten Wong	5	4				6		5				3	8			35
Jeff McNeil	10		10	10	9			9			7	8		5	7	24
Luis Guillorme					10	7	10	9				2	7		8	24

Others receiving points: Santiago Espinal 20, Adam Frazier 19, Gavin Lux 11, Nicky Lopez 9, Tony Kemp 8, Christian Arroyo 6, Josh Harrison 3, Cavan Biggio 2, Jose Altuve 2

Third Basemen

Third Basemen	Alyson	Bill	Bobby	Chris	Dan	Eduardo	Emma	Hal	Joe	John	Mark	Moses	Peter	SIS Video Scouts	Travis	Total Points
Nolan Arenado	1	1	2	1	1	2	1	2	1	2	2	1	2	2	2	142
Ke'Bryan Hayes	3	2	1	2	2	1	2	1	2	1	1	4	1	1	1	140
Matt Chapman	2	4	7		3	3	4	5	6	4	6	2	3	3	3	99
Ryan McMahon	4		5	8	8	5	9	4	3	3	7	8	7	6	66
Austin Riley	5	7	8	9	4		6			6	7	5	5	9	5	56
Ramon Urias	9	8	3		5		4	5	5	4	10		4			53
Manny Machado	10	3		3		5		3	3		3		5			53
Josh Donaldson		5	6	4		7	8	7	7	7	9		10	8	7	47
Jace Peterson	8		4	6	9	9	7		10	8	5	9	7	6	10	45
Alex Bregman	6	9	9	7	6	4		8			8	8	9	10	8	40

Others receiving points: Luis Urias 34, Jose Ramirez 24, Gio Urshela 8, Rafael Devers 6, DJ LeMahieu 5, Max Muncy 4, Emmanuel Rivera 1, Isaac Paredes 1, Eugenio Suarez 1

Shortstops

Shortstops	Alyson	Bill	Bobby	Chris	Dan	Eduardo	Emma	Hal	Joe	John	Mark	Moses	Peter	SIS Video Scouts	Travis	Total Points
Jorge Mateo	6	4	3	5	3	1	1	2	2	6	3	1	2	1	2	123
Miguel Rojas	1	7	2	4	1	2	3	7	7	1	1	4	1	2	1	121
Jeremy Pena	4	5	1	9	6	4	2	9	3	4	2	2	4	4	3	103
Ha-seong Kim	5	9	5		5	3	5	10	8	3	4	3	7	5	6	76
Dansby Swanson		3		3	2		10	1	1		5			3	9	62
Isiah Kiner-Falefa	3	2	4		8		7		9	2			3	9	5	58
Nico Hoerner	10	6	7	2			6	5	4	9	7		8	6	4	58
Taylor Walls		1	6		9	7	4		6	5	9	9	6	8		51
Andrew Velazquez	9	8	8		7	8	8		5	7	6				7	37
Tommy Edman	7			6	4			8		10	8	7	9	7	8	36

Others receiving points: Willy Adames 24, Francisco Lindor 23, Carlos Correa 17, J.P. Crawford 9, Brandon Crawford 7, Nick Allen 6, CJ Abrams 6, Jose Iglesias 5, Xander Bogaerts 2, Amed Rosario 1

Left Fielders

Left Fielders	Alyson	Bill	Bobby	Chris	Dan	Eduardo	Emma	Hal	Joe	John	Mark	Moses	Peter	SIS Video Scouts	Travis	Total Points
Steven Kwan	1	1	1	1	1	1	1	1	1	1	1	1	1	1	1	150
Ian Happ	5	2	2	5	2	3	2	8	2	2	2	2	2	2	2	122
Austin Hays	2		5	4	2	4	6	3	3	6	3	3		4	3	95
Brandon Marsh	9		3	2	3		3	4	6		3		4	3	5	76
Andrew Benintendi	7	4		6				2	4	5	4	4	8		10	56
A.J. Pollock		3	6		6		6		7	8	8	6	6	5	7	53
Connor Joe	4		4	10	7	8	5			4		5		9	4	50
Lourdes Gurriel Jr.	6	9	8		9		7		8	7	5	9	9	10	6	39
Tyler O'Neill	3		9					3		6	10		7	7		32
Joey Gallo		8		4		5		5						10		23

Others receiving points: David Peralta 19, Randy Arozarena 15, Tommy Pham 13, Jack Suwinski 13, Jurickson Profar 11, Mark Canha 8, Sam Hilliard 8, Alex Verdugo 8, Christian Yelich 7, Nick Gordon 6, Andrew Vaughn 6, Yadiel Hernandez 4, Ben Gamel 4, Raimel Tapia 3, Chris Taylor 2, Kyle Schwarber 1, Chad Pinder 1

Center Fielders

Center Fielders	Alyson	Bill	Bobby	Chris	Dan	Eduardo	Emma	Hal	Joe	John	Mark	Moses	Peter	SIS Video Scouts	Travis	Total Points
Myles Straw	2	5	2	3	1	2	2	2	2	2	1	1	1	1	1	137
Michael A. Taylor	1	1	1	8	2	1	1	1	1	1	2	8	2	4	2	129
Victor Robles	3	2	5	4	5	10	3	8	5	3	3	6	4	6	4	94
Jose Siri	8		6	1	4	7	4	3		4	6	2	3	2	3	90
Michael Harris II		7	3	6			5	4	3	6	4	3	5	5	5	76
Trent Grisham	7	9	4	2		5	9	5	4	5	5	9	8	3	8	71
Alek Thomas	4		7		7		6			7	4	6		7	6	45
Dylan Carlson	5		8	8			7	10	8	8	10	5	7		7	38
Harrison Bader	6	8		9	6	10	6	9						8		26
Cedric Mullins II		3						7	6		8		9	10	10	24

Others receiving points: Julio Rodriguez 19, Tyrone Taylor 15, Kike Hernandez 12, Brandon Nimmo 12, Cody Bellinger 10, Aaron Judge 7, Cristian Pache 6, Mike Trout 5, Riley Greene 5, George Springer 3, Adam Engel 1

Right Fielders

Right Fielders	Alyson	Bill	Bobby	Chris	Dan	Eduardo	Emma	Hal	Joe	John	Mark	Moses	Peter	SIS Video Scouts	Travis	Total Points
Mookie Betts	2	1	1	1	5	2	4	1	1	1	1	2	3	2	1	137
Kyle Tucker	1	5	3		1	1	1	4	3	2	2	1	1	1	2	126
Daulton Varsho	7	9	6	3	3	4	3	6	8	4	5	3	4	3	4	93
Aristides Aquino	4		2	5	4		2	7	7	3	3	4	2	5	6	89
Max Kepler	6	2	5	2	9	10	7	3	2	6	4		8	4		75
Jackie Bradley Jr.	10	3	8	10	6		6	2	5	7	6	5	5	6	3	72
Adolis Garcia	3		9		10	3	10	5	6	8	8	9	10	7	9	46
Oswaldo Cabrera	5		4		2		5			5	10	10			10	37
Starling Marte		6		9		5		8	9		7		6		5	33
Lars Nootbaar	9		10	8	7		9			9		7	7	8	8	28

Others receiving points: Wil Myers 20, Hunter Renfroe 15, Manuel Margot 10, Kyle Isbel 8, Ronald Acuna Jr. 7, Teoscar Hernandez 5, Tyler Naquin 4, Gavin Sheets 4, Randal Grichuk 4, Juan Soto 4, Seiya Suzuki 3, Anthony Santander 3, Ramon Laureano 2

Pitchers

Pitchers	Alyson	Bill	Bobby	Chris	Dan	Eduardo	Emma	Hal	Joe	John	Mark	Moses	Peter	SIS Video Scouts	Travis	Total Points
Ranger Suarez	1	3	1	4	2	2	1	2	3	1	1	1	1	1	1	140
Taijuan Walker	2	7	2		1		2	4	2	2	2	2		2	2	102
Tyler Anderson	4		3	5	4		3	6	5	3	3	3	4	3	3	94
Max Fried	3	1	6				5	3	1	4	6	8	2	5		77
Corbin Burnes	5	4	4		5	9	4	8	8	8	5	4	8	4	4	74
Zack Greinke	8	5	7	9	6		6	1	4	5	8	6	6	7	6	70
Shane Bieber		2	8	6		8	9	9	6		7				8	36
Zach Davies	10		5				7	5		6	4	10			7	34
Max Scherzer	6				7		8					5	9	6	5	31
Marcus Stroman					3	1				10			7	10		24

Others receiving points: Jose Berrios 22, Martin Perez 15, Zack Wheeler 14, Adam Wainwright 12, Zac Gallen 11, Framber Valdez 10, Alex Cobb 10, Jameson Taillon 8, Dylan Cease 7, Cal Quantrill 5, Nick Pivetta 5, Zach Plesac 4, Gerrit Cole 4, Sandy Alcantara 3, Joe Ryan 3, Johnny Cueto 3, Logan Webb 3, Justin Verlander 3, Aaron Nola 1

Catchers

Catchers	Alyson	Bill	Bobby	Chris	Dan	Eduardo	Emma	Hal	Joe	John	Mark	Moses	Peter	SIS Video Scouts	Travis	Total Points
Jose Trevino	1	2	1	2	1	1	1	5	3	1	1	2	1	1	1	141
Adley Rutschman	2	4	2	6	2	2	2	6	1	2	2	1	2	3	2	126
J.T. Realmuto	3	3	4	4	4	3	3	1	2	9	3	3	3	4	4	112
Cal Raleigh	4		3	1	5	5	4	7	4	4	4	4	5	2	3	99
Austin Hedges	6	6	7		3	6	6	2	10	3	8	5	4	8	6	74
Christian Vazquez	9	5	6	7	7	7	5	4		5	6	7		6		58
Alejandro Kirk	5	8	5	8	6	9	7			10	7	6	6	5	9	52
Yadier Molina	7	9	8	5	10		9		6	7	5	8		7	5	46
Jonah Heim	10	10	9	3	9	10	8	9	7	6		9	9	9	8	38
Will Smith	8		10		8	8			5				7	10		21

Others receiving points: Martin Maldonado 16, Tomas Nido 16, Sean Murphy 10, Travis d'Arnaud 7, Keibert Ruiz 4, Kyle Higashioka 2, Danny Jansen 1, Victor Caratini 1, Salvador Perez 1

Multi-Position

Fielders	Alyson	Bill	Bobby	Chris	Dan	Eduardo	Emma	Hal	Joe	John	Mark	Moses	Peter	SIS Video Scouts	Travis	Total Points
Tommy Edman	1	1	2	1	1	2	1	2	2	1	1	1	1	1	1	146
Daulton Varsho	5	2	1	8	3	3	4	1	1	7	3	3	2	3	2	117
Taylor Walls	4	4	3	9	2	1	2	6	3	2	4	2	3	2	3	115
Marwin Gonzalez	6		4	3	4	6	3	8	5	3	2	4	10	6	4	86
Brendan Donovan	8	8	5	5	6		5	10	8	4	5	5	5	4	5	71
Mauricio Dubon	7	5	6	10	8	7	6	3		6	7	7	7	5	7	63
Whit Merrifield	2	9			7		10	5	9	9		8	8		8	35
Dylan Moore	3	7				9		4		5			6	8		35
Nicky Lopez		10		2		5		7	4			9		7		33
Matt Reynolds	9		7		5		9			10	9	6		9	6	29

Others receiving points: Christopher Morel 23, Luis Rengifo 22, Willi Castro 20, Leury Garcia 17, Nick Gordon 13

Why Michael Harris Impresses Me

Bobby L. Scales II

In today's baseball we often see rookies come up and have immediate impact, but rarely do we see a rookie have sustainable impact on a good major league club. The overwhelming majority of players come up, have some modicum of success, then go through an adjustment period.

Depending on just how difficult that struggle may be will often determine just how long that player stays on the major league roster. There is NO shame in that!!

Playing in the major leagues is hard…really hard, and now with the amount of information available at a moment's notice, the ceremonial lap around the league that rookies and young players used to enjoy before they got exposed is no more. The opposition will have information about the player's tendencies before the name gets stitched on the back of his jersey.

The biggest jump that any ballplayer will make is the one from Triple-A to the big leagues. The Atlanta Braves' Michael Harris II made an even more remarkable leap to the major leagues from Double-A Mississippi in late May and now should be the National League Rookie of the Year.

There are a few plays that will serve as an illustration as to why this young man had the impact he had on the Atlanta Braves and what led a really intelligent front office group to sign him to an eight-year pact worth up to $72 million. (You can watch the play by scanning the QR code below.)

Harris II made some absolute highlight reel catches in his first year in the major leagues. While spectacular, those don't move the needle for me. I spoke with a veteran National League evaluator and asked him what sticks out about Harris II. "This young man has intelligence, elite athleticism and an ability to make difficult things look very easy".

Padres (then Nationals) slugger Josh Bell has an unorthodox approach that yields the ability to impact the baseball from line to line from both sides of the plate. Atlanta's information has Harris shading oppo. On the play in question, the ball was hit at 101 mph/28-degree launch angle in the right-center field gap.

We had it as a 55% catch probability; other sources had it higher, but Harris II covered 100 feet at 30 ft/sec to catch the baseball like it was a routine can of corn. On the surface it doesn't look like a difficult play; Michael Harris II made a difficult play look easy, running this ball down with room to spare.

Of course there is a 'how' attached to everything, and when you look at how Michael achieves this, it's evident how he makes the difficult look routine. His jumps are elite, both by the eye test and by Baseball Savant (scan the QR code and you'll see he's top-tier in the "Burst" stat). More often than not he's on the correct route, decisive and, as we alluded to, has tremendous "burst" right out of the gate. The scary part for the rest of the league is he's still learning how to be a major league center fielder.

On our podcast last year (which you can listen to by scanning the following QR code), he talked about how he learned to play the outfield from Marquis Grissom. Who better to learn from than a fellow Atlantan who won a World Series as a Brave.

By the way, he also went 4-for-4 with a home run in the same game. That brings us to his offensive impact on this club. Harris II performed in most every way and all year long. .297/19 HR/64 RBI, yep you're getting a dose of cough medicine to start. He finished with a 135 OPS+, he hit right-handed pitching (.943 OPS) and held his own against left-handed pitching (.649 OPS).

The fact that he was better on the road (.965 OPS away) wasn't entirely surprising given Atlanta is his hometown (.721 OPS at home) and certainly there is probably some level of pressure involved playing in front of friends and family every night. More intriguing was the lack of power production in a very hitter friendly Truist Park. Fifteen of his 19 home runs were hit on the road.

Late in the year, the hits kept coming... August (.990 OPS) and September (.838 OPS). Finally, my personal favorite stat on the planet, how he did with runners in scoring position with two outs...(.845 OPS compared to the MLB average, .712).

He was above average in Hard Hit Percentage at 41%, above average in Barrels at 10%, and his K% was a tick below average at 24.3%. Some will point to his BABIP of .361 and say he was extremely lucky. Good hitters create their own luck by barreling the baseball more than most and using the entire field.

Harris does a really nice job of staying in the middle of the field with his approach and was above average at 43.5% of balls in play going up the middle. He has shown the propensity to chase pitches, especially offspeed.

I would anticipate him improving his pitch recognition as well as his walk percentage from 4.8% as he grows in experience as well.

The one thing that Harris II didn't do this year was go 20/20. He just missed. He finished with 19 homers and was 20-for-22 in stolen base attempts this year.

Harris II is more than a flash in the pan—he's a young player that passes the eyeball test but also gives key indicators of success on both sides of the ball that he is here to stay. He's with a franchise that has done an unbelievable job of identifying the right young men, developing them quickly and then putting them in positions to succeed at the major league level. He certainly exceeded expectations and will find himself in the middle, literally, of another great run in Atlanta.

SIS VP, Baseball Bobby Scales played 14 seasons of pro baseball (2 with the Cubs) and worked in the Pirates' and Angels' front offices.

Welcome To The Show

Others in this extraordinary 2022 class of rookie position players included:

Julio Rodriguez had 28 home runs and 25 stolen bases in his debut season for the Mariners. He may have had only 1 Defensive Run Saved, but that was a *huge* improvement on the Mariners center field defense last season. And he did all this at age 21. Rodriguez and **Bobby Witt Jr.** became the fourth and fifth players to go 20 homers/20 steals in their debut season.

Adley Rutschman's presence at catcher will shape the future of the Orioles. He easily led the Orioles in Offensive Winning Percentage* and ranked second among catchers in Defensive Runs Saved. Baltimore was 60-47 when he started, 23-32 when he didn't.

 Offensive winning percentage measures how often a lineup of 9 of that hitter would win with average pitching and defense.

Jeremy Peña showed both power (22 home runs) and speed (11 stolen bases) to go along with finishing third at shortstop in The Fielding Bible Awards.

Steven Kwan was an elite contact hitter, hit .298 with 19 stolen bases, and won a Fielding Bible Award in left field. He had an all-time start to his season, with 10 hits and seven walks in his first five games, in which he hit .667.

Defensive Runs Saved Leaders

Sarah Thompson

The top of the Defensive Runs Saved leaderboard this year is full of newcomers—Brendan Rodgers and Adley Rutschman to name a couple. One other notable is Reds right fielder Aristides Aquino, who led all outfielders in MLB with 20 Defensive Runs Saved. Prior to 2022, he had only 1 Run Saved to his name in just under 1,000 innings of work.

Aquino earned his 20 Runs Saved in a variety of ways. He had no issue getting to balls quickly this season, earning 11 of his 20 Runs Saved due to his range. What's just as impressive as his range is his 8 Runs Saved with his arm this season.

Scan the QR code below with your phone to watch a play that showcases both aspects of his stellar defense this year.

On that play, Aquino makes an over-the-shoulder catch nearly on the warning track to convert a near-certain double from Alec Bohm to an out. With all his momentum bringing him towards the outfield wall, he takes more than a few steps to slow down, turn, and throw a dart to first baseman Matt Reynolds. He doubles up Rhys Hoskins, who ran on contact and was a few feet away from second base when Aquino made the catch.

Aquino had 10 kills (thrown out runners without the help of a cutoff man) in 561⅓ innings from right field, which led the position in MLB. In 2019, his most recent year with substantial innings in right, he had only 3.

Whether Aquino will become a mainstay of the Runs Saved leaderboard remains to be seen, but for 2022 he's among the elite.

Infield Runs Saved Leaders

First Basemen 3-Year Leaders		Second Basemen 3-Year Leaders		Third Basemen 3-Year Leaders		Shortstops 3-Year Leaders	
Walker, Christian	20	Semien, Marcus	22	Hayes, Ke'Bryan	44	Correa, Carlos	30
Diaz, Lewin	16	Edman, Tommy	20	Arenado, Nolan	38	Kiner-Falefa, Isiah	23
Olson, Matt	15	Fletcher, David	17	McMahon, Ryan	26	Walls, Taylor	21
Goldschmidt, Paul	12	Rodgers, Brendan	16	Urias, Ramon	16	Rojas, Miguel	21
Santana, Carlos	10	Gimenez, Andres	15	Chapman, Matt	14	Kim, Ha-seong	19
White, Evan	9	Wendle, Joey	13	Peterson, Jace	10	Simmons, Andrelton	17
Fuentes, Joshua	8	Frazier, Adam	12	Fuentes, Joshua	10	Pena, Jeremy	16
Cron, C.J.	8	Lux, Gavin	12	Urias, Luis	10	Story, Trevor	15
France, Ty	7	Arroyo, Christian	11	Machado, Manny	10	Velazquez, Andrew	14
Rivas, Alfonso	6	Wong, Kolten	10	Gonzalez, Erik	10	2 tied with	13

First Basemen 3-Year Trailers		Second Basemen 3-Year Trailers		Third Basemen 3-Year Trailers		Shortstops 3-Year Trailers	
Dalbec, Bobby	-13	Altuve, Jose	-21	Bohm, Alec	-36	Iglesias, Jose	-28
Tellez, Rowdy	-11	Odor, Rougned	-17	Diaz, Yandy	-24	Garcia, Luis	-21
Lowe, Nathaniel	-10	India, Jonathan	-14	Devers, Rafael	-23	Torres, Gleyber	-19
Sano, Miguel	-10	Hernandez, Cesar	-13	Franco, Maikel	-18	Witt Jr., Bobby	-18
Hoskins, Rhys	-9	3 tied with	-12	Dozier, Hunter	-17	Gregorius, Didi	-17
6 tied with	-6			Davis, J.D.	-16	Andrus, Elvis	-17

First Basemen 2022 Leaders		Second Basemen 2022 Leaders		Third Basemen 2022 Leaders		Shortstops 2022 Leaders	
Walker, Christian	17	Rodgers, Brendan	22	Hayes, Ke'Bryan	24	Pena, Jeremy	16
Olson, Matt	6	Gimenez, Andres	16	Arenado, Nolan	19	Rojas, Miguel	15
Rivas, Alfonso	6	Edman, Tommy	12	Urias, Ramon	14	Mateo, Jorge	14
Diaz, Lewin	5	Semien, Marcus	11	Peterson, Jace	11	Velazquez, Andrew	11
Solano, Donovan	5	Torres, Gleyber	9	McMahon, Ryan	10	Walls, Taylor	11
Cron, C.J.	5	Wendle, Joey	9	Donovan, Brendan	8	Hoerner, Nico	10
Arraez, Luis	4	Schoop, Jonathan	8	Vargas, Ildemaro	8	Kim, Ha-seong	10
5 tied with	3	Story, Trevor	6	Muncy, Max	7	Kiner-Falefa, Isiah	10
		5 tied with	4	Donaldson, Josh	7	Adames, Willy	9
				LeMahieu, DJ	7	Swanson, Dansby	9

First Basemen 2022 Trailers		Second Basemen 2022 Trailers		Third Basemen 2022 Trailers		Shortstops 2022 Trailers	
Lowe, Nathaniel	-9	Altuve, Jose	-15	Bohm, Alec	-17	Witt Jr., Bobby	-18
Dalbec, Bobby	-6	India, Jonathan	-14	Diaz, Yandy	-14	Garcia, Luis	-17
Miranda, Jose	-6	Estrada, Thairo	-12	Escobar, Eduardo	-11	Bichette, Bo	-16
Tellez, Rowdy	-6	Flores, Wilmer	-9	Franco, Maikel	-10	Anderson, Tim	-7
3 tied with	-5	Odor, Rougned	-9	Castro, Harold	-9	Crawford, Brandon	-6
		2 tied with	-8	4 tied with	-6	6 tied with	-5

Outfield Runs Saved Leaders

Left Fielders 3-Year Leaders		Center Fielders 3-Year Leaders		Right Fielders 3-Year Leaders	
O'Neill, Tyler	21	Taylor, Michael A.	38	Betts, Mookie	30
Kwan, Steven	21	Buxton, Byron	29	Gallo, Joey	27
Happ, Ian	16	Kiermaier, Kevin	25	Tucker, Kyle	27
Verdugo, Alex	15	Grisham, Trent	23	Kepler, Max	21
Benintendi, Andrew	11	Straw, Myles	21	Phillips, Brett	17
Hays, Austin	11	Hernandez, Kike	18	Aquino, Aristides	16
Hilliard, Sam	11	Bader, Harrison	15	Varsho, Daulton	16
White, Eli	11	Bradley Jr., Jackie	11	Garcia, Adolis	16
4 tied with	9	Taveras, Leody	10	Judge, Aaron	16
		Cain, Lorenzo	10	Bradley Jr., Jackie	10

Left Fielders 3-Year Trailers		Center Fielders 3-Year Trailers		Right Fielders 3-Year Trailers	
Schwarber, Kyle	-22	Reynolds, Bryan	-17	Castellanos, Nick	-19
Winker, Jesse	-20	Hicks, Aaron	-16	Dozier, Hunter	-19
Pederson, Joc	-18	Kelenic, Jarred	-16	Soler, Jorge	-12
Canha, Mark	-16	Marte, Ketel	-15	Sheets, Gavin	-10
Upton, Justin	-15	Duran, Jarren	-14	4 tied with	-9
Dickerson, Alex	-13	3 tied with	-13		

Left Fielders 2022 Leaders		Center Fielders 2022 Leaders		Right Fielders 2022 Leaders	
Kwan, Steven	21	Taylor, Michael A.	19	Aquino, Aristides	16
Happ, Ian	13	Straw, Myles	17	Betts, Mookie	15
Hilliard, Sam	11	Robles, Victor	12	Varsho, Daulton	14
Baddoo, Akil	8	Grisham, Trent	8	Tucker, Kyle	14
Hicks, Aaron	8	Harris II, Michael	8	Kepler, Max	10
Haggerty, Sam	7	Buxton, Byron	8	Phillips, Brett	9
Marsh, Brandon	6	5 tied with	6	Cabrera, Oswaldo	9
Reyes, Victor	6			Bradley Jr., Jackie	8
Larnach, Trevor	6			Eaton, Nate	6
5 tied with	5			Myers, Wil	6

Left Fielders 2022 Trailers		Center Fielders 2022 Trailers		Right Fielders 2022 Trailers	
Winker, Jesse	-16	Reynolds, Bryan	-14	Castellanos, Nick	-8
Schwarber, Kyle	-14	Senzel, Nick	-11	Sheets, Gavin	-8
Pederson, Joc	-12	Duran, Jarren	-9	Rosario, Eddie	-7
Santander, Anthony	-8	Slater, Austin	-9	4 tied with	-6
Vaughn, Andrew	-8	Daza, Yonathan	-8		
Ruf, Darin	-7	Vierling, Matt	-7		

Pitcher/Catcher Runs Saved Leaders

Pitchers 3-Year Leaders		Catchers 3-Year Leaders	
Suarez, Ranger	15	Trevino, Jose	29
Fried, Max	14	Hedges, Austin	20
Walker, Taijuan	13	Stallings, Jacob	19
Keuchel, Dallas	13	Nido, Tomas	18
Davies, Zach	10	Rutschman, Adley	18
Anderson, Tyler	9	Vazquez, Christian	17
Greinke, Zack	9	Molina, Yadier	16
Wheeler, Zack	9	Heim, Jonah	16
4 tied with	7	3 tied with	13

Pitchers 3-Year Trailers		Catchers 3-Year Trailers	
Ottavino, Adam	-9	Suzuki, Kurt	-24
Stammen, Craig	-9	Collins, Zack	-19
Valdez, Framber	-9	Melendez, MJ	-18
Cease, Dylan	-9	Chirinos, Robinson	-17
Manaea, Sean	-8	Plawecki, Kevin	-14
Rodon, Carlos	-7	Torrens, Luis	-14

Pitchers 2022 Leaders		Catchers 2022 Leaders	
Suarez, Ranger	9	Trevino, Jose	21
Walker, Taijuan	6	Rutschman, Adley	18
Anderson, Tyler	5	Raleigh, Cal	14
Kikuchi, Yusei	4	Vazquez, Christian	11
Burnes, Corbin	4	Realmuto, J.T.	11
Davies, Zach	4	Kirk, Alejandro	9
Peralta, Wandy	4	Molina, Yadier	9
Severino, Luis	4	Heim, Jonah	8
14 tied with	3	Hedges, Austin	8
		Nido, Tomas	8

Pitchers 2022 Trailers		Catchers 2022 Trailers	
Syndergaard, Noah	-6	Melendez, MJ	-18
Steele, Justin	-5	Diaz, Elias	-15
Stephan, Trevor	-4	Plawecki, Kevin	-10
Manaea, Sean	-4	Chirinos, Robinson	-10
15 tied with	-3	3 tied with	-9

Fielding Statistics

Brian Reiff

There are some times where you don't want to see how something gets made. See: sausage. Defensive Runs Saved, though, isn't generally one of those things. Because of the black-boxy nature of the defensive metrics as a whole, people seem to appreciate any details that help provide more context as to why a player's defense was worth X amount of runs.

This section is for those people. For fielders with regular playing time—750 innings at an infield or outfield position, or 600 innings at catcher—the individual components that comprise their DRS are broken down and reported.

All the positions report Runs Saved from Good Fielding Plays and Defensive Misplays. For infielders, DRS is additionally composed of ART (Air, Range, and Throwing), Bunts (for corner infielders) and Double Plays; in the outfield, Range and Positioning replaces ART, and Throwing is its own component; and at catcher, there's also Stolen Base Runs Saved and Strike Zone Runs Saved.

One place where this breakdown can be truly appreciated is at right field. The two leaders among those with regular playing time, Mookie Betts of the Dodgers and Kyle Tucker of the Astros, finished one run apart in aggregate but got there in vastly different ways. Betts saved 13 runs with his Range and Positioning and two with his arm. Tucker's Range and Positioning was worth just seven runs, but he more than made up for that with six Runs Saved from Good Fielding Plays. (You can read more about his excellence in that area in the Home Robberies section.)

Be sure to check out the All Other Fielders tables in this section as well. Just because a player didn't meet the above criteria doesn't mean their numbers weren't noteworthy. Case in point: Aristides Aquino, who actually saved more runs (16) than either Betts or Tucker to lead all right fielders, despite only playing 561⅓ innings.

First Basemen - Regulars

Player	Tm	G	GS	Inn	PO	A	E	DP	Pct.	Bases Saved	Runs Saved			
											ART	GFP/ DME	Bunts/ GDP	Total
Walker, Christian	Ari	150	146	1292	1109	78	5	106	.996	+13	17	0	0	17
Olson, Matt	Atl	162	161	1441	1209	101	8	104	.994	0	8	-2	0	6
Cron, C.J.	Col	121	120	1028	1033	59	7	113	.994	+5	5	0	0	5
Hoskins, Rhys	Phi	151	150	1298	1098	103	12	103	.990	+2	4	-1	0	3
Guerrero Jr., Vladimir	Tor	128	126	1119	969	47	10	80	.990	0	4	0	-1	3
Chavis, Michael	Pit	107	82	755	679	39	3	66	.996	0	2	1	-1	2
France, Ty	Sea	127	124	1084	816	72	3	73	.997	-4	1	2	-1	2
Goldschmidt, Paul	StL	128	127	1104	1071	91	1	118	.999	+1	0	2	0	2
Abreu, Jose	CWS	128	128	1136	954	51	11	96	.989	0	3	-2	0	1
Mountcastle, Ryan	Bal	124	123	1079	963	75	5	112	.995	-8	-1	2	0	1
Bell, Josh	TOT	124	120	1044	868	83	9	78	.991	-2	-2	0	1	-1
Alonso, Pete	NYM	134	133	1142	912	92	8	102	.992	-2	-1	0	-1	-2
Walsh, Jared	LAA	118	106	959	842	46	5	83	.994	-1	-2	0	0	-2
Choi, Ji-Man	TB	98	92	793	706	30	3	62	.996	-1	-2	-1	1	-2
Freeman, Freddie	LAD	159	159	1378	1155	91	5	100	.996	-4	-4	2	0	-2
Gurriel, Yuli	Hou	142	138	1226	1057	45	4	106	.996	-2	-4	2	0	-2
Torkelson, Spencer	Det	109	105	925	805	51	2	76	.998	-1	-2	-1	0	-3
Rizzo, Anthony	NYY	120	115	1034	919	72	5	71	.995	-1	-5	2	0	-3
Hosmer, Eric	TOT	102	101	856	690	77	6	67	.992	-5	-5	0	0	-5
Tellez, Rowdy	Mil	139	126	1144	946	81	2	86	.998	+2	-5	0	-1	-6
Lowe, Nathaniel	Tex	153	150	1327	1252	70	9	125	.993	-4	-9	1	-1	-9

Second Basemen - Regulars

Player	Tm	G	GS	Inn	PO	A	E	DP	Pct.	Range	Bases Saved	Runs Saved		
												ART	GFP/ DME	GDP	Total
Rodgers, Brendan	Col	134	133	1168	218	411	10	99	.984	4.85	+17	21	-1	2	22
Gimenez, Andres	Cle	125	120	1073	226	317	9	70	.984	4.55	+16	15	0	1	16
Semien, Marcus	Tex	148	148	1293	252	398	7	89	.989	4.52	+11	14	-1	-2	11
Torres, Gleyber	NYY	124	121	1083	192	270	7	50	.985	3.84	+14	11	0	-2	9
Schoop, Jonathan	Det	129	127	1106	207	313	3	86	.994	4.23	0	2	2	4	8
Story, Trevor	Bos	94	92	814	157	215	6	50	.984	4.11	+2	7	0	-1	6
Espinal, Santiago	Tor	120	105	945	148	255	4	56	.990	3.84	-7	5	0	-1	4
Lux, Gavin	LAD	102	93	820	148	180	9	45	.973	3.60	+5	3	0	0	3
McNeil, Jeff	NYM	106	95	844	160	223	3	55	.992	4.08	-1	3	0	0	3
Cronenworth, Jake	SD	147	142	1240	205	308	4	77	.992	3.72	+1	1	0	1	2
Wong, Kolten	Mil	131	115	1031	182	255	17	60	.963	3.82	+4	0	0	-1	-1
Segura, Jean	Phi	97	96	823	168	216	4	57	.990	4.20	-3	0	1	-2	-1
Polanco, Jorge	Min	97	96	833	167	215	8	55	.979	4.13	-5	-3	2	0	-1
Frazier, Adam	Sea	124	113	992	191	238	6	61	.986	3.89	-1	-3	1	1	-1
Marte, Ketel	Ari	94	91	806	135	196	8	49	.976	3.69	-4	-5	0	-1	-6
Hernandez, Cesar	Was	126	124	1080	191	284	4	70	.992	3.96	0	-6	-1	-1	-8
Odor, Rougned	Bal	129	111	1019	209	296	16	74	.969	4.46	-4	-8	-1	0	-9
Estrada, Thairo	SF	102	88	776	159	205	5	59	.986	4.22	-2	-9	-1	-2	-12
Altuve, Jose	Hou	135	134	1150	159	269	9	67	.979	3.35	+1	-15	-1	1	-15

Third Basemen - Regulars

Player	Tm	G	GS	Inn	PO	A	E	DP	Pct.	Range	Bases Saved	Runs Saved		
												ART	GFP/ DME	Bunts/ GDP	Total
Hayes, Ke'Bryan	Pit	133	128	1103	109	307	12	36	.972	3.40	+15	20	0	4	24
Arenado, Nolan	StL	131	131	1119	84	283	12	42	.968	2.95	+17	17	2	0	19
Urias, Ramon	Bal	98	84	769	54	197	8	26	.969	2.94	+10	13	0	1	14
McMahon, Ryan	Col	145	132	1176	88	257	17	29	.953	2.64	+9	9	0	1	10
Donaldson, Josh	NYY	104	102	903	78	220	12	18	.961	2.97	+1	9	-1	-1	7
Riley, Austin	Atl	159	157	1408	97	283	14	20	.964	2.43	-11	5	1	0	6
Urshela, Gio	Min	136	131	1145	100	237	6	25	.983	2.65	+1	4	0	0	4
Ramirez, Jose	Cle	127	127	1110	91	234	10	27	.970	2.64	+10	3	-1	0	2
Moncada, Yoan	CWS	101	98	860	82	163	5	18	.980	2.56	0	3	-1	0	2
Chapman, Matt	Tor	153	151	1344	164	263	5	41	.988	2.86	-1	3	-1	0	2
Candelario, Jeimer	Det	117	112	974	75	197	11	17	.961	2.51	+1	-3	0	2	-1
Suarez, Eugenio	Sea	130	129	1144	112	226	10	23	.971	2.66	+4	-2	0	0	-2
Machado, Manny	SD	134	132	1143	94	217	11	27	.966	2.45	-7	-4	1	0	-3
Bregman, Alex	Hou	154	153	1360	144	263	7	39	.983	2.69	0	-6	2	0	-4
Devers, Rafael	Bos	138	137	1186	124	255	14	29	.964	2.88	+5	-4	-1	-1	-6
Wisdom, Patrick	ChC	105	103	903	66	187	14	28	.948	2.52	-8	-5	-2	1	-6
Franco, Maikel	Was	99	95	828	59	196	11	15	.959	2.77	-5	-8	0	-2	-10
Escobar, Eduardo	NYM	130	125	1109	91	184	12	19	.958	2.23	-8	-11	1	-1	-11

Player	Tm	G	GS	Inn	PO	A	E	DP	Pct.	Range	Bases Saved	ART	GFP/ DME	Bunts/ GDP	Total
Diaz, Yandy	TB	102	97	839	63	163	5	18	.978	2.42	-9	-16	2	0	-14
Bohm, Alec	Phi	135	132	1147	92	241	13	22	.962	2.61	-15	-16	0	-1	-17

Shortstops - Regulars

Player	Tm	G	GS	Inn	PO	A	E	DP	Pct.	Range	Bases Saved	ART	GFP/ DME	GDP	Total
Pena, Jeremy	Hou	134	132	1165	146	347	19	64	.963	3.81	+3	13	0	3	16
Rojas, Miguel	Mia	136	132	1114	184	340	7	74	.987	4.23	+4	11	2	2	15
Mateo, Jorge	Bal	149	142	1257	181	417	17	91	.972	4.28	+9	10	2	2	14
Velazquez, Andrew	LAA	124	100	906	106	271	8	44	.979	3.75	+11	10	1	0	11
Kim, Ha-seong	SD	131	125	1092	119	327	8	59	.982	3.68	+10	10	0	0	10
Kiner-Falefa, Isiah	NYY	138	131	1185	149	331	15	51	.970	3.65	+8	9	1	0	10
Hoerner, Nico	ChC	133	128	1118	127	359	13	58	.974	3.91	+8	9	0	1	10
Adames, Willy	Mil	136	136	1200	178	334	14	68	.973	3.84	+10	9	0	0	9
Swanson, Dansby	Atl	161	161	1433	193	391	8	77	.986	3.67	+1	7	3	-1	9
Rosario, Amed	Cle	140	139	1241	151	357	12	61	.977	3.68	+10	8	-1	-1	6
Bogaerts, Xander	Bos	146	146	1250	171	401	10	78	.983	4.12	-3	5	-1	1	5
Correa, Carlos	Min	132	129	1113	157	307	8	51	.983	3.75	0	3	0	0	3
Farmer, Kyle	Cin	98	97	842	106	214	7	49	.979	3.42	-12	-3	2	1	0
Turner, Trea	LAD	160	160	1387	174	334	16	54	.969	3.30	+6	0	0	-1	-1
Lindor, Francisco	NYM	159	159	1379	198	385	9	83	.985	3.81	+9	-4	0	2	-2
Perdomo, Geraldo	Ari	140	131	1160	169	329	14	83	.973	3.86	-7	-5	2	0	-3
Andrus, Elvis	TOT	143	139	1220	172	366	10	65	.982	3.97	+9	-1	-2	-1	-4
Seager, Corey	Tex	144	144	1259	176	407	17	91	.972	4.17	+10	-3	-1	0	-4
Crawford, J.P.	Sea	144	143	1254	162	326	14	70	.972	3.50	-10	-5	1	0	-4
Iglesias, Jose	Col	116	116	976	123	298	8	73	.981	3.88	-4	-5	0	1	-4
Baez, Javier	Det	133	132	1123	187	354	26	76	.954	4.34	-3	-5	0	1	-4
Crawford, Brandon	SF	116	113	979	163	287	16	68	.966	4.14	-4	-7	3	-2	-6
Bichette, Bo	Tor	157	157	1374	166	363	23	58	.958	3.46	-8	-15	0	-1	-16
Witt Jr., Bobby	KC	98	96	826	113	259	16	51	.959	4.05	-8	-19	0	1	-18

Left Fielders - Regulars

Player	Tm	G	GS	Inn	PO	A	E	DP	Pct.	Range	Bases Saved	R/P	GFP/ DME	Throws	Total
Kwan, Steven	Cle	123	110	1020	224	2	2	2	.991	2.04	+29	19	0	2	21
Happ, Ian	ChC	146	142	1233	274	8	3	1	.989	2.06	+20	11	1	1	13
Pollock, A.J.	CWS	107	77	752	147	6	3	3	.981	1.83	+1	0	2	2	4
Gurriel Jr., Lourdes	Tor	105	104	897	185	7	3	2	.985	1.93	+5	0	2	1	3
Benintendi, Andrew	TOT	124	119	1041	214	4	0	0	1.000	1.88	+11	5	0	-3	2
Profar, Jurickson	SD	146	141	1238	229	10	4	2	.984	1.74	-6	-3	0	5	2
Verdugo, Alex	Bos	102	98	874	154	4	3	0	.981	1.63	+1	-1	1	0	0
Pham, Tommy	TOT	134	133	1135	227	15	7	1	.972	1.92	-8	-4	2	2	0
Yelich, Christian	Mil	115	114	1009	189	2	1	1	.995	1.70	+7	1	-1	-2	-2
Arozarena, Randy	TB	104	98	876	157	4	5	0	.970	1.65	-9	-4	0	0	-4
Peralta, David	TOT	113	106	927	215	2	2	1	.991	2.11	+4	0	-2	-3	-5
Canha, Mark	NYM	123	113	982	169	2	0	1	1.000	1.57	+1	-1	-1	-3	-5
Schwarber, Kyle	Phi	139	138	1167	182	3	1	0	.995	1.43	-19	-10	-2	-2	-14
Winker, Jesse	Sea	118	113	972	176	5	4	0	.978	1.68	-16	-13	-2	-1	-16

Center Fielders - Regulars

Player	Tm	G	GS	Inn	PO	A	E	DP	Pct.	Range	Bases Saved	R/P	GFP/ DME	Throws	Total
Taylor, Michael A.	KC	123	114	1010	289	8	3	0	.990	2.65	+17	12	3	4	19
Straw, Myles	Cle	152	144	1309	371	12	2	2	.995	2.63	+19	7	3	7	17
Robles, Victor	Was	128	110	972	340	7	6	3	.983	3.21	+3	7	-1	6	12
Grisham, Trent	SD	148	124	1143	341	3	2	1	.994	2.71	+13	9	2	-3	8
Harris II, Michael	Atl	114	114	1021	252	3	2	0	.992	2.25	+9	6	1	1	8
Siri, Jose	TOT	95	84	750	234	1	1	0	.996	2.82	+17	7	-1	0	6
Thomas, Alek	Ari	112	102	907	311	4	3	0	.991	3.12	+14	4	3	-1	6
Mullins II, Cedric	Bal	150	140	1260	358	9	0	4	1.000	2.62	+13	3	1	1	5
Rodriguez, Julio	Sea	130	130	1127	357	3	6	0	.984	2.88	+16	6	-1	-2	3
Greene, Riley	Det	93	93	814	241	0	2	0	.992	2.66	+12	4	1	-3	2
Trout, Mike	LAA	111	110	938	250	2	1	0	.996	2.42	+6	2	-1	-1	0
Bellinger, Cody	LAD	144	135	1223	322	2	3	0	.991	2.38	+14	2	-2	0	0
Taveras, Leody	Tex	93	86	766	211	3	2	1	.991	2.52	-9	-1	-2	1	-2
Nimmo, Brandon	NYM	151	148	1282	304	4	0	1	1.000	2.16	-7	-3	3	-3	-3

Player	Tm	G	GS	Inn	PO	A	E	DP	Pct.	Range	Bases Saved	Runs Saved R/P	GFP/ DME	Throws	Total
Robert, Luis	CWS	91	89	782	208	1	2	0	.991	2.41	+2	-3	0	-1	-4
Senzel, Nick	Cin	101	98	847	236	3	4	2	.984	2.54	-14	-4	-3	-4	-11
Reynolds, Bryan	Pit	127	125	1063	277	2	2	1	.993	2.36	-11	-12	0	-2	-14

Right Fielders - Regulars

Player	Tm	G	GS	Inn	PO	A	E	DP	Pct.	Range	Bases Saved	Runs Saved R/P	GFP/ DME	Throws	Total
Betts, Mookie	LAD	136	133	1154	298	8	2	4	.994	2.39	+27	13	0	2	15
Tucker, Kyle	Hou	147	145	1276	287	8	3	1	.990	2.08	+13	7	6	1	14
Kepler, Max	Min	110	103	891	222	5	2	1	.991	2.29	+8	10	-1	1	10
Marte, Starling	NYM	116	116	994	209	9	1	2	.995	1.97	+3	3	1	0	4
Garcia, Adolis	Tex	93	88	750	164	8	4	1	.977	2.06	-4	-1	0	4	3
Renfroe, Hunter	Mil	118	118	1044	210	11	4	2	.982	1.91	-5	0	1	1	2
Acuna Jr., Ronald	Atl	92	88	792	150	4	4	0	.975	1.75	0	0	0	0	0
Soto, Juan	TOT	151	151	1298	304	3	3	0	.990	2.13	-4	1	-1	-2	-2
Ward, Taylor	LAA	125	122	1069	263	5	5	1	.982	2.26	+3	2	-2	-3	-3
Hernandez, Teoscar	Tor	117	115	967	227	10	4	1	.983	2.21	+9	-5	0	2	-3
Suzuki, Seiya	ChC	106	104	905	201	3	4	2	.981	2.03	-8	-4	-1	1	-4
Castellanos, Nick	Phi	121	119	1009	217	8	0	3	1.000	2.01	-8	-7	0	-1	-8

Catchers - Regulars

Player	Tm	G	GS	Inn	PO	A	E	DP	PB	Pct.	SB Att	CS	Pit CS	CS Pct	Cat ERA	Stk Sav	Runs Saved GFP/ DME	SB	SZ	Other	Total
Trevino, Jose	NYY	112	89	820	828	32	6	1	2	.993	39	9	6	.23	3.09	104	2	3	12	4	21
Rutschman, Adley	Bal	93	84	762	670	35	8	3	2	.989	36	11	0	.31	3.79	80	4	0	9	5	18
Raleigh, Cal	Sea	115	99	917	911	28	6	3	3	.994	69	16	9	.23	3.30	68	1	2	8	3	14
Vazquez, Christian	TOT	108	96	870	863	40	8	5	3	.991	67	16	3	.24	3.90	29	2	2	3	4	11
Realmuto, J.T.	Phi	133	130	1132	1151	49	8	11	2	.993	65	27	3	.42	3.90	11	3	9	1	-2	11
Molina, Yadier	StL	77	71	628	512	25	3	6	1	.994	29	9	4	.31	3.54	22	3	1	3	2	9
Kirk, Alejandro	Tor	78	74	654	655	31	3	7	1	.996	47	12	0	.26	3.48	42	3	1	5	0	9
Heim, Jonah	Tex	111	102	901	839	37	3	3	3	.997	69	12	1	.17	3.90	43	-2	-1	5	6	8
Nido, Tomas	NYM	96	86	766	859	27	5	3	3	.994	62	12	1	.19	3.65	57	4	1	7	-4	8
Hedges, Austin	Cle	105	97	840	824	35	5	5	1	.994	56	9	4	.16	3.37	28	5	-2	3	2	8
Smith, Will	LAD	109	106	956	968	32	3	6	4	.997	52	6	4	.12	2.58	14	0	-3	2	8	7
d'Arnaud, Travis	Atl	99	99	876	956	23	2	2	3	.998	54	10	5	.19	3.35	53	1	1	6	-2	6
Higashioka, Kyle	NYY	82	72	622	669	21	5	2	6	.993	28	9	4	.32	3.56	28	0	2	3	-2	3
Narvaez, Omar	Mil	83	80	681	704	32	5	3	5	.993	44	9	1	.20	3.81	26	0	-2	3	1	2
Caratini, Victor	Mil	90	73	691	737	38	4	3	5	.995	52	12	3	.23	3.88	31	1	0	4	-3	2
McGuire, Reese	TOT	84	70	628	624	31	3	4	3	.995	46	14	2	.30	4.49	15	-2	3	2	-1	2
Maldonado, Martin	Hou	113	110	949	1025	49	2	3	9	.998	62	16	0	.26	2.91	9	1	2	1	-2	2
Sanchez, Gary	Min	91	80	714	678	37	4	4	4	.994	48	12	2	.25	4.27	17	0	1	2	-2	1
Murphy, Sean	Oak	116	116	1004	878	40	8	4	2	.991	52	10	9	.19	4.70	44	-1	1	5	-4	1
Mejia, Francisco	TB	83	70	638	619	27	2	2	5	.997	44	8	3	.18	3.20	-12	-2	0	-1	3	0
Stassi, Max	LAA	97	92	829	826	26	7	7	8	.992	54	10	2	.19	3.60	28	-2	0	3	-1	0
Contreras, Willson	ChC	72	72	625	606	45	4	7	7	.994	33	9	2	.27	3.96	-22	0	2	-3	0	-1
Kelly, Carson	Ari	100	86	772	707	35	0	4	3	1.000	59	11	3	.19	3.82	-30	1	-2	-4	4	-1
Perez, Salvador	KC	77	74	622	548	30	3	3	1	.995	28	9	1	.32	4.65	-65	1	0	-8	3	-4
Ruiz, Keibert	Was	106	97	865	794	37	7	5	4	.992	69	18	2	.26	5.11	-18	0	4	-2	-7	-5
Bart, Joey	SF	93	80	699	656	34	8	4	4	.989	55	9	3	.16	4.03	-39	-1	-1	-5	1	-6
Nola, Austin	SD	101	94	835	833	27	6	3	5	.993	61	5	3	.08	3.38	-59	1	-4	-7	4	-6
Barnhart, Tucker	Det	92	90	778	653	29	3	3	3	.996	67	16	4	.24	4.05	-39	2	-2	-5	-3	-8
Knizner, Andrew	StL	90	78	685	577	21	6	6	3	.990	27	6	1	.22	3.94	-74	1	-1	-9	0	-9
Haase, Eric	Det	84	68	609	527	23	7	2	6	.987	38	11	2	.29	4.05	-44	-3	0	-5	-1	-9
Stallings, Jacob	Mia	110	103	906	918	24	2	2	0	.998	71	10	4	.14	3.79	-8	2	-4	-1	-6	-9
Diaz, Elias	Col	104	94	833	672	52	11	3	3	.985	60	12	3	.20	5.15	-109	-1	0	-13	-1	-15

All Other Fielders

Player	Pos	G	GS	Inn	Pct.	DRS
Abrams, C	2B	13	6	66	.946	0
	SS	75	71	619	.955	-5
	RF	3	1	12	1.000	0
Acuna Jr., R	CF	1	0	1	-	0
Adams, R	1B	1	0	9	1.000	0
Adell, J	LF	69	59	477	.963	-1
	RF	15	12	113	.976	0
Adrianza, E	2B	8	7	61	1.000	1
	3B	19	16	137	.976	0
	SS	3	1	12	1.000	-1
	LF	9	2	32	1.000	-1
Aguilar, J	1B	63	60	532	.992	-5
	3B	4	0	5	1.000	1
Aguilar, R	1B	1	0	2	1.000	0
	LF	2	2	18	1.000	0
	CF	1	1	7	1.000	0
	RF	5	3	31	1.000	-1
Ahmed, N	SS	16	15	134	.983	-3
Alberto, H	1B	3	0	10	1.000	0
	2B	37	21	186	.966	1
	3B	20	13	124	1.000	0
	SS	5	2	28	1.000	0
	RF	1	1	6	-	0
Albies, O	2B	64	63	554	.987	-1
Alcantara, S	2B	25	11	120	.963	-2
	3B	41	32	291	.946	-4
	SS	28	15	142	.983	2
Alford, A	LF	1	1	6	1.000	0
	CF	1	0	2	-	0
	RF	1	0	1	-	0
Allen, G	LF	23	16	140	1.000	3
	CF	11	10	92	1.000	-1
	RF	13	6	61	1.000	0
Allen, N	2B	43	35	307	.975	4
	SS	60	57	502	.978	6
Almonte, A	LF	3	2	23	1.000	1
	CF	5	4	34	1.000	-3
	RF	1	1	8	-	0
Almora Jr., A	LF	17	15	131	1.000	2
	CF	23	19	168	1.000	4
	RF	28	25	224	.967	2
Alvarez, E	3B	5	2	23	1.000	0
	SS	1	0	2	-	0
	LF	1	1	6	1.000	0
	RF	5	4	29	.909	-1
Alvarez, Y	LF	56	56	468	.977	5
Anderson, B	2B	1	0	2	1.000	0
	3B	48	42	371	.937	-4
	LF	8	6	52	1.000	1
	RF	36	35	307	.972	1
Anderson, T	SS	79	79	691	.962	-7
Andujar, M	1B	1	0	0	-	0
	LF	23	22	189	1.000	3
Aquino, A	LF	7	3	36	1.000	4
	CF	2	1	11	1.000	0
	RF	69	66	561	.964	16
Aranda, J	1B	11	4	45	1.000	0
	2B	13	11	79	.917	0
	3B	6	5	37	1.000	-1
	LF	1	1	5	-	0
Arauz, J	2B	4	4	30	1.000	0
	3B	6	6	48	.889	-1
	SS	4	2	18	1.000	-1
Arcia, O	2B	50	43	399	.979	0
	3B	4	4	32	.875	-1
	SS	1	0	3	1.000	0
	LF	6	6	47	1.000	-2
Arias, G	1B	1	1	9	1.000	0
	2B	3	3	29	.938	0
	3B	9	8	73	.882	-2
	SS	3	2	20	.750	0
Arozarena, R	RF	25	25	208	1.000	-1
Arraez, L	1B	65	60	529	1.000	4
	2B	41	31	278	.992	3
	3B	7	4	41	.941	-2
Arroyo, C	1B	9	6	51	1.000	-1
	2B	40	35	310	.993	4
	3B	10	8	72	1.000	0
	SS	14	7	77	.939	1
	RF	17	16	108	1.000	-5
Astudillo, W	1B	3	0	5	1.000	0
	2B	8	6	52	.842	-2

All Other Fielders

Player	Pos	G	GS	Inn	Pct.	DRS
	3B	10	5	49	1.000	-3
Azocar, J	LF	21	5	66	1.000	1
	CF	35	31	241	.978	2
	RF	49	18	227	.966	0
Baddoo, A	LF	50	47	404	.992	8
	CF	16	16	135	.978	-2
Bader, H	CF	85	77	698	1.000	-1
Bae, J	2B	4	4	35	1.000	0
	LF	1	1	8	.750	0
	CF	5	4	40	.857	0
Bannon, R	2B	1	0	2	-	0
	3B	3	3	26	1.000	-1
Barnes, A	2B	1	0	1	-	0
Barnhart, T	3B	1	0	1	-	0
Barrera, L	LF	16	11	99	.913	1
	CF	1	0	1	1.000	0
	RF	16	11	101	.962	1
Barrero, S	SS	48	46	407	.965	-2
Batten, M	2B	5	1	15	1.000	0
	3B	7	3	31	1.000	0
	LF	1	1	6	1.000	0
Baty, B	3B	11	11	93	.933	-3
Beaty, M	1B	3	0	10	1.000	0
	LF	2	2	13	1.000	0
	RF	10	9	58	1.000	-1
Beckham, T	1B	2	1	11	1.000	0
	LF	4	1	14	1.000	0
Beer, S	1B	5	5	35	.974	-1
Belt, B	1B	63	58	506	.988	2
Benson, W	LF	4	3	32	1.000	2
	CF	10	9	73	1.000	-2
	RF	6	1	19	.800	0
Bernard, W	LF	1	1	8	1.000	0
	CF	10	9	86	1.000	1
	RF	1	0	4	1.000	0
Berti, J	2B	47	37	341	.994	1
	3B	37	34	288	.975	1
	SS	10	5	54	1.000	0
	LF	16	14	112	1.000	2
	CF	3	1	12	1.000	-1
Bethancourt, C	1B	37	28	249	.996	-1
	3B	1	0	3	1.000	0
Betts, M	2B	7	5	46	1.000	0
Biggio, C	1B	33	32	262	.992	2
	2B	49	36	320	.987	0
	3B	1	1	8	1.000	0
	LF	2	2	16	1.000	0
	RF	7	6	45	1.000	0
Blackmon, C	RF	51	49	403	.957	-6
Blanco, D	CF	3	2	17	1.000	0
Bleday, J	LF	22	15	147	1.000	-1
	CF	38	37	330	.988	-3
	RF	4	4	36	1.000	1
Bohm, A	1B	10	5	57	1.000	0
Bolt, S	LF	2	0	4	1.000	0
	CF	36	28	253	1.000	-2
	RF	5	2	23	1.000	-1
Bote, D	1B	6	5	37	1.000	1
	2B	18	14	119	1.000	-1
	3B	16	15	133	.975	4
Bouchard, S	LF	26	25	218	1.000	0
Bradley, B	1B	7	5	41	.969	-1
Bradley Jr., J	CF	55	32	307	.978	-3
	RF	91	66	614	1.000	8
Brantley, M	LF	29	29	249	1.000	2
Brennan, W	LF	5	5	45	1.000	-1
	CF	1	1	10	1.000	0
	RF	4	3	29	1.000	1
Bride, J	1B	5	2	20	1.000	0
	2B	32	28	234	.990	2
	3B	21	14	133	.930	-1
Brinson, L	LF	1	0	1	-	0
	CF	15	9	87	1.000	-3
Brosseau, M	1B	3	2	15	1.000	0
	3B	55	40	321	.934	-6
	SS	4	2	20	.917	0
Brown, S	1B	84	72	636	.993	0
	LF	38	18	190	.974	0
	CF	17	15	122	.969	-5
	RF	32	25	217	1.000	-1
Brujan, V	2B	31	25	236	.965	1
	3B	1	0	5	1.000	0

All Other Fielders

Player	Pos	G	GS	Inn	Pct.	DRS
	SS	5	4	36	1.000	0
	LF	1	0	2	-	0
	CF	1	1	5	-	0
	RF	19	10	91	.952	0
Bryant, K	LF	30	30	252	.955	-5
Burdick, P	LF	14	12	108	1.000	-4
	CF	13	13	113	1.000	0
	RF	4	3	30	1.000	2
Burger, J	2B	3	0	5	1.000	0
	3B	37	36	326	.934	-5
Burleson, A	1B	6	1	28	1.000	0
	LF	2	2	11	1.000	0
	RF	9	9	61	1.000	0
Buxton, B	CF	57	51	445	1.000	8
Cabrera, O	1B	3	0	13	1.000	0
	2B	3	3	19	.929	2
	3B	3	3	28	1.000	1
	SS	4	3	28	1.000	2
	LF	9	8	70	1.000	0
	RF	27	24	209	1.000	9
Cain, L	CF	42	40	358	.976	3
Calhoun, K	LF	29	24	212	1.000	-1
	CF	1	0	2	-	0
	RF	75	61	560	1.000	-2
Calhoun, W	LF	5	3	26	1.000	0
Call, A	LF	28	23	209	1.000	-2
	CF	4	4	39	1.000	0
	RF	8	2	31	1.000	1
Camargo, J	1B	5	3	26	1.000	0
	2B	9	5	55	1.000	-1
	3B	13	10	91	.974	3
	SS	26	20	186	1.000	-3
Cameron, D	CF	7	7	58	1.000	0
	RF	14	12	109	1.000	0
Canha, M	1B	1	0	1	1.000	0
	3B	1	0	8	1.000	0
	CF	11	7	71	1.000	0
	RF	6	4	41	1.000	1
Cano, R	2B	20	19	150	.986	-5
Capel, C	LF	2	1	7	-	0
	RF	18	15	130	1.000	-2
Capra, V	2B	1	0	1	1.000	0
	LF	1	1	6	-	0
	RF	1	1	5	-	0
Caratini, V	1B	2	1	9	1.000	0
Carlson, D	CF	73	62	530	.993	6
	RF	62	47	448	.987	-5
Carpenter, K	LF	12	10	89	1.000	-1
	RF	8	7	61	1.000	0
Carpenter, M	1B	5	3	25	1.000	-1
	3B	2	2	16	1.000	1
	LF	3	3	21	1.000	0
	RF	12	11	85	1.000	0
Carroll, C	LF	25	18	176	.971	3
	CF	5	4	31	1.000	0
	RF	2	2	18	1.000	0
Casali, C	1B	3	0	4	1.000	0
Casas, T	1B	27	22	198	.995	-2
Castellanos, N	LF	3	3	25	1.000	0
Castillo, D	1B	7	3	32	.943	0
	2B	28	18	175	1.000	0
	3B	4	1	16	.750	-2
	SS	33	30	255	.950	0
	RF	22	18	137	.972	-3
Castro, H	1B	50	48	412	.990	-1
	2B	14	13	113	.952	-1
	3B	25	24	210	.935	-9
	SS	19	13	121	.957	-2
	LF	3	2	17	1.000	1
	CF	1	0	1	-	0
Castro, R	2B	32	28	236	.966	-2
	3B	34	21	190	.950	4
	SS	19	17	155	.934	-1
Castro, W	2B	16	11	98	1.000	1
	3B	6	3	34	.909	0
	SS	16	7	75	.943	0
	LF	27	23	207	.959	1
	CF	16	14	121	1.000	0
	RF	40	36	312	1.000	3
Cave, J	LF	45	34	314	.985	2
	CF	4	2	15	1.000	0
	RF	10	7	66	1.000	1

All Other Fielders

Player	Pos	G	GS	Inn	Pct.	DRS
Celestino, G	LF	28	14	128	.973	0
	CF	90	68	637	.985	2
	RF	8	5	44	1.000	-1
Chang, Y	1B	9	6	53	1.000	0
	2B	43	27	257	.984	1
	3B	7	2	26	1.000	1
	SS	16	11	99	1.000	-1
Chavis, M	2B	14	7	65	1.000	0
	3B	9	5	45	.842	0
Chisholm Jr., J	2B	60	56	476	.982	2
Clemens, K	1B	13	8	73	1.000	2
	2B	9	7	69	1.000	0
	3B	8	11	96	.962	2
	LF	9	5	44	1.000	0
Clement, E	1B	5	1	15	1.000	0
	2B	15	10	93	.936	-2
	3B	30	20	201	.987	4
	SS	1	1	9	1.000	-1
	LF	12	8	78	1.000	1
Collins, Z	1B	9	7	62	1.000	1
Contreras, M	LF	3	0	10	1.000	0
	CF	13	9	84	.970	1
	RF	9	6	57	1.000	2
Contreras, W	LF	1	1	9	-	-1
Cooper, G	1B	59	56	469	.995	-4
Cordero, F	1B	53	47	362	.977	-4
	LF	12	8	82	.923	-1
	CF	2	1	7	1.000	0
	RF	26	11	124	.971	0
Cronenworth, J	1B	20	5	73	1.000	-1
	SS	9	6	55	.966	-3
Crook, N	CF	1	1	5	1.000	0
	RF	2	1	13	1.000	-1
Cruz, O	SS	79	77	678	.953	1
	LF	1	0	1	-	0
Culberson, C	1B	1	0	1	1.000	1
	2B	11	7	66	.971	0
	3B	25	22	157	.907	-3
	SS	1	0	1	-	0
	LF	12	8	70	.941	2
Dalbec, B	1B	89	64	635	.997	-6
	2B	2	0	5	1.000	0
	3B	24	14	140	.933	-1
	SS	1	1	10	1.000	-1
Davidson, M	1B	1	1	5	1.000	-1
	3B	9	8	63	.875	-3
Davis, B	3B	1	1	9	1.000	-1
	RF	2	2	16	1.000	-1
Davis, J	1B	18	12	113	.991	-2
	3B	30	18	172	.958	-1
	LF	2	0	2	-	0
Davis, J	LF	1	1	8	1.000	0
	CF	4	2	19	1.000	-1
	RF	3	3	24	1.000	0
Davis, J	CF	34	26	228	.982	-2
Daza, Y	LF	27	23	195	.918	3
	CF	92	71	644	.991	-8
	RF	1	0	1	-	0
De La Cruz, B	LF	39	23	212	.982	2
	CF	42	34	307	.970	-1
	RF	41	28	276	.963	-2
Dean, A	LF	3	2	18	1.000	0
	RF	1	0	1	-	0
DeJong, P	2B	1	1	7	.875	1
	SS	75	57	537	.978	5
DeLuzio, B	CF	18	4	65	1.000	0
Demeritte, T	LF	6	6	49	1.000	-2
	RF	20	19	167	1.000	1
Diaz, A	1B	6	5	45	1.000	1
	2B	22	18	166	1.000	3
	3B	10	8	71	1.000	0
	SS	18	16	144	.966	-1
	LF	28	22	189	.974	-1
	RF	1	0	3	-	0
Diaz, J	1B	1	1	8	1.000	0
	2B	12	11	89	.956	1
Diaz, L	1B	56	47	410	1.000	5
Diaz, Y	1B	17	15	133	.992	0
Diaz, Y	RF	1	0	1	1.000	0
Dickerson, A	RF	1	0	1	-	0
Dickerson, C	LF	60	53	453	.988	-3
	RF	10	5	41	1.000	-2
Difo, W	2B	1	1	8	1.000	1
	SS	2	1	10	1.000	-1
Dixon, B	3B	2	1	12	1.000	1
	RF	1	1	6	1.000	0
Donovan, B	1B	16	6	58	.971	0
	2B	38	32	264	1.000	0
	3B	31	21	189	.960	8
	SS	7	6	56	.967	-1
	LF	19	16	144	1.000	2
	RF	20	16	143	1.000	1
Downs, J	2B	8	7	56	.952	-1
	3B	6	3	32	.929	-1
	SS	3	0	8	1.000	-1
Dozier, H	1B	42	38	332	.997	-1
	3B	27	25	212	.920	-5
	LF	9	7	59	1.000	0
	RF	35	27	230	1.000	-6
Drury, B	1B	30	24	222	1.000	-2
	2B	27	23	190	1.000	1
	3B	67	58	513	.959	-4
	SS	2	0	4	1.000	0
	RF	1	0	1	-	0
Dubon, M	2B	17	5	65	.964	2
	3B	3	2	20	1.000	0
	SS	21	14	144	.974	2
	LF	9	5	47	.917	1
	CF	59	33	326	.989	-1
	RF	3	1	12	1.000	0
Duffy, M	1B	21	14	122	.991	0
	2B	17	7	75	.953	0
	3B	42	37	329	.969	-3
Duggar, S	LF	14	5	73	1.000	0
	CF	18	15	120	1.000	-1
Dunand, J	2B	2	1	15	1.000	0
	3B	1	1	9	1.000	0
Duran, E	2B	9	6	57	.957	0
	3B	51	48	427	.933	-1
Duran, J	CF	51	48	416	1.000	-9
	RF	7	5	46	.941	2
Duvall, A	LF	35	26	237	.980	-2
	CF	44	43	382	.991	0
	RF	11	11	90	1.000	-1
Eaton, N	3B	15	13	113	.966	-4
	LF	6	3	29	.857	0
	CF	5	4	37	1.000	1
	RF	20	13	116	1.000	6
Edman, T	2B	89	67	615	.991	12
	3B	8	1	26	.938	0
	SS	80	74	622	.994	6
	CF	1	0	5	1.000	0
	RF	2	0	3	1.000	0
Ellis, D	3B	7	6	45	.938	-2
Encarnacion, J	LF	10	10	85	.923	1
	RF	10	9	84	.958	1
Engel, A	LF	3	0	7	.667	0
	CF	57	33	345	.979	2
	RF	55	27	298	1.000	1
Escobar, A	2B	2	0	4	1.000	-1
	SS	37	36	308	.965	-4
Escobar, E	2B	2	0	2	1.000	0
Espinal, S	3B	11	10	83	.920	-1
	SS	11	4	50	1.000	1
Estrada, T	3B	3	1	16	1.000	0
	SS	37	32	286	.961	-2
	LF	18	8	84	1.000	-3
	CF	1	0	2	-	0
Fairchild, S	LF	22	15	130	1.000	2
	CF	20	12	117	1.000	0
	RF	4	2	17	1.000	0
Farmer, K	1B	2	0	2	-	0
	3B	36	35	299	.979	-2
Fletcher, D	2B	44	30	286	.993	4
	SS	36	23	207	1.000	3
Flores, W	1B	45	31	301	.990	1
	2B	61	50	441	1.000	-9
	3B	34	28	235	.941	-1
Florial, E	LF	2	0	5	1.000	1
	CF	14	9	116	1.000	-3
Ford, M	1B	29	26	224	1.000	0
Fortes, N	1B	1	0	1	1.000	0
Fox, L	3B	4	1	14	.857	-1
	SS	6	6	52	.944	-2
Fraley, J	LF	29	21	191	1.000	0
	CF	7	7	56	1.000	-2
	RF	16	14	127	.933	-4
France, T	2B	1	0	1	1.000	0
	3B	6	6	47	1.000	-2
Franco, M	1B	4	1	14	1.000	1
Franco, W	SS	73	71	604	.980	0
Frazier, A	SS	4	2	19	.909	0
	LF	16	9	99	1.000	-1
	CF	2	1	5	1.000	0
	RF	21	8	91	1.000	3
Frazier, C	LF	5	3	26	.875	0
	RF	2	2	14	1.000	0
Freeman, T	2B	4	4	33	.933	0
	3B	11	10	95	.850	-5
	SS	7	7	65	1.000	0
Friedl, T	LF	25	22	182	.975	-1
	CF	24	21	183	1.000	-3
	RF	15	11	101	1.000	0
Gallo, J	1B	1	0	1	1.000	0
	LF	77	68	579	.981	0
	CF	1	0	6	1.000	0
	RF	48	31	314	1.000	-4
Garcia, A	CF	57	45	427	.991	1
Garcia, A	1B	5	0	8	1.000	0
Garcia, A	RF	86	83	702	.985	-3
Garcia, D	1B	35	28	249	1.000	2
	LF	1	1	8	.667	0
Garcia, L	2B	47	45	395	.983	-1
	3B	6	6	53	.938	0
	SS	19	13	132	.932	0
	LF	9	5	46	.909	1
	CF	4	2	20	.909	0
	RF	15	5	62	1.000	0
Garcia, L	2B	33	33	286	.977	3
	SS	58	58	503	.938	-17
Garcia, M	SS	8	6	53	.917	-1
Garlick, K	LF	27	18	135	.975	-1
	RF	23	12	120	1.000	-2
Garrett, S	LF	13	13	98	1.000	0
Gimenez, A	SS	18	14	130	1.000	1
Gonzalez, E	1B	1	0	1	1.000	0
	2B	2	2	15	1.000	1
	3B	7	4	48	1.000	1
	SS	8	3	36	1.000	0
Gonzalez, L	LF	52	24	241	.982	0
	CF	6	5	34	1.000	0
	RF	69	57	449	.973	-1
Gonzalez, M	1B	14	12	98	.976	3
	2B	3	0	3	1.000	0
	3B	12	8	77	1.000	0
	SS	20	16	135	1.000	0
	LF	16	9	92	1.000	0
	RF	20	9	98	1.000	4
Gonzalez, O	RF	84	82	735	.963	0
Gonzalez, R	2B	25	24	217	.989	-1
	SS	3	3	27	1.000	0
	LF	1	0	2	-	0
	RF	2	1	7	1.000	0
Goodrum, N	1B	4	4	34	1.000	0
	2B	10	6	60	.970	0
Gordon, N	2B	36	29	258	.966	-3
	3B	1	0	4	1.000	0
	SS	17	7	76	.933	-3
	LF	62	47	418	.990	0
	CF	38	31	244	.971	0
Gore, T	LF	3	0	5	1.000	0
	CF	3	1	15	1.000	0
Gorman, N	2B	68	62	549	.975	-5
	LF	1	0	1	-	0
Gosselin, P	1B	3	3	21	1.000	0
	2B	10	6	59	.964	2
	3B	17	12	103	1.000	-2
	RF	1	0	1	-	0
Grandal, Y	1B	5	3	30	.969	0
Gregorius, D	SS	61	58	506	.991	-5
Grichuk, R	CF	52	48	406	.991	-3
	RF	106	80	737	.974	-1

Player	Pos	G	GS	Inn	Pct.	DRS
Grissom, V	2B	40	39	347	.973	-3
	SS	2	1	10	1.000	0
Groshans, J	3B	17	17	154	.981	-1
Grossman, R	LF	69	62	531	.976	1
	RF	59	52	459	1.000	2
Guerrero Jr., V	3B	1	0	2	-	0
Guillorme, L	2B	67	61	543	.996	1
	3B	22	19	160	.979	1
	SS	15	3	52	.955	0
Gurriel Jr., L	1B	8	2	27	1.000	1
Guthrie, D	2B	1	0	1	1.000	0
	3B	1	1	7	1.000	0
	RF	12	5	62	1.000	0
Gutierrez, K	3B	10	8	68	.960	-1
Guzman, R	1B	3	1	16	1.000	0
Haase, E	LF	11	4	48	1.000	2
Hager, J	2B	16	9	85	1.000	0
	3B	7	5	41	1.000	-1
	SS	4	3	25	1.000	-1
Haggerty, S	2B	4	1	12	1.000	2
	LF	33	21	210	.984	7
	CF	6	3	31	1.000	0
	RF	37	24	229	1.000	2
Hall, D	1B	7	4	39	1.000	0
Hamilton, B	2B	3	0	5	1.000	0
	3B	1	0	1	-	0
	LF	12	3	36	1.000	0
	CF	5	3	29	1.000	0
Hamilton, C	1B	6	1	19	1.000	-1
Hampson, G	2B	10	8	69	.976	-5
	3B	7	6	50	1.000	1
	SS	32	20	211	.968	0
	CF	36	23	201	1.000	-5
Haniger, M	RF	47	45	396	.981	3
Happ, I	CF	3	1	12	1.000	1
Harper, B	RF	8	8	68	1.000	-1
Harrison, J	2B	90	85	749	.971	3
	3B	23	20	188	.926	3
	SS	2	0	3	-	0
	LF	2	1	8	-	0
Harrison, M	LF	6	4	30	1.000	1
	CF	3	0	6	.500	0
Haseley, A	LF	4	2	13	1.000	0
	CF	3	2	18	1.000	0
	RF	5	1	22	1.000	1
Hayes, K	SS	3	0	5	1.000	0
Hays, A	LF	86	82	744	1.000	3
	CF	6	3	28	1.000	0
	RF	58	51	439	.991	1
Henderson, G	2B	3	3	26	1.000	-2
	3B	24	18	173	1.000	1
	SS	7	6	48	.970	1
Hensley, D	2B	5	0	10	1.000	0
	3B	3	1	12	1.000	0
	SS	2	2	18	1.000	-1
	LF	1	0	3	1.000	0
Heredia, G	LF	35	6	105	1.000	0
	CF	5	4	44	1.000	0
	RF	23	9	97	.966	1
Hermosillo, M	LF	1	0	1	1.000	0
	CF	28	19	172	.943	-2
	RF	2	0	5	-	0
Hernandez, C	3B	9	8	69	.957	1
	LF	10	10	80	.960	3
Hernandez, E	1B	1	1	7	1.000	0
	LF	7	5	44	1.000	0
	RF	1	1	7	1.000	0
Hernandez, K	2B	11	10	87	1.000	0
	SS	10	4	45	1.000	2
	CF	80	77	669	1.000	4
Hernandez, T	LF	8	3	33	1.000	1
Hernandez, Y	LF	79	75	599	.993	-3
	RF	1	0	2	-	0
Hernandez, Y	2B	2	1	11	1.000	0
	3B	10	6	57	1.000	2
Herrera, O	LF	11	2	34	1.000	1
	CF	48	43	377	.992	-3
	RF	7	3	32	1.000	1
Heyward, J	CF	26	23	182	1.000	-2
	RF	21	18	166	1.000	-1
Hicklen, B	LF	2	0	2	-	0
	CF	1	1	7	1.000	0
	RF	2	0	3	1.000	0
Hicks, A	LF	55	46	413	1.000	8
	CF	81	64	582	.992	-4
Higgins, P	1B	38	25	244	1.000	1
	3B	4	2	25	.727	-1
Hill, D	CF	30	26	236	1.000	4
Hilliard, S	LF	59	40	377	1.000	11
	CF	14	11	88	1.000	-1
	RF	3	0	5	1.000	0
Hiura, K	1B	33	30	246	.986	-1
	2B	14	9	83	.921	-2
	LF	5	4	37	.900	0
Hoerner, N	3B	1	0	1	-	0
Huff, S	1B	6	3	32	1.000	0
Hummel, C	LF	21	17	154	.970	1
	RF	2	0	1	-	0
Ibanez, A	1B	6	6	44	.949	0
	2B	2	1	12	1.000	0
	3B	25	22	197	.961	2
Inciarte, E	LF	6	1	14	1.000	0
	CF	2	0	4	-	0
	RF	2	0	5	1.000	1
India, J	2B	86	85	720	.966	-14
Isbel, K	LF	29	19	172	.978	5
	CF	30	25	205	.981	0
	RF	49	28	279	.978	4
Jackson, D	3B	1	0	1	-	0
	LF	1	0	2	-	0
	RF	2	1	7	1.000	0
Jankowski, T	LF	19	2	43	1.000	0
	CF	11	6	57	1.000	2
	RF	12	9	84	1.000	-1
Jimenez, E	LF	30	30	232	1.000	-2
Joe, C	1B	24	17	162	.988	3
	LF	50	43	375	1.000	5
	RF	16	16	132	1.000	-5
Johnson, B	LF	1	0	6	1.000	-1
	CF	7	3	30	1.000	-1
	RF	4	3	19	1.000	0
Jones, N	RF	22	21	169	1.000	1
Judge, A	CF	78	74	633	1.000	1
	RF	73	54	492	1.000	2
Jung, J	3B	25	25	219	.974	0
Katoh, G	1B	3	2	21	1.000	0
	2B	2	2	13	1.000	0
Kelenic, J	LF	3	3	18	1.000	0
	CF	24	19	190	.981	0
	RF	24	20	180	1.000	3
Kemp, T	2B	89	67	612	.990	-2
	LF	65	61	507	.991	0
Kennedy, B	2B	22	22	174	.973	-1
	3B	2	1	8	1.000	0
Kepler, M	CF	3	0	9	1.000	-1
Kiermaier, K	CF	60	56	482	.993	2
Kim, H	3B	24	17	171	1.000	2
Kiner-Falefa, I	3B	6	4	42	.909	0
Kingery, S	2B	1	0	1	-	0
Kirilloff, A	1B	18	14	132	1.000	-2
	LF	21	19	152	.975	0
	RF	8	3	37	1.000	0
Knizner, A	1B	5	0	7	1.000	0
Kreidler, R	2B	2	2	18	1.000	0
	3B	13	11	94	.971	3
	SS	13	9	86	1.000	2
	CF	1	0	2	-	0
Krizan, J	LF	3	3	23	1.000	0
Kwan, S	CF	7	4	30	1.000	-2
	RF	20	19	153	.944	-4
La Stella, T	1B	3	1	19	1.000	0
	2B	3	2	20	.900	-2
	3B	6	4	37	1.000	-1
Lagares, J	LF	5	5	44	1.000	0
	CF	8	5	53	1.000	0
	RF	9	7	56	.889	-4
Lamb, J	1B	4	0	19	1.000	0
	3B	4	2	22	.875	-1
	LF	14	6	66	1.000	0
	RF	6	3	24	1.000	0
Larnach, T	LF	33	27	247	1.000	6
	RF	11	10	84	1.000	3
Larsen, J	RF	1	1	4	-	0
Laureano, R	CF	34	29	240	1.000	-5
	RF	71	58	502	.984	4
Leblanc, C	1B	8	4	40	1.000	0
	2B	26	25	218	1.000	2
	3B	13	13	109	.964	-3
Lee, K	CF	2	0	3	-	-1
LeMahieu, D	1B	35	31	265	.996	2
	2B	41	35	313	.986	-1
	3B	47	43	386	.992	7
Lester, J	3B	1	0	1	1.000	0
Lewis, K	LF	1	1	9	1.000	1
	RF	3	3	22	1.000	0
Lewis, R	SS	11	11	99	.952	0
	CF	1	1	3	1.000	0
Liberato, L	LF	1	0	2	-	0
	CF	1	0	1	-	0
	RF	1	0	1	-	0
Locastro, T	LF	11	3	38	1.000	-1
	CF	9	3	35	1.000	0
	RF	7	4	34	1.000	-1
Longoria, E	3B	68	59	512	.966	-4
Lopes, C	2B	2	1	11	1.000	0
	LF	1	1	6		0
	RF	1	0	3	1.000	0
Lopez, A	2B	33	22	213	.976	-4
	3B	8	4	38	1.000	-1
	LF	4	1	15	1.000	0
	RF	2	0	3	1.000	0
Lopez, N	2B	68	62	537	.989	-8
	3B	30	20	176	1.000	1
	SS	52	45	406	.982	0
Lopez, O	2B	1	1	4	1.000	0
	SS	5	1	17	1.000	0
	CF	1	0	1		0
Lowe, B	2B	53	51	438	.969	2
	RF	1	0	3	-	-1
Lowe, J	LF	10	9	75	1.000	4
	CF	9	7	57	1.000	-1
	RF	33	25	235	1.000	-1
Lowrie, J	1B	3	3	25	1.000	0
	2B	2	2	16	1.000	-1
Luplow, J	1B	1	0	3	1.000	0
	3B	1	0	0	1.000	0
	LF	22	18	152	.976	0
	CF	5	4	32	.909	0
	RF	41	25	229	1.000	2
Lux, G	SS	9	0	31	1.000	1
	LF	28	24	205	1.000	-3
Machado, D	SS	5	5	45	1.000	2
Machin, V	2B	1	0	1	-	0
	3B	68	62	538	.964	-6
	SS	1	0	1	.000	-1
MacKinnon, D	1B	12	9	76	1.000	1
	3B	5	4	33	1.000	-1
Madrigal, N	2B	59	53	487	.996	4
Madris, B	1B	9	8	59	1.000	0
	LF	5	4	38	1.000	1
	CF	2	0	2	-	0
	RF	19	17	150	1.000	-5
Mancini, T	1B	39	36	323	1.000	2
	LF	20	20	162	1.000	2
	RF	11	11	86	.967	0
Marcano, T	2B	23	18	157	.989	-1
	SS	1	0	2	1.000	0
	LF	30	26	225	.977	-1
	RF	1	0	1	-	0
Margot, M	LF	8	7	62	1.000	2
	CF	18	13	114	1.000	1
	RF	53	49	429	.980	0
Marisnick, J	LF	12	7	70	1.000	3
	CF	14	12	105	1.000	-2
	RF	4	2	21	1.000	0
Marrero, D	3B	1	1	3	1.000	0
	SS	3	0	7	1.000	0
Marsh, B	LF	77	67	594	.979	6
	CF	59	50	432	1.000	-1
	RF	2	2	17	1.000	1
Marte, S	CF	2	0	5	-	0
Martin, R	2B	10	7	60	.963	1
	SS	2	2	17	.900	0
Massey, M	2B	48	46	402	.982	1
	3B	1	1	8	1.000	-1
Mastrobuoni, M	2B	6	3	31	1.000	-1

Player	Pos	G	GS	Inn	Pct.	DRS
	RF	3	1	10	1.000	0
Mathias, M	1B	3	2	24	1.000	0
	2B	6	5	39	1.000	1
	3B	2	1	11	1.000	0
	LF	2	2	15	1.000	0
	RF	2	1	6	1.000	0
Matijevic, J	1B	10	6	56	1.000	0
	LF	1	0	1	-	0
Maton, N	2B	10	7	62	1.000	0
	3B	2	1	11	1.000	0
	SS	2	2	14	1.000	0
	LF	10	4	49	1.000	0
	RF	10	8	64	1.000	1
Mayfield, J	2B	11	6	59	.970	-1
	3B	8	6	54	1.000	0
	LF	2	2	14	1.000	0
	RF	4	4	28	1.000	1
Mazara, N	LF	3	0	9	1.000	0
	RF	48	41	339	.989	-2
Mazeika, P	1B	2	0	2	1.000	0
McCann, J	1B	3	1	15	1.000	-1
McCarthy, J	LF	32	27	243	1.000	-1
	CF	12	10	81	1.000	1
	RF	47	34	312	.988	-1
McCormick, C	LF	64	32	340	.984	-1
	CF	60	54	456	1.000	0
	RF	17	12	119	1.000	-1
McCutchen, A	LF	31	31	268	1.000	5
	CF	3	2	13	1.000	0
	RF	19	16	153	1.000	0
McDonald, M	CF	1	1	7	1.000	0
	RF	1	1	9	1.000	0
McKenna, R	LF	39	15	170	.950	1
	CF	21	19	146	1.000	0
	RF	31	9	107	1.000	2
McKinney, B	1B	7	4	37	1.000	-1
	LF	4	3	22	1.000	0
	RF	10	7	62	1.000	1
McKinstry, Z	2B	21	18	160	1.000	0
	3B	22	16	146	.938	0
	SS	10	6	66	1.000	1
	LF	1	1	9	1.000	1
	RF	3	0	10	1.000	0
McMahon, R	1B	1	0	1	1.000	0
	2B	10	9	81	1.000	-1
McNeil, J	3B	1	0	1	1.000	0
	LF	34	33	271	.986	2
	RF	13	11	92	1.000	0
Meadows, A	LF	15	14	123	1.000	3
	RF	18	17	141	1.000	1
Mejia, F	1B	2	0	4	1.000	0
Melendez, M	LF	23	23	198	.957	-3
	RF	15	14	114	1.000	-2
Mendick, D	2B	6	4	38	1.000	-2
	3B	2	2	21	1.000	0
	SS	22	20	182	1.000	-1
	LF	1	0	1	-	0
Meneses, J	1B	40	32	285	.996	-4
	LF	3	1	11	1.000	0
	RF	22	22	183	.944	-6
Mercado, O	LF	12	9	70	.952	0
	CF	5	3	26	1.000	-1
	RF	36	20	211	1.000	2
Mercedes, Y	1B	4	1	15	1.000	-1
	LF	8	7	48	.875	-1
Merrifield, W	1B	2	0	8	1.000	0
	2B	83	72	634	.987	-5
	LF	5	3	26	1.000	0
	CF	18	15	120	1.000	-2
	RF	40	34	287	1.000	-1
Meyers, J	CF	51	44	403	.983	4
Miller, B	3B	27	12	137	.946	-4
	LF	28	24	199	1.000	-4
	RF	3	0	9	1.000	-1
Miller, O	1B	80	71	638	.989	-1
	2B	25	23	211	.952	-2
	3B	4	0	7	1.000	0
Miranda, J	1B	77	69	595	.994	-6
	3B	34	27	247	.952	0
Mitchell, C	RF	54	50	428	.978	-4
Mitchell, G	CF	28	19	176	.976	1
Molina, Y	1B	1	0	1	-	0

Player	Pos	G	GS	Inn	Pct.	DRS
Mondesi, A	SS	15	15	131	1.000	1
Mondou, N	2B	1	1	8	-	0
Moniak, M	LF	13	11	93	1.000	-1
	CF	21	19	168	1.000	-4
	RF	4	0	4	-	0
Montero, E	1B	16	12	115	.991	0
	3B	23	22	182	.943	0
Moore, D	1B	8	3	34	1.000	1
	2B	12	8	64	1.000	1
	3B	2	0	2	-	0
	SS	26	17	174	.984	-5
	LF	18	9	80	1.000	0
	CF	7	7	58	1.000	-1
	RF	39	20	202	1.000	3
Moran, C	1B	25	20	176	1.000	-1
	3B	14	9	81	1.000	0
Morel, C	2B	33	28	242	.990	0
	3B	18	16	141	.918	-3
	SS	13	10	91	.953	-1
	LF	1	1	9	-	0
	CF	57	50	458	.975	-6
Moreno, G	2B	1	0	1	-	0
	3B	1	0	4	1.000	0
	LF	1	1	4	-	0
Motter, T	2B	1	0	2	1.000	0
	3B	2	2	12	.500	-1
Moustakas, M	1B	24	21	184	1.000	-2
	3B	25	22	178	.978	-1
Muncy, M	1B	3	0	5	1.000	0
	2B	31	25	223	.981	0
	3B	84	80	713	.955	7
Munoz, Y	2B	14	11	95	1.000	-1
	3B	8	4	44	1.000	0
	LF	1	0	1	.000	0
	RF	2	1	10	1.000	-1
Naquin, T	LF	14	11	96	.950	-1
	CF	3	0	4	1.000	0
	RF	68	55	507	.991	-5
Naylor, J	1B	88	84	748	.991	1
	RF	5	5	37	1.000	0
Neuse, S	1B	13	10	89	.980	0
	2B	23	17	147	.931	-5
	3B	44	39	332	.935	2
	SS	2	2	16	1.000	-1
Nevin, T	1B	8	7	65	1.000	0
	3B	44	40	327	.960	-4
	LF	2	2	17	.750	0
	RF	1	1	7	1.000	0
Newman, K	2B	42	37	332	.994	0
	SS	33	31	272	.955	-2
Nola, A	2B	2	0	3	1.000	0
	3B	1	0	1	-	0
Nootbaar, L	LF	11	2	46	1.000	1
	CF	11		80	1.000	0
	RF	79	66	585	.987	3
Odor, R	3B	2	2	12	1.000	0
O'Hearn, R	1B	13	6	66	1.000	0
	RF	13	9	77	1.000	-2
Olivares, E	LF	12	11	90	1.000	-1
	CF	1	0	2	1.000	0
	RF	27	24	197	.982	-4
O'Neill, T	LF	83	67	609	.992	1
	CF	21	20	167	1.000	-3
	RF	19	12	120	1.000	1
Ortega, R	LF	11	7	63	1.000	0
	CF	67	47	410	.990	-3
	RF	19	12	120	1.000	1
Outman, J	LF	3	2	21	1.000	0
	RF	1	1	6	-	0
Owings, C	2B	11	10	82	1.000	1
	3B	2	1	10	1.000	0
	SS	8	7	63	.931	-2
	LF	1	1	8	1.000	0
Ozuna, M	LF	52	52	420	.988	-6
Pache, C	CF	90	70	646	.995	5
Padlo, K	1B	7	4	36	1.000	0
	3B	5	5	40	1.000	-1

Player	Pos	G	GS	Inn	Pct.	DRS
Palacios, J	1B	1	0	3	1.000	0
	2B	12	6	64	.864	-3
	3B	1	0	1	-	0
	SS	14	12	115	.930	1
Palacios, J	LF	9	4	36	1.000	0
	RF	12	7	62	1.000	0
Palacios, R	2B	2	0	3	1.000	0
	LF	25	20	156	1.000	1
Papierski, M	1B	1	0	2	1.000	0
Paredes, I	1B	29	17	160	.994	-1
	2B	43	33	280	.992	1
	3B	50	38	362	.977	5
	SS	1	0	2	1.000	0
Park, H	2B	11	8	61	.974	-2
	3B	6	4	39	.889	-2
	SS	3	3	22	1.000	0
	RF	2	2	12	.800	0
Pasquantino, V	1B	37	37	307	.993	-2
Payton, M	LF	6	5	45	1.000	-1
	CF	1	1	6	1.000	0
	RF	3	0	7	-	0
Pederson, J	LF	102	84	685	.984	-12
	RF	18	12	94	1.000	-3
Peguero, L	SS	1	1	9	1.000	1
Peraza, O	2B	4	3	34	1.000	0
	SS	12	11	89	1.000	-1
Perdomo, G	2B	2	2	18	1.000	1
	3B	6	5	43	1.000	0
Perez, J	3B	1	0	2	1.000	0
Peterson, J	1B	5	3	28	1.000	0
	2B	3	0	8	1.000	0
	3B	86	67	615	.980	11
	LF	3	2	18	1.000	0
	RF	12	9	78	1.000	0
Phillips, B	LF	5	3	26	1.000	1
	CF	42	30	287	.988	-3
	RF	38	27	247	.985	9
Pillar, K	LF	4	3	25	1.000	1
	CF	1	1	7	-	0
Pinder, C	1B	3	2	20	1.000	0
	2B	1	0	1	-	0
	3B	9	2	31	1.000	-2
	LF	64	54	478	1.000	-5
	RF	30	20	187	.981	0
Piscotty, S	LF	5	4	34	1.000	1
	RF	28	26	217	1.000	-5
Plummer, N	LF	4	2	24	1.000	0
	RF	5	1	17	1.000	0
Polanco, J	SS	6	3	30	1.000	0
Pollock, A	CF	37	35	277	.976	-2
	RF	14	11	91	1.000	-2
Pratto, N	1B	43	39	340	1.000	0
	LF	7	6	51	1.000	0
	RF	1	1	7	1.000	0
Proctor, F	2B	6	6	49	1.000	-1
Pujols, A	1B	22	20	163	1.000	0
Quinn, R	LF	11	2	26	1.000	-1
	CF	28	16	155	.979	3
	RF	8	4	40	1.000	0
Quiroz, E	2B	12	10	93	.982	2
Raley, L	1B	3	1	17	1.000	0
	LF	7	6	50	1.000	0
	RF	8	7	57	.938	3
Ramirez, H	1B	32	29	248	.982	-4
	LF	5	2	21	1.000	0
	RF	24	15	132	1.000	0
Ramos, H	LF	3	2	17	-	-1
	RF	6	5	41	1.000	-2
Realmuto, J	1B	3	0	6	.857	0
Refsnyder, R	LF	6	2	25	1.000	0
	CF	17	13	115	.971	-2
	RF	28	16	163	.967	-4
Reks, Z	LF	13	7	73	1.000	0
	RF	3	0	8	1.000	0
Rendon, A	3B	47	46	395	.948	2
Renfroe, H	1B	1	0	2	-	0
Rengifo, L	2B	99	77	693	.978	-1
	3B	39	26	251	.941	3
	SS	19	16	99	.941	0
	LF	1	0	1	-	0
	RF	5	1	14	1.000	1
Reyes, F	LF	2	1	9	1.000	-1

All Other Fielders

Player	Pos	G	GS	Inn	Pct.	DRS
	RF	13	11	86	1.000	0
Reyes, P	3B	2	1	11	1.000	0
	SS	3	2	25	.750	-1
Reyes, V	LF	19	14	127	1.000	6
	CF	8	6	52	1.000	-1
	RF	63	57	502	.985	-5
Reynolds, B	LF	1	1	10	1.000	0
Reynolds, M	1B	13	6	64	1.000	1
	2B	36	29	258	.956	-4
	3B	14	6	69	1.000	0
	SS	23	19	170	.988	4
	LF	3	2	16	1.000	0
	CF	1	0	2	-	0
	RF	11	5	47	1.000	1
Riddle, J	3B	1	1	9	1.000	0
Riley, A	1B	1	1	7	.818	0
Rios, E	1B	4	0	9	1.000	0
	3B	4	1	11	1.000	1
Rivas, A	1B	92	73	646	.998	6
	LF	2	0	4	1.000	0
	RF	1	0	2	1.000	0
Rivera, E	1B	5	3	27	1.000	0
	3B	86	80	702	.983	6
Robertson, K	SS	1	0	1	.000	-1
Rojas, J	3B	12	8	70	1.000	-1
	LF	1	1	8	1.000	0
	RF	6	5	43	.900	-2
Rojas, J	2B	26	26	230	.972	0
	3B	89	84	741	.946	-1
Rojas, M	1B	10	0	28	1.000	2
Rooker, B	LF	8	5	42	1.000	1
	RF	1	0	2	-	-1
Rosario, A	LF	6	6	45	.818	-2
Rosario, E	LF	54	46	410	.987	-2
	RF	15	14	119	.852	-7
Rosario, E	3B	4	0	4	-	0
	SS	2	0	3	1.000	1
Ruf, D	1B	45	35	306	.993	-5
	LF	29	17	158	1.000	-7
	RF	9	7	52	1.000	-2
Ruiz, E	LF	7	4	38	1.000	-2
	CF	6	3	26	1.000	-1
	RF	6	2	22	1.000	1
Sanchez, G	1B	1	0	1	1.000	0
Sanchez, J	LF	12	10	87	1.000	1
	CF	78	74	646	.994	2
	RF	1	0	1	-	0
Sanchez, Y	2B	14	12	109	.984	0
	3B	2	0	2	1.000	0
	SS	1	0	1	.500	-1
Sano, M	1B	19	17	147	.986	0
Santana, C	1B	76	74	655	.997	3
	RF	1	0	1	-	0
Santander, A	LF	38	37	299	.962	-8
	RF	84	79	696	.994	3
Schoop, J	1B	2	1	10	1.000	0
Schrock, M	2B	2	1	10	1.000	0
	LF	2	1	9	1.000	1
	RF	3	1	11	1.000	0
Schwindel, F	1B	48	45	385	1.000	-2
Segura, J	SS	1	0	1	1.000	0
Semien, M	SS	17	13	128	.971	-1
Senzel, N	2B	1	0	2	1.000	0
	3B	2	1	13	1.000	0
Serven, B	1B	1	0	2	1.000	0
Severino, P	1B	2	0	3	1.000	0
Shaw, T	1B	3	3	26	1.000	-1
Sheets, G	1B	13	9	86	1.000	-1
	LF	3	2	12	1.000	0
	RF	85	78	646	.976	-8
Short, Z	2B	2	2	16	1.000	0
	SS	4	1	15	1.000	0
Siani, M	CF	9	7	63	1.000	0
Sierra, M	LF	17	4	67	1.000	1
	CF	28	18	176	1.000	0
	RF	2	0	2	1.000	0
Simmons, A	2B	18	11	106	1.000	-1
	SS	18	11	104	.980	4
Siri, J	LF	2	1	9	1.000	0
	RF	3	3	27	.875	1
Slater, A	LF	16	5	60	1.000	0
	CF	106	53	538	.978	-9

All Other Fielders

Player	Pos	G	GS	Inn	Pct.	DRS
	RF	14	3	40	1.000	0
Smith, D	1B	37	20	196	1.000	0
Smith, J	2B	2	0	6	1.000	-1
	3B	36	32	288	.989	6
	SS	6	5	47	1.000	0
	LF	24	21	183	1.000	0
Smith, K	3B	39	36	312	.991	5
	SS	10	5	50	.962	0
Smith, P	1B	10	8	74	1.000	1
	RF	43	40	328	.976	0
Smith-Njigba, C	LF	2	2	14	1.000	-1
Solak, N	2B	1	0	1	-	0
	LF	22	16	133	1.000	-3
Solano, D	1B	26	25	215	1.000	5
	2B	7	5	50	.952	1
	3B	16	16	140	.977	-2
Soler, J	LF	57	56	469	1.000	-1
Sosa, E	2B	1	0	1	-	0
	3B	22	13	137	1.000	1
	SS	42	32	283	.971	5
	LF	2	0	3	1.000	0
Sosa, L	2B	6	4	40	1.000	0
	SS	5	5	41	1.000	-2
Soto, L	3B	1	1	7	1.000	0
	SS	18	14	135	.963	0
Souza Jr., S	RF	5	5	40	1.000	0
Spangenberg, C	3B	1	0	1	-	0
Springer, G	CF	86	84	677	.995	-4
	RF	26	2	60	1.000	0
Stanton, G	LF	4	4	32	1.000	0
	RF	34	34	281	.982	-4
Steer, S	1B	9	9	71	1.000	1
	2B	5	4	36	.960	0
	3B	14	12	108	.960	0
Stefanic, M	2B	22	19	131	1.000	2
Stephenson, T	1B	1	0	0	1.000	0
Stevenson, C	LF	1	0	2	1.000	0
	CF	22	19	157	1.000	-1
	RF	2	0	4	1.000	0
Stott, B	2B	47	41	372	1.000	1
	3B	2	2	15	.857	-1
	SS	83	75	658	.975	-5
Stowers, K	LF	13	10	83	1.000	-3
	RF	12	10	88	1.000	0
Strange-Gordon, D	SS	13	11	103	.963	-5
	LF	3	2	13	1.000	0
	CF	4	2	19	.833	1
Stubbs, G	LF	1	0	1	-	0
Suwinski, J	LF	56	46	418	.987	2
	CF	19	10	107	1.000	1
	RF	38	34	294	.984	-1
Suzuki, K	1B	1	0	2	1.000	0
Swaggerty, T	LF	3	2	15	.500	0
	CF	1	1	9	-	0
Tapia, R	LF	64	48	459	1.000	0
	CF	38	33	250	.987	0
	RF	32	25	227	.966	-4
Taylor, C	2B	22	18	170	1.000	1
	3B	3	0	4	1.000	0
	SS	1	0	1	-	-1
	LF	80	71	646	.993	-4
	CF	10	9	75	.955	0
	RF	10	7	56	1.000	2
Taylor, T	LF	20	9	97	1.000	1
	CF	84	75	669	1.000	6
	RF	23	19	171	1.000	-1
Thaiss, M	1B	11	8	69	1.000	-1
	3B	3	0	4	1.000	0
Thomas, C	LF	10	9	74	1.000	-2
Thomas, D	LF	5	1	15	1.000	0
	RF	5	2	19	1.000	1
Thomas, L	LF	73	45	434	.990	-4
	CF	56	47	392	.991	2
	RF	43	33	299	1.000	1
Thompson, B	LF	35	32	283	.983	0
	CF	9	9	77	1.000	2
	RF	10	10	86	1.000	-2
Thompson, T	LF	36	24	228	1.000	0
	CF	18	17	146	1.000	0
	RF	29	14	160	1.000	2
Toglia, M	1B	15	13	117	1.000	2
	RF	17	17	143	1.000	-3

All Other Fielders

Player	Pos	G	GS	Inn	Pct.	DRS
Tom, K	RF	1	0	1	-	0
Toro, A	1B	1	1	8	1.000	0
	2B	55	39	367	.988	-2
	3B	31	24	223	.940	0
	RF	1	0	1	-	0
Torrens, L	2B	2	1	11	1.000	0
Torres, G	SS	6	1	15	.889	0
Tovar, E	SS	9	9	78	.971	-3
Trammell, T	LF	3	3	22	1.000	0
	CF	7	2	33	1.000	1
	RF	34	29	225	1.000	1
Trejo, A	2B	13	12	107	1.000	1
	3B	2	2	17	1.000	1
	SS	20	17	161	.949	-5
Tsutsugo, Y	1B	35	34	285	.993	-4
Tucker, C	2B	6	5	42	1.000	0
	SS	3	3	23	.750	-2
	RF	12	8	74	1.000	0
Turner, J	3B	66	66	574	.961	1
Upton, J	LF	2	2	12	1.000	0
	RF	4	3	23	1.000	0
Urias, L	2B	46	33	285	.992	1
	3B	73	54	499	.940	2
	SS	24	22	201	.966	-1
Urias, R	2B	21	19	147	1.000	0
	SS	8	4	40	.933	-1
Urshela, G	SS	2	0	3	1.000	0
VanMeter, J	1B	21	17	137	.974	-1
	2B	39	31	260	.969	0
	3B	2	1	10	1.000	0
	RF	1	0	2	-	0
Vargas, I	2B	4	2	23	1.000	-1
	3B	43	43	372	.971	8
	SS	15	12	121	.983	-2
Vargas, M	1B	8	3	41	1.000	1
	3B	1	0	1	-	0
	LF	7	4	46	.900	-2
Varsho, D	CF	54	42	379	.981	5
	RF	71	61	542	.994	14
Vaughn, A	1B	23	22	191	1.000	-3
	2B	2	0	3	1.000	0
	LF	44	40	330	.971	-8
	RF	45	39	315	.970	-6
Vavra, T	2B	15	11	90	.978	-1
	LF	11	9	65	1.000	0
	RF	1	1	6	1.000	0
Vazquez, C	1B	9	5	47	1.000	0
	2B	1	0	1	1.000	0
Velazquez, N	LF	14	6	74	1.000	1
	CF	32	21	198	.955	-6
	RF	23	18	164	.951	-3
Verdugo, A	RF	52	51	432	.980	-5
Vientos, M	3B	2	1	13	1.000	0
Vierling, M	1B	2	0	2	1.000	0
	2B	4	2	19	1.000	1
	3B	5	5	42	.923	-1
	LF	30	15	147	1.000	0
	CF	61	50	435	1.000	-7
	RF	37	18	175	1.000	1
Villar, D	1B	11	9	69	.986	0
	2B	6	4	39	.944	0
	3B	27	25	219	.932	2
Villar, J	2B	29	27	225	.958	-7
	3B	28	23	203	.912	-3
	SS	2	2	17	.833	-2
Vogelbach, D	1B	5	0	5	.857	0
Vogt, S	1B	17	12	95	1.000	0
Voit, L	1B	37	37	306	.982	0
Vosler, J	1B	2	1	12	1.000	0
	2B	1	1	6	1.000	0
	3B	29	25	216	.984	-5
	SS	1	0	4	1.000	-1
	LF	3	2	14	1.000	-2
	RF	1	0	1	-	0
Votto, J	1B	76	76	650	.998	-2
Wade, T	2B	31	23	192	.978	-1
	3B	12	9	80	.935	-2
	SS	19	9	89	.978	0
	LF	7	2	23	1.000	-1
	CF	2	1	11	1.000	-1
	RF	5	4	36	1.000	-1
Wade Jr., L	1B	22	18	154	.982	2

All Other Fielders

Player	Pos	G	GS	Inn	Pct.	DRS
	LF	19	7	70	1.000	-2
	CF	1	0	1	1.000	0
	RF	33	28	209	1.000	-1
Walker, S	LF	4	3	29	1.000	-1
	RF	1	1	8	1.000	0
Wallner, M	RF	16	16	139	.935	-3
Walls, T	2B	35	23	209	.983	3
	3B	25	20	166	.966	5
	SS	92	79	726	.972	11
Walsh, J	LF	2	0	4	1.000	0
Walton, D	2B	14	10	96	1.000	3
	3B	1	0	1	-	0
	SS	12	10	93	.962	0
Ward, T	3B	2	0	2	-	0
	LF	2	2	12	1.000	0
	CF	7	5	50	1.000	0
Waters, D	LF	4	2	25	1.000	2
	CF	12	10	89	1.000	-4
	RF	17	16	139	1.000	0
Wendle, J	2B	33	26	225	.990	9
	3B	43	37	305	.955	-3
	SS	34	22	233	.975	6
White, E	LF	21	15	142	1.000	5
	CF	22	20	148	1.000	2
	RF	1	0	1	1.000	0
Whitefield, A	LF	1	0	1	-	0
	CF	2	2	17	1.000	0
	RF	3	0	7	1.000	0
Williams, L	1B	1	0	1	1.000	0
	2B	14	9	91	1.000	0
	3B	31	11	128	1.000	-1
	LF	26	16	155	1.000	1
Wilson, M	CF	1	0	1	-	0
	RF	2	1	9	1.000	0
Wisdom, P	1B	18	12	115	1.000	0
	LF	5	3	33	1.000	-3
	CF	2	0	7	1.000	-1
	RF	7	6	46	1.000	-1
Witt Jr., B	3B	55	50	444	.976	-4
Wolters, T	2B	1	0	1	-	0
Wong, C	2B	2	0	5	-	0
	3B	1	0	1	-	0
Wong, K	SS	1	0	1	1.000	0
Yastrzemski, M	CF	93	74	572	.994	4
	RF	104	51	556	.983	-1
Yepez, J	1B	15	8	75	1.000	0
	3B	6	3	36	1.000	0
	LF	23	21	165	.920	-4
	RF	17	15	120	1.000	0
Young, J	1B	2	2	16	1.000	0
	RF	1	0	3	-	0
Zavala, S	1B	2	0	4	1.000	1
Zimmer, B	CF	97	26	355	.982	6
	RF	2	2	15	1.000	0

All Other Catchers

Player	Tm	G	GS	Inn	PO	A	E	DP	PB	Pct.	SB Att	CS	Pit CS	CS Pct	Cat ERA	Stk Sav	GFP/ DME	SB	SZ	Other	Total
Adams, Riley	Was	44	43	367	319	15	2	1	1	.994	34	2	3	.06	4.54	-47	0	-3	-6	3	-6
Alfaro, Jorge	SD	65	59	531	544	27	2	4	7	.997	28	3	2	.11	4.12	-18	-1	-1	-2	0	-4
Allen, Austin	Oak	4	4	34	24	3	0	1	0	1.000	1	1	0	1.00	2.65	-1	1	1	0	0	2
Alvarez, Francisco	NYM	2	1	13	12	0	0	0	0	1.000	0	0	0	-	1.38	0	0	0	0	0	0
Barnes, Austin	LAD	55	55	487	521	12	4	3	2	.993	24	3	6	.13	3.20	31	2	0	4	-3	3
Barrera, Tres	Was	19	18	146	109	4	0	1	0	1.000	13	1	1	.08	5.30	-3	-1	-1	0	1	-1
Bemboom, Anthony	Bal	21	15	143	121	4	3	0	0	.977	6	1	2	.17	3.40	1	0	-1	0	1	0
Bethancourt, Christian	TOT	49	47	406	362	22	3	0	2	.992	29	12	1	.41	3.88	28	-2	4	3	-1	4
Brantly, Rob	NYY	1	1	9	9	0	0	0	0	1.000	0	0	0	-	5.00	0	0	0	0	0	0
Campusano, Luis	SD	10	9	78	81	2	1	0	1	.988	8	0	0	.00	6.35	-2	1	-1	0	-1	-1
Casali, Curt	TOT	54	49	421	399	24	3	1	1	.993	26	4	0	.15	3.42	-20	1	-1	-3	5	2
Castro, Jason	Hou	30	22	201	200	10	3	2	1	.986	16	4	0	.25	2.46	-14	-1	0	-2	0	-3
Chirinos, Robinson	Bal	66	63	528	459	21	3	3	3	.994	30	8	2	.27	4.39	-97	1	-1	-11	1	-10
Collins, Zack	TOT	13	8	76	74	7	1	0	0	.988	8	3	0	.38	3.45	-6	0	0	-1	0	-1
Contreras, William	Atl	60	57	519	559	10	8	1	3	.986	40	4	2	.10	3.52	-28	0	-1	-3	0	-4
Delay, Jason	Pit	57	49	437	393	15	9	2	0	.978	46	9	0	.20	4.60	29	0	0	3	-1	2
Diaz, Yainer	Hou	2	0	2	2	1	0	0	0	1.000	0	0	0	-	0.00	0	0	0	0	0	0
Feliciano, Mario	Mil	2	2	14	12	2	0	1	0	1.000	3	1	0	.33	2.57	1	0	0	0	0	0
Fermin, Freddy	KC	3	2	19	16	1	0	0	0	1.000	1	1	0	1.00	4.26	1	0	0	0	0	0
Fortes, Nick	Mia	59	48	441	464	19	0	3	1	1.000	34	9	1	.26	3.92	18	1	1	2	0	4
Gallagher, Cam	KC	18	14	124	108	6	1	0	1	.991	8	2	0	.25	4.14	3	-1	-1	0	0	-2
Garcia, Aramis	Cin	41	34	294	303	12	2	1	0	.994	24	6	0	.25	5.84	14	0	1	2	-3	0
Garneau, Dustin	Det	7	4	33	23	1	0	0	0	1.000	1	0	0	.00	3.55	-3	0	0	0	0	0
Garver, Mitch	Tex	14	14	124	119	4	1	0	2	.992	11	1	1	.09	4.21	-4	-1	-1	0	0	-2
Godoy, Jose	TOT	10	7	59	50	3	0	0	0	1.000	7	2	0	.29	3.94	2	0	0	0	0	0
Gomes, Yan	ChC	69	66	582	576	35	7	5	2	.989	53	16	2	.30	3.72	-3	1	3	0	1	5
Grandal, Yasmani	CWS	71	64	554	546	17	4	1	8	.993	53	7	1	.13	4.21	27	-4	-3	3	-1	-5
Greiner, Grayson	Ari	2	2	18	15	1	1	0	0	.941	1	0	0	.00	5.00	-1	0	0	0	0	0
Hamilton, Caleb	Min	11	3	38	31	0	0	0	0	1.000	6	0	0	.00	5.92	5	0	-1	1	0	0
Heineman, Tyler	TOT	59	50	436	390	29	5	2	4	.988	37	10	2	.27	4.81	31	1	1	3	0	5
Henry, Payton	Mia	15	11	90	78	8	0	0	1	1.000	7	1	2	.14	4.18	3	0	-1	0	0	-1
Herrera, Ivan	StL	11	6	59	49	8	0	0	1	1.000	1	0	0	.00	4.27	3	-1	0	0	0	-1
Herrera, Jose	Ari	46	42	347	275	18	5	1	3	.983	26	10	2	.38	4.23	-20	-1	3	-2	-1	-1
Higgins, P.J.	ChC	34	24	236	200	10	2	2	3	.991	19	3	0	.16	4.96	-18	-1	-1	-2	-2	-6
Huff, Sam	Tex	29	25	228	208	11	3	0	5	.986	26	3	1	.12	5.06	4	-1	-1	0	-1	-3
Hummel, Cooper	Ari	18	14	118	94	3	0	0	4	1.000	7	0	0	.00	4.87	-22	-2	0	-3	0	-5
Jackson, Alex	Mil	4	3	27	34	0	0	0	0	1.000	0	0	0	-	2.33	1	0	0	0	0	0
Jansen, Danny	Tor	63	58	524	501	18	7	3	1	.987	39	9	2	.23	3.74	0	2	2	0	1	5
Jeffers, Ryan	Min	59	56	496	475	14	3	2	5	.994	36	5	2	.14	3.59	28	0	-1	3	2	4
Knapp, Andrew	TOT	16	13	115	91	4	2	0	1	.979	14	2	0	.14	4.23	-17	0	0	-1	0	-1
Kolozsvary, Mark	Cin	9	6	60	53	0	0	0	2	1.000	4	0	1	.00	5.70	-2	0	0	0	0	0
Langeliers, Shea	Oak	17	14	133	126	10	1	2	0	.993	19	3	0	.16	4.93	-6	0	0	-1	0	-1
Lavastida, Bryan	Cle	6	4	36	36	1	0	0	0	1.000	2	0	0	.00	3.50	-2	0	0	0	0	0
Lee, Korey	Hou	12	7	67	73	0	1	0	2	.986	4	0	0	.00	3.63	-6	-2	-1	-1	0	-4
Leon, Sandy	TOT	33	28	231	233	5	2	0	3	.992	26	2	1	.08	3.94	8	-1	-2	1	0	-2
Maile, Luke	Cle	76	55	513	484	23	0	2	1	1.000	48	12	2	.25	3.47	-10	0	2	-1	-1	0
Mazeika, Patrick	NYM	22	18	162	159	3	1	1	1	.994	10	2	2	.20	4.23	2	1	0	0	-1	0
McCann, James	NYM	60	53	461	524	16	4	4	1	.993	34	8	0	.24	3.26	18	-2	1	2	1	2
Melendez, MJ	KC	78	65	578	467	27	5	3	6	.990	38	9	2	.24	4.81	-87	-6	-1	-10	0	-18
Mercedes, Yermin	SF	1	0	1	0	0	0	0	0	-	0	0	0	-	18.00	0	0	0	0	0	0
Moreno, Gabriel	Tor	19	17	148	134	12	2	1	0	.986	17	7	0	.41	5.79	3	1	2	0	-1	2
Murphy, Tom	Sea	12	11	91	96	2	0	0	1	1.000	4	0	0	.00	3.87	2	0	0	0	0	0
Naylor, Bo	Cle	4	0	14	15	3	0	0	0	1.000	4	1	0	.25	3.86	-1	0	0	0	0	0
Nunez, Dom	Col	14	13	108	93	5	1	0	0	.990	13	1	2	.08	5.50	-6	0	-1	-1	0	-2
O'Hoppe, Logan	LAA	5	4	39	43	1	0	0	0	1.000	3	0	0	.00	2.29	-1	-1	0	0	0	-1
O'Keefe, Brian	Sea	1	0	1	1	0	0	0	0	1.000	0	0	0	-	36.00	0	0	0	0	0	0
Okey, Chris	Cin	7	3	34	30	0	1	0	1	.968	6	0	1	.00	5.08	-2	0	-1	0	0	-1
Papierski, Michael	TOT	38	30	277	268	15	1	1	2	.996	38	3	2	.08	4.72	-3	0	-1	-1	1	-1
Perez, Carlos	CWS	6	5	46	50	2	1	0	1	.981	3	0	0	.00	4.30	-2	-1	-1	0	0	-2
Perez, Michael	TOT	44	38	332	294	16	1	1	2	.997	23	6	2	.26	4.88	-15	2	0	-2	0	0
Perez, Roberto	Pit	20	19	159	163	4	1	0	1	.994	7	1	2	.14	4.19	9	1	0	1	1	3
Pina, Manny	Atl	5	5	44	50	2	0	0	1	1.000	1	0	1	.00	5.11	-2	0	0	0	0	0
Pineda, Israel	Was	4	4	34	26	3	0	0	2	1.000	3	1	0	.33	6.09	-1	-1	0	0	0	0
Pinto, Rene	TB	25	23	203	215	3	3	0	1	.986	13	0	1	.00	3.95	11	0	-1	1	0	0
Plawecki, Kevin	TOT	61	49	447	416	14	1	1	1	.998	49	3	2	.06	4.41	-8	-2	-5	-1	-2	-10
Proctor, Ford	SF	1	0	1	1	0	0	0	0	1.000	0	0	0	-	9.00	0	0	0	0	0	0
Rivero, Sebastian	KC	17	7	73	70	2	0	0	0	1.000	5	1	0	.20	5.67	4	1	-1	1	0	1
Robinson, Chuckie	Cin	25	20	169	140	5	1	0	1	.993	17	3	0	.18	4.15	1	0	-1	0	0	0
Romine, Austin	TOT	50	39	350	372	17	1	2	1	.997	37	4	2	.11	4.40	-12	1	-1	-1	0	-1
Sands, Donny	Phi	1	0	2	1	0	0	0	0	1.000	0	0	0	-	4.50	0	0	0	0	0	0
Serven, Brian	Col	59	55	484	415	26	5	2	2	.989	51	10	0	.20	4.85	40	0	-1	5	1	5
Severino, Pedro	Mil	4	4	33	38	3	0	1	2	1.000	3	1	1	.33	4.86	0	0	0	0	0	0
Stephenson, Tyler	Cin	45	43	352	385	16	0	1	0	1.000	36	9	1	.25	4.89	-16	0	0	-2	-1	-3
Stubbs, Garrett	Phi	41	32	295	285	10	3	1	3	.990	24	6	1	.25	4.28	-23	0	-1	-3	1	-3
Suzuki, Kurt	LAA	44	42	351	341	10	1	1	2	.997	39	4	3	.10	4.13	-37	0	-2	-4	-1	-7
Thaiss, Matt	LAA	14	11	99	96	3	0	0	0	1.000	6	1	2	.17	5.00	-3	-1	0	0	0	-1
Torrens, Luis	Sea	42	35	304	271	16	1	1	0	.997	26	7	2	.27	4.20	-28	0	1	-3	-1	-3
Tromp, Chadwick	Atl	1	1	9	6	0	1	0	0	.857	1	0	0	.00	2.00	0	0	0	0	0	0
VanMeter, Josh	Pit	1	0	1	1	0	0	0	0	1.000	0	0	0	-	27.00	0	0	0	0	0	0

Player	Tm	G	GS	Inn	PO	A	E	DP	PB	Pct.	SB Att	CS	Pit CS	CS Pct	Cat ERA	Stk Sav	Runs Saved GFP/ DME	SB	SZ	Other	Total
Varsho, Daulton	Ari	31	18	175	140	10	3	2	3	.980	18	6	0	.33	5.71	-15	-1	1	-2	-1	-3
Viloria, Meibrys	Tex	20	18	157	151	10	5	0	1	.970	15	7	0	.47	4.60	7	-1	3	1	0	3
Vogt, Stephen	Oak	19	16	144	115	8	1	2	0	.992	15	2	1	.13	3.75	-11	-1	0	-1	0	-2
Wallach, Chad	LAA	12	10	93	80	3	0	0	0	1.000	9	1	0	.11	3.39	2	0	0	0	0	0
Wolters, Tony	LAD	1	1	8	5	1	0	0	0	1.000	1	0	0	.00	4.50	0	0	0	0	0	0
Wong, Connor	Bos	20	17	138	129	7	2	0	1	.986	21	3	0	.14	3.72	-2	-1	-1	0	0	-2
Wynns, Austin	SF	57	43	391	423	19	6	0	2	.987	24	3	2	.13	3.76	2	1	-1	0	-1	-1
Zavala, Seby	CWS	58	49	449	474	24	2	5	4	.996	29	7	0	.24	4.01	40	0	0	5	-2	3
Zunino, Mike	TB	35	34	299	283	9	1	0	2	.997	19	3	1	.16	3.16	18	-3	-1	2	0	-2

Strike Zone Runs Saved

Mark Simon

We often hear that one of the challenges for a catcher is learning his pitching staff. It's difficult, and you can imagine that for someone traded to a team a week before the season starts or a rookie called up 40 games into the season, it's even more difficult.

That's why Jose Trevino of the Yankees and Adley Rutschman of the Orioles deserve considerable props for finishing 1-2 in Defensive Runs Saved among catchers in 2022.

The key to that was a steady hand. They were the top two catchers in our pitch-framing stat, Strike Zone Runs Saved.

Trevino's acquisition in a series of moves by the Yankees changed the look of their defense. The team finished with the most Defensive Runs Saved in a season in the 20-year history of the stat. That came one year after they finished 29th in Runs Saved.

Trevino excelled at catching the pitch at or just below the bottom of the strike zone. He made sure that he got calls with an approach in which he brought his glove down just above the dirt and then caught the pitches with his glove hand moving up. As such, his 12 Strike Zone Runs Saved in 2022 were the second most by any catcher in the last five seasons.

Rutschman validated every expectation that the Orioles had for him in his debut season, both at the plate and in the field. He was not only one of the game's best pitch framers, but one of its best pitch blockers as well.

The impact Rutschman made was evident in basic numbers for the Orioles pitching staff. Orioles pitchers had a 3.2-to-1 strikeout-to-walk ratio when Rutschman caught and a 2.4-to-1 ratio when anyone else caught. If Rutschman was this good in his debut season, learning the major leagues as he went, we can only imagine how good he'll be once he's fully entrenched.

2022 Catcher Strike Zone Runs Saved Leaders

Catcher	Called Pitches	Called Strikes			Runs Saved	
		Actual	Expected	Extra	Per 1,000 Called Pitches	Total
Trevino, Jose	6897	2284	2180	104	1.74	12
Rutschman, Adley	6252	2025	1945	80	1.44	9
Raleigh, Cal	7185	2235	2167	68	1.11	8
Nido, Tomas	6309	2061	2004	57	1.11	7
d'Arnaud, Travis	7369	2370	2317	53	0.81	6
Murphy, Sean	8643	2672	2628	44	0.58	5
Heim, Jonah	7797	2417	2374	43	0.64	5
Kirk, Alejandro	5202	1775	1733	42	0.96	5
Serven, Brian	4171	1287	1247	40	1.20	5
Zavala, Seby	3979	1246	1206	40	1.26	5
Caratini, Victor	6360	2064	2033	31	0.63	4
Barnes, Austin	3707	1256	1225	31	1.08	4
Heineman, Tyler	3914	1206	1175	31	0.77	3
Vazquez, Christian	7482	2401	2372	29	0.40	3
Delay, Jason	3964	1246	1217	29	0.76	3
Jeffers, Ryan	4099	1303	1275	28	0.73	3
Bethancourt, Christian	3349	1033	1005	28	0.90	3
Stassi, Max	6878	2101	2073	28	0.44	3
Higashioka, Kyle	5142	1631	1603	28	0.58	3
Hedges, Austin	6447	2074	2046	28	0.47	3
Grandal, Yasmani	4686	1388	1361	27	0.64	3
Narvaez, Omar	6237	2060	2034	26	0.48	3
Molina, Yadier	5388	1788	1766	22	0.56	3
McCann, James	3795	1201	1183	18	0.53	2
Zunino, Mike	2285	751	733	18	0.88	2
Fortes, Nick	3943	1297	1279	18	0.51	2
Sanchez, Gary	6059	1934	1917	17	0.33	2
McGuire, Reese	5730	1763	1748	15	0.35	2
Smith, Will	7572	2459	2445	14	0.26	2
Realmuto, J.T.	9633	3074	3063	11	0.10	1
Maldonado, Martin	7672	2406	2397	9	0.13	1
Wynns, Austin	3473	1159	1157	2	0.00	0
Jansen, Danny	4226	1345	1345	0	0.00	0
Gomes, Yan	5110	1617	1620	-3	0.00	0
Plawecki, Kevin	3735	1228	1236	-8	-0.27	-1
Stallings, Jacob	7453	2339	2347	-8	-0.13	-1
Maile, Luke	4147	1201	1211	-10	-0.24	-1
Romine, Austin	3170	955	967	-12	-0.32	-1
Mejia, Francisco	5088	1688	1700	-12	-0.20	-1
Perez, Michael	3048	904	919	-15	-0.66	-2
Stephenson, Tyler	3341	1036	1052	-16	-0.60	-2
Ruiz, Keibert	7976	2430	2448	-18	-0.25	-2
Alfaro, Jorge	4580	1446	1464	-18	-0.44	-2
Herrera, Jose	3078	966	986	-20	-0.65	-2
Casali, Curt	3344	1113	1133	-20	-0.90	-3
Contreras, Willson	5541	1722	1744	-22	-0.54	-3
Torrens, Luis	2514	689	717	-28	-1.19	-3
Contreras, William	4355	1319	1347	-28	-0.69	-3
Kelly, Carson	6515	2113	2143	-30	-0.61	-4
Suzuki, Kurt	3069	933	970	-37	-1.30	-4
Barnhart, Tucker	6745	2060	2099	-39	-0.74	-5
Bart, Joey	6069	1970	2009	-39	-0.82	-5
Haase, Eric	5177	1543	1587	-44	-0.97	-5
Adams, Riley	3210	997	1044	-47	-1.87	-6
Nola, Austin	7081	2313	2372	-59	-0.99	-7
Perez, Salvador	5774	1740	1805	-65	-1.39	-8
Knizner, Andrew	6067	1883	1957	-74	-1.48	-9
Melendez, MJ	5322	1571	1658	-87	-1.88	-10
Chirinos, Robinson	4482	1333	1430	-97	-2.45	-11
Diaz, Elias	7509	2199	2308	-109	-1.73	-13

Pitchers Fielding & Holding Runners, and Hitters Pitching

Brian Reiff

You'd be forgiven for not knowing the rule. Heck, even Dodgers manager Dave Roberts didn't.

Prior to the 2020 MLB season, MLB and the MLB Players Association agreed on new rules regarding who is allowed to pitch in games. Teams would have to designate certain players on their teams as pitchers or position players prior to their debut each season, and as long as neither team is leading by more than five runs, only players designated as pitchers would be able to pitch during the regularly scheduled innings of a game.

Of course, something happened just before the season started that threw everything into chaos. *Gestures vaguely at ongoing global pandemic*

That rule, though, was finally implemented this year, and when Roberts attempted to bring in a position player to pitch in a June game with his team only up five runs, he was prevented from doing so by the umpires.

All that said, you'd probably expect to have seen a decline in position players pitching this season. And you'd be wrong.

In 2022, 65 different position players pitched in a game. Those players combined for 132⅓ innings pitched over 132 games. All of those are the highest in at least the last 21 years. (SIS began collecting data in 2002.)

If you're wondering, "Why the increase?", the answer is likely because of the other rule that went into effect this year. As mentioned above, teams had to designate everyone on the roster as either a pitcher or a position player. Starting June 20, teams were restricted to only carrying 13 pitchers on their roster at any one time. With fewer arms available out of the bullpen, teams seemed to become more willing to put a position player on the mound whenever the opportunity arose.

While no position player hit the 20-inning threshold—which would have qualified them for two-way player status and made them eligible to pitch in any game next season—there was still plenty to note.

Dodgers utility infielder Hanser Alberto led all other players with 11 innings pitched in 10 games. He was reasonably effective as well, pitching to a 4.09 ERA compared to an overall position player average of 10.00.

Christian Bethancourt, meanwhile, made his long-awaited return to the majors this year—long-awaited, that is, by two-way player enthusiasts. In 2017, Bethancourt played in 44 games as a hitter and 34 as a pitcher for the Padres' Triple-A affiliate. Five years later, he only managed to make a pitching appearance in four games across stints for A's and Rays, but made the most of them allowing only one run in four innings.

This section also includes stats on pitchers fielding and holding runners, something that is likely more of a focus now that they no longer have responsibilities at the plate.

The Phillies' Ranger Suárez led pitchers in Defensive Runs Saved with nine. He was above average fielding balls in play, as he's been throughout his career, and the only two baserunners who attempted a stolen base against him were both thrown out.

Taijuan Walker of the Mets finished a close second behind Suárez with six runs saved. Walker similarly excelled at limiting baserunning, allowing just eight stolen bases and picking off an MLB-leading five baserunners.

On the other side of the leaderboard, Angels and Phillies pitcher Noah Syndergaard cost his teams six runs with his defense, including four in the realm of holding baserunners. The 30 stolen bases he allowed were the most in MLB, although that total was an improvement by his standards. Syndergaard has now allowed the most stolen bases in MLB in four of the past seven seasons, having allowed 42, 32 and 48 in 2019, 2018 and 2016, respectively.

Pitchers Fielding and Holding Runners

	2022 Fielding and Holding Runners											
Pitcher	Inn	PO	A	E	DP	Pct	SBA	CS	PCS	PPO	CS%	RS
Abbott, Cory	48.0	2	1	0	0	1.000	5	1	0	0	.20	0
Abreu, Albert	38.2	2	5	2	1	.778	3	2	0	1	.67	0
Abreu, Bryan	60.1	2	6	0	0	1.000	8	1	0	0	.13	0
Acevedo, D.	67.2	3	3	3	0	.667	4	0	0	1	.00	-1
Adam, Jason	63.1	1	2	0	0	1.000	12	0	0	0	.00	-3
Adams, Austin L	2.1	1	0	0	0	1.000	0	0	0	0	-	0
Adon, Joan	64.2	8	7	2	0	.882	4	1	0	0	.25	0
Akin, Keegan	81.2	3	11	0	2	1.000	2	2	0	0	1.00	0
Alcala, Jorge	2.1	0	0	0	0	-	0	0	0	0	-	0
Alcantara, Sandy	228.2	20	28	0	2	1.000	28	4	1	2	.14	-2
Alexander, Jason	71.2	2	14	1	2	.941	7	4	0	0	.57	0
Alexander, Scott	17.1	2	5	0	1	1.000	0	0	0	0	-	1
Alexander, Tyler	101.0	2	7	1	0	.900	10	3	1	0	.30	0
Alexy, A.J.	7.0	0	1	1	0	.500	0	0	0	0	-	-1
Allard, Kolby	21.0	1	2	0	0	1.000	1	1	0	0	1.00	0
Alldred, Cam	1.0	0	0	0	0	-	0	0	0	0	-	0
Allen, Logan	7.2	0	2	0	0	1.000	0	0	0	0	-	0
Almonte, Yency	35.1	4	3	1	0	.875	2	0	0	0	.00	-1
Alvarado, Jose	51.0	3	6	0	1	1.000	7	1	1	0	.14	0
Alvarez, Jose	15.1	1	2	0	0	1.000	0	0	0	0	-	0
Alvarez, R.J.	2.1	1	0	0	0	1.000	0	0	0	0	-	0
Alzolay, Adbert	13.1	1	2	0	0	1.000	0	0	0	0	-	1
Anderson, Chase	24.0	0	2	0	0	1.000	4	2	0	0	.50	0
Anderson, Ian	111.2	8	10	0	0	1.000	7	3	1	0	.43	2
Anderson, Shaun	1.0	0	0	0	0	-	0	0	0	0	-	0
Anderson, Tyler	178.2	13	31	3	2	.936	5	1	1	0	.20	5
Appel, Mark	10.1	0	0	0	0	-	1	1	0	0	1.00	-1
Arano, Victor	42.0	0	2	1	0	.667	7	2	1	0	.29	-2
Archer, Chris	102.2	2	6	0	1	1.000	4	1	0	0	.25	-1
Arihara, Kohei	20.0	1	1	0	0	1.000	1	0	0	0	.00	0
Armstrong, Shawn	61.2	0	5	0	0	1.000	5	1	0	0	.20	0
Ashby, Aaron	107.1	6	8	0	0	1.000	7	0	0	0	.00	-3
Ashcraft, Graham	105.0	17	11	0	1	1.000	7	1	0	0	.14	0
Assad, Javier	37.2	3	3	0	0	1.000	7	2	1	0	.29	0
Avila, Pedro	4.0	1	0	0	0	1.000	0	0	0	0	-	0
Baez, Michel	2.0	0	0	0	0	-	0	0	0	0	-	0
Baez, Pedro	2.1	0	0	0	0	-	0	0	0	0	-	0
Baker, Bryan	69.2	2	4	0	0	1.000	2	0	0	1	.00	-1
Banda, Anthony	26.2	1	1	0	0	1.000	4	1	0	0	.25	-1
Banks, Tanner	53.0	2	5	0	0	1.000	3	3	1	0	1.00	1
Banuelos, Manny	41.0	2	12	0	1	1.000	6	1	1	0	.17	3
Bard, Daniel	60.1	2	6	0	0	1.000	5	0	0	0	.00	-2
Bard, Luke	15.0	1	3	0	0	1.000	10	1	0	0	.10	0
Barker, Luke	4.0	1	1	0	0	1.000	0	0	0	0	-	0
Barlow, Joe	35.0	1	2	0	0	1.000	2	1	0	0	.50	0
Barlow, Scott	74.1	7	2	0	0	1.000	5	1	0	0	.20	1
Barnes, Jacob	22.1	1	5	0	1	1.000	1	0	0	0	.00	1
Barnes, Matt	39.2	2	2	0	0	1.000	5	0	0	0	.00	-2
Barraclough, Kyle	9.0	1	1	0	0	1.000	2	1	0	0	.50	0
Barria, Jaime	79.1	3	10	0	1	1.000	2	0	0	1	.00	1
Bass, Anthony	70.1	6	7	2	1	.867	6	3	0	0	.50	1
Bassitt, Chris	181.2	16	16	0	3	1.000	10	3	0	1	.30	2
Baumann, Mike	34.1	2	4	1	0	.857	4	3	0	0	.75	1
Bautista, Felix	65.2	4	4	0	0	1.000	8	2	0	0	.25	0
Baz, Shane	27.0	3	0	0	0	1.000	1	0	0	0	.00	0
Bazardo, Eduard	16.1	2	3	0	0	1.000	2	1	0	1	.50	0
Beasley, Jeremy	15.0	2	1	0	0	1.000	2	2	1	0	1.00	0
Bednar, David	51.2	0	2	0	1	1.000	4	0	0	0	.00	-1
Beede, Tyler	61.1	3	4	0	0	1.000	9	2	0	0	.22	-2
Beeks, Jalen	61.0	1	7	0	0	1.000	0	0	0	0	-	0
Bellatti, Andrew	54.1	1	3	0	0	1.000	5	2	1	1	.40	1
Bello, Brayan	57.1	5	3	0	2	1.000	7	1	0	0	.14	-2
Bender, Anthony	19.1	3	1	0	0	1.000	2	0	0	1	.00	-1
Bernardino, B.	2.1	0	1	1	0	.500	0	0	0	0	-	-1
Berrios, Jose	172.0	6	16	1	1	.957	11	5	1	2	.45	1
Bickford, Phil	61.0	1	3	0	0	1.000	9	2	1	0	.22	-1
Bieber, Shane	200.0	15	16	1	1	.969	13	4	1	0	.31	3
Bielak, Brandon	12.1	0	0	0	0	-	0	0	0	0	-	0
Bird, Jake	47.2	2	5	0	0	1.000	4	0	0	0	.00	0
Blach, Ty	44.1	5	3	0	0	1.000	0	0	0	0	-	1
Blackburn, Paul	111.1	9	12	0	2	1.000	15	2	1	0	.13	-1

	2022 Fielding and Holding Runners											
Pitcher	Inn	PO	A	E	DP	Pct	SBA	CS	PCS	PPO	CS%	RS
Blanco, Ronel	6.1	1	0	0	0	1.000	0	0	0	0	-	0
Bleier, Richard	50.2	6	7	0	0	1.000	4	1	1	1	.25	1
Bolanos, Ronald	18.1	2	3	0	0	1.000	2	2	0	0	1.00	2
Borucki, Ryan	25.1	0	5	0	0	1.000	4	1	1	0	.25	0
Boxberger, Brad	64.0	3	2	1	0	.833	7	0	0	0	.00	-2
Boyd, Matthew	13.1	2	2	0	0	1.000	1	0	0	0	.00	0
Bracho, Silvino	4.1	0	1	0	0	1.000	0	0	0	0	-	0
Bradish, Kyle	117.2	7	10	0	0	1.000	1	0	0	0	.00	0
Bradley, Archie	18.2	0	0	0	0	-	4	0	0	0	.00	-2
Brash, Matt	50.2	3	5	1	1	.889	3	3	0	0	1.00	1
Brasier, Ryan	62.1	0	6	1	1	.857	7	0	0	1	.00	-1
Brault, Steven	9.0	0	0	0	0	-	1	0	0	0	.00	0
Brazoban, H.	32.0	2	4	1	0	.857	4	2	0	0	.50	0
Brebbia, John	68.0	4	10	0	0	1.000	8	4	0	0	.50	2
Brentz, Jake	5.1	0	0	0	0	-	0	0	0	0	-	0
Brice, Austin	6.2	0	1	0	0	1.000	0	0	0	0	-	0
Brieske, Beau	81.2	5	11	2	1	.889	4	2	1	0	.50	3
Brigham, Jeff	24.0	2	2	0	0	1.000	6	1	0	0	.17	-1
Britton, Zack	0.2	0	0	0	0	-	0	0	0	0	-	0
Brogdon, Connor	44.0	2	1	0	0	1.000	3	1	0	0	.33	0
Brooks, Aaron	9.1	0	2	0	0	1.000	1	0	0	0	.00	0
Brown, Hunter	20.1	1	2	0	0	1.000	2	1	0	0	.50	0
Brubaker, JT	144.0	5	14	3	2	.864	8	3	2	0	.38	2
Bruihl, Justin	23.2	2	4	1	0	.857	2	1	1	0	.50	-1
Bubic, Kris	129.0	5	14	2	1	.905	6	2	0	0	.33	0
Buehler, Walker	65.0	5	6	0	0	1.000	8	2	0	0	.25	1
Bumgarner, M.	158.2	2	11	0	3	1.000	20	5	2	0	.25	-2
Bummer, Aaron	26.2	0	2	0	0	1.000	3	1	1	0	.33	-1
Bundy, Dylan	140.0	4	6	0	0	1.000	10	1	0	0	.10	-3
Burke, Brock	82.1	2	8	0	2	1.000	4	2	0	0	.50	0
Burnes, Corbin	202.0	32	17	2	3	.961	9	4	1	1	.44	4
Burr, Ryan	9.0	1	0	1	0	.500	1	0	0	0	.00	-1
Bush, Matt	59.2	5	6	2	1	.846	5	0	0	1	.00	0
Butto, Jose	4.0	0	0	0	0	-	1	0	0	0	.00	0
Cabrera, Edward	71.2	6	4	0	2	1.000	5	1	0	0	.20	-1
Cabrera, Genesis	44.2	3	11	0	0	1.000	2	1	1	0	.50	2
Cano, Yennier	18.0	2	3	0	0	1.000	1	0	0	0	.00	0
Carlton, Drew	8.2	0	0	0	0	-	0	0	0	0	-	0
Carrasco, Carlos	152.0	15	18	1	3	.971	9	1	0	1	.11	2
Castano, Daniel	35.2	3	3	0	0	1.000	1	1	0	0	1.00	0
Castellani, Ryan	2.2	0	0	0	0	-	0	0	0	0	-	0
Castellanos, H.	44.1	2	0	0	1	1.000	1	0	0	0	.00	0
Castillo, Diego	54.1	7	4	1	0	.917	11	1	0	0	.09	-2
Castillo, Jose	1.0	0	0	0	0	-	0	0	0	0	-	0
Castillo, Luis	3.2	0	0	0	0	-	0	0	0	0	-	0
Castillo, Luis	150.1	11	7	0	0	1.000	12	1	0	1	.08	-3
Castillo, Max	39.1	1	2	0	0	1.000	4	1	0	0	.25	-1
Castro, Anthony	13.1	0	2	0	0	1.000	3	1	0	0	.33	0
Castro, Kervin	12.1	0	1	1	0	.500	1	0	0	0	.00	0
Castro, Miguel	29.0	0	3	0	0	1.000	5	2	0	0	.40	-1
Cavalli, Cade	4.1	1	0	0	0	1.000	1	1	0	0	1.00	0
Cease, Dylan	184.0	2	8	2	0	.833	15	5	0	1	.33	-2
Cessa, Luis	80.2	9	11	1	2	.952	7	1	0	0	.14	0
Chacin, Jhoulys	47.1	1	8	0	3	1.000	1	0	0	0	.00	2
Chafin, Andrew	57.1	5	5	2	1	.833	3	1	1	0	.33	-2
Chapman, Aroldis	36.1	2	6	0	0	1.000	5	3	3	1	.60	3
Chargois, JT	22.1	1	3	0	0	1.000	1	0	0	0	.00	0
Chavez, Jesse	69.1	2	5	0	0	1.000	4	1	0	0	.25	1
Chirinos, Yonny	7.0	0	0	0	0	-	0	0	0	0	-	0
Cimber, Adam	70.2	2	11	1	1	.929	7	0	0	0	.00	-2
Cishek, Steve	66.1	2	2	0	0	1.000	5	2	0	0	.40	-1
Cisneros, Jose	25.0	0	2	0	0	1.000	0	0	0	1	-	0
Civale, Aaron	97.0	11	5	2	0	.889	9	1	0	1	.11	-1
Clarke, Taylor	49.0	5	3	0	0	1.000	1	0	0	1	.00	0
Clase, Emmanuel	72.2	7	6	0	1	1.000	4	0	0	0	.00	-2
Claudio, Alex	3.1	0	0	0	0	-	0	0	0	0	-	0
Clay, Sam	5.1	0	1	0	0	1.000	0	0	0	0	-	0
Cleavinger, Garret	23.0	0	1	0	0	1.000	0	0	0	0	-	0
Clevinger, Mike	114.1	6	8	3	0	.824	14	1	0	0	.07	-2
Clippard, Tyler	5.0	0	0	0	0	-	1	0	0	0	.00	0
Cobb, Alex	149.2	19	27	0	4	1.000	17	2	1	0	.12	3

2022 Fielding and Holding Runners

Pitcher	Inn	PO	A	E	DP	Pct	SBA	CS	PCS	PPO	CS%	RS
Cole, Gerrit	200.2	12	16	0	0	1.000	16	5	1	0	.31	1
Coleman, Dylan	68.0	3	3	3	0	.667	5	3	0	0	.60	-1
Colome, Alex	47.0	3	5	0	0	1.000	8	1	0	0	.13	-2
Contreras, Roansy	95.0	5	4	0	0	1.000	10	3	0	0	.30	0
Coonrod, Sam	12.2	1	0	1	0	.500	0	0	0	0	-	0
Corbin, Patrick	152.2	9	17	0	0	1.000	19	5	3	0	.26	-1
Cortes, Nestor	158.1	5	8	1	0	.929	5	2	1	1	.40	1
Cotton, Jharel	43.0	2	2	0	0	1.000	6	1	0	0	.17	-1
Coulombe, Danny	12.1	1	1	0	0	1.000	3	0	0	0	.00	0
Cousins, Jake	13.1	2	1	0	0	1.000	1	0	0	0	.00	0
Crawford, Kutter	77.1	7	4	3	2	.786	9	4	0	0	.44	-1
Crick, Kyle	15.2	1	4	1	1	.833	2	2	1	0	1.00	2
Crismatt, Nabil	67.1	4	5	0	1	1.000	9	0	0	0	.00	-1
Criswell, Cooper	3.1	0	0	0	0	-	0	0	0	0	-	0
Crowe, Wil	76.0	5	6	2	1	.846	0	0	0	0	-	0
Cruz, Fernando	14.2	0	1	0	0	1.000	2	0	0	0	.00	-1
Cruz, Jesus	8.2	1	0	0	0	1.000	1	0	0	0	.00	0
Cuas, Jose	37.2	0	8	0	0	1.000	4	1	0	0	.25	1
Cueto, Johnny	158.1	11	15	1	2	.963	6	2	0	1	.33	1
Curry, Xzavion	9.1	1	1	0	0	1.000	1	1	0	0	1.00	0
Cyr, Tyler	13.1	1	1	0	0	1.000	1	0	0	0	.00	0
Danish, Tyler	40.1	2	4	0	0	1.000	2	0	0	1	.00	0
Darvish, Yu	194.2	15	5	1	0	.952	16	2	0	0	.13	-2
Davidson, Tucker	52.0	2	5	0	0	1.000	4	1	1	0	.25	-1
Davies, Zach	134.1	17	16	1	1	.971	12	5	2	1	.42	4
Davis, Austin	56.0	1	5	1	0	.857	4	0	0	0	.00	-1
Davis, Noah	1.0	0	0	0	0	-	0	0	0	0	-	0
De Jesus, Angel	12.2	1	2	0	0	1.000	0	0	0	0	-	0
De Jong, Chase	71.2	3	4	1	0	.875	5	2	0	0	.40	0
De Los Santos, E.	53.1	3	4	1	0	.875	4	0	0	0	.00	-1
De Los Santos, Y.	25.2	0	4	0	0	1.000	5	1	0	0	.20	1
deGrom, Jacob	64.1	5	1	0	0	1.000	3	0	0	0	.00	0
Dermody, Matt	1.0	0	0	0	0	-	0	0	0	0	-	0
DeSclafani, A.	19.0	1	0	0	0	1.000	1	1	0	0	1.00	-1
Detmers, Reid	129.0	2	12	2	0	.875	17	4	2	0	.24	-1
Detwiler, Ross	26.1	1	0	0	0	1.000	0	0	0	0	-	0
Devenski, Chris	14.2	0	0	0	0	-	4	0	0	0	.00	-1
Diaz, Alexis	63.2	2	6	1	1	.889	8	0	0	0	.00	0
Diaz, Edwin	62.0	4	1	1	0	.833	11	2	0	0	.18	-3
Diaz, Jhonathan	15.1	0	0	0	0	-	1	0	0	0	.00	0
Diaz, Miguel	3.2	0	0	0	0	-	1	0	0	0	.00	0
Diehl, Phillip	5.2	0	0	0	0	-	0	0	0	0	-	0
Diekman, Jake	57.2	3	4	0	0	1.000	8	2	0	0	.25	0
Diplan, Marcos	5.2	1	0	0	0	1.000	0	0	0	0	-	0
Dominguez, S.	51.0	5	0	0	0	1.000	4	1	0	0	.25	-1
Doolittle, Sean	5.1	0	0	0	0	-	0	0	0	0	-	0
Doval, Camilo	67.2	9	8	1	0	.944	3	1	0	0	.33	-2
Dowdy, Kyle	6.1	0	2	0	0	1.000	0	0	0	0	-	0
Duarte, Daniel	2.2	0	0	0	0	-	0	0	0	0	-	0
Duffey, Tyler	44.0	2	3	0	0	1.000	2	1	0	0	.50	0
Dugger, Robert	16.0	1	0	0	0	1.000	3	1	0	0	.33	0
Dunn, Justin	31.0	1	3	0	0	1.000	7	2	1	0	.29	-1
Dunning, Dane	153.1	5	14	1	1	.950	12	5	0	0	.42	-1
Duran, Jhoan	67.2	1	6	1	1	.875	6	2	0	0	.33	-1
Duron, Nick	1.0	0	0	0	0	-	0	0	0	0	-	0
Edwards Jr., Carl	62.0	5	6	0	0	1.000	4	3	0	1	.75	1
Effross, Scott	56.2	0	6	0	0	1.000	4	2	0	0	.50	-1
Eflin, Zach	75.2	3	13	0	0	1.000	2	0	0	0	.00	3
Eickhoff, Jerad	4.1	1	1	0	0	1.000	0	0	0	0	-	0
Elder, Bryce	54.0	3	4	0	1	1.000	7	1	0	0	.14	-1
Elias, Roenis	7.2	0	2	0	0	1.000	0	0	0	0	-	0
Ellis, Chris	4.1	1	0	0	0	1.000	2	0	0	0	.00	0
Eovaldi, Nathan	109.1	12	7	1	2	.950	6	1	0	0	.17	-1
Erlin, Robbie	2.0	0	0	0	0	-	0	0	0	0	-	0
Espinal, Raynel	4.2	0	1	0	0	1.000	0	0	0	0	-	0
Espino, Paolo	113.1	15	13	2	0	.933	3	2	0	0	.67	1
Espinoza, A.	18.1	0	0	0	0	-	1	0	0	0	.00	-1
Estevez, Carlos	57.0	6	5	0	1	1.000	0	0	0	0	-	1
Estrada, Jeremiah	5.2	1	0	0	0	1.000	1	0	0	0	.00	0
Faedo, Alex	53.2	3	2	0	0	1.000	10	3	0	0	.30	0
Fairbanks, Pete	24.0	7	1	0	0	1.000	3	0	0	0	.00	0
Falter, Bailey	84.0	4	4	0	0	1.000	7	4	2	0	.57	0
Familia, Jeurys	44.1	3	1	2	0	.667	5	3	0	0	.60	0
Farmer, Buck	47.0	6	6	1	0	.923	6	3	1	0	.50	0
Farrell, Luke	15.0	0	1	0	0	1.000	1	0	0	0	.00	0
Faucher, Calvin	21.1	0	1	0	0	1.000	4	0	0	0	.00	-1
Fedde, Erick	127.0	14	11	0	1	1.000	19	2	0	0	.11	-2
Feliz, Michael	3.1	1	0	0	0	1.000	2	0	0	0	.00	0
Feltner, Ryan	97.1	8	7	0	0	1.000	11	1	0	0	.09	-1
Ferguson, Caleb	34.2	0	2	0	0	1.000	2	1	1	0	.50	0
Fernandez, Junior	18.2	0	1	0	0	1.000	0	0	0	0	-	0
Festa, Matthew	54.0	5	5	0	1	1.000	6	1	0	0	.17	-1
Feyereisen, J.P.	24.1	1	0	0	0	1.000	0	0	0	0	-	0
Finnegan, Kyle	66.2	3	9	0	0	1.000	4	0	0	0	.00	2
Fisher, Nate	3.0	0	1	0	0	1.000	1	1	1	0	1.00	0
Fishman, Jake	11.0	0	1	0	0	1.000	0	0	0	0	-	0
Flaherty, Jack	36.0	3	3	2	0	.750	1	0	0	0	.00	-1
Fleming, Josh	35.0	4	3	1	1	.875	2	2	0	0	1.00	-1
Fletcher, Aaron	11.2	0	1	0	0	1.000	0	0	0	0	-	0
Flexen, Chris	137.2	9	9	1	1	.947	6	0	0	0	.00	-2
Floro, Dylan	53.2	0	4	0	0	1.000	1	0	0	0	.00	1
Foley, Jason	60.1	2	8	0	1	1.000	8	3	0	0	.38	0
Foster, Matt	45.0	1	1	0	0	1.000	3	0	0	0	.00	0
Francis, Bowden	0.2	0	0	0	0	-	0	0	0	0	-	0
Freeland, Kyle	174.2	2	14	0	0	1.000	21	6	0	1	.29	0
Frias, Luis	17.0	0	0	0	0	-	0	0	0	0	-	0
Fried, Max	185.1	15	26	1	0	.976	7	4	2	1	.57	3
Fry, Paul	13.0	1	1	0	0	1.000	1	0	0	0	.00	0
Fulmer, Michael	63.2	1	5	0	0	1.000	7	1	1	0	.14	0
Gaddis, Hunter	7.1	0	2	0	0	1.000	0	0	0	0	-	1
Gage, Matt	13.0	0	0	0	0	-	0	0	0	0	-	0
Gallegos, G.	59.0	3	6	0	0	1.000	3	0	0	0	.00	1
Gallen, Zac	184.0	10	16	1	3	.963	9	3	0	0	.33	2
Garcia, Bryan	20.1	0	1	0	0	1.000	1	1	0	0	1.00	0
Garcia, Jarlin	65.0	1	3	0	0	1.000	3	0	0	0	.00	-1
Garcia, Luis	61.0	2	5	4	2	.636	6	0	0	0	.00	-3
Garcia, Luis	157.1	4	8	1	2	.923	5	0	0	0	.00	-1
Garcia, Rico	8.0	0	0	0	0	-	1	0	0	0	.00	-1
Garcia, Rony	51.0	0	3	0	0	1.000	4	1	0	0	.25	0
Garcia, Yimi	61.0	0	5	0	0	1.000	6	1	0	0	.17	-2
Garrett, Amir	45.1	1	2	0	0	1.000	6	0	0	0	.00	-1
Garrett, Braxton	88.0	6	11	1	1	.944	13	3	0	0	.23	1
Garrett, Reed	9.1	0	0	1	0	.000	1	1	0	0	1.00	0
Garza, Ralph	35.0	1	3	0	0	1.000	0	0	0	0	-	0
Gausman, Kevin	174.2	3	12	1	0	.938	22	4	0	1	.18	-1
German, Domingo	72.1	5	1	1	0	.857	1	0	0	0	.00	-2
German, Frank	4.0	1	0	0	0	1.000	0	0	0	0	-	0
Gibaut, Ian	36.0	2	1	0	0	1.000	3	1	0	0	.33	0
Gibson, Kyle	167.2	12	17	1	1	.967	6	3	0	2	.50	2
Gil, Luis	4.0	0	1	0	0	1.000	0	0	0	1	-	0
Gilbert, Logan	185.2	15	13	1	1	.966	11	5	1	0	.45	-1
Gilbert, Tyler	34.1	1	5	0	0	1.000	1	0	0	0	.00	0
Gilbreath, Lucas	43.0	1	6	1	2	.875	6	2	0	0	.33	1
Giles, Ken	4.1	0	0	0	0	-	0	0	0	0	-	0
Gillaspie, Logan	17.1	0	1	0	0	1.000	0	0	0	0	-	0
Ginkel, Kevin	29.1	1	4	0	0	1.000	1	0	0	0	.00	0
Giolito, Lucas	161.2	5	12	0	1	1.000	7	1	0	1	.14	-1
Givens, Mychal	61.1	1	10	1	2	.917	6	3	0	2	.50	1
Glasnow, Tyler	6.2	0	0	0	0	-	0	0	0	0	-	0
Gomber, Austin	124.2	7	9	0	2	1.000	12	4	2	0	.33	0
Gonsolin, Tony	130.1	9	10	0	0	1.000	7	2	1	0	.29	2
Gonzales, Marco	183.0	7	9	0	1	1.000	11	2	0	1	.18	-2
Gonzalez, Chi Chi	23.0	1	3	0	0	1.000	1	1	0	1	1.00	-1
Gore, MacKenzie	70.0	2	7	0	0	1.000	2	1	1	0	.50	2
Gose, Anthony	21.0	2	0	0	0	1.000	0	0	0	0	-	0
Gott, Trevor	45.2	2	3	0	0	1.000	6	1	0	0	.17	0
Goudeau, Ashton	20.1	0	0	0	0	-	3	0	0	0	.00	-1
Graterol, Brusdar	49.2	13	10	0	0	1.000	1	0	0	0	.00	3
Graveman, K.	65.0	3	6	1	0	.900	5	0	0	0	.00	0
Gray, Jon	127.1	6	10	0	2	1.000	17	2	1	0	.12	-1
Gray, Josiah	148.2	4	8	0	0	1.000	15	4	0	0	.27	-1
Gray, Sonny	119.2	5	12	1	1	.944	9	1	1	1	.11	0
Green, Chad	15.0	0	1	0	0	1.000	0	0	0	0	-	0
Greene, Hunter	125.2	6	5	1	0	.917	12	2	0	0	.17	-2
Greene, Shane	3.0	0	0	0	0	-	0	0	0	0	-	0
Greinke, Zack	137.0	20	17	0	1	1.000	8	2	0	2	.25	3

2022 Fielding and Holding Runners

Pitcher	Inn	PO	A	E	DP	Pct	SBA	CS	PCS	PPO	CS%	RS
Griffin, Foster	6.1	0	2	0	0	1.000	1	0	0	0	.00	0
Grimm, Justin	15.1	1	3	0	0	1.000	2	1	1	1	.50	1
Grove, Michael	29.1	1	4	0	0	1.000	6	0	0	0	.00	0
Gsellman, Robert	15.1	1	2	0	0	1.000	0	0	0	0	-	0
Guerra, Javy	18.0	1	2	0	0	1.000	0	0	0	0	-	0
Gustave, Jandel	28.0	1	1	0	0	1.000	1	1	0	0	1.00	0
Gutierrez, Vladimir	36.2	5	3	2	1	.800	4	1	0	0	.25	0
Hader, Josh	50.0	1	4	1	0	.833	5	0	0	0	.00	-1
Hall, DL	13.2	0	0	0	0	-	2	0	0	0	.00	-1
Hamilton, Ian	2.2	0	1	0	0	1.000	0	0	0	0	-	0
Hand, Brad	45.0	4	1	1	0	.833	3	0	0	0	.00	1
Harvey, Hunter	39.1	2	2	0	0	1.000	5	0	0	0	.00	-1
Hatch, Thomas	4.2	0	0	0	0	-	0	0	0	0	-	-1
Head, Louis	28.2	2	2	0	0	1.000	1	0	0	0	.00	1
Heaney, Andrew	72.2	2	2	1	0	.800	1	1	0	0	1.00	-1
Hearn, Taylor	100.0	2	3	2	0	.714	5	2	1	0	.40	-1
Heasley, Jon	104.0	4	5	1	1	.900	2	1	0	1	.50	1
Helsley, Ryan	64.2	7	2	0	1	1.000	1	0	0	0	.00	2
Hembree, Heath	22.0	0	1	0	0	1.000	8	1	0	0	.13	-1
Hendricks, Kyle	84.1	5	8	1	0	.929	11	2	0	0	.18	0
Hendriks, Liam	57.2	1	5	1	0	.857	7	0	0	0	.00	-2
Hendrix, Ryan	8.1	0	1	0	0	1.000	3	1	0	0	.33	0
Henriquez, Ronny	11.2	3	1	1	0	.800	2	0	0	0	.00	1
Henry, Tommy	47.0	1	1	0	0	1.000	2	0	0	0	.00	0
Hentges, Sam	62.0	3	11	1	1	.933	7	1	0	0	.14	1
Herget, Jimmy	69.0	5	6	0	0	1.000	6	0	0	0	.00	-2
Herget, Kevin	7.0	0	1	0	0	1.000	0	0	0	0	-	0
Hernandez, Carlos	56.0	3	6	0	0	1.000	5	1	0	0	.20	1
Hernandez, D.	6.2	0	1	0	0	1.000	1	1	1	0	1.00	0
Hernandez, E.	62.1	1	5	0	0	1.000	8	3	0	0	.38	1
Hernandez, J.	30.1	1	1	1	0	.667	2	2	0	0	1.00	0
Hicks, Jordan	61.1	4	9	0	0	1.000	6	1	0	0	.17	1
Hill, Garrett	60.1	3	2	1	0	.833	5	1	0	0	.20	0
Hill, Rich	124.1	3	9	1	1	.923	9	2	0	1	.22	-1
Hill, Tim	48.0	6	7	2	0	.867	1	0	0	0	.00	0
Hjelle, Sean	25.0	1	2	2	1	.600	0	0	0	0	-	0
Hoeing, Bryan	12.2	1	3	0	0	1.000	1	0	0	0	.00	1
Hoffman, Jeff	44.2	2	0	1	0	.667	9	4	0	0	.44	-1
Holderman, Colin	28.1	5	0	0	0	1.000	0	0	0	0	-	0
Holland, Greg	4.2	0	0	0	0	-	1	0	0	0	.00	0
Holloway, Jordan	2.2	0	1	0	0	1.000	0	0	0	0	-	0
Hollowell, Gavin	7.0	1	0	0	0	1.000	0	0	0	0	-	0
Holmes, Clay	63.2	8	8	0	0	1.000	1	0	0	0	.00	0
Holton, Tyler	9.0	0	0	0	0	-	0	0	0	0	-	0
Houck, Tanner	60.0	5	10	1	0	.938	6	1	0	0	.17	1
Houser, Adrian	102.2	12	8	0	0	1.000	9	2	0	1	.22	1
Howard, Sam	2.0	0	0	0	0	-	0	0	0	0	-	0
Howard, Spencer	37.2	1	4	0	0	1.000	4	0	0	1	.00	0
Hudson, Dakota	139.2	13	14	1	1	.964	11	4	0	0	.36	-2
Hudson, Daniel	24.1	1	0	0	0	1.000	0	0	0	0	-	-1
Hughes, Brandon	57.2	3	1	0	0	1.000	0	0	0	0	-	0
Hunter, Tommy	22.1	1	4	0	0	1.000	2	0	0	0	.00	0
Hutchison, Drew	105.1	6	8	1	1	.933	9	1	0	1	.11	0
Iglesias, Raisel	62.0	3	5	0	1	1.000	1	0	0	0	.00	0
Irvin, Cole	181.0	6	9	1	2	.938	2	2	1	0	1.00	1
Jackson, Andre	9.2	1	1	0	0	1.000	0	0	0	0	-	0
Jackson, Jay	1.1	0	0	0	0	-	0	0	0	0	-	0
Jackson, Zach	48.0	2	1	0	0	1.000	4	1	0	0	.25	0
Jameson, Drey	24.1	2	2	0	0	1.000	2	0	0	0	.00	0
Jansen, Kenley	64.0	1	3	0	0	1.000	12	2	0	0	.17	-1
Javier, Cristian	148.2	2	3	0	0	1.000	12	3	0	1	.25	-1
Jax, Griffin	72.1	2	3	1	0	.833	4	0	0	0	.00	-1
Jefferies, Daulton	39.1	8	1	0	0	1.000	2	1	0	0	.50	-1
Jimenez, Dany	34.1	1	1	0	0	1.000	9	0	0	0	.00	-1
Jimenez, Joe	56.2	1	1	0	0	1.000	7	1	0	0	.14	-2
Johnson, Pierce	14.1	1	1	0	0	1.000	2	0	0	0	.00	0
Jones, Damon	4.2	0	0	0	0	-	0	0	0	0	-	0
Junis, Jakob	112.0	7	12	1	0	.950	12	1	0	2	.08	-1
Junk, Janson	8.1	1	0	0	0	1.000	0	0	0	0	-	0
Kahnle, Tommy	12.2	4	2	0	0	1.000	0	0	0	0	-	0
Kaprielian, James	134.0	10	6	1	1	.941	8	3	0	0	.38	-1
Karinchak, James	39.0	1	1	0	0	1.000	10	1	0	0	.10	-1
Kay, Anthony	2.0	0	0	0	0	-	0	0	0	0	-	0

2022 Fielding and Holding Runners

Pitcher	Inn	PO	A	E	DP	Pct	SBA	CS	PCS	PPO	CS%	RS
Keller, Brad	139.2	13	11	1	0	.960	7	2	0	0	.29	-2
Keller, Mitch	159.0	10	15	1	2	.962	20	3	0	0	.15	-1
Kelley, Trevor	23.2	0	2	0	0	1.000	2	0	0	0	.00	0
Kelly, Joe	37.0	3	4	0	1	1.000	4	0	0	1	.00	-1
Kelly, Merrill	200.1	15	19	1	2	.971	20	5	0	4	.25	2
Kelly, Michael	4.0	1	0	0	0	1.000	0	0	0	0	-	0
Kelly, Zack	13.2	1	2	0	0	1.000	2	1	0	0	.50	0
Kennedy, Ian	50.1	1	0	0	0	1.000	5	1	0	0	.20	-1
Kerr, Ray	5.0	0	1	0	0	1.000	0	0	0	0	-	0
Kershaw, Clayton	126.1	3	10	2	0	.867	5	2	1	1	.40	-1
Keuchel, Dallas	60.2	6	8	0	2	1.000	2	2	0	0	1.00	1
Kikuchi, Yusei	100.2	4	11	1	1	.938	4	3	0	1	.75	4
Kilian, Caleb	11.1	0	2	0	0	1.000	3	1	0	0	.33	0
Kimbrel, Craig	60.0	3	3	0	0	1.000	4	1	0	0	.25	-1
King, John	51.1	1	7	0	0	1.000	4	0	0	0	.00	0
King, Michael	51.0	2	7	2	1	.818	2	0	0	0	.00	1
Kinley, Tyler	24.0	2	1	1	0	.750	5	0	0	0	.00	-2
Kirby, George	130.0	7	10	0	1	1.000	15	5	1	0	.33	-1
Kittredge, Andrew	20.0	0	2	0	0	1.000	0	0	0	0	-	0
Kluber, Corey	164.0	7	9	1	1	.941	10	5	0	0	.50	-1
Knebel, Corey	44.2	4	7	0	0	1.000	6	2	0	1	.33	1
Knehr, Reiss	13.2	1	2	0	0	1.000	0	0	0	0	-	1
Knight, Dusten	11.0	0	3	0	0	1.000	0	0	0	0	-	0
Koch, Matt	4.1	0	1	0	0	1.000	0	0	0	0	-	0
Koenig, Jared	39.1	0	3	1	0	.750	1	1	0	0	1.00	0
Kolarek, Adam	17.2	2	3	0	0	1.000	3	1	0	0	.33	1
Kopech, Michael	119.1	0	3	1	0	.750	19	4	0	0	.21	-3
Kowar, Jackson	15.2	0	4	0	0	1.000	0	0	0	0	-	0
Kranick, Max	5.0	1	2	0	1	1.000	0	0	0	0	-	1
Krehbiel, Joey	57.2	4	8	1	1	.923	4	2	1	0	.50	1
Kremer, Dean	125.1	6	6	1	1	.923	8	3	0	1	.38	0
Kuhl, Chad	137.0	12	9	1	0	.955	11	5	0	0	.45	1
Kuhnel, Joel	58.0	9	4	1	0	.929	4	2	1	0	.50	1
Ladwig, A.J.	3.1	0	0	0	0	-	0	0	0	0	-	0
Lakins Sr., Travis	10.1	1	1	0	0	1.000	1	0	0	0	.00	0
Lambert, Jimmy	47.0	1	4	0	0	1.000	9	1	0	0	.11	0
Lamet, Dinelson	32.1	2	4	0	0	1.000	4	0	0	0	.00	-2
Lange, Alex	63.1	5	7	1	0	.923	7	1	0	0	.14	1
Lauer, Eric	158.2	9	10	1	0	.950	9	3	1	1	.33	0
Law, Derek	19.2	2	2	1	1	.800	1	0	0	0	.00	-1
Lawrence, Casey	18.0	2	2	0	0	1.000	0	0	0	0	-	0
Lawrence, Justin	42.2	0	11	0	1	1.000	4	1	0	0	.25	3
Leclerc, Jose	47.2	1	1	0	0	1.000	4	0	0	0	.00	-1
Lee, Dylan	50.2	2	2	0	0	1.000	1	0	0	0	.00	0
Lee, Evan	8.2	0	1	0	0	1.000	0	0	0	0	-	0
Leiter Jr., Mark	67.2	2	9	0	2	1.000	8	2	0	0	.25	1
Lemoine, Jacob	16.1	0	1	0	0	1.000	0	0	0	0	-	0
Leone, Dominic	49.1	3	7	2	0	.833	4	2	0	0	.50	2
Liberatore, M.	34.2	0	2	0	0	1.000	1	0	0	0	.00	-1
Littell, Zack	44.1	5	2	0	0	1.000	0	0	0	0	-	0
Little, Brendon	0.2	0	0	0	0	-	0	0	0	0	-	0
Llovera, Mauricio	16.1	0	2	0	0	1.000	2	0	0	0	.00	0
Loaisiga, Jonathan	48.0	4	13	0	0	1.000	3	0	0	0	.00	3
Lodolo, Nick	103.1	2	10	0	0	1.000	9	3	1	0	.33	0
Logue, Zach	57.0	3	5	0	0	1.000	4	1	0	0	.25	-1
Long, Sammy	42.1	0	5	0	0	1.000	1	0	0	0	.00	0
Lopez, Jorge	71.0	4	7	2	0	.846	7	1	0	0	.14	-1
Lopez, Pablo	180.0	13	12	2	2	.926	8	2	1	0	.25	0
Lopez, Reynaldo	65.1	6	6	1	0	.923	8	1	0	0	.13	-1
Lopez, Yoan	11.0	2	0	0	0	1.000	2	0	0	0	.00	0
Lorenzen, Michael	97.2	8	9	1	0	.944	5	1	0	0	.20	-1
Loup, Aaron	58.2	0	9	0	0	1.000	7	2	2	0	.29	0
Lowther, Zac	5.1	0	0	0	0	-	0	0	0	0	-	0
Luetge, Lucas	57.1	1	3	2	2	.667	0	0	0	0	-	0
Lugo, Seth	65.0	3	8	0	0	1.000	3	1	0	0	.33	2
Luzardo, Jesus	100.1	1	13	1	2	.933	3	1	1	0	.33	3
Lyles, Jordan	179.0	13	15	0	2	1.000	8	1	0	0	.13	0
Lynch, Daniel	131.2	3	10	1	0	.929	8	2	1	0	.25	-1
Lynn, Lance	121.2	2	5	0	0	1.000	3	2	0	0	.67	-1
Machado, Andres	59.1	3	7	1	0	.909	8	0	0	0	.00	-1
Mahle, Tyler	120.2	9	7	2	1	.889	10	4	1	0	.40	-1
Manaea, Sean	158.0	5	5	0	0	1.000	5	0	0	0	.00	-4
Manning, Matt	63.0	4	6	0	0	1.000	4	2	0	0	.50	0

161

2022 Fielding and Holding Runners

Pitcher	Inn	PO	A	E	DP	Pct	SBA	CS	PCS	PPO	CS%	RS
Manoah, Alek	196.2	5	14	1	1	.950	13	5	0	0	.38	1
Mantiply, Joe	60.0	2	5	0	0	1.000	2	0	0	0	.00	1
Marinaccio, Ron	44.0	4	2	0	1	1.000	5	1	0	0	.20	0
Markel, Parker	3.0	0	0	0	0	-	0	0	0	0	-	0
Marquez, German	181.2	6	15	2	1	.913	12	2	1	1	.17	0
Marte, Jose	11.0	0	0	0	0	-	2	0	0	0	.00	0
Marte, Yunior	48.0	0	7	0	1	1.000	2	1	0	0	.50	1
Martin, Brett	50.0	4	7	0	2	1.000	3	0	0	0	.00	0
Martin, Chris	56.0	2	8	1	0	.909	9	3	1	0	.33	2
Martin, Corbin	22.1	2	1	0	0	1.000	5	2	0	0	.40	-1
Martin, Davis	63.1	5	8	0	3	1.000	4	0	0	1	.00	1
Martinez, Adrian	57.2	1	2	0	1	1.000	5	2	0	0	.40	0
Martinez, Nick	106.1	13	11	3	2	.889	7	1	0	1	.14	0
Martinez, Seth	38.2	1	5	0	1	1.000	3	1	0	0	.33	0
Maton, Phil	65.2	2	6	1	0	.889	3	1	0	0	.33	0
Matz, Steven	48.0	2	7	1	0	.900	0	0	0	0	-	1
Matzek, Tyler	43.2	0	3	0	1	1.000	4	1	0	0	.25	0
May, Dustin	30.0	2	6	2	0	.800	5	0	0	0	.00	-1
May, Trevor	25.0	2	1	0	0	1.000	2	0	0	0	.00	0
Mayers, Mike	50.2	0	3	0	0	1.000	3	0	0	0	.00	1
Mayza, Tim	48.2	3	6	0	0	1.000	2	0	0	0	.00	-1
Mazza, Chris	5.1	1	1	0	0	1.000	3	0	0	0	.00	-1
McCarty, Kirk	37.2	2	4	0	0	1.000	2	2	1	0	1.00	0
McClanahan, S.	166.1	1	12	1	1	.929	7	1	1	1	.14	-2
McCullers Jr., L	47.2	2	2	0	0	1.000	4	2	0	0	.50	-1
McFarland, T.J.	32.2	3	6	0	0	1.000	2	1	1	0	.50	1
McGee, Easton	3.0	0	0	0	0	-	0	0	0	0	-	0
McGee, Jake	37.0	0	2	0	0	1.000	1	0	0	0	.00	0
McHugh, Collin	69.1	5	3	0	1	1.000	1	0	0	0	.00	0
McKay, David	6.2	1	0	0	1	1.000	0	0	0	0	-	0
McKenzie, Triston	191.1	12	9	1	1	.955	11	5	0	0	.45	0
Means, John	8.0	0	0	0	0	-	0	0	0	0	-	0
Mears, Nick	2.0	0	0	0	0	-	0	0	0	0	-	0
Medina, Adonis	23.2	5	5	1	0	.909	6	2	1	0	.33	0
Megill, Trevor	45.0	1	2	2	0	.600	9	3	0	1	.33	-1
Megill, Tylor	47.1	3	5	0	0	1.000	3	1	0	0	.33	0
Mejia, JC	2.1	0	1	0	0	1.000	0	0	0	0	-	0
Melancon, Mark	56.0	5	6	0	2	1.000	4	1	0	0	.25	1
Menez, Conner	1.0	0	0	0	0	-	0	0	0	0	-	0
Mengden, Daniel	7.0	3	0	0	0	1.000	0	0	0	0	-	0
Merryweather, J	26.2	0	1	0	0	1.000	2	0	0	0	.00	-1
Meyer, .Max	6.0	1	0	0	0	1.000	1	1	0	0	1.00	0
Middleton, Keynan	17.0	1	2	0	0	1.000	3	0	0	0	.00	0
Mikolas, Miles	202.1	17	14	0	1	1.000	6	3	0	0	.50	0
Miley, Wade	37.0	0	3	1	0	.750	3	1	0	0	.33	-1
Miller, Shelby	7.0	0	0	0	0	-	0	0	0	0	-	0
Miller, Tyson	10.2	1	2	0	1	1.000	2	0	0	0	.00	1
Mills, Alec	17.2	1	1	0	0	1.000	1	1	0	0	1.00	1
Mills, Wyatt	29.1	1	6	0	0	1.000	3	1	1	0	.33	0
Milner, Hoby	64.2	4	10	0	1	1.000	1	0	0	1	.00	1
Milone, Tommy	16.2	1	0	0	1	1.000	1	1	0	0	1.00	0
Minaya, Juan	9.2	1	0	0	0	1.000	1	0	0	0	.00	0
Minor, Mike	98.0	4	5	0	1	1.000	16	0	0	0	.00	0
Minter, A.J.	70.0	2	4	0	0	1.000	10	3	3	0	.30	-1
Misiewicz, A.	29.0	1	2	0	0	1.000	0	0	0	0	-	0
Mize, Casey	10.0	0	3	0	0	1.000	3	0	0	0	.00	-1
Moll, Sam	43.1	2	4	2	0	.750	4	2	1	0	.50	1
Montas, Frankie	144.1	10	8	1	1	.947	6	3	0	0	.50	0
Montero, Rafael	68.1	2	6	1	0	.889	8	0	0	0	.00	-1
Montes de Oca, B.	3.1	2	1	0	0	1.000	1	0	0	0	.00	0
Montgomery, J.	178.1	7	21	0	1	1.000	8	3	3	0	.38	1
Moore, Matt	74.0	2	2	0	0	1.000	10	2	1	0	.20	-1
Morales, F.	5.0	0	0	0	0	-	0	0	0	0	-	0
Moran, Brian	0.1	0	0	0	0	-	0	0	0	0	-	0
Moran, Jovani	40.2	0	5	0	0	1.000	5	0	0	0	.00	-1
Morejon, Adrian	34.0	1	3	1	1	.800	2	0	0	0	.00	0
Moreta, Dauri	38.1	1	3	0	0	1.000	0	0	0	0	-	0
Morgan, Eli	66.2	3	6	0	0	1.000	8	2	0	1	.25	1
Moronta, Reyes	37.2	0	2	1	0	.667	3	0	0	0	.00	-1
Morris, Cody	23.2	2	1	0	1	1.000	7	2	0	0	.29	0
Morton, Charlie	172.0	7	15	2	2	.917	12	2	0	3	.17	1
Muller, Kyle	12.1	0	1	0	0	1.000	4	0	0	0	.00	-1
Munoz, Andres	65.0	3	4	0	0	1.000	6	1	0	0	.17	-1

2022 Fielding and Holding Runners

Pitcher	Inn	PO	A	E	DP	Pct	SBA	CS	PCS	PPO	CS%	RS
Murfee, Penn	69.1	2	4	0	1	1.000	3	0	0	0	.00	1
Murphy, Patrick	5.2	0	2	0	0	1.000	0	0	0	0	-	0
Musgrove, Joe	181.0	19	17	1	2	.973	7	0	0	0	.00	0
Mushinski, Parker	7.1	1	0	0	0	1.000	0	0	0	0	-	0
Naile, James	9.0	3	2	0	0	1.000	1	0	0	0	.00	0
Nance, Tommy	43.2	1	4	0	0	1.000	8	0	0	0	.00	-3
Nardi, Andrew	14.2	0	0	0	0	-	0	0	0	0	-	-1
Naughton, Packy	32.0	2	3	0	0	1.000	0	0	0	0	-	0
Neidert, Nick	5.0	2	0	0	0	1.000	0	0	0	0	-	0
Nelson, Kyle	37.0	3	4	1	1	.875	2	1	1	0	.50	0
Nelson, Nick	68.2	3	5	1	0	.889	6	2	0	0	.33	-2
Nelson, Ryne	18.1	1	2	1	0	.750	0	0	0	0	-	1
Neris, Hector	65.1	2	2	1	1	.800	4	1	0	0	.25	-1
Newcomb, Sean	27.2	1	5	0	1	1.000	4	1	0	0	.25	0
Nittoli, Vinny	2.0	0	0	0	0	-	0	0	0	0	-	0
Nogosek, Stephen	22.0	4	1	0	0	1.000	1	0	0	0	.00	0
Nola, Aaron	205.0	9	14	2	0	.920	19	8	0	0	.42	0
Norris, Daniel	58.2	4	3	1	0	.875	1	1	0	0	1.00	0
Norwood, James	17.1	1	0	0	0	1.000	1	0	0	0	.00	0
Ober, Bailey	56.0	1	3	0	0	1.000	1	0	0	0	.00	0
O'Brien, Riley	1.0	0	0	0	0	-	0	0	0	0	-	0
O'Day, Darren	21.2	1	2	0	1	1.000	4	0	0	0	.00	0
Odorizzi, Jake	106.1	5	10	2	1	.882	9	4	0	1	.44	2
Ogando, Cristofer	4.1	0	0	0	0	-	1	1	0	0	1.00	0
Ohtani, Shohei	166.0	6	5	0	0	1.000	5	1	0	0	.20	1
Okert, Steven	51.1	1	2	2	0	.600	2	0	0	0	.00	-2
Oller, Adam	74.1	4	5	2	0	.818	4	2	2	1	.50	1
Ort, Kaleb	28.1	1	1	0	1	1.000	6	1	0	0	.17	-1
Ortega, Oliver	34.0	1	2	0	0	1.000	6	2	0	0	.33	0
Ortiz, Luis	8.2	0	2	0	0	1.000	1	0	0	0	.00	0
Ortiz, Luis	16.0	0	1	0	0	1.000	0	0	0	0	-	0
Ottavino, Adam	65.2	3	6	3	0	.750	22	3	0	1	.14	-3
Otto, Glenn	135.2	10	7	2	0	.895	18	2	0	0	.11	-3
Overton, Connor	33.0	6	3	0	1	1.000	3	2	1	0	.67	1
Oviedo, Johan	56.0	3	3	1	1	.857	6	1	0	0	.17	0
Paddack, Chris	22.1	0	1	1	0	.500	1	0	0	0	.00	-1
Padilla, Nicholas	1.2	0	0	0	0	-	0	0	0	0	-	0
Pagan, Emilio	63.0	2	3	1	1	.833	2	1	0	0	.50	0
Pallante, Andre	108.0	12	15	0	1	1.000	7	2	1	0	.29	1
Paredes, Enoli	3.0	0	0	0	0	-	0	0	0	0	-	0
Patino, Luis	20.0	3	2	0	0	1.000	4	2	0	0	.50	0
Patton, Spencer	7.0	1	0	0	0	1.000	2	0	0	0	.00	0
Payamps, Joel	55.2	6	7	1	0	.929	4	1	0	0	.25	0
Peacock, Matt	10.0	0	1	0	0	1.000	0	0	0	0	-	0
Peguero, Elvis	17.1	0	2	0	0	1.000	1	0	0	0	.00	0
Pepiot, Ryan	36.1	2	1	0	1	1.000	1	0	0	0	.00	0
Peralta, Freddy	78.0	4	8	0	1	1.000	7	3	0	0	.43	2
Peralta, Wandy	56.1	3	14	1	2	.944	0	0	0	1	-	4
Peralta, Wily	38.1	5	2	0	2	1.000	2	0	0	0	.00	0
Perdomo, Luis	23.2	2	3	1	0	.833	2	0	0	0	.00	-1
Perez, Cionel	57.2	5	5	1	0	.909	3	1	0	0	.33	0
Perez, Francisco	8.2	1	0	0	0	1.000	1	0	0	0	.00	0
Perez, Martin	196.1	6	19	2	1	.926	11	1	1	0	.09	1
Perez, Oliver	4.0	1	0	0	0	1.000	1	0	0	0	.00	0
Peters, Dillon	39.1	5	5	0	1	1.000	2	1	1	0	.50	1
Peterson, David	105.2	11	12	3	1	.813	1	0	0	3	.00	2
Phelps, David	63.2	1	6	0	0	1.000	4	2	0	0	.50	1
Phillips, Evan	63.0	3	8	0	0	1.000	4	1	1	0	.25	0
Pilkington, Konnor	58.0	1	6	2	0	.778	3	3	2	0	1.00	0
Pineda, Michael	46.2	1	2	0	0	1.000	7	2	0	0	.29	0
Pivetta, Nick	179.2	11	8	0	1	1.000	25	6	0	0	.24	-3
Plassmeyer, M.	7.1	0	1	0	1	1.000	0	0	0	0	-	0
Plesac, Zach	131.2	10	13	2	1	.920	3	2	0	1	.67	0
Poche, Colin	58.2	0	2	0	0	1.000	3	1	1	0	.33	-1
Pop, Zach	39.0	2	3	1	0	.833	2	1	0	0	.50	-3
Poppen, Sean	28.2	2	2	0	0	1.000	2	1	0	1	.50	0
Poteet, Cody	28.0	1	2	0	0	1.000	3	2	1	0	.67	1
Pressly, Ryan	48.1	2	3	0	0	1.000	1	1	0	0	1.00	0
Price, David	40.1	1	6	0	0	1.000	2	0	0	0	.00	-1
Pruitt, Austin	55.1	6	4	0	0	1.000	5	2	0	0	.40	1
Puk, A.J.	66.1	0	7	1	1	.875	7	0	0	0	.00	0
Quantrill, Cal	186.1	11	16	2	0	.931	20	4	2	0	.20	-1
Quijada, Jose	40.2	0	3	1	0	.750	2	1	0	0	.50	-1

	2022 Fielding and Holding Runners											
Pitcher	Inn	PO	A	E	DP	Pct	SBA	CS	PCS	PPO	CS%	RS
Quintana, Jose	165.2	4	19	0	0	1.000	10	4	1	0	.40	0
Ragans, Cole	40.0	1	0	0	0	1.000	5	2	0	0	.40	-1
Rainey, Tanner	30.0	1	1	0	0	1.000	3	0	0	0	.00	0
Raley, Brooks	53.2	2	4	1	0	.857	0	0	0	0	-	-1
Ramirez, Erasmo	86.1	4	9	1	0	.929	1	0	0	0	.00	1
Ramirez, Noe	50.0	3	4	0	1	1.000	10	4	0	1	.40	0
Ramirez, Yohan	37.1	5	5	0	1	1.000	1	0	0	1	.00	2
Rasmussen, Drew	146.0	9	10	1	0	.950	12	4	0	0	.33	0
Ray, Robbie	189.0	6	18	0	1	1.000	26	9	6	0	.35	1
Reed, Jake	16.2	0	2	1	0	.667	0	0	0	0	-	0
Reid-Foley, Sean	10.0	0	0	0	0	-	2	0	0	0	.00	0
Reyes, Denyi	7.2	0	1	0	0	1.000	0	0	0	0	-	0
Reyes, Gerardo	2.0	0	0	0	0	-	0	0	0	0	-	0
Richards, Garrett	42.2	2	1	0	0	1.000	5	1	0	0	.20	-1
Richards, Trevor	64.0	3	2	0	1	1.000	8	3	0	0	.38	0
Roberts, Ethan	7.2	0	1	0	0	1.000	0	0	0	0	-	0
Robertson, David	63.2	3	4	0	0	1.000	2	1	0	0	.50	1
Robles, Hansel	24.2	0	0	0	0	-	4	1	0	0	.25	-1
Rodon, Carlos	178.0	3	9	0	0	1.000	20	2	2	0	.10	-3
Rodriguez, Dereck	7.2	1	0	0	0	1.000	0	0	0	0	-	0
Rodriguez, E.	91.0	4	7	2	1	.846	4	0	0	0	.00	-1
Rodriguez, Elvin	29.2	2	1	0	1	1.000	0	0	0	0	-	0
Rodriguez, Joely	50.1	0	2	1	0	.667	3	0	0	0	.00	-1
Rodriguez, Manue	13.2	0	1	0	0	1.000	0	0	0	0	-	0
Rodriguez, Yerry	1.0	0	0	0	0	-	0	0	0	0	-	0
Rogers, Josh	26.1	0	3	0	0	1.000	1	1	1	0	1.00	1
Rogers, Taylor	64.1	3	7	0	0	1.000	6	1	1	0	.17	0
Rogers, Trevor	107.0	1	12	2	0	.867	8	0	0	1	.00	-1
Rogers, Tyler	75.2	5	21	1	1	.963	3	0	0	0	.00	2
Romano, Jordan	64.0	2	5	0	0	1.000	6	0	0	0	.00	-2
Romero, Jhon	5.0	0	2	0	1	1.000	0	0	0	0	-	0
Romero, JoJo	16.1	0	2	0	1	1.000	1	1	1	0	1.00	1
Romero, Tommy	8.1	0	1	0	0	1.000	0	0	0	1	-	0
Romo, Sergio	18.0	0	2	0	0	1.000	4	0	0	0	.00	0
Rondon, Angel	5.0	0	0	0	0	-	1	0	0	0	.00	0
Rosenberg, Kenny	10.2	0	0	0	0	-	1	1	0	0	1.00	0
Rossman, Bubby	1.0	0	0	0	0	-	0	0	0	0	-	0
Rucker, Michael	54.2	3	6	0	1	1.000	1	0	0	0	.00	0
Ruiz, Jose	60.2	2	5	0	1	1.000	10	1	0	0	.10	-1
Ruiz, Norge	19.0	1	1	0	0	1.000	1	0	0	0	.00	0
Ryan, Joe	147.0	2	11	1	0	.929	14	3	2	0	.21	2
Ryu, Hyun-Jin	27.0	0	2	0	0	1.000	0	0	0	0	-	0
Sadzeck, Connor	3.0	0	0	0	0	-	1	0	0	0	.00	0
Sale, Chris	5.2	1	0	0	0	1.000	0	0	0	0	-	0
Sampson, Adrian	104.1	5	13	0	0	1.000	5	2	0	0	.40	3
Sanchez, Aaron	60.0	3	8	0	0	1.000	9	4	1	0	.44	1
Sanchez, Anibal	69.1	4	4	2	0	.800	9	0	0	0	.00	-1
Sanchez, C.	40.0	3	6	0	0	1.000	2	1	0	0	.50	0
Sanchez, Miguel	13.1	2	1	0	1	1.000	0	0	0	0	-	0
Sanders, Phoenix	14.2	0	0	0	0	-	0	0	0	0	-	0
Sandlin, Nick	44.0	2	6	1	2	.889	5	0	0	0	.00	-1
Sandoval, Patrick	148.2	7	14	0	1	1.000	5	2	1	1	.40	2
Sands, Cole	30.2	1	3	1	0	.800	5	0	0	0	.00	-2
Sanmartin, Reiver	57.0	3	5	0	1	1.000	1	0	0	0	.00	-2
Santana, Dennis	58.2	1	8	1	1	.900	3	0	0	1	.00	2
Santillan, Tony	19.2	0	2	1	0	.667	0	0	0	0	-	-1
Santos, Gregory	3.2	0	0	0	0	-	0	0	0	0	-	0
Saucedo, Tayler	2.2	0	0	0	0	-	0	0	0	0	-	0
Sawamura, H.	50.2	1	8	1	1	.900	2	1	0	0	.50	0
Sborz, Josh	18.1	0	1	0	0	1.000	7	2	0	0	.29	-1
Scherzer, Max	145.1	6	12	0	1	1.000	8	4	0	0	.50	2
Schmidt, Clarke	57.2	4	6	0	1	1.000	3	2	0	0	.67	0
Schreiber, John	65.0	7	8	0	2	1.000	3	2	1	0	.67	0
Scott, Tanner	62.2	1	2	1	0	.750	2	1	0	0	.50	-1
Scott, Tayler	12.0	0	1	0	0	1.000	0	0	0	0	-	0
Seabold, Connor	18.1	0	1	0	0	1.000	1	0	0	0	.00	0
Sears, JP	70.0	0	5	0	0	1.000	8	3	2	0	.38	0
Sedlock, Cody	3.0	0	0	0	0	-	0	0	0	0	-	0
Selman, Sam	18.1	3	2	0	0	1.000	2	1	0	0	.50	0
Senzatela, Antonio	92.1	7	15	1	1	.957	2	0	0	1	.00	2
Severino, A.	7.1	0	2	1	0	.667	0	0	0	0	-	1
Severino, Luis	102.0	6	13	0	0	1.000	5	4	1	0	.80	4
Sewald, Paul	64.0	3	13	0	0	1.000	6	2	1	0	.33	2

	2022 Fielding and Holding Runners											
Pitcher	Inn	PO	A	E	DP	Pct	SBA	CS	PCS	PPO	CS%	RS
Shaw, Bryan	58.1	7	2	0	0	1.000	2	0	0	0	.00	0
Sheffield, Jordan	2.0	1	1	0	1	1.000	1	1	1	0	1.00	0
Sheffield, Justus	11.2	0	0	0	0	-	0	0	0	0	-	0
Shreve, Chasen	26.1	1	2	0	0	1.000	3	2	1	0	.67	1
Silseth, Chase	28.2	1	1	0	0	1.000	3	0	0	0	.00	0
Sims, Lucas	6.2	0	2	0	0	1.000	0	0	0	0	-	0
Singer, Brady	153.1	7	17	1	0	.960	7	5	2	1	.71	0
Skubal, Tarik	117.2	2	13	1	1	.938	7	5	2	1	.71	0
Small, Ethan	6.1	0	0	0	0	-	0	0	0	0	-	0
Smeltzer, Devin	70.1	1	4	1	0	.833	2	2	1	0	1.00	-1
Smith, Caleb	70.0	2	7	0	1	1.000	3	2	0	1	.67	1
Smith, Chad	18.0	0	0	1	0	.000	3	2	0	0	.67	-3
Smith, Drew	46.0	2	2	0	0	1.000	1	1	0	0	1.00	0
Smith, Joe	27.1	1	4	0	0	1.000	2	0	0	0	.00	1
Smith, Will	59.0	2	3	0	0	1.000	6	2	0	0	.33	0
Smyly, Drew	106.1	2	9	0	0	1.000	10	1	1	0	.10	0
Snead, Kirby	44.2	1	6	1	1	.875	9	2	2	0	.22	0
Snell, Blake	128.0	4	10	0	0	1.000	15	4	3	0	.27	-1
Snider, Collin	34.1	4	1	0	1	1.000	0	0	0	0	-	-1
Snyder, Nicklaus	1.0	0	0	0	0	-	0	0	0	0	-	0
Solomon, Jared	8.1	0	0	0	0	-	0	0	0	0	-	0
Soto, Gregory	60.1	0	7	1	1	.875	3	0	0	0	.00	-1
Sousa, Bennett	20.1	0	0	2	0	.000	3	1	0	0	.33	-2
Speier, Gabe	19.1	2	1	0	1	1.000	1	0	0	0	.00	0
Springs, Jeffrey	135.1	4	10	0	1	1.000	8	4	3	0	.50	1
St. John, Locke	2.0	0	0	0	0	-	0	0	0	0	-	0
Stammen, Craig	40.2	3	3	0	0	1.000	6	1	0	0	.17	-2
Stanek, Ryne	54.2	0	1	0	0	1.000	6	2	0	0	.33	-1
Stashak, Cody	16.1	0	2	0	0	1.000	0	0	0	0	-	1
Staumont, Josh	37.2	2	3	0	0	1.000	4	1	0	0	.25	1
Steckenrider, Drew	14.1	3	2	0	0	1.000	2	1	0	0	.50	0
Steele, Justin	119.0	4	3	1	1	.875	8	2	0	0	.25	-5
Stephan, Trevor	63.2	5	2	2	0	.778	11	0	0	0	.00	-4
Stephens, Jackson	53.2	3	8	0	0	1.000	8	0	0	0	.00	-1
Stephenson, R.	58.0	2	4	1	0	.857	8	3	0	0	.38	0
Stout, Eric	22.1	0	1	1	0	.500	2	0	0	0	.00	0
Strahm, Matt	44.2	1	4	2	0	.714	3	0	0	0	.00	0
Strasburg, S.	4.2	0	0	0	0	-	1	0	0	0	.00	0
Stratton, Chris	63.1	2	4	1	3	.857	1	0	0	0	.00	-1
Strickland, Hunter	62.1	3	5	0	0	1.000	14	0	0	0	.00	-1
Strider, Spencer	131.2	5	8	0	1	1.000	5	1	1	0	.20	-2
Stripling, Ross	134.1	6	9	0	0	1.000	10	3	0	0	.30	1
Stroman, Marcus	138.2	12	21	0	2	1.000	12	5	0	0	.42	2
Strzelecki, Peter	35.0	2	5	0	1	1.000	2	0	0	0	.00	1
Suarez, Jose	109.0	2	5	1	0	.875	3	2	1	0	.67	-1
Suarez, Ranger	155.1	13	31	0	0	1.000	2	2	0	0	1.00	9
Suarez, Robert	47.2	3	1	0	0	1.000	3	2	0	0	.67	-1
Sulser, Beau	22.1	2	1	1	0	.750	1	0	0	0	.00	0
Sulser, Cole	34.0	3	4	0	1	1.000	4	2	2	0	.50	0
Suter, Brent	66.2	2	9	1	0	.917	5	2	0	2	.40	1
Swanson, Erik	53.2	3	4	0	0	1.000	4	1	0	1	.25	0
Swarmer, Matt	34.0	1	1	0	0	1.000	4	1	0	0	.25	0
Syndergaard, N.	134.2	7	11	2	2	.900	33	3	1	0	.09	-6
Szapucki, Thomas	15.0	0	2	0	1	1.000	4	2	2	0	.50	0
Taillon, Jameson	177.1	8	18	1	2	.963	8	2	0	0	.25	2
Tapia, Domingo	17.0	0	3	0	1	1.000	1	0	0	0	.00	-1
Tarnok, Freddy	0.2	0	0	0	0	-	1	0	0	0	.00	0
Tate, Dillon	73.2	4	6	2	0	.833	5	1	0	0	.20	-1
Taylor, Blake	16.0	1	0	0	0	1.000	0	0	0	0	-	0
Tepera, Ryan	57.1	1	4	0	0	1.000	7	1	0	0	.14	-1
Tetreault, Jackson	21.0	0	2	0	0	1.000	1	0	0	0	.00	0
Thielbar, Caleb	59.1	3	3	1	0	.857	4	1	0	1	.25	0
Thompson, K.	115.0	6	3	0	0	1.000	4	3	0	0	.75	0
Thompson, Mason	24.2	5	1	0	0	1.000	1	0	0	0	.00	0
Thompson, Ryan	42.2	5	8	2	1	.867	4	0	0	0	.00	-2
Thompson, Zach	121.2	5	5	0	0	1.000	12	2	0	0	.17	-3
Thompson, Zack	34.2	4	3	0	0	1.000	1	0	0	0	.00	1
Thornburg, Tyler	19.0	1	2	0	0	1.000	0	0	0	0	-	0
Thornton, Trent	46.0	1	2	1	0	.750	3	0	0	0	.00	0
Tinoco, Jesus	20.2	1	2	0	1	1.000	2	0	0	0	.00	1
Topa, Justin	7.1	1	4	0	0	1.000	2	1	1	0	.50	-1
Toussaint, Touki	25.1	0	0	0	0	-	3	1	0	0	.33	0
Treinen, Blake	5.0	0	0	0	0	-	0	0	0	0	-	0

	2022 Fielding and Holding Runners											
Pitcher	Inn	PO	A	E	DP	Pct	SBA	CS	PCS	PPO	CS%	RS
Trivino, Lou	53.2	4	6	1	0	.909	1	1	1	0	1.00	1
Tully, Tanner	6.0	0	1	0	0	1.000	0	0	0	0	-	1
Tyler, Kyle	4.0	1	0	0	0	1.000	0	0	0	0	-	0
Uceta, Edwin	17.0	1	2	0	0	1.000	0	0	0	0	-	1
Uelmen, Erich	27.0	2	0	1	0	.667	2	0	0	0	.00	-2
Underwood Jr., D.	57.1	3	5	0	1	1.000	6	2	0	0	.33	1
Urena, Jose	97.0	16	13	1	0	.967	11	2	1	0	.18	1
Urias, Julio	175.0	3	11	1	0	.933	9	4	2	0	.44	0
Urquidy, Jose	164.1	6	11	0	1	1.000	14	3	0	0	.21	-1
Valdez, Cesar	1.0	0	0	0	0	-	0	0	0	0	-	0
Valdez, Framber	201.1	6	23	1	0	.967	7	0	0	0	.00	0
Valdez, Phillips	16.1	1	2	0	0	1.000	2	0	0	0	.00	0
Varland, Louie	26.0	0	2	0	0	1.000	0	0	0	0	-	0
Vasquez, Andrew	8.2	1	0	0	0	1.000	1	0	0	0	.00	-1
Velasquez, Vince	75.1	2	2	3	0	.571	4	1	0	0	.25	-1
VerHagen, Drew	21.2	1	3	0	0	1.000	3	0	0	0	.00	1
Verlander, Justin	175.0	4	15	1	2	.950	13	3	0	0	.23	0
Vesia, Alex	54.1	1	4	2	0	.714	4	1	1	0	.25	-2
Vespi, Nick	26.1	1	3	0	1	1.000	3	0	0	0	.00	0
Vest, Will	63.0	5	6	1	0	.917	5	4	0	0	.80	-1
Vieaux, Cam	8.2	0	0	0	0	-	0	0	0	0	-	0
Vizcaino, Arodys	5.2	0	0	0	0	-	1	0	0	0	.00	0
Voth, Austin	101.2	6	9	0	0	1.000	2	1	0	0	.50	2
Wacha, Michael	127.1	8	13	0	0	1.000	4	0	0	0	.00	2
Wainwright, Adam	191.2	18	16	0	0	1.000	14	6	0	0	.43	2
Waites, Cole	5.2	0	0	0	0	-	1	0	0	0	.00	0
Waldichuk, Ken	34.2	1	2	0	1	1.000	2	0	0	0	.00	0
Walker, Taijuan	157.1	15	24	2	1	.951	10	2	0	5	.20	6
Walsh, Jake	2.2	0	0	0	0	-	0	0	0	0	-	0
Walters, Nash	0.1	0	0	0	0	-	0	0	0	0	-	0
Wantz, Andrew	50.1	2	3	0	0	1.000	4	2	0	0	.50	0
Warren, Art	36.0	1	2	0	0	1.000	10	1	0	0	.10	-1
Warren, Austin	16.0	1	2	0	0	1.000	1	0	0	0	.00	0
Watkins, Spenser	105.1	6	6	2	0	.857	5	3	1	0	.60	-1
Weathers, Ryan	3.2	1	0	0	0	1.000	0	0	0	0	-	0
Weaver, Luke	35.2	2	3	1	0	.833	2	0	0	0	.00	0
Webb, Logan	192.1	22	22	0	2	1.000	19	5	2	0	.26	1
Weber, Ryan	10.2	3	1	0	0	1.000	1	1	0	1	1.00	1
Weems, Jordan	39.2	2	2	0	0	1.000	0	0	0	0	-	-1
Weiss, Zack	13.1	1	0	1	0	.500	2	0	0	0	.00	0
Weissert, Greg	11.1	1	0	1	0	.500	2	0	0	0	.00	-1
Wells, Alex	3.2	0	0	0	0	-	0	0	0	0	-	0
Wells, Tyler	103.2	12	8	0	0	1.000	10	5	2	0	.50	2
Wendelken, J.B.	29.0	1	4	0	2	1.000	4	2	0	0	.50	0
Wentz, Joey	32.2	1	5	0	0	1.000	1	1	1	0	1.00	3
Wesneski, Hayden	33.0	5	0	1	0	.833	5	2	0	0	.40	-1
Wheeler, Zack	153.0	11	11	0	1	1.000	9	4	0	1	.44	2
White, Mitch	99.0	9	10	0	0	1.000	12	2	0	0	.17	1
Whitley, Kodi	12.2	2	2	0	0	1.000	0	0	0	0	-	0
Whitlock, Garrett	78.1	6	6	0	0	1.000	7	1	1	0	.14	1
Wick, Rowan	64.0	4	7	1	0	.917	6	1	0	0	.17	-1
Widener, Taylor	17.1	1	0	0	0	1.000	2	0	0	0	.00	0
Wiles, Collin	9.2	1	0	0	0	1.000	1	0	0	0	.00	-1
Williams, Devin	60.2	3	5	0	0	1.000	8	2	0	1	.25	1
Williams, Trevor	89.2	6	4	0	1	1.000	3	2	0	0	.67	1
Wilson, Bryse	115.2	4	3	0	0	1.000	9	3	0	0	.33	-1
Wilson, Justin	3.2	1	0	0	0	1.000	0	0	0	0	-	0
Wilson, Steven	53.0	2	3	1	0	.833	2	0	0	0	.00	0
Winckowski, Josh	70.1	9	7	1	0	.941	5	1	1	0	.20	-1
Winder, Josh	67.0	1	2	0	0	1.000	12	2	0	0	.17	-2
Wisler, Matt	44.0	2	2	0	0	1.000	3	0	0	0	.00	0
Wittgren, Nick	29.0	2	2	0	1	1.000	0	0	0	0	-	1
Wood, Alex	130.2	3	14	1	1	.944	3	2	0	0	.67	0
Woodford, Jake	48.1	3	0	0	0	1.000	1	0	0	0	.00	-2
Woodruff, Brandon	153.1	8	13	0	1	1.000	14	5	2	0	.36	1
Woods, William	2.0	0	0	0	0	-	0	0	0	0	-	0
Woods Richardson, S.	5.0	0	0	0	0	-	1	0	0	0	.00	0
Wright, Kyle	180.1	23	23	0	1	1.000	5	2	1	0	.40	2
Yacabonis, Jimmy	14.0	1	0	1	1	.500	1	1	0	0	1.00	0
Yajure, Miguel	24.1	3	2	0	0	1.000	2	1	0	0	.50	0
Yarbrough, Ryan	80.1	2	9	2	1	.846	9	3	1	0	.33	1
Yates, Kirby	7.0	1	0	0	0	1.000	0	0	0	0	-	0
Ynoa, Huascar	6.2	1	2	0	0	1.000	1	0	0	0	.00	1

	2022 Fielding and Holding Runners											
Pitcher	Inn	PO	A	E	DP	Pct	SBA	CS	PCS	PPO	CS%	RS
Young, Alex	26.2	3	1	0	1	1.000	1	0	0	0	.00	-1
Young, Danny	6.1	0	0	0	0	-	0	0	0	0	-	-1
Zabala, Aneurys	2.2	0	0	0	0	-	1	0	0	0	.00	0
Zastryzny, Rob	4.0	0	0	0	0	-	1	0	0	0	.00	0
Zerpa, Angel	11.0	0	1	1	0	.500	0	0	0	0	-	-1
Zeuch, T.J.	10.2	3	2	0	0	1.000	2	0	0	0	.00	0
Zimmermann, B.	73.2	1	5	0	0	1.000	2	0	0	0	.00	-1

Hitters Pitching

Player	2022 Pitching											Career Pitching										
	G	W	L	Sv	IP	H	R	ER	BB	SO	ERA	G	W	L	Sv	IP	H	R	ER	BB	SO	ERA
Adrianza, Ehire	1	-	-	-	1.0	-	-	-	1	1	0.00	3	0	0	0	3.0	6	4	4	1	2	12.00
Alberto, Hanser	10	-	-	-	11.0	10	5	5	3	1	4.09	12	0	0	0	12.1	11	7	7	5	1	5.11
Alcantara, Sergio	-	-	-	-	-	-	-	-	-	-		1	0	0	0	0.1	0	0	0	0	0	0.00
Almora Jr., Albert	-	-	-	-	-	-	-	-	-	-		1	0	0	0	1.0	1	3	3	1	0	27.00
Arauz, Jonathan	-	-	-	-	-	-	-	-	-	-		1	0	0	0	1.0	2	1	1	0	0	9.00
Arcia, Orlando	1	-	-	-	1.0	-	-	-	1	-	0.00	3	0	0	0	3.0	4	4	4	2	0	12.00
Arroyo, Christian	-	-	-	-	-	-	-	-	-	-		1	0	0	0	1.0	1	2	0	1	0	0.00
Astudillo, Willians	2	-	-	-	2.0	-	-	-	2	-	0.00	7	0	0	0	7.0	6	6	6	4	0	7.71
Barnhart, Tucker	1	-	-	-	1.0	3	1	1	-	-	9.00	1	0	0	0	1.0	3	1	1	0	0	9.00
Batten, Matt	2	-	-	-	2.0	2	1	1	-	1	4.50	2	0	0	0	2.0	2	1	1	0	1	4.50
Bemboom, Anthony	-	-	-	-	-	-	-	-	-	-		2	0	0	0	2.0	3	2	2	1	0	9.00
Bethancourt, Christian	4	-	-	-	4.0	6	1	1	1	1	2.25	10	0	0	0	9.1	13	10	7	12	4	6.75
Bradley Jr., Jackie	1	-	-	-	1.0	1	1	1	3	1	9.00	1	0	0	0	1.0	1	1	1	3	1	9.00
Brantly, Rob	-	-	-	-	-	-	-	-	-	-		1	0	0	0	1.0	1	1	1	0	0	9.00
Brosseau, Mike	3	-	-	-	3.0	2	-	-	1	-	0.00	7	0	0	0	7.1	7	2	2	1	1	2.45
Caratini, Victor	1	-	-	-	1.0	2	3	3	1	-	27.00	5	0	0	0	5.0	7	7	7	2	0	12.60
Carpenter, Matt	-	-	-	-	-	-	-	-	-	-		1	0	0	0	1.1	2	0	0	0	0	0.00
Castillo, Diego	2	-	-	-	2.0	6	8	8	3	1	36.00	2	0	0	0	2.0	6	8	8	3	1	36.00
Castro, Harold	4	-	-	-	4.0	6	2	2	1	1	4.50	7	0	0	0	6.2	6	2	2	4	1	2.70
Chang, Yu	2	-	-	-	2.0	6	3	3	-	-	13.50	2	0	0	0	2.0	6	3	3	0	0	13.50
Clemens, Kody	7	-	-	-	7.0	12	3	3	1	1	3.86	7	0	0	0	7.0	12	3	3	1	1	3.86
Clement, Ernie	2	-	-	-	2.0	6	4	4	-	-	18.00	2	0	0	0	2.0	6	4	4	0	0	18.00
Cronenworth, Jake	-	-	-	-	-	-	-	-	-	-		1	0	0	0	0.2	1	0	0	0	1	0.00
Culberson, Charlie	2	-	-	-	2.0	1	-	-	1	-	0.00	8	0	0	0	7.1	7	1	1	3	1	1.23
Davidson, Matt	-	-	-	-	-	-	-	-	-	-		6	0	0	0	6.1	5	2	2	3	3	2.84
Davis, J.D.	-	-	-	-	-	-	-	-	-	-		3	0	0	0	2.2	2	1	1	1	4	3.38
Demeritte, Travis	-	-	-	-	-	-	-	-	-	-		1	0	0	0	1.0	4	4	4	0	0	36.00
Dickerson, Corey	1	-	-	-	1.0	2	-	-	1	-	0.00	1	0	0	0	1.0	2	0	0	1	0	0.00
Difo, Wilmer	-	-	-	-	-	-	-	-	-	-		2	0	0	0	2.0	9	8	8	3	1	36.00
Dixon, Brandon	-	-	-	-	-	-	-	-	-	-		4	0	0	0	3.1	1	2	2	0	2	5.40
Dozier, Hunter	1	-	-	-	1.0	2	2	2	1	-	18.00	1	0	0	0	1.0	2	2	2	1	0	18.00
Drury, Brandon	-	-	-	-	-	-	-	-	-	-		1	0	0	0	0.2	3	2	2	1	0	27.00
Duffy, Matt	-	-	-	-	-	-	-	-	-	-		1	0	0	0	0.1	0	0	0	0	0	0.00
Escobar, Alcides	2	-	-	-	1.2	3	2	2	1	-	10.80	2	0	0	0	1.2	3	2	2	1	0	10.80
Escobar, Eduardo	-	-	-	-	-	-	-	-	-	-		1	0	0	0	1.0	1	0	0	0	0	0.00
Espinal, Santiago	-	-	-	-	-	-	-	-	-	-		2	0	0	0	2.0	3	2	2	1	0	9.00
Farmer, Kyle	-	-	-	-	-	-	-	-	-	-		1	0	0	0	1.1	1	0	0	0	0	0.00
Ford, Mike	1	-	-	-	1.0	1	2	2	1	-	18.00	2	0	0	0	3.0	7	7	7	1	1	21.00
France, Ty	-	-	-	-	-	-	-	-	-	-		2	0	0	0	2.0	2	1	1	0	0	4.50
Garcia, Leury	-	-	-	-	-	-	-	-	-	-		2	0	1	0	2.0	2	2	2	2	1	9.00
Garver, Mitch	-	-	-	-	-	-	-	-	-	-		1	0	0	0	1.0	1	0	0	0	0	0.00
Gonzalez, Luis	5	-	-	-	6.1	9	4	4	1	-	5.68	5	0	0	0	6.1	9	4	4	1	0	5.68
Gonzalez, Marwin	1	-	-	-	0.1	-	-	-	-	-	0.00	2	0	0	0	1.1	0	0	0	0	0	0.00
Gonzalez, Romy	-	-	-	-	-	-	-	-	-	-		1	0	0	0	0.1	0	0	0	0	1	0.00
Gordon, Nick	4	-	-	-	3.2	10	9	9	4	-	22.09	4	0	0	0	3.2	10	9	9	4	0	22.09
Gosselin, Phil	1	-	-	-	1.0	-	-	-	-	-	0.00	1	0	0	0	1.0	0	0	0	0	0	0.00
Grichuk, Randal	1	-	-	-	1.0	-	-	-	-	-	0.00	1	0	0	0	1.0	0	0	0	0	0	0.00
Guillorme, Luis	-	-	-	-	-	-	-	-	-	-		2	0	0	0	2.0	3	2	2	1	0	9.00
Hager, Jake	3	-	-	-	2.1	3	2	2	-	1	7.71	3	0	0	0	2.1	3	2	2	0	1	7.71
Hall, Darick	1	-	-	-	0.1	1	-	-	-	-	0.00	1	0	0	0	0.1	1	0	0	0	0	0.00
Happ, Ian	-	-	-	-	-	-	-	-	-	-		1	0	0	0	1.0	1	0	0	0	0	0.00
Harrison, Josh	3	-	-	-	3.0	9	6	6	2	2	18.00	4	0	0	0	3.1	9	6	6	2	2	16.20
Heineman, Tyler	-	-	-	-	-	-	-	-	-	-		1	0	0	0	1.0	1	0	0	0	0	0.00
Hernandez, Kike	-	-	-	-	-	-	-	-	-	-		1	0	1	0	0.1	1	3	3	2	0	81.00
Kelly, Carson	4	-	-	-	4.2	9	4	4	2	-	7.71	5	0	0	0	5.2	10	4	4	2	0	6.35
Kingery, Scott	-	-	-	-	-	-	-	-	-	-		1	0	0	0	1.1	4	2	2	0	0	13.50
Knapp, Andrew	-	-	-	-	-	-	-	-	-	-		1	0	0	0	0.1	0	0	0	0	0	0.00
Knizner, Andrew	1	-	-	-	0.2	1	-	-	-	-	0.00	1	0	0	0	0.2	1	0	0	0	0	0.00
La Stella, Tommy	-	-	-	-	-	-	-	-	-	-		1	0	0	0	1.1	3	1	1	0	0	6.75
Leon, Sandy	1	-	-	-	2.0	-	-	-	-	-	0.00	7	0	0	0	8.0	7	5	5	1	2	5.63
Lopez, Alejo	3	-	-	-	2.2	2	2	2	-	-	6.75	3	0	0	0	2.2	2	2	2	0	0	6.75
Lopez, Nicky	1	-	-	-	1.0	3	2	2	-	-	18.00	1	0	0	0	1.0	3	2	2	0	0	18.00
Luplow, Jordan	-	-	-	-	-	-	-	-	-	-		1	0	0	0	1.0	2	1	1	0	0	9.00
Maile, Luke	-	-	-	-	-	-	-	-	-	-		3	0	0	0	3.0	3	1	1	0	3	3.00
Maldonado, Martin	-	-	-	-	-	-	-	-	-	-		1	0	0	0	1.0	1	0	0	0	0	0.00
Maton, Nick	2	-	-	-	1.1	4	3	3	-	-	20.25	3	0	0	0	1.2	4	3	3	0	1	16.20
Mayfield, Jack	1	-	-	-	1.0	1	-	-	-	-	0.00	2	0	0	0	1.1	1	0	0	0	0	0.00
McGuire, Reese	1	-	-	-	1.0	-	-	-	-	-	0.00	1	0	0	0	1.0	0	0	0	0	0	0.00

Hitters Pitching

Player	2022 Pitching											Career Pitching										
	G	W	L	Sv	IP	H	R	ER	BB	SO	ERA	G	W	L	Sv	IP	H	R	ER	BB	SO	ERA
McKenna, Ryan	2	-	-	-	1.1	5	2	2	1	-	13.50	2	0	0	0	1.1	5	2	2	1	0	13.50
Mejia, Francisco	-	-	-	-	-	-	-	-	-	-		2	0	0	0	2.0	6	6	6	0	0	27.00
Mendick, Danny	-	-	-	-	-	-	-	-	-	-		1	0	0	0	1.0	1	0	0	0	1	0.00
Mercedes, Yermin	-	-	-	-	-	-	-	-	-	-		1	0	0	0	1.0	3	1	1	2	0	9.00
Merrifield, Whit	1	-	-	-	1.0	2	2	2	-	-	18.00	1	0	0	0	1.0	2	2	2	0	0	18.00
Molina, Yadier	2	-	-	-	2.0	6	4	4	-	1	18.00	2	0	0	0	2.0	6	4	4	0	1	18.00
Moore, Dylan	-	-	-	-	-	-	-	-	-	-		1	0	0	0	1.0	5	4	4	2	0	36.00
Motter, Taylor	-	-	-	-	-	-	-	-	-	-		2	0	0	0	1.1	2	1	1	1	1	6.75
Murphy, Tom	-	-	-	-	-	-	-	-	-	-		3	0	0	0	3.0	1	2	2	1	2	6.00
Myers, Wil	4	-	-	-	3.2	4	3	3	-	-	7.36	4	0	0	0	3.2	4	3	3	0	0	7.36
Neuse, Sheldon	3	-	-	-	3.2	1	-	-	-	-	0.00	3	0	0	0	3.2	1	0	0	0	0	0.00
Owings, Chris	1	-	-	-	1.0	2	1	1	-	-	9.00	2	0	0	0	2.2	8	5	5	1	0	16.88
Palacios, Jermaine	2	-	-	-	0.2	1	-	-	-	1	0.00	2	0	0	0	0.2	1	0	0	0	1	0.00
Peralta, David	-	-	-	-	-	-	-	-	-	-		1	0	0	0	1.0	4	3	3	0	1	27.00
Peterson, Jace	1	-	-	-	1.0	-	-	-	-	-	0.00	4	0	0	0	4.0	10	6	6	1	3	13.50
Phillips, Brett	3	-	-	-	4.0	9	8	8	2	-	18.00	4	0	0	0	5.0	11	9	9	4	0	16.20
Pillar, Kevin	-	-	-	-	-	-	-	-	-	-		1	0	0	0	0.1	0	0	0	0	0	0.00
Pinder, Chad	1	-	-	-	1.0	2	3	3	2	-	27.00	1	0	0	0	1.0	2	3	3	2	0	27.00
Plawecki, Kevin	1	-	-	-	1.0	1	-	-	-	-	0.00	7	0	0	0	7.2	6	4	4	1	0	4.70
Pujols, Albert	1	-	-	-	1.0	3	4	4	1	-	36.00	1	0	0	0	1.0	3	4	4	1	0	36.00
Quinn, Roman	-	-	-	-	-	-	-	-	-	-		3	0	1	0	5.0	13	10	10	5	1	18.00
Reyes, Franmil	1	-	-	-	1.0	-	-	-	-	1	0.00	1	0	0	0	1.0	0	0	0	0	1	0.00
Reyes, Pablo	1	-	-	-	1.0	-	-	-	-	-	0.00	1	0	0	0	1.0	0	0	0	0	0	0.00
Reynolds, Matt	2	-	-	-	1.1	3	1	1	-	-	6.75	2	0	0	0	1.1	3	1	1	0	0	6.75
Rizzo, Anthony	-	-	-	-	-	-	-	-	-	-		2	0	0	0	1.0	0	0	0	1	1	0.00
Romine, Austin	-	-	-	-	-	-	-	-	-	-		1	0	0	0	1.0	4	3	3	0	0	27.00
Ruf, Darin	1	-	-	-	2.0	1	-	-	-	-	0.00	2	0	0	0	3.0	4	2	2	0	0	6.00
Sanchez, Yolmer	1	-	-	-	1.0	3	1	1	-	-	9.00	2	0	0	0	2.0	5	2	2	0	0	9.00
Schrock, Max	1	-	-	-	1.0	7	5	5	-	-	45.00	4	0	0	0	3.2	7	5	5	0	1	12.27
Schwindel, Frank	3	-	-	-	3.0	8	6	6	1	-	18.00	3	0	0	0	3.0	8	6	6	1	0	18.00
Serven, Brian	1	-	-	-	1.0	-	-	-	1	-	0.00	1	0	0	0	1.0	0	0	0	1	0	0.00
Simmons, Andrelton	1	-	-	-	1.0	5	5	5	1	-	45.00	1	0	0	0	1.0	5	5	5	1	0	45.00
Slater, Austin	-	-	-	-	-	-	-	-	-	-		1	0	0	0	0.1	0	0	0	1	0	0.00
Spangenberg, Cory	-	-	-	-	-	-	-	-	-	-		2	0	0	0	2.0	4	3	3	3	0	13.50
Stallings, Jacob	-	-	-	-	-	-	-	-	-	-		1	0	0	0	1.0	0	0	0	0	0	0.00
Stassi, Max	-	-	-	-	-	-	-	-	-	-		1	0	0	0	0.1	0	0	0	0	0	0.00
Strange-Gordon, Dee	1	-	-	-	1.0	2	3	3	3	-	27.00	1	0	0	0	1.0	2	3	3	3	0	27.00
Stubbs, Garrett	4	-	-	-	3.2	7	7	7	1	1	17.18	4	0	0	0	3.2	7	7	7	1	1	17.18
Taylor, Michael A.	1	-	-	-	2.0	5	2	2	2	2	9.00	1	0	0	0	2.0	5	2	2	2	2	9.00
Tom, Ka'ai	-	-	-	-	-	-	-	-	-	-		1	0	0	0	1.0	1	0	0	0	0	0.00
Torrens, Luis	2	1	-	-	2.0	3	2	1	-	-	4.50	2	1	0	0	2.0	3	2	1	0	0	4.50
Turner, Justin	-	-	-	-	-	-	-	-	-	-		1	0	0	0	1.0	2	0	0	0	0	0.00
VanMeter, Josh	3	-	-	-	3.0	15	13	13	2	-	39.00	3	0	0	0	3.0	15	13	13	2	0	39.00
Vargas, Ildemaro	1	-	-	-	1.0	-	-	-	-	-	0.00	1	0	0	0	1.0	0	0	0	0	0	0.00
Walsh, Jared	-	-	-	-	-	-	-	-	-	-		5	0	0	0	5.0	3	1	1	6	5	1.80
Walton, Donovan	1	-	-	-	1.0	3	3	3	1	-	27.00	1	0	0	0	1.0	3	3	3	1	0	27.00
Wynns, Austin	2	-	-	-	2.0	3	3	3	1	-	13.50	3	0	0	0	3.0	4	4	4	1	0	12.00

Shift Update: Goodbye Full Shifts

Sarah Thompson and Mark Simon

In 2023, MLB will be placing restrictions on where infielders can play, requiring two infielders on each side of second base and for those infielders to be situated on the infield dirt rather than the grass.

This is a major change given that more than 38,000 balls were hit into play against full infield shifts in 2022, those in which three defenders were on the pull side of second base.

So how is this going to impact the game on the whole?

For one thing, some teams are going to have to adjust more than others. The Dodgers led the way in full shift usage in 2022, with 53% of balls in play against Los Angeles coming against such an alignment. Five other teams had a rate of 40% or higher—the Blue Jays (51%), Astros (49%), Twins (45%), Marlins (44%), and Mariners (44%).

In contrast, six teams shifted against no more than 25% of balls in play—the Rockies (18%), Guardians (22%), Orioles (23%), Padres (23%), Yankees (25%) and Brewers (25%).

Percentage of Full Shifts on Balls in Play
MLB Teams – 2022 Season

Team	Percentage
Dodgers	53%
Blue Jays	51%
Astros	49%
Twins	45%
Marlins	44%
Mariners	44%
White Sox	39%
Cubs	38%
Mets	37%
Red Sox	37%
Tigers	36%
Angels	35%
Rangers	34%

Percentage of Full Shifts on Balls in Play
MLB Teams – 2022 Season

Team	Percentage
Nationals	32%
Giants	32%
Athletics	32%
Pirates	31%
Braves	29%
Reds	29%
Cardinals	29%
Rays	28%
Phillies	28%
Diamondbacks	27%
Royals	26%
Brewers	25%
Yankees	25%
Padres	23%
Orioles	23%
Guardians	22%
Rockies	18%

For another thing, the hitters who pull almost all of their ground balls will have better opportunities to get hits since there are only two infielders on each side of the field, rather than the three they often face on the pull side. You can see the list of the most shifted hitters at the end of this essay.

But in sum, how much will the game change?

Given that next season's shift rules preclude three infielders standing on one side of second base, one way to answer this question is to compare historical batted ball outcomes when a full shift is on vs. when the infield is aligned in any way other than a full shift.

To do this reliably, we take a weighted approach, rather than straight-up comparing batting averages with and without the shift. This is because players who get shifted on most of their plate appearances, like Matt Olson or Kyle Schwarber, would be over-represented in the shift group and under-represented in the non-shift group, potentially skewing results. The weighted approach weights each player by the lesser of their shifted and unshifted count, and from there we can derive proper shift and no-shift batting averages.

Using the weighted approach, SIS estimates that in 2022, full shifts suppressed batting averages by approximately 22 points on ground balls and short line drives (GSL) versus any other alignment.

The effect of full shifts is magnified when we consider only batters who are worthy of one. Right-handed batters who pull at least 80% of GSLs and left-handed batters who pull at least 75% of GSLs are considered by SIS to be shift-worthy.

In 2022, shift-worthy batters saw a 39-point decrease in batting average on GSLs when facing a full shift as opposed to any other alignment (.237 to .198). However, non-shift-worthy batters saw just a 10-point decrease.

Weighted Batting Average on Ground Balls and Short Line Drives, 2022

SIS Recommendation	No Shift	Shift	Difference
Shift Candidate	.237	.198	Helps by 39 points
Non-Shift Candidates	.253	.243	Helps by 10 points

If we expand our scope to batted balls of all kinds (besides home runs), full shifts suppressed batting averages by a mere 8 points in 2022.

With all of this in mind, there are a couple of ways to look at the effect of banning full shifts. From a league-wide, game-wide perspective, viewers may enjoy a couple more ground balls and short line drives land for hits than in years past, but probably not enough to change the complexion of league-wide offense.

However, it's certainly possible that the right type of player, specifically extreme pull-hitters on ground balls and short liners, can see a non-insignificant bump in their BABIP.

And that's why we suggest reading the Hits Lost and Gained to the Shift section introduction.

Shifts by Team

American League

Team	2021	2022	Change
Detroit Tigers	2627	2777	150
Minnesota Twins	3012	2754	-258
Toronto Blue Jays	1756	2740	984
Houston Astros	2308	2594	286
Tampa Bay Rays	2349	2515	166
Oakland Athletics	1935	2452	517
Seattle Mariners	2356	2404	48
Los Angeles Angels	2289	2374	85
Chicago White Sox	1194	2264	1070
Boston Red Sox	2037	2173	136
Kansas City Royals	1899	2168	269
Texas Rangers	2321	2038	-283
New York Yankees	1442	2022	580
Baltimore Orioles	1623	1759	136
Cleveland Guardians	1520	1664	144
Total	30668	34698	4030
Average	2045	2313	268

National League

Team	2021	2022	Change
Los Angeles Dodgers	2751	3026	275
Pittsburgh Pirates	2223	2811	588
Cincinnati Reds	2081	2706	625
Atlanta Braves	2599	2657	58
Washington Nationals	2293	2562	269
Miami Marlins	2091	2519	428
San Francisco Giants	2226	2450	224
Arizona Diamondbacks	2045	2411	366
Chicago Cubs	1947	2279	332
San Diego Padres	1614	2263	649
Milwaukee Brewers	1751	2217	466
New York Mets	2588	2169	-419
St Louis Cardinals	1920	2136	216
Colorado Rockies	1644	2047	403
Philadelphia Phillies	1446	1902	456
Total	31219	36155	4936
Average	2081	2410	329

Top 30 Shifted Batters

Batter	Shifted PA	Shift Percent	Shift GSL BA	No Shift GSL BA
Olson, Matt	657	94.4	.232	.111
Schwarber, Kyle	648	97.4	.160	.333
Seager, Corey	643	97.9	.155	.750
Semien, Marcus	635	88.2	.253	.320
Ohtani, Shohei	635	96.8	.272	.600
Ramirez, Jose	587	87.1	.288	.500
Tucker, Kyle	580	95.7	.183	.333
Freeman, Freddie	578	82.5	.286	.378
Soto, Juan	573	87.7	.206	.160
Hoskins, Rhys	573	85.7	.230	.211
Tellez, Rowdy	566	96.1	.144	.333
Suarez, Eugenio	564	89.8	.264	.364
Lindor, Francisco	539	77.2	.263	.339
Muncy, Max	538	95.6	.179	.286
Devers, Rafael	534	88.3	.280	.273
Alvarez, Yordan	531	95.7	.169	.857
Yastrzemski, Mike	529	95.0	.163	.333
Brown, Seth	528	96.4	.212	.200
Betts, Mookie	528	82.9	.228	.172
Mullins II, Cedric	527	79.1	.290	.298
Bellinger, Cody	527	95.8	.231	.400
Santander, Anthony	521	81.0	.213	.300
Blackmon, Charlie	515	89.7	.207	.263
Voit, Luke	514	91.0	.218	.286
Bell, Josh	512	79.8	.240	.235
Judge, Aaron	508	74.9	.248	.357
Winker, Jesse	505	92.7	.225	.143
Yelich, Christian	504	75.9	.266	.288
Rizzo, Anthony	502	92.6	.190	.214
Bregman, Alex	498	76.1	.239	.163

Hits Lost and Gained to the Shift

Mark Simon

The happiest hitter to see the disappearance of the full defensive shift?

That's an easy one based on data from the 2022 season. It's Rangers shortstop Corey Seager.

Full shifts (those with three infielders on the pull side) completely vexed Seager in 2022.

Seager went 18-for-161 on ground balls and short line drives hit between first base and second base (not including balls fielded by the pitcher). That's a .112 batting average. That helps explain why Seager hit .245 last season, 52 points lower than his batting average with the Dodgers from 2015 to 2021.

At Sports Info Solutions, we track shift effectiveness on an at-bat by at-bat basis through a system that credits and debits hitters by comparing the result of a play on a ball hit against a full or partial shift to the expected result of the play with an unshifted defense, knowing where the ball was hit and how hard it was hit. Summing each ground ball and short line drive produces a season total of hits gained and hits lost.

By our calculations, Seager had a net loss of 30 hits against all defensive shifts this season (both full shifts and partial shifts, the latter of which will still be allowed in 2023).

If we look solely at his balls hit against full shifts and compare those to how he would have fared under next season's defensive rules (straight-up defenses and partial shifts), Seager would gain 29 hits (29 rather than 30, because Seager lost 29 hits to full shifts, 1 to partial shifts). Add 29 hits to Seager's 2022 ledger and he's basically the same hitter he had been for his Dodgers career.

Seager was by far the hitter most impacted in the aggregate in 2022. Other prominent hitters whose batting average was dampened by repeatedly making outs on shifts include Kyle Schwarber, Carlos Santana, and Rowdy Tellez.

One name worth pointing out on this list is Christian Walker, a right-handed hitter, who was in a similar boat to Seager in the first four months of the season. Walker's batting average was .199 entering August 6. But he hit .315 in his last 57 games of the season to raise his overall batting average by 43 points.

Walker countered defensive shifts with 10 hits on grounders/liners hit to the right of second base in that span, compared to the seven he had in the 103 games before it. He changed the narrative of his season with the way he played in the last third of it.

"That was honestly something that's just been happening," Walker said when we talked to him about it on *The Sports Info Solutions Baseball Podcast*. "I didn't want to lose slug to gain average points. I still wanted to do what I do well and help the team win. I can drive the ball and put a point on the board. But understanding what a team needs, and when I get to two strikes and I'm getting sliders away, does it make more sense for me to drive the ball out of the park, or does my team need me to poke a single the other way and pass the baton to the next guy. It's me understanding what I can do to help the team without launching the ball out of the ballpark."

The tables in the section that follows have two halves. The first half is for 2022 only and the second shows aggregated data since 2010 (the first season SIS began collecting shift data). In both cases, you will find listed the number of shifts on balls in play that a player saw, how many hits he lost, how many hits he gained, and the net of his hits lost and gained.

Hits Lost and Gained to the Shift for Batters

Player	2022 Season				Career Since 2010			
	Shifts	Lost	Gained	Net	Shifts	Lost	Gained	Net
Seager, Corey	454	48	18	30	1440	131	86	45
Schwarber, Kyle	322	33	10	23	1486	154	97	57
Santana, Carlos	289	33	13	20	2644	245	149	96
Alvarez, Yordan	319	35	17	18	815	88	42	46
Yastrzemski, Mike	318	27	11	16	871	63	40	23
Blackmon, Charlie	364	41	25	16	1673	138	122	16
Tellez, Rowdy	362	31	15	16	872	84	48	36
Marte, Ketel	323	31	15	16	834	68	53	15
Naylor, Josh	336	37	22	15	682	68	52	16
Bradley Jr., Jackie	236	27	12	15	1540	157	111	46
Tucker, Kyle	401	35	20	15	970	80	51	29
Carlson, Dylan	267	24	10	14	625	51	35	16
Olson, Matt	398	35	22	13	1647	140	97	43
Bregman, Alex	341	26	13	13	925	71	46	25
Ruiz, Keibert	293	28	16	12	340	31	18	13
Pache, Cristian	123	18	7	11	142	20	8	12
Walker, Christian	280	27	16	11	618	51	43	8
Soler, Jorge	147	16	5	11	832	72	53	19
Melendez, MJ	293	27	16	11	293	27	16	11
Reynolds, Bryan	308	31	21	10	826	75	58	17
Winker, Jesse	314	31	21	10	1021	91	65	26
Murphy, Sean	256	22	12	10	429	33	22	11
Narvaez, Omar	189	15	5	10	819	61	40	21
Kelly, Carson	171	17	7	10	464	39	18	21
Riley, Austin	284	25	15	10	712	58	45	13
Rizzo, Anthony	308	25	15	10	2971	255	148	107
Profar, Jurickson	316	29	19	10	998	92	64	28
Votto, Joey	213	20	11	9	1769	155	113	42
Betts, Mookie	357	29	20	9	1155	91	75	16
Ruf, Darin	155	15	6	9	323	28	19	9
Rutschman, Adley	278	23	14	9	278	23	14	9
Calhoun, Kole	239	21	12	9	1849	179	110	69
Candelario, Jeimer	251	26	17	9	963	88	53	35
Ozuna, Marcell	256	20	11	9	744	59	44	15
Heim, Jonah	238	21	12	9	412	34	19	15
Toro, Abraham	195	13	4	9	442	37	24	13
Brantley, Michael	180	18	9	9	1243	116	89	27
Nootbaar, Lars	178	16	7	9	244	21	9	12
Raleigh, Cal	202	18	9	9	272	24	11	13
Suwinski, Jack	180	19	11	8	180	19	11	8
Soto, Juan	354	32	24	8	1006	94	82	12
Muncy, Max	297	21	13	8	1253	110	56	54
Brown, Seth	319	23	15	8	529	34	23	11
Sanchez, Gary	219	21	13	8	916	86	51	35
De La Cruz, Bryan	105	10	3	7	164	16	9	7
Taylor, Tyrone	186	15	8	7	306	26	18	8
Hedges, Austin	141	12	5	7	469	34	20	14
Frazier, Adam	241	20	13	7	770	62	47	15
Kiermaier, Kevin	88	11	4	7	759	69	70	-1
Vogelbach, Daniel	243	17	10	7	771	71	34	37
Moncada, Yoan	228	17	10	7	931	74	72	2
Guerrero Jr., Vladimir	197	19	12	7	630	57	44	13
Caratini, Victor	138	13	6	7	509	52	34	18
VanMeter, Josh	115	12	5	7	437	36	20	16
Arenado, Nolan	233	16	9	7	976	68	64	4
Perdomo, Geraldo	173	14	7	7	173	14	7	7
McMahon, Ryan	285	28	21	7	829	76	62	14
Smith, Dominic	88	10	3	7	737	73	38	35
Lowe, Brandon	159	13	6	7	728	56	42	14
Stanton, Giancarlo	143	16	9	7	1000	98	79	19
Thomas, Alek	200	24	17	7	200	24	17	7
Judge, Aaron	255	22	16	6	855	76	66	10
Maldonado, Martin	158	14	8	6	524	51	24	27
Mejia, Francisco	150	14	8	6	407	37	26	11
Harrison, Josh	98	8	2	6	485	38	22	16
Crawford, Brandon	238	20	14	6	1153	88	83	5
Contreras, Willson	149	16	10	6	472	44	33	11
Rengifo, Luis	278	27	21	6	483	45	34	11
Arraez, Luis	199	16	10	6	353	24	22	2
Kirk, Alejandro	110	12	6	6	176	17	10	7
Bleday, J.J.	127	8	2	6	127	8	2	6
Peterson, Jace	161	15	9	6	458	38	27	11
Sanchez, Jesus	167	16	10	6	269	25	16	9

Hits Lost and Gained to the Shift for Batters

Player	2022 Season				Career Since 2010			
	Shifts	Lost	Gained	Net	Shifts	Lost	Gained	Net
Franco, Wander	193	17	11	6	326	27	20	7
Rendon, Anthony	53	6	0	6	412	36	16	20
Hilliard, Sam	111	13	7	6	309	29	24	5
Moran, Colin	75	9	3	6	842	82	51	31
Alonso, Pete	302	23	17	6	800	65	53	12
Ortega, Rafael	194	11	5	6	404	26	21	5
Gregorius, Didi	146	12	6	6	1020	77	52	25
Schoop, Jonathan	153	11	6	5	716	60	56	4
Suzuki, Kurt	76	5	0	5	525	43	23	20
Cabrera, Miguel	78	10	5	5	479	49	39	10
Wade Jr., LaMonte	144	9	4	5	348	24	13	11
Knizner, Andrew	84	7	2	5	120	9	3	6
Castellanos, Nick	284	26	21	5	1148	83	89	-6
Arroyo, Christian	63	7	2	5	126	11	6	5
O'Hearn, Ryan	93	11	6	5	533	56	37	19
Peralta, David	249	18	13	5	1169	106	97	9
Serven, Brian	66	6	1	5	66	6	1	5
Urias, Ramon	61	7	2	5	94	9	6	3
Rojas, Josh	203	16	11	5	520	41	34	7
Wong, Kolten	261	20	15	5	970	79	73	6
Gamel, Ben	210	18	13	5	590	54	34	20
Biggio, Cavan	159	13	8	5	626	47	31	16
Franco, Maikel	196	15	10	5	923	85	56	29
Adrianza, Ehire	50	6	1	5	299	26	10	16
Hoskins, Rhys	336	25	20	5	1179	85	65	20
McKinstry, Zach	74	7	2	5	150	14	5	9
Duvall, Adam	151	11	6	5	978	66	57	9
Reyes, Victor	97	8	3	5	286	19	18	1
Gonzalez, Marwin	100	9	4	5	824	60	53	7
Collins, Zack	52	5	0	5	219	15	10	5
Bellinger, Cody	329	28	23	5	1588	127	119	8
Vogt, Stephen	118	9	4	5	1099	76	59	17
Flores, Wilmer	251	20	15	5	587	43	29	14
Diaz, Lewin	99	10	5	5	195	16	10	6
Miller, Brad	138	10	15	-5	738	70	70	0
Diaz, Aledmys	114	7	12	-5	396	24	31	-7
Leblanc, Charles	53	2	7	-5	53	2	7	-5
Contreras, William	88	6	11	-5	132	11	14	-3
Hernandez, Cesar	222	15	20	-5	678	57	60	-3
Benintendi, Andrew	319	24	29	-5	1328	103	104	-1
Taylor, Michael A.	134	8	13	-5	409	28	36	-8
Robles, Victor	136	6	11	-5	371	21	25	-4
Mateo, Jorge	78	5	10	-5	127	9	12	-3
Hiura, Keston	70	2	7	-5	192	12	20	-8
Alfaro, Jorge	66	4	9	-5	171	13	16	-3
Ramirez, Harold	70	6	11	-5	148	10	20	-10
Nola, Austin	129	7	12	-5	257	16	20	-4
Harris II, Michael	157	15	21	-6	157	15	21	-6
Iglesias, Jose	125	9	15	-6	260	20	25	-5
Haniger, Mitch	125	10	16	-6	743	58	60	-2
Hays, Austin	204	13	19	-6	428	31	38	-7
Bogaerts, Xander	184	13	19	-6	613	40	61	-21
Baddoo, Akil	76	4	10	-6	253	18	25	-7
Pena, Jeremy	209	13	20	-7	209	13	20	-7
Swanson, Dansby	288	18	25	-7	775	58	54	4
Suzuki, Seiya	99	5	12	-7	99	5	12	-7
Goldschmidt, Paul	178	10	18	-8	820	58	77	-19
Rodriguez, Julio	181	13	21	-8	181	13	21	-8
Semien, Marcus	456	26	36	-10	1380	85	100	-15

Outs Gained and Lost to the Shift for Pitchers

Player	2022 Season				Career Since 2010			
	Shifts	Gained	Lost	Net	Shifts	Gained	Lost	Net
Taillon, Jameson	317	29	10	19	1013	86	56	30
Gonsolin, Tony	290	33	15	18	576	54	27	27
Wright, Kyle	359	37	20	17	464	47	27	20
Lopez, Pablo	347	32	17	15	836	69	48	21
Mikolas, Miles	339	32	17	15	774	68	42	26
Gallen, Zac	265	28	14	14	654	62	39	23
Alcantara, Sandy	460	40	28	12	1232	107	88	19
Verlander, Justin	321	29	17	12	1049	81	53	28
Musgrove, Joe	362	31	19	12	1304	115	78	37
Pivetta, Nick	301	25	13	12	819	62	57	5
Gilbert, Logan	306	27	15	12	500	40	25	15
Manaea, Sean	230	20	9	11	696	65	42	23
Thompson, Zach	273	26	15	11	415	36	24	12
Castillo, Luis	228	24	14	10	1044	100	83	17
Montgomery, Jordan	179	22	12	10	530	49	49	0
Kikuchi, Yusei	164	19	9	10	609	59	40	19
Wacha, Michael	238	23	13	10	946	92	63	29
Ashcraft, Graham	222	26	16	10	222	26	16	10
Feltner, Ryan	149	16	7	9	159	17	7	10
Singer, Brady	224	22	13	9	505	44	40	4
Darvish, Yu	347	21	12	9	1109	79	59	20
Kelly, Merrill	350	25	16	9	939	86	49	37
Odorizzi, Jake	202	16	7	9	1575	120	78	42
Cueto, Johnny	319	31	22	9	1136	96	59	37
Festa, Matthew	76	10	1	9	107	11	3	8
Burnes, Corbin	281	26	17	9	635	56	47	9
Irvin, Cole	300	21	13	8	576	43	34	9
Ryan, Joe	282	19	11	8	328	20	13	7
Gomber, Austin	164	14	6	8	305	26	14	12
Kaprielian, James	274	22	14	8	447	33	21	12
Morton, Charlie	299	22	14	8	1578	145	98	47
Hendricks, Kyle	150	13	5	8	979	86	65	21
Stripling, Ross	278	27	19	8	920	88	61	27
Gray, Sonny	231	20	12	8	1332	113	80	33
Fried, Max	349	27	19	8	902	80	53	27
Holmes, Clay	94	14	6	8	292	34	28	6
Mayza, Tim	77	11	3	8	248	30	11	19
Skubal, Tarik	212	20	12	8	511	40	29	11
Garcia, Luis	304	22	14	8	595	45	32	13
Elder, Bryce	96	12	4	8	96	12	4	8
Brieske, Beau	178	15	8	7	178	15	8	7
Senzatela, Antonio	163	16	9	7	890	90	60	30
Blackburn, Paul	227	19	12	7	373	35	22	13
Gray, Jon	174	18	11	7	1030	93	64	29
Smyly, Drew	183	16	9	7	758	52	51	1
Archer, Chris	209	16	9	7	1207	100	74	26
Espino, Paolo	242	20	13	7	509	45	23	22
Wainwright, Adam	345	26	19	7	1270	107	70	37
Pineda, Michael	112	11	4	7	1141	94	69	25
German, Domingo	146	13	6	7	641	52	35	17
Severino, Luis	159	13	6	7	657	57	41	16
Anderson, Ian	277	28	21	7	586	58	45	13
Plesac, Zach	224	18	12	6	599	48	27	21
Bieber, Shane	233	23	17	6	658	60	41	19
Akin, Keegan	97	12	6	6	247	20	19	1
Civale, Aaron	131	13	7	6	459	43	19	24
Martin, Brett	92	13	7	6	293	35	25	10
Fedde, Erick	271	22	16	6	753	71	56	15
Javier, Cristian	246	17	11	6	490	35	20	15
Barria, Jaime	152	13	7	6	495	41	22	19
Urquidy, Jose	345	27	21	6	655	51	36	15
Webb, Logan	386	38	32	6	789	80	73	7
Hearn, Taylor	144	14	8	6	302	27	19	8
Price, David	83	10	4	6	648	60	46	14
Pressly, Ryan	72	9	3	6	395	45	29	16
McHugh, Collin	128	11	5	6	1162	102	63	39
Syndergaard, Noah	257	24	18	6	668	61	48	13
Sanchez, Aaron	127	16	10	6	637	65	45	20
Almonte, Yency	69	10	4	6	206	19	13	6
Giolito, Lucas	263	24	18	6	998	94	58	36
Montero, Rafael	118	12	6	6	350	35	25	10
Junis, Jakob	250	24	18	6	834	75	67	8
Duffey, Tyler	94	11	5	6	522	46	28	18

Outs Gained and Lost to the Shift for Pitchers

Player	2022 Season				Career Since 2010			
	Shifts	Gained	Lost	Net	Shifts	Gained	Lost	Net
Manoah, Alek	380	28	22	6	501	38	32	6
Rasmussen, Drew	223	21	15	6	305	27	20	7
Martin, Davis	130	14	8	6	130	14	8	6
McClanahan, Shane	255	25	20	5	480	38	41	-3
Brown, Hunter	36	6	1	5	36	6	1	5
Thompson, Zack	50	5	0	5	50	5	0	5
Koenig, Jared	72	9	4	5	72	9	4	5
Henry, Tommy	64	7	2	5	64	7	2	5
Suarez, Robert	52	6	1	5	52	6	1	5
Suter, Brent	110	11	6	5	479	46	39	7
Barnes, Matt	55	7	2	5	241	21	16	5
Anderson, Tyler	432	31	26	5	1013	71	56	15
Bundy, Dylan	327	27	22	5	1292	98	72	26
De Jong, Chase	121	9	4	5	286	21	11	10
Urias, Julio	363	25	20	5	996	78	59	19
Bard, Luke	29	6	1	5	79	11	4	7
Lugo, Seth	98	10	5	5	427	44	24	20
Gibson, Kyle	256	23	18	5	1662	156	120	36
Phelps, David	128	12	7	5	387	28	27	1
Banuelos, Manny	70	9	4	5	125	13	7	6
Kershaw, Clayton	277	25	20	5	1269	118	97	21
Gilbert, Tyler	68	6	1	5	109	10	5	5
Garcia, Jarlin	105	10	5	5	418	38	20	18
Crismatt, Nabil	161	14	9	5	310	26	23	3
Cortes, Nestor	144	10	5	5	314	20	15	5
Overton, Connor	81	8	3	5	107	10	5	5
Quantrill, Cal	243	19	14	5	615	51	38	13
Herget, Jimmy	119	12	7	5	181	17	10	7
Mahle, Tyler	243	18	13	5	830	68	54	14
Alexander, Jason	150	13	8	5	150	13	8	5
Crowe, Wil	147	14	9	5	346	32	22	10
Bolanos, Ronald	31	5	0	5	75	9	3	6
Wentz, Joey	67	7	2	5	67	7	2	5
Hicks, Jordan	64	8	3	5	91	11	5	6
Sandlin, Nick	45	7	2	5	70	9	3	6
Peterson, David	151	10	15	-5	319	26	26	0
Wilson, Bryse	262	17	22	-5	488	32	33	-1
Hernandez, Elieser	128	6	11	-5	441	31	21	10
Scherzer, Max	205	8	13	-5	1115	66	72	-6
Garcia, Luis	75	4	9	-5	247	20	28	-8
Minor, Mike	187	8	13	-5	731	48	53	-5
Goudeau, Ashton	41	2	7	-5	121	10	11	-1
Pilkington, Konnor	59	2	7	-5	59	2	7	-5
Kirby, George	232	15	20	-5	232	15	20	-5
Cobb, Alex	308	29	35	-6	1315	128	110	18
Abbott, Cory	77	3	9	-6	101	4	10	-6
Sandoval, Patrick	237	17	23	-6	445	36	41	-5
Gausman, Kevin	297	20	27	-7	1343	99	103	-4
Lynch, Daniel	155	10	17	-7	233	14	24	-10
Kuhnel, Joel	125	9	17	-8	138	9	19	-10
Snead, Kirby	88	4	12	-8	103	5	13	-8
Fleming, Josh	63	3	13	-10	273	27	28	-1

Hits Lost and Gained to the Shift by Batting Team

Team	2022 Season				Totals Since 2010			
	Shifts	Lost	Gained	Net	Shifts	Lost	Gained	Net
Houston Astros	2643	219	160	59	11954	995	745	250
Arizona Diamondbacks	2657	225	172	53	10460	885	716	169
Oakland Athletics	2263	186	136	50	13141	1025	836	189
Seattle Mariners	2476	205	159	46	13021	1101	815	286
Milwaukee Brewers	2723	208	163	45	10421	853	664	189
San Francisco Giants	2568	191	146	45	10208	779	605	174
Philadelphia Phillies	2476	197	153	44	11595	1024	725	299
Pittsburgh Pirates	2342	192	148	44	10052	895	678	217
Miami Marlins	1927	162	121	41	7641	645	559	86
Toronto Blue Jays	1778	153	117	36	12628	1100	765	335
New York Yankees	2221	180	146	34	13210	1142	817	325
Tampa Bay Rays	2069	167	134	33	11877	961	816	145
St Louis Cardinals	2571	194	161	33	10400	790	675	115
Texas Rangers	2846	225	193	32	12907	1125	915	210
Cleveland Guardians	2189	177	146	31	12130	995	791	204
Colorado Rockies	2080	185	154	31	9800	812	786	26
Washington Nationals	2430	195	164	31	10325	864	700	164
Los Angeles Dodgers	2645	193	163	30	12861	1052	834	218
Los Angeles Angels	2271	189	159	30	12129	1087	829	258
New York Mets	2541	207	181	26	12666	1107	792	315
Chicago Cubs	2098	164	141	23	12585	1071	851	220
Cincinnati Reds	2124	159	136	23	11271	920	722	198
Detroit Tigers	2233	184	161	23	10052	810	701	109
Kansas City Royals	2530	197	174	23	11792	967	813	154
Minnesota Twins	2353	183	161	22	12885	1030	865	165
Boston Red Sox	2355	186	165	21	14411	1224	970	254
Baltimore Orioles	2322	165	146	19	11767	954	788	166
Atlanta Braves	2588	200	183	17	12039	966	798	168
San Diego Padres	2505	193	184	9	9996	847	716	131
Chicago White Sox	2029	151	150	1	8741	731	642	89

Outs Gained and Lost to the Shift by Defensive Team

Team	2022 Season				Totals Since 2010			
	Shifts	Gained	Lost	Net	Shifts	Gained	Lost	Net
New York Yankees	2022	177	108	69	12495	1051	864	187
Atlanta Braves	2657	218	153	65	11178	964	740	224
Los Angeles Dodgers	3026	252	194	58	12832	1106	857	249
Houston Astros	2594	215	158	57	16385	1411	1059	352
Arizona Diamondbacks	2411	182	134	48	11377	983	721	262
Boston Red Sox	2173	178	130	48	10448	857	684	173
St Louis Cardinals	2136	171	127	44	9008	755	566	189
Chicago Cubs	2279	194	151	43	8436	746	545	201
Toronto Blue Jays	2740	227	185	42	12605	1061	806	255
Detroit Tigers	2777	224	184	40	11142	912	757	155
Minnesota Twins	2754	205	168	37	14084	1108	909	199
San Diego Padres	2263	165	129	36	8869	750	558	192
Milwaukee Brewers	2217	173	137	36	13156	1135	914	221
Colorado Rockies	2047	173	138	35	10872	964	724	240
Cleveland Guardians	1664	135	100	35	9689	807	544	263
Los Angeles Angels	2374	189	158	31	11021	891	736	155
Seattle Mariners	2404	189	158	31	12966	1075	878	197
Pittsburgh Pirates	2811	226	196	30	14829	1241	1037	204
Miami Marlins	2519	197	169	28	11062	854	747	107
Texas Rangers	2038	182	156	26	10723	925	708	217
Chicago White Sox	2264	186	162	24	11192	969	750	219
Tampa Bay Rays	2515	182	160	22	16668	1385	1125	260
San Francisco Giants	2450	213	192	21	10863	895	718	177
Baltimore Orioles	1759	143	128	15	12565	1048	820	228
Kansas City Royals	2168	179	165	14	10555	862	787	75
Oakland Athletics	2452	182	168	14	10039	817	649	168
Cincinnati Reds	2706	189	181	8	11527	910	753	157
Philadelphia Phillies	1902	142	137	5	8842	719	631	88
Washington Nationals	2562	192	191	1	9899	786	684	102
New York Mets	2169	150	162	-12	9638	769	661	108

Four-Outfielder Alignments

Jackson Lewis

When it comes to the four-outfielder alignment, teams this season did not hold back. This season's 294 balls in play against a four-outfielder set is more than all previous seasons combined (since SIS began tracking such alignments in 2018). While the league-wide rate is up, we can attribute most of this spike to the AL East. Two hundred sixty of the 294 were deployed by these teams, with the Blue Jays accounting for nearly 60% of all occurrences. With the shift ban looming for the 2023 season, no division will feel its absence more.

On a batter level, Anthony Rizzo (41 BIP), Rafael Devers (26 BIP), and last year's leader, Joey Gallo (17 BIP), topped the leaderboard in encounters with this shift. AL East teams, for good reason, took full advantage of Rizzo's first full season with the Yankees, as his 33% groundball rate and 79% pulled-groundball rate made him a prime candidate for the four-outfielder arrangement.

Devers' presence on this list, however, is a bit head scratching. His relatively high ground ball rate (42%) and low pulled-groundball rate (66%) don't exactly scream four outfielders. And, as seen in the second table on the next page, he's had success against this alignment. Both his BABIP and SlgBIP are significantly higher when facing four-outfielders than when not. While this is a small sample size, you'd think teams would like to see results if they're employing this shift on a player that doesn't fit the typical mold.

Four-Outfielder Alignments Employed
On Balls In Play

Team	2018	2019	2020	2021	2022	Total
Toronto Blue Jays	0	4	1	38	174	217
Tampa Bay Rays	2	51	30	48	54	185
Cincinnati Reds	0	36	0	0	2	38
New York Yankees	0	0	0	0	30	30
Minnesota Twins	27	3	0	0	0	30
Detroit Tigers	0	0	0	2	15	17
Texas Rangers	0	0	0	2	15	17
Pittsburgh Pirates	0	0	7	0	1	8
Arizona Diamondbacks	0	5	0	0	0	5
San Francisco Giants	0	5	0	0	0	5
Houston Astros	5	0	0	0	0	5
Baltimore Orioles	0	0	0	0	2	2
Los Angeles Dodgers	0	1	0	0	1	2
Chicago Cubs	2	0	0	0	0	2
New York Mets	0	0	0	1	0	1
St Louis Cardinals	0	0	1	0	0	1
Seattle Mariners	0	1	0	0	0	1
Colorado Rockies	1	0	0	0	0	1
MLB	37	106	39	91	294	567

Four-Outfielder Alignments By Batter, Career
On Balls In Play (Minimum 4 BIP)

Batter	AB	H	2B	3B	BABIP	SlgBIP
Gallo, Joey	48	18	1	0	.375	.396
Rizzo, Anthony	43	8	1	0	.186	.209
Biggio, Cavan	28	13	3	0	.464	.571
Devers, Rafael	26	11	4	0	.423	.577
Smoak, Justin	25	6	1	0	.240	.280
Carpenter, Matt	18	7	1	1	.389	.556
Polanco, Jorge	18	8	1	0	.444	.500
Olson, Matt	16	5	2	0	.313	.438
Seager, Corey	16	10	1	0	.625	.688
Meadows, Austin	14	1	0	0	.071	.071
Ramirez, Jose	14	3	0	0	.214	.214
Tucker, Kyle	14	9	1	0	.643	.714
Belt, Brandon	12	2	1	0	.167	.250
Trout, Mike	12	2	1	0	.167	.250
Alvarez, Yordan	11	4	0	0	.364	.364
Duda, Lucas	11	3	0	0	.273	.273
Lowe, Brandon	11	4	0	1	.364	.545
Grossman, Robbie	10	2	0	0	.200	.200
Rutschman, Adley	9	7	2	0	.778	1.000
Santana, Carlos	8	3	0	0	.375	.375
Winker, Jesse	8	1	0	0	.125	.125
Freeman, Freddie	7	5	0	0	.714	.714
Kepler, Max	7	1	0	0	.143	.143
Sanchez, Gary	7	2	0	0	.286	.286
Arenado, Nolan	6	3	1	0	.500	.667
Shaw, Travis	6	0	0	0	.000	.000
Bellinger, Cody	5	3	2	0	.600	1.000
Grandal, Yasmani	5	3	0	0	.600	.600
Moreland, Mitch	5	0	0	0	.000	.000
Muncy, Max	5	1	0	0	.200	.200
Ohtani, Shohei	5	2	0	0	.400	.400
Schwarber, Kyle	5	0	0	0	.000	.000
Seager, Kyle	5	1	0	0	.200	.200
Lowrie, Jed	4	2	0	0	.500	.500
Perez, Michael	4	1	0	0	.250	.250
Semien, Marcus	4	0	0	0	.000	.000
Voit, Luke	4	2	0	0	.500	.500
Zunino, Mike	4	0	0	0	.000	.000

Home Run Robberies

Jackson Lewis

Fortunately for batters (and somewhat unfortunately for us fans), home run robberies were down this year, with 49 marking the lowest total since the 2016 season. However, we still have plenty of things to explore here…

Let's start with Mr. Home Run Robbery himself, Kyle Tucker, who twice took advantage of the short right field wall at Minute Maid Park and nabbed another over the even shorter one at Fenway.

While right field in Houston and Boston have been popular places for robberies over the past few years, left field at Detroit's Comerica Park topped MLB this season with five, including three from Tigers defenders. Interestingly, all three were by different players, as Akil Baddoo, Austin Meadows, and Victor Reyes each snagged one during their time in left.

Speaking of the Tigers, their September series with the White Sox was an up-and-down affair for Chicago's Andrew Vaughn. Vaughn started the series by bringing one back off the bat of Javier Báez. Then, two days later, Detroit's Riley Greene returned the favor, robbing what would have been a two-run shot for Vaughn.

Not to be topped by that, the Braves and Marlins recorded robberies in back-to-back *innings* in their October 5th meeting, with Peyton Burdick and Robbie Grossman trading thefts in the 4th and 5th.

As for which one was best, I'm going with Mets center fielder Brandon Nimmo's against Justin Turner of the Dodgers. Nimmo's robbery in their August 31st meeting was the only one all season that preserved a lead in the 7th inning or later. That lead was especially important to the Mets, as their once double-digit lead in the NL East had been shrinking by the day.

There's no denying that play meant something. And even though the Mets didn't pull things out in the East (or the playoffs), you could tell that catch served as a spark for a team that desperately needed one.

Home Run Robberies

Date	Matchup	Fielder	Pos	Pitcher	Batter	Inn.	Outs	Men On	Score
08/05/2022	Braves@Mets	Ronald Acuna Jr.	9	Ian Anderson	Pete Alonso	1	2	2_	4-0
04/10/2022	Astros@Angels	Jo Adell	7	Jimmy Herget	Niko Goodrum	8	2	12_	4-1
08/07/2022	Rays@Tigers	Randy Arozarena	7	Jalen Beeks	Harold Castro	4	2	1_	0-0
07/23/2022	Twins@Tigers	Akil Baddoo	7	Joe Jimenez	Carlos Correa	7	2	1_	5-1
09/10/2022	Guardians@Twins	Will Benson	7	Nick Sandlin	Max Kepler	8	2	___	6-0
10/05/2022	Braves@Marlins	Peyton Burdick	9	Elieser Hernandez	Matt Olson	4	0	___	2-3
08/19/2022	Blue Jays@Yankees	Oswaldo Cabrera	9	Jameson Taillon	Lourdes Gurriel Jr.	1	0	___	0-0
05/22/2022	Tigers@Guardians	Daz Cameron	8	Alex Faedo	Amed Rosario	5	1	1_	3-2
06/12/2022	Rockies@Padres	Yonathan Daza	7	German Marquez	Ha-seong Kim	6	0	___	2-1
04/13/2022	Mariners@White Sox	Adam Engel	9	Kyle Crick	Jesse Winker	6	0	___	3-4
05/28/2022	Cubs@White Sox	Adam Engel	8	Jose Ruiz	Willson Contreras	9	1	___	5-1
09/25/2022	Cardinals@Dodgers	Joey Gallo	7	Michael Grove	Brendan Donovan	1	0	___	0-0
05/28/2022	Pirates@Padres	Ben Gamel	7	JT Brubaker	Eric Hosmer	3	0	___	0-1
06/13/2022	Astros@Rangers	Adolis Garcia	9	Taylor Hearn	Yordan Alvarez	5	2	1_	3-1
07/31/2022	Cubs@Giants	Luis Gonzalez	7	Carlos Rodon	Christopher Morel	1	0	___	0-0
07/24/2022	Twins@Tigers	Nick Gordon	7	Jharel Cotton	Riley Greene	8	1	___	8-1
08/14/2022	Twins@Angels	Nick Gordon	8	Emilio Pagan	Kurt Suzuki	8	2	___	2-4
09/25/2022	Tigers@White Sox	Riley Greene	8	Tyler Alexander	Andrew Vaughn	4	0	1_	0-1
04/12/2022	Rockies@Rangers	Randal Grichuk	8	Jhoulys Chacin	Corey Seager	5	2	12_	3-1
04/16/2022	Braves@Padres	Trent Grisham	8	Nick Martinez	Manny Pina	2	2	3_	1-0
10/05/2022	Braves@Marlins	Robbie Grossman	9	Tyler Matzek	Charles Leblanc	5	2	1_	3-5
08/02/2022	Cubs@Cardinals	Ian Happ	7	Keegan Thompson	Paul DeJong	4	0	___	0-2
05/04/2022	Braves@Mets	Guillermo Heredia	9	Ian Anderson	Jeff McNeil	2	0	___	0-0
09/10/2022	Red Sox@Orioles	Kike Hernandez	8	Michael Wacha	Ryan Mountcastle	4	1	___	8-1
06/01/2022	Marlins@Rockies	Sam Hilliard	7	Antonio Senzatela	Jorge Soler	3	0	___	1-0
08/04/2022	Rockies@Padres	Sam Hilliard	7	Kyle Freeland	Brandon Drury	2	0	1_	0-0
07/29/2022	Royals@Yankees	Aaron Judge	9	Gerrit Cole	MJ Melendez	1	0	___	0-0
04/17/2022	Rays@White Sox	Josh Lowe	7	J.P. Feyereisen	Tim Anderson	1	0	___	4-0
10/03/2022	Rays@Red Sox	Manuel Margot	9	Tyler Glasnow	Alex Verdugo	4	0	___	3-0
09/27/2022	Diamondbacks@Astros	Jake McCarthy	9	Luis Frias	David Hensley	8	0	___	2-10
06/15/2022	White Sox@Tigers	Austin Meadows	7	Kody Clemens	Seby Zavala	8	1	12_	12-0
05/11/2022	Cubs@Padres	Wil Myers	9	Nabil Crismatt	Jason Heyward	7	0	___	5-3
08/31/2022	Dodgers@Mets	Brandon Nimmo	8	Jacob deGrom	Justin Turner	7	1	___	1-2
04/16/2022	Rays@White Sox	Brett Phillips	8	Corey Kluber	Yasmani Grandal	4	1	___	1-2
06/12/2022	Rangers@White Sox	A.J. Pollock	7	Michael Kopech	Marcus Semien	1	0	___	0-0
07/26/2022	Rays@Orioles	Luke Raley	9	Shane McClanahan	Ryan Mountcastle	1	1	___	0-1
08/04/2022	Rays@Tigers	Victor Reyes	7	Drew Hutchison	Christian Bethancourt	6	1	___	4-2
06/04/2022	Nationals@Reds	Juan Soto	9	Erick Fedde	Joey Votto	1	1	12_	0-0
05/07/2022	Pirates@Reds	Jack Suwinski	9	Mitch Keller	Colin Moran	1	1	1_	4-2
05/02/2022	Royals@Cardinals	Michael A. Taylor	8	Zack Greinke	Andrew Knizner	5	2	___	0-1
08/09/2022	Rays@Brewers	Tyrone Taylor	8	Freddy Peralta	David Peralta	2	0	___	0-1
06/08/2022	Diamondbacks@Reds	Alek Thomas	8	Merrill Kelly	Joey Votto	1	2	2_	0-0
08/13/2022	Diamondbacks@Rockies	Alek Thomas	8	Ian Kennedy	C.J. Cron	9	2	2_	6-0
05/08/2022	Tigers@Astros	Kyle Tucker	9	Hector Neris	Javier Baez	9	0	___	0-5
05/18/2022	Astros@Red Sox	Kyle Tucker	9	Luis Garcia	J.D. Martinez	1	1	3_	1-0
07/28/2022	Mariners@Astros	Kyle Tucker	9	Jose Urquidy	Adam Frazier	5	0	___	2-2
09/23/2022	Tigers@White Sox	Andrew Vaughn	9	Lucas Giolito	Javier Baez	5	0	1_	3-1
05/30/2022	Rays@Rangers	Eli White	8	Glenn Otto	Ji-Man Choi	1	1	12_	0-0
08/09/2022	Giants@Padres	Mike Yastrzemski	8	Alex Cobb	Brandon Drury	4	2	___	1-1

Minor League Prospects

Mark Simon

You're probably figuring that we're going to write about Gunnar Henderson or Francisco Álvarez here. But those guys are going to get plenty of hype and ink this offseason, as are most of the other top-tier prospects. How about we share someone that you're probably not familiar with?

Washington Nationals minor league infielder Jake Alu was a 24th-round pick in 2019 as a senior out of Boston College.

Upon being promoted to Double-A in the middle of 2021, Alu's primary position switched from second base to third base (he'd played both in college). But things didn't come easily there. He finished the season with -7 Defensive Runs Saved.

"I was having trouble getting throws over to first base with some oomph on the ball, and when I did do that, I kind of sailed it," Alu said when we talked to him on our podcast in September.

"I wasn't very accurate. One of the things I worked on this offseason was with (infield coordinator) Mark Harrison my throwing motion and first-step quickness. Third base is a lot about footwork and getting yourself in position to make a throw because the ball comes at you hot."

The ball came at Alu plenty hot in 2022 and Alu was up to the challenge. He finished with 15 Runs Saved at third base, the most for any infielder, and earned a promotion to Triple-A.

A word about the minor league version of Defensive Runs Saved. It's calculated using the same basis as the major league version, meaning that Alu is essentially being judged against the same standard as Nolan Arenado, Ke'Bryan Hayes, and Matt Chapman. The latter is an example of a player whose minor league Runs Saved foreshadowed his MLB numbers.

We should also note that Alu thrived both in the field and at the plate, hitting a combined .299 with 20 home runs and 15 stolen bases between the two levels.

Alu was a late bloomer with both his defense and his power. At 5-foot-10, 175 pounds, he had never hit more than four home runs in a season in college. But with both his hitting and fielding in 2022, he's put himself on the Nationals' radar for 2023.

So what's on the agenda for Alu this offseason?

Improving his hitting approach and defensive versatility.

"There's times where I'm a pitch behind in an at-bat," Alu said. "Sometimes when I'm hitting, if I took that one pitch, I'd be in a better count to hit, rather than being in a two-strike at-bat. Defensively, I'm going to Florida in January to work with the guys, getting in the outfield there too. Anything I can do to get on the big league club, I'll be all-in to do."

A few years ago, Alex Vigderman built a "Synthetic Statcast" model that we provide to our clients. It uses SIS-collected data to replicate select Statcast metrics at the minor league level and allows us to track player exit velocities, launch angles, and hard-hit rates (percentage of batted balls that result in a 95+ MPH exit velocity).

This year's Synthetic Statcast hard-hit rate leader was Matt Wallner of the Twins, who recorded a hard-hit ball on 51% of his batted balls. He was the only player to have at least 125 batted balls who had a hard-hit ball on more than half of them.

Wallner got a late look with the Twins this season, hitting .228 with 2 home runs in 57 at-bats.

Career Register

Brian Reiff

If you like numbers, then you're in the right place. The next hundred-plus pages comprise the core of this book, the Career Register.

In it, you'll find the career statistics of every player who played in MLB in 2022. Minor league statistics are also included where it's relevant, as are career postseason stats from before this season. We even have data for some of the game's top prospects who haven't yet reached the big leagues.

The Register is a trove of information for anyone willing to get lost in it.

Take Aaron Judge, who is coming off one of the best offensive seasons of all time. Note how many statistics he led the American League in (indicated by **boldface**): total bases, runs, Runs Batted In, Runs Created, walks, On-Base Percentage, Slugging Percentage and On-Base Plus Slugging percentage, not to mention other stats not listed in this book like extra-base hits, times on base, Wins Above Replacement and Win Probability Added. Oh, and he also hit a bunch of home runs. Not that any Yankee fan would let you forget.

What about a less historic season? Flipping through the pages, we find Andrés Giménez, for example. After coming up through the Mets farm system, he had a couple of fine years in the majors before exploding in a big way in 2022. Giménez set new career highs in almost every stat, including a .371 OBP that ranked 11th among qualified AL players. He was also hit by more pitches than anyone else in the league.

Just following Giménez are two big-name pitchers: Lucas Giolito and Tyler Glasnow. Giolito will look to regain his form after a rough season in which he pitched to a 4.90 ERA, his highest mark since his first full season in 2018. Glasnow, meanwhile, spent the year recovering from Tommy John surgery and managed to make just two late-season starts, but he looked as good as ever and will also hope to get back to his dominating self in 2023.

Cory Abbott

Pitches: R Bats: R Pos: SP-9; RP-7   Ht: 6'1" Wt: 210 Born: 9/20/1995 Age: 27

		HOW MUCH PITCHED				WHAT HE GAVE UP										THE RESULTS						
Year	Team	Lg	G	GS	GF	IP	BFP	H	R	ER	HR	SH	SF	HB	TBB	IBB	SO	WP	W	L	Pct	Sv-Op	Hld	Vel	OPS	ERC	ERA
2022	Roch	AAA	10	6	0	28.1	133	30	20	16	4	0	3	0	17	0	34	4	0	4	.000	0- -	-	-	.769	5.37	5.08
2021	ChC	NL	7	1	2	17.1	82	20	15	13	7	1	0	0	11	0	12	2	0	0	-	0-0	0	93	1.026	8.39	6.75
2022	Was	NL	16	9	7	48.0	216	44	30	28	12	0	2	5	25	0	45	2	0	5	.000	0-0	0	91	.843	5.56	5.25
	2 ML YEARS		23	10	9	65.1	298	64	45	41	19	1	2	5	36	0	57	4	0	5	.000	0-0	0	92	.893	6.28	5.65

Mick Abel

Pitches: R Bats: R Pos: P   Ht: 6'5" Wt: 190 Born: 8/18/2001 Age: 21

		HOW MUCH PITCHED				WHAT HE GAVE UP										THE RESULTS						
Year	Team	Lg	G	GS	GF	IP	BFP	H	R	ER	HR	SH	SF	HB	TBB	IBB	SO	WP	W	L	Pct	Sv-Op	Hld	Vel	OPS	ERC	ERA
2021	Clrwtr	A	14	14	0	44.2	189	27	23	22	5	0	1	6	27	0	66	2	1	3	.250	0- -	-	-	-	3.33	4.43
2022	Rdng	AA	5	5	0	23.0	99	19	9	9	5	0	0	2	12	0	27	0	1	3	.250	0- -	-	-	.745	4.82	3.52
2022	JrsyShr	A+	18	0	0	85.1	372	75	42	38	6	0	0	6	38	0	103	3	7	8	.467	0- -	-	-	-	3.59	4.01

CJ Abrams

Bats: L Throws: R Pos: SS-75;2B-13;RF-3;PH-3;PR-3;DH-2   Ht: 6'2" Wt: 185 Born: 10/3/2000 Age: 22

			BATTING																		RUNNING			AVERAGES			
Year	Team	Lg	G	AB	H	2B	3B	HR	(Hm	Rd)	TB	R	RBI	RC	TBB	IBB	SO	HBP	SH	SF	SB	CS	GDP	Avg	OBP	Slg	OPS
2019	2 Tms	Low	34	150	59	13	8	3	(-	-)	97	41	22	41	11	0	14	2	0	2	15	6	3	.393	.436	.647	1.083
2021	SnAnt	AA	42	162	48	14	0	2	(-	-)	68	26	23	27	15	0	36	3	1	2	13	2	3	.296	.363	.420	.782
2022	ElPaso	AAA	30	140	44	4	1	7	(-	-)	71	35	28	26	8	0	25	3	0	0	10	3	3	.314	.364	.507	.871
2022	2 Tms	NL	90	284	70	12	2	2	(1	1)	92	33	21	26	5	0	50	9	2	2	7	4	5	.246	.280	.324	.604
22	SD	NL	46	125	29	5	0	2	(1	1)	40	16	11	12	4	0	27	6	2	2	1	2	4	.232	.285	.320	.605
22	Was	NL	44	159	41	7	2	0	(0	0)	52	17	10	14	1	0	23	3	0	0	6	2	1	.258	.276	.327	.603

Albert Abreu

Pitches: R Bats: R Pos: RP-33   Ht: 6'2" Wt: 190 Born: 9/26/1995 Age: 27

		HOW MUCH PITCHED				WHAT HE GAVE UP										THE RESULTS						
Year	Team	Lg	G	GS	GF	IP	BFP	H	R	ER	HR	SH	SF	HB	TBB	IBB	SO	WP	W	L	Pct	Sv-Op	Hld	Vel	OPS	ERC	ERA
2020	NYY	AL	2	0	1	1.1	11	4	4	3	1	0	0	1	2	0	2	0	0	0	.000	0-0	0	96	1.511	36.34	20.25
2021	NYY	AL	28	0	14	36.2	156	27	21	21	8	0	3	3	19	1	35	3	2	0	1.000	1-1	3	98	.749	4.18	5.15
2022	3 Tms	AL	33	0	11	38.2	172	35	15	14	5	1	2	3	22	0	38	6	2	2	.500	0-1	1	98	.733	4.74	3.26
22	Tex	AL	7	0	0	8.2	42	4	3	3	2	0	0	1	12	0	9	0	0	0	-	0-0	0	97	.750	6.43	3.12
22	KC	AL	4	0	3	4.1	22	6	2	2	1	0	0	1	4	0	3	1	0	0	-	0-0	0	98	1.088	11.84	4.15
22	NYY	AL	22	0	8	25.2	108	25	10	9	2	1	2	1	6	0	26	5	2	2	.500	0-1	1	99	.656	3.26	3.16
	3 ML YEARS		63	0	26	76.2	339	66	40	38	14	1	5	7	43	1	75	9	4	3	.571	1-2	4	98	.764	4.88	4.46

Bryan Abreu

Pitches: R Bats: R Pos: RP-55   Ht: 6'1" Wt: 225 Born: 4/22/1997 Age: 26

		HOW MUCH PITCHED				WHAT HE GAVE UP										THE RESULTS						
Year	Team	Lg	G	GS	GF	IP	BFP	H	R	ER	HR	SH	SF	HB	TBB	IBB	SO	WP	W	L	Pct	Sv-Op	Hld	Vel	OPS	ERC	ERA
2019	Hou	AL	7	0	2	8.2	32	4	1	1	0	0	0	0	3	0	13	0	0	0	-	0-0	0	95	.391	1.05	1.04
2020	Hou	AL	4	0	1	3.1	20	1	2	1	0	0	0	2	7	0	3	0	0	0	-	0-0	0	93	.682	7.75	2.70
2021	Hou	AL	31	0	3	36.0	161	35	26	23	4	0	2	3	18	0	36	4	3	3	.500	1-5	7	96	.754	4.71	5.75
2022	Hou	AL	55	0	18	60.1	248	45	16	13	2	0	1	4	26	0	88	7	4	0	1.000	2-2	8	97	.570	2.69	1.94
	Postseason		1	0	0	0.2	6	2	2	2	1	0	0	0	2	0	0	0	0	0	-	0-0	0	96	1.917	51.61	27.00
	4 ML YEARS		97	0	24	108.1	461	85	45	38	6	0	3	9	54	0	140	11	7	3	.700	3-7	15	96	.627	3.30	3.16

Jose Abreu

Bats: R Throws: R Pos: 1B-128;DH-29   Ht: 6'3" Wt: 235 Born: 1/29/1987 Age: 36

			BATTING																		RUNNING			AVERAGES			
Year	Team	Lg	G	AB	H	2B	3B	HR	(Hm	Rd)	TB	R	RBI	RC	TBB	IBB	SO	HBP	SH	SF	SB	CS	GDP	Avg	OBP	Slg	OPS
2014	CWS	AL	145	556	176	35	2	36	(15	21)	323	80	107	113	51	15	131	11	0	4	3	1	14	.317	.383	.581	.964
2015	CWS	AL	154	613	178	34	3	30	(16	14)	308	88	101	105	39	11	140	15	0	1	0	0	16	.290	.347	.502	.850
2016	CWS	AL	159	624	183	32	1	25	(15	10)	292	67	100	92	47	7	125	15	0	9	0	2	21	.293	.353	.468	.820
2017	CWS	AL	156	621	189	43	6	33	(16	17)	343	95	102	116	35	6	119	15	0	4	3	0	21	.304	.354	.552	.906
2018	CWS	AL	128	499	132	36	1	22	(11	11)	236	68	78	78	37	7	109	11	0	6	2	0	14	.265	.325	.473	.798
2019	CWS	AL	159	634	180	38	1	33	(15	18)	319	85	123	103	36	4	152	13	0	10	2	2	24	.284	.330	.503	.834
2020	CWS	AL	60	240	76	15	0	19	(8	11)	148	43	60	49	18	1	59	3	0	1	0	0	10	.317	.370	.617	.987
2021	CWS	AL	152	566	148	30	2	30	(18	12)	272	86	117	95	61	3	143	22	0	10	1	0	28	.261	.351	.481	.831
2022	CWS	AL	157	601	183	40	0	15	(7	8)	268	85	75	90	62	2	110	12	0	0	0	0	19	.304	.378	.446	.824
	Postseason		7	28	9	1	0	1	(0	1)	13	2	5	4	2	0	4	2	0	0	0	0	2	.321	.406	.464	.871
	9 ML YEARS		1270	4954	1445	303	16	243	(121	122)	2509	697	863	841	386	56	1088	117	0	49	11	5	167	.292	.354	.506	.860

Domingo Acevedo

Pitches: R Bats: R Pos: RP-70   Ht: 6'7" Wt: 240 Born: 3/6/1994 Age: 29

		HOW MUCH PITCHED				WHAT HE GAVE UP										THE RESULTS						
Year	Team	Lg	G	GS	GF	IP	BFP	H	R	ER	HR	SH	SF	HB	TBB	IBB	SO	WP	W	L	Pct	Sv-Op	Hld	Vel	OPS	ERC	ERA
2021	Oak	AL	10	0	7	11.0	44	9	4	4	3	0	0	0	4	0	9	0	0	0	-	0-0	0	93	.770	4.18	3.27
2022	Oak	AL	70	0	12	67.2	266	50	26	25	9	2	1	3	17	4	58	1	4	4	.500	4-8	20	93	.636	2.48	3.33
	2 ML YEARS		80	0	19	78.2	310	59	30	29	12	2	1	3	21	4	67	1	4	4	.500	4-8	20	93	.655	2.70	3.32

186

Ronald Acuna Jr.

Bats: R Throws: R Pos: RF-92;DH-27;PH-4;CF-1   Ht: 6'0" Wt: 205 Born: 12/18/1997 Age: 25

Year	Team	Lg	G	AB	H	2B	3B	HR	(Hm	Rd)	TB	R	RBI	RC	TBB	IBB	SO	HBP	SH	SF	SB	CS	GDP	Avg	OBP	Slg	OPS
2018	Atl	NL	111	433	127	26	4	26	(14	12)	239	78	64	83	45	2	123	6	0	3	16	5	4	.293	.366	.552	.917
2019	Atl	NL	156	626	175	22	2	41	(18	23)	324	127	101	122	76	4	188	9	0	1	37	9	8	.280	.365	.518	.883
2020	Atl	NL	46	160	40	11	0	14	(8	6)	93	46	29	37	38	2	60	4	0	0	8	1	3	.250	.406	.581	.987
2021	Atl	NL	82	297	84	19	1	24	(16	8)	177	72	52	63	49	2	85	9	0	5	17	6	0	.283	.394	.596	.990
2022	Atl	NL	119	467	124	24	0	15	(10	5)	193	71	50	67	53	4	126	10	0	3	29	11	8	.266	.351	.413	.764
	Postseason		21	80	21	8	1	3	(3	0)	40	12	9	13	12	0	27	2	0	0	3	2	1	.263	.372	.500	.872
5 ML YEARS			514	1983	550	102	7	120	(66	54)	1026	394	296	372	261	14	582	38	0	12	107	32	23	.277	.370	.517	.887

Jason Adam

Pitches: R Bats: R Pos: RP-67   Ht: 6'3" Wt: 229 Born: 8/4/1991 Age: 31

Year	Team	Lg	G	GS	GF	IP	BFP	H	R	ER	HR	SH	SF	HB	TBB	IBB	SO	WP	W	L	Pct	Sv-Op	Hld	Vel	OPS	ERC	ERA
2018	KC	AL	31	0	14	32.1	142	30	22	22	9	0	2	3	15	1	37	4	0	3	.000	0-2	2	94	.871	5.56	6.12
2019	Tor	AL	23	0	2	21.2	91	15	8	7	1	0	3	3	10	1	18	1	3	0	1.000	0-1	4	94	.601	2.75	2.91
2020	ChC	NL	13	0	5	13.2	58	9	7	5	2	0	0	0	8	0	21	0	2	1	.667	0-0	0	95	.673	3.19	3.29
2021	ChC	NL	12	0	4	10.2	50	10	7	7	1	0	0	3	6	0	19	0	1	0	1.000	0-0	2	94	.795	5.42	5.91
2022	TB	AL	67	0	16	63.1	237	31	12	11	5	0	2	6	17	2	75	2	2	3	.400	8-12	21	95	.471	1.42	1.56
5 ML YEARS			146	0	41	141.2	578	95	56	52	18	0	7	15	56	4	170	7	8	7	.533	8-15	29	94	.636	2.86	3.30

Willy Adames

Bats: R Throws: R Pos: SS-136;DH-2;PH-1   Ht: 6'0" Wt: 210 Born: 9/2/1995 Age: 27

Year	Team	Lg	G	AB	H	2B	3B	HR	(Hm	Rd)	TB	R	RBI	RC	TBB	IBB	SO	HBP	SH	SF	SB	CS	GDP	Avg	OBP	Slg	OPS
2018	TB	AL	85	288	80	7	0	10	(7	3)	117	43	34	34	31	3	95	1	1	2	6	5	6	.278	.348	.406	.754
2019	TB	AL	152	531	135	25	1	20	(5	15)	222	69	52	60	46	1	153	3	3	1	4	2	9	.254	.317	.418	.735
2020	TB	AL	54	185	48	15	1	8	(1	7)	89	29	23	31	20	0	74	0	0	0	2	1	4	.259	.332	.481	.813
2021	2 Tms		140	497	130	32	1	25	(13	12)	239	77	73	84	57	1	156	0	0	1	5	4	9	.262	.337	.481	.818
2022	Mil	NL	139	563	134	31	0	31	(18	13)	258	83	98	92	49	3	166	1	0	4	8	3	11	.238	.298	.458	.756
21	TB	AL	41	132	26	6	1	5	(3	2)	49	16	15	11	10	0	51	0	0	0	1	2	1	.197	.254	.371	.625
21	Mil	NL	99	365	104	26	0	20	(10	10)	190	61	58	73	47	1	105	0	0	1	4	2	8	.285	.366	.521	.886
	Postseason		30	93	18	6	0	2	(2	0)	30	6	6	8	16	0	39	1	0	0	1	2	1	.194	.318	.323	.641
5 ML YEARS			570	2064	527	110	3	94	(44	50)	925	301	280	301	203	8	644	5	4	8	25	15	39	.255	.322	.448	.771

Austin L Adams

Pitches: R Bats: R Pos: RP-2   Ht: 6'3" Wt: 220 Born: 5/5/1991 Age: 32

Year	Team	Lg	G	GS	GF	IP	BFP	H	R	ER	HR	SH	SF	HB	TBB	IBB	SO	WP	W	L	Pct	Sv-Op	Hld	Vel	OPS	ERC	ERA
2017	Was	NL	6	0	3	5.0	29	4	4	2	0	0	1	1	8	0	10	1	0	0	-	0-0	0	95	.711	7.11	3.60
2018	Was	NL	2	0	0	1.0	7	1	0	0	0	0	0	0	3	0	0	0	0	0	-	0-0	0	95	.821	13.82	0.00
2019	2 Tms		30	2	3	32.0	130	20	14	14	4	0	1	1	16	0	53	4	2	2	.500	0-2	10	95	.615	2.77	3.94
2020	SD	NL	3	0	1	4.0	17	3	2	2	1	0	0	0	2	0	7	1	0	0	-	0-0	1	93	.694	4.02	4.50
2021	SD	NL	65	0	18	52.2	241	28	28	24	1	3	3	24	35	2	76	4	3	2	.600	0-1	10	94	.610	3.49	4.10
2022	SD	NL	2	0	0	2.1	9	0	0	0	0	0	0	0	3	0	2	0	1	0	1.000	0-0	0	93	.333	1.62	0.00
19	Was	NL	1	0	0	1.0	6	0	1	1	0	0	0	1	2	0	2	2	0	0	-	0-0	0		.500	7.00	9.00
19	Sea	AL	29	2	3	31.0	124	20	13	13	4	0	1	0	14	0	51	2	2	2	.500	0-2	10	95	.614	2.62	3.77
	Postseason		4	0	0	1.2	9	0	1	1	0	0	0	2	2	0	1	0	1	0	1.000	0-0	0	92	.444	4.82	5.40
6 ML YEARS			108	2	25	97.0	433	56	48	42	6	3	5	26	67	2	148	10	6	4	.600	0-3	21	95	.624	3.53	3.90

Riley Adams

Bats: R Throws: R Pos: C-44;PH-3;DH-2;1B-1   Ht: 6'4" Wt: 249 Born: 6/26/1996 Age: 27

Year	Team	Lg	G	AB	H	2B	3B	HR	(Hm	Rd)	TB	R	RBI	RC	TBB	IBB	SO	HBP	SH	SF	SB	CS	GDP	Avg	OBP	Slg	OPS
2022	Roch	AAA	29	107	24	8	0	4	(-	-)	44	11	17	14	11	1	41	4	0	1	0	0	3	.224	.317	.411	.728
2021	2 Tms		47	99	22	8	1	2	(1	1)	38	13	10	14	15	0	40	6	0	0	0	0	2	.222	.358	.384	.742
2022	Was	NL	48	142	25	4	0	5	(4	1)	44	14	10	11	12	0	46	1	0	0	0	1	2	.176	.245	.310	.555
21	Tor	AL	12	28	3	2	0	0	(0	0)	5	2	0	0	2	0	12	0	0	0	0	0	1	.107	.167	.179	.345
21	Was	NL	35	71	19	6	1	2	(1	1)	33	11	10	14	13	0	28	6	0	0	0	0	1	.268	.422	.465	.887
2 ML YEARS			95	241	47	12	1	7	(5	2)	82	27	20	25	27	0	86	7	0	0	0	1	4	.195	.295	.340	.635

Jo Adell

Bats: R Throws: R Pos: LF-69;RF-15;PH-13;DH-1;PR-1   Ht: 6'3" Wt: 215 Born: 4/8/1999 Age: 24

Year	Team	Lg	G	AB	H	2B	3B	HR	(Hm	Rd)	TB	R	RBI	RC	TBB	IBB	SO	HBP	SH	SF	SB	CS	GDP	Avg	OBP	Slg	OPS
2022	Salt Lk	AAA	40	155	37	15	0	13	(-	-)	91	35	33	34	20	0	56	3	0	2	3	2	2	.239	.333	.587	.920
2020	LAA	AL	38	124	20	4	0	3	(3	0)	33	9	7	7	7	0	55	1	0	0	0	1	3	.161	.212	.266	.478
2021	LAA	AL	35	130	32	5	2	4	(2	2)	53	17	26	21	8	0	32	1	1	0	2	1	3	.246	.295	.408	.703
2022	LAA	AL	88	268	60	12	2	8	(5	3)	100	22	27	21	11	0	107	4	0	1	4	2	6	.224	.264	.373	.637
3 ML YEARS			161	522	112	21	4	15	(10	5)	186	48	60	43	26	0	194	6	1	1	6	4	12	.215	.259	.356	.616

Joan Adon

Pitches: R **Bats:** R **Pos:** SP-14　　　　　　**Ht:** 6'2" **Wt:** 246 **Born:** 8/12/1998 **Age:** 24

			HOW MUCH PITCHED					WHAT HE GAVE UP										THE RESULTS							
Year	Team	Lg	G	GS	GF	IP	BFP	H	R	ER	HR	SH	SF	HB	TBB	IBB	SO	WP	W	L	Pct	Sv-Op	Hld	Vel	OPS	ERC	ERA
2022	Roch	AAA	10	10	0	42.1	189	41	26	22	5	0	3	3	24	0	43	2	2	2	.500	0- -	-	-	.781	5.03	4.68
2021	Was	NL	1	1	0	5.1	24	6	2	2	1	0	0	1	3	0	9	1	0	0	-	0-0	0	95	.867	7.44	3.38
2022	Was	NL	14	14	0	64.2	310	76	53	51	8	1	2	6	39	1	55	7	1	12	.077	0-0	0	95	.873	6.45	7.10
	2 ML YEARS		15	15	0	70.0	334	82	55	53	9	1	2	7	42	1	64	8	1	12	.077	0-0	0	95	.872	6.52	6.81

Ehire Adrianza

Bats: B **Throws:** R **Pos:** 3B-19;LF-9;2B-8;PH-5;SS-3;DH-1　　eh-EE-ray ah-dree-AHN-zah　　**Ht:** 6'1" **Wt:** 198 **Born:** 8/21/1989 **Age:** 33

						BATTING												RUNNING			AVERAGES			
Year	Team	Lg	G	AB	H	2B	3B	HR	(Hm | Rd)	TB	R	RBI	RC	TBB	IBB	SO	HBP	SH	SF	SB	CS	GDP	Avg	OBP	Slg	OPS
2013	SF	NL	9	18	4	1	0	1	(0 | 1)	8	3	3	1	1	0	5	0	1	0	0	0	1	.222	.263	.444	.708
2014	SF	NL	53	97	23	6	0	0	(0 | 0)	29	10	5	6	5	1	22	1	2	1	1	1	2	.237	.279	.299	.578
2015	SF	NL	52	113	21	7	1	0	(0 | 0)	30	11	11	12	15	0	20	4	2	0	3	2	2	.186	.303	.265	.569
2016	SF	NL	40	63	16	2	0	2	(1 | 1)	24	3	7	6	2	0	13	2	4	0	0	1	0	.254	.299	.381	.679
2017	Min	AL	70	162	43	9	2	2	(0 | 2)	62	30	24	24	16	1	25	1	1	6	8	1	0	.265	.304	.383	.707
2018	Min	AL	114	335	84	23	1	6	(2 | 4)	127	42	39	38	24	2	82	1	4	2	5	1	4	.251	.301	.379	.680
2019	Min	AL	84	202	55	8	3	5	(3 | 2)	84	34	22	31	20	1	40	6	2	4	0	2	2	.272	.349	.416	.765
2020	Min	AL	44	89	17	7	0	0	(0 | 0)	24	10	3	4	11	0	23	1	0	0	1	0	3	.191	.287	.270	.557
2021	Atl	NL	109	182	45	9	2	5	(4 | 1)	73	32	28	28	21	0	42	2	1	3	0	0	4	.247	.327	.401	.728
2022	2 Tms	NL	37	97	17	3	0	0	(0 | 0)	20	8	7	5	11	0	25	1	0	1	1	0	2	.175	.264	.206	.470
22	Was	NL	31	84	15	2	0	0	(0 | 0)	17	5	7	4	8	0	22	1	0	1	1	0	2	.179	.255	.202	.458
22	Atl	NL	6	13	2	1	0	0	(0 | 0)	3	3	0	1	3	0	3	0	0	0	0	0	0	.154	.313	.231	.543
	Postseason		11	11	1	1	0	0	(0 | 0)	2	1	0	0	0	0	3	0	0	0	0	0	0	.091	.091	.182	.273
	10 ML YEARS		612	1358	325	75	9	21	(10 | 11)	481	183	149	155	126	5	297	19	17	17	19	8	20	.239	.309	.354	.663

Jesus Aguilar

Bats: R **Throws:** R **Pos:** 1B-63;DH-60;PH-10;3B-4　　AGG-you-lahr　　**Ht:** 6'3" **Wt:** 277 **Born:** 6/30/1990 **Age:** 33

						BATTING												RUNNING			AVERAGES			
Year	Team	Lg	G	AB	H	2B	3B	HR	(Hm | Rd)	TB	R	RBI	RC	TBB	IBB	SO	HBP	SH	SF	SB	CS	GDP	Avg	OBP	Slg	OPS
2014	Cle	AL	19	33	4	0	0	0	(0 | 0)	4	2	3	0	4	0	13	0	0	1	0	0	1	.121	.211	.121	.332
2015	Cle	AL	7	19	6	1	0	0	(0 | 0)	7	0	2	4	0	0	7	1	0	0	0	0	0	.316	.350	.368	.718
2016	Cle	AL	9	6	0	0	0	0	(0 | 0)	0	0	0	0	0	0	1	0	0	0	0	0	0	.000	.000	.000	.000
2017	Mil	NL	133	279	74	15	2	16	(4 | 12)	141	40	52	47	25	1	94	4	0	3	0	0	8	.265	.331	.505	.837
2018	Mil	NL	149	492	135	25	0	35	(18 | 17)	265	80	108	82	58	3	143	6	0	10	0	0	19	.274	.352	.539	.890
2019	2 Tms	NL	131	314	74	12	0	12	(5 | 7)	122	39	50	43	43	0	81	2	0	7	0	0	12	.236	.325	.389	.714
2020	Mia	NL	51	188	52	10	0	8	(1 | 7)	86	31	34	31	23	0	40	1	0	4	0	1	5	.277	.352	.457	.809
2021	Mia	NL	131	449	117	23	0	22	(5 | 17)	206	49	93	78	46	4	93	3	0	7	0	0	11	.261	.329	.459	.788
2022	2 Tms	NL	129	464	109	19	0	16	(6 | 10)	176	39	51	56	28	1	119	4	0	5	1	0	8	.235	.281	.379	.661
19	Mil	NL	94	222	50	9	0	8	(3 | 5)	83	26	34	28	31	0	59	2	0	4	0	0	11	.225	.320	.374	.694
19	TB	AL	37	92	24	3	0	4	(2 | 2)	39	13	16	15	12	0	22	0	0	3	0	0	1	.261	.336	.424	.760
22	Mia	NL	113	415	98	18	0	15	(6 | 9)	161	37	49	52	27	1	106	4	0	5	1	0	8	.236	.286	.388	.674
22	Bal	AL	16	49	11	1	0	1	(0 | 1)	15	2	2	4	1	0	13	0	0	0	0	0	0	.224	.240	.306	.546
	Postseason		15	58	12	4	0	3	(1 | 2)	25	6	7	4	3	1	22	1	0	0	0	0	2	.207	.258	.431	.689
	9 ML YEARS		759	2244	571	105	2	109	(39 | 70)	1007	280	393	341	227	9	591	21	0	37	1	1	64	.254	.324	.449	.773

Ryan Aguilar

Bats: L **Throws:** L **Pos:** RF-5;LF-2;1B-1;CF-1　　　　　　**Ht:** 6'2" **Wt:** 168 **Born:** 9/11/1994 **Age:** 28

						BATTING												RUNNING			AVERAGES			
Year	Team	Lg	G	AB	H	2B	3B	HR	(Hm | Rd)	TB	R	RBI	RC	TBB	IBB	SO	HBP	SH	SF	SB	CS	GDP	Avg	OBP	Slg	OPS
2022	Rock	AA	93	291	79	13	3	15	(- | -)	143	56	50	65	66	0	103	6	0	1	11	3	2	.271	.415	.491	.906
2022	LAA	AL	7	22	3	1	0	0	(0 | 0)	4	2	2	1	2	0	14	1	0	1	0	0	0	.136	.231	.182	.413

Nick Ahmed

Bats: R **Throws:** R **Pos:** SS-16;PH-2;DH-1　　　　　　**Ht:** 6'2" **Wt:** 201 **Born:** 3/15/1990 **Age:** 33

						BATTING												RUNNING			AVERAGES			
Year	Team	Lg	G	AB	H	2B	3B	HR	(Hm | Rd)	TB	R	RBI	RC	TBB	IBB	SO	HBP	SH	SF	SB	CS	GDP	Avg	OBP	Slg	OPS
2014	Ari	NL	25	70	14	2	0	1	(1 | 0)	19	9	4	3	3	0	10	0	2	0	1	2	2	.200	.233	.271	.504
2015	Ari	NL	134	421	95	17	6	9	(4 | 5)	151	49	34	38	29	1	81	1	5	3	4	5	4	.226	.275	.359	.634
2016	Ari	NL	90	284	62	9	1	4	(1 | 3)	85	26	20	18	15	3	58	4	2	3	5	2	9	.218	.265	.299	.564
2017	Ari	NL	53	167	42	8	1	6	(3 | 3)	70	24	21	18	10	3	39	1	0	0	3	4	6	.251	.298	.419	.717
2018	Ari	NL	153	516	121	33	5	16	(7 | 9)	212	61	70	62	40	2	109	2	1	5	5	4	15	.234	.290	.411	.700
2019	Ari	NL	158	556	141	33	6	19	(8 | 11)	243	79	82	73	52	2	113	4	1	12	8	2	15	.254	.316	.437	.753
2020	Ari	NL	57	199	53	10	1	5	(2 | 3)	80	29	29	32	16	0	46	0	0	4	0	3	3	.266	.327	.402	.729
2021	Ari	NL	129	434	96	30	3	5	(4 | 1)	147	46	38	41	34	3	104	2	2	1	7	2	9	.221	.280	.339	.619
2022	Ari	NL	17	52	12	2	0	3	(1 | 2)	23	7	7	7	2	0	15	0	0	0	0	1	2	.231	.259	.442	.702
	9 ML YEARS		816	2699	636	144	23	68	(31 | 37)	1030	330	305	292	203	14	575	14	13	24	36	21	65	.236	.290	.382	.672

Keegan Akin

Pitches: L Bats: L Pos: RP-44; SP-1   Ht: 5'11" Wt: 235 Born: 4/1/1995 Age: 28

| | | | HOW MUCH PITCHED | | | WHAT HE GAVE UP | | | | | | | | | | | THE RESULTS | | | | | | |
Year Team	Lg	G	GS	GF	IP	BFP	H	R	ER	HR	SH	SF	HB	TBB	IBB	SO	WP	W	L	Pct	Sv-Op	Hld	Vel	OPS	ERC	ERA
2020 Bal	AL	8	6	0	25.2	116	27	17	13	3	0	2	1	10	0	35	0	1	2	.333	0-0	0	92	.755	4.45	4.56
2021 Bal	AL	24	17	1	95.0	427	110	70	70	17	1	5	2	40	1	82	5	2	10	.167	0-0	0	92	.848	5.76	6.63
2022 Bal	AL	45	1	10	81.2	329	69	35	29	10	1	2	1	20	0	77	1	3	3	.500	2-2	3	94	.650	2.85	3.20
3 ML YEARS		77	24	11	202.1	872	206	122	112	30	2	9	4	70	1	194	6	6	15	.286	2-2	3	93	.760	4.36	4.98

Hanser Alberto

HAHN-zer al-BAIR-tow

Bats: R Throws: R Pos: 2B-37;3B-20;PH-17;SS-5;DH-5;1B-3;RF-1;PR-1   Ht: 5'11" Wt: 215 Born: 10/17/1992 Age: 30

| | | BATTING | | | | | | | | | | | | | | | | | | | | | RUNNING | | | AVERAGES | | | |
Year Team	Lg	G	AB	H	2B	3B	HR	(Hm	Rd)	TB	R	RBI	RC	TBB	IBB	SO	HBP	SH	SF	SB	CS	GDP	Avg	OBP	Slg	OPS
2015 Tex	AL	41	99	22	2	1	0	(0	0)	26	12	4	3	2	0	17	0	3	0	1	0	2	.222	.238	.263	.500
2016 Tex	AL	35	56	8	1	0	0	(0	0)	9	2	5	1	0	0	17	0	2	0	1	0	1	.143	.143	.161	.304
2018 Tex	AL	13	27	5	2	0	0	(0	0)	7	0	0	0	2	0	4	0	1	0	0	1	0	.185	.241	.259	.501
2019 Bal	AL	139	524	160	21	2	12	(9	3)	221	62	51	64	16	1	50	4	3	3	4	4	9	.305	.329	.422	.751
2020 Bal	AL	54	219	62	15	0	3	(3	0)	86	35	22	23	5	0	30	3	2	2	3	0	6	.283	.306	.393	.698
2021 KC	AL	103	241	65	20	3	2	(1	1)	97	25	24	28	4	0	26	4	4	2	3	1	1	.270	.291	.402	.693
2022 2 Tms	NL	73	156	38	9	2	2	(1	1)	57	13	15	8	3	0	25	0	0	0	0	0	7	.244	.258	.365	.623
Postseason		3	10	2	1	0	0	(0	0)	3	0	2	1	0	0	2	0	0	1	0	0	0	.200	.182	.300	.482
7 ML YEARS		458	1322	360	70	8	19	(14	5)	503	149	121	127	32	1	169	11	15	7	12	7	26	.272	.294	.380	.674

Ozzie Albies

Bats: B Throws: R Pos: 2B-64;PH-1   Ht: 5'8" Wt: 165 Born: 1/7/1997 Age: 26

| | | BATTING | | | | | | | | | | | | | | | | | | | | | RUNNING | | | AVERAGES | | | |
Year Team	Lg	G	AB	H	2B	3B	HR	(Hm	Rd)	TB	R	RBI	RC	TBB	IBB	SO	HBP	SH	SF	SB	CS	GDP	Avg	OBP	Slg	OPS
2017 Atl	NL	57	217	62	9	5	6	(1	5)	99	34	28	36	21	0	36	3	1	2	8	1	3	.286	.354	.456	.810
2018 Atl	NL	158	639	167	40	5	24	(9	15)	289	105	72	82	36	0	116	5	1	3	14	3	9	.261	.305	.452	.757
2019 Atl	NL	160	640	189	43	8	24	(12	12)	320	102	86	113	54	6	112	4	0	4	15	4	4	.295	.352	.500	.852
2020 Atl	NL	29	118	32	5	0	6	(2	4)	55	21	19	20	5	0	30	1	0	0	3	1	0	.271	.306	.466	.773
2021 Atl	NL	156	629	163	40	7	30	(17	13)	307	103	106	107	47	2	128	3	0	7	20	4	4	.259	.310	.488	.799
2022 Atl	NL	64	247	61	16	0	8	(4	4)	101	36	35	29	16	0	47	2	0	4	3	5	0	.247	.294	.409	.703
Postseason		37	145	37	5	0	3	(0	3)	51	24	9	11	12	0	27	0	0	2	5	0	0	.255	.308	.352	.660
6 ML YEARS		624	2490	674	153	25	98	(45	53)	1171	401	346	387	179	8	469	18	2	20	63	18	18	.271	.322	.470	.792

Jorge Alcala

Pitches: R Bats: R Pos: RP-2   Ht: 6'3" Wt: 205 Born: 7/28/1995 Age: 27

| | | | HOW MUCH PITCHED | | | WHAT HE GAVE UP | | | | | | | | | | | THE RESULTS | | | | | | |
Year Team	Lg	G	GS	GF	IP	BFP	H	R	ER	HR	SH	SF	HB	TBB	IBB	SO	WP	W	L	Pct	Sv-Op	Hld	Vel	OPS	ERC	ERA
2019 Min	AL	2	0	2	1.2	7	1	0	0	0	0	0	0	1	0	1	0	0	0	-	0-0	0	94	.452	2.03	0.00
2020 Min	AL	16	0	8	24.0	94	21	8	7	3	0	0	0	8	0	27	1	2	1	.667	0-1	0	97	.681	3.52	2.63
2021 Min	AL	59	0	15	59.2	229	45	29	26	10	1	3	2	13	1	61	1	3	6	.333	1-5	11	97	.644	2.70	3.92
2022 Min	AL	2	0	0	2.1	10	2	0	0	0	0	0	0	2	0	2	0	0	0	-	0-0	0	94	.650	4.61	0.00
4 ML YEARS		79	0	25	87.2	340	69	37	33	13	1	3	2	24	1	91	2	5	7	.417	1-6	11	97	.651	2.96	3.39

Sandy Alcantara

Pitches: R Bats: R Pos: SP-32   Ht: 6'5" Wt: 200 Born: 9/7/1995 Age: 27

| | | | HOW MUCH PITCHED | | | WHAT HE GAVE UP | | | | | | | | | | | THE RESULTS | | | | | | |
Year Team	Lg	G	GS	GF	IP	BFP	H	R	ER	HR	SH	SF	HB	TBB	IBB	SO	WP	W	L	Pct	Sv-Op	Hld	Vel	OPS	ERC	ERA
2017 StL	NL	8	0	3	8.1	39	9	6	4	2	0	0	0	6	0	10	0	0	0	-	0-0	0	98	.869	7.04	4.32
2018 Mia	NL	6	6	0	34.0	146	25	13	13	3	2	2	2	23	0	30	0	2	3	.400	0-0	0	95	.706	3.90	3.44
2019 Mia	NL	32	32	0	197.1	838	179	94	85	23	5	1	8	81	5	151	4	6	14	.300	0-0	0	96	.719	3.86	3.88
2020 Mia	NL	7	7	0	42.0	172	35	22	14	4	1	0	1	15	0	39	1	3	2	.600	0-0	0	97	.653	3.11	3.00
2021 Mia	NL	33	33	0	205.2	837	171	85	73	21	6	3	10	50	2	201	6	9	15	.375	0-0	0	98	.643	2.76	3.19
2022 Mia	NL	32	32	0	228.2	886	174	67	58	16	1	6	9	50	1	207	3	14	9	.609	0-0	0	98	.588	2.19	2.28
Postseason		2	2	0	12.2	55	11	6	6	2	0	0	2	4	0	12	0	1	1	.500	0-0	0	97	.697	3.95	4.26
6 ML YEARS		118	110	3	716.0	2918	593	287	247	69	15	12	30	225	8	638	14	34	43	.442	0-0	0	97	.654	2.98	3.10

Sergio Alcantara

Bats: B Throws: R Pos: 3B-41;SS-28;2B-25;PR-10;PH-4;DH-3   Ht: 5'9" Wt: 151 Born: 7/10/1996 Age: 26

| | | BATTING | | | | | | | | | | | | | | | | | | | | | RUNNING | | | AVERAGES | | | |
Year Team	Lg	G	AB	H	2B	3B	HR	(Hm	Rd)	TB	R	RBI	RC	TBB	IBB	SO	HBP	SH	SF	SB	CS	GDP	Avg	OBP	Slg	OPS
2020 Det	AL	10	21	3	0	1	1	(0	1)	8	2	1	1	2	0	4	0	0	0	0	0	0	.143	.217	.381	.598
2021 ChC	NL	89	220	45	6	3	5	(2	3)	72	30	17	21	30	2	74	2	1	2	3	0	3	.205	.303	.327	.630
2022 2 Tms	NL	93	205	45	8	1	6	(3	3)	73	26	29	21	12	0	57	1	2	4	1	2	6	.220	.261	.356	.617
22 Ari	NL	71	170	41	8	1	6	(3	3)	69	23	26	21	10	0	45	1	2	3	1	0	6	.241	.283	.406	.688
22 SD	NL	22	35	4	0	0	0	(0	0)	4	3	3	0	2	0	12	0	0	1	0	2	0	.114	.158	.114	.272
3 ML YEARS		192	446	93	14	5	12	(5	7)	153	58	47	43	44	2	135	3	3	6	4	2	9	.209	.281	.343	.624

Jason Alexander

Pitches: R Bats: R Pos: SP-11; RP-7   Ht: 6'3" Wt: 200 Born: 3/1/1993 Age: 30

			HOW MUCH PITCHED					WHAT HE GAVE UP										THE RESULTS							
Year	Team	Lg	G	GS	GF	IP	BFP	H	R	ER	HR	SH	SF	HB	TBB	IBB	SO	WP	W	L	Pct	Sv-Op	Hld	Vel	OPS	ERC	ERA
2022	Nashv	AAA	13	10	0	63.1	260	58	22	20	5	0	0	5	17	0	47	2	8	2	.800	0- -	-	-	.648	3.35	2.84
2022	Mil	NL	18	11	3	71.2	321	88	47	43	12	0	7	4	28	0	46	1	2	3	.400	0-0	0	92	.888	6.27	5.40

Scott Alexander

Pitches: L Bats: L Pos: RP-13; SP-4   Ht: 6'2" Wt: 195 Born: 7/10/1989 Age: 33

			HOW MUCH PITCHED					WHAT HE GAVE UP										THE RESULTS							
Year	Team	Lg	G	GS	GF	IP	BFP	H	R	ER	HR	SH	SF	HB	TBB	IBB	SO	WP	W	L	Pct	Sv-Op	Hld	Vel	OPS	ERC	ERA
2022	Scrmto	AAA	7	0	1	7.2	27	2	0	0	0	0	0	0	4	0	8	0	1	0	1.000	0- -	-	-	.353	0.88	0.00
2022	2 Tms	Low	6	0	0	6.0	24	6	1	1	0	0	0	1	0	0	5	0	2	0	1.000	0- -	-	-		2.62	1.50
2015	KC	AL	4	0	3	6.0	25	5	3	3	0	0	0	1	3	0	3	1	0	0	-	0-0	0	93	.598	3.67	4.50
2016	KC	AL	17	0	4	19.0	84	24	7	7	1	0	1	0	7	0	16	0	0	0	-	0-1	0	91	.790	5.24	3.32
2017	KC	AL	58	0	9	69.0	283	62	23	19	3	1	2	0	28	0	59	3	5	4	.556	4-6	9	93	.645	3.27	2.48
2018	LAD	NL	73	1	8	66.0	268	57	28	27	4	1	0	2	27	2	56	2	2	1	.667	3-6	21	93	.667	3.32	3.68
2019	LAD	NL	28	0	4	17.1	76	17	7	7	2	0	0	1	7	2	9	0	3	2	.600	0-0	6	93	.741	4.09	3.63
2020	LAD	NL	13	0	1	12.1	52	9	6	4	2	1	0	0	9	1	9	0	2	0	1.000	0-2	3	93	.710	4.35	2.92
2021	LAD	NL	18	0	6	15.1	67	15	6	5	2	0	0	1	4	1	8	1	0	2	.000	0-1	2	92	.669	3.62	2.93
2022	SF	NL	17	4	3	17.1	63	12	2	2	1	0	0	0	1	0	10	0	0	0	-	2-2	5	92	.481	1.32	1.04
	Postseason		4	0	1	2.1	10	1	2	2	0	0	0	0	2	0	2	1	0	0	-	0-0	0	92	.425	2.03	7.71
	8 ML YEARS		228	5	38	222.1	918	201	82	74	15	3	3	5	86	6	170	7	12	9	.571	9-18	46	93	.665	3.42	3.00

Tyler Alexander

Pitches: L Bats: R Pos: SP-17; RP-10   Ht: 6'2" Wt: 203 Born: 7/14/1994 Age: 28

			HOW MUCH PITCHED					WHAT HE GAVE UP										THE RESULTS							
Year	Team	Lg	G	GS	GF	IP	BFP	H	R	ER	HR	SH	SF	HB	TBB	IBB	SO	WP	W	L	Pct	Sv-Op	Hld	Vel	OPS	ERC	ERA
2022	Toledo	AAA	5	1	0	9.0	41	12	8	8	1	0	0	1	1	0	8	0	1	1	.500	0- -	-	-	.803	5.23	8.00
2019	Det	AL	13	8	1	53.2	235	68	30	29	9	0	1	2	7	0	47	1	1	4	.200	0-0	0	91	.834	5.10	4.86
2020	Det	AL	14	2	0	36.1	152	39	16	16	8	0	1	4	9	0	34	0	2	3	.400	0-0	0	91	.849	5.40	3.96
2021	Det	AL	41	15	7	106.1	451	106	47	45	16	0	4	4	28	0	87	2	2	4	.333	0-0	3	90	.735	3.98	3.81
2022	Det	AL	27	17	1	101.0	427	108	58	54	18	2	6	1	25	1	61	0	4	11	.267	0-0	1	90	.789	4.43	4.81
	4 ML YEARS		95	42	9	297.1	1265	321	151	144	51	2	12	11	69	1	229	3	9	22	.290	0-0	4	90	.785	4.50	4.36

A.J. Alexy

Pitches: R Bats: R Pos: RP-4   Ht: 6'4" Wt: 195 Born: 4/21/1998 Age: 25

			HOW MUCH PITCHED					WHAT HE GAVE UP										THE RESULTS							
Year	Team	Lg	G	GS	GF	IP	BFP	H	R	ER	HR	SH	SF	HB	TBB	IBB	SO	WP	W	L	Pct	Sv-Op	Hld	Vel	OPS	ERC	ERA
2022	RdRck	AAA	31	16	3	96.0	437	108	67	63	25	0	2	1	56	0	103	5	6	6	.500	0- -	-	-	.923	7.00	5.91
2021	Tex	AL	5	4	0	23.0	97	13	12	12	4	0	1	1	17	0	17	0	3	1	.750	0-0	0	93	.666	3.74	4.70
2022	Tex	AL	4	0	0	7.0	38	10	9	9	1	0	0	0	9	0	6	1	1	1	.500	0-0	0	94	1.017	11.43	11.57
	2 ML YEARS		9	4	0	30.0	135	23	21	21	5	0	1	1	26	0	23	1	4	2	.667	0-0	0	94	.763	5.33	6.30

Jorge Alfaro

Bats: R Throws: R Pos: C-65;DH-11;PH-10   Ht: 6'3" Wt: 230 Born: 6/11/1993 Age: 30

			BATTING																		RUNNING			AVERAGES			
Year	Team	Lg	G	AB	H	2B	3B	HR	(Hm	Rd)	TB	R	RBI	RC	TBB	IBB	SO	HBP	SH	SF	SB	CS	GDP	Avg	OBP	Slg	OPS
2016	Phi	NL	6	16	2	0	0	0	(0	0)	2	0	0	0	1	1	8	0	0	0	0	0	0	.125	.176	.125	.301
2017	Phi	NL	29	107	34	6	0	5	(3	2)	55	12	14	20	3	1	33	4	0	0	0	0	2	.318	.360	.514	.874
2018	Phi	NL	108	344	90	16	2	10	(8	2)	140	35	37	44	18	6	138	14	0	1	3	0	2	.262	.324	.407	.731
2019	Mia	NL	130	431	113	14	1	18	(7	11)	183	44	57	53	22	1	154	10	0	4	4	4	12	.262	.312	.425	.736
2020	Mia	NL	31	93	21	2	0	3	(2	1)	32	12	16	14	4	1	36	3	0	0	2	0	2	.226	.280	.344	.624
2021	Mia	NL	92	295	72	15	1	4	(2	2)	101	22	30	31	11	0	99	5	0	0	8	1	8	.244	.283	.342	.625
2022	SD	NL	82	256	63	14	0	7	(3	4)	98	25	40	30	11	0	98	4	0	3	1	0	6	.246	.285	.383	.667
	Postseason		2	3	0	0	0	0	(0	0)	0	0	0	0	0	0	1	0	0	0	0	0	0	.000	.000	.000	.000
	7 ML YEARS		478	1542	395	67	4	47	(25	22)	611	150	194	192	70	10	566	40	0	6	18	5	31	.256	.305	.396	.701

Anthony Alford

Bats: R Throws: R Pos: LF-1;CF-1;RF-1   Ht: 6'1" Wt: 215 Born: 7/20/1994 Age: 28

			BATTING																		RUNNING			AVERAGES			
Year	Team	Lg	G	AB	H	2B	3B	HR	(Hm	Rd)	TB	R	RBI	RC	TBB	IBB	SO	HBP	SH	SF	SB	CS	GDP	Avg	OBP	Slg	OPS
2017	Tor	AL	4	8	1	1	0	0	(0	0)	2	0	0	0	0	0	3	0	0	0	0	0	0	.125	.125	.250	.375
2018	Tor	AL	13	19	2	0	0	0	(0	0)	2	3	1	1	2	0	9	0	0	0	1	0	0	.105	.190	.105	.296
2019	Tor	AL	16	28	5	0	0	1	(1	0)	8	3	1	2	1	0	11	1	0	0	2	0	0	.179	.233	.286	.519
2020	2 Tms		18	28	6	0	1	2	(2	0)	14	5	7	3	1	0	8	0	0	0	3	0	0	.214	.241	.500	.741
2021	Pit	NL	49	133	31	6	1	5	(2	3)	54	14	11	10	12	1	58	3	0	0	5	6	4	.233	.311	.406	.717
2022	Pit	NL	2	4	1	0	0	0	(0	0)	1	0	0	0	0	0	2	0	0	0	0	0	0	.250	.250	.250	.500
20	Tor	AL	13	16	3	0	0	1	(1	0)	6	3	3	2	0	0	7	0	0	0	3	0	0	.188	.188	.375	.563
20	Pit	NL	5	12	3	0	1	1	(1	0)	8	2	4	1	1	0	1	0	0	0	0	0	0	.250	.308	.667	.974
	6 ML YEARS		102	220	46	7	2	8	(5	3)	81	25	20	16	16	1	91	4	0	0	11	6	4	.209	.275	.368	.643

Kolby Allard

Pitches: L Bats: L Pos: RP-10   Ht: 6'1" Wt: 195 Born: 8/13/1997 Age: 25

		HOW MUCH PITCHED					WHAT HE GAVE UP										THE RESULTS							
Year	Team	Lg	G	GS	GF	IP	BFP	H	R	ER	HR	SH	SF	HB	TBB	IBB	SO	WP	W	L	Pct	Sv-Op Hld	Vel	OPS	ERC	ERA
2022	RdRck	AAA	20	20	0	89.0	383	81	50	46	21	0	1	2	38	1	113	7	3	3	.500	0- - -	-	.810	4.67	4.65
2018	Atl	NL	3	1	0	8.0	47	19	12	11	3	1	0	1	4	0	3	0	1	1	.500	0-0 0	89	1.253	17.45	12.38
2019	Tex	AL	9	9	0	45.1	208	52	26	25	3	0	1	2	19	0	33	1	4	2	.667	0-0 0	92	.742	4.82	4.96
2020	Tex	AL	11	8	2	33.2	152	31	29	29	4	0	1	1	20	0	32	1	0	6	.000	0-0 0	92	.734	4.58	7.75
2021	Tex	AL	32	17	3	124.2	534	128	80	75	29	0	3	4	31	0	104	4	3	12	.200	0-0 1	92	.779	4.58	5.41
2022	Tex	AL	10	0	4	21.0	87	21	17	17	9	0	0	1	6	1	19	0	1	2	.333	1-1 0	91	.972	6.17	7.29
	5 ML YEARS		65	35	9	232.2	1028	251	164	157	48	1	5	9	80	1	191	6	9	23	.281	1-1 1	92	.803	5.16	6.07

Cam Alldred

Pitches: L Bats: L Pos: RP-1   Ht: 6'3" Wt: 205 Born: 7/25/1996 Age: 26

		HOW MUCH PITCHED					WHAT HE GAVE UP										THE RESULTS							
Year	Team	Lg	G	GS	GF	IP	BFP	H	R	ER	HR	SH	SF	HB	TBB	IBB	SO	WP	W	L	Pct	Sv-Op Hld	Vel	OPS	ERC	ERA
2022	Indy	AAA	42	2	5	66.1	284	66	33	30	5	1	1	3	25	0	62	6	3	3	.500	1- - -	-	.706	4.00	4.07
2022	Pit	NL	1	0	0	1.0	4	1	0	0	0	0	0	0	0	0	1	0	0	0	-	0-0 0	87	.500	1.95	0.00

Austin Allen

Bats: L Throws: R Pos: C-4;DH-1   Ht: 6'2" Wt: 219 Born: 1/16/1994 Age: 29

						BATTING															RUNNING			AVERAGES			
Year	Team	Lg	G	AB	H	2B	3B	HR	(Hm	Rd)	TB	R	RBI	RC	TBB	IBB	SO	HBP	SH	SF	SB	CS	GDP	Avg	OBP	Slg	OPS
2022	LsVgs	AAA	35	129	35	11	0	5	(-	-)	61	17	26	22	12	0	37	4	1	1	0	0	2	.271	.349	.473	.822
2022	Memp	AAA	20	66	21	4	0	2	(-	-)	31	7	14	12	9	0	19	0	0	1	0	0	1	.318	.395	.470	.864
2019	SD	NL	34	65	14	4	0	0	(0	0)	18	4	3	4	6	3	21	0	0	0	0	0	2	.215	.282	.277	.559
2020	Oak	AL	14	31	6	1	0	1	(1	0)	10	1	3	2	1	0	14	0	0	0	0	0	0	.194	.219	.323	.541
2021	Oak	AL	4	8	2	0	0	1	(1	0)	5	2	1	1	0	0	3	0	0	0	0	0	0	.250	.250	.625	.875
2022	Oak	AL	5	14	1	0	0	0	(0	0)	1	1	0	0	1	0	9	1	0	0	0	0	1	.071	.188	.071	.259
	4 ML YEARS		57	118	23	5	0	2	(2	0)	34	8	7	7	8	3	47	1	0	0	0	0	3	.195	.252	.288	.540

Greg Allen

Bats: B Throws: R Pos: LF-23;RF-13;CF-11;PR-6;PH-5;DH-1   Ht: 6'0" Wt: 185 Born: 3/15/1993 Age: 30

						BATTING															RUNNING			AVERAGES			
Year	Team	Lg	G	AB	H	2B	3B	HR	(Hm	Rd)	TB	R	RBI	RC	TBB	IBB	SO	HBP	SH	SF	SB	CS	GDP	Avg	OBP	Slg	OPS
2017	Cle	AL	25	35	8	1	0	1	(0	1)	12	7	6	4	2	0	8	1	0	1	1	0	0	.229	.282	.343	.625
2018	Cle	AL	91	265	68	11	3	2	(1	1)	91	36	20	26	14	1	58	7	4	1	21	4	5	.257	.310	.343	.654
2019	Cle	AL	89	231	53	9	3	4	(0	4)	80	30	27	24	11	1	53	9	4	1	8	2	3	.229	.290	.346	.636
2020	2 Tms		16	26	4	1	0	1	(1	0)	8	4	4	3	3	0	10	2	0	1	2	0	0	.154	.281	.308	.589
2021	NYY	AL	15	37	10	4	1	0	(0	0)	16	9	2	7	5	0	13	5	0	1	5	0	0	.270	.417	.432	.849
2022	Pit	NL	46	118	22	4	0	2	(1	1)	32	17	8	6	10	0	42	2	3	1	8	2	2	.186	.260	.271	.531
20	Cle	AL	15	25	4	1	0	1	(1	0)	8	3	4	2	1	0	9	1	0	1	1	0	0	.160	.214	.320	.534
20	SD	NL	1	1	0	0	0	0	(0	0)	0	1	0	1	2	0	1	1	0	0	1	0	0	.000	.750	.000	.750
	Postseason		4	1	0	0	0	0	(0	0)	0	0	0	0	0	0	0	0	0	0	0	0	1	.000	.000	.000	.000
	6 ML YEARS		282	712	165	30	7	10	(3	7)	239	103	67	70	45	2	184	26	11	6	45	8	10	.232	.299	.336	.635

Logan Allen

Pitches: L Bats: R Pos: RP-7   Ht: 6'3" Wt: 200 Born: 5/23/1997 Age: 26

		HOW MUCH PITCHED					WHAT HE GAVE UP										THE RESULTS							
Year	Team	Lg	G	GS	GF	IP	BFP	H	R	ER	HR	SH	SF	HB	TBB	IBB	SO	WP	W	L	Pct	Sv-Op Hld	Vel	OPS	ERC	ERA
2022	Norfolk	AAA	21	0	3	24.1	123	38	28	23	4	0	2	4	11	0	21	2	1	0	1.000	0- - -	-	1.025	9.10	8.51
2022	Albq	AAA	6	6	0	28.0	124	33	20	20	8	0	2	2	9	0	25	1	1	3	.250	0- - -	-	.904	6.58	6.43
2019	2 Tms		9	4	3	27.2	127	36	20	19	4	2	1	2	13	0	17	0	2	3	.400	0-0 0	93	.958	7.07	6.18
2020	Cle	AL	3	0	2	10.2	49	12	4	4	1	0	0	1	7	0	7	1	0	0	-	0-0 0	94	.847	6.44	3.38
2021	Cle	AL	14	11	1	50.1	222	58	39	35	12	0	2	4	17	0	37	4	2	7	.222	0-0 0	93	.873	6.18	6.26
2022	2 Tms		7	0	0	7.2	40	12	5	5	0	0	0	1	5	0	7	0	1	0	1.000	0-0 0	91	.919	8.30	5.87
19	SD	NL	8	4	2	25.1	118	33	20	19	4	2	1	2	13	0	14	0	2	3	.400	0-0 0	93	.974	7.39	6.75
19	Cle	AL	1	0	1	2.1	9	3	0	0	0	0	0	0	0	0	3	0	0	0	-	0-0 0	94	.778	3.75	0.00
22	Bal	AL	4	0	0	6.0	30	9	3	3	0	0	0	1	3	0	6	0	1	0	1.000	0-0 0	91	.973	7.43	4.50
22	Bal	AL	3	0	0	1.2	10	3	2	2	0	0	0	0	2	0	1	0	0	0	-	0-0 0	92	1.125	11.51	10.80
	4 ML YEARS		33	15	6	96.1	438	118	68	63	17	2	3	8	42	0	68	5	5	10	.333	0-0 0	93	.905	6.65	5.89

Nick Allen

Bats: R Throws: R Pos: SS-60;2B-43;PH-1   Ht: 5'8" Wt: 166 Born: 10/8/1998 Age: 24

						BATTING															RUNNING			AVERAGES			
Year	Team	Lg	G	AB	H	2B	3B	HR	(Hm	Rd)	TB	R	RBI	RC	TBB	IBB	SO	HBP	SH	SF	SB	CS	GDP	Avg	OBP	Slg	OPS
2022	LsVgs	AAA	46	173	46	10	0	2	(-	-)	62	31	16	24	27	0	34	2	4	0	10	2	2	.266	.371	.358	.730
2022	Oak	AL	100	299	62	13	0	4	(1	3)	87	31	19	18	19	0	64	1	6	1	3	2	5	.207	.256	.291	.547

Abraham Almonte

Bats: B Throws: R Pos: PH-6;CF-5;LF-3;DH-2;RF-1;PR-1   Ht: 5'10" Wt: 223 Born: 6/27/1989 Age: 34

Year	Team	Lg	G	AB	H	2B	3B	HR	(Hm	Rd)	TB	R	RBI	RC	TBB	IBB	SO	HBP	SH	SF	SB	CS	GDP	Avg	OBP	Slg	OPS
2022	Nashv	AAA	48	184	54	11	0	11	(-	-)	98	36	42	38	25	0	48	2	0	2	1	0	6	.293	.380	.533	.913
2022	Wrcstr	AAA	32	110	32	4	1	7	(-	-)	59	30	24	29	36	0	29	1	0	0	5	2	3	.291	.469	.536	1.006
2013	Sea	AL	25	72	19	4	0	2	(1	1)	29	10	9	9	6	0	21	0	2	2	1	0	2	.264	.313	.403	.715
2014	2 Tms		59	204	47	10	1	3	(2	1)	68	19	15	18	12	0	60	1	2	1	4	3	5	.230	.275	.333	.609
2015	2 Tms		82	232	58	12	5	5	(4	1)	95	36	24	28	21	0	52	0	3	2	7	1	5	.250	.310	.409	.719
2016	Cle	AL	67	182	48	20	1	1	(1	0)	73	24	22	20	8	1	42	1	0	3	8	0	5	.264	.294	.401	.695
2017	Cle	AL	69	172	40	8	3	3	(2	1)	63	26	14	19	20	0	46	1	1	1	2	1	2	.233	.314	.366	.681
2018	KC	AL	50	134	24	1	2	3	(1	2)	38	15	9	5	15	0	36	0	1	1	2	2	6	.179	.260	.284	.544
2019	Ari	NL	17	31	9	3	1	1	(1	0)	17	11	4	6	7	0	8	0	0	0	0	0	1	.290	.421	.548	.969
2020	SD	NL	7	11	1	0	0	0	(0	0)	1	0	0	0	2	0	4	0	0	0	1	1	0	.091	.231	.091	.322
2021	Atl	NL	64	148	32	12	0	5	(1	4)	59	20	19	18	26	0	38	0	0	1	1	1	1	.216	.331	.399	.730
2022	Bos	AL	15	35	9	2	0	1	(1	0)	14	7	2	4	1	0	12	1	0	0	1	0	1	.257	.297	.400	.697
14	Sea	AL	27	106	21	5	1	1	(0	1)	31	10	8	10	6	0	40	1	0	0	3	1	1	.198	.248	.292	.540
14	SD		32	98	26	5	0	2	(2	0)	37	9	7	8	6	0	20	0	2	1	1	2	4	.265	.305	.378	.682
15	SD	NL	31	54	11	3	0	0	(0	0)	14	6	4	3	5	0	19	0	3	0	1	1	1	.204	.271	.259	.530
15	Cle	AL	51	178	47	9	5	5	(4	1)	81	30	20	25	16	0	33	0	0	2	6	0	4	.264	.321	.455	.776
10 ML YEARS			455	1221	287	72	13	24	(14	10)	457	168	118	127	118	1	319	4	9	11	27	9	29	.235	.302	.374	.676

Yency Almonte

Pitches: R Bats: R Pos: RP-33   Ht: 6'5" Wt: 223 Born: 6/4/1994 Age: 29

Year	Team	Lg	G	GS	GF	IP	BFP	H	R	ER	HR	SH	SF	HB	TBB	IBB	SO	WP	W	L	Pct	Sv-Op	Hld	Vel	OPS	ERC	ERA
2022	OkCity	AAA	14	0	5	18.0	69	14	8	8	3	0	0	1	1	0	28	0	0	1	.000	3- -	-	-	.605	2.23	4.00
2018	Col	NL	14	0	3	14.2	60	15	5	3	1	0	1	0	4	0	14	1	0	0	-	0-0	3	95	.735	3.61	1.84
2019	Col	NL	28	0	6	34.0	157	39	22	21	7	1	1	1	14	0	29	1	0	1	.000	0-1	1	96	.860	5.73	5.56
2020	Col	NL	24	0	4	27.2	113	25	13	9	2	0	1	3	6	0	23	0	3	0	1.000	1-3	4	95	.670	3.14	2.93
2021	Col	NL	48	0	15	47.2	217	47	42	40	9	0	3	4	29	1	47	3	1	3	.250	0-3	3	94	.844	5.87	7.55
2022	LAD	NL	33	0	3	35.1	135	18	4	4	2	1	1	4	10	1	33	0	0	0	-	1-2	8	96	.470	1.46	1.02
5 ML YEARS			147	0	31	159.1	682	144	86	77	21	1	7	12	63	2	146	5	4	4	.500	2-9	19	95	.734	4.03	4.35

Albert Almora Jr.

Bats: R Throws: R Pos: RF-28;CF-23;LF-17;DH-1;PH-1;PR-1   Ht: 6'2" Wt: 190 Born: 4/16/1994 Age: 29

Year	Team	Lg	G	AB	H	2B	3B	HR	(Hm	Rd)	TB	R	RBI	RC	TBB	IBB	SO	HBP	SH	SF	SB	CS	GDP	Avg	OBP	Slg	OPS
2022	Lsvlle	AAA	20	81	24	4	0	0	(-	-)	28	9	7	6	2	0	8	0	0	0	0	0	4	.296	.313	.346	.659
2016	ChC	NL	47	112	31	9	1	3	(1	2)	51	14	14	16	5	0	20	0	0	0	0	0	5	.277	.308	.455	.763
2017	ChC	NL	132	299	89	18	1	8	(4	4)	133	39	46	44	19	1	53	0	3	2	1	0	8	.298	.338	.445	.782
2018	ChC	NL	152	444	127	24	1	5	(3	2)	168	62	41	51	24	1	83	3	2	6	1	3	12	.286	.323	.378	.701
2019	ChC	NL	130	339	80	11	1	12	(6	6)	129	41	32	25	16	4	62	1	5	2	2	1	8	.236	.271	.381	.651
2020	ChC	NL	28	30	5	1	0	0	(0	0)	6	4	1	1	3	0	9	1	0	0	0	0	0	.167	.256	.200	.465
2021	NYM	NL	47	52	6	3	0	0	(0	0)	9	3	0	0	2	0	17	0	0	0	0	0	1	.115	.148	.173	.321
2022	Cin	NL	64	215	48	10	1	5	(5	0)	75	26	29	23	17	0	46	1	1	1	3	2	9	.223	.282	.349	.631
Postseason			19	37	7	1	0	1	(0	1)	11	2	3	3	1	0	7	0	2	0	0	0	1	.189	.211	.297	.508
7 ML YEARS			600	1491	386	76	5	33	(19	14)	571	189	163	160	86	6	290	6	11	11	7	6	43	.259	.300	.383	.683

Pete Alonso

Bats: R Throws: R Pos: 1B-134;DH-27   Ht: 6'3" Wt: 245 Born: 12/7/1994 Age: 28

Year	Team	Lg	G	AB	H	2B	3B	HR	(Hm	Rd)	TB	R	RBI	RC	TBB	IBB	SO	HBP	SH	SF	SB	CS	GDP	Avg	OBP	Slg	OPS
2019	NYM	NL	161	597	155	30	2	53	(27	26)	348	103	120	112	72	6	183	21	0	3	1	0	13	.260	.358	.583	.941
2020	NYM	NL	57	208	48	6	0	16	(7	9)	102	31	35	31	24	4	61	6	0	1	1	0	4	.231	.326	.490	.817
2021	NYM	NL	152	561	147	27	3	37	(12	25)	291	81	94	91	60	6	127	12	0	4	3	0	20	.262	.344	.519	.863
2022	NYM	NL	160	597	162	27	4	40	(17	23)	309	95	131	125	67	16	128	12	0	9	5	1	17	.271	.352	.518	.869
4 ML YEARS			530	1963	512	90	5	146	(63	83)	1050	310	380	359	223	32	499	51	0	17	10	1	54	.261	.349	.535	.884

Dan Altavilla

Pitches: R Bats: R Pos: P   all-ta-VILL-ah   Ht: 5'11" Wt: 226 Born: 9/8/1992 Age: 30

Year	Team	Lg	G	GS	GF	IP	BFP	H	R	ER	HR	SH	SF	HB	TBB	IBB	SO	WP	W	L	Pct	Sv-Op	Hld	Vel	OPS	ERC	ERA
2016	Sea	AL	15	0	7	12.1	48	11	1	1	0	0	1	1	1	0	10	1	0	0	-	0-1	1	-	.560	2.09	0.73
2017	Sea	AL	41	0	13	46.2	203	43	27	22	9	0	4	1	20	1	52	9	1	1	.500	0-4	2	-	.765	4.38	4.24
2018	Sea	AL	22	0	3	20.2	85	11	7	6	0	2	0	2	15	0	23	4	3	2	.600	0-1	5	-	.609	3.27	2.61
2019	Sea	AL	17	0	3	14.2	64	9	9	9	1	1	1	0	12	1	18	2	2	1	.667	0-2	1	-	.613	3.20	5.52
2020	2 Tms		22	0	7	20.1	89	18	14	13	3	0	0	0	12	0	24	2	2	3	.400	1-3	3	-	.779	4.54	5.75
2021	SD	NL	2	0	1	1.1	5	1	1	1	1	0	0	0	0	0	2	0	0	0	-	0-0	0	-	1.000	4.25	6.75
20	Sea	AL	13	0	5	11.2	54	12	11	10	3	0	0	0	7	0	14	0	1	2	.333	1-1	1	-	.884	6.13	7.71
20	SD	NL	9	0	2	8.2	35	6	3	3	0	0	0	0	5	0	10	2	1	1	.500	0-2	2	-	.614	2.54	3.12
Postseason			2	0	1	2.0	9	2	1	1	0	0	1	0	1	0	2	0	0	0	-	0-0	0	-	.619	3.63	4.50
6 ML YEARS			119	0	34	116.0	494	93	59	52	16	1	6	4	60	2	129	18	8	7	.533	1-9	12	-	.706	3.82	4.03

Jose Altuve

Bats: R Throws: R Pos: 2B-135;PH-4;DH-2   al-TOO-vay   Ht: 5'6" Wt: 166 Born: 5/6/1990 Age: 33

Year	Team	Lg	G	AB	H	2B	3B	HR	(Hm	Rd)	TB	R	RBI	RC	TBB	IBB	SO	HBP	SH	SF	SB	CS	GDP	Avg	OBP	Slg	OPS
2011	Hou	NL	57	221	61	10	1	2	(2	0)	79	26	12	18	5	0	29	2	5	1	7	3	5	.276	.297	.357	.654
2012	Hou	NL	147	576	167	34	4	7	(4	3)	230	80	37	76	40	0	74	6	4	4	33	11	8	.290	.340	.399	.740
2013	Hou	AL	152	626	177	31	2	5	(4	1)	227	64	52	67	32	5	85	2	4	8	35	13	24	.283	.316	.363	.678
2014	Hou	AL	158	660	225	47	3	7	(4	3)	299	85	59	106	36	7	53	5	1	5	56	9	20	.341	.377	.453	.830
2015	Hou	AL	154	638	200	40	4	15	(9	6)	293	86	66	98	33	8	67	9	3	6	38	13	17	.313	.353	.459	.812
2016	Hou	AL	161	640	216	42	5	24	(15	9)	340	108	96	132	60	11	70	7	3	7	30	10	15	.338	.396	.531	.928
2017	Hou	AL	153	590	204	39	4	24	(9	15)	323	112	81	118	58	3	84	9	1	4	32	6	19	.346	.410	.547	.957
2018	Hou	AL	137	534	169	29	2	13	(7	6)	241	84	61	91	55	4	79	6	3	1	17	4	17	.316	.386	.451	.837
2019	Hou	AL	124	500	149	27	3	31	(18	13)	275	89	74	81	41	0	82	3	1	3	6	5	19	.298	.353	.550	.903
2020	Hou	AL	48	192	42	9	0	5	(1	4)	66	32	18	14	17	0	39	1	0	0	2	3	5	.219	.286	.344	.629
2021	Hou	AL	146	601	167	32	1	31	(19	12)	294	117	83	109	66	3	91	4	1	6	5	3	9	.278	.350	.489	.839
2022	Hou	AL	141	527	158	39	0	28	(13	15)	281	103	57	101	66	2	87	10	0	1	18	1	13	.300	.387	.533	.921
	Postseason		79	322	92	15	0	23	(16	7)	176	70	49	53	37	2	55	2	0	2	7	4	11	.286	.361	.547	.907
	12 ML YEARS		1578	6305	1935	379	29	192	(105	87)	2948	986	696	1011	509	43	840	64	26	46	279	81	171	.307	.362	.468	.830

Jose Alvarado

Pitches: L Bats: L Pos: RP-59   Ht: 6'2" Wt: 245 Born: 5/21/1995 Age: 28

	HOW MUCH PITCHED					WHAT HE GAVE UP											THE RESULTS						
Year	Team	Lg	G	GS	GF	IP	BFP	H	R	ER	HR	SH	SF	HB	TBB	IBB	SO	WP	W	L	Pct	Sv-Op Hld	Vel	OPS	ERC	ERA
2017	TB	AL	35	0	6	29.2	123	24	12	12	1	2	1	0	9	1	29	2	0	3	.000	0-0 7	98	.570	2.19	3.64
2018	TB	AL	70	0	17	64.0	263	42	21	17	1	2	2	1	29	4	80	2	1	6	.143	8-12 32	97	.525	1.90	2.39
2019	TB	AL	35	1	16	30.0	146	29	18	16	2	3	2	0	27	3	39	8	1	6	.143	7-9 8	98	.751	5.28	4.80
2020	TB	AL	9	0	3	9.0	45	9	7	6	2	0	1	2	6	0	13	3	0	0		0-0 1	97	.850	6.78	6.00
2021	Phi	NL	64	0	10	55.2	251	42	30	26	5	0	0	7	47	5	68	9	7	1	.875	5-8 16	99	.707	4.79	4.20
2022	Phi	NL	59	0	8	51.0	214	38	21	18	2	1	1	1	24	4	81	5	4	2	.667	2-4 22	100	.585	2.51	3.18
	Postseason		2	0	0	1.2	9	1	0	0	0	0	0	0	3	0	4	0	0	0		0-0 0	98	.611	6.15	0.00
	6 ML YEARS		272	1	60	239.1	1042	184	109	95	13	8	7	11	142	17	310	29	13	18	.419	22-33 86	98	.630	3.25	3.57

Eddy Alvarez

Bats: L Throws: R Pos: 3B-5;RF-5;DH-2;PH-2;PR-2;SS-1;LF-1   Ht: 5'9" Wt: 185 Born: 1/30/1990 Age: 33

							BATTING													RUNNING			AVERAGES			
Year	Team	Lg	G	AB	H	2B	3B	HR	(Hm	Rd)	TB	R	RBI	RC	TBB	IBB	SO	HBP	SH	SF	SB	CS	GDP	Avg	OBP	Slg	OPS
2022	OkCity	AAA	47	177	57	9	4	8	(-	-)	98	40	29	42	28	0	55	9	1	0	3	3	2	.322	.439	.554	.993
2020	Mia	NL	12	37	7	1	0	0	(0	0)	8	6	2	3	3	0	16	1	0	0	2	0	0	.189	.268	.216	.485
2021	Mia	NL	24	64	12	4	1	1	(0	1)	21	8	6	7	4	1	18	6	0	0	1	0	2	.188	.297	.328	.625
2022	LAD	NL	14	25	4	0	0	0	(0	0)	4	1	3	0	0	0	9	0	1	1	1	0	1	.160	.154	.160	.314
	3 ML YEARS		50	126	23	5	1	1	(0	1)	33	15	11	10	7	1	43	7	1	1	4	0	3	.183	.262	.262	.524

Francisco Alvarez

Bats: R Throws: R Pos: DH-3;C-2;PH-2   Ht: 5'10" Wt: 233 Born: 11/19/2001 Age: 21

							BATTING													RUNNING			AVERAGES			
Year	Team	Lg	G	AB	H	2B	3B	HR	(Hm	Rd)	TB	R	RBI	RC	TBB	IBB	SO	HBP	SH	SF	SB	CS	GDP	Avg	OBP	Slg	OPS
2021	2 Tms	Low	99	327	89	18	1	24	(-	-)	181	67	70	0	55	0	89	11	0	7	8	5	12	.272	.388	.554	.941
2022	Bnghtn	AA	67	253	70	16	0	18	(-	-)	140	43	47	54	36	1	71	3	0	4	0	0	9	.277	.368	.553	.922
2022	Syrcse	AAA	45	158	37	6	0	9	(-	-)	70	31	31	30	34	2	52	5	0	2	0	0	4	.234	.382	.443	.825
2022	NYM	NL	5	12	2	1	0	1	(1	0)	6	3	1	1	2	0	4	0	0	0	0	0	1	.167	.286	.500	.786

Jose Alvarez

Pitches: L Bats: L Pos: RP-21   Ht: 5'11" Wt: 195 Born: 5/6/1989 Age: 34

	HOW MUCH PITCHED					WHAT HE GAVE UP											THE RESULTS						
Year	Team	Lg	G	GS	GF	IP	BFP	H	R	ER	HR	SH	SF	HB	TBB	IBB	SO	WP	W	L	Pct	Sv-Op Hld	Vel	OPS	ERC	ERA
2013	Det	AL	14	6	0	38.2	172	42	26	25	7	2	2	2	16	1	31	0	1	5	.167	0-0 2	89	.866	5.41	5.82
2014	LAA	AL	2	0	1	0.2	3	1	0	0	0	0	0	0	0	1	0	0	0	0		0-0 0	89	.667	4.47	0.00
2015	LAA	AL	64	0	18	67.0	283	58	29	26	5	0	1	5	23	4	59	1	4	3	.571	0-1 7	91	.642	3.13	3.49
2016	LAA	AL	64	0	12	57.1	256	71	29	22	4	1	1	1	15	4	51	2	1	3	.250	0-1 11	91	.745	4.55	3.45
2017	LAA	AL	64	0	12	48.2	203	50	23	21	7	1	0	0	12	5	45	1	0	3	.000	1-3 13	91	.733	3.78	3.88
2018	LAA	AL	76	0	5	63.0	261	51	20	19	3	2	0	2	22	2	59	1	6	4	.600	1-4 14	92	.613	2.59	2.71
2019	Phi	NL	67	1	11	59.0	255	66	25	22	8	1	3	1	18	4	51	3	3	4	.429	1-3 16	91	.766	4.61	3.36
2020	Phi	NL	8	0	1	6.1	27	7	1	1	0	0	0	0	3	0	6	0	0	0		0-0 1	92	.745	4.44	1.42
2021	SF	NL	67	1	12	64.2	266	53	23	17	2	1	1	0	19	1	42	1	5	2	.714	0-0 8	91	.551	2.23	2.37
2022	SF	NL	21	0	6	15.1	76	17	10	9	3	1	0	2	9	1	15	1	2	1	.667	1-3 1	91	.870	6.34	5.28
	Postseason		2	0	0	3.1	11	0	0	0	0	0	0	0	1	0	3	0	0	0		0-0 0	91	.091	0.10	0.00
	10 ML YEARS		447	8	78	420.2	1802	416	186	162	39	9	8	13	137	22	360	10	22	25	.468	4-15 73	91	.699	3.68	3.47

R.J. Alvarez

Pitches: R Bats: R Pos: RP-1   Ht: 6'1" Wt: 230 Born: 6/8/1991 Age: 32

	HOW MUCH PITCHED					WHAT HE GAVE UP											THE RESULTS						
Year	Team	Lg	G	GS	GF	IP	BFP	H	R	ER	HR	SH	SF	HB	TBB	IBB	SO	WP	W	L	Pct	Sv-Op Hld	Vel	OPS	ERC	ERA
2022	Syrcse	AAA	40	0	22	45.2	202	34	23	18	3	0	2	7	29	3	44	5	4	3	.571	4- -	-	.686	3.80	3.55

Year	Team	Lg	G	GS	GF	IP	BFP	H	R	ER	HR	SH	SF	HB	TBB	IBB	SO	WP	W	L	Pct	Sv-Op	Hld	Vel	OPS	ERC	ERA
						HOW MUCH PITCHED					WHAT HE GAVE UP											THE RESULTS					
2014	SD	NL	10	0	4	8.0	33	3	1	1	0	0	1	1	5	1	9	1	0	0	-	0-0	1	95	.388	1.42	1.13
2015	Oak	AL	21	0	11	20.0	100	27	23	22	7	0	2	0	13	1	23	5	0	0	-	0-1	0	94	1.035	9.16	9.90
2022	NYM	NL	1	0	0	2.1	13	4	3	3	2	0	0	0	3	0	2	0	0	1	.000	0-0	0	93	1.538	22.36	11.57
3 ML YEARS			32	0	15	30.1	146	34	27	26	9	0	3	1	21	2	34	6	0	1	.000	0-1	1	94	.937	7.54	7.71

Yordan Alvarez

Bats: L Throws: R Pos: DH-77;LF-56;PH-2   **Ht: 6'5" Wt: 225 Born: 6/27/1997 Age: 26**

Year	Team	Lg	G	AB	H	2B	3B	HR	(Hm	Rd)	TB	R	RBI	RC	TBB	IBB	SO	HBP	SH	SF	SB	CS	GDP	Avg	OBP	Slg	OPS
						BATTING															RUNNING			AVERAGES			
2019	Hou	AL	87	313	98	26	0	27	(14	13)	205	58	78	72	52	4	94	2	0	2	0	0	9	.313	.412	.655	1.067
2020	Hou	AL	2	8	2	0	0	1	(1	0)	5	2	4	2	0	0	1	1	0	0	0	0	1	.250	.333	.625	.958
2021	Hou	AL	144	537	149	35	1	33	(15	18)	285	92	104	96	50	3	145	4	0	3	1	0	16	.277	.346	.531	.877
2022	Hou	AL	135	470	144	29	2	37	(20	17)	288	95	97	105	78	9	106	6	0	7	1	1	12	.306	.406	.613	1.019
Postseason			34	112	31	7	2	3	(1	2)	51	18	12	18	20	1	38	1	0	1	0	0	1	.277	.388	.455	.843
4 ML YEARS			368	1328	393	90	3	98	(50	48)	783	247	283	275	180	16	346	17	0	12	2	1	38	.296	.384	.590	.973

Adbert Alzolay

Pitches: R Bats: R Pos: RP-6   **Ht: 6'1" Wt: 208 Born: 3/1/1995 Age: 28**

Year	Team	Lg	G	GS	GF	IP	BFP	H	R	ER	HR	SH	SF	HB	TBB	IBB	SO	WP	W	L	Pct	Sv-Op	Hld	Vel	OPS	ERC	ERA
						HOW MUCH PITCHED					WHAT HE GAVE UP											THE RESULTS					
2019	ChC	NL	4	2	1	12.1	60	13	10	10	4	0	0	1	9	0	13	0	1	1	.500	0-0	0	94	.923	7.80	7.30
2020	ChC	NL	6	4	0	21.1	87	12	8	7	1	0	2	1	13	0	29	1	1	1	.500	0-0	0	95	.566	2.43	2.95
2021	ChC	NL	29	21	1	125.2	519	112	66	64	25	5	1	5	34	2	128	2	5	13	.278	1-1	0	94	.733	3.75	4.58
2022	ChC	NL	6	0	1	13.1	52	9	5	5	1	0	0	1	2	0	19	0	2	1	.667	0-0	1	95	.578	1.66	3.38
4 ML YEARS			45	27	3	172.2	718	146	89	86	31	5	3	8	58	2	189	3	9	16	.360	1-1	1	94	.718	3.67	4.48

Brian Anderson

Bats: R Throws: R Pos: 3B-48;RF-36;DH-9;LF-8;PH-6;2B-1   **Ht: 6'3" Wt: 208 Born: 5/19/1993 Age: 30**

Year	Team	Lg	G	AB	H	2B	3B	HR	(Hm	Rd)	TB	R	RBI	RC	TBB	IBB	SO	HBP	SH	SF	SB	CS	GDP	Avg	OBP	Slg	OPS
						BATTING															RUNNING			AVERAGES			
2017	Mia	NL	25	84	22	7	1	0	(0	0)	31	11	8	11	10	0	28	0	0	1	0	0	1	.262	.337	.369	.706
2018	Mia	NL	156	590	161	34	4	11	(7	4)	236	87	65	94	62	2	129	16	0	2	2	4	18	.273	.357	.400	.757
2019	Mia	NL	126	459	120	33	1	20	(10	10)	215	57	66	72	44	1	114	14	0	3	5	1	15	.261	.342	.468	.811
2020	Mia	NL	59	200	51	7	1	11	(4	7)	93	27	38	40	22	1	66	6	0	1	0	0	2	.255	.345	.465	.810
2021	Mia	NL	67	233	58	9	0	7	(4	3)	88	24	28	35	26	2	65	5	0	0	5	0	4	.249	.337	.378	.715
2022	Mia	NL	98	338	75	16	1	8	(6	2)	117	43	28	32	37	2	101	7	0	1	1	0	7	.222	.311	.346	.657
Postseason			5	19	4	1	0	0	(0	0)	5	1	1	2	1	0	7	1	0	0	0	0	1	.211	.286	.263	.549
6 ML YEARS			531	1904	487	106	8	57	(31	26)	780	249	233	284	201	8	503	48	0	8	13	5	47	.256	.341	.410	.750

Chase Anderson

Pitches: R Bats: R Pos: SP-7; RP-2   **Ht: 6'1" Wt: 210 Born: 11/30/1987 Age: 35**

Year	Team	Lg	G	GS	GF	IP	BFP	H	R	ER	HR	SH	SF	HB	TBB	IBB	SO	WP	W	L	Pct	Sv-Op	Hld	Vel	OPS	ERC	ERA
						HOW MUCH PITCHED					WHAT HE GAVE UP											THE RESULTS					
2022	Toledo	AAA	17	15	1	70.0	305	70	41	36	14	0	1	2	27	0	62	4	4	3	.571	0- -	-	-	.805	4.81	4.63
2022	Drham	AAA	10	1	3	10.0	40	7	6	4	2	0	0	0	2	0	10	0	3	0	1.000	1- -	-	-	.646	2.24	3.60
2014	Ari	NL	21	21	0	114.1	486	117	56	51	16	4	4	2	40	2	105	4	9	7	.563	0-0	0	91	.779	4.39	4.01
2015	Ari	NL	27	27	0	152.2	640	158	75	73	18	3	9	7	40	2	111	3	6	6	.500	0-0	0	92	.754	4.08	4.30
2016	Mil	NL	31	30	1	151.2	647	155	83	74	28	4	3	4	53	0	120	4	9	11	.450	0-0	0	91	.819	4.76	4.39
2017	Mil	NL	25	25	0	141.1	569	113	47	43	14	5	2	7	41	1	133	0	12	4	.750	0-0	0	93	.647	2.80	2.74
2018	Mil	NL	30	30	0	158.0	644	131	71	69	30	4	1	7	57	0	128	1	9	8	.529	0-0	0	92	.731	3.85	3.93
2019	Mil	NL	32	27	1	139.0	592	126	67	65	23	6	2	8	50	2	124	1	8	4	.667	0-0	0	93	.763	4.03	4.21
2020	Tor	AL	10	7	0	33.2	154	45	29	27	11	0	0	1	10	0	38	1	1	2	.333	0-0	0	92	.986	7.54	7.22
2021	Phi	NL	14	9	2	48.0	215	51	36	36	10	1	1	3	20	1	35	0	2	4	.333	0-0	0	92	.867	5.49	6.75
2022	Cin	NL	9	7	1	24.0	103	17	18	17	3	0	2	3	15	0	23	0	2	4	.333	0-0	0	92	.701	4.08	6.38
9 ML YEARS			199	183	5	962.2	4050	913	482	455	153	27	24	42	326	8	817	14	58	50	.537	0-0	0	92	.764	4.16	4.25

Ian Anderson

Pitches: R Bats: R Pos: SP-22   **Ht: 6'3" Wt: 170 Born: 5/2/1998 Age: 25**

Year	Team	Lg	G	GS	GF	IP	BFP	H	R	ER	HR	SH	SF	HB	TBB	IBB	SO	WP	W	L	Pct	Sv-Op	Hld	Vel	OPS	ERC	ERA
						HOW MUCH PITCHED					WHAT HE GAVE UP											THE RESULTS					
2020	Atl	NL	6	6	0	32.1	138	21	11	7	1	0	0	2	14	0	41	4	3	2	.600	0-0	0	94	.498	2.04	1.95
2021	Atl	NL	24	24	0	128.1	535	105	51	51	16	5	1	1	53	2	124	7	9	5	.643	0-0	0	95	.671	3.31	3.58
2022	Atl	NL	22	22	0	111.2	493	115	63	62	12	0	2	1	54	0	97	4	10	6	.625	0-0	0	94	.753	4.68	5.00
Postseason			8	8	0	35.2	145	20	5	5	1	0	0	2	17	0	40	1	4	0	1.000	0-0	0	94	.483	1.84	1.26
3 ML YEARS			52	52	0	272.1	1166	241	125	120	29	5	3	4	121	2	262	15	22	13	.629	0-0	0	94	.685	3.68	3.97

Nick Anderson

Pitches: R Bats: R Pos: P   Ht: 6'4" Wt: 205 Born: 7/5/1990 Age: 32

			HOW MUCH PITCHED					WHAT HE GAVE UP											THE RESULTS						
Year	Team	Lg	G	GS	GF	IP	BFP	H	R	ER	HR	SH	SF	HB	TBB	IBB	SO	WP	W	L	Pct	Sv-Op	Hld	Vel	OPS	ERC	ERA
2022	Drhm	AAA	17	0	1	16.0	69	20	11	10	5	0	0	1	3	0	12	2	1	0	1.000	1--	-	-	.902	6.64	5.63
2019	2 Tms		68	0	3	65.0	264	52	24	24	8	0	1	2	18	4	110	4	5	4	.556	1-5	16	-	.647	2.71	3.32
2020	TB	AL	19	0	9	16.1	58	5	2	1	1	0	0	0	3	0	26	0	2	1	.667	6-6	6	-	.320	0.55	0.55
2021	TB	AL	6	0	2	6.0	24	4	3	3	2	0	1	0	2	0	1	0	0	1	.000	1-1	0	-	.726	3.37	4.50
19	Mia	NL	45	0	3	43.2	186	40	19	19	5	0	1	1	16	3	69	2	2	4	.333	1-2	7	-	.705	3.53	3.92
19	TB	AL	23	0	0	21.1	78	12	5	5	3	0	0	1	2	1	41	2	3	0	1.000	0-3	9	-	.512	1.33	2.11
	Postseason		14	0	3	20.1	82	21	10	10	3	0	1	0	4	1	17	2	1	2	.333	1-3	3	-	.733	3.82	4.43
	3 ML YEARS		93	0	14	87.1	346	61	29	28	11	0	2	2	23	4	137	4	7	6	.538	8-12	22	-	.597	2.17	2.89

Shaun Anderson

Pitches: R Bats: R Pos: RP-1   Ht: 6'6" Wt: 228 Born: 10/29/1994 Age: 28

			HOW MUCH PITCHED					WHAT HE GAVE UP											THE RESULTS						
Year	Team	Lg	G	GS	GF	IP	BFP	H	R	ER	HR	SH	SF	HB	TBB	IBB	SO	WP	W	L	Pct	Sv-Op	Hld	Vel	OPS	ERC	ERA
2022	Buffalo	AAA	36	15	1	88.0	369	75	39	35	11	2	0	2	32	0	76	5	3	3	.500	1--	-	-	.669	3.36	3.58
2019	SF	NL	28	16	4	96.0	427	111	61	58	13	4	1	2	38	3	70	6	3	5	.375	2-2		93	.818	5.29	5.44
2020	SF	NL	18	0	4	15.1	67	10	6	6	3	0	0	0	12	0	18	2	0	0	-	0-0	2	95	.710	4.30	3.52
2021	3 Tms		16	0	6	23.1	124	36	30	22	4	0	1	2	12	1	19	3	0	0	-	0-0	0	93	.917	8.35	8.49
2022	Tor	AL	1	0	1	1.0	7	4	2	2	0	0	1	0	0	0	0	0	0	0	-	0-0	0	92	1.238	22.42	18.00
21	Min	AL	4	0	0	8.2	47	13	12	9	1	0	0	1	5	0	8	0	0	0	-	0-0	0	93	.868	7.97	9.35
21	Bal	AL	7	0	5	10.0	55	17	15	10	3	0	0	1	5	0	7	3	0	0	-	0-0	0	94	1.051	10.61	9.00
21	SD	NL	5	0	1	4.2	22	6	3	3	0	0	1	0	2	1	4	0	0	0	-	0-0	0	94	.679	4.53	5.79
	4 ML YEARS		63	16	15	135.2	625	161	99	88	20	4	3	4	62	4	107	11	3	5	.375	2-2	3	93	.831	5.79	5.84

Tim Anderson

Bats: R Throws: R Pos: SS-79   Ht: 6'1" Wt: 185 Born: 6/23/1993 Age: 30

			BATTING																	RUNNING			AVERAGES			
Year	Team	Lg	G	AB	H	2B	3B	HR	(Hm	Rd)	TB	R	RBI	RC	TBB	IBB	SO	HBP	SH	SF	SB	CS	GDP	Avg	OBP	Slg	OPS
2016	CWS	AL	99	410	116	22	6	9	(5	4)	177	57	30	45	13	0	117	1	6	1	10	2	15	.283	.306	.432	.738
2017	CWS	AL	146	587	151	26	4	17	(7	10)	236	72	56	59	13	0	162	3	2	1	15	1	13	.257	.276	.402	.679
2018	CWS	AL	153	567	136	28	3	20	(10	10)	230	77	64	58	30	2	149	4	2	3	26	8	15	.240	.281	.406	.687
2019	CWS	AL	123	498	167	32	0	18	(9	9)	253	81	56	77	15	0	109	3	0	2	17	5	12	.335	.357	.508	.865
2020	CWS	AL	49	208	67	11	1	10	(5	5)	110	45	21	31	10	0	50	2	0	1	5	2	4	.322	.357	.529	.886
2021	CWS	AL	123	527	163	29	2	17	(9	8)	247	94	61	82	22	1	119	1	0	1	18	7	5	.309	.338	.469	.806
2022	CWS	AL	79	332	100	13	0	6	(2	4)	131	50	25	35	14	1	55	5	0	0	13	0	10	.301	.339	.395	.734
	Postseason		7	33	16	2	0	0	(0	0)	18	6	1	7	0	0	5	0	0	0	0	0	0	.485	.485	.545	1.030
	7 ML YEARS		772	3129	900	161	16	97	(47	50)	1384	476	313	387	117	4	761	19	10	9	104	25	74	.288	.316	.442	.759

Tyler Anderson

Pitches: L Bats: L Pos: SP-28; RP-2   Ht: 6'2" Wt: 220 Born: 12/30/1989 Age: 33

			HOW MUCH PITCHED					WHAT HE GAVE UP											THE RESULTS						
Year	Team	Lg	G	GS	GF	IP	BFP	H	R	ER	HR	SH	SF	HB	TBB	IBB	SO	WP	W	L	Pct	Sv-Op	Hld	Vel	OPS	ERC	ERA
2016	Col	NL	19	19	0	114.1	478	119	50	45	12	6	3	3	28	2	99	4	5	6	.455	0-0	0	91	.742	3.85	3.54
2017	Col	NL	17	15	1	86.0	362	88	48	46	16	5	2	2	26	0	81	6	6	6	.500	0-0	0	92	.820	4.57	4.81
2018	Col	NL	32	32	0	176.0	737	165	94	89	30	3	7	3	59	1	164	9	7	9	.438	0-0	0	92	.757	4.04	4.55
2019	Col	NL	5	5	0	20.2	106	33	27	27	8	2	2	0	11	0	23	0	0	3	.000	0-0	0	91	1.159	10.75	11.76
2020	SF	NL	13	11	0	59.2	260	59	32	29	5	1	3	4	25	0	41	1	4	3	.571	0-0	0	90	.746	4.15	4.37
2021	2 Tms		31	31	0	167.0	703	170	87	84	27	9	7	1	38	2	134	1	7	11	.389	0-0	0	91	.753	3.87	4.53
2022	LAD	NL	30	28	0	178.2	707	145	57	51	14	3	4	9	34	0	138	6	15	5	.750	0-0	0	91	.617	2.39	2.57
21	Pit	NL	18	18	0	103.1	430	99	52	50	16	6	4	1	25	0	86	0	5	8	.385	0-0	0	90	.719	3.60	4.35
21	Sea	AL	13	13	0	63.2	273	71	35	34	11	3	3	0	13	2	48	1	2	3	.400	0-0	0	91	.807	4.33	4.81
	Postseason		2	1	0	7.0	28	6	3	3	1	0	0	0	2	0	6	0	0	1	.000	0-0	0	92	.709	3.21	3.86
	7 ML YEARS		147	141	1	802.1	3353	778	395	371	112	29	28	22	221	5	680	27	44	43	.506	0-0	0	91	.742	3.80	4.16

Elvis Andrus

Bats: R Throws: R Pos: SS-143;DH-4;PH-4;PR-1   AHN-droos   Ht: 6'0" Wt: 210 Born: 8/26/1988 Age: 34

			BATTING																	RUNNING			AVERAGES			
Year	Team	Lg	G	AB	H	2B	3B	HR	(Hm	Rd)	TB	R	RBI	RC	TBB	IBB	SO	HBP	SH	SF	SB	CS	GDP	Avg	OBP	Slg	OPS
2009	Tex	AL	145	480	128	17	8	6	(3	3)	179	72	40	65	40	0	77	6	12	3	33	6	4	.267	.329	.373	.702
2010	Tex	AL	148	588	156	15	3	0	(0	0)	177	88	35	79	64	0	96	5	17	2	32	15	3	.265	.342	.301	.643
2011	Tex	AL	150	587	164	27	3	5	(2	3)	212	96	60	76	56	0	74	5	16	1	37	12	17	.279	.347	.361	.708
2012	Tex	AL	158	629	180	31	9	3	(1	2)	238	85	62	92	57	0	96	5	17	3	21	10	15	.286	.349	.378	.727
2013	Tex	AL	156	620	168	17	4	4	(0	4)	205	91	67	72	52	1	97	4	16	6	42	8	19	.271	.328	.331	.659
2014	Tex	AL	157	619	163	35	1	2	(1	1)	206	72	41	59	46	0	96	3	9	7	27	15	21	.263	.314	.333	.647
2015	Tex	AL	160	596	154	34	2	7	(4	3)	213	69	62	68	46	1	78	2	8	9	25	9	14	.258	.309	.357	.667
2016	Tex	AL	147	506	153	31	7	8	(3	5)	222	75	69	87	47	2	70	4	4	7	24	8	18	.302	.362	.439	.800
2017	Tex	AL	158	643	191	44	4	20	(7	13)	303	100	88	104	38	0	101	3	1	4	25	10	18	.297	.337	.471	.808
2018	Tex	AL	97	395	101	20	3	6	(6	0)	145	53	33	44	28	0	66	3	0	2	5	3	8	.256	.308	.367	.675
2019	Tex	AL	147	600	165	27	4	12	(4	8)	236	81	72	76	34	1	96	4	0	10	31	8	16	.275	.313	.393	.707
2020	Tex	AL	29	103	20	5	0	3	(2	1)	34	11	7	6	8	0	15	0	0	0	3	1	5	.194	.252	.330	.582
2021	Oak	AL	146	497	121	25	2	3	(1	2)	159	60	37	45	31	2	81	6	3	4	12	2	14	.243	.294	.320	.614
2022	2 Tms	AL	149	535	133	32	0	17	(4	13)	216	66	58	67	39	0	92	3	0	11	18	4	11	.249	.303	.404	.707

BATTING																					RUNNING			AVERAGES			
Year	Team	Lg	G	AB	H	2B	3B	HR	(Hm	Rd)	TB	R	RBI	RC	TBB	IBB	SO	HBP	SH	SF	SB	CS	GDP	Avg	OBP	Slg	OPS
22	Oak	AL	106	354	84	24	0	8	(1	7)	132	41	30	35	30	0	62	2	0	0	7	4	10	.237	.301	.373	.673
22	CWS	AL	43	181	49	8	0	9	(3	6)	84	25	28	32	9	0	30	1	0	0	11	0	1	.271	.309	.464	.773
	Postseason		42	173	46	4	1	1	(0	1)	55	21	7	15	12	0	24	1	4	1	9	5	6	.266	.316	.318	.633
	14 ML YEARS		1947	7398	1997	360	50	96	(38	58)	2745	1019	731	940	586	7	1135	53	103	56	335	111	186	.270	.326	.371	.697

Miguel Andujar

Bats: R **Throws:** R **Pos:** LF-23;DH-13;PH-2;1B-1 **Ht:** 6'0" **Wt:** 211 **Born:** 3/2/1995 **Age:** 28

BATTING																					RUNNING			AVERAGES			
Year	Team	Lg	G	AB	H	2B	3B	HR	(Hm	Rd)	TB	R	RBI	RC	TBB	IBB	SO	HBP	SH	SF	SB	CS	GDP	Avg	OBP	Slg	OPS
2022	S-WB	AAA	71	277	79	17	0	13	(-	-)	135	42	51	47	17	1	35	2	0	1	5	0	3	.285	.330	.487	.817
2017	NYY	AL	5	7	4	2	0	0	(0	0)	6	0	4	4	1	0	0	0	0	0	1	0	0	.571	.625	.857	1.482
2018	NYY	AL	149	573	170	47	2	27	(16	11)	302	83	92	99	25	2	97	4	0	4	2	1	9	.297	.328	.527	.855
2019	NYY	AL	12	47	6	0	0	0	(0	0)	6	1	1	0	1	0	11	0	0	1	0	0	4	.128	.143	.128	.271
2020	NYY	AL	21	62	15	2	1	1	(0	1)	22	5	5	4	3	0	9	0	0	0	0	0	1	.242	.277	.355	.632
2021	NYY	AL	45	154	39	2	0	6	(4	2)	59	19	12	8	7	0	28	0	0	1	0	1	8	.253	.284	.383	.667
2022	2 Tms		36	132	31	5	1	1	(1	0)	41	13	17	9	5	0	27	0	0	3	4	1	1	.235	.257	.311	.568
22	NYY	AL	27	96	22	2	0	1	(1	0)	27	9	8	7	3	0	22	0	0	1	4	0	0	.229	.250	.281	.531
22	Pit	NL	9	36	9	3	1	0	(0	0)	14	4	9	2	2	0	5	0	0	2	0	1	1	.250	.275	.389	.664
	Postseason		4	10	2	0	0	0	(0	0)	2	0	0	1	2	0	2	0	0	0	0	0	1	.200	.333	.200	.533
	6 ML YEARS		268	975	265	58	4	35	(21	14)	436	121	131	124	42	2	172	4	0	9	7	3	23	.272	.302	.447	.749

Tejay Antone

Pitches: R **Bats:** R **Pos:** P **Ht:** 6'4" **Wt:** 230 **Born:** 12/5/1993 **Age:** 29

HOW MUCH PITCHED						WHAT HE GAVE UP											THE RESULTS							
Year	Team	Lg	G	GS	GF	IP	BFP	H	R	ER	HR	SH	SF	HB	TBB	IBB	SO	WP	W	L	Pct	Sv-Op	Hld	Vel	OPS	ERC	ERA
2020	Cin	NL	13	4	1	35.1	141	20	11	11	4	0	2	2	16	0	45	2	0	3	.000	0-1	-		.584	2.34	2.80
2021	Cin	NL	23	0	4	33.2	128	17	8	8	3	0	0	3	13	0	42	1	2	0	1.000	3-7	8	-	.508	1.87	2.14
	2 ML YEARS		36	4	5	69.0	269	37	19	19	7	0	2	5	29	0	87	3	2	3	.400	3-8	9	-	.547	2.11	2.48

Mark Appel

Pitches: R **Bats:** R **Pos:** RP-6 **Ht:** 6'5" **Wt:** 220 **Born:** 7/15/1991 **Age:** 31

HOW MUCH PITCHED						WHAT HE GAVE UP											THE RESULTS							
Year	Team	Lg	G	GS	GF	IP	BFP	H	R	ER	HR	SH	SF	HB	TBB	IBB	SO	WP	W	L	Pct	Sv-Op	Hld	Vel	OPS	ERC	ERA
2022	LV	AAA	31	0	10	40.0	171	33	17	14	4	0	0	6	17	0	36	3	6	0	1.000	5--	-	-	.652	3.83	3.15
2022	Phi	NL	6	0	3	10.1	40	9	2	2	0	0	0	0	3	0	5	0	0	0	-	0-0	0	95	.597	2.51	1.74

Aristides Aquino

Bats: R **Throws:** R **Pos:** RF-69;LF-7;PH-4;CF-2;PR-2;DH-1 **Ht:** 6'4" **Wt:** 220 **Born:** 4/22/1994 **Age:** 29

BATTING																					RUNNING			AVERAGES			
Year	Team	Lg	G	AB	H	2B	3B	HR	(Hm	Rd)	TB	R	RBI	RC	TBB	IBB	SO	HBP	SH	SF	SB	CS	GDP	Avg	OBP	Slg	OPS
2022	Lsvlle	AAA	22	77	24	6	0	8	(-	-)	54	18	19	23	9	0	33	4	0	1	2	1	1	.312	.407	.701	1.108
2018	Cin	NL	1	1	0	0	0	0	(0	0)	0	0	0	0	0	0	1	0	0	0	0	0	0	.000	.000	.000	.000
2019	Cin	NL	56	205	53	8	0	19	(11	8)	118	31	47	39	16	2	60	2	0	2	7	0	5	.259	.316	.576	.891
2020	Cin	NL	23	47	8	1	0	2	(1	1)	15	7	8	9	6	0	18	3	0	0	1	0	1	.170	.304	.319	.623
2021	Cin	NL	84	174	33	6	1	10	(6	4)	71	25	23	21	27	2	75	1	0	2	2	2	2	.190	.299	.408	.707
2022	Cin	NL	80	259	51	13	0	10	(5	5)	94	24	30	27	17	0	101	0	0	0	2	3	1	.197	.246	.363	.609
	Postseason		1	6	2	0	0	0	(0	0)	2	0	0	0	0	0	2	0	0	0	0	1	0	.333	.333	.333	.667
	5 ML YEARS		244	686	145	28	1	41	(23	18)	298	87	108	96	66	4	255	6	0	4	12	5	7	.211	.285	.434	.719

Jonathan Aranda

Bats: L **Throws:** R **Pos:** 2B-13;1B-11;PH-8;3B-6;LF-1;DH-1 **Ht:** 6'0" **Wt:** 210 **Born:** 5/23/1998 **Age:** 25

BATTING																					RUNNING			AVERAGES			
Year	Team	Lg	G	AB	H	2B	3B	HR	(Hm	Rd)	TB	R	RBI	RC	TBB	IBB	SO	HBP	SH	SF	SB	CS	GDP	Avg	OBP	Slg	OPS
2022	Drham	AAA	104	403	128	26	1	18	(-	-)	210	71	85	83	45	0	100	10	0	7	5	0	10	.318	.394	.521	.915
2022	TB	AL	32	78	15	4	0	2	(1	1)	25	10	6	8	8	1	23	1	0	0	0	0	1	.192	.276	.321	.596

Victor Arano

Pitches: R **Bats:** R **Pos:** RP-43 **Ht:** 6'2" **Wt:** 228 **Born:** 2/7/1995 **Age:** 28

HOW MUCH PITCHED						WHAT HE GAVE UP											THE RESULTS							
Year	Team	Lg	G	GS	GF	IP	BFP	H	R	ER	HR	SH	SF	HB	TBB	IBB	SO	WP	W	L	Pct	Sv-Op	Hld	Vel	OPS	ERC	ERA
2017	Phi	NL	10	0	2	10.2	42	6	2	2	0	0	0	0	4	0	13	0	1	0	1.000	0-0	2	93	.475	1.35	1.69
2018	Phi	NL	60	0	14	59.1	246	54	19	18	6	0	2	1	17	4	60	1	1	2	.333	3-5	10	94	.673	3.12	2.73
2019	Phi	NL	3	0	1	4.2	16	2	2	2	1	0	0	0	2	0	7	0	1	0	1.000	0-0	0	93	.635	2.23	3.86
2022	Was	NL	43	0	7	42.0	187	47	30	21	5	1	1	4	12	0	44	6	1	1	.500	1-2	7	94	.747	4.76	4.50
	4 ML YEARS		116	0	24	116.2	491	109	53	43	12	1	4	5	35	4	124	7	4	3	.571	4-7	19	94	.683	3.45	3.32

Jonathan Arauz

Bats: B Throws: R Pos: 3B-6;2B-4;SS-4;PH-1;PR-1   Ht: 6'0" Wt: 195 Born: 8/3/1998 Age: 24

Year	Team	Lg	G	AB	H	2B	3B	HR	(Hm	Rd)	TB	R	RBI	RC	TBB	IBB	SO	HBP	SH	SF	SB	CS	GDP	Avg	OBP	Slg	OPS
2022	Wrcstr	AAA	24	92	17	5	0	0	(-	-)	22	11	3	3	7	0	13	0	0	0	1	0	2	.185	.242	.239	.482
2022	Norfolk	AAA	11	40	10	3	0	0	(-	-)	13	4	6	3	4	0	9	1	0	0	1	0	0	.250	.333	.325	.658
2020	Bos	AL	25	72	18	2	0	1	(0	1)	23	8	9	12	8	0	21	0	0	0	0	0	0	.250	.325	.319	.644
2021	Bos	AL	28	65	12	3	0	3	(2	1)	24	9	8	6	8	0	15	0	2	0	0	0	2	.185	.274	.369	.643
2022	2 Tms	AL	15	38	5	0	0	1	(0	1)	8	3	5	1	1	0	12	0	1	1	0	0	2	.132	.150	.211	.361
22	Bos	AL	6	10	0	0	0	0	(0	0)	0	1	1	0	0	0	3	0	1	1	0	0	0	.000	.000	.000	.000
22	Bal	AL	9	28	5	0	0	1	(0	1)	8	2	4	1	1	0	9	0	0	0	0	0	0	.179	.207	.286	.493
3 ML YEARS			68	175	35	5	0	5	(2	3)	55	20	22	19	17	0	48	0	3	1	0	0	2	.200	.269	.314	.584

Chris Archer

Pitches: R Bats: R Pos: SP-25   Ht: 6'2" Wt: 195 Born: 9/26/1988 Age: 34

Year	Team	Lg	G	GS	GF	IP	BFP	H	R	ER	HR	SH	SF	HB	TBB	IBB	SO	WP	W	L	Pct	Sv-Op	Hld	Vel	OPS	ERC	ERA
2012	TB	AL	6	4	1	29.1	122	23	17	15	3	1	0	1	13	0	36	2	1	3	.250	0-0	0	94	.624	3.24	4.60
2013	TB	AL	23	23	0	128.2	525	107	49	46	15	1	5	8	38	2	101	7	9	7	.563	0-0	0	95	.660	3.13	3.22
2014	TB	AL	32	32	0	194.2	822	177	85	72	12	4	9	8	72	1	173	8	10	9	.526	0-0	0	95	.650	3.36	3.33
2015	TB	AL	34	34	0	212.0	868	175	85	76	19	2	2	3	66	0	252	13	12	13	.480	0-0	0	95	.613	2.79	3.23
2016	TB	AL	33	33	0	201.1	850	183	100	90	30	6	4	3	67	0	233	11	9	19	.321	0-0	0	94	.703	3.66	4.02
2017	TB	AL	34	34	0	201.0	852	193	101	91	27	1	2	5	60	0	249	15	10	12	.455	0-0	0	95	.710	3.75	4.07
2018	2 Tms		27	27	0	148.1	638	155	77	71	19	1	3	6	49	3	162	6	6	8	.429	0-0	0	95	.767	4.41	4.31
2019	Pit	NL	23	23	0	119.2	526	114	73	69	26	6	3	4	55	2	143	6	3	9	.250	0-0	0	94	.793	4.89	5.19
2021	TB	AL	6	5	0	19.1	83	18	11	10	3	0	0	0	8	0	21	1	1	1	.500	0-0	0	92	.727	4.09	4.66
2022	Min	AL	25	25	0	102.2	437	87	56	52	12	0	4	3	48	0	84	3	2	8	.200	0-0	0	93	.708	3.73	4.56
18	TB	AL	17	17	0	96.0	413	102	50	46	11	0	1	4	31	0	102	3	3	5	.375	0-0	0	95	.751	4.43	4.31
18	Pit	NL	10	10	0	52.1	225	53	27	25	8	1	2	2	18	3	60	3	3	3	.500	0-0	0	95	.796	4.36	4.30
Postseason			2	0	0	1.2	6	1	0	0	0	0	1	0	0	0	2	0	0	0	-	0-0	0	96	.367	0.75	0.00
10 ML YEARS			243	240	1	1357.0	5723	1232	654	592	165	22	32	41	476	8	1454	72	63	89	.414	0-0	0	95	.693	3.62	3.93

Orlando Arcia

Bats: R Throws: R Pos: 2B-50;DH-7;LF-6;3B-4;PH-2;SS-1   ARR-see-ya   Ht: 6'0" Wt: 187 Born: 8/4/1994 Age: 28

Year	Team	Lg	G	AB	H	2B	3B	HR	(Hm	Rd)	TB	R	RBI	RC	TBB	IBB	SO	HBP	SH	SF	SB	CS	GDP	Avg	OBP	Slg	OPS
2016	Mil	NL	55	201	44	10	3	4	(2	2)	72	21	17	20	15	0	47	0	0	0	8	0	6	.219	.273	.358	.631
2017	Mil	NL	153	506	140	17	2	15	(8	7)	206	56	53	63	36	9	100	1	2	3	14	7	10	.277	.324	.407	.731
2018	Mil	NL	119	348	82	16	0	3	(2	1)	107	32	30	26	15	0	87	1	1	1	7	4	9	.236	.268	.307	.576
2019	Mil	NL	152	494	110	16	1	15	(6	9)	173	51	59	48	43	5	109	1	2	6	8	5	15	.223	.283	.350	.633
2020	Mil	NL	59	173	45	10	1	5	(2	3)	72	22	20	19	14	0	32	1	0	1	2	0	10	.260	.317	.416	.734
2021	2 Tms	NL	36	81	16	3	0	2	(0	2)	25	9	14	9	7	1	19	0	0	1	1	0	2	.198	.258	.309	.567
2022	Atl	NL	68	209	51	9	0	9	(4	5)	87	25	30	29	21	0	51	2	0	2	0	0	7	.244	.316	.416	.733
21	Mil	NL	4	11	1	0	0	0	(0	0)	1	0	1	0	0	0	3	0	0	0	0	0	0	.091	.091	.091	.182
21	Atl	NL	32	70	15	3	0	2	(0	2)	24	9	13	9	7	1	16	0	0	1	1	0	2	.214	.282	.343	.625
Postseason			19	48	13	0	0	4	(1	3)	25	8	6	5	2	1	10	0	0	0	0	0	1	.271	.300	.521	.821
7 ML YEARS			642	2012	488	81	7	53	(24	29)	742	216	223	214	151	15	445	6	5	14	40	16	59	.243	.295	.369	.664

Nolan Arenado

Bats: R Throws: R Pos: 3B-131;DH-17;PH-1   ahr-eh-NOD-oh   Ht: 6'2" Wt: 215 Born: 4/16/1991 Age: 32

Year	Team	Lg	G	AB	H	2B	3B	HR	(Hm	Rd)	TB	R	RBI	RC	TBB	IBB	SO	HBP	SH	SF	SB	CS	GDP	Avg	OBP	Slg	OPS
2013	Col	NL	133	486	130	29	4	10	(5	5)	197	49	52	48	23	1	72	1	2	2	2	0	16	.267	.301	.405	.706
2014	Col	NL	111	432	124	34	2	18	(16	2)	216	58	61	60	25	1	58	4	1	5	2	1	13	.287	.328	.500	.828
2015	Col	NL	157	616	177	43	4	42	(20	22)	354	97	130	116	34	13	110	4	0	11	2	5	17	.287	.323	.575	.898
2016	Col	NL	160	618	182	35	6	41	(25	16)	352	116	133	118	68	10	103	2	0	8	2	3	17	.294	.362	.570	.932
2017	Col	NL	159	606	187	43	7	37	(19	18)	355	100	130	130	62	9	106	4	1	6	3	2	21	.309	.373	.586	.959
2018	Col	NL	156	590	175	38	2	38	(23	15)	331	104	110	117	73	10	122	3	1	6	2	2	16	.297	.374	.561	.935
2019	Col	NL	155	588	185	31	2	41	(21	20)	343	102	118	123	62	11	93	4	0	8	3	2	14	.315	.379	.583	.962
2020	Col	NL	48	182	46	9	0	8	(7	1)	79	23	26	18	15	3	20	0	0	4	0	0	7	.253	.303	.434	.738
2021	StL	NL	157	593	151	34	3	34	(14	20)	293	81	105	94	50	8	96	3	0	7	2	0	20	.255	.312	.494	.807
2022	StL	NL	148	557	163	42	1	30	(14	16)	297	73	103	106	52	3	72	7	0	4	5	3	15	.293	.358	.533	.891
Postseason			6	25	4	0	0	1	(0	1)	7	2	3	0	0	0	7	0	0	2	0	0	0	.160	.148	.280	.428
10 ML YEARS			1384	5268	1520	338	31	299	(164	135)	2817	803	968	940	464	69	852	32	5	61	23	18	156	.289	.346	.535	.881

Gabriel Arias

Bats: R Throws: R Pos: 3B-9;2B-3;SS-3;1B-1;PR-1   Ht: 6'1" Wt: 217 Born: 2/27/2000 Age: 23

Year	Team	Lg	G	AB	H	2B	3B	HR	(Hm	Rd)	TB	R	RBI	RC	TBB	IBB	SO	HBP	SH	SF	SB	CS	GDP	Avg	OBP	Slg	OPS
2022	Clmbs	AAA	77	288	69	9	0	13	(-	-)	117	46	36	39	25	0	78	6	0	4	5	1	6	.240	.310	.406	.716
2022	Cle	AL	16	47	9	1	1	1	(1	0)	15	9	5	5	8	0	16	1	1	0	1	0	1	.191	.321	.319	.641

Kohei Arihara

Pitches: R Bats: R Pos: SP-4; RP-1   Ht: 6'2" Wt: 210 Born: 8/11/1992 Age: 30

Year	Team	Lg	G	GS	GF	IP	BFP	H	R	ER	HR	SH	SF	HB	TBB	IBB	SO	WP	W	L	Pct	Sv-Op	Hld	Vel	OPS	ERC	ERA
2022	RdRck	AAA	19	15	0	74.0	320	80	44	40	10	0	2	6	19	0	64	2	3	6	.333	0- -	-	-	.762	4.54	4.86
2021	Tex	AL	10	10	0	40.2	178	45	31	30	11	0	1	4	13	0	24	1	2	4	.333	0-0	0	91	.948	6.12	6.64
2022	Tex	AL	5	4	0	20.0	108	36	22	21	4	1	0	3	11	0	14	0	1	3	.250	0-0	0	91	1.112	11.49	9.45
	2 ML YEARS		15	14	0	60.2	286	81	53	51	15	1	1	7	24	0	38	1	3	7	.300	0-0	0	91	1.010	7.83	7.57

Shawn Armstrong

Pitches: R Bats: R Pos: RP-47; SP-3   Ht: 6'2" Wt: 225 Born: 9/11/1990 Age: 32

Year	Team	Lg	G	GS	GF	IP	BFP	H	R	ER	HR	SH	SF	HB	TBB	IBB	SO	WP	W	L	Pct	Sv-Op	Hld	Vel	OPS	ERC	ERA
2022	Drham	AAA	7	0	3	7.0	27	5	2	2	0	0	0	0	2	0	10	0	0	0	-	2- -	-	-	.539	1.68	2.57
2015	Cle	AL	8	0	5	8.0	30	5	2	2	1	0	0	0	2	0	11	0	0	0	-	0-0	0	94	.590	1.84	2.25
2016	Cle	AL	10	0	2	10.2	44	9	3	3	1	1	0	0	5	2	7	1	0	0	-	0-0	0	92	.668	3.25	2.53
2017	Cle	AL	21	0	14	24.2	108	23	12	12	5	0	0	1	10	0	20	1	0	0	1.000	0-0	0	93	.737	4.50	4.38
2018	Sea	AL	14	0	3	14.2	57	9	2	2	1	0	2	3	3	1	15	0	0	1	.000	1-1	2	94	.569	1.91	1.23
2019	2 Tms	AL	55	0	10	58.0	271	66	38	37	8	1	3	4	29	1	63	4	1	1	.500	4-9	9	93	.815	5.74	5.74
2020	Bal	AL	14	0	2	15.0	57	9	6	3	1	0	0	1	3	0	14	2	2	0	1.000	0-0	3	94	.530	1.51	1.80
2021	2 Tms	AL	31	0	11	36.0	165	39	28	27	10	0	1	2	15	0	44	0	1	0	1.000	0-1	2	94	.870	6.02	6.75
2022	2 Tms	AL	50	3	19	61.2	269	66	32	30	7	1	5	4	17	2	66	3	2	3	.400	2-3	2	96	.754	4.23	4.38
19	Sea	AL	4	0	1	3.2	23	8	6	6	1	0	1	0	3	1	3	0	0	1	.000	0-0	0	93	1.268	16.16	14.73
19	Bal	AL	51	0	9	54.1	248	58	32	31	7	0	3	3	26	0	60	4	1	0	1.000	4-9	9	93	.777	5.14	5.13
21	Bal	AL	20	0	8	20.0	100	28	20	19	5	0	1	1	10	0	22	0	0	0	-	0-1	1	93	.970	8.15	8.55
21	TB	AL	11	0	3	16.0	65	11	8	8	5	0	0	1	5	0	22	0	1	0	1.000	0-0	1	94	.719	3.54	4.50
22	Mia	NL	7	0	1	6.2	34	10	10	8	1	0	1	0	3	0	5	1	0	0	-	0-0	0	95	.982	7.33	10.80
22	TB	AL	43	3	18	55.0	235	56	22	22	6	1	4	4	14	2	61	2	2	3	.400	2-3	2	96	.722	3.88	3.60
	8 ML YEARS		203	3	66	228.2	1001	226	123	116	34	3	11	15	84	6	240	11	7	5	.583	7-14	18	94	.756	4.39	4.57

Randy Arozarena

Bats: R Throws: R Pos: LF-104;DH-27;RF-25;PH-3   ah-row-sah-RAY-nah   Ht: 5'11" Wt: 185 Born: 2/28/1995 Age: 28

Year	Team	Lg	G	AB	H	2B	3B	HR	(Hm	Rd)	TB	R	RBI	RC	TBB	IBB	SO	HBP	SH	SF	SB	CS	GDP	Avg	OBP	Slg	OPS
2019	StL	NL	19	20	6	1	0	1	(0	1)	10	4	2	3	2	0	4	1	0	0	2	1	0	.300	.391	.500	.891
2020	TB	AL	23	64	18	2	0	7	(2	5)	41	15	11	15	6	0	22	5	0	1	4	0	2	.281	.382	.641	1.022
2021	TB	AL	141	529	145	32	3	20	(13	7)	243	94	69	91	56	4	170	14	0	5	20	10	9	.274	.356	.459	.815
2022	TB	AL	153	586	154	41	3	20	(9	11)	261	72	89	86	46	2	156	11	0	2	32	12	17	.263	.327	.445	.773
	Postseason		29	96	34	4	1	11	(7	4)	73	23	17	23	12	2	26	2	0	0	3	2	0	.354	.436	.760	1.197
	4 ML YEARS		336	1199	323	76	6	48	(24	24)	555	185	171	195	110	6	352	31	0	8	58	23	28	.269	.344	.463	.807

Luis Arraez

Bats: L Throws: R Pos: 1B-65;2B-41;DH-38;PH-13;3B-7   ah-RYE-ez   Ht: 5'10" Wt: 175 Born: 4/9/1997 Age: 26

Year	Team	Lg	G	AB	H	2B	3B	HR	(Hm	Rd)	TB	R	RBI	RC	TBB	IBB	SO	HBP	SH	SF	SB	CS	GDP	Avg	OBP	Slg	OPS
2019	Min	AL	92	326	109	20	1	4	(1	3)	143	54	28	59	36	1	29	1	0	3	2	2	2	.334	.399	.439	.838
2020	Min	AL	32	112	36	9	0	0	(0	0)	45	16	13	22	8	0	11	0	0	1	0	0	2	.321	.364	.402	.765
2021	Min	AL	121	428	126	17	6	2	(2	0)	161	58	42	63	43	2	48	2	0	6	2	2	9	.294	.357	.376	.733
2022	Min	AL	144	547	173	31	1	8	(7	1)	230	88	49	84	50	2	43	3	0	3	4	4	6	.316	.375	.420	.795
	Postseason		5	17	5	4	0	0	(0	0)	9	1	1	2	2	0	3	0	0	0	0	0	1	.294	.368	.529	.898
	4 ML YEARS		389	1413	444	77	8	14	(10	4)	579	216	132	228	137	5	131	6	0	13	8	8	19	.314	.374	.410	.784

Christian Arroyo

Bats: R Throws: R Pos: 2B-40;RF-17;SS-14;3B-10;1B-9;DH-5;PH-3;PR-2   Ht: 6'1" Wt: 210 Born: 5/30/1995 Age: 28

Year	Team	Lg	G	AB	H	2B	3B	HR	(Hm	Rd)	TB	R	RBI	RC	TBB	IBB	SO	HBP	SH	SF	SB	CS	GDP	Avg	OBP	Slg	OPS
2017	SF	NL	34	125	24	5	0	3	(2	1)	38	9	14	7	8	1	32	1	0	1	1	2	4	.192	.244	.304	.548
2018	TB	AL	20	53	14	2	1	1	(1	0)	21	5	6	9	6	0	16	0	0	0	0	0	0	.264	.339	.396	.735
2019	TB	AL	16	50	11	2	0	2	(2	0)	19	8	7	6	5	0	18	1	1	0	0	0	0	.220	.304	.380	.684
2020	2 Tms	AL	15	50	12	1	0	3	(1	2)	22	7	8	10	4	0	11	0	0	0	0	0	2	.240	.296	.440	.736
2021	Bos	AL	57	164	43	12	0	6	(2	4)	73	22	25	26	8	0	44	7	1	0	1	0	1	.262	.324	.445	.769
2022	Bos	AL	87	280	80	16	1	6	(3	3)	116	32	36	36	13	2	49	3	2	2	5	1	7	.286	.322	.414	.736
20	Cle	AL	1	0	0	0	0	0	(0	0)	0	0	0	0	0	0	0	0	0	0	0	0	0	-	-	-	-
20	Bos	AL	14	50	12	1	0	3	(1	2)	22	7	8	10	4	0	11	0	0	0	0	0	2	.240	.296	.440	.736
	Postseason		11	38	9	1	1	1	(1	0)	15	4	3	3	0	0	7	0	2	0	0	0	1	.237	.237	.395	.632
	6 ML YEARS		229	722	184	38	2	21	(11	10)	289	83	96	94	44	3	170	12	4	3	7	3	14	.255	.307	.400	.708

Aaron Ashby

Pitches: L Bats: R Pos: SP-19; RP-8   Ht: 6'2" Wt: 181 Born: 5/24/1998 Age: 25

Year	Team	Lg	G	GS	GF	IP	BFP	H	R	ER	HR	SH	SF	HB	TBB	IBB	SO	WP	W	L	Pct	Sv-Op	Hld	Vel	OPS	ERC	ERA
2018	2 Tms	Low	13	10	1	57.2	242	58	24	23	4	0	0	2	17	0	66	4	3	2	.400	1- -	-	-	.704	3.67	3.59
2019	2 Tms	Low	24	23	0	126.0	530	101	60	49	4	2	6	8	60	0	135	6	5	10	.333	0- -	-	-	.648	3.15	3.50
2021	Nashv	AAA	21	12	0	63.1	276	55	35	31	4	0	0	2	32	0	100	4	5	4	.556	0- -	-	-	.637	3.58	4.41

Year	Team	Lg	G	GS	GF	IP	BFP	H	R	ER	HR	SH	SF	HB	TBB	IBB	SO	WP	W	L	Pct	Sv-Op	Hld	Vel	OPS	ERC	ERA
2021	Mil	NL	13	4	3	31.2	133	25	20	16	4	0	1	1	12	0	39	1	3	2	.600	1-1	0	97	.613	3.09	4.55
2022	Mil	NL	27	19	2	107.1	475	106	62	53	15	1	3	6	47	0	126	7	2	10	.167	1-1	1	96	.752	4.62	4.44
Postseason			2	0	0	2.2	16	5	2	2	0	0	0	1	2	0	3	0	0	0	-	0-0	0	97	.885	11.70	6.75
2 ML YEARS			40	23	5	139.0	608	131	82	69	19	1	4	7	59	0	165	8	5	12	.294	2-2	1	96	.721	4.26	4.47

Graham Ashcraft

Pitches: R **Bats:** L **Pos:** SP-19   **Ht:** 6'2" **Wt:** 240 **Born:** 2/11/1998 **Age:** 25

Year	Team	Lg	G	GS	GF	IP	BFP	H	R	ER	HR	SH	SF	HB	TBB	IBB	SO	WP	W	L	Pct	Sv-Op	Hld	Vel	OPS	ERC	ERA
2022	Lsvlle	AAA	8	8	0	35.1	171	42	24	9	0	0	2	2	17	0	35	3	3	2	.600	0--	-	-	.663	4.67	2.29
2022	Cin	NL	19	19	0	105.0	464	119	61	57	11	0	3	8	30	1	71	9	5	6	.455	0-0	0	97	.743	4.68	4.89

Javier Assad

Pitches: R **Bats:** R **Pos:** SP-8; RP-1   **Ht:** 6'1" **Wt:** 200 **Born:** 7/30/1997 **Age:** 25

Year	Team	Lg	G	GS	GF	IP	BFP	H	R	ER	HR	SH	SF	HB	TBB	IBB	SO	WP	W	L	Pct	Sv-Op	Hld	Vel	OPS	ERC	ERA
2022	Tenn	AA	15	14	0	71.2	299	68	24	20	6	0	0	3	28	0	74	5	4	1	.800	0--	-	-	.712	3.93	2.51
2022	Iowa	AAA	8	7	0	36.2	149	31	13	12	4	0	0	3	7	0	37	1	1	2	.333	0--	-	-	.613	2.82	2.95
2022	ChC	NL	9	8	0	37.2	166	35	14	13	4	0	0	0	20	0	30	1	2	2	.500	0-0	0	93	.701	4.20	3.11

Willians Astudillo

Bats: R **Throws:** R **Pos:** 3B-10;2B-8;1B-3;PH-3;DH-1;PR-1   **Ht:** 5'9" **Wt:** 225 **Born:** 10/14/1991 **Age:** 31

Year	Team	Lg	G	AB	H	2B	3B	HR	(Hm	Rd)	TB	R	RBI	RC	TBB	IBB	SO	HBP	SH	SF	SB	CS	GDP	Avg	OBP	Slg	OPS
2022	Jaxnvl	AAA	75	283	87	18	0	16	(-	-)	153	36	53	56	17	0	16	13	0	2	4	1	10	.307	.371	.541	.912
2018	Min	AL	30	93	33	4	1	3	(1	2)	48	9	21	17	2	0	3	1	0	1	0	0	4	.355	.371	.516	.887
2019	Min	AL	58	190	51	9	0	4	(1	3)	72	28	21	19	5	0	8	5	0	4	0	0	6	.268	.299	.379	.678
2020	Min	AL	8	16	4	1	0	1	(1	0)	8	4	3	1	0	0	2	0	0	0	0	0	0	.250	.250	.500	.750
2021	Min	AL	73	208	49	8	0	7	(4	3)	78	17	21	13	3	0	12	4	0	1	0	0	12	.236	.259	.375	.634
2022	Mia	NL	21	54	13	0	0	1	(0	1)	16	5	4	2	1	0	3	0	0	0	1	0	2	.241	.255	.296	.551
Postseason			1	1	0	0	0	0	(0	0)	0	0	0	0	0	0	0	0	0	0	0	0	1	.000	.000	.000	.000
5 ML YEARS			190	561	150	22	1	16	(7	9)	222	63	70	52	11	0	28	10	0	6	1	0	24	.267	.291	.396	.687

Pedro Avila

Pitches: R **Bats:** R **Pos:** RP-2   AH-vee-lah   **Ht:** 5'11" **Wt:** 210 **Born:** 1/14/1997 **Age:** 26

Year	Team	Lg	G	GS	GF	IP	BFP	H	R	ER	HR	SH	SF	HB	TBB	IBB	SO	WP	W	L	Pct	Sv-Op	Hld	Vel	OPS	ERC	ERA
2022	ElPaso	AAA	30	24	2	112.0	475	98	64	57	16	0	1	3	49	0	124	4	7	2	.778	0--	-	-	.745	3.95	4.58
2019	SD	NL	1	1	0	5.1	23	4	1	1	0	0	0	1	2	0	5	0	0	0		0-0	0	94	.504	2.60	1.69
2021	SD	NL	1	1	0	4.0	20	4	2	1	1	0	0	0	3	0	5	0	0	1	.000	0-0	0	93	.762	6.21	2.25
2022	SD	NL	2	0	1	4.0	18	3	3	2	1	0	0	1	1	0	5	1	0	0		0-0	0	93	.653	3.76	4.50
3 ML YEARS			4	2	1	13.1	61	11	6	4	2	0	0	2	6	0	15	1	0	1	.000	0-0	0	93	.632	3.99	2.70

Jose Azocar

Bats: R **Throws:** R **Pos:** RF-49;CF-35;LF-21;PH-11;PR-11;DH-3   **Ht:** 5'11" **Wt:** 181 **Born:** 5/11/1996 **Age:** 27

Year	Team	Lg	G	AB	H	2B	3B	HR	(Hm	Rd)	TB	R	RBI	RC	TBB	IBB	SO	HBP	SH	SF	SB	CS	GDP	Avg	OBP	Slg	OPS
2022	ElPaso	AAA	23	98	30	6	0	5	(-	-)	51	11	16	19	7	0	24	0	0	0	3	1	0	.306	.352	.520	.873
2022	SD	NL	98	202	52	9	3	0	(0	0)	67	24	10	10	12	0	44	0	1	1	5	6	1	.257	.298	.332	.629

Akil Baddoo

Bats: L **Throws:** L **Pos:** LF-50;CF-16;PR-6;PH-4;DH-2   uh-KEEL buh-DOO   **Ht:** 6'1" **Wt:** 214 **Born:** 8/16/1998 **Age:** 24

Year	Team	Lg	G	AB	H	2B	3B	HR	(Hm	Rd)	TB	R	RBI	RC	TBB	IBB	SO	HBP	SH	SF	SB	CS	GDP	Avg	OBP	Slg	OPS
2022	Toledo	AAA	30	110	33	9	2	3	(-	-)	55	14	15	22	19	0	26	1	0	1	7	4	0	.300	.405	.500	.905
2021	Det	AL	124	413	107	20	7	13	(6	7)	180	60	55	71	45	1	122	0	0	3	18	4	5	.259	.330	.436	.766
2022	Det	AL	73	201	41	3	2	2	(1	1)	54	30	9	15	24	0	64	0	0	0	9	6	2	.204	.289	.269	.558
2 ML YEARS			197	614	148	23	9	15	(7	8)	234	90	64	86	69	1	186	0	0	3	27	10	7	.241	.316	.381	.697

Harrison Bader

Bats: R **Throws:** R **Pos:** CF-85;PH-4   **Ht:** 6'0" **Wt:** 210 **Born:** 6/3/1994 **Age:** 29

Year	Team	Lg	G	AB	H	2B	3B	HR	(Hm	Rd)	TB	R	RBI	RC	TBB	IBB	SO	HBP	SH	SF	SB	CS	GDP	Avg	OBP	Slg	OPS
2017	StL	NL	32	85	20	3	0	3	(0	3)	32	10	10	10	5	1	24	1	0	1	2	1	1	.235	.283	.376	.659
2018	StL	NL	138	379	100	20	2	12	(2	10)	160	61	37	54	31	3	125	11	2	4	15	3	1	.264	.334	.422	.756
2019	StL	NL	128	347	71	14	3	12	(5	7)	127	54	39	41	46	4	117	10	1	2	11	3	3	.205	.314	.366	.680
2020	StL	NL	50	106	24	7	2	4	(4	0)	47	21	11	16	13	0	40	5	0	1	3	1	2	.226	.336	.443	.779
2021	StL	NL	103	367	98	21	1	16	(3	13)	169	45	50	53	27	6	85	5	0	2	9	4	4	.267	.324	.460	.785
2022	2 Tms		86	292	73	10	3	5	(2	3)	104	38	30	36	15	0	62	4	0	4	17	3	4	.250	.294	.356	.650

Year	Team	Lg	G	AB	H	2B	3B	HR	(Hm	Rd)	TB	R	RBI	RC	TBB	IBB	SO	HBP	SH	SF	SB	CS	GDP	Avg	OBP	Slg	OPS
22	StL	NL	72	246	63	7	3	5	(2	3)	91	35	21	29	13	0	47	4	0	1	15	2	4	.256	.303	.370	.673
22	NYY	AL	14	46	10	3	0	0	(0	0)	13	3	9	7	2	0	15	0	0	1	2	1	0	.217	.245	.283	.528
Postseason			10	22	3	0	0	0	(0	0)	3	3	3	0	2	0	14	3	0	1	1	1	0	.136	.286	.136	.422
6 ML YEARS			537	1576	386	75	11	52	(16	36)	639	229	177	210	137	14	453	36	3	12	57	15	15	.245	.317	.405	.723

Ji Hwan Bae

Bats: L **Throws:** R **Pos:** CF-5;2B-4;LF-1 gee-WAHN bay **Ht:** 6'1" **Wt:** 185 **Born:** 7/26/1999 **Age:** 23

Year	Team	Lg	G	AB	H	2B	3B	HR	(Hm	Rd)	TB	R	RBI	RC	TBB	IBB	SO	HBP	SH	SF	SB	CS	GDP	Avg	OBP	Slg	OPS
2022	Indy	AAA	108	419	121	23	6	8	(-	-)	180	81	53	65	48	1	80	2	1	3	30	8	5	.289	.362	.430	.792
2022	Pit	NL	10	33	11	3	0	0	(0	0)	14	5	6	6	2	0	6	2	0	0	3	0	0	.333	.405	.424	.830

Javier Baez

Bats: R **Throws:** R **Pos:** SS-133;DH-10;PH-2 BYE-ezz **Ht:** 6'0" **Wt:** 190 **Born:** 12/1/1992 **Age:** 30

Year	Team	Lg	G	AB	H	2B	3B	HR	(Hm	Rd)	TB	R	RBI	RC	TBB	IBB	SO	HBP	SH	SF	SB	CS	GDP	Avg	OBP	Slg	OPS
2014	ChC	NL	52	213	36	6	0	9	(3	6)	69	25	20	12	15	0	95	1	0	0	5	1	5	.169	.227	.324	.551
2015	ChC	NL	28	76	22	6	0	1	(1	0)	31	4	4	5	4	1	24	0	0	0	1	2	0	.289	.325	.408	.733
2016	ChC	NL	142	421	115	19	1	14	(8	6)	178	50	59	53	15	3	108	11	1	2	12	3	8	.273	.314	.423	.737
2017	ChC	NL	145	469	128	24	2	23	(13	10)	225	75	75	69	30	15	144	1	6	2	10	3	10	.273	.317	.480	.796
2018	ChC	NL	160	606	176	40	9	34	(13	21)	336	101	**111**	96	29	8	167	5	1	4	21	9	10	.290	.326	.554	.881
2019	ChC	NL	138	531	149	38	4	29	(15	14)	282	89	85	82	28	3	156	0	0	2	11	7	16	.281	.316	.531	.847
2020	ChC	NL	59	222	45	9	1	8	(2	6)	80	27	24	15	7	0	75	4	0	2	3	0	8	.203	.238	.360	.599
2021	2 Tms	NL	138	502	133	18	2	31	(19	12)	248	80	87	77	28	2	**184**	13	0	3	18	5	12	.265	.319	.494	.813
2022	Det	AL	144	555	132	27	4	17	(7	10)	218	64	67	74	26	1	147	6	0	3	9	2	13	.238	.278	.393	.671
21	ChC	NL	91	335	83	9	2	22	(14	8)	162	48	65	52	15	1	131	7	0	3	13	3	7	.248	.292	.484	.775
21	NYM	NL	47	167	50	9	0	9	(5	4)	86	32	22	25	13	1	53	6	0	0	5	2	5	.299	.371	.515	.886
Postseason			36	122	27	5	0	5	(4	1)	47	12	14	13	5	0	41	0	0	1	7	0	3	.221	.250	.385	.635
9 ML YEARS			1006	3595	936	187	23	166	(81	85)	1667	515	532	483	182	33	1100	41	8	18	90	32	82	.260	.302	.464	.766

Michel Baez

Pitches: R **Bats:** R **Pos:** RP-2 BYE-ezz **Ht:** 6'8" **Wt:** 220 **Born:** 1/21/1996 **Age:** 27

Year	Team	Lg	G	GS	GF	IP	BFP	H	R	ER	HR	SH	SF	HB	TBB	IBB	SO	WP	W	L	Pct	Sv-Op	Hld	Vel	OPS	ERC	ERA
2022	SnAnt	AA	13	0	3	18.2	74	10	5	5	3	0	0	5	4	0	24	3	4	1	.800	1--	-	-	.564	2.35	2.41
2022	ElPaso	AAA	24	0	3	21.1	108	27	21	20	3	0	0	3	18	0	24	7	1	2	.333	0--	-	-	.927	8.67	8.44
2019	SD	NL	24	1	8	29.2	131	25	10	10	3	1	1	3	14	2	28	1	1	1	.500	0-0	0	96	.689	3.69	3.03
2020	SD	NL	3	1	1	4.2	23	7	4	4	0	0	0	0	2	0	7	0	0	0	-	0-1	0	95	.820	6.19	7.71
2022	SD	NL	2	0	2	2.0	7	1	0	0	0	0	0	0	0	0	2	1	0	0	-	0-0	0	95	.286	0.54	0.00
3 ML YEARS			29	2	11	36.1	161	33	14	14	3	1	1	3	16	2	37	2	1	1	.500	0-1	0	96	.689	3.74	3.47

Pedro Baez

Pitches: R **Bats:** R **Pos:** RP-3 BYE-ezz **Ht:** 6'0" **Wt:** 232 **Born:** 3/11/1988 **Age:** 35

Year	Team	Lg	G	GS	GF	IP	BFP	H	R	ER	HR	SH	SF	HB	TBB	IBB	SO	WP	W	L	Pct	Sv-Op	Hld	Vel	OPS	ERC	ERA
2022	OkCity	AAA	7	0	0	5.2	32	13	9	9	1	0	0	0	2	0	3	0	0	1	.000	0--	-	-	1.135	12.90	14.29
2022	Ddgrs	R	5	4	0	5.1	21	3	2	2	0	0	0	0	2	0	4	0	0	0	-	0--	-	-	-	1.35	3.38
2014	LAD	NL	20	0	8	24.0	92	16	7	7	3	1	1	0	5	1	18	0	0	0	-	0-0	5	95	.537	1.79	2.63
2015	LAD	NL	52	0	8	51.0	208	47	22	19	4	3	3	1	11	1	60	1	4	2	.667	0-3	11	97	.693	2.87	3.35
2016	LAD	NL	73	0	10	74.0	295	52	27	25	11	1	2	2	22	0	83	3	3	2	.600	0-2	23	97	.615	2.52	3.04
2017	LAD	NL	66	0	6	64.0	280	56	24	21	9	0	0	2	29	2	64	1	3	6	.333	0-3	23	97	.728	3.84	2.95
2018	LAD	NL	55	0	8	56.1	237	46	19	18	4	2	2	1	23	2	62	0	4	3	.571	0-1	7	96	.652	2.91	2.88
2019	LAD	NL	71	0	9	69.2	276	43	30	24	6	2	0	4	23	1	69	0	7	2	.778	1-7	25	96	.543	1.97	3.10
2020	LAD	NL	18	0	2	17.0	70	10	8	6	2	0	0	0	7	0	13	0	0	0	-	2-2	6	94	.529	2.01	3.18
2021	Hou	AL	4	0	3	4.1	15	2	1	1	1	0	0	0	1	0	5	1	0	0	-	0-0	0	90	.557	1.63	2.08
2022	Hou	AL	3	0	1	2.1	16	5	6	3	0	0	1	0	3	0	2	0	0	0	-	0-0	0	90	1.083	13.45	11.57
Postseason			31	0	1	29.1	125	22	17	13	6	1	1	2	16	1	33	0	1	0	1.000	0-1	4	97	.732	4.23	3.99
9 ML YEARS			362	0	55	362.2	1489	277	144	124	40	9	9	10	124	7	376	6	21	15	.583	3-18	100	96	.635	2.72	3.08

Bryan Baker

Pitches: R **Bats:** R **Pos:** RP-64; SP-2 **Ht:** 6'6" **Wt:** 245 **Born:** 12/2/1994 **Age:** 28

Year	Team	Lg	G	GS	GF	IP	BFP	H	R	ER	HR	SH	SF	HB	TBB	IBB	SO	WP	W	L	Pct	Sv-Op	Hld	Vel	OPS	ERC	ERA
2021	Tor	AL	1	0	0	1.0	4	1	0	0	0	0	0	0	0	0	1	2	0	0	-	0-0	0	95	.500	1.95	0.00
2022	Bal	AL	66	2	11	69.2	291	60	29	27	3	0	1	3	26	1	76	2	4	3	.571	1-3	9	96	.616	3.00	3.49
2 ML YEARS			67	2	11	70.2	295	61	29	27	3	0	1	3	26	1	77	4	4	3	.571	1-3	9	96	.615	2.98	3.44

Anthony Banda

Pitches: L Bats: L Pos: RP-31; SP-1   Ht: 6'2" Wt: 220 Born: 8/10/1993 Age: 29

			HOW MUCH PITCHED				WHAT HE GAVE UP										THE RESULTS						
Year Team	Lg	G	GS	GF	IP	BFP	H	R	ER	HR	SH	SF	HB	TBB	IBB	SO	WP	W	L	Pct	Sv-Op	Hld	Vel	OPS	ERC	ERA
2022 S-WB	AAA	6	1	1	7.1	36	7	6	5	0	1	0	2	6	0	8	0	0	3	.000	0- -	-	-	.762	5.73	6.14
2017 Ari	NL	8	4	1	25.2	115	26	17	17	1	0	0	3	10	1	25	2	2	3	.400	0-0	0	94	.771	3.98	5.96
2018 TB	AL	3	1	1	14.2	56	12	6	6	1	1	1	0	3	0	10	0	1	0	1.000	0-0	0	95	.665	2.32	3.68
2019 TB	AL	3	0	1	4.0	18	6	3	3	0	0	0	0	0	0	2	0	0	0	-	0-0	0	93	.889	4.47	6.75
2020 TB	AL	4	0	3	7.0	36	10	9	8	1	0	0	2	5	0	4	0	1	0	1.000	1-1	0	92	1.127	10.08	10.29
2021 2 Tms	NL	30	0	5	33.2	153	39	18	16	6	0	2	2	13	1	32	3	2	2	.500	0-3	4	94	.831	5.67	4.28
2022 3 Tms	AL	32	1	3	26.2	135	43	20	20	4	0	1	2	13	2	30	1	1	1	.500	0-0	2	94	.967	8.88	6.75
21 NYM	NL	5	0	3	7.1	37	14	8	6	2	0	1	0	1	0	7	1	1	0	1.000	0-1	0	94	1.063	9.93	7.36
21 Pit	NL	25	0	2	26.1	116	25	10	10	4	0	1	2	12	1	25	2	1	2	.333	0-2	4	94	.752	4.61	3.42
22 Pit	NL	23	0	1	19.2	98	34	14	14	3	0	1	1	5	2	22	1	1	0	1.000	0-0	2	95	.969	8.32	6.41
22 Tor	AL	7	1	2	6.1	27	7	3	3	1	0	0	0	3	0	7	0	0	1	.000	0-0	0	94	.829	5.73	4.26
22 NYY	AL	2	0	0	0.2	10	2	3	3	0	0	0	1	5	0	1	0	0	0	-	0-0	0	93	1.300	59.85	40.50
6 ML YEARS		80	6	14	111.2	513	136	73	70	13	1	4	9	44	4	103	6	7	6	.538	1-4	6	94	.857	5.71	5.64

Tanner Banks

Pitches: L Bats: R Pos: RP-35   Ht: 6'1" Wt: 210 Born: 10/24/1991 Age: 31

			HOW MUCH PITCHED				WHAT HE GAVE UP										THE RESULTS						
Year Team	Lg	G	GS	GF	IP	BFP	H	R	ER	HR	SH	SF	HB	TBB	IBB	SO	WP	W	L	Pct	Sv-Op	Hld	Vel	OPS	ERC	ERA
2022 Charlit	AAA	9	2	1	17.0	73	17	5	5	1	1	0	1	5	0	24	0	2	0	1.000	0- -	-	-	.668	3.58	2.65
2022 CWS	AL	35	0	15	53.0	217	42	25	18	5	0	1	1	18	0	49	2	2	0	1.000	0-0	1	93	.596	2.77	3.06

Rylan Bannon

Bats: R Throws: R Pos: 3B-3;2B-1;DH-1   Ht: 5'8" Wt: 180 Born: 4/22/1996 Age: 27

								BATTING												RUNNING			AVERAGES			
Year Team	Lg	G	AB	H	2B	3B	HR	(Hm Rd)	TB	R	RBI	RC	TBB	IBB	SO	HBP	SH	SF		SB	CS	GDP	Avg	OBP	Slg	OPS
2022 Norfolk	AAA	78	275	63	14	1	11	(- -)	112	45	58	41	45	0	87	5	0	1		6	1	9	.229	.347	.407	.754
2022 Gwnntt	AAA	21	67	22	4	0	2	(- -)	32	12	19	14	14	0	13	2	0	2		4	0	2	.328	.447	.478	.925
2022 2 Tms		5	14	2	0	0	0	(0 0)	2	0	0	0	0	0	5	1	0	0		0	0	0	.143	.200	.143	.343
22 Bal	AL	4	14	2	0	0	0	(0 0)	2	0	0	0	0	0	5	1	0	0		0	0	0	.143	.200	.143	.343
22 Atl	NL	1	0	0	0	0	0	(0 0)	0	0	0	0	0	0	0	0	0	0		0	0	0	-	-	-	-

Manny Banuelos

Pitches: L Bats: R Pos: RP-35   ban-yoo-WAY-lohss   Ht: 5'10" Wt: 215 Born: 3/13/1991 Age: 32

			HOW MUCH PITCHED				WHAT HE GAVE UP										THE RESULTS						
Year Team	Lg	G	GS	GF	IP	BFP	H	R	ER	HR	SH	SF	HB	TBB	IBB	SO	WP	W	L	Pct	Sv-Op	Hld	Vel	OPS	ERC	ERA
2022 S-WB	AAA	7	5	0	30.2	124	22	10	8	0	0	1	2	12	0	30	4	0	2	.000	0- -	-	-	.538	2.20	2.35
2015 Atl	NL	7	6	0	26.1	121	30	17	15	4	0	0	3	12	0	19	1	1	4	.200	0-0	0	89	.825	6.01	5.13
2019 CWS	AL	16	8	4	50.2	235	60	39	39	12	1	2	1	33	3	44	2	3	4	.429	0-0	0	92	.932	7.52	6.93
2022 2 Tms		35	0	7	41.0	175	32	23	20	2	1	1	3	21	1	42	0	2	1	.667	1-2	5	94	.637	3.20	4.39
22 NYY	AL	4	0	3	8.1	35	7	2	2	0	0	0	0	3	0	8	0	0	0	-	1-1	0	94	.567	2.37	2.16
22 Pit	NL	31	0	4	32.2	140	25	21	18	2	1	1	3	18	1	34	0	2	1	.667	0-1	5	94	.656	3.42	4.96
3 ML YEARS		58	14	11	118.0	531	122	79	74	18	2	3	7	66	4	105	3	6	9	.400	1-2	5	92	.810	5.57	5.64

Daniel Bard

Pitches: R Bats: R Pos: RP-57   Ht: 6'4" Wt: 215 Born: 6/25/1985 Age: 38

			HOW MUCH PITCHED				WHAT HE GAVE UP										THE RESULTS						
Year Team	Lg	G	GS	GF	IP	BFP	H	R	ER	HR	SH	SF	HB	TBB	IBB	SO	WP	W	L	Pct	Sv-Op	Hld	Vel	OPS	ERC	ERA
2009 Bos	AL	49	0	12	49.1	212	41	24	20	5	4	3	3	22	3	63	1	2	2	.500	1-4	13	97	.690	3.43	3.65
2010 Bos	AL	73	0	14	74.2	295	45	18	16	6	2	5	2	30	3	76	2	1	2	.333	3-10	32	98	.540	1.99	1.93
2011 Bos	AL	70	0	10	73.0	288	46	29	27	5	5	0	2	24	3	74	2	2	9	.182	1-6	34	97	.546	1.80	3.33
2012 Bos	AL	17	10	2	59.1	277	60	42	41	9	2	3	8	43	1	38	1	5	6	.455	0-0	0	93	.852	6.55	6.22
2013 Bos	AL	2	0	1	1.0	6	1	1	1	0	0	0	0	2	0	1	0	0	0	-	0-0	0	94	.750	9.51	9.00
2020 Col	NL	23	0	10	24.2	106	22	10	10	2	0	0	3	10	2	27	1	4	2	.667	6-6	2	97	.674	3.73	3.65
2021 Col	NL	67	0	44	65.2	304	69	41	38	8	1	0	7	36	1	80	4	7	8	.467	20-28	4	97	.800	5.51	5.21
2022 Col	NL	57	0	48	60.1	245	35	15	12	3	0	1	3	25	1	69	3	6	4	.600	34-37	0	98	.503	1.80	1.79
Postseason		2	0	1	3.0	8	0	0	0	0	0	0	0	0	0	4	0	0	0	-	0-0	1		.000	0.00	0.00
8 ML YEARS		358	10	139	408.0	1733	319	180	165	38	14	12	28	192	14	428	14	27	33	.450	65-91	85	97	.657	3.31	3.64

Luke Bard

Pitches: R Bats: R Pos: RP-9   Ht: 6'3" Wt: 200 Born: 11/13/1990 Age: 32

			HOW MUCH PITCHED				WHAT HE GAVE UP										THE RESULTS						
Year Team	Lg	G	GS	GF	IP	BFP	H	R	ER	HR	SH	SF	HB	TBB	IBB	SO	WP	W	L	Pct	Sv-Op	Hld	Vel	OPS	ERC	ERA
2022 Drham	AAA	19	1	5	24.0	94	18	13	13	7	0	0	1	5	0	27	1	0	0	-	0- -	-	-	.721	3.32	4.88
2022 S-WB	AAA	9	0	4	11.2	53	12	8	4	2	0	0	2	5	1	11	2	1	1	.500	2- -	-	-	.793	5.43	3.09
2018 LAA	AL	8	0	4	11.2	53	10	7	7	4	0	0	3	5	1	13	1	0	0	-	0-0	0	92	.829	5.95	5.40
2019 LAA	AL	32	3	5	49.0	199	41	27	26	8	0	1	5	13	1	40	5	3	3	.500	0-1	1	94	.691	3.52	4.78
2020 LAA	AL	6	0	3	5.1	23	7	4	4	2	0	0	0	4	0	7	0	0	0	-	0-0	1	94	1.000	5.96	6.75
2022 2 Tms	AL	9	0	5	15.0	59	7	3	3	0	1	0	2	7	0	8	0	1	1	.500	0-0	0	94	.480	1.57	1.80
22 TB	AL	8	0	4	14.0	56	7	3	3	0	1	0	2	7	0	8	0	1	1	.500	0-0	0	94	.508	1.80	1.93
22 NYY	AL	1	0	1	1.0	3	0	0	0	0	0	0	0	0	0	0	0	0	0	-	0-0	0	94	.000	0.00	0.00
4 ML YEARS		55	3	16	81.0	334	65	41	40	14	1	1	10	25	2	68	6	4	4	.500	0-1	2	94	.701	3.61	4.44

Luke Barker

Pitches: R Bats: R Pos: RP-3   Ht: 6'3" Wt: 230 Born: 3/11/1992 Age: 31

		HOW MUCH PITCHED					WHAT HE GAVE UP										THE RESULTS							
Year	Team	Lg	G	GS	GF	IP	BFP	H	R	ER	HR	SH	SF	HB	TBB	IBB	SO	WP	W	L	Pct	Sv-Op	Hld	Vel	OPS	ERC	ERA
2022	Nashv	AAA	23	0	12	25.0	106	20	11	10	2	0	2	0	10	0	28	2	5	0	1.000	3- -	-	-	.602	2.78	3.60
2022	Mil	NL	3	0	2	4.0	19	7	5	5	2	0	0	0	0	0	3	1	0	0	-	0-0	0	91	1.158	9.97	11.25

Joe Barlow

Pitches: R Bats: R Pos: RP-35   Ht: 6'2" Wt: 210 Born: 9/28/1995 Age: 27

		HOW MUCH PITCHED					WHAT HE GAVE UP										THE RESULTS							
Year	Team	Lg	G	GS	GF	IP	BFP	H	R	ER	HR	SH	SF	HB	TBB	IBB	SO	WP	W	L	Pct	Sv-Op	Hld	Vel	OPS	ERC	ERA
2021	Tex	AL	31	0	18	29.0	111	12	9	5	2	0	2	0	12	0	27	1	0	2	.000	11-12	3	94	.433	1.26	1.55
2022	Tex	AL	35	0	26	35.0	146	27	18	15	5	0	2	4	13	0	28	0	3	1	.750	13-17	0	95	.679	3.46	3.86
	2 ML YEARS		66	0	44	64.0	257	39	27	20	7	0	4	4	25	0	55	1	3	3	.500	24-29	3	95	.573	2.30	2.81

Scott Barlow

Pitches: R Bats: R Pos: RP-69   Ht: 6'3" Wt: 210 Born: 12/18/1992 Age: 30

		HOW MUCH PITCHED					WHAT HE GAVE UP										THE RESULTS							
Year	Team	Lg	G	GS	GF	IP	BFP	H	R	ER	HR	SH	SF	HB	TBB	IBB	SO	WP	W	L	Pct	Sv-Op	Hld	Vel	OPS	ERC	ERA
2018	KC	AL	6	0	3	15.0	65	16	7	6	2	0	0	0	3	0	15	0	1	1	.500	0-0	0	91	.679	3.73	3.60
2019	KC	AL	61	0	7	70.1	310	64	33	33	6	2	1	3	37	3	92	5	3	3	.500	1-3	14	94	.735	4.03	4.22
2020	KC	AL	32	0	7	30.0	125	27	14	14	4	0	1	2	9	2	39	2	2	1	.667	2-2	7	95	.693	3.54	4.20
2021	KC	AL	71	0	28	74.1	306	61	20	20	4	0	2	2	28	2	91	4	5	3	.625	16-22	14	95	.626	2.81	2.42
2022	KC	AL	69	0	47	74.1	290	52	23	18	9	0	3	3	22	1	77	5	7	4	.636	24-28	6	94	.590	2.45	2.18
	5 ML YEARS		239	0	92	264.0	1096	220	97	91	25	2	7	10	99	8	314	16	18	12	.600	43-55	41	94	.658	3.16	3.10

Austin Barnes

Bats: R Throws: R Pos: C-55;DH-5;PH-3;PR-3;2B-1   Ht: 5'10" Wt: 187 Born: 12/28/1989 Age: 33

			BATTING																				RUNNING			AVERAGES			
Year	Team	Lg	G	AB	H	2B	3B	HR	(Hm	Rd)	TB	R	RBI	RC	TBB	IBB	SO	HBP	SH	SF	SB	CS	GDP	Avg	OBP	Slg	OPS
2015	LAD	NL	20	29	6	2	0	0	(0	0)	8	4	1	3	6	0	6	1	1	0	1	0	2	.207	.361	.276	.637
2016	LAD	NL	21	32	5	1	0	0	(0	0)	6	3	2	3	5	0	9	0	0	0	0	0	0	.156	.270	.188	.458
2017	LAD	NL	102	218	63	15	2	8	(6	2)	106	35	38	46	39	1	43	5	0	4	1	6		.289	.408	.486	.895
2018	LAD	NL	100	200	41	5	0	4	(2	2)	58	32	14	15	31	4	67	6	1	0	4	3	7	.205	.329	.290	.619
2019	LAD	NL	75	212	43	12	1	5	(4	1)	72	28	25	18	23	3	56	5	0	2	3	0	8	.203	.293	.340	.633
2020	LAD	NL	29	86	21	3	0	1	(1	0)	27	14	9	12	13	0	24	2	2	1	3	0	0	.244	.353	.314	.667
2021	LAD	NL	77	200	43	8	0	6	(3	3)	69	28	23	19	20	1	56	4	1	0	1	0	6	.215	.299	.345	.644
2022	LAD	NL	62	179	38	6	0	8	(3	5)	68	31	26	21	27	0	37	3	2	1	2	1	5	.212	.324	.380	.704
	Postseason		40	103	20	2	0	2	(0	2)	28	13	10	7	10	0	32	1	2	1	1	1	2	.194	.270	.272	.541
	8 ML YEARS		486	1156	260	52	3	32	(19	13)	414	175	138	137	164	9	298	26	7	4	18	5	34	.225	.333	.358	.691

Jacob Barnes

Pitches: R Bats: R Pos: RP-23   Ht: 6'2" Wt: 231 Born: 4/14/1990 Age: 33

		HOW MUCH PITCHED					WHAT HE GAVE UP										THE RESULTS							
Year	Team	Lg	G	GS	GF	IP	BFP	H	R	ER	HR	SH	SF	HB	TBB	IBB	SO	WP	W	L	Pct	Sv-Op	Hld	Vel	OPS	ERC	ERA
2022	Toledo	AAA	5	0	1	6.0	27	7	2	2	0	0	0	0	2	0	12	1	0	0	-	0- -	-	-	.613	3.91	3.00
2022	S-WB	AAA	10	0	5	8.0	32	4	3	2	0	0	0	0	4	1	8	1	1	1	.500	0- -	-	-	.500	1.30	2.25
2016	Mil	NL	27	0	7	26.2	106	24	9	8	1	1	0	0	6	1	26	2	0	1	.000	1-1	0	95	.612	2.50	2.70
2017	Mil	NL	73	0	8	72.0	304	57	35	32	8	0	3	3	33	4	80	6	3	4	.429	2-7	24	97	.664	3.31	4.00
2018	Mil	NL	49	0	19	48.2	217	51	24	18	4	1	1	0	23	2	47	4	0	1	.000	2-4	4	95	.723	4.39	3.33
2019	2 Tms		33	1	6	32.2	160	36	30	27	7	0	2	0	22	1	32	3	1	5	.167	0-0	1	94	.840	6.34	7.44
2020	LAA	AL	18	0	5	18.0	78	19	13	11	1	2	2	2	4	0	24	0	0	2	.000	0-0	1	95	.716	3.77	5.50
2021	2 Tms		29	0	7	28.2	128	31	20	20	7	1	0	1	11	0	33	0	1	2	.333	2-2	1	95	.843	5.60	6.28
2022	2 Tms	AL	23	0	3	22.1	97	23	14	14	3	1	0	2	9	0	12	1	3	1	.750	0-1	2	95	.825	4.97	5.64
	19 Mil	NL	18	1	3	19.2	95	22	17	15	7	0	1	0	11	1	22	1	1	1	.500	0-0	1	94	.769	5.40	6.86
	19 KC	AL	15	0	3	13.0	65	14	13	12	0	0	1	0	11	0	10	2	0	4	.000	0-0	0	94	.951	7.85	8.31
	21 NYM	NL	19	0	6	18.2	79	19	13	13	6	1	0	0	5	0	18	0	1	1	.500	2-2	1	94	.856	5.11	6.27
	21 Tor	AL	10	0	1	10.0	49	12	7	7	1	0	0	1	6	0	15	0	0	1	.000	0-0	0	95	.816	6.34	6.30
	22 Det	AL	22	0	2	20.2	89	21	14	14	3	1	0	1	9	0	10	1	3	1	.750	0-1	2	95	.827	4.96	6.10
	22 NYY	AL	1	0	1	1.2	8	2	0	0	0	0	0	1	0	0	2	0	0	0	-	0-0	0	94	.804	5.10	0.00
	7 ML YEARS		252	1	55	249.0	1090	241	145	130	31	5	9	8	108	8	254	16	7-15		.333	7-15	33	95	.735	4.24	4.70

Matt Barnes

Pitches: R Bats: R Pos: RP-44   Ht: 6'4" Wt: 208 Born: 6/17/1990 Age: 33

		HOW MUCH PITCHED					WHAT HE GAVE UP										THE RESULTS							
Year	Team	Lg	G	GS	GF	IP	BFP	H	R	ER	HR	SH	SF	HB	TBB	IBB	SO	WP	W	L	Pct	Sv-Op	Hld	Vel	OPS	ERC	ERA
2014	Bos	AL	5	0	3	9.0	39	11	4	4	1	0	1	0	2	0	8	0	0	0	-	0-0	0	94	.861	4.72	4.00
2015	Bos	AL	32	2	7	43.0	199	56	28	26	9	2	0	2	15	0	39	4	3	4	.429	0-0	3	95	.887	6.66	5.44
2016	Bos	AL	62	0	13	66.2	287	62	32	30	6	2	1	3	31	1	71	4	4	3	.571	1-2	16	97	.709	4.06	4.05
2017	Bos	AL	70	0	15	69.2	300	57	31	30	7	1	3	1	28	0	83	3	7	3	.700	1-3	21	95	.655	3.20	3.88
2018	Bos	AL	62	0	8	61.2	265	47	25	25	5	0	2	2	31	1	96	8	6	4	.600	0-3	25	97	.624	3.08	3.65
2019	Bos	AL	70	0	14	64.1	285	51	29	27	8	0	1	2	38	2	110	13	5	4	.556	4-12	26	97	.666	3.81	3.78
2020	Bos	AL	24	0	14	23.0	102	18	13	11	4	1	1	2	14	1	31	4	1	3	.250	9-13	4	96	.706	4.43	4.30

Year	Team	Lg	G	GS	GF	IP	BFP	H	R	ER	HR	SH	SF	HB	TBB	IBB	SO	WP	W	L	Pct	Sv-Op	Hld	Vel	OPS	ERC	ERA
												WHAT HE GAVE UP										**THE RESULTS**					
2021	Bos	AL	60	0	44	54.2	222	41	25	23	8	0	1	2	20	2	84	3	6	5	.545	24-30	0	96	.641	3.02	3.79
2022	Bos	AL	44	0	16	39.2	176	36	22	19	2	1	1	3	21	1	34	4	0	4	.000	8-10	4	95	.676	3.92	4.31
	Postseason		12	0	1	11.1	48	7	2	1	1	0	0	0	8	0	11	2	2	0	1.000	0-0	3	96	.563	3.10	0.79
	9 ML YEARS		429	2	134	431.2	1862	379	209	195	50	7	11	17	200	8	556	43	32	30	.516	47-73	99	96	.694	3.86	4.07

Tucker Barnhart

Bats: B Throws: R Pos: C-92;3B-1   Ht: 5'11" Wt: 192 Born: 1/7/1991 Age: 32

							BATTING													**RUNNING**			**AVERAGES**			
Year	Team	Lg	G	AB	H	2B	3B	HR	(Hm Rd)	TB	R	RBI	RC	TBB	IBB	SO	HBP	SH	SF	SB	CS	GDP	Avg	OBP	Slg	OPS
2014	Cin	NL	21	54	10	0	0	1	(1 0)	13	3	1	2	4	1	10	0	2	0	0	0	0	.185	.241	.241	.482
2015	Cin	NL	81	242	61	9	0	3	(2 1)	79	23	18	22	25	5	45	2	2	3	0	1	10	.252	.324	.326	.650
2016	Cin	NL	115	377	97	23	1	7	(6 1)	143	34	51	51	36	8	72	2	2	3	1	0	12	.257	.323	.379	.702
2017	Cin	NL	121	370	100	24	2	7	(2 5)	149	26	44	50	42	11	68	3	5	3	4	0	12	.270	.347	.403	.750
2018	Cin	NL	138	460	114	21	3	10	(7 3)	171	50	46	48	54	2	96	2	3	3	0	4	13	.248	.328	.372	.699
2019	Cin	NL	114	316	73	14	0	11	(5 6)	120	32	40	40	44	7	83	2	1	1	1	0	5	.231	.328	.380	.708
2020	Cin	NL	38	98	20	3	0	5	(4 1)	38	10	13	11	12	0	28	0	0	0	0	0	2	.204	.291	.388	.679
2021	Cin	NL	116	348	86	21	0	7	(6 1)	128	41	48	44	29	1	100	8	0	3	0	0	8	.247	.317	.368	.685
2022	Det	AL	94	281	62	10	0	1	(1 0)	75	16	16	18	25	0	74	1	1	0	0	0	7	.221	.287	.267	.554
	Postseason		2	5	0	0	0	0	(0 0)	0	0	0	0	0	0	3	0	0	0	0	0	0	.000	.000	.000	.000
	9 ML YEARS		838	2546	623	125	6	52	(34 18)	916	235	277	286	271	35	576	20	16	16	6	5	69	.245	.320	.360	.680

Kyle Barraclough

Pitches: R Bats: R Pos: RP-8   BAIR-ah-claw   Ht: 6'3" Wt: 229 Born: 5/23/1990 Age: 33

			HOW MUCH PITCHED					**WHAT HE GAVE UP**											**THE RESULTS**								
Year	Team	Lg	G	GS	GF	IP	BFP	H	R	ER	HR	SH	SF	HB	TBB	IBB	SO	WP	W	L	Pct	Sv-Op	Hld	Vel	OPS	ERC	ERA
2022	Salt Lk	AAA	41	0	8	45.0	193	31	16	15	3	0	1	3	28	0	61	6	4	3	.571	2- -	-		.619	3.25	3.00
2015	Mia	NL	25	0	5	24.1	98	12	8	7	1	0	2	0	18	2	30	1	2	1	.667	0-1	6	96	.563	2.25	2.59
2016	Mia	NL	75	0	6	72.2	306	45	24	23	1	2	2	2	44	1	113	8	6	3	.667	0-4	29	96	.538	2.31	2.85
2017	Mia	NL	66	0	12	66.0	286	53	25	22	5	3	4	2	38	3	76	6	6	2	.750	1-5	22	95	.638	3.53	3.00
2018	Mia	NL	61	0	25	55.2	245	40	27	26	8	2	1	5	34	3	60	4	1	6	.143	10-17	10	94	.675	3.84	4.20
2019	2 Tms	NL	43	0	9	33.2	164	38	24	21	9	1	1	2	21	2	40	3	1	2	.333	0-3	8	94	.892	7.02	5.61
2021	Min	AL	10	0	3	13.0	60	12	8	8	4	0	1	2	8	0	18	0	2	0	1.000	0-0	1	93	.877	6.74	5.54
2022	LAA	AL	8	0	3	9.0	37	7	3	3	0	0	1	0	4	0	9	2	0	1	.000	0-2	2	93	.610	2.43	3.00
19	Was	NL	33	0	6	25.2	124	33	21	19	8	0	1	2	12	2	30	2	1	2	.333	0-2	8	93	.948	7.83	6.66
19	SF	NL	10	0	3	8.0	40	5	3	2	1	1	0	0	9	0	10	1	0	0	-	0-1	0	94	.692	4.59	2.25
	7 ML YEARS		288	0	62	274.1	1196	207	119	110	28	8	12	13	167	11	346	24	18	15	.545	11-30	78	94	.660	3.63	3.61

Luis Barrera

Bats: L Throws: L Pos: LF-16;RF-16;PH-6;CF-1;PR-1   Ht: 6'0" Wt: 195 Born: 11/15/1995 Age: 27

							BATTING													**RUNNING**			**AVERAGES**			
Year	Team	Lg	G	AB	H	2B	3B	HR	(Hm Rd)	TB	R	RBI	RC	TBB	IBB	SO	HBP	SH	SF	SB	CS	GDP	Avg	OBP	Slg	OPS
2022	LsVgs	AAA	85	312	82	16	7	8	(- -)	136	55	45	45	29	0	68	3	1	3	9	3	5	.263	.329	.436	.764
2021	Oak	AL	6	8	2	0	0	0	(0 0)	2	1	0	1	0	0	2	0	0	0	0	0	0	.250	.250	.250	.500
2022	Oak	AL	32	77	18	5	0	1	(1 0)	26	3	7	8	6	0	17	1	0	1	3	0	2	.234	.294	.338	.632
	2 ML YEARS		38	85	20	5	0	1	(1 0)	28	4	7	9	6	0	19	1	0	1	3	0	2	.235	.290	.329	.620

Tres Barrera

Bats: R Throws: R Pos: C-19   Ht: 6'0" Wt: 215 Born: 9/15/1994 Age: 28

							BATTING													**RUNNING**			**AVERAGES**			
Year	Team	Lg	G	AB	H	2B	3B	HR	(Hm Rd)	TB	R	RBI	RC	TBB	IBB	SO	HBP	SH	SF	SB	CS	GDP	Avg	OBP	Slg	OPS
2022	Roch	AAA	55	177	45	7	1	7	(- -)	75	25	25	27	20	0	41	3	1	1	0	2	1	.254	.338	.424	.762
2019	Was	NL	2	2	0	0	0	0	(0 0)	0	0	0	0	0	0	0	0	0	0	0	0	0	.000	.000	.000	.000
2021	Was	NL	30	91	24	3	1	2	(1 1)	35	8	10	14	12	2	22	4	0	0	0	0	3	.264	.374	.385	.758
2022	Was	NL	19	50	9	1	0	0	(0 0)	10	2	4	1	2	0	16	0	1	0	0	0	1	.180	.212	.200	.412
	3 ML YEARS		51	143	33	4	1	2	(1 1)	45	10	14	15	14	2	38	4	1	0	0	0	4	.231	.317	.315	.631

Jose Barrero

Bats: R Throws: R Pos: SS-48   Ht: 6'2" Wt: 175 Born: 4/5/1998 Age: 25

							BATTING													**RUNNING**			**AVERAGES**			
Year	Team	Lg	G	AB	H	2B	3B	HR	(Hm Rd)	TB	R	RBI	RC	TBB	IBB	SO	HBP	SH	SF	SB	CS	GDP	Avg	OBP	Slg	OPS
2022	Lsvlle	AAA	55	220	46	8	1	9	(- -)	83	27	24	22	11	0	89	5	0	1	5	2	5	.209	.262	.377	.639
2020	Cin	NL	24	67	13	0	0	0	(0 0)	13	4	2	0	1	0	26	0	0	0	1	1	1	.194	.206	.194	.400
2021	Cin	NL	21	50	10	4	1	0	(0 0)	16	4	3	5	3	0	17	3	0	0	1	0	2	.200	.286	.320	.606
2022	Cin	NL	48	165	25	3	0	2	(0 2)	34	13	10	1	9	0	76	0	0	0	4	1	4	.152	.195	.206	.401
	Postseason		1	1	0	0	0	0	(0 0)	0	0	0	0	0	0	0	0	0	0	0	0	0	.000	.000	.000	.000
	3 ML YEARS		93	282	48	7	1	2	(0 2)	63	21	15	6	13	0	119	3	0	0	6	2	7	.170	.215	.223	.438

Jaime Barria

Pitches: R Bats: R Pos: RP-34; SP-1　　　　　HIGH-may　　　　　Ht: 6'1" Wt: 210 Born: 7/18/1996 Age: 26

Year	Team	Lg	G	GS	GF	IP	BFP	H	R	ER	HR	SH	SF	HB	TBB	IBB	SO	WP	W	L	Pct	Sv-Op	Hld	Vel	OPS	ERC	ERA
2018	LAA	AL	26	26	0	129.1	537	117	50	49	17	0	0	6	47	0	98	3	10	9	.526	0-0	0	91	.719	3.89	3.41
2019	LAA	AL	19	13	1	82.2	365	92	61	59	24	0	2	2	27	0	75	1	4	10	.286	0-0	0	92	.903	5.85	6.42
2020	LAA	AL	7	5	2	32.1	132	27	13	13	3	0	1	1	9	1	27	0	1	0	1.000	0-0	0	92	.685	2.76	3.62
2021	LAA	AL	13	11	0	56.2	250	70	29	29	8	0	1	2	19	0	35	0	2	4	.333	0-0	0	93	.838	5.77	4.61
2022	LAA	AL	35	1	21	79.1	316	63	29	23	11	3	1	3	19	0	54	3	3	3	.500	0-3	5	92	.665	2.78	2.61
5 ML YEARS			100	56	24	380.1	1600	369	182	173	63	3	5	14	121	1	289	7	20	26	.435	0-3	5	92	.766	4.22	4.09

Joey Bart

Bats: R Throws: R Pos: C-93;DH-3;PR-3;PH-1　　　　　Ht: 6'2" Wt: 238 Born: 12/15/1996 Age: 26

Year	Team	Lg	G	AB	H	2B	3B	HR	(Hm	Rd)	TB	R	RBI	RC	TBB	IBB	SO	HBP	SH	SF	SB	CS	GDP	Avg	OBP	Slg	OPS
2020	SF	NL	33	103	24	5	2	0	(0	0)	33	15	7	8	3	0	41	5	0	0	0	0	1	.233	.288	.320	.609
2021	SF	NL	2	6	2	0	0	0	(0	0)	2	1	1	1	0	0	2	0	0	0	0	0	0	.333	.333	.333	.667
2022	SF	NL	97	261	56	6	0	11	(6	5)	95	34	25	29	26	0	112	4	0	0	2	1	5	.215	.296	.364	.660
3 ML YEARS			132	370	82	11	2	11	(6	5)	130	50	33	38	29	0	155	9	0	0	2	1	6	.222	.294	.351	.645

Anthony Bass

Pitches: R Bats: R Pos: RP-73　　　　　Ht: 6'2" Wt: 205 Born: 11/1/1987 Age: 35

Year	Team	Lg	G	GS	GF	IP	BFP	H	R	ER	HR	SH	SF	HB	TBB	IBB	SO	WP	W	L	Pct	Sv-Op	Hld	Vel	OPS	ERC	ERA
2011	SD	NL	27	3	6	48.1	198	41	9	9	3	2	0	1	21	1	24	1	2	0	1.000	0-0	4	93	.655	3.28	1.68
2012	SD	NL	24	15	3	97.0	411	89	59	51	10	2	2	1	39	3	80	5	2	8	.200	1-1	1	92	.719	3.65	4.73
2013	SD	NL	24	0	9	42.0	193	51	26	25	4	1	0	0	20	4	31	5	0	0	-	0-0	0	92	.829	5.41	5.36
2014	Hou	AL	21	0	8	27.0	119	32	20	19	6	0	1	2	7	1	7	2	1	1	.500	2-4	4	94	.840	5.74	6.33
2015	Tex	AL	33	0	9	64.0	272	66	33	32	5	3	3	1	20	1	45	1	0	0	-	0-1	0	93	.756	3.81	4.50
2017	Tex	AL	2	0	1	5.2	31	14	9	9	1	0	1	0	0	0	1	1	0	0	-	0-0	0	92	1.152	12.41	14.29
2018	ChC	NL	16	0	3	15.1	62	18	6	5	1	0	0	0	3	0	14	2	0	0	-	0-0	3	94	.729	4.26	2.93
2019	Sea	AL	44	0	14	48.0	189	30	20	19	5	2	1	1	17	2	43	6	2	4	.333	5-10	6	95	.560	2.04	3.56
2020	Tor	AL	26	0	14	25.2	100	17	13	10	2	1	0	0	9	2	21	0	2	3	.400	7-9	3	95	.563	1.97	3.51
2021	Mia	NL	70	1	12	61.1	260	55	33	26	11	2	3	3	24	6	58	0	3	9	.250	0-4	19	95	.743	4.07	3.82
2022	2 Tms		73	0	12	70.1	275	51	15	12	6	0	1	0	20	1	73	2	4	3	.571	0-3	23	95	.569	2.16	1.54
22	Mia	NL	45	0	7	44.2	173	32	10	7	1	0	1	0	10	0	45	1	2	3	.400	0-3	16	95	.514	1.61	1.41
22	Tor	AL	28	0	5	25.2	102	19	5	5	5	0	0	0	10	1	28	1	2	0	1.000	0-0	7	95	.665	3.28	1.75
Postseason			1	0	0	1.0	4	0	0	0	0	0	0	0	2	0	1	0	0	0	-	0-0	0	95	.500	4.48	0.00
11 ML YEARS			360	19	91	504.2	2110	464	243	217	54	13	12	9	180	21	397	25	16	28	.364	15-32	63	94	.703	3.55	3.87

Chris Bassitt

Pitches: R Bats: R Pos: SP-30　　　　　Ht: 6'5" Wt: 217 Born: 2/22/1989 Age: 34

Year	Team	Lg	G	GS	GF	IP	BFP	H	R	ER	HR	SH	SF	HB	TBB	IBB	SO	WP	W	L	Pct	Sv-Op	Hld	Vel	OPS	ERC	ERA
2014	CWS	AL	6	5	1	29.2	137	34	13	13	0	1	1	3	13	1	21	0	1	1	.500	0-0	0	93	.721	4.57	3.94
2015	Oak	AL	18	13	3	86.0	361	78	36	34	5	1	1	9	30	0	64	5	1	8	.111	0-0	0	93	.684	3.55	3.56
2016	Oak	AL	5	5	0	28.0	133	35	20	19	5	0	0	0	14	0	23	2	0	2	.000	0-0	0	93	.856	6.44	6.11
2018	Oak	AL	11	7	0	47.2	204	40	21	16	4	0	0	4	19	0	41	2	2	3	.400	0-0	0	92	.624	3.37	3.02
2019	Oak	AL	28	25	2	144.0	612	125	66	61	21	2	5	13	47	0	141	3	10	5	.667	0-0	0	94	.698	3.68	3.81
2020	Oak	AL	11	11	0	63.0	261	56	18	16	6	1	1	2	17	0	55	2	5	2	.714	0-0	0	93	.659	3.05	2.29
2021	Oak	AL	27	27	0	157.1	637	127	55	55	15	0	4	11	39	1	159	5	12	4	.750	0-0	0	93	.626	2.71	3.15
2022	NYM	NL	30	30	0	181.2	745	159	71	69	19	0	2	13	49	0	167	5	15	9	.625	0-0	0	93	.656	3.24	3.42
Postseason			2	2	0	11.0	48	15	4	4	2	0	0	0	1	0	9	1	1	0	1.000	0-0	0	93	.780	5.49	3.27
8 ML YEARS			136	123	6	737.1	3090	654	300	283	75	5	14	55	228	2	671	24	46	34	.575	0-0	0	93	.671	3.40	3.45

Matthew Batten

Bats: R Throws: R Pos: 3B-7;2B-5;PH-5;PR-2;LF-1;DH-1　　　　　Ht: 5'11" Wt: 180 Born: 6/22/1995 Age: 28

Year	Team	Lg	G	AB	H	2B	3B	HR	(Hm	Rd)	TB	R	RBI	RC	TBB	IBB	SO	HBP	SH	SF	SB	CS	GDP	Avg	OBP	Slg	OPS
2022	ElPaso	AAA	85	325	94	17	1	12	(-	-)	149	63	46	60	47	0	73	3	1	2	18	2	5	.289	.382	.458	.840
2022	SD	NL	15	19	2	1	0	0	(0	0)	3	0	1	0	2	0	6	1	0	0	0	0	0	.105	.227	.158	.385

Brett Baty

Bats: L Throws: R Pos: 3B-11　　　　　Ht: 6'3" Wt: 210 Born: 11/13/1999 Age: 23

Year	Team	Lg	G	AB	H	2B	3B	HR	(Hm	Rd)	TB	R	RBI	RC	TBB	IBB	SO	HBP	SH	SF	SB	CS	GDP	Avg	OBP	Slg	OPS
2021	Bklyn	A+	51	181	56	14	1	7	(-	-)	93	27	34	0	24	0	53	3	0	1	4	3	3	.309	.397	.514	.911
2021	Bnghtn	AA	41	153	41	8	0	5	(-	-)	64	16	22	0	22	0	46	1	0	2	2	0	8	.268	.360	.418	.778
2022	Bnghtn	AA	89	340	106	22	0	19	(-	-)	185	73	59	74	46	0	98	8	0	0	2	3	8	.312	.406	.544	.950
2022	NYM	NL	11	38	7	0	0	2	(1	1)	13	4	5	4	2	0	8	1	0	0	0	0	0	.184	.244	.342	.586

Trevor Bauer

Pitches: R Bats: R Pos: P   Ht: 6'1" Wt: 205 Born: 1/17/1991 Age: 32

			HOW MUCH PITCHED					WHAT HE GAVE UP											THE RESULTS						
Year	Team	Lg	G	GS	GF	IP	BFP	H	R	ER	HR	SH	SF	HB	TBB	IBB	SO	WP	W	L	Pct	Sv-Op	Hld	Vel	OPS	ERC	ERA
2012	Ari	NL	4	4	0	16.1	77	14	13	11	2	1	1	1	13	0	17	2	1	2	.333	0-0	0	-	.795	5.12	6.06
2013	Cle	AL	4	4	0	17.0	81	15	11	10	2	0	1	1	16	0	11	1	1	2	.333	0-0	0	-	.840	6.47	5.29
2014	Cle	AL	26	26	0	153.0	663	151	76	71	16	1	8	11	60	4	143	6	5	8	.385	0-0	0	-	.737	4.27	4.18
2015	Cle	AL	31	30	1	176.0	744	152	90	89	23	4	1	5	79	1	170	7	11	12	.478	0-0	0	-	.713	3.86	4.55
2016	Cle	AL	35	28	3	190.0	811	179	96	90	20	4	7	9	70	1	168	3	12	8	.600	0-0	0	-	.712	3.85	4.26
2017	Cle	AL	32	31	1	176.1	749	181	84	82	25	1	3	5	60	0	196	3	17	9	.654	0-0	0	-	.774	4.46	4.19
2018	Cle	AL	28	27	1	175.1	717	134	51	43	9	3	3	9	57	2	221	12	12	6	.667	1-1	0	-	.582	2.41	2.21
2019	2 Tms		34	34	0	213.0	911	184	118	106	34	5	5	19	82	0	253	10	11	13	.458	0-0	0	-	.743	4.00	4.48
2020	Cin	NL	11	11	0	73.0	278	41	17	14	9	0	0	3	17	1	100	3	5	4	.556	0-0	0	-	.522	1.59	1.73
2021	LAD	NL	17	17	0	107.2	432	71	36	31	19	2	0	3	37	1	137	3	8	5	.615	0-0	0	-	.632	2.61	2.59
19	Cle	AL	24	24	0	156.2	664	127	76	66	22	2	3	14	63	0	185	8	9	8	.529	0-0	0	-	.707	3.65	3.79
19	Cin	NL	10	10	0	56.1	247	57	42	40	12	3	2	5	19	0	68	2	2	5	.286	0-0	0	-	.841	5.02	6.39
	Postseason		11	7	1	33.2	143	33	16	11	4	0	1	1	8	1	44	1	1	4	.200	0-1	0	-	.715	3.45	2.94
	10 ML YEARS		222	212	6	1297.2	5463	1122	592	547	160	21	29	66	491	10	1416	50	83	69	.546	1-1	0	-	.699	3.60	3.79

Mike Baumann

Pitches: R Bats: R Pos: RP-9; SP-4   Ht: 6'4" Wt: 235 Born: 9/10/1995 Age: 27

			HOW MUCH PITCHED					WHAT HE GAVE UP											THE RESULTS						
Year	Team	Lg	G	GS	GF	IP	BFP	H	R	ER	HR	SH	SF	HB	TBB	IBB	SO	WP	W	L	Pct	Sv-Op	Hld	Vel	OPS	ERC	ERA
2022	Norfolk	AAA	20	9	3	60.0	260	54	33	28	6	0	0	1	25	0	81	5	2	6	.250	1--	-	-	.650	3.57	4.20
2021	Bal	AL	4	0	0	10.0	50	13	12	11	2	0	0	1	6	0	5	0	1	1	.500	0-0	1	94	.958	7.84	9.90
2022	Bal	AL	13	4	2	34.1	149	43	19	18	3	0	1	2	9	0	23	1	1	3	.250	0-0	1	96	.808	5.28	4.72
	2 ML YEARS		17	4	2	44.1	199	56	31	29	5	0	1	3	15	0	28	1	2	4	.333	0-0	2	95	.844	5.84	5.89

Felix Bautista

Pitches: R Bats: R Pos: RP-65   Ht: 6'5" Wt: 190 Born: 6/20/1995 Age: 28

			HOW MUCH PITCHED					WHAT HE GAVE UP											THE RESULTS						
Year	Team	Lg	G	GS	GF	IP	BFP	H	R	ER	HR	SH	SF	HB	TBB	IBB	SO	WP	W	L	Pct	Sv-Op	Hld	Vel	OPS	ERC	ERA
2022	Bal	AL	65	0	30	65.2	253	38	18	16	7	0	2	1	23	1	88	2	4	4	.500	15-17	13	99	.536	1.87	2.19

Shane Baz

Pitches: R Bats: R Pos: SP-6   Ht: 6'2" Wt: 190 Born: 6/17/1999 Age: 24

			HOW MUCH PITCHED					WHAT HE GAVE UP											THE RESULTS						
Year	Team	Lg	G	GS	GF	IP	BFP	H	R	ER	HR	SH	SF	HB	TBB	IBB	SO	WP	W	L	Pct	Sv-Op	Hld	Vel	OPS	ERC	ERA
2018	2 Tms	Low	12	12	0	52.1	244	56	30	26	3	0	1	4	29	0	59	12	4	5	.444	0--	-	-	.790	4.98	4.47
2019	BG	A	17	17	0	81.1	342	63	30	27	5	1	3	5	37	0	87	10	3	2	.600	0--	-	-	.393	3.04	2.99
2021	Mont	AA	7	7	0	32.2	120	22	9	9	3	0	0	2	2	0	49	1	4	3	.333	0--	-	-	.510	1.53	2.48
2021	Drham	AAA	10	10	0	46.0	178	28	10	9	6	1	0	5	11	0	64	2	3	0	1.000	0--	-	-	.553	2.09	1.76
2021	TB	AL	3	3	0	13.1	49	6	3	3	3	0	0	0	3	0	18	1	2	0	1.000	0-0	0	97	.531	1.46	2.03
2022	TB	AL	6	6	0	27.0	117	27	15	15	5	0	0	1	9	0	30	2	1	2	.333	0-0	0	96	.765	4.50	5.00
	Postseason		1	1	0	2.1	13	6	3	3	1	0	0	0	1	0	2	0	0	0	-	0-0	0	97	1.372	19.60	11.57
	2 ML YEARS		9	9	0	40.1	166	33	18	18	8	0	0	1	12	0	48	3	3	2	.600	0-0	0	96	.695	3.38	4.02

Eduard Bazardo

Pitches: R Bats: R Pos: RP-12   Ht: 6'0" Wt: 165 Born: 9/1/1995 Age: 27

			HOW MUCH PITCHED					WHAT HE GAVE UP											THE RESULTS						
Year	Team	Lg	G	GS	GF	IP	BFP	H	R	ER	HR	SH	SF	HB	TBB	IBB	SO	WP	W	L	Pct	Sv-Op	Hld	Vel	OPS	ERC	ERA
2022	Wrcstr	AAA	37	4	4	57.1	255	65	28	22	5	0	3	1	19	0	60	2	2	4	.333	1--	-	-	.734	4.46	3.45
2021	Bos	AL	2	0	1	3.0	12	1	0	0	0	0	0	0	2	0	3	0	0	0	-	0-0	0	94	.450	1.26	0.00
2022	Bos	AL	12	0	4	16.1	65	12	5	5	4	0	0	2	4	0	11	1	1	0	1.000	0-0	0	94	.718	3.49	2.76
	2 ML YEARS		14	0	5	19.1	77	13	5	5	4	0	0	2	6	0	14	1	1	0	1.000	0-0	0	94	.679	3.09	2.33

Jeremy Beasley

Pitches: R Bats: R Pos: RP-9   Ht: 6'2" Wt: 235 Born: 11/20/1995 Age: 27

			HOW MUCH PITCHED					WHAT HE GAVE UP											THE RESULTS						
Year	Team	Lg	G	GS	GF	IP	BFP	H	R	ER	HR	SH	SF	HB	TBB	IBB	SO	WP	W	L	Pct	Sv-Op	Hld	Vel	OPS	ERC	ERA
2022	Buffalo	AAA	19	3	4	38.0	143	20	9	8	5	0	0	1	11	0	43	1	2	1	.667	1--	-	-	.529	1.64	1.89
2020	Ari	NL	1	0	1	0.1	3	2	0	0	0	0	0	0	0	0	1	0	0	0	-	0-0	0	92	1.667	39.65	0.00
2021	Tor	AL	8	0	6	9.1	47	7	9	8	3	0	1	2	9	2	13	2	0	1	.000	0-0	0	95	.869	6.90	7.71
2022	Tor	AL	9	0	5	15.0	64	14	9	8	4	0	1	2	5	0	19	0	0	0	-	0-0	0	95	.846	5.21	4.80
	3 ML YEARS		18	0	12	24.2	114	23	18	16	7	0	2	4	14	2	33	2	0	1	.000	0-0	0	95	.881	6.23	5.84

Matt Beaty

Bats: L Throws: R Pos: RF-10;PH-4;1B-3;DH-3;LF-2   Ht: 6'0" Wt: 215 Born: 4/28/1993 Age: 30

			BATTING																			RUNNING			AVERAGES			
Year	Team	Lg	G	AB	H	2B	3B	HR	(Hm	Rd)	TB	R	RBI	RC	TBB	IBB	SO	HBP	SH	SF	SB	CS	GDP	Avg	OBP	Slg	OPS
2022	ElPaso	AAA	35	126	34	2	1	2	(-	-)	44	19	13	14	14	0	27	5	0	0	0	0	6	.270	.366	.349	.715
2019	LAD	NL	99	249	66	19	1	9	(5	4)	114	36	46	42	17	2	33	2	0	0	5	0	6	.265	.317	.458	.775
2020	LAD	NL	21	50	11	1	0	2	(0	2)	18	8	5	5	2	0	14	2	0	0	0	0	3	.220	.278	.360	.638

Year	Team	Lg	G	AB	H	2B	3B	HR	(Hm	Rd)	TB	R	RBI	RC	TBB	IBB	SO	HBP	SH	SF	SB	CS	GDP	Avg	OBP	Slg	OPS
2021	LAD	NL	120	204	55	4	1	7	(4	3)	82	35	40	37	20	0	44	10	0	0	2	2	3	.270	.363	.402	.765
2022	SD	NL	20	43	4	1	1	0	(0	0)	7	6	1	0	2	0	8	2	0	0	0	0	3	.093	.170	.163	.333
	Postseason		15	19	4	0	0	0	(0	0)	4	1	1	1	1	0	2	1	0	0	0	0	0	.211	.318	.211	.529
	4 ML YEARS		260	546	136	25	3	18	(9	9)	221	85	92	84	41	2	99	16	0	0	7	2	15	.249	.320	.405	.725

Tim Beckham

Bats: R **Throws:** R **Pos:** PH-5;LF-4;DH-3;1B-2;PR-1 **Ht:** 6'0" **Wt:** 215 **Born:** 1/27/1990 **Age:** 33

Year	Team	Lg	G	AB	H	2B	3B	HR	(Hm	Rd)	TB	R	RBI	RC	TBB	IBB	SO	HBP	SH	SF	SB	CS	GDP	Avg	OBP	Slg	OPS
2022	StPaul	AAA	34	126	52	6	0	5	(-	-)	73	18	31	32	14	0	31	3	0	0	2	1	2	.413	.483	.579	1.062
2013	TB	AL	5	7	3	0	0	0	(0	0)	3	1	1	1	0	0	0	0	0	1	0	0	0	.429	.375	.429	.804
2015	TB	AL	83	203	45	7	4	9	(3	6)	87	24	37	26	13	0	69	3	0	4	3	1	3	.222	.274	.429	.702
2016	TB	AL	64	198	49	12	5	5	(1	4)	86	25	16	23	14	0	67	1	2	0	2	1	3	.247	.300	.434	.735
2017	2 Tms	AL	137	533	148	18	5	22	(9	13)	242	67	62	81	36	0	167	4	1	1	6	5	10	.278	.328	.454	.782
2018	Bal	AL	96	369	85	17	0	12	(6	6)	138	45	35	39	27	0	100	3	1	2	1	2	10	.230	.287	.374	.661
2019	Sea	AL	88	304	72	21	1	15	(9	6)	140	39	47	44	21	0	102	3	1	3	1	3	7	.237	.293	.461	.753
2022	Min	AL	12	25	2	0	0	0	(0	0)	2	1	1	0	0	0	9	0	0	0	0	0	2	.080	.080	.080	.160
17	TB	AL	87	317	82	5	3	12	(5	7)	129	31	36	39	24	0	110	2	1	1	5	4	8	.259	.314	.407	.721
17	Bal	AL	50	216	66	13	2	10	(4	6)	113	36	26	42	12	0	57	2	0	0	1	1	2	.306	.348	.523	.871
	7 ML YEARS		485	1639	404	75	15	63	(28	35)	698	202	199	214	111	0	514	14	4	8	13	12	35	.246	.299	.426	.724

David Bednar

Pitches: R **Bats:** L **Pos:** RP-45 **Ht:** 6'1" **Wt:** 250 **Born:** 10/10/1994 **Age:** 28

Year	Team	Lg	G	GS	GF	IP	BFP	H	R	ER	HR	SH	SF	HB	TBB	IBB	SO	WP	W	L	Pct	Sv-Op	Hld	Vel	OPS	ERC	ERA
2019	SD	NL	13	0	4	11.0	48	10	8	8	3	2	1	0	5	0	14	0	0	2	.000	0-0	2	95	.876	4.89	6.55
2020	SD	NL	4	0	3	6.1	32	11	6	5	1	0	0	0	2	0	5	0	0	0		0-0	0	96	.973	8.59	7.11
2021	Pit	NL	61	0	24	60.2	237	40	15	15	5	0	1	1	19	2	77	1	3	1	.750	3-5	13	97	.577	1.96	2.23
2022	Pit	NL	45	0	34	51.2	210	42	19	15	4	0	0	1	16	2	69	2	3	4	.429	19-23	4	96	.618	2.63	2.61
	4 ML YEARS		123	0	65	129.2	527	103	48	43	13	2	2	2	42	4	165	3	6	7	.462	22-28	19	96	.643	2.72	2.98

Tyler Beede

Pitches: R **Bats:** R **Pos:** RP-26; SP-5 **Ht:** 6'2" **Wt:** 216 **Born:** 5/23/1993 **Age:** 30

Year	Team	Lg	G	GS	GF	IP	BFP	H	R	ER	HR	SH	SF	HB	TBB	IBB	SO	WP	W	L	Pct	Sv-Op	Hld	Vel	OPS	ERC	ERA
2018	SF	NL	2	2	0	7.2	40	9	7	7	0	0	0	1	8	0	9	0	0	1	.000	0-0	0	92	.869	7.41	8.22
2019	SF	NL	24	22	0	117.0	523	127	70	66	22	1	3	5	46	1	113	9	5	10	.333	0-0	0	96	.803	5.29	5.08
2021	SF	NL	1	0	0	1.0	6	2	3	3	0	0	0	1	0	0	2	1	0	0	-	0-0	0	96	1.300	12.01	27.00
2022	2 Tms	NL	31	5	6	61.1	285	71	37	35	7	0	1	5	29	2	39	5	2	5	.286	0-0	3	96	.808	5.62	5.14
22	SF	NL	6	0	3	9.2	48	14	5	5	1	0	0	0	6	0	4	1	0	0	-	0-0	0	96	.845	7.76	4.66
22	Pit	NL	25	5	3	51.2	237	57	32	30	6	0	1	5	23	2	35	4	2	5	.286	0-0	3	96	.801	5.24	5.23
	4 ML YEARS		58	29	6	187.0	854	209	117	111	29	1	4	12	83	3	163	15	7	16	.304	0-0	3	95	.811	5.54	5.34

Jalen Beeks

Pitches: L **Bats:** L **Pos:** RP-35; SP-7 **Ht:** 5'11" **Wt:** 215 **Born:** 7/10/1993 **Age:** 29

Year	Team	Lg	G	GS	GF	IP	BFP	H	R	ER	HR	SH	SF	HB	TBB	IBB	SO	WP	W	L	Pct	Sv-Op	Hld	Vel	OPS	ERC	ERA
2018	2 Tms	AL	14	1	0	50.2	223	52	31	31	6	1	1	3	24	0	42	0	1	1	.833	0-0	0	92	.794	4.97	5.51
2019	TB	AL	33	3	5	104.1	464	115	56	50	12	1	5	9	40	1	89	3	6	3	.667	1-1	2	92	.789	5.07	4.31
2020	TB	AL	12	0	3	19.1	81	21	9	7	1	1	0	0	4	0	26	2	1	1	.500	1-1	2	93	.694	3.48	3.26
2022	TB	AL	42	7	8	61.0	250	49	22	19	7	1	1	2	22	0	70	3	2	3	.400	2-6	4	95	.673	3.11	2.80
18	Bos	AL	2	1	0	6.1	34	11	9	9	1	0	0	1	4	0	5	0	0	1	.000	0-0	0	91	1.160	11.16	12.79
18	TB	AL	12	0	0	44.1	189	41	22	22	5	1	1	2	20	0	37	0	5	0	1.000	0-0	0	92	.729	4.20	4.47
	4 ML YEARS		101	11	16	235.1	1018	237	118	107	26	4	7	14	90	1	227	8	14	8	.636	4-8	8	93	.754	4.38	4.09

Seth Beer

Bats: L **Throws:** R **Pos:** DH-28;1B-5;PH-5 **Ht:** 6'3" **Wt:** 213 **Born:** 9/18/1996 **Age:** 26

Year	Team	Lg	G	AB	H	2B	3B	HR	(Hm	Rd)	TB	R	RBI	RC	TBB	IBB	SO	HBP	SH	SF	SB	CS	GDP	Avg	OBP	Slg	OPS
2022	Reno	AAA	90	331	80	20	1	14	(-	-)	144	56	62	53	44	1	68	21	0	6	0	1	10	.242	.361	.435	.796
2021	Ari	NL	5	9	4	1	0	1	(0	1)	8	4	3	4	1	0	3	0	0	0	0	0	0	.444	.500	.889	1.389
2022	Ari	NL	38	111	21	3	0	1	(1	0)	27	4	9	8	11	1	31	3	0	1	0	0	3	.189	.278	.243	.521
	2 ML YEARS		43	120	25	4	0	2	(1	1)	35	8	12	12	12	1	34	3	0	1	0	0	3	.208	.294	.292	.586

Josh Bell

Bats: B **Throws:** R **Pos:** 1B-124;DH-32;PH-4 **Ht:** 6'4" **Wt:** 261 **Born:** 8/14/1992 **Age:** 30

Year	Team	Lg	G	AB	H	2B	3B	HR	(Hm	Rd)	TB	R	RBI	RC	TBB	IBB	SO	HBP	SH	SF	SB	CS	GDP	Avg	OBP	Slg	OPS
2016	Pit	NL	45	128	35	8	0	3	(2	1)	52	18	19	18	21	0	19	0	0	3	0	1	4	.273	.368	.406	.775
2017	Pit	NL	159	549	140	26	6	26	(11	15)	256	75	90	86	66	4	117	1	0	4	2	4	15	.255	.334	.466	.800
2018	Pit	NL	148	501	131	31	4	12	(5	7)	206	74	62	73	77	2	104	0	0	5	2	5	12	.261	.357	.411	.768
2019	Pit	NL	143	527	146	37	3	37	(17	20)	300	94	116	112	74	13	118	5	0	7	0	1	11	.277	.367	.569	.936
2020	Pit	NL	57	195	44	3	0	8	(2	6)	71	22	22	25	22	4	59	2	0	4	0	0	3	.226	.305	.364	.669

Year	Team	Lg	G	AB	H	2B	3B	HR	(Hm	Rd)	TB	R	RBI	RC	TBB	IBB	SO	HBP	SH	SF	SB	CS	GDP	Avg	OBP	Slg	OPS
2021	Was	NL	144	498	130	24	1	27	(12	15)	237	75	88	69	65	2	101	2	0	3	0	0	22	.261	.347	.476	.823
2022	2 Tms	NL	156	552	147	29	3	17	(13	4)	233	78	71	76	81	4	102	5	0	6	0	1	22	.266	.362	.422	.784
22	Was	NL	103	375	113	24	3	14	(10	4)	185	52	57	61	49	4	61	5	0	6	0	1	19	.301	.384	.493	.877
22	SD	NL	53	177	34	5	0	3	(3	0)	48	26	14	15	32	0	41	0	0	0	0	0	3	.192	.316	.271	.587
7 ML YEARS			852	2950	773	158	17	130	(62	68)	1355	436	468	459	406	29	620	15	0	32	4	12	89	.262	.351	.459	.810

Andrew Bellatti

Pitches: R **Bats:** R **Pos:** RP-58; SP-1   bell-LAH-tee   **Ht:** 6'1" **Wt:** 190 **Born:** 8/5/1991 **Age:** 31

			HOW MUCH PITCHED					WHAT HE GAVE UP											THE RESULTS							
Year	Team	Lg	G	GS	GF	IP	BFP	H	R	ER	HR	SH	SF	HB	TBB	IBB	SO	WP	W	L	Pct	Sv-Op	Hld	Vel	OPS	ERC	ERA
2015	TB	AL	17	0	6	23.1	95	16	7	6	4	2	1	1	10	0	18	0	3	1	.750	0-0	2	93	.685	3.15	2.31
2021	Mia	NL	3	0	0	3.1	19	6	5	5	0	0	0	0	2	0	4	0	0	0	-	0-0	0	94	.833	8.33	13.50
2022	Phi	NL	59	1	16	54.1	230	47	25	20	5	0	3	1	25	1	78	1	4	4	.500	2-3	9	94	.700	3.58	3.31
3 ML YEARS			79	1	22	81.0	344	69	37	31	9	2	4	2	37	1	100	1	7	5	.583	2-3	11	94	.704	3.64	3.44

Cody Bellinger

Bats: L **Throws:** L **Pos:** CF-144;PH-4   **Ht:** 6'4" **Wt:** 203 **Born:** 7/13/1995 **Age:** 27

			BATTING																		RUNNING			AVERAGES			
Year	Team	Lg	G	AB	H	2B	3B	HR	(Hm	Rd)	TB	R	RBI	RC	TBB	IBB	SO	HBP	SH	SF	SB	CS	GDP	Avg	OBP	Slg	OPS
2017	LAD	NL	132	480	128	26	4	39	(19	20)	279	87	97	94	64	13	146	1	0	3	10	3	5	.267	.352	.581	.933
2018	LAD	NL	162	557	145	28	7	25	(11	14)	262	84	76	88	69	9	151	3	0	3	14	1	7	.260	.343	.470	.814
2019	LAD	NL	156	558	170	34	3	47	(27	20)	351	121	115	124	95	21	108	3	0	4	15	5	10	.305	.406	.629	1.035
2020	LAD	NL	56	213	51	10	0	12	(3	9)	97	33	30	34	30	2	42	0	0	0	6	1	4	.239	.333	.455	.789
2021	LAD	NL	95	315	52	9	2	10	(7	3)	95	39	36	23	31	2	94	1	0	3	3	1	2	.165	.240	.302	.542
2022	LAD	NL	144	504	106	27	3	19	(12	7)	196	70	68	56	38	0	150	2	0	6	14	3	7	.210	.265	.389	.654
Postseason			66	235	50	7	3	9	(4	5)	90	29	33	28	25	3	83	0	0	0	14	1	1	.213	.288	.383	.671
6 ML YEARS			745	2627	652	134	19	152	(79	73)	1280	434	422	419	327	47	691	10	0	19	62	14	35	.248	.332	.487	.819

Brayan Bello

Pitches: R **Bats:** R **Pos:** SP-11; RP-2   **Ht:** 6'1" **Wt:** 170 **Born:** 5/17/1999 **Age:** 24

			HOW MUCH PITCHED					WHAT HE GAVE UP											THE RESULTS							
Year	Team	Lg	G	GS	GF	IP	BFP	H	R	ER	HR	SH	SF	HB	TBB	IBB	SO	WP	W	L	Pct	Sv-Op	Hld	Vel	OPS	ERC	ERA
2019	Grnvlle	A	25	25	0	117.2	526	135	77	71	9	3	4	9	38	0	119	5	5	10	.333	0--	-		.506	4.71	5.43
2021	Grnvlle	A+	6	6	0	31.2	122	25	10	8	3	0	0	0	7	0	45	1	5	0	1.000	0--	-		.584	2.36	2.27
2021	Portlnd	AA	15	15	0	63.2	280	66	34	33	5	0	4	4	24	0	87	10	2	3	.400	0--	-		.739	4.26	4.66
2022	Portlnd	AA	7	7	0	37.1	142	18	8	7	3	0	0	0	12	0	48	2	4	2	.667	0--	-		.461	1.30	1.69
2022	Wrcstr	AAA	11	10	0	58.2	240	46	18	18	3	0	1	0	24	0	81	1	6	2	.750	0--	-		.617	2.67	2.76
2022	Bos	AL	13	11	0	57.1	268	75	34	30	1	0	1	2	27	1	55	2	2	8	.200	0-0	0	97	.804	5.65	4.71

Brandon Belt

Bats: L **Throws:** L **Pos:** 1B-63;DH-11;PH-10   **Ht:** 6'3" **Wt:** 231 **Born:** 4/20/1988 **Age:** 35

			BATTING																		RUNNING			AVERAGES			
Year	Team	Lg	G	AB	H	2B	3B	HR	(Hm	Rd)	TB	R	RBI	RC	TBB	IBB	SO	HBP	SH	SF	SB	CS	GDP	Avg	OBP	Slg	OPS
2011	SF	NL	63	187	42	6	1	9	(2	7)	79	21	18	20	20	1	57	2	0	0	3	2	3	.225	.306	.422	.718
2012	SF	NL	145	411	113	27	6	7	(5	2)	173	47	56	63	54	5	106	3	0	4	12	2	4	.275	.360	.421	.781
2013	SF	NL	150	509	147	39	4	17	(6	11)	245	76	67	82	52	4	125	6	1	3	5	2	4	.289	.360	.481	.841
2014	SF	NL	61	214	52	8	0	12	(2	10)	96	30	27	24	18	2	64	2	0	1	3	1	4	.243	.306	.449	.755
2015	SF	NL	137	492	138	33	5	18	(5	13)	235	73	68	78	56	2	147	4	0	4	9	3	3	.280	.356	.478	.834
2016	SF	NL	156	542	149	41	8	17	(6	11)	257	77	82	105	104	4	148	5	0	4	0	4	7	.275	.394	.474	.868
2017	SF	NL	104	382	92	27	3	18	(8	10)	179	63	51	60	66	2	104	2	0	1	3	2	5	.241	.355	.469	.823
2018	SF	NL	112	399	101	18	2	14	(8	6)	165	50	46	63	49	6	107	6	0	2	4	0	2	.253	.342	.414	.756
2019	SF	NL	156	526	123	32	3	17	(5	12)	212	76	57	72	83	3	127	3	0	4	4	3	6	.234	.339	.403	.742
2020	SF	NL	51	149	46	13	1	9	(7	2)	88	25	30	32	30	1	36	0	0	0	0	0	5	.309	.425	.591	1.015
2021	SF	NL	97	325	89	14	2	29	(13	16)	194	65	59	68	48	3	103	7	0	1	3	2	9	.274	.378	.597	.975
2022	SF	NL	78	254	54	9	1	8	(5	3)	89	25	23	26	37	2	81	6	0	1	1	0	9	.213	.326	.350	.676
Postseason			37	127	29	2	2	2	(1	1)	41	14	13	16	21	1	40	0	0	3	1	2	0	.228	.331	.323	.654
12 ML YEARS			1310	4390	1146	267	36	175	(72	103)	2010	628	584	693	617	35	1205	46	1	25	47	21	59	.261	.356	.458	.814

Anthony Bemboom

Bats: L **Throws:** R **Pos:** C-21;PH-2;PR-2   **Ht:** 6'2" **Wt:** 200 **Born:** 1/18/1990 **Age:** 33

			BATTING																		RUNNING			AVERAGES			
Year	Team	Lg	G	AB	H	2B	3B	HR	(Hm	Rd)	TB	R	RBI	RC	TBB	IBB	SO	HBP	SH	SF	SB	CS	GDP	Avg	OBP	Slg	OPS
2022	Norfolk	AAA	34	123	28	6	0	3	(-	-)	43	18	15	13	10	0	28	2	0	2	0	0	1	.228	.292	.350	.642
2019	2 Tms	AL	25	54	7	1	0	1	(1	0)	11	2	4	1	1	0	21	0	1	0	0	0	0	.130	.145	.204	.349
2020	LAA	AL	21	48	10	1	0	3	(0	3)	20	9	5	5	7	0	13	2	2	1	0	1	0	.208	.328	.417	.744
2021	LAA	AL	8	27	6	0	0	0	(0	0)	6	2	2	0	1	0	10	0	0	0	0	0	0	.222	.250	.222	.472
2022	Bal	AL	22	52	6	2	0	1	(0	1)	11	4	1	0	6	0	17	0	1	0	0	0	0	.115	.207	.212	.418
19	TB	AL	3	5	2	1	0	0	(0	0)	3	0	1	1	0	0	2	0	0	0	0	0	0	.400	.400	.600	1.000
19	LAA	AL	22	49	5	0	0	1	(1	0)	8	2	3	0	1	0	19	0	1	0	0	0	0	.102	.120	.163	.283
4 ML YEARS			76	181	29	4	0	5	(1	4)	48	17	12	6	15	0	61	2	4	1	0	1	2	.160	.231	.265	.496

Anthony Bender

Pitches: R Bats: R Pos: RP-22   Ht: 6'4" Wt: 205 Born: 2/3/1995 Age: 28

			HOW MUCH PITCHED					WHAT HE GAVE UP												THE RESULTS						
Year	Team	Lg	G	GS	GF	IP	BFP	H	R	ER	HR	SH	SF	HB	TBB	IBB	SO	WP	W	L	Pct	Sv-Op	Hld	Vel	OPS	ERC	ERA
2021	Mia	NL	60	1	13	61.1	247	45	22	19	5	0	4	6	20	3	71	4	3	2	.600	3-5	12	97	.638	2.62	2.79
2022	Mia	NL	22	0	11	19.1	78	17	7	7	3	0	1	1	8	0	17	1	1	3	.250	6-8	3	98	.716	4.31	3.26
	2 ML YEARS		82	1	24	80.2	325	62	29	26	8	0	5	7	28	3	88	5	4	5	.444	9-13	15	97	.656	2.99	2.90

Andrew Benintendi

Bats: L Throws: L Pos: LF-124;PH-4;DH-1   Ht: 5'9" Wt: 180 Born: 7/6/1994 Age: 28

					BATTING																RUNNING			AVERAGES			
Year	Team	Lg	G	AB	H	2B	3B	HR	(Hm	Rd)	TB	R	RBI	RC	TBB	IBB	SO	HBP	SH	SF	SB	CS	GDP	Avg	OBP	Slg	OPS
2016	Bos	AL	34	105	31	11	1	2	(0	2)	50	16	14	20	10	0	25	1	1	1	1	0	0	.295	.359	.476	.835
2017	Bos	AL	151	573	155	26	1	20	(7	13)	243	84	90	96	70	7	112	6	1	8	20	5	16	.271	.352	.424	.776
2018	Bos	AL	148	579	168	41	6	16	(7	9)	269	103	87	105	71	1	106	2	2	7	21	3	9	.290	.366	.465	.830
2019	Bos	AL	138	541	144	40	5	13	(8	5)	233	72	68	88	59	1	140	7	3	5	10	3	6	.266	.343	.431	.774
2020	Bos	AL	14	39	4	1	0	0	(0	0)	5	4	1	1	11	0	17	1	1	0	1	2	1	.103	.314	.128	.442
2021	KC	AL	134	493	136	27	2	17	(5	12)	218	63	73	78	36	0	97	2	1	6	8	9	2	.276	.324	.442	.766
2022	2 Tms	AL	126	461	140	23	3	5	(2	3)	184	54	51	67	52	0	77	2	1	5	8	3	7	.304	.373	.399	.772
22	KC	AL	93	347	111	14	2	3	(1	2)	138	40	39	50	39	0	52	1	0	3	4	2	6	.320	.387	.398	.785
22	NYY	AL	33	114	29	9	1	2	(1	1)	46	14	12	17	13	0	25	1	1	2	4	1	1	.254	.331	.404	.734
	Postseason		21	81	22	5	0	2	(1	1)	33	18	9	13	5	0	17	1	0	0	2	0	2	.272	.322	.407	.729
	7 ML YEARS		745	2791	778	169	18	73	(29	44)	1202	396	384	455	309	9	574	21	10	32	69	25	41	.279	.351	.431	.782

Will Benson

Bats: L Throws: L Pos: CF-10;RF-6;PH-6;LF-4;DH-2;PR-2   Ht: 6'5" Wt: 230 Born: 6/16/1998 Age: 25

					BATTING																RUNNING			AVERAGES			
Year	Team	Lg	G	AB	H	2B	3B	HR	(Hm	Rd)	TB	R	RBI	RC	TBB	IBB	SO	HBP	SH	SF	SB	CS	GDP	Avg	OBP	Slg	OPS
2022	Clmbs	AAA	89	316	88	20	3	17	(-	-)	165	75	45	75	75	3	91	7	2	1	16	4	5	.278	.426	.522	.948
2022	Cle	AL	28	55	10	1	0	0	(0	0)	11	8	3	3	3	0	19	2	1	0	0	0	1	.182	.250	.200	.450

Wynton Bernard

Bats: R Throws: R Pos: CF-10;LF-1;RF-1;DH-1;PR-1   Ht: 6'2" Wt: 195 Born: 9/24/1990 Age: 32

					BATTING																RUNNING			AVERAGES			
Year	Team	Lg	G	AB	H	2B	3B	HR	(Hm	Rd)	TB	R	RBI	RC	TBB	IBB	SO	HBP	SH	SF	SB	CS	GDP	Avg	OBP	Slg	OPS
2022	Albq	AAA	108	429	143	31	8	21	(-	-)	253	95	92	98	39	0	67	2	0	5	30	5	7	.333	.387	.590	.977
2022	Col	NL	12	42	12	1	0	0	(0	0)	13	9	3	3	0	0	8	0	0	0	3	1	1	.286	.286	.310	.595

Brennan Bernardino

Pitches: L Bats: L Pos: RP-2   Ht: 6'4" Wt: 180 Born: 1/15/1992 Age: 31

			HOW MUCH PITCHED					WHAT HE GAVE UP												THE RESULTS						
Year	Team	Lg	G	GS	GF	IP	BFP	H	R	ER	HR	SH	SF	HB	TBB	IBB	SO	WP	W	L	Pct	Sv-Op	Hld	Vel	OPS	ERC	ERA
2022	Tacom	AAA	23	0	4	32.2	125	18	10	8	1	0	0	3	10	0	35	0	2	0	1.000	2- -	-	-	.507	1.53	2.20
2022	Sea	AL	2	0	2	2.1	13	3	3	1	0	0	1	0	2	1	0	0	0	1	.000	0-0	0	93	.685	5.24	3.86

Jose Berrios

Pitches: R Bats: R Pos: SP-32   beh-REE-ohs   Ht: 6'0" Wt: 205 Born: 5/27/1994 Age: 29

			HOW MUCH PITCHED					WHAT HE GAVE UP												THE RESULTS						
Year	Team	Lg	G	GS	GF	IP	BFP	H	R	ER	HR	SH	SF	HB	TBB	IBB	SO	WP	W	L	Pct	Sv-Op	Hld	Vel	OPS	ERC	ERA
2016	Min	AL	14	14	0	58.1	281	74	56	52	12	2	0	5	35	0	49	1	3	7	.300	0-0	0	93	.932	7.85	8.02
2017	Min	AL	26	25	0	145.2	616	131	71	63	15	3	4	13	48	0	139	7	14	8	.636	0-0	0	93	.693	3.62	3.89
2018	Min	AL	32	32	0	192.1	797	159	83	82	25	2	4	6	61	1	202	2	12	11	.522	0-0	0	93	.665	3.26	3.84
2019	Min	AL	32	32	0	200.1	842	194	94	82	26	2	6	9	51	0	195	8	14	8	.636	0-0	0	93	.707	3.69	3.68
2020	Min	AL	12	12	0	63.0	271	57	28	28	8	0	2	3	26	0	68	5	5	4	.556	0-0	0	94	.701	3.95	4.00
2021	2 Tms	AL	32	32	0	192.0	781	159	83	75	22	2	5	15	45	0	204	3	12	9	.571	0-0	0	94	.661	2.92	3.52
2022	Tor	AL	32	32	0	172.0	753	199	103	100	29	0	3	11	45	0	149	3	12	7	.632	0-0	0	94	.805	5.19	5.23
21	Min	AL	20	20	0	121.2	490	95	53	47	14	2	3	8	32	0	126	3	7	5	.583	0-0	0	94	.641	2.76	3.48
21	Tor	AL	12	12	0	70.1	291	64	30	28	8	0	2	7	13	0	78	0	5	4	.556	0-0	0	94	.694	3.22	3.58
	Postseason		3	2	0	12.0	52	11	7	5	1	0	0	0	5	0	14	0	0	1	.000	0-0	0	95	.669	3.49	3.75
	7 ML YEARS		180	179	0	1023.2	4341	973	518	482	137	11	24	69	311	1	1006	29	72	54	.571	0-0	0	93	.720	3.92	4.24

Jon Berti

Bats: R Throws: R Pos: 2B-47;3B-37;LF-16;SS-10;PR-6;CF-3;DH-3;PH-3   Ht: 5'10" Wt: 190 Born: 1/22/1990 Age: 33

					BATTING																RUNNING			AVERAGES			
Year	Team	Lg	G	AB	H	2B	3B	HR	(Hm	Rd)	TB	R	RBI	RC	TBB	IBB	SO	HBP	SH	SF	SB	CS	GDP	Avg	OBP	Slg	OPS
2018	Tor	AL	4	15	4	1	1	0	(0	0)	7	2	2	2	0	0	4	0	0	0	1	0	0	.267	.267	.467	.733
2019	Mia	NL	73	256	70	14	1	6	(3	3)	104	52	24	37	24	0	73	6	0	1	17	3	2	.273	.348	.406	.755
2020	Mia	NL	39	120	31	5	0	2	(1	1)	42	21	14	22	23	0	37	3	2	1	9	2	1	.258	.388	.350	.738
2021	Mia	NL	85	233	49	10	1	4	(1	3)	73	35	19	22	32	0	61	3	1	2	8	4	7	.210	.311	.313	.624
2022	Mia	NL	102	358	86	17	3	4	(4	0)	121	47	28	37	42	0	89	3	0	1	41	5	6	.240	.324	.338	.662
	Postseason		5	17	3	0	0	0	(0	0)	3	1	0	1	2	0	5	2	0	0	2	0	0	.176	.333	.176	.510
	5 ML YEARS		303	982	240	47	6	16	(9	7)	347	157	87	120	121	0	264	15	3	5	76	14	16	.244	.335	.353	.688

Christian Bethancourt

Bats: R Throws: R Pos: C-49;1B-37;PH-13;DH-10;PR-2;3B-1   BETH-an-court   Ht: 6'3" Wt: 205 Born: 9/2/1991 Age: 31

Year	Team	Lg	G	AB	H	2B	3B	HR	(Hm	Rd)	TB	R	RBI	RC	TBB	IBB	SO	HBP	SH	SF	SB	CS	GDP	Avg	OBP	Slg	OPS
2013	Atl	NL	1	1	0	0	0	0	(0	0)	0	0	0	0	0	0	1	0	0	0	0	0	0	.000	.000	.000	.000
2014	Atl	NL	31	113	28	3	0	0	(0	0)	31	7	9	8	3	0	26	1	0	0	1	1	3	.248	.274	.274	.548
2015	Atl	NL	48	155	31	8	0	2	(1	1)	45	16	12	4	5	1	33	0	0	0	1	1	7	.200	.225	.290	.515
2016	SD	NL	73	193	44	9	0	6	(4	2)	71	20	25	15	10	0	56	0	0	1	1	2	9	.228	.265	.368	.633
2017	SD	NL	8	7	1	0	0	0	(0	0)	1	0	0	0	0	0	3	0	0	0	0	0	0	.143	.143	.143	.286
2022	2 Tms	AL	101	318	80	17	0	11	(8	3)	130	39	34	41	12	0	80	2	1	0	5	1	6	.252	.283	.409	.692
22	Oak	AL	56	169	42	11	0	4	(1	3)	65	23	19	22	10	0	41	2	1	0	4	1	3	.249	.298	.385	.683
22	TB	AL	45	149	38	6	0	7	(7	0)	65	16	15	19	2	0	39	0	0	0	1	0	3	.255	.265	.436	.701
	6 ML YEARS		262	787	184	37	0	19	(13	6)	278	82	80	68	30	1	199	3	1	1	8	5	25	.234	.264	.353	.618

Mookie Betts

Bats: R Throws: R Pos: RF-136;2B-7;PH-3;DH-1   Ht: 5'9" Wt: 180 Born: 10/7/1992 Age: 30

Year	Team	Lg	G	AB	H	2B	3B	HR	(Hm	Rd)	TB	R	RBI	RC	TBB	IBB	SO	HBP	SH	SF	SB	CS	GDP	Avg	OBP	Slg	OPS
2014	Bos	AL	52	189	55	12	1	5	(1	4)	84	34	18	30	21	0	31	2	1	0	7	3	2	.291	.368	.444	.812
2015	Bos	AL	145	597	174	42	8	18	(9	9)	286	92	77	100	46	1	82	2	3	6	21	6	2	.291	.341	.479	.820
2016	Bos	AL	158	**672**	214	42	5	31	(17	14)	359	122	113	130	49	1	80	2	0	7	26	4	12	.318	.363	.534	.897
2017	Bos	AL	153	628	166	46	2	24	(8	16)	288	101	102	115	77	9	79	2	0	5	26	3	9	.264	.344	.459	.803
2018	Bos	AL	136	520	180	47	5	32	(13	19)	333	**129**	80	134	81	8	91	8	0	5	30	6	5	**.346**	.438	**.640**	1.078
2019	Bos	AL	150	597	176	40	5	29	(17	12)	313	**135**	80	118	97	6	101	3	0	9	16	3	11	.295	.391	.524	.915
2020	LAD	NL	55	219	64	9	1	16	(11	5)	123	47	39	52	24	1	38	2	0	1	10	2	2	.292	.366	.562	.927
2021	LAD	NL	122	466	123	29	3	23	(15	8)	227	93	58	80	68	2	86	11	0	5	10	5	5	.264	.367	.487	.854
2022	LAD	NL	142	572	154	40	3	35	(16	19)	305	**117**	82	106	55	0	104	8	0	4	12	2	8	.269	.340	.533	.873
	Postseason		51	206	56	16	0	4	(3	1)	84	37	17	27	25	4	38	1	0	2	14	0	3	.272	.350	.408	.758
	9 ML YEARS		1113	4460	1306	307	33	213	(107	106)	2318	870	649	865	518	28	692	40	4	42	158	34	56	.293	.368	.520	.888

Bo Bichette

Bats: R Throws: R Pos: SS-157;DH-1;PH-1   Ht: 6'0" Wt: 190 Born: 3/5/1998 Age: 25

Year	Team	Lg	G	AB	H	2B	3B	HR	(Hm	Rd)	TB	R	RBI	RC	TBB	IBB	SO	HBP	SH	SF	SB	CS	GDP	Avg	OBP	Slg	OPS
2019	Tor	AL	46	196	61	18	0	11	(3	8)	112	32	21	32	14	0	50	1	0	1	4	4	2	.311	.358	.571	.930
2020	Tor	AL	29	123	37	9	1	5	(3	2)	63	18	23	23	5	1	27	0	0	0	4	1	2	.301	.328	.512	.840
2021	Tor	AL	159	640	**191**	30	1	29	(15	14)	310	121	102	114	40	0	137	6	0	4	25	1	10	.298	.343	.484	.828
2022	Tor	AL	159	652	**189**	43	1	24	(8	16)	306	91	93	91	41	0	155	2	0	2	13	8	21	.290	.333	.469	.802
	Postseason		2	6	0	0	0	0	(0	0)	0	0	1	0	1	0	1	0	0	1	0	0	0	.000	.125	.000	.125
	4 ML YEARS		393	1611	478	100	3	69	(29	40)	791	262	239	260	100	1	369	9	0	7	46	14	35	.297	.340	.491	.831

Phil Bickford

Pitches: R Bats: R Pos: RP-60   Ht: 6'4" Wt: 200 Born: 7/10/1995 Age: 27

Year	Team	Lg	G	GS	GF	IP	BFP	H	R	ER	HR	SH	SF	HB	TBB	IBB	SO	WP	W	L	Pct	Sv-Op	Hld	Vel	OPS	ERC	ERA
2022	OkCity	AAA	6	0	4	5.0	22	4	5	5	2	0	1	0	3	0	6	0	0	0	-	0--	-	-	.985	5.76	9.00
2020	Mil	NL	1	0	0	1.0	9	4	4	4	0	0	0	2	1	0	2	1	0	0	-	0-0	0	89	1.831	32.97	36.00
2021	2 Tms	NL	57	0	8	51.1	207	36	18	16	7	0	2	3	19	7	59	0	4	2	.667	1-3	9	94	.630	2.67	2.81
2022	LAD	NL	60	0	13	61.0	247	53	33	32	12	0	4	2	14	0	67	0	2	1	.667	0-1	6	94	.729	3.46	4.72
21	Mil	NL	1	0	0	1.0	7	2	2	2	1	0	1	1	1	0	0	0	0	0	-	0-0	0	93	1.821	29.25	18.00
21	LAD	NL	56	0	8	50.1	200	34	16	14	6	0	1	2	18	7	59	0	4	2	.667	1-3	9	94	.600	2.33	2.50
	Postseason		6	0	3	6.0	21	4	0	0	0	0	0	0	0	0	4	0	0	0	-	0-0	0	93	.381	0.96	0.00
	3 ML YEARS		118	0	21	113.1	463	93	55	52	19	0	6	7	33	7	128	1	6	3	.667	1-4	15	94	.697	3.29	4.13

Shane Bieber

Pitches: R Bats: R Pos: SP-31   Ht: 6'3" Wt: 200 Born: 5/31/1995 Age: 28

Year	Team	Lg	G	GS	GF	IP	BFP	H	R	ER	HR	SH	SF	HB	TBB	IBB	SO	WP	W	L	Pct	Sv-Op	Hld	Vel	OPS	ERC	ERA
2018	Cle	AL	20	19	0	114.2	485	130	60	58	13	0	4	2	23	0	118	5	11	5	.688	0-0	0	93	.787	4.23	4.55
2019	Cle	AL	34	33	1	214.1	859	186	86	78	31	2	1	6	40	1	259	6	15	8	.652	0-0	0	93	.663	2.94	3.28
2020	Cle	AL	12	12	0	77.1	297	46	15	14	7	0	0	1	21	0	**122**	5	8	1	**.889**	0-0	0	94	.494	1.61	**1.63**
2021	Cle	AL	16	16	0	96.2	405	84	36	34	11	0	1	4	33	0	134	5	7	4	.636	0-0	0	93	.672	3.37	3.17
2022	Cle	AL	31	31	0	200.0	791	172	70	64	18	3	3	2	36	0	198	5	13	8	.619	0-0	0	91	.613	2.51	2.88
	Postseason		1	1	0	4.2	25	9	7	7	2	0	0	2	2	0	7	0	0	1	.000	0-0	0	94	1.179	13.07	13.50
	5 ML YEARS		113	111	1	703.0	2837	618	267	248	80	5	9	15	153	1	831	26	54	26	.675	0-0	0	93	.654	2.91	3.17

Brandon Bielak

Pitches: R Bats: L Pos: RP-5   BEE-lak   Ht: 6'2" Wt: 208 Born: 4/2/1996 Age: 27

Year	Team	Lg	G	GS	GF	IP	BFP	H	R	ER	HR	SH	SF	HB	TBB	IBB	SO	WP	W	L	Pct	Sv-Op	Hld	Vel	OPS	ERC	ERA
2022	SgrLnd	AAA	23	14	3	88.2	388	82	39	31	5	1	3	3	43	0	86	2	3	6	.333	0--	-		.698	3.78	3.15
2020	Hou	AL	12	6	3	32.0	148	39	26	24	9	1	0	2	17	0	26	0	3	1	.500	0-0	0	93	.784	7.84	6.75
2021	Hou	AL	28	2	6	50.0	218	48	29	25	5	2	3	3	21	0	46	4	3	4	.429	1-2	2	94	.714	4.15	4.50
2022	Hou	AL	5	0	2	12.1	54	11	5	5	2	0	0	3	4	0	12	1	0	0	-	0-0	1	93	.716	4.57	3.65
	3 ML YEARS		45	8	11	94.1	420	98	60	54	16	3	3	8	42	0	84	5	6	7	.462	1-2	3	94	.805	5.38	5.15

Cavan Biggio

Bats: L **Throws:** R **Pos:** 2B-49;1B-33;PH-18;RF-7;DH-3;LF-2;PR-2;3B-1   **Ht:** 6'2" **Wt:** 200 **Born:** 4/11/1995 **Age:** 28

								BATTING											RUNNING			AVERAGES			
Year	Team	Lg	G	AB	H	2B	3B	HR	(Hm | Rd)	TB	R	RBI	RC	TBB	IBB	SO	HBP	SH	SF	SB	CS	GDP	Avg	OBP	Slg	OPS
2022	Buffalo	AAA	10	29	8	3	0	0	(- | -)	11	9	3	5	10	1	6	0	0	0	2	0	1	.276	.462	.379	.841
2019	Tor	AL	100	354	83	17	2	16	(9 | 7)	152	66	48	65	71	0	123	2	0	2	14	0	0	.234	.364	.429	.793
2020	Tor	AL	59	220	55	16	0	8	(3 | 5)	95	41	28	42	41	0	61	3	0	0	6	0	2	.250	.375	.432	.807
2021	Tor	AL	79	250	56	10	1	7	(3 | 4)	89	27	27	31	37	2	78	1	1	4	3	1	4	.224	.322	.356	.678
2022	Tor	AL	97	257	52	18	1	6	(1 | 5)	90	43	24	32	38	0	85	6	1	1	2	0	2	.202	.318	.350	.668
	Postseason		2	8	1	1	0	0	(0 | 0)	2	0	0	0	0	0	6	0	0	0	0	0	0	.125	.125	.250	.375
	4 ML YEARS		335	1081	246	61	4	37	(16 | 21)	426	177	127	170	187	2	347	12	2	7	25	1	8	.228	.346	.394	.740

Jake Bird

Pitches: R **Bats:** R **Pos:** RP-38   **Ht:** 6'3" **Wt:** 200 **Born:** 12/4/1995 **Age:** 27

			HOW MUCH PITCHED					WHAT HE GAVE UP										THE RESULTS						
Year	Team	Lg	G	GS	GF	IP	BFP	H	R	ER	HR	SH	SF	HB	TBB	IBB	SO	WP	W	L	Pct	Sv-Op	Hld	Vel	OPS	ERC	ERA
2022	Albq	AAA	22	0	4	26.0	106	16	10	8	3	0	0	3	9	0	34	1	2	2	.500	2- -	-	-	.562	2.36	2.77
2022	Col	NL	38	0	11	47.2	211	45	29	26	7	1	2	4	23	3	42	4	2	4	.333	0-1	5	95	.763	4.65	4.91

Ty Blach

Pitches: L **Bats:** R **Pos:** RP-23; SP-1   block   **Ht:** 6'1" **Wt:** 215 **Born:** 10/20/1990 **Age:** 32

			HOW MUCH PITCHED					WHAT HE GAVE UP										THE RESULTS						
Year	Team	Lg	G	GS	GF	IP	BFP	H	R	ER	HR	SH	SF	HB	TBB	IBB	SO	WP	W	L	Pct	Sv-Op	Hld	Vel	OPS	ERC	ERA
2022	Albq	AAA	15	1	0	36.0	158	44	23	18	3	3	1	0	8	0	20	0	1	5	.167	0- -	-	-	.760	4.46	4.50
2016	SF	NL	4	2	2	17.0	62	8	2	2	1	1	0	0	5	0	10	0	1	0	1.000	0-0	0	91	.445	1.18	1.06
2017	SF	NL	34	24	3	163.2	692	179	91	87	17	10	5	1	43	2	73	3	8	12	.400	0-0	0	90	.766	4.14	4.78
2018	SF	NL	47	13	13	118.2	512	133	62	56	8	8	1	1	41	4	75	1	6	7	.462	0-0	3	90	.746	4.35	4.25
2019	2 Tms		7	5	1	27.0	139	46	37	36	8	0	0	0	17	0	20	2	1	3	.250	0-0	0	90	1.125	11.59	12.00
2022	Col	NL	24	1	10	44.1	193	51	29	29	4	1	4	2	11	2	29	1	1	0	1.000	1-2	0	91	.796	4.35	5.89
19	SF	NL	2	0	1	6.1	36	14	10	10	2	0	0	0	4	0	3	0	0	0	-	0-0	0	91	1.188	15.61	14.21
19	Bal	AL	5	5	0	20.2	103	32	27	26	6	0	0	0	13	0	17	2	1	3	.250	0-0	0	90	1.104	10.41	11.32
	Postseason		2	0	1	3.1	11	2	0	0	0	0	0	0	0	0	3	0	1	0	1.000	0-0	0	92	.364	0.82	0.00
	5 ML YEARS		116	45	29	370.2	1598	417	221	210	38	20	10	4	117	8	207	7	17	22	.436	1-2	3	90	.782	4.52	5.10

Paul Blackburn

Pitches: R **Bats:** R **Pos:** SP-21   **Ht:** 6'1" **Wt:** 196 **Born:** 12/4/1993 **Age:** 29

			HOW MUCH PITCHED					WHAT HE GAVE UP										THE RESULTS						
Year	Team	Lg	G	GS	GF	IP	BFP	H	R	ER	HR	SH	SF	HB	TBB	IBB	SO	WP	W	L	Pct	Sv-Op	Hld	Vel	OPS	ERC	ERA
2017	Oak	AL	10	10	0	58.2	238	58	22	21	5	0	1	0	16	0	22	1	3	1	.750	0-0	0	90	.686	3.62	3.22
2018	Oak	AL	6	6	0	27.2	119	33	23	22	2	0	2	2	6	0	19	1	2	3	.400	0-0	0	90	.794	4.62	7.16
2019	Oak	AL	4	1	1	11.0	57	19	14	13	3	1	1	1	4	0	8	1	0	2	.000	0-0	0	91	1.089	10.24	10.64
2020	Oak	AL	1	1	0	2.1	14	5	7	7	0	0	0	0	2	0	2	1	0	1	.000	0-0	0	90	1.083	12.37	27.00
2021	Oak	AL	9	9	0	38.1	175	52	26	25	8	0	0	2	10	0	26	1	1	4	.200	0-0	0	91	.899	6.68	5.87
2022	Oak	AL	21	21	0	111.1	467	110	53	53	15	1	0	5	30	2	89	1	7	6	.538	0-0	0	92	.752	3.91	4.28
	6 ML YEARS		51	48	1	249.1	1070	277	145	141	33	2	3	11	68	2	166	6	13	17	.433	0-0	0	91	.788	4.64	5.09

Charlie Blackmon

Bats: L **Throws:** L **Pos:** DH-80;RF-51;PH-7   **Ht:** 6'3" **Wt:** 221 **Born:** 7/1/1986 **Age:** 36

								BATTING											RUNNING			AVERAGES			
Year	Team	Lg	G	AB	H	2B	3B	HR	(Hm	Rd)	TB	R	RBI	RC	TBB	IBB	SO	HBP	SH	SF	SB	CS	GDP	Avg	OBP	Slg	OPS
2011	Col	NL	27	98	25	1	0	1	(1	0)	29	9	8	10	3	1	8	0	1	0	5	1	2	.255	.277	.296	.573
2012	Col	NL	42	113	32	8	0	2	(1	1)	46	15	9	11	4	0	17	3	1	0	1	2	4	.283	.325	.407	.732
2013	Col	NL	82	246	76	17	2	6	(3	3)	115	35	22	35	7	0	49	3	2	0	7	0	1	.309	.336	.467	.803
2014	Col	NL	154	593	171	27	3	19	(13	6)	261	82	72	87	31	5	96	13	6	5	28	10	3	.288	.335	.440	.775
2015	Col	NL	157	614	176	31	9	17	(7	10)	276	93	58	90	46	2	112	13	5	4	43	13	4	.287	.347	.450	.797
2016	Col	NL	143	578	187	35	5	29	(12	17)	319	111	82	110	43	4	102	13	3	4	17	9	2	.324	.381	.552	.933
2017	Col	NL	159	644	213	35	14	37	(24	13)	387	137	104	151	65	9	135	10	3	3	14	10	4	.331	.399	.601	1.000
2018	Col	NL	156	626	182	31	7	29	(14	15)	314	119	70	110	59	2	134	8	1	2	12	4	10	.291	.358	.502	.860
2019	Col	NL	140	580	182	42	7	32	(22	10)	334	112	86	115	40	1	104	9	0	5	2	5	11	.314	.364	.576	.940
2020	Col	NL	59	221	67	12	1	6	(3	3)	99	31	42	36	19	4	44	2	0	5	2	1	4	.303	.356	.448	.804
2021	Col	NL	150	514	139	25	4	13	(11	2)	211	76	78	86	54	1	91	11	0	3	3	0	8	.270	.351	.411	.761
2022	Col	NL	135	530	140	22	6	16	(9	7)	222	60	78	79	32	4	109	8	4	3	4	1	10	.264	.314	.419	.733
	Postseason		5	19	2	0	0	0	(0	0)	2	1	2	0	1	0	2	0	1	0	0	0	0	.105	.150	.105	.255
	12 ML YEARS		1404	5357	1590	286	58	207	(120	87)	2613	880	709	925	403	33	1001	93	26	34	138	56	63	.297	.354	.488	.842

Dairon Blanco

Bats: R **Throws:** R **Pos:** CF-3;PR-2;DH-1;PH-1   **Ht:** 6'0" **Wt:** 170 **Born:** 4/26/1993 **Age:** 30

								BATTING											RUNNING			AVERAGES			
Year	Team	Lg	G	AB	H	2B	3B	HR	(Hm	Rd)	TB	R	RBI	RC	TBB	IBB	SO	HBP	SH	SF	SB	CS	GDP	Avg	OBP	Slg	OPS
2022	Omha	AAA	107	366	110	20	3	14	(-	-)	178	63	61	69	35	0	98	6	2	5	45	7	5	.301	.367	.486	.853
2022	KC	AL	5	7	2	0	0	0	(0	0)	2	1	2	1	0	0	4	0	0	0	1	0	0	.286	.286	.286	.571

Ronel Blanco

Pitches: R **Bats:** R **Pos:** RP-7   **Ht:** 6'0" **Wt:** 180 **Born:** 8/31/1993 **Age:** 29

			HOW MUCH PITCHED					WHAT HE GAVE UP											THE RESULTS							
Year	Team	Lg	G	GS	GF	IP	BFP	H	R	ER	HR	SH	SF	HB	TBB	IBB	SO	WP	W	L	Pct	Sv-Op	Hld	Vel	OPS	ERC	ERA
2022	SgrLnd	AAA	44	0	28	44.2	185	35	23	18	8	1	0	0	19	0	58	6	4	7	.364	5- -	-	-	.706	3.51	3.63
2022	Hou	AL	7	0	3	6.1	32	8	5	5	1	0	0	1	4	0	7	0	0	0		0-0	0	95	.962	7.63	7.11

Travis Blankenhorn

Bats: L **Throws:** R **Pos:** DH-1   **Ht:** 6'2" **Wt:** 235 **Born:** 8/3/1996 **Age:** 26

						BATTING															RUNNING			AVERAGES			
Year	Team	Lg	G	AB	H	2B	3B	HR	(Hm	Rd)	TB	R	RBI	RC	TBB	IBB	SO	HBP	SH	SF	SB	CS	GDP	Avg	OBP	Slg	OPS
2022	Syrcse	AAA	91	329	88	20	0	15	(-	-)	153	44	55	55	32	1	88	6	1	1	10	1	7	.267	.342	.465	.807
2020	Min	AL	1	3	1	1	0	0	(0	0)	2	0	0	1	0	0	0	1	0	0	0	0	0	.333	.500	.667	1.167
2021	2 Tms		24	23	4	2	0	1	(0	1)	9	4	4	2	1	0	8	0	0	0	0	0	0	.174	.208	.391	.600
2022	NYM	NL	1	3	0	0	0	0	(0	0)	0	0	0	0	0	0	1	0	0	0	0	0	0	.000	.000	.000	.000
21	Min	AL	1	0	0	0	0	0	(0	0)	0	1	0	0	0	0	0	0	0	0	0	0	0	-	-	-	-
21	NYM	NL	23	23	4	2	0	1	(0	1)	9	3	4	2	1	0	8	0	0	0	0	0	0	.174	.208	.391	.600
3 ML YEARS			26	29	5	3	0	1	(0	1)	11	4	4	3	1	0	9	1	0	0	0	0	0	.172	.226	.379	.605

J.J. Bleday

Bats: L **Throws:** L **Pos:** CF-38;LF-22;PH-6;RF-4   **Ht:** 6'3" **Wt:** 205 **Born:** 11/10/1997 **Age:** 25

						BATTING															RUNNING			AVERAGES			
Year	Team	Lg	G	AB	H	2B	3B	HR	(Hm	Rd)	TB	R	RBI	RC	TBB	IBB	SO	HBP	SH	SF	SB	CS	GDP	Avg	OBP	Slg	OPS
2022	Jaxnvl	AAA	85	302	69	13	0	20	(-	-)	142	54	52	60	60	0	99	5	0	0	1	1	2	.228	.365	.470	.835
2022	Mia	NL	65	204	34	10	2	5	(1	4)	63	21	16	20	30	0	67	2	0	2	4	1	5	.167	.277	.309	.586

Richard Bleier

Pitches: L **Bats:** L **Pos:** RP-54; SP-1   BLY-er   **Ht:** 6'3" **Wt:** 215 **Born:** 4/16/1987 **Age:** 36

			HOW MUCH PITCHED					WHAT HE GAVE UP											THE RESULTS							
Year	Team	Lg	G	GS	GF	IP	BFP	H	R	ER	HR	SH	SF	HB	TBB	IBB	SO	WP	W	L	Pct	Sv-Op	Hld	Vel	OPS	ERC	ERA
2016	NYY	AL	23	0	8	23.0	92	20	6	5	0	0	1	1	4	0	13	0	0	0	-	0-0	2	89	.586	2.11	1.96
2017	Bal	AL	57	0	14	63.1	265	62	23	14	6	3	4	4	13	3	26	5	2	1	.667	0-0	3	89	.671	3.33	1.99
2018	Bal	AL	31	0	4	32.2	133	36	7	7	0	0	2	1	4	1	15	1	3	0	1.000	0-1	9	88	.673	3.05	1.93
2019	Bal	AL	53	1	13	55.1	235	65	34	33	6	1	2	4	8	2	30	1	3	0	1.000	4-5	5	89	.802	4.39	5.37
2020	2 Tms		21	0	1	16.2	67	14	6	4	0	0	1	4	4	1	11	2	1	1	.500	0-0	6	88	.590	2.18	2.16
2021	Mia	NL	68	0	6	58.0	225	51	20	19	4	1	3	3	6	3	44	1	3	2	.600	0-6	20	90	.603	2.34	2.95
2022	Mia	NL	55	1	12	50.2	222	63	22	20	3	1	1	1	10	3	32	3	2	2	.500	1-3	7	90	.794	4.31	3.55
20	Bal	AL	2	0	0	3.0	11	1	0	0	0	0	1	0	0	0	4	1	0	0	-	0-0	0	89	.282	0.69	0.00
20	Mia	NL	19	0	1	13.2	56	13	6	4	0	0	0	4	4	1	7	1	1	1	.500	0-0	6	88	.650	2.68	2.63
Postseason			3	0	0	2.0	6	0	0	0	0	0	0	0	0	0	0	0	0	0	-	0-0	1	91	.000	0.00	0.00
7 ML YEARS			308	2	58	299.2	1239	311	118	102	19	6	13	15	49	13	171	13	14	6	.700	5-15	52	89	.695	3.28	3.06

Xander Bogaerts

Bats: R **Throws:** R **Pos:** SS-146;DH-4;PH-2   ZAN-derr BO-garts   **Ht:** 6'2" **Wt:** 218 **Born:** 10/1/1992 **Age:** 30

						BATTING															RUNNING			AVERAGES			
Year	Team	Lg	G	AB	H	2B	3B	HR	(Hm	Rd)	TB	R	RBI	RC	TBB	IBB	SO	HBP	SH	SF	SB	CS	GDP	Avg	OBP	Slg	OPS
2013	Bos	AL	18	44	11	2	0	1	(0	1)	16	7	5	4	5	0	13	0	0	1	1	0	1	.250	.320	.364	.684
2014	Bos	AL	144	538	129	28	1	12	(7	5)	195	60	46	43	39	1	138	8	2	7	2	3	11	.240	.297	.362	.660
2015	Bos	AL	156	613	196	35	3	7	(5	2)	258	84	81	88	32	1	101	3	3	3	10	2	16	.320	.355	.421	.776
2016	Bos	AL	157	652	192	34	1	21	(11	10)	291	115	89	98	58	0	123	6	0	3	13	4	14	.294	.356	.446	.802
2017	Bos	AL	148	571	156	32	6	10	(4	6)	230	94	62	81	56	6	116	6	0	2	15	1	17	.273	.343	.403	.746
2018	Bos	AL	136	513	148	45	3	23	(15	8)	268	72	103	100	55	4	102	6	0	6	8	2	14	.288	.360	.522	.883
2019	Bos	AL	155	614	190	52	0	33	(17	16)	341	110	117	124	76	12	122	2	0	4	4	2	11	.309	.384	.555	.939
2020	Bos	AL	56	203	61	8	0	11	(5	6)	102	36	28	32	21	2	41	0	0	1	8	0	3	.300	.364	.502	.867
2021	Bos	AL	144	529	156	34	1	23	(15	8)	261	90	79	97	62	2	113	5	0	7	5	1	13	.295	.370	.493	.863
2022	Bos	AL	150	557	171	38	0	15	(10	5)	254	84	73	94	57	2	118	10	0	7	8	2	14	.307	.377	.456	.833
Postseason			44	160	37	7	1	5	(4	1)	61	24	16	18	19	1	39	0	0	2	0	0	5	.231	.309	.381	.691
10 ML YEARS			1264	4834	1410	308	15	156	(89	67)	2216	752	683	761	461	20	987	46	5	43	74	17	114	.292	.356	.458	.814

Alec Bohm

Bats: R **Throws:** R **Pos:** 3B-135;1B-10;DH-9;PH-3;PR-1   **Ht:** 6'5" **Wt:** 218 **Born:** 8/3/1996 **Age:** 26

						BATTING															RUNNING			AVERAGES			
Year	Team	Lg	G	AB	H	2B	3B	HR	(Hm	Rd)	TB	R	RBI	RC	TBB	IBB	SO	HBP	SH	SF	SB	CS	GDP	Avg	OBP	Slg	OPS
2020	Phi	NL	44	160	54	11	0	4	(2	2)	77	24	23	33	16	0	36	2	0	2	1	1	4	.338	.400	.481	.881
2021	Phi	NL	115	380	94	15	0	7	(5	2)	130	46	47	42	31	0	111	2	0	4	4	0	12	.247	.305	.342	.647
2022	Phi	NL	152	586	164	24	3	13	(6	7)	233	79	72	67	31	1	110	4	0	10	2	3	18	.280	.315	.398	.713
3 ML YEARS			311	1126	312	50	3	24	(13	11)	440	149	142	142	78	1	257	8	0	16	7	4	34	.277	.324	.391	.715

Ronald Bolanos

Pitches: R Bats: R Pos: RP-8   boh-LAHN-yos   Ht: 6'2" Wt: 230 Born: 8/23/1996 Age: 26

Year	Team	Lg	G	GS	GF	IP	BFP	H	R	ER	HR	SH	SF	HB	TBB	IBB	SO	WP	W	L	Pct	Sv-Op	Hld	Vel	OPS	ERC	ERA
2022	Omha	AAA	28	4	7	41.2	194	59	32	29	6	0	0	4	18	0	34	7	0	4	.000	0- -	-	-	.947	7.82	6.26
2019	SD	NL	5	3	0	19.2	88	17	13	13	3	0	1	1	12	0	19	1	0	2	.000	0-0	0	94	.800	4.68	5.95
2020	KC	AL	2	2	0	3.2	21	8	7	5	2	0	0	1	3	0	2	2	0	2	.000	0-0	0	95	1.395	21.97	12.27
2021	KC	AL	3	0	0	6.1	25	4	1	1	0	0	0	0	2	0	10	0	0	0	-	0-0	0	95	.414	1.43	1.42
2022	KC	AL	8	0	4	18.1	87	20	9	9	2	0	2	3	12	1	12	1	0	0	-	0-0	0	93	.845	6.37	4.42
	4 ML YEARS		18	5	4	48.0	221	49	30	28	7	0	3	5	29	1	43	4	0	4	.000	0-0	0	94	.827	5.80	5.25

Skye Bolt

Bats: B Throws: R Pos: CF-36;RF-5;PH-5;LF-2;PR-1   Ht: 6'2" Wt: 180 Born: 1/15/1994 Age: 29

Year	Team	Lg	G	AB	H	2B	3B	HR	(Hm	Rd)	TB	R	RBI	RC	TBB	IBB	SO	HBP	SH	SF	SB	CS	GDP	Avg	OBP	Slg	OPS
2022	LsVgs	AAA	24	95	31	7	0	4	(-	-)	50	15	23	18	7	0	23	2	0	0	1	1	2	.326	.385	.526	.911
2019	Oak	AL	5	10	1	1	0	0	(0	0)	2	1	0	0	1	0	3	0	0	0	0	0	0	.100	.182	.200	.382
2021	2 Tms		34	57	5	1	0	1	(1	0)	9	5	4	0	1	0	15	0	2	0	2	0	0	.088	.103	.158	.261
2022	Oak	AL	42	106	21	2	0	4	(2	2)	35	10	13	14	7	0	30	2	0	1	5	0	1	.198	.259	.330	.589
21	SF	NL	2	1	0	0	0	0	(0	0)	0	0	0	0	0	0	1	0	0	0	0	0	0	.000	.000	.000	.000
21	Oak	AL	32	56	5	1	0	1	(1	0)	9	5	4	0	1	0	14	0	2	0	2	0	0	.089	.105	.161	.266
	3 ML YEARS		81	173	27	4	0	5	(3	2)	46	16	17	14	9	0	48	2	2	1	7	0	1	.156	.205	.266	.471

Ryan Borucki

Pitches: L Bats: L Pos: RP-32   Ht: 6'4" Wt: 210 Born: 3/31/1994 Age: 29

Year	Team	Lg	G	GS	GF	IP	BFP	H	R	ER	HR	SH	SF	HB	TBB	IBB	SO	WP	W	L	Pct	Sv-Op	Hld	Vel	OPS	ERC	ERA
2018	Tor	AL	17	17	0	97.2	415	96	48	42	7	3	2	2	33	3	67	2	4	6	.400	0-0	0	92	.705	3.58	3.87
2019	Tor	AL	2	2	0	6.2	40	15	10	8	2	0	0	0	6	0	6	0	0	1	.000	0-0	0	92	1.319	17.16	10.80
2020	Tor	AL	21	0	1	16.2	73	12	5	5	1	0	1	0	12	1	21	0	1	1	.500	0-1	3	95	.629	3.35	2.70
2021	Tor	AL	24	0	6	23.2	98	18	14	13	5	1	1	1	11	0	21	2	3	1	.750	0-1	1	95	.738	3.98	4.94
2022	2 Tms		32	0	4	25.1	111	24	16	16	6	1	0	2	11	0	21	5	2	0	1.000	0-0	6	95	.800	5.21	5.68
22	Tor	AL	11	0	2	6.1	33	7	7	7	2	1	0	1	5	0	8	0	0	0	-	0-0	2	95	.945	8.43	9.95
22	Sea	AL	21	0	2	19.0	78	17	9	9	4	0	0	1	6	0	13	5	2	0	1.000	0-0	4	95	.744	4.20	4.26
	Postseason		1	0	0	0.2	2	0	0	0	0	0	0	0	1	0	1	0	0	0	-	0-0	0	94	.000	0.00	0.00
	5 ML YEARS		96	19	11	170.0	737	165	93	84	21	5	4	5	73	4	136	9	10	9	.526	0-2	10	93	.749	4.28	4.45

David Bote

Bats: R Throws: R Pos: 2B-18;3B-16;1B-6;PH-2;DH-1;PR-1   BOH-tee   Ht: 6'1" Wt: 205 Born: 4/7/1993 Age: 30

Year	Team	Lg	G	AB	H	2B	3B	HR	(Hm	Rd)	TB	R	RBI	RC	TBB	IBB	SO	HBP	SH	SF	SB	CS	GDP	Avg	OBP	Slg	OPS
2022	Iowa	AAA	38	143	36	8	1	3	(-	-)	55	14	22	16	10	0	39	5	0	2	5	1	5	.252	.319	.385	.703
2018	ChC	NL	74	184	44	9	2	6	(5	1)	75	23	33	26	19	1	60	4	0	3	3	4	3	.239	.319	.408	.727
2019	ChC	NL	127	303	78	17	0	11	(3	8)	128	47	41	44	44	4	93	7	0	2	5	1	11	.257	.362	.422	.785
2020	ChC	NL	45	125	25	3	1	7	(1	6)	51	15	29	23	17	0	40	2	0	1	2	0	6	.200	.303	.408	.711
2021	ChC	NL	97	291	58	10	2	8	(6	2)	96	32	35	24	27	0	73	5	1	3	0	1	13	.199	.276	.330	.606
2022	ChC	NL	41	116	30	8	0	4	(0	4)	50	15	12	15	6	0	45	4	0	1	1	0	3	.259	.315	.431	.746
	Postseason		2	6	0	0	0	0	(0	0)	0	0	0	0	0	0	4	0	0	0	0	0	0	.000	.000	.000	.000
	5 ML YEARS		384	1019	235	47	5	36	(15	21)	400	132	150	132	113	5	311	22	1	10	11	6	36	.231	.318	.393	.710

Sean Bouchard

Bats: R Throws: R Pos: LF-26;PH-1   Ht: 6'3" Wt: 215 Born: 5/16/1996 Age: 27

Year	Team	Lg	G	AB	H	2B	3B	HR	(Hm	Rd)	TB	R	RBI	RC	TBB	IBB	SO	HBP	SH	SF	SB	CS	GDP	Avg	OBP	Slg	OPS
2022	Albq	AAA	69	260	78	15	6	20	(-	-)	165	61	56	71	44	0	70	4	0	4	12	2	3	.300	.404	.635	1.038
2022	Col	NL	27	74	22	6	0	3	(0	3)	37	9	11	17	21	0	25	1	0	1	0	0	1	.297	.454	.500	.954

Brad Boxberger

Pitches: R Bats: R Pos: RP-70   Ht: 5'10" Wt: 211 Born: 5/27/1988 Age: 35

Year	Team	Lg	G	GS	GF	IP	BFP	H	R	ER	HR	SH	SF	HB	TBB	IBB	SO	WP	W	L	Pct	Sv-Op	Hld	Vel	OPS	ERC	ERA
2012	SD	NL	24	0	4	27.2	120	22	12	8	3	0	1	2	18	1	33	0	0	0	-	0-0	1	92	.734	4.28	2.60
2013	SD	NL	18	0	6	22.0	94	19	9	7	3	3	2	0	13	0	24	0	0	1	.000	1-1	0	92	.760	4.43	2.86
2014	TB	AL	63	0	10	64.2	247	34	17	17	9	2	2	4	20	0	104	3	5	2	.714	2-5	18	93	.538	1.84	2.37
2015	TB	AL	69	0	53	63.0	271	54	29	26	9	2	1	2	32	5	74	5	4	10	.286	41-47	2	93	.703	4.01	3.71
2016	TB	AL	27	0	3	24.1	114	23	13	13	3	0	1	2	19	1	22	0	4	3	.571	0-3	7	92	.734	5.75	4.81
2017	TB	AL	30	0	10	29.1	121	23	11	11	4	1	1	1	11	3	40	1	4	4	.500	0-2	5	92	.665	3.03	3.38
2018	Ari	NL	60	0	45	53.1	235	44	30	26	9	2	1	1	32	4	71	3	3	7	.300	32-40	1	91	.732	4.27	4.39
2019	KC	AL	29	0	9	26.2	122	25	16	16	3	0	1	1	17	0	27	1	1	3	.250	1-4	0	90	.751	4.83	5.40
2020	Mia	NL	23	0	0	18.0	79	17	7	6	3	0	1	1	8	0	18	0	1	0	1.000	0-1	5	93	.749	4.60	3.00
2021	Mil	NL	71	0	12	64.2	266	44	26	24	8	3	2	6	25	1	83	3	5	4	.556	4-9	23	94	.618	2.79	3.34
2022	Mil	NL	70	0	9	64.0	268	52	23	21	6	3	3	2	27	1	68	0	4	3	.571	1-8	29	93	.649	3.20	2.95
	Postseason		5	0	1	5.1	19	0	0	0	0	0	0	0	3	0	4	0	1	0	1.000	0-0	0	93	.158	0.34	0.00
	11 ML YEARS		484	0	161	457.2	1937	357	193	175	60	16	16	22	222	16	564	16	31	37	.456	82-120	91	92	.675	3.55	3.44

Matthew Boyd

Pitches: L **Bats:** L **Pos:** RP-10 **Ht:** 6'3" **Wt:** 223 **Born:** 2/2/1991 **Age:** 32

			HOW MUCH PITCHED					WHAT HE GAVE UP											THE RESULTS								
Year	Team	Lg	G	GS	GF	IP	BFP	H	R	ER	HR	SH	SF	HB	TBB	IBB	SO	WP	W	L	Pct	Sv-Op	Hld	Vel	OPS	ERC	ERA
2022	Tacom	AAA	6	0	1	8.0	29	4	2	2	1	0	0	1	0	0	14	0	1	1	.500	0--	-	-	.565	1.09	2.25
2015	2 Tms	AL	13	12	0	57.1	252	71	50	48	17	1	3	1	20	0	43	4	1	6	.143	0-0	0	91	.979	7.04	7.53
2016	Det	AL	20	18	1	97.1	412	97	51	49	17	0	3	4	29	0	82	1	6	5	.545	0-0	0	91	.765	4.35	4.53
2017	Det	AL	26	25	0	135.0	605	157	84	79	18	3	6	3	53	3	110	2	6	11	.353	0-0	0	92	.826	5.28	5.27
2018	Det	AL	31	31	0	170.1	709	146	87	83	27	2	6	11	51	0	159	6	9	13	.409	0-0	0	90	.704	3.53	4.39
2019	Det	AL	32	32	0	185.1	788	178	101	94	**39**	4	4	8	50	1	238	6	9	12	.429	0-0	0	92	.766	4.18	4.56
2020	Det	AL	12	12	0	60.1	271	67	46	**45**	**15**	1	2	5	22	0	60	5	3	**7**	.300	0-0	0	92	.900	5.99	6.71
2021	Det	AL	15	15	0	78.2	337	77	37	34	9	1	4	7	23	0	67	4	3	8	.273	0-0	0	92	.716	3.97	3.89
2022	Sea	AL	10	0	1	13.1	53	5	2	2	0	1	0	1	8	3	13	0	2	0	1.000	0-0	1	92	.386	1.20	1.35
15	Tor	AL	2	2	0	6.2	36	15	11	11	5	0	1	0	1	0	7	2	0	2	.000	0-0	0	91	1.327	17.16	14.85
15	Det	AL	11	10	0	50.2	216	56	39	37	12	1	2	1	19	0	36	2	1	4	.200	0-0	0	91	.918	5.88	6.57
8 ML YEARS			159	145	2	797.2	3427	798	458	434	142	13	28	40	256	7	772	28	39	62	.386	0-0	1	91	.780	4.48	4.90

Silvino Bracho

Pitches: R **Bats:** R **Pos:** RP-3 BRAH-cho **Ht:** 5'10" **Wt:** 190 **Born:** 7/17/1992 **Age:** 30

			HOW MUCH PITCHED					WHAT HE GAVE UP											THE RESULTS								
Year	Team	Lg	G	GS	GF	IP	BFP	H	R	ER	HR	SH	SF	HB	TBB	IBB	SO	WP	W	L	Pct	Sv-Op	Hld	Vel	OPS	ERC	ERA
2022	Wrcstr	AAA	18	1	2	31.1	123	29	12	11	2	0	1	2	4	0	36	1	0	3	.000	0--	-	-	.698	2.76	3.16
2022	Gwnntt	AAA	20	4	0	26.0	107	21	6	6	2	0	1	2	6	0	34	0	2	1	.667	0--	-	-	.628	2.52	2.08
2015	Ari	NL	13	0	3	12.1	50	9	2	2	2	0	0	1	4	1	17	1	0	0	-	1-1	0	93	.680	2.95	1.46
2016	Ari	NL	26	0	11	24.2	119	31	22	20	7	0	1	3	10	1	17	3	0	2	.000	0-0	0	93	.951	7.32	7.30
2017	Ari	NL	21	0	10	20.2	87	18	14	13	5	0	0	0	7	0	25	1	0	0	-	0-0	0	94	.725	3.98	5.66
2018	Ari	NL	31	0	7	31.0	129	25	12	11	2	1	1	3	12	2	34	2	2	0	1.000	0-4	2	93	.670	3.05	3.19
2020	Ari	NL	1	0	0	1.0	5	2	2	2	1	0	0	0	0	0	1	0	0	0	-	0-0	0	92	1.400	16.28	18.00
2022	Atl	NL	3	0	2	4.1	18	3	3	3	2	0	0	1	1	0	4	0	0	0	-	0-0	0	94	.840	4.84	6.23
6 ML YEARS			95	0	33	94.0	408	88	55	51	19	1	2	8	34	4	98	7	2	2	.500	1-5	2	93	.782	4.50	4.88

Kyle Bradish

Pitches: R **Bats:** R **Pos:** SP-23 **Ht:** 6'4" **Wt:** 220 **Born:** 9/12/1996 **Age:** 26

			HOW MUCH PITCHED					WHAT HE GAVE UP											THE RESULTS								
Year	Team	Lg	G	GS	GF	IP	BFP	H	R	ER	HR	SH	SF	HB	TBB	IBB	SO	WP	W	L	Pct	Sv-Op	Hld	Vel	OPS	ERC	ERA
2022	Bal	AL	23	23	0	117.2	509	119	68	64	17	2	4	7	46	0	111	7	4	7	.364	0-0	0	95	.759	4.72	4.90

Archie Bradley

Pitches: R **Bats:** R **Pos:** RP-21 **Ht:** 6'4" **Wt:** 215 **Born:** 8/10/1992 **Age:** 30

			HOW MUCH PITCHED					WHAT HE GAVE UP											THE RESULTS								
Year	Team	Lg	G	GS	GF	IP	BFP	H	R	ER	HR	SH	SF	HB	TBB	IBB	SO	WP	W	L	Pct	Sv-Op	Hld	Vel	OPS	ERC	ERA
2015	Ari	NL	8	8	0	35.2	161	36	23	23	3	1	1	2	22	1	23	0	2	3	.400	0-0	0	92	.768	5.12	5.80
2016	Ari	NL	26	26	0	141.2	638	154	84	79	16	2	7	4	67	**8**	143	7	8	9	.471	0-0	0	92	.802	4.96	5.02
2017	Ari	NL	63	0	13	73.0	290	55	14	14	4	1	1	1	21	2	79	0	3	3	.500	1-7	25	96	.567	2.14	1.73
2018	Ari	NL	76	0	8	71.2	296	62	30	29	9	1	0	4	20	1	75	2	4	5	.444	3-11	**34**	96	.672	3.24	3.64
2019	Ari	NL	66	1	32	71.2	317	67	30	28	5	2	2	5	36	2	87	0	4	5	.444	18-21	7	96	.714	4.10	3.52
2020	2 Tms	NL	16	0	10	18.1	73	17	6	6	1	0	0	1	3	0	18	0	2	0	1.000	6-7	2	94	.635	2.78	2.95
2021	Phi	NL	53	0	11	51.0	224	51	24	21	5	0	1	3	22	1	40	1	7	3	.700	2-5	13	94	.743	4.39	3.71
2022	LAA	AL	21	0	6	18.2	78	17	13	10	1	0	0	0	7	1	15	1	0	1	.000	2-4	4	93	.632	3.12	4.82
20	Ari	NL	10	0	9	10.2	45	13	5	5	0	0	0	1	3	0	12	0	1	0	1.000	6-7	0	94	.792	4.78	4.22
20	Cin	NL	6	0	1	7.2	28	4	1	1	1	0	0	0	0	0	6	0	1	0	1.000	0-0	2	94	.393	0.87	1.17
Postseason			4	0	1	6.1	31	8	4	3	2	0	0	0	3	0	5	0	0	1	.000	0-0	1	96	.891	7.26	4.26
8 ML YEARS			329	35	80	481.2	2077	459	224	210	44	7	12	20	198	16	480	11	30	29	.508	32-55	85	94	.715	3.91	3.92

Bobby Bradley

Bats: L **Throws:** R **Pos:** 1B-7;PH-2 **Ht:** 6'1" **Wt:** 225 **Born:** 5/29/1996 **Age:** 27

			BATTING																		RUNNING			AVERAGES			
Year	Team	Lg	G	AB	H	2B	3B	HR	(Hm	Rd)	TB	R	RBI	RC	TBB	IBB	SO	HBP	SH	SF	SB	CS	GDP	Avg	OBP	Slg	OPS
2022	Clmbs	AAA	47	167	29	10	0	7	(-	-)	60	24	30	19	19	0	74	5	0	7	0	1	0	.174	.268	.359	.627
2019	Cle	AL	15	45	8	5	0	1	(1	0)	16	4	4	1	4	0	20	0	0	0	0	0	2	.178	.245	.356	.600
2021	Cle	AL	74	245	51	10	0	16	(10	6)	109	36	41	36	25	1	99	6	0	3	0	0	3	.208	.294	.445	.739
2022	Cle	AL	8	17	2	0	0	0	(0	0)	2	1	0	0	0	0	9	0	0	0	0	0	0	.118	.118	.118	.235
3 ML YEARS			97	307	61	15	0	17	(11	6)	127	41	45	37	29	1	128	6	0	3	0	0	5	.199	.278	.414	.692

Jackie Bradley Jr.

Bats: L **Throws:** R **Pos:** RF-91;CF-55;PH-3;PR-1 **Ht:** 5'10" **Wt:** 196 **Born:** 4/19/1990 **Age:** 33

			BATTING																		RUNNING			AVERAGES			
Year	Team	Lg	G	AB	H	2B	3B	HR	(Hm	Rd)	TB	R	RBI	RC	TBB	IBB	SO	HBP	SH	SF	SB	CS	GDP	Avg	OBP	Slg	OPS
2013	Bos	AL	37	95	18	5	0	3	(2	1)	32	18	10	8	10	0	31	2	0	0	2	0	1	.189	.280	.337	.617
2014	Bos	AL	127	384	76	19	2	1	(1	0)	102	45	30	27	31	1	121	5	1	2	8	0	10	.198	.265	.266	.531
2015	Bos	AL	74	221	55	17	4	10	(5	5)	110	43	43	41	27	0	69	3	1	3	3	0	5	.249	.335	.498	.832
2016	Bos	AL	156	558	149	30	7	26	(12	14)	271	94	87	86	63	5	143	10	0	5	9	2	10	.267	.349	.486	.835
2017	Bos	AL	133	482	118	19	3	17	(6	11)	194	58	63	70	48	4	124	9	0	2	8	3	8	.245	.323	.402	.726
2018	Bos	AL	144	474	111	33	4	13	(4	9)	191	76	59	67	46	3	137	11	0	4	17	1	6	.234	.314	.403	.717
2019	Bos	AL	147	494	111	28	3	21	(10	11)	208	69	62	61	56	3	155	12	3	2	8	6	6	.225	.317	.421	.738
2020	Bos	AL	55	191	54	11	0	7	(3	4)	86	32	22	28	23	1	48	2	0	1	5	2	2	.283	.364	.450	.814

Year	Team	Lg	G	AB	H	2B	3B	HR	(Hm	Rd)	TB	R	RBI	RC	TBB	IBB	SO	HBP	SH	SF	SB	CS	GDP	Avg	OBP	Slg	OPS
2021	Mil	NL	134	387	63	14	3	6	(3	3)	101	39	29	18	28	0	132	10	0	3	7	1	8	.163	.236	.261	.497
2022	2 Tms	AL	132	344	70	23	1	4	(3	1)	107	30	38	29	24	0	77	0	2	0	2	3	5	.203	.255	.311	.566
22	Bos	AL	92	271	57	19	1	3	(3	0)	87	21	29	24	17	0	58	0	2	0	2	3	3	.210	.257	.321	.578
22	Tor	AL	40	73	13	4	0	1	(0	1)	20	9	9	5	7	0	19	0	0	0	0	0	2	.178	.250	.274	.524
	Postseason		22	65	12	2	0	4	(1	3)	26	7	15	12	9	0	22	2	0	0	1	2	2	.185	.303	.400	.703
	10 ML YEARS		1139	3630	825	199	27	108	(49	59)	1402	504	443	435	356	17	1037	64	7	22	69	18	61	.227	.306	.386	.692

Michael Brantley

Bats: L **Throws:** L **Pos:** DH-35;LF-29   **Ht:** 6'2" **Wt:** 209 **Born:** 5/15/1987 **Age:** 36

Year	Team	Lg	G	AB	H	2B	3B	HR	(Hm	Rd)	TB	R	RBI	RC	TBB	IBB	SO	HBP	SH	SF	SB	CS	GDP	Avg	OBP	Slg	OPS
2009	Cle	AL	28	112	35	4	0	0	(0	0)	39	10	11	16	8	0	19	0	1	0	4	4	3	.313	.358	.348	.707
2010	Cle	AL	72	297	73	9	3	3	(2	1)	97	38	22	32	22	0	38	0	4	2	10	2	6	.246	.296	.327	.623
2011	Cle	AL	114	451	120	24	4	7	(4	3)	173	63	46	56	34	2	76	3	3	5	13	5	11	.266	.318	.384	.702
2012	Cle	AL	149	552	159	37	4	6	(3	3)	222	63	60	76	53	12	56	0	4	6	12	9	7	.288	.348	.402	.750
2013	Cle	AL	151	556	158	26	3	10	(9	1)	220	66	73	86	40	1	67	4	3	8	17	4	11	.284	.332	.396	.728
2014	Cle	AL	156	611	200	45	2	20	(11	9)	309	94	97	114	52	4	56	8	0	5	23	1	16	.327	.385	.506	.890
2015	Cle	AL	137	529	164	45	0	15	(9	6)	254	68	84	94	60	8	51	2	0	5	15	1	14	.310	.379	.480	.859
2016	Cle	AL	11	39	9	2	0	0	(0	0)	11	5	7	5	3	1	6	0	0	1	1	0	1	.231	.279	.282	.561
2017	Cle	AL	90	338	101	20	1	9	(6	3)	150	47	52	51	31	3	50	2	0	4	11	1	8	.299	.357	.444	.801
2018	Cle	AL	143	570	176	36	2	17	(9	8)	267	89	76	86	48	0	60	5	1	6	12	3	15	.309	.364	.468	.832
2019	Hou	AL	148	575	179	40	2	22	(12	10)	289	88	90	103	51	3	66	7	0	4	3	2	21	.311	.372	.503	.875
2020	Hou	AL	46	170	51	15	0	5	(3	2)	81	24	22	35	17	0	28	0	0	0	2	0	3	.300	.364	.476	.840
2021	Hou	AL	121	469	146	29	3	8	(2	6)	205	68	47	71	33	1	53	5	0	1	1	0	11	.311	.362	.437	.799
2022	Hou	AL	64	243	70	14	1	5	(3	2)	101	28	26	37	31	2	30	1	1	1	1	1	1	.288	.370	.416	.785
	Postseason		54	216	64	6	0	4	(4	0)	82	21	25	31	20	2	40	1	1	1	3	0	6	.296	.357	.380	.737
	14 ML YEARS		1430	5512	1641	346	25	127	(73	54)	2418	751	713	862	483	37	656	37	13	46	125	33	128	.298	.356	.439	.794

Rob Brantly

Bats: L **Throws:** R **Pos:** C-1   **Ht:** 6'0" **Wt:** 191 **Born:** 7/14/1989 **Age:** 33

Year	Team	Lg	G	AB	H	2B	3B	HR	(Hm	Rd)	TB	R	RBI	RC	TBB	IBB	SO	HBP	SH	SF	SB	CS	GDP	Avg	OBP	Slg	OPS
2022	S-WB	AAA	59	182	49	10	1	1	(-	-)	64	18	22	18	11	0	32	7	0	1	1	0	5	.269	.333	.352	.685
2012	Mia	NL	31	100	29	8	0	3	(1	2)	46	14	8	14	13	2	16	0	0	0	1	1	1	.290	.372	.460	.832
2013	Mia	NL	67	223	47	9	0	1	(1	0)	59	11	18	14	15	1	53	2	0	3	0	0	8	.211	.263	.265	.528
2015	CWS	AL	14	33	4	1	0	1	(1	0)	8	3	6	1	2	0	8	0	0	1	0	0	0	.121	.167	.242	.409
2017	CWS	AL	14	31	9	1	0	2	(1	1)	16	4	5	7	3	0	14	2	0	0	0	0	0	.290	.389	.516	.905
2019	Phi	NL	1	1	0	0	0	0	(0	0)	0	0	0	0	0	0	1	0	0	0	0	0	0	.000	.000	.000	.000
2020	SF	NL	1	3	0	0	0	0	(0	0)	0	0	0	0	0	0	0	0	0	0	0	0	0	.000	.000	.000	.000
2021	NYY	AL	6	20	3	1	0	0	(0	0)	4	0	0	0	0	0	4	1	0	0	0	0	0	.150	.190	.200	.390
2022	NYY	AL	1	3	1	1	0	0	(0	0)	2	0	0	1	0	0	0	0	0	0	0	0	0	.333	.333	.667	1.000
	8 ML YEARS		135	414	93	21	0	7	(4	3)	135	32	37	37	33	3	96	5	0	4	1	1	10	.225	.287	.326	.613

Matt Brash

Pitches: R **Bats:** R **Pos:** RP-34; SP-5   **Ht:** 6'1" **Wt:** 173 **Born:** 5/12/1998 **Age:** 25

			HOW MUCH PITCHED					WHAT HE GAVE UP											THE RESULTS							
Year	Team	Lg	G	GS	GF	IP	BFP	H	R	ER	HR	SH	SF	HB	TBB	IBB	SO	WP	W	L	Pct	Sv-Op	Hld	Vel	OPS	ERC	ERA
2019	2 Tms	Low	5	1	1	5.1	20	4	1	1	0	0	0	0	0	0	8	0	0	0	-	0- -	-	-	1.000	1.13	1.69
2021	Ark	AA	10	10	0	55.0	222	32	15	13	3	0	0	0	23	0	80	2	3	2	.600	0- -	-	-	.486	1.71	2.13
2021	Everett	A+	10	9	1	42.1	183	31	16	12	3	0	0	4	25	0	62	0	3	2	.600	1- -	-	-	.350	2.55
2022	Tacom	AAA	22	0	10	26.0	107	19	14	10	4	1	0	0	14	0	41	3	0	1	.000	3- -	-	-	.692	3.59	3.46
2022	Sea	AL	39	5	3	50.2	222	46	25	25	3	1	0	2	33	1	62	3	4	4	.500	0-0	9	97	.694	4.48	4.44

Ryan Brasier

Pitches: R **Bats:** R **Pos:** RP-68   BRAY-zhur   **Ht:** 6'0" **Wt:** 227 **Born:** 8/26/1987 **Age:** 35

			HOW MUCH PITCHED					WHAT HE GAVE UP											THE RESULTS							
Year	Team	Lg	G	GS	GF	IP	BFP	H	R	ER	HR	SH	SF	HB	TBB	IBB	SO	WP	W	L	Pct	Sv-Op	Hld	Vel	OPS	ERC	ERA
2013	LAA	AL	7	0	7	9.0	35	7	2	2	1	0	1	0	4	0	7	0	0	0	-	0-0	0	94	.648	3.37	2.00
2018	Bos	AL	34	0	5	33.2	124	19	6	6	2	1	5	0	7	0	29	1	2	0	1.000	0-2	10	97	.482	1.26	1.60
2019	Bos	AL	62	0	15	55.2	241	51	33	30	9	0	3	3	21	1	61	3	4	4	.333	7-11	9	96	.722	4.06	4.85
2020	Bos	AL	25	1	1	25.0	110	24	12	11	2	0	1	0	11	1	30	1	1	0	1.000	0-2	10	96	.696	3.71	3.96
2021	Bos	AL	13	0	2	12.0	50	12	5	2	2	0	1	0	4	0	9	0	1	1	.500	0-0	3	95	.742	4.37	1.50
2022	Bos	AL	68	0	11	62.1	263	68	43	40	9	0	6	1	13	1	64	1	0	3	.000	1-4	13	96	.793	4.18	5.78
	Postseason		16	0	1	12.2	58	15	5	5	0	0	1	1	5	0	12	1	0	0	-	0-1	8	96	.735	4.61	3.55
	6 ML YEARS		209	1	41	197.2	823	181	101	91	25	1	17	4	60	3	200	6	6	8	.429	8-19	45	96	.704	3.47	4.14

Steven Brault

Pitches: L **Bats:** L **Pos:** RP-9   **Ht:** 6'0" **Wt:** 195 **Born:** 4/29/1992 **Age:** 31

			HOW MUCH PITCHED					WHAT HE GAVE UP											THE RESULTS							
Year	Team	Lg	G	GS	GF	IP	BFP	H	R	ER	HR	SH	SF	HB	TBB	IBB	SO	WP	W	L	Pct	Sv-Op	Hld	Vel	OPS	ERC	ERA
2022	Iowa	AAA	7	0	1	6.0	36	11	8	8	1	0	0	3	5	0	6	1	2	0	1.000	0- -	-	-	1.135	14.65	12.00
2016	Pit	NL	8	7	0	33.1	166	45	26	18	5	3	0	2	17	1	29	1	0	3	.000	0-0	0	91	.893	6.99	4.86
2017	Pit	NL	11	4	2	34.2	162	41	21	18	3	2	1	2	14	1	23	0	1	0	1.000	1-1	0	92	.790	5.06	4.67
2018	Pit	NL	45	5	6	91.2	413	84	51	47	10	3	1	8	57	4	82	9	6	3	.667	0-0	3	93	.747	4.84	4.61
2019	Pit	NL	25	19	1	113.1	505	117	69	65	15	0	7	5	53	2	100	7	4	6	.400	0-0	0	92	.791	5.00	5.16

Year	Team	Lg	HOW MUCH PITCHED					WHAT HE GAVE UP											THE RESULTS							
			G	GS	GF	IP	BFP	H	R	ER	HR	SH	SF	HB	TBB	IBB	SO	WP	W	L	Pct	Sv-Op	Hld	Vel	OPS	ERC	ERA
2020	Pit	NL	11	10	0	42.2	178	29	17	16	2	0	2	5	22	0	38	3	1	3	.250	0-0	0	92	.563	2.92	3.38
2021	Pit	NL	7	7	0	27.2	127	33	18	18	3	1	0	1	12	2	19	0	0	3	.000	0-0	0	91	.870	5.37	5.86
2022	ChC	NL	9	0	1	9.0	39	8	4	3	0	0	0	1	5	0	8	1	0	0	-	0-1	1	91	.753	3.85	3.00
7 ML YEARS			116	52	10	352.1	1590	357	206	185	38	12	4	26	180	10	299	21	12	18	.400	1-2	4	92	.771	4.88	4.73

Huascar Brazoban

Pitches: R Bats: R Pos: RP-27   Ht: 6'3" Wt: 155 Born: 10/15/1989 Age: 33

Year	Team	Lg	HOW MUCH PITCHED					WHAT HE GAVE UP											THE RESULTS							
			G	GS	GF	IP	BFP	H	R	ER	HR	SH	SF	HB	TBB	IBB	SO	WP	W	L	Pct	Sv-Op	Hld	Vel	OPS	ERC	ERA
2022	Jaxnvl	AAA	27	0	8	45.1	181	32	16	16	6	0	2	1	16	0	59	6	2	0	1.000	0--	-	-	.623	2.66	3.18
2022	Mia	NL	27	0	2	32.0	141	26	13	11	3	1	0	2	21	1	40	7	1	1	.500	0-1	4	97	.700	4.20	3.09

John Brebbia

Pitches: R Bats: L Pos: RP-65; SP-11   Ht: 6'1" Wt: 200 Born: 5/30/1990 Age: 33

Year	Team	Lg	HOW MUCH PITCHED					WHAT HE GAVE UP											THE RESULTS							
			G	GS	GF	IP	BFP	H	R	ER	HR	SH	SF	HB	TBB	IBB	SO	WP	W	L	Pct	Sv-Op	Hld	Vel	OPS	ERC	ERA
2017	StL	NL	50	0	13	51.2	209	37	15	14	8	1	0	5	11	3	51	2	0	1		0-1	5	94	.264	2.45	2.44
2018	StL	NL	45	0	17	50.2	209	43	18	18	5	1	2	0	16	2	60	1	3	3	.500	2-2	5	95	.647	2.85	3.20
2019	StL	NL	66	0	22	72.2	304	59	31	29	6	0	1	3	27	2	87	0	3	4	.429	0-1	12	93	.626	2.93	3.59
2021	SF	NL	18	0	6	18.1	87	25	13	12	4	1	1	2	4	2	22	0	0	1	1.000	0-0	1	93	.917	6.43	5.89
2022	SF	NL	76	11	4	68.0	288	71	27	24	5	2	2	1	18	2	54	0	6	2	.750	0-4	18	94	.737	3.62	3.18
Postseason			5	0	0	3.0	17	7	2	2	1	0	0	0	1	0	3	0	0	0	-	0-0	0	93	1.408	14.72	6.00
5 ML YEARS			255	11	62	261.1	1097	235	104	97	28	5	6	11	76	11	274	3	12	10	.545	2-8	41	94	.685	3.22	3.34

Alex Bregman

Bats: R Throws: R Pos: 3B-154;PH-1   Ht: 6'0" Wt: 192 Born: 3/30/1994 Age: 29

Year	Team	Lg	BATTING																				RUNNING			AVERAGES			
			G	AB	H	2B	3B	HR	(Hm	Rd)	TB	R	RBI	RC	TBB	IBB	SO	HBP	SH	SF	SB	CS	GDP	Avg	OBP	Slg	OPS
2016	Hou	AL	49	201	53	13	3	8	(3	5)	96	31	34	37	15	0	52	0	0	1	2	0	1	.264	.313	.478	.791
2017	Hou	AL	155	556	158	39	5	19	(9	10)	264	88	71	87	55	2	97	7	1	7	17	5	15	.284	.352	.475	.827
2018	Hou	AL	157	594	170	51	1	31	(16	15)	316	105	103	135	96	2	85	12	0	3	10	4	15	.286	.394	.532	.926
2019	Hou	AL	156	554	164	37	2	41	(16	25)	328	122	112	126	119	2	83	9	0	8	5	1	9	.296	.423	.592	1.015
2020	Hou	AL	42	153	37	12	1	6	(2	4)	69	19	22	28	24	1	26	2	0	1	0	0	2	.242	.350	.451	.801
2021	Hou	AL	91	348	94	17	0	12	(5	7)	147	54	55	56	44	4	53	4	0	4	1	0	13	.270	.355	.422	.777
2022	Hou	AL	155	548	142	38	0	23	(16	7)	249	93	93	95	87	1	77	11	0	10	1	2	18	.259	.366	.454	.820
Postseason			73	270	61	11	0	12	(7	5)	108	46	36	32	40	4	48	7	0	2	2	1	8	.226	.339	.400	.739
7 ML YEARS			805	2954	818	207	12	140	(67	73)	1469	512	490	564	440	12	473	45	1	34	36	12	73	.277	.375	.497	.872

Will Brennan

Bats: L Throws: L Pos: LF-5;RF-4;CF-1;DH-1;PH-1   Ht: 6'0" Wt: 200 Born: 2/2/1998 Age: 25

Year	Team	Lg	BATTING																				RUNNING			AVERAGES			
			G	AB	H	2B	3B	HR	(Hm	Rd)	TB	R	RBI	RC	TBB	IBB	SO	HBP	SH	SF	SB	CS	GDP	Avg	OBP	Slg	OPS
2022	Akron	AA	36	135	42	12	1	4	(-	-)	68	16	39	26	17	0	16	1	0	4	5	2	1	.311	.382	.504	.886
2022	Clmbs	AAA	93	393	124	28	3	9	(-	-)	185	53	68	66	33	0	53	2	0	5	15	1	8	.316	.367	.471	.838
2022	Cle	AL	11	42	15	1	1	1	(1	0)	21	6	8	10	2	1	4	1	0	0	2	1	0	.357	.400	.500	.900

Jake Brentz

Pitches: L Bats: L Pos: RP-8   Ht: 6'1" Wt: 205 Born: 9/14/1994 Age: 28

Year	Team	Lg	HOW MUCH PITCHED					WHAT HE GAVE UP											THE RESULTS							
			G	GS	GF	IP	BFP	H	R	ER	HR	SH	SF	HB	TBB	IBB	SO	WP	W	L	Pct	Sv-Op	Hld	Vel	OPS	ERC	ERA
2021	KC	AL	72	0	10	64.0	278	45	32	26	7	2	3	6	37	1	76	8	5	2	.714	2-7	15	97	.665	3.49	3.66
2022	KC	AL	8	0	1	5.1	38	11	15	14	1	1	0	1	10	0	9	2	0	3	.000	0-0	2	96	1.210	19.85	23.63
2 ML YEARS			80	0	11	69.1	316	56	47	40	8	3	3	7	47	1	85	10	5	5	.500	2-7	17	97	.725	4.49	5.19

Austin Brice

Pitches: R Bats: R Pos: RP-4   Ht: 6'4" Wt: 238 Born: 6/19/1992 Age: 31

Year	Team	Lg	HOW MUCH PITCHED					WHAT HE GAVE UP											THE RESULTS							
			G	GS	GF	IP	BFP	H	R	ER	HR	SH	SF	HB	TBB	IBB	SO	WP	W	L	Pct	Sv-Op	Hld	Vel	OPS	ERC	ERA
2022	Indy	AAA	37	2	15	43.2	199	42	32	27	7	0	3	6	18	4	53	3	3	4	.429	6--	-	-	.779	4.58	5.56
2016	Mia	NL	15	0	2	14.0	59	9	12	11	2	0	0	2	5	1	14	0	0	1	.000	0-0	1	94	.598	2.63	7.07
2017	Cin	NL	22	0	4	32.2	137	33	18	18	6	1	1	3	7	0	26	0	0	0	-	0-0	1	94	.756	4.38	4.96
2018	Cin	NL	33	0	8	37.1	162	39	26	24	9	1	1	3	13	6	32	1	2	3	.400	0-0	3	94	.876	5.26	5.79
2019	Mia	NL	36	0	10	44.2	199	37	21	17	7	0	1	7	18	2	46	2	1	0	1.000	0-1	6	93	.676	3.92	3.43
2020	Bos	AL	21	1	2	19.2	87	17	13	13	3	0	0	2	13	0	25	1	1	0	1.000	0-0	4	93	.826	5.28	5.95
2021	Bos	AL	13	0	4	13.2	64	14	10	10	2	0	0	4	7	0	12	0	0	0	-	0-0	0	93	.843	6.30	6.59
2022	Pit	NL	4	0	2	6.2	27	4	3	3	0	0	0	0	3	0	5	0	0	0	-	0-0	0	94	.509	1.61	4.05
7 ML YEARS			144	1	32	168.2	735	153	103	96	29	2	3	21	66	9	160	4	4	4	.500	0-1	15	94	.755	4.41	5.12

Jonah Bride

Bats: R Throws: R Pos: 2B-32;3B-21;PH-8;1B-5;DH-2   Ht: 5'10" Wt: 200 Born: 12/27/1995 Age: 27

Year	Team	Lg	G	AB	H	2B	3B	HR	(Hm	Rd)	TB	R	RBI	RC	TBB	IBB	SO	HBP	SH	SF	SB	CS	GDP	Avg	OBP	Slg	OPS
2022	Mdlnd	AA	19	73	23	9	0	4	(-	-)	44	18	22	16	11	0	11	1	0	2	0	0	4	.315	.402	.603	1.005
2022	LsVgs	AAA	18	61	24	6	0	2	(-	-)	36	14	10	16	13	0	12	4	0	0	0	0	3	.393	.526	.590	1.116
2022	Oak	AL	58	162	33	4	0	1	(1	0)	40	17	6	7	19	0	32	4	1	1	1	0	4	.204	.301	.247	.548

Beau Brieske

Pitches: R Bats: R Pos: SP-15   bris-KEE   Ht: 6'3" Wt: 200 Born: 4/5/1998 Age: 25

			HOW MUCH PITCHED				WHAT HE GAVE UP									THE RESULTS							
Year	Team	Lg	G	GS	GF	IP	BFP	H	R	ER	HR	SH	SF	HB	TBB	IBB	SO	WP	W	L	Pct	Sv-Op	Hld	Vel	OPS	ERC	ERA
2022	Det	AL	15	15	0	81.2	339	73	39	38	14	1	3	1	25	0	54	2	3	6	.333	0-0	0	94	.704	3.63	4.19

Jeff Brigham

Pitches: R Bats: R Pos: RP-16   Ht: 6'0" Wt: 195 Born: 2/16/1992 Age: 31

			HOW MUCH PITCHED				WHAT HE GAVE UP									THE RESULTS							
Year	Team	Lg	G	GS	GF	IP	BFP	H	R	ER	HR	SH	SF	HB	TBB	IBB	SO	WP	W	L	Pct	Sv-Op	Hld	Vel	OPS	ERC	ERA
2022	Jaxnvl	AAA	30	1	9	43.0	183	35	21	19	8	0	2	2	21	0	69	1	3	3	.500	1--	-	-	.747	4.18	3.98
2018	Mia	NL	4	4	0	16.1	77	16	11	11	2	0	3	2	13	0	12	0	0	4	.000	0-0	0	93	.860	6.35	6.06
2019	Mia	NL	32	0	10	38.1	161	36	20	19	8	0	1	1	14	2	39	6	3	2	.600	1-2	4	97	.765	4.43	4.46
2020	Mia	NL	1	0	0	1.0	5	2	1	1	0	0	0	0	0	0	0	0	0	0	-	0-0	0	94	1.000	7.48	9.00
2022	Mia	NL	16	0	2	24.0	101	22	10	9	3	1	0	0	10	0	28	1	0	1	.000	1-1	2	95	.731	3.90	3.38
	4 ML YEARS		53	4	12	79.2	344	76	42	40	13	1	4	3	37	2	79	7	3	7	.300	2-3	6	95	.780	4.69	4.52

Lewis Brinson

Bats: R Throws: R Pos: CF-15;PH-6;LF-1   Ht: 6'5" Wt: 212 Born: 5/8/1994 Age: 29

Year	Team	Lg	G	AB	H	2B	3B	HR	(Hm	Rd)	TB	R	RBI	RC	TBB	IBB	SO	HBP	SH	SF	SB	CS	GDP	Avg	OBP	Slg	OPS
2022	SgrLnd	AAA	85	331	99	21	2	22	(-	-)	190	61	63	69	26	0	102	4	2	1	5	3	8	.299	.356	.574	.930
2017	Mil	NL	21	47	5	0	1	2	(0	2)	13	2	3	4	7	1	17	1	0	1	1	0	0	.106	.236	.277	.513
2018	Mia	NL	109	382	76	10	5	11	(2	9)	129	31	42	29	17	2	120	4	0	2	2	1	6	.199	.240	.338	.577
2019	Mia	NL	75	226	39	9	1	0	(0	0)	50	15	15	10	13	1	74	6	2	1	1	1	8	.173	.236	.221	.457
2020	Mia	NL	47	106	24	6	0	3	(2	1)	39	14	12	12	6	0	30	0	0	4	0	2	2	.226	.268	.368	.636
2021	Mia	NL	89	274	62	14	0	9	(5	4)	103	24	33	23	13	0	72	1	1	1	1	1	5	.226	.263	.376	.639
2022	SF	NL	16	36	6	2	0	3	(0	3)	17	5	4	5	2	0	14	0	1	0	1	0	0	.167	.211	.472	.683
	Postseason		5	6	0	0	0	0	(0	0)	0	1	0	0	0	0	2	0	0	0	0	0	0	.000	.000	.000	.000
	6 ML YEARS		357	1071	212	41	7	28	(9	19)	351	91	109	83	58	4	327	12	4	4	10	3	21	.198	.246	.328	.574

Zack Britton

Pitches: L Bats: L Pos: RP-3   Ht: 6'1" Wt: 200 Born: 12/22/1987 Age: 35

			HOW MUCH PITCHED				WHAT HE GAVE UP									THE RESULTS							
Year	Team	Lg	G	GS	GF	IP	BFP	H	R	ER	HR	SH	SF	HB	TBB	IBB	SO	WP	W	L	Pct	Sv-Op	Hld	Vel	OPS	ERC	ERA
2011	Bal	AL	28	28	0	154.1	666	162	93	79	12	8	7	1	62	3	97	7	11	11	.500	0-0	0	92	.735	4.24	4.61
2012	Bal	AL	12	11	0	60.1	270	61	37	34	6	0	1	2	32	3	53	4	5	3	.625	0-0	0	92	.756	4.70	5.07
2013	Bal	AL	8	7	0	40.0	182	52	23	22	4	1	1	1	17	1	18	1	2	3	.400	0-0	0	92	.837	6.14	4.95
2014	Bal	AL	71	0	49	76.1	285	46	17	14	4	3	0	1	23	0	62	0	3	2	.600	37-41	7	95	.500	1.62	1.65
2015	Bal	AL	64	0	58	65.2	253	51	16	14	3	0	0	1	14	1	79	5	4	1	.800	36-40	0	96	.547	2.02	1.92
2016	Bal	AL	69	0	63	67.0	254	38	7	4	1	1	0	0	18	3	74	10	2	1	.667	47-47	0	96	.430	1.18	0.54
2017	Bal	AL	38	0	30	37.1	161	39	12	12	1	1	1	0	18	1	29	4	2	1	.667	15-17	0	96	.690	4.18	2.89
2018	2 Tms	AL	41	0	21	40.2	169	26	14	14	3	0	1	3	21	0	34	7	2	0	1.000	7-10	9	95	.605	3.13	3.10
2019	NYY	AL	66	0	15	61.1	245	38	13	13	3	1	2	1	32	1	53	3	3	1	.750	3-7	29	95	.545	2.32	1.91
2020	NYY	AL	20	0	10	19.0	76	12	6	4	0	0	0	0	7	0	16	4	1	2	.333	8-8	3	95	.482	1.54	1.89
2021	NYY	AL	22	0	4	18.1	82	17	14	12	2	0	1	2	14	0	16	2	1	0	1.000	1-4	11	93	.564	5.93	5.89
2022	NYY	AL	3	0	0	0.2	9	1	1	1	0	0	0	0	6	0	1	1	0	0	-	0-0	2	93	1.111	46.45	13.50
18	Bal	AL	16	0	11	15.2	63	11	6	6	1	0	0	1	10	0	13	2	1	0	1.000	4-5	1	94	.676	3.63	3.45
18	NYY	AL	25	0	10	25.0	106	18	10	8	2	0	1	2	11	0	21	5	1	0	1.000	3-5	8	95	.564	2.84	2.88
	Postseason		21	0	4	23.0	99	13	8	8	3	1	1	0	17	3	22	2	0	0	-	2-2	7	95	.631	2.96	3.13
	12 ML YEARS		442	46	250	641.0	2652	546	255	223	39	15	14	12	264	13	532	48	35	26	.574	154-174	61	94	.638	3.15	3.13

Connor Brogdon

Pitches: R Bats: R Pos: RP-47   Ht: 6'6" Wt: 205 Born: 1/29/1995 Age: 28

			HOW MUCH PITCHED				WHAT HE GAVE UP									THE RESULTS							
Year	Team	Lg	G	GS	GF	IP	BFP	H	R	ER	HR	SH	SF	HB	TBB	IBB	SO	WP	W	L	Pct	Sv-Op	Hld	Vel	OPS	ERC	ERA
2022	LV	AAA	10	1	3	9.1	43	8	3	3	0	0	1	1	6	0	17	2	0	1	.000	2--	-	-	.663	3.76	2.89
2020	Phi	NL	9	0	3	11.1	44	5	5	5	3	0	0	0	5	1	17	0	1	0	1.000	0-0	0	95	.612	2.17	3.97
2021	Phi	NL	56	1	8	57.2	235	47	27	22	6	1	2	1	18	2	50	2	5	4	.556	1-5	10	96	.644	2.80	3.43
2022	Phi	NL	47	0	11	44.0	188	44	16	16	6	1	1	1	11	0	50	3	2	2	.500	2-4	6	95	.713	3.74	3.27
	3 ML YEARS		112	1	22	113.0	467	96	48	43	15	2	3	2	34	3	117	5	8	6	.571	3-9	16	96	.669	3.09	3.42

Aaron Brooks

Pitches: R Bats: R Pos: RP-5   Ht: 6'4" Wt: 230 Born: 4/27/1990 Age: 33

			HOW MUCH PITCHED					WHAT HE GAVE UP											THE RESULTS						
Year	Team	Lg	G	GS	GF	IP	BFP	H	R	ER	HR	SH	SF	HB	TBB	IBB	SO	WP	W	L	Pct	Sv-Op	Hld	Vel	OPS	ERC	ERA
2022	Memp	AAA	15	13	1	69.2	300	81	45	43	9	0	4	2	20	0	54	3	5	4	.556	0--	-		.803	4.97	5.56
2014	KC	AL	2	1	1	2.2	24	12	13	13	1	0	1	2	3	0	2	0	0	1	.000	0-0	0	92	1.764	44.02	43.88
2015	2 Tms	AL	13	9	3	55.1	250	73	41	41	9	3	2	4	14	0	38	0	3	4	.429	0-0	0	92	.888	6.17	6.67
2018	Oak	AL	3	0	2	2.2	10	1	0	0	0	0	0	0	2	0	1	0	0	0	-	0-0	0	92	.425	1.70	0.00
2019	2 Tms	AL	29	18	8	110.0	482	118	72	69	21	1	1	10	34	0	82	4	6	8	.429	0-0	0	92	.830	5.15	5.65
2022	StL	NL	5	0	3	9.1	43	11	8	8	3	0	0	1	2	0	7	0	0	0	-	0-0	0	93	.926	6.13	7.71
15	KC	AL	2	0	2	4.1	18	6	3	3	0	0	0	0	0	0	3	0	0	0	-	0-0	0	91	1.000	4.08	6.23
15	Oak	AL	11	9	1	51.0	232	67	38	38	9	3	2	4	14	0	35	0	3	4	.429	0-0	0	92	.878	6.35	6.71
19	Oak	AL	15	6	7	50.1	215	49	29	28	12	0	0	4	14	0	43	1	2	3	.400	0-0	0	92	.799	4.68	5.01
19	Bal	AL	14	12	1	59.2	267	69	43	41	9	1	1	6	20	0	39	3	4	5	.444	0-0	0	92	.855	5.54	6.18
5 ML YEARS			52	28	17	180.0	809	215	134	131	34	4	4	17	55	0	130	4	9	13	.409	0-0	0	92	.874	5.89	6.55

Mike Brosseau

Bats: R Throws: R Pos: 3B-55;PH-20;SS-4;1B-3;PR-2;DH-1   Ht: 5'10" Wt: 205 Born: 3/15/1994 Age: 29

							BATTING													RUNNING			AVERAGES			
Year	Team	Lg	G	AB	H	2B	3B	HR	(Hm	Rd)	TB	R	RBI	RC	TBB	IBB	SO	HBP	SH	SF	SB	CS	GDP	Avg	OBP	Slg	OPS
2019	TB	AL	51	132	36	7	0	6	(2	4)	61	17	16	18	7	0	39	2	1	0	1	0	3	.273	.319	.462	.781
2020	TB	AL	37	86	26	5	1	5	(1	4)	48	12	12	16	8	0	31	3	0	1	2	0	1	.302	.378	.558	.936
2021	TB	AL	57	150	28	9	0	5	(3	2)	52	21	18	14	15	0	53	2	0	2	2	0	1	.187	.266	.347	.613
2022	Mil	NL	70	141	36	5	0	6	(2	4)	59	15	23	24	14	0	48	5	0	0	2	0	0	.255	.344	.418	.762
Postseason			15	26	6	0	0	1	(1	0)	9	2	2	3	3	0	12	1	0	0	0	0	1	.231	.333	.346	.679
4 ML YEARS			215	509	126	26	1	22	(8	14)	220	65	69	72	44	0	171	12	1	3	7	0	5	.248	.320	.432	.753

Hunter Brown

Pitches: R Bats: R Pos: RP-5; SP-2   Ht: 6'2" Wt: 212 Born: 8/29/1998 Age: 24

			HOW MUCH PITCHED					WHAT HE GAVE UP											THE RESULTS						
Year	Team	Lg	G	GS	GF	IP	BFP	H	R	ER	HR	SH	SF	HB	TBB	IBB	SO	WP	W	L	Pct	Sv-Op	Hld	Vel	OPS	ERC	ERA
2019	TriCity	A-	12	6	1	23.2	102	13	12	12	0	0	0	4	18	0	33	5	2	2	.500	0--	-		.324	2.28	4.56
2021	CpChr	AA	13	11	1	49.1	217	45	23	23	6	1	1	2	29	0	76	2	1	4	.200	1--	-		.749	4.70	4.20
2021	SgrLnd	AAA	10	8	0	48.0	206	47	24	22	6	1	2	0	20	0	51	1	5	1	.833	0--	-		.748	4.22	4.13
2022	SgrLnd	AAA	23	14	5	106.0	426	70	35	30	5	0	2	4	45	0	134	4	9	4	.692	1--	-		.540	2.16	2.55
2022	Hou	AL	7	2	0	20.1	80	15	2	2	0	0	0	0	7	0	22	0	2	0	1.000	0-0	1	97	.563	1.96	0.89

Seth Brown

Bats: L Throws: L Pos: 1B-84;LF-38;RF-32;CF-17;PH-14;DH-2;PR-1   Ht: 6'1" Wt: 223 Born: 7/13/1992 Age: 30

							BATTING													RUNNING			AVERAGES			
Year	Team	Lg	G	AB	H	2B	3B	HR	(Hm	Rd)	TB	R	RBI	RC	TBB	IBB	SO	HBP	SH	SF	SB	CS	GDP	Avg	OBP	Slg	OPS
2019	Oak	AL	26	75	22	8	2	0	(0	0)	34	11	13	13	7	0	23	1	0	0	1	0	2	.293	.361	.453	.815
2020	Oak	AL	7	5	0	0	0	0	(0	0)	0	0	0	0	0	0	2	0	0	0	0	0	0	.000	.000	.000	.000
2021	Oak	AL	111	281	60	13	1	20	(7	13)	135	43	48	31	23	2	89	1	0	2	4	1	1	.214	.274	.480	.754
2022	Oak	AL	150	500	115	26	3	25	(8	17)	222	55	73	79	51	3	146	3	0	1	11	2	7	.230	.305	.444	.749
Postseason			1	1	0	0	0	0	(0	0)	0	0	0	0	0	0	0	0	0	0	0	0	0	.000	.000	.000	.000
4 ML YEARS			294	861	197	47	6	45	(15	30)	391	109	134	123	81	5	260	5	0	3	16	3	10	.229	.298	.454	.752

JT Brubaker

Pitches: R Bats: R Pos: SP-28   Ht: 6'3" Wt: 185 Born: 11/17/1993 Age: 29

			HOW MUCH PITCHED					WHAT HE GAVE UP											THE RESULTS						
Year	Team	Lg	G	GS	GF	IP	BFP	H	R	ER	HR	SH	SF	HB	TBB	IBB	SO	WP	W	L	Pct	Sv-Op	Hld	Vel	OPS	ERC	ERA
2020	Pit	NL	11	9	0	47.1	205	48	27	26	6	0	2	3	17	0	48	4	1	3	.250	0-0	1	94	.758	4.45	4.94
2021	Pit	NL	24	24	0	124.1	538	123	75	74	28	5	1	9	38	1	129	3	5	13	.278	0-0	0	93	.799	4.74	5.36
2022	Pit	NL	28	28	0	144.0	646	157	85	75	17	0	3	9	54	0	147	6	3	12	.200	0-0	0	93	.773	4.81	4.69
3 ML YEARS			63	61	0	315.2	1389	328	187	175	51	5	6	21	109	1	324	13	9	28	.243	0-0	1	93	.781	4.73	4.99

Justin Bruihl

Pitches: L Bats: L Pos: RP-24   Ht: 6'2" Wt: 215 Born: 6/26/1997 Age: 26

			HOW MUCH PITCHED					WHAT HE GAVE UP											THE RESULTS						
Year	Team	Lg	G	GS	GF	IP	BFP	H	R	ER	HR	SH	SF	HB	TBB	IBB	SO	WP	W	L	Pct	Sv-Op	Hld	Vel	OPS	ERC	ERA
2022	OkCity	AAA	25	1	4	30.1	144	32	15	12	2	0	1	2	20	0	24	1	3	1	.750	0--	-		.788	5.33	3.56
2021	LAD	NL	21	2	2	18.2	73	13	7	6	1	1	0	1	7	2	11	3	0	1	.000	0-0	3	90	.542	2.26	2.89
2022	LAD	NL	24	0	11	23.2	100	22	11	10	4	3	1	3	6	2	13	0	1	1	.500	1-2	3	89	.756	3.95	3.80
Postseason			3	0	0	2.0	7	1	0	0	0	0	0	0	0	0	5	0	0	0	-	0-0	0	91	.286	0.54	0.00
2 ML YEARS			45	2	13	42.1	173	35	18	16	5	4	1	4	13	4	24	3	1	2	.333	1-2	6	89	.665	3.18	3.40

Vidal Brujan

Bats: B Throws: R Pos: 2B-31;RF-19;SS-5;PR-4;PH-3;3B-1;LF-1;CF-1;DH-1   Ht: 5'10" Wt: 180 Born: 2/9/1998 Age: 25

							BATTING													RUNNING			AVERAGES			
Year	Team	Lg	G	AB	H	2B	3B	HR	(Hm	Rd)	TB	R	RBI	RC	TBB	IBB	SO	HBP	SH	SF	SB	CS	GDP	Avg	OBP	Slg	OPS
2018	2 Tms	Low	122	475	152	25	7	9	(--	--)	218	112	53	60	63	0	68	5	2	3	55	19	3	.320	.403	.459	.862
2019	Mont	AA	55	207	55	9	4	3	(--	--)	81	28	25	30	20	0	35	3	1	2	23	8	2	.266	.336	.391	.728
2019	Charltt	A+	44	176	51	8	3	1	(--	--)	68	28	15	30	17	1	26	2	0	1	24	5	6	.290	.357	.386	.744
2021	Drham	AAA	99	372	98	30	1	11	(--	--)	163	73	54	65	47	1	67	1	1	1	43	6	7	.263	.347	.438	.785

Year	Team	Lg	G	AB	H	2B	3B	HR	(Hm	Rd)	TB	R	RBI	RC	TBB	IBB	SO	HBP	SH	SF	SB	CS	GDP	Avg	OBP	Slg	OPS
									BATTING												RUNNING			AVERAGES			
2022	Drham	AAA	63	257	75	14	3	6	(-	-)	113	56	21	39	27	0	48	5	0	1	26	12	5	.292	.369	.440	.809
2021	TB	AL	10	26	2	0	0	0	(0	0)	2	3	2	0	0	0	8	0	0	0	1	0	0	.077	.077	.077	.154
2022	TB	AL	52	147	24	5	0	3	(1	2)	38	13	16	8	12	0	37	1	0	2	5	5	2	.163	.228	.259	.487
	2 ML YEARS		62	173	26	5	0	3	(1	2)	40	16	18	8	12	0	45	1	0	2	6	5	2	.150	.207	.231	.439

Kris Bryant

Bats: R **Throws:** R **Pos:** LF-30;DH-12   **Ht:** 6'5" **Wt:** 230 **Born:** 1/4/1992 **Age:** 31

Year	Team	Lg	G	AB	H	2B	3B	HR	(Hm	Rd)	TB	R	RBI	RC	TBB	IBB	SO	HBP	SH	SF	SB	CS	GDP	Avg	OBP	Slg	OPS
2015	ChC	NL	151	559	154	31	5	26	(21	5)	273	87	99	104	77	0	199	9	0	5	13	4	7	.275	.369	.488	.858
2016	ChC	NL	155	603	176	35	3	39	(17	22)	334	121	102	120	75	5	154	18	0	3	8	5	3	.292	.385	.554	.939
2017	ChC	NL	151	549	162	38	4	29	(18	11)	295	111	73	113	95	5	128	15	0	6	7	5	8	.295	.409	.537	.946
2018	ChC	NL	102	389	106	28	3	13	(7	6)	179	59	52	65	48	6	107	17	0	3	2	4	5	.272	.374	.460	.834
2019	ChC	NL	147	543	153	35	1	31	(15	16)	283	108	77	107	74	1	145	15	0	2	4	0	10	.282	.382	.521	.903
2020	ChC	NL	34	131	27	5	1	4	(1	3)	46	20	11	15	12	0	40	4	0	0	0	0	1	.206	.293	.351	.644
2021	2 Tms	NL	144	513	136	32	2	25	(11	14)	247	86	73	83	62	4	135	9	0	2	10	2	9	.265	.353	.481	.835
2022	Col	NL	42	160	49	12	0	5	(0	5)	76	28	14	17	17	0	27	2	0	2	0	0	7	.306	.376	.475	.851
21	ChC	NL	93	326	87	19	2	18	(7	11)	164	58	51	57	39	1	89	8	0	1	4	2	6	.267	.358	.503	.861
21	SF	NL	51	187	49	13	0	7	(4	3)	83	28	22	26	23	3	46	1	0	1	6	0	3	.262	.344	.444	.788
	Postseason		44	170	43	8	1	7	(5	2)	74	18	18	21	14	0	55	1	0	0	1	0	3	.253	.314	.435	.749
	8 ML YEARS		926	3447	963	216	19	172	(90	82)	1733	620	501	624	460	21	935	89	0	23	44	20	50	.279	.376	.503	.879

Kris Bubic

Pitches: L **Bats:** L **Pos:** SP-27; RP-1   **Ht:** 6'3" **Wt:** 225 **Born:** 8/19/1997 **Age:** 25

Year	Team	Lg	G	GS	GF	IP	BFP	H	R	ER	HR	SH	SF	HB	TBB	IBB	SO	WP	W	L	Pct	Sv-Op	Hld	Vel	OPS	ERC	ERA
						HOW MUCH PITCHED					WHAT HE GAVE UP											THE RESULTS					
2020	KC	AL	10	10	0	50.0	222	52	29	24	8	0	2	2	22	1	49	0	1	6	.143	0-0	0	91	.777	5.02	4.32
2021	KC	AL	29	20	3	130.0	556	121	67	64	22	0	3	7	59	0	114	0	6	7	.462	0-0	0	91	.780	4.70	4.43
2022	KC	AL	28	27	1	129.0	587	156	87	80	18	1	9	4	63	0	110	4	3	13	.188	0-0	0	92	.855	6.22	5.58
	3 ML YEARS		67	57	4	309.0	1365	329	183	168	48	1	12	13	144	1	273	4	10	26	.278	0-0	0	91	.812	5.37	4.89

Walker Buehler

Pitches: R **Bats:** R **Pos:** SP-12   **Ht:** 6'2" **Wt:** 185 **Born:** 7/28/1994 **Age:** 28

Year	Team	Lg	G	GS	GF	IP	BFP	H	R	ER	HR	SH	SF	HB	TBB	IBB	SO	WP	W	L	Pct	Sv-Op	Hld	Vel	OPS	ERC	ERA
						HOW MUCH PITCHED					WHAT HE GAVE UP											THE RESULTS					
2017	LAD	NL	8	0	2	9.1	44	11	8	8	2	0	0	0	8	1	12	1	1	0	1.000	0-0	1	98	.932	8.22	7.71
2018	LAD	NL	24	23	0	137.1	541	95	43	40	12	2	3	6	37	1	151	4	8	5	.615	0-1	0	96	.556	2.10	2.62
2019	LAD	NL	30	30	0	182.1	737	153	77	66	20	2	6	7	37	0	215	4	14	4	.778	0-0	0	97	.636	2.66	3.26
2020	LAD	NL	8	8	0	36.2	147	24	18	14	7	0	0	1	11	0	42	4	1	0	1.000	0-0	0	97	.600	2.48	3.44
2021	LAD	NL	33	33	0	207.2	815	149	61	57	19	7	3	6	52	2	212	5	16	4	.800	0-0	0	95	.586	2.13	2.47
2022	LAD	NL	12	12	0	65.0	274	67	30	29	8	0	0	2	17	0	58	1	6	3	.667	0-0	0	95	.726	4.00	4.02
	Postseason		15	15	0	79.2	325	61	28	26	8	1	0	1	31	1	101	2	3	3	.500	0-0	0	97	.623	2.84	2.94
	6 ML YEARS		115	106	2	638.1	2558	499	237	214	68	11	12	22	162	4	690	19	46	16	.742	0-1	1	96	.616	2.54	3.02

Madison Bumgarner

Pitches: L **Bats:** R **Pos:** SP-30   **Ht:** 6'4" **Wt:** 257 **Born:** 8/1/1989 **Age:** 33

Year	Team	Lg	G	GS	GF	IP	BFP	H	R	ER	HR	SH	SF	HB	TBB	IBB	SO	WP	W	L	Pct	Sv-Op	Hld	Vel	OPS	ERC	ERA
						HOW MUCH PITCHED					WHAT HE GAVE UP											THE RESULTS					
2009	SF	NL	4	1	1	10.0	40	8	2	2	2	1	1	0	3	1	10	0	0	0	-	0-0	0	89	.739	3.14	1.80
2010	SF	NL	18	18	0	111.0	472	119	40	37	11	0	4	5	26	2	86	1	7	6	.538	0-0	0	91	.732	3.98	3.00
2011	SF	NL	33	33	0	204.2	844	202	82	73	12	12	4	5	46	5	191	0	13	13	.500	0-0	0	92	.670	3.14	3.21
2012	SF	NL	32	32	0	208.1	849	183	87	78	23	7	4	7	49	4	191	4	16	11	.593	0-0	0	91	.670	2.95	3.37
2013	SF	NL	31	31	0	201.1	803	146	68	62	15	10	4	6	62	6	199	6	13	9	.591	0-0	0	91	.577	2.23	2.77
2014	SF	NL	33	33	0	217.1	873	194	81	72	21	9	5	6	43	3	219	4	18	10	.643	0-0	0	92	.653	2.83	2.98
2015	SF	NL	32	32	0	218.1	869	181	73	71	21	5	4	7	39	2	234	1	18	9	.667	0-0	0	91	.612	2.43	2.93
2016	SF	NL	34	34	0	226.2	912	179	79	69	26	3	6	8	54	0	251	4	15	9	.625	0-0	0	91	.619	2.57	2.74
2017	SF	NL	17	17	0	111.0	450	101	41	41	17	2	1	3	20	3	101	0	4	9	.308	0-0	0	91	.704	3.14	3.32
2018	SF	NL	21	21	0	129.2	551	118	51	47	14	5	3	5	43	3	109	3	6	7	.462	0-0	0	91	.694	3.44	3.26
2019	SF	NL	34	34	0	207.2	844	191	99	90	30	5	5	10	43	3	203	3	9	9	.500	0-0	0	91	.717	3.38	3.90
2020	Ari	NL	9	9	0	41.2	190	47	31	30	13	0	1	6	13	2	30	0	1	4	.200	0-0	0	88	.924	6.48	6.48
2021	Ari	NL	26	26	0	146.1	613	134	82	76	24	3	7	11	39	2	124	2	7	10	.412	0-0	0	90	.741	3.78	4.67
2022	Ari	NL	30	30	0	158.2	698	179	97	86	25	1	2	9	49	0	112	2	7	15	.318	0-0	0	91	.827	5.09	4.88
	Postseason		16	14	1	102.1	398	74	25	24	8	6	1	1	18	2	87	0	8	3	.727	1-1	0	92	.544	1.88	2.11
	14 ML YEARS		354	351	1	2192.2	9008	1982	913	834	254	63	51	88	529	38	2060	29	134	121	.525	0-0	0	91	.683	3.18	3.42

Aaron Bummer

Pitches: L **Bats:** L **Pos:** RP-32   **Ht:** 6'3" **Wt:** 215 **Born:** 9/21/1993 **Age:** 29

Year	Team	Lg	G	GS	GF	IP	BFP	H	R	ER	HR	SH	SF	HB	TBB	IBB	SO	WP	W	L	Pct	Sv-Op	Hld	Vel	OPS	ERC	ERA
						HOW MUCH PITCHED					WHAT HE GAVE UP											THE RESULTS					
2017	CWS	AL	30	0	3	22.0	91	13	11	11	4	1	1	1	15	1	17	1	1	3	.250	0-1	5	93	.692	3.70	4.50
2018	CWS	AL	37	0	9	31.2	144	40	19	15	1	0	0	1	10	0	35	7	0	1	.000	0-1	2	93	.730	4.80	4.26
2019	CWS	AL	58	0	5	67.2	262	43	17	16	4	1	0	3	24	2	60	4	0	0	-	1-3	27	96	.520	1.99	2.13
2020	CWS	AL	9	0	1	9.1	38	5	1	1	0	0	0	0	5	0	14	0	1	0	1.000	0-0	3	96	.415	1.60	0.96

Year	Team	Lg	G	GS	GF	IP	BFP	H	R	ER	HR	SH	SF	HB	TBB	IBB	SO	WP	W	L	Pct	Sv-Op	Hld	Vel	OPS	ERC	ERA
												WHAT HE GAVE UP								THE RESULTS						
2021	CWS	AL	62	0	6	56.1	242	42	28	22	3	0	1	4	29	3	75	5	5	5	.500	2-8	21	95	.560	2.96	3.51
2022	CWS	AL	32	0	3	26.2	117	30	11	7	2	0	1	2	10	0	30	0	2	1	.667	2-6	10	95	.734	4.91	2.36
	Postseason		5	0	0	4.2	22	6	3	3	0	0	0	0	2	0	8	0	0	1	.000	0-0	2	95	.664	4.93	5.79
	6 ML YEARS		228	0	27	213.2	894	173	87	72	14	2	3	11	93	6	231	17	9	10	.474	5-19	70	95	.606	3.12	3.03

Dylan Bundy

Pitches: R Bats: B Pos: SP-29 Ht: 6'1" Wt: 225 Born: 11/15/1992 Age: 30

Year	Team	Lg	G	GS	GF	IP	BFP	H	R	ER	HR	SH	SF	HB	TBB	IBB	SO	WP	W	L	Pct	Sv-Op	Hld	Vel	OPS	ERC	ERA
2012	Bal	AL	2	0	2	1.2	6	1	0	0	0	0	0	0	1	0	0	0	0	0	-	0-0	0	94	.533	2.46	0.00
2016	Bal	AL	36	14	6	109.2	474	109	52	49	18	1	1	6	42	4	104	0	10	6	.625	0-0	3	94	.766	4.61	4.02
2017	Bal	AL	28	28	0	169.2	698	152	82	80	26	0	7	7	51	0	152	0	13	9	.591	0-0	0	92	.721	3.68	4.24
2018	Bal	AL	31	31	0	171.2	750	188	116	104	41	3	2	6	54	1	184	6	8	16	.333	0-0	0	92	.855	5.39	5.45
2019	Bal	AL	30	30	0	161.2	700	161	95	86	29	1	7	6	58	0	162	7	7	14	.333	0-0	0	91	.784	4.57	4.79
2020	LAA	AL	11	11	0	65.2	267	51	27	24	5	0	0	4	17	1	72	2	6	3	.667	0-0	0	90	.614	2.41	3.29
2021	LAA	AL	23	19	1	90.2	397	89	64	61	20	2	3	6	34	0	84	1	2	9	.182	0-0	0	91	.818	4.94	6.06
2022	Min	AL	29	29	0	140.0	595	151	79	76	24	0	6	3	28	0	94	3	8	8	.500	0-0	0	89	.765	4.25	4.89
	8 ML YEARS		190	162	9	910.2	3887	902	515	480	163	7	26	38	285	6	852	19	54	65	.454	0-0	3	92	.772	4.37	4.74

Peyton Burdick

Bats: R Throws: R Pos: LF-14;CF-13;RF-4;PH-1;PR-1 Ht: 6'0" Wt: 205 Born: 2/26/1997 Age: 26

Year	Team	Lg	G	AB	H	2B	3B	HR	(Hm	Rd)	TB	R	RBI	RC	TBB	IBB	SO	HBP	SH	SF	SB	CS	GDP	Avg	OBP	Slg	OPS
2022	Jaxnvl	AAA	99	364	78	16	5	15	(-	-)	149	74	58	53	53	0	120	9	0	3	13	3	8	.214	.326	.409	.736
2022	Mia	NL	32	92	19	4	0	4	(2	2)	35	8	11	11	8	0	35	2	0	0	1	0	1	.207	.284	.380	.665

Jake Burger

Bats: R Throws: R Pos: 3B-37;DH-9;2B-3;PH-3;PR-1 Ht: 6'2" Wt: 230 Born: 4/10/1996 Age: 27

Year	Team	Lg	G	AB	H	2B	3B	HR	(Hm	Rd)	TB	R	RBI	RC	TBB	IBB	SO	HBP	SH	SF	SB	CS	GDP	Avg	OBP	Slg	OPS
2022	Charltt	AAA	39	146	37	0	2	5	(-	-)	56	22	16	19	18	0	34	4	0	0	0	1	4	.253	.351	.384	.735
2021	CWS	AL	15	38	10	3	1	1	(1	0)	18	5	3	6	4	0	15	0	0	0	0	0	2	.263	.333	.474	.807
2022	CWS	AL	51	168	42	9	1	8	(7	1)	77	20	26	23	10	1	56	3	1	0	0	0	7	.250	.302	.458	.761
	2 ML YEARS		66	206	52	12	2	9	(8	1)	95	25	29	29	14	1	71	3	1	1	0	0	9	.252	.308	.461	.769

Brock Burke

Pitches: L Bats: L Pos: RP-52 Ht: 6'4" Wt: 210 Born: 8/4/1996 Age: 26

Year	Team	Lg	G	GS	GF	IP	BFP	H	R	ER	HR	SH	SF	HB	TBB	IBB	SO	WP	W	L	Pct	Sv-Op	Hld	Vel	OPS	ERC	ERA
2019	Tex	AL	6	6	0	26.2	120	30	22	22	6	1	1	2	11	0	14	0	0	2	.000	0-0	0	92	.876	6.15	7.43
2022	Tex	AL	52	0	5	82.1	328	63	25	18	9	4	0	2	24	1	90	2	7	5	.583	0-5	9	95	.630	2.59	1.97
	2 ML YEARS		58	6	5	109.0	448	93	47	40	15	5	1	4	35	1	104	2	7	7	.500	0-5	9	94	.695	3.38	3.30

Alec Burleson

Bats: L Throws: L Pos: RF-9;1B-6;DH-3;LF-2;PH-2 Ht: 6'2" Wt: 212 Born: 11/25/1998 Age: 24

Year	Team	Lg	G	AB	H	2B	3B	HR	(Hm	Rd)	TB	R	RBI	RC	TBB	IBB	SO	HBP	SH	SF	SB	CS	GDP	Avg	OBP	Slg	OPS
2022	Memp	AAA	109	432	143	25	1	20	(-	-)	230	68	87	84	29	0	67	3	0	6	4	0	13	.331	.372	.532	.905
2022	StL	NL	16	48	9	1	0	1	(0	1)	13	4	3	3	5	0	9	0	0	1	1	0	1	.188	.264	.271	.535

Corbin Burnes

Pitches: R Bats: R Pos: SP-33 Ht: 6'3" Wt: 225 Born: 10/22/1994 Age: 28

Year	Team	Lg	G	GS	GF	IP	BFP	H	R	ER	HR	SH	SF	HB	TBB	IBB	SO	WP	W	L	Pct	Sv-Op	Hld	Vel	OPS	ERC	ERA
2018	Mil	NL	30	0	6	38.0	152	27	11	11	4	1	1	3	11	2	35	2	7	0	1.000	1-2	3	95	.595	2.42	2.61
2019	Mil	NL	32	4	8	49.0	235	70	52	48	17	3	0	0	20	0	70	2	1	5	.167	1-1	4	95	1.011	8.65	8.82
2020	Mil	NL	12	9	2	59.2	240	37	15	14	2	0	0	3	24	0	88	5	4	1	.800	0-0	0	96	.515	1.91	2.11
2021	Mil	NL	28	28	0	167.0	657	123	47	45	7	1	4	6	34	0	234	5	11	5	.688	0-0	0	97	.521	1.81	2.43
2022	Mil	NL	33	33	0	202.0	797	144	73	66	23	0	2	13	51	0	243	10	12	8	.600	0-0	0	96	.602	2.38	2.94
	Postseason		7	1	1	15.0	52	6	2	2	0	0	1	0	4	0	17	1	1	0	1.000	0-0	1	96	.382	0.90	1.20
	5 ML YEARS		135	74	16	515.2	2081	401	198	184	53	5	7	25	140	2	670	24	35	19	.648	2-3	7	96	.611	2.61	3.21

Ryan Burr

Pitches: R Bats: R Pos: RP-8 Ht: 6'4" Wt: 220 Born: 5/28/1994 Age: 29

Year	Team	Lg	G	GS	GF	IP	BFP	H	R	ER	HR	SH	SF	HB	TBB	IBB	SO	WP	W	L	Pct	Sv-Op	Hld	Vel	OPS	ERC	ERA
2018	CWS	AL	8	0	1	9.2	44	12	8	8	3	1	0	1	6	1	6	0	0	0	-	0-0	0	95	1.109	9.13	7.45
2019	CWS	AL	16	1	2	19.2	86	17	13	10	3	1	2	0	8	0	20	0	1	1	.500	0-0	0	95	.707	3.54	4.58
2021	CWS	AL	34	1	8	36.2	151	28	11	10	3	2	2	1	21	0	33	5	2	1	.667	0-1	3	95	.656	3.58	2.45
2022	CWS	AL	8	0	2	9.0	39	8	7	6	3	0	0	0	4	0	7	0	1	1	.500	0-0	1	94	.851	5.13	6.00
	4 ML YEARS		66	2	13	75.0	320	65	39	34	12	4	4	2	39	1	66	5	4	3	.571	0-1	4	95	.756	4.38	4.08

219

Matt Bush

Pitches: R Bats: R Pos: RP-59; SP-6   Ht: 5'9" Wt: 180 Born: 2/8/1986 Age: 37

Year	Team	Lg	HOW MUCH PITCHED					WHAT HE GAVE UP											THE RESULTS							
			G	GS	GF	IP	BFP	H	R	ER	HR	SH	SF	HB	TBB	IBB	SO	WP	W	L	Pct	Sv-Op	Hld	Vel	OPS	ERC	ERA
2016	Tex	AL	58	0	15	61.2	243	44	18	17	4	1	3	1	14	0	61	2	7	2	.778	1-4	22	97	.525	1.83	2.48
2017	Tex	AL	57	0	22	52.1	240	57	30	22	7	0	1	4	19	0	58	2	3	4	.429	10-15	10	97	.750	4.81	3.78
2018	Tex	AL	21	0	6	23.0	108	23	13	12	3	0	2	2	14	0	19	1	0	0	-	0-0	3	96	.828	5.37	4.70
2021	Tex	AL	4	0	1	4.0	17	4	3	3	3	0	0	0	1	0	5	0	0	0	-	0-0	2	95	1.107	7.62	6.75
2022	2 Tms		65	6	11	59.2	244	43	31	23	11	2	2	3	18	2	74	4	2	3	.400	3-10	18	97	.630	2.82	3.47
22	Tex	AL	40	5	7	36.2	151	27	16	12	5	2	1	2	10	0	45	3	2	1	.667	1-4	9	97	.585	2.55	2.95
22	Mil	NL	25	1	4	23.0	93	16	15	11	6	0	1	1	8	2	29	1	0	2	.000	2-6	9	97	.703	3.27	4.30
	Postseason		2	0	1	3.2	14	1	1	0	0	0	0	0	2	1	6	0	0	1	.000	0-0	0	98	.381	0.66	0.00
	5 ML YEARS		205	6	55	200.2	852	171	95	77	28	3	8	10	66	2	217	9	12	9	.571	14-29	55	97	.667	3.35	3.45

Jose Butto

Pitches: R Bats: R Pos: SP-1   Ht: 6'1" Wt: 202 Born: 3/19/1998 Age: 25

Year	Team	Lg	HOW MUCH PITCHED					WHAT HE GAVE UP											THE RESULTS							
			G	GS	GF	IP	BFP	H	R	ER	HR	SH	SF	HB	TBB	IBB	SO	WP	W	L	Pct	Sv-Op	Hld	Vel	OPS	ERC	ERA
2022	Bnghtn	AA	20	18	1	92.1	397	86	44	41	14	0	0	9	35	0	108	6	6	5	.545	0-	-	-	.769	4.38	4.00
2022	Syrcse	AAA	8	7	0	36.2	143	26	10	10	3	0	1	2	9	0	30	1	1	1	.500	0-	-	-	.602	2.14	2.45
2022	NYM	NL	1	1	0	4.0	23	9	7	7	2	0	0	0	2	0	5	0	0	0	-	0-0	0	95	1.240	16.72	15.75

Byron Buxton

Bats: R Throws: R Pos: CF-57;DH-34;PH-5;PR-1   Ht: 6'2" Wt: 190 Born: 12/18/1993 Age: 29

Year	Team	Lg	BATTING																		RUNNING			AVERAGES			
			G	AB	H	2B	3B	HR	(Hm	Rd)	TB	R	RBI	RC	TBB	IBB	SO	HBP	SH	SF	SB	CS	GDP	Avg	OBP	Slg	OPS
2015	Min	AL	46	129	27	7	1	2	(0	2)	42	16	6	10	6	0	44	1	2	0	2	2	1	.209	.250	.326	.576
2016	Min	AL	92	298	67	19	6	10	(6	4)	128	44	38	33	23	0	118	3	4	3	10	2	2	.225	.284	.430	.714
2017	Min	AL	140	462	117	14	6	16	(8	8)	191	69	51	63	38	2	150	4	5	2	29	1	1	.253	.314	.413	.728
2018	Min	AL	28	90	14	4	0	0	(0	0)	18	8	4	4	3	0	28	0	1	0	5	0	1	.156	.183	.200	.383
2019	Min	AL	87	271	71	30	4	10	(4	6)	139	48	46	44	19	1	68	2	2	1	14	3	3	.262	.314	.513	.827
2020	Min	AL	39	130	33	3	0	13	(4	9)	75	19	27	17	2	0	36	1	0	2	2	1	2	.254	.267	.577	.844
2021	Min	AL	61	235	72	23	0	19	(9	10)	152	50	32	50	13	0	62	6	0	0	9	1	0	.306	.358	.647	1.005
2022	Min	AL	92	340	76	13	3	28	(15	13)	179	61	51	61	34	0	116	7	0	1	6	0	0	.224	.306	.526	.833
	Postseason		3	6	1	0	0	0	(0	0)	1	0	1	0	0	0	4	0	0	0	2	1	0	.167	.167	.167	.333
	8 ML YEARS		585	1955	477	113	20	98	(46	52)	924	315	255	281	138	3	622	24	14	9	77	10	10	.244	.301	.473	.773

Edward Cabrera

Pitches: R Bats: R Pos: SP-14   Ht: 6'5" Wt: 217 Born: 4/13/1998 Age: 25

Year	Team	Lg	HOW MUCH PITCHED					WHAT HE GAVE UP											THE RESULTS							
			G	GS	GF	IP	BFP	H	R	ER	HR	SH	SF	HB	TBB	IBB	SO	WP	W	L	Pct	Sv-Op	Hld	Vel	OPS	ERC	ERA
2018	Grnsbr	A	22	22	0	100.1	440	105	57	47	11	0	0	6	42	0	93	17	8	8	.333	0-	-	-	.870	4.77	4.22
2019	Jaxnvl	AA	8	8	0	38.2	156	28	12	11	6	0	0	3	13	0	43	11	4	1	.800	0-	-	-	.653	3.04	2.56
2019	Jupiter	A+	11	11	0	58.0	227	37	16	13	1	1	0	5	18	0	73	0	5	3	.625	0-	-	-	.564	1.76	2.02
2021	Pnscla	AA	5	5	0	26.0	97	19	10	8	3	1	0	0	6	0	33	3	2	1	.667	0-	-	-	.605	2.29	2.77
2021	Jaxnvl	AAA	6	6	0	29.1	129	22	13	12	4	0	2	1	19	0	48	5	1	3	.250	0-	-	-	.737	3.99	3.68
2022	Jaxnvl	AAA	6	6	0	28.2	116	21	13	12	2	0	0	0	19	0	39	1	2	2	.500	0-	-	-	.611	2.57	3.77
2021	Mia	NL	7	7	0	26.1	120	24	20	17	6	0	0	4	28	0	28	3	0	3	.000	0-0	0	97	.897	6.71	5.81
2022	Mia	NL	14	14	0	71.2	291	44	24	24	10	0	0	9	33	0	75	2	6	4	.600	0-0	0	96	.621	3.04	3.01
	2 ML YEARS		21	21	0	98.0	411	68	44	41	16	0	0	13	52	0	103	5	6	7	.462	0-0	0	96	.699	3.94	3.77

Genesis Cabrera

Pitches: L Bats: L Pos: RP-39   heh-NEH-sees   Ht: 6'2" Wt: 180 Born: 10/10/1996 Age: 26

Year	Team	Lg	HOW MUCH PITCHED					WHAT HE GAVE UP											THE RESULTS							
			G	GS	GF	IP	BFP	H	R	ER	HR	SH	SF	HB	TBB	IBB	SO	WP	W	L	Pct	Sv-Op	Hld	Vel	OPS	ERC	ERA
2022	Memp	AAA	10	0	6	13.0	58	14	11	11	1	0	1	0	4	0	15	2	1	1	.500	2-	-	-	.707	3.81	7.62
2019	StL	NL	13	2	5	20.1	99	23	16	11	2	1	1	2	11	0	19	1	0	2	.000	1-1	1	96	.760	5.53	4.87
2020	StL	NL	19	0	1	22.1	96	10	9	6	3	0	0	4	16	0	32	3	4	1	.800	1-1	2	96	.589	3.18	2.42
2021	StL	NL	71	0	5	70.0	296	52	31	29	3	4	2	5	36	2	77	9	4	5	.444	0-3	28	98	.628	2.96	3.73
2022	StL	NL	39	0	4	44.2	194	39	24	23	8	0	1	4	20	3	32	1	4	2	.667	1-2	13	96	.745	4.34	4.63
	Postseason		4	0	1	2.2	13	2	2	2	0	0	1	1	3	0	2	0	0	0	-	0-0	1	98	.712	6.41	6.75
	4 ML YEARS		142	2	15	157.1	685	124	80	69	16	5	4	15	83	5	160	14	12	10	.545	3-7	44	97	.676	3.70	3.95

Miguel Cabrera

Bats: R Throws: R Pos: DH-109;PH-3   Ht: 6'4" Wt: 267 Born: 4/18/1983 Age: 40

Year	Team	Lg	BATTING																		RUNNING			AVERAGES			
			G	AB	H	2B	3B	HR	(Hm	Rd)	TB	R	RBI	RC	TBB	IBB	SO	HBP	SH	SF	SB	CS	GDP	Avg	OBP	Slg	OPS
2003	Fla	NL	87	314	84	21	3	12	(7	5)	147	39	62	51	25	3	84	2	4	1	0	2	12	.268	.325	.468	.793
2004	Fla	NL	160	603	177	31	1	33	(14	19)	309	101	112	92	68	5	148	6	0	8	5	2	20	.294	.366	.512	.879
2005	Fla	NL	158	613	198	43	2	33	(11	22)	344	106	116	108	64	12	125	2	0	20	1	0	20	.323	.385	.561	.947
2006	Fla	NL	158	576	195	50	2	26	(15	11)	327	112	114	132	86	27	108	10	0	4	9	6	18	.339	.430	.568	.998
2007	Fla	NL	157	588	188	38	2	34	(19	15)	332	91	119	122	79	23	127	5	1	7	2	1	17	.320	.401	.565	.965
2008	Det	AL	160	616	180	36	2	37	(19	18)	331	85	127	109	56	6	126	3	0	4	1	0	22	.292	.349	.537	.887
2009	Det	AL	160	611	198	34	0	34	(19	15)	334	96	103	114	68	14	107	5	0	1	6	2	22	.324	.396	.547	.942
2010	Det	AL	150	548	180	45	1	38	(17	21)	341	111	126	122	89	32	95	3	0	8	3	3	17	.328	.420	.622	1.042
2011	Det	AL	161	572	197	48	0	30	(15	15)	335	111	105	141	108	22	89	3	0	5	2	1	24	.344	.448	.586	1.033

Year	Team	Lg	G	AB	H	2B	3B	HR	(Hm	Rd)	TB	R	RBI	RC	TBB	IBB	SO	HBP	SH	SF	SB	CS	GDP	Avg	OBP	Slg	OPS
2012 Det	AL		161	622	205	40	0	44	(28	16)	377	109	139	123	66	17	98	3	0	6	4	1	28	.330	.393	.606	.999
2013 Det	AL		148	555	193	26	1	44	(17	27)	353	103	137	146	90	19	94	5	0	2	3	0	19	.348	.442	.636	1.078
2014 Det	AL		159	611	191	52	1	25	(13	12)	320	101	109	110	60	10	117	3	0	11	1	1	21	.313	.371	.524	.895
2015 Det	AL		119	429	145	28	1	18	(7	11)	229	64	76	93	77	15	82	3	0	2	1	1	19	.338	.440	.534	.974
2016 Det	AL		158	595	188	31	1	38	(20	18)	335	92	108	106	75	15	116	4	0	5	0	0	26	.316	.393	.563	.956
2017 Det	AL		130	469	117	22	0	16	(11	5)	187	50	60	55	54	6	110	3	0	3	0	1	15	.249	.329	.399	.728
2018 Det	AL		38	134	40	11	0	3	(2	1)	60	17	22	23	22	4	27	0	0	1	0	0	6	.299	.395	.448	.843
2019 Det	AL		136	493	139	21	0	12	(5	7)	196	41	59	72	48	4	108	3	0	5	0	0	18	.282	.346	.398	.744
2020 Det	AL		57	204	51	4	0	10	(5	5)	85	28	35	39	24	1	51	1	0	2	1	0	3	.250	.329	.417	.746
2021 Det	AL		130	472	121	16	0	15	(5	10)	182	48	75	58	40	0	118	5	0	9	0	0	21	.256	.316	.386	.701
2022 Det	AL		112	397	101	10	0	5	(4	1)	126	25	43	41	28	3	101	3	0	5	1	0	16	.254	.305	.317	.622
Postseason			55	205	57	10	0	13	(4	9)	106	29	38	34	27	7	48	2	1	0	3	0	7	.278	.368	.517	.885
20 ML YEARS			2699	10022	3088	607	17	507	(253	254)	5250	1530	1847	1857	1227	238	2031	72	5	100	40	21	353	.308	.384	.524	.908

Oswaldo Cabrera

Bats: B Throws: R Pos: RF-27;LF-9;SS-4;1B-3;2B-3;3B-3;PH-2;PR-1   Ht: 6'0" Wt: 200 Born: 3/1/1999 Age: 24

Year	Team	Lg	G	AB	H	2B	3B	HR	(Hm	Rd)	TB	R	RBI	RC	TBB	IBB	SO	HBP	SH	SF	SB	CS	GDP	Avg	OBP	Slg	OPS
2022 S-WB	AAA		47	183	48	12	3	8	(-	-)	90	29	29	32	19	0	55	3	2	1	10	3	2	.262	.340	.492	.832
2022 NYY	AL		44	154	38	8	1	6	(4	2)	66	21	19	20	15	0	44	0	1	1	3	2	1	.247	.312	.429	.740

Lorenzo Cain

Bats: R Throws: R Pos: CF-42;PH-2;PR-1   Ht: 6'2" Wt: 214 Born: 4/13/1986 Age: 37

Year	Team	Lg	G	AB	H	2B	3B	HR	(Hm	Rd)	TB	R	RBI	RC	TBB	IBB	SO	HBP	SH	SF	SB	CS	GDP	Avg	OBP	Slg	OPS
2010 Mil	NL		43	147	45	11	1	1	(1	0)	61	17	13	23	9	0	28	1	0	1	7	1	1	.306	.348	.415	.763
2011 KC	AL		6	22	6	1	0	0	(0	0)	7	4	1	2	1	0	4	0	0	0	0	0	0	.273	.304	.318	.623
2012 KC	AL		61	222	59	9	2	7	(3	4)	93	27	31	32	15	0	56	3	0	4	10	0	4	.266	.316	.419	.734
2013 KC	AL		115	399	100	21	3	4	(3	1)	139	54	46	46	33	2	90	4	0	6	14	6	10	.251	.310	.348	.658
2014 KC	AL		133	471	142	29	4	5	(3	2)	194	55	53	67	24	2	108	4	0	3	28	5	9	.301	.339	.412	.751
2015 KC	AL		140	551	169	34	6	16	(9	7)	263	101	72	90	37	4	98	12	0	4	28	6	16	.307	.361	.477	.838
2016 KC	AL		103	397	114	19	1	9	(3	6)	162	56	56	53	31	3	84	2	0	4	14	5	15	.287	.339	.408	.747
2017 KC	AL		155	584	175	27	5	15	(3	12)	257	86	49	90	54	1	100	5	0	2	26	2	20	.300	.363	.440	.803
2018 Mil	NL		141	539	166	25	2	10	(4	6)	225	90	38	94	71	1	94	8	0	2	30	7	10	.308	.395	.417	.813
2019 Mil	NL		148	562	146	30	0	11	(7	4)	209	75	48	61	50	0	106	6	0	4	18	8	14	.260	.325	.372	.697
2020 Mil	NL		5	18	6	1	0	0	(0	0)	7	4	2	5	3	1	2	0	0	0	0	0	0	.333	.429	.389	.817
2021 Mil	NL		78	257	66	13	0	8	(1	7)	103	40	36	37	26	0	48	2	0	1	13	2	5	.257	.329	.401	.729
2022 Mil	NL		43	145	26	5	0	1	(0	1)	34	17	9	5	8	0	36	2	0	1	2	2	4	.179	.234	.241	.465
Postseason			46	184	51	11	0	1	(0	1)	65	28	21	30	20	3	38	1	1	2	9	2	1	.277	.348	.353	.701
13 ML YEARS			1171	4314	1220	225	24	87	(37	50)	1754	626	454	605	362	14	854	49	0	32	190	44	109	.283	.343	.407	.749

Kole Calhoun

Bats: L Throws: L Pos: RF-75;LF-29;PH-23;DH-20;CF-1   Ht: 5'10" Wt: 205 Born: 10/14/1987 Age: 35

Year	Team	Lg	G	AB	H	2B	3B	HR	(Hm	Rd)	TB	R	RBI	RC	TBB	IBB	SO	HBP	SH	SF	SB	CS	GDP	Avg	OBP	Slg	OPS
2012 LAA	AL		21	23	4	1	0	0	(0	0)	5	2	1	0	2	1	6	0	0	0	1	0	0	.174	.240	.217	.457
2013 LAA	AL		58	195	55	7	2	8	(5	3)	90	29	32	33	21	0	41	1	0	5	2	2	6	.282	.347	.462	.808
2014 LAA	AL		127	493	134	31	3	17	(7	10)	222	90	58	75	38	0	104	2	2	2	5	3	6	.272	.325	.450	.776
2015 LAA	AL		159	630	161	23	2	26	(16	10)	266	78	83	85	45	1	164	5	2	4	4	1	6	.256	.308	.422	.731
2016 LAA	AL		157	594	161	35	5	18	(7	11)	260	91	75	93	67	0	118	6	0	5	2	3	10	.271	.348	.438	.786
2017 LAA	AL		155	569	139	23	2	19	(8	11)	223	77	71	85	71	4	134	8	0	6	5	1	10	.244	.333	.392	.725
2018 LAA	AL		137	491	102	18	2	19	(9	10)	181	71	57	53	53	2	133	1	0	6	6	2	9	.208	.283	.369	.652
2019 LAA	AL		152	552	128	29	1	33	(16	17)	258	92	74	77	70	7	162	7	0	2	4	1	14	.232	.325	.467	.792
2020 Ari	NL		54	190	43	9	0	16	(7	9)	100	35	40	37	28	0	50	6	0	4	1	1	6	.226	.338	.526	.864
2021 Ari	NL		51	166	39	8	0	5	(2	3)	62	17	17	13	15	0	41	0	0	1	1	0	2	.235	.297	.373	.670
2022 LAA	AL		125	388	76	14	1	12	(7	5)	128	36	49	39	27	0	136	6	0	3	3	2	6	.196	.257	.330	.587
Postseason			3	15	5	0	0	0	(0	0)	5	1	0	1	0	0	1	0	0	0	0	0	0	.333	.333	.333	.667
11 ML YEARS			1196	4291	1042	198	18	173	(84	89)	1795	618	557	590	437	15	1089	42	4	38	34	16	74	.243	.316	.418	.735

Willie Calhoun

Bats: L Throws: R Pos: DH-16;LF-5;PH-5   Ht: 5'8" Wt: 200 Born: 11/4/1994 Age: 28

Year	Team	Lg	G	AB	H	2B	3B	HR	(Hm	Rd)	TB	R	RBI	RC	TBB	IBB	SO	HBP	SH	SF	SB	CS	GDP	Avg	OBP	Slg	OPS
2022 RdRck	AAA		21	83	18	1	0	5	(-	-)	34	18	20	10	6	0	13	0	0	2	0	0	3	.217	.264	.410	.673
2022 Scrmto	AAA		42	148	43	9	0	5	(-	-)	67	24	23	25	19	0	22	2	0	1	0	0	3	.291	.376	.453	.829
2017 Tex	AL		13	34	9	0	0	1	(1	0)	12	3	4	6	2	0	7	1	0	0	0	0	0	.265	.324	.353	.677
2018 Tex	AL		35	99	22	5	0	2	(1	1)	33	8	11	11	6	0	24	1	0	2	0	0	2	.222	.269	.333	.602
2019 Tex	AL		83	309	83	14	1	21	(8	13)	162	51	48	49	23	0	53	3	0	2	0	0	5	.269	.323	.524	.848
2020 Tex	AL		29	100	19	2	1	1	(1	0)	26	3	13	9	5	0	17	1	0	2	0	0	1	.190	.231	.260	.491
2021 Tex	AL		75	260	65	10	3	6	(3	3)	99	26	25	29	21	0	34	2	0	1	0	2	6	.250	.310	.381	.691
2022 2 Tms			22	52	7	3	0	1	(1	0)	13	7	3	1	9	0	8	1	0	0	0	0	2	.135	.274	.250	.524
22 Tex	AL		18	44	6	3	0	1	(1	0)	12	7	2	1	8	0	6	1	0	0	0	0	1	.136	.283	.273	.556
22 SF	NL		4	8	1	0	0	0	(0	0)	1	0	1	0	1	0	2	0	0	0	0	0	1	.125	.222	.125	.347
6 ML YEARS			257	854	205	34	5	32	(15	17)	345	98	104	105	66	0	143	9	0	7	0	2	16	.240	.299	.404	.703

Alex Call

Bats: R **Throws:** R **Pos:** LF-28;RF-8;PH-7;CF-6;PR-5;DH-3   **Ht:** 5'11" **Wt:** 188 **Born:** 9/27/1994 **Age:** 28

Year	Team	Lg	G	AB	H	2B	3B	HR	(Hm	Rd)	TB	R	RBI	RC	TBB	IBB	SO	HBP	SH	SF	SB	CS	GDP	Avg	OBP	Slg	OPS
2022	Clmbs	AAA	71	239	67	16	1	11	(-	-)	118	56	46	54	49	0	50	11	1	5	6	0	2	.280	.418	.494	.911
2022	2 Tms		47	114	27	3	1	5	(1	4)	47	18	13	19	15	0	30	2	0	0	3	3	2	.237	.336	.412	.748
22	Cle	AL	12	12	2	0	0	0	(0	0)	2	2	0	1	4	0	4	0	0	0	0	0	0	.167	.375	.167	.542
22	Was	NL	35	102	25	3	1	5	(1	4)	45	16	13	18	11	0	26	2	0	0	3	3	2	.245	.330	.441	.772

Johan Camargo

Bats: B **Throws:** R **Pos:** SS-26;3B-13;PH-10;2B-9;1B-5;DH-2;PR-1   **Ht:** 6'0" **Wt:** 195 **Born:** 12/13/1993 **Age:** 29

Year	Team	Lg	G	AB	H	2B	3B	HR	(Hm	Rd)	TB	R	RBI	RC	TBB	IBB	SO	HBP	SH	SF	SB	CS	GDP	Avg	OBP	Slg	OPS
2022	LV	AAA	41	141	30	6	0	2	(-	-)	42	19	23	12	21	0	25	1	0	4	0	0	4	.213	.311	.298	.609
2017	Atl	NL	82	241	72	21	2	4	(2	2)	109	30	27	32	12	2	51	0	2	1	0	0	5	.299	.331	.452	.783
2018	Atl	NL	134	464	126	27	1	19	(7	12)	212	63	76	72	51	4	108	6	0	3	1	1	13	.272	.349	.457	.806
2019	Atl	NL	98	232	54	12	1	7	(2	5)	89	31	32	27	15	2	43	0	1	0	1	0	5	.233	.279	.384	.663
2020	Atl	NL	35	120	24	8	0	4	(1	3)	44	16	9	7	6	0	35	1	0	0	0	0	1	.200	.244	.367	.611
2021	Atl	NL	15	16	0	0	0	0	(0	0)	0	1	0	0	2	0	6	0	0	0	0	0	0	.000	.111	.000	.111
2022	Phi	NL	52	152	36	3	0	3	(0	3)	48	8	15	16	13	0	37	0	1	0	0	0	1	.237	.297	.316	.613
Postseason			12	27	2	1	0	0	(0	0)	3	1	1	2	3	0	10	0	0	0	0	0	1	.074	.167	.111	.278
6 ML YEARS			416	1225	312	71	4	37	(12	25)	502	149	159	154	99	8	280	7	4	4	2	1	25	.255	.313	.410	.723

Daz Cameron

Bats: R **Throws:** R **Pos:** RF-14;CF-7;PH-1;PR-1   **Ht:** 6'2" **Wt:** 185 **Born:** 1/15/1997 **Age:** 26

Year	Team	Lg	G	AB	H	2B	3B	HR	(Hm	Rd)	TB	R	RBI	RC	TBB	IBB	SO	HBP	SH	SF	SB	CS	GDP	Avg	OBP	Slg	OPS
2022	Toledo	AAA	98	383	92	24	2	10	(-	-)	150	56	50	49	37	0	123	5	0	5	19	4	5	.240	.312	.392	.703
2020	Det	AL	17	57	11	2	1	0	(0	0)	15	4	3	3	2	0	19	0	0	1	1	0	1	.193	.220	.263	.483
2021	Det	AL	35	103	20	5	0	4	(2	2)	37	16	13	11	10	0	38	2	0	0	6	0	2	.194	.278	.359	.637
2022	Det	AL	21	64	14	3	1	1	(1	0)	22	6	8	9	5	0	20	1	0	0	2	0	1	.219	.286	.344	.629
3 ML YEARS			73	224	45	10	2	5	(3	2)	74	26	24	23	17	0	77	3	0	0	9	0	4	.201	.266	.330	.597

Luis Campusano

Bats: R **Throws:** R **Pos:** C-10;DH-5;PH-4   **Ht:** 5'11" **Wt:** 232 **Born:** 9/29/1998 **Age:** 24

Year	Team	Lg	G	AB	H	2B	3B	HR	(Hm	Rd)	TB	R	RBI	RC	TBB	IBB	SO	HBP	SH	SF	SB	CS	GDP	Avg	OBP	Slg	OPS
2022	ElPaso	AAA	81	319	95	15	1	14	(-	-)	154	62	60	55	33	0	62	2	0	4	0	0	12	.298	.363	.483	.846
2020	SD	NL	1	3	1	0	0	1	(0	1)	4	2	1	1	0	0	2	1	0	0	0	0	0	.333	.500	1.333	1.833
2021	SD	NL	11	34	3	0	0	0	(0	0)	3	0	1	0	4	0	11	0	0	0	0	0	2	.088	.184	.088	.272
2022	SD	NL	16	48	12	1	0	1	(0	1)	16	4	5	3	1	0	11	0	0	1	0	0	0	.250	.260	.333	.593
Postseason			1	1	0	0	0	0	(0	0)	0	0	0	0	0	0	1	0	0	0	0	0	0	.000	.000	.000	.000
3 ML YEARS			28	85	16	1	0	2	(0	2)	23	6	7	4	5	0	24	1	0	1	0	0	4	.188	.239	.271	.510

Jeimer Candelario

Bats: B **Throws:** R **Pos:** 3B-117;DH-8;PH-3;PR-1   **Ht:** 6'1" **Wt:** 216 **Born:** 11/24/1993 **Age:** 29

Year	Team	Lg	G	AB	H	2B	3B	HR	(Hm	Rd)	TB	R	RBI	RC	TBB	IBB	SO	HBP	SH	SF	SB	CS	GDP	Avg	OBP	Slg	OPS
2016	ChC	NL	5	11	1	0	0	0	(0	0)	1	0	0	0	2	1	5	1	0	0	0	0	0	.091	.286	.091	.377
2017	2 Tms		38	127	36	9	0	3	(2	1)	54	18	16	19	13	0	30	2	0	0	0	0	3	.283	.359	.425	.784
2018	Det	AL	144	539	121	28	3	19	(10	9)	212	78	54	64	66	1	160	9	0	5	3	2	4	.224	.317	.393	.710
2019	Det	AL	94	335	68	17	2	8	(4	4)	113	33	32	35	43	1	99	7	0	1	3	1	3	.203	.306	.337	.643
2020	Det	AL	52	185	55	11	3	7	(3	4)	93	30	29	36	20	0	49	1	0	0	1	1	3	.297	.369	.503	.872
2021	Det	AL	149	557	151	**42**	3	16	(6	10)	247	75	67	93	65	1	135	4	0	0	0	0	10	.271	.351	.443	.795
2022	Det	AL	124	429	93	19	2	13	(4	9)	155	49	50	50	28	1	109	6	0	4	0	0	9	.217	.272	.361	.633
17	ChC	NL	11	33	5	2	0	1	(0	1)	10	2	3	1	1	0	12	2	0	0	0	0	2	.152	.222	.303	.525
17	Det	AL	27	94	31	7	0	2	(2	0)	44	16	13	18	12	0	18	0	0	0	0	0	2	.330	.406	.468	.874
7 ML YEARS			606	2183	525	126	13	66	(29	37)	875	283	248	297	237	5	587	30	0	10	7	5	32	.240	.322	.401	.723

Mark Canha

Bats: R **Throws:** R **Pos:** LF-123;CF-11;PH-10;RF-6;DH-3;PR-3;1B-1;3B-1   CAN-uh   **Ht:** 6'2" **Wt:** 209 **Born:** 2/15/1989 **Age:** 34

Year	Team	Lg	G	AB	H	2B	3B	HR	(Hm	Rd)	TB	R	RBI	RC	TBB	IBB	SO	HBP	SH	SF	SB	CS	GDP	Avg	OBP	Slg	OPS
2015	Oak	AL	124	441	112	22	3	16	(8	8)	188	61	70	62	33	0	96	8	0	3	7	2	9	.254	.315	.426	.742
2016	Oak	AL	16	41	5	0	0	3	(1	2)	14	4	6	0	0	0	20	1	1	1	0	1	1	.122	.140	.341	.481
2017	Oak	AL	57	173	36	13	1	5	(3	2)	66	16	14	13	7	0	56	6	0	1	2	0	5	.208	.262	.382	.644
2018	Oak	AL	122	365	91	22	0	17	(8	9)	164	60	52	52	34	3	88	10	0	2	1	2	11	.249	.328	.449	.778
2019	Oak	AL	126	410	112	16	3	26	(15	11)	212	80	58	80	67	1	107	18	0	2	3	2	10	.273	.396	.517	.913
2020	Oak	AL	59	191	47	12	2	5	(3	2)	78	32	33	43	37	1	54	10	0	5	4	0	2	.246	.387	.408	.795
2021	Oak	AL	141	519	120	22	4	17	(7	10)	201	93	61	90	77	0	128	**27**	0	2	12	2	9	.231	.358	.387	.746
2022	NYM	NL	140	462	123	24	0	13	(5	8)	186	71	61	72	48	1	97	**28**	0	4	3	1	3	.266	.367	.403	.770
Postseason			9	29	4	0	0	1	(0	1)	7	3	3	0	3	0	10	0	0	0	0	0	0	.138	.212	.241	.454
8 ML YEARS			785	2602	646	131	13	102	(50	52)	1109	417	355	412	303	6	646	108	1	20	32	10	50	.248	.348	.426	.775

Griffin Canning

Pitches: R Bats: R Pos: P   Ht: 6'2" Wt: 180 Born: 5/11/1996 Age: 27

Year	Team	Lg	G	GS	GF	IP	BFP	H	R	ER	HR	SH	SF	HB	TBB	IBB	SO	WP	W	L	Pct	Sv-Op	Hld	Vel	OPS	ERC	ERA
2019 LAA		AL	18	17	1	90.1	384	80	46	46	14	1	4	8	30	0	96	9	5	6	.455	0-0	0	-	.739	3.87	4.58
2020 LAA		AL	11	11	0	56.1	238	54	29	25	8	0	4	1	23	0	56	5	2	3	.400	0-0	0	-	.771	4.33	3.99
2021 LAA		AL	14	13	0	62.2	277	65	41	39	14	0	1	1	28	0	62	3	5	4	.556	0-0	0	-	.841	5.44	5.60
3 ML YEARS			43	41	1	209.1	899	199	116	110	36	1	9	10	81	0	214	17	12	13	.480	0-0	0	-	.779	4.45	4.73

Robinson Cano

Bats: L Throws: R Pos: 2B-20;DH-8;PH-6   kuh-NOE   Ht: 6'0" Wt: 212 Born: 10/22/1982 Age: 40

Year	Team	Lg	G	AB	H	2B	3B	HR	(Hm	Rd)	TB	R	RBI	RC	TBB	IBB	SO	HBP	SH	SF	SB	CS	GDP	Avg	OBP	Slg	OPS
2022 ElPaso		AAA	21	96	32	5	0	3	(-	-)	46	20	20	16	7	0	22	0	0	1	0	0	3	.333	.375	.479	.854
2005 NYY		AL	132	522	155	34	4	14	(5	9)	239	78	62	59	16	1	68	1	3	3	1	3	16	.297	.320	.458	.778
2006 NYY		AL	122	482	165	41	1	15	(9	6)	253	62	78	74	18	3	54	2	1	5	5	2	19	.342	.365	.525	.890
2007 NYY		AL	160	617	189	41	7	19	(10	9)	301	93	97	94	39	5	85	8	1	4	4	5	19	.306	.353	.488	.841
2008 NYY		AL	159	597	162	35	3	14	(7	7)	245	70	72	64	26	3	65	5	1	5	2	4	15	.271	.305	.410	.715
2009 NYY		AL	161	637	204	48	2	25	(14	11)	331	103	85	79	30	2	63	3	0	4	5	7	22	.320	.352	.520	.871
2010 NYY		AL	160	626	200	41	3	29	(16	13)	334	103	109	118	57	14	77	8	0	5	3	2	19	.319	.381	.534	.914
2011 NYY		AL	159	623	188	46	7	28	(16	12)	332	104	118	111	38	11	96	12	0	8	8	2	18	.302	.349	.533	.882
2012 NYY		AL	161	627	196	48	1	33	(22	11)	345	105	94	110	61	10	96	7	0	2	3	2	22	.313	.379	.550	.929
2013 NYY		AL	160	605	190	41	0	27	(11	16)	312	81	107	120	65	16	85	6	0	5	7	1	18	.314	.383	.516	.899
2014 Sea		AL	157	595	187	37	2	14	(9	5)	270	77	82	106	61	20	68	6	0	3	10	3	19	.314	.382	.454	.836
2015 Sea		AL	156	624	179	34	1	21	(11	10)	278	82	79	84	43	5	107	3	0	4	2	6	26	.287	.334	.446	.779
2016 Sea		AL	161	655	195	33	2	39	(17	22)	349	107	103	100	47	8	100	8	0	5	0	1	18	.298	.350	.533	.882
2017 Sea		AL	150	592	166	33	4	23	(11	12)	268	79	97	96	49	8	85	4	0	3	1	0	18	.280	.338	.453	.791
2018 Sea		AL	80	310	94	22	0	10	(5	5)	146	44	50	55	32	2	47	4	0	2	0	0	9	.303	.374	.471	.845
2019 NYM		NL	107	390	100	28	0	13	(6	7)	167	46	39	40	25	3	69	5	0	3	0	0	16	.256	.307	.428	.736
2020 NYM		NL	49	171	54	9	0	10	(3	7)	93	23	30	27	9	1	24	1	0	1	0	0	7	.316	.352	.544	.896
2022 3 Tms		NL	33	100	15	1	0	1	(1	0)	19	5	4	1	4	0	25	0	0	0	0	0	2	.150	.183	.190	.373
22 NYM		NL	12	41	8	0	0	1	(1	0)	11	3	3	1	2	0	11	0	0	0	0	0	0	.195	.233	.268	.501
22 SD		NL	12	33	3	0	0	0	(0	0)	3	1	1	0	1	0	10	0	0	0	0	0	0	.091	.118	.091	.209
22 Atl		NL	9	26	4	1	0	0	(0	0)	5	1	0	0	1	0	4	0	0	0	0	0	2	.154	.185	.192	.377
Postseason			51	203	45	10	3	8	(5	3)	85	22	33	23	11	3	28	2	0	1	0	2	7	.222	.267	.419	.686
17 ML YEARS			2267	8773	2639	572	33	335	(173	162)	4282	1262	1306	1338	620	112	1214	85	10	62	51	38	286	.301	.351	.488	.839

Yennier Cano

Pitches: R Bats: R Pos: RP-13   Ht: 6'4" Wt: 185 Born: 3/9/1994 Age: 29

Year	Team	Lg	G	GS	GF	IP	BFP	H	R	ER	HR	SH	SF	HB	TBB	IBB	SO	WP	W	L	Pct	Sv-Op	Hld	Vel	OPS	ERC	ERA
2022 StPaul		AAA	20	0	14	23.2	89	16	6	5	2	1	2	1	6	0	25	0	1	1	.500	3--	-	-	.565	2.06	1.90
2022 Norfolk		AAA	11	0	3	16.2	75	17	11	8	3	0	0	0	8	0	20	2	0	1	.000	1--	-	-	.751	4.98	4.32
2022 2 Tms		AL	13	0	3	18.0	97	26	23	23	3	0	2	1	16	0	21	2	1	1	.500	0-0	0	95	.956	9.61	11.50
22 Min		AL	10	0	2	13.2	70	17	14	14	3	0	2	1	11	0	14	2	1	0	1.000	0-0	0	95	.968	8.45	9.22
22 Bal		AL	3	0	1	4.1	27	9	9	9	0	0	0	0	5	0	7	0	0	1	.000	0-0	0	96	.928	13.28	18.69

Conner Capel

Bats: L Throws: L Pos: RF-18;LF-2;DH-2;PH-2;PR-1   Ht: 6'1" Wt: 185 Born: 5/19/1997 Age: 26

Year	Team	Lg	G	AB	H	2B	3B	HR	(Hm	Rd)	TB	R	RBI	RC	TBB	IBB	SO	HBP	SH	SF	SB	CS	GDP	Avg	OBP	Slg	OPS
2022 Memp		AAA	87	325	84	18	3	10	(-	-)	138	52	38	49	50	0	62	2	0	0	19	8	10	.258	.361	.425	.785
2022 2 Tms		AL	22	52	16	0	1	3	(2	1)	27	7	11	10	5	0	10	0	0	2	1	1	2	.308	.356	.519	.875
22 StL		NL	9	17	3	0	1	0	(0	1)	6	1	2	1	1	0	2	0	0	1	0	0	0	.176	.211	.353	.563
22 Oak		AL	13	35	13	0	1	2	(2	0)	21	6	9	9	4	0	8	0	0	1	1	1	2	.371	.425	.600	1.025

Vinny Capra

Bats: R Throws: R Pos: PH-3;DH-2;PR-2;2B-1;LF-1;RF-1   Ht: 5'8" Wt: 175 Born: 7/7/1996 Age: 26

Year	Team	Lg	G	AB	H	2B	3B	HR	(Hm	Rd)	TB	R	RBI	RC	TBB	IBB	SO	HBP	SH	SF	SB	CS	GDP	Avg	OBP	Slg	OPS
2022 Buffalo		AAA	52	191	54	6	1	5	(-	-)	77	31	28	29	29	0	29	1	0	1	5	2	4	.283	.378	.403	.782
2022 Tor		AL	8	5	1	0	0	0	(0	0)	1	2	0	1	2	0	1	0	0	0	0	0	0	.200	.429	.200	.629

Victor Caratini

Bats: B Throws: R Pos: C-90;PH-11;1B-2;DH-1   Ht: 6'1" Wt: 215 Born: 8/17/1993 Age: 29

Year	Team	Lg	G	AB	H	2B	3B	HR	(Hm	Rd)	TB	R	RBI	RC	TBB	IBB	SO	HBP	SH	SF	SB	CS	GDP	Avg	OBP	Slg	OPS
2017 ChC		NL	31	59	15	3	0	1	(0	1)	21	6	2	3	4	1	13	3	0	0	0	0	3	.254	.333	.356	.689
2018 ChC		NL	76	181	42	7	0	2	(1	1)	55	21	21	15	12	0	42	4	2	1	0	0	5	.232	.293	.304	.597
2019 ChC		NL	95	244	65	11	0	11	(4	7)	109	31	34	35	29	0	59	3	0	3	1	0	5	.266	.348	.447	.794
2020 ChC		NL	44	116	28	7	0	1	(0	1)	38	10	16	15	12	1	31	4	0	0	1	4	1	.241	.333	.328	.661
2021 SD		NL	116	313	71	9	0	7	(4	3)	101	33	39	30	35	8	82	4	0	4	2	0	13	.227	.309	.323	.632
2022 Mil		NL	96	272	54	12	0	9	(2	7)	93	26	34	29	31	1	67	9	1	0	0	0	11	.199	.300	.342	.642
Postseason			3	7	1	0	0	0	(0	0)	1	0	0	0	0	0	1	0	0	0	0	0	0	.143	.143	.143	.286
6 ML YEARS			458	1185	275	49	0	31	(11	20)	417	127	146	127	123	11	294	27	3	9	3	1	42	.232	.316	.352	.668

Dylan Carlson

Bats: B **Throws:** L **Pos:** CF-73;RF-62;PH-10;PR-3;DH-2 **Ht:** 6'2" **Wt:** 205 **Born:** 10/23/1998 **Age:** 24

								BATTING														RUNNING			AVERAGES			
Year	Team	Lg	G	AB	H	2B	3B	HR	(Hm	Rd)	TB	R	RBI	RC	TBB	IBB	SO	HBP	SH	SF	SB	CS	GDP	Avg	OBP	Slg	OPS
2020	StL	NL	35	110	22	7	1	3	(2	1)	40	11	16	11	8	0	35	0	0	1	1	1	3	.200	.252	.364	.616
2021	StL	NL	149	542	144	31	4	18	(9	9)	237	79	65	82	57	2	152	11	1	8	2	1	5	.266	.343	.437	.780
2022	StL	NL	128	432	102	30	4	8	(5	3)	164	56	42	50	45	1	94	7	0	4	5	2	6	.236	.316	.380	.695
	Postseason		4	13	4	1	0	0	(0	0)	5	2	0	3	4	0	4	1	0	0	1	0	0	.308	.500	.385	.885
3 ML YEARS			312	1084	268	68	9	29	(16	13)	441	146	123	143	110	3	281	18	1	13	8	4	14	.247	.323	.407	.730

Drew Carlton

Pitches: R **Bats:** R **Pos:** RP-5 **Ht:** 6'1" **Wt:** 215 **Born:** 9/8/1995 **Age:** 27

			HOW MUCH PITCHED					WHAT HE GAVE UP									THE RESULTS						
Year	Team	Lg	G	GS	GF	IP	BFP	H	R	ER	HR	SH	SF	HB	TBB	IBB	SO	WP	W	L	Pct	Sv-Op Hld	Vel	OPS	ERC	ERA
2022	Toledo	AAA	46	2	17	58.1	245	58	33	31	9	1	3	2	11	1	67	2	4	3	.571	2- - -	-	.734	3.62	4.78
2021	Det	AL	4	0	1	3.2	19	6	2	2	1	0	1	0	4	0	1	0	0	0	-	0-0 0	90	1.312	14.15	4.91
2022	Det	AL	5	0	4	8.2	32	4	4	2	1	0	1	0	0	0	7	1	0	0	-	0-0 0	91	.351	0.67	2.08
2 ML YEARS			9	0	5	12.1	51	10	6	4	2	0	2	0	4	0	8	1	0	0	-	0-0 0	91	.675	3.10	2.92

Kerry Carpenter

Bats: L **Throws:** R **Pos:** LF-12;DH-12;RF-8;PH-2 **Ht:** 6'2" **Wt:** 220 **Born:** 9/2/1997 **Age:** 25

								BATTING														RUNNING			AVERAGES			
Year	Team	Lg	G	AB	H	2B	3B	HR	(Hm	Rd)	TB	R	RBI	RC	TBB	IBB	SO	HBP	SH	SF	SB	CS	GDP	Avg	OBP	Slg	OPS
2022	Erie	AA	63	240	73	16	0	22	(-	-)	155	43	48	58	16	3	72	5	0	1	3	4	.304	.359	.646	1.005
2022	Toledo	AAA	35	118	39	11	1	8	(-	-)	76	17	27	29	17	0	17	2	0	1	2	7	3	.331	.420	.644	1.064
2022	Det	AL	31	103	26	4	1	6	(0	6)	50	16	10	16	6	0	32	3	0	1	0	0	.252	.310	.485	.795

Matt Carpenter

Bats: L **Throws:** R **Pos:** DH-16;RF-12;PH-12;1B-5;LF-3;3B-2 **Ht:** 6'4" **Wt:** 210 **Born:** 11/26/1985 **Age:** 37

								BATTING														RUNNING			AVERAGES			
Year	Team	Lg	G	AB	H	2B	3B	HR	(Hm	Rd)	TB	R	RBI	RC	TBB	IBB	SO	HBP	SH	SF	SB	CS	GDP	Avg	OBP	Slg	OPS
2022	RdRck	AAA	21	80	22	5	2	6	(-	-)	49	15	19	19	14	0	20	0	0	1	1	1	1	.275	.379	.613	.991
2011	StL	NL	7	15	1	1	0	0	(0	0)	2	0	0	0	4	0	4	0	0	0	0	0	0	.067	.263	.133	.396
2012	StL	NL	114	296	87	22	5	6	(3	3)	137	44	46	46	34	2	63	3	0	7	1	1	10	.294	.365	.463	.828
2013	StL	NL	157	626	199	55	7	11	(6	5)	301	126	78	119	72	1	98	9	3	7	3	3	4	.318	.392	.481	.873
2014	StL	NL	158	595	162	33	2	8	(4	4)	223	99	59	93	95	2	111	8	2	9	5	3	4	.272	.375	.375	.750
2015	StL	NL	154	574	156	44	3	28	(13	15)	290	101	84	108	81	5	151	6	0	4	4	3	5	.272	.365	.505	.871
2016	StL	NL	129	473	128	36	6	21	(9	12)	239	81	68	87	81	6	108	5	3	4	0	4	4	.271	.380	.505	.885
2017	StL	NL	145	497	120	31	2	23	(9	14)	224	91	69	94	109	4	125	9	2	5	2	1	5	.241	.384	.451	.835
2018	StL	NL	156	564	145	42	0	36	(13	23)	295	111	81	107	102	17	158	6	0	4	4	1	0	.257	.374	.523	.897
2019	StL	NL	129	416	94	20	2	15	(8	7)	163	59	46	61	63	0	129	7	1	5	6	1	3	.226	.334	.392	.726
2020	StL	NL	50	140	26	6	0	4	(1	3)	44	22	24	18	23	1	48	6	0	0	0	0	1	.186	.325	.314	.640
2021	StL	NL	130	207	35	11	1	3	(2	1)	57	18	21	22	35	1	77	6	0	1	2	0	1	.169	.305	.275	.581
2022	NYY	AL	47	128	39	9	0	15	(9	6)	93	28	37	43	19	1	35	5	1	1	0	0	2	.305	.412	.727	1.138
	Postseason		50	158	36	9	1	6	(4	2)	65	24	21	23	17	0	49	2	0	4	1	0	1	.228	.304	.411	.715
12 ML YEARS			1376	4531	1192	310	28	170	(77	93)	2068	780	613	798	718	40	1107	70	12	47	27	17	38	.263	.369	.456	.825

Carlos Carrasco

Pitches: R **Bats:** R **Pos:** SP-29 **Ht:** 6'4" **Wt:** 224 **Born:** 3/21/1987 **Age:** 36

			HOW MUCH PITCHED					WHAT HE GAVE UP									THE RESULTS						
Year	Team	Lg	G	GS	GF	IP	BFP	H	R	ER	HR	SH	SF	HB	TBB	IBB	SO	WP	W	L	Pct	Sv-Op Hld	Vel	OPS	ERC	ERA
2009	Cle	AL	5	5	0	22.1	112	40	23	22	6	0	1	0	11	1	11	0	0	4	.000	0-0 0	92	1.125	11.36	8.87
2010	Cle	AL	7	7	0	44.2	188	47	20	19	6	2	1	1	14	1	38	1	2	2	.500	0-0 0	93	.816	4.42	3.83
2011	Cle	AL	21	21	0	124.2	536	130	68	64	15	3	7	4	40	3	85	3	8	9	.471	0-0 0	92	.754	4.24	4.62
2013	Cle	AL	15	7	5	46.2	218	64	36	35	4	2	3	1	18	2	30	2	1	4	.200	0-0 0	95	.864	6.11	6.75
2014	Cle	AL	40	14	12	134.0	529	103	40	38	7	2	3	3	29	1	140	4	8	7	.533	1-1 0	95	.543	2.00	2.55
2015	Cle	AL	30	30	0	183.2	730	154	75	74	18	1	6	5	43	2	216	5	14	12	.538	0-0 0	95	.646	2.72	3.63
2016	Cle	AL	25	25	0	146.1	599	134	64	54	21	1	6	3	34	2	150	4	11	8	.579	0-0 0	94	.711	3.31	3.32
2017	Cle	AL	32	32	0	200.0	798	173	73	73	21	1	6	10	46	2	226	10	18	6	.750	0-0 0	94	.674	2.99	3.29
2018	Cle	AL	32	30	1	192.0	784	173	78	72	21	4	5	6	43	4	231	9	17	10	.630	0-0 0	93	.669	3.02	3.38
2019	Cle	AL	23	12	3	80.0	341	92	48	47	18	2	2	2	16	1	96	2	6	7	.462	1-2 0	93	.867	5.11	5.29
2020	Cle	AL	12	12	0	68.0	280	55	22	22	8	1	1	2	27	0	82	6	3	4	.429	0-0 0	94	.663	3.30	2.91
2021	NYM	NL	12	12	0	53.2	237	59	39	36	12	0	2	0	18	0	50	1	1	5	.167	0-0 0	93	.827	5.18	6.04
2022	NYM	NL	29	29	0	152.0	645	161	71	67	17	0	2	8	41	2	152	5	15	7	.682	0-0 0	93	.751	4.21	3.97
	Postseason		3	3	0	14.0	58	11	6	6	1	1	0	1	7	0	16	0	0	1	.000	0-0 0	94	.660	3.49	3.86
13 ML YEARS			283	236	21	1448.0	5997	1385	657	623	174	19	42	45	380	21	1507	52	104	85	.550	2-3 0	94	.713	3.56	3.87

Corbin Carroll

Bats: L **Throws:** L **Pos:** LF-25;CF-5;PH-5;RF-2;DH-2 **Ht:** 5'10" **Wt:** 165 **Born:** 8/21/2000 **Age:** 22

								BATTING														RUNNING			AVERAGES			
Year	Team	Lg	G	AB	H	2B	3B	HR	(Hm	Rd)	TB	R	RBI	RC	TBB	IBB	SO	HBP	SH	SF	SB	CS	GDP	Avg	OBP	Slg	OPS
2019	2 Tms	Low	42	154	46	9	7	2	(-	-)	75	36	20	35	29	1	41	1	0	2	18	1	1	.299	.409	.487	.896
2022	Amrillo	AA	58	227	71	11	8	16	(-	-)	146	62	39	66	41	2	68	7	0	2	20	3	0	.313	.430	.643	1.073
2022	Reno	AAA	33	129	37	11	0	7	(-	-)	69	25	22	30	24	0	36	3	0	1	11	2	2	.287	.408	.535	.943
2022	Ari	NL	32	104	27	9	2	4	(1	3)	52	13	14	15	8	0	31	3	0	0	2	1	1	.260	.330	.500	.830

Curt Casali

Bats: R **Throws:** R **Pos:** C-54;1B-3;DH-1;PH-1   cuh-SAL-ee   **Ht:** 6'2" **Wt:** 220 **Born:** 11/9/1988 **Age:** 34

Year	Team	Lg	G	AB	H	2B	3B	HR	(Hm	Rd)	TB	R	RBI	RC	TBB	IBB	SO	HBP	SH	SF	SB	CS	GDP	Avg	OBP	Slg	OPS
2014	TB	AL	30	72	12	3	0	0	(0	0)	15	10	3	3	8	0	23	2	2	0	0	0	2	.167	.268	.208	.477
2015	TB	AL	38	101	24	6	0	10	(7	3)	60	13	18	14	8	0	34	2	1	1	0	0	2	.238	.304	.594	.898
2016	TB	AL	84	226	42	10	0	8	(3	5)	76	23	25	18	25	1	82	2	3	0	0	0	2	.186	.273	.336	.609
2017	TB	AL	9	9	3	0	0	1	(1	0)	6	2	3	2	3	0	3	0	0	0	0	0	0	.333	.462	.667	1.128
2018	Cin	NL	52	140	41	10	0	4	(2	2)	63	15	16	17	12	1	32	1	1	1	0	2	5	.293	.355	.450	.805
2019	Cin	NL	84	207	52	9	0	8	(2	6)	85	24	32	24	25	1	59	1	0	3	0	0	1	.251	.331	.411	.741
2020	Cin	NL	31	76	17	3	0	6	(4	2)	38	10	8	12	14	0	29	3	0	0	2	0	0	.224	.366	.500	.866
2021	SF	NL	77	200	42	11	1	5	(4	1)	70	20	26	23	26	4	66	4	1	0	0	0	3	.210	.313	.350	.663
2022	2 Tms		57	148	30	4	0	5	(1	4)	49	20	17	18	24	0	50	2	0	2	0	0	1	.203	.318	.331	.649
22	SF	NL	41	108	25	3	0	4	(0	4)	40	13	14	16	15	0	36	1	0	2	0	0	1	.231	.325	.370	.696
22	Sea	AL	16	40	5	1	0	1	(1	0)	9	7	3	2	9	0	14	1	0	0	0	0	0	.125	.300	.225	.525
	Postseason		3	3	0	0	0	0	(0	0)	0	0	0	0	0	0	2	0	0	0	0	0	0	.000	.000	.000	.000
	9 ML YEARS		462	1179	263	56	1	47	(24	23)	462	137	148	131	145	7	378	18	8	8	2	2	18	.223	.316	.392	.707

Triston Casas

Bats: L **Throws:** R **Pos:** 1B-27;PH-4   **Ht:** 6'4" **Wt:** 252 **Born:** 1/15/2000 **Age:** 23

Year	Team	Lg	G	AB	H	2B	3B	HR	(Hm	Rd)	TB	R	RBI	RC	TBB	IBB	SO	HBP	SH	SF	SB	CS	GDP	Avg	OBP	Slg	OPS
2019	2 Tms	Low	120	429	110	26	5	20	(-	-)	206	66	81	76	58	3	118	7	0	6	3	2	11	.256	.350	.480	.830
2021	Portlnd	AA	78	277	78	12	2	13	(-	-)	133	57	52	55	49	0	64	3	0	2	6	3	6	.282	.393	.480	.873
2022	Wrcstr	AAA	72	264	72	20	1	11	(-	-)	127	45	38	51	46	4	68	3	0	4	0	0	4	.273	.382	.481	.863
2022	Bos	AL	27	76	15	1	0	5	(2	3)	31	11	12	17	19	0	23	0	0	0	1	0	4	.197	.358	.408	.766

Daniel Castano

Pitches: L **Bats:** L **Pos:** SP-7; RP-3   **Ht:** 6'3" **Wt:** 231 **Born:** 9/17/1994 **Age:** 28

Year	Team	Lg	G	GS	GF	IP	BFP	H	R	ER	HR	SH	SF	HB	TBB	IBB	SO	WP	W	L	Pct	Sv-Op	Hld	Vel	OPS	ERC	ERA
2022	Jaxnvl	AAA	7	6	0	34.0	144	33	19	16	1	0	0	1	11	0	38	1	3	0	1.000	0- -	-		.843	5.07	4.24
2020	Mia	NL	7	6	0	29.2	126	30	12	10	3	0	1	0	11	0	12	1	1	2	.333	0-0	0	89	.729	4.08	3.03
2021	Mia	NL	5	4	0	20.1	92	22	12	11	3	1	0	1	8	0	13	0	0	2	.000	0-0	0	90	.792	4.95	4.87
2022	Mia	NL	10	7	3	35.2	156	42	20	16	5	1	0	2	9	0	20	2	1	3	.250	0-0	0	91	.849	5.04	4.04
	3 ML YEARS		22	17	3	85.2	374	94	44	37	11	2	1	3	28	0	45	3	2	7	.222	0-0	0	90	.795	4.68	3.89

Ryan Castellani

Pitches: R **Bats:** R **Pos:** RP-3   **Ht:** 6'4" **Wt:** 218 **Born:** 4/1/1996 **Age:** 27

Year	Team	Lg	G	GS	GF	IP	BFP	H	R	ER	HR	SH	SF	HB	TBB	IBB	SO	WP	W	L	Pct	Sv-Op	Hld	Vel	OPS	ERC	ERA
2022	LsVgs	AAA	26	0	8	29.1	174	40	45	39	6	1	0	8	40	0	25	10	2	1	.667	3- -	-		1.061	12.82	11.97
2020	Col	NL	10	9	0	43.1	189	37	30	28	12	0	1	5	26	0	25	1	1	4	.200	0-0	0	92	.882	6.02	5.82
2021	Col	NL	1	1	0	3.1	17	5	2	2	1	0	0	1	4	0	2	0	0	0		0-0	0	90	1.422	16.64	5.40
2022	Oak	AL	3	0	1	2.2	11	2	1	0	0	0	0	0	0	0	1	2	0	0		0-0	1	93	.364	1.03	0.00
	3 ML YEARS		14	10	1	49.1	217	44	33	30	13	0	1	6	30	0	28	3	1	4	.200	0-0	1	92	.891	6.24	5.47

Humberto Castellanos

Pitches: R **Bats:** R **Pos:** SP-9; RP-2   **Ht:** 5'11" **Wt:** 222 **Born:** 4/3/1998 **Age:** 25

Year	Team	Lg	G	GS	GF	IP	BFP	H	R	ER	HR	SH	SF	HB	TBB	IBB	SO	WP	W	L	Pct	Sv-Op	Hld	Vel	OPS	ERC	ERA
2020	Hou	AL	8	0	4	10.2	51	12	8	8	2	0	0	2	5	0	12	0	0	1	.000	0-1	0	90	.850	6.42	6.75
2021	Ari	NL	14	7	2	45.2	196	48	26	25	7	5	0	2	15	0	29	0	2	2	.500	0-1	1	90	.805	4.68	4.93
2022	Ari	NL	11	9	1	44.1	194	50	29	28	7	0	4	4	12	0	32	2	3	2	.600	0-0	0	90	.822	5.10	5.68
	3 ML YEARS		33	16	7	100.2	441	110	63	61	16	5	4	8	32	0	73	2	5	5	.500	0-2	1	90	.817	5.05	5.45

Nick Castellanos

Bats: R **Throws:** R **Pos:** RF-121;DH-12;LF-3;PH-2   cahs-teh-YAHN-ohs   **Ht:** 6'4" **Wt:** 203 **Born:** 3/4/1992 **Age:** 31

Year	Team	Lg	G	AB	H	2B	3B	HR	(Hm	Rd)	TB	R	RBI	RC	TBB	IBB	SO	HBP	SH	SF	SB	CS	GDP	Avg	OBP	Slg	OPS
2013	Det	AL	11	18	5	0	0	0	(0	0)	5	1	0	1	0	0	1	0	0	0	0	0	0	.278	.278	.278	.556
2014	Det	AL	148	533	138	31	4	11	(6	5)	210	50	66	63	36	3	140	3	0	7	2	2	7	.259	.306	.394	.700
2015	Det	AL	154	549	140	33	6	15	(6	9)	230	42	73	66	39	1	152	1	0	6	0	3	21	.255	.303	.419	.721
2016	Det	AL	110	411	117	25	4	18	(5	13)	204	54	58	67	28	1	111	3	0	5	1	1	4	.285	.331	.496	.827
2017	Det	AL	157	614	167	36	10	26	(14	12)	301	73	101	97	41	0	142	5	0	5	4	5	12	.272	.320	.490	.811
2018	Det	AL	157	620	185	46	5	23	(10	13)	310	88	89	110	49	5	151	6	0	3	2	1	8	.298	.354	.500	.854
2019	2 Tms		151	615	178	58	3	27	(11	16)	323	100	73	94	41	1	143	5	0	3	2	2	12	.289	.337	.525	.863
2020	Cin	NL	60	218	49	11	2	14	(7	7)	106	37	34	29	19	1	69	4	0	1	0	2	5	.225	.298	.486	.784
2021	Cin	NL	138	531	164	38	1	34	(23	11)	306	95	100	101	41	5	121	7	0	6	3	1	16	.309	.362	.576	.939
2022	Phi	NL	136	524	138	27	0	13	(7	6)	204	56	62	60	29	0	130	3	0	2	7	1	15	.263	.305	.389	.694
19	Det	AL	100	403	110	37	3	11	(3	8)	186	57	37	54	31	1	96	3	0	2	1	1	7	.273	.328	.462	.790
19	ChC	NL	51	212	68	21	0	16	(8	8)	137	43	36	40	10	0	47	2	0	1	1	1	5	.321	.356	.646	1.002
	Postseason		5	20	4	1	0	1	(0	1)	8	1	1	0	2	1	5	0	0	0	0	0	0	.200	.273	.400	.673
	10 ML YEARS		1222	4633	1281	305	35	181	(89	92)	2199	596	656	688	323	17	1160	37	0	38	21	18	100	.276	.326	.475	.801

Diego Castillo

Pitches: R **Bats:** R **Pos:** RP-59   **Ht:** 6'3" **Wt:** 268 **Born:** 1/18/1994 **Age:** 29

Year	Team	Lg	G	GS	GF	IP	BFP	H	R	ER	HR	SH	SF	HB	TBB	IBB	SO	WP	W	L	Pct	Sv-Op	Hld	Vel	OPS	ERC	ERA
2018	TB	AL	43	11	5	56.2	222	36	21	20	6	0	0	2	18	0	65	5	4	2	.667	0-2	10	98	.554	2.09	3.18
2019	TB	AL	65	6	18	68.2	290	59	32	26	8	1	1	5	26	4	81	5	5	8	.385	8-10	17	98	.685	3.53	3.41
2020	TB	AL	22	0	5	21.2	89	12	4	4	3	0	0	1	11	0	23	0	3	0	1.000	4-5	5	96	.581	2.52	1.66
2021	2 Tms	AL	61	0	32	58.1	233	40	23	18	9	2	3	5	17	2	75	2	5	5	.500	16-22	10	95	.623	2.64	2.78
2022	Sea	AL	59	0	23	54.1	222	40	27	22	5	0	1	2	22	4	53	1	7	3	.700	7-7	9	95	.588	2.69	3.64
21	TB	AL	37	0	26	36.1	145	26	14	11	5	2	2	1	10	2	49	1	2	4	.333	14-16	3	95	.613	2.37	2.72
21	Sea	AL	24	0	6	22.0	88	14	9	7	4	0	1	4	7	0	26	1	3	1	.750	2-6	7	94	.639	3.11	2.86
	Postseason		14	1	5	16.2	69	12	3	2	0	1	0	1	9	0	20	0	1	0	1.000	3-3	2	98	.565	2.71	1.08
	5 ML YEARS		250	17	83	259.2	1056	187	107	90	31	3	5	15	94	10	297	13	24	18	.571	35-46	51	97	.614	2.74	3.12

Diego Castillo

Bats: R **Throws:** R **Pos:** SS-32;2B-28;RF-22;PH-19;1B-7;3B-4;DH-1;PR-1   **Ht:** 5'11" **Wt:** 185 **Born:** 10/28/1997 **Age:** 25

Year	Team	Lg	G	AB	H	2B	3B	HR	(Hm	Rd)	TB	R	RBI	RC	TBB	IBB	SO	HBP	SH	SF	SB	CS	GDP	Avg	OBP	Slg	OPS
2022	Indy	AAA	35	134	33	6	0	3	(-	-)	48	21	12	14	14	0	33	3	0	0	1	1	7	.246	.331	.358	.689
2022	2 Pit	NL	96	262	54	13	0	11	(2	9)	100	28	29	24	14	1	75	3	0	4	1	1	7	.206	.251	.382	.633

Jose Castillo

Pitches: L **Bats:** L **Pos:** RP-1   **Ht:** 6'6" **Wt:** 252 **Born:** 1/10/1996 **Age:** 27

Year	Team	Lg	G	GS	GF	IP	BFP	H	R	ER	HR	SH	SF	HB	TBB	IBB	SO	WP	W	L	Pct	Sv-Op	Hld	Vel	OPS	ERC	ERA
2022	Lk Els	A	5	0	0	5.1	22	4	1	0	0	0	0	0	1	0	7	0	0	0	-	0- -	-	-		1.45	0.00
2022	ElPaso	AAA	43	0	10	43.1	184	43	16	14	3	0	1	2	20	0	58	1	3	2	.600	3- -	-	-	.745	4.41	2.91
2018	SD	NL	37	0	5	38.1	150	23	14	14	3	0	0	3	12	1	52	1	3	3	.500	0-1	12	95	.520	1.87	3.29
2019	SD	NL	1	0	0	0.2	4	0	0	0	0	0	0	1	1	0	2	1	0	0	-	0-0	0	95	.500	7.00	0.00
2022	SD	NL	1	0	0	1.0	5	1	1	1	0	0	1	0	1	0	1	0	0	0	-	0-0	0	95	.733	5.48	9.00
	3 ML YEARS		39	0	5	40.0	159	24	15	15	3	0	1	4	14	1	55	2	3	3	.500	0-1	12	95	.528	2.03	3.38

Luis Castillo

Pitches: R **Bats:** R **Pos:** RP-3   **Ht:** 6'3" **Wt:** 212 **Born:** 3/10/1995 **Age:** 28

Year	Team	Lg	G	GS	GF	IP	BFP	H	R	ER	HR	SH	SF	HB	TBB	IBB	SO	WP	W	L	Pct	Sv-Op	Hld	Vel	OPS	ERC	ERA
2022	Toledo	AAA	40	0	2	41.1	167	39	10	8	2	1	0	1	11	0	39	0	4	1	.800	0- -	-	-	.658	3.11	1.74
2022	Det	AL	3	0	1	3.2	14	2	0	0	0	0	0	0	0	0	4	0	0	0	-	0-0	0	94	.286	0.59	0.00

Luis Castillo

Pitches: R **Bats:** R **Pos:** SP-25   **Ht:** 6'2" **Wt:** 200 **Born:** 12/12/1992 **Age:** 30

Year	Team	Lg	G	GS	GF	IP	BFP	H	R	ER	HR	SH	SF	HB	TBB	IBB	SO	WP	W	L	Pct	Sv-Op	Hld	Vel	OPS	ERC	ERA
2017	Cin	NL	15	15	0	89.1	359	64	32	31	11	4	3	3	32	1	98	2	3	7	.300	0-0	0	97	.638	2.70	3.12
2018	Cin	NL	31	31	0	169.2	708	158	89	81	28	3	6	5	49	1	165	4	10	12	.455	0-0	0	96	.732	3.80	4.30
2019	Cin	NL	32	32	0	190.2	781	139	76	72	22	6	1	7	79	0	226	5	15	8	.652	0-0	0	96	.633	2.94	3.40
2020	Cin	NL	12	12	0	70.0	292	62	31	25	5	0	1	1	24	0	89	1	4	6	.400	0-0	0	97	.663	3.10	3.21
2021	Cin	NL	33	33	0	187.2	803	181	94	83	19	8	2	7	75	4	192	1	8	16	.333	0-0	0	97	.733	4.03	3.98
2022	2 Tms		25	25	0	150.1	615	118	56	50	13	1	3	8	45	0	167	0	8	6	.571	0-0	0	97	.611	2.66	2.99
22	Cin	NL	14	14	0	85.0	349	63	30	27	7	1	1	4	28	0	90	0	4	4	.500	0-0	0	97	.592	2.48	2.86
22	Sea	AL	11	11	0	65.1	266	55	26	23	6	0	2	4	17	0	77	0	4	2	.667	0-0	0	97	.636	2.90	3.17
	Postseason		1	1	0	5.1	23	6	1	1	0	0	0	1	1	1	7	0	0	1	.000	0-0	0	98	.623	2.88	1.69
	6 ML YEARS		148	148	0	857.2	3558	722	378	342	98	22	16	31	304	6	937	13	48	55	.466	0-0	0	97	.675	3.27	3.59

Max Castillo

Pitches: R **Bats:** R **Pos:** RP-8; SP-6   **Ht:** 6'2" **Wt:** 280 **Born:** 5/4/1999 **Age:** 24

Year	Team	Lg	G	GS	GF	IP	BFP	H	R	ER	HR	SH	SF	HB	TBB	IBB	SO	WP	W	L	Pct	Sv-Op	Hld	Vel	OPS	ERC	ERA
2022	Nham	AA	6	6	0	29.0	122	21	10	10	3	1	1	0	14	0	35	2	3	1	.750	0- -	-	-	.667	2.88	3.10
2022	Buffalo	AAA	5	3	0	27.1	100	10	2	2	2	0	0	1	10	0	29	0	2	0	1.000	0- -	-	-	.423	1.15	0.66
2022	Omha	AAA	7	6	0	21.1	113	35	24	20	8	0	3	2	9	0	22	0	1	1	.500	0- -	-	-	.973	8.47	8.44
2022	2 Tms	AL	14	6	4	39.1	170	38	28	26	8	1	1	2	15	0	37	2	0	2	.000	0-0	0	93	.776	4.73	5.95
22	Tor	AL	9	2	4	20.2	81	15	9	7	4	0	0	0	5	0	20	1	0	0	-	0-0	0	94	.628	2.59	3.05
22	KC	AL	5	4	0	18.2	89	23	19	19	4	1	1	2	10	0	17	1	0	2	.000	0-0	0	92	.918	7.44	9.16

Anthony Castro

Pitches: R **Bats:** R **Pos:** RP-12   **Ht:** 6'2" **Wt:** 185 **Born:** 4/13/1995 **Age:** 28

Year	Team	Lg	G	GS	GF	IP	BFP	H	R	ER	HR	SH	SF	HB	TBB	IBB	SO	WP	W	L	Pct	Sv-Op	Hld	Vel	OPS	ERC	ERA
2022	Clmbs	AAA	28	0	18	29.2	132	25	15	13	2	0	0	2	20	2	39	3	1	3	.250	3- -	-	-	.692	4.19	3.94
2022	Norfolk	AAA	8	0	2	8.1	37	8	2	2	0	0	0	0	6	0	8	0	0	0	-	0- -	-	-	.701	4.46	2.16
2020	Det	AL	1	0	1	1.0	5	1	2	2	1	0	0	0	1	0	1	0	0	0	-	0-0	0	92	1.400	14.27	18.00
2021	Tor	AL	25	0	7	24.2	109	23	15	13	4	0	1	3	8	2	32	4	1	2	.333	1-2	1	95	.745	4.05	4.74
2022	Cle	AL	12	0	2	13.1	65	19	15	11	5	0	0	0	10	0	12	1	0	0	-	0-1	0	95	1.101	11.20	7.43
	3 ML YEARS		38	0	10	39.0	179	43	32	26	10	0	1	3	19	2	45	5	1	2	.333	1-3	1	95	.889	6.45	6.00

Harold Castro

Bats: L **Throws:** R **Pos:** 1B-50;3B-25;SS-19;2B-14;DH-9;PH-9;LF-3;CF-1;PR-1   **Ht:** 5'10" **Wt:** 195 **Born:** 11/30/1993 **Age:** 29

									BATTING									RUNNING			AVERAGES			
Year	Team	Lg	G	AB	H	2B	3B	HR	(Hm | Rd)	TB	R	RBI	RC	TBB	IBB	SO	HBP	SH	SF	SB	CS	GDP	Avg	OBP	Slg	OPS
2018	Det	AL	6	10	3	0	0	0	(0 | 0)	3	2	0	1	0	0	2	0	0	0	1	0	0	.300	.300	.300	.600
2019	Det	AL	97	354	103	10	4	5	(2 | 3)	136	30	38	44	9	0	86	0	2	4	4	2	6	.291	.305	.384	.689
2020	Det	AL	22	49	17	4	0	0	(0 | 0)	21	6	3	8	5	0	11	0	0	0	0	0	1	.347	.407	.429	.836
2021	Det	AL	106	315	89	13	1	3	(3 | 0)	113	35	37	36	14	0	72	1	4	5	1	1	7	.283	.310	.359	.669
2022	Det	AL	120	420	114	21	2	7	(2 | 5)	160	37	47	52	17	1	79	1	3	2	0	1	5	.271	.300	.381	.681
	5 ML YEARS		351	1148	326	48	7	15	(7 | 8)	433	110	125	141	45	1	250	2	9	11	6	4	19	.284	.309	.377	.686

Jason Castro

Bats: L **Throws:** R **Pos:** C-30;PH-7   **Ht:** 6'3" **Wt:** 215 **Born:** 6/18/1987 **Age:** 36

									BATTING									RUNNING			AVERAGES			
Year	Team	Lg	G	AB	H	2B	3B	HR	(Hm | Rd)	TB	R	RBI	RC	TBB	IBB	SO	HBP	SH	SF	SB	CS	GDP	Avg	OBP	Slg	OPS
2010	Hou	NL	67	195	40	8	1	2	(1 | 1)	56	26	8	12	22	2	41	0	0	0	0	0	4	.205	.286	.287	.573
2012	Hou	NL	87	257	66	15	2	6	(3 | 3)	103	29	29	33	31	2	61	1	2	4	0	0	8	.257	.334	.401	.735
2013	Hou	AL	120	435	120	35	1	18	(13 | 5)	211	63	56	76	50	3	130	2	0	4	2	1	4	.276	.350	.485	.835
2014	Hou	AL	126	465	103	21	2	14	(10 | 4)	170	43	56	45	34	1	151	9	1	3	1	0	11	.222	.286	.366	.651
2015	Hou	AL	104	337	71	19	0	11	(8 | 3)	123	38	31	29	33	1	115	2	0	3	0	0	5	.211	.283	.365	.648
2016	Hou	AL	113	329	69	16	3	11	(5 | 6)	124	41	32	34	45	0	123	1	1	0	2	1	9	.210	.307	.377	.684
2017	Min	AL	110	356	86	22	0	10	(6 | 4)	138	49	47	45	45	1	108	4	1	1	0	0	10	.242	.333	.388	.720
2018	Min	AL	19	63	9	3	0	1	(0 | 1)	15	4	3	1	9	0	26	1	0	1	0	0	2	.143	.257	.238	.495
2019	Min	AL	79	237	55	9	0	13	(7 | 6)	103	39	30	31	33	0	88	3	1	1	0	0	2	.232	.332	.435	.767
2020	2 Tms		27	80	15	9	0	2	(1 | 1)	30	8	9	11	12	0	33	0	0	0	0	0	2	.188	.293	.375	.668
2021	Hou	AL	66	149	35	7	0	8	(4 | 4)	66	22	21	23	25	1	54	3	2	0	0	0	4	.235	.356	.443	.799
2022	Hou	AL	34	78	9	2	0	1	(0 | 1)	14	6	3	0	8	0	40	1	0	1	1	0	1	.115	.205	.179	.384
20	LAA	AL	18	52	10	4	0	2	(1 | 1)	20	5	6	8	10	0	23	0	0	0	0	0	1	.192	.323	.385	.707
20	SD	NL	9	28	5	5	0	0	(0 | 0)	10	3	3	3	2	0	10	0	0	0	0	0	1	.179	.233	.357	.590
	Postseason		14	27	3	0	0	1	(1 | 0)	6	3	4	3	4	0	13	0	0	0	0	0	2	.111	.226	.222	.448
	12 ML YEARS		952	2981	678	166	9	97	(58 | 39)	1153	368	325	340	347	11	970	27	8	18	6	2	60	.227	.312	.387	.699

Kervin Castro

Pitches: R **Bats:** R **Pos:** RP-10   **Ht:** 6'0" **Wt:** 185 **Born:** 2/7/1999 **Age:** 24

			HOW MUCH PITCHED					WHAT HE GAVE UP									THE RESULTS							
Year	Team	Lg	G	GS	GF	IP	BFP	H	R	ER	HR	SH	SF	HB	TBB	IBB	SO	WP	W	L	Pct	Sv-Op Hld	Vel	OPS	ERC	ERA
2022	Scrmto	AAA	29	0	6	32.1	151	31	21	20	4	1	1	3	24	0	32	2	0	4	.000	0-- -	-	.797	5.80	5.57
2022	Iowa	AAA	8	0	1	13.2	51	7	2	2	0	0	1	0	7	1	18	3	2	0	1.000	1-- -	-	.507	1.52	1.32
2021	SF	NL	10	0	4	13.1	56	13	1	0	1	1	0	0	4	1	13	0	1	0	.500	0-0 0	95	.609	2.76	0.00
2022	2 Tms	NL	10	0	6	12.1	57	15	14	14	3	0	0	0	7	0	11	0	0	1	.000	0-0 0	93	.966	7.33	10.22
22	SF	NL	2	0	1	1.2	11	4	5	5	0	0	0	0	2	0	4	0	0	0	-	0-0 0	94	1.212	15.90	27.00
22	ChC	NL	8	0	5	10.2	46	11	9	9	3	0	0	0	5	0	7	0	0	1	.000	0-0 0	93	.909	6.02	7.59
	Postseason		2	0	1	1.1	6	0	0	0	0	0	0	0	2	0	0	0	0	0	-	0-0 0	95	.333	1.96	0.00
	2 ML YEARS		20	0	10	25.2	113	28	15	14	3	1	0	1	11	1	24	0	1	2	.333	0-0 0	94	.788	4.79	4.91

Miguel Castro

Pitches: R **Bats:** R **Pos:** RP-34   **Ht:** 6'7" **Wt:** 201 **Born:** 12/24/1994 **Age:** 28

			HOW MUCH PITCHED					WHAT HE GAVE UP									THE RESULTS							
Year	Team	Lg	G	GS	GF	IP	BFP	H	R	ER	HR	SH	SF	HB	TBB	IBB	SO	WP	W	L	Pct	Sv-Op Hld	Vel	OPS	ERC	ERA
2015	2 Tms		18	0	12	17.2	83	21	13	12	4	0	2	0	10	2	18	2	0	3	.000	4-6 1	96	.937	6.61	6.11
2016	Col	NL	19	0	4	14.2	67	18	10	10	3	1	0	1	9	0	12	0	0	0	-	0-1 7	96	.880	6.21	6.14
2017	Bal	AL	39	1	8	66.1	274	53	29	26	8	3	4	2	28	4	38	2	3	3	.500	0-0 1	96	.682	3.27	3.53
2018	Bal	AL	63	1	16	86.1	376	75	41	38	9	0	3	5	50	7	57	9	2	7	.222	0-2 5	96	.714	4.22	3.96
2019	Bal	AL	65	0	28	73.1	319	63	42	38	10	0	6	0	41	3	71	11	1	3	.250	2-5 9	97	.712	4.08	4.66
2020	2 Tms		26	0	5	24.2	115	28	12	11	4	0	0	1	13	0	38	0	2	2	.500	1-3 5	98	.821	5.95	4.01
2021	NYM	NL	69	2	7	70.1	303	48	30	27	7	0	0	6	43	0	77	8	3	4	.429	0-2 9	98	.619	3.46	3.45
2022	NYY	AL	34	0	2	29.0	131	27	16	13	2	0	0	4	15	0	31	2	5	0	1.000	0-1 9	98	.741	4.42	4.03
15	Tor	AL	13	0	9	12.1	57	15	7	6	2	0	2	0	6	2	12	2	0	2	.000	4-6 1	96	.858	5.86	4.38
15	Col	NL	5	0	3	5.1	26	6	6	6	2	0	0	0	4	0	6	0	0	1	.000	0-0 0	96	1.112	8.41	10.13
20	Bal	AL	16	0	4	15.2	70	17	7	7	3	0	0	1	5	0	24	0	1	0	1.000	1-3 4	98	.782	5.04	4.02
20	NYM	NL	10	0	1	9.0	45	11	5	4	1	0	0	0	8	0	14	0	1	2	.333	0-0 1	99	.882	7.55	4.00
	8 ML YEARS		333	4	82	382.1	1668	333	193	175	47	4	15	19	205	16	342	34	16	22	.421	7-20 46	97	.719	4.18	4.12

Rodolfo Castro

Bats: B **Throws:** R **Pos:** 2B-32;3B-24;SS-19;DH-2;PH-1;PR-1   **Ht:** 6'0" **Wt:** 205 **Born:** 5/21/1999 **Age:** 24

									BATTING									RUNNING			AVERAGES			
Year	Team	Lg	G	AB	H	2B	3B	HR	(Hm | Rd)	TB	R	RBI	RC	TBB	IBB	SO	HBP	SH	SF	SB	CS	GDP	Avg	OBP	Slg	OPS
2022	Indy	AAA	75	272	67	13	2	12	(- | -)	120	37	40	42	32	0	86	6	0	4	6	3	6	.246	.334	.441	.776
2021	Pit	NL	31	86	17	2	0	5	(2 | 3)	34	9	8	5	6	0	27	1	0	0	0	0	4	.198	.258	.395	.653
2022	Pit	NL	71	253	59	8	4	11	(3 | 8)	108	25	27	35	22	0	74	2	0	1	5	3	6	.233	.299	.427	.725
	2 ML YEARS		102	339	76	10	4	16	(5 | 11)	142	34	35	40	28	0	101	3	0	1	5	3	10	.224	.288	.419	.707

Willi Castro

Bats: B **Throws:** R **Pos:** RF-40;LF-27;2B-16;SS-16;CF-16;PH-8;3B-6;PR-6;DH-5   **Ht:** 6'1" **Wt:** 206 **Born:** 4/24/1997 **Age:** 26

						BATTING													RUNNING			AVERAGES			
Year	Team	Lg	G	AB	H	2B	3B	HR	(Hm | Rd)	TB	R	RBI	RC	TBB	IBB	SO	HBP	SH	SF	SB	CS	GDP	Avg	OBP	Slg	OPS
2019	Det	AL	30	100	23	6	1	1	(1 | 0)	34	10	8	9	6	0	34	2	1	1	0	1	4	.230	.284	.340	.624
2020	Det	AL	36	129	45	4	2	6	(3 | 3)	71	21	24	30	7	0	38	1	1	2	0	1	0	.349	.381	.550	.932
2021	Det	AL	125	413	91	15	6	9	(5 | 4)	145	56	38	36	23	1	109	8	3	3	9	4	5	.220	.273	.351	.624
2022	Det	AL	112	365	88	18	2	8	(5 | 3)	134	47	31	31	15	0	82	8	1	3	9	4	4	.241	.284	.367	.651
	4 ML YEARS		303	1007	247	43	11	24	(14 | 10)	384	134	101	106	51	1	263	19	6	9	18	10	13	.245	.292	.381	.673

Cade Cavalli

Pitches: R **Bats:** R **Pos:** SP-1   **Ht:** 6'4" **Wt:** 240 **Born:** 8/14/1998 **Age:** 24

			HOW MUCH PITCHED				WHAT HE GAVE UP									THE RESULTS							
Year	Team	Lg	G	GS	GF	IP	BFP	H	R	ER	HR	SH	SF	HB	TBB	IBB	SO	WP	W	L	Pct	Sv-Op	Hld	Vel	OPS	ERC	ERA
2021	Hrsbrg	AA	11	11	0	58.0	243	39	19	18	2	0	0	0	35	0	80	5	3	3	.500	0- -	-	-	.571	2.66	2.79
2021	Roch	AAA	5	5	0	24.0	114	31	17	16	2	0	0	4	10	0	23	1	1	4	.200	0- -	-	-	.795	6.45	6.00
2021	Wilmg	A+	7	7	0	40.2	158	24	9	8	1	0	0	2	12	0	71	0	3	1	.750	0- -	-	-	-	1.48	1.77
2022	Roch	AAA	20	20	0	97.0	401	75	43	40	3	0	4	9	39	0	104	4	6	4	.600	0- -	-	-	.602	2.80	3.71
2022	Was	NL	1	1	0	4.1	23	6	7	7	0	0	0	3	2	0	6	0	0	1	.000	0-0	0	96	.978	8.88	14.54

Jake Cave

Bats: L **Throws:** L **Pos:** LF-45;RF-10;PH-7;CF-4;PR-1   **Ht:** 6'0" **Wt:** 200 **Born:** 12/4/1992 **Age:** 30

						BATTING													RUNNING			AVERAGES			
Year	Team	Lg	G	AB	H	2B	3B	HR	(Hm	Rd)	TB	R	RBI	RC	TBB	IBB	SO	HBP	SH	SF	SB	CS	GDP	Avg	OBP	Slg	OPS
2022	StPaul	AAA	85	322	88	20	7	14	(-	-)	164	63	57	61	43	3	93	7	0	1	10	0	10	.273	.370	.509	.879
2018	Min	AL	91	283	75	16	2	13	(6	7)	134	54	45	46	18	2	102	3	2	3	2	1	2	.265	.313	.473	.786
2019	Min	AL	72	198	51	11	2	8	(3	5)	90	28	25	27	21	0	71	8	0	1	0	0	5	.258	.351	.455	.805
2020	Min	AL	42	113	25	3	2	4	(3	1)	44	17	15	15	5	0	44	5	0	0	0	2	0	.221	.285	.389	.674
2021	Min	AL	76	164	31	6	1	3	(1	2)	48	14	13	13	10	0	62	3	1	0	1	1	0	.189	.249	.293	.541
2022	Min	AL	54	164	35	7	3	5	(3	2)	63	17	20	17	11	0	49	0	0	2	2	0	2	.213	.260	.384	.644
	Postseason		3	5	1	0	0	0	(0	0)	1	0	0	0	0	0	3	0	0	0	0	0	0	.200	.200	.200	.400
	5 ML YEARS		335	922	217	43	10	33	(16	17)	379	130	118	118	65	2	328	19	3	6	5	4	9	.235	.297	.411	.708

Dylan Cease

Pitches: R **Bats:** R **Pos:** SP-32   **Ht:** 6'2" **Wt:** 195 **Born:** 12/28/1995 **Age:** 27

			HOW MUCH PITCHED				WHAT HE GAVE UP									THE RESULTS							
Year	Team	Lg	G	GS	GF	IP	BFP	H	R	ER	HR	SH	SF	HB	TBB	IBB	SO	WP	W	L	Pct	Sv-Op	Hld	Vel	OPS	ERC	ERA
2019	CWS	AL	14	14	0	73.0	326	78	51	47	15	0	1	2	35	1	81	4	4	7	.364	0-0	0	97	.839	5.70	5.79
2020	CWS	AL	12	12	0	58.1	255	50	30	26	12	0	1	5	34	1	44	1	5	4	.556	0-0	0	97	.827	5.17	4.01
2021	CWS	AL	32	32	0	165.2	708	139	77	72	20	1	7	9	68	0	226	13	13	7	.650	0-0	0	97	.670	3.54	3.91
2022	CWS	AL	32	32	0	184.0	747	126	55	45	16	2	1	3	78	2	227	7	14	8	.636	0-0	0	97	.584	2.48	2.20
	Postseason		2	1	0	2.2	13	2	3	3	0	0	0	0	3	0	2	0	0	0	-	0-0	0	99	.685	4.52	10.13
	4 ML YEARS		90	90	0	481.0	2036	393	213	190	63	3	10	19	215	4	578	25	36	26	.581	0-0	0	97	.684	3.60	3.56

Gilberto Celestino

Bats: R **Throws:** L **Pos:** CF-90;LF-28;PH-14;PR-9;RF-8   **Ht:** 6'0" **Wt:** 170 **Born:** 2/13/1999 **Age:** 24

						BATTING													RUNNING			AVERAGES			
Year	Team	Lg	G	AB	H	2B	3B	HR	(Hm	Rd)	TB	R	RBI	RC	TBB	IBB	SO	HBP	SH	SF	SB	CS	GDP	Avg	OBP	Slg	OPS
2021	Min	AL	23	59	8	3	0	2	(0	2)	17	7	3	1	3	0	14	0	0	0	0	0	2	.136	.177	.288	.466
2022	Min	AL	122	311	74	12	1	2	(1	1)	94	30	24	24	32	0	77	2	2	0	4	1	13	.238	.313	.302	.615
	2 ML YEARS		145	370	82	15	1	4	(1	3)	111	37	27	25	35	0	91	2	2	0	4	1	15	.222	.292	.300	.592

Luis Cessa

Pitches: R **Bats:** R **Pos:** RP-36; SP-10   SESS-uh   **Ht:** 6'0" **Wt:** 208 **Born:** 4/25/1992 **Age:** 31

			HOW MUCH PITCHED				WHAT HE GAVE UP									THE RESULTS							
Year	Team	Lg	G	GS	GF	IP	BFP	H	R	ER	HR	SH	SF	HB	TBB	IBB	SO	WP	W	L	Pct	Sv-Op	Hld	Vel	OPS	ERC	ERA
2016	NYY	AL	17	9	5	70.1	285	64	36	34	16	1	1	3	14	0	46	2	4	4	.500	0-0	0	95	.744	3.81	4.35
2017	NYY	AL	10	5	2	36.0	160	36	21	19	7	0	0	3	17	0	30	2	0	3	.000	0-0	0	96	.829	5.43	4.75
2018	NYY	AL	16	5	6	44.2	195	51	27	26	5	1	0	0	13	0	39	7	1	4	.200	2-2	0	95	.761	4.50	5.24
2019	NYY	AL	43	0	14	81.0	343	75	42	37	14	0	4	3	31	1	75	1	2	1	.667	1-1	4	94	.751	4.26	4.11
2020	NYY	AL	16	0	6	21.2	93	20	10	8	2	0	0	0	7	0	17	1	0	0	-	1-1	1	94	.693	3.20	3.32
2021	2 Tms		53	0	15	64.2	261	55	24	18	5	2	0	0	19	1	54	1	5	2	.714	0-0	4	94	.627	2.74	2.51
2022	Cin	NL	46	10	1	80.2	336	76	44	41	14	0	2	2	28	0	59	3	4	4	.500	0-1	5	94	.753	4.22	4.57
21	NYY	AL	29	0	13	38.1	161	31	17	12	2	2	0	0	17	1	31	0	3	1	.750	0-0	1	93	.605	2.83	2.82
21	Cin	NL	24	0	2	26.1	100	24	7	6	3	0	0	0	2	0	23	1	2	1	.667	0-0	3	94	.658	2.57	2.05
	Postseason		5	0	3	8.0	32	5	2	2	0	0	1	0	3	0	7	0	0	0	-	0-0	0	94	.531	1.92	2.25
	7 ML YEARS		201	29	49	399.0	1673	377	204	183	63	4	7	11	129	2	320	17	16	18	.471	4-5	14	94	.736	3.99	4.13

Jhoulys Chacin

Pitches: R Bats: R Pos: RP-35 yoo-LEES cha-SEEN Ht: 6'3" Wt: 215 Born: 1/7/1988 Age: 35

Year	Team	Lg	G	GS	GF	IP	BFP	H	R	ER	HR	SH	SF	HB	TBB	IBB	SO	WP	W	L	Pct	Sv-Op	Hld	Vel	OPS	ERC	ERA
2009	Col	NL	9	1	3	11.0	48	6	6	6	1	1	0	0	11	0	13	2	0	1	.000	0-0	0	91	.667	3.87	4.91
2010	Col	NL	28	21	2	137.1	583	114	64	50	10	6	5	9	61	5	138	4	9	11	.450	0-0	0	91	.650	3.33	3.28
2011	Col	NL	31	31	0	194.0	827	168	87	78	20	5	3	4	87	1	150	7	11	14	.440	0-0	0	91	.707	3.61	3.62
2012	Col	NL	14	14	0	69.0	314	80	35	34	10	1	1	2	32	0	45	3	3	5	.375	0-0	0	91	.821	5.73	4.43
2013	Col	NL	31	31	0	197.1	816	188	82	76	11	3	7	3	61	3	126	5	14	10	.583	0-0	0	90	.685	3.26	3.47
2014	Col	NL	11	11	0	63.1	272	63	38	38	8	2	3	1	28	1	42	4	1	7	.125	0-0	0	88	.790	4.52	5.40
2015	Ari	NL	5	4	0	26.2	111	24	11	10	4	1	0	0	10	0	21	0	2	1	.667	0-0	0	89	.729	3.80	3.38
2016	2 Tms		34	22	5	144.0	632	153	81	77	14	4	6	5	55	4	119	8	6	8	.429	0-0	0	91	.745	4.42	4.81
2017	SD	NL	32	32	0	180.1	765	157	82	78	19	6	6	14	72	5	153	7	13	10	.565	0-0	0	91	.693	3.67	3.89
2018	Mil	NL	35	35	0	192.2	796	153	83	75	18	8	9	11	71	3	156	5	15	8	.652	0-0	0	90	.655	3.01	3.50
2019	2 Tms		25	24	0	103.1	470	115	73	69	25	4	4	5	46	1	101	3	3	12	.200	0-0	0	91	.877	6.13	6.01
2020	Atl	NL	2	0	0	5.0	24	6	4	4	1	0	0	0	3	0	3	0	1	0	1.000	0-0	0	91	.851	6.75	7.20
2021	Col	NL	46	1	3	64.1	269	53	32	31	8	1	1	0	28	0	47	1	3	2	.600	0-2	17	93	.708	3.42	4.34
2022	Col	NL	35	0	7	47.1	219	55	44	40	7	0	1	2	21	0	37	3	4	2	.667	0-0	2	93	.848	5.63	7.61
16	Atl	NL	5	5	0	26.2	117	29	17	16	4	2	1	0	8	0	27	0	1	2	.333	0-0	0	89	.756	4.42	5.40
16	LAA	AL	29	17	5	117.1	515	124	64	61	10	2	5	5	47	4	92	8	5	6	.455	0-0	0	91	.742	4.42	4.68
19	Mil	NL	19	19	0	88.2	403	99	61	57	19	4	4	5	39	1	80	3	3	10	.231	0-0	0	90	.857	5.96	5.79
19	Bos	AL	6	5	0	14.2	67	16	12	12	6	0	0	0	7	0	21	0	0	2	.000	0-0	0	90	.993	7.12	7.36
	Postseason		3	3	0	12.1	51	9	2	2	1	0	0	0	6	1	9	0	2	1	.667	0-0	0	91	.627	2.72	1.46
	14 ML YEARS		338	227	20	1435.2	6146	1335	722	666	156	42	46	56	586	23	1151	52	85	91	.483	0-2	19	91	.723	3.91	4.18

Andrew Chafin

Pitches: L Bats: R Pos: RP-64 Ht: 6'2" Wt: 235 Born: 6/17/1990 Age: 33

Year	Team	Lg	G	GS	GF	IP	BFP	H	R	ER	HR	SH	SF	HB	TBB	IBB	SO	WP	W	L	Pct	Sv-Op	Hld	Vel	OPS	ERC	ERA
2014	Ari	NL	3	3	0	14.0	60	13	6	6	0	2	0	1	8	1	10	2	0	1	.000	0-0	0	91	.685	3.92	3.86
2015	Ari	NL	66	0	6	75.0	306	56	23	23	3	3	2	1	30	6	58	2	5	1	.833	2-2	16	92	.587	2.30	2.76
2016	Ari	NL	32	0	1	22.2	98	22	18	17	1	1	0	1	11	1	28	2	0	1	.000	0-1	6	93	.703	4.01	6.75
2017	Ari	NL	71	0	12	51.1	221	48	21	20	5	2	1	2	21	3	61	1	1	0	1.000	0-0	17	94	.699	3.78	3.51
2018	Ari	NL	77	0	13	49.1	211	41	18	17	0	0	3	2	25	1	53	3	1	6	.143	0-0	17	94	.621	2.99	3.10
2019	Ari	NL	77	0	6	52.2	225	52	23	22	6	3	0	2	18	0	68	2	2	2	.500	0-4	23	94	.691	4.03	3.76
2020	2 Tms	NL	15	0	5	9.2	45	11	7	7	2	0	0	0	5	1	13	0	1	2	.333	1-3	3	94	.856	5.87	6.52
2021	2 Tms	NL	71	0	11	68.2	266	45	14	14	4	0	3	2	19	1	64	3	2	4	.333	5-8	22	92	.521	1.76	1.83
2022	Det	AL	64	0	10	57.1	243	48	26	18	4	3	1	3	19	0	67	4	2	3	.400	3-4	19	92	.619	2.97	2.83
20	Ari	NL	11	0	1	6.2	33	9	6	6	1	0	0	0	4	0	10	0	1	1	.500	0-2	3	94	.877	7.28	8.10
20	ChC	NL	4	0	4	3.0	12	2	1	1	1	0	0	0	1	1	3	0	0	1	.000	1-1	0	94	.795	2.95	3.00
21	ChC	NL	43	0	1	39.1	150	21	9	9	1	0	2	2	12	1	37	2	0	2	.000	0-1	17	93	.461	1.33	2.06
21	Oak	AL	28	0	10	29.1	116	24	5	5	3	0	3	0	7	0	27	1	2	2	.500	5-7	5	91	.597	2.56	1.53
	Postseason		4	0	1	1.0	4	2	1	1	0	0	0	0	0	0	0	1	1	0	1.000	0-0	0	94	1.000	9.49	9.00
	9 ML YEARS		476	3	64	400.2	1675	336	156	144	26	13	12	14	156	14	422	19	14	20	.412	11-22	123	93	.631	3.01	3.23

Yu Chang

Bats: R Throws: R Pos: 2B-43;SS-16;1B-9;3B-7;PH-5;DH-3 Ht: 6'1" Wt: 180 Born: 8/18/1995 Age: 27

Year	Team	Lg	G	AB	H	2B	3B	HR	(Hm	Rd)	TB	R	RBI	RC	TBB	IBB	SO	HBP	SH	SF	SB	CS	GDP	Avg	OBP	Slg	OPS
2019	Cle	AL	28	73	13	2	1	1	(0	1)	20	8	6	5	11	0	22	0	0	0	0	0	4	.178	.286	.274	.560
2020	Cle	AL	10	11	2	0	0	0	(0	0)	2	1	1	0	2	0	4	0	0	0	0	0	0	.182	.308	.182	.490
2021	Cle	AL	89	237	54	14	3	9	(4	5)	101	32	39	32	11	0	69	2	0	1	1	0	4	.228	.267	.426	.693
2022	4 Tms		69	168	35	6	0	4	(1	3)	53	19	15	15	16	0	59	4	0	2	0	1	5	.208	.289	.315	.605
22	Cle	AL	4	10	0	0	0	0	(0	0)	0	0	0	0	0	0	7	0	0	0	0	0	0	.000	.000	.000	.000
22	Pit	NL	18	42	7	1	0	1	(0	1)	11	5	2	2	4	0	18	3	0	0	0	1	1	.167	.286	.262	.548
22	TB	AL	36	96	25	3	0	3	(1	2)	37	11	12	12	7	0	27	0	0	2	0	0	3	.260	.305	.385	.690
22	Bos	AL	11	20	3	2	0	0	(0	0)	5	3	1	1	5	0	7	1	0	0	0	0	1	.150	.346	.250	.596
	4 ML YEARS		196	489	104	22	4	14	(5	9)	176	60	61	52	40	0	154	6	0	3	1	1	15	.213	.279	.360	.639

Aroldis Chapman

Pitches: L Bats: L Pos: RP-43 ah-ROLL-diss Ht: 6'4" Wt: 218 Born: 2/28/1988 Age: 35

Year	Team	Lg	G	GS	GF	IP	BFP	H	R	ER	HR	SH	SF	HB	TBB	IBB	SO	WP	W	L	Pct	Sv-Op	Hld	Vel	OPS	ERC	ERA
2010	Cin	NL	15	0	3	13.1	51	9	4	3	0	0	0	0	5	0	19	2	2	2	.500	0-1	4	100	.492	1.82	2.03
2011	Cin	NL	54	0	15	50.0	207	24	21	20	2	1	0	2	41	0	71	4	4	1	.800	1-3	13	98	.534	2.69	3.60
2012	Cin	NL	68	0	52	71.2	276	35	13	12	4	0	1	4	23	0	122	4	5	5	.500	38-43	0	98	.450	1.35	1.51
2013	Cin	NL	68	0	55	63.2	258	37	18	18	7	1	0	3	29	0	112	6	4	5	.444	38-43	0	98	.544	2.33	2.54
2014	Cin	NL	54	0	44	54.0	202	21	12	12	1	1	1	2	24	0	106	4	0	3	.000	36-38	0	100	.406	1.18	2.00
2015	Cin	NL	65	0	54	66.1	278	43	13	12	3	0	2	5	33	1	116	7	4	4	.500	33-36	0	99	.527	2.45	1.63
2016	2 Tms		59	0	52	58.0	222	32	12	10	2	0	1	0	18	0	90	8	4	1	.800	36-39	0	100	.452	1.33	1.55
2017	NYY	AL	52	0	42	50.1	210	37	20	18	3	0	1	3	20	2	69	5	4	3	.571	22-26	1	100	.584	2.53	3.22
2018	NYY	AL	55	0	43	51.1	212	24	15	14	2	0	1	3	30	0	93	9	3	0	1.000	32-34	1	99	.493	1.94	2.45
2019	NYY	AL	60	0	53	57.0	235	38	18	14	3	0	3	1	25	0	85	6	3	2	.600	37-42	0	98	.537	2.21	2.21
2020	NYY	AL	13	0	8	11.2	45	6	4	4	2	0	0	1	8	0	22	0	1	1	.500	3-5	0	98	.619	2.15	3.09
2021	NYY	AL	61	0	46	56.1	243	36	23	21	9	2	2	3	38	2	97	7	6	4	.600	30-34	1	99	.678	3.69	3.36
2022	NYY	AL	43	0	19	36.1	160	24	18	18	4	0	2	3	28	0	43	6	4	4	.500	9-9	1	98	.654	3.77	4.46
16	NYY	AL	31	0	29	31.1	120	20	8	7	2	0	0	0	8	0	44	2	3	0	1.000	20-21	0	100	.519	1.59	2.01
16	ChC	NL	28	0	23	26.2	102	12	4	3	0	0	1	0	10	0	46	6	1	1	.500	16-18	0	101	.370	1.04	1.01
	Postseason		35	0	27	41.1	168	28	14	11	3	1	1	2	16	1	62	2	3	4	.429	10-14	0	100	.566	2.31	2.40
	13 ML YEARS		667	0	484	640.0	2599	366	191	176	42	5	13	30	318	5	1045	68	44	35	.557	315-353	27	99	.530	2.16	2.48

Matt Chapman

Bats: R Throws: R Pos: 3B-153;PH-2;DH-1   Ht: 6'0" Wt: 215 Born: 4/28/1993 Age: 30

									BATTING													RUNNING			AVERAGES			
Year	Team	Lg	G	AB	H	2B	3B	HR	(Hm	Rd)	TB	R	RBI	RC	TBB	IBB	SO	HBP	SH	SF	SB	CS	GDP	Avg	OBP	Slg	OPS
2017	Oak	AL	84	290	68	23	2	14	(8	6)	137	39	40	42	32	0	92	2	0	2	0	3	2	.234	.313	.472	.785
2018	Oak	AL	145	547	152	42	6	24	(8	16)	278	100	68	94	58	0	146	9	0	2	1	2	18	.278	.356	.508	.864
2019	Oak	AL	156	583	145	36	3	36	(21	15)	295	102	91	109	73	0	147	11	0	3	1	1	12	.249	.342	.506	.848
2020	Oak	AL	37	142	33	9	2	10	(7	3)	76	22	25	20	8	0	54	1	0	1	0	0	2	.232	.276	.535	.812
2021	Oak	AL	151	529	111	15	3	27	(10	17)	213	75	72	68	80	0	202	4	0	9	3	2	6	.210	.314	.403	.716
2022	Tor	AL	155	538	123	27	1	27	(19	8)	233	83	76	83	68	1	170	10	0	5	2	2	7	.229	.324	.433	.757
	Postseason		2	8	2	0	0	0	(0	0)	2	0	0	0	1	0	0	0	0	0	0	0	0	.250	.333	.250	.583
	6 ML YEARS		728	2629	632	152	17	138	(73	65)	1232	421	372	416	319	1	811	37	0	22	7	10	47	.240	.329	.469	.797

JT Chargois

Pitches: R Bats: B Pos: RP-18; SP-3   SHAHG-wah   Ht: 6'3" Wt: 200 Born: 12/3/1990 Age: 32

				HOW MUCH PITCHED			WHAT HE GAVE UP										THE RESULTS						
Year	Team	Lg	G	GS	GF	IP	BFP	H	R	ER	HR	SH	SF	HB	TBB	IBB	SO	WP	W	L	Pct	Sv-Op	Hld	Vel	OPS	ERC	ERA
2022	Drham	AAA	10	0	0	5.2	35	10	13	13	1	0	0	2	7	0	4	0	1	2	.333	0--	-	-	1.235	15.52	20.65
2016	Min	AL	25	0	10	23.0	100	25	12	12	0	0	1	1	12	0	17	3	1	1	.500	0-0	2	96	.752	4.67	4.70
2018	LAD	NL	39	0	4	32.1	135	26	13	12	4	1	0	2	15	3	40	3	2	4	.333	0-4	7	95	.697	3.58	3.34
2019	LAD	NL	21	0	9	21.1	88	21	16	15	4	0	4	2	5	2	28	0	1	0	1.000	0-0	0	96	.825	4.28	6.33
2021	2 Tms	AL	56	0	3	53.2	216	38	16	15	5	0	2	6	20	3	53	2	6	1	.857	0-5	15	96	.642	2.80	2.52
2022	TB	AL	21	3	3	22.1	86	16	7	6	3	0	0	2	5	0	17	0	2	0	1.000	0-0	3	96	.673	2.58	2.42
21	Sea	AL	31	0	0	30.0	118	23	11	10	2	0	1	5	6	0	29	2	1	0	1.000	0-2	9	96	.618	2.62	3.00
21	TB	AL	25	0	3	23.2	98	15	5	5	3	0	1	1	14	3	24	0	5	1	.833	0-3	6	97	.672	3.03	1.90
	Postseason		4	0	1	3.1	13	3	0	0	0	0	0	0	1	0	2	0	0	0	-	0-0	0	97	.641	2.69	0.00
	5 ML YEARS		162	3	29	152.2	625	126	64	60	16	1	7	13	57	8	155	8	12	6	.667	0-9	27	96	.702	3.41	3.54

Jesse Chavez

Pitches: R Bats: R Pos: RP-59; SP-1   CHAH-vezz   Ht: 6'1" Wt: 175 Born: 8/21/1983 Age: 39

				HOW MUCH PITCHED			WHAT HE GAVE UP										THE RESULTS						
Year	Team	Lg	G	GS	GF	IP	BFP	H	R	ER	HR	SH	SF	HB	TBB	IBB	SO	WP	W	L	Pct	Sv-Op	Hld	Vel	OPS	ERC	ERA
2008	Pit	NL	15	0	6	15.0	74	20	11	11	2	3	1	0	9	2	16	2	0	1	.000	0-2	0	94	.900	6.76	6.60
2009	Pit	NL	73	0	24	67.1	286	69	33	30	11	1	1	1	22	3	47	5	1	4	.200	0-4	15	94	.783	4.39	4.01
2010	2 Tms	AL	51	0	26	62.2	280	69	44	41	11	5	3	1	23	7	45	2	5	5	.500	0-1	6	95	.834	4.85	5.89
2011	KC	AL	4	0	3	7.2	39	12	9	9	3	0	0	0	5	0	8	0	0	0	-	0-0	0	93	1.112	11.48	10.57
2012	KC	AL	13	2	3	24.2	123	34	29	27	7	0	1	3	11	1	30	1	1	1	.500	0-0	0	93	.983	8.32	9.85
2013	Oak	AL	35	0	16	57.1	248	50	27	25	3	6	2	3	20	4	55	5	2	4	.333	1-2	1	92	.620	2.85	3.92
2014	Oak	AL	32	21	5	146.0	621	142	64	56	17	4	5	4	49	3	136	7	8	8	.500	0-0	0	91	.692	3.89	3.45
2015	Oak	AL	30	26	3	157.0	672	164	78	73	18	4	6	2	48	2	136	3	7	15	.318	1-1	0	91	.730	4.08	4.18
2016	2 Tms	AL	62	0	9	67.0	282	71	36	33	12	0	1	2	18	3	63	1	2	2	.500	0-3	10	93	.779	4.56	4.43
2017	LAA	AL	38	21	6	138.0	586	148	83	82	28	0	2	2	45	2	119	1	7	11	.389	0-1	1	92	.826	5.06	5.35
2018	2 Tms	AL	62	0	26	95.1	377	84	28	27	13	0	2	0	17	1	92	1	5	2	.714	5-6	7	93	.645	2.84	2.55
2019	Tex	AL	48	9	5	78.0	337	82	48	42	12	1	2	5	22	0	72	1	3	5	.375	1-2	8	91	.787	4.52	4.85
2020	Tex	AL	18	0	5	17.0	77	20	13	13	6	0	3	1	7	0	13	0	0	0	-	0-3	2	91	.985	7.42	6.88
2021	Atl	NL	30	4	6	33.2	133	23	9	8	0	0	2	0	11	1	36	3	3	2	.600	0-1	3	91	.522	1.60	2.14
2022	3 Tms	AL	60	1	14	69.1	292	71	34	29	8	1	1	1	20	0	74	2	4	3	.571	0-5	10	91	.747	3.96	3.76
10	Atl	NL	28	0	16	36.2	162	40	24	24	6	3	2	1	12	3	29	0	3	2	.600	0-0	0	95	.812	4.65	5.89
10	KC	AL	23	0	10	26.0	118	29	20	17	5	2	1	0	11	4	16	2	2	3	.400	0-1	6	94	.864	5.13	5.88
12	Tor	AL	9	2	2	21.1	102	25	22	20	6	0	1	2	10	1	27	0	1	1	.500	0-0	0	93	.925	6.90	8.44
12	Oak	AL	4	0	1	3.1	21	9	7	7	1	0	0	1	1	0	3	1	0	0	-	0-0	0	93	1.261	18.70	18.90
16	Tor	AL	39	0	6	41.1	173	43	22	21	9	0	1	2	10	0	42	1	1	2	.333	0-2	7	93	.799	4.75	4.57
16	LAD	NL	23	0	3	25.2	109	28	14	12	3	0	0	0	8	3	21	0	1	0	1.000	0-1	3	93	.746	4.24	4.21
18	Tex	AL	30	0	15	56.1	234	58	23	22	10	0	1	0	12	1	50	1	3	1	.750	1-1	3	93	.747	4.00	3.51
18	ChC	NL	32	0	11	39.0	143	26	5	5	3	0	1	0	5	0	42	0	2	1	.667	4-5	4	93	.480	1.47	1.15
22	ChC	NL	3	0	0	5.2	24	7	4	4	1	0	0	0	2	0	3	0	0	0	-	0-1	0	90	.920	6.22	6.35
22	Atl	NL	46	1	8	53.0	218	49	18	16	5	1	1	1	14	0	61	2	3	3	.500	0-2	10	91	.678	3.20	2.72
22	LAA	AL	11	0	6	10.2	50	15	12	9	2	0	0	0	4	0	10	0	1	0	1.000	0-2	0	91	.967	7.10	7.59
	Postseason		8	1	1	7.1	30	6	0	0	0	1	0	0	3	1	2	0	0	0	-	0-0	1	91	.618	2.32	0.00
	15 ML YEARS		571	84	157	1036.0	4427	1059	546	506	151	22	31	26	327	29	942	34	48	63	.432	8-31	62	92	.754	4.24	4.40

Michael Chavis

Bats: R Throws: R Pos: 1B-107;PH-17;2B-14;3B-9;DH-6;PR-5   Ht: 5'10" Wt: 190 Born: 8/11/1995 Age: 27

									BATTING													RUNNING			AVERAGES			
Year	Team	Lg	G	AB	H	2B	3B	HR	(Hm	Rd)	TB	R	RBI	RC	TBB	IBB	SO	HBP	SH	SF	SB	CS	GDP	Avg	OBP	Slg	OPS
2019	Bos	AL	95	347	88	10	1	18	(10	8)	154	46	58	47	31	2	127	4	0	0	2	1	11	.254	.322	.444	.766
2020	Bos	AL	42	146	31	5	2	5	(2	3)	55	16	19	13	8	0	50	0	2	3	3	0	6	.212	.259	.377	.636
2021	2 Tms		43	121	30	7	1	3	(1	2)	48	16	11	8	1	0	42	1	0	1	1	2	2	.248	.258	.397	.655
2022	Pit	NL	129	401	92	16	3	14	(5	9)	156	39	49	43	19	1	126	2	0	4	1	1	4	.229	.265	.389	.654
21	Bos	AL	31	79	15	4	1	2	(0	2)	27	12	6	1	1	0	32	1	0	1	1	1	2	.190	.207	.342	.549
21	Pit	NL	12	42	15	3	0	1	(1	0)	21	4	5	7	0	0	10	0	0	0	0	1	2	.357	.357	.500	.857
	4 ML YEARS		309	1015	241	38	7	40	(18	22)	413	117	137	111	59	3	345	9	0	7	7	4	25	.237	.283	.407	.690

Robinson Chirinos

Bats: R **Throws:** R **Pos:** C-66;PH-1 · chee-REE-nos · **Ht:** 6'1" **Wt:** 220 **Born:** 6/5/1984 **Age:** 39

Year Team	Lg	G	AB	H	2B	3B	HR	(Hm	Rd)	TB	R	RBI	RC	TBB	IBB	SO	HBP	SH	SF	SB	CS	GDP	Avg	OBP	Slg	OPS
2011 TB	AL	20	55	12	2	0	1	(1	0)	17	4	7	5	5	0	13	0	0	0	0	0	0	.218	.283	.309	.592
2013 Tex	AL	13	28	5	3	0	0	(0	0)	8	3	0	0	2	0	6	0	0	0	0	0	1	.179	.233	.286	.519
2014 Tex	AL	93	306	73	15	0	13	(6	7)	127	36	40	38	17	1	71	7	4	4	0	1	4	.239	.290	.415	.705
2015 Tex	AL	78	233	54	16	1	10	(4	6)	102	33	34	28	28	0	62	5	5	2	0	0	4	.232	.325	.438	.762
2016 Tex	AL	57	147	33	11	0	9	(1	8)	71	21	20	21	15	0	44	5	1	2	0	1	4	.224	.314	.483	.797
2017 Tex	AL	88	263	67	13	1	17	(10	7)	133	46	38	44	34	0	79	10	1	1	1	0	5	.255	.360	.506	.866
2018 Tex	AL	113	360	80	15	1	18	(10	8)	151	48	65	66	45	0	140	19	0	2	2	0	7	.222	.338	.419	.757
2019 Hou	AL	114	366	87	22	1	17	(10	7)	162	57	58	55	51	1	125	13	2	5	1	2	11	.238	.347	.443	.790
2020 2 Tms		26	74	12	3	0	1	(0	1)	18	4	7	2	6	0	21	1	0	1	0	0	5	.162	.232	.243	.475
2021 ChC	NL	45	97	22	5	1	5	(3	2)	44	13	15	14	9	0	36	5	1	0	0	0	4	.227	.324	.454	.778
2022 Bal	AL	67	195	35	9	0	4	(1	3)	56	10	22	18	19	0	67	4	1	1	1	0	4	.179	.265	.287	.552
20 Tex	AL	14	42	5	1	0	0	(0	0)	6	3	2	0	5	0	12	1	0	1	0	0	3	.119	.224	.143	.367
20 NYM	NL	12	32	7	2	0	1	(0	1)	12	1	5	2	1	0	9	0	0	0	0	0	2	.219	.242	.375	.617
Postseason		18	52	9	1	0	4	(0	4)	22	5	7	5	4	0	19	1	0	0	0	0	2	.173	.246	.423	.669
11 ML YEARS		714	2124	480	114	5	95	(46	49)	889	275	306	291	231	2	664	69	15	18	5	4	47	.226	.319	.419	.738

Yonny Chirinos

Pitches: R **Bats:** R **Pos:** SP-1; RP-1 · chih-REE-nos · **Ht:** 6'2" **Wt:** 225 **Born:** 12/26/1993 **Age:** 29

Year Team	Lg	G	GS	GF	IP	BFP	H	R	ER	HR	SH	SF	HB	TBB	IBB	SO	WP	W	L	Pct	Sv-Op	Hld	Vel	OPS	ERC	ERA
2022 Drham	AAA	5	5	0	16.0	63	11	5	5	2	1	0	0	6	0	13	1	0	0	0--	-	-		.578	2.56	2.81
2018 TB	AL	18	7	2	89.2	370	84	40	35	7	2	7	5	25	2	75	5	5	5	.500	0-0	0	94	.687	3.36	3.51
2019 TB	AL	26	18	0	133.1	530	112	61	57	23	0	1	3	28	1	114	4	9	5	.643	0-0	0	94	.683	3.05	3.85
2020 TB	AL	3	3	0	11.1	52	14	4	3	2	0	0	2	4	0	10	0	0	0		0-0	0	93	.863	6.73	2.38
2022 TB	AL	2	1	0	7.0	30	7	0	0	0	0	0	1	1	0	6	1	1	0	1.000	0-0	0	94	.621	2.89	0.00
4 ML YEARS		49	29	2	241.1	982	217	105	95	32	2	8	11	58	3	205	10	15	10	.600	0-0	0	94	.693	3.32	3.54

Jazz Chisholm Jr.

Bats: L **Throws:** R **Pos:** 2B-60;PH-3 · **Ht:** 5'11" **Wt:** 184 **Born:** 2/1/1998 **Age:** 25

Year Team	Lg	G	AB	H	2B	3B	HR	(Hm	Rd)	TB	R	RBI	RC	TBB	IBB	SO	HBP	SH	SF	SB	CS	GDP	Avg	OBP	Slg	OPS
2020 Mia	NL	21	56	9	1	1	2	(0	2)	18	8	6	3	5	0	19	1	0	0	2	2	0	.161	.242	.321	.563
2021 Mia	NL	124	464	115	20	4	18	(11	7)	197	70	53	64	34	0	145	4	2	3	23	8	3	.248	.303	.425	.728
2022 Mia	NL	60	213	54	10	4	14	(5	9)	114	39	45	51	21	0	66	3	0	3	12	5	0	.254	.325	.535	.860
Postseason		1	3	1	1	0	0	(0	0)	2	0	1	0	1	0	0	0	0	0	0	0	0	.333	.500	.667	1.167
3 ML YEARS		205	733	178	31	9	34	(16	18)	329	117	104	118	60	0	230	8	2	6	37	15	3	.243	.305	.449	.754

Ji-Man Choi

Bats: L **Throws:** R **Pos:** 1B-98;DH-12;PH-11 · gee-man choy · **Ht:** 6'1" **Wt:** 260 **Born:** 5/19/1991 **Age:** 32

Year Team	Lg	G	AB	H	2B	3B	HR	(Hm	Rd)	TB	R	RBI	RC	TBB	IBB	SO	HBP	SH	SF	SB	CS	GDP	Avg	OBP	Slg	OPS
2016 LAA	AL	54	112	19	4	0	5	(3	2)	38	9	12	8	16	1	27	0	0	1	2	4	2	.170	.271	.339	.611
2017 NYY	AL	6	15	4	1	0	2	(2	0)	11	2	5	3	2	0	5	0	0	1	0	0	1	.267	.333	.733	1.067
2018 2 Tms		61	190	50	14	1	10	(5	5)	96	25	32	30	26	1	55	3	0	2	2	0	1	.263	.357	.505	.863
2019 TB	AL	127	410	107	20	2	19	(8	11)	188	54	63	68	64	2	108	6	0	7	2	3	7	.261	.363	.459	.822
2020 TB	AL	42	122	28	13	0	3	(1	2)	50	16	16	17	20	2	36	0	0	3	0	0	1	.230	.331	.410	.741
2021 TB	AL	83	258	59	14	0	11	(4	7)	106	36	45	47	45	0	87	2	0	0	0	0	5	.229	.348	.411	.758
2022 TB	AL	113	356	83	22	0	11	(5	6)	138	36	52	63	58	3	123	2	0	3	0	0	3	.233	.341	.388	.729
18 Mil	NL	12	30	7	2	0	2	(0	2)	15	4	5	5	2	1	14	0	0	0	0	0	0	.233	.281	.500	.781
18 Tor	AL	49	160	43	12	1	8	(5	3)	81	21	27	25	24	0	41	3	0	2	2	0	0	.269	.370	.506	.877
Postseason		27	63	15	1	0	4	(3	1)	28	11	6	13	17	1	23	1	0	0	0	0	1	.238	.407	.444	.852
7 ML YEARS		486	1463	350	88	3	61	(28	33)	627	178	225	236	231	9	441	13	0	17	6	7	20	.239	.345	.429	.773

Adam Cimber

Pitches: R **Bats:** R **Pos:** RP-77 · **Ht:** 6'3" **Wt:** 195 **Born:** 8/15/1990 **Age:** 32

Year Team	Lg	G	GS	GF	IP	BFP	H	R	ER	HR	SH	SF	HB	TBB	IBB	SO	WP	W	L	Pct	Sv-Op	Hld	Vel	OPS	ERC	ERA
2018 2 Tms		70	0	16	68.1	284	68	28	26	5	2	2	6	17	9	58	1	3	8	.273	0-1	12	87	.743	3.49	3.42
2019 Cle	AL	68	0	12	56.2	244	56	29	28	6	1	2	4	19	2	41	0	6	3	.667	1-3	19	85	.720	4.01	4.45
2020 Cle	AL	14	0	5	11.1	49	13	5	5	1	0	2	0	2	0	5	0	0	1	.000	0-0	3	86	.751	3.84	3.97
2021 2 Tms		72	0	10	71.2	286	61	24	18	2	0	2	7	16	4	51	1	3	4	.429	1-1	5	87	.604	2.53	2.26
2022 Tor	AL	77	0	15	70.2	293	66	28	22	6	4	2	8	13	1	58	1	10	6	.625	4-8	19	87	.669	3.21	2.80
18 SD	NL	42	0	10	48.1	192	42	19	17	2	1	2	2	10	3	51	0	3	5	.375	0-1	5	86	.644	2.42	3.17
18 Cle	AL	28	0	6	20.0	92	26	9	9	3	1	0	4	7	6	7	1	0	3	.000	0-0	7	87	.957	6.53	4.05
21 Mia	NL	33	0	10	34.1	140	30	14	11	0	0	0	5	11	4	21	1	1	2	.333	0-0	0	87	.643	2.90	2.88
21 Tor	AL	39	0	9	37.1	146	31	10	7	2	0	2	2	5	0	30	0	2	2	.500	1-1	5	87	.567	2.17	1.69
Postseason		3	0	1	2.2	13	4	4	4	0	0	0	0	2	0	0	0	0	0	-	0-0	0	87	.862	8.14	13.50
5 ML YEARS		301	0	67	278.2	1156	264	114	99	20	7	10	25	67	16	213	3	22	22	.500	6-13	58	86	.685	3.28	3.20

Steve Cishek

Pitches: R Bats: R Pos: RP-69   SEE-sheck   Ht: 6'6" Wt: 220 Born: 6/18/1986 Age: 37

Year	Team	Lg	G	GS	GF	IP	BFP	H	R	ER	HR	SH	SF	HB	TBB	IBB	SO	WP	W	L	Pct	Sv-Op	Hld	Vel	OPS	ERC	ERA
2010	Fla	NL	3	0	2	4.1	15	1	0	0	0	0	0	0	1	0	3	0	0	0	-	0-0	0	93	.276	0.35	0.00
2011	Fla	NL	45	0	21	54.2	229	45	18	16	1	3	0	3	19	7	55	5	2	1	.667	3-3	2	93	.591	2.38	2.63
2012	Mia	NL	68	0	36	63.2	275	54	26	19	3	3	2	6	29	6	68	1	5	2	.714	15-19	13	92	.663	3.28	2.69
2013	Mia	NL	69	0	62	69.2	281	53	19	18	3	3	3	2	22	6	74	1	4	6	.400	34-36	1	92	.568	2.15	2.33
2014	Mia	NL	67	0	55	65.1	275	58	26	23	3	5	3	1	21	2	84	1	4	5	.444	39-43	0	92	.643	2.78	3.17
2015	2 Tms	NL	59	0	23	55.1	243	55	26	22	4	1	2	1	27	3	48	1	2	6	.250	4-9	6	91	.720	4.17	3.58
2016	Sea	AL	62	0	40	64.0	258	44	21	20	8	1	0	4	21	2	76	4	4	6	.400	25-32	9	91	.600	2.51	2.81
2017	2 Tms	AL	49	0	11	44.2	174	26	10	10	3	0	1	3	14	1	41	3	3	2	.600	1-4	15	90	.491	1.70	2.01
2018	ChC	AL	80	0	10	70.1	288	45	19	17	5	2	1	9	28	4	78	2	4	3	.571	4-7	25	90	.593	2.39	2.18
2019	ChC	AL	70	0	23	64.0	267	48	22	21	7	0	2	7	29	1	57	4	4	6	.400	7-11	11	91	.642	3.44	2.95
2020	CWS	AL	22	0	8	20.0	93	21	12	12	4	0	2	4	9	0	21	0	0	0	-	0-1	0	90	.853	6.10	5.40
2021	LAA	AL	74	0	9	68.1	308	61	32	26	2	1	4	6	41	5	64	4	0	2	.000	0-4	21	90	.668	3.90	3.42
2022	Was	NL	69	0	12	66.1	287	54	33	31	11	4	4	13	27	1	74	3	1	4	.200	1-3	6	90	.709	4.29	4.21
15	Mia	NL	32	0	15	32.0	144	37	19	16	2	1	2	0	14	3	28	0	2	6	.250	3-7	3	91	.782	4.66	4.50
15	StL	AL	27	0	8	23.1	99	18	7	6	2	0	0	1	13	0	20	1	0	0	-	1-2	3	91	.629	3.53	2.31
17	Sea	AL	23	0	8	20.0	80	13	7	7	3	0	1	1	7	1	15	1	1	1	.500	1-4	6	90	.601	2.48	3.15
17	TB	AL	26	0	3	24.2	94	13	3	3	0	0	0	2	7	0	26	2	2	1	.667	0-0	9	91	.399	1.25	1.09
	Postseason		1	0	0	0.2	1	0	0	0	0	0	0	0	0	0	0	0	0	0	-	0-0	0	92	.000	0.00	0.00
13 ML YEARS			737	0	312	710.2	2993	565	264	235	54	20	24	59	288	38	743	29	33	43	.434	133-172	109	91	.636	3.05	2.98

Jose Cisnero

Pitches: R Bats: R Pos: RP-28   siss-NEHR-oh   Ht: 6'3" Wt: 258 Born: 4/11/1989 Age: 34

Year	Team	Lg	G	GS	GF	IP	BFP	H	R	ER	HR	SH	SF	HB	TBB	IBB	SO	WP	W	L	Pct	Sv-Op	Hld	Vel	OPS	ERC	ERA
2022	Toledo	AAA	6	0	0	5.2	22	3	2	2	0	0	1	0	6	0	6	0	1	0	1.000	0- -	-		.477	1.21	3.18
2013	Hou	AL	28	0	11	43.2	198	49	23	20	5	0	2	1	22	5	41	1	2	2	.500	0-2	5	93	.826	5.21	4.12
2014	Hou	AL	5	0	1	4.2	25	8	5	5	0	0	1	0	4	0	5	0	0	0	-	0-1	0	94	.930	9.79	9.64
2019	Det	AL	35	0	10	35.1	162	35	21	17	5	2	2	3	19	3	40	1	0	4	.000	0-2	4	96	.805	4.99	4.33
2020	Det	AL	29	0	2	29.2	123	23	10	10	1	0	0	3	10	0	34	0	3	3	.500	0-2	6	96	.584	2.58	3.03
2021	Det	AL	67	0	11	61.2	265	51	34	25	6	2	2	4	31	1	62	4	4	4	.500	4-8	18	97	.672	3.73	3.65
2022	Det	AL	28	0	6	25.0	105	15	4	3	0	0	0	1	19	0	23	1	1	0	1.000	0-0	5	95	.545	2.79	1.08
6 ML YEARS			192	0	41	200.0	878	181	97	80	17	4	7	12	105	9	205	7	10	13	.435	4-15	38	95	.712	4.09	3.60

Aaron Civale

Pitches: R Bats: R Pos: SP-20   Ht: 6'2" Wt: 215 Born: 6/12/1995 Age: 28

Year	Team	Lg	G	GS	GF	IP	BFP	H	R	ER	HR	SH	SF	HB	TBB	IBB	SO	WP	W	L	Pct	Sv-Op	Hld	Vel	OPS	ERC	ERA
2019	Cle	AL	10	10	0	57.2	227	44	18	15	4	1	5	1	16	0	46	2	3	4	.429	0-0	0	93	.638	2.31	2.34
2020	Cle	AL	12	12	0	74.0	312	82	39	39	11	0	2	3	16	0	69	0	4	6	.400	0-0	0	92	.798	4.52	4.74
2021	Cle	AL	21	21	0	124.1	498	108	56	53	23	1	4	4	31	0	99	3	12	5	.706	0-0	0	92	.731	3.52	3.84
2022	Cle	AL	20	20	0	97.0	407	93	58	53	14	0	5	7	22	1	98	1	5	6	.455	0-0	0	91	.723	3.72	4.92
4 ML YEARS			63	63	0	353.0	1444	327	171	160	52	2	16	15	85	1	312	6	24	21	.533	0-0	0	92	.729	3.57	4.08

Taylor Clarke

Pitches: R Bats: R Pos: RP-47   Ht: 6'4" Wt: 217 Born: 5/13/1993 Age: 30

Year	Team	Lg	G	GS	GF	IP	BFP	H	R	ER	HR	SH	SF	HB	TBB	IBB	SO	WP	W	L	Pct	Sv-Op	Hld	Vel	OPS	ERC	ERA
2019	Ari	NL	23	15	3	84.2	369	86	55	50	23	1	5	6	30	0	68	3	5	5	.500	1-1	0	94	.882	5.50	5.31
2020	Ari	NL	12	5	2	43.1	183	35	23	21	8	0	1	0	21	2	40	0	3	0	1.000	0-0	0	94	.728	3.84	4.36
2021	Ari	NL	43	0	10	43.1	194	52	28	24	4	0	1	0	14	2	39	2	1	3	.250	0-1	7	96	.776	4.71	4.98
2022	KC	AL	47	0	8	49.0	203	50	25	22	6	0	2	1	8	0	48	3	3	1	.750	3-8	10	96	.718	3.47	4.04
4 ML YEARS			125	20	23	220.1	949	223	131	117	41	1	9	7	73	4	195	8	12	9	.571	4-10	17	95	.795	4.55	4.78

Emmanuel Clase

Pitches: R Bats: R Pos: RP-77   Ht: 6'2" Wt: 206 Born: 3/18/1998 Age: 25

Year	Team	Lg	G	GS	GF	IP	BFP	H	R	ER	HR	SH	SF	HB	TBB	IBB	SO	WP	W	L	Pct	Sv-Op	Hld	Vel	OPS	ERC	ERA
2019	Tex	AL	21	1	7	23.1	94	20	8	6	2	0	0	1	6	0	21	1	2	3	.400	1-4	4	99	.678	2.89	2.31
2021	Cle	AL	71	0	51	69.2	279	51	18	10	2	1	0	0	16	3	74	3	4	5	.444	24-29	6	100	.481	1.61	1.29
2022	Cle	AL	77	0	67	72.2	271	43	18	11	3	1	1	1	10	2	77	4	3	4	.429	42-46	0	100	.425	1.12	1.36
3 ML YEARS			169	1	125	165.2	644	114	44	27	7	2	1	2	32	5	172	8	9	12	.429	67-76	10	100	.486	1.50	1.47

Alex Claudio

Pitches: L Bats: L Pos: RP-3   Ht: 6'3" Wt: 188 Born: 1/31/1992 Age: 31

Year	Team	Lg	G	GS	GF	IP	BFP	H	R	ER	HR	SH	SF	HB	TBB	IBB	SO	WP	W	L	Pct	Sv-Op	Hld	Vel	OPS	ERC	ERA
2022	Syrcse	AAA	34	0	9	48.1	208	46	27	21	7	0	6	2	15	0	42	3	3	2	.600	2- -	-		.730	3.84	3.91
2014	Tex	AL	15	0	5	12.1	54	14	4	4	0	0	0	0	4	0	14	0	0	0	-	0-0	0	84	.693	3.79	2.92
2015	Tex	AL	18	0	6	15.2	66	12	6	5	4	0	2	1	6	2	13	0	1	1	.500	0-1	3	84	.762	3.74	2.87
2016	Tex	AL	39	0	15	51.2	217	55	19	16	2	0	2	1	10	0	34	0	4	1	.800	0-0	2	85	.662	3.28	2.79
2017	Tex	AL	70	1	38	82.2	323	71	26	23	5	1	3	2	15	4	56	0	4	2	.667	11-15	7	87	.591	2.37	2.50
2018	Tex	AL	66	1	20	68.1	299	91	35	34	4	3	3	3	13	3	41	0	4	2	.667	1-3	14	86	.827	5.03	4.48

Year	Team	Lg	G	GS	GF	IP	BFP	H	R	ER	HR	SH	SF	HB	TBB	IBB	SO	WP	W	L	Pct	Sv-Op	Hld	Vel	OPS	ERC	ERA
2019	Mil	NL	83	0	9	62.0	267	57	29	28	8	1	3	6	24	2	44	1	2	2	.500	0-3	22	86	.751	4.12	4.06
2020	Mil	NL	20	0	7	19.0	81	18	10	9	2	0	0	1	6	0	15	2	0	0	-	1-1	1	86	.687	3.67	4.26
2021	LAA	AL	41	0	11	32.2	148	37	22	20	6	0	0	0	15	1	30	1	1	2	.333	1-1	2	85	.840	5.62	5.51
2022	NYM	NL	3	0	2	3.1	13	1	0	0	0	0	0	0	2	0	2	0	0	0	-	0-0	0	85	.322	1.05	0.00
Postseason			2	0	0	5.0	18	3	0	0	0	0	0	0	3	0	0	0	0	0	-	0-0	0	86	.600	2.46	0.00
9 ML YEARS			355	2	113	347.2	1468	356	151	139	31	5	13	14	95	12	249	5	16	10	.615	14-24	51	86	.717	3.77	3.60

Sam Clay

Pitches: L Bats: L Pos: RP-7   Ht: 6'3" Wt: 238 Born: 6/21/1993 Age: 30

Year	Team	Lg	G	GS	GF	IP	BFP	H	R	ER	HR	SH	SF	HB	TBB	IBB	SO	WP	W	L	Pct	Sv-Op	Hld	Vel	OPS	ERC	ERA
2022	Roch	AAA	21	0	3	20.1	92	22	7	7	2	0	0	2	7	0	20	1	1	2	.333	0- -	-	-	.735	4.59	3.10
2022	Syrcse	AAA	19	0	4	22.2	95	22	11	10	1	1	0	1	10	0	25	3	4	1	.800	0- -	-	-	.713	4.02	3.97
2021	Was	NL	58	0	9	45.0	214	55	32	28	4	0	1	5	22	5	34	3	0	5	.000	0-1	11	92	.792	5.84	5.60
2022	2 Tms	NL	7	0	1	5.1	29	4	6	5	1	1	0	4	4	0	5	0	0	0	-	0-0	0	92	.779	7.39	8.44
22	Was	NL	6	0	0	4.1	23	3	5	5	1	1	0	4	3	0	3	0	0	0	-	0-0	0	91	.855	8.21	10.38
22	NYM	NL	1	0	1	1.0	6	1	1	0	0	0	0	0	1	0	2	0	0	0	-	0-0	0	93	.533	4.47	0.00
2 ML YEARS			65	0	10	50.1	243	59	38	33	5	1	1	9	26	5	39	3	0	5	.000	0-1	11	92	.791	6.01	5.90

Garrett Cleavinger

Pitches: L Bats: R Pos: RP-17   Ht: 6'1" Wt: 220 Born: 4/23/1994 Age: 29

Year	Team	Lg	G	GS	GF	IP	BFP	H	R	ER	HR	SH	SF	HB	TBB	IBB	SO	WP	W	L	Pct	Sv-Op	Hld	Vel	OPS	ERC	ERA
2022	OkCity	AAA	22	1	9	29.0	124	20	9	9	4	0	0	3	17	0	47	2	0	2	.000	1- -	-	-	.669	3.78	2.79
2022	Drham	AAA	9	0	3	9.0	33	2	2	1	0	0	0	1	3	0	17	0	0	0	-	2- -	-	-	.285	0.61	1.00
2020	Phi	NL	1	0	1	0.2	4	2	1	1	1	0	0	0	0	0	1	0	0	0	-	0-0	0	94	1.750	31.01	13.50
2021	LAD	NL	22	1	7	18.0	84	20	11	6	4	1	1	1	12	1	21	0	2	4	.333	0-1	0	96	.890	7.07	3.00
2022	2 Tms	NL	17	0	3	23.0	92	14	12	10	2	1	1	1	7	0	32	0	1	1	.500	0-1	0	96	.559	1.78	3.91
22	LAD	NL	4	0	1	4.1	24	6	7	5	1	1	1	1	3	0	7	0	0	1	.000	0-1	0	96	1.101	9.29	10.38
22	TB	AL	13	0	2	18.2	68	8	5	5	1	0	0	0	4	0	25	0	1	0	1.000	0-0	0	96	.395	0.87	2.41
3 ML YEARS			40	1	11	41.2	180	36	24	17	7	2	2	2	19	1	54	0	3	5	.375	0-2	0	96	.740	4.13	3.67

Kody Clemens

Bats: L Throws: R Pos: 3B-17;1B-13;2B-9;LF-9;PR-9;DH-6;PH-6   Ht: 6'1" Wt: 200 Born: 5/15/1996 Age: 27

Year	Team	Lg	G	AB	H	2B	3B	HR	(Hm	Rd)	TB	R	RBI	RC	TBB	IBB	SO	HBP	SH	SF	SB	CS	GDP	Avg	OBP	Slg	OPS
2022	Toledo	AAA	60	241	66	12	6	13	(-	-)	129	41	43	45	20	1	71	0	1	2	5	2	2	.274	.327	.535	.862
2022	Det	AL	57	117	17	4	0	5	(3	2)	36	13	17	10	8	0	33	0	0	2	1	0	1	.145	.197	.308	.505

Ernie Clement

Bats: R Throws: R Pos: 3B-30;2B-15;PR-15;LF-12;PH-7;DH-6;1B-5;SS-1   Ht: 6'0" Wt: 170 Born: 3/22/1996 Age: 27

Year	Team	Lg	G	AB	H	2B	3B	HR	(Hm	Rd)	TB	R	RBI	RC	TBB	IBB	SO	HBP	SH	SF	SB	CS	GDP	Avg	OBP	Slg	OPS
2022	Clmbs	AAA	21	80	19	2	1	4	(-	-)	35	13	17	10	6	0	8	0	1	0	0	0	3	.238	.291	.438	.728
2021	Cle	AL	40	121	28	4	0	3	(1	2)	41	16	9	7	7	0	19	2	3	0	1	3	3	.231	.285	.339	.623
2022	2 Tms	AL	70	163	30	4	0	0	(0	0)	34	19	6	6	11	0	26	2	2	1	0	1	3	.184	.243	.209	.452
22	Cle	AL	64	145	29	3	0	0	(0	0)	32	18	6	6	11	0	24	2	2	1	0	1	3	.200	.264	.221	.485
22	Oak	AL	6	18	1	1	0	0	(0	0)	2	1	0	0	0	0	2	0	0	0	0	0	0	.056	.056	.111	.167
2 ML YEARS			110	284	58	8	0	3	(1	2)	75	35	15	13	18	0	45	4	5	1	0	2	6	.204	.261	.264	.525

Mike Clevinger

Pitches: R Bats: R Pos: SP-22; RP-1   Ht: 6'4" Wt: 215 Born: 12/21/1990 Age: 32

Year	Team	Lg	G	GS	GF	IP	BFP	H	R	ER	HR	SH	SF	HB	TBB	IBB	SO	WP	W	L	Pct	Sv-Op	Hld	Vel	OPS	ERC	ERA
2016	Cle	AL	17	10	3	53.0	233	50	31	31	8	0	1	0	29	0	50	2	3	3	.500	0-0	0	93	.768	4.72	5.26
2017	Cle	AL	27	21	1	121.2	502	92	46	42	13	1	0	3	60	2	137	3	12	6	.667	0-0	0	92	.667	3.29	3.11
2018	Cle	AL	32	32	0	200.0	810	164	71	67	21	0	1	4	67	0	207	4	13	8	.619	0-0	0	94	.655	3.02	3.02
2019	Cle	AL	21	21	0	126.0	499	96	38	38	10	0	1	2	37	0	169	0	13	4	.765	0-0	0	95	.602	2.41	2.71
2020	2 Tms	AL	8	8	0	41.2	162	34	14	14	6	0	0	0	14	0	40	2	3	2	.600	0-0	0	95	.713	3.31	3.02
2022	SD	NL	23	22	0	114.1	485	102	56	55	20	1	2	10	35	0	91	3	7	7	.500	0-0	0	95	.716	3.93	4.33
20	Cle	AL	4	4	0	22.2	93	20	8	8	5	0	0	0	11	0	21	0	1	1	.500	0-0	0	95	.818	4.83	3.18
20	SD	AL	4	4	0	19.0	69	14	6	6	1	0	0	0	3	0	19	2	2	1	.667	0-0	0	96	.580	1.75	2.84
Postseason			8	2	3	13.0	63	8	7	7	4	0	1	0	15	0	16	2	0	0	-	0-0	0	95	.837	6.09	4.15
6 ML YEARS			128	114	4	656.2	2691	538	256	247	78	2	5	19	242	2	694	14	51	30	.630	0-0	0	94	.671	3.25	3.39

Tyler Clippard

Pitches: R Bats: R Pos: RP-4   Ht: 6'3" Wt: 200 Born: 2/14/1985 Age: 38

Year	Team	Lg	G	GS	GF	IP	BFP	H	R	ER	HR	SH	SF	HB	TBB	IBB	SO	WP	W	L	Pct	Sv-Op	Hld	Vel	OPS	ERC	ERA
2022	Roch	AAA	36	0	8	40.1	168	30	11	10	1	0	0	0	18	0	53	3	4	1	.800	1- -	-	-	.539	2.37	2.23
2007	NYY	AL	6	6	0	27.0	124	29	19	19	6	0	0	0	17	1	18	2	3	1	.750	0-0	0	88	.876	6.37	6.33
2008	Was	NL	2	2	0	10.1	48	12	5	5	2	0	0	0	7	1	8	1	1	1	.500	0-0	0	89	.957	6.90	4.35
2009	Was	NL	41	0	8	60.1	246	36	20	18	9	3	1	1	32	1	67	1	4	2	.667	0-1	3	90	.633	2.79	2.69

			HOW MUCH PITCHED					WHAT HE GAVE UP											THE RESULTS								
Year	Team	Lg	G	GS	GF	IP	BFP	H	R	ER	HR	SH	SF	HB	TBB	IBB	SO	WP	W	L	Pct	Sv-Op	Hld	Vel	OPS	ERC	ERA
2010	Was	NL	78	0	18	91.0	378	69	33	31	8	3	7	2	41	4	112	1	11	8	.579	1-11	23	92	.646	2.91	3.07
2011	Was	NL	72	0	8	88.1	329	48	18	18	11	4	3	0	26	2	104	1	3	0	1.000	0-7	**38**	93	.535	1.61	1.83
2012	Was	NL	74	0	42	72.2	307	55	32	30	7	3	4	2	29	2	84	5	2	6	.250	32-37	13	93	.621	2.73	3.72
2013	Was	NL	72	0	6	71.0	275	37	19	19	9	2	1	4	24	1	73	2	6	3	.667	0-3	**33**	92	.517	1.79	2.41
2014	Was	NL	75	0	6	70.1	278	47	22	17	5	2	2	1	23	1	82	0	7	4	.636	1-7	**40**	92	.541	1.98	2.18
2015	2 Tms		69	0	36	71.0	301	49	25	23	8	1	2	4	31	2	64	6	5	4	.556	19-25	8	92	.599	2.72	2.92
2016	2 Tms		69	0	17	63.0	262	54	27	25	10	1	0	1	26	2	72	5	4	6	.400	3-6	25	91	.716	3.80	3.57
2017	3 Tms	AL	67	0	23	60.1	264	47	33	32	10	3	3	2	31	1	72	11	2	8	.200	5-11	9	91	.711	3.73	4.77
2018	Tor	AL	73	1	22	68.2	285	57	29	28	13	2	2	2	23	0	85	7	4	3	.571	7-13	15	91	.719	3.57	3.67
2019	Cle	AL	53	3	7	62.0	241	38	20	20	8	2	1	7	15	0	64	3	1	0	1.000	0-0	8	90	.608	2.13	2.90
2020	Min	AL	26	2	1	26.0	98	19	9	8	2	0	0	0	4	0	26	2	2	1	.667	0-2	7	89	.543	1.74	2.77
2021	Ari	NL	26	0	15	25.1	111	22	12	9	3	1	1	3	11	1	21	1	1	1	.500	6-9	3	89	.727	3.95	3.20
2022	Was	NL	4	0	3	5.0	28	6	4	4	1	0	0	3	4	0	4	0	0	0	-	0-0	0	88	.988	10.36	7.20
15	Oak	AL	37	0	30	38.2	167	25	12	12	3	0	1	2	21	1	38	1	1	3	.250	17-21	0	91	.567	2.62	2.79
15	NYM	NL	32	0	6	32.1	134	24	13	11	5	1	1	2	10	1	26	5	4	1	.800	2-4	8	92	.637	2.82	3.06
16	Ari	NL	40	0	10	37.2	155	34	18	18	7	1	0	0	15	0	46	1	2	3	.400	1-3	13	91	.764	4.23	4.30
16	NYY	AL	29	0	7	25.1	107	20	9	7	3	0	0	1	11	2	26	4	2	3	.400	2-3	12	92	.646	3.19	2.49
17	NYY	AL	40	0	7	36.1	158	28	21	20	7	3	1	1	19	1	42	5	1	5	.167	1-6	8	91	.735	3.88	4.95
17	CWS	AL	11	0	7	10.0	44	8	2	2	0	0	1	0	5	0	12	3	1	1	.500	2-2	0	91	.585	2.56	1.80
17	Hou	AL	16	0	9	14.0	62	11	10	10	3	0	1	1	7	0	18	3	0	2	.000	2-3	1	90	.740	4.19	6.43
Postseason			14	0	1	12.2	53	9	6	6	2	1	0	0	5	0	11	1	0	1	.000	0-0	8	92	.673	2.77	4.26
16 ML YEARS			807	14	212	872.1	3575	625	327	306	112	27	27	32	344	19	956	48	56	48	.538	74-132	225	91	.638	2.82	3.16

Alex Cobb

Pitches: R **Bats:** R **Pos:** SP-28 **Ht:** 6'3" **Wt:** 205 **Born:** 10/7/1987 **Age:** 35

			HOW MUCH PITCHED					WHAT HE GAVE UP											THE RESULTS								
Year	Team	Lg	G	GS	GF	IP	BFP	H	R	ER	HR	SH	SF	HB	TBB	IBB	SO	WP	W	L	Pct	Sv-Op	Hld	Vel	OPS	ERC	ERA
2011	TB	AL	9	9	0	52.2	224	49	21	20	3	0	1	1	21	1	37	2	3	2	.600	0-0	0	91	.655	3.44	3.42
2012	TB	AL	23	23	0	136.1	569	130	67	61	11	3	6	9	40	2	106	8	11	9	.550	0-0	0	90	.690	3.56	4.03
2013	TB	AL	22	22	0	143.1	578	120	46	44	13	1	2	3	45	4	134	5	11	3	.786	0-0	0	91	.644	2.92	2.76
2014	TB	AL	27	27	0	166.1	681	142	56	53	11	4	4	10	47	1	149	8	10	9	.526	0-0	0	92	.619	2.87	2.87
2016	TB	AL	5	5	0	22.0	104	32	22	21	5	1	1	0	7	0	16	0	1	2	.333	0-0	0	90	.968	7.40	8.59
2017	TB	AL	29	29	0	179.1	742	175	78	73	22	2	1	6	44	2	128	8	12	10	.545	0-0	0	92	.709	3.64	3.66
2018	Bal	AL	28	28	0	152.1	661	172	93	83	24	2	6	4	43	5	102	4	5	15	.250	0-0	0	92	.814	4.81	4.90
2019	Bal	AL	3	3	0	12.1	60	21	16	15	9	0	0	0	2	0	8	0	0	2	.000	0-0	0	92	1.297	12.47	10.95
2020	Bal	AL	10	10	0	52.1	226	52	27	25	8	0	0	2	18	0	38	1	2	5	.286	0-0	0	93	.736	4.31	4.30
2021	LAA	AL	18	18	0	93.1	393	85	46	39	5	1	2	3	33	0	98	4	8	3	.727	0-0	0	93	.645	3.22	3.76
2022	SF	NL	28	28	0	149.2	631	152	72	62	9	1	3	3	43	0	151	4	7	8	.467	0-0	0	95	.665	3.54	3.73
Postseason			2	2	0	11.2	51	13	3	2	0	0	0	1	3	0	10	1	1	0	1.000	0-0	0	92	.695	3.75	1.54
11 ML YEARS			202	202	0	1160.0	4869	1130	544	496	120	15	26	41	343	15	967	44	70	68	.507	0-0	0	92	.702	3.69	3.85

Gerrit Cole

Pitches: R **Bats:** R **Pos:** SP-33 **Ht:** 6'4" **Wt:** 220 **Born:** 9/8/1990 **Age:** 32

			HOW MUCH PITCHED					WHAT HE GAVE UP											THE RESULTS								
Year	Team	Lg	G	GS	GF	IP	BFP	H	R	ER	HR	SH	SF	HB	TBB	IBB	SO	WP	W	L	Pct	Sv-Op	Hld	Vel	OPS	ERC	ERA
2013	Pit	NL	19	19	0	117.1	469	109	43	42	7	5	2	3	28	0	100	4	10	7	.588	0-0	0	96	.638	3.02	3.22
2014	Pit	NL	22	22	0	138.0	571	127	58	56	11	10	0	9	40	1	138	9	11	5	.688	0-0	0	95	.693	3.37	3.65
2015	Pit	NL	32	32	0	208.0	832	183	71	60	11	7	6	10	44	1	202	7	19	8	.704	0-0	0	96	.623	2.66	2.60
2016	Pit	NL	21	21	0	116.0	506	131	57	50	7	4	6	6	36	3	98	5	7	10	.412	0-0	0	95	.754	4.35	3.88
2017	Pit	NL	33	**33**	0	203.0	849	199	98	96	31	5	1	4	55	1	196	7	12	12	.500	0-0	0	96	.739	3.89	4.26
2018	Hou	AL	32	32	0	200.1	799	143	68	64	19	2	3	7	64	0	276	9	15	5	.750	0-0	0	97	.600	2.40	2.88
2019	Hou	AL	33	33	0	212.1	817	142	66	59	29	1	3	3	48	0	**326**	4	20	5	.800	0-0	0	97	.579	2.02	**2.50**
2020	NYY	AL	12	12	0	73.0	288	53	27	23	14	0	0	2	17	0	94	2	7	3	.700	0-0	0	97	.655	2.65	2.84
2021	NYY	AL	30	30	0	181.1	726	151	69	65	24	0	6	2	41	0	243	5	**16**	8	.667	0-0	0	98	.639	**2.77**	3.23
2022	NYY	AL	33	**33**	0	200.2	793	154	81	78	**33**	0	2	2	50	0	**257**	2	13	8	.619	0-0	0	98	.650	2.72	3.50
Postseason			14	14	0	86.0	336	58	29	28	15	0	0	1	22	1	111	1	8	5	.615	0-0	0	97	.602	2.31	2.93
10 ML YEARS			267	267	0	1650.0	6650	1392	638	593	186	34	29	48	423	6	1930	54	130	71	.647	0-0	0	96	.653	2.91	3.23

Dylan Coleman

Pitches: R **Bats:** R **Pos:** RP-68 **Ht:** 6'5" **Wt:** 230 **Born:** 9/16/1996 **Age:** 26

			HOW MUCH PITCHED					WHAT HE GAVE UP											THE RESULTS								
Year	Team	Lg	G	GS	GF	IP	BFP	H	R	ER	HR	SH	SF	HB	TBB	IBB	SO	WP	W	L	Pct	Sv-Op	Hld	Vel	OPS	ERC	ERA
2021	KC	AL	5	0	1	6.1	25	5	1	1	0	0	0	0	1	0	7	1	0	0	-	0-0	0	98	.532	1.57	1.42
2022	KC	AL	68	0	9	68.0	289	47	26	21	5	0	4	6	37	1	71	7	5	2	.714	0-3	16	98	.617	3.08	2.78
2 ML YEARS			73	0	10	74.1	314	52	27	22	5	0	4	6	38	1	78	8	5	2	.714	0-3	16	98	.610	2.93	2.66

Zack Collins

Bats: L **Throws:** R **Pos:** C-13;DH-13;1B-9;PH-4 **Ht:** 6'3" **Wt:** 220 **Born:** 2/6/1995 **Age:** 28

			BATTING																		RUNNING			AVERAGES			
Year	Team	Lg	G	AB	H	2B	3B	HR	(Hm	Rd)	TB	R	RBI	RC	TBB	IBB	SO	HBP	SH	SF	SB	CS	GDP	Avg	OBP	Slg	OPS
2022	Buffalo	AAA	36	118	23	7	1	5	(-	-)	47	15	28	20	32	0	40	1	0	4	3	0	2	.195	.361	.398	.760
2019	CWS	AL	27	86	16	3	1	3	(0	3)	30	10	12	11	14	1	39	1	0	0	0	0	1	.186	.307	.349	.656
2020	CWS	AL	9	16	1	1	0	0	(0	0)	2	1	0	0	2	0	5	0	0	0	0	0	0	.063	.167	.125	.292
2021	CWS	AL	78	195	41	13	0	4	(2	2)	66	25	26	25	34	1	69	1	1	0	1	1	4	.210	.330	.338	.669
2022	2 Tms		36	97	15	4	0	4	(1	3)	31	9	11	10	9	0	41	1	0	1	0	0	0	.155	.231	.320	.551

Year	Team	Lg	G	AB	H	2B	3B	HR	(Hm	Rd)	TB	R	RBI	RC	TBB	IBB	SO	HBP	SH	SF	SB	CS	GDP	Avg	OBP	Slg	OPS
22	Tor	AL	26	72	14	4	0	4	(1	3)	30	7	10	10	6	0	31	1	0	0	0	0	0	.194	.266	.417	.682
22	Pit	NL	10	25	1	0	0	0	(0	0)	1	2	1	0	3	0	10	0	0	1	0	0	0	.040	.138	.040	.178
	Postseason		1	1	0	0	0	0	(0	0)	0	0	0	0	0	0	1	0	0	0	0	0	0	.000	.000	.000	.000
	4 ML YEARS		150	394	73	21	1	11	(3	8)	129	45	49	46	59	2	154	3	1	1	1	1	5	.185	.295	.327	.623

Alex Colome

Pitches: R Bats: R Pos: RP-53   COH-loh-may   **Ht: 6'1" Wt: 225 Born: 12/31/1988 Age: 34**

			HOW MUCH PITCHED					WHAT HE GAVE UP											THE RESULTS							
Year	Team	Lg	G	GS	GF	IP	BFP	H	R	ER	HR	SH	SF	HB	TBB	IBB	SO	WP	W	L	Pct	Sv-Op	Hld	Vel	OPS	ERC	ERA
2013	TB	AL	3	3	0	16.0	71	14	8	4	2	0	0	1	9	0	12	1	1	1	.500	0-0	0	95	.715	4.41	2.25
2014	TB	AL	5	3	1	23.2	97	19	7	7	1	0	1	0	10	0	13	3	2	0	1.000	0-0	0	94	.590	2.77	2.66
2015	TB	AL	43	13	5	109.2	457	112	50	48	9	2	7	4	31	4	88	8	8	5	.615	0-5	8	94	.698	3.78	3.94
2016	TB	AL	57	0	48	56.2	226	43	12	12	6	0	0	2	15	1	71	1	2	4	.333	37-40	1	95	.572	2.46	1.91
2017	TB	AL	65	0	53	66.2	281	57	27	24	4	3	6	3	23	7	58	4	2	3	.400	**47-53**	1	95	.636	2.79	3.24
2018	2 Tms	AL	70	0	24	68.0	282	59	26	23	7	0	1	3	21	2	72	10	7	5	.583	12-17	30	95	.645	3.15	3.04
2019	CWS	AL	62	0	54	61.0	249	42	28	19	7	2	3	1	23	2	55	4	4	5	.444	30-33	0	94	.617	2.43	2.80
2020	CWS	AL	21	0	18	22.1	90	13	3	2	0	0	0	1	8	0	16	0	2	0	1.000	12-13	0	94	.460	1.45	0.81
2021	Min	AL	67	0	31	65.0	290	68	41	30	8	1	4	4	23	1	58	2	4	4	.500	17-24	5	94	.740	4.43	4.15
2022	Col	NL	53	0	13	47.0	215	57	36	30	5	0	2	0	22	2	32	4	2	7	.222	4-7	7	95	.853	5.57	5.74
18	TB	AL	23	0	21	21.2	97	24	12	10	1	0	1	0	8	1	23	4	2	5	.286	11-13	0	95	.728	3.99	4.15
18	Sea	AL	47	0	3	46.1	185	35	14	13	6	0	0	3	13	1	49	6	5	0	1.000	1-4	30	95	.601	2.77	2.53
	Postseason		2	0	2	2.0	7	0	0	0	0	0	0	0	1	0	1	0	0	0	-	1-1	0	95	.143	0.27	0.00
	10 ML YEARS		446	19	247	536.0	2258	484	238	199	49	8	24	19	185	19	475	37	34	34	.500	159-192	52	94	.668	3.35	3.34

Michael Conforto

Bats: L Throws: R Pos: OF   **Ht: 6'1" Wt: 215 Born: 3/1/1993 Age: 30**

			BATTING																RUNNING			AVERAGES			
Year	Team	Lg	G	AB	H	2B	3B	HR	(Hm	Rd)	TB	R	RBI	RC	TBB	IBB	SO	HBP	SH	SF	SB	CS	GDP	Avg	OBP	Slg	OPS
2015	NYM	NL	56	174	47	14	0	9	(4	5)	88	30	26	29	17	0	39	1	0	2	0	1	4	.270	.335	.506	.841
2016	NYM	NL	109	304	67	21	1	12	(7	5)	126	38	42	35	36	2	89	5	0	3	2	1	6	.220	.310	.414	.725
2017	NYM	NL	109	373	104	20	1	27	(16	11)	207	72	68	77	57	5	113	8	0	2	2	0	3	.279	.384	.555	.939
2018	NYM	NL	153	543	132	25	1	28	(11	17)	243	78	82	87	84	8	159	7	0	4	3	4	10	.243	.350	.448	.797
2019	NYM	NL	151	549	141	29	1	33	(18	15)	271	90	92	97	84	5	149	10	0	5	7	2	11	.257	.363	.494	.856
2020	NYM	NL	54	202	65	12	0	9	(4	5)	104	40	31	39	24	0	57	7	0	0	3	3	6	.322	.412	.515	.927
2021	NYM	NL	125	406	94	20	0	14	(6	8)	156	52	55	58	59	3	104	12	0	2	1	0	14	.232	.344	.384	.729
	Postseason		12	30	6	0	0	3	(2	1)	15	3	6	5	1	0	8	1	0	2	0	0	0	.200	.235	.500	.735
	7 ML YEARS		757	2551	650	141	4	132	(66	66)	1195	400	396	422	361	23	710	50	0	18	18	11	54	.255	.356	.468	.824

Mark Contreras

Bats: L Throws: R Pos: CF-13;RF-9;PH-4;LF-3;PR-3   **Ht: 6'0" Wt: 195 Born: 1/24/1995 Age: 28**

			BATTING																RUNNING			AVERAGES			
Year	Team	Lg	G	AB	H	2B	3B	HR	(Hm	Rd)	TB	R	RBI	RC	TBB	IBB	SO	HBP	SH	SF	SB	CS	GDP	Avg	OBP	Slg	OPS
2022	StPaul	AAA	102	376	89	21	1	15	(-	-)	157	64	59	56	37	1	125	8	0	2	24	2	3	.237	.317	.418	.734
2022	Min	AL	28	58	7	1	0	3	(2	1)	17	9	6	0	1	0	21	1	0	1	1	0	2	.121	.148	.293	.441

Roansy Contreras

Pitches: R Bats: R Pos: SP-18; RP-3   **Ht: 6'0" Wt: 175 Born: 11/7/1999 Age: 23**

			HOW MUCH PITCHED					WHAT HE GAVE UP											THE RESULTS							
Year	Team	Lg	G	GS	GF	IP	BFP	H	R	ER	HR	SH	SF	HB	TBB	IBB	SO	WP	W	L	Pct	Sv-Op	Hld	Vel	OPS	ERC	ERA
2018	2 Tms	Low	12	12	0	63.1	250	44	19	17	5	2	1	1	21	0	60	5	0	2	.000	0- -	-		.662	2.20	2.42
2019	CtnSC	A	24	24	0	132.1	536	105	55	49	10	4	12	6	36	0	113	16	12	5	.706	0- -	-		.413	2.52	3.33
2021	Altna	AA	12	12	0	54.1	218	37	21	16	5	2	1	3	12	0	76	1	3	2	.600	0- -	-		.536	1.89	2.65
2022	Indy	AAA	9	9	0	34.1	141	29	13	12	4	0	0	0	13	0	46	2	1	1	.500	0- -	-		.681	3.30	3.15
2021	Pit	NL	1	1	0	3.0	12	3	0	0	0	0	0	0	1	0	4	0	0	0	-	0-0	0	96	.697	3.35	0.00
2022	Pit	NL	21	18	1	95.0	408	82	45	40	13	0	2	2	39	1	86	11	5	5	.500	0-0	0	96	.715	3.60	3.79
	2 ML YEARS		22	19	1	98.0	420	85	45	40	13	0	2	2	40	1	90	11	5	5	.500	0-0	0	96	.715	3.60	3.67

William Contreras

Bats: R Throws: R Pos: C-60;DH-34;PH-7;LF-1   **Ht: 6'0" Wt: 180 Born: 12/24/1997 Age: 25**

			BATTING																RUNNING			AVERAGES			
Year	Team	Lg	G	AB	H	2B	3B	HR	(Hm	Rd)	TB	R	RBI	RC	TBB	IBB	SO	HBP	SH	SF	SB	CS	GDP	Avg	OBP	Slg	OPS
2022	Gwnntt	AAA	13	48	14	3	0	0	(-	-)	17	2	8	5	3	0	10	0	0	0	0	0	0	.292	.333	.354	.688
2020	Atl	NL	4	10	4	1	0	0	(0	0)	5	0	1	2	0	0	4	0	0	0	0	0	0	.400	.400	.500	.900
2021	Atl	NL	52	163	35	4	1	8	(4	4)	65	19	23	19	19	1	54	2	0	1	0	0	3	.215	.303	.399	.701
2022	Atl	NL	97	334	93	14	1	20	(12	8)	169	51	45	56	39	1	104	1	0	2	2	0	5	.278	.354	.506	.860
	Postseason		1	1	0	0	0	0	(0	0)	0	0	0	0	0	0	0	0	0	0	0	0	0	.000	.000	.000	.000
	3 ML YEARS		153	507	132	19	2	28	(16	12)	239	70	69	77	58	2	162	3	0	3	2	0	8	.260	.338	.471	.809

Willson Contreras

Bats: R Throws: R Pos: C-72;DH-39;PH-2　　　　Ht: 6'1" Wt: 225 Born: 5/13/1992 Age: 31

									BATTING										RUNNING			AVERAGES			
Year	Team	Lg	G	AB	H	2B	3B	HR	(Hm | Rd)	TB	R	RBI	RC	TBB	IBB	SO	HBP	SH	SF	SB	CS	GDP	Avg	OBP	Slg	OPS
2016	ChC	NL	76	252	71	14	1	12	(8 | 4)	123	33	35	41	26	0	67	4	0	1	2	2	7	.282	.357	.488	.845
2017	ChC	NL	117	377	104	21	0	21	(10 | 11)	188	50	74	76	45	2	98	3	1	2	5	4	13	.276	.356	.499	.855
2018	ChC	NL	138	474	118	27	5	10	(6 | 4)	185	50	54	58	53	2	121	13	2	2	4	1	14	.249	.339	.390	.730
2019	ChC	NL	105	360	98	18	2	24	(15 | 9)	192	57	64	62	38	2	102	9	0	2	1	2	4	.272	.355	.533	.888
2020	ChC	NL	57	189	46	10	0	7	(3 | 4)	77	37	26	32	20	1	57	14	0	2	1	2	6	.243	.356	.407	.763
2021	ChC	NL	128	413	98	20	0	21	(14 | 7)	181	61	57	63	52	1	138	14	0	4	5	4	11	.237	.340	.438	.778
2022	ChC	NL	113	416	101	23	2	22	(10 | 12)	194	65	55	70	45	0	103	24	0	2	4	2	14	.243	.349	.466	.815
	Postseason		30	78	18	3	0	3	(2 | 1)	30	9	7	11	13	1	21	3	0	0	0	0	0	.231	.362	.385	.746
	7 ML YEARS		734	2481	636	133	10	117	(66 | 51)	1140	353	365	402	279	8	686	81	3	15	22	17	69	.256	.349	.459	.808

Sam Coonrod

Pitches: R Bats: R Pos: RP-12　　　　Ht: 6'1" Wt: 225 Born: 9/22/1992 Age: 30

				HOW MUCH PITCHED						WHAT HE GAVE UP										THE RESULTS					
Year	Team	Lg	G	GS	GF	IP	BFP	H	R	ER	HR	SH	SF	HB	TBB	IBB	SO	WP	W	L	Pct	Sv-Op	Hld	Vel	OPS	ERC	ERA
2022	LV	AAA	9	0	0	9.0	45	12	9	8	1	0	0	1	6	0	5	1	1	0	1.000	0- -	-	-	.870	7.79	8.00
2019	SF	NL	33	0	9	27.2	114	19	11	11	3	1	0	4	15	1	20	2	5	1	.833	0-1	0	97	.655	3.63	3.58
2020	SF	NL	18	0	5	14.2	71	17	16	16	2	0	1	2	7	0	15	1	0	2	.000	3-5	2	98	.871	5.94	9.82
2021	Phi	NL	42	2	7	42.1	185	41	21	19	5	0	1	3	15	1	48	4	2	2	.500	2-6	8	98	.692	4.02	4.04
2022	Phi	NL	12	0	3	12.2	58	12	12	11	1	0	3	3	12	0	12	1	0	0	-	0-0	3	97	.802	5.22	7.82
	4 ML YEARS		105	2	24	97.1	428	89	60	57	11	1	5	12	44	2	95	8	7	5	.583	5-12	13	97	.727	4.34	5.27

Garrett Cooper

Bats: R Throws: R Pos: 1B-59;DH-56;PH-6　　　　Ht: 6'5" Wt: 235 Born: 12/25/1990 Age: 32

									BATTING										RUNNING			AVERAGES			
Year	Team	Lg	G	AB	H	2B	3B	HR	(Hm	Rd)	TB	R	RBI	RC	TBB	IBB	SO	HBP	SH	SF	SB	CS	GDP	Avg	OBP	Slg	OPS
2017	NYY	AL	13	43	14	5	1	0	(0	0)	21	3	6	6	1	0	12	0	0	1	0	0	0	.326	.333	.488	.822
2018	Mia	NL	14	33	7	1	0	0	(0	0)	8	2	2	3	4	0	12	1	0	0	0	0	1	.212	.316	.242	.558
2019	Mia	NL	107	381	107	16	1	15	(6	9)	170	52	50	57	33	0	110	5	0	2	0	0	10	.281	.344	.446	.791
2020	Mia	NL	34	120	34	8	0	6	(3	3)	60	20	20	22	11	0	31	2	0	0	0	0	5	.283	.353	.500	.853
2021	Mia	NL	71	215	61	10	1	9	(6	3)	100	30	33	30	30	0	68	4	0	1	1	1	6	.284	.380	.465	.845
2022	Mia	NL	119	414	108	33	2	9	(5	4)	172	37	50	57	40	0	119	10	0	5	0	0	6	.261	.337	.415	.752
	Postseason		5	18	3	1	0	1	(0	1)	7	2	3	2	3	0	5	0	0	0	0	0	0	.167	.286	.389	.675
	6 ML YEARS		358	1206	331	73	5	39	(20	19)	531	144	161	184	119	0	352	22	0	9	1	1	28	.274	.348	.440	.788

Patrick Corbin

Pitches: L Bats: L Pos: SP-31　　　　Ht: 6'4" Wt: 222 Born: 7/19/1989 Age: 33

				HOW MUCH PITCHED						WHAT HE GAVE UP										THE RESULTS					
Year	Team	Lg	G	GS	GF	IP	BFP	H	R	ER	HR	SH	SF	HB	TBB	IBB	SO	WP	W	L	Pct	Sv-Op	Hld	Vel	OPS	ERC	ERA
2012	Ari	NL	22	17	3	107.0	454	117	56	54	14	2	5	4	25	2	86	1	6	8	.429	1-1	0	91	.782	4.31	4.54
2013	Ari	NL	32	32	0	208.1	860	189	81	79	19	8	1	9	54	1	178	13	14	8	.636	0-0	0	92	.671	3.14	3.41
2015	Ari	NL	16	16	0	85.0	357	91	34	34	9	2	1	2	17	0	78	4	6	5	.545	0-0	0	92	.743	3.82	3.60
2016	Ari	NL	36	24	6	155.2	701	177	109	89	24	6	5	5	66	2	131	9	5	13	.278	1-1	2	92	.825	5.47	5.15
2017	Ari	NL	33	32	0	189.2	826	208	97	85	26	4	5	3	61	8	178	10	14	13	.519	0-0	0	92	.792	4.55	4.03
2018	Ari	NL	33	33	0	200.0	800	162	70	70	15	3	2	5	48	3	246	8	11	7	.611	0-0	0	91	.607	2.41	3.15
2019	Was	NL	33	33	0	202.0	835	169	81	73	24	8	8	3	70	2	238	4	14	7	.667	0-0	0	92	.668	3.15	3.25
2020	Was	NL	11	11	0	65.2	295	85	35	34	10	0	1	0	18	1	60	1	2	7	.222	0-0	0	90	.838	5.61	4.66
2021	Was	NL	31	31	0	171.2	751	192	114	111	37	10	5	3	60	2	143	0	9	16	.360	0-0	0	93	.855	5.47	5.82
2022	Was	NL	31	31	0	152.2	713	210	119	107	27	1	1	7	49	1	128	2	6	19	.240	0-0	0	93	.887	6.73	6.31
	Postseason		8	3	0	23.1	103	21	16	15	2	0	0	1	12	1	36	0	2	3	.400	0-1	2	93	.663	3.90	5.79
	10 ML YEARS		278	260	9	1537.2	6592	1600	796	736	205	44	34	41	468	22	1466	52	87	103	.458	2-2	2	92	.758	4.24	4.31

Franchy Cordero

Bats: L Throws: R Pos: 1B-53;RF-26;LF-12;PH-11;DH-3;CF-2;PR-1　　　　Ht: 6'3" Wt: 226 Born: 9/2/1994 Age: 28

									BATTING										RUNNING			AVERAGES			
Year	Team	Lg	G	AB	H	2B	3B	HR	(Hm	Rd)	TB	R	RBI	RC	TBB	IBB	SO	HBP	SH	SF	SB	CS	GDP	Avg	OBP	Slg	OPS
2022	Wrcstr	AAA	31	117	38	10	0	7	(-	-)	69	23	36	27	15	0	42	1	0	3	4	2	2	.325	.397	.590	.987
2017	SD	NL	30	92	21	3	3	3	(3	0)	39	15	9	9	6	0	44	0	1	0	1	1	0	.228	.276	.424	.699
2018	SD	NL	40	139	33	5	1	7	(3	4)	61	19	19	19	14	0	55	0	1	0	5	2	1	.237	.307	.439	.746
2019	SD	NL	9	15	5	1	0	0	(0	0)	6	2	1	3	4	0	7	0	0	1	1	0	0	.333	.450	.400	.850
2020	KC	AL	16	38	8	3	0	2	(2	0)	17	7	7	7	4	0	4	0	0	1	1	0	1	.211	.286	.447	.733
2021	Bos	AL	48	127	24	6	0	1	(0	1)	33	12	9	7	8	0	51	0	1	0	1	1	1	.189	.237	.260	.497
2022	Bos	AL	84	242	53	17	1	8	(6	2)	96	36	29	33	28	1	92	1	2	4	4	1	1	.219	.300	.397	.697
	6 ML YEARS		227	653	144	35	5	21	(14	7)	252	91	74	78	64	1	253	1	5	3	13	5	4	.221	.290	.386	.676

Carlos Correa

Bats: R Throws: R Pos: SS-132;DH-4;PH-3　　　　coh-RAY-uh　　　　Ht: 6'4" Wt: 220 Born: 9/22/1994 Age: 28

									BATTING										RUNNING			AVERAGES			
Year	Team	Lg	G	AB	H	2B	3B	HR	(Hm	Rd)	TB	R	RBI	RC	TBB	IBB	SO	HBP	SH	SF	SB	CS	GDP	Avg	OBP	Slg	OPS
2015	Hou	AL	99	387	108	22	1	22	(12	10)	198	52	68	68	40	2	78	1	0	4	14	4	10	.279	.345	.512	.857
2016	Hou	AL	153	577	158	36	3	20	(8	12)	260	76	96	93	75	5	139	5	0	3	13	3	12	.274	.361	.451	.811
2017	Hou	AL	109	422	133	25	1	24	(11	13)	232	82	84	86	53	5	92	2	0	4	2	1	12	.315	.391	.550	.941
2018	Hou	AL	110	402	96	20	1	15	(7	8)	163	60	65	49	53	3	111	2	0	11	3	0	17	.239	.323	.405	.728

236

Year Team	Lg	G	AB	H	2B	3B	HR	(Hm	Rd)	TB	R	RBI	RC	TBB	IBB	SO	HBP	SH	SF	SB	CS	GDP	Avg	OBP	Slg	OPS
								BATTING												**RUNNING**			**AVERAGES**			
2019 Hou	AL	75	280	78	16	1	21	(11	10)	159	42	59	52	35	0	75	2	0	4	1	0	8	.279	.358	.568	.926
2020 Hou	AL	58	201	53	9	0	5	(1	4)	77	22	25	23	16	2	49	3	0	1	0	0	4	.264	.326	.383	.709
2021 Hou	AL	148	555	155	34	1	26	(14	12)	269	104	92	94	75	2	116	4	0	6	0	0	16	.279	.366	.485	.850
2022 Min	AL	136	522	152	24	1	22	(11	11)	244	70	64	87	61	2	121	3	0	4	0	1	18	.291	.366	.467	.834
Postseason		79	301	82	16	0	18	(9	9)	152	37	59	51	30	2	79	3	0	0	1	0	8	.272	.344	.505	.849
8 ML YEARS		888	3346	933	186	9	155	(75	80)	1602	508	553	552	408	21	781	22	0	37	33	9	97	.279	.357	.479	.836

Nestor Cortes

Pitches: L **Bats:** R **Pos:** SP-28 **Ht:** 5'11" **Wt:** 210 **Born:** 12/10/1994 **Age:** 28

Year Team	Lg	G	GS	GF	IP	BFP	H	R	ER	HR	SH	SF	HB	TBB	IBB	SO	WP	W	L	Pct	Sv-Op	Hld	Vel	OPS	ERC	ERA
					HOW MUCH PITCHED					**WHAT HE GAVE UP**										**THE RESULTS**						
2018 Bal	AL	4	0	3	4.2	26	10	4	4	2	0	0	0	4	0	3	0	0	0	-	0-0	0	88	1.357	18.44	7.71
2019 NYY	AL	33	1	7	66.2	298	75	44	42	16	0	2	1	28	1	69	1	5	1	.833	0-1	1	90	.843	5.97	5.67
2020 Sea	AL	5	1	2	7.2	44	12	14	13	6	0	0	2	6	0	8	0	0	1	.000	0-0	0	88	1.379	16.80	15.26
2021 NYY	AL	22	14	3	93.0	374	75	32	30	14	1	1	2	25	0	103	2	2	3	.400	0-0	0	91	.659	2.95	2.90
2022 NYY	AL	28	28	0	158.1	615	108	44	43	16	0	3	2	38	0	163	1	12	4	.750	0-0	0	92	.554	1.93	2.44
5 ML YEARS		92	44	15	330.1	1357	280	138	132	54	1	6	7	101	1	346	4	19	9	.679	0-1	1	91	.684	3.37	3.60

Jharel Cotton

Pitches: R **Bats:** R **Pos:** RP-30 JUH-rel **Ht:** 5'11" **Wt:** 200 **Born:** 1/19/1992 **Age:** 31

Year Team	Lg	G	GS	GF	IP	BFP	H	R	ER	HR	SH	SF	HB	TBB	IBB	SO	WP	W	L	Pct	Sv-Op	Hld	Vel	OPS	ERC	ERA
					HOW MUCH PITCHED					**WHAT HE GAVE UP**										**THE RESULTS**						
2022 StPaul	AAA	22	0	11	25.0	105	17	8	8	4	0	1	3	10	1	39	3	4	1	.800	1--	-		.648	3.09	2.88
2016 Oak	AL	5	5	0	29.1	112	20	10	7	4	0	0	0	4	0	23	1	2	0	1.000	0-0	0	92	.538	1.70	2.15
2017 Oak	AL	24	24	0	129.0	566	133	91	80	28	4	5	4	53	1	105	9	9	10	.474	0-0	0	93	.833	5.26	5.58
2021 Tex	AL	23	0	5	30.2	137	28	12	12	2	0	2	2	15	0	30	1	2	0	1.000	0-0	3	93	.659	3.84	3.52
2022 2 Tms		30	0	9	43.0	181	34	20	17	7	0	3	2	20	0	39	3	4	2	.667	0-2	5	93	.713	3.80	3.56
22 Min	AL	25	0	7	35.0	144	23	13	11	7	0	2	2	16	0	31	2	2	2	.500	0-2	2	93	.680	3.31	2.83
22 SF	NL	5	0	2	8.0	37	11	7	6	0	0	1	0	4	0	8	1	2	0	1.000	0-0	3	93	.843	6.07	6.75
4 ML YEARS		82	29	14	232.0	996	215	133	116	41	4	10	8	92	1	197	14	17	12	.586	0-2	5	93	.753	4.30	4.50

Danny Coulombe

Pitches: L **Bats:** L **Pos:** RP-10 KOO-lohm **Ht:** 5'10" **Wt:** 190 **Born:** 10/26/1989 **Age:** 33

Year Team	Lg	G	GS	GF	IP	BFP	H	R	ER	HR	SH	SF	HB	TBB	IBB	SO	WP	W	L	Pct	Sv-Op	Hld	Vel	OPS	ERC	ERA
					HOW MUCH PITCHED					**WHAT HE GAVE UP**										**THE RESULTS**						
2014 LAD	NL	5	0	0	4.1	22	5	3	2	1	0	0	0	2	0	4	2	0	0	-	0-0	0	91	.768	5.49	4.15
2015 2 Tms		14	0	4	16.0	72	17	10	10	0	0	0	0	9	0	11	2	0	1	-	0-1	0	90	.742	4.32	5.63
2016 Oak	AL	35	0	4	47.2	193	37	24	24	6	2	3	0	17	2	54	3	3	1	.750	0-1	2	90	.634	2.84	4.53
2017 Oak	AL	72	0	10	51.2	219	46	22	20	4	0	1	4	22	1	39	5	2	2	.500	0-1	13	91	.714	3.74	3.48
2018 Oak	AL	27	0	3	23.2	98	24	13	12	5	0	1	0	11	0	26	2	1	1	.500	0-0	0	90	.846	5.58	4.56
2020 Min	AL	2	0	2	2.2	13	2	0	0	0	0	0	0	3	0	3	0	0	0	-	0-0	0	90	.585	4.52	0.00
2021 Min	AL	29	1	13	34.1	139	35	17	14	5	1	0	0	7	1	33	0	3	2	.600	0-0	7	91	.747	3.77	3.67
2022 Min	AL	10	0	3	12.1	53	7	3	2	0	1	0	0	9	0	9	1	0	0	-	0-0	0	91	.511	2.27	1.46
15 LAD	NL	5	0	3	8.1	40	9	7	7	0	0	0	0	6	0	7	1	0	0	-	0-0	0	90	.816	4.97	7.56
15 Oak	AL	9	0	1	7.2	32	8	3	3	0	0	0	0	3	0	4	1	0	1	-	0-1	0	89	.654	3.72	3.52
8 ML YEARS		194	1	46	192.2	809	173	92	84	21	3	6	4	80	4	179	15	9	6	.600	0-4	17	90	.707	3.73	3.92

Jake Cousins

Pitches: R **Bats:** R **Pos:** RP-12 **Ht:** 6'4" **Wt:** 185 **Born:** 7/14/1994 **Age:** 28

Year Team	Lg	G	GS	GF	IP	BFP	H	R	ER	HR	SH	SF	HB	TBB	IBB	SO	WP	W	L	Pct	Sv-Op	Hld	Vel	OPS	ERC	ERA
					HOW MUCH PITCHED					**WHAT HE GAVE UP**										**THE RESULTS**						
2022 Nashv	AAA	21	0	3	22.2	97	15	8	7	2	0	0	3	11	0	31	2	1	0	1.000	1--	-	-	.552	2.94	2.78
2021 Mil	NL	30	0	3	30.0	125	16	9	9	3	1	0	4	19	1	44	2	1	0	1.000	0-0	7	96	.582	2.95	2.70
2022 Mil	NL	12	0	6	13.1	59	10	4	4	1	0	0	2	8	1	21	4	2	1	.667	0-1	1	96	.706	3.71	2.70
Postseason		1	0	1	1.0	5	1	0	0	0	0	0	0	1	1	1	1	0	0	-	0-0	0	95	.900	3.46	0.00
2 ML YEARS		42	0	9	43.1	184	26	13	13	4	1	0	6	27	2	65	6	3	1	.750	0-1	8	96	.622	3.18	2.70

Brandon Crawford

Bats: L **Throws:** R **Pos:** SS-116;PH-5 **Ht:** 6'1" **Wt:** 223 **Born:** 1/21/1987 **Age:** 36

Year Team	Lg	G	AB	H	2B	3B	HR	(Hm	Rd)	TB	R	RBI	RC	TBB	IBB	SO	HBP	SH	SF	SB	CS	GDP	Avg	OBP	Slg	OPS
								BATTING												**RUNNING**			**AVERAGES**			
2011 SF	NL	66	196	40	5	2	3	(0	3)	58	22	21	20	23	1	31	0	1	0	1	3	4	.204	.288	.296	.584
2012 SF	NL	143	435	108	26	3	4	(1	3)	152	44	45	40	33	6	95	3	2	3	1	4	6	.248	.304	.349	.653
2013 SF	NL	149	499	124	24	3	9	(2	7)	181	52	43	42	42	6	96	5	1	3	1	2	10	.248	.311	.363	.674
2014 SF	NL	153	491	121	20	10	10	(4	6)	191	54	69	72	59	10	129	2	3	3	5	3	4	.246	.324	.389	.713
2015 SF	NL	143	507	130	33	4	21	(8	13)	234	65	84	69	39	9	119	11	0	4	6	4	18	.256	.321	.462	.782
2016 SF	NL	155	553	152	28	11	12	(4	8)	238	67	84	82	57	10	115	4	0	9	7	0	13	.275	.342	.430	.772
2017 SF	NL	144	518	131	34	1	14	(6	8)	209	58	77	61	42	3	113	1	0	9	3	5	18	.253	.305	.403	.709
2018 SF	NL	151	531	135	28	2	14	(7	7)	209	63	54	60	50	13	122	8	0	5	4	5	12	.254	.325	.394	.719
2019 SF	NL	147	500	114	24	2	11	(2	9)	175	58	59	55	53	5	117	3	0	4	3	2	10	.228	.304	.350	.654
2020 SF	NL	54	169	43	8	0	5	(3	2)	66	28	26	27	15	2	47	4	0	2	1	2	3	.256	.326	.465	.792
2021 SF	NL	138	483	144	30	3	24	(11	13)	252	79	90	100	56	6	105	11	3	8	11	3	8	.298	.373	.522	.895
2022 SF	NL	118	407	94	15	2	9	(3	6)	140	50	52	45	39	3	98	8	0	4	1	1	12	.231	.308	.344	.652
Postseason		43	147	35	7	1	2	(1	1)	50	15	19	15	15	2	36	0	1	2	2	0	2	.238	.305	.340	.645
12 ML YEARS		1561	5292	1337	279	43	139	(53	86)	2119	638	706	673	508	74	1187	54	6	58	44	34	116	.253	.321	.400	.722

J.P. Crawford

Bats: L Throws: R Pos: SS-144;PR-1   Ht: 6'2" Wt: 202 Born: 1/11/1995 Age: 28

Year Team	Lg	G	AB	H	2B	3B	HR	(Hm Rd)	TB	R	RBI	RC	TBB	IBB	SO	HBP	SH	SF	SB	CS	GDP	Avg	OBP	Slg	OPS
2017 Phi	NL	23	70	15	4	1	0	(0 0)	21	8	6	9	16	0	22	1	0	1	1	0	1	.214	.356	.300	.656
2018 Phi	NL	49	117	25	6	3	3	(2 1)	46	17	12	17	13	0	37	5	2	0	2	0	2	.214	.319	.393	.712
2019 Sea	AL	93	345	78	21	4	7	(4 3)	128	43	46	46	43	0	83	2	3	3	5	3	4	.226	.313	.371	.684
2020 Sea	AL	53	204	52	7	2	2	(1 1)	69	33	24	30	23	0	39	3	0	2	6	3	4	.255	.336	.338	.674
2021 Sea	AL	160	619	169	37	0	9	(5 4)	233	89	54	85	58	1	114	5	1	4	3	6	10	.273	.338	.376	.715
2022 Sea	AL	145	518	126	24	3	6	(3 3)	174	57	42	53	68	0	80	10	2	5	3	2	11	.243	.339	.336	.675
6 ML YEARS		523	1873	465	99	13	27	(15 12)	671	247	184	240	221	1	375	25	8	15	20	14	32	.248	.333	.358	.691

Kutter Crawford

Pitches: R Bats: R Pos: SP-12; RP-9   Ht: 6'1" Wt: 209 Born: 4/1/1996 Age: 27

Year Team	Lg	G	GS	GF	IP	BFP	H	R	ER	HR	SH	SF	HB	TBB	IBB	SO	WP	W	L	Pct	Sv-Op	Hld	Vel	OPS	ERC	ERA
2022 Wrcstr	AAA	6	4	0	24.1	111	29	16	14	5	0	1	1	6	0	23	2	1	0	1.000	0- -	-	-	.800	5.26	5.18
2021 Bos	AL	1	1	0	2.0	13	5	5	5	1	0	2	0	2	0	2	0	0	0	.000	0-0	0	94	1.538	21.61	22.50
2022 Bos	AL	21	12	3	77.1	334	81	49	47	12	0	2	2	29	1	77	4	3	6	.333	0-0	0	95	.794	4.77	5.47
2 ML YEARS		22	13	3	79.1	347	86	54	52	13	0	4	2	31	1	79	4	3	7	.300	0-0	0	95	.817	5.11	5.90

Kyle Crick

Pitches: R Bats: L Pos: RP-14   Ht: 6'4" Wt: 225 Born: 11/30/1992 Age: 30

Year Team	Lg	G	GS	GF	IP	BFP	H	R	ER	HR	SH	SF	HB	TBB	IBB	SO	WP	W	L	Pct	Sv-Op	Hld	Vel	OPS	ERC	ERA
2022 Charltt	AAA	6	0	1	6.2	28	3	3	2	1	0	0	0	4	0	9	0	1	0	1.000	0- -	-	-	.607	2.15	2.70
2017 SF	NL	30	0	14	32.1	134	22	13	11	2	1	0	1	17	1	28	6	0	0	-	0-0	1	96	.596	2.68	3.06
2018 Pit	NL	64	0	13	60.1	255	45	18	16	3	1	1	7	23	3	65	9	3	2	.600	2-3	16	96	.569	2.63	2.39
2019 Pit	NL	52	0	9	49.0	226	41	30	27	10	0	1	7	35	1	61	1	3	7	.300	0-6	13	95	.579	5.73	4.96
2020 Pit	NL	7	0	2	5.2	29	7	6	1	0	0	0	0	4	0	7	0	1	0	1.000	0-1	0	91	.699	5.50	1.59
2021 Pit	NL	27	0	6	24.1	107	14	14	12	0	1	2	5	19	0	21	6	1	1	.500	0-1	6	93	.558	3.26	4.44
2022 CWS	AL	14	0	3	15.2	66	10	7	7	0	0	0	2	11	0	19	0	2	0	1.000	0-0	3	92	.575	3.13	4.02
6 ML YEARS		194	0	47	187.1	817	139	88	74	15	3	4	22	109	5	201	22	9	11	.450	2-11	39	95	.641	3.61	3.56

Nabil Crismatt

Pitches: R Bats: R Pos: RP-49; SP-1   Ht: 6'1" Wt: 220 Born: 12/25/1994 Age: 28

Year Team	Lg	G	GS	GF	IP	BFP	H	R	ER	HR	SH	SF	HB	TBB	IBB	SO	WP	W	L	Pct	Sv-Op	Hld	Vel	OPS	ERC	ERA
2020 StL	NL	6	0	6	8.1	31	6	3	3	2	0	0	1	1	0	8	0	0	0	-	0-0	0	90	.692	2.27	3.24
2021 SD	NL	45	0	14	81.1	351	87	40	34	10	2	0	8	24	2	71	3	3	1	.750	0-0	1	90	.761	4.63	3.76
2022 SD	NL	50	1	14	67.1	280	57	29	22	5	0	4	2	22	1	65	0	5	2	.714	0-4	5	90	.650	2.87	2.94
3 ML YEARS		101	1	34	157.0	662	150	72	59	17	2	4	10	47	3	144	3	8	3	.727	0-4	6	90	.711	3.72	3.38

Cooper Criswell

Pitches: R Bats: R Pos: SP-1   Ht: 6'6" Wt: 200 Born: 7/24/1996 Age: 26

Year Team	Lg	G	GS	GF	IP	BFP	H	R	ER	HR	SH	SF	HB	TBB	IBB	SO	WP	W	L	Pct	Sv-Op	Hld	Vel	OPS	ERC	ERA
2022 Angels	R	5	0	0	13.0	52	11	3	3	0	0	0	1	2	0	19	1	0	0	-	0- -	-	-	-	2.04	2.08
2022 Drham	AAA	11	3	0	36.2	145	31	19	17	3	1	0	1	6	0	33	3	2	1	.667	0- -	-	-	.607	2.39	4.17
2021 LAA	AL	1	1	0	1.1	10	6	3	3	0	0	0	0	0	0	0	0	0	1	.000	0-0	0	87	1.500	26.58	20.25
2022 TB	AL	1	1	0	3.1	13	2	1	1	0	0	0	0	1	0	4	0	0	0	-	0-0	0	90	.397	1.31	2.70
2 ML YEARS		2	2	0	4.2	23	8	4	4	0	0	0	0	1	0	4	0	0	1	.000	0-0	0	89	.891	6.61	7.71

Garrett Crochet

CROH-shay

Pitches: L Bats: L Pos: P   Ht: 6'6" Wt: 230 Born: 6/21/1999 Age: 24

Year Team	Lg	G	GS	GF	IP	BFP	H	R	ER	HR	SH	SF	HB	TBB	IBB	SO	WP	W	L	Pct	Sv-Op	Hld	Vel	OPS	ERC	ERA
2020 CWS	AL	5	0	1	6.0	22	3	0	0	0	0	0	0	1	0	8	0	0	0	-	0-0	0	-	.325	0.80	0.00
2021 CWS	AL	54	0	12	54.1	230	42	22	17	2	2	2	1	27	2	65	4	3	5	.375	0-1	12	-	.598	2.79	2.82
Postseason		4	0	0	3.0	14	5	0	0	0	0	0	0	1	0	6	0	0	0	-	0-0	0	-	.890	7.34	0.00
2 ML YEARS		59	0	13	60.1	252	45	22	17	2	2	2	1	27	2	73	4	3	5	.375	0-1	12	-	.572	2.52	2.54

C.J. Cron

CROHN

Bats: R Throws: R Pos: 1B-121;DH-28;PH-2   Ht: 6'4" Wt: 235 Born: 1/5/1990 Age: 33

Year Team	Lg	G	AB	H	2B	3B	HR	(Hm Rd)	TB	R	RBI	RC	TBB	IBB	SO	HBP	SH	SF	SB	CS	GDP	Avg	OBP	Slg	OPS
2014 LAA	AL	79	242	62	12	1	11	(5 6)	109	28	37	35	10	0	61	1	0	0	0	0	10	.256	.289	.450	.739
2015 LAA	AL	113	378	99	17	1	16	(11 5)	166	37	51	46	17	1	82	5	0	3	3	1	9	.262	.300	.439	.739
2016 LAA	AL	116	407	113	25	2	16	(7 9)	190	51	69	66	24	1	75	7	0	5	2	3	9	.278	.325	.467	.792
2017 LAA	AL	100	339	84	14	1	16	(8 8)	148	39	56	51	22	0	96	3	2	5	3	2	5	.248	.305	.437	.741
2018 TB	AL	140	501	127	28	1	30	(11 19)	247	68	74	65	37	2	145	17	0	5	1	2	11	.253	.323	.493	.816
2019 Min	AL	125	458	116	24	0	25	(10 15)	215	51	78	66	29	3	107	10	0	2	0	0	13	.253	.311	.469	.780
2020 Det	AL	13	42	8	3	0	4	(0 4)	23	9	8	7	9	0	16	1	0	0	0	0	2	.190	.346	.548	.894

Year	Team	Lg	G	AB	H	2B	3B	HR	(Hm	Rd)	TB	R	RBI	RC	TBB	IBB	SO	HBP	SH	SF	SB	CS	GDP	Avg	OBP	Slg	OPS
2021	Col	NL	142	470	132	31	1	28	(19	9)	249	70	92	95	60	3	117	13	0	4	1	0	11	.281	.375	.530	.905
2022	Col	NL	150	575	148	28	3	29	(22	7)	269	79	102	100	43	6	164	8	0	5	0	0	16	.257	.315	.468	.783
Postseason			5	14	2	1	0	0	(0	0)	3	0	0	0	3	0	5	0	0	0	0	0	0	.143	.294	.214	.508
9 ML YEARS			978	3412	889	182	10	175	(93	82)	1616	432	567	531	251	16	863	69	0	27	10	8	86	.261	.322	.474	.795

Jake Cronenworth

Bats: L Throws: R Pos: 2B-147;1B-20;SS-9;PH-3;DH-2   Ht: 6'0" Wt: 187 Born: 1/21/1994 Age: 29

Year	Team	Lg	G	AB	H	2B	3B	HR	(Hm	Rd)	TB	R	RBI	RC	TBB	IBB	SO	HBP	SH	SF	SB	CS	GDP	Avg	OBP	Slg	OPS
2020	SD	NL	54	172	49	15	3	4	(3	1)	82	26	20	28	18	0	30	1	0	1	3	1	4	.285	.354	.477	.831
2021	SD	NL	152	567	151	33	7	21	(13	8)	261	94	71	88	55	6	90	10	3	3	4	3	8	.266	.340	.460	.800
2022	SD	NL	158	587	140	30	4	17	(9	8)	229	88	88	91	70	3	131	16	0	8	3	0	2	.239	.332	.390	.722
Postseason			6	18	7	0	1	1	(1	0)	12	5	3	6	4	0	5	2	0	0	1	0	0	.389	.542	.667	1.208
3 ML YEARS			364	1326	340	78	14	42	(25	17)	572	208	179	207	143	9	251	27	3	12	10	4	14	.256	.338	.431	.770

Narciso Crook

Bats: R Throws: R Pos: RF-2;PH-2;CF-1   Ht: 6'3" Wt: 220 Born: 7/12/1995 Age: 27

Year	Team	Lg	G	AB	H	2B	3B	HR	(Hm	Rd)	TB	R	RBI	RC	TBB	IBB	SO	HBP	SH	SF	SB	CS	GDP	Avg	OBP	Slg	OPS
2022	Iowa	AAA	101	362	94	21	3	19	(-	-)	178	61	67	64	36	0	124	11	0	0	13	6	5	.260	.345	.492	.836
2022	ChC	NL	4	8	2	1	0	0	(0	0)	3	1	2	1	0	0	3	0	0	1	0	0	1	.250	.222	.375	.597

Wil Crowe

Pitches: R Bats: R Pos: RP-59; SP-1   Ht: 6'2" Wt: 245 Born: 9/9/1994 Age: 28

Year	Team	Lg	G	GS	GF	IP	BFP	H	R	ER	HR	SH	SF	HB	TBB	IBB	SO	WP	W	L	Pct	Sv-Op	Hld	Vel	OPS	ERC	ERA
2020	Was	NL	3	3	0	8.1	46	14	13	11	5	0	0	1	8	0	8	0	0	2	.000	0-0	0	91	1.338	17.20	11.88
2021	Pit	NL	26	25	0	116.2	524	126	75	71	25	3	1	6	57	1	111	3	4	8	.333	0-0	0	94	.864	6.02	5.48
2022	Pit	NL	60	1	20	76.0	332	68	40	37	8	1	1	3	38	0	68	3	6	10	.375	4-10	16	95	.686	4.05	4.38
3 ML YEARS			89	29	20	201.0	902	208	128	119	38	4	2	10	103	1	187	6	10	20	.333	4-10	16	94	.821	5.62	5.33

Fernando Cruz

Pitches: R Bats: R Pos: RP-12; SP-2   Ht: 6'2" Wt: 205 Born: 3/28/1990 Age: 33

Year	Team	Lg	G	GS	GF	IP	BFP	H	R	ER	HR	SH	SF	HB	TBB	IBB	SO	WP	W	L	Pct	Sv-Op	Hld	Vel	OPS	ERC	ERA
2022	Lsvlle	AAA	51	0	42	56.0	225	39	22	18	4	1	4	4	19	0	66	2	4	4	.500	23--	-	-	.576	2.37	2.89
2022	Cin	NL	14	2	1	14.2	64	9	3	2	1	0	0	1	9	0	21	1	0	1	.000	0-0	1	94	.556	2.74	1.23

Jesus Cruz

Pitches: R Bats: R Pos: RP-7   Ht: 6'1" Wt: 230 Born: 4/15/1995 Age: 28

Year	Team	Lg	G	GS	GF	IP	BFP	H	R	ER	HR	SH	SF	HB	TBB	IBB	SO	WP	W	L	Pct	Sv-Op	Hld	Vel	OPS	ERC	ERA
2022	Gwnntt	AAA	28	0	12	27.2	121	20	13	13	4	0	0	1	16	0	39	3	2	1	.667	1--	-	-	.681	3.58	4.23
2020	StL	NL	1	0	0	1.0	7	3	2	2	0	0	1	0	1	0	2	0	0	0	-	0-0	0	91	1.371	19.55	18.00
2022	Atl	NL	7	0	4	8.2	39	8	6	6	3	0	0	1	4	0	6	0	0	0	-	0-0	0	95	.863	6.04	6.23
2 ML YEARS			8	0	4	9.2	46	11	8	8	3	0	1	1	5	0	8	0	0	0	-	0-0	0	94	.934	7.35	7.45

Nelson Cruz

Bats: R Throws: R Pos: DH-123;PH-2   Ht: 6'2" Wt: 230 Born: 7/1/1980 Age: 42

Year	Team	Lg	G	AB	H	2B	3B	HR	(Hm	Rd)	TB	R	RBI	RC	TBB	IBB	SO	HBP	SH	SF	SB	CS	GDP	Avg	OBP	Slg	OPS
2005	Mil	NL	8	5	1	1	0	0	(0	0)	2	1	0	1	2	0	0	0	0	0	0	0	0	.200	.429	.400	.829
2006	Tex	AL	41	130	29	3	0	6	(3	3)	50	15	22	18	7	0	32	0	0	1	1	0	1	.223	.261	.385	.645
2007	Tex	AL	96	307	72	15	2	9	(4	5)	118	35	34	32	21	1	87	2	1	1	2	4	5	.235	.287	.384	.671
2008	Tex	AL	31	115	38	9	1	7	(4	3)	70	19	26	30	17	2	28	1	0	0	3	1	1	.330	.421	.609	1.030
2009	Tex	AL	128	462	120	21	1	33	(18	15)	242	75	76	72	49	6	118	2	0	2	20	4	9	.260	.332	.524	.856
2010	Tex	AL	108	399	127	31	3	22	(13	9)	230	60	78	77	38	5	81	1	1	6	17	4	12	.318	.374	.576	.950
2011	Tex	AL	124	475	125	28	1	29	(19	10)	242	64	87	79	33	1	116	2	0	3	9	5	8	.263	.312	.509	.821
2012	Tex	AL	159	585	152	45	0	24	(18	6)	269	86	90	80	48	2	140	5	0	4	8	4	7	.260	.319	.460	.779
2013	Tex	AL	109	413	110	18	0	27	(13	14)	209	49	76	69	35	2	109	4	0	4	5	1	14	.266	.327	.506	.833
2014	Bal	AL	159	613	166	32	2	40	(15	25)	322	87	108	93	55	8	140	5	0	5	4	5	17	.271	.333	.525	.859
2015	Sea	AL	152	590	178	22	1	44	(17	27)	334	90	93	108	59	9	164	5	0	1	3	2	6	.302	.369	.566	.936
2016	Sea	AL	155	589	169	27	1	43	(17	26)	327	96	105	101	62	5	159	9	0	7	2	0	15	.287	.360	.555	.915
2017	Sea	AL	155	556	160	28	0	39	(19	20)	305	91	119	112	70	7	140	12	0	7	1	1	15	.288	.375	.549	.924
2018	Sea	AL	144	519	133	18	1	37	(21	16)	264	70	97	90	55	5	122	14	0	3	1	0	15	.256	.342	.509	.850
2019	Min	AL	120	454	141	26	0	41	(21	20)	290	81	108	102	56	8	131	7	0	0	1	0	14	.311	.392	.639	1.031
2020	Min	AL	53	185	56	6	0	16	(6	10)	110	33	33	38	25	5	58	4	0	0	0	0	14	.303	.397	.595	.992
2021	2 Tms	AL	140	536	136	21	1	32	(12	20)	255	79	86	81	51	10	126	7	0	9	3	0	14	.265	.334	.497	.832
2022	Was	NL	124	448	105	16	0	10	(6	4)	151	50	64	48	49	1	119	4	0	3	4	0	16	.234	.313	.337	.651
21 Min		AL	85	296	87	13	1	19	(9	10)	159	44	50	53	35	6	63	5	0	7	3	0	10	.294	.370	.537	.907
21 TB		AL	55	217	49	8	0	13	(3	10)	96	35	36	28	16	4	63	2	0	2	0	0	4	.226	.283	.442	.725
Postseason			50	187	52	12	0	18	(11	7)	118	35	38	38	19	2	45	1	0	0	1	1	5	.278	.348	.631	.979
18 ML YEARS			2006	7358	2018	367	14	459	(226	233)	3790	1081	1302	1231	732	77	1870	84	2	59	83	32	177	.274	.344	.515	.859

Oneil Cruz

Bats: L Throws: R Pos: SS-79;DH-8;PH-2;LF-1   Ht: 6'7" Wt: 220 Born: 10/4/1998 Age: 24

Year Team	Lg	G	AB	H	2B	3B	HR	(Hm Rd)	TB	R	RBI	RC	TBB	IBB	SO	HBP	SH	SF	SB	CS	GDP	Avg	OBP	Slg	OPS
2018 WV	A	103	402	115	25	7	14	(- -)	196	66	59	68	34	2	100	3	0	4	11	5	6	.286	.343	.488	.831
2019 Altna	AA	35	119	32	8	3	1	(- -)	49	14	17	18	15	1	35	0	0	2	3	1	1	.269	.346	.412	.757
2019 2 Tms	Low	38	146	47	7	1	7	(- -)	77	21	17	28	9	1	39	1	0	0	8	0	0	.322	.365	.527	.893
2021 Altna	AA	62	250	73	15	5	12	(- -)	134	51	40	48	20	0	64	1	0	1	18	3	3	.292	.346	.536	.882
2022 Indy	AAA	55	211	49	7	3	9	(- -)	89	40	35	32	30	0	56	4	0	2	11	6	1	.232	.336	.422	.758
2021 Pit	NL	2	9	3	0	0	1	(1 0)	6	2	3	2	0	0	4	0	0	0	0	0	0	.333	.333	.667	1.000
2022 Pit	NL	87	331	77	13	4	17	(9 8)	149	45	54	57	28	1	126	1	0	1	10	4	3	.233	.294	.450	.744
2 ML YEARS		89	340	80	13	4	18	(10 8)	155	47	57	59	28	1	130	1	0	1	10	4	3	.235	.295	.456	.750

Jose Cuas

Pitches: R Bats: R Pos: RP-47   Ht: 6'3" Wt: 195 Born: 6/28/1994 Age: 29

Year Team	Lg	G	GS	GF	IP	BFP	H	R	ER	HR	SH	SF	HB	TBB	IBB	SO	WP	W	L	Pct	Sv-Op	Hld	Vel	OPS	ERC	ERA
2022 Omha	AAA	22	0	15	22.1	95	17	7	4	1	2	0	3	7	1	21	1	0	3	.000	3- -	-	-	.555	2.47	1.61
2022 KC	AL	47	0	4	37.2	180	39	18	15	2	1	1	6	24	2	34	1	4	2	.667	1-1	11	93	.757	5.31	3.58

Johnny Cueto

Pitches: R Bats: R Pos: SP-24; RP-1   KWAY-toe   Ht: 5'11" Wt: 229 Born: 2/15/1986 Age: 37

Year Team	Lg	G	GS	GF	IP	BFP	H	R	ER	HR	SH	SF	HB	TBB	IBB	SO	WP	W	L	Pct	Sv-Op	Hld	Vel	OPS	ERC	ERA
2008 Cin	NL	31	31	0	174.0	769	178	101	93	29	9	5	14	68	1	158	6	9	14	.391	0-0	0	93	.803	4.95	4.81
2009 Cin	NL	30	30	0	171.1	740	172	90	84	24	5	3	14	61	0	132	4	11	11	.500	0-0	0	93	.780	4.57	4.41
2010 Cin	NL	31	31	0	185.2	780	181	79	75	19	9	3	9	56	5	138	5	12	7	.632	0-0	0	93	.727	3.75	3.64
2011 Cin	NL	24	24	0	156.0	631	123	51	40	8	10	4	10	47	0	104	5	9	5	.643	0-0	0	93	.593	2.55	2.31
2012 Cin	NL	33	33	0	217.0	888	205	73	67	15	6	6	12	49	5	170	1	19	9	.679	0-0	0	93	.667	3.13	2.78
2013 Cin	NL	11	11	0	60.2	242	46	20	19	7	2	1	1	18	1	51	1	5	2	.714	0-0	0	92	.607	2.57	2.82
2014 Cin	NL	34	34	0	243.2	961	169	69	61	22	7	1	15	65	2	242	1	20	9	.690	0-0	0	93	.574	2.18	2.25
2015 2 Tms		32	32	0	212.0	866	194	87	81	21	5	4	8	46	1	176	0	11	13	.458	0-0	0	92	.675	3.06	3.44
2016 SF	NL	32	32	0	219.2	881	195	71	68	15	7	3	8	45	1	198	3	18	5	.783	0-0	0	91	.633	2.71	2.79
2017 SF	NL	25	25	0	147.1	648	160	77	74	22	7	3	8	53	2	136	4	8	8	.500	0-0	0	91	.814	4.97	4.52
2018 SF	NL	9	9	0	53.0	214	46	19	19	8	3	0	5	13	0	38	2	3	2	.600	0-0	0	89	.702	3.55	3.23
2019 SF	NL	4	4	0	16.0	67	11	9	9	3	2	0	0	9	0	13	1	1	2	.333	0-0	0	91	.754	3.58	5.06
2020 SF	NL	12	12	0	63.1	277	61	41	38	9	0	2	3	26	0	56	1	2	3	.400	0-0	0	91	.748	4.35	5.40
2021 SF	NL	22	21	0	114.2	490	127	57	52	15	10	1	4	30	1	98	0	7	7	.500	0-0	0	92	.801	4.52	4.08
2022 CWS	AL	25	24	0	158.1	651	161	66	59	15	1	7	6	33	2	102	2	8	10	.444	0-0	0	91	.717	3.58	3.35
15 Cin	NL	19	19	0	130.2	516	93	42	38	11	4	3	6	29	1	120	0	7	6	.538	0-0	0	93	.577	2.00	2.62
15 Cin	AL	13	13	0	81.1	350	101	45	43	10	1	1	2	17	0	56	0	4	7	.364	0-0	0	92	.818	5.05	4.76
Postseason		8	8	0	41.2	170	33	22	21	7	1	1	1	12	0	32	0	2	4	.333	0-0	0	93	.646	3.02	4.54
15 ML YEARS		355	353	0	2192.2	9105	2029	910	839	232	83	43	117	619	21	1812	36	143	107	.572	0-0	0	92	.699	3.47	3.44

Charlie Culberson

Bats: R Throws: R Pos: 3B-25;PR-16;LF-12;2B-11;DH-9;PH-7;1B-1;SS-1   Ht: 6'1" Wt: 200 Born: 4/10/1989 Age: 34

Year Team	Lg	G	AB	H	2B	3B	HR	(Hm Rd)	TB	R	RBI	RC	TBB	IBB	SO	HBP	SH	SF	SB	CS	GDP	Avg	OBP	Slg	OPS
2012 SF	NL	6	22	3	0	0	0	(0 0)	3	0	1	0	0	0	7	0	1	0	0	0	0	.136	.136	.136	.273
2013 Col	NL	47	99	29	5	0	2	(0 2)	40	12	12	13	4	1	23	0	0	1	5	1	5	.293	.317	.404	.721
2014 Col	NL	95	210	41	7	2	3	(2 1)	61	17	24	14	12	2	62	5	4	2	2	2	6	.195	.253	.290	.544
2016 LAD	NL	34	67	20	3	0	1	(1 0)	26	6	7	9	1	0	13	0	0	0	1	0	2	.299	.309	.388	.697
2017 LAD	NL	15	13	2	1	0	0	(0 0)	3	0	1	0	2	0	4	0	0	0	0	0	2	.154	.267	.231	.497
2018 Atl	NL	113	296	80	18	2	12	(5 7)	138	47	45	50	21	5	85	4	0	1	4	2	5	.270	.326	.466	.792
2019 Atl	NL	108	135	35	5	2	5	(3 2)	59	14	20	11	6	0	44	1	1	1	0	1	5	.259	.294	.437	.731
2020 Atl	NL	10	7	1	1	0	0	(0 0)	2	2	1	1	0	0	4	0	0	0	0	0	0	.143	.143	.286	.429
2021 Tex	AL	91	247	60	15	2	5	(1 4)	94	23	22	30	17	1	64	2	4	1	7	1	3	.243	.296	.381	.676
2022 Tex	AL	70	115	29	6	0	2	(1 1)	41	19	12	9	5	0	31	0	4	0	2	3	5	.252	.283	.357	.640
Postseason		21	38	12	2	1	1	(1 0)	19	5	2	5	1	1	10	0	1	1	0	0	0	.316	.325	.500	.825
10 ML YEARS		589	1211	300	61	8	30	(13 17)	467	140	145	137	68	9	337	12	14	6	21	10	33	.248	.293	.386	.679

Xzavion Curry

Pitches: R Bats: R Pos: SP-2   Ht: 6'0" Wt: 195 Born: 7/27/1998 Age: 24

Year Team	Lg	G	GS	GF	IP	BFP	H	R	ER	HR	SH	SF	HB	TBB	IBB	SO	WP	W	L	Pct	Sv-Op	Hld	Vel	OPS	ERC	ERA
2022 Akron	AA	13	11	0	69.0	282	56	32	28	9	0	3	3	19	0	80	5	5	3	.625	0- -	-	-	.677	2.93	3.65
2022 Clmbs	AAA	12	10	0	53.0	230	50	29	27	9	0	1	0	23	0	54	3	4	1	.800	0- -	-	-	.748	4.33	4.58
2022 Cle	AL	2	2	0	9.1	47	13	7	6	1	0	0	1	6	0	3	0	0	1	.000	0-0	0	92	.876	8.01	5.79

Tyler Cyr

Pitches: R Bats: R Pos: RP-12   Ht: 6'1" Wt: 205 Born: 5/5/1993 Age: 30

			HOW MUCH PITCHED					WHAT HE GAVE UP											THE RESULTS					
Year	Team	Lg	G	GS	GF	IP	BFP	H	R	ER	HR	SH	SF	HB	TBB	IBB	SO	WP	W	L	Pct	Sv-Op Hld	Vel	OPS	ERC	ERA
2022 LV		AAA	35	0	16	36.0	149	26	13	10	0	0	1	1	18	0	37	2	2	3	.400	6- -	-	.550	2.44	2.50
2022 2 Tms			12	0	3	13.1	55	11	4	4	2	0	0	1	5	0	16	0	1	0	1.000	0-0	1	95	.697	3.72	2.70
22 Phi		NL	1	0	1	0.1	3	2	1	1	1	0	0	0	0	0	0	0	0	0	-	0-0	0	95	2.667	83.63	27.00
22 Oak		AL	11	0	2	13.0	52	9	3	3	1	0	0	1	5	0	16	0	1	0	1.000	0-0	1	95	.571	2.61	2.08

Bobby Dalbec

Bats: R Throws: R Pos: 1B-89;3B-24;PH-17;2B-2;PR-2;SS-1;DH-1   Ht: 6'4" Wt: 227 Born: 6/29/1995 Age: 28

			BATTING																			RUNNING			AVERAGES			
Year	Team	Lg	G	AB	H	2B	3B	HR	(Hm	Rd)	TB	R	RBI	RC	TBB	IBB	SO	HBP	SH	SF	SB	CS	GDP	Avg	OBP	Slg	OPS
2022 Wrcstr		AAA	13	48	12	0	0	5	(-	-)	27	8	8	10	3	0	14	1	0	1	0	0	0	.250	.302	.563	.864
2020 Bos		AL	23	80	21	3	0	8	(4	4)	48	13	16	15	10	0	39	2	0	0	0	0	0	.263	.359	.600	.959
2021 Bos		AL	133	417	100	21	5	25	(14	11)	206	50	78	67	28	1	156	7	0	1	2	0	3	.240	.298	.494	.792
2022 Bos		AL	117	317	68	9	2	12	(6	6)	117	40	39	31	29	0	118	3	0	4	3	0	5	.215	.283	.369	.652
Postseason			8	12	0	0	0	0	(0	0)	0	0	0	0	0	0	5	0	0	0	0	0	0	.000	.000	.000	.000
3 ML YEARS			273	814	189	33	7	45	(24	21)	371	103	133	113	67	1	313	12	0	5	5	0	8	.232	.298	.456	.754

Tyler Danish

Pitches: R Bats: R Pos: RP-32   Ht: 6'0" Wt: 200 Born: 9/12/1994 Age: 28

			HOW MUCH PITCHED					WHAT HE GAVE UP											THE RESULTS					
Year	Team	Lg	G	GS	GF	IP	BFP	H	R	ER	HR	SH	SF	HB	TBB	IBB	SO	WP	W	L	Pct	Sv-Op Hld	Vel	OPS	ERC	ERA
2022 Wrcstr		AAA	6	0	0	6.1	27	8	4	4	0	0	0	0	3	0	9	0	0	0	-	0- -	-	.782	5.59	5.68
2016 CWS		AL	3	0	2	1.2	12	6	2	2	0	0	0	0	3	1	0	0	0	0	-	0-0	0	92	1.417	31.12	10.80
2017 CWS		AL	1	1	0	5.0	23	3	0	0	0	0	0	0	6	0	6	0	1	0	1.000	0-0	0	90	.627	4.17	0.00
2018 CWS		AL	7	0	0	6.1	31	8	5	5	2	0	1	1	4	0	5	0	1	0	1.000	0-0	0	89	.979	9.35	7.11
2022 Bos		AL	32	0	10	40.1	173	40	24	23	7	0	0	4	12	0	32	1	3	1	.750	0-0	3	91	.763	4.55	5.13
4 ML YEARS			43	1	12	53.1	239	57	31	30	9	0	1	5	25	1	43	1	5	1	.833	0-0	3	91	.811	5.70	5.06

Travis d'Arnaud

Bats: R Throws: R Pos: C-99;DH-5;PH-3   dar-NO   Ht: 6'2" Wt: 210 Born: 2/10/1989 Age: 34

			BATTING																			RUNNING			AVERAGES			
Year	Team	Lg	G	AB	H	2B	3B	HR	(Hm	Rd)	TB	R	RBI	RC	TBB	IBB	SO	HBP	SH	SF	SB	CS	GDP	Avg	OBP	Slg	OPS
2013 NYM		NL	31	99	20	3	0	1	(1	0)	26	4	5	6	12	0	21	0	0	1	0	0	3	.202	.286	.263	.548
2014 NYM		NL	108	385	93	22	3	13	(5	8)	160	48	41	39	32	5	64	2	1	1	1	0	15	.242	.302	.416	.718
2015 NYM		NL	67	239	64	14	1	12	(6	6)	116	31	41	36	23	0	49	4	0	2	0	0	7	.268	.340	.485	.825
2016 NYM		NL	75	251	62	7	0	4	(4	0)	81	27	15	17	19	1	50	3	2	1	0	0	7	.247	.307	.323	.629
2017 NYM		NL	112	348	85	19	1	16	(5	11)	154	39	57	41	23	3	59	2	0	3	0	0	12	.244	.293	.443	.735
2018 NYM		NL	4	15	3	0	0	1	(1	0)	6	1	3	2	1	0	5	0	0	0	0	0	0	.200	.250	.400	.650
2019 3 Tms			103	351	88	16	0	16	(6	10)	152	52	69	59	32	0	85	2	0	6	0	1	4	.251	.312	.433	.745
2020 Atl		NL	44	165	53	8	0	9	(5	4)	88	19	34	31	16	0	50	2	0	1	1	0	8	.321	.386	.533	.919
2021 Atl		NL	60	209	46	14	0	7	(0	7)	81	21	26	21	17	0	53	2	0	1	0	0	7	.220	.284	.388	.671
2022 Atl		NL	107	396	106	25	1	18	(7	11)	187	61	60	61	19	0	90	11	0	0	0	0	5	.268	.319	.472	.791
19 NYM		NL	10	23	2	0	0	0	(0	0)	2	2	2	0	2	0	5	0	0	0	0	0	1	.087	.160	.087	.247
19 LAD		NL	1	1	0	0	0	0	(0	0)	0	0	0	0	0	0	0	0	0	0	0	0	0	.000	.000	.000	.000
19 TB		AL	92	327	86	16	0	16	(6	10)	150	50	67	59	30	0	80	2	0	6	0	1	3	.263	.323	.459	.782
Postseason			48	171	37	4	0	7	(5	2)	62	17	22	13	14	0	58	3	0	3	0	0	7	.216	.283	.363	.645
10 ML YEARS			711	2458	620	128	6	97	(40	57)	1051	303	351	313	194	9	526	28	3	16	2	1	75	.252	.312	.428	.740

Yu Darvish

Pitches: R Bats: R Pos: SP-30   YOO DARR-vish   Ht: 6'5" Wt: 220 Born: 8/16/1986 Age: 36

			HOW MUCH PITCHED					WHAT HE GAVE UP											THE RESULTS					
Year	Team	Lg	G	GS	GF	IP	BFP	H	R	ER	HR	SH	SF	HB	TBB	IBB	SO	WP	W	L	Pct	Sv-Op Hld	Vel	OPS	ERC	ERA
2012 Tex		AL	29	29	0	191.1	816	156	89	83	14	2	7	10	89	1	221	8	16	9	.640	0-0	0	93	.659	3.31	3.90
2013 Tex		AL	32	32	0	209.2	841	145	68	66	26	0	5	8	80	1	277	7	13	9	.591	0-0	0	93	.611	2.70	2.83
2014 Tex		AL	22	22	0	144.1	605	133	54	49	13	1	2	2	49	1	182	14	10	7	.588	0-0	0	92	.679	3.39	3.06
2016 Tex		AL	17	17	0	100.1	416	81	43	38	12	0	4	3	31	1	132	6	7	5	.583	0-0	0	93	.636	2.87	3.41
2017 2 Tms			31	31	0	186.2	766	159	83	80	27	2	3	6	58	1	209	12	10	12	.455	0-0	0	94	.689	3.35	3.86
2018 ChC		NL	8	8	0	40.0	180	36	24	22	7	1	1	4	21	0	49	2	1	3	.250	0-0	0	94	.766	4.88	4.95
2019 ChC		NL	31	31	0	178.2	731	140	82	79	33	3	4	11	56	1	229	11	6	8	.429	0-0	0	94	.695	3.35	3.98
2020 ChC		NL	12	12	0	76.0	297	59	18	17	5	0	0	2	14	1	93	3	8	3	.727	0-0	0	96	.575	2.03	2.01
2021 SD		NL	30	30	0	166.1	681	138	81	78	28	1	5	8	44	1	199	9	8	11	.421	0-0	0	95	.708	3.23	4.22
2022 SD		NL	30	30	0	194.2	771	148	67	67	22	1	6	12	37	0	197	4	16	8	.667	0-0	0	95	.587	2.35	3.10
17 Tex		AL	22	22	0	137.0	564	115	63	61	20	1	3	5	45	0	148	9	6	9	.400	0-0	0	94	.689	3.39	4.01
17 LAD		NL	9	9	0	49.2	202	44	20	19	7	1	0	1	13	1	61	3	4	3	.571	0-0	0	94	.690	3.27	3.44
Postseason			7	7	0	33.0	140	32	21	19	9	1	2	4	6	1	31	0	2	5	.286	0-0	0	94	.814	4.58	5.18
10 ML YEARS			242	242	0	1488.0	6104	1195	609	579	187	11	37	66	479	8	1788	76	95	75	.559	0-0	0	94	.656	3.05	3.50

Matt Davidson

Bats: R **Throws:** R **Pos:** 3B-9;DH-2;PH-2;1B-1   **Ht:** 6'3" **Wt:** 230 **Born:** 3/26/1991 **Age:** 32

Year	Team	Lg	G	AB	H	2B	3B	HR	(Hm	Rd)	TB	R	RBI	RC	TBB	IBB	SO	HBP	SH	SF	SB	CS	GDP	Avg	OBP	Slg	OPS
2022	Reno	AAA	11	44	17	1	0	8	(-	-)	42	8	12	20	6	0	14	1	0	0	0	0	0	.386	.471	.955	1.425
2022	LsVgs	AAA	75	279	83	9	1	24	(-	-)	166	59	54	71	38	1	88	13	0	1	0	0	6	.297	.405	.595	1.000
2013	Ari	NL	31	76	18	6	0	3	(1	2)	33	8	12	12	10	1	24	1	0	0	0	1	1	.237	.333	.434	.768
2016	CWS	AL	1	2	1	0	0	0	(0	0)	1	1	1	0	0	0	1	0	0	0	0	0	0	.500	.500	.500	1.000
2017	CWS	AL	118	414	91	16	1	26	(15	11)	187	43	68	48	19	0	165	5	0	5	0	1	12	.220	.260	.452	.711
2018	CWS	AL	126	434	99	23	0	20	(5	15)	182	51	62	64	52	0	165	7	0	3	0	0	8	.228	.319	.419	.738
2020	Cin	NL	22	43	7	1	0	3	(1	2)	17	3	11	8	4	0	13	0	0	0	0	0	2	.163	.234	.395	.629
2022	2 Tms		13	34	5	0	0	2	(0	2)	11	3	3	2	3	0	13	0	0	0	0	1	0	.147	.216	.324	.540
22	Ari	NL	5	10	1	0	0	1	(0	1)	4	1	1	1	3	0	3	0	0	0	0	0	0	.100	.308	.400	.708
22	Oak	AL	8	24	4	0	0	1	(0	1)	7	2	2	1	0	0	10	0	0	0	0	1	0	.167	.167	.292	.458
	Postseason		1	0	0	0	0	0	(0	0)	0	0	0	0	0	0	0	0	0	0	0	0	0	-	-	-	-
	6 ML YEARS		311	1003	221	46	1	54	(22	32)	431	109	157	134	88	1	381	13	0	8	0	3	23	.220	.290	.430	.719

Tucker Davidson

Pitches: L **Bats:** L **Pos:** SP-11; RP-1   **Ht:** 6'2" **Wt:** 215 **Born:** 3/25/1996 **Age:** 27

Year	Team	Lg	G	GS	GF	IP	BFP	H	R	ER	HR	SH	SF	HB	TBB	IBB	SO	WP	W	L	Pct	Sv-Op	Hld	Vel	OPS	ERC	ERA
2022	Gwnntt	AAA	15	15	0	80.1	345	82	43	41	14	1	2	2	24	0	96	1	3	7	.300	0-	-	-	.792	4.36	4.59
2020	Atl	NL	1	1	0	1.2	13	3	7	2	1	0	0	0	4	0	2	0	0	1	1.000	0-0	0	92	1.205	22.80	10.80
2021	Atl	NL	4	4	0	20.0	83	15	8	8	3	1	1	0	8	0	18	0	0	0	-	0-0	0	93	.664	3.00	3.60
2022	2 Tms		12	11	1	52.0	243	54	39	39	7	0	2	3	35	0	33	1	2	7	.222	0-0	0	93	.827	5.91	6.75
22	Atl	NL	4	3	1	15.1	74	15	11	11	0	0	1	1	13	0	10	0	1	2	.333	0-0	0	94	.714	5.10	6.46
22	LAA	AL	8	8	0	36.2	169	39	28	28	7	0	1	2	22	0	23	1	1	5	.167	0-0	0	93	.873	6.22	6.87
	Postseason		1	1	0	2.0	11	2	4	2	0	0	1	0	3	0	1	0	0	0	-	0-0	0	93	.883	7.45	9.00
	3 ML YEARS		17	16	1	73.2	339	72	54	49	11	1	3	3	47	0	53	1	2	8	.200	0-0	0	93	.800	5.39	5.99

Zach Davies

Pitches: R **Bats:** R **Pos:** SP-27   **Ht:** 6'0" **Wt:** 180 **Born:** 2/7/1993 **Age:** 30

Year	Team	Lg	G	GS	GF	IP	BFP	H	R	ER	HR	SH	SF	HB	TBB	IBB	SO	WP	W	L	Pct	Sv-Op	Hld	Vel	OPS	ERC	ERA
2015	Mil	NL	6	6	0	34.0	139	26	14	14	2	1	0	0	15	0	24	0	3	2	.600	0-0	0	89	.614	2.74	3.71
2016	Mil	NL	28	28	0	163.1	682	166	79	72	20	3	4	6	38	0	135	3	11	7	.611	0-0	0	89	.728	3.83	3.97
2017	Mil	NL	33	33	0	191.1	817	204	90	83	20	7	5	9	55	3	124	2	17	9	.654	0-0	0	90	.755	4.24	3.90
2018	Mil	NL	13	13	0	66.0	280	67	36	35	8	0	5	4	21	3	49	1	2	7	.222	0-0	0	90	.768	4.22	4.77
2019	Mil	NL	31	31	0	159.2	672	155	73	63	20	7	5	2	51	0	102	4	10	7	.588	0-0	0	88	.729	3.83	3.55
2020	SD	NL	12	12	0	69.1	276	55	26	21	9	1	1	0	19	0	63	2	7	4	.636	0-0	0	89	.630	2.71	2.73
2021	ChC	NL	32	32	0	148.0	668	162	99	95	25	8	2	5	75	2	114	0	6	12	.333	0-0	0	88	.852	5.73	5.78
2022	Ari	NL	27	27	0	134.1	570	122	66	61	21	1	8	2	52	0	102	1	2	5	.286	0-0	0	90	.722	3.95	4.09
	Postseason		3	2	1	8.0	39	15	8	8	2	0	0	0	1	0	7	0	0	1	.000	0-0	0	89	1.068	9.69	9.00
	8 ML YEARS		182	182	0	966.0	4104	957	483	444	125	28	30	28	326	8	713	13	58	53	.523	0-0	0	89	.744	4.11	4.14

Austin Davis

Pitches: L **Bats:** L **Pos:** RP-49; SP-3   **Ht:** 6'4" **Wt:** 235 **Born:** 2/3/1993 **Age:** 30

Year	Team	Lg	G	GS	GF	IP	BFP	H	R	ER	HR	SH	SF	HB	TBB	IBB	SO	WP	W	L	Pct	Sv-Op	Hld	Vel	OPS	ERC	ERA
2018	Phi	NL	32	0	10	34.2	151	35	20	16	4	1	4	2	12	1	38	4	1	2	.333	0-0	2	93	.812	4.17	4.15
2019	Phi	NL	14	0	7	20.2	98	22	15	15	6	0	0	3	14	1	24	0	0	0	-	0-0	0	93	.929	7.79	6.53
2020	2 Tms	NL	9	0	3	6.2	32	11	8	8	1	0	0	0	2	0	5	0	0	0	-	0-0	1	93	.906	8.13	10.80
2021	2 Tms		29	0	7	26.1	117	24	17	15	4	0	2	1	12	2	28	1	1	2	.333	0-3	4	94	.748	4.06	5.13
2022	2 Tms	AL	52	3	12	56.0	264	57	39	36	5	2	3	5	33	1	64	1	2	1	.667	0-1	3	94	.747	5.03	5.79
20	Phi	NL	4	0	1	3.0	20	10	7	7	1	0	0	0	1	0	2	0	0	0	-	0-0	0	94	1.287	22.82	21.00
20	Pit	NL	5	0	2	3.2	12	1	1	1	0	0	0	0	1	0	3	0	0	0	-	0-0	1	93	.258	0.51	2.45
21	Pit	NL	10	0	2	9.2	42	6	7	6	2	0	1	0	5	0	11	0	0	1	.000	0-1	2	94	.702	3.42	5.59
21	Bos	AL	19	0	5	16.2	75	18	10	9	2	0	2	0	7	2	17	1	1	1	.500	0-2	2	94	.773	4.44	4.86
22	Bos	AL	50	3	10	54.1	254	56	36	33	5	2	3	5	29	1	61	1	2	1	.667	0-1	3	94	.743	4.91	5.47
22	Min	AL	2	0	2	1.2	10	1	3	3	0	0	0	0	4	0	3	0	0	0	-	0-0	0	95	.833	8.50	16.20
	Postseason		1	0	0	0.1	2	0	0	0	0	0	0	0	1	0	0	0	0	0	-	0-0	1	94	.500	7.00	0.00
	5 ML YEARS		136	3	39	144.1	662	149	99	90	20	3	9	11	73	5	159	6	4	5	.444	0-4	10	94	.797	5.14	5.61

Brendon Davis

Bats: R **Throws:** R **Pos:** RF-2;3B-1   **Ht:** 6'4" **Wt:** 185 **Born:** 7/28/1997 **Age:** 25

Year	Team	Lg	G	AB	H	2B	3B	HR	(Hm	Rd)	TB	R	RBI	RC	TBB	IBB	SO	HBP	SH	SF	SB	CS	GDP	Avg	OBP	Slg	OPS
2022	Salt Lk	AAA	36	136	33	10	1	6	(-	-)	63	24	25	20	18	0	31	2	0	3	2	2	7	.243	.333	.463	.797
2022	Toledo	AAA	103	367	85	19	2	14	(-	-)	150	54	47	54	55	2	104	7	0	1	6	4	5	.232	.342	.409	.751
2022	Det	AL	3	10	2	0	0	0	(0	0)	2	2	0	0	1	0	3	1	0	0	1	0	0	.200	.273	.200	.473

Brennen Davis

Bats: R Throws: R Pos: OF   Ht: 6'4" Wt: 210 Born: 11/2/1999 Age: 23

Year Team	Lg	G	AB	H	2B	3B	HR	(Hm Rd)	TB	R	RBI	RC	TBB	IBB	SO	HBP	SH	SF	SB	CS	GDP	Avg	OBP	Slg	OPS
2018 Cubs2	R	18	57	17	2	0	0	(- -)	19	9	3	11	10	0	12	4	0	1	6	1	0	.298	.431	.333	.764
2019 Sbend	A	50	177	54	9	3	8	(- -)	93	33	30	37	18	0	38	5	2	2	4	1	3	.305	.381	.525	.907
2021 Tenn	AA	77	267	67	20	0	13	(- -)	126	50	36	48	36	0	97	13	0	1	6	4	5	.251	.366	.472	.838
2021 Iowa	AAA	11	43	14	2	0	4	(- -)	28	9	9	10	5	0	12	0	0	1	0	0	1	.326	.396	.651	1.047
2022 Iowa	AAA	43	141	27	6	0	4	(- -)	45	16	13	16	23	0	52	6	0	4	0	1	0	.191	.322	.319	.641
2022 2 Tms	Low	10	37	5	0	0	1	(- -)	8	2	4	1	2	0	13	1	0	0	0	0	0	.135	.200	.216	.416

Henry Davis

Bats: R Throws: R Pos: C   Ht: 6'2" Wt: 210 Born: 9/21/1999 Age: 23

Year Team	Lg	G	AB	H	2B	3B	HR	(Hm Rd)	TB	R	RBI	RC	TBB	IBB	SO	HBP	SH	SF	SB	CS	GDP	Avg	OBP	Slg	OPS
2022 Altna	AA	31	116	24	8	0	4	(- -)	44	19	18	13	12	0	30	8	0	0	3	1	7	.207	.324	.379	.703
2022 2 Tms	Low	27	93	32	4	1	6	(- -)	56	20	24	23	9	0	20	11	0	2	6	1	4	.344	.452	.602	1.054

J.D. Davis

Bats: R Throws: R Pos: DH-56;3B-30;PH-28;1B-18;PR-3;LF-2   Ht: 6'3" Wt: 218 Born: 4/27/1993 Age: 30

Year Team	Lg	G	AB	H	2B	3B	HR	(Hm Rd)	TB	R	RBI	RC	TBB	IBB	SO	HBP	SH	SF	SB	CS	GDP	Avg	OBP	Slg	OPS
2017 Hou	AL	25	62	14	4	0	4	(2 2)	30	8	7	4	4	0	20	1	0	1	1	1	3	.226	.279	.484	.763
2018 Hou	AL	42	103	18	2	0	1	(0 1)	23	9	5	3	10	0	29	0	0	0	0	0	3	.175	.248	.223	.471
2019 NYM	NL	140	410	126	22	1	22	(16 6)	216	65	57	66	38	2	97	3	0	2	3	0	14	.307	.369	.527	.895
2020 NYM	NL	56	190	47	9	0	6	(2 4)	74	26	19	25	31	1	56	7	0	1	0	0	8	.247	.371	.389	.760
2021 NYM	NL	73	179	51	12	0	5	(1 4)	78	18	23	30	24	1	68	6	0	2	1	0	6	.285	.384	.436	.820
2022 2 Tms	NL	115	318	79	16	1	12	(5 7)	133	46	35	42	39	1	122	6	0	2	1	1	13	.248	.340	.418	.758
22 NYM	NL	66	181	43	8	1	4	(1 3)	65	26	21	21	20	0	66	4	0	2	1	1	9	.238	.324	.359	.683
22 SF	NL	49	137	36	8	0	8	(4 4)	68	20	14	21	19	1	56	2	0	0	0	0	4	.263	.361	.496	.857
6 ML YEARS		451	1262	335	65	2	50	(26 24)	554	172	146	170	146	5	392	23	0	8	6	2	45	.265	.350	.439	.789

Jaylin Davis

Bats: R Throws: R Pos: CF-4;RF-3;PH-3;PR-2;LF-1   Ht: 5'11" Wt: 205 Born: 7/1/1994 Age: 28

Year Team	Lg	G	AB	H	2B	3B	HR	(Hm Rd)	TB	R	RBI	RC	TBB	IBB	SO	HBP	SH	SF	SB	CS	GDP	Avg	OBP	Slg	OPS
2022 Scrmto	AAA	10	44	13	3	0	2	(- -)	22	10	7	7	3	1	14	0	0	0	3	1	0	.295	.340	.500	.840
2022 Wrcstr	AAA	88	296	60	12	3	7	(- -)	99	43	24	30	43	0	107	5	0	2	1	3	7	.203	.312	.334	.647
2019 SF	NL	17	42	7	0	0	1	(1 0)	10	2	3	1	3	0	11	2	0	1	2	1	0	.167	.255	.238	.493
2020 SF	NL	4	12	2	0	0	1	(0 1)	5	2	1	0	0	0	6	0	0	0	0	0	0	.167	.167	.417	.583
2021 SF	NL	5	9	1	1	0	0	(0 0)	2	1	0	0	0	0	1	0	0	0	0	0	1	.111	.111	.222	.333
2022 Bos	AL	12	24	8	1	0	0	(0 0)	9	4	2	4	3	0	11	0	0	0	0	0	0	.333	.407	.375	.782
4 ML YEARS		38	87	18	2	0	2	(1 1)	26	9	6	5	6	0	29	2	0	0	1	2	2	.207	.274	.299	.573

Jonathan Davis

Bats: R Throws: R Pos: CF-34;PR-4;PH-1   Ht: 5'8" Wt: 190 Born: 5/12/1992 Age: 31

Year Team	Lg	G	AB	H	2B	3B	HR	(Hm Rd)	TB	R	RBI	RC	TBB	IBB	SO	HBP	SH	SF	SB	CS	GDP	Avg	OBP	Slg	OPS
2022 Nashv	AAA	48	184	54	11	1	4	(- -)	79	27	22	33	28	0	44	5	1	3	14	1	2	.293	.395	.429	.825
2018 Tor	AL	20	25	5	1	0	0	(0 0)	6	3	0	0	1	0	6	1	0	0	3	0	2	.200	.259	.240	.499
2019 Tor	AL	37	83	15	1	0	2	(1 1)	22	8	6	5	5	0	24	5	1	1	3	1	1	.181	.266	.265	.531
2020 Tor	AL	13	27	7	2	0	1	(1 0)	12	4	6	7	3	0	11	2	0	1	1	0	1	.259	.364	.444	.808
2021 2 Tms	AL	64	87	11	1	0	1	(0 1)	15	20	4	5	12	0	26	3	0	1	4	1	1	.126	.252	.172	.425
2022 Mil	NL	37	76	17	1	0	0	(0 0)	18	9	4	8	14	0	26	0	1	0	7	1	1	.224	.344	.237	.581
21 Tor	AL	52	70	10	1	0	1	(0 1)	14	16	4	5	11	0	21	3	0	1	4	1	1	.143	.282	.200	.482
21 NYY	AL	12	17	1	0	0	0	(0 0)	1	4	0	0	1	0	5	0	0	0	0	0	0	.059	.111	.059	.170
5 ML YEARS		171	298	55	6	0	4	(2 2)	73	44	20	25	35	0	93	11	2	3	18	3	6	.185	.291	.245	.536

Noah Davis

Pitches: R Bats: R Pos: RP-1   Ht: 6'2" Wt: 195 Born: 4/22/1997 Age: 26

Year Team	Lg	G	GS	GF	IP	BFP	H	R	ER	HR	SH	SF	HB	TBB	IBB	SO	WP	W	L	Pct	Sv-Op	Hld	Vel	OPS	ERC	ERA
2022 Hrtfrd	AA	26	26	0	133.1	588	133	86	82	26	2	2	13	60	0	152	3	8	8	.500	0--	-	-	.817	5.42	5.54
2022 Col	NL	1	0	0	1.0	7	3	2	2	1	0	0	0	1	0	2	0	0	0	-	0-0	0	-	1.571	32.12	18.00

Ronnie Dawson

Bats: L Throws: R Pos: DH-1   Ht: 6'2" Wt: 217 Born: 5/19/1995 Age: 28

Year Team	Lg	G	AB	H	2B	3B	HR	(Hm Rd)	TB	R	RBI	RC	TBB	IBB	SO	HBP	SH	SF	SB	CS	GDP	Avg	OBP	Slg	OPS
2022 Lsvlle	AAA	116	393	99	23	0	11	(- -)	155	58	43	54	42	1	112	11	0	2	11	3	7	.252	.339	.394	.734
2021 Hou	AL	3	5	1	0	0	0	(0 0)	1	2	0	0	1	0	0	0	0	0	0	0	1	.200	.333	.200	.533
2022 Cin	NL	1	3	0	0	0	0	(0 0)	0	0	0	0	0	0	2	0	0	0	0	0	0	.000	.000	.000	.000
2 ML YEARS		4	8	1	0	0	0	(0 0)	1	2	0	0	1	0	2	0	0	0	0	0	1	.125	.222	.125	.347

Yonathan Daza

Bats: R Throws: R Pos: CF-92;LF-27;PH-4;PR-2;RF-1 YOHN-uh-tuhn DAH-za Ht: 6'2" Wt: 207 Born: 2/28/1994 Age: 29

							BATTING													RUNNING			AVERAGES			
Year	Team	Lg	G	AB	H	2B	3B	HR	(Hm | Rd)	TB	R	RBI	RC	TBB	IBB	SO	HBP	SH	SF	SB	CS	GDP	Avg	OBP	Slg	OPS
2019	Col	NL	44	97	20	1	1	0	(0 | 0)	23	7	3	5	7	0	21	0	0	1	1	0	2	.206	.257	.237	.494
2021	Col	NL	107	301	85	12	2	2	(2 | 0)	107	26	30	36	21	0	60	2	6	1	2	1	9	.282	.332	.355	.688
2022	Col	NL	113	372	112	21	2	2	(1 | 1)	143	56	34	43	26	0	58	4	1	5	0	3	12	.301	.349	.384	.733
	3 ML YEARS		264	770	217	34	5	4	(3 | 1)	273	89	67	84	54	0	139	6	7	7	3	4	23	.282	.331	.355	.685

Angel De Jesus

Pitches: R Bats: R Pos: RP-8 Ht: 6'4" Wt: 200 Born: 2/13/1997 Age: 26

			HOW MUCH PITCHED				WHAT HE GAVE UP										THE RESULTS							
Year	Team	Lg	G	GS	GF	IP	BFP	H	R	ER	HR	SH	SF	HB	TBB	IBB	SO	WP	W	L	Pct	Sv-Op	Hld	Vel	OPS	ERC	ERA
2022	Toledo	AAA	44	0	11	47.2	199	34	26	22	4	0	2	3	20	0	44	3	5	1	.833	1--	-	-	.643	2.72	4.15
2022	Det	AL	8	0	3	12.2	54	9	3	3	2	0	0	2	4	0	7	2	0	0	-	0-0	0	94	.611	3.05	2.13

Chase De Jong

Pitches: R Bats: L Pos: RP-42 de-YUNG Ht: 6'4" Wt: 230 Born: 12/29/1993 Age: 29

			HOW MUCH PITCHED				WHAT HE GAVE UP										THE RESULTS							
Year	Team	Lg	G	GS	GF	IP	BFP	H	R	ER	HR	SH	SF	HB	TBB	IBB	SO	WP	W	L	Pct	Sv-Op	Hld	Vel	OPS	ERC	ERA
2017	Sea	AL	7	4	2	28.1	125	31	20	20	5	1	1	0	13	0	13	0	0	3	.000	0-1	0	90	.837	5.49	6.35
2018	Min	AL	4	4	0	17.2	74	18	9	7	3	0	0	0	6	0	13	2	1	1	.500	0-0	0	89	.810	4.53	3.57
2019	Min	AL	1	0	1	1.0	9	3	4	4	1	0	0	0	3	0	0	0	0	0	-	0-0	0	91	1.667	44.28	36.00
2020	Hou	AL	3	2	0	7.1	38	12	12	12	2	0	1	1	4	0	9	0	0	1	.000	0-0	0	93	1.010	11.02	14.73
2021	Pit	NL	9	9	0	43.2	196	49	28	28	11	1	0	1	19	2	39	0	1	4	.200	0-0	0	93	.942	6.09	5.77
2022	Pit	NL	42	0	16	71.2	293	52	24	21	10	1	1	5	30	1	59	4	6	3	.667	1-4	3	93	.679	3.23	2.64
	6 ML YEARS		66	19	19	169.2	735	165	97	92	32	3	3	7	75	3	133	6	8	12	.400	1-5	3	92	.818	4.91	4.88

Bryan De La Cruz

Bats: R Throws: R Pos: CF-42;RF-41;LF-39;PH-8;DH-6;PR-6 Ht: 6'2" Wt: 175 Born: 12/16/1996 Age: 26

							BATTING													RUNNING			AVERAGES			
Year	Team	Lg	G	AB	H	2B	3B	HR	(Hm	Rd)	TB	R	RBI	RC	TBB	IBB	SO	HBP	SH	SF	SB	CS	GDP	Avg	OBP	Slg	OPS
2022	Jaxnvl	AAA	13	50	16	3	0	4	(-	-)	31	10	10	12	4	0	13	0	0	0	1	0	1	.320	.370	.620	.990
2021	Mia	NL	58	199	59	7	2	5	(2	3)	85	17	19	24	18	1	53	1	0	1	1	1	8	.296	.356	.427	.783
2022	Mia	NL	115	329	83	20	0	13	(8	5)	142	38	43	39	19	0	90	2	0	4	4	0	8	.252	.294	.432	.725
	2 ML YEARS		173	528	142	27	2	18	(10	8)	227	55	62	63	37	1	143	3	0	5	5	1	16	.269	.318	.430	.748

Enyel De Los Santos

Pitches: R Bats: R Pos: RP-50 Ht: 6'3" Wt: 235 Born: 12/25/1995 Age: 27

			HOW MUCH PITCHED				WHAT HE GAVE UP										THE RESULTS							
Year	Team	Lg	G	GS	GF	IP	BFP	H	R	ER	HR	SH	SF	HB	TBB	IBB	SO	WP	W	L	Pct	Sv-Op	Hld	Vel	OPS	ERC	ERA
2018	Phi	NL	7	2	2	19.0	81	19	10	10	2	1	1	1	8	0	15	1	1	0	1.000	0-0	0	95	.836	4.54	4.74
2019	Phi	NL	5	1	3	11.0	46	13	9	9	4	0	0	0	5	0	9	1	0	1	.000	0-0	0	93	1.001	8.11	7.36
2021	2 Tms	NL	33	0	13	35.1	173	43	32	25	8	3	0	4	18	4	48	5	2	1	.667	0-2	2	95	.916	6.87	6.37
2022	Cle	AL	50	0	11	53.1	215	40	18	18	3	0	4	2	17	1	61	3	5	0	1.000	1-2	3	95	.603	2.32	3.04
21	Phi	NL	26	0	10	28.0	137	34	28	21	7	2	0	3	14	3	42	5	1	1	.500	0-2	1	95	.929	6.97	6.75
21	Pit	NL	7	0	3	7.1	36	9	4	4	1	1	0	1	4	1	6	0	1	0	1.000	0-0	1	95	.867	6.47	4.91
	4 ML YEARS		95	3	29	118.2	515	115	69	62	17	4	5	7	48	5	133	10	8	2	.800	1-4	5	95	.778	4.40	4.70

Yerry De Los Santos

Pitches: R Bats: R Pos: RP-26 Ht: 6'2" Wt: 215 Born: 12/12/1997 Age: 25

			HOW MUCH PITCHED				WHAT HE GAVE UP										THE RESULTS							
Year	Team	Lg	G	GS	GF	IP	BFP	H	R	ER	HR	SH	SF	HB	TBB	IBB	SO	WP	W	L	Pct	Sv-Op	Hld	Vel	OPS	ERC	ERA
2022	Indy	AAA	12	0	10	15.2	58	8	3	3	1	1	0	2	0	20	0	2	0	1.000	3--	-	-	.398	0.93	1.72
2022	Pit	NL	26	0	13	25.2	112	22	18	14	3	1	0	1	11	1	26	0	0	3	.000	3-5	2	95	.676	3.49	4.91

Austin Dean

Bats: R Throws: R Pos: LF-3;RF-1;PH-1 Ht: 6'0" Wt: 215 Born: 10/14/1993 Age: 29

							BATTING													RUNNING			AVERAGES			
Year	Team	Lg	G	AB	H	2B	3B	HR	(Hm	Rd)	TB	R	RBI	RC	TBB	IBB	SO	HBP	SH	SF	SB	CS	GDP	Avg	OBP	Slg	OPS
2022	Scrmto	AAA	115	392	105	17	5	17	(-	-)	183	68	55	64	38	3	94	8	0	0	10	2	9	.268	.345	.467	.812
2018	Mia	NL	34	113	25	4	0	4	(2	2)	41	16	14	12	7	0	22	2	0	0	1	0	1	.221	.279	.363	.642
2019	Mia	NL	64	178	40	14	0	6	(4	2)	72	17	21	16	9	1	47	0	1	1	0	2	5	.225	.261	.404	.665
2020	StL	NL	3	4	1	1	0	0	(0	0)	2	1	0	1	3	0	2	0	0	0	0	0	0	.250	.571	.500	1.071
2021	StL	NL	22	30	7	2	0	1	(1	0)	12	5	7	5	6	0	11	0	0	2	0	0	0	.233	.342	.400	.742
2022	SF	NL	3	8	3	0	0	0	(0	0)	3	1	0	1	1	0	0	0	0	0	1	0	0	.375	.444	.375	.819
	Postseason		1	1	0	0	0	0	(0	0)	0	0	0	0	0	0	1	0	0	0	0	0	0	.000	.000	.000	.000
	5 ML YEARS		126	333	76	21	0	11	(7	4)	130	40	42	35	26	1	82	2	1	3	1	2	6	.228	.286	.390	.676

Jacob deGrom

Pitches: R **Bats:** L **Pos:** SP-11   duh-GRAHM   **Ht:** 6'4" **Wt:** 180 **Born:** 6/19/1988 **Age:** 35

			HOW MUCH PITCHED					WHAT HE GAVE UP										THE RESULTS							
Year	Team	Lg	G	GS	GF	IP	BFP	H	R	ER	HR	SH	SF	HB	TBB	IBB	SO	WP	W	L	Pct	Sv-Op	Hld	Vel	OPS	ERC	ERA
2014	NYM	NL	22	22	0	140.1	565	117	44	42	7	5	3	1	43	2	144	1	9	6	.600	0-0	0	93	.613	2.57	2.69
2015	NYM	NL	30	30	0	191.0	751	149	59	54	16	10	7	2	38	2	205	6	14	8	.636	0-0	0	95	.574	2.13	2.54
2016	NYM	NL	24	24	0	148.0	604	142	53	50	15	5	3	3	36	0	143	4	7	8	.467	0-0	0	93	.685	3.40	3.04
2017	NYM	NL	31	31	0	201.1	827	180	87	79	28	3	5	2	59	5	239	7	15	10	.600	0-0	0	95	.682	3.36	3.53
2018	NYM	NL	32	32	0	217.0	835	152	48	41	10	3	5	5	46	3	269	2	10	9	.526	0-0	0	96	.521	**1.67**	**1.70**
2019	NYM	NL	32	32	0	204.0	804	154	59	55	19	5	3	7	44	1	**255**	2	11	8	.579	0-0	0	97	.580	**2.21**	2.43
2020	NYM	NL	12	12	0	68.0	268	47	21	18	7	0	2	0	18	0	104	4	4	2	.667	0-0	0	99	.565	2.00	2.38
2021	NYM	NL	15	15	0	92.0	324	40	14	11	6	0	2	1	11	0	146	0	7	2	.778	0-0	0	99	.402	0.78	1.08
2022	NYM	NL	11	11	0	64.1	239	40	22	22	9	1	0	0	8	0	102	0	5	4	.556	0-0	0	99	.525	1.50	3.08
	Postseason		4	4	0	25.0	105	21	8	8	2	2	0	0	8	1	29	0	3	1	.750	0-0	0	96	.608	2.65	2.88
	9 ML YEARS		209	209	0	1326.0	5217	1021	407	372	117	32	31	21	303	13	1607	26	82	57	.590	0-0	0	96	.587	2.24	2.54

Paul DeJong

Bats: R **Throws:** R **Pos:** SS-75;PH-6;2B-1   de-YUNG   **Ht:** 6'0" **Wt:** 205 **Born:** 8/2/1993 **Age:** 29

						BATTING															RUNNING			AVERAGES			
Year	Team	Lg	G	AB	H	2B	3B	HR	(Hm	Rd)	TB	R	RBI	RC	TBB	IBB	SO	HBP	SH	SF	SB	CS	GDP	Avg	OBP	Slg	OPS
2022	Memp	AAA	51	201	50	10	0	17	(-	-)	111	36	54	40	20	0	52	2	0	7	1	1	4	.249	.313	.552	.865
2017	StL	NL	108	417	119	26	1	25	(11	14)	222	55	65	57	21	1	124	4	0	1	1	0	8	.285	.325	.532	.857
2018	StL	NL	115	436	105	25	1	19	(4	15)	189	68	68	67	36	2	123	12	0	5	1	1	6	.241	.313	.433	.746
2019	StL	NL	159	583	136	31	1	30	(10	20)	259	97	78	76	62	1	149	13	0	6	9	5	15	.233	.318	.444	.762
2020	StL	NL	45	152	38	6	0	3	(1	2)	53	17	25	23	17	0	50	1	0	4	1	0	4	.250	.322	.349	.671
2021	StL	NL	113	356	70	10	1	19	(5	14)	139	44	45	39	35	0	103	9	0	2	4	1	6	.197	.284	.390	.674
2022	StL	NL	77	210	33	9	0	6	(2	4)	60	19	25	18	21	0	79	4	0	2	3	2	2	.157	.245	.286	.530
	Postseason		13	41	9	2	0	0	(0	0)	11	5	3	6	6	2	17	1	0	0	0	0	0	.220	.333	.268	.602
	6 ML YEARS		617	2154	501	107	4	102	(33	69)	922	300	306	280	192	4	628	43	0	20	19	9	41	.233	.306	.428	.734

Jason Delay

Bats: R **Throws:** R **Pos:** C-57   **Ht:** 5'11" **Wt:** 200 **Born:** 3/7/1995 **Age:** 28

						BATTING															RUNNING			AVERAGES			
Year	Team	Lg	G	AB	H	2B	3B	HR	(Hm	Rd)	TB	R	RBI	RC	TBB	IBB	SO	HBP	SH	SF	SB	CS	GDP	Avg	OBP	Slg	OPS
2022	Indy	AAA	28	82	18	5	1	0	(-	-)	25	10	8	6	8	0	15	0	2	1	1	0	2	.220	.286	.305	.591
2022	Pit	NL	57	155	33	6	0	1	(1	0)	42	17	11	10	9	0	50	2	1	0	0	2	4	.213	.265	.271	.536

Ben DeLuzio

Bats: R **Throws:** R **Pos:** CF-18;PH-3;PR-3;DH-2   **Ht:** 6'3" **Wt:** 200 **Born:** 8/9/1994 **Age:** 28

						BATTING															RUNNING			AVERAGES			
Year	Team	Lg	G	AB	H	2B	3B	HR	(Hm	Rd)	TB	R	RBI	RC	TBB	IBB	SO	HBP	SH	SF	SB	CS	GDP	Avg	OBP	Slg	OPS
2022	Memp	AAA	94	364	101	16	6	9	(-	-)	156	60	49	56	36	0	91	7	0	1	29	6	5	.277	.353	.429	.782
2022	StL	NL	22	20	3	1	0	0	(0	0)	4	3	0	0	3	0	5	1	1	0	1	1	0	.150	.292	.200	.492

Travis Demeritte

Bats: R **Throws:** R **Pos:** RF-20;LF-6;PH-1   **Ht:** 6'0" **Wt:** 180 **Born:** 9/30/1994 **Age:** 28

						BATTING															RUNNING			AVERAGES			
Year	Team	Lg	G	AB	H	2B	3B	HR	(Hm	Rd)	TB	R	RBI	RC	TBB	IBB	SO	HBP	SH	SF	SB	CS	GDP	Avg	OBP	Slg	OPS
2022	Gwnntt	AAA	38	140	29	11	2	2	(-	-)	50	14	13	14	17	0	54	0	0	1	6	0	5	.207	.291	.357	.648
2019	Det	AL	48	169	38	7	2	3	(2	1)	58	24	10	13	14	0	63	1	1	1	3	0	3	.225	.286	.343	.630
2020	Det	AL	18	29	5	1	0	0	(0	0)	6	5	4	3	3	0	14	1	0	0	0	0	0	.172	.273	.207	.480
2022	Atl	NL	26	89	19	2	0	3	(2	1)	30	9	6	7	6	0	32	0	0	1	0	0	2	.213	.260	.337	.597
	3 ML YEARS		92	287	62	10	2	6	(4	2)	94	38	20	23	23	0	109	2	1	2	3	0	5	.216	.277	.328	.605

Matt Dermody

Pitches: L **Bats:** R **Pos:** RP-1   **Ht:** 6'5" **Wt:** 190 **Born:** 7/4/1990 **Age:** 32

				HOW MUCH PITCHED					WHAT HE GAVE UP										THE RESULTS							
Year	Team	Lg	G	GS	GF	IP	BFP	H	R	ER	HR	SH	SF	HB	TBB	IBB	SO	WP	W	L	Pct	Sv-Op	Hld	Vel	OPS	ERC	ERA
2022	Iowa	AAA	20	13	1	79.1	344	85	33	33	11	0	2	8	18	0	70	2	6	3	.667	0--	-	-	.769	4.43	3.74
2016	Tor	AL	5	0	1	3.0	16	6	4	4	1	0	0	1	0	0	5	1	0	0		0-0	0	91	1.104	12.18	12.00
2017	Tor	AL	23	0	3	22.1	95	23	13	11	6	0	1	2	5	1	15	1	2	0	1.000	0-0	1	92	.822	5.00	4.43
2020	ChC	NL	1	0	1	1.0	3	0	0	0	0	0	0	0	0	0	1	0	0	0		0-0	0	95	.000	0.00	0.00
2022	ChC	NL	1	0	1	1.0	7	2	2	2	0	0	0	0	2	1	1	0	0	0		0-0	0	92	1.371	13.81	18.00
	4 ML YEARS		30	0	6	27.1	121	31	19	17	7	0	1	3	7	2	22	2	2	0	1.000	0-0	1	92	.866	5.71	5.60

Anthony DeSclafani

Pitches: R **Bats:** R **Pos:** SP-5   DEE-skla-fa-nee   **Ht:** 6'2" **Wt:** 195 **Born:** 4/18/1990 **Age:** 33

				HOW MUCH PITCHED					WHAT HE GAVE UP										THE RESULTS							
Year	Team	Lg	G	GS	GF	IP	BFP	H	R	ER	HR	SH	SF	HB	TBB	IBB	SO	WP	W	L	Pct	Sv-Op	Hld	Vel	OPS	ERC	ERA
2014	Mia	NL	13	5	4	33.0	146	40	23	23	4	4	3	2	5	0	26	2	2	2	.500	0-0	0	93	.801	4.56	6.27
2015	Cin	NL	31	31	0	184.2	785	194	93	83	17	10	5	5	55	5	151	6	9	13	.409	0-0	0	93	.742	4.00	4.05
2016	Cin	NL	20	20	0	123.1	507	120	51	45	16	7	3	4	30	2	105	6	9	5	.643	0-0	0	93	.723	3.67	3.28
2018	Cin	NL	21	21	0	115.0	484	118	68	63	24	5	4	2	30	2	108	4	7	8	.467	0-0	0	94	.792	4.47	4.93
2019	Cin	NL	31	31	0	166.2	696	151	77	72	29	5	3	4	49	5	167	2	9	9	.500	0-0	0	95	.717	3.66	3.89
2020	Cin	NL	9	7	1	33.2	158	41	27	27	7	0	3	6	16	0	25	1	1	2	.333	0-0	0	95	.909	6.91	7.22

			HOW MUCH PITCHED				WHAT HE GAVE UP											THE RESULTS						
Year	Team	Lg	G	GS	GF	IP	BFP	H	R	ER	HR	SH	SF	HB	TBB	IBB	SO	WP	W	L	Pct	Sv-Op	Hld	Vel	OPS	ERC	ERA
2021	SF	NL	31	31	0	167.2	676	141	61	59	19	6	0	2	42	1	152	7	13	7	.650	0-0	0	94	.634	2.79	3.17
2022	SF	NL	5	5	0	19.0	94	34	21	14	4	1	3	1	4	0	17	0	0	2	.000	0-0	0	92	1.078	9.37	6.63
	Postseason		1	1	0	1.2	10	5	2	2	0	0	1	0	0	0	2	0	0	1	.000	0-0	0	94	1.167	14.52	10.80
	8 ML YEARS		161	151	5	843.0	3546	839	421	386	120	38	24	23	231	15	751	28	50	48	.510	0-0	0	94	.739	3.93	4.12

Reid Detmers

Pitches: L Bats: L Pos: SP-25

Ht: 6'2" Wt: 210 Born: 7/8/1999 Age: 23

			HOW MUCH PITCHED				WHAT HE GAVE UP											THE RESULTS						
Year	Team	Lg	G	GS	GF	IP	BFP	H	R	ER	HR	SH	SF	HB	TBB	IBB	SO	WP	W	L	Pct	Sv-Op	Hld	Vel	OPS	ERC	ERA
2021	Rock	AA	12	12	0	54.0	225	45	24	21	10	2	2	1	18	0	97	3	2	4	.333	0--	-	-	.688	3.49	3.50
2021	LAA	AL	5	5	0	20.2	101	26	17	17	5	0	0	2	11	1	19	1	1	3	.250	0-0	0	93	.920	7.51	7.40
2022	LAA	AL	25	25	0	129.0	539	110	56	54	13	1	7	8	46	1	122	2	7	6	.538	0-0	0	93	.682	3.35	3.77
	2 ML YEARS		30	30	0	149.2	640	136	73	71	18	1	7	10	57	2	141	3	8	9	.471	0-0	0	93	.719	3.87	4.27

Ross Detwiler

Pitches: L Bats: R Pos: RP-30

DETT-why-lerr

Ht: 6'5" Wt: 210 Born: 3/6/1986 Age: 37

			HOW MUCH PITCHED				WHAT HE GAVE UP											THE RESULTS						
Year	Team	Lg	G	GS	GF	IP	BFP	H	R	ER	HR	SH	SF	HB	TBB	IBB	SO	WP	W	L	Pct	Sv-Op	Hld	Vel	OPS	ERC	ERA
2022	Lsvlle	AAA	7	0	0	7.0	32	6	3	3	0	1	2	1	5	0	7	0	1	0	1.000	0--	-	-	.735	4.29	3.86
2007	Was	NL	1	0	1	1.0	4	0	0	0	0	0	0	0	0	0	1	0	0	0		0-0	0	93	.000	0.00	0.00
2009	Was	NL	15	14	0	75.2	341	87	43	42	3	4	1	2	33	3	43	4	1	6	.143	0-0	0	91	.767	4.65	5.00
2010	Was	NL	8	5	1	29.2	135	34	22	14	5	2	0	1	14	1	17	1	1	3	.250	0-0	0	90	.826	5.83	4.25
2011	Was	NL	15	10	0	66.0	277	63	26	22	7	7	3	3	20	2	41	2	4	5	.444	0-0	1	92	.704	3.64	3.00
2012	Was	NL	33	27	1	164.1	686	149	75	62	15	8	3	5	52	0	105	4	10	8	.556	0-0	1	92	.681	3.30	3.40
2013	Was	NL	13	13	0	71.1	316	92	37	32	5	4	1	5	14	2	39	0	2	7	.222	0-0	0	92	.811	4.96	4.04
2014	Was	NL	47	0	15	63.0	274	68	34	28	5	4	3	5	21	4	39	3	2	3	.400	1-2	3	93	.734	4.36	4.00
2015	2 Tms		41	7	7	58.1	288	82	51	47	10	1	4	6	36	1	41	3	1	5	.167	0-2	2	92	.984	8.67	7.25
2016	2 Tms	AL	16	7	0	48.2	220	59	34	33	5	0	1	1	19	0	26	3	2	4	.333	0-1	0	92	.806	5.37	6.10
2018	Sea	AL	1	0	0	6.0	23	8	3	3	1	0	1	0	2	0	2	0	0	1	1.000	0-0	0	90	.985	7.59	4.50
2019	CWS	AL	18	12	2	69.2	315	86	54	51	20	2	1	3	27	3	46	1	3	5	.375	0-0	0	92	.942	7.05	6.59
2020	CWS	AL	16	0	4	19.2	81	19	8	7	2	0	0	1	5	1	15	1	1	1	.500	0-0	1	92	.695	3.52	3.20
2021	2 Tms	AL	53	5	10	52.1	229	44	28	27	10	0	3	8	20	1	62	2	3	1	.750	0-0	1	92	.764	4.24	4.64
2022	Cin	NL	30	0	7	26.1	122	31	13	13	5	0	1	3	10	2	28	0	0	2	.000	1-1	1	92	.851	5.97	4.44
15	Tex	AL	17	7	4	43.0	208	62	37	34	9	1	3	3	20	0	28	3	0	5	.000	0-1	1	91	.991	8.35	7.12
15	Atl	NL	24	0	3	15.1	80	20	14	13	1	0	1	3	16	1	13	0	1	0	1.000	0-1	1	93	.954	9.42	7.63
16	Cle	AL	7	0	0	4.2	21	3	3	3	1	0	1	0	4	0	3	0	0	0	-	0-1	0	91	.833	4.60	5.79
16	Oak	AL	9	7	0	44.0	199	56	31	30	4	0	0	1	15	0	23	3	2	4	.333	0-0	0	92	.804	5.46	6.14
21	Mia	NL	46	5	6	45.1	200	41	26	25	8	0	3	7	15	0	56	1	2	1	.667	0-0	1	92	.766	4.30	4.96
21	SD	NL	7	0	4	7.0	29	3	2	2	2	0	0	1	5	1	6	1	1	0	1.000	0-0	0	90	.745	3.84	2.57
	Postseason		1	1	0	6.0	25	3	1	0	0	1	1	0	3	1	2	0	0	0	-	0-0	0	92	.400	1.21	0.00
	14 ML YEARS		307	100	48	752.0	3311	822	428	381	93	32	22	43	273	20	505	24	30	51	.370	2-6	10	92	.787	4.83	4.56

Chris Devenski

Pitches: R Bats: R Pos: RP-13

Ht: 6'3" Wt: 211 Born: 11/13/1990 Age: 32

			HOW MUCH PITCHED				WHAT HE GAVE UP											THE RESULTS						
Year	Team	Lg	G	GS	GF	IP	BFP	H	R	ER	HR	SH	SF	HB	TBB	IBB	SO	WP	W	L	Pct	Sv-Op	Hld	Vel	OPS	ERC	ERA
2022	Reno	AAA	6	0	1	7.1	30	7	6	6	3	0	0	0	2	0	9	0	0	0	-	0--	-	-	.907	5.43	7.36
2022	LV	AAA	9	0	3	8.2	33	4	1	1	1	0	0	0	3	0	11	0	0	0	-	0--	-	-	.445	1.42	1.04
2016	Hou	AL	48	5	16	108.1	408	79	26	26	4	1	1	3	20	0	104	2	4	4	.500	1-1	5	92	.551	1.74	2.16
2017	Hou	AL	62	0	14	80.2	316	50	26	24	11	0	1	2	26	3	100	2	8	5	.615	4-10	24	94	.588	2.10	2.68
2018	Hou	AL	50	1	8	47.1	196	42	23	22	9	1	1	3	13	1	51	0	2	3	.400	2-5	18	94	.719	3.79	4.18
2019	Hou	AL	61	1	19	69.0	298	69	39	37	13	1	3	3	21	0	72	2	2	3	.400	0-1	7	95	.784	4.42	4.83
2020	Hou	AL	4	0	0	3.2	21	7	6	6	1	0	0	0	3	0	5	0	0	1	.000	0-1	0	93	1.143	13.40	14.73
2021	Ari	NL	8	0	2	7.1	35	11	7	7	2	0	1	2	2	0	5	0	1	0	1.000	1-3	1	91	.994	8.69	8.59
2022	2 Tms	NL	13	0	1	14.2	67	21	14	14	3	0	3	1	1	0	12	0	2	1	.667	0-0	1	94	.988	6.16	8.59
22	Ari	NL	10	0	0	10.2	48	14	9	9	2	0	2	1	1	0	9	0	2	1	.667	0-0	0	94	.992	5.53	7.59
22	Phi	NL	3	0	1	4.0	19	7	5	5	1	0	1	0	0	0	3	0	0	0	-	0-0	0	95	.980	7.95	11.25
	Postseason		13	0	5	11.0	50	12	11	11	3	0	1	1	4	0	11	0	1	0	1.000	0-1	3	95	.954	5.99	9.00
	7 ML YEARS		246	7	56	331.0	1341	279	141	136	43	3	9	13	86	4	349	7	19	17	.528	8-21	55	94	.678	3.04	3.70

Rafael Devers

Bats: L Throws: R Pos: 3B-138;DH-3;PH-1

Ht: 6'0" Wt: 240 Born: 10/24/1996 Age: 26

			BATTING																	RUNNING			AVERAGES			
Year	Team	Lg	G	AB	H	2B	3B	HR	(Hm	Rd)	TB	R	RBI	RC	TBB	IBB	SO	HBP	SH	SF	SB	CS	GDP	Avg	OBP	Slg	OPS
2017	Bos	AL	58	222	63	14	0	10	(6	4)	107	34	30	34	18	3	57	0	0	0	3	1	5	.284	.338	.482	.819
2018	Bos	AL	121	450	108	24	0	21	(9	12)	195	59	66	47	38	6	121	0	0	2	5	2	9	.240	.298	.433	.731
2019	Bos	AL	156	647	201	54	4	32	(13	19)	359	129	115	119	48	7	119	4	1	2	8	8	8	.311	.361	.555	.916
2020	Bos	AL	57	232	61	16	1	11	(5	6)	112	32	43	34	13	0	67	3	0	0	0	0	8	.263	.310	.483	.793
2021	Bos	AL	156	591	165	37	1	38	(16	22)	318	101	113	111	62	7	143	7	0	4	5	5	13	.279	.352	.538	.890
2022	Bos	AL	141	555	164	42	1	27	(11	16)	289	84	88	102	50	11	114	6	0	3	3	1	14	.295	.358	.521	.879
	Postseason		26	89	27	0	0	8	(5	3)	51	21	26	21	12	0	25	0	0	1	1	0	1	.303	.382	.573	.955
	6 ML YEARS		689	2697	762	187	7	139	(60	79)	1380	439	455	447	229	34	621	20	1	11	24	17	57	.283	.342	.512	.854

Aledmys Diaz
ah-LED-mees

Bats: R **Throws:** R **Pos:** LF-28;2B-22;SS-18;3B-10;PH-9;DH-7;1B-6;PR-2;RF-1   **Ht:** 6'1" **Wt:** 195 **Born:** 8/1/1990 **Age:** 32

												BATTING										RUNNING			AVERAGES			
Year	Team	Lg	G	AB	H	2B	3B	HR	(Hm	Rd)	TB	R	RBI	RC	TBB	IBB	SO	HBP	SH	SF	SB	CS	GDP	Avg	OBP	Slg	OPS
2016	StL	NL	111	404	121	28	3	17	(7	10)	206	71	65	75	41	6	60	7	2	6	4	4	10	.300	.369	.510	.879
2017	StL	NL	79	286	74	17	0	7	(5	2)	112	31	20	27	13	1	42	0	1	1	4	1	9	.259	.290	.392	.682
2018	Tor	AL	130	422	111	26	0	18	(7	11)	191	55	55	50	23	2	62	3	0	4	3	4	9	.263	.303	.453	.756
2019	Hou	AL	69	210	57	12	1	9	(5	4)	98	36	40	36	26	1	28	5	0	6	2	0	10	.271	.356	.467	.823
2020	Hou	AL	17	58	14	5	0	3	(1	2)	28	8	6	5	1	0	12	0	0	0	0	0	1	.241	.254	.483	.737
2021	Hou	AL	84	294	76	19	0	8	(1	7)	119	28	45	42	16	3	62	9	0	0	0	1	7	.259	.317	.405	.721
2022	Hou	AL	92	305	74	13	0	12	(9	3)	123	35	38	37	18	0	53	2	0	2	1	1	7	.243	.287	.403	.691
	Postseason		24	32	7	0	0	1	(1	0)	10	3	2	4	3	0	10	0	0	0	0	0	0	.219	.286	.313	.598
7 ML YEARS			582	1979	527	120	4	74	(35	39)	877	264	269	272	138	13	319	26	3	19	14	11	53	.266	.320	.443	.763

Alexis Diaz

Pitches: R **Bats:** R **Pos:** RP-59   **Ht:** 6'2" **Wt:** 224 **Born:** 9/28/1996 **Age:** 26

			HOW MUCH PITCHED				WHAT HE GAVE UP										THE RESULTS							
Year	Team	Lg	G	GS	GF	IP	BFP	H	R	ER	HR	SH	SF	HB	TBB	IBB	SO	WP	W	L	Pct	Sv-Op	Hld	Vel	OPS	ERC	ERA
2022	Cin	NL	59	0	20	63.2	255	28	18	13	5	1	3	5	33	3	83	7	7	3	.700	10-14	13	96	.476	1.75	1.84

Edwin Diaz

Pitches: R **Bats:** R **Pos:** RP-61   **Ht:** 6'3" **Wt:** 165 **Born:** 3/22/1994 **Age:** 29

			HOW MUCH PITCHED				WHAT HE GAVE UP										THE RESULTS							
Year	Team	Lg	G	GS	GF	IP	BFP	H	R	ER	HR	SH	SF	HB	TBB	IBB	SO	WP	W	L	Pct	Sv-Op	Hld	Vel	OPS	ERC	ERA
2016	Sea	AL	49	0	23	51.2	217	45	16	16	5	0	0	3	15	2	88	6	0	4	.000	18-21	13	97	.627	3.05	2.79
2017	Sea	AL	66	0	52	66.0	278	44	28	24	10	1	2	3	32	2	89	3	4	6	.400	34-39	2	97	.619	3.01	3.27
2018	Sea	AL	73	0	65	73.1	280	41	17	16	5	0	0	6	17	0	124	3	0	4	.000	57-61	0	97	.470	1.49	1.96
2019	NYM	NL	66	0	48	58.0	254	58	36	36	15	1	2	4	22	3	99	3	2	7	.222	26-33	1	97	.834	5.31	5.59
2020	NYM	NL	26	0	19	25.2	110	18	6	5	2	0	0	2	14	0	50	1	2	1	.667	6-9	2	98	.596	3.12	1.75
2021	NYM	NL	63	0	51	62.2	257	43	27	24	3	3	1	9	23	1	89	5	5	6	.455	32-38	0	99	.580	2.49	3.45
2022	NYM	NL	61	0	49	62.0	235	34	9	9	3	0	2	2	18	1	118	2	3	1	.750	32-35	4	99	.446	1.40	1.31
7 ML YEARS			404	0	307	399.1	1631	283	139	130	43	5	7	29	141	9	657	23	16	29	.356	205-236	22	98	.595	2.64	2.93

Elias Diaz
eh-LEE-ahs

Bats: R **Throws:** R **Pos:** C-104;PH-7   **Ht:** 6'1" **Wt:** 223 **Born:** 11/17/1990 **Age:** 32

												BATTING										RUNNING			AVERAGES			
Year	Team	Lg	G	AB	H	2B	3B	HR	(Hm	Rd)	TB	R	RBI	RC	TBB	IBB	SO	HBP	SH	SF	SB	CS	GDP	Avg	OBP	Slg	OPS
2015	Pit	NL	2	2	0	0	0	0	(0	0)	0	0	0	0	0	0	1	0	0	0	0	0	0	.000	.000	.000	.000
2016	Pit	NL	1	4	0	0	0	0	(0	0)	0	0	1	0	0	0	1	0	0	0	0	0	0	.000	.000	.000	.000
2017	Pit	NL	64	188	42	14	0	1	(0	1)	59	18	19	15	11	0	38	0	0	1	1	0	8	.223	.265	.314	.579
2018	Pit	NL	82	252	72	12	0	10	(3	7)	114	33	34	36	21	1	40	1	0	3	0	1	4	.286	.339	.452	.792
2019	Pit	NL	101	303	73	14	0	2	(2	0)	93	31	28	30	23	0	56	2	1	3	0	0	11	.241	.296	.307	.603
2020	Col	NL	26	68	16	2	0	2	(1	1)	24	4	9	6	5	0	15	0	0	0	0	0	4	.235	.288	.353	.641
2021	Col	NL	106	338	83	18	1	18	(9	9)	157	52	44	32	30	1	60	2	0	1	0	0	15	.246	.310	.464	.774
2022	Col	NL	105	351	80	18	2	9	(7	2)	129	29	51	39	25	0	82	2	0	3	2	1	8	.228	.281	.368	.648
8 ML YEARS			487	1506	366	78	3	42	(22	20)	576	167	186	158	115	2	293	7	1	11	1	2	50	.243	.298	.382	.680

Jhonathan Diaz

Pitches: L **Bats:** L **Pos:** SP-3; RP-1   **Ht:** 6'0" **Wt:** 170 **Born:** 9/13/1996 **Age:** 26

			HOW MUCH PITCHED				WHAT HE GAVE UP										THE RESULTS							
Year	Team	Lg	G	GS	GF	IP	BFP	H	R	ER	HR	SH	SF	HB	TBB	IBB	SO	WP	W	L	Pct	Sv-Op	Hld	Vel	OPS	ERC	ERA
2022	Salt Lk	AAA	10	10	0	47.0	207	44	28	26	4	1	0	6	20	0	46	0	3	1	.750	0- -	-	-	.721	4.20	4.98
2021	LAA	AL	3	2	1	13.0	59	11	6	6	1	0	1	1	7	0	9	0	1	0	1.000	0-0	0	89	.682	3.72	4.15
2022	LAA	AL	4	3	1	15.1	66	13	5	5	1	0	1	0	10	0	11	0	1	1	.500	0-0	0	90	.730	4.06	2.93
2 ML YEARS			7	5	2	28.1	125	24	11	11	2	0	2	1	17	0	20	0	2	1	.667	0-0	0	89	.707	3.90	3.49

Jordan Diaz

Bats: R **Throws:** R **Pos:** 2B-12;DH-2;1B-1   **Ht:** 5'10" **Wt:** 175 **Born:** 8/13/2000 **Age:** 22

												BATTING										RUNNING			AVERAGES			
Year	Team	Lg	G	AB	H	2B	3B	HR	(Hm	Rd)	TB	R	RBI	RC	TBB	IBB	SO	HBP	SH	SF	SB	CS	GDP	Avg	OBP	Slg	OPS
2022	Mdlnd	AA	94	379	121	26	0	15	(-	-)	192	48	58	65	22	0	61	4	0	2	0	0	15	.319	.361	.507	.868
2022	LsVgs	AAA	26	112	39	8	1	4	(-	-)	61	19	25	21	6	0	15	1	0	1	0	0	3	.348	.383	.545	.928
2022	Oak	AL	15	49	13	3	0	0	(0	0)	16	3	1	4	2	0	7	0	0	0	0	0	1	.265	.294	.327	.621

Lewin Diaz

Bats: L **Throws:** L **Pos:** 1B-56;DH-2;PH-1   **Ht:** 6'4" **Wt:** 217 **Born:** 11/19/1996 **Age:** 26

												BATTING										RUNNING			AVERAGES			
Year	Team	Lg	G	AB	H	2B	3B	HR	(Hm	Rd)	TB	R	RBI	RC	TBB	IBB	SO	HBP	SH	SF	SB	CS	GDP	Avg	OBP	Slg	OPS
2022	Jaxnvl	AAA	82	325	82	19	1	19	(-	-)	160	55	64	57	32	0	75	5	0	6	0	0	5	.252	.323	.492	.816
2020	Mia	NL	14	39	6	2	0	0	(0	0)	8	2	3	2	2	0	12	0	0	0	0	0	2	.154	.195	.205	.400
2021	Mia	NL	40	122	25	4	1	8	(2	6)	55	16	13	9	6	1	33	0	0	0	0	0	1	.205	.242	.451	.693
2022	Mia	NL	58	160	27	4	0	5	(2	3)	46	12	11	8	11	0	54	1	0	2	1	0	3	.169	.224	.288	.512
3 ML YEARS			112	321	58	10	1	13	(4	9)	109	30	27	19	19	1	99	1	0	2	1	0	6	.181	.227	.340	.567

Miguel Diaz

Pitches: R Bats: R Pos: RP-3   Ht: 6'0" Wt: 224 Born: 11/28/1994 Age: 28

| | | | HOW MUCH PITCHED | | | | | WHAT HE GAVE UP | | | | | | | | | | | THE RESULTS | | | | | | | | |
Year	Team	Lg	G	GS	GF	IP	BFP	H	R	ER	HR	SH	SF	HB	TBB	IBB	SO	WP	W	L	Pct	Sv-Op	Hld	Vel	OPS	ERC	ERA
2022	Toledo	AAA	58	0	16	65.0	285	59	39	31	5	3	3	3	30	0	69	8	4	5	.444	7- -	-	-	.704	3.76	4.29
2017	SD	NL	31	3	8	41.2	192	44	35	34	11	2	2	3	25	0	33	5	1	1	.500	0-0	0	96	.929	6.87	7.34
2018	SD	NL	11	0	4	18.2	85	16	11	10	2	0	2	0	12	2	30	1	1	0	1.000	0-0	0	96	.738	3.94	4.82
2019	SD	NL	5	0	2	6.1	29	9	5	5	1	0	0	2	1	0	4	1	0	0	-	0-0	1	95	1.068	7.78	7.11
2021	SD	NL	25	2	10	42.0	172	31	19	17	8	1	0	0	19	0	46	0	3	1	.750	1-1	1	94	.727	3.48	3.64
2022	Det	AL	3	0	0	3.2	14	1	1	1	0	0	0	0	2	0	3	1	0	0	-	0-0	0	96	.298	0.88	2.45
	5 ML YEARS		75	5	24	112.1	492	101	71	67	22	3	4	5	59	2	116	8	5	2	.714	1-1	2	95	.815	4.85	5.37

Yainer Diaz

Bats: R Throws: R Pos: DH-3;C-2;PH-2   Ht: 6'0" Wt: 195 Born: 9/21/1998 Age: 24

| | | | BATTING | | | | | | | | | | | | | | RUNNING | | | AVERAGES | | | |
Year	Team	Lg	G	AB	H	2B	3B	HR	(Hm	Rd)	TB	R	RBI	RC	TBB	IBB	SO	HBP	SH	SF	SB	CS	GDP	Avg	OBP	Slg	OPS
2022	CpChr	AA	57	244	77	13	3	9	(-	-)	123	37	43	42	21	0	40	0	0	2	1	0	11	.316	.367	.504	.871
2022	SgrLnd	AAA	48	201	59	9	1	16	(-	-)	118	38	48	41	13	0	39	3	0	2	1	0	0	.294	.342	.587	.930
2022	Hou	AL	6	8	1	1	0	0	(0	0)	2	0	1	0	1	0	2	0	0	0	0	0	0	.125	.222	.250	.472

Yandy Diaz

Bats: R Throws: R Pos: 3B-102;1B-17;DH-14;PH-9;PR-1   Ht: 6'2" Wt: 215 Born: 8/8/1991 Age: 31

| | | | BATTING | | | | | | | | | | | | | | RUNNING | | | AVERAGES | | | |
Year	Team	Lg	G	AB	H	2B	3B	HR	(Hm	Rd)	TB	R	RBI	RC	TBB	IBB	SO	HBP	SH	SF	SB	CS	GDP	Avg	OBP	Slg	OPS
2017	Cle	AL	49	156	41	8	1	0	(0	0)	51	25	13	18	21	0	35	1	0	1	2	0	5	.263	.352	.327	.679
2018	Cle	AL	39	109	34	5	2	1	(1	0)	46	15	15	16	11	1	19	0	0	0	0	0	6	.312	.375	.422	.797
2019	TB	AL	79	307	82	20	1	14	(7	7)	146	53	38	38	35	1	61	1	0	4	2	2	9	.267	.340	.476	.816
2020	TB	AL	34	114	35	3	0	2	(1	1)	44	16	11	21	23	1	17	1	0	0	0	0	6	.307	.428	.386	.814
2021	TB	AL	134	465	119	20	1	13	(5	8)	180	62	64	73	69	4	85	3	0	4	1	1	11	.256	.353	.387	.740
2022	TB	AL	137	473	140	33	0	9	(4	5)	200	71	57	77	78	2	60	6	0	3	3	3	10	.296	.401	.423	.824
	Postseason		22	67	14	1	1	2	(0	2)	23	6	5	11	12	0	17	0	0	0	0	0	0	.209	.329	.343	.672
	6 ML YEARS		472	1624	451	89	5	39	(18	21)	667	242	198	243	237	9	277	12	0	10	8	6	47	.278	.372	.411	.782

Yusniel Diaz

Bats: R Throws: R Pos: RF-1;PH-1   Ht: 6'1" Wt: 215 Born: 10/7/1996 Age: 26

| | | | BATTING | | | | | | | | | | | | | | RUNNING | | | AVERAGES | | | |
Year	Team	Lg	G	AB	H	2B	3B	HR	(Hm	Rd)	TB	R	RBI	RC	TBB	IBB	SO	HBP	SH	SF	SB	CS	GDP	Avg	OBP	Slg	OPS
2022	Norfolk	AAA	70	247	62	9	0	6	(-	-)	89	40	34	30	36	1	66	1	0	2	9	4	7	.251	.346	.360	.706
2022	Bal	AL	1	1	0	0	0	0	(0	0)	0	0	0	0	0	0	1	0	0	0	0	0	0	.000	.000	.000	.000

Alex Dickerson

Bats: L Throws: L Pos: DH-10;PH-3;RF-1   Ht: 6'2" Wt: 226 Born: 5/26/1990 Age: 33

| | | | BATTING | | | | | | | | | | | | | | RUNNING | | | AVERAGES | | | |
Year	Team	Lg	G	AB	H	2B	3B	HR	(Hm	Rd)	TB	R	RBI	RC	TBB	IBB	SO	HBP	SH	SF	SB	CS	GDP	Avg	OBP	Slg	OPS
2022	Gwnntt	AAA	92	322	77	20	2	12	(-	-)	137	36	43	43	29	0	76	3	0	3	1	0	6	.239	.305	.425	.731
2015	SD	NL	11	8	2	0	0	0	(0	0)	2	0	0	0	0	0	3	0	0	0	0	0	1	.250	.250	.250	.500
2016	SD	NL	84	253	65	16	2	10	(5	5)	115	39	37	40	26	2	44	4	0	2	5	1	5	.257	.333	.455	.788
2019	2 Tms	NL	68	174	48	13	3	6	(4	2)	85	29	28	27	13	1	42	2	0	1	1	1	5	.276	.332	.489	.820
2020	SF	NL	52	151	45	10	1	10	(5	5)	87	28	27	27	16	2	30	2	0	1	0	0	5	.298	.371	.576	.947
2021	SF	NL	111	283	66	10	2	13	(6	7)	119	37	38	40	23	1	76	6	0	0	1	1	7	.233	.304	.420	.725
2022	Atl	NL	13	33	4	0	0	1	(1	0)	7	3	2	0	3	0	9	0	0	0	0	0	0	.121	.194	.212	.407
	19 SD	NL	12	19	3	0	0	0	(0	0)	3	1	2	2	0	0	7	0	0	0	0	0	0	.158	.158	.158	.316
	19 SF	NL	56	155	45	13	3	6	(4	2)	82	28	26	25	13	1	35	2	0	1	1	1	5	.290	.351	.529	.880
	Postseason		4	4	0	0	0	0	(0	0)	0	0	0	0	0	0	3	0	0	0	0	0	0	.000	.000	.000	.000
	6 ML YEARS		339	902	230	49	8	40	(21	19)	415	136	132	134	81	6	204	14	0	4	7	2	26	.255	.325	.460	.785

Corey Dickerson

Bats: L Throws: R Pos: LF-60;DH-20;PH-14;RF-10;PR-4   Ht: 6'1" Wt: 200 Born: 5/22/1989 Age: 34

| | | | BATTING | | | | | | | | | | | | | | RUNNING | | | AVERAGES | | | |
Year	Team	Lg	G	AB	H	2B	3B	HR	(Hm	Rd)	TB	R	RBI	RC	TBB	IBB	SO	HBP	SH	SF	SB	CS	GDP	Avg	OBP	Slg	OPS
2013	Col	NL	69	194	51	13	5	5	(4	1)	89	32	17	23	16	0	41	0	1	2	2	2	1	.263	.316	.459	.775
2014	Col	NL	131	436	136	27	6	24	(15	9)	247	74	76	79	37	6	101	1	0	4	8	7	6	.312	.364	.567	.931
2015	Col	NL	65	224	68	18	2	10	(5	5)	120	30	31	39	10	0	56	0	0	0	1	3	3	.304	.333	.536	.869
2016	TB	AL	148	510	125	36	3	24	(7	17)	239	57	70	59	33	6	134	2	0	2	0	2	12	.245	.293	.469	.761
2017	TB	AL	150	588	166	33	4	27	(14	13)	288	84	62	87	35	6	152	3	0	2	4	3	11	.282	.325	.490	.815
2018	Pit	NL	135	504	151	35	7	13	(4	9)	239	65	55	69	21	4	80	4	0	4	8	3	14	.300	.330	.474	.804
2019	2 Tms	NL	78	260	79	28	2	12	(6	6)	147	33	59	50	16	4	56	1	0	3	1	0	3	.304	.341	.565	.906
2020	Mia	NL	52	194	50	5	1	7	(2	5)	78	25	17	20	15	1	35	0	0	0	1	1	5	.258	.311	.402	.713
2021	2 Tms	NL	109	336	91	18	5	6	(2	4)	137	43	29	34	25	1	68	3	0	1	6	5	9	.271	.326	.408	.734
2022	StL	NL	97	281	75	17	1	6	(2	4)	112	28	36	34	12	1	48	2	0	2	0	0	4	.267	.300	.399	.698
	19 Pit	NL	44	127	40	18	0	4	(0	4)	70	20	25	24	13	4	23	0	0	2	1	0	2	.315	.373	.551	.924
	19 Phi	NL	34	133	39	10	2	8	(6	2)	77	13	34	26	3	0	33	0	0	1	0	0	1	.293	.307	.579	.886
	21 Mia	NL	63	205	54	12	3	2	(0	2)	78	27	14	17	16	0	45	3	0	1	2	4	5	.263	.324	.380	.705
	21 Tor	AL	46	131	37	6	2	4	(2	2)	59	16	15	17	9	1	23	0	0	0	4	1	3	.282	.329	.450	.779
	Postseason		5	19	4	0	0	1	(0	1)	7	1	3	2	2	0	5	0	0	0	0	0	0	.211	.286	.368	.654
	10 ML YEARS		1034	3527	992	230	36	134	(61	73)	1696	471	452	494	220	29	771	15	1	20	30	24	68	.281	.324	.481	.805

248

Phillip Diehl

Pitches: L Bats: L Pos: RP-5   Ht: 6'2" Wt: 169 Born: 7/16/1994 Age: 28

			HOW MUCH PITCHED				WHAT HE GAVE UP									THE RESULTS					
Year	Team	Lg	G	GS	GF	IP	BFP	H	R	ER	HR	SH	SF	HB	TBB	IBB	SO	WP	W	L	Pct	Sv-Op	Hld	Vel	OPS	ERC	ERA
2022	Lsvlle	AAA	25	0	2	23.1	98	18	12	11	4	0	3	1	8	0	30	0	2	1	.667	0- -	-	-	.706	3.15	4.24
2022	Syrcse	AAA	13	0	6	16.1	79	21	17	15	4	0	2	0	10	1	9	0	0	2	.000	1- -	-	-	.900	7.71	8.27
2019	Col	NL	10	0	2	7.1	35	10	6	6	1	0	0	1	2	0	8	1	0	0	-	0-0	0	91	.934	6.41	7.36
2020	Col	NL	6	0	2	6.0	25	7	7	7	2	0	0	0	1	0	4	0	0	0	-	0-0	0	90	.945	5.81	10.50
2022	Cin	NL	5	0	1	5.2	28	8	7	7	3	0	0	0	3	1	3	1	0	0	-	0-0	0	91	1.193	10.29	11.12
	3 ML YEARS		21	0	5	19.0	88	25	20	20	6	0	0	1	6	1	15	2	0	0	-	0-0	0	91	1.018	7.35	9.47

Jake Diekman

Pitches: L Bats: R Pos: RP-70   DEEK-man   Ht: 6'4" Wt: 195 Born: 1/21/1987 Age: 36

			HOW MUCH PITCHED				WHAT HE GAVE UP									THE RESULTS					
Year	Team	Lg	G	GS	GF	IP	BFP	H	R	ER	HR	SH	SF	HB	TBB	IBB	SO	WP	W	L	Pct	Sv-Op	Hld	Vel	OPS	ERC	ERA
2012	Phi	NL	32	0	7	27.1	131	25	17	12	1	1	0	3	20	3	35	1	1	1	.500	0-1	4	95	.696	4.45	3.95
2013	Phi	NL	45	0	11	38.1	164	34	15	11	1	2	1	0	16	2	41	2	1	4	.200	0-1	11	96	.598	2.89	2.58
2014	Phi	NL	73	0	19	71.0	313	66	36	30	4	2	7	3	35	5	100	7	5	5	.500	0-4	35	97	.692	3.73	3.80
2015	2 Tms		67	0	7	58.1	260	53	28	26	5	0	0	3	31	0	69	2	2	1	.667	0-3	16	96	.689	4.11	4.01
2016	Tex	AL	66	0	14	53.0	221	36	22	20	4	0	2	3	26	1	59	3	4	2	.667	4-5	26	95	.544	2.72	3.40
2017	Tex	AL	11	0	2	10.2	45	4	3	3	1	0	2	0	10	1	13	0	0	0	-	1-1	5	95	.523	2.58	2.53
2018	2 Tms		71	0	15	53.1	243	49	33	28	4	0	2	6	31	2	66	3	1	2	.333	2-3	17	95	.717	4.46	4.73
2019	2 Tms		76	0	5	62.0	282	49	34	32	3	1	3	11	39	1	84	6	1	7	.125	0-2	31	96	.668	4.00	4.65
2020	Oak	AL	21	0	2	21.1	84	8	2	1	1	1	0	1	12	1	31	0	2	0	1.000	0-1	13	95	.410	1.43	0.42
2021	Oak	AL	67	0	17	60.2	262	47	29	26	10	0	1	4	34	2	83	8	3	3	.500	7-14	14	95	.715	4.11	3.86
2022	2 Tms		70	0	10	57.2	269	52	40	32	9	0	3	8	42	2	79	7	5	4	.556	1-4	16	96	.796	5.77	4.99
15	Phi	NL	41	0	6	36.2	175	40	23	21	3	0	0	2	24	0	49	1	2	1	.667	0-2	6	96	.773	5.60	5.15
15	Tex	AL	26	0	1	21.2	85	13	5	5	2	0	0	1	7	0	20	1	0	0	-	0-1	10	97	.520	1.89	2.08
18	Tex	AL	47	0	10	39.0	172	31	18	16	2	0	2	3	23	1	48	0	1	1	.500	2-3	14	95	.651	3.53	3.69
18	Ari	NL	24	0	5	14.1	71	18	15	12	2	0	0	3	8	1	18	3	0	1	.000	0-0	3	96	.875	7.29	7.53
19	KC	AL	48	0	4	41.2	188	33	23	22	3	0	1	8	23	0	63	4	0	6	.000	0-2	18	96	.667	3.97	4.75
19	Oak	AL	28	0	1	20.1	94	16	11	10	0	1	2	3	16	1	21	2	1	1	.500	0-0	13	96	.668	4.05	4.43
22	Bos	AL	44	0	8	38.1	171	27	22	18	5	0	2	6	30	1	51	5	5	1	.833	1-4	12	96	.744	4.80	4.23
22	CWS	AL	26	0	2	19.1	98	25	18	14	4	0	1	2	12	1	28	2	0	3	.000	0-0	4	96	.880	7.77	6.52
	Postseason		13	0	4	12.0	50	10	6	6	2	0	0	1	4	1	11	0	0	0	-	1-1	2	96	.700	3.56	4.50
	11 ML YEARS		599	0	109	513.2	2274	423	259	221	43	7	21	42	296	20	660	39	25	29	.463	15-39	171	96	.676	3.87	3.87

Wilmer Difo

Bats: B Throws: R Pos: SS-2;2B-1   DEE-fo   Ht: 5'11" Wt: 200 Born: 4/2/1992 Age: 31

			BATTING																RUNNING			AVERAGES			
Year	Team	Lg	G	AB	H	2B	3B	HR	(Hm | Rd)	TB	R	RBI	RC	TBB	IBB	SO	HBP	SH	SF	SB	CS	GDP	Avg	OBP	Slg	OPS
2022	Reno	AAA	72	279	75	15	0	7	(- | -)	111	33	43	32	20	0	41	0	1	6	4	2	10	.269	.311	.398	.709
2015	Was	NL	15	11	2	0	0	0	(0 | 0)	2	1	0	0	0	0	2	0	0	0	0	0	0	.182	.182	.182	.364
2016	Was	NL	31	58	16	3	0	1	(1 | 0)	22	14	7	9	8	1	12	0	0	0	3	0	0	.276	.364	.379	.743
2017	Was	NL	124	332	90	10	4	5	(3 | 2)	123	47	21	34	24	6	74	1	5	3	10	1	7	.271	.319	.370	.690
2018	Was	NL	148	408	94	14	7	7	(5 | 2)	143	55	42	38	39	5	82	2	3	4	10	3	8	.230	.298	.350	.649
2019	Was	NL	43	131	33	2	0	2	(1 | 1)	41	15	8	15	12	3	29	0	1	0	1	2	2	.252	.315	.313	.628
2020	Was	NL	12	14	1	0	0	0	(0 | 0)	1	1	1	0	3	0	4	0	0	1	0	0	0	.071	.222	.071	.294
2021	Pit	NL	116	219	59	7	3	4	(3 | 1)	84	25	24	29	20	0	54	0	0	1	0	0	2	.269	.329	.384	.713
2022	Ari	NL	3	6	0	0	0	0	(0 | 0)	0	0	0	0	0	0	1	0	0	0	0	0	0	.000	.000	.000	.000
	Postseason		3	3	0	0	0	0	(0 | 0)	0	0	0	0	0	0	1	0	0	0	0	0	0	.000	.000	.000	.000
	8 ML YEARS		492	1179	295	36	14	19	(13 | 6)	416	158	103	125	106	15	258	3	9	9	24	5	19	.250	.311	.353	.664

Marcos Diplan

Pitches: R Bats: R Pos: RP-5   Ht: 6'0" Wt: 200 Born: 9/18/1996 Age: 26

			HOW MUCH PITCHED				WHAT HE GAVE UP									THE RESULTS					
Year	Team	Lg	G	GS	GF	IP	BFP	H	R	ER	HR	SH	SF	HB	TBB	IBB	SO	WP	W	L	Pct	Sv-Op	Hld	Vel	OPS	ERC	ERA
2022	Norfolk	AAA	20	0	5	26.2	118	20	9	6	2	0	1	2	17	0	28	0	2	0	1.000	2- -	-	-	.626	3.66	2.03
2021	Bal	AL	23	0	4	30.0	123	22	16	15	6	0	1	0	15	0	24	3	2	0	1.000	0-0	1	94	.712	3.74	4.50
2022	Bal	AL	5	0	2	5.2	27	4	2	1	0	0	0	0	5	0	8	0	0	0	-	0-0	0	93	.561	3.29	1.59
	2 ML YEARS		28	0	6	35.2	150	26	18	16	6	0	1	0	20	0	32	3	2	0	1.000	0-0	1	94	.687	3.69	4.04

Brandon Dixon

Bats: R Throws: R Pos: 3B-2;DH-2;RF-1;PR-1   Ht: 6'2" Wt: 215 Born: 1/29/1992 Age: 31

			BATTING																RUNNING			AVERAGES			
Year	Team	Lg	G	AB	H	2B	3B	HR	(Hm | Rd)	TB	R	RBI	RC	TBB	IBB	SO	HBP	SH	SF	SB	CS	GDP	Avg	OBP	Slg	OPS
2022	ElPaso	AAA	25	97	36	9	0	13	(- | -)	84	24	32	37	14	3	27	1	0	2	3	1	1	.371	.447	.866	1.313
2022	SnAnt	AA	25	98	36	7	2	10	(- | -)	77	23	42	34	12	0	25	1	0	3	6	0	1	.367	.430	.786	1.216
2018	Cin	NL	74	118	21	6	0	5	(2 | 3)	42	14	10	2	6	0	43	0	0	0	0	0	2	.178	.218	.356	.574
2019	Det	AL	118	391	97	20	4	15	(5 | 10)	170	41	52	50	21	0	136	4	0	4	5	1	5	.248	.290	.435	.725
2020	Det	AL	5	13	1	1	0	0	(0 | 0)	2	0	1	0	1	0	4	0	0	0	0	0	0	.077	.143	.154	.297
2022	SD	NL	5	14	3	1	0	0	(0 | 0)	4	1	1	0	0	0	5	0	0	0	0	0	0	.214	.214	.286	.500
	4 ML YEARS		202	536	122	28	4	20	(7 | 13)	218	56	65	52	28	0	188	4	0	4	5	1	9	.228	.269	.407	.676

Seranthony Dominguez

Pitches: R Bats: R Pos: RP-54 Ht: 6'1" Wt: 225 Born: 11/25/1994 Age: 28

Year	Team	Lg	G	GS	GF	IP	BFP	H	R	ER	HR	SH	SF	HB	TBB	IBB	SO	WP	W	L	Pct	Sv-Op	Hld	Vel	OPS	ERC	ERA
2018	Phi	NL	53	0	24	58.0	231	32	19	19	4	0	1	4	22	2	74	10	2	5	.286	16-20	14	98	.501	1.74	2.95
2019	Phi	NL	27	0	2	24.2	110	24	13	11	3	1	0	1	12	0	29	1	3	0	1.000	0-2	9	97	.725	4.52	4.01
2021	Phi	NL	1	0	0	1.0	3	0	0	0	0	0	0	0	0	0	1	0	0	0	—	0-0	0	95	.000	0.00	0.00
2022	Phi	NL	54	0	16	51.0	207	36	18	17	4	0	1	1	22	1	61	3	6	5	.545	9-11	15	98	.596	2.57	3.00
4 ML YEARS			135	0	42	134.2	551	92	50	47	11	1	2	6	56	3	165	14	11	10	.524	25-33	38	98	.578	2.48	3.14

Josh Donaldson

Bats: R Throws: R Pos: 3B-104;DH-23;PH-6;PR-1 Ht: 6'1" Wt: 210 Born: 12/8/1985 Age: 37

Year	Team	Lg	G	AB	H	2B	3B	HR	(Hm	Rd)	TB	R	RBI	RC	TBB	IBB	SO	HBP	SH	SF	SB	CS	GDP	Avg	OBP	Slg	OPS
2010	Oak	AL	14	32	5	1	0	1	(0	1)	9	1	4	3	2	0	12	0	0	0	0	0	0	.156	.206	.281	.487
2012	Oak	AL	75	274	66	16	0	9	(3	6)	109	34	33	33	14	0	61	5	0	1	4	1	6	.241	.289	.398	.687
2013	Oak	AL	158	579	174	37	3	24	(13	11)	289	89	93	112	76	2	110	6	1	6	5	2	15	.301	.384	.499	.883
2014	Oak	AL	158	608	155	31	2	29	(11	18)	277	93	98	105	76	5	130	7	0	4	8	0	16	.255	.342	.456	.798
2015	Tor	AL	158	620	184	41	2	41	(24	17)	**352**	**122**	**123**	**131**	73	0	133	6	2	**10**	6	0	16	.297	.371	.568	.939
2016	Tor	AL	155	577	164	32	5	37	(21	16)	317	122	99	121	109	6	119	9	2	3	7	1	16	.284	.404	.549	.953
2017	Tor	AL	113	415	112	21	0	33	(14	19)	232	65	78	98	76	1	111	3	0	2	2	2	5	.270	.385	.559	.944
2018	2 Tms	AL	52	187	46	14	0	8	(4	4)	84	30	23	32	31	2	54	0	0	1	2	0	3	.246	.352	.449	.801
2019	Atl	NL	155	549	142	33	0	37	(22	15)	286	96	94	103	100	2	155	8	0	2	4	2	13	.259	.379	.521	.900
2020	Min	AL	28	81	18	2	0	6	(3	3)	38	14	11	14	18	1	24	2	0	1	0	0	4	.222	.373	.469	.842
2021	Min	AL	135	457	113	26	0	26	(10	16)	217	73	72	77	74	2	114	4	0	8	0	0	22	.247	.352	.475	.827
2022	NYY	AL	132	478	106	28	0	15	(4	11)	179	59	62	59	54	1	148	8	0	6	2	2	13	.222	.308	.374	.682
18	Tor	AL	36	137	32	11	0	5	(2	3)	58	22	16	24	21	2	44	0	0	1	2	0	1	.234	.333	.423	.757
18	Cle	AL	16	50	14	3	0	3	(2	1)	26	8	7	8	10	0	10	0	0	0	0	0	2	.280	.400	.520	.920
	Postseason		39	150	39	11	0	5	(4	1)	65	19	16	22	15	2	39	2	0	0	1	0	2	.260	.335	.433	.769
12 ML YEARS			1333	4857	1285	282	12	266	(129	137)	2389	798	790	888	703	22	1171	58	5	44	40	10	129	.265	.361	.492	.853

Brendan Donovan

Bats: L Throws: R Pos: 2B-38;3B-31;RF-20;LF-19;1B-16;DH-16;SS-7;PH-7;PR-5 Ht: 6'1" Wt: 195 Born: 1/16/1997 Age: 26

Year	Team	Lg	G	AB	H	2B	3B	HR	(Hm	Rd)	TB	R	RBI	RC	TBB	IBB	SO	HBP	SH	SF	SB	CS	GDP	Avg	OBP	Slg	OPS
2022	Memp	AAA	16	57	17	3	0	1	(-	-)	23	12	6	8	8	0	8	0	0	0	0	0	2	.298	.385	.404	.788
2022	StL	NL	126	391	110	21	1	5	(3	2)	148	64	45	58	60	1	70	14	1	2	2	3	8	.281	.394	.379	.773

Sean Doolittle

Pitches: L Bats: L Pos: RP-6 Ht: 6'2" Wt: 227 Born: 9/26/1986 Age: 36

Year	Team	Lg	G	GS	GF	IP	BFP	H	R	ER	HR	SH	SF	HB	TBB	IBB	SO	WP	W	L	Pct	Sv-Op	Hld	Vel	OPS	ERC	ERA
2012	Oak	AL	44	0	7	47.1	191	40	18	16	3	2	2	0	11	1	60	0	2	1	.667	1-2	18	94	.611	2.36	3.04
2013	Oak	AL	70	0	11	69.0	266	53	24	24	4	3	0	2	13	1	60	2	5	5	.500	2-7	26	94	.573	2.00	3.13
2014	Oak	AL	61	0	40	62.2	236	38	19	19	5	2	1	0	8	1	89	0	2	4	.333	22-26	5	94	.459	1.23	2.73
2015	Oak	AL	12	0	7	13.2	57	12	6	6	1	0	1	0	5	0	15	0	1	0	1.000	4-5	1	92	.651	3.10	3.95
2016	Oak	AL	44	0	13	39.0	155	34	13	14	6	4	0	0	8	2	45	1	2	3	.400	4-6	10	95	.705	2.79	3.23
2017	2 Tms		53	0	34	51.1	197	34	18	16	5	0	3	0	10	1	62	3	2	1	.667	24-26	9	95	.517	1.62	2.81
2018	Was	NL	43	0	35	45.0	163	21	8	8	3	0	0	2	6	1	60	1	3	3	.500	25-26	1	94	.391	0.93	1.60
2019	Was	NL	63	0	55	60.0	260	63	27	27	11	1	0	2	15	2	66	0	6	5	.545	29-35	2	93	.772	4.32	4.05
2020	Was	NL	11	0	3	7.2	36	9	6	5	1	1	0	0	4	2	6	0	0	2	.000	0-0	3	93	1.005	7.28	5.87
2021	2 Tms		56	0	13	49.2	223	50	27	25	7	2	2	2	23	3	53	2	3	1	.750	1-5	9	93	.793	4.64	4.53
2022	Was	NL	6	0	0	5.1	17	1	0	0	0	0	0	0	0	0	6	0	0	0	—	0-0	2	93	.176	0.08	0.00
17	Oak	AL	23	0	6	21.1	79	12	8	8	3	0	1	0	2	0	31	1	1	0	1.000	3-4	8	94	.467	1.23	3.38
17	Was	NL	30	0	28	30.0	118	22	10	8	2	0	2	0	8	1	31	2	1	0	1.000	21-22	1	95	.551	1.99	2.40
21	Cin	NL	45	0	11	38.1	173	40	21	19	6	2	2	1	18	3	41	0	3	1	.750	1-5	4	93	.832	4.91	4.46
21	Sea	AL	11	0	2	11.1	50	10	6	6	1	0	0	1	5	0	12	2	0	0	—	0-0	1	94	.661	3.75	4.76
	Postseason		20	0	8	22.1	87	17	8	6	2	3	1	0	3	0	23	0	0	1	.000	3-6	5	95	.563	1.81	2.42
11 ML YEARS			463	0	218	450.2	1801	354	167	160	48	15	10	8	103	14	522	9	26	24	.520	112-138	82	94	.612	2.36	3.20

Camilo Doval

Pitches: R Bats: R Pos: RP-68 Ht: 6'2" Wt: 185 Born: 7/4/1997 Age: 25

Year	Team	Lg	G	GS	GF	IP	BFP	H	R	ER	HR	SH	SF	HB	TBB	IBB	SO	WP	W	L	Pct	Sv-Op	Hld	Vel	OPS	ERC	ERA
2021	SF	NL	29	0	9	27.0	109	19	10	9	4	0	0	1	9	2	37	2	5	1	.833	3-6	5	99	.599	2.59	3.00
2022	SF	NL	68	0	51	67.2	286	54	27	19	4	1	4	3	30	2	80	4	6	6	.500	27-30	1	99	.624	2.98	2.53
	Postseason		3	0	2	3.2	14	2	1	1	0	0	0	0	0	0	2	0	0	0	.000	1-1	0	100	.368	1.10	2.45
2 ML YEARS			97	0	60	94.2	395	73	37	28	8	1	4	4	39	4	117	6	11	7	.611	30-36	6	99	.617	2.87	2.66

Kyle Dowdy

Pitches: R Bats: R Pos: RP-2   Ht: 6'1" Wt: 195 Born: 2/3/1993 Age: 30

		HOW MUCH PITCHED					WHAT HE GAVE UP										THE RESULTS						
Year	Team	Lg	G	GS	GF	IP	BFP	H	R	ER	HR	SH	SF	HB	TBB	IBB	SO	WP	W	L	Pct	Sv-Op	Hld	Vel	OPS	ERC	ERA
2022	Lsville	AAA	48	0	9	52.1	233	47	29	23	3	1	3	2	31	1	56	5	1	3	.250	1--	-	-	.707	4.03	3.96
2019	Tex	AL	13	1	2	22.1	110	26	20	18	4	1	2	1	18	1	17	3	2	1	.667	0-1	0	95	.890	7.50	7.25
2022	Cin	NL	2	0	0	6.1	27	5	0	0	0	0	0	1	3	0	3	0	0	0	-	0-0	0	96	.551	3.15	0.00
	2 ML YEARS		15	1	2	28.2	137	31	20	18	4	1	2	2	21	1	20	3	2	1	.667	0-1	0	95	.820	6.46	5.65

Jeter Downs

Bats: R Throws: R Pos: 2B-8;3B-6;SS-3;PH-2;PR-2;DH-1   Ht: 5'11" Wt: 195 Born: 7/27/1998 Age: 24

			BATTING																	RUNNING			AVERAGES			
Year	Team	Lg	G	AB	H	2B	3B	HR	(Hm	Rd)	TB	R	RBI	RC	TBB	IBB	SO	HBP	SH	SF	SB	CS	GDP	Avg	OBP	Slg	OPS
2022	Wrcstr	AAA	81	284	56	11	1	16	(-	-)	117	56	33	43	38	0	99	12	0	1	18	4	3	.197	.316	.412	.728
2022	Bos	AL	14	39	6	1	0	1	(0	1)	10	4	4	3	1	0	21	0	0	1	0	0	0	.154	.171	.256	.427

Hunter Dozier

Bats: R Throws: R Pos: 1B-42;RF-35;3B-27;DH-25;LF-9;PH-4;PR-1   DOE-zhur   Ht: 6'4" Wt: 220 Born: 8/22/1991 Age: 31

			BATTING																	RUNNING			AVERAGES			
Year	Team	Lg	G	AB	H	2B	3B	HR	(Hm	Rd)	TB	R	RBI	RC	TBB	IBB	SO	HBP	SH	SF	SB	CS	GDP	Avg	OBP	Slg	OPS
2016	KC	AL	8	19	4	1	0	0	(0	0)	5	4	1	1	2	0	8	0	0	0	0	0	0	.211	.286	.263	.549
2018	KC	AL	102	362	83	19	4	11	(5	6)	143	36	34	26	24	0	109	1	0	1	2	3	12	.229	.278	.395	.673
2019	KC	AL	139	523	146	29	10	26	(8	18)	273	75	84	91	55	2	148	3	0	5	2	2	9	.279	.348	.522	.870
2020	KC	AL	44	158	36	4	2	6	(4	2)	62	29	12	20	27	0	48	1	0	0	4	0	3	.228	.344	.392	.736
2021	KC	AL	144	487	105	27	6	16	(9	7)	192	55	54	52	43	0	154	7	0	6	5	4	12	.216	.285	.394	.680
2022	KC	AL	129	462	109	26	4	12	(5	7)	179	51	41	44	34	0	125	3	0	1	4	3	14	.236	.292	.387	.679
	6 ML YEARS		566	2011	483	106	26	71	(31	40)	854	250	226	234	185	2	592	15	0	13	17	12	50	.240	.307	.425	.732

Brandon Drury

Bats: R Throws: R Pos: 3B-67;1B-30;2B-27;DH-26;PH-5;SS-2;RF-1;PR-1   DROO-ree   Ht: 6'2" Wt: 230 Born: 8/21/1992 Age: 30

			BATTING																	RUNNING			AVERAGES			
Year	Team	Lg	G	AB	H	2B	3B	HR	(Hm	Rd)	TB	R	RBI	RC	TBB	IBB	SO	HBP	SH	SF	SB	CS	GDP	Avg	OBP	Slg	OPS
2015	Ari	NL	20	56	12	3	0	2	(0	2)	21	3	8	4	2	0	8	1	0	0	0	0	5	.214	.254	.375	.629
2016	Ari	NL	134	461	130	31	1	16	(12	4)	211	59	53	59	31	2	100	3	0	4	1	1	14	.282	.329	.458	.786
2017	Ari	NL	135	445	119	37	2	13	(7	6)	199	41	63	62	28	1	103	5	0	2	1	1	9	.267	.317	.447	.764
2018	2 Tms	AL	26	77	13	4	0	1	(0	1)	20	5	10	7	7	0	20	2	0	0	0	0	5	.169	.256	.260	.516
2019	Tor	AL	120	418	91	21	1	15	(9	6)	159	43	41	37	25	0	113	1	0	3	0	1	6	.218	.262	.380	.642
2020	Tor	AL	21	46	7	1	0	0	(0	0)	8	3	1	0	2	0	9	0	0	1	0	0	0	.152	.184	.174	.358
2021	NYM	NL	51	84	23	5	0	4	(4	0)	40	7	14	11	3	0	22	1	0	0	0	0	3	.274	.307	.476	.783
2022	2 Tms	NL	138	518	136	31	2	28	(14	14)	255	87	87	93	38	0	126	8	0	4	2	3	8	.263	.320	.492	.813
18	NYY	AL	18	51	9	2	0	1	(0	1)	14	2	7	5	5	0	12	1	0	0	0	0	4	.176	.263	.275	.538
18	Tor	AL	8	26	4	2	0	0	(0	0)	6	3	3	2	2	0	8	1	0	0	0	0	1	.154	.241	.231	.472
22	Cin	NL	92	350	96	22	2	20	(12	8)	182	62	59	69	29	0	84	4	0	2	2	2	6	.274	.335	.520	.855
22	SD	NL	46	168	40	9	0	8	(2	6)	73	25	28	24	9	0	42	4	0	2	0	1	2	.238	.290	.435	.724
	Postseason		3	6	1	0	0	1	(0	1)	4	1	3	1	0	0	2	0	0	0	0	0	0	.167	.167	.667	.833
	8 ML YEARS		645	2105	531	133	6	79	(46	33)	913	248	277	273	136	3	501	21	0	14	4	6	50	.252	.302	.434	.736

Daniel Duarte

Pitches: R Bats: R Pos: RP-3   Ht: 6'0" Wt: 170 Born: 12/4/1996 Age: 26

			HOW MUCH PITCHED					WHAT HE GAVE UP										THE RESULTS						
Year	Team	Lg	G	GS	GF	IP	BFP	H	R	ER	HR	SH	SF	HB	TBB	IBB	SO	WP	W	L	Pct	Sv-Op	Hld	Vel	OPS	ERC	ERA
2022	Lsville	AAA	10	0	1	7.2	35	8	8	8	1	0	0	0	6	0	7	1	0	1	.000	0--	-	-	.883	6.36	9.39
2022	Cin	NL	3	0	1	2.2	14	3	3	3	1	0	1	0	3	0	2	0	0	0	-	0-0	0	96	1.129	10.25	10.13

Mauricio Dubon

Bats: R Throws: R Pos: CF-59;SS-21;2B-17;PH-11;LF-9;PR-4;3B-3;RF-3;DH-1   Ht: 6'0" Wt: 173 Born: 7/19/1994 Age: 28

			BATTING																	RUNNING			AVERAGES			
Year	Team	Lg	G	AB	H	2B	3B	HR	(Hm	Rd)	TB	R	RBI	RC	TBB	IBB	SO	HBP	SH	SF	SB	CS	GDP	Avg	OBP	Slg	OPS
2019	2 Tms	NL	30	106	29	5	0	4	(2	2)	46	12	9	11	5	0	20	0	0	0	3	1	3	.274	.306	.434	.740
2020	SF	NL	54	157	43	4	1	4	(3	1)	61	21	19	22	15	0	36	1	1	2	2	3	4	.274	.337	.389	.726
2021	SF	NL	74	175	42	9	0	5	(1	4)	66	20	20	12	9	2	41	1	0	2	2	1	5	.240	.278	.377	.655
2022	2 Tms	NL	104	243	52	9	0	5	(5	0)	76	31	24	15	13	0	30	1	3	5	2	3	7	.214	.252	.313	.565
19	Mil	NL	2	2	0	0	0	0	(0	0)	0	0	0	0	0	0	1	0	0	0	0	0	0	.000	.000	.000	.000
19	SF	NL	28	104	29	5	0	4	(2	2)	46	12	9	11	5	0	19	0	0	0	3	1	3	.279	.312	.442	.754
22	SF	NL	21	46	11	1	0	2	(2	0)	18	10	8	5	1	0	4	0	0	2	0	0	0	.239	.245	.391	.636
22	Hou	AL	83	197	41	8	0	3	(3	0)	58	21	16	10	12	0	26	1	3	3	2	3	7	.208	.254	.294	.548
	4 ML YEARS		262	681	166	27	1	18	(11	7)	249	84	74	60	42	2	127	3	4	9	9	8	19	.244	.287	.366	.653

Tyler Duffey

Pitches: R **Bats:** R **Pos:** RP-40   **Ht:** 6'3" **Wt:** 220 **Born:** 12/27/1990 **Age:** 32

			HOW MUCH PITCHED					WHAT HE GAVE UP											THE RESULTS							
Year	Team	Lg	G	GS	GF	IP	BFP	H	R	ER	HR	SH	SF	HB	TBB	IBB	SO	WP	W	L	Pct	Sv-Op	Hld	Vel	OPS	ERC	ERA
2022	S-WB	AAA	7	0	3	6.0	32	11	7	7	1	0	0	2	1	0	8	1	1	1	.500	1--	-	-	1.093	10.21	10.50
2015	Min	AL	10	10	0	58.0	242	56	20	20	4	3	0	0	20	0	53	1	5	1	.833	0-0	0	90	.702	3.51	3.10
2016	Min	AL	26	26	0	133.0	596	167	103	95	25	2	2	6	32	3	114	9	9	12	.429	0-0	0	90	.876	5.66	6.43
2017	Min	AL	56	0	7	71.0	310	79	41	39	9	1	3	1	18	5	67	4	2	3	.400	1-3	12	92	.721	4.17	4.94
2018	Min	AL	19	1	4	25.0	107	26	22	20	6	0	2	1	4	0	19	2	2	2	.500	0-0	2	93	.830	4.29	7.20
2019	Min	AL	58	0	12	57.2	238	44	23	16	8	1	1	3	14	1	82	3	5	1	.833	0-2	15	94	.595	2.55	2.50
2020	Min	AL	22	0	1	24.0	92	13	6	5	2	0	0	1	6	0	31	0	1	1	.500	0-2	12	93	.488	1.43	1.88
2021	Min	AL	64	0	6	62.1	254	48	25	22	4	1	1	2	28	1	61	5	3	3	.500	3-5	22	93	.619	2.97	3.18
2022	Min	AL	40	0	10	44.0	185	45	24	24	8	0	1	1	15	1	39	2	2	4	.333	2-5	9	92	.800	4.71	4.91
	Postseason		4	0	1	3.2	20	6	5	5	1	0	1	1	3	0	6	1	0	0	-	0-1	0	93	1.167	13.41	12.27
	8 ML YEARS		295	37	40	475.0	2024	478	264	241	66	8	10	15	137	11	466	26	29	27	.518	6-17	72	92	.740	4.01	4.57

Danny Duffy

Pitches: L **Bats:** L **Pos:** P   **Ht:** 6'3" **Wt:** 205 **Born:** 12/21/1988 **Age:** 34

			HOW MUCH PITCHED					WHAT HE GAVE UP											THE RESULTS							
Year	Team	Lg	G	GS	GF	IP	BFP	H	R	ER	HR	SH	SF	HB	TBB	IBB	SO	WP	W	L	Pct	Sv-Op	Hld	Vel	OPS	ERC	ERA
2011	KC	AL	20	20	0	105.1	474	119	66	66	15	2	2	5	51	1	87	4	4	8	.333	0-0	0	-	.864	5.76	5.64
2012	KC	AL	6	6	0	27.2	121	26	13	12	2	0	0	0	18	1	28	0	2	2	.500	0-0	0	-	.771	4.58	3.90
2013	KC	AL	5	5	0	24.1	104	19	5	5	0	0	0	1	14	0	22	2	2	0	1.000	0-0	0	-	.608	3.02	1.85
2014	KC	AL	31	25	1	149.1	606	113	52	42	12	3	4	5	53	2	113	5	9	12	.429	0-0	1	-	.605	2.62	2.53
2015	KC	AL	30	24	1	136.2	588	137	64	62	15	3	5	9	53	0	102	11	7	8	.467	1-1	2	-	.746	4.44	4.08
2016	KC	AL	42	26	5	179.2	731	163	71	70	27	4	2	7	42	0	188	4	12	3	.800	0-0	1	-	.710	3.44	3.51
2017	KC	AL	24	24	0	146.1	609	143	67	62	13	6	2	4	41	0	130	2	9	10	.474	0-0	1	-	.709	3.55	3.81
2018	KC	AL	28	28	0	155.0	692	161	86	84	23	2	6	4	70	1	141	14	8	12	.400	0-0	1	-	.767	4.90	4.88
2019	KC	AL	23	23	0	130.2	555	125	69	63	21	0	3	8	46	0	115	4	7	6	.538	0-0	1	-	.760	4.35	4.34
2020	KC	AL	12	11	0	56.1	242	53	33	31	10	1	4	2	22	0	57	3	4	4	.500	0-0	1	-	.756	4.37	4.95
2021	KC	AL	13	12	0	61.0	252	52	19	17	6	0	0	0	22	1	65	3	4	3	.571	0-0	0	-	.650	3.10	2.51
	Postseason		9	0	1	10.2	44	10	6	6	2	1	1	0	4	0	14	0	2	0	1.000	0-0	0	-	.878	4.35	5.06
	11 ML YEARS		234	204	7	1172.1	4974	1111	545	514	144	21	28	45	432	6	1048	52	68	68	.500	1-1	5	-	.728	3.99	3.95

Matt Duffy

Bats: R **Throws:** R **Pos:** 3B-42;1B-21;2B-17;PH-15   **Ht:** 6'2" **Wt:** 190 **Born:** 1/15/1991 **Age:** 32

			BATTING																		RUNNING			AVERAGES			
Year	Team	Lg	G	AB	H	2B	3B	HR	(Hm	Rd)	TB	R	RBI	RC	TBB	IBB	SO	HBP	SH	SF	SB	CS	GDP	Avg	OBP	Slg	OPS
2022	Salt Lk	AAA	10	35	6	0	0	1	(-	-)	9	4	2	2	2	0	8	1	0	0	0	0	0	.171	.237	.257	.494
2014	SF	NL	34	60	16	2	0	0	(0	0)	18	5	8	8	1	0	14	2	1	0	0	1	1	.267	.302	.300	.602
2015	SF	NL	149	573	169	28	6	12	(7	5)	245	77	77	84	30	0	96	5	2	2	12	0	22	.295	.334	.428	.762
2016	2 Tms		91	333	86	14	2	5	(1	4)	119	41	28	30	23	0	53	4	2	4	8	5	13	.258	.310	.357	.668
2018	TB	AL	132	503	148	22	1	4	(0	4)	184	59	44	72	47	1	93	7	1	2	12	6	12	.294	.361	.366	.727
2019	TB	AL	46	147	37	8	0	1	(0	1)	48	12	12	19	19	0	29	2	0	1	0	1	4	.252	.343	.327	.670
2021	ChC	NL	97	289	83	12	0	5	(2	3)	110	45	30	40	25	0	63	7	0	1	8	1	16	.287	.357	.381	.738
2022	LAA	AL	77	228	57	8	0	2	(0	2)	71	14	16	23	17	0	50	2	0	0	0	0	6	.250	.308	.311	.619
16	SF	NL	70	257	65	11	2	4	(1	3)	92	32	21	23	20	0	40	4	2	3	8	4	9	.253	.313	.358	.671
16	TB	AL	21	76	21	3	0	1	(0	1)	27	9	7	7	3	0	13	0	0	1	0	1	4	.276	.300	.355	.655
	Postseason		11	11	4	0	0	0	(0	0)	4	4	0	0	0	0	2	0	1	0	0	0	0	.364	.364	.364	.727
	7 ML YEARS		626	2133	596	94	9	29	(10	19)	795	253	215	276	162	1	398	29	6	10	40	14	74	.279	.337	.373	.710

Steven Duggar

Bats: L **Throws:** R **Pos:** CF-18;LF-14;PR-1   **Ht:** 6'1" **Wt:** 187 **Born:** 11/4/1993 **Age:** 29

			BATTING																		RUNNING			AVERAGES			
Year	Team	Lg	G	AB	H	2B	3B	HR	(Hm	Rd)	TB	R	RBI	RC	TBB	IBB	SO	HBP	SH	SF	SB	CS	GDP	Avg	OBP	Slg	OPS
2022	Scrmto	AAA	14	49	10	1	0	1	(-	-)	14	8	5	3	3	0	18	1	0	0	2	0	0	.204	.264	.286	.550
2022	RdRck	AAA	11	38	7	2	0	1	(-	-)	12	5	5	5	11	0	13	0	0	0	3	0	1	.184	.360	.316	.676
2022	Salt Lk	AAA	10	34	5	1	0	2	(-	-)	12	3	2	3	3	0	14	0	0	0	1	0	1	.147	.216	.353	.569
2018	SF	NL	41	141	36	11	1	2	(1	1)	55	20	17	19	10	1	44	0	0	1	5	1	0	.255	.303	.390	.693
2019	SF	NL	73	261	61	12	2	4	(1	3)	89	26	28	29	16	0	78	1	0	3	1	4	1	.234	.278	.341	.619
2020	SF	NL	21	34	6	2	0	0	(0	0)	8	3	3	1	1	0	11	1	0	0	0	0	1	.176	.222	.235	.458
2021	SF	NL	107	268	69	14	5	8	(5	3)	117	45	35	37	27	3	88	2	0	0	7	0	4	.257	.330	.437	.767
2022	3 Tms		29	72	11	3	1	0	(0	0)	16	7	4	2	7	0	41	0	0	1	5	1	0	.153	.225	.222	.447
22	SF	NL	12	36	7	3	0	0	(0	0)	10	2	4	2	2	0	16	0	0	1	4	0	0	.194	.231	.278	.509
22	Tex	AL	8	17	3	0	0	0	(0	0)	3	2	0	0	2	0	12	0	0	0	1	1	0	.176	.263	.176	.440
22	LAA	AL	9	19	1	0	1	0	(0	0)	3	3	0	0	3	0	13	0	0	0	0	0	0	.053	.182	.158	.340
	Postseason		3	3	0	0	0	0	(0	0)	0	0	0	0	1	0	2	0	0	0	0	0	0	.000	.250	.000	.250
	5 ML YEARS		271	776	183	42	9	14	(7	7)	285	101	87	88	61	4	262	4	0	5	19	6	6	.236	.293	.367	.660

Robert Dugger

Pitches: R **Bats:** R **Pos:** RP-3; SP-1   **Ht:** 6'0" **Wt:** 198 **Born:** 7/3/1995 **Age:** 27

			HOW MUCH PITCHED					WHAT HE GAVE UP											THE RESULTS							
Year	Team	Lg	G	GS	GF	IP	BFP	H	R	ER	HR	SH	SF	HB	TBB	IBB	SO	WP	W	L	Pct	Sv-Op	Hld	Vel	OPS	ERC	ERA
2022	Drhm	AAA	5	5	0	16.0	68	13	9	7	2	0	0	2	7	0	13	0	0	2	.000	0--	-	-	.730	3.89	3.94
2022	Lsvlle	AAA	14	7	1	50.1	215	49	28	26	5	0	3	0	26	0	39	2	2	1	.667	0--	-	-	.800	4.52	4.65
2019	Mia	NL	7	7	0	34.1	156	33	26	22	6	1	3	5	17	1	25	2	0	4	.000	0-0	0	90	.824	5.29	5.77
2020	Mia	NL	4	1	2	10.2	56	21	16	15	5	0	0	0	3	0	4	1	0	0	-	0-0	0	92	1.315	12.95	12.66
2021	Sea	AL	12	4	5	25.2	121	34	24	21	4	0	2	1	12	0	19	1	0	2	.000	0-0	0	91	.925	6.94	7.36

Year	Team	Lg	G	GS	GF	IP	BFP	H	R	ER	HR	SH	SF	HB	TBB	IBB	SO	WP	W	L	Pct	Sv-Op	Hld	Vel	OPS	ERC	ERA
2022	2 Tms		4	1	1	16.0	72	19	11	11	3	0	0	0	7	0	19	2	0	1	.000	0-0	0	90	.869	6.04	6.19
22	TB	AL	1	0	1	5.1	24	8	3	3	0	0	0	0	0	0	7	1	0	0	-	0-0	0	90	.750	4.47	5.06
22	Cin	NL	3	1	0	10.2	48	11	8	8	3	0	0	0	7	0	12	1	0	1	.000	0-0	0	90	.936	6.89	6.75
	4 ML YEARS		27	13	8	86.2	405	107	77	69	18	1	5	6	39	1	67	6	0	7	.000	0-0	0	91	.935	6.77	7.17

Joe Dunand

Bats: R Throws: R Pos: 2B-2;3B-1   Ht: 6'2" Wt: 205 Born: 9/20/1995 Age: 27

Year	Team	Lg	G	AB	H	2B	3B	HR	(Hm	Rd)	TB	R	RBI	RC	TBB	IBB	SO	HBP	SH	SF	SB	CS	GDP	Avg	OBP	Slg	OPS
2022	Jaxnvl	AAA	20	66	16	6	0	2	(-	-)	28	15	9	10	10	0	27	2	0	1	2	0	2	.242	.354	.424	.779
2022	Gwnntt	AAA	70	229	47	12	1	4	(-	-)	73	28	15	21	27	0	78	4	0	0	4	1	6	.205	.300	.319	.619
2022	Mia	NL	3	10	3	1	0	1	(0	1)	7	2	1	1	0	0	3	1	0	0	0	0	0	.300	.364	.700	1.064

Justin Dunn

Pitches: R Bats: R Pos: SP-7   Ht: 6'2" Wt: 185 Born: 9/22/1995 Age: 27

Year	Team	Lg	G	GS	GF	IP	BFP	H	R	ER	HR	SH	SF	HB	TBB	IBB	SO	WP	W	L	Pct	Sv-Op	Hld	Vel	OPS	ERC	ERA
2022	Lsvlle	AAA	8	8	0	29.0	140	31	26	20	4	0	1	5	18	0	27	0	0	3	.000	0- -	-		.834	6.30	6.21
2019	Sea	AL	4	4	0	6.2	30	2	2	2	0	0	2	0	9	0	5	0	0	0	-	0-0	0	92	.472	3.04	2.70
2020	Sea	AL	10	10	0	45.2	198	31	23	22	10	0	1	2	31	1	38	0	4	1	.800	0-0	0	91	.732	4.34	4.34
2021	Sea	AL	11	11	0	50.1	218	37	21	21	6	0	1	4	29	0	49	1	1	3	.250	0-0	0	94	.653	3.72	3.75
2022	Cin	NL	7	7	0	31.0	138	32	21	21	11	1	1	3	17	0	21	0	1	3	.250	0-0	0	92	1.009	7.52	6.10
	4 ML YEARS		32	32	0	133.2	584	102	67	66	27	1	5	9	86	1	113	1	6	7	.462	0-0	0	92	.758	4.72	4.44

Dane Dunning

Pitches: R Bats: R Pos: SP-29   Ht: 6'4" Wt: 225 Born: 12/20/1994 Age: 28

Year	Team	Lg	G	GS	GF	IP	BFP	H	R	ER	HR	SH	SF	HB	TBB	IBB	SO	WP	W	L	Pct	Sv-Op	Hld	Vel	OPS	ERC	ERA
2020	CWS	AL	7	7	0	34.0	142	25	17	15	4	0	0	2	13	0	35	5	2	0	1.000	0-0	0	92	.597	2.88	3.97
2021	Tex	AL	27	25	0	117.2	511	126	61	59	13	1	1	7	43	0	114	8	5	10	.333	0-0	0	90	.772	4.72	4.51
2022	Tex	AL	29	29	0	153.1	671	158	80	76	20	0	8	11	62	0	137	6	4	8	.333	0-0	0	90	.788	4.82	4.46
	Postseason		1	1	0	0.2	4	2	0	0	0	0	0	0	0	0	0	0	0	0	-	0-0	0	92	1.000	14.52	0.00
	3 ML YEARS		63	61	0	305.0	1324	309	158	150	37	1	9	20	118	0	286	19	11	18	.379	0-0	0	90	.761	4.55	4.43

Ezequiel Duran

Bats: R Throws: R Pos: 3B-51;2B-9;PH-2;DH-1   Ht: 5'11" Wt: 185 Born: 5/22/1999 Age: 24

Year	Team	Lg	G	AB	H	2B	3B	HR	(Hm	Rd)	TB	R	RBI	RC	TBB	IBB	SO	HBP	SH	SF	SB	CS	GDP	Avg	OBP	Slg	OPS
2018	Pulski	R+	53	219	44	8	2	4	(-	-)	68	34	20	18	9	0	65	6	0	1	7	0	4	.201	.251	.311	.562
2019	Stnlld	A-	66	246	63	12	4	13	(-	-)	122	49	37	43	25	1	77	3	0	3	11	4	1	.256	.329	.496	.824
2021	2 Tms	Low	105	416	111	22	6	19	(-	-)	202	67	79	74	40	3	130	10	0	5	19	9	7	.267	.342	.486	.827
2022	Frisco	AA	45	183	58	24	1	7	(-	-)	105	34	31	37	14	0	36	1	0	2	7	2	4	.317	.365	.574	.939
2022	RdRck	AAA	33	145	41	9	0	9	(-	-)	77	18	26	24	7	0	43	1	0	2	7	5	4	.283	.316	.531	.847
2022	Tex	AL	58	208	49	10	1	5	(4	1)	76	25	25	22	12	0	54	0	0	0	4	1	3	.236	.277	.365	.643

Jarren Duran

Bats: L Throws: R Pos: CF-51;RF-7;PH-2;DH-1   Ht: 6'2" Wt: 212 Born: 9/5/1996 Age: 26

Year	Team	Lg	G	AB	H	2B	3B	HR	(Hm	Rd)	TB	R	RBI	RC	TBB	IBB	SO	HBP	SH	SF	SB	CS	GDP	Avg	OBP	Slg	OPS
2022	Wrcstr	AAA	68	279	79	16	6	10	(-	-)	137	49	38	50	26	1	73	2	0	0	18	3	2	.283	.349	.491	.840
2021	Bos	AL	33	107	23	3	2	2	(0	2)	36	17	10	9	4	0	40	0	0	1	2	1	1	.215	.241	.336	.578
2022	Bos	AL	58	204	45	14	3	3	(1	2)	74	23	17	23	14	0	63	4	0	1	7	1	1	.221	.283	.363	.645
	2 ML YEARS		91	311	68	17	5	5	(1	4)	110	40	27	32	18	0	103	4	0	2	9	2	2	.219	.269	.354	.622

Jhoan Duran

Pitches: R Bats: R Pos: RP-57   Ht: 6'5" Wt: 230 Born: 1/8/1998 Age: 25

Year	Team	Lg	G	GS	GF	IP	BFP	H	R	ER	HR	SH	SF	HB	TBB	IBB	SO	WP	W	L	Pct	Sv-Op	Hld	Vel	OPS	ERC	ERA
2022	Min	AL	57	0	18	67.2	266	50	15	14	6	2	2	4	16	3	89	6	2	4	.333	8-8	18	101	.571	2.24	1.86

Nick Duron

Pitches: R Bats: R Pos: RP-1   Ht: 6'4" Wt: 190 Born: 1/30/1996 Age: 27

Year	Team	Lg	G	GS	GF	IP	BFP	H	R	ER	HR	SH	SF	HB	TBB	IBB	SO	WP	W	L	Pct	Sv-Op	Hld	Vel	OPS	ERC	ERA
2022	LV	AAA	52	0	32	48.2	213	45	21	15	3	2	2	2	29	6	63	4	4	7	.364	7- -	-		.714	4.16	2.77
2022	Phi	NL	1	0	0	1.0	4	2	0	0	0	0	0	0	1	0	1	0	0	0	-	0-0	0	97	1.000	9.49	0.00

Adam Duvall

Bats: R **Throws:** R **Pos:** CF-44;LF-35;RF-11;PH-2   **Ht:** 6'1" **Wt:** 215 **Born:** 9/4/1988 **Age:** 34

							BATTING													RUNNING			AVERAGES			
Year	Team	Lg	G	AB	H	2B	3B	HR	(Hm | Rd)	TB	R	RBI	RC	TBB	IBB	SO	HBP	SH	SF	SB	CS	GDP	Avg	OBP	Slg	OPS
2014	SF	NL	28	73	14	2	0	3	(2 | 1)	25	8	5	4	3	0	20	1	0	0	0	0	0	.192	.234	.342	.576
2015	Cin	NL	27	64	14	2	0	5	(3 | 2)	31	6	9	9	6	1	26	2	0	0	0	0	0	.219	.306	.484	.790
2016	Cin	NL	150	552	133	31	6	33	(16 | 17)	275	85	103	80	41	1	164	6	0	8	6	5	7	.241	.297	.498	.795
2017	Cin	NL	157	587	146	37	3	31	(12 | 19)	282	78	99	75	39	1	170	10	0	11	5	3	11	.249	.301	.480	.782
2018	2 Tms	NL	138	384	75	20	0	15	(8 | 7)	140	48	61	37	37	3	117	5	0	1	2	2	9	.195	.274	.365	.639
2019	Atl	NL	41	120	32	4	1	10	(4 | 6)	68	17	19	19	7	0	39	2	0	1	0	0	0	.267	.315	.567	.882
2020	Atl	NL	57	190	45	8	0	16	(7 | 9)	101	34	33	24	15	0	54	3	0	1	0	0	0	.237	.301	.532	.833
2021	2 Tms	NL	146	513	117	17	2	38	(16 | 22)	252	67	113	89	35	1	174	4	0	3	5	0	7	.228	.281	.491	.772
2022	Atl	NL	86	287	61	16	1	12	(6 | 6)	115	39	36	33	21	0	101	5	0	2	0	2	2	.213	.276	.401	.677
18	Cin	NL	105	331	68	19	0	15	(8 | 7)	132	40	61	37	34	3	100	4	0	1	2	2	8	.205	.286	.399	.685
18	Atl	NL	33	53	7	1	0	0	(0 | 0)	8	8	0	0	3	0	17	1	0	0	0	0	1	.132	.193	.151	.344
21	Mia	NL	91	314	72	10	1	22	(8 | 14)	150	41	68	54	21	0	105	1	0	3	5	0	4	.229	.277	.478	.755
21	Atl	NL	55	199	45	7	1	16	(8 | 8)	102	26	45	35	14	1	69	3	0	0	0	0	3	.226	.287	.513	.800
	Postseason		27	90	18	1	1	5	(3 | 2)	36	7	18	10	5	2	32	1	0	1	0	0	0	.200	.247	.400	.647
	9 ML YEARS		830	2770	637	137	13	163	(74 | 89)	1289	382	478	370	204	7	865	38	0	27	18	12	38	.230	.289	.465	.755

Nate Eaton

Bats: R **Throws:** R **Pos:** RF-20;3B-15;LF-6;PR-6;CF-5;PH-4   **Ht:** 5'11" **Wt:** 185 **Born:** 12/22/1996 **Age:** 26

							BATTING													RUNNING			AVERAGES			
Year	Team	Lg	G	AB	H	2B	3B	HR	(Hm | Rd)	TB	R	RBI	RC	TBB	IBB	SO	HBP	SH	SF	SB	CS	GDP	Avg	OBP	Slg	OPS
2022	NWArk	AA	37	140	38	4	1	4	(- | -)	56	23	19	20	11	0	29	3	2	3	12	1	1	.271	.331	.400	.731
2022	Omha	AAA	54	200	59	10	3	9	(- | -)	102	33	32	39	21	0	48	6	0	2	11	4	1	.295	.376	.510	.886
2022	KC	AL	44	106	28	4	3	1	(0 | 1)	41	16	12	11	10	0	30	2	1	3	11	1	2	.264	.331	.387	.717

Tommy Edman

Bats: B **Throws:** R **Pos:** 2B-89;SS-80;3B-8;PH-4;RF-2;PR-2;CF-1   **Ht:** 5'10" **Wt:** 180 **Born:** 5/9/1995 **Age:** 28

							BATTING													RUNNING			AVERAGES			
Year	Team	Lg	G	AB	H	2B	3B	HR	(Hm | Rd)	TB	R	RBI	RC	TBB	IBB	SO	HBP	SH	SF	SB	CS	GDP	Avg	OBP	Slg	OPS
2019	StL	NL	92	326	99	17	7	11	(4 | 7)	163	59	36	52	16	0	61	7	0	0	15	1	3	.304	.350	.500	.850
2020	StL	NL	55	204	51	7	1	5	(3 | 2)	75	29	26	26	16	0	48	5	0	2	2	4	5	.250	.317	.368	.685
2021	StL	NL	159	641	168	41	3	11	(2 | 9)	248	91	56	81	38	1	95	6	2	4	30	5	4	.262	.308	.387	.695
2022	StL	NL	153	577	153	31	4	13	(8 | 5)	231	95	57	77	46	2	111	5	1	1	32	3	10	.265	.324	.400	.725
	Postseason		13	52	12	3	1	0	(0 | 0)	17	6	3	4	3	0	11	0	0	0	2	0	1	.231	.273	.327	.600
	4 ML YEARS		459	1748	471	96	15	40	(17 | 23)	717	274	175	236	116	3	315	23	3	7	79	13	22	.269	.322	.410	.732

Carl Edwards Jr.

Pitches: R **Bats:** R **Pos:** RP-57   **Ht:** 6'3" **Wt:** 170 **Born:** 9/3/1991 **Age:** 31

			HOW MUCH PITCHED						WHAT HE GAVE UP										THE RESULTS							
Year	Team	Lg	G	GS	GF	IP	BFP	H	R	ER	HR	SH	SF	HB	TBB	IBB	SO	WP	W	L	Pct	Sv-Op	Hld	Vel	OPS	ERC	ERA
2022	Roch	AAA	13	0	8	14.1	50	3	1	1	0	1	1	0	4	0	17	0	1	0	1.000	3- -	-	-	.211	0.37	0.63
2015	ChC	NL	5	0	3	4.2	19	3	3	2	0	0	0	0	3	0	4	0	0	0	-	0-0	0	93	.566	2.50	3.86
2016	ChC	NL	36	0	10	36.0	138	15	15	15	4	0	2	0	14	1	52	5	0	1	.000	2-3	6	95	.456	1.33	3.75
2017	ChC	NL	73	0	8	66.1	262	29	22	22	6	1	1	4	38	2	94	4	5	4	.556	0-4	25	95	.503	1.99	2.98
2018	ChC	NL	58	0	2	52.0	222	36	17	15	4	2	1	0	32	1	67	4	3	2	.600	0-2	23	95	.583	2.75	2.60
2019	2 Tms	AL	22	0	4	17.0	78	12	17	16	3	0	1	1	13	0	19	4	1	1	.500	0-2	4	94	.683	4.48	8.47
2020	Sea	AL	5	0	1	4.2	17	2	1	1	0	0	0	0	1	0	6	0	0	0	-	1-1	1	93	.489	0.71	1.93
2021	2 Tms		7	0	1	5.2	31	11	7	7	3	0	1	0	3	0	6	2	0	0	-	0-1	0	94	1.303	14.71	11.12
2022	Was	NL	57	0	8	62.0	256	51	22	19	8	0	2	1	25	0	56	2	6	3	.667	2-5	13	95	.652	3.42	2.76
19	ChC	NL	20	0	3	15.1	64	8	11	10	3	0	1	1	9	0	17	2	1	1	.500	0-2	4	94	.621	3.05	5.87
19	SD	NL	2	0	1	1.2	14	4	6	6	0	0	0	0	4	0	2	2	0	0	-	0-0	0	94	.971	20.14	32.40
21	Atl	NL	1	0	0	0.1	5	3	3	3	1	0	0	0	1	0	1	1	0	0	-	0-0	0	93	2.550	136.7	81.00
21	Tor	AL	6	0	1	5.1	26	8	4	4	2	0	1	0	2	0	5	1	0	0	-	0-1	0	94	1.080	9.14	6.75
	Postseason		15	0	0	11.0	48	7	8	8	1	1	0	0	10	0	12	2	1	2	.333	0-1	5	95	.632	4.04	6.55
	8 ML YEARS		263	0	37	248.1	1023	159	104	97	26	2	7	6	129	4	304	21	15	11	.577	5-18	72	95	.591	2.72	3.52

Scott Effross

Pitches: R **Bats:** R **Pos:** RP-59; SP-1   **Ht:** 6'2" **Wt:** 202 **Born:** 12/28/1993 **Age:** 29

			HOW MUCH PITCHED						WHAT HE GAVE UP										THE RESULTS							
Year	Team	Lg	G	GS	GF	IP	BFP	H	R	ER	HR	SH	SF	HB	TBB	IBB	SO	WP	W	L	Pct	Sv-Op	Hld	Vel	OPS	ERC	ERA
2021	ChC	NL	14	0	2	14.2	58	13	6	6	2	0	2	3	1	0	18	1	2	1	.667	0-1	3	91	.716	3.33	3.68
2022	2 Tms		60	1	11	56.2	229	45	23	16	3	1	1	1	15	3	62	0	1	4	.200	4-6	16	91	.564	2.18	2.54
22	ChC	NL	47	1	6	44.0	178	36	19	13	2	1	1	0	11	3	50	0	1	4	.200	1-3	13	90	.566	2.12	2.66
22	NYY	AL	13	0	5	12.2	51	9	4	3	1	0	0	1	4	0	12	0	0	0	-	3-3	3	91	.557	2.42	2.13
	2 ML YEARS		74	1	13	71.1	287	58	29	22	5	1	3	4	16	3	80	1	3	5	.375	4-7	19	91	.594	2.41	2.78

Zach Eflin

Pitches: R Bats: R Pos: SP-13; RP-7   Ht: 6'6" Wt: 220 Born: 4/8/1994 Age: 29

		HOW MUCH PITCHED					WHAT HE GAVE UP									THE RESULTS							
Year	Team	Lg	G	GS	GF	IP	BFP	H	R	ER	HR	SH	SF	HB	TBB	IBB	SO	WP	W	L	Pct	Sv-Op	Hld	Vel	OPS	ERC	ERA
2016	Phi	NL	11	11	0	63.1	272	67	42	39	12	1	4	1	17	1	31	1	3	5	.375	0-0	0	92	.828	4.49	5.54
2017	Phi	NL	11	11	0	64.1	280	79	45	44	16	2	5	5	12	0	35	2	1	5	.167	0-0	0	93	.896	6.00	6.16
2018	Phi	NL	24	24	0	128.0	548	130	69	62	16	5	4	3	37	4	123	4	11	8	.579	0-0	0	94	.746	3.90	4.36
2019	Phi	NL	32	28	3	163.1	705	172	88	75	28	6	3	6	48	5	129	1	10	13	.435	0-0	0	94	.775	4.53	4.13
2020	Phi	NL	11	10	0	59.0	245	60	28	26	8	1	0	1	15	0	70	1	4	2	.667	0-0	0	94	.759	3.96	3.97
2021	Phi	NL	18	18	0	105.2	442	116	52	49	15	1	1	3	16	2	99	2	4	7	.364	0-0	0	93	.767	4.01	4.17
2022	Phi	NL	20	13	2	75.2	313	70	38	34	8	0	3	5	15	1	65	0	3	5	.375	1-1	0	93	.681	3.15	4.04
	7 ML YEARS		127	115	5	659.1	2805	694	362	329	103	16	20	24	160	13	552	11	36	45	.444	1-1	2	93	.773	4.24	4.49

Jerad Eickhoff

Pitches: R Bats: R Pos: SP-1   Ht: 6'4" Wt: 246 Born: 7/2/1990 Age: 32

EYE-koff

		HOW MUCH PITCHED					WHAT HE GAVE UP									THE RESULTS							
Year	Team	Lg	G	GS	GF	IP	BFP	H	R	ER	HR	SH	SF	HB	TBB	IBB	SO	WP	W	L	Pct	Sv-Op	Hld	Vel	OPS	ERC	ERA
2022	Indy	AAA	28	20	0	114.1	475	102	68	63	17	2	2	8	30	0	107	2	6	7	.462	0--	-	-	.696	3.54	4.96
2015	Phi	NL	8	8	0	51.0	203	40	16	15	5	0	1	0	13	0	49	1	3	3	.500	0-0	0	91	.621	2.40	2.65
2016	Phi	NL	33	33	0	197.1	811	187	88	80	30	6	10	8	42	2	167	6	11	14	.440	0-0	0	91	.740	3.56	3.65
2017	Phi	NL	24	24	0	128.0	576	142	74	67	16	3	9	5	53	4	118	6	4	8	.333	0-0	0	90	.794	5.00	4.71
2018	Phi	NL	3	1	1	5.1	26	10	4	4	1	0	0	0	0	0	11	0	0	1	.000	0-0	0	91	1.038	8.28	6.75
2019	Phi	NL	12	10	1	58.1	245	58	37	37	18	3	0	2	18	0	51	0	3	4	.429	1-1	0	89	.885	5.33	5.71
2021	NYM	NL	5	4	0	19.2	104	30	24	19	9	0	1	3	10	2	13	0	0	2	.000	0-0	0	90	1.136	11.11	8.69
2022	Pit	NL	1	1	0	4.1	27	10	10	10	2	0	1	3	1	0	4	0	0	1	.000	0-0	0	89	1.428	19.14	20.77
	7 ML YEARS		86	81	2	464.0	1992	477	253	232	81	12	22	21	137	8	413	13	21	33	.389	1-1	0	91	.794	4.48	4.50

Bryce Elder

Pitches: R Bats: R Pos: SP-9; RP-1   Ht: 6'2" Wt: 220 Born: 5/19/1999 Age: 24

		HOW MUCH PITCHED					WHAT HE GAVE UP									THE RESULTS							
Year	Team	Lg	G	GS	GF	IP	BFP	H	R	ER	HR	SH	SF	HB	TBB	IBB	SO	WP	W	L	Pct	Sv-Op	Hld	Vel	OPS	ERC	ERA
2022	Gwnntt	AAA	18	17	1	105.0	436	93	55	52	14	1	1	5	32	0	97	4	6	5	.545	0--	-	-	.697	3.50	4.46
2022	Atl	NL	10	9	1	54.0	227	44	19	19	4	1	2	3	23	1	47	0	2	4	.333	0-0	0	91	.643	3.19	3.17

Roenis Elias

Pitches: L Bats: L Pos: RP-7   Ht: 6'1" Wt: 205 Born: 8/1/1988 Age: 34

roh-EN-ees ehl-LEE-us

		HOW MUCH PITCHED					WHAT HE GAVE UP									THE RESULTS							
Year	Team	Lg	G	GS	GF	IP	BFP	H	R	ER	HR	SH	SF	HB	TBB	IBB	SO	WP	W	L	Pct	Sv-Op	Hld	Vel	OPS	ERC	ERA
2022	Tacom	AAA	37	9	3	65.0	278	70	39	37	8	0	4	0	19	0	55	2	3	3	.500	0--	-	-	.763	4.24	5.12
2014	Sea	AL	29	29	0	163.2	693	151	77	70	16	4	4	11	64	3	143	6	10	12	.455	0-0	0	92	.713	3.89	3.85
2015	Sea	AL	22	20	0	115.1	490	106	57	53	15	1	4	9	44	1	97	1	5	8	.385	0-0	1	92	.730	4.10	4.14
2016	Bos	AL	3	1	2	7.2	41	15	11	11	2	0	0	0	5	1	3	0	1	0	1.000	0-0	0	93	1.210	13.11	12.91
2017	Bos	AL	1	0	1	0.1	2	0	0	0	0	0	0	0	1	0	1	0	0	0	-	0-0	0	92	.500	7.00	0.00
2018	Sea	AL	23	4	13	51.0	210	46	17	15	1	0	3	1	16	1	34	3	3	1	.750	0-0	4	94	.642	2.76	2.65
2019	2 Tms		48	0	28	50.0	216	46	32	22	10	1	1	1	18	1	47	1	4	2	.667	14-17	2	94	.728	4.09	3.96
2022	Sea	AL	7	0	5	7.2	33	7	3	3	1	0	0	0	3	0	6	0	0	0	-	0-0	0	94	.670	3.69	3.52
19	Sea	AL	44	0	28	47.0	203	41	28	19	8	1	1	1	17	1	45	1	4	2	.667	14-16	1	94	.686	3.61	3.64
19	Was	NL	4	0	0	3.0	13	5	4	3	2	0	0	0	1	0	2	0	0	0	-	0-1	1	94	1.378	14.71	9.00
	7 ML YEARS		133	54	49	395.2	1685	371	197	174	45	6	12	22	151	7	331	11	22	24	.478	14-17	3	92	.722	3.97	3.96

Chris Ellis

Pitches: R Bats: L Pos: SP-2   Ht: 6'5" Wt: 205 Born: 9/22/1992 Age: 30

		HOW MUCH PITCHED					WHAT HE GAVE UP									THE RESULTS							
Year	Team	Lg	G	GS	GF	IP	BFP	H	R	ER	HR	SH	SF	HB	TBB	IBB	SO	WP	W	L	Pct	Sv-Op	Hld	Vel	OPS	ERC	ERA
2019	KC	AL	1	0	1	1.0	5	1	0	0	0	0	0	0	1	0	0	0	0	0	-	0-0	0	93	.650	5.48	0.00
2021	2 Tms	AL	7	6	1	29.1	121	21	7	7	3	0	0	2	14	0	23	3	1	0	1.000	0-0	0	94	.630	3.17	2.15
2022	Bal	AL	2	2	0	4.1	25	5	5	5	0	0	0	1	6	0	2	0	0	0	-	0-0	0	94	.758	8.92	10.38
21	TB	AL	1	0	1	4.0	16	3	0	0	0	0	0	0	1	0	7	1	1	0	1.000	0-0	0	94	.517	1.65	0.00
21	Bal	AL	6	6	0	25.1	105	18	7	7	3	0	0	2	13	0	16	2	0	0	-	0-0	0	94	.648	3.44	2.49
	3 ML YEARS		10	8	2	34.2	151	27	12	12	3	0	0	3	21	0	25	3	1	0	1.000	0-0	0	94	.653	3.91	3.12

Drew Ellis

Bats: R Throws: R Pos: 3B-7   Ht: 6'3" Wt: 205 Born: 12/1/1995 Age: 27

			BATTING																RUNNING			AVERAGES			
Year	Team	Lg	G	AB	H	2B	3B	HR	(Hm Rd)	TB	R	RBI	RC	TBB	IBB	SO	HBP	SH	SF	SB	CS	GDP	Avg	OBP	Slg	OPS
2022	Reno	AAA	42	143	31	12	1	4	(- -)	57	27	27	21	33	0	38	2	0	1	2	0	6	.217	.369	.399	.767
2022	Tacom	AAA	70	242	56	15	1	15	(- -)	118	34	39	45	41	1	79	3	0	3	4	3	5	.231	.346	.488	.834
2021	Ari	NL	28	69	9	2	0	1	(1 0)	14	10	5	5	10	1	27	4	0	0	0	0	1	.130	.277	.203	.480
2022	2 Tms		7	16	3	1	0	0	(0 0)	4	2	1	1	1	0	7	0	0	0	0	0	0	.188	.235	.250	.485
22	Ari	NL	6	13	2	1	0	0	(0 0)	3	2	1	1	1	0	6	0	0	0	0	0	0	.154	.214	.231	.445
22	Sea	AL	1	3	1	0	0	0	(0 0)	1	0	0	0	0	0	1	0	0	0	0	0	0	.333	.333	.333	.667
	2 ML YEARS		35	85	12	3	0	1	(1 0)	18	12	6	6	11	1	34	4	0	0	0	0	1	.141	.270	.212	.482

Jerar Encarnacion

Bats: R **Throws:** R **Pos:** LF-10;RF-10;DH-2;PR-1   **Ht:** 6'4" **Wt:** 250 **Born:** 10/22/1997 **Age:** 25

								BATTING											RUNNING			AVERAGES			
Year	Team	Lg	G	AB	H	2B	3B	HR	(Hm | Rd)	TB	R	RBI	RC	TBB	IBB	SO	HBP	SH	SF	SB	CS	GDP	Avg	OBP	Slg	OPS
2022	Pnscla	AA	31	120	43	3	0	8	(- | -)	70	26	18	30	13	0	35	2	0	1	4	2	1	.358	.426	.583	1.010
2022	Jaxnvl	AAA	68	264	70	12	0	14	(- | -)	124	43	40	45	29	1	87	0	0	4	1	1	4	.265	.333	.470	.803
2022	Mia	NL	23	77	14	3	0	3	(0 | 3)	26	7	14	7	3	0	32	0	0	1	2	0	3	.182	.210	.338	.548

Adam Engel

Bats: R **Throws:** R **Pos:** CF-57;RF-55;PR-17;PH-8;LF-3;DH-2   **Ht:** 6'2" **Wt:** 215 **Born:** 12/9/1991 **Age:** 31

								BATTING											RUNNING			AVERAGES			
Year	Team	Lg	G	AB	H	2B	3B	HR	(Hm | Rd)	TB	R	RBI	RC	TBB	IBB	SO	HBP	SH	SF	SB	CS	GDP	Avg	OBP	Slg	OPS
2017	CWS	AL	97	301	50	11	3	6	(4 | 2)	85	34	21	16	19	0	117	8	8	0	8	1	1	.166	.235	.282	.517
2018	CWS	AL	143	429	101	17	4	6	(4 | 2)	144	49	29	31	18	0	129	8	7	1	16	8	1	.235	.279	.336	.614
2019	CWS	AL	89	227	55	10	2	6	(3 | 3)	87	26	26	26	14	0	78	6	1	0	3	3	5	.242	.304	.383	.687
2020	CWS	AL	36	88	26	5	1	3	(2 | 1)	42	11	12	14	3	0	19	2	0	0	1	0	1	.295	.333	.477	.811
2021	CWS	AL	39	123	31	9	0	7	(3 | 4)	61	21	18	21	11	0	31	5	0	1	7	1	4	.252	.336	.496	.832
2022	CWS	AL	119	245	55	13	1	2	(1 | 1)	76	32	17	20	11	1	76	4	0	0	12	4	2	.224	.269	.310	.579
	Postseason		7	19	3	1	0	1	(0 | 1)	7	1	1	0	0	0	6	0	0	0	0	0	0	.158	.158	.368	.526
	6 ML YEARS		523	1413	318	65	11	30	(17 | 13)	495	173	123	128	76	1	450	33	16	2	47	17	14	.225	.280	.350	.631

Nathan Eovaldi

Pitches: R **Bats:** R **Pos:** SP-20   ee-VAUL-dee   **Ht:** 6'2" **Wt:** 217 **Born:** 2/13/1990 **Age:** 33

			HOW MUCH PITCHED					WHAT HE GAVE UP										THE RESULTS							
Year	Team	Lg	G	GS	GF	IP	BFP	H	R	ER	HR	SH	SF	HB	TBB	IBB	SO	WP	W	L	Pct	Sv-Op	Hld	Vel	OPS	ERC	ERA
2011	LAD	NL	10	6	1	34.2	146	28	14	14	2	2	0	2	20	0	23	0	1	2	.333	0-0	1	94	.667	3.75	3.63
2012	2 Tms	NL	22	22	0	119.1	526	133	59	57	10	1	6	3	47	3	78	1	4	13	.235	0-0	0	94	.771	4.67	4.30
2013	Mia	NL	18	18	0	106.1	451	100	44	40	7	6	1	1	40	3	78	3	4	6	.400	0-0	0	96	.681	3.41	3.39
2014	Mia	NL	33	33	0	199.2	854	223	107	97	14	9	5	7	43	5	142	6	6	14	.300	0-0	0	96	.732	3.89	4.37
2015	NYY	AL	27	27	0	154.1	673	175	72	72	10	3	3	3	49	0	121	8	14	3	.824	0-0	0	97	.716	4.34	4.20
2016	NYY	AL	24	21	2	124.2	525	123	66	66	23	1	1	1	40	2	97	5	9	8	.529	0-0	0	97	.778	4.30	4.76
2018	2 Tms	AL	22	21	0	111.0	455	105	55	47	14	1	4	3	20	1	101	4	6	7	.462	0-0	0	97	.685	3.18	3.81
2019	Bos	AL	23	12	2	67.2	302	72	46	45	16	1	2	3	35	0	70	6	2	1	.667	0-1	4	98	.875	6.26	5.99
2020	Bos	AL	9	9	0	48.1	199	51	20	20	8	1	0	4	7	0	52	2	4	2	.667	0-0	0	97	.789	4.24	3.72
2021	Bos	AL	32	32	0	182.1	764	182	81	76	15	1	2	7	35	2	195	6	11	9	.550	0-0	0	97	.696	3.24	3.75
2022	Bos	AL	20	20	0	109.1	460	115	55	47	21	2	1	2	20	0	103	2	6	3	.667	0-0	0	96	.754	4.10	3.87
12	LAD	NL	10	10	0	56.1	241	63	27	26	5	0	3	0	20	2	34	1	1	6	.143	0-0	0	94	.771	4.54	4.15
12	Mia	NL	12	12	0	63.0	285	70	32	31	5	1	3	3	27	1	44	0	3	7	.300	0-0	0	94	.770	4.79	4.43
18	TB	AL	10	10	0	57.0	224	48	27	27	11	0	2	1	8	1	53	1	3	4	.429	0-0	0	97	.682	2.85	4.26
18	Bos	AL	12	11	0	54.0	231	57	28	20	3	1	2	2	12	0	48	3	3	3	.500	0-0	0	97	.687	3.48	3.33
	Postseason		11	6	1	43.0	172	34	16	15	3	1	0	0	8	2	41	0	4	3	.571	0-0	2	98	.546	1.93	3.14
	11 ML YEARS		240	221	5	1257.2	5355	1307	619	581	140	28	26	35	356	16	1060	43	67	68	.496	0-1	5	96	.735	4.01	4.16

Robbie Erlin

Pitches: L **Bats:** R **Pos:** RP-2   **Ht:** 5'11" **Wt:** 200 **Born:** 10/8/1990 **Age:** 32

			HOW MUCH PITCHED					WHAT HE GAVE UP										THE RESULTS							
Year	Team	Lg	G	GS	GF	IP	BFP	H	R	ER	HR	SH	SF	HB	TBB	IBB	SO	WP	W	L	Pct	Sv-Op	Hld	Vel	OPS	ERC	ERA
2022	OkCity	AAA	21	14	2	77.0	362	95	63	60	14	0	3	3	35	0	69	3	5	4	.556	0--	-	-	.881	6.38	7.01
2013	SD	NL	11	9	2	54.2	227	53	26	25	6	3	1	0	15	0	40	3	3	3	.500	0-0	0	90	.698	3.50	4.12
2014	SD	NL	13	11	1	61.1	264	71	34	34	6	2	4	1	15	1	46	4	4	5	.444	0-0	0	90	.787	4.39	4.99
2015	SD	NL	3	3	0	17.0	65	16	9	9	1	0	0	1	2	0	10	1	1	2	.333	0-0	0	88	.663	2.84	4.76
2016	SD	NL	3	2	0	15.2	58	12	7	7	3	0	0	1	3	0	13	2	1	2	.333	0-0	0	88	.750	2.77	4.02
2018	SD	NL	39	12	8	109.0	439	112	57	51	12	3	5	0	12	0	88	2	4	7	.364	0-0	1	90	.695	3.20	4.21
2019	SD	NL	37	1	10	55.1	251	72	36	33	6	1	3	1	15	0	52	3	0	1	.000	0-1	5	91	.789	5.37	5.37
2020	2 Tms	NL	9	5	1	26.2	122	33	24	24	8	0	1	2	7	1	25	1	0	0	-	0-0	0	89	.987	6.51	8.10
2022	LAD	NL	2	0	2	2.0	9	2	2	2	1	0	0	0	1	0	1	0	0	0	-	0-0	0	89	1.083	7.30	9.00
20	Pit	NL	2	0	1	3.1	17	5	2	2	0	0	0	1	1	1	4	0	0	0	-	0-0	0	89	1.012	6.27	5.40
20	Atl	NL	7	5	0	23.1	105	28	22	22	8	0	1	1	6	0	21	1	0	0	-	0-0	0	89	.983	6.48	8.49
	8 ML YEARS		117	43	24	341.2	1435	371	195	185	43	9	14	5	70	2	275	16	13	20	.394	0-1	6	90	.756	4.03	4.87

Alcides Escobar

Bats: R **Throws:** R **Pos:** SS-37;PR-4;2B-2   al-SEE-dess   **Ht:** 6'1" **Wt:** 205 **Born:** 12/16/1986 **Age:** 36

								BATTING											RUNNING			AVERAGES			
Year	Team	Lg	G	AB	H	2B	3B	HR	(Hm	Rd)	TB	R	RBI	RC	TBB	IBB	SO	HBP	SH	SF	SB	CS	GDP	Avg	OBP	Slg	OPS
2008	Mil	NL	9	4	2	0	0	0	(0	0)	2	2	0	0	0	0	1	0	0	0	0	0	0	.500	.500	.500	1.000
2009	Mil	NL	38	125	38	3	1	1	(0	1)	46	20	11	16	4	0	18	2	2	1	4	2	0	.304	.333	.368	.701
2010	Mil	NL	145	506	119	14	10	4	(3	1)	165	57	41	51	36	7	70	3	4	3	10	4	8	.235	.288	.326	.614
2011	KC	AL	158	548	139	21	8	4	(0	4)	188	69	46	46	25	1	73	4	18	3	26	9	10	.254	.290	.343	.633
2012	KC	AL	155	605	177	30	7	5	(5	0)	236	68	52	72	27	2	100	2	9	5	35	5	14	.293	.331	.390	.721
2013	KC	AL	158	607	142	20	4	4	(1	3)	182	57	52	51	19	1	84	3	9	4	22	0	12	.234	.259	.300	.559
2014	KC	AL	162	579	165	34	5	3	(2	1)	218	74	50	68	23	1	83	6	8	4	31	6	12	.285	.317	.377	.694
2015	KC	AL	148	612	157	20	5	3	(0	3)	196	76	47	60	26	1	75	8	11	5	17	5	10	.257	.293	.320	.614
2016	KC	AL	162	637	166	24	6	7	(5	2)	223	57	55	66	27	2	96	3	10	5	17	4	16	.261	.292	.350	.642
2017	KC	AL	162	599	150	36	5	6	(2	4)	214	71	54	58	15	1	102	4	7	4	4	7	14	.250	.272	.357	.629
2018	KC	AL	140	485	112	22	3	4	(2	2)	152	54	34	40	29	1	74	5	8	4	8	2	14	.231	.279	.313	.593

Year	Team	Lg	G	AB	H	2B	3B	HR	(Hm	Rd)	TB	R	RBI	RC	TBB	IBB	SO	HBP	SH	SF	SB	CS	GDP	Avg	OBP	Slg	OPS
2021	Was	NL	75	319	92	21	2	4	(3	1)	129	53	28	49	17	0	56	9	2	2	3	0	2	.288	.340	.404	.744
2022	Was	NL	42	124	27	4	2	0	(0	0)	35	12	8	11	5	0	32	2	0	0	1	1	1	.218	.260	.282	.542
	Postseason		31	135	42	9	3	2	(1	1)	63	21	14	24	1	0	21	3	6	2	2	1	2	.311	.326	.467	.793
13 ML YEARS			1554	5750	1486	249	58	45	(23	22)	1986	670	478	588	253	17	864	57	87	35	178	45	113	.258	.295	.345	.640

Eduardo Escobar

Bats: B Throws: R Pos: 3B-130;DH-6;PH-3;2B-2;PR-1   Ht: 5'10" Wt: 193 Born: 1/5/1989 Age: 34

Year	Team	Lg	G	AB	H	2B	3B	HR	(Hm	Rd)	TB	R	RBI	RC	TBB	IBB	SO	HBP	SH	SF	SB	CS	GDP	Avg	OBP	Slg	OPS
2011	CWS	AL	9	7	2	0	0	0	(0	0)	2	0	0	1	0	0	1	0	0	0	0	0	0	.286	.286	.286	.571
2012	2 Tms	AL	50	131	28	4	1	0	(0	0)	34	18	9	12	11	0	31	1	2	1	3	0	0	.214	.278	.260	.537
2013	Min	AL	66	165	39	5	2	3	(2	1)	57	23	10	14	11	0	34	0	2	1	0	2	0	.236	.282	.345	.628
2014	Min	AL	133	433	119	35	2	6	(2	4)	176	52	37	53	24	1	93	2	4	2	1	1	6	.275	.315	.406	.721
2015	Min	AL	127	409	107	31	4	12	(2	10)	182	48	58	55	28	1	86	2	2	5	2	3	7	.262	.309	.445	.754
2016	Min	AL	105	352	83	14	2	6	(3	3)	119	32	37	38	21	1	72	1	2	1	1	3	7	.236	.280	.338	.618
2017	Min	AL	129	457	116	16	5	21	(12	9)	205	62	73	72	33	3	98	5	1	3	5	1	5	.254	.309	.449	.758
2018	2 Tms		151	566	154	48	3	23	(9	14)	277	75	84	93	52	8	126	5	0	8	2	4	12	.272	.334	.489	.824
2019	Ari	NL	158	636	171	29	10	35	(18	17)	325	94	118	108	50	3	130	3	0	10	5	1	8	.269	.320	.511	.831
2020	Ari	NL	54	203	43	7	3	4	(3	1)	68	22	20	19	15	4	41	2	0	2	1	0	5	.212	.270	.335	.605
2021	2 Tms	NL	146	549	139	26	5	28	(15	13)	259	77	90	89	48	1	124	1	0	1	1	0	3	.253	.314	.472	.786
2022	NYM	NL	136	495	119	26	4	20	(11	9)	213	58	69	63	40	3	129	1	0	6	0	2	4	.240	.295	.430	.726
12	CWS	AL	36	87	18	4	1	0	(0	0)	24	14	3	7	9	0	23	0	1	0	2	0	0	.207	.281	.276	.557
12	Min	AL	14	44	10	0	0	0	(0	0)	10	4	6	5	2	0	8	1	1	1	1	0	0	.227	.271	.227	.498
18	Min	AL	97	368	101	37	3	15	(7	8)	189	45	63	70	34	6	91	3	0	3	1	3	7	.274	.338	.514	.852
18	Ari	NL	54	198	53	11	0	8	(2	6)	88	30	21	23	18	2	35	2	0	5	1	1	5	.268	.327	.444	.772
21	Ari	NL	98	370	91	14	3	22	(12	10)	177	50	65	60	29	1	85	0	0	1	1	0	1	.246	.300	.478	.778
21	Mil	NL	48	179	48	12	2	6	(3	3)	82	27	25	29	19	0	39	1	0	0	0	0	2	.268	.342	.458	.800
	Postseason		5	14	5	1	0	0	(0	0)	6	0	0	0	0	0	5	0	0	0	0	0	0	.357	.357	.429	.786
12 ML YEARS			1264	4403	1120	241	41	158	(77	81)	1917	561	605	617	333	25	965	23	13	40	21	17	57	.254	.308	.435	.743

Raynel Espinal

Pitches: R Bats: R Pos: RP-2   Ht: 6'3" Wt: 215 Born: 10/6/1991 Age: 31

Year	Team	Lg	G	GS	GF	IP	BFP	H	R	ER	HR	SH	SF	HB	TBB	IBB	SO	WP	W	L	Pct	Sv-Op	Hld	Vel	OPS	ERC	ERA
2022	Scrmto	AAA	19	18	0	83.1	370	87	51	49	16	1	1	5	38	1	102	3	5	5	.500	0- -	-		.857	5.50	5.29
2022	Lsvlle	AAA	6	3	0	19.2	83	17	10	10	3	0	0	5	7	0	22	2	0	1	.000	0- -	-		.800	4.72	4.58
2021	Bos	AL	1	0	1	2.0	8	2	2	2	0	0	0	0	1	0	0	0	0	0	-	0-0	0	93	.804	4.15	9.00
2022	Cin	NL	2	0	0	4.2	21	6	4	4	1	1	0	0	1	0	5	0	0	1	.000	0-0	0	93	.982	5.68	7.71
2 ML YEARS			3	0	1	6.2	29	8	6	6	1	1	0	0	2	0	5	0	0	1	.000	0-0	0	93	.934	5.26	8.10

Santiago Espinal

Bats: R Throws: R Pos: 2B-120;PH-14;3B-11;SS-11   Ht: 5'10" Wt: 187 Born: 11/13/1994 Age: 28

Year	Team	Lg	G	AB	H	2B	3B	HR	(Hm	Rd)	TB	R	RBI	RC	TBB	IBB	SO	HBP	SH	SF	SB	CS	GDP	Avg	OBP	Slg	OPS
2020	Tor	AL	27	60	16	4	0	0	(0	0)	20	10	6	6	4	0	16	0	1	1	0	0	1	.267	.308	.333	.641
2021	Tor	AL	92	222	69	13	1	2	(2	0)	90	32	17	29	22	0	30	1	1	0	6	1	4	.311	.376	.405	.781
2022	Tor	AL	135	449	120	25	0	7	(3	4)	166	51	51	43	36	1	68	2	1	3	6	6	12	.267	.322	.370	.692
3 ML YEARS			254	731	205	42	1	9	(5	4)	276	93	74	78	62	1	114	3	3	4	13	7	17	.280	.338	.378	.715

Daniel Espino

Pitches: R Bats: R Pos: P   Ht: 6'2" Wt: 225 Born: 1/5/2001 Age: 22

Year	Team	Lg	G	GS	GF	IP	BFP	H	R	ER	HR	SH	SF	HB	TBB	IBB	SO	WP	W	L	Pct	Sv-Op	Hld	Vel	OPS	ERC	ERA
2019	2 Tms	Low	9	9	0	23.2	98	16	11	10	2	2	0	1	10	0	34	3	0	3	.000	0- -	-		.333	2.47	3.80
2021	2 Tms	Low	20	20	0	91.2	375	64	40	38	9	0	0	1	39	0	152	10	3	8	.273	0- -	-		.260	2.60	3.73

Paolo Espino

Pitches: R Bats: R Pos: RP-23; SP-19   Ht: 5'10" Wt: 211 Born: 1/10/1987 Age: 36

Year	Team	Lg	G	GS	GF	IP	BFP	H	R	ER	HR	SH	SF	HB	TBB	IBB	SO	WP	W	L	Pct	Sv-Op	Hld	Vel	OPS	ERC	ERA
2017	2 Tms		12	2	7	24.0	109	23	17	16	7	1	0	3	10	0	20	0	0	0	-	0-0	1	89	.870	5.64	6.00
2020	Was	NL	2	1	1	6.0	27	8	3	3	1	0	0	0	2	0	7	0	0	0	-	0-0	0	90	.850	6.38	4.50
2021	Was	NL	35	19	11	109.2	455	108	53	52	19	4	3	1	25	2	92	1	5	5	.500	1-1	0	89	.757	3.80	4.27
2022	Was	NL	42	19	18	113.1	487	131	64	61	24	0	5	2	24	0	92	1	0	9	.000	0-0	0	89	.816	5.06	4.84
17	Mil	NL	6	2	3	17.2	82	17	13	12	5	1	0	3	8	0	13	0	0	0	-	0-0	0	88	.860	5.94	6.11
17	Tex	AL	6	0	4	6.1	27	6	4	4	2	0	0	0	2	0	7	0	0	0	-	0-0	1	90	.896	4.79	5.68
4 ML YEARS			91	41	37	253.0	1078	270	137	132	51	5	8	6	61	2	211	2	5	14	.263	1-1	1	89	.797	4.58	4.70

Anderson Espinoza

Pitches: R **Bats:** R **Pos:** RP-7   **Ht:** 6'0" **Wt:** 190 **Born:** 3/9/1998 **Age:** 25

		HOW MUCH PITCHED					WHAT HE GAVE UP												THE RESULTS							
Year	Team	Lg	G	GS	GF	IP	BFP	H	R	ER	HR	SH	SF	HB	TBB	IBB	SO	WP	W	L	Pct	Sv-Op	Hld	Vel	OPS	ERC	ERA
2022	Tenn	AA	13	12	0	44.1	194	40	37	35	10	0	0	5	25	0	54	5	1	4	.200	0- -	-	-	.872	5.73	7.11
2022	Iowa	AAA	8	6	1	26.0	123	32	25	24	7	0	1	1	19	0	24	1	1	5	.167	1- -	-	-	1.031	8.81	8.31
2022	ChC	NL	7	0	2	18.1	85	14	11	11	4	0	0	4	16	0	19	1	0	2	.000	0-0	0	94	.831	6.63	5.40

Carlos Estevez

Pitches: R **Bats:** R **Pos:** RP-62   **Ht:** 6'6" **Wt:** 277 **Born:** 12/28/1992 **Age:** 30

		HOW MUCH PITCHED					WHAT HE GAVE UP												THE RESULTS							
Year	Team	Lg	G	GS	GF	IP	BFP	H	R	ER	HR	SH	SF	HB	TBB	IBB	SO	WP	W	L	Pct	Sv-Op	Hld	Vel	OPS	ERC	ERA
2016	Col	NL	63	0	26	55.0	246	50	32	32	6	1	4	5	28	4	59	3	3	7	.300	11-18	11	97	.728	4.23	5.24
2017	Col	NL	35	0	9	32.1	149	39	21	20	3	1	0	1	14	2	31	1	5	0	1.000	0-0	6	97	.778	5.31	5.57
2019	Col	NL	71	0	13	72.0	308	70	34	30	12	1	3	1	23	1	81	1	2	2	.500	0-2	11	98	.756	4.03	3.75
2020	Col	NL	26	0	6	24.0	116	33	21	20	6	0	0	3	9	0	27	2	1	3	.250	1-4	6	97	1.003	7.91	7.50
2021	Col	NL	64	0	22	61.2	270	71	32	30	8	1	4	2	21	0	60	5	3	5	.375	11-17	15	97	.804	5.12	4.38
2022	Col	NL	62	0	20	57.0	235	44	27	22	7	0	2	1	23	1	54	6	4	4	.500	2-6	13	98	.663	3.06	3.47
	Postseason		1	0	0	0.1	2	1	1	1	0	0	0	0	0	0	1	0	0	0	-	0-0	0	99	1.000	14.52	27.00
	6 ML YEARS		321	0	96	302.0	1324	307	167	154	42	4	13	13	118	8	312	18	18	21	.462	25-47	62	97	.769	4.51	4.59

Jeremiah Estrada

Pitches: R **Bats:** B **Pos:** RP-5   **Ht:** 6'1" **Wt:** 185 **Born:** 11/1/1998 **Age:** 24

		HOW MUCH PITCHED					WHAT HE GAVE UP												THE RESULTS							
Year	Team	Lg	G	GS	GF	IP	BFP	H	R	ER	HR	SH	SF	HB	TBB	IBB	SO	WP	W	L	Pct	Sv-Op	Hld	Vel	OPS	ERC	ERA
2022	Tenn	AA	13	0	7	19.1	77	11	5	4	0	0	1	1	9	1	27	3	1	0	1.000	2- -	-	-	.470	1.65	1.86
2022	Sbend	A+	15	0	13	23.0	91	14	6	3	1	0	0	1	10	1	39	1	2	2	.500	5- -	-	-		1.99	1.17
2022	Iowa	AAA	6	0	3	6.0	25	6	0	0	0	0	0	0	1	0	12	1	0	0	-	2- -	-	-	.530	2.49	0.00
2022	ChC	NL	5	0	3	5.2	25	6	2	2	1	0	1	0	3	0	8	1	0	0	-	0-0	0	97	.931	5.63	3.18

Thairo Estrada

Bats: R **Throws:** R **Pos:** 2B-102;SS-37;LF-18;PH-7;3B-3;PR-3;CF-1   **Ht:** 5'10" **Wt:** 185 **Born:** 2/22/1996 **Age:** 27

			BATTING																		RUNNING			AVERAGES			
Year	Team	Lg	G	AB	H	2B	3B	HR	(Hm	Rd)	TB	R	RBI	RC	TBB	IBB	SO	HBP	SH	SF	SB	CS	GDP	Avg	OBP	Slg	OPS
2019	NYY	AL	35	64	16	3	0	3	(1	2)	28	12	12	12	3	0	15	1	1	0	4	0	1	.250	.294	.438	.732
2020	NYY	AL	26	48	8	0	0	1	(1	0)	11	8	3	1	1	0	19	3	0	0	1	0	0	.167	.231	.229	.460
2021	SF	NL	52	121	33	4	0	7	(3	4)	58	19	22	20	9	1	23	2	0	2	1	0	2	.273	.333	.479	.813
2022	SF	NL	140	488	127	22	2	14	(6	8)	195	71	62	63	33	0	89	14	1	5	21	6	10	.260	.322	.400	.722
	4 ML YEARS		253	721	184	29	2	25	(11	14)	292	110	99	96	46	1	146	20	2	5	27	6	13	.255	.316	.405	.721

Alex Faedo

Pitches: R **Bats:** R **Pos:** SP-12   **Ht:** 6'5" **Wt:** 225 **Born:** 11/12/1995 **Age:** 27

		HOW MUCH PITCHED					WHAT HE GAVE UP												THE RESULTS							
Year	Team	Lg	G	GS	GF	IP	BFP	H	R	ER	HR	SH	SF	HB	TBB	IBB	SO	WP	W	L	Pct	Sv-Op	Hld	Vel	OPS	ERC	ERA
2022	Det	AL	12	12	0	53.2	244	63	34	33	7	0	3	1	25	0	44	2	1	5	.167	0-0	0	93	.830	5.68	5.53

Pete Fairbanks

Pitches: R **Bats:** R **Pos:** RP-24   **Ht:** 6'6" **Wt:** 225 **Born:** 12/16/1993 **Age:** 29

		HOW MUCH PITCHED					WHAT HE GAVE UP												THE RESULTS							
Year	Team	Lg	G	GS	GF	IP	BFP	H	R	ER	HR	SH	SF	HB	TBB	IBB	SO	WP	W	L	Pct	Sv-Op	Hld	Vel	OPS	ERC	ERA
2022	Drham	AAA	6	0	0	4.2	25	5	5	2	1	0	0	0	3	0	7	1	0	1	.000	0- -	-	-	.729	5.43	3.86
2019	2 Tms	AL	21	0	3	21.0	99	25	20	16	5	0	0	0	10	0	28	2	2	3	.400	2-2	3	97	.882	6.37	6.86
2020	TB	AL	27	2	2	26.2	117	23	9	8	2	0	0	2	14	0	39	6	6	3	.667	0-2	7	97	.640	3.89	2.70
2021	TB	AL	47	0	17	42.2	189	40	22	17	2	0	1	1	21	1	56	3	3	6	.333	5-7	14	97	.659	3.68	3.59
2022	TB	AL	24	0	10	24.0	87	13	3	3	1	0	1	0	3	0	38	0	0	0	-	8-8	6	99	.393	0.96	1.13
19	Tex	AL	8	0	0	8.2	41	8	10	9	4	0	0	0	7	0	15	1	0	2	.000	0-0	0	97	.954	8.04	9.35
19	TB	AL	13	0	3	12.1	58	17	10	7	1	0	0	0	3	0	13	1	2	1	.667	2-2	3	98	.836	5.26	5.11
	Postseason		11	0	3	15.0	63	13	6	6	4	0	0	0	7	1	19	3	0	0	-	3-3	3	99	.817	4.71	3.60
	4 ML YEARS		119	2	32	114.1	492	101	54	44	10	0	2	3	48	1	161	11	11	12	.478	15-19	30	98	.652	3.46	3.46

Stuart Fairchild

Bats: R **Throws:** R **Pos:** LF-22;CF-20;PR-5;RF-4;PH-4   **Ht:** 6'0" **Wt:** 205 **Born:** 3/17/1996 **Age:** 27

			BATTING																		RUNNING			AVERAGES			
Year	Team	Lg	G	AB	H	2B	3B	HR	(Hm	Rd)	TB	R	RBI	RC	TBB	IBB	SO	HBP	SH	SF	SB	CS	GDP	Avg	OBP	Slg	OPS
2022	Reno	AAA	10	37	6	2	0	2	(-	-)	14	3	3	3	4	1	15	2	0	1	0	1	1	.162	.279	.378	.657
2022	Lsvlle	AAA	34	121	33	6	1	7	(-	-)	62	23	16	23	10	0	34	3	0	2	5	1	1	.273	.338	.512	.851
2021	Ari	NL	12	15	2	1	0	0	(0	0)	3	3	2	1	0	0	3	1	0	0	0	0	1	.133	.235	.200	.435
2022	3 Tms		46	97	24	4	1	5	(1	4)	45	14	6	13	8	0	34	5	0	0	0	2	1	.247	.336	.464	.800
22	Sea	AL	3	3	0	0	0	0	(0	0)	0	0	0	0	0	0	2	0	0	0	0	0	0	.000	.000	.000	.000
22	SF	NL	5	8	0	0	0	0	(0	0)	0	1	0	0	0	0	3	0	0	0	0	0	0	.000	.000	.000	.000
22	Cin	NL	38	86	24	4	1	5	(1	4)	45	13	6	13	8	0	29	5	0	0	0	2	1	.279	.374	.523	.897
	2 ML YEARS		58	112	26	5	1	5	(1	4)	48	17	8	14	9	0	37	6	0	0	0	2	2	.232	.323	.429	.751

Bailey Falter

Pitches: L Bats: R Pos: SP-16; RP-4   Ht: 6'4" Wt: 175 Born: 4/24/1997 Age: 26

			HOW MUCH PITCHED				WHAT HE GAVE UP											THE RESULTS						
Year	Team	Lg	G	GS	GF	IP	BFP	H	R	ER	HR	SH	SF	HB	TBB	IBB	SO	WP	W	L	Pct	Sv-Op	Hld	Vel	OPS	ERC	ERA
2022	LV	AAA	9	9	0	47.0	170	25	10	10	4	2	1	2	6	0	49	0	4	1	.800	0- -	-	-	.479	1.18	1.91
2021	Phi	NL	22	1	6	33.2	139	34	21	21	5	0	1	2	6	0	34	2	2	1	.667	0-0	2	92	.725	3.86	5.61
2022	Phi	NL	20	16	3	84.0	349	85	39	36	16	0	3	6	17	0	74	2	6	4	.600	0-0	0	91	.786	4.31	3.86
	2 ML YEARS		42	17	9	117.2	488	119	60	57	21	0	4	8	23	0	108	4	8	5	.615	0-0	2	91	.769	4.18	4.36

Jeurys Familia

Pitches: R Bats: R Pos: RP-48   jer-ISS fa-MEAL-ya   Ht: 6'3" Wt: 240 Born: 10/10/1989 Age: 33

			HOW MUCH PITCHED				WHAT HE GAVE UP											THE RESULTS						
Year	Team	Lg	G	GS	GF	IP	BFP	H	R	ER	HR	SH	SF	HB	TBB	IBB	SO	WP	W	L	Pct	Sv-Op	Hld	Vel	OPS	ERC	ERA
2012	NYM	NL	8	1	4	12.1	52	10	8	8	0	0	0	0	9	0	10	0	0	0	-	0-0	0	96	.644	3.76	5.84
2013	NYM	NL	9	0	3	10.2	52	12	5	5	2	2	0	0	9	1	8	3	0	0	-	1-1	0	95	.908	7.20	4.22
2014	NYM	NL	76	0	16	77.1	322	59	26	19	3	4	2	2	32	5	73	9	2	5	.286	5-10	23	96	.587	2.45	2.21
2015	NYM	NL	76	0	65	78.0	308	59	16	16	6	1	1	2	19	1	86	4	2	2	.500	43-48	1	97	.569	2.19	1.85
2016	NYM	NL	78	0	67	77.2	321	63	25	22	1	2	1	1	31	6	84	3	3	4	.429	51-56	0	96	.574	2.44	2.55
2017	NYM	NL	26	0	15	24.2	111	21	14	12	1	2	2	1	15	3	25	1	2	2	.500	6-7	2	96	.636	3.48	4.38
2018	2 Tms		70	0	36	72.0	302	60	26	25	3	0	1	2	28	1	83	2	8	6	.571	18-24	7	96	.601	2.81	3.13
2019	NYM	NL	66	0	14	60.0	274	62	39	38	7	2	1	3	42	4	63	3	4	2	.667	0-4	14	96	.831	5.84	5.70
2020	NYM	NL	25	0	4	26.2	120	20	11	11	2	0	0	3	19	2	23	1	2	0	1.000	0-1	5	97	.687	3.98	3.71
2021	NYM	NL	65	0	16	59.1	262	57	31	26	10	2	0	2	27	2	72	4	9	4	.692	1-7	11	97	.767	4.58	3.94
2022	2 Tms		48	0	8	44.1	204	58	34	30	7	0	0	2	22	2	41	1	2	3	.400	0-3	7	95	.908	7.13	6.09
18	NYM	NL	40	0	29	40.2	171	36	13	13	1	0	1	2	14	1	43	1	4	4	.500	17-21	1	96	.616	2.88	2.88
18	Oak	AL	30	0	7	31.1	131	24	13	12	2	0	0	0	14	0	40	1	4	2	.667	1-3	6	97	.581	2.73	3.45
22	Phi	NL	38	0	5	34.0	158	48	26	23	6	0	0	1	15	1	33	1	1	1	.500	0-2	5	95	.933	7.66	6.09
22	Bos	AL	10	0	3	10.1	46	10	8	7	1	0	0	1	7	1	8	0	1	2	.333	0-1	1	95	.812	5.42	6.10
	Postseason		14	0	11	16.2	60	7	5	4	2	0	0	0	3	0	11	0	0	1	.000	5-8	0	96	.412	0.97	2.16
	11 ML YEARS		547	1	248	543.0	2328	481	235	212	42	15	8	18	253	27	568	31	34	28	.548	125-161	70	96	.676	3.60	3.51

Buck Farmer

Pitches: R Bats: L Pos: RP-44   Ht: 6'4" Wt: 232 Born: 2/20/1991 Age: 32

			HOW MUCH PITCHED				WHAT HE GAVE UP											THE RESULTS						
Year	Team	Lg	G	GS	GF	IP	BFP	H	R	ER	HR	SH	SF	HB	TBB	IBB	SO	WP	W	L	Pct	Sv-Op	Hld	Vel	OPS	ERC	ERA
2022	Lsville	AAA	20	0	4	22.1	92	18	9	9	4	0	0	0	9	0	34	1	0	3	.000	1- -	-	-	.667	3.57	3.63
2014	Det	AL	4	2	1	9.1	46	12	12	12	2	0	0	2	5	0	11	0	0	1	.000	0-0	0	93	1.054	8.29	11.57
2015	Det	AL	14	5	0	40.1	186	53	35	33	10	1	1	3	17	2	24	1	0	4	.000	0-0	0	93	.986	7.65	7.36
2016	Det	AL	14	1	7	29.1	131	25	15	15	4	1	1	1	20	1	27	2	0	1	.000	0-0	0	93	.771	4.71	4.60
2017	Det	AL	11	11	0	48.0	219	55	38	36	9	0	2	4	20	0	49	1	5	5	.500	0-0	0	92	.843	5.99	6.75
2018	Det	AL	66	1	12	69.1	308	67	34	32	6	1	2	1	41	1	57	2	3	4	.429	0-0	7	94	.754	4.41	4.15
2019	Det	AL	73	1	8	67.2	288	62	32	28	8	4	4	5	24	2	73	4	6	6	.500	0-3	15	95	.743	3.81	3.72
2020	Det	AL	23	0	9	21.1	89	20	9	9	3	1	1	0	5	0	14	1	1	0	1.000	0-1	7	93	.674	3.29	3.80
2021	Det	AL	36	0	8	35.1	171	40	25	25	9	0	1	5	21	1	37	2	0	0	-	0-1	2	94	.886	7.37	6.37
2022	Cin	NL	44	0	10	47.0	199	36	21	20	2	1	1	1	25	0	54	4	2	2	.500	2-3	5	95	.611	3.00	3.83
	9 ML YEARS		285	21	55	367.2	1637	370	221	210	53	9	13	22	178	7	346	17	17	23	.425	2-8	36	94	.793	4.99	5.14

Kyle Farmer

Bats: R Throws: R Pos: SS-98;3B-36;DH-10;PH-3;1B-2   Ht: 6'0" Wt: 205 Born: 8/17/1990 Age: 32

			BATTING																	RUNNING			AVERAGES			
Year	Team	Lg	G	AB	H	2B	3B	HR	(Hm	Rd)	TB	R	RBI	RC	TBB	IBB	SO	HBP	SH	SF	SB	CS	GDP	Avg	OBP	Slg	OPS
2017	LAD	NL	20	20	6	1	0	0	(0	0)	7	1	2	1	0	0	3	0	0	0	0	0	2	.300	.300	.350	.650
2018	LAD	NL	39	68	16	4	1	0	(0	0)	22	1	9	7	5	1	15	3	0	1	0	0	1	.235	.312	.324	.635
2019	Cin	NL	97	183	42	6	0	9	(6	3)	75	22	27	22	10	1	59	3	0	1	4	1	3	.230	.279	.410	.689
2020	Cin	NL	32	64	17	3	0	0	(0	0)	20	4	4	7	5	0	13	1	0	0	1	0	0	.266	.329	.313	.641
2021	Cin	NL	147	483	121	22	2	16	(9	7)	201	60	63	64	22	1	97	18	1	5	2	3	16	.250	.316	.416	.732
2022	Cin	NL	145	526	134	25	1	14	(7	7)	203	58	78	66	33	0	99	16	2	6	4	3	20	.255	.315	.386	.701
	Postseason		6	9	0	0	0	0	(0	0)	0	0	1	0	0	0	4	0	0	1	0	0	0	.000	.000	.000	.000
	6 ML YEARS		480	1344	342	61	4	39	(22	17)	528	146	183	167	75	3	286	41	3	13	11	7	40	.254	.311	.393	.704

Luke Farrell

Pitches: R Bats: L Pos: RP-4; SP-2   Ht: 6'6" Wt: 200 Born: 6/7/1991 Age: 32

			HOW MUCH PITCHED				WHAT HE GAVE UP											THE RESULTS						
Year	Team	Lg	G	GS	GF	IP	BFP	H	R	ER	HR	SH	SF	HB	TBB	IBB	SO	WP	W	L	Pct	Sv-Op	Hld	Vel	OPS	ERC	ERA
2022	Iowa	AAA	17	11	2	59.0	258	58	33	33	10	0	1	4	28	0	49	2	3	4	.429	0- -	-	-	.802	5.14	5.03
2017	2 Tms		10	1	3	13.0	61	12	8	8	2	0	0	0	10	0	9	0	0	0	-	0-0	1	91	.753	5.40	5.54
2018	ChC	NL	20	2	8	31.1	141	30	22	18	7	0	1	1	16	2	39	1	3	4	.429	0-1	5	92	.797	5.09	5.17
2019	Tex	AL	9	1	3	13.1	48	6	4	4	3	0	0	1	3	0	12	0	1	0	1.000	0-0	0	92	.574	1.49	2.70
2020	Tex	AL	4	0	1	5.1	27	5	5	5	1	0	1	0	5	0	8	2	0	0	-	0-0	0	91	.923	7.27	8.44
2021	Min	AL	20	1	3	24.2	113	28	13	13	4	0	0	0	13	0	25	0	1	1	.500	0-0	0	91	.843	5.84	4.74
2022	2 Tms	NL	6	2	1	15.0	70	18	10	9	3	1	0	0	7	0	14	0	0	0	-	0-0	0	91	.833	6.16	5.40
17	KC	AL	1	1	0	2.2	18	7	5	5	2	0	0	0	3	0	2	0	0	0	-	0-0	0	90	1.289	21.83	16.88
17	Cin	NL	9	0	3	10.1	43	5	3	3	0	0	0	0	7	0	7	0	0	0	-	0-0	1	91	.529	2.34	2.61
22	ChC	NL	4	1	1	11.0	48	12	5	5	2	0	0	0	3	0	9	0	0	0	-	0-0	0	91	.757	4.55	4.09
22	Cin	NL	2	0	1	4.0	22	6	5	4	1	0	0	0	4	0	5	0	0	0	-	0-0	0	92	1.010	11.08	9.00
	6 ML YEARS		69	7	20	102.2	460	99	62	57	20	1	2	2	54	2	107	3	5	5	.500	0-1	3	92	.792	5.04	5.00

Calvin Faucher

Pitches: R Bats: R Pos: RP-22 Ht: 6'1" Wt: 190 Born: 9/22/1995 Age: 27

Year	Team	Lg	G	GS	GF	IP	BFP	H	R	ER	HR	SH	SF	HB	TBB	IBB	SO	WP	W	L	Pct	Sv-Op	Hld	Vel	OPS	ERC	ERA
2022	Drham	AAA	34	4	7	43.0	192	44	19	17	7	0	1	0	21	1	52	5	3	3	.500	1--	-	-	.790	4.93	3.56
2022	TB	AL	22	0	7	21.1	101	26	16	13	4	0	0	1	10	0	21	2	2	3	.400	1-2	1	95	.811	6.39	5.48

Erick Fedde

Pitches: R Bats: R Pos: SP-27 Ht: 6'4" Wt: 203 Born: 2/25/1993 Age: 30

Year	Team	Lg	G	GS	GF	IP	BFP	H	R	ER	HR	SH	SF	HB	TBB	IBB	SO	WP	W	L	Pct	Sv-Op	Hld	Vel	OPS	ERC	ERA
2017	Was	NL	3	3	0	15.1	76	25	16	16	5	2	0	1	8	2	15	0	0	1	.000	0-0	0	93	1.106	11.01	9.39
2018	Was	NL	11	11	0	50.1	217	55	31	31	8	1	2	0	22	1	46	0	2	4	.333	0-0	0	94	.846	5.32	5.54
2019	Was	NL	21	12	3	78.0	334	81	39	39	11	4	2	2	33	2	41	1	4	2	.667	0-0	0	92	.802	4.88	4.50
2020	Was	NL	11	8	1	50.1	222	47	25	24	10	1	1	3	22	2	28	2	2	4	.333	0-0	0	93	.767	4.65	4.29
2021	Was	NL	29	27	1	133.1	590	144	90	81	23	8	5	4	48	6	128	1	7	9	.438	0-1	0	94	.803	4.88	5.47
2022	Was	NL	27	27	0	127.0	573	149	84	82	21	1	6	0	58	0	94	6	6	13	.316	0-0	0	93	.832	5.85	5.81
	6 ML YEARS		102	88	5	454.1	2012	501	285	273	78	17	16	10	191	13	352	10	21	33	.389	0-1	0	93	.823	5.35	5.41

Mario Feliciano

Bats: R Throws: R Pos: C-2 Ht: 6'1" Wt: 200 Born: 11/20/1998 Age: 24

Year	Team	Lg	G	AB	H	2B	3B	HR	(Hm	Rd)	TB	R	RBI	RC	TBB	IBB	SO	HBP	SH	SF	SB	CS	GDP	Avg	OBP	Slg	OPS
2022	Nashv	AAA	77	285	78	14	0	6	(-	-)	110	31	38	31	18	0	52	5	0	2	2	2	13	.274	.326	.386	.712
2021	Mil	NL	1	0	0	0	0	0	(0	0)	0	1	0	0	1	0	0	0	0	0	0	0	0	-	1.000	-	-
2022	Mil	NL	2	4	1	0	0	0	(0	0)	1	0	0	0	1	0	1	0	0	0	0	0	0	.250	.400	.250	.650
	2 ML YEARS		3	4	1	0	0	0	(0	0)	1	1	0	0	2	0	1	0	0	0	0	0	0	.250	.500	.250	.750

Michael Feliz

Pitches: R Bats: R Pos: RP-1 Ht: 6'4" Wt: 250 Born: 6/28/1993 Age: 30

Year	Team	Lg	G	GS	GF	IP	BFP	H	R	ER	HR	SH	SF	HB	TBB	IBB	SO	WP	W	L	Pct	Sv-Op	Hld	Vel	OPS	ERC	ERA
2022	Wrcstr	AAA	18	3	0	24.2	101	20	10	9	1	0	2	0	9	0	28	1	0	1	.000	0--	-	-	.605	2.56	3.28
2022	StPaul	AAA	18	0	8	24.2	96	12	8	6	0	0	1	2	10	0	24	1	3	1	.750	2--	-	-	.407	1.38	2.19
2015	Hou	AL	5	0	5	8.0	38	9	7	7	2	0	0	1	4	0	7	0	0	0	-	0-0	0	94	.884	6.79	7.88
2016	Hou	AL	47	0	17	65.0	270	55	33	32	10	0	2	0	22	0	95	6	8	1	.889	0-3	5	94	.659	3.32	4.43
2017	Hou	AL	46	0	13	48.0	218	53	31	30	8	0	4	0	22	1	70	7	4	2	.667	0-2	2	96	.854	5.28	5.63
2018	Pit	NL	47	0	7	47.2	217	49	33	30	6	0	3	3	23	0	55	3	1	2	.333	0-2	12	95	.776	4.92	5.66
2019	Pit	NL	58	1	5	56.1	239	44	27	25	11	1	1	2	27	1	73	0	4	4	.500	0-1	3	95	.720	3.91	3.99
2020	Pit	NL	3	0	0	1.2	12	4	6	6	1	0	0	1	2	0	2	0	0	0	-	0-0	0	94	1.361	26.50	32.40
2021	4 Tms		21	0	7	20.0	90	26	17	16	4	0	0	0	7	0	22	2	0	0	-	1-1	0	94	.873	6.49	7.20
2022	Bos	AL	1	0	0	3.1	13	1	2	1	1	0	0	0	2	0	4	0	0	0	-	0-0	0	94	.594	2.36	2.70
21	Pit	NL	7	0	2	7.2	31	8	3	2	0	0	0	0	1	0	8	1	0	0	-	0-0	0	93	.690	2.68	2.35
21	Cin	NL	9	0	5	6.2	37	13	12	12	2	0	0	0	4	0	9	1	0	0	-	1-1	0	94	1.035	12.87	16.20
21	Bos	AL	4	0	0	5.1	19	4	2	2	2	0	0	0	1	0	5	0	0	0	-	0-0	0	95	.819	3.84	3.38
21	Oak	AL	1	0	0	0.1	3	1	0	0	0	0	0	0	1	0	0	0	0	0	-	0-0	0	93	1.167	29.63	0.00
	8 ML YEARS		228	1	54	250.0	1097	241	156	147	43	1	10	7	109	2	328	18	17	9	.654	1-9	22	95	.766	4.57	5.29

Ryan Feltner

Pitches: R Bats: R Pos: SP-19; RP-1 Ht: 6'4" Wt: 190 Born: 9/2/1996 Age: 26

Year	Team	Lg	G	GS	GF	IP	BFP	H	R	ER	HR	SH	SF	HB	TBB	IBB	SO	WP	W	L	Pct	Sv-Op	Hld	Vel	OPS	ERC	ERA
2022	Albq	AAA	11	11	0	51.2	221	49	25	22	5	1	1	2	18	0	60	0	5	1	.833	0--	-	-	.721	3.69	3.83
2021	Col	NL	2	2	0	6.1	33	9	8	8	3	0	1	0	5	0	6	0	0	1	.000	0-0	0	92	1.185	12.84	11.37
2022	Col	NL	20	19	0	97.1	428	102	65	63	16	0	4	5	35	0	84	4	4	9	.308	0-0	0	94	.792	4.82	5.83
	2 ML YEARS		22	21	0	103.2	461	111	73	71	19	0	5	6	40	0	90	4	4	10	.286	0-0	0	94	.818	5.24	6.16

Caleb Ferguson

Pitches: L Bats: R Pos: RP-36; SP-1 Ht: 6'3" Wt: 226 Born: 7/2/1996 Age: 26

Year	Team	Lg	G	GS	GF	IP	BFP	H	R	ER	HR	SH	SF	HB	TBB	IBB	SO	WP	W	L	Pct	Sv-Op	Hld	Vel	OPS	ERC	ERA
2022	OkCity	AAA	10	2	0	7.1	37	10	8	6	1	0	0	1	4	0	13	0	0	1	.000	0--	-	-	.905	7.61	7.36
2018	LAD	NL	29	3	7	49.0	202	43	21	19	8	0	0	3	12	1	59	1	7	2	.778	2-3	5	94	.688	3.42	3.49
2019	LAD	NL	46	2	5	44.2	204	39	26	24	7	1	3	6	27	2	54	1	1	2	.333	0-0	4	94	.774	4.99	4.84
2020	LAD	NL	21	0	3	18.2	75	16	7	6	4	0	0	0	3	0	27	0	2	1	.667	0-2	5	95	.670	3.02	2.89
2022	LAD	NL	37	1	3	34.2	142	23	9	7	1	0	0	2	17	0	37	0	1	0	1.000	0-0	7	95	.572	2.42	1.82
	Postseason		6	0	0	3.0	10	0	0	0	0	0	0	0	1	0	3	0	0	0	-	0-0	1	95	.100	0.13	0.00
	4 ML YEARS		133	7	15	147.0	623	121	63	56	20	1	3	11	59	3	177	2	11	5	.688	2-5	21	94	.688	3.60	3.43

Freddy Fermin

Bats: R Throws: R Pos: C-3 Ht: 5'10" Wt: 200 Born: 5/16/1995 Age: 28

Year	Team	Lg	G	AB	H	2B	3B	HR	(Hm	Rd)	TB	R	RBI	RC	TBB	IBB	SO	HBP	SH	SF	SB	CS	GDP	Avg	OBP	Slg	OPS
2022	Omha	AAA	87	296	80	17	0	15	(-	-)	142	44	56	55	46	0	62	1	0	5	1	0	8	.270	.365	.480	.845
2022	KC	AL	3	7	0	0	0	0	(0	0)	0	1	0	0	0	0	3	0	0	0	0	1	0	.000	.000	.000	.000

Junior Fernandez

Pitches: R Bats: R Pos: RP-16   Ht: 6'3" Wt: 215 Born: 3/2/1997 Age: 26

			HOW MUCH PITCHED					WHAT HE GAVE UP										THE RESULTS						
Year	Team	Lg	G	GS	GF	IP	BFP	H	R	ER	HR	SH	SF	HB	TBB	IBB	SO	WP	W	L	Pct	Sv-Op Hld	Vel	OPS	ERC	ERA
2022	Memp	AAA	35	0	21	36.1	171	47	24	22	4	0	1	3	17	1	43	6	1	3	.250	5-- -	-	.845	6.52	5.45
2022	Indy	AAA	6	0	0	8.0	32	2	2	2	0	0	1	0	6	0	8	0	1	0	1.000	0-- -	-	.370	1.18	2.25
2019	StL	NL	13	0	5	11.2	54	9	7	7	2	0	0	4	6	0	16	2	0	1	.000	0-3	0	97	.693	5.01	5.40
2020	StL	NL	3	0	2	3.0	16	6	6	6	1	0	0	0	2	0	2	0	0	0	-	0-0	0	94	1.286	14.84	18.00
2021	StL	NL	18	0	11	20.2	97	25	13	13	2	0	0	0	15	1	15	1	1	0	1.000	0-0	0	98	.864	6.74	5.66
2022	2 Tms	NL	16	0	2	18.2	84	18	6	5	3	0	0	1	12	0	14	2	0	0	-	0-1	3	99	.788	5.62	2.41
22	StL	NL	13	0	2	15.1	70	17	6	5	3	0	0	1	8	0	12	1	0	0	-	0-1	3	99	.843	6.28	2.93
22	Pit	NL	3	0	0	3.1	14	1	0	0	0	0	0	0	4	0	2	1	0	0	-	0-0	0	99	.457	2.68	0.00
4 ML YEARS			50	0	20	54.0	251	58	32	31	8	0	0	5	35	1	47	5	1	1	.500	0-4	3	98	.830	6.35	5.17

Matthew Festa

Pitches: R Bats: R Pos: RP-53   Ht: 6'1" Wt: 195 Born: 3/11/1993 Age: 30

			HOW MUCH PITCHED					WHAT HE GAVE UP										THE RESULTS						
Year	Team	Lg	G	GS	GF	IP	BFP	H	R	ER	HR	SH	SF	HB	TBB	IBB	SO	WP	W	L	Pct	Sv-Op Hld	Vel	OPS	ERC	ERA
2022	Tacom	AAA	6	0	1	6.2	24	2	2	0	0	0	0	0	2	0	11	0	1	0	1.000	0-- -	-	.258	0.57	0.00
2018	Sea	AL	8	1	0	8.1	40	13	2	2	0	0	0	1	2	0	4	2	0	0	-	0-0	1	93	.859	6.44	2.16
2019	Sea	AL	20	0	10	22.1	101	20	15	14	5	1	2	2	12	1	21	1	0	2	.000	0-2	3	93	.874	5.12	5.64
2022	Sea	AL	53	0	13	54.0	219	43	26	25	10	2	0	2	18	0	64	1	2	0	1.000	2-3	6	93	.717	3.45	4.17
3 ML YEARS			81	1	23	84.2	360	76	43	41	15	3	2	5	32	1	89	4	2	2	.500	2-5	10	93	.775	4.17	4.36

J.P. Feyereisen

Pitches: R Bats: R Pos: RP-20; SP-2   FIRE-eye-zehn   Ht: 6'2" Wt: 215 Born: 2/7/1993 Age: 30

			HOW MUCH PITCHED					WHAT HE GAVE UP										THE RESULTS						
Year	Team	Lg	G	GS	GF	IP	BFP	H	R	ER	HR	SH	SF	HB	TBB	IBB	SO	WP	W	L	Pct	Sv-Op Hld	Vel	OPS	ERC	ERA
2020	Mil	NL	6	0	4	9.1	37	6	3	3	0	2	1	0	5	0	7	0	0	0	-	0-0	0	93	.719	3.39	5.79
2021	2 Tms		55	0	14	56.0	234	36	23	17	5	2	2	0	33	0	53	3	4	4	.500	3-6	15	93	.617	2.80	2.73
2022	TB	AL	22	2	3	24.1	86	7	1	0	0	0	0	0	5	0	25	0	4	0	1.000	1-2	7	92	.226	0.41	0.00
21	Mil	NL	21	0	4	19.1	77	10	9	7	2	1	0	0	11	0	20	1	0	2	.000	0-2	9	94	.538	2.26	3.26
21	TB	AL	34	0	10	36.2	157	26	14	10	3	1	2	0	22	0	33	2	4	2	.667	3-4	6	93	.656	3.09	2.45
Postseason			3	0	2	3.2	17	6	1	1	0	2	1	0	0	0	2	0	0	1	.000	0-0	0	92	.829	5.25	2.45
3 ML YEARS			83	2	21	89.2	357	47	30	23	8	2	4	1	43	0	85	3	8	4	.667	4-8	22	93	.527	1.91	2.31

Kyle Finnegan

Pitches: R Bats: R Pos: RP-66   Ht: 6'2" Wt: 197 Born: 9/4/1991 Age: 31

			HOW MUCH PITCHED					WHAT HE GAVE UP										THE RESULTS						
Year	Team	Lg	G	GS	GF	IP	BFP	H	R	ER	HR	SH	SF	HB	TBB	IBB	SO	WP	W	L	Pct	Sv-Op Hld	Vel	OPS	ERC	ERA
2020	Was	NL	25	0	4	24.2	107	21	10	8	2	0	0	1	13	4	27	2	1	0	1.000	0-1	4	95	.639	3.49	2.92
2021	Was	NL	68	0	24	66.0	294	64	39	26	9	2	0	2	34	4	68	8	5	9	.357	11-14	13	96	.748	4.61	3.55
2022	Was	NL	66	0	24	66.2	268	54	28	26	9	0	2	0	22	2	70	0	6	4	.600	11-15	14	97	.665	3.02	3.51
3 ML YEARS			159	0	52	157.1	669	139	77	60	20	2	2	3	69	10	165	10	12	13	.480	22-30	31	96	.697	3.75	3.43

Nate Fisher

Pitches: L Bats: L Pos: RP-1   Ht: 6'1" Wt: 205 Born: 5/28/1996 Age: 27

			HOW MUCH PITCHED					WHAT HE GAVE UP										THE RESULTS						
Year	Team	Lg	G	GS	GF	IP	BFP	H	R	ER	HR	SH	SF	HB	TBB	IBB	SO	WP	W	L	Pct	Sv-Op Hld	Vel	OPS	ERC	ERA
2022	Bnghtn	AA	12	2	1	28.2	118	19	14	12	3	0	1	1	11	0	40	2	0	1	.000	0-- -	-	.596	2.35	3.77
2022	Syrcse	AAA	18	11	0	56.0	246	60	29	27	6	0	1	5	23	0	40	5	1	2	.333	0-- -	-	.768	5.04	4.34
2022	NYM	NL	1	0	0	3.0	11	1	0	0	0	0	0	0	2	0	1	0	0	0	-	0-0	0	93	.384	1.37	0.00

Jake Fishman

Pitches: L Bats: L Pos: RP-7   Ht: 6'3" Wt: 195 Born: 2/8/1995 Age: 28

			HOW MUCH PITCHED					WHAT HE GAVE UP										THE RESULTS						
Year	Team	Lg	G	GS	GF	IP	BFP	H	R	ER	HR	SH	SF	HB	TBB	IBB	SO	WP	W	L	Pct	Sv-Op Hld	Vel	OPS	ERC	ERA
2022	Jaxnvl	AAA	33	0	11	56.0	234	39	21	14	4	1	2	10	20	0	54	1	4	1	.800	1-- -	-	.595	2.76	2.25
2022	Mia	NL	7	0	2	11.0	48	13	5	5	0	0	0	3	0	0	6	0	0	0	-	0-0	2	88	.733	3.86	4.09

Jack Flaherty

Pitches: R Bats: R Pos: SP-8; RP-1   Ht: 6'4" Wt: 225 Born: 10/15/1995 Age: 27

			HOW MUCH PITCHED					WHAT HE GAVE UP										THE RESULTS						
Year	Team	Lg	G	GS	GF	IP	BFP	H	R	ER	HR	SH	SF	HB	TBB	IBB	SO	WP	W	L	Pct	Sv-Op Hld	Vel	OPS	ERC	ERA
2017	StL	NL	6	5	0	21.1	94	23	15	15	4	0	2	1	10	1	20	0	0	2	.000	0-0	0	93	.843	5.71	6.33
2018	StL	NL	28	28	0	151.0	615	108	59	56	20	2	1	11	59	3	182	6	8	9	.471	0-0	0	93	.635	3.01	3.34
2019	StL	NL	33	33	0	196.1	772	135	62	60	25	3	3	7	55	2	231	6	11	8	.579	0-0	0	94	.591	2.31	2.75
2020	StL	NL	9	9	0	40.1	170	33	22	22	6	1	1	3	16	0	49	1	4	3	.571	0-0	0	94	.677	3.68	4.91
2021	StL	NL	17	15	0	78.1	322	57	35	28	12	2	2	6	26	1	85	4	9	2	.818	0-0	0	93	.642	2.94	3.22
2022	StL	NL	9	8	0	36.0	167	36	18	17	4	1	0	5	22	0	33	0	2	1	.667	0-0	0	93	.804	5.58	4.25
Postseason			4	4	0	23.0	98	23	9	9	2	2	0	1	6	0	30	3	1	3	.250	0-0	0	94	.695	3.57	3.52
6 ML YEARS			102	98	0	523.1	2140	392	211	198	71	9	9	33	188	7	600	17	34	25	.576	0-0	0	93	.645	3.04	3.41

Josh Fleming

Pitches: L Bats: L Pos: RP-7; SP-3   Ht: 6'2" Wt: 220 Born: 5/18/1996 Age: 27

Year	Team	Lg	G	GS	GF	IP	BFP	H	R	ER	HR	SH	SF	HB	TBB	IBB	SO	WP	W	L	Pct	Sv-Op	Hld	Vel	OPS	ERC	ERA
2022	Drham	AAA	15	10	0	64.2	260	73	23	22	4	0	1	2	14	0	46	2	9	2	.818	0- -	-	-	.733	4.22	3.06
2020	TB	AL	7	5	0	32.1	130	28	10	10	5	0	0	1	7	0	25	0	5	0	1.000	0-0	0	91	.670	3.14	2.78
2021	TB	AL	26	11	1	104.1	448	110	60	59	11	3	1	3	31	5	65	0	10	8	.556	1-1	3	91	.731	4.04	5.09
2022	TB	AL	10	3	1	35.0	169	54	36	25	5	0	1	1	12	1	29	0	2	5	.286	0-0	0	92	.938	7.52	6.43
	Postseason		4	0	0	6.2	31	11	4	4	1	0	0	0	2	0	4	0	0	0	-	0-0	0	93	1.006	8.41	5.40
	3 ML YEARS		43	19	2	171.2	747	192	106	94	21	3	2	5	50	6	119	0	17	13	.567	1-1	3	91	.767	4.52	4.93

Aaron Fletcher

Pitches: L Bats: L Pos: RP-9   Ht: 6'0" Wt: 220 Born: 2/25/1996 Age: 27

Year	Team	Lg	G	GS	GF	IP	BFP	H	R	ER	HR	SH	SF	HB	TBB	IBB	SO	WP	W	L	Pct	Sv-Op	Hld	Vel	OPS	ERC	ERA
2022	Indy	AAA	14	0	4	18.2	82	20	6	3	0	0	1	0	6	0	9	1	1	1	.500	1- -	-	-	.597	3.37	1.45
2022	Scrmto	AAA	15	0	2	13.2	83	22	26	23	4	0	3	4	14	0	12	1	0	1	.000	0- -	-	-	1.076	13.01	15.15
2020	Sea	AL	6	0	0	4.1	29	7	6	6	1	0	0	2	7	0	7	0	0	0	-	0-0	1	93	1.102	16.97	12.46
2021	Sea	AL	4	0	2	3.2	20	7	5	5	1	0	0	1	1	0	2	0	0	0	-	0-0	0	92	.979	10.06	12.27
2022	Pit	NL	9	0	4	11.2	52	10	9	9	2	0	2	3	4	0	6	1	0	1	.000	0-0	0	91	.746	4.48	6.94
	3 ML YEARS		19	0	6	19.2	101	24	20	20	4	0	2	6	12	0	15	1	0	1	.000	0-0	1	92	.894	8.00	9.15

David Fletcher

Bats: R Throws: R Pos: 2B-44;SS-36;PH-4;PR-2   Ht: 5'9" Wt: 185 Born: 5/31/1994 Age: 29

Year	Team	Lg	G	AB	H	2B	3B	HR	(Hm	Rd)	TB	R	RBI	RC	TBB	IBB	SO	HBP	SH	SF	SB	CS	GDP	Avg	OBP	Slg	OPS
2022	Salt Lk	AAA	13	49	10	1	0	0	(-	-)	11	3	1	1	2	0	7	0	0	0	1	0	1	.204	.235	.224	.460
2018	LAA	AL	80	284	78	18	2	1	(1	0)	103	35	25	35	15	0	34	3	3	2	3	0	7	.275	.316	.363	.678
2019	LAA	AL	154	596	173	30	4	6	(3	3)	229	83	49	89	55	2	64	0	1	1	8	3	8	.290	.350	.384	.734
2020	LAA	AL	49	207	66	13	0	3	(1	2)	88	31	18	38	20	0	25	0	1	2	2	1	4	.319	.376	.425	.801
2021	LAA	AL	157	626	164	27	3	2	(0	2)	203	74	47	70	31	1	60	1	6	1	15	3	10	.262	.297	.324	.622
2022	LAA	AL	61	216	55	9	1	2	(1	1)	72	20	17	18	7	0	16	3	2	0	1	0	6	.255	.288	.333	.621
	5 ML YEARS		501	1929	536	97	10	14	(6	8)	695	243	156	250	128	3	199	7	13	6	29	7	35	.278	.324	.360	.684

Chris Flexen

Pitches: R Bats: R Pos: SP-22; RP-11   Ht: 6'3" Wt: 219 Born: 7/1/1994 Age: 28

Year	Team	Lg	G	GS	GF	IP	BFP	H	R	ER	HR	SH	SF	HB	TBB	IBB	SO	WP	W	L	Pct	Sv-Op	Hld	Vel	OPS	ERC	ERA
2017	NYM	NL	14	9	1	48.0	233	62	44	42	11	1	2	2	35	0	36	1	3	6	.333	0-0	0	92	.981	8.75	7.88
2018	NYM	NL	4	1	2	6.1	40	14	13	9	2	0	0	1	6	1	3	0	0	2	.000	0-0	0	93	1.283	17.26	12.79
2019	NYM	NL	9	1	4	13.2	70	15	12	10	1	0	1	0	13	2	10	1	0	3	.000	0-0	0	94	.829	6.12	6.59
2021	Sea	AL	31	31	0	179.2	741	185	74	72	19	0	7	4	40	0	125	2	14	6	.700	0-0	0	92	.724	3.74	3.61
2022	Sea	AL	33	22	11	137.2	590	132	61	57	17	3	5	2	51	3	95	7	8	9	.471	2-2	0	92	.723	3.89	3.73
	5 ML YEARS		91	64	18	385.1	1674	408	204	190	50	4	15	9	145	6	269	11	25	26	.490	2-2	0	92	.775	4.62	4.44

Wilmer Flores

Bats: R Throws: R Pos: 2B-61;1B-45;3B-34;DH-26;PH-18   Ht: 6'2" Wt: 213 Born: 8/6/1991 Age: 31

Year	Team	Lg	G	AB	H	2B	3B	HR	(Hm	Rd)	TB	R	RBI	RC	TBB	IBB	SO	HBP	SH	SF	SB	CS	GDP	Avg	OBP	Slg	OPS
2013	NYM	NL	27	95	20	5	0	1	(0	1)	28	8	13	7	5	0	23	0	0	0	0	0	1	.211	.248	.295	.542
2014	NYM	NL	78	259	65	13	1	6	(4	2)	98	28	29	25	12	2	31	1	1	1	1	0	6	.251	.286	.378	.664
2015	NYM	NL	137	483	127	22	0	16	(8	8)	197	55	59	58	19	2	63	4	2	2	0	1	12	.263	.295	.408	.703
2016	NYM	NL	103	307	82	14	0	16	(12	4)	144	38	49	39	23	0	48	2	0	3	1	1	9	.267	.319	.469	.788
2017	NYM	NL	110	336	91	17	1	18	(9	9)	164	42	52	39	17	1	54	3	0	6	1	1	14	.271	.307	.488	.795
2018	NYM	NL	126	386	103	25	0	11	(4	7)	161	43	51	51	29	1	42	5	0	9	0	0	8	.267	.319	.417	.736
2019	Ari	NL	89	265	84	18	0	9	(6	3)	129	31	37	38	15	0	31	4	0	1	0	0	9	.317	.361	.487	.848
2020	SF	NL	55	198	53	11	1	12	(7	5)	102	30	32	30	13	1	36	1	0	1	0	0	5	.268	.315	.515	.830
2021	SF	NL	139	389	102	16	1	18	(8	10)	174	57	53	56	41	0	56	3	0	3	1	0	11	.262	.335	.447	.782
2022	SF	NL	151	525	120	28	1	19	(11	8)	207	72	71	79	59	1	103	11	0	7	0	0	7	.229	.316	.394	.710
	Postseason		17	53	9	2	1	0	(0	0)	13	5	0	5	6	2	11	1	1	0	1	0	1	.170	.267	.245	.512
	10 ML YEARS		1015	3243	847	169	5	126	(69	57)	1404	404	446	422	233	8	487	34	3	34	5	3	82	.261	.314	.433	.747

Estevan Florial

Bats: L Throws: R Pos: CF-14;LF-2;DH-2;PR-2;PH-1   Ht: 6'1" Wt: 195 Born: 11/25/1997 Age: 25

Year	Team	Lg	G	AB	H	2B	3B	HR	(Hm	Rd)	TB	R	RBI	RC	TBB	IBB	SO	HBP	SH	SF	SB	CS	GDP	Avg	OBP	Slg	OPS
2022	S-WB	AAA	101	403	114	31	2	15	(-	-)	194	66	46	76	54	3	140	1	2	1	39	10	0	.283	.368	.481	.850
2020	NYY	AL	1	3	1	0	0	0	(0	0)	1	0	0	0	0	0	2	0	0	0	0	0	0	.333	.333	.333	.667
2021	NYY	AL	11	20	6	2	0	1	(1	0)	11	3	2	3	5	0	6	0	0	0	1	0	0	.300	.440	.550	.990
2022	NYY	AL	17	31	3	0	0	0	(0	0)	3	4	1	1	3	0	13	1	0	0	2	0	0	.097	.200	.097	.297
	3 ML YEARS		29	54	10	2	0	1	(1	0)	15	7	3	4	8	0	21	1	0	0	3	0	0	.185	.302	.278	.579

Dylan Floro

Pitches: R Bats: L Pos: RP-56　　　　　　　　　　　　　　　　Ht: 6'2" Wt: 203 Born: 12/27/1990 Age: 32

			HOW MUCH PITCHED					WHAT HE GAVE UP										THE RESULTS							
Year	Team	Lg	G	GS	GF	IP	BFP	H	R	ER	HR	SH	SF	HB	TBB	IBB	SO	WP	W	L	Pct	Sv-Op	Hld	Vel	OPS	ERC	ERA
2016	TB	AL	12	0	4	15.0	72	23	8	7	0	0	1	0	5	1	14	2	0	1	.000	0-0	0	93	.813	5.96	4.20
2017	ChC	NL	3	0	2	9.2	45	15	7	7	2	0	0	1	2	0	6	0	0	0	-	0-0	0	91	.971	8.12	6.52
2018	2 Tms	NL	54	0	20	64.0	271	57	17	16	3	3	3	1	23	6	58	1	6	3	.667	0-0	7	93	.634	2.85	2.25
2019	LAD	NL	50	0	4	46.2	201	46	25	22	4	2	1	2	14	5	42	1	5	3	.625	0-3	6	94	.685	3.44	4.24
2020	LAD	NL	25	0	4	24.1	98	23	7	7	1	0	2	0	4	1	19	1	3	0	1.000	0-0	4	93	.623	2.48	2.59
2021	Mia	NL	68	0	32	64.0	270	53	25	20	2	0	1	0	25	3	62	1	6	6	.500	15-21	11	94	.576	2.54	2.81
2022	Mia	NL	56	0	23	53.2	220	48	23	18	4	0	1	0	15	3	48	1	1	3	.250	10-14	5	93	.625	2.81	3.02
18	Cin	NL	25	0	13	36.1	159	39	12	11	2	2	3	0	12	3	27	0	3	2	.600	0-0	1	93	.726	3.69	2.72
18	LAD	NL	29	0	7	27.2	112	18	5	5	1	0	1	1	11	3	31	1	3	1	.750	0-0	6	94	.503	1.84	1.63
	Postseason		14	0	3	12.1	51	11	8	6	1	0	0	0	5	2	15	0	1	0	1.000	0-0	0	93	.705	3.20	4.38
	7 ML YEARS		268	0	89	277.1	1177	265	112	97	16	5	9	4	88	19	249	7	21	16	.568	25-38	33	93	.651	3.14	3.15

Jason Foley

Pitches: R Bats: R Pos: RP-60　　　　　　　　　　　　　　　　Ht: 6'4" Wt: 215 Born: 11/1/1995 Age: 27

			HOW MUCH PITCHED					WHAT HE GAVE UP										THE RESULTS							
Year	Team	Lg	G	GS	GF	IP	BFP	H	R	ER	HR	SH	SF	HB	TBB	IBB	SO	WP	W	L	Pct	Sv-Op	Hld	Vel	OPS	ERC	ERA
2021	Det	AL	11	0	1	10.1	45	8	3	3	1	0	0	3	5	0	6	3	0	0	-	0-0	2	96	.761	4.35	2.61
2022	Det	AL	60	0	15	60.1	256	72	27	26	2	1	0	2	11	0	43	0	1	0	1.000	0-1	4	96	.697	4.03	3.88
	2 ML YEARS		71	0	16	70.2	301	80	30	29	3	1	0	5	16	0	49	3	1	0	1.000	0-1	6	96	.706	4.07	3.69

Mike Ford

Bats: L Throws: R Pos: 1B-29;DH-12;PH-10　　　　　　　　　　Ht: 6'0" Wt: 225 Born: 7/4/1992 Age: 30

					BATTING																RUNNING			AVERAGES			
Year	Team	Lg	G	AB	H	2B	3B	HR	(Hm	Rd)	TB	R	RBI	RC	TBB	IBB	SO	HBP	SH	SF	SB	CS	GDP	Avg	OBP	Slg	OPS
2022	Tacom	AAA	11	41	13	1	0	2	(-	-)	20	10	5	7	5	0	4	1	0	0	0	0	2	.317	.404	.488	.892
2022	Gwnntt	AAA	14	42	10	6	0	0	(-	-)	16	2	3	6	11	0	7	0	0	0	0	0	1	.238	.396	.381	.777
2019	NYY	AL	50	143	37	7	0	12	(2	10)	80	30	25	27	17	2	28	3	0	0	0	0	0	.259	.350	.559	.909
2020	NYY	AL	29	74	10	4	0	2	(1	1)	20	5	11	3	7	0	16	2	0	1	0	0	4	.135	.226	.270	.496
2021	NYY	AL	22	60	8	0	0	3	(1	2)	17	6	5	3	11	1	23	1	0	0	0	0	1	.133	.278	.283	.561
2022	4 Tms		50	131	27	5	0	3	(3	0)	41	9	10	11	17	0	40	1	0	0	0	0	1	.206	.302	.313	.615
22	SF	NL	1	4	1	0	0	0	(0	0)	1	0	2	1	0	0	0	0	0	0	0	0	0	.250	.250	.250	.500
22	Sea	AL	16	29	5	1	0	0	(0	0)	6	1	3	4	8	0	12	1	0	0	0	0	0	.172	.368	.207	.575
22	Atl	NL	5	7	0	0	0	0	(0	0)	0	0	0	0	1	0	2	0	0	0	0	0	0	.000	.125	.000	.125
22	LAA	AL	28	91	21	4	0	3	(3	0)	34	8	5	6	8	0	26	0	0	0	0	0	1	.231	.293	.374	.667
	Postseason		3	2	0	0	0	0	(0	0)	0	0	0	0	0	0	1	0	0	0	0	0	0	.000	.000	.000	.000
	4 ML YEARS		151	408	82	16	0	20	(7	13)	158	50	51	44	52	3	107	7	0	1	0	0	6	.201	.301	.387	.689

Nick Fortes

Bats: R Throws: R Pos: C-59;DH-13;PH-8;PR-3;1B-1　　　　Ht: 5'11" Wt: 198 Born: 11/11/1996 Age: 26

					BATTING																RUNNING			AVERAGES			
Year	Team	Lg	G	AB	H	2B	3B	HR	(Hm	Rd)	TB	R	RBI	RC	TBB	IBB	SO	HBP	SH	SF	SB	CS	GDP	Avg	OBP	Slg	OPS
2022	Jaxnvl	AAA	28	105	27	4	0	3	(-	-)	40	13	13	13	11	0	17	3	0	1	1	0	5	.257	.342	.381	.723
2021	Mia	NL	14	31	9	0	0	4	(4	0)	21	6	7	8	3	0	8	0	0	0	1	0	1	.290	.353	.677	1.030
2022	Mia	NL	72	217	50	6	1	9	(7	2)	85	41	24	26	18	0	45	5	0	0	5	3	5	.230	.304	.392	.696
	2 ML YEARS		86	248	59	6	1	13	(11	2)	106	47	31	34	21	0	53	5	0	0	6	3	6	.238	.310	.427	.738

Matt Foster

Pitches: R Bats: R Pos: RP-48　　　　　　　　　　　　　　　　Ht: 6'0" Wt: 215 Born: 1/27/1995 Age: 28

			HOW MUCH PITCHED					WHAT HE GAVE UP										THE RESULTS							
Year	Team	Lg	G	GS	GF	IP	BFP	H	R	ER	HR	SH	SF	HB	TBB	IBB	SO	WP	W	L	Pct	Sv-Op	Hld	Vel	OPS	ERC	ERA
2022	Charltt	AAA	11	0	3	11.0	42	7	1	1	0	0	0	1	2	0	14	1	1	0	1.000	2--	-	-	.418	1.39	0.82
2020	CWS	AL	23	2	4	28.2	109	16	8	7	2	1	0	0	9	0	31	0	6	1	.857	0-1	2	94	.504	1.50	2.20
2021	CWS	AL	37	0	17	39.0	174	43	27	26	9	0	2	2	13	0	40	1	2	1	.667	1-2	5	94	.811	5.47	6.00
2022	CWS	AL	48	0	12	45.0	193	43	25	22	6	1	1	0	17	1	42	1	1	2	.333	1-1	5	94	.703	3.89	4.40
	Postseason		1	0	0	0.1	3	0	0	0	0	0	0	0	2	0	0	0	0	0	-	0-0	0	95	.667	19.60	0.00
	3 ML YEARS		108	2	33	112.2	476	102	60	55	17	2	3	2	39	1	113	2	9	4	.692	2-4	9	94	.697	3.71	4.39

Lucius Fox

Bats: B Throws: R Pos: SS-6;3B-4;PR-1　　　　　　　　　　Ht: 6'1" Wt: 192 Born: 7/2/1997 Age: 25

					BATTING																RUNNING			AVERAGES			
Year	Team	Lg	G	AB	H	2B	3B	HR	(Hm	Rd)	TB	R	RBI	RC	TBB	IBB	SO	HBP	SH	SF	SB	CS	GDP	Avg	OBP	Slg	OPS
2022	Roch	AAA	55	206	47	7	2	4	(-	-)	70	28	25	21	22	1	61	1	2	0	12	4	4	.228	.306	.340	.645
2022	Was	NL	10	25	2	0	0	0	(0	0)	2	2	2	0	1	0	9	0	2	0	1	0	1	.080	.115	.080	.195

Jake Fraley

Bats: L **Throws:** L **Pos:** LF-29;RF-16;DH-14;PH-12;CF-7   **Ht:** 6'0" **Wt:** 195 **Born:** 5/25/1995 **Age:** 28

Year	Team	Lg	G	AB	H	2B	3B	HR	(Hm	Rd)	TB	R	RBI	RC	TBB	IBB	SO	HBP	SH	SF	SB	CS	GDP	Avg	OBP	Slg	OPS
2022	Lsvlle	AAA	12	41	11	0	0	1	(-	-)	14	8	4	6	7	0	14	0	0	0	1	0	0	.268	.375	.341	.716
2019	Sea	AL	12	40	6	2	0	0	(0	0)	8	3	1	2	0	0	14	1	0	0	0	0	0	.150	.171	.200	.371
2020	Sea	AL	7	26	4	1	1	0	(0	0)	7	3	0	1	2	0	11	1	0	0	2	1	0	.154	.241	.269	.511
2021	Sea	AL	78	214	45	7	0	9	(3	6)	79	27	36	40	46	1	71	2	1	2	10	2	3	.210	.352	.369	.721
2022	Cin	NL	68	216	56	9	0	12	(5	7)	101	33	28	39	26	1	54	3	0	2	4	1	1	.259	.344	.468	.812
	4 ML YEARS		165	496	111	19	1	21	(8	13)	195	66	65	82	74	2	150	7	1	4	16	4	4	.224	.330	.393	.724

Ty France

Bats: R **Throws:** R **Pos:** 1B-127;DH-8;3B-6;PH-2;2B-1   **Ht:** 5'11" **Wt:** 215 **Born:** 7/13/1994 **Age:** 28

Year	Team	Lg	G	AB	H	2B	3B	HR	(Hm	Rd)	TB	R	RBI	RC	TBB	IBB	SO	HBP	SH	SF	SB	CS	GDP	Avg	OBP	Slg	OPS
2019	SD	NL	69	184	43	8	1	7	(4	3)	74	20	24	25	9	0	49	7	0	1	0	2	8	.234	.294	.402	.696
2020	2 Tms		43	141	43	9	1	4	(2	2)	66	19	23	29	11	0	37	3	0	0	0	0	3	.305	.368	.468	.836
2021	Sea	AL	152	571	166	32	1	18	(6	12)	254	85	73	100	46	1	106	27	0	6	0	0	13	.291	.368	.445	.813
2022	Sea	AL	140	551	151	27	1	20	(10	10)	240	65	83	79	35	3	94	21	0	5	0	0	18	.274	.338	.436	.774
20	SD	NL	20	55	17	4	0	2	(2	0)	27	9	10	11	5	0	15	1	0	0	0	0	1	.309	.377	.491	.868
20	Sea	AL	23	86	26	5	1	2	(0	2)	39	10	13	18	6	0	22	2	0	0	0	0	2	.302	.362	.453	.815
	4 ML YEARS		404	1447	403	76	4	49	(22	27)	634	189	203	233	101	4	286	58	0	12	0	2	42	.279	.347	.438	.785

Bowden Francis

Pitches: R **Bats:** R **Pos:** RP-1   **Ht:** 6'5" **Wt:** 220 **Born:** 4/22/1996 **Age:** 27

			HOW MUCH PITCHED				WHAT HE GAVE UP										THE RESULTS							
Year	Team	Lg	G	GS	GF	IP	BFP	H	R	ER	HR	SH	SF	HB	TBB	IBB	SO	WP	W	L	Pct	Sv-Op	Hld	Vel	OPS	ERC	ERA
2022	Buffalo	AAA	37	23	0	98.1	452	108	77	72	23	2	6	13	43	0	110	3	5	10	.333	0- --	-		.908	6.35	6.59
2022	Tor	AL	1	0	1	0.2	3	1	0	0	0	0	0	0	0	0	1	0	0	0	-	0-0	0	92	1.000	4.47	0.00

Maikel Franco

Bats: R **Throws:** R **Pos:** 3B-99;1B-4;PH-4;DH-3   MY-kell   **Ht:** 6'1" **Wt:** 225 **Born:** 8/26/1992 **Age:** 30

Year	Team	Lg	G	AB	H	2B	3B	HR	(Hm	Rd)	TB	R	RBI	RC	TBB	IBB	SO	HBP	SH	SF	SB	CS	GDP	Avg	OBP	Slg	OPS
2014	Phi	NL	16	56	10	2	0	0	(0	0)	12	5	5	1	1	0	13	0	0	1	0	0	1	.179	.190	.214	.404
2015	Phi	NL	80	304	85	22	1	14	(7	7)	151	45	50	48	26	2	52	4	0	1	1	0	8	.280	.343	.497	.840
2016	Phi	NL	152	581	148	23	1	25	(10	15)	248	67	88	74	40	7	106	5	0	4	1	1	13	.255	.306	.427	.733
2017	Phi	NL	154	575	132	29	1	24	(14	10)	235	66	76	53	41	3	95	2	0	5	0	0	21	.230	.281	.409	.690
2018	Phi	NL	131	433	117	17	1	22	(10	12)	202	48	68	55	29	7	62	0	0	3	1	0	15	.270	.314	.467	.780
2019	Phi	NL	123	389	91	17	0	17	(13	4)	159	48	56	44	36	19	61	0	0	3	0	0	14	.234	.297	.409	.705
2020	KC	AL	60	223	62	16	0	8	(3	5)	102	23	38	36	16	1	38	0	0	4	1	0	4	.278	.321	.457	.778
2021	Bal	AL	104	377	79	22	0	11	(7	4)	134	31	47	30	20	0	67	3	0	3	0	0	12	.210	.253	.355	.609
2022	Was	NL	103	371	85	15	0	9	(7	2)	127	31	39	29	12	0	75	2	0	3	1	0	18	.229	.255	.342	.597
	9 ML YEARS		923	3309	809	163	4	130	(71	59)	1370	364	467	370	221	39	569	16	0	27	5	1	106	.244	.293	.414	.707

Wander Franco

Bats: B **Throws:** R **Pos:** SS-73;DH-10;PH-3   **Ht:** 5'10" **Wt:** 189 **Born:** 3/1/2001 **Age:** 22

Year	Team	Lg	G	AB	H	2B	3B	HR	(Hm	Rd)	TB	R	RBI	RC	TBB	IBB	SO	HBP	SH	SF	SB	CS	GDP	Avg	OBP	Slg	OPS
2021	TB	AL	70	281	81	18	5	7	(2	5)	130	53	39	51	24	0	37	2	0	1	2	1	2	.288	.347	.463	.810
2022	TB	AL	83	314	87	20	3	6	(3	3)	131	46	33	44	26	1	33	0	0	4	8	0	5	.277	.328	.417	.746
	Postseason		4	19	7	2	0	2	(0	2)	15	5	4	5	0	0	3	0	0	0	0	0	0	.368	.368	.789	1.158
	2 ML YEARS		153	595	168	38	8	13	(5	8)	261	99	72	95	50	1	70	2	0	5	10	1	7	.282	.337	.439	.776

Adam Frazier

Bats: L **Throws:** R **Pos:** 2B-124;RF-21;LF-16;PH-14;DH-8;SS-4;CF-2;PR-1   **Ht:** 5'10" **Wt:** 181 **Born:** 12/14/1991 **Age:** 31

Year	Team	Lg	G	AB	H	2B	3B	HR	(Hm	Rd)	TB	R	RBI	RC	TBB	IBB	SO	HBP	SH	SF	SB	CS	GDP	Avg	OBP	Slg	OPS
2016	Pit	NL	66	146	44	8	1	2	(2	0)	60	21	11	23	12	0	26	1	0	1	4	1	0	.301	.356	.411	.767
2017	Pit	NL	121	406	112	20	6	6	(2	4)	162	55	53	61	36	2	57	8	1	3	9	5	9	.276	.344	.399	.743
2018	Pit	NL	113	318	88	23	2	10	(6	4)	145	52	35	49	29	2	53	3	1	1	1	3	3	.277	.342	.456	.798
2019	Pit	NL	152	554	154	33	7	10	(5	5)	231	80	50	72	40	4	75	9	4	1	5	5	6	.278	.336	.417	.753
2020	Pit	NL	58	209	48	7	0	7	(5	2)	76	22	23	23	17	0	35	3	1	3	1	3	3	.230	.297	.364	.661
2021	2 Tms		155	577	176	36	5	5	(4	1)	237	83	43	84	48	2	69	10	3	1	10	5	10	.305	.368	.411	.779
2022	Sea	AL	156	541	129	22	4	3	(1	2)	168	61	42	42	46	1	73	5	4	6	11	6	15	.238	.301	.311	.612
21	Pit	NL	98	386	125	28	4	4	(3	1)	173	58	32	64	35	1	46	6	0	1	5	4	6	.324	.388	.448	.836
21	SD	NL	57	191	51	8	1	1	(1	0)	64	25	11	20	13	1	23	4	3	0	5	1	4	.267	.327	.335	.662
	7 ML YEARS		821	2751	751	149	25	43	(25	18)	1079	374	257	354	228	11	388	39	14	13	41	28	46	.273	.336	.392	.728

Jackson Frazier

Bats: R **Throws:** R **Pos:** DH-8;PH-6;LF-5;RF-2;PR-2   **Ht:** 5'11" **Wt:** 212 **Born:** 9/6/1994 **Age:** 28

								BATTING											RUNNING			AVERAGES			
Year	Team	Lg	G	AB	H	2B	3B	HR	(Hm | Rd)	TB	R	RBI	RC	TBB	IBB	SO	HBP	SH	SF	SB	CS	GDP	Avg	OBP	Slg	OPS
2022	Iowa	AAA	66	232	44	8	0	6	(- | -)	70	26	35	21	25	0	92	6	0	2	5	0	3	.190	.283	.302	.585
2017	NYY	AL	39	134	31	9	4	4	(3 | 1)	60	16	17	17	7	0	43	0	0	1	1	0	2	.231	.268	.448	.715
2018	NYY	AL	15	34	9	3	0	0	(0 | 0)	12	9	1	3	5	0	13	2	0	0	0	0	3	.265	.390	.353	.743
2019	NYY	AL	69	225	60	14	0	12	(5 | 7)	110	31	38	40	16	1	70	2	0	3	1	2	2	.267	.317	.489	.806
2020	NYY	AL	39	131	35	6	1	8	(6 | 2)	67	24	26	29	25	0	44	3	0	1	3	0	5	.267	.394	.511	.905
2021	NYY	AL	66	183	34	9	0	5	(3 | 2)	58	20	15	18	32	0	65	3	0	0	2	0	8	.186	.317	.317	.633
2022	ChC	NL	19	37	8	3	0	0	(0 | 0)	11	4	1	5	7	0	11	1	0	0	1	0	1	.216	.356	.297	.653
Postseason			4	7	2	0	0	1	(0 | 1)	5	1	1	0	0	0	5	0	0	0	0	0	0	.286	.286	.714	1.000
6 ML YEARS			247	744	177	44	5	29	(17 | 12)	318	104	98	112	92	1	246	11	0	5	8	2	21	.238	.329	.427	.756

Kyle Freeland

Pitches: L **Bats:** L **Pos:** SP-31   **Ht:** 6'4" **Wt:** 204 **Born:** 5/14/1993 **Age:** 30

			HOW MUCH PITCHED					WHAT HE GAVE UP										THE RESULTS							
Year	Team	Lg	G	GS	GF	IP	BFP	H	R	ER	HR	SH	SF	HB	TBB	IBB	SO	WP	W	L	Pct	Sv-Op	Hld	Vel	OPS	ERC	ERA
2017	Col	NL	33	28	0	156.0	688	169	78	71	17	14	7	8	63	4	107	1	11	11	.500	0-0	0	92	.792	4.83	4.10
2018	Col	NL	33	33	0	202.1	844	182	64	64	17	5	6	6	70	2	173	2	17	7	.708	0-0	0	92	.666	3.33	2.85
2019	Col	NL	22	22	0	104.1	473	126	85	78	25	2	4	2	39	3	79	4	3	11	.214	0-0	0	92	.909	6.23	6.73
2020	Col	NL	13	13	0	70.2	304	77	34	34	9	0	1	3	23	0	46	0	2	3	.400	0-0	0	92	.772	4.73	4.33
2021	Col	NL	23	23	0	120.2	515	133	59	58	20	3	4	4	38	1	105	1	7	8	.467	0-0	0	91	.813	5.03	4.33
2022	Col	NL	31	31	0	174.2	766	193	96	88	19	1	9	16	53	0	131	4	9	11	.450	0-0	0	90	.798	4.74	4.53
Postseason			1	1	0	6.2	24	4	0	0	0	0	0	0	1	0	6	0	0	0	-	0-0	0	93	.382	1.06	0.00
6 ML YEARS			155	150	0	828.2	3590	880	416	393	107	25	28	39	286	10	641	12	49	51	.490	0-0	0	91	.780	4.62	4.27

Freddie Freeman

Bats: L **Throws:** R **Pos:** 1B-159   **Ht:** 6'5" **Wt:** 220 **Born:** 9/12/1989 **Age:** 33

								BATTING											RUNNING			AVERAGES			
Year	Team	Lg	G	AB	H	2B	3B	HR	(Hm	Rd)	TB	R	RBI	RC	TBB	IBB	SO	HBP	SH	SF	SB	CS	GDP	Avg	OBP	Slg	OPS
2010	Atl	NL	20	24	4	1	0	1	(0	1)	8	3	1	0	0	0	8	0	0	0	0	0	1	.167	.167	.333	.500
2011	Atl	NL	157	571	161	32	0	21	(9	12)	256	67	76	79	53	3	142	6	0	5	4	4	15	.282	.346	.448	.795
2012	Atl	NL	147	540	140	33	2	23	(12	11)	246	91	94	82	64	4	129	7	0	9	2	0	10	.259	.340	.456	.796
2013	Atl	NL	147	551	176	27	2	23	(16	7)	276	89	109	124	66	10	121	7	0	5	1	0	10	.319	.396	.501	.897
2014	Atl	NL	162	607	175	43	4	18	(7	11)	280	93	78	101	90	4	145	8	0	3	3	4	13	.288	.386	.461	.847
2015	Atl	NL	118	416	115	27	0	18	(5	13)	196	62	66	77	56	4	98	7	0	2	3	1	6	.276	.370	.471	.841
2016	Atl	NL	158	589	178	43	6	34	(15	19)	335	102	91	119	89	18	171	10	0	5	6	1	12	.302	.400	.569	.968
2017	Atl	NL	117	440	135	35	2	28	(11	17)	258	84	71	93	65	14	95	7	0	4	8	5	9	.307	.403	.586	.989
2018	Atl	NL	162	618	191	44	4	23	(13	10)	312	94	98	115	76	12	132	7	0	6	10	3	11	.309	.388	.505	.892
2019	Atl	NL	158	597	176	34	2	38	(22	16)	328	113	121	126	87	11	127	6	0	2	6	3	17	.295	.389	.549	.938
2020	Atl	NL	60	214	73	23	1	13	(9	4)	137	51	53	68	45	7	37	3	0	2	2	0	6	.341	.462	.640	1.102
2021	Atl	NL	159	600	180	25	2	31	(15	16)	302	120	83	122	85	15	107	8	0	2	8	3	11	.300	.393	.503	.896
2022	LAD	NL	159	612	199	47	2	21	(9	12)	313	117	100	129	84	12	102	5	0	7	13	3	6	.325	.407	.511	.918
Postseason			42	155	45	9	0	9	(4	5)	81	23	20	28	24	2	37	3	0	1	1	0	3	.290	.393	.523	.916
13 ML YEARS			1724	6379	1903	414	27	292	(143	149)	3247	1086	1041	1235	860	114	1414	81	0	48	66	27	132	.298	.386	.509	.895

Tyler Freeman

Bats: R **Throws:** R **Pos:** 3B-11;SS-7;2B-4;PH-2;DH-1;PR-1   **Ht:** 6'0" **Wt:** 190 **Born:** 5/21/1999 **Age:** 24

								BATTING											RUNNING			AVERAGES			
Year	Team	Lg	G	AB	H	2B	3B	HR	(Hm	Rd)	TB	R	RBI	RC	TBB	IBB	SO	HBP	SH	SF	SB	CS	GDP	Avg	OBP	Slg	OPS
2018	MhVlly	A-	72	270	95	29	4	2	(-	-)	138	49	38	57	8	1	22	19	0	4	14	3	9	.352	.405	.511	.916
2019	2 Tms	Low	123	493	151	32	5	3	(-	-)	202	89	44	80	26	0	53	24	1	3	19	5	8	.306	.368	.410	.778
2021	Akron	AA	41	164	53	14	2	2	(-	-)	77	26	19	29	8	0	21	6	0	2	4	2	1	.323	.372	.470	.842
2022	Clmbs	AAA	72	297	83	7	0	6	(-	-)	108	51	44	36	25	0	32	19	1	1	6	2	14	.279	.371	.364	.735
2022	Cle	AL	24	77	19	3	0	0	(0	0)	22	9	3	2	4	0	11	4	0	1	1	0	2	.247	.314	.286	.600

Luis Frias

Pitches: R **Bats:** R **Pos:** RP-15   **Ht:** 6'3" **Wt:** 245 **Born:** 5/23/1998 **Age:** 25

			HOW MUCH PITCHED					WHAT HE GAVE UP										THE RESULTS							
Year	Team	Lg	G	GS	GF	IP	BFP	H	R	ER	HR	SH	SF	HB	TBB	IBB	SO	WP	W	L	Pct	Sv-Op	Hld	Vel	OPS	ERC	ERA
2022	Reno	AAA	27	3	8	47.1	211	44	26	21	6	0	0	0	26	0	74	3	3	2	.600	0- -	-		.732	4.38	3.99
2021	Ari	NL	3	0	1	3.1	16	2	1	1	0	0	1	0	5	0	3	0	0	0	-	0-0	1	97	.738	5.39	2.70
2022	Ari	NL	15	0	6	17.0	90	23	20	20	1	0	0	1	17	0	14	4	1	1	.500	0-0	3	97	.914	8.66	10.59
2 ML YEARS			18	0	7	20.1	106	25	21	21	1	0	1	1	22	0	17	4	1	1	.500	0-0	4	97	.892	8.11	9.30

Max Fried

Pitches: L **Bats:** L **Pos:** SP-30   FREED   **Ht:** 6'4" **Wt:** 190 **Born:** 1/18/1994 **Age:** 29

			HOW MUCH PITCHED					WHAT HE GAVE UP										THE RESULTS							
Year	Team	Lg	G	GS	GF	IP	BFP	H	R	ER	HR	SH	SF	HB	TBB	IBB	SO	WP	W	L	Pct	Sv-Op	Hld	Vel	OPS	ERC	ERA
2017	Atl	NL	9	4	4	26.0	121	30	15	11	3	0	0	4	12	1	22	0	1	1	.500	0-0	0	92	.818	5.92	3.81
2018	Atl	NL	14	5	5	33.2	142	26	12	11	3	2	2	2	20	0	44	2	1	4	.200	0-0	1	93	.738	3.84	2.94
2019	Atl	NL	33	30	1	165.2	702	174	80	74	21	3	2	5	47	3	173	11	17	6	.739	0-0	0	94	.743	4.22	4.02
2020	Atl	NL	11	11	0	56.0	224	42	14	14	2	0	2	4	19	0	50	1	7	0	1.000	0-0	0	93	.622	2.46	2.25

Year Team	Lg	G	GS	GF	IP	BFP	H	R	ER	HR	SH	SF	HB	TBB	IBB	SO	WP	W	L	Pct	Sv-Op	Hld	Vel	OPS	ERC	ERA
					HOW MUCH PITCHED					WHAT HE GAVE UP										THE RESULTS						
2021 Atl	NL	28	28	0	165.2	667	139	61	56	15	4	3	7	41	0	158	7	14	7	.667	0-0	0	94	.635	2.77	3.04
2022 Atl	NL	30	30	0	185.1	733	156	55	51	12	0	5	4	32	2	170	9	14	7	.667	0-0	0	94	.581	2.27	2.48
Postseason		17	9	0	57.2	243	60	26	26	8	0	1	2	13	0	59	3	2	3	.400	0-0	2	94	.727	4.01	4.06
6 ML YEARS		125	108	10	632.1	2589	567	237	217	56	9	14	26	171	6	617	30	54	25	.684	0-0	1	94	.659	3.12	3.09

T.J. Friedl

Bats: L **Throws:** L **Pos:** LF-25;CF-24;RF-15;PH-12;DH-5;PR-2   FREE-duhl   **Ht:** 5'10" **Wt:** 180 **Born:** 8/14/1995 **Age:** 27

Year Team	Lg	G	AB	H	2B	3B	HR	(Hm Rd)	TB	R	RBI	RC	TBB	IBB	SO	HBP	SH	SF	SB	CS	GDP	Avg	OBP	Slg	OPS
						BATTING													RUNNING			AVERAGES			
2022 Lsvlle	AAA	64	205	57	9	3	8	(- -)	96	33	38	38	28	0	48	3	4	1	10	2	1	.278	.371	.468	.840
2021 Cin	NL	14	31	9	1	0	1	(1 0)	13	9	2	4	4	0	2	0	0	1	0	0	0	.290	.361	.419	.780
2022 Cin	NL	72	225	54	10	5	8	(4 4)	98	33	25	31	20	0	40	7	0	6	7	2	3	.240	.314	.436	.750
2 ML YEARS		86	256	63	11	5	9	(5 4)	111	42	27	35	24	0	42	7	0	7	7	2	3	.246	.320	.434	.753

Paul Fry

Pitches: L **Bats:** L **Pos:** RP-13   **Ht:** 6'0" **Wt:** 205 **Born:** 7/26/1992 **Age:** 30

Year Team	Lg	G	GS	GF	IP	BFP	H	R	ER	HR	SH	SF	HB	TBB	IBB	SO	WP	W	L	Pct	Sv-Op	Hld	Vel	OPS	ERC	ERA
					HOW MUCH PITCHED					WHAT HE GAVE UP										THE RESULTS						
2022 Reno	AAA	29	0	4	28.2	131	27	15	14	2	0	0	5	15	0	28	2	1	0	1.000	0- -	-	-	.737	4.65	4.40
2018 Bal	AL	35	0	11	37.2	159	33	20	14	1	0	0	4	15	0	36	3	1	2	.333	2-4	9	91	.613	3.34	3.35
2019 Bal	AL	66	0	8	57.1	255	54	39	34	7	1	0	6	29	1	55	2	1	9	.100	3-8	11	91	.752	4.72	5.34
2020 Bal	AL	22	0	4	22.0	98	22	7	6	3	0	0	1	9	0	29	3	1	0	1.000	0-0	4	93	.724	4.45	2.45
2021 Bal	AL	52	0	12	47.1	215	37	34	32	3	1	1	4	35	0	60	4	4	5	.444	2-4	11	93	.637	4.18	6.08
2022 2 Tms		13	0	7	13.0	61	11	10	9	1	0	1	2	9	0	14	2	0	0	-	0-0	1	92	.721	4.66	6.23
22 Bal	AL	12	0	6	12.0	54	9	9	8	1	0	1	2	7	0	12	2	0	0	-	0-0	1	92	.688	3.82	6.00
22 Ari	NL	1	0	1	1.0	7	2	1	1	0	0	0	0	2	0	2	0	0	0	-	0-0	0	91	.971	16.69	9.00
5 ML YEARS		188	0	42	177.1	788	157	110	95	15	2	2	17	97	1	194	14	7	16	.304	7-16	36	92	.688	4.24	4.82

Michael Fulmer

Pitches: R **Bats:** R **Pos:** RP-67   **Ht:** 6'3" **Wt:** 224 **Born:** 3/15/1993 **Age:** 30

Year Team	Lg	G	GS	GF	IP	BFP	H	R	ER	HR	SH	SF	HB	TBB	IBB	SO	WP	W	L	Pct	Sv-Op	Hld	Vel	OPS	ERC	ERA
					HOW MUCH PITCHED					WHAT HE GAVE UP										THE RESULTS						
2016 Det	AL	26	26	0	159.0	647	136	57	54	16	4	2	9	42	1	132	1	11	7	.611	0-0	0	95	.652	3.02	3.06
2017 Det	AL	25	25	0	164.2	676	150	80	70	13	3	8	8	40	2	114	3	10	12	.455	0-0	0	96	.644	3.04	3.83
2018 Det	AL	24	24	0	132.1	558	128	75	69	19	1	2	5	46	1	110	1	3	12	.200	0-0	0	96	.758	4.18	4.69
2020 Det	AL	10	10	0	27.2	136	45	27	27	8	1	2	1	12	0	20	0	0	2	.000	0-0	0	95	1.046	10.13	8.78
2021 Det	AL	52	4	21	69.2	297	69	27	23	7	0	2	5	20	2	73	2	5	6	.455	14-18	9	96	.694	3.82	2.97
2022 2 Tms		67	0	11	63.2	276	59	27	24	4	0	4	5	28	6	61	3	5	6	.455	3-7	25	94	.697	3.72	3.39
22 Det	AL	41	0	7	39.1	169	29	17	14	1	0	3	3	20	4	39	1	3	4	.429	2-6	18	94	.580	2.64	3.20
22 Min	AL	26	0	4	24.1	107	30	10	10	3	0	1	2	8	2	22	2	2	2	.500	1-1	7	95	.874	5.71	3.70
6 ML YEARS		204	89	32	617.0	2590	587	293	267	67	9	20	33	188	12	510	10	34	45	.430	17-25	34	95	.703	3.70	3.89

Kyle Funkhouser

Pitches: R **Bats:** R **Pos:** P   **Ht:** 6'3" **Wt:** 229 **Born:** 3/16/1994 **Age:** 29

Year Team	Lg	G	GS	GF	IP	BFP	H	R	ER	HR	SH	SF	HB	TBB	IBB	SO	WP	W	L	Pct	Sv-Op	Hld	Vel	OPS	ERC	ERA
					HOW MUCH PITCHED					WHAT HE GAVE UP										THE RESULTS						
2020 Det	AL	13	0	4	17.1	81	22	14	14	3	0	1	0	11	0	12	1	1	1	.500	0-0	0	-	.929	7.49	7.27
2021 Det	AL	57	2	7	68.1	298	58	32	26	6	2	2	3	38	0	63	9	7	4	.636	1-5	9	-	.674	3.92	3.42
2 ML YEARS		70	2	11	85.2	379	80	46	40	9	2	3	3	49	0	75	10	8	5	.615	1-5	9	-	.729	4.58	4.20

Hunter Gaddis

Pitches: R **Bats:** R **Pos:** SP-2   **Ht:** 6'6" **Wt:** 260 **Born:** 4/9/1998 **Age:** 25

Year Team	Lg	G	GS	GF	IP	BFP	H	R	ER	HR	SH	SF	HB	TBB	IBB	SO	WP	W	L	Pct	Sv-Op	Hld	Vel	OPS	ERC	ERA
					HOW MUCH PITCHED					WHAT HE GAVE UP										THE RESULTS						
2022 Akron	AA	15	14	0	76.1	312	63	37	36	12	0	1	2	26	0	102	1	4	3	.571	0- -	-		.715	3.41	4.24
2022 Clmbs	AAA	9	9	0	45.0	181	27	20	18	5	0	1	6	15	0	56	4	4	3	.571	0- -	-		.570	2.31	3.60
2022 Cle	AL	2	2	0	7.1	40	15	15	15	7	0	0	0	3	0	5	0	0	2	.000	0-0	0	93	1.504	19.07	18.41

Matt Gage

Pitches: L **Bats:** L **Pos:** RP-11   **Ht:** 6'3" **Wt:** 265 **Born:** 2/11/1993 **Age:** 30

Year Team	Lg	G	GS	GF	IP	BFP	H	R	ER	HR	SH	SF	HB	TBB	IBB	SO	WP	W	L	Pct	Sv-Op	Hld	Vel	OPS	ERC	ERA
					HOW MUCH PITCHED					WHAT HE GAVE UP										THE RESULTS						
2022 Buffalo	AAA	41	0	33	42.1	168	30	13	11	1	0	0	0	16	1	46	2	2	2	.500	12- -	-	-	.517	2.02	2.34
2022 Tor	AL	11	0	5	13.0	50	6	4	2	1	1	1	1	6	1	12	0	0	1	.000	0-1	0	93	.509	1.69	1.38

Cam Gallagher

Bats: R Throws: R Pos: C-18   Ht: 6'3" Wt: 230 Born: 12/6/1992 Age: 30

							BATTING											RUNNING			AVERAGES			
Year	Team	Lg	G	AB	H	2B	3B	HR	(Hm | Rd)	TB	R	RBI	RC	TBB	IBB	SO	HBP	SH	SF	SB	CS	GDP	Avg	OBP	Slg	OPS
2022 Omha	AAA	10	33	6	1	0	2	(- | -)	13	3	5	3	3	0	12	0	0	0	0	0	1	.182	.250	.394	.644
2022 ElPaso	AAA	16	55	14	4	0	1	(- | -)	21	9	10	5	6	0	11	0	0	2	0	0	4	.255	.317	.382	.699
2017 KC	AL	13	24	6	1	0	1	(0 | 1)	10	2	5	4	3	0	4	0	0	0	0	0	1	.250	.333	.417	.750
2018 KC	AL	22	63	13	3	0	1	(1 | 0)	19	5	7	5	3	0	15	1	1	1	0	0	1	.206	.250	.302	.552
2019 KC	AL	45	126	30	7	0	3	(2 | 1)	46	14	12	14	11	0	28	3	1	1	0	1	3	.238	.312	.365	.677
2020 KC	AL	25	53	15	5	0	1	(0 | 1)	23	10	3	6	6	0	11	0	1	0	0	0	0	.283	.356	.434	.790
2021 KC	AL	48	112	28	6	0	1	(0 | 1)	37	9	7	13	8	0	20	0	2	1	0	0	2	.250	.298	.330	.628
2022 KC	AL	18	42	9	5	0	0	(0 | 0)	14	1	5	3	3	0	13	0	2	0	0	0	0	.214	.267	.333	.600
6 ML YEARS		171	420	101	27	0	7	(3 | 4)	149	41	39	45	34	0	91	4	7	3	0	1	7	.240	.302	.355	.656

Giovanny Gallegos

Pitches: R Bats: R Pos: RP-57   gah-YAY-gohss   Ht: 6'2" Wt: 215 Born: 8/14/1991 Age: 31

			HOW MUCH PITCHED					WHAT HE GAVE UP										THE RESULTS						
Year	Team	Lg	G	GS	GF	IP	BFP	H	R	ER	HR	SH	SF	HB	TBB	IBB	SO	WP	W	L	Pct	Sv-Op	Hld	Vel	OPS	ERC	ERA
2017 NYY	AL	16	0	7	20.1	88	21	12	11	3	1	1	0	5	1	22	1	0	1	.000	0-1	0	94	.740	3.76	4.87
2018 2 Tms		6	0	4	11.1	45	11	5	5	2	1	0	0	3	0	12	0	0	0	-	1-1	0	94	.782	4.10	3.97
2019 StL	NL	66	0	10	74.0	279	44	19	19	9	0	1	3	16	2	93	3	3	2	.600	1-4	19	94	.546	1.66	2.31
2020 StL	NL	16	0	7	15.0	57	9	6	6	1	0	0	4	0	21	1	2	2	.500	4-4	1	94	.473	1.51	3.60
2021 StL	NL	73	0	20	80.1	310	51	28	27	6	1	5	6	20	2	95	4	6	5	.545	14-22	24	94	.551	1.81	3.02
2022 StL	NL	57	0	30	59.0	235	42	23	20	6	1	3	0	18	1	73	2	3	6	.333	14-20	12	94	.594	2.21	3.05
18 NYY	AL	4	0	2	10.0	40	10	5	5	2	1	0	0	3	0	10	0	0	0	-	1-1	0	94	.833	4.63	4.50
18 StL	NL	2	0	2	1.1	5	1	0	0	0	0	0	0	0	2	0	0	0	-	0-0	0	95	.400	1.13	0.00
Postseason		8	0	0	7.1	33	7	3	3	2	0	0	0	4	1	11	0	1	0	1.000	0-1	0	94	.885	5.32	3.68
6 ML YEARS		234	0	78	260.0	1014	178	93	88	27	4	10	9	66	6	316	11	14	16	.467	34-52	56	94	.582	2.06	3.05

Zac Gallen

Pitches: R Bats: R Pos: SP-31   Ht: 6'2" Wt: 189 Born: 8/3/1995 Age: 27

			HOW MUCH PITCHED					WHAT HE GAVE UP										THE RESULTS						
Year	Team	Lg	G	GS	GF	IP	BFP	H	R	ER	HR	SH	SF	HB	TBB	IBB	SO	WP	W	L	Pct	Sv-Op	Hld	Vel	OPS	ERC	ERA
2019 2 Tms	NL	15	15	0	80.0	334	62	26	25	8	0	1	4	36	1	96	3	3	6	.333	0-0	0	93	.660	3.24	2.81
2020 Ari	NL	12	12	0	72.0	291	55	24	22	9	1	0	2	25	0	82	4	3	2	.600	0-0	0	93	.620	2.91	2.75
2021 Ari	NL	23	23	0	121.1	523	108	61	58	19	3	3	5	49	1	139	6	4	10	.286	0-0	0	93	.724	3.96	4.30
2022 Ari	NL	31	31	0	184.0	714	121	56	52	15	1	3	12	47	0	192	5	12	4	.750	0-0	0	94	.560	1.97	2.54
19 Mia	NL	7	7	0	36.1	151	25	12	11	3	0	0	2	18	1	43	1	1	3	.250	0-0	0	92	.603	2.83	2.72
19 Ari	NL	8	8	0	43.2	183	37	14	14	5	0	1	2	18	0	53	2	2	3	.400	0-0	0	93	.707	3.60	2.89
4 ML YEARS		81	81	0	457.1	1862	346	167	157	51	5	7	23	157	2	509	18	22	22	.500	0-0	0	94	.633	2.84	3.09

Joey Gallo

Bats: L Throws: R Pos: LF-77;RF-48;PH-6;DH-5;PR-4;1B-1;CF-1   Ht: 6'5" Wt: 250 Born: 11/19/1993 Age: 29

							BATTING											RUNNING			AVERAGES			
Year	Team	Lg	G	AB	H	2B	3B	HR	(Hm | Rd)	TB	R	RBI	RC	TBB	IBB	SO	HBP	SH	SF	SB	CS	GDP	Avg	OBP	Slg	OPS
2015 Tex	AL	36	108	22	3	1	6	(4	2)	45	16	14	13	15	3	57	0	0	0	3	0	0	.204	.301	.417	.717
2016 Tex	AL	17	25	1	0	0	1	(1	0)	4	2	1	0	5	0	19	0	0	0	1	0	0	.040	.200	.160	.360
2017 Tex	AL	145	449	94	18	3	41	(22	19)	241	85	80	84	75	1	196	8	0	0	7	2	3	.209	.333	.537	.869
2018 Tex	AL	148	500	103	24	1	40	(23	17)	249	82	92	80	74	4	207	3	0	0	3	4	3	.206	.312	.498	.810
2019 Tex	AL	70	241	61	15	1	22	(13	9)	144	54	49	50	52	4	114	2	1	1	4	2	0	.253	.389	.598	.986
2020 Tex	AL	57	193	35	8	0	10	(5	5)	73	23	26	29	29	2	79	4	0	1	2	0	0	.181	.301	.378	.679
2021 2 Tms	AL	153	498	99	13	1	38	(22	16)	228	90	77	84	111	5	213	6	0	1	6	0	6	.199	.351	.458	.808
2022 2 Tms		126	350	56	8	2	19	(8	11)	125	48	47	44	56	0	163	3	0	1	3	0	0	.160	.280	.357	.638
21 Tex	AL	95	310	69	6	1	25	(15	10)	152	57	55	63	74	4	125	4	0	0	6	0	3	.223	.379	.490	.869
21 NYY	AL	58	188	30	7	0	13	(7	6)	76	33	22	21	37	1	88	2	0	1	0	0	3	.160	.303	.404	.707
22 Tex	AL	82	233	37	4	1	12	(4	8)	79	32	24	27	40	0	106	0	0	0	2	0	0	.159	.282	.339	.621
22 LAD	NL	44	117	19	4	1	7	(4	3)	46	16	23	17	16	0	57	3	0	1	1	0	0	.162	.277	.393	.671
Postseason		1	4	0	0	0	0	(0	0)	0	0	0	0	0	0	1	0	0	0	0	0	0	.000	.000	.000	.000
8 ML YEARS		752	2364	471	89	9	177	(98	79)	1109	400	386	384	417	19	1048	26	1	3	29	8	12	.199	.325	.469	.794

Ben Gamel

Bats: L Throws: L Pos: LF-57;RF-39;DH-21;PH-9;1B-5;CF-1;PR-1   Ht: 5'11" Wt: 180 Born: 5/17/1992 Age: 31

							BATTING											RUNNING			AVERAGES			
Year	Team	Lg	G	AB	H	2B	3B	HR	(Hm | Rd)	TB	R	RBI	RC	TBB	IBB	SO	HBP	SH	SF	SB	CS	GDP	Avg	OBP	Slg	OPS
2016 2 Tms	AL	33	48	9	2	0	1	(0	1)	14	9	5	4	6	0	16	0	3	0	0	0	1	.188	.278	.292	.569
2017 Sea	AL	134	509	140	27	5	11	(5	6)	210	68	59	68	36	1	122	1	1	3	4	1	8	.275	.322	.413	.735
2018 Sea	AL	101	257	70	14	4	1	(1	0)	95	37	19	38	31	1	61	4	0	1	7	3	4	.272	.358	.370	.728
2019 Mil	NL	134	311	77	18	0	7	(4	3)	116	47	33	40	40	2	104	3	0	2	2	2	0	.248	.337	.373	.710
2020 Mil	NL	40	114	27	8	1	3	(1	2)	46	13	10	15	13	0	39	0	0	0	2	0	4	.237	.315	.404	.718
2021 2 Tms		122	340	84	18	3	8	(5	3)	132	43	26	43	51	2	105	3	2	4	3	6	7	.247	.347	.388	.735
2022 Pit	NL	115	371	86	20	2	9	(3	6)	137	42	46	53	48	2	98	3	0	1	5	1	5	.232	.324	.369	.693
16 NYY	AL	6	8	1	0	0	0	(0	0)	1	1	0	0	1	0	1	0	1	0	0	0	1	.125	.222	.125	.347
16 Sea	AL	27	40	8	2	0	1	(0	1)	13	8	5	4	5	0	15	0	2	0	0	0	0	.200	.289	.325	.614
21 Cle	AL	11	14	1	1	0	0	(0	0)	2	1	0	0	3	0	6	0	0	0	0	0	1	.071	.235	.143	.378
21 Pit	NL	111	326	83	17	3	8	(5	3)	130	42	26	43	48	2	99	3	2	4	3	6	6	.255	.352	.399	.750
Postseason		2	2	0	0	0	0	(0	0)	0	0	0	0	0	0	0	0	0	0	0	0	0	.000	.000	.000	.000
7 ML YEARS		679	1950	493	107	15	40	(19	21)	750	259	198	261	225	8	545	14	6	11	21	15	29	.253	.333	.385	.717

Adolis Garcia

Bats: R Throws: R Pos: RF-93;CF-57;DH-21;PH-2 Ht: 6'1" Wt: 205 Born: 3/2/1993 Age: 30

									BATTING												RUNNING			AVERAGES			
Year	Team	Lg	G	AB	H	2B	3B	HR	(Hm	Rd)	TB	R	RBI	RC	TBB	IBB	SO	HBP	SH	SF	SB	CS	GDP	Avg	OBP	Slg	OPS
2018	StL	NL	21	17	2	1	0	0	(0	0)	3	3	1	0	0	0	7	0	0	0	0	0	0	.118	.118	.176	.294
2020	Tex	AL	3	6	0	0	0	0	(0	0)	0	0	0	0	1	0	4	0	0	0	0	0	0	.000	.143	.000	.143
2021	Tex	AL	149	581	141	26	2	31	(19	12)	264	77	90	72	32	0	194	5	0	4	16	5	15	.243	.286	.454	.741
2022	Tex	AL	156	605	151	34	5	27	(15	12)	276	88	101	98	40	2	183	6	0	6	25	6	9	.250	.300	.456	.756
4 ML YEARS			329	1209	294	61	7	58	(34	24)	543	168	192	170	73	2	388	11	0	10	41	11	24	.243	.290	.449	.739

Aramis Garcia

Bats: R Throws: R Pos: C-41;1B-5;PH-3;DH-1 Ht: 6'1" Wt: 228 Born: 1/12/1993 Age: 30

									BATTING												RUNNING			AVERAGES			
Year	Team	Lg	G	AB	H	2B	3B	HR	(Hm	Rd)	TB	R	RBI	RC	TBB	IBB	SO	HBP	SH	SF	SB	CS	GDP	Avg	OBP	Slg	OPS
2018	SF	NL	19	63	18	1	0	4	(2	2)	31	8	9	8	2	0	31	0	0	0	0	0	1	.286	.308	.492	.800
2019	SF	NL	18	42	6	1	0	2	(2	0)	13	5	5	2	4	1	21	0	0	0	0	0	1	.143	.217	.310	.527
2021	Oak	AL	32	88	18	1	0	3	(1	2)	28	8	7	6	1	0	28	3	2	0	0	0	4	.205	.239	.318	.557
2022	Cin	NL	47	108	23	2	0	1	(0	1)	28	6	4	4	3	0	34	2	2	0	0	1	4	.213	.248	.259	.507
4 ML YEARS			116	301	65	5	0	10	(5	5)	100	27	25	20	10	1	114	5	4	0	0	1	10	.216	.253	.332	.585

Avisail Garcia

Bats: R Throws: R Pos: RF-86;DH-11;PH-3 ah-vee-SAH-eel Ht: 6'4" Wt: 250 Born: 6/12/1991 Age: 32

									BATTING												RUNNING			AVERAGES			
Year	Team	Lg	G	AB	H	2B	3B	HR	(Hm	Rd)	TB	R	RBI	RC	TBB	IBB	SO	HBP	SH	SF	SB	CS	GDP	Avg	OBP	Slg	OPS
2012	Det	AL	23	47	15	0	0	0	(0	0)	15	7	3	5	3	1	10	1	0	0	0	2	1	.319	.373	.319	.692
2013	2 Tms	AL	72	244	69	7	3	7	(3	4)	103	31	31	30	9	0	59	1	0	2	3	3	8	.283	.309	.422	.731
2014	CWS	AL	46	172	42	8	0	7	(2	5)	71	19	29	20	14	1	44	2	0	2	4	1	5	.244	.305	.413	.718
2015	CWS	AL	148	553	142	17	2	13	(8	5)	202	66	59	58	36	3	141	8	0	4	7	7	13	.257	.309	.365	.675
2016	CWS	AL	120	413	101	18	2	12	(5	7)	159	59	51	56	34	0	115	4	0	2	4	4	9	.245	.307	.385	.692
2017	CWS	AL	136	518	171	27	5	18	(9	9)	262	75	80	96	33	5	111	9	0	1	5	3	14	.330	.380	.506	.885
2018	TB	AL	93	356	84	11	2	19	(6	13)	156	47	49	38	20	2	102	4	0	5	3	1	9	.236	.281	.438	.719
2019	TB	AL	125	489	138	25	2	20	(13	7)	227	61	72	70	31	2	125	7	0	3	10	4	15	.282	.332	.464	.796
2020	Mil	NL	53	181	43	10	0	2	(1	1)	59	20	15	21	20	2	49	6	0	0	1	3	2	.238	.333	.326	.659
2021	Mil	NL	135	461	121	18	0	29	(14	15)	226	68	86	79	38	5	121	11	0	5	8	4	12	.262	.330	.490	.820
2022	Mia	NL	98	357	80	9	0	8	(3	5)	113	31	35	28	17	0	109	4	0	2	4	0	12	.224	.266	.317	.582
13	Det	AL	30	83	20	3	1	2	(1	1)	31	12	10	7	4	0	21	0	0	1	0	1	3	.241	.273	.373	.646
13	CWS	AL	42	161	49	4	2	5	(2	3)	72	19	21	23	5	0	38	1	0	1	3	2	5	.304	.327	.447	.775
Postseason			23	66	18	1	0	1	(0	1)	22	6	7	5	2	0	21	1	0	0	1	0	1	.273	.304	.333	.638
11 ML YEARS			1049	3791	1006	150	16	135	(64	71)	1593	484	510	501	255	21	986	57	0	26	49	32	100	.265	.319	.420	.739

Bryan Garcia

Pitches: R Bats: R Pos: SP-4 Ht: 6'1" Wt: 205 Born: 4/19/1995 Age: 28

			HOW MUCH PITCHED					WHAT HE GAVE UP											THE RESULTS							
Year	Team	Lg	G	GS	GF	IP	BFP	H	R	ER	HR	SH	SF	HB	TBB	IBB	SO	WP	W	L	Pct	Sv-Op	Hld	Vel	OPS	ERC	ERA
2022	Toledo	AAA	39	11	7	85.1	355	77	36	36	11	0	1	2	34	0	69	4	5	3	.625	1--	-	-	.724	3.91	3.80
2019	Det	AL	7	0	1	6.2	33	9	9	9	1	0	0	0	5	1	7	1	0	0	-	0-1	1	94	.924	7.88	12.15
2020	Det	AL	26	0	12	21.2	93	18	6	4	0	0	1	1	10	0	12	1	2	1	.667	4-6	3	94	.559	2.84	1.66
2021	Det	AL	39	0	10	39.1	192	48	38	33	10	2	0	2	25	1	32	7	3	2	.600	2-3	5	94	.947	7.72	7.55
2022	Det	AL	4	4	0	20.1	84	14	8	8	3	0	1	3	10	0	17	1	2	0	1.000	0-0	0	93	.650	3.74	3.54
4 ML YEARS			76	4	23	88.0	402	89	61	54	14	2	2	6	50	2	68	10	7	3	.700	6-10	7	94	.792	5.48	5.52

Dermis Garcia

Bats: R Throws: R Pos: 1B-35;PH-5;DH-2;LF-1 Ht: 6'3" Wt: 200 Born: 1/7/1998 Age: 25

									BATTING												RUNNING			AVERAGES			
Year	Team	Lg	G	AB	H	2B	3B	HR	(Hm	Rd)	TB	R	RBI	RC	TBB	IBB	SO	HBP	SH	SF	SB	CS	GDP	Avg	OBP	Slg	OPS
2022	LsVgs	AAA	68	239	63	15	1	13	(-	-)	119	51	44	46	32	0	83	2	0	5	4	1	1	.264	.349	.498	.847
2022	Oak	AL	39	116	24	6	0	5	(1	4)	45	13	20	17	8	0	55	1	0	0	0	0	1	.207	.264	.388	.652

Jarlin Garcia

Pitches: L Bats: L Pos: RP-58 HAR-lin Ht: 6'3" Wt: 215 Born: 1/18/1993 Age: 30

			HOW MUCH PITCHED					WHAT HE GAVE UP											THE RESULTS							
Year	Team	Lg	G	GS	GF	IP	BFP	H	R	ER	HR	SH	SF	HB	TBB	IBB	SO	WP	W	L	Pct	Sv-Op	Hld	Vel	OPS	ERC	ERA
2017	Mia	NL	68	0	14	53.1	225	47	29	28	6	2	2	4	17	0	42	5	1	2	.333	0-1	15	94	.695	3.46	4.73
2018	Mia	NL	29	7	3	66.0	278	59	37	36	16	1	2	0	28	3	40	0	3	3	.500	0-0	2	92	.792	4.52	4.91
2019	Mia	NL	53	0	11	50.2	206	40	17	17	4	1	2	2	16	2	39	4	4	2	.667	0-1	6	93	.602	2.61	3.02
2020	SF	NL	19	0	5	18.1	73	11	6	1	0	0	3	2	7	1	14	0	2	1	.667	0-0	6	94	.487	1.70	0.49
2021	SF	NL	58	0	13	68.2	269	48	26	20	9	3	1	2	18	3	68	2	6	3	.667	1-3	11	93	.635	2.26	2.62
2022	SF	NL	58	0	14	65.0	270	60	34	27	10	2	1	1	18	1	56	2	1	4	.200	1-3	4	94	.710	3.55	3.74
Postseason			2	0	0	1.1	8	2	2	1	1	0	0	0	1	0	1	0	0	0	-	0-0	0	93	1.089	12.70	6.75
6 ML YEARS			285	7	60	322.0	1321	265	149	129	45	9	11	11	104	10	259	13	17	15	.531	2-8	44	93	.681	3.18	3.61

Leury Garcia

lay-OOH-ree

Bats: B Throws: R Pos: 2B-47;SS-19;RF-15;LF-9;PR-9;3B-6;PH-6;DH-5;CF-4 Ht: 5'8" Wt: 190 Born: 3/18/1991 Age: 32

								BATTING															RUNNING			AVERAGES			
Year	Team	Lg	G	AB	H	2B	3B	HR	(Hm | Rd)	TB	R	RBI	RC	TBB	IBB	SO	HBP	SH	SF				SB	CS	GDP	Avg	OBP	Slg	OPS
2013	2 Tms	AL	45	101	20	1	1	0	(0 | 0)	23	10	2	4	7	0	34	0	2	1				7	2	0	.198	.248	.228	.475
2014	CWS	AL	74	145	24	3	0	1	(0 | 1)	30	13	6	0	5	1	48	0	4	1				11	1	6	.166	.192	.207	.399
2015	CWS	AL	18	14	3	0	0	0	(0 | 0)	3	0	1	2	1	0	7	0	0	0				1	0	0	.214	.267	.214	.481
2016	CWS	AL	18	48	11	1	1	1	(1 | 0)	17	6	5	5	1	0	13	1	0	0				2	1	0	.229	.260	.354	.614
2017	CWS	AL	87	300	81	15	2	9	(5 | 4)	127	41	33	39	13	0	69	8	3	2				8	5	4	.270	.316	.423	.739
2018	CWS	AL	82	258	70	7	4	4	(2 | 2)	97	23	32	38	9	0	69	3	4	1				12	1	2	.271	.303	.376	.679
2019	CWS	AL	140	577	161	27	3	8	(6 | 2)	218	93	40	60	21	0	139	6	11	3				15	5	6	.279	.310	.378	.688
2020	CWS	AL	16	59	16	1	0	3	(3 | 0)	26	6	8	9	4	0	9	0	0	0				0	0	0	.271	.317	.441	.758
2021	CWS	AL	126	415	111	22	4	5	(2 | 3)	156	60	54	60	41	0	97	4	9	5				6	2	12	.267	.335	.376	.711
2022	CWS	AL	97	300	63	8	0	3	(2 | 1)	80	38	20	15	7	0	65	3	2	3				2	0	6	.210	.233	.267	.500
13	Tex	AL	25	52	10	0	1	0	(0 | 0)	12	8	1	2	3	0	16	0	2	0				1	0	0	.192	.236	.231	.467
13	CWS	AL	20	49	10	1	0	0	(0 | 0)	11	2	1	2	4	0	18	0	0	1				6	2	0	.204	.259	.224	.484
	Postseason		6	21	3	1	0	1	(1 | 0)	7	3	4	4	1	0	10	0	0	0				0	0	0	.143	.182	.333	.515
	10 ML YEARS		703	2217	560	85	15	34	(21 | 13)	777	290	201	232	109	1	550	25	35	16				64	17	36	.253	.293	.350	.644

Luis Garcia

Pitches: R Bats: R Pos: RP-64 Ht: 6'2" Wt: 240 Born: 1/30/1987 Age: 36

			HOW MUCH PITCHED					WHAT HE GAVE UP										THE RESULTS							
Year	Team	Lg	G	GS	GF	IP	BFP	H	R	ER	HR	SH	SF	HB	TBB	IBB	SO	WP	W	L	Pct	Sv-Op	Hld	Vel	OPS	ERC	ERA
2013	Phi	NL	24	0	6	31.1	138	27	15	13	3	0	0	1	23	0	23	3	1	1	.500	0-0	1	94	.764	4.85	3.73
2014	Phi	NL	13	0	5	14.0	69	14	12	10	2	1	0	0	13	0	12	4	1	0	1.000	0-0	0	95	.815	6.43	6.43
2015	Phi	NL	72	0	14	66.2	304	72	28	26	4	3	2	0	37	8	63	6	4	6	.400	2-4	16	96	.748	4.59	3.51
2016	Phi	NL	17	0	7	15.1	76	21	11	11	2	0	1	1	8	1	14	2	1	1	.500	0-1	1	97	.895	7.04	6.46
2017	Phi	NL	66	0	16	71.1	295	61	22	21	3	1	2	0	26	5	60	9	2	5	.286	2-7	14	97	.593	2.69	2.65
2018	Phi	NL	59	0	7	46.0	204	49	31	31	4	0	1	4	18	1	51	7	3	1	.750	1-4	13	97	.773	4.63	6.07
2019	LAA	AL	64	2	18	62.0	278	61	35	30	13	1	2	5	33	1	57	7	2	1	.667	1-3	6	97	.800	5.68	4.35
2020	Tex	AL	11	2	3	8.1	45	10	9	7	1	0	0	0	9	1	11	2	0	2	.000	0-0	0	97	.839	7.69	7.56
2021	StL	NL	34	0	6	33.1	135	25	12	12	2	0	2	1	8	1	34	3	1	1	.500	2-3	11	99	.550	1.98	3.24
2022	SD	NL	64	0	11	61.0	259	57	28	23	3	1	1	5	17	0	68	7	4	6	.400	3-4	19	99	.617	3.19	3.39
	Postseason		1	0	0	1.2	7	1	0	0	0	0	0	0	0	0	0	0	0	0	—	0-0	0	98	.452	2.03	0.00
	10 ML YEARS		424	4	93	409.1	1803	397	203	184	37	7	11	17	192	18	393	50	19	24	.442	11-26	81	97	.711	4.18	4.05

Luis Garcia

Bats: L Throws: R Pos: SS-59;2B-33;PH-2 Ht: 6'2" Wt: 212 Born: 5/16/2000 Age: 23

								BATTING															RUNNING			AVERAGES			
Year	Team	Lg	G	AB	H	2B	3B	HR	(Hm | Rd)	TB	R	RBI	RC	TBB	IBB	SO	HBP	SH	SF				SB	CS	GDP	Avg	OBP	Slg	OPS
2022	Roch	AAA	45	185	57	7	4	8	(- | -)	96	39	32	36	18	2	36	0	0	2				3	0	2	.308	.366	.519	.885
2020	Was	NL	40	134	37	6	0	2	(0 | 2)	49	18	16	16	5	0	29	0	0	0				1	1	3	.276	.302	.366	.668
2021	Was	NL	70	236	57	18	2	6	(3 | 3)	97	29	22	22	11	1	43	0	0	0				0	2	8	.242	.275	.411	.686
2022	Was	NL	93	360	99	23	2	7	(4 | 3)	147	29	45	44	11	1	84	1	1	4				3	4	5	.275	.295	.408	.704
	3 ML YEARS		203	730	193	47	4	15	(7 | 8)	293	76	83	82	27	2	156	1	1	4				4	7	16	.264	.290	.401	.691

Luis Garcia

Pitches: R Bats: R Pos: SP-28 Ht: 6'1" Wt: 244 Born: 12/13/1996 Age: 26

			HOW MUCH PITCHED					WHAT HE GAVE UP										THE RESULTS							
Year	Team	Lg	G	GS	GF	IP	BFP	H	R	ER	HR	SH	SF	HB	TBB	IBB	SO	WP	W	L	Pct	Sv-Op	Hld	Vel	OPS	ERC	ERA
2020	Hou	AL	5	1	1	12.1	49	7	4	4	1	0	1	1	5	0	9	1	0	1	.000	0-0	0	94	.622	2.08	2.92
2021	Hou	AL	30	28	1	155.1	633	133	62	60	19	2	5	3	50	1	167	9	11	8	.579	0-0	0	93	.687	3.26	3.48
2022	Hou	AL	28	28	0	157.1	643	131	70	65	23	1	5	1	47	0	157	8	15	8	.652	0-0	0	94	.678	3.09	3.72
	Postseason		6	6	0	17.2	82	13	14	14	3	0	0	1	14	1	22	0	1	3	.250	0-0	0	95	.744	4.60	7.13
	3 ML YEARS		63	57	2	325.0	1325	271	136	129	43	3	11	5	102	1	333	18	26	17	.605	0-0	0	94	.680	3.13	3.57

Maikel Garcia

Bats: R Throws: R Pos: SS-8;PH-1 Ht: 6'0" Wt: 145 Born: 3/3/2000 Age: 23

								BATTING															RUNNING			AVERAGES			
Year	Team	Lg	G	AB	H	2B	3B	HR	(Hm | Rd)	TB	R	RBI	RC	TBB	IBB	SO	HBP	SH	SF				SB	CS	GDP	Avg	OBP	Slg	OPS
2022	NWArk	AA	78	323	94	24	1	4	(- | -)	132	63	33	49	41	0	60	0	3	2				27	3	7	.291	.369	.409	.778
2022	Omha	AAA	40	164	45	10	0	7	(- | -)	76	41	28	27	17	1	42	1	1	3				12	5	3	.274	.341	.463	.804
2022	KC	AL	9	22	7	1	0	0	(0 | 0)	8	1	2	1	1	0	5	0	0	0				0	0	0	.318	.348	.364	.711

Rico Garcia

Pitches: R Bats: R Pos: RP-6 Ht: 5'9" Wt: 201 Born: 1/10/1994 Age: 29

			HOW MUCH PITCHED					WHAT HE GAVE UP										THE RESULTS							
Year	Team	Lg	G	GS	GF	IP	BFP	H	R	ER	HR	SH	SF	HB	TBB	IBB	SO	WP	W	L	Pct	Sv-Op	Hld	Vel	OPS	ERC	ERA
2022	Norfolk	AAA	18	2	3	34.2	141	25	10	9	6	0	0	6	14	0	40	5	3	1	.750	3- -	-	-	.639	3.06	2.34
2019	Col	NL	2	1	1	6.0	30	9	7	7	3	0	0	0	5	0	2	0	0	1	.000	0-0	0	90	1.307	13.57	10.50
2020	SF	NL	12	0	2	10.0	44	13	6	6	1	0	1	0	4	0	7	2	1	0	.500	0-1	2	96	.874	6.12	5.40
2022	Bal	AL	6	0	4	8.0	35	8	4	4	2	0	0	0	3	0	2	0	0	0	—	0-0	0	95	.783	4.92	4.50
	3 ML YEARS		20	1	7	24.0	109	30	17	17	6	0	1	0	12	0	11	2	1	2	.333	0-1	2	94	.958	7.37	6.38

Rony Garcia

Pitches: R **Bats:** R **Pos:** SP-8; RP-8   **Ht:** 6'3" **Wt:** 200 **Born:** 12/19/1997 **Age:** 25

Year	Team	Lg	G	GS	GF	IP	BFP	H	R	ER	HR	SH	SF	HB	TBB	IBB	SO	WP	W	L	Pct	Sv-Op	Hld	Vel	OPS	ERC	ERA
2020	Det	AL	15	2	7	21.0	96	25	20	19	7	0	0	0	9	0	14	1	1	0	1.000	0-0	0	93	.940	7.04	8.14
2021	Det	AL	2	0	0	3.2	12	1	1	1	1	0	0	0	2	0	2	0	0	0	-	0-1	0	92	.650	2.31	2.45
2022	Det	AL	16	8	2	51.0	206	40	27	25	9	0	1	4	13	0	48	3	3	3	.500	0-0	0	93	.692	3.16	4.41
	3 ML YEARS		33	10	9	75.2	314	66	48	45	17	0	1	4	24	0	64	4	4	3	.571	0-1	0	93	.766	4.10	5.35

Yimi Garcia

Pitches: R **Bats:** R **Pos:** RP-61   yee-mee   **Ht:** 6'1" **Wt:** 230 **Born:** 8/18/1990 **Age:** 32

Year	Team	Lg	G	GS	GF	IP	BFP	H	R	ER	HR	SH	SF	HB	TBB	IBB	SO	WP	W	L	Pct	Sv-Op	Hld	Vel	OPS	ERC	ERA
2014	LAD	NL	8	0	5	10.0	36	6	2	2	2	0	0	0	9	0	9	0	0	0	-	0-0	1	92	.537	1.59	1.80
2015	LAD	NL	59	1	15	56.2	225	44	23	21	8	0	2	2	10	1	68	1	3	5	.375	1-6	11	93	.595	2.40	3.34
2016	LAD	NL	9	0	1	8.1	35	9	3	3	0	2	2	1	1	0	4	0	0	0	-	0-2	1	93	.644	3.23	3.24
2018	LAD	NL	25	0	3	22.1	101	29	18	14	7	0	0	2	4	1	19	0	1	2	.333	0-1	2	94	.957	6.74	5.64
2019	LAD	NL	64	0	22	62.1	247	40	28	25	15	1	1	6	14	2	66	1	1	4	.200	0-3	4	94	.671	2.65	3.61
2020	Mia	NL	14	0	4	15.0	60	9	1	1	0	0	0	0	5	0	19	0	3	0	1.000	1-2	4	94	.452	1.35	0.60
2021	2 Tms		62	0	38	57.2	237	49	33	27	8	2	3	1	18	5	60	0	4	9	.308	15-18	4	96	.698	3.12	4.21
2022	Tor	AL	61	0	9	61.0	247	48	26	21	6	0	4	4	16	3	58	1	4	5	.444	1-5	22	95	.621	2.60	3.10
21	Mia	NL	39	0	30	36.1	151	31	18	14	5	1	3	1	13	5	35	0	3	7	.300	15-18	2	96	.729	3.27	3.47
21	Hou	AL	23	0	8	21.1	86	18	15	13	3	1	0	0	5	0	25	0	1	2	.333	0-0	2	96	.646	2.85	5.48
	Postseason		15	0	1	13.1	60	13	10	10	3	0	1	2	5	0	14	2	1	1	.500	0-1	1	94	.756	5.24	6.75
	8 ML YEARS		302	1	97	293.1	1188	234	134	114	46	5	12	16	69	12	303	3	16	25	.390	18-37	49	94	.660	2.86	3.50

Kyle Garlick

Bats: R **Throws:** R **Pos:** LF-27;RF-23;PH-19;DH-8;PR-1   **Ht:** 6'1" **Wt:** 210 **Born:** 1/26/1992 **Age:** 31

Year	Team	Lg	G	AB	H	2B	3B	HR	(Hm	Rd)	TB	R	RBI	RC	TBB	IBB	SO	HBP	SH	SF	SB	CS	GDP	Avg	OBP	Slg	OPS
2022	StPaul	AAA	11	40	10	1	1	3	(-	-)	22	5	7	8	6	0	16	0	0	0	0	0	2	.250	.348	.550	.898
2019	LAD	NL	30	48	12	4	0	3	(2	1)	25	8	6	7	5	1	19	0	0	0	0	0	0	.250	.321	.521	.842
2020	Phi	NL	12	22	3	1	0	0	(0	0)	4	0	3	0	0	0	7	1	0	0	0	0	0	.136	.174	.182	.356
2021	Min	AL	36	99	23	8	0	5	(1	4)	46	17	10	10	6	0	32	1	0	1	1	0	2	.232	.280	.465	.745
2022	Min	AL	66	150	35	3	0	9	(2	7)	65	23	18	16	8	0	48	3	0	1	0	0	2	.233	.284	.433	.717
	4 ML YEARS		144	319	73	16	0	17	(5	12)	140	48	37	33	19	1	106	5	0	2	1	0	4	.229	.281	.439	.720

Dustin Garneau

Bats: R **Throws:** R **Pos:** C-7;PH-1   GARR-noh   **Ht:** 6'2" **Wt:** 205 **Born:** 8/13/1987 **Age:** 35

Year	Team	Lg	G	AB	H	2B	3B	HR	(Hm	Rd)	TB	R	RBI	RC	TBB	IBB	SO	HBP	SH	SF	SB	CS	GDP	Avg	OBP	Slg	OPS
2022	Toledo	AAA	52	164	32	9	0	7	(-	-)	62	21	21	20	17	0	52	8	0	2	1	0	2	.195	.298	.378	.676
2015	Col	NL	22	70	11	3	0	2	(0	2)	20	6	8	5	6	2	14	0	0	0	0	0	2	.157	.224	.286	.509
2016	Col	NL	24	68	16	6	0	1	(0	1)	25	7	6	6	6	0	22	0	0	1	0	0	1	.235	.293	.368	.661
2017	2 Tms		41	112	21	8	0	2	(1	1)	35	10	9	6	12	0	36	1	1	0	0	0	3	.188	.272	.313	.585
2018	CWS	AL	1	2	1	0	0	0	(0	0)	1	0	1	1	1	0	0	0	0	0	0	0	0	.500	.667	.500	1.167
2019	2 Tms		35	86	21	5	0	3	(1	2)	35	14	14	15	10	0	22	4	0	0	0	0	1	.244	.350	.407	.757
2020	Hou	AL	17	38	6	0	1	1	(1	0)	11	4	4	2	6	0	15	0	2	0	0	0	1	.158	.273	.289	.562
2021	Det	AL	20	62	13	5	0	6	(2	4)	36	9	11	5	3	0	18	1	0	2	0	0	2	.210	.250	.581	.831
2022	Det	AL	8	10	3	1	0	0	(0	0)	4	1	2	1	0	0	4	0	0	0	0	0	0	.300	.364	.400	.764
17	Col	NL	22	68	14	7	0	1	(1	0)	24	5	6	4	4	0	24	1	1	0	0	0	1	.206	.253	.353	.613
17	Oak	AL	19	44	7	1	0	1	(0	1)	11	5	3	2	8	0	12	0	0	0	0	0	2	.159	.288	.250	.538
19	LAA	AL	28	69	16	3	0	2	(1	1)	25	11	7	9	8	0	18	4	0	0	0	0	1	.232	.346	.362	.708
19	Oak	AL	7	17	5	2	0	1	(0	1)	10	3	7	6	2	0	4	0	0	0	0	0	0	.294	.368	.588	.957
	Postseason		2	2	0	0	0	0	(0	0)	0	0	0	0	0	0	2	0	0	0	0	0	0	.000	.000	.000	.000
	8 ML YEARS		168	448	92	28	1	15	(5	10)	167	51	54	42	45	2	131	6	3	3	0	0	10	.205	.285	.373	.658

Amir Garrett

Pitches: L **Bats:** R **Pos:** RP-60   **Ht:** 6'5" **Wt:** 239 **Born:** 5/3/1992 **Age:** 31

Year	Team	Lg	G	GS	GF	IP	BFP	H	R	ER	HR	SH	SF	HB	TBB	IBB	SO	WP	W	L	Pct	Sv-Op	Hld	Vel	OPS	ERC	ERA
2017	Cin	NL	16	14	0	70.2	321	74	60	58	23	1	3	2	40	2	63	1	3	8	.273	0-0	1	92	.937	6.86	7.39
2018	Cin	NL	66	0	7	63.0	264	56	30	30	8	1	1	3	25	3	71	3	1	2	.333	0-2	21	94	.734	3.81	4.29
2019	Cin	NL	69	0	4	56.0	246	44	22	20	7	0	0	4	35	1	78	5	5	3	.625	0-3	22	95	.695	4.19	3.21
2020	Cin	NL	21	0	1	18.1	69	10	5	5	4	0	0	0	7	0	26	0	1	0	1.000	1-2	6	95	.601	2.45	2.45
2021	Cin	NL	63	0	22	47.2	215	46	34	32	9	1	0	0	29	4	61	5	0	4	.000	7-11	7	95	.799	5.19	6.04
2022	KC	AL	60	0	3	45.1	196	28	26	25	0	0	1	5	32	0	49	7	3	1	.750	0-1	10	94	.572	2.86	4.96
	Postseason		1	0	1	0.0	1	1	0	0	0	0	0	0	0	0	0	0	0	0	-	0-0	0	-	2.000	-	-
	6 ML YEARS		295	14	37	301.0	1311	258	177	170	51	3	5	14	168	10	348	21	13	18	.419	8-19	67	94	.757	4.55	5.08

Braxton Garrett

Pitches: L Bats: R Pos: SP-17   Ht: 6'2" Wt: 202 Born: 8/5/1997 Age: 25

			HOW MUCH PITCHED					WHAT HE GAVE UP											THE RESULTS						
Year	Team	Lg	G	GS	GF	IP	BFP	H	R	ER	HR	SH	SF	HB	TBB	IBB	SO	WP	W	L	Pct	Sv-Op	Hld	Vel	OPS	ERC	ERA
2022	Jaxnvl	AAA	7	7	0	34.1	141	28	13	12	3	0	3	1	9	0	29	3	2	3	.400	0- -	-	-	.598	2.56	3.15
2020	Mia	NL	2	2	0	7.2	34	8	6	5	3	0	0	0	5	0	8	1	1	1	.500	0-0	0	90	1.003	8.00	5.87
2021	Mia	NL	8	7	1	34.0	159	42	20	19	3	4	1	2	20	0	32	4	1	2	.333	0-0	0	90	.860	6.53	5.03
2022	Mia	NL	17	17	0	88.0	373	86	38	35	9	1	0	10	24	1	90	2	3	7	.300	0-0	0	91	.725	3.93	3.58
	3 ML YEARS		27	26	1	129.2	566	136	64	59	15	5	1	12	49	1	130	7	5	10	.333	0-0	0	91	.778	4.81	4.10

Reed Garrett

Pitches: R Bats: R Pos: RP-7   Ht: 6'2" Wt: 196 Born: 1/2/1993 Age: 30

			HOW MUCH PITCHED					WHAT HE GAVE UP											THE RESULTS						
Year	Team	Lg	G	GS	GF	IP	BFP	H	R	ER	HR	SH	SF	HB	TBB	IBB	SO	WP	W	L	Pct	Sv-Op	Hld	Vel	OPS	ERC	ERA
2022	Roch	AAA	42	0	21	47.1	196	40	20	16	5	2	0	6	18	1	53	4	4	4	.500	3- -	-	-	.674	3.18	3.04
2019	Det	AL	13	0	5	15.1	77	24	15	14	3	0	0	1	13	0	10	0	0	0	-	0-1	0	96	1.144	11.60	8.22
2022	Was	NL	7	0	0	9.1	49	13	8	7	1	0	0	1	8	1	6	1	0	1	.000	0-0	0	96	.874	8.72	6.75
	2 ML YEARS		20	0	5	24.2	126	37	23	21	4	0	0	2	21	1	16	1	0	1	.000	0-1	0	96	1.039	10.46	7.66

Stone Garrett

Bats: R Throws: R Pos: LF-13;DH-9;PH-5;PR-1   Ht: 6'2" Wt: 195 Born: 11/22/1995 Age: 27

			BATTING																	RUNNING			AVERAGES			
Year	Team	Lg	G	AB	H	2B	3B	HR	(Hm	Rd)	TB	R	RBI	RC	TBB	IBB	SO	HBP	SH	SF	SB	CS	GDP	Avg	OBP	Slg	OPS
2022	Reno	AAA	103	389	107	22	4	28	(-	-)	221	73	96	82	33	2	105	3	0	6	15	2	6	.275	.332	.568	.900
2022	Ari	NL	27	76	21	8	0	4	(2	2)	41	13	10	12	3	0	27	1	0	1	3	1	1	.276	.309	.539	.848

Mitch Garver

Bats: R Throws: R Pos: DH-36;C-14;PH-5   Ht: 6'1" Wt: 220 Born: 1/15/1991 Age: 32

			BATTING																	RUNNING			AVERAGES			
Year	Team	Lg	G	AB	H	2B	3B	HR	(Hm	Rd)	TB	R	RBI	RC	TBB	IBB	SO	HBP	SH	SF	SB	CS	GDP	Avg	OBP	Slg	OPS
2017	Min	AL	23	46	9	1	3	0	(0	0)	16	5	3	5	6	0	15	0	0	0	0	0	1	.196	.288	.348	.636
2018	Min	AL	103	302	81	19	2	7	(4	3)	125	38	45	45	29	2	72	2	1	1	0	0	8	.268	.335	.414	.749
2019	Min	AL	93	311	85	16	1	31	(16	15)	196	70	67	71	41	0	87	5	0	2	0	0	1	.273	.365	.630	.995
2020	Min	AL	23	72	12	1	0	2	(2	0)	19	8	5	3	7	0	37	1	0	1	0	0	1	.167	.247	.264	.511
2021	Min	AL	68	207	53	15	0	13	(5	8)	107	29	34	36	31	0	71	3	0	2	1	1	4	.256	.358	.517	.875
2022	Tex	AL	54	188	39	7	0	10	(2	8)	76	23	24	24	23	0	53	2	0	2	1	1	3	.207	.298	.404	.702
	Postseason		4	13	2	0	0	0	(0	0)	2	1	1	1	1	0	6	0	0	0	0	0	0	.154	.214	.154	.368
	6 ML YEARS		364	1126	279	59	6	63	(29	34)	539	173	178	184	137	2	335	13	1	8	2	2	22	.248	.334	.479	.813

Ralph Garza

Pitches: R Bats: R Pos: RP-19   Ht: 6'2" Wt: 220 Born: 4/6/1994 Age: 29

			HOW MUCH PITCHED					WHAT HE GAVE UP											THE RESULTS						
Year	Team	Lg	G	GS	GF	IP	BFP	H	R	ER	HR	SH	SF	HB	TBB	IBB	SO	WP	W	L	Pct	Sv-Op	Hld	Vel	OPS	ERC	ERA
2022	Drham	AAA	21	3	6	30.1	124	31	21	19	6	1	0	3	4	0	22	0	3	2	.600	1- -	-	-	.792	4.28	5.64
2021	Min	AL	27	0	16	30.1	127	24	15	12	5	0	0	1	14	1	29	1	1	4	.200	1-2	2	91	.718	3.71	3.56
2022	TB	AL	19	0	10	35.0	153	38	14	13	4	1	0	2	16	2	17	2	2	2	.500	0-2	0	89	.794	5.20	3.34
	21 Hou	AL	9	0	8	11.0	49	11	6	5	2	0	0	0	7	1	14	1	1	2	.333	0-0	0	92	.867	5.61	4.09
	21 Min	AL	18	0	8	19.1	78	13	9	7	3	0	0	1	7	0	15	0	0	2	.000	1-2	2	91	.626	2.74	3.26
	2 ML YEARS		46	0	26	65.1	280	62	29	25	9	1	0	3	30	3	46	3	3	6	.333	1-4	2	90	.759	4.49	3.44

Kevin Gausman

Pitches: R Bats: L Pos: SP-31   Gauze-min   Ht: 6'2" Wt: 205 Born: 1/6/1991 Age: 32

			HOW MUCH PITCHED					WHAT HE GAVE UP											THE RESULTS						
Year	Team	Lg	G	GS	GF	IP	BFP	H	R	ER	HR	SH	SF	HB	TBB	IBB	SO	WP	W	L	Pct	Sv-Op	Hld	Vel	OPS	ERC	ERA
2013	Bal	AL	20	5	3	47.2	201	51	30	30	8	2	1	0	13	2	49	4	3	5	.375	0-2	0	96	.792	4.41	5.66
2014	Bal	AL	20	20	0	113.1	476	111	48	45	7	3	7	1	38	0	88	9	7	7	.500	0-0	0	95	.685	3.52	3.57
2015	Bal	AL	25	17	1	112.1	470	109	56	53	17	2	3	2	29	1	103	7	4	7	.364	0-0	1	95	.739	3.74	4.25
2016	Bal	AL	30	30	0	179.2	757	183	76	72	28	4	3	5	47	1	174	8	9	12	.429	0-0	0	95	.742	4.13	3.61
2017	Bal	AL	34	34	0	186.2	816	208	99	97	29	1	3	5	71	0	179	8	11	12	.478	0-0	0	95	.808	5.24	4.68
2018	2 Tms		31	31	0	192.0	776	189	85	80	26	0	4	7	50	1	148	6	10	11	.476	0-0	0	94	.753	4.19	3.92
2019	2 Tms	NL	31	17	6	102.1	451	113	71	65	15	7	6	5	32	3	114	2	3	9	.250	0-0	2	94	.792	4.76	5.72
2020	SF	NL	12	10	1	59.2	245	50	26	24	8	0	2	0	16	0	79	4	3	3	.500	0-0	0	95	.660	2.87	3.62
2021	SF	NL	33	33	0	192.0	775	150	66	60	20	2	4	4	50	1	227	7	14	6	.700	0-0	0	95	.609	2.48	2.81
2022	Tor	AL	31	31	0	174.2	725	188	72	65	15	1	5	1	28	0	205	2	12	10	.545	0-0	0	95	.700	3.49	3.35
	18 Bal	AL	21	21	0	124.0	534	139	62	61	21	0	2	5	32	0	104	6	5	8	.385	0-0	0	94	.806	4.88	4.43
	18 Atl	NL	10	10	0	59.2	242	50	23	19	5	0	2	2	18	1	44	0	5	3	.625	0-0	0	94	.635	2.87	2.87
	19 Atl	NL	16	16	0	80.0	360	92	60	55	12	6	6	4	27	2	85	2	3	7	.300	0-0	0	94	.814	5.14	6.19
	19 Cin	NL	15	1	6	22.1	91	21	11	10	3	1	0	1	5	1	29	0	0	2	.000	0-0	2	95	.705	3.46	4.03
	Postseason		6	1	2	16.0	62	10	7	7	1	0	1	0	7	1	18	0	1	0	.000	0-0	0	96	.570	2.06	3.94
	10 ML YEARS		267	228	11	1352.0	5692	1352	629	591	173	22	38	30	374	9	1366	57	76	82	.481	0-2	5	95	.726	3.86	3.93

Domingo German

Pitches: R Bats: R Pos: SP-14; RP-1   hair-MAHN   Ht: 6'2" Wt: 181 Born: 8/4/1992 Age: 30

Year	Team	Lg	G	GS	GF	IP	BFP	H	R	ER	HR	SH	SF	HB	TBB	IBB	SO	WP	W	L	Pct	Sv-Op	Hld	Vel	OPS	ERC	ERA
2017	NYY	AL	7	0	5	14.1	62	11	6	5	1	1	1	0	9	0	18	3	0	1	.000	0-0	0	96	.661	3.44	3.14
2018	NYY	AL	21	14	2	85.2	375	81	55	53	15	0	2	5	33	0	102	7	2	6	.250	0-0	0	95	.774	4.39	5.57
2019	NYY	AL	27	24	0	143.0	594	125	69	64	30	1	1	5	39	0	153	5	18	4	.818	0-0	0	94	.727	3.69	4.03
2021	NYY	AL	22	18	0	98.1	410	89	52	50	17	0	1	2	27	0	98	3	4	5	.444	0-0	1	94	.714	3.58	4.58
2022	NYY	AL	15	14	0	72.1	298	65	31	29	11	0	0	4	19	0	58	0	2	5	.286	0-0	0	93	.713	3.57	3.61
5 ML YEARS			92	70	7	413.2	1739	371	213	201	74	2	5	16	127	0	429	18	26	21	.553	0-0	1	94	.730	3.78	4.37

Frank German

Pitches: R Bats: R Pos: RP-5   Ht: 6'2" Wt: 195 Born: 9/22/1997 Age: 25

Year	Team	Lg	G	GS	GF	IP	BFP	H	R	ER	HR	SH	SF	HB	TBB	IBB	SO	WP	W	L	Pct	Sv-Op	Hld	Vel	OPS	ERC	ERA
2022	Portlnd	AA	11	0	7	11.1	46	6	7	4	0	0	1	4	3	0	18	3	3	1	.750	0- -	-	-	.493	1.82	3.18
2022	Wrcstr	AAA	32	0	24	38.1	151	20	11	11	2	0	1	4	16	0	46	4	2	1	.667	7- -	-	-	.496	1.83	2.58
2022	Bos	AL	5	0	3	4.0	23	7	8	8	2	0	0	0	4	0	4	0	0	0	-	0-0	0	98	1.215	15.52	18.00

Ian Gibaut

Pitches: R Bats: R Pos: RP-34   jih-BOH   Ht: 6'3" Wt: 250 Born: 11/19/1993 Age: 29

Year	Team	Lg	G	GS	GF	IP	BFP	H	R	ER	HR	SH	SF	HB	TBB	IBB	SO	WP	W	L	Pct	Sv-Op	Hld	Vel	OPS	ERC	ERA
2022	Clmbs	AAA	17	0	8	19.2	79	16	8	7	0	0	1	0	8	0	19	2	2	0	1.000	3- -	-	-	.604	2.55	3.20
2019	2 Tms	AL	10	0	1	14.1	64	12	9	9	1	0	2	1	10	1	16	1	1	1	.500	0-0	0	95	.732	4.28	5.65
2020	Tex	AL	14	0	0	12.1	59	11	10	9	2	1	0	1	9	0	14	2	1	0	1.000	0-1	2	95	.779	5.35	6.57
2021	Min	AL	3	0	0	6.2	28	7	2	2	2	0	0	1	2	0	4	0	0	0	-	0-0	0	95	.917	6.38	2.70
2022	2 Tms	AL	34	0	3	36.0	160	39	18	18	3	0	0	1	18	0	48	0	1	2	.333	1-3	3	96	.802	5.02	4.50
19	TB	AL	1	0	1	2.0	9	1	2	2	0	0	1	0	2	0	2	0	0	0	-	0-0	0	95	.667	2.80	9.00
19	Tex	AL	9	0	0	12.1	55	11	7	7	1	0	1	1	8	1	14	1	1	1	.500	0-0	0	95	.741	4.54	5.11
22	Cle	AL	1	0	0	1.1	6	1	0	0	0	0	0	1	0	0	0	0	0	0	-	0-0	0	97	.533	3.21	0.00
22	Cin	NL	33	0	3	34.2	154	38	18	18	3	0	0	0	18	0	48	0	1	2	.333	1-3	3	96	.812	5.09	4.67
4 ML YEARS			61	0	4	69.1	311	69	39	38	8	1	2	4	39	1	82	3	2	4	.333	1-4	5	96	.795	5.06	4.93

Kyle Gibson

Pitches: R Bats: R Pos: SP-31   Ht: 6'6" Wt: 215 Born: 10/23/1987 Age: 35

Year	Team	Lg	G	GS	GF	IP	BFP	H	R	ER	HR	SH	SF	HB	TBB	IBB	SO	WP	W	L	Pct	Sv-Op	Hld	Vel	OPS	ERC	ERA
2013	Min	AL	10	10	0	51.0	238	69	38	37	7	0	2	5	20	0	29	4	2	4	.333	0-0	0	92	.874	6.98	6.53
2014	Min	AL	31	31	0	179.1	757	178	91	89	12	4	3	2	57	0	107	11	13	12	.520	0-0	0	91	.679	3.54	4.47
2015	Min	AL	32	32	0	194.2	821	186	88	83	18	6	6	7	65	6	145	7	11	11	.500	0-0	0	92	.698	3.63	3.84
2016	Min	AL	25	25	0	147.1	653	175	89	83	20	3	4	4	55	3	104	9	6	11	.353	0-0	0	91	.820	5.47	5.07
2017	Min	AL	29	29	0	158.0	693	182	93	89	24	1	2	6	60	0	121	4	12	10	.545	0-0	0	92	.826	5.53	5.07
2018	Min	AL	32	32	0	196.2	826	177	88	79	23	3	7	4	79	2	179	8	10	13	.435	0-0	0	93	.701	3.75	3.62
2019	Min	AL	34	29	0	160.0	706	175	99	86	23	3	2	7	56	0	160	8	13	7	.650	0-1	2	93	.782	4.88	4.84
2020	Tex	AL	12	12	0	67.1	301	73	44	40	12	0	0	6	30	1	58	1	2	6	.250	0-0	0	92	.823	5.75	5.35
2021	2 Tms		31	30	0	182.0	754	158	78	75	17	2	5	8	64	2	155	2	10	9	.526	0-0	0	92	.669	3.32	3.71
2022	Phi	NL	31	31	0	167.2	718	176	98	94	24	1	4	9	48	0	144	4	10	8	.556	0-0	0	92	.759	4.44	5.05
21	Tex	AL	19	19	0	113.0	460	92	38	36	9	0	3	5	41	0	94	2	6	3	.667	0-0	0	93	.626	3.04	2.87
21	Phi	NL	12	11	0	69.0	294	66	40	39	8	2	2	3	23	2	61	0	4	6	.400	0-0	0	92	.736	3.80	5.09
Postseason			1	0	0	1.0	7	1	3	3	0	0	0	0	3	0	1	0	0	0	-	0-0	0	94	1.071	13.82	27.00
10 ML YEARS			267	261	0	1504.0	6467	1549	806	755	180	23	35	58	534	14	1202	58	89	91	.494	0-1	2	92	.747	4.38	4.52

Luis Gil

Pitches: R Bats: R Pos: SP-1   HEEL   Ht: 6'2" Wt: 185 Born: 6/3/1998 Age: 25

Year	Team	Lg	G	GS	GF	IP	BFP	H	R	ER	HR	SH	SF	HB	TBB	IBB	SO	WP	W	L	Pct	Sv-Op	Hld	Vel	OPS	ERC	ERA
2022	S-WB	AAA	6	6	0	21.2	103	21	20	19	6	0	2	0	15	0	31	2	0	3	.000	0- -	-	-	.896	6.19	7.89
2021	NYY	AL	6	6	0	29.1	129	20	11	10	4	0	0	1	19	0	38	1	1	1	.500	0-0	0	96	.613	3.56	3.07
2022	NYY	AL	1	1	0	4.0	19	5	4	4	0	0	0	0	2	0	5	1	0	0	-	0-0	0	97	.721	5.00	9.00
2 ML YEARS			7	7	0	33.1	148	25	15	14	4	0	0	1	21	0	43	2	1	1	.500	0-0	0	96	.627	3.73	3.78

Logan Gilbert

Pitches: R Bats: R Pos: SP-32   Ht: 6'6" Wt: 215 Born: 5/5/1997 Age: 26

Year	Team	Lg	G	GS	GF	IP	BFP	H	R	ER	HR	SH	SF	HB	TBB	IBB	SO	WP	W	L	Pct	Sv-Op	Hld	Vel	OPS	ERC	ERA
2021	Sea	AL	24	24	0	119.1	503	112	63	62	17	2	3	6	28	2	128	9	6	5	.545	0-0	0	95	.716	3.48	4.68
2022	Sea	AL	32	32	0	185.2	766	170	71	66	19	4	5	6	49	2	174	5	13	6	.684	0-0	0	96	.686	3.23	3.20
2 ML YEARS			56	56	0	305.0	1269	282	134	128	36	6	8	12	77	4	302	14	19	11	.633	0-0	0	96	.698	3.33	3.78

Tyler Gilbert

Pitches: L **Bats:** L **Pos:** SP-7; RP-1   **Ht:** 6'3" **Wt:** 223 **Born:** 12/22/1993 **Age:** 29

			HOW MUCH PITCHED						WHAT HE GAVE UP									THE RESULTS						
Year	Team	Lg	G	GS	GF	IP	BFP	H	R	ER	HR	SH	SF	HB	TBB	IBB	SO	WP	W	L	Pct	Sv-Op Hld	Vel	OPS	ERC	ERA
2022	Reno	AAA	11	10	0	44.0	206	55	37	37	11	0	3	1	24	0	26	0	4	4	.500	0- -	-	.961	7.57	7.57
2021	Ari	NL	9	6	0	40.0	157	28	17	14	4	1	2	1	13	0	25	0	2	2	.500	0-0	1	90	.612	2.38	3.15
2022	Ari	NL	8	7	1	34.1	146	33	21	20	8	1	1	1	10	1	20	0	0	3	.000	0-0	0	90	.775	4.34	5.24
2 ML YEARS			17	13	1	74.1	303	61	38	34	12	2	3	2	23	1	45	0	2	5	.286	0-0	1	90	.691	3.25	4.12

Lucas Gilbreath

Pitches: L **Bats:** L **Pos:** RP-47   **Ht:** 6'1" **Wt:** 185 **Born:** 3/5/1996 **Age:** 27

			HOW MUCH PITCHED						WHAT HE GAVE UP									THE RESULTS						
Year	Team	Lg	G	GS	GF	IP	BFP	H	R	ER	HR	SH	SF	HB	TBB	IBB	SO	WP	W	L	Pct	Sv-Op Hld	Vel	OPS	ERC	ERA
2022	Albq	AAA	5	0	0	4.2	25	8	5	5	0	0	0	1	2	0	6	0	1	1	.500	0- -	-	.849	8.45	9.64
2021	Col	NL	47	1	9	42.2	185	33	18	16	5	0	2	1	23	0	44	4	3	2	.600	1-1	4	93	.635	3.50	3.38
2022	Col	NL	47	0	9	43.0	187	37	22	20	2	1	3	4	26	0	49	2	2	0	1.000	0-2	12	94	.680	4.17	4.19
2 ML YEARS			94	1	18	85.2	372	70	40	36	7	1	5	5	49	0	93	6	5	2	.714	1-3	16	94	.658	3.84	3.78

Ken Giles

Pitches: R **Bats:** R **Pos:** RP-5   **Ht:** 6'3" **Wt:** 197 **Born:** 9/20/1990 **Age:** 32

			HOW MUCH PITCHED						WHAT HE GAVE UP									THE RESULTS						
Year	Team	Lg	G	GS	GF	IP	BFP	H	R	ER	HR	SH	SF	HB	TBB	IBB	SO	WP	W	L	Pct	Sv-Op Hld	Vel	OPS	ERC	ERA
2022	Tacom	AAA	8	0	7	7.0	38	10	9	8	3	0	0	0	7	0	6	1	0	1	.000	0- -	-	1.189	12.33	10.29
2022	2 Tms	Low	7	0	0	6.1	33	9	11	7	1	0	0	0	4	0	11	0	0	0	-	0- -	-	-	7.69	9.95
2014	Phi	NL	44	0	11	45.2	166	25	7	6	1	2	1	0	11	1	64	1	3	1	.750	1-1	13	97	.450	1.15	1.18
2015	Phi	NL	69	0	28	70.0	298	59	23	14	2	1	2	1	25	2	87	1	6	3	.667	15-20	12	97	.569	2.53	1.80
2016	Hou	AL	69	0	24	65.2	286	60	32	30	8	2	1	2	25	1	102	14	2	5	.286	15-20	18	97	.709	3.66	4.11
2017	Hou	AL	63	0	55	62.2	247	44	16	16	4	1	2	1	21	0	83	3	1	3	.250	34-38	2	98	.566	2.17	2.30
2018	2 Tms	AL	55	0	42	50.1	212	54	28	26	6	1	0	1	7	0	53	2	0	3	.000	26-26	1	97	.722	3.59	4.65
2019	Tor	AL	53	0	44	53.0	208	36	11	11	5	0	0	0	17	1	83	2	2	3	.400	23-24	0	97	.574	2.10	1.87
2020	Tor	AL	4	0	1	3.2	19	4	4	4	2	0	0	0	6	0	6	0	0	0	-	1-1	1	94	1.154	11.42	9.82
2022	Sea	AL	5	0	3	4.1	18	1	0	0	0	0	0	0	4	0	6	1	0	0	-	0-0	0	95	.421	1.45	0.00
18	Hou	AL	34	0	24	30.2	129	36	17	17	2	0	0	0	3	0	31	1	0	2	.000	12-12	1	97	.723	3.59	4.99
18	Tor	AL	21	0	18	19.2	83	18	11	9	4	1	0	1	4	0	22	1	0	1	.000	14-14	0	97	.722	3.58	4.12
Postseason			7	0	4	7.2	40	12	10	10	3	0	0	0	5	1	10	3	0	2	.000	2-3	0	98	1.111	10.90	11.74
8 ML YEARS			362	0	208	355.1	1454	283	121	107	28	7	6	5	114	5	484	24	14	18	.438	115-130	47	97	.611	2.58	2.71

Logan Gillaspie

Pitches: R **Bats:** R **Pos:** RP-17   **Ht:** 6'2" **Wt:** 220 **Born:** 4/17/1997 **Age:** 26

			HOW MUCH PITCHED						WHAT HE GAVE UP									THE RESULTS						
Year	Team	Lg	G	GS	GF	IP	BFP	H	R	ER	HR	SH	SF	HB	TBB	IBB	SO	WP	W	L	Pct	Sv-Op Hld	Vel	OPS	ERC	ERA
2022	Bowie	AA	6	0	2	8.0	36	7	3	3	0	1	0	1	4	0	11	2	1	0	1.000	0- -	-	.633	3.42	3.38
2022	Norfolk	AAA	22	0	4	35.1	153	39	20	20	2	2	1	1	9	0	38	1	5	3	.625	1- -	-	.710	3.85	5.09
2022	Bal	AL	17	0	6	17.1	74	20	8	6	1	0	1	2	3	0	10	1	1	0	1.000	0-1	0	95	.750	4.28	3.12

Andres Gimenez

Bats: L **Throws:** R **Pos:** 2B-125; SS-18; PH-8   **Ht:** 5'11" **Wt:** 161 **Born:** 9/4/1998 **Age:** 24

			BATTING																		RUNNING			AVERAGES			
Year	Team	Lg	G	AB	H	2B	3B	HR	(Hm	Rd)	TB	R	RBI	RC	TBB	IBB	SO	HBP	SH	SF	SB	CS	GDP	Avg	OBP	Slg	OPS
2020	NYM	NL	49	118	31	3	2	3	(2	1)	47	22	12	15	7	0	28	6	0	1	8	1	0	.263	.333	.398	.732
2021	Cle	AL	68	188	41	10	0	5	(3	2)	66	23	16	21	11	0	54	7	1	3	11	0	1	.218	.282	.351	.633
2022	Cle	AL	146	491	146	26	3	17	(6	11)	229	66	69	94	34	4	112	25	4	3	20	3	9	.297	.371	.466	.837
3 ML YEARS			263	797	218	39	5	25	(11	14)	342	111	97	130	52	4	194	38	5	7	39	4	10	.274	.345	.429	.774

Kevin Ginkel

Pitches: R **Bats:** L **Pos:** RP-30   **Ht:** 6'4" **Wt:** 235 **Born:** 3/24/1994 **Age:** 29

			HOW MUCH PITCHED						WHAT HE GAVE UP									THE RESULTS						
Year	Team	Lg	G	GS	GF	IP	BFP	H	R	ER	HR	SH	SF	HB	TBB	IBB	SO	WP	W	L	Pct	Sv-Op Hld	Vel	OPS	ERC	ERA
2022	Reno	AAA	30	0	23	30.2	123	23	6	4	1	0	1	0	12	1	45	0	2	1	.667	9- -	-	.580	2.30	1.17
2019	Ari	NL	25	0	4	24.1	96	15	7	4	2	0	0	0	9	0	28	2	3	0	1.000	2-2	8	94	.532	1.91	1.48
2020	Ari	NL	19	0	2	16.0	79	21	13	12	3	0	0	0	13	2	18	4	0	2	.000	1-2	0	96	.961	8.38	6.75
2021	Ari	NL	32	0	9	28.1	129	30	24	20	7	1	0	2	14	0	31	3	0	1	.000	0-1	6	95	.904	6.19	6.35
2022	Ari	NL	30	0	3	29.1	124	27	14	11	1	0	1	1	11	0	30	1	1	1	.500	1-3	4	96	.648	3.23	3.38
4 ML YEARS			106	0	18	98.0	428	93	58	47	13	1	1	3	47	2	107	10	4	4	.500	4-8	18	95	.754	4.43	4.32

Lucas Giolito

Pitches: R **Bats:** R **Pos:** SP-30   jee-oh-LEE-toh   **Ht:** 6'6" **Wt:** 245 **Born:** 7/14/1994 **Age:** 28

			HOW MUCH PITCHED						WHAT HE GAVE UP									THE RESULTS						
Year	Team	Lg	G	GS	GF	IP	BFP	H	R	ER	HR	SH	SF	HB	TBB	IBB	SO	WP	W	L	Pct	Sv-Op Hld	Vel	OPS	ERC	ERA
2016	Was	NL	6	4	1	21.1	101	26	18	16	7	0	0	1	12	0	11	1	0	1	.000	0-0	0	93	.988	8.14	6.75
2017	CWS	AL	7	7	0	45.1	179	31	14	12	8	1	0	3	12	0	34	2	3	3	.500	0-0	0	92	.645	2.63	2.38
2018	CWS	AL	32	32	0	173.1	775	166	123	118	27	1	5	15	90	2	125	13	10	13	.435	0-0	0	92	.794	5.05	6.13
2019	CWS	AL	29	29	0	176.2	705	131	69	67	24	4	3	4	57	1	228	6	14	9	.609	0-0	0	94	.646	2.75	3.41
2020	CWS	AL	12	12	0	72.1	288	47	31	28	8	0	3	2	28	0	97	3	4	3	.571	0-0	0	94	.577	2.40	3.48

Year	Team	Lg	G	GS	GF	IP	BFP	H	R	ER	HR	SH	SF	HB	TBB	IBB	SO	WP	W	L	Pct	Sv-Op	Hld	Vel	OPS	ERC	ERA
2021	CWS	AL	31	31	0	178.2	720	145	74	70	27	1	3	2	52	1	201	12	11	9	.550	0-0	0	94	.671	3.03	3.53
2022	CWS	AL	30	30	0	161.2	698	171	92	88	24	0	5	4	61	1	177	3	11	9	.550	0-0	0	93	.794	4.81	4.90
	Postseason		2	2	0	11.1	45	5	5	5	0	0	1	0	6	0	12	1	1	0	1.000	0-0	0	95	.402	1.30	3.97
	7 ML YEARS		147	145	1	829.1	3466	717	421	399	125	4	19	31	312	5	873	40	53	47	.530	0-0	0	93	.718	3.74	4.33

Mychal Givens

Pitches: R Bats: R Pos: RP-58; SP-1   michael   **Ht: 6'0" Wt: 230 Born: 5/13/1990 Age: 33**

Year	Team	Lg	G	GS	GF	IP	BFP	H	R	ER	HR	SH	SF	HB	TBB	IBB	SO	WP	W	L	Pct	Sv-Op	Hld	Vel	OPS	ERC	ERA
2015	Bal	AL	22	0	5	30.0	117	20	7	6	1	1	1	1	6	0	38	0	2	0	1.000	0-0	4	94	.538	1.49	1.80
2016	Bal	AL	66	0	8	74.2	313	59	28	26	6	2	1	6	36	2	96	3	8	2	.800	0-1	13	94	.664	3.44	3.13
2017	Bal	AL	69	0	8	78.2	315	57	24	24	10	0	0	5	25	1	88	2	8	1	.889	0-5	21	96	.617	2.74	2.75
2018	Bal	AL	69	0	32	76.2	317	61	37	34	4	1	3	3	30	4	79	4	0	7	.000	9-13	15	95	.622	2.72	3.99
2019	Bal	AL	58	0	33	63.0	260	49	35	32	13	0	2	2	26	1	86	5	2	6	.250	11-19	7	95	.722	3.74	4.57
2020	2 Tms		22	0	5	22.1	93	16	10	9	5	0	1	2	10	0	25	2	1	1	.500	1-3	6	95	.751	3.91	3.63
2021	2 Tms	NL	54	0	22	51.0	216	43	22	19	7	0	3	2	27	4	54	2	4	3	.571	8-11	11	95	.746	4.09	3.35
2022	2 Tms	NL	59	1	12	61.1	260	56	27	23	8	0	3	5	25	4	71	2	7	3	.700	2-6	7	94	.727	4.13	3.38
20	Bal	AL	12	0	3	13.0	51	7	2	2	1	0	1	0	6	0	19	0	0	1	.000	0-0	5	95	.573	1.84	1.38
20	Col	NL	10	0	2	9.1	42	9	8	7	4	0	0	2	4	0	6	2	1	0	1.000	1-3	1	95	.968	7.42	6.75
21	Col	NL	31	0	9	29.2	124	25	11	9	5	0	1	2	14	2	34	2	3	2	.600	0-1	8	94	.751	4.25	2.73
21	Cin	NL	23	0	13	21.1	92	18	11	10	2	0	2	0	13	2	20	0	1	1	.500	8-10	3	95	.740	3.87	4.22
22	ChC	NL	40	0	5	40.2	172	32	15	12	5	0	2	3	19	3	51	1	6	2	.750	2-5	6	94	.652	3.51	2.66
22	NYM	NL	19	1	7	20.2	88	24	12	11	3	0	1	2	6	1	20	1	1	1	.500	0-1	1	93	.870	5.47	4.79
	Postseason		1	0	0	2.1	6	0	0	0	0	0	0	0	0	0	3	0	0	0	-	0-0	0	96	.000	0.00	0.00
	8 ML YEARS		419	1	125	457.2	1891	361	190	173	54	4	14	26	185	16	537	20	32	23	.582	31-58	84	95	.671	3.27	3.40

Tyler Glasnow

Pitches: R Bats: L Pos: SP-2   **Ht: 6'8" Wt: 225 Born: 8/23/1993 Age: 29**

Year	Team	Lg	G	GS	GF	IP	BFP	H	R	ER	HR	SH	SF	HB	TBB	IBB	SO	WP	W	L	Pct	Sv-Op	Hld	Vel	OPS	ERC	ERA
2016	Pit	NL	7	4	0	23.1	105	22	13	11	2	1	0	3	13	0	24	2	0	2	.000	0-0	0	94	.774	4.80	4.24
2017	Pit	NL	15	13	0	62.0	305	81	61	53	13	4	1	2	44	2	56	3	2	7	.222	0-0	1	95	.997	8.32	7.69
2018	2 Tms		45	11	9	111.2	468	89	55	53	15	0	1	4	53	3	136	12	2	7	.222	0-0	4	97	.688	3.62	4.27
2019	TB	AL	12	12	0	60.2	230	40	13	12	4	0	1	0	14	0	76	2	6	1	.857	0-0	0	97	.509	1.63	1.78
2020	TB	AL	11	11	0	57.1	238	43	26	26	11	0	1	0	22	0	91	7	5	1	.833	0-0	0	97	.673	3.18	4.08
2021	TB	AL	14	14	0	88.0	340	55	26	26	10	0	0	0	27	0	123	8	5	2	.714	0-0	0	97	.561	1.93	2.66
2022	TB	AL	2	2	0	6.2	26	4	1	1	1	0	0	0	2	0	10	1	0	0	-	0-0	0	97	.522	1.94	1.35
18	Pit	NL	34	0	9	56.0	243	47	28	27	5	0	0	1	34	2	72	7	1	2	.333	0-0	4	97	.698	3.95	4.34
18	TB	AL	11	11	0	55.2	225	42	27	26	10	0	1	3	19	1	64	5	1	5	.167	0-0	0	97	.676	3.26	4.20
	Postseason		8	8	0	35.2	159	35	26	26	10	0	0	0	20	0	48	6	2	5	.286	0-0	0	98	.835	5.96	6.56
	7 ML YEARS		106	67	9	409.2	1712	334	195	182	56	5	4	9	175	5	516	35	20	20	.500	0-0	5	96	.691	3.50	4.00

Jose Godoy

Bats: L Throws: R Pos: C-10   **Ht: 5'11" Wt: 200 Born: 10/13/1994 Age: 28**

Year	Team	Lg	G	AB	H	2B	3B	HR	(Hm	Rd)	TB	R	RBI	RC	TBB	IBB	SO	HBP	SH	SF	SB	CS	GDP	Avg	OBP	Slg	OPS
2022	StPaul	AAA	43	137	27	5	0	3	(-	-)	41	13	14	10	13	2	41	1	0	0	0	0	3	.197	.272	.299	.571
2022	Indy	AAA	10	39	13	1	0	3	(-	-)	23	7	12	8	1	0	7	1	0	1	0	0	0	.333	.357	.590	.947
2021	Sea	AL	16	37	6	1	0	0	(0	0)	7	2	3	2	3	0	14	0	0	0	0	0	2	.162	.225	.189	.414
2022	2 Tms		10	20	1	0	0	0	(0	0)	1	3	1	0	2	0	9	0	0	0	0	0	0	.050	.136	.050	.186
22	Min	AL	2	3	0	0	0	0	(0	0)	0	2	0	0	2	0	2	0	0	0	0	0	0	.000	.400	.000	.400
22	Pit	NL	8	17	1	0	0	0	(0	0)	1	1	1	0	0	0	7	0	0	0	0	0	0	.059	.059	.059	.118
	2 ML YEARS		26	57	7	1	0	0	(0	0)	8	5	4	2	5	0	23	0	0	0	0	0	2	.123	.194	.140	.334

Paul Goldschmidt

Bats: R Throws: R Pos: 1B-128;DH-23;PH-1   **Ht: 6'3" Wt: 220 Born: 9/10/1987 Age: 35**

Year	Team	Lg	G	AB	H	2B	3B	HR	(Hm	Rd)	TB	R	RBI	RC	TBB	IBB	SO	HBP	SH	SF	SB	CS	GDP	Avg	OBP	Slg	OPS
2011	Ari	NL	48	156	39	9	1	8	(2	6)	74	28	26	26	20	0	53	0	0	1	4	0	4	.250	.333	.474	.808
2012	Ari	NL	145	514	147	43	1	20	(10	10)	252	82	82	86	60	4	130	4	0	9	18	3	9	.286	.359	.490	.850
2013	Ari	NL	160	602	182	36	3	36	(17	19)	332	103	125	131	99	19	145	3	0	5	15	7	25	.302	.401	.551	.952
2014	Ari	NL	109	406	122	39	1	19	(10	9)	220	75	69	83	64	10	110	2	0	3	9	3	10	.300	.396	.542	.938
2015	Ari	NL	159	567	182	38	2	33	(13	20)	323	103	110	135	118	29	151	2	0	7	21	5	16	.321	.435	.570	1.005
2016	Ari	NL	158	579	172	33	3	24	(15	9)	283	106	95	113	110	15	150	7	0	8	32	5	14	.297	.411	.489	.899
2017	Ari	NL	155	558	166	34	3	36	(20	16)	314	117	120	131	94	13	147	8	0	4	18	5	14	.297	.404	.563	.966
2018	Ari	NL	158	593	172	35	5	33	(12	21)	316	95	83	118	90	11	173	6	0	0	7	4	7	.290	.389	.533	.922
2019	StL	NL	161	597	155	25	1	34	(17	17)	284	97	97	103	78	2	166	4	0	3	3	1	11	.260	.346	.476	.821
2020	StL	NL	58	191	58	13	0	6	(4	2)	89	31	21	38	37	0	43	1	0	1	1	0	4	.304	.417	.466	.883
2021	StL	NL	158	603	177	36	2	31	(14	17)	310	102	99	107	67	2	136	4	0	4	12	0	13	.294	.365	.514	.879
2022	StL	NL	151	561	178	41	0	35	(22	13)	324	106	115	132	79	1	141	5	0	4	7	0	7	.317	.404	.578	.981
	Postseason		21	85	24	5	0	8	(3	5)	53	13	16	16	8	1	23	1	0	0	1	0	1	.282	.351	.624	.975
	12 ML YEARS		1620	5927	1750	382	22	315	(156	159)	3121	1045	1042	1203	916	108	1545	44	0	50	147	33	134	.295	.391	.527	.917

Austin Gomber

Pitches: L Bats: L Pos: SP-17; RP-16
Ht: 6'5" Wt: 220 Born: 11/23/1993 Age: 29

		HOW MUCH PITCHED						WHAT HE GAVE UP											THE RESULTS						
Year	Team	Lg	G	GS	GF	IP	BFP	H	R	ER	HR	SH	SF	HB	TBB	IBB	SO	WP	W	L	Pct	Sv-Op	Hld	Vel	OPS	ERC	ERA
2018	StL	NL	29	11	1	75.0	334	81	40	37	7	4	2	4	32	4	67	3	6	2	.750	0-0	7	92	.786	4.72	4.44
2020	StL	NL	14	4	2	29.0	119	19	6	6	1	0	2	2	15	0	27	1	1	1	.500	0-0	1	93	.563	2.56	1.86
2021	Col	NL	23	23	0	115.1	488	102	64	58	20	2	2	3	41	2	113	1	9	9	.500	0-0	0	92	.721	3.79	4.53
2022	Col	NL	33	17	2	124.2	529	137	80	77	20	1	4	2	34	1	95	4	5	7	.417	0-0	0	91	.807	4.67	5.56
Postseason			1	0	0	1.1	7	2	0	0	0	0	0	0	1	0	2	0	0	0	-	0-0	0	94	.762	7.52	0.00
4 ML YEARS			99	55	5	344.0	1470	339	190	178	48	7	10	11	122	7	302	9	21	19	.525	0-0	8	92	.755	4.20	4.66

Yan Gomes

Bats: R Throws: R Pos: C-69;DH-9;PH-9
YAHN GOHMS

Ht: 6'2" Wt: 212 Born: 7/19/1987 Age: 35

			BATTING															RUNNING			AVERAGES			
Year	Team	Lg	G	AB	H	2B	3B	HR	(Hm | Rd)	TB	R	RBI	RC	TBB	IBB	SO	HBP	SH	SF	SB	CS	GDP	Avg	OBP	Slg	OPS
2012	Tor	AL	43	98	20	4	0	4	(3 | 1)	36	9	13	11	6	0	32	3	1	3	0	0	3	.204	.264	.367	.631
2013	Cle	AL	88	293	86	18	2	11	(6 | 5)	141	45	38	42	18	0	67	7	0	4	2	0	12	.294	.345	.481	.826
2014	Cle	AL	135	485	135	25	3	21	(9 | 12)	229	61	74	65	24	3	120	3	0	6	0	0	13	.278	.313	.472	.785
2015	Cle	AL	95	363	84	22	0	12	(5 | 7)	142	38	45	25	13	1	104	7	0	6	0	0	11	.231	.267	.391	.659
2016	Cle	AL	74	251	42	11	1	9	(4 | 5)	82	22	34	18	9	0	69	2	0	2	0	0	7	.167	.201	.327	.527
2017	Cle	AL	105	341	79	15	0	14	(5 | 9)	136	43	56	41	31	0	99	8	1	2	0	0	9	.232	.309	.399	.708
2018	Cle	AL	112	403	107	26	0	16	(5 | 11)	181	52	48	47	21	2	119	8	0	3	0	0	4	.266	.313	.449	.762
2019	Was	NL	97	314	70	16	0	12	(8 | 4)	122	36	43	39	38	6	84	5	0	1	2	0	7	.223	.316	.389	.704
2020	Was	NL	30	109	31	6	1	4	(4 | 0)	51	14	13	12	6	0	22	1	0	3	1	0	1	.284	.319	.468	.787
2021	2 Tms		103	349	88	15	1	14	(9 | 5)	147	49	52	42	19	3	78	6	0	1	0	0	15	.252	.301	.421	.723
2022	ChC	NL	86	277	65	12	0	8	(3 | 5)	101	23	31	21	8	0	47	3	1	4	2	0	15	.235	.260	.365	.625
21	Was	NL	63	218	59	11	1	9	(6 | 3)	99	30	35	30	13	3	47	4	0	0	0	0	12	.271	.323	.454	.778
21	Oak	AL	40	131	29	4	0	5	(3 | 2)	48	19	17	12	6	0	31	2	0	1	0	0	3	.221	.264	.366	.631
Postseason			22	51	13	4	0	0	(0 | 0)	17	6	4	6	5	2	17	0	0	0	0	0	1	.255	.321	.333	.655
11 ML YEARS			968	3283	807	170	8	125	(61 | 64)	1368	392	447	363	193	15	841	53	3	35	7	0	97	.246	.295	.417	.712

Tony Gonsolin

Pitches: R Bats: R Pos: SP-24
Ht: 6'3" Wt: 205 Born: 5/14/1994 Age: 29

			HOW MUCH PITCHED						WHAT HE GAVE UP											THE RESULTS						
Year	Team	Lg	G	GS	GF	IP	BFP	H	R	ER	HR	SH	SF	HB	TBB	IBB	SO	WP	W	L	Pct	Sv-Op	Hld	Vel	OPS	ERC	ERA
2019	LAD	NL	11	6	1	40.0	163	26	15	13	4	0	1	4	15	0	37	2	4	2	.667	1-1	0	94	.580	2.21	2.93
2020	LAD	NL	9	8	1	46.2	176	32	13	12	2	1	1	1	7	0	46	3	2	2	.500	0-0	0	95	.518	1.48	2.31
2021	LAD	NL	15	13	0	55.2	239	41	20	20	8	2	0	0	34	0	65	4	4	1	.800	0-0	0	94	.686	3.72	3.23
2022	LAD	NL	24	24	0	130.1	498	79	32	31	11	0	1	4	35	1	119	5	16	1	.941	0-0	0	95	.536	1.67	2.14
Postseason			7	3	1	13.1	65	14	14	14	6	0	0	0	10	0	17	0	1	2	.333	0-0	0	95	1.006	8.39	9.45
4 ML YEARS			59	51	2	272.2	1076	178	80	76	25	3	3	6	91	1	267	14	26	6	.813	1-1	0	94	.572	2.09	2.51

Marco Gonzales

Pitches: L Bats: L Pos: SP-32
Ht: 6'1" Wt: 205 Born: 2/16/1992 Age: 31

			HOW MUCH PITCHED						WHAT HE GAVE UP											THE RESULTS						
Year	Team	Lg	G	GS	GF	IP	BFP	H	R	ER	HR	SH	SF	HB	TBB	IBB	SO	WP	W	L	Pct	Sv-Op	Hld	Vel	OPS	ERC	ERA
2014	StL	NL	10	5	0	34.2	156	32	16	16	4	0	1	1	21	1	31	0	4	2	.667	0-0	1	90	.737	4.59	4.15
2015	StL	NL	1	1	0	2.2	16	7	4	4	1	0	1	0	1	0	1	0	0	0	-	0-0	0	89	1.286	17.70	13.50
2017	2 Tms		11	8	1	40.0	185	59	27	27	8	0	1	1	11	0	32	2	1	1	.500	0-0	0	92	.924	7.40	6.08
2018	Sea	AL	29	29	0	166.2	686	172	76	74	17	1	4	6	32	0	145	2	13	9	.591	0-0	0	90	.720	3.65	4.00
2019	Sea	AL	34	34	0	203.0	866	210	106	90	23	1	9	6	56	1	147	2	16	13	.552	0-0	0	89	.736	3.96	3.99
2020	Sea	AL	11	11	0	69.2	277	59	27	24	8	0	0	4	7	0	64	0	7	2	.778	0-0	0	88	.614	2.43	3.10
2021	Sea	AL	25	25	0	143.1	585	125	64	63	29	1	2	5	42	3	108	1	10	6	.625	0-0	0	88	.760	3.78	3.96
2022	Sea	AL	32	32	0	183.0	783	194	97	84	30	3	6	7	50	1	103	1	10	15	.400	0-0	0	88	.779	4.51	4.13
17	StL	NL	1	1	0	3.1	16	6	5	5	3	0	0	0	0	0	2	0	0	0	-	0-0	0	91	1.500	13.65	13.50
17	Sea	AL	10	7	1	36.2	169	53	22	22	5	0	1	1	11	0	30	2	1	1	.500	0-0	0	92	.865	6.82	5.40
Postseason			6	0	1	6.0	24	4	3	3	0	1	0	0	2	0	4	0	2	1	.667	0-1	0	91	.451	1.57	4.50
8 ML YEARS			153	145	1	843.0	3554	858	417	382	120	6	24	30	220	6	631	8	61	48	.560	0-0	1	89	.749	4.06	4.08

Chi Chi Gonzalez

Pitches: R Bats: R Pos: SP-5; RP-2
Ht: 6'3" Wt: 210 Born: 1/15/1992 Age: 31

			HOW MUCH PITCHED						WHAT HE GAVE UP											THE RESULTS						
Year	Team	Lg	G	GS	GF	IP	BFP	H	R	ER	HR	SH	SF	HB	TBB	IBB	SO	WP	W	L	Pct	Sv-Op	Hld	Vel	OPS	ERC	ERA
2022	StPaul	AAA	8	5	0	36.2	151	32	16	14	3	1	1	0	14	0	35	0	2	2	.500	0- -	-		.655	3.25	3.44
2022	Toledo	AAA	5	4	0	21.1	93	24	13	13	4	1	1	1	8	0	18	2	0	1	.000	0- -	-		.822	5.67	5.48
2022	S-WB	AAA	5	5	0	22.1	98	26	9	9	1	0	0	5	5	0	18	1	0	0	-	0- -	-		.725	3.81	3.63
2015	Tex	AL	14	10	1	67.0	280	49	33	29	6	1	2	3	32	1	30	2	4	6	.400	0-0	0	91	.632	3.00	3.90
2016	Tex	AL	3	3	0	10.1	62	21	13	10	1	0	1	0	9	0	7	0	0	2	.000	0-0	0	91	.984	12.48	8.71
2019	Col	NL	14	12	0	63.0	278	59	39	37	11	3	1	1	33	0	46	1	2	6	.250	0-0	0	92	.784	4.78	5.29
2020	Col	NL	6	4	0	19.2	91	22	16	15	3	1	1	3	10	0	16	2	0	2	.000	0-0	0	92	.889	6.34	6.86
2021	Col	NL	24	18	1	101.2	448	127	74	73	18	3	2	6	28	0	56	2	3	7	.300	0-0	0	92	.900	5.96	6.46
2022	3 Tms		7	5	2	23.0	99	28	15	15	5	0	0	0	7	0	15	0	1	0	1.000	0-0	0	92	.897	6.00	5.87
22	Min	AL	2	2	0	7.0	31	12	6	6	2	0	0	0	4	0	4	0	0	0	-	0-0	0	93	1.000	8.54	7.71
22	Mil	NL	4	2	2	11.1	48	12	8	8	3	0	0	0	4	0	8	0	1	0	1.000	0-0	0	93	.879	5.52	6.35
22	NYY	AL	1	1	0	4.2	20	4	1	1	0	0	0	0	3	0	3	0	0	0	-	0-0	0	93	.762	3.59	1.93
Postseason			1	0	0	1.2	8	2	1	1	1	0	0	0	0	0	2	0	0	0	-	0-0	0	93	1.333	15.09	5.40
6 ML YEARS			68	52	4	284.2	1258	306	190	179	44	8	7	13	119	1	170	7	9	24	.273	0-0	0	92	.819	5.19	5.66

Erik Gonzalez

Bats: R Throws: R Pos: SS-8;3B-7;2B-2;1B-1   Ht: 6'3" Wt: 205 Born: 8/31/1991 Age: 31

							BATTING												RUNNING			AVERAGES			
Year Team	Lg	G	AB	H	2B	3B	HR	(Hm | Rd)	TB	R	RBI	RC	TBB	IBB	SO	HBP	SH	SF	SB	CS	GDP	Avg	OBP	Slg	OPS
2022 Jaxnvl	AAA	99	370	105	19	1	4	(- | -)	138	42	38	44	28	0	86	2	0	2	9	2	6	.284	.336	.373	.709
2016 Cle	AL	21	16	5	0	0	0	(0 | 0)	5	2	0	1	1	0	8	0	0	0	0	1	0	.313	.353	.313	.665
2017 Cle	AL	60	110	28	6	0	4	(1 | 3)	46	18	11	9	3	0	37	0	1	1	1	2	1	.255	.272	.418	.690
2018 Cle	AL	81	136	36	10	1	1	(0 | 1)	51	17	16	14	5	0	34	2	0	0	3	0	0	.265	.301	.375	.676
2019 Pit	NL	53	142	36	4	1	1	(1 | 0)	45	15	6	7	9	3	37	1	3	1	4	1	5	.254	.301	.317	.618
2020 Pit	NL	50	181	41	13	1	3	(1 | 2)	65	14	20	21	8	0	51	0	1	3	2	3	5	.227	.255	.359	.614
2021 Pit	NL	71	220	51	7	1	2	(1 | 1)	66	17	21	18	8	0	40	0	0	1	2	2	4	.232	.258	.300	.558
2022 Mia	NL	16	37	7	1	0	0	(0 | 0)	8	4	3	2	4	0	12	0	0	0	1	0	1	.189	.268	.216	.485
Postseason		2	2	0	0	0	0	(0 | 0)	0	0	0	0	0	0	0	0	0	0	0	0	0	.000	.000	.000	.000
7 ML YEARS		352	842	204	41	4	11	(4 | 7)	286	87	77	72	38	3	219	3	5	6	13	9	16	.242	.276	.340	.615

Luis Gonzalez

Bats: L Throws: L Pos: RF-69;LF-52;PH-8;CF-6;DH-3   Ht: 6'1" Wt: 185 Born: 9/10/1995 Age: 27

							BATTING												RUNNING			AVERAGES			
Year Team	Lg	G	AB	H	2B	3B	HR	(Hm	Rd)	TB	R	RBI	RC	TBB	IBB	SO	HBP	SH	SF	SB	CS	GDP	Avg	OBP	Slg	OPS
2022 Scrmto	AAA	20	76	22	1	0	6	(-	-)	41	15	13	18	15	0	22	0	0	1	4	2	0	.289	.402	.539	.942
2020 CWS	AL	3	1	0	0	0	0	(0	0)	0	1	0	0	0	0	1	1	0	0	0	0	0	.000	.500	.000	.500
2021 CWS	AL	6	8	2	2	0	0	(0	0)	4	2	0	1	3	0	2	0	0	0	0	0	1	.250	.455	.500	.955
2022 SF	NL	98	311	79	17	2	4	(1	3)	112	31	36	40	30	1	75	4	0	5	10	2	5	.254	.323	.360	.683
3 ML YEARS		107	320	81	19	2	4	(1	3)	116	34	36	41	33	1	78	5	0	5	10	2	6	.253	.328	.363	.690

Marwin Gonzalez

MARR-win

Bats: B Throws: R Pos: SS-20;RF-20;LF-16;1B-14;3B-12;PR-7;PH-6;2B-3;DH-2   Ht: 6'1" Wt: 205 Born: 3/14/1989 Age: 34

							BATTING												RUNNING			AVERAGES			
Year Team	Lg	G	AB	H	2B	3B	HR	(Hm	Rd)	TB	R	RBI	RC	TBB	IBB	SO	HBP	SH	SF	SB	CS	GDP	Avg	OBP	Slg	OPS
2012 Hou	NL	80	205	48	13	0	2	(1	1)	67	21	12	12	13	0	29	0	1	0	3	3	9	.234	.280	.327	.607
2013 Hou	AL	72	204	45	8	0	4	(2	2)	65	22	14	10	9	0	37	0	8	1	6	2	5	.221	.252	.319	.571
2014 Hou	AL	103	285	79	15	1	6	(3	3)	114	33	23	26	17	0	58	4	4	0	2	4	6	.277	.327	.400	.727
2015 Hou	AL	120	344	96	18	1	12	(6	6)	152	44	34	39	16	0	74	3	7	0	4	5	9	.279	.317	.442	.759
2016 Hou	AL	141	484	123	26	3	13	(8	5)	194	55	51	47	22	1	118	5	6	1	12	6	16	.254	.293	.401	.694
2017 Hou	AL	134	455	138	34	0	23	(15	8)	241	67	90	93	49	4	99	6	3	2	8	3	8	.303	.377	.530	.907
2018 Hou	AL	145	489	121	25	3	16	(5	11)	200	61	68	61	53	3	126	3	5	2	2	3	14	.247	.324	.409	.733
2019 Min	AL	114	425	112	19	0	15	(10	5)	176	52	55	58	31	2	98	6	0	1	1	0	7	.264	.322	.414	.736
2020 Min	AL	53	175	37	4	0	5	(3	2)	56	15	22	21	17	0	41	3	0	4	0	0	1	.211	.286	.320	.606
2021 2 Tms	AL	91	276	55	14	0	5	(2	3)	84	30	28	22	20	0	78	9	1	1	3	2	8	.199	.275	.304	.579
2022 NYY	AL	86	184	34	7	0	6	(2	4)	59	20	18	13	14	0	54	4	3	2	3	0	8	.185	.255	.321	.576
21 Bos	AL	77	242	49	14	0	2	(1	1)	69	25	20	18	19	0	70	8	1	1	3	2	5	.202	.281	.285	.567
21 Hou	AL	14	34	6	0	0	3	(1	2)	15	5	8	4	1	0	8	1	0	0	0	0	3	.176	.222	.441	.663
Postseason		39	117	27	7	0	3	(1	2)	43	11	15	9	8	2	32	4	0	0	0	2	1	.231	.302	.368	.670
11 ML YEARS		1139	3526	888	183	8	107	(57	50)	1408	420	415	402	261	10	812	43	38	14	44	28	91	.252	.310	.399	.709

Oscar Gonzalez

Bats: R Throws: R Pos: RF-84;DH-7;PH-2   Ht: 6'4" Wt: 240 Born: 1/10/1998 Age: 25

							BATTING												RUNNING			AVERAGES			
Year Team	Lg	G	AB	H	2B	3B	HR	(Hm	Rd)	TB	R	RBI	RC	TBB	IBB	SO	HBP	SH	SF	SB	CS	GDP	Avg	OBP	Slg	OPS
2022 Clmbs	AAA	41	174	49	8	2	9	(-	-)	88	21	33	28	6	2	26	1	0	1	0	0	4	.282	.308	.506	.813
2022 Cle	AL	91	362	107	27	0	11	(3	8)	167	39	43	49	15	2	75	3	0	2	1	2	6	.296	.327	.461	.789

Romy Gonzalez

Bats: R Throws: R Pos: 2B-25;SS-3;PH-3;RF-2;LF-1   Ht: 6'1" Wt: 215 Born: 9/6/1996 Age: 26

							BATTING												RUNNING			AVERAGES			
Year Team	Lg	G	AB	H	2B	3B	HR	(Hm	Rd)	TB	R	RBI	RC	TBB	IBB	SO	HBP	SH	SF	SB	CS	GDP	Avg	OBP	Slg	OPS
2022 Charltt	AAA	33	121	24	5	0	4	(-	-)	41	15	10	12	13	0	45	1	0	0	5	2	2	.198	.281	.339	.620
2021 CWS	AL	10	32	8	3	0	0	(0	0)	11	4	2	3	1	0	11	0	0	0	0	0	1	.250	.273	.344	.616
2022 CWS	AL	32	105	25	4	1	2	(1	1)	37	15	11	11	2	0	39	1	0	1	0	1	3	.238	.257	.352	.609
2 ML YEARS		42	137	33	7	1	2	(1	1)	48	19	13	14	3	0	50	1	0	1	0	1	4	.241	.261	.350	.611

Niko Goodrum

Bats: B Throws: R Pos: 2B-10;1B-4;DH-1;PH-1   Ht: 6'3" Wt: 215 Born: 2/28/1992 Age: 31

							BATTING												RUNNING			AVERAGES			
Year Team	Lg	G	AB	H	2B	3B	HR	(Hm	Rd)	TB	R	RBI	RC	TBB	IBB	SO	HBP	SH	SF	SB	CS	GDP	Avg	OBP	Slg	OPS
2022 SgrLnd	AAA	13	45	14	3	0	2	(-	-)	23	12	5	13	17	0	14	0	0	0	2	0	0	.311	.500	.511	1.011
2017 Min	AL	11	17	1	0	0	0	(0	0)	1	1	0	0	1	0	10	0	0	0	0	0	0	.059	.111	.059	.170
2018 Det	AL	131	444	109	29	3	16	(8	8)	192	55	53	63	42	1	132	4	0	2	12	4	9	.245	.315	.432	.747
2019 Det	AL	112	423	105	27	5	12	(4	8)	178	61	45	50	46	1	138	1	0	2	12	3	7	.248	.322	.421	.743
2020 Det	AL	43	158	29	7	1	5	(2	3)	53	15	20	13	18	0	69	0	0	3	7	1	4	.184	.263	.335	.598
2021 Det	AL	90	290	62	11	2	9	(1	8)	104	39	33	32	29	0	107	4	0	2	14	5	6	.214	.292	.359	.651
2022 Hou	AL	15	43	5	2	0	0	(0	0)	7	2	1	0	2	0	23	0	0	0	1	0	0	.116	.156	.163	.318
6 ML YEARS		402	1375	311	76	11	42	(15	27)	535	173	152	158	138	2	479	9	0	9	46	13	26	.226	.299	.389	.688

Nick Gordon

Bats: L Throws: R Pos: LF-62;CF-38;2B-36;SS-17;PR-8;PH-6;3B-1;DH-1   Ht: 6'0" Wt: 160 Born: 10/24/1995 Age: 27

							BATTING															RUNNING			AVERAGES			
Year	Team	Lg	G	AB	H	2B	3B	HR	(Hm	Rd)	TB	R	RBI	RC	TBB	IBB	SO	HBP	SH	SF	SB	CS	GDP	Avg	OBP	Slg	OPS
2021	Min	AL	73	200	48	9	1	4	(2	2)	71	19	23	26	12	0	55	3	0	1	10	1	7	.240	.292	.355	.647
2022	Min	AL	138	405	110	28	4	9	(6	3)	173	45	50	52	19	1	105	10	3	6	6	4	8	.272	.316	.427	.743
	2 ML YEARS		211	605	158	37	5	13	(8	5)	244	64	73	78	31	1	160	13	3	7	16	5	15	.261	.308	.403	.711

MacKenzie Gore

Pitches: L Bats: L Pos: SP-13; RP-3   Ht: 6'2" Wt: 197 Born: 2/24/1999 Age: 24

			HOW MUCH PITCHED					WHAT HE GAVE UP										THE RESULTS							
Year	Team	Lg	G	GS	GF	IP	BFP	H	R	ER	HR	SH	SF	HB	TBB	IBB	SO	WP	W	L	Pct	Sv-Op	Hld	Vel	OPS	ERC	ERA
2018	FtWyn	A	16	16	0	60.2	261	61	35	30	5	0	2	5	18	0	74	9	2	5	.286	0--	-	-	.888	3.89	4.45
2019	Lk Els	A+	15	15	0	79.1	288	36	9	9	4	1	3	2	20	0	110	4	7	1	.875	0--	-	-	.420	1.07	1.02
2019	Amrillo	AA	5	5	0	21.2	90	20	10	10	3	0	1	1	8	0	25	2	2	1	.667	0--	-	-	.735	4.09	4.15
2021	ElPaso	AAA	6	6	0	20.0	96	24	17	13	3	0	0	1	12	0	18	1	0	2	.000	0--	-	-	.891	6.62	5.85
2022	SD	NL	16	13	0	70.0	309	66	35	35	7	0	2	4	37	0	72	6	4	4	.500	0-0	1	95	.722	4.51	4.50

Terrance Gore

Bats: R Throws: R Pos: PR-5;LF-3;CF-3;DH-2   Ht: 5'7" Wt: 160 Born: 6/8/1991 Age: 32

							BATTING															RUNNING			AVERAGES			
Year	Team	Lg	G	AB	H	2B	3B	HR	(Hm	Rd)	TB	R	RBI	RC	TBB	IBB	SO	HBP	SH	SF	SB	CS	GDP	Avg	OBP	Slg	OPS
2022	Syrcse	AAA	26	58	14	0	0	0	(-	-)	14	15	4	4	6	0	19	0	2	0	9	2	0	.241	.313	.241	.554
2014	KC	AL	11	1	0	0	0	0	(0	0)	0	5	0	1	0	0	0	1	0	0	5	0	0	.000	.500	.000	.500
2015	KC	AL	9	3	0	0	0	0	(0	0)	0	1	0	0	0	0	1	1	0	0	3	0	0	.000	.250	.000	.250
2016	KC	AL	17	3	0	0	0	0	(0	0)	0	6	0	0	0	0	1	0	0	0	11	2	0	.000	.000	.000	.000
2017	KC	AL	12	4	0	0	0	0	(0	0)	0	2	0	0	1	0	2	0	0	0	2	2	0	.000	.200	.000	.200
2018	ChC	NL	14	5	1	0	0	0	(0	0)	1	5	0	1	0	0	1	0	0	0	6	0	0	.200	.200	.200	.400
2019	KC	AL	37	51	14	2	1	0	(0	0)	18	13	1	8	6	0	18	1	0	0	13	5	0	.275	.362	.353	.715
2020	LAD	NL	2	0	0	0	0	0	(0	0)	0	0	0	0	0	0	0	0	0	0	0	0	0	-	-	-	-
2022	NYM	NL	10	7	1	0	0	0	(0	0)	1	1	0	0	0	0	3	0	1	0	3	0	0	.143	.143	.143	.286
	Postseason		10	2	0	0	0	0	(0	0)	0	3	0	0	0	0	2	0	0	0	5	1	0	.000	.000	.000	.000
	8 ML YEARS		112	74	16	2	1	0	(0	0)	20	33	1	10	7	0	26	3	1	0	43	9	0	.216	.310	.270	.580

Nolan Gorman

Bats: L Throws: R Pos: 2B-68;DH-16;PH-12;LF-1   Ht: 6'1" Wt: 210 Born: 5/10/2000 Age: 23

							BATTING															RUNNING			AVERAGES			
Year	Team	Lg	G	AB	H	2B	3B	HR	(Hm	Rd)	TB	R	RBI	RC	TBB	IBB	SO	HBP	SH	SF	SB	CS	GDP	Avg	OBP	Slg	OPS
2018	2 Tms	Low	63	237	69	13	1	17	(-	-)	135	49	44	49	34	0	76	1	0	2	1	5	1	.291	.380	.570	.949
2019	2 Tms	Low	125	456	113	30	6	15	(-	-)	200	65	62	67	45	3	152	9	0	2	2	1	5	.248	.326	.439	.765
2021	Sprgfld	AA	43	177	51	6	0	11	(-	-)	90	26	27	32	18	0	52	0	0	2	4	0	2	.288	.354	.508	.862
2021	Memp	AAA	74	294	81	13	1	14	(-	-)	138	44	48	45	19	2	60	2	0	3	3	0	5	.276	.321	.469	.790
2022	Memp	AAA	43	171	47	5	0	16	(-	-)	100	35	26	39	14	0	69	1	0	2	3	0	0	.275	.330	.585	.915
2022	StL	NL	89	283	64	13	0	14	(6	8)	119	44	35	37	28	0	103	2	0	0	1	0	2	.226	.300	.420	.721

Anthony Gose

Pitches: L Bats: L Pos: RP-22   GOASE   Ht: 6'0" Wt: 200 Born: 8/10/1990 Age: 32

			HOW MUCH PITCHED					WHAT HE GAVE UP										THE RESULTS							
Year	Team	Lg	G	GS	GF	IP	BFP	H	R	ER	HR	SH	SF	HB	TBB	IBB	SO	WP	W	L	Pct	Sv-Op	Hld	Vel	OPS	ERC	ERA
2021	Cle	AL	6	0	0	6.2	24	2	1	1	0	0	0	0	2	0	9	0	0	0	-	0-0	0	99	.303	0.57	1.35
2022	Cle	AL	22	0	3	21.0	92	15	13	11	4	0	1	1	14	1	28	2	3	0	1.000	0-1	0	97	.760	4.24	4.71
	2 ML YEARS		28	0	3	27.2	116	17	14	12	4	0	1	1	16	1	37	2	3	0	1.000	0-1	0	98	.660	3.04	3.90

Phil Gosselin

Bats: R Throws: R Pos: 3B-17;2B-10;PH-6;1B-3;PR-3;RF-1;DH-1   GOSS-lin   Ht: 6'1" Wt: 188 Born: 10/3/1988 Age: 34

							BATTING															RUNNING			AVERAGES			
Year	Team	Lg	G	AB	H	2B	3B	HR	(Hm	Rd)	TB	R	RBI	RC	TBB	IBB	SO	HBP	SH	SF	SB	CS	GDP	Avg	OBP	Slg	OPS
2022	Gwnntt	AAA	49	182	54	13	2	5	(-	-)	86	25	24	30	16	0	40	3	0	3	4	0	3	.297	.358	.473	.830
2013	Atl	NL	4	6	2	0	0	0	(0	0)	2	2	0	1	1	1	2	0	0	0	0	0	0	.333	.429	.333	.762
2014	Atl	NL	46	128	34	4	0	1	(1	0)	41	17	3	10	5	0	27	2	1	0	2	1	2	.266	.304	.320	.624
2015	2 Tms	NL	44	106	33	9	1	3	(2	1)	53	19	15	22	9	0	16	2	0	1	2	1	2	.311	.373	.500	.873
2016	Ari	NL	122	220	61	12	1	2	(1	1)	81	26	13	24	15	0	46	1	2	2	3	0	0	.277	.324	.368	.692
2017	2 Tms	NL	40	48	7	2	0	0	(0	0)	9	3	2	0	2	0	12	0	0	0	0	1	1	.146	.180	.188	.368
2018	Cin	NL	20	24	3	0	0	1	(1	0)	6	5	2	2	4	1	8	0	0	0	0	0	1	.125	.250	.250	.500
2019	Phi	NL	44	65	17	3	0	0	(0	0)	20	5	7	8	3	0	16	0	0	0	0	0	1	.262	.294	.308	.602
2020	Phi	NL	39	92	23	5	0	3	(2	1)	37	14	12	11	11	0	27	0	0	0	0	0	0	.250	.324	.402	.726
2021	LAA	AL	104	345	90	14	0	7	(3	4)	125	40	47	48	24	0	81	3	0	1	4	2	3	.261	.314	.362	.676
2022	2 Tms	AL	34	74	11	0	1	0	(0	0)	13	6	2	0	2	0	24	1	0	0	0	0	1	.149	.182	.176	.357
	15 Atl	NL	20	40	13	4	0	0	(0	0)	17	2	2	6	5	0	5	0	0	0	2	0	0	.325	.357	.425	.782
	15 Ari	NL	24	66	20	5	1	3	(2	1)	36	17	13	16	7	0	11	2	0	1	0	1	2	.303	.382	.545	.927
	17 Pit	NL	28	40	6	1	0	0	(0	0)	7	3	2	0	2	0	9	0	0	0	0	1	1	.150	.190	.175	.365
	17 Tex	NL	12	8	1	1	0	0	(0	0)	2	0	0	0	0	0	3	0	0	0	0	0	0	.125	.125	.250	.375
	22 Atl	NL	12	23	6	0	0	0	(0	0)	6	4	0	0	1	0	6	0	0	0	0	0	0	.261	.292	.261	.553
	22 LAA	AL	22	51	5	0	1	0	(0	0)	7	2	2	0	1	0	18	1	0	0	0	0	1	.098	.132	.137	.269
	10 ML YEARS		497	1108	281	49	3	17	(10	7)	387	137	103	126	75	3	259	9	3	4	11	6	13	.254	.305	.349	.654

Trevor Gott

Pitches: R Bats: R Pos: RP-45 Ht: 5'10" Wt: 182 Born: 8/26/1992 Age: 30

			HOW MUCH PITCHED				WHAT HE GAVE UP										THE RESULTS						
Year	Team	Lg	G	GS	GF	IP	BFP	H	R	ER	HR	SH	SF	HB	TBB	IBB	SO	WP	W	L	Pct	Sv-Op	Hld	Vel	OPS	ERC	ERA
2015	LAA	AL	48	0	7	47.2	202	43	18	16	2	2	3	3	16	3	27	1	4	2	.667	0-4	14	96	.625	3.03	3.02
2016	Was	NL	9	0	1	6.0	28	6	1	1	0	0	0	1	3	1	6	0	0	0	-	0-0	1	94	.690	3.93	1.50
2017	Was	NL	4	0	1	3.0	23	11	10	10	1	0	0	0	3	1	3	1	1	0	1.000	0-0	0	95	1.359	28.38	30.00
2018	Was	NL	20	0	5	19.0	84	19	13	12	4	0	2	2	10	1	15	2	0	2	.000	0-0	2	95	.869	5.94	5.68
2019	SF	NL	50	0	6	52.2	214	41	26	26	4	1	4	2	17	0	57	1	7	0	1.000	1-2	5	95	.597	2.61	4.44
2020	SF	NL	15	0	5	11.2	57	13	13	13	7	0	0	1	8	0	8	0	1	2	.333	4-6	3	96	1.198	10.36	10.03
2022	Mil	NL	45	0	3	45.2	186	35	25	21	8	0	3	3	12	0	44	0	3	4	.429	0-4	11	95	.661	2.99	4.14
	7 ML YEARS		191	0	28	185.2	794	168	106	99	26	3	9	12	69	6	160	5	16	10	.615	5-16	32	95	.714	3.90	4.80

Ashton Goudeau

Pitches: R Bats: R Pos: RP-12 Ht: 6'6" Wt: 220 Born: 7/23/1992 Age: 30

			HOW MUCH PITCHED				WHAT HE GAVE UP										THE RESULTS						
Year	Team	Lg	G	GS	GF	IP	BFP	H	R	ER	HR	SH	SF	HB	TBB	IBB	SO	WP	W	L	Pct	Sv-Op	Hld	Vel	OPS	ERC	ERA
2022	Albq	AAA	20	15	2	64.1	313	101	71	68	15	0	4	3	23	0	44	3	0	7	.000	0-	-	-	1.052	8.75	9.51
2020	Col	NL	4	0	2	8.1	39	15	7	7	3	0	2	1	2	0	2	1	0	0	-	0-0	0	93	1.226	12.28	7.56
2021	2 Tms	NL	16	1	3	34.1	141	24	16	16	4	3	0	2	17	3	22	1	2	1	.667	0-0	0	93	.681	3.08	4.19
2022	Col	NL	12	0	4	20.1	94	25	18	16	3	0	2	0	10	0	16	3	1	0	1.000	1-1	0	92	.836	6.17	7.08
21	Cin	NL	5	0	2	9.0	44	8	4	4	1	1	0	0	9	3	5	0	0	0	-	0-0	0	92	.837	5.13	4.00
21	Col	NL	11	1	1	25.1	97	16	12	12	3	2	0	2	8	0	17	1	2	1	.667	0-0	0	93	.615	2.37	4.26
	3 ML YEARS		32	1	9	63.0	274	64	41	39	10	3	4	3	29	3	40	5	3	1	.750	1-1	0	93	.814	5.05	5.57

Yasmani Grandal

Bats: B Throws: R Pos: C-71;DH-25;1B-5;PH-4 yahz-MAH-nee gran-DAHL Ht: 6'2" Wt: 225 Born: 11/8/1988 Age: 34

			BATTING																	RUNNING			AVERAGES			
Year	Team	Lg	G	AB	H	2B	3B	HR	(Hm	Rd)	TB	R	RBI	RC	TBB	IBB	SO	HBP	SH	SF	SB	CS	GDP	Avg	OBP	Slg	OPS
2012	SD	NL	60	192	57	7	1	8	(3	5)	90	28	36	37	31	1	39	1	0	2	0	0	8	.297	.394	.469	.863
2013	SD	NL	28	88	19	8	0	1	(1	0)	30	13	9	12	18	2	18	1	0	1	0	0	1	.216	.352	.341	.693
2014	SD	NL	128	377	85	19	1	15	(7	8)	151	47	49	45	58	1	115	2	0	6	3	0	7	.225	.327	.401	.728
2015	LAD	NL	115	355	83	12	0	16	(8	8)	143	43	47	47	65	1	92	2	1	3	0	1	16	.234	.353	.403	.756
2016	LAD	NL	126	390	89	14	1	27	(20	7)	186	49	72	63	64	1	116	2	0	1	1	3	11	.228	.339	.477	.816
2017	LAD	NL	129	438	108	27	0	22	(13	9)	201	50	58	48	40	0	130	0	1	3	0	1	10	.247	.308	.459	.767
2018	LAD	NL	140	440	106	23	2	24	(11	13)	205	65	68	65	72	1	124	3	0	3	2	1	12	.241	.349	.466	.815
2019	Mil	NL	153	513	126	26	2	28	(13	15)	240	79	77	94	109	2	139	5	0	5	5	1	16	.246	.380	.468	.848
2020	CWS	AL	46	161	37	7	0	8	(3	5)	68	27	27	29	30	0	58	1	0	2	0	0	4	.230	.351	.422	.773
2021	CWS	AL	93	279	67	9	0	23	(14	9)	145	60	62	67	87	0	82	3	1	5	0	0	15	.240	.420	.520	.939
2022	CWS	AL	99	327	66	7	0	5	(1	4)	88	15	27	27	45	1	79	2	0	2	1	0	8	.202	.301	.269	.570
	Postseason		40	102	13	1	0	6	(3	3)	32	7	16	7	23	0	42	1	1	1	0	0	4	.127	.291	.314	.605
	11 ML YEARS		1117	3560	843	159	7	177	(94	83)	1547	476	532	534	619	10	992	22	3	33	12	7	108	.237	.350	.435	.785

Brusdar Graterol

Pitches: R Bats: R Pos: RP-45; SP-1 BROOS-dar Ht: 6'1" Wt: 265 Born: 8/26/1998 Age: 24

			HOW MUCH PITCHED				WHAT HE GAVE UP										THE RESULTS						
Year	Team	Lg	G	GS	GF	IP	BFP	H	R	ER	HR	SH	SF	HB	TBB	IBB	SO	WP	W	L	Pct	Sv-Op	Hld	Vel	OPS	ERC	ERA
2019	Min	AL	10	0	4	9.2	40	10	5	5	1	0	1	1	2	1	10	2	1	1	.500	0-0	1	99	.714	3.90	4.66
2020	LAD	NL	23	2	1	23.1	88	18	9	8	1	0	2	3	3	0	13	0	1	2	.333	0-1	5	99	.560	2.17	3.09
2021	LAD	NL	34	1	6	33.1	150	34	18	17	2	0	0	5	13	6	27	2	3	0	1.000	0-2	4	100	.738	4.08	4.59
2022	LAD	NL	46	1	12	49.2	197	39	20	18	3	0	3	3	10	1	43	0	2	4	.333	4-5	10	100	.584	2.20	3.26
	Postseason		18	0	2	17.2	66	10	4	4	0	0	0	2	1	0	13	0	0	1	.000	1-1	3	100	.372	0.97	2.04
	4 ML YEARS		113	4	23	116.0	475	101	52	48	7	0	6	12	28	8	93	4	7	7	.500	4-8	20	100	.639	2.84	3.72

Kendall Graveman

Pitches: R Bats: R Pos: RP-65 Ht: 6'2" Wt: 200 Born: 12/21/1990 Age: 32

			HOW MUCH PITCHED				WHAT HE GAVE UP										THE RESULTS						
Year	Team	Lg	G	GS	GF	IP	BFP	H	R	ER	HR	SH	SF	HB	TBB	IBB	SO	WP	W	L	Pct	Sv-Op	Hld	Vel	OPS	ERC	ERA
2014	Tor	AL	5	0	1	4.2	18	4	2	2	0	0	0	0	4	1	4	1	0	0	-	0-0	0	93	.556	1.44	3.86
2015	Oak	AL	21	21	0	115.2	502	126	57	52	15	1	2	5	38	0	77	4	6	9	.400	0-0	0	91	.761	4.72	4.05
2016	Oak	AL	31	31	0	186.0	786	196	87	85	22	2	6	7	47	2	108	2	10	11	.476	0-0	0	93	.734	4.08	4.11
2017	Oak	AL	19	19	0	105.1	444	114	50	49	12	0	1	4	32	1	70	5	6	4	.600	0-0	0	93	.780	4.53	4.19
2018	Oak	AL	7	7	0	34.1	158	44	32	29	9	0	0	1	13	0	27	2	1	5	.167	0-0	0	95	.909	7.04	7.60
2020	Sea	AL	11	2	1	18.2	77	15	13	12	2	0	1	0	8	0	15	0	1	3	.250	0-1	5	95	.710	3.20	5.79
2021	2 Tms	AL	53	0	17	56.0	222	35	15	11	3	0	0	8	20	1	61	3	5	1	.833	10-15	11	97	.536	2.25	1.77
2022	CWS	AL	65	0	14	65.0	285	65	29	23	5	0	3	3	26	2	66	3	3	4	.429	6-12	27	97	.693	4.00	3.18
21	Sea	AL	30	0	14	33.0	121	15	7	3	2	0	0	3	8	0	34	2	4	0	1.000	10-12	4	97	.424	1.22	0.82
21	Hou	AL	23	0	3	23.0	101	20	8	8	1	0	0	5	12	1	27	1	1	1	.500	0-3	7	97	.676	4.28	3.13
	Postseason		9	0	4	11.0	44	7	2	2	1	0	0	1	4	0	11	0	1	0	1.000	0-0	2	96	.529	2.35	1.64
	8 ML YEARS		212	80	33	585.2	2492	599	285	263	68	3	13	28	184	6	428	20	32	37	.464	16-28	43	93	.735	4.19	4.04

Jon Gray

Pitches: R **Bats:** R **Pos:** SP-24   **Ht:** 6'4" **Wt:** 225 **Born:** 11/5/1991 **Age:** 31

Year	Team	Lg	G	GS	GF	IP	BFP	H	R	ER	HR	SH	SF	HB	TBB	IBB	SO	WP	W	L	Pct	Sv-Op	Hld	Vel	OPS	ERC	ERA
2015	Col	NL	9	9	0	40.2	185	52	26	25	4	2	4	2	14	2	40	3	0	2	.000	0-0	0	94	.856	5.60	5.53
2016	Col	NL	29	29	0	168.0	712	153	92	86	18	5	5	12	59	2	185	7	10	10	.500	0-0	0	95	.703	3.71	4.61
2017	Col	NL	20	20	0	110.1	461	113	47	45	10	2	2	2	30	0	112	3	10	4	.714	0-0	0	96	.716	3.76	3.67
2018	Col	NL	31	31	0	172.1	743	180	102	98	27	4	3	6	52	1	183	6	12	9	.571	0-0	0	95	.773	4.44	5.12
2019	Col	NL	26	25	1	150.0	637	147	70	64	19	7	3	4	56	4	150	7	11	8	.579	0-0	0	96	.766	4.16	3.84
2020	Col	NL	8	8	0	39.0	174	45	31	29	6	0	1	2	11	0	22	2	2	4	.333	0-0	0	94	.815	4.99	6.69
2021	Col	NL	29	29	0	149.0	644	140	83	76	21	2	4	8	58	2	157	7	8	12	.400	0-0	0	95	.740	4.15	4.59
2022	Tex	AL	24	24	0	127.1	521	105	61	56	17	0	4	6	39	0	134	4	7	7	.500	0-0	0	96	.663	3.18	3.96
	Postseason		1	1	0	1.1	11	7	4	4	1	0	0	0	0	0	2	0	0	1	.000	0-0	0	97	1.818	43.52	27.00
	8 ML YEARS		176	175	1	956.2	4077	935	512	479	122	22	26	42	319	11	983	39	60	56	.517	0-0	0	95	.740	4.04	4.51

Josiah Gray

Pitches: R **Bats:** R **Pos:** SP-28   **Ht:** 6'1" **Wt:** 199 **Born:** 12/21/1997 **Age:** 25

Year	Team	Lg	G	GS	GF	IP	BFP	H	R	ER	HR	SH	SF	HB	TBB	IBB	SO	WP	W	L	Pct	Sv-Op	Hld	Vel	OPS	ERC	ERA
2021	2 Tms	NL	14	13	0	70.2	307	63	44	43	19	5	2	2	33	3	76	7	2	2	.500	0-0	0	95	.830	4.92	5.48
2022	Was	NL	28	28	0	148.2	649	136	84	83	38	0	5	8	66	1	154	7	7	10	.412	0-0	0	94	.813	5.03	5.02
21	LAD	NL	2	1	0	8.0	35	7	6	6	4	0	0	0	5	1	13	1	0	0	-	0-0	0	95	.976	7.09	6.75
21	Was	NL	12	12	0	62.2	272	56	38	37	15	5	2	2	28	2	63	6	2	2	.500	0-0	0	95	.811	4.66	5.31
	2 ML YEARS		42	41	0	219.1	956	199	128	126	57	5	7	10	99	4	230	14	9	12	.429	0-0	0	95	.818	5.00	5.17

Sonny Gray

Pitches: R **Bats:** R **Pos:** SP-24   **Ht:** 5'10" **Wt:** 195 **Born:** 11/7/1989 **Age:** 33

Year	Team	Lg	G	GS	GF	IP	BFP	H	R	ER	HR	SH	SF	HB	TBB	IBB	SO	WP	W	L	Pct	Sv-Op	Hld	Vel	OPS	ERC	ERA
2013	Oak	AL	12	10	0	64.0	261	51	22	19	4	0	3	0	20	0	67	2	5	3	.625	0-0	0	93	.570	2.42	2.67
2014	Oak	AL	33	33	0	219.0	899	187	84	75	15	8	5	7	74	2	183	15	14	10	.583	0-0	0	93	.627	2.99	3.08
2015	Oak	AL	31	31	0	208.0	831	166	71	63	17	1	4	2	59	0	169	13	14	7	.667	0-0	0	93	.590	2.53	2.73
2016	Oak	AL	22	22	0	117.0	517	133	80	74	18	0	7	2	42	0	94	15	5	11	.313	0-0	0	93	.818	5.16	5.69
2017	2 Tms	AL	27	27	0	162.1	678	139	79	64	19	1	2	3	57	1	153	11	10	12	.455	0-0	0	93	.668	3.26	3.55
2018	NYY	AL	30	23	2	130.1	582	138	73	71	14	1	5	8	57	0	123	9	11	9	.550	0-0	0	93	.768	4.85	4.90
2019	Cin	NL	31	31	0	175.1	708	122	59	56	17	6	5	7	68	1	205	7	11	8	.579	0-0	0	93	.605	2.57	2.87
2020	Cin	NL	11	11	0	56.0	235	42	26	23	4	0	0	2	26	0	72	7	5	3	.625	0-0	0	93	.607	2.90	3.70
2021	Cin	NL	26	26	0	135.1	575	115	67	63	19	2	2	8	50	1	155	9	7	9	.438	0-0	0	92	.687	3.58	4.19
2022	Min	AL	24	24	0	119.2	488	99	44	41	11	1	4	6	36	0	117	3	8	5	.615	0-0	0	92	.639	2.94	3.08
17	Oak	AL	16	16	0	97.0	400	84	48	37	8	0	2	1	30	0	94	7	6	5	.545	0-0	0	93	.644	2.93	3.43
17	NYY	AL	11	11	0	65.1	278	55	31	27	11	1	0	2	27	1	59	4	4	7	.364	0-0	0	93	.702	3.77	3.72
	Postseason		4	4	0	21.1	90	14	8	7	2	1	0	2	12	1	18	2	0	2	.000	0-0	0	93	.615	3.09	2.95
	10 ML YEARS		247	238	2	1387.0	5774	1192	605	549	138	20	37	45	489	5	1338	91	90	77	.539	0-0	0	93	.659	3.25	3.56

Chad Green

Pitches: R **Bats:** L **Pos:** RP-14   **Ht:** 6'3" **Wt:** 215 **Born:** 5/24/1991 **Age:** 32

Year	Team	Lg	G	GS	GF	IP	BFP	H	R	ER	HR	SH	SF	HB	TBB	IBB	SO	WP	W	L	Pct	Sv-Op	Hld	Vel	OPS	ERC	ERA
2016	NYY	AL	12	8	4	45.2	198	49	26	24	12	1	1	1	15	0	52	1	2	4	.333	1-1	0	94	.852	5.46	4.73
2017	NYY	AL	40	1	4	69.0	253	34	14	14	4	2	1	2	17	0	103	3	5	0	1.000	0-1	9	96	.454	1.20	1.83
2018	NYY	AL	63	0	3	75.2	298	64	22	21	9	0	3	1	15	2	94	3	8	3	.727	0-4	12	96	.641	2.67	2.50
2019	NYY	AL	54	15	10	69.0	295	66	35	32	10	0	3	6	19	0	98	2	4	4	.500	2-2	4	96	.735	3.95	4.17
2020	NYY	AL	22	0	5	25.2	100	13	13	10	5	1	1	0	8	2	32	3	3	3	.500	1-3	6	95	.534	1.66	3.51
2021	NYY	AL	67	0	15	83.2	315	57	32	29	14	1	2	0	17	2	99	5	10	7	.588	6-12	18	96	.622	2.13	3.12
2022	NYY	AL	14	0	2	15.0	62	13	6	5	1	0	2	0	5	0	16	0	1	1	.500	1-4	3	95	.647	2.88	3.00
	Postseason		18	1	2	26.0	110	23	13	12	4	1	1	1	9	1	27	0	3	0	1.000	0-0	2	96	.742	3.65	4.15
	7 ML YEARS		272	24	43	383.2	1521	296	148	135	55	5	13	10	96	6	494	17	33	22	.600	11-27	52	96	.645	2.67	3.17

Hunter Greene

Pitches: R **Bats:** R **Pos:** SP-24   **Ht:** 6'5" **Wt:** 230 **Born:** 8/6/1999 **Age:** 23

Year	Team	Lg	G	GS	GF	IP	BFP	H	R	ER	HR	SH	SF	HB	TBB	IBB	SO	WP	W	L	Pct	Sv-Op	Hld	Vel	OPS	ERC	ERA
2018	Dayton	A	18	18	0	68.1	294	66	35	34	6	1	0	6	23	0	89	6	3	7	.300	0- -	-	-	.739	3.89	4.48
2021	Chatt	AA	7	7	0	41.0	162	27	9	9	2	0	0	3	14	0	60	2	5	0	1.000	0- -	-	-	.534	2.10	1.98
2021	Lsvlle	AAA	14	14	0	65.1	276	59	35	30	11	0	1	4	25	0	79	2	5	8	.385	0- -	-	-	.733	4.23	4.13
2022	Cin	NL	24	24	0	125.2	531	104	64	62	24	0	4	10	48	0	164	4	5	13	.278	0-0	0	99	.725	3.97	4.44

Riley Greene

Bats: L **Throws:** L **Pos:** CF-93   **Ht:** 6'3" **Wt:** 200 **Born:** 9/28/2000 **Age:** 22

Year	Team	Lg	G	AB	H	2B	3B	HR	(Hm	Rd)	TB	R	RBI	RC	TBB	IBB	SO	HBP	SH	SF	SB	CS	GDP	Avg	OBP	Slg	OPS
2019	3 Tms	Low	57	221	60	8	3	5	(-	-)	89	34	28	33	22	0	63	5	0	3	5	0	4	.271	.347	.403	.749
2021	Erie	AA	84	326	97	16	5	16	(-	-)	171	59	54	67	41	1	102	4	0	3	12	1	3	.298	.381	.525	.905
2021	Toledo	AAA	36	145	42	7	3	7	(-	-)	76	32	27	29	19	2	47	2	0	1	3	0	3	.290	.377	.524	.901
2022	Toledo	AAA	15	62	17	4	0	1	(-	-)	24	10	6	8	6	0	14	0	0	0	3	0	1	.274	.338	.387	.725
2022	Det	AL	93	376	95	18	4	5	(3	2)	136	46	42	46	36	0	120	3	0	3	1	4	8	.253	.321	.362	.682

Shane Greene

Pitches: R Bats: R Pos: RP-2 | Ht: 6'4" Wt: 200 Born: 11/17/1988 Age: 34

Year	Team	Lg	G	GS	GF	IP	BFP	H	R	ER	HR	SH	SF	HB	TBB	IBB	SO	WP	W	L	Pct	Sv-Op	Hld	Vel	OPS	ERC	ERA
2022	OkCity	AAA	7	0	1	7.2	42	13	5	5	1	0	0	0	4	0	9	0	0	1	.000	0--	-	-	.783	7.40	5.87
2022	S-WB	AAA	20	0	6	26.2	121	26	16	16	3	0	0	3	15	0	30	1	2	1	.667	3--	-	-	.781	5.14	5.40
2014	NYY	AL	15	14	0	78.2	345	81	38	33	8	0	1	6	29	0	81	1	5	4	.556	0-0	0	93	.715	4.43	3.78
2015	Det	AL	18	16	1	83.2	373	103	67	64	13	2	4	6	27	4	50	1	4	8	.333	0-0	0	92	.897	5.83	6.88
2016	Det	AL	50	3	4	60.1	256	58	39	39	3	2	2	4	22	1	59	0	5	4	.556	2-3	16	94	.680	3.65	5.82
2017	Det	AL	71	0	26	67.2	283	50	21	20	6	0	1	4	34	4	73	1	4	3	.571	9-13	14	95	.631	3.14	2.66
2018	Det	AL	66	0	58	63.1	279	68	39	36	12	0	3	3	19	1	65	3	4	6	.400	32-38	0	94	.787	4.80	5.12
2019	2 Tms	AL	65	0	37	62.2	252	46	22	16	8	1	1	3	17	1	64	0	0	3	.000	23-28	10	93	.598	2.51	2.30
2020	Atl	NL	28	0	6	27.2	109	22	9	8	2	1	1	2	9	1	21	0	1	0	1.000	0-0	9	92	.639	2.89	2.60
2021	2 Tms	NL	28	0	7	23.2	113	25	19	19	6	0	0	4	14	0	24	1	1	0	1.000	1-2	2	93	.886	7.06	7.23
2022	2 Tms		2	0	2	3.0	13	3	2	2	1	0	0	0	1	0	2	0	1	0	1.000	0-0	0	91	.808	5.31	6.00
19	Det	AL	38	0	32	38.0	151	21	11	5	5	1	0	1	12	1	43	0	0	2	.000	22-25	0	93	.504	1.70	1.18
19	Atl	NL	27	0	5	24.2	101	25	11	11	3	0	1	2	5	0	21	0	0	1	.000	1-3	10	92	.736	3.97	4.01
21	Atl	NL	19	0	5	17.0	83	22	16	16	5	0	0	1	9	0	17	0	0	1	.000	0-1	2	93	.947	8.09	8.47
21	LAD	NL	9	0	2	6.2	30	3	3	3	1	0	0	3	5	0	7	1	0	0	-	1-1	0	92	.685	4.53	4.05
22	LAD	NL	1	0	1	2.0	8	2	0	0	0	0	0	0	0	0	1	0	1	0	1.000	0-0	0	92	.500	1.95	0.00
22	NYY	AL	1	0	1	1.0	5	1	2	2	1	0	0	0	1	0	1	0	0	0	-	0-0	0	91	1.400	14.27	18.00
Postseason			8	0	3	8.2	37	10	2	2	0	0	0	0	2	1	9	1	0	0	-	0-1	0	93	.696	3.39	2.08
9 ML YEARS			343	33	141	470.2	2023	456	256	237	59	6	13	32	172	12	439	7	24	29	.453	67-84	51	93	.734	4.19	4.53

Didi Gregorius

Bats: L Throws: R Pos: SS-61;PH-3 | dee-dee greh-GORE-ee-us | Ht: 6'3" Wt: 205 Born: 2/18/1990 Age: 33

Year	Team	Lg	G	AB	H	2B	3B	HR	(Hm	Rd)	TB	R	RBI	RC	TBB	IBB	SO	HBP	SH	SF	SB	CS	GDP	Avg	OBP	Slg	OPS
2012	Cin	NL	8	20	6	0	0	0	(0	0)	6	1	2	2	0	0	5	0	1	0	0	0	0	.300	.300	.300	.600
2013	Ari	NL	103	357	90	16	3	7	(3	4)	133	47	28	42	37	5	65	6	2	1	0	2	4	.252	.332	.373	.704
2014	Ari	NL	80	270	61	9	5	6	(3	3)	98	35	27	37	22	3	52	3	2	2	3	0	1	.226	.290	.363	.653
2015	NYY	AL	155	525	139	24	2	9	(6	3)	194	57	56	64	33	0	85	11	3	6	5	3	4	.265	.318	.370	.688
2016	NYY	AL	153	562	155	32	2	20	(11	9)	251	68	70	71	19	2	82	6	5	5	7	1	9	.276	.304	.447	.751
2017	NYY	AL	136	534	153	27	0	25	(12	13)	255	73	87	84	25	1	70	3	0	7	3	1	7	.287	.318	.478	.796
2018	NYY	AL	134	504	135	23	5	27	(19	8)	249	89	86	79	48	3	69	7	1	9	10	6	8	.268	.335	.494	.829
2019	NYY	AL	82	324	77	14	2	16	(6	10)	143	47	61	45	17	1	53	1	0	2	2	1	5	.238	.276	.441	.718
2020	Phi	NL	60	215	61	10	2	10	(7	3)	105	34	40	38	15	3	28	4	1	2	3	2	4	.284	.339	.488	.827
2021	Phi	NL	103	368	77	16	2	13	(9	4)	136	35	54	31	25	1	67	8	0	7	3	0	8	.209	.270	.370	.639
2022	Phi	NL	63	214	45	9	4	1	(0	1)	65	17	19	19	13	0	36	3	0	2	1	0	0	.210	.263	.304	.567
Postseason			28	101	26	3	1	4	(2	2)	43	11	16	16	9	3	22	0	1	1	0	0	0	.257	.315	.426	.741
11 ML YEARS			1077	3893	999	180	27	134	(76	58)	1635	503	530	512	254	19	612	52	15	43	37	16	50	.257	.308	.420	.728

Grayson Greiner

Bats: R Throws: R Pos: C-2 | Ht: 6'6" Wt: 238 Born: 10/11/1992 Age: 30

Year	Team	Lg	G	AB	H	2B	3B	HR	(Hm	Rd)	TB	R	RBI	RC	TBB	IBB	SO	HBP	SH	SF	SB	CS	GDP	Avg	OBP	Slg	OPS
2022	Reno	AAA	45	151	35	6	0	6	(-	-)	59	20	20	20	18	1	67	1	0	0	1	0	2	.232	.318	.391	.708
2018	Det	AL	30	96	21	6	0	0	(0	0)	27	9	12	13	17	0	32	0	0	3	0	1	0	.219	.328	.281	.609
2019	Det	AL	58	208	42	5	1	5	(1	4)	64	18	19	15	13	0	70	1	1	1	0	0	5	.202	.251	.308	.559
2020	Det	AL	18	51	6	2	0	3	(0	3)	17	8	8	3	3	0	20	1	0	0	0	0	2	.118	.182	.333	.515
2021	Det	AL	31	72	17	4	0	1	(0	1)	24	7	7	14	9	0	31	0	1	0	0	0	0	.236	.321	.333	.654
2022	Ari	NL	2	6	1	0	0	0	(0	0)	1	0	0	0	2	0	3	0	0	0	0	0	0	.167	.375	.167	.542
5 ML YEARS			139	433	87	17	1	9	(1	8)	133	42	46	45	44	0	156	2	2	4	0	1	7	.201	.275	.307	.583

Zack Greinke

Pitches: R Bats: R Pos: SP-26 | GRAIN-key | Ht: 6'2" Wt: 200 Born: 10/21/1983 Age: 39

Year	Team	Lg	G	GS	GF	IP	BFP	H	R	ER	HR	SH	SF	HB	TBB	IBB	SO	WP	W	L	Pct	Sv-Op	Hld	Vel	OPS	ERC	ERA
2004	KC	AL	24	24	0	145.0	599	143	64	64	26	3	2	8	26	3	100	1	8	11	.421	0-0	0	89	.752	3.85	3.97
2005	KC	AL	33	33	0	183.0	829	233	125	118	23	4	4	13	53	0	114	4	5	17	.227	0-0	0	90	.846	5.71	5.80
2006	KC	AL	3	0	1	6.1	28	7	3	3	1	0	0	0	3	2	5	0	1	0	1.000	0-0	0	93	.757	4.93	4.26
2007	KC	AL	52	14	7	122.0	507	122	52	50	12	3	4	3	36	5	106	3	7	7	.500	1-1	12	94	.747	3.77	3.69
2008	KC	AL	32	32	0	202.1	851	202	87	78	21	2	4	4	56	1	183	8	13	10	.565	0-0	0	93	.715	3.68	3.47
2009	KC	AL	33	33	0	229.1	915	195	64	55	11	8	3	4	51	0	242	5	16	8	.667	0-0	0	94	.611	2.39	2.16
2010	KC	AL	33	33	0	220.0	919	219	114	102	18	6	7	7	55	1	181	4	10	14	.417	0-0	0	93	.696	3.48	4.17
2011	Mil	NL	28	28	0	171.2	715	161	82	73	19	6	1	4	45	0	201	10	16	6	.727	0-0	0	93	.708	3.35	3.83
2012	2 Tms		34	34	0	212.1	868	200	84	82	18	7	2	2	54	0	200	8	15	5	.750	0-0	0	92	.663	3.17	3.48
2013	LAD	NL	28	28	0	177.2	717	152	54	52	13	13	1	7	46	1	148	5	15	4	.789	0-0	0	92	.647	2.78	2.63
2014	LAD	NL	32	32	0	202.1	821	190	69	61	19	2	4	2	43	3	207	12	17	8	.680	0-0	0	91	.660	3.03	2.71
2015	LAD	NL	32	32	0	222.2	843	148	43	41	14	6	2	5	40	1	200	7	19	3	.864	0-0	0	92	.507	1.56	1.66
2016	Ari	NL	26	26	0	158.2	667	161	80	77	23	7	4	0	41	3	134	1	13	7	.650	0-0	0	91	.750	3.86	4.37
2017	Ari	NL	32	32	0	202.1	801	172	80	72	25	4	3	0	45	0	215	12	17	7	.708	0-0	0	92	.659	2.79	3.20
2018	Ari	NL	33	33	0	207.2	839	181	77	74	28	3	3	6	43	3	199	4	15	11	.577	0-0	0	90	.665	2.96	3.21
2019	2 Tms		33	33	0	208.2	810	175	73	68	21	5	4	4	30	2	187	2	18	5	.783	0-0	0	90	.623	2.39	2.93
2020	Hou	AL	12	12	0	67.0	273	67	30	30	6	0	1	1	9	0	67	3	3	3	.500	0-0	0	87	.687	3.04	4.03
2021	Hou	AL	30	29	0	171.0	697	164	82	79	30	2	5	2	40	0	120	3	11	6	.647	0-0	1	89	.725	3.68	4.16
2022	KC	AL	26	26	0	137.0	585	157	65	56	14	1	5	3	27	0	73	7	4	9	.308	0-0	0	89	.737	4.19	3.68
12	Mil	NL	21	21	0	123.0	504	120	49	47	7	3	0	0	28	0	122	4	9	3	.750	0-0	0	92	.653	3.02	3.44
12	LAA	AL	13	13	0	89.1	364	80	35	35	11	4	2	2	26	0	78	4	6	2	.750	0-0	0	92	.679	3.38	3.53

Year	Team	Lg	G	GS	GF	IP	BFP	H	R	ER	HR	SH	SF	HB	TBB	IBB	SO	WP	W	L	Pct	Sv-Op	Hld	Vel	OPS	ERC	ERA
19 Ari		NL	23	23	0	146.0	562	117	48	47	15	4	3	3	21	2	135	1	10	4	.714	0-0	0	90	.614	2.22	2.90
19 Hou		AL	10	10	0	62.2	248	58	25	21	6	1	1	1	9	0	52	1	8	1	.889	0-0	0	90	.644	2.79	3.02
Postseason			22	21	0	113.0	469	103	55	52	19	3	1	3	33	0	100	2	4	6	.400	0-0	0	91	.723	3.73	4.14
19 ML YEARS			556	514	8	3247.0	13284	3049	1328	1235	342	82	59	75	739	25	2882	99	223	141	.613	1-1	13	92	.684	3.21	3.42

Randal Grichuk

Bats: R **Throws:** R **Pos:** RF-106;CF-52;PH-3;DH-1;PR-1   GRICH-ick   **Ht:** 6'2" **Wt:** 216 **Born:** 8/13/1991 **Age:** 31

								BATTING												RUNNING			AVERAGES			
Year	Team	Lg	G	AB	H	2B	3B	HR	(Hm | Rd)	TB	R	RBI	RC	TBB	IBB	SO	HBP	SH	SF	SB	CS	GDP	Avg	OBP	Slg	OPS
2014	StL	NL	47	110	27	6	1	3	(2 | 1)	44	11	8	7	5	0	31	0	1	0	0	2	4	.245	.278	.400	.678
2015	StL	NL	103	323	89	23	7	17	(10 | 7)	177	49	47	47	22	2	110	4	0	1	4	2	6	.276	.329	.548	.877
2016	StL	NL	132	446	107	29	3	24	(12 | 12)	214	66	68	62	28	0	141	3	0	1	5	4	9	.240	.289	.480	.769
2017	StL	NL	122	412	98	25	3	22	(13 | 9)	195	53	59	47	26	3	133	2	0	2	6	1	9	.238	.285	.473	.758
2018	Tor	AL	124	424	104	32	1	25	(17 | 8)	213	60	61	61	27	0	122	8	0	3	3	2	5	.245	.301	.502	.803
2019	Tor	AL	151	586	136	29	5	31	(19 | 12)	268	75	80	68	35	0	163	5	0	2	2	1	20	.232	.280	.457	.738
2020	Tor	AL	55	216	59	9	0	12	(7 | 5)	104	38	35	35	13	1	49	0	0	2	1	1	5	.273	.312	.481	.793
2021	Tor	AL	149	511	123	25	1	22	(11 | 11)	216	59	81	61	27	0	114	3	0	4	0	3	17	.241	.281	.423	.703
2022	Col	NL	141	506	131	21	3	19	(13 | 6)	215	60	73	72	24	0	127	6	0	2	4	0	12	.259	.299	.425	.724
Postseason			15	50	9	0	0	3	(1 | 2)	18	5	4	2	2	0	22	0	0	0	0	0	0	.180	.212	.360	.572
9 ML YEARS			1024	3534	874	199	24	175	(104 | 71)	1646	471	512	460	207	6	990	31	1	17	25	16	87	.247	.293	.466	.759

Foster Griffin

Pitches: L **Bats:** R **Pos:** RP-6   **Ht:** 6'3" **Wt:** 225 **Born:** 7/27/1995 **Age:** 27

				HOW MUCH PITCHED				WHAT HE GAVE UP										THE RESULTS								
Year	Team	Lg	G	GS	GF	IP	BFP	H	R	ER	HR	SH	SF	HB	TBB	IBB	SO	WP	W	L	Pct	Sv-Op	Hld	Vel	OPS	ERC	ERA
2022	Omha	AAA	20	0	2	28.0	109	22	14	14	2	0	1	1	6	0	32	1	4	0	1.000	0- -	-		.516	1.74	1.93
2022	Buffalo	AAA	18	0	7	23.1	101	21	6	6	1	0	0	1	9	1	25	3	2	0	1.000	1- -	-		.637	3.10	2.31
2020	KC	AL	1	0	0	1.2	6	0	0	0	0	0	0	0	0	0	1	0	1	0	1.000	0-0	0	92	.000	0.00	0.00
2022	2 Tms	AL	6	0	4	6.1	32	7	7	6	0	2	1	1	5	0	4	0	0	0	-	0-0	0	94	.955	5.89	8.53
22 KC		AL	5	0	3	4.1	24	6	7	6	0	2	1	1	4	0	2	0	0	0	-	0-0	0	94	1.125	8.48	12.46
22 Tor		AL	1	0	1	2.0	8	1	0	0	0	0	0	0	1	0	2	0	0	0	-	0-0	0	93	.536	1.41	0.00
2 ML YEARS			7	0	4	8.0	38	7	7	6	0	2	1	1	5	0	5	0	1	0	1.000	0-0	0	93	.775	3.74	6.75

Justin Grimm

Pitches: R **Bats:** R **Pos:** RP-15   **Ht:** 6'3" **Wt:** 210 **Born:** 8/16/1988 **Age:** 34

				HOW MUCH PITCHED				WHAT HE GAVE UP										THE RESULTS								
Year	Team	Lg	G	GS	GF	IP	BFP	H	R	ER	HR	SH	SF	HB	TBB	IBB	SO	WP	W	L	Pct	Sv-Op	Hld	Vel	OPS	ERC	ERA
2012	Tex	AL	5	2	3	14.0	65	22	14	14	1	0	2	0	3	0	13	3	1	1	.500	0-0	0	92	.935	6.54	9.00
2013	2 Tms		27	17	3	98.0	442	120	70	65	15	4	2	2	34	1	76	4	7	9	.438	0-0	3	92	.846	5.61	5.97
2014	ChC	NL	73	0	19	69.0	292	59	32	29	4	1	3	4	27	2	70	8	5	2	.714	0-1	11	94	.632	3.14	3.78
2015	ChC	NL	62	0	11	49.2	204	31	18	11	4	0	3	1	26	1	67	8	3	5	.375	3-6	15	95	.572	2.48	1.99
2016	ChC	NL	68	0	11	52.2	225	47	24	24	5	0	0	1	23	2	65	7	2	1	.667	0-0	10	94	.679	3.59	4.10
2017	ChC	NL	50	0	13	55.1	232	47	34	34	12	1	1	1	27	0	59	4	1	2	.333	1-3	4	95	.760	4.57	5.53
2018	2 Tms	AL	21	0	5	17.1	83	19	20	20	3	2	3	0	14	1	11	1	1	3	.250	0-2	3	93	.907	6.84	10.38
2020	Mil	NL	4	0	2	4.2	27	9	9	9	4	0	0	0	4	0	6	0	0	0	-	0-0	0	93	1.395	19.93	17.36
2022	Oak	AL	15	0	5	15.1	71	18	8	7	1	0	1	2	7	0	11	0	0	0	-	0-0	3	93	.807	5.60	4.11
13 Tex		AL	17	17	0	89.0	406	116	67	63	15	2	2	1	31	1	68	4	7	7	.500	0-0	0	91	.883	6.21	6.37
13 ChC		NL	10	0	3	9.0	36	4	3	2	0	2	0	1	3	0	8	0	0	2	.000	0-0	3	94	.402	1.12	2.00
18 KC		AL	16	0	3	12.2	67	17	19	19	2	2	2	0	14	1	8	1	1	3	.250	0-2	3	93	1.008	9.68	13.50
18 Sea		AL	5	0	2	4.2	16	2	1	1	1	0	1	0	0	0	3	0	0	0	-	0-0	0	94	.525	0.85	1.93
Postseason			9	0	0	6.1	28	7	6	6	0	0	1	0	1	0	7	1	0	0	-	0-0	0	95	.706	3.52	8.53
9 ML YEARS			325	19	72	376.0	1641	372	229	213	49	8	15	11	165	7	378	35	20	23	.465	4-12	49	94	.753	4.47	5.10

Trent Grisham

Bats: L **Throws:** L **Pos:** CF-148;PH-14;PR-3   **Ht:** 5'11" **Wt:** 224 **Born:** 11/1/1996 **Age:** 26

								BATTING												RUNNING			AVERAGES			
Year	Team	Lg	G	AB	H	2B	3B	HR	(Hm	Rd)	TB	R	RBI	RC	TBB	IBB	SO	HBP	SH	SF	SB	CS	GDP	Avg	OBP	Slg	OPS
2019	Mil	NL	51	156	36	6	2	6	(3	3)	64	24	24	20	20	0	48	4	0	3	1	0	3	.231	.328	.410	.738
2020	SD	NL	59	215	54	8	3	10	(6	4)	98	42	26	35	31	0	64	3	1	1	10	1	1	.251	.352	.456	.808
2021	SD	NL	132	462	112	28	3	15	(4	11)	191	61	62	68	54	2	119	6	1	4	13	5	10	.242	.327	.413	.740
2022	SD	NL	152	451	83	16	2	17	(9	8)	154	58	53	56	57	1	150	7	7	2	7	1	3	.184	.284	.341	.626
Postseason			7	25	3	1	0	0	(0	0)	4	2	2	4	5	0	13	1	0	0	0	0	0	.120	.290	.160	.450
4 ML YEARS			394	1284	285	58	10	48	(22	26)	507	185	165	179	162	3	381	20	9	10	31	7	17	.222	.316	.395	.711

Vaughn Grissom

Bats: R **Throws:** R **Pos:** 2B-40;SS-2   **Ht:** 6'3" **Wt:** 210 **Born:** 1/5/2001 **Age:** 22

								BATTING												RUNNING			AVERAGES			
Year	Team	Lg	G	AB	H	2B	3B	HR	(Hm	Rd)	TB	R	RBI	RC	TBB	IBB	SO	HBP	SH	SF	SB	CS	GDP	Avg	OBP	Slg	OPS
2022	Rome	A+	74	298	93	17	1	11	(-	-)	145	62	55	56	32	0	40	14	0	0	20	4	11	.312	.404	.487	.891
2022	Missi	AA	22	91	33	3	1	3	(-	-)	47	10	12	19	4	0	14	3	0	1	7	1	0	.363	.408	.516	.925
2022	Atl	NL	41	141	41	6	0	5	(2	3)	62	24	18	21	11	1	34	3	0	1	5	2	0	.291	.353	.440	.792

Jordan Groshans

Bats: R Throws: R Pos: 3B-17   Ht: 6'3" Wt: 200 Born: 11/10/1999 Age: 23

Year	Team	Lg	G	AB	H	2B	3B	HR	(Hm	Rd)	TB	R	RBI	RC	TBB	IBB	SO	HBP	SH	SF	SB	CS	GDP	Avg	OBP	Slg	OPS
2022	Buffalo	AAA	67	240	60	8	0	1	(-	-)	71	30	24	24	35	0	46	2	0	2	2	0	6	.250	.348	.296	.644
2022	Jaxnvl	AAA	31	113	34	7	0	2	(-	-)	47	14	10	19	19	0	19	0	0	1	1	0	0	.301	.398	.416	.814
2022	Mia	NL	17	61	16	0	0	1	(1	0)	19	9	2	3	4	0	13	0	0	0	0	0	2	.262	.308	.311	.619

Robbie Grossman

Bats: B Throws: L Pos: LF-69;RF-59;PH-10;DH-3   Ht: 6'0" Wt: 209 Born: 9/16/1989 Age: 33

Year	Team	Lg	G	AB	H	2B	3B	HR	(Hm	Rd)	TB	R	RBI	RC	TBB	IBB	SO	HBP	SH	SF	SB	CS	GDP	Avg	OBP	Slg	OPS
2013	Hou	AL	63	257	69	14	0	4	(3	1)	95	29	21	37	23	0	70	2	5	1	6	7	2	.268	.332	.370	.702
2014	Hou	AL	103	360	84	14	2	6	(2	4)	120	42	37	48	55	1	105	4	3	4	9	3	7	.233	.337	.333	.670
2015	Hou	AL	24	49	7	2	0	1	(1	0)	12	7	5	4	5	0	17	0	0	0	0	0	0	.143	.222	.245	.467
2016	Min	AL	99	332	93	19	1	11	(8	3)	147	49	37	52	55	0	96	2	0	0	2	3	3	.280	.386	.443	.828
2017	Min	AL	119	382	94	22	1	9	(5	4)	145	62	45	58	67	0	79	3	2	0	3	1	6	.246	.361	.380	.741
2018	Min	AL	129	396	108	27	1	5	(2	3)	152	50	48	62	60	0	83	2	2	5	0	1	2	.273	.367	.384	.751
2019	Oak	AL	138	420	101	21	3	6	(2	4)	146	57	38	58	59	2	86	1	0	2	9	4	7	.240	.334	.348	.682
2020	Oak	AL	51	166	40	12	2	8	(4	4)	80	23	23	27	21	2	38	5	0	0	8	1	1	.241	.344	.482	.826
2021	Det	AL	156	557	133	23	3	23	(12	11)	231	88	67	96	98	3	155	8	2	6	20	5	8	.239	.357	.415	.772
2022	2 Tms		129	411	86	19	1	7	(5	2)	128	40	45	46	56	0	129	6	0	4	6	2	3	.209	.310	.311	.622
22	Det	AL	83	273	56	13	1	2	(2	0)	77	24	23	26	38	0	90	6	0	3	3	1	2	.205	.313	.282	.595
22	Atl	NL	46	138	30	6	0	5	(3	2)	51	16	22	20	18	0	39	0	0	1	3	1	1	.217	.306	.370	.675
Postseason			8	25	5	2	0	0	(0	0)	7	3	0	2	3	0	8	0	0	0	0	0	0	.200	.286	.280	.566
10 ML YEARS			1011	3330	815	173	14	80	(44	36)	1256	447	366	488	499	8	858	31	14	22	63	27	39	.245	.346	.377	.724

Michael Grove

Pitches: R Bats: R Pos: SP-6; RP-1   Ht: 6'3" Wt: 200 Born: 12/18/1996 Age: 26

Year	Team	Lg	G	GS	GF	IP	BFP	H	R	ER	HR	SH	SF	HB	TBB	IBB	SO	WP	W	L	Pct	Sv-Op	Hld	Vel	OPS	ERC	ERA
2022	Tulsa	AA	5	5	0	16.1	67	11	8	5	1	0	0	0	5	0	22	3	0	1	.000	0-	-	-	.567	1.75	2.76
2022	OkCity	AAA	14	12	0	59.2	255	56	32	27	10	0	6	1	21	0	68	5	1	4	.200	0-	-	-	.764	4.02	4.07
2022	LAD	NL	7	6	1	29.1	133	32	21	15	6	0	0	0	10	1	24	2	1	0	1.000	0-0	0	94	.779	4.81	4.60

Robert Gsellman

Pitches: R Bats: R Pos: RP-8   guh-ZELL-man   Ht: 6'4" Wt: 200 Born: 7/18/1993 Age: 29

Year	Team	Lg	G	GS	GF	IP	BFP	H	R	ER	HR	SH	SF	HB	TBB	IBB	SO	WP	W	L	Pct	Sv-Op	Hld	Vel	OPS	ERC	ERA
2022	Iowa	AAA	10	9	0	29.0	127	29	22	20	3	1	3	3	11	0	22	1	1	4	.200	0-	-	-	.724	4.44	6.21
2016	NYM	NL	8	7	0	44.2	185	42	12	12	1	4	2	1	15	2	42	1	4	2	.667	0-0	0	94	.639	3.05	2.42
2017	NYM	NL	25	22	1	119.2	549	138	85	69	17	4	2	8	42	3	82	4	8	7	.533	0-1	1	93	.807	5.16	5.19
2018	NYM	NL	68	0	24	80.0	345	76	44	38	8	3	5	5	28	6	70	1	6	3	.667	13-19	15	94	.700	3.69	4.28
2019	NYM	NL	52	0	9	63.2	277	64	36	33	7	1	2	6	23	2	60	4	2	3	.400	1-5	7	95	.766	4.36	4.66
2020	NYM	NL	6	4	0	14.0	71	22	15	15	4	0	1	1	8	0	9	2	0	0	-	0-0	1	94	1.109	10.49	9.64
2021	NYM	NL	17	1	1	28.2	119	27	14	12	3	0	0	2	7	0	17	0	0	1	.000	0-0	1	94	.690	3.48	3.77
2022	ChC	NL	8	0	5	15.1	64	17	10	8	2	0	0	0	3	0	9	0	0	2	.000	1-2	0	93	.788	4.13	4.60
7 ML YEARS			184	34	40	366.0	1610	386	216	187	42	12	12	23	126	13	289	12	20	18	.526	15-27	25	94	.762	4.42	4.60

Deolis Guerra

Pitches: R Bats: R Pos: P   day-OH-lis   Ht: 6'5" Wt: 245 Born: 4/17/1989 Age: 34

Year	Team	Lg	G	GS	GF	IP	BFP	H	R	ER	HR	SH	SF	HB	TBB	IBB	SO	WP	W	L	Pct	Sv-Op	Hld	Vel	OPS	ERC	ERA
2015	Pit	NL	10	0	4	16.2	74	26	12	12	5	0	0	1	3	0	17	2	2	0	1.000	0-0	0	-	1.077	8.96	6.48
2016	LAA	AL	44	0	11	53.1	220	52	23	19	6	1	1	2	7	0	36	2	3	0	1.000	0-4	5	-	.671	3.08	3.21
2017	LAA	AL	19	0	5	25.0	105	20	13	13	4	0	1	0	12	0	22	2	2	2	.500	0-1	0	-	.729	3.70	4.68
2019	Mil	NL	1	0	0	0.2	6	4	4	4	1	0	1	0	0	0	0	0	0	0	-	0-0	0	-	2.067	61.64	54.00
2020	Phi	NL	9	0	5	7.1	36	10	9	7	3	0	0	2	2	0	8	0	1	3	.250	0-0	0	-	1.014	9.34	8.59
2021	Oak	AL	53	0	14	65.2	269	53	34	30	8	1	1	4	20	0	62	1	4	1	.800	0-0	3	-	.645	3.06	4.11
6 ML YEARS			136	0	39	168.2	710	165	95	85	27	2	4	9	44	0	145	7	12	6	.667	0-5	8	-	.741	4.03	4.54

Javy Guerra

Pitches: R Bats: L Pos: RP-18   Ht: 6'0" Wt: 185 Born: 9/25/1995 Age: 27

Year	Team	Lg	G	GS	GF	IP	BFP	H	R	ER	HR	SH	SF	HB	TBB	IBB	SO	WP	W	L	Pct	Sv-Op	Hld	Vel	OPS	ERC	ERA
2022	Drham	AAA	43	0	30	41.1	163	20	10	8	1	1	1	2	16	0	52	3	2	0	1.000	9-	-	-	.450	1.33	1.74
2019	SD	NL	8	0	1	8.2	36	7	5	5	3	0	1	0	3	0	6	0	0	0	-	0-0	0	98	.840	4.29	5.19
2020	SD	NL	14	0	5	13.1	67	25	16	15	1	0	1	1	5	0	12	2	1	0	1.000	0-2	2	98	.979	9.97	10.13
2021	SD	NL	4	0	0	3.2	18	4	2	2	0	0	0	0	2	0	3	0	0	0	-	0-0	0	98	.646	4.01	4.91
2022	2 Tms		18	0	4	18.0	82	16	11	10	3	1	0	1	11	2	10	2	2	1	.667	0-0	0	97	.766	4.70	5.00
22	Det	NL	1	0	1	2.0	12	3	4	4	1	0	0	0	3	0	1	0	0	0	-	0-0	0	97	1.167	16.26	18.00
22	TB	AL	17	0	3	16.0	70	13	7	6	2	1	0	1	8	2	9	2	2	1	.667	0-0	0	98	.702	3.56	3.38
4 ML YEARS			44	0	10	43.2	203	52	34	32	7	1	2	2	21	2	31	4	3	1	.750	0-0	4	98	.840	6.06	6.60

Vladimir Guerrero Jr.

Bats: R Throws: R Pos: 1B-128;DH-32;PH-2;3B-1   Ht: 6'2" Wt: 240 Born: 3/16/1999 Age: 24

							BATTING													RUNNING			AVERAGES			
Year	Team	Lg	G	AB	H	2B	3B	HR	(Hm | Rd)	TB	R	RBI	RC	TBB	IBB	SO	HBP	SH	SF	SB	CS	GDP	Avg	OBP	Slg	OPS
2019	Tor	AL	123	464	126	26	2	15	(5 | 10)	201	52	69	67	46	0	91	2	0	2	0	1	17	.272	.339	.433	.772
2020	Tor	AL	60	221	58	13	2	9	(5 | 4)	102	34	33	30	20	1	38	2	0	0	1	0	6	.262	.329	.462	.791
2021	Tor	AL	161	604	188	29	1	48	(31 | 17)	363	123	111	136	86	7	110	6	0	2	4	1	20	.311	.401	.601	1.002
2022	Tor	AL	160	638	175	35	0	32	(19 | 13)	306	90	97	101	58	6	116	6	0	4	8	3	26	.274	.339	.480	.818
	Postseason		2	7	1	0	0	0	(0 | 0)	1	0	0	0	0	0	4	1	0	0	0	0	0	.143	.250	.143	.393
	4 ML YEARS		504	1927	547	103	5	104	(60 | 44)	972	299	310	334	210	14	355	16	0	8	13	5	69	.284	.358	.504	.862

Luis Guillorme

Bats: L Throws: R Pos: 2B-67;3B-22;SS-15;PH-8;DH-3;PR-1   ghee-YOR-may   Ht: 5'10" Wt: 190 Born: 9/27/1994 Age: 28

							BATTING													RUNNING			AVERAGES			
Year	Team	Lg	G	AB	H	2B	3B	HR	(Hm	Rd)	TB	R	RBI	RC	TBB	IBB	SO	HBP	SH	SF	SB	CS	GDP	Avg	OBP	Slg	OPS
2018	NYM	NL	35	67	14	2	0	0	(0	0)	16	4	5	6	7	0	3	0	0	0	1	0	1	.209	.284	.239	.523
2019	NYM	NL	45	61	15	4	0	1	(1	0)	22	8	3	5	7	0	14	0	2	0	0	0	2	.246	.324	.361	.684
2020	NYM	NL	30	57	19	6	0	0	(0	0)	25	6	9	11	10	0	17	0	0	1	2	0	0	.333	.426	.439	.865
2021	NYM	NL	69	132	35	3	0	1	(0	1)	41	13	5	15	23	2	23	0	1	0	0	2	2	.265	.374	.311	.685
2022	NYM	NL	102	297	81	12	1	2	(1	1)	101	33	17	22	34	1	46	2	2	0	1	0	15	.273	.351	.340	.691
	5 ML YEARS		281	614	164	27	1	4	(2	2)	205	64	39	59	81	3	103	2	5	1	4	2	23	.267	.354	.334	.688

Yuli Gurriel

Bats: R Throws: R Pos: 1B-142;DH-3;PH-3   yoo-lee goo-REE-el   Ht: 6'0" Wt: 215 Born: 6/9/1984 Age: 39

							BATTING													RUNNING			AVERAGES			
Year	Team	Lg	G	AB	H	2B	3B	HR	(Hm	Rd)	TB	R	RBI	RC	TBB	IBB	SO	HBP	SH	SF	SB	CS	GDP	Avg	OBP	Slg	OPS
2016	Hou	AL	36	130	34	7	0	3	(1	2)	50	13	15	13	5	0	12	1	0	1	1	1	7	.262	.292	.385	.677
2017	Hou	AL	139	529	158	43	1	18	(8	10)	257	69	75	83	22	1	62	7	0	6	3	2	12	.299	.332	.486	.817
2018	Hou	AL	136	537	156	33	1	13	(10	3)	230	70	85	88	23	0	63	6	0	7	5	1	22	.291	.323	.428	.751
2019	Hou	AL	144	564	168	40	2	31	(19	12)	305	85	104	98	37	2	65	5	0	6	5	3	12	.298	.343	.541	.884
2020	Hou	AL	57	211	49	12	1	6	(3	3)	81	27	22	18	12	0	27	2	0	5	0	1	6	.232	.274	.384	.658
2021	Hou	AL	143	530	169	31	0	15	(8	7)	245	83	81	94	59	2	68	4	0	12	1	1	16	.319	.383	.462	.846
2022	Hou	AL	146	545	132	40	0	8	(2	6)	196	53	53	47	30	0	73	6	0	3	8	0	13	.242	.288	.360	.647
	Postseason		73	277	70	13	1	6	(5	1)	103	27	35	33	24	5	33	2	0	2	3	0	6	.253	.315	.372	.687
	7 ML YEARS		801	3046	866	206	5	94	(51	43)	1364	400	435	441	188	5	370	31	0	40	23	9	88	.284	.328	.448	.776

Lourdes Gurriel Jr.

Bats: R Throws: R Pos: LF-105;DH-13;1B-8;PH-2   goo-REE-el   Ht: 6'4" Wt: 215 Born: 10/10/1993 Age: 29

							BATTING													RUNNING			AVERAGES			
Year	Team	Lg	G	AB	H	2B	3B	HR	(Hm	Rd)	TB	R	RBI	RC	TBB	IBB	SO	HBP	SH	SF	SB	CS	GDP	Avg	OBP	Slg	OPS
2018	Tor	AL	65	249	70	8	0	11	(6	5)	111	30	35	30	9	1	59	2	1	2	1	2	2	.281	.309	.446	.755
2019	Tor	AL	84	314	87	19	2	20	(10	10)	170	52	50	51	20	0	86	5	1	3	6	4	4	.277	.327	.541	.869
2020	Tor	AL	57	208	64	14	0	11	(3	8)	111	28	33	37	14	0	48	0	0	2	3	1	7	.308	.348	.534	.882
2021	Tor	AL	141	500	138	28	2	21	(10	11)	233	62	84	82	32	1	102	2	1	6	1	3	8	.276	.319	.466	.785
2022	Tor	AL	121	453	132	32	1	5	(3	2)	181	52	52	53	31	1	83	6	0	2	3	4	11	.291	.343	.400	.743
	Postseason		2	8	2	1	0	0	(0	0)	3	0	0	1	0	0	1	0	0	0	0	0	0	.250	.250	.375	.625
	5 ML YEARS		468	1724	491	101	5	68	(32	36)	806	224	254	253	106	3	378	15	3	15	14	14	32	.285	.329	.468	.797

Jandel Gustave

Pitches: R Bats: R Pos: RP-27   yahn-DELL goo-STAH-vay   Ht: 6'3" Wt: 220 Born: 10/12/1992 Age: 30

			HOW MUCH PITCHED					WHAT HE GAVE UP									THE RESULTS							
Year	Team	Lg	G	GS	GF	IP	BFP	H	R	ER	HR	SH	SF	HB	TBB	IBB	SO	WP	W	L	Pct	Sv-Op	Hld	Vel	OPS	ERC	ERA
2016	Hou	AL	14	0	4	15.1	60	13	6	6	2	0	0	0	4	0	16	2	1	0	1.000	0-0	0	97	.676	3.04	3.52
2017	Hou	AL	6	0	2	5.0	25	5	4	3	0	0	0	0	7	0	2	0	0	0	-	0-0	0	96	.813	7.65	5.40
2019	SF	NL	23	0	4	24.1	99	18	11	8	1	1	3	0	9	0	14	0	0	0	-	1-2	4	96	.566	2.22	2.96
2021	Mil	NL	14	0	7	18.1	79	15	10	7	2	0	3	4	5	2	13	2	1	2	.333	0-1	0	97	.632	3.25	3.44
2022	Mil	NL	27	0	6	28.0	120	25	13	12	4	0	1	2	11	0	27	2	2	0	1.000	0-0	2	96	.675	4.02	3.86
	5 ML YEARS		84	0	23	91.0	383	76	44	36	9	1	7	6	36	2	72	6	4	2	.667	1-3	6	96	.648	3.38	3.56

Dalton Guthrie

Bats: R Throws: R Pos: RF-12;PH-2;PR-2;2B-1;3B-1   Ht: 5'11" Wt: 160 Born: 12/23/1995 Age: 27

							BATTING													RUNNING			AVERAGES			
Year	Team	Lg	G	AB	H	2B	3B	HR	(Hm	Rd)	TB	R	RBI	RC	TBB	IBB	SO	HBP	SH	SF	SB	CS	GDP	Avg	OBP	Slg	OPS
2022	LV	AAA	92	338	102	27	1	10	(-	-)	161	64	53	58	24	0	73	9	2	1	21	6	4	.302	.363	.476	.839
2022	Phi	NL	14	21	7	0	0	1	(1	0)	10	3	5	7	6	0	7	1	0	0	1	0	0	.333	.500	.476	.976

Kelvin Gutierrez

Bats: R Throws: R Pos: 3B-10;PH-4;DH-1   Ht: 6'2" Wt: 215 Born: 8/28/1994 Age: 28

							BATTING													RUNNING			AVERAGES			
Year	Team	Lg	G	AB	H	2B	3B	HR	(Hm	Rd)	TB	R	RBI	RC	TBB	IBB	SO	HBP	SH	SF	SB	CS	GDP	Avg	OBP	Slg	OPS
2022	Norfolk	AAA	60	211	51	8	2	6	(-	-)	81	34	26	24	24	0	51	0	0	3	5	2	9	.242	.315	.384	.699
2019	KC	AL	20	73	19	2	1	1	(1	0)	26	4	11	9	5	0	24	0	0	1	1	0	2	.260	.304	.356	.660
2020	KC	AL	4	9	1	0	0	0	(0	0)	1	0	0	0	3	0	6	0	0	0	0	0	0	.111	.333	.111	.444
2021	2 Tms	AL	85	272	63	8	3	3	(1	2)	86	23	20	24	19	0	76	4	0	0	0	1	4	.232	.292	.316	.608

Year Team	Lg	G	AB	H	2B	3B	HR	(Hm Rd)	TB	R	RBI	RC	TBB	IBB	SO	HBP	SH	SF	SB	CS	GDP	Avg	OBP	Slg	OPS
2022 Bal	AL	12	28	4	1	0	0	(0 0)	5	2	3	2	4	0	8	0	0	0	1	0	1	.143	.250	.179	.429
21 KC	AL	38	135	29	4	2	1	(0 1)	40	9	8	7	6	0	31	1	0	0	0	1	3	.215	.254	.296	.550
21 Bal	AL	47	137	34	4	1	2	(1 1)	46	14	12	17	13	0	45	3	0	0	0	0	1	.248	.327	.336	.663
4 ML YEARS		121	382	87	11	4	4	(2 2)	118	29	34	35	31	0	114	4	0	1	2	1	7	.228	.292	.309	.601

Vladimir Gutierrez

Pitches: R **Bats:** R **Pos:** SP-8; RP-2   **Ht:** 6'1" **Wt:** 190 **Born:** 9/18/1995 **Age:** 27

		HOW MUCH PITCHED					WHAT HE GAVE UP										THE RESULTS							
Year Team	Lg	G	GS	GF	IP	BFP	H	R	ER	HR	SH	SF	HB	TBB	IBB	SO	WP	W	L	Pct	Sv-Op	Hld	Vel	OPS	ERC	ERA
2021 Cin	NL	22	22	0	114.0	496	115	61	60	20	4	4	4	46	0	88	3	9	6	.600	0-0	0	93	.805	4.83	4.74
2022 Cin	NL	10	8	0	36.2	179	46	31	31	8	0	2	6	24	1	29	2	1	6	.143	0-0	0	93	1.037	8.52	7.61
2 ML YEARS		32	30	0	150.2	675	161	92	91	28	4	6	10	70	1	117	5	10	12	.455	0-0	0	93	.865	5.68	5.44

Ronald Guzman

Bats: L **Throws:** L **Pos:** 1B-3   **Ht:** 6'5" **Wt:** 235 **Born:** 10/20/1994 **Age:** 28

								BATTING									RUNNING			AVERAGES			
Year Team	Lg	G	AB	H	2B	3B	HR	(Hm Rd)	TB	R	RBI	RC	TBB	IBB	SO	HBP	SH	SF	SB	CS	GDP	Avg	OBP	Slg	OPS
2022 S-WB	AAA	105	322	82	24	0	16	(- -)	154	51	53	58	41	0	100	5	0	4	2	0	3	.255	.344	.478	.822
2018 Tex	AL	123	387	91	18	2	16	(7 9)	161	46	58	55	33	2	121	7	0	1	1	0	8	.235	.306	.416	.722
2019 Tex	AL	87	256	56	20	0	10	(2 8)	106	34	36	36	32	1	87	3	0	4	1	2	7	.219	.308	.414	.723
2020 Tex	AL	26	78	19	1	1	4	(3 1)	34	10	9	12	7	0	24	1	0	0	1	0	0	.244	.314	.436	.750
2021 Tex	AL	7	16	1	0	0	1	(1 0)	4	1	1	0	1	0	6	0	0	0	0	0	0	.063	.118	.250	.368
2022 NYY	AL	3	6	0	0	0	0	(0 0)	0	0	0	0	0	0	5	0	0	0	0	0	1	.000	.000	.000	.000
5 ML YEARS		246	743	167	39	3	31	(13 18)	305	91	104	103	73	3	243	11	0	5	3	2	16	.225	.302	.410	.712

Eric Haase

Bats: R **Throws:** R **Pos:** C-84; PH-23; DH-12; LF-11; PR-1   **Ht:** 5'10" **Wt:** 210 **Born:** 12/18/1992 **Age:** 30

								BATTING									RUNNING			AVERAGES			
Year Team	Lg	G	AB	H	2B	3B	HR	(Hm Rd)	TB	R	RBI	RC	TBB	IBB	SO	HBP	SH	SF	SB	CS	GDP	Avg	OBP	Slg	OPS
2018 Cle	AL	9	16	2	0	0	0	(0 0)	2	0	1	1	0	0	6	1	0	0	0	0	1	.125	.176	.125	.301
2019 Cle	AL	10	16	1	0	0	1	(0 1)	4	1	3	1	1	0	8	0	0	0	0	0	0	.063	.118	.250	.368
2020 Det	AL	7	17	3	0	0	0	(0 0)	3	1	2	1	1	0	6	0	0	1	0	0	0	.176	.211	.176	.387
2021 Det	AL	98	351	81	12	1	22	(8 14)	161	48	61	43	26	0	119	2	0	2	2	0	11	.231	.286	.459	.745
2022 Det	AL	110	323	82	17	1	14	(8 6)	143	41	44	50	24	1	97	1	0	3	0	0	9	.254	.305	.443	.748
5 ML YEARS		234	723	169	29	2	37	(16 21)	313	91	111	96	52	1	236	4	0	6	2	0	21	.234	.287	.433	.720

Josh Hader

Pitches: L **Bats:** L **Pos:** RP-56   **Ht:** 6'3" **Wt:** 180 **Born:** 4/7/1994 **Age:** 29

		HOW MUCH PITCHED					WHAT HE GAVE UP										THE RESULTS							
Year Team	Lg	G	GS	GF	IP	BFP	H	R	ER	HR	SH	SF	HB	TBB	IBB	SO	WP	W	L	Pct	Sv-Op	Hld	Vel	OPS	ERC	ERA
2017 Mil	NL	35	0	2	47.2	188	25	11	11	4	1	1	4	22	1	68	0	2	3	.400	0-1	12	94	.554	2.09	2.08
2018 Mil	NL	55	0	14	81.1	306	36	23	22	9	1	2	1	30	1	143	0	6	1	.857	12-17	21	95	.484	1.45	2.43
2019 Mil	NL	61	0	46	75.2	289	41	24	22	15	0	0	4	20	2	138	0	3	5	.375	37-44	6	96	.591	1.98	2.62
2020 Mil	NL	21	0	17	19.0	78	8	8	8	3	0	0	3	10	0	31	2	1	2	.333	13-15	0	95	.562	2.44	3.79
2021 Mil	NL	60	0	42	58.2	224	25	8	8	3	0	1	2	24	0	102	3	4	2	.667	34-35	0	96	.421	1.30	1.23
2022 2 Tms	NL	56	0	45	50.0	219	43	30	29	8	0	3	4	21	0	81	5	2	5	.286	36-40	0	97	.714	4.00	5.22
22 Mil	NL	37	0	34	34.0	141	26	16	16	7	0	1	1	12	0	59	2	1	4	.200	29-31	0	97	.698	3.35	4.24
22 SD	NL	19	0	11	16.0	78	17	14	13	1	0	3	3	9	0	22	3	1	1	.500	7-9	0	98	.737	5.33	7.31
Postseason		11	0	4	14.1	54	9	4	3	1	1	0	1	3	0	23	0	0	2	.000	1-2	2	96	.490	1.67	1.88
6 ML YEARS		288	0	166	332.1	1304	178	104	100	42	2	7	18	127	3	563	10	18	18	.500	132-152	39	95	.551	2.00	2.71

Jake Hager

Bats: R **Throws:** R **Pos:** 2B-16; 3B-7; SS-4; PR-2; DH-1   **Ht:** 6'1" **Wt:** 170 **Born:** 3/4/1993 **Age:** 30

								BATTING									RUNNING			AVERAGES			
Year Team	Lg	G	AB	H	2B	3B	HR	(Hm Rd)	TB	R	RBI	RC	TBB	IBB	SO	HBP	SH	SF	SB	CS	GDP	Avg	OBP	Slg	OPS
2022 Reno	AAA	72	260	68	19	0	5	(- -)	102	38	45	36	32	0	60	3	2	6	8	2	4	.262	.342	.392	.735
2021 2 Tms	NL	14	26	3	0	0	0	(0 0)	3	2	2	1	4	0	14	0	0	0	0	0	0	.115	.233	.115	.349
2022 Ari	NL	28	50	12	2	0	0	(0 0)	14	4	3	7	8	0	17	0	1	0	0	0	0	.240	.345	.280	.625
21 NYM	NL	5	8	1	0	0	0	(0 0)	1	1	0	1	0	0	3	0	0	0	0	0	0	.125	.125	.125	.250
21 Ari	NL	9	18	2	0	0	0	(0 0)	2	1	2	0	4	0	11	0	0	0	0	0	0	.111	.273	.111	.384
2 ML YEARS		42	76	15	2	0	0	(0 0)	17	6	5	8	12	0	31	0	1	0	0	0	0	.197	.307	.224	.531

Sam Haggerty

Bats: B **Throws:** R **Pos:** RF-37; LF-33; PR-14; PH-9; CF-6; DH-6; 2B-4   **Ht:** 5'11" **Wt:** 175 **Born:** 5/26/1994 **Age:** 29

								BATTING									RUNNING			AVERAGES			
Year Team	Lg	G	AB	H	2B	3B	HR	(Hm Rd)	TB	R	RBI	RC	TBB	IBB	SO	HBP	SH	SF	SB	CS	GDP	Avg	OBP	Slg	OPS
2022 Tacom	AAA	39	152	43	11	2	6	(- -)	76	28	25	30	18	0	34	4	3	2	15	1	2	.283	.369	.500	.869
2019 NYM	NL	11	4	0	0	0	0	(0 0)	0	2	0	0	0	0	3	0	0	0	0	0	0	.000	.000	.000	.000
2020 Sea	AL	13	50	13	4	0	1	(1 0)	20	7	6	10	4	0	16	0	0	0	4	0	0	.260	.315	.400	.715
2021 Sea	AL	35	86	16	3	0	2	(0 2)	25	15	5	5	6	0	28	1	1	0	5	1	1	.186	.247	.291	.538
2022 Sea	AL	83	176	45	9	1	5	(2 3)	71	29	23	24	18	3	53	4	1	2	13	1	4	.256	.335	.403	.738
4 ML YEARS		142	316	74	16	1	8	(3 5)	116	53	34	39	28	3	100	5	2	2	22	2	5	.234	.305	.367	.672

Darick Hall

Bats: L **Throws:** R **Pos:** DH-31;1B-7;PH-6   **Ht:** 6'4" **Wt:** 232 **Born:** 7/25/1995 **Age:** 27

								BATTING													RUNNING			AVERAGES			
Year	Team	Lg	G	AB	H	2B	3B	HR	(Hm	Rd)	TB	R	RBI	RC	TBB	IBB	SO	HBP	SH	SF	SB	CS	GDP	Avg	OBP	Slg	OPS
2022	LV	AAA	101	394	100	24	0	28	(-	-)	208	59	88	74	42	4	100	4	0	3	6	1	14	.254	.330	.528	.857
2022	Phi	NL	42	136	34	8	1	9	(8	1)	71	19	16	18	5	0	44	1	0	0	0	0	3	.250	.282	.522	.804

DL Hall

Pitches: L **Bats:** L **Pos:** RP-10; SP-1   **Ht:** 6'2" **Wt:** 195 **Born:** 9/19/1998 **Age:** 24

			HOW MUCH PITCHED				WHAT HE GAVE UP											THE RESULTS						
Year	Team	Lg	G	GS	GF	IP	BFP	H	R	ER	HR	SH	SF	HB	TBB	IBB	SO	WP	W	L	Pct	Sv-Op Hld	Vel	OPS	ERC	ERA
2018	Dlmrva	A	22	20	0	94.1	391	68	31	22	6	6	2	5	42	0	100	7	2	7	.222	0- - -	-	.612	2.72	2.10
2019	Frdrck	A+	19	17	1	80.2	346	53	33	31	3	1	5	6	54	0	116	4	4	5	.444	1- - -	-	.592	3.09	3.46
2021	Bowie	AA	7	7	0	31.2	128	16	11	11	4	0	0	2	16	0	56	2	2	0	1.000	0- - -	-	.538	2.29	3.13
2022	Norfolk	AAA	22	18	2	76.2	346	62	47	40	10	0	1	2	49	0	125	10	3	7	.300	0- - -	-	.686	4.13	4.70
2022	Bal	AL	11	1	1	13.2	64	17	9	9	0	0	1	0	6	0	19	2	1	1	.500	1-1 0	96	.710	4.73	5.93

Billy Hamilton

Bats: R **Throws:** R **Pos:** PR-23;LF-12;CF-5;DH-5;2B-3;PH-2;3B-1   **Ht:** 6'0" **Wt:** 160 **Born:** 9/9/1990 **Age:** 32

								BATTING													RUNNING			AVERAGES			
Year	Team	Lg	G	AB	H	2B	3B	HR	(Hm	Rd)	TB	R	RBI	RC	TBB	IBB	SO	HBP	SH	SF	SB	CS	GDP	Avg	OBP	Slg	OPS
2022	Tacom	AAA	22	86	16	2	0	0	(-	-)	18	11	5	4	9	0	25	0	0	0	4	0	0	.186	.263	.209	.472
2013	Cin	NL	13	19	7	2	0	0	(0	0)	9	9	1	5	2	0	4	0	1	0	13	1	0	.368	.429	.474	.902
2014	Cin	NL	152	563	141	25	8	6	(3	3)	200	72	48	64	34	0	117	1	9	4	56	23	1	.250	.292	.355	.648
2015	Cin	NL	114	412	93	8	3	4	(2	2)	119	56	28	32	28	0	75	1	9	4	57	8	5	.226	.274	.289	.563
2016	Cin	NL	119	411	107	19	3	3	(2	1)	141	69	17	46	36	0	93	1	11	1	58	8	5	.260	.321	.343	.664
2017	Cin	NL	139	582	144	17	11	4	(3	1)	195	85	38	62	44	0	133	0	5	2	59	13	5	.247	.299	.335	.634
2018	Cin	NL	153	504	119	16	9	4	(4	0)	165	74	29	51	46	0	132	1	1	4	34	10	1	.236	.299	.327	.626
2019	2 Tms		119	316	69	14	2	0	(0	0)	87	41	15	29	32	1	87	0	3	2	22	6	1	.218	.289	.275	.564
2020	2 Tms	NL	31	32	4	0	0	1	(0	1)	7	10	2	2	2	0	7	0	1	1	6	2	0	.125	.171	.219	.390
2021	CWS	AL	71	127	28	8	3	2	(2	0)	48	23	11	9	4	0	47	0	3	1	9	0	1	.220	.242	.378	.620
2022	2 Tms		37	20	1	0	0	0	(0	0)	1	13	0	0	2	0	12	0	1	0	10	1	0	.050	.136	.050	.186
19	KC	AL	93	275	58	12	2	0	(0	0)	74	32	12	22	25	0	74	0	3	2	18	5	1	.211	.275	.269	.544
19	Atl	NL	26	41	11	2	0	0	(0	0)	13	9	3	7	7	1	13	0	0	0	4	1	0	.268	.375	.317	.692
20	NYM	NL	17	22	1	0	0	0	(0	0)	1	4	1	0	1	0	3	0	1	1	3	1	0	.045	.083	.045	.129
20	ChC	NL	14	10	3	0	0	1	(0	1)	6	6	1	2	1	0	4	0	0	0	3	1	0	.300	.364	.600	.964
22	Mia	NL	20	13	1	0	0	0	(0	0)	1	9	0	0	1	0	8	0	1	0	7	0	0	.077	.143	.077	.220
22	Min	AL	17	7	0	0	0	0	(0	0)	0	4	0	0	1	0	4	0	0	0	3	1	0	.000	.125	.000	.125
	Postseason		3	0	0	0	0	0	(0	0)	0	2	0	0	1	0	0	0	0	0	1	0	0	-	1.000	-	-
10 ML YEARS			948	2986	713	109	39	24	(16	8)	972	452	189	300	230	1	707	4	44	19	324	72	19	.239	.292	.326	.618

Caleb Hamilton

Bats: R **Throws:** R **Pos:** C-11;1B-6;PR-5;PH-2   **Ht:** 6'0" **Wt:** 185 **Born:** 2/5/1995 **Age:** 28

								BATTING													RUNNING			AVERAGES			
Year	Team	Lg	G	AB	H	2B	3B	HR	(Hm	Rd)	TB	R	RBI	RC	TBB	IBB	SO	HBP	SH	SF	SB	CS	GDP	Avg	OBP	Slg	OPS
2022	StPaul	AAA	62	206	48	10	0	11	(-	-)	91	34	43	38	43	1	67	1	0	1	1	0	3	.233	.367	.442	.808
2022	Min	AL	22	18	1	0	0	1	(1	0)	4	5	1	1	4	0	14	0	1	0	0	0	0	.056	.227	.222	.449

Ian Hamilton

Pitches: R **Bats:** R **Pos:** RP-1   **Ht:** 6'1" **Wt:** 200 **Born:** 6/16/1995 **Age:** 28

			HOW MUCH PITCHED				WHAT HE GAVE UP											THE RESULTS						
Year	Team	Lg	G	GS	GF	IP	BFP	H	R	ER	HR	SH	SF	HB	TBB	IBB	SO	WP	W	L	Pct	Sv-Op Hld	Vel	OPS	ERC	ERA
2022	StPaul	AAA	23	0	15	28.2	112	16	9	6	3	0	1	2	8	0	36	3	2	3	.400	1- - -	-	.509	1.68	1.88
2022	Clmbs	AAA	15	0	7	18.2	84	17	14	13	3	1	0	0	11	0	24	1	0	4	.000	1- - -	-	.768	4.66	6.27
2018	CWS	AL	10	0	3	8.0	33	6	5	4	2	0	1	1	2	0	5	0	1	2	.333	0-1 1	97	.687	3.51	4.50
2020	CWS	AL	4	0	0	4.0	20	4	2	2	0	0	0	0	5	0	4	2	0	0	-	0-0 0	94	.717	6.80	4.50
2022	Min	AL	1	0	0	2.2	11	3	2	2	1	0	0	0	1	0	0	0	0	0	-	0-0 0	94	1.064	7.24	6.75
3 ML YEARS			15	0	3	14.2	64	13	9	8	3	0	1	1	8	0	9	2	1	2	.333	0-1 1	95	.770	5.11	4.91

Garrett Hampson

Bats: R **Throws:** R **Pos:** CF-36;SS-32;PR-15;2B-10;3B-7;DH-3;PH-1   **Ht:** 5'11" **Wt:** 196 **Born:** 10/10/1994 **Age:** 28

								BATTING													RUNNING			AVERAGES			
Year	Team	Lg	G	AB	H	2B	3B	HR	(Hm	Rd)	TB	R	RBI	RC	TBB	IBB	SO	HBP	SH	SF	SB	CS	GDP	Avg	OBP	Slg	OPS
2018	Col	NL	24	40	11	3	1	0	(0	0)	16	3	4	9	7	0	12	1	0	0	2	0	0	.275	.396	.400	.796
2019	Col	NL	105	299	74	9	4	8	(1	7)	115	40	27	29	24	1	88	0	2	2	15	3	2	.247	.302	.385	.686
2020	Col	NL	53	167	39	4	3	5	(3	2)	64	25	11	16	13	0	60	0	3	1	6	1	1	.234	.287	.383	.671
2021	Col	NL	147	453	106	21	6	11	(7	4)	172	69	33	49	33	2	118	3	3	2	17	7	6	.234	.289	.380	.669
2022	Col	NL	90	199	42	7	3	2	(2	0)	61	29	15	19	21	0	63	1	3	2	12	2	3	.211	.287	.307	.594
	Postseason		2	0	0	0	0	0	(0	0)	0	1	0	0	0	0	0	0	0	0	0	0	0	.000	.000	.000	.000
5 ML YEARS			419	1158	272	44	17	26	(13	13)	428	166	90	122	98	3	341	5	11	7	52	13	12	.235	.296	.370	.665

285

Brad Hand

Pitches: L Bats: L Pos: RP-55   Ht: 6'3" Wt: 224 Born: 3/20/1990 Age: 33

			HOW MUCH PITCHED				WHAT HE GAVE UP											THE RESULTS							
Year	Team	Lg	G	GS	GF	IP	BFP	H	R	ER	HR	SH	SF	HB	TBB	IBB	SO	WP	W	L	Pct	Sv-Op	Hld	Vel	OPS	ERC	ERA
2011	Fla	NL	12	12	0	60.0	263	53	32	28	10	4	3	1	35	1	38	0	1	8	.111	0-0	0	90	.789	4.68	4.20
2012	Mia	NL	1	1	0	3.2	23	6	7	7	1	0	0	0	6	1	3	0	0	1	.000	0-0	0	90	1.169	14.74	17.18
2013	Mia	NL	7	2	2	20.2	82	13	7	7	2	0	0	0	8	0	15	1	1	1	.500	0-0	0	93	.553	2.10	3.05
2014	Mia	NL	32	16	5	111.0	474	112	56	54	10	6	2	2	39	3	67	5	3	8	.273	1-1	0	92	.732	3.91	4.38
2015	Mia	NL	38	12	7	93.1	408	107	55	55	9	5	2	3	32	1	67	2	4	7	.364	0-0	2	92	.784	4.83	5.30
2016	SD	NL	82	0	16	89.1	364	63	32	29	8	2	2	1	36	4	111	7	4	4	.500	1-7	21	93	.589	2.44	2.92
2017	SD	NL	72	0	32	79.1	311	54	20	19	9	1	1	7	20	1	104	4	3	4	.429	21-26	16	94	.580	2.30	2.16
2018	2 Tms		69	0	42	72.0	301	52	28	22	8	2	0	9	28	2	106	2	2	5	.286	32-39	10	94	.656	3.03	2.75
2019	Cle	AL	60	0	54	57.1	242	53	21	21	6	1	0	4	18	5	84	0	6	4	.600	34-39	0	93	.695	3.50	3.30
2020	Cle	AL	23	0	21	22.0	86	13	8	5	0	0	1	2	4	0	29	1	2	1	.667	16-16	1	91	.486	1.21	2.05
2021	3 Tms		68	0	45	64.2	278	56	39	28	9	3	5	6	26	4	61	3	6	7	.462	21-29	3	93	.728	3.86	3.90
2022	Phi	NL	55	0	15	45.0	198	37	18	14	2	1	2	6	23	1	38	1	3	2	.600	5-7	13	93	.654	3.57	2.80
18	SD	NL	41	0	31	44.1	186	33	21	15	5	1	0	7	15	1	65	1	2	4	.333	24-29	3	94	.672	3.09	3.05
18	Cle	AL	28	0	11	27.2	115	19	7	7	3	1	0	2	13	1	41	1	0	1	.000	8-10	7	93	.632	2.94	2.28
21	Was	NL	41	0	36	42.2	182	31	22	17	5	3	3	5	18	4	42	1	5	5	.500	21-26	0	93	.655	3.04	3.59
21	Tor	AL	11	0	5	8.2	41	13	10	7	3	0	1	0	3	0	5	1	0	2	.000	0-1	0	93	1.012	8.98	7.27
21	NYM	NL	16	0	4	13.1	55	12	7	4	1	0	1	1	5	0	14	1	1	0	1.000	0-2	3	93	.744	3.68	2.70
	Postseason		3	0	1	2.1	15	6	4	4	1	0	1	0	2	1	5	1	0	1	.000	0-1	0	92	1.283	19.40	15.43
	12 ML YEARS		519	43	239	718.1	3030	619	323	289	74	25	18	41	275	23	723	26	35	52	.402	131-164	66	92	.686	3.45	3.62

Mitch Haniger

Bats: R Throws: R Pos: RF-47;DH-12   Ht: 6'2" Wt: 214 Born: 12/23/1990 Age: 32

			BATTING															RUNNING			AVERAGES			
Year	Team	Lg	G	AB	H	2B	3B	HR	(Hm | Rd)	TB	R	RBI	RC	TBB	IBB	SO	HBP	SH	SF	SB	CS	GDP	Avg	OBP	Slg	OPS
2016	Ari	NL	34	109	25	2	1	5	(4 | 1)	44	9	17	16	12	2	27	1	0	1	0	0	3	.229	.309	.404	.713
2017	Sea	AL	96	369	104	25	2	16	(6 | 10)	181	58	47	55	31	0	93	9	1	0	5	4	9	.282	.352	.491	.843
2018	Sea	AL	157	596	170	38	4	26	(12 | 14)	294	90	93	102	70	4	148	10	0	7	8	2	8	.285	.366	.493	.859
2019	Sea	AL	63	246	54	13	1	15	(7 | 8)	114	46	32	35	30	1	81	5	0	2	4	0	3	.220	.314	.463	.778
2021	Sea	AL	157	620	157	23	2	39	(19 | 20)	301	110	100	105	54	2	169	5	0	12	1	0	12	.253	.318	.485	.804
2022	Sea	AL	57	224	55	8	0	11	(7 | 4)	96	31	34	33	20	1	65	1	0	2	0	0	7	.246	.308	.429	.736
	6 ML YEARS		564	2164	565	109	10	112	(55 | 57)	1030	344	323	346	217	10	583	35	1	20	18	6	42	.261	.335	.476	.811

Ian Happ

Bats: B Throws: R Pos: LF-146;DH-10;PH-6;CF-3   Ht: 6'0" Wt: 205 Born: 8/12/1994 Age: 28

			BATTING															RUNNING			AVERAGES			
Year	Team	Lg	G	AB	H	2B	3B	HR	(Hm | Rd)	TB	R	RBI	RC	TBB	IBB	SO	HBP	SH	SF	SB	CS	GDP	Avg	OBP	Slg	OPS
2017	ChC	NL	115	364	92	17	3	24	(15 | 9)	187	62	68	57	39	5	129	4	2	4	8	4	12	.253	.328	.514	.842
2018	ChC	NL	142	387	90	19	2	15	(7 | 8)	158	56	44	56	70	9	167	3	0	2	8	4	6	.233	.353	.408	.761
2019	ChC	NL	58	140	37	7	1	11	(4 | 7)	79	25	30	30	15	0	39	0	0	1	2	0	1	.264	.333	.564	.898
2020	ChC	NL	57	198	51	11	1	12	(8 | 4)	100	27	28	35	30	1	63	2	1	0	1	3	1	.258	.361	.505	.866
2021	ChC	NL	148	465	105	20	1	25	(13 | 12)	202	63	66	75	62	0	156	5	2	1	9	2	12	.226	.323	.434	.757
2022	ChC	NL	158	573	155	42	2	17	(6 | 11)	252	72	72	83	58	4	149	6	0	4	9	4	11	.271	.342	.440	.781
	Postseason		8	15	5	0	0	1	(1 | 0)	8	1	1	0	2	0	6	0	0	0	0	0	0	.333	.412	.533	.945
	6 ML YEARS		678	2127	530	116	10	104	(53 | 51)	978	305	308	336	274	19	703	20	5	12	37	17	43	.249	.339	.460	.798

Bryce Harper

Bats: L Throws: R Pos: DH-90;RF-8;PH-1   Ht: 6'3" Wt: 210 Born: 10/16/1992 Age: 30

			BATTING															RUNNING			AVERAGES			
Year	Team	Lg	G	AB	H	2B	3B	HR	(Hm | Rd)	TB	R	RBI	RC	TBB	IBB	SO	HBP	SH	SF	SB	CS	GDP	Avg	OBP	Slg	OPS
2012	Was	NL	139	533	144	26	9	22	(10 | 12)	254	98	59	82	56	0	120	2	3	3	18	6	4	.270	.340	.477	.817
2013	Was	NL	118	424	116	24	3	20	(13 | 7)	206	71	58	73	61	4	94	5	3	4	11	4	4	.274	.368	.486	.854
2014	Was	NL	100	352	96	10	2	13	(5 | 8)	149	41	32	43	38	4	104	1	3	1	2	2	6	.273	.344	.423	.768
2015	Was	NL	153	521	172	38	1	42	(23 | 19)	338	118	99	138	124	15	131	5	0	4	6	4	15	.330	.460	.649	1.109
2016	Was	NL	147	506	123	24	2	24	(12 | 12)	223	84	86	90	108	20	117	3	0	10	21	10	11	.243	.373	.441	.814
2017	Was	NL	111	420	134	27	1	29	(12 | 17)	250	95	87	93	68	11	99	1	0	3	4	2	15	.319	.413	.595	1.008
2018	Was	NL	159	550	137	34	0	34	(17 | 17)	273	103	100	111	130	16	169	6	0	9	13	3	7	.249	.393	.496	.889
2019	Phi	NL	157	573	149	36	1	35	(20 | 15)	292	98	114	125	99	11	178	6	0	4	15	3	10	.260	.372	.510	.882
2020	Phi	NL	58	190	51	9	2	13	(7 | 6)	103	41	33	44	49	8	43	2	1	2	8	2	5	.268	.420	.542	.962
2021	Phi	NL	141	488	151	42	1	35	(19 | 16)	300	101	84	120	100	14	134	5	2	4	13	3	12	.309	.429	.615	1.044
2022	Phi	NL	99	370	106	28	1	18	(9 | 9)	190	63	65	70	46	9	87	3	0	7	11	4	13	.286	.364	.514	.877
	Postseason		19	76	16	4	1	5	(3 | 2)	37	12	10	12	11	1	23	1	0	1	4	0	0	.211	.315	.487	.801
	11 ML YEARS		1382	4927	1379	298	23	285	(147 | 138)	2578	913	817	989	879	112	1276	39	12	51	122	43	106	.280	.390	.523	.913

Michael Harris II

Bats: L Throws: L Pos: CF-114   Ht: 6'0" Wt: 195 Born: 3/7/2001 Age: 22

			BATTING															RUNNING			AVERAGES			
Year	Team	Lg	G	AB	H	2B	3B	HR	(Hm | Rd)	TB	R	RBI	RC	TBB	IBB	SO	HBP	SH	SF	SB	CS	GDP	Avg	OBP	Slg	OPS
2019	2 Tms	Low	53	191	53	8	4	2	(- | -)	75	26	27	28	18	0	42	2	0	1	8	2	4	.277	.344	.393	.737
2021	Rome	A+	101	374	110	26	3	7	(- | -)	163	55	64	66	35	4	76	7	0	4	27	0	7	.294	.362	.436	.798
2022	Missi	AA	43	174	53	16	2	5	(- | -)	88	33	33	32	17	0	39	3	0	2	11	3	3	.305	.372	.506	.878
2022	Atl	NL	114	414	123	27	3	19	(4 | 15)	213	75	64	78	21	0	107	5	1	0	20	2	7	.297	.339	.514	.853

Josh Harrison

Bats: R **Throws:** R **Pos:** 2B-90;3B-23;DH-4;PH-4;SS-2;LF-2;PR-2 **Ht:** 5'8" **Wt:** 190 **Born:** 7/8/1987 **Age:** 35

Year	Team	Lg	G	AB	H	2B	3B	HR	(Hm	Rd)	TB	R	RBI	RC	TBB	IBB	SO	HBP	SH	SF	SB	CS	GDP	Avg	OBP	Slg	OPS
2011	Pit	NL	65	195	53	13	2	1	(1	0)	73	21	16	19	3	0	24	0	5	1	4	1	6	.272	.281	.374	.656
2012	Pit	NL	104	249	58	9	5	3	(1	2)	86	34	16	22	10	0	37	7	7	3	7	3	3	.233	.279	.345	.624
2013	Pit	NL	60	88	22	1	2	3	(1	2)	36	10	14	11	2	0	10	3	2	0	2	0	4	.250	.290	.409	.699
2014	Pit	NL	143	520	164	38	7	13	(4	9)	255	77	52	84	22	1	81	4	2	2	18	7	6	.315	.347	.490	.837
2015	Pit	NL	114	418	120	29	1	4	(2	2)	163	57	28	48	19	1	71	7	3	2	10	8	4	.287	.327	.390	.717
2016	Pit	NL	131	487	138	25	7	4	(2	2)	189	57	59	61	18	0	76	5	4	8	19	4	10	.283	.311	.388	.699
2017	Pit	NL	128	486	132	26	2	16	(9	7)	210	66	47	65	28	2	90	23	2	3	12	4	5	.272	.339	.432	.771
2018	Pit	NL	97	344	86	13	1	8	(3	5)	125	41	37	42	18	1	68	5	2	5	3	0	8	.250	.293	.363	.656
2019	Det	AL	36	137	24	7	1	1	(1	0)	36	10	8	3	6	0	27	2	0	2	4	2	0	.175	.218	.263	.480
2020	Was	NL	33	79	22	2	0	3	(1	2)	33	11	14	12	6	0	12	4	0	2	1	2	2	.278	.352	.418	.769
2021	2 Tms		138	505	141	33	2	8	(4	4)	202	58	60	69	31	0	75	18	0	3	9	5	9	.279	.341	.400	.741
2022	CWS	AL	119	386	99	19	2	7	(3	4)	143	50	27	40	21	0	71	14	2	2	2	1	9	.256	.317	.370	.687
21	Was		90	320	94	23	2	6	(2	4)	139	39	38	52	25	0	50	12	0	1	5	2	4	.294	.366	.434	.800
21	Oak	AL	48	185	47	10	0	2	(2	0)	63	19	22	17	6	0	25	6	0	2	4	3	5	.254	.296	.341	.637
	Postseason		4	7	2	0	0	0	(0	0)	2	1	0	0	0	0	2	1	0	0	0	1	0	.286	.375	.286	.661
12 ML YEARS			1168	3894	1059	215	32	71	(32	39)	1551	492	378	476	184	5	642	92	29	33	91	37	66	.272	.318	.398	.716

Monte Harrison

Bats: R **Throws:** R **Pos:** LF-6;CF-3;PR-1 **Ht:** 6'3" **Wt:** 225 **Born:** 8/10/1995 **Age:** 27

Year	Team	Lg	G	AB	H	2B	3B	HR	(Hm	Rd)	TB	R	RBI	RC	TBB	IBB	SO	HBP	SH	SF	SB	CS	GDP	Avg	OBP	Slg	OPS
2022	Salt Lk	AAA	82	288	68	13	2	9	(-	-)	112	52	40	41	39	0	113	1	0	3	28	4	4	.236	.326	.389	.715
2020	Mia	NL	32	47	8	1	0	1	(1	0)	12	8	3	1	4	0	26	0	0	0	6	0	0	.170	.235	.255	.491
2021	Mia	NL	9	10	2	1	0	0	(0	0)	3	0	0	0	0	0	3	0	1	0	0	1	0	.200	.200	.300	.500
2022	LAA	AL	9	11	2	0	0	1	(0	1)	5	5	3	3	2	0	8	1	0	1	1	0	1	.182	.357	.455	.812
	Postseason		2	0	0	0	0	0	(0	0)	0	0	0	0	0	0	0	0	0	0	1	0	0	-	-	-	-
3 ML YEARS			50	68	12	2	0	2	(1	1)	20	13	6	4	6	0	37	1	1	0	7	1	1	.176	.253	.294	.547

Hunter Harvey

Pitches: R **Bats:** R **Pos:** RP-38 **Ht:** 6'2" **Wt:** 225 **Born:** 12/9/1994 **Age:** 28

Year	Team	Lg	G	GS	GF	IP	BFP	H	R	ER	HR	SH	SF	HB	TBB	IBB	SO	WP	W	L	Pct	Sv-Op	Hld	Vel	OPS	ERC	ERA
2019	Bal	AL	7	0	1	6.1	26	3	1	1	1	0	0	0	4	0	11	0	1	0	1.000	0-1	1	98	.678	2.51	1.42
2020	Bal	AL	10	0	2	8.2	37	8	6	4	2	0	1	1	2	0	6	2	0	2	.000	0-0	4	97	.722	4.23	4.15
2021	Bal	AL	9	0	0	8.2	36	8	4	4	1	0	0	0	3	0	6	0	0	0	-	0-0	2	97	.760	3.58	4.15
2022	Was	NL	38	0	7	39.1	157	33	12	11	1	0	4	0	12	0	45	2	2	1	.667	0-1	6	98	.620	2.46	2.52
4 ML YEARS			64	0	10	63.0	256	52	23	20	5	0	5	1	21	0	68	4	3	3	.500	0-2	13	98	.660	2.85	2.86

Adam Haseley

Bats: L **Throws:** L **Pos:** RF-5;PR-5;LF-4;CF-3;DH-2;PH-2 **Ht:** 6'1" **Wt:** 190 **Born:** 4/12/1996 **Age:** 27

Year	Team	Lg	G	AB	H	2B	3B	HR	(Hm	Rd)	TB	R	RBI	RC	TBB	IBB	SO	HBP	SH	SF	SB	CS	GDP	Avg	OBP	Slg	OPS
2022	Charllt	AAA	110	418	100	19	4	15	(-	-)	172	59	63	56	32	0	78	9	1	3	18	3	6	.239	.305	.411	.717
2019	Phi	NL	67	222	59	14	0	5	(3	2)	88	30	26	28	14	1	60	5	1	0	4	0	7	.266	.324	.396	.720
2020	Phi	NL	40	79	22	5	0	0	(0	0)	27	7	13	12	7	1	17	2	3	1	0	0	3	.278	.348	.342	.690
2021	Phi	NL	9	21	4	1	0	0	(0	0)	5	2	0	0	0	0	4	0	0	0	0	0	0	.190	.190	.238	.429
2022	CWS	AL	14	21	5	0	0	0	(0	0)	5	4	2	1	3	0	7	0	1	0	0	0	0	.238	.333	.238	.571
4 ML YEARS			130	343	90	20	0	5	(3	2)	125	43	41	41	24	2	88	7	5	1	4	0	10	.262	.323	.364	.687

Thomas Hatch

Pitches: R **Bats:** R **Pos:** SP-1 **Ht:** 6'1" **Wt:** 195 **Born:** 9/29/1994 **Age:** 28

Year	Team	Lg	G	GS	GF	IP	BFP	H	R	ER	HR	SH	SF	HB	TBB	IBB	SO	WP	W	L	Pct	Sv-Op	Hld	Vel	OPS	ERC	ERA
2022	Buffalo	AAA	28	22	0	131.0	558	127	73	68	16	3	4	12	38	0	113	5	8	7	.533	0- -	-	-	.734	3.99	4.67
2020	Tor	AL	17	1	1	26.1	109	18	11	8	2	0	0	2	13	0	23	0	3	1	.750	0-0	3	95	.601	2.90	2.73
2021	Tor	AL	3	2	0	9.1	45	11	7	7	2	0	0	1	6	0	8	2	0	1	.000	0-0	0	94	.953	7.58	6.75
2022	Tor	AL	1	1	0	4.2	26	12	10	10	3	0	0	1	2	0	4	0	0	1	.000	0-0	0	95	1.577	24.38	19.29
	Postseason		2	0	1	2.0	6	0	0	0	0	0	0	0	0	0	1	0	0	0	-	0-0	0	95	.000	0.00	0.00
3 ML YEARS			21	4	1	40.1	180	41	28	25	7	0	0	4	21	0	35	2	3	3	.500	0-0	3	95	.831	5.73	5.58

Ke'Bryan Hayes

Bats: R **Throws:** R **Pos:** 3B-133;PH-4;SS-3;DH-2 **Ht:** 5'10" **Wt:** 205 **Born:** 1/28/1997 **Age:** 26

Year	Team	Lg	G	AB	H	2B	3B	HR	(Hm	Rd)	TB	R	RBI	RC	TBB	IBB	SO	HBP	SH	SF	SB	CS	GDP	Avg	OBP	Slg	OPS
2020	Pit	NL	24	85	32	7	2	5	(3	2)	58	17	11	24	9	2	20	1	0	0	5	0	0	.376	.442	.682	1.124
2021	Pit	NL	96	362	93	20	2	6	(2	4)	135	49	38	48	31	0	87	1	0	2	9	1	11	.257	.316	.373	.689
2022	Pit	NL	136	505	123	24	3	7	(3	4)	174	55	41	52	48	0	122	5	0	2	20	5	12	.244	.314	.345	.659
3 ML YEARS			256	952	248	51	7	18	(8	10)	367	121	90	124	88	2	229	7	0	4	30	6	25	.261	.326	.386	.712

Austin Hays

Bats: R Throws: R Pos: LF-86;RF-58;CF-6;DH-3;PH-1;PR-1   Ht: 6'0" Wt: 205 Born: 7/5/1995 Age: 27

							BATTING													RUNNING			AVERAGES			
Year	Team	Lg	G	AB	H	2B	3B	HR	(Hm | Rd)	TB	R	RBI	RC	TBB	IBB	SO	HBP	SH	SF	SB	CS	GDP	Avg	OBP	Slg	OPS
2017	Bal	AL	20	60	13	3	0	1	(0 | 1)	19	4	8	5	2	0	16	0	0	1	0	0	2	.217	.238	.317	.555
2019	Bal	AL	21	68	21	6	0	4	(2 | 2)	39	12	13	16	7	0	13	0	0	0	2	0	0	.309	.373	.574	.947
2020	Bal	AL	33	122	34	2	0	4	(1 | 3)	48	20	9	14	8	0	25	2	0	2	2	3	1	.279	.328	.393	.722
2021	Bal	AL	131	488	125	26	4	22	(13 | 9)	225	73	71	76	28	0	107	9	3	1	4	3	9	.256	.308	.461	.769
2022	Bal	AL	145	535	134	35	2	16	(6 | 10)	221	66	60	64	34	0	114	10	0	3	2	4	11	.250	.306	.413	.719
	5 ML YEARS		350	1273	327	72	6	47	(22 | 25)	552	175	161	175	79	0	275	21	3	7	10	10	23	.257	.309	.434	.743

Louis Head

Pitches: R Bats: R Pos: RP-28   Ht: 6'1" Wt: 180 Born: 4/23/1990 Age: 33

			HOW MUCH PITCHED					WHAT HE GAVE UP										THE RESULTS						
Year	Team	Lg	G	GS	GF	IP	BFP	H	R	ER	HR	SH	SF	HB	TBB	IBB	SO	WP	W	L	Pct	Sv-Op	Hld	Vel	OPS	ERC	ERA
2022	Norfolk	AAA	14	0	4	15.1	71	11	12	12	1	0	0	2	17	0	19	2	1	1	.500	0--	-		.788	5.73	7.04
2021	TB	AL	27	2	12	35.0	134	21	10	9	2	0	2	3	9	0	32	1	2	0	1.000	0-0	0	94	.496	1.67	2.31
2022	2 Tms		28	0	9	28.2	138	32	20	20	4	0	0	5	15	1	26	2	0	0	-	1-1	1	94	.867	6.08	6.28
22	Mia	NL	23	0	7	23.2	111	26	19	19	4	0	0	4	11	1	23	1	0	0	-	1-1	1	94	.890	5.99	7.23
22	Bal	AL	5	0	2	5.0	27	6	1	1	0	0	0	1	4	0	3	1	0	0	-	0-0	0	94	.756	6.41	1.80
	2 ML YEARS		55	2	21	63.2	272	53	30	29	6	0	2	8	24	1	58	3	2	0	1.000	1-1	1	94	.681	3.47	4.10

Andrew Heaney

Pitches: L Bats: L Pos: SP-14; RP-2   HEE-nee   Ht: 6'2" Wt: 200 Born: 6/5/1991 Age: 32

			HOW MUCH PITCHED					WHAT HE GAVE UP										THE RESULTS						
Year	Team	Lg	G	GS	GF	IP	BFP	H	R	ER	HR	SH	SF	HB	TBB	IBB	SO	WP	W	L	Pct	Sv-Op	Hld	Vel	OPS	ERC	ERA
2014	Mia	NL	7	5	2	29.1	126	32	19	19	6	2	0	3	7	0	20	2	0	3	.000	0-0	0	90	.847	5.17	5.83
2015	LAA	AL	18	18	0	105.2	438	99	41	41	9	1	3	6	28	1	78	4	6	4	.600	0-0	0	91	.679	3.35	3.49
2016	LAA	AL	1	1	0	6.0	25	7	4	4	2	0	0	0	0	0	7	0	1	0	1.000	0-0	0	91	.840	4.78	6.00
2017	LAA	AL	5	5	0	21.2	101	27	17	17	12	2	0	0	9	0	27	2	1	2	.333	0-0	0	92	1.108	8.99	7.06
2018	LAA	AL	30	30	0	180.0	749	171	91	83	27	2	5	8	45	0	180	9	9	10	.474	0-0	0	92	.719	3.73	4.15
2019	LAA	AL	18	18	0	95.1	409	93	53	52	20	0	2	7	30	1	118	4	4	6	.400	0-0	0	93	.772	4.63	4.91
2020	LAA	AL	12	12	0	66.2	279	63	35	33	9	0	2	2	19	1	70	2	4	3	.571	0-0	0	92	.715	3.65	4.46
2021	2 Tms	AL	30	23	2	129.2	558	130	85	84	29	4	0	6	41	0	150	4	8	9	.471	0-1	0	92	.804	4.78	5.83
2022	LAD	NL	16	14	1	72.2	310	60	34	25	14	1	1	9	19	0	110	0	4	4	.500	0-0	0	93	.713	3.55	3.10
21	LAA	AL	18	18	0	94.0	401	92	56	55	16	0	0	3	31	0	113	3	6	7	.462	0-0	0	92	.744	4.28	5.27
21	NYY	AL	12	5	2	35.2	157	38	29	29	13	0	2	3	10	0	37	1	2	2	.500	0-1	0	92	.959	6.12	7.32
	9 ML YEARS		137	126	5	707.0	2995	682	379	358	128	8	17	41	198	3	760	27	36	42	.462	0-1	0	92	.755	4.16	4.56

Taylor Hearn

Pitches: L Bats: L Pos: RP-18; SP-13   Ht: 6'6" Wt: 230 Born: 8/30/1994 Age: 28

			HOW MUCH PITCHED					WHAT HE GAVE UP										THE RESULTS						
Year	Team	Lg	G	GS	GF	IP	BFP	H	R	ER	HR	SH	SF	HB	TBB	IBB	SO	WP	W	L	Pct	Sv-Op	Hld	Vel	OPS	ERC	ERA
2019	Tex	AL	1	1	0	0.1	8	3	5	4	0	0	0	4	0	0	0	0	0	1	.000	0-0	0	92	1.875	131.5	108.0
2020	Tex	AL	14	0	3	17.1	76	13	8	7	2	0	1	1	11	0	23	2	0	0	-	0-0	0	95	.646	3.90	3.63
2021	Tex	AL	42	11	10	104.1	441	96	58	54	17	1	5	3	42	1	92	6	6	6	.500	0-1	1	95	.745	4.22	4.66
2022	Tex	AL	31	13	3	100.0	449	107	60	57	11	1	2	3	43	0	97	3	6	8	.429	1-2	2	95	.769	4.72	5.13
	4 ML YEARS		88	25	16	222.0	974	219	131	122	30	2	8	7	100	1	212	11	12	15	.444	1-3	3	95	.756	4.56	4.95

Jon Heasley

Pitches: R Bats: R Pos: SP-21   Ht: 6'3" Wt: 225 Born: 1/27/1997 Age: 26

			HOW MUCH PITCHED					WHAT HE GAVE UP										THE RESULTS						
Year	Team	Lg	G	GS	GF	IP	BFP	H	R	ER	HR	SH	SF	HB	TBB	IBB	SO	WP	W	L	Pct	Sv-Op	Hld	Vel	OPS	ERC	ERA
2022	Omha	AAA	9	9	0	39.1	160	35	22	19	7	1	1	0	10	0	45	3	1	2	.333	0--	-		.729	3.42	4.35
2021	KC	AL	3	3	0	14.2	59	15	8	8	3	0	0	2	3	0	6	0	1	1	.500	0-0	0	94	.876	5.03	4.91
2022	KC	AL	21	21	0	104.0	465	108	67	61	19	0	8	6	47	0	70	9	4	10	.286	0-0	0	93	.824	5.33	5.28
	2 ML YEARS		24	24	0	118.2	524	123	75	69	22	0	8	8	50	0	76	9	5	11	.313	0-0	0	93	.830	5.30	5.23

Austin Hedges

Bats: R Throws: R Pos: C-105   Ht: 6'1" Wt: 223 Born: 8/18/1992 Age: 30

							BATTING													RUNNING			AVERAGES			
Year	Team	Lg	G	AB	H	2B	3B	HR	(Hm	Rd)	TB	R	RBI	RC	TBB	IBB	SO	HBP	SH	SF	SB	CS	GDP	Avg	OBP	Slg	OPS
2015	SD	NL	56	137	23	2	0	3	(2	1)	34	13	11	7	8	1	38	1	3	3	0	0	1	.168	.215	.248	.463
2016	SD	NL	8	24	3	1	0	0	(0	0)	4	2	1	0	0	0	7	1	0	1	0	1	0	.125	.154	.167	.321
2017	SD	NL	120	387	83	17	0	18	(9	9)	154	36	55	39	23	3	122	3	1	3	4	1	10	.214	.262	.398	.660
2018	SD	NL	91	303	70	14	2	14	(5	9)	130	29	37	28	21	3	90	1	0	1	3	0	9	.231	.282	.429	.711
2019	SD	NL	102	312	55	9	0	11	(3	8)	97	28	36	28	27	3	109	4	1	0	1	0	5	.176	.252	.311	.563
2020	2 Tms		35	69	10	1	0	3	(1	2)	20	7	6	3	6	0	23	2	5	1	1	1	3	.145	.231	.290	.521
2021	Cle	AL	88	286	51	7	0	10	(5	5)	88	32	31	20	15	1	87	1	7	3	1	0	7	.178	.220	.308	.527
2022	Cle	AL	105	294	48	4	0	7	(1	6)	73	26	30	16	25	0	78	6	10	3	2	0	12	.163	.241	.248	.489
20	SD	NL	29	57	9	1	0	3	(1	2)	19	7	6	3	6	0	18	2	5	1	1	1	3	.158	.258	.333	.591
20	Cle	AL	6	12	1	0	0	0	(0	0)	1	0	0	0	0	0	5	0	0	0	0	0	0	.083	.083	.083	.167
	Postseason		1	1	0	0	0	0	(0	0)	0	0	0	0	0	0	1	0	0	0	0	0	0	.000	.000	.000	.000
	8 ML YEARS		605	1812	343	55	2	66	(26	40)	600	173	207	141	125	11	554	20	28	16	12	3	45	.189	.247	.331	.578

Jonah Heim

Bats: B **Throws:** R **Pos:** C-111;PH-18;DH-7   **Ht:** 6'4" **Wt:** 220 **Born:** 6/27/1995 **Age:** 28

								BATTING												RUNNING			AVERAGES			
Year	Team	Lg	G	AB	H	2B	3B	HR	(Hm | Rd)	TB	R	RBI	RC	TBB	IBB	SO	HBP	SH	SF	SB	CS	GDP	Avg	OBP	Slg	OPS
2020	Oak	AL	13	38	8	0	0	0	(0 | 0)	8	5	5	5	3	0	3	0	0	0	0	0	1	.211	.268	.211	.479
2021	Tex	AL	82	265	52	13	0	10	(7 | 3)	95	22	32	23	15	0	58	1	1	3	3	1	8	.196	.239	.358	.598
2022	Tex	AL	127	406	92	20	1	16	(8 | 8)	162	51	48	50	41	0	87	1	0	2	2	0	10	.227	.298	.399	.697
	3 ML YEARS		222	709	152	33	1	26	(15 | 11)	265	78	85	78	59	0	148	2	1	5	5	1	19	.214	.275	.374	.649

Tyler Heineman

Bats: B **Throws:** R **Pos:** C-59;PH-4;DH-1;PR-1   **Ht:** 5'10" **Wt:** 190 **Born:** 6/19/1991 **Age:** 32

								BATTING												RUNNING			AVERAGES			
Year	Team	Lg	G	AB	H	2B	3B	HR	(Hm	Rd)	TB	R	RBI	RC	TBB	IBB	SO	HBP	SH	SF	SB	CS	GDP	Avg	OBP	Slg	OPS
2019	Mia	NL	5	11	3	1	0	1	(0	1)	7	1	2	3	0	0	4	0	1	0	0	0	0	.273	.273	.636	.909
2020	SF	NL	15	42	8	1	0	0	(0	0)	9	3	1	3	4	0	6	2	2	0	1	0	0	.190	.292	.214	.506
2022	2 Tms		62	157	34	8	0	0	(0	0)	42	16	9	9	8	0	17	5	4	0	1	0	3	.217	.276	.268	.544
22	Tor	AL	10	15	4	2	0	0	(0	0)	6	2	1	1	0	0	4	0	1	0	0	0	1	.267	.267	.400	.667
22	Pit	NL	52	142	30	6	0	0	(0	0)	36	14	8	8	8	0	13	5	3	0	1	0	2	.211	.277	.254	.531
	3 ML YEARS		82	210	45	10	0	1	(0	1)	58	20	12	15	12	0	27	7	7	0	2	0	3	.214	.279	.276	.556

Ryan Helsley

Pitches: R **Bats:** R **Pos:** RP-54   **Ht:** 6'2" **Wt:** 230 **Born:** 7/18/1994 **Age:** 28

			HOW MUCH PITCHED				WHAT HE GAVE UP											THE RESULTS						
Year	Team	Lg	G	GS	GF	IP	BFP	H	R	ER	HR	SH	SF	HB	TBB	IBB	SO	WP	W	L	Pct	Sv-Op	Hld	Vel	OPS	ERC	ERA
2019	StL	NL	24	0	4	36.2	153	34	13	12	5	1	1	0	12	2	32	2	2	0	1.000	0-1	1	98	.734	3.56	2.95
2020	StL	NL	12	0	4	12.0	52	8	8	7	3	0	0	1	8	1	10	0	1	1	.500	1-3	2	97	.769	4.53	5.25
2021	StL	NL	51	0	7	47.1	206	40	24	24	4	1	2	0	27	2	47	7	6	4	.600	1-3	10	97	.668	3.67	4.56
2022	StL	NL	54	0	33	64.2	239	28	11	9	6	0	0	0	20	1	94	1	9	1	.900	19-23	7	100	.438	1.19	1.25
	Postseason		7	0	1	7.0	24	2	1	1	0	0	0	0	1	0	10	0	0	0	-	0-0	0	98	.255	0.34	1.29
	4 ML YEARS		141	0	48	160.2	650	110	56	52	18	3	3	1	67	6	183	10	18	6	.750	21-30	20	98	.606	2.53	2.91

Heath Hembree

Pitches: R **Bats:** R **Pos:** RP-26   HEHM-bree   **Ht:** 6'4" **Wt:** 220 **Born:** 1/13/1989 **Age:** 34

			HOW MUCH PITCHED				WHAT HE GAVE UP											THE RESULTS						
Year	Team	Lg	G	GS	GF	IP	BFP	H	R	ER	HR	SH	SF	HB	TBB	IBB	SO	WP	W	L	Pct	Sv-Op	Hld	Vel	OPS	ERC	ERA
2022	OkCity	AAA	10	0	4	9.1	39	6	5	5	2	2	0	0	2	0	14	0	1	0	1.000	1--	-	-	.616	1.95	4.82
2013	SF	NL	9	0	2	7.2	29	4	0	0	0	0	0	0	2	0	12	0	0	0	-	0-0	0	92	.392	1.02	0.00
2014	Bos	AL	6	0	3	10.0	43	11	5	5	1	0	0	0	5	2	6	1	0	0	-	0-0	0	92	.846	4.94	4.50
2015	Bos	AL	22	0	9	25.1	106	25	10	10	5	0	0	0	9	2	15	1	2	0	1.000	0-0	1	94	.795	4.46	3.55
2016	Bos	AL	38	0	8	51.0	223	51	23	15	6	0	1	0	17	1	47	0	4	1	.800	0-2	5	94	.695	3.78	2.65
2017	Bos	AL	62	0	8	62.0	271	72	29	25	10	1	2	1	18	0	70	2	2	3	.400	0-3	14	95	.803	5.07	3.63
2018	Bos	AL	67	0	10	60.0	260	53	30	28	10	0	5	1	27	1	76	4	4	1	.800	0-3	20	95	.734	4.05	4.20
2019	Bos	AL	45	0	14	39.2	173	34	20	17	7	0	0	3	18	2	46	2	1	0	1.000	2-3	4	94	.772	4.18	3.86
2020	2 Tms		22	0	2	19.0	90	26	19	19	9	0	1	2	8	0	20	0	3	0	1.000	0-1	3	94	1.159	10.17	9.00
2021	2 Tms	NL	60	0	21	58.0	243	45	39	36	12	0	0	2	24	1	83	2	2	7	.222	9-11	7	95	.712	3.68	5.59
2022	2 Tms	NL	26	0	6	22.0	107	26	19	18	6	0	3	0	17	2	17	1	3	1	.750	0-1	2	94	1.000	8.01	7.36
20	Bos	AL	11	0	1	9.2	40	9	6	6	2	0	0	0	3	0	10	0	2	0	1.000	0-1	1	94	.786	4.08	5.59
20	Phi	NL	11	0	1	9.1	50	17	13	13	7	0	1	2	5	0	10	0	1	0	1.000	0-0	2	94	1.480	17.96	12.54
21	NYM	NL	15	0	5	15.2	64	13	6	6	2	0	0	0	5	1	15	1	0	0	-	1-1	1	95	.637	2.94	3.45
21	Cin	NL	45	0	16	42.1	179	32	33	30	10	0	0	2	19	0	68	1	2	7	.222	8-10	6	95	.739	3.97	6.38
22	Pit	NL	20	0	3	16.1	78	17	13	13	5	0	2	0	14	1	12	1	2	0	1.000	0-1	2	94	1.010	7.87	7.16
22	LAD	NL	6	0	3	5.2	29	9	6	5	1	0	1	0	3	1	5	0	1	1	.500	0-0	0	95	.974	8.39	7.94
	Postseason		4	0	2	4.2	16	0	0	0	0	0	0	0	5	0	3	0	0	0	-	0-0	0	94	.313	1.27	0.00
	10 ML YEARS		357	0	83	354.2	1545	347	194	173	66	1	12	9	145	11	392	13	21	13	.618	11-24	56	94	.784	4.62	4.39

Gunnar Henderson

Bats: L **Throws:** R **Pos:** 3B-24;SS-7;DH-4;PH-4;2B-3   **Ht:** 6'2" **Wt:** 210 **Born:** 6/29/2001 **Age:** 22

								BATTING												RUNNING			AVERAGES			
Year	Team	Lg	G	AB	H	2B	3B	HR	(Hm	Rd)	TB	R	RBI	RC	TBB	IBB	SO	HBP	SH	SF	SB	CS	GDP	Avg	OBP	Slg	OPS
2019	Orioles	R	29	108	28	5	2	1	(-	-)	40	21	11	14	11	0	28	1	0	1	2	2	2	.259	.331	.370	.701
2021	2 Tms	Low	100	384	100	27	4	17	(-	-)	186	64	74	69	54	0	133	3	0	5	16	2	5	.260	.352	.484	.836
2022	Bowie	AA	47	157	49	11	3	8	(-	-)	90	41	35	43	41	0	38	4	0	6	12	2	3	.312	.452	.573	1.025
2022	Norfolk	AAA	65	250	72	13	4	11	(-	-)	126	60	41	53	38	0	78	5	0	2	10	1	0	.288	.390	.504	.894
2022	Bal	AL	34	116	30	7	1	4	(1	3)	51	12	18	20	16	1	34	0	0	0	1	1	1	.259	.348	.440	.788

Kyle Hendricks

Pitches: R **Bats:** R **Pos:** SP-16   **Ht:** 6'3" **Wt:** 190 **Born:** 12/7/1989 **Age:** 33

			HOW MUCH PITCHED				WHAT HE GAVE UP											THE RESULTS						
Year	Team	Lg	G	GS	GF	IP	BFP	H	R	ER	HR	SH	SF	HB	TBB	IBB	SO	WP	W	L	Pct	Sv-Op	Hld	Vel	OPS	ERC	ERA
2014	ChC	NL	13	13	0	80.1	321	72	24	22	4	4	1	4	15	2	47	0	7	2	.778	0-0	0	88	.610	2.61	2.46
2015	ChC	NL	32	32	0	180.0	739	166	82	79	17	6	0	8	43	1	167	3	8	7	.533	0-0	0	88	.677	3.18	3.95
2016	ChC	NL	31	30	0	190.0	745	142	53	45	15	4	3	8	44	3	170	5	16	8	.667	0-0	0	88	.581	**2.19**	**2.13**
2017	ChC	NL	24	24	0	139.2	570	126	49	47	17	6	1	2	40	1	123	0	7	5	.583	0-0	0	88	.670	3.34	3.03
2018	ChC	NL	33	33	0	199.0	812	184	82	76	22	7	7	9	44	4	161	0	14	11	.560	0-0	0	87	.685	3.22	3.44
2019	ChC	NL	30	30	0	177.0	730	168	78	68	19	8	5	9	32	1	150	1	11	10	.524	0-0	0	87	.683	3.17	3.46
2020	ChC	NL	12	12	0	81.1	315	73	26	24	10	0	2	1	6	1	64	1	6	5	.545	0-0	0	87	.632	2.62	2.88

Year	Team	Lg	G	GS	GF	IP	BFP	H	R	ER	HR	SH	SF	HB	TBB	IBB	SO	WP	W	L	Pct	Sv-Op	Hld	Vel	OPS	ERC	ERA
			HOW MUCH PITCHED					WHAT HE GAVE UP											THE RESULTS								
2021	ChC	NL	32	32	0	181.0	785	200	101	96	31	6	3	13	44	3	131	2	14	7	.667	0-0	0	87	.811	4.80	4.77
2022	ChC	NL	16	16	0	84.1	356	85	45	45	15	1	0	3	24	0	66	0	4	6	.400	0-0	0	87	.787	4.37	4.80
	Postseason		12	11	0	57.2	242	53	22	20	10	2	1	3	16	1	51	0	2	4	.333	0-0	0	88	.726	3.79	3.12
	9 ML YEARS		223	222	0	1312.2	5373	1216	540	504	150	42	22	57	294	16	1079	12	87	61	.588	0-0	0	87	.686	3.26	3.46

Liam Hendriks

Pitches: R Bats: R Pos: RP-58   Ht: 6'0" Wt: 235 Born: 2/10/1989 Age: 34

Year	Team	Lg	G	GS	GF	IP	BFP	H	R	ER	HR	SH	SF	HB	TBB	IBB	SO	WP	W	L	Pct	Sv-Op	Hld	Vel	OPS	ERC	ERA
2011	Min	AL	4	4	0	23.1	100	29	16	16	3	0	1	0	6	0	16	1	0	2	.000	0-0	0	90	.866	5.26	6.17
2012	Min	AL	16	16	0	85.1	381	106	61	53	17	3	1	4	26	3	50	4	1	8	.111	0-0	0	90	.890	6.03	5.59
2013	Min	AL	10	8	1	47.1	224	67	39	36	10	0	2	3	14	1	34	1	1	3	.250	0-0	0	91	.907	7.16	6.85
2014	2 Tms	AL	9	6	0	32.2	143	38	21	19	3	0	2	3	7	0	23	1	1	2	.333	0-0	1	91	.786	4.56	5.23
2015	Tor	AL	58	0	14	64.2	261	59	23	21	3	0	2	2	11	1	71	4	5	0	1.000	0-2	5	95	.605	2.51	2.92
2016	Oak	AL	53	0	10	64.2	275	69	31	27	6	0	4	1	14	3	71	3	0	4	.000	0-1	10	94	.704	3.63	3.76
2017	Oak	AL	70	0	13	64.0	273	57	34	30	7	0	1	0	23	0	78	6	4	2	.667	1-4	16	95	.663	3.30	4.22
2018	Oak	AL	25	8	1	24.0	104	25	11	11	3	0	1	0	10	0	22	1	0	1	.000	0-0	0	94	.759	4.82	4.13
2019	Oak	AL	75	2	41	85.0	332	61	18	17	5	2	3	2	21	5	124	7	4	4	.500	25-32	8	96	.564	1.86	1.80
2020	Oak	AL	24	0	20	25.1	92	14	6	5	1	1	1	0	3	1	37	0	3	1	.750	14-15	0	96	.405	0.95	1.78
2021	CWS	AL	69	0	58	71.0	267	45	23	20	11	0	0	1	7	1	113	6	8	3	.727	**38-44**	0	98	.517	1.53	2.54
2022	CWS	AL	58	0	51	57.2	235	44	22	18	7	3	4	2	16	1	85	8	4	4	.500	37-41	0	98	.620	2.56	2.81
14	Tor	AL	3	3	0	13.1	57	12	9	9	3	0	0	2	4	0	8	0	1	0	1.000	0-0	0	91	.767	4.58	6.08
14	KC	AL	6	3	0	19.1	86	26	12	10	0	0	2	1	3	0	15	1	0	2	.000	0-0	1	92	.799	4.52	4.66
	Postseason		11	1	7	15.2	64	15	10	10	3	0	1	0	3	0	22	0	1	1	.500	1-1	0	97	.709	3.60	5.74
	12 ML YEARS		471	44	209	645.0	2687	614	305	273	76	9	22	19	158	16	724	42	31	34	.477	115-139	40	94	.692	3.39	3.81

Ryan Hendrix

Pitches: R Bats: R Pos: RP-9   Ht: 6'3" Wt: 215 Born: 12/16/1994 Age: 28

Year	Team	Lg	G	GS	GF	IP	BFP	H	R	ER	HR	SH	SF	HB	TBB	IBB	SO	WP	W	L	Pct	Sv-Op	Hld	Vel	OPS	ERC	ERA
2022	Lsvlle	AAA	42	0	9	38.2	177	33	23	22	3	0	0	1	31	0	53	4	1	1	.500	0- -	-	-	.698	4.75	5.12
2021	Cin	NL	36	0	9	31.2	142	33	23	21	8	0	2	1	16	2	35	6	5	1	.833	0-1	3	96	.881	5.93	5.97
2022	Cin	NL	9	0	7	8.1	38	9	5	5	0	0	0	2	6	1	9	3	0	0	-	0-0	0	94	.847	6.19	5.40
	2 ML YEARS		45	0	16	40.0	180	42	28	26	8	0	2	3	22	3	44	9	5	1	.833	0-1	3	96	.875	6.04	5.85

Ronny Henriquez

Pitches: R Bats: R Pos: RP-3   Ht: 5'10" Wt: 155 Born: 6/20/2000 Age: 23

Year	Team	Lg	G	GS	GF	IP	BFP	H	R	ER	HR	SH	SF	HB	TBB	IBB	SO	WP	W	L	Pct	Sv-Op	Hld	Vel	OPS	ERC	ERA
2022	StPaul	AAA	24	14	2	95.1	412	99	60	60	19	1	1	5	33	0	106	5	3	4	.429	1- -	-	-	.806	5.04	5.66
2022	Min	AL	3	0	1	11.2	50	8	4	3	1	0	0	2	3	0	9	0	0	1	.000	0-0	0	93	.616	2.28	2.31

Payton Henry

Bats: R Throws: R Pos: C-15;PH-1   Ht: 6'2" Wt: 215 Born: 6/24/1997 Age: 26

Year	Team	Lg	G	AB	H	2B	3B	HR	(Hm	Rd)	TB	R	RBI	RC	TBB	IBB	SO	HBP	SH	SF	SB	CS	GDP	Avg	OBP	Slg	OPS
2022	Jaxnvl	AAA	21	71	17	3	0	1	(-	-)	23	13	9	7	7	0	28	3	0	2	0	0	1	.239	.325	.324	.649
2021	Mia	NL	5	15	4	1	0	0	(0	0)	5	0	0	1	1	0	5	0	0	0	0	0	0	.267	.313	.333	.646
2022	Mia	NL	15	28	4	0	0	0	(0	0)	4	2	4	2	5	0	8	2	0	0	0	0	0	.143	.314	.143	.457
	2 ML YEARS		20	43	8	1	0	0	(0	0)	9	2	4	3	6	0	13	2	0	0	0	0	1	.186	.314	.209	.523

Tommy Henry

Pitches: L Bats: L Pos: SP-9   Ht: 6'3" Wt: 205 Born: 7/29/1997 Age: 25

Year	Team	Lg	G	GS	GF	IP	BFP	H	R	ER	HR	SH	SF	HB	TBB	IBB	SO	WP	W	L	Pct	Sv-Op	Hld	Vel	OPS	ERC	ERA
2022	Reno	AAA	21	21	0	113.0	474	103	47	47	11	1	1	2	45	0	103	4	4	4	.500	0- -	-	-	.682	3.68	3.74
2022	Ari	NL	9	9	0	47.0	205	47	28	28	10	1	1	3	21	1	36	3	3	4	.429	0-0	0	92	.823	5.40	5.36

David Hensley

Bats: R Throws: R Pos: DH-6;2B-5;3B-3;PH-3;SS-2;LF-1   Ht: 6'6" Wt: 190 Born: 3/28/1996 Age: 27

Year	Team	Lg	G	AB	H	2B	3B	HR	(Hm	Rd)	TB	R	RBI	RC	TBB	IBB	SO	HBP	SH	SF	SB	CS	GDP	Avg	OBP	Slg	OPS
2022	SgrLnd	AAA	104	379	113	30	4	10	(-	-)	181	80	57	76	80	0	103	2	0	3	20	7	8	.298	.420	.478	.898
2022	Hou	AL	16	29	10	2	1	1	(1	0)	17	7	5	6	5	0	6	0	0	0	0	0	3	.345	.441	.586	1.027

Sam Hentges

Pitches: L Bats: L Pos: RP-57   Ht: 6'6" Wt: 245 Born: 7/18/1996 Age: 26

Year	Team	Lg	G	GS	GF	IP	BFP	H	R	ER	HR	SH	SF	HB	TBB	IBB	SO	WP	W	L	Pct	Sv-Op	Hld	Vel	OPS	ERC	ERA
2021	Cle	AL	30	12	6	68.2	318	90	54	51	10	1	2	0	32	0	68	11	1	4	.200	0-0	0	94	.876	6.62	6.68
2022	Cle	AL	57	0	15	62.0	245	41	17	16	3	1	1	3	19	1	72	3	3	2	.600	1-1	8	96	.516	1.86	2.32
	2 ML YEARS		87	12	21	130.2	563	131	71	67	13	2	3	3	51	1	140	14	4	6	.400	1-1	8	95	.719	4.14	4.61

Guillermo Heredia

Bats: R Throws: L Pos: LF-35;RF-23;PR-10;CF-6;DH-6;PH-3   ghee-YAIR-moh   Ht: 5'10" Wt: 195 Born: 1/31/1991 Age: 32

Year	Team	Lg	G	AB	H	2B	3B	HR	(Hm	Rd)	TB	R	RBI	RC	TBB	IBB	SO	HBP	SH	SF	SB	CS	GDP	Avg	OBP	Slg	OPS
2016	Sea	AL	45	92	23	3	0	1	(1	0)	29	12	12	12	12	0	15	2	1	0	1	1	1	.250	.349	.315	.664
2017	Sea	AL	123	386	96	16	0	6	(4	2)	130	43	24	37	27	2	64	11	1	1	1	5	9	.249	.315	.337	.652
2018	Sea	AL	125	292	69	14	1	5	(1	4)	100	29	19	33	32	0	52	4	7	2	2	4	4	.236	.318	.342	.661
2019	TB	AL	89	204	46	13	0	5	(1	4)	74	31	20	20	18	0	60	6	2	1	2	2	4	.225	.306	.363	.668
2020	2 Tms	NL	15	33	7	0	0	2	(1	1)	13	6	5	4	3	0	9	0	0	0	1	0	0	.212	.278	.394	.672
2021	Atl	NL	120	305	67	26	0	5	(2	3)	108	46	26	34	32	3	81	9	0	1	0	0	5	.220	.311	.354	.665
2022	Atl	NL	74	76	12	3	1	3	(1	2)	26	12	8	7	6	0	32	0	0	0	0	0	1	.158	.220	.342	.562
20	Pit	NL	8	16	3	0	0	0	(0	0)	3	2	2	2	2	0	4	0	0	0	1	0	0	.188	.278	.188	.465
20	NYM	NL	7	17	4	0	0	2	(1	1)	10	4	3	2	1	0	5	0	0	0	0	0	0	.235	.278	.588	.866
	Postseason		10	3	0	0	0	0	(0	0)	0	0	0	0	0	0	0	1	0	0	0	0	0	.000	.250	.000	.250
	7 ML YEARS		591	1388	320	75	2	27	(11	16)	480	179	114	147	130	5	313	32	11	5	7	12	24	.231	.310	.346	.656

Jimmy Herget

Pitches: R Bats: R Pos: RP-48; SP-1   Ht: 6'3" Wt: 170 Born: 9/9/1993 Age: 29

Year	Team	Lg	G	GS	GF	IP	BFP	H	R	ER	HR	SH	SF	HB	TBB	IBB	SO	WP	W	L	Pct	Sv-Op	Hld	Vel	OPS	ERC	ERA
2019	Cin	NL	5	0	4	6.1	26	8	3	3	2	0	0	0	3	0	0	0	0	0	-	0-0	0	93	1.119	8.76	4.26
2020	Tex	AL	20	1	6	19.2	87	13	7	7	2	1	1	2	14	1	17	0	1	0	1.000	0-1	1	93	.671	3.68	3.20
2021	2 Tms	AL	18	0	3	18.2	78	20	12	11	1	0	1	3	4	1	20	0	2	3	.400	0-2	1	91	.789	4.14	5.30
2022	LAA	AL	49	1	13	69.0	266	48	20	19	4	2	1	3	15	3	63	0	2	1	.667	9-12	6	91	.564	1.76	2.48
21	Tex	AL	4	0	1	4.0	18	5	5	4	1	0	0	1	0	0	2	0	0	1	.000	0-0	1	91	.922	5.88	9.00
21	LAA	AL	14	0	2	14.2	60	15	7	7	0	0	1	2	4	1	18	0	2	2	.500	0-2	0	91	.746	3.64	4.30
	4 ML YEARS		92	2	26	113.2	457	89	42	40	9	3	3	8	36	5	100	0	5	4	.556	9-15	8	92	.654	2.74	3.17

Kevin Herget

Pitches: R Bats: L Pos: RP-3   Ht: 5'10" Wt: 185 Born: 4/3/1991 Age: 32

Year	Team	Lg	G	GS	GF	IP	BFP	H	R	ER	HR	SH	SF	HB	TBB	IBB	SO	WP	W	L	Pct	Sv-Op	Hld	Vel	OPS	ERC	ERA
2022	Drham	AAA	21	17	0	97.2	406	105	35	32	13	0	4	0	17	0	99	5	8	1	.889	0- -		-	.747	3.83	2.95
2022	TB	AL	3	0	3	7.0	30	9	6	6	0	0	2	0	0	0	4	0	0	1	.000	0-0	0	92	.800	3.32	7.71

Michael Hermosillo

Bats: R Throws: R Pos: CF-28;PH-7;RF-2;LF-1;PR-1   air-moh-SEE-yo   Ht: 6'0" Wt: 205 Born: 1/17/1995 Age: 28

Year	Team	Lg	G	AB	H	2B	3B	HR	(Hm	Rd)	TB	R	RBI	RC	TBB	IBB	SO	HBP	SH	SF	SB	CS	GDP	Avg	OBP	Slg	OPS
2018	LAA	AL	31	57	12	4	0	1	(1	0)	19	7	1	3	3	0	17	2	0	0	0	1	0	.211	.274	.333	.608
2019	LAA	AL	18	36	5	1	1	0	(0	0)	8	7	3	3	5	0	19	4	0	1	2	0	1	.139	.304	.222	.527
2020	LAA	AL	7	8	2	0	0	0	(0	0)	2	0	2	1	1	0	1	0	0	1	1	0	0	.250	.300	.250	.550
2021	ChC	NL	16	36	7	2	0	3	(1	2)	18	5	7	3	1	0	12	1	0	0	0	0	3	.194	.237	.500	.737
2022	ChC	NL	31	61	7	2	0	0	(0	0)	9	7	4	3	7	0	27	4	1	0	1	0	0	.115	.250	.148	.398
	5 ML YEARS		103	198	33	9	1	4	(2	2)	56	26	17	13	17	0	76	11	1	2	4	1	4	.167	.268	.283	.550

Carlos Hernandez

Pitches: R Bats: R Pos: RP-20; SP-7   Ht: 6'4" Wt: 245 Born: 3/11/1997 Age: 26

Year	Team	Lg	G	GS	GF	IP	BFP	H	R	ER	HR	SH	SF	HB	TBB	IBB	SO	WP	W	L	Pct	Sv-Op	Hld	Vel	OPS	ERC	ERA
2022	Omha	AAA	12	11	0	50.0	208	39	24	21	7	0	1	0	19	0	44	1	2	4	.333	0- -		-	.646	3.02	3.78
2020	KC	AL	5	3	0	14.2	67	19	9	8	4	0	1	0	6	0	13	0	0	1	.000	0-0	0	96	.955	7.75	4.91
2021	KC	AL	24	11	1	85.2	358	69	36	35	7	0	3	4	41	1	74	6	6	2	.750	0-0	0	97	.651	3.41	3.68
2022	KC	AL	27	7	4	56.0	266	72	48	46	7	0	5	1	31	1	35	3	0	5	.000	0-0	1	97	.876	6.66	7.39
	3 ML YEARS		56	21	5	156.1	691	160	93	89	18	0	8	6	78	2	122	9	6	8	.429	0-0	1	97	.767	4.90	5.12

Cesar Hernandez

Bats: B Throws: R Pos: 2B-126;LF-10;3B-9;PH-4;PR-1   Ht: 5'10" Wt: 183 Born: 5/23/1990 Age: 33

Year	Team	Lg	G	AB	H	2B	3B	HR	(Hm	Rd)	TB	R	RBI	RC	TBB	IBB	SO	HBP	SH	SF	SB	CS	GDP	Avg	OBP	Slg	OPS
2013	Phi	NL	34	121	35	5	0	0	(0	0)	40	17	10	13	9	0	26	1	0	0	0	3	2	.289	.344	.331	.674
2014	Phi	NL	66	114	27	2	0	1	(1	0)	32	13	4	7	9	1	33	0	1	1	1	1	1	.237	.290	.281	.571
2015	Phi	NL	127	405	110	20	4	1	(1	0)	141	57	35	52	40	1	86	2	4	1	19	5	6	.272	.339	.348	.687
2016	Phi	NL	155	547	161	14	11	6	(4	2)	215	67	39	82	66	4	116	2	5	2	17	13	6	.294	.371	.393	.764
2017	Phi	NL	128	511	150	26	6	9	(6	3)	215	85	34	80	61	1	104	4	0	1	15	5	8	.294	.373	.421	.793
2018	Phi	NL	161	605	153	15	3	15	(7	8)	219	91	60	85	95	4	155	4	1	3	19	6	12	.253	.356	.362	.718
2019	Phi	NL	161	612	171	31	3	14	(7	7)	250	77	71	82	45	4	100	6	0	4	9	2	9	.279	.333	.408	.741
2020	Cle	AL	58	233	66	20	0	3	(3	0)	95	35	20	36	24	0	57	2	1	0	0	0	3	.283	.355	.408	.763
2021	2 Tms	AL	149	570	132	21	2	18	(12	6)	220	84	62	73	59	2	135	5	0	3	1	1	11	.232	.308	.386	.694
2022	Was	NL	147	560	139	28	4	1	(0	1)	178	64	34	52	45	0	114	7	3	2	10	4	9	.248	.311	.318	.629
21	Cle	AL	96	376	87	17	2	18	(12	6)	162	60	47	56	38	0	90	4	0	0	0	0	6	.231	.307	.431	.738
21	CWS	AL	53	194	45	4	0	3	(0	3)	58	24	15	17	21	2	45	1	0	1	1	1	5	.232	.309	.299	.608
	Postseason		5	15	5	1	0	0	(0	0)	6	2	1	4	5	0	6	0	0	0	0	0	0	.333	.500	.400	.900
	10 ML YEARS		1186	4278	1144	182	33	71	(41	30)	1605	590	369	562	453	17	926	33	15	17	91	40	67	.267	.341	.375	.716

Darwinzon Hernandez

Pitches: L Bats: L Pos: RP-7   Ht: 6'2" Wt: 255 Born: 12/17/1996 Age: 26

		HOW MUCH PITCHED					WHAT HE GAVE UP											THE RESULTS							
Year Team	Lg	G	GS	GF	IP	BFP	H	R	ER	HR	SH	SF	HB	TBB	IBB	SO	WP	W	L	Pct	Sv-Op	Hld	Vel	OPS	ERC	ERA
2022 Wrcstr	AAA	23	7	1	33.0	153	22	23	21	3	1	1	7	27	0	51	3	0	3	.000	0- -	-		.693	4.53	5.73
2019 Bos	AL	29	1	2	30.1	147	27	18	15	1	1	0	3	26	1	57	4	0	1	.000	0-0	2	96	.725	4.90	4.45
2020 Bos	AL	7	0	0	8.1	40	5	2	2	0	0	0	1	8	0	13	1	1	0	1.000	0-0	2	94	.511	3.46	2.16
2021 Bos	AL	48	0	5	40.0	182	29	17	15	5	1	2	5	31	0	54	3	2	2	.500	0-4	12	95	.702	4.64	3.38
2022 Bos	AL	7	0	2	6.2	43	14	17	16	4	0	0	2	8	0	9	0	0	1	.000	0-0	0	94	1.376	22.81	21.60
Postseason		2	0	0	1.1	7	2	2	2	2	0	0	0	1	0	3	0	0	0	-	0-0	0	94	1.762	21.66	13.50
4 ML YEARS		91	1	9	85.1	412	75	54	48	10	2	2	11	73	1	133	8	3	4	.429	0-4	16	95	.761	5.74	5.06

Elier Hernandez

Bats: R Throws: R Pos: LF-7;DH-5;1B-1;RF-1;PH-1;PR-1   Ht: 6'3" Wt: 197 Born: 11/21/1994 Age: 28

		BATTING																	RUNNING			AVERAGES			
Year Team	Lg	G	AB	H	2B	3B	HR	(Hm Rd)	TB	R	RBI	RC	TBB	IBB	SO	HBP	SH	SF	SB	CS	GDP	Avg	OBP	Slg	OPS
2022 RdRck	AAA	89	319	95	20	6	13	(- -)	166	56	57	57	24	0	64	6	0	2	10	2	11	.298	.356	.520	.877
2022 Tex	AL	14	33	6	2	0	0	(0 0)	8	4	3	1	1	0	15	0	0	1	0	0	1	.182	.200	.242	.442

Elieser Hernandez

Pitches: R Bats: R Pos: SP-10; RP-10   eh-LEE-eh-ser   Ht: 6'0" Wt: 214 Born: 5/3/1995 Age: 28

		HOW MUCH PITCHED					WHAT HE GAVE UP											THE RESULTS							
Year Team	Lg	G	GS	GF	IP	BFP	H	R	ER	HR	SH	SF	HB	TBB	IBB	SO	WP	W	L	Pct	Sv-Op	Hld	Vel	OPS	ERC	ERA
2022 Jaxnvl	AAA	12	11	0	57.0	236	51	31	26	8	0	1	2	17	0	68	1	4	4	.500	0- -	-		.681	3.52	4.11
2018 Mia	NL	32	6	6	65.2	284	68	38	38	11	3	2	2	27	3	45	1	2	7	.222	0-0	2	91	.809	4.94	5.21
2019 Mia	NL	21	15	1	82.1	353	76	49	46	20	3	1	9	26	1	85	2	3	5	.375	0-0	0	91	.820	4.69	5.03
2020 Mia	NL	6	6	0	25.2	106	21	10	9	5	0	0	2	5	0	34	0	1	0	1.000	0-0	0	91	.678	3.11	3.16
2021 Mia	NL	11	11	0	51.2	225	54	26	24	13	2	2	3	14	2	53	1	1	3	.250	0-0	0	91	.848	4.96	4.18
2022 Mia	NL	20	10	4	62.1	278	67	48	44	19	0	3	4	22	1	60	1	3	6	.333	0-1	0	92	.921	5.97	6.35
5 ML YEARS		90	48	11	287.2	1246	286	171	161	68	8	8	20	94	7	277	5	10	21	.323	0-1	2	91	.833	4.92	5.04

Jonathan Hernandez

Pitches: R Bats: R Pos: RP-29   Ht: 6'3" Wt: 190 Born: 7/6/1996 Age: 26

		HOW MUCH PITCHED					WHAT HE GAVE UP											THE RESULTS							
Year Team	Lg	G	GS	GF	IP	BFP	H	R	ER	HR	SH	SF	HB	TBB	IBB	SO	WP	W	L	Pct	Sv-Op	Hld	Vel	OPS	ERC	ERA
2022 RdRck	AAA	15	0	2	13.1	65	13	7	6	1	0	3	0	13	0	16	1	0	2	.000	0- -	-		.765	5.99	4.05
2019 Tex	AL	9	2	1	16.2	78	14	10	8	3	0	1	0	13	0	19	1	2	1	.667	0-0	1	97	.721	5.09	4.32
2020 Tex	AL	27	0	5	31.0	125	24	10	10	2	1	2	4	8	0	31	0	5	1	.833	0-0	5	98	.618	2.65	2.90
2022 Tex	AL	29	0	16	30.1	131	26	14	10	2	1	0	1	17	3	27	5	2	3	.400	4-6	3	98	.669	3.66	2.97
3 ML YEARS		65	2	22	78.0	334	64	34	28	7	2	3	5	38	3	77	6	9	5	.643	4-6	9	98	.661	3.54	3.23

Kike Hernandez

Bats: R Throws: R Pos: CF-80;2B-11;SS-10;PH-1;PR-1   KEE-kay   Ht: 5'11" Wt: 190 Born: 8/24/1991 Age: 31

		BATTING																	RUNNING			AVERAGES			
Year Team	Lg	G	AB	H	2B	3B	HR	(Hm Rd)	TB	R	RBI	RC	TBB	IBB	SO	HBP	SH	SF	SB	CS	GDP	Avg	OBP	Slg	OPS
2014 2 Tms		42	121	30	6	3	3	(1 2)	51	13	14	18	12	0	21	1	0	0	0	0	1	.248	.321	.421	.742
2015 LAD	NL	76	202	62	12	2	7	(2 5)	99	24	22	32	11	0	46	2	1	2	0	2	3	.307	.346	.490	.836
2016 LAD	NL	109	216	41	8	0	7	(5 2)	70	25	18	16	28	1	64	0	0	0	2	0	3	.190	.283	.324	.607
2017 LAD	NL	140	297	64	24	2	11	(7 4)	125	46	37	39	41	2	80	0	1	3	3	0	4	.215	.308	.421	.729
2018 LAD	NL	145	402	103	17	3	21	(14 7)	189	67	52	58	50	5	78	1	4	5	3	0	3	.256	.336	.470	.806
2019 LAD	NL	130	414	98	19	1	17	(8 9)	170	57	64	57	36	3	97	6	4	4	4	0	5	.237	.304	.411	.715
2020 LAD	NL	48	139	32	8	1	5	(4 1)	57	20	20	18	6	0	31	2	0	1	0	1	5	.230	.270	.410	.680
2021 Bos	AL	134	508	127	35	3	20	(10 10)	228	84	60	80	61	0	110	9	0	7	1	0	4	.250	.337	.449	.786
2022 Bos	AL	93	361	80	24	0	6	(2 4)	122	48	45	40	34	0	71	3	0	4	0	2	11	.222	.291	.338	.629
14 Hou	AL	24	81	23	4	2	1	(1 0)	34	10	8	14	8	0	11	0	0	0	0	0	0	.284	.348	.420	.768
14 Mia	NL	18	40	7	2	1	2	(0 2)	17	3	6	4	4	0	10	1	0	0	0	0	1	.175	.267	.425	.692
Postseason		69	171	46	7	1	13	(6 7)	94	26	27	28	19	2	40	3	0	1	3	2	1	.269	.351	.550	.900
9 ML YEARS		917	2660	637	153	15	97	(53 44)	1111	384	332	358	279	11	598	24	6	26	13	5	43	.239	.314	.418	.732

Teoscar Hernandez

Bats: R Throws: R Pos: RF-117;DH-10;LF-8;PH-3   tay-OH-skar   Ht: 6'2" Wt: 215 Born: 10/15/1992 Age: 30

		BATTING																	RUNNING			AVERAGES			
Year Team	Lg	G	AB	H	2B	3B	HR	(Hm Rd)	TB	R	RBI	RC	TBB	IBB	SO	HBP	SH	SF	SB	CS	GDP	Avg	OBP	Slg	OPS
2016 Hou	AL	41	100	23	7	0	4	(1 3)	42	15	11	11	11	1	28	0	0	1	0	2	5	.230	.304	.420	.724
2017 2 Tms	AL	27	88	23	6	0	8	(5 3)	53	16	20	15	6	0	36	0	0	1	0	1	0	.261	.305	.602	.908
2018 Tor	AL	134	476	114	29	7	22	(9 13)	223	67	57	60	41	0	163	3	0	3	5	5	14	.239	.302	.468	.771
2019 Tor	AL	125	417	96	19	2	26	(15 11)	197	58	65	67	45	1	153	1	0	1	6	3	4	.230	.306	.472	.778
2020 Tor	AL	50	190	55	7	0	16	(6 10)	110	33	34	31	14	0	63	1	0	1	6	1	4	.289	.340	.579	.919
2021 Tor	AL	143	550	163	29	0	32	(12 20)	288	92	116	104	36	1	148	7	0	2	12	4	5	.296	.346	.524	.870
2022 Tor	AL	131	499	133	35	1	25	(15 10)	245	71	77	79	34	0	152	2	0	0	6	3	18	.267	.316	.491	.807
17 Hou	AL	1	0	0	0	0	0	(0 0)	0	0	0	0	0	0	0	0	0	0	0	0	0	---	---	---	---
17 Tor	AL	26	88	23	6	0	8	(5 3)	53	16	20	15	6	0	36	0	0	1	0	1	0	.261	.305	.602	.908
Postseason		2	7	1	0	0	0	(0 0)	1	0	1	1	0	0	4	0	0	0	0	0	0	.143	.250	.143	.393
7 ML YEARS		651	2320	607	132	10	133	(63 70)	1158	352	380	367	187	3	743	14	0	9	35	19	54	.262	.319	.499	.819

Yadiel Hernandez

Bats: L **Throws:** R **Pos:** LF-79;DH-10;PH-10;RF-1   **Ht:** 5'10" **Wt:** 197 **Born:** 10/9/1987 **Age:** 35

Year Team	Lg	G	AB	H	2B	3B	HR	(Hm	Rd)	TB	R	RBI	RC	TBB	IBB	SO	HBP	SH	SF	SB	CS	GDP	Avg	OBP	Slg	OPS
2020 Was	NL	12	26	5	3	0	1	(1	0)	11	3	6	4	1	0	12	0	0	1	0	0	0	.192	.214	.423	.637
2021 Was	NL	112	264	72	8	1	9	(3	6)	109	33	32	26	22	1	59	1	0	2	3	0	11	.273	.329	.413	.742
2022 Was	NL	94	305	82	16	0	9	(6	3)	125	30	41	38	19	0	74	1	0	2	2	1	9	.269	.312	.410	.722
3 ML YEARS		218	595	159	27	1	19	(10	9)	245	66	79	68	42	1	145	2	0	5	5	1	20	.267	.315	.412	.727

Yonny Hernandez

Bats: B **Throws:** R **Pos:** 3B-10;2B-2;PH-2   **Ht:** 5'9" **Wt:** 140 **Born:** 5/4/1998 **Age:** 25

Year Team	Lg	G	AB	H	2B	3B	HR	(Hm	Rd)	TB	R	RBI	RC	TBB	IBB	SO	HBP	SH	SF	SB	CS	GDP	Avg	OBP	Slg	OPS
2022 Reno	AAA	70	250	61	6	6	1	(-	-)	56	49	31	28	35	0	47	7	3	0	30	5	9	.244	.353	.328	.681
2021 Tex	AL	43	143	31	5	0	0	(0	0)	36	15	6	13	17	0	32	4	1	1	11	2	2	.217	.315	.252	.567
2022 Ari	NL	12	24	2	0	0	0	(0	0)	2	2	0	0	2	0	4	0	2	0	2	0	0	.083	.154	.083	.237
2 ML YEARS		55	167	33	5	0	0	(0	0)	38	17	6	13	19	0	36	4	3	1	13	2	2	.198	.293	.228	.521

Ivan Herrera

Bats: R **Throws:** R **Pos:** C-11   **Ht:** 5'11" **Wt:** 220 **Born:** 6/1/2000 **Age:** 23

Year Team	Lg	G	AB	H	2B	3B	HR	(Hm	Rd)	TB	R	RBI	RC	TBB	IBB	SO	HBP	SH	SF	SB	CS	GDP	Avg	OBP	Slg	OPS
2018 Cards	R	28	112	39	6	4	1	(-	-)	56	23	25	21	11	0	20	5	0	2	1	1	2	.348	.423	.500	.923
2019 2 Tms	Low	87	306	87	10	0	9	(-	-)	124	48	47	50	40	0	72	6	0	4	1	0	19	.284	.374	.405	.779
2021 Sprgfld	AA	98	363	84	13	0	17	(-	-)	148	50	63	56	60	0	96	7	0	7	2	3	10	.231	.346	.408	.753
2022 Memp	AAA	65	235	63	10	1	6	(-	-)	93	41	34	33	38	0	52	3	0	2	5	1	12	.268	.374	.396	.770
2022 StL	NL	11	18	2	0	0	0	(0	0)	2	0	1	0	2	0	8	0	1	1	0	0	0	.111	.190	.111	.302

Jose Herrera

Bats: B **Throws:** R **Pos:** C-46;DH-1;PH-1   **Ht:** 5'10" **Wt:** 217 **Born:** 2/24/1997 **Age:** 26

Year Team	Lg	G	AB	H	2B	3B	HR	(Hm	Rd)	TB	R	RBI	RC	TBB	IBB	SO	HBP	SH	SF	SB	CS	GDP	Avg	OBP	Slg	OPS
2022 Reno	AAA	26	91	31	3	0	2	(-	-)	40	16	14	15	12	0	10	1	0	0	0	0	4	.341	.423	.440	.863
2022 Ari	NL	47	111	21	2	0	0	(0	0)	23	9	5	1	9	0	34	0	4	0	0	0	1	.189	.250	.207	.457

Odubel Herrera

Bats: L **Throws:** R **Pos:** CF-48;LF-11;PH-10;RF-7   oh-DOO-bull   **Ht:** 5'11" **Wt:** 205 **Born:** 12/29/1991 **Age:** 31

Year Team	Lg	G	AB	H	2B	3B	HR	(Hm	Rd)	TB	R	RBI	RC	TBB	IBB	SO	HBP	SH	SF	SB	CS	GDP	Avg	OBP	Slg	OPS
2015 Phi	NL	147	495	147	30	3	8	(4	4)	207	64	41	66	28	0	129	8	5	1	16	8	6	.297	.344	.418	.762
2016 Phi	NL	159	583	167	21	6	15	(7	8)	245	87	49	93	63	7	134	6	2	2	25	7	6	.286	.361	.420	.781
2017 Phi	NL	138	526	148	42	3	14	(8	6)	238	67	56	63	31	4	126	4	0	2	8	5	13	.281	.325	.452	.778
2018 Phi	NL	148	550	140	19	3	22	(13	9)	231	64	71	71	38	3	122	7	1	1	5	2	11	.255	.310	.420	.730
2019 Phi	NL	39	126	28	10	1	1	(1	0)	43	12	16	13	11	0	33	1	0	1	2	2	0	.222	.288	.341	.629
2021 Phi	NL	124	450	117	27	2	13	(3	10)	187	59	51	58	29	0	77	6	1	5	6	1	6	.260	.310	.416	.726
2022 Phi	NL	62	185	44	9	1	5	(2	3)	70	23	21	17	11	0	42	0	0	1	6	0	3	.238	.279	.378	.658
7 ML YEARS		817	2915	791	158	19	78	(38	40)	1221	376	305	381	211	14	663	32	9	13	68	25	45	.271	.326	.419	.745

Codi Heuer

Pitches: R **Bats:** R **Pos:** P   **Ht:** 6'5" **Wt:** 200 **Born:** 7/3/1996 **Age:** 26

Year Team	Lg	G	GS	GF	IP	BFP	H	R	ER	HR	SH	SF	HB	TBB	IBB	SO	WP	W	L	Pct	Sv-Op	Hld	Vel	OPS	ERC	ERA
2020 CWS	AL	21	0	4	23.2	92	12	4	4	1	0	0	5	9	0	25	0	3	0	1.000	1-1	5	-	.433	1.36	1.52
2021 2 Tms		65	0	11	67.1	281	65	34	32	7	4	3	2	23	3	56	6	7	4	.636	2-5	17	-	.731	3.81	4.28
21 CWS	AL	40	0	2	38.2	166	45	22	22	5	2	1	1	10	0	39	3	4	1	.800	0-0	13	-	.802	4.83	5.12
21 ChC	NL	25	0	9	28.2	115	20	12	10	2	2	2	1	13	3	17	3	3	3	.500	2-5	4	-	.620	2.54	3.14
Postseason		2	0	1	2.1	10	2	2	2	1	0	0	0	1	0	2	0	0	0	-	0-0	0	-	.856	5.50	7.71
2 ML YEARS		86	0	15	91.0	373	77	38	36	8	4	3	2	32	3	81	6	10	4	.714	3-6	22	-	.656	3.06	3.56

Jason Heyward

Bats: L **Throws:** L **Pos:** CF-26;RF-21;PH-3   **Ht:** 6'5" **Wt:** 240 **Born:** 8/9/1989 **Age:** 33

Year Team	Lg	G	AB	H	2B	3B	HR	(Hm	Rd)	TB	R	RBI	RC	TBB	IBB	SO	HBP	SH	SF	SB	CS	GDP	Avg	OBP	Slg	OPS
2010 Atl	NL	142	520	144	29	5	18	(9	9)	237	83	72	96	91	2	128	10	0	2	11	6	13	.277	.393	.456	.849
2011 Atl	NL	128	396	90	18	2	14	(5	9)	154	50	42	49	51	4	93	4	0	3	9	2	7	.227	.319	.389	.708
2012 Atl	NL	158	587	158	30	6	27	(9	18)	281	93	82	87	58	1	152	2	0	3	21	8	4	.269	.335	.479	.814
2013 Atl	NL	104	382	97	22	1	14	(10	4)	163	67	38	55	48	1	73	8	1	0	2	4	7	.254	.349	.427	.776
2014 Atl	NL	149	573	155	26	3	11	(5	6)	220	74	58	84	67	3	98	6	0	3	20	4	2	.271	.351	.384	.735
2015 StL	NL	154	547	160	33	4	13	(5	8)	240	79	60	78	56	4	90	2	0	3	23	3	13	.293	.359	.439	.797
2016 ChC	NL	142	530	122	27	1	7	(3	4)	172	61	49	53	54	0	93	5	1	2	11	4	12	.230	.306	.325	.631
2017 ChC	NL	126	432	112	15	4	11	(4	7)	168	59	59	60	41	1	67	3	2	2	4	4	8	.259	.326	.389	.715
2018 ChC	NL	127	440	119	23	4	8	(5	3)	174	67	57	67	42	1	60	2	2	2	1	1	7	.270	.335	.395	.731
2019 ChC	NL	147	513	129	20	4	21	(8	13)	220	78	62	74	68	5	110	5	0	3	8	3	12	.251	.343	.429	.772
2020 ChC	NL	50	147	39	6	2	6	(1	5)	67	20	22	30	30	1	37	2	0	1	2	0	1	.265	.392	.456	.848

Year Team	Lg	G	AB	H	2B	3B	HR	(Hm	Rd)	TB	R	RBI	RC	TBB	IBB	SO	HBP	SH	SF	SB	CS	GDP	Avg	OBP	Slg	OPS
2021 ChC	NL	104	323	69	15	2	8	(7	1)	112	35	30	32	27	1	68	3	0	0	5	1	4	.214	.280	.347	.627
2022 ChC	NL	48	137	28	5	1	1	(0	1)	38	15	10	7	11	0	32	3	0	0	1	0	3	.204	.278	.277	.556
Postseason		40	128	20	4	1	2	(0	2)	32	8	7	5	7	2	36	3	0	0	4	0	2	.156	.217	.250	.467
13 ML YEARS		1579	5527	1422	269	39	159	(71	88)	2246	781	641	772	644	24	1101	55	6	25	118	40	93	.257	.339	.406	.746

Brewer Hicklen

Bats: R **Throws:** R **Pos:** PR-3;LF-2;RF-2;CF-1;PH-1   **Ht:** 6'2" **Wt:** 208 **Born:** 2/9/1996 **Age:** 27

Year Team	Lg	G	AB	H	2B	3B	HR	(Hm	Rd)	TB	R	RBI	RC	TBB	IBB	SO	HBP	SH	SF	SB	CS	GDP	Avg	OBP	Slg	OPS
2022 Omha	AAA	130	480	119	30	4	28	(-	-)	241	85	85	94	58	1	202	17	1	3	35	2	7	.248	.348	.502	.850
2022 KC	AL	6	4	0	0	0	0	(0	0)	0	1	0	0	0	0	4	0	0	0	0	0	0	.000	.000	.000	.000

Aaron Hicks

Bats: B **Throws:** R **Pos:** CF-81;LF-55;PH-10;PR-3;DH-1   **Ht:** 6'1" **Wt:** 205 **Born:** 10/2/1989 **Age:** 33

Year Team	Lg	G	AB	H	2B	3B	HR	(Hm	Rd)	TB	R	RBI	RC	TBB	IBB	SO	HBP	SH	SF	SB	CS	GDP	Avg	OBP	Slg	OPS
2013 Min	AL	81	281	54	11	3	8	(3	5)	95	37	27	25	24	0	84	2	4	2	9	3	0	.192	.259	.338	.597
2014 Min	AL	69	186	40	8	0	1	(0	1)	51	22	18	22	36	0	56	0	2	1	4	3	2	.215	.341	.274	.615
2015 Min	AL	97	352	90	11	3	11	(6	5)	140	48	33	45	34	2	66	2	0	2	13	3	6	.256	.323	.398	.721
2016 NYY	AL	123	327	71	13	1	8	(7	1)	110	32	31	28	30	1	68	0	1	3	3	4	7	.217	.281	.336	.617
2017 NYY	AL	88	301	80	18	0	15	(12	3)	143	54	52	52	51	0	67	3	1	5	10	5	8	.266	.372	.475	.847
2018 NYY	AL	137	480	119	18	3	27	(15	12)	224	90	79	94	90	1	111	3	2	6	11	2	1	.248	.366	.467	.833
2019 NYY	AL	59	221	52	10	0	12	(4	8)	98	41	36	34	31	0	72	0	0	3	1	2	2	.235	.325	.443	.769
2020 NYY	AL	54	169	38	10	2	6	(4	2)	70	28	21	32	41	1	38	1	0	0	4	1	4	.225	.379	.414	.793
2021 NYY	AL	32	108	21	3	0	4	(1	3)	36	13	14	10	14	0	30	2	0	2	0	0	3	.194	.294	.333	.627
2022 NYY	AL	130	384	83	9	2	8	(3	5)	120	54	40	37	62	3	109	4	1	2	10	3	10	.216	.330	.313	.642
Postseason		28	94	21	4	1	2	(1	1)	33	13	12	15	15	0	25	0	0	1	1	0	1	.223	.327	.351	.678
10 ML YEARS		870	2809	648	111	14	100	(55	45)	1087	419	351	379	413	8	701	17	11	26	65	26	43	.231	.330	.387	.717

Jordan Hicks

Pitches: R **Bats:** R **Pos:** RP-27; SP-8   **Ht:** 6'2" **Wt:** 220 **Born:** 9/6/1996 **Age:** 26

		HOW MUCH PITCHED					WHAT HE GAVE UP											THE RESULTS							
Year Team	Lg	G	GS	GF	IP	BFP	H	R	ER	HR	SH	SF	HB	TBB	IBB	SO	WP	W	L	Pct	Sv-Op	Hld	Vel	OPS	ERC	ERA
2018 StL	NL	73	0	20	77.2	339	59	33	31	2	0	2	8	45	2	70	9	3	4	.429	6-13	24	101	.587	3.24	3.59
2019 StL	NL	29	0	21	28.2	110	16	10	10	2	0	0	1	11	0	31	2	2	2	.500	14-15	3	101	.510	1.80	3.14
2021 StL	NL	10	0	1	10.0	44	5	6	6	0	0	0	0	10	0	10	3	0	0	-	0-0	3	99	.576	2.87	5.40
2022 StL	NL	35	8	2	61.1	263	46	33	33	5	0	2	7	35	0	63	5	3	6	.333	0-1	8	99	.659	3.72	4.84
4 ML YEARS		147	8	44	177.2	756	126	82	80	9	0	4	16	101	2	174	19	8	12	.400	20-29	38	100	.600	3.14	4.05

Kyle Higashioka

Bats: R **Throws:** R **Pos:** C-82;PH-2;DH-1;PR-1   he-gah-shi-oh-kah   **Ht:** 6'1" **Wt:** 202 **Born:** 4/20/1990 **Age:** 33

Year Team	Lg	G	AB	H	2B	3B	HR	(Hm	Rd)	TB	R	RBI	RC	TBB	IBB	SO	HBP	SH	SF	SB	CS	GDP	Avg	OBP	Slg	OPS
2017 NYY	AL	9	18	0	0	0	0	(0	0)	0	2	0	0	2	0	6	0	0	0	0	0	0	.000	.100	.000	.100
2018 NYY	AL	29	72	12	2	0	3	(3	0)	23	6	6	2	6	0	16	1	0	0	0	0	2	.167	.241	.319	.560
2019 NYY	AL	18	56	12	5	0	3	(0	3)	26	8	11	7	0	0	26	0	0	1	0	0	1	.214	.211	.464	.675
2020 NYY	AL	16	48	12	1	0	4	(4	0)	25	7	10	8	0	0	11	0	0	0	0	0	0	.250	.250	.521	.771
2021 NYY	AL	67	193	35	10	0	10	(3	7)	75	20	29	20	17	0	59	0	0	1	0	0	4	.181	.246	.389	.635
2022 NYY	AL	83	229	52	7	0	10	(6	4)	89	27	31	21	12	0	52	1	2	4	0	1	5	.227	.264	.389	.653
Postseason		6	20	5	0	0	1	(0	1)	8	2	2	3	1	0	5	0	0	0	0	0	0	.250	.286	.400	.686
6 ML YEARS		222	616	123	25	0	30	(16	14)	238	70	87	58	37	0	170	2	2	6	0	1	12	.200	.245	.386	.631

P.J. Higgins

Bats: R **Throws:** R **Pos:** 1B-38;C-34;PH-9;3B-4;DH-1;PR-1   **Ht:** 5'10" **Wt:** 195 **Born:** 5/10/1993 **Age:** 30

Year Team	Lg	G	AB	H	2B	3B	HR	(Hm	Rd)	TB	R	RBI	RC	TBB	IBB	SO	HBP	SH	SF	SB	CS	GDP	Avg	OBP	Slg	OPS
2022 Iowa	AAA	22	72	30	8	0	1	(-	-)	41	9	17	18	12	0	16	1	0	1	1	0	1	.417	.500	.569	1.069
2021 ChC	NL	9	23	1	0	0	0	(0	0)	1	1	0	0	2	0	8	0	0	0	0	0	2	.043	.120	.043	.163
2022 ChC	NL	74	201	46	11	1	6	(4	2)	77	23	30	29	22	0	58	2	3	1	0	0	2	.229	.310	.383	.693
2 ML YEARS		83	224	47	11	1	6	(4	2)	78	24	30	29	24	0	66	2	3	1	0	0	4	.210	.291	.348	.639

Derek Hill

Bats: R **Throws:** R **Pos:** CF-30;PR-2   **Ht:** 6'2" **Wt:** 190 **Born:** 12/30/1995 **Age:** 27

Year Team	Lg	G	AB	H	2B	3B	HR	(Hm	Rd)	TB	R	RBI	RC	TBB	IBB	SO	HBP	SH	SF	SB	CS	GDP	Avg	OBP	Slg	OPS
2022 Toledo	AAA	31	121	27	5	2	2	(-	-)	42	19	10	11	9	0	32	0	1	1	2	1	0	.223	.275	.347	.622
2022 Tacom	AAA	34	106	25	5	2	5	(-	-)	49	19	19	17	13	0	36	1	1	2	6	1	1	.236	.320	.462	.782
2020 Det	AL	15	11	1	0	0	0	(0	0)	1	3	0	1	1	0	6	0	0	0	0	0	0	.091	.167	.091	.258
2021 Det	AL	49	139	36	3	3	3	(2	1)	54	19	14	18	10	0	42	1	0	0	6	3	2	.259	.313	.388	.702
2022 Det	AL	31	83	19	2	0	1	(1	0)	24	8	3	7	5	0	28	0	3	1	3	0	0	.229	.270	.289	.559
3 ML YEARS		95	233	56	5	3	4	(3	1)	79	30	17	26	16	0	76	1	3	1	9	3	2	.240	.291	.339	.630

Garrett Hill

Pitches: R Bats: R Pos: RP-9; SP-8   Ht: 6'0" Wt: 185 Born: 1/16/1996 Age: 27

		HOW MUCH PITCHED					WHAT HE GAVE UP										THE RESULTS						
Year	Team	Lg	G	GS	GF	IP	BFP	H	R	ER	HR	SH	SF	HB	TBB	IBB	SO	WP	W	L	Pct	Sv-Op Hld	Vel	OPS	ERC	ERA
2022	Erie	AA	7	7	0	32.0	127	19	9	8	3	0	0	3	10	0	52	1	2	0	1.000	0- - -	-	.550	1.98	2.25
2022	Toledo	AAA	8	8	0	37.2	160	31	20	17	4	0	1	3	15	0	46	0	2	2	.500	0- - -	-	.689	3.43	4.06
2022	Det	AL	17	8	1	60.1	263	53	29	27	8	0	1	4	29	0	40	2	3	3	.500	0-0 1	92	.707	4.18	4.03

Rich Hill

Pitches: L Bats: L Pos: SP-26   Ht: 6'5" Wt: 221 Born: 3/11/1980 Age: 43

		HOW MUCH PITCHED					WHAT HE GAVE UP										THE RESULTS						
Year	Team	Lg	G	GS	GF	IP	BFP	H	R	ER	HR	SH	SF	HB	TBB	IBB	SO	WP	W	L	Pct	Sv-Op Hld	Vel	OPS	ERC	ERA
2005	ChC	NL	10	4	1	23.2	115	25	24	24	3	1	0	1	17	1	21	0	0	2	.000	0-0 0	90	.794	5.81	9.13
2006	ChC	NL	17	16	1	99.1	417	83	51	46	16	8	3	2	39	1	90	3	6	7	.462	0-0 0	90	.725	3.59	4.17
2007	ChC	NL	32	32	0	195.0	812	170	89	85	27	9	4	12	63	3	183	1	11	8	.579	0-0 0	89	.699	3.56	3.92
2008	ChC	NL	5	5	0	19.2	89	13	9	9	2	0	2	1	18	0	15	1	1	0	1.000	0-0 0	88	.683	4.38	4.12
2009	Bal	AL	14	13	0	57.2	275	68	53	50	7	2	2	1	40	2	46	1	3	3	.500	0-0 0	88	.886	6.55	7.80
2010	Bos	AL	6	0	0	4.0	18	5	0	0	0	0	0	0	1	0	3	0	1	0	1.000	0-0 1	89	.627	4.05	0.00
2011	Bos	AL	9	0	3	8.0	30	3	0	0	0	0	0	1	3	0	12	1	0	0	-	0-0 3	91	.349	1.10	0.00
2012	Bos	AL	25	0	3	19.2	83	17	4	4	0	0	0	0	11	1	21	0	1	0	1.000	0-6 6	92	.685	3.24	1.83
2013	Cle	AL	63	0	3	38.2	182	38	30	27	3	1	2	2	29	6	51	6	1	2	.333	0-2 13	91	.719	5.07	6.28
2014	2 Tms	AL	16	0	2	5.1	29	7	2	2	0	0	0	1	6	1	9	0	0	0	-	0-0 1	90	.801	8.55	3.38
2015	2 Tms	AL	4	4	0	29.0	106	14	5	5	2	0	0	2	5	0	36	0	2	1	.667	0-0 0	90	.410	1.13	1.55
2016	2 Tms	AL	20	20	0	110.1	439	77	29	26	4	1	2	8	33	0	129	0	12	5	.706	0-0 0	90	.530	2.04	2.12
2017	LAD	NL	25	25	0	135.2	552	99	51	50	18	4	2	9	49	1	166	2	12	8	.600	0-0 0	89	.639	2.96	3.32
2018	LAD	NL	25	24	0	132.2	547	108	57	54	20	4	1	8	41	3	150	2	11	5	.688	0-0 0	89	.689	3.24	3.66
2019	LAD	NL	13	13	0	58.2	242	48	20	16	10	4	1	4	18	2	72	0	4	1	.800	0-0 0	88	.689	3.40	2.45
2020	Min	AL	8	8	0	38.2	156	28	13	13	3	0	1	1	17	0	31	1	2	2	.500	0-0 0	88	.601	2.78	3.03
2021	2 Tms	AL	32	31	0	158.2	661	137	70	68	21	3	5	16	55	0	150	3	7	8	.467	0-0 0	88	.718	3.80	3.86
2022	Bos	AL	26	26	0	124.1	526	125	67	59	15	0	1	4	37	0	109	1	8	7	.533	0-0 0	88	.747	3.99	4.27
14	LAA	AL	2	0	0	0.0	4	1	1	1	0	0	0	0	3	0	0	1	0	0	-	0-0 0	92	2.000		
14	NYY	AL	14	0	2	5.1	25	6	1	1	0	0	0	1	3	1	9	0	0	0	-	0-0 1	90	.686	5.10	1.69
16	Oak	AL	14	14	0	76.0	311	55	22	19	2	0	1	8	28	0	90	0	9	3	.750	0-0 0	90	.559	2.44	2.25
16	LAD	NL	6	6	0	34.1	128	22	7	7	2	1	1	0	5	0	39	0	3	2	.600	0-0 0	90	.461	1.34	1.83
21	TB	AL	19	19	0	95.1	389	75	41	41	14	1	3	8	36	0	91	3	6	4	.600	0-0 0	88	.703	3.56	3.87
21	NYM	NL	13	12	0	63.1	272	62	29	27	7	2	2	8	19	0	59	0	1	4	.200	0-0 0	88	.740	4.16	3.84
	Postseason		13	12	1	53.0	234	41	18	18	5	3	1	4	32	3	65	1	1	2	.333	0-0 0	90	.643	3.71	3.06
	18 ML YEARS		350	221	13	1259.0	5279	1065	574	538	151	37	26	73	482	21	1294	22	82	59	.582	0-2 24	89	.688	3.51	3.85

Tim Hill

Pitches: L Bats: R Pos: RP-55   Ht: 6'4" Wt: 200 Born: 2/10/1990 Age: 33

		HOW MUCH PITCHED					WHAT HE GAVE UP										THE RESULTS						
Year	Team	Lg	G	GS	GF	IP	BFP	H	R	ER	HR	SH	SF	HB	TBB	IBB	SO	WP	W	L	Pct	Sv-Op Hld	Vel	OPS	ERC	ERA
2018	KC	AL	70	0	9	45.2	198	46	28	23	4	2	1	2	14	0	42	0	1	4	.200	2-4 13	91	.691	3.77	4.53
2019	KC	AL	46	0	4	39.2	161	31	17	16	4	1	0	4	13	2	39	0	2	0	1.000	1-2 9	91	.636	3.01	3.63
2020	SD	NL	23	0	3	18.0	79	17	9	9	3	0	0	2	6	1	20	1	3	0	1.000	0-0 5	91	.739	4.22	4.50
2021	SD	NL	78	0	10	59.2	255	51	34	24	9	2	2	6	23	5	56	1	6	6	.500	1-5 17	92	.704	3.81	3.62
2022	SD	NL	55	0	21	48.0	199	45	20	19	1	0	2	4	14	1	25	1	3	0	1.000	0-0 7	90	.629	3.13	3.56
	Postseason		3	0	0	2.1	10	1	1	0	0	0	0	1	1	0	3	0	0	0	-	0-0 0	91	.425	2.03	0.00
	5 ML YEARS		272	0	47	211.0	892	190	108	91	21	5	5	18	70	9	182	3	15	10	.600	4-11 51	91	.675	3.53	3.88

Sam Hilliard

Bats: L Throws: L Pos: LF-59;CF-14;PR-9;RF-3   Ht: 6'5" Wt: 236 Born: 2/21/1994 Age: 29

			BATTING																RUNNING			AVERAGES			
Year	Team	Lg	G	AB	H	2B	3B	HR	(Hm | Rd)	TB	R	RBI	RC	TBB	IBB	SO	HBP	SH	SF	SB	CS	GDP	Avg	OBP	Slg	OPS
2022	Albq	AAA	37	133	41	5	2	13	(- | -)	89	27	32	37	21	0	39	2	0	2	4	1	4	.308	.405	.669	1.074
2019	Col	NL	27	77	21	4	2	7	(5 | 2)	50	13	13	17	9	0	23	1	0	0	2	0	1	.273	.356	.649	1.006
2020	Col	NL	36	105	22	2	2	6	(1 | 5)	46	13	10	12	9	0	42	0	0	0	3	0	0	.210	.272	.438	.710
2021	Col	NL	81	214	46	7	2	14	(6 | 8)	99	32	34	33	23	3	87	1	0	0	5	0	0	.215	.294	.463	.757
2022	Col	NL	70	174	32	6	1	2	(2 | 0)	46	26	14	13	23	0	57	1	0	2	5	1	2	.184	.280	.264	.544
	4 ML YEARS		214	570	121	19	7	29	(14 | 15)	241	84	71	75	64	3	209	3	0	2	15	1	3	.212	.294	.423	.717

Keston Hiura

Bats: R Throws: R Pos: 1B-33;DH-26;2B-14;PH-7;LF-5;PR-2   Ht: 6'0" Wt: 202 Born: 8/2/1996 Age: 26

			BATTING																RUNNING			AVERAGES			
Year	Team	Lg	G	AB	H	2B	3B	HR	(Hm | Rd)	TB	R	RBI	RC	TBB	IBB	SO	HBP	SH	SF	SB	CS	GDP	Avg	OBP	Slg	OPS
2022	Nashv	AAA	13	47	15	1	0	6	(- | -)	34	8	18	15	9	0	15	3	0	0	0	3	0	.319	.458	.723	1.181
2019	Mil	NL	84	314	95	23	2	19	(10 | 9)	179	51	49	53	25	1	107	8	0	1	9	3	6	.303	.368	.570	.938
2020	Mil	NL	59	217	46	4	0	13	(6 | 7)	89	30	32	28	16	2	85	11	0	2	3	2	7	.212	.297	.410	.707
2021	Mil	NL	61	173	29	9	1	4	(3 | 1)	52	16	19	17	14	0	77	7	2	1	3	0	6	.168	.256	.301	.557
2022	Mil	NL	80	234	53	8	1	14	(7 | 7)	105	34	32	35	23	0	111	8	0	1	5	2	3	.226	.316	.449	.765
	Postseason		3	10	2	1	0	0	(0 | 0)	3	0	0	0	1	0	5	0	0	0	0	0	0	.200	.273	.300	.573
	4 ML YEARS		284	938	223	44	4	50	(26 | 24)	425	131	132	133	78	3	380	34	2	5	20	7	22	.238	.318	.453	.771

Sean Hjelle

Pitches: R Bats: R Pos: RP-8

JEL-ee

Ht: 6'11" Wt: 228 Born: 5/7/1997 Age: 26

Year	Team	Lg	G	GS	GF	IP	BFP	H	R	ER	HR	SH	SF	HB	TBB	IBB	SO	WP	W	L	Pct	Sv-Op	Hld	Vel	OPS	ERC	ERA
2022	Scrmto	AAA	22	22	0	97.0	443	112	62	53	11	1	3	11	38	0	80	6	6	8	.429	0- -	-	-	.810	5.49	4.92
2022	SF	NL	8	0	0	25.0	115	33	19	16	3	0	0	1	8	0	28	1	1	2	.333	0-0	0	94	.790	5.91	5.76

Header groups: HOW MUCH PITCHED | WHAT HE GAVE UP | THE RESULTS

Bryan Hoeing

Pitches: R Bats: R Pos: RP-7; SP-1

Ht: 6'6" Wt: 210 Born: 10/19/1996 Age: 26

Year	Team	Lg	G	GS	GF	IP	BFP	H	R	ER	HR	SH	SF	HB	TBB	IBB	SO	WP	W	L	Pct	Sv-Op	Hld	Vel	OPS	ERC	ERA
2022	Jaxnvl	AAA	18	17	0	94.0	406	100	56	53	14	2	6	6	35	0	49	2	7	5	.583	0- -	-	-	.817	5.05	5.07
2022	Mia	NL	8	1	0	12.2	61	19	17	17	5	1	1	0	5	0	6	1	1	1	.500	0-0	0	93	1.122	9.57	12.08

Nico Hoerner

Bats: R Throws: R Pos: SS-133;PH-3;3B-1;DH-1

Ht: 6'1" Wt: 200 Born: 5/13/1997 Age: 26

Year	Team	Lg	G	AB	H	2B	3B	HR	(Hm	Rd)	TB	R	RBI	RC	TBB	IBB	SO	HBP	SH	SF	SB	CS	GDP	Avg	OBP	Slg	OPS
2019	ChC	NL	20	78	22	1	1	3	(3	0)	34	13	17	14	3	1	11	0	0	1	0	0	3	.282	.305	.436	.741
2020	ChC	NL	48	108	24	4	0	0	(0	0)	28	19	13	14	12	0	24	3	0	2	3	2	3	.222	.312	.259	.571
2021	ChC	NL	44	149	45	10	0	0	(0	0)	55	13	16	26	17	3	25	3	0	1	5	3	3	.302	.382	.369	.751
2022	ChC	NL	135	481	135	22	5	10	(4	6)	197	60	55	65	28	4	57	6	0	2	20	2	11	.281	.327	.410	.736
	4 ML YEARS		247	816	226	37	6	13	(7	6)	314	105	101	119	60	8	117	12	0	6	28	7	20	.277	.333	.385	.718

Header groups: BATTING | RUNNING | AVERAGES

Jeff Hoffman

Pitches: R Bats: R Pos: RP-34; SP-1

Ht: 6'5" Wt: 235 Born: 1/8/1993 Age: 30

Year	Team	Lg	G	GS	GF	IP	BFP	H	R	ER	HR	SH	SF	HB	TBB	IBB	SO	WP	W	L	Pct	Sv-Op	Hld	Vel	OPS	ERC	ERA
2016	Col	NL	8	6	0	31.1	147	37	29	17	7	1	0	0	17	1	22	4	0	4	.000	0-0	0	94	.881	6.55	4.88
2017	Col	NL	23	16	3	99.1	440	106	66	65	15	3	5	4	40	1	82	2	6	5	.545	0-0	0	94	.833	4.97	5.89
2018	Col	NL	6	1	1	8.2	44	15	9	9	0	0	0	0	7	1	5	1	0	0	-	0-0	1	93	.986	9.88	9.35
2019	Col	NL	15	15	0	70.0	315	77	51	51	21	3	2	4	34	3	68	2	2	6	.250	0-0	0	94	.957	6.81	6.56
2020	Col	NL	16	0	5	21.1	104	32	23	22	3	0	2	2	9	1	20	4	2	1	.667	1-1	0	94	.985	7.93	9.28
2021	Cin	NL	31	11	7	73.0	335	70	41	37	12	1	2	5	45	2	79	9	3	5	.375	0-0	2	94	.795	5.37	4.56
2022	Cin	NL	35	1	7	44.2	197	40	22	19	5	0	1	3	23	1	45	3	2	0	1.000	0-1	1	94	.741	4.23	3.83
	7 ML YEARS		134	50	23	348.1	1582	377	241	220	63	8	12	18	175	10	321	25	15	21	.417	1-2	4	94	.857	5.75	5.68

Colin Holderman

Pitches: R Bats: R Pos: RP-24

Ht: 6'7" Wt: 240 Born: 10/8/1995 Age: 27

Year	Team	Lg	G	GS	GF	IP	BFP	H	R	ER	HR	SH	SF	HB	TBB	IBB	SO	WP	W	L	Pct	Sv-Op	Hld	Vel	OPS	ERC	ERA
2022	Syrcse	AAA	11	0	5	14.1	56	9	5	4	2	0	1	3	3	0	17	1	1	0	1.000	3- -	-	-	.546	1.94	2.51
2022	2 Tms	NL	24	0	6	28.1	118	20	14	12	0	1	2	4	14	1	24	0	5	0	1.000	0-0	2	96	.572	2.70	3.81
22	NYM	NL	15	0	5	17.2	67	11	6	4	0	0	1	0	7	0	18	0	4	0	1.000	0-0	1	96	.489	1.66	2.04
22	Pit	NL	9	0	1	10.2	51	9	8	8	0	1	1	4	7	1	6	0	1	0	1.000	0-0	1	97	.689	4.62	6.75

Greg Holland

Pitches: R Bats: R Pos: RP-5

Ht: 5'10" Wt: 210 Born: 11/20/1985 Age: 37

Year	Team	Lg	G	GS	GF	IP	BFP	H	R	ER	HR	SH	SF	HB	TBB	IBB	SO	WP	W	L	Pct	Sv-Op	Hld	Vel	OPS	ERC	ERA
2010	KC	AL	15	0	10	18.2	87	23	15	14	3	1	0	0	8	0	23	2	0	1	.000	0-0	0	96	.835	5.88	6.75
2011	KC	AL	46	0	15	60.0	233	37	13	12	3	1	1	1	19	3	74	7	5	1	.833	4-6	18	96	.521	1.60	1.80
2012	KC	AL	67	0	36	67.0	289	58	22	22	2	4	3	0	34	7	91	3	7	4	.636	16-20	9	96	.653	3.07	2.96
2013	KC	AL	68	0	61	67.0	255	40	11	9	3	1	1	0	18	1	103	2	2	1	.667	47-50	1	96	.479	1.41	1.21
2014	KC	AL	65	0	60	62.1	240	37	13	10	3	1	1	0	20	0	90	9	1	3	.250	46-48	0	96	.472	1.54	1.44
2015	KC	AL	48	0	40	44.2	193	37	20	19	2	3	1	0	26	1	49	7	3	2	.600	32-37	0	94	.692	3.68	3.83
2017	Col	NL	61	0	58	57.1	235	40	24	23	7	0	1	1	26	1	70	7	3	6	.333	41-45	1	93	.623	2.86	3.61
2018	2 Tms	NL	56	0	13	46.1	212	43	30	24	2	1	0	1	32	2	47	0	2	2	.500	3-6	6	93	.697	4.33	4.66
2019	Ari	NL	40	0	27	35.2	152	25	18	18	5	0	2	0	24	2	41	6	1	2	.333	17-22	0	92	.687	3.71	4.54
2020	KC	AL	28	0	9	28.1	112	20	8	6	1	1	1	3	7	1	31	1	3	0	1.000	6-6	2	93	.580	1.98	1.91
2021	KC	AL	57	0	24	55.2	243	49	32	30	9	1	1	2	26	2	53	6	3	5	.375	8-12	8	93	.721	4.03	4.85
2022	KC	AL	5	0	2	4.2	20	6	5	4	3	0	1	0	1	0	5	0	0	1	.000	0-0	0	94	1.183	9.29	7.71
18	StL	NL	32	0	7	25.0	132	34	28	22	1	1	0	0	22	2	22	0	0	2	.000	0-3	2	93	.859	7.32	7.92
18	Was	NL	24	0	6	21.1	80	9	2	2	1	0	0	1	10	0	25	0	2	0	1.000	3-3	4	93	.438	1.48	0.84
	Postseason		12	0	11	11.2	49	7	3	3	0	0	0	0	6	2	15	1	0	0	-	7-7	0	95	.475	1.54	2.31
	12 ML YEARS		556	0	355	547.2	2271	417	211	191	43	14	13	7	241	20	677	50	30	28	.517	220-252	45	95	.622	2.80	3.14

Jackson Holliday

Bats: L Throws: R Pos: SS

Ht: 6'1" Wt: 175 Born: 12/4/2003 Age: 19

Year	Team	Lg	G	AB	H	2B	3B	HR	(Hm	Rd)	TB	R	RBI	RC	TBB	IBB	SO	HBP	SH	SF	SB	CS	GDP	Avg	OBP	Slg	OPS
2022	Dlmrva	A	12	42	10	4	0	0	(-	-)	14	8	6	6	15	1	10	0	0	0	1	1	1	.238	.439	.333	.772

Jordan Holloway

Pitches: R Bats: R Pos: RP-1   Ht: 6'6" Wt: 230 Born: 6/13/1996 Age: 27

	HOW MUCH PITCHED					WHAT HE GAVE UP											THE RESULTS							
Year Team	Lg	G	GS	GF	IP	BFP	H	R	ER	HR	SH	SF	HB	TBB	IBB	SO	WP	W	L	Pct	Sv-Op	Hld	Vel	OPS	ERC	ERA
2022 Jaxnvl	AAA	8	2	0	17.2	78	12	13	13	4	0	1	0	16	0	24	2	0	1	.000	0- -	-	-	.802	5.32	6.62
2020 Mia	NL	1	0	0	0.1	4	2	0	0	0	0	0	0	1	0	0	0	0	0	-	0-0	0	97	1.417	56.02	0.00
2021 Mia	NL	13	4	2	36.0	158	23	19	16	3	0	2	0	26	0	36	2	2	3	.400	0-0	0	96	.626	3.13	4.00
2022 Mia	NL	1	0	0	2.2	11	3	1	1	0	0	0	0	1	0	2	0	0	0	-	0-0	0	96	.764	4.24	3.38
3 ML YEARS		15	4	2	39.0	173	28	20	17	3	0	2	0	28	0	38	2	2	3	.400	0-0	0	96	.652	3.49	3.92

Gavin Hollowell

Pitches: R Bats: R Pos: RP-6   Ht: 6'7" Wt: 215 Born: 11/4/1997 Age: 25

	HOW MUCH PITCHED					WHAT HE GAVE UP											THE RESULTS							
Year Team	Lg	G	GS	GF	IP	BFP	H	R	ER	HR	SH	SF	HB	TBB	IBB	SO	WP	W	L	Pct	Sv-Op	Hld	Vel	OPS	ERC	ERA
2022 Hrtfrd	AA	42	0	37	48.2	188	30	18	17	3	0	1	5	14	1	64	2	4	2	.667	16- -	-	-	.540	1.89	3.14
2022 Col	NL	6	0	3	7.0	32	7	7	6	1	0	1	0	4	0	8	0	0	2	.000	0-0	0	93	.751	4.97	7.71

Clay Holmes

Pitches: R Bats: R Pos: RP-62   Ht: 6'5" Wt: 245 Born: 3/27/1993 Age: 30

	HOW MUCH PITCHED					WHAT HE GAVE UP											THE RESULTS							
Year Team	Lg	G	GS	GF	IP	BFP	H	R	ER	HR	SH	SF	HB	TBB	IBB	SO	WP	W	L	Pct	Sv-Op	Hld	Vel	OPS	ERC	ERA
2018 Pit	NL	11	4	6	26.1	129	30	21	20	2	0	1	2	23	1	21	4	1	3	.250	0-1	0	94	.824	6.99	6.84
2019 Pit	NL	35	0	10	50.0	240	45	36	31	5	0	0	9	36	1	56	4	1	2	.333	0-1	1	94	.743	5.32	5.58
2020 Pit	NL	1	0	0	1.1	6	2	0	0	0	0	0	0	0	0	1	0	0	0	-	0-0	0	92	.667	4.47	0.00
2021 2 Tms		69	0	15	70.0	292	53	32	28	5	1	1	4	29	2	78	9	8	4	.667	0-2	11	96	.580	2.80	3.60
2022 NYY	AL	62	0	32	63.2	260	45	21	18	2	0	0	9	20	2	65	1	7	4	.636	20-25	7	97	.547	2.27	2.54
21 Pit	NL	44	0	10	42.0	189	35	24	23	3	1	0	4	25	2	44	5	3	2	.600	0-0	6	96	.649	3.91	4.93
21 NYY	AL	25	0	5	28.0	103	18	8	5	2	0	1	0	4	0	34	4	5	2	.714	0-2	5	97	.458	1.40	1.61
Postseason		1	0	0	2.0	5	1	0	0	0	0	0	0	0	0	1	0	0	0	-	0-0	0	97	.400	0.75	0.00
5 ML YEARS		178	4	63	211.1	927	175	110	97	14	1	2	24	108	6	221	18	17	13	.567	20-29	19	96	.645	3.67	4.13

Tyler Holton

Pitches: L Bats: L Pos: RP-10   Ht: 6'2" Wt: 200 Born: 6/13/1996 Age: 27

	HOW MUCH PITCHED					WHAT HE GAVE UP											THE RESULTS							
Year Team	Lg	G	GS	GF	IP	BFP	H	R	ER	HR	SH	SF	HB	TBB	IBB	SO	WP	W	L	Pct	Sv-Op	Hld	Vel	OPS	ERC	ERA
2022 Reno	AAA	24	2	3	44.2	183	39	23	22	5	1	1	0	17	0	43	3	5	0	1.000	1- -	-	-	.674	3.47	4.43
2022 Ari	NL	10	0	5	9.0	39	8	3	3	1	0	0	1	2	0	6	1	0	0	-	0-0	0	91	.615	3.12	3.00

Rhys Hoskins

Bats: R Throws: R Pos: 1B-151;DH-4;PH-2   REES   Ht: 6'4" Wt: 245 Born: 3/17/1993 Age: 30

		BATTING																		RUNNING			AVERAGES			
Year Team	Lg	G	AB	H	2B	3B	HR	(Hm	Rd)	TB	R	RBI	RC	TBB	IBB	SO	HBP	SH	SF	SB	CS	GDP	Avg	OBP	Slg	OPS
2017 Phi	NL	50	170	44	7	0	18	(10	8)	105	37	48	45	37	1	46	3	0	2	2	0	2	.259	.396	.618	1.014
2018 Phi	NL	153	558	137	38	0	34	(20	14)	277	89	96	97	87	2	150	9	0	5	5	3	7	.246	.354	.496	.850
2019 Phi	NL	160	570	129	33	5	29	(16	13)	259	86	85	97	116	6	173	11	0	6	2	2	10	.226	.364	.454	.819
2020 Phi	NL	41	151	37	9	0	10	(4	6)	76	35	26	29	29	0	43	5	0	0	1	0	4	.245	.384	.503	.887
2021 Phi	NL	107	389	96	29	0	27	(9	18)	206	64	71	62	47	0	108	5	0	2	3	2	7	.247	.334	.530	.864
2022 Phi	NL	156	589	145	33	2	30	(18	12)	272	81	79	96	72	0	169	6	0	1	2	1	12	.246	.332	.462	.794
6 ML YEARS		667	2427	588	149	7	148	(77	71)	1195	392	405	426	388	9	689	39	0	19	15	8	42	.242	.353	.492	.846

Eric Hosmer

Bats: L Throws: L Pos: 1B-102;DH-2   HOZ-mur   Ht: 6'4" Wt: 226 Born: 10/24/1989 Age: 33

		BATTING																		RUNNING			AVERAGES			
Year Team	Lg	G	AB	H	2B	3B	HR	(Hm	Rd)	TB	R	RBI	RC	TBB	IBB	SO	HBP	SH	SF	SB	CS	GDP	Avg	OBP	Slg	OPS
2011 KC	AL	128	523	153	27	3	19	(3	16)	243	66	78	71	34	7	82	1	0	5	11	5	13	.293	.334	.465	.799
2012 KC	AL	152	535	124	22	2	14	(8	6)	192	65	60	61	56	4	95	2	0	5	16	1	10	.232	.304	.359	.663
2013 KC	AL	159	623	188	34	3	17	(10	7)	279	86	79	88	51	4	100	1	1	4	11	4	15	.302	.353	.448	.801
2014 KC	AL	131	503	136	35	1	9	(5	4)	200	54	58	62	35	4	93	3	0	6	4	2	12	.270	.318	.398	.716
2015 KC	AL	158	599	178	33	5	18	(10	8)	275	98	93	94	61	6	108	3	1	3	7	3	16	.297	.363	.459	.822
2016 KC	AL	158	605	161	24	1	25	(8	17)	262	80	104	87	57	5	132	1	0	4	5	3	18	.266	.328	.433	.761
2017 KC	AL	162	603	192	31	1	25	(16	9)	300	98	94	116	66	3	104	0	0	2	6	1	20	.318	.385	.498	.882
2018 SD	NL	157	613	155	31	2	18	(10	8)	244	72	69	77	62	10	142	1	0	1	7	4	18	.253	.322	.398	.720
2019 SD	NL	160	619	164	29	2	22	(11	11)	263	72	99	87	40	3	163	0	3	5	0	3	15	.265	.310	.425	.735
2020 SD	NL	38	143	41	6	0	9	(4	5)	74	23	36	27	9	0	28	2	0	2	4	0	3	.287	.333	.517	.851
2021 SD	NL	151	509	137	28	0	12	(7	5)	201	53	65	70	48	2	99	5	1	2	5	4	13	.269	.337	.395	.732
2022 2 Tms		104	380	102	19	0	8	(4	4)	145	38	44	41	37	5	64	1	0	1	0	0	10	.268	.334	.382	.716
22 SD	NL	90	335	91	16	0	8	(4	4)	131	32	40	36	33	5	55	0	0	1	0	0	10	.272	.336	.391	.727
22 Bos	AL	14	45	11	3	0	0	(0	0)	14	6	4	5	4	0	9	1	0	0	0	0	2	.244	.320	.311	.631
Postseason		37	148	38	6	1	4	(1	3)	58	21	33	22	13	2	38	0	0	4	1	1	2	.257	.309	.392	.701
12 ML YEARS		1658	6255	1731	319	20	196	(96	100)	2678	805	879	881	556	53	1210	23	3	40	76	30	162	.277	.336	.428	.764

Tanner Houck

Pitches: R **Bats:** R **Pos:** RP-28; SP-4   **Ht:** 6'5" **Wt:** 230 **Born:** 6/29/1996 **Age:** 27

Year	Team	Lg	G	GS	GF	IP	BFP	H	R	ER	HR	SH	SF	HB	TBB	IBB	SO	WP	W	L	Pct	Sv-Op	Hld	Vel	OPS	ERC	ERA
2020	Bos	AL	3	3	0	17.0	63	6	2	1	1	0	0	1	9	0	21	1	3	0	1.000	0-0	0	92	.443	1.49	0.53
2021	Bos	AL	18	13	2	69.0	285	57	32	27	4	1	1	6	21	1	87	3	1	5	.167	1-1	1	94	.608	2.82	3.52
2022	Bos	AL	32	4	14	60.0	247	49	22	21	3	1	1	6	22	3	56	3	5	4	.556	8-9	1	95	.608	3.00	3.15
	Postseason		5	0	0	10.1	38	7	6	6	3	0	0	0	0	0	10	0	1	0	1.000	0-1	1	95	.643	2.32	5.23
	3 ML YEARS		53	20	16	146.0	595	112	56	49	8	2	2	13	52	4	164	7	9	9	.500	9-10	2	94	.591	2.72	3.02

Adrian Houser

Pitches: R **Bats:** R **Pos:** SP-21; RP-1   HOW-zer   **Ht:** 6'3" **Wt:** 222 **Born:** 2/2/1993 **Age:** 30

Year	Team	Lg	G	GS	GF	IP	BFP	H	R	ER	HR	SH	SF	HB	TBB	IBB	SO	WP	W	L	Pct	Sv-Op	Hld	Vel	OPS	ERC	ERA
2015	Mil	NL	2	0	2	2.0	8	1	0	0	0	0	0	0	2	0	0	0	0	0	-	0-0	0	94	.542	3.21	0.00
2018	Mil	NL	7	0	5	13.2	59	13	5	5	0	0	0	1	7	0	8	1	0	0	-	0-0	0	94	.728	3.89	3.29
2019	Mil	NL	35	18	7	111.1	462	101	49	46	14	3	3	5	37	2	117	2	6	7	.462	0-0	1	94	.710	3.68	3.72
2020	Mil	NL	12	11	1	56.0	246	63	41	33	8	0	4	4	21	0	44	1	1	6	.143	0-0	0	93	.815	5.41	5.30
2021	Mil	NL	28	26	0	142.1	599	118	61	51	12	6	1	9	64	0	105	9	10	6	.625	0-0	0	94	.662	3.51	3.22
2022	Mil	NL	22	21	1	102.2	455	103	66	54	8	0	6	2	47	1	69	2	6	10	.375	0-0	0	94	.722	4.17	4.73
	Postseason		3	0	1	5.0	21	5	4	4	2	0	0	0	2	0	2	0	1	1	.500	0-0	0	94	.912	6.39	7.20
	6 ML YEARS		106	76	16	428.0	1829	399	222	189	42	9	10	21	178	3	343	15	23	29	.442	0-0	1	94	.712	3.96	3.97

Sam Howard

Pitches: L **Bats:** R **Pos:** RP-3   **Ht:** 6'4" **Wt:** 195 **Born:** 3/5/1993 **Age:** 30

Year	Team	Lg	G	GS	GF	IP	BFP	H	R	ER	HR	SH	SF	HB	TBB	IBB	SO	WP	W	L	Pct	Sv-Op	Hld	Vel	OPS	ERC	ERA
2022	Toledo	AAA	40	0	1	34.0	144	25	15	12	6	0	1	0	20	0	41	0	2	1	.667	0- -	-	-	.711	3.89	3.18
2018	Col	NL	4	0	4	4.0	20	5	1	1	0	0	0	1	3	0	1	0	0	0	-	0-0	0	92	.888	7.36	2.25
2019	Col	NL	20	0	3	19.0	91	21	16	14	5	2	0	3	10	0	23	2	2	0	1.000	0-0	0	93	.895	7.04	6.63
2020	Pit	NL	22	0	4	21.0	90	17	10	9	4	0	1	3	9	0	27	0	2	3	.400	0-2	4	92	.764	4.34	3.86
2021	Pit	NL	54	1	5	45.0	199	34	29	28	7	1	2	3	32	1	60	2	3	4	.429	0-1	11	93	.727	4.58	5.60
2022	Pit	NL	3	0	2	2.0	12	2	2	2	1	0	0	1	4	0	1	0	0	0	-	0-0	0	91	1.298	19.07	9.00
	5 ML YEARS		103	1	18	91.0	412	79	58	54	17	3	3	11	58	1	112	4	7	7	.500	0-3	15	93	.795	5.40	5.34

Spencer Howard

Pitches: R **Bats:** R **Pos:** SP-8; RP-2   **Ht:** 6'3" **Wt:** 210 **Born:** 7/28/1996 **Age:** 26

Year	Team	Lg	G	GS	GF	IP	BFP	H	R	ER	HR	SH	SF	HB	TBB	IBB	SO	WP	W	L	Pct	Sv-Op	Hld	Vel	OPS	ERC	ERA
2022	RdRck	AAA	14	12	0	59.0	254	53	35	31	6	0	1	3	25	0	73	4	3	6	.333	0- -	-	-	.697	3.80	4.73
2020	Phi	NL	6	6	0	24.1	113	30	17	16	6	0	2	1	10	0	23	0	1	2	.333	0-0	0	94	.893	6.73	5.92
2021	2 Tms		19	15	1	49.2	229	53	45	41	7	0	2	3	27	0	52	5	0	5	.000	0-0	0	94	.814	5.55	7.43
2022	Tex	AL	10	8	0	37.2	179	50	33	31	12	0	1	1	15	1	32	1	2	4	.333	0-0	0	94	.986	7.68	7.41
21	Phi	NL	11	7	1	28.1	127	25	19	18	2	0	1	3	17	0	31	2	0	2	.000	0-0	0	95	.751	4.39	5.72
21	Tex	AL	8	8	0	21.1	102	28	26	23	5	0	1	0	10	0	21	3	0	3	.000	0-0	0	94	.889	7.16	9.70
	3 ML YEARS		35	29	1	111.2	521	133	95	88	25	0	5	5	52	1	107	6	3	11	.214	0-0	0	94	.892	6.52	7.09

Dakota Hudson

Pitches: R **Bats:** R **Pos:** SP-26; RP-1   **Ht:** 6'5" **Wt:** 215 **Born:** 9/15/1994 **Age:** 28

Year	Team	Lg	G	GS	GF	IP	BFP	H	R	ER	HR	SH	SF	HB	TBB	IBB	SO	WP	W	L	Pct	Sv-Op	Hld	Vel	OPS	ERC	ERA
2018	StL	NL	26	0	2	27.1	118	19	9	8	0	0	2	1	18	0	19	2	4	1	.800	0-0	11	96	.559	2.82	2.63
2019	StL	NL	33	32	1	174.2	757	160	80	65	22	3	7	9	86	8	136	5	16	7	.696	1-1	0	94	.742	4.32	3.35
2020	StL	NL	8	8	0	39.0	151	24	13	12	5	0	0	1	15	1	31	0	3	2	.600	0-0	0	93	.583	2.34	2.77
2021	StL	NL	2	1	0	8.2	34	7	2	2	0	0	0	1	1	0	6	1	1	0	1.000	0-0	0	92	.546	1.90	2.08
2022	StL	NL	27	26	0	139.2	596	141	71	69	9	3	6	9	61	0	78	4	8	7	.533	0-0	0	92	.731	4.43	4.45
	Postseason		2	2	0	5.0	28	10	11	5	1	0	2	0	3	1	2	0	0	1	.000	0-0	0	93	1.160	11.75	9.00
	5 ML YEARS		96	67	3	389.1	1656	351	175	156	36	6	15	21	181	9	270	12	32	17	.653	1-1	11	93	.706	3.98	3.61

Daniel Hudson

Pitches: R **Bats:** R **Pos:** RP-25   **Ht:** 6'3" **Wt:** 215 **Born:** 3/9/1987 **Age:** 36

Year	Team	Lg	G	GS	GF	IP	BFP	H	R	ER	HR	SH	SF	HB	TBB	IBB	SO	WP	W	L	Pct	Sv-Op	Hld	Vel	OPS	ERC	ERA
2009	CWS	AL	6	2	1	18.2	82	16	9	7	3	0	1	1	9	0	14	1	1	1	.500	0-0	0	93	.711	4.15	3.38
2010	2 Tms		14	14	0	95.1	372	68	26	26	8	2	2	4	27	1	84	5	8	2	.800	0-0	0	93	.579	2.26	2.45
2011	Ari	NL	33	33	0	222.0	921	217	98	86	17	6	6	8	50	1	169	4	16	12	.571	0-0	0	93	.694	3.26	3.49
2012	Ari	NL	9	9	0	45.1	202	62	37	37	9	2	1	6	12	0	37	2	3	2	.600	0-0	0	93	.910	6.56	7.35
2014	Ari	NL	3	0	0	2.2	13	4	4	4	0	0	0	0	0	0	2	0	0	1	.000	0-0	0	95	.769	4.08	13.50
2015	Ari	NL	64	1	13	67.2	290	64	34	29	7	1	3	0	25	2	71	5	4	3	.571	4-6	20	96	.691	3.58	3.86
2016	Ari	NL	70	0	17	60.1	268	65	40	35	6	0	4	4	23	3	58	5	3	2	.600	5-7	17	96	.753	4.51	5.22
2017	Pit	NL	71	0	18	61.2	271	57	34	30	7	1	2	5	33	1	66	4	2	7	.222	0-2	21	96	.761	4.63	4.38
2018	LAD	NL	40	1	11	46.0	197	38	25	21	6	0	4	4	18	1	44	3	3	2	.600	0-1	3	95	.653	3.54	4.11
2019	2 Tms		69	1	25	73.0	304	56	25	20	8	1	5	4	27	2	71	2	9	3	.750	8-12	11	96	.650	2.91	2.47
2020	Was	NL	21	0	15	20.2	92	15	15	14	6	1	0	3	11	0	28	0	3	2	.600	10-15	0	96	.786	4.83	6.10
2021	2 Tms		54	0	18	51.2	210	40	22	19	8	0	4	1	16	1	75	3	5	3	.625	0-3	16	97	.672	2.81	3.31
2022	LAD	NL	25	0	8	24.1	97	17	7	6	1	1	4	2	5	0	30	4	2	3	.400	5-6	9	97	.511	1.76	2.22

Year	Team	Lg	G	GS	GF	IP	BFP	H	R	ER	HR	SH	SF	HB	TBB	IBB	SO	WP	W	L	Pct	Sv-Op	Hld	Vel	OPS	ERC	ERA
10	CWS	AL	3	3	0	15.2	71	17	11	11	1	1	0	1	11	0	14	2	1	1	.500	0-0	0	93	.797	5.69	6.32
10	Ari	NL	11	11	0	79.2	301	51	15	15	7	1	1	4	16	1	70	3	7	1	.875	0-0	0	92	.531	1.70	1.69
19	Tor	AL	45	1	11	48.0	207	38	18	16	5	1	3	3	23	0	48	1	6	3	.667	2-4	8	96	.678	3.45	3.00
19	Was	NL	24	0	14	25.0	97	18	7	4	3	0	2	1	4	2	23	1	3	0	1.000	6-8	3	96	.593	1.93	1.44
21	Was	NL	31	0	2	32.2	127	23	9	8	4	0	2	0	7	0	48	1	4	1	.800	0-2	14	97	.575	2.00	2.20
21	SD	NL	23	0	6	19.0	83	17	13	11	4	0	2	0	9	1	27	2	1	2	.333	0-1	2	97	.827	4.37	5.21
Postseason			10	1	6	15.0	69	20	9	9	2	0	0	1	4	2	16	0	1	1	.500	4-4	1	96	.878	5.72	5.40
13 ML YEARS			479	61	116	789.1	3319	719	376	334	86	15	25	35	255	12	749	38	59	43	.578	32-52	97	95	.694	3.49	3.81

Sam Huff

Bats: R Throws: R Pos: C-29;PH-7;1B-6;DH-4 Ht: 6'5" Wt: 240 Born: 1/14/1998 Age: 25

									BATTING											RUNNING			AVERAGES			
Year	Team	Lg	G	AB	H	2B	3B	HR	(Hm | Rd)	TB	R	RBI	RC	TBB	IBB	SO	HBP	SH	SF	SB	CS	GDP	Avg	OBP	Slg	OPS
2022	RdRck	AAA	63	246	64	4	0	21	(- | -)	131	46	50	48	25	1	85	3	0	0	0	0	8	.260	.336	.533	.868
2020	Tex	AL	10	31	11	3	0	3	(2 | 1)	23	5	4	7	2	0	11	0	0	0	0	0	0	.355	.394	.742	1.136
2022	Tex	AL	44	121	29	4	0	4	(3 | 1)	45	9	10	14	11	1	42	0	0	0	1	0	1	.240	.303	.372	.675
2 ML YEARS			54	152	40	7	0	7	(5 | 2)	68	14	14	21	13	1	53	0	0	0	1	0	1	.263	.321	.447	.769

Brandon Hughes

Pitches: L Bats: B Pos: RP-57 Ht: 6'2" Wt: 215 Born: 12/1/1995 Age: 27

Year	Team	Lg	G	GS	GF	IP	BFP	H	R	ER	HR	SH	SF	HB	TBB	IBB	SO	WP	W	L	Pct	Sv-Op	Hld	Vel	OPS	ERC	ERA
2022	Tenn	AA	5	0	4	6.1	22	1	0	0	0	0	0	0	1	0	10	0	0	0	-	1- -	-	-	.186	0.16	0.00
2022	Iowa	AAA	5	0	0	10.1	36	4	0	0	0	0	0	0	2	0	12	0	1	0	1.000	0- -	-	-	.314	0.61	0.00
2022	ChC	NL	57	0	16	57.2	239	42	22	20	11	0	2	6	21	3	68	3	2	3	.400	8-12	8	93	.684	3.37	3.12

Cooper Hummel

Bats: B Throws: R Pos: LF-21;PH-20;C-18;DH-16;RF-2 Ht: 5'10" Wt: 198 Born: 11/28/1994 Age: 28

									BATTING											RUNNING			AVERAGES			
Year	Team	Lg	G	AB	H	2B	3B	HR	(Hm	Rd)	TB	R	RBI	RC	TBB	IBB	SO	HBP	SH	SF	SB	CS	GDP	Avg	OBP	Slg	OPS
2022	Reno	AAA	33	129	40	8	1	6	(-	-)	68	31	19	27	24	1	40	2	0	1	3	4	5	.310	.423	.527	.950
2022	Ari	NL	66	176	31	8	3	3	(1	2)	54	20	17	15	23	0	64	1	0	1	4	1	4	.176	.274	.307	.580

Tommy Hunter

Pitches: R Bats: R Pos: RP-18 Ht: 6'3" Wt: 250 Born: 7/3/1986 Age: 36

Year	Team	Lg	G	GS	GF	IP	BFP	H	R	ER	HR	SH	SF	HB	TBB	IBB	SO	WP	W	L	Pct	Sv-Op	Hld	Vel	OPS	ERC	ERA
2022	Syrcse	AAA	8	0	2	13.2	61	16	9	7	2	0	0	0	1	0	14	1	1	0	1.000	0- -	-	-	.729	3.72	4.61
2008	Tex	AL	3	3	0	11.0	63	23	20	20	4	0	0	1	3	0	9	0	0	2	.000	0-0	0	91	1.144	12.66	16.36
2009	Tex	AL	19	19	0	112.0	475	113	55	51	13	2	1	2	33	2	64	6	9	6	.600	0-0	0	89	.736	3.86	4.10
2010	Tex	AL	23	22	0	128.0	536	126	55	53	21	3	2	3	33	0	68	1	13	4	.765	0-0	0	90	.740	3.95	3.73
2011	2 Tms	AL	20	11	2	84.2	367	100	50	44	12	2	2	4	15	1	45	0	4	4	.500	0-1	9	92	.782	4.65	4.68
2012	Bal	AL	33	20	5	133.2	573	161	85	81	32	3	6	4	27	2	77	0	7	8	.467	0-1	0	92	.864	5.63	5.45
2013	Bal	AL	68	0	20	86.1	336	71	28	27	11	1	0	2	14	1	68	0	6	5	.545	4-6	21	96	.617	2.53	2.81
2014	Bal	AL	60	0	24	60.2	241	55	22	20	4	1	2	1	12	3	45	2	3	2	.600	11-17	12	96	.643	2.65	2.97
2015	2 Tms	AL	58	0	17	60.1	249	61	29	28	7	1	3	1	14	2	47	2	4	2	.667	1-2	7	96	.711	3.65	4.18
2016	2 Tms	AL	33	0	8	34.0	139	35	13	12	1	1	0	2	8	1	23	0	2	2	.500	0-1	1	94	.678	3.43	3.18
2017	TB	AL	61	0	18	58.2	228	43	18	17	6	0	0	1	14	0	64	2	3	5	.375	1-1	25	96	.588	2.21	2.61
2018	Phi	NL	65	0	10	64.0	270	65	28	27	6	1	1	3	15	1	51	1	5	4	.556	4-6	25	96	.745	3.62	3.80
2019	Phi	NL	5	0	1	5.1	18	2	0	0	0	0	0	0	0	0	5	0	0	0	-	0-0	1	94	.222	0.31	0.00
2020	Phi	NL	24	0	3	24.2	102	22	11	11	2	1	0	3	6	0	25	0	0	1	.000	1-3	8	93	.698	3.27	4.01
2021	NYM	NL	4	1	0	8.0	33	4	0	0	0	1	0	1	3	0	6	1	0	0	-	0-0	0	92	.443	1.37	0.00
2022	NYM	NL	18	0	7	22.1	94	21	8	6	4	1	0	0	6	0	22	1	0	1	.000	0-0	1	93	.727	3.68	2.42
11	Tex	AL	8	0	2	15.1	62	12	6	5	1	1	1	0	5	0	10	0	1	1	.500	0-1	0	93	.570	2.44	2.93
11	Bal	AL	12	11	0	69.1	305	88	44	39	11	1	1	4	10	1	35	0	3	3	.500	0-0	1	92	.823	5.19	5.06
15	Bal	AL	39	0	12	44.2	180	41	19	18	3	1	3	1	11	2	32	2	2	2	.500	0-1	6	96	.650	2.92	3.63
15	ChC	AL	19	0	5	15.2	69	20	10	10	4	0	0	0	3	0	15	0	2	0	1.000	1-1	1	97	.864	5.91	5.74
16	Cle	AL	21	0	5	21.2	90	21	10	9	1	1	0	2	5	1	17	0	2	2	.500	0-0	1	94	.668	3.22	3.74
16	Bal	AL	12	0	3	12.1	49	14	3	3	0	0	0	0	3	0	6	0	0	0	-	0-0	1	95	.695	3.82	2.19
Postseason			7	3	2	14.1	65	19	8	7	2	0	2	1	2	0	15	0	0	2	.000	0-0	0	92	.888	5.35	4.40
15 ML YEARS			494	76	106	893.2	3724	902	422	397	123	18	17	28	203	13	619	16	56	46	.549	22-38	102	93	.732	3.82	4.00

Drew Hutchison

Pitches: R Bats: L Pos: SP-18; RP-10 Ht: 6'3" Wt: 215 Born: 8/22/1990 Age: 32

Year	Team	Lg	G	GS	GF	IP	BFP	H	R	ER	HR	SH	SF	HB	TBB	IBB	SO	WP	W	L	Pct	Sv-Op	Hld	Vel	OPS	ERC	ERA
2022	Toledo	AAA	6	3	0	13.2	53	11	6	6	2	0	0	0	3	0	19	0	1	1	.500	0- -	-	-	.664	2.72	3.95
2012	Tor	AL	11	11	0	58.2	257	59	31	30	8	1	5	5	20	0	49	1	5	3	.625	0-0	0	91	.759	4.43	4.60
2014	Tor	AL	32	32	0	184.2	786	173	92	92	23	4	10	7	60	1	184	4	11	13	.458	0-0	0	92	.723	3.70	4.48
2015	Tor	AL	30	28	0	150.1	664	179	103	93	22	0	6	11	44	0	129	7	13	5	.722	0-0	0	92	.825	5.44	5.57
2016	2 Tms	AL	9	3	3	24.0	104	28	14	14	6	1	2	2	7	0	22	0	1	0	1.000	0-1	0	92	.903	6.24	5.25
2018	2 Tms	AL	16	5	6	42.2	199	50	32	32	9	3	4	2	26	0	31	5	2	2	.500	0-0	0	90	.922	7.17	6.75
2021	Det	AL	9	2	0	21.1	91	20	11	5	1	1	2	0	11	0	10	1	3	1	.750	0-1	0	92	.682	3.89	2.11
2022	Det	AL	28	18	3	105.1	464	114	58	53	15	1	2	2	42	1	68	3	3	9	.250	0-0	0	93	.773	4.91	4.53
16	Tor	AL	3	2	0	12.2	53	13	7	7	4	0	1	1	4	0	12	0	1	0	1.000	0-1	0	92	.923	5.98	4.97

			HOW MUCH PITCHED					WHAT HE GAVE UP											THE RESULTS							
Year	Team	Lg	G	GS	GF	IP	BFP	H	R	ER	HR	SH	SF	HB	TBB	IBB	SO	WP	W	L	Pct	Sv-Op	Hld	Vel	OPS	ERC	ERA
16	Pit	NL	6	1	3	11.1	51	15	7	7	2	1	2	1	3	0	10	0	0	0	-	0-0	0	92	.880	6.50	5.56
18	Phi	NL	11	0	6	21.1	94	21	11	11	4	1	2	1	13	0	19	4	1	1	.500	0-0	0	91	.857	5.89	4.64
18	Tex	AL	5	5	0	21.1	105	29	21	21	5	2	2	1	13	0	12	1	1	1	.500	0-0	0	90	.981	8.50	8.86
7 ML YEARS			135	99	12	587.0	2565	623	341	319	84	11	27	29	210	2	493	21	38	33	.535	0-2	0	92	.783	4.77	4.89

Andy Ibanez

Bats: R **Throws:** R **Pos:** 3B-25;DH-8;1B-6;2B-2;PH-2   **Ht:** 5'11" **Wt:** 205 **Born:** 4/3/1993 **Age:** 30

			BATTING																		RUNNING			AVERAGES			
Year	Team	Lg	G	AB	H	2B	3B	HR	(Hm	Rd)	TB	R	RBI	RC	TBB	IBB	SO	HBP	SH	SF	SB	CS	GDP	Avg	OBP	Slg	OPS
2022	RdRck	AAA	73	282	72	18	1	6	(-	-)	110	38	33	36	28	0	48	4	0	1	5	2	3	.255	.330	.390	.720
2021	Tex	AL	76	253	70	15	2	7	(5	2)	110	31	25	33	15	0	35	2	1	1	0	0	6	.277	.321	.435	.756
2022	Tex	AL	40	119	26	4	0	1	(0	1)	33	13	9	6	9	0	21	0	0	0	3	0	0	.218	.273	.277	.551
2 ML YEARS			116	372	96	19	2	8	(5	3)	143	44	34	39	24	0	56	2	1	1	3	0	6	.258	.306	.384	.690

Jose Iglesias

Bats: R **Throws:** R **Pos:** SS-116;DH-2   ee-GLAY-see-us   **Ht:** 5'11" **Wt:** 195 **Born:** 1/5/1990 **Age:** 33

			BATTING																		RUNNING			AVERAGES			
Year	Team	Lg	G	AB	H	2B	3B	HR	(Hm	Rd)	TB	R	RBI	RC	TBB	IBB	SO	HBP	SH	SF	SB	CS	GDP	Avg	OBP	Slg	OPS
2011	Bos	AL	10	6	2	0	0	0	(0	0)	2	3	0	0	0	0	2	0	0	0	0	0	0	.333	.333	.333	.667
2012	Bos	AL	25	68	8	2	0	1	(0	1)	13	5	2	0	4	0	16	3	2	0	1	0	2	.118	.200	.191	.391
2013	2 Tms	AL	109	350	106	16	2	3	(1	2)	135	39	29	45	15	0	60	11	4	2	5	2	7	.303	.349	.386	.735
2015	Det	AL	120	416	125	17	3	2	(1	1)	154	44	23	47	25	2	44	6	4	3	11	8	10	.300	.347	.370	.717
2016	Det	AL	137	467	119	26	0	4	(1	3)	157	57	32	47	28	1	50	8	7	3	7	4	12	.255	.306	.336	.643
2017	Det	AL	130	463	118	33	1	6	(4	2)	171	56	54	54	21	0	65	1	3	1	7	4	6	.255	.288	.369	.658
2018	Det	AL	125	432	116	31	3	5	(3	2)	168	43	48	60	19	0	47	8	3	2	15	6	11	.269	.310	.389	.699
2019	Cin	NL	146	504	145	21	3	11	(9	2)	205	62	59	61	20	3	70	3	1	2	6	6	17	.288	.318	.407	.724
2020	Bal	AL	39	142	53	17	0	3	(1	2)	79	16	24	32	3	0	17	4	0	1	0	0	1	.373	.400	.556	.956
2021	2 Tms	AL	137	483	131	27	2	9	(5	4)	189	65	48	58	21	0	75	6	0	1	5	2	10	.271	.309	.391	.701
2022	Col	NL	118	439	128	30	0	3	(2	1)	167	48	47	54	17	0	56	8	0	3	2	3	11	.292	.328	.380	.708
13	Bos	AL	63	215	71	10	2	1	(0	1)	88	27	19	34	11	0	30	6	0	2	3	1	4	.330	.376	.409	.785
13	Det	AL	46	135	35	6	0	2	(1	1)	47	12	10	11	4	0	30	5	4	0	2	1	3	.259	.306	.348	.654
21	LAA	AL	114	424	110	23	1	8	(5	3)	159	57	41	46	18	0	66	4	0	1	5	2	10	.259	.295	.375	.670
21	Bos	AL	23	59	21	4	1	1	(0	1)	30	8	7	12	3	0	9	2	0	0	0	0	0	.356	.406	.508	.915
Postseason			11	26	6	0	0	0	(0	0)	6	2	1	0	1	0	5	1	3	0	0	1	1	.231	.286	.231	.516
11 ML YEARS			1096	3770	1051	220	14	47	(27	20)	1440	438	366	458	173	6	502	58	24	18	59	35	87	.279	.319	.382	.701

Raisel Iglesias

Pitches: R **Bats:** R **Pos:** RP-67   rye-SELL   **Ht:** 6'2" **Wt:** 190 **Born:** 1/4/1990 **Age:** 33

			HOW MUCH PITCHED					WHAT HE GAVE UP											THE RESULTS							
Year	Team	Lg	G	GS	GF	IP	BFP	H	R	ER	HR	SH	SF	HB	TBB	IBB	SO	WP	W	L	Pct	Sv-Op	Hld	Vel	OPS	ERC	ERA
2015	Cin	NL	18	16	1	95.1	395	81	45	44	11	4	0	7	28	0	104	2	3	7	.300	0-0	0	92	.682	3.24	4.15
2016	Cin	NL	37	5	15	78.1	325	63	22	22	7	1	2	5	26	1	83	3	3	2	.600	6-8	7	93	.623	2.90	2.53
2017	Cin	NL	63	0	57	76.0	306	57	22	21	5	1	1	1	27	1	92	1	3	3	.500	28-30	0	96	.576	2.43	2.49
2018	Cin	NL	66	0	57	72.0	291	52	22	19	12	1	2	2	25	2	80	2	2	5	.286	30-34	0	95	.644	2.88	2.38
2019	Cin	NL	68	0	55	67.0	279	61	31	31	12	1	1	2	21	4	89	3	3	12	.200	34-40	3	95	.743	3.81	4.16
2020	Cin	NL	22	0	17	23.0	91	16	11	7	1	1	1	1	5	1	31	0	4	3	.571	8-10	2	96	.510	1.64	2.74
2021	LAA	AL	65	0	59	70.0	273	53	25	20	11	1	3	1	12	0	103	2	7	5	.583	34-39	0	95	.610	2.34	2.57
2022	2 Tms	AL	67	0	39	62.0	246	46	20	17	5	2	1	3	14	1	78	3	2	6	.250	17-21	15	95	.572	2.14	2.47
22	LAA	AL	39	0	32	35.2	146	29	18	16	5	1	0	2	9	1	48	3	2	6	.250	16-19	0	95	.656	2.91	4.04
22	Atl	NL	28	0	7	26.1	100	17	2	1	0	1	1	1	5	0	30	0	0	0	-	1-2	15	95	.450	1.32	0.34
Postseason			2	0	0	1.2	10	2	4	3	2	0	0	0	3	0	5	0	0	0	-	0-0	0	98	1.643	23.20	16.20
8 ML YEARS			406	21	300	543.2	2206	429	198	181	64	12	11	22	158	10	660	16	27	43	.386	157-182	27	95	.633	2.78	3.00

Ender Inciarte

Bats: L **Throws:** L **Pos:** LF-6;PR-4;CF-2;RF-2;DH-1;PH-1   END-er in-see-ARR-tay   **Ht:** 5'11" **Wt:** 190 **Born:** 10/29/1990 **Age:** 32

			BATTING																		RUNNING			AVERAGES			
Year	Team	Lg	G	AB	H	2B	3B	HR	(Hm	Rd)	TB	R	RBI	RC	TBB	IBB	SO	HBP	SH	SF	SB	CS	GDP	Avg	OBP	Slg	OPS
2022	S-WB	AAA	34	103	26	2	1	4	(-	-)	42	12	11	14	13	0	17	0	0	0	4	2	2	.252	.336	.408	.744
2014	Ari	NL	118	418	116	18	2	4	(1	3)	150	54	27	49	25	0	53	0	4	0	19	3	3	.278	.318	.359	.677
2015	Ari	NL	132	524	159	27	5	6	(1	5)	214	73	45	69	26	0	58	4	2	5	21	10	8	.303	.338	.408	.747
2016	Atl	NL	131	522	152	24	7	3	(1	2)	199	85	29	58	45	5	68	4	5	2	16	7	8	.291	.351	.381	.732
2017	Atl	NL	158	662	201	27	5	11	(6	5)	271	93	57	95	49	3	94	0	3	4	22	9	8	.304	.350	.409	.759
2018	Atl	NL	156	597	158	27	6	10	(3	7)	227	83	61	70	49	1	86	6	4	6	28	14	6	.265	.325	.380	.705
2019	Atl	NL	65	199	49	11	2	5	(2	3)	79	30	24	32	26	2	41	4	0	1	7	1	1	.246	.343	.397	.740
2020	Atl	NL	46	116	22	2	1	1	(0	1)	29	17	10	9	12	0	25	0	1	2	4	1	0	.190	.262	.250	.512
2021	Atl	NL	52	79	17	2	0	2	(0	2)	25	11	10	7	7	0	22	0	2	1	1	0	1	.215	.276	.316	.592
2022	NYM	NL	11	8	1	0	0	0	(0	0)	1	1	0	0	0	0	0	0	0	0	0	0	0	.125	.125	.125	.250
Postseason			4	13	3	0	0	0	(0	0)	3	0	1	0	0	0	4	1	0	0	0	0	0	.231	.231	.231	.462
9 ML YEARS			869	3125	875	138	28	42	(14	28)	1195	447	263	389	239	11	447	18	21	19	118	45	35	.280	.333	.382	.715

Jonathan India

Bats: R **Throws:** R **Pos:** 2B-86;DH-13;PH-5 **Ht:** 6'0" **Wt:** 200 **Born:** 12/15/1996 **Age:** 26

									BATTING											RUNNING			AVERAGES			
Year	Team	Lg	G	AB	H	2B	3B	HR	(Hm | Rd)	TB	R	RBI	RC	TBB	IBB	SO	HBP	SH	SF	SB	CS	GDP	Avg	OBP	Slg	OPS
2021	Cin	NL	150	532	143	34	2	21	(9 | 12)	244	98	69	99	71	1	141	23	1	4	12	3	13	.269	.376	.459	.835
2022	Cin	NL	103	386	96	16	2	10	(7 | 3)	146	48	41	53	31	1	94	14	0	0	3	4	5	.249	.327	.378	.705
	2 ML YEARS		253	918	239	50	4	31	(16 | 15)	390	146	110	152	102	2	235	37	1	4	15	7	18	.260	.356	.425	.781

Cole Irvin

Pitches: L **Bats:** L **Pos:** SP-30 **Ht:** 6'4" **Wt:** 217 **Born:** 1/31/1994 **Age:** 29

			HOW MUCH PITCHED				WHAT HE GAVE UP										THE RESULTS						
Year	Team	Lg	G	GS	GF	IP	BFP	H	R	ER	HR	SH	SF	HB	TBB	IBB	SO	WP	W	L	Pct	Sv-Op Hld	Vel	OPS	ERC	ERA
2019	Phi	NL	16	3	1	41.2	181	45	28	27	7	1	2	3	13	1	31	1	2	1	.667	1-1 0	90	.796	4.96	5.83
2020	Phi	NL	3	0	1	3.2	22	11	7	7	1	0	0	0	1	0	4	0	0	1	.000	0-0 0	92	1.355	19.91	17.18
2021	Oak	AL	32	32	0	178.1	768	195	94	84	23	4	2	9	42	1	125	3	10	15	.400	0-0 0	91	.746	4.33	4.24
2022	Oak	AL	30	30	0	181.0	741	174	87	80	25	1	4	7	36	3	128	3	9	13	.409	0-0 0	91	.709	3.49	3.98
	4 ML YEARS		81	65	2	404.2	1712	425	216	198	56	6	8	19	92	4	288	7	21	30	.412	1-1 0	91	.743	4.12	4.40

Kyle Isbel

Bats: L **Throws:** R **Pos:** RF-49;CF-30;LF-29;PR-13;PH-4;DH-2 **Ht:** 5'11" **Wt:** 190 **Born:** 3/3/1997 **Age:** 26

									BATTING											RUNNING			AVERAGES			
Year	Team	Lg	G	AB	H	2B	3B	HR	(Hm	Rd)	TB	R	RBI	RC	TBB	IBB	SO	HBP	SH	SF	SB	CS	GDP	Avg	OBP	Slg	OPS
2021	KC	AL	28	76	21	5	2	1	(1	0)	33	16	7	13	7	0	23	0	0	0	2	0	0	.276	.337	.434	.772
2022	KC	AL	106	256	54	10	4	5	(3	2)	87	32	28	20	16	0	75	3	1	2	9	6	5	.211	.264	.340	.603
	2 ML YEARS		134	332	75	15	6	6	(4	2)	120	48	35	33	23	0	98	3	1	2	11	6	5	.226	.281	.361	.642

Alex Jackson

Bats: R **Throws:** R **Pos:** C-4;PH-1 **Ht:** 6'2" **Wt:** 215 **Born:** 12/25/1995 **Age:** 27

									BATTING											RUNNING			AVERAGES			
Year	Team	Lg	G	AB	H	2B	3B	HR	(Hm	Rd)	TB	R	RBI	RC	TBB	IBB	SO	HBP	SH	SF	SB	CS	GDP	Avg	OBP	Slg	OPS
2022	Nashv	AAA	31	102	23	8	1	2	(-	-)	39	9	18	13	12	0	28	3	0	2	1	0	1	.225	.319	.382	.702
2019	Atl	NL	4	13	0	0	0	0	(0	0)	0	0	0	0	1	1	5	1	0	0	0	0	1	.000	.133	.000	.133
2020	Atl	NL	5	7	2	1	0	0	(0	0)	3	0	0	0	0	0	4	0	0	0	0	0	0	.286	.286	.429	.714
2021	2 Tms	NL	52	131	18	4	0	3	(2	1)	31	13	12	11	13	1	73	7	0	0	0	0	0	.137	.252	.237	.488
2022	Mil	NL	5	12	3	0	0	0	(0	0)	3	0	0	0	0	0	7	0	0	0	0	0	0	.250	.250	.250	.500
	21 Atl	NL	10	23	1	0	0	0	(0	0)	1	2	0	0	2	1	13	3	0	0	0	0	0	.043	.214	.043	.258
	21 Mia	NL	42	108	17	4	0	3	(2	1)	30	11	12	11	11	0	60	4	0	0	0	0	0	.157	.260	.278	.538
	4 ML YEARS		66	163	23	5	0	3	(2	1)	37	13	12	11	14	2	89	8	0	0	0	0	2	.141	.243	.227	.470

Andre Jackson

Pitches: R **Bats:** R **Pos:** RP-4 **Ht:** 6'3" **Wt:** 210 **Born:** 5/1/1996 **Age:** 27

			HOW MUCH PITCHED				WHAT HE GAVE UP										THE RESULTS						
Year	Team	Lg	G	GS	GF	IP	BFP	H	R	ER	HR	SH	SF	HB	TBB	IBB	SO	WP	W	L	Pct	Sv-Op Hld	Vel	OPS	ERC	ERA
2022	OkCity	AAA	21	19	1	75.2	355	68	48	42	10	0	2	1	61	0	76	11	2	7	.222	1-- -	-	.748	5.32	5.00
2021	LAD	NL	3	0	1	11.2	50	10	3	3	1	2	0	0	6	0	10	0	1	0	1.000	1-1 0	92	.714	3.63	2.31
2022	LAD	NL	4	0	3	9.2	42	9	3	2	0	1	0	0	4	0	9	0	0	0	-	1-1 1	95	.641	2.98	1.86
	2 ML YEARS		7	0	4	21.1	92	19	6	5	1	3	0	0	10	0	19	0	0	1	.000	2-2 1	93	.680	3.33	2.11

Drew Jackson

Bats: R **Throws:** R **Pos:** RF-2;3B-1;LF-1;PH-1 **Ht:** 6'2" **Wt:** 200 **Born:** 7/28/1993 **Age:** 29

									BATTING											RUNNING			AVERAGES			
Year	Team	Lg	G	AB	H	2B	3B	HR	(Hm	Rd)	TB	R	RBI	RC	TBB	IBB	SO	HBP	SH	SF	SB	CS	GDP	Avg	OBP	Slg	OPS
2022	LsVgs	AAA	50	148	36	5	0	1	(-	-)	44	19	14	14	23	0	56	2	0	0	8	1	6	.243	.353	.297	.650
2022	Scrmto	AAA	10	30	6	1	0	3	(-	-)	16	7	5	4	1	0	15	0	0	1	0	0	1	.200	.226	.533	.759
2019	Bal	AL	3	3	0	0	0	0	(0 | 0)	0	0	0	0	0	1	0	1	0	0	0	0	0	0	.000	.250	.000	.250
2022	Oak	AL	3	3	0	0	0	0	(0	0)	0	0	0	0	0	0	1	0	0	0	0	0	0	.000	.000	.000	.000
	2 ML YEARS		6	6	0	0	0	0	(0	0)	0	0	0	0	1	0	2	0	0	0	0	0	0	.000	.143	.000	.143

Jay Jackson

Pitches: R **Bats:** R **Pos:** RP-2 **Ht:** 6'1" **Wt:** 195 **Born:** 10/27/1987 **Age:** 35

			HOW MUCH PITCHED				WHAT HE GAVE UP										THE RESULTS						
Year	Team	Lg	G	GS	GF	IP	BFP	H	R	ER	HR	SH	SF	HB	TBB	IBB	SO	WP	W	L	Pct	Sv-Op Hld	Vel	OPS	ERC	ERA
2022	Gwnntt	AAA	19	0	4	19.2	80	18	5	5	2	0	1	0	4	0	25	1	2	0	1.000	1-- -	-	.635	2.87	2.29
2015	SD	NL	6	0	1	4.1	20	7	3	3	0	0	0	0	1	0	4	0	0	0	-	0-0 0	95	.874	6.40	6.23
2019	Mil	NL	28	0	9	30.1	132	22	15	15	6	1	2	2	18	1	47	0	1	0	1.000	0-0 2	94	.724	4.15	4.45
2021	SF	NL	23	1	4	21.2	90	15	9	9	3	1	1	0	12	0	28	0	2	1	.667	0-2 3	95	.685	3.28	3.74
2022	Atl	NL	2	0	1	1.1	5	1	0	0	0	0	0	0	0	0	1	0	0	0	-	0-0 0	95	.400	1.13	0.00
	4 ML YEARS		59	1	15	57.2	247	45	27	27	9	2	3	2	31	1	80	0	3	1	.750	0-2 5	95	.715	3.88	4.21

Luke Jackson

Pitches: R Bats: R Pos: P

Ht: 6'2" Wt: 210 Born: 8/24/1991 Age: 31

Year	Team	Lg	G	GS	GF	IP	BFP	H	R	ER	HR	SH	SF	HB	TBB	IBB	SO	WP	W	L	Pct	Sv-Op	Hld	Vel	OPS	ERC	ERA
			HOW MUCH PITCHED					**WHAT HE GAVE UP**											**THE RESULTS**								
2015	Tex	AL	7	0	4	6.1	27	5	3	3	1	0	0	0	2	0	6	1	0	0	-	0-0	0	-	.619	2.81	4.26
2016	Tex	AL	8	0	2	11.2	62	22	14	14	4	0	1	0	8	0	3	0	0	0	-	0-0	0	-	1.201	13.93	10.80
2017	Atl	NL	43	0	17	50.2	224	55	26	26	4	1	2	4	19	4	33	4	2	0	1.000	0-0	1	-	.759	4.50	4.62
2018	Atl	NL	35	0	11	40.2	184	41	22	20	3	1	2	2	21	3	46	6	1	2	.333	1-2	3	-	.742	4.39	4.43
2019	Atl	NL	70	0	35	72.2	315	76	34	31	10	1	0	2	26	4	106	3	9	2	.818	18-25	9	-	.733	4.46	3.84
2020	Atl	NL	19	0	3	26.1	132	39	23	20	2	0	4	2	13	0	20	3	2	0	1.000	0-0	1	-	.852	7.39	6.84
2021	Atl	NL	71	0	5	63.2	261	45	15	14	6	1	2	2	29	2	70	3	2	2	.500	0-4	31	-	.609	2.78	1.98
Postseason			14	0	0	11.1	58	17	9	8	2	0	0	2	6	1	15	0	0	1	.000	0-1	5	-	.971	8.95	6.35
7 ML YEARS			253	0	77	272.0	1205	283	137	128	30	4	11	12	118	13	284	20	16	6	.727	19-31	45	-	.747	4.60	4.24

Zach Jackson

Pitches: R Bats: R Pos: RP-54

Ht: 6'4" Wt: 230 Born: 12/25/1994 Age: 28

Year	Team	Lg	G	GS	GF	IP	BFP	H	R	ER	HR	SH	SF	HB	TBB	IBB	SO	WP	W	L	Pct	Sv-Op	Hld	Vel	OPS	ERC	ERA
			HOW MUCH PITCHED					**WHAT HE GAVE UP**											**THE RESULTS**								
2022	Oak	AL	54	0	10	48.0	202	28	18	16	1	2	1	2	33	3	67	9	2	3	.400	3-6	26	95	.547	2.46	3.00

Drey Jameson

Pitches: R Bats: R Pos: SP-4

Ht: 6'0" Wt: 165 Born: 8/17/1997 Age: 25

Year	Team	Lg	G	GS	GF	IP	BFP	H	R	ER	HR	SH	SF	HB	TBB	IBB	SO	WP	W	L	Pct	Sv-Op	Hld	Vel	OPS	ERC	ERA
			HOW MUCH PITCHED					**WHAT HE GAVE UP**											**THE RESULTS**								
2019	Hlsbro	A-	8	8	0	11.2	58	14	8	8	1	0	0	1	9	0	12	1	0	0	-	0- --		-	.424	7.00	6.17
2021	Hlsbro	A+	13	12	0	64.1	270	60	31	28	9	2	2	4	18	0	77	3	2	4	.333	0- --		-	-	3.74	3.92
2021	Amrllo	AA	8	8	0	46.1	194	38	22	21	6	0	3	4	18	0	68	6	3	2	.600	0- --		-	.676	3.61	4.08
2022	Reno	AAA	22	21	1	114.0	514	139	91	88	21	0	1	6	42	0	109	3	5	12	.294	0- --		-	.897	6.14	6.95
2022	Ari	NL	4	4	0	24.1	98	20	4	4	2	0	0	1	7	0	24	1	3	0	1.000	0-0	0	95	.619	2.79	1.48

Travis Jankowski

Bats: L Throws: R Pos: LF-19;PR-13;RF-12;CF-11;DH-2;PH-1

Ht: 6'2" Wt: 190 Born: 6/15/1991 Age: 32

Year	Team	Lg	G	AB	H	2B	3B	HR	(Hm	Rd)	TB	R	RBI	RC	TBB	IBB	SO	HBP	SH	SF	SB	CS	GDP	Avg	OBP	Slg	OPS
			BATTING																		**RUNNING**			**AVERAGES**			
2022	Syrcse	AAA	36	131	31	3	1	1	(-	-)	39	27	6	17	33	0	36	1	1	0	15	1	3	.237	.387	.298	.684
2015	SD	NL	34	90	19	2	2	2	(0	2)	31	9	12	10	4	0	24	0	2	0	2	1	1	.211	.245	.344	.589
2016	SD	NL	131	335	82	13	2	2	(1	1)	105	53	12	34	42	0	100	2	3	0	30	12	5	.245	.332	.313	.646
2017	SD	NL	27	75	14	2	0	0	(0	0)	16	10	1	5	9	0	28	1	2	0	4	0	2	.187	.282	.213	.496
2018	SD	NL	117	347	90	12	3	4	(3	1)	120	45	17	42	37	0	73	1	2	0	24	7	7	.259	.332	.346	.678
2019	SD	NL	25	22	4	0	0	0	(0	0)	4	4	0	0	2	0	4	0	0	0	2	2	0	.182	.250	.182	.432
2020	Cin	NL	16	15	1	0	0	0	(0	0)	1	3	0	0	2	0	7	0	0	0	2	1	1	.067	.176	.067	.243
2021	Phi	NL	76	131	33	6	2	1	(1	0)	46	24	10	22	22	4	29	1	2	0	5	0	1	.252	.364	.351	.715
2022	2 Tms		44	55	9	0	0	0	(0	0)	9	11	2	2	8	0	10	1	0	0	3	0	0	.164	.281	.164	.445
22	NYM	NL	43	54	9	0	0	0	(0	0)	9	11	2	2	8	0	9	1	0	0	3	0	0	.167	.286	.167	.452
22	Sea	AL	1	1	0	0	0	0	(0	0)	0	0	0	0	0	0	1	0	0	0	0	0	0	.000	.000	.000	.000
Postseason			1	0	0	0	0	0	(0	0)	0	0	0	0	0	0	0	0	0	0	1	0	0	-	-	-	-
8 ML YEARS			470	1070	252	35	9	9	(5	8)	332	159	54	115	126	4	275	6	11	0	72	23	17	.236	.319	.310	.630

Danny Jansen

Bats: R Throws: R Pos: C-63;PH-5;DH-3;PR-1

Ht: 6'2" Wt: 215 Born: 4/15/1995 Age: 28

Year	Team	Lg	G	AB	H	2B	3B	HR	(Hm	Rd)	TB	R	RBI	RC	TBB	IBB	SO	HBP	SH	SF	SB	CS	GDP	Avg	OBP	Slg	OPS
			BATTING																		**RUNNING**			**AVERAGES**			
2018	Tor	AL	31	81	20	6	0	3	(1	2)	35	12	8	14	9	0	17	4	0	1	0	0	1	.247	.347	.432	.779
2019	Tor	AL	107	347	72	12	1	13	(8	5)	125	41	43	40	31	1	79	4	1	8	0	1	8	.207	.279	.360	.640
2020	Tor	AL	43	120	22	3	0	6	(4	2)	43	18	20	17	21	0	31	2	3	1	0	0	1	.183	.313	.358	.671
2021	Tor	AL	70	184	41	13	0	11	(5	6)	87	32	28	24	17	0	44	3	1	0	0	0	4	.223	.299	.473	.772
2022	Tor	AL	72	215	56	10	0	15	(7	8)	111	34	44	45	25	1	44	3	0	5	1	0	1	.260	.339	.516	.855
Postseason			2	5	2	0	0	2	(0	2)	8	2	2	1	0	0	0	0	0	0	0	0	0	.400	.400	1.600	2.000
5 ML YEARS			323	947	211	44	1	48	(25	23)	401	137	143	140	103	2	215	16	5	8	1	1	15	.223	.307	.423	.731

Kenley Jansen

Pitches: R Bats: B Pos: RP-65

KEN-lee JANN-sen

Ht: 6'5" Wt: 265 Born: 9/30/1987 Age: 35

Year	Team	Lg	G	GS	GF	IP	BFP	H	R	ER	HR	SH	SF	HB	TBB	IBB	SO	WP	W	L	Pct	Sv-Op	Hld	Vel	OPS	ERC	ERA
			HOW MUCH PITCHED					**WHAT HE GAVE UP**											**THE RESULTS**								
2010	LAD	NL	25	0	8	27.0	109	12	2	2	0	1	0	1	15	1	41	1	1	0	1.000	4-4	4	94	.422	1.40	0.67
2011	LAD	NL	51	0	13	53.2	218	30	17	17	3	0	1	2	26	0	96	0	2	1	.667	5-6	9	94	.494	1.96	2.85
2012	LAD	NL	65	0	40	65.0	252	33	18	17	6	0	1	3	22	1	99	3	5	3	.625	25-32	5	92	.504	1.55	2.35
2013	LAD	NL	75	0	45	76.2	292	48	16	16	6	0	0	3	18	1	111	2	4	3	.571	28-32	16	94	.509	1.65	1.88
2014	LAD	NL	68	0	57	65.1	268	55	20	20	5	1	2	0	19	2	101	2	2	3	.400	44-49	0	94	.610	2.60	2.76
2015	LAD	NL	54	0	50	52.1	200	33	14	14	6	0	2	2	8	0	80	0	2	1	.667	36-38	1	93	.513	1.58	2.41
2016	LAD	NL	71	0	63	68.2	251	35	14	14	3	1	2	1	11	2	104	1	3	2	.600	47-53	0	94	.446	1.03	1.83
2017	LAD	NL	65	0	57	68.1	258	44	11	10	5	0	0	2	7	0	109	2	5	0	1.000	41-42	1	94	.476	1.35	1.32
2018	LAD	NL	69	0	59	71.2	289	54	28	24	13	0	1	2	17	1	82	0	1	5	.167	38-42	25	94	.635	2.68	3.01
2019	LAD	NL	62	0	51	63.0	263	51	28	26	9	0	3	4	16	0	80	2	5	3	.625	33-41	5	93	.653	2.92	3.71
2020	LAD	NL	27	0	24	24.1	102	19	11	9	2	0	0	3	9	0	33	0	3	1	.750	11-13	0	92	.615	3.13	3.33

Year	Team	Lg	G	GS	GF	IP	BFP	H	R	ER	HR	SH	SF	HB	TBB	IBB	SO	WP	W	L	Pct	Sv-Op	Hld	Vel	OPS	ERC	ERA
2021	LAD	NL	69	0	52	69.0	278	36	21	17	4	1	2	2	36	4	86	4	4	4	.500	38-43	0	94	.501	1.84	2.22
2022	Atl	NL	65	0	54	64.0	260	45	25	24	8	0	2	2	22	3	85	1	5	2	.714	**41-48**	0	94	.612	2.48	3.38
	Postseason		57	0	45	63.1	243	33	17	15	6	0	0	3	18	3	92	0	3	2	.600	19-23	2	94	.488	1.46	2.13
	13 ML YEARS		766	0	573	769.0	3040	495	225	210	71	6	15	28	226	15	1107	18	42	28	.600	391-443	39	94	.543	1.92	2.46

Cristian Javier

Pitches: R Bats: R Pos: SP-25; RP-5　　　　　　　Ht: 6'1" Wt: 213 Born: 3/26/1997 Age: 26

Year	Team	Lg	G	GS	GF	IP	BFP	H	R	ER	HR	SH	SF	HB	TBB	IBB	SO	WP	W	L	Pct	Sv-Op	Hld	Vel	OPS	ERC	ERA
2020	Hou	AL	12	10	0	54.1	214	36	21	21	11	0	2	2	18	0	54	4	5	2	.714	0-0	0	92	.652	2.83	3.48
2021	Hou	AL	36	9	5	101.1	424	67	41	40	16	1	2	7	53	1	130	6	4	1	.800	2-4	5	94	.655	3.35	3.55
2022	Hou	AL	30	25	0	148.2	585	89	44	42	17	2	1	6	52	0	194	5	11	9	.550	0-0	0	94	.557	2.08	2.54
	Postseason		11	0	0	20.0	84	12	7	7	4	0	0	2	11	0	32	1	2	1	.667	0-1	3	94	.734	3.52	3.15
	3 ML YEARS		78	44	5	304.1	1223	192	106	103	44	3	5	15	123	1	378	15	20	12	.625	2-4	5	93	.608	2.62	3.05

Griffin Jax

Pitches: R Bats: R Pos: RP-65　　　　　　　Ht: 6'2" Wt: 195 Born: 11/22/1994 Age: 28

Year	Team	Lg	G	GS	GF	IP	BFP	H	R	ER	HR	SH	SF	HB	TBB	IBB	SO	WP	W	L	Pct	Sv-Op	Hld	Vel	OPS	ERC	ERA
2021	Min	AL	18	14	2	82.0	360	82	62	58	23	0	6	5	29	1	65	6	4	5	.444	0-0	0	93	.501	5.32	6.37
2022	Min	AL	65	0	10	72.1	290	56	29	27	7	1	2	3	20	3	78	2	7	4	.636	1-7	18	95	.607	2.52	3.36
	2 ML YEARS		83	14	12	154.1	650	138	91	85	30	1	8	8	49	4	143	8	11	9	.550	1-7	18	94	.746	3.94	4.96

Daulton Jefferies

Pitches: R Bats: L Pos: SP-8　　　　　　　Ht: 6'0" Wt: 182 Born: 8/2/1995 Age: 27

Year	Team	Lg	G	GS	GF	IP	BFP	H	R	ER	HR	SH	SF	HB	TBB	IBB	SO	WP	W	L	Pct	Sv-Op	Hld	Vel	OPS	ERC	ERA
2020	Oak	AL	1	1	0	2.0	13	5	5	5	2	0	0	0	2	0	1	0	0	1	.000	0-0	0	94	1.538	27.53	22.50
2021	Oak	AL	5	1	1	15.0	58	11	6	6	1	0	0	1	4	0	8	1	1	0	1.000	0-0	0	94	.634	2.34	3.60
2022	Oak	AL	8	8	0	39.1	172	46	26	25	4	0	1	2	8	0	28	3	1	7	.125	0-0	0	92	.767	4.41	5.72
	3 ML YEARS		14	10	1	56.1	243	62	37	36	7	0	1	3	14	0	37	4	2	8	.200	0-0	0	93	.774	4.42	5.75

Ryan Jeffers

Bats: R Throws: R Pos: C-59; DH-7; PH-4　　　　　　　Ht: 6'4" Wt: 235 Born: 6/3/1997 Age: 26

Year	Team	Lg	G	AB	H	2B	3B	HR	(Hm	Rd)	TB	R	RBI	RC	TBB	IBB	SO	HBP	SH	SF	SB	CS	GDP	Avg	OBP	Slg	OPS
2020	Min	AL	26	55	15	0	0	3	(3	0)	24	5	7	8	5	0	19	2	0	0	0	0	0	.273	.355	.436	.791
2021	Min	AL	85	267	53	10	1	14	(8	6)	107	28	35	30	22	0	108	4	0	0	0	1	6	.199	.270	.401	.670
2022	Min	AL	67	212	44	10	1	7	(3	4)	77	25	27	28	23	0	62	0	1	0	0	0	6	.208	.285	.363	.648
	Postseason		2	5	0	0	0	0	(0	0)	0	0	0	0	0	0	2	0	0	0	0	0	0	.000	.000	.000	.000
	3 ML YEARS		178	534	112	20	2	24	(14	10)	208	58	69	66	50	0	189	6	1	0	0	1	12	.210	.285	.390	.674

Dany Jimenez

Pitches: R Bats: R Pos: RP-34　　　　　　　Ht: 6'1" Wt: 182 Born: 12/23/1993 Age: 29

Year	Team	Lg	G	GS	GF	IP	BFP	H	R	ER	HR	SH	SF	HB	TBB	IBB	SO	WP	W	L	Pct	Sv-Op	Hld	Vel	OPS	ERC	ERA
2020	SF	NL	2	0	1	1.1	8	1	1	1	0	0	0	0	3	0	1	0	0	0	-	0-0	0	93	.700	8.88	6.75
2022	Oak	AL	34	0	22	34.1	145	23	16	13	2	0	1	0	18	4	34	2	3	4	.429	11-14	4	94	.537	2.29	3.41
	2 ML YEARS		36	0	23	35.2	153	24	17	14	2	0	1	0	21	4	35	2	3	4	.429	11-14	4	94	.546	2.50	3.53

Eloy Jimenez

Bats: R Throws: R Pos: DH-50; LF-30; PH-4　　eh-LOY he-MEN-ez　　　Ht: 6'4" Wt: 240 Born: 11/27/1996 Age: 26

Year	Team	Lg	G	AB	H	2B	3B	HR	(Hm	Rd)	TB	R	RBI	RC	TBB	IBB	SO	HBP	SH	SF	SB	CS	GDP	Avg	OBP	Slg	OPS
2022	Charlit	AAA	17	57	14	0	0	2	(-	-)	20	8	6	5	6	0	12	0	0	0	0	0	5	.246	.317	.351	.668
2019	CWS	AL	122	468	125	18	2	31	(12	19)	240	69	79	68	30	0	134	4	0	2	0	0	11	.267	.315	.513	.828
2020	CWS	AL	55	213	63	14	0	14	(8	6)	119	26	41	44	12	0	56	0	0	1	0	0	4	.296	.332	.559	.891
2021	CWS	AL	55	213	53	10	0	10	(2	8)	93	23	37	27	16	0	57	1	0	1	0	0	8	.249	.303	.437	.740
2022	CWS	AL	84	292	86	12	0	16	(9	7)	146	40	54	57	28	0	72	3	0	4	0	0	8	.295	.358	.500	.858
	Postseason		5	19	6	1	0	0	(0	0)	7	0	3	1	0	0	5	0	0	0	0	0	1	.316	.316	.368	.684
	4 ML YEARS		316	1186	327	54	2	71	(31	40)	598	158	211	196	86	0	319	8	0	8	0	0	31	.276	.327	.504	.831

Joe Jimenez

Pitches: R Bats: R Pos: RP-62　　he-MEN-ez　　　Ht: 6'3" Wt: 277 Born: 1/17/1995 Age: 28

Year	Team	Lg	G	GS	GF	IP	BFP	H	R	ER	HR	SH	SF	HB	TBB	IBB	SO	WP	W	L	Pct	Sv-Op	Hld	Vel	OPS	ERC	ERA
2017	Det	AL	24	0	6	19.0	99	31	28	26	4	0	1	2	9	0	17	0	0	2	.000	0-1	0	95	.999	9.60	12.32
2018	Det	AL	68	0	17	62.2	267	53	34	30	5	0	2	3	22	3	78	3	5	4	.556	3-7	23	96	.645	2.95	4.31
2019	Det	AL	66	0	29	59.2	257	56	33	29	13	0	0	4	23	1	82	1	4	7	.364	9-14	15	95	.797	4.74	4.37

Year	Team	Lg	G	GS	GF	IP	BFP	H	R	ER	HR	SH	SF	HB	TBB	IBB	SO	WP	W	L	Pct	Sv-Op	Hld	Vel	OPS	ERC	ERA
2020	Det	AL	25	0	9	22.2	101	25	19	18	7	0	2	5	6	0	22	1	1	3	.250	5-6	4	94	.936	6.68	7.15
2021	Det	AL	52	0	12	45.1	210	34	33	30	6	0	2	8	35	1	57	6	6	1	.857	1-2	5	95	.755	4.98	5.96
2022	Det	AL	62	0	12	56.2	231	49	24	22	4	0	1	0	13	0	77	0	3	2	.600	2-4	11	96	.609	2.50	3.49
6 ML YEARS			297	0	85	266.0	1165	248	171	155	39	0	8	22	108	5	333	11	19	19	.500	20-34	58	95	.746	4.30	5.24

Connor Joe

Bats: R **Throws:** R **Pos:** LF-50;DH-27;1B-24;RF-16;PH-7;PR-3   **Ht:** 6'0" **Wt:** 205 **Born:** 8/16/1992 **Age:** 30

Year	Team	Lg	G	AB	H	2B	3B	HR	(Hm	Rd)	TB	R	RBI	RC	TBB	IBB	SO	HBP	SH	SF	SB	CS	GDP	Avg	OBP	Slg	OPS
2019	SF	NL	8	15	1	0	0	0	(0	0)	1	1	0	1	1	0	5	0	0	0	0	0	1	.067	.125	.067	.192
2021	Col	NL	63	179	51	9	0	8	(5	3)	84	23	35	41	41	0	41	3	0	3	0	0	1	.285	.379	.469	.848
2022	Col	NL	111	404	96	20	4	7	(2	5)	145	56	28	41	55	0	97	7	0	1	6	2	8	.238	.338	.359	.697
3 ML YEARS			182	598	148	29	4	15	(7	8)	230	80	63	82	82	0	143	10	0	4	6	2	10	.247	.346	.385	.730

Bryce Johnson

Bats: B **Throws:** R **Pos:** CF-7;RF-4;LF-1;PR-1   **Ht:** 6'1" **Wt:** 195 **Born:** 10/27/1995 **Age:** 27

Year	Team	Lg	G	AB	H	2B	3B	HR	(Hm	Rd)	TB	R	RBI	RC	TBB	IBB	SO	HBP	SH	SF	SB	CS	GDP	Avg	OBP	Slg	OPS
2022	Scrmto	AAA	94	307	89	11	4	5	(-	-)	123	41	36	47	33	0	90	7	2	3	31	5	3	.290	.369	.401	.769
2022	SF	NL	11	18	2	0	0	0	(0	0)	2	1	2	1	1	0	7	0	0	0	0	0	0	.111	.158	.111	.269

Pierce Johnson

Pitches: R **Bats:** R **Pos:** RP-15   **Ht:** 6'2" **Wt:** 202 **Born:** 5/10/1991 **Age:** 32

Year	Team	Lg	G	GS	GF	IP	BFP	H	R	ER	HR	SH	SF	HB	TBB	IBB	SO	WP	W	L	Pct	Sv-Op	Hld	Vel	OPS	ERC	ERA
2022	ElPaso	AAA	5	0	1	5.0	17	2	1	1	0	0	0	0	0	0	6	2	0	0	-	1--	-		.353	0.35	1.80
2017	ChC	NL	1	0	0	1.0	7	2	2	0	0	0	0	0	1	0	2	0	0	0	-	0-0	0	92	.762	10.22	0.00
2018	SF	NL	37	0	7	43.2	186	38	27	27	5	1	2	0	22	1	36	1	3	2	.600	0-0	1	94	.740	3.86	5.56
2020	SD	NL	24	0	7	20.0	80	15	7	6	2	0	1	0	9	0	27	1	3	1	.750	0-0	1	96	.643	3.04	2.70
2021	SD	NL	63	2	7	58.2	244	47	21	21	6	0	2	1	27	3	77	6	3	4	.429	0-2	9	96	.677	3.27	3.22
2022	SD	NL	15	0	1	14.1	64	14	8	8	1	0	0	0	8	0	21	1	1	2	.333	0-1	6	95	.683	4.31	5.02
Postseason			5	0	0	4.0	18	3	2	2	0	0	0	1	2	0	7	0	0	0	-	0-0	0	96	.533	3.21	4.50
5 ML YEARS			140	2	22	137.2	581	116	65	62	14	1	5	1	67	4	163	9	10	9	.526	0-3	17	95	.694	3.57	4.05

Termarr Johnson

Bats: L **Throws:** R **Pos:** SS   **Ht:** 5'7" **Wt:** 175 **Born:** 6/11/2004 **Age:** 19

Year	Team	Lg	G	AB	H	2B	3B	HR	(Hm	Rd)	TB	R	RBI	RC	TBB	IBB	SO	HBP	SH	SF	SB	CS	GDP	Avg	OBP	Slg	OPS
2022	Bradtn	A	14	40	11	4	0	1	(-	-)	18	7	6	7	10	0	13	0	0	3	4	1	1	.275	.396	.450	.846

Damon Jones

Pitches: L **Bats:** L **Pos:** RP-4   **Ht:** 6'5" **Wt:** 233 **Born:** 9/30/1994 **Age:** 28

Year	Team	Lg	G	GS	GF	IP	BFP	H	R	ER	HR	SH	SF	HB	TBB	IBB	SO	WP	W	L	Pct	Sv-Op	Hld	Vel	OPS	ERC	ERA
2021	Phi	NL	1	0	0	0.1	4	1	0	0	0	0	0	0	2	0	0	0	0	0	-	0-0	0	94	1.250	44.74	0.00
2022	Phi	NL	4	0	3	4.2	26	4	5	5	0	0	0	3	5	0	5	1	0	0	-	0-0	0	93	.795	7.40	9.64
2 ML YEARS			5	0	3	5.0	30	5	5	5	0	0	0	3	7	0	5	1	0	0	-	0-0	0	93	.850	9.51	9.00

Nolan Jones

Bats: L **Throws:** R **Pos:** RF-22;DH-4;PH-3   **Ht:** 6'4" **Wt:** 195 **Born:** 5/7/1998 **Age:** 25

Year	Team	Lg	G	AB	H	2B	3B	HR	(Hm	Rd)	TB	R	RBI	RC	TBB	IBB	SO	HBP	SH	SF	SB	CS	GDP	Avg	OBP	Slg	OPS
2018	2 Tms	Low	120	427	121	21	0	19	(-	-)	199	69	66	53	89	1	131	0	0	3	2	1	7	.283	.405	.466	.871
2019	Akron	AA	49	178	45	10	2	8	(-	-)	83	33	22	32	31	1	63	2	0	2	2	0	4	.253	.370	.466	.836
2019	Lynbrg	A+	77	252	72	12	1	7	(-	-)	107	48	41	54	65	0	85	4	0	3	5	3	5	.286	.435	.425	.860
2021	Clmbs	AAA	99	341	81	25	1	13	(-	-)	147	60	48	57	59	1	122	5	0	2	10	2	7	.238	.356	.431	.787
2022	Clmbs	AAA	55	214	59	11	1	9	(-	-)	99	44	43	38	31	0	64	1	1	1	4	1	5	.276	.368	.463	.831
2022	Cle	AL	28	86	21	5	0	2	(0	2)	32	10	13	9	8	1	31	0	0	2	0	0	2	.244	.309	.372	.681

Taylor Jones

Bats: R **Throws:** R **Pos:** PH-1   **Ht:** 6'7" **Wt:** 230 **Born:** 12/6/1993 **Age:** 29

Year	Team	Lg	G	AB	H	2B	3B	HR	(Hm	Rd)	TB	R	RBI	RC	TBB	IBB	SO	HBP	SH	SF	SB	CS	GDP	Avg	OBP	Slg	OPS
2022	SgrLnd	AAA	74	274	72	17	0	12	(-	-)	125	52	43	48	35	1	78	12	0	1	0	0	6	.263	.370	.456	.826
2020	Hou	AL	7	21	4	1	0	1	(0	1)	8	3	3	1	1	0	7	0	0	0	0	0	2	.190	.227	.381	.608
2021	Hou	AL	35	102	25	8	1	2	(2	0)	41	11	16	12	4	0	29	0	0	2	0	0	5	.245	.269	.402	.670
2022	Hou	AL	1	1	0	0	0	0	(0	0)	0	0	0	0	0	0	0	0	0	0	0	0	0	.000	.000	.000	.000
3 ML YEARS			43	124	29	9	1	3	(2	1)	49	14	19	13	5	0	36	0	0	2	0	0	7	.234	.260	.395	.655

Aaron Judge

Bats: R Throws: R Pos: CF-78;RF-73;DH-25;PH-4   Ht: 6'7" Wt: 282 Born: 4/26/1992 Age: 31

						BATTING													RUNNING			AVERAGES			
Year	Team	Lg	G	AB	H	2B	3B	HR	(Hm | Rd)	TB	R	RBI	RC	TBB	IBB	SO	HBP	SH	SF	SB	CS	GDP	Avg	OBP	Slg	OPS
2016 NYY	AL	27	84	15	2	0	4	(3 | 1)	29	10	10	6	9	0	42	1	0	1	0	1	2	.179	.263	.345	.608
2017 NYY	AL	155	542	154	24	3	52	(33 | 19)	340	128	114	131	127	11	208	5	0	4	9	4	15	.284	.422	.627	1.049
2018 NYY	AL	112	413	115	22	0	27	(18 | 9)	218	77	67	82	76	3	152	4	0	5	6	3	10	.278	.392	.528	.919
2019 NYY	AL	102	378	103	18	1	27	(11 | 16)	204	75	55	70	64	4	141	3	0	1	3	2	11	.272	.381	.540	.921
2020 NYY	AL	28	101	26	3	0	9	(5 | 4)	56	23	22	19	10	0	32	2	0	0	0	1	5	.257	.336	.554	.891
2021 NYY	AL	148	550	158	24	0	39	(15 | 24)	299	89	98	115	75	2	158	3	0	5	6	1	16	.287	.373	.544	.916
2022 NYY	AL	157	570	177	28	0	62	(30 | 32)	391	133	131	173	111	19	175	6	0	5	16	3	14	.311	.425	.686	1.111
Postseason		35	135	31	4	0	11	(4 | 7)	68	24	22	22	23	0	51	0	0	1	2	1	2	.230	.340	.504	.843
7 ML YEARS		729	2638	748	121	4	220	(115 | 105)	1537	535	497	596	472	39	908	24	0	21	40	15	73	.284	.394	.583	.977

Josh Jung

Bats: R Throws: R Pos: 3B-25;DH-1   Ht: 6'2" Wt: 214 Born: 2/12/1998 Age: 25

						BATTING													RUNNING			AVERAGES			
Year	Team	Lg	G	AB	H	2B	3B	HR	(Hm | Rd)	TB	R	RBI	RC	TBB	IBB	SO	HBP	SH	SF	SB	CS	GDP	Avg	OBP	Slg	OPS
2019 2 Tms	Low	44	174	55	14	1	2	(- | -)	77	23	28	31	18	1	32	4	0	2	4	1	3	.316	.389	.443	.831
2021 Frisco	AA	43	169	52	8	1	10	(- | -)	92	25	40	32	13	0	42	3	0	1	2	2	2	.308	.366	.544	.910
2021 RdRck	AAA	31	122	40	13	0	7	(- | -)	74	25	19	29	16	1	30	1	0	0	0	0	2	.328	.410	.607	1.017
2022 RdRck	AAA	23	99	27	7	0	6	(- | -)	52	15	24	18	4	0	30	3	0	0	1	0	1	.273	.321	.525	.846
2022 Tex	AL	26	98	20	4	1	5	(1 | 4)	41	9	14	12	4	0	39	0	0	0	2	0	2	.204	.235	.418	.654

Jakob Junis

Pitches: R Bats: R Pos: SP-17; RP-6   Ht: 6'3" Wt: 220 Born: 9/16/1992 Age: 30

			HOW MUCH PITCHED				WHAT HE GAVE UP										THE RESULTS							
Year	Team	Lg	G	GS	GF	IP	BFP	H	R	ER	HR	SH	SF	HB	TBB	IBB	SO	WP	W	L	Pct	Sv-Op	Hld	Vel	OPS	ERC	ERA
2017 KC	AL	20	16	1	98.1	422	101	52	47	15	3	3	9	25	1	80	3	9	3	.750	0-0	0	91	.762	4.36	4.30
2018 KC	AL	30	30	0	177.0	758	182	94	86	32	4	8	15	43	1	164	9	9	12	.429	0-0	0	91	.773	4.49	4.37
2019 KC	AL	31	31	0	175.1	771	192	108	102	31	0	5	11	58	1	164	4	9	14	.391	0-0	0	92	.807	5.14	5.24
2020 KC	AL	8	6	0	25.1	114	35	18	18	7	0	1	2	6	1	19	2	0	2	.000	0-0	1	91	.958	7.50	6.39
2021 KC	AL	16	6	1	39.1	168	43	24	23	7	0	2	0	12	0	41	2	2	4	.333	0-2	0	91	.788	4.82	5.26
2022 SF	NL	23	17	0	112.0	478	120	57	55	13	2	1	4	25	0	98	1	5	7	.417	0-0	0	92	.757	4.00	4.42
6 ML YEARS		128	106	2	627.1	2711	673	353	331	105	9	20	41	169	4	566	21	34	42	.447	0-2	1	91	.787	4.69	4.75

Janson Junk

Pitches: R Bats: R Pos: SP-2; RP-1   Ht: 6'1" Wt: 177 Born: 1/15/1996 Age: 27

			HOW MUCH PITCHED				WHAT HE GAVE UP										THE RESULTS							
Year	Team	Lg	G	GS	GF	IP	BFP	H	R	ER	HR	SH	SF	HB	TBB	IBB	SO	WP	W	L	Pct	Sv-Op	Hld	Vel	OPS	ERC	ERA
2022 Salt Lk	AAA	16	15	0	73.2	312	77	41	38	9	0	2	1	18	0	69	0	1	7	.125	0--	-	-	.754	3.90	4.64
2021 LAA	AL	4	4	0	16.1	71	20	11	7	5	1	0	0	2	0	10	0	1	0	1.000	0-0	0	93	.844	5.53	3.86
2022 LAA	AL	3	2	1	8.1	37	10	6	6	1	0	0	0	3	0	11	0	1	1	.500	0-0	0	93	.793	5.24	6.48
2 ML YEARS		7	6	1	24.2	108	30	17	13	6	1	0	0	5	0	21	0	1	2	.333	0-0	0	93	.827	5.47	4.74

Tommy Kahnle

KAIN-lee

Pitches: R Bats: R Pos: RP-13   Ht: 6'1" Wt: 230 Born: 8/7/1989 Age: 33

			HOW MUCH PITCHED				WHAT HE GAVE UP										THE RESULTS							
Year	Team	Lg	G	GS	GF	IP	BFP	H	R	ER	HR	SH	SF	HB	TBB	IBB	SO	WP	W	L	Pct	Sv-Op	Hld	Vel	OPS	ERC	ERA
2022 OkCity	AAA	10	0	0	9.2	40	8	4	4	2	0	0	0	3	0	10	1	1	0	1.000	0--	-	-	.653	3.41	3.72
2022 Rcuca	A	5	0	0	3.2	16	5	1	1	0	0	0	0	0	0	4	0	0	0	-	0--	-	-	.372	3.72	2.45
2014 Col	NL	54	0	7	68.2	285	51	39	32	7	2	3	1	31	2	63	7	2	1	.667	0-2	8	95	.628	2.91	4.19
2015 Col	NL	36	0	8	33.1	155	31	22	18	3	1	2	0	28	1	39	3	0	1	.000	2-3	10	96	.778	5.31	4.86
2016 CWS	AL	29	0	12	27.1	119	21	8	8	2	0	0	0	20	3	25	3	0	0	-	1-2	4	97	.678	3.74	2.63
2017 2 Tms	AL	69	0	17	62.2	256	53	20	18	4	1	4	2	17	1	96	5	2	4	.333	0-6	15	98	.606	2.63	2.59
2018 NYY	AL	24	0	7	23.1	107	23	22	17	3	0	2	0	15	0	30	2	2	0	1.000	1-2	2	95	.811	5.11	6.56
2019 NYY	AL	72	0	5	61.1	248	45	27	25	9	0	1	2	20	0	88	8	3	2	.600	0-5	27	96	.635	2.79	3.67
2020 NYY	AL	1	0	0	1.0	6	1	0	0	0	0	0	0	1	1	3	0	0	0	-	0-0	1	98	.733	2.79	0.00
2022 LAD	NL	13	0	2	12.2	46	5	4	4	2	0	1	3	3	0	14	1	0	0	-	1-1	1	96	.521	1.79	2.84
17 CWS	AL	37	0	10	36.0	141	28	12	10	3	1	2	0	7	1	60	2	1	3	.250	0-4	7	98	.571	2.04	2.50
17 NYY	AL	32	0	7	26.2	115	25	8	8	1	0	2	2	10	0	36	3	1	1	.500	0-2	8	98	.648	3.47	2.70
Postseason		15	0	3	19.1	71	10	5	5	2	0	0	0	5	0	18	0	1	0	1.000	1-1	2	98	.484	1.39	2.33
8 ML YEARS		298	0	58	290.1	1222	230	142	122	30	4	13	8	135	8	358	29	9	9	.500	5-21	68	96	.660	3.28	3.78

James Kaprielian

ka-PRELL-ee-an

Pitches: R Bats: R Pos: SP-26   Ht: 6'3" Wt: 225 Born: 3/2/1994 Age: 29

			HOW MUCH PITCHED				WHAT HE GAVE UP										THE RESULTS							
Year	Team	Lg	G	GS	GF	IP	BFP	H	R	ER	HR	SH	SF	HB	TBB	IBB	SO	WP	W	L	Pct	Sv-Op	Hld	Vel	OPS	ERC	ERA
2020 Oak	AL	2	0	0	3.2	17	4	3	3	2	0	0	0	2	0	4	0	0	0	-	0-0	0	95	1.020	8.51	7.36
2021 Oak	AL	24	21	0	119.1	502	105	55	54	19	2	3	5	41	0	123	1	8	5	.615	0-0	0	93	.732	3.74	4.07
2022 Oak	AL	26	26	0	134.0	577	121	68	63	16	1	5	5	59	0	98	2	5	9	.357	0-0	0	94	.735	3.96	4.23
3 ML YEARS		52	47	0	257.0	1096	230	126	120	37	3	8	10	102	0	225	3	13	14	.481	0-0	0	94	.738	3.92	4.20

James Karinchak

Pitches: R Bats: R Pos: RP-38   Ht: 6'3" Wt: 215 Born: 9/22/1995 Age: 27

		HOW MUCH PITCHED					WHAT HE GAVE UP											THE RESULTS						
Year	Team	Lg	G	GS	GF	IP	BFP	H	R	ER	HR	SH	SF	HB	TBB	IBB	SO	WP	W	L	Pct	Sv-Op	Hld	Vel	OPS	ERC	ERA
2022	Clmbs	AAA	12	0	1	11.0	53	10	7	7	0	0	1	0	11	0	17	2	1	0	1.000	0- -	-	-	.689	5.06	5.73
2019	Cle	AL	5	0	4	5.1	22	3	1	1	0	0	1	0	1	0	8	2	0	0	-	0-0	0	97	.382	0.90	1.69
2020	Cle	AL	27	0	4	27.0	109	14	9	8	1	1	4	0	16	1	53	5	1	2	.333	1-4	8	96	.505	1.87	2.67
2021	Cle	AL	60	0	26	55.1	235	35	27	25	9	0	2	2	32	0	78	3	7	4	.636	11-16	13	96	.645	3.27	4.07
2022	Cle	AL	38	0	9	39.0	160	22	9	9	2	0	1	1	21	0	62	4	2	0	1.000	3-4	8	95	.516	2.09	2.08
	Postseason		1	0	0	0.0	3	1	1	1	1	0	0	0	2	0	0	0	0	0	-	0-0	0	96	5.000	-	-
	4 ML YEARS		130	0	43	126.2	526	74	46	43	12	1	8	3	70	1	201	14	10	6	.625	15-24	29	96	.566	2.46	3.06

Gosuke Katoh

Bats: L Throws: R Pos: 1B-3;PR-3;2B-2;DH-1   gohs-kay kah-toe   Ht: 6'1" Wt: 200 Born: 10/8/1994 Age: 28

			BATTING																	RUNNING			AVERAGES			
Year	Team	Lg	G	AB	H	2B	3B	HR	(Hm	Rd)	TB	R	RBI	RC	TBB	IBB	SO	HBP	SH	SF	SB	CS	GDP	Avg	OBP	Slg	OPS
2022	Syrcse	AAA	80	287	64	15	2	9	(-	-)	110	42	32	35	32	2	72	4	1	0	7	1	5	.223	.310	.383	.693
2022	Tor	AL	8	7	1	1	0	0	(0	0)	2	2	0	1	3	0	1	0	1	0	0	0	0	.143	.400	.286	.686

Anthony Kay

Pitches: L Bats: L Pos: RP-1   Ht: 6'0" Wt: 225 Born: 3/21/1995 Age: 28

			HOW MUCH PITCHED					WHAT HE GAVE UP											THE RESULTS						
Year	Team	Lg	G	GS	GF	IP	BFP	H	R	ER	HR	SH	SF	HB	TBB	IBB	SO	WP	W	L	Pct	Sv-Op	Hld	Vel	OPS	ERC	ERA
2022	Buffalo	AAA	8	1	1	14.0	70	18	14	13	4	0	1	1	11	0	15	3	1	3	.250	0- -	-	-	1.043	9.52	8.36
2019	Tor	AL	3	2	0	14.0	63	15	9	9	0	0	0	1	5	0	13	1	1	0	1.000	0-0	0	93	.649	3.75	5.79
2020	Tor	AL	13	0	0	21.0	98	22	13	12	3	0	2	0	14	1	22	0	2	0	1.000	0-0	2	94	.867	5.61	5.14
2021	Tor	AL	11	5	0	33.2	156	38	22	21	7	0	0	3	18	0	39	2	1	2	.333	0-0	0	95	.897	6.65	5.61
2022	Tor	AL	1	0	1	2.0	10	2	1	1	0	0	1	1	1	0	3	0	0	0	-	0-0	2	94	.971	5.48	4.50
	4 ML YEARS		28	7	1	70.2	327	77	45	43	10	0	3	5	38	1	77	3	4	2	.667	0-0	2	94	.840	5.70	5.48

Jarred Kelenic

Bats: L Throws: L Pos: CF-24;RF-24;PH-6;LF-3;DH-2   KELL-nick   Ht: 6'1" Wt: 206 Born: 7/16/1999 Age: 23

			BATTING																	RUNNING			AVERAGES			
Year	Team	Lg	G	AB	H	2B	3B	HR	(Hm	Rd)	TB	R	RBI	RC	TBB	IBB	SO	HBP	SH	SF	SB	CS	GDP	Avg	OBP	Slg	OPS
2022	Tacom	AAA	86	352	104	32	3	18	(-	-)	196	58	65	73	35	3	82	5	0	2	9	4	3	.295	.365	.557	.922
2021	Sea	AL	93	337	61	13	1	14	(5	9)	118	41	43	29	36	0	106	3	0	1	6	4	5	.181	.265	.350	.615
2022	Sea	AL	54	163	23	5	1	7	(4	3)	51	20	17	13	16	0	61	1	0	1	5	2	3	.141	.221	.313	.534
	2 ML YEARS		147	500	84	18	2	21	(9	12)	169	61	60	42	52	0	167	4	0	2	11	6	8	.168	.251	.338	.589

Brad Keller

Pitches: R Bats: R Pos: SP-22; RP-13   Ht: 6'5" Wt: 255 Born: 7/27/1995 Age: 27

			HOW MUCH PITCHED					WHAT HE GAVE UP											THE RESULTS						
Year	Team	Lg	G	GS	GF	IP	BFP	H	R	ER	HR	SH	SF	HB	TBB	IBB	SO	WP	W	L	Pct	Sv-Op	Hld	Vel	OPS	ERC	ERA
2018	KC	AL	41	20	2	140.1	583	133	50	48	7	0	3	2	50	1	96	8	9	6	.600	0-2	5	94	.653	3.39	3.08
2019	KC	AL	28	28	0	165.1	709	154	80	77	15	1	5	9	70	2	122	9	7	14	.333	0-0	0	93	.711	3.94	4.19
2020	KC	AL	9	9	0	54.2	215	39	16	15	2	0	3	2	17	0	35	1	5	3	.625	0-0	0	93	.513	2.06	2.47
2021	KC	AL	26	26	0	133.2	613	158	89	80	18	1	9	7	64	1	120	5	8	12	.400	0-0	0	94	.831	5.97	5.39
2022	KC	AL	35	22	4	139.2	617	153	86	79	17	1	4	2	57	1	102	11	6	14	.300	1-1	1	94	.771	4.86	5.09
	5 ML YEARS		139	105	6	633.2	2737	637	321	299	59	3	24	22	258	5	475	34	35	49	.417	1-3	6	94	.723	4.24	4.25

Mitch Keller

Pitches: R Bats: R Pos: SP-29; RP-2   Ht: 6'2" Wt: 220 Born: 4/4/1996 Age: 27

			HOW MUCH PITCHED					WHAT HE GAVE UP											THE RESULTS						
Year	Team	Lg	G	GS	GF	IP	BFP	H	R	ER	HR	SH	SF	HB	TBB	IBB	SO	WP	W	L	Pct	Sv-Op	Hld	Vel	OPS	ERC	ERA
2019	Pit	NL	11	11	0	48.0	227	72	41	38	6	1	2	1	16	0	65	2	1	5	.167	0-0	0	95	.940	7.13	7.13
2020	Pit	NL	5	5	0	21.2	87	9	7	7	4	0	0	1	18	0	16	2	1	1	.500	0-0	0	94	.660	3.51	2.91
2021	Pit	NL	23	23	0	100.2	470	131	69	69	10	3	4	7	49	1	92	2	5	11	.313	0-0	0	95	.877	6.61	6.17
2022	Pit	NL	31	29	0	159.0	687	162	77	69	14	2	4	12	60	1	138	2	5	12	.294	0-0	0	95	.729	4.35	3.91
	4 ML YEARS		70	68	0	329.1	1471	374	194	183	34	6	10	21	143	2	311	8	12	29	.293	0-0	0	95	.806	5.35	5.00

Trevor Kelley

Pitches: R Bats: R Pos: RP-18   Ht: 6'2" Wt: 210 Born: 10/20/1992 Age: 30

			HOW MUCH PITCHED					WHAT HE GAVE UP											THE RESULTS						
Year	Team	Lg	G	GS	GF	IP	BFP	H	R	ER	HR	SH	SF	HB	TBB	IBB	SO	WP	W	L	Pct	Sv-Op	Hld	Vel	OPS	ERC	ERA
2022	Nashv	AAA	34	0	22	34.1	140	29	11	9	2	1	0	0	10	0	42	1	3	3	.500	9- -	-	-	.560	2.57	2.36
2019	Bos	AL	10	0	3	8.1	40	9	8	8	2	0	4	0	5	0	6	2	0	3	.000	0-0	0	89	.963	6.15	8.64
2020	Phi	NL	4	0	2	3.1	19	8	4	4	2	0	0	0	1	0	5	1	0	0	-	0-0	0	90	1.307	17.83	10.80
2022	Mil	NL	18	0	8	23.2	107	25	17	16	7	0	0	2	9	0	23	0	1	0	1.000	0-1	2	90	.868	5.99	6.08
	3 ML YEARS		32	0	13	35.1	166	42	29	28	11	0	4	2	15	0	34	3	1	3	.250	0-1	2	90	.942	6.98	7.13

Carson Kelly

Bats: R **Throws:** R **Pos:** C-100;PH-7;DH-2   **Ht:** 6'2" **Wt:** 212 **Born:** 7/14/1994 **Age:** 28

Year Team	Lg	G	AB	H	2B	3B	HR	(Hm	Rd)	TB	R	RBI	RC	TBB	IBB	SO	HBP	SH	SF	SB	CS	GDP	Avg	OBP	Slg	OPS
2016 StL	NL	10	13	2	1	0	0	(0	0)	3	1	1	0	0	0	2	1	0	0	0	0	0	.154	.214	.231	.445
2017 StL	NL	34	69	12	3	0	0	(0	0)	15	5	6	4	5	0	11	1	0	0	0	0	3	.174	.240	.217	.457
2018 StL	NL	19	35	4	0	0	0	(0	0)	4	1	3	1	3	0	7	1	3	0	0	0	0	.114	.205	.114	.319
2019 Ari	NL	111	314	77	19	0	18	(4	14)	150	46	47	46	48	10	79	2	0	1	0	0	11	.245	.348	.478	.826
2020 Ari	NL	39	122	27	5	0	5	(2	3)	47	11	19	16	6	0	29	1	0	0	0	0	4	.221	.264	.385	.649
2021 Ari	NL	98	304	73	11	1	13	(5	8)	125	41	46	45	44	1	74	6	0	5	0	0	10	.240	.343	.417	.754
2022 Ari	NL	104	317	67	18	0	7	(4	3)	106	40	35	27	29	0	71	4	0	4	2	0	10	.211	.282	.334	.617
7 ML YEARS		415	1174	262	57	1	43	(15	28)	450	145	157	139	135	11	273	16	3	10	2	0	38	.223	.309	.383	.693

Joe Kelly

Pitches: R **Bats:** R **Pos:** RP-42; SP-1   **Ht:** 6'1" **Wt:** 174 **Born:** 6/9/1988 **Age:** 35

Year Team	Lg	G	GS	GF	IP	BFP	H	R	ER	HR	SH	SF	HB	TBB	IBB	SO	WP	W	L	Pct	Sv-Op	Hld	Vel	OPS	ERC	ERA
2012 StL	NL	24	16	4	107.0	457	112	50	42	10	4	1	3	36	2	75	4	5	7	.417	0-0	0	94	.740	4.17	3.53
2013 StL	NL	37	15	8	124.0	532	124	42	37	10	2	2	5	44	4	79	3	10	5	.667	0-1	2	95	.694	3.88	2.69
2014 2 Tms		17	17	0	96.1	415	88	48	45	8	2	4	7	42	0	66	3	6	4	.600	0-0	0	95	.693	3.92	4.20
2015 Bos	AL	25	25	0	134.1	587	145	76	72	15	0	5	6	49	0	110	9	10	6	.625	0-0	0	95	.769	4.68	4.82
2016 Bos	AL	20	6	6	40.0	188	44	23	23	5	0	4	2	24	0	48	0	4	0	1.000	0-1	2	96	.828	5.80	5.18
2017 Bos	AL	54	0	14	58.0	238	42	19	18	3	0	2	1	27	1	52	4	4	1	.800	0-4	13	99	.573	2.61	2.79
2018 Bos	AL	73	0	9	65.2	285	57	34	32	4	0	4	5	32	0	68	4	4	2	.667	2-7	21	98	.662	3.70	4.39
2019 LAD	NL	55	0	13	51.1	226	49	31	26	6	0	0	3	22	2	62	10	5	4	.556	1-6	8	98	.711	4.16	4.56
2020 LAD	NL	12	1	2	10.0	42	8	3	2	0	0	1	0	7	0	9	3	0	0	-	0-0	3	97	.681	3.57	1.80
2021 LAD	NL	48	0	7	44.0	182	28	16	14	3	0	2	4	15	1	50	0	2	0	1.000	2-3	10	98	.544	2.01	2.86
2022 CWS	AL	43	1	4	37.0	170	36	26	25	2	0	1	3	23	0	53	4	1	3	.250	1-1	15	98	.721	4.73	6.08
14 StL		7	7	0	35.0	156	41	19	17	3	1	3		10	0	25	3	2	2	.500	0-0	0	95	.774	4.82	4.37
14 Bos	AL	10	10	0	61.1	259	47	29	28	5	1	3	4	32	0	41	0	4	2	.667	0-0	0	95	.641	3.43	4.11
Postseason		40	5	4	58.1	247	52	25	23	4	1	1	2	21	2	53	6	4	3	.571	1-1	2	97	.625	3.17	3.55
11 ML YEARS		408	81	67	767.2	3322	733	368	336	66	8	26	39	321	10	672	44	51	32	.614	6-23	74	96	.704	3.98	3.94

Merrill Kelly

Pitches: R **Bats:** R **Pos:** SP-33   **Ht:** 6'2" **Wt:** 202 **Born:** 10/14/1988 **Age:** 34

Year Team	Lg	G	GS	GF	IP	BFP	H	R	ER	HR	SH	SF	HB	TBB	IBB	SO	WP	W	L	Pct	Sv-Op	Hld	Vel	OPS	ERC	ERA
2019 Ari	NL	32	32	0	183.1	777	184	95	90	29	2	5	2	57	4	158	4	13	14	.481	0-0	0	92	.761	4.16	4.42
2020 Ari	NL	5	5	0	31.1	125	26	9	9	5	0	0	1	5	1	29	0	3	2	.600	0-0	0	92	.651	2.68	2.59
2021 Ari	NL	27	27	0	158.0	667	163	82	78	21	6	4	4	41	3	130	2	7	11	.389	0-0	0	92	.748	4.00	4.44
2022 Ari	NL	33	33	0	200.1	804	167	77	75	21	1	1	2	61	2	177	4	13	8	.619	0-0	0	93	.657	2.94	3.37
4 ML YEARS		97	97	0	573.0	2373	540	263	252	76	9	10	9	164	10	494	10	36	35	.507	0-0	0	92	.716	3.59	3.96

Michael Kelly

Pitches: R **Bats:** R **Pos:** RP-4   **Ht:** 6'4" **Wt:** 185 **Born:** 9/6/1992 **Age:** 30

Year Team	Lg	G	GS	GF	IP	BFP	H	R	ER	HR	SH	SF	HB	TBB	IBB	SO	WP	W	L	Pct	Sv-Op	Hld	Vel	OPS	ERC	ERA
2022 LV	AAA	47	1	12	51.0	227	56	34	30	8	0	1	1	24	0	66	1	2	2	.500	1--	-	-	.824	5.49	5.29
2022 Phi	NL	4	0	3	4.0	16	3	1	1	1	0	0	1	1	0	4	0	0	0	-	0-0	0	94	.741	4.30	2.25

Zack Kelly

Pitches: R **Bats:** R **Pos:** RP-13   **Ht:** 6'3" **Wt:** 205 **Born:** 3/3/1995 **Age:** 28

Year Team	Lg	G	GS	GF	IP	BFP	H	R	ER	HR	SH	SF	HB	TBB	IBB	SO	WP	W	L	Pct	Sv-Op	Hld	Vel	OPS	ERC	ERA
2022 Wrcstr	AAA	44	0	21	49.2	209	34	23	15	2	1	2	3	25	3	72	4	6	3	.667	3--	-	-	.545	2.50	2.72
2022 Bos	AL	13	0	2	13.2	59	14	6	6	2	0	1	0	4	0	11	0	1	0	1.000	0-0	1	95	.731	4.01	3.95

Tony Kemp

Bats: L **Throws:** R **Pos:** 2B-89;LF-65;PH-15;DH-2   **Ht:** 5'6" **Wt:** 160 **Born:** 10/31/1991 **Age:** 31

Year Team	Lg	G	AB	H	2B	3B	HR	(Hm	Rd)	TB	R	RBI	RC	TBB	IBB	SO	HBP	SH	SF	SB	CS	GDP	Avg	OBP	Slg	OPS
2016 Hou	AL	59	120	26	4	3	1	(1	0)	39	15	7	11	14	0	27	0	1	1	2	1	5	.217	.296	.325	.621
2017 Hou	AL	17	37	8	1	0	0	(0	0)	9	6	4	4	1	0	5	1	0	0	1	0	0	.216	.256	.243	.500
2018 Hou	AL	97	255	67	15	0	6	(1	5)	100	37	30	41	32	1	44	3	3	1	9	3	7	.263	.351	.392	.743
2019 2 Tms		110	245	52	9	4	8	(7	1)	93	31	29	28	23	1	47	6	1	4	4	4	4	.212	.291	.380	.671
2020 Oak	AL	49	93	23	5	0	0	(0	0)	28	15	4	11	15	0	14	3	1	2	3	1	1	.247	.363	.301	.664
2021 Oak	AL	131	330	92	16	3	8	(2	6)	138	54	37	65	52	0	51	6	4	5	8	2	2	.279	.382	.418	.800
2022 Oak	AL	147	497	117	24	2	7	(4	3)	166	61	46	59	45	0	69	8	5	3	11	1	5	.235	.307	.334	.641
19 Hou	AL	66	163	37	6	2	7	(6	1)	68	23	17	18	16	1	29	4	1	2	4	3	2	.227	.308	.417	.725
19 ChC	NL	44	82	15	3	2	1	(1	0)	25	8	12	10	7	0	18	2	0	2	0	1	2	.183	.258	.305	.563
Postseason		6	14	4	1	0	1	(1	0)	8	3	1	3	5	0	3	0	0	0	0	0	0	.286	.474	.571	1.045
7 ML YEARS		610	1577	385	74	12	30	(15	15)	573	219	157	219	182	2	257	27	15	16	38	12	23	.244	.330	.363	.693

Buddy Kennedy

Bats: R **Throws:** R **Pos:** 2B-22;DH-3;PH-3;3B-2;PR-1 **Ht:** 6'1" **Wt:** 190 **Born:** 10/5/1998 **Age:** 24

							BATTING													RUNNING			AVERAGES			
Year	Team	Lg	G	AB	H	2B	3B	HR	(Hm | Rd)	TB	R	RBI	RC	TBB	IBB	SO	HBP	SH	SF	SB	CS	GDP	Avg	OBP	Slg	OPS
2022	Reno	AAA	93	330	86	14	3	7	(- | -)	127	55	40	45	54	0	76	3	0	7	8	4	12	.261	.363	.385	.748
2022	Ari	NL	30	83	18	2	2	1	(1 | 0)	27	10	12	12	8	0	23	1	0	2	0	0	1	.217	.287	.325	.613

Ian Kennedy

Pitches: R **Bats:** R **Pos:** RP-57 **Ht:** 6'0" **Wt:** 210 **Born:** 12/19/1984 **Age:** 38

			HOW MUCH PITCHED					WHAT HE GAVE UP										THE RESULTS							
Year	Team	Lg	G	GS	GF	IP	BFP	H	R	ER	HR	SH	SF	HB	TBB	IBB	SO	WP	W	L	Pct	Sv-Op	Hld	Vel	OPS	ERC	ERA
2007	NYY	AL	3	3	0	19.0	77	13	6	4	1	0	0	0	9	0	15	0	1	0	1.000	0-0	0	89	.565	2.42	1.89
2008	NYY	AL	10	9	1	39.2	194	50	37	36	5	1	4	1	26	0	27	3	0	4	.000	0-0	0	89	.917	6.93	8.17
2009	NYY	AL	1	0	0	1.0	6	0	0	0	0	0	0	1	2	0	1	0	0	0	-	0-0	1	92	.500	7.00	0.00
2010	Ari	NL	32	32	0	194.0	810	163	87	82	26	11	5	10	70	2	168	16	9	10	.474	0-0	0	89	.696	3.47	3.80
2011	Ari	NL	33	33	0	222.0	900	186	73	71	19	9	9	9	55	0	198	11	21	4	.840	0-0	0	90	.641	2.71	2.88
2012	Ari	NL	33	33	0	208.1	899	216	101	93	28	13	5	14	55	4	187	5	15	12	.556	0-0	0	90	.775	4.18	4.02
2013	2 Tms	NL	31	31	0	181.1	794	180	108	99	27	8	5	12	73	1	163	10	7	10	.412	0-0	0	92	.781	4.64	4.91
2014	SD	NL	33	33	0	201.0	846	189	85	81	16	9	8	4	70	4	207	11	13	13	.500	0-0	0	92	.698	3.47	3.63
2015	SD	NL	30	30	0	168.1	713	166	95	80	31	8	2	7	52	4	174	5	9	15	.375	0-0	0	91	.816	4.37	4.28
2016	KC	AL	33	33	0	195.2	818	173	81	80	33	1	5	13	66	1	184	4	11	11	.500	0-0	0	92	.722	3.94	3.68
2017	KC	AL	30	30	0	154.0	655	143	99	92	34	1	6	5	61	2	131	4	5	13	.278	0-0	0	92	.804	4.64	5.38
2018	KC	AL	22	22	0	119.2	518	125	66	62	20	4	2	1	40	2	105	4	3	9	.250	0-0	0	92	.779	4.51	4.66
2019	KC	AL	63	0	51	63.1	266	64	24	24	6	3	0	1	17	1	73	3	3	2	.600	30-34	1	94	.675	3.63	3.41
2020	KC	AL	15	1	1	14.0	69	20	17	14	7	1	0	1	5	1	15	0	0	2	.000	0-0	2	94	1.076	9.67	9.00
2021	2 Tms		55	0	44	56.1	228	45	21	20	12	1	0	2	17	3	62	0	3	1	.750	26-30	0	94	.700	3.41	3.20
2022	Ari	NL	57	0	21	50.1	232	57	33	30	11	0	3	1	22	3	44	3	4	7	.364	10-16	10	93	.849	5.71	5.36
13	Ari	NL	21	21	0	124.0	549	128	79	72	18	8	5	10	48	1	108	9	3	8	.273	0-0	0	90	.798	4.82	5.23
13	SD	NL	10	10	0	57.1	245	52	29	27	9	0	0	2	25	0	55	1	4	2	.667	0-0	0	94	.744	4.26	4.24
21	Tex	AL	32	0	25	32.1	126	27	9	9	5	0	0	0	7	2	35	0	0	0	-	16-17	0	94	.656	2.83	2.51
21	Phi	NL	23	0	19	24.0	102	18	12	11	7	1	0	2	10	1	27	0	3	1	.750	10-13	0	94	.758	4.22	4.13
	Postseason		2	2	0	12.2	57	13	6	6	1	0	2	3	3	0	8	1	0	1	.000	0-0	0	92	.782	4.25	4.26
	16 ML YEARS		481	290	118	1888.0	8025	1790	933	868	276	70	54	82	640	28	1754	79	104	113	.479	66-80	14	91	.746	4.01	4.14

Max Kepler

Bats: L **Throws:** L **Pos:** RF-110;PH-9;CF-3;DH-2 **Ht:** 6'4" **Wt:** 225 **Born:** 2/10/1993 **Age:** 30

							BATTING													RUNNING			AVERAGES			
Year	Team	Lg	G	AB	H	2B	3B	HR	(Hm	Rd)	TB	R	RBI	RC	TBB	IBB	SO	HBP	SH	SF	SB	CS	GDP	Avg	OBP	Slg	OPS
2015	Min	AL	3	7	1	0	0	0	(0	0)	1	0	0	0	0	0	3	0	0	0	0	0	0	.143	.143	.143	.286
2016	Min	AL	113	396	93	20	2	17	(8	9)	168	52	63	52	42	3	93	3	1	5	6	2	2	.235	.309	.424	.734
2017	Min	AL	147	511	124	32	2	19	(9	10)	217	67	69	68	47	2	114	6	1	3	6	1	5	.243	.312	.425	.737
2018	Min	AL	156	532	119	30	4	20	(12	8)	217	80	58	65	71	2	96	5	0	3	4	5	8	.224	.319	.408	.727
2019	Min	AL	134	524	132	32	0	36	(17	19)	272	98	90	90	60	0	99	8	0	4	1	5	5	.252	.336	.519	.855
2020	Min	AL	48	171	39	9	0	9	(3	6)	75	27	23	27	22	0	36	2	0	1	3	0	1	.228	.321	.439	.760
2021	Min	AL	121	426	90	21	4	19	(11	8)	176	61	54	57	54	3	96	6	0	4	10	0	2	.211	.306	.413	.719
2022	Min	AL	115	388	88	18	1	9	(6	3)	135	54	43	39	49	1	66	5	0	4	3	2	7	.227	.318	.348	.666
	Postseason		6	18	1	1	0	0	(0	0)	2	1	0	1	7	0	4	0	0	0	0	0	0	.056	.320	.111	.431
	8 ML YEARS		837	2955	686	162	13	129	(66	63)	1261	439	400	398	345	11	603	35	2	24	33	15	30	.232	.317	.427	.744

Ray Kerr

Pitches: L **Bats:** L **Pos:** RP-7 **Ht:** 6'3" **Wt:** 185 **Born:** 9/10/1994 **Age:** 28

			HOW MUCH PITCHED					WHAT HE GAVE UP										THE RESULTS							
Year	Team	Lg	G	GS	GF	IP	BFP	H	R	ER	HR	SH	SF	HB	TBB	IBB	SO	WP	W	L	Pct	Sv-Op	Hld	Vel	OPS	ERC	ERA
2022	ElPaso	AAA	46	0	10	44.1	205	45	29	25	4	0	1	1	36	0	67	3	5	0	1.000	3- -		-	.831	6.00	5.08
2022	SD	NL	7	0	6	5.0	21	3	5	5	1	0	1	0	4	0	3	1	0	0	-	0-0	0	96	.771	4.26	9.00

Clayton Kershaw

Pitches: L **Bats:** L **Pos:** SP-22 **Ht:** 6'4" **Wt:** 225 **Born:** 3/19/1988 **Age:** 35

			HOW MUCH PITCHED					WHAT HE GAVE UP										THE RESULTS							
Year	Team	Lg	G	GS	GF	IP	BFP	H	R	ER	HR	SH	SF	HB	TBB	IBB	SO	WP	W	L	Pct	Sv-Op	Hld	Vel	OPS	ERC	ERA
2008	LAD	NL	22	21	0	107.2	470	109	51	51	11	3	3	1	52	3	100	7	5	5	.500	0-0	1	94	.756	4.53	4.26
2009	LAD	NL	31	30	1	171.0	701	119	55	53	7	11	2	1	91	4	185	11	8	8	.500	0-0	0	94	.588	2.60	2.79
2010	LAD	NL	32	32	0	204.1	848	160	73	66	13	8	4	7	81	9	212	5	13	10	.565	0-0	0	93	.615	2.72	2.91
2011	LAD	NL	33	33	0	233.1	912	174	66	59	15	11	2	3	54	2	248	5	21	5	.808	0-0	0	93	.554	2.00	2.28
2012	LAD	NL	33	33	0	227.2	901	170	70	64	16	18	4	5	63	5	229	6	14	9	.609	0-0	0	93	.593	2.20	2.53
2013	LAD	NL	33	33	0	236.0	908	164	55	48	11	8	3	3	52	2	232	12	16	9	.640	0-0	0	93	.521	1.65	1.83
2014	LAD	NL	27	27	0	198.1	749	139	42	39	9	6	1	2	31	0	239	7	21	3	.875	0-0	0	93	.521	1.53	1.77
2015	LAD	NL	33	33	0	232.2	890	163	62	55	15	4	0	5	42	1	301	9	16	7	.696	0-0	0	94	.521	1.67	2.13
2016	LAD	NL	21	21	0	149.0	544	97	31	28	8	4	1	2	11	1	172	5	12	4	.750	0-0	0	93	.472	1.23	1.69
2017	LAD	NL	27	27	0	175.0	679	136	49	45	23	4	3	0	30	0	202	4	18	4	.818	0-0	0	93	.604	2.27	2.31
2018	LAD	NL	26	26	0	161.1	650	139	55	49	17	3	2	2	29	0	155	10	9	5	.643	0-0	0	91	.630	2.56	2.73
2019	LAD	NL	29	28	0	178.1	706	145	63	60	28	6	1	2	41	0	189	7	16	5	.762	0-0	0	90	.664	2.86	3.03
2020	LAD	NL	10	10	0	58.1	221	41	18	14	8	0	1	1	8	0	62	0	6	2	.750	0-0	0	92	.591	1.90	2.16
2021	LAD	NL	22	22	0	121.2	488	103	51	48	15	3	0	3	21	0	144	7	10	8	.556	0-0	0	91	.636	2.62	3.55
2022	LAD	NL	22	22	0	126.1	493	96	36	32	10	1	2	2	23	0	137	0	12	3	.800	0-0	0	91	.556	1.99	2.28
	Postseason		37	30	2	189.0	759	153	93	88	28	6	5	4	50	5	207	10	13	12	.520	1-2	1	93	.656	2.90	4.19
	15 ML YEARS		401	398	1	2581.0	10160	1955	777	711	206	90	29	39	629	27	2807	95	197	87	.694	0-0	1	93	.582	2.18	2.48

Dallas Keuchel

Pitches: L **Bats:** L **Pos:** SP-14   KY-kull   **Ht:** 6'2" **Wt:** 205 **Born:** 1/1/1988 **Age:** 35

Year Team	Lg	G	GS	GF	IP	BFP	H	R	ER	HR	SH	SF	HB	TBB	IBB	SO	WP	W	L	Pct	Sv-Op	Hld	Vel	OPS	ERC	ERA
2012 Hou	NL	16	16	0	85.1	377	93	56	50	14	9	3	1	39	1	38	2	3	8	.273	0-0	0	88	.823	5.39	5.27
2013 Hou	AL	31	22	2	153.2	682	184	96	88	20	2	3	5	52	3	123	7	6	10	.375	0-0	0	89	.812	5.33	5.15
2014 Hou	AL	29	29	0	200.0	808	187	71	65	11	4	5	7	48	2	146	7	12	9	.571	0-0	0	90	.655	3.02	2.93
2015 Hou	AL	33	33	0	**232.0**	**911**	185	68	64	17	1	3	2	51	0	216	9	**20**	8	.714	0-0	0	90	.575	**2.26**	2.48
2016 Hou	AL	26	26	0	168.0	701	168	88	85	20	2	1	2	48	1	144	9	9	12	.429	0-0	0	89	.736	3.84	4.55
2017 Hou	AL	23	23	0	145.2	584	116	50	47	15	1	0	2	47	0	125	1	14	5	.737	0-0	0	89	.619	2.82	2.90
2018 Hou	AL	34	**34**	0	204.2	**874**	**211**	92	85	18	3	**9**	2	58	0	153	9	12	11	.522	0-0	0	89	.704	3.71	3.74
2019 Atl	NL	19	19	0	112.2	487	115	50	47	16	5	0	9	39	1	91	6	8	8	.500	0-0	0	88	.764	4.62	3.75
2020 CWS	AL	11	11	0	63.1	257	52	15	14	2	**2**	0	0	17	0	42	0	6	2	.750	0-0	0	87	.556	2.21	1.99
2021 CWS	AL	32	30	0	162.0	720	189	**105**	95	25	0	1	7	59	1	95	5	9	9	.500	0-0	0	88	.827	5.51	5.28
2022 3 Tms		14	14	0	60.2	303	94	69	62	11	0	3	0	31	2	45	3	2	9	.182	0-0	0	87	.985	8.50	9.20
22 CWS	AL	8	8	0	32.0	164	49	33	28	6	0	1	0	20	2	20	3	2	5	.286	0-0	0	87	.945	8.84	7.88
22 Ari	NL	4	4	0	18.2	89	27	22	20	4	0	0	0	7	0	18	0	0	2	.000	0-0	0	88	1.016	7.52	9.64
22 Tex	AL	2	2	0	10.0	50	18	14	14	1	0	2	0	4	0	7	0	0	2	.000	0-0	0	87	1.054	9.26	12.60
Postseason		13	12	1	63.0	264	58	29	26	10	4	1	0	20	3	56	1	4	3	.571	0-0	0	90	.727	3.61	3.71
11 ML YEARS		268	257	2	1588.0	6704	1594	760	702	169	29	28	37	489	11	1218	58	101	91	.526	0-0	2	89	.718	3.89	3.98

Carter Kieboom

Bats: R **Throws:** R **Pos:** IF   **Ht:** 6'2" **Wt:** 200 **Born:** 9/3/1997 **Age:** 25

Year Team	Lg	G	AB	H	2B	3B	HR	(Hm	Rd)	TB	R	RBI	RC	TBB	IBB	SO	HBP	SH	SF	SB	CS	GDP	Avg	OBP	Slg	OPS
2019 Was	NL	11	39	5	0	0	2	(2	0)	11	4	2	0	4	1	16	0	0	0	0	0	0	.128	.209	.282	.491
2020 Was	NL	33	99	20	1	0	0	(0	0)	21	15	9	10	17	0	33	5	0	1	0	1	6	.202	.344	.212	.556
2021 Was	NL	62	217	45	6	0	6	(5	1)	69	26	20	14	25	2	62	5	0	2	0	0	9	.207	.301	.318	.619
3 ML YEARS		106	355	70	7	0	8	(7	1)	101	45	31	24	46	3	111	10	0	3	0	1	15	.197	.304	.285	.589

Kevin Kiermaier

Bats: L **Throws:** R **Pos:** CF-60;DH-2;PR-2   KEER-my-urr   **Ht:** 6'1" **Wt:** 210 **Born:** 4/22/1990 **Age:** 33

Year Team	Lg	G	AB	H	2B	3B	HR	(Hm	Rd)	TB	R	RBI	RC	TBB	IBB	SO	HBP	SH	SF	SB	CS	GDP	Avg	OBP	Slg	OPS
2013 TB	AL	1	0	0	0	0	0	(0	0)	0	0	0	0	0	0	0	0	0	0	0	0	0	-	-	-	-
2014 TB	AL	108	331	87	16	8	10	(4	6)	149	35	35	37	23	2	71	3	5	2	5	4	3	.263	.315	.450	.765
2015 TB	AL	151	505	133	25	12	10	(5	5)	212	62	40	66	24	0	95	2	2	2	18	5	7	.263	.298	.420	.718
2016 TB	AL	105	366	90	20	2	12	(5	7)	150	55	37	54	40	1	74	7	0	1	21	3	5	.246	.331	.410	.741
2017 TB	AL	98	380	105	15	3	15	(8	7)	171	56	39	53	31	2	99	5	4	1	16	7	3	.276	.338	.450	.788
2018 TB	AL	88	332	72	12	9	7	(4	3)	123	44	29	30	25	2	91	6	2	2	10	5	4	.217	.282	.370	.653
2019 TB	AL	129	447	102	20	7	14	(7	7)	178	60	55	56	26	2	104	5	1	1	19	5	8	.228	.278	.398	.676
2020 TB	AL	49	138	30	5	3	3	(0	3)	50	16	22	20	20	1	42	1	0	0	8	1	2	.217	.321	.362	.683
2021 TB	AL	122	348	90	19	7	4	(2	2)	135	54	37	47	33	2	99	5	0	4	9	5	4	.259	.328	.388	.716
2022 TB	AL	63	206	47	8	0	7	(4	3)	76	28	22	27	14	0	61	1	0	0	6	1	2	.228	.281	.369	.649
Postseason		29	91	20	9	0	4	(2	2)	41	11	11	11	3	1	28	1	0	1	0	1	1	.220	.253	.451	.703
10 ML YEARS		914	3053	756	140	51	82	(39	43)	1244	410	316	390	236	12	736	35	14	13	112	36	38	.248	.308	.407	.715

Yusei Kikuchi

Pitches: L **Bats:** L **Pos:** SP-20; RP-12   **Ht:** 6'0" **Wt:** 205 **Born:** 6/17/1991 **Age:** 32

Year Team	Lg	G	GS	GF	IP	BFP	H	R	ER	HR	SH	SF	HB	TBB	IBB	SO	WP	W	L	Pct	Sv-Op	Hld	Vel	OPS	ERC	ERA
2019 Sea	AL	32	32	0	161.2	721	195	109	98	36	0	5	6	50	0	116	5	6	11	.353	0-0	0	92	.888	5.97	5.46
2020 Sea	AL	9	9	0	47.0	194	41	27	27	3	0	2	0	20	0	47	3	2	4	.333	0-0	0	95	.681	3.31	5.17
2021 Sea	AL	29	29	0	157.0	666	145	82	77	27	1	1	5	62	0	163	6	7	9	.438	0-0	0	95	.751	4.28	4.41
2022 Tor	AL	32	20	4	100.2	454	93	67	58	23	1	3	9	58	0	124	3	6	7	.462	1-1	0	95	.847	5.67	5.19
4 ML YEARS		102	90	4	466.1	2035	474	285	260	89	2	11	20	190	0	450	17	21	31	.404	1-1	0	94	.814	5.05	5.02

Caleb Kilian

Pitches: R **Bats:** R **Pos:** SP-3   **Ht:** 6'4" **Wt:** 180 **Born:** 6/2/1997 **Age:** 26

Year Team	Lg	G	GS	GF	IP	BFP	H	R	ER	HR	SH	SF	HB	TBB	IBB	SO	WP	W	L	Pct	Sv-Op	Hld	Vel	OPS	ERC	ERA
2022 Iowa	AAA	26	26	0	106.2	478	108	56	50	7	1	2	3	59	0	125	7	5	4	.556	0--	-	-	.756	4.61	4.22
2022 ChC	NL	3	3	0	11.1	56	11	15	13	0	0	1	1	12	1	9	3	0	2	.000	0-0	0	94	.786	5.91	10.32

Ha-seong Kim

Bats: R **Throws:** R **Pos:** SS-131;3B-24;PH-3;PR-1   **Ht:** 5'9" **Wt:** 168 **Born:** 10/17/1995 **Age:** 27

Year Team	Lg	G	AB	H	2B	3B	HR	(Hm	Rd)	TB	R	RBI	RC	TBB	IBB	SO	HBP	SH	SF	SB	CS	GDP	Avg	OBP	Slg	OPS
2021 SD	NL	117	267	54	12	2	8	(5	3)	94	27	34	24	22	1	71	4	2	3	6	1	6	.202	.270	.352	.622
2022 SD	NL	150	517	130	29	3	11	(5	6)	198	58	59	66	51	0	100	7	3	4	12	2	9	.251	.325	.383	.708
2 ML YEARS		267	784	184	41	5	19	(10	9)	292	85	93	90	73	1	171	11	5	7	18	3	15	.235	.306	.372	.679

Craig Kimbrel

Pitches: R Bats: R Pos: RP-63
KIM-brull
Ht: 6'0" Wt: 215 Born: 5/28/1988 Age: 35

Year Team	Lg	G	GS	GF	IP	BFP	H	R	ER	HR	SH	SF	HB	TBB	IBB	SO	WP	W	L	Pct	Sv-Op	Hld	Vel	OPS	ERC	ERA
2010 Atl	NL	21	0	7	20.2	88	9	2	1	0	0	0	0	16	1	40	4	4	0	1.000	1-1	2	95	.437	1.72	0.44
2011 Atl	NL	79	0	64	77.0	306	48	19	18	3	1	2	1	32	1	127	4	4	3	.571	46-54	0	96	.499	1.88	2.10
2012 Atl	NL	63	0	56	62.2	231	27	7	7	3	0	0	2	14	0	116	5	3	1	.750	42-45	0	97	.358	0.93	1.01
2013 Atl	NL	68	0	60	67.0	258	39	10	9	4	0	0	3	20	2	98	3	4	3	.571	50-54	0	97	.487	1.58	1.21
2014 Atl	NL	63	0	54	61.2	244	30	13	11	2	3	0	2	26	0	95	6	0	3	.000	47-51	0	97	.430	1.41	1.61
2015 SD	NL	61	0	53	59.1	239	40	19	17	6	0	0	1	22	1	87	4	4	2	.667	39-43	0	97	.569	2.31	2.58
2016 Bos	AL	57	0	47	53.0	220	28	22	20	4	1	1	4	30	0	83	6	2	6	.250	31-33	1	97	.533	2.32	3.40
2017 Bos	AL	67	0	51	69.0	254	33	11	11	6	1	0	4	14	0	126	5	5	0	1.000	35-39	1	98	.444	1.21	1.43
2018 Bos	AL	63	0	57	62.1	247	31	19	19	7	1	0	2	31	0	96	7	5	1	.833	42-47	0	97	.565	2.07	2.74
2019 ChC	NL	23	0	17	20.2	96	21	15	15	9	0	1	2	12	0	30	0	0	4	.000	13-16	0	96	1.019	7.90	6.53
2020 ChC	NL	18	0	11	15.1	69	10	9	9	2	0	0	2	12	1	28	4	0	1	.000	2-3	3	97	.693	4.20	5.28
2021 2 Tms		63	0	43	59.2	235	31	19	15	6	0	3	3	23	1	100	8	4	5	.444	24-29	6	97	.514	1.76	2.26
2022 LAD	NL	63	0	47	60.0	260	51	31	25	4	1	1	5	28	2	72	7	6	7	.462	22-27	2	96	.675	3.52	3.75
21 ChC	NL	39	0	35	36.2	137	13	6	2	1	0	1	0	13	0	64	3	2	3	.400	23-25	0	97	.336	0.85	0.49
21 CWS	AL	24	0	8	23.0	98	18	13	13	5	0	2	3	10	1	36	5	2	2	.500	1-4	6	96	.774	4.27	5.09
Postseason		23	0	15	24.0	103	17	13	11	3	0	1	3	15	0	27	3	1	0	1.000	7-7	2	98	.709	4.08	4.13
13 ML YEARS		709	0	567	688.1	2747	398	196	177	56	8	8	31	280	9	1098	63	41	36	.532	394-442	15	97	.528	1.97	2.31

Isiah Kiner-Falefa

Bats: R Throws: R Pos: SS-138;3B-6;PR-2;PH-1
Ht: 5'11" Wt: 190 Born: 3/23/1995 Age: 28

Year Team	Lg	G	AB	H	2B	3B	HR	(Hm	Rd)	TB	R	RBI	RC	TBB	IBB	SO	HBP	SH	SF	SB	CS	GDP	Avg	OBP	Slg	OPS
2018 Tex	AL	111	356	93	18	2	4	(0	4)	127	43	34	34	28	1	62	6	5	1	7	5	14	.261	.325	.357	.682
2019 Tex	AL	65	202	48	12	1	1	(0	1)	65	23	21	18	14	0	49	4	1	1	3	0	9	.238	.299	.322	.620
2020 Tex	AL	58	211	59	4	3	3	(1	2)	78	28	10	26	14	0	32	2	0	1	8	5	6	.280	.329	.370	.699
2021 Tex	AL	158	635	172	25	3	8	(6	2)	227	74	53	72	28	2	90	11	1	2	20	5	11	.271	.312	.357	.670
2022 NYY	AL	142	483	126	20	0	4	(2	2)	158	66	48	53	35	2	72	5	3	5	22	4	13	.261	.314	.327	.642
5 ML YEARS		534	1887	498	79	9	20	(9	11)	655	234	166	203	119	5	305	28	10	10	60	19	53	.264	.316	.347	.663

John King

Pitches: L Bats: L Pos: RP-39
Ht: 6'2" Wt: 215 Born: 9/14/1994 Age: 28

Year Team	Lg	G	GS	GF	IP	BFP	H	R	ER	HR	SH	SF	HB	TBB	IBB	SO	WP	W	L	Pct	Sv-Op	Hld	Vel	OPS	ERC	ERA
2022 RdRck	AAA	14	0	0	17.1	80	20	16	14	5	0	1	1	7	0	18	2	2	1	.667	0--	-	-	.871	6.53	7.27
2020 Tex	AL	6	0	0	10.1	51	13	8	7	2	0	0	2	4	0	9	0	1	0	1.000	0-1	0	93	.839	6.83	6.10
2021 Tex	AL	27	0	6	46.0	193	41	24	18	3	1	0	4	12	1	40	2	7	5	.583	0-1	4	92	.626	3.00	3.52
2022 Tex	AL	39	0	5	51.1	222	61	27	23	5	1	1	1	14	3	30	2	1	4	.200	0-5	8	92	.754	4.67	4.03
3 ML YEARS		72	0	11	107.2	466	115	59	48	10	2	1	7	30	4	79	4	9	9	.500	0-7	12	92	.710	4.11	4.01

Michael King

Pitches: R Bats: R Pos: RP-34
Ht: 6'3" Wt: 210 Born: 5/25/1995 Age: 28

Year Team	Lg	G	GS	GF	IP	BFP	H	R	ER	HR	SH	SF	HB	TBB	IBB	SO	WP	W	L	Pct	Sv-Op	Hld	Vel	OPS	ERC	ERA
2019 NYY	AL	1	0	0	2.0	9	2	1	0	0	0	0	0	1	0	1	0	0	0	-	0-0	0	92	.444	1.68	0.00
2020 NYY	AL	9	4	1	26.2	121	30	23	23	5	0	0	2	11	0	26	0	1	2	.333	0-0	0	93	.846	5.80	7.76
2021 NYY	AL	22	6	3	63.1	275	57	29	25	6	1	1	6	24	1	62	5	2	4	.333	0-0	2	94	.674	3.69	3.55
2022 NYY	AL	34	0	10	51.0	199	35	15	13	3	0	1	0	16	2	66	2	6	3	.667	1-3	16	96	.547	1.89	2.29
Postseason		1	0	1	2.0	6	0	0	0	0	0	0	0	0	0	1	0	0	0	-	0-0	0	94	.000	0.00	0.00
4 ML YEARS		66	10	14	143.0	604	124	68	61	14	1	2	8	51	3	155	7	9	9	.500	1-3	18	94	.663	3.33	3.84

Scott Kingery

Bats: R Throws: R Pos: 2B-1
Ht: 5'10" Wt: 180 Born: 4/29/1994 Age: 29

Year Team	Lg	G	AB	H	2B	3B	HR	(Hm	Rd)	TB	R	RBI	RC	TBB	IBB	SO	HBP	SH	SF	SB	CS	GDP	Avg	OBP	Slg	OPS
2022 LV	AAA	95	305	70	14	4	7	(-	-)	113	51	34	45	54	0	108	2	4	1	18	2	1	.230	.348	.370	.719
2018 Phi	NL	147	452	102	23	4	8	(6	2)	153	55	35	39	24	1	126	1	3	5	10	3	2	.226	.267	.338	.605
2019 Phi	NL	126	458	118	34	4	19	(10	9)	217	64	55	63	34	1	147	5	1	2	15	4	3	.258	.315	.474	.788
2020 Phi	NL	36	113	18	5	0	3	(1	2)	32	12	6	6	9	0	35	1	1	0	0	0	1	.159	.228	.283	.511
2021 Phi	NL	15	19	1	0	0	0	(0	0)	1	1	0	0	0	0	12	0	0	0	0	0	0	.053	.053	.053	.105
2022 Phi	NL	1	0	0	0	0	0	(0	0)	0	0	0	0	0	0	0	0	0	0	0	0	0	.-	.-	.-	.-
5 ML YEARS		325	1042	239	62	6	30	(17	13)	403	132	96	108	67	2	320	9	2	7	25	7	6	.229	.280	.387	.667

Tyler Kinley

Pitches: R Bats: R Pos: RP-25
Ht: 6'4" Wt: 220 Born: 1/31/1991 Age: 32

Year Team	Lg	G	GS	GF	IP	BFP	H	R	ER	HR	SH	SF	HB	TBB	IBB	SO	WP	W	L	Pct	Sv-Op	Hld	Vel	OPS	ERC	ERA
2018 2 Tms		13	0	4	11.0	57	15	15	15	2	0	0	1	8	2	13	3	0	0	-	0-0	0	97	.942	8.25	12.27
2019	NL	52	0	13	49.1	221	43	20	20	5	1	2	1	36	2	46	3	3	1	.750	1-3	1	95	.723	4.71	3.65
2020 Col	NL	24	0	4	23.2	96	13	15	14	2	1	2	3	12	0	26	4	0	2	.000	0-0	0	96	.564	2.52	5.32
2021 Col	NL	70	0	7	70.1	295	59	37	37	12	1	2	2	26	1	68	4	3	2	.600	0-4	10	96	.720	3.60	4.73

Year	Team	Lg	G	GS	GF	IP	BFP	H	R	ER	HR	SH	SF	HB	TBB	IBB	SO	WP	W	L	Pct	Sv-Op	Hld	Vel	OPS	ERC	ERA
						HOW MUCH PITCHED					**WHAT HE GAVE UP**										**THE RESULTS**						
2022	Col	NL	25	0	3	24.0	100	21	5	2	0	0	0	1	6	0	27	2	1	1	.500	0-0	10	95	.560	2.31	0.75
18	Min	AL	4	0	3	3.1	23	9	9	9	2	0	0	0	4	0	4	2	0	0	-	0-0	0	96	1.407	25.66	24.30
18	Mia	NL	9	0	1	7.2	34	6	6	6	0	0	0	1	4	2	9	1	0	0	-	0-0	0	97	.634	2.62	7.04
	5 ML YEARS		184	0	31	178.1	769	151	92	88	21	3	6	8	88	5	180	16	7	6	.538	1-7	25	96	.697	3.83	4.44

George Kirby

Pitches: R Bats: R Pos: SP-25　　　　Ht: 6'4" Wt: 215 Born: 2/4/1998 Age: 25

Year	Team	Lg	G	GS	GF	IP	BFP	H	R	ER	HR	SH	SF	HB	TBB	IBB	SO	WP	W	L	Pct	Sv-Op	Hld	Vel	OPS	ERC	ERA
						HOW MUCH PITCHED					**WHAT HE GAVE UP**										**THE RESULTS**						
2019	Everett	A-	9	8	0	23.0	89	24	6	6	1	0	0	0	0	0	25	0	0	0	-	0- -	-	-	.674	2.53	2.35
2021	Everett	A+	9	9	0	41.2	164	33	15	11	1	1	0	1	8	0	52	1	4	2	.667	0- -	-	-	.569	1.89	2.38
2021	Ark	AA	6	6	0	26.0	110	25	8	8	0	0	1	1	7	0	28	2	1	1	.500	0- -	-	-	.627	2.81	2.77
2022	Ark	AA	5	5	0	24.2	93	17	6	5	3	0	0	1	5	0	32	0	2	0	1.000	0- -	-	-	.604	2.12	1.82
2022	Sea	AL	25	25	0	130.0	542	135	54	49	13	1	3	5	22	0	133	4	8	5	.615	0-0	0	95	.693	3.53	3.39

Alex Kirilloff

Bats: L Throws: L Pos: LF-21;1B-18;RF-8;DH-3;PH-2　　　　Ht: 6'2" Wt: 195 Born: 11/9/1997 Age: 25

Year	Team	Lg	G	AB	H	2B	3B	HR	(Hm	Rd)	TB	R	RBI	RC	TBB	IBB	SO	HBP	SH	SF	SB	CS	GDP	Avg	OBP	Slg	OPS
						BATTING															**RUNNING**			**AVERAGES**			
2022	StPaul	AAA	35	131	47	7	0	10	(-	-)	84	33	32	38	22	0	26	4	0	0	1	0	2	.359	.465	.641	1.106
2021	Min	AL	59	215	54	11	1	8	(6	2)	91	23	34	31	14	2	52	1	0	1	1	1	3	.251	.299	.423	.722
2022	Min	AL	45	144	36	7	0	3	(0	3)	52	14	21	16	5	0	36	4	0	2	0	0	5	.250	.290	.361	.651
	Postseason		1	4	1	0	0	0	(0	0)	1	0	0	0	0	0	0	0	0	0	0	0	0	.250	.250	.250	.500
	2 ML YEARS		104	359	90	18	1	11	(6	5)	143	37	55	47	19	2	88	5	0	3	1	1	8	.251	.295	.398	.694

Alejandro Kirk

Bats: R Throws: R Pos: C-78;DH-50;PH-16　　　　Ht: 5'8" Wt: 245 Born: 11/6/1998 Age: 24

Year	Team	Lg	G	AB	H	2B	3B	HR	(Hm	Rd)	TB	R	RBI	RC	TBB	IBB	SO	HBP	SH	SF	SB	CS	GDP	Avg	OBP	Slg	OPS
						BATTING															**RUNNING**			**AVERAGES**			
2020	Tor	AL	9	24	9	2	0	1	(1	0)	14	4	3	5	1	0	4	0	0	0	0	0	0	.375	.400	.583	.983
2021	Tor	AL	60	165	40	8	0	8	(4	4)	72	19	24	22	19	0	22	3	0	2	0	0	7	.242	.328	.436	.764
2022	Tor	AL	139	470	134	19	0	14	(8	6)	195	59	63	72	63	2	58	4	0	4	0	0	11	.285	.372	.415	.786
	Postseason		1	3	1	0	0	0	(0	0)	1	0	0	0	0	0	0	0	0	0	0	0	0	.333	.333	.333	.667
	3 ML YEARS		208	659	183	29	0	23	(13	10)	281	82	90	99	83	2	84	7	0	6	0	0	18	.278	.362	.426	.788

Andrew Kittredge

Pitches: R Bats: R Pos: RP-17　　　　Ht: 6'1" Wt: 230 Born: 3/17/1990 Age: 33

Year	Team	Lg	G	GS	GF	IP	BFP	H	R	ER	HR	SH	SF	HB	TBB	IBB	SO	WP	W	L	Pct	Sv-Op	Hld	Vel	OPS	ERC	ERA
						HOW MUCH PITCHED					**WHAT HE GAVE UP**										**THE RESULTS**						
2017	TB	AL	15	0	2	15.1	66	13	4	3	2	1	0	0	6	1	14	1	0	1	.000	0-0	1	94	.665	3.19	1.76
2018	TB	AL	33	3	4	38.1	181	54	34	33	7	1	2	1	17	5	30	1	3	2	.600	0-0	0	93	.956	7.35	7.75
2019	TB	AL	37	7	10	49.2	210	51	25	23	7	0	2	2	12	0	58	2	1	0	1.000	0-0	2	95	.717	4.03	4.17
2020	TB	AL	8	1	1	8.0	31	8	2	2	0	0	0	0	2	0	3	0	0	0	-	1-1	0	94	.667	3.09	2.25
2021	TB	AL	57	4	15	71.2	282	55	21	15	7	1	1	3	15	5	77	5	9	3	.750	8-9	7	95	.592	2.23	1.88
2022	TB	AL	17	0	9	20.0	75	15	7	7	4	0	0	0	2	0	14	0	3	1	.750	5-8	0	95	.638	2.26	3.15
	Postseason		2	0	0	3.1	11	2	0	0	0	0	0	0	0	0	2	0	0	0	-	0-0	0	94	.364	0.82	0.00
	6 ML YEARS		167	15	41	203.0	845	196	93	83	27	3	5	6	54	11	196	9	16	7	.696	14-18	11	95	.712	3.64	3.68

Corey Kluber

Pitches: R Bats: R Pos: SP-31　　　　CLUE-burr　　　　Ht: 6'4" Wt: 215 Born: 4/10/1986 Age: 37

Year	Team	Lg	G	GS	GF	IP	BFP	H	R	ER	HR	SH	SF	HB	TBB	IBB	SO	WP	W	L	Pct	Sv-Op	Hld	Vel	OPS	ERC	ERA
						HOW MUCH PITCHED					**WHAT HE GAVE UP**										**THE RESULTS**						
2011	Cle	AL	3	0	2	4.1	25	6	4	4	0	0	0	2	3	0	5	1	0	0	-	0-0	0	92	.740	8.12	8.31
2012	Cle	AL	12	12	0	63.0	281	76	44	36	9	1	0	4	18	0	54	2	2	5	.286	0-0	0	93	.834	5.38	5.14
2013	Cle	AL	26	24	1	147.1	608	153	67	63	15	4	2	5	33	0	136	1	11	5	.688	0-0	0	93	.729	3.83	3.85
2014	Cle	AL	34	34	0	235.2	951	207	72	64	14	5	2	6	51	3	269	3	18	9	.667	0-0	0	93	.624	2.57	2.44
2015	Cle	AL	32	32	0	222.0	886	189	92	86	22	7	4	11	45	3	245	6	9	16	.360	0-0	0	92	.650	2.74	3.49
2016	Cle	AL	32	32	0	215.0	860	170	82	75	22	6	2	7	57	1	227	5	18	9	.667	0-0	0	92	.631	2.62	3.14
2017	Cle	AL	29	29	0	203.2	777	141	56	51	21	3	1	5	36	2	265	4	18	4	.818	0-0	0	93	.556	1.83	2.25
2018	Cle	AL	33	33	0	215.0	842	179	75	69	25	2	2	3	34	0	222	2	20	7	.741	0-0	0	92	.624	2.47	2.89
2019	Cle	AL	7	7	0	35.2	168	44	26	23	4	1	1	3	15	0	38	1	2	3	.400	0-0	0	92	.824	5.87	5.80
2020	Tex	AL	1	1	0	1.0	3	0	0	0	0	0	0	0	0	0	1	0	0	0	-	0-0	0	92	.333	1.26	0.00
2021	NYY	AL	16	16	0	80.0	341	74	37	34	8	1	3	5	33	0	82	3	5	3	.625	0-0	0	91	.704	4.00	3.83
2022	TB	AL	31	31	0	164.0	689	178	82	79	20	2	6	10	21	0	139	2	10	10	.500	0-0	0	89	.729	3.85	4.34
	Postseason		9	9	0	45.1	194	44	20	20	10	0	1	5	13	0	47	0	4	3	.571	0-0	0	92	.787	4.75	3.97
	12 ML YEARS		256	251	3	1586.2	6431	1417	637	584	160	32	23	61	347	9	1683	30	113	71	.614	0-0	0	92	.660	2.98	3.31

Andrew Knapp

Bats: B Throws: R Pos: C-16;PH-1   Ht: 6'1" Wt: 189 Born: 11/9/1991 Age: 31

Year	Team	Lg	G	AB	H	2B	3B	HR	(Hm	Rd)	TB	R	RBI	RC	TBB	IBB	SO	HBP	SH	SF	SB	CS	GDP	Avg	OBP	Slg	OPS
2022	Tacom	AAA	22	81	16	7	0	4	(-	-)	35	8	11	10	4	0	22	0	0	1	0	0	1	.198	.250	.432	.682
2022	Scrmto	AAA	34	127	35	7	0	8	(-	-)	66	20	26	24	13	0	35	2	0	0	1	1	2	.276	.352	.520	.872
2017	Phi	NL	56	171	44	8	1	3	(2	1)	63	26	13	20	31	4	56	0	0	2	1	0	5	.257	.368	.368	.736
2018	Phi	NL	84	187	37	6	2	4	(1	3)	59	19	15	15	24	1	75	2	1	1	1	0	2	.198	.294	.316	.610
2019	Phi	NL	74	136	29	9	0	2	(0	2)	44	12	8	11	18	2	51	3	3	0	0	0	2	.213	.318	.324	.642
2020	Phi	NL	33	72	20	4	1	2	(0	2)	32	9	15	17	15	0	19	1	0	1	0	0	1	.278	.404	.444	.849
2021	Phi	NL	62	145	22	3	0	2	(1	1)	31	13	11	6	10	0	61	2	1	1	0	0	1	.152	.215	.214	.429
2022	3 Tms		16	39	5	1	0	0	(0	0)	6	4	4	1	5	0	12	1	0	1	0	0	0	.128	.239	.154	.393
22	Pit	NL	11	31	4	1	0	0	(0	0)	5	2	2	0	3	0	9	1	0	0	0	0	0	.129	.229	.161	.390
22	Sea	AL	2	4	0	0	0	0	(0	0)	0	0	0	0	0	0	3	0	0	0	0	0	0	.000	.000	.000	.000
22	SF	NL	3	4	1	0	0	0	(0	0)	1	2	2	1	2	0	0	0	0	1	0	0	0	.250	.429	.250	.679
	6 ML YEARS		325	750	157	31	4	13	(4	9)	235	83	66	70	103	7	274	9	5	6	2	0	11	.209	.310	.313	.623

Corey Knebel

Pitches: R Bats: R Pos: RP-46   kuh-NAY-bull   Ht: 6'3" Wt: 224 Born: 11/26/1991 Age: 31

Year	Team	Lg	G	GS	GF	IP	BFP	H	R	ER	HR	SH	SF	HB	TBB	IBB	SO	WP	W	L	Pct	Sv-Op	Hld	Vel	OPS	ERC	ERA
2014	Det	AL	8	0	4	8.2	39	11	7	6	0	0	0	0	3	0	11	1	0	0	-	0-0	0	94	.776	4.65	6.23
2015	Mil	NL	48	0	15	50.1	209	44	18	18	8	0	0	2	17	1	58	1	0	1	3	0-1	3	95	.744	3.69	3.22
2016	Mil	NL	35	0	7	32.2	145	32	20	17	3	0	1	1	16	3	38	1	1	4	.200	2-4	13	95	.708	4.18	4.68
2017	Mil	NL	76	0	48	76.0	309	48	15	15	6	0	0	2	40	5	126	2	1	4	.200	39-45	11	97	.568	2.51	1.78
2018	Mil	NL	57	0	29	55.1	223	38	23	22	7	0	1	4	22	0	88	0	4	3	.571	16-19	6	97	.659	2.90	3.58
2020	Mil	NL	15	0	2	13.1	62	15	9	9	4	0	0	0	8	0	15	0	0	0	-	0-2	0	94	.927	7.20	6.08
2021	LAD	NL	27	4	3	25.2	101	16	8	7	2	0	1	0	9	1	30	0	4	0	1.000	3-5	7	96	.522	1.80	2.45
2022	Phi	NL	46	0	29	44.2	194	33	22	17	4	0	1	2	28	3	41	2	3	5	.375	12-16	2	96	.662	3.48	3.43
	Postseason		16	2	1	15.2	56	7	3	3	0	0	0	1	4	0	25	1	1	0	1.000	1-1	3	97	.410	0.98	1.72
	8 ML YEARS		312	4	137	306.2	1282	237	122	111	34	0	4	11	143	13	407	7	13	16	.448	72-92	42	96	.664	3.26	3.26

Reiss Knehr

Pitches: R Bats: L Pos: RP-4; SP-1   Ht: 6'2" Wt: 205 Born: 11/3/1996 Age: 26

Year	Team	Lg	G	GS	GF	IP	BFP	H	R	ER	HR	SH	SF	HB	TBB	IBB	SO	WP	W	L	Pct	Sv-Op	Hld	Vel	OPS	ERC	ERA
2022	ElPaso	AAA	32	15	1	87.2	403	89	68	67	18	0	1	3	55	1	92	7	4	4	.500	1- -	-	-	.850	6.00	6.88
2021	SD	NL	12	5	1	29.0	129	23	16	16	2	0	3	2	20	1	20	3	1	2	.333	0-0	0	94	.714	4.02	4.97
2022	SD	NL	5	1	2	13.2	59	11	6	6	1	0	0	4	4	0	10	0	0	0	-	0-0	0	93	.714	3.51	3.95
	2 ML YEARS		17	6	3	42.2	188	34	22	22	3	0	3	6	24	1	30	3	1	2	.333	0-0	0	93	.715	3.86	4.64

Dusten Knight

Pitches: R Bats: R Pos: RP-6   Ht: 6'0" Wt: 200 Born: 9/7/1990 Age: 32

Year	Team	Lg	G	GS	GF	IP	BFP	H	R	ER	HR	SH	SF	HB	TBB	IBB	SO	WP	W	L	Pct	Sv-Op	Hld	Vel	OPS	ERC	ERA
2022	Drham	AAA	48	1	25	55.1	238	40	23	21	7	0	0	0	32	0	66	6	4	4	.500	12- -	-	-	.637	3.36	3.42
2021	Bal	AL	7	0	3	8.2	44	11	10	9	1	0	1	0	5	0	11	3	0	0	-	0-0	0	91	.837	6.06	9.35
2022	TB	AL	6	0	3	11.0	49	11	8	7	4	1	0	0	4	1	9	1	0	1	.000	0-0	0	90	.881	5.39	5.73
	2 ML YEARS		13	0	6	19.2	93	22	18	16	5	1	1	0	9	1	20	4	0	1	.000	0-0	0	90	.861	5.74	7.32

Andrew Knizner

Bats: R Throws: R Pos: C-90;1B-5;PH-5;PR-2;DH-1   KIZZ-ner   Ht: 6'1" Wt: 225 Born: 2/3/1995 Age: 28

Year	Team	Lg	G	AB	H	2B	3B	HR	(Hm	Rd)	TB	R	RBI	RC	TBB	IBB	SO	HBP	SH	SF	SB	CS	GDP	Avg	OBP	Slg	OPS
2019	StL	NL	18	53	12	2	0	2	(1	1)	20	7	7	7	4	0	14	1	0	0	2	0	3	.226	.293	.377	.670
2020	StL	NL	8	16	4	1	0	0	(0	0)	5	1	4	2	0	0	5	0	0	1	0	0	2	.250	.235	.313	.548
2021	StL	NL	63	161	28	7	0	1	(1	0)	38	18	9	6	20	2	39	4	0	0	0	0	5	.174	.281	.236	.517
2022	StL	NL	97	260	56	10	0	4	(2	2)	78	28	25	18	26	0	62	6	1	0	0	1	9	.215	.301	.300	.601
	4 ML YEARS		186	490	100	20	0	7	(4	3)	141	54	45	33	50	2	120	11	1	1	2	1	21	.204	.292	.288	.579

Matt Koch

Pitches: R Bats: L Pos: RP-4   cook   Ht: 6'3" Wt: 215 Born: 11/2/1990 Age: 32

Year	Team	Lg	G	GS	GF	IP	BFP	H	R	ER	HR	SH	SF	HB	TBB	IBB	SO	WP	W	L	Pct	Sv-Op	Hld	Vel	OPS	ERC	ERA
2022	Tacom	AAA	38	0	20	38.1	156	27	14	13	6	1	1	3	13	1	50	1	4	1	.800	4- -	-	-	.669	2.88	3.05
2016	Ari	NL	7	2	4	18.0	69	9	4	4	1	1	0	2	4	0	10	0	1	1	.500	1-1	0	92	.463	1.29	2.00
2017	Ari	NL	1	0	0	0.0	3	2	3	3	0	0	0	0	1	0	0	0	0	0	-	0-0	0	92	2.500		
2018	Ari	NL	19	14	4	86.2	360	88	43	40	19	2	1	6	22	1	50	3	5	5	.500	0-0	0	91	.816	4.79	4.15
2019	Ari	NL	9	0	5	20.2	96	29	21	21	8	0	0	5	4	0	9	1	0	0	-	0-0	0	92	1.097	9.26	9.15
2022	Sea	AL	4	0	2	4.1	19	5	4	4	2	0	0	0	1	0	3	0	0	0	-	0-0	0	94	.927	6.67	8.31
	5 ML YEARS		40	16	15	129.2	547	133	75	72	30	3	1	13	32	1	72	4	6	6	.500	1-1	0	92	.833	5.01	5.00

Jared Koenig

Pitches: L Bats: R Pos: SP-5; RP-5   Ht: 6'5" Wt: 235 Born: 1/24/1994 Age: 29

		HOW MUCH PITCHED			WHAT HE GAVE UP											THE RESULTS						
Year Team	Lg	G GS GF	IP	BFP	H	R	ER	HR	SH	SF	HB	TBB	IBB	SO	WP	W L	Pct	Sv-Op Hld	Vel	OPS	ERC	ERA
2022 LsVgs	AAA	20 18 1	107.0	450	112	57	56	13	2	1	0	30	0	104	4	6 6	.500	0- - 0	-	.753	4.05	4.71
2022 Oak	AL	10 5 4	39.1	177	40	25	25	4	1	2	5	15	0	22	4	1 3	.250	0-0 0	89	.756	4.53	5.72

Adam Kolarek

Pitches: L Bats: L Pos: RP-15   Ht: 6'3" Wt: 215 Born: 1/14/1989 Age: 34

		HOW MUCH PITCHED			WHAT HE GAVE UP											THE RESULTS						
Year Team	Lg	G GS GF	IP	BFP	H	R	ER	HR	SH	SF	HB	TBB	IBB	SO	WP	W L	Pct	Sv-Op Hld	Vel	OPS	ERC	ERA
2022 LsVgs	AAA	37 0 10	41.1	179	42	29	28	4	0	2	5	16	0	39	4	2 3	.400	2- - -	-	.769	4.69	6.10
2017 TB	AL	12 0 5	8.1	40	9	6	6	2	1	0	4	4	2	4	1	1 0	1.000	0-0 2	88	.984	7.84	6.48
2018 TB	AL	31 0 5	34.1	141	38	15	15	0	0	1	1	5	1	19	0	1 0	1.000	2-4 10	90	.685	3.14	3.93
2019 2 Tms	NL	80 0 18	55.0	229	48	22	20	7	0	0	3	16	4	45	1	6 3	.667	1-1 17	89	.669	3.23	3.27
2020 LAD	NL	20 0 3	19.0	72	11	2	2	1	0	1	0	4	0	13	2	3 0	1.000	1-1 3	89	.432	1.26	0.95
2021 Oak	AL	12 0 2	9.0	51	15	10	8	2	1	0	1	5	0	4	1	0 0	-	0-0 0	89	.943	9.73	8.00
2022 Oak	AL	15 0 7	17.2	79	20	9	9	1	0	0	3	8	0	9	0	0 1	.000	0-0 0	88	.804	5.63	4.58
19 TB	AL	54 0 15	43.1	184	39	19	19	6	0	0	3	14	4	36	1	4 3	.571	1-1 14	89	.700	3.58	3.95
19 LAD	NL	26 0 3	11.2	45	9	3	1	1	0	0	0	2	0	9	0	2 0	1.000	0-0 3	89	.547	2.01	0.77
Postseason		7 0 2	4.1	25	9	5	5	1	0	0	0	3	1	5	0	0 0	-	0-0 2	90	1.116	13.01	10.38
6 ML YEARS		170 0 40	143.1	612	141	64	60	13	2	2	12	42	7	94	5	11 4	.733	4-6 32	89	.702	3.75	3.77

Mark Kolozsvary

Bats: R Throws: R Pos: C-9;PR-1   KOLS-vary   Ht: 5'8" Wt: 180 Born: 9/4/1995 Age: 27

		BATTING																	RUNNING			AVERAGES			
Year Team	Lg	G	AB	H	2B	3B	HR	(Hm Rd)	TB	R	RBI	RC	TBB	IBB	SO	HBP	SH	SF	SB	CS	GDP	Avg	OBP	Slg	OPS
2022 Lsvlle	AAA	42	119	20	6	0	3	(- -)	35	14	7	10	13	0	44	8	2	0	0	0	2	.168	.293	.294	.587
2022 Cin	NL	10	20	4	2	0	1	(1 0)	9	3	3	3	1	0	9	0	0	0	0	0	1	.200	.238	.450	.688

Michael Kopech

Pitches: R Bats: R Pos: SP-25   Ht: 6'3" Wt: 210 Born: 4/30/1996 Age: 27

		HOW MUCH PITCHED			WHAT HE GAVE UP											THE RESULTS						
Year Team	Lg	G GS GF	IP	BFP	H	R	ER	HR	SH	SF	HB	TBB	IBB	SO	WP	W L	Pct	Sv-Op Hld	Vel	OPS	ERC	ERA
2018 CWS	AL	4 4 0	14.1	68	20	8	8	4	0	0	5	2	0	15	1	1 1	.500	0-0 0	95	1.004	8.42	5.02
2021 CWS	AL	44 4 1	69.1	285	54	27	27	9	0	3	1	24	1	103	3	4 3	.571	0-1 13	97	.651	2.88	3.50
2022 CWS	AL	25 25 0	119.1	494	85	53	47	15	0	5	3	57	0	105	2	5 9	.357	0-0 0	95	.641	3.10	3.54
Postseason		2 0 0	3.0	17	7	6	6	1	0	0	0	1	0	5	0	1 0	1.000	0-0 0	98	1.096	14.72	18.00
3 ML YEARS		73 33 1	203.0	847	159	88	82	28	0	8	9	83	1	223	6	10 13	.435	0-1 13	96	.674	3.34	3.64

Jackson Kowar

Pitches: R Bats: R Pos: RP-7   Ht: 6'5" Wt: 200 Born: 10/4/1996 Age: 26

		HOW MUCH PITCHED			WHAT HE GAVE UP											THE RESULTS						
Year Team	Lg	G GS GF	IP	BFP	H	R	ER	HR	SH	SF	HB	TBB	IBB	SO	WP	W L	Pct	Sv-Op Hld	Vel	OPS	ERC	ERA
2022 Omha	AAA	20 20 0	83.1	387	95	67	57	14	1	4	8	43	0	88	10	4 10	.286	0- - -	-	.831	6.32	6.16
2021 KC	AL	9 8 1	30.1	154	43	38	38	7	0	4	2	20	0	29	8	0 6	.000	0-0 0	96	1.008	9.14	11.27
2022 KC	AL	7 0 3	15.2	82	27	17	17	4	0	0	0	11	0	17	0	0 0	-	0-0 2	96	1.139	11.71	9.77
2 ML YEARS		16 8 4	46.0	236	70	55	55	11	0	4	2	31	0	46	8	0 6	.000	0-0 2	96	1.055	9.99	10.76

Max Kranick

Pitches: R Bats: R Pos: RP-2   Ht: 6'3" Wt: 220 Born: 7/21/1997 Age: 25

		HOW MUCH PITCHED			WHAT HE GAVE UP											THE RESULTS						
Year Team	Lg	G GS GF	IP	BFP	H	R	ER	HR	SH	SF	HB	TBB	IBB	SO	WP	W L	Pct	Sv-Op Hld	Vel	OPS	ERC	ERA
2021 Pit	NL	9 9 0	38.2	182	47	28	27	4	1	2	4	19	3	32	2	2 3	.400	0-0 0	95	.855	6.02	6.28
2022 Pit	NL	2 0 0	5.0	19	3	0	0	0	0	0	0	3	0	4	1	0 0	-	0-0 1	95	.628	2.30	0.00
2 ML YEARS		11 9 0	43.2	201	50	28	27	4	1	2	4	22	3	36	3	2 3	.400	0-0 1	94	.833	5.56	5.56

Joey Krehbiel

Pitches: R Bats: R Pos: RP-56   KRAY-bull   Ht: 6'3" Wt: 240 Born: 12/20/1992 Age: 30

		HOW MUCH PITCHED			WHAT HE GAVE UP											THE RESULTS						
Year Team	Lg	G GS GF	IP	BFP	H	R	ER	HR	SH	SF	HB	TBB	IBB	SO	WP	W L	Pct	Sv-Op Hld	Vel	OPS	ERC	ERA
2018 Ari	NL	2 0 1	3.0	12	1	0	0	0	0	0	0	2	0	0	0	0 0	-	0-0 0	96	.350	1.26	0.00
2021 2 Tms	AL	6 0 1	8.1	34	5	4	4	1	0	0	0	5	0	7	1	0 0	-	0-0 2	96	.639	2.88	4.32
2022 Bal	AL	56 0 8	57.2	244	53	28	25	9	0	4	3	18	1	45	1	5 5	.500	1-1 10	94	.737	3.81	3.90
21 TB	AL	1 0 1	1.0	4	0	0	0	0	0	0	0	1	0	2	0	0 0	-	0-0 0	96	.250	0.95	0.00
21 Bal	AL	5 0 0	7.1	30	5	4	4	1	0	0	0	4	0	5	1	0 0	-	0-0 2	96	.685	3.22	4.91
3 ML YEARS		64 0 10	69.0	290	59	32	29	10	0	4	3	25	1	52	2	5 5	.500	1-1 12	95	.711	3.57	3.78

Ryan Kreidler

Bats: R Throws: R Pos: 3B-13;SS-13;2B-2;PH-2;CF-1;PR-1   Ht: 6'4" Wt: 208 Born: 11/12/1997 Age: 25

							BATTING													RUNNING			AVERAGES			
Year	Team	Lg	G	AB	H	2B	3B	HR	(Hm | Rd)	TB	R	RBI	RC	TBB	IBB	SO	HBP	SH	SF	SB	CS	GDP	Avg	OBP	Slg	OPS
2022	Toledo	AAA	56	202	43	12	2	8	(- | -)	83	29	22	35	36	0	72	9	0	3	15	1	0	.213	.352	.411	.763
2022	Det	AL	26	73	13	1	0	1	(0 | 1)	17	8	6	4	6	0	22	1	2	2	0	1	0	.178	.244	.233	.477

Dean Kremer

Pitches: R Bats: R Pos: SP-21; RP-1   Ht: 6'2" Wt: 200 Born: 1/7/1996 Age: 27

			HOW MUCH PITCHED					WHAT HE GAVE UP									THE RESULTS							
Year	Team	Lg	G	GS	GF	IP	BFP	H	R	ER	HR	SH	SF	HB	TBB	IBB	SO	WP	W	L	Pct	Sv-Op	Hld	Vel	OPS	ERC	ERA
2020	Bal	AL	4	4	0	18.2	83	15	10	10	0	0	1	0	12	0	22	0	1	1	.500	0-0	0	93	.711	3.12	4.82
2021	Bal	AL	13	13	0	53.2	245	63	46	45	17	0	3	1	25	0	47	5	0	7	.000	0-0	0	93	.951	7.14	7.55
2022	Bal	AL	22	21	0	125.1	512	123	48	45	11	1	2	5	34	0	87	5	8	7	.533	0-0	0	93	.708	3.67	3.23
	3 ML YEARS		39	38	0	197.2	840	201	104	100	28	1	6	6	71	0	156	10	9	15	.375	0-0	0	93	.778	4.50	4.55

Jason Krizan

Bats: L Throws: R Pos: LF-3   Ht: 6'0" Wt: 185 Born: 6/28/1989 Age: 34

							BATTING													RUNNING			AVERAGES			
Year	Team	Lg	G	AB	H	2B	3B	HR	(Hm | Rd)	TB	R	RBI	RC	TBB	IBB	SO	HBP	SH	SF	SB	CS	GDP	Avg	OBP	Slg	OPS
2022	Scrmto	AAA	97	357	95	30	2	15	(- | -)	174	58	55	59	35	0	61	0	0	3	1	1	7	.266	.329	.487	.817
2022	SF	NL	3	8	1	0	0	0	(0 | 0)	1	0	0	0	2	0	3	0	0	0	0	0	0	.125	.300	.125	.425

Chad Kuhl

Pitches: R Bats: R Pos: SP-27   cool   Ht: 6'3" Wt: 205 Born: 9/10/1992 Age: 30

			HOW MUCH PITCHED					WHAT HE GAVE UP									THE RESULTS							
Year	Team	Lg	G	GS	GF	IP	BFP	H	R	ER	HR	SH	SF	HB	TBB	IBB	SO	WP	W	L	Pct	Sv-Op	Hld	Vel	OPS	ERC	ERA
2016	Pit	NL	14	14	0	70.2	301	73	34	33	7	2	2	4	20	0	53	2	5	4	.556	0-0	0	93	.757	4.04	4.20
2017	Pit	NL	31	31	0	157.1	680	159	81	76	17	6	4	6	72	7	142	8	8	11	.421	0-0	0	96	.793	4.60	4.35
2018	Pit	NL	16	16	0	85.0	373	89	47	43	14	6	6	4	33	1	81	7	5	5	.500	0-0	0	95	.806	4.94	4.55
2020	Pit	NL	11	9	0	46.1	197	35	26	22	8	1	0	2	28	0	44	1	2	3	.400	0-0	0	94	.727	4.27	4.27
2021	Pit	NL	28	14	2	80.1	349	73	50	43	13	2	6	9	42	0	75	9	5	7	.417	0-2	4	94	.802	5.09	4.82
2022	Col	NL	27	27	0	137.0	617	155	91	87	25	3	5	5	58	1	110	5	6	11	.353	0-0	0	93	.855	5.68	5.72
	6 ML YEARS		127	111	2	576.2	2517	584	329	304	84	20	23	30	253	9	505	32	31	41	.431	0-2	4	94	.802	4.87	4.74

Joel Kuhnel

Pitches: R Bats: R Pos: RP-53   Ht: 6'4" Wt: 280 Born: 2/19/1995 Age: 28

			HOW MUCH PITCHED					WHAT HE GAVE UP									THE RESULTS							
Year	Team	Lg	G	GS	GF	IP	BFP	H	R	ER	HR	SH	SF	HB	TBB	IBB	SO	WP	W	L	Pct	Sv-Op	Hld	Vel	OPS	ERC	ERA
2022	Lsvlle	AAA	10	0	7	10.1	42	9	3	3	1	0	0	0	1	0	7	0	0	1	.000	3- -	-	-	.580	2.15	2.61
2019	Cin	NL	11	0	2	9.2	42	8	5	5	1	0	0	0	5	0	9	0	1	0	1.000	0-0	1	96	.634	3.53	4.66
2020	Cin	NL	3	0	1	3.0	13	4	2	2	2	0	0	0	0	3	0	1	0	1.000	0-0	0	95	1.077	8.07	6.00
2022	Cin	NL	53	0	13	58.0	255	67	41	41	8	2	4	5	14	1	56	1	2	3	.400	1-3	5	96	.805	4.91	6.36
	3 ML YEARS		67	0	16	70.2	310	79	48	48	11	2	4	5	19	1	68	1	4	3	.571	1-3	6	96	.795	4.86	6.11

Steven Kwan

Bats: L Throws: L Pos: LF-123;RF-20;CF-7;PH-7;DH-6   Ht: 5'9" Wt: 170 Born: 9/5/1997 Age: 25

							BATTING													RUNNING			AVERAGES			
Year	Team	Lg	G	AB	H	2B	3B	HR	(Hm	Rd)	TB	R	RBI	RC	TBB	IBB	SO	HBP	SH	SF	SB	CS	GDP	Avg	OBP	Slg	OPS
2018	2 Tms	Low	17	52	18	3	1	0	(-	-)	23	9	5	11	11	0	5	1	0	0	3	0	1	.346	.469	.442	.911
2019	Lynbrg	A+	123	479	134	26	7	3	(-	-)	183	68	39	72	53	1	51	4	1	5	11	7	1	.280	.353	.382	.735
2021	Akron	AA	51	193	65	12	3	7	(-	-)	104	42	31	42	22	0	23	3	2	1	4	2	2	.337	.411	.539	.950
2021	Clmbs	AAA	22	87	26	3	1	4	(-	-)	43	21	11	17	11	0	8	1	2	0	2	0	0	.299	.384	.494	.878
2022	Cle	AL	147	563	168	25	7	6	(1	5)	225	89	52	83	62	2	60	7	2	4	19	5	9	.298	.373	.400	.772

Tommy La Stella

Bats: L Throws: R Pos: DH-43;PH-13;3B-6;1B-3;2B-3   Ht: 5'11" Wt: 180 Born: 1/31/1989 Age: 34

							BATTING													RUNNING			AVERAGES			
Year	Team	Lg	G	AB	H	2B	3B	HR	(Hm	Rd)	TB	R	RBI	RC	TBB	IBB	SO	HBP	SH	SF	SB	CS	GDP	Avg	OBP	Slg	OPS
2022	Scrmto	AAA	12	38	12	2	0	2	(-	-)	20	8	7	9	9	0	7	1	0	0	0	0	2	.316	.458	.526	.985
2014	Atl	NL	93	319	80	16	1	1	(1	0)	101	22	31	36	36	2	40	1	3	1	2	1	8	.251	.328	.317	.644
2015	ChC	NL	33	67	18	6	0	1	(1	0)	27	4	11	10	5	0	7	1	0	1	2	0	1	.269	.324	.403	.727
2016	ChC	NL	74	148	40	12	1	2	(1	1)	60	17	11	20	18	1	27	2	0	0	0	1	2	.270	.357	.405	.763
2017	ChC	NL	73	125	36	8	0	5	(0	5)	59	18	22	24	20	1	18	2	0	2	0	0	2	.288	.389	.472	.861
2018	ChC	NL	123	169	45	8	0	1	(0	1)	56	23	19	17	17	1	27	2	0	0	0	1	5	.266	.340	.331	.672
2019	LAA	AL	80	292	86	8	0	16	(11	5)	142	49	44	43	20	0	28	3	0	0	0	0	6	.295	.346	.486	.832
2020	2 Tms	AL	55	196	55	14	2	5	(2	3)	88	31	25	36	27	0	12	2	1	2	1	0	6	.281	.370	.449	.819
2021	SF	NL	76	220	55	11	1	7	(2	5)	89	26	27	31	18	1	26	1	0	1	0	0	4	.250	.308	.405	.713
2022	SF	NL	60	180	43	14	0	2	(1	1)	63	17	14	15	11	0	30	1	0	3	0	0	4	.239	.282	.350	.632
	20	LAA	AL	28	99	27	8	0	4	(2 | 2)	47	15	14	19	15	0	7	1	1	1	1	0	3	.273	.371	.475	.846
	20	Oak	AL	27	97	28	6	2	1	(0 | 1)	41	16	11	17	12	0	5	1	0	1	0	0	3	.289	.369	.423	.792
	Postseason		24	49	11	1	0	1	(0	1)	15	6	2	6	5	0	9	1	0	0	0	0	2	.224	.309	.306	.615
	9 ML YEARS		667	1716	458	97	5	40	(19	21)	685	207	204	232	172	6	215	15	4	10	5	3	41	.267	.337	.399	.736

A.J. Ladwig

Pitches: R Bats: R Pos: RP-1 Ht: 6'5" Wt: 220 Born: 12/24/1992 Age: 30

		HOW MUCH PITCHED			WHAT HE GAVE UP							THE RESULTS							
Year Team	Lg	G GS GF	IP	BFP	H	R	ER	HR SH SF HB	TBB IBB	SO WP	W	L	Pct	Sv-Op Hld	Vel	OPS	ERC	ERA
2022 Pnscla	AA	16 15 0	89.1	382	112	49	41	11 0 3 4	7 0	63 0	8	5	.615	0-- -	-	.817	4.57	4.13
2022 Mia	NL	1 0 0	3.1	15	6	4	4	2 0 0 0	0 0	0 0	0	0	-	0-0 0	91	1.333	11.95	10.80

Juan Lagares

Bats: R Throws: R Pos: RF-9;CF-8;LF-5;PH-1;PR-1 luh-GAR-ess Ht: 6'2" Wt: 219 Born: 3/17/1989 Age: 34

		BATTING																	RUNNING			AVERAGES			
Year Team	Lg	G	AB	H	2B	3B	HR	(Hm Rd)	TB	R	RBI	RC	TBB	IBB	SO	HBP	SH	SF	SB	CS	GDP	Avg	OBP	Slg	OPS
2013 NYM	NL	121	392	95	21	5	4	(1 3)	138	35	34	36	20	4	96	2	5	2	6	3	6	.242	.281	.352	.633
2014 NYM	NL	116	416	117	24	3	4	(2 2)	159	46	47	53	20	1	87	7	3	6	13	4	6	.281	.321	.382	.703
2015 NYM	NL	143	441	114	16	5	6	(2 4)	158	47	41	51	16	2	87	4	1	3	7	3	6	.259	.289	.358	.647
2016 NYM	NL	79	142	34	7	2	3	(2 1)	54	15	9	12	11	1	27	2	4	1	4	2	4	.239	.301	.380	.682
2017 NYM	NL	94	252	63	16	2	3	(1 2)	92	37	15	20	14	0	56	3	2	1	7	3	6	.250	.296	.365	.661
2018 NYM	NL	30	59	20	1	1	0	(0 0)	23	9	6	10	3	1	9	1	0	1	3	1	2	.339	.375	.390	.765
2019 NYM	NL	133	258	55	12	1	5	(2 3)	84	38	27	23	22	4	75	2	2	1	4	1	8	.213	.279	.326	.605
2020 NYM	NL	2	0	0	0	0	0	(0 0)	0	0	0	0	0	0	0	0	0	0	0	0	0	-	-	-	-
2021 LAA	AL	112	309	73	20	2	6	(1 5)	115	39	38	31	12	0	76	1	4	1	1	2	8	.236	.266	.372	.638
2022 LAA	AL	20	60	11	2	1	0	(0 0)	15	4	0	0	2	0	15	0	0	0	0	0	0	.183	.210	.250	.460
Postseason		13	23	8	2	0	0	(0 0)	10	7	0	3	1	0	3	0	1	0	2	0	0	.348	.375	.435	.810
10 ML YEARS		850	2329	582	119	22	31	(11 20)	838	270	217	236	120	13	528	22	21	16	45	19	46	.250	.291	.360	.651

Travis Lakins Sr.

Pitches: R Bats: R Pos: RP-6 Ht: 6'1" Wt: 220 Born: 6/29/1994 Age: 29

		HOW MUCH PITCHED			WHAT HE GAVE UP							THE RESULTS							
Year Team	Lg	G GS GF	IP	BFP	H	R	ER	HR SH SF HB	TBB IBB	SO WP	W	L	Pct	Sv-Op Hld	Vel	OPS	ERC	ERA
2022 Norfolk	AAA	5 2 1	9.1	49	15	9	9	3 0 1 0	8 0	7 1	0	1	.000	0-- -	-	1.144	12.37	8.68
2019 Bos	AL	16 3 4	23.1	102	23	11	10	1 0 2 1	10 1	18 1	0	1	.000	0-0 -	94	.738	3.78	3.86
2020 Bal	AL	22 0 5	25.2	116	25	11	8	2 0 1 2	13 0	25 3	3	2	.600	1-1 1	93	.725	4.42	2.81
2021 Bal	AL	24 1 3	28.0	123	23	20	18	4 0 1 1	17 0	24 4	1	4	.200	0-1 3	93	.689	4.32	5.79
2022 Bal	AL	6 0 3	10.1	50	14	11	11	3 0 0 1	6 0	8 1	0	1	.000	0-0 -	94	1.048	9.28	9.58
4 ML YEARS		68 4 15	87.1	391	85	53	47	10 0 4 5	46 1	75 9	4	8	.333	1-2 5	94	.759	4.72	4.84

Jake Lamb

Bats: L Throws: R Pos: DH-15;LF-14;PH-8;RF-6;1B-4;3B-4;PR-1 Ht: 6'3" Wt: 215 Born: 10/9/1990 Age: 32

		BATTING																	RUNNING			AVERAGES			
Year Team	Lg	G	AB	H	2B	3B	HR	(Hm Rd)	TB	R	RBI	RC	TBB	IBB	SO	HBP	SH	SF	SB	CS	GDP	Avg	OBP	Slg	OPS
2022 OkCity	AAA	61	231	67	12	0	15	(- -)	124	44	50	51	39	0	74	3	0	3	1	1	6	.290	.395	.537	.932
2014 Ari	NL	37	126	29	4	1	4	(2 2)	47	15	11	7	6	0	37	0	0	1	1	1	4	.230	.263	.373	.636
2015 Ari	NL	107	350	92	15	5	6	(1 5)	135	38	34	39	36	3	97	1	0	3	3	2	5	.263	.331	.386	.716
2016 Ari	NL	151	523	130	31	9	29	(19 10)	266	81	91	84	64	5	154	3	0	4	6	1	13	.249	.332	.509	.840
2017 Ari	NL	149	536	133	30	4	30	(16 14)	261	89	105	90	87	13	152	7	0	5	6	4	15	.248	.357	.487	.844
2018 Ari	NL	56	207	46	8	0	6	(3 3)	72	34	31	26	26	0	65	1	0	4	1	2	4	.222	.307	.348	.655
2019 Ari	NL	78	187	36	8	2	6	(3 3)	66	26	30	27	32	1	55	5	0	2	1	0	4	.193	.323	.353	.676
2020 2 Tms		31	88	17	5	0	3	(2 1)	31	7	10	11	8	0	25	3	0	0	0	1	1	.193	.283	.352	.635
2021 2 Tms	AL	55	144	28	4	0	7	(4 3)	53	25	19	14	22	0	51	2	0	2	0	0	4	.194	.306	.368	.674
2022 2 Tms		41	97	21	6	1	3	(3 0)	38	13	6	7	11	0	38	3	0	0	0	1	4	.216	.315	.392	.707
20 Ari	NL	18	43	5	1	0	0	(0 0)	6	2	1	1	6	0	17	1	0	0	0	1	0	.116	.240	.140	.380
20 Oak	AL	13	45	12	4	0	3	(2 1)	25	5	9	10	2	0	8	2	0	0	0	0	1	.267	.327	.556	.882
21 CWS	AL	43	113	24	2	0	6	(4 2)	44	20	13	12	17	0	38	1	0	0	0	0	4	.212	.321	.389	.710
21 Tor	AL	12	31	4	2	0	1	(0 1)	9	5	6	2	5	0	13	1	0	2	0	0	0	.129	.256	.290	.547
22 LAD	NL	25	67	16	5	1	2	(2 0)	29	10	4	5	8	0	24	2	0	0	0	1	4	.239	.338	.433	.770
22 Sea	AL	16	30	5	1	0	1	(1 0)	9	3	2	2	3	0	14	1	0	0	0	0	0	.167	.265	.300	.565
Postseason		8	20	7	0	0	0	(0 0)	7	4	0	1	0	0	3	0	0	0	0	0	1	.350	.350	.350	.700
9 ML YEARS		705	2258	532	111	22	94	(53 41)	969	328	337	305	292	22	674	25	0	21	18	12	54	.236	.327	.429	.756

Jimmy Lambert

Pitches: R Bats: R Pos: RP-40; SP-2 Ht: 6'2" Wt: 190 Born: 11/18/1994 Age: 28

		HOW MUCH PITCHED			WHAT HE GAVE UP							THE RESULTS							
Year Team	Lg	G GS GF	IP	BFP	H	R	ER	HR SH SF HB	TBB IBB	SO WP	W	L	Pct	Sv-Op Hld	Vel	OPS	ERC	ERA
2022 Charltt	AAA	5 5 0	12.2	62	21	14	13	8 0 0 0	5 0	12 1	0	3	.000	0-- -	-	1.279	13.09	9.24
2020 CWS	AL	2 0 1	2.0	8	2	0	0	0 0 0 0	0 0	2 0	0	0	-	0-0 0	93	.500	1.95	0.00
2021 CWS	AL	4 3 0	13.0	60	16	9	9	3 0 1 2	6 0	10 0	1	1	.500	0-0 0	94	.948	7.66	6.23
2022 CWS	AL	42 2 7	47.0	204	40	18	17	4 1 2 1	24 0	45 5	1	2	.333	0-1 10	94	.672	3.62	3.26
3 ML YEARS		48 5 8	62.0	272	58	27	26	7 1 3 3	30 0	57 5	2	3	.400	0-1 10	94	.727	4.31	3.77

Dinelson Lamet

Pitches: R Bats: R Pos: RP-32 dee-NEL-sun luh-MET Ht: 6'3" Wt: 228 Born: 7/18/1992 Age: 30

		HOW MUCH PITCHED			WHAT HE GAVE UP							THE RESULTS							
Year Team	Lg	G GS GF	IP	BFP	H	R	ER	HR SH SF HB	TBB IBB	SO WP	W	L	Pct	Sv-Op Hld	Vel	OPS	ERC	ERA
2022 SnAnt	AA	6 0 2	7.0	32	10	3	3	2 0 0 0	1 0	9 1	0	0	-	0-- -	-	.957	6.78	3.86
2022 ElPaso	AAA	11 0 4	11.2	49	8	2	1	0 0 0 0	5 1	18 3	0	1	.000	0-- -	-	.538	1.73	0.77
2017 SD	NL	21 21 0	114.1	485	88	63	58	18 1 5 6	54 2	139 9	7	8	.467	0-0 0	95	.707	3.64	4.57
2019 SD	NL	14 14 0	73.0	313	62	38	33	12 2 2 5	30 0	105 6	3	5	.375	0-0 0	96	.721	3.95	4.07

			HOW MUCH PITCHED					WHAT HE GAVE UP										THE RESULTS						
Year	Team	Lg	G	GS	GF	IP	BFP	H	R	ER	HR	SH	SF	HB	TBB	IBB	SO	WP	W	L	Pct	Sv-Op Hld	Vel	OPS	ERC	ERA
2020	SD	NL	12	12	0	69.0	267	39	18	16	5	0	1	4	20	0	93	1	3	1	.750	0-0 0	97	.496	1.60	2.09
2021	SD	NL	22	9	1	47.0	209	48	24	23	6	1	1	2	22	0	57	3	2	4	.333	0-0 1	96	.761	4.83	4.40
2022	2 Tms	NL	32	0	8	32.1	149	30	23	22	4	0	2	4	19	0	45	6	1	2	.333	0-2 4	95	.775	5.00	6.12
22	SD		13	0	3	12.1	62	16	14	13	2	0	2	1	9	0	16	3	0	1	.000	0-0 1	95	.979	8.12	9.49
22	Col	NL	19	0	5	20.0	87	14	9	9	2	0	0	3	10	0	29	3	1	1	.500	0-2 3	95	.635	3.32	4.05
5 ML YEARS			101	56	9	335.2	1423	267	166	152	45	4	11	21	145	2	439	25	16	20	.444	0-2 5	96	.684	3.52	4.08

Alex Lange

Pitches: R Bats: R Pos: RP-71   Ht: 6'3" Wt: 202 Born: 10/2/1995 Age: 27

			HOW MUCH PITCHED					WHAT HE GAVE UP										THE RESULTS						
Year	Team	Lg	G	GS	GF	IP	BFP	H	R	ER	HR	SH	SF	HB	TBB	IBB	SO	WP	W	L	Pct	Sv-Op Hld	Vel	OPS	ERC	ERA
2021	Det	AL	36	0	6	35.2	162	37	18	16	5	0	0	3	16	0	39	6	1	3	.250	1-3 6	96	.765	5.04	4.04
2022	Det	AL	71	0	11	63.1	271	47	30	24	5	2	2	5	31	1	82	15	7	4	.636	0-4 21	96	.620	3.11	3.41
2 ML YEARS			107	0	17	99.0	433	84	48	40	10	2	2	8	47	1	121	21	8	7	.533	1-7 27	96	.675	3.77	3.64

Shea Langeliers

Bats: R Throws: R Pos: DH-24;C-17   Ht: 6'0" Wt: 205 Born: 11/18/1997 Age: 25

			BATTING																RUNNING			AVERAGES			
Year	Team	Lg	G	AB	H	2B	3B	HR	(Hm | Rd)	TB	R	RBI	RC	TBB	IBB	SO	HBP	SH	SF	SB	CS	GDP	Avg	OBP	Slg	OPS
2019	Rome	A	54	216	55	13	0	2	(- | -)	74	27	34	24	17	0	55	2	0	4	0	0	5	.255	.310	.343	.652
2021	Missi	AA	92	329	85	13	0	22	(- | -)	164	56	52	56	36	3	97	4	0	1	1	0	5	.258	.338	.498	.836
2022	LsVgs	AAA	92	353	100	19	2	19	(- | -)	180	62	56	69	43	0	88	4	0	2	5	1	6	.283	.366	.510	.876
2022	Oak	AL	40	142	31	10	1	6	(1 | 5)	61	14	22	21	9	0	53	0	0	2	0	0	4	.218	.261	.430	.691

Trevor Larnach

Bats: L Throws: R Pos: LF-33;RF-11;DH-7;PH-4;PR-1   Ht: 6'4" Wt: 223 Born: 2/26/1997 Age: 26

			BATTING																RUNNING			AVERAGES			
Year	Team	Lg	G	AB	H	2B	3B	HR	(Hm | Rd)	TB	R	RBI	RC	TBB	IBB	SO	HBP	SH	SF	SB	CS	GDP	Avg	OBP	Slg	OPS
2022	StPaul	AAA	10	36	8	0	0	0	(- | -)	8	1	2	1	4	0	11	0	0	1	0	0	1	.222	.293	.222	.515
2021	Min	AL	79	260	58	12	0	7	(4 | 3)	91	29	28	26	31	0	104	8	0	2	1	0	3	.223	.322	.350	.672
2022	Min	AL	51	160	37	13	0	5	(4 | 1)	65	22	18	19	18	1	57	0	0	2	0	0	1	.231	.306	.406	.712
2 ML YEARS			130	420	95	25	0	12	(8 | 4)	156	51	46	45	49	1	161	8	0	4	1	0	4	.226	.316	.371	.687

Jack Larsen

Bats: L Throws: L Pos: RF-1   Ht: 6'1" Wt: 195 Born: 1/13/1995 Age: 28

			BATTING																RUNNING			AVERAGES			
Year	Team	Lg	G	AB	H	2B	3B	HR	(Hm | Rd)	TB	R	RBI	RC	TBB	IBB	SO	HBP	SH	SF	SB	CS	GDP	Avg	OBP	Slg	OPS
2022	Ark	AA	116	450	121	24	4	10	(- | -)	183	88	57	70	72	1	107	3	0	3	8	2	6	.269	.371	.407	.778
2022	Sea	AL	1	1	0	0	0	0	(0 | 0)	0	0	0	0	0	0	1	0	0	0	0	0	0	.000	.000	.000	.000

Eric Lauer

Pitches: L Bats: R Pos: SP-29   Ht: 6'3" Wt: 228 Born: 6/3/1995 Age: 28

			HOW MUCH PITCHED					WHAT HE GAVE UP										THE RESULTS						
Year	Team	Lg	G	GS	GF	IP	BFP	H	R	ER	HR	SH	SF	HB	TBB	IBB	SO	WP	W	L	Pct	Sv-Op Hld	Vel	OPS	ERC	ERA
2018	SD	NL	23	23	0	112.0	504	127	61	54	15	4	2	6	46	2	100	2	6	7	.462	0-0 0	91	.800	5.33	4.34
2019	SD	NL	30	29	0	149.2	651	158	82	74	20	3	3	5	51	4	138	4	8	10	.444	0-0 0	92	.760	4.47	4.45
2020	Mil	NL	4	2	0	11.0	61	17	16	16	2	0	1	2	9	0	12	1	0	2	.000	0-0 0	92	1.030	10.72	13.09
2021	Mil	NL	24	20	0	118.2	489	94	46	42	16	6	2	2	41	1	117	2	7	5	.583	0-0 0	93	.640	3.00	3.19
2022	Mil	NL	29	29	0	158.2	661	135	71	65	27	0	4	2	59	0	157	5	11	7	.611	0-0 0	93	.709	3.66	3.69
Postseason			1	1	0	3.2	17	4	2	2	0	0	0	1	2	0	2	0	0	0	-	0-0 0	94	.840	5.65	4.91
5 ML YEARS			110	103	0	550.0	2366	531	276	251	80	13	12	17	206	7	524	14	32	31	.508	0-0 0	92	.736	4.18	4.11

Ramon Laureano

Bats: R Throws: R Pos: RF-71;CF-34;DH-5;PR-1   Ht: 5'11" Wt: 203 Born: 7/15/1994 Age: 28

			BATTING																RUNNING			AVERAGES			
Year	Team	Lg	G	AB	H	2B	3B	HR	(Hm | Rd)	TB	R	RBI	RC	TBB	IBB	SO	HBP	SH	SF	SB	CS	GDP	Avg	OBP	Slg	OPS
2022	LsVgs	AAA	10	37	5	2	0	0	(- | -)	7	10	2	1	5	0	11	2	0	0	2	0	1	.135	.273	.189	.462
2018	Oak	AL	48	156	45	12	1	5	(4 | 1)	74	27	19	29	16	0	50	2	0	2	7	1	0	.288	.358	.474	.832
2019	Oak	AL	123	434	125	29	0	24	(13 | 11)	226	79	67	69	27	0	123	11	1	8	13	2	7	.288	.340	.521	.860
2020	Oak	AL	54	183	39	8	1	6	(3 | 3)	67	27	25	28	24	0	58	12	0	3	2	1	7	.213	.338	.366	.704
2021	Oak	AL	88	341	84	21	2	14	(8 | 6)	151	43	39	49	27	0	98	9	0	1	12	5	4	.246	.317	.443	.760
2022	Oak	AL	94	346	73	18	0	13	(5 | 8)	130	49	34	39	25	0	104	12	0	0	11	6	6	.211	.287	.376	.663
Postseason			9	32	6	1	0	2	(0 | 2)	13	4	6	3	2	0	10	0	0	1	0	0	1	.188	.229	.406	.635
5 ML YEARS			407	1460	366	88	4	62	(33 | 29)	648	225	184	214	119	0	433	46	1	14	45	15	24	.251	.324	.444	.768

Bryan Lavastida

Bats: R Throws: R Pos: C-6   Ht: 6'0" Wt: 200 Born: 11/27/1998 Age: 24

			BATTING																RUNNING			AVERAGES			
Year	Team	Lg	G	AB	H	2B	3B	HR	(Hm | Rd)	TB	R	RBI	RC	TBB	IBB	SO	HBP	SH	SF	SB	CS	GDP	Avg	OBP	Slg	OPS
2022	Clmbs	AAA	39	147	33	6	2	4	(- | -)	55	24	16	16	16	0	35	4	0	1	2	1	5	.224	.315	.374	.690
2022	Akron	AA	45	174	34	4	2	5	(- | -)	57	22	14	14	12	0	45	3	0	2	5	1	3	.195	.257	.328	.584
2022	Cle	AL	6	12	1	0	0	0	(0 | 0)	1	0	0	0	3	0	4	0	0	0	0	0	0	.083	.267	.083	.350

Derek Law

Pitches: R Bats: R Pos: RP-17   Ht: 6'3" Wt: 225 Born: 9/14/1990 Age: 32

		HOW MUCH PITCHED					WHAT HE GAVE UP										THE RESULTS					
Year	Team	Lg	G	GS	GF	IP	BFP	H	R	ER	HR	SH	SF	HB	TBB	IBB	SO	WP	W	L	Pct	Sv-Op	Hld	Vel	OPS	ERC	ERA
2022	Toledo	AAA	33	0	29	39.0	162	37	15	14	2	0	3	1	10	2	44	1	1	3	.250	15--	-	-	.654	2.94	3.23
2022	Lsvlle	AAA	6	0	1	8.0	28	4	1	1	0	0	0	0	3	0	3	1	0	0	-	0--	-	-	.450	1.30	1.13
2016	SF	NL	61	0	12	55.0	214	44	13	13	3	0	0	0	9	0	50	1	4	2	.667	1-2	14	93	.570	1.93	2.13
2017	SF	NL	41	0	12	37.1	168	45	21	21	5	2	2	2	14	2	35	5	4	1	.800	4-6	5	94	.840	5.60	5.06
2018	SF	NL	7	0	4	13.1	66	16	13	11	2	0	1	1	8	0	12	1	1	0	1.000	0-0	0	94	.861	6.55	7.43
2019	Tor	AL	58	4	18	60.2	285	61	36	33	8	2	2	3	40	3	67	7	1	2	.333	5-6	8	94	.804	5.40	4.90
2021	Min	AL	9	0	4	15.0	67	16	7	7	2	0	1	0	8	0	14	1	0	0	-	0-0	0	94	.824	5.29	4.20
2022	2 Tms		17	0	2	19.2	92	23	13	9	3	1	2	2	8	0	17	1	2	3	.400	0-1	3	95	.831	5.78	4.12
22	Det	AL	2	0	1	2.0	13	4	5	1	1	0	2	1	1	0	2	1	0	1	.000	0-1	0	96	1.239	16.12	4.50
22	Cin	NL	15	0	1	17.2	79	19	8	8	2	1	0	1	7	0	15	0	2	2	.500	0-0	3	95	.775	4.77	4.08
	Postseason		3	0	0	2.1	11	1	1	1	1	0	0	0	1	0	3	0	0	0	-	0-0	0	94	.282	0.88	3.86
	6 ML YEARS		193	4	52	201.0	892	205	103	94	23	5	8	8	87	5	195	16	12	8	.600	10-15	30	94	.760	4.49	4.21

Casey Lawrence

Pitches: R Bats: R Pos: RP-6   Ht: 6'0" Wt: 170 Born: 10/28/1987 Age: 35

		HOW MUCH PITCHED					WHAT HE GAVE UP										THE RESULTS					
Year	Team	Lg	G	GS	GF	IP	BFP	H	R	ER	HR	SH	SF	HB	TBB	IBB	SO	WP	W	L	Pct	Sv-Op	Hld	Vel	OPS	ERC	ERA
2022	Buffalo	AAA	23	23	0	126.0	483	95	41	39	18	0	2	3	17	0	106	1	9	5	.643	0--	-	-	.607	2.18	2.79
2017	2 Tms	AL	27	2	12	55.1	264	77	41	39	11	1	2	1	25	4	52	1	2	3	.400	0-1	0	91	.907	7.38	6.34
2018	Sea	AL	11	0	5	23.1	106	28	19	19	2	0	0	2	10	1	14	1	1	0	1.000	0-0	0	90	.867	5.60	7.33
2022	Tor	AL	6	0	2	18.0	79	23	15	15	5	0	1	1	4	0	11	0	0	1	.000	0-0	0	91	.930	6.65	7.50
17	Tor	AL	4	2	2	13.1	72	21	14	13	2	1	1	0	11	3	7	0	0	3	.000	0-0	0	91	.993	9.29	8.78
17	Sea	AL	23	0	10	42.0	192	56	27	26	9	0	1	1	14	1	45	1	2	0	1.000	0-1	0	91	.875	6.76	5.57
	3 ML YEARS		44	2	19	96.2	449	128	75	73	18	1	3	4	39	5	77	2	3	4	.429	0-1	0	91	.902	6.82	6.80

Justin Lawrence

Pitches: R Bats: R Pos: RP-38   Ht: 6'3" Wt: 213 Born: 11/25/1994 Age: 28

		HOW MUCH PITCHED					WHAT HE GAVE UP										THE RESULTS					
Year	Team	Lg	G	GS	GF	IP	BFP	H	R	ER	HR	SH	SF	HB	TBB	IBB	SO	WP	W	L	Pct	Sv-Op	Hld	Vel	OPS	ERC	ERA
2022	Albq	AAA	28	0	4	29.1	118	17	11	10	2	0	0	2	13	0	49	4	1	0	1.000	1--	-	-	.533	2.13	3.07
2021	Col	NL	19	0	4	16.2	72	21	16	16	0	1	3	0	19	1	17	2	1	0	1.000	0-1	2	97	.883	7.86	8.64
2022	Col	NL	38	0	11	42.2	191	44	27	27	3	0	2	1	22	0	48	1	3	1	.750	1-3	7	95	.736	4.57	5.70
	2 ML YEARS		57	0	15	59.1	277	65	43	43	3	1	5	1	41	1	65	3	4	1	.800	1-4	9	96	.781	5.47	6.52

Charles Leblanc

Bats: R Throws: R Pos: 2B-26;3B-13;1B-8;PH-5;DH-1;PR-1   Ht: 6'3" Wt: 195 Born: 6/3/1996 Age: 27

			BATTING																RUNNING			AVERAGES			
Year	Team	Lg	G	AB	H	2B	3B	HR	(Hm | Rd)	TB	R	RBI	RC	TBB	IBB	SO	HBP	SH	SF	SB	CS	GDP	Avg	OBP	Slg	OPS
2022	Jaxnvl	AAA	87	318	96	20	1	14	(- | -)	160	47	45	62	35	1	98	6	0	1	6	0	5	.302	.381	.503	.884
2022	Mia	NL	48	156	41	10	0	4	(3 | 1)	63	18	11	19	12	0	53	1	0	0	4	2	0	.263	.320	.404	.723

Jose Leclerc

Pitches: R Bats: R Pos: RP-39   leh-KLURK   Ht: 6'0" Wt: 195 Born: 12/19/1993 Age: 29

		HOW MUCH PITCHED					WHAT HE GAVE UP										THE RESULTS					
Year	Team	Lg	G	GS	GF	IP	BFP	H	R	ER	HR	SH	SF	HB	TBB	IBB	SO	WP	W	L	Pct	Sv-Op	Hld	Vel	OPS	ERC	ERA
2022	RdRck	AAA	7	0	1	6.2	31	5	4	4	0	0	0	1	5	0	8	0	0	1	.000	0--	-	-	.658	3.72	5.40
2016	Tex	AL	12	0	5	15.0	66	11	4	3	0	0	1	0	13	2	15	1	0	0	-	0-0	0	94	.710	3.46	1.80
2017	Tex	AL	47	0	15	45.2	200	23	21	20	4	0	0	3	40	1	60	5	2	3	.400	2-3	10	96	.585	3.28	3.94
2018	Tex	AL	59	0	21	57.2	223	24	16	10	1	4	0	3	25	1	85	2	2	3	.400	12-16	15	95	.431	1.21	1.56
2019	Tex	AL	70	3	40	68.2	299	52	34	33	7	3	2	6	39	1	100	7	2	4	.333	14-18	7	97	.701	3.68	4.33
2020	Tex	AL	2	0	2	2.0	10	2	1	1	0	0	0	0	2	0	3	0	0	0	-	1-1	0	95	.775	5.48	4.50
2022	Tex	AL	39	0	20	47.2	198	33	17	15	5	0	2	3	21	0	54	2	0	3	.000	7-9	4	96	.625	2.84	2.83
	6 ML YEARS		229	3	103	236.2	996	145	93	82	17	7	5	15	140	5	317	17	6	13	.316	36-47	36	96	.604	2.73	3.12

Brooks Lee

Bats: B Throws: R Pos: SS   Ht: 6'2" Wt: 205 Born: 2/14/2001 Age: 22

			BATTING																RUNNING			AVERAGES			
Year	Team	Lg	G	AB	H	2B	3B	HR	(Hm | Rd)	TB	R	RBI	RC	TBB	IBB	SO	HBP	SH	SF	SB	CS	GDP	Avg	OBP	Slg	OPS
2022	Crpds	A+	25	97	28	4	0	4	(- | -)	44	14	12	17	16	0	18	1	0	0	0	2	2	.289	.395	.454	.848

Dylan Lee

Pitches: L Bats: L Pos: RP-46   Ht: 6'3" Wt: 214 Born: 8/1/1994 Age: 28

		HOW MUCH PITCHED					WHAT HE GAVE UP										THE RESULTS					
Year	Team	Lg	G	GS	GF	IP	BFP	H	R	ER	HR	SH	SF	HB	TBB	IBB	SO	WP	W	L	Pct	Sv-Op	Hld	Vel	OPS	ERC	ERA
2022	Gwnntt	AAA	14	0	7	15.2	61	14	5	4	2	0	0	0	2	0	23	0	1	1	.500	2--	-	-	.686	2.70	2.30
2021	Atl	NL	2	0	2	2.0	9	3	2	2	1	0	0	0	0	0	3	0	0	0	-	0-0	0	93	1.222	8.13	9.00
2022	Atl	NL	46	0	5	50.2	201	40	16	12	5	0	2	0	10	1	59	0	5	1	.833	0-3	9	92	.572	2.18	2.13
	Postseason		3	1	0	3.0	16	4	2	2	1	0	0	0	2	0	4	0	0	0	-	0-0	0	93	.875	8.47	6.00
	2 ML YEARS		48	0	5	52.2	210	43	18	14	6	0	2	0	10	1	62	0	5	1	.833	0-3	9	92	.601	2.36	2.39

Evan Lee

Pitches: L Bats: L Pos: RP-3; SP-1   Ht: 6'1" Wt: 210 Born: 6/18/1997 Age: 26

			HOW MUCH PITCHED					WHAT HE GAVE UP										THE RESULTS						
Year	Team	Lg	G	GS	GF	IP	BFP	H	R	ER	HR	SH	SF	HB	TBB	IBB	SO	WP	W	L	Pct	Sv-Op	Hld	Vel	OPS	ERC	ERA
2022	Hrsbrg	AA	7	7	0	30.0	126	25	13	12	2	0	1	1	15	0	37	0	0	3	.000	0- -	-	-	.674	3.52	3.60
2022	Was	NL	4	1	1	8.2	43	9	5	4	1	0	0	1	7	0	7	2	0	1	.000	0-0	0	92	.738	6.41	4.15

Khalil Lee

Bats: L Throws: L Pos: CF-2   Ht: 5'10" Wt: 170 Born: 6/26/1998 Age: 25

						BATTING																RUNNING			AVERAGES			
Year	Team	Lg	G	AB	H	2B	3B	HR	(Hm	Rd)	TB	R	RBI	RC	TBB	IBB	SO	HBP	SH	SF	SB	CS	GDP	Avg	OBP	Slg	OPS
2022	Syrcse	AAA	100	355	75	25	0	10	(-	-)	130	48	37	45	47	0	139	14	0	1	14	3	4	.211	.326	.366	.692
2021	NYM	NL	11	18	1	1	0	0	(0	0)	2	2	1	0	0	0	13	0	0	0	0	0	0	.056	.056	.111	.167
2022	NYM	NL	2	2	1	0	0	1	(0	1)	4	1	3	3	0	0	0	0	0	0	0	0	0	.500	.500	2.000	2.500
	2 ML YEARS		13	20	2	1	0	1	(0	1)	6	3	4	3	0	0	13	0	0	0	0	0	0	.100	.100	.300	.400

Korey Lee

Bats: R Throws: R Pos: C-12;PH-4;PR-1   Ht: 6'2" Wt: 210 Born: 7/25/1998 Age: 24

						BATTING																RUNNING			AVERAGES			
Year	Team	Lg	G	AB	H	2B	3B	HR	(Hm	Rd)	TB	R	RBI	RC	TBB	IBB	SO	HBP	SH	SF	SB	CS	GDP	Avg	OBP	Slg	OPS
2022	SgrLnd	AAA	104	404	96	20	2	25	(-	-)	195	74	76	67	36	0	127	5	0	1	12	1	10	.238	.307	.483	.790
2022	Hou	AL	12	25	4	2	0	0	(0	0)	6	1	4	1	1	0	9	0	0	0	0	0	1	.160	.192	.240	.432

Jack Leiter

Pitches: R Bats: R Pos: P   Ht: 6'1" Wt: 205 Born: 4/21/2000 Age: 23

			HOW MUCH PITCHED					WHAT HE GAVE UP										THE RESULTS						
Year	Team	Lg	G	GS	GF	IP	BFP	H	R	ER	HR	SH	SF	HB	TBB	IBB	SO	WP	W	L	Pct	Sv-Op	Hld	Vel	OPS	ERC	ERA
2022	Frisco	AA	23	22	0	92.2	425	88	69	57	11	0	2	8	56	0	109	5	3	10	.231	0- -	-	-	.740	5.03	5.54

Mark Leiter Jr.

Pitches: R Bats: R Pos: RP-31; SP-4   Ht: 6'0" Wt: 210 Born: 3/13/1991 Age: 32

			HOW MUCH PITCHED					WHAT HE GAVE UP										THE RESULTS						
Year	Team	Lg	G	GS	GF	IP	BFP	H	R	ER	HR	SH	SF	HB	TBB	IBB	SO	WP	W	L	Pct	Sv-Op	Hld	Vel	OPS	ERC	ERA
2022	Iowa	AAA	6	6	0	22.0	94	21	13	13	4	0	0	1	6	0	32	1	0	3	.000	0- -	-	-	.712	3.97	5.32
2017	Phi	NL	27	11	5	90.2	395	90	59	50	18	1	2	7	31	2	84	3	3	6	.333	0-0	0	91	.785	4.74	4.96
2018	2 Tms		20	0	4	23.1	123	35	28	20	7	0	2	2	12	3	22	2	0	1	.000	0-0	1	91	.987	9.02	7.71
2022	ChC	NL	35	4	11	67.2	282	52	32	30	10	0	2	7	25	2	73	5	2	7	.222	3-5	4	91	.673	3.37	3.99
18	Phi	NL	12	0	2	16.2	84	22	17	10	5	0	1	1	8	2	13	0	0	1	.000	0-0	0	91	.937	7.55	5.40
18	Tor	AL	8	0	2	6.2	39	13	11	10	2	0	1	1	4	1	9	2	0	0	-	0-0	1	91	1.098	12.93	13.50
	3 ML YEARS		82	15	20	181.2	800	177	119	100	35	1	6	16	68	7	179	10	5	14	.263	3-5	5	91	.777	4.71	4.95

DJ LeMahieu

Bats: R Throws: R Pos: 3B-47;2B-41;1B-35;PH-8;DH-7   la-MAY-hugh   Ht: 6'4" Wt: 220 Born: 7/13/1988 Age: 34

						BATTING																RUNNING			AVERAGES			
Year	Team	Lg	G	AB	H	2B	3B	HR	(Hm	Rd)	TB	R	RBI	RC	TBB	IBB	SO	HBP	SH	SF	SB	CS	GDP	Avg	OBP	Slg	OPS
2011	ChC	NL	37	60	15	2	0	0	(0	0)	17	3	4	3	1	0	12	0	1	0	1	2	2	.250	.262	.283	.546
2012	Col	NL	81	229	68	12	4	2	(1	1)	94	26	22	28	13	4	42	0	3	2	1	2	8	.297	.332	.410	.742
2013	Col	NL	109	404	113	21	3	2	(1	1)	146	39	28	42	19	2	67	1	7	3	18	7	13	.280	.311	.361	.673
2014	Col	NL	149	494	132	15	5	5	(2	3)	172	59	42	47	33	7	97	2	7	2	10	10	13	.267	.315	.348	.663
2015	Col	NL	150	564	170	21	5	6	(3	3)	219	85	61	75	50	4	107	1	3	2	23	3	20	.301	.358	.388	.746
2016	Col	NL	146	552	192	32	8	11	(7	4)	273	104	66	104	66	2	80	3	8	6	11	7	19	.348	.416	.495	.911
2017	Col	NL	155	609	189	28	4	8	(3	5)	249	95	64	87	59	1	90	6	3	5	6	5	14	.310	.374	.409	.783
2018	Col	NL	128	533	147	32	2	15	(4	11)	228	90	62	72	37	0	82	2	2	7	6	5	14	.276	.321	.428	.749
2019	NYY	AL	145	602	197	33	2	26	(19	7)	312	109	102	122	46	0	90	2	1	4	5	2	14	.327	.375	.518	.893
2020	NYY	AL	50	195	71	10	2	10	(8	2)	115	41	27	46	18	0	21	2	0	1	3	0	3	.364	.421	.590	1.011
2021	NYY	AL	150	597	160	24	1	10	(5	5)	216	84	57	84	73	2	94	4	0	5	4	2	16	.268	.349	.362	.711
2022	NYY	AL	125	467	122	18	0	12	(7	5)	176	74	46	57	67	0	71	4	1	2	4	3	12	.261	.357	.377	.734
	Postseason		21	92	25	5	0	3	(2	1)	39	14	11	13	10	0	15	0	0	1	0	1	2	.272	.340	.424	.764
	12 ML YEARS		1425	5306	1576	248	36	107	(60	47)	2217	809	581	767	482	22	853	27	36	39	91	46	158	.297	.356	.418	.774

Jacob Lemoine

Pitches: R Bats: R Pos: RP-9   Ht: 6'5" Wt: 220 Born: 11/28/1993 Age: 29

			HOW MUCH PITCHED					WHAT HE GAVE UP										THE RESULTS						
Year	Team	Lg	G	GS	GF	IP	BFP	H	R	ER	HR	SH	SF	HB	TBB	IBB	SO	WP	W	L	Pct	Sv-Op	Hld	Vel	OPS	ERC	ERA
2022	LsVgs	AAA	26	2	4	36.1	168	42	21	20	5	1	2	0	22	0	26	3	2	1	.667	1- -	-	-	.866	6.18	4.95
2022	Oak	AL	9	0	2	16.1	74	18	15	14	4	1	0	1	7	1	13	1	0	0	-	0-0	0	93	.838	5.63	7.71

Sandy Leon

Bats: B **Throws:** R **Pos:** C-33 lay-OHN **Ht:** 5'10" **Wt:** 235 **Born:** 3/13/1989 **Age:** 34

Year	Team	Lg	G	AB	H	2B	3B	HR	(Hm	Rd)	TB	R	RBI	RC	TBB	IBB	SO	HBP	SH	SF	SB	CS	GDP	Avg	OBP	Slg	OPS
2022	Lsvlle	AAA	26	72	16	3	0	1	(-	1)	22	5	7	7	10	0	12	1	0	1	0	0	0	.222	.321	.306	.627
2012	Was	NL	12	30	8	2	0	0	(0	0)	10	2	2	2	4	0	11	2	0	0	0	0	1	.267	.389	.333	.722
2013	Was	NL	2	1	0	0	0	0	(0	0)	0	0	0	0	0	0	1	0	0	0	0	0	0	.000	.000	.000	.000
2014	Was	NL	20	64	10	1	0	1	(0	1)	14	7	3	2	6	0	20	0	0	0	0	0	1	.156	.229	.219	.447
2015	Bos	AL	41	114	21	2	0	0	(0	0)	23	8	3	1	7	1	28	1	6	0	0	1	4	.184	.238	.202	.439
2016	Bos	AL	78	252	78	17	2	7	(2	5)	120	36	35	44	23	1	66	2	4	2	0	0	4	.310	.369	.476	.845
2017	Bos	AL	85	271	61	14	0	7	(3	4)	96	32	39	32	25	1	74	1	1	3	0	0	5	.225	.290	.354	.644
2018	Bos	AL	89	265	47	12	0	5	(2	3)	74	30	22	17	15	0	75	4	3	1	1	0	6	.177	.232	.279	.511
2019	Bos	AL	65	172	33	3	0	5	(4	1)	51	14	19	15	13	0	47	1	4	1	0	0	0	.192	.251	.297	.548
2020	Cle	AL	25	66	9	1	0	2	(1	1)	16	4	4	3	14	0	21	1	0	0	0	0	2	.136	.296	.242	.539
2021	Mia	NL	84	202	37	5	0	4	(1	3)	54	15	14	5	12	0	65	3	1	2	0	0	2	.183	.237	.267	.505
2022	2 Tms	AL	34	71	12	3	0	0	(0	0)	15	6	4	3	13	0	27	0	2	0	0	0	2	.169	.298	.211	.509
22	Cle	AL	9	15	2	0	0	0	(0	0)	2	0	0	1	6	0	4	0	0	0	0	0	1	.133	.381	.133	.514
22	Min	AL	25	56	10	3	0	0	(0	0)	13	6	4	2	7	0	23	0	2	0	0	0	1	.179	.270	.232	.502
	Postseason		17	32	8	1	0	1	(0	1)	12	2	3	4	2	0	11	0	1	0	0	0	0	.250	.294	.375	.669
	11 ML YEARS		535	1508	316	60	2	31	(13	18)	473	154	145	124	132	3	435	15	21	9	1	1	27	.210	.278	.314	.592

Dominic Leone

Pitches: R **Bats:** R **Pos:** RP-55 LEE-own **Ht:** 5'10" **Wt:** 215 **Born:** 10/26/1991 **Age:** 31

Year	Team	Lg	G	GS	GF	IP	BFP	H	R	ER	HR	SH	SF	HB	TBB	IBB	SO	WP	W	L	Pct	Sv-Op	Hld	Vel	OPS	ERC	ERA
2014	Sea	AL	57	0	3	66.1	272	52	18	16	4	1	3	3	25	3	70	4	8	2	.800	0-2	7	95	.624	2.71	2.17
2015	2 Tms		13	0	6	15.0	74	19	15	14	2	0	1	1	9	2	9	2	0	5	.000	0-1	1	93	.884	6.63	8.40
2016	Ari	NL	25	0	8	27.0	131	45	21	19	7	0	3	1	12	1	23	4	0	1	.000	0-1	0	93	1.095	10.37	6.33
2017	Tor	NL	65	0	6	70.1	279	51	22	20	6	0	3	0	23	3	81	8	3	0	1.000	1-5	11	94	.625	2.25	2.56
2018	StL	NL	29	0	8	24.0	106	27	12	12	3	1	3	0	8	3	26	0	1	2	.333	0-2	5	94	.727	4.43	4.50
2019	StL	NL	40	0	11	40.2	180	39	28	25	9	1	1	0	22	2	46	1	1	0	1.000	1-2	0	94	.822	5.20	5.53
2020	Cle	AL	12	0	4	9.2	47	14	9	9	3	0	0	0	5	0	16	1	0	0	-	0-0	3	95	1.023	9.14	8.38
2021	SF	NL	57	4	11	53.2	219	37	15	9	2	3	2	1	22	1	50	2	4	5	.444	2-4	15	95	.547	2.13	1.51
2022	SF	NL	55	0	8	49.1	222	55	24	22	6	1	1	0	24	5	52	3	4	5	.444	3-7	11	96	.822	5.07	4.01
15	Sea	AL	10	0	5	11.1	54	11	9	8	1	0	0	0	9	2	7	2	0	4	.000	0-0	1	93	.770	4.93	6.35
15	Ari	NL	3	0	1	3.2	20	8	6	6	1	0	1	1	0	0	2	0	0	1	.000	0-1	0	93	1.172	12.63	14.73
	Postseason		2	0	0	1.2	11	4	3	3	0	0	0	0	2	0	1	0	0	0	-	0-0	0	95	1.323	15.90	16.20
	9 ML YEARS		353	4	65	356.0	1530	339	164	146	42	7	17	6	150	20	373	25	21	20	.512	7-24	53	94	.737	4.00	3.69

Josh Lester

Bats: L **Throws:** R **Pos:** 3B-1;DH-1;PH-1 **Ht:** 6'3" **Wt:** 180 **Born:** 7/17/1994 **Age:** 28

Year	Team	Lg	G	AB	H	2B	3B	HR	(Hm	Rd)	TB	R	RBI	RC	TBB	IBB	SO	HBP	SH	SF	SB	CS	GDP	Avg	OBP	Slg	OPS
2022	Toledo	AAA	145	557	137	39	2	29	(-	-)	267	84	99	90	51	3	137	5	0	7	7	3	10	.246	.311	.479	.791
2022	Det	AL	2	5	0	0	0	0	(0	0)	0	0	0	0	0	0	3	0	0	0	0	0	0	.000	.000	.000	.000

Kyle Lewis

Bats: R **Throws:** R **Pos:** DH-11;RF-3;PH-3;LF-1 **Ht:** 6'4" **Wt:** 222 **Born:** 7/13/1995 **Age:** 27

Year	Team	Lg	G	AB	H	2B	3B	HR	(Hm	Rd)	TB	R	RBI	RC	TBB	IBB	SO	HBP	SH	SF	SB	CS	GDP	Avg	OBP	Slg	OPS
2022	Tacom	AAA	42	147	36	4	0	12	(-	-)	76	29	34	30	26	0	45	1	0	0	0	0	0	.245	.362	.517	.879
2019	Sea	AL	18	71	19	5	0	6	(4	2)	42	10	13	13	3	0	29	0	0	0	0	0	0	.268	.293	.592	.885
2020	Sea	AL	58	206	54	3	0	11	(5	6)	90	37	28	31	34	0	71	0	0	2	5	1	5	.262	.364	.437	.801
2021	Sea	AL	36	130	32	4	0	5	(2	3)	51	15	11	21	16	0	37	1	0	0	2	0	1	.246	.333	.392	.726
2022	Sea	AL	18	56	8	0	0	3	(2	1)	17	6	5	3	5	0	19	1	0	0	0	0	2	.143	.226	.304	.529
	4 ML YEARS		130	463	113	12	0	25	(13	12)	200	68	57	68	58	0	156	2	0	3	7	1	8	.244	.329	.432	.761

Royce Lewis

Bats: R **Throws:** R **Pos:** SS-11;CF-1 **Ht:** 6'2" **Wt:** 200 **Born:** 6/5/1999 **Age:** 24

Year	Team	Lg	G	AB	H	2B	3B	HR	(Hm	Rd)	TB	R	RBI	RC	TBB	IBB	SO	HBP	SH	SF	SB	CS	GDP	Avg	OBP	Slg	OPS
2018	Low	Low	121	483	141	29	3	14	(-	-)	218	83	74	65	43	1	84	4	1	4	28	8	8	.292	.352	.451	.803
2019	FtMyrs	A+	94	383	91	17	3	10	(-	-)	144	55	35	46	27	1	90	3	0	5	16	8	5	.238	.289	.376	.665
2019	Pnscla	AA	33	134	31	9	1	2	(-	-)	48	18	14	15	11	0	33	1	0	2	6	2	0	.231	.291	.358	.649
2022	StPaul	AAA	34	131	41	12	1	5	(-	-)	70	30	14	29	18	0	32	3	0	1	12	2	1	.313	.405	.534	.940
2022	Min	AL	12	40	12	4	0	2	(1	1)	22	5	5	7	1	0	5	0	0	0	0	0	2	.300	.317	.550	.867

Luis Liberato

Bats: L **Throws:** L **Pos:** DH-3;PH-3;PR-3;LF-1;CF-1;RF-1 **Ht:** 6'1" **Wt:** 175 **Born:** 12/18/1995 **Age:** 27

Year	Team	Lg	G	AB	H	2B	3B	HR	(Hm	Rd)	TB	R	RBI	RC	TBB	IBB	SO	HBP	SH	SF	SB	CS	GDP	Avg	OBP	Slg	OPS
2022	ElPaso	AAA	99	329	86	28	2	20	(-	-)	178	68	59	68	48	0	99	2	6	5	6	1	9	.261	.354	.541	.895
2022	SD	NL	7	5	0	0	0	0	(0	0)	0	0	0	0	0	0	3	0	0	0	0	0	0	.000	.000	.000	.000

Matthew Liberatore

Pitches: L **Bats:** L **Pos:** SP-7; RP-2   **Ht:** 6'4" **Wt:** 200 **Born:** 11/6/1999 **Age:** 23

Year	Team	Lg	G	GS	GF	IP	BFP	H	R	ER	HR	SH	SF	HB	TBB	IBB	SO	WP	W	L	Pct	Sv-Op	Hld	Vel	OPS	ERC	ERA
2018	2 Tms	Low	9	9	0	32.2	127	21	9	5	0	0	0	3	13	0	37	1	2	2	.500	0--	-	-	.802	2.04	1.38
2019	BG	A	16	15	0	78.1	332	70	33	27	2	1	1	4	31	0	76	6	6	2	.750	0--	-	-	.555	3.17	3.10
2021	Memp	AAA	21	18	0	121.1	510	122	66	56	19	3	2	4	33	0	119	3	8	9	.471	0--	-	-	.752	4.14	4.15
2022	Memp	AAA	22	22	0	115.0	495	118	68	66	16	1	4	10	41	0	116	5	7	9	.438	0--	-	-	.770	4.77	5.17
2022	StL	NL	9	7	1	34.2	161	42	23	23	5	2	2	1	18	0	28	5	2	2	.500	0-0	0	93	.913	6.30	5.97

Francisco Lindor

Bats: B **Throws:** R **Pos:** SS-159;DH-2   lin-DOHR   **Ht:** 5'11" **Wt:** 190 **Born:** 11/14/1993 **Age:** 29

Year	Team	Lg	G	AB	H	2B	3B	HR	(Hm	Rd)	TB	R	RBI	RC	TBB	IBB	SO	HBP	SH	SF	SB	CS	GDP	Avg	OBP	Slg	OPS
2015	Cle	AL	99	390	122	22	4	12	(8	4)	188	50	51	64	27	0	69	1	13	7	12	2	12	.313	.353	.482	.835
2016	Cle	AL	158	604	182	30	3	15	(6	9)	263	99	78	87	57	3	88	5	3	15	19	5	18	.301	.358	.435	.794
2017	Cle	AL	159	651	178	44	4	33	(16	17)	329	99	89	107	60	6	93	4	5	3	15	3	11	.273	.337	.505	.842
2018	Cle	AL	158	661	183	42	2	38	(20	18)	343	129	92	117	70	7	107	8	3	3	25	10	3	.277	.352	.519	.871
2019	Cle	AL	143	598	170	40	2	32	(14	18)	310	101	74	89	46	9	98	3	1	6	22	5	13	.284	.335	.518	.854
2020	Cle	AL	60	236	61	13	0	8	(3	5)	98	30	27	29	24	2	41	4	0	2	6	2	8	.258	.335	.415	.750
2021	NYM	NL	125	452	104	16	3	20	(12	8)	186	73	63	70	58	4	96	5	6	3	10	4	7	.230	.322	.412	.734
2022	NYM	NL	161	630	170	25	5	26	(12	14)	283	98	107	101	59	2	133	10	0	7	16	6	11	.270	.339	.449	.788
	Postseason		25	95	25	4	0		(4	1)	44	11	12	14	9	2	27	0	1	0	1	3	3	.263	.327	.463	.790
	8 ML YEARS		1063	4222	1170	232	23	184	(91	93)	2000	679	581	664	401	33	725	40	31	46	125	37	85	.277	.342	.474	.816

Zack Littell

Pitches: R **Bats:** R **Pos:** RP-39   lah-TELL   **Ht:** 6'4" **Wt:** 220 **Born:** 10/5/1995 **Age:** 27

Year	Team	Lg	G	GS	GF	IP	BFP	H	R	ER	HR	SH	SF	HB	TBB	IBB	SO	WP	W	L	Pct	Sv-Op	Hld	Vel	OPS	ERC	ERA
2022	Scrmto	AAA	13	1	2	13.1	56	14	10	10	3	0	0	0	4	0	13	0	0	1	.000	0--	-	-	.821	4.91	6.75
2018	Min	AL	8	2	1	20.1	101	25	17	14	3	1	1	4	11	0	14	0	0	2	.000	0-0	0	92	.924	7.09	6.20
2019	Min	AL	29	0	7	37.0	146	34	12	11	4	1	0	0	9	1	32	0	6	0	1.000	0-1	1	94	.708	3.18	2.68
2020	Min	AL	6	0	3	6.1	31	12	7	7	5	0	0	1	3	0	3	1	0	0	-	0-0	0	94	1.516	19.87	9.95
2021	SF	NL	63	2	10	61.2	252	46	24	20	7	2	2	2	24	1	63	3	4	0	1.000	2-6	5	95	.662	2.88	2.92
2022	SF	NL	39	0	7	44.1	190	48	25	25	8	0	2	1	13	0	39	1	3	3	.500	1-1	5	95	.783	4.81	5.08
	Postseason		4	0	1	3.0	17	6	5	5	1	0	0	1	1	0	5	1	0	1	.000	0-0	0	95	1.071	13.93	15.00
	5 ML YEARS		145	4	28	169.2	720	165	85	77	27	4	5	8	60	2	151	5	13	5	.722	3-8	11	94	.783	4.37	4.08

Brendon Little

Pitches: L **Bats:** L **Pos:** RP-1   **Ht:** 6'2" **Wt:** 195 **Born:** 8/11/1996 **Age:** 26

Year	Team	Lg	G	GS	GF	IP	BFP	H	R	ER	HR	SH	SF	HB	TBB	IBB	SO	WP	W	L	Pct	Sv-Op	Hld	Vel	OPS	ERC	ERA
2022	Iowa	AAA	36	0	9	50.1	223	50	26	24	4	1	3	2	26	1	49	7	4	5	.444	1--	-	-	.723	4.49	4.29
2022	ChC	NL	1	0	0	0.2	6	2	3	3	1	0	0	1	1	0	0	0	0	1	.000	0-1	0	95	1.917	51.61	40.50

Mauricio Llovera

Pitches: R **Bats:** R **Pos:** RP-16; SP-1   yo-VAIR-uh   **Ht:** 5'11" **Wt:** 224 **Born:** 4/17/1996 **Age:** 27

Year	Team	Lg	G	GS	GF	IP	BFP	H	R	ER	HR	SH	SF	HB	TBB	IBB	SO	WP	W	L	Pct	Sv-Op	Hld	Vel	OPS	ERC	ERA
2022	Scrmto	AAA	15	0	4	20.0	78	13	1	0	0	0	0	1	4	1	28	0	2	0	1.000	1--	-	-	.436	1.31	0.00
2020	Phi	NL	1	0	0	1.0	10	5	4	4	0	0	0	1	1	0	1	0	0	0	-	0-0	0	93	1.575	41.68	36.00
2021	Phi	NL	6	0	4	6.2	35	10	7	7	5	0	0	1	4	0	7	1	1	0	1.000	0-0	0	95	1.262	14.59	9.45
2022	SF	NL	17	1	5	16.1	72	14	8	8	2	0	0	0	8	1	20	1	0	0	-	0-0	1	95	.665	3.56	4.41
	3 ML YEARS		24	1	9	24.0	117	29	19	19	7	0	0	2	13	1	28	2	1	0	1.000	0-0	1	95	.915	7.53	7.13

Jonathan Loaisiga

Pitches: R **Bats:** R **Pos:** RP-50   loh-AYE-sig-ah   **Ht:** 5'11" **Wt:** 165 **Born:** 11/2/1994 **Age:** 28

Year	Team	Lg	G	GS	GF	IP	BFP	H	R	ER	HR	SH	SF	HB	TBB	IBB	SO	WP	W	L	Pct	Sv-Op	Hld	Vel	OPS	ERC	ERA
2018	NYY	AL	9	4	2	24.2	108	26	17	14	3	0	0	0	12	0	33	0	2	0	1.000	0-0	0	96	.789	4.97	5.11
2019	NYY	AL	15	4	3	31.2	139	31	16	16	6	0	4	1	16	0	37	1	2	2	.500	0-1	0	97	.820	5.21	4.55
2020	NYY	AL	12	3	2	23.0	100	21	11	9	3	1	0	4	7	1	22	1	3	0	1.000	0-2	2	97	.740	4.00	3.52
2021	NYY	AL	57	0	8	70.2	283	56	19	17	3	2	2	3	16	0	69	4	9	4	.692	5-9	17	98	.548	2.16	2.17
2022	NYY	AL	50	0	9	48.0	203	43	25	22	3	0	0	0	19	1	37	0	2	3	.400	2-3	10	98	.599	3.19	4.13
	Postseason		7	0	2	5.2	32	6	6	5	1	0	0	1	8	0	6	2	0	0	-	0-1	0	97	.947	10.00	7.94
	5 ML YEARS		143	11	24	198.0	833	177	88	78	18	3	6	8	70	2	198	6	18	9	.667	7-15	29	98	.658	3.40	3.55

Tim Locastro

Bats: R **Throws:** R **Pos:** PR-18;LF-11;CF-9;RF-7;DH-4;PH-3   **Ht:** 6'1" **Wt:** 200 **Born:** 7/14/1992 **Age:** 30

Year	Team	Lg	G	AB	H	2B	3B	HR	(Hm	Rd)	TB	R	RBI	RC	TBB	IBB	SO	HBP	SH	SF	SB	CS	GDP	Avg	OBP	Slg	OPS
2022	S-WB	AAA	47	167	40	13	2	3	(-	-)	66	27	18	21	12	0	38	11	0	0	7	1	2	.240	.332	.395	.727
2017	LAD	NL	3	1	0	0	0	0	(0	0)	0	0	0	0	0	0	0	0	0	0	1	0	0	.000	.000	.000	.000
2018	LAD	NL	18	11	2	1	0	0	(0	0)	3	6	0	2	2	0	5	1	0	0	4	0	0	.182	.357	.273	.630
2019	Ari	NL	91	212	53	12	2	1	(0	1)	72	38	17	35	14	0	44	22	1	1	17	0	1	.250	.357	.340	.697

Year Team	Lg	G	AB	H	2B	3B	HR	(Hm	Rd)	TB	R	RBI	RC	TBB	IBB	SO	HBP	SH	SF	SB	CS	GDP	Avg	OBP	Slg	OPS
2020 Ari	NL	33	69	20	4	1	2	(1	1)	32	15	7	15	8	0	14	4	1	0	4	0	0	.290	.395	.464	.859
2021 2 Tms		64	139	25	4	0	2	(0	2)	35	15	7	7	7	0	33	9	0	1	5	3	0	.180	.263	.252	.515
2022 NYY	AL	38	43	8	1	0	2	(2	0)	15	13	4	5	2	0	7	1	0	0	8	2	0	.186	.239	.349	.588
21 Ari	NL	55	118	21	2	0	1	(0	1)	26	11	5	6	6	0	26	9	0	0	5	3	2	.178	.271	.220	.491
21 NYY	AL	9	21	4	2	0	1	(0	1)	9	4	2	1	1	0	7	0	0	1	0	0	0	.190	.217	.429	.646
6 ML YEARS		247	475	108	22	3	7	(3	4)	157	87	35	64	33	0	103	37	2	2	39	5	3	.227	.325	.331	.656

Nick Lodolo

Pitches: L Bats: L Pos: SP-19　　　　Ht: 6'6" Wt: 205 Born: 2/5/1998 Age: 25

	HOW MUCH PITCHED					WHAT HE GAVE UP											THE RESULTS								
Year Team	Lg	G	GS	GF	IP	BFP	H	R	ER	HR	SH	SF	HB	TBB	IBB	SO	WP	W	L	Pct	Sv-Op	Hld	Vel	OPS	ERC	ERA
2021 Chatt	AA	10	10	0	44.0	173	31	9	9	1	0	0	6	9	0	68	4	2	1	.667	0- -	-	-	.513	1.91	1.84
2022 Cin	NL	19	19	0	103.1	441	90	44	42	13	0	0	19	39	0	131	6	4	7	.364	0-0	0	94	.727	4.26	3.66

Zach Logue

Pitches: L Bats: L Pos: SP-10; RP-4　　　　Ht: 6'0" Wt: 165 Born: 4/23/1996 Age: 27

	HOW MUCH PITCHED					WHAT HE GAVE UP											THE RESULTS								
Year Team	Lg	G	GS	GF	IP	BFP	H	R	ER	HR	SH	SF	HB	TBB	IBB	SO	WP	W	L	Pct	Sv-Op	Hld	Vel	OPS	ERC	ERA
2022 LsVgs	AAA	17	17	0	78.2	385	119	74	71	25	1	0	7	38	1	59	2	3	6	.333	0- -	-	-	1.097	10.09	8.12
2022 Oak	AL	14	10	1	57.0	257	68	44	43	13	2	1	2	20	0	42	0	3	8	.273	0-0	0	90	.918	6.08	6.79

Sammy Long

Pitches: L Bats: L Pos: RP-22; SP-6　　　　Ht: 6'1" Wt: 185 Born: 7/8/1995 Age: 27

	HOW MUCH PITCHED					WHAT HE GAVE UP											THE RESULTS								
Year Team	Lg	G	GS	GF	IP	BFP	H	R	ER	HR	SH	SF	HB	TBB	IBB	SO	WP	W	L	Pct	Sv-Op	Hld	Vel	OPS	ERC	ERA
2022 Scrmto	AAA	8	3	1	16.2	78	11	8	8	2	0	1	0	16	0	16	3	1	0	1.000	0- -	-	-	.674	4.32	4.32
2021 SF	NL	12	5	2	40.2	176	37	27	25	5	0	3	15	0	38	5		2	1	.667	0-0	0	93	.723	3.84	5.53
2022 SF	NL	28	6	12	42.1	181	39	23	17	8	1	1	1	14	1	33	3	1	3	.250	1-1	0	95	.770	3.94	3.61
2 ML YEARS		40	11	14	83.0	357	76	50	42	13	1	3	4	29	1	71	8	3	4	.429	1-1	0	94	.747	3.90	4.55

Evan Longoria

Bats: R Throws: R Pos: 3B-68;PH-19;DH-17　　　　Ht: 6'1" Wt: 213 Born: 10/7/1985 Age: 37

								BATTING												RUNNING			AVERAGES			
Year Team	Lg	G	AB	H	2B	3B	HR	(Hm	Rd)	TB	R	RBI	RC	TBB	IBB	SO	HBP	SH	SF	SB	CS	GDP	Avg	OBP	Slg	OPS
2008 TB	AL	122	448	122	31	2	27	(18	9)	238	67	85	72	46	4	122	6	0	8	7	0	8	.272	.343	.531	.874
2009 TB	AL	157	584	164	44	0	33	(16	17)	307	100	113	102	72	11	140	8	0	7	9	0	27	.281	.364	.526	.889
2010 TB	AL	151	574	169	46	5	22	(10	12)	291	96	104	99	72	12	124	5	0	10	15	5	15	.294	.372	.507	.879
2011 TB	AL	133	483	118	26	1	31	(14	17)	239	78	99	91	80	6	93	6	0	5	3	2	11	.244	.355	.495	.850
2012 TB	AL	74	273	79	14	0	17	(8	9)	144	39	55	55	33	6	61	3	0	3	2	3	14	.289	.369	.527	.896
2013 TB	AL	160	614	165	39	3	32	(15	17)	306	91	88	90	70	10	162	3	0	6	1	0	16	.269	.343	.498	.842
2014 TB	AL	162	624	158	26	1	22	(12	10)	252	83	91	83	57	11	133	9	1	9	5	0	15	.253	.320	.404	.724
2015 TB	AL	160	604	163	35	1	21	(10	11)	263	74	73	77	51	8	132	6	0	9	3	1	11	.270	.328	.435	.764
2016 TB	AL	160	633	173	41	4	36	(17	19)	330	81	98	95	42	6	144	3	0	7	0	3	13	.273	.318	.521	.840
2017 TB	AL	156	613	160	36	2	20	(10	10)	260	71	86	81	46	3	109	6	0	12	6	1	18	.261	.313	.424	.737
2018 SF	NL	125	480	117	25	4	16	(4	12)	198	51	54	46	22	3	101	5	0	5	3	1	14	.244	.281	.413	.694
2019 SF	NL	129	453	115	19	2	20	(6	14)	198	59	69	63	43	1	112	7	0	5	3	1	14	.254	.325	.437	.762
2020 SF	NL	53	193	49	10	1	7	(6	1)	82	26	28	16	11	0	39	2	0	3	0	1	10	.254	.297	.425	.722
2021 SF	NL	81	253	66	17	0	13	(5	8)	122	45	46	37	35	4	68	1	0	2	1	1	9	.261	.351	.482	.833
2022 SF	NL	89	266	65	13	0	14	(8	6)	120	31	42	42	27	2	83	2	0	3	0	0	6	.244	.315	.451	.767
Postseason		35	132	24	5	0	10	(4	6)	59	18	22	13	11	0	42	0	0	0	1	0	5	.182	.245	.447	.692
15 ML YEARS		1912	7095	1883	422	26	331	(159	172)	3350	992	1131	1049	707	87	1623	72	1	94	58	19	198	.265	.334	.472	.806

Christian Lopes

Bats: R Throws: R Pos: 2B-2;PH-2;LF-1;RF-1;DH-1　　　　Ht: 6'0" Wt: 211 Born: 10/1/1992 Age: 30

								BATTING												RUNNING			AVERAGES			
Year Team	Lg	G	AB	H	2B	3B	HR	(Hm	Rd)	TB	R	RBI	RC	TBB	IBB	SO	HBP	SH	SF	SB	CS	GDP	Avg	OBP	Slg	OPS
2022 LsVgs	AAA	53	187	48	14	1	2	(-	-)	70	24	22	24	23	0	56	4	0	2	4	1	2	.257	.347	.374	.722
2022 Oak	AL	4	9	0	0	0	0	(0	0)	0	0	0	0	1	0	5	0	0	0	0	0	0	.000	.100	.000	.100

Alejo Lopez

Bats: B Throws: R Pos: 2B-33;PH-16;3B-8;DH-4;LF-4;PR-3;RF-2　　　　Ht: 5'10" Wt: 170 Born: 5/5/1996 Age: 27

								BATTING												RUNNING			AVERAGES			
Year Team	Lg	G	AB	H	2B	3B	HR	(Hm	Rd)	TB	R	RBI	RC	TBB	IBB	SO	HBP	SH	SF	SB	CS	GDP	Avg	OBP	Slg	OPS
2022 Lsvlle	AAA	46	160	41	8	0	3	(-	-)	58	14	22	17	17	0	21	2	0	3	2	0	9	.256	.330	.363	.692
2021 Cin	NL	14	23	6	0	0	0	(0	0)	6	3	0	0	0	0	5	0	0	0	0	0	1	.261	.261	.261	.522
2022 Cin	NL	61	145	38	5	1	1	(0	1)	48	15	10	13	9	1	21	2	0	0	3	1	1	.262	.314	.331	.645
2 ML YEARS		75	168	44	5	1	1	(0	1)	54	18	10	13	9	1	26	2	0	0	3	1	2	.262	.307	.321	.629

Jorge Lopez

Pitches: R **Bats:** R **Pos:** RP-67   **Ht:** 6'3" **Wt:** 200 **Born:** 2/10/1993 **Age:** 30

Year	Team	Lg	G	GS	GF	IP	BFP	H	R	ER	HR	SH	SF	HB	TBB	IBB	SO	WP	W	L	Pct	Sv-Op	Hld	Vel	OPS	ERC	ERA
2015	Mil	NL	2	2	0	10.0	46	14	6	6	0	0	0	1	5	0	10	1	1	1	.500	0-0	0	94	.860	6.87	5.40
2017	Mil	NL	1	0	1	2.0	10	4	1	1	0	0	0	0	1	0	0	0	0	0	-	0-0	0	95	1.056	10.75	4.50
2018	2 Tms		17	7	8	53.2	234	57	30	30	6	0	2	1	22	1	38	3	2	5	.286	0-0	0	94	.763	4.64	5.03
2019	KC	AL	39	18	8	123.2	548	140	94	87	27	0	7	10	42	0	109	6	4	9	.308	1-2	0	94	.864	5.85	6.33
2020	2 Tms	AL	10	6	1	39.0	174	46	32	29	7	1	3	3	12	1	28	4	2	2	.500	0-0	0	94	.817	5.61	6.69
2021	Bal	AL	33	25	2	121.2	555	142	83	82	21	1	3	10	56	2	112	9	3	14	.176	0-1	2	95	.860	6.25	6.07
2022	2 Tms	AL	67	0	47	71.0	298	53	26	20	4	1	2	7	31	5	72	5	4	7	.364	23-29	1	98	.606	2.83	2.54
18	Mil	NL	10	0	8	19.2	85	16	6	6	1	0	1	0	13	1	15	1	0	1	.000	0-0	0	94	.665	3.66	2.75
18	KC	AL	7	7	0	34.0	149	41	24	24	5	0	1	1	9	0	23	2	2	4	.333	0-0	0	93	.813	5.20	6.35
20	KC	AL	1	0	0	0.2	5	3	2	2	0	0	0	0	0	0	0	0	0	0	-	0-0	0	94	1.400	26.58	27.00
20	Bal	AL	9	6	1	38.1	169	43	30	27	7	1	3	3	12	1	28	4	2	2	.500	0-0	0	94	.799	5.32	6.34
22	Bal	AL	44	0	35	48.1	196	30	15	9	3	1	2	4	17	1	54	2	4	6	.400	19-23	0	98	.529	1.96	1.68
22	Min	AL	23	0	12	22.2	102	23	11	11	1	0	0	3	14	4	18	3	0	1	.000	4-6	1	97	.757	4.95	4.37
7 ML YEARS			169	58	67	421.0	1865	456	272	255	65	3	17	32	169	9	369	28	16	38	.296	24-32	3	95	.806	5.28	5.45

Nicky Lopez

Bats: L **Throws:** R **Pos:** 2B-68;SS-52;3B-30;PR-7;PH-3   **Ht:** 5'11" **Wt:** 180 **Born:** 3/13/1995 **Age:** 28

Year	Team	Lg	G	AB	H	2B	3B	HR	(Hm	Rd)	TB	R	RBI	RC	TBB	IBB	SO	HBP	SH	SF	SB	CS	GDP	Avg	OBP	Slg	OPS
2019	KC	AL	103	379	91	22	2	2	(1	1)	123	44	30	38	18	0	51	1	4	0	1	1	5	.240	.276	.325	.601
2020	KC	AL	56	169	34	8	0	1	(1	0)	45	15	13	12	18	0	41	2	3	0	0	5	1	.201	.286	.266	.552
2021	KC	AL	151	497	149	21	6	2	(1	1)	188	78	43	82	49	0	74	4	12	3	22	1	9	.300	.365	.378	.744
2022	KC	AL	142	436	99	12	4	0	(0	0)	119	51	20	22	29	0	63	4	10	1	13	3	8	.227	.281	.273	.554
4 ML YEARS			452	1481	373	63	12	5	(3	2)	475	188	106	154	114	0	229	11	29	4	36	10	23	.252	.309	.321	.630

Otto Lopez

Bats: R **Throws:** R **Pos:** SS-5;PR-2;2B-1;CF-1;PH-1   **Ht:** 5'10" **Wt:** 185 **Born:** 10/1/1998 **Age:** 24

Year	Team	Lg	G	AB	H	2B	3B	HR	(Hm	Rd)	TB	R	RBI	RC	TBB	IBB	SO	HBP	SH	SF	SB	CS	GDP	Avg	OBP	Slg	OPS
2022	Buffalo	AAA	91	340	101	19	6	3	(-	-)	141	53	34	49	41	2	61	5	2	3	14	5	10	.297	.378	.415	.793
2021	Tor	AL	1	1	0	0	0	0	(0	0)	0	0	0	0	0	0	1	0	0	0	0	0	0	.000	.000	.000	.000
2022	Tor	AL	8	9	6	0	0	0	(0	0)	6	0	3	3	1	0	1	0	0	0	0	1	0	.667	.700	.667	1.367
2 ML YEARS			9	10	6	0	0	0	(0	0)	6	0	3	3	1	0	2	0	0	0	0	1	0	.600	.636	.600	1.236

Pablo Lopez

Pitches: R **Bats:** L **Pos:** SP-32   **Ht:** 6'4" **Wt:** 225 **Born:** 3/7/1996 **Age:** 27

Year	Team	Lg	G	GS	GF	IP	BFP	H	R	ER	HR	SH	SF	HB	TBB	IBB	SO	WP	W	L	Pct	Sv-Op	Hld	Vel	OPS	ERC	ERA
2018	Mia	NL	10	10	0	58.2	247	56	28	27	8	1	2	4	18	5	46	2	2	4	.333	0-0	0	92	.745	3.88	4.14
2019	Mia	NL	21	21	0	111.1	469	111	64	63	15	4	2	11	27	3	95	6	5	8	.385	0-0	0	94	.756	4.07	5.09
2020	Mia	NL	11	11	0	57.1	240	50	27	23	4	0	3	2	18	1	59	0	6	4	.600	0-0	0	94	.637	2.93	3.61
2021	Mia	NL	20	20	0	102.2	418	89	37	35	11	1	2	7	26	1	115	3	5	5	.500	0-0	0	94	.677	3.13	3.07
2022	Mia	NL	32	32	0	180.0	736	157	78	75	21	0	4	8	53	1	174	4	10	10	.500	0-0	0	94	.700	3.29	3.75
Postseason			1	1	0	5.0	19	3	2	2	2	0	0	0	0	0	7	0	0	1	.000	0-0	0	95	.684	1.78	3.60
5 ML YEARS			94	94	0	510.0	2110	463	234	223	59	6	13	32	142	11	489	15	28	31	.475	0-0	0	94	.706	3.45	3.94

Reynaldo Lopez

Pitches: R **Bats:** R **Pos:** RP-60; SP-1   ray-NAHL-doh   **Ht:** 6'1" **Wt:** 225 **Born:** 1/4/1994 **Age:** 29

Year	Team	Lg	G	GS	GF	IP	BFP	H	R	ER	HR	SH	SF	HB	TBB	IBB	SO	WP	W	L	Pct	Sv-Op	Hld	Vel	OPS	ERC	ERA
2016	Was	NL	11	6	1	44.0	201	47	27	24	4	3	2	0	22	2	42	5	5	3	.625	0-0	1	96	.772	4.60	4.91
2017	CWS	AL	8	8	0	47.2	207	49	29	25	7	0	2	1	14	0	30	3	3	3	.500	0-0	0	94	.741	4.12	4.72
2018	CWS	AL	32	32	0	188.2	799	165	88	82	25	0	9	10	75	1	151	7	7	10	.412	0-0	0	95	.713	3.80	3.91
2019	CWS	AL	33	33	0	184.0	809	203	119	110	35	2	5	8	65	0	169	5	10	15	.400	0-0	0	95	.833	5.33	5.38
2020	CWS	AL	8	8	0	26.1	121	28	21	19	9	1	0	1	15	0	24	1	1	3	.250	0-0	0	96	.944	7.17	6.49
2021	CWS	AL	20	9	3	57.2	222	42	27	22	10	0	4	1	13	0	55	1	4	4	.500	0-0	0	96	.667	2.48	3.43
2022	CWS	AL	61	1	8	65.1	254	51	24	20	1	3	4	1	11	1	63	4	6	4	.600	0-5	9	97	.564	1.68	2.76
Postseason			2	0	0	4.0	17	3	2	2	1	0	0	0	2	0	5	0	0	0	-	0-0	0	96	.761	4.02	4.50
7 ML YEARS			173	97	12	613.2	2613	585	335	302	91	9	26	21	215	4	534	26	36	42	.462	0-5	10	96	.749	4.07	4.43

Yoan Lopez

Pitches: R **Bats:** R **Pos:** RP-8   **Ht:** 6'3" **Wt:** 208 **Born:** 1/2/1993 **Age:** 30

Year	Team	Lg	G	GS	GF	IP	BFP	H	R	ER	HR	SH	SF	HB	TBB	IBB	SO	WP	W	L	Pct	Sv-Op	Hld	Vel	OPS	ERC	ERA
2022	Syrcse	AAA	29	0	11	35.0	160	41	22	20	4	0	1	0	15	0	38	3	2	2	.500	2- -	-	-	.787	5.20	5.14
2018	Ari	NL	10	0	5	9.0	35	7	3	3	2	1	0	0	1	0	11	0	0	0	-	0-0	1	97	.720	2.47	3.00
2019	Ari	NL	70	0	13	60.2	246	52	27	23	11	1	4	0	17	2	42	1	2	7	.222	1-4	21	96	.728	3.32	3.41
2020	Ari	NL	20	0	7	19.2	87	21	15	13	4	0	0	0	9	2	16	0	1	0	1.000	0-0	1	95	.870	5.30	5.95
2021	Ari	NL	13	0	5	12.1	61	18	10	9	3	0	1	0	6	2	13	0	0	0	-	0-3	2	96	1.005	7.96	6.57
2022	NYM	NL	8	0	5	11.0	51	14	8	7	2	0	0	1	5	1	10	0	1	0	1.000	0-0	0	96	.948	6.92	5.73
5 ML YEARS			121	0	35	112.2	480	112	63	55	22	2	5	1	38	7	92	1	3	8	.273	1-7	25	96	.811	4.38	4.39

Michael Lorenzen

Pitches: R Bats: R Pos: SP-18   Ht: 6'3" Wt: 217 Born: 1/4/1992 Age: 31

Year	Team	Lg	G	GS	GF	IP	BFP	H	R	ER	HR	SH	SF	HB	TBB	IBB	SO	WP	W	L	Pct	Sv-Op	Hld	Vel	OPS	ERC	ERA
2015	Cin	NL	27	21	1	113.1	515	131	70	68	18	2	1	6	57	6	83	4	4	9	.308	0-0	1	94	.882	6.09	5.40
2016	Cin	NL	35	0	4	50.0	202	41	16	16	5	0	0	6	13	0	48	2	2	1	.667	0-2	10	96	.630	3.11	2.88
2017	Cin	NL	70	0	14	83.0	361	78	43	41	9	2	1	4	34	5	80	12	8	4	.667	2-7	18	96	.695	3.89	4.45
2018	Cin	NL	45	3	10	81.0	344	78	32	28	6	2	3	3	34	2	54	2	4	2	.667	1-2	8	95	.707	3.95	3.11
2019	Cin	NL	73	0	16	83.1	343	68	29	27	9	4	2	2	28	1	85	2	1	4	.200	7-11	21	97	.644	2.96	2.92
2020	Cin	NL	18	2	3	33.2	147	30	17	16	3	1	1	1	17	1	35	2	3	1	.750	0-1	2	97	.691	3.84	4.28
2021	Cin	NL	27	0	5	29.0	125	26	18	18	2	1	1	1	14	0	21	5	1	2	.333	4-4	11	96	.673	3.75	5.59
2022	LAA	AL	18	18	0	97.2	411	81	48	46	11	0	1	4	44	0	85	3	8	6	.571	0-0	0	94	.679	3.61	4.24
	Postseason		2	0	1	2.2	11	2	0	0	0	0	0	1	0	0	6	1	0	0	-	0-0	0	97	.473	2.01	0.00
	8 ML YEARS		313	44	52	571.0	2448	533	273	260	63	12	10	27	241	15	491	32	31	29	.517	14-27	71	95	.719	4.03	4.10

Aaron Loup

Pitches: L Bats: L Pos: RP-65   LOOP   Ht: 5'11" Wt: 210 Born: 12/19/1987 Age: 35

Year	Team	Lg	G	GS	GF	IP	BFP	H	R	ER	HR	SH	SF	HB	TBB	IBB	SO	WP	W	L	Pct	Sv-Op	Hld	Vel	OPS	ERC	ERA
2012	Tor	AL	33	0	3	30.2	117	26	10	9	0	2	1	0	2	0	21	1	0	0	.000	0-1	6	92	.547	1.59	2.64
2013	Tor	AL	64	0	12	69.1	282	66	23	19	5	2	4	7	13	4	53	2	4	6	.400	2-3	8	92	.670	3.20	2.47
2014	Tor	AL	71	0	15	68.2	283	50	25	24	4	3	3	6	30	5	56	5	4	4	.500	4-8	13	92	.647	2.75	3.15
2015	Tor	AL	60	0	6	42.1	186	47	24	21	6	2	0	6	7	0	46	0	2	5	.286	0-4	9	93	.776	4.54	4.46
2016	Tor	AL	21	0	2	14.1	62	15	8	8	2	0	3	3	4	0	15	3	0	0	-	0-1	1	91	.855	5.13	5.02
2017	Tor	AL	70	0	8	57.2	265	59	27	24	4	5	0	6	29	5	64	3	2	3	.400	0-0	6	92	.722	4.56	3.75
2018	2 Tms		59	0	8	39.2	183	48	23	20	4	0	3	4	14	0	44	0	0	0	-	0-0	11	92	.805	5.45	4.54
2019	SD	NL	4	0	1	3.1	14	2	0	0	0	1	0	1	1	0	5	0	0	0	-	0-0	1	92	.558	2.03	0.00
2020	TB	AL	24	0	6	25.0	96	17	9	7	3	2	1	3	4	0	22	0	3	2	.600	0-1	4	92	.635	2.16	2.52
2021	NYM	NL	65	2	6	56.2	218	37	9	6	1	1	4	4	16	0	57	0	6	0	1.000	0-4	16	92	.501	1.72	0.95
2022	LAA	AL	65	0	7	58.2	260	54	38	25	4	0	0	8	23	3	52	0	0	5	.000	1-6	18	91	.671	3.66	3.84
18	Tor	AL	50	0	7	35.2	166	44	21	18	4	0	3	3	13	0	42	0	0	0	-	0-0	9	92	.824	5.63	4.54
18	Phi	NL	9	0	1	4.0	17	4	2	2	0	0	0	1	1	0	2	0	0	0	-	0-0	2	91	.620	3.88	4.50
	Postseason		13	0	0	7.1	31	6	3	3	0	0	0	1	4	0	7	1	0	0	-	0-0	5	93	.624	3.58	3.68
	11 ML YEARS		536	2	74	466.1	1966	421	196	163	33	17	20	48	142	17	435	14	21	27	.438	7-28	93	92	.674	3.33	3.15

Richard Lovelady

Pitches: L Bats: L Pos: P   Ht: 6'0" Wt: 185 Born: 7/7/1995 Age: 27

Year	Team	Lg	G	GS	GF	IP	BFP	H	R	ER	HR	SH	SF	HB	TBB	IBB	SO	WP	W	L	Pct	Sv-Op	Hld	Vel	OPS	ERC	ERA
2019	KC	AL	25	0	5	20.0	96	30	17	17	2	1	1	1	8	2	17	1	0	3	.000	0-1	2	-	.952	7.18	7.65
2020	KC	AL	1	0	0	1.0	4	1	1	1	1	0	0	0	1	0	0	0	0	0	-	0-0	0	-	1.833	17.98	9.00
2021	KC	AL	20	0	2	20.2	84	16	9	8	3	0	1	1	6	1	23	1	2	0	1.000	1-1	4	-	.616	2.85	3.48
	3 ML YEARS		46	0	7	41.2	184	47	27	26	6	1	2	2	15	3	40	2	2	3	.400	1-2	6	-	.813	5.07	5.62

Brandon Lowe

Bats: L Throws: R Pos: 2B-53;DH-11;PH-4;RF-1   LAOW   Ht: 5'10" Wt: 185 Born: 7/6/1994 Age: 28

Year	Team	Lg	G	AB	H	2B	3B	HR	(Hm	Rd)	TB	R	RBI	RC	TBB	IBB	SO	HBP	SH	SF	SB	CS	GDP	Avg	OBP	Slg	OPS
2018	TB	AL	43	129	30	6	2	6	(2	4)	58	16	25	21	16	0	38	2	0	1	2	1	3	.233	.324	.450	.774
2019	TB	AL	82	296	80	17	2	17	(8	9)	152	42	51	50	25	0	113	5	0	1	5	0	1	.270	.336	.514	.850
2020	TB	AL	56	193	52	9	2	14	(6	8)	107	36	37	39	25	0	58	4	0	2	3	0	4	.269	.362	.554	.916
2021	TB	AL	149	535	132	31	0	39	(19	20)	280	97	99	110	68	4	167	9	0	3	7	1	2	.247	.340	.523	.863
2022	TB	AL	65	235	52	10	2	8	(4	4)	90	31	25	32	27	0	61	3	0	1	1	0	1	.221	.308	.383	.691
	Postseason		29	113	13	1	0	5	(2	3)	29	8	9	5	7	0	47	0	0	0	0	0	0	.115	.167	.257	.423
	5 ML YEARS		395	1388	346	73	8	84	(39	45)	687	222	237	252	161	4	437	23	0	8	18	2	9	.249	.335	.495	.830

Josh Lowe

Bats: L Throws: R Pos: RF-33;LF-10;CF-9;DH-7;PH-2   Ht: 6'4" Wt: 205 Born: 2/2/1998 Age: 25

Year	Team	Lg	G	AB	H	2B	3B	HR	(Hm	Rd)	TB	R	RBI	RC	TBB	IBB	SO	HBP	SH	SF	SB	CS	GDP	Avg	OBP	Slg	OPS
2022	Drham	AAA	80	302	95	27	2	14	(-	-)	168	51	67	70	44	1	115	2	0	3	25	2	4	.315	.402	.556	.958
2021	TB	AL	2	1	1	0	0	0	(0	0)	1	0	0	1	0	0	0	0	0	0	1	0	0	1.000	1.000	1.000	2.000
2022	TB	AL	52	181	40	12	2	2	(1	1)	62	24	13	18	15	1	66	1	1	0	3	0	1	.221	.284	.343	.627
	2 ML YEARS		54	182	41	12	2	2	(1	1)	63	24	13	19	16	1	66	1	1	0	4	0	1	.225	.291	.346	.638

Nathaniel Lowe

Bats: L Throws: R Pos: 1B-153;DH-4;PH-3   Ht: 6'4" Wt: 220 Born: 7/7/1995 Age: 27

Year	Team	Lg	G	AB	H	2B	3B	HR	(Hm	Rd)	TB	R	RBI	RC	TBB	IBB	SO	HBP	SH	SF	SB	CS	GDP	Avg	OBP	Slg	OPS
2019	TB	AL	50	152	40	8	0	7	(4	3)	69	24	19	19	13	0	50	2	0	2	0	0	4	.263	.325	.454	.779
2020	TB	AL	21	67	15	2	0	4	(3	1)	29	10	11	8	9	2	28	0	0	0	1	0	2	.224	.316	.433	.749
2021	Tex	AL	157	557	147	24	3	18	(8	10)	231	75	72	96	80	2	162	2	0	3	8	0	13	.264	.357	.415	.771
2022	Tex	AL	157	593	179	26	3	27	(10	17)	292	74	76	107	48	2	147	4	0	0	2	2	10	.302	.358	.492	.851
	Postseason		1	3	0	0	0	0	(0	0)	0	0	0	0	0	0	2	0	0	0	0	0	0	.000	.000	.000	.000
	4 ML YEARS		385	1369	381	60	6	56	(25	31)	621	183	178	230	150	6	387	8	0	5	11	2	29	.278	.352	.454	.805

Jed Lowrie

Bats: B **Throws:** R **Pos:** DH-39;PH-8;1B-3;2B-2 LAU-ree **Ht:** 6'0" **Wt:** 180 **Born:** 4/17/1984 **Age:** 39

								BATTING												RUNNING			AVERAGES			
Year Team	Lg	G	AB	H	2B	3B	HR	(Hm Rd)	TB	R	RBI	RC	TBB	IBB	SO	HBP	SH	SF	SB	CS	GDP	Avg	OBP	Slg	OPS
2008 Bos	AL	81	260	67	25	3	2	(0 2)	104	34	46	35	35	0	68	1	2	8	1	0	8	.258	.339	.400	.739
2009 Bos	AL	32	68	10	2	0	2	(1 1)	18	5	11	5	6	0	20	0	0	2	0	0	0	.147	.211	.265	.475
2010 Bos	AL	55	171	49	14	0	9	(3 6)	90	31	24	32	25	0	25	1	0	0	1	1	2	.287	.381	.526	.907
2011 Bos	AL	88	309	78	14	4	6	(3 3)	118	40	36	33	23	2	60	2	1	6	1	1	6	.252	.303	.382	.685
2012 Hou	NL	97	340	83	18	0	16	(9 7)	149	43	42	45	43	0	65	2	0	2	2	0	3	.244	.331	.438	.769
2013 Oak	AL	154	603	175	45	2	15	(7 8)	269	80	75	88	50	3	91	2	3	4	1	0	17	.290	.344	.446	.791
2014 Oak	AL	136	502	125	29	3	6	(4 2)	178	59	50	52	51	5	79	5	2	6	0	0	14	.249	.321	.355	.676
2015 Hou	AL	69	230	51	14	0	9	(5 4)	92	35	30	29	28	5	43	3	0	2	1	0	3	.222	.312	.400	.712
2016 Oak	AL	87	338	89	12	1	2	(1 1)	109	30	27	36	26	0	65	1	0	4	0	0	10	.263	.314	.322	.637
2017 Oak	AL	153	567	157	49	3	14	(8 6)	254	86	69	94	73	2	100	2	0	3	0	1	10	.277	.360	.448	.808
2018 Oak	AL	157	596	159	37	1	23	(4 19)	267	78	99	106	78	1	128	3	0	3	0	0	8	.267	.353	.448	.801
2019 NYM	NL	9	7	0	0	0	0	(0 0)	0	0	0	0	1	0	4	0	0	0	0	0	0	.000	.125	.000	.125
2021 Oak	AL	139	457	112	28	0	14	(5 9)	182	55	69	72	49	1	108	2	0	4	0	0	4	.245	.318	.398	.717
2022 Oak	AL	50	167	30	5	0	3	(0 3)	44	14	16	10	15	0	39	0	0	2	1	0	5	.180	.245	.263	.508
Postseason		23	64	9	2	0	1	(0 1)	14	7	5	4	7	0	17	1	1	1	0	0	1	.141	.233	.219	.452
14 ML YEARS		1307	4615	1185	292	17	121	(50 71)	1874	590	594	637	503	19	895	24	8	46	8	3	94	.257	.330	.406	.736

Zac Lowther

Pitches: L **Bats:** L **Pos:** RP-1 **Ht:** 6'2" **Wt:** 235 **Born:** 4/30/1996 **Age:** 27

		HOW MUCH PITCHED					WHAT HE GAVE UP											THE RESULTS							
Year Team	Lg	G	GS	GF	IP	BFP	H	R	ER	HR	SH	SF	HB	TBB	IBB	SO	WP	W	L	Pct	Sv-Op	Hld	Vel	OPS	ERC	ERA
2022 Norfolk	AAA	17	9	2	43.2	228	75	53	50	10	1	3	4	23	0	46	4	1	5	.167	0--	-	-	1.084	10.81	10.31
2021 Bal	AL	10	6	2	29.2	138	36	23	22	6	1	3	4	13	0	30	1	1	3	.250	0-0	0	91	.880	6.94	6.67
2022 Bal	AL	1	0	0	5.1	28	8	6	5	0	0	2	1	2	0	1	0	0	0	-	0-0	0	91	.871	6.48	8.44
2 ML YEARS		11	6	2	35.0	166	44	29	27	6	1	5	5	15	0	31	1	1	3	.250	0-0	0	91	.879	6.88	6.94

Joey Lucchesi

Pitches: L **Bats:** L **Pos:** P loo-KAY-zee **Ht:** 6'5" **Wt:** 225 **Born:** 6/6/1993 **Age:** 30

		HOW MUCH PITCHED					WHAT HE GAVE UP											THE RESULTS							
Year Team	Lg	G	GS	GF	IP	BFP	H	R	ER	HR	SH	SF	HB	TBB	IBB	SO	WP	W	L	Pct	Sv-Op	Hld	Vel	OPS	ERC	ERA
2018 SD	NL	26	26	0	130.0	548	125	63	59	23	3	4	4	43	2	145	4	8	9	.471	0-0	0	-	.766	4.24	4.08
2019 SD	NL	30	30	0	163.2	686	144	78	76	23	5	4	2	56	0	158	8	10	10	.500	0-0	0	-	.702	3.48	4.18
2020 SD	NL	3	2	0	5.2	32	13	5	5	0	0	1	1	2	0	5	0	0	1	.000	0-0	0	-	1.036	12.30	7.94
2021 NYM	NL	11	8	1	38.1	157	34	20	19	4	2	2	2	11	0	41	1	1	4	.200	0-0	0	-	.722	3.31	4.46
4 ML YEARS		70	66	1	337.2	1423	316	166	159	50	10	11	9	112	2	349	13	19	24	.442	0-0	0	-	.737	3.87	4.24

Marco Luciano

Bats: R **Throws:** R **Pos:** SS **Ht:** 6'2" **Wt:** 178 **Born:** 9/10/2001 **Age:** 21

								BATTING												RUNNING			AVERAGES			
Year Team	Lg	G	AB	H	2B	3B	HR	(Hm Rd)	TB	R	RBI	RC	TBB	IBB	SO	HBP	SH	SF	SB	CS	GDP	Avg	OBP	Slg	OPS
2019 2 Tms	Low	47	179	54	13	2	10	(- -)	101	52	42	44	32	0	45	4	0	1	9	6	4	.302	.417	.564	.981
2021 2 Tms	Low	106	395	102	17	5	19	(- -)	186	68	71	0	48	0	122	6	0	4	6	5	7	.258	.344	.471	.815
2022 2 Tms	Low	65	227	61	12	0	11	(- -)	106	33	36	38	26	0	58	3	0	1	0	0	6	.269	.350	.467	.817

Lucas Luetge

Pitches: L **Bats:** L **Pos:** RP-50 LIT-key **Ht:** 6'4" **Wt:** 205 **Born:** 3/24/1987 **Age:** 36

		HOW MUCH PITCHED					WHAT HE GAVE UP											THE RESULTS							
Year Team	Lg	G	GS	GF	IP	BFP	H	R	ER	HR	SH	SF	HB	TBB	IBB	SO	WP	W	L	Pct	Sv-Op	Hld	Vel	OPS	ERC	ERA
2012 Sea	AL	63	0	16	40.2	178	37	20	18	3	1	3	1	24	6	38	5	2	2	.500	2-3	12	89	.693	4.01	3.98
2013 Sea	AL	35	0	15	37.0	165	42	22	20	2	2	3	2	16	2	27	4	1	3	.250	0-0	1	91	.784	4.81	4.86
2014 Sea	AL	12	0	4	9.0	38	6	5	5	3	0	0	0	5	0	7	1	0	0	-	0-0	0	91	.744	4.31	5.00
2015 Sea	AL	1	0	1	2.1	8	0	0	0	0	0	0	0	2	0	2	0	0	0	-	0-0	0	91	.500	0.81	0.00
2021 NYY	AL	57	1	13	72.1	301	67	30	22	6	0	1	3	15	1	78	8	4	2	.667	1-3	3	88	.643	2.92	2.74
2022 NYY	AL	50	0	18	57.1	251	63	19	17	4	0	2	4	17	1	60	1	4	4	.500	2-3	6	88	.721	4.24	2.67
6 ML YEARS		218	1	67	218.2	941	215	96	82	18	3	9	10	79	10	212	19	11	11	.500	5-9	22	90	.699	3.81	3.38

Seth Lugo

Pitches: R **Bats:** R **Pos:** RP-62 **Ht:** 6'4" **Wt:** 225 **Born:** 11/17/1989 **Age:** 33

		HOW MUCH PITCHED					WHAT HE GAVE UP											THE RESULTS							
Year Team	Lg	G	GS	GF	IP	BFP	H	R	ER	HR	SH	SF	HB	TBB	IBB	SO	WP	W	L	Pct	Sv-Op	Hld	Vel	OPS	ERC	ERA
2016 NYM	NL	17	8	2	64.0	260	49	19	19	7	8	4	4	21	3	45	1	5	2	.714	0-0	0	92	.666	2.81	2.67
2017 NYM	NL	19	18	1	101.1	436	114	57	53	13	2	5	2	25	1	85	2	7	5	.583	0-0	0	91	.770	4.43	4.71
2018 NYM	NL	54	5	13	101.1	410	81	36	30	9	1	5	2	28	4	103	2	3	4	.429	3-4	11	94	.595	2.49	2.66
2019 NYM	NL	61	0	14	80.0	314	56	28	24	8	1	1	5	16	4	104	2	7	4	.636	6-11	21	94	.562	1.97	2.70
2020 NYM	NL	16	7	6	36.2	160	40	22	21	8	0	2	2	10	1	47	1	3	4	.429	3-5	0	93	.825	5.05	5.15
2021 NYM	NL	46	0	10	46.1	195	41	18	18	6	0	2	1	19	2	55	0	4	3	.571	1-4	13	94	.712	3.73	3.50
2022 NYM	NL	62	0	20	65.0	272	58	26	26	9	0	2	3	18	1	69	2	3	2	.600	3-6	16	94	.668	3.38	3.60
7 ML YEARS		275	38	66	494.2	2047	439	206	191	60	12	21	19	137	16	508	10	32	24	.571	16-30	61	93	.675	3.22	3.48

Jordan Luplow

Bats: R **Throws:** R **Pos:** RF-41;PH-27;LF-22;DH-6;CF-5;1B-1;3B-1   **Ht:** 6'1" **Wt:** 195 **Born:** 9/26/1993 **Age:** 29

Year	Team	Lg	G	AB	H	2B	3B	HR	(Hm	Rd)	TB	R	RBI	RC	TBB	IBB	SO	HBP	SH	SF	SB	CS	GDP	Avg	OBP	Slg	OPS
2022	Reno	AAA	10	45	13	3	0	6	(-	-)	34	10	14	12	2	0	9	1	0	0	0	0	2	.289	.333	.756	1.089
2017	Pit	NL	27	78	16	3	1	3	(3	0)	30	6	11	8	6	0	22	2	0	1	0	1	4	.205	.276	.385	.660
2018	Pit	NL	37	92	17	1	3	3	(3	0)	33	16	7	4	10	0	18	1	0	0	2	2	7	.185	.272	.359	.631
2019	Cle	AL	85	225	62	15	1	15	(8	7)	124	42	38	42	33	0	61	2	0	1	3	2	7	.276	.372	.551	.923
2020	Cle	AL	29	78	15	5	1	2	(1	1)	28	8	8	8	12	0	19	1	0	1	0	1	3	.192	.304	.359	.663
2021	2 Tms	AL	62	163	33	8	0	11	(5	6)	74	23	28	31	28	0	57	2	0	1	2	2	2	.202	.326	.454	.780
2022	Ari	NL	83	205	36	5	0	11	(6	5)	74	26	28	25	25	1	60	3	0	1	5	1	5	.176	.274	.361	.634
21	Cle	AL	36	98	17	5	0	7	(3	4)	43	12	20	22	21	0	31	2	0	0	0	2	1	.173	.331	.439	.769
21	TB	AL	26	65	16	3	0	4	(2	2)	31	11	8	9	7	0	26	0	0	0	1	0	1	.246	.319	.477	.796
	Postseason		5	9	3	2	0	1	(1	0)	8	2	6	4	1	0	4	0	0	0	0	0	0	.333	.400	.889	1.289
	6 ML YEARS		323	841	179	37	6	45	(26	19)	363	121	120	118	114	1	237	11	0	4	11	9	28	.213	.313	.432	.745

Gavin Lux

Bats: L **Throws:** R **Pos:** 2B-102;LF-28;SS-9;PH-8;DH-1   **Ht:** 6'2" **Wt:** 190 **Born:** 11/23/1997 **Age:** 25

Year	Team	Lg	G	AB	H	2B	3B	HR	(Hm	Rd)	TB	R	RBI	RC	TBB	IBB	SO	HBP	SH	SF	SB	CS	GDP	Avg	OBP	Slg	OPS
2019	LAD	NL	23	75	18	4	1	2	(0	2)	30	12	9	10	7	0	24	0	0	0	2	0	0	.240	.305	.400	.705
2020	LAD	NL	19	63	11	2	0	3	(0	3)	22	8	8	8	6	0	19	1	0	0	1	0	0	.175	.246	.349	.596
2021	LAD	NL	102	335	81	12	4	7	(5	2)	122	49	46	48	41	3	83	3	0	2	4	1	3	.242	.328	.364	.692
2022	LAD	NL	129	421	116	20	7	6	(1	5)	168	66	42	53	47	0	95	0	0	3	7	2	3	.276	.346	.399	.745
	Postseason		14	24	5	0	0	1	(1	0)	8	2	1	2	5	0	10	0	0	0	1	0	0	.208	.345	.333	.678
	4 ML YEARS		273	894	226	38	12	18	(6	12)	342	135	105	119	101	3	221	3	0	5	14	3	6	.253	.329	.383	.712

Jesus Luzardo

Pitches: L **Bats:** L **Pos:** SP-18   **Ht:** 6'0" **Wt:** 218 **Born:** 9/30/1997 **Age:** 25

Year	Team	Lg	G	GS	GF	IP	BFP	H	R	ER	HR	SH	SF	HB	TBB	IBB	SO	WP	W	L	Pct	Sv-Op	Hld	Vel	OPS	ERC	ERA
2019	Oak	AL	6	0	2	12.0	46	5	2	2	1	0	0	1	3	0	16	2	0	0	-	2-2	2	96	.434	1.13	1.50
2020	Oak	AL	12	9	1	59.0	248	58	27	27	9	1	1	3	17	1	59	3	3	2	.600	0-0	0	96	.745	4.11	4.12
2021	2 Tms		25	18	1	95.1	437	106	73	70	20	2	5	4	48	1	98	8	6	9	.400	0-0	1	96	.887	6.12	6.61
2022	Mia	NL	18	18	0	100.1	400	96	40	37	10	1	1	2	35	0	120	5	4	7	.364	0-0	0	96	.601	2.35	3.32
21	Oak	AL	13	6	1	38.0	173	46	32	29	11	1	0	0	16	0	40	3	2	4	.333	0-0	1	96	.915	6.84	6.87
21	Mia	NL	12	12	0	57.1	264	60	41	41	9	1	4	4	32	1	58	5	4	5	.444	0-0	0	95	.867	5.64	6.44
	Postseason		3	2	0	10.2	46	12	7	7	4	0	0	0	4	0	11	0	0	1	1.000	0-0	0	96	.943	6.90	5.91
	4 ML YEARS		61	45	4	266.2	1131	238	142	136	40	4	7	10	103	2	293	18	13	18	.419	2-2	3	96	.734	3.90	4.59

Jordan Lyles

Pitches: R **Bats:** R **Pos:** SP-32   **Ht:** 6'5" **Wt:** 230 **Born:** 10/19/1990 **Age:** 32

Year	Team	Lg	G	GS	GF	IP	BFP	H	R	ER	HR	SH	SF	HB	TBB	IBB	SO	WP	W	L	Pct	Sv-Op	Hld	Vel	OPS	ERC	ERA
2011	Hou	NL	20	15	2	94.0	415	107	61	56	14	7	1	5	26	1	67	0	2	8	.200	0-0	0	90	.817	4.87	5.36
2012	Hou	NL	25	25	0	141.1	628	159	97	80	20	6	4	5	42	4	99	2	5	12	.294	0-0	0	92	.772	4.67	5.09
2013	Hou	NL	27	25	1	141.2	642	165	98	88	17	0	3	11	49	1	93	4	7	9	.438	1-1	1	92	.801	5.20	5.59
2014	Col	NL	22	22	0	126.2	546	127	64	61	12	4	3	8	46	1	90	6	7	4	.636	0-0	0	91	.750	4.17	4.33
2015	Col	NL	10	10	0	49.0	212	54	32	28	2	3	1	3	19	1	30	2	2	5	.286	0-0	0	92	.751	4.51	5.14
2016	Col	NL	40	5	17	58.2	273	69	46	38	4	1	2	4	28	2	32	5	4	5	.444	1-4	3	93	.790	5.32	5.83
2017	2 Tms	NL	38	5	12	69.2	324	96	61	60	16	2	1	4	22	1	55	4	1	5	.167	0-0	2	94	.948	7.24	7.75
2018	2 Tms	NL	35	8	10	87.2	371	83	42	40	12	3	4	3	28	3	84	5	3	4	.429	0-0	2	94	.718	3.78	4.11
2019	2 Tms	NL	28	28	0	141.0	599	131	72	65	25	2	3	1	55	2	146	4	12	8	.600	0-0	0	93	.767	4.18	4.15
2020	Tex	AL	12	9	0	57.2	266	67	49	45	12	1	5	2	23	0	36	3	1	6	.143	0-0	0	93	.841	5.82	7.02
2021	Tex	AL	32	30	1	180.0	769	194	104	103	38	2	7	7	56	0	146	9	10	13	.435	0-0	0	93	.834	5.20	5.15
2022	Bal	AL	32	32	0	179.0	774	196	94	88	26	0	4	8	52	0	144	5	12	11	.522	0-0	0	91	.784	4.70	4.42
17	Col	NL	33	0	12	46.2	211	61	37	36	11	1	1	4	12	1	33	2	0	2	.000	0-0	2	94	.921	6.72	6.94
17	SD	NL	5	5	0	23.0	113	35	24	24	5	1	0	0	10	0	22	2	1	3	.250	0-0	0	93	1.000	8.31	9.39
18	SD	NL	24	8	5	71.1	300	71	35	34	12	3	3	1	19	0	62	4	2	4	.333	0-0	2	93	.741	4.03	4.29
18	Mil	NL	11	0	5	16.1	71	12	7	6	0	0	1	2	9	3	22	1	1	0	1.000	0-0	0	94	.612	2.63	3.31
19	Pit	NL	17	17	0	82.1	361	88	53	49	16	1	1	1	33	1	90	4	5	7	.417	0-0	0	93	.853	5.20	5.36
19	Mil	NL	11	11	0	58.2	238	43	19	16	9	1	2	0	22	1	56	0	7	1	.875	0-0	0	93	.636	2.87	2.45
	12 ML YEARS		321	214	33	1326.1	5819	1448	820	752	198	31	38	61	446	16	1022	50	66	90	.423	2-5	8	92	.796	4.86	5.10

Daniel Lynch

Pitches: L **Bats:** L **Pos:** SP-27   **Ht:** 6'6" **Wt:** 200 **Born:** 11/17/1996 **Age:** 26

Year	Team	Lg	G	GS	GF	IP	BFP	H	R	ER	HR	SH	SF	HB	TBB	IBB	SO	WP	W	L	Pct	Sv-Op	Hld	Vel	OPS	ERC	ERA
2021	KC	AL	15	15	0	68.0	311	80	46	43	9	1	4	4	31	0	55	4	4	6	.400	0-0	0	94	.836	5.85	5.69
2022	KC	AL	27	27	0	131.2	600	155	79	75	21	2	6	5	52	2	122	7	4	13	.235	0-0	0	94	.811	5.60	5.13
	2 ML YEARS		42	42	0	199.2	911	235	125	118	30	3	10	9	83	2	177	11	8	19	.296	0-0	0	94	.819	5.69	5.32

Lance Lynn

Pitches: R **Bats:** B **Pos:** SP-21   **Ht:** 6'5" **Wt:** 270 **Born:** 5/12/1987 **Age:** 36

Year	Team	Lg	G	GS	GF	IP	BFP	H	R	ER	HR	SH	SF	HB	TBB	IBB	SO	WP	W	L	Pct	Sv-Op	Hld	Vel	OPS	ERC	ERA
2011	StL	NL	18	2	2	34.2	136	25	12	12	3	1	0	1	11	1	40	1	1	1	.500	1-2	3	93	.591	2.37	3.12
2012	StL	NL	35	29	2	176.0	744	168	76	74	16	4	3	10	64	3	180	3	18	7	.720	0-0	1	93	.728	3.87	3.78
2013	StL	NL	33	33	0	201.2	856	189	92	89	14	11	8	11	76	0	198	6	15	10	.600	0-0	0	92	.701	3.67	3.97
2014	StL	NL	33	33	0	203.2	866	185	72	62	13	6	4	7	72	1	181	7	15	10	.600	0-0	0	92	.662	3.24	2.74
2015	StL	NL	31	31	0	175.1	751	172	66	59	13	9	2	5	68	5	167	2	12	11	.522	0-0	0	92	.708	3.83	3.03
2017	StL	NL	33	33	0	186.1	776	151	80	71	27	9	3	10	78	5	153	2	11	8	.579	0-0	0	92	.707	3.62	3.43
2018	2 Tms		31	29	0	156.2	700	163	87	83	14	0	2	6	76	3	161	5	10	10	.500	0-0	0	93	.744	4.68	4.77
2019	Tex	AL	33	33	0	208.1	875	195	89	85	21	1	6	8	59	0	246	18	16	11	.593	0-0	0	94	.689	3.41	3.67
2020	Tex	AL	13	13	0	84.0	344	64	34	31	13	1	1	6	25	0	89	2	6	3	.667	0-0	0	93	.663	3.01	3.32
2021	CWS	AL	28	28	0	157.0	641	123	52	47	18	2	2	2	45	2	176	5	11	6	.647	0-0	0	93	.605	2.58	2.69
2022	CWS	AL	21	21	0	121.2	512	119	65	54	19	0	2	10	19	0	124	4	8	7	.533	0-0	0	93	.697	3.62	3.99
18	Min	AL	20	20	0	102.1	469	105	61	58	12	0	2	6	62	3	100	3	7	8	.467	0-0	0	93	.780	5.38	5.10
18	NYY	AL	11	9	0	54.1	231	58	26	25	2	0	0	0	14	0	61	2	3	2	.600	0-0	0	93	.676	3.44	4.14
	Postseason		27	8	3	58.0	264	65	38	34	6	3	3	1	30	5	56	1	5	5	.500	0-0	3	94	.800	5.19	5.28
	11 ML YEARS		309	285	4	1705.1	7201	1554	725	667	171	44	33	76	593	20	1715	55	123	84	.594	1-2	4	93	.691	3.54	3.52

Andres Machado

Pitches: R **Bats:** R **Pos:** RP-51   muh-CHAH-doe   **Ht:** 6'0" **Wt:** 235 **Born:** 4/22/1993 **Age:** 30

Year	Team	Lg	G	GS	GF	IP	BFP	H	R	ER	HR	SH	SF	HB	TBB	IBB	SO	WP	W	L	Pct	Sv-Op	Hld	Vel	OPS	ERC	ERA
2022	Roch	AAA	13	0	1	17.0	72	18	11	11	0	0	0	1	5	0	18	0	0	0	-	0- -	-		.712	3.58	5.82
2017	KC	AL	2	0	1	3.2	24	10	9	9	2	0	0	0	3	0	1	0	0	0	-	0-0	0	96	1.399	23.02	22.09
2021	Was	NL	40	0	6	35.2	154	30	17	14	4	0	1	5	15	1	30	3	1	2	.333	0-3	10	95	.701	3.86	3.53
2022	Was	NL	51	0	14	59.1	261	55	32	22	7	0	5	2	26	0	46	3	2	0	1.000	0-0	3	95	.722	3.98	3.34
	3 ML YEARS		93	0	21	98.2	439	95	58	45	13	0	6	7	44	1	77	6	3	2	.600	0-3	13	95	.751	4.47	4.10

Dixon Machado

Bats: R **Throws:** R **Pos:** SS-5   muh-CHAH-doe   **Ht:** 6'1" **Wt:** 190 **Born:** 2/22/1992 **Age:** 31

Year	Team	Lg	G	AB	H	2B	3B	HR	(Hm	Rd)	TB	R	RBI	RC	TBB	IBB	SO	HBP	SH	SF	SB	CS	GDP	Avg	OBP	Slg	OPS
2022	Iowa	AAA	86	340	106	20	1	2	(-	-)	134	46	31	50	46	0	41	5	0	0	10	3	9	.312	.402	.394	.796
2022	Scrmto	AAA	35	121	28	6	0	4	(-	-)	46	14	15	11	7	0	23	2	0	1	2	0	1	.231	.282	.380	.663
2015	Det	AL	24	68	16	3	0	0	(0	0)	19	6	5	5	7	0	14	0	3	0	1	0	3	.235	.307	.279	.586
2016	Det	AL	8	10	1	0	0	0	(0	0)	1	1	0	0	3	0	4	0	0	0	0	0	0	.100	.308	.100	.408
2017	Det	AL	73	166	43	5	1	1	(1	0)	53	17	11	11	10	0	32	1	2	2	1	0	6	.259	.302	.319	.621
2018	Det	AL	67	214	44	13	1	1	(1	0)	62	20	21	14	14	1	41	3	1	1	1	1	2	.206	.263	.290	.553
2022	SF	NL	5	15	3	0	0	0	(0	0)	3	1	0	1	1	0	5	1	0	0	0	0	0	.200	.294	.200	.494
	5 ML YEARS		177	473	107	21	2	2	(2	0)	138	45	37	30	35	1	96	5	6	3	3	1	11	.226	.285	.292	.577

Manny Machado

Bats: R **Throws:** R **Pos:** 3B-134;DH-15;PH-2   muh-CHAH-doe   **Ht:** 6'3" **Wt:** 218 **Born:** 7/6/1992 **Age:** 30

Year	Team	Lg	G	AB	H	2B	3B	HR	(Hm	Rd)	TB	R	RBI	RC	TBB	IBB	SO	HBP	SH	SF	SB	CS	GDP	Avg	OBP	Slg	OPS
2012	Bal	AL	51	191	50	8	3	7	(7	0)	85	24	26	29	9	0	38	0	1	0	2	0	6	.262	.294	.445	.739
2013	Bal	AL	156	667	189	51	3	14	(5	9)	288	88	71	87	29	0	113	2	9	3	6	7	15	.283	.314	.432	.746
2014	Bal	AL	82	327	91	14	0	12	(9	3)	141	38	32	44	20	2	68	3	2	2	2	0	13	.278	.324	.431	.755
2015	Bal	AL	162	633	181	30	1	35	(21	14)	318	102	86	107	70	2	111	4	2	4	20	8	14	.286	.359	.502	.861
2016	Bal	AL	157	640	188	40	1	37	(18	19)	341	105	96	103	48	9	120	3	0	5	0	3	14	.294	.343	.533	.876
2017	Bal	AL	156	630	163	33	1	33	(22	11)	297	81	95	94	50	3	115	1	0	9	9	4	17	.259	.310	.471	.782
2018	2 Tms		162	632	188	35	3	37	(24	13)	340	84	107	115	70	18	104	2	0	5	14	2	14	.297	.367	.538	.905
2019	SD	NL	156	587	150	21	2	32	(15	17)	271	81	85	86	65	3	128	6	0	3	5	3	24	.256	.334	.462	.796
2020	SD	NL	60	224	68	12	1	16	(13	3)	130	44	47	46	26	4	37	0	0	4	6	3	9	.304	.370	.580	.950
2021	SD	NL	153	564	157	31	2	28	(17	11)	276	92	106	102	63	10	102	2	0	11	12	3	10	.278	.347	.489	.836
2022	SD	NL	150	578	172	37	1	32	(17	15)	307	100	102	118	63	10	133	1	0	2	9	1	12	.298	.366	.531	.898
18	Bal	AL	96	365	115	21	1	24	(17	7)	210	48	65	74	45	12	51	0	0	3	8	1	14	.315	.387	.575	.963
18	LAD	NL	66	267	73	14	2	13	(7	6)	130	36	42	41	25	6	53	2	0	2	6	1	12	.273	.338	.487	.825
	Postseason		29	115	23	3	0	6	(2	4)	44	14	16	9	7	2	28	1	2	1	1	0	6	.200	.250	.383	.633
	11 ML YEARS		1445	5673	1597	312	18	283	(168	115)	2794	839	853	938	513	61	1069	24	14	49	85	34	163	.282	.341	.493	.833

Vimael Machin

Bats: L **Throws:** R **Pos:** 3B-68;PH-10;2B-1;SS-1;DH-1   vee-MAL mah-CHEEN   **Ht:** 5'11" **Wt:** 185 **Born:** 9/25/1993 **Age:** 29

Year	Team	Lg	G	AB	H	2B	3B	HR	(Hm	Rd)	TB	R	RBI	RC	TBB	IBB	SO	HBP	SH	SF	SB	CS	GDP	Avg	OBP	Slg	OPS
2022	LsVgs	AAA	64	256	83	16	3	4	(-	-)	117	41	49	42	33	0	30	1	0	2	0	0	10	.324	.401	.457	.858
2020	Oak	AL	24	63	13	2	0	0	(0	0)	15	11	0	8	10	0	8	0	0	0	0	0	0	.206	.296	.238	.534
2021	Oak	AL	15	32	4	0	0	0	(0	0)	4	1	1	0	3	0	10	0	2	0	0	0	2	.125	.200	.125	.325
2022	Oak	AL	73	223	49	12	0	1	(1	0)	64	26	13	21	25	0	47	2	0	3	1	1	6	.220	.300	.287	.587
	3 ML YEARS		112	318	66	14	0	1	(1	0)	83	38	14	21	36	0	67	2	2	3	1	1	12	.208	.290	.261	.551

David MacKinnon

Bats: R Throws: R Pos: 1B-12;PH-8;3B-5   Ht: 6'2" Wt: 200 Born: 12/15/1994 Age: 28

								BATTING												RUNNING			AVERAGES			
Year	Team	Lg	G	AB	H	2B	3B	HR	(Hm | Rd)	TB	R	RBI	RC	TBB	IBB	SO	HBP	SH	SF	SB	CS	GDP	Avg	OBP	Slg	OPS
2022	Salt Lk	AAA	63	225	73	19	4	14	(- | -)	142	47	45	60	42	3	51	2	0	4	2	2	5	.324	.429	.631	1.060
2022	LsVgs	AAA	16	64	19	5	0	1	(- | -)	27	6	9	9	7	0	12	1	0	1	0	0	1	.297	.370	.422	.792
2022	2 Tms	AL	22	50	7	0	0	0	(0 | 0)	7	2	6	2	6	0	17	0	0	1	0	0	2	.140	.228	.140	.368
22	LAA	AL	16	37	7	0	0	0	(0 | 0)	7	0	6	2	5	0	12	0	0	1	0	0	2	.189	.279	.189	.468
22	Oak	AL	6	13	0	0	0	0	(0 | 0)	0	2	0	0	1	0	5	0	0	0	0	0	0	.000	.071	.000	.071

Nick Madrigal

Bats: R Throws: R Pos: 2B-59;PH-5   Ht: 5'8" Wt: 175 Born: 3/5/1997 Age: 26

								BATTING												RUNNING			AVERAGES			
Year	Team	Lg	G	AB	H	2B	3B	HR	(Hm	Rd)	TB	R	RBI	RC	TBB	IBB	SO	HBP	SH	SF	SB	CS	GDP	Avg	OBP	Slg	OPS
2022	Iowa	AAA	12	40	13	1	0	0	(-	-)	14	8	5	4	3	0	5	1	0	0	0	0	2	.325	.386	.350	.736
2020	CWS	AL	29	103	35	3	0	0	(0	0)	38	8	11	16	4	0	7	2	0	0	2	1	5	.340	.376	.369	.745
2021	CWS	AL	54	200	61	10	4	2	(1	1)	85	30	21	30	11	0	17	3	0	1	1	2	3	.305	.349	.425	.774
2022	ChC	NL	59	209	52	7	0	0	(0	0)	59	19	7	8	14	0	27	3	2	0	3	1	6	.249	.305	.282	.588
	Postseason		3	12	3	0	0	0	(0	0)	3	1	0	0	0	0	0	0	0	0	0	0	0	.250	.250	.250	.500
	3 ML YEARS		142	512	148	20	4	2	(1	1)	182	57	39	54	29	0	51	8	2	1	6	4	14	.289	.336	.355	.692

Bligh Madris

Bats: L Throws: R Pos: RF-19;1B-9;LF-5;PH-4;DH-3;CF-2;PR-1   Ht: 6'0" Wt: 208 Born: 2/29/1996 Age: 27

								BATTING												RUNNING			AVERAGES			
Year	Team	Lg	G	AB	H	2B	3B	HR	(Hm	Rd)	TB	R	RBI	RC	TBB	IBB	SO	HBP	SH	SF	SB	CS	GDP	Avg	OBP	Slg	OPS
2022	Indy	AAA	71	255	75	19	4	7	(-	-)	123	34	34	43	29	0	63	1	1	2	4	2	7	.294	.366	.482	.848
2022	Drham	AAA	10	41	13	3	0	4	(-	-)	28	11	15	11	4	0	11	0	0	1	0	0	0	.317	.370	.683	1.052
2022	Pit	NL	39	113	20	7	0	1	(1	0)	30	10	7	6	10	0	31	0	0	0	2	1	0	.177	.244	.265	.509

Kenta Maeda

Pitches: R Bats: R Pos: P   mah-AY-duh   Ht: 6'1" Wt: 185 Born: 4/11/1988 Age: 35

			HOW MUCH PITCHED				WHAT HE GAVE UP										THE RESULTS						
Year	Team	Lg	G	GS	GF	IP	BFP	H	R	ER	HR	SH	SF	HB	TBB	IBB	SO	WP	W	L	Pct	Sv-Op	Hld	Vel	OPS	ERC	ERA
2016	LAD	NL	32	32	0	175.2	716	150	72	68	20	0	3	8	50	6	179	6	16	11	.593	0-0	0	-	.649	3.09	3.48
2017	LAD	NL	29	25	1	134.1	557	121	68	63	22	6	4	5	34	1	140	4	13	6	.684	1-1	0	-	.714	3.48	4.22
2018	LAD	NL	39	20	4	125.1	532	115	58	53	13	2	3	5	43	4	153	2	8	10	.444	2-2	5	-	.706	3.51	3.81
2019	LAD	NL	37	26	3	153.2	624	114	70	69	22	2	3	4	51	1	169	3	10	8	.556	3-3	4	-	.642	2.79	4.04
2020	Min	AL	11	11	0	66.2	248	40	20	20	9	0	0	0	10	0	80	0	6	1	.857	0-0	0	-	.508	1.48	2.70
2021	Min	AL	21	21	0	106.1	453	106	60	55	16	1	1	7	32	1	113	3	6	5	.545	0-0	0	-	.755	4.28	4.66
	Postseason		25	4	2	37.2	159	29	12	12	2	0	0	2	15	2	44	2	2	1	.667	0-0	4	-	.620	2.60	2.87
	6 ML YEARS		169	135	8	762.0	3130	646	348	328	102	11	14	29	220	13	834	18	59	41	.590	6-6	9	-	.673	3.16	3.87

Tyler Mahle

Pitches: R Bats: R Pos: SP-23   Ht: 6'3" Wt: 210 Born: 9/29/1994 Age: 28

			HOW MUCH PITCHED				WHAT HE GAVE UP										THE RESULTS						
Year	Team	Lg	G	GS	GF	IP	BFP	H	R	ER	HR	SH	SF	HB	TBB	IBB	SO	WP	W	L	Pct	Sv-Op	Hld	Vel	OPS	ERC	ERA
2017	Cin	NL	4	4	0	20.0	92	19	6	6	0	2	0	4	11	1	14	1	1	2	.333	0-0	0	93	.684	4.27	2.70
2018	Cin	NL	23	23	0	112.0	507	125	68	62	22	5	3	5	53	7	110	1	7	9	.438	0-0	0	92	.848	5.77	4.98
2019	Cin	NL	25	25	0	129.2	556	136	82	74	25	2	2	6	34	0	129	2	3	12	.200	0-0	0	93	.775	4.61	5.14
2020	Cin	NL	10	9	0	47.2	201	34	21	19	6	0	4	4	21	0	60	2	2	2	.500	0-0	0	94	.666	3.13	3.59
2021	Cin	NL	33	33	0	180.0	759	158	78	75	24	9	2	10	64	0	210	4	13	6	.684	0-0	0	94	.705	3.67	3.75
2022	2 Tms		23	23	0	120.2	503	104	61	59	16	1	5	2	43	0	126	3	6	8	.429	0-0	0	93	.693	3.43	4.40
22	Cin	NL	19	19	0	104.1	440	91	53	51	12	1	5	2	39	0	114	3	5	7	.417	0-0	0	93	.690	3.42	4.40
22	Min	AL	4	4	0	16.1	63	13	8	8	4	0	0	0	4	0	12	0	1	1	.500	0-0	0	92	.711	3.39	4.41
	6 ML YEARS		118	117	0	610.0	2618	576	316	295	93	19	16	29	226	8	649	13	32	39	.451	0-0	0	93	.742	4.16	4.35

Luke Maile

Bats: R Throws: R Pos: C-76   MAY-lee   Ht: 6'3" Wt: 225 Born: 2/6/1991 Age: 32

								BATTING												RUNNING			AVERAGES			
Year	Team	Lg	G	AB	H	2B	3B	HR	(Hm	Rd)	TB	R	RBI	RC	TBB	IBB	SO	HBP	SH	SF	SB	CS	GDP	Avg	OBP	Slg	OPS
2015	TB	AL	15	35	6	3	0	0	(0	0)	9	2	2	0	0	0	8	0	0	0	0	0	3	.171	.171	.257	.429
2016	TB	AL	42	119	27	7	0	3	(2	1)	43	10	15	11	4	1	36	0	3	0	0	0	2	.227	.252	.361	.613
2017	Tor	AL	46	130	19	5	0	2	(1	1)	30	10	7	2	3	0	35	2	0	1	0	0	2	.146	.176	.231	.407
2018	Tor	AL	68	202	50	13	1	3	(2	1)	74	22	27	28	25	0	67	2	0	2	2	0	4	.248	.333	.366	.700
2019	Tor	AL	45	119	18	2	1	2	(2	0)	28	9	9	4	8	0	33	0	2	0	1	0	1	.151	.205	.235	.440
2021	Mil	NL	15	30	9	4	0	0	(0	0)	13	6	3	4	3	0	7	1	0	0	0	0	1	.300	.382	.433	.816
2022	Cle	AL	76	181	40	10	0	3	(3	0)	59	19	17	12	19	0	54	3	0	3	0	0	6	.221	.301	.326	.627
	Postseason		2	2	0	0	0	0	(0	0)	0	0	0	0	0	0	1	0	0	0	0	0	1	.000	.000	.000	.000
	7 ML YEARS		307	816	169	44	2	13	(10	3)	256	78	80	61	62	1	240	8	5	6	4	0	19	.207	.268	.314	.582

Martin Maldonado

Bats: R Throws: R Pos: C-113   mar-TEEN   Ht: 6'0" Wt: 230 Born: 8/16/1986 Age: 36

Year	Team	Lg	G	AB	H	2B	3B	HR	(Hm	Rd)	TB	R	RBI	RC	TBB	IBB	SO	HBP	SH	SF	SB	CS	GDP	Avg	OBP	Slg	OPS
2011	Mil	NL	3	1	0	0	0	0	(0	0)	0	0	0	0	0	0	1	0	0	0	0	0	0	.000	.000	.000	.000
2012	Mil	NL	78	233	62	9	0	8	(6	2)	95	22	30	28	17	0	56	2	4	0	1	1	5	.266	.321	.408	.729
2013	Mil	NL	67	183	31	7	1	4	(1	3)	52	13	22	14	13	1	53	3	3	0	0	0	2	.169	.236	.284	.520
2014	Mil	NL	52	111	26	5	0	4	(2	2)	43	14	16	14	11	1	32	3	1	0	0	0	4	.234	.320	.387	.707
2015	Mil	NL	79	229	48	7	0	4	(4	0)	67	19	22	20	23	3	65	1	1	2	0	1	6	.210	.282	.293	.575
2016	Mil	NL	76	208	42	7	0	8	(6	2)	73	21	21	23	35	9	56	6	3	1	0	0	6	.202	.332	.351	.683
2017	LAA	AL	138	429	95	19	1	14	(5	9)	158	43	38	37	15	1	119	18	8	1	0	2	12	.221	.276	.368	.645
2018	2 Tms	AL	119	373	84	18	1	9	(2	7)	131	39	44	38	16	0	98	11	2	2	0	1	3	.225	.276	.351	.627
2019	3 Tms		105	333	71	19	0	12	(8	4)	126	46	27	29	32	1	86	6	2	1	0	0	11	.213	.293	.378	.671
2020	Hou	AL	47	135	29	4	0	6	(4	2)	51	19	24	27	27	0	51	1	2	0	1	0	4	.215	.350	.378	.727
2021	Hou	AL	125	373	64	10	1	12	(5	7)	112	40	36	28	47	1	127	5	0	1	0	0	9	.172	.272	.300	.573
2022	Hou	AL	113	344	64	12	0	15	(7	8)	121	40	45	32	22	0	116	7	4	2	0	0	6	.186	.248	.352	.600
18	LAA	AL	78	265	59	14	0	5	(2	3)	88	24	32	30	13	0	73	10	1	1	0	1	3	.223	.284	.332	.616
18	Hou	AL	41	108	25	4	1	4	(0	4)	43	15	12	8	3	0	25	1	1	1	0	0	0	.231	.257	.398	.655
19	KC	AL	74	238	54	15	0	6	(2	4)	87	26	17	21	17	0	55	5	2	1	0	0	9	.227	.291	.366	.657
19	ChC	NL	4	11	0	0	0	0	(0	0)	0	0	0	0	2	1	5	0	0	0	0	0	0	.000	.154	.000	.154
19	Hou	AL	27	84	17	4	0	6	(6	0)	39	20	10	8	13	0	26	1	0	0	0	0	2	.202	.316	.464	.781
Postseason			43	120	20	4	0	3	(2	1)	33	13	9	7	7	0	47	4	3	1	0	0	3	.167	.235	.275	.510
12 ML YEARS			1002	2952	616	117	4	96	(50	46)	1029	316	325	290	258	17	860	63	30	10	3	5	71	.209	.285	.349	.634

Sean Manaea

Pitches: L Bats: R Pos: SP-28; RP-2   muh-NIE-uh   Ht: 6'5" Wt: 245 Born: 2/1/1992 Age: 31

Year	Team	Lg	G	GS	GF	IP	BFP	H	R	ER	HR	SH	SF	HB	TBB	IBB	SO	WP	W	L	Pct	Sv-Op	Hld	Vel	OPS	ERC	ERA
2016	Oak	AL	25	24	0	144.2	594	135	65	62	20	4	4	4	37	1	124	3	7	9	.438	0-0	0	92	.713	3.53	3.86
2017	Oak	AL	29	29	0	158.2	692	167	88	77	18	1	2	10	55	1	140	8	12	10	.545	0-0	0	92	.763	4.51	4.37
2018	Oak	AL	27	27	0	160.2	654	141	67	64	21	4	2	8	32	1	108	9	12	9	.571	0-0	0	90	.663	3.02	3.59
2019	Oak	AL	5	5	0	29.2	109	16	4	4	3	0	0	2	7	0	30	1	4	0	1.000	0-0	0	90	.509	1.58	1.21
2020	Oak	AL	11	11	0	54.0	222	57	32	27	7	0	2	1	8	0	45	1	4	3	.571	0-0	0	90	.724	3.69	4.50
2021	Oak	AL	32	32	0	179.1	754	179	79	78	25	1	1	9	41	0	194	5	11	10	.524	0-0	0	92	.719	3.85	3.91
2022	SD	NL	30	28	1	158.0	671	155	95	87	29	2	5	3	50	1	156	0	8	9	.471	0-0	0	91	.766	4.26	4.96
Postseason			2	2	0	6.1	28	9	8	8	5	0	0	1	0	7	0	0	2	.000	0-0	0	91	1.283	11.03	11.37
7 ML YEARS			159	156	1	885.0	3696	850	430	399	123	12	16	37	230	4	797	27	58	50	.537	0-0	0	91	.719	3.73	4.06

Trey Mancini

Bats: R Throws: R Pos: DH-71;1B-39;LF-20;RF-11;PH-6   Ht: 6'3" Wt: 230 Born: 3/18/1992 Age: 31

Year	Team	Lg	G	AB	H	2B	3B	HR	(Hm	Rd)	TB	R	RBI	RC	TBB	IBB	SO	HBP	SH	SF	SB	CS	GDP	Avg	OBP	Slg	OPS
2016	Bal	AL	5	14	5	1	0	3	(3	0)	15	3	5	5	0	0	4	1	0	0	0	0	0	.357	.400	1.071	1.471
2017	Bal	AL	147	543	159	26	4	24	(11	13)	265	65	78	90	33	1	139	6	0	4	1	0	12	.293	.338	.488	.826
2018	Bal	AL	156	582	141	23	3	24	(13	11)	242	69	58	55	44	1	153	5	0	5	0	1	17	.242	.299	.416	.715
2019	Bal	AL	154	602	175	38	2	35	(18	17)	322	106	97	101	63	3	143	9	0	5	1	0	22	.291	.364	.535	.899
2021	Bal	AL	147	556	142	33	1	21	(14	7)	240	77	71	73	51	4	143	8	0	1	0	0	19	.255	.326	.432	.758
2022	2 Tms	AL	143	519	124	23	1	18	(10	8)	203	56	63	67	53	2	135	10	0	5	0	0	12	.239	.319	.391	.710
22	Bal	AL	92	354	95	16	1	10	(5	5)	143	39	41	50	35	2	86	9	0	3	0	0	4	.268	.347	.404	.751
22	Hou	AL	51	165	29	7	0	8	(5	3)	60	17	22	17	18	0	49	1	0	2	0	0	8	.176	.258	.364	.622
6 ML YEARS			752	2816	746	144	11	125	(69	56)	1287	376	372	391	244	11	717	39	0	20	2	1	82	.265	.330	.457	.787

Matt Manning

Pitches: R Bats: R Pos: SP-12   Ht: 6'6" Wt: 195 Born: 1/28/1998 Age: 25

Year	Team	Lg	G	GS	GF	IP	BFP	H	R	ER	HR	SH	SF	HB	TBB	IBB	SO	WP	W	L	Pct	Sv-Op	Hld	Vel	OPS	ERC	ERA
2022	Toledo	AAA	6	6	0	20.1	87	19	6	6	0	0	2	1	10	0	23	1	1	1	.500	0- -	-	-	.642	3.62	2.66
2021	Det	AL	18	18	0	85.1	385	96	59	55	10	0	4	3	33	0	57	1	4	7	.364	0-0	0	94	.789	4.93	5.80
2022	Det	AL	12	12	0	63.0	263	55	27	24	6	0	5	1	19	0	48	2	2	3	.400	0-0	0	93	.621	3.00	3.43
2 ML YEARS			30	30	0	148.1	648	151	86	79	16	0	9	4	52	0	105	3	6	10	.375	0-0	0	93	.720	4.07	4.79

Alek Manoah

Pitches: R Bats: R Pos: SP-31   Ht: 6'6" Wt: 285 Born: 1/9/1998 Age: 25

Year	Team	Lg	G	GS	GF	IP	BFP	H	R	ER	HR	SH	SF	HB	TBB	IBB	SO	WP	W	L	Pct	Sv-Op	Hld	Vel	OPS	ERC	ERA
2021	Tor	AL	20	20	0	111.2	459	77	44	40	12	0	2	16	40	0	127	0	9	2	.818	0-0	0	93	.604	2.87	3.22
2022	Tor	AL	31	31	0	196.2	786	144	55	49	16	1	5	15	51	0	180	5	16	7	.696	0-0	0	94	.582	2.34	2.24
2 ML YEARS			51	51	0	308.1	1245	221	99	89	28	1	7	31	91	0	307	5	25	9	.735	0-0	0	94	.590	2.52	2.60

Joe Mantiply

Pitches: L **Bats:** R **Pos:** RP-69   **Ht:** 6'4" **Wt:** 219 **Born:** 3/1/1991 **Age:** 32

		HOW MUCH PITCHED					WHAT HE GAVE UP									THE RESULTS							
Year	Team	Lg	G	GS	GF	IP	BFP	H	R	ER	HR	SH	SF	HB	TBB	IBB	SO	WP	W	L	Pct	Sv-Op	Hld	Vel	OPS	ERC	ERA
2016	Det	AL	5	0	3	2.2	16	7	5	5	1	1	0	0	2	1	2	0	0	0	-	0-0	0	88	1.446	19.98	16.88
2019	NYY	AL	1	0	0	3.0	14	3	3	3	1	0	0	0	2	0	2	0	1	0	1.000	0-0	0	89	1.024	6.85	9.00
2020	Ari	NL	4	0	1	2.1	15	3	4	4	0	0	0	0	4	0	2	0	0	0	-	0-0	0	91	.830	9.50	15.43
2021	Ari	NL	57	0	7	39.2	177	45	24	15	1	1	4	1	17	3	38	2	0	3	.000	0-2	11	91	.806	4.37	3.40
2022	Ari	NL	69	0	9	60.0	243	59	22	19	6	1	2	3	6	0	61	3	2	5	.286	2-8	22	91	.640	3.03	2.85
	5 ML YEARS		136	0	20	107.2	465	117	58	46	9	3	6	4	31	4	105	5	3	8	.273	2-10	33	91	.745	4.09	3.85

Tucupita Marcano

Bats: L **Throws:** R **Pos:** LF-30;2B-23;PH-4;SS-1;RF-1   **Ht:** 6'0" **Wt:** 180 **Born:** 9/16/1999 **Age:** 23

			BATTING																		RUNNING			AVERAGES			
Year	Team	Lg	G	AB	H	2B	3B	HR	(Hm	Rd)	TB	R	RBI	RC	TBB	IBB	SO	HBP	SH	SF	SB	CS	GDP	Avg	OBP	Slg	OPS
2022	Altna	AA	31	99	30	7	2	2	(-	-)	47	22	13	20	20	1	25	0	1	2	4	2	0	.303	.413	.475	.888
2022	Indy	AAA	25	101	29	5	0	3	(-	-)	43	16	9	14	13	0	16	0	0	1	1	5	2	.287	.365	.426	.791
2021	SD	NL	25	44	8	1	0	0	(0	0)	9	7	3	1	6	0	9	0	0	0	1	1	2	.182	.280	.205	.485
2022	Pit	NL	49	160	33	6	2	2	(0	2)	49	18	13	12	10	0	44	1	5	1	2	1	1	.206	.256	.306	.562
	2 ML YEARS		74	204	41	7	2	2	(0	2)	58	25	16	13	16	0	53	1	5	1	2	2	3	.201	.261	.284	.546

Manuel Margot

Bats: R **Throws:** R **Pos:** RF-53;CF-18;DH-16;LF-8;PH-3   mar-GOH   **Ht:** 5'11" **Wt:** 180 **Born:** 9/28/1994 **Age:** 28

			BATTING																		RUNNING			AVERAGES			
Year	Team	Lg	G	AB	H	2B	3B	HR	(Hm	Rd)	TB	R	RBI	RC	TBB	IBB	SO	HBP	SH	SF	SB	CS	GDP	Avg	OBP	Slg	OPS
2016	SD	NL	10	37	9	4	1	0	(0	0)	15	4	3	5	0	0	7	0	0	0	2	0	0	.243	.243	.405	.649
2017	SD	NL	126	487	128	18	7	13	(7	6)	199	53	39	55	35	0	106	2	1	4	17	7	6	.263	.313	.409	.721
2018	SD	NL	141	477	117	26	8	8	(5	3)	183	50	51	56	32	4	88	2	1	7	11	10	9	.245	.292	.384	.675
2019	SD	NL	151	398	93	19	3	12	(3	9)	154	59	37	47	38	1	88	2	3	0	20	4	6	.234	.304	.387	.691
2020	TB	AL	47	145	39	9	0	1	(1	0)	51	19	11	17	13	0	25	0	0	1	12	4	0	.269	.327	.352	.679
2021	TB	AL	125	421	107	18	3	10	(4	6)	161	55	57	57	37	2	70	1	1	4	13	8	4	.254	.313	.382	.696
2022	TB	AL	89	336	92	18	2	4	(0	4)	126	36	47	41	24	1	68	0	0	7	7	3	7	.274	.325	.375	.700
	Postseason		22	65	17	1	0	5	(5	0)	33	11	11	11	6	0	22	1	1	0	2	2	0	.262	.333	.508	.841
	7 ML YEARS		689	2301	585	112	24	48	(20	28)	889	276	245	278	179	8	452	9	6	17	82	36	32	.254	.308	.386	.695

Ron Marinaccio

Pitches: R **Bats:** R **Pos:** RP-40   **Ht:** 6'2" **Wt:** 205 **Born:** 7/1/1995 **Age:** 27

			HOW MUCH PITCHED					WHAT HE GAVE UP											THE RESULTS							
Year	Team	Lg	G	GS	GF	IP	BFP	H	R	ER	HR	SH	SF	HB	TBB	IBB	SO	WP	W	L	Pct	Sv-Op	Hld	Vel	OPS	ERC	ERA
2022	S-WB	AAA	8	0	2	9.2	44	10	3	3	3	0	0	0	4	0	21	0	1	0	1.000	0- -	-	-	.868	5.58	2.79
2022	NYY	AL	40	0	8	44.0	181	22	12	10	2	0	2	6	24	0	56	5	1	0	1.000	0-0	6	95	.525	2.16	2.05

Jake Marisnick

Bats: R **Throws:** R **Pos:** CF-14;LF-12;RF-4;PH-3;PR-1   muh-RIZ-nick   **Ht:** 6'4" **Wt:** 220 **Born:** 3/30/1991 **Age:** 32

			BATTING																		RUNNING			AVERAGES			
Year	Team	Lg	G	AB	H	2B	3B	HR	(Hm	Rd)	TB	R	RBI	RC	TBB	IBB	SO	HBP	SH	SF	SB	CS	GDP	Avg	OBP	Slg	OPS
2022	Gwnntt	AAA	17	68	16	1	1	1	(-	-)	22	8	3	6	3	0	18	3	0	0	7	1	0	.235	.297	.324	.621
2013	Mia	NL	40	109	20	2	1	1	(1	0)	27	6	5	7	6	0	27	1	1	1	3	1	1	.183	.231	.248	.478
2014	2 Tms		65	221	55	8	0	3	(3	0)	72	21	19	19	8	3	67	3	2	3	11	3	2	.249	.281	.326	.607
2015	Hou	AL	133	339	80	15	4	9	(4	5)	130	46	36	40	18	0	105	5	6	4	24	9	2	.236	.281	.383	.665
2016	Hou	AL	118	287	60	18	1	5	(1	4)	95	40	21	23	16	0	83	3	4	1	10	5	4	.209	.257	.331	.588
2017	Hou	AL	106	230	56	10	0	16	(10	6)	114	50	35	31	20	1	90	6	2	1	9	4	5	.243	.319	.496	.815
2018	Hou	AL	103	213	45	8	1	10	(2	8)	85	34	28	24	15	1	84	4	1	1	6	2	6	.211	.275	.399	.674
2019	Hou	AL	120	292	68	16	3	10	(5	5)	120	46	34	31	17	0	95	6	3	0	10	3	6	.233	.289	.411	.700
2020	NYM	NL	16	33	11	3	0	2	(1	1)	20	4	5	6	1	0	10	0	0	0	0	0	0	.333	.353	.606	.959
2021	2 Tms	NL	99	176	38	7	3	5	(4	1)	66	21	24	20	11	0	65	7	2	2	4	1	4	.216	.286	.375	.661
2022	Pit	NL	31	77	18	6	0	2	(0	2)	30	9	6	8	4	1	24	0	1	0	2	1	2	.234	.272	.390	.661
	14 Mia	NL	14	48	8	0	0	0	(0	0)	8	3	0	1	3	1	19	0	0	0	5	0	0	.167	.216	.167	.382
	14 Hou	AL	51	173	47	8	0	3	(3	0)	64	18	19	18	5	2	48	3	2	3	6	3	2	.272	.299	.370	.669
	21 ChC	NL	65	128	29	6	3	5	(4	1)	56	17	22	18	9	0	43	4	1	2	3	1	2	.227	.294	.438	.731
	21 SD	NL	34	48	9	1	0	0	(0	0)	10	4	2	2	2	0	22	3	1	0	1	0	2	.188	.264	.208	.472
	Postseason		23	21	7	1	0	0	(0	0)	8	1	0	3	1	0	8	0	0	0	2	0	0	.333	.364	.381	.745
	10 ML YEARS		831	1977	451	93	13	63	(31	32)	759	277	213	209	116	6	650	35	22	13	79	29	32	.228	.281	.384	.665

Parker Markel

Pitches: R **Bats:** R **Pos:** RP-3   **Ht:** 6'5" **Wt:** 240 **Born:** 9/15/1990 **Age:** 32

			HOW MUCH PITCHED					WHAT HE GAVE UP											THE RESULTS							
Year	Team	Lg	G	GS	GF	IP	BFP	H	R	ER	HR	SH	SF	HB	TBB	IBB	SO	WP	W	L	Pct	Sv-Op	Hld	Vel	OPS	ERC	ERA
2022	LsVgs	AAA	17	0	11	19.0	79	13	5	4	2	0	0	1	10	0	28	1	3	0	1.000	1- -	-	-	.598	3.12	1.89
2022	Charltt	AAA	24	0	4	21.0	111	28	26	24	5	1	0	2	18	0	27	7	1	3	.250	1- -	-	-	.970	9.58	10.29
2019	2 Tms		20	0	8	22.0	110	26	21	19	6	0	0	3	17	1	24	2	0	1	.000	0-0	0	96	.985	8.74	7.77
2022	Oak	AL	3	0	1	3.0	13	1	0	0	0	0	0	0	5	0	3	0	0	0	-	0-0	0	95	.712	4.86	0.00
	19 Sea	AL	5	0	0	4.2	28	10	9	8	3	0	0	1	4	0	3	1	0	0	-	0-0	0	96	1.449	21.44	15.43
	19 Pit	NL	15	0	8	17.1	82	16	12	11	3	0	0	2	13	1	21	1	0	1	.000	0-0	0	96	.826	5.93	5.71
	2 ML YEARS		23	0	9	25.0	123	27	21	19	6	0	0	3	22	1	27	2	0	1	.000	0-0	0	96	.964	8.31	6.84

German Marquez

Pitches: R Bats: R Pos: SP-31   hair-MAHN   Ht: 6'1" Wt: 230 Born: 2/22/1995 Age: 28

		HOW MUCH PITCHED					WHAT HE GAVE UP											THE RESULTS						
Year	Team	Lg	G	GS	GF	IP	BFP	H	R	ER	HR	SH	SF	HB	TBB	IBB	SO	WP	W	L	Pct	Sv-Op	Hld	Vel	OPS	ERC	ERA
2016	Col	NL	6	3	0	20.2	98	28	12	12	2	2	1	3	6	0	15	0	1	1	.500	0-0	0	93	.932	6.21	5.23
2017	Col	NL	29	29	0	162.0	701	174	82	79	25	5	4	8	49	3	147	6	11	7	.611	0-0	0	95	.806	4.67	4.39
2018	Col	NL	33	33	0	196.0	817	179	90	82	24	2	6	8	57	5	230	8	14	11	.560	0-0	0	95	.698	3.45	3.77
2019	Col	NL	28	28	0	174.0	721	174	96	92	29	6	4	5	35	0	175	14	12	5	.706	0-0	0	95	.740	3.86	4.76
2020	Col	NL	13	13	0	81.2	344	78	41	34	6	0	3	0	25	0	73	4	4	6	.400	0-0	0	96	.673	3.26	3.75
2021	Col	NL	32	32	0	180.0	756	165	92	88	21	5	0	4	64	5	176	15	12	11	.522	0-0	0	95	.699	3.61	4.40
2022	Col	NL	31	31	0	181.2	779	185	109	100	30	1	7	4	63	0	150	8	9	13	.409	0-0	0	95	.791	4.53	4.95
	Postseason		1	1	0	5.0	22	7	2	2	1	0	0	0	1	0	5	0	0	1	.000	0-0	0	96	.840	6.52	3.60
	7 ML YEARS		172	169	0	996.0	4216	983	522	487	137	21	25	32	299	13	966	55	63	54	.538	0-0	0	95	.744	3.98	4.40

Deven Marrero

Bats: R Throws: R Pos: SS-3;3B-1;PR-1   Ht: 6'0" Wt: 190 Born: 8/25/1990 Age: 32

							BATTING														RUNNING			AVERAGES			
Year	Team	Lg	G	AB	H	2B	3B	HR	(Hm	Rd)	TB	R	RBI	RC	TBB	IBB	SO	HBP	SH	SF	SB	CS	GDP	Avg	OBP	Slg	OPS
2022	Syrcse	AAA	44	144	33	1	2	3	(-	-)	47	23	19	16	20	0	34	0	2	0	5	1	1	.229	.323	.326	.650
2015	Bos	AL	25	53	12	0	0	1	(0	1)	15	8	3	4	3	0	19	0	0	0	2	1	0	.226	.268	.283	.551
2016	Bos	AL	13	12	1	0	0	0	(0	0)	1	0	0	0	2	0	5	0	0	0	0	0	0	.083	.214	.083	.298
2017	Bos	AL	71	171	36	9	0	4	(1	3)	57	32	27	18	12	0	61	0	3	2	5	0	8	.211	.259	.333	.593
2018	Ari	NL	49	78	13	1	1	0	(0	0)	16	11	7	4	6	0	23	0	0	1	3	0	5	.167	.224	.205	.429
2019	Mia	NL	5	5	0	0	0	0	(0	0)	0	0	0	0	0	0	3	0	0	0	0	0	0	.000	.000	.000	.000
2021	Mia	NL	10	16	3	0	0	1	(1	0)	6	4	1	1	3	0	6	0	0	0	1	0	2	.188	.316	.375	.691
2022	NYM	NL	5	6	0	0	0	0	(0	0)	0	0	0	0	0	0	3	0	0	0	0	0	0	.000	.000	.000	.000
	Postseason		1	2	0	0	0	0	(0	0)	0	0	0	0	0	0	2	0	0	0	0	0	0	.000	.000	.000	.000
	7 ML YEARS		178	341	65	10	1	6	(2	4)	95	55	38	27	26	0	120	0	3	3	12	1	15	.191	.246	.279	.525

Brandon Marsh

Bats: L Throws: R Pos: LF-77;CF-59;PH-8;PR-3;RF-2   Ht: 6'4" Wt: 215 Born: 12/18/1997 Age: 25

							BATTING														RUNNING			AVERAGES			
Year	Team	Lg	G	AB	H	2B	3B	HR	(Hm	Rd)	TB	R	RBI	RC	TBB	IBB	SO	HBP	SH	SF	SB	CS	GDP	Avg	OBP	Slg	OPS
2021	LAA	AL	70	236	60	12	3	2	(0	2)	84	27	19	26	20	0	91	2	1	1	6	1	3	.254	.317	.356	.673
2022	2 Tms		134	424	104	18	4	11	(8	3)	163	49	52	53	28	1	158	3	3	3	10	4	4	.245	.295	.384	.679
22	LAA	AL	93	292	66	9	2	8	(7	1)	103	34	37	34	22	1	117	3	3	3	8	2	2	.226	.284	.353	.637
22	Phi	NL	41	132	38	9	2	3	(1	2)	60	15	15	19	6	0	41	0	0	0	2	2	2	.288	.319	.455	.773
	2 ML YEARS		204	660	164	30	7	13	(8	5)	247	76	71	79	48	1	249	5	4	4	16	5	7	.248	.303	.374	.677

Jose Marte

Pitches: R Bats: R Pos: RP-11   Ht: 6'3" Wt: 180 Born: 6/14/1996 Age: 27

			HOW MUCH PITCHED					WHAT HE GAVE UP										THE RESULTS							
Year	Team	Lg	G	GS	GF	IP	BFP	H	R	ER	HR	SH	SF	HB	TBB	IBB	SO	WP	W	L	Pct	Sv-Op	Hld	Vel	OPS	ERC	ERA
2022	Salt Lk	AAA	34	0	14	34.2	156	27	23	21	4	0	0	5	23	0	46	7	0	2	.000	3- -	-	-	.704	4.53	5.45
2021	LAA	AL	4	0	2	4.0	18	4	5	4	1	0	0	0	3	0	5	0	1	0	1.000	0-1	0	97	.922	6.96	9.00
2022	LAA	AL	11	0	4	11.0	58	8	9	9	2	0	0	0	18	0	15	1	0	0	-	0-0	0	97	.848	8.21	7.36
	2 ML YEARS		15	0	6	15.0	76	12	14	13	3	0	0	0	21	0	20	1	0	1	.000	0-1	0	97	.871	7.91	7.80

Ketel Marte

Bats: B Throws: R Pos: 2B-94;DH-37;PH-9   kuh-TELL marr-TAY   Ht: 6'1" Wt: 210 Born: 10/12/1993 Age: 29

							BATTING														RUNNING			AVERAGES			
Year	Team	Lg	G	AB	H	2B	3B	HR	(Hm	Rd)	TB	R	RBI	RC	TBB	IBB	SO	HBP	SH	SF	SB	CS	GDP	Avg	OBP	Slg	OPS
2015	Sea	AL	57	219	62	14	3	2	(1	1)	88	25	17	33	24	0	43	0	2	2	8	4	1	.283	.351	.402	.753
2016	Sea	AL	119	437	113	21	2	1	(1	0)	141	55	33	41	18	0	84	2	3	6	11	5	10	.259	.287	.323	.610
2017	Ari	NL	73	223	58	11	2	5	(1	4)	88	30	18	27	29	3	37	1	0	2	3	1	3	.260	.345	.395	.740
2018	Ari	NL	153	520	135	26	12	14	(8	6)	227	68	59	67	54	3	79	3	1	2	6	1	12	.260	.332	.437	.768
2019	Ari	NL	144	569	187	36	9	32	(13	19)	337	97	92	121	53	2	86	4	0	3	10	2	7	.329	.389	.592	.981
2020	Ari	NL	45	181	52	14	1	2	(1	1)	74	19	17	27	7	0	21	0	0	3	1	0	2	.287	.323	.409	.732
2021	Ari	NL	90	340	108	29	1	14	(7	7)	181	52	50	68	31	3	60	2	0	1	2	0	8	.318	.377	.532	.909
2022	Ari	NL	137	492	118	42	2	12	(5	7)	200	68	52	62	55	3	101	6	0	5	5	1	12	.240	.321	.407	.727
	Postseason		4	17	7	0	2	1	(0	1)	14	4	2	4	0	0	5	0	0	0	0	0	0	.412	.412	.824	1.235
	8 ML YEARS		818	2981	833	193	32	82	(37	45)	1336	414	338	446	271	14	511	22	6	23	46	14	55	.279	.342	.448	.790

Noelvi Marte

Bats: R Throws: R Pos: SS   Ht: 6'1" Wt: 181 Born: 10/16/2001 Age: 21

							BATTING														RUNNING			AVERAGES			
Year	Team	Lg	G	AB	H	2B	3B	HR	(Hm	Rd)	TB	R	RBI	RC	TBB	IBB	SO	HBP	SH	SF	SB	CS	GDP	Avg	OBP	Slg	OPS
2021	2 Tms	Low	107	444	121	28	2	17	(-	-)	204	91	71	0	60	1	117	6	0	1	24	7	6	.273	.366	.459	.825
2022	2 Tms	Low	115	448	125	23	0	19	(-	-)	205	74	68	79	59	1	107	9	0	4	23	9	6	.279	.371	.458	.829

Starling Marte

Bats: R Throws: R Pos: RF-116;CF-2;DH-1;PH-1;PR-1 marr-TAY Ht: 6'1" Wt: 195 Born: 10/9/1988 Age: 34

								BATTING												RUNNING			AVERAGES			
Year	Team	Lg	G	AB	H	2B	3B	HR	(Hm | Rd)	TB	R	RBI	RC	TBB	IBB	SO	HBP	SH	SF	SB	CS	GDP	Avg	OBP	Slg	OPS
2012	Pit	NL	47	167	43	3	6	5	(3 | 2)	73	18	17	21	4	0	50	3	2	2	12	5	5	.257	.300	.437	.737
2013	Pit	NL	135	510	143	26	10	12	(5 | 7)	225	83	35	74	25	2	138	24	6	1	41	15	6	.280	.343	.441	.784
2014	Pit	NL	135	495	144	29	6	13	(5 | 8)	224	73	56	70	33	0	131	17	0	0	30	11	5	.291	.356	.453	.808
2015	Pit	NL	153	579	166	30	2	19	(10 | 9)	257	84	81	81	27	3	123	19	3	5	30	10	14	.287	.337	.444	.780
2016	Pit	NL	129	489	152	34	5	9	(2 | 7)	223	71	46	77	23	5	104	16	1	0	47	12	8	.311	.362	.456	.818
2017	Pit	NL	77	309	85	7	2	7	(5 | 2)	117	48	31	46	20	0	63	8	0	2	21	4	5	.275	.333	.379	.712
2018	Pit	NL	145	559	155	32	5	20	(8 | 12)	257	81	72	83	35	2	109	8	1	3	33	14	11	.277	.327	.460	.787
2019	Pit	NL	132	539	159	31	6	23	(9 | 14)	271	97	82	95	25	1	94	16	2	4	25	6	15	.295	.342	.503	.845
2020	2 Tms	NL	61	228	64	14	1	6	(2 | 4)	98	36	27	32	12	1	41	9	0	1	10	2	5	.281	.340	.430	.770
2021	2 Tms		120	467	145	27	3	12	(7 | 5)	214	89	55	89	43	2	99	13	1	2	47	5	6	.310	.383	.458	.841
2022	NYM	NL	118	466	136	24	5	16	(10 | 6)	218	76	63	70	26	0	97	13	0	0	18	9	18	.292	.347	.468	.814
20	Ari	NL	33	122	38	8	1	2	(0 | 2)	54	23	14	21	10	1	19	5	0	1	5	2	3	.311	.384	.443	.827
20	Mia	NL	28	106	26	6	0	4	(2 | 2)	44	13	13	11	2	0	22	4	0	0	5	0	2	.245	.286	.415	.701
21	Mia	NL	64	233	71	11	1	7	(3 | 4)	105	52	25	46	32	2	57	8	1	1	22	3	2	.305	.405	.451	.856
21	Oak	AL	56	234	74	16	2	5	(4 | 1)	109	37	30	43	11	0	42	5	0	1	25	2	4	.316	.359	.466	.824
	Postseason		9	36	6	2	0	1	(0 | 1)	11	3	1	2	1	0	7	2	0	0	1	0	2	.167	.231	.306	.536
	11 ML YEARS		1252	4808	1392	257	51	142	(66 | 76)	2177	756	565	738	277	16	1049	146	16	20	314	93	98	.290	.346	.453	.798

Yunior Marte

Pitches: R Bats: R Pos: RP-39 Ht: 6'2" Wt: 180 Born: 2/2/1995 Age: 28

			HOW MUCH PITCHED					WHAT HE GAVE UP										THE RESULTS						
Year	Team	Lg	G	GS	GF	IP	BFP	H	R	ER	HR	SH	SF	HB	TBB	IBB	SO	WP	W	L	Pct	Sv-Op	Hld	Vel	OPS	ERC	ERA
2022	Scrmto	AAA	25	0	14	25.2	94	9	11	9	4	0	0	0	9	0	35	1	1	1	.500	3- -	-	-	.474	1.25	3.16
2022	SF	NL	39	0	10	48.0	214	47	32	29	5	0	2	6	22	0	44	3	1	1	.500	0-0	2	97	.742	4.72	5.44

Brett Martin

Pitches: L Bats: L Pos: RP-54; SP-1 Ht: 6'4" Wt: 200 Born: 4/28/1995 Age: 28

			HOW MUCH PITCHED					WHAT HE GAVE UP										THE RESULTS						
Year	Team	Lg	G	GS	GF	IP	BFP	H	R	ER	HR	SH	SF	HB	TBB	IBB	SO	WP	W	L	Pct	Sv-Op	Hld	Vel	OPS	ERC	ERA
2019	Tex	AL	51	2	7	62.1	280	72	38	33	7	0	3	2	18	2	62	3	2	3	.400	0-1	4	94	.745	4.54	4.76
2020	Tex	AL	15	0	4	14.2	61	8	5	3	2	0	1	0	9	0	8	1	1	1	.500	0-0	2	94	.612	2.67	1.84
2021	Tex	AL	66	0	24	62.1	264	67	31	22	5	4	0	0	14	4	42	4	4	4	.500	0-2	11	93	.686	3.54	3.18
2022	Tex	AL	55	1	20	50.0	212	50	27	23	4	1	1	0	18	3	40	7	1	7	.125	3-6	7	94	.718	3.71	4.14
	4 ML YEARS		187	3	55	189.1	817	197	101	81	18	5	5	2	59	9	152	15	8	15	.348	3-9	24	94	.709	3.84	3.85

Chris Martin

Pitches: R Bats: R Pos: RP-60 Ht: 6'8" Wt: 225 Born: 6/2/1986 Age: 37

			HOW MUCH PITCHED					WHAT HE GAVE UP										THE RESULTS						
Year	Team	Lg	G	GS	GF	IP	BFP	H	R	ER	HR	SH	SF	HB	TBB	IBB	SO	WP	W	L	Pct	Sv-Op	Hld	Vel	OPS	ERC	ERA
2014	Col	NL	16	0	1	15.2	69	22	12	12	2	0	0	0	4	0	14	1	0	0	-	0-0	3	94	.915	6.30	6.89
2015	NYY	AL	24	0	8	20.2	99	28	13	13	2	0	0	1	6	1	18	3	0	2	.000	1-1	5	94	.777	5.52	5.66
2018	Tex	AL	46	0	8	41.2	177	46	21	21	5	0	1	3	5	2	37	4	1	5	.167	0-3	14	95	.722	3.85	4.54
2019	2 Tms		58	0	20	55.2	216	52	23	21	9	0	2	0	5	0	65	0	1	3	.250	4-6	18	96	.675	2.98	3.40
2020	Atl	NL	19	0	3	18.0	66	8	3	2	1	0	0	1	3	1	20	0	1	1	.500	1-1	6	94	.375	0.89	1.00
2021	Atl	NL	46	0	8	43.1	181	49	20	19	4	2	1	3	6	1	33	0	2	4	.333	1-5	13	95	.726	4.03	3.95
2022	2 Tms		60	0	6	56.0	225	50	20	19	6	0	2	1	5	1	74	7	4	1	.800	2-4	9	95	.622	2.37	3.05
19	Tex	AL	38	0	15	38.0	147	35	13	13	8	0	1	0	4	0	43	0	0	2	.000	4-5	12	96	.716	3.27	3.08
19	Atl	NL	20	0	5	17.2	69	17	10	8	1	0	1	0	1	0	22	0	1	1	.500	0-1	6	95	.589	2.36	4.08
22	ChC	NL	34	0	4	31.1	133	38	16	15	5	0	1	0	4	1	40	6	1	0	1.000	0-1	6	95	.816	4.55	4.31
22	LAD	NL	26	0	2	24.2	92	12	4	4	1	0	1	1	1	0	34	1	3	1	.750	2-3	3	96	.343	0.71	1.46
	Postseason		13	0	1	12.1	49	9	3	3	2	0	1	1	2	0	9	0	0	1	.000	0-0	1	95	.578	2.41	2.19
	7 ML YEARS		269	0	54	251.0	1033	255	112	107	29	2	6	9	34	6	261	15	9	16	.360	9-20	68	95	.687	3.33	3.84

Corbin Martin

Pitches: R Bats: R Pos: RP-5; SP-2 Ht: 6'2" Wt: 225 Born: 12/28/1995 Age: 27

			HOW MUCH PITCHED					WHAT HE GAVE UP										THE RESULTS						
Year	Team	Lg	G	GS	GF	IP	BFP	H	R	ER	HR	SH	SF	HB	TBB	IBB	SO	WP	W	L	Pct	Sv-Op	Hld	Vel	OPS	ERC	ERA
2022	Reno	AAA	17	17	0	77.0	340	86	60	52	15	0	6	1	30	0	79	4	6	7	.462	0- -	-	-	.846	5.48	6.08
2019	Hou	AL	5	5	0	19.1	92	23	14	12	8	0	0	0	12	0	19	1	1	1	.500	0-0	0	95	1.030	8.64	5.59
2021	Ari	NL	5	3	0	16.0	86	23	19	19	5	2	1	1	14	0	13	0	0	3	.000	0-0	0	94	1.114	10.95	10.69
2022	Ari	NL	7	2	1	22.1	101	25	14	12	3	1	2	0	12	0	21	2	0	1	.000	0-0	0	94	.835	5.64	4.84
	3 ML YEARS		17	10	1	57.2	279	71	47	43	16	3	3	1	38	0	53	3	1	5	.167	0-0	0	95	.984	8.07	6.71

Davis Martin

Pitches: R Bats: L Pos: SP-9; RP-5 Ht: 6'2" Wt: 200 Born: 1/4/1997 Age: 26

			HOW MUCH PITCHED					WHAT HE GAVE UP										THE RESULTS						
Year	Team	Lg	G	GS	GF	IP	BFP	H	R	ER	HR	SH	SF	HB	TBB	IBB	SO	WP	W	L	Pct	Sv-Op	Hld	Vel	OPS	ERC	ERA
2022	Brham	AA	5	5	0	24.0	102	23	9	8	4	0	0	0	7	0	33	4	2	1	.667	0- -	-	-	.747	3.78	3.00
2022	Charllt	AAA	13	13	0	53.0	233	60	40	36	11	0	1	3	18	0	66	2	3	5	.375	0- -	-	-	.893	5.68	6.11
2022	CWS	AL	14	9	1	63.1	269	63	36	34	8	2	1	3	19	1	48	3	3	6	.333	0-1	0	94	.748	4.01	4.83

Richie Martin

Bats: R **Throws:** R **Pos:** 2B-10;SS-2;DH-1;PH-1;PR-1 **Ht:** 6'0" **Wt:** 190 **Born:** 12/22/1994 **Age:** 28

Year	Team	Lg	G	AB	H	2B	3B	HR	(Hm	Rd)	TB	R	RBI	RC	TBB	IBB	SO	HBP	SH	SF	SB	CS	GDP	Avg	OBP	Slg	OPS
2022	Norfolk	AAA	80	292	73	20	6	2	(-	-)	111	51	25	36	32	0	66	9	0	1	29	5	9	.250	.341	.380	.721
2019	Bal	AL	120	283	59	8	3	6	(3	3)	91	29	23	17	14	0	83	6	5	1	10	1	6	.208	.260	.322	.581
2021	Bal	AL	37	98	23	2	0	1	(0	1)	28	9	8	5	4	0	28	1	1	1	0	2	1	.235	.269	.286	.555
2022	Bal	AL	13	30	5	0	2	0	(0	0)	9	4	3	3	3	0	10	0	0	0	3	1	0	.167	.242	.300	.542
	3 ML YEARS		170	411	87	10	5	7	(3	4)	128	42	34	25	21	0	121	7	6	2	13	4	7	.212	.261	.311	.572

Adrian Martinez

Pitches: R **Bats:** R **Pos:** SP-12 **Ht:** 6'2" **Wt:** 215 **Born:** 12/10/1996 **Age:** 26

Year	Team	Lg	G	GS	GF	IP	BFP	H	R	ER	HR	SH	SF	HB	TBB	IBB	SO	WP	W	L	Pct	Sv-Op	Hld	Vel	OPS	ERC	ERA
2022	LsVgs	AAA	18	18	0	89.2	389	94	64	57	24	0	3	5	33	0	100	11	5	7	.417	0- -	-	-	.880	5.74	5.72
2022	Oak	AL	12	12	0	57.2	259	69	42	40	13	0	3	3	19	1	53	6	4	6	.400	0-0	0	94	.856	6.05	6.24

J.D. Martinez

Bats: R **Throws:** R **Pos:** DH-139 **Ht:** 6'3" **Wt:** 230 **Born:** 8/21/1987 **Age:** 35

Year	Team	Lg	G	AB	H	2B	3B	HR	(Hm	Rd)	TB	R	RBI	RC	TBB	IBB	SO	HBP	SH	SF	SB	CS	GDP	Avg	OBP	Slg	OPS
2011	Hou	NL	53	208	57	13	0	6	(3	3)	88	29	35	30	13	1	48	2	0	3	0	1	4	.274	.319	.423	.742
2012	Hou	NL	113	395	95	14	3	11	(5	6)	148	34	55	45	40	0	96	1	0	2	0	2	18	.241	.311	.375	.685
2013	Hou	AL	86	296	74	17	0	7	(4	3)	112	24	36	29	10	0	82	0	0	3	2	0	9	.250	.272	.378	.650
2014	Det	AL	123	441	139	30	3	23	(13	10)	244	57	76	75	30	5	126	3	0	6	6	3	8	.315	.358	.553	.912
2015	Det	AL	158	596	168	33	2	38	(20	18)	319	93	102	100	53	7	178	5	0	3	3	2	11	.282	.344	.535	.879
2016	Det	AL	120	460	141	35	2	22	(13	9)	246	69	68	77	49	2	128	1	0	5	1	2	13	.307	.373	.535	.908
2017	2 Tms		119	432	131	26	3	45	(27	18)	298	85	104	92	53	8	128	0	0	4	4	0	23	.303	.376	.690	1.066
2018	Bos	AL	150	569	188	37	2	43	(26	17)	358	111	130	138	69	11	146	4	0	7	6	1	19	.330	.402	.629	1.031
2019	Bos	AL	146	575	175	33	2	36	(18	18)	320	98	105	117	72	9	138	4	0	5	2	0	19	.304	.383	.557	.939
2020	Bos	AL	54	211	45	16	0	7	(4	3)	82	22	27	23	22	3	59	2	0	2	1	0	6	.213	.291	.389	.680
2021	Bos	AL	148	570	163	42	3	28	(14	14)	295	92	99	105	55	6	150	3	0	5	0	0	18	.286	.349	.518	.867
2022	Bos	AL	139	533	146	43	1	16	(9	7)	239	76	62	68	52	1	145	5	0	5	0	0	20	.274	.341	.448	.790
17	Det	AL	57	200	61	13	2	16	(11	5)	126	38	39	39	29	5	54	0	0	3	2	0	10	.305	.388	.630	1.018
17	Ari	NL	62	232	70	13	1	29	(16	13)	172	47	65	53	24	3	74	0	0	1	2	0	13	.302	.366	.741	1.107
	Postseason		30	109	33	5	0	9	(2	7)	65	14	30	28	16	3	31	1	0	2	0	1	1	.303	.391	.596	.987
	12 ML YEARS		1409	5286	1522	339	21	282	(156	126)	2749	790	899	899	518	53	1424	32	0	50	25	11	167	.288	.352	.520	.872

Nick Martinez

Pitches: R **Bats:** L **Pos:** RP-37; SP-10 **Ht:** 6'1" **Wt:** 200 **Born:** 8/5/1990 **Age:** 32

Year	Team	Lg	G	GS	GF	IP	BFP	H	R	ER	HR	SH	SF	HB	TBB	IBB	SO	WP	W	L	Pct	Sv-Op	Hld	Vel	OPS	ERC	ERA
2014	Tex	AL	29	24	3	140.1	610	150	79	71	18	1	6	3	55	1	77	7	5	12	.294	0-0	2	91	.795	4.76	4.55
2015	Tex	AL	24	21	1	125.0	558	135	66	55	16	1	5	13	46	2	77	4	7	7	.500	0-0	0	90	.799	4.99	3.96
2016	Tex	AL	12	5	2	38.2	179	45	24	24	8	0	0	5	19	1	16	0	2	3	.400	0-0	0	92	.908	6.86	5.59
2017	Tex	AL	23	18	2	111.1	478	124	74	70	26	2	1	2	28	0	67	3	3	8	.273	0-0	0	92	.838	5.14	5.66
2022	SD	NL	47	10	15	106.1	448	96	44	41	15	0	1	4	41	0	95	4	4	4	.500	8-9	8	93	.713	3.94	3.47
	5 ML YEARS		135	78	23	521.2	2273	550	287	261	83	4	13	27	189	4	332	18	21	34	.382	8-9	10	91	.798	4.88	4.50

Seth Martinez

Pitches: R **Bats:** R **Pos:** RP-29 **Ht:** 6'2" **Wt:** 200 **Born:** 8/29/1994 **Age:** 28

Year	Team	Lg	G	GS	GF	IP	BFP	H	R	ER	HR	SH	SF	HB	TBB	IBB	SO	WP	W	L	Pct	Sv-Op	Hld	Vel	OPS	ERC	ERA
2022	SgrLnd	AAA	14	0	2	15.0	61	10	7	6	2	0	0	1	6	1	15	0	2	1	.667	0- -	-	-	.594	2.69	3.60
2021	Hou	AL	3	0	3	3.0	16	5	5	5	0	0	0	0	3	0	3	0	0	0	-	0-0	0	90	1.038	10.34	15.00
2022	Hou	AL	29	0	7	38.2	155	26	10	9	3	1	0	1	14	1	38	0	1	1	.500	0-0	2	92	.532	2.16	2.09
	2 ML YEARS		32	0	10	41.2	171	31	15	14	3	1	0	1	17	1	41	0	1	1	.500	0-0	2	91	.578	2.63	3.02

Michael Massey

Bats: L **Throws:** R **Pos:** 2B-48;PH-3;DH-2;3B-1;PR-1 **Ht:** 6'0" **Wt:** 190 **Born:** 3/22/1998 **Age:** 25

Year	Team	Lg	G	AB	H	2B	3B	HR	(Hm	Rd)	TB	R	RBI	RC	TBB	IBB	SO	HBP	SH	SF	SB	CS	GDP	Avg	OBP	Slg	OPS
2022	NWArk	AA	54	220	67	15	0	9	(-	-)	109	36	48	41	21	2	54	1	0	6	9	2	1	.305	.359	.495	.854
2022	Omha	AAA	33	126	41	13	0	7	(-	-)	75	21	29	29	13	0	35	2	0	3	4	0	3	.325	.392	.595	.987
2022	KC	AL	52	173	42	9	1	4	(2	2)	65	16	17	17	9	0	46	8	2	2	3	0	1	.243	.307	.376	.683

Miles Mastrobuoni

Bats: L **Throws:** R **Pos:** 2B-6;RF-3;PH-1;PR-1 **Ht:** 5'11" **Wt:** 185 **Born:** 10/31/1995 **Age:** 27

Year	Team	Lg	G	AB	H	2B	3B	HR	(Hm	Rd)	TB	R	RBI	RC	TBB	IBB	SO	HBP	SH	SF	SB	CS	GDP	Avg	OBP	Slg	OPS
2022	Drham	AAA	129	507	152	32	3	16	(-	-)	238	92	64	91	63	0	95	1	0	2	23	3	8	.300	.377	.469	.846
2022	TB	AL	8	16	3	0	0	0	(0	0)	3	1	0	0	1	0	6	0	0	0	1	0	0	.188	.235	.188	.423

Jorge Mateo

Bats: R Throws: R Pos: SS-149;PR-5;PH-2   Ht: 6'0" Wt: 182 Born: 6/23/1995 Age: 28

							BATTING														RUNNING			AVERAGES			
Year	Team	Lg	G	AB	H	2B	3B	HR	(Hm	Rd)	TB	R	RBI	RC	TBB	IBB	SO	HBP	SH	SF	SB	CS	GDP	Avg	OBP	Slg	OPS
2020	SD	NL	22	26	4	3	0	0	(0	0)	7	4	2	2	1	0	11	0	1	0	1	0	1	.154	.185	.269	.454
2021	2 Tms		89	194	48	11	1	4	(1	3)	73	19	14	22	9	0	55	4	1	1	10	3	1	.247	.293	.376	.670
2022	Bal	AL	150	494	109	25	7	13	(5	8)	187	63	50	50	27	0	147	5	3	2	35	9	8	.221	.267	.379	.646
21	SD	NL	57	87	18	4	0	2	(0	2)	28	10	6	7	2	0	27	3	1	0	5	0	1	.207	.250	.322	.572
21	Bal	AL	32	107	30	7	1	2	(1	1)	45	9	8	15	7	0	28	1	0	1	5	3	0	.280	.328	.421	.748
	3 ML YEARS		261	714	161	39	8	17	(6	11)	267	86	66	74	37	0	213	9	5	3	46	12	10	.225	.271	.374	.645

Mark Mathias

Bats: R Throws: R Pos: DH-14;PH-7;2B-6;1B-3;3B-2;LF-2;RF-2;PR-1   Ht: 6'0" Wt: 200 Born: 8/2/1994 Age: 28

							BATTING														RUNNING			AVERAGES			
Year	Team	Lg	G	AB	H	2B	3B	HR	(Hm	Rd)	TB	R	RBI	RC	TBB	IBB	SO	HBP	SH	SF	SB	CS	GDP	Avg	OBP	Slg	OPS
2022	Nashv	AAA	50	170	54	8	1	8	(-	-)	88	20	30	36	27	1	48	4	0	1	8	3	5	.318	.421	.518	.938
2020	Mil	NL	16	36	10	3	0	0	(0	0)	13	2	4	3	0	0	7	0	0	0	1	0	0	.278	.278	.361	.639
2022	2 Tms		30	81	20	3	0	6	(5	1)	41	13	20	19	9	0	30	0	0	1	3	0	0	.247	.319	.506	.825
22	Mil	NL	6	16	2	0	0	1	(0	1)	5	2	4	2	0	0	4	0	0	1	1	0	0	.125	.118	.313	.430
22	Tex	AL	24	65	18	3	0	5	(5	0)	36	11	16	17	9	0	26	0	0	0	2	0	0	.277	.365	.554	.919
	2 ML YEARS		46	117	30	6	0	6	(5	1)	54	15	24	22	9	0	37	0	0	1	4	0	0	.256	.307	.462	.769

J.J. Matijevic

Bats: L Throws: R Pos: PH-16;DH-12;1B-10;LF-1   mah-ti-JEH-vic   Ht: 6'0" Wt: 206 Born: 11/14/1995 Age: 27

							BATTING														RUNNING			AVERAGES			
Year	Team	Lg	G	AB	H	2B	3B	HR	(Hm	Rd)	TB	R	RBI	RC	TBB	IBB	SO	HBP	SH	SF	SB	CS	GDP	Avg	OBP	Slg	OPS
2022	SgrLnd	AAA	64	246	70	16	2	16	(-	-)	138	46	54	55	33	3	68	2	0	1	10	2	3	.285	.372	.561	.933
2022	Hou	AL	32	67	14	2	0	2	(1	1)	22	7	5	5	2	0	25	2	0	0	1	0	1	.209	.254	.328	.582

Nick Maton

Bats: L Throws: R Pos: 2B-10;LF-10;RF-10;PH-3;3B-2;SS-2   Ht: 6'2" Wt: 178 Born: 2/18/1997 Age: 26

							BATTING														RUNNING			AVERAGES			
Year	Team	Lg	G	AB	H	2B	3B	HR	(Hm	Rd)	TB	R	RBI	RC	TBB	IBB	SO	HBP	SH	SF	SB	CS	GDP	Avg	OBP	Slg	OPS
2022	LV	AAA	57	211	55	20	1	5	(-	-)	92	33	35	34	34	0	55	3	0	2	3	1	4	.261	.368	.436	.804
2021	Phi	NL	52	117	30	7	1	2	(0	2)	45	16	14	17	10	0	39	2	1	1	2	0	0	.256	.323	.385	.708
2022	Phi	NL	35	72	18	2	1	5	(4	1)	37	13	17	16	10	0	29	1	0	2	0	0	0	.250	.341	.514	.855
	2 ML YEARS		87	189	48	9	2	7	(4	3)	82	29	31	33	20	0	68	3	1	3	2	0	0	.254	.330	.434	.764

Phil Maton

Pitches: R Bats: R Pos: RP-67   Ht: 6'2" Wt: 206 Born: 3/25/1993 Age: 30

			HOW MUCH PITCHED				WHAT HE GAVE UP											THE RESULTS						
Year	Team	Lg	G	GS	GF	IP	BFP	H	R	ER	HR	SH	SF	HB	TBB	IBB	SO	WP	W	L	Pct	Sv-Op	Hld	Vel	OPS	ERC	ERA
2017	SD	NL	46	0	12	43.0	180	41	23	20	10	0	0	1	14	0	46	0	3	2	.600	1-1	8	93	.778	4.56	4.19
2018	SD	NL	45	0	12	47.1	214	50	25	23	3	2	1	2	23	1	55	4	0	2	.000	0-1	3	91	.757	4.55	4.37
2019	2 Tms		30	0	13	36.2	163	38	27	25	7	2	0	2	12	0	33	3	0	0	-	0-0	2	91	.806	4.72	6.14
2020	Cle	AL	23	0	4	21.2	96	23	14	11	1	0	0	4	6	1	32	1	3	3	.500	0-1	4	94	.716	4.18	4.57
2021	2 Tms		65	1	5	66.2	297	65	36	35	6	0	5	6	32	0	85	0	6	0	1.000	0-4	5	92	.772	4.52	4.73
2022	Hou	AL	67	0	10	65.2	281	58	34	28	10	1	3	8	24	2	73	0	0	2	.000	0-2	14	91	.730	4.09	3.84
19	SD	NL	21	0	5	24.1	115	34	22	21	6	2	0	1	6	0	20	1	0	0	-	0-0	2	91	.948	6.90	7.77
19	Cle	AL	9	0	8	12.1	48	4	5	4	1	0	0	1	6	0	13	2	0	0	-	0-0	0	90	.449	1.36	2.92
21	Cle	AL	38	1	3	41.1	178	36	21	21	4	0	3	3	20	0	61	0	2	0	1.000	0-1	3	92	.766	3.98	4.57
21	Hou	AL	27	0	2	25.1	119	29	15	14	2	0	2	3	12	0	24	0	4	0	1.000	0-3	2	91	.782	5.44	4.97
	Postseason		14	0	0	15.2	61	10	2	2	1	1	1	0	4	1	15	0	0	0	-	0-0	2	92	.524	1.51	1.15
	6 ML YEARS		276	1	56	281.0	1231	275	159	142	37	5	9	23	111	4	324	8	12	9	.571	1-9	36	92	.761	4.45	4.55

Steven Matz

Pitches: L Bats: R Pos: SP-10; RP-5   Ht: 6'2" Wt: 201 Born: 5/29/1991 Age: 32

			HOW MUCH PITCHED				WHAT HE GAVE UP											THE RESULTS						
Year	Team	Lg	G	GS	GF	IP	BFP	H	R	ER	HR	SH	SF	HB	TBB	IBB	SO	WP	W	L	Pct	Sv-Op	Hld	Vel	OPS	ERC	ERA
2022	Memp	AAA	6	4	0	14.2	56	9	3	3	1	0	1	1	3	0	19	0	0	0	-	0- -	-		.467	1.57	1.84
2015	NYM	NL	6	6	0	35.2	149	34	9	9	4	1	1	1	10	1	34	0	4	0	1.000	0-0	0	94	.650	3.55	2.27
2016	NYM	NL	22	22	0	132.1	547	129	53	50	14	8	1	5	31	2	129	3	9	8	.529	0-0	0	94	.689	3.49	3.40
2017	NYM	NL	13	13	0	66.2	298	83	46	45	12	3	1	3	19	2	48	1	2	7	.222	0-0	0	93	.860	5.78	6.08
2018	NYM	NL	30	30	0	154.0	654	134	77	68	25	6	2	10	58	2	152	0	5	11	.313	0-0	0	93	.730	3.91	3.97
2019	NYM	NL	32	30	0	160.1	691	163	83	75	27	5	1	7	52	7	153	3	11	10	.524	0-0	1	93	.777	4.44	4.21
2020	NYM	NL	9	6	1	30.2	142	42	33	33	14	1	1	0	10	0	36	2	0	5	.000	0-0	0	95	1.069	8.76	9.68
2021	Tor	AL	29	29	0	150.2	647	158	70	64	18	0	1	6	43	0	144	5	14	7	.667	0-0	0	95	.725	4.18	3.82
2022	StL	NL	15	10	1	48.0	207	50	28	28	8	0	0	2	10	0	54	1	5	3	.625	0-0	2	95	.730	4.05	5.25
	Postseason		3	3	0	14.2	64	17	6	6	0	0	0	0	4	1	13	0	0	1	.000	0-0	0	94	.678	3.60	3.68
	8 ML YEARS		156	146	2	778.1	3335	793	399	372	122	24	8	34	233	13	750	15	50	51	.495	0-0	3	94	.755	4.31	4.30

Tyler Matzek

Pitches: L Bats: L Pos: RP-42 — MATT-zick — Ht: 6'3" Wt: 230 Born: 10/19/1990 Age: 32

Year	Team	Lg	G	GS	GF	IP	BFP	H	R	ER	HR	SH	SF	HB	TBB	IBB	SO	WP	W	L	Pct	Sv-Op	Hld	Vel	OPS	ERC	ERA
2014	Col	NL	20	19	1	117.2	503	120	53	53	7	4	2	3	44	1	91	3	6	11	.353	0-0	0	93	.749	4.06	4.05
2015	Col	NL	5	5	0	22.0	102	21	10	10	2	1	1	3	19	0	15	2	2	1	.667	0-0	0	92	.823	6.45	4.09
2020	Atl	NL	21	0	3	29.0	121	23	9	9	1	0	0	2	10	0	43	1	4	3	.571	0-2	1	94	.574	2.57	2.79
2021	Atl	NL	69	0	13	63.0	264	40	19	18	3	4	1	2	37	5	77	6	0	4	.000	0-0	24	96	.581	2.48	2.57
2022	Atl	NL	42	0	6	43.2	184	26	21	17	3	0	3	2	29	2	36	7	4	2	.667	1-1	8	94	.590	2.80	3.50
	Postseason		20	0	1	24.1	94	16	4	4	1	1	0	0	7	1	38	1	4	0	1.000	0-0	6	97	.526	1.61	1.48
	5 ML YEARS		157	24	23	275.1	1174	230	112	107	18	9	8	12	139	8	262	19	16	21	.432	1-3	33	94	.676	3.48	3.50

Dustin May

Pitches: R Bats: R Pos: SP-6 — Ht: 6'6" Wt: 180 Born: 9/6/1997 Age: 25

Year	Team	Lg	G	GS	GF	IP	BFP	H	R	ER	HR	SH	SF	HB	TBB	IBB	SO	WP	W	L	Pct	Sv-Op	Hld	Vel	OPS	ERC	ERA
2022	OkCity	AAA	5	5	0	19.0	79	14	4	4	2	0	0	0	6	0	33	1	1	0	1.000	0- -	-	-	.609	2.30	1.89
2019	LAD	NL	14	4	0	34.2	141	33	17	14	2	0	0	4	5	0	32	0	2	3	.400	0-1	4	96	.639	3.06	3.63
2020	LAD	NL	12	10	0	56.0	224	45	18	16	9	1	1	1	16	0	44	2	3	1	.750	0-0	0	98	.649	3.08	2.57
2021	LAD	NL	5	5	0	23.0	93	16	8	7	4	0	0	0	6	0	35	0	1	1	.500	0-0	0	98	.596	2.49	2.74
2022	LAD	NL	6	6	0	30.0	127	21	17	15	3	0	0	5	14	0	29	0	2	3	.400	0-0	0	98	.611	3.35	4.50
	Postseason		9	3	1	14.0	59	13	7	6	1	1	1	1	7	1	14	0	1	0	1.000	0-0	1	99	.770	4.22	3.86
	4 ML YEARS		37	25	0	143.2	585	115	60	52	18	1	1	11	41	0	140	2	8	8	.500	0-1	4	97	.631	3.04	3.26

Trevor May

Pitches: R Bats: R Pos: RP-26 — Ht: 6'5" Wt: 240 Born: 9/23/1989 Age: 33

Year	Team	Lg	G	GS	GF	IP	BFP	H	R	ER	HR	SH	SF	HB	TBB	IBB	SO	WP	W	L	Pct	Sv-Op	Hld	Vel	OPS	ERC	ERA
2014	Min	AL	10	9	0	45.2	213	59	41	40	7	0	1	2	22	1	44	3	3	6	.333	0-0	0	92	.900	6.80	7.88
2015	Min	AL	48	16	9	114.2	492	127	53	51	11	3	4	4	26	2	110	4	8	9	.471	0-2	7	93	.752	4.06	4.00
2016	Min	AL	44	0	10	42.2	187	39	26	25	7	0	0	2	17	1	60	10	2	2	.500	0-2	6	94	.757	4.07	5.27
2018	Min	AL	24	1	6	25.1	103	21	9	9	4	2	0	1	5	0	36	1	4	1	.800	3-3	5	94	.646	2.85	3.20
2019	Min	AL	65	0	13	64.1	266	43	24	21	8	0	3	3	26	1	79	3	5	3	.625	2-4	17	96	.587	2.59	2.94
2020	Min	AL	24	0	4	23.1	96	20	11	10	5	0	1	0	7	0	38	2	1	0	1.000	2-2	8	96	.679	3.61	3.86
2021	NYM	NL	68	0	19	62.2	266	55	29	25	10	0	0	6	24	4	83	7	7	3	.700	4-7	16	97	.698	3.58	3.59
2022	NYM	NL	26	0	6	25.0	111	27	14	14	4	0	0	0	9	0	30	0	2	0	1.000	1-1	6	96	.756	4.69	5.04
	Postseason		4	0	1	3.0	10	1	0	0	0	0	0	0	0	0	2	0	0	0	-	0-0	1	96	.200	0.25	0.00
	8 ML YEARS		309	26	67	403.2	1734	391	207	195	56	5	9	12	136	9	480	30	32	24	.571	12-21	65	94	.727	3.95	4.35

Marcelo Mayer

Bats: L Throws: R Pos: SS — Ht: 6'3" Wt: 188 Born: 12/12/2002 Age: 20

Year	Team	Lg	G	AB	H	2B	3B	HR	(Hm	Rd)	TB	R	RBI	RC	TBB	IBB	SO	HBP	SH	SF	SB	CS	GDP	Avg	OBP	Slg	OPS
2021	RedSx	R	26	91	25	4	1	3	(-	-)	40	25	17	0	15	0	27	0	0	0	7	1	1	.275	.377	.440	.817
2022	2 Tms	Low	91	350	98	30	2	13	(-	-)	171	61	53	71	68	3	107	3	0	3	17	0	7	.280	.399	.489	.887

Mike Mayers

Pitches: R Bats: R Pos: RP-21; SP-3 — MY-erz — Ht: 6'2" Wt: 220 Born: 12/6/1991 Age: 31

Year	Team	Lg	G	GS	GF	IP	BFP	H	R	ER	HR	SH	SF	HB	TBB	IBB	SO	WP	W	L	Pct	Sv-Op	Hld	Vel	OPS	ERC	ERA
2022	Salt Lk	AAA	8	8	0	33.0	148	30	27	23	7	0	2	2	17	0	34	4	0	3	.000	0- -	-	-	.788	4.97	6.27
2016	StL	NL	4	1	0	5.1	35	16	16	16	3	0	1	1	3	0	2	0	1	1	.500	0-0	0	93	1.438	25.90	27.00
2017	StL	NL	3	0	1	4.2	25	8	8	6	2	0	2	0	4	1	3	0	0	0	-	0-0	0	94	1.427	13.79	11.57
2018	StL	NL	50	0	15	51.2	226	59	28	27	7	3	3	1	15	1	49	4	2	1	.667	1-1	6	96	.822	4.72	4.70
2019	StL	NL	16	0	4	19.0	88	21	14	14	3	0	0	1	11	2	16	1	0	1	.000	0-0	1	95	.888	5.90	6.63
2020	LAA	AL	29	0	4	30.0	121	18	10	7	2	0	0	1	9	0	43	0	2	0	1.000	2-4	5	94	.484	1.59	2.10
2021	LAA	AL	72	2	9	75.0	315	71	32	32	11	1	1	3	26	0	90	0	5	5	.500	2-5	17	95	.748	4.10	3.84
2022	LAA	AL	24	3	7	50.2	223	52	35	32	15	0	2	2	18	0	45	3	1	1	.500	0-1	1	94	.840	5.52	5.68
	7 ML YEARS		198	6	40	236.1	1033	245	143	134	43	4	9	9	86	4	248	8	11	9	.550	5-11	30	95	.802	4.83	5.10

Jack Mayfield

Bats: R Throws: R Pos: 2B-11;3B-8;RF-4;PH-4;LF-2;DH-1 — Ht: 5'11" Wt: 190 Born: 9/30/1990 Age: 32

Year	Team	Lg	G	AB	H	2B	3B	HR	(Hm	Rd)	TB	R	RBI	RC	TBB	IBB	SO	HBP	SH	SF	SB	CS	GDP	Avg	OBP	Slg	OPS
2022	Salt Lk	AAA	54	223	55	14	3	6	(-	-)	93	31	31	24	12	0	47	3	1	2	6	3	11	.247	.292	.417	.709
2019	Hou	AL	26	64	10	5	0	2	(0	2)	21	8	5	3	1	0	16	0	0	0	0	0	0	.156	.169	.328	.497
2020	Hou	AL	21	42	8	1	0	0	(0	0)	9	5	3	1	2	0	14	1	1	0	0	0	1	.190	.239	.214	.453
2021	2 Tms	AL	87	266	58	15	0	10	(5	5)	103	30	39	29	17	0	68	3	3	1	5	0	6	.218	.272	.387	.659
2022	LAA	AL	23	70	13	1	1	1	(1	0)	19	8	6	5	3	0	17	1	0	1	1	0	1	.186	.230	.271	.501
21	LAA	AL	75	232	52	14	0	10	(5	5)	96	28	36	29	16	0	58	3	3	1	5	0	4	.224	.282	.414	.696
21	Sea	AL	12	34	6	1	0	0	(0	0)	7	2	3	0	1	0	10	0	0	0	0	0	2	.176	.200	.206	.406
	4 ML YEARS		157	442	89	22	1	13	(6	7)	152	51	53	38	23	0	115	5	4	2	6	0	8	.201	.248	.344	.592

Tim Mayza

Pitches: L Bats: L Pos: RP-63   Ht: 6'3" Wt: 213 Born: 1/15/1992 Age: 31

			HOW MUCH PITCHED					WHAT HE GAVE UP										THE RESULTS							
Year	Team	Lg	G	GS	GF	IP	BFP	H	R	ER	HR	SH	SF	HB	TBB	IBB	SO	WP	W	L	Pct	Sv-Op	Hld	Vel	OPS	ERC	ERA
2017	Tor	AL	19	0	7	17.0	79	24	15	13	3	0	0	0	4	0	27	0	1	0	1.000	0-0	2	94	.874	6.27	6.88
2018	Tor	AL	37	0	9	35.2	151	33	13	13	3	0	0	2	14	4	40	2	2	0	1.000	0-0	1	94	.695	3.61	3.28
2019	Tor	AL	68	0	5	51.1	227	45	29	28	8	1	2	1	27	2	55	4	1	3	.250	0-1	18	94	.741	4.20	4.91
2021	Tor	AL	61	0	10	53.0	210	40	21	20	5	1	0	3	12	0	57	2	5	2	.714	1-4	18	94	.572	2.34	3.40
2022	Tor	AL	63	0	9	48.2	193	42	19	17	7	1	2	1	12	2	44	2	8	1	.889	2-6	16	94	.688	3.14	3.14
	5 ML YEARS		248	0	40	205.2	860	184	97	91	26	3	4	7	69	8	223	10	17	6	.739	3-11	55	94	.692	3.50	3.98

Nomar Mazara

Bats: L Throws: L Pos: RF-48;PH-12;LF-3;PR-1   Ht: 6'4" Wt: 224 Born: 4/26/1995 Age: 28

					BATTING																	RUNNING			AVERAGES			
Year	Team	Lg	G	AB	H	2B	3B	HR	(Hm	Rd)	TB	R	RBI	RC	TBB	IBB	SO	HBP	SH	SF	SB	CS	GDP	Avg	OBP	Slg	OPS
2022	ElPaso	AAA	35	128	47	14	0	7	(-	-)	82	32	27	36	21	0	29	1	0	2	0	0	1	.367	.454	.641	1.095
2016	Tex	AL	145	516	137	13	3	20	(7	13)	216	59	64	67	39	6	112	6	0	7	0	2	12	.266	.320	.419	.739
2017	Tex	AL	148	554	140	30	2	20	(11	9)	234	64	101	87	55	6	127	4	0	3	2	2	12	.253	.323	.422	.745
2018	Tex	AL	128	489	126	25	1	20	(15	5)	213	61	77	67	40	2	116	4	0	3	1	0	13	.258	.317	.436	.753
2019	Tex	AL	116	429	115	27	1	19	(8	11)	201	69	66	60	28	2	108	6	0	6	4	1	5	.268	.318	.469	.786
2020	CWS	AL	42	136	31	6	0	1	(0	1)	40	13	15	16	10	0	44	3	0	0	0	1	0	.228	.295	.294	.589
2021	Det	AL	50	165	35	5	2	3	(2	1)	53	12	19	19	15	0	45	0	0	1	0	0	4	.212	.276	.321	.597
2022	SD	NL	55	159	42	8	0	2	(0	2)	56	16	18	20	10	0	40	2	0	0	0	0	3	.264	.316	.352	.668
	Postseason		4	12	4	1	0	0	(0	0)	5	1	2	2	1	0	6	0	0	0	0	0	0	.333	.385	.417	.801
	7 ML YEARS		684	2448	626	114	9	85	(43	42)	1013	294	360	336	197	11	592	25	0	20	7	6	49	.256	.315	.414	.729

Patrick Mazeika

Bats: L Throws: R Pos: C-22;PH-3;1B-2   Ht: 6'3" Wt: 210 Born: 10/14/1993 Age: 29

					BATTING																	RUNNING			AVERAGES			
Year	Team	Lg	G	AB	H	2B	3B	HR	(Hm	Rd)	TB	R	RBI	RC	TBB	IBB	SO	HBP	SH	SF	SB	CS	GDP	Avg	OBP	Slg	OPS
2022	Syrcse	AAA	33	111	29	2	0	2	(-	-)	37	10	12	13	15	0	18	7	0	0	0	0	5	.261	.383	.333	.717
2022	Scrmto	AAA	13	51	12	2	0	2	(-	-)	20	9	6	6	3	0	5	1	0	0	0	0	0	.235	.291	.392	.683
2021	NYM	NL	37	79	15	3	0	1	(0	1)	21	6	6	3	4	1	18	3	0	1	0	0	2	.190	.253	.266	.519
2022	NYM	NL	24	68	13	4	0	1	(1	0)	20	4	6	5	2	0	9	0	2	0	0	0	0	.191	.214	.294	.508
	2 ML YEARS		61	147	28	7	0	2	(1	1)	41	10	12	8	6	1	27	3	2	1	0	0	2	.190	.236	.279	.515

Chris Mazza

Pitches: R Bats: R Pos: RP-2   Ht: 6'4" Wt: 190 Born: 10/17/1989 Age: 33

			HOW MUCH PITCHED					WHAT HE GAVE UP										THE RESULTS							
Year	Team	Lg	G	GS	GF	IP	BFP	H	R	ER	HR	SH	SF	HB	TBB	IBB	SO	WP	W	L	Pct	Sv-Op	Hld	Vel	OPS	ERC	ERA
2022	Drham	AAA	8	0	0	13.0	63	16	9	7	0	0	2	2	6	0	18	1	1	0	1.000	0- -	-	-	.758	5.33	4.85
2022	Tacoma	AAA	15	7	0	33.2	156	44	29	28	9	0	0	3	13	0	28	4	4	3	.571	0- -	-	-	.999	7.68	7.49
2019	NYM	NL	9	0	6	16.1	74	21	10	10	0	0	1	4	5	0	11	0	1	1	.500	0-0	0	92	.905	5.81	5.51
2020	Bos	AL	9	6	0	30.0	136	34	18	16	3	0	1	2	15	0	29	4	1	2	.333	0-0	0	92	.790	5.61	4.80
2021	TB	AL	14	0	7	27.1	112	26	14	14	3	0	2	2	7	1	21	3	0	0	-	1-1	0	90	.718	3.64	4.61
2022	TB	AL	2	0	0	5.1	35	9	10	7	3	0	2	2	6	0	5	1	1	0	1.000	0-0	0	89	1.152	17.36	11.81
	4 ML YEARS		34	6	13	79.0	357	90	52	47	9	0	4	10	33	1	66	8	3	3	.500	1-1	0	91	.824	5.64	5.35

James McCann

Bats: R Throws: R Pos: C-60;1B-3;PH-1   Ht: 6'3" Wt: 220 Born: 6/13/1990 Age: 33

					BATTING																	RUNNING			AVERAGES			
Year	Team	Lg	G	AB	H	2B	3B	HR	(Hm	Rd)	TB	R	RBI	RC	TBB	IBB	SO	HBP	SH	SF	SB	CS	GDP	Avg	OBP	Slg	OPS
2014	Det	AL	9	12	3	1	0	0	(0	0)	4	2	0	1	0	0	2	0	0	0	1	0	0	.250	.250	.333	.583
2015	Det	AL	114	401	106	18	5	7	(5	2)	155	32	41	34	16	0	90	3	4	1	0	1	17	.264	.297	.387	.683
2016	Det	AL	105	344	76	9	1	12	(7	5)	123	31	48	30	23	0	109	2	1	3	0	1	12	.221	.272	.358	.629
2017	Det	AL	106	352	89	14	2	13	(8	5)	146	39	49	46	26	0	89	9	1	3	1	0	8	.253	.318	.415	.733
2018	Det	AL	118	427	94	16	0	8	(5	3)	134	31	39	31	26	0	116	2	0	2	0	3	9	.220	.267	.314	.581
2019	CWS	AL	118	439	120	26	1	18	(8	10)	202	62	60	67	30	1	137	6	1	0	4	1	10	.273	.328	.460	.789
2020	CWS	AL	31	97	28	3	0	7	(4	3)	52	20	15	16	8	0	30	4	0	2	1	1	2	.289	.360	.536	.896
2021	NYM	NL	121	375	87	12	1	10	(4	6)	131	29	46	37	32	1	115	2	0	3	1	2	12	.232	.294	.349	.643
2022	NYM	NL	61	174	34	6	0	3	(2	1)	49	19	18	13	11	0	46	4	0	2	3	0	5	.195	.257	.282	.538
	Postseason		2	6	1	0	0	0	(0	0)	1	1	0	0	0	0	3	1	0	0	0	0	0	.167	.286	.167	.452
	9 ML YEARS		783	2621	637	105	10	78	(43	35)	996	265	316	275	172	2	734	32	7	16	11	9	75	.243	.296	.380	.676

Jake McCarthy

Bats: L Throws: L Pos: RF-47;LF-32;CF-12;DH-11;PH-9;PR-3   Ht: 6'2" Wt: 215 Born: 7/30/1997 Age: 25

					BATTING																	RUNNING			AVERAGES			
Year	Team	Lg	G	AB	H	2B	3B	HR	(Hm	Rd)	TB	R	RBI	RC	TBB	IBB	SO	HBP	SH	SF	SB	CS	GDP	Avg	OBP	Slg	OPS
2022	Reno	AAA	36	141	52	11	3	5	(-	-)	84	33	27	36	19	0	22	4	1	0	11	4	1	.369	.457	.596	1.053
2021	Ari	NL	24	59	13	3	0	2	(1	1)	22	11	4	5	8	0	23	2	1	0	3	2	0	.220	.333	.373	.706
2022	Ari	NL	99	321	91	16	3	8	(4	4)	137	53	43	60	23	0	76	6	3	1	23	3	3	.283	.342	.427	.769
	2 ML YEARS		123	380	104	19	3	10	(5	5)	159	64	47	65	31	0	99	8	4	1	26	5	3	.274	.340	.418	.759

Kirk McCarty

Pitches: L Bats: L Pos: RP-11; SP-2   Ht: 5'8" Wt: 185 Born: 10/12/1995 Age: 27

			HOW MUCH PITCHED					WHAT HE GAVE UP											THE RESULTS						
Year	Team	Lg	G	GS	GF	IP	BFP	H	R	ER	HR	SH	SF	HB	TBB	IBB	SO	WP	W	L	Pct	Sv-Op	Hld	Vel	OPS	ERC	ERA
2022	Clmbs	AAA	17	8	2	61.1	257	57	27	23	11	2	2	1	23	1	53	2	4	1	.800	0- -	-	-	.754	4.22	3.38
2022	Cle	AL	13	2	6	37.2	159	37	23	19	11	0	2	1	13	1	26	0	4	3	.571	0-0	0	93	.838	5.22	4.54

Shane McClanahan

Pitches: L Bats: L Pos: SP-28   Ht: 6'1" Wt: 200 Born: 4/28/1997 Age: 26

			HOW MUCH PITCHED					WHAT HE GAVE UP											THE RESULTS						
Year	Team	Lg	G	GS	GF	IP	BFP	H	R	ER	HR	SH	SF	HB	TBB	IBB	SO	WP	W	L	Pct	Sv-Op	Hld	Vel	OPS	ERC	ERA
2021	TB	AL	25	25	0	123.1	517	120	49	47	14	2	0	2	37	0	141	9	10	6	.625	0-0	0	96	.697	3.71	3.43
2022	TB	AL	28	28	0	166.1	641	116	52	47	19	1	1	3	38	1	194	9	12	8	.600	0-0	0	97	.562	2.07	2.54
	Postseason		6	1	2	10.0	52	18	10	9	3	0	1	0	3	0	7	0	1	0	1.000	0-0	0	97	1.008	10.02	8.10
	2 ML YEARS		53	53	0	289.2	1158	236	101	94	33	3	1	5	75	1	335	18	22	14	.611	0-0	0	97	.622	2.73	2.92

Chas McCormick

Bats: R Throws: L Pos: LF-64;CF-60;RF-17;PH-2;DH-1;PR-1   Ht: 6'0" Wt: 208 Born: 4/19/1995 Age: 28

			BATTING																		RUNNING			AVERAGES			
Year	Team	Lg	G	AB	H	2B	3B	HR	(Hm	Rd)	TB	R	RBI	RC	TBB	IBB	SO	HBP	SH	SF	SB	CS	GDP	Avg	OBP	Slg	OPS
2021	Hou	AL	108	284	73	12	0	14	(7	7)	127	47	50	45	25	0	104	4	0	7	4	2	5	.257	.319	.447	.766
2022	Hou	AL	119	359	88	12	2	14	(7	7)	146	47	44	51	46	0	106	1	0	1	4	3	5	.245	.332	.407	.738
	Postseason		9	23	6	0	0	0	(0	0)	6	3	2	2	3	0	10	0	0	1	0	0	0	.261	.333	.261	.594
	2 ML YEARS		227	643	161	24	2	28	(14	14)	273	94	94	96	71	0	210	5	0	8	8	5	10	.250	.326	.425	.751

Lance McCullers Jr.

Pitches: R Bats: L Pos: SP-8   Ht: 6'1" Wt: 202 Born: 10/2/1993 Age: 29

			HOW MUCH PITCHED					WHAT HE GAVE UP											THE RESULTS						
Year	Team	Lg	G	GS	GF	IP	BFP	H	R	ER	HR	SH	SF	HB	TBB	IBB	SO	WP	W	L	Pct	Sv-Op	Hld	Vel	OPS	ERC	ERA
2015	Hou	AL	22	22	0	125.2	520	106	49	45	10	0	3	5	43	2	129	8	6	7	.462	0-0	0	94	.659	3.02	3.22
2016	Hou	AL	14	14	0	81.0	352	80	29	29	5	0	0	0	45	1	106	9	6	5	.545	0-0	0	94	.736	4.42	3.22
2017	Hou	AL	22	22	0	118.2	512	114	61	56	8	2	2	11	40	1	132	8	7	4	.636	0-0	0	94	.696	3.71	4.25
2018	Hou	AL	25	22	0	128.1	527	100	60	55	12	1	4	7	50	0	142	14	10	6	.625	0-0	1	94	.653	3.05	3.86
2020	Hou	AL	11	11	0	55.0	227	44	29	24	5	1	1	5	20	0	56	0	3	3	.500	0-0	0	94	.710	3.19	3.93
2021	Hou	AL	28	28	0	162.1	684	122	59	57	13	1	1	10	76	0	185	7	13	5	.722	0-0	0	94	.628	3.08	3.16
2022	Hou	AL	8	8	0	47.2	195	37	12	12	4	0	1	0	22	0	50	1	4	2	.667	0-0	0	93	.640	3.06	2.27
	Postseason		16	9	1	57.1	234	44	23	18	10	0	0	9	18	0	62	2	2	2	.500	1-1	0	94	.685	3.66	2.83
	7 ML YEARS		130	127	0	718.2	3017	603	299	278	57	5	12	38	296	4	800	47	49	32	.605	0-0	1	94	.669	3.32	3.48

Andrew McCutchen

Bats: R Throws: R Pos: DH-82;LF-31;RF-19;CF-3;PH-3   Ht: 5'11" Wt: 195 Born: 10/10/1986 Age: 36

			BATTING																		RUNNING			AVERAGES			
Year	Team	Lg	G	AB	H	2B	3B	HR	(Hm	Rd)	TB	R	RBI	RC	TBB	IBB	SO	HBP	SH	SF	SB	CS	GDP	Avg	OBP	Slg	OPS
2009	Pit	NL	108	433	124	26	9	12	(8	4)	204	74	54	78	54	2	83	2	0	4	22	5	3	.286	.365	.471	.836
2010	Pit	NL	154	570	163	35	5	16	(8	8)	256	94	56	86	70	1	89	5	1	7	33	10	6	.286	.365	.449	.814
2011	Pit	NL	158	572	148	34	5	23	(10	13)	261	87	89	102	89	3	126	9	2	6	23	10	7	.259	.364	.456	.820
2012	Pit	NL	157	593	194	29	6	31	(15	16)	328	107	96	125	70	13	132	5	0	5	20	12	9	.327	.400	.553	.953
2013	Pit	NL	157	583	185	38	5	21	(9	12)	296	97	84	105	78	12	101	9	0	4	27	10	13	.317	.404	.508	.911
2014	Pit	NL	146	548	172	38	6	25	(10	15)	297	89	83	109	84	8	115	10	0	6	18	3	9	.314	.410	.542	.952
2015	Pit	NL	157	566	165	36	3	23	(13	10)	276	91	96	120	98	12	133	12	0	9	11	5	9	.292	.401	.488	.889
2016	Pit	NL	153	598	153	26	3	24	(10	14)	257	81	79	83	69	7	143	5	0	3	6	7	15	.256	.336	.430	.766
2017	Pit	NL	156	570	159	30	2	28	(9	19)	277	94	88	98	73	5	116	4	0	3	11	5	10	.279	.363	.486	.849
2018	2 Tms		155	569	145	30	3	20	(7	13)	241	83	65	88	95	1	145	11	0	7	14	9	12	.255	.368	.424	.792
2019	Phi	NL	59	219	56	12	1	10	(5	5)	100	45	29	41	43	0	55	0	0	0	2	1	1	.256	.378	.457	.834
2020	Phi	NL	57	217	55	9	0	10	(5	5)	94	32	34	34	22	0	48	1	0	1	4	0	4	.253	.324	.433	.757
2021	Phi	NL	144	482	107	24	1	27	(12	15)	214	78	80	80	81	2	132	4	0	7	6	1	10	.222	.334	.444	.778
2022	Mil	NL	134	515	122	25	0	17	(10	7)	198	66	69	65	57	1	124	4	0	4	8	6	10	.237	.316	.384	.700
18	SF	NL	130	482	123	28	2	15	(5	10)	200	65	55	70	73	1	123	7	0	6	13	6	11	.255	.357	.415	.772
18	NYY	AL	25	87	22	2	1	5	(2	3)	41	18	10	18	22	0	22	4	0	1	1	3	1	.253	.421	.471	.892
	Postseason		13	46	11	1	0	0	(0	0)	12	5	1	3	7	1	7	0	0	0	0	0	0	.239	.340	.261	.600
	14 ML YEARS		1895	7035	1948	392	49	287	(131	156)	3299	1118	1002	1214	983	67	1542	81	3	66	205	84	118	.277	.369	.469	.838

Mickey McDonald

Bats: L Throws: R Pos: CF-1;RF-1;DH-1;PH-1;PR-1   Ht: 6'2" Wt: 175 Born: 6/2/1995 Age: 28

			BATTING																		RUNNING			AVERAGES			
Year	Team	Lg	G	AB	H	2B	3B	HR	(Hm	Rd)	TB	R	RBI	RC	TBB	IBB	SO	HBP	SH	SF	SB	CS	GDP	Avg	OBP	Slg	OPS
2022	LsVgs	AAA	67	210	56	9	1	2	(-	-)	73	37	17	27	32	0	55	4	5	1	7	4	3	.267	.372	.348	.720
2022	Mdlnd	AA	16	62	20	4	0	1	(-	-)	27	10	6	11	6	0	15	3	2	0	4	0	0	.323	.408	.435	.844
2022	Oak	AL	4	4	0	0	0	0	(0	0)	0	0	0	0	2	0	3	0	0	0	0	0	0	.000	.333	.000	.333

T.J. McFarland

Pitches: L Bats: L Pos: RP-28   Ht: 6'3" Wt: 200 Born: 6/8/1989 Age: 34

Year	Team	Lg	G	GS	GF	IP	BFP	H	R	ER	HR	SH	SF	HB	TBB	IBB	SO	WP	W	L	Pct	Sv-Op	Hld	Vel	OPS	ERC	ERA
			HOW MUCH PITCHED					**WHAT HE GAVE UP**											**THE RESULTS**								
2022	Memp	AAA	17	0	5	18.0	72	17	9	8	2	0	0	1	4	0	15	1	0	2	.000	0--	-		.679	3.52	4.00
2013	Bal	AL	38	1	8	74.2	331	83	37	35	7	2	1	0	28	5	58	2	4	1	.800	0-0	0	88	.737	4.40	4.22
2014	Bal	AL	37	1	14	58.2	255	70	22	18	2	5	0	4	13	2	34	0	4	2	.667	0-0	5	91	.739	4.23	2.76
2015	Bal	AL	30	0	7	40.1	188	52	26	22	4	0	0	0	18	5	26	3	2	2	.500	0-0	3	92	.814	5.68	4.91
2016	Bal	AL	16	0	2	24.2	112	33	19	19	3	0	3	2	10	2	7	1	2	2	.500	0-3	0	92	.928	6.74	6.93
2017	Ari	NL	43	1	22	54.0	241	65	42	32	4	2	3	2	17	6	29	2	4	5	.444	0-0	2	92	.757	4.65	5.33
2018	Ari	NL	47	0	21	72.0	292	64	18	16	4	1	1	0	22	3	42	2	2	2	.500	1-1	0	91	.631	2.82	2.00
2019	Ari	NL	51	0	13	56.0	250	71	35	30	6	2	2	1	20	5	35	1	0	0	-	0-0	9	89	.842	5.53	4.82
2020	Oak	NL	23	0	2	20.2	92	26	10	10	5	0	0	1	5	0	9	1	2	0	1.000	0-0	6	88	.894	6.20	4.35
2021	StL	NL	38	0	7	38.2	144	32	11	11	3	0	0	0	9	1	21	0	4	1	.800	0-1	15	89	.655	2.59	2.56
2022	StL	NL	28	0	11	32.2	145	42	26	24	5	1	1	2	11	0	16	2	0	0	-	0-0	1	89	.874	6.38	6.61
	Postseason		3	0	2	2.2	10	0	1	1	0	0	1	0	2	0	2	0	0	1	.000	0-0	0	90	.200	0.57	3.38
	10 ML YEARS		351	3	107	472.1	2050	538	246	217	43	13	11	12	153	29	277	14	24	15	.615	1-5	42	90	.765	4.55	4.13

Easton McGee

Pitches: R Bats: R Pos: RP-1   Ht: 6'6" Wt: 205 Born: 12/26/1997 Age: 25

Year	Team	Lg	G	GS	GF	IP	BFP	H	R	ER	HR	SH	SF	HB	TBB	IBB	SO	WP	W	L	Pct	Sv-Op	Hld	Vel	OPS	ERC	ERA
			HOW MUCH PITCHED					**WHAT HE GAVE UP**											**THE RESULTS**								
2022	Drham	AAA	27	22	0	107.2	470	122	71	65	24	0	3	10	20	0	82	4	6	9	.400	0--	-		.827	5.16	5.43
2022	TB	AL	1	0	1	3.0	14	4	1	0	0	0	0	0	1	0	1	0	0	0	-	0-0	0	93	.571	3.27	0.00

Jake McGee

Pitches: L Bats: L Pos: RP-42   Ht: 6'4" Wt: 229 Born: 8/6/1986 Age: 36

Year	Team	Lg	G	GS	GF	IP	BFP	H	R	ER	HR	SH	SF	HB	TBB	IBB	SO	WP	W	L	Pct	Sv-Op	Hld	Vel	OPS	ERC	ERA
			HOW MUCH PITCHED					**WHAT HE GAVE UP**											**THE RESULTS**								
2010	TB	AL	8	0	3	5.0	20	2	1	1	0	0	0	0	3	0	6	0	0	0	-	0-0	0	94	.426	1.32	1.80
2011	TB	AL	37	0	9	28.0	124	30	14	14	5	1	0	0	12	1	27	0	5	2	.714	0-0	4	95	.801	5.09	4.50
2012	TB	AL	69	0	13	55.1	212	33	13	12	3	0	2	1	11	4	73	4	5	2	.714	0-2	19	96	.452	1.26	1.95
2013	TB	AL	71	0	6	62.2	260	52	28	28	8	1	3	1	22	5	75	4	5	3	.625	1-5	27	96	.659	3.07	4.02
2014	TB	AL	73	0	31	71.1	274	48	15	15	4	1	2	1	16	1	90	1	5	2	.714	19-23	14	96	.486	1.55	1.89
2015	TB	AL	39	0	6	37.1	147	27	11	10	3	0	1	1	8	1	48	1	1	2	.333	6-10	19	95	.544	1.92	2.41
2016	Col	NL	57	0	25	45.2	205	56	25	24	9	0	0	3	16	1	38	4	2	3	.400	15-19	4	93	.887	6.26	4.73
2017	Col	NL	62	0	13	57.1	229	47	23	23	4	1	1	1	16	0	58	5	0	2	.000	3-6	20	94	.624	2.59	3.61
2018	Col	NL	61	0	9	51.1	227	59	39	37	10	2	0	2	16	1	47	5	2	4	.333	1-3	14	94	.883	5.38	6.49
2019	Col	NL	45	0	10	41.1	180	47	25	20	11	0	3	3	11	1	35	0	0	2	.000	0-2	4	94	.903	5.83	4.35
2020	LAD	NL	24	0	4	20.1	79	14	6	6	2	1	0	0	3	0	33	0	3	1	.750	0-0	4	95	.565	1.59	2.66
2021	SF	NL	62	0	42	59.2	239	44	25	18	7	0	3	2	10	1	58	0	3	2	.600	31-36	8	95	.565	2.00	2.72
2022	3 Tms	NL	42	0	11	37.0	163	41	29	28	6	1	1	0	12	1	25	1	1	3	.250	3-7	4	94	.810	4.71	6.81
22	SF	NL	24	0	8	21.1	96	27	18	17	2	0	1	0	6	1	11	1	1	2	.333	3-6	4	95	.838	4.93	7.17
22	Mil	NL	6	0	0	5.2	25	7	4	4	2	0	0	0	1	0	4	0	0	0	-	0-1	0	94	.903	6.18	6.35
22	Was	NL	12	0	3	10.0	42	7	7	7	2	1	0	0	5	0	10	0	0	1	.000	0-0	0	94	.682	3.43	6.30
	Postseason		13	0	5	9.0	41	9	5	5	2	1	0	1	4	1	8	0	0	1	.000	0-0	3	96	.779	5.31	5.00
	13 ML YEARS		650	0	182	572.1	2359	500	254	236	70	8	15	16	156	17	613	24	32	28	.533	79-113	141	95	.672	3.10	3.71

Reese McGuire

Bats: L Throws: R Pos: C-84;PH-8;PR-2;DH-1   Ht: 6'0" Wt: 218 Born: 3/2/1995 Age: 28

Year	Team	Lg	G	AB	H	2B	3B	HR	(Hm	Rd)	TB	R	RBI	RC	TBB	IBB	SO	HBP	SH	SF	SB	CS	GDP	Avg	OBP	Slg	OPS
			BATTING																		**RUNNING**			**AVERAGES**			
2018	Tor	AL	14	31	9	3	0	2	(1	1)	18	5	4	5	2	0	9	0	0	0	1	0	0	.290	.333	.581	.914
2019	Tor	AL	30	97	29	7	0	5	(4	1)	51	14	11	14	7	0	18	0	0	0	0	0	1	.299	.346	.526	.872
2020	Tor	AL	19	41	3	0	0	1	(0	1)	6	2	1	0	0	0	11	0	4	0	0	0	1	.073	.073	.146	.220
2021	Tor	AL	78	198	50	15	0	1	(0	1)	68	22	10	16	15	0	44	2	1	0	0	0	4	.253	.310	.343	.654
2022	2 Tms	AL	89	249	67	14	1	3	(1	2)	92	25	22	27	12	0	56	3	6	3	1	0	6	.269	.307	.369	.677
22	CWS	AL	53	151	34	9	0	0	(0	0)	43	12	10	11	6	0	33	2	5	2	0	0	2	.225	.261	.285	.546
22	Bos	AL	36	98	33	5	1	3	(1	2)	49	13	12	16	6	0	23	1	1	1	1	0	4	.337	.377	.500	.877
	Postseason		1	0	0	0	0	0	(0	0)	0	0	0	0	0	0	0	0	0	0	0	0	0	-	-	-	-
	5 ML YEARS		230	616	158	39	1	12	(6	6)	235	68	48	62	36	0	138	5	11	4	2	0	12	.256	.301	.381	.683

Collin McHugh

mick-HYOO

Pitches: R Bats: R Pos: RP-58   Ht: 6'2" Wt: 191 Born: 6/19/1987 Age: 36

Year	Team	Lg	G	GS	GF	IP	BFP	H	R	ER	HR	SH	SF	HB	TBB	IBB	SO	WP	W	L	Pct	Sv-Op	Hld	Vel	OPS	ERC	ERA
			HOW MUCH PITCHED					**WHAT HE GAVE UP**											**THE RESULTS**								
2012	NYM	NL	8	4	1	21.1	99	27	21	18	5	2	1	2	8	2	17	0	0	4	.000	0-0	0	90	1.044	6.83	7.59
2013	2 Tms	NL	7	5	2	26.0	125	45	29	29	6	2	2	0	6	0	11	0	0	4	.000	0-0	0	90	1.053	8.82	10.04
2014	Hou	AL	25	25	0	154.2	619	117	53	47	13	6	4	6	41	1	157	6	11	9	.550	0-0	0	90	.588	2.34	2.73
2015	Hou	AL	32	32	0	203.2	859	207	89	88	19	5	4	9	53	2	171	5	19	7	.731	0-0	0	90	.705	3.75	3.89
2016	Hou	AL	33	33	0	184.2	796	206	92	89	25	1	5	5	54	1	177	9	13	10	.565	0-0	0	90	.790	4.69	4.34
2017	Hou	AL	12	12	0	63.1	271	62	27	25	7	0	2	0	20	0	62	4	5	2	.714	0-0	0	90	.747	4.02	3.55
2018	Hou	AL	58	0	18	72.1	283	45	18	16	6	1	1	5	21	0	94	0	6	2	.750	0-1	12	92	.542	1.92	1.99
2019	Hou	AL	35	8	8	74.2	317	62	41	39	12	0	3	3	30	0	82	0	4	5	.444	0-0	4	91	.733	3.67	4.70
2021	TB	AL	37	7	11	64.0	247	48	15	11	3	1	0	2	12	2	74	2	6	1	.857	1-3	6	91	.541	1.83	1.55
2022	Atl	NL	58	0	3	69.1	272	51	20	20	5	0	2	5	14	0	75	3	3	2	.600	0-5	17	89	.556	2.09	2.60

HOW MUCH PITCHED						WHAT HE GAVE UP											THE RESULTS								
Year	Team	Lg	G	GS	GF	IP	BFP	H	R	ER	HR	SH	SF	HB	TBB	IBB	SO	WP	W	L	Pct	Sv-Op	Hld	Vel	OPS	ERC	ERA
13	NYM	NL	3	1	2	7.0	34	12	8	8	2	0	1	0	3	0	3	0	0	1	.000	0-0	0	91	1.141	10.77	10.29
13	Col	NL	4	4	0	19.0	91	33	21	21	4	2	1	0	2	0	8	0	0	3	.000	0-0	0	90	1.021	8.14	9.95
	Postseason		10	3	3	23.2	92	14	11	11	5	0	0	2	7	0	16	0	2	2	.500	0-0	0	91	.611	2.57	4.18
	10 ML YEARS		305	126	43	934.0	3888	870	405	382	101	18	22	42	258	9	920	29	67	46	.593	1-9	39	91	.696	3.45	3.68

David McKay

Pitches: R Bats: R Pos: RP-4 **Ht: 6'3" Wt: 205 Born: 3/31/1995 Age: 28**

HOW MUCH PITCHED						WHAT HE GAVE UP											THE RESULTS								
Year	Team	Lg	G	GS	GF	IP	BFP	H	R	ER	HR	SH	SF	HB	TBB	IBB	SO	WP	W	L	Pct	Sv-Op	Hld	Vel	OPS	ERC	ERA
2022	S-WB	AAA	17	0	4	21.2	88	15	7	7	3	0	0	0	11	0	26	1	3	0	1.000	1- -	-	-	.659	3.15	2.91
2022	LsVgs	AAA	5	0	0	6.1	28	9	5	5	2	0	1	0	2	0	5	1	0	0		0- -	-	-	1.153	8.41	7.11
2019	2 Tms	AL	25	0	11	26.1	115	20	17	16	3	0	0	1	17	1	34	2	0	1		0-1	1	94	.681	3.87	5.47
2020	Det	AL	1	0	0	0.1	3	1	2	2	1	0	0	0	1	0	0	0	0	0		0-0	0	92	2.667	73.60	54.00
2022	3 Tms	AL	4	0	2	6.2	32	8	5	5	1	0	1	0	4	0	3	0	0	0		0-0	0	92	.856	6.33	6.75
19	Det	AL	18	0	6	19.1	81	15	12	12	2	0	0	1	9	1	29	2	0	1		0-1	1	94	.647	3.27	5.59
19	Sea	AL	7	0	5	7.0	34	5	5	4	1	0	0	0	8	0	5	0	0	0		0-0	0	93	.767	5.59	5.14
22	NYY	AL	2	0	2	2.0	9	1	0	0	0	0	0	0	2	0	1	0	0	0		0-0	0	93	.476	2.80	0.00
22	TB	AL	1	0	0	2.0	11	3	4	4	1	0	0	0	2	0	0	0	0	0		0-0	0	93	1.121	13.58	18.00
22	Oak	AL	1	0	0	2.2	12	4	1	1	0	0	1	0	0	0	2	0	0	0		0-0	0	92	.879	4.47	3.38
	3 ML YEARS		30	0	13	33.1	150	29	24	23	5	0	1	1	22	1	37	2	0	0		0-1	1	94	.751	4.77	6.21

Ryan McKenna

Bats: R Throws: R Pos: LF-39;RF-31;CF-21;PR-18;PH-13;DH-5 **Ht: 5'11" Wt: 195 Born: 2/14/1997 Age: 26**

BATTING																	RUNNING			AVERAGES			
Year	Team	Lg	G	AB	H	2B	3B	HR	(Hm | Rd)	TB	R	RBI	RC	TBB	IBB	SO	HBP	SH	SF	SB	CS	GDP	Avg	OBP	Slg	OPS
2021	Bal	AL	90	169	31	6	1	2	(2 | 0)	45	20	14	16	24	0	74	2	2	1	0	1		.183	.292	.266	.559
2022	Bal	AL	105	156	37	10	0	2	(1 | 1)	53	23	11	14	11	1	55	2	2	1	2	1	3	.237	.294	.340	.634
	2 ML YEARS		195	325	68	16	1	4	(3 | 1)	98	43	25	30	35	1	129	4	4	1	3	1	4	.209	.293	.302	.595

Triston McKenzie

Pitches: R Bats: R Pos: SP-30; RP-1 **Ht: 6'5" Wt: 165 Born: 8/2/1997 Age: 25**

HOW MUCH PITCHED						WHAT HE GAVE UP											THE RESULTS								
Year	Team	Lg	G	GS	GF	IP	BFP	H	R	ER	HR	SH	SF	HB	TBB	IBB	SO	WP	W	L	Pct	Sv-Op	Hld	Vel	OPS	ERC	ERA
2020	Cle	AL	8	6	0	33.1	127	21	12	12	6	0	0	1	9	0	42	0	2	1	.667	0-0	0	93	.612	2.32	3.24
2021	Cle	AL	25	24	0	120.0	495	84	66	66	21	0	1	3	58	0	136	2	5	9	.357	0-0	0	92	.676	3.38	4.95
2022	Cle	AL	31	30	1	191.1	741	138	65	63	25	2	2	5	44	0	190	8	11	11	.500	0-0	0	93	.611	2.32	2.96
	Postseason		1	0	0	1.2	9	1	2	2	1	0	0	0	2	0	2	0	0	0		0-0	0	93	.905	7.86	10.80
	3 ML YEARS		64	60	1	344.2	1363	243	143	141	52	2	3	9	111	0	368	10	18	21	.462	0-0	0	92	.634	2.68	3.68

Billy McKinney

Bats: L Throws: L Pos: RF-10;1B-7;LF-4;PH-4;DH-1;PR-1 **Ht: 6'1" Wt: 205 Born: 8/23/1994 Age: 28**

BATTING																	RUNNING			AVERAGES			
Year	Team	Lg	G	AB	H	2B	3B	HR	(Hm | Rd)	TB	R	RBI	RC	TBB	IBB	SO	HBP	SH	SF	SB	CS	GDP	Avg	OBP	Slg	OPS
2022	LsVgs	AAA	69	251	74	13	5	12	(- | -)	133	48	49	55	36	1	83	6	0	0	2	0	1	.295	.396	.530	.926
2018	2 Tms	AL	38	119	30	7	0	6	(5 | 1)	55	14	13	14	11	0	33	1	0	1	1	0	0	.252	.318	.462	.780
2019	Tor	AL	84	251	54	14	1	12	(7 | 5)	106	37	28	35	19	0	73	2	2	2	0	2	0	.215	.274	.422	.696
2020	Tor	AL	3	3	2	0	0	0	(0 | 0)	2	1	0	0	0	0	0	0	0	0	0	0	0	.667	.667	.667	1.333
2021	3 Tms	NL	116	265	51	11	3	9	(2 | 7)	95	32	27	25	32	2	79	1	0	2	2	0	3	.192	.280	.358	.638
2022	Oak	AL	23	52	5	1	0	1	(0 | 1)	9	3	4	0	4	1	16	0	0	1	0	0	0	.096	.158	.173	.331
18	NYY	AL	2	4	1	0	0	0	(0 | 0)	1	0	0	0	0	0	1	0	0	0	0	0	0	.250	.250	.250	.500
18	Tor	AL	36	115	29	7	0	6	(5 | 1)	54	14	13	14	11	0	32	1	0	1	1	0	0	.252	.320	.470	.790
21	Mil	NL	40	92	19	3	1	3	(0 | 3)	33	9	6	5	7	1	24	0	0	1	1	0	1	.207	.260	.359	.619
21	NYM	NL	39	91	20	6	1	5	(1 | 4)	43	15	14	14	11	0	31	1	0	0	1	0	1	.220	.304	.473	.776
21	LAD	NL	37	82	12	2	1	1	(1 | 0)	19	8	7	6	14	1	24	0	0	1	0	0	1	.146	.276	.232	.507
	Postseason		4	1	0	0	0	0	(0 | 0)	0	0	0	0	0	0	1	0	0	0	0	0	0	.000	.000	.000	.000
	5 ML YEARS		263	690	142	33	4	28	(14 | 14)	267	87	72	74	66	3	201	4	2	6	3	2	3	.206	.277	.387	.664

Zach McKinstry

Bats: L Throws: R Pos: 3B-22;2B-21;SS-10;PH-4;RF-3;DH-3;PR-2;LF-1 **Ht: 6'0" Wt: 180 Born: 4/29/1995 Age: 28**

BATTING																	RUNNING			AVERAGES			
Year	Team	Lg	G	AB	H	2B	3B	HR	(Hm | Rd)	TB	R	RBI	RC	TBB	IBB	SO	HBP	SH	SF	SB	CS	GDP	Avg	OBP	Slg	OPS
2022	OkCity	AAA	48	191	64	9	4	4	(- | -)	93	36	25	37	27	1	33	2	0	3	0	3	1	.335	.417	.487	.904
2020	LAD	NL	4	7	2	1	0	0	(0 | 0)	3	1	0	1	0	0	3	0	0	0	0	0	0	.286	.286	.429	.714
2021	LAD	NL	60	158	34	9	0	7	(5 | 2)	64	19	29	17	10	1	50	1	1	2	1	1	3	.215	.263	.405	.668
2022	2 Tms	NL	57	166	33	6	3	5	(3 | 2)	60	21	14	19	16	0	52	1	2	0	7	0	0	.199	.273	.361	.635
22	LAD	NL	10	11	1	0	0	1	(1 | 0)	4	4	2	2	3	0	4	0	0	0	0	0	0	.091	.286	.364	.649
22	ChC	NL	47	155	32	6	3	4	(2 | 2)	56	17	12	17	13	0	48	1	2	0	7	0	0	.206	.272	.361	.633
	3 ML YEARS		121	331	69	16	3	12	(8 | 4)	127	41	43	37	26	1	105	2	3	2	8	1	4	.208	.269	.384	.652

Ryan McMahon

Bats: L **Throws:** R **Pos:** 3B-145;2B-10;PR-2;1B-1;DH-1   **Ht:** 6'2" **Wt:** 219 **Born:** 12/14/1994 **Age:** 28

								BATTING												RUNNING			AVERAGES			
Year Team	Lg	G	AB	H	2B	3B	HR	(Hm Rd)	TB	R	RBI	RC	TBB	IBB	SO	HBP	SH	SF	SB	CS	GDP	Avg	OBP	Slg	OPS
2017 Col	NL	17	19	3	1	0	0	(0 0)	4	2	1	1	5	0	5	0	0	1	0	0	1	.158	.333	.211	.544
2018 Col	NL	91	181	42	9	1	5	(4 1)	68	17	19	23	18	2	64	2	0	1	1	0	0	.232	.307	.376	.683
2019 Col	NL	141	480	120	22	1	24	(18 6)	216	70	83	69	56	1	160	1	1	1	5	1	14	.250	.329	.450	.779
2020 Col	NL	52	172	37	6	1	9	(6 3)	72	23	26	24	18	0	66	2	0	1	0	1	4	.215	.295	.419	.714
2021 Col	NL	151	528	134	32	1	23	(12 11)	237	80	86	79	59	2	147	4	0	5	6	2	14	.254	.331	.449	.779
2022 Col	NL	153	529	130	23	3	20	(14 6)	219	67	67	70	60	0	158	5	0	3	7	3	7	.246	.327	.414	.741
Postseason		4	3	0	0	0	0	(0 0)	0	0	0	0	1	0	1	0	0	0	0	1	0	.000	.250	.000	.250
6 ML YEARS		605	1909	466	93	7	81	(54 27)	816	259	282	266	216	5	600	14	1	11	19	7	40	.244	.324	.427	.751

Jeff McNeil

Bats: L **Throws:** R **Pos:** 2B-106;LF-34;RF-13;DH-4;PH-3;3B-1;PR-1   **Ht:** 6'1" **Wt:** 195 **Born:** 4/8/1992 **Age:** 31

								BATTING												RUNNING			AVERAGES			
Year Team	Lg	G	AB	H	2B	3B	HR	(Hm Rd)	TB	R	RBI	RC	TBB	IBB	SO	HBP	SH	SF	SB	CS	GDP	Avg	OBP	Slg	OPS
2018 NYM	NL	63	225	74	11	6	3	(1 2)	106	35	19	39	14	1	24	5	4	0	7	1	2	.329	.381	.471	.852
2019 NYM	NL	133	510	162	38	1	23	(9 14)	271	83	75	103	35	2	75	21	0	1	5	6	5	.318	.384	.531	.916
2020 NYM	NL	52	183	57	14	0	4	(4 0)	83	19	23	30	22	2	24	3	0	3	0	2	3	.311	.383	.454	.836
2021 NYM	NL	120	386	97	19	1	7	(6 1)	139	48	35	36	29	0	58	10	0	1	3	0	10	.251	.319	.360	.679
2022 NYM	NL	148	533	174	39	1	9	(5 4)	242	73	62	88	40	1	61	11	0	5	4	0	6	**.326**	.382	.454	.836
5 ML YEARS		516	1837	564	121	9	46	(25 21)	841	258	214	296	138	6	242	50	4	10	19	9	26	.307	.370	.458	.827

Austin Meadows

Bats: L **Throws:** L **Pos:** RF-18;LF-15;DH-4;PH-1   **Ht:** 6'3" **Wt:** 225 **Born:** 5/3/1995 **Age:** 28

								BATTING												RUNNING			AVERAGES			
Year Team	Lg	G	AB	H	2B	3B	HR	(Hm Rd)	TB	R	RBI	RC	TBB	IBB	SO	HBP	SH	SF	SB	CS	GDP	Avg	OBP	Slg	OPS
2022 Toledo	AAA	10	34	5	0	0	1	(- -)	8	4	4	2	4	0	7	0	0	1	0	0	0	.147	.231	.235	.466
2018 2 Tms		59	178	51	9	2	6	(3 3)	82	19	17	23	10	2	40	1	0	2	5	1	1	.287	.325	.461	.785
2019 TB	AL	138	530	154	29	7	33	(13 20)	296	83	89	103	54	6	131	7	0	0	12	7	3	.291	.364	.558	.922
2020 TB	AL	36	132	27	8	1	4	(1 3)	49	19	13	13	17	0	50	1	0	2	2	1	0	.205	.296	.371	.667
2021 TB	AL	142	518	121	29	3	27	(10 17)	237	79	106	98	59	3	122	6	0	8	4	3	4	.234	.315	.458	.772
2022 Det	AL	36	128	32	6	2	0	(0 0)	42	9	11	13	16	0	17	3	0	0	0	1	2	.250	.347	.328	.675
18 Pit	NL	49	154	45	8	2	5	(2 3)	72	16	13	20	8	2	35	1	0	2	4	1	1	.292	.327	.468	.795
18 TB	AL	10	24	6	1	0	1	(1 0)	10	3	4	3	2	0	5	0	0	0	1	0	0	.250	.308	.417	.724
Postseason		25	83	12	3	0	3	(2 1)	24	7	8	4	5	0	30	0	0	0	0	0	1	.145	.193	.289	.482
5 ML YEARS		411	1486	385	81	15	70	(27 43)	706	209	236	250	156	11	360	18	0	12	23	13	10	.259	.334	.475	.809

John Means

Pitches: L **Bats:** L **Pos:** SP-2   **Ht:** 6'3" **Wt:** 235 **Born:** 4/24/1993 **Age:** 30

		HOW MUCH PITCHED					WHAT HE GAVE UP											THE RESULTS							
Year Team	Lg	G	GS	GF	IP	BFP	H	R	ER	HR	SH	SF	HB	TBB	IBB	SO	WP	W	L	Pct	Sv-Op	Hld	Vel	OPS	ERC	ERA
2018 Bal	AL	1	0	0	3.1	16	6	5	5	1	0	0	0	0	0	4	0				0-0	0	90	1.125	8.70	13.50
2019 Bal	AL	31	27	1	155.0	637	138	68	62	23	0	3	5	38	0	121	5	12	11	.522	0-0	0	90	.702	3.31	3.60
2020 Bal	AL	10	10	0	43.2	176	36	22	22	12	0	1	4	7	0	42	2	2	4	.333	0-0	0	94	.718	3.61	4.53
2021 Bal	AL	26	26	0	146.2	590	125	64	59	30	1	2	4	26	0	134	3	6	9	.400	0-0	0	93	.690	3.14	3.62
2022 Bal	AL	2	2	0	8.0	34	8	3	3	0	1	0	1	2	0	7	0			-	0-0	0	92	.584	2.77	3.38
5 ML YEARS		70	65	1	356.2	1453	313	162	151	66	1	7	13	73	0	308	10	20	24	.455	0-0	0	92	.701	3.31	3.81

Nick Mears

Pitches: R **Bats:** R **Pos:** RP-2   **Ht:** 6'2" **Wt:** 200 **Born:** 10/7/1996 **Age:** 26

		HOW MUCH PITCHED					WHAT HE GAVE UP											THE RESULTS							
Year Team	Lg	G	GS	GF	IP	BFP	H	R	ER	HR	SH	SF	HB	TBB	IBB	SO	WP	W	L	Pct	Sv-Op	Hld	Vel	OPS	ERC	ERA
2022 Indy	AAA	23	0	4	24.2	106	19	14	13	2	0	0	0	17	0	27	3	1	1	.500	0- -	-		.699	3.85	4.74
2022 Bradtn	A	6	1	1	5.1	23	4	3	3	0	0	0	0	2	0	7	0	1	0	1.000	0- -	-			1.90	5.06
2020 Pit	NL	4	0	2	5.0	26	4	3	3	1	0	1	0	7	0	7	1	0	0		0-0	0	96	.868	7.69	5.40
2021 Pit	NL	30	0	6	23.1	107	25	14	13	5	0	1	0	13	1	23	3	1	0	1.000	0-5	3	96	.818	5.86	5.01
2022 Pit	NL	2	0	0	2.0	8	1	0	0	0	0	0	0	1	0	2	0	0	0	-	0-0	1	97	.393	1.41	0.00
3 ML YEARS		36	0	8	30.1	141	30	17	16	6	0	2	0	21	1	32	4	1	0	1.000	0-5	4	96	.802	5.81	4.75

Adonis Medina

Pitches: R **Bats:** R **Pos:** RP-14   **Ht:** 6'1" **Wt:** 187 **Born:** 12/18/1996 **Age:** 26

		HOW MUCH PITCHED					WHAT HE GAVE UP											THE RESULTS							
Year Team	Lg	G	GS	GF	IP	BFP	H	R	ER	HR	SH	SF	HB	TBB	IBB	SO	WP	W	L	Pct	Sv-Op	Hld	Vel	OPS	ERC	ERA
2022 Syrcse	AAA	18	2	1	31.0	149	36	19	16	4	0	1	4	17	0	33	1	1	0	1.000	1- -	-		.816	6.30	4.65
2020 Phi	NL	1	1	0	4.0	18	3	2	2	0	0	0	0	3	0	4	0	0	0	-	0-0	0	92	.600	3.21	4.50
2021 Phi	NL	4	1	2	7.2	36	9	3	3	0	0	0	3	4	0	6	0	0	0	-	0-0	0	93	.858	6.73	3.52
2022 NYM	NL	14	0	6	23.2	110	30	18	16	2	0	0	4	6	0	17	0	1	0	1.000	1-1	0	93	.809	5.52	6.08
3 ML YEARS		19	2	8	35.1	164	42	23	21	2	0	0	7	13	0	27	0	1	1	.500	1-1	0	93	.798	5.51	5.35

Trevor Megill

Pitches: R Bats: L Pos: RP-39   Ht: 6'8" Wt: 250 Born: 12/5/1993 Age: 29

			HOW MUCH PITCHED					WHAT HE GAVE UP										THE RESULTS						
Year	Team	Lg	G	GS	GF	IP	BFP	H	R	ER	HR	SH	SF	HB	TBB	IBB	SO	WP	W	L	Pct	Sv-Op	Hld	Vel	OPS	ERC	ERA
2022	StPaul	AAA	10	0	3	12.0	47	11	6	4	2	2	2	0	4	1	16	2	0	2	.000	2- -	-	-	.821	3.95	3.00
2021	ChC	NL	28	0	3	23.2	115	36	24	22	7	1	0	1	8	1	30	5	1	2	.333	0-0	1	96	1.014	8.63	8.37
2022	Min	AL	39	0	11	45.0	196	50	29	24	4	0	1	1	17	0	49	2	4	3	.571	0-2	3	98	.748	4.69	4.80
	2 ML YEARS		67	0	14	68.2	311	86	53	46	11	1	1	2	25	1	79	7	5	5	.500	0-2	4	97	.847	5.99	6.03

Tylor Megill

Pitches: R Bats: R Pos: SP-9; RP-6   Ht: 6'7" Wt: 230 Born: 7/28/1995 Age: 27

			HOW MUCH PITCHED					WHAT HE GAVE UP										THE RESULTS						
Year	Team	Lg	G	GS	GF	IP	BFP	H	R	ER	HR	SH	SF	HB	TBB	IBB	SO	WP	W	L	Pct	Sv-Op	Hld	Vel	OPS	ERC	ERA
2021	NYM	NL	18	18	0	89.2	379	88	46	45	19	2	2	2	27	0	99	1	4	6	.400	0-0	0	95	.778	4.43	4.52
2022	NYM	NL	15	9	2	47.1	200	46	27	27	7	2	2	1	13	0	51	1	4	2	.667	0-0	0	96	.721	3.79	5.13
	2 ML YEARS		33	27	2	137.0	579	134	73	72	26	4	4	3	40	0	150	2	8	8	.500	0-0	0	95	.758	4.20	4.73

Francisco Mejia

Bats: B Throws: R Pos: C-83; PH-13; DH-3; 1B-2   Ht: 5'8" Wt: 188 Born: 10/27/1995 Age: 27

			BATTING																			RUNNING			AVERAGES			
Year	Team	Lg	G	AB	H	2B	3B	HR	(Hm	Rd)	TB	R	RBI	RC	TBB	IBB	SO	HBP	SH	SF	SB	CS	GDP	Avg	OBP	Slg	OPS
2017	Cle	AL	11	13	2	0	0	0	(0	0)	2	1	1	0	1	1	3	0	0	0	0	0	0	.154	.214	.154	.368
2018	2 Tms		21	56	10	2	0	3	(1	2)	21	6	8	5	5	0	19	1	0	0	0	0	2	.179	.258	.375	.633
2019	SD	NL	79	226	60	11	2	8	(3	5)	99	27	22	27	13	1	56	4	0	1	1	1	6	.265	.316	.438	.754
2020	SD	NL	17	39	3	1	0	1	(1	0)	7	5	2	0	1	0	9	2	0	0	0	0	1	.077	.143	.179	.322
2021	TB	AL	84	250	65	15	3	6	(2	4)	104	31	35	42	17	0	49	7	1	2	0	0	4	.260	.322	.416	.738
2022	TB	AL	93	289	70	22	0	6	(2	4)	110	32	31	30	7	0	65	2	0	1	0	0	6	.242	.264	.381	.645
18	Cle	AL	1	2	0	0	0	0	(0	0)	0	0	0	0	2	0	0	0	0	0	0	0	0	.000	.500	.000	.500
18	SD	NL	20	54	10	2	0	3	(1	2)	21	6	8	5	3	0	19	1	0	0	0	0	2	.185	.241	.389	.630
	Postseason		1	0	0	0	0	0	(0	0)	0	0	0	0	1	0	0	0	0	0	0	0	0	-	1.000		
	6 ML YEARS		305	873	210	51	5	24	(9	15)	343	102	99	104	44	2	201	16	1	4	1	1	19	.241	.288	.393	.681

JC Mejia

Pitches: R Bats: R Pos: RP-2   Ht: 6'5" Wt: 240 Born: 8/26/1996 Age: 26

			HOW MUCH PITCHED					WHAT HE GAVE UP										THE RESULTS						
Year	Team	Lg	G	GS	GF	IP	BFP	H	R	ER	HR	SH	SF	HB	TBB	IBB	SO	WP	W	L	Pct	Sv-Op	Hld	Vel	OPS	ERC	ERA
2022	Nashv	AAA	24	0	5	29.1	117	15	11	9	3	0	1	3	13	0	33	1	0	3	.000	1- -	-	-	.535	2.13	2.76
2021	Cle	AL	17	11	1	52.1	238	60	48	48	13	1	0	3	24	0	47	2	1	7	.125	0-0	0	93	.905	6.60	8.25
2022	Mil	NL	2	0	1	2.1	16	5	6	6	0	0	0	0	5	0	1	0	0	0	-	0-0	0	96	1.170	19.65	23.14
	2 ML YEARS		19	11	2	54.2	254	65	54	54	13	1	0	3	29	0	48	2	1	7	.125	0-0	0	93	.922	7.13	8.89

Mark Melancon

Pitches: R Bats: R Pos: RP-62   muh-LANN-sun   Ht: 6'1" Wt: 215 Born: 3/28/1985 Age: 38

			HOW MUCH PITCHED					WHAT HE GAVE UP										THE RESULTS						
Year	Team	Lg	G	GS	GF	IP	BFP	H	R	ER	HR	SH	SF	HB	TBB	IBB	SO	WP	W	L	Pct	Sv-Op	Hld	Vel	OPS	ERC	ERA
2009	NYY	AL	13	0	4	16.1	74	13	8	7	0	0	0	4	10	0	10	3	0	1	.000	0-1	0	93	.665	3.94	3.86
2010	2 Tms		22	0	4	21.1	90	19	13	10	2	0	1	1	8	0	22	2	2	0	1.000	0-1	8	93	.674	3.53	4.22
2011	Hou	NL	71	0	47	74.1	309	65	28	23	5	2	0	2	26	6	66	1	8	4	.667	20-25	3	93	.631	2.98	2.78
2012	Bos	AL	41	0	17	45.0	194	45	31	31	8	1	2	3	12	1	41	2	0	2	.000	1-2	3	93	.754	4.24	6.20
2013	Pit	NL	72	0	24	71.0	279	60	15	11	1	0	1	1	8	0	70	6	3	2	.600	16-21	26	93	.511	1.78	1.39
2014	Pit	NL	72	0	48	71.0	277	51	15	15	2	1	1	3	11	1	71	3	3	5	.375	33-37	14	93	.473	1.54	1.90
2015	Pit	NL	78	0	63	76.2	293	57	22	19	4	1	1	2	14	2	62	3	3	2	.600	51-53	1	92	.541	1.82	2.23
2016	2 Tms		75	0	67	71.1	270	52	16	13	3	0	2	1	12	0	65	4	2	2	.500	47-51	0	92	.511	1.66	1.64
2017	SF	NL	32	0	18	30.0	130	37	16	15	3	0	0	1	6	0	29	2	1	2	.333	11-16	5	92	.794	4.78	4.50
2018	SF	NL	41	0	8	39.0	174	48	18	14	2	0	0	1	14	2	31	4	1	4	.200	3-7	8	92	.771	4.94	3.23
2019	2 Tms	NL	66	0	34	67.1	284	71	28	27	4	0	1	2	18	2	68	4	5	2	.714	12-12	5	92	.678	3.69	3.61
2020	Atl	NL	23	0	19	22.2	95	22	8	7	1	1	1	2	7	3	14	1	2	1	.667	11-13	0	92	.639	3.38	2.78
2021	SD	NL	64	0	53	64.2	265	54	21	16	4	0	2	1	25	4	59	3	4	3	.571	39-45	0	92	.618	2.90	2.23
2022	Ari	NL	62	0	48	56.0	247	63	37	29	5	1	0	1	21	2	35	6	3	10	.231	18-21	1	91	.738	4.63	4.66
10	NYY	AL	2	0	2	4.0	19	7	5	4	1	0	1	0	0	0	3	0	0	0	-	0-0	0	93	.980	7.95	9.00
10	Hou	NL	20	0	2	17.1	71	12	8	6	1	0	0	1	8	0	19	2	2	0	1.000	0-1	8	93	.586	2.65	3.12
16	Pit	NL	45	0	39	41.2	163	31	10	7	2	0	2	1	9	0	38	1	1	1	.500	30-33	0	92	.516	1.89	1.51
16	Was	NL	30	0	28	29.2	107	21	6	6	1	0	0	0	3	0	27	3	1	1	.500	17-18	0	92	.503	1.41	1.82
19	SF	NL	43	0	16	46.1	195	49	19	18	3	0	1	2	16	2	44	3	4	2	.667	1-1	5	92	.724	4.18	3.50
19	Atl	NL	23	0	18	21.0	89	22	9	9	1	0	0	0	2	0	24	1	1	0	1.000	11-11	0	93	.580	2.69	3.86
	Postseason		20	0	15	19.1	80	19	9	8	2	0	0	0	5	3	17	0	1	1	.500	5-7	0	93	.713	3.24	3.72
	14 ML YEARS		732	0	454	726.2	2981	657	276	237	44	7	12	25	192	23	643	44	37	40	.481	262-305	73	93	.623	2.89	2.94

MJ Melendez

Bats: L Throws: R Pos: C-78; LF-23; DH-23; RF-15; PH-3; PR-1   Ht: 6'1" Wt: 190 Born: 11/29/1998 Age: 24

			BATTING																			RUNNING			AVERAGES			
Year	Team	Lg	G	AB	H	2B	3B	HR	(Hm	Rd)	TB	R	RBI	RC	TBB	IBB	SO	HBP	SH	SF	SB	CS	GDP	Avg	OBP	Slg	OPS
2018	Lxngtn	A	111	419	105	26	9	19	(-	-)	206	52	73	67	43	0	143	4	0	6	4	6	3	.251	.322	.492	.814
2019	Wilmg	A+	110	363	59	23	2	9	(-	-)	113	34	54	31	44	0	165	5	3	4	7	5	3	.163	.260	.311	.571

Year	Team	Lg	G	AB	H	2B	3B	HR	(Hm	Rd)	TB	R	RBI	RC	TBB	IBB	SO	HBP	SH	SF	SB	CS	GDP	Avg	OBP	Slg	OPS
2021	NWArk	AA	79	298	85	18	0	28	(-	-)	187	58	65	68	43	0	76	1	0	5	2	4	3	.285	.372	.628	.999
2021	Omha	AAA	40	131	37	2	2	13	(-	-)	82	31	32	33	30	0	34	0	0	0	1	2	0	.282	.411	.626	1.037
2022	Omha	AAA	21	78	13	4	0	2	(-	-)	23	7	6	7	13	0	22	0	0	0	3	0	1	.167	.286	.295	.581
2022	KC	AL	129	460	100	21	3	18	(11	7)	181	57	62	70	66	1	131	1	0	7	2	3	2	.217	.313	.393	.706

Danny Mendick

Bats: R **Throws:** R **Pos:** SS-22;2B-6;3B-2;LF-1;PR-1   **Ht:** 5'10" **Wt:** 195 **Born:** 9/28/1993 **Age:** 29

Year	Team	Lg	G	AB	H	2B	3B	HR	(Hm	Rd)	TB	R	RBI	RC	TBB	IBB	SO	HBP	SH	SF	SB	CS	GDP	Avg	OBP	Slg	OPS
2019	CWS	AL	16	39	12	0	0	2	(2	0)	18	6	4	6	1	0	11	0	0	0	0	0	1	.308	.325	.462	.787
2020	CWS	AL	33	107	26	4	1	3	(2	1)	41	11	6	6	6	0	25	0	0	1	0	1	3	.243	.281	.383	.664
2021	CWS	AL	71	164	36	5	0	2	(0	2)	47	14	20	22	18	0	42	2	1	1	0	1	1	.220	.303	.287	.589
2022	CWS	AL	31	97	28	4	1	3	(1	2)	43	22	15	15	7	0	23	1	1	0	1	0	2	.289	.343	.443	.786
	4 ML YEARS		151	407	102	13	2	10	(5	5)	149	53	45	49	32	0	101	3	2	2	1	2	7	.251	.309	.366	.675

Joey Meneses

Bats: R **Throws:** R **Pos:** 1B-40;RF-22;LF-3;PH-1   **Ht:** 6'3" **Wt:** 215 **Born:** 5/6/1992 **Age:** 31

Year	Team	Lg	G	AB	H	2B	3B	HR	(Hm	Rd)	TB	R	RBI	RC	TBB	IBB	SO	HBP	SH	SF	SB	CS	GDP	Avg	OBP	Slg	OPS
2022	Roch	AAA	96	374	107	14	1	20	(-	-)	183	51	64	62	32	2	89	2	0	6	1	0	17	.286	.341	.489	.830
2022	Was	NL	56	222	72	14	0	13	(5	8)	125	33	34	37	15	2	52	1	0	2	1	0	13	.324	.367	.563	.930

Conner Menez

Pitches: L **Bats:** L **Pos:** RP-1   **Ht:** 6'2" **Wt:** 206 **Born:** 5/29/1995 **Age:** 28

Year	Team	Lg		HOW MUCH PITCHED					WHAT HE GAVE UP										THE RESULTS							
			G	GS	GF	IP	BFP	H	R	ER	HR	SH	SF	HB	TBB	IBB	SO	WP	W	L	Pct	Sv-Op	Hld	Vel	OPS	ERC	ERA
2022	Iowa	AAA	11	1	1	21.0	87	16	8	5	0	0	0	0	8	1	25	4	2	0	1.000	0- -	-	-	.529	2.02	2.14
2019	SF	NL	8	3	2	17.0	73	13	10	10	4	1	1	0	12	0	22	2	0	1	.000	0-0	0	91	.805	5.06	5.29
2020	SF	NL	7	0	3	11.1	45	6	4	3	2	1	0	1	5	0	8	0	1	0	1.000	0-0	0	92	.641	2.61	2.38
2021	SF	NL	8	1	0	14.0	62	16	10	6	2	0	1	0	3	0	15	0	1	0	1.000	0-0	1	91	.772	4.25	3.86
2022	ChC	NL	1	0	0	1.0	5	1	0	0	0	0	1	0	0	0	1	0	0	0	-	0-0	0	91	.650	5.48	0.00
	4 ML YEARS		24	4	5	43.1	185	36	24	19	8	2	2	2	20	0	46	2	2	1	.667	0-0	1	91	.751	4.13	3.95

Daniel Mengden

Pitches: R **Bats:** R **Pos:** RP-4; SP-1   MENG-den   **Ht:** 6'1" **Wt:** 215 **Born:** 2/19/1993 **Age:** 30

Year	Team	Lg		HOW MUCH PITCHED					WHAT HE GAVE UP										THE RESULTS							
			G	GS	GF	IP	BFP	H	R	ER	HR	SH	SF	HB	TBB	IBB	SO	WP	W	L	Pct	Sv-Op	Hld	Vel	OPS	ERC	ERA
2022	Omha	AAA	25	20	0	109.0	473	106	65	63	24	0	1	3	56	0	93	5	7	7	.500	0- -	-	-	.826	5.49	5.20
2016	Oak	AL	14	14	0	72.0	332	83	54	52	9	2	1	4	33	0	71	5	2	9	.182	0-0	0	92	.819	5.56	6.50
2017	Oak	AL	7	7	0	43.0	169	36	16	15	6	1	2	0	9	0	29	2	3	2	.600	0-0	0	92	.650	2.78	3.14
2018	Oak	AL	22	17	0	115.2	476	103	58	52	18	4	2	3	26	0	72	6	7	6	.538	0-0	0	92	.699	3.22	4.05
2019	Oak	AL	13	9	2	59.2	260	59	32	32	7	0	1	0	27	0	42	1	5	2	.714	1-1	0	91	.753	4.34	4.83
2020	Oak	AL	4	1	2	12.1	58	14	5	5	2	0	1	1	7	0	10	0	0	1	.000	0-0	0	90	.869	6.36	3.65
2022	KC	AL	5	1	1	7.0	32	10	5	4	1	0	1	0	1	0	8	1	0	1	.000	1-1	0	93	.844	5.70	5.14
	6 ML YEARS		65	49	5	309.2	1327	305	170	160	43	7	8	8	103	0	232	15	17	21	.447	2-2	0	92	.744	4.07	4.65

Oscar Mercado

Bats: R **Throws:** R **Pos:** RF-36;LF-12;PR-6;CF-5;PH-5   **Ht:** 6'2" **Wt:** 197 **Born:** 12/16/1994 **Age:** 28

Year	Team	Lg	G	AB	H	2B	3B	HR	(Hm	Rd)	TB	R	RBI	RC	TBB	IBB	SO	HBP	SH	SF	SB	CS	GDP	Avg	OBP	Slg	OPS
2022	Clmbs	AAA	49	167	47	7	3	5	(-	-)	75	25	31	27	18	0	28	4	0	1	9	4	3	.281	.363	.449	.812
2019	Cle	AL	115	438	118	25	3	15	(11	4)	194	70	54	69	28	0	84	5	7	4	15	4	9	.269	.318	.443	.761
2020	Cle	AL	36	86	11	1	0	1	(0	1)	15	6	6	1	5	0	27	0	1	1	3	0	0	.128	.174	.174	.348
2021	Cle	AL	72	214	48	11	1	6	(4	2)	79	27	19	29	21	0	42	2	1	0	7	1	1	.224	.300	.369	.669
2022	2 Tms		55	121	25	6	1	4	(0	4)	45	17	16	10	5	0	29	1	0	1	2	2	4	.207	.242	.372	.614
22	Cle	AL	54	120	25	6	1	4	(0	4)	45	17	16	10	5	0	28	1	0	1	2	2	4	.208	.244	.375	.619
22	Phi	NL	1	1	0	0	0	0	(0	0)	0	0	0	0	0	0	1	0	0	0	0	0	0	.000	.000	.000	.000
	Postseason		1	1	0	0	0	0	(0	0)	0	0	0	0	0	0	1	0	0	0	0	0	0	.000	.000	.000	.000
	4 ML YEARS		278	859	202	43	5	26	(15	11)	333	120	95	109	59	0	182	8	9	6	27	7	14	.235	.289	.388	.676

Yermin Mercedes

Bats: R **Throws:** R **Pos:** DH-15;PH-9;LF-8;1B-4;C-1   **Ht:** 5'11" **Wt:** 245 **Born:** 2/14/1993 **Age:** 30

Year	Team	Lg	G	AB	H	2B	3B	HR	(Hm	Rd)	TB	R	RBI	RC	TBB	IBB	SO	HBP	SH	SF	SB	CS	GDP	Avg	OBP	Slg	OPS
2022	Charltt	AAA	25	87	20	5	0	4	(-	-)	37	14	13	16	20	0	24	1	0	1	5	1	1	.230	.376	.425	.801
2022	Scrmto	AAA	37	142	38	5	0	8	(-	-)	67	17	19	23	13	1	34	1	0	2	2	0	5	.268	.329	.472	.801
2020	CWS	AL	1	1	0	0	0	0	(0	0)	0	0	0	0	0	0	0	0	0	0	0	0	0	.000	.000	.000	.000
2021	CWS	AL	68	240	65	9	1	7	(4	3)	97	26	37	29	20	1	46	1	0	1	0	1	7	.271	.328	.404	.732
2022	SF	NL	31	73	17	5	0	1	(1	0)	25	9	8	7	9	0	17	1	0	0	0	0	1	.233	.325	.342	.668
	3 ML YEARS		100	314	82	14	1	8	(5	3)	122	35	45	36	29	1	63	2	0	1	0	1	8	.261	.327	.389	.715

Whit Merrifield

Bats: R Throws: R Pos: 2B-83;RF-40;CF-18;LF-5;DH-5;PR-5;PH-3;1B-2   Ht: 6'1" Wt: 195 Born: 1/24/1989 Age: 34

																			RUNNING			AVERAGES			
Year Team	Lg	G	AB	H	2B	3B	HR	(Hm | Rd)	TB	R	RBI	RC	TBB	IBB	SO	HBP	SH	SF	SB	CS	GDP	Avg	OBP	Slg	OPS
2016 KC	AL	81	311	88	22	3	2	(2 | 0)	122	44	29	38	19	1	72	0	1	1	8	3	1	.283	.323	.392	.716
2017 KC	AL	145	587	169	32	6	19	(13 | 6)	270	80	78	88	29	0	88	6	1	7	34	8	13	.288	.324	.460	.784
2018 KC	AL	158	632	192	43	3	12	(5 | 7)	277	88	60	103	61	2	114	6	2	6	45	10	12	.304	.367	.438	.806
2019 KC	AL	162	681	206	41	10	16	(4 | 12)	315	105	74	114	45	5	126	5	0	4	20	10	8	.302	.348	.463	.811
2020 KC	AL	60	248	70	12	0	9	(3 | 6)	109	38	30	41	12	0	33	4	0	1	12	3	3	.282	.325	.440	.764
2021 KC	AL	162	664	184	42	3	10	(5 | 5)	262	97	74	92	40	1	103	4	0	12	40	4	12	.277	.317	.395	.711
2022 2 Tms	AL	139	504	126	28	1	11	(2 | 9)	189	70	58	53	38	0	85	0	0	8	16	5	11	.250	.298	.375	.673
22 KC	AL	95	383	92	23	1	6	(1 | 5)	135	51	42	39	30	0	61	0	0	7	15	3	8	.240	.290	.352	.643
22 Tor	AL	44	121	34	5	0	5	(1 | 4)	54	19	16	14	8	0	24	0	0	1	1	2	3	.281	.323	.446	.769
7 ML YEARS		907	3627	1035	220	26	79	(34 | 45)	1544	522	403	529	244	9	621	25	4	39	175	43	60	.285	.331	.426	.757

Julian Merryweather

Pitches: R Bats: R Pos: RP-25; SP-1   Ht: 6'4" Wt: 215 Born: 10/14/1991 Age: 31

		HOW MUCH PITCHED					WHAT HE GAVE UP											THE RESULTS							
Year Team	Lg	G	GS	GF	IP	BFP	H	R	ER	HR	SH	SF	HB	TBB	IBB	SO	WP	W	L	Pct	Sv-Op	Hld	Vel	OPS	ERC	ERA
2022 Buffalo	AAA	13	0	2	14.1	55	5	1	0	0	0	0	0	6	0	18	0	2	0	1.000	0- -	-	-	.343	0.84	0.00
2020 Tor	AL	8	3	0	13.0	55	11	6	6	0	0	0	0	6	0	15	0	0	0	-	0-0	1	97	.595	2.79	4.15
2021 Tor	AL	13	1	4	13.0	55	13	7	7	4	0	1	1	4	0	12	2	0	1	.000	2-2	1	97	.837	5.58	4.85
2022 Tor	AL	26	1	6	26.2	119	31	20	20	4	2	2	2	7	1	23	1	0	3	.000	0-1	1	97	.832	4.98	6.75
3 ML YEARS		47	5	10	52.2	229	55	33	33	8	2	3	3	17	1	50	3	0	4	.000	2-3	3	97	.776	4.57	5.64

Max Meyer

Pitches: R Bats: L Pos: SP-2   Ht: 6'0" Wt: 196 Born: 3/12/1999 Age: 24

		HOW MUCH PITCHED					WHAT HE GAVE UP											THE RESULTS							
Year Team	Lg	G	GS	GF	IP	BFP	H	R	ER	HR	SH	SF	HB	TBB	IBB	SO	WP	W	L	Pct	Sv-Op	Hld	Vel	OPS	ERC	ERA
2022 Jaxnvl	AAA	12	12	0	58.0	229	39	25	24	5	0	0	2	19	0	65	4	3	4	.429	0- -	-	-	.565	2.19	3.72
2022 Mia	NL	2	2	0	6.0	26	7	5	5	2	0	0	0	2	0	6	0	0	1	.000	0-0	0	95	1.013	6.62	7.50

Jake Meyers

Bats: R Throws: L Pos: CF-51;PH-2;PR-1   Ht: 6'0" Wt: 200 Born: 6/18/1996 Age: 27

																			RUNNING			AVERAGES			
Year Team	Lg	G	AB	H	2B	3B	HR	(Hm	Rd)	TB	R	RBI	RC	TBB	IBB	SO	HBP	SH	SF	SB	CS	GDP	Avg	OBP	Slg	OPS
2022 SgrLnd	AAA	38	144	44	6	1	7	(-	-)	73	26	18	30	25	1	30	0	0	1	2	0	5	.306	.406	.507	.913
2021 Hou	AL	49	146	38	6	0	6	(3	3)	64	22	28	22	10	0	50	4	2	1	3	0	0	.260	.323	.438	.761
2022 Hou	AL	52	150	34	6	2	1	(1	0)	47	13	15	12	7	0	54	2	0	1	2	1	1	.227	.269	.313	.582
Postseason		4	8	3	0	0	0	(0	0)	3	1	2	3	0	0	2	0	0	0	1	0	0	.375	.375	.375	.750
2 ML YEARS		101	296	72	14	2	7	(4	3)	111	35	43	34	17	0	104	6	2	2	5	1	1	.243	.296	.375	.671

Keynan Middleton

Pitches: R Bats: R Pos: RP-18   Ht: 6'3" Wt: 215 Born: 9/12/1993 Age: 29

		HOW MUCH PITCHED					WHAT HE GAVE UP											THE RESULTS							
Year Team	Lg	G	GS	GF	IP	BFP	H	R	ER	HR	SH	SF	HB	TBB	IBB	SO	WP	W	L	Pct	Sv-Op	Hld	Vel	OPS	ERC	ERA
2022 Reno	AAA	17	0	4	17.0	66	8	4	4	1	0	2	0	7	0	24	1	2	0	1.000	1- -	-	-	.455	1.38	2.12
2017 LAA	AL	64	0	17	58.1	246	60	25	25	11	0	2	0	18	2	63	2	6	1	.857	3-5	10	97	.791	4.47	3.86
2018 LAA	AL	16	0	9	17.2	71	14	4	4	1	0	1	1	9	1	16	1	0	0	-	6-7	2	96	.688	3.42	2.04
2019 LAA	AL	11	0	0	7.2	33	4	1	1	0	0	0	0	7	0	6	1	0	0	-	0-0	0	94	.572	2.72	1.17
2020 LAA	AL	13	0	4	12.0	53	12	8	7	2	0	3	0	6	0	11	1	0	1	.000	0-0	2	97	.817	4.95	5.25
2021 Sea	AL	32	1	10	31.0	140	30	20	17	2	0	0	2	19	1	24	0	1	2	.333	4-4	3	95	.734	4.69	4.94
2022 Ari	NL	18	0	2	17.0	69	16	13	10	5	1	0	1	3	0	15	1	1	2	.333	0-2	1	95	.841	4.40	5.29
6 ML YEARS		154	1	42	143.2	612	136	71	64	21	1	6	4	62	4	135	6	8	6	.571	13-18	18	96	.765	4.36	4.01

Miles Mikolas

Pitches: R Bats: R Pos: SP-32; RP-1   MIKE-uh-liss   Ht: 6'4" Wt: 230 Born: 8/23/1988 Age: 34

		HOW MUCH PITCHED					WHAT HE GAVE UP											THE RESULTS							
Year Team	Lg	G	GS	GF	IP	BFP	H	R	ER	HR	SH	SF	HB	TBB	IBB	SO	WP	W	L	Pct	Sv-Op	Hld	Vel	OPS	ERC	ERA
2012 SD	NL	25	0	9	32.1	144	32	15	13	4	2	0	2	15	0	23	2	2	1	.667	0-1	1	93	.761	4.65	3.62
2013 SD	NL	2	0	1	1.2	7	0	0	0	0	0	0	1	1	0	1	0	0	0	-	0-0	0	94	.286	1.30	0.00
2014 Tex	AL	10	10	0	57.1	255	64	43	41	8	1	2	4	18	2	38	0	2	5	.286	0-0	0	93	.769	4.85	6.44
2018 StL	NL	32	32	0	200.2	808	186	70	63	16	8	4	7	29	4	146	2	18	4	.818	0-0	0	94	.628	2.70	2.83
2019 StL	NL	32	32	0	184.0	764	193	90	85	27	3	7	12	32	1	144	5	9	14	.391	0-0	0	94	.761	4.08	4.16
2021 StL	NL	9	9	0	44.2	186	43	24	21	6	2	1	2	11	0	31	1	2	3	.400	0-0	0	93	.710	3.68	4.23
2022 StL	NL	33	32	0	202.1	805	170	81	74	25	0	8	6	39	0	153	1	12	13	.480	0-0	0	93	.640	2.72	3.29
Postseason		3	2	1	12.0	50	10	2	2	0	0	0	4	1	0	9	0	1	1	.500	0-0	0	94	.606	2.14	1.50
7 ML YEARS		143	115	10	723.0	2969	688	323	297	86	16	22	34	145	7	536	11	45	40	.529	0-1	1	93	.688	3.35	3.70

Wade Miley

Pitches: L **Bats:** L **Pos:** SP-8; RP-1   MY-lee   **Ht:** 6'2" **Wt:** 220 **Born:** 11/13/1986 **Age:** 36

			HOW MUCH PITCHED					WHAT HE GAVE UP												THE RESULTS						
Year	Team	Lg	G	GS	GF	IP	BFP	H	R	ER	HR	SH	SF	HB	TBB	IBB	SO	WP	W	L	Pct	Sv-Op	Hld	Vel	OPS	ERC	ERA
2011	Ari	NL	8	7	0	40.0	180	48	20	20	6	3	1	0	18	0	25	1	4	2	.667	0-0	0	90	.873	5.90	4.50
2012	Ari	NL	32	29	0	194.2	807	193	79	72	14	8	3	2	37	0	144	6	16	11	.593	0-0	0	91	.685	3.05	3.33
2013	Ari	NL	33	33	0	202.2	847	201	88	80	21	6	2	4	66	4	147	13	10	10	.500	0-0	0	91	.727	3.88	3.55
2014	Ari	NL	33	33	0	201.1	866	207	103	97	23	8	9	4	75	3	183	9	8	12	.400	0-0	0	91	.746	4.31	4.34
2015	Bos	AL	32	32	0	193.2	831	201	98	96	17	3	2	4	64	0	147	10	11	11	.500	0-0	0	91	.740	4.01	4.46
2016	2 Tms	AL	30	30	0	166.0	711	187	100	99	25	2	5	6	49	1	137	8	7	13	.409	0-0	0	90	.808	4.98	5.37
2017	Bal	AL	32	32	0	157.1	728	179	104	98	25	1	6	4	93	1	142	1	8	15	.348	0-0	0	91	.841	6.27	5.61
2018	Mil	NL	16	16	0	80.2	338	71	28	23	3	5	1	5	27	1	50	1	5	2	.714	0-0	0	91	.636	2.98	2.57
2019	Hou	AL	33	33	0	167.1	720	164	83	74	23	2	5	5	61	0	140	4	14	6	.700	0-0	0	90	.726	4.19	3.98
2020	Cin	NL	6	4	2	14.1	67	15	10	9	1	0	0	2	9	0	12	0	0	3	.000	0-0	0	90	.799	5.62	5.65
2021	Cin	NL	28	28	0	163.0	690	166	64	61	17	8	2	3	50	0	125	2	12	7	.632	0-0	0	90	.729	3.94	3.37
2022	ChC	NL	9	8	0	37.0	159	31	20	13	3	0	1	2	14	0	28	1	2	2	.500	0-0	0	89	.627	3.10	3.16
16	Sea	AL	19	19	0	112.0	469	117	62	62	18	2	3	3	34	1	82	5	7	8	.467	0-0	0	90	.786	4.58	4.98
16	Bal	AL	11	11	0	54.0	242	70	38	37	7	0	2	3	15	0	55	3	2	5	.286	0-0	0	90	.850	5.83	6.17
	Postseason		5	4	0	17.1	72	14	5	4	2	0	0	0	5	0	10	0	0	0	-	0-0	0	91	.607	2.64	2.08
	12 ML YEARS		292	285	2	1618.0	6944	1663	797	742	178	46	37	41	563	10	1280	56	99	94	.513	0-0	0	91	.744	4.21	4.13

Brad Miller

Bats: L **Throws:** R **Pos:** LF-28;3B-27;DH-22;PH-20;RF-3;PR-1   **Ht:** 6'2" **Wt:** 195 **Born:** 10/18/1989 **Age:** 33

			BATTING															RUNNING			AVERAGES			
Year	Team	Lg	G	AB	H	2B	3B	HR	(Hm | Rd)	TB	R	RBI	RC	TBB	IBB	SO	HBP	SH	SF	SB	CS	GDP	Avg	OBP	Slg	OPS
2013	Sea	AL	76	306	81	11	6	8	(3 | 5)	128	41	36	41	24	0	52	1	2	2	5	3	2	.265	.318	.418	.737
2014	Sea	AL	123	367	81	15	4	10	(4 | 6)	134	47	36	41	34	2	95	2	3	3	4	2	2	.221	.288	.365	.653
2015	Sea	AL	144	438	113	22	4	11	(6 | 5)	176	44	46	58	47	0	101	2	4	6	13	4	7	.258	.329	.402	.730
2016	TB	AL	152	548	133	29	6	30	(22 | 8)	264	73	81	74	47	0	149	3	0	3	6	4	5	.243	.304	.482	.786
2017	TB	AL	110	338	68	13	3	9	(6 | 3)	114	43	40	37	63	4	110	2	1	1	5	3	5	.201	.327	.337	.664
2018	2 Tms		75	230	57	13	2	7	(5 | 2)	95	21	29	27	22	1	82	0	0	2	0	0	4	.248	.311	.413	.724
2019	2 Tms		79	154	40	6	1	13	(6 | 7)	87	26	25	26	15	0	45	1	0	0	2	0	2	.260	.329	.565	.894
2020	StL	NL	48	142	33	8	1	7	(1 | 6)	64	21	25	25	25	1	46	3	0	1	1	0	2	.232	.357	.451	.807
2021	Phi	NL	140	331	75	9	3	20	(10 | 10)	150	53	49	52	45	2	112	1	0	0	3	0	7	.227	.321	.453	.774
2022	Tex	AL	81	222	47	3	0	7	(3 | 4)	71	20	32	25	18	0	70	0	1	4	2	3	3	.212	.270	.320	.590
18	TB	AL	48	156	40	10	1	5	(3 | 2)	67	16	21	18	16	0	51	0	0	2	0	0	2	.256	.322	.429	.751
18	Mil	NL	27	74	17	3	1	2	(2 | 0)	28	5	8	9	6	1	31	0	0	0	0	0	2	.230	.288	.378	.666
19	Cle	AL	13	36	9	3	0	1	(0 | 1)	15	4	4	7	4	0	10	0	0	0	1	0	0	.250	.325	.417	.742
19	Phi	NL	66	118	31	3	1	12	(6 | 6)	72	22	21	19	11	0	35	1	0	0	1	0	2	.263	.331	.610	.941
	Postseason		1	1	0	0	0	0	(0 | 0)	0	0	0	0	0	0	0	0	0	0	0	0	0	.000	.000	.000	.000
	10 ML YEARS		1028	3076	728	129	30	122	(66 | 56)	1283	389	399	406	340	10	862	15	9	22	43	18	39	.237	.314	.417	.731

Owen Miller

Bats: R **Throws:** R **Pos:** 1B-80;2B-25;DH-22;PH-12;PR-6;3B-4   **Ht:** 6'0" **Wt:** 185 **Born:** 11/15/1996 **Age:** 26

			BATTING															RUNNING			AVERAGES			
Year	Team	Lg	G	AB	H	2B	3B	HR	(Hm | Rd)	TB	R	RBI	RC	TBB	IBB	SO	HBP	SH	SF	SB	CS	GDP	Avg	OBP	Slg	OPS
2021	Cle	AL	60	191	39	8	0	4	(2 | 2)	59	17	18	8	9	0	54	1	0	1	2	0	7	.204	.243	.309	.551
2022	Cle	AL	130	424	103	26	1	6	(4 | 2)	149	53	51	47	32	1	93	7	0	9	2	0	8	.243	.301	.351	.652
	2 ML YEARS		190	615	142	34	1	10	(6 | 4)	208	70	69	55	41	1	147	8	0	10	4	0	15	.231	.283	.338	.622

Shelby Miller

Pitches: R **Bats:** R **Pos:** RP-4   **Ht:** 6'3" **Wt:** 225 **Born:** 10/10/1990 **Age:** 32

			HOW MUCH PITCHED					WHAT HE GAVE UP												THE RESULTS						
Year	Team	Lg	G	GS	GF	IP	BFP	H	R	ER	HR	SH	SF	HB	TBB	IBB	SO	WP	W	L	Pct	Sv-Op	Hld	Vel	OPS	ERC	ERA
2022	S-WB	AAA	16	0	9	21.0	85	13	6	4	1	1	0	1	6	0	25	1	2	2	.500	4- -	-	-	.491	1.58	1.71
2022	Scrmto	AAA	27	1	14	32.1	136	25	17	13	3	1	1	1	15	0	44	2	0	2	.000	8- -	-	-	.668	3.15	3.62
2012	StL	NL	6	1	1	13.2	54	9	2	2	0	0	1	1	4	0	16	0	1	0	1.000	0-0	1	93	.463	1.65	1.32
2013	StL	NL	31	31	0	173.1	722	152	65	59	20	7	3	5	57	0	169	2	15	9	.625	0-0	0	94	.670	3.34	3.06
2014	StL	NL	32	31	0	183.0	764	160	78	76	22	7	4	2	73	4	127	4	10	9	.526	0-0	0	93	.698	3.56	3.74
2015	Atl	NL	33	33	0	205.1	860	183	82	69	13	8	4	6	73	8	171	5	6	17	.261	0-0	0	93	.663	3.12	3.02
2016	Ari	NL	20	20	0	101.0	460	127	72	69	14	3	3	2	42	3	70	3	3	12	.200	0-0	0	93	.867	6.03	6.15
2017	Ari	NL	4	4	0	22.0	99	22	10	10	1	0	0	0	12	1	20	1	2	2	.500	0-0	0	94	.668	3.53	4.09
2018	Ari	NL	5	4	0	16.0	79	24	21	19	5	0	1	0	8	0	19	1	0	4	.000	0-0	1	94	1.048	9.35	10.69
2019	Tex	AL	19	8	4	44.0	220	58	46	42	8	0	4	3	29	1	30	1	1	3	.250	0-1	1	94	.908	7.95	8.59
2021	2 Tms	NL	13	0	4	12.2	62	16	13	13	3	0	1	1	11	0	8	0	0	1	.000	0-0	1	94	1.023	9.68	9.24
2022	SF	NL	4	0	0	7.0	30	6	5	5	0	0	0	0	3	1	14	0	0	1	.000	0-0	1	94	.633	2.46	6.43
21	ChC	NL	3	0	1	2.0	18	7	7	7	0	0	1	0	5	0	1	0	0	0	-	0-0	0	94	1.417	31.30	31.50
21	Pit	NL	10	0	3	10.2	44	9	6	6	3	0	0	1	6	0	7	0	0	1	.000	0-0	1	94	.877	5.98	5.06
	Postseason		5	2	0	13.2	61	16	8	8	1	1	1	1	6	0	12	0	0	0	-	0-0	0	94	.768	5.46	5.27
	10 ML YEARS		167	132	9	778.0	3350	755	394	364	86	25	20	20	312	18	644	17	38	58	.396	0-1	5	94	.728	4.05	4.21

Tyson Miller

Pitches: R Bats: R Pos: SP-2; RP-2 **Ht:** 6'4" **Wt:** 225 **Born:** 7/29/1995 **Age:** 27

Year	Team	Lg	G	GS	GF	IP	BFP	H	R	ER	HR	SH	SF	HB	TBB	IBB	SO	WP	W	L	Pct	Sv-Op	Hld	Vel	OPS	ERC	ERA
2022	RdRck	AAA	29	16	2	89.2	398	91	51	45	14	0	1	6	40	0	114	2	4	7	.364	1--	-	-	.774	5.02	4.52
2020	ChC	NL	2	1	1	5.0	20	2	3	3	1	0	1	0	3	0	0	0	0	0	-	0-0	0	93	.625	2.30	5.40
2022	Tex	AL	4	2	0	10.2	56	16	14	13	1	0	0	2	8	0	8	0	1	2	.333	0-0	0	91	.943	9.59	10.97
	2 ML YEARS		6	3	1	15.2	76	18	17	16	2	0	1	2	11	0	8	0	1	2	.333	0-0	0	92	.860	7.00	9.19

Alec Mills

Pitches: R Bats: R Pos: RP-5; SP-2 **Ht:** 6'4" **Wt:** 205 **Born:** 11/30/1991 **Age:** 31

Year	Team	Lg	G	GS	GF	IP	BFP	H	R	ER	HR	SH	SF	HB	TBB	IBB	SO	WP	W	L	Pct	Sv-Op	Hld	Vel	OPS	ERC	ERA
2016	KC	AL	3	0	2	3.1	19	3	5	5	0	0	0	1	5	0	4	0	0	0	-	0-0	0	92	.858	8.02	13.50
2018	ChC	NL	7	2	1	18.0	71	11	8	8	1	0	0	0	7	0	23	1	0	1	.000	0-0	0	91	.550	1.80	4.00
2019	ChC	NL	9	4	3	36.0	152	31	11	11	5	0	0	7	11	0	42	0	1	0	1.000	1-1	0	90	.718	4.03	2.75
2020	ChC	NL	11	11	0	62.1	252	53	31	31	13	0	1	2	19	0	46	0	5	5	.500	0-0	0	89	.741	3.80	4.48
2021	ChC	NL	32	20	4	119.0	517	137	75	67	16	4	2	7	34	2	87	4	6	7	.462	1-1	0	89	.798	5.01	5.07
2022	ChC	NL	7	2	2	17.2	84	28	20	19	7	0	1	3	3	1	11	0	0	1	.000	0-0	0	89	1.171	9.99	9.68
	6 ML YEARS		69	39	12	256.1	1095	263	150	141	42	4	4	20	79	3	213	5	12	14	.462	2-2	0	89	.788	4.66	4.95

Wyatt Mills

Pitches: R Bats: R Pos: RP-27 **Ht:** 6'4" **Wt:** 214 **Born:** 1/25/1995 **Age:** 28

Year	Team	Lg	G	GS	GF	IP	BFP	H	R	ER	HR	SH	SF	HB	TBB	IBB	SO	WP	W	L	Pct	Sv-Op	Hld	Vel	OPS	ERC	ERA
2022	Tacom	AAA	16	0	2	19.2	76	12	4	4	1	0	0	0	7	0	17	0	1	0	1.000	0--	-	-	.496	1.70	1.83
2022	Omha	AAA	13	0	8	14.0	58	7	5	4	2	0	0	2	9	2	23	1	2	1	.667	1--	-	-	.693	2.98	2.57
2021	Sea	AL	11	0	4	12.2	64	19	14	14	1	0	2	1	7	0	11	1	0	0	-	0-0	0	93	.940	7.88	9.95
2022	2 Tms	AL	27	0	3	29.1	128	26	15	15	1	1	2	5	13	2	26	3	0	1	.000	0-0	4	92	.702	3.71	4.60
22	Sea	AL	8	0	1	8.2	34	5	4	4	0	0	1	2	3	0	6	1	0	0	-	0-0	0	92	.580	2.00	4.15
22	KC	AL	19	0	2	20.2	94	21	11	11	1	1	1	3	10	2	20	2	0	1	.000	0-0	4	91	.745	4.49	4.79
	2 ML YEARS		38	0	7	42.0	192	45	29	29	2	1	4	6	20	2	37	4	0	1	.000	0-0	4	92	.782	4.88	6.21

Hoby Milner

Pitches: L Bats: L Pos: RP-67 **Ht:** 6'3" **Wt:** 175 **Born:** 1/13/1991 **Age:** 32

Year	Team	Lg	G	GS	GF	IP	BFP	H	R	ER	HR	SH	SF	HB	TBB	IBB	SO	WP	W	L	Pct	Sv-Op	Hld	Vel	OPS	ERC	ERA
2017	Phi	NL	37	0	5	31.1	139	30	7	7	2	2	1	4	16	3	22	0	0	0	-	0-1	7	89	.736	4.39	2.01
2018	2 Tms		14	0	3	7.1	38	9	8	6	3	0	0	1	5	1	8	0	0	0	-	0-0	1	89	.988	9.22	7.36
2019	TB	AL	4	0	1	3.2	17	4	3	3	0	0	0	1	1	0	3	0	0	0	-	0-0	1	88	.820	4.28	7.36
2020	LAA	AL	19	0	4	13.1	59	13	12	12	5	0	0	1	6	0	13	0	0	0	-	0-0	1	88	.897	6.45	8.10
2021	Mil	NL	19	0	10	21.2	99	30	15	13	8	1	0	2	3	0	30	0	0	0	-	0-0	1	89	.970	7.64	5.40
2022	Mil	NL	67	0	9	64.2	272	61	29	27	5	3	3	7	15	0	64	1	3	3	.500	0-1	9	89	.686	3.38	3.76
18	Phi	NL	10	0	2	4.2	25	6	4	4	1	0	0	1	3	1	4	0	0	0	-	0-0	0	89	.829	7.79	7.71
18	TB	AL	4	0	1	2.2	13	3	4	2	2	0	0	0	2	0	4	0	0	0	-	0-0	1	89	1.294	11.59	6.75
	6 ML YEARS		160	0	32	142.0	624	147	74	68	23	6	4	16	46	4	140	1	3	3	.500	0-2	20	89	.786	4.81	4.31

Tommy Milone

Pitches: L Bats: L Pos: RP-7

mah-LONE

Ht: 6'0" **Wt:** 215 **Born:** 2/16/1987 **Age:** 36

Year	Team	Lg	G	GS	GF	IP	BFP	H	R	ER	HR	SH	SF	HB	TBB	IBB	SO	WP	W	L	Pct	Sv-Op	Hld	Vel	OPS	ERC	ERA
2022	Tacom	AAA	11	10	0	40.1	156	30	12	12	3	0	1	0	11	0	38	0	3	1	.750	0--	-	-	.582	2.20	2.68
2011	Was	NL	5	5	0	26.0	110	28	11	11	2	3	2	2	4	2	15	0	1	0	1.000	0-0	0	88	.742	3.55	3.81
2012	Oak	AL	31	31	0	190.0	791	207	90	79	24	3	3	4	36	2	137	2	13	10	.565	0-0	0	88	.738	4.04	3.74
2013	Oak	AL	28	26	0	156.1	667	160	83	72	25	0	6	2	39	2	126	1	12	9	.571	0-0	0	87	.738	3.98	4.14
2014	2 Tms	AL	22	21	1	118.0	519	128	63	55	16	1	2	5	37	2	75	0	6	4	.600	0-0	0	87	.763	4.55	4.19
2015	Min	AL	24	23	1	128.2	543	128	64	56	17	6	7	1	36	1	91	3	9	5	.643	1-1	0	88	.731	3.79	3.92
2016	Min	AL	19	12	3	69.1	311	84	53	44	15	4	3	1	22	3	49	3	3	5	.375	0-0	1	88	.857	5.77	5.71
2017	2 Tms	NL	17	8	2	48.1	221	65	43	41	15	2	0	0	14	3	38	0	1	3	.250	1-1	0	88	.970	7.12	7.63
2018	Was	NL	5	4	1	26.1	118	37	17	17	7	2	2	1	1	0	23	0	1	1	.500	0-0	0	88	.917	6.17	5.81
2019	Sea	AL	23	6	0	111.2	453	102	61	59	24	0	5	2	23	2	94	1	4	10	.286	0-0	0	87	.765	3.63	4.76
2020	2 Tms		9	9	0	39.0	181	55	34	29	9	1	2	2	6	0	40	1	1	4	.200	0-0	0	86	.950	6.50	6.69
2021	Tor	AL	6	1	1	14.0	65	20	10	10	3	0	0	2	3	0	17	0	1	0	1.000	1-1	0	88	.934	6.57	6.43
2022	Sea	AL	7	0	3	16.2	69	14	10	10	4	0	2	1	6	0	5	0	1	1	.500	0-0	0	87	.804	4.26	5.40
14	Oak	AL	16	16	0	96.1	405	91	42	38	12	1	2	4	26	2	61	0	6	3	.667	0-0	0	87	.705	3.53	3.55
14	Min	AL	6	5	1	21.2	114	37	21	17	4	0	0	1	11	0	14	0	0	1	.000	0-0	0	87	.969	9.76	7.06
17	Mil	NL	6	3	1	21.0	93	29	15	15	6	0	0	0	2	0	16	0	1	0	1.000	1-1	0	88	.905	6.32	6.43
17	NYM	NL	11	5	1	27.1	128	36	28	26	9	2	0	0	12	3	22	0	0	3	.000	0-0	0	87	1.021	7.74	8.56
20	Bal	AL	6	6	0	29.1	129	33	18	13	5	1	1	2	4	0	31	1	1	4	.200	0-0	0	86	.776	4.30	3.99
20	Atl	NL	3	3	0	9.2	52	22	16	16	4	0	1	0	2	0	9	0	0	0	-	0-0	0	86	1.380	14.68	14.90
	Postseason		1	1	0	6.0	25	5	1	1	0	0	0	1	1	0	6	1	0	0	-	0-0	0	88	.584	2.26	1.50
	12 ML YEARS		196	146	12	944.1	4048	1028	539	483	161	22	34	21	227	17	710	11	53	52	.505	3-3	1	87	.784	4.46	4.60

Juan Minaya

Pitches: R Bats: R Pos: RP-6   Ht: 6'4" Wt: 210 Born: 9/18/1990 Age: 32

Year	Team	Lg	G	GS	GF	IP	BFP	H	R	ER	HR	SH	SF	HB	TBB	IBB	SO	WP	W	L	Pct	Sv-Op	Hld	Vel	OPS	ERC	ERA
2022	StPaul	AAA	29	1	12	40.0	187	41	33	31	6	1	1	10	20		36	3	1	5	.167	4--	-	-	.814	6.04	6.98
2022	Roch	AAA	6	0	1	8.2	36	5	4	3	2	1	0	0	6	1	6	1	0	2	.000	0--	-	-	.694	3.65	3.12
2016	CWS	AL	11	0	3	10.1	47	10	6	5	0	0	0	2	5	0	6	0	1	0	1.000	0-0	0	94	.712	4.19	4.35
2017	CWS	AL	40	0	20	43.2	184	38	22	22	7	0	1	4	20	0	51	2	3	2	.600	9-10	2	94	.765	4.51	4.53
2018	CWS	AL	52	0	9	46.2	209	39	19	17	3	0	0	3	29	3	58	9	2	2	.500	1-4	8	95	.673	3.84	3.28
2019	CWS	AL	22	0	8	27.2	126	31	13	12	4	0	0	2	12	0	27	3	0	0	-	0-0	0	93	.857	5.51	3.90
2021	Min	AL	29	0	9	40.0	167	27	12	11	4	1	1	2	20	0	43	3	2	1	.667	0-0	7	94	.624	2.89	2.48
2022	Min	AL	6	0	2	9.2	45	8	6	6	0	0	0	3	5	0	11	2	1	0	1.000	0-0	0	94	.599	3.88	5.59
6 ML YEARS			160	0	51	178.0	778	153	78	73	18	1	2	16	91	3	196	19	9	5	.643	10-14	17	94	.713	4.05	3.69

Mike Minor

Pitches: L Bats: R Pos: SP-19   Ht: 6'4" Wt: 210 Born: 12/26/1987 Age: 35

Year	Team	Lg	G	GS	GF	IP	BFP	H	R	ER	HR	SH	SF	HB	TBB	IBB	SO	WP	W	L	Pct	Sv-Op	Hld	Vel	OPS	ERC	ERA
2010	Atl	NL	9	8	1	40.2	185	53	28	27	6	1	3	1	11	0	43	0	3	2	.600	0-0	0	91	.880	5.71	5.98
2011	Atl	NL	15	15	0	82.2	361	93	39	38	7	3	1	1	30	5	77	2	5	3	.625	0-0	0	91	.785	4.51	4.14
2012	Atl	NL	30	30	0	179.1	728	151	88	82	26	8	8	5	56	7	145	3	11	10	.524	0-0	0	90	.702	3.28	4.12
2013	Atl	NL	32	32	0	204.2	820	177	79	73	22	5	6	1	46	2	181	5	13	9	.591	0-0	0	90	.657	2.76	3.21
2014	Atl	NL	25	25	0	145.1	637	165	77	77	21	6	2	6	44	2	120	5	6	12	.333	0-0	0	90	.798	4.93	4.77
2017	KC	AL	65	0	13	77.2	307	57	23	22	5	3	1	1	22	3	88	5	6	6	.500	6-9	17	94	.585	2.07	2.55
2018	KC	AL	28	28	0	157.0	640	138	76	73	25	1	6	8	38	1	132	3	12	8	.600	0-0	0	93	.733	3.40	4.18
2019	Tex	AL	32	32	0	208.1	863	190	86	83	30	3	6	7	68	1	200	2	14	10	.583	0-0	0	91	.704	3.78	3.59
2020	2 Tms	AL	12	11	0	56.2	239	50	36	35	11	0	1	1	20	0	62	0	1	6	.143	0-0	0	91	.712	3.90	5.56
2021	KC	AL	28	28	0	158.2	669	156	92	89	26	2	2	5	41	0	149	4	8	12	.400	0-0	0	91	.750	3.95	5.05
2022	Cin	NL	19	19	0	98.0	455	120	72	66	24	0	3	7	40	4	76	2	4	12	.250	0-0	0	90	.903	6.75	6.06
20	Tex	AL	7	7	0	35.1	155	35	23	22	7	0	1	0	13	0	35	0	0	5	.000	0-0	0	91	.742	4.45	5.60
20	Oak	AL	5	4	0	21.1	84	15	13	13	4	0	0	1	7	0	27	0	1	1	.500	0-0	0	91	.655	3.02	5.48
Postseason			4	1	0	10.0	40	10	1	1	0	1	0	2	2	0	7	0	1	0	1.000	0-0	0	92	.702	3.66	0.90
11 ML YEARS			295	228	14	1409.0	5904	1350	696	665	203	32	39	43	416	25	1273	31	83	90	.480	6-9	17	91	.735	3.84	4.25

A.J. Minter

Pitches: L Bats: L Pos: RP-75   Ht: 6'0" Wt: 215 Born: 9/2/1993 Age: 29

Year	Team	Lg	G	GS	GF	IP	BFP	H	R	ER	HR	SH	SF	HB	TBB	IBB	SO	WP	W	L	Pct	Sv-Op	Hld	Vel	OPS	ERC	ERA
2017	Atl	NL	16	0	3	15.0	60	13	5	5	1	0	0	0	2	0	26	0	0	1	.000	0-0	5	96	.595	2.15	3.00
2018	Atl	NL	65	0	31	61.1	260	57	23	22	3	1	1	2	22	1	69	5	4	3	.571	15-17	12	97	.642	3.27	3.23
2019	Atl	NL	36	0	12	29.1	147	36	23	23	3	1	1	1	23	5	35	5	3	4	.429	5-7	5	96	.857	6.73	7.06
2020	Atl	NL	22	0	6	21.2	85	15	3	2	1	1	0	0	9	2	24	1	1	1	.500	0-0	5	96	.606	2.15	0.83
2021	Atl	NL	61	0	4	52.1	221	44	27	22	2	0	4	1	20	0	57	0	3	6	.333	0-6	23	96	.644	2.77	3.78
2022	Atl	NL	75	0	13	70.0	271	49	21	16	5	2	3	3	15	0	94	3	5	4	.556	5-9	34	97	.556	1.89	2.06
Postseason			15	1	2	20.0	80	13	6	6	2	0	0	1	6	2	31	1	2	1	.667	0-1	4	96	.565	1.94	2.70
6 ML YEARS			275	0	69	249.2	1044	214	102	90	15	5	9	7	91	8	305	14	16	19	.457	25-39	84	96	.643	2.95	3.24

Jose Miranda

Bats: R Throws: R Pos: 1B-77;3B-34;DH-21;PH-4;PR-1   Ht: 6'2" Wt: 210 Born: 6/29/1998 Age: 25

Year	Team	Lg	G	AB	H	2B	3B	HR	(Hm	Rd)	TB	R	RBI	RC	TBB	IBB	SO	HBP	SH	SF	SB	CS	GDP	Avg	OBP	Slg	OPS
2018	2 Tms	Low	131	503	133	27	1	16	(-	-)	210	61	82	41	31	0	62	12	0	6	0	3	19	.264	.319	.417	.736
2019	FtMyrs	A+	118	440	109	25	1	8	(-	-)	160	48	55	50	24	0	54	10	0	4	0	0	18	.248	.299	.364	.663
2021	Wich	AA	47	194	67	8	0	13	(-	-)	114	36	38	44	17	2	25	5	0	2	2	2	5	.345	.408	.588	.996
2021	StPaul	AAA	75	320	109	21	0	16	(-	-)	178	57	54	67	24	1	48	5	0	1	0	1	7	.341	.394	.556	.951
2022	StPaul	AAA	21	86	22	10	0	2	(-	-)	38	10	12	11	5	0	14	1	0	3	0	0	1	.256	.295	.442	.737
2022	Min	AL	125	444	119	25	0	15	(6	9)	189	45	66	56	28	0	91	10	0	1	1	1	19	.268	.325	.426	.751

Anthony Misiewicz

Pitches: L Bats: R Pos: RP-32   mih-SEV-itch   Ht: 6'1" Wt: 196 Born: 11/1/1994 Age: 28

Year	Team	Lg	G	GS	GF	IP	BFP	H	R	ER	HR	SH	SF	HB	TBB	IBB	SO	WP	W	L	Pct	Sv-Op	Hld	Vel	OPS	ERC	ERA
2022	Tacom	AAA	13	0	3	12.1	55	10	5	5	2	0	0	0	6	0	13	0	0	0	-	0--	-	-	.684	3.95	3.65
2022	Omha	AAA	8	0	3	6.2	24	3	3	3	2	0	1	0	1	0	7	0	2	1	.667	0--	-	-	.576	1.48	4.05
2020	Sea	AL	21	0	1	20.0	83	20	9	9	2	0	0	1	6	1	25	2	0	2	.000	0-1	8	94	.746	3.92	4.05
2021	Sea	AL	66	0	11	54.2	236	61	30	28	7	1	1	1	15	2	53	6	5	5	.500	0-5	19	94	.759	4.44	4.61
2022	2 Tms	AL	32	0	10	29.0	121	27	15	14	4	1	1	0	10	2	27	1	1	2	.333	0-0	4	93	.730	3.65	4.34
22	Sea	AL	17	0	3	13.2	57	14	7	7	1	0	0	0	6	0	8	0	1	0	1.000	0-0	3	92	.782	4.39	4.61
22	KC	AL	15	0	7	15.1	64	13	8	7	3	1	1	0	4	2	19	1	1	1	.500	0-0	1	93	.684	3.02	4.11
3 ML YEARS			119	0	22	103.2	440	108	54	51	13	2	2	2	31	5	105	9	6	9	.400	0-6	31	94	.749	4.12	4.43

Calvin Mitchell

Bats: L **Throws:** L **Pos:** RF-54;DH-11;PH-7;PR-1   **Ht:** 6'0" **Wt:** 205 **Born:** 3/8/1999 **Age:** 24

							BATTING												RUNNING			AVERAGES			
Year	Team	Lg	G	AB	H	2B	3B	HR	(Hm | Rd)	TB	R	RBI	RC	TBB	IBB	SO	HBP	SH	SF	SB	CS	GDP	Avg	OBP	Slg	OPS
2022 Indy	AAA	63	236	80	18	2	9	(- | -)	129	33	49	49	17	1	38	5	0	3	8	1	3	.339	.391	.547	.937
2022 Pit	NL	69	212	48	11	0	5	(4 | 1)	74	21	17	21	18	0	52	0	1	3	3	1	3	.226	.286	.349	.635

Garrett Mitchell

Bats: L **Throws:** R **Pos:** CF-28;PH-2;PR-1   **Ht:** 6'3" **Wt:** 215 **Born:** 9/4/1998 **Age:** 24

Year	Team	Lg	G	AB	H	2B	3B	HR	(Hm	Rd)	TB	R	RBI	RC	TBB	IBB	SO	HBP	SH	SF	SB	CS	GDP	Avg	OBP	Slg	OPS
2022 Biloxi	AA	44	166	46	9	2	4	(-	-)	71	29	25	24	16	0	52	4	0	1	7	1	4	.277	.353	.428	.781
2022 Nashv	AAA	20	73	25	6	0	1	(-	-)	34	15	9	15	10	0	18	2	0	0	9	0	0	.342	.435	.466	.901
2022 Mil	NL	28	61	19	3	0	2	(2	0)	28	9	9	10	6	0	28	0	1	0	8	0	0	.311	.373	.459	.832

Casey Mize

Pitches: R **Bats:** R **Pos:** SP-2   **Ht:** 6'3" **Wt:** 212 **Born:** 5/1/1997 **Age:** 26

			HOW MUCH PITCHED					WHAT HE GAVE UP										THE RESULTS						
Year	Team	Lg	G	GS	GF	IP	BFP	H	R	ER	HR	SH	SF	HB	TBB	IBB	SO	WP	W	L	Pct	Sv-Op	Hld	Vel	OPS	ERC	ERA
2020 Det	AL	7	7	0	28.1	133	29	25	22	7	0	0	5	13	0	26	2	0	3	.000	0-0	0	94	.832	6.13	6.99
2021 Det	AL	30	30	0	150.1	612	130	64	62	24	1	4	11	41	0	118	7	7	9	.438	0-0	0	94	.716	3.59	3.71
2022 Det	AL	2	2	0	10.0	45	13	6	6	1	0	0	0	2	0	4	0	0	1	.000	0-0	0	93	.868	4.87	5.40
3 ML YEARS		39	39	0	188.2	790	172	95	90	32	1	4	16	56	0	148	9	7	13	.350	0-0	0	94	.744	4.02	4.29

Yadier Molina

Bats: R **Throws:** R **Pos:** C-77;1B-1;DH-1;PH-1   YAH-dee-air   **Ht:** 5'11" **Wt:** 225 **Born:** 7/13/1982 **Age:** 40

							BATTING												RUNNING			AVERAGES			
Year	Team	Lg	G	AB	H	2B	3B	HR	(Hm | Rd)	TB	R	RBI	RC	TBB	IBB	SO	HBP	SH	SF	SB	CS	GDP	Avg	OBP	Slg	OPS
2004 StL	NL	51	135	36	6	0	2	(1	1)	48	12	15	15	13	3	20	0	2	1	0	1	4	.267	.329	.356	.684
2005 StL	NL	114	385	97	15	1	8	(6	2)	138	36	49	46	23	3	30	2	8	3	2	3	10	.252	.295	.358	.654
2006 StL	NL	129	417	90	26	0	6	(2	4)	134	29	49	35	26	2	41	8	8	2	1	2	15	.216	.274	.321	.595
2007 StL	NL	111	353	97	15	0	6	(4	2)	130	30	40	38	34	5	43	3	2	4	1	1	18	.275	.340	.368	.708
2008 StL	NL	124	444	135	18	0	7	(2	5)	174	37	56	57	32	4	29	1	3	5	0	2	15	.304	.349	.392	.740
2009 StL	NL	140	481	141	23	1	6	(5	1)	184	45	54	64	50	2	39	6	6	1	9	3	27	.293	.366	.383	.749
2010 StL	NL	136	465	122	19	0	6	(1	5)	159	34	62	55	42	6	51	7	2	5	8	4	19	.262	.329	.342	.671
2011 StL	NL	139	475	145	32	1	14	(5	9)	221	55	65	64	33	4	44	1	5	4	4	5	21	.305	.349	.465	.814
2012 StL	NL	138	505	159	28	0	22	(9	13)	253	65	76	91	45	4	55	5	3	5	12	3	10	.315	.373	.501	.874
2013 StL	NL	136	505	161	44	0	12	(5	7)	241	68	80	84	30	4	55	3	0	3	3	2	14	.319	.359	.477	.836
2014 StL	NL	110	404	114	21	0	7	(3	4)	156	40	38	47	28	4	55	6	1	6	1	1	14	.282	.333	.386	.719
2015 StL	NL	136	488	132	23	2	4	(3	1)	171	34	61	48	32	3	59	0	1	9	3	1	16	.270	.310	.350	.660
2016 StL	NL	147	534	164	38	1	8	(4	4)	228	56	58	74	39	1	63	6	0	2	3	2	22	.307	.360	.427	.787
2017 StL	NL	136	501	137	27	1	18	(7	11)	220	60	82	67	28	4	74	4	1	9	9	4	14	.273	.312	.439	.751
2018 StL	NL	123	459	120	20	0	20	(3	17)	200	55	74	70	29	0	66	9	0	6	4	3	15	.261	.314	.436	.750
2019 StL	NL	113	419	113	24	0	10	(4	6)	167	45	57	56	23	0	58	5	0	5	6	1	14	.270	.312	.399	.711
2020 StL	NL	42	145	38	2	0	4	(2	2)	52	12	16	16	6	0	21	3	1	1	0	0	7	.262	.303	.359	.662
2021 StL	NL	121	440	111	19	0	11	(5	6)	163	45	66	53	24	1	79	5	0	3	3	0	16	.252	.297	.370	.667
2022 StL	NL	80	262	56	8	0	5	(4	1)	79	19	24	16	5	0	40	2	0	1	2	0	10	.214	.233	.302	.535
Postseason		102	365	101	19	0	4	(2	2)	132	29	36	36	27	6	42	3	1	2	1	1	13	.277	.330	.362	.692
19 ML YEARS		2226	7817	2168	408	7	176	(75	101)	3118	777	1022	991	542	50	922	76	43	75	71	37	287	.277	.327	.399	.726

Sam Moll

Pitches: L **Bats:** L **Pos:** RP-53   **Ht:** 5'9" **Wt:** 190 **Born:** 1/3/1992 **Age:** 31

			HOW MUCH PITCHED					WHAT HE GAVE UP										THE RESULTS						
Year	Team	Lg	G	GS	GF	IP	BFP	H	R	ER	HR	SH	SF	HB	TBB	IBB	SO	WP	W	L	Pct	Sv-Op	Hld	Vel	OPS	ERC	ERA
2017 Oak	AL	11	0	1	6.2	35	13	8	8	2	0	0	0	3	0	7	0	0	0	-	0-0	3	92	1.176	12.45	10.80
2021 Oak	AL	8	0	1	10.1	44	8	4	4	1	0	0	2	5	0	8	0	0	0	-	0-0	0	94	.638	3.98	3.48
2022 Oak	AL	53	0	7	43.1	187	33	16	14	5	0	1	3	22	6	46	2	2	1	.667	0-2	16	93	.646	3.29	2.91
3 ML YEARS		72	0	9	60.1	266	54	28	26	8	0	1	5	30	6	61	2	2	1	.667	0-2	19	93	.717	4.24	3.88

Yoan Moncada

Bats: B **Throws:** R **Pos:** 3B-101;PH-4   yo-AHN   **Ht:** 6'2" **Wt:** 225 **Born:** 5/27/1995 **Age:** 28

							BATTING												RUNNING			AVERAGES			
Year	Team	Lg	G	AB	H	2B	3B	HR	(Hm | Rd)	TB	R	RBI	RC	TBB	IBB	SO	HBP	SH	SF	SB	CS	GDP	Avg	OBP	Slg	OPS
2016 Bos	AL	8	19	4	1	0	0	(0	0)	5	3	1	0	1	0	12	0	0	0	0	0	0	.211	.250	.263	.513
2017 CWS	AL	54	199	46	8	2	8	(4	4)	82	31	22	27	29	0	74	3	0	0	3	2	0	.231	.338	.412	.750
2018 CWS	AL	149	578	136	32	6	17	(10	7)	231	73	61	73	67	1	217	1	2	2	12	6	4	.235	.315	.400	.714
2019 CWS	AL	132	511	161	34	5	25	(16	9)	280	83	79	94	40	2	154	4	1	3	10	3	1	.315	.367	.548	.915
2020 CWS	AL	52	200	45	8	3	6	(5	1)	77	28	24	30	28	0	72	1	0	2	0	0	2	.225	.320	.385	.705
2021 CWS	AL	144	520	137	33	1	14	(12	2)	214	74	61	89	84	1	157	10	0	3	3	2	6	.263	.375	.412	.787
2022 CWS	AL	104	397	84	18	1	12	(5	7)	140	41	51	47	32	2	114	2	1	1	2	0	5	.212	.273	.353	.626
Postseason		7	29	5	0	0	0	(0	0)	5	3	0	0	2	0	7	0	0	0	1	0	1	.172	.226	.172	.398
7 ML YEARS		643	2424	613	134	18	82	(52	30)	1029	333	299	360	281	6	800	21	4	10	30	13	17	.253	.334	.425	.759

Adalberto Mondesi

Bats: B Throws: R Pos: SS-15   Ht: 6'1" Wt: 200 Born: 7/27/1995 Age: 27

Year	Team	Lg	G	AB	H	2B	3B	HR	(Hm	Rd)	TB	R	RBI	RC	TBB	IBB	SO	HBP	SH	SF	SB	CS	GDP	Avg	OBP	Slg	OPS
2016	KC	AL	47	135	25	1	3	2	(0	2)	38	16	13	9	6	0	48	0	1	0	9	1	1	.185	.231	.281	.512
2017	KC	AL	25	53	9	1	0	1	(1	0)	13	4	3	0	3	0	22	0	4	0	5	2	2	.170	.214	.245	.460
2018	KC	AL	75	275	76	13	3	14	(7	7)	137	47	37	39	11	0	77	1	3	1	32	7	2	.276	.306	.498	.804
2019	KC	AL	102	415	109	20	10	9	(4	5)	176	58	62	60	19	0	132	6	1	3	43	7	6	.263	.291	.424	.715
2020	KC	AL	59	219	56	11	3	6	(4	2)	91	33	22	24	11	0	70	1	2	0	24	8	4	.256	.294	.416	.710
2021	KC	AL	35	126	29	8	1	6	(4	2)	57	19	17	17	6	0	43	1	3	0	15	1	2	.230	.271	.452	.723
2022	KC	AL	15	50	7	0	0	0	(0	0)	7	3	3	1	4	0	20	0	0	0	5	0	0	.140	.204	.140	.344
	Postseason		1	1	0	0	0	0	(0	0)	0	0	0	0	0	0	1	0	0	0	0	0	0	.000	.000	.000	.000
7 ML YEARS			358	1273	311	54	20	38	(20	18)	519	180	157	150	60	0	412	5	21	7	133	26	19	.244	.280	.408	.687

Nate Mondou

Bats: L Throws: R Pos: 2B-1   Ht: 5'10" Wt: 205 Born: 3/24/1995 Age: 28

Year	Team	Lg	G	AB	H	2B	3B	HR	(Hm	Rd)	TB	R	RBI	RC	TBB	IBB	SO	HBP	SH	SF	SB	CS	GDP	Avg	OBP	Slg	OPS
2022	LsVgs	AAA	108	385	109	30	3	7	(-	-)	166	59	64	61	46	1	83	13	0	5	1	1	5	.283	.374	.431	.805
2022	Oak	AL	1	2	0	0	0	0	(0	0)	0	0	0	0	1	0	1	0	0	0	0	0	0	.000	.333	.000	.333

Mickey Moniak

Bats: L Throws: R Pos: CF-21;LF-13;RF-4;PR-3;PH-2;DH-1   Ht: 6'2" Wt: 195 Born: 5/13/1998 Age: 25

Year	Team	Lg	G	AB	H	2B	3B	HR	(Hm	Rd)	TB	R	RBI	RC	TBB	IBB	SO	HBP	SH	SF	SB	CS	GDP	Avg	OBP	Slg	OPS
2022	LV	AAA	20	83	23	5	0	5	(-	-)	43	14	8	15	8	0	22	0	0	0	5	3	0	.277	.341	.518	.859
2020	Phi	NL	8	14	3	0	0	0	(0	0)	3	3	0	1	4	0	6	0	0	0	0	0	0	.214	.389	.214	.603
2021	Phi	NL	21	33	3	0	0	1	(1	0)	6	3	3	1	3	1	16	0	1	0	0	0	0	.091	.167	.182	.348
2022	2 Tms		37	106	18	3	1	3	(1	2)	32	13	8	8	4	0	44	1	1	0	1	0	0	.170	.207	.302	.509
22	Phi	NL	18	46	6	1	0	0	(0	0)	7	4	2	2	3	0	19	0	1	0	0	0	0	.130	.184	.152	.336
22	LAA	AL	19	60	12	2	1	3	(1	2)	25	9	6	6	1	0	25	1	0	0	1	0	0	.200	.226	.417	.642
3 ML YEARS			66	153	24	3	1	4	(2	2)	41	19	11	10	11	1	66	1	2	0	1	0	0	.157	.218	.268	.486

Frankie Montas

Pitches: R Bats: R Pos: SP-27   MOHN-tahs   Ht: 6'2" Wt: 255 Born: 3/21/1993 Age: 30

Year	Team	Lg	G	GS	GF	IP	BFP	H	R	ER	HR	SH	SF	HB	TBB	IBB	SO	WP	W	L	Pct	Sv-Op	Hld	Vel	OPS	ERC	ERA
2015	CWS	AL	7	2	2	15.0	66	14	8	8	1	0	0	0	9	1	20	0	0	2	.000	0-0	0	97	.699	4.16	4.80
2017	Oak	AL	23	0	5	32.0	152	39	25	25	10	0	0	3	20	0	36	1	1	1	.500	0-0	1	98	.974	8.72	7.03
2018	Oak	AL	13	11	1	65.0	283	74	34	28	5	2	3	2	21	0	43	5	5	4	.556	0-0	0	96	.796	4.55	3.88
2019	Oak	AL	16	16	0	96.0	394	84	35	28	8	0	2	4	23	1	103	5	9	2	.818	0-0	0	97	.646	2.82	2.63
2020	Oak	AL	11	11	0	53.0	237	57	35	33	10	0	2	1	23	0	60	2	3	5	.375	0-0	0	96	.806	5.33	5.60
2021	Oak	AL	32	32	0	187.0	778	164	79	70	20	2	4	7	57	1	207	11	13	9	.591	0-0	0	96	.666	3.21	3.37
2022	2 Tms		27	27	0	144.1	608	137	72	65	18	2	5	6	43	3	142	7	5	12	.294	0-0	0	96	.710	3.69	4.05
22	Oak	AL	19	19	0	104.2	423	91	44	37	12	1	3	1	28	3	109	4	4	9	.308	0-0	0	96	.656	2.99	3.18
22	NYY	AL	8	8	0	39.2	185	46	28	28	6	1	2	5	15	0	33	3	1	3	.250	0-0	0	96	.838	5.69	6.35
	Postseason		2	1	0	5.2	27	9	6	6	2	0	0	0	1	0	5	0	1	1	.500	0-0	0	97	.947	8.56	9.53
7 ML YEARS			129	99	8	592.1	2518	569	288	257	72	6	16	23	196	6	611	31	36	35	.507	0-0	1	96	.720	3.87	3.90

Elehuris Montero

Bats: R Throws: R Pos: 3B-23;1B-16;DH-12;PH-2;PR-1   el-her-EES   Ht: 6'3" Wt: 235 Born: 8/17/1998 Age: 24

Year	Team	Lg	G	AB	H	2B	3B	HR	(Hm	Rd)	TB	R	RBI	RC	TBB	IBB	SO	HBP	SH	SF	SB	CS	GDP	Avg	OBP	Slg	OPS
2022	Albq	AAA	65	255	79	10	2	15	(-	-)	138	44	54	54	27	0	63	10	0	4	4	2	7	.310	.392	.541	.933
2022	Col	NL	53	176	41	15	1	6	(5	1)	76	21	20	20	8	0	60	1	0	0	0	0	4	.233	.270	.432	.702

Rafael Montero

Pitches: R Bats: R Pos: RP-71   Ht: 6'0" Wt: 190 Born: 10/17/1990 Age: 32

Year	Team	Lg	G	GS	GF	IP	BFP	H	R	ER	HR	SH	SF	HB	TBB	IBB	SO	WP	W	L	Pct	Sv-Op	Hld	Vel	OPS	ERC	ERA
2014	NYM	NL	10	8	1	44.1	194	44	21	20	8	0	0	0	23	0	42	0	1	3	.250	0-0	0	92	.825	5.16	4.06
2015	NYM	NL	5	1	1	10.0	46	9	6	5	0	1	0	0	5	3	13	0	0	1	.000	0-0	1	92	.661	2.50	4.50
2016	NYM	NL	9	3	1	19.0	93	23	17	17	4	0	0	0	16	1	20	2	0	1	.000	0-0	0	93	.965	8.15	8.05
2017	NYM	NL	34	18	4	119.0	550	141	75	73	12	9	8	5	67	5	114	6	5	11	.313	0-0	0	94	.832	6.01	5.52
2019	Tex	AL	22	0	16	29.0	113	23	8	8	5	0	0	2	5	0	34	0	2	0	1.000	0-1	7	96	.671	2.89	2.48
2020	Tex	AL	17	0	16	17.2	72	12	11	8	2	1	0	1	6	0	19	0	1	0	1.000	8-8	0	96	.652	2.43	4.08
2021	2 Tms	AL	44	0	18	49.1	225	59	40	35	4	1	3	5	17	1	42	4	5	4	.556	7-13	4	96	.784	5.18	6.39
2022	Hou	AL	71	0	25	68.1	270	47	22	18	3	1	1	2	23	2	73	1	5	2	.714	14-16	23	96	.535	1.99	2.37
21	Sea	AL	40	0	17	43.1	204	56	39	35	4	1	3	5	15	1	37	4	5	3	.625	7-13	4	96	.819	5.86	7.27
21	Hou	AL	4	0	1	6.0	21	3	1	0	0	0	0	0	2	0	5	0	0	1	.000	0-0	0	95	.449	1.20	0.00
8 ML YEARS			212	30	72	356.2	1563	358	200	184	38	13	12	15	162	12	357	13	18	23	.439	29-38	35	94	.754	4.49	4.64

Bryce Montes de Oca

Pitches: R Bats: R Pos: RP-3
Ht: 6'7" Wt: 265 Born: 4/23/1996 Age: 27

Year Team	Lg	G	GS	GF	IP	BFP	H	R	ER	HR	SH	SF	HB	TBB	IBB	SO	WP	W	L	Pct	Sv-Op	Hld	Vel	OPS	ERC	ERA
2022 Bnghtn AA		14	1	11	17.1	77	11	8	6	0	0	0	0	14	1	24	0	1	1	.500	3- -	-	-	.567	2.97	3.12
2022 Syrcse AAA		30	0	14	34.0	154	24	14	13	0	0	1	6	24	0	56	6	2	2	.500	8- -	-	-	.603	3.49	3.44
2022 NYM NL		3	0	1	3.1	19	7	4	4	0	0	0	0	2	0	6	1	0	0	-	0-0	0	100	.885	10.87	10.80

Jordan Montgomery

Pitches: L Bats: L Pos: SP-32
Ht: 6'6" Wt: 228 Born: 12/27/1992 Age: 30

Year Team	Lg	G	GS	GF	IP	BFP	H	R	ER	HR	SH	SF	HB	TBB	IBB	SO	WP	W	L	Pct	Sv-Op	Hld	Vel	OPS	ERC	ERA
2017 NYY AL		29	29	0	155.1	649	140	72	67	21	2	3	1	51	0	144	7	9	7	.563	0-0	0	92	.684	3.50	3.88
2018 NYY AL		6	6	0	27.1	116	25	11	11	3	0	0	0	12	0	23	0	2	0	1.000	0-0	0	90	.675	3.85	3.62
2019 NYY AL		2	1	0	4.0	19	7	3	3	1	0	0	0	0	0	5	0	0	0	-	0-0	0	92	1.053	7.95	6.75
2020 NYY AL		10	10	0	44.0	193	48	27	25	7	0	0	2	9	0	47	3	2	3	.400	0-0	0	93	.749	4.25	5.11
2021 NYY AL		30	30	0	157.1	661	150	73	67	19	1	7	2	51	0	162	12	6	7	.462	0-0	0	93	.688	3.72	3.83
2022 2 Tms		32	32	0	178.1	724	159	72	69	21	2	1	8	36	0	158	4	9	6	.600	0-0	0	93	.665	3.03	3.48
22 NYY AL		21	21	0	114.2	469	103	48	47	15	2	1	7	23	0	97	3	3	3	.500	0-0	0	93	.670	3.19	3.69
22 StL NL		11	11	0	63.2	255	56	24	22	6	0	0	1	13	0	61	1	6	3	.667	0-0	0	93	.656	2.74	3.11
Postseason		1	1	0	4.0	17	3	1	1	0	0	0	0	3	0	4	0	0	0	-	0-0	0	92	.639	3.44	2.25
6 ML YEARS		109	108	0	566.1	2362	529	258	242	72	5	11	13	159	0	539	26	28	23	.549	0-0	0	92	.687	3.51	3.85

Dylan Moore

Bats: R Throws: R Pos: RF-39;SS-26;LF-18;PH-16;2B-12;PR-10;1B-8;CF-7;3B-2;DH-2
Ht: 6'0" Wt: 205 Born: 8/2/1992 Age: 30

Year Team	Lg	G	AB	H	2B	3B	HR	(Hm Rd)	TB	R	RBI	RC	TBB	IBB	SO	HBP	SH	SF	SB	CS	GDP	Avg	OBP	Slg	OPS
2019 Sea AL		113	247	51	14	2	9	(6 3)	96	31	28	29	25	0	93	9	1	0	11	9	6	.206	.302	.389	.691
2020 Sea AL		38	137	35	9	0	8	(4 4)	68	26	17	22	14	0	43	8	0	0	12	5	4	.255	.358	.496	.855
2021 Sea AL		126	332	60	11	2	12	(7 5)	111	42	43	40	40	0	111	4	0	1	21	5	6	.181	.276	.334	.610
2022 Sea AL		104	205	46	11	2	6	(4 2)	79	41	24	30	34	2	75	13	1	1	21	8	5	.224	.368	.385	.753
4 ML YEARS		381	921	192	45	6	35	(21 14)	354	140	112	121	113	2	322	34	2	2	65	27	21	.208	.317	.384	.701

Matt Moore

Pitches: L Bats: L Pos: RP-63
Ht: 6'3" Wt: 210 Born: 6/18/1989 Age: 34

Year Team	Lg	G	GS	GF	IP	BFP	H	R	ER	HR	SH	SF	HB	TBB	IBB	SO	WP	W	L	Pct	Sv-Op	Hld	Vel	OPS	ERC	ERA
2011 TB AL		3	1	0	9.1	40	9	3	3	1	0	0	0	3	0	15	2	1	0	1.000	0-0	1	96	.651	3.54	2.89
2012 TB AL		31	31	0	177.1	759	158	85	75	18	3	4	7	81	5	175	8	11	11	.500	0-0	0	94	.706	3.83	3.81
2013 TB AL		27	27	0	150.1	642	119	58	55	14	5	6	4	76	1	143	17	17	4	.810	0-0	0	92	.655	3.36	3.29
2014 TB AL		2	2	0	10.0	44	10	3	3	1	0	0	0	5	0	6	0	2	0	.000	0-0	0	92	.777	4.48	2.70
2015 TB AL		12	12	0	63.0	278	74	40	38	9	0	3	4	23	1	46	6	3	4	.429	0-0	0	93	.839	5.63	5.43
2016 2 Tms		33	33	0	198.1	838	184	93	90	25	4	4	6	72	1	178	6	13	12	.520	0-0	0	93	.694	3.83	4.08
2017 SF NL		32	31	1	174.1	790	200	116	107	27	6	4	7	67	3	148	10	6	15	.286	0-0	0	93	.835	5.33	5.52
2018 Tex AL		39	12	10	102.0	471	128	82	77	19	1	4	5	41	1	86	6	3	8	.273	0-1	2	92	.911	6.43	6.79
2019 Det AL		2	2	0	10.0	33	3	0	0	0	0	0	0	1	0	9	0	0	0	-	0-0	0	93	.215	0.32	0.00
2021 Phi NL		24	13	5	73.0	334	78	54	51	15	8	1	2	38	4	63	3	4	4	.333	0-0	1	92	.871	5.71	6.29
2022 Tex AL		63	0	18	74.0	304	49	20	16	3	0	3	1	38	2	83	8	5	2	.714	5-6	14	94	.564	2.35	1.95
16 TB AL		21	21	0	130.0	549	125	62	59	20	3	2	5	40	0	109	3	7	7	.500	0-0	0	93	.716	4.02	4.08
16 SF NL		12	12	0	68.1	289	59	31	31	5	1	2	1	32	1	69	3	6	5	.545	0-0	0	93	.651	3.47	4.08
Postseason		5	3	0	24.1	97	14	11	9	2	0	1	2	8	1	25	2	1	1	.500	0-0	0	93	.550	1.78	3.33
11 ML YEARS		268	164	34	1041.2	4533	1012	554	515	132	27	29	36	445	18	952	66	61	62	.496	5-7	18	93	.748	4.31	4.45

Francisco Morales

Pitches: R Bats: R Pos: RP-3
Ht: 6'4" Wt: 185 Born: 10/27/1999 Age: 23

Year Team	Lg	G	GS	GF	IP	BFP	H	R	ER	HR	SH	SF	HB	TBB	IBB	SO	WP	W	L	Pct	Sv-Op	Hld	Vel	OPS	ERC	ERA
2022 Rdng AA		23	0	4	30.1	116	9	5	5	0	0	0	1	17	0	54	9	2	0	1.000	1- -	-	-	.355	1.04	1.48
2022 LV AAA		22	0	6	20.2	113	24	23	22	1	0	1	1	28	0	16	4	3	3	.500	2- -	-	-	.879	8.73	9.58
2022 Phi NL		3	0	2	5.0	21	2	5	4	1	0	0	1	6	0	3	0	0	0	-	1-1	0	95	.786	6.07	7.20

Brian Moran

Pitches: L Bats: L Pos: RP-1
Ht: 6'4" Wt: 225 Born: 9/30/1988 Age: 34

Year Team	Lg	G	GS	GF	IP	BFP	H	R	ER	HR	SH	SF	HB	TBB	IBB	SO	WP	W	L	Pct	Sv-Op	Hld	Vel	OPS	ERC	ERA
2022 Salt Lk AAA		45	1	10	48.2	211	49	25	22	7	0	0	6	14	0	52	2	5	2	.714	0- -	-	-	.777	4.46	4.07
2019 Mia NL		10	0	0	6.1	29	6	3	3	1	1	0	2	2	1	10	0	1	0	1.000	0-1	2	84	.857	4.74	4.26
2020 2 Tms		7	0	2	4.2	26	6	5	5	1	0	0	0	6	0	7	0	1	0	1.000	0-1	0	84	1.012	10.57	9.64
2022 LAA AL		1	0	0	0.1	5	3	2	2	1	0	0	0	1	1	0	0	0	0	-	0-0	0	84	2.550	124.6	54.00
20 Tor AL		2	0	1	1.0	4	1	0	0	0	0	0	0	0	0	1	0	0	0	-	0-1	0	81	.500	1.95	0.00
20 Mia NL		5	0	1	3.2	22	5	5	5	1	0	0	0	6	0	6	0	1	0	1.000	0-0	0	82	1.125	13.42	12.27
3 ML YEARS		18	0	2	11.1	60	15	10	10	3	1	0	2	9	2	17	0	2	0	1.000	0-2	2	83	1.066	9.46	7.94

Colin Moran

Bats: L **Throws:** R **Pos:** 1B-25;3B-14;PH-9;DH-2   **Ht:** 6'4" **Wt:** 225 **Born:** 10/1/1992 **Age:** 30

								BATTING												RUNNING			AVERAGES			
Year Team	Lg	G	AB	H	2B	3B	HR	(Hm Rd)	TB	R	RBI	RC	TBB	IBB	SO	HBP	SH	SF	SB	CS	GDP	Avg	OBP	Slg	OPS
2022 Lsvlle	AAA	53	193	48	11	0	7	(- -)	80	21	26	25	18	0	54	1	0	2	0	0	5	.249	.310	.415	.724
2016 Hou	AL	9	23	3	1	0	0	(0 0)	4	1	2	0	1	0	8	1	0	0	0	0	4	.130	.200	.174	.374
2017 Hou	AL	7	11	4	0	1	1	(0 1)	9	3	3	4	1	0	1	0	0	0	0	0	0	.364	.417	.818	1.235
2018 Pit	NL	144	415	115	19	1	11	(5 6)	169	49	58	55	39	4	82	4	0	7	0	2	6	.277	.340	.407	.747
2019 Pit	NL	149	466	129	30	1	13	(6 7)	200	46	80	69	30	4	117	3	0	4	0	1	13	.277	.322	.429	.751
2020 Pit	NL	52	178	44	10	0	10	(4 6)	84	28	23	22	19	0	52	2	0	1	0	0	9	.247	.325	.472	.797
2021 Pit	NL	99	318	82	12	0	10	(4 6)	124	29	50	42	36	0	87	2	0	3	1	0	6	.258	.334	.390	.724
2022 Cin	NL	42	109	23	3	0	5	(4 1)	41	11	23	17	16	0	30	0	0	3	0	0	4	.211	.305	.376	.681
7 ML YEARS		502	1520	400	75	3	50	(23 27)	631	167	239	209	142	8	377	12	0	18	1	3	42	.263	.327	.415	.743

Jovani Moran

Pitches: L **Bats:** L **Pos:** RP-31   **Ht:** 6'1" **Wt:** 167 **Born:** 4/24/1997 **Age:** 26

		HOW MUCH PITCHED					WHAT HE GAVE UP											THE RESULTS							
Year Team	Lg	G	GS	GF	IP	BFP	H	R	ER	HR	SH	SF	HB	TBB	IBB	SO	WP	W	L	Pct	Sv-Op	Hld	Vel	OPS	ERC	ERA
2022 StPaul	AAA	20	0	2	24.0	112	25	16	16	2	0	0	2	14	0	43	5	1	2	.333	0- -	-	-	.772	5.17	6.00
2021 Min	AL	5	0	0	8.0	38	9	7	7	0	0	0	0	7	0	10	1	0	0	-	0-0	0	93	.744	6.06	7.88
2022 Min	AL	31	0	16	40.2	164	25	11	10	0	0	1	0	18	0	54	2	0	1	.000	1-1	2	93	.490	1.65	2.21
2 ML YEARS		36	0	16	48.2	202	34	18	17	0	0	1	0	25	0	64	3	0	1	.000	1-1	2	93	.536	2.25	3.14

Adrian Morejon

Pitches: L **Bats:** L **Pos:** RP-26   moh-ray-HOHN   **Ht:** 5'11" **Wt:** 224 **Born:** 2/27/1999 **Age:** 24

		HOW MUCH PITCHED					WHAT HE GAVE UP											THE RESULTS							
Year Team	Lg	G	GS	GF	IP	BFP	H	R	ER	HR	SH	SF	HB	TBB	IBB	SO	WP	W	L	Pct	Sv-Op	Hld	Vel	OPS	ERC	ERA
2022 SnAnt	AA	5	0	0	7.0	22	1	0	0	0	0	0	0	2	0	8	0	0	0	-	0- -	-	-	.186	0.29	0.00
2019 SD	NL	5	2	1	8.0	42	15	9	9	1	0	0	0	3	0	9	0	0	0	-	0-0	0	96	1.044	9.51	10.13
2020 SD	NL	9	4	0	19.1	79	20	11	10	7	0	0	0	4	0	25	0	2	2	.500	0-0	0	97	.877	5.33	4.66
2021 SD	NL	2	2	0	4.2	20	5	2	2	2	0	0	0	2	0	3	0	0	0	-	0-0	0	96	.961	7.26	3.86
2022 SD	NL	26	0	6	34.0	141	31	18	16	4	0	1	1	9	1	28	0	5	1	.833	0-0	5	97	.652	3.25	4.24
Postseason		3	1	0	5.0	23	3	3	3	0	0	0	1	2	0	4	1	0	1	.000	0-0	0	97	.461	1.80	5.40
4 ML YEARS		42	8	7	66.0	282	71	40	37	14	0	1	1	18	1	65	0	7	3	.700	0-0	5	97	.796	4.82	5.05

Christopher Morel

Bats: R **Throws:** R **Pos:** CF-57;2B-33;3B-18;SS-13;PR-3;DH-2;PH-2;LF-1   **Ht:** 5'11" **Wt:** 145 **Born:** 6/24/1999 **Age:** 24

								BATTING												RUNNING			AVERAGES			
Year Team	Lg	G	AB	H	2B	3B	HR	(Hm Rd)	TB	R	RBI	RC	TBB	IBB	SO	HBP	SH	SF	SB	CS	GDP	Avg	OBP	Slg	OPS
2022 Tenn	AA	28	108	33	5	1	7	(- -)	61	22	20	22	10	0	30	3	1	0	3	3	3	.306	.380	.565	.945
2022 ChC	NL	113	379	89	19	4	16	(11 5)	164	55	47	50	38	0	137	3	3	2	10	7	6	.235	.308	.433	.741

Gabriel Moreno

Bats: R **Throws:** R **Pos:** C-19;PH-4;DH-2;2B-1;3B-1;LF-1;PR-1   **Ht:** 5'11" **Wt:** 195 **Born:** 2/14/2000 **Age:** 23

								BATTING												RUNNING			AVERAGES			
Year Team	Lg	G	AB	H	2B	3B	HR	(Hm Rd)	TB	R	RBI	RC	TBB	IBB	SO	HBP	SH	SF	SB	CS	GDP	Avg	OBP	Slg	OPS
2018 2 Tms	Low	40	153	55	17	2	4	(- -)	88	24	36	33	7	1	20	4	0	3	2	1	4	.359	.395	.575	.970
2019 Lnsng	A	82	307	86	17	5	12	(- -)	149	47	52	53	22	1	38	7	0	5	7	1	3	.280	.337	.485	.823
2021 Nham	AA	32	126	47	9	1	8	(- -)	82	29	45	33	14	0	22	3	0	2	1	2	3	.373	.441	.651	1.092
2022 Buffalo	AAA	62	238	75	16	0	3	(- -)	100	35	39	36	24	0	45	4	0	1	7	1	7	.315	.386	.420	.806
2022 Tor	AL	25	69	22	1	0	1	(0 1)	26	10	7	10	4	0	8	0	0	0	0	0	2	.319	.356	.377	.733

Dauri Moreta

Pitches: R **Bats:** R **Pos:** RP-34; SP-1   DOW-ree   **Ht:** 6'2" **Wt:** 185 **Born:** 4/15/1996 **Age:** 27

		HOW MUCH PITCHED					WHAT HE GAVE UP											THE RESULTS							
Year Team	Lg	G	GS	GF	IP	BFP	H	R	ER	HR	SH	SF	HB	TBB	IBB	SO	WP	W	L	Pct	Sv-Op	Hld	Vel	OPS	ERC	ERA
2022 Lsvlle	AAA	28	0	15	27.1	120	31	16	12	6	2	0	1	12	0	28	1	3	4	.429	1- -	-	-	.906	6.27	3.95
2021 Cin	NL	4	0	3	3.2	14	2	1	1	1	0	0	0	1	0	4	0	0	0	-	0-0	0	95	.599	2.19	2.45
2022 Cin	NL	35	1	17	38.1	160	32	24	23	10	0	2	4	13	1	39	1	0	2	.000	1-1	1	96	.803	4.41	5.40
2 ML YEARS		39	1	20	42.0	174	34	25	24	11	0	2	4	14	1	43	1	0	2	.000	1-1	1	96	.786	4.20	5.14

Eli Morgan

Pitches: R **Bats:** R **Pos:** RP-49; SP-1   **Ht:** 5'10" **Wt:** 190 **Born:** 5/13/1996 **Age:** 27

		HOW MUCH PITCHED					WHAT HE GAVE UP											THE RESULTS							
Year Team	Lg	G	GS	GF	IP	BFP	H	R	ER	HR	SH	SF	HB	TBB	IBB	SO	WP	W	L	Pct	Sv-Op	Hld	Vel	OPS	ERC	ERA
2021 Cle	AL	18	18	0	89.1	379	90	54	53	20	2	1	4	22	0	81	0	5	7	.417	0-0	0	90	.809	4.50	5.34
2022 Cle	AL	50	1	7	66.2	256	46	29	25	10	0	2	2	13	0	72	0	5	3	.625	0-4	10	91	.619	2.15	3.38
2 ML YEARS		68	19	7	156.0	635	136	83	78	30	2	3	6	35	0	153	0	10	10	.500	0-4	10	91	.732	3.43	4.50

Reyes Moronta

Pitches: R Bats: R Pos: RP-39　　　　　　　　　　Ht: 5'10" Wt: 265 Born: 1/6/1993 Age: 30

		HOW MUCH PITCHED					WHAT HE GAVE UP										THE RESULTS						
Year Team	Lg	G	GS	GF	IP	BFP	H	R	ER	HR	SH	SF	HB	TBB	IBB	SO	WP	W	L	Pct	Sv-Op	Hld	Vel	OPS	ERC	ERA
2022 OkCity	AAA	11	0	5	10.0	46	8	3	3	1	0	0	0	9	0	17	2	1	0	1.000	2--	-	-	.694	4.90	2.70
2017 SF	NL	7	0	1	6.2	29	6	2	2	1	0	0	0	3	1	11	0	0	0	-	0-1	0	96	.656	3.74	2.70
2018 SF	NL	69	0	9	65.0	262	34	20	18	4	1	3	0	37	4	79	5	5	2	.714	1-6	12	97	.507	1.93	2.49
2019 SF	NL	56	0	5	56.2	246	41	19	18	4	1	1	3	33	1	70	3	3	7	.300	0-5	15	97	.612	3.18	2.86
2021 SF	NL	4	0	0	4.0	13	1	1	1	1	0	0	0	0	0	2	0	0	0	-	0-0	2	94	.385	0.46	2.25
2022 2 Tms	NL	39	0	14	37.2	161	30	20	18	5	0	1	2	18	1	38	8	2	2	.500	2-4	4	95	.682	3.62	4.30
22 LAD	NL	22	0	6	23.2	98	17	11	11	5	0	0	2	10	0	27	4	0	0	-	0-0	0	95	.703	3.71	4.18
22 Ari	NL	17	0	8	14.0	63	13	9	7	0	0	1	0	8	1	11	4	2	2	.500	2-4	4	96	.648	3.39	4.50
5 ML YEARS		175	0	29	170.0	711	112	62	57	15	2	5	5	91	7	200	16	10	11	.476	3-16	33	97	.588	2.72	3.02

Cody Morris

Pitches: R Bats: R Pos: SP-5; RP-2　　　　　　　　Ht: 6'4" Wt: 205 Born: 11/4/1996 Age: 26

		HOW MUCH PITCHED					WHAT HE GAVE UP										THE RESULTS						
Year Team	Lg	G	GS	GF	IP	BFP	H	R	ER	HR	SH	SF	HB	TBB	IBB	SO	WP	W	L	Pct	Sv-Op	Hld	Vel	OPS	ERC	ERA
2022 Clmbs	AAA	6	3	1	15.1	58	5	4	4	2	0	0	0	6	0	30	3	0	0	-	1--	-	-	.420	1.15	2.35
2022 Cle	AL	7	5	0	23.2	100	21	8	6	3	0	1	0	12	0	23	1	1	2	.333	0-0	1	95	.709	4.15	2.28

Charlie Morton

Pitches: R Bats: R Pos: SP-31　　　　　　　　　　Ht: 6'5" Wt: 215 Born: 11/12/1983 Age: 39

		HOW MUCH PITCHED					WHAT HE GAVE UP										THE RESULTS						
Year Team	Lg	G	GS	GF	IP	BFP	H	R	ER	HR	SH	SF	HB	TBB	IBB	SO	WP	W	L	Pct	Sv-Op	Hld	Vel	OPS	ERC	ERA
2008 Atl	NL	16	15	0	74.2	345	80	56	51	9	5	4	2	41	2	48	2	4	8	.333	0-0	0	91	.816	5.21	6.15
2009 Pit	NL	18	18	0	97.0	416	102	49	49	7	1	1	5	40	0	62	4	5	9	.357	0-0	0	91	.761	4.56	4.55
2010 Pit	NL	17	17	0	79.2	382	112	79	67	15	6	6	7	26	3	59	5	2	12	.143	0-0	0	93	.908	7.10	7.57
2011 Pit	NL	29	29	0	171.2	769	186	82	73	6	12	6	13	77	5	110	9	10	10	.500	0-0	0	91	.737	4.52	3.83
2012 Pit	NL	9	9	0	50.1	223	62	30	26	5	5	2	2	11	1	25	4	2	6	.250	0-0	0	90	.812	4.74	4.65
2013 Pit	NL	20	20	0	116.0	493	113	51	42	6	6	2	16	36	1	85	5	7	4	.636	0-0	0	93	.683	3.84	3.26
2014 Pit	NL	26	26	0	157.1	666	143	76	65	9	7	5	19	57	2	126	8	6	12	.333	0-0	0	91	.682	3.64	3.72
2015 Pit	NL	23	23	0	129.0	563	137	77	69	13	4	0	12	41	6	96	2	9	9	.500	0-0	0	92	.769	4.41	4.81
2016 Phi	NL	4	4	0	17.1	71	15	8	8	1	1	0	0	8	0	19	1	1	1	.500	0-0	0	94	.651	3.42	4.15
2017 Hou	AL	25	25	0	146.2	617	125	65	59	14	2	2	13	50	1	163	4	14	7	.667	0-0	0	96	.692	3.34	3.62
2018 Hou	AL	30	30	0	167.0	695	130	63	58	18	1	4	16	64	0	201	4	15	3	.833	0-0	0	96	.659	3.25	3.13
2019 TB	AL	33	33	0	194.2	790	154	71	66	15	1	3	12	57	0	240	5	16	6	.727	0-0	0	94	.623	2.67	3.05
2020 TB	AL	9	9	0	38.0	170	43	21	20	4	0	2	4	10	0	42	1	2	2	.500	0-0	0	95	.764	4.65	4.74
2021 Atl	NL	33	33	0	185.2	756	136	77	69	16	6	6	17	58	1	216	5	14	6	.700	0-0	0	95	.591	2.58	3.34
2022 Atl	NL	31	31	0	172.0	728	149	85	83	28	1	6	18	63	0	205	4	9	6	.600	0-0	0	95	.727	4.07	4.34
Postseason		17	16	1	78.0	332	63	31	29	7	2	2	7	32	0	89	5	7	4	.636	0-0	0	95	.634	3.31	3.35
15 ML YEARS		323	322	0	1797.0	7684	1687	890	805	166	58	49	156	639	22	1697	63	116	101	.535	0-0	0	93	.709	3.84	4.03

Taylor Motter

Bats: R Throws: R Pos: 3B-2;2B-1　　　　　　　　Ht: 6'1" Wt: 195 Born: 9/18/1989 Age: 33

		BATTING																	RUNNING			AVERAGES			
Year Team	Lg	G	AB	H	2B	3B	HR	(Hm	Rd)	TB	R	RBI	RC	TBB	IBB	SO	HBP	SH	SF	SB	CS	GDP	Avg	OBP	Slg	OPS
2022 Lsvlle	AAA	39	132	33	4	0	8	(-	-)	61	12	18	23	19	0	34	0	0	2	0	0	3	.250	.340	.462	.802
2022 Gwnntt	AAA	42	147	38	11	0	12	(-	-)	85	30	36	34	29	0	39	0	0	4	2	0	6	.259	.372	.578	.950
2016 TB	AL	34	80	15	3	0	2	(0	2)	24	11	9	7	11	0	19	1	0	1	0	1	1	.188	.290	.300	.590
2017 Sea	AL	92	258	51	12	0	7	(5	2)	84	29	26	21	21	0	62	0	0	1	12	1	9	.198	.257	.326	.583
2018 2 Tms	AL	17	34	5	0	0	1	(1	0)	8	2	2	2	4	0	8	0	0	0	1	0	0	.147	.237	.235	.472
2021 2 Tms	AL	16	26	5	1	1	0	(0	0)	8	5	1	2	3	0	8	0	0	0	0	0	1	.192	.276	.308	.584
2022 Cin	NL	2	6	1	0	0	0	(0	0)	1	0	0	0	0	0	3	0	0	0	0	0	0	.167	.167	.167	.333
18 Sea	AL	8	15	4	0	0	1	(1	0)	7	2	1	2	2	0	5	0	0	0	0	0	0	.267	.353	.467	.820
18 Min	AL	9	19	1	0	0	0	(0	0)	1	0	1	0	2	0	3	0	0	0	1	0	0	.053	.143	.053	.195
21 Col	NL	13	20	3	0	0	0	(0	0)	3	2	0	0	2	0	6	0	0	0	0	0	1	.150	.227	.150	.377
21 Bos	AL	3	6	2	1	1	0	(0	0)	5	3	1	2	1	0	2	0	0	0	0	0	0	.333	.429	.833	1.262
5 ML YEARS		161	404	77	16	1	10	(6	4)	125	47	38	32	39	0	100	1	0	2	13	2	11	.191	.262	.309	.572

Ryan Mountcastle

Bats: R Throws: R Pos: 1B-124;DH-21;PH-1　　　　Ht: 6'4" Wt: 230 Born: 2/18/1997 Age: 26

		BATTING																	RUNNING			AVERAGES			
Year Team	Lg	G	AB	H	2B	3B	HR	(Hm	Rd)	TB	R	RBI	RC	TBB	IBB	SO	HBP	SH	SF	SB	CS	GDP	Avg	OBP	Slg	OPS
2020 Bal	AL	35	126	42	5	0	5	(2	3)	62	12	23	25	11	0	30	1	0	2	0	1	2	.333	.386	.492	.878
2021 Bal	AL	144	534	136	23	1	33	(22	11)	260	77	89	78	41	2	161	4	0	7	4	3	12	.255	.309	.487	.796
2022 Bal	AL	145	555	139	28	1	22	(11	11)	235	62	85	73	43	1	154	4	0	7	4	1	12	.250	.305	.423	.729
3 ML YEARS		324	1215	317	56	2	60	(35	25)	557	151	197	176	95	3	345	9	0	16	8	5	26	.261	.315	.458	.774

Mike Moustakas

Bats: L **Throws:** R **Pos:** DH-30;3B-25;1B-24;PH-6   moo-STOCK-us   **Ht:** 6'0" **Wt:** 225 **Born:** 9/11/1988 **Age:** 34

Year	Team	Lg	G	AB	H	2B	3B	HR	(Hm	Rd)	TB	R	RBI	RC	TBB	IBB	SO	HBP	SH	SF	SB	CS	GDP	Avg	OBP	Slg	OPS
2011	KC	AL	89	338	89	18	1	5	(3	2)	124	26	30	31	22	0	51	1	2	2	2	0	5	.263	.309	.367	.675
2012	KC	AL	149	563	136	34	1	20	(10	10)	232	69	73	64	39	4	124	7	0	5	5	2	4	.242	.296	.412	.708
2013	KC	AL	136	472	110	26	0	12	(5	7)	172	42	42	35	32	1	83	5	1	4	2	4	13	.233	.287	.364	.651
2014	KC	AL	140	457	97	21	1	15	(5	10)	165	45	54	44	35	1	74	3	1	4	1	0	12	.212	.271	.361	.632
2015	KC	AL	147	549	156	34	1	22	(9	13)	258	73	82	85	43	1	76	13	4	5	1	2	14	.284	.348	.470	.817
2016	KC	AL	27	104	25	6	0	7	(4	3)	52	12	13	10	9	0	13	0	0	0	0	1	5	.240	.301	.500	.801
2017	KC	AL	148	555	151	24	0	38	(14	24)	289	75	85	77	34	7	94	3	0	6	0	0	18	.272	.314	.521	.835
2018	2 Tms		152	573	144	33	1	28	(14	14)	263	66	95	89	49	5	103	7	0	6	4	1	13	.251	.315	.459	.774
2019	Mil	NL	143	523	133	30	1	35	(14	21)	270	80	87	82	53	5	98	6	0	2	3	0	12	.254	.329	.516	.845
2020	Cin	NL	44	139	32	9	0	8	(4	4)	65	13	27	26	18	1	36	4	0	2	1	0	5	.230	.331	.468	.799
2021	Cin	NL	62	183	38	12	0	6	(3	3)	68	21	22	20	18	0	46	2	0	3	0	0	6	.208	.282	.372	.653
2022	Cin	NL	78	252	54	12	0	7	(2	5)	87	30	25	26	24	0	75	6	0	3	2	0	8	.214	.295	.345	.640
18	KC	AL	98	378	94	21	1	20	(9	11)	177	46	62	54	30	3	63	5	0	4	3	0	10	.249	.309	.468	.778
18	Mil	NL	54	195	50	12	0	8	(5	3)	86	20	33	35	19	2	40	2	0	2	1	1	3	.256	.326	.441	.767
	Postseason		44	169	34	5	0	6	(3	3)	57	17	18	15	10	3	33	1	1	1	0	0	2	.201	.249	.337	.586
	12 ML YEARS		1315	4708	1165	259	6	203	(87	116)	2045	552	635	589	376	25	873	57	8	42	21	10	115	.247	.308	.434	.743

Kyle Muller

Pitches: L **Bats:** R **Pos:** SP-3   **Ht:** 6'7" **Wt:** 250 **Born:** 10/7/1997 **Age:** 25

Year	Team	Lg	G	GS	GF	IP	BFP	H	R	ER	HR	SH	SF	HB	TBB	IBB	SO	WP	W	L	Pct	Sv-Op	Hld	Vel	OPS	ERC	ERA
2022	Gwnntt	AAA	23	23	0	134.2	542	119	53	51	14	0	1	6	40	0	159	5	6	8	.429	0- -	-		.694	3.36	3.41
2021	Atl	NL	9	8	0	36.2	155	26	17	17	2	2	2	2	20	1	37	9	2	4	.333	0-0	0	93	.608	2.91	4.17
2022	Atl	NL	3	3	0	12.1	59	13	11	11	2	1	0	0	8	0	12	2	1	1	.500	0-0	0	94	.782	5.64	8.03
	2 ML YEARS		12	11	0	49.0	214	39	28	28	4	3	2	2	28	1	49	11	3	5	.375	0-0	0	94	.657	3.56	5.14

Cedric Mullins II

Bats: L **Throws:** L **Pos:** CF-150;PH-8;DH-4   **Ht:** 5'8" **Wt:** 175 **Born:** 10/1/1994 **Age:** 28

Year	Team	Lg	G	AB	H	2B	3B	HR	(Hm	Rd)	TB	R	RBI	RC	TBB	IBB	SO	HBP	SH	SF	SB	CS	GDP	Avg	OBP	Slg	OPS
2018	Bal	AL	45	170	40	9	0	4	(1	3)	61	23	11	17	17	0	37	2	2	0	2	3	1	.235	.312	.359	.671
2019	Bal	AL	22	64	6	0	2	0	(0	0)	10	7	4	1	4	0	14	3	2	1	1	0	2	.094	.181	.156	.337
2020	Bal	AL	48	140	38	4	3	3	(2	1)	57	16	12	17	8	0	37	1	4	0	7	2	0	.271	.315	.407	.723
2021	Bal	AL	159	602	175	37	5	30	(22	8)	312	91	59	109	59	3	125	8	1	4	30	8	2	.291	.360	.518	.878
2022	Bal	AL	156	608	157	32	4	16	(10	6)	245	89	64	84	47	2	126	9	1	5	34	10	4	.258	.318	.403	.721
	5 ML YEARS		430	1584	416	82	14	53	(35	18)	685	226	150	228	135	5	339	23	10	10	74	23	9	.263	.328	.432	.760

Max Muncy

Bats: L **Throws:** R **Pos:** 3B-84;2B-31;DH-25;PH-5;1B-3   **Ht:** 6'0" **Wt:** 215 **Born:** 8/25/1990 **Age:** 32

Year	Team	Lg	G	AB	H	2B	3B	HR	(Hm	Rd)	TB	R	RBI	RC	TBB	IBB	SO	HBP	SH	SF	SB	CS	GDP	Avg	OBP	Slg	OPS
2015	Oak	AL	45	102	21	8	1	3	(1	2)	40	14	9	9	9	0	31	0	0	1	0	0	0	.206	.268	.392	.660
2016	Oak	AL	51	113	21	2	0	2	(1	1)	29	13	8	10	20	1	24	0	0	0	0	0	2	.186	.308	.257	.565
2018	LAD	NL	137	395	104	17	2	35	(20	15)	230	75	79	87	79	6	131	5	0	2	3	0	4	.263	.391	.582	.973
2019	LAD	NL	141	487	122	22	1	35	(13	22)	251	101	98	93	90	1	149	8	0	4	4	1	5	.251	.374	.515	.889
2020	LAD	NL	58	203	39	4	0	12	(7	5)	79	36	27	28	39	2	60	4	0	3	2	0	3	.192	.331	.389	.720
2021	LAD	NL	144	497	124	26	2	36	(23	13)	262	95	94	109	83	5	120	11	0	1	2	1	7	.249	.368	.527	.895
2022	LAD	NL	136	464	91	22	1	21	(11	10)	178	69	69	73	90	1	141	5	0	6	2	0	2	.196	.329	.384	.713
	Postseason		39	129	30	5	0	9	(5	4)	62	26	27	29	36	2	46	0	0	0	2	0	1	.233	.400	.481	.881
	7 ML YEARS		712	2261	522	101	7	144	(76	68)	1069	403	384	409	410	16	656	33	0	16	12	2	23	.231	.355	.473	.828

Andres Munoz

Pitches: R **Bats:** R **Pos:** RP-64   ahn-DRAYS MOO-nyohs   **Ht:** 6'2" **Wt:** 222 **Born:** 1/16/1999 **Age:** 24

Year	Team	Lg	G	GS	GF	IP	BFP	H	R	ER	HR	SH	SF	HB	TBB	IBB	SO	WP	W	L	Pct	Sv-Op	Hld	Vel	OPS	ERC	ERA
2019	SD	NL	22	0	3	23.0	97	16	10	10	2	1	0	0	11	0	30	1	1	1	.500	1-2	8	100	.611	2.59	3.91
2021	Sea	AL	1	0	0	0.2	4	0	0	0	0	0	0	0	2	0	1	0	0	0	-	0-0	0	100	.500	7.00	0.00
2022	Sea	AL	64	0	12	65.0	248	43	20	18	5	0	2	4	15	3	96	4	2	5	.286	4-8	22	100	.523	1.84	2.49
	3 ML YEARS		87	0	15	88.2	349	59	30	28	7	1	2	4	28	3	127	5	3	6	.333	5-10	30	100	.548	2.07	2.84

Yairo Munoz

Bats: R **Throws:** R **Pos:** 2B-14;3B-8;PH-5;RF-2;PR-2;LF-1   JYE-roh MOON-yohs   **Ht:** 5'11" **Wt:** 200 **Born:** 1/23/1995 **Age:** 28

Year	Team	Lg	G	AB	H	2B	3B	HR	(Hm	Rd)	TB	R	RBI	RC	TBB	IBB	SO	HBP	SH	SF	SB	CS	GDP	Avg	OBP	Slg	OPS
2022	LV	AAA	72	277	86	15	1	6	(-	-)	121	41	37	39	9	0	48	3	2	1	13	3	5	.310	.338	.437	.775
2018	StL	NL	108	293	81	16	4	8	(1	7)	121	39	42	46	30	7	71	4	3	5	5	6	5	.276	.350	.413	.763
2019	StL	NL	88	172	46	7	1	2	(0	2)	61	20	13	19	7	0	37	1	0	1	8	3	5	.267	.298	.355	.653
2020	Bos	AL	12	45	15	5	0	1	(1	0)	23	6	4	7	0	0	11	0	0	0	2	0	1	.333	.333	.511	.844
2021	Bos	AL	5	11	1	0	0	0	(0	0)	1	0	1	0	0	0	2	0	0	0	0	0	0	.091	.091	.091	.182
2022	Phi	NL	29	57	12	2	0	3	(0	3)	23	7	7	6	3	0	10	0	0	0	1	0	0	.211	.250	.404	.654
	Postseason		1	1	0	0	0	0	(0	0)	0	0	0	0	0	0	0	0	0	0	0	0	0	.000	.000	.000	.000
	5 ML YEARS		242	578	155	30	5	14	(2	12)	229	72	66	78	40	7	131	5	0	3	16	9	9	.268	.319	.396	.716

Penn Murfee

Pitches: R Bats: R Pos: RP-63; SP-1 **Ht: 6'2" Wt: 195 Born: 5/2/1994 Age: 29**

Year	Team	Lg	G	GS	GF	IP	BFP	H	R	ER	HR	SH	SF	HB	TBB	IBB	SO	WP	W	L	Pct	Sv-Op	Hld	Vel	OPS	ERC	ERA
2022	Tacom	AAA	5	0	4	8.0	27	1	0	0	0	1	0	1	2	0	10	0	2	0	1.000	2- -	-	-	.197	0.35	0.00
2022	Sea	AL	64	1	15	69.1	272	48	23	23	7	0	2	2	18	1	76	2	4	0	1.000	0-0	7	89	.570	2.08	2.99

Patrick Murphy

Pitches: R Bats: R Pos: RP-6 **Ht: 6'5" Wt: 211 Born: 6/10/1995 Age: 28**

Year	Team	Lg	G	GS	GF	IP	BFP	H	R	ER	HR	SH	SF	HB	TBB	IBB	SO	WP	W	L	Pct	Sv-Op	Hld	Vel	OPS	ERC	ERA
2022	Roch	AAA	40	7	9	63.0	280	59	41	35	6	1	1	2	33	1	73	4	3	3	.500	2- -	-	-	.707	4.22	5.00
2020	Tor	AL	4	0	2	6.0	25	6	1	1	0	0	0	0	2	0	5	0	0	0	-	0-0	0	97	.711	3.19	1.50
2021	2 Tms		25	0	4	28.0	128	31	18	16	3	0	0	4	10	0	29	3	0	3	.000	0-0	5	97	.764	5.07	5.14
2022	Was	NL	6	0	1	5.2	34	8	6	4	0	0	1	0	8	0	4	1	0	0	-	0-0	0	96	.791	9.47	6.35
21	Tor	AL	8	0	1	9.1	44	12	6	5	1	0	0	2	4	0	6	1	0	1	.000	0-0	1	97	.856	7.02	4.82
21	Was	NL	17	0	3	18.2	84	19	12	11	2	0	0	2	6	0	23	2	0	2	.000	0-0	4	97	.716	4.18	5.30
	3 ML YEARS		35	0	7	39.2	187	45	25	21	3	0	1	4	20	0	38	4	0	3	.000	0-0	5	96	.764	5.39	4.76

Sean Murphy

Bats: R Throws: R Pos: C-116;DH-30;PH-2 **Ht: 6'3" Wt: 228 Born: 10/4/1994 Age: 28**

Year	Team	Lg	G	AB	H	2B	3B	HR	(Hm	Rd)	TB	R	RBI	RC	TBB	IBB	SO	HBP	SH	SF	SB	CS	GDP	Avg	OBP	Slg	OPS
2019	Oak	AL	20	53	13	5	0	4	(1	3)	30	14	8	7	6	0	16	1	0	0	0	0	3	.245	.333	.566	.899
2020	Oak	AL	43	116	27	5	0	7	(3	4)	53	21	14	15	24	0	37	0	0	0	0	0	6	.233	.364	.457	.821
2021	Oak	AL	119	393	85	23	0	17	(6	11)	159	47	59	53	40	0	114	12	0	3	0	0	7	.216	.306	.405	.710
2022	Oak	AL	148	537	134	37	2	18	(7	11)	229	67	66	81	56	2	124	13	0	5	1	0	14	.250	.332	.426	.759
	Postseason		8	23	5	0	0	2	(2	0)	11	4	4	5	2	0	4	0	0	1	0	0	1	.217	.269	.478	.747
	4 ML YEARS		330	1099	259	70	2	46	(17	29)	471	149	147	156	126	2	291	26	0	8	1	0	30	.236	.326	.429	.755

Tom Murphy

Bats: R Throws: R Pos: C-12;PH-2;DH-1 **Ht: 6'1" Wt: 206 Born: 4/3/1991 Age: 32**

Year	Team	Lg	G	AB	H	2B	3B	HR	(Hm	Rd)	TB	R	RBI	RC	TBB	IBB	SO	HBP	SH	SF	SB	CS	GDP	Avg	OBP	Slg	OPS
2015	Col	NL	11	35	9	1	0	3	(3	0)	19	5	9	9	4	1	10	0	0	0	0	0	0	.257	.333	.543	.876
2016	Col	NL	21	44	12	2	0	5	(5	0)	29	8	13	10	4	0	19	1	0	0	1	0	0	.273	.347	.659	1.006
2017	Col	NL	12	24	1	1	0	0	(0	0)	2	1	1	0	2	1	9	0	0	0	0	0	0	.042	.115	.083	.199
2018	Col	NL	37	93	21	7	1	2	(1	1)	36	5	11	8	3	1	44	0	0	0	0	1	2	.226	.250	.387	.637
2019	Sea	AL	76	260	71	12	1	18	(6	12)	139	32	40	43	19	0	87	1	0	1	2	0	0	.273	.324	.535	.858
2021	Sea	AL	97	277	56	8	0	11	(10	1)	97	35	34	34	40	0	99	2	0	3	0	0	8	.202	.304	.350	.655
2022	Sea	AL	14	33	10	2	0	1	(0	1)	15	9	1	5	8	0	13	0	0	0	0	0	1	.303	.439	.455	.894
	7 ML YEARS		268	766	180	33	2	40	(25	15)	337	95	109	109	80	3	281	4	0	4	3	1	13	.235	.309	.440	.749

Joe Musgrove

Pitches: R Bats: R Pos: SP-30 **Ht: 6'5" Wt: 230 Born: 12/4/1992 Age: 30**

Year	Team	Lg	G	GS	GF	IP	BFP	H	R	ER	HR	SH	SF	HB	TBB	IBB	SO	WP	W	L	Pct	Sv-Op	Hld	Vel	OPS	ERC	ERA
2016	Hou	AL	11	10	1	62.0	256	59	28	28	9	0	1	3	16	0	55	0	4	4	.500	0-0	0	92	.758	3.80	4.06
2017	Hou	AL	38	15	5	109.1	462	117	59	58	18	5	2	4	28	1	98	4	7	8	.467	2-4	5	93	.798	4.54	4.77
2018	Pit	NL	19	19	0	115.1	486	113	56	52	12	3	5	8	23	3	100	5	6	9	.400	0-0	0	93	.687	3.40	4.06
2019	Pit	NL	32	31	0	170.1	718	168	98	84	21	1	6	9	39	1	157	2	11	12	.478	0-0	1	92	.738	3.66	4.44
2020	Pit	NL	8	8	0	39.2	166	33	17	17	5	0	2	2	16	0	55	1	1	5	.167	0-0	0	92	.711	3.56	3.86
2021	SD	NL	32	31	1	181.1	748	142	68	64	22	3	6	18	54	3	203	3	11	9	.550	0-0	0	93	.652	3.00	3.18
2022	SD	NL	30	30	0	181.0	740	154	67	59	22	0	4	14	42	1	184	4	10	7	.588	0-0	0	93	.667	3.06	2.93
	Postseason		7	0	3	6.2	27	6	6	6	3	0	1	0	1	1	3	0	1	0	1.000	0-0	1	95	.859	4.35	8.10
	7 ML YEARS		170	144	7	859.0	3576	786	393	362	109	12	26	58	218	9	852	19	50	54	.481	2-4	6	93	.707	3.47	3.79

Parker Mushinski

Pitches: L Bats: L Pos: RP-7 **Ht: 6'0" Wt: 218 Born: 11/22/1995 Age: 27**

Year	Team	Lg	G	GS	GF	IP	BFP	H	R	ER	HR	SH	SF	HB	TBB	IBB	SO	WP	W	L	Pct	Sv-Op	Hld	Vel	OPS	ERC	ERA
2022	SgrLnd	AAA	38	0	8	40.2	172	28	17	12	3	2	3	3	19	0	41	4	2	2	.500	0- -	-	-	.570	2.72	2.66
2022	Hou	AL	7	0	1	7.1	30	5	3	3	0	0	0	1	3	0	8	0	0	0	-	0-0	1	92	.569	2.32	3.68

Simon Muzziotti

Bats: L Throws: L Pos: CF-8;PR-1 **Ht: 6'1" Wt: 175 Born: 12/27/1998 Age: 24**

Year	Team	Lg	G	AB	H	2B	3B	HR	(Hm	Rd)	TB	R	RBI	RC	TBB	IBB	SO	HBP	SH	SF	SB	CS	GDP	Avg	OBP	Slg	OPS
2022	Rdng	AA	38	143	37	5	4	5	(-	-)	65	23	20	22	19	0	31	0	0	3	7	3	4	.259	.339	.455	.794
2022	Phi	NL	9	7	1	0	0	0	(0	0)	1	0	0	0	0	0	2	1	1	0	0	0	0	.143	.250	.143	.393

Wil Myers

Bats: R Throws: R Pos: RF-36;1B-25;LF-10;CF-6;PH-6;3B-1   Ht: 6'3" Wt: 207 Born: 12/10/1990 Age: 32

								BATTING													RUNNING			AVERAGES			
Year	Team	Lg	G	AB	H	2B	3B	HR	(Hm	Rd)	TB	R	RBI	RC	TBB	IBB	SO	HBP	SH	SF	SB	CS	GDP	Avg	OBP	Slg	OPS
2013	TB	AL	88	335	98	23	0	13	(5	8)	160	50	53	52	33	6	91	1	0	4	5	2	10	.293	.354	.478	.831
2014	TB	AL	87	325	72	14	0	6	(2	4)	104	37	35	32	34	3	90	0	0	2	6	1	10	.222	.294	.320	.614
2015	SD	NL	60	225	57	13	1	8	(3	5)	96	40	29	35	27	0	55	1	0	0	5	2	2	.253	.336	.427	.763
2016	SD	NL	157	599	155	29	4	28	(18	10)	276	99	94	97	68	1	160	4	0	5	28	6	12	.259	.336	.461	.797
2017	SD	NL	155	567	138	29	3	30	(8	22)	263	80	74	80	70	3	180	5	0	7	20	6	15	.243	.328	.464	.792
2018	SD	NL	83	312	79	25	1	11	(6	5)	139	39	39	45	30	1	94	0	0	1	13	1	10	.253	.318	.446	.763
2019	SD	NL	155	435	104	22	1	18	(9	9)	182	58	53	54	51	0	168	2	1	1	16	7	12	.239	.321	.418	.739
2020	SD	NL	55	198	57	14	2	15	(11	4)	120	34	40	44	18	0	56	2	0	0	2	1	5	.288	.353	.606	.959
2021	SD	NL	146	442	113	24	2	17	(6	11)	192	56	63	65	54	2	141	0	0	4	8	5	9	.256	.334	.434	.768
2022	SD	NL	77	261	68	15	0	7	(3	4)	104	29	41	35	21	1	86	1	0	3	2	1	7	.261	.315	.398	.713
	Postseason		11	42	7	1	0	2	(2	0)	14	4	5	3	5	1	15	0	0	0	1	0	0	.167	.255	.333	.589
	10 ML YEARS		1063	3699	941	208	14	153	(71	82)	1636	522	521	539	406	17	1121	16	1	27	105	32	87	.254	.329	.442	.771

James Naile

Pitches: R Bats: R Pos: RP-7   Ht: 6'4" Wt: 185 Born: 2/8/1993 Age: 30

			HOW MUCH PITCHED				WHAT HE GAVE UP										THE RESULTS							
Year	Team	Lg	G	GS	GF	IP	BFP	H	R	ER	HR	SH	SF	HB	TBB	IBB	SO	WP	W	L	Pct	Sv-Op	Hld	Vel	OPS	ERC	ERA
2022	Memp	AAA	44	3	8	73.1	317	80	31	27	5	1	0	5	21	0	64	6	4	3	.571	0- -	-	-	.694	4.21	3.31
2022	StL	NL	7	0	4	9.0	37	8	5	5	2	0	0	0	2	0	5	0	0	0	-	0-0	0	92	.670	3.48	5.00

Tommy Nance

Pitches: R Bats: R Pos: RP-33; SP-2   Ht: 6'6" Wt: 235 Born: 3/19/1991 Age: 32

			HOW MUCH PITCHED				WHAT HE GAVE UP										THE RESULTS							
Year	Team	Lg	G	GS	GF	IP	BFP	H	R	ER	HR	SH	SF	HB	TBB	IBB	SO	WP	W	L	Pct	Sv-Op	Hld	Vel	OPS	ERC	ERA
2021	ChC	NL	27	0	6	28.2	127	25	23	23	5	0	1	3	13	0	30	7	1	1	.500	0-0	5	95	.741	4.42	7.22
2022	Mia	NL	35	2	8	43.2	196	45	22	21	5	1	0	4	21	3	57	5	2	3	.400	0-2	2	94	.777	4.95	4.33
	2 ML YEARS		62	2	14	72.1	323	70	45	44	10	1	1	7	34	3	87	12	3	4	.429	0-2	7	95	.763	4.74	5.47

Tyler Naquin

Bats: L Throws: R Pos: RF-68;DH-15;LF-14;PH-13;PR-4;CF-3   NAY-kwin   Ht: 6'2" Wt: 195 Born: 4/24/1991 Age: 32

								BATTING													RUNNING			AVERAGES			
Year	Team	Lg	G	AB	H	2B	3B	HR	(Hm	Rd)	TB	R	RBI	RC	TBB	IBB	SO	HBP	SH	SF	SB	CS	GDP	Avg	OBP	Slg	OPS
2016	Cle	AL	116	321	95	18	5	14	(9	5)	165	52	43	53	36	4	112	4	2	2	6	3	4	.296	.372	.514	.886
2017	Cle	AL	19	37	8	2	0	0	(0	0)	10	4	1	2	2	0	9	0	0	1	1	1	1	.216	.250	.270	.520
2018	Cle	AL	61	174	46	7	0	3	(0	3)	62	22	23	21	6	1	42	2	0	1	1	1	1	.264	.295	.356	.651
2019	Cle	AL	89	274	79	19	0	10	(6	4)	128	34	34	36	14	2	66	2	2	2	4	2	8	.288	.325	.467	.792
2020	Cle	AL	40	133	29	8	1	4	(0	4)	51	15	20	14	5	0	40	1	0	2	0	1	3	.218	.248	.383	.632
2021	Cin	NL	127	411	111	24	2	19	(13	6)	196	52	70	67	35	1	106	5	0	3	5	3	5	.270	.333	.477	.809
2022	2 Tms	NL	105	310	71	19	4	11	(7	4)	131	47	46	40	19	2	93	4	1	0	4	2	3	.229	.282	.423	.705
22	Cin	NL	56	187	46	12	2	7	(4	3)	83	29	33	28	13	2	53	3	1	0	3	2	1	.246	.305	.444	.749
22	NYM	NL	49	123	25	7	2	4	(3	1)	48	18	13	12	6	0	40	1	0	0	1	0	2	.203	.246	.390	.636
	Postseason		13	31	5	2	0	0	(0	0)	7	0	3	1	1	1	18	0	1	0	0	0	0	.161	.188	.226	.413
	7 ML YEARS		557	1660	439	97	12	61	(35	26)	743	226	237	233	117	10	468	18	5	11	20	13	29	.264	.318	.448	.765

Andrew Nardi

Pitches: L Bats: L Pos: RP-13   Ht: 6'3" Wt: 215 Born: 8/18/1998 Age: 24

			HOW MUCH PITCHED				WHAT HE GAVE UP										THE RESULTS							
Year	Team	Lg	G	GS	GF	IP	BFP	H	R	ER	HR	SH	SF	HB	TBB	IBB	SO	WP	W	L	Pct	Sv-Op	Hld	Vel	OPS	ERC	ERA
2022	Pnscla	AA	13	0	5	19.1	75	15	4	3	1	0	0	1	4	0	31	4	2	2	.500	2- -	-	-	.567	2.17	1.40
2022	Jaxnvl	AAA	24	0	15	31.2	124	14	10	10	3	0	1	2	14	0	45	0	3	0	1.000	7- -	-	-	.494	1.65	2.84
2022	Mia	NL	13	0	5	14.2	83	25	17	16	5	0	0	0	14	0	24	1	1	1	.500	0-0	1	95	1.151	13.27	9.82

Omar Narvaez

Bats: L Throws: R Pos: C-83;DH-1;PH-1   nahr-VIE-ez   Ht: 5'11" Wt: 220 Born: 2/10/1992 Age: 31

								BATTING													RUNNING			AVERAGES			
Year	Team	Lg	G	AB	H	2B	3B	HR	(Hm	Rd)	TB	R	RBI	RC	TBB	IBB	SO	HBP	SH	SF	SB	CS	GDP	Avg	OBP	Slg	OPS
2016	CWS	AL	34	101	27	4	0	1	(1	0)	34	13	10	15	14	1	14	0	0	2	0	0	0	.267	.350	.337	.687
2017	CWS	AL	90	253	70	10	0	2	(2	0)	86	23	14	33	38	1	45	1	3	0	0	0	8	.277	.373	.340	.713
2018	CWS	AL	97	280	77	14	1	9	(4	5)	120	30	30	43	38	1	65	2	2	0	0	2	5	.275	.366	.429	.794
2019	Sea	AL	132	428	119	12	0	22	(13	9)	197	63	55	66	47	1	92	4	0	3	0	0	5	.278	.353	.460	.813
2020	Mil	NL	40	108	19	4	0	2	(2	0)	29	8	10	13	16	0	39	2	0	0	0	0	1	.176	.294	.269	.562
2021	Mil	NL	123	391	104	20	0	11	(4	7)	157	54	49	59	41	3	84	1	0	6	0	0	13	.266	.342	.402	.743
2022	Mil	NL	84	262	54	12	1	4	(1	3)	80	21	23	23	29	1	57	3	1	1	0	0	4	.206	.292	.305	.597
	Postseason		5	9	3	1	0	0	(0	0)	4	0	1	1	0	0	1	0	0	0	0	0	1	.333	.333	.444	.778
	7 ML YEARS		600	1823	470	76	2	51	(27	24)	703	212	191	252	223	8	396	19	6	12	0	2	36	.258	.343	.386	.728

Packy Naughton

Pitches: L Bats: R Pos: RP-23; SP-3   Ht: 6'2" Wt: 195 Born: 4/16/1996 Age: 27

Year	Team	Lg	G	GS	GF	IP	BFP	H	R	ER	HR	SH	SF	HB	TBB	IBB	SO	WP	W	L	Pct	Sv-Op	Hld	Vel	OPS	ERC	ERA
2022	Memp	AAA	11	0	2	21.2	89	21	6	5	2	1	0	1	5	0	25	0	2	1	.667	0- -	-	-	.721	3.43	2.08
2021	LAA	AL	7	5	0	22.2	108	27	18	16	3	0	0	1	14	1	12	0	0	4	.000	0-0	0	91	.808	6.44	6.35
2022	StL	NL	26	3	5	32.0	141	39	17	17	3	1	0	1	7	1	31	1	0	2	.000	1-2	3	93	.775	4.58	4.78
	2 ML YEARS		33	8	5	54.2	249	66	35	33	6	1	0	2	21	2	43	1	0	6	.000	1-2	3	92	.790	5.33	5.43

Bo Naylor

Bats: L Throws: R Pos: C-4;DH-1   Ht: 6'0" Wt: 205 Born: 2/21/2000 Age: 23

							BATTING														RUNNING			AVERAGES			
Year	Team	Lg	G	AB	H	2B	3B	HR	(Hm	Rd)	TB	R	RBI	RC	TBB	IBB	SO	HBP	SH	SF	SB	CS	GDP	Avg	OBP	Slg	OPS
2018	Indians2	R	33	117	32	3	3	2	(-	-)	47	17	17	20	21	0	28	0	0	1	5	1	0	.274	.381	.402	.783
2019	Lk Cty	A	107	399	97	18	10	11	(-	-)	168	60	65	57	43	1	104	1	3	7	7	5	8	.243	.313	.421	.734
2021	Akron	AA	87	313	59	13	1	10	(-	-)	104	41	44	32	37	1	112	3	1	1	10	0	3	.188	.280	.332	.612
2022	Akron	AA	52	170	46	12	2	6	(-	-)	80	29	21	37	45	0	46	3	0	2	11	3	3	.271	.427	.471	.898
2022	Clmbs	AAA	66	245	63	14	2	15	(-	-)	126	44	47	50	37	0	75	6	0	2	9	1	5	.257	.366	.514	.880
2022	Cle	AL	5	8	0	0	0	0	(0	0)	0	0	0	0	0	0	5	0	0	0	0	0	0	.000	.000	.000	.000

Josh Naylor

Bats: L Throws: L Pos: 1B-88;DH-27;PH-6;RF-5   Ht: 5'11" Wt: 250 Born: 6/22/1997 Age: 26

							BATTING														RUNNING			AVERAGES			
Year	Team	Lg	G	AB	H	2B	3B	HR	(Hm	Rd)	TB	R	RBI	RC	TBB	IBB	SO	HBP	SH	SF	SB	CS	GDP	Avg	OBP	Slg	OPS
2019	SD	NL	94	253	63	15	0	8	(4	4)	102	29	32	36	25	1	64	0	0	1	1	1	4	.249	.315	.403	.719
2020	2 Tms		40	97	24	3	1	1	(0	1)	32	13	6	9	5	0	12	1	0	2	1	0	2	.247	.291	.330	.621
2021	Cle	AL	69	233	59	13	0	7	(1	6)	93	28	21	24	14	1	45	2	0	0	1	0	7	.253	.301	.399	.700
2022	Cle	AL	122	449	115	28	0	20	(9	11)	203	47	79	76	38	4	80	6	0	5	6	1	13	.256	.319	.452	.771
20	SD	NL	18	36	10	0	1	1	(0	1)	15	4	4	4	1	0	4	1	0	0	1	0	2	.278	.316	.417	.732
20	Cle	AL	22	61	14	3	0	0	(0	0)	17	9	2	5	4	0	8	0	0	0	0	0	0	.230	.277	.279	.556
	Postseason		2	7	5	3	0	1	(1	0)	11	3	3	3	0	0	0	0	0	0	0	0	0	.714	.714	1.571	2.286
	4 ML YEARS		325	1032	261	59	1	36	(14	22)	430	117	138	145	82	6	201	9	0	6	9	2	26	.253	.312	.417	.728

Nick Neidert

Pitches: R Bats: R Pos: SP-1   NY-dert   Ht: 6'1" Wt: 202 Born: 11/20/1996 Age: 26

Year	Team	Lg	G	GS	GF	IP	BFP	H	R	ER	HR	SH	SF	HB	TBB	IBB	SO	WP	W	L	Pct	Sv-Op	Hld	Vel	OPS	ERC	ERA
2022	Jaxnvl	AAA	14	8	1	46.0	184	39	15	10	6	0	0	3	9	0	48	0	4	0	1.000	1- -	-	-	.643	2.96	1.96
2020	Mia	NL	4	0	1	8.1	34	10	5	5	1	0	0	0	4	0	4	0	0	0	-	0-0	0	92	.853	5.06	5.40
2021	Mia	NL	8	7	1	35.2	157	31	18	18	4	1	2	5	23	1	21	3	1	2	.333	0-0	0	92	.783	5.08	4.54
2022	Mia	NL	1	1	0	5.0	20	5	2	2	1	0	0	0	0	0	3	0	0	1	.000	0-0	0	92	.700	3.05	3.60
	3 ML YEARS		13	8	2	49.0	211	46	25	25	6	1	2	5	25	1	28	3	1	3	.250	0-0	0	92	.789	4.88	4.59

Jimmy Nelson

Pitches: R Bats: R Pos: P   Ht: 6'6" Wt: 250 Born: 6/5/1989 Age: 34

Year	Team	Lg	G	GS	GF	IP	BFP	H	R	ER	HR	SH	SF	HB	TBB	IBB	SO	WP	W	L	Pct	Sv-Op	Hld	Vel	OPS	ERC	ERA
2013	Mil	NL	4	1	0	10.0	37	2	1	1	0	0	1	0	5	0	8	1	0	0	-	0-0	0	-	.286	0.64	0.90
2014	Mil	NL	14	12	1	69.1	311	82	42	38	6	1	2	8	19	0	57	4	2	9	.182	0-0	0	-	.793	4.96	4.93
2015	Mil	NL	30	30	0	177.1	752	163	89	81	18	4	7	13	65	4	148	11	11	13	.458	0-0	0	-	.704	3.79	4.11
2016	Mil	NL	32	32	0	179.1	807	186	108	92	25	7	4	17	86	2	140	8	8	16	.333	0-0	0	-	.791	5.29	4.62
2017	Mil	NL	29	29	0	175.1	728	171	75	68	16	4	2	9	48	1	199	6	12	6	.667	0-0	0	-	.689	3.64	3.49
2019	Mil	NL	10	3	2	22.0	105	25	18	17	4	0	0	2	17	1	26	1	0	2	.000	0-0	0	-	.966	7.63	6.95
2021	LAD	NL	28	1	5	29.0	116	14	8	6	0	1	0	4	13	0	44	4	1	2	.333	0-1	6	-	.453	1.56	1.86
	7 ML YEARS		147	108	8	662.1	2856	643	341	303	69	17	16	53	253	8	622	35	34	48	.415	0-1	6	-	.728	4.20	4.12

Kyle Nelson

Pitches: L Bats: L Pos: RP-42; SP-1   Ht: 6'1" Wt: 175 Born: 7/8/1996 Age: 26

Year	Team	Lg	G	GS	GF	IP	BFP	H	R	ER	HR	SH	SF	HB	TBB	IBB	SO	WP	W	L	Pct	Sv-Op	Hld	Vel	OPS	ERC	ERA
2020	Cle	AL	1	0	0	0.2	6	3	4	4	1	0	0	1	1	0	0	0	0	0	-	0-0	0	90	1.867	56.63	54.00
2021	Cle	AL	10	0	4	9.2	49	10	10	10	0	0	0	2	8	0	8	0	0	0	-	0-0	0	93	.716	5.81	9.31
2022	Ari	NL	43	1	4	37.0	151	26	10	9	1	0	0	3	14	0	30	1	2	1	.667	0-0	11	92	.583	2.28	2.19
	3 ML YEARS		54	1	8	47.1	206	39	24	23	2	0	0	5	23	0	38	1	2	1	.667	0-0	11	92	.651	3.41	4.37

Nick Nelson

Pitches: R Bats: R Pos: RP-45; SP-2   Ht: 6'1" Wt: 205 Born: 12/5/1995 Age: 27

Year	Team	Lg	G	GS	GF	IP	BFP	H	R	ER	HR	SH	SF	HB	TBB	IBB	SO	WP	W	L	Pct	Sv-Op	Hld	Vel	OPS	ERC	ERA
2020	NYY	AL	11	0	4	20.2	90	20	13	11	4	0	0	1	11	0	18	0	1	0	1.000	0-0	0	96	.780	5.18	4.79
2021	NYY	AL	11	2	3	14.1	78	15	16	14	0	0	2	3	16	0	22	5	0	2	.000	0-1	0	96	.857	6.94	8.79
2022	Phi	NL	47	2	10	68.2	306	66	38	37	1	0	9	4	36	0	69	13	3	2	.600	1-1	3	96	.697	3.91	4.85
	Postseason		2	0	1	2.0	7	1	0	0	0	0	0	0	0	0	2	0	0	0	-	0-0	0	-	.286	0.54	0.00
	3 ML YEARS		69	4	17	103.2	474	101	67	62	5	0	12	7	63	0	109	18	4	4	.500	1-2	3	96	.738	4.58	5.38

Ryne Nelson

Pitches: R Bats: R Pos: SP-3   Ht: 6'3" Wt: 184 Born: 2/1/1998 Age: 25

Year Team	Lg	G	GS	GF	IP	BFP	H	R	ER	HR	SH	SF	HB	TBB	IBB	SO	WP	W	L	Pct	Sv-Op	Hld	Vel	OPS	ERC	ERA
2022 Reno	AAA	26	26	0	136.0	593	142	88	82	25	0	4	4	47	0	128	3	10	5	.667	0- -	-	-	.803	4.79	5.43
2022 Ari	NL	3	3	0	18.1	69	9	4	3	2	0	1	0	6	1	16	0	1	1	.500	0-0	0	95	.524	1.42	1.47

Hector Neris

Pitches: R Bats: R Pos: RP-70   NAIR-ess   Ht: 6'2" Wt: 227 Born: 6/14/1989 Age: 34

Year Team	Lg	G	GS	GF	IP	BFP	H	R	ER	HR	SH	SF	HB	TBB	IBB	SO	WP	W	L	Pct	Sv-Op	Hld	Vel	OPS	ERC	ERA
2014 Phi	NL	1	0	1	1.0	3	0	0	0	0	0	0	0	0	0	1	0	1	0	1.000	0-0	0	93	.000	0.00	0.00
2015 Phi	NL	32	0	8	40.1	170	38	19	17	8	1	0	4	10	0	41	3	2	2	.500	0-0	2	93	.772	4.21	3.79
2016 Phi	NL	79	0	13	80.1	328	59	26	23	9	1	2	3	30	3	102	4	4	4	.500	2-6	28	94	.620	2.73	2.58
2017 Phi	NL	74	0	56	74.2	320	68	26	25	9	1	2	6	26	3	86	2	4	5	.444	26-29	4	95	.689	3.74	3.01
2018 Phi	NL	53	0	28	47.2	203	46	27	27	11	2	0	1	16	1	76	5	1	3	.250	11-14	4	95	.803	4.55	5.10
2019 Phi	NL	68	0	49	67.2	275	45	24	22	10	1	2	6	24	1	89	2	3	6	.333	28-34	2	95	.613	2.74	2.93
2020 Phi	NL	24	0	13	21.2	103	24	15	11	0	0	0	0	13	2	27	3	2	2	.500	5-8	4	94	.670	4.36	4.57
2021 Phi	NL	74	0	29	74.1	310	55	34	30	12	1	1	4	32	3	98	4	4	7	.364	12-19	11	94	.677	3.32	3.63
2022 Hou	AL	70	0	26	65.1	263	49	29	27	3	1	0	6	17	0	79	6	6	4	.600	3-7	25	94	.580	2.27	3.72
9 ML YEARS		475	0	223	473.0	1975	384	200	182	62	8	7	30	168	13	599	29	27	33	.450	87-117	80	94	.668	3.28	3.46

Sheldon Neuse

Bats: R Throws: R Pos: 3B-44;2B-23;1B-13;DH-9;PH-8;PR-3;SS-2   Ht: 6'0" Wt: 232 Born: 12/10/1994 Age: 28

Year Team	Lg	G	AB	H	2B	3B	HR	(Hm	Rd)	TB	R	RBI	RC	TBB	IBB	SO	HBP	SH	SF	SB	CS	GDP	Avg	OBP	Slg	OPS
2022 LsVgs	AAA	25	108	43	6	1	5	(-	-)	66	14	20	24	3	0	22	0	0	2	2	0	3	.398	.407	.611	1.018
2019 Oak	AL	25	56	14	3	0	0	(0	0)	17	3	7	5	4	0	19	0	0	1	0	0	2	.250	.295	.304	.599
2021 LAD	NL	33	65	11	1	0	3	(2	1)	21	6	4	0	1	0	26	0	0	0	1	1	2	.169	.182	.323	.505
2022 Oak	AL	89	271	58	4	2	4	(1	3)	78	25	26	25	20	0	80	2	0	6	6	1	5	.214	.273	.288	.561
3 ML YEARS		147	392	83	8	2	7	(3	4)	116	34	37	30	25	0	125	2	0	7	7	2	9	.212	.262	.296	.558

Tyler Nevin

Bats: R Throws: R Pos: 3B-44;1B-8;DH-3;LF-2;RF-1   Ht: 6'4" Wt: 225 Born: 5/29/1997 Age: 26

Year Team	Lg	G	AB	H	2B	3B	HR	(Hm	Rd)	TB	R	RBI	RC	TBB	IBB	SO	HBP	SH	SF	SB	CS	GDP	Avg	OBP	Slg	OPS
2022 Norfolk	AAA	44	165	48	8	1	7	(-	-)	79	30	36	29	21	0	36	4	0	1	4	0	8	.291	.382	.479	.861
2021 Bal	AL	6	14	4	2	0	1	(0	1)	9	3	3	4	4	0	5	0	0	0	0	0	0	.286	.444	.643	1.087
2022 Bal	AL	58	157	31	4	0	2	(0	2)	41	17	16	12	20	0	46	4	0	3	0	0	4	.197	.299	.261	.560
2 ML YEARS		64	171	35	6	0	3	(0	3)	50	20	19	16	24	0	51	4	0	3	0	0	4	.205	.312	.292	.604

Sean Newcomb

Pitches: L Bats: L Pos: RP-19; SP-1   Ht: 6'5" Wt: 255 Born: 6/12/1993 Age: 30

Year Team	Lg	G	GS	GF	IP	BFP	H	R	ER	HR	SH	SF	HB	TBB	IBB	SO	WP	W	L	Pct	Sv-Op	Hld	Vel	OPS	ERC	ERA
2022 Iowa	AAA	12	1	3	24.0	101	12	10	9	1	0	0	2	18	0	31	2	1	1	.500	1- -	-	-	.539	2.65	3.38
2017 Atl	NL	19	19	0	100.0	456	100	51	48	10	5	3	6	57	6	108	3	4	9	.308	0-0	0	94	.780	4.85	4.32
2018 Atl	NL	31	30	0	164.0	696	137	74	71	18	4	3	1	81	1	160	4	12	9	.571	0-0	0	93	.679	3.62	3.90
2019 Atl	NL	55	4	4	68.1	293	61	28	24	8	0	2	3	29	1	65	4	6	3	.667	1-3	16	94	.692	3.83	3.16
2020 Atl	NL	4	4	0	13.2	70	20	17	17	4	0	1	3	6	0	10	1	0	2	.000	0-0	0	93	.998	9.58	11.20
2021 Atl	NL	32	0	5	32.1	150	28	17	17	1	1	1	2	27	1	43	5	2	0	1.000	1-2	2	96	.719	4.66	4.73
2022 2 Tms	NL	20	1	2	27.2	134	33	28	27	8	0	0	0	19	0	28	2	2	1	.667	0-0	2	94	.927	7.90	8.78
22 Atl	NL	3	0	0	5.0	26	7	4	4	1	0	0	0	4	0	4	1	0	0	-	0-0	0	95	.969	8.96	7.20
22 ChC	NL	17	1	2	22.2	108	26	24	23	7	0	0	0	15	0	24	1	2	1	.667	0-0	2	94	.917	7.66	9.13
Postseason		6	1	1	8.1	28	2	2	1	0	1	0	0	3	0	6	0	1	0	1.000	0-0	1	96	.269	0.57	1.08
6 ML YEARS		161	58	11	406.0	1799	379	215	204	49	10	10	15	219	9	414	19	26	24	.520	2-5	20	94	.741	4.49	4.52

Kevin Newman

Bats: R Throws: R Pos: 2B-42;SS-33;PH-6;DH-3   Ht: 6'0" Wt: 195 Born: 8/4/1993 Age: 29

Year Team	Lg	G	AB	H	2B	3B	HR	(Hm	Rd)	TB	R	RBI	RC	TBB	IBB	SO	HBP	SH	SF	SB	CS	GDP	Avg	OBP	Slg	OPS
2022 Indy	AAA	13	48	19	3	0	0	(-	-)	22	6	6	8	3	0	6	1	0	1	0	0	2	.396	.434	.458	.892
2018 Pit	NL	31	91	19	2	0	0	(0	0)	21	7	6	5	4	1	23	1	0	1	0	1	2	.209	.247	.231	.478
2019 Pit	NL	130	493	152	20	6	12	(3	9)	220	61	64	73	28	2	62	7	2	1	16	8	5	.308	.353	.446	.800
2020 Pit	NL	44	156	35	5	0	1	(0	1)	43	12	10	15	12	0	21	1	1	2	0	1	1	.224	.281	.276	.556
2021 Pit	NL	148	517	117	22	3	5	(2	3)	160	50	39	35	27	3	41	1	6	3	6	1	7	.226	.265	.309	.574
2022 Pit	NL	78	288	79	18	2	2	(2	0)	107	31	24	33	16	0	48	2	1	6	8	2	6	.274	.316	.372	.687
5 ML YEARS		431	1545	402	67	11	20	(7	13)	551	161	143	161	87	6	195	12	11	8	30	13	21	.260	.303	.357	.660

Tomas Nido

Bats: R Throws: R Pos: C-96;PH-3   Ht: 6'0" Wt: 211 Born: 4/12/1994 Age: 29

Year	Team	Lg	G	AB	H	2B	3B	HR	(Hm	Rd)	TB	R	RBI	RC	TBB	IBB	SO	HBP	SH	SF	SB	CS	GDP	Avg	OBP	Slg	OPS
2017	NYM	NL	5	10	3	1	0	0	(0	0)	4	0	3	2	0	0	2	0	0	0	0	0	0	.300	.300	.400	.700
2018	NYM	NL	34	84	14	3	0	1	(1	0)	20	10	9	2	4	0	27	0	0	2	0	0	4	.167	.200	.238	.438
2019	NYM	NL	50	136	26	5	0	4	(2	2)	43	9	14	5	7	2	37	0	1	0	0	0	4	.191	.231	.316	.547
2020	NYM	NL	7	24	7	1	0	2	(2	0)	14	4	6	4	2	0	6	0	0	0	0	0	0	.292	.346	.583	.929
2021	NYM	NL	58	153	34	5	1	3	(1	2)	50	16	13	12	5	1	44	3	0	0	1	0	4	.222	.261	.327	.588
2022	NYM	NL	98	284	68	15	0	3	(1	2)	92	31	28	22	14	0	76	1	12	2	0	0	14	.239	.276	.324	.600
	6 ML YEARS		252	691	152	30	1	13	(7	6)	223	70	73	47	32	3	192	4	13	4	1	0	28	.220	.257	.323	.580

Brandon Nimmo

Bats: L Throws: R Pos: CF-151   NIH-moe   Ht: 6'3" Wt: 206 Born: 3/27/1993 Age: 30

Year	Team	Lg	G	AB	H	2B	3B	HR	(Hm	Rd)	TB	R	RBI	RC	TBB	IBB	SO	HBP	SH	SF	SB	CS	GDP	Avg	OBP	Slg	OPS
2016	NYM	NL	32	73	20	1	0	1	(1	0)	24	12	6	9	6	0	20	1	0	0	0	0	0	.274	.338	.329	.666
2017	NYM	NL	69	177	46	11	1	5	(3	2)	74	26	21	26	33	1	60	2	1	2	2	0	3	.260	.379	.418	.797
2018	NYM	NL	140	433	114	28	8	17	(8	9)	209	77	47	84	80	2	140	22	0	0	9	6	8	.263	.404	.483	.886
2019	NYM	NL	69	199	44	11	1	8	(2	6)	81	34	29	38	46	2	71	5	1	3	3	0	1	.221	.375	.407	.783
2020	NYM	NL	55	186	52	8	3	8	(5	3)	90	33	18	33	33	0	43	6	0	0	1	2	1	.280	.404	.484	.888
2021	NYM	NL	92	325	95	17	3	8	(4	4)	142	51	28	58	54	0	79	5	2	0	5	4	3	.292	.401	.437	.838
2022	NYM	NL	151	580	159	30	7	16	(4	12)	251	102	64	98	71	0	116	16	3	3	3	2	9	.274	.367	.433	.800
	7 ML YEARS		608	1973	530	106	23	63	(27	36)	871	335	213	346	323	5	529	57	7	8	23	14	25	.269	.385	.441	.827

Vinny Nittoli

Pitches: R Bats: R Pos: RP-2   Ht: 6'1" Wt: 210 Born: 11/11/1990 Age: 32

Year	Team	Lg	G	GS	GF	IP	BFP	H	R	ER	HR	SH	SF	HB	TBB	IBB	SO	WP	W	L	Pct	Sv-Op	Hld	Vel	OPS	ERC	ERA
2022	S-WB	AAA	22	4	4	36.2	147	26	15	14	5	1	2	2	13	0	44	1	4	1	.800	0- -	-	-	.653	2.84	3.44
2022	Buffalo	AAA	10	0	4	9.2	37	6	3	3	0	0	0	1	1	0	15	0	0	0	-	2- -	-	-	.416	1.18	2.79
2022	LV	AAA	5	0	0	5.2	24	8	5	5	2	0	0	0	0	0	5	0	0	0	-	0- -	-	-	1.000	6.76	7.94
2021	Sea	AL	1	0	0	1.0	6	1	2	2	1	0	0	0	2	0	1	0	0	0	-	0-0	0	93	1.500	20.50	18.00
2022	Phi	NL	2	0	0	2.0	8	0	0	0	0	0	0	1	1	0	1	0	0	0	-	0-0	1	93	.250	0.95	0.00
	2 ML YEARS		3	0	0	3.0	14	1	2	2	1	0	0	1	3	0	2	0	0	0	-	0-0	1	93	.757	5.65	6.00

Stephen Nogosek

Pitches: R Bats: R Pos: RP-12   Ht: 6'2" Wt: 205 Born: 1/11/1995 Age: 28

Year	Team	Lg	G	GS	GF	IP	BFP	H	R	ER	HR	SH	SF	HB	TBB	IBB	SO	WP	W	L	Pct	Sv-Op	Hld	Vel	OPS	ERC	ERA
2022	Syrcse	AAA	31	0	9	43.0	176	31	13	11	2	0	2	3	15	0	53	1	2	0	1.000	4- -	-	-	.570	2.33	2.30
2019	NYM	NL	7	0	0	6.2	34	12	8	8	2	0	1	0	2	0	6	0	0	1	.000	0-0	0	95	1.057	10.23	10.80
2021	NYM	NL	1	0	0	3.0	12	3	2	2	2	0	0	0	0	0	5	0	0	1	.000	0-0	0	94	1.000	5.62	6.00
2022	NYM	NL	12	0	3	22.0	95	20	10	6	4	0	0	1	7	0	21	1	1	1	.500	0-0	0	95	.697	3.85	2.45
	3 ML YEARS		20	0	9	31.2	141	35	20	16	8	0	1	1	9	0	32	1	1	3	.250	0-0	0	95	.811	5.27	4.55

Aaron Nola

Pitches: R Bats: R Pos: SP-32   Ht: 6'2" Wt: 200 Born: 6/4/1993 Age: 30

Year	Team	Lg	G	GS	GF	IP	BFP	H	R	ER	HR	SH	SF	HB	TBB	IBB	SO	WP	W	L	Pct	Sv-Op	Hld	Vel	OPS	ERC	ERA
2015	Phi	NL	13	13	0	77.2	318	74	31	31	11	1	1	2	19	1	68	0	6	2	.750	0-0	0	91	.703	3.62	3.59
2016	Phi	NL	20	20	0	111.0	483	116	68	59	10	5	4	6	29	3	121	2	6	9	.400	0-0	0	90	.712	3.80	4.78
2017	Phi	NL	27	27	0	168.0	693	154	67	66	18	2	0	2	49	2	184	1	12	11	.522	0-0	0	92	.679	3.30	3.54
2018	Phi	NL	33	33	0	212.1	831	149	57	56	17	6	4	7	58	3	224	4	17	6	.739	0-0	0	92	.570	2.09	2.37
2019	Phi	NL	34	34	0	202.1	852	176	91	87	27	4	2	11	80	3	229	3	12	7	.632	0-0	0	93	.708	3.79	3.87
2020	Phi	NL	12	12	0	71.1	289	54	31	26	9	0	1	2	23	2	96	1	5	5	.500	0-0	0	92	.627	2.72	3.28
2021	Phi	NL	32	32	0	180.2	749	165	95	93	26	3	2	9	39	1	223	0	9	9	.500	0-0	0	93	.691	3.32	4.63
2022	Phi	NL	32	32	0	205.0	807	168	75	74	19	3	0	9	29	1	235	2	11	13	.458	0-0	0	93	.603	2.30	3.25
	8 ML YEARS		203	203	0	1228.1	5022	1056	515	492	137	24	14	48	326	16	1380	13	78	62	.557	0-0	0	92	.657	3.02	3.60

Austin Nola

Bats: R Throws: R Pos: C-101;DH-6;PH-3;2B-2;3B-1   Ht: 6'0" Wt: 197 Born: 12/28/1989 Age: 33

Year	Team	Lg	G	AB	H	2B	3B	HR	(Hm	Rd)	TB	R	RBI	RC	TBB	IBB	SO	HBP	SH	SF	SB	CS	GDP	Avg	OBP	Slg	OPS
2019	Sea	AL	79	238	64	12	1	10	(1	9)	108	37	31	34	23	1	63	4	1	1	1	0	8	.269	.342	.454	.796
2020	2 Tms		48	161	44	9	1	7	(4	3)	76	24	28	27	18	1	34	3	0	2	0	0	3	.273	.353	.472	.825
2021	SD	NL	56	173	47	12	0	2	(2	0)	65	15	29	32	14	0	19	5	0	2	0	1	2	.272	.340	.376	.716
2022	SD	NL	110	347	87	15	0	4	(1	3)	114	40	40	36	34	1	60	6	1	9	2	1	5	.251	.321	.329	.649
20	Sea	AL	29	98	30	5	1	5	(3	2)	52	15	19	19	9	1	17	2	0	1	0	0	1	.306	.373	.531	.903
20	SD	NL	19	63	14	4	0	2	(1	1)	24	9	9	8	9	0	17	1	0	1	0	0	2	.222	.324	.381	.705
	Postseason		6	17	2	0	0	0	(0	0)	2	2	3	1	4	0	7	0	0	2	0	0	0	.118	.261	.118	.379
	4 ML YEARS		293	919	242	48	2	23	(8	15)	363	116	128	129	89	3	176	18	2	14	3	2	18	.263	.336	.395	.731

Lars Nootbaar

Bats: L Throws: R Pos: RF-79;CF-12;PH-12;LF-11;DH-8;PR-6   Ht: 6'3" Wt: 210 Born: 9/8/1997 Age: 25

							BATTING												RUNNING			AVERAGES			
Year	Team	Lg	G	AB	H	2B	3B	HR	(Hm | Rd)	TB	R	RBI	RC	TBB	IBB	SO	HBP	SH	SF	SB	CS	GDP	Avg	OBP	Slg	OPS
2022	Memp	AAA	17	63	14	4	0	4	(- | -)	30	13	14	11	10	0	19	1	0	3	2	0	1	.222	.325	.476	.801
2021	StL	NL	58	109	26	3	1	5	(1 | 4)	46	15	15	16	13	1	28	0	1	1	2	1	0	.239	.317	.422	.739
2022	StL	NL	108	290	66	16	3	14	(6 | 8)	130	53	40	50	51	1	71	1	0	5	4	1	3	.228	.340	.448	.788
	2 ML YEARS		166	399	92	19	4	19	(7 | 12)	176	68	55	66	64	2	99	1	1	6	6	2	3	.231	.334	.441	.775

Daniel Norris

Pitches: L Bats: L Pos: RP-38; SP-3   Ht: 6'2" Wt: 207 Born: 4/25/1993 Age: 30

			HOW MUCH PITCHED					WHAT HE GAVE UP										THE RESULTS							
Year	Team	Lg	G	GS	GF	IP	BFP	H	R	ER	HR	SH	SF	HB	TBB	IBB	SO	WP	W	L	Pct	Sv-Op	Hld	Vel	OPS	ERC	ERA
2014	Tor	AL	5	1	2	6.2	30	5	4	4	1	0	1	0	5	0	4	0	0	0	1	0-0	1	91	.667	4.31	5.40
2015	2 Tms	AL	13	13	0	60.0	251	53	31	25	9	1	4	2	19	0	45	3	3	2	.600	0-0	0	92	.732	3.55	3.75
2016	Det	AL	14	13	1	69.1	302	75	30	26	10	0	3	0	22	0	71	1	4	2	.667	0-0	0	93	.762	4.46	3.38
2017	Det	AL	22	18	1	101.2	460	120	64	60	12	2	3	3	44	3	86	1	5	8	.385	0-0	0	93	.840	5.48	5.31
2018	Det	AL	11	8	0	44.1	200	46	28	28	8	1	2	2	19	0	51	2	0	5	.000	0-0	0	90	.791	5.06	5.68
2019	Det	AL	32	29	0	144.1	610	154	75	72	25	5	3	4	38	0	125	5	3	13	.188	0-0	0	91	.797	4.58	4.49
2020	Det	AL	14	1	1	27.2	116	25	10	10	2	0	0	0	7	0	28	0	3	1	.750	0-0	0	93	.639	2.74	3.25
2021	2 Tms		56	0	13	57.0	248	55	41	39	9	1	0	2	30	1	58	5	2	3	.400	1-4	7	93	.780	5.02	6.16
2022	2 Tms		41	3	17	58.2	250	45	39	34	11	0	0	7	29	0	66	2	2	4	.333	0-2	2	91	.754	4.28	5.22
15	Tor	AL	5	5	0	23.1	103	23	11	10	3	1	2	2	12	0	18	2	1	1	.500	0-0	0	91	.816	5.10	3.86
15	Det	AL	8	8	0	36.2	148	30	20	15	6	0	2	0	7	0	27	1	2	1	.667	0-0	0	92	.674	2.64	3.68
21	Det	AL	38	0	10	36.2	157	38	25	24	4	0	0	2	15	1	40	3	1	3	.250	1-3	6	93	.757	4.70	5.89
21	Mil	NL	18	0	3	20.1	91	17	16	15	5	1	0	0	15	0	18	2	1	0	1.000	0-1	1	93	.822	5.60	6.64
22	ChC	NL	27	1	12	30.0	134	23	28	23	7	0	0	2	21	0	43	1	0	4	.000	0-0	2	92	.821	5.17	6.90
22	Det	AL	14	2	5	28.2	116	22	11	11	4	0	0	5	8	0	23	1	2	0	1.000	0-0	0	91	.680	3.38	3.45
	9 ML YEARS		208	86	35	569.2	2467	578	322	298	87	10	16	20	213	4	534	19	22	38	.367	1-4	10	92	.779	4.56	4.71

James Norwood

Pitches: R Bats: R Pos: RP-20   Ht: 6'2" Wt: 215 Born: 12/24/1993 Age: 29

			HOW MUCH PITCHED					WHAT HE GAVE UP										THE RESULTS							
Year	Team	Lg	G	GS	GF	IP	BFP	H	R	ER	HR	SH	SF	HB	TBB	IBB	SO	WP	W	L	Pct	Sv-Op	Hld	Vel	OPS	ERC	ERA
2022	Wrcstr		15	0	2	20.1	88	19	13	11	0	0	0	0	11	0	24	4	0	1	.000	0- -	-		.705	3.57	4.87
2018	ChC	NL	11	0	5	11.0	54	14	7	5	0	0	2	0	5	0	10	1	0	1	.000	0-0	2	98	.714	4.75	4.09
2019	ChC	NL	9	0	3	9.1	44	9	4	3	1	0	0	0	8	0	11	1	0	1	.000	0-0	0	96	.803	5.76	2.89
2020	ChC	NL	3	0	0	1.2	9	4	3	3	0	0	0	0	1	0	1	0	0	0	-	0-0	0	97	1.181	14.52	16.20
2021	SD	NL	5	0	2	5.0	23	6	0	0	0	0	0	0	3	0	3	0	0	0	-	0-0	0	97	.741	5.34	0.00
2022	Phi	NL	20	0	5	17.1	85	24	17	16	2	0	0	0	9	0	22	0	1	0	1.000	0-0	1	97	.822	6.84	8.31
	5 ML YEARS		48	0	15	44.1	215	57	31	27	3	0	2	0	26	0	46	3	1	2	.333	0-0	3	97	.798	6.14	5.48

Dom Nunez

Bats: L Throws: R Pos: C-14   Ht: 6'1" Wt: 212 Born: 1/17/1995 Age: 28

							BATTING												RUNNING			AVERAGES			
Year	Team	Lg	G	AB	H	2B	3B	HR	(Hm | Rd)	TB	R	RBI	RC	TBB	IBB	SO	HBP	SH	SF	SB	CS	GDP	Avg	OBP	Slg	OPS
2022	Albq	AAA	62	247	55	13	3	5	(- | -)	89	36	29	30	34	0	70	2	0	2	1	1	1	.223	.319	.360	.680
2019	Col	NL	16	39	7	3	0	2	(2 | 0)	16	4	4	2	3	0	17	0	1	0	0	0	0	.179	.233	.410	.643
2021	Col	NL	81	228	43	12	3	10	(6 | 4)	91	31	33	27	34	4	91	0	0	1	0	0	0	.189	.293	.399	.692
2022	Col	NL	14	33	4	1	0	0	(0 | 0)	5	3	2	1	6	0	10	0	0	2	0	0	0	.121	.244	.152	.395
	3 ML YEARS		111	300	54	16	3	12	(8 | 4)	112	38	39	30	43	4	118	0	1	4	0	0	0	.180	.280	.373	.653

Bailey Ober

Pitches: R Bats: R Pos: SP-11   Ht: 6'9" Wt: 260 Born: 7/12/1995 Age: 27

			HOW MUCH PITCHED					WHAT HE GAVE UP										THE RESULTS							
Year	Team	Lg	G	GS	GF	IP	BFP	H	R	ER	HR	SH	SF	HB	TBB	IBB	SO	WP	W	L	Pct	Sv-Op	Hld	Vel	OPS	ERC	ERA
2021	Min	AL	20	20	0	92.1	379	92	45	43	20	0	3	1	19	0	96	1	3	3	.500	0-0	0	92	.784	4.13	4.19
2022	Min	AL	11	11	0	56.0	227	48	22	20	4	1	2	2	11	0	51	0	2	3	.400	0-0	0	92	.621	2.49	3.21
	2 ML YEARS		31	31	0	148.1	606	140	67	63	24	1	5	3	30	0	147	1	5	6	.455	0-0	0	92	.723	3.48	3.82

Riley O'Brien

Pitches: R Bats: R Pos: RP-1   Ht: 6'4" Wt: 180 Born: 2/6/1995 Age: 28

			HOW MUCH PITCHED					WHAT HE GAVE UP										THE RESULTS							
Year	Team	Lg	G	GS	GF	IP	BFP	H	R	ER	HR	SH	SF	HB	TBB	IBB	SO	WP	W	L	Pct	Sv-Op	Hld	Vel	OPS	ERC	ERA
2022	Tacom	AAA	32	1	4	36.2	184	43	36	29	4	0	0	5	29	0	43	3	1	3	.250	0- -	-		.872	7.33	7.12
2021	Cin	NL	1	1	0	1.1	9	2	2	2	2	0	0	0	3	0	2	0	0	1	.000	0-0	0	92	1.889	32.44	13.50
2022	Sea	AL	1	0	1	1.0	5	1	0	0	0	0	0	0	1	0	1	0	0	0	-	0-0	0	92	.650	5.48	0.00
	2 ML YEARS		2	1	1	2.1	14	3	2	2	2	0	0	0	4	0	3	0	0	1	.000	0-0	0	92	1.400	19.65	7.71

Darren O'Day

Pitches: R Bats: R Pos: RP-28 Ht: 6'4" Wt: 220 Born: 10/22/1982 Age: 40

Year	Team	Lg	G	GS	GF	IP	BFP	H	R	ER	HR	SH	SF	HB	TBB	IBB	SO	WP	W	L	Pct	Sv-Op	Hld	Vel	OPS	ERC	ERA
2022	Gwnntt	AAA	7	0	0	7.0	29	3	2	2	2	0	0	1	4	0	8	0	0	0	0- -	-		-	.651	3.35	2.57
2008	LAA	AL	30	0	17	43.1	194	49	24	22	2	2	1	4	14	6	29	1	0	1	.000	0-0	1	87	.719	4.20	4.57
2009	2 Tms		68	0	15	58.2	233	41	14	12	3	1	3	5	18	1	56	1	2	1	.667	2-2	20	85	.543	2.20	1.84
2010	Tex	AL	72	0	14	62.0	240	43	15	14	5	1	3	5	12	2	45	0	6	2	.750	0-2	22	86	.548	1.93	2.03
2011	Tex	AL	16	0	7	16.2	74	17	10	10	7	1	1	2	5	0	18	0	0	1	.000	0-0	3	84	.929	6.45	5.40
2012	Bal	AL	69	0	10	67.0	263	49	17	17	6	3	1	3	14	2	69	0	7	1	.875	0-2	15	85	.613	2.06	2.28
2013	Bal	AL	68	0	18	62.0	247	47	16	15	7	1	1	5	15	1	59	1	5	3	.625	2-6	20	86	.617	2.60	2.18
2014	Bal	AL	68	0	18	68.2	271	42	14	13	6	1	2	8	19	4	73	0	5	2	.714	4-8	25	87	.550	1.92	1.70
2015	Bal	AL	68	0	19	65.1	257	47	13	11	5	0	1	5	14	1	82	0	6	2	.750	6-11	18	87	.540	2.09	1.52
2016	Bal	AL	34	0	6	31.0	131	25	13	13	6	0	0	1	13	2	38	0	3	1	.750	3-5	10	86	.717	3.70	3.77
2017	Bal	AL	64	0	16	60.1	240	41	24	23	8	0	1	3	24	2	76	0	2	3	.400	2-4	17	88	.609	2.79	3.43
2018	Bal	AL	20	0	10	20.0	83	18	9	8	3	0	0	3	4	1	27	0	0	2	.000	2-4	4	87	.722	3.61	3.60
2019	Atl	NL	8	0	0	5.1	21	3	1	1	0	0	1	0	1	0	6	0	0	0	-	0-0	0	87	.554	1.35	1.69
2020	Atl	NL	19	0	1	16.1	67	8	3	2	1	0	0	3	5	0	22	0	4	0	1.000	0-1	2	86	.442	1.57	1.10
2021	NYY	AL	12	0	1	10.2	46	9	4	4	2	0	0	1	4	0	11	0	0	0	-	0-0	4	86	.695	4.00	3.38
2022	Atl	NL	28	0	3	21.2	94	19	12	10	3	0	3	1	10	2	26	0	2	2	.500	0-1	5	86	.757	3.89	4.15
09	NYM	NL	4	0	1	3.0	17	5	2	0	0	0	1	1	1	0	2	0	0	0	-	0-0	0	84	.769	7.72	0.00
09	Tex	AL	64	0	14	55.2	216	36	12	12	3	1	2	4	17	1	54	1	2	1	.667	2-2	20	85	.526	1.95	1.94
	Postseason		30	0	1	20.1	82	16	10	10	4	1	0	2	6	1	21	0	0	3	.000	0-0	6	86	.694	3.53	4.43
	15 ML YEARS		644	0	155	609.0	2461	458	189	175	64	10	17	50	172	24	637	3	42	21	.667	21-46	166	86	.614	2.62	2.59

Rougned Odor

Bats: L Throws: R Pos: 2B-129;PH-18;3B-2;DH-1   ROOG-ned oh-DORE   Ht: 5'11" Wt: 200 Born: 2/3/1994 Age: 29

							BATTING														RUNNING			AVERAGES		
Year	Team	Lg	G	AB	H	2B	3B	HR	(Hm	Rd)	TB	R	RBI	RC	TBB	IBB	SO	HBP	SH	SF	SB	CS	GDP	Avg	OBP	Slg	OPS
2014	Tex	AL	114	386	100	14	7	9	(4	5)	155	39	48	46	17	1	71	5	6	3	4	7	7	.259	.297	.402	.698
2015	Tex	AL	120	426	111	21	9	16	(7	9)	198	54	61	62	23	2	79	14	2	5	6	7	3	.261	.316	.465	.781
2016	Tex	AL	150	605	164	33	4	33	(17	16)	304	89	88	77	19	0	135	4	0	4	14	7	6	.271	.296	.502	.798
2017	Tex	AL	162	607	124	21	3	30	(18	12)	241	79	75	61	32	5	162	8	0	4	15	6	13	.204	.252	.397	.649
2018	Tex	AL	129	474	120	23	2	18	(10	8)	201	76	63	67	43	2	127	11	2	5	12	12	5	.253	.326	.424	.751
2019	Tex	AL	145	522	107	30	1	30	(15	15)	229	77	93	77	52	2	178	11	9	4	11	9	4	.205	.283	.439	.721
2020	Tex	AL	38	138	23	4	0	10	(6	4)	57	15	30	16	7	0	47	1	0	2	0	1	2	.167	.209	.413	.623
2021	NYY	AL	102	322	65	12	0	15	(7	8)	122	42	39	38	27	2	100	11	1	0	1	1	3	.202	.286	.379	.665
2022	Bal	AL	135	426	88	19	3	13	(8	5)	152	49	53	50	32	1	109	10	0	4	6	1	9	.207	.275	.357	.632
	Postseason		9	30	7	1	0	2	(0	2)	14	9	4	5	3	0	6	2	0	0	0	0	0	.233	.343	.467	.810
	9 ML YEARS		1095	3906	902	177	29	174	(92	82)	1659	520	550	494	252	15	1008	69	12	28	68	51	52	.231	.287	.425	.712

Jake Odorizzi

Pitches: R Bats: R Pos: SP-22   oh-duh-RIZZ-ee   Ht: 6'2" Wt: 190 Born: 3/27/1990 Age: 33

Year	Team	Lg	G	GS	GF	IP	BFP	H	R	ER	HR	SH	SF	HB	TBB	IBB	SO	WP	W	L	Pct	Sv-Op	Hld	Vel	OPS	ERC	ERA
2012	KC	AL	2	2	0	7.1	34	8	4	4	1	0	0	0	4	0	4	0	0	1	.000	0-0	0	90	.820	5.34	4.91
2013	TB	AL	7	4	2	29.2	122	28	13	13	3	0	1	2	8	0	22	1	0	1	.000	1-1	0	91	.744	3.62	3.94
2014	TB	AL	31	31	0	168.0	719	156	79	77	20	3	8	5	59	0	174	3	11	13	.458	0-0	0	91	.692	3.68	4.13
2015	TB	AL	28	28	0	169.1	700	149	65	63	18	4	3	3	46	0	150	5	9	9	.500	0-0	0	91	.680	3.02	3.35
2016	TB	AL	33	33	0	187.2	773	170	80	77	29	3	6	4	54	3	166	3	10	6	.625	0-0	0	92	.715	3.56	3.69
2017	TB	AL	28	28	0	143.1	604	117	80	66	30	2	7	2	61	1	127	1	10	8	.556	0-0	0	92	.736	3.91	4.14
2018	Min	AL	32	32	0	164.1	711	150	89	82	20	4	4	8	70	3	162	1	7	10	.412	0-0	0	91	.743	4.02	4.49
2019	Min	AL	30	30	0	159.0	658	139	65	62	16	4	4	4	53	0	178	4	15	7	.682	0-0	0	93	.671	3.25	3.51
2020	Min	AL	4	4	0	13.2	60	16	10	10	4	0	0	1	3	0	12	0	0	1	.000	0-0	0	93	.903	6.00	6.59
2021	Hou	AL	24	23	0	104.2	441	97	51	49	16	4	1	3	34	1	91	0	6	7	.462	0-0	0	92	.735	3.82	4.21
2022	2 Tms		22	22	0	106.1	453	106	58	52	14	1	3	3	35	1	86	2	6	6	.500	0-0	0	92	.720	4.10	4.40
22	Hou	AL	12	12	0	60.0	245	52	29	25	5	1	0	2	17	0	46	2	4	3	.571	0-0	0	92	.629	2.96	3.75
22	Atl	NL	10	10	0	46.1	208	54	29	27	9	0	3	1	18	1	40	0	2	3	.400	0-0	0	92	.829	5.74	5.24
	Postseason		3	1	0	11.1	48	13	6	6	3	0	0	0	6	0	15	1	0	1	.000	0-0	0	93	.787	4.14	4.76
	11 ML YEARS		241	237	2	1253.1	5275	1137	594	555	171	25	37	35	427	9	1172	20	74	69	.517	1-1	0	92	.714	3.67	3.99

Cristofer Ogando

Pitches: R Bats: R Pos: RP-3 Ht: 6'3" Wt: 195 Born: 10/23/1993 Age: 29

Year	Team	Lg	G	GS	GF	IP	BFP	H	R	ER	HR	SH	SF	HB	TBB	IBB	SO	WP	W	L	Pct	Sv-Op	Hld	Vel	OPS	ERC	ERA
2022	Drham	AAA	41	0	11	53.1	226	41	31	27	8	0	2	8	26	1	53	5	2	1	.667	3- -	-		.721	4.13	4.56
2022	TB	AL	3	0	2	4.1	17	4	2	2	0	0	1	1	1	0	2	0	0	0	-	0-0	0	95	.853	3.54	4.15

Ryan O'Hearn

Bats: L Throws: L Pos: PH-33;DH-15;1B-13;RF-13;PR-1 Ht: 6'3" Wt: 220 Born: 7/26/1993 Age: 29

							BATTING														RUNNING			AVERAGES		
Year	Team	Lg	G	AB	H	2B	3B	HR	(Hm	Rd)	TB	R	RBI	RC	TBB	IBB	SO	HBP	SH	SF	SB	CS	GDP	Avg	OBP	Slg	OPS
2018	KC	AL	44	149	39	10	2	12	(5	7)	89	23	30	33	20	0	45	1	0	0	0	0	0	.262	.353	.597	.950
2019	KC	AL	105	328	64	13	1	14	(6	8)	121	32	38	25	39	1	99	1	0	2	0	1	7	.195	.281	.369	.650
2020	KC	AL	42	113	22	6	0	2	(0	2)	34	7	18	14	18	2	37	0	0	1	0	0	4	.195	.303	.301	.604
2021	KC	AL	84	236	53	5	1	9	(1	8)	87	23	29	24	13	0	71	2	0	3	0	0	7	.225	.268	.369	.636
2022	KC	AL	67	134	32	6	1	1	(0	1)	43	14	16	13	8	0	35	2	0	1	0	0	2	.239	.290	.321	.611
	5 ML YEARS		342	960	210	40	5	38	(12	26)	374	99	131	109	98	3	287	6	0	7	0	1	21	.219	.293	.390	.683

Logan O'Hoppe

Bats: R **Throws:** R **Pos:** C-5 — **Ht:** 6'2" **Wt:** 185 **Born:** 2/9/2000 **Age:** 23

Year	Team	Lg	G	AB	H	2B	3B	HR	(Hm	Rd)	TB	R	RBI	RC	TBB	IBB	SO	HBP	SH	SF	SB	CS	GDP	Avg	OBP	Slg	OPS
2018	PhilliesW	R	34	109	40	10	1	2	(-	-)	58	19	21	23	10	0	28	1	0	4	2	1	2	.367	.411	.532	.943
2019	Wmspt	A-	45	162	35	12	2	5	(-	-)	66	20	26	18	12	0	49	0	0	3	3	0	7	.216	.266	.407	.673
2021	Rdng	AA	13	54	16	1	0	3	(-	-)	26	6	7	8	1	0	9	2	0	0	0	0	0	.296	.333	.481	.815
2021	JrsyShr	A+	85	318	86	17	2	13	(-	-)	146	43	48	52	30	0	63	4	0	6	6	3	2	.270	.335	.459	.794
2022	Rdng	AA	75	262	72	11	1	15	(-	-)	130	48	45	55	41	1	52	11	0	2	6	2	3	.275	.392	.496	.889
2022	Rock	AA	29	98	30	3	0	11	(-	-)	66	24	33	33	29	1	22	3	0	1	1	2	1	.306	.473	.673	1.147
2022	LAA	AL	5	14	4	0	0	0	(0	0)	4	1	2	2	2	0	3	0	0	0	0	0	0	.286	.375	.286	.661

Shohei Ohtani

Bats: L **Throws:** R **Pos:** DH-152;PH-4 — **Ht:** 6'4" **Wt:** 210 **Born:** 7/5/1994 **Age:** 28

Year	Team	Lg	G	AB	H	2B	3B	HR	(Hm	Rd)	TB	R	RBI	RC	TBB	IBB	SO	HBP	SH	SF	SB	CS	GDP	Avg	OBP	Slg	OPS
2018	LAA	AL	114	326	93	21	2	22	(15	7)	184	59	61	70	37	2	102	2	0	1	10	4	2	.285	.361	.564	.925
2019	LAA	AL	106	384	110	20	5	18	(11	7)	194	51	62	68	33	1	110	2	0	4	12	3	6	.286	.343	.505	.848
2020	LAA	AL	46	153	29	6	0	7	(4	3)	56	23	24	16	22	0	50	0	0	0	7	1	3	.190	.291	.366	.657
2021	LAA	AL	158	537	138	26	8	46	(26	20)	318	103	100	119	96	20	189	4	0	2	26	10	7	.257	.372	.592	.965
2022	LAA	AL	157	586	160	30	6	34	(21	13)	304	90	95	113	72	14	161	5	0	3	11	9	6	.273	.356	.519	.875
	5 ML YEARS		581	1986	530	103	21	127	(77	50)	1056	326	342	386	260	37	612	13	0	10	66	27	24	.267	.354	.532	.886

Shohei Ohtani

Pitches: R **Bats:** L **Pos:** SP-28 — **Ht:** 6'4" **Wt:** 210 **Born:** 7/5/1994 **Age:** 28

Year	Team	Lg	G	GS	GF	IP	BFP	H	R	ER	HR	SH	SF	HB	TBB	IBB	SO	WP	W	L	Pct	Sv-Op	Hld	Vel	OPS	ERC	ERA
2018	LAA	AL	10	10	0	51.2	211	38	19	19	6	0	1	1	22	0	63	5	4	2	.667	0-0	0	97	.621	2.96	3.31
2020	LAA	AL	2	2	0	1.2	16	3	7	7	0	0	0	0	8	0	3	1	0	1	.000	0-0	0	94	1.063	28.51	37.80
2021	LAA	AL	23	23	0	130.1	533	98	48	46	15	2	4	10	44	2	156	10	9	2	.818	0-0	0	96	.637	2.89	3.18
2022	LAA	AL	28	28	0	166.0	660	124	45	43	14	0	3	2	44	0	219	14	15	9	.625	0-0	0	97	.574	2.21	2.33
	4 ML YEARS		63	63	0	349.2	1420	263	119	115	35	2	8	13	118	2	441	30	28	14	.667	0-0	0	96	.610	2.66	2.96

Brian O'Keefe

Bats: R **Throws:** R **Pos:** C-1;DH-1 — **Ht:** 6'1" **Wt:** 210 **Born:** 7/15/1993 **Age:** 29

Year	Team	Lg	G	AB	H	2B	3B	HR	(Hm	Rd)	TB	R	RBI	RC	TBB	IBB	SO	HBP	SH	SF	SB	CS	GDP	Avg	OBP	Slg	OPS
2022	Tacom	AAA	83	316	80	19	2	13	(-	-)	142	42	40	48	32	0	80	4	0	0	1	1	7	.253	.330	.449	.779
2022	Sea	AL	2	3	1	0	0	0	(0	0)	1	0	0	1	1	0	2	0	0	0	0	0	0	.333	.500	.333	.833

Steven Okert

Pitches: L **Bats:** L **Pos:** RP-60 — **Ht:** 6'2" **Wt:** 202 **Born:** 7/9/1991 **Age:** 31

Year	Team	Lg	G	GS	GF	IP	BFP	H	R	ER	HR	SH	SF	HB	TBB	IBB	SO	WP	W	L	Pct	Sv-Op	Hld	Vel	OPS	ERC	ERA
2016	SF	NL	16	0	3	14.0	58	14	5	5	2	0	0	0	4	1	14	0	0	0		0-1	2	92	.699	3.87	3.21
2017	SF	NL	44	0	3	27.0	118	24	18	17	3	3	2	3	11	2	22	0	1	1	.500	0-0	11	92	.755	3.83	5.67
2018	SF	NL	10	0	4	7.1	27	4	1	1	1	0	0	0	8	0	8	0	0	0		0-0	0	92	.444	0.94	1.23
2021	Mia	NL	34	0	5	36.0	142	22	12	11	5	1	2	4	15	2	40	4	3	1	.750	0-0	1	92	.649	2.78	2.75
2022	Mia	NL	60	0	5	51.1	221	34	19	17	7	4	1	7	26	2	63	1	5	5	.500	0-4	19	94	.648	3.29	2.98
	5 ML YEARS		164	0	20	135.2	566	98	55	51	18	8	5	14	56	7	147	5	9	7	.563	0-5	33	93	.665	3.16	3.38

Chris Okey

Bats: R **Throws:** R **Pos:** C-7 — **Ht:** 5'11" **Wt:** 200 **Born:** 12/29/1994 **Age:** 28

Year	Team	Lg	G	AB	H	2B	3B	HR	(Hm	Rd)	TB	R	RBI	RC	TBB	IBB	SO	HBP	SH	SF	SB	CS	GDP	Avg	OBP	Slg	OPS
2022	Lsvlle	AAA	41	118	26	4	3	2	(-	-)	42	18	14	10	10	0	39	0	0	1	0	1	4	.220	.279	.356	.635
2022	Cin	NL	7	12	2	0	0	0	(0	0)	2	3	0	0	0	0	5	1	0	0	0	0	0	.167	.231	.167	.397

Edward Olivares

Bats: R **Throws:** R **Pos:** RF-27;LF-12;DH-8;PH-7;PR-4;CF-1 — **Ht:** 6'2" **Wt:** 190 **Born:** 3/6/1996 **Age:** 27

Year	Team	Lg	G	AB	H	2B	3B	HR	(Hm	Rd)	TB	R	RBI	RC	TBB	IBB	SO	HBP	SH	SF	SB	CS	GDP	Avg	OBP	Slg	OPS
2022	Omha	AAA	21	78	21	7	0	1	(-	-)	31	13	11	9	8	0	14	0	0	0	2	1	3	.269	.337	.397	.735
2020	2 Tms		31	96	23	2	1	3	(2	1)	36	9	10	8	4	0	25	0	0	1	0	2	1	.240	.267	.375	.642
2021	KC	AL	39	101	24	2	0	5	(1	4)	41	14	12	11	5	0	19	3	1	1	2	2	2	.238	.291	.406	.697
2022	KC	AL	53	161	46	8	0	4	(3	1)	66	24	15	20	10	0	36	2	0	1	2	3	1	.286	.333	.410	.743
20	SD	NL	13	34	6	1	0	1	(1	0)	10	4	3	2	2	0	14	0	0	0	0	1	0	.176	.222	.294	.516
20	KC	AL	18	62	17	1	1	2	(1	1)	26	5	7	6	2	0	11	0	0	1	0	1	1	.274	.292	.419	.712
	3 ML YEARS		123	358	93	12	1	12	(6	6)	143	47	37	39	19	0	80	5	1	3	4	7	4	.260	.304	.399	.703

Adam Oller

Pitches: R **Bats:** R **Pos:** SP-14; RP-5   **Ht:** 6'4" **Wt:** 225 **Born:** 10/17/1994 **Age:** 28

Year	Team	Lg	G	GS	GF	IP	BFP	H	R	ER	HR	SH	SF	HB	TBB	IBB	SO	WP	W	L	Pct	Sv-Op	Hld	Vel	OPS	ERC	ERA
2022	LsVgs	AAA	7	7	0	31.2	139	29	17	13	0	1	0	1	17	0	32	1	3	0	1.000	0--	-	-	.649	3.52	3.69
2022	Oak	AL	19	14	3	74.1	337	82	55	52	17	0	2	2	39	0	46	4	2	8	.200	0-0	1	93	.916	6.34	6.30

Matt Olson

Bats: L **Throws:** R **Pos:** 1B-162   **Ht:** 6'5" **Wt:** 225 **Born:** 3/29/1994 **Age:** 29

Year	Team	Lg	G	AB	H	2B	3B	HR	(Hm	Rd)	TB	R	RBI	RC	TBB	IBB	SO	HBP	SH	SF	SB	CS	GDP	Avg	OBP	Slg	OPS
2016	Oak	AL	11	21	2	1	0	0	(0	0)	3	3	0	1	7	0	4	0	0	0	0	0	1	.095	.321	.143	.464
2017	Oak	AL	59	189	49	2	0	24	(12	12)	123	33	45	40	22	1	60	5	0	0	0	0	6	.259	.352	.651	1.003
2018	Oak	AL	162	580	143	33	0	29	(14	15)	263	85	84	86	70	3	163	8	0	2	2	1	13	.247	.335	.453	.788
2019	Oak	AL	127	483	129	26	0	36	(13	23)	263	73	91	92	51	7	138	12	0	1	0	0	11	.267	.351	.545	.896
2020	Oak	AL	60	210	41	4	1	14	(9	5)	89	28	42	34	34	2	77	1	0	0	1	0	2	.195	.310	.424	.734
2021	Oak	AL	156	565	153	35	0	39	(18	21)	305	101	111	107	88	12	113	9	0	11	4	1	17	.271	.371	.540	.911
2022	Atl	NL	162	616	148	44	0	34	(16	18)	294	86	103	103	75	6	170	4	0	4	0	0	13	.240	.325	.477	.802
	Postseason		9	28	4	0	0	2	(1	1)	10	4	3	1	8	0	11	0	0	0	0	0	2	.143	.333	.357	.690
	7 ML YEARS		737	2664	665	145	1	176	(82	94)	1340	409	476	463	347	31	725	39	0	18	7	2	63	.250	.343	.503	.846

Tyler O'Neill

Bats: R **Throws:** R **Pos:** LF-83; CF-21; PH-2; DH-1   **Ht:** 5'11" **Wt:** 200 **Born:** 6/22/1995 **Age:** 28

Year	Team	Lg	G	AB	H	2B	3B	HR	(Hm	Rd)	TB	R	RBI	RC	TBB	IBB	SO	HBP	SH	SF	SB	CS	GDP	Avg	OBP	Slg	OPS
2018	StL	NL	61	130	33	5	0	9	(6	3)	65	29	23	24	7	0	57	3	0	2	2	0	0	.254	.303	.500	.803
2019	StL	NL	60	141	37	6	0	5	(4	1)	58	18	16	19	10	0	53	0	0	0	1	0	3	.262	.311	.411	.723
2020	StL	NL	50	139	24	5	0	7	(2	5)	50	20	19	15	15	0	43	2	0	1	3	1	3	.173	.261	.360	.621
2021	StL	NL	138	482	138	26	2	34	(15	19)	270	89	80	84	38	0	168	13	0	4	15	4	8	.286	.352	.560	.912
2022	StL	NL	96	334	76	11	1	14	(6	8)	131	56	58	49	38	0	103	4	0	7	14	4	7	.228	.308	.392	.700
	Postseason		4	4	0	0	0	0	(0	0)	0	0	0	0	1	0	3	0	0	0	1	0	0	.000	.200	.000	.200
	5 ML YEARS		405	1226	308	53	3	69	(33	36)	574	212	196	191	108	0	424	22	0	14	35	9	23	.251	.320	.468	.788

Kaleb Ort

Pitches: R **Bats:** R **Pos:** RP-25   **Ht:** 6'4" **Wt:** 240 **Born:** 2/5/1992 **Age:** 31

Year	Team	Lg	G	GS	GF	IP	BFP	H	R	ER	HR	SH	SF	HB	TBB	IBB	SO	WP	W	L	Pct	Sv-Op	Hld	Vel	OPS	ERC	ERA
2022	Wrcstr	AAA	39	0	39	40.2	168	28	16	13	1	2	1	2	18	2	53	1	2	2	.500	16--	-	-	.572	2.21	2.88
2021	Bos	AL	1	0	0	0.1	3	1	0	0	0	0	0	0	1	0	0	0	0	0	-	0-0	-	96	1.167	29.63	0.00
2022	Bos	AL	25	0	6	28.1	134	35	23	20	4	0	1	2	15	2	27	1	1	2	.333	1-2	1	96	.845	6.50	6.35
	2 ML YEARS		26	0	6	28.2	137	36	23	20	4	0	1	2	16	2	27	1	1	2	.333	1-2	1	96	.852	6.73	6.28

Oliver Ortega

Pitches: R **Bats:** R **Pos:** RP-27   **Ht:** 6'0" **Wt:** 165 **Born:** 10/2/1996 **Age:** 26

Year	Team	Lg	G	GS	GF	IP	BFP	H	R	ER	HR	SH	SF	HB	TBB	IBB	SO	WP	W	L	Pct	Sv-Op	Hld	Vel	OPS	ERC	ERA
2022	Salt Lk	AAA	23	0	4	25.2	121	34	18	17	3	0	3	4	8	0	27	2	2	1	.667	2--	-	-	.899	6.38	5.96
2021	LAA	AL	8	0	1	9.1	39	12	5	5	1	0	0	1	2	0	4	0	1	0	1.000	0-0	0	97	.829	5.94	4.82
2022	LAA	AL	27	0	7	34.0	148	32	18	14	5	1	0	1	18	0	33	5	1	3	.250	1-1	5	96	.745	4.79	3.71
	2 ML YEARS		35	0	8	43.1	187	44	23	19	6	1	0	2	20	0	37	5	2	3	.400	1-1	5	96	.763	5.02	3.95

Rafael Ortega

Bats: L **Throws:** R **Pos:** CF-67; DH-22; PH-22; RF-19; LF-11; PR-2   **Ht:** 5'11" **Wt:** 180 **Born:** 5/15/1991 **Age:** 32

Year	Team	Lg	G	AB	H	2B	3B	HR	(Hm	Rd)	TB	R	RBI	RC	TBB	IBB	SO	HBP	SH	SF	SB	CS	GDP	Avg	OBP	Slg	OPS
2012	Col	NL	2	4	2	0	0	0	(0	0)	2	0	0	2	1	0	2	1	0	0	1	0	0	.500	.667	.500	1.167
2016	LAA	AL	66	185	43	8	0	1	(0	1)	54	24	16	19	13	0	23	0	3	0	8	3	5	.232	.283	.292	.575
2018	Mia	NL	41	133	31	3	1	0	(0	0)	36	10	7	10	10	0	23	0	0	0	5	2	5	.233	.287	.271	.557
2019	Atl	NL	34	88	18	3	0	2	(1	1)	27	7	10	8	8	0	22	0	0	0	3	0	2	.205	.271	.307	.578
2021	ChC	NL	103	296	86	14	2	11	(4	7)	137	44	33	56	30	1	70	2	2	0	12	6	3	.291	.360	.463	.823
2022	ChC	NL	118	316	76	14	1	7	(3	4)	113	35	35	33	44	2	74	2	1	7	12	7	10	.241	.331	.358	.688
	Postseason		4	3	0	0	0	0	(0	0)	0	1	0	0	0	0	1	0	0	0	0	0	0	.000	.000	.000	.000
	6 ML YEARS		364	1022	256	42	4	21	(8	13)	369	120	101	128	106	3	214	5	6	7	41	18	25	.250	.322	.361	.683

Luis Ortiz

Pitches: R **Bats:** R **Pos:** RP-6   **Ht:** 6'3" **Wt:** 230 **Born:** 9/22/1995 **Age:** 27

Year	Team	Lg	G	GS	GF	IP	BFP	H	R	ER	HR	SH	SF	HB	TBB	IBB	SO	WP	W	L	Pct	Sv-Op	Hld	Vel	OPS	ERC	ERA
2022	Scrmto	AAA	35	4	4	67.1	283	68	38	34	8	2	3	3	13	0	72	1	4	3	.571	2--	-	-	.700	3.58	4.54
2018	Bal	AL	2	1	0	2.1	18	7	6	4	0	0	1	0	3	0	1	0	0	1	.000	0-0	0	92	1.341	19.79	15.43
2019	Bal	AL	1	1	0	3.1	18	4	4	4	2	0	0	0	5	0	3	0	0	1	.000	0-0	0	94	1.346	15.85	10.80
2022	SF	NL	6	0	4	8.2	33	5	1	1	0	0	0	0	3	0	6	0	0	0	-	0-0	0	95	.409	1.37	1.04
	3 ML YEARS		9	2	4	14.1	69	16	11	9	2	0	1	0	11	0	9	1	0	2	.000	0-0	0	94	.865	6.55	5.65

Luis Ortiz

Pitches: R **Bats:** R **Pos:** SP-4   **Ht:** 6'2" **Wt:** 240 **Born:** 1/27/1999 **Age:** 24

		HOW MUCH PITCHED					WHAT HE GAVE UP									THE RESULTS						
Year	Team	Lg	G	GS	GF	IP	BFP	H	R	ER	HR	SH	SF	HB	TBB	IBB	SO	WP	W	L	Pct	Sv-Op	Hld	Vel	OPS	ERC	ERA
2022	Altna	AA	24	23	0	114.1	468	100	63	59	19	0	5	7	34	0	126	5	5	9	.357	0--	-		.725	3.73	4.64
2022	Pit	NL	4	4	0	16.0	69	8	9	8	1	0	0	0	10	0	17	0	0	2	.000	0-0	0	99	.481	1.93	4.50

Adam Ottavino

Pitches: R **Bats:** B **Pos:** RP-66   ott-tah-VEE-no   **Ht:** 6'5" **Wt:** 246 **Born:** 11/22/1985 **Age:** 37

		HOW MUCH PITCHED					WHAT HE GAVE UP									THE RESULTS						
Year	Team	Lg	G	GS	GF	IP	BFP	H	R	ER	HR	SH	SF	HB	TBB	IBB	SO	WP	W	L	Pct	Sv-Op	Hld	Vel	OPS	ERC	ERA
2010	StL	NL	5	3	0	22.1	110	37	21	21	5	1	0	0	9	1	12	1	0	2	.000	0-0	0	93	1.072	9.22	8.46
2012	Col	NL	53	0	6	79.0	339	76	42	40	9	3	1	1	34	7	81	8	5	1	.833	0-2	6	94	.717	4.01	4.56
2013	Col	NL	51	0	5	78.1	335	73	27	23	5	6	4	2	31	5	78	9	1	3	.250	0-0	8	91	.672	3.42	2.64
2014	Col	NL	75	0	16	65.0	272	67	26	26	6	2	3	4	16	1	70	4	1	4	.200	1-6	21	94	.735	3.87	3.60
2015	Col	NL	10	0	5	10.1	35	3	0	0	0	0	0	1	2	0	13	0	1	0	1.000	3-3	3	96	.265	0.56	0.00
2016	Col	NL	34	0	19	27.0	107	18	9	8	3	0	0	2	7	0	35	4	1	3	.250	7-12	6	94	.528	2.17	2.67
2017	Col	NL	63	0	11	53.1	243	48	30	30	8	0	3	4	39	2	63	8	2	3	.400	0-2	21	94	.786	5.51	5.06
2018	Col	NL	75	0	16	77.2	309	41	25	21	5	1	5	6	36	5	112	7	6	4	.600	6-11	34	94	.509	1.89	2.43
2019	NYY	AL	73	0	7	66.1	283	47	17	14	5	0	3	2	40	3	88	3	6	5	.545	2-9	28	94	.624	3.13	1.90
2020	NYY	AL	24	0	4	18.1	85	20	12	12	7	0	1	1	9	0	25	1	2	3	.400	0-3	2	93	.772	5.13	5.89
2021	Bos	AL	69	0	15	62.0	276	55	31	29	5	2	2	7	35	2	71	4	7	3	.700	11-17	22	95	.728	4.34	4.21
2022	NYM	NL	66	0	19	65.2	258	48	15	15	6	0	2	5	16	2	79	7	6	3	.667	3-6	18	94	.591	2.33	2.06
	Postseason		17	0	3	11.2	57	13	8	7	2	0	0	0	7	1	10	3	0	1	.000	0-1	1	94	.806	5.60	5.40
	12 ML YEARS		598	3	123	625.1	2652	533	255	239	59	15	24	35	274	28	727	56	38	34	.528	33-71	167	94	.677	3.54	3.44

Glenn Otto

Pitches: R **Bats:** R **Pos:** SP-27   **Ht:** 6'3" **Wt:** 240 **Born:** 3/11/1996 **Age:** 27

		HOW MUCH PITCHED					WHAT HE GAVE UP									THE RESULTS						
Year	Team	Lg	G	GS	GF	IP	BFP	H	R	ER	HR	SH	SF	HB	TBB	IBB	SO	WP	W	L	Pct	Sv-Op	Hld	Vel	OPS	ERC	ERA
2021	Tex	AL	6	6	0	23.1	111	32	24	24	2	1	0	2	8	0	28	1	0	3	.000	0-0	0	93	.872	6.19	9.26
2022	Tex	AL	27	27	0	135.2	587	119	74	70	21	1	5	13	62	0	107	5	7	10	.412	0-0	0	92	.734	4.40	4.64
	2 ML YEARS		33	33	0	159.0	698	151	98	94	23	2	5	15	70	0	135	6	7	13	.350	0-0	0	92	.756	4.65	5.32

James Outman

Bats: L **Throws:** R **Pos:** LF-3;RF-1;DH-1   **Ht:** 6'3" **Wt:** 215 **Born:** 5/14/1997 **Age:** 26

						BATTING												RUNNING			AVERAGES			
Year	Team	Lg	G	AB	H	2B	3B	HR	(Hm | Rd)	TB	R	RBI	RC	TBB	IBB	SO	HBP	SH	SF	SB	CS	GDP	Avg	OBP	Slg	OPS
2022	Tulsa	AA	68	261	77	17	1	16	(- | -)	144	59	45	60	38	1	89	6	0	2	7	3	6	.295	.394	.552	.946
2022	OkCity	AAA	57	212	62	14	6	15	(- | -)	133	42	61	55	32	0	63	4	0	3	6	1	1	.292	.390	.627	1.018
2022	LAD	NL	4	13	6	2	0	1	(0 | 1)	11	6	3	4	2	0	7	1	0	0	0	0	0	.462	.563	.846	1.409

Connor Overton

Pitches: R **Bats:** L **Pos:** SP-4; RP-2   **Ht:** 6'0" **Wt:** 190 **Born:** 7/24/1993 **Age:** 29

		HOW MUCH PITCHED					WHAT HE GAVE UP									THE RESULTS						
Year	Team	Lg	G	GS	GF	IP	BFP	H	R	ER	HR	SH	SF	HB	TBB	IBB	SO	WP	W	L	Pct	Sv-Op	Hld	Vel	OPS	ERC	ERA
2022	Lsville	AAA	6	4	0	26.2	107	22	12	8	4	0	1	0	5	0	31	0	2	3	.400	0--	-		.658	2.60	2.70
2021	2 Tms		9	3	2	15.1	63	14	8	8	2	0	2	0	5	0	15	1	0	1	.000	0-0	0	92	.712	3.57	4.70
2022	Cin	NL	6	4	1	33.0	124	21	10	10	1	0	1	0	11	0	14	0	1	0	1.000	0-0	0	91	.499	1.70	2.73
21	Tor	AL	4	0	2	6.2	24	4	0	0	0	0	0	0	2	0	4	1	0	0		0-0	0	93	.432	1.41	0.00
21	Pit	NL	5	3	0	8.2	39	10	8	8	2	0	2	0	3	0	11	0	0	1	.000	0-0	0	91	.892	5.58	8.31
	2 ML YEARS		15	7	3	48.1	187	35	18	18	3	0	3	0	16	0	29	1	1	1	.500	0-0	0	91	.570	2.25	3.35

Johan Oviedo

Pitches: R **Bats:** R **Pos:** RP-13; SP-8   **Ht:** 6'5" **Wt:** 245 **Born:** 3/2/1998 **Age:** 25

		HOW MUCH PITCHED					WHAT HE GAVE UP									THE RESULTS						
Year	Team	Lg	G	GS	GF	IP	BFP	H	R	ER	HR	SH	SF	HB	TBB	IBB	SO	WP	W	L	Pct	Sv-Op	Hld	Vel	OPS	ERC	ERA
2022	Memp	AAA	10	10	0	50.0	214	43	33	31	14	0	1	4	23	0	51	5	4	2	.667	0--	-		.822	5.17	5.58
2022	Indy	AAA	5	4	0	11.1	45	8	1	1	0	0	0	1	3	0	13	2	0	0		0--	-		.511	1.81	0.79
2020	StL	NL	5	5	0	24.2	112	24	18	15	3	0	2	5	10	0	16	4	0	3	.000	0-0	0	95	.780	4.84	5.47
2021	StL	NL	14	13	0	62.1	288	61	39	34	8	1	1	6	37	2	51	2	0	5	.000	0-0	0	95	.774	5.21	4.91
2022	2 Tms	NL	21	8	3	56.0	242	49	21	20	5	0	0	3	23	0	54	2	4	3	.571	0-0	0	96	.653	3.50	3.21
22	StL	NL	14	1	3	25.1	108	26	9	9	4	0	0	1	7	0	26	1	2	1	.667	0-0	0	96	.775	4.28	3.20
22	Pit	NL	7	7	0	30.2	134	23	12	11	1	0	0	2	16	0	28	1	2	2	.500	0-0	0	96	.547	2.87	3.23
	3 ML YEARS		40	26	3	143.0	642	134	78	69	16	1	3	14	70	2	121	8	4	11	.267	0-0	0	95	.728	4.46	4.34

Chris Owings

Bats: R **Throws:** R **Pos:** 2B-11;SS-8;PH-5;3B-2;PR-2;LF-1   **Ht:** 5'10" **Wt:** 185 **Born:** 8/12/1991 **Age:** 31

						BATTING												RUNNING			AVERAGES			
Year	Team	Lg	G	AB	H	2B	3B	HR	(Hm | Rd)	TB	R	RBI	RC	TBB	IBB	SO	HBP	SH	SF	SB	CS	GDP	Avg	OBP	Slg	OPS
2022	S-WB	AAA	59	187	44	7	1	8	(- | -)	77	27	30	26	18	0	52	1	0	2	5	2	1	.235	.303	.412	.715
2013	Ari	NL	20	55	16	5	0	0	(0 | 0)	21	5	5	7	6	1	10	0	0	0	2	0	0	.291	.361	.382	.742
2014	Ari	NL	91	310	81	15	6	6	(1 | 5)	126	34	26	38	16	0	67	2	2	2	8	1	6	.261	.300	.406	.706
2015	Ari	NL	147	515	117	27	5	4	(3 | 1)	166	59	43	41	26	3	144	1	7	3	16	4	9	.227	.264	.322	.587
2016	Ari	NL	119	437	121	24	11	5	(5 | 0)	182	52	49	60	20	4	87	5	2	2	21	2	8	.277	.315	.416	.731

Year	Team	Lg	G	AB	H	2B	3B	HR	(Hm	Rd)	TB	R	RBI	RC	TBB	IBB	SO	HBP	SH	SF	SB	CS	GDP	Avg	OBP	Slg	OPS
2017	Ari	NL	97	362	97	25	1	12	(8	4)	160	41	51	48	17	0	87	1	2	4	12	2	3	.268	.299	.442	.741
2018	Ari	NL	106	281	58	15	0	4	(3	1)	85	34	22	25	24	4	75	2	0	2	11	4	4	.206	.272	.302	.574
2019	2 Tms	AL	67	180	25	6	1	3	(0	3)	42	13	14	7	14	0	78	2	0	0	5	2	2	.139	.209	.233	.443
2020	Col	NL	17	41	11	1	0	2	(2	0)	18	9	5	6	3	0	11	0	0	0	1	0	0	.268	.318	.439	.757
2021	Col	NL	21	43	14	4	3	1	(0	1)	27	9	5	11	7	1	15	0	0	0	2	1	0	.326	.420	.628	1.048
2022	Bal	AL	27	56	6	2	0	0	(0	0)	8	6	0	0	10	0	24	1	1	0	1	0	3	.107	.254	.143	.397
19	KC	AL	41	135	18	4	1	2	(0	2)	30	9	9	4	8	0	55	2	0	0	4	1	1	.133	.193	.222	.415
19	Bos	AL	26	45	7	2	0	1	(0	1)	12	4	5	3	6	0	23	0	0	0	1	1	1	.156	.255	.267	.522
10 ML YEARS			712	2280	546	124	27	37	(22	15)	835	262	220	243	143	13	598	14	14	13	79	16	33	.239	.287	.366	.653

Marcell Ozuna

Bats: R Throws: R Pos: DH-72;LF-52   oh-ZUNE-uh   Ht: 6'1" Wt: 225 Born: 11/12/1990 Age: 32

Year	Team	Lg	G	AB	H	2B	3B	HR	(Hm	Rd)	TB	R	RBI	RC	TBB	IBB	SO	HBP	SH	SF	SB	CS	GDP	Avg	OBP	Slg	OPS
2013	Mia	NL	70	275	73	17	4	3	(0	3)	107	31	32	35	13	0	57	2	1	0	5	1	6	.265	.303	.389	.693
2014	Mia	NL	153	565	152	26	5	23	(12	11)	257	72	85	74	41	1	164	1	0	5	3	1	12	.269	.317	.455	.772
2015	Mia	NL	123	459	119	27	0	10	(2	8)	176	47	44	48	30	1	110	3	0	2	2	3	10	.259	.308	.383	.691
2016	Mia	NL	148	557	148	23	6	23	(12	11)	252	75	76	69	43	2	115	4	0	4	0	3	11	.266	.321	.452	.773
2017	Mia	NL	159	613	191	30	2	37	(22	15)	336	93	124	117	64	4	144	0	0	2	1	3	18	.312	.376	.548	.924
2018	StL	NL	148	582	163	16	2	23	(13	10)	252	69	88	86	38	2	110	3	0	4	3	0	10	.280	.325	.433	.758
2019	StL	NL	130	485	117	23	1	29	(13	16)	229	80	89	73	62	2	114	1	0	1	12	2	21	.241	.328	.472	.800
2020	Atl	NL	60	228	77	14	0	18	(8	10)	145	38	56	58	38	3	60	0	0	1	0	0	3	.338	.431	.636	1.067
2021	Atl	NL	48	188	40	6	0	7	(5	2)	67	21	26	21	19	0	46	1	0	0	0	0	5	.213	.288	.356	.645
2022	Atl	NL	124	470	106	19	0	23	(11	12)	194	56	56	47	31	0	122	2	0	4	2	1	12	.226	.274	.413	.687
Postseason			21	88	25	7	0	5	(5	0)	47	14	16	13	3	0	27	1	0	0	0	0	2	.284	.315	.534	.849
10 ML YEARS			1163	4422	1186	201	20	196	(98	98)	2015	582	676	628	379	15	1042	17	1	23	28	14	109	.268	.327	.456	.782

Cristian Pache

Bats: R Throws: R Pos: CF-90;PR-4;PH-3   PAH-chay   Ht: 6'2" Wt: 215 Born: 11/19/1998 Age: 24

Year	Team	Lg	G	AB	H	2B	3B	HR	(Hm	Rd)	TB	R	RBI	RC	TBB	IBB	SO	HBP	SH	SF	SB	CS	GDP	Avg	OBP	Slg	OPS
2022	LsVgs	AAA	41	157	39	8	1	4	(-	-)	61	15	20	17	11	0	39	1	0	2	1	1	5	.248	.298	.389	.687
2020	Atl	NL	2	4	1	0	0	0	(0	0)	1	0	0	0	0	0	2	0	0	0	0	0	0	.250	.250	.250	.500
2021	Atl	NL	22	63	7	3	0	1	(0	1)	13	6	4	1	2	0	25	1	2	0	0	0	1	.111	.152	.206	.358
2022	Oak	AL	91	241	40	5	2	3	(1	2)	58	18	18	12	15	0	70	1	3	0	2	2	5	.166	.218	.241	.459
Postseason			14	22	4	1	0	1	(1	0)	8	4	4	2	3	0	4	0	0	0	0	0	0	.182	.280	.364	.644
3 ML YEARS			115	308	48	8	2	4	(1	3)	72	24	22	13	17	0	97	2	5	0	2	2	6	.156	.205	.234	.439

Chris Paddack

Pitches: R Bats: R Pos: SP-5   Ht: 6'5" Wt: 217 Born: 1/8/1996 Age: 27

Year	Team	Lg	G	GS	GF	IP	BFP	H	R	ER	HR	SH	SF	HB	TBB	IBB	SO	WP	W	L	Pct	Sv-Op	Hld	Vel	OPS	ERC	ERA
2019	SD	NL	26	26	0	140.2	568	107	58	52	23	4	3	6	31	1	153	1	9	7	.563	0-0	0	94	.635	2.62	3.33
2020	SD	NL	12	12	0	59.0	245	60	33	31	14	0	2	2	12	0	58	0	4	5	.444	0-0	0	94	.817	4.46	4.73
2021	SD	NL	23	22	0	108.1	459	115	67	61	15	7	2	1	22	1	99	2	7	7	.500	0-0	0	95	.750	3.87	5.07
2022	Min	AL	5	5	0	22.1	93	25	10	10	0	0	2	1	2	0	20	1	1	2	.333	0-0	0	93	.687	3.03	4.03
Postseason			1	1	0	2.1	15	8	6	6	1	0	1	0	0	0	1	0	0	1	.000	0-0	0	94	1.533	22.85	23.14
4 ML YEARS			66	65	0	330.1	1365	307	168	154	52	11	9	10	67	2	330	4	21	21	.500	0-0	0	94	.710	3.36	4.20

Nicholas Padilla

Pitches: R Bats: R Pos: RP-1   Ht: 6'2" Wt: 220 Born: 12/24/1996 Age: 26

Year	Team	Lg	G	GS	GF	IP	BFP	H	R	ER	HR	SH	SF	HB	TBB	IBB	SO	WP	W	L	Pct	Sv-Op	Hld	Vel	OPS	ERC	ERA
2022	Tenn	AA	15	0	9	22.1	98	16	9	7	0	0	1	1	14	0	25	3	1	1	.500	2--	-		.597	2.79	2.82
2022	Sbend	A+	7	0	5	10.0	40	4	3	2	0	0	0	0	5	0	18	4	1	0	1.000	1--	-			1.10	1.80
2022	Iowa	AAA	10	0	4	14.2	59	8	2	2	0	1	0	0	8	0	17	0	1	0	1.000	1--	-		.491	1.67	1.23
2022	Charllt	AAA	7	0	1	6.0	27	4	3	2	1	0	0	2	4	0	6	1	0	0	-	0--	-		.751	5.15	3.00
2022	ChC	NL	1	0	0	1.2	9	2	1	1	0	0	0	0	2	0	1	1	0	0	-	0-0	0	94	.873	7.49	5.40

Kevin Padlo

Bats: R Throws: R Pos: 1B-7;3B-5;PH-4   Ht: 6'2" Wt: 210 Born: 7/15/1996 Age: 26

Year	Team	Lg	G	AB	H	2B	3B	HR	(Hm	Rd)	TB	R	RBI	RC	TBB	IBB	SO	HBP	SH	SF	SB	CS	GDP	Avg	OBP	Slg	OPS
2022	Tacom	AAA	38	140	32	6	1	4	(-	-)	52	18	20	17	18	0	41	2	0	1	7	2	3	.229	.323	.371	.694
2022	Scrmto	AAA	22	80	22	3	1	7	(-	-)	48	16	16	17	5	0	18	2	0	0	3	0	2	.275	.333	.600	.933
2022	Indy	AAA	22	86	24	7	0	1	(-	-)	34	15	15	10	9	0	31	0	0	1	3	0	4	.279	.344	.395	.739
2021	2 Tms	AL	10	13	1	1	0	0	(0	0)	2	1	0	0	2	0	9	0	0	0	0	0	0	.077	.200	.154	.354
2022	3 Tms		13	33	4	1	0	0	(0	0)	5	0	3	1	1	0	10	0	0	0	0	0	2	.121	.147	.152	.299
21	TB	AL	9	12	1	1	0	0	(0	0)	2	1	0	0	2	0	8	0	0	0	0	0	0	.083	.214	.167	.381
21	Sea	AL	1	1	0	0	0	0	(0	0)	0	0	0	0	0	0	1	0	0	0	0	0	0	.000	.000	.000	.000
22	SF	NL	4	12	2	0	0	0	(0	0)	2	0	0	0	0	0	4	0	0	0	0	0	1	.167	.167	.167	.333
22	Sea	AL	6	10	2	1	0	0	(0	0)	3	0	3	1	1	0	5	0	0	0	0	0	0	.200	.273	.300	.573
22	Pit	NL	3	11	0	0	0	0	(0	0)	0	0	0	0	0	0	1	0	0	0	0	0	1	.000	.000	.000	.000
2 ML YEARS			23	46	5	2	0	0	(0	0)	7	1	3	1	3	0	19	0	0	0	0	0	2	.109	.163	.152	.315

Emilio Pagan

Pitches: R **Bats:** L **Pos:** RP-59　　　　　　　　**Ht:** 6'2" **Wt:** 208 **Born:** 5/7/1991 **Age:** 32

			HOW MUCH PITCHED						WHAT HE GAVE UP										THE RESULTS						
Year	Team	Lg	G	GS	GF	IP	BFP	H	R	ER	HR	SH	SF	HB	TBB	IBB	SO	WP	W	L	Pct	Sv-Op	Hld	Vel	OPS	ERC	ERA
2017	Sea	AL	34	0	9	50.1	196	39	20	18	7	1	2	1	8	0	56	1	2	3	.400	0-1	8	94	.610	2.32	3.22
2018	Oak	AL	55	0	17	62.0	262	55	30	30	13	0	1	3	19	1	63	3	3	1	.750	0-0	6	94	.767	3.92	4.35
2019	TB	AL	66	0	29	70.0	267	45	19	18	12	0	1	1	13	1	96	3	4	2	.667	20-28	7	96	.590	1.91	2.31
2020	SD	NL	22	0	5	22.0	87	14	11	11	4	0	1	0	9	0	23	0	1	0	.000	2-7	5	95	.641	2.73	4.50
2021	SD	NL	67	0	10	63.1	263	56	35	34	16	0	1	2	18	0	69	0	4	3	.571	0-5	17	95	.801	4.07	4.83
2022	Min	AL	59	0	27	63.0	274	60	36	31	12	1	1	1	26	2	84	3	4	6	.400	9-16	7	94	.776	4.44	4.43
	Postseason		9	0	1	8.0	36	7	3	2	2	0	0	0	4	0	5	0	1	0	1.000	0-0	2	97	.774	4.58	2.25
	6 ML YEARS		303	0	97	330.2	1349	269	151	142	64	2	7	8	93	4	391	10	17	16	.515	31-57	52	95	.709	3.26	3.86

Jermaine Palacios

Bats: R **Throws:** R **Pos:** SS-14;2B-12;PR-3;PH-2;1B-1;3B-1　　　　**Ht:** 6'0" **Wt:** 145 **Born:** 7/19/1996 **Age:** 26

							BATTING													RUNNING			AVERAGES			
Year	Team	Lg	G	AB	H	2B	3B	HR	(Hm | Rd)	TB	R	RBI	RC	TBB	IBB	SO	HBP	SH	SF	SB	CS	GDP	Avg	OBP	Slg	OPS
2022	StPaul	AAA	102	392	111	28	0	14	(- | -)	181	70	60	59	34	0	102	1	0	1	12	9	11	.283	.341	.462	.803
2022	Min	AL	30	70	10	0	0	2	(0 | 2)	16	8	6	1	4	0	27	0	1	2	0	0	2	.143	.184	.229	.413

Josh Palacios

Bats: L **Throws:** R **Pos:** RF-12;LF-9;PH-8;PR-5;DH-3　　　　**Ht:** 6'1" **Wt:** 200 **Born:** 7/30/1995 **Age:** 27

							BATTING													RUNNING			AVERAGES			
Year	Team	Lg	G	AB	H	2B	3B	HR	(Hm | Rd)	TB	R	RBI	RC	TBB	IBB	SO	HBP	SH	SF	SB	CS	GDP	Avg	OBP	Slg	OPS
2022	Roch	AAA	76	275	82	12	2	7	(- | -)	119	43	44	46	33	0	50	5	2	1	19	7	3	.298	.382	.433	.815
2021	Tor	AL	13	35	7	0	0	0	(0 | 0)	7	7	4	3	3	0	11	2	1	0	0	0	0	.200	.263	.200	.493
2022	Was	NL	29	47	10	2	0	0	(0 | 0)	12	8	2	2	1	0	15	1	0	0	1	0	0	.213	.245	.255	.500
	2 ML YEARS		42	82	17	2	0	0	(0 | 0)	19	15	6	5	4	0	26	3	1	1	1	0	0	.207	.267	.232	.498

Richie Palacios

Bats: L **Throws:** R **Pos:** LF-25;PH-22;DH-11;2B-2;PR-1　　　　**Ht:** 5'10" **Wt:** 180 **Born:** 5/16/1997 **Age:** 26

							BATTING													RUNNING			AVERAGES			
Year	Team	Lg	G	AB	H	2B	3B	HR	(Hm | Rd)	TB	R	RBI	RC	TBB	IBB	SO	HBP	SH	SF	SB	CS	GDP	Avg	OBP	Slg	OPS
2022	Clmbs	AAA	45	179	50	10	5	4	(- | -)	82	34	36	30	24	1	43	2	1	0	12	2	4	.279	.371	.458	.829
2022	Cle	AL	54	112	26	6	0	0	(0 | 0)	32	7	10	8	9	1	20	1	0	1	2	0	2	.232	.293	.286	.578

Andre Pallante

Pitches: R **Bats:** R **Pos:** RP-37; SP-10　　　　　　　　**Ht:** 6'0" **Wt:** 203 **Born:** 9/18/1998 **Age:** 24

			HOW MUCH PITCHED						WHAT HE GAVE UP										THE RESULTS						
Year	Team	Lg	G	GS	GF	IP	BFP	H	R	ER	HR	SH	SF	HB	TBB	IBB	SO	WP	W	L	Pct	Sv-Op	Hld	Vel	OPS	ERC	ERA
2022	StL	NL	47	10	4	108.0	457	113	39	38	9	2	1	1	40	2	73	4	6	5	.545	0-1	9	95	.726	4.22	3.17

Michael Papierski

Bats: B **Throws:** R **Pos:** C-38;1B-1;PH-1　　　　　　　　**Ht:** 6'3" **Wt:** 224 **Born:** 2/26/1996 **Age:** 27

							BATTING													RUNNING			AVERAGES			
Year	Team	Lg	G	AB	H	2B	3B	HR	(Hm | Rd)	TB	R	RBI	RC	TBB	IBB	SO	HBP	SH	SF	SB	CS	GDP	Avg	OBP	Slg	OPS
2022	SgrLnd	AAA	26	90	19	3	0	1	(- | -)	25	12	15	8	14	1	9	2	0	2	0	0	1	.211	.324	.278	.602
2022	Scrmto	AAA	14	53	11	2	0	2	(- | -)	19	5	13	5	3	0	18	0	0	1	0	0	0	.208	.246	.358	.604
2022	Lsvlle	AAA	17	47	14	2	0	3	(- | -)	25	6	13	11	9	0	12	1	0	0	0	0	0	.298	.421	.532	.953
2022	2 Tms	NL	39	91	13	1	0	1	(0 | 1)	17	7	4	3	10	0	26	0	2	0	0	0	4	.143	.228	.187	.415
22	SF	NL	5	9	0	0	0	0	(0 | 0)	0	1	0	0	1	0	4	0	0	0	0	0	0	.000	.100	.000	.100
22	Cin	NL	34	82	13	1	0	1	(0 | 1)	17	6	4	3	9	0	22	0	2	0	0	0	4	.159	.242	.207	.449

Enoli Paredes

Pitches: R **Bats:** R **Pos:** RP-3　　　　　pah-RAY-deez　　　　**Ht:** 5'11" **Wt:** 171 **Born:** 9/28/1995 **Age:** 27

			HOW MUCH PITCHED						WHAT HE GAVE UP										THE RESULTS						
Year	Team	Lg	G	GS	GF	IP	BFP	H	R	ER	HR	SH	SF	HB	TBB	IBB	SO	WP	W	L	Pct	Sv-Op	Hld	Vel	OPS	ERC	ERA
2022	SgrLnd	AAA	50	0	26	54.2	230	34	24	16	4	2	2	2	31	2	81	3	5	4	.556	12--	-	-	.589	2.56	2.63
2020	Hou	AL	22	0	4	20.2	90	18	9	7	1	1	1	1	11	0	20	0	3	3	.500	0-2	4	96	.666	3.69	3.05
2021	Hou	AL	12	0	1	8.2	53	7	10	6	0	0	1	2	17	0	15	1	0	0	-	0-0	2	95	.763	8.84	6.23
2022	Hou	AL	3	0	3	3.0	14	3	1	1	0	0	0	0	3	0	2	0	0	0	-	0-0	0	95	.701	5.91	3.00
	Postseason		7	0	1	7.0	29	3	4	4	1	1	0	2	4	0	9	0	0	0	-	0-1	2	96	.594	3.09	5.14
	3 ML YEARS		37	0	8	32.1	157	28	20	14	1	1	2	3	31	0	37	1	3	3	.500	0-2	6	96	.706	5.24	3.90

Isaac Paredes

Bats: R **Throws:** R **Pos:** 3B-50;2B-43;1B-29;PH-16;SS-1　　ee-ZACK pah-RAY-deez　　**Ht:** 5'11" **Wt:** 213 **Born:** 2/18/1999 **Age:** 24

							BATTING													RUNNING			AVERAGES			
Year	Team	Lg	G	AB	H	2B	3B	HR	(Hm | Rd)	TB	R	RBI	RC	TBB	IBB	SO	HBP	SH	SF	SB	CS	GDP	Avg	OBP	Slg	OPS
2022	Drham	AAA	25	95	25	7	1	4	(- | -)	46	15	18	17	13	0	19	2	0	3	0	1	0	.263	.354	.484	.838
2020	Det	AL	34	100	22	4	0	1	(0 | 1)	29	7	6	8	8	0	24	0	0	0	0	0	0	.220	.278	.290	.568
2021	Det	AL	23	72	15	3	1	1	(1 | 0)	23	7	5	5	10	1	11	1	0	2	0	0	4	.208	.306	.319	.625
2022	TB	AL	111	331	68	16	0	20	(11 | 9)	144	48	45	42	44	0	67	4	0	2	0	1	12	.205	.304	.435	.740
	3 ML YEARS		168	503	105	23	1	22	(12 | 10)	196	62	56	55	62	1	102	5	0	4	0	1	17	.209	.300	.390	.689

Hoy Park

Bats: L Throws: R Pos: 2B-11;3B-6;SS-3;RF-2;PH-2;PR-2   Ht: 6'1" Wt: 200 Born: 4/7/1996 Age: 27

									BATTING									RUNNING			AVERAGES			
Year	Team	Lg	G	AB	H	2B	3B	HR	(Hm	Rd)	TB	R	RBI	RC	TBB	IBB	SO	HBP	SH	SF	SB	CS	GDP	Avg	OBP	Slg	OPS
2022	Indy	AAA	89	316	71	11	0	10	(- | -)	112	48	37	42	52	2	99		0	1	2	14	0	4	.225	.332	.354	.687
2021	2 Tms		45	128	25	5	2	3	(1	2)	43	16	14	14	18	1	38	1	1	1	1	1	4	.195	.297	.336	.633
2022	Pit	NL	23	51	11	2	0	2	(1	1)	19	7	6	7	4	0	15	1	2	2	1	0	0	.216	.276	.373	.648
21	NYY	AL	1	1	0	0	0	0	(0	0)	0	0	0	0	0	0	0	0	0	0	0	0	0	.000	.000	.000	.000
21	Pit	NL	44	127	25	5	2	3	(1	2)	43	16	14	14	18	1	38	1	1	1	1	1	4	.197	.299	.339	.638
	2 ML YEARS		68	179	36	7	2	5	(2	3)	62	23	20	21	22	1	53	2	3	3	2	1	4	.201	.291	.346	.638

Vinnie Pasquantino

Bats: L Throws: L Pos: 1B-37;DH-35   pass-kwin-tee-no   Ht: 6'4" Wt: 245 Born: 10/10/1997 Age: 25

									BATTING									RUNNING			AVERAGES			
Year	Team	Lg	G	AB	H	2B	3B	HR	(Hm	Rd)	TB	R	RBI	RC	TBB	IBB	SO	HBP	SH	SF	SB	CS	GDP	Avg	OBP	Slg	OPS
2021	QuadC	A+	61	237	69	20	3	13	(-	-)	134	44	42	52	33	0	38	4	0	2	4	0	3	.291	.384	.565	.949
2021	NWArk	AA	55	200	62	17	0	11	(-	-)	112	35	42	46	31	3	26	3	0	3	2	0	3	.310	.405	.560	.965
2022	Omha	AAA	73	264	73	17	2	18	(-	-)	148	52	70	58	40	2	39	3	0	6	3	1	7	.277	.371	.561	.931
2022	KC	AL	72	258	76	10	0	10	(6	4)	116	25	26	42	35	1	34	3	0	2	1	0	5	.295	.383	.450	.832

Luis Patino

Pitches: R Bats: R Pos: SP-6   Ht: 6'1" Wt: 192 Born: 10/26/1999 Age: 23

						HOW MUCH PITCHED			WHAT HE GAVE UP										THE RESULTS							
Year	Team	Lg	G	GS	GF	IP	BFP	H	R	ER	HR	SH	SF	HB	TBB	IBB	SO	WP	W	L	Pct	Sv-Op	Hld	Vel	OPS	ERC	ERA
2022	Drham	AAA	9	9	0	34.0	145	32	19	17	6	0	1	1	13	0	34	6	3	2	.600	0- -	-	-	.756	4.33	4.50
2020	SD	NL	11	1	1	17.1	85	18	10	10	3	0	0	1	14	0	21	1	1	0	1.000	0-0	1	97	.788	6.66	5.19
2021	TB	AL	19	15	0	77.1	333	69	40	37	12	0	3	3	29	2	74	7	5	3	.625	0-0	0	96	.696	3.79	4.31
2022	TB	AL	6	6	0	20.0	98	26	18	18	6	0	1	1	13	1	11	0	1	2	.333	0-0	0	94	1.011	8.80	8.10
	Postseason		5	0	2	5.0	22	4	3	3	1	0	0	0	3	0	2	0	0	1	.000	0-0	1	97	.792	4.36	5.40
	3 ML YEARS		36	22	1	114.2	516	113	68	65	21	0	4	5	56	3	106	8	7	5	.583	0-0	1	96	.770	5.00	5.10

Spencer Patton

Pitches: R Bats: R Pos: RP-7   Ht: 6'1" Wt: 200 Born: 2/20/1988 Age: 35

						HOW MUCH PITCHED			WHAT HE GAVE UP										THE RESULTS							
Year	Team	Lg	G	GS	GF	IP	BFP	H	R	ER	HR	SH	SF	HB	TBB	IBB	SO	WP	W	L	Pct	Sv-Op	Hld	Vel	OPS	ERC	ERA
2022	RdRck	AAA	24	0	6	29.1	137	33	24	21	8	1	0	2	17	0	40	3	4	2	.667	1- -	-	-	.920	7.25	6.44
2014	Tex	AL	9	0	2	9.1	35	6	1	1	0	0	0	0	2	0	8	0	1	0	1.000	0-0	2	92	.441	1.29	0.96
2015	Tex	AL	27	0	6	24.0	109	24	24	24	5	1	0	4	12	0	28	1	1	1	.500	0-0	3	92	.870	6.04	9.00
2016	ChC	NL	16	0	7	21.1	101	20	16	13	3	0	0	1	14	0	22	0	1	1	.500	0-0	1	92	.719	5.01	5.48
2021	Tex	AL	42	0	13	42.1	172	36	20	18	4	0	0	0	15	0	48	1	2	2	.500	2-5	11	93	.653	3.12	3.83
2022	Tex	AL	7	0	1	7.0	29	4	3	3	1	0	1	2	3	0	5	1	0	0	-	0-0	1	92	.615	3.31	3.86
	5 ML YEARS		101	0	29	104.0	446	90	64	59	13	1	1	7	46	0	111	3	5	4	.556	2-5	18	93	.700	3.93	5.11

James Paxton

Pitches: L Bats: L Pos: P   Ht: 6'4" Wt: 227 Born: 11/6/1988 Age: 34

						HOW MUCH PITCHED			WHAT HE GAVE UP										THE RESULTS							
Year	Team	Lg	G	GS	GF	IP	BFP	H	R	ER	HR	SH	SF	HB	TBB	IBB	SO	WP	W	L	Pct	Sv-Op	Hld	Vel	OPS	ERC	ERA
2013	Sea	AL	4	4	0	24.0	94	15	5	4	2	0	0	0	7	2	21	0	3	0	1.000	0-0	0	-	.533	1.61	1.50
2014	Sea	AL	13	13	0	74.0	303	60	29	25	3	3	1	1	29	2	59	7	6	4	.600	0-0	0	-	.612	2.69	3.04
2015	Sea	AL	13	13	0	67.0	297	67	34	29	8	0	3	0	29	1	56	5	3	4	.429	0-0	0	-	.704	4.22	3.90
2016	Sea	AL	20	20	0	121.0	511	134	62	51	9	0	6	1	24	3	117	5	6	7	.462	0-0	0	-	.717	3.70	3.79
2017	Sea	AL	24	24	0	136.0	552	113	47	45	9	1	5	3	37	1	156	15	12	5	.706	0-0	0	-	.602	2.56	2.98
2018	Sea	AL	28	28	0	160.1	645	134	67	67	23	2	2	1	42	0	208	8	11	6	.647	0-0	0	-	.662	2.98	3.76
2019	NYY	AL	29	29	0	150.2	633	138	71	64	23	2	4	2	55	0	186	7	15	6	.714	0-0	0	-	.732	3.90	3.82
2020	NYY	AL	5	5	0	20.1	90	23	17	15	4	0	1	0	7	0	26	2	1	1	.500	0-0	0	-	.875	5.53	6.64
2021	Sea	AL	1	1	0	1.1	5	0	1	1	0	0	0	0	1	0	2	1	0	0	-	0-0	0	-	.200	0.57	6.75
	Postseason		3	3	0	13.0	58	13	5	5	2	0	0	0	7	0	20	1	1	0	1.000	0-0	0	-	.776	5.01	3.46
	9 ML YEARS		137	137	0	754.2	3130	684	333	301	81	8	22	9	231	9	831	50	57	33	.633	0-0	0	-	.675	3.28	3.59

Joel Payamps

Pitches: R Bats: R Pos: RP-41   Ht: 6'2" Wt: 225 Born: 4/7/1994 Age: 29

						HOW MUCH PITCHED			WHAT HE GAVE UP										THE RESULTS							
Year	Team	Lg	G	GS	GF	IP	BFP	H	R	ER	HR	SH	SF	HB	TBB	IBB	SO	WP	W	L	Pct	Sv-Op	Hld	Vel	OPS	ERC	ERA
2019	Ari	NL	2	0	1	4.0	17	4	2	2	0	1	0	0	3	0	3	0	0	0	-	0-0	0	93	.745	5.14	4.50
2020	Ari	NL	2	0	1	3.0	13	2	2	1	0	0	0	0	3	0	2	0	0	0	-	0-0	0	94	.685	3.96	3.00
2021	2 Tms	AL	37	1	9	50.1	205	44	22	19	6	0	1	1	14	2	38	1	1	3	.250	0-0	0	95	.667	3.10	3.40
2022	2 Tms	AL	41	0	16	55.2	241	60	24	20	7	1	2	2	16	2	41	3	3	6	.333	0-2	3	95	.752	4.31	3.23
21	Tor	AL	22	0	8	30.0	119	21	10	9	3	0	1	1	11	2	22	0	0	2	.000	0-0	0	95	.586	2.47	2.70
21	KC	AL	15	1	1	20.1	86	23	12	10	3	0	0	0	3	0	16	1	1	1	.500	0-0	0	95	.772	4.08	4.43
22	KC	AL	29	0	14	42.2	188	46	19	15	5	1	1	2	16	2	33	2	2	3	.400	0-2	2	95	.771	4.65	3.16
22	Oak	AL	12	0	2	13.0	53	14	5	5	2	0	1	0	0	0	8	1	1	3	.250	0-0	1	94	.687	3.19	3.46
	4 ML YEARS		82	1	27	113.0	476	110	50	42	13	2	3	3	36	4	84	4	4	9	.308	0-2	3	95	.714	3.78	3.35

Mark Payton

Bats: L **Throws:** L **Pos:** LF-6;RF-3;CF-1;PH-1   **Ht:** 5'8" **Wt:** 180 **Born:** 12/7/1991 **Age:** 31

								BATTING												RUNNING			AVERAGES			
Year	Team	Lg	G	AB	H	2B	3B	HR	(Hm | Rd)	TB	R	RBI	RC	TBB	IBB	SO	HBP	SH	SF	SB	CS	GDP	Avg	OBP	Slg	OPS
2022	Charllt	AAA	119	471	138	31	5	25	(- | 0)	254	85	95	97	54	1	76	6	2	6	15	6	7	.293	.369	.539	.908
2020	Cin	NL	8	18	3	1	0	0	(0 | 0)	4	0	0	0	2	0	5	0	0	0	1	0	1	.167	.250	.222	.472
2021	Cin	NL	24	22	4	0	0	0	(0 | 0)	4	2	0	1	2	0	7	0	0	0	0	0	0	.182	.250	.182	.432
2022	CWS	AL	8	21	3	0	0	0	(0 | 0)	3	3	1	1	4	0	4	0	0	0	0	0	0	.143	.280	.143	.423
	3 ML YEARS		40	61	10	1	0	0	(0 | 0)	11	5	1	2	8	0	16	0	0	0	1	0	1	.164	.261	.180	.441

Matt Peacock

Pitches: R **Bats:** R **Pos:** RP-9   **Ht:** 6'1" **Wt:** 185 **Born:** 2/27/1994 **Age:** 29

			HOW MUCH PITCHED					WHAT HE GAVE UP										THE RESULTS							
Year	Team	Lg	G	GS	GF	IP	BFP	H	R	ER	HR	SH	SF	HB	TBB	IBB	SO	WP	W	L	Pct	Sv-Op	Hld	Vel	OPS	ERC	ERA
2022	Omha	AAA	8	0	1	10.0	47	13	7	5	2	0	0	0	3	0	8	0	0	1	.000	0- -	-	-	.772	5.90	4.50
2022	Buffalo	AAA	14	0	2	15.2	68	17	9	7	3	1	0	0	4	0	15	2	1	2	.333	0- -	-	-	.790	4.51	4.02
2021	Ari	NL	35	8	12	86.1	386	107	55	47	13	2	3	1	28	5	50	2	5	7	.417	0-0	0	93	.848	5.49	4.90
2022	2 Tms		9	0	7	10.0	46	12	6	6	1	0	0	0	4	0	6	1	0	0	-	0-0	0	93	.729	5.10	5.40
22	Ari	NL	2	0	2	2.2	13	3	2	2	1	0	0	0	2	0	2	0	0	0	-	0-0	0	92	.930	8.41	6.75
22	KC	AL	7	0	5	7.1	33	9	4	4	0	0	0	0	2	0	4	1	0	0	-	0-0	0	93	.656	4.01	4.91
	2 ML YEARS		44	8	19	96.1	432	119	61	53	14	2	3	1	32	5	56	3	5	7	.417	0-0	0	93	.836	5.45	4.95

Joc Pederson

Bats: L **Throws:** L **Pos:** LF-102;PH-28;RF-18;DH-14   JOCK   **Ht:** 6'1" **Wt:** 220 **Born:** 4/21/1992 **Age:** 31

								BATTING												RUNNING			AVERAGES			
Year	Team	Lg	G	AB	H	2B	3B	HR	(Hm	Rd)	TB	R	RBI	RC	TBB	IBB	SO	HBP	SH	SF	SB	CS	GDP	Avg	OBP	Slg	OPS
2014	LAD	NL	18	28	4	0	0	0	(0	0)	4	1	0	1	9	0	11	0	1	0	0	0	1	.143	.351	.143	.494
2015	LAD	NL	151	480	101	19	1	26	(13	13)	200	67	54	62	92	6	170	9	2	2	4	7	5	.210	.346	.417	.763
2016	LAD	NL	137	406	100	26	0	25	(13	12)	201	64	68	71	63	4	130	4	1	2	6	2	5	.246	.352	.495	.847
2017	LAD	NL	102	273	58	20	0	11	(8	3)	111	44	35	35	39	1	68	10	0	1	4	3	7	.212	.331	.407	.738
2018	LAD	NL	148	395	98	27	3	25	(13	12)	206	65	56	55	40	3	85	4	1	3	1	5	6	.248	.321	.522	.843
2019	LAD	NL	149	450	112	16	3	36	(24	12)	242	83	74	82	50	2	111	12	0	2	1	1	4	.249	.339	.538	.876
2020	LAD	NL	43	121	23	4	0	7	(2	5)	48	21	16	15	11	0	34	5	0	0	1	0	5	.190	.285	.397	.681
2021	2 Tms	NL	137	429	102	19	3	18	(7	11)	181	55	61	59	39	0	117	8	0	5	2	3	9	.238	.310	.422	.732
2022	SF	NL	134	380	104	19	3	23	(10	13)	198	57	70	83	42	3	100	7	0	4	3	2	5	.274	.353	.521	.874
21	ChC	NL	73	256	59	11	2	11	(5	6)	107	35	39	34	22	0	74	5	0	4	2	3	5	.230	.300	.418	.718
21	Atl	NL	64	173	43	8	1	7	(2	5)	74	20	22	25	17	0	43	3	0	1	0	0	4	.249	.325	.428	.752
	Postseason		79	195	50	8	0	12	(7	5)	94	29	29	32	17	4	61	5	1	0	2	0	4	.256	.332	.482	.814
	9 ML YEARS		1019	2962	702	150	13	171	(90	81)	1391	457	434	463	385	19	826	59	5	19	22	23	47	.237	.335	.470	.804

Elvis Peguero

Pitches: R **Bats:** R **Pos:** RP-13   **Ht:** 6'5" **Wt:** 208 **Born:** 3/20/1997 **Age:** 26

			HOW MUCH PITCHED					WHAT HE GAVE UP										THE RESULTS							
Year	Team	Lg	G	GS	GF	IP	BFP	H	R	ER	HR	SH	SF	HB	TBB	IBB	SO	WP	W	L	Pct	Sv-Op	Hld	Vel	OPS	ERC	ERA
2022	Salt Lk	AAA	38	0	13	44.1	182	34	18	14	2	0	3	4	13	0	50	7	4	1	.800	5- -	-	-	.558	2.42	2.84
2021	LAA	AL	3	0	0	2.1	17	7	7	7	0	0	0	1	3	0	0	0	0	1	.000	0-0	0	96	1.493	24.54	27.00
2022	LAA	AL	13	0	6	17.1	77	23	16	13	4	0	0	0	5	0	12	3	0	0	-	0-0	0	96	.933	6.66	6.75
	2 ML YEARS		16	0	6	19.2	94	30	23	20	4	0	0	1	8	0	12	3	0	1	.000	0-0	0	96	1.027	8.61	9.15

Liover Peguero

Bats: R **Throws:** R **Pos:** SS-1   **Ht:** 6'2" **Wt:** 200 **Born:** 12/31/2000 **Age:** 22

								BATTING												RUNNING			AVERAGES			
Year	Team	Lg	G	AB	H	2B	3B	HR	(Hm	Rd)	TB	R	RBI	RC	TBB	IBB	SO	HBP	SH	SF	SB	CS	GDP	Avg	OBP	Slg	OPS
2018	Dbcks	R	19	66	13	0	0	0	(-	-)	13	8	5	3	5	0	17	0	0	0	3	2	2	.197	.254	.197	.450
2019	Hlsbro	A-	22	84	22	4	2	0	(-	-)	30	13	11	11	8	0	17	1	0	0	3	1	2	.262	.333	.357	.690
2021	Grnsbr	A+	90	374	101	19	2	14	(-	-)	166	67	45	61	33	0	105	3	4	3	28	6	0	.270	.332	.444	.776
2022	Altna	AA	121	483	125	22	5	10	(-	-)	187	65	58	57	29	1	111	4	3	2	28	6	8	.259	.305	.387	.692
2022	Pit	NL	1	3	1	0	0	0	(0	0)	1	0	0	1	0	0	2	0	0	0	0	0	0	.333	.500	.333	.833

Jeremy Pena

Bats: R **Throws:** R **Pos:** SS-134;PH-2;PR-1   **Ht:** 6'0" **Wt:** 202 **Born:** 9/22/1997 **Age:** 25

								BATTING												RUNNING			AVERAGES			
Year	Team	Lg	G	AB	H	2B	3B	HR	(Hm	Rd)	TB	R	RBI	RC	TBB	IBB	SO	HBP	SH	SF	SB	CS	GDP	Avg	OBP	Slg	OPS
2018	TriCity	A-	36	136	34	5	0	1	(-	-)	42	22	10	16	18	0	19	1	0	1	3	0	0	.250	.340	.309	.649
2019	2 Tms	Low	109	409	124	21	7	7	(-	-)	180	72	54	76	47	0	90	11	0	6	20	10	4	.303	.385	.440	.825
2021	SgrLnd	AAA	25	102	34	4	2	9	(-	-)	69	19	18	25	5	0	29	5	0	0	5	1	0	.333	.393	.676	1.069
2022	Hou	AL	136	521	132	20	2	22	(14	8)	222	72	63	69	22	0	135	6	1	5	11	2	5	.253	.289	.426	.715

Ryan Pepiot

Pitches: R **Bats:** R **Pos:** SP-7; RP-2   PEP-ee-oh   **Ht:** 6'3" **Wt:** 215 **Born:** 8/21/1997 **Age:** 25

			HOW MUCH PITCHED					WHAT HE GAVE UP										THE RESULTS							
Year	Team	Lg	G	GS	GF	IP	BFP	H	R	ER	HR	SH	SF	HB	TBB	IBB	SO	WP	W	L	Pct	Sv-Op	Hld	Vel	OPS	ERC	ERA
2022	OkCity	AAA	19	17	1	91.1	369	62	27	26	10	0	1	10	36	0	114	1	9	1	.900	0- -	-	-	.621	2.88	2.56
2022	LAD	NL	9	7	0	36.1	160	26	15	14	6	0	0	3	27	0	42	1	3	0	1.000	0-0	0	94	.719	4.69	3.47

David Peralta

Bats: L **Throws:** L **Pos:** LF-113;PH-18;DH-11   **Ht:** 6'1" **Wt:** 210 **Born:** 8/14/1987 **Age:** 35

Year	Team	Lg	G	AB	H	2B	3B	HR	(Hm	Rd)	TB	R	RBI	RC	TBB	IBB	SO	HBP	SH	SF	SB	CS	GDP	Avg	OBP	Slg	OPS
2014	Ari	NL	88	329	94	12	9	8	(5	3)	148	40	36	38	16	0	60	1	1	1	6	3	9	.286	.320	.450	.770
2015	Ari	NL	149	462	144	26	10	17	(8	9)	241	61	78	83	44	2	107	4	0	7	9	4	7	.312	.371	.522	.893
2016	Ari	NL	48	171	43	9	5	4	(3	1)	74	23	15	15	8	1	42	3	0	1	2	0	3	.251	.295	.433	.728
2017	Ari	NL	140	525	154	31	3	14	(8	6)	233	82	57	77	43	1	94	6	0	3	8	4	7	.293	.352	.444	.796
2018	Ari	NL	146	560	164	25	5	30	(16	14)	289	75	87	104	48	4	124	4	0	2	4	0	14	.293	.352	.516	.868
2019	Ari	NL	99	382	105	29	3	12	(6	6)	176	48	57	62	35	3	87	5	0	1	0	0	9	.275	.343	.461	.804
2020	Ari	NL	54	203	61	10	1	5	(2	3)	88	19	34	33	13	0	45	0	0	2	1	0	4	.300	.339	.433	.773
2021	Ari	NL	150	487	126	30	8	8	(5	3)	196	57	63	69	46	3	92	3	0	2	2	1	9	.259	.325	.402	.728
2022	2 Tms		134	439	110	30	3	12	(5	7)	182	39	59	64	41	5	114	4	0	6	1	3	8	.251	.316	.415	.731
22	Ari	NL	87	278	69	19	2	12	(5	7)	128	29	41	46	27	4	74	2	0	3	1	2	6	.248	.316	.460	.777
22	TB	AL	47	161	41	11	1	0	(0	0)	54	10	18	18	14	1	40	2	0	3	0	1	2	.255	.317	.335	.652
	Postseason		4	18	4	0	0	0	(0	0)	4	2	0	1	1	0	1	0	0	0	0	0	1	.222	.263	.222	.485
	9 ML YEARS		1008	3558	1001	202	47	110	(58	52)	1627	444	486	545	294	19	765	30	1	25	33	15	70	.281	.339	.457	.796

Freddy Peralta

Pitches: R **Bats:** R **Pos:** SP-17; RP-1   **Ht:** 5'11" **Wt:** 199 **Born:** 6/4/1996 **Age:** 27

			HOW MUCH PITCHED				WHAT HE GAVE UP										THE RESULTS							
Year	Team	Lg	G	GS	GF	IP	BFP	H	R	ER	HR	SH	SF	HB	TBB	IBB	SO	WP	W	L	Pct	Sv-Op	Hld	Vel	OPS	ERC	ERA
2018	Mil	NL	16	14	1	78.1	321	49	37	37	8	1	1	4	40	1	96	3	6	4	.600	0-0	0	91	.622	2.71	4.25
2019	Mil	NL	39	8	3	85.0	382	87	58	50	15	3	1	2	37	1	115	3	7	3	.700	1-2	5	94	.790	4.86	5.29
2020	Mil	NL	15	1	2	29.1	125	22	14	13	2	1	1	3	12	0	47	2	3	1	.750	0-1	3	93	.622	2.88	3.99
2021	Mil	NL	28	27	0	144.1	580	84	47	45	14	2	1	11	56	1	195	4	10	5	.667	0-0	0	93	.561	2.12	2.81
2022	Mil	NL	18	17	0	78.0	317	54	31	31	6	1	2	3	27	0	86	1	4	4	.500	0-1	0	93	.569	2.25	3.58
	Postseason		3	1	0	8.0	31	4	1	1	1	0	0	0	4	0	12	0	0	0	-	0-0	0	93	.591	2.10	1.13
	5 ML YEARS		116	67	6	415.0	1725	296	187	176	45	8	6	23	172	3	539	13	30	17	.638	1-4	8	93	.629	2.82	3.82

Wandy Peralta

Pitches: L **Bats:** L **Pos:** RP-56   **Ht:** 6'0" **Wt:** 227 **Born:** 7/27/1991 **Age:** 31

			HOW MUCH PITCHED				WHAT HE GAVE UP										THE RESULTS							
Year	Team	Lg	G	GS	GF	IP	BFP	H	R	ER	HR	SH	SF	HB	TBB	IBB	SO	WP	W	L	Pct	Sv-Op	Hld	Vel	OPS	ERC	ERA
2016	Cin	NL	10	0	3	7.1	39	11	7	7	1	0	0	1	7	0	5	0	0	0	-	0-0	2	95	1.036	10.93	8.59
2017	Cin	NL	69	0	10	64.2	263	53	28	27	8	2	3	1	24	1	57	4	3	4	.429	0-2	16	96	.681	3.24	3.76
2018	Cin	NL	59	0	6	45.1	227	58	32	27	2	1	1	2	31	2	31	0	2	2	.500	0-0	7	96	.783	6.37	5.36
2019	2 Tms	NL	47	0	11	39.2	172	40	25	25	11	0	3	2	16	3	32	0	1	1	.500	0-1	3	95	.860	5.56	5.67
2020	SF	NL	25	0	9	27.1	114	22	13	10	3	0	1	2	11	0	25	0	1	1	.500	0-1	1	95	.657	3.40	3.29
2021	2 Tms		56	1	14	51.0	219	49	24	19	6	0	2	1	21	1	43	4	5	4	.556	5-6	5	95	.709	4.08	3.35
2022	NYY	AL	56	0	18	56.1	223	42	19	17	2	2	1	1	17	1	47	2	3	4	.429	4-9	9	95	.534	2.08	2.72
19	Cin	NL	39	0	11	34.0	151	36	23	23	10	0	3	2	15	3	27	0	1	1	.500	0-1	2	95	.893	6.17	6.09
19	SF	NL	8	0	0	5.2	21	4	2	2	1	0	0	0	1	0	5	0	0	0	-	0-0	1	95	.638	2.27	3.18
21	SF	NL	10	0	6	8.1	37	11	5	5	1	0	1	0	3	0	8	1	2	1	.667	2-3	0	96	.863	6.15	5.40
21	NYY	AL	46	1	8	42.2	182	38	19	14	5	0	1	1	18	1	35	3	3	3	.500	3-3	5	95	.677	3.72	2.95
	7 ML YEARS		322	1	71	291.2	1257	275	148	132	33	5	11	10	127	8	240	10	15	16	.484	9-19	43	96	.710	4.09	4.07

Wily Peralta

Pitches: R **Bats:** R **Pos:** RP-27; SP-1   **Ht:** 6'1" **Wt:** 255 **Born:** 5/8/1989 **Age:** 34

			HOW MUCH PITCHED				WHAT HE GAVE UP										THE RESULTS							
Year	Team	Lg	G	GS	GF	IP	BFP	H	R	ER	HR	SH	SF	HB	TBB	IBB	SO	WP	W	L	Pct	Sv-Op	Hld	Vel	OPS	ERC	ERA
2022	Toledo	AAA	5	0	1	5.1	26	7	2	2	0	0	0	0	3	0	8	1	0	0	-	1- -	-	-	.863	5.60	3.38
2012	Mil	NL	6	5	1	29.0	113	24	8	8	3	0	0	0	11	0	23	1	2	1	.667	0-0	0	96	.601	2.61	2.48
2013	Mil	NL	32	32	0	183.1	802	187	107	89	19	11	3	7	73	3	129	12	11	15	.423	0-0	0	96	.722	4.32	4.37
2014	Mil	NL	32	32	0	198.2	838	198	88	78	23	9	3	7	61	0	154	7	17	11	.607	0-0	0	96	.714	3.98	3.53
2015	Mil	NL	20	20	0	108.2	478	130	60	57	14	4	3	4	37	2	60	5	5	10	.333	0-0	0	94	.844	5.40	4.72
2016	Mil	NL	23	23	0	127.2	554	152	73	69	19	6	4	3	43	1	93	0	7	11	.389	0-0	0	95	.855	5.52	4.86
2017	Mil	NL	19	8	4	57.1	269	73	51	50	10	1	3	1	32	2	52	5	5	4	.556	0-0	0	96	.947	7.07	7.85
2018	KC	AL	37	0	30	34.1	149	28	14	14	4	1	2	1	23	1	35	4	1	0	1.000	14-14	1	96	.737	4.37	3.67
2019	KC	AL	42	0	23	40.1	176	45	28	26	7	1	2	2	19	1	24	0	2	4	.333	2-5	5	94	.864	6.01	5.80
2021	Det	AL	19	18	0	93.2	402	87	41	32	12	2	5	4	38	0	58	1	4	5	.444	0-0	1	94	.738	4.07	3.07
2022	Det	AL	28	1	6	38.1	168	34	12	11	2	2	1	2	24	0	32	1	2	0	1.000	0-0	2	95	.677	4.13	2.58
	10 ML YEARS		258	139	64	911.1	3949	958	482	434	110	38	27	30	361	10	660	36	56	61	.479	16-19	9	95	.773	4.68	4.29

Oswald Peraza

Bats: R **Throws:** R **Pos:** SS-12;2B-4;PH-2;PR-2   **Ht:** 6'0" **Wt:** 200 **Born:** 6/15/2000 **Age:** 23

Year	Team	Lg	G	AB	H	2B	3B	HR	(Hm	Rd)	TB	R	RBI	RC	TBB	IBB	SO	HBP	SH	SF	SB	CS	GDP	Avg	OBP	Slg	OPS
2018	Pulski	R+	36	140	35	3	2	1	(-	-)	45	25	11	17	14	0	41	4	0	1	8	1	2	.250	.333	.321	.655
2019	2 Tms	Low	65	262	69	6	1	4	(-	-)	89	38	20	36	21	0	37	7	1	2	23	7	6	.263	.332	.340	.672
2021	Smrst	AA	79	326	96	16	2	12	(-	-)	152	51	40	54	23	0	82	4	0	0	20	8	6	.294	.348	.466	.815
2021	HudVal	A+	28	111	34	10	0	5	(-	-)	59	20	16	26	12	0	24	3	0	1	16	1	1	.306	.386	.532	.917
2022	S-WB	AAA	99	386	100	16	0	19	(-	-)	173	57	50	65	34	0	100	7	1	1	33	5	2	.259	.329	.448	.778
2022	NYY	AL	18	49	15	3	0	1	(0	1)	21	8	2	5	6	0	9	2	0	0	2	0	3	.306	.404	.429	.832

Geraldo Perdomo

Bats: B **Throws:** R **Pos:** SS-140;3B-6;2B-2;PR-2;PH-1   **Ht:** 6'2" **Wt:** 203 **Born:** 10/22/1999 **Age:** 23

Year Team	Lg	G	AB	H	2B	3B	HR	(Hm	Rd)	TB	R	RBI	RC	TBB	IBB	SO	HBP	SH	SF	SB	CS	GDP	Avg	OBP	Slg	OPS
2018 3 Tms	Low	57	211	68	7	5	4	(-	-)	97	43	24	48	39	3	44	5	1		24	6	3	.322	.438	.460	.897
2019 2 Tms	Low	116	407	112	21	3	3	(-	-)	148	63	47	73	70	0	67	15	3	4	26	13	8	.275	.397	.364	.761
2021 Amrillo	AA	82	286	66	8	5	6	(-	-)	102	51	32	40	47	0	81	7	2	2	8	4	5	.231	.351	.357	.708
2021 Ari	NL	11	31	8	3	1	0	(0	0)	13	5	1	3	6	2	6	0	0	0	0	0	0	.258	.378	.419	.798
2022 Ari	NL	148	431	84	10	2	5	(1	4)	113	58	40	46	50	0	103	5	12	2	9	2	3	.195	.285	.262	.547
2 ML YEARS		159	462	92	13	3	5	(1	4)	126	63	41	49	56	2	109	5	12	2	9	2	3	.199	.291	.273	.564

Luis Perdomo

Pitches: R **Bats:** R **Pos:** RP-14   **Ht:** 6'2" **Wt:** 201 **Born:** 5/9/1993 **Age:** 30

Year Team	Lg	G	GS	GF	IP	BFP	H	R	ER	HR	SH	SF	HB	TBB	IBB	SO	WP	W	L	Pct	Sv-Op	Hld	Vel	OPS	ERC	ERA
2022 Nashv	AAA	24	3	7	30.1	115	21	9	9	2	0	0	2	4	0	33	0	2	0	1.000	4--	-		.510	1.66	2.67
2016 SD	NL	35	20	8	146.2	662	187	99	93	23	0	4	7	46	7	105	10	9	10	.474	0-0	0	94	.847	5.91	5.71
2017 SD	NL	29	29	0	163.2	716	182	97	85	17	3	2	8	65	3	118	11	8	11	.421	0-0	0	94	.784	5.00	4.67
2018 SD	NL	12	10	2	44.2	217	62	37	35	4	1	2	3	22	2	39	4	1	6	.143	0-0	0	93	.895	6.86	7.05
2019 SD	NL	47	1	13	72.0	296	69	34	32	6	2	0	2	18	1	55	3	2	4	.333	0-1	7	94	.675	3.29	4.00
2020 SD	NL	10	1	3	17.1	74	13	12	11	3	0	0	0	10	0	16	0	0	0	-	0-0	0	94	.717	3.87	5.71
2022 Mil	NL	14	0	3	23.2	96	24	10	10	4	0	0	1	3	0	12	0	3	0	1.000	0-0	1	94	.716	3.75	3.80
6 ML YEARS		147	61	29	468.0	2061	537	289	266	57	6	8	21	164	13	345	28	23	31	.426	0-1	8	94	.794	5.07	5.12

Carlos Perez

Bats: R **Throws:** R **Pos:** C-6;PH-1;PR-1   **Ht:** 5'11" **Wt:** 205 **Born:** 9/10/1996 **Age:** 26

Year Team	Lg	G	AB	H	2B	3B	HR	(Hm	Rd)	TB	R	RBI	RC	TBB	IBB	SO	HBP	SH	SF	SB	CS	GDP	Avg	OBP	Slg	OPS
2022 Charllt	AAA	109	418	106	17	1	21	(-	-)	188	53	76	61	34	0	40	7	0	6	1	2	15	.254	.316	.450	.766
2022 CWS	AL	7	18	4	2	0	0	(0	0)	6	0	2	2	0	0	2	0	0	0	0	0	1	.222	.222	.333	.556

Cionel Perez

Pitches: L **Bats:** R **Pos:** RP-66   see-oh-NEHL   **Ht:** 5'11" **Wt:** 162 **Born:** 4/21/1996 **Age:** 27

Year Team	Lg	G	GS	GF	IP	BFP	H	R	ER	HR	SH	SF	HB	TBB	IBB	SO	WP	W	L	Pct	Sv-Op	Hld	Vel	OPS	ERC	ERA
2018 Hou	AL	8	0	3	11.1	45	6	5	5	3	0	0	0	7	0	12	0	0	0	-	0-0	0	95	.684	3.56	3.97
2019 Hou	AL	5	0	3	9.0	40	11	10	10	3	0	0	0	2	0	7	0	1	1	.500	0-0	0	95	.904	6.18	10.00
2020 Hou	AL	7	0	1	6.1	32	7	2	2	0	0	0	0	6	1	8	0	0	0	-	0-0	2	95	.675	5.57	2.84
2021 Cin	NL	25	0	5	24.0	111	21	21	17	5	0	1	0	20	1	25	1	1	2	.333	0-0	0	96	.814	5.85	6.38
2022 Bal	AL	66	0	8	57.2	234	46	11	9	2	0	3	1	21	1	55	4	7	1	.875	1-1	24	97	.568	2.53	1.40
5 ML YEARS		111	0	20	108.1	462	91	49	43	13	0	4	1	56	3	107	5	9	4	.692	1-1	26	96	.674	3.80	3.57

Eury Perez

Pitches: R **Bats:** R **Pos:** P   **Ht:** 6'8" **Wt:** 220 **Born:** 4/15/2003 **Age:** 20

Year Team	Lg	G	GS	GF	IP	BFP	H	R	ER	HR	SH	SF	HB	TBB	IBB	SO	WP	W	L	Pct	Sv-Op	Hld	Vel	OPS	ERC	ERA
2021 2 Tms	Low	20	20	0	78.0	305	43	24	17	7	0	0	7	26	0	108	5	3	5	.375	0--	-	-	-	1.84	1.96
2022 Pnscla	AA	17	17	0	75.0	311	62	36	34	9	0	3	5	25	0	106	5	3	3	.500	0--	-	-	.681	3.28	4.08

Francisco Perez

Pitches: L **Bats:** B **Pos:** RP-10   **Ht:** 6'2" **Wt:** 217 **Born:** 7/20/1997 **Age:** 25

Year Team	Lg	G	GS	GF	IP	BFP	H	R	ER	HR	SH	SF	HB	TBB	IBB	SO	WP	W	L	Pct	Sv-Op	Hld	Vel	OPS	ERC	ERA
2022 Roch	AAA	45	0	8	46.2	204	34	29	25	3	1	4	1	32	2	61	5	1	3	.250	1--	-		.649	3.41	4.82
2021 Cle	AL	4	0	1	6.2	28	6	3	3	0	0	0	0	3	0	5	0	0	0	-	0-0	0	93	.613	3.08	4.05
2022 Was	NL	10	0	4	8.2	48	13	7	7	2	0	0	0	9	0	7	1	0	0	-	0-0	0	93	.997	11.08	7.27
2 ML YEARS		14	0	5	15.1	76	19	10	10	2	0	1	0	12	0	12	1	0	0	-	0-0	0	93	.852	7.30	5.87

Joe Perez

Bats: R **Throws:** R **Pos:** 3B-1;PH-1   **Ht:** 6'2" **Wt:** 198 **Born:** 8/12/1999 **Age:** 23

Year Team	Lg	G	AB	H	2B	3B	HR	(Hm	Rd)	TB	R	RBI	RC	TBB	IBB	SO	HBP	SH	SF	SB	CS	GDP	Avg	OBP	Slg	OPS
2022 CpChr	AA	64	257	68	16	0	6	(-	-)	102	30	28	34	26	1	70	1	0	0	3	0	5	.265	.335	.397	.731
2022 Hou	AL	1	1	0	0	0	0	(0	0)	0	0	0	0	0	0	0	0	0	0	0	0	0	.000	.000	.000	.000

Martin Perez

Pitches: L **Bats:** L **Pos:** SP-32   mar-TEEN   **Ht:** 6'0" **Wt:** 200 **Born:** 4/4/1991 **Age:** 32

Year Team	Lg	G	GS	GF	IP	BFP	H	R	ER	HR	SH	SF	HB	TBB	IBB	SO	WP	W	L	Pct	Sv-Op	Hld	Vel	OPS	ERC	ERA
2012 Tex	AL	12	6	2	38.0	177	47	26	23	3	1	1	2	15	1	25	5	1	4	.200	0-0	0	92	.819	5.33	5.45
2013 Tex	AL	20	20	0	124.1	529	129	55	50	15	2	3	3	37	0	84	9	10	6	.625	0-0	0	93	.728	4.14	3.62
2014 Tex	AL	8	8	0	51.1	207	50	25	25	3	1	0	1	19	1	35	1	4	3	.571	0-0	0	90	.743	3.82	4.38
2015 Tex	AL	14	14	0	78.2	339	88	45	39	3	0	3	2	24	1	48	1	3	6	.333	0-0	0	92	.729	4.04	4.46

Year	Team	Lg	G	GS	GF	IP	BFP	H	R	ER	HR	SH	SF	HB	TBB	IBB	SO	WP	W	L	Pct	Sv-Op	Hld	Vel	OPS	ERC	ERA
2016	Tex	AL	33	33	0	198.2	855	205	110	97	18	9	8	4	76	0	103	3	10	11	.476	0-0	0	93	.741	4.24	4.39
2017	Tex	AL	32	32	0	185.0	811	221	108	99	23	4	3	6	63	3	115	4	13	12	.520	0-0	0	93	.812	5.35	4.82
2018	Tex	AL	22	15	3	85.1	397	116	68	59	16	1	5	2	36	1	52	3	2	7	.222	0-1	2	93	.916	7.19	6.22
2019	Min	AL	32	29	0	165.1	737	184	104	94	23	3	5	3	67	1	135	3	10	7	.588	0-0	0	94	.785	5.07	5.12
2020	Bos	AL	12	12	0	62.0	262	55	33	31	8	1	1	3	28	0	46	2	3	5	.375	0-0	0	92	.744	4.13	4.50
2021	Bos	AL	36	22	6	114.0	509	136	71	60	19	1	4	9	36	2	97	2	7	8	.467	0-0	1	93	.838	5.68	4.74
2022	Tex	AL	32	32	0	196.1	821	178	70	63	11	4	3	6	69	0	169	6	12	8	.600	0-0	0	93	.646	3.22	2.89
Postseason			5	1	3	8.0	38	12	9	8	0	1	0	0	7	3	2	0	0	1	.000	0-0	0	93	1.014	8.24	9.00
11 ML YEARS			253	223	11	1299.0	5644	1409	715	640	142	27	36	41	470	10	909	39	75	77	.493	0-1	3	93	.765	4.63	4.43

Michael Perez

Bats: L Throws: R Pos: C-44;PH-1

Ht: 5'10" Wt: 195 Born: 8/7/1992 Age: 30

Year	Team	Lg	G	AB	H	2B	3B	HR	(Hm	Rd)	TB	R	RBI	RC	TBB	IBB	SO	HBP	SH	SF	SB	CS	GDP	Avg	OBP	Slg	OPS
2022	Syrcse	AAA	17	60	11	2	0	2	(-	-)	19	3	10	2	3	0	18	1	0	1	0	0	5	.183	.231	.317	.547
2018	TB	AL	24	74	21	5	0	1	(0	1)	29	9	11	9	3	0	19	0	1	2	0	0	0	.284	.304	.392	.696
2019	TB	AL	22	46	10	5	0	0	(0	0)	15	6	2	6	8	0	19	1	0	0	0	0	0	.217	.345	.326	.672
2020	TB	AL	38	84	14	3	0	1	(1	0)	20	7	13	5	7	0	27	1	0	1	0	0	3	.167	.237	.238	.475
2021	Pit	NL	70	210	30	8	1	7	(4	3)	61	19	21	8	19	1	68	2	0	0	0	1	4	.143	.221	.290	.511
2022	2 Tms	NL	45	121	18	0	0	6	(5	1)	36	10	14	10	10	0	32	1	0	2	1	0	2	.149	.214	.298	.511
22	Pit	NL	39	107	16	0	0	6	(5	1)	34	8	11	8	8	0	26	1	0	0	1	0	2	.150	.209	.318	.526
22	NYM	NL	6	14	2	0	0	0	(0	0)	2	2	3	2	2	0	6	0	0	0	0	0	0	.143	.250	.143	.393
Postseason			8	7	2	0	0	1	(0	1)	5	1	3	3	0	0	2	0	0	0	0	0	0	.286	.286	.714	1.000
5 ML YEARS			199	535	93	21	1	15	(10	5)	161	51	61	38	47	1	165	4	2	3	1	1	9	.174	.244	.301	.545

Oliver Perez

Pitches: L Bats: L Pos: RP-7

Ht: 6'3" Wt: 225 Born: 8/15/1981 Age: 41

Year	Team	Lg	G	GS	GF	IP	BFP	H	R	ER	HR	SH	SF	HB	TBB	IBB	SO	WP	W	L	Pct	Sv-Op	Hld	Vel	OPS	ERC	ERA
2002	SD	NL	16	15	0	90.0	387	71	37	35	13	5	3	5	48	1	94	3	4	5	.444	0-0	0	91	.702	3.93	3.50
2003	2 Tms	NL	24	24	0	126.2	579	129	80	77	22	5	2	4	77	3	141	7	4	10	.286	0-0	0	93	.830	5.66	5.47
2004	Pit	NL	30	30	0	196.0	805	145	71	65	22	9	5	9	81	2	239	2	12	10	.545	0-0	0	93	.655	2.99	2.98
2005	Pit	NL	20	20	0	103.0	471	102	68	67	23	5	4	6	70	1	97	3	7	5	.583	0-0	0	90	.874	6.44	5.85
2006	2 Tms	NL	22	22	0	112.2	529	129	90	82	20	5	10	6	68	0	102	5	3	13	.188	0-0	0	90	.865	6.62	6.55
2007	NYM	NL	29	29	0	177.0	765	153	90	70	22	4	7	7	79	1	174	6	15	10	.600	0-0	0	91	.696	3.76	3.56
2008	NYM	NL	34	34	0	194.0	847	167	100	91	24	9	7	11	105	4	180	9	10	7	.588	0-0	0	91	.725	4.21	4.22
2009	NYM	NL	14	14	0	66.0	324	69	51	50	12	5	4	4	58	2	62	2	3	4	.429	0-0	0	90	.897	7.16	6.82
2010	NYM	NL	17	7	4	46.1	234	54	37	35	9	1	3	4	42	3	37	4	0	5	.000	0-0	0	88	.953	8.27	6.80
2012	Sea	AL	33	0	6	29.2	123	27	7	7	1	1	1	0	10	2	24	2	1	3	.250	0-2	5	94	.628	2.82	2.12
2013	Sea	AL	61	0	22	53.0	229	50	23	22	6	1	0	1	26	3	74	1	3	3	.500	2-3	8	92	.731	4.23	3.74
2014	Ari	NL	68	0	11	58.2	256	50	25	19	5	4	0	7	24	2	76	3	3	4	.429	0-1	15	91	.679	3.53	2.91
2015	2 Tms	NL	70	0	15	41.0	183	39	24	19	4	1	0	4	15	2	51	3	2	4	.333	0-3	10	92	.681	3.81	4.17
2016	Was	NL	64	0	7	40.0	182	38	22	22	4	1	1	7	20	3	46	5	2	3	.400	0-1	15	92	.751	4.72	4.95
2017	Was	NL	50	0	8	33.0	143	32	17	17	4	0	1	4	12	2	39	1	0	0		1-1	12	93	.772	4.32	4.64
2018	Cle	AL	51	0	1	32.1	120	17	6	5	1	0	1	2	7	3	43	1	1	1	.500	0-0	15	92	.417	1.12	1.39
2019	Cle	AL	67	0	4	40.2	173	38	20	18	5	0	1	3	12	2	48	1	2	4	.333	1-5	22	92	.733	3.64	3.98
2020	Cle	AL	21	0	2	18.0	72	13	5	4	0	0	1	3	6	3	14	0	1	1	.500	1-2	3	90	.564	2.17	2.00
2021	Cle	AL	5	0	3	3.2	18	5	1	0	0	0	0	0	1	1	4	0	0	1	.000	0-0	0	89	.627	4.01	0.00
2022	Ari	NL	7	0	1	4.0	24	8	9	7	1	0	3	1	1	0	1	0	1	1	.500	0-0	0	88	1.101	11.16	15.75
03	SD	NL	19	19	0	103.2	473	103	65	62	20	4	2	3	65	2	117	6	4	7	.364	0-0	0	92	.836	5.74	5.38
03	Pit	NL	5	5	0	23.0	106	26	15	15	2	1	0	1	12	1	24	1	0	3	.000	0-0	0	92	.806	5.29	5.87
06	Pit	NL	15	15	0	76.0	364	88	64	56	13	5	8	3	51	0	61	4	2	10	.167	0-0	0	90	.877	6.85	6.63
06	NYM	NL	7	7	0	36.2	165	41	26	26	7	0	2	3	17	0	41	1	1	3	.250	0-0	0	91	.838	6.16	6.38
15	Ari	NL	48	0	11	29.0	128	25	12	10	2	1	0	4	11	1	37	2	2	1	.667	0-3	7	92	.627	3.38	3.10
15	Hou	NL	22	0	4	12.0	55	14	12	9	2	0	0	0	4	1	14	1	0	3	.000	0-0	3	92	.798	4.89	6.75
Postseason			11	2	2	16.2	71	18	7	7	3	3	0	2	5	1	10	0	2	0	1.000	0-0	3	93	.859	5.30	3.78
20 ML YEARS			703	195	84	1465.2	6464	1336	783	712	198	56	54	88	762	40	1546	58	74	94	.440	5-18	105	91	.748	4.49	4.37

Roberto Perez

Bats: R Throws: R Pos: C-20;PH-2

Ht: 5'11" Wt: 220 Born: 12/23/1988 Age: 34

Year	Team	Lg	G	AB	H	2B	3B	HR	(Hm	Rd)	TB	R	RBI	RC	TBB	IBB	SO	HBP	SH	SF	SB	CS	GDP	Avg	OBP	Slg	OPS
2014	Cle	AL	29	85	23	5	0	1	(1	0)	31	10	4	8	5	0	26	0	5	0	0	0	1	.271	.311	.365	.676
2015	Cle	AL	70	184	42	9	1	7	(4	3)	74	30	21	24	33	1	64	2	5	2	0	0	9	.228	.348	.402	.751
2016	Cle	AL	61	153	28	6	1	3	(1	2)	45	14	17	17	23	0	44	0	5	3	0	0	4	.183	.285	.294	.579
2017	Cle	AL	73	217	45	12	0	8	(6	2)	81	22	38	26	26	0	71	4	4	1	0	1	4	.207	.291	.373	.664
2018	Cle	AL	62	179	30	9	1	2	(1	1)	47	16	19	12	21	0	70	1	7	2	1	0	6	.168	.256	.263	.519
2019	Cle	AL	119	389	93	9	1	24	(12	12)	176	46	63	56	45	1	127	4	7	4	0	0	12	.239	.321	.452	.774
2020	Cle	AL	32	97	16	2	0	1	(0	1)	21	6	5	5	11	0	38	2	0	0	0	0	3	.165	.264	.216	.480
2021	Cle	AL	44	141	21	3	0	7	(3	4)	45	13	17	13	17	0	56	1	2	0	1	0	1	.149	.245	.319	.564
2022	Pit	NL	21	60	14	2	0	2	(0	2)	22	8	6	6	9	0	25	0	0	0	0	0	0	.233	.333	.367	.700
Postseason			21	59	13	1	0	4	(3	1)	26	6	10	8	9	0	20	1	2	0	0	0	2	.220	.333	.441	.774
9 ML YEARS			511	1505	312	57	4	55	(28	27)	542	165	192	167	190	2	521	10	35	12	2	1	41	.207	.298	.360	.658

Salvador Perez

Bats: R Throws: R Pos: C-77;DH-40   Ht: 6'3" Wt: 255 Born: 5/10/1990 Age: 33

								BATTING													RUNNING			AVERAGES			
Year	Team	Lg	G	AB	H	2B	3B	HR	(Hm	Rd)	TB	R	RBI	RC	TBB	IBB	SO	HBP	SH	SF	SB	CS	GDP	Avg	OBP	Slg	OPS
2011	KC	AL	39	148	49	8	2	3	(1	2)	70	20	21	26	7	0	20	1	0	2	0	0	5	.331	.361	.473	.834
2012	KC	AL	76	289	87	16	0	11	(3	8)	136	38	39	36	12	3	27	1	0	3	0	0	14	.301	.328	.471	.798
2013	KC	AL	138	496	145	25	3	13	(6	7)	215	48	79	77	21	2	63	4	0	5	0	0	13	.292	.323	.433	.757
2014	KC	AL	150	578	150	28	2	17	(8	9)	233	57	70	55	22	2	85	3	0	3	1	0	22	.260	.289	.403	.692
2015	KC	AL	142	531	138	25	2	21	(9	12)	226	52	70	60	13	4	82	4	0	5	1	0	23	.260	.280	.426	.706
2016	KC	AL	139	514	127	28	2	22	(11	11)	225	57	64	61	22	3	119	8	0	2	0	0	12	.247	.288	.438	.725
2017	KC	AL	129	471	126	24	1	27	(6	21)	233	57	80	65	17	3	95	5	0	5	1	0	23	.268	.297	.495	.792
2018	KC	AL	129	510	120	23	0	27	(11	16)	224	52	80	58	17	0	108	12	0	5	1	1	19	.235	.274	.439	.713
2020	KC	AL	37	150	50	12	0	11	(5	6)	95	22	32	29	3	0	36	2	0	1	1	0	0	.333	.353	.633	.986
2021	KC	AL	161	620	169	24	1	48	(27	21)	337	88	121	103	28	4	170	13	0	4	1	0	14	.273	.316	.544	.859
2022	KC	AL	114	445	113	23	1	23	(10	13)	207	48	76	74	18	2	109	7	0	3	0	0	9	.254	.292	.465	.757
	Postseason		31	116	27	4	0	5	(3	2)	46	14	14	10	5	0	19	3	0	0	0	0	3	.233	.282	.397	.679
	11 ML YEARS		1254	4752	1274	236	11	223	(97	126)	2201	539	732	644	180	23	914	60	0	38	6	1	154	.268	.301	.463	.764

Dillon Peters

Pitches: L Bats: L Pos: RP-18; SP-4   Ht: 5'11" Wt: 195 Born: 8/31/1992 Age: 30

			HOW MUCH PITCHED					WHAT HE GAVE UP										THE RESULTS						
Year	Team	Lg	G	GS	GF	IP	BFP	H	R	ER	HR	SH	SF	HB	TBB	IBB	SO	WP	W	L	Pct	Sv-Op	Hld	Vel	OPS	ERC	ERA
2022	Indy	AAA	5	0	0	7.2	31	5	1	1	0	0	1	0	3	0	7	2	0	0	-	0--	-	-	.443	1.65	1.17
2017	Mia	NL	6	6	0	31.1	139	32	18	18	3	0	2	3	19	1	27	3	1	2	.333	0-0	0	91	.771	5.38	5.17
2018	Mia	NL	7	5	2	27.2	129	34	22	22	4	1	1	1	15	0	17	3	2	2	.500	0-0	0	91	.868	6.59	7.16
2019	LAA	AL	17	12	1	72.0	327	85	50	43	18	1	2	5	26	1	55	1	4	4	.500	0-0	0	91	.926	6.34	5.38
2020	LAA	AL	1	1	0	1.2	9	3	4	3	2	0	0	0	0	0	2	0	0	0	-	0-0	0	91	1.333	14.27	16.20
2021	Pit	NL	6	6	0	26.2	117	26	12	11	2	0	0	1	10	0	23	0	1	2	.333	0-0	0	91	.731	3.72	3.71
2022	Pit	NL	22	4	2	39.1	165	35	20	20	5	1	2	0	17	0	26	1	5	2	.714	0-0	3	93	.710	3.83	4.58
	6 ML YEARS		59	34	5	198.2	886	215	126	117	34	3	5	9	87	2	150	8	13	12	.520	0-0	3	91	.833	5.42	5.30

David Peterson

Pitches: L Bats: L Pos: SP-19; RP-9   Ht: 6'6" Wt: 240 Born: 9/3/1995 Age: 27

			HOW MUCH PITCHED					WHAT HE GAVE UP										THE RESULTS						
Year	Team	Lg	G	GS	GF	IP	BFP	H	R	ER	HR	SH	SF	HB	TBB	IBB	SO	WP	W	L	Pct	Sv-Op	Hld	Vel	OPS	ERC	ERA
2022	Syrcse	AAA	6	6	0	26.0	119	33	16	14	1	0	0	0	10	0	34	4	2	3	.400	0--	-	-	.774	5.06	4.85
2020	NYM	NL	10	9	0	49.2	205	36	20	19	5	0	0	3	24	0	40	1	6	2	.750	0-0	0	92	.644	3.20	3.44
2021	NYM	NL	15	15	0	66.2	287	64	44	41	11	2	0	5	29	0	69	6	2	6	.250	0-0	0	93	.798	4.85	5.54
2022	NYM	NL	28	19	0	105.2	454	93	50	45	11	2	3	7	48	1	126	3	7	5	.583	0-1	1	94	.706	3.91	3.83
	3 ML YEARS		53	43	0	222.0	946	193	114	105	27	4	3	15	101	1	235	10	15	13	.536	0-1	1	93	.720	4.02	4.26

Jace Peterson

Bats: L Throws: R Pos: 3B-86;PH-21;RF-12;1B-5;2B-3;LF-3;PR-2;DH-1 JAYCE   Ht: 6'0" Wt: 215 Born: 5/9/1990 Age: 33

								BATTING													RUNNING			AVERAGES			
Year	Team	Lg	G	AB	H	2B	3B	HR	(Hm	Rd)	TB	R	RBI	RC	TBB	IBB	SO	HBP	SH	SF	SB	CS	GDP	Avg	OBP	Slg	OPS
2014	SD	NL	27	53	6	0	0	0	(0	0)	6	3	0	0	2	1	18	1	2	0	2	0	1	.113	.161	.113	.274
2015	Atl	NL	152	528	126	23	5	6	(1	5)	177	55	52	56	56	4	120	3	7	3	12	10	5	.239	.314	.335	.649
2016	Atl	NL	115	350	89	16	1	7	(3	4)	128	45	29	42	52	2	69	1	2	3	5	5	9	.254	.350	.366	.715
2017	Atl	NL	89	186	40	9	2	2	(2	0)	59	15	17	20	27	3	48	1	1	0	3	0	4	.215	.318	.317	.635
2018	2 Tms	AL	96	210	42	13	2	3	(2	1)	68	21	28	26	31	0	58	3	1	1	13	3	8	.200	.310	.324	.634
2019	Bal	AL	29	100	22	3	1	2	(2	0)	33	14	11	13	6	0	24	1	0	1	4	1	1	.220	.269	.330	.599
2020	Mil	NL	26	45	9	1	0	2	(1	1)	16	6	5	10	15	0	20	0	0	1	1	0	0	.200	.393	.356	.749
2021	Mil	NL	94	259	64	11	1	6	(1	5)	95	36	31	41	38	0	68	3	0	2	10	1	1	.247	.348	.367	.714
2022	Mil	NL	113	288	68	14	2	8	(1	7)	110	44	34	33	33	2	85	2	2	3	12	1	8	.236	.316	.382	.698
18	NYY	AL	3	10	3	0	0	0	(0	0)	3	0	0	1	1	0	3	0	0	0	0	1	0	.300	.364	.300	.664
18	Bal	AL	93	200	39	13	2	3	(2	1)	65	21	28	25	30	0	55	3	1	1	13	2	8	.195	.308	.325	.633
	Postseason		3	0	0	0	0	0	(0	0)	0	0	0	0	0	0	0	0	0	0	0	0	0	-	1.000		
	9 ML YEARS		741	2019	466	90	14	36	(13	23)	692	239	207	241	260	12	510	15	15	14	62	21	37	.231	.321	.343	.664

Tommy Pham

Bats: R Throws: R Pos: LF-134;DH-10;PH-1   FAM   Ht: 6'1" Wt: 223 Born: 3/8/1988 Age: 35

								BATTING													RUNNING			AVERAGES			
Year	Team	Lg	G	AB	H	2B	3B	HR	(Hm	Rd)	TB	R	RBI	RC	TBB	IBB	SO	HBP	SH	SF	SB	CS	GDP	Avg	OBP	Slg	OPS
2014	StL	NL	6	2	0	0	0	0	(0	0)	0	0	0	0	0	0	2	0	0	0	0	0	0	.000	.000	.000	.000
2015	StL	NL	52	153	41	7	5	5	(1	4)	73	28	18	26	19	1	41	0	0	1	2	0	1	.268	.347	.477	.824
2016	StL	NL	78	159	36	7	0	9	(3	6)	70	26	17	21	20	1	71	3	1	0	2	2	3	.226	.324	.440	.764
2017	StL	NL	128	444	136	22	2	23	(6	17)	231	95	73	93	71	0	117	10	2	3	25	7	18	.306	.411	.520	.931
2018	2 Tms	NL	137	494	136	18	6	21	(9	12)	229	102	63	76	67	2	140	6	0	3	15	7	18	.275	.367	.464	.830
2019	TB	AL	145	567	155	33	4	21	(11	10)	255	77	68	86	81	4	123	5	0	1	25	4	22	.273	.369	.450	.818
2020	SD	NL	31	109	23	2	0	3	(0	3)	34	13	12	14	15	0	27	1	0	0	6	0	2	.211	.312	.312	.624
2021	SD	NL	155	475	109	24	3	15	(10	5)	184	74	49	55	78	3	128	4	0	4	14	6	10	.229	.340	.383	.724
2022	2 Tms	AL	144	554	131	23	1	17	(9	8)	207	89	63	64	56	0	167	7	0	5	8	3	6	.236	.312	.374	.686
18	StL	NL	98	351	87	11	0	14	(6	8)	140	67	41	45	42	1	97	2	0	1	10	6	12	.248	.331	.399	.730
18	TB	AL	39	143	49	7	6	7	(3	4)	89	35	22	31	25	1	43	4	0	2	5	1	6	.343	.448	.622	1.071
22	Cin	NL	91	340	81	11	1	11	(6	5)	127	57	39	42	42	0	100	1	0	4	7	2	5	.238	.320	.374	.694
22	Bos	AL	53	214	50	12	0	6	(3	3)	80	32	24	22	14	0	67	6	0	1	1	1	7	.234	.298	.374	.672
	Postseason		15	54	19	2	0	3	(2	1)	30	5	6	9	2	0	11	0	0	0	4	0	3	.352	.375	.556	.931
	9 ML YEARS		876	2957	767	136	18	114	(44	70)	1281	504	363	435	407	11	816	36	3	17	97	29	94	.259	.354	.433	.787

David Phelps

Pitches: R **Bats:** R **Pos:** RP-64; SP-1   Ht: 6'2" **Wt:** 200 **Born:** 10/9/1986 **Age:** 36

			HOW MUCH PITCHED				WHAT HE GAVE UP										THE RESULTS						
Year	Team	Lg	G	GS	GF	IP	BFP	H	R	ER	HR	SH	SF	HB	TBB	IBB	SO	WP	W	L	Pct	Sv-Op	Hld	Vel	OPS	ERC	ERA
2012 NYY		AL	33	11	5	99.2	414	81	38	37	14	4	3	6	38	2	96	2	4	4	.500	0-0	2	91	.682	3.48	3.34
2013 NYY		AL	22	12	3	86.2	376	88	50	48	8	1	2	5	35	1	79	2	6	5	.545	0-1	1	90	.749	4.38	4.98
2014 NYY		AL	32	17	5	113.0	497	115	62	55	13	4	3	7	46	2	92	2	5	5	.500	1-1	5	90	.753	4.52	4.38
2015 Mia		NL	23	19	1	112.0	482	119	59	56	11	2	5	4	33	0	77	2	4	8	.333	0-0	0	90	.729	4.13	4.50
2016 Mia		NL	64	5	6	86.2	352	61	23	22	6	1	2	2	38	6	114	0	7	6	.538	4-10	25	94	.582	2.47	2.28
2017 2 Tms			54	0	5	55.2	238	51	23	21	5	2	2	1	26	3	62	0	4	5	.444	0-8	21	94	.693	3.82	3.40
2019 2 Tms			41	1	4	34.1	147	31	14	13	5	0	1	1	17	1	36	3	2	1	.667	1-5	5	93	.755	4.36	3.41
2020 2 Tms		NL	22	0	4	20.2	85	19	16	15	7	0	0	1	5	0	31	1	2	4	.333	0-2	6	94	.813	4.78	6.53
2021 Tor		AL	11	1	1	10.1	42	8	2	1	0	0	0	1	4	0	15	0	0	0		0-0	4	94	.553	2.60	0.87
2022 Tor		AL	65	1	11	63.2	272	52	22	20	2	1	0	4	31	0	64	3	0	2	.000	1-2	9	93	.617	3.17	2.83
17 Mia		NL	44	0	4	47.0	197	42	20	18	5	2	1	0	21	3	51	0	2	4	.333	0-6	18	94	.699	3.68	3.45
17 Sea		AL	10	0	1	8.2	41	9	3	3	0	0	1	1	5	0	11	0	2	1	.667	0-2	3	94	.660	4.54	3.12
19 Tor		AL	17	1	1	17.1	71	14	7	7	3	0	1	0	7	1	18	1	0	0	-	0-2	4	92	.754	3.77	3.63
19 ChC		NL	24	0	3	17.0	76	17	7	6	2	0	1	0	10	0	18	2	2	1	.667	1-3	1	93	.755	4.98	3.18
20 Mil		NL	12	0	3	13.0	48	7	5	4	2	0	0	1	2	0	20	1	2	3	.400	0-1	4	94	.497	1.56	2.77
20 Phi		NL	10	0	1	7.2	37	12	11	11	5	0	0	0	3	0	11	0	0	1	.000	0-1	2	94	1.229	12.43	12.91
Postseason			3	0	1	3.1	19	7	4	3	0	0	0	0	1	0	2	0	0	2	.000	0-0	0	90	1.032	8.97	8.10
10 ML YEARS			367	67	45	682.2	2905	625	309	288	71	15	18	32	273	15	666	15	34	40	.459	7-29	78	92	.700	3.80	3.80

Brett Phillips

Bats: L **Throws:** R **Pos:** CF-42;RF-38;PR-7;LF-5;PH-4;DH-2   Ht: 6'0" **Wt:** 195 **Born:** 5/30/1994 **Age:** 29

			BATTING																		RUNNING			AVERAGES			
Year	Team	Lg	G	AB	H	2B	3B	HR	(Hm	Rd)	TB	R	RBI	RC	TBB	IBB	SO	HBP	SH	SF	SB	CS	GDP	Avg	OBP	Slg	OPS
2022 Norfolk		AAA	24	65	18	1	2	6	(-	-)	41	16	17	20	17	0	25	3	0	3	1	0	0	.277	.432	.631	1.063
2017 Mil		NL	37	87	24	3	0	4	(2	2)	39	9	12	14	9	2	34	1	1	0	5	0	0	.276	.351	.448	.799
2018 2 Tms			51	134	25	4	3	2	(1	1)	41	15	11	10	11	0	61	1	0	1	1	1	2	.187	.252	.306	.558
2019 KC		AL	30	65	9	2	0	2	(1	1)	17	7	6	2	10	0	23	0	2	2	3	0	1	.138	.247	.262	.508
2020 2 Tms		AL	35	51	10	0	2	2	(1	1)	20	10	5	6	8	0	15	0	0	0	6	1	0	.196	.305	.392	.697
2021 TB		AL	119	253	52	9	4	13	(6	7)	108	50	44	40	33	0	113	2	2	2	14	3	0	.206	.300	.427	.727
2022 2 Tms		AL	83	201	29	6	0	5	(4	1)	50	22	15	13	16	0	94	3	4	1	7	0	0	.144	.217	.249	.466
18 Mil		NL	15	22	4	0	1	0	(0	0)	6	2	4	2	2	0	11	0	0	0	0	0	1	.182	.250	.273	.523
18 KC		AL	36	112	21	4	2	2	(1	1)	35	13	7	8	9	0	50	1	0	1	1	1	1	.188	.252	.313	.565
20 KC		AL	18	31	7	0	1	1	(0	1)	12	8	2	3	3	0	8	0	0	0	3	1	0	.226	.294	.387	.681
20 TB		AL	17	20	3	0	1	1	(1	0)	8	2	3	3	5	0	7	0	0	0	3	0	0	.150	.320	.400	.720
22 TB		AL	75	184	27	4	0	5	(4	1)	46	21	14	13	16	0	85	3	4	1	7	0	0	.147	.225	.250	.475
22 Bal		AL	8	17	2	2	0	0	(0	0)	4	1	1	0	0	0	9	0	0	0	0	0	0	.118	.118	.235	.353
Postseason			7	3	1	0	0	0	(0	0)	1	0	1	1	0	0	1	0	0	0	0	0	0	.333	.333	.333	.667
6 ML YEARS			355	791	149	24	9	28	(15	13)	275	113	93	85	87	2	340	7	9	6	36	5	6	.188	.273	.348	.620

Evan Phillips

Pitches: R **Bats:** R **Pos:** RP-64   Ht: 6'2" **Wt:** 215 **Born:** 9/11/1994 **Age:** 28

			HOW MUCH PITCHED				WHAT HE GAVE UP										THE RESULTS						
Year	Team	Lg	G	GS	GF	IP	BFP	H	R	ER	HR	SH	SF	HB	TBB	IBB	SO	WP	W	L	Pct	Sv-Op	Hld	Vel	OPS	ERC	ERA
2018 2 Tms			9	1	4	11.2	59	13	19	17	5	0	0	1	10	0	8	1	0	1	.000	0-0	0	94	1.073	9.76	13.11
2019 Bal		AL	25	0	2	28.0	140	32	20	20	2	1	2	5	20	0	40	2	0	1	.000	0-0	3	94	.821	6.59	6.43
2020 Bal		AL	14	0	3	14.1	69	14	8	8	1	0	0	3	10	0	20	1	1	1	.500	0-0	2	95	.567	5.67	5.02
2021 2 Tms			8	0	5	13.1	58	11	6	5	1	0	0	1	5	1	11	1	1	1	.500	1-1	0	95	.601	2.91	3.38
2022 LAD		NL	64	0	9	63.0	233	33	11	8	2	0	2	3	15	1	77	0	7	3	.700	2-4	19	96	.430	1.20	1.14
18 Atl		NL	4	0	4	6.1	29	6	6	6	3	0	0	0	4	0	3	0	0	0	-	0-0	0	94	.985	7.41	8.53
18 Bal		AL	5	1	0	5.1	30	7	13	11	2	0	0	1	6	0	5	1	0	1	.000	0-0	0	94	1.162	12.53	18.56
21 TB		AL	1	0	1	3.0	12	3	1	1	1	0	0	0	0	0	2	0	0	0	-	1-1	0	96	.750	3.79	3.00
21 LAD		NL	7	0	4	10.1	46	8	5	4	0	0	0	1	5	1	9	1	1	1	.500	0-0	0	95	.554	2.55	3.48
Postseason			2	0	0	3.0	12	1	0	0	0	0	0	0	2	0	6	0	1	0	1.000	0-0	0	95	.350	1.26	0.00
5 ML YEARS			120	1	23	130.1	559	103	64	58	11	1	4	13	60	2	156	5	9	7	.563	3-5	24	95	.640	3.39	4.01

Konnor Pilkington

Pitches: L **Bats:** L **Pos:** SP-11; RP-4   Ht: 6'3" **Wt:** 240 **Born:** 9/12/1997 **Age:** 25

			HOW MUCH PITCHED				WHAT HE GAVE UP										THE RESULTS						
Year	Team	Lg	G	GS	GF	IP	BFP	H	R	ER	HR	SH	SF	HB	TBB	IBB	SO	WP	W	L	Pct	Sv-Op	Hld	Vel	OPS	ERC	ERA
2022 Clmbs		AAA	13	12	0	56.2	252	59	40	37	8	0	1	3	26	0	58	4	3	5	.375	0- -	-	-	.786	5.08	5.88
2022 Cle		AL	15	11	3	58.0	258	53	30	25	6	0	1	2	32	0	50	1	1	2	.333	0-0	0	92	.700	4.30	3.88

Kevin Pillar

Bats: R **Throws:** R **Pos:** LF-4;CF-1   pih-LAHR   Ht: 6'0" **Wt:** 200 **Born:** 1/4/1989 **Age:** 34

			BATTING																		RUNNING			AVERAGES			
Year	Team	Lg	G	AB	H	2B	3B	HR	(Hm	Rd)	TB	R	RBI	RC	TBB	IBB	SO	HBP	SH	SF	SB	CS	GDP	Avg	OBP	Slg	OPS
2022 OkCity		AAA	42	149	47	7	3	10	(-	-)	90	42	40	36	20	0	22	3	0	4	2	1	5	.315	.398	.604	1.002
2013 Tor		AL	36	102	21	4	0	3	(1	2)	34	11	13	9	4	0	29	2	2	0	1	0	1	.206	.250	.333	.583
2014 Tor		AL	53	116	31	9	0	2	(2	0)	46	19	7	8	4	0	28	1	0	1	1	2	3	.267	.295	.397	.692
2015 Tor		AL	159	586	163	31	2	12	(6	6)	234	76	56	73	28	1	85	5	4	5	25	4	9	.278	.314	.399	.713
2016 Tor		AL	146	548	146	35	2	7	(3	4)	206	59	53	66	24	0	90	6	3	3	14	6	12	.266	.303	.376	.679
2017 Tor		AL	154	587	150	37	1	16	(6	10)	237	72	42	58	33	0	95	6	3	3	15	6	13	.256	.300	.404	.704
2018 Tor		AL	142	512	129	40	2	15	(11	4)	218	65	59	59	18	0	98	6	0	6	14	3	8	.252	.282	.426	.708
2019 2 Tms			161	611	158	37	3	21	(11	10)	264	83	88	76	18	4	89	9	0	7	14	5	15	.259	.287	.432	.719

Year	Team	Lg	G	AB	H	2B	3B	HR	(Hm	Rd)	TB	R	RBI	RC	TBB	IBB	SO	HBP	SH	SF	SB	CS	GDP	Avg	OBP	Slg	OPS
2020	2 Tms		54	208	60	12	3	6	(2	4)	96	34	26	29	13	1	41	2	0	0	5	2	4	.288	.336	.462	.798
2021	NYM	NL	124	325	75	11	2	15	(6	9)	135	40	47	40	11	0	81	10	0	1	4	3	5	.231	.277	.415	.692
2022	LAD	NL	4	12	1	1	0	0	(0	0)	2	1	0	0	1	0	4	0	0	0	0	0	1	.083	.154	.167	.321
19	Tor	AL	5	16	1	0	0	0	(0	0)	1	1	1	0	0	0	3	0	0	1	0	0	0	.063	.059	.063	.121
19	SF	NL	156	595	157	37	3	21	(11	10)	263	82	87	76	18	4	86	9	0	6	14	5	15	.264	.293	.442	.735
20	Bos	AL	30	117	32	7	2	4	(2	2)	55	20	13	14	8	0	23	1	0	0	1	1	4	.274	.325	.470	.795
20	Col	NL	24	91	28	5	1	2	(0	2)	41	14	13	15	5	1	18	1	0	0	4	1	0	.308	.351	.451	.801
	Postseason		20	74	15	6	0	2	(0	2)	27	7	8	8	5	1	14	0	0	1	3	1	1	.203	.250	.365	.615
	10 ML YEARS		1033	3607	934	217	15	97	(48	49)	1472	460	391	418	154	6	640	47	12	26	92	32	70	.259	.296	.408	.704

Manny Pina

Bats: R **Throws:** R **Pos:** C-5 PEEN-yah **Ht:** 6'0" **Wt:** 222 **Born:** 6/5/1987 **Age:** 36

Year	Team	Lg	G	AB	H	2B	3B	HR	(Hm	Rd)	TB	R	RBI	RC	TBB	IBB	SO	HBP	SH	SF	SB	CS	GDP	Avg	OBP	Slg	OPS
2011	KC	AL	4	14	3	2	0	0	(0	0)	5	2	0	1	1	0	2	0	0	0	0	0	1	.214	.267	.357	.624
2012	KC	AL	1	2	0	0	0	0	(0	0)	0	0	0	0	0	0	0	0	0	0	0	0	0	.000	.000	.000	.000
2016	Mil	NL	33	71	18	4	0	2	(1	1)	28	4	12	8	10	0	15	0	0	0	0	1	2	.254	.346	.394	.740
2017	Mil	NL	107	330	92	21	0	9	(6	3)	140	45	43	46	20	0	79	5	1	3	2	0	8	.279	.327	.424	.751
2018	Mil	NL	98	306	77	13	2	9	(6	3)	121	39	28	27	21	3	62	5	1	4	2	0	13	.252	.307	.395	.702
2019	Mil	NL	76	158	36	8	0	7	(5	2)	65	10	25	20	16	1	50	4	0	1	0	0	1	.228	.313	.411	.724
2020	Mil	NL	15	39	9	1	0	2	(2	0)	16	4	5	6	3	0	11	3	0	0	0	0	0	.231	.333	.410	.744
2021	Mil	NL	75	180	34	6	0	13	(4	9)	79	27	33	28	22	0	38	5	0	1	0	0	4	.189	.293	.439	.732
2022	Atl	NL	5	14	2	0	0	0	(0	0)	2	2	1	1	1	0	1	1	0	1	0	0	0	.143	.235	.143	.378
	Postseason		8	11	3	1	0	0	(0	0)	4	1	0	3	5	0	4	0	0	0	0	0	0	.273	.500	.364	.864
	9 ML YEARS		414	1114	271	55	2	42	(24	18)	456	132	148	137	94	4	258	23	2	10	4	1	29	.243	.313	.409	.722

Chad Pinder

Bats: R **Throws:** R **Pos:** LF-64;RF-30;PH-20;DH-12;3B-9;1B-3;2B-1 **Ht:** 6'2" **Wt:** 210 **Born:** 3/29/1992 **Age:** 31

Year	Team	Lg	G	AB	H	2B	3B	HR	(Hm	Rd)	TB	R	RBI	RC	TBB	IBB	SO	HBP	SH	SF	SB	CS	GDP	Avg	OBP	Slg	OPS
2016	Oak	AL	22	51	12	4	0	1	(0	1)	19	4	4	5	3	0	14	0	0	1	0	0	1	.235	.273	.373	.645
2017	Oak	AL	87	282	67	15	1	15	(10	5)	129	36	42	37	18	0	92	5	0	3	2	1	7	.238	.292	.457	.750
2018	Oak	AL	110	298	77	12	1	13	(6	7)	130	43	27	35	27	1	88	6	2	0	0	2	4	.258	.332	.436	.769
2019	Oak	AL	124	341	82	21	0	13	(6	7)	142	45	47	43	20	0	88	5	1	3	0	1	11	.240	.290	.416	.706
2020	Oak	AL	24	56	13	3	0	2	(0	2)	22	8	8	8	5	0	13	0	0	0	0	0	3	.232	.295	.393	.688
2021	Oak	AL	75	214	52	16	1	6	(2	4)	88	30	27	25	16	0	62	2	0	1	1	0	6	.243	.300	.411	.712
2022	Oak	AL	111	361	85	18	0	12	(5	7)	139	38	42	39	14	0	118	0	1	2	2	0	10	.235	.263	.385	.648
	Postseason		7	22	7	1	0	2	(1	1)	14	2	7	7	3	1	6	0	0	1	0	0	1	.318	.385	.636	1.021
	7 ML YEARS		553	1603	388	89	3	62	(29	33)	669	204	197	192	103	1	475	18	4	10	5	4	42	.242	.294	.417	.711

Israel Pineda

Bats: R **Throws:** R **Pos:** C-4 **Ht:** 5'11" **Wt:** 188 **Born:** 4/3/2000 **Age:** 23

Year	Team	Lg	G	AB	H	2B	3B	HR	(Hm	Rd)	TB	R	RBI	RC	TBB	IBB	SO	HBP	SH	SF	SB	CS	GDP	Avg	OBP	Slg	OPS
2022	Hrsbrg	AA	26	93	26	3	0	7	(-	-)	50	15	21	17	9	0	18	0	0	1	1	0	5	.280	.340	.538	.877
2022	Wilmg	A+	67	246	65	16	2	8	(-	-)	109	31	45	35	22	0	70	1	0	2	2	2	6	.264	.325	.443	.768
2022	Was	NL	4	13	1	0	0	0	(0	0)	1	1	0	0	1	0	7	0	0	0	0	0	0	.077	.143	.077	.220

Michael Pineda

Pitches: R **Bats:** R **Pos:** SP-11 pah-NAY-dah **Ht:** 6'7" **Wt:** 280 **Born:** 1/18/1989 **Age:** 34

			HOW MUCH PITCHED					WHAT HE GAVE UP											THE RESULTS							
Year	Team	Lg	G	GS	GF	IP	BFP	H	R	ER	HR	SH	SF	HB	TBB	IBB	SO	WP	W	L	Pct	Sv-Op	Hld	Vel	OPS	ERC	ERA
2022	Toledo	AAA	7	6	0	25.0	106	30	13	13	2	0	0	0	5	0	21	2	1	2	.333	0- -	-	-	.736	4.34	4.68
2011	Sea	AL	28	28	0	171.0	696	133	76	71	18	4	3	5	55	1	173	9	9	10	.474	0-0	0	95	.621	2.73	3.74
2014	NYY	AL	13	13	0	76.1	290	56	18	16	5	2	1	0	7	0	59	3	5	5	.500	0-0	0	92	.526	1.51	1.89
2015	NYY	AL	27	27	0	160.2	668	176	83	78	21	4	6	3	21	0	156	4	12	10	.545	0-0	0	93	.752	3.82	4.37
2016	NYY	AL	32	32	0	175.2	756	184	98	94	27	0	3	6	53	1	207	7	6	12	.333	0-0	0	94	.784	4.45	4.82
2017	NYY	AL	17	17	0	96.1	410	103	55	47	20	0	4	2	21	0	92	5	8	4	.667	0-0	0	94	.769	4.52	4.39
2019	Min	AL	26	26	0	146.0	600	141	68	65	23	2	7	5	28	1	140	8	11	5	.688	0-0	0	93	.721	3.58	4.01
2020	Min	AL	5	5	0	26.2	111	25	10	10	0	0	2	1	7	0	25	0	2	0	1.000	0-0	0	92	.604	2.69	3.38
2021	Min	AL	22	21	0	109.1	458	114	49	44	17	3	2	2	21	1	88	1	9	8	.529	0-0	0	91	.755	3.90	3.62
2022	Det	AL	11	11	0	46.2	200	58	31	30	13	0	1	0	8	0	26	0	2	7	.222	0-0	0	90	.906	5.87	5.79
	9 ML YEARS		181	180	0	1008.2	4189	990	488	455	144	15	29	24	221	4	966	37	64	61	.512	0-0	0	93	.722	3.63	4.06

Rene Pinto

Bats: R **Throws:** R **Pos:** C-25 **Ht:** 5'10" **Wt:** 195 **Born:** 11/2/1996 **Age:** 26

Year	Team	Lg	G	AB	H	2B	3B	HR	(Hm	Rd)	TB	R	RBI	RC	TBB	IBB	SO	HBP	SH	SF	SB	CS	GDP	Avg	OBP	Slg	OPS
2022	Drham	AAA	73	282	75	26	2	14	(-	-)	147	39	54	48	22	1	82	1	0	1	1	0	8	.266	.320	.521	.842
2022	TB	AL	25	80	17	3	0	2	(1	1)	26	5	10	6	2	0	35	1	0	0	0	0	3	.213	.241	.325	.566

Stephen Piscotty

Bats: R **Throws:** R **Pos:** RF-28;DH-8;LF-5;PH-3   **Ht:** 6'4" **Wt:** 211 **Born:** 1/14/1991 **Age:** 32

Year	Team	Lg	G	AB	H	2B	3B	HR	(Hm	Rd)	TB	R	RBI	RC	TBB	IBB	SO	HBP	SH	SF	SB	CS	GDP	Avg	OBP	Slg	OPS
2022	Lsvlle	AAA	24	88	22	3	0	5	(-	-)	40	8	14	13	7	0	24	1	0	3	0	0	3	.250	.313	.455	.767
2015	StL	NL	63	233	71	15	4	7	(4	3)	115	29	39	41	20	2	56	1	0	2	2	1	7	.305	.359	.494	.853
2016	StL	NL	153	582	159	35	3	22	(13	9)	266	86	85	97	51	0	133	12	1	2	7	5	14	.273	.343	.457	.800
2017	StL	NL	107	341	80	16	1	9	(1	8)	125	40	39	43	52	2	87	5	0	3	3	6	11	.235	.342	.367	.708
2018	Oak	AL	151	546	146	41	0	27	(10	17)	268	78	88	87	42	0	114	12	0	5	2	0	21	.267	.331	.491	.821
2019	Oak	AL	93	357	89	17	1	13	(8	5)	147	46	44	42	29	0	84	3	1	3	2	0	13	.249	.309	.412	.720
2020	Oak	AL	45	159	36	6	0	5	(1	4)	57	17	29	21	9	0	53	1	1	1	4	0	4	.226	.271	.358	.629
2021	Oak	AL	72	173	38	8	0	5	(2	3)	61	14	16	21	13	0	48	2	0	0	1	0	2	.220	.282	.353	.635
2022	Oak	AL	42	126	24	4	0	5	(4	1)	43	12	14	16	9	1	48	2	0	2	2	0	2	.190	.252	.341	.593
	Postseason		8	26	7	1	0	3	(1	2)	17	5	6	8	3	0	11	0	0	0	0	0	1	.269	.345	.654	.999
	8 ML YEARS		726	2517	643	142	9	93	(43	50)	1082	322	354	368	225	5	623	38	3	18	23	12	74	.255	.324	.430	.754

Nick Pivetta

Pitches: R **Bats:** R **Pos:** SP-33   **Ht:** 6'5" **Wt:** 214 **Born:** 2/14/1993 **Age:** 30

Year	Team	Lg	G	GS	GF	IP	BFP	H	R	ER	HR	SH	SF	HB	TBB	IBB	SO	WP	W	L	Pct	Sv-Op	Hld	Vel	OPS	ERC	ERA
2017	Phi	NL	26	26	0	133.0	584	144	91	89	25	4	7	4	57	0	140	11	8	10	.444	0-0	0	94	.846	5.52	6.02
2018	Phi	NL	33	32	1	164.0	694	163	91	87	24	8	5	5	51	0	188	8	7	14	.333	0-0	0	95	.743	4.15	4.77
2019	Phi	NL	30	13	8	93.2	421	103	64	56	20	4	4	4	39	2	89	4	4	6	.400	1-1	1	95	.866	5.67	5.38
2020	2 Tms		5	2	0	15.2	71	18	12	12	4	0	1	1	6	0	17	1	2	0	1.000	0-0	1	93	.924	6.28	6.89
2021	Bos	AL	31	30	1	155.0	661	137	80	78	24	2	4	5	65	2	175	9	9	8	.529	1-1	0	95	.731	3.98	4.53
2022	Bos	AL	33	33	0	179.2	773	175	91	91	27	0	4	5	73	0	175	10	10	12	.455	0-0	0	93	.753	4.44	4.56
20	Phi	NL	3	0	0	5.2	29	10	10	10	3	0	1	1	1	0	4	1	0	0	-	0-0	1	94	1.375	12.33	15.88
20	Bos	AL	2	2	0	10.0	42	8	2	2	1	0	0	0	5	0	13	0	2	0	1.000	0-0	0	92	.607	3.39	1.80
	Postseason		3	1	1	13.2	53	9	4	4	3	0	0	0	5	0	14	1	1	0	1.000	0-0	0	95	.681	2.95	2.63
	6 ML YEARS		158	136	10	741.0	3204	740	429	413	124	18	25	24	291	4	784	43	40	50	.444	2-2	2	94	.782	4.65	5.02

Michael Plassmeyer

Pitches: L **Bats:** L **Pos:** RP-2   **Ht:** 6'2" **Wt:** 197 **Born:** 11/5/1996 **Age:** 26

Year	Team	Lg	G	GS	GF	IP	BFP	H	R	ER	HR	SH	SF	HB	TBB	IBB	SO	WP	W	L	Pct	Sv-Op	Hld	Vel	OPS	ERC	ERA
2022	Scrmto	AAA	11	10	1	46.1	212	50	39	38	15	0	0	9	24	0	47	1	0	6	.000	0- -	-	-	.989	7.88	7.38
2022	LV	AAA	16	16	0	82.0	330	63	26	22	12	0	0	8	23	0	82	2	6	3	.667	0- -	-	-	.659	3.10	2.41
2022	Phi	NL	2	0	0	7.1	29	9	3	3	1	0	0	0	1	0	7	0	0	1	.000	0-0	0	91	.845	4.97	3.68

Kevin Plawecki

Bats: R **Throws:** R **Pos:** C-61;PH-4   plah-WEH-kee   **Ht:** 6'2" **Wt:** 208 **Born:** 2/26/1991 **Age:** 32

Year	Team	Lg	G	AB	H	2B	3B	HR	(Hm	Rd)	TB	R	RBI	RC	TBB	IBB	SO	HBP	SH	SF	SB	CS	GDP	Avg	OBP	Slg	OPS
2015	NYM	NL	73	233	51	9	0	3	(1	2)	69	18	21	22	17	4	60	4	1	3	0	0	4	.219	.280	.296	.576
2016	NYM	NL	48	132	26	6	0	1	(0	1)	35	6	11	11	17	2	33	2	0	0	0	0	5	.197	.298	.265	.563
2017	NYM	NL	37	100	26	5	0	3	(3	0)	40	11	13	15	14	2	17	3	0	1	1	0	2	.260	.364	.400	.764
2018	NYM	NL	79	238	50	13	2	7	(5	2)	88	33	30	25	28	2	65	9	1	1	0	1	12	.210	.315	.370	.685
2019	Cle	AL	60	158	35	10	0	3	(3	0)	54	13	17	14	12	0	31	3	0	1	0	1	4	.222	.287	.342	.629
2020	Bos	AL	24	82	28	5	1	1	(1	0)	38	8	17	17	5	0	14	2	0	0	1	0	4	.341	.393	.463	.857
2021	Bos	AL	64	157	45	7	0	3	(3	0)	61	15	15	12	12	0	26	3	1	0	0	0	4	.287	.349	.389	.737
2022	2 Tms	AL	64	168	37	8	0	1	(0	1)	48	15	13	13	14	0	32	2	1	1	0	0	6	.220	.286	.286	.572
22	Bos	AL	61	157	34	8	0	1	(0	1)	45	15	12	12	14	0	28	2	1	1	0	0	5	.217	.287	.287	.574
22	Tex	AL	3	11	3	0	0	0	(0	0)	3	0	1	1	0	0	4	0	0	0	0	0	1	.273	.273	.273	.545
	Postseason		5	7	1	1	0	0	(0	0)	2	1	0	0	1	0	0	0	0	0	0	0	0	.143	.250	.286	.536
	8 ML YEARS		449	1268	298	63	3	22	(16	6)	433	119	137	138	119	10	278	28	4	7	2	2	37	.235	.313	.341	.654

Zach Plesac

Pitches: R **Bats:** R **Pos:** SP-24; RP-1   **Ht:** 6'3" **Wt:** 220 **Born:** 1/21/1995 **Age:** 28

Year	Team	Lg	G	GS	GF	IP	BFP	H	R	ER	HR	SH	SF	HB	TBB	IBB	SO	WP	W	L	Pct	Sv-Op	Hld	Vel	OPS	ERC	ERA
2019	Cle	AL	21	21	0	115.2	475	102	52	49	19	2	0	3	40	0	88	1	8	6	.571	0-0	0	94	.744	3.82	3.81
2020	Cle	AL	8	8	0	55.1	206	38	14	14	8	0	0	1	6	0	57	0	4	2	.667	0-0	0	93	.565	1.78	2.28
2021	Cle	AL	25	25	0	142.2	598	137	79	74	23	1	3	7	34	1	100	5	10	6	.625	0-0	0	93	.735	3.79	4.67
2022	Cle	AL	25	24	0	131.2	568	136	74	63	19	0	1	5	38	0	100	4	3	12	.200	0-0	0	92	.741	4.23	4.31
	4 ML YEARS		79	78	0	445.1	1847	413	219	200	69	3	4	16	118	1	345	10	25	26	.490	0-0	0	93	.720	3.66	4.04

Nick Plummer

Bats: L **Throws:** L **Pos:** RF-5;DH-5;LF-4;PR-2   **Ht:** 5'10" **Wt:** 200 **Born:** 7/31/1996 **Age:** 26

Year	Team	Lg	G	AB	H	2B	3B	HR	(Hm	Rd)	TB	R	RBI	RC	TBB	IBB	SO	HBP	SH	SF	SB	CS	GDP	Avg	OBP	Slg	OPS
2022	Syrcse	AAA	65	235	56	11	0	7	(-	-)	88	29	41	31	25	0	80	8	0	2	8	4	0	.238	.330	.374	.704
2022	NYM	NL	14	29	4	1	0	2	(2	0)	11	4	6	2	1	0	12	1	0	0	0	0	1	.138	.194	.379	.573

Colin Poche

Pitches: L **Bats:** L **Pos:** RP-65 poh-SHAY **Ht:** 6'3" **Wt:** 225 **Born:** 1/17/1994 **Age:** 29

			HOW MUCH PITCHED				WHAT HE GAVE UP										THE RESULTS					
Year	Team	Lg	G	GS	GF	IP	BFP	H	R	ER	HR	SH	SF	HB	TBB	IBB	SO	WP	W	L	Pct	Sv-Op	Hld	Vel	OPS	ERC	ERA
2022	Drham	AAA	6	0	3	6.0	21	1	0	0	0	0	0	0	2	0	11	1	0	0	-	1- -	-		.195	0.36	0.00
2019	TB	AL	51	0	8	51.2	207	33	27	27	9	1	0	5	19	1	72	2	5	5	.500	2-6	16	93	.650	2.88	4.70
2022	TB	AL	65	0	13	58.2	245	46	30	26	11	0	4	1	22	0	64	4	4	2	.667	7-13	23	93	.690	3.38	3.99
	Postseason		5	0	3	4.1	15	2	1	1	0	0	0	0	0	0	6	0	0	0	-	0-0	0	93	.467	0.97	2.08
	2 ML YEARS		116	0	21	110.1	452	79	57	53	20	1	4	6	41	1	136	6	9	7	.563	9-19	39	93	.672	3.14	4.32

Jorge Polanco

Bats: B **Throws:** R **Pos:** 2B-97;SS-6;DH-5;PH-1 poh-LAHN-koh **Ht:** 5'11" **Wt:** 208 **Born:** 7/5/1993 **Age:** 29

			BATTING																	RUNNING			AVERAGES			
Year	Team	Lg	G	AB	H	2B	3B	HR	(Hm	Rd)	TB	R	RBI	RC	TBB	IBB	SO	HBP	SH	SF	SB	CS	GDP	Avg	OBP	Slg	OPS
2014	Min	AL	5	6	2	1	1	0	(0	0)	5	2	3	4	2	0	2	0	0	0	0	0	0	.333	.500	.833	1.333
2015	Min	AL	4	10	3	0	0	0	(0	0)	3	1	1	3	2	0	1	0	0	0	1	0	0	.300	.417	.300	.717
2016	Min	AL	69	245	69	15	4	4	(1	3)	104	24	27	36	17	0	46	3	2	3	4	3	3	.282	.332	.424	.757
2017	Min	AL	133	488	125	30	3	13	(4	9)	200	60	74	68	41	1	78	2	7	6	13	5	7	.256	.313	.410	.723
2018	Min	AL	77	302	87	18	3	6	(1	5)	129	38	42	50	25	0	62	2	3	1	7	7	5	.288	.345	.427	.773
2019	Min	AL	153	631	186	40	7	22	(9	13)	306	107	79	112	60	2	116	4	2	7	4	3	11	.295	.356	.485	.841
2020	Min	AL	55	209	54	8	0	4	(2	2)	74	22	19	23	13	0	35	1	2	1	4	2	7	.258	.304	.354	.658
2021	Min	AL	152	588	158	35	2	33	(11	22)	296	97	98	112	45	0	118	5	0	6	11	6	4	.269	.323	.503	.826
2022	Min	AL	104	375	88	16	0	16	(8	8)	152	54	56	61	64	1	95	2	0	4	3	3	4	.235	.346	.405	.751
	Postseason		6	22	5	0	0	1	(0	1)	8	3	2	3	4	0	5	1	0	0	1	0	0	.227	.370	.364	.734
	9 ML YEARS		752	2854	772	163	20	98	(36	62)	1269	405	399	469	269	4	553	19	16	28	47	29	41	.270	.334	.445	.779

A.J. Pollock

Bats: R **Throws:** R **Pos:** LF-107;CF-37;RF-14;PR-5;PH-2 **Ht:** 6'1" **Wt:** 210 **Born:** 12/5/1987 **Age:** 35

			BATTING																	RUNNING			AVERAGES			
Year	Team	Lg	G	AB	H	2B	3B	HR	(Hm	Rd)	TB	R	RBI	RC	TBB	IBB	SO	HBP	SH	SF	SB	CS	GDP	Avg	OBP	Slg	OPS
2012	Ari	NL	31	81	20	4	1	2	(2	0)	32	8	8	9	9	1	11	0	1	2	1	2	2	.247	.315	.395	.710
2013	Ari	NL	137	443	119	28	5	8	(3	5)	181	64	38	58	33	1	82	2	3	1	12	3	5	.269	.322	.409	.730
2014	Ari	NL	75	265	80	19	6	7	(7	0)	132	41	24	43	19	0	46	2	1	0	14	3	4	.302	.353	.498	.851
2015	Ari	NL	157	609	192	39	6	20	(9	11)	303	111	76	106	53	0	89	2	0	9	39	7	19	.315	.367	.498	.865
2016	Ari	NL	12	41	10	0	0	2	(0	2)	16	9	4	5	5	0	8	0	0	0	4	0	1	.244	.326	.390	.716
2017	Ari	NL	112	425	113	33	6	14	(9	5)	200	73	49	66	35	1	71	6	0	0	20	6	8	.266	.330	.471	.801
2018	Ari	NL	113	413	106	21	5	21	(11	10)	200	61	65	57	31	2	100	8	1	7	13	2	6	.257	.316	.484	.800
2019	LAD	NL	86	308	82	15	1	15	(9	6)	144	49	47	50	23	1	74	7	0	4	5	1	7	.266	.327	.468	.795
2020	LAD	NL	55	196	54	9	0	16	(9	7)	111	30	34	29	12	1	45	0	0	2	2	2	5	.276	.314	.566	.881
2021	LAD	NL	117	384	114	27	1	21	(12	9)	206	53	69	73	30	4	80	6	0	2	9	1	4	.297	.355	.536	.892
2022	CWS	NL	138	449	120	26	1	14	(9	5)	190	61	56	53	32	0	98	2	0	4	3	1	13	.245	.292	.389	.681
	Postseason		34	103	23	7	1	3	(2	1)	41	15	14	10	6	1	31	1	0	0	1	0	3	.223	.273	.398	.671
	11 ML YEARS		1033	3654	1010	221	32	140	(80	60)	1715	560	470	549	282	11	704	35	6	31	122	28	75	.276	.332	.469	.801

Drew Pomeranz

Pitches: L **Bats:** R **Pos:** P POMM-er-anze **Ht:** 6'5" **Wt:** 246 **Born:** 11/22/1988 **Age:** 34

			HOW MUCH PITCHED				WHAT HE GAVE UP											THE RESULTS								
Year	Team	Lg	G	GS	GF	IP	BFP	H	R	ER	HR	SH	SF	HB	TBB	IBB	SO	WP	W	L	Pct	Sv-Op	Hld	Vel	OPS	ERC	ERA
2011	Col	NL	4	4	0	18.1	77	19	11	11	0	1	0	1	5	0	13	1	2	1	.667	0-0	0	-	.700	3.36	5.40
2012	Col	NL	22	22	0	96.2	434	97	57	53	14	8	4	4	46	2	83	8	2	9	.182	0-0	0	-	.775	4.78	4.93
2013	Col	NL	8	4	0	21.2	105	25	15	15	4	1	1	1	19	1	19	0	0	4	.000	0-0	0	-	.951	8.04	6.23
2014	Oak	AL	20	10	4	69.0	278	51	22	18	7	1	0	1	26	0	64	0	5	4	.556	0-0	0	-	.586	2.70	2.35
2015	Oak	AL	53	9	9	86.0	357	71	44	35	8	4	5	3	31	1	82	2	5	6	.455	3-6	12	-	.651	3.05	3.66
2016	2 Tms		31	30	1	170.2	703	137	65	63	22	3	3	1	65	3	186	10	11	12	.478	0-0	0	-	.658	3.13	3.32
2017	Bos	AL	32	32	0	173.2	740	166	69	64	19	2	6	4	69	0	174	6	17	6	.739	0-0	0	-	.712	4.00	3.32
2018	Bos	AL	26	11	5	74.0	344	87	53	50	12	0	3	4	47	1	66	4	2	6	.250	0-0	1	-	.894	6.73	6.08
2019	2 Tms	NL	46	18	4	104.0	455	105	58	56	21	2	2	4	44	0	137	1	2	10	.167	2-2	12	-	.804	5.13	4.85
2020	SD	NL	20	0	5	18.2	73	9	3	3	1	0	1	0	10	0	29	0	1	0	1.000	4-5	9	-	.454	1.71	1.45
2021	SD	NL	27	0	2	25.2	102	19	6	5	2	0	2	0	10	1	30	1	1	0	1.000	0-0	13	-	.618	2.55	1.75
16	SD	NL	17	17	0	102.0	411	67	30	28	8	2	3	1	41	2	115	7	8	7	.533	0-0	0	-	.555	2.17	2.47
16	Bos	AL	14	13	1	68.2	292	70	35	35	14	1	0	0	24	1	71	3	3	5	.375	0-0	0	-	.799	4.73	4.59
19	SF	NL	21	17	0	77.2	355	89	51	49	17	2	1	4	36	0	92	1	2	9	.182	0-0	0	-	.872	6.32	5.68
19	Mil	NL	25	1	4	26.1	100	16	7	7	4	0	1	0	8	0	45	0	0	1	.000	2-2	12	-	.570	2.07	2.39
	Postseason		9	1	0	11.2	54	12	8	6	3	1	3	1	6	1	14	0	0	1	.000	0-0	3	-	.893	5.98	4.63
	11 ML YEARS		289	140	30	858.1	3668	786	403	373	110	22	27	23	369	9	883	33	48	58	.453	9-13	47	-	.720	4.02	3.91

Zach Pop

Pitches: R **Bats:** R **Pos:** RP-35 **Ht:** 6'4" **Wt:** 220 **Born:** 9/20/1996 **Age:** 26

			HOW MUCH PITCHED				WHAT HE GAVE UP											THE RESULTS								
Year	Team	Lg	G	GS	GF	IP	BFP	H	R	ER	HR	SH	SF	HB	TBB	IBB	SO	WP	W	L	Pct	Sv-Op	Hld	Vel	OPS	ERC	ERA
2022	Jaxnvl	AAA	19	0	4	24.1	103	28	8	6	0	0	0	1	8	0	20	2	0	1	.000	0- -	-		.753	4.26	2.22
2021	Mia	NL	50	0	10	54.2	246	54	29	25	3	1	0	8	24	2	51	2	1	0	1.000	0-1	5	95	.713	4.30	4.12
2022	2 Tms		35	0	8	39.0	157	41	13	12	2	0	0	2	4	0	25	1	4	0	1.000	0-0	3	97	.650	3.17	2.77
22	Mia	NL	18	0	6	20.0	83	23	9	8	1	0	0	1	2	0	14	1	2	0	1.000	0-0	1	97	.688	3.64	3.60
22	Tor	AL	17	0	2	19.0	74	18	4	4	1	0	0	1	2	0	11	0	2	0	1.000	0-0	2	97	.608	2.70	1.89
	2 ML YEARS		85	0	18	93.2	403	95	42	37	5	1	0	10	28	2	76	3	5	0	1.000	0-1	4	96	.688	3.83	3.56

Sean Poppen

Pitches: R Bats: R Pos: RP-29   Ht: 6'3" Wt: 210 Born: 3/15/1994 Age: 29

			HOW MUCH PITCHED					WHAT HE GAVE UP											THE RESULTS						
Year	Team	Lg	G	GS	GF	IP	BFP	H	R	ER	HR	SH	SF	HB	TBB	IBB	SO	WP	W	L	Pct	Sv-Op	Hld	Vel	OPS	ERC	ERA
2022	Reno	AAA	21	0	10	25.1	112	26	15	13	1	0	3	7	7	1	19	1	0	3	.000	1--	-	-	.789	4.36	4.62
2019	Min	AL	4	0	3	8.1	36	10	7	7	1	0	0	0	5	0	9	0	0	0	-	0-0	0	95	.997	6.83	7.56
2020	Min	AL	6	0	4	7.2	35	9	4	4	0	0	0	0	4	0	10	3	0	0	-	0-0	1	94	.759	4.80	4.70
2021	3 Tms		24	0	6	22.2	110	31	18	13	2	0	3	9	2	26	2	1	1	.500	1-1	1	94	.860	6.44	5.16
2022	Ari	NL	29	0	6	28.2	120	27	15	14	5	1	4	1	12	3	22	2	2	2	.500	0-1	4	95	.826	4.46	4.40
21	Pit	NL	3	0	1	4.2	26	11	7	4	1	0	0	1	2	0	4	0	0	0	-	0-0	0	94	1.278	16.48	7.71
21	TB	AL	1	0	1	0.2	2	0	0	0	0	0	0	0	0	0	1	0	0	0	-	0-0	0	93	.000	0.00	0.00
21	Ari	NL	20	0	4	17.1	82	20	11	9	1	0	0	2	7	2	21	2	1	1	.500	1-1	1	94	.751	4.71	4.67
	4 ML YEARS		63	0	19	67.1	301	77	44	38	8	1	4	4	30	5	67	7	3	3	.500	1-2	6	94	.851	5.44	5.08

Cody Poteet

Pitches: R Bats: R Pos: RP-10; SP-2   Ht: 6'1" Wt: 190 Born: 7/30/1994 Age: 28

			HOW MUCH PITCHED					WHAT HE GAVE UP											THE RESULTS						
Year	Team	Lg	G	GS	GF	IP	BFP	H	R	ER	HR	SH	SF	HB	TBB	IBB	SO	WP	W	L	Pct	Sv-Op	Hld	Vel	OPS	ERC	ERA
2021	Mia	NL	7	7	0	30.2	132	25	17	17	7	0	0	0	16	0	32	1	2	3	.400	0-0	0	94	.768	4.36	4.99
2022	Mia	NL	12	2	2	28.0	114	23	12	12	4	0	0	0	11	0	21	1	0	1	.000	0-0	1	95	.716	3.43	3.86
	2 ML YEARS		19	9	2	58.2	246	48	29	29	11	0	0	0	27	0	53	2	2	4	.333	0-0	1	94	.743	3.91	4.45

Nick Pratto

Bats: L Throws: L Pos: 1B-43;LF-7;PH-2;RF-1   Ht: 6'1" Wt: 215 Born: 10/6/1998 Age: 24

			BATTING													RUNNING			AVERAGES		
Year	Team	Lg	G	AB	H	2B	3B	HR	(Hm | Rd)	TB	R	RBI	RC	TBB	IBB	SO	HBP	SH	SF	SB	CS	GDP	Avg	OBP	Slg	OPS
2018	Lxngtn	A	127	485	136	33	2	14	(- | -)	215	79	62	78	45	1	150	3	0	4	22	5	2	.280	.343	.443	.786
2019	Wilmg	A+	124	419	80	21	1	9	(- | -)	130	48	46	40	49	0	164	2	0	2	17	7	2	.191	.278	.310	.588
2021	NWArk	AA	61	221	60	13	4	15	(- | -)	126	44	43	51	46	1	80	5	0	3	7	5	1	.271	.404	.570	.974
2021	Omha	AAA	59	212	54	14	3	19	(- | -)	131	47	49	47	32	0	72	3	0	4	4	0	0	.255	.355	.618	.973
2022	Omha	AAA	82	303	69	10	3	17	(- | -)	136	57	47	56	59	1	114	10	0	2	8	2	7	.228	.369	.449	.818
2022	KC	AL	49	158	29	9	1	7	(3 | 4)	61	18	20	16	19	0	66	1	1	3	0	0	6	.184	.271	.386	.657

Ryan Pressly

Pitches: R Bats: R Pos: RP-50   Ht: 6'2" Wt: 206 Born: 12/15/1988 Age: 34

			HOW MUCH PITCHED					WHAT HE GAVE UP											THE RESULTS						
Year	Team	Lg	G	GS	GF	IP	BFP	H	R	ER	HR	SH	SF	HB	TBB	IBB	SO	WP	W	L	Pct	Sv-Op	Hld	Vel	OPS	ERC	ERA
2013	Min	AL	49	0	18	76.2	315	71	37	33	5	2	3	0	27	1	49	7	3	3	.500	0-0	1	93	.677	3.31	3.87
2014	Min	AL	25	0	5	28.1	122	30	10	9	3	2	1	0	8	2	14	1	2	0	1.000	0-1	2	93	.779	3.98	2.86
2015	Min	AL	27	0	6	27.2	119	27	9	9	0	1	1	0	12	1	22	2	3	2	.600	0-0	4	95	.645	3.31	2.93
2016	Min	AL	72	0	10	75.1	328	79	34	31	8	4	2	2	23	2	67	7	6	7	.462	1-6	13	95	.725	4.01	3.70
2017	Min	AL	57	0	10	61.1	252	52	34	32	10	2	1	3	19	5	61	5	2	3	.400	0-1	6	96	.697	3.41	4.70
2018	2 Tms	AL	77	0	11	71.0	292	57	21	20	6	1	2	3	22	1	101	8	2	1	.667	2-8	21	96	.604	2.71	2.54
2019	Hou	AL	55	0	34	54.1	211	37	15	14	6	0	1	0	12	0	72	4	2	3	.400	3-8	31	96	.543	1.85	2.32
2020	Hou	AL	23	0	15	21.0	91	21	10	8	2	0	0	1	7	1	29	1	1	3	.250	12-16	1	95	.728	3.85	3.43
2021	Hou	AL	64	0	49	64.0	250	49	19	16	4	1	0	1	13	1	81	3	5	3	.625	26-28	1	95	.546	1.92	2.25
2022	Hou	AL	50	0	43	48.1	182	30	17	16	4	2	1	0	13	0	65	0	3	3	.500	33-37	0	95	.516	1.67	2.98
18	Min	AL	51	0	7	47.2	208	46	19	18	5	1	2	2	19	1	69	6	1	1	.500	0-4	8	96	.699	3.99	3.40
18	Hou	AL	26	0	4	23.1	84	11	2	2	1	0	0	1	3	0	32	2	1	0	1.000	2-4	13	96	.379	0.88	0.77
	Postseason		31	0	14	27.2	118	26	12	11	1	1	0	1	9	1	35	5	2	0	1.000	5-5	3	95	.597	3.06	3.58
	10 ML YEARS		499	0	175	528.0	2162	453	206	188	48	15	14	10	156	14	561	38	29	28	.509	77-105	79	95	.640	2.90	3.20

David Price

Pitches: L Bats: L Pos: RP-40   Ht: 6'5" Wt: 215 Born: 8/26/1985 Age: 37

			HOW MUCH PITCHED					WHAT HE GAVE UP											THE RESULTS						
Year	Team	Lg	G	GS	GF	IP	BFP	H	R	ER	HR	SH	SF	HB	TBB	IBB	SO	WP	W	L	Pct	Sv-Op	Hld	Vel	OPS	ERC	ERA
2008	TB	AL	5	1	0	14.0	57	9	4	3	1	0	1	1	4	0	12	0	0	0	-	0-0	1	94	.501	1.86	1.93
2009	TB	AL	23	23	0	128.1	557	119	72	63	17	3	2	4	54	0	102	2	10	7	.588	0-0	0	93	.716	4.05	4.42
2010	TB	AL	32	31	0	208.2	861	170	71	63	15	4	3	5	79	1	188	5	19	6	.760	0-0	0	95	.637	2.91	2.72
2011	TB	AL	34	34	0	224.1	918	192	93	87	22	4	7	9	63	5	218	2	12	13	.480	0-0	0	96	.659	2.97	3.49
2012	TB	AL	31	31	0	211.0	836	173	63	60	16	2	3	5	59	2	205	8	20	5	.800	0-0	0	96	.602	2.67	2.56
2013	TB	AL	27	27	0	186.2	740	178	78	69	16	1	2	3	27	0	151	6	10	8	.556	0-0	0	96	.661	2.89	3.33
2014	2 Tms	AL	34	34	0	248.1	1009	230	100	90	25	4	5	3	38	1	271	2	15	12	.556	0-0	0	93	.647	2.79	3.26
2015	2 Tms	AL	32	32	0	220.1	888	190	70	60	17	4	8	3	47	2	225	4	18	5	.783	0-0	0	94	.621	2.54	2.45
2016	Bos	AL	35	35	0	230.0	951	227	106	102	30	8	7	7	50	1	228	4	17	9	.654	0-0	0	93	.721	3.63	3.99
2017	Bos	AL	16	11	0	74.2	317	65	30	28	8	0	2	4	24	0	76	2	6	3	.667	0-0	0	95	.652	3.25	3.38
2018	Bos	AL	30	30	0	176.0	722	151	75	70	25	1	4	10	50	0	177	1	16	7	.696	0-0	0	93	.691	3.38	3.58
2019	Bos	AL	22	22	0	107.1	458	109	57	51	15	0	1	3	32	0	128	3	7	5	.583	0-0	0	93	.755	4.13	4.28
2021	LAD	NL	39	11	5	73.2	326	79	35	33	8	3	2	4	26	2	58	1	5	2	.714	1-1	0	93	.766	4.48	4.03
2022	LAD	NL	40	0	13	40.1	167	38	11	11	6	1	0	0	9	2	37	0	2	0	1.000	2-4	4	92	.704	3.27	2.45
14	TB	AL	23	23	0	170.2	689	156	68	59	20	3	3	5	23	1	189	2	11	8	.579	0-0	0	93	.647	2.79	3.11
14	Det	AL	11	11	0	77.2	320	74	32	31	5	1	0	0	15	0	82	0	4	4	.500	0-0	0	93	.647	2.77	3.59
15	Det	AL	21	21	0	146.0	592	133	50	41	13	4	5	3	29	2	138	3	9	4	.692	0-0	0	94	.654	2.83	2.53
15	Tor	AL	11	11	0	74.1	296	57	20	19	4	0	3	0	18	0	87	1	9	1	.900	0-0	0	95	.555	2.00	2.30
	Postseason		23	14	5	99.1	414	91	53	51	16	0	2	3	28	1	91	1	5	9	.357	1-1	0	94	.707	3.65	4.62
	14 ML YEARS		400	322	19	2143.2	8807	1930	865	790	221	35	45	63	562	16	2076	40	157	82	.657	3-5	7	94	.668	3.14	3.32

Ford Proctor

Bats: L **Throws:** R **Pos:** 2B-6;C-1;PH-1 **Ht:** 6'1" **Wt:** 195 **Born:** 12/4/1996 **Age:** 26

								BATTING											RUNNING			AVERAGES			
Year	Team	Lg	G	AB	H	2B	3B	HR	(Hm | Rd)	TB	R	RBI	RC	TBB	IBB	SO	HBP	SH	SF	SB	CS	GDP	Avg	OBP	Slg	OPS
2022	Drham	AAA	79	268	57	7	0	6	(- | -)	82	27	28	29	44	0	95	3	1	1	3	2	3	.213	.329	.306	.635
2022	Scrmto	AAA	34	116	31	3	0	6	(- | -)	52	19	14	22	24	1	38	0	1	1	0	0	2	.267	.390	.448	.838
2022	SF	NL	7	18	2	0	0	1	(1 | 0)	5	3	6	2	2	0	3	0	0	2	0	0	0	.111	.182	.278	.460

Jurickson Profar

Bats: B **Throws:** R **Pos:** LF-146;DH-6;PH-4   JURR-ick-sun PRO-farr   **Ht:** 6'0" **Wt:** 184 **Born:** 2/20/1993 **Age:** 30

								BATTING											RUNNING			AVERAGES			
Year	Team	Lg	G	AB	H	2B	3B	HR	(Hm | Rd)	TB	R	RBI	RC	TBB	IBB	SO	HBP	SH	SF	SB	CS	GDP	Avg	OBP	Slg	OPS
2012	Tex	AL	9	17	3	2	0	1	(0 | 1)	8	2	2	1	0	0	4	0	0	0	0	0	1	.176	.176	.471	.647
2013	Tex	AL	85	286	67	11	0	6	(3 | 3)	96	30	26	30	26	0	63	5	6	1	2	4	1	.234	.308	.336	.644
2016	Tex	AL	90	272	65	6	3	5	(4 | 1)	92	35	20	30	30	0	61	3	2	0	2	1	7	.239	.321	.338	.660
2017	Tex	AL	22	58	10	2	0	0	(0 | 0)	12	8	5	5	9	0	14	1	2	0	1	1	0	.172	.294	.207	.501
2018	Tex	AL	146	524	133	35	6	20	(11 | 9)	240	82	77	88	54	1	88	12	0	4	10	0	4	.254	.335	.458	.793
2019	Oak	AL	139	459	100	24	2	20	(11 | 9)	188	65	67	58	48	2	75	8	0	3	9	1	12	.218	.301	.410	.711
2020	SD	NL	56	180	50	6	0	7	(2 | 5)	77	28	25	30	15	0	28	4	1	2	7	1	1	.278	.343	.428	.771
2021	SD	NL	137	353	80	17	2	4	(2 | 2)	113	47	33	36	49	1	65	6	1	2	10	5	12	.227	.329	.320	.649
2022	SD	NL	152	575	140	36	2	15	(9 | 6)	225	82	58	79	73	0	103	4	3	3	5	1	12	.243	.331	.391	.723
	Postseason		8	20	7	0	0	0	(0 | 0)	7	1	0	2	0	0	3	0	0	0	0	0	0	.350	.350	.350	.700
	9 ML YEARS		836	2724	648	139	15	78	(42 | 36)	1051	379	313	357	304	4	501	43	15	15	46	14	55	.238	.322	.386	.708

Austin Pruitt

Pitches: R **Bats:** R **Pos:** RP-38; SP-1   **Ht:** 5'10" **Wt:** 185 **Born:** 8/31/1989 **Age:** 33

				HOW MUCH PITCHED					WHAT HE GAVE UP									THE RESULTS						
Year	Team	Lg	G	GS	GF	IP	BFP	H	R	ER	HR	SH	SF	HB	TBB	IBB	SO	WP	W	L	Pct	Sv-Op Hld	Vel	OPS	ERC	ERA
2022	LsVgs	AAA	12	0	3	22.0	91	20	10	8	0	1	1	3	2	0	20	0	1	0	1.000	1- -	-	.599	2.27	3.27
2017	TB	AL	30	8	7	83.0	371	103	55	49	11	1	0	5	22	2	66	4	7	5	.583	1-2	92	.827	5.36	5.31
2018	TB	AL	23	0	11	69.2	291	72	40	36	7	1	4	1	16	0	42	1	2	3	.400	4-5 0	92	.712	3.67	4.65
2019	TB	AL	14	2	4	47.0	193	47	23	23	7	2	2	0	12	2	39	1	3	0	1.000	0-0 0	92	.761	3.84	4.40
2021	2 Tms		6	0	3	7.1	29	7	3	3	2	0	0	0	0	0	5	0	0	1	.000	0-0 0	92	.776	3.93	3.68
2022	Oak	AL	39	1	14	55.1	224	48	29	26	11	0	2	1	9	0	38	0	0	1	.000	1-3 2	91	.698	3.07	4.23
21	Hou	AL	2	0	1	2.2	12	3	2	2	2	0	0	0	0	0	1	0	0	1	.000	0-0 0	92	1.152	9.34	6.75
21	Mia	NL	4	0	2	4.2	17	4	1	1	0	0	0	0	0	0	4	0	0	0	-	0-0 0	92	.529	1.52	1.93
	5 ML YEARS		112	11	39	262.1	1108	277	150	137	38	4	8	8	59	4	190	6	12	10	.545	6-10 3	92	.758	4.10	4.70

Albert Pujols

Bats: R **Throws:** R **Pos:** DH-68;PH-28;1B-22   POO-holes   **Ht:** 6'3" **Wt:** 235 **Born:** 1/16/1980 **Age:** 43

								BATTING											RUNNING			AVERAGES			
Year	Team	Lg	G	AB	H	2B	3B	HR	(Hm	Rd)	TB	R	RBI	RC	TBB	IBB	SO	HBP	SH	SF	SB	CS	GDP	Avg	OBP	Slg	OPS
2001	StL	NL	161	590	194	47	4	37	(18	19)	360	112	130	132	69	6	93	9	1	7	1	3	21	.329	.403	.610	1.013
2002	StL	NL	157	590	185	40	2	34	(14	20)	331	118	127	121	72	13	69	9	0	4	2	4	20	.314	.394	.561	.955
2003	StL	NL	157	591	212	51	1	43	(21	22)	394	137	124	160	79	12	65	10	0	5	5	1	13	.359	.439	.667	1.106
2004	StL	NL	154	592	196	51	2	46	(18	28)	389	133	123	143	84	12	52	7	0	9	5	5	21	.331	.415	.657	1.072
2005	StL	NL	161	591	195	38	2	41	(23	18)	360	129	117	139	97	27	65	9	0	3	16	2	19	.330	.430	.609	1.039
2006	StL	NL	143	535	177	33	1	49	(24	25)	359	119	137	146	92	28	50	4	0	3	7	2	20	.331	.431	.671	1.102
2007	StL	NL	158	565	185	38	1	32	(12	20)	321	99	103	118	99	22	58	7	0	8	2	6	27	.327	.429	.568	.997
2008	StL	NL	148	524	187	44	0	37	(19	18)	342	100	116	130	104	34	54	5	0	8	7	3	16	.357	.462	.653	1.114
2009	StL	NL	160	568	186	45	1	47	(22	25)	374	124	135	145	115	44	64	9	0	8	16	4	23	.327	.443	.658	1.101
2010	StL	NL	159	587	183	39	1	42	(17	25)	350	115	118	131	103	38	76	4	0	6	14	4	23	.312	.414	.596	1.011
2011	StL	NL	147	579	173	29	0	37	(16	21)	313	105	99	100	61	15	58	4	0	7	9	1	29	.299	.366	.541	.906
2012	LAA	AL	154	607	173	50	0	30	(14	16)	313	85	105	105	52	16	76	5	0	8	8	1	19	.285	.343	.516	.859
2013	LAA	AL	99	391	101	19	0	17	(8	9)	171	49	64	54	40	8	55	5	0	7	1	1	18	.258	.330	.437	.767
2014	LAA	AL	159	633	172	37	1	28	(13	15)	295	89	105	86	48	11	71	5	0	9	5	1	28	.272	.324	.466	.790
2015	LAA	AL	157	602	147	22	0	40	(20	20)	289	85	95	91	50	10	72	6	0	3	5	3	15	.244	.307	.480	.787
2016	LAA	AL	152	593	159	19	0	31	(18	13)	271	71	119	91	49	6	75	2	0	6	4	0	24	.268	.323	.457	.780
2017	LAA	AL	149	593	143	17	0	23	(13	10)	229	53	101	66	37	5	93	2	0	4	3	0	26	.241	.286	.386	.672
2018	LAA	AL	117	465	114	20	0	19	(10	9)	191	50	64	55	28	3	65	2	0	3	1	0	12	.245	.289	.411	.700
2019	LAA	AL	131	491	120	22	0	23	(9	14)	211	55	93	64	43	1	68	3	0	9	3	0	21	.244	.305	.430	.734
2020	LAA	AL	39	152	34	8	0	6	(4	2)	60	15	25	15	9	1	25	1	0	1	0	0	4	.224	.270	.395	.665
2021	2 Tms		109	275	65	3	0	17	(10	7)	119	29	50	36	14	3	45	4	0	2	0	0	14	.236	.284	.433	.717
2022	StL	NL	109	307	83	14	0	24	(10	14)	169	42	68	62	28	1	55	10	0	6	1	2	13	.270	.345	.550	.895
21	LAA	AL	24	86	17	0	0	5	(2	3)	32	9	12	9	3	1	13	3	0	1	0	0	4	.198	.250	.372	.622
21	LAD	NL	85	189	48	3	0	12	(8	4)	87	20	38	24	11	2	32	1	0	1	0	0	10	.254	.299	.460	.759
	Postseason		86	296	95	18	1	19	(7	12)	172	57	54	69	50	20	45	5	0	1	1	2	6	.321	.426	.581	1.007
	22 ML YEARS		3080	11421	3384	686	16	703	(333	370)	6211	1914	2218	2181	1373	316	1404	123	1	123	117	43	426	.296	.374	.544	.918

A.J. Puk

Pitches: L **Bats:** L **Pos:** RP-62   **Ht:** 6'7" **Wt:** 248 **Born:** 4/25/1995 **Age:** 28

				HOW MUCH PITCHED					WHAT HE GAVE UP									THE RESULTS						
Year	Team	Lg	G	GS	GF	IP	BFP	H	R	ER	HR	SH	SF	HB	TBB	IBB	SO	WP	W	L	Pct	Sv-Op Hld	Vel	OPS	ERC	ERA
2019	Oak	AL	10	0	0	11.1	47	10	4	4	1	0	0	0	5	0	13	2	2	0	1.000	0-1 2	97	.652	3.60	3.18
2021	Oak	AL	12	0	3	13.1	65	18	9	9	1	0	0	1	6	0	16	2	0	3	.000	0-2 0	96	.764	6.31	6.08
2022	Oak	AL	62	0	9	66.1	281	53	27	23	7	3	0	10	23	3	76	6	4	3	.571	4-9 20	97	.667	3.31	3.12
	3 ML YEARS		84	0	12	91.0	393	81	40	36	9	3	0	11	34	3	105	10	6	6	.500	4-12 22	97	.681	3.75	3.56

Cal Quantrill

Pitches: R Bats: L Pos: SP-32 **Ht: 6'3" Wt: 195 Born: 2/10/1995 Age: 28**

			HOW MUCH PITCHED					WHAT HE GAVE UP											THE RESULTS						
Year Team	Lg	G	GS	GF	IP	BFP	H	R	ER	HR	SH	SF	HB	TBB	IBB	SO	WP	W	L	Pct	Sv-Op	Hld	Vel	OPS	ERC	ERA
2019 SD	NL	23	18	0	103.0	443	106	61	59	15	2	3	3	28	2	89	3	6	8	.429	0-0	1	94	.741	4.07	5.16
2020 2 Tms		18	3	2	32.0	135	31	12	8	4	1	0	3	8	1	31	0	2	0	1.000	1-2	2	95	.701	3.81	2.25
2021 Cle	AL	40	22	2	149.2	616	129	55	48	16	4	4	9	47	0	121	3	8	3	.727	0-0	1	94	.675	3.31	2.89
2022 Cle	AL	32	32	0	186.1	770	178	78	70	21	4	7	10	47	0	128	1	15	5	.750	0-0	0	94	.696	3.60	3.38
20 SD	NL	10	1	1	17.1	74	17	6	5	2	1	0	2	6	1	18	0	2	0	1.000	1-1	1	95	.727	4.32	2.60
20 Cle	AL	8	2	1	14.2	61	14	6	3	2	0	0	1	2	0	13	0	0	0	-	0-1	1	95	.669	3.24	1.84
Postseason		1	0	1	0.1	2	0	0	0	0	0	0	0	1	0	1	0	0	0	-	0-0	0	95	.500	7.00	0.00
4 ML YEARS		113	75	4	471.0	1964	444	206	185	56	11	14	25	130	3	369	9	31	16	.660	1-2	4	94	.700	3.62	3.54

Jose Quijada

Pitches: L Bats: L Pos: RP-42 kee-HAH-dah **Ht: 5'11" Wt: 215 Born: 11/9/1995 Age: 27**

			HOW MUCH PITCHED					WHAT HE GAVE UP											THE RESULTS						
Year Team	Lg	G	GS	GF	IP	BFP	H	R	ER	HR	SH	SF	HB	TBB	IBB	SO	WP	W	L	Pct	Sv-Op	Hld	Vel	OPS	ERC	ERA
2019 Mia	NL	34	0	9	29.2	144	27	20	19	10	1	0	4	26	3	44	2	2	3	.400	1-2	1	93	.974	7.81	5.76
2020 LAA	AL	6	0	1	3.2	20	6	4	3	1	0	1	1	2	0	6	0	0	1	.000	0-1	1	93	1.013	11.40	7.36
2021 LAA	AL	26	0	2	25.2	110	20	14	13	2	0	0	1	15	1	38	1	0	2	.000	0-0	4	94	.657	3.53	4.56
2022 LAA	AL	42	0	11	40.2	169	25	19	18	5	0	1	2	21	4	52	1	0	5	.000	3-5	12	95	.636	2.63	3.98
4 ML YEARS		108	0	23	99.2	443	78	57	53	18	1	2	8	64	8	140	4	2	11	.154	4-8	21	94	.763	4.54	4.79

Roman Quinn

Bats: B Throws: R Pos: CF-28;LF-11;RF-8;PR-8;PH-2 **Ht: 5'10" Wt: 175 Born: 5/14/1993 Age: 30**

					BATTING															RUNNING			AVERAGES			
Year Team	Lg	G	AB	H	2B	3B	HR	(Hm	Rd)	TB	R	RBI	RC	TBB	IBB	SO	HBP	SH	SF	SB	CS	GDP	Avg	OBP	Slg	OPS
2016 Phi	NL	15	57	15	4	0	0	(0	0)	19	10	6	9	8	0	19	2	2	0	5	1	0	.263	.373	.333	.706
2018 Phi	NL	50	131	34	6	4	2	(1	1)	54	13	12	15	10	0	35	1	1	0	10	4	1	.260	.317	.412	.729
2019 Phi	NL	44	108	23	3	1	4	(3	1)	40	18	11	15	12	0	34	1	1	0	8	0	2	.213	.298	.370	.668
2020 Phi	NL	41	108	23	3	1	2	(2	0)	34	14	7	9	5	0	39	2	1	0	12	0	0	.213	.261	.315	.576
2021 Phi	NL	28	52	9	2	2	0	(0	0)	15	8	2	4	6	0	19	4	0	0	4	3	0	.173	.306	.288	.595
2022 2 Tms		44	79	17	3	2	0	(0	0)	24	15	7	7	7	0	36	1	0	0	4	3	0	.215	.287	.304	.591
22 Phi	NL	23	37	6	1	0	0	(0	0)	7	8	3	1	3	0	15	0	0	0	4	1	0	.162	.225	.189	.414
22 TB	AL	21	42	11	2	2	0	(0	0)	17	7	4	6	4	0	21	1	0	0	0	2	0	.262	.340	.405	.745
6 ML YEARS		222	535	121	21	10	8	(6	2)	186	78	45	59	48	0	182	11	5	0	43	11	3	.226	.303	.348	.651

Jose Quintana

Pitches: L Bats: R Pos: SP-32 KIN-tahn-ah **Ht: 6'1" Wt: 220 Born: 1/24/1989 Age: 34**

			HOW MUCH PITCHED					WHAT HE GAVE UP											THE RESULTS						
Year Team	Lg	G	GS	GF	IP	BFP	H	R	ER	HR	SH	SF	HB	TBB	IBB	SO	WP	W	L	Pct	Sv-Op	Hld	Vel	OPS	ERC	ERA
2012 CWS	AL	25	22	2	136.1	568	142	62	57	14	5	1	3	42	4	81	10	6	6	.500	0-0	0	90	.754	4.13	3.76
2013 CWS	AL	33	33	0	200.0	832	188	83	78	23	3	6	5	56	2	164	2	9	7	.563	0-0	0	91	.695	3.47	3.51
2014 CWS	AL	32	32	0	200.1	830	197	87	74	10	4	6	2	52	3	178	7	9	11	.450	0-0	0	92	.662	3.15	3.32
2015 CWS	AL	32	32	0	206.1	862	218	81	77	16	4	4	8	44	4	177	5	9	10	.474	0-0	0	92	.722	3.67	3.36
2016 CWS	AL	32	32	0	208.0	837	192	76	74	22	2	2	4	50	1	181	10	13	12	.520	0-0	0	92	.687	3.23	3.20
2017 2 Tms		32	32	0	188.2	790	170	92	87	23	1	3	10	61	4	207	8	11	11	.500	0-0	0	92	.701	3.57	4.15
2018 ChC	NL	32	32	0	174.1	739	162	81	78	25	8	2	3	68	3	158	3	13	11	.542	0-0	0	92	.737	4.00	4.03
2019 ChC	NL	32	31	0	171.0	745	191	100	89	20	5	13	2	46	0	152	11	13	9	.591	0-0	0	91	.763	4.32	4.68
2020 ChC	NL	4	1	0	10.0	41	10	5	5	1	0	0	0	3	0	12	1	0	0	-	0-0	0	91	.738	3.80	4.50
2021 2 Tms		29	10	5	63.0	297	74	50	45	12	0	2	1	35	1	85	7	0	3	.000	0-0	2	92	.853	6.40	6.43
2022 2 Tms	NL	32	32	0	165.2	679	154	61	54	8	1	1	3	47	1	137	1	6	7	.462	0-0	0	91	.645	3.01	2.93
17 CWS	AL	18	18	0	104.1	444	98	55	52	14	1	2	2	40	1	109	7	4	8	.333	0-0	0	92	.735	3.97	4.49
17 ChC	NL	14	14	0	84.1	346	72	37	35	9	0	1	8	21	3	98	1	7	3	.700	0-0	0	91	.659	3.08	3.74
21 LAA	AL	24	10	5	53.1	254	66	45	40	9	0	2	1	29	0	73	5	0	3	.000	0-0	2	92	.860	6.62	6.75
21 SF	NL	5	0	0	9.2	43	8	5	5	3	0	0	0	6	1	12	2	0	0	-	0-0	0	92	.812	5.22	4.66
22 Pit	NL	20	20	0	103.0	432	100	43	40	7	0	0	2	31	1	89	1	3	5	.375	0-0	0	91	.679	3.39	3.50
22 StL	NL	12	12	0	62.2	247	54	18	14	1	1	1	1	16	0	48	0	3	2	.600	0-0	0	92	.585	2.42	2.01
Postseason		4	3	0	13.1	57	11	9	8	1	0	2	0	5	0	12	0	1	0	1.000	0-0	1	92	.621	2.76	5.40
11 ML YEARS		315	289	7	1723.2	7220	1698	778	718	174	33	40	41	504	23	1532	65	89	87	.506	0-0	2	92	.712	3.68	3.75

Esteban Quiroz

Bats: L Throws: R Pos: 2B-12;PH-3 **Ht: 5'6" Wt: 199 Born: 2/17/1992 Age: 31**

					BATTING															RUNNING			AVERAGES			
Year Team	Lg	G	AB	H	2B	3B	HR	(Hm	Rd)	TB	R	RBI	RC	TBB	IBB	SO	HBP	SH	SF	SB	CS	GDP	Avg	OBP	Slg	OPS
2022 Iowa	AAA	40	118	25	4	0	3	(-	-)	38	13	13	14	24	2	35	4	0	2	0	0	3	.212	.358	.322	.680
2022 ChC	NL	14	40	11	0	0	0	(0	0)	11	3	3	5	4	0	9	2	1	0	1	1	0	.275	.370	.275	.645

Cole Ragans

Pitches: L Bats: L Pos: SP-9 **Ht: 6'4" Wt: 190 Born: 12/12/1997 Age: 25**

			HOW MUCH PITCHED					WHAT HE GAVE UP											THE RESULTS						
Year Team	Lg	G	GS	GF	IP	BFP	H	R	ER	HR	SH	SF	HB	TBB	IBB	SO	WP	W	L	Pct	Sv-Op	Hld	Vel	OPS	ERC	ERA
2022 Frisco	AA	10	10	0	51.1	208	41	18	16	6	0	1	1	19	0	65	3	5	3	.625	0- -	-	-	.641	3.12	2.81
2022 RdRck	AAA	8	8	0	43.1	178	34	18	16	4	0	1	4	12	0	48	2	3	2	.600	0- -	-	-	.616	2.75	3.32
2022 Tex	AL	9	9	0	40.0	174	43	24	22	6	0	0	0	16	0	27	2	0	3	.000	0-0	0	92	.795	4.91	4.95

Tanner Rainey

Pitches: R Bats: R Pos: RP-29   Ht: 6'2" Wt: 244 Born: 12/25/1992 Age: 30

		HOW MUCH PITCHED					WHAT HE GAVE UP										THE RESULTS						
Year	Team	Lg	G	GS	GF	IP	BFP	H	R	ER	HR	SH	SF	HB	TBB	IBB	SO	WP	W	L	Pct	Sv-Op	Hld	Vel	OPS	ERC	ERA
2018	Cin	NL	8	0	2	7.0	45	13	19	19	4	0	1	0	12	1	7	0	0	0	-	0-0	0	98	1.462	21.19	24.43
2019	Was	NL	52	0	7	48.1	214	32	22	21	6	2	0	4	38	2	74	7	2	3	.400	0-3	9	98	.696	4.13	3.91
2020	Was	NL	20	0	1	20.1	75	8	6	6	4	0	0	1	7	1	32	3	1	1	.500	0-0	9	97	.542	1.60	2.66
2021	Was	NL	38	0	8	31.2	151	29	27	26	6	0	1	3	25	1	42	0	1	3	.250	3-6	10	96	.836	6.11	7.39
2022	Was	NL	29	0	20	30.0	128	26	16	11	5	0	1	0	13	0	36	1	1	3	.250	12-16	1	97	.691	3.88	3.30
	Postseason		9	0	1	6.2	28	3	5	5	1	0	0	0	5	0	6	1	0	0	-	0-0	2	99	.547	2.75	6.75
	5 ML YEARS		147	0	38	137.1	613	108	90	83	25	2	3	8	95	5	191	11	5	10	.333	15-25	29	97	.761	4.78	5.44

Cal Raleigh

Bats: B Throws: R Pos: C-115;PH-16;DH-1   Ht: 6'3" Wt: 235 Born: 11/26/1996 Age: 26

								BATTING												RUNNING			AVERAGES			
Year	Team	Lg	G	AB	H	2B	3B	HR	(Hm | Rd)	TB	R	RBI	RC	TBB	IBB	SO	HBP	SH	SF	SB	CS	GDP	Avg	OBP	Slg	OPS
2021	Sea	AL	47	139	25	12	0	2	(1 | 1)	43	6	13	7	7	0	52	1	0	1	0	0	3	.180	.223	.309	.532
2022	Sea	AL	119	370	78	20	1	27	(9 | 18)	181	46	63	60	38	0	122	2	0	5	1	0	5	.211	.284	.489	.774
	2 ML YEARS		166	509	103	32	1	29	(10 | 19)	224	52	76	67	45	0	174	3	0	6	1	0	8	.202	.268	.440	.708

Brooks Raley

Pitches: L Bats: L Pos: RP-60   RAIL-ee   Ht: 6'3" Wt: 200 Born: 6/29/1988 Age: 35

				HOW MUCH PITCHED					WHAT HE GAVE UP											THE RESULTS						
Year	Team	Lg	G	GS	GF	IP	BFP	H	R	ER	HR	SH	SF	HB	TBB	IBB	SO	WP	W	L	Pct	Sv-Op	Hld	Vel	OPS	ERC	ERA
2012	ChC	NL	5	5	0	24.1	116	33	23	22	7	1	0	0	11	0	16	0	1	2	.333	0-0	0	88	.931	7.87	8.14
2013	ChC	NL	9	0	1	14.0	61	11	9	8	2	1	1	2	8	0	14	0	0	0	-	0-0	0	89	.758	4.48	5.14
2020	2 Tms		21	0	7	20.0	84	13	12	11	3	1	0	4	6	0	27	0	0	1	.000	1-1	6	90	.633	2.82	4.95
2021	Hou	AL	58	0	9	49.0	205	43	30	26	6	1	0	3	16	0	65	1	2	3	.400	2-5	9	91	.666	3.51	4.78
2022	TB	AL	60	0	12	53.2	219	37	19	16	3	1	1	6	15	0	61	3	1	2	.333	6-9	22	91	.542	2.12	2.68
20	Cin	NL	4	0	2	4.0	22	5	4	4	0	0	0	3	2	0	6	0	0	0	-	0-0	0	90	.866	8.02	9.00
20	Hou	AL	17	0	5	16.0	62	8	8	7	3	1	0	1	4	0	21	0	0	1	.000	1-1	6	90	.552	1.69	3.94
	Postseason		14	0	3	12.1	56	11	7	7	0	0	3	1	8	1	13	0	0	1	.000	0-0	2	91	.744	3.81	5.11
	5 ML YEARS		153	5	29	161.0	685	137	93	83	21	5	2	15	56	0	183	4	4	8	.333	9-15	37	90	.675	3.58	4.64

Luke Raley

Bats: L Throws: R Pos: RF-8;LF-7;DH-4;1B-3;PH-3   Ht: 6'4" Wt: 235 Born: 9/19/1994 Age: 28

								BATTING												RUNNING			AVERAGES			
Year	Team	Lg	G	AB	H	2B	3B	HR	(Hm	Rd)	TB	R	RBI	RC	TBB	IBB	SO	HBP	SH	SF	SB	CS	GDP	Avg	OBP	Slg	OPS
2022	Drham	AAA	63	227	68	8	1	14	(-	-)	120	39	50	51	27	0	73	12	1	1	7	2	2	.300	.401	.529	.929
2021	LAD	NL	33	66	12	1	0	2	(0	2)	19	5	4	4	2	1	25	4	0	0	0	0	1	.182	.250	.288	.538
2022	TB	AL	22	61	12	2	0	1	(0	1)	17	7	4	5	7	0	24	3	0	1	0	0	1	.197	.306	.279	.584
	Postseason		1	1	0	0	0	0	(0	0)	0	0	0	0	0	0	1	0	0	0	0	0	0	.000	.000	.000	.000
	2 ML YEARS		55	127	24	3	0	3	(0	3)	36	12	8	9	9	1	49	7	0	1	0	0	2	.189	.278	.283	.561

Erasmo Ramirez

Pitches: R Bats: R Pos: RP-58; SP-2   eh-RASS-moh   Ht: 6'0" Wt: 217 Born: 5/2/1990 Age: 33

				HOW MUCH PITCHED					WHAT HE GAVE UP											THE RESULTS						
Year	Team	Lg	G	GS	GF	IP	BFP	H	R	ER	HR	SH	SF	HB	TBB	IBB	SO	WP	W	L	Pct	Sv-Op	Hld	Vel	OPS	ERC	ERA
2022	Roch	AAA	5	0	1	7.0	26	4	0	0	0	0	0	0	1	0	12	0	0	0	-	0- -	-	-	.432	0.93	0.00
2012	Sea	AL	16	8	2	59.0	238	47	26	22	6	1	5	3	12	1	48	0	1	3	.250	0-0	0	93	.616	2.42	3.36
2013	Sea	AL	14	13	0	72.1	321	79	44	40	12	0	3	3	26	0	57	0	5	3	.625	0-0	0	91	.772	5.04	4.98
2014	Sea	AL	17	14	0	75.1	338	82	44	44	13	1	1	6	34	2	60	3	1	6	.143	0-0	0	91	.815	5.68	5.26
2015	TB	AL	34	27	5	163.1	666	145	73	68	16	1	1	9	40	0	126	3	11	6	.647	0-0	0	91	.655	3.11	3.75
2016	TB	AL	64	1	13	90.2	378	90	39	38	14	7	2	4	26	5	63	7	7	11	.389	2-6	15	91	.766	4.13	3.77
2017	2 Tms		37	19	4	131.1	539	123	70	64	22	2	7	2	31	2	109	1	5	6	.455	1-2	6	92	.733	3.58	4.39
2018	Sea	AL	10	10	0	45.2	202	52	35	33	14	0	4	3	12	0	33	0	2	4	.333	0-0	0	90	.916	6.02	6.50
2019	Bos	AL	1	0	1	3.0	15	4	4	4	2	1	0	1	1	0	1	0	0	0	-	0-0	0	90	1.345	12.01	12.00
2020	NYM	NL	6	0	3	14.1	53	8	1	1	0	0	0	0	4	0	9	0	0	0	-	1-1	0	90	.471	1.45	0.63
2021	Det	AL	17	0	3	26.2	109	24	17	17	4	0	2	1	5	0	20	0	1	1	.500	0-0	0	92	.681	3.15	5.74
2022	Was	NL	60	2	10	86.1	347	79	31	28	11	1	3	6	14	1	61	1	4	2	.667	0-0	5	89	.676	3.18	2.92
17	TB	AL	26	8	4	69.1	282	66	39	37	10	1	2	1	16	1	55	1	4	3	.571	1-2	6	92	.719	3.53	4.80
17	Sea	AL	11	11	0	62.0	257	57	31	27	12	1	5	1	15	1	54	0	1	3	.250	0-0	0	92	.749	3.62	3.92
	11 ML YEARS		276	94	41	768.0	3206	733	384	359	115	14	28	38	205	11	587	15	37	42	.468	4-9	26	92	.726	3.83	4.21

Harold Ramirez

Bats: R Throws: R Pos: DH-52;1B-32;RF-24;PH-21;LF-5   Ht: 5'10" Wt: 232 Born: 9/6/1994 Age: 28

								BATTING												RUNNING			AVERAGES			
Year	Team	Lg	G	AB	H	2B	3B	HR	(Hm	Rd)	TB	R	RBI	RC	TBB	IBB	SO	HBP	SH	SF	SB	CS	GDP	Avg	OBP	Slg	OPS
2019	Mia	NL	119	421	116	20	3	11	(5	6)	175	54	50	52	18	1	91	5	0	1	2	1	8	.276	.312	.416	.728
2020	Mia	NL	3	10	2	0	0	0	(0	0)	2	2	1	1	0	0	2	0	0	0	0	1	0	.200	.273	.200	.473
2021	Cle	AL	99	339	91	21	1	7	(1	6)	135	33	41	48	14	1	56	5	0	3	3	1	10	.268	.305	.398	.703
2022	TB	AL	120	403	121	24	0	6	(3	3)	163	46	58	53	19	1	72	9	0	4	3	5	5	.300	.343	.404	.747
	4 ML YEARS		341	1173	330	65	4	24	(9	15)	475	135	150	154	52	3	221	19	0	8	8	8	23	.281	.320	.405	.725

Jose Ramirez

Bats: B Throws: R Pos: 3B-127;DH-30   Ht: 5'9" Wt: 190 Born: 9/17/1992 Age: 30

Year	Team	Lg	G	AB	H	2B	3B	HR	(Hm	Rd)	TB	R	RBI	RC	TBB	IBB	SO	HBP	SH	SF	SB	CS	GDP	Avg	OBP	Slg	OPS
2013	Cle	AL	15	12	4	0	1	0	(0	0)	6	5	0	2	2	0	2	0	0	0	0	1	0	.333	.429	.500	.929
2014	Cle	AL	68	237	62	10	2	2	(1	1)	82	27	17	25	13	0	35	1	13	2	10	1	3	.262	.300	.346	.646
2015	Cle	AL	97	315	69	14	3	6	(1	5)	107	50	27	28	32	0	39	1	5	2	10	4	5	.219	.291	.340	.631
2016	Cle	AL	152	565	176	46	3	11	(8	3)	261	84	76	101	44	1	62	4	1	4	22	7	10	.312	.363	.462	.825
2017	Cle	AL	152	585	186	56	6	29	(10	19)	341	107	83	113	52	5	69	3	0	5	17	5	13	.318	.374	.583	.957
2018	Cle	AL	157	578	156	38	4	39	(19	20)	319	110	105	130	106	15	80	8	0	6	34	6	2	.270	.387	.552	.939
2019	Cle	AL	129	482	123	33	3	23	(8	15)	231	68	83	80	52	3	74	2	0	6	24	4	8	.255	.327	.479	.806
2020	Cle	AL	58	219	64	16	1	17	(8	9)	133	45	46	52	31	0	43	3	0	1	10	3	2	.292	.386	.607	.993
2021	Cle	AL	152	552	147	32	5	36	(21	15)	297	111	103	116	72	10	87	7	0	5	27	4	13	.266	.355	.538	.893
2022	Cle	AL	157	601	168	44	5	29	(11	18)	309	90	126	129	69	20	82	6	0	9	20	7	5	.280	.355	.514	.869
	Postseason		25	94	20	5	0	1	(0	1)	28	9	8	7	8	1	19	0	0	0	0	1	2	.213	.275	.298	.572
10 ML YEARS			1137	4146	1155	289	33	192	(87	105)	2086	697	666	776	473	54	573	35	19	40	174	42	61	.279	.354	.503	.857

Noe Ramirez

Pitches: R Bats: R Pos: RP-55   no-EH   Ht: 6'3" Wt: 205 Born: 12/22/1989 Age: 33

Year	Team	Lg	G	GS	GF	IP	BFP	H	R	ER	HR	SH	SF	HB	TBB	IBB	SO	WP	W	L	Pct	Sv-Op	Hld	Vel	OPS	ERC	ERA
2015	Bos	AL	17	0	3	13.0	61	13	12	6	3	0	0	2	7	0	13	1	0	1	.000	0-0	4	90	.803	6.15	4.15
2016	Bos	AL	14	0	7	13.0	61	16	9	9	4	0	2	2	8	1	15	0	0	0	-	0-0	0	90	1.059	9.08	6.23
2017	2 Tms	AL	12	0	1	13.0	49	6	5	4	2	0	0	0	5	0	14	0	0	0	-	0-0	0	90	.520	1.68	2.77
2018	LAA	AL	69	1	12	83.1	353	75	43	42	15	0	0	6	30	3	95	4	7	5	.583	1-4	5	90	.750	4.16	4.54
2019	LAA	AL	51	7	10	67.2	280	59	30	30	9	0	1	5	20	1	79	2	5	4	.556	0-0	3	89	.698	3.48	3.99
2020	LAA	AL	21	0	3	21.0	85	15	7	7	2	0	1	1	9	2	14	1	1	0	1.000	0-1	0	89	.618	2.73	3.00
2021	2 Tms	AL	38	0	7	36.0	147	23	14	12	3	1	2	3	12	0	29	2	0	2	.000	1-3	10	89	.547	2.12	3.00
2022	Ari	NL	55	0	3	50.0	215	45	32	29	9	1	1	3	26	2	51	2	5	4	.556	0-4	10	90	.797	4.85	5.22
17	Bos	AL	2	0	1	4.2	18	3	2	2	2	0	0	0	1	0	4	0	0	0	-	0-0	0	89	.752	3.21	3.86
17	LAA	AL	10	0	0	8.1	31	3	3	2	0	0	0	0	4	0	10	0	0	0	-	0-0	0	90	.374	1.02	2.16
21	LAA	AL	2	0	1	3.1	15	5	2	2	1	0	0	0	1	0	0	0	0	0	-	0-0	0	89	1.114	8.71	5.40
21	Ari	NL	36	0	6	32.2	132	18	12	10	2	1	2	3	11	0	29	2	0	2	.000	1-3	10	89	.479	1.64	2.76
8 ML YEARS			277	8	46	297.0	1251	252	152	139	47	2	7	22	117	9	310	12	18	16	.529	2-12	32	90	.721	3.88	4.21

Yohan Ramirez

Pitches: R Bats: R Pos: RP-30   Ht: 6'4" Wt: 212 Born: 5/6/1995 Age: 28

Year	Team	Lg	G	GS	GF	IP	BFP	H	R	ER	HR	SH	SF	HB	TBB	IBB	SO	WP	W	L	Pct	Sv-Op	Hld	Vel	OPS	ERC	ERA
2022	Clmbs	AAA	11	0	3	10.1	44	3	5	5	0	0	0	3	10	1	13	0	1	0	1.000	0--	-	-	.493	2.63	4.35
2022	Indy	AAA	5	0	1	5.1	19	1	0	0	0	0	0	0	2	0	4	0	1	0	1.000	0--	-	-	.217	0.45	0.00
2020	Sea	AL	16	0	7	20.2	94	9	6	6	3	0	1	4	20	1	26	2	0	0	-	3-3	1	96	.626	4.07	2.61
2021	Sea	AL	25	0	15	27.2	114	18	14	12	6	3	0	3	12	0	35	2	1	3	.250	2-2	0	95	.693	3.50	3.90
2022	3 Tms	AL	30	0	16	37.1	167	32	19	19	4	2	0	6	20	1	32	2	4	1	.800	1-2	2	95	.718	4.42	4.58
22	Sea	AL	7	0	3	8.1	40	7	7	7	3	0	0	2	6	0	10	1	1	0	1.000	0-1	0	94	.938	7.39	7.56
22	Cle	AL	1	0	1	2.0	11	3	1	1	0	0	0	1	1	0	1	1	0	0	-	0-0	0	95	.899	8.58	4.50
22	Pit	NL	22	0	12	27.0	116	22	11	11	1	2	0	3	13	1	21	0	3	1	.750	1-1	2	96	.629	3.31	3.67
3 ML YEARS			71	0	38	85.2	375	59	39	37	13	5	1	13	52	2	93	6	5	4	.556	6-7	3	96	.690	4.06	3.89

Heliot Ramos

Bats: R Throws: R Pos: RF-6;LF-3;PH-1   Ht: 6'1" Wt: 188 Born: 9/7/1999 Age: 23

Year	Team	Lg	G	AB	H	2B	3B	HR	(Hm	Rd)	TB	R	RBI	RC	TBB	IBB	SO	HBP	SH	SF	SB	CS	GDP	Avg	OBP	Slg	OPS
2022	Scrmto	AAA	108	427	97	17	1	11	(-	-)	149	61	45	42	41	1	112	7	0	0	6	6	13	.227	.305	.349	.654
2022	SF	NL	9	20	2	0	0	0	(0	0)	2	4	0	0	2	0	6	0	0	0	0	0	1	.100	.182	.100	.282

Drew Rasmussen

Pitches: R Bats: R Pos: SP-28   Ht: 6'1" Wt: 211 Born: 7/27/1995 Age: 27

Year	Team	Lg	G	GS	GF	IP	BFP	H	R	ER	HR	SH	SF	HB	TBB	IBB	SO	WP	W	L	Pct	Sv-Op	Hld	Vel	OPS	ERC	ERA
2020	Mil	NL	12	0	3	15.1	71	17	10	10	3	0	0	0	9	0	21	0	1	0	1.000	0-0	0	98	.834	6.18	5.87
2021	2 Tms		35	10	9	76.0	307	57	27	24	5	1	1	0	25	2	73	4	4	1	.800	1-1	1	97	.575	2.25	2.84
2022	TB	AL	28	28	0	146.0	584	121	51	46	13	1	2	3	31	0	125	10	11	7	.611	0-0	0	95	.614	2.48	2.84
21	Mil	NL	15	0	7	17.0	77	13	11	8	2	0	0	0	12	2	25	2	0	1	.000	1-1	0	97	.679	3.74	4.24
21	TB	AL	20	10	2	59.0	230	44	16	16	3	1	1	0	13	0	48	2	4	0	1.000	0-0	1	97	.542	1.85	2.44
	Postseason		2	1	1	3.0	15	7	3	3	1	0	0	0	0	0	3	0	0	0	-	0-0	0		1.200	13.81	9.00
3 ML YEARS			75	38	12	237.1	962	195	88	80	21	2	3	3	65	2	219	14	16	8	.667	1-1	1	96	.617	2.61	3.03

Robbie Ray

Pitches: L Bats: L Pos: SP-32   Ht: 6'2" Wt: 225 Born: 10/1/1991 Age: 31

Year	Team	Lg	G	GS	GF	IP	BFP	H	R	ER	HR	SH	SF	HB	TBB	IBB	SO	WP	W	L	Pct	Sv-Op	Hld	Vel	OPS	ERC	ERA
2014	Det	AL	9	6	1	28.2	136	43	26	26	5	1	1	0	11	0	19	2	1	4	.200	0-0	1	91	.993	7.72	8.16
2015	Ari	NL	23	23	0	127.2	545	121	56	50	9	7	6	8	49	3	119	2	5	12	.294	0-0	0	93	.731	3.75	3.52
2016	Ari	NL	32	32	0	174.1	776	185	105	95	24	3	2	6	71	4	218	8	8	15	.348	0-0	0	94	.770	4.78	4.90
2017	Ari	NL	28	28	0	162.0	665	116	57	52	23	4	3	5	71	3	218	8	15	5	.750	0-0	0	94	.646	3.08	2.89

Year	Team	Lg	G	GS	GF	IP	BFP	H	R	ER	HR	SH	SF	HB	TBB	IBB	SO	WP	W	L	Pct	Sv-Op	Hld	Vel	OPS	ERC	ERA
2018	Ari	NL	24	24	0	123.2	526	97	55	54	19	1	1	5	70	3	165	5	6	2	.750	0-0	0	94	.706	4.08	3.93
2019	Ari	NL	33	33	0	174.1	747	150	91	84	30	11	4	5	84	5	235	7	12	8	.600	0-0	0	92	.766	4.19	4.34
2020	2 Tms		12	11	0	51.2	251	53	40	38	13	0	2	1	45	1	68	6	2	5	.286	0-0	0	94	.917	7.42	6.62
2021	Tor	AL	32	32	0	193.1	773	150	62	61	33	1	2	4	52	0	248	5	13	7	.650	0-0	0	95	.667	2.91	2.84
2022	Sea	AL	32	32	0	189.0	775	163	80	78	32	0	1	7	62	0	212	5	12	12	.500	0-0	0	93	.722	3.70	3.71
20	Ari	NL	7	7	0	31.0	154	31	27	27	9	0	2	1	31	1	43	6	1	4	.200	0-0	0	94	.967	8.23	7.84
20	Tor	AL	5	4	0	20.2	97	22	13	11	4	0	0	0	14	0	25	0	1	1	.500	0-0	0	94	.841	6.26	4.79
	Postseason		3	1	0	9.2	41	7	6	6	0	0	0	1	5	0	14	5	0	2	.000	0-0	0	94	.603	2.74	5.59
	9 ML YEARS		225	221	1	1224.2	5194	1078	572	538	188	28	22	41	515	19	1502	48	74	70	.514	0-0	1	94	.733	3.98	3.95

J.T. Realmuto

Bats: R Throws: R Pos: C-133;PH-7;1B-3;DH-3 reel-MYOO-toh **Ht: 6'1" Wt: 212 Born: 3/18/1991 Age: 32**

Year	Team	Lg	G	AB	H	2B	3B	HR	(Hm	Rd)	TB	R	RBI	RC	TBB	IBB	SO	HBP	SH	SF	SB	CS	GDP	Avg	OBP	Slg	OPS
2014	Mia	NL	11	29	7	1	1	0	(0	0)	10	4	9	4	1	0	8	0	0	2	0	0	2	.241	.267	.345	.611
2015	Mia	NL	126	441	114	21	7	10	(6	4)	179	49	47	44	19	2	70	2	1	4	8	4	11	.259	.290	.406	.696
2016	Mia	NL	137	509	154	31	0	11	(3	8)	218	60	48	63	28	1	100	5	0	3	12	4	12	.303	.343	.428	.771
2017	Mia	NL	141	532	148	31	5	17	(5	12)	240	68	65	74	36	4	106	8	0	3	8	2	13	.278	.332	.451	.783
2018	Mia	NL	125	477	132	30	3	21	(8	13)	231	74	74	74	38	0	104	10	0	4	3	2	9	.277	.340	.484	.825
2019	Phi	NL	145	538	148	36	3	25	(16	9)	265	92	83	78	41	2	123	5	0	8	9	1	12	.275	.328	.493	.820
2020	Phi	NL	47	173	46	6	0	11	(8	3)	85	33	32	28	16	0	48	6	0	4	4	1	3	.266	.349	.491	.840
2021	Phi	NL	134	476	125	25	4	17	(12	5)	209	64	73	80	48	5	129	11	0	2	13	3	8	.263	.343	.439	.782
2022	Phi	NL	139	504	139	26	5	22	(12	10)	241	75	84	83	41	1	119	12	0	5	21	1	5	.276	.342	.478	.820
	9 ML YEARS		1005	3679	1013	207	28	134	(70	64)	1678	519	515	528	268	15	807	59	1	29	78	18	77	.275	.332	.456	.788

Jake Reed

Pitches: R Bats: R Pos: RP-18 **Ht: 6'2" Wt: 195 Born: 9/29/1992 Age: 30**

Year	Team	Lg	G	GS	GF	IP	BFP	H	R	ER	HR	SH	SF	HB	TBB	IBB	SO	WP	W	L	Pct	Sv-Op	Hld	Vel	OPS	ERC	ERA
2022	Syrcse	AAA	8	0	0	11.0	53	11	8	7	1	0	0	3	5	0	11	0	0	0	-	0- -	-		.714	5.07	5.73
2022	OkCity	AAA	10	0	1	10.1	42	8	1	1	0	0	0	1	3	1	11	0	2	0	1.000	0- -	-		.549	2.08	0.87
2021	2 Tms	NL	10	1	3	10.0	43	10	6	4	1	1	0	0	2	1	10	0	0	1	.000	0-1	0	88	.636	3.00	3.60
2022	3 Tms	NL	18	0	5	16.2	77	17	15	13	2	0	0	3	8	0	13	0	2	1	1.000	1-1	0	92	.818	5.34	7.02
21	LAD	NL	6	1	2	5.1	24	5	3	2	1	1	0	0	2	1	5	0	0	0	-	0-1	0	88	.733	3.67	3.38
21	NYM	NL	4	0	1	4.2	19	5	3	2	0	0	0	0	0	0	5	0	0	1	.000	0-0	0	88	.526	2.27	3.86
22	NYM	NL	5	0	1	6.1	30	4	8	8	2	0	0	1	6	0	6	0	1	0	1.000	0-0	0	91	.845	6.36	11.37
22	LAD	NL	5	0	2	4.2	20	6	1	1	0	0	0	1	0	0	2	0	0	0	-	1-1	0	92	.824	4.34	1.93
22	Bal	AL	8	0	2	5.2	27	7	6	4	0	0	0	2	1	0	5	0	1	0	1.000	0-0	0	92	.787	5.03	6.35
	2 ML YEARS		28	1	8	26.2	120	27	21	17	3	1	0	3	10	1	23	0	2	1	.667	1-2	0	91	.751	4.41	5.74

Rob Refsnyder

Bats: R Throws: R Pos: RF-28;CF-17;PH-17;DH-7;LF-6;PR-1 REF-snide-er **Ht: 6'0" Wt: 205 Born: 3/26/1991 Age: 32**

Year	Team	Lg	G	AB	H	2B	3B	HR	(Hm	Rd)	TB	R	RBI	RC	TBB	IBB	SO	HBP	SH	SF	SB	CS	GDP	Avg	OBP	Slg	OPS
2022	Wrcstr	AAA	42	147	45	14	0	6	(-	-)	77	31	28	34	28	0	42	5	0	2	4	0	2	.306	.429	.524	.952
2015	NYY	AL	16	43	13	3	0	2	(1	1)	22	3	5	6	3	1	7	0	0	0	2	0	3	.302	.348	.512	.859
2016	NYY	AL	58	152	38	9	0	0	(0	0)	47	25	12	14	18	2	30	1	0	3	2	1	5	.250	.328	.309	.637
2017	2 Tms	AL	52	88	15	2	1	0	(0	0)	19	8	0	0	8	1	17	1	0	0	4	1	2	.170	.247	.216	.463
2018	TB	AL	40	84	14	3	0	2	(0	2)	23	10	5	5	18	0	26	0	0	0	0	2	5	.167	.314	.274	.588
2020	Tex	AL	15	30	6	1	0	0	(0	0)	7	4	1	2	2	0	11	1	0	1	0	0	0	.200	.265	.233	.498
2021	Min	AL	51	139	34	7	0	2	(1	1)	47	21	12	16	17	0	40	1	0	1	1	0	4	.245	.325	.338	.663
2022	Bos	AL	57	153	47	11	0	6	(4	2)	76	25	21	27	15	0	46	6	0	3	1	1	1	.307	.384	.497	.881
17	NYY	AL	20	37	5	1	1	0	(0	0)	8	3	0	0	3	0	8	0	0	0	2	0	0	.135	.200	.216	.416
17	Tor	AL	32	51	10	1	0	0	(0	0)	11	5	0	0	5	1	9	1	0	0	2	1	2	.196	.281	.216	.496
	Postseason		1	3	0	0	0	0	(0	0)	0	0	0	0	0	0	0	0	0	0	0	0	0	.000	.000	.000	.000
	7 ML YEARS		289	689	167	36	1	12	(6	6)	241	96	56	71	81	4	177	9	0	8	10	5	20	.242	.327	.350	.676

Sean Reid-Foley

Pitches: R Bats: R Pos: RP-7 **Ht: 6'3" Wt: 230 Born: 8/30/1995 Age: 27**

Year	Team	Lg	G	GS	GF	IP	BFP	H	R	ER	HR	SH	SF	HB	TBB	IBB	SO	WP	W	L	Pct	Sv-Op	Hld	Vel	OPS	ERC	ERA
2018	Tor	AL	7	7	0	33.1	150	31	23	19	6	0	1	1	21	0	42	3	2	4	.333	0-0	0	94	.794	5.32	5.13
2019	Tor	AL	9	6	0	31.2	150	33	20	15	5	0	1	2	21	0	28	3	2	4	.333	0-0	0	94	.818	6.01	4.26
2020	Tor	AL	5	0	2	6.2	30	3	3	1	0	0	0	0	6	1	6	0	1	0	1.000	0-0	0	95	.425	1.93	1.35
2021	NYM	NL	12	0	1	20.2	92	22	15	12	3	0	0	0	9	2	26	1	2	1	.667	0-0	0	94	.771	4.70	5.23
2022	NYM	NL	7	0	3	10.0	44	7	6	6	1	0	0	1	7	0	8	0	0	0	-	0-0	0	96	.758	3.96	5.40
	5 ML YEARS		40	13	6	102.1	466	96	67	53	15	0	2	4	64	3	110	7	7	9	.438	0-0	0	94	.771	5.02	4.66

Zach Reks

Bats: L **Throws:** R **Pos:** LF-13;PH-6;RF-3;PR-1   **Ht:** 6'2" **Wt:** 190 **Born:** 11/12/1993 **Age:** 29

							BATTING													RUNNING			AVERAGES			
Year	Team	Lg	G	AB	H	2B	3B	HR	(Hm | Rd)	TB	R	RBI	RC	TBB	IBB	SO	HBP	SH	SF	SB	CS	GDP	Avg	OBP	Slg	OPS
2022	RdRck	AAA	34	121	40	10	1	6	(- | -)	70	24	21	29	15	0	36	4	0	0	1	1	1	.331	.421	.579	1.000
2021	LAD	NL	6	10	0	0	0	0	(0 | 0)	0	2	0	0	0	0	7	0	0	0	0	0	0	.000	.000	.000	.000
2022	Tex	AL	16	34	9	1	0	0	(0 | 0)	10	3	3	4	0	0	10	0	0	0	0	1	0	.265	.265	.294	.559
	2 ML YEARS		22	44	9	1	0	0	(0 | 0)	10	5	3	4	0	0	17	0	0	0	0	1	0	.205	.205	.227	.432

Anthony Rendon

Bats: R **Throws:** R **Pos:** 3B-47;PH-1   ren-DOAN   **Ht:** 6'1" **Wt:** 200 **Born:** 6/6/1990 **Age:** 33

							BATTING													RUNNING			AVERAGES			
Year	Team	Lg	G	AB	H	2B	3B	HR	(Hm	Rd)	TB	R	RBI	RC	TBB	IBB	SO	HBP	SH	SF	SB	CS	GDP	Avg	OBP	Slg	OPS
2013	Was	NL	98	351	93	23	1	7	(3	4)	139	40	35	43	31	3	69	5	2	5	1	1	7	.265	.329	.396	.725
2014	Was	NL	153	613	176	39	6	21	(10	11)	290	111	83	97	58	2	104	5	2	5	17	3	11	.287	.351	.473	.824
2015	Was	NL	80	311	82	16	0	5	(3	2)	113	43	25	39	36	0	70	4	0	4	1	2	8	.264	.344	.363	.707
2016	Was	NL	156	567	153	38	2	20	(11	9)	255	91	85	95	65	2	117	7	0	8	12	6	5	.270	.348	.450	.797
2017	Was	NL	147	508	153	41	1	25	(14	11)	271	81	100	115	84	6	82	7	0	6	7	2	7	.301	.403	.533	.937
2018	Was	NL	136	529	163	44	2	24	(10	14)	283	88	92	99	55	5	82	5	0	8	2	1	5	.308	.374	.535	.909
2019	Was	NL	146	545	174	44	3	34	(20	14)	326	117	126	130	80	8	86	12	0	9	5	1	13	.319	.412	.598	1.010
2020	LAA	AL	52	189	54	11	1	9	(9	0)	94	29	31	38	38	2	31	5	0	0	0	0	10	.286	.418	.497	.915
2021	LAA	AL	58	217	52	13	0	6	(2	4)	83	24	34	23	29	2	41	1	0	2	0	0	11	.240	.329	.382	.712
2022	LAA	AL	47	166	38	10	0	5	(3	2)	63	15	24	22	23	0	35	2	0	2	2	0	7	.229	.326	.380	.706
	Postseason		31	117	33	8	0	5	(1	4)	56	16	21	22	18	3	19	0	0	3	1	0	0	.282	.370	.479	.848
	10 ML YEARS		1073	3996	1138	279	16	156	(85	71)	1917	639	635	701	499	30	717	53	4	49	47	16	84	.285	.368	.480	.847

Hunter Renfroe

Bats: R **Throws:** R **Pos:** RF-118;DH-7;1B-1   **Ht:** 6'1" **Wt:** 230 **Born:** 1/28/1992 **Age:** 31

							BATTING													RUNNING			AVERAGES			
Year	Team	Lg	G	AB	H	2B	3B	HR	(Hm	Rd)	TB	R	RBI	RC	TBB	IBB	SO	HBP	SH	SF	SB	CS	GDP	Avg	OBP	Slg	OPS
2016	SD	NL	11	35	13	3	0	4	(4	0)	28	8	14	10	1	1	5	0	0	0	0	0	1	.371	.389	.800	1.189
2017	SD	NL	122	445	103	25	1	26	(14	12)	208	51	58	48	27	1	140	6	0	1	3	0	4	.231	.284	.467	.751
2018	SD	NL	117	403	100	23	1	26	(13	13)	203	53	68	58	30	2	109	3	0	5	2	1	9	.248	.302	.504	.805
2019	SD	NL	140	440	95	19	1	33	(14	19)	215	64	64	57	46	1	154	2	0	6	5	0	6	.216	.289	.489	.778
2020	TB	AL	42	122	19	5	0	8	(5	3)	48	18	22	13	14	0	37	2	0	1	2	0	3	.156	.252	.393	.645
2021	Bos	AL	144	521	135	33	0	31	(14	17)	261	89	96	78	44	0	130	1	0	6	1	2	6	.259	.315	.501	.816
2022	Mil	NL	125	474	121	23	1	29	(11	18)	233	62	72	77	39	1	121	4	2	3	1	1	11	.255	.315	.492	.807
	Postseason		23	59	11	3	0	2	(2	0)	20	6	8	4	8	0	23	0	0	0	1	0	5	.186	.284	.339	.623
	7 ML YEARS		701	2440	586	131	4	157	(75	82)	1196	345	394	341	201	6	696	18	2	22	14	4	40	.240	.300	.490	.790

Luis Rengifo

Bats: B **Throws:** R **Pos:** 2B-99;3B-39;SS-19;RF-5;PH-5;LF-1   ren-HEE-foh   **Ht:** 5'10" **Wt:** 195 **Born:** 2/26/1997 **Age:** 26

							BATTING													RUNNING			AVERAGES			
Year	Team	Lg	G	AB	H	2B	3B	HR	(Hm	Rd)	TB	R	RBI	RC	TBB	IBB	SO	HBP	SH	SF	SB	CS	GDP	Avg	OBP	Slg	OPS
2022	Salt Lk	AAA	24	99	31	5	2	4	(-	-)	52	19	15	18	12	1	24	0	0	1	2	2	4	.313	.384	.525	.909
2019	LAA	AL	108	357	85	18	3	7	(1	6)	130	44	33	45	40	0	93	5	1	3	2	5	6	.238	.321	.364	.685
2020	LAA	AL	33	90	14	1	0	1	(0	1)	18	12	3	2	14	0	26	0	2	0	3	1	2	.156	.269	.200	.469
2021	LAA	AL	54	174	35	1	0	6	(3	3)	54	22	18	10	9	0	38	2	3	2	1	0	3	.201	.246	.310	.556
2022	LAA	AL	127	489	129	22	4	17	(12	5)	210	45	52	50	17	0	79	4	1	0	6	2	11	.264	.294	.429	.724
	4 ML YEARS		322	1110	263	42	7	31	(16	15)	412	123	106	107	80	0	236	11	7	5	12	8	22	.237	.294	.371	.665

Alex Reyes

Pitches: R **Bats:** R **Pos:** P   **Ht:** 6'4" **Wt:** 220 **Born:** 8/29/1994 **Age:** 28

			HOW MUCH PITCHED					WHAT HE GAVE UP									THE RESULTS							
Year	Team	Lg	G	GS	GF	IP	BFP	H	R	ER	HR	SH	SF	HB	TBB	IBB	SO	WP	W	L	Pct	Sv-Op	Hld	Vel	OPS	ERC	ERA
2016	StL	NL	12	5	3	46.0	189	33	8	8	1	1	1	0	23	1	52	3	4	1	.800	1-1	1	-	.578	2.43	1.57
2018	StL	NL	1	1	0	4.0	15	3	0	0	0	0	0	1	2	0	2	0	0	0	-	0-0	0	-	.650	3.97	0.00
2019	StL	NL	4	0	0	3.0	17	2	5	5	1	0	1	0	6	0	1	1	0	1	.000	0-0	2	-	.971	10.79	15.00
2020	StL	NL	15	1	5	19.2	86	14	10	7	1	1	0	0	14	1	27	2	2	1	.667	1-1	2	-	.611	3.22	3.20
2021	StL	NL	69	0	54	72.1	317	46	32	26	9	0	1	2	52	1	95	10	10	8	.556	29-34	3	-	.609	3.48	3.24
	Postseason		3	0	3	3.1	16	3	4	2	2	0	0	0	2	1	3	0	0	0	-	1-1	0	-	.955	6.86	5.40
	5 ML YEARS		101	7	62	145.0	624	98	55	46	12	2	3	3	97	3	177	16	16	11	.593	31-36	8	-	.609	3.24	2.86

Denyi Reyes

Pitches: R **Bats:** R **Pos:** RP-2; SP-1   **Ht:** 6'4" **Wt:** 255 **Born:** 11/2/1996 **Age:** 26

			HOW MUCH PITCHED					WHAT HE GAVE UP									THE RESULTS							
Year	Team	Lg	G	GS	GF	IP	BFP	H	R	ER	HR	SH	SF	HB	TBB	IBB	SO	WP	W	L	Pct	Sv-Op	Hld	Vel	OPS	ERC	ERA
2022	Norfolk	AAA	15	10	4	54.0	246	74	46	43	13	2	5	2	8	0	54	3	0	7	.000	1- -	-	-	.929	6.27	7.17
2022	Bal	AL	3	1	1	7.2	31	8	2	2	0	0	0	0	1	0	3	0	0	0	-	0-0	0	93	.624	2.68	2.35

Franmil Reyes

Bats: R **Throws:** R **Pos:** DH-100;RF-13;PH-6;LF-2   **Ht:** 6'5" **Wt:** 265 **Born:** 7/7/1995 **Age:** 27

Year	Team	Lg	G	AB	H	2B	3B	HR	(Hm	Rd)	TB	R	RBI	RC	TBB	IBB	SO	HBP	SH	SF	SB	CS	GDP	Avg	OBP	Slg	OPS
2018	SD	NL	87	261	73	9	0	16	(8	8)	130	36	31	37	24	0	80	0	0	0	0	0	5	.280	.340	.498	.838
2019	2 Tms		150	494	123	19	0	37	(25	12)	253	69	81	71	47	1	156	0	0	7	0	0	15	.249	.310	.512	.822
2020	Cle	AL	59	211	58	10	0	9	(2	7)	95	27	34	32	24	0	69	1	0	5	0	0	6	.275	.344	.450	.795
2021	Cle	AL	115	418	106	18	2	30	(16	14)	218	57	85	70	43	3	149	2	0	3	4	1	13	.254	.324	.522	.846
2022	2 Tms		118	438	97	17	2	14	(4	10)	160	43	47	43	30	0	157	2	0	3	2	1	12	.221	.273	.365	.638
19	SD	NL	99	321	82	9	0	27	(17	10)	172	43	46	41	29	1	93	0	0	4	0	0	12	.255	.314	.536	.849
19	Cle	AL	51	173	41	10	0	10	(8	2)	81	26	35	30	18	0	63	0	0	3	0	0	3	.237	.304	.468	.772
22	Cle	AL	70	263	56	9	0	9	(4	5)	92	24	28	20	14	0	104	1	0	2	2	0	8	.213	.254	.350	.603
22	ChC	NL	48	175	41	8	2	5	(0	5)	68	19	19	23	16	0	53	1	0	1	0	1	4	.234	.301	.389	.689
	Postseason		2	7	0	0	0	0	(0	0)	0	2	0	0	2	0	5	0	0	0	0	0	0	.000	.222	.000	.222
	5 ML YEARS		529	1822	457	73	4	106	(55	51)	856	232	278	253	168	4	611	5	0	18	6	2	51	.251	.313	.470	.783

Gerardo Reyes

Pitches: R **Bats:** R **Pos:** RP-2   **Ht:** 5'11" **Wt:** 195 **Born:** 5/13/1993 **Age:** 30

Year	Team	Lg	G	GS	GF	IP	BFP	H	R	ER	HR	SH	SF	HB	TBB	IBB	SO	WP	W	L	Pct	Sv-Op Hld	Vel	OPS	ERC	ERA
2022	Salt Lk	AAA	46	0	21	45.2	207	35	23	19	5	0	2	6	33	2	58	2	3	4	.429	6- - -	-	.701	4.51	3.74
2019	SD	NL	27	0	9	26.0	117	24	22	22	3	1	2	3	11	1	38	3	4	0	1.000	0-1 1	97	.738	4.10	7.62
2022	LAA	AL	2	0	1	2.0	12	3	1	1	1	0	0	0	3	0	0	0	0	0	-	0-0 0	97	1.278	16.26	4.50
	2 ML YEARS		29	0	10	28.0	129	27	23	23	4	1	2	3	14	1	38	3	4	0	1.000	0-1 1	97	.784	4.80	7.39

Pablo Reyes

Bats: R **Throws:** R **Pos:** SS-3;3B-2   **Ht:** 5'8" **Wt:** 175 **Born:** 9/5/1993 **Age:** 29

Year	Team	Lg	G	AB	H	2B	3B	HR	(Hm	Rd)	TB	R	RBI	RC	TBB	IBB	SO	HBP	SH	SF	SB	CS	GDP	Avg	OBP	Slg	OPS
2022	Nashv	AAA	99	385	105	27	2	11	(-	-)	169	63	59	58	39	0	67	6	1	1	15	7	7	.273	.348	.439	.787
2018	Pit	NL	18	58	17	2	0	3	(0	3)	28	9	7	7	5	0	11	0	0	0	0	1	2	.293	.349	.483	.832
2019	Pit	NL	71	143	29	7	2	1	(1	1)	46	18	19	16	13	0	36	1	0	0	1	1	0	.203	.274	.322	.596
2021	Mil	NL	53	78	20	5	0	1	(1	0)	28	12	3	8	9	1	15	0	0	0	4	0	2	.256	.333	.359	.692
2022	Mil	NL	6	15	4	0	0	0	(0	0)	4	1	0	1	1	0	2	0	0	0	0	0	0	.267	.313	.267	.579
	4 ML YEARS		148	294	70	14	2	6	(2	4)	106	40	29	32	28	1	64	1	0	0	5	2	4	.238	.307	.361	.667

Victor Reyes

Bats: B **Throws:** R **Pos:** RF-63;LF-19;CF-8;PH-8;DH-4;PR-3   **Ht:** 6'5" **Wt:** 194 **Born:** 10/5/1994 **Age:** 28

Year	Team	Lg	G	AB	H	2B	3B	HR	(Hm	Rd)	TB	R	RBI	RC	TBB	IBB	SO	HBP	SH	SF	SB	CS	GDP	Avg	OBP	Slg	OPS
2018	Det	AL	100	212	47	5	3	1	(0	1)	61	35	12	12	5	0	46	0	1	1	9	1	4	.222	.239	.288	.526
2019	Det	AL	69	276	84	16	5	3	(2	1)	119	29	25	35	14	0	64	0	0	2	9	3	5	.304	.336	.431	.767
2020	Det	AL	57	202	56	7	2	4	(1	3)	79	30	14	23	9	0	45	2	0	0	8	2	4	.277	.315	.391	.706
2021	Det	AL	76	209	54	10	4	5	(4	1)	87	26	22	25	8	0	55	0	2	1	5	1	2	.258	.284	.416	.701
2022	Det	AL	92	315	80	19	3	3	(2	1)	114	27	34	31	13	0	77	4	0	4	2	2	7	.254	.289	.362	.651
	5 ML YEARS		394	1214	321	57	17	16	(9	7)	460	147	107	126	49	0	287	6	3	8	33	9	22	.264	.294	.379	.673

Bryan Reynolds

Bats: B **Throws:** R **Pos:** CF-127;DH-18;LF-1;PH-1   **Ht:** 6'3" **Wt:** 205 **Born:** 1/27/1995 **Age:** 28

Year	Team	Lg	G	AB	H	2B	3B	HR	(Hm	Rd)	TB	R	RBI	RC	TBB	IBB	SO	HBP	SH	SF	SB	CS	GDP	Avg	OBP	Slg	OPS
2019	Pit	NL	134	491	154	37	4	16	(8	8)	247	83	68	89	46	0	121	6	0	3	3	2	9	.314	.377	.503	.880
2020	Pit	NL	55	185	35	6	2	7	(4	3)	66	24	19	22	21	0	57	1	0	0	1	1	2	.189	.275	.357	.632
2021	Pit	NL	159	559	169	35	8	24	(12	12)	292	93	90	112	75	9	119	8	0	4	5	2	10	.302	.390	.522	.912
2022	Pit	NL	145	542	142	19	4	27	(10	17)	250	74	62	88	56	6	141	14	0	2	7	3	13	.262	.345	.461	.807
	4 ML YEARS		493	1777	500	97	18	74	(34	40)	855	274	239	311	198	15	438	29	0	9	16	8	34	.281	.361	.481	.842

Matt Reynolds

Bats: R **Throws:** R **Pos:** 2B-36;SS-23;3B-14;1B-13;RF-11;PH-8;PR-6;LF-3;CF-1;DH-1   **Ht:** 6'1" **Wt:** 200 **Born:** 12/3/1990 **Age:** 32

Year	Team	Lg	G	AB	H	2B	3B	HR	(Hm	Rd)	TB	R	RBI	RC	TBB	IBB	SO	HBP	SH	SF	SB	CS	GDP	Avg	OBP	Slg	OPS
2016	NYM	NL	47	89	20	8	0	3	(2	1)	37	11	13	10	4	0	34	1	2	0	0	1	2	.225	.266	.416	.682
2017	NYM	NL	68	113	26	1	2	1	(1	0)	34	12	5	11	14	1	37	2	1	0	0	1	2	.230	.326	.301	.626
2018	Was	NL	12	13	2	0	0	0	(0	0)	2	1	1	0	1	0	4	0	0	0	0	0	0	.154	.214	.154	.368
2020	KC	AL	3	11	0	0	0	0	(0	0)	0	1	0	0	0	0	7	0	0	0	0	0	0	.000	.000	.000	.000
2022	2 Tms	NL	93	244	60	10	1	3	(3	0)	81	31	23	28	26	0	78	1	0	1	5	0	7	.246	.320	.332	.652
22	NYM	NL	1	0	0	0	0	0	(0	0)	0	0	0	0	0	0	0	0	0	0	0	0	0	-	-	-	-
22	Cin	NL	92	244	60	10	1	3	(3	0)	81	31	23	28	26	0	78	1	0	1	5	0	7	.246	.320	.332	.652
	5 ML YEARS		223	470	108	19	3	7	(6	1)	154	56	42	49	45	1	160	4	3	1	5	2	11	.230	.302	.328	.630

Garrett Richards

Pitches: R **Bats:** R **Pos:** RP-30; SP-2   **Ht:** 6'2" **Wt:** 210 **Born:** 5/27/1988 **Age:** 35

			HOW MUCH PITCHED				WHAT HE GAVE UP												THE RESULTS								
Year	Team	Lg	G	GS	GF	IP	BFP	H	R	ER	HR	SH	SF	HB	TBB	IBB	SO	WP	W	L	Pct	Sv-Op	Hld	Vel	OPS	ERC	ERA
2011	LAA	AL	7	3	2	14.0	62	16	11	9	4	0	0	0	7	0	9	2	0	2	.000	0-0	0	95	.989	6.97	5.79
2012	LAA	AL	30	9	4	71.0	318	77	46	37	7	2	4	3	34	1	47	2	4	3	.571	1-3	5	95	.793	5.04	4.69
2013	LAA	AL	47	17	6	145.0	620	151	73	67	12	9	3	1	44	4	101	11	7	8	.467	1-2	5	95	.699	3.78	4.16
2014	LAA	AL	26	26	0	168.2	678	124	51	49	5	0	3	7	51	1	164	22	13	4	.765	0-0	0	96	.529	2.06	2.61
2015	LAA	AL	32	32	0	207.1	865	181	94	84	20	6	10	5	76	2	176	17	15	12	.556	0-0	0	95	.664	3.32	3.65
2016	LAA	AL	6	6	0	34.2	148	31	16	9	2	2	0	1	15	1	34	3	1	3	.250	0-0	0	96	.683	3.39	2.34
2017	LAA	AL	6	6	0	27.2	108	18	8	7	1	1	0	0	7	0	27	2	0	2	.000	0-0	0	96	.494	1.49	2.28
2018	LAA	AL	16	16	0	76.1	324	64	43	31	11	1	0	1	34	0	87	15	5	4	.556	0-0	0	96	.688	3.69	3.66
2019	SD	NL	3	3	0	8.2	41	10	8	8	2	1	0	0	6	0	11	1	0	1	.000	0-0	0	95	1.076	7.31	8.31
2020	SD	NL	14	10	2	51.1	213	47	23	23	7	0	1	2	17	0	46	3	2	2	.500	0-0	1	95	.724	3.80	4.03
2021	Bos	AL	40	22	4	136.2	617	158	86	74	19	0	5	5	60	1	115	7	7	8	.467	3-3	2	94	.829	5.60	4.87
2022	Tex	AL	32	2	11	42.2	185	44	28	25	3	0	1	3	13	0	36	2	1	1	.500	1-1	3	94	.723	3.92	5.27
	Postseason		5	0	0	3.0	13	1	2	2	0	0	0	0	2	0	4	1	0	1	.000	0-0	0	95	.413	1.16	6.00
	12 ML YEARS		259	152	29	984.0	4179	921	487	423	93	22	27	28	364	10	853	87	55	50	.524	6-9	16	95	.694	3.66	3.87

Trevor Richards

Pitches: R **Bats:** R **Pos:** RP-58; SP-4   **Ht:** 6'2" **Wt:** 205 **Born:** 5/15/1993 **Age:** 30

			HOW MUCH PITCHED				WHAT HE GAVE UP												THE RESULTS								
Year	Team	Lg	G	GS	GF	IP	BFP	H	R	ER	HR	SH	SF	HB	TBB	IBB	SO	WP	W	L	Pct	Sv-Op	Hld	Vel	OPS	ERC	ERA
2018	Mia	NL	25	25	0	126.1	547	121	65	62	15	5	4	5	54	5	130	8	4	9	.308	0-0	0	91	.754	4.18	4.42
2019	2 Tms		30	23	1	135.1	580	127	63	61	19	5	4	5	56	6	127	4	6	12	.333	0-0	1	91	.749	4.16	4.06
2020	TB	AL	9	4	1	32.0	150	44	24	21	6	1	1	0	11	0	27	1	0	0	-	0-0	0	91	.880	6.66	5.91
2021	3 Tms		53	0	10	64.1	251	40	26	25	12	1	0	0	22	1	78	8	7	2	.778	1-6	6	93	.612	2.40	3.50
2022	Tor		62	4	10	64.0	281	57	41	38	9	1	4	1	35	1	82	3	3	2	.600	0-1	8	93	.728	4.34	5.34
19	Mia	NL	23	20	1	112.0	483	104	56	56	16	4	4	5	51	6	103	4	3	12	.200	0-0	1	91	.759	4.32	4.50
19	TB	AL	7	3	0	23.1	97	23	7	5	3	1	0	0	5	0	24	0	3	0	1.000	0-0	0	90	.698	3.43	1.93
21	TB	AL	6	0	2	12.0	47	9	6	6	2	0	0	0	3	0	16	1	0	0	-	1-1	1	92	.642	2.62	4.50
21	Mil	NL	15	0	3	19.2	82	15	7	7	3	1	0	0	9	1	25	6	3	0	1.000	0-2	0	93	.685	3.27	3.20
21	Tor	AL	32	0	5	32.2	122	16	13	12	7	0	0	0	10	0	37	1	4	2	.667	0-3	5	93	.552	1.82	3.31
	5 ML YEARS		179	56	22	422.0	1809	389	219	207	61	13	13	11	178	13	444	24	20	25	.444	1-7	15	92	.739	4.09	4.41

JT Riddle

Bats: L **Throws:** R **Pos:** 3B-1;PH-1   **Ht:** 6'1" **Wt:** 190 **Born:** 10/12/1991 **Age:** 31

			BATTING																		RUNNING			AVERAGES			
Year	Team	Lg	G	AB	H	2B	3B	HR	(Hm	Rd)	TB	R	RBI	RC	TBB	IBB	SO	HBP	SH	SF	SB	CS	GDP	Avg	OBP	Slg	OPS
2022	Lsvlle	AAA	27	96	20	4	1	3	(-	-)	35	7	5	8	5	0	22	1	0	2	0	0	2	.208	.250	.365	.615
2022	Syrcse	AAA	61	236	60	17	1	8	(-	-)	103	32	30	29	5	0	49	3	0	2	0	0	4	.254	.276	.436	.713
2017	Mia	NL	70	228	57	13	1	3	(2	1)	81	20	31	24	12	2	50	0	2	5	0	2	6	.250	.282	.355	.637
2018	Mia	NL	102	308	71	10	4	9	(4	5)	116	28	36	31	20	1	67	0	3	1	0	3	4	.231	.277	.377	.653
2019	Mia	NL	51	132	25	6	0	6	(3	3)	49	15	12	7	5	1	42	2	0	0	0	0	3	.189	.230	.371	.601
2020	Pit	NL	23	67	10	2	0	1	(0	1)	15	8	1	0	2	0	13	0	0	0	1	0	0	.149	.174	.224	.398
2021	Min	AL	4	6	2	0	0	0	(0	0)	2	1	0	0	0	0	0	0	0	0	0	0	0	.333	.333	.333	.667
2022	Cin	NL	2	4	1	0	0	0	(0	0)	1	0	0	0	0	0	1	0	0	0	0	0	0	.250	.250	.250	.500
	6 ML YEARS		252	745	166	31	5	19	(9	10)	264	72	80	62	39	4	173	2	5	6	1	5	13	.223	.261	.354	.616

Austin Riley

Bats: R **Throws:** R **Pos:** 3B-159;1B-1;PH-1   **Ht:** 6'3" **Wt:** 240 **Born:** 4/2/1997 **Age:** 26

			BATTING																		RUNNING			AVERAGES			
Year	Team	Lg	G	AB	H	2B	3B	HR	(Hm	Rd)	TB	R	RBI	RC	TBB	IBB	SO	HBP	SH	SF	SB	CS	GDP	Avg	OBP	Slg	OPS
2019	Atl	NL	80	274	62	11	1	18	(11	7)	129	41	49	38	16	3	108	5	0	2	0	2	4	.226	.279	.471	.750
2020	Atl	NL	51	188	45	7	1	8	(3	5)	78	24	27	24	16	1	49	1	0	1	0	0	5	.239	.301	.415	.716
2021	Atl	NL	160	590	179	33	1	33	(13	20)	313	91	107	111	52	2	168	12	0	8	0	1	11	.303	.367	.531	.898
2022	Atl	NL	159	615	168	39	2	38	(24	14)	325	90	93	108	57	1	168	17	0	4	2	0	13	.273	.349	.528	.878
	Postseason		28	110	26	5	0	3	(1	2)	40	11	12	10	6	1	43	1	0	0	0	0	0	.236	.282	.364	.646
	4 ML YEARS		450	1667	454	90	5	97	(51	46)	845	246	276	281	141	7	493	35	0	15	2	3	33	.272	.339	.507	.846

Edwin Rios

Bats: L **Throws:** R **Pos:** DH-20;PH-5;1B-4;3B-4   **Ht:** 6'3" **Wt:** 220 **Born:** 4/21/1994 **Age:** 29

			BATTING																		RUNNING			AVERAGES			
Year	Team	Lg	G	AB	H	2B	3B	HR	(Hm	Rd)	TB	R	RBI	RC	TBB	IBB	SO	HBP	SH	SF	SB	CS	GDP	Avg	OBP	Slg	OPS
2022	OkCity	AAA	48	189	49	17	0	9	(-	-)	93	32	39	33	20	0	66	5	0	4	0	1	4	.259	.339	.492	.832
2019	LAD	NL	28	47	13	2	1	4	(0	4)	29	10	8	10	9	0	21	0	0	0	0	0	0	.277	.393	.617	1.010
2020	LAD	NL	32	76	19	6	0	8	(4	4)	49	13	17	15	4	0	18	2	0	0	0	0	2	.250	.301	.645	.946
2021	LAD	NL	25	51	4	0	1	0	(0	1)	7	4	1	0	7	0	18	2	0	0	0	0	3	.078	.217	.137	.354
2022	LAD	NL	27	86	21	1	0	7	(3	4)	43	12	17	14	5	1	36	1	0	0	0	1	2	.244	.293	.500	.793
	Postseason		7	14	2	0	0	2	(0	2)	8	2	3	1	3	0	8	0	0	1	0	0	0	.143	.278	.571	.849
	4 ML YEARS		112	260	57	9	1	20	(7	13)	128	39	43	39	25	1	93	5	0	1	0	1	8	.219	.299	.492	.791

Alfonso Rivas

Bats: L Throws: L Pos: 1B-92;PH-13;DH-3;LF-2;RF-1;PR-1   Ht: 5'11" Wt: 190 Born: 9/13/1996 Age: 26

Year Team	Lg	G	AB	H	2B	3B	HR	Hm	Rd	TB	R	RBI	RC	TBB	IBB	SO	HBP	SH	SF	SB	CS	GDP	Avg	OBP	Slg	OPS
2022 Iowa	AAA	26	94	28	6	1	1	-	-	39	15	10	13	10	0	28	1	0	1	0	0	1	.298	.368	.415	.783
2021 ChC	NL	18	44	14	1	0	1	0	1	18	7	3	6	4	0	16	1	0	0	0	0	1	.318	.388	.409	.797
2022 ChC	NL	101	251	59	5	2	3	1	2	77	27	25	31	29	1	87	4	1	2	6	1	1	.235	.322	.307	.628
2 ML YEARS		119	295	73	6	2	4	1	3	95	34	28	37	33	1	103	5	1	2	6	1	2	.247	.331	.322	.653

Emmanuel Rivera

Bats: R Throws: R Pos: 3B-86;PH-10;DH-8;1B-5   Ht: 6'2" Wt: 225 Born: 6/29/1996 Age: 27

Year Team	Lg	G	AB	H	2B	3B	HR	Hm	Rd	TB	R	RBI	RC	TBB	IBB	SO	HBP	SH	SF	SB	CS	GDP	Avg	OBP	Slg	OPS
2022 Omha	AAA	20	75	23	5	1	3	-	-	39	12	5	14	10	0	16	0	0	0	1	0	2	.307	.388	.520	.908
2021 KC	AL	29	90	23	4	0	1	0	1	30	13	5	9	8	0	21	0	0	0	2	0	2	.256	.316	.333	.650
2022 2 Tms		102	330	77	16	3	12	5	7	135	46	40	37	23	0	83	5	0	1	1	2	8	.233	.292	.409	.702
22 KC	AL	63	198	47	8	3	6	2	4	79	24	22	19	11	0	46	2	0	0	0	0	7	.237	.284	.399	.683
22 Ari	NL	39	132	30	8	0	6	3	3	56	22	18	18	12	0	37	3	0	1	1	2	1	.227	.304	.424	.728
2 ML YEARS		131	420	100	20	3	13	5	8	165	59	45	46	31	0	104	5	0	1	3	2	10	.238	.298	.393	.690

Sebastian Rivero

Bats: R Throws: R Pos: C-17;PR-1   Ht: 6'1" Wt: 210 Born: 11/16/1998 Age: 24

Year Team	Lg	G	AB	H	2B	3B	HR	Hm	Rd	TB	R	RBI	RC	TBB	IBB	SO	HBP	SH	SF	SB	CS	GDP	Avg	OBP	Slg	OPS
2022 NWArk	AA	42	156	34	15	0	5	-	-	64	22	27	19	15	0	38	3	1	3	1	0	3	.218	.294	.410	.704
2021 KC	AL	17	40	7	2	0	0	0	0	9	1	3	0	3	0	15	1	0	0	0	0	1	.175	.250	.225	.475
2022 KC	AL	17	26	4	0	0	0	0	0	4	2	1	1	2	0	10	0	1	0	0	0	0	.154	.214	.154	.368
2 ML YEARS		34	66	11	2	0	0	0	0	13	3	4	1	5	0	25	1	1	0	0	0	1	.167	.236	.197	.433

Anthony Rizzo

Bats: L Throws: L Pos: 1B-120;DH-9;PH-5   Ht: 6'3" Wt: 240 Born: 8/8/1989 Age: 33

Year Team	Lg	G	AB	H	2B	3B	HR	Hm	Rd	TB	R	RBI	RC	TBB	IBB	SO	HBP	SH	SF	SB	CS	GDP	Avg	OBP	Slg	OPS
2011 SD	NL	49	128	18	8	1	1	1	0	31	9	9	7	21	1	46	4	0	0	2	1	2	.141	.281	.242	.523
2012 ChC	NL	87	337	96	15	0	15	7	8	156	44	48	57	27	1	62	3	0	1	3	2	7	.285	.342	.463	.805
2013 ChC	NL	160	606	141	40	2	23	13	10	254	71	80	74	76	7	127	6	0	2	6	5	12	.233	.323	.419	.742
2014 ChC	NL	140	524	150	28	1	32	14	**18**	276	89	78	99	73	7	116	15	0	4	5	4	8	.286	.386	.527	.913
2015 ChC	NL	160	586	163	38	3	31	11	20	300	94	101	115	78	9	105	**30**	0	7	17	6	9	.278	.387	.512	.899
2016 ChC	NL	155	583	170	43	4	32	12	20	317	94	109	119	74	8	108	16	0	3	3	5	13	.292	.385	.544	.928
2017 ChC	NL	157	572	156	32	3	32	15	17	290	99	109	116	91	11	90	**24**	0	4	10	4	21	.273	.392	.507	.899
2018 ChC	NL	153	566	160	29	1	25	11	14	266	74	101	97	70	15	80	20	0	9	6	4	11	.283	.376	.470	.846
2019 ChC	NL	146	512	150	29	3	27	13	14	266	89	94	111	71	3	86	**27**	0	3	5	2	15	.293	.405	.520	.924
2020 ChC	NL	58	203	45	6	0	11	4	7	84	26	24	25	28	4	38	10	0	2	3	1	6	.222	.342	.414	.755
2021 2 Tms		141	496	123	23	3	22	10	12	218	73	61	75	52	2	59	23	0	5	6	2	15	.248	.344	.440	.783
2022 NYY	AL	130	465	104	21	1	32	19	13	223	77	75	76	58	6	101	23	0	2	6	5	13	.224	.338	.480	.817
21 ChC	NL	92	323	80	16	3	14	7	7	144	41	40	49	36	2	43	14	0	3	4	2	10	.248	.346	.446	.792
21 NYY	AL	49	173	43	7	0	8	3	5	74	32	21	26	16	0	16	9	0	2	2	0	5	.249	.340	.428	.768
Postseason		40	150	31	6	0	7	3	4	58	17	19	17	12	2	40	4	0	0	2	0	4	.207	.283	.387	.670
12 ML YEARS		1536	5578	1476	312	22	283	132	151	2681	839	889	971	719	74	1046	201	0	42	72	41	132	.265	.366	.481	.847

Luis Robert

Bats: R Throws: R Pos: CF-91;PR-5;DH-4   Ht: 6'2" Wt: 220 Born: 8/3/1997 Age: 25

Year Team	Lg	G	AB	H	2B	3B	HR	Hm	Rd	TB	R	RBI	RC	TBB	IBB	SO	HBP	SH	SF	SB	CS	GDP	Avg	OBP	Slg	OPS
2020 CWS	AL	56	202	47	8	0	11	6	5	88	33	31	30	20	0	73	1	0	2	9	2	4	.233	.302	.436	.738
2021 CWS	AL	68	275	93	22	1	13	8	5	156	42	43	53	14	1	61	5	0	2	6	1	4	.338	.378	.567	.946
2022 CWS	AL	98	380	108	18	0	12	6	6	162	54	56	56	17	1	77	3	0	1	11	3	6	.284	.319	.426	.746
Postseason		7	28	11	0	0	1	0	1	14	6	3	4	2	0	6	1	0	0	0	1	0	.393	.452	.500	.952
3 ML YEARS		222	857	248	48	1	36	20	16	406	129	130	139	51	2	211	9	0	5	26	6	14	.289	.334	.474	.808

Ethan Roberts

Pitches: R Bats: R Pos: RP-9   Ht: 5'10" Wt: 180 Born: 7/4/1997 Age: 25

Year Team	Lg	G	GS	GF	IP	BFP	H	R	ER	HR	SH	SF	HB	TBB	IBB	SO	WP	W	L	Pct	Sv-Op	Hld	Vel	OPS	ERC	ERA
2022 ChC	NL	9	0	3	7.2	38	10	7	7	3	0	0	1	6	0	9	0	0	1	.000	0-0	1	94	1.189	11.21	8.22

David Robertson

Pitches: R Bats: R Pos: RP-58   Ht: 5'11" Wt: 195 Born: 4/9/1985 Age: 38

Year Team	Lg	G	GS	GF	IP	BFP	H	R	ER	HR	SH	SF	HB	TBB	IBB	SO	WP	W	L	Pct	Sv-Op	Hld	Vel	OPS	ERC	ERA
2008 NYY	AL	25	0	8	30.1	131	29	18	18	3	0	3	0	15	2	36	6	4	0	1.000	0-0	0	91	.690	4.12	5.34
2009 NYY	AL	45	0	20	43.2	191	36	19	16	4	0	0	1	23	1	63	6	2	1	.667	1-1	5	92	.685	3.51	3.30
2010 NYY	AL	64	0	10	61.1	273	59	26	26	5	5	3	3	33	6	71	7	4	5	.444	1-3	14	92	.721	4.29	3.82
2011 NYY	AL	70	0	8	66.2	272	40	9	8	1	1	0	1	35	6	100	6	4	0	1.000	1-4	34	93	.506	1.85	1.08
2012 NYY	AL	65	0	17	60.2	248	52	19	18	5	0	1	1	19	0	81	1	2	7	.222	2-5	30	92	.638	2.95	2.67

Year	Team	Lg	G	GS	GF	IP	BFP	H	R	ER	HR	SH	SF	HB	TBB	IBB	SO	WP	W	L	Pct	Sv-Op	Hld	Vel	OPS	ERC	ERA
2013	NYY	AL	70	0	9	66.1	262	51	15	15	5	3	0	2	18	1	77	1	5	1	.833	3-5	33	92	.584	2.37	2.04
2014	NYY	AL	63	0	55	64.1	259	45	23	22	7	1	0	1	23	2	96	0	4	5	.444	39-44	5	92	.588	2.41	3.08
2015	CWS	AL	60	0	53	63.1	250	46	27	24	7	0	0	1	13	2	86	4	6	5	.545	34-41	0	92	.573	2.00	3.41
2016	CWS	AL	62	0	48	62.1	267	53	24	24	6	3	2	1	32	4	75	1	5	3	.625	37-44	0	91	.684	3.63	3.47
2017	2 Tms	AL	61	0	34	68.1	264	35	14	14	6	0	1	3	23	5	98	7	9	2	.818	14-16	8	91	.488	1.50	1.84
2018	NYY	AL	69	0	11	69.2	283	46	30	25	7	4	1	0	26	1	91	1	8	3	.727	5-9	21	92	.595	2.15	3.23
2019	Phi	NL	7	0	3	6.2	33	8	4	4	1	0	0	0	6	0	6	0	0	1	.000	0-0	2	92	.869	7.88	5.40
2021	TB	AL	12	1	1	12.0	50	11	7	6	2	0	0	4	4	0	16	0	0	0	-	0-2	2	92	.713	3.81	4.50
2022	2 Tms	NL	58	0	33	63.2	264	39	18	17	6	0	1	3	35	1	81	4	4	3	.571	20-28	3	93	.589	2.69	2.40
17	CWS	AL	31	0	28	33.1	132	21	10	10	4	0	0	2	11	3	47	3	4	2	.667	13-14	0	91	.577	2.14	2.70
17	NYY	AL	30	0	6	35.0	132	14	4	4	2	0	1	1	12	2	51	4	5	0	1.000	1-2	8	92	.399	1.05	1.03
22	ChC	NL	36	0	22	40.1	165	23	10	10	4	0	1	3	19	0	51	2	3	0	1.000	14-19	0	93	.554	2.35	2.23
22	Phi	NL	22	0	11	23.1	99	16	8	7	2	0	0	0	16	1	30	2	1	3	.250	6-9	3	92	.649	3.32	2.70
	Postseason		33	0	9	37.2	152	29	13	13	4	1	0	1	11	3	42	2	5	0	1.000	0-1	3	92	.631	2.48	3.11
	14 ML YEARS		731	1	310	739.1	3047	550	253	237	65	17	12	17	305	31	977	44	57	36	.613	157-202	152	92	.611	2.70	2.89

Kramer Robertson

Bats: R **Throws:** R **Pos:** SS-1;PH-1;PR-1   **Ht:** 5'10" **Wt:** 166 **Born:** 9/20/1994 **Age:** 28

						BATTING										RUNNING			AVERAGES			
Year	Team	Lg	G	AB	H	2B	3B	HR	(Hm Rd)	TB	R	RBI	RC	TBB	IBB	SO	HBP	SH	SF	SB	CS	GDP	Avg	OBP	Slg	OPS

Year	Team	Lg	G	AB	H	2B	3B	HR	(Hm	Rd)	TB	R	RBI	RC	TBB	IBB	SO	HBP	SH	SF	SB	CS	GDP	Avg	OBP	Slg	OPS
2022	Memp	AAA	81	285	65	13	0	9	(-	-)	105	56	34	46	60	0	79	15	0	0	22	3	7	.228	.389	.368	.757
2022	Gwnntt	AAA	13	50	15	3	0	1	(-	-)	21	9	6	7	7	0	10	1	0	0	4	3	2	.300	.397	.420	.817
2022	Syrcse	AAA	22	75	18	0	1	1	(-	-)	23	16	7	10	17	0	14	4	0	0	4	2	1	.240	.406	.307	.713
2022	StL	NL	2	1	0	0	0	0	(0	0)	0	0	1	0	0	0	0	0	0	0	0	0	0	.000	.000	.000	.000

Chuckie Robinson

Bats: R **Throws:** R **Pos:** C-25   **Ht:** 5'11" **Wt:** 221 **Born:** 12/14/1994 **Age:** 28

Year	Team	Lg	G	AB	H	2B	3B	HR	(Hm	Rd)	TB	R	RBI	RC	TBB	IBB	SO	HBP	SH	SF	SB	CS	GDP	Avg	OBP	Slg	OPS
2022	Lsvlle	AAA	27	87	22	5	1	2	(-	-)	35	11	12	10	5	0	19	1	0	0	0	0	1	.253	.301	.402	.703
2022	Chatt	AA	31	116	32	5	0	3	(-	-)	46	13	13	14	9	0	30	1	0	0	4	2	3	.276	.333	.397	.730
2022	Cin	NL	25	59	8	2	0	2	(2	0)	16	3	5	0	0	0	17	0	1	0	0	0	5	.136	.136	.271	.407

Hansel Robles

Pitches: R **Bats:** R **Pos:** RP-26   **Ht:** 6'0" **Wt:** 220 **Born:** 8/13/1990 **Age:** 32

Year	Team	Lg	G	GS	GF	IP	BFP	H	R	ER	HR	SH	SF	HB	TBB	IBB	SO	WP	W	L	Pct	Sv-Op	Hld	Vel	OPS	ERC	ERA
2022	OkCity	AAA	20	1	1	18.0	85	16	16	16	2	0	1	1	14	0	18	1	1	0	1.000	0- -	-	-	.742	5.12	8.00
2015	NYM	NL	57	0	7	54.0	217	37	27	22	8	1	1	2	18	1	61	2	4	3	.571	0-4	12	96	.659	2.57	3.67
2016	NYM	NL	68	0	15	77.2	331	69	32	30	7	1	5	1	36	4	85	3	6	4	.600	1-3	13	95	.703	3.62	3.48
2017	NYM	NL	46	0	9	56.2	247	47	31	31	10	3	2	5	29	2	60	2	7	5	.583	0-2	5	95	.750	4.38	4.92
2018	2 Tms		53	0	14	56.0	242	53	26	23	9	2	3	2	25	1	59	2	2	3	.400	2-3	8	96	.771	4.53	3.70
2019	LAA	AL	71	1	51	72.2	283	58	20	20	6	2	3	0	16	1	75	4	5	1	.833	23-27	2	97	.595	2.28	2.48
2020	LAA	AL	18	0	5	16.2	80	19	20	19	4	1	1	1	10	0	20	1	0	2	.000	1-3	0	96	.917	6.96	10.26
2021	2 Tms	AL	72	0	21	69.0	297	58	39	34	8	1	0	5	37	3	76	4	3	5	.375	14-16	17	97	.735	4.10	4.43
2022	Bos	AL	26	0	8	24.2	111	25	19	16	5	0	1	0	14	1	21	0	1	3	.250	2-8	7	96	.831	5.52	5.84
18	NYM	NL	16	0	3	19.2	88	21	11	11	7	1	1	1	10	1	23	1	2	2	.500	0-0	2	95	.981	7.12	5.03
18	LAA	AL	37	0	11	36.1	154	32	15	12	2	1	2	1	15	0	36	1	0	1	.000	2-3	6	97	.654	3.27	2.97
21	Min	AL	45	0	16	44.0	188	37	28	24	6	1	0	3	24	1	43	2	3	4	.429	10-12	14	97	.761	4.35	4.91
21	Bos	AL	27	0	5	25.0	109	21	11	10	2	0	0	2	13	2	33	2	0	1	.000	4-4	3	97	.692	3.68	3.60
	Postseason		9	0	2	8.1	31	7	4	3	2	0	0	0	1	0	9	0	0	1	.000	0-1	0	97	.758	3.14	3.24
	8 ML YEARS		411	1	130	427.1	1808	366	214	195	57	11	16	16	185	13	457	18	28	26	.519	43-66	64	96	.718	3.76	4.11

Victor Robles

Bats: R **Throws:** R **Pos:** CF-128;PR-7;DH-2   **Ht:** 6'0" **Wt:** 195 **Born:** 5/19/1997 **Age:** 26

Year	Team	Lg	G	AB	H	2B	3B	HR	(Hm	Rd)	TB	R	RBI	RC	TBB	IBB	SO	HBP	SH	SF	SB	CS	GDP	Avg	OBP	Slg	OPS
2017	Was	NL	13	24	6	1	2	0	(0	0)	11	2	4	3	0	0	6	2	1	0	0	1	2	.250	.308	.458	.766
2018	Was	NL	21	59	17	3	1	3	(2	1)	31	8	10	10	4	0	12	2	0	1	3	2	2	.288	.348	.525	.874
2019	Was	NL	155	546	139	33	3	17	(10	7)	229	86	65	79	35	3	140	25	6	5	28	9	6	.255	.326	.419	.745
2020	Was	NL	52	168	37	5	1	3	(2	1)	53	20	15	18	9	0	53	9	1	2	4	1	0	.220	.293	.315	.608
2021	Was	NL	107	316	64	21	1	2	(2	0)	93	37	19	30	33	3	85	16	4	1	6	6	7	.203	.310	.295	.605
2022	Was	NL	132	366	82	10	2	6	(5	1)	114	42	33	28	17	0	104	9	11	4	15	4	3	.224	.273	.311	.584
	Postseason		14	42	9	1	1	1	(1	0)	15	9	3	3	2	0	16	1	1	0	1	0	2	.214	.267	.357	.624
	6 ML YEARS		480	1478	345	73	10	31	(21	10)	531	195	146	168	98	6	400	63	23	13	58	23	20	.233	.306	.359	.666

Brendan Rodgers

Bats: R **Throws:** R **Pos:** 2B-134;DH-2   **Ht:** 6'0" **Wt:** 204 **Born:** 8/9/1996 **Age:** 26

Year	Team	Lg	G	AB	H	2B	3B	HR	(Hm	Rd)	TB	R	RBI	RC	TBB	IBB	SO	HBP	SH	SF	SB	CS	GDP	Avg	OBP	Slg	OPS
2019	Col	NL	25	76	17	2	0	0	(0	0)	19	8	7	5	4	0	27	1	0	0	0	0	2	.224	.272	.250	.522
2020	Col	NL	7	21	2	1	0	0	(0	0)	3	1	2	0	0	0	6	0	0	0	0	0	0	.095	.095	.143	.238
2021	Col	NL	102	387	110	21	3	15	(3	12)	182	49	51	58	19	0	84	7	0	2	0	0	8	.284	.328	.470	.798
2022	Col	NL	137	527	140	30	3	13	(10	3)	215	72	63	64	46	0	101	3	0	5	0	0	25	.266	.325	.408	.733
	4 ML YEARS		271	1011	269	54	6	28	(13	15)	419	130	123	127	69	0	218	11	0	7	0	0	35	.266	.318	.414	.732

Carlos Rodon

Pitches: L Bats: L Pos: SP-31   roh-DON   Ht: 6'3" Wt: 245 Born: 12/10/1992 Age: 30

Year	Team	Lg	G	GS	GF	IP	BFP	H	R	ER	HR	SH	SF	HB	TBB	IBB	SO	WP	W	L	Pct	Sv-Op	Hld	Vel	OPS	ERC	ERA
2015	CWS	AL	26	23	1	139.1	607	130	63	58	11	6	5	8	71	0	139	7	9	6	.600	0-0	0	93	.725	4.25	3.75
2016	CWS	AL	28	28	0	165.0	715	176	82	74	23	4	6	6	54	3	168	11	9	10	.474	0-0	0	93	.763	4.57	4.04
2017	CWS	AL	12	12	0	69.1	297	64	35	32	12	1	2	3	31	0	76	4	2	5	.286	0-0	0	93	.770	4.57	4.15
2018	CWS	AL	20	20	0	120.2	511	97	61	56	15	0	2	12	55	1	90	4	6	8	.429	0-0	0	93	.698	3.80	4.18
2019	CWS	AL	7	7	0	34.2	158	33	22	20	4	0	2	1	17	0	46	5	3	2	.600	0-0	0	92	.714	4.19	5.19
2020	CWS	AL	4	2	0	7.2	35	9	7	7	1	0	0	1	3	0	6	1	0	2	.000	0-1	0	93	.920	5.87	8.22
2021	CWS	AL	24	24	0	132.2	534	91	39	35	13	3	5	8	36	1	185	7	13	5	.722	0-0	0	95	.560	2.14	2.37
2022	SF	NL	31	31	0	178.0	710	131	59	57	12	2	3	3	52	0	237	10	14	8	.636	0-0	0	96	.571	2.17	2.88
	Postseason		2	1	0	2.2	17	4	4	4	0	0	0	1	4	1	3	0	0	1	.000	0-0	0	96	1.113	11.43	13.50
	8 ML YEARS		152	147	1	847.1	3567	731	368	339	91	16	25	42	319	5	947	49	56	46	.549	0-1	0	94	.678	3.47	3.60

Dereck Rodriguez

Pitches: R Bats: R Pos: RP-2   Ht: 6'0" Wt: 208 Born: 6/5/1992 Age: 31

Year	Team	Lg	G	GS	GF	IP	BFP	H	R	ER	HR	SH	SF	HB	TBB	IBB	SO	WP	W	L	Pct	Sv-Op	Hld	Vel	OPS	ERC	ERA
2022	StPaul	AAA	23	16	1	94.2	405	93	54	50	13	1	3	3	32	0	92	6	8	4	.667	0- -	-		.757	4.10	4.75
2018	SF	NL	21	19	1	118.1	487	98	43	37	9	2	3	7	36	2	89	1	6	4	.600	0-0	0	91	.667	2.84	2.81
2019	SF	NL	28	16	4	99.0	439	108	74	62	21	3	0	2	36	0	71	1	6	11	.353	0-0	0	91	.827	5.28	5.64
2020	SF	NL	2	0	0	4.0	24	10	6	6	2	0	0	0	3	0	2	0	0	0		0-0	0	93	1.399	21.06	13.50
2022	Min	AL	2	0	1	7.2	34	7	5	3	3	2	0	0	4	1	4	0	0	1	.000	0-0	0	92	.915	5.83	3.52
	4 ML YEARS		53	35	6	229.0	984	223	128	108	35	7	3	9	79	3	166	2	12	16	.429	0-0	0	91	.764	4.19	4.24

Eduardo Rodriguez

Pitches: L Bats: L Pos: SP-17   Ht: 6'2" Wt: 231 Born: 4/7/1993 Age: 30

Year	Team	Lg	G	GS	GF	IP	BFP	H	R	ER	HR	SH	SF	HB	TBB	IBB	SO	WP	W	L	Pct	Sv-Op	Hld	Vel	OPS	ERC	ERA
2015	Bos	AL	21	21	0	121.2	522	120	55	52	13	5	4	4	37	1	98	4	10	6	.625	0-0	0	94	.701	3.73	3.85
2016	Bos	AL	20	20	0	107.0	458	99	58	56	16	1	4	3	40	1	100	0	3	7	.300	0-0	0	93	.728	3.96	4.71
2017	Bos	AL	25	24	0	137.1	582	126	66	64	19	1	3	5	50	1	150	1	6	7	.462	0-0	0	93	.736	3.87	4.19
2018	Bos	AL	27	23	0	129.2	553	119	56	55	16	0	3	4	45	1	146	1	13	5	.722	0-0	0	93	.681	3.63	3.82
2019	Bos	AL	34	34	0	203.1	859	195	88	86	24	2	5	7	75	2	213	3	19	6	.760	0-0	0	93	.714	4.03	3.81
2021	Bos	AL	32	31	0	157.2	675	172	87	83	19	2	2	2	47	0	185	0	13	8	.619	0-0	0	93	.766	4.41	4.74
2022	Det	AL	17	17	0	91.0	391	87	49	41	12	2	1	2	34	0	72	1	5	5	.500	0-0	0	92	.720	4.00	4.05
	Postseason		11	4	2	22.2	94	17	16	16	3	0	0	2	7	1	25	0	1	1	.500	0-0	1	93	.630	2.82	6.35
	7 ML YEARS		176	170	1	947.2	4040	918	459	437	119	13	22	27	328	6	964	10	69	44	.611	0-0	0	93	.722	3.96	4.15

Elvin Rodriguez

Pitches: R Bats: R Pos: SP-5; RP-2   Ht: 6'3" Wt: 160 Born: 3/31/1998 Age: 25

Year	Team	Lg	G	GS	GF	IP	BFP	H	R	ER	HR	SH	SF	HB	TBB	IBB	SO	WP	W	L	Pct	Sv-Op	Hld	Vel	OPS	ERC	ERA
2022	Toledo	AAA	23	21	0	99.1	441	115	58	55	17	0	7	4	36	0	91	4	6	4	.600	0- -	-		.841	5.57	4.98
2022	Det	AL	7	5	0	29.2	143	42	35	35	12	0	0	1	15	1	25	1	0	4	.000	0-0	0	93	1.091	9.85	10.62

Grayson Rodriguez

Pitches: R Bats: L Pos: P   Ht: 6'5" Wt: 220 Born: 11/16/1999 Age: 23

Year	Team	Lg	G	GS	GF	IP	BFP	H	R	ER	HR	SH	SF	HB	TBB	IBB	SO	WP	W	L	Pct	Sv-Op	Hld	Vel	OPS	ERC	ERA
2018	Orioles	R	9	8	0	19.1	80	17	6	3	0	0	1	0	7	0	20	1	0	2	.000	0- -	-		.674	2.64	1.40
2019	Dlmrva	A	20	20	0	94.0	377	57	30	28	4	0	4	6	36	0	129	6	10	4	.714	0- -	-		.340	1.88	2.68
2021	Abrdn	A+	5	5	0	23.1	88	11	4	4	2	0	0	3	5	0	40	1	3	0	1.000	0- -	-			1.35	1.54
2021	Bowie	AA	18	18	0	79.2	310	47	26	23	8	0	0	3	22	0	121	3	6	1	.857	0- -	-		.539	1.70	2.60
2022	Norfolk	AAA	14	14	0	69.2	271	44	17	17	2	0	2	1	21	0	97	2	6	1	.857	0- -	-		.507	1.57	2.20

Joely Rodriguez

Pitches: L Bats: L Pos: RP-55   joe-EL-ee   Ht: 6'1" Wt: 200 Born: 11/14/1991 Age: 31

Year	Team	Lg	G	GS	GF	IP	BFP	H	R	ER	HR	SH	SF	HB	TBB	IBB	SO	WP	W	L	Pct	Sv-Op	Hld	Vel	OPS	ERC	ERA
2016	Phi	NL	12	0	1	9.2	39	8	3	3	0	0	0	1	4	1	7	0	0	0	-	0-0	3	95	.598	2.91	2.79
2017	Phi	NL	26	0	4	27.0	134	37	26	19	4	1	0	4	15	3	18	0	1	2	.333	0-2	3	95	.930	7.81	6.33
2020	Tex	AL	12	0	2	12.2	52	8	3	3	0	1	0	0	5	0	17	1	0	0	-	0-1	3	95	.494	1.56	2.13
2021	2 Tms	AL	52	0	8	46.1	207	53	27	24	4	2	5	0	18	1	47	3	2	3	.400	1-3	13	94	.739	4.67	4.66
2022	NYM	NL	55	0	9	50.1	216	42	28	25	3	2	1	1	26	1	57	2	4	4	.333	0-0	9	93	.634	3.37	4.47
21	Tex	AL	31	0	6	27.1	128	32	19	18	3	1	2	0	12	1	30	1	1	3	.250	1-2	9	94	.748	5.01	5.93
21	NYY	AL	21	0	2	19.0	79	21	8	6	1	1	3	0	6	0	17	2	1	0	1.000	0-1	4	94	.723	4.18	2.84
	5 ML YEARS		157	0	24	146.0	648	148	87	74	11	6	6	6	68	6	146	6	5	9	.357	1-6	31	94	.715	4.30	4.56

Julio Rodriguez

Bats: R Throws: R Pos: CF-130;DH-1;PH-1   Ht: 6'3" Wt: 228 Born: 12/29/2000 Age: 22

Year	Team	Lg	G	AB	H	2B	3B	HR	(Hm	Rd)	TB	R	RBI	RC	TBB	IBB	SO	HBP	SH	SF	SB	CS	GDP	Avg	OBP	Slg	OPS
2019	2 Tms	Low	84	328	107	26	4	12	(-	-)	177	63	69	68	25	1	76	11	0	3	1	3	10	.326	.390	.540	.929
2021	Ark	AA	46	174	63	11	0	7	(-	-)	95	35	26	44	29	1	37	3	0	0	16	4	2	.362	.461	.546	1.007
2021	Everett	A+	28	117	38	8	2	6	(-	-)	68	29	21	0	14	0	29	3	0	0	5	1	3	.325	.410	.581	.992
2022	Sea	AL	132	511	145	25	3	28	(15	13)	260	84	75	92	40	4	145	8	0	1	25	7	7	.284	.345	.509	.853

Manuel Rodriguez

Pitches: R Bats: R Pos: RP-14   Ht: 5'11" Wt: 210 Born: 8/6/1996 Age: 26

Year	Team	Lg	G	GS	GF	IP	BFP	H	R	ER	HR	SH	SF	HB	TBB	IBB	SO	WP	W	L	Pct	Sv-Op	Hld	Vel	OPS	ERC	ERA
2022	Iowa	AAA	5	0	2	5.0	23	8	5	5	2	0	0	1	1	0	10	1	0	1	1.000	1- -	-	-	1.197	11.13	9.00
2021	ChC	NL	20	0	8	17.2	83	18	18	12	3	0	0	1	12	1	16	1	3	3	.500	1-1	1	97	.816	5.94	6.11
2022	ChC	NL	14	0	5	13.2	57	10	6	5	1	0	0	0	9	0	8	2	2	0	1.000	4-6	2	96	.687	3.53	3.29
	2 ML YEARS		34	0	13	31.1	140	28	24	17	4	0	0	1	21	1	24	3	5	3	.625	5-7	3	97	.764	4.86	4.88

Yerry Rodriguez

Pitches: R Bats: R Pos: RP-1   Ht: 6'2" Wt: 198 Born: 10/15/1997 Age: 25

Year	Team	Lg	G	GS	GF	IP	BFP	H	R	ER	HR	SH	SF	HB	TBB	IBB	SO	WP	W	L	Pct	Sv-Op	Hld	Vel	OPS	ERC	ERA
2022	RdRck	AAA	49	5	16	59.0	268	60	31	28	9	0	4	2	32	0	73	2	4	1	.800	4- -	-	-	.794	5.22	4.27
2022	Tex	AL	1	0	0	1.0	4	1	0	0	0	0	0	0	0	0	1	1	0	0		0-0	1	-	.500	1.95	0.00

Jake Rogers

Bats: R Throws: R Pos: C   Ht: 6'1" Wt: 201 Born: 4/18/1995 Age: 28

Year	Team	Lg	G	AB	H	2B	3B	HR	(Hm	Rd)	TB	R	RBI	RC	TBB	IBB	SO	HBP	SH	SF	SB	CS	GDP	Avg	OBP	Slg	OPS
2019	Det	AL	35	112	14	3	0	4	(3	1)	29	11	8	4	13	0	51	1	2	0	0	0	3	.125	.222	.259	.481
2021	Det	AL	38	113	27	5	3	6	(3	3)	56	17	17	17	11	0	46	0	3	0	1	0	0	.239	.306	.496	.802
	2 ML YEARS		73	225	41	8	3	10	(6	4)	85	28	25	21	24	0	97	1	5	0	1	0	3	.182	.264	.378	.642

Josh Rogers

Pitches: L Bats: L Pos: RP-13; SP-3   Ht: 6'3" Wt: 211 Born: 7/10/1994 Age: 28

Year	Team	Lg	G	GS	GF	IP	BFP	H	R	ER	HR	SH	SF	HB	TBB	IBB	SO	WP	W	L	Pct	Sv-Op	Hld	Vel	OPS	ERC	ERA
2022	Jaxnvl	AAA	9	9	0	47.1	207	47	26	25	6	0	1	3	21	0	32	0	4	4	.500	0- -	-	-	.777	4.70	4.75
2018	Bal	AL	3	3	0	11.2	56	17	11	11	2	0	1	0	5	0	6	0	1	2	.333	0-0	0	90	.953	7.52	8.49
2019	Bal	AL	5	0	1	14.1	69	18	14	14	7	0	0	4	6	0	5	0	0	1	.000	0-0	0	89	1.118	10.35	8.79
2021	Was	NL	6	6	0	35.2	151	32	13	13	7	1	1	2	14	0	22	0	2	2	.500	0-0	0	90	.756	4.40	3.28
2022	Was	NL	16	3	4	26.1	113	24	15	15	6	1	0	0	11	0	12	0	2	2	.500	0-0	1	90	.758	4.48	5.13
	4 ML YEARS		30	12	5	88.0	389	91	53	53	22	2	2	6	36	0	45	0	5	7	.417	0-0	1	90	.848	5.70	5.42

Taylor Rogers

Pitches: L Bats: L Pos: RP-66   Ht: 6'3" Wt: 190 Born: 12/17/1990 Age: 32

Year	Team	Lg	G	GS	GF	IP	BFP	H	R	ER	HR	SH	SF	HB	TBB	IBB	SO	WP	W	L	Pct	Sv-Op	Hld	Vel	OPS	ERC	ERA
2016	Min	AL	57	0	8	61.1	264	63	29	27	7	0	1	5	16	3	64	1	3	1	.750	0-0	9	93	.719	3.99	3.96
2017	Min	AL	69	0	7	55.2	237	52	20	19	6	2	0	3	21	5	49	1	7	3	.700	0-4	30	93	.693	3.76	3.07
2018	Min	AL	72	0	6	68.1	260	49	20	20	3	1	3	2	16	3	75	0	1	2	.333	2-4	18	93	.553	1.83	2.63
2019	Min	AL	60	0	36	69.0	278	58	20	20	8	3	0	6	11	2	90	2	2	4	.333	30-36	10	95	.625	2.70	2.61
2020	Min	AL	21	0	16	20.0	91	26	14	9	2	0	0	1	4	0	24	1	2	4	.333	9-11	2	95	.806	5.07	4.05
2021	Min	AL	40	0	15	40.1	166	38	18	15	4	2	2	0	8	2	59	3	2	4	.333	9-13	8	96	.651	2.88	3.35
2022	2 Tms	NL	66	0	40	64.1	274	57	38	34	7	1	4	11	19	2	84	1	4	8	.333	31-41	4	94	.725	3.72	4.76
22	SD	NL	42	0	35	41.1	174	37	22	20	1	0	2	8	9	1	48	0	1	5	.167	28-35	0	95	.659	3.00	4.35
22	Mil	NL	24	0	5	23.0	100	20	16	14	6	1	2	3	10	1	36	1	3	3	.500	3-6	4	94	.845	5.09	5.48
	Postseason		4	0	0	3.1	14	4	2	2	0	0	0	0	1	0	4	0	0	0		0-0	0	95	.742	4.29	5.40
	7 ML YEARS		385	0	128	379.0	1570	343	159	144	37	9	10	28	95	17	445	9	21	26	.447	81-109	81	94	.670	3.20	3.42

Trevor Rogers

Pitches: L Bats: L Pos: SP-23   Ht: 6'5" Wt: 217 Born: 11/13/1997 Age: 25

Year	Team	Lg	G	GS	GF	IP	BFP	H	R	ER	HR	SH	SF	HB	TBB	IBB	SO	WP	W	L	Pct	Sv-Op	Hld	Vel	OPS	ERC	ERA
2020	Mia	NL	7	7	0	28.0	130	32	20	19	5	0	2	2	13	0	39	0	1	2	.333	0-0	0	94	.866	5.99	6.11
2021	Mia	NL	25	25	0	133.0	550	107	46	39	6	6	2	5	46	2	157	4	7	8	.467	0-0	0	95	.609	2.58	2.64
2022	Mia	NL	23	23	0	107.0	477	116	69	65	15	0	4	5	45	0	106	5	4	11	.267	0-0	0	95	.816	5.12	5.47
	Postseason		1	0	0	1.2	10	4	3	2	0	0	0	1	1	0	2	0	0	0		0-0	0	96	1.167	13.02	10.80
	3 ML YEARS		55	55	0	268.0	1157	255	135	123	26	6	8	12	104	2	302	9	12	21	.364	0-0	0	94	.723	3.88	4.13

Tyler Rogers

Pitches: R Bats: R Pos: RP-68   Ht: 6'3" Wt: 181 Born: 12/17/1990 Age: 32

			HOW MUCH PITCHED					WHAT HE GAVE UP										THE RESULTS						
Year	Team	Lg	G	GS	GF	IP	BFP	H	R	ER	HR	SH	SF	HB	TBB	IBB	SO	WP	W	L	Pct	Sv-Op	Hld	Vel	OPS	ERC	ERA
2019	SF	NL	17	0	4	17.2	70	12	3	2	0	1	0	1	3	0	16	1	2	0	1.000	0-2	5	82	.463	1.37	1.02
2020	SF	NL	29	0	6	28.0	123	31	16	14	2	1	0	4	6	0	27	0	3	3	.500	3-6	10	83	.711	4.27	4.50
2021	SF	NL	80	0	18	81.0	326	74	23	20	5	1	2	5	13	0	55	0	7	1	.875	13-19	30	83	.611	2.73	2.22
2022	SF	NL	68	0	8	75.2	319	73	34	30	3	0	2	5	23	0	49	1	3	4	.429	0-1	15	83	.682	3.38	3.57
Postseason			4	0	0	3.1	16	5	0	0	0	0	1	0	1	0	1	0	1	0	1.000	0-0	1	82	.732	5.66	0.00
4 ML YEARS			194	0	36	202.1	838	190	76	66	10	3	4	15	45	0	147	2	15	8	.652	16-28	60	83	.640	3.03	2.94

Jose Rojas

Bats: L Throws: R Pos: 3B-12;RF-6;PH-6;LF-1;PR-1   Ht: 6'0" Wt: 200 Born: 2/24/1993 Age: 30

									BATTING											RUNNING			AVERAGES			
Year	Team	Lg	G	AB	H	2B	3B	HR	(Hm	Rd)	TB	R	RBI	RC	TBB	IBB	SO	HBP	SH	SF	SB	CS	GDP	Avg	OBP	Slg	OPS
2022	Salt Lk	AAA	62	247	68	13	3	18	(-	-)	141	46	50	54	29	0	58	1	0	3	5	2	2	.275	.350	.571	.921
2021	LAA	AL	61	168	35	14	0	6	(4	2)	67	26	15	18	15	0	50	1	0	0	2	1	2	.208	.277	.399	.676
2022	LAA	AL	22	56	7	2	0	0	(0	0)	9	1	1	0	0	0	19	1	0	0	0	0	1	.125	.140	.161	.301
2 ML YEARS			83	224	42	16	0	6	(4	2)	76	27	16	18	15	0	69	2	0	0	2	1	3	.188	.245	.339	.584

Josh Rojas

Bats: L Throws: R Pos: 3B-89;2B-26;PH-7;DH-5   Ht: 6'1" Wt: 207 Born: 6/30/1994 Age: 29

									BATTING											RUNNING			AVERAGES			
Year	Team	Lg	G	AB	H	2B	3B	HR	(Hm	Rd)	TB	R	RBI	RC	TBB	IBB	SO	HBP	SH	SF	SB	CS	GDP	Avg	OBP	Slg	OPS
2019	Ari	NL	41	138	30	7	0	2	(2	0)	43	17	16	15	18	0	41	1	0	0	4	2	3	.217	.312	.312	.624
2020	Ari	NL	17	61	11	0	0	0	(0	0)	11	9	2	2	7	0	16	0	0	0	1	1	1	.180	.257	.180	.437
2021	Ari	NL	139	484	128	32	3	11	(6	5)	199	69	44	66	58	1	137	0	1	3	9	4	7	.264	.341	.411	.752
2022	Ari	NL	125	443	119	25	1	9	(2	7)	173	66	56	69	55	2	98	2	5	5	23	3	7	.269	.349	.391	.739
4 ML YEARS			322	1126	288	64	4	22	(10	12)	426	161	118	152	138	3	292	3	6	10	37	10	18	.256	.336	.378	.714

Miguel Rojas

Bats: R Throws: R Pos: SS-136;1B-10;PH-3;PR-1   Ht: 6'0" Wt: 188 Born: 2/24/1989 Age: 34

									BATTING											RUNNING			AVERAGES			
Year	Team	Lg	G	AB	H	2B	3B	HR	(Hm	Rd)	TB	R	RBI	RC	TBB	IBB	SO	HBP	SH	SF	SB	CS	GDP	Avg	OBP	Slg	OPS
2014	LAD	NL	85	149	27	3	0	1	(0	1)	33	16	9	6	10	1	28	2	1	0	0	0	5	.181	.242	.221	.464
2015	Mia	NL	60	142	40	7	1	1	(1	0)	52	13	17	15	11	1	16	0	2	3	0	1	4	.282	.329	.366	.695
2016	Mia	NL	123	194	48	12	0	1	(0	1)	63	27	14	14	11	2	27	1	6	2	2	1	10	.247	.288	.325	.613
2017	Mia	NL	90	272	79	16	2	1	(1	0)	102	37	26	32	27	5	32	4	1	2	2	1	6	.290	.361	.375	.736
2018	Mia	NL	153	488	123	13	0	11	(4	7)	169	44	53	51	24	2	69	9	2	4	6	3	23	.252	.297	.346	.643
2019	Mia	NL	132	483	137	29	1	5	(3	2)	183	52	46	63	32	2	62	5	1	5	9	5	15	.284	.331	.379	.710
2020	Mia	NL	40	125	38	10	1	4	(2	2)	62	20	20	28	16	2	18	2	0	0	5	1	1	.304	.392	.496	.888
2021	Mia	NL	132	495	131	30	3	9	(4	5)	194	66	48	64	37	0	74	5	1	1	13	3	10	.265	.322	.392	.713
2022	Mia	NL	140	471	111	19	2	6	(3	3)	152	34	36	43	26	1	61	6	1	3	9	3	12	.236	.283	.323	.605
Postseason			6	19	3	0	0	1	(0	1)	6	2	1	0	1	1	3	1	0	0	0	0	0	.158	.238	.316	.554
9 ML YEARS			955	2819	734	139	10	39	(18	21)	1010	309	269	316	194	16	387	34	15	19	46	18	86	.260	.314	.358	.672

Jordan Romano

Pitches: R Bats: R Pos: RP-63   Ht: 6'5" Wt: 210 Born: 4/21/1993 Age: 30

			HOW MUCH PITCHED					WHAT HE GAVE UP										THE RESULTS						
Year	Team	Lg	G	GS	GF	IP	BFP	H	R	ER	HR	SH	SF	HB	TBB	IBB	SO	WP	W	L	Pct	Sv-Op	Hld	Vel	OPS	ERC	ERA
2019	Tor	AL	17	0	2	15.1	75	17	14	13	4	0	0	4	9	0	21	0	0	2	.000	0-0	5	95	.884	7.90	7.63
2020	Tor	AL	15	0	3	14.2	57	8	3	2	2	0	0	0	5	0	21	0	2	1	.667	2-3	5	97	.517	1.77	1.23
2021	Tor	AL	62	0	43	63.0	253	41	17	15	7	1	0	1	25	0	85	2	7	1	.875	23-24	5	98	.576	2.37	2.14
2022	Tor	AL	63	0	52	64.0	258	44	18	15	4	0	0	4	21	4	73	0	5	4	.556	36-42	2	97	.531	2.10	2.11
4 ML YEARS			157	0	100	157.0	643	110	52	45	17	1	0	9	60	4	200	2	14	8	.636	61-69	17	97	.587	2.64	2.58

Jhon Romero

Pitches: R Bats: R Pos: RP-4   Ht: 5'10" Wt: 195 Born: 1/17/1995 Age: 28

			HOW MUCH PITCHED					WHAT HE GAVE UP										THE RESULTS						
Year	Team	Lg	G	GS	GF	IP	BFP	H	R	ER	HR	SH	SF	HB	TBB	IBB	SO	WP	W	L	Pct	Sv-Op	Hld	Vel	OPS	ERC	ERA
2021	Was	NL	5	0	1	4.0	17	5	2	2	0	0	1	0	0	0	3	0	0	0	-	0-0	0	95	.857	3.14	4.50
2022	Min	AL	4	0	3	5.0	24	9	2	2	0	0	0	0	1	0	6	0	0	0	-	0-0	0	94	.895	7.40	3.60
2 ML YEARS			9	0	4	9.0	41	14	4	4	0	0	1	0	1	0	9	0	0	0	-	0-0	0	94	.879	5.37	4.00

JoJo Romero

Pitches: L Bats: L Pos: RP-17   Ht: 5'11" Wt: 200 Born: 9/9/1996 Age: 26

			HOW MUCH PITCHED					WHAT HE GAVE UP										THE RESULTS						
Year	Team	Lg	G	GS	GF	IP	BFP	H	R	ER	HR	SH	SF	HB	TBB	IBB	SO	WP	W	L	Pct	Sv-Op	Hld	Vel	OPS	ERC	ERA
2022	LV	AAA	5	0	1	4.0	15	3	0	0	0	0	0	0	0	0	3	0	0	0	-	0- -			.467	1.13	0.00
2020	Phi	NL	12	0	2	10.2	47	13	10	9	1	1	0	2	2	0	10	0	0	0	-	0-0	4	95	.822	5.30	7.59
2021	Phi	NL	11	0	1	9.0	44	12	8	7	4	0	0	1	4	1	8	0	0	0	-	0-0	3	94	1.053	9.26	7.00
2022	2 Tms	NL	17	0	5	16.1	67	13	9	9	3	1	0	0	10	0	17	0	0	0	-	0-0	0	95	.777	4.63	4.96
22	Phi	NL	2	0	1	2.0	10	4	3	3	1	0	0	0	1	0	1	0	0	0	-	0-0	0	95	1.278	16.25	13.50
22	StL	NL	15	0	4	14.1	57	9	6	6	2	1	0	0	9	0	16	0	0	0	-	0-0	0	95	.683	3.40	3.77
3 ML YEARS			40	0	8	36.0	158	38	27	25	8	2	0	3	16	1	35	0	0	0	-	0-0	7	95	.869	5.94	6.25

Tommy Romero

Pitches: R **Bats:** R **Pos:** SP-2; RP-2   **Ht:** 6'2" **Wt:** 225 **Born:** 7/8/1997 **Age:** 25

			HOW MUCH PITCHED					WHAT HE GAVE UP										THE RESULTS						
Year	Team	Lg	G	GS	GF	IP	BFP	H	R	ER	HR	SH	SF	HB	TBB	IBB	SO	WP	W	L	Pct	Sv-Op Hld	Vel	OPS	ERC	ERA
2022	Drhm	AAA	23	13	2	66.2	277	57	29	26	12	2	1	1	25	0	58	0	6	5	.545	1- -	-	.701	3.79	3.51
2022	Roch	AAA	6	2	1	19.1	79	13	5	5	4	0	1	0	9	0	14	0	3	1	.750	0- -	-	.655	3.24	2.33
2022	2 Tms		4	2	1	8.1	44	11	12	10	7	0	0	0	9	0	7	0	1	1	.500	0-0	0	90	1.426	16.34	10.80
22	TB	AL	3	1	1	4.2	21	3	4	4	2	0	0	0	5	0	5	0	1	0	1.000	0-0	0	90	.943	7.55	7.71
22	Was	NL	1	1	0	3.2	23	8	8	6	5	0	0	0	4	0	2	0	0	1	.000	0-0	0	91	1.838	29.40	14.73

Austin Romine

Bats: R **Throws:** R **Pos:** C-50;DH-1;PH-1   ROW-mine   **Ht:** 6'1" **Wt:** 216 **Born:** 11/22/1988 **Age:** 34

						BATTING																	RUNNING			AVERAGES			
Year	Team	Lg	G	AB	H	2B	3B	HR	(Hm	Rd)	TB	R	RBI	RC	TBB	IBB	SO	HBP	SH	SF	SB	CS	GDP	Avg	OBP	Slg	OPS
2022	Salt Lk	AAA	10	33	9	1	0	1	(-	-)	13	7	4	5	5	0	8	0	1	0		0	0	0	.273	.368	.394	.762
2011	NYY	AL	9	19	3	0	0	0	(0	0)	3	2	0	0	1	0	5	0	0	0		0	0	0	.158	.200	.158	.358
2013	NYY	AL	60	135	28	9	0	1	(0	1)	40	15	10	8	8	0	37	1	3	1		1	0	7	.207	.255	.296	.551
2014	NYY	AL	7	13	3	1	0	0	(0	0)	4	2	1	2	0	0	4	0	0	0		0	0	0	.231	.231	.308	.538
2015	NYY	AL	1	2	0	0	0	0	(0	0)	0	0	0	0	0	0	0	0	0	0		0	0	0	.000	.000	.000	.000
2016	NYY	AL	62	165	40	11	0	4	(1	3)	63	17	26	19	7	1	31	0	1	3		1	0	4	.242	.269	.382	.650
2017	NYY	AL	80	229	50	9	1	2	(2	0)	67	19	21	18	16	0	57	2	2	3		0	0	7	.218	.272	.293	.565
2018	NYY	AL	77	242	59	12	0	10	(3	7)	101	30	42	32	17	0	67	2	1	3		1	0	10	.244	.295	.417	.713
2019	NYY	AL	73	228	64	12	0	8	(2	6)	100	29	35	30	10	0	50	0	1	1		1	1	7	.281	.310	.439	.748
2020	Det	AL	37	130	31	5	0	2	(1	1)	42	12	17	13	4	0	47	0	0	1		0	0	3	.238	.259	.323	.582
2021	ChC	NL	28	60	13	2	0	1	(1	0)	18	5	5	2	2	0	22	0	0	0		0	0	4	.217	.242	.300	.542
2022	3 Tms		51	129	20	3	0	3	(2	1)	32	10	9	3	4	0	46	1	2	0		0	0	2	.155	.187	.248	.435
22	LAA	AL	3	8	2	0	0	0	(0	0)	2	0	0	1	0	0	3	0	1	0		0	0	0	.250	.250	.250	.500
22	StL	NL	11	26	4	1	0	0	(0	0)	5	2	0	0	2	0	7	0	0	0		0	0	0	.154	.214	.192	.407
22	Cin	NL	37	95	14	2	0	3	(2	1)	25	8	9	2	2	0	36	1	1	0		0	0	2	.147	.173	.263	.437
	Postseason		3	2	0	0	0	0	(0	0)	0	0	0	0	0	0	0	0	0	0		0	0	0	.000	.000	.000	.000
	11 ML YEARS		485	1352	311	64	1	31	(12	19)	470	141	166	127	69	1	366	6	10	12		4	1	47	.230	.268	.348	.616

Sergio Romo

Pitches: R **Bats:** R **Pos:** RP-23   **Ht:** 5'11" **Wt:** 185 **Born:** 3/4/1983 **Age:** 40

			HOW MUCH PITCHED					WHAT HE GAVE UP										THE RESULTS						
Year	Team	Lg	G	GS	GF	IP	BFP	H	R	ER	HR	SH	SF	HB	TBB	IBB	SO	WP	W	L	Pct	Sv-Op Hld	Vel	OPS	ERC	ERA
2008	SF	NL	29	0	8	34.0	130	16	13	8	3	2	1	3	8	1	33	0	3	1	.750	0-0 5	89	.470	1.27	2.12
2009	SF	NL	45	0	9	34.0	143	30	15	15	1	2	0	1	11	0	41	2	5	2	.714	2-2 10	90	.631	2.76	3.97
2010	SF	NL	68	0	13	62.0	247	46	16	15	6	2	2	4	14	2	70	0	5	3	.625	0-4 21	89	.599	2.26	2.18
2011	SF	NL	65	0	16	48.0	175	29	8	8	2	2	0	0	5	1	70	0	3	1	.750	1-2 23	89	.458	1.08	1.50
2012	SF	NL	69	0	27	55.1	215	37	11	11	5	2	0	3	10	1	63	2	4	2	.667	14-15 23	88	.525	1.72	1.79
2013	SF	NL	65	0	52	60.1	250	53	20	17	5	1	1	1	12	3	58	1	5	8	.385	38-43 0	88	.614	2.47	2.54
2014	SF	NL	64	0	35	58.0	230	43	24	24	9	2	0	4	12	2	59	2	6	4	.600	23-28 11	88	.622	2.54	3.72
2015	SF	NL	70	0	14	57.1	230	51	20	19	3	2	0	1	10	2	71	4	0	5	.000	2-4 34	87	.622	2.37	2.98
2016	SF	NL	40	0	13	30.2	117	26	9	9	5	0	0	0	7	1	33	1	1	0	1.000	4-4 14	86	.709	3.13	2.64
2017	2 Tms		55	0	12	55.2	224	42	23	22	9	0	1	1	19	2	59	2	3	1	.750	0-1 11	86	.661	2.97	3.56
2018	TB	AL	73	5	38	67.1	284	65	31	31	11	2	2	2	20	0	75	2	3	4	.429	25-33 9	86	.718	4.02	4.14
2019	2 Tms		65	0	33	60.1	249	50	27	23	7	0	4	2	17	3	60	3	2	1	.667	20-23 17	86	.649	2.83	3.43
2020	Min	AL	24	0	7	20.0	87	16	9	9	3	0	1	3	7	0	23	0	1	2	.333	5-6 10	86	.667	3.58	4.05
2021	Oak	AL	66	0	18	61.2	259	56	33	32	9	0	1	2	21	2	60	1	1	1	.500	3-7 12	86	.709	3.73	4.67
2022	2 Tms		23	0	5	18.0	79	19	16	15	7	0	1	0	6	1	14	2	0	1	.000	0-0 4	85	.926	5.95	7.50
17	LAD	NL	30	0	8	25.0	108	23	17	17	7	0	0	0	12	1	31	0	1	1	.500	0-0 7	87	.845	5.15	6.12
17	TB	AL	25	0	4	30.2	116	19	6	5	2	0	1	1	7	1	28	2	2	0	1.000	0-1 4	86	.494	1.54	1.47
19	Mia	NL	38	0	28	37.2	156	33	18	15	4	0	3	0	13	3	33	2	2	0	1.000	17-18 1	86	.673	3.12	3.58
19	Min	AL	27	0	5	22.2	93	17	9	8	3	0	1	2	4	0	27	1	0	1	.000	3-5 16	86	.608	2.35	3.18
22	Sea	AL	17	0	3	14.1	65	18	13	13	6	0	1	0	4	0	11	2	0	0	-	0-0 4	85	1.005	7.30	8.16
22	Tor	AL	6	0	2	3.2	14	1	3	2	1	0	0	0	2	1	3	0	0	1	.000	0-0 0	85	.548	1.63	4.91
	Postseason		30	0	13	26.0	106	22	13	10	4	0	0	0	6	0	23	1	3	2	.600	4-7 4	88	.634	2.89	3.46
	15 ML YEARS		821	5	300	722.2	2919	579	275	258	85	17	14	27	179	21	789	22	42	36	.538	137-172 204	87	.631	2.65	3.21

Angel Rondon

Pitches: R **Bats:** R **Pos:** RP-1   **Ht:** 6'1" **Wt:** 205 **Born:** 12/1/1997 **Age:** 25

			HOW MUCH PITCHED					WHAT HE GAVE UP										THE RESULTS						
Year	Team	Lg	G	GS	GF	IP	BFP	H	R	ER	HR	SH	SF	HB	TBB	IBB	SO	WP	W	L	Pct	Sv-Op Hld	Vel	OPS	ERC	ERA
2022	Memp	AAA	18	5	1	49.0	215	39	25	22	7	2	1	0	33	0	52	2	3	1	.750	0- -	-	.724	4.31	4.04
2021	StL	NL	2	0	1	2.0	7	1	0	0	0	0	0	0	1	0	1	0	0	0	-	0-0 0	93	.452	1.62	0.00
2022	StL	NL	1	0	0	5.0	20	1	0	0	0	0	0	0	3	0	4	0	1	0	1.000	0-0 0	93	.259	0.76	0.00
	2 ML YEARS		3	0	1	7.0	27	2	0	0	0	0	0	0	4	0	5	0	1	0	1.000	0-0 0	93	.309	0.96	0.00

Brent Rooker

Bats: R **Throws:** R **Pos:** LF-8;PH-7;DH-5;RF-1   **Ht:** 6'4" **Wt:** 225 **Born:** 11/1/1994 **Age:** 28

						BATTING																	RUNNING			AVERAGES			
Year	Team	Lg	G	AB	H	2B	3B	HR	(Hm	Rd)	TB	R	RBI	RC	TBB	IBB	SO	HBP	SH	SF	SB	CS	GDP	Avg	OBP	Slg	OPS
2022	ElPaso	AAA	61	228	62	19	0	19	(-	-)	138	55	55	57	37	2	78	6	0	2		5	1	5	.272	.385	.605	.990
2022	Omha	AAA	20	80	27	8	0	9	(-	-)	62	16	32	25	9	0	25	3	0	0		0	1	4	.338	.424	.775	1.199
2020	Min	AL	7	19	6	2	0	1	(0	1)	11	4	5	5	0	0	5	2	0	0		0	0	0	.316	.381	.579	.960
2021	Min	AL	58	189	38	10	0	9	(6	3)	75	25	16	18	15	0	70	9	0	0		0	0	1	.201	.291	.397	.688

Year Team	Lg	G	AB	H	2B	3B	HR	(Hm Rd)	TB	R	RBI	RC	TBB	IBB	SO	HBP	SH	SF	SB	CS	GDP	Avg	OBP	Slg	OPS
2022 2 Tms		16	32	4	1	0	0	(0 0)	5	1	2	1	3	0	11	1	0	0	0	0	2	.125	.222	.156	.378
22 SD	NL	2	7	0	0	0	0	(0 0)	0	0	0	0	0	0	4	0	0	0	0	0	0	.000	.000	.000	.000
22 KC	AL	14	25	4	1	0	0	(0 0)	5	1	2	1	3	0	7	1	0	0	0	0	2	.160	.276	.200	.476
3 ML YEARS		81	240	48	13	0	10	(6 4)	91	30	23	24	18	0	86	12	0	0	0	0	3	.200	.289	.379	.668

Amed Rosario

Bats: R **Throws:** R **Pos:** SS-140;LF-6;DH-6;PH-2   **Ht:** 6'2" **Wt:** 190 **Born:** 11/20/1995 **Age:** 27

Year Team	Lg	G	AB	H	2B	3B	HR	(Hm Rd)	TB	R	RBI	RC	TBB	IBB	SO	HBP	SH	SF	SB	CS	GDP	Avg	OBP	Slg	OPS
2017 NYM	NL	46	165	41	4	4	4	(1 3)	65	16	10	14	3	0	49	2	0	0	7	3	3	.248	.271	.394	.665
2018 NYM	NL	154	554	142	26	8	9	(4 5)	211	76	51	60	29	4	119	3	3	3	24	11	9	.256	.295	.381	.676
2019 NYM	NL	157	616	177	30	7	15	(8 7)	266	75	72	79	31	2	124	3	2	3	19	10	13	.287	.323	.432	.755
2020 NYM	NL	46	143	36	3	1	4	(0 4)	53	20	15	10	4	0	34	0	0	0	1	1	5	.252	.272	.371	.643
2021 Cle	AL	141	550	155	25	6	11	(5 6)	225	77	57	82	31	0	120	3	0	4	13	0	12	.282	.321	.409	.731
2022 Cle	AL	153	637	180	26	9	11	(6 5)	257	86	71	77	25	0	111	4	0	4	18	4	19	.283	.312	.403	.715
6 ML YEARS		697	2665	731	114	35	54	(24 30)	1077	350	276	322	123	6	557	15	5	14	81	29	61	.274	.308	.404	.713

Eddie Rosario

Bats: L **Throws:** R **Pos:** LF-54;RF-15;PH-13;DH-9   **Ht:** 6'1" **Wt:** 180 **Born:** 9/28/1991 **Age:** 31

Year Team	Lg	G	AB	H	2B	3B	HR	(Hm Rd)	TB	R	RBI	RC	TBB	IBB	SO	HBP	SH	SF	SB	CS	GDP	Avg	OBP	Slg	OPS
2015 Min	AL	122	453	121	18	15	13	(10 3)	208	60	50	58	15	3	118	0	3	3	11	6	5	.267	.289	.459	.748
2016 Min	AL	92	335	90	17	2	10	(4 6)	141	52	32	35	12	2	91	2	2	3	5	2	4	.269	.295	.421	.716
2017 Min	AL	151	542	157	33	2	27	(20 7)	275	79	78	77	35	1	106	0	4	8	9	8	10	.290	.328	.507	.836
2018 Min	AL	138	559	161	31	2	24	(15 9)	268	87	77	79	30	5	104	0	1	2	8	2	4	.288	.323	.479	.803
2019 Min	AL	137	562	155	28	1	32	(12 20)	281	91	109	88	22	2	86	0	0	6	3	1	10	.276	.300	.500	.800
2020 Min	AL	57	210	54	7	0	13	(6 7)	100	31	42	37	19	2	34	0	0	3	3	1	3	.257	.316	.476	.792
2021 2 Tms		111	379	98	19	3	14	(6 8)	165	42	62	55	26	0	61	1	2	4	11	3	4	.259	.305	.435	.740
2022 Atl	NL	80	250	53	12	1	5	(4 1)	82	27	24	20	17	0	68	0	0	3	3	0	3	.212	.259	.328	.587
21 Cle	AL	78	283	72	15	1	7	(2 5)	110	29	46	38	17	0	47	1	2	3	9	2	3	.254	.296	.389	.685
21 Atl	NL	33	96	26	4	2	7	(4 3)	55	13	16	17	9	0	14	0	0	1	2	1	1	.271	.330	.573	.903
Postseason		22	83	28	4	1	5	(2 3)	49	13	14	14	9	1	16	0	0	0	1	1	1	.337	.402	.590	.993
8 ML YEARS		888	3290	889	165	26	138	(77 61)	1520	469	474	449	176	15	668	3	12	31	53	23	43	.270	.305	.462	.767

Eguy Rosario

Bats: R **Throws:** R **Pos:** PH-5;3B-4;SS-2;PR-1   **Ht:** 5'9" **Wt:** 150 **Born:** 8/25/1999 **Age:** 23

Year Team	Lg	G	AB	H	2B	3B	HR	(Hm Rd)	TB	R	RBI	RC	TBB	IBB	SO	HBP	SH	SF	SB	CS	GDP	Avg	OBP	Slg	OPS
2022 ElPaso	AAA	124	490	141	34	4	22	(- -)	249	98	81	93	59	0	109	7	1	7	21	8	10	.288	.368	.508	.876
2022 SD	NL	7	5	1	0	0	0	(0 0)	1	0	0	0	1	0	2	0	0	0	0	0	0	.200	.333	.200	.533

Kenny Rosenberg

Pitches: L **Bats:** L **Pos:** RP-2; SP-1   **Ht:** 6'1" **Wt:** 195 **Born:** 7/9/1995 **Age:** 27

Year Team	Lg	G	GS	GF	IP	BFP	H	R	ER	HR	SH	SF	HB	TBB	IBB	SO	WP	W	L	Pct	Sv-Op	Hld	Vel	OPS	ERC	ERA
2022 Salt Lk	AAA	14	13	0	62.2	265	50	27	22	9	2	1	4	27	0	62	2	2	5	.286	0- -	-	-	.685	3.62	3.16
2022 LAA	AL	3	1	1	10.2	47	9	5	5	1	0	1	0	6	0	8	0	0	0	-	0-0	0	91	.669	3.71	4.22

Joe Ross

Pitches: R **Bats:** R **Pos:** P   **Ht:** 6'4" **Wt:** 223 **Born:** 5/21/1993 **Age:** 30

Year Team	Lg	G	GS	GF	IP	BFP	H	R	ER	HR	SH	SF	HB	TBB	IBB	SO	WP	W	L	Pct	Sv-Op	Hld	Vel	OPS	ERC	ERA
2015 Was	NL	16	13	1	76.2	314	64	33	31	7	3	1	2	21	0	69	1	5	5	.500	0-0	0	-	.628	2.74	3.64
2016 Was	NL	19	19	0	105.0	447	108	43	40	9	7	3	6	29	3	93	2	7	5	.583	0-0	0	-	.713	3.84	3.43
2017 Was	NL	13	13	0	73.2	323	88	44	41	16	5	0	1	20	2	68	2	5	3	.625	0-0	0	-	.867	5.54	5.01
2018 Was	NL	3	3	0	16.0	68	17	10	9	3	0	0	2	4	0	7	0	0	2	.000	0-0	0	-	.870	5.09	5.06
2019 Was	NL	27	9	0	64.0	295	74	41	39	7	3	1	4	33	1	57	2	4	4	.500	0-2	2	-	.829	5.79	5.48
2021 Was	NL	20	19	0	108.0	460	98	57	50	17	3	2	8	34	4	109	0	5	9	.357	0-0	0	-	.708	3.81	4.17
Postseason		3	2	0	9.2	42	9	8	8	3	0	0	2	4	0	4	1	0	1	.000	0-0	0	-	.885	6.34	7.45
6 ML YEARS		98	76	4	443.1	1907	449	228	210	59	21	7	23	141	10	403	7	26	28	.481	0-2	2	-	.748	4.22	4.26

Bubby Rossman

Pitches: R **Bats:** B **Pos:** RP-1   **Ht:** 6'5" **Wt:** 220 **Born:** 6/29/1992 **Age:** 31

Year Team	Lg	G	GS	GF	IP	BFP	H	R	ER	HR	SH	SF	HB	TBB	IBB	SO	WP	W	L	Pct	Sv-Op	Hld	Vel	OPS	ERC	ERA
2022 Rdng	AA	29	6	9	44.2	182	29	18	15	3	0	0	6	25	0	56	4	2	2	.500	1- -	-	-	.583	2.74	3.02
2022 LV	AAA	15	5	2	25.1	121	29	18	17	2	0	1	1	17	0	27	3	3	3	.500	0- -	-	-	.751	5.98	6.04
2022 Phi	NL	1	0	1	1.0	5	1	2	2	1	0	0	0	1	0	1	0	0	0	-	0-0	0	97	1.400	14.27	18.00

Michael Rucker

Pitches: R Bats: R Pos: RP-41   Ht: 6'1" Wt: 195 Born: 4/27/1994 Age: 29

			HOW MUCH PITCHED					WHAT HE GAVE UP											THE RESULTS					
Year	Team	Lg	G	GS	GF	IP	BFP	H	R	ER	HR	SH	SF	HB	TBB	IBB	SO	WP	W	L	Pct	Sv-Op Hld	Vel	OPS	ERC	ERA
2022	Iowa	AAA	10	0	4	15.1	68	15	3	2	0	0	0	0	8	1	13	1	1	0	1.000	0- -	-	.638	3.54	1.17
2021	ChC	NL	20	0	6	28.1	126	32	25	22	5	0	1	2	11	0	30	0	0	0	-	1-2	0	95	.839	5.71	6.99
2022	ChC	NL	41	0	9	54.2	229	50	25	24	8	0	2	0	20	0	50	4	3	1	.750	0-0	4	95	.702	3.80	3.95
	2 ML YEARS		61	0	15	83.0	355	82	50	46	13	0	3	2	31	0	80	4	3	1	.750	1-2	4	95	.750	4.42	4.99

Darin Ruf

Bats: R Throws: R Pos: 1B-45;DH-36;PH-34;LF-29;RF-9;PR-1   ROUGH   Ht: 6'2" Wt: 232 Born: 7/28/1986 Age: 36

			BATTING																	RUNNING			AVERAGES			
Year	Team	Lg	G	AB	H	2B	3B	HR	(Hm	Rd)	TB	R	RBI	RC	TBB	IBB	SO	HBP	SH	SF	SB	CS	GDP	Avg	OBP	Slg	OPS
2012	Phi	NL	12	33	11	2	1	3	(1	2)	24	4	10	5	2	1	12	0	0	2	0	0	1	.333	.351	.727	1.079
2013	Phi	NL	73	251	62	11	0	14	(11	3)	115	36	30	33	33	1	91	7	0	2	0	0	4	.247	.348	.458	.806
2014	Phi	NL	52	102	24	8	0	3	(3	0)	41	13	8	9	8	0	32	4	1	2	0	0	2	.235	.310	.402	.712
2015	Phi	NL	106	268	63	12	0	12	(6	6)	111	30	39	34	21	0	69	5	0	3	1	0	7	.235	.300	.414	.714
2016	Phi	NL	43	83	17	2	0	3	(1	2)	28	8	9	4	4	0	25	0	0	2	0	1	1	.205	.236	.337	.573
2020	SF	NL	40	87	24	6	0	5	(4	1)	45	11	18	18	13	0	23	0	0	0	1	0	1	.276	.370	.517	.887
2021	SF	NL	117	262	71	13	2	16	(5	11)	136	41	43	45	46	2	87	3	0	1	2	0	8	.271	.385	.519	.904
2022	2 Tms	NL	119	334	68	12	0	11	(7	4)	113	52	45	41	45	0	105	6	0	3	2	0	11	.204	.307	.338	.645
22	SF	NL	90	268	58	9	0	11	(7	4)	100	46	38	41	40	0	85	5	0	1	2	0	8	.216	.328	.373	.701
22	NYM	NL	29	66	10	3	0	0	(0	0)	13	6	7	0	5	0	20	1	0	2	0	0	3	.152	.216	.197	.413
	Postseason		3	11	1	0	0	1	(1	0)	4	1	2	0	0	0	5	0	0	0	0	0	0	.091	.091	.364	.455
	8 ML YEARS		562	1420	340	66	3	67	(38	29)	613	195	202	189	172	4	444	25	1	15	6	1	39	.239	.329	.432	.761

Esteury Ruiz

Bats: R Throws: R Pos: LF-7;CF-6;RF-6;PH-3   est-AIR-ee   Ht: 6'0" Wt: 169 Born: 2/15/1999 Age: 24

			BATTING																	RUNNING			AVERAGES			
Year	Team	Lg	G	AB	H	2B	3B	HR	(Hm	Rd)	TB	R	RBI	RC	TBB	IBB	SO	HBP	SH	SF	SB	CS	GDP	Avg	OBP	Slg	OPS
2022	SnAnt	AA	49	180	62	17	2	9	(-	-)	110	54	37	54	32	0	40	14	3	2	37	5	1	.344	.474	.611	1.085
2022	ElPaso	AAA	28	111	35	6	0	4	(-	-)	53	30	9	26	20	0	25	9	2	0	23	4	1	.315	.457	.477	.935
2022	Nashv	AAA	37	146	48	10	0	3	(-	-)	67	30	19	27	14	0	29	4	3	0	25	5	3	.329	.402	.459	.861
2022	2 Tms	NL	17	35	6	1	1	0	(0	0)	9	3	2	1	1	0	7	0	0	0	1	2	0	.171	.194	.257	.452
22	SD	NL	14	27	6	1	1	0	(0	0)	9	1	2	2	1	0	5	0	0	0	1	2	0	.222	.222	.333	.556
22	Mil	NL	3	8	0	0	0	0	(0	0)	0	2	0	0	1	0	2	0	0	0	0	0	0	.000	.111	.000	.111

Jose Ruiz

Pitches: R Bats: R Pos: RP-63   Ht: 6'1" Wt: 245 Born: 10/21/1994 Age: 28

			HOW MUCH PITCHED					WHAT HE GAVE UP											THE RESULTS					
Year	Team	Lg	G	GS	GF	IP	BFP	H	R	ER	HR	SH	SF	HB	TBB	IBB	SO	WP	W	L	Pct	Sv-Op Hld	Vel	OPS	ERC	ERA
2017	SD	NL	1	0	1	1.0	4	0	0	0	0	0	0	0	1	0	1	0	0	0	-	0-0	0	95	.250	0.95	0.00
2018	CWS	AL	6	0	2	4.1	21	5	2	2	1	0	0	0	3	0	6	2	0	0	-	0-0	0	96	.825	7.12	4.15
2019	CWS	AL	40	1	16	40.0	198	56	27	25	6	2	2	2	24	2	35	4	1	4	.200	0-1	1	96	.924	7.89	5.63
2020	CWS	AL	5	0	4	4.0	14	2	1	1	0	0	0	0	0	0	5	0	0	0	-	0-1	0	97	.500	1.13	2.25
2021	CWS	AL	59	0	23	65.0	271	51	26	22	8	1	2	0	25	1	63	2	1	3	.250	0-1	4	97	.648	2.93	3.05
2022	CWS	AL	63	0	21	60.2	265	53	32	31	9	0	3	0	33	0	68	4	1	0	1.000	0-0	11	97	.735	4.24	4.60
	Postseason		1	0	1	1.1	4	0	0	0	0	0	0	0	0	0	1	0	0	0	-	0-0	0	97	.000	0.00	0.00
	6 ML YEARS		174	1	67	175.0	773	167	88	81	25	3	7	2	86	3	178	12	3	7	.300	0-3	16	97	.747	4.45	4.17

Keibert Ruiz

Bats: B Throws: R Pos: C-106;PH-13;DH-1   Ht: 6'0" Wt: 225 Born: 7/20/1998 Age: 24

			BATTING																	RUNNING			AVERAGES			
Year	Team	Lg	G	AB	H	2B	3B	HR	(Hm	Rd)	TB	R	RBI	RC	TBB	IBB	SO	HBP	SH	SF	SB	CS	GDP	Avg	OBP	Slg	OPS
2020	LAD	NL	2	8	2	0	0	1	(0	1)	5	1	1	1	0	0	3	0	0	0	0	0	0	.250	.250	.625	.875
2021	2 Tms	NL	29	88	24	3	0	3	(0	3)	36	10	15	9	6	0	9	2	0	0	0	0	3	.273	.333	.409	.742
2022	Was	NL	112	394	99	22	0	7	(3	4)	142	33	36	38	30	0	50	6	1	2	6	1	9	.251	.313	.360	.673
21	LAD	NL	6	7	1	0	0	1	(0	1)	4	1	1	0	0	0	5	0	0	0	0	0	0	.143	.143	.571	.714
21	Was	NL	23	81	23	3	0	2	(0	2)	32	9	14	9	6	0	4	2	0	0	0	0	3	.284	.348	.395	.743
	3 ML YEARS		143	490	125	25	0	11	(3	8)	183	44	52	48	36	0	62	8	1	2	6	1	12	.255	.315	.373	.689

Norge Ruiz

Pitches: R Bats: R Pos: RP-14   Ht: 5'10" Wt: 180 Born: 3/15/1994 Age: 29

			HOW MUCH PITCHED					WHAT HE GAVE UP											THE RESULTS					
Year	Team	Lg	G	GS	GF	IP	BFP	H	R	ER	HR	SH	SF	HB	TBB	IBB	SO	WP	W	L	Pct	Sv-Op Hld	Vel	OPS	ERC	ERA
2022	LsVgs	AAA	31	0	13	41.0	173	36	18	17	5	0	0	0	16	1	39	2	5	1	.833	2- -	-	.695	3.45	3.73
2022	Oak	AL	14	0	6	19.0	94	30	16	15	4	0	2	2	7	0	18	2	0	1	.000	0-1	1	93	.981	8.94	7.11

Adley Rutschman

Bats: B Throws: R Pos: C-93;DH-23;PH-6   Ht: 6'2" Wt: 220 Born: 2/6/1998 Age: 25

								BATTING											RUNNING			AVERAGES			
Year	Team	Lg	G	AB	H	2B	3B	HR	(Hm | Rd)	TB	R	RBI	RC	TBB	IBB	SO	HBP	SH	SF	SB	CS	GDP	Avg	OBP	Slg	OPS
2019	3 Tms	Low	37	130	33	8	1	4	(-- | --)	55	19	26	20	20	1	27	1	0	3	1	0	2	.254	.351	.423	.774
2021	Bowie	AA	80	295	80	16	0	18	(-- | --)	150	61	55	61	55	2	57	5	1	1	1	1	5	.271	.392	.508	.901
2021	Norfolk	AAA	38	138	44	9	2	5	(-- | --)	72	22	20	30	22	0	29	2	0	2	2	2	1	.319	.415	.522	.936
2022	Norfolk	AAA	12	43	10	0	0	3	(-- | --)	19	5	7	7	7	0	6	3	0	0	0	0	2	.233	.377	.442	.819
2022	Bal	AL	113	398	101	35	1	13	(5 | 8)	177	70	42	65	65	0	86	4	0	3	4	0	4	.254	.362	.445	.806

Joe Ryan

Pitches: R Bats: R Pos: SP-27   Ht: 6'2" Wt: 205 Born: 6/5/1996 Age: 27

			HOW MUCH PITCHED				WHAT HE GAVE UP										THE RESULTS						
Year	Team	Lg	G	GS	GF	IP	BFP	H	R	ER	HR	SH	SF	HB	TBB	IBB	SO	WP	W	L	Pct	Sv-Op	Hld	Vel	OPS	ERC	ERA
2021	Min	AL	5	5	0	26.2	100	16	12	12	4	0	0	0	5	0	30	1	2	1	.667	0-0	0	91	.557	1.62	4.05
2022	Min	AL	27	27	0	147.0	604	115	60	58	20	1	0	10	47	0	151	2	13	8	.619	0-0	0	92	.664	3.09	3.55
	2 ML YEARS		32	32	0	173.2	704	131	72	70	24	1	0	10	52	0	181	3	15	9	.625	0-0	0	92	.649	2.85	3.63

Hyun-Jin Ryu

Pitches: L Bats: R Pos: SP-6   he-YUN-jin ree-YOO   Ht: 6'3" Wt: 250 Born: 3/25/1987 Age: 36

			HOW MUCH PITCHED				WHAT HE GAVE UP										THE RESULTS						
Year	Team	Lg	G	GS	GF	IP	BFP	H	R	ER	HR	SH	SF	HB	TBB	IBB	SO	WP	W	L	Pct	Sv-Op	Hld	Vel	OPS	ERC	ERA
2013	LAD	NL	30	30	0	192.0	783	182	67	64	15	7	3	1	49	4	154	5	14	8	.636	0-0	0	90	.660	3.13	3.00
2014	LAD	NL	26	26	0	152.0	631	152	60	57	8	6	2	3	29	2	139	2	14	7	.667	0-0	0	91	.658	3.00	3.38
2016	LAD	NL	1	1	0	4.2	24	8	6	6	1	0	0	0	2	1	4	0	0	1	.000	0-0	0	90	1.144	9.03	11.57
2017	LAD	NL	25	24	1	126.2	541	128	58	53	22	4	1	4	45	3	116	4	5	9	.357	1-1	0	90	.792	4.61	3.77
2018	LAD	NL	15	15	0	82.1	324	68	23	18	9	1	0	1	15	1	89	0	7	3	.700	0-0	0	90	.622	2.45	1.97
2019	LAD	NL	29	29	0	182.2	723	160	53	47	17	8	2	4	24	2	163	0	14	5	.737	0-0	0	91	.622	2.45	2.32
2020	Tor	AL	12	12	0	67.0	275	60	22	20	6	1	0	1	17	0	72	1	5	2	.714	0-0	0	90	.636	2.94	2.69
2021	Tor	AL	31	31	0	169.0	701	170	85	82	24	1	3	2	37	1	143	2	14	10	.583	0-0	0	90	.733	3.73	4.37
2022	Tor	AL	6	6	0	27.0	113	32	17	17	5	0	0	0	4	0	16	0	2	0	1.000	0-0	0	89	.860	4.77	5.67
	Postseason		9	9	0	41.2	180	49	25	21	5	0	0	0	9	2	35	0	3	3	.500	0-0	0	92	.749	4.37	4.54
	9 ML YEARS		175	174	1	1003.1	4115	960	391	364	107	28	11	16	222	13	896	14	75	45	.625	1-1	0	90	.686	3.25	3.27

Casey Sadler

Pitches: R Bats: R Pos: P   Ht: 6'3" Wt: 223 Born: 7/13/1990 Age: 32

			HOW MUCH PITCHED				WHAT HE GAVE UP										THE RESULTS						
Year	Team	Lg	G	GS	GF	IP	BFP	H	R	ER	HR	SH	SF	HB	TBB	IBB	SO	WP	W	L	Pct	Sv-Op	Hld	Vel	OPS	ERC	ERA
2014	Pit	NL	6	1	2	10.1	49	12	9	9	0	0	2	1	5	0	7	1	0	1	.000	0-0	0	--	.782	4.80	7.84
2015	Pit	NL	1	1	0	5.0	19	4	2	2	1	0	0	0	1	0	5	0	1	0	1.000	0-0	0	--	.763	2.98	3.60
2018	Pit	NL	2	0	1	4.1	25	9	7	4	0	0	0	0	3	0	3	1	0	0	--	0-0	0	--	1.116	11.14	8.31
2019	2 Tms		33	1	16	46.1	194	41	14	11	5	2	1	4	13	2	31	0	4	0	1.000	1-2	2	--	.664	3.30	2.14
2020	2 Tms		17	0	2	19.1	86	15	13	11	3	1	0	0	12	0	21	5	1	2	.333	0-0	5	--	.715	3.94	5.12
2021	Sea	AL	42	0	2	40.1	145	19	4	3	1	0	1	1	10	0	37	2	0	1	.000	0-0	15	--	.402	1.03	0.67
19	TB	AL	9	0	8	19.1	79	16	5	4	2	0	0	1	5	0	11	0	0	0	--	0-0	0	--	.621	2.83	1.86
19	LAD	NL	24	1	8	27.0	115	25	9	7	3	2	1	3	8	2	20	0	4	0	1.000	1-2	2	--	.695	3.64	2.33
20	ChC	NL	10	0	1	9.1	44	8	6	6	2	1	0	0	8	0	9	3	0	0	--	0-0	4	--	.801	5.86	5.79
20	Sea	AL	7	0	1	10.0	42	7	7	5	1	0	0	0	4	0	12	2	1	2	.333	0-0	1	--	.630	2.39	4.50
	6 ML YEARS		101	2	23	125.2	518	100	49	40	10	3	4	6	44	2	104	9	6	4	.600	1-2	22	--	.634	2.82	2.86

Connor Sadzeck

Pitches: R Bats: R Pos: RP-2   Ht: 6'7" Wt: 235 Born: 10/1/1991 Age: 31

			HOW MUCH PITCHED				WHAT HE GAVE UP										THE RESULTS						
Year	Team	Lg	G	GS	GF	IP	BFP	H	R	ER	HR	SH	SF	HB	TBB	IBB	SO	WP	W	L	Pct	Sv-Op	Hld	Vel	OPS	ERC	ERA
2022	Nashv	AAA	24	0	10	28.0	114	17	5	3	2	0	1	2	12	0	35	2	1	1	.500	3--	--	--	.565	2.21	0.96
2022	Roch	AAA	17	0	3	21.0	87	17	9	9	6	0	1	1	8	1	21	0	0	3	.000	0--	--	--	.805	4.32	3.86
2018	Tex	AL	13	2	1	9.1	45	6	2	1	0	0	1	1	11	1	7	1	0	0	--	0-0	5	97	.612	4.40	0.96
2019	Sea	AL	20	0	10	23.2	107	18	10	7	3	0	0	2	15	1	27	4	0	1	.000	1-2	1	96	.672	3.97	2.66
2022	Mil	NL	2	0	2	3.0	13	4	3	3	2	0	0	0	1	0	2	1	0	0	--	0-0	0	95	1.301	10.88	9.00
	3 ML YEARS		35	2	13	36.0	165	28	15	11	5	0	3	4	27	2	36	6	0	1	.000	1-2	6	96	.714	4.64	2.75

Chris Sale

Pitches: L Bats: L Pos: SP-2   SAIL   Ht: 6'6" Wt: 183 Born: 3/30/1989 Age: 34

			HOW MUCH PITCHED				WHAT HE GAVE UP										THE RESULTS						
Year	Team	Lg	G	GS	GF	IP	BFP	H	R	ER	HR	SH	SF	HB	TBB	IBB	SO	WP	W	L	Pct	Sv-Op	Hld	Vel	OPS	ERC	ERA
2010	CWS	AL	21	0	8	23.1	92	15	5	5	2	1	0	0	10	0	32	1	2	1	.667	4-4	2	96	.546	2.30	1.93
2011	CWS	AL	58	0	17	71.0	288	52	22	22	6	3	0	2	27	3	79	2	2	2	.500	8-10	16	95	.612	2.55	2.79
2012	CWS	AL	30	29	0	192.0	772	167	66	65	19	1	3	6	51	5	192	6	17	8	.680	0-1	0	92	.660	3.00	3.05
2013	CWS	AL	30	30	0	214.1	866	184	81	73	23	2	4	14	46	2	226	8	11	14	.440	0-0	0	93	.636	2.92	3.07
2014	CWS	AL	26	26	0	174.0	685	129	48	42	13	2	3	11	39	2	208	3	12	4	.750	0-0	0	94	.567	2.18	2.17
2015	CWS	AL	31	31	0	208.2	854	185	88	79	23	2	3	13	42	0	274	7	13	11	.542	0-0	0	94	.649	3.00	3.41
2016	CWS	AL	32	32	0	226.2	907	190	88	84	27	5	3	17	45	2	233	2	17	10	.630	0-0	0	93	.651	2.88	3.34
2017	Bos	AL	32	32	0	214.1	851	165	73	69	24	2	4	8	43	0	308	3	17	8	.680	0-0	0	94	.603	2.33	2.90
2018	Bos	AL	27	27	0	158.0	617	102	39	37	11	0	4	14	34	0	237	4	12	4	.750	0-0	0	95	.532	1.76	2.11
2019	Bos	AL	25	25	0	147.1	612	123	80	72	24	4	4	13	37	0	218	2	6	11	.353	0-0	0	93	.695	3.31	4.40

Year	Team	Lg	G	GS	GF	IP	BFP	H	R	ER	HR	SH	SF	HB	TBB	IBB	SO	WP	W	L	Pct	Sv-Op	Hld	Vel	OPS	ERC	ERA
2021	Bos	AL	9	9	0	42.2	183	45	19	15	6	0	0	4	12	1	52	0	5	1	.833	0-0	0	94	.752	4.60	3.16
2022	Bos	AL	2	2	0	5.2	25	5	3	2	0	0	0	1	1	0	5	0	0	1	.000	0-0	0	95	.584	2.42	3.18
	Postseason		10	7	1	34.0	152	36	26	24	7	0	1	2	13	0	47	1	1	3	.250	0-0	1	94	.784	5.28	6.35
	12 ML YEARS		323	243	25	1678.0	6752	1362	612	565	178	20	28	103	387	15	2064	38	114	75	.603	12-15	18	94	.628	2.71	3.03

Adrian Sampson

Pitches: R **Bats:** R **Pos:** SP-19; RP-2   **Ht:** 6'2" **Wt:** 210 **Born:** 10/7/1991 **Age:** 31

			HOW MUCH PITCHED					WHAT HE GAVE UP											THE RESULTS								
Year	Team	Lg	G	GS	GF	IP	BFP	H	R	ER	HR	SH	SF	HB	TBB	IBB	SO	WP	W	L	Pct	Sv-Op	Hld	Vel	OPS	ERC	ERA
2022	Iowa	AAA	8	6	0	28.1	123	29	15	12	6	0	1	3	7	0	18	3	0	3	.000	0- -	-	-	.808	4.74	3.81
2016	Sea	AL	1	1	0	4.2	21	8	4	4	2	0	0	0	1	0	2	0	0	1	.000	0-0	0	91	1.129	11.33	7.71
2018	Tex	AL	5	4	0	23.0	96	24	13	11	6	0	1	2	4	0	15	2	0	3	.000	0-0	0	91	.829	4.92	4.30
2019	Tex	AL	35	15	4	125.1	563	156	86	82	29	0	2	9	36	1	101	4	6	8	.429	0-0	0	93	.925	6.36	5.89
2021	ChC	NL	10	5	0	35.1	145	30	15	11	8	1	0	6	8	0	28	1	1	2	.333	0-0	0	92	.767	4.15	2.80
2022	ChC	NL	21	19	2	104.1	428	101	40	36	10	0	0	2	27	0	73	0	4	5	.444	0-0	0	92	.687	3.46	3.11
	5 ML YEARS		72	44	6	292.2	1253	319	158	144	55	1	3	19	76	1	219	7	11	19	.367	0-0	0	92	.821	4.96	4.43

Aaron Sanchez

Pitches: R **Bats:** R **Pos:** SP-10; RP-5   **Ht:** 6'4" **Wt:** 212 **Born:** 7/1/1992 **Age:** 30

			HOW MUCH PITCHED					WHAT HE GAVE UP											THE RESULTS								
Year	Team	Lg	G	GS	GF	IP	BFP	H	R	ER	HR	SH	SF	HB	TBB	IBB	SO	WP	W	L	Pct	Sv-Op	Hld	Vel	OPS	ERC	ERA
2022	StPaul	AAA	10	10	0	47.1	202	43	24	20	7	1	2	9	15	0	33	1	3	2	.600	0- -	-	-	.762	4.40	3.80
2014	Tor	AL	24	0	6	33.0	121	14	5	4	1	2	0	1	9	0	27	1	2	2	.500	3-3	7	97	.367	0.96	1.09
2015	Tor	AL	41	11	4	92.1	380	74	35	33	9	2	1	3	44	2	61	8	7	6	.538	0-1	10	95	.666	3.47	3.22
2016	Tor	AL	30	30	0	192.0	790	161	69	64	15	1	2	5	63	0	161	5	15	2	**.882**	0-0	0	95	.625	2.90	**3.00**
2017	Tor	AL	8	8	0	36.0	167	42	24	17	6	0	0	1	20	0	24	1	1	3	.250	0-0	0	95	.836	6.36	4.25
2018	Tor	AL	20	20	0	105.0	474	106	62	57	11	0	4	7	58	2	86	4	4	6	.400	0-0	0	94	.768	5.02	4.89
2019	2 Tms		27	27	0	131.1	605	145	92	86	20	0	4	11	68	2	115	7	5	14	.263	0-0	0	94	.828	5.88	5.89
2021	SF	NL	9	7	1	35.1	156	32	12	12	2	0	0	4	15	0	26	0	1	1	.500	0-0	0	92	.655	3.71	3.06
2022	2 Tms		15	10	2	60.0	265	78	46	44	8	1	3	5	15	1	41	2	3	4	.429	0-0	0	92	.861	5.95	6.60
19	Tor	AL	23	23	0	112.2	524	131	82	76	15	0	3	10	59	2	99	7	3	14	.176	0-0	0	94	.835	6.16	6.07
19	Hou	AL	4	4	0	18.2	81	14	10	10	5	0	1	1	9	0	16	0	2	0	1.000	0-0	0	92	.782	4.22	4.82
22	Was	NL	7	7	0	31.1	141	47	30	29	6	1	3	1	8	1	16	1	3	3	.500	0-0	0	92	.978	7.61	8.33
22	Min	AL	8	3	2	28.2	124	31	16	15	2	0	0	4	7	0	25	1	0	1	.000	0-0	0	93	.728	4.30	4.71
	Postseason		11	2	1	19.0	77	12	8	7	2	2	0	0	8	0	16	1	2	0	1.000	0-0	0	96	.565	2.24	3.32
	8 ML YEARS		174	113	13	685.0	2958	652	345	317	72	6	14	37	292	7	541	28	38	38	.500	3-4	17	94	.718	4.17	4.16

Anibal Sanchez

Pitches: R **Bats:** R **Pos:** SP-14   ah-NEE-bahl   **Ht:** 6'0" **Wt:** 207 **Born:** 2/27/1984 **Age:** 39

			HOW MUCH PITCHED					WHAT HE GAVE UP											THE RESULTS								
Year	Team	Lg	G	GS	GF	IP	BFP	H	R	ER	HR	SH	SF	HB	TBB	IBB	SO	WP	W	L	Pct	Sv-Op	Hld	Vel	OPS	ERC	ERA
2006	Fla	NL	18	17	0	114.1	469	90	39	36	9	3	1	4	46	1	72	4	10	3	.769	0-0	0	91	.635	2.96	2.83
2007	Fla	NL	6	6	0	30.0	151	43	17	16	3	2	2	2	19	1	14	3	2	1	.667	0-0	0	90	.930	7.90	4.80
2008	Fla	NL	10	10	0	51.2	241	54	35	32	7	4	2	6	27	2	50	1	2	5	.286	0-0	0	90	.788	5.40	5.57
2009	Fla	NL	16	16	0	86.0	383	84	39	37	10	2	2	1	46	5	71	0	4	8	.333	0-0	0	91	.756	4.51	3.87
2010	Fla	NL	32	32	0	195.0	841	192	89	77	10	13	3	7	70	5	157	7	13	12	.520	0-0	0	91	.680	3.56	3.55
2011	Fla	NL	32	32	0	196.1	830	187	85	80	20	12	1	5	64	8	202	4	8	9	.471	0-0	0	92	.711	3.57	3.67
2012	2 Tms		31	31	0	195.2	820	200	95	84	20	5	7	5	48	3	167	2	9	13	.409	0-0	0	92	.716	3.70	3.86
2013	Det	AL	29	29	0	182.0	746	156	56	52	9	4	4	2	54	1	202	7	14	8	.636	0-0	0	93	.616	2.63	**2.57**
2014	Det	AL	22	21	0	126.0	514	108	55	48	4	3	4	3	30	1	102	5	8	5	.615	0-0	0	92	.599	2.35	3.43
2015	Det	AL	25	25	0	157.0	660	152	89	87	29	5	2	1	49	1	138	5	10	10	.500	0-0	0	92	.768	4.14	4.99
2016	Det	AL	35	26	3	153.1	668	171	108	100	30	4	6	5	53	1	135	7	7	13	.350	0-0	0	91	.828	5.40	5.87
2017	Det	AL	28	17	6	105.1	482	139	81	75	26	2	3	4	29	1	104	5	3	7	.300	0-0	0	91	.906	6.66	6.41
2018	Atl	NL	25	24	0	136.2	553	106	48	43	15	7	3	4	42	0	135	4	7	6	.538	0-0	0	91	.633	2.71	2.83
2019	Was	NL	30	30	0	166.0	712	153	77	71	22	1	2	4	58	10	134	1	11	8	.579	0-0	0	90	.709	3.59	3.85
2020	Was	NL	11	11	0	53.0	245	70	40	39	11	0	0	3	18	2	43	0	4	5	.444	0-0	0	90	.907	6.74	6.62
2022	Was	NL	14	14	0	69.1	292	55	34	33	13	1	1	4	33	2	48	2	4	6	.400	0-0	0	90	.731	4.05	4.28
12	Mia	NL	19	19	0	121.0	504	119	59	53	12	4	5	2	33	2	110	4	5	7	.417	0-0	0	91	.717	3.55	3.94
12	Det	AL	12	12	0	74.2	316	81	36	31	8	1	2	3	15	1	57	3	4	6	.400	0-0	0	93	.714	3.95	3.74
	Postseason		11	10	0	61.1	256	51	22	20	9	1	1	2	19	1	64	4	3	6	.333	0-0	1	92	.677	3.16	2.93
	16 ML YEARS		364	341	9	2017.2	8607	1960	987	910	238	68	43	60	686	44	1774	62	116	119	.494	0-0	0	91	.723	3.88	4.06

Cristopher Sanchez

Pitches: L **Bats:** L **Pos:** RP-12; SP-3   **Ht:** 6'1" **Wt:** 165 **Born:** 12/12/1996 **Age:** 26

			HOW MUCH PITCHED					WHAT HE GAVE UP											THE RESULTS								
Year	Team	Lg	G	GS	GF	IP	BFP	H	R	ER	HR	SH	SF	HB	TBB	IBB	SO	WP	W	L	Pct	Sv-Op	Hld	Vel	OPS	ERC	ERA
2022	LV	AAA	15	14	0	57.1	238	48	24	20	1	1	1	4	20	0	58	2	2	2	.500	0- -	-	-	.606	2.74	3.14
2021	Phi	NL	7	1	0	12.2	59	16	8	7	1	2	0	0	7	0	13	0	1	0	1.000	0-0	0	94	.864	6.15	4.97
2022	Phi	NL	15	3	3	40.0	177	38	25	25	5	0	0	4	17	1	35	0	2	2	.500	1-1	1	93	.731	4.38	5.63
	2 ML YEARS		22	4	3	52.2	236	54	33	32	6	2	0	4	24	1	48	0	3	2	.600	1-1	1	93	.763	4.79	5.47

Gary Sanchez

Bats: R **Throws**: R **Pos**: C-91;DH-32;PH-11;1B-1   **Ht**: 6'2" **Wt**: 230 **Born**: 12/2/1992 **Age**: 30

Year Team	Lg	G	AB	H	2B	3B	HR	(Hm	Rd)	TB	R	RBI	RC	TBB	IBB	SO	HBP	SH	SF	SB	CS	GDP	Avg	OBP	Slg	OPS
2015 NYY	AL	2	2	0	0	0	0	(0	0)	0	0	0	0	0	0	1	0	0	0	0	0	0	.000	.000	.000	.000
2016 NYY	AL	53	201	60	12	0	20	(10	10)	132	34	42	40	24	2	57	2	0	2	1	0	5	.299	.376	.657	1.032
2017 NYY	AL	122	471	131	20	0	33	(15	18)	250	79	90	81	40	1	120	10	0	4	2	1	9	.278	.345	.531	.876
2018 NYY	AL	89	323	60	17	0	18	(8	10)	131	51	53	41	46	0	94	3	0	2	1	0	10	.186	.291	.406	.697
2019 NYY	AL	106	396	92	12	1	34	(19	15)	208	62	77	64	40	3	125	9	0	1	0	1	3	.232	.316	.525	.841
2020 NYY	AL	49	156	23	4	0	10	(7	3)	57	19	24	12	18	0	64	4	0	0	0	0	6	.147	.253	.365	.618
2021 NYY	AL	117	383	78	13	1	23	(15	8)	162	54	54	50	52	3	121	5	0	0	0	0	14	.204	.307	.423	.730
2022 Min	AL	128	419	86	24	0	16	(5	11)	158	42	61	51	40	0	136	7	0	5	2	0	12	.205	.282	.377	.659
Postseason		31	111	19	3	0	7	(3	4)	43	11	19	10	6	0	44	1	0	3	0	0	3	.171	.215	.387	.602
8 ML YEARS		666	2351	530	102	2	154	(79	75)	1098	341	401	339	260	9	718	40	0	14	6	2	59	.225	.311	.467	.778

Jesus Sanchez

Bats: L **Throws**: R **Pos**: CF-78;LF-12;PH-7;DH-2;RF-1;PR-1   **Ht**: 6'3" **Wt**: 222 **Born**: 10/7/1997 **Age**: 25

Year Team	Lg	G	AB	H	2B	3B	HR	(Hm	Rd)	TB	R	RBI	RC	TBB	IBB	SO	HBP	SH	SF	SB	CS	GDP	Avg	OBP	Slg	OPS
2022 Jaxnvl	AAA	42	159	49	7	0	6	(-	-)	74	30	27	29	21	0	39	3	0	0	4	1	5	.308	.399	.465	.864
2020 Mia	NL	10	25	1	1	0	0	(0	0)	2	1	2	0	4	0	11	0	0	0	0	0	1	.040	.172	.080	.252
2021 Mia	NL	64	227	57	8	2	14	(7	7)	111	27	36	38	20	3	78	3	0	1	0	1	2	.251	.319	.489	.808
2022 Mia	NL	98	313	67	14	3	13	(7	6)	126	38	36	36	26	0	92	3	0	1	0	0	7	.214	.280	.403	.682
3 ML YEARS		172	565	125	23	5	27	(14	13)	239	66	74	74	50	3	181	6	0	2	1	1	10	.221	.291	.423	.714

Miguel Sanchez

Pitches: R **Bats**: R **Pos**: RP-12   **Ht**: 6'3" **Wt**: 205 **Born**: 12/31/1993 **Age**: 29

Year Team	Lg	G	GS	GF	IP	BFP	H	R	ER	HR	SH	SF	HB	TBB	IBB	SO	WP	W	L	Pct	Sv-Op	Hld	Vel	OPS	ERC	ERA
2022 Nashv	AAA	17	0	4	19.0	76	16	8	8	2	0	0	2	6	0	18	1	4	2	.667	1--	-	-	.683	3.51	3.79
2021 Mil	NL	28	0	11	26.0	120	27	14	12	4	1	2	2	14	2	23	2	2	1	.667	0-1	0	94	.807	5.37	4.15
2022 Mil	NL	12	0	3	13.1	58	12	7	6	3	0	1	0	8	2	9	0	1	1	.500	0-0	2	94	.855	5.05	4.05
2 ML YEARS		40	0	14	39.1	178	39	21	18	7	1	3	2	22	4	32	2	3	2	.600	0-1	2	94	.823	5.26	4.12

Yolmer Sanchez

Bats: B **Throws**: R **Pos**: 2B-14;3B-2;SS-1;PR-1   **Ht**: 6'0" **Wt**: 210 **Born**: 6/29/1992 **Age**: 31

Year Team	Lg	G	AB	H	2B	3B	HR	(Hm	Rd)	TB	R	RBI	RC	TBB	IBB	SO	HBP	SH	SF	SB	CS	GDP	Avg	OBP	Slg	OPS
2022 Wrcstr	AAA	78	247	61	12	1	9	(-	-)	102	43	33	43	50	2	67	3	1	2	6	1	2	.247	.377	.413	.790
2022 Syrcse	AAA	22	78	19	4	0	1	(-	-)	26	6	7	8	10	0	19	4	0	1	0	0	4	.244	.355	.333	.688
2014 CWS	AL	28	100	25	5	0	0	(0	0)	30	6	5	5	3	0	25	0	0	1	1	1	1	.250	.269	.300	.569
2015 CWS	AL	120	389	87	23	1	5	(2	3)	127	40	31	30	19	0	81	5	6	1	2	2	9	.224	.268	.326	.595
2016 CWS	AL	53	154	32	9	1	4	(2	2)	55	15	21	14	5	0	42	1	2	1	0	1	1	.208	.236	.357	.593
2017 CWS	AL	141	484	129	19	8	12	(8	4)	200	63	59	68	35	2	111	4	7	4	8	9	10	.267	.319	.413	.732
2018 CWS	AL	155	600	145	34	10	8	(4	4)	223	62	55	72	49	0	138	8	2	3	14	6	9	.242	.306	.372	.678
2019 CWS	AL	149	496	125	20	4	2	(0	2)	159	59	43	55	44	1	117	5	7	3	5	4	7	.252	.318	.321	.638
2020 CWS	AL	12	16	5	3	0	1	(0	1)	11	7	1	4	5	0	5	0	0	0	0	0	1	.313	.476	.688	1.164
2022 2 Tms		17	37	4	0	0	0	(0	0)	4	1	2	1	5	0	13	0	2	0	0	2	0	.108	.214	.108	.322
22 Bos	AL	14	37	4	0	0	0	(0	0)	4	1	2	1	5	0	13	0	2	0	0	2	0	.108	.214	.108	.322
22 NYM	NL	3	0	0	0	0	0	(0	0)	0	0	0	0	0	0	0	0	0	0	0	0	0	-	-	-	-
Postseason		1	0	0	0	0	0	(0	0)	0	0	0	0	0	0	0	0	0	0	0	0	0	-	-	-	-
8 ML YEARS		675	2276	552	113	24	32	(16	16)	809	253	217	249	165	3	532	23	26	13	30	25	38	.243	.299	.355	.654

Phoenix Sanders

Pitches: R **Bats**: R **Pos**: RP-8   **Ht**: 5'10" **Wt**: 205 **Born**: 6/5/1995 **Age**: 28

Year Team	Lg	G	GS	GF	IP	BFP	H	R	ER	HR	SH	SF	HB	TBB	IBB	SO	WP	W	L	Pct	Sv-Op	Hld	Vel	OPS	ERC	ERA
2022 Drham	AAA	25	1	4	30.0	129	39	19	18	6	0	1	0	2	0	36	3	0	0	-	1--	-	-	.834	5.10	5.40
2022 TB	AL	8	0	3	14.2	57	12	5	5	0	0	1	0	3	0	12	0	0	0	-	0-0	0	89	.603	1.88	3.07

Nick Sandlin

Pitches: R **Bats**: R **Pos**: RP-46   **Ht**: 5'11" **Wt**: 175 **Born**: 1/10/1997 **Age**: 26

Year Team	Lg	G	GS	GF	IP	BFP	H	R	ER	HR	SH	SF	HB	TBB	IBB	SO	WP	W	L	Pct	Sv-Op	Hld	Vel	OPS	ERC	ERA
2022 Clmbs	AAA	5	0	0	4.1	19	3	4	4	1	1	0	0	4	1	3	0	0	0	-	0--	-	-	.889	5.16	8.31
2021 Cle	AL	34	0	4	33.2	141	21	15	11	2	0	1	0	17	0	48	1	1	1	.500	0-1	5	95	.584	2.63	2.94
2022 Cle	AL	46	0	11	44.0	180	27	13	11	2	0	0	3	24	3	41	1	5	2	.714	0-3	7	94	.548	2.42	2.25
2 ML YEARS		80	0	15	77.2	321	48	28	22	4	0	1	7	41	3	89	2	6	3	.667	0-4	12	94	.564	2.51	2.55

Patrick Sandoval

Pitches: L Bats: L Pos: SP-27   Ht: 6'3" Wt: 190 Born: 10/18/1996 Age: 26

Year Team	Lg	G	GS	GF	IP	BFP	H	R	ER	HR	SH	SF	HB	TBB	IBB	SO	WP	W	L	Pct	Sv-Op	Hld	Vel	OPS	ERC	ERA
2019 LAA	AL	10	9	0	39.1	169	35	22	22	6	2	1	1	19	0	42	4	0	4	.000	0-0	0	93	.754	4.28	5.03
2020 LAA	AL	9	6	0	36.2	159	37	26	23	10	0	0	0	12	0	33	2	1	5	.167	0-0	0	93	.818	4.92	5.65
2021 LAA	AL	17	14	2	87.0	363	69	38	35	11	0	2	4	36	0	94	3	3	6	.333	1-1	0	93	.649	3.36	3.62
2022 LAA	AL	27	27	0	148.2	638	139	56	48	8	3	4	5	60	0	151	6	6	9	.400	0-0	0	93	.655	3.53	2.91
4 ML YEARS		63	56	2	311.2	1329	280	142	128	35	5	7	10	127	0	320	15	10	24	.294	1-1	0	93	.686	3.74	3.70

Cole Sands

Pitches: R Bats: R Pos: RP-8; SP-3   Ht: 6'3" Wt: 215 Born: 7/17/1997 Age: 25

Year Team	Lg	G	GS	GF	IP	BFP	H	R	ER	HR	SH	SF	HB	TBB	IBB	SO	WP	W	L	Pct	Sv-Op	Hld	Vel	OPS	ERC	ERA
2022 StPaul	AAA	19	13	0	61.2	284	78	42	38	9	2	3	3	24	0	72	4	3	6	.333	0- -	-	-	.868	6.14	5.55
2022 Min	AL	11	3	5	30.2	145	35	21	20	4	0	0	5	13	0	28	1	0	3	.000	1-1	0	92	.806	5.76	5.87

Donny Sands

Bats: R Throws: R Pos: PH-3;C-1;DH-1   Ht: 6'2" Wt: 190 Born: 5/16/1996 Age: 27

Year Team	Lg	G	AB	H	2B	3B	HR	(Hm	Rd)	TB	R	RBI	RC	TBB	IBB	SO	HBP	SH	SF	SB	CS	GDP	Avg	OBP	Slg	OPS
2022 LV	AAA	57	201	62	9	0	5	(-	-)	86	41	34	34	38	1	44	0	0	3	1	0	10	.308	.413	.428	.841
2022 Phi	NL	3	3	0	0	0	0	(0	0)	0	0	0	0	1	0	1	0	0	0	0	0	1	.000	.250	.000	.250

Reiver Sanmartin

Pitches: L Bats: L Pos: RP-41; SP-4   Ht: 6'2" Wt: 160 Born: 4/15/1996 Age: 27

Year Team	Lg	G	GS	GF	IP	BFP	H	R	ER	HR	SH	SF	HB	TBB	IBB	SO	WP	W	L	Pct	Sv-Op	Hld	Vel	OPS	ERC	ERA
2022 Lsvlle	AAA	7	2	0	18.1	81	24	16	15	2	0	0	1	4	0	26	0	2	2	.500	0- -	-	-	.805	5.50	7.36
2021 Cin	NL	2	2	0	11.2	47	12	2	2	0	0	0	0	2	0	11	1	2	0	1.000	0-0	0	89	.653	2.78	1.54
2022 Cin	NL	45	4	3	57.0	256	66	43	40	8	1	1	0	29	2	47	2	4	4	.500	0-0	7	91	.848	5.79	6.32
2 ML YEARS		47	6	3	68.2	303	78	45	42	8	1	1	0	31	2	58	3	6	4	.600	0-0	7	90	.816	5.24	5.50

Miguel Sano

Bats: R Throws: R Pos: 1B-19;DH-2   sah-NO   Ht: 6'4" Wt: 272 Born: 5/11/1993 Age: 30

Year Team	Lg	G	AB	H	2B	3B	HR	(Hm	Rd)	TB	R	RBI	RC	TBB	IBB	SO	HBP	SH	SF	SB	CS	GDP	Avg	OBP	Slg	OPS
2015 Min	AL	80	279	75	17	1	18	(10	8)	148	46	52	62	53	1	119	1	0	2	1	1	4	.269	.385	.530	.916
2016 Min	AL	116	437	103	22	1	25	(11	14)	202	57	66	62	54	1	178	1	0	3	1	0	3	.236	.319	.462	.781
2017 Min	AL	114	424	112	15	2	28	(12	16)	215	75	77	71	54	5	173	4	0	1	0	0	12	.264	.352	.507	.859
2018 Min	AL	71	266	53	14	0	13	(7	6)	106	32	41	28	31	0	115	0	0	2	0	0	7	.199	.281	.398	.679
2019 Min	AL	105	380	94	19	2	34	(14	20)	219	76	79	74	55	0	159	3	0	1	0	1	5	.247	.346	.576	.923
2020 Min	AL	53	186	38	12	0	13	(6	7)	89	31	25	22	18	1	90	1	0	0	0	0	3	.204	.278	.478	.757
2021 Min	AL	135	470	105	24	0	30	(17	13)	219	68	75	60	59	2	183	2	0	1	2	1	13	.223	.312	.466	.778
2022 Min	AL	20	60	5	0	0	1	(0	1)	8	1	3	2	9	0	25	1	0	1	1	0	0	.083	.211	.133	.345
Postseason		5	19	2	0	0	1	(0	1)	5	1	1	0	1	0	9	0	0	0	0	0	0	.105	.150	.263	.413
8 ML YEARS		694	2502	585	123	6	162	(77	85)	1206	386	418	381	333	10	1042	13	0	11	5	3	52	.234	.326	.482	.808

Carlos Santana

Bats: B Throws: R Pos: 1B-76;DH-50;PH-8;RF-1;PR-1   Ht: 5'11" Wt: 215 Born: 4/8/1986 Age: 37

Year Team	Lg	G	AB	H	2B	3B	HR	(Hm	Rd)	TB	R	RBI	RC	TBB	IBB	SO	HBP	SH	SF	SB	CS	GDP	Avg	OBP	Slg	OPS
2010 Cle	AL	46	150	39	13	0	6	(2	4)	70	23	22	25	37	2	29	1	0	4	3	0	3	.260	.401	.467	.868
2011 Cle	AL	155	552	132	35	2	27	(14	13)	252	84	79	81	97	7	133	2	0	7	5	3	15	.239	.351	.457	.808
2012 Cle	AL	143	507	128	27	2	18	(7	11)	213	72	76	77	91	4	101	3	0	8	3	5	21	.252	.365	.420	.785
2013 Cle	AL	154	541	145	39	1	20	(12	8)	246	75	74	93	93	6	110	4	0	4	3	1	7	.268	.377	.455	.832
2014 Cle	AL	152	541	125	25	0	27	(13	14)	231	68	85	88	113	5	124	3	0	3	5	2	13	.231	.365	.427	.792
2015 Cle	AL	154	550	127	29	2	19	(6	13)	217	72	85	80	108	4	122	3	0	5	11	3	20	.231	.357	.395	.752
2016 Cle	AL	158	582	151	31	3	34	(20	14)	290	89	87	104	99	0	99	2	0	5	5	2	18	.259	.366	.498	.865
2017 Cle	AL	154	571	148	37	3	23	(11	12)	260	90	79	89	88	6	94	2	0	2	5	1	11	.259	.363	.455	.818
2018 Phi	NL	161	560	128	28	2	24	(13	11)	232	82	86	87	110	6	93	1	0	8	2	1	12	.229	.352	.414	.766
2019 Cle	AL	158	573	161	30	1	34	(19	15)	295	110	93	114	108	12	108	3	0	2	4	0	13	.281	.397	.515	.911
2020 Cle	AL	60	206	41	7	0	8	(5	3)	72	34	30	35	47	1	43	1	0	1	0	0	6	.199	.349	.350	.699
2021 KC	AL	158	565	121	15	0	19	(7	12)	193	66	69	66	86	3	102	3	0	5	2	0	12	.214	.319	.342	.660
2022 2 Tms	AL	131	431	87	18	0	19	(10	9)	162	52	60	60	71	2	88	2	0	2	0	0	9	.202	.316	.376	.692
22 KC	AL	52	176	38	10	0	4	(2	2)	60	17	21	26	36	1	28	0	0	0	0	0	1	.216	.349	.341	.690
22 Sea	AL	79	255	49	8	0	15	(8	7)	102	35	39	34	35	1	60	2	0	2	0	0	8	.192	.293	.400	.693
Postseason		23	83	16	2	0	4	(1	3)	30	9	8	10	12	0	19	1	0	0	0	0	1	.193	.302	.361	.664
13 ML YEARS		1784	6329	1533	334	16	278	(139	139)	2733	917	925	999	1148	62	1246	34	0	56	48	18	159	.242	.359	.432	.791

Dennis Santana

Pitches: R Bats: R Pos: RP-62; SP-1   Ht: 6'2" Wt: 190 Born: 4/12/1996 Age: 27

			HOW MUCH PITCHED					WHAT HE GAVE UP									THE RESULTS						
Year	Team	Lg	G	GS	GF	IP	BFP	H	R	ER	HR	SH	SF	HB	TBB	IBB	SO	WP	W	L	Pct	Sv-Op	Hld	Vel	OPS	ERC	ERA
2018	LAD	NL	1	0	0	3.2	19	6	5	5	0	1	0	1	1	0	4	1	1	0	1.000	0-0	0	93	1.007	7.52	12.27
2019	LAD	NL	3	0	1	5.0	27	6	4	4	1	0	1	2	4	0	6	1	0	0	-	0-0	0	93	.994	9.44	7.20
2020	LAD	NL	12	0	7	17.0	73	15	11	10	4	0	0	2	7	0	18	1	1	2	.333	0-1	0	94	.782	4.93	5.29
2021	2 Tms		55	0	12	54.2	237	48	31	26	4	1	1	3	32	2	46	4	2	4	.333	0-2	6	95	.692	4.16	4.28
2022	Tex	AL	63	1	13	58.2	255	50	39	34	2	0	4	4	28	1	54	3	3	8	.273	1-3	19	97	.637	3.29	5.22
21	LAD	NL	16	0	5	15.0	74	18	11	10	0	0	0	3	11	1	8	2	0	0	-	0-0	1	95	.766	6.55	6.00
21	Tex	AL	39	0	7	39.2	163	30	20	16	4	1	1	0	21	1	38	2	2	4	.333	0-2	5	96	.658	3.31	3.63
	5 ML YEARS		134	1	33	139.0	611	125	90	79	11	2	6	12	72	3	128	10	7	14	.333	1-6	25	96	.702	4.13	5.12

Anthony Santander

Bats: B Throws: R Pos: RF-84;LF-38;DH-34;PH-1   sahn-tahn-DARE   Ht: 6'2" Wt: 235 Born: 10/19/1994 Age: 28

			BATTING																		RUNNING			AVERAGES			
Year	Team	Lg	G	AB	H	2B	3B	HR	(Hm	Rd)	TB	R	RBI	RC	TBB	IBB	SO	HBP	SH	SF	SB	CS	GDP	Avg	OBP	Slg	OPS
2017	Bal	AL	13	30	8	3	0	0	(0	0)	11	1	2	2	0	0	8	0	0	1	0	0	0	.267	.258	.367	.625
2018	Bal	AL	33	101	20	5	1	1	(0	1)	30	8	6	10	6	0	21	1	0	0	1	0	1	.198	.250	.297	.547
2019	Bal	AL	93	380	99	20	1	20	(10	10)	181	46	59	55	19	0	86	2	1	3	1	2	11	.261	.297	.476	.773
2020	Bal	AL	37	153	40	13	1	11	(8	3)	88	24	32	28	10	3	25	2	0	0	0	1	2	.261	.315	.575	.890
2021	Bal	AL	110	406	98	24	0	18	(15	3)	176	54	50	40	23	0	101	4	1	4	1	1	11	.241	.286	.433	.720
2022	Bal	AL	152	574	138	24	0	33	(15	18)	261	78	89	89	55	1	122	13	0	5	0	2	14	.240	.318	.455	.773
	6 ML YEARS		438	1644	403	89	3	83	(48	35)	747	211	238	224	113	4	363	22	2	13	3	6	29	.245	.300	.454	.755

Hector Santiago

Pitches: L Bats: R Pos: P   Ht: 6'0" Wt: 215 Born: 12/16/1987 Age: 35

			HOW MUCH PITCHED					WHAT HE GAVE UP									THE RESULTS						
Year	Team	Lg	G	GS	GF	IP	BFP	H	R	ER	HR	SH	SF	HB	TBB	IBB	SO	WP	W	L	Pct	Sv-Op	Hld	Vel	OPS	ERC	ERA
2011	CWS	AL	2	0	1	5.1	18	1	0	0	0	0	0	0	1	1	2	1	0	0	-	0-0	0	-	.170	0.16	0.00
2012	CWS	AL	42	4	19	70.1	306	54	26	26	10	2	1	7	40	1	79	5	4	1	.800	4-6	4	-	.680	4.11	3.33
2013	CWS	AL	34	23	4	149.0	656	137	69	59	17	3	3	15	72	2	137	2	4	9	.308	0-0	0	-	.739	4.43	3.56
2014	LAA	AL	30	24	2	127.1	544	120	63	53	15	1	3	3	53	3	108	5	6	9	.400	0-0	1	-	.698	4.02	3.75
2015	LAA	AL	33	32	0	180.2	776	156	80	72	29	4	4	10	71	5	162	1	9	9	.500	0-0	0	-	.723	3.82	3.59
2016	2 Tms		33	33	0	182.0	785	169	100	95	33	5	6	5	79	0	144	3	13	10	.565	0-0	0	-	.774	4.48	4.70
2017	Min	AL	15	14	1	70.1	311	70	44	44	15	0	1	5	31	0	51	0	4	8	.333	0-0	0	-	.782	5.33	5.63
2018	CWS	AL	49	7	27	102.0	460	101	54	50	16	1	3	5	60	3	103	1	6	3	.667	2-2	0	-	.807	5.38	4.41
2019	2 Tms		19	2	11	33.2	163	42	26	25	8	1	0	1	22	0	40	0	1	1	.500	0-0	0	-	.950	7.71	6.68
2021	Sea	AL	13	1	6	26.1	117	27	10	10	2	0	1	0	11	0	30	0	1	1	.500	0-0	0	-	.715	4.01	3.42
16	LAA	AL	22	22	0	120.2	515	104	61	57	20	3	4	4	57	0	107	2	10	4	.714	0-0	0	-	.736	4.20	4.25
16	Min	AL	11	11	0	61.1	270	65	39	38	13	2	2	1	22	0	37	1	3	6	.333	0-0	0	-	.843	5.05	5.58
19	NYM	NL	8	0	6	8.0	38	10	6	6	1	0	0	0	5	0	6	0	1	0	1.000	0-0	0	-	.940	6.73	6.75
19	CWS	AL	11	2	5	25.2	125	32	20	19	7	1	0	1	17	0	34	0	0	1	.000	0-0	0	-	.953	8.01	6.66
	Postseason		1	0	0	1.1	7	1	2	2	1	0	0	0	2	0	0	0	0	0	-	0-0	0	-	1.229	12.98	13.50
	10 ML YEARS		270	140	71	947.0	4136	877	472	434	145	16	23	50	440	15	856	18	48	51	.485	6-8	5	-	.749	4.47	4.12

Tony Santillan

Pitches: R Bats: R Pos: RP-21   Ht: 6'3" Wt: 240 Born: 4/15/1997 Age: 26

			HOW MUCH PITCHED					WHAT HE GAVE UP									THE RESULTS						
Year	Team	Lg	G	GS	GF	IP	BFP	H	R	ER	HR	SH	SF	HB	TBB	IBB	SO	WP	W	L	Pct	Sv-Op	Hld	Vel	OPS	ERC	ERA
2021	Cin	NL	26	4	5	43.1	190	34	15	14	7	1	4	7	21	0	56	1	1	3	.250	0-0	0	95	.729	4.24	2.91
2022	Cin	NL	21	0	4	19.2	96	23	14	12	1	1	2	4	12	1	21	4	0	1	.000	4-7	6	96	.839	6.23	5.49
	2 ML YEARS		47	4	9	63.0	286	57	29	26	8	2	6	11	33	1	77	5	1	4	.200	4-7	6	95	.766	4.85	3.71

Gregory Santos

Pitches: R Bats: R Pos: RP-2   Ht: 6'2" Wt: 190 Born: 8/28/1999 Age: 23

			HOW MUCH PITCHED					WHAT HE GAVE UP									THE RESULTS						
Year	Team	Lg	G	GS	GF	IP	BFP	H	R	ER	HR	SH	SF	HB	TBB	IBB	SO	WP	W	L	Pct	Sv-Op	Hld	Vel	OPS	ERC	ERA
2022	Scrmto	AAA	33	0	3	33.0	148	29	22	18	4	0	2	3	20	0	34	2	1	2	.333	1--	-	98	.766	4.71	4.91
2021	SF	NL	3	0	1	2.0	13	5	6	5	3	0	0	2	2	0	3	0	0	2	.000	0-0	1	98	1.811	33.45	22.50
2022	SF	NL	2	0	1	3.2	17	3	2	2	0	0	0	3	3	0	2	0	0	0	-	0-0	0	99	.639	3.80	4.91
	2 ML YEARS		5	0	2	5.2	30	8	8	7	3	0	0	5	5	0	5	0	0	2	.000	0-0	1	98	1.153	12.56	11.12

Tayler Saucedo

Pitches: L Bats: L Pos: RP-4   Ht: 6'4" Wt: 205 Born: 6/18/1993 Age: 30

			HOW MUCH PITCHED					WHAT HE GAVE UP									THE RESULTS						
Year	Team	Lg	G	GS	GF	IP	BFP	H	R	ER	HR	SH	SF	HB	TBB	IBB	SO	WP	W	L	Pct	Sv-Op	Hld	Vel	OPS	ERC	ERA
2022	Buffalo	AAA	20	0	4	19.0	82	14	5	5	1	0	0	2	10	0	28	2	1	0	1.000	1--	-	94	.603	3.16	2.37
2021	Tor	AL	29	0	9	25.2	109	22	14	13	1	0	1	2	10	0	19	2	0	0	-	0-2	1	94	.666	3.13	4.91
2022	Tor	AL	4	0	0	2.2	15	6	4	4	3	0	0	0	1	0	0	0	0	0	-	0-0	0	93	1.610	22.42	13.50
	2 ML YEARS		33	0	9	28.1	124	28	18	17	4	0	1	2	11	0	19	2	0	0	-	0-2	1	94	.785	4.52	5.40

Hirokazu Sawamura

Pitches: R Bats: R Pos: RP-49 **Ht: 6'0" Wt: 212 Born: 4/3/1988 Age: 35**

		HOW MUCH PITCHED					WHAT HE GAVE UP										THE RESULTS						
Year	Team	Lg	G	GS	GF	IP	BFP	H	R	ER	HR	SH	SF	HB	TBB	IBB	SO	WP	W	L	Pct	Sv-Op	Hld	Vel	OPS	ERC	ERA
2021	Bos	AL	55	0	4	53.0	233	45	24	18	9	0	1	2	32	6	61	8	5	1	.833	0-1	10	96	.768	4.50	3.06
2022	Bos	AL	49	0	11	50.2	221	45	23	21	4	0	5	0	27	2	40	8	1	1	.500	0-0	3	96	.664	3.72	3.73
	Postseason		3	0	1	2.0	11	2	1	1	0	0	1	1	2	0	2	1	0	0	-	0-0	0	97	.740	7.45	4.50
	2 ML YEARS		104	0	15	103.2	454	90	47	39	13	0	6	2	59	8	101	16	6	2	.750	0-1	13	96	.718	4.12	3.39

Josh Sborz

Pitches: R Bats: R Pos: RP-18; SP-1 **Ht: 6'3" Wt: 215 Born: 12/17/1993 Age: 29**

		HOW MUCH PITCHED					WHAT HE GAVE UP										THE RESULTS						
Year	Team	Lg	G	GS	GF	IP	BFP	H	R	ER	HR	SH	SF	HB	TBB	IBB	SO	WP	W	L	Pct	Sv-Op	Hld	Vel	OPS	ERC	ERA
2022	RdRck	AAA	19	1	5	22.1	89	11	6	4	2	1	1	0	11	0	30	3	3	0	1.000	1- -	-	-	.493	1.76	1.61
2019	LAD	NL	7	0	6	9.0	40	10	8	8	2	0	1	0	4	0	7	0	0	1	.000	0-0	0	95	.921	5.84	8.00
2020	LAD	NL	4	0	3	4.1	16	2	1	1	1	0	0	0	1	0	2	0	0	0	-	0-0	0	96	.588	1.53	2.08
2021	Tex	AL	63	0	16	59.0	257	52	29	26	7	0	3	0	32	1	69	8	4	3	.571	1-4	9	97	.710	4.05	3.97
2022	Tex	AL	19	1	6	22.1	100	25	16	16	4	0	1	0	11	1	32	2	1	0	1.000	0-0	1	97	.849	5.72	6.45
	4 ML YEARS		93	1	31	94.2	413	89	54	51	14	0	5	0	48	2	110	10	5	4	.556	1-4	10	97	.759	4.47	4.85

Max Scherzer

Pitches: R Bats: R Pos: SP-23 SHERR-zer **Ht: 6'3" Wt: 208 Born: 7/27/1984 Age: 38**

		HOW MUCH PITCHED					WHAT HE GAVE UP										THE RESULTS						
Year	Team	Lg	G	GS	GF	IP	BFP	H	R	ER	HR	SH	SF	HB	TBB	IBB	SO	WP	W	L	Pct	Sv-Op	Hld	Vel	OPS	ERC	ERA
2008	Ari	NL	16	7	2	56.0	237	48	24	19	5	4	2	5	21	1	66	2	0	4	.000	0-0	0	94	.649	3.45	3.05
2009	Ari	NL	30	30	0	170.1	741	166	94	78	20	5	6	10	63	1	174	5	9	11	.450	0-0	0	94	.751	4.12	4.12
2010	Det	AL	31	31	0	195.2	800	174	84	76	20	5	5	7	70	1	184	8	12	11	.522	0-0	0	94	.700	3.56	3.50
2011	Det	AL	33	33	0	195.0	833	207	101	96	29	3	7	7	56	1	174	12	15	9	.625	0-0	0	93	.781	4.48	4.43
2012	Det	AL	32	32	0	187.2	787	179	82	78	23	5	1	5	60	2	231	2	16	7	.696	0-0	0	94	.721	3.77	3.74
2013	Det	AL	32	32	0	214.1	836	152	73	69	18	2	8	4	56	0	240	6	21	3	.875	0-0	0	93	.583	2.07	2.90
2014	Det	AL	33	33	0	220.1	904	196	80	77	18	4	8	4	63	1	252	10	18	5	.783	0-0	0	93	.663	3.04	3.15
2015	Was	NL	33	33	0	228.2	899	176	74	71	27	11	2	5	34	2	276	10	14	12	.538	0-0	0	94	.600	2.11	2.79
2016	Was	NL	34	34	0	228.1	902	165	77	75	31	7	3	6	56	2	284	2	20	7	.741	0-0	0	94	.619	2.35	2.96
2017	Was	NL	31	31	0	200.2	780	126	62	56	22	4	1	11	55	2	268	4	16	6	.727	0-0	0	94	.566	1.98	2.51
2018	Was	NL	33	33	0	220.2	866	150	66	62	23	4	2	12	51	4	300	4	18	7	.720	0-0	0	94	.580	2.02	2.53
2019	Was	NL	27	27	0	172.1	693	144	59	56	18	0	2	7	33	2	243	0	11	7	.611	0-0	0	95	.637	2.58	2.92
2020	Was	NL	12	12	0	67.1	295	70	30	28	10	0	2	1	23	1	92	6	5	4	.556	0-0	0	95	.742	4.36	3.74
2021	2 Tms	NL	30	30	0	179.1	693	119	53	49	23	2	1	10	36	0	236	2	15	4	.789	0-0	0	94	.570	2.01	2.46
2022	NYM	NL	23	23	0	145.1	565	108	39	37	13	3	4	11	24	0	173	1	11	5	.688	0-0	0	94	.574	2.14	2.29
21	Was	NL	19	19	0	111.0	428	71	36	34	18	1	1	8	28	0	147	0	8	4	.667	0-0	0	94	.604	2.35	2.76
21	LAD	NL	11	11	0	68.1	265	48	17	15	5	1	0	2	8	0	89	2	7	0	1.000	0-0	0	95	.515	1.54	1.98
	Postseason		26	21	1	128.2	531	91	49	46	14	4	0	8	51	3	160	6	7	6	.538	1-1	2	94	.621	2.74	3.22
	15 ML YEARS		430	421	2	2682.0	10831	2180	998	927	300	59	54	107	701	20	3193	74	201	102	.663	0-0	0	94	.646	2.78	3.11

Clarke Schmidt

Pitches: R Bats: R Pos: RP-26; SP-3 **Ht: 6'1" Wt: 200 Born: 2/20/1996 Age: 27**

		HOW MUCH PITCHED					WHAT HE GAVE UP										THE RESULTS						
Year	Team	Lg	G	GS	GF	IP	BFP	H	R	ER	HR	SH	SF	HB	TBB	IBB	SO	WP	W	L	Pct	Sv-Op	Hld	Vel	OPS	ERC	ERA
2022	S-WB	AAA	8	8	0	33.0	139	26	13	12	1	1	0	2	9	0	46	0	2	1	.667	0- -	-	-	.544	2.17	3.27
2020	NYY	AL	3	1	2	6.1	33	7	5	5	0	0	0	2	5	0	7	1	0	1	.000	0-0	0	95	.770	6.52	7.11
2021	NYY	AL	2	1	1	6.1	38	11	8	4	1	1	0	1	5	0	6	0	0	0	-	0-0	0	95	.976	10.94	5.68
2022	NYY	AL	29	3	7	57.2	236	46	23	20	5	3	1	2	23	3	56	0	5	5	.500	2-3	4	95	.648	3.00	3.12
	3 ML YEARS		34	5	10	70.1	307	64	36	29	6	4	1	5	33	3	69	1	5	6	.455	2-3	4	95	.700	3.94	3.71

Jonathan Schoop

Bats: R Throws: R Pos: 2B-129;1B-2;PH-2;DH-1 SCOPE **Ht: 6'1" Wt: 247 Born: 10/16/1991 Age: 31**

			BATTING																			RUNNING			AVERAGES			
Year	Team	Lg	G	AB	H	2B	3B	HR	(Hm	Rd)	TB	R	RBI	RC	TBB	IBB	SO	HBP	SH	SF	SB	CS	GDP	Avg	OBP	Slg	OPS
2013	Bal	AL	5	14	4	0	0	1	(1	0)	7	5	1	1	0	2	0	0	0	0	2	.286	.333	.500	.833
2014	Bal	AL	137	455	95	18	0	16	(5	11)	161	48	45	32	13	0	122	8	5	0	2	0	12	.209	.244	.354	.598
2015	Bal	AL	86	305	85	17	0	15	(9	6)	147	34	39	40	9	0	79	4	1	2	2	0	6	.279	.306	.482	.788
2016	Bal	AL	162	615	164	38	1	25	(13	12)	279	82	82	72	21	0	137	6	0	3	1	2	16	.267	.298	.454	.752
2017	Bal	AL	160	622	182	35	0	32	(18	14)	313	92	105	100	35	0	142	10	1	7	1	0	20	.293	.338	.503	.841
2018	2 Tms		131	473	110	22	1	21	(12	9)	197	61	61	45	19	2	115	4	1	4	1	1	11	.233	.266	.416	.682
2019	Min	AL	121	433	111	23	1	23	(7	16)	205	61	59	52	20	1	116	10	0	1	1	1	13	.256	.304	.473	.777
2020	Det	AL	44	162	45	4	2	8	(6	2)	77	26	23	23	4	0	39	4	0	2	0	0	8	.278	.324	.475	.799
2021	Det	AL	156	623	173	30	1	22	(11	11)	271	85	84	86	37	0	133	6	0	8	2	0	15	.278	.320	.435	.755
2022	Det	AL	131	481	97	23	1	11	(5	6)	155	48	38	30	19	1	107	6	0	4	5	0	15	.202	.239	.322	.561
18	Bal	AL	85	349	85	18	1	17	(9	8)	156	45	40	34	12	1	74	3	1	2	1	0	8	.244	.273	.447	.720
18	Mil	NL	46	124	25	4	0	4	(3	1)	41	16	21	11	7	1	41	1	0	2	1	0	3	.202	.246	.331	.577
	Postseason		14	35	4	1	0	0	(0	0)	5	3	2	2	3	0	10	0	0	0	2	0	1	.114	.184	.143	.327
	10 ML YEARS		1133	4183	1066	210	7	174	(87	87)	1812	542	537	481	182	4	992	61	7	31	15	4	121	.255	.294	.433	.727

John Schreiber

Pitches: R Bats: R Pos: RP-64 Ht: 6'2" Wt: 210 Born: 3/5/1994 Age: 29

			HOW MUCH PITCHED					WHAT HE GAVE UP											THE RESULTS						
Year	Team	Lg	G	GS	GF	IP	BFP	H	R	ER	HR	SH	SF	HB	TBB	IBB	SO	WP	W	L	Pct	Sv-Op	Hld	Vel	OPS	ERC	ERA
2022	Wrcstr	AAA	7	0	1	12.1	49	9	4	2	2	0	0	1	3	0	15	0	2	1	.667	0- -	-		.643	2.77	1.46
2019	Det	AL	13	0	3	13.0	59	16	9	9	3	0	0	1	4	0	19	1	2	0	1.000	0-1	1	92	.837	6.34	6.23
2020	Det	AL	15	0	2	15.2	70	19	11	11	2	0	1	1	4	1	14	0	0	1	.000	0-1	1	90	.827	5.02	6.32
2021	Bos	AL	1	0	0	3.0	13	4	1	1	0	0	0	0	1	0	5	0	0	0	-	0-0	0	92	.885	5.24	3.00
2022	Bos	AL	64	0	13	65.0	257	45	19	16	3	1	2	4	19	0	74	4	4	4	.500	8-10	22	94	.577	2.02	2.22
	4 ML YEARS		93	0	18	96.2	399	84	40	37	8	1	3	6	28	1	112	5	6	5	.545	8-12	24	93	.670	3.07	3.44

Max Schrock

Bats: L Throws: R Pos: PH-8;RF-3;2B-2;LF-2;DH-1 Ht: 5'9" Wt: 185 Born: 10/12/1994 Age: 28

								BATTING													RUNNING			AVERAGES			
Year	Team	Lg	G	AB	H	2B	3B	HR	(Hm	Rd)	TB	R	RBI	RC	TBB	IBB	SO	HBP	SH	SF	SB	CS	GDP	Avg	OBP	Slg	OPS
2022	Lsvlle	AAA	20	69	21	3	0	2	(-	-)	30	14	9	10	3	0	10	1	0	0	0	0	0	.304	.342	.435	.777
2020	StL	NL	11	17	3	0	0	1	(0	1)	6	1	1	0	0	0	6	0	0	0	0	0	0	.176	.176	.353	.529
2021	Cin	NL	53	125	36	7	2	3	(2	1)	56	19	14	20	8	1	24	0	0	1	1	1	0	.288	.328	.448	.776
2022	Cin	NL	13	26	4	0	0	0	(0	0)	4	1	1	0	1	0	6	0	0	0	0	0	0	.154	.185	.154	.339
	3 ML YEARS		77	168	43	7	2	4	(2	2)	66	21	16	20	9	1	36	0	0	1	1	1	0	.256	.292	.393	.685

Kyle Schwarber

Bats: L Throws: R Pos: LF-139;DH-15;PH-2   SHWAR-burr   Ht: 6'0" Wt: 229 Born: 3/5/1993 Age: 30

								BATTING													RUNNING			AVERAGES			
Year	Team	Lg	G	AB	H	2B	3B	HR	(Hm	Rd)	TB	R	RBI	RC	TBB	IBB	SO	HBP	SH	SF	SB	CS	GDP	Avg	OBP	Slg	OPS
2015	ChC	NL	69	232	57	6	1	16	(7	9)	113	52	43	39	36	1	77	4	0	1	3	3	4	.246	.355	.487	.842
2016	ChC	NL	2	4	0	0	0	0	(0	0)	0	0	0	0	1	0	2	0	0	0	0	0	0	.000	.200	.000	.200
2017	ChC	NL	129	422	89	16	1	30	(18	12)	197	67	59	55	59	1	150	5	0	0	1	1	6	.211	.315	.467	.782
2018	ChC	NL	137	428	102	14	3	26	(11	15)	200	64	61	65	78	20	140	1	1	2	4	3	6	.238	.356	.467	.823
2019	ChC	NL	155	529	132	29	3	38	(18	20)	281	82	92	92	70	5	156	5	0	0	2	3	6	.250	.339	.531	.871
2020	ChC	NL	59	191	36	6	0	11	(5	6)	75	30	24	27	30	1	66	3	0	0	1	0	3	.188	.308	.393	.701
2021	2 Tms		113	399	106	19	0	32	(21	11)	221	76	71	83	64	1	127	6	0	2	1	1	4	.266	.374	.554	.928
2022	Phi	NL	155	577	126	21	3	46	(21	25)	291	100	94	108	86	3	200	4	0	2	10	1	10	.218	.323	.504	.827
21	Was	NL	72	265	67	9	0	25	(17	8)	151	42	53	49	31	1	88	5	0	2	1	1	4	.253	.340	.570	.910
21	Bos	AL	41	134	39	10	0	7	(4	3)	70	34	18	34	33	0	39	1	0	0	0	0	0	.291	.435	.522	.957
	Postseason		35	110	28	2	0	9	(7	2)	57	18	17	18	18	0	30	0	0	0	2	0	2	.255	.359	.518	.878
	8 ML YEARS		819	2782	648	111	11	199	(101	98)	1378	471	444	469	424	32	918	28	1	13	22	12	39	.233	.339	.495	.834

Frank Schwindel

Bats: R Throws: R Pos: 1B-48;DH-26;PH-6 Ht: 6'1" Wt: 220 Born: 6/29/1992 Age: 31

								BATTING													RUNNING			AVERAGES			
Year	Team	Lg	G	AB	H	2B	3B	HR	(Hm	Rd)	TB	R	RBI	RC	TBB	IBB	SO	HBP	SH	SF	SB	CS	GDP	Avg	OBP	Slg	OPS
2022	Iowa	AAA	10	37	8	3	0	1	(-	-)	14	5	4	2	0	0	8	0	0	0	0	0	2	.216	.216	.378	.595
2019	KC	AL	6	15	1	0	0	0	(0	0)	1	0	0	0	0	0	2	0	0	0	0	0	0	.067	.067	.067	.133
2021	2 Tms		64	242	79	20	1	14	(7	7)	143	44	43	48	16	2	41	1	0	0	2	1	4	.326	.371	.591	.962
2022	ChC	NL	75	271	62	11	0	8	(5	3)	97	23	36	22	19	1	58	0	0	2	0	0	12	.229	.277	.358	.635
21	Oak	AL	8	20	3	1	0	1	(1	0)	7	2	3	2	0	0	5	0	0	0	0	0	0	.150	.150	.350	.500
21	ChC	NL	56	222	76	19	1	13	(6	7)	136	42	40	46	16	2	36	1	0	0	2	1	4	.342	.389	.613	1.002
	3 ML YEARS		145	528	142	31	1	22	(12	10)	241	67	79	70	35	3	101	1	0	2	2	1	16	.269	.314	.456	.771

Tanner Scott

Pitches: L Bats: R Pos: RP-67 Ht: 6'0" Wt: 235 Born: 7/22/1994 Age: 28

			HOW MUCH PITCHED					WHAT HE GAVE UP											THE RESULTS						
Year	Team	Lg	G	GS	GF	IP	BFP	H	R	ER	HR	SH	SF	HB	TBB	IBB	SO	WP	W	L	Pct	Sv-Op	Hld	Vel	OPS	ERC	ERA
2017	Bal	AL	2	0	1	1.2	9	2	2	2	0	0	0	0	2	0	2	0	0	0	-	0-0	0	98	.873	7.49	10.80
2018	Bal	AL	53	0	8	53.1	240	55	33	32	6	1	1	1	28	1	76	7	3	3	.500	0-3	5	97	.777	4.86	5.40
2019	Bal	AL	28	0	5	26.1	122	28	17	14	4	0	0	2	19	2	37	2	1	1	.500	0-1	2	96	.847	6.54	4.78
2020	Bal	AL	25	0	6	20.2	86	12	5	3	0	0	0	2	10	0	23	4	0	0	-	1-2	5	96	.524	2.37	1.31
2021	Bal	AL	62	0	12	54.0	251	48	34	31	6	0	3	6	37	1	70	10	5	4	.556	0-2	16	97	.714	4.99	5.17
2022	Mia	NL	67	0	35	62.2	289	55	34	30	5	0	6	4	46	1	90	3	5	4	.444	20-27	4	97	.711	4.71	4.31
	6 ML YEARS		237	0	67	218.2	997	200	125	112	22	1	10	16	142	5	298	26	13	13	.500	21-35	32	97	.730	4.80	4.61

Tayler Scott

Pitches: R Bats: R Pos: RP-8 Ht: 6'3" Wt: 185 Born: 6/1/1992 Age: 31

			HOW MUCH PITCHED					WHAT HE GAVE UP											THE RESULTS						
Year	Team	Lg	G	GS	GF	IP	BFP	H	R	ER	HR	SH	SF	HB	TBB	IBB	SO	WP	W	L	Pct	Sv-Op	Hld	Vel	OPS	ERC	ERA
2022	ElPaso	AAA	33	0	9	40.2	171	41	22	17	5	0	2	1	11	0	52	7	2	1	.667	3- -	-		.737	3.88	3.76
2019	2 Tms	AL	13	2	6	16.1	93	31	28	26	6	0	0	4	11	0	14	2	0	0	-	0-0	0	95	1.174	15.16	14.33
2022	SD	NL	8	0	2	12.0	59	19	10	9	1	0	0	0	6	0	13	0	0	1	.000	0-0	0	94	.895	8.03	6.75
19	Sea	AL	5	2	1	7.2	41	11	10	8	1	0	0	2	6	0	7	0	0	0	-	0-0	0	95	.948	9.89	9.39
19	Bal	AL	8	0	5	8.2	52	20	18	18	5	0	0	2	5	0	7	2	0	0	-	0-0	0	94	1.341	20.19	18.69
	2 ML YEARS		21	2	8	28.1	152	50	38	35	7	0	0	4	17	0	27	2	0	1	.000	0-0	0	94	1.063	12.01	11.12

Connor Seabold

Pitches: R Bats: R Pos: SP-5   **Ht: 6'2" Wt: 190 Born: 1/24/1996 Age: 27**

			HOW MUCH PITCHED				WHAT HE GAVE UP									THE RESULTS							
Year	Team	Lg	G	GS	GF	IP	BFP	H	R	ER	HR	SH	SF	HB	TBB	IBB	SO	WP	W	L	Pct	Sv-Op	Hld	Vel	OPS	ERC	ERA
2022	Wrcstr	AAA	19	19	0	86.2	360	79	35	32	7	1	1	6	19	0	89	5	8	2	.800	0- -	-		.656	3.02	3.32
2021	Bos	AL	1	1	0	3.0	12	3	2	2	1	0	0	0	2	0	0	0	0	0	-	0-0	0	90	1.117	8.08	6.00
2022	Bos	AL	5	5	0	18.1	98	35	24	23	5	0	0	3	8	0	19	4	0	4	.000	0-0	0	92	1.194	12.68	11.29
	2 ML YEARS		6	6	0	21.1	110	38	26	25	6	0	0	3	10	0	19	4	0	4	.000	0-0	0	92	1.185	12.03	10.55

Corey Seager

Bats: L Throws: R Pos: SS-144;DH-7   SEE-gurr   **Ht: 6'4" Wt: 215 Born: 4/27/1994 Age: 29**

			BATTING																	RUNNING			AVERAGES			
Year	Team	Lg	G	AB	H	2B	3B	HR	(Hm	Rd)	TB	R	RBI	RC	TBB	IBB	SO	HBP	SH	SF	SB	CS	GDP	Avg	OBP	Slg	OPS
2015	LAD	NL	27	98	33	8	1	4	(3	1)	55	17	17	19	14	1	19	1	0	0	2	0	2	.337	.425	.561	.986
2016	LAD	NL	157	627	193	40	5	26	(18	8)	321	105	72	110	54	5	133	4	0	2	3	3	12	.308	.365	.512	.877
2017	LAD	NL	145	539	159	33	0	22	(12	10)	258	85	77	104	67	5	131	4	0	3	4	2	14	.295	.375	.479	.854
2018	LAD	NL	26	101	27	5	1	2	(1	1)	40	13	13	17	11	1	17	2	0	1	0	0	2	.267	.348	.396	.744
2019	LAD	NL	134	489	133	44	1	19	(9	10)	236	82	87	81	44	3	98	4	0	4	1	0	8	.272	.335	.483	.817
2020	LAD	NL	52	212	65	12	1	15	(7	8)	124	38	41	36	17	0	37	1	0	2	1	0	8	.307	.358	.585	.943
2021	LAD	NL	95	353	108	22	3	16	(9	7)	184	54	57	74	48	2	66	5	0	3	1	1	8	.306	.394	.521	.915
2022	Tex	AL	151	593	145	24	1	33	(22	11)	270	91	83	94	58	7	103	7	0	5	3	0	14	.245	.317	.455	.772
	Postseason		61	233	55	11	1	13	(6	7)	107	37	36	32	27	1	67	2	0	2	3	0	6	.236	.318	.459	.777
	8 ML YEARS		787	3012	863	188	13	137	(81	56)	1488	485	447	535	313	24	604	28	0	20	15	6	68	.287	.357	.494	.851

JP Sears

Pitches: L Bats: R Pos: SP-11; RP-6   **Ht: 5'11" Wt: 180 Born: 2/19/1996 Age: 27**

			HOW MUCH PITCHED					WHAT HE GAVE UP										THE RESULTS								
Year	Team	Lg	G	GS	GF	IP	BFP	H	R	ER	HR	SH	SF	HB	TBB	IBB	SO	WP	W	L	Pct	Sv-Op	Hld	Vel	OPS	ERC	ERA
2022	S-WB	AAA	11	9	1	43.0	163	24	12	8	3	0	0	1	7	0	55	1	1	1	.500	0- -	-		.429	1.19	1.67
2022	2 Tms	AL	17	11	1	70.0	288	67	31	30	8	1	0	2	23	1	51	0	6	3	.667	0-0	0	93	.716	3.87	3.86
22	NYY	AL	7	2	1	22.0	83	14	5	5	1	0	1	1	5	0	15	0	3	0	1.000	0-0	0	94	.504	1.59	2.05
22	Oak	AL	10	9	0	48.0	205	53	26	25	7	0	0	1	18	1	36	0	3	3	.500	0-0	0	93	.803	5.13	4.69

Cody Sedlock

Pitches: R Bats: R Pos: RP-1   **Ht: 6'4" Wt: 220 Born: 6/19/1995 Age: 28**

			HOW MUCH PITCHED					WHAT HE GAVE UP										THE RESULTS								
Year	Team	Lg	G	GS	GF	IP	BFP	H	R	ER	HR	SH	SF	HB	TBB	IBB	SO	WP	W	L	Pct	Sv-Op	Hld	Vel	OPS	ERC	ERA
2022	Norfolk	AAA	14	10	1	54.1	245	55	39	33	4	1	3	6	28	0	62	1	4	1	.800	0- -	-		.761	4.87	5.47
2022	Toledo	AAA	14	2	0	25.2	110	20	11	10	3	0	0	1	16	0	19	0	1	2	.333	0- -	-		.734	4.06	3.51
2022	Bal	AL	1	0	0	3.0	16	6	5	5	0	0	0	0	1	0	3	0	0	0	-	0-0	0	91	.971	8.97	15.00

Jean Segura

Bats: R Throws: R Pos: 2B-97;PH-2;SS-1   JEEN seh-GOO-ruh   **Ht: 5'10" Wt: 220 Born: 3/17/1990 Age: 33**

			BATTING																	RUNNING			AVERAGES			
Year	Team	Lg	G	AB	H	2B	3B	HR	(Hm	Rd)	TB	R	RBI	RC	TBB	IBB	SO	HBP	SH	SF	SB	CS	GDP	Avg	OBP	Slg	OPS
2012	2 Tms		45	151	39	4	3	0	(0	0)	49	19	14	16	13	3	23	0	1	1	7	1	1	.258	.315	.325	.640
2013	Mil	NL	146	588	173	20	10	12	(7	5)	249	74	49	72	25	1	84	6	2	2	44	13	17	.294	.329	.423	.752
2014	Mil	NL	146	513	126	14	6	5	(3	2)	167	61	31	45	28	5	70	4	10	2	20	9	13	.246	.289	.326	.614
2015	Mil	NL	142	560	144	16	5	6	(4	2)	188	57	50	57	13	2	93	6	3	2	25	6	14	.257	.281	.336	.616
2016	Ari	NL	153	637	203	41	7	20	(12	8)	318	102	64	107	39	1	101	12	4	2	33	10	6	.319	.368	.499	.867
2017	Sea	AL	125	524	157	30	2	11	(7	4)	224	80	45	71	34	3	83	6	0	1	22	8	14	.300	.349	.427	.776
2018	Sea	AL	144	586	178	29	3	10	(7	3)	243	91	63	77	32	2	69	4	4	6	20	11	17	.304	.341	.415	.755
2019	Phi	NL	144	576	161	37	4	12	(9	3)	242	79	60	79	30	1	73	8	1	3	10	2	11	.280	.323	.420	.743
2020	Phi	NL	54	192	51	5	2	7	(5	2)	81	28	25	28	23	2	45	1	1	0	2	2	5	.266	.347	.422	.769
2021	Phi	NL	131	514	149	27	3	14	(6	8)	224	76	58	75	39	5	78	9	1	4	9	3	16	.290	.348	.436	.784
2022	Phi	NL	98	354	98	9	0	10	(6	4)	137	45	33	38	25	1	58	7	0	1	13	6	16	.277	.336	.387	.723
12	LAA	AL	1	3	0	0	0	0	(0	0)	0	0	0	0	0	0	2	0	0	0	0	0	0	.000	.000	.000	.000
12	Mil	NL	44	148	39	4	3	0	(0	0)	49	19	14	16	13	3	21	0	1	1	7	1	1	.264	.321	.331	.652
	11 ML YEARS		1328	5195	1479	232	45	107	(66	41)	2122	712	492	665	301	24	777	63	27	24	205	71	131	.285	.330	.408	.739

Sam Selman

Pitches: L Bats: R Pos: RP-16   **Ht: 6'2" Wt: 198 Born: 11/14/1990 Age: 32**

			HOW MUCH PITCHED					WHAT HE GAVE UP										THE RESULTS								
Year	Team	Lg	G	GS	GF	IP	BFP	H	R	ER	HR	SH	SF	HB	TBB	IBB	SO	WP	W	L	Pct	Sv-Op	Hld	Vel	OPS	ERC	ERA
2022	LsVgs	AAA	28	0	9	35.0	144	20	11	11	2	0	0	4	18	1	36	2	2	0	1.000	6- -	-		.546	2.36	2.83
2019	SF	NL	10	0	3	10.1	44	6	5	5	2	1	0	2	6	0	10	0	0	0	-	0-1	1	90	.697	3.89	4.35
2020	SF	NL	24	0	8	19.1	82	13	8	8	1	2	1	0	9	0	23	2	1	1	.500	1-1	3	91	.611	2.92	3.72
2021	2 Tms	AL	25	0	9	25.0	110	20	17	16	3	0	3	5	12	1	19	0	0	1	.000	0-1	1	91	.692	4.12	5.76
2022	Oak	AL	16	0	7	18.1	75	16	10	10	4	0	0	1	5	0	18	0	0	0	-	0-1	0	89	.757	3.90	4.91
21	SF	NL	7	0	2	8.0	33	4	4	4	2	0	0	1	4	0	8	0	0	0	-	0-1	0	91	.666	3.17	4.50
21	LAA	AL	18	0	7	17.0	77	16	13	12	1	0	3	4	8	1	11	0	0	1	.000	0-0	1	91	.702	4.54	6.35
	4 ML YEARS		75	0	27	73.0	311	55	40	39	11	2	3	10	32	1	70	2	1	2	.333	1-4	5	91	.689	3.72	4.81

Marcus Semien

Bats: R **Throws:** R **Pos:** 2B-148;SS-17   SIM-ee-inn   **Ht:** 6'0" **Wt:** 195 **Born:** 9/17/1990 **Age:** 32

Year	Team	Lg	G	AB	H	2B	3B	HR	(Hm	Rd)	TB	R	RBI	RC	TBB	IBB	SO	HBP	SH	SF	SB	CS	GDP	Avg	OBP	Slg	OPS
2013	CWS	AL	21	69	18	4	0	2	(2	0)	28	7	7	7	1	0	22	0	0	1	2	2	1	.261	.268	.406	.673
2014	CWS	AL	64	231	54	10	2	6	(4	2)	86	30	28	31	21	0	70	1	2	0	3	0	6	.234	.300	.372	.673
2015	Oak	AL	155	556	143	23	7	15	(5	10)	225	65	45	57	42	1	132	1	1	1	11	5	16	.257	.310	.405	.715
2016	Oak	AL	159	568	135	27	2	27	(10	17)	247	72	75	77	51	1	139	0	1	1	10	2	12	.238	.300	.435	.735
2017	Oak	AL	85	342	85	19	1	10	(5	5)	136	53	40	48	38	0	85	2	1	3	12	1	3	.249	.325	.398	.722
2018	Oak	AL	159	632	161	35	2	15	(6	9)	245	89	70	85	61	1	131	1	2	7	14	6	12	.255	.318	.388	.706
2019	Oak	AL	162	657	187	43	7	33	(15	18)	343	123	92	136	87	2	102	2	0	1	10	8	11	.285	.369	.522	.892
2020	Oak	AL	53	211	47	9	1	7	(2	5)	79	28	23	30	25	0	50	0	0	0	4	0	3	.223	.305	.374	.679
2021	Tor	AL	162	652	173	39	2	45	(22	23)	351	115	102	112	66	0	146	3	0	3	15	1	9	.265	.334	.538	.873
2022	Tex	AL	161	657	163	31	5	26	(10	16)	282	101	83	95	53	0	120	4	0	10	25	8	10	.248	.304	.429	.733
	Postseason		9	35	13	1	0	2	(1	1)	20	7	4	9	5	0	4	0	0	0	0	0	0	.371	.450	.571	1.021
	10 ML YEARS		1181	4575	1166	240	29	186	(81	105)	2022	683	565	678	445	5	997	14	7	27	106	33	80	.255	.321	.442	.763

Antonio Senzatela

Pitches: R **Bats:** R **Pos:** SP-19   **Ht:** 6'1" **Wt:** 236 **Born:** 1/21/1995 **Age:** 28

			HOW MUCH PITCHED					WHAT HE GAVE UP										THE RESULTS							
Year	Team	Lg	G	GS	GF	IP	BFP	H	R	ER	HR	SH	SF	HB	TBB	IBB	SO	WP	W	L	Pct	Sv-Op	Hld	Vel	OPS	ERC	ERA
2017	Col	NL	36	20	3	134.2	564	128	72	70	18	4	5	4	47	1	102	1	10	5	.667	0-0	1	94	.756	4.00	4.68
2018	Col	NL	23	13	2	90.1	390	94	45	44	10	1	3	3	30	1	69	1	6	6	.500	0-0	0	94	.763	4.22	4.38
2019	Col	NL	25	25	0	124.2	582	161	99	93	19	4	4	4	57	5	76	1	11	11	.500	0-0	0	94	.890	6.53	6.71
2020	Col	NL	12	12	0	73.1	303	71	29	28	9	0	2	4	18	0	41	0	5	3	.625	0-0	0	94	.716	3.72	3.44
2021	Col	NL	28	28	0	156.2	670	178	84	77	12	3	6	9	32	1	105	4	4	10	.286	0-0	0	95	.749	4.14	4.42
2022	Col	NL	19	19	0	92.1	413	133	56	52	9	3	3	3	23	0	54	1	3	7	.300	0-0	0	94	.892	6.39	5.07
	Postseason		1	1	0	5.0	19	3	2	2	1	0	0	0	2	0	1	2	0	0	-	0-0	0	94	.616	2.72	3.60
	6 ML YEARS		143	117	5	672.0	2922	765	385	364	77	15	22	27	207	8	447	8	39	42	.481	0-0	1	94	.797	4.79	4.88

Nick Senzel

Bats: R **Throws:** R **Pos:** CF-101;DH-5;PH-3;3B-2;PR-2;2B-1   **Ht:** 6'1" **Wt:** 205 **Born:** 6/29/1995 **Age:** 28

Year	Team	Lg	G	AB	H	2B	3B	HR	(Hm	Rd)	TB	R	RBI	RC	TBB	IBB	SO	HBP	SH	SF	SB	CS	GDP	Avg	OBP	Slg	OPS
2019	Cin	NL	104	375	96	20	4	12	(7	5)	160	55	42	49	30	0	101	3	0	1	14	5	6	.256	.315	.427	.742
2020	Cin	NL	23	70	13	6	0	2	(2	0)	25	8	8	7	6	0	15	0	0	1	2	1	2	.186	.247	.357	.604
2021	Cin	NL	36	111	28	4	0	1	(1	0)	35	18	8	12	12	0	16	0	0	1	2	5	3	.252	.323	.315	.638
2022	Cin	NL	110	373	86	13	0	5	(3	2)	114	45	25	33	30	0	76	5	2	1	8	5	7	.231	.296	.306	.601
	Postseason		2	7	2	0	0	0	(0	0)	2	0	0	0	0	0	2	0	0	0	0	0	0	.286	.286	.286	.571
	4 ML YEARS		273	929	223	43	4	20	(13	7)	334	126	83	101	78	0	208	8	2	4	26	16	18	.240	.303	.360	.663

Brian Serven

Bats: R **Throws:** R **Pos:** C-59;1B-1;PR-1   **Ht:** 6'0" **Wt:** 207 **Born:** 5/5/1995 **Age:** 28

Year	Team	Lg	G	AB	H	2B	3B	HR	(Hm	Rd)	TB	R	RBI	RC	TBB	IBB	SO	HBP	SH	SF	SB	CS	GDP	Avg	OBP	Slg	OPS
2022	Albq	AAA	23	77	21	3	0	5	(-	-)	39	18	11	17	16	0	15	2	0	1	0	0	1	.273	.406	.506	.913
2022	Col	NL	62	187	38	4	1	6	(6	0)	62	19	16	15	13	0	44	2	2	1	0	0	7	.203	.261	.332	.593

Anderson Severino

Pitches: L **Bats:** L **Pos:** RP-6   **Ht:** 5'10" **Wt:** 190 **Born:** 9/17/1994 **Age:** 28

			HOW MUCH PITCHED					WHAT HE GAVE UP										THE RESULTS							
Year	Team	Lg	G	GS	GF	IP	BFP	H	R	ER	HR	SH	SF	HB	TBB	IBB	SO	WP	W	L	Pct	Sv-Op	Hld	Vel	OPS	ERC	ERA
2022	Charltt	AAA	37	0	4	30.0	167	37	40	38	6	0	0	2	42	0	34	2	3	4	.429	0- -	-	-	1.013	11.17	11.40
2022	CWS	AL	6	0	4	7.1	34	7	5	5	0	0	0	2	4	0	9	2	0	0	-	0-0	0	96	.704	4.69	6.14

Luis Severino

Pitches: R **Bats:** R **Pos:** SP-19   **Ht:** 6'2" **Wt:** 218 **Born:** 2/20/1994 **Age:** 29

			HOW MUCH PITCHED					WHAT HE GAVE UP										THE RESULTS							
Year	Team	Lg	G	GS	GF	IP	BFP	H	R	ER	HR	SH	SF	HB	TBB	IBB	SO	WP	W	L	Pct	Sv-Op	Hld	Vel	OPS	ERC	ERA
2015	NYY	AL	11	11	0	62.1	255	53	21	20	9	0	0	2	22	0	56	2	5	3	.625	0-0	0	95	.705	3.57	2.89
2016	NYY	AL	22	11	3	71.0	312	78	48	46	11	0	0	3	25	1	66	3	3	8	.273	0-0	1	96	.812	5.00	5.83
2017	NYY	AL	31	31	0	193.1	783	150	73	64	21	3	2	6	51	0	230	6	14	6	.700	0-0	0	98	.603	2.53	2.98
2018	NYY	AL	32	32	0	191.1	780	173	76	72	19	1	2	5	46	0	220	8	19	8	.704	0-0	0	96	.666	3.06	3.39
2019	NYY	AL	3	3	0	12.0	48	6	2	2	0	0	0	1	6	0	17	0	1	1	.500	0-0	0	96	.442	1.62	1.50
2021	NYY	AL	4	0	1	6.0	22	2	0	0	0	0	0	1	1	0	8	0	1	0	1.000	0-0	1	95	.332	0.69	0.00
2022	NYY	AL	19	19	0	102.0	405	72	37	36	14	2	1	4	30	0	112	1	7	3	.700	0-0	0	96	.616	2.53	3.18
	Postseason		9	8	0	32.2	150	32	19	19	7	0	1	0	20	0	32	0	1	3	.250	0-0	0	97	.796	5.56	5.23
	7 ML YEARS		122	107	4	638.0	2605	534	257	240	74	6	5	22	181	1	709	20	50	29	.633	0-0	2	97	.654	2.99	3.39

Pedro Severino

Bats: R Throws: R Pos: C-4;PH-3;1B-2;DH-2   Ht: 6'1" Wt: 235 Born: 7/20/1993 Age: 29

Year	Team	Lg	G	AB	H	2B	3B	HR	(Hm	Rd)	TB	R	RBI	RC	TBB	IBB	SO	HBP	SH	SF	SB	CS	GDP	Avg	OBP	Slg	OPS
2022	Nashv	AAA	31	117	36	10	0	4	(-	-)	58	20	17	19	6	0	27	2	0	1	2	0	4	.308	.349	.496	.845
2015	Was	NL	2	4	1	1	0	0	(0	0)	2	1	0	0	0	0	1	0	0	0	0	0	0	.250	.250	.500	.750
2016	Was	NL	16	28	9	2	0	2	(1	1)	17	6	4	5	5	0	3	1	0	0	0	0	0	.321	.441	.607	1.048
2017	Was	NL	17	29	5	1	0	0	(0	0)	6	0	3	2	2	1	10	0	0	0	0	0	0	.172	.226	.207	.433
2018	Was	NL	70	190	32	9	0	2	(2	0)	47	14	15	12	18	4	47	4	0	1	1	0	3	.168	.254	.247	.501
2019	Bal	AL	96	305	76	13	0	13	(7	6)	128	37	44	39	29	0	73	4	1	2	3	1	5	.249	.321	.420	.740
2020	Bal	AL	48	160	40	5	1	5	(3	2)	62	17	21	20	16	0	40	1	1	0	0	0	3	.250	.322	.388	.710
2021	Bal	AL	113	379	94	18	0	11	(8	3)	145	32	46	48	34	1	109	1	0	5	0	0	9	.248	.308	.383	.690
2022	Mil	NL	8	18	4	2	0	0	(0	0)	6	0	1	3	3	0	7	0	0	0	0	0	0	.222	.333	.333	.667
	Postseason		4	10	1	1	0	0	(0	0)	2	1	0	0	0	0	3	0	0	0	0	0	0	.100	.100	.200	.300
	8 ML YEARS		370	1113	261	51	1	33	(21	12)	413	107	134	129	107	6	290	11	2	8	5	1	20	.235	.306	.371	.677

Paul Sewald

Pitches: R Bats: R Pos: RP-65   Ht: 6'3" Wt: 219 Born: 5/26/1990 Age: 33

Year	Team	Lg	G	GS	GF	IP	BFP	H	R	ER	HR	SH	SF	HB	TBB	IBB	SO	WP	W	L	Pct	Sv-Op	Hld	Vel	OPS	ERC	ERA
2017	NYM	NL	57	0	12	65.1	275	58	36	33	8	3	3	3	21	2	69	3	0	6	.000	0-3	13	91	.706	3.41	4.55
2018	NYM	NL	46	0	9	56.1	253	62	39	38	8	2	3	1	23	2	58	1	0	7	.000	2-4	2	90	.820	4.93	6.07
2019	NYM	NL	17	0	6	19.2	80	18	10	10	3	1	1	1	3	0	22	0	1	1	.500	1-1	0	91	.724	3.17	4.58
2020	NYM	NL	5	0	1	6.0	35	12	9	9	1	0	1	1	4	0	2	0	0	0	-	0-0	0	92	1.072	13.03	13.50
2021	Sea	AL	62	0	18	64.2	264	42	24	22	10	0	0	0	24	5	104	2	10	3	.769	11-16	16	92	.590	2.29	3.06
2022	Sea	AL	65	0	37	64.0	242	32	21	19	10	1	1	4	17	4	72	1	5	4	.556	20-25	8	93	.521	1.61	2.67
	6 ML YEARS		252	0	83	276.0	1149	224	139	131	40	7	9	10	92	13	327	7	16	21	.432	34-49	39	92	.677	3.12	4.27

Bryan Shaw

Pitches: R Bats: B Pos: RP-58; SP-2   Ht: 6'1" Wt: 226 Born: 11/8/1987 Age: 35

Year	Team	Lg	G	GS	GF	IP	BFP	H	R	ER	HR	SH	SF	HB	TBB	IBB	SO	WP	W	L	Pct	Sv-Op	Hld	Vel	OPS	ERC	ERA
2011	Ari	NL	33	0	8	28.1	122	30	9	8	2	0	0	4	8	1	24	1	1	0	1.000	0-0	5	91	.699	4.31	2.54
2012	Ari	NL	64	0	19	59.1	252	60	29	23	4	4	2	2	24	3	41	4	1	6	.143	2-4	10	92	.747	4.08	3.49
2013	Cle	AL	70	0	11	75.0	316	60	31	27	4	4	2	4	28	2	73	5	7	3	.700	1-5	12	91	.586	2.71	3.24
2014	Cle	AL	80	0	16	76.1	313	61	26	22	6	5	2	2	22	4	64	4	5	5	.500	2-9	24	93	.602	2.45	2.59
2015	Cle	AL	74	0	19	64.0	265	59	24	21	8	1	0	1	19	1	54	3	3	3	.500	2-6	23	92	.693	3.47	2.95
2016	Cle	AL	75	0	9	66.2	275	56	26	24	8	2	1	1	28	3	69	2	2	5	.286	1-4	25	93	.686	3.47	3.24
2017	Cle	AL	79	0	16	76.2	312	71	36	30	5	1	1	0	22	3	73	3	4	6	.400	3-6	26	94	.653	3.01	3.52
2018	Col	NL	61	0	14	54.2	257	70	43	36	9	1	3	1	28	1	54	8	4	6	.400	0-5	13	93	.896	6.79	5.93
2019	Col	NL	70	0	18	72.0	311	69	44	43	12	1	1	5	29	1	58	1	3	2	.600	1-6	12	93	.798	4.61	5.38
2020	Sea	AL	6	0	1	6.0	38	13	12	12	1	0	1	1	6	0	4	0	1	0	1.000	0-1	0	93	1.293	15.93	18.00
2021	Cle	AL	81	0	10	77.1	334	69	33	30	10	1	0	1	38	0	71	6	6	7	.462	2-8	20	93	.712	4.08	3.49
2022	Cle	AL	60	2	11	58.1	261	58	38	35	9	0	1	4	26	1	52	2	6	2	.750	1-1	5	93	.755	4.80	5.40
	Postseason		19	0	2	22.0	89	19	8	6	2	0	1	0	6	3	22	1	2	1	.667	0-0	5	95	.622	2.63	2.45
	12 ML YEARS		753	2	152	714.2	3056	676	351	311	78	20	14	26	278	20	637	39	43	45	.489	15-55	179	93	.714	3.90	3.92

Travis Shaw

Bats: L Throws: R Pos: 1B-3;DH-3;PH-2   Ht: 6'4" Wt: 230 Born: 4/16/1990 Age: 33

Year	Team	Lg	G	AB	H	2B	3B	HR	(Hm	Rd)	TB	R	RBI	RC	TBB	IBB	SO	HBP	SH	SF	SB	CS	GDP	Avg	OBP	Slg	OPS
2015	Bos	AL	65	226	61	10	0	13	(8	5)	110	31	36	35	18	1	57	2	0	2	0	1	1	.270	.327	.487	.813
2016	Bos	AL	145	480	116	34	2	16	(7	9)	202	63	71	64	43	4	133	3	0	4	5	1	10	.242	.306	.421	.726
2017	Mil	NL	144	538	147	34	1	31	(13	18)	276	84	101	93	60	6	138	4	1	3	10	0	20	.273	.349	.513	.862
2018	Mil	NL	152	498	120	23	0	32	(16	16)	239	73	86	84	78	6	108	4	1	6	5	2	7	.241	.345	.480	.825
2019	Mil	NL	86	230	36	5	0	7	(3	4)	62	22	16	11	36	3	89	4	0	0	0	0	5	.157	.281	.270	.551
2020	Tor	AL	50	163	39	10	0	6	(3	3)	67	17	17	19	16	0	50	0	0	1	0	0	6	.239	.306	.411	.717
2021	2 Tms		84	220	44	11	0	9	(6	3)	82	20	39	24	24	0	68	3	2	1	0	0	2	.200	.286	.373	.659
2022	Bos	AL	7	19	0	0	0	0	(0	0)	0	0	0	0	0	0	7	0	0	0	0	0	0	.000	.000	.000	.000
21	Mil	NL	56	178	34	8	0	6	(4	2)	60	14	28	15	19	0	51	3	1	1	0	0	2	.191	.279	.337	.616
21	Bos	AL	28	42	10	3	0	3	(2	1)	22	6	11	9	5	0	17	0	1	0	0	0	0	.238	.319	.524	.843
	Postseason		18	41	11	2	1	1	(1	0)	18	2	2	3	5	1	14	0	0	0	1	0	0	.268	.348	.439	.787
	8 ML YEARS		733	2374	563	127	3	114	(56	58)	1038	310	366	330	275	20	650	20	4	17	20	4	49	.237	.319	.437	.757

Gavin Sheets

Bats: L Throws: L Pos: RF-85;PH-18;DH-15;1B-13;LF-3   Ht: 6'5" Wt: 230 Born: 4/23/1996 Age: 27

Year	Team	Lg	G	AB	H	2B	3B	HR	(Hm	Rd)	TB	R	RBI	RC	TBB	IBB	SO	HBP	SH	SF	SB	CS	GDP	Avg	OBP	Slg	OPS
2021	CWS	AL	54	160	40	8	0	11	(8	3)	81	23	34	30	16	0	40	2	0	1	0	0	6	.250	.324	.506	.830
2022	CWS	AL	124	377	91	19	0	15	(14	1)	155	34	53	49	27	0	86	3	0	3	0	0	9	.241	.295	.411	.706
	Postseason		3	12	4	1	0	1	(1	0)	8	2	1	2	0	0	5	0	0	0	0	0	0	.333	.333	.667	1.000
	2 ML YEARS		178	537	131	27	0	26	(22	4)	236	57	87	79	43	0	126	5	0	4	0	0	13	.244	.304	.439	.743

Jordan Sheffield

Pitches: R **Bats:** R **Pos:** RP-2   **Ht:** 5'10" **Wt:** 190 **Born:** 6/1/1995 **Age:** 28

			HOW MUCH PITCHED					WHAT HE GAVE UP										THE RESULTS							
Year Team	Lg	G	GS	GF	IP	BFP	H	R	ER	HR	SH	SF	HB	TBB	IBB	SO	WP	W	L	Pct	Sv-Op	Hld	Vel	OPS	ERC	ERA
2022 Albq	AAA	27	1	2	22.2	115	32	32	28	12	0	0	2	20	0	19	2	0	0	-	0- -	-	-	1.200	13.13	11.12
2021 Col	NL	30	0	12	29.1	116	19	11	11	2	0	1	2	13	0	20	4	0	0	-	0-0	4	96	.563	2.54	3.38
2022 Col	NL	2	0	2	2.0	8	2	0	0	0	0	0	0	2	0	1	0	0	0	-	0-0	0	94	.833	6.99	0.00
2 ML YEARS		32	0	14	31.1	124	21	11	11	2	0	1	2	15	0	21	4	0	0	-	0-0	4	96	.580	2.77	3.16

Justus Sheffield

Pitches: L **Bats:** L **Pos:** RP-5; SP-1   **Ht:** 5'10" **Wt:** 224 **Born:** 5/13/1996 **Age:** 27

			HOW MUCH PITCHED					WHAT HE GAVE UP										THE RESULTS							
Year Team	Lg	G	GS	GF	IP	BFP	H	R	ER	HR	SH	SF	HB	TBB	IBB	SO	WP	W	L	Pct	Sv-Op	Hld	Vel	OPS	ERC	ERA
2022 Tacom	AAA	24	24	0	103.0	490	138	85	80	19	0	3	11	47	0	86	9	6	8	.429	0- -	-	-	.924	7.58	6.99
2018 NYY	AL	3	0	2	2.2	14	4	3	3	1	0	0	0	3	0	1	1	0	0	-	0-0	0	94	1.227	13.94	10.13
2019 Sea	AL	8	7	0	36.0	168	44	22	22	5	1	0	3	18	0	37	3	0	1	.000	0-0	0	93	.881	6.51	5.50
2020 Sea	AL	10	10	0	55.1	232	52	23	22	2	0	2	3	20	0	48	1	4	3	.571	0-0	0	92	.628	3.43	3.58
2021 Sea	AL	21	15	3	80.1	385	105	69	61	14	1	4	5	43	1	63	5	7	8	.467	0-0	0	92	.913	7.36	6.83
2022 Sea	AL	6	1	3	11.2	51	9	5	5	1	0	1	1	6	0	7	0	1	0	1.000	0-0	0	92	.593	3.41	3.86
5 ML YEARS		48	33	5	186.0	850	214	122	113	23	2	7	12	90	1	155	10	12	12	.500	0-0	0	92	.813	5.77	5.47

Zack Short

Bats: R **Throws:** R **Pos:** SS-4; 2B-2; DH-1; PR-1   **Ht:** 5'10" **Wt:** 180 **Born:** 5/29/1995 **Age:** 28

				BATTING															RUNNING			AVERAGES			
Year Team	Lg	G	AB	H	2B	3B	HR	(Hm	Rd)	TB	R	RBI	RC	TBB	IBB	SO	HBP	SH	SF	SB	CS	GDP	Avg	OBP	Slg	OPS
2022 Toledo	AAA	128	459	105	31	1	11	(-	-)	171	79	60	65	88	2	149	5	1	6	11	5	6	.229	.355	.373	.727
2021 Det	AL	61	156	22	4	0	6	(4	2)	44	21	20	9	22	1	59	0	0	6	2	0	4	.141	.239	.282	.521
2022 Det	AL	6	9	0	0	0	0	(0	0)	0	2	2	0	2	0	5	0	0	2	1	0	0	.000	.154	.000	.154
2 ML YEARS		67	165	22	4	0	6	(4	2)	44	23	22	9	24	1	64	0	0	8	3	0	4	.133	.234	.267	.500

Chasen Shreve

Pitches: L **Bats:** L **Pos:** RP-25   CHAY-sen shreev   **Ht:** 6'4" **Wt:** 180 **Born:** 7/12/1990 **Age:** 32

			HOW MUCH PITCHED					WHAT HE GAVE UP										THE RESULTS							
Year Team	Lg	G	GS	GF	IP	BFP	H	R	ER	HR	SH	SF	HB	TBB	IBB	SO	WP	W	L	Pct	Sv-Op	Hld	Vel	OPS	ERC	ERA
2022 S-WB	AAA	5	0	0	4.2	17	1	1	1	0	0	1	0	1	0	5	1	1	0	1.000	0- -	-	-	.184	0.29	1.93
2014 Atl	NL	15	0	4	12.1	50	10	1	1	0	1	0	0	3	0	15	1	0	0	-	0-0	2	91	.526	1.88	0.73
2015 NYY	AL	59	0	13	58.1	251	49	21	20	10	2	0	1	33	2	64	4	6	2	.750	0-1	10	91	.738	4.39	3.09
2016 NYY	AL	37	0	11	33.0	142	29	19	19	8	1	0	3	13	0	33	0	2	1	.667	1-1	1	92	.823	4.70	5.18
2017 NYY	AL	44	0	15	45.1	198	35	20	19	8	0	2	0	25	3	58	4	4	1	.800	0-1	1	93	.712	3.71	3.77
2018 2 Tms		60	0	20	52.2	235	53	28	23	11	0	4	1	27	0	62	2	3	4	.429	1-1	6	92	.832	5.43	3.93
2019 StL	NL	3	0	0	2.0	10	2	2	2	0	0	0	1	1	0	2	0	1	0	1.000	0-0	1	91	.900	5.48	9.00
2020 NYM	NL	17	0	1	25.0	102	17	12	11	4	0	1	0	12	0	34	0	1	0	1.000	0-0	1	92	.655	3.07	3.96
2021 Pit	NL	57	0	5	56.1	235	43	20	20	7	0	3	1	28	0	45	0	3	3	.500	0-2	11	92	.681	3.42	3.20
2022 NYM	NL	25	0	4	26.1	114	27	19	19	6	0	1	0	10	1	29	2	1	1	.500	0-1	4	91	.781	4.97	6.49
18 NYY	AL	40	0	17	38.0	170	39	23	18	8	0	2	1	18	0	46	2	2	2	.500	1-1	3	92	.831	5.40	4.26
18 StL	NL	20	0	3	14.2	65	14	5	5	3	0	2	0	9	0	16	0	1	2	.333	0-0	3	92	.835	5.52	3.07
9 ML YEARS		317	0	73	311.1	1337	265	142	134	54	4	11	7	152	6	342	13	21	12	.636	2-7	37	92	.740	4.15	3.87

Mike Siani

Bats: L **Throws:** L **Pos:** CF-9; PR-2   **Ht:** 6'1" **Wt:** 188 **Born:** 7/16/1999 **Age:** 23

				BATTING															RUNNING			AVERAGES			
Year Team	Lg	G	AB	H	2B	3B	HR	(Hm	Rd)	TB	R	RBI	RC	TBB	IBB	SO	HBP	SH	SF	SB	CS	GDP	Avg	OBP	Slg	OPS
2022 Chatt	AA	121	456	115	19	7	12	(-	-)	184	76	49	68	64	0	90	7	1	3	49	12	8	.252	.351	.404	.754
2022 Cin	NL	9	24	4	0	0	0	(0	0)	4	1	0	0	0	0	7	0	0	0	0	1	1	.167	.167	.167	.333

Magneuris Sierra

Bats: L **Throws:** L **Pos:** CF-28; LF-17; PR-6; RF-2; PH-2   mag-NEW-rees   **Ht:** 5'11" **Wt:** 178 **Born:** 4/7/1996 **Age:** 27

				BATTING															RUNNING			AVERAGES			
Year Team	Lg	G	AB	H	2B	3B	HR	(Hm	Rd)	TB	R	RBI	RC	TBB	IBB	SO	HBP	SH	SF	SB	CS	GDP	Avg	OBP	Slg	OPS
2022 Salt Lk	AAA	76	279	83	10	4	7	(-	-)	122	49	45	44	24	0	51	4	1	3	22	5	3	.297	.358	.437	.795
2017 StL	NL	22	60	19	0	0	0	(0	0)	19	10	5	10	2	0	14	0	0	0	2	2	0	.317	.359	.317	.676
2018 Mia	NL	54	147	28	3	0	0	(0	0)	31	10	7	6	6	1	39	0	3	0	3	2	0	.190	.222	.211	.433
2019 Mia	NL	15	40	14	1	1	0	(0	0)	17	5	1	5	2	0	7	0	0	0	3	3	0	.350	.381	.425	.806
2020 Mia	NL	19	44	11	3	1	0	(0	0)	16	8	7	8	5	0	9	1	2	1	4	1	0	.250	.333	.364	.697
2021 Mia	NL	123	209	48	6	1	0	(0	0)	56	27	5	15	15	4	50	0	1	0	11	0	1	.230	.281	.268	.549
2022 LAA	AL	45	91	15	1	3	0	(0	0)	22	7	5	3	4	0	25	0	1	0	6	1	0	.165	.200	.242	.442
Postseason		5	11	3	1	0	0	(0	0)	4	1	1	1	0	0	4	0	0	0	0	0	0	.273	.273	.364	.636
6 ML YEARS		278	591	135	14	6	0	(0	0)	161	67	30	47	36	5	144	1	7	1	29	9	1	.228	.273	.272	.546

Chase Silseth

Pitches: R **Bats:** R **Pos:** SP-7   **Ht:** 6'0" **Wt:** 217 **Born:** 5/18/2000 **Age:** 23

			HOW MUCH PITCHED					WHAT HE GAVE UP										THE RESULTS							
Year Team	Lg	G	GS	GF	IP	BFP	H	R	ER	HR	SH	SF	HB	TBB	IBB	SO	WP	W	L	Pct	Sv-Op	Hld	Vel	OPS	ERC	ERA
2022 Rock	AA	15	15	0	83.0	320	52	23	21	11	1	2	4	27	0	110	5	7	0	1.000	0- -	-	-	.587	2.32	2.28
2022 LAA	AL	7	7	0	28.2	129	33	21	21	7	1	0	1	12	0	24	2	1	3	.250	0-0	0	95	.899	6.30	6.59

Andrelton Simmons

Bats: R Throws: R Pos: 2B-18;SS-18;DH-2;PR-2   ANN-drel-ton   Ht: 6'2" Wt: 195 Born: 9/4/1989 Age: 33

Year	Team	Lg	G	AB	H	2B	3B	HR	(Hm	Rd)	TB	R	RBI	RC	TBB	IBB	SO	HBP	SH	SF	SB	CS	GDP	Avg	OBP	Slg	OPS
2022	Iowa	AAA	12	45	6	0	0	1	(-	-)	9	3	2	0	4	0	13	1	0	0	1	2	1	.133	.220	.200	.420
2012	Atl	NL	49	166	48	8	2	3	(3	0)	69	17	19	23	12	1	21	1	0	3	1	0	5	.289	.335	.416	.751
2013	Atl	NL	157	606	150	27	6	17	(5	12)	240	76	59	60	40	1	55	3	5	6	5	5	16	.248	.296	.396	.692
2014	Atl	NL	146	540	132	18	4	7	(3	4)	179	44	46	41	32	4	60	0	2	2	4	5	25	.244	.286	.331	.617
2015	Atl	NL	147	535	142	23	2	4	(2	2)	181	60	44	48	39	6	48	6	1	2	5	3	19	.265	.321	.338	.660
2016	LAA	AL	124	448	126	22	2	4	(4	0)	164	48	44	52	28	0	38	2	1	4	10	1	16	.281	.324	.366	.690
2017	LAA	AL	158	589	164	38	2	14	(10	4)	248	77	69	91	47	0	67	3	0	8	19	6	20	.278	.331	.421	.752
2018	LAA	AL	146	554	162	26	5	11	(1	10)	231	68	75	80	35	2	44	5	1	5	10	2	17	.292	.337	.417	.754
2019	LAA	AL	103	398	105	19	0	7	(5	2)	145	47	40	36	24	1	37	2	0	0	10	2	21	.264	.309	.364	.673
2020	LAA	AL	30	118	35	7	0	0	(0	0)	42	19	10	15	8	0	16	1	0	0	2	0	5	.297	.346	.356	.702
2021	Min	AL	131	412	92	12	0	3	(3	0)	113	37	31	35	32	0	62	3	3	1	1	0	14	.223	.283	.274	.558
2022	ChC	NL	35	75	13	1	0	0	(0	0)	14	8	7	7	7	0	13	0	3	0	4	0	5	.173	.244	.187	.431
Postseason			5	16	4	1	0	0	(0	0)	5	0	2	1	2	0	3	0	1	0	0	0		.250	.333	.313	.646
11 ML YEARS			1226	4441	1169	201	23	70	(36	34)	1626	501	444	483	304	15	461	26	16	29	72	24	163	.263	.312	.366	.678

Lucas Sims

Pitches: R Bats: R Pos: RP-6   Ht: 6'2" Wt: 225 Born: 5/10/1994 Age: 29

Year	Team	Lg	G	GS	GF	IP	BFP	H	R	ER	HR	SH	SF	HB	TBB	IBB	SO	WP	W	L	Pct	Sv-Op	Hld	Vel	OPS	ERC	ERA
2017	Atl	NL	14	10	1	57.2	255	64	37	36	9	5	1	4	23	2	44	0	3	6	.333	0-0	1	92	.869	5.43	5.62
2018	2 Tms	NL	9	0	2	15.2	77	15	13	13	3	0	0	2	13	1	16	0	0	0	-	0-1	0	92	.825	6.59	7.47
2019	Cin	NL	24	4	2	43.0	177	31	22	22	8	1	1	2	19	0	57	1	2	1	.667	0-0	3	94	.711	3.49	4.60
2020	Cin	NL	20	0	5	25.2	103	13	10	7	3	0	0	3	11	0	34	0	3	0	1.000	0-2	5	94	.554	2.17	2.45
2021	Cin	NL	47	0	13	47.0	195	34	26	23	6	0	3	4	18	3	76	2	5	3	.625	7-10	9	95	.658	2.92	4.40
2022	Cin	NL	6	0	1	6.2	31	5	7	7	0	0	1	1	6	0	5	0	1	0	1.000	1-1	0	94	.691	4.41	9.45
18	Atl	NL	6	0	2	10.1	52	12	9	9	2	0	0	1	8	1	10	0	0	0	-	0-1	0	93	.869	7.45	7.84
18	Cin	NL	3	0	0	5.1	25	3	4	4	1	0	0	1	5	0	6	0	0	0	-	0-0	0	92	.728	5.00	6.75
Postseason			2	0	0	2.2	9	0	0	0	0	0	0	0	1	0	5	0	0	0	-	0-0	0	95	.111	0.16	0.00
6 ML YEARS			120	14	24	195.2	838	162	115	108	29	6	6	16	90	6	232	3	14	10	.583	8-14	18	93	.737	3.97	4.97

Brady Singer

Pitches: R Bats: R Pos: SP-24; RP-3   Ht: 6'5" Wt: 215 Born: 8/4/1996 Age: 26

Year	Team	Lg	G	GS	GF	IP	BFP	H	R	ER	HR	SH	SF	HB	TBB	IBB	SO	WP	W	L	Pct	Sv-Op	Hld	Vel	OPS	ERC	ERA
2020	KC	AL	12	12	0	64.1	263	52	29	29	8	0	2	2	23	0	61	5	4	5	.444	0-0	0	93	.649	3.19	4.06
2021	KC	AL	27	27	0	128.1	586	146	81	70	14	0	3	11	53	1	131	3	5	10	.333	0-0	0	94	.773	5.28	4.91
2022	KC	AL	27	24	2	153.1	621	140	58	55	18	4	2	11	35	0	150	3	10	5	.667	0-0	0	94	.679	3.42	3.23
3 ML YEARS			66	63	2	346.0	1470	338	168	154	40	4	7	24	111	1	342	11	19	20	.487	0-0	0	94	.711	4.05	4.01

Jose Siri

Bats: R Throws: R Pos: CF-95;PR-6;RF-3;LF-2;DH-2;PH-1   Ht: 6'2" Wt: 175 Born: 7/22/1995 Age: 27

Year	Team	Lg	G	AB	H	2B	3B	HR	(Hm	Rd)	TB	R	RBI	RC	TBB	IBB	SO	HBP	SH	SF	SB	CS	GDP	Avg	OBP	Slg	OPS
2022	SgrLnd	AAA	16	71	21	3	2	9	(-	-)	55	17	22	21	6	0	20	0	0	1	2	0	2	.296	.346	.775	1.121
2021	Hou	AL	21	46	14	0	1	4	(1	3)	28	10	9	11	1	0	17	2	0	0	3	1	0	.304	.347	.609	.956
2022	2 Tms	AL	104	301	64	13	2	7	(2	5)	102	53	24	23	20	0	108	3	0	1	14	2	3	.213	.268	.339	.607
22	Hou	AL	48	135	24	4	2	3	(1	2)	41	18	10	7	9	0	48	2	0	1	6	1	2	.178	.238	.304	.542
22	TB	AL	56	166	40	9	0	4	(1	3)	61	35	14	16	11	0	60	1	0	0	8	1	1	.241	.292	.367	.660
Postseason			7	14	2	0	0	0	(0	0)	2	1	3	1	0	0	4	0	0	0	1	0	0	.143	.143	.143	.286
2 ML YEARS			125	347	78	13	3	11	(3	8)	130	63	33	34	21	0	125	5	0	1	17	3	3	.225	.278	.375	.653

Tarik Skubal

Pitches: L Bats: R Pos: SP-21   Ht: 6'3" Wt: 240 Born: 11/20/1996 Age: 26

Year	Team	Lg	G	GS	GF	IP	BFP	H	R	ER	HR	SH	SF	HB	TBB	IBB	SO	WP	W	L	Pct	Sv-Op	Hld	Vel	OPS	ERC	ERA
2020	Det	AL	8	7	0	32.0	134	28	21	20	9	0	2	2	11	0	37	0	1	4	.200	0-0	0	94	.802	4.65	5.63
2021	Det	AL	31	29	1	149.1	634	141	76	72	35	1	4	6	47	0	164	4	8	12	.400	0-0	0	94	.782	4.47	4.34
2022	Det	AL	21	21	0	117.2	477	104	53	46	9	2	4	1	32	0	117	1	7	8	.467	0-0	0	94	.661	2.88	3.52
3 ML YEARS			60	57	1	299.0	1245	273	150	138	53	3	10	9	90	0	318	5	16	24	.400	0-0	0	94	.737	3.85	4.15

Austin Slater

Bats: R Throws: R Pos: CF-106;PH-44;LF-16;RF-14;PR-7;DH-2   Ht: 6'1" Wt: 204 Born: 12/13/1992 Age: 30

Year	Team	Lg	G	AB	H	2B	3B	HR	(Hm	Rd)	TB	R	RBI	RC	TBB	IBB	SO	HBP	SH	SF	SB	CS	GDP	Avg	OBP	Slg	OPS
2017	SF	NL	34	117	33	3	1	1	(0	1)	47	15	16	17	8	0	29	2	0	0	0	0	3	.282	.339	.402	.740
2018	SF	NL	74	199	50	6	1	1	(0	1)	61	21	23	23	20	2	69	5	0	1	7	0	6	.251	.333	.307	.640
2019	SF	NL	68	168	40	9	3	5	(2	3)	70	20	21	28	22	1	59	2	0	1	1	0	1	.238	.333	.417	.750
2020	SF	NL	31	85	24	2	1	5	(2	3)	43	18	7	18	16	0	22	2	1	0	8	1	2	.282	.408	.506	.914
2021	SF	NL	129	274	66	12	1	12	(5	7)	116	39	32	37	28	2	84	4	0	0	15	2	7	.241	.320	.423	.744
2022	SF	NL	125	277	73	15	2	7	(3	4)	113	49	34	41	40	0	89	6	0	2	12	1	9	.264	.366	.408	.774
Postseason			3	5	2	1	0	0	(0	0)	3	0	0	0	0	0	0	0	0	0	1	0	0	.400	.400	.600	1.000
6 ML YEARS			461	1120	286	47	9	33	(12	21)	450	162	133	164	134	5	352	21	1	3	43	4	27	.255	.345	.402	.747

Ethan Small

Pitches: L Bats: L Pos: SP-2   Ht: 6'4" Wt: 215 Born: 2/14/1997 Age: 26

			HOW MUCH PITCHED				WHAT HE GAVE UP										THE RESULTS					
Year	Team	Lg	G	GS	GF	IP	BFP	H	R	ER	HR	SH	SF	HB	TBB	IBB	SO	WP	W	L	Pct	Sv-Op Hld	Vel	OPS	ERC	ERA
2022	Nashv	AAA	27	21	2	103.0	446	82	57	51	8	0	6	4	58	0	114	14	7	6	.538	0- - - -		.664	3.55	4.46
2022	Mil	NL	2	2	0	6.1	33	8	5	5	1	0	0	0	8	0	7	0	0	0	-	0-0 0	91	1.085	10.37	7.11

Devin Smeltzer

Pitches: L Bats: R Pos: SP-12; RP-3   Ht: 6'3" Wt: 195 Born: 9/7/1995 Age: 27

			HOW MUCH PITCHED				WHAT HE GAVE UP										THE RESULTS					
Year	Team	Lg	G	GS	GF	IP	BFP	H	R	ER	HR	SH	SF	HB	TBB	IBB	SO	WP	W	L	Pct	Sv-Op Hld	Vel	OPS	ERC	ERA
2022	StPaul	AAA	15	9	0	50.0	231	64	44	42	10	1	3	2	16	0	47	2	3	4	.429	0- - - -		.930	6.21	7.56
2019	Min	AL	11	6	2	49.0	202	50	23	21	8	0	0	1	12	0	38	1	2	2	.500	1-1 1	89	.777	4.18	3.86
2020	Min	AL	7	1	2	16.0	72	19	12	12	2	1	0	1	5	0	15	0	2	0	1.000	0-0 0	88	.829	5.20	6.75
2021	Min	AL	1	0	1	4.2	17	1	1	0	0	0	1	2	1	0	3	0	0	0	-	0-0 0	86	.312	0.95	0.00
2022	Min	AL	15	12	1	70.1	287	67	30	29	13	1	1	1	19	0	40	2	5	2	.714	0-0 0	89	.753	4.01	3.71
	Postseason		1	0	0	3.1	14	2	0	0	0	0	0	0	3	0	4	0	0	0	-	0-0 0	89	.539	3.21	0.00
4 ML YEARS			34	19	6	140.0	578	137	66	62	23	2	2	5	37	0	96	3	9	4	.692	1-1 1	89	.760	4.07	3.99

Caleb Smith

Pitches: L Bats: R Pos: RP-43; SP-1   Ht: 6'0" Wt: 207 Born: 7/28/1991 Age: 31

			HOW MUCH PITCHED				WHAT HE GAVE UP										THE RESULTS					
Year	Team	Lg	G	GS	GF	IP	BFP	H	R	ER	HR	SH	SF	HB	TBB	IBB	SO	WP	W	L	Pct	Sv-Op Hld	Vel	OPS	ERC	ERA
2017	NYY	AL	9	2	6	18.2	86	21	16	16	4	0	1	0	10	1	18	1	0	1	.000	0-0 0	94	.854	6.09	7.71
2018	Mia	NL	16	16	0	77.1	326	63	36	36	10	2	2	3	33	2	88	0	5	6	.455	0-0 0	93	.694	3.46	4.19
2019	Mia	NL	28	28	0	153.1	646	128	82	77	33	2	5	6	60	2	168	6	10	11	.476	0-0 0	92	.755	4.01	4.52
2020	2 Tms	NL	5	4	0	14.0	60	6	4	4	3	0	0	0	12	0	15	0	0	0	-	0-0 0	92	.613	3.44	2.57
2021	Ari	NL	45	13	4	113.2	500	93	64	61	20	1	0	6	63	3	124	2	4	9	.308	0-2 2	91	.726	4.31	4.83
2022	Ari	NL	44	1	14	70.0	302	57	35	32	14	1	0	1	39	1	65	1	1	3	.250	0-0 4	92	.751	4.38	4.11
20	Mia	NL	1	1	0	3.0	15	1	1	1	1	0	0	0	6	0	3	0	0	0	-	0-0 0	92	.911	9.13	3.00
20	Ari	NL	4	3	0	11.0	45	5	3	3	2	0	0	0	6	0	12	0	0	0	-	0-0 0	92	.526	2.21	2.45
6 ML YEARS			147	64	24	447.0	1920	368	237	226	84	6	8	16	217	9	478	10	20	30	.400	0-2 6	92	.737	4.11	4.55

Chad Smith

Pitches: R Bats: R Pos: RP-15   Ht: 6'4" Wt: 200 Born: 6/8/1995 Age: 28

			HOW MUCH PITCHED				WHAT HE GAVE UP										THE RESULTS					
Year	Team	Lg	G	GS	GF	IP	BFP	H	R	ER	HR	SH	SF	HB	TBB	IBB	SO	WP	W	L	Pct	Sv-Op Hld	Vel	OPS	ERC	ERA
2022	Albq	AAA	32	0	24	35.0	136	27	13	12	6	0	0	0	11	1	40	3	1	2	.333	12- - - -		.671	3.06	3.09
2022	Col	NL	15	0	2	18.0	85	16	15	15	2	0	1	2	15	0	23	3	0	1	.000	0-1 0	96	.791	5.71	7.50

Dominic Smith

Bats: L Throws: L Pos: 1B-37; DH-16; PH-13; PR-1   Ht: 6'0" Wt: 239 Born: 6/15/1995 Age: 28

			BATTING																	RUNNING			AVERAGES		
Year	Team	Lg	G	AB	H	2B	3B	HR	(Hm | Rd)	TB	R	RBI	RC	TBB	IBB	SO	HBP	SH	SF	SB	CS	GDP	Avg	OBP	Slg	OPS
2022	Syrcse	AAA	54	218	62	11	0	10	(- | -)	103	42	38	39	25	2	39	4	0	1	4	1	3	.284	.367	.472	.839
2017	NYM	NL	49	167	33	6	0	9	(4 | 5)	66	17	26	19	14	0	49	1	0	0	0	0	5	.198	.262	.395	.658
2018	NYM	NL	56	143	32	11	1	5	(4 | 1)	60	14	11	9	4	0	47	2	0	0	0	0	2	.224	.255	.420	.675
2019	NYM	NL	89	177	50	10	0	11	(3 | 8)	93	35	25	26	19	0	44	1	0	0	1	2	5	.282	.355	.525	.881
2020	NYM	NL	50	177	56	21	1	10	(5 | 5)	109	27	42	35	14	0	45	5	0	3	0	0	3	.316	.377	.616	.993
2021	NYM	NL	145	446	109	20	0	11	(3 | 8)	162	43	58	48	32	2	112	9	0	6	2	1	13	.244	.304	.363	.667
2022	NYM	NL	58	134	26	10	1	0	(0 | 0)	38	11	17	13	12	0	37	4	0	2	0	0	0	.194	.276	.284	.560
6 ML YEARS			447	1244	306	78	3	46	(19 | 27)	528	147	179	150	95	2	334	22	0	12	3	3	27	.246	.308	.424	.733

Drew Smith

Pitches: R Bats: R Pos: RP-44   Ht: 6'2" Wt: 190 Born: 9/24/1993 Age: 29

			HOW MUCH PITCHED				WHAT HE GAVE UP										THE RESULTS					
Year	Team	Lg	G	GS	GF	IP	BFP	H	R	ER	HR	SH	SF	HB	TBB	IBB	SO	WP	W	L	Pct	Sv-Op Hld	Vel	OPS	ERC	ERA
2018	NYM	NL	27	0	8	28.0	120	34	11	11	2	0	2	2	6	0	18	1	1	1	.500	0-2 4	96	.795	4.77	3.54
2020	NYM	NL	8	0	3	7.0	29	6	6	5	2	0	0	0	2	1	7	1	0	1	.000	0-0 2	95	.757	3.75	6.43
2021	NYM	NL	31	1	10	41.1	165	28	13	11	7	0	1	2	16	4	41	0	3	1	.750	0-0 1	96	.676	2.85	2.40
2022	NYM	NL	44	0	6	46.0	187	38	17	17	9	0	1	0	15	0	53	0	3	3	.500	0-2 14	96	.687	3.48	3.33
4 ML YEARS			110	1	27	122.1	501	106	47	44	20	0	4	4	39	5	119	2	7	6	.538	0-4 21	96	.714	3.57	3.24

Joe Smith

Pitches: R Bats: R Pos: RP-34   Ht: 6'2" Wt: 211 Born: 3/22/1984 Age: 39

			HOW MUCH PITCHED				WHAT HE GAVE UP										THE RESULTS					
Year	Team	Lg	G	GS	GF	IP	BFP	H	R	ER	HR	SH	SF	HB	TBB	IBB	SO	WP	W	L	Pct	Sv-Op Hld	Vel	OPS	ERC	ERA
2007	NYM	NL	54	0	14	44.1	205	48	18	17	3	2	0	7	21	4	45	2	3	2	.600	0-0 10	86	.757	5.04	3.45
2008	NYM	NL	82	0	12	63.1	271	51	28	25	4	4	0	4	31	4	52	1	6	3	.667	0-3 18	89	.658	3.23	3.55
2009	Cle	AL	37	0	5	34.0	142	30	16	13	4	1	1	0	13	0	30	2	0	0	-	0-1 10	90	.707	3.49	3.44
2010	Cle	AL	53	0	7	40.0	170	30	18	17	4	1	0	1	24	2	32	0	2	2	.500	0-1 17	91	.659	3.53	3.83
2011	Cle	AL	71	0	13	67.0	267	52	16	15	1	2	2	2	21	1	45	2	3	3	.500	0-3 16	90	.541	2.19	2.01
2012	Cle	AL	72	0	12	67.0	278	53	27	22	4	1	1	2	25	4	53	1	7	4	.636	0-3 21	89	.594	2.60	2.96
2013	Cle	AL	70	0	20	63.0	259	54	17	16	4	0	0	3	23	2	54	3	6	2	.750	3-8 25	90	.643	3.23	2.29
2014	LAA	AL	76	0	26	74.2	285	45	16	15	4	0	3	6	15	3	68	4	7	2	.778	15-19 18	89	.491	1.47	1.81

Year	Team	Lg	G	GS	GF	IP	BFP	H	R	ER	HR	SH	SF	HB	TBB	IBB	SO	WP	W	L	Pct	Sv-Op	Hld	Vel	OPS	ERC	ERA
						HOW MUCH PITCHED				**WHAT HE GAVE UP**											**THE RESULTS**						
2015	LAA	AL	70	0	13	65.1	271	64	26	26	4	2	1	2	19	4	57	1	5	5	.500	5-9	32	88	.684	3.36	3.58
2016	2 Tms	AL	54	0	19	52.0	217	47	20	20	8	1	1	6	18	3	40	0	2	5	.286	6-9	7	88	.716	4.19	3.46
2017	2 Tms	AL	59	0	3	54.0	214	46	20	20	4	1	1	1	10	1	71	0	3	0	1.000	1-2	21	89	.601	2.40	3.33
2018	Hou	AL	56	0	13	45.2	180	34	20	19	7	0	2	2	12	0	46	1	5	1	.833	0-2	11	88	.645	2.75	3.74
2019	Hou	AL	28	0	4	25.0	96	19	6	5	2	0	0	0	5	0	22	0	1	0	1.000	0-1	4	88	.569	2.04	1.80
2021	2 Tms	AL	50	0	12	39.2	173	47	23	22	5	2	2	3	8	2	34	2	4	4	.500	0-3	4	86	.801	4.75	4.99
2022	Min	AL	34	0	3	27.1	122	33	18	14	7	0	1	1	9	1	17	0	1	1	.500	0-2	14	85	.893	6.29	4.61
16	LAA	AL	38	0	16	37.2	160	36	16	16	4	1	1	5	13	3	25	0	1	4	.200	6-9	6	88	.697	4.15	3.82
16	ChC	NL	16	0	3	14.1	57	11	4	4	4	0	0	1	5	0	15	0	1	1	.500	0-0	1	89	.769	4.20	2.51
17	Tor	AL	38	0	1	35.2	144	30	13	13	3	1	1	1	10	1	51	0	3	0	1.000	0-1	13	89	.623	2.78	3.28
17	Cle	AL	21	0	2	18.1	70	16	7	7	1	0	0	0	0	0	20	0	0	0	-	1-1	8	89	.557	1.72	3.44
21	Hou	AL	27	0	10	21.2	103	35	18	18	4	2	1	3	4	0	17	2	1	1	.500	0-0	1	87	.996	8.38	7.48
21	Sea	AL	23	0	2	18.0	70	12	5	4	1	0	1	0	4	2	17	0	3	3	.500	0-3	3	86	.521	1.45	2.00
	Postseason		18	0	4	14.0	54	8	4	4	2	0	1	0	3	1	13	0	0	1	.000	0-0	2	89	.484	1.47	2.57
	15 ML YEARS		866	0	176	762.1	3150	653	289	266	66	23	12	40	254	31	666	19	55	34	.618	30-66	228	89	.651	3.12	3.14

Josh Smith

Bats: L Throws: R Pos: 3B-36;LF-24;PH-11;SS-6;DH-5;2B-2;PR-1   Ht: 5'10" Wt: 172 Born: 8/7/1997 Age: 25

Year	Team	Lg	G	AB	H	2B	3B	HR	(Hm	Rd)	TB	R	RBI	RC	TBB	IBB	SO	HBP	SH	SF	SB	CS	GDP	Avg	OBP	Slg	OPS
						BATTING															**RUNNING**			**AVERAGES**			
2019	Stnlld	A-	33	111	36	6	1	3	(-	-)	53	17	15	27	25	2	17	2	1	2	6	3	3	.324	.450	.477	.927
2021	Frisco	AA	30	102	30	5	0	3	(-	-)	44	12	10	21	18	0	20	6	0	1	7	2	2	.294	.425	.431	.857
2021	3 Tms	Low	48	186	59	15	3	10	(-	-)	110	54	31	49	25	0	42	12	1	0	19	0	0	.317	.430	.591	1.022
2022	RdRck	AAA	55	221	64	13	4	6	(-	-)	103	45	45	40	33	0	54	6	0	1	9	4	4	.290	.395	.466	.861
2022	Tex	AL	73	213	42	5	0	2	(2	0)	53	23	16	17	28	0	50	7	2	3	4	3	1	.197	.307	.249	.556

Kevin Smith

Bats: R Throws: R Pos: 3B-39;SS-10;PH-2   Ht: 6'0" Wt: 190 Born: 7/4/1996 Age: 26

Year	Team	Lg	G	AB	H	2B	3B	HR	(Hm	Rd)	TB	R	RBI	RC	TBB	IBB	SO	HBP	SH	SF	SB	CS	GDP	Avg	OBP	Slg	OPS
						BATTING															**RUNNING**			**AVERAGES**			
2022	LsVgs	AAA	86	332	89	16	2	13	(-	-)	148	44	49	52	29	1	112	4	1	4	6	1	4	.268	.331	.446	.776
2021	Tor	AL	18	32	3	0	0	1	(0	1)	6	2	1	0	3	0	11	1	0	0	0	0	0	.094	.194	.188	.382
2022	Oak	AL	47	139	25	9	1	2	(2	0)	42	9	13	10	7	0	42	0	3	2	4	0	5	.180	.216	.302	.518
	2 ML YEARS		65	171	28	9	1	3	(2	1)	48	11	14	10	10	0	53	1	3	2	4	0	5	.164	.212	.281	.493

Pavin Smith

Bats: L Throws: L Pos: RF-43;DH-22;1B-10;PH-9   Ht: 6'2" Wt: 208 Born: 2/6/1996 Age: 27

Year	Team	Lg	G	AB	H	2B	3B	HR	(Hm	Rd)	TB	R	RBI	RC	TBB	IBB	SO	HBP	SH	SF	SB	CS	GDP	Avg	OBP	Slg	OPS
						BATTING															**RUNNING**			**AVERAGES**			
2020	Ari	NL	12	37	10	0	1	1	(1	0)	15	7	4	5	5	0	8	0	0	2	1	0	0	.270	.341	.405	.746
2021	Ari	NL	145	498	133	27	4	11	(6	5)	201	68	49	66	42	1	106	4	0	1	1	0	11	.267	.328	.404	.732
2022	Ari	NL	75	245	54	9	0	9	(4	5)	90	24	33	32	28	1	67	1	0	3	1	0	1	.220	.300	.367	.667
	3 ML YEARS		232	780	197	36	5	21	(11	10)	306	99	86	103	75	2	181	5	0	6	3	0	13	.253	.320	.392	.712

Will Smith

Pitches: L Bats: R Pos: RP-65   Ht: 6'5" Wt: 255 Born: 7/10/1989 Age: 33

Year	Team	Lg	G	GS	GF	IP	BFP	H	R	ER	HR	SH	SF	HB	TBB	IBB	SO	WP	W	L	Pct	Sv-Op	Hld	Vel	OPS	ERC	ERA
						HOW MUCH PITCHED				**WHAT HE GAVE UP**											**THE RESULTS**						
2012	KC	AL	16	16	0	89.2	396	111	54	53	12	2	5	1	33	1	59	4	6	9	.400	0-0	0	90	.853	5.75	5.32
2013	KC	AL	19	1	4	33.1	131	24	16	12	6	0	4	1	7	0	43	0	2	1	.667	0-3	6	91	.631	2.47	3.24
2014	Mil	NL	78	0	6	65.2	286	62	31	27	6	1	1	3	31	6	86	7	1	3	.250	1-6	30	93	.737	4.02	3.70
2015	Mil	NL	76	0	11	63.1	264	52	23	19	5	1	2	1	24	1	91	5	7	2	.778	0-4	20	93	.649	2.91	2.70
2016	2 Tms	NL	53	0	4	40.1	167	31	19	15	3	1	1	1	18	1	48	3	2	4	.333	0-5	23	92	.637	2.92	3.35
2018	SF	NL	54	0	27	53.0	210	37	18	15	3	2	2	0	15	4	71	2	2	3	.400	14-18	0	93	.533	1.74	2.55
2019	SF	NL	63	0	52	65.1	257	46	20	20	10	0	1	0	21	2	96	3	6	0	1.000	34-38	0	93	.618	2.54	2.76
2020	Atl	NL	18	0	1	16.0	62	11	8	8	7	0	0	0	4	0	18	0	2	2	.500	0-1	5	93	.794	3.74	4.50
2021	Atl	NL	71	0	60	68.0	283	49	27	26	11	0	2	5	28	2	87	3	3	7	.300	37-43	0	93	.693	3.24	3.44
2022	2 Tms	NL	65	0	18	59.0	261	58	35	26	9	0	3	2	25	3	65	2	0	3	.000	5-8	16	92	.763	4.42	3.97
16	Mil	NL	27	0	3	22.0	92	18	13	9	3	1	1	1	9	1	22	3	1	3	.250	0-4	12	92	.708	3.48	3.68
16	SF	NL	26	0	1	18.1	75	13	6	6	0	0	0	0	9	0	26	0	1	1	.500	0-1	11	92	.551	2.26	2.95
22	Atl	NL	41	0	12	37.0	171	35	25	18	7	0	2	2	21	3	41	2	0	1	.000	5-8	10	92	.764	5.00	4.38
22	Hou	NL	24	0	6	22.0	90	23	10	8	2	0	1	0	4	0	24	0	0	2	.000	0-0	6	92	.759	3.47	3.27
	Postseason		20	0	11	18.1	68	8	4	3	1	0	0	0	6	0	16	0	4	2	.667	6-8	2	94	.383	1.12	1.47
	10 ML YEARS		513	17	183	553.2	2317	481	251	221	72	7	21	14	206	20	664	29	31	34	.477	91-126	106	92	.701	3.50	3.59

Will Smith

Bats: R Throws: R Pos: C-109;DH-25;PH-6   Ht: 5'10" Wt: 195 Born: 3/28/1995 Age: 28

Year	Team	Lg	G	AB	H	2B	3B	HR	(Hm	Rd)	TB	R	RBI	RC	TBB	IBB	SO	HBP	SH	SF	SB	CS	GDP	Avg	OBP	Slg	OPS
						BATTING															**RUNNING**			**AVERAGES**			
2019	LAD	NL	54	170	43	9	0	15	(7	8)	97	30	42	38	18	1	52	5	0	3	2	0	3	.253	.337	.571	.907
2020	LAD	NL	37	114	33	9	0	8	(7	1)	66	23	25	27	20	1	22	2	0	1	0	0	0	.289	.401	.579	.980
2021	LAD	NL	130	414	107	19	2	25	(13	12)	205	71	76	73	58	4	101	18	0	11	3	0	11	.258	.365	.495	.860
2022	LAD	NL	137	508	132	26	3	24	(10	14)	236	68	87	84	56	4	96	10	0	4	1	0	11	.260	.343	.465	.807
	Postseason		34	126	26	6	0	5	(2	3)	47	13	17	15	17	4	37	0	0	0	0	0	0	.206	.301	.373	.674
	4 ML YEARS		358	1206	315	63	5	72	(37	35)	604	192	230	222	152	10	271	35	0	19	6	0	27	.261	.356	.501	.856

Canaan Smith-Njigba

Bats: L Throws: R Pos: LF-2;PH-1   in-JIG-buh   Ht: 6'0" Wt: 230 Born: 4/30/1999 Age: 24

Year Team	Lg	G	AB	H	2B	3B	HR	(Hm	Rd)	TB	R	RBI	RC	TBB	IBB	SO	HBP	SH	SF	SB	CS	GDP	Avg	OBP	Slg	OPS
2022 Indy	AAA	52	184	51	15	3	1	(-	-)	75	31	19	28	33	0	52	0	1	0	8	3	2	.277	.387	.408	.795
2022 Pit	NL	3	5	1	1	0	0	(0	0)	2	1	0	1	1	0	0	1	0	0	0	0	0	.200	.429	.400	.829

Drew Smyly

Pitches: L Bats: L Pos: SP-22   SMY-lee   Ht: 6'2" Wt: 188 Born: 6/13/1989 Age: 34

Year Team	Lg	G	GS	GF	IP	BFP	H	R	ER	HR	SH	SF	HB	TBB	IBB	SO	WP	W	L	Pct	Sv-Op	Hld	Vel	OPS	ERC	ERA
2012 Det	AL	23	18	0	99.1	416	93	49	44	12	2	3	2	33	1	94	3	4	3	.571	0-0	1	92	.732	3.68	3.99
2013 Det	AL	63	0	9	76.0	303	62	20	20	4	0	1	1	17	1	81	5	6	0	1.000	2-6	21	91	.601	2.21	2.37
2014 2 Tms	AL	28	25	0	153.0	618	136	57	55	18	1	3	1	42	2	133	8	9	10	.474	0-0	1	90	.688	3.17	3.24
2015 TB	AL	12	12	0	66.2	275	58	24	23	11	1	1	1	20	0	77	2	5	2	.714	0-0	0	90	.701	3.45	3.11
2016 TB	AL	30	30	0	175.1	738	174	103	95	32	5	11	2	49	2	167	10	7	12	.368	0-0	0	90	.763	4.13	4.88
2019 2 Tms	NL	25	21	1	114.0	514	126	83	79	32	2	2	2	55	0	120	7	4	7	.364	1-1	0	91	.916	6.49	6.24
2020 SF	NL	7	5	0	26.1	111	20	11	10	2	0	1	0	9	0	42	1	0	1	.000	0-0	0	94	.558	2.32	3.42
2021 Atl	NL	29	23	2	126.2	546	133	69	63	27	5	3	2	41	3	117	5	11	4	.733	0-0	0	92	.806	4.87	4.48
2022 ChC	NL	22	22	0	106.1	447	101	46	41	16	0	1	5	26	0	91	3	7	8	.467	0-0	0	90	.717	3.67	3.47
14 Det	AL	21	18	0	105.1	445	111	48	46	14	0	3	1	31	1	89	4	6	9	.400	0-0	1	90	.770	4.26	3.93
14 TB	AL	7	7	0	47.2	173	25	9	9	4	1	0	0	11	1	44	4	3	1	.750	0-0	0	90	.476	1.28	1.70
19 Tex	AL	13	9	1	51.1	251	64	49	48	19	0	2	1	34	0	52	5	1	5	.167	1-1	0	91	1.021	8.95	8.42
19 Phi	NL	12	12	0	62.2	263	62	34	31	13	2	0	1	21	0	68	2	3	2	.600	0-0	0	92	.820	4.64	4.45
Postseason		13	0	2	14.1	64	12	8	7	1	0	0	1	8	1	15	1	2	0	1.000	0-0	2	91	.655	3.63	4.40
9 ML YEARS		239	156	12	943.2	3968	903	462	430	154	16	26	16	292	9	922	44	53	47	.530	3-7	23	91	.745	3.96	4.10

Kirby Snead

Pitches: L Bats: L Pos: RP-46   Ht: 6'1" Wt: 218 Born: 10/7/1994 Age: 28

Year Team	Lg	G	GS	GF	IP	BFP	H	R	ER	HR	SH	SF	HB	TBB	IBB	SO	WP	W	L	Pct	Sv-Op	Hld	Vel	OPS	ERC	ERA
2022 LsVgs	AAA	11	0	7	13.2	57	13	7	7	1	0	0	1	3	1	20	0	2	0	1.000	1- -	-		.638	3.10	4.61
2021 Tor	AL	7	0	2	7.2	30	7	3	2	0	1	2	0	1	0	7	1	0	1	.000	0-0	0	93	.667	3.16	2.35
2022 Oak	AL	46	0	14	44.2	210	56	31	29	5	1	3	2	23	3	35	3	1	1	.500	1-3	5	93	.861	6.08	5.84
2 ML YEARS		53	0	16	52.1	240	63	34	31	5	1	3	2	24	3	42	4	1	2	.333	1-3	5	93	.836	5.63	5.33

Blake Snell

Pitches: L Bats: L Pos: SP-24   Ht: 6'4" Wt: 225 Born: 12/4/1992 Age: 30

Year Team	Lg	G	GS	GF	IP	BFP	H	R	ER	HR	SH	SF	HB	TBB	IBB	SO	WP	W	L	Pct	Sv-Op	Hld	Vel	OPS	ERC	ERA
2016 TB	AL	19	19	0	89.0	401	93	44	35	5	2	2	0	51	0	98	6	6	8	.429	0-0	0	94	.728	4.69	3.54
2017 TB	AL	24	24	0	129.1	547	113	65	58	15	4	1	0	59	1	119	8	5	7	.417	0-0	0	94	.707	3.71	4.04
2018 TB	AL	31	31	0	180.2	700	112	41	38	16	2	3	1	64	2	221	13	21	5	.808	0-0	0	96	.554	1.95	1.89
2019 TB	AL	23	23	0	107.0	441	96	53	51	14	0	1	1	40	1	147	11	6	8	.429	0-0	0	96	.702	3.72	4.29
2020 TB	AL	11	11	0	50.0	203	42	19	18	10	1	0	0	18	0	63	7	4	2	.667	0-0	0	95	.726	3.77	3.24
2021 SD	NL	27	27	0	128.2	550	101	61	60	16	5	1	3	69	1	170	7	7	6	.538	0-0	0	95	.692	3.66	4.20
2022 SD	NL	24	24	0	128.0	535	103	51	48	11	1	5	2	51	0	171	6	8	10	.444	0-0	0	96	.635	2.96	3.38
Postseason		9	7	1	35.0	138	24	11	11	6	0	1	0	14	0	44	2	2	3	.400	1-1	0	96	.633	2.93	2.83
7 ML YEARS		159	159	0	812.2	3377	660	334	308	87	15	13	7	352	5	989	58	57	46	.553	0-0	0	95	.664	3.28	3.41

Collin Snider

Pitches: R Bats: R Pos: RP-42   Ht: 6'4" Wt: 195 Born: 10/10/1995 Age: 27

Year Team	Lg	G	GS	GF	IP	BFP	H	R	ER	HR	SH	SF	HB	TBB	IBB	SO	WP	W	L	Pct	Sv-Op	Hld	Vel	OPS	ERC	ERA
2022 Omha	AAA	20	0	3	21.2	100	18	15	13	1	0	3	3	16	1	13	0	2	1	.667	0- -	-		.716	4.45	5.40
2022 KC	AL	42	0	2	34.1	151	40	25	25	3	1	0	2	15	0	22	0	4	2	.667	0-2	7	96	.824	5.53	6.55

Nicklaus Snyder

Pitches: R Bats: R Pos: RP-2   Ht: 6'4" Wt: 190 Born: 10/10/1995 Age: 27

Year Team	Lg	G	GS	GF	IP	BFP	H	R	ER	HR	SH	SF	HB	TBB	IBB	SO	WP	W	L	Pct	Sv-Op	Hld	Vel	OPS	ERC	ERA
2022 RdRck	AAA	41	1	17	38.0	165	36	23	21	5	0	2	2	18	1	51	7	2	2	.500	2- -	-		.731	4.51	4.97
2021 Tex	AL	4	0	2	3.2	15	3	2	2	0	0	0	0	3	0	1	0	0	0	-	0-0	1	99	.733	4.38	4.91
2022 Tex	AL	2	0	0	1.0	7	1	2	2	0	0	0	0	3	0	0	0	0	0	-	0-0	0	97	.821	13.82	18.00
2 ML YEARS		6	0	2	4.2	22	4	4	4	0	0	0	0	6	0	1	0	0	0	-	0-0	1	98	.767	6.30	7.71

Nick Solak

Bats: R Throws: R Pos: LF-22;DH-11;PH-9;2B-1   Ht: 5'11" Wt: 185 Born: 1/11/1995 Age: 28

Year Team	Lg	G	AB	H	2B	3B	HR	(Hm	Rd)	TB	R	RBI	RC	TBB	IBB	SO	HBP	SH	SF	SB	CS	GDP	Avg	OBP	Slg	OPS
2022 RdRck	AAA	57	223	62	15	1	10	(-	-)	109	38	45	42	30	0	51	4	0	2	6	0	4	.278	.371	.489	.859
2019 Tex	AL	33	116	34	6	1	5	(3	2)	57	19	17	25	15	1	29	4	0	0	2	0	2	.293	.393	.491	.884

Year	Team	Lg	G	AB	H	2B	3B	HR	(Hm	Rd)	TB	R	RBI	RC	TBB	IBB	SO	HBP	SH	SF	SB	CS	GDP	Avg	OBP	Slg	OPS
2020	Tex	AL	58	209	56	10	0	2	(0	2)	72	27	23	30	18	0	42	2	0	4	7	1	6	.268	.326	.344	.671
2021	Tex	AL	127	458	111	18	2	11	(6	5)	166	57	49	53	34	0	107	15	2	2	7	5	11	.242	.314	.362	.677
2022	Tex	AL	35	82	17	1	0	3	(1	2)	27	14	4	7	7	0	19	5	1	0	3	2	1	.207	.309	.329	.638
4 ML YEARS			253	865	218	35	3	21	(10	11)	322	117	93	115	74	1	197	26	3	6	19	8	20	.252	.327	.372	.700

Donovan Solano

Bats: R **Throws:** R **Pos:** 1B-26;DH-26;3B-16;PH-9;2B-7   sol-ON-oh   **Ht:** 5'8" **Wt:** 210 **Born:** 12/17/1987 **Age:** 35

Year	Team	Lg	G	AB	H	2B	3B	HR	(Hm	Rd)	TB	R	RBI	RC	TBB	IBB	SO	HBP	SH	SF	SB	CS	GDP	Avg	OBP	Slg	OPS
2012	Mia	NL	93	285	84	11	3	2	(0	2)	107	29	28	35	21	1	58	2	3	5	7	0	5	.295	.342	.375	.717
2013	Mia	NL	102	361	90	13	1	3	(0	3)	114	33	34	38	23	3	57	7	2	2	3	1	11	.249	.305	.316	.621
2014	Mia	NL	111	310	78	11	1	3	(1	2)	100	26	28	35	19	0	61	3	7	1	1	2	5	.252	.300	.323	.623
2015	Mia	NL	55	90	17	3	1	0	(0	0)	22	6	7	3	1	0	18	2	1	0	0	0	4	.189	.215	.244	.459
2016	NYY	AL	9	22	5	2	0	1	(0	1)	10	5	2	3	1	0	3	0	0	0	0	0	0	.227	.261	.455	.715
2019	SF	NL	81	215	71	13	1	4	(0	4)	98	27	23	36	10	0	49	1	0	2	0	1	4	.330	.360	.456	.815
2020	SF	NL	54	190	62	15	1	3	(3	0)	88	22	29	36	10	0	39	2	0	1	0	0	2	.326	.365	.463	.828
2021	SF	NL	101	307	86	17	0	7	(3	4)	124	35	31	40	25	2	58	7	1	4	2	0	8	.280	.344	.404	.748
2022	Cin	NL	80	278	79	16	0	4	(3	1)	107	22	24	35	19	1	61	5	0	2	0	0	5	.284	.339	.385	.724
Postseason			5	8	0	0	0	0	(0	0)	0	0	0	0	0	0	3	0	0	1	0	0	0	.000	.000	.000	.000
9 ML YEARS			686	2058	572	101	8	27	(10	17)	770	205	206	261	129	7	404	29	14	17	13	4	44	.278	.327	.374	.701

Jorge Soler

Bats: R **Throws:** R **Pos:** LF-57;DH-14;PH-2   HOR-hay so-LAIR   **Ht:** 6'4" **Wt:** 235 **Born:** 2/25/1992 **Age:** 31

Year	Team	Lg	G	AB	H	2B	3B	HR	(Hm	Rd)	TB	R	RBI	RC	TBB	IBB	SO	HBP	SH	SF	SB	CS	GDP	Avg	OBP	Slg	OPS
2014	ChC	NL	24	89	26	8	1	5	(1	4)	51	11	20	15	6	0	24	0	0	2	1	0	3	.292	.330	.573	.903
2015	ChC	NL	101	366	96	18	1	10	(7	3)	146	39	47	43	32	5	121	3	0	3	3	1	9	.262	.324	.399	.723
2016	ChC	NL	86	227	54	9	0	12	(6	6)	99	37	31	31	31	0	66	3	0	3	0	0	5	.238	.333	.436	.769
2017	KC	AL	35	97	14	5	0	2	(2	0)	25	7	6	5	12	1	36	1	0	0	0	0	5	.144	.245	.258	.503
2018	KC	AL	61	223	59	18	0	9	(5	4)	104	27	28	32	28	0	69	4	0	2	3	1	6	.265	.354	.466	.820
2019	KC	AL	162	589	156	33	1	48	(21	27)	335	95	117	109	73	3	178	10	0	4	3	1	16	.265	.354	.569	.922
2020	KC	AL	43	149	34	8	0	8	(4	4)	66	17	24	24	19	0	60	3	0	1	0	0	3	.228	.326	.443	.769
2021	2 Tms		149	516	115	27	0	27	(13	14)	223	74	70	66	67	0	142	6	0	5	0	0	12	.223	.316	.432	.749
2022	Mia	NL	72	270	56	13	0	13	(8	5)	108	32	34	35	31	1	90	3	0	1	0	2	9	.207	.295	.400	.695
21	KC	AL	94	308	59	16	0	13	(7	6)	114	38	37	29	38	0	97	5	0	3	0	0	9	.192	.288	.370	.658
21	Atl	NL	55	208	56	11	0	14	(6	8)	109	36	33	37	29	0	45	1	0	2	0	0	3	.269	.358	.524	.882
Postseason			26	65	19	6	1	6	(3	3)	45	11	11	16	14	0	21	0	0	0	0	0	1	.292	.418	.692	1.110
9 ML YEARS			733	2526	610	139	3	134	(67	67)	1157	339	377	360	299	10	786	33	0	21	10	5	68	.241	.327	.458	.785

Jared Solomon

Pitches: R **Bats:** R **Pos:** RP-9   **Ht:** 6'2" **Wt:** 200 **Born:** 6/10/1997 **Age:** 26

			HOW MUCH PITCHED					WHAT HE GAVE UP										THE RESULTS							
Year	Team	Lg	G	GS	GF	IP	BFP	H	R	ER	HR	SH	SF	HB	TBB	IBB	SO	WP	W	L	Pct	Sv-Op	Hld	Vel	OPS	ERC	ERA
2022	Chatt	AA	5	0	4	7.0	23	2	0	0	0	0	0	1	0	6	0					3- -	-	-	.221	0.35	0.00
2022	Lsvlle	AAA	41	0	10	40.1	195	48	42	40	12	0	0	3	29	0	44	3	3	2	.600	0- -	-	-	.981	8.67	8.93
2022	Cin	NL	9	0	5	8.1	39	8	10	10	3	0	0	1	5	0	9	0	0	0	-	0-0	0	96	.904	7.05	10.80

Edmundo Sosa

Bats: R **Throws:** R **Pos:** SS-42;3B-22;PH-13;PR-8;DH-4;LF-2;2B-1   **Ht:** 6'0" **Wt:** 210 **Born:** 3/6/1996 **Age:** 27

Year	Team	Lg	G	AB	H	2B	3B	HR	(Hm	Rd)	TB	R	RBI	RC	TBB	IBB	SO	HBP	SH	SF	SB	CS	GDP	Avg	OBP	Slg	OPS
2018	StL	NL	3	2	0	0	0	0	(0	0)	0	1	0	0	1	0	1	0	0	0	0	0	0	.000	.333	.000	.333
2019	StL	NL	8	8	2	0	0	0	(0	0)	2	2	0	1	1	0	2	1	0	0	1	0	0	.250	.400	.250	.650
2021	StL	NL	113	288	78	8	4	6	(2	4)	112	39	27	36	17	2	63	17	1	2	4	4	8	.271	.346	.389	.735
2022	2 Tms	NL	78	176	40	11	4	2	(2	0)	65	26	21	15	5	0	50	7	1	1	6	1	6	.227	.275	.369	.644
22	StL	NL	53	122	23	4	3	0	(0	0)	33	17	8	4	4	0	38	5	0	0	3	1	3	.189	.244	.270	.515
22	Phi	NL	25	54	17	7	1	2	(2	0)	32	9	13	11	1	0	12	2	1	1	3	0	3	.315	.345	.593	.937
Postseason			1	4	0	0	0	0	(0	0)	0	0	0	0	0	0	1	0	0	0	0	0	0	.000	.000	.000	.000
4 ML YEARS			202	474	120	19	8	8	(4	4)	179	68	48	52	24	2	116	25	2	3	11	5	14	.253	.321	.378	.699

Lenyn Sosa

Bats: R **Throws:** R **Pos:** 2B-6;SS-5;PH-1   **Ht:** 6'0" **Wt:** 180 **Born:** 1/25/2000 **Age:** 23

Year	Team	Lg	G	AB	H	2B	3B	HR	(Hm	Rd)	TB	R	RBI	RC	TBB	IBB	SO	HBP	SH	SF	SB	CS	GDP	Avg	OBP	Slg	OPS
2022	Brham	AA	62	257	85	10	2	14	(-	-)	141	47	44	54	21	1	40	5	0	6	0	0	7	.331	.384	.549	.933
2022	Charllt	AAA	57	226	67	12	0	9	(-	-)	106	30	31	35	18	0	43	2	0	1	3	4	7	.296	.352	.469	.821
2022	CWS	AL	11	35	4	1	0	1	(0	1)	8	3	1	0	1	0	12	0	0	0	0	0	0	.114	.139	.229	.367

Gregory Soto

Pitches: L Bats: L Pos: RP-64

Ht: 6'1" Wt: 234 Born: 2/11/1995 Age: 28

			HOW MUCH PITCHED					WHAT HE GAVE UP											THE RESULTS						
Year	Team	Lg	G	GS	GF	IP	BFP	H	R	ER	HR	SH	SF	HB	TBB	IBB	SO	WP	W	L	Pct	Sv-Op	Hld	Vel	OPS	ERC	ERA
2019	Det	AL	33	7	9	57.2	276	74	39	37	9	0	3	0	33	1	45	5	0	5	.000	0-1	2	95	.884	6.86	5.77
2020	Det	AL	27	0	6	23.0	98	16	11	11	2	0	0	2	13	0	29	3	0	1	.000	2-3	4	97	.605	3.30	4.30
2021	Det	AL	62	0	38	63.2	276	46	30	24	7	1	2	1	40	2	76	11	6	3	.667	18-19	7	98	.635	3.46	3.39
2022	Det	AL	64	0	54	60.1	263	49	32	22	2	1	3	7	34	1	60	3	2	11	.154	30-33	5	98	.660	3.63	3.28
	4 ML YEARS		186	7	107	204.2	913	185	112	94	20	2	8	10	120	4	210	22	8	20	.286	50-56	15	97	.716	4.39	4.13

Juan Soto

Bats: L Throws: L Pos: RF-151;DH-1;PH-1

Ht: 6'2" Wt: 224 Born: 10/25/1998 Age: 24

						BATTING															RUNNING			AVERAGES			
Year	Team	Lg	G	AB	H	2B	3B	HR	(Hm	Rd)	TB	R	RBI	RC	TBB	IBB	SO	HBP	SH	SF	SB	CS	GDP	Avg	OBP	Slg	OPS
2018	Was	NL	116	414	121	25	1	22	(6	16)	214	77	70	73	79	10	99	0	1	0	5	2	9	.292	.406	.517	.923
2019	Was	NL	150	542	153	32	5	34	(18	16)	297	110	110	117	108	3	132	3	0	6	12	1	11	.282	.401	.548	.949
2020	Was	NL	47	154	54	14	0	13	(4	9)	107	39	37	53	41	12	28	1	0	0	6	2	1	.351	.490	.695	1.185
2021	Was	NL	151	502	157	20	2	29	(10	19)	268	111	95	127	145	23	93	2	0	5	9	7	23	.313	.465	.534	.999
2022	2 Tms	NL	153	524	127	25	2	27	(14	13)	237	93	62	97	135	6	96	4	0	0	6	2	12	.242	.401	.452	.853
22	Was	NL	101	342	84	17	1	21	(11	10)	166	62	46	67	91	4	62	3	0	0	6	2	11	.246	.408	.485	.894
22	SD	NL	52	182	43	8	1	6	(3	3)	71	31	16	30	44	2	34	1	0	0	0	0	1	.236	.388	.390	.778
	Postseason		17	65	18	3	0	5	(2	3)	36	12	14	12	9	2	21	1	0	0	1	0	0	.277	.373	.554	.927
	5 ML YEARS		617	2136	612	116	10	125	(52	73)	1123	430	374	467	508	54	448	10	1	11	38	14	56	.287	.424	.526	.950

Livan Soto

Bats: L Throws: R Pos: SS-18;3B-1;PR-1

Ht: 6'0" Wt: 160 Born: 6/22/2000 Age: 23

						BATTING															RUNNING			AVERAGES			
Year	Team	Lg	G	AB	H	2B	3B	HR	(Hm	Rd)	TB	R	RBI	RC	TBB	IBB	SO	HBP	SH	SF	SB	CS	GDP	Avg	OBP	Slg	OPS
2022	Rock	AA	119	456	128	17	1	6	(-	-)	165	69	57	63	71	0	102	5	5	6	18	8	10	.281	.379	.362	.741
2022	LAA	AL	18	55	22	5	1	1	(1	0)	32	9	9	11	2	0	13	0	1	1	1	1	1	.400	.414	.582	.996

Bennett Sousa

Pitches: L Bats: L Pos: RP-25

Ht: 6'3" Wt: 220 Born: 4/6/1995 Age: 28

			HOW MUCH PITCHED					WHAT HE GAVE UP											THE RESULTS						
Year	Team	Lg	G	GS	GF	IP	BFP	H	R	ER	HR	SH	SF	HB	TBB	IBB	SO	WP	W	L	Pct	Sv-Op	Hld	Vel	OPS	ERC	ERA
2022	Charlt	AAA	28	0	13	27.1	116	22	14	12	4	0	2	2	12	1	35	2	2	1	.667	6- -	-	-	.703	3.69	3.95
2022	CWS	AL	25	0	2	20.1	96	25	20	19	3	0	2	1	10	1	12	4	3	0	1.000	1-2	5	94	.833	6.22	8.41

Steven Souza Jr.

Bats: R Throws: R Pos: RF-5;DH-1

SOO-zuh

Ht: 6'4" Wt: 225 Born: 4/24/1989 Age: 34

						BATTING															RUNNING			AVERAGES			
Year	Team	Lg	G	AB	H	2B	3B	HR	(Hm	Rd)	TB	R	RBI	RC	TBB	IBB	SO	HBP	SH	SF	SB	CS	GDP	Avg	OBP	Slg	OPS
2022	Tacom	AAA	22	75	20	5	0	5	(-	-)	40	17	17	18	19	0	25	1	0	1	3	1	1	.267	.417	.533	.950
2014	Was	NL	21	23	3	0	0	2	(1	1)	9	2	2	1	3	0	7	0	0	0	0	0	0	.130	.231	.391	.622
2015	TB	AL	110	373	84	15	1	16	(6	10)	149	59	40	40	46	0	144	5	1	1	12	6	7	.225	.318	.399	.717
2016	TB	AL	120	430	106	17	1	17	(7	10)	176	58	49	53	31	0	159	5	0	2	7	6	5	.247	.303	.409	.713
2017	TB	AL	148	523	125	21	2	30	(14	16)	240	78	78	85	84	2	179	7	2	1	16	4	9	.239	.351	.459	.810
2018	Ari	NL	72	241	53	15	3	5	(3	2)	89	21	29	29	28	0	75	3	0	0	6	1	4	.220	.309	.369	.678
2020	ChC	NL	11	27	4	2	0	1	(1	0)	9	3	5	3	4	0	15	0	0	0	1	0	0	.148	.258	.333	.591
2021	LAD	NL	17	33	5	1	1	1	(0	1)	11	2	3	1	2	0	14	1	0	0	0	0	2	.152	.222	.333	.556
2022	Sea	AL	6	19	3	0	0	0	(0	0)	3	0	1	0	0	0	8	0	0	0	0	0	0	.158	.158	.158	.316
	Postseason		10	8	1	0	0	0	(0	0)	1	0	0	1	1	0	4	0	0	0	0	0	0	.125	.222	.125	.347
	8 ML YEARS		505	1669	383	71	8	72	(32	40)	686	223	207	212	198	2	601	21	3	4	42	17	30	.229	.318	.411	.729

Cory Spangenberg

Bats: L Throws: R Pos: 3B-1

SPAN-jen-burg

Ht: 6'0" Wt: 195 Born: 3/16/1991 Age: 32

						BATTING															RUNNING			AVERAGES			
Year	Team	Lg	G	AB	H	2B	3B	HR	(Hm	Rd)	TB	R	RBI	RC	TBB	IBB	SO	HBP	SH	SF	SB	CS	GDP	Avg	OBP	Slg	OPS
2022	Memp	AAA	106	382	90	17	5	10	(-	-)	147	53	42	44	27	0	135	3	0	2	14	3	4	.236	.290	.385	.675
2014	SD	NL	20	62	18	2	1	2	(1	1)	28	7	9	9	2	0	14	0	1	0	4	2	1	.290	.313	.452	.764
2015	SD	NL	108	303	82	17	5	4	(3	1)	121	38	21	40	28	1	75	2	8	3	9	4	4	.271	.333	.399	.733
2016	SD	NL	14	48	11	1	1	1	(0	1)	17	6	8	7	4	0	13	1	0	1	1	0	0	.229	.302	.354	.656
2017	SD	NL	129	444	117	18	2	13	(6	7)	178	57	46	58	34	1	128	5	2	1	11	3	2	.264	.322	.401	.723
2018	SD	NL	116	298	70	9	4	7	(5	2)	108	35	25	32	25	0	108	2	4	0	6	1	6	.235	.298	.362	.661
2019	Mil	NL	32	95	22	2	2	2	(1	1)	34	11	10	10	6	1	36	0	1	0	3	0	1	.232	.277	.358	.635
2022	StL	NL	1	0	0	0	0	0	(0	0)	0	0	0	0	0	0	0	0	0	0	0	0	0	-	-	-	-
	Postseason		1	0	0	0	0	0	(0	0)	0	0	0	0	0	0	0	0	0	0	0	0	0	-	-	-	-
	7 ML YEARS		420	1250	320	49	15	29	(16	13)	486	154	119	156	99	3	374	10	16	4	34	10	14	.256	.315	.389	.704

Gabe Speier

Pitches: L Bats: L Pos: RP-16; SP-1   Ht: 5'11" Wt: 200 Born: 4/12/1995 Age: 28

			HOW MUCH PITCHED					WHAT HE GAVE UP										THE RESULTS						
Year	Team	Lg	G	GS	GF	IP	BFP	H	R	ER	HR	SH	SF	HB	TBB	IBB	SO	WP	W	L	Pct	Sv-Op	Hld	Vel	OPS	ERC	ERA
2022	Omha	AAA	30	0	5	26.2	145	51	44	43	11	2	1	3	12	1	34	2	1	3	.250	0--	-	-	1.210	13.52	14.51
2019	KC	AL	9	0	1	7.1	33	5	6	6	2	0	0	0	6	0	10	1	0	0	-	0-0	1	95	.778	5.10	7.36
2020	KC	AL	8	0	3	5.2	30	9	5	5	1	0	0	0	4	0	6	0	0	1	.000	0-0	1	92	.972	9.58	7.94
2021	KC	AL	7	0	1	7.2	33	10	3	1	0	0	0	1	0	0	5	0	0	0	-	0-0	0	94	.646	4.03	1.17
2022	KC	AL	17	1	5	19.1	77	16	5	5	2	0	1	0	5	0	14	1	0	1	.000	0-1	2	94	.625	2.68	2.33
	4 ML YEARS		41	1	10	40.0	173	40	19	17	5	0	1	1	15	0	35	2	0	2	.000	0-1	4	94	.715	4.24	3.83

George Springer

Bats: R Throws: R Pos: CF-86;DH-40;RF-26;PH-7   Ht: 6'3" Wt: 220 Born: 9/19/1989 Age: 33

			BATTING																RUNNING			AVERAGES			
Year	Team	Lg	G	AB	H	2B	3B	HR	(Hm | Rd)	TB	R	RBI	RC	TBB	IBB	SO	HBP	SH	SF	SB	CS	GDP	Avg	OBP	Slg	OPS
2014	Hou	AL	78	295	68	8	1	20	(5 | 15)	138	45	51	45	39	4	114	9	0	2	5	2	4	.231	.336	.468	.804
2015	Hou	AL	102	388	107	19	2	16	(9 | 7)	178	59	41	60	50	0	109	8	2	3	16	4	4	.276	.367	.459	.826
2016	Hou	AL	162	644	168	29	5	29	(13 | 16)	294	116	82	100	88	2	178	11	0	1	9	10	12	.261	.359	.457	.815
2017	Hou	AL	140	548	155	29	0	34	(16 | 18)	286	112	85	99	64	1	111	11	0	4	5	7	11	.283	.367	.522	.889
2018	Hou	AL	140	544	144	26	0	22	(12 | 10)	236	102	71	84	64	0	122	5	0	3	6	4	12	.265	.346	.434	.780
2019	Hou	AL	122	479	140	20	3	39	(18 | 21)	283	96	96	103	67	1	113	6	0	4	6	2	12	.292	.383	.591	.974
2020	Hou	AL	51	189	50	6	2	14	(6 | 8)	102	37	32	42	24	0	38	5	0	2	1	2	3	.265	.359	.540	.899
2021	Tor	AL	78	299	79	19	1	22	(15 | 7)	166	59	50	55	37	1	79	4	0	1	4	1	6	.264	.352	.555	.907
2022	Tor	AL	133	513	137	22	4	25	(15 | 10)	242	89	76	86	54	1	100	7	0	5	14	2	7	.267	.342	.472	.814
	Postseason		63	260	70	15	0	19	(9 | 10)	142	43	38	48	31	1	71	1	0	0	4	1	4	.269	.349	.546	.895
	9 ML YEARS		1006	3899	1048	178	18	221	(109 | 112)	1925	715	584	674	487	10	964	66	2	25	66	34	71	.269	.358	.494	.851

Jeffrey Springs

Pitches: L Bats: L Pos: SP-25; RP-8   Ht: 6'3" Wt: 218 Born: 9/20/1992 Age: 30

			HOW MUCH PITCHED					WHAT HE GAVE UP										THE RESULTS						
Year	Team	Lg	G	GS	GF	IP	BFP	H	R	ER	HR	SH	SF	HB	TBB	IBB	SO	WP	W	L	Pct	Sv-Op	Hld	Vel	OPS	ERC	ERA
2018	Tex	AL	18	2	4	32.0	141	32	14	12	4	1	0	1	14	1	31	3	1	1	.500	0-1	2	91	.744	4.44	3.38
2019	Tex	AL	25	0	7	32.1	155	38	23	23	4	0	2	0	23	0	32	0	4	1	.800	0-0	1	92	.884	6.57	6.40
2020	Bos	AL	16	0	8	20.1	99	30	18	16	5	0	1	1	7	1	28	2	0	2	.000	0-1	1	92	.973	7.87	7.08
2021	TB	AL	43	0	9	44.2	179	35	21	17	9	1	2	0	14	1	63	3	5	1	.833	2-4	10	93	.720	3.21	3.43
2022	TB	AL	33	25	0	135.1	549	114	42	37	14	0	2	1	31	0	144	1	9	5	.643	0-0	0	91	.620	2.61	2.46
	5 ML YEARS		135	27	28	264.2	1123	249	118	105	36	2	7	3	89	3	298	9	19	10	.655	2-6	14	92	.717	3.73	3.57

Locke St. John

Pitches: L Bats: L Pos: RP-1   Ht: 6'3" Wt: 180 Born: 1/31/1993 Age: 30

			HOW MUCH PITCHED					WHAT HE GAVE UP										THE RESULTS						
Year	Team	Lg	G	GS	GF	IP	BFP	H	R	ER	HR	SH	SF	HB	TBB	IBB	SO	WP	W	L	Pct	Sv-Op	Hld	Vel	OPS	ERC	ERA
2022	Iowa	AAA	5	0	0	7.0	38	7	4	4	1	0	1	3	6	0	8	0	0	1	.000	0--	-	-	.885	7.72	5.14
2022	Syrcse	AAA	29	1	6	42.0	192	37	33	28	8	2	3	7	23	1	35	2	2	5	.286	1--	-	-	.816	5.21	6.00
2019	Tex	AL	7	0	4	6.2	33	7	4	4	0	0	0	4	0	5	0	0	0	-	0-0	2	90	.678	3.97	5.40
2022	ChC	NL	1	0	1	2.0	9	3	3	3	2	0	0	0	0	0	4	0	0	0	-	0-0	0	89	1.444	11.80	13.50
	2 ML YEARS		8	0	5	8.2	42	10	7	7	2	0	0	4	0	0	9	0	0	0	-	0-0	2	90	.860	5.77	7.27

Jacob Stallings

Bats: R Throws: R Pos: C-110;PH-3;DH-1   Ht: 6'5" Wt: 225 Born: 12/22/1989 Age: 33

			BATTING																RUNNING			AVERAGES			
Year	Team	Lg	G	AB	H	2B	3B	HR	(Hm	Rd)	TB	R	RBI	RC	TBB	IBB	SO	HBP	SH	SF	SB	CS	GDP	Avg	OBP	Slg	OPS
2016	Pit	NL	5	15	6	1	0	0	(0	0)	7	0	2	3	0	0	4	0	0	0	1	0	0	.400	.400	.467	.867
2017	Pit	NL	5	14	5	2	0	0	(0	0)	7	3	3	3	2	1	2	0	0	0	0	0	0	.357	.438	.500	.938
2018	Pit	NL	14	37	8	0	0	0	(0	0)	8	2	5	3	3	0	9	0	0	1	0	0	2	.216	.268	.216	.485
2019	Pit	NL	71	191	50	5	0	6	(1	5)	73	26	13	18	16	5	40	2	1	0	0	0	3	.262	.325	.382	.708
2020	Pit	NL	42	125	31	7	0	3	(3	0)	47	13	18	18	15	0	40	0	2	1	0	0	0	.248	.326	.376	.702
2021	Pit	NL	112	374	92	20	1	8	(5	3)	138	38	53	49	49	0	85	2	0	2	0	0	10	.246	.335	.369	.704
2022	Mia	NL	114	346	77	12	0	4	(0	4)	101	25	34	28	29	0	83	6	1	2	0	1	15	.223	.292	.292	.584
	7 ML YEARS		363	1102	269	47	1	21	(9	12)	381	107	128	122	114	6	263	10	4	6	1	1	32	.244	.319	.346	.665

Craig Stammen

Pitches: R Bats: R Pos: RP-32; SP-1   Ht: 6'2" Wt: 228 Born: 3/9/1984 Age: 39
STAMM-enn

			HOW MUCH PITCHED					WHAT HE GAVE UP										THE RESULTS						
Year	Team	Lg	G	GS	GF	IP	BFP	H	R	ER	HR	SH	SF	HB	TBB	IBB	SO	WP	W	L	Pct	Sv-Op	Hld	Vel	OPS	ERC	ERA
2009	Was	NL	19	19	0	105.2	448	112	67	60	14	4	3	3	24	1	48	7	4	7	.364	0-0	0	89	.774	4.03	5.11
2010	Was	NL	35	19	3	128.0	562	151	78	73	13	5	6	1	41	4	85	3	4	4	.500	0-0	1	90	.814	4.79	5.13
2011	Was	NL	7	0	2	10.1	38	3	1	1	0	0	0	0	4	0	12	1	1	1	.500	0-0	1	91	.272	0.67	0.87
2012	Was	NL	59	0	15	88.1	370	70	27	23	7	5	1	2	36	4	87	3	6	1	.857	1-2	10	92	.636	2.84	2.34
2013	Was	NL	55	0	14	81.2	339	78	30	25	4	8	4	2	27	3	79	2	7	6	.538	0-1	7	92	.682	3.32	2.76
2014	Was	NL	49	0	15	72.2	304	78	34	31	5	3	1	3	14	2	56	1	4	5	.444	0-0	7	92	.708	3.61	3.84
2015	Was	NL	5	0	0	4.0	17	2	0	0	0	0	1	0	3	1	3	0	0	0	-	0-0	0	92	.525	1.66	0.00
2017	SD	NL	60	0	9	80.1	329	68	29	28	12	2	0	2	28	3	74	2	2	3	.400	0-2	11	92	.684	3.46	3.14
2018	SD	NL	73	0	7	79.0	317	65	25	24	3	2	1	3	17	3	88	3	8	3	.727	0-5	23	92	.583	2.17	2.73
2019	SD	NL	76	0	12	82.0	339	80	36	30	13	0	3	2	15	2	73	0	8	7	.533	4-13	31	93	.719	3.51	3.29
2020	SD	NL	24	0	6	24.0	105	27	16	15	2	2	0	2	4	0	20	0	4	2	.667	0-1	5	92	.702	3.97	5.63

	HOW MUCH PITCHED					WHAT HE GAVE UP										THE RESULTS						
Year Team	Lg	G	GS	GF	IP	BFP	H	R	ER	HR	SH	SF	HB	TBB	IBB	SO	WP	W	L	Pct	Sv-Op	Hld	Vel	OPS	ERC	ERA
2021 SD	NL	67	4	4	88.1	355	79	31	30	13	1	2	3	13	1	83	3	6	3	.667	1-2	7	92	.652	2.94	3.06
2022 SD	NL	33	1	9	40.2	177	45	22	20	9	0	3	2	10	0	35	3	1	2	.333	0-1	2	91	.796	5.07	4.43
Postseason		10	1	0	11.2	55	13	7	7	1	1	1	3	4	1	9	1	0	0	-	0-0	1	92	.805	5.14	5.40
13 ML YEARS		562	43	96	885.0	3700	858	396	360	95	32	25	25	236	24	743	28	55	44	.556	6-27	107	91	.704	3.51	3.66

Ryne Stanek

Pitches: R **Bats:** R **Pos:** RP-59   **Ht:** 6'4" **Wt:** 226 **Born:** 7/26/1991 **Age:** 31

	HOW MUCH PITCHED					WHAT HE GAVE UP										THE RESULTS						
Year Team	Lg	G	GS	GF	IP	BFP	H	R	ER	HR	SH	SF	HB	TBB	IBB	SO	WP	W	L	Pct	Sv-Op	Hld	Vel	OPS	ERC	ERA
2017 TB	AL	21	0	4	20.0	95	26	13	13	6	0	1	0	12	2	29	4	0	0		0-1	4	98	.985	8.31	5.85
2018 TB	AL	59	29	16	66.1	263	45	23	22	8	0	0	1	27	1	81	5	2	3	.400	0-0	8	98	.618	2.64	2.98
2019 2 Tms		63	27	12	77.0	327	61	39	34	11	0	3	0	39	3	89	5	0	4	.000	1-5	7	98	.688	3.56	3.97
2020 Mia	NL	9	0	3	10.0	48	11	8	8	3	0	0	0	8	1	11	0	0	0		0-0	0	96	.921	7.82	7.20
2021 Hou	AL	72	0	13	68.1	290	46	32	26	8	0	1	5	37	3	83	6	3	5	.375	2-4	21	98	.615	3.15	3.42
2022 Hou	AL	59	0	10	54.2	224	36	8	7	2	0	2	0	31	1	62	4	2	1	.667	1-5	17	98	.556	2.49	1.15
19 TB	AL	41	27	3	55.2	228	44	24	21	7	0	2	0	20	1	61	2	0	2	.000	0-0	2	98	.654	2.93	3.40
19 Mia	NL	22	0	9	21.1	99	17	15	13	4	0	1	0	19	2	28	3	0	2	.000	1-5	5	98	.769	5.31	5.48
Postseason		15	0	4	13.0	47	5	3	3	2	0	0	0	5	0	14	1	2	0	1.000	0-0	2	97	.498	1.47	2.08
6 ML YEARS		283	56	52	296.1	1247	225	123	110	38	0	7	6	154	11	355	24	7	13	.350	4-15	57	98	.664	3.45	3.34

Giancarlo Stanton

Bats: R **Throws:** R **Pos:** DH-65;RF-34;PH-7;LF-4   john-CAHR-loh   **Ht:** 6'6" **Wt:** 245 **Born:** 11/8/1989 **Age:** 33

	BATTING																	RUNNING			AVERAGES			
Year Team	Lg	G	AB	H	2B	3B	HR	(Hm | Rd)	TB	R	RBI	RC	TBB	IBB	SO	HBP	SH	SF	SB	CS	GDP	Avg	OBP	Slg	OPS
2010 Fla	NL	100	359	93	21	1	22	(7 | 15)	182	45	59	56	34	6	123	2	0	1	5	2	7	.259	.326	.507	.833
2011 Fla	NL	150	516	135	30	5	34	(16 | 18)	277	79	87	81	70	6	166	9	0	6	5	5	11	.262	.356	.537	.893
2012 Mia	NL	123	449	130	30	1	37	(16 | 21)	273	75	86	79	46	9	143	5	0	1	6	2	5	.290	.361	.608	.969
2013 Mia	NL	116	425	106	26	0	24	(15 | 9)	204	62	62	66	74	5	140	4	0	1	1	0	10	.249	.365	.480	.845
2014 Mia	NL	145	539	155	31	1	37	(24 | 13)	299	89	105	109	94	24	170	3	0	2	13	1	16	.288	.395	.555	.950
2015 Mia	NL	74	279	74	12	1	27	(13 | 14)	169	47	67	54	34	6	95	2	0	3	4	2	5	.265	.346	.606	.952
2016 Mia	NL	119	413	99	20	1	27	(13 | 14)	202	56	74	56	50	5	140	4	0	2	0	0	6	.240	.326	.489	.815
2017 Mia	NL	159	597	168	32	0	59	(31 | 28)	377	123	132	117	85	13	163	7	0	3	2	2	13	.281	.376	.631	1.007
2018 NYY	AL	158	617	164	34	1	38	(20 | 18)	314	102	100	98	70	5	211	8	0	10	5	0	17	.266	.343	.509	.852
2019 NYY	AL	18	59	17	3	0	3	(2 | 1)	29	8	13	14	12	0	24	0	0	1	0	0	1	.288	.403	.492	.894
2020 NYY	AL	23	76	19	7	0	4	(1 | 3)	38	12	11	14	15	1	27	2	0	0	1	1	4	.250	.387	.500	.887
2021 NYY	AL	139	510	139	19	0	35	(15 | 20)	263	64	97	91	63	1	157	3	0	3	0	0	22	.273	.354	.516	.870
2022 NYY	AL	110	398	84	7	0	31	(18 | 13)	184	53	78	69	50	2	137	0	0	3	0	0	8	.211	.297	.462	.759
Postseason		18	64	19	1	0	9	(2 | 7)	47	13	17	13	9	0	23	0	0	2	1	0	3	.297	.373	.734	1.108
13 ML YEARS		1434	5237	1383	272	11	378	(191 | 187)	2811	815	971	904	697	83	1696	49	0	36	42	15	125	.264	.354	.537	.890

Cody Stashak

Pitches: R **Bats:** R **Pos:** RP-11   **Ht:** 6'2" **Wt:** 180 **Born:** 6/4/1994 **Age:** 29

	HOW MUCH PITCHED					WHAT HE GAVE UP										THE RESULTS						
Year Team	Lg	G	GS	GF	IP	BFP	H	R	ER	HR	SH	SF	HB	TBB	IBB	SO	WP	W	L	Pct	Sv-Op	Hld	Vel	OPS	ERC	ERA
2019 Min	AL	18	1	4	25.0	104	29	9	9	3	0	1	1	1	0	25	0	0	1	.000	0-0	1	92	.773	3.82	3.24
2020 Min	AL	11	0	1	15.0	57	11	5	5	2	0	0	0	3	0	17	1	1	0	1.000	0-0	5	92	.635	2.22	3.00
2021 Min	AL	15	0	1	15.2	75	16	12	12	2	0	2	1	10	0	26	1	0	0	-	0-0	2	91	.779	5.42	6.89
2022 Min	AL	11	0	4	16.1	65	16	7	7	1	0	1	0	0	0	15	0	3	0	1.000	0-0	1	91	.621	2.20	3.86
Postseason		3	0	0	3.2	16	4	3	3	3	0	0	0	1	0	1	0	0	1	.000	0-0	0	92	1.179	8.92	7.36
4 ML YEARS		55	1	10	72.0	301	72	33	33	8	0	4	2	14	0	83	2	4	1	.800	0-0	9	91	.716	3.42	4.13

Max Stassi

Bats: R **Throws:** R **Pos:** C-97;PH-6;DH-1   STASS-ee   **Ht:** 5'10" **Wt:** 200 **Born:** 3/15/1991 **Age:** 32

	BATTING																	RUNNING			AVERAGES			
Year Team	Lg	G	AB	H	2B	3B	HR	(Hm | Rd)	TB	R	RBI	RC	TBB	IBB	SO	HBP	SH	SF	SB	CS	GDP	Avg	OBP	Slg	OPS
2013 Hou	AL	3	7	2	0	0	0	(0 | 0)	2	0	1	0	0	0	2	1	0	0	0	0	1	.286	.375	.286	.661
2014 Hou	AL	7	20	7	2	0	0	(0 | 0)	9	2	4	4	0	0	6	0	0	0	0	0	0	.350	.350	.450	.800
2015 Hou	AL	11	15	6	0	0	1	(1 | 0)	9	4	2	3	1	0	5	0	1	0	0	0	1	.400	.438	.600	1.038
2016 Hou	AL	9	13	1	0	0	0	(0 | 0)	1	1	0	0	0	0	5	0	0	0	0	0	0	.077	.077	.077	.154
2017 Hou	AL	14	24	4	1	0	2	(1 | 1)	11	5	4	3	6	0	4	0	0	1	0	0	2	.167	.323	.458	.781
2018 Hou	AL	88	221	50	13	0	8	(1 | 7)	87	28	27	33	23	0	74	6	0	0	0	0	6	.226	.316	.394	.710
2019 2 Tms	AL	51	132	18	1	0	1	(0 | 1)	22	7	5	2	12	0	49	1	0	2	0	0	2	.136	.211	.167	.378
2020 LAA	AL	31	90	25	2	0	7	(3 | 4)	48	12	20	18	11	0	21	1	0	3	0	0	5	.278	.352	.533	.886
2021 LAA	AL	87	282	68	11	1	13	(9 | 4)	120	45	35	40	28	0	101	8	0	1	0	0	8	.241	.326	.426	.752
2022 LAA	AL	102	333	60	12	1	9	(3 | 6)	101	32	30	24	38	0	112	2	1	1	0	0	12	.180	.267	.303	.571
19 Hou	AL	31	90	15	1	0	1	(0 | 1)	19	4	3	2	7	0	34	1	0	0	0	0	1	.167	.235	.211	.446
19 LAA	AL	20	42	3	0	0	0	(0 | 0)	3	3	2	0	5	0	15	0	0	2	0	0	2	.071	.163	.071	.235
10 ML YEARS		403	1137	241	42	2	41	(18 | 23)	410	136	128	127	119	0	379	19	2	8	0	0	38	.212	.295	.361	.656

Josh Staumont

Pitches: R Bats: R Pos: RP-42
Ht: 6'3" Wt: 200 Born: 12/21/1993 Age: 29

			HOW MUCH PITCHED					WHAT HE GAVE UP												THE RESULTS						
Year	Team	Lg	G	GS	GF	IP	BFP	H	R	ER	HR	SH	SF	HB	TBB	IBB	SO	WP	W	L	Pct	Sv-Op	Hld	Vel	OPS	ERC	ERA
2019	KC	AL	16	0	7	19.1	88	21	13	8	4	0	0	1	10	1	15	0	0	0	-	0-1	0	96	.870	6.01	3.72
2020	KC	AL	26	0	3	25.2	112	20	8	7	2	0	0	3	16	0	37	1	2	1	.667	0-0	8	98	.639	4.06	2.45
2021	KC	AL	64	0	19	65.2	264	43	24	21	6	0	0	2	27	1	72	4	4	3	.571	5-5	16	97	.566	2.37	2.88
2022	KC	AL	42	0	15	37.2	176	37	28	27	3	1	3	1	29	0	43	5	3	3	.500	3-6	5	96	.805	5.39	6.45
	4 ML YEARS		148	0	44	148.1	640	121	73	63	15	1	3	7	82	2	167	10	9	7	.563	8-12	29	97	.685	3.83	3.82

Drew Steckenrider

Pitches: R Bats: R Pos: RP-16
Ht: 6'4" Wt: 235 Born: 1/10/1991 Age: 32

			HOW MUCH PITCHED					WHAT HE GAVE UP												THE RESULTS						
Year	Team	Lg	G	GS	GF	IP	BFP	H	R	ER	HR	SH	SF	HB	TBB	IBB	SO	WP	W	L	Pct	Sv-Op	Hld	Vel	OPS	ERC	ERA
2022	Tacom	AAA	23	0	9	25.1	123	29	14	13	6	0	0	0	17	0	21	1	4	0	1.000	3- --	-	-	.912	6.96	4.62
2017	Mia	NL	37	0	7	34.2	151	30	13	9	4	0	1	0	18	1	54	1	1	1	.500	1-1	10	95	.674	3.80	2.34
2018	Mia	NL	71	0	17	64.2	272	55	29	28	7	0	1	2	27	5	74	0	4	4	.500	5-10	19	95	.664	3.39	3.90
2019	Mia	NL	15	0	4	14.1	58	9	10	10	6	0	0	1	5	0	14	0	0	2	.000	0-1	3	95	.778	4.00	6.28
2021	Sea	AL	62	0	20	67.2	267	52	16	15	5	1	2	4	17	2	58	0	5	2	.714	14-17	7	94	.608	2.38	2.00
2022	Sea	AL	16	0	3	14.1	68	21	9	9	2	0	0	0	5	0	10	0	0	2	.000	2-4	4	94	.922	6.92	5.65
	5 ML YEARS		201	0	51	195.2	816	167	77	71	24	1	4	7	72	8	210	1	10	11	.476	22-33	43	95	.678	3.39	3.27

Justin Steele

Pitches: L Bats: L Pos: SP-24
Ht: 6'2" Wt: 205 Born: 7/11/1995 Age: 27

			HOW MUCH PITCHED					WHAT HE GAVE UP												THE RESULTS						
Year	Team	Lg	G	GS	GF	IP	BFP	H	R	ER	HR	SH	SF	HB	TBB	IBB	SO	WP	W	L	Pct	Sv-Op	Hld	Vel	OPS	ERC	ERA
2021	ChC	NL	20	9	2	57.0	248	50	29	27	12	1	0	5	27	2	59	0	4	4	.500	0-0	1	93	.769	4.76	4.26
2022	ChC	NL	24	24	0	119.0	512	111	53	42	8	0	4	3	50	0	126	4	4	7	.364	0-0	0	92	.660	3.64	3.18
	2 ML YEARS		44	33	2	176.0	760	161	82	69	20	1	4	8	77	2	185	4	8	11	.421	0-0	1	92	.695	3.99	3.53

Spencer Steer

Bats: R Throws: R Pos: 3B-14;1B-9;2B-5;DH-2;PH-1
Ht: 5'11" Wt: 185 Born: 12/7/1997 Age: 25

					BATTING															RUNNING			AVERAGES			
Year	Team	Lg	G	AB	H	2B	3B	HR	(Hm	Rd)	TB	R	RBI	RC	TBB	IBB	SO	HBP	SH	SF	SB	CS	GDP	Avg	OBP	Slg	OPS
2022	Wich	AA	35	137	42	13	1	8	(-	-)	81	27	30	31	14	0	23	4	0	1	1	3	1	.307	.385	.591	.976
2022	StPaul	AAA	48	198	48	10	1	12	(-	-)	96	39	32	35	28	1	43	4	0	2	2	0	3	.242	.345	.485	.830
2022	Lsvlle	AAA	23	92	27	7	0	3	(-	-)	43	14	13	15	9	0	23	3	0	0	1	0	2	.293	.375	.467	.842
2022	Cin	NL	28	95	20	5	0	2	(2	0)	31	12	8	10	11	0	26	2	0	0	0	1	2	.211	.306	.326	.632

Michael Stefanic

Bats: R Throws: R Pos: 2B-22;PH-4;PR-1
Ht: 5'10" Wt: 180 Born: 2/24/1996 Age: 27

					BATTING															RUNNING			AVERAGES			
Year	Team	Lg	G	AB	H	2B	3B	HR	(Hm	Rd)	TB	R	RBI	RC	TBB	IBB	SO	HBP	SH	SF	SB	CS	GDP	Avg	OBP	Slg	OPS
2022	Salt Lk	AAA	77	287	90	14	3	4	(-	-)	122	50	37	48	48	1	22	8	0	3	4	2	12	.314	.422	.425	.847
2022	LAA	AL	25	61	12	2	0	0	(0	0)	14	5	0	1	5	0	12	2	1	0	0	0	1	.197	.279	.230	.509

Trevor Stephan

Pitches: R Bats: R Pos: RP-66
Ht: 6'5" Wt: 225 Born: 11/25/1995 Age: 27

			HOW MUCH PITCHED					WHAT HE GAVE UP												THE RESULTS						
Year	Team	Lg	G	GS	GF	IP	BFP	H	R	ER	HR	SH	SF	HB	TBB	IBB	SO	WP	W	L	Pct	Sv-Op	Hld	Vel	OPS	ERC	ERA
2021	Cle	AL	43	0	13	63.1	282	58	32	31	15	0	1	3	31	1	75	0	3	1	.750	1-1	3	96	.796	5.00	4.41
2022	Cle	AL	66	0	8	63.2	267	57	24	19	3	3	2	4	18	2	82	3	6	5	.545	3-5	19	97	.628	2.88	2.69
	2 ML YEARS		109	0	21	127.0	549	115	56	50	18	3	3	7	49	3	157	3	9	6	.600	4-6	22	96	.714	3.90	3.54

Jackson Stephens

Pitches: R Bats: R Pos: RP-38; SP-1
Ht: 6'2" Wt: 220 Born: 5/11/1994 Age: 29

			HOW MUCH PITCHED					WHAT HE GAVE UP												THE RESULTS						
Year	Team	Lg	G	GS	GF	IP	BFP	H	R	ER	HR	SH	SF	HB	TBB	IBB	SO	WP	W	L	Pct	Sv-Op	Hld	Vel	OPS	ERC	ERA
2017	Cin	NL	7	4	1	25.0	101	19	13	13	6	0	0	1	9	0	21	1	2	1	.667	0-0	0	93	.727	3.73	4.68
2018	Cin	NL	29	0	12	38.1	183	50	30	21	7	2	0	3	15	3	33	3	2	3	.400	0-0	0	94	.891	6.54	4.93
2022	Atl	NL	39	1	24	53.2	235	49	32	22	3	2	1	3	23	4	47	1	3	3	.500	2-3	2	94	.647	3.42	3.69
	3 ML YEARS		75	5	37	117.0	519	118	75	56	16	4	1	7	47	7	101	5	7	7	.500	2-3	2	94	.749	4.47	4.31

Robert Stephenson

Pitches: R Bats: R Pos: RP-58
Ht: 6'3" Wt: 205 Born: 2/24/1993 Age: 30

			HOW MUCH PITCHED					WHAT HE GAVE UP												THE RESULTS						
Year	Team	Lg	G	GS	GF	IP	BFP	H	R	ER	HR	SH	SF	HB	TBB	IBB	SO	WP	W	L	Pct	Sv-Op	Hld	Vel	OPS	ERC	ERA
2016	Cin	NL	8	8	0	37.0	170	41	26	25	9	0	0	4	19	1	31	2	2	3	.400	0-0	0	93	.893	6.78	6.08
2017	Cin	NL	25	11	6	84.2	383	81	52	44	12	5	6	2	53	3	86	5	5	6	.455	1-1	0	94	.805	5.06	4.68
2018	Cin	NL	4	3	0	11.2	63	17	12	12	2	0	0	0	12	3	11	2	0	2	.000	0-0	0	93	1.040	9.71	9.26
2019	Cin	NL	57	0	16	64.2	262	43	30	27	9	0	1	0	24	4	81	3	3	2	.600	0-4	11	95	.634	2.33	3.76
2020	Cin	NL	10	0	4	10.0	43	11	11	11	8	0	0	1	3	0	13	0	0	0	-	0-0	1	95	1.246	10.14	9.90
2021	Col	NL	49	0	10	46.0	197	42	20	16	5	1	2	2	18	0	52	3	2	1	.667	1-2	4	97	.724	3.77	3.13

Year Team	Lg	G	GS	GF	IP	BFP	H	R	ER	HR	SH	SF	HB	TBB	IBB	SO	WP	W	L	Pct	Sv-Op	Hld	Vel	OPS	ERC	ERA
		HOW MUCH PITCHED					**WHAT HE GAVE UP**											**THE RESULTS**								
2022 2 Tms	NL	58	0	13	58.0	247	63	39	35	10	1	2	1	14	1	55	4	2	2	.500	0-3	8	97	.819	4.47	5.43
22 Col	NL	45	0	9	44.2	197	53	34	30	8	0	2	0	13	1	37	3	2	1	.667	0-2	6	97	.862	5.21	6.04
22 Pit	NL	13	0	4	13.1	50	10	5	5	2	1	0	1	1	0	18	1	0	1	.000	0-1	2	96	.649	2.22	3.38
7 ML YEARS		211	22	49	312.0	1365	298	190	170	55	7	12	10	143	12	329	19	14	16	.467	2-10	24	95	.799	4.65	4.90

Tyler Stephenson

Bats: R Throws: R Pos: C-45;DH-3;PH-3;1B-1   Ht: 6'4" Wt: 225 Born: 8/16/1996 Age: 26

Year Team	Lg	G	AB	H	2B	3B	HR	(Hm	Rd)	TB	R	RBI	RC	TBB	IBB	SO	HBP	SH	SF	SB	CS	GDP	Avg	OBP	Slg	OPS
							BATTING													**RUNNING**			**AVERAGES**			
2020 Cin	NL	8	17	5	0	0	2	(2	0)	11	4	6	3	2	0	9	1	0	0	0	0	0	.294	.400	.647	1.047
2021 Cin	NL	132	350	100	21	0	10	(5	5)	151	56	45	52	41	1	75	6	0	5	0	0	11	.286	.366	.431	.797
2022 Cin	NL	50	166	53	9	0	6	(3	3)	80	24	35	34	12	0	47	3	0	2	1	0	4	.319	.372	.482	.854
3 ML YEARS		190	533	158	30	0	18	(10	8)	242	84	86	89	55	1	131	10	0	7	1	0	15	.296	.369	.454	.823

Cal Stevenson

Bats: L Throws: L Pos: CF-22;RF-2;PH-2;LF-1   Ht: 5'10" Wt: 175 Born: 9/12/1996 Age: 26

Year Team	Lg	G	AB	H	2B	3B	HR	(Hm	Rd)	TB	R	RBI	RC	TBB	IBB	SO	HBP	SH	SF	SB	CS	GDP	Avg	OBP	Slg	OPS
							BATTING													**RUNNING**			**AVERAGES**			
2022 Drham	AAA	57	170	45	7	1	2	(-	-)	60	29	17	23	31	0	42	0	1	1	9	2	3	.265	.376	.353	.729
2022 LsVgs	AAA	24	87	28	2	2	4	(-	-)	46	23	19	20	14	0	12	1	0	2	7	1	1	.322	.413	.529	.942
2022 Oak	AL	23	60	10	3	0	0	(0	0)	13	5	1	2	8	0	23	0	2	1	1	1	1	.167	.261	.217	.478

D.J. Stewart

Bats: L Throws: R Pos: PH-3   Ht: 6'0" Wt: 210 Born: 11/30/1993 Age: 29

Year Team	Lg	G	AB	H	2B	3B	HR	(Hm	Rd)	TB	R	RBI	RC	TBB	IBB	SO	HBP	SH	SF	SB	CS	GDP	Avg	OBP	Slg	OPS
							BATTING													**RUNNING**			**AVERAGES**			
2022 Norfolk	AAA	29	86	22	2	0	6	(-	-)	42	18	17	18	16	0	28	3	0	0	2	0	1	.256	.390	.488	.879
2018 Bal	AL	17	40	10	3	0	3	(2	1)	22	8	10	8	4	0	12	2	0	1	2	1	0	.250	.340	.550	.890
2019 Bal	AL	44	126	30	6	0	4	(1	3)	48	15	15	17	14	1	26	1	0	1	1	2	3	.238	.317	.381	.698
2020 Bal	AL	31	88	17	2	0	7	(4	3)	40	13	15	18	20	0	38	2	2	0	0	0	0	.193	.355	.455	.809
2021 Bal	AL	100	270	55	10	0	12	(7	5)	101	39	33	35	44	1	89	4	0	0	0	0	3	.204	.324	.374	.698
2022 Bal	AL	3	3	0	0	0	0	(0	0)	0	0	0	0	0	0	2	0	0	0	0	0	0	.000	.000	.000	.000
5 ML YEARS		195	527	112	21	0	26	(14	12)	211	75	73	78	82	2	167	9	2	2	3	3	6	.213	.327	.400	.728

Trevor Story

Bats: R Throws: R Pos: 2B-94;PR-1   Ht: 6'2" Wt: 213 Born: 11/15/1992 Age: 30

Year Team	Lg	G	AB	H	2B	3B	HR	(Hm	Rd)	TB	R	RBI	RC	TBB	IBB	SO	HBP	SH	SF	SB	CS	GDP	Avg	OBP	Slg	OPS
							BATTING													**RUNNING**			**AVERAGES**			
2016 Col	NL	97	372	101	21	4	27	(16	11)	211	67	72	67	35	2	130	5	2	1	8	5	5	.272	.341	.567	.909
2017 Col	NL	145	503	120	32	3	24	(13	11)	230	68	82	66	49	4	191	2	0	1	7	2	12	.239	.308	.457	.765
2018 Col	NL	157	598	174	42	6	37	(26	11)	339	88	108	107	47	3	168	7	0	4	27	6	12	.291	.348	.567	.914
2019 Col	NL	145	588	173	38	6	35	(11	24)	326	111	85	113	58	0	174	7	0	3	23	8	3	.294	.363	.554	.917
2020 Col	NL	59	235	68	13	4	11	(5	6)	122	41	28	35	24	1	63	0	0	0	15	3	5	.289	.355	.519	.874
2021 Col	NL	142	526	132	34	5	24	(11	13)	248	88	75	83	53	2	139	11	0	5	20	6	7	.251	.329	.471	.801
2022 Bos	AL	94	357	85	22	0	16	(12	4)	155	53	66	57	32	4	122	3	0	4	13	0	9	.238	.303	.434	.737
Postseason		5	22	7	2	0	1	(0	1)	12	3	1	2	0	0	7	0	0	0	0	0	0	.318	.318	.545	.864
7 ML YEARS		839	3179	853	202	27	174	(107	67)	1631	516	516	528	298	16	987	35	2	18	113	30	53	.268	.336	.513	.849

Bryson Stott

Bats: L Throws: R Pos: SS-83;2B-47;PH-6;3B-2;PR-1   Ht: 6'3" Wt: 200 Born: 10/6/1997 Age: 25

Year Team	Lg	G	AB	H	2B	3B	HR	(Hm	Rd)	TB	R	RBI	RC	TBB	IBB	SO	HBP	SH	SF	SB	CS	GDP	Avg	OBP	Slg	OPS
							BATTING													**RUNNING**			**AVERAGES**			
2019 2 Tms	Low	48	166	49	9	3	6	(-	-)	82	30	27	33	24	1	39	2	1	0	5	3	0	.295	.391	.494	.885
2021 Rdng	AA	80	312	94	22	2	10	(-	-)	150	49	36	56	35	1	78	6	3	4	5	2	4	.301	.368	.481	.848
2021 JrsyShr	A+	22	73	21	4	0	5	(-	-)	40	18	10	19	22	0	22	0	0	0	3	2	0	.288	.453	.548	1.001
2022 Phi	NL	127	427	100	19	2	10	(5	5)	153	58	49	47	36	0	89	1	1	1	12	4	3	.234	.295	.358	.653

Eric Stout

Pitches: L Bats: L Pos: RP-20   Ht: 6'3" Wt: 205 Born: 3/27/1993 Age: 30

Year Team	Lg	G	GS	GF	IP	BFP	H	R	ER	HR	SH	SF	HB	TBB	IBB	SO	WP	W	L	Pct	Sv-Op	Hld	Vel	OPS	ERC	ERA
		HOW MUCH PITCHED					**WHAT HE GAVE UP**											**THE RESULTS**								
2022 Iowa	AAA	16	1	6	29.2	131	18	13	13	4	0	0	2	22	0	48	3	2	2	.500	2--	-	-	.685	3.65	3.94
2022 Indy	AAA	11	0	6	13.1	56	11	1	1	0	0	0	0	7	0	15	0	1	0	1.000	3--	-	-	.566	2.96	0.68
2018 KC	AL	3	0	0	2.1	16	7	7	6	2	0	0	0	2	0	2	0	0	0		0-0	0	91	1.634	29.43	23.14
2022 2 Tms	NL	20	0	4	22.1	110	25	15	14	2	0	0	3	16	1	25	2	0	0		1-2	1	92	.840	6.35	5.64
22 ChC	NL	2	0	1	3.2	15	3	2	2	1	0	0	0	1	0	6	0	0	0		0-0	0	93	.767	3.60	4.91
22 Pit	NL	18	0	3	18.2	95	22	13	12	1	0	0	3	15	1	19	2	0	0		1-2	1	92	.850	6.86	5.79
2 ML YEARS		23	0	4	24.2	126	32	22	20	4	0	0	3	18	1	27	2	0	0		1-2	1	92	.944	8.14	7.30

Kyle Stowers

Bats: L Throws: L Pos: LF-13;RF-12;DH-6;PH-6;PR-2   Ht: 6'3" Wt: 200 Born: 1/2/1998 Age: 25

							BATTING										RUNNING			AVERAGES			
Year	Team	Lg	G	AB	H	2B	3B	HR	(Hm | Rd)	TB	R	RBI	RC	TBB	IBB	SO	HBP	SH	SF	SB	CS	GDP	Avg	OBP	Slg	OPS
2022	Norfolk	AAA	95	349	92	29	3	19	(- | -)	184	54	78	69	45	1	104	8	1	4	3	2	6	.264	.357	.527	.884
2022	Bal	AL	34	91	23	4	1	3	(2 | 1)	38	11	11	10	5	0	29	2	0	0	0	0	3	.253	.306	.418	.724

Matt Strahm

Pitches: L Bats: R Pos: RP-50   Ht: 6'2" Wt: 190 Born: 11/12/1991 Age: 31

			HOW MUCH PITCHED				WHAT HE GAVE UP									THE RESULTS						
Year	Team	Lg	G	GS	GF	IP	BFP	H	R	ER	HR	SH	SF	HB	TBB	IBB	SO	WP	W	L	Pct	Sv-Op	Hld	Vel	OPS	ERC	ERA
2016	KC	AL	21	0	1	22.0	88	13	4	3	0	0	1	1	11	1	30	1	2	2	.500	0-0	6	94	.484	1.84	1.23
2017	KC	AL	24	3	3	34.2	154	30	22	21	6	2	0	3	22	2	37	3	2	5	.286	0-0	5	94	.779	5.10	5.45
2018	SD	NL	41	5	5	61.1	245	39	16	14	6	1	1	3	21	1	69	2	3	4	.429	0-0	7	93	.564	2.12	2.05
2019	SD	NL	46	16	4	114.2	487	121	61	60	22	4	1	7	22	4	118	3	6	11	.353	0-1	6	92	.787	4.35	4.71
2020	SD	NL	19	0	2	20.2	83	14	6	6	3	0	0	5	4	0	15	1	0	1	.000	0-2	3	93	.615	2.82	2.61
2021	SD	NL	6	1	0	6.2	36	15	6	6	0	1	0	0	1	0	4	0	0	1	.000	0-1	0	93	1.045	9.49	8.10
2022	Bos	AL	50	0	10	44.2	193	38	24	19	5	0	1	5	17	1	52	2	4	4	.500	4-9	12	94	.664	3.60	3.83
	Postseason		4	0	0	2.1	16	7	3	3	0	0	1	0	2	1	2	0	0	0	-	0-0	0	94	1.255	17.62	11.57
	7 ML YEARS		207	25	25	304.2	1286	270	139	129	42	8	4	24	98	10	325	12	17	28	.378	4-13	39	93	.703	3.64	3.81

Dee Strange-Gordon

Bats: L Throws: R Pos: SS-13;CF-4;LF-3;PR-2;DH-1;PH-1   Ht: 5'11" Wt: 166 Born: 4/22/1988 Age: 35

							BATTING										RUNNING			AVERAGES			
Year	Team	Lg	G	AB	H	2B	3B	HR	(Hm | Rd)	TB	R	RBI	RC	TBB	IBB	SO	HBP	SH	SF	SB	CS	GDP	Avg	OBP	Slg	OPS
2011	LAD	NL	56	224	68	9	2	0	(0 | 0)	81	34	11	25	7	0	27	0	2	0	24	7	1	.304	.325	.362	.686
2012	LAD	NL	87	303	69	9	2	1	(0 | 1)	85	38	17	22	20	0	62	3	2	2	32	10	5	.228	.280	.281	.561
2013	LAD	NL	38	94	22	1	1	1	(1 | 0)	28	9	6	9	10	2	21	1	1	0	10	2	0	.234	.314	.298	.612
2014	LAD	NL	148	609	176	24	12	2	(2 | 0)	230	92	34	76	31	0	107	4	3	3	64	19	3	.289	.326	.378	.704
2015	Mia	NL	145	615	205	24	8	4	(2 | 2)	257	88	46	94	25	2	91	2	6	5	58	20	6	.333	.359	.418	.776
2016	Mia	NL	79	325	87	7	6	1	(1 | 0)	109	47	14	33	18	1	55	0	1	1	30	7	4	.268	.305	.335	.641
2017	Mia	NL	158	653	201	20	9	2	(0 | 2)	245	114	33	81	25	0	93	10	2	4	60	16	7	.308	.341	.375	.716
2018	Sea	AL	141	556	149	17	8	4	(2 | 2)	194	62	36	50	9	0	80	9	9	5	30	12	10	.268	.288	.349	.637
2019	Sea	AL	117	393	108	12	6	3	(0 | 3)	141	36	34	51	18	1	61	1	3	6	22	5	8	.275	.304	.359	.663
2020	Sea	AL	33	75	15	1	0	0	(0 | 0)	16	12	3	5	5	0	13	2	0	0	3	2	1	.200	.268	.213	.482
2022	Was	NL	23	59	18	1	1	0	(0 | 0)	21	6	2	5	0	0	8	0	0	0	3	2	1	.305	.305	.356	.661
	Postseason		6	17	3	0	0	0	(0 | 0)	3	0	2	0	2	0	6	0	0	0	1	1	0	.176	.263	.176	.440
	11 ML YEARS		1025	3906	1118	125	55	18	(8 | 10)	1407	538	236	451	168	6	618	32	29	26	336	102	46	.286	.319	.360	.679

Stephen Strasburg

Pitches: R Bats: R Pos: SP-1   Ht: 6'5" Wt: 239 Born: 7/20/1988 Age: 34

			HOW MUCH PITCHED				WHAT HE GAVE UP									THE RESULTS						
Year	Team	Lg	G	GS	GF	IP	BFP	H	R	ER	HR	SH	SF	HB	TBB	IBB	SO	WP	W	L	Pct	Sv-Op	Hld	Vel	OPS	ERC	ERA
2010	Was	NL	12	12	0	68.0	274	56	25	22	5	2	2	0	17	0	92	2	5	3	.625	0-0	0	97	.596	2.41	2.91
2011	Was	NL	5	5	0	24.0	88	15	5	4	0	1	1	0	2	0	24	0	1	1	.500	0-0	0	96	.398	0.97	1.50
2012	Was	NL	28	28	0	159.1	653	136	62	56	15	6	4	4	48	1	197	5	15	6	.714	0-0	0	96	.649	2.97	3.16
2013	Was	NL	30	30	0	183.0	731	136	71	61	16	5	1	12	56	1	191	7	8	9	.471	0-0	0	95	.588	2.58	3.00
2014	Was	NL	34	34	0	215.0	868	198	86	75	23	9	4	5	43	4	242	7	14	11	.560	0-0	0	95	.672	3.02	3.14
2015	Was	NL	23	23	0	127.1	523	115	56	49	14	5	1	3	26	0	155	4	11	7	.611	0-0	0	95	.653	2.92	3.46
2016	Was	NL	24	24	0	147.2	598	119	59	59	15	5	1	2	44	1	183	2	15	4	.789	0-0	0	95	.637	2.72	3.60
2017	Was	NL	28	28	0	175.1	701	131	55	49	13	2	4	7	47	5	204	3	15	4	.789	0-0	0	96	.581	2.22	2.52
2018	Was	NL	22	22	0	130.0	544	118	59	54	18	1	5	8	38	2	156	5	10	7	.588	0-0	0	95	.711	3.62	3.74
2019	Was	NL	33	33	0	209.0	841	161	79	77	24	3	4	10	56	4	251	8	18	6	.750	0-0	0	94	.620	2.62	3.32
2020	Was	NL	2	2	0	5.0	23	8	6	6	1	0	0	0	1	0	2	0	0	1	.000	0-0	0	95	.937	7.85	10.80
2021	Was	NL	5	5	0	21.2	95	16	12	11	4	0	0	1	14	2	21	0	1	2	.333	0-0	0	92	.714	4.17	4.57
2022	Was	NL	1	1	0	4.2	23	8	7	7	1	0	0	1	2	0	5	1	0	1	.000	0-0	0	90	1.178	11.48	13.50
	Postseason		9	8	0	55.1	218	44	13	9	4	2	2	1	8	1	71	1	6	2	.750	0-0	0	95	.562	1.95	1.46
	13 ML YEARS		247	247	0	1470.0	5962	1217	582	530	149	39	27	53	394	20	1723	44	113	62	.646	0-0	0	95	.636	2.79	3.24

Chris Stratton

Pitches: R Bats: R Pos: RP-59; SP-1   Ht: 6'2" Wt: 205 Born: 8/22/1990 Age: 32

			HOW MUCH PITCHED				WHAT HE GAVE UP									THE RESULTS						
Year	Team	Lg	G	GS	GF	IP	BFP	H	R	ER	HR	SH	SF	HB	TBB	IBB	SO	WP	W	L	Pct	Sv-Op	Hld	Vel	OPS	ERC	ERA
2016	SF	NL	7	0	7	10.0	43	11	4	4	1	0	0	0	5	0	6	0	1	0	1.000	0-0	0	91	.767	5.31	3.60
2017	SF	NL	13	10	1	58.2	256	59	25	24	5	2	3	1	28	0	51	2	4	4	.500	1-2	0	92	.738	4.42	3.68
2018	SF	NL	28	26	1	145.0	625	153	87	82	19	3	6	2	54	1	112	6	10	10	.500	0-0	0	91	.791	4.59	5.09
2019	2 Tms	NL	35	5	7	76.0	344	93	50	47	13	0	1	0	33	1	69	2	1	3	.250	0-0	0	92	.873	6.10	5.57
2020	Pit	NL	27	0	3	30.0	131	26	19	13	3	0	2	0	13	0	39	1	2	1	.667	0-2	5	93	.651	3.34	3.90
2021	Pit	NL	68	0	18	79.1	337	70	34	32	9	0	3	1	33	2	86	3	7	1	.875	8-13	9	93	.675	3.57	3.63
2022	2 Tms	NL	60	1	23	63.1	279	72	34	30	4	1	4	2	25	2	60	4	10	4	.714	2-7	8	93	.761	4.69	4.26
	19	LAA	AL	7	5	0	29.1	144	43	28	26	6	0	1	0	18	0	22	1	0	2	.000	0-0	0	91	1.000	8.90	8.59
	19	Pit	NL	28	0	7	46.2	200	50	22	19	7	0	0	0	15	1	47	1	1	1	.500	0-0	0	93	.784	4.50	3.66
	22	Pit	NL	40	1	14	40.2	181	50	26	23	4	1	3	1	13	2	37	3	5	4	.556	2-7	8	93	.816	5.10	5.09
	22	StL	NL	20	0	9	22.2	98	22	8	7	0	0	1	1	12	0	23	1	5	0	1.000	0-0	0	93	.655	3.96	2.78
	7 ML YEARS		238	42	60	462.1	2015	484	253	232	54	6	19	6	191	6	423	18	35	23	.603	11-24	20	92	.766	4.57	4.52

Myles Straw

Bats: R Throws: R Pos: CF-152;PH-3;PR-1

Ht: 5'10" Wt: 178 Born: 10/17/1994 Age: 28

									BATTING											RUNNING			AVERAGES			
Year	Team	Lg	G	AB	H	2B	3B	HR	(Hm	Rd)	TB	R	RBI	RC	TBB	IBB	SO	HBP	SH	SF	SB	CS	GDP	Avg	OBP	Slg	OPS
2018	Hou	AL	9	9	3	0	0	1	(0	1)	6	4	1	2	1	0	0	0	0	0	2	0	0	.333	.400	.667	1.067
2019	Hou	AL	56	108	29	4	2	0	(0	0)	37	27	7	17	19	0	24	0	1	0	8	1	2	.269	.378	.343	.721
2020	Hou	AL	33	82	17	4	0	0	(0	0)	21	8	8	8	4	0	22	0	0	0	6	2	0	.207	.244	.256	.500
2021	2 Tms	AL	158	564	153	29	1	4	(2	2)	196	86	48	72	67	0	121	2	1	4	30	6	13	.271	.349	.348	.696
2022	Cle	AL	152	535	118	22	3	0	(0	0)	146	72	32	39	54	0	87	1	2	4	21	1	4	.221	.291	.273	.564
21	Hou	AL	98	325	85	13	1	2	(1	1)	106	44	34	39	38	0	71	2	1	4	17	5	7	.262	.339	.326	.665
21	Cle	AL	60	239	68	16	0	2	(1	1)	90	42	14	33	29	0	50	0	0	0	13	1	6	.285	.362	.377	.739
	Postseason		8	0	0	0	0	0	(0	0)	0	1	0	0	0	0	0	0	0	0	1	0	0	-	-	-	-
	5 ML YEARS		408	1298	320	59	6	5	(2	3)	406	197	96	138	145	0	254	3	4	8	67	10	19	.247	.322	.313	.635

Hunter Strickland

Pitches: R Bats: R Pos: RP-66

Ht: 6'3" Wt: 225 Born: 9/24/1988 Age: 34

			HOW MUCH PITCHED					WHAT HE GAVE UP										THE RESULTS						
Year	Team	Lg	G	GS	GF	IP	BFP	H	R	ER	HR	SH	SF	HB	TBB	IBB	SO	WP	W	L	Pct	Sv-Op	Hld	Vel	OPS	ERC	ERA
2014	SF	NL	9	0	5	7.0	25	5	0	0	0	0	0	0	0	0	9	0	1	0	1.000	1-1	1	98	.440	1.08	0.00
2015	SF	NL	55	0	11	51.1	191	34	14	14	4	0	0	2	10	1	50	1	3	3	.500	0-2	20	97	.543	1.72	2.45
2016	SF	NL	72	0	14	61.0	250	50	21	21	4	0	3	2	19	3	57	3	3	3	.500	3-8	18	97	.589	2.61	3.10
2017	SF	NL	68	0	17	61.1	268	59	20	18	4	1	3	2	29	4	58	3	4	3	.571	1-3	21	96	.702	3.91	2.64
2018	SF	NL	49	0	35	45.1	201	43	25	20	5	2	3	1	21	2	37	4	3	5	.375	14-18	0	95	.758	4.03	3.97
2019	2 Tms		28	0	3	24.1	105	22	15	15	6	0	1	3	8	0	18	1	2	1	.667	2-3	10	95	.809	4.72	5.55
2020	NYM	NL	4	0	2	3.1	16	5	4	3	0	0	0	0	1	0	4	0	0	1	.000	0-0	0	95	.842	5.66	8.10
2021	3 Tms		57	0	19	58.2	242	46	21	17	8	1	1	2	22	0	58	3	3	2	.600	0-0	2	95	.670	3.18	2.61
2022	Cin	NL	66	0	35	62.1	284	61	37	34	8	0	3	7	33	1	60	1	3	3	.500	7-11	4	95	.791	5.06	4.91
19	Sea	AL	4	0	2	3.1	13	2	3	3	1	0	0	1	0	0	3	0	0	1	.000	2-3	0	96	.731	2.70	8.10
19	Was	AL	24	0	1	21.0	92	20	12	12	5	0	1	2	8	0	15	1	2	0	1.000	0-0	10	96	.820	5.05	5.14
21	TB	AL	13	0	7	16.0	66	14	4	3	1	0	0	0	6	0	16	1	0	0	-	0-0	1	95	.653	3.09	1.69
21	LAA	AL	9	0	2	6.1	34	11	9	7	3	1	0	0	4	0	4	0	0	0	-	0-0	0	95	1.248	13.14	9.95
21	Mil	AL	35	0	10	36.1	142	21	8	7	4	0	1	2	12	0	38	2	3	2	.600	0-0	1	95	.546	1.95	1.73
	Postseason		16	0	7	15.1	64	17	11	11	9	0	0	0	4	0	16	1	1	0	1.000	1-2	1	97	1.095	7.76	6.46
	9 ML YEARS		408	0	141	374.2	1582	325	157	142	39	4	14	19	143	11	351	16	22	21	.512	28-46	76	96	.686	3.45	3.41

Spencer Strider

Pitches: R Bats: R Pos: SP-20; RP-11

Ht: 6'0" Wt: 195 Born: 10/28/1998 Age: 24

			HOW MUCH PITCHED					WHAT HE GAVE UP										THE RESULTS						
Year	Team	Lg	G	GS	GF	IP	BFP	H	R	ER	HR	SH	SF	HB	TBB	IBB	SO	WP	W	L	Pct	Sv-Op	Hld	Vel	OPS	ERC	ERA
2021	Atl	NL	2	0	0	2.1	9	2	1	1	1	0	0	0	1	0	0	0	1	0	1.000	0-0	0	98	.958	6.17	3.86
2022	Atl	NL	31	20	3	131.2	528	86	42	39	7	0	2	3	45	1	202	6	11	5	.688	0-1	2	98	.517	1.86	2.67
	2 ML YEARS		33	20	3	134.0	537	88	43	40	8	0	2	3	46	1	202	6	12	5	.706	0-1	2	98	.525	1.92	2.69

Ross Stripling

Pitches: R Bats: R Pos: SP-24; RP-8

Ht: 6'1" Wt: 215 Born: 11/23/1989 Age: 33

			HOW MUCH PITCHED					WHAT HE GAVE UP										THE RESULTS						
Year	Team	Lg	G	GS	GF	IP	BFP	H	R	ER	HR	SH	SF	HB	TBB	IBB	SO	WP	W	L	Pct	Sv-Op	Hld	Vel	OPS	ERC	ERA
2016	LAD	NL	22	14	4	100.0	419	96	46	44	10	3	1	1	30	3	74	6	5	9	.357	0-0	0	90	.709	3.46	3.96
2017	LAD	NL	49	2	12	74.1	304	69	31	31	10	2	3	0	19	4	74	2	3	5	.375	2-5	4	93	.691	3.29	3.75
2018	LAD	NL	33	21	2	122.0	503	123	42	41	18	2	0	1	22	2	136	3	8	6	.571	0-0	3	92	.722	3.58	3.02
2019	LAD	NL	32	15	4	90.2	370	84	40	35	11	0	4	2	20	0	93	4	4	4	.500	0-0	3	91	.699	3.22	3.47
2020	2 Tms		12	9	1	49.1	220	56	37	32	13	2	0	1	18	0	40	1	3	3	.500	1-1	0	92	.882	5.97	5.84
2021	Tor	AL	24	19	1	101.1	431	99	55	54	23	1	3	2	30	0	94	0	5	7	.417	0-0	0	92	.793	4.43	4.80
2022	Tor	AL	32	24	2	134.1	536	117	49	45	12	0	3	2	20	0	111	0	10	4	.714	1-1	0	92	.614	2.43	3.01
20	LAD	NL	7	7	0	33.2	150	38	26	21	12	2	0	1	11	0	27	1	3	1	.750	0-0	0	92	.933	6.43	5.61
20	Tor	AL	5	2	1	15.2	70	18	11	11	1	0	0	0	7	0	13	0	0	2	.000	1-1	0	92	.770	4.87	6.32
	Postseason		12	0	4	9.2	43	14	7	6	0	0	2	0	2	0	5	1	0	0	-	0-0	0	92	.834	5.25	5.59
	7 ML YEARS		204	104	26	672.0	2783	644	300	282	97	10	14	9	159	9	622	16	38	38	.500	4-7	10	91	.716	3.52	3.78

Marcus Stroman

Pitches: R Bats: R Pos: SP-25

Ht: 5'7" Wt: 180 Born: 5/1/1991 Age: 32

			HOW MUCH PITCHED					WHAT HE GAVE UP										THE RESULTS						
Year	Team	Lg	G	GS	GF	IP	BFP	H	R	ER	HR	SH	SF	HB	TBB	IBB	SO	WP	W	L	Pct	Sv-Op	Hld	Vel	OPS	ERC	ERA
2014	Tor	AL	26	20	1	130.2	534	125	56	53	7	0	2	3	28	1	111	9	11	6	.647	1-1	0	94	.633	2.93	3.65
2015	Tor	AL	4	4	0	27.0	103	20	5	5	2	0	0	1	6	0	18	2	4	0	1.000	0-0	0	92	.554	2.16	1.67
2016	Tor	AL	32	32	0	204.0	855	209	104	99	21	2	2	4	54	0	166	9	9	10	.474	0-0	0	92	.720	3.81	4.37
2017	Tor	AL	33	33	0	201.0	834	201	82	69	21	0	4	6	62	1	164	3	13	9	.591	0-0	0	93	.715	3.97	3.09
2018	Tor	AL	19	19	0	102.1	449	115	68	63	9	2	3	2	36	0	77	3	4	9	.308	0-0	0	92	.759	4.59	5.54
2019	2 Tms		32	32	0	184.1	774	183	77	66	18	1	2	1	58	1	159	7	10	13	.435	0-0	0	92	.697	3.73	3.22
2021	NYM	NL	33	33	0	179.0	730	161	70	60	17	6	8	7	44	2	158	7	10	13	.435	0-0	0	92	.655	3.07	3.02
2022	ChC	NL	25	25	0	138.2	569	123	61	54	16	1	3	4	36	0	119	2	6	7	.462	0-0	0	93	.664	3.14	3.50
19	Tor	AL	21	21	0	124.2	513	118	50	41	10	0	1	0	35	0	99	4	6	11	.353	0-0	0	92	.656	3.23	2.96
19	NYM	NL	11	11	0	59.2	261	65	27	25	8	1	1	1	23	1	60	3	4	2	.667	0-0	0	92	.781	4.84	3.77
	Postseason		5	5	0	30.2	128	29	16	15	4	0	1	0	7	0	21	2	1	1	.500	0-0	0	93	.690	3.24	4.40
	8 ML YEARS		204	198	1	1167.0	4848	1137	523	469	111	12	24	28	324	5	972	42	67	67	.500	1-1	0	93	.690	3.55	3.62

Peter Strzelecki

Pitches: R Bats: R Pos: RP-30   Ht: 6'2" Wt: 195 Born: 10/24/1994 Age: 28

		HOW MUCH PITCHED				WHAT HE GAVE UP										THE RESULTS							
Year	Team	Lg	G	GS	GF	IP	BFP	H	R	ER	HR	SH	SF	HB	TBB	IBB	SO	WP	W	L	Pct	Sv-Op	Hld	Vel	OPS	ERC	ERA
2022	Nashv	AAA	27	0	8	31.2	120	18	10	10	4	0	1	2	10	0	50	1	4	0	1.000	3- -	-	-	.596	2.04	2.84
2022	Mil	NL	30	0	13	35.0	148	28	13	11	2	2	3	1	15	2	40	0	2	1	.667	1-3	4	94	.632	2.80	2.83

Garrett Stubbs

Bats: L Throws: R Pos: C-41;DH-4;PR-4;PH-2;LF-1   Ht: 5'10" Wt: 170 Born: 5/26/1993 Age: 30

			BATTING																	RUNNING			AVERAGES			
Year	Team	Lg	G	AB	H	2B	3B	HR	(Hm	Rd)	TB	R	RBI	RC	TBB	IBB	SO	HBP	SH	SF	SB	CS	GDP	Avg	OBP	Slg	OPS
2019	Hou	AL	19	35	7	3	0	0	(0	0)	10	8	2	1	4	0	7	0	0	0	1	0	1	.200	.282	.286	.568
2020	Hou	AL	14	8	1	0	0	0	(0	0)	1	1	1	0	0	0	0	0	1	1	0	1	0	.125	.111	.125	.236
2021	Hou	AL	18	34	6	2	0	0	(0	0)	8	2	3	2	2	0	7	0	2	0	0	0	0	.176	.222	.235	.458
2022	Phi	NL	50	106	28	4	1	5	(3	2)	49	19	16	20	14	0	30	0	1	0	2	0	2	.264	.350	.462	.812
	Postseason		2	0	0	0	0	0	(0	0)	0	0	0	0	0	0	0	0	0	0	0	0	0	-	-	-	-
	4 ML YEARS		101	183	42	9	1	5	(3	2)	68	30	22	23	20	0	44	0	4	1	3	1	3	.230	.304	.372	.676

Eugenio Suarez

Bats: R Throws: R Pos: 3B-130;DH-19;PH-3   ay-yoo-HAY-nee-oh SWAH-rez   Ht: 5'11" Wt: 213 Born: 7/18/1991 Age: 31

			BATTING																	RUNNING			AVERAGES			
Year	Team	Lg	G	AB	H	2B	3B	HR	(Hm	Rd)	TB	R	RBI	RC	TBB	IBB	SO	HBP	SH	SF	SB	CS	GDP	Avg	OBP	Slg	OPS
2014	Det	AL	85	244	59	9	1	4	(2	2)	82	33	23	30	22	1	67	5	5	1	3	2	3	.242	.316	.336	.652
2015	Cin	NL	97	372	104	19	2	13	(4	9)	166	42	48	49	17	0	94	3	4	2	4	1	7	.280	.315	.446	.761
2016	Cin	NL	159	565	140	25	2	21	(10	11)	232	78	70	77	51	0	155	8	0	3	11	5	10	.248	.317	.411	.728
2017	Cin	NL	156	534	139	25	2	26	(21	5)	246	87	82	81	84	1	147	9	0	5	4	5	16	.260	.367	.461	.828
2018	Cin	NL	143	527	149	22	2	34	(19	15)	277	79	104	95	64	7	142	9	0	6	1	1	20	.283	.366	.526	.892
2019	Cin	NL	159	575	156	22	2	49	(24	25)	329	87	103	103	70	4	189	11	0	6	3	2	12	.271	.358	.572	.930
2020	Cin	NL	57	198	40	8	0	15	(5	10)	93	29	38	32	30	1	67	2	0	1	2	0	5	.202	.312	.470	.781
2021	Cin	NL	145	505	100	23	0	31	(15	16)	216	71	79	53	56	0	171	8	0	1	0	1	14	.198	.286	.428	.713
2022	Sea	AL	150	543	128	24	2	31	(16	15)	249	76	87	99	73	0	196	8	0	5	0	0	12	.236	.332	.459	.791
	Postseason		3	10	2	0	0	0	(0	0)	2	0	0	0	1	0	4	0	0	0	0	0	0	.200	.273	.200	.473
	9 ML YEARS		1151	4063	1015	177	13	224	(116	108)	1890	582	634	619	467	14	1228	63	9	34	28	17	99	.250	.334	.465	.799

Jose Suarez

Pitches: L Bats: L Pos: SP-20; RP-2   Ht: 5'10" Wt: 225 Born: 1/3/1998 Age: 25

			HOW MUCH PITCHED					WHAT HE GAVE UP										THE RESULTS							
Year	Team	Lg	G	GS	GF	IP	BFP	H	R	ER	HR	SH	SF	HB	TBB	IBB	SO	WP	W	L	Pct	Sv-Op	Hld	Vel	OPS	ERC	ERA
2019	LAA	AL	19	15	0	81.0	375	100	67	64	23	1	2	10	33	1	72	5	2	6	.250	0-0	0	92	.948	7.55	7.11
2020	LAA	AL	2	2	0	2.1	23	10	10	10	1	0	0	1	5	0	2	1	0	2	.000	0-0	0	93	1.578	44.98	38.57
2021	LAA	AL	23	14	2	98.1	413	85	45	41	11	2	2	4	36	1	85	4	8	8	.500	0-0	0	93	.686	3.42	3.75
2022	LAA	AL	22	20	0	109.0	462	103	49	48	14	1	1	4	33	2	103	1	8	8	.500	0-0	0	93	.708	3.66	3.96
	4 ML YEARS		66	51	2	290.2	1273	298	171	163	49	4	5	19	107	4	262	11	18	24	.429	0-0	0	92	.785	4.81	5.05

Ranger Suarez

Pitches: L Bats: L Pos: SP-29   Ht: 6'1" Wt: 217 Born: 8/26/1995 Age: 27

			HOW MUCH PITCHED				WHAT HE GAVE UP										THE RESULTS							
Year	Team	Lg	G	GS	GF	IP	BFP	H	R	ER	HR	SH	SF	HB	TBB	IBB	SO	WP	W	L	Pct	Sv-Op	Hld	Vel	OPS	ERC	ERA
2018	Phi	NL	4	3	0	15.0	69	21	14	9	3	1	0	0	6	1	11	0	1	1	.500	0-0	0	92	.945	7.33	5.40
2019	Phi	NL	37	0	8	48.2	205	52	18	17	6	3	2	1	12	2	42	1	6	1	.857	0-1	6	92	.739	4.07	3.14
2020	Phi	NL	3	0	1	4.0	26	10	9	9	1	0	0	1	4	0	1	0	0	1	.000	0-0	0	91	1.291	20.74	20.25
2021	Phi	NL	39	12	13	106.0	418	73	20	16	4	3	1	5	33	3	107	1	8	5	.615	4-7	9	93	.523	1.94	1.36
2022	Phi	NL	29	29	0	155.1	662	149	74	63	15	2	2	2	58	0	129	4	10	7	.588	0-0	0	93	.713	3.77	3.65
	5 ML YEARS		112	44	22	329.0	1380	305	135	114	29	9	5	9	113	6	290	6	25	15	.625	4-8	6	93	.681	3.47	3.12

Robert Suarez

Pitches: R Bats: R Pos: RP-45   Ht: 6'2" Wt: 210 Born: 3/1/1991 Age: 32

			HOW MUCH PITCHED				WHAT HE GAVE UP										THE RESULTS							
Year	Team	Lg	G	GS	GF	IP	BFP	H	R	ER	HR	SH	SF	HB	TBB	IBB	SO	WP	W	L	Pct	Sv-Op	Hld	Vel	OPS	ERC	ERA
2022	SD	NL	45	0	6	47.2	191	29	13	12	4	1	0	4	21	0	61	2	5	1	.833	1-4	11	98	.569	2.44	2.27

Beau Sulser

Pitches: R Bats: R Pos: RP-10   Ht: 6'2" Wt: 195 Born: 5/5/1994 Age: 29

			HOW MUCH PITCHED				WHAT HE GAVE UP										THE RESULTS							
Year	Team	Lg	G	GS	GF	IP	BFP	H	R	ER	HR	SH	SF	HB	TBB	IBB	SO	WP	W	L	Pct	Sv-Op	Hld	Vel	OPS	ERC	ERA
2022	Norfolk	AAA	17	3	3	44.0	195	53	24	23	4	1	6	1	12	0	46	3	2	2	.500	0- -	-	-	.809	4.72	4.70
2022	2 Tms		10	0	6	22.1	99	24	14	9	3	0	1	1	9	2	19	0	0	0	-	0-0	0	93	.843	4.78	3.63
22	Pit	NL	4	0	2	9.2	46	8	9	4	1	0	1	1	6	2	10	0	0	0	-	0-0	0	93	.773	3.74	3.72
22	Bal	AL	6	0	4	12.2	53	16	5	5	2	0	0	0	3	0	9	0	0	0	-	0-0	0	93	.898	5.66	3.55

Cole Sulser

Pitches: R Bats: R Pos: RP-39   Ht: 6'1" Wt: 190 Born: 3/12/1990 Age: 33

			HOW MUCH PITCHED						WHAT HE GAVE UP											THE RESULTS						
Year	Team	Lg	G	GS	GF	IP	BFP	H	R	ER	HR	SH	SF	HB	TBB	IBB	SO	WP	W	L	Pct	Sv-Op	Hld	Vel	OPS	ERC	ERA
2022	Jaxnvl	AAA	6	0	0	6.1	30	8	4	4	2	0	1	0	2	0	10	0	0	1	.000	0- -	-		1.037	6.52	5.68
2019	TB	AL	7	0	4	7.1	29	5	0	0	0	0	0	0	3	0	9	0	0	0	-	0-0	0	93	.507	1.90	0.00
2020	Bal	AL	19	0	9	22.2	100	17	18	14	2	2	0	0	17	1	19	1	1	5	.167	5-8	1	94	.705	3.87	5.56
2021	Bal	AL	60	0	18	63.1	257	48	20	19	5	1	1	0	23	0	73	6	5	4	.556	8-11	6	93	.596	2.53	2.70
2022	Mia	NL	39	0	14	34.0	149	39	23	20	6	1	0	0	16	1	38	0	1	4	.200	2-5	5	92	.864	5.95	5.29
	4 ML YEARS		125	0	45	127.1	535	109	61	53	13	4	1	0	59	2	139	7	7	13	.350	15-24	12	93	.686	3.56	3.75

Brent Suter

Pitches: L Bats: L Pos: RP-54   SOO-ter   Ht: 6'4" Wt: 213 Born: 8/29/1989 Age: 33

			HOW MUCH PITCHED						WHAT HE GAVE UP											THE RESULTS						
Year	Team	Lg	G	GS	GF	IP	BFP	H	R	ER	HR	SH	SF	HB	TBB	IBB	SO	WP	W	L	Pct	Sv-Op	Hld	Vel	OPS	ERC	ERA
2016	Mil	NL	14	2	4	21.2	91	25	8	8	3	1	0	1	5	0	15	1	2	2	.500	0-0	2	84	.773	4.90	3.32
2017	Mil	NL	22	14	1	81.2	341	83	33	31	8	1	1	2	22	2	64	1	3	2	.600	0-0	0	86	.702	3.75	3.42
2018	Mil	NL	20	18	0	101.1	424	102	55	50	18	5	1	4	19	2	84	1	8	7	.533	0-0	0	87	.754	3.88	4.44
2019	Mil	NL	9	0	0	18.1	65	10	1	1	0	0	0	0	1	0	15	0	4	0	1.000	0-0	2	88	.435	0.88	0.49
2020	Mil	NL	16	4	1	31.2	129	30	13	11	4	0	0	1	5	0	38	0	2	0	1.000	0-0	2	86	.645	3.14	3.13
2021	Mil	NL	61	1	9	73.1	313	72	34	25	9	2	0	1	24	3	69	1	12	5	.706	1-9	8	87	.714	3.80	3.07
2022	Mil	NL	54	0	17	66.2	272	58	32	28	9	1	0	3	22	0	53	0	5	3	.625	0-0	1	87	.713	3.59	3.78
	Postseason		2	1	0	2.2	18	4	3	3	0	0	0	0	5	0	0	0	0	1	.000	0-0	0	86	1.038	11.70	10.13
	7 ML YEARS		196	39	32	394.2	1635	380	176	154	52	10	2	12	98	7	338	4	36	19	.655	1-9	15	86	.708	3.60	3.51

Jack Suwinski

Bats: L Throws: L Pos: LF-56;RF-38;CF-19;PH-6;PR-3;DH-1   Ht: 6'2" Wt: 215 Born: 7/29/1998 Age: 24

			BATTING														RUNNING			AVERAGES			
Year	Team	Lg	G	AB	H	2B	3B	HR	(Hm | Rd)	TB	R	RBI	RC	TBB	IBB	SO	HBP	SH	SF	SB	CS	GDP	Avg	OBP	Slg	OPS
2022	Altna	AA	13	51	18	8	0	3	(- | -)	35	13	13	13	5	0	14	1	0	0	1	0	1	.353	.421	.686	1.107
2022	Indy	AAA	31	117	25	5	0	6	(- | -)	48	19	18	15	11	0	49	1	0	1	1	0	2	.214	.285	.410	.695
2022	Pit	NL	106	326	66	11	0	19	(16 | 3)	134	45	38	43	41	1	114	4	0	1	4	2	5	.202	.298	.411	.709

Kurt Suzuki

Bats: R Throws: R Pos: C-44;PH-7;DH-2;1B-1   Ht: 5'11" Wt: 210 Born: 10/4/1983 Age: 39

			BATTING														RUNNING			AVERAGES			
Year	Team	Lg	G	AB	H	2B	3B	HR	(Hm | Rd)	TB	R	RBI	RC	TBB	IBB	SO	HBP	SH	SF	SB	CS	GDP	Avg	OBP	Slg	OPS
2007	Oak	AL	68	213	53	13	0	7	(4 | 3)	87	27	39	33	24	0	39	3	3	5	0	0	4	.249	.327	.408	.735
2008	Oak	AL	148	530	148	25	1	7	(5 | 2)	196	54	42	66	44	2	69	11	2	1	2	3	20	.279	.346	.370	.716
2009	Oak	AL	147	570	156	37	1	15	(8 | 7)	240	74	88	77	28	0	59	8	1	7	8	2	14	.274	.313	.421	.734
2010	Oak	AL	131	495	120	18	2	13	(8 | 5)	181	55	71	54	33	3	49	12	0	4	3	2	22	.242	.303	.366	.669
2011	Oak	AL	134	460	109	26	0	14	(8 | 6)	177	54	44	42	38	1	64	7	3	7	2	2	14	.237	.301	.385	.686
2012	2 Tms		118	408	96	20	0	6	(3 | 3)	134	36	43	39	20	3	73	5	4	5	2	0	5	.235	.276	.328	.605
2013	2 Tms		94	285	66	13	1	5	(2 | 3)	96	25	32	34	22	6	35	3	2	4	2	0	2	.232	.290	.337	.627
2014	Min	AL	131	452	130	34	0	3	(1 | 2)	173	37	61	65	34	0	46	9	1	7	0	1	9	.288	.345	.383	.727
2015	Min	AL	131	433	104	17	0	5	(3 | 2)	136	36	50	46	29	4	59	7	6	4	0	0	14	.240	.296	.314	.610
2016	Min	AL	106	345	89	24	1	8	(4 | 4)	139	34	49	45	18	0	48	5	1	4	0	0	9	.258	.301	.403	.704
2017	Atl	NL	81	276	78	13	0	19	(8 | 11)	148	38	50	49	17	2	39	13	1	2	0	0	5	.283	.351	.536	.887
2018	Atl	NL	105	347	94	24	0	12	(5 | 7)	154	45	50	45	22	0	43	13	0	6	0	0	6	.271	.332	.444	.776
2019	Was	NL	85	280	74	11	0	17	(10 | 7)	136	37	63	53	20	1	36	6	0	3	0	1	10	.264	.324	.486	.809
2020	Was	NL	33	111	30	8	0	2	(0 | 2)	44	15	17	11	11	0	19	4	0	3	1	0	4	.270	.349	.396	.745
2021	LAA	AL	72	219	49	8	0	6	(3 | 3)	75	17	16	21	12	0	44	11	2	3	0	0	7	.224	.294	.342	.636
2022	LAA	AL	51	139	25	4	0	4	(2 | 2)	41	10	15	11	15	0	29	2	1	2	1	0	3	.180	.266	.295	.561
	12 Oak	AL	75	262	57	15	0	1	(1 | 0)	75	19	18	16	9	0	53	3	2	2	1	0	3	.218	.250	.286	.536
	12 Was	NL	43	146	39	5	0	5	(2 | 3)	59	17	25	23	11	3	20	2	2	3	1	0	2	.267	.321	.404	.725
	13 Was	NL	79	252	56	11	1	3	(0 | 3)	78	19	25	26	20	6	32	3	2	4	2	0	2	.222	.283	.310	.593
	13 Oak	AL	15	33	10	2	0	2	(2 | 0)	18	6	7	8	2	0	3	0	0	0	0	0	0	.303	.343	.545	.888
	Postseason		19	55	9	0	0	1	(0 | 1)	12	2	5	4	6	0	16	1	0	0	0	0	3	.164	.258	.218	.476
	16 ML YEARS		1635	5563	1421	295	6	143	(74 | 69)	2157	594	730	691	387	22	751	119	27	67	20	11	148	.255	.314	.388	.702

Seiya Suzuki

Bats: R Throws: R Pos: RF-106;PH-5;DH-1   Ht: 5'11" Wt: 182 Born: 8/18/1994 Age: 28

			BATTING														RUNNING			AVERAGES			
Year	Team	Lg	G	AB	H	2B	3B	HR	(Hm | Rd)	TB	R	RBI	RC	TBB	IBB	SO	HBP	SH	SF	SB	CS	GDP	Avg	OBP	Slg	OPS
2022	ChC	NL	111	397	104	22	2	14	(8 | 6)	172	54	46	58	42	3	110	4	0	3	9	5	8	.262	.336	.433	.770

Travis Swaggerty

Bats: L Throws: L Pos: LF-3;CF-1;PH-1;PR-1   Ht: 5'10" Wt: 200 Born: 8/19/1997 Age: 25

			BATTING														RUNNING			AVERAGES			
Year	Team	Lg	G	AB	H	2B	3B	HR	(Hm | Rd)	TB	R	RBI	RC	TBB	IBB	SO	HBP	SH	SF	SB	CS	GDP	Avg	OBP	Slg	OPS
2022	Indy	AAA	107	398	101	15	8	9	(- | -)	159	55	55	59	57	0	117	1	1	1	20	5	1	.254	.348	.399	.747
2022	Pit	NL	5	9	1	0	0	0	(0 | 0)	1	0	0	0	0	0	4	0	0	0	0	0	0	.111	.111	.111	.222

Dansby Swanson

Bats: R **Throws:** R **Pos:** SS-161   **Ht:** 6'1" **Wt:** 190 **Born:** 2/11/1994 **Age:** 29

							BATTING												RUNNING			AVERAGES			
Year Team	Lg	G	AB	H	2B	3B	HR	(Hm | Rd)	TB	R	RBI	RC	TBB	IBB	SO	HBP	SH	SF	SB	CS	GDP	Avg	OBP	Slg	OPS
2016 Atl	NL	38	129	39	7	1	3	(1 | 2)	57	20	17	17	13	5	34	0	1	2	3	0	2	.302	.361	.442	.803
2017 Atl	NL	144	488	113	23	2	6	(2 | 4)	158	59	51	55	59	10	120	0	0	4	3	3	7	.232	.312	.324	.636
2018 Atl	NL	136	478	114	25	4	14	(7 | 7)	189	51	59	59	44	15	122	2	6	3	10	4	5	.238	.304	.395	.699
2019 Atl	NL	127	483	121	26	3	17	(8 | 9)	204	77	65	61	51	2	124	5	1	5	10	5	7	.251	.325	.422	.748
2020 Atl	NL	60	237	65	15	0	10	(6 | 4)	110	49	35	40	22	0	71	4	0	1	5	0	1	.274	.345	.464	.809
2021 Atl	NL	160	588	146	33	2	27	(14 | 13)	264	78	88	85	52	4	167	5	1	7	9	3	7	.248	.311	.449	.760
2022 Atl	NL	162	640	177	32	1	25	(14 | 11)	286	99	96	99	49	0	182	8	1	4	18	7	12	.277	.329	.447	.776
Postseason		33	121	32	6	1	5	(3 | 2)	55	15	15	19	9	2	38	0	0	1	3	0	1	.264	.313	.455	.768
7 ML YEARS		827	3043	775	161	13	102	(52 | 50)	1268	433	411	416	290	36	820	19	9	26	58	22	40	.255	.321	.417	.738

Erik Swanson

Pitches: R **Bats:** R **Pos:** RP-56; SP-1   **Ht:** 6'3" **Wt:** 222 **Born:** 9/4/1993 **Age:** 29

		HOW MUCH PITCHED					WHAT HE GAVE UP										THE RESULTS						
Year Team	Lg	G	GS	GF	IP	BFP	H	R	ER	HR	SH	SF	HB	TBB	IBB	SO	WP	W	L	Pct	Sv-Op	Hld	Vel	OPS	ERC	ERA
2019 Sea	AL	27	8	7	58.0	245	56	41	37	17	0	1	2	12	1	52	2	1	5	.167	2-2	1	93	.803	4.38	5.74
2020 Sea	AL	9	0	2	7.2	37	11	12	11	3	0	1	2	2	0	9	1	0	2	.000	0-1	1	96	1.093	9.84	12.91
2021 Sea	AL	33	2	5	35.1	144	28	18	13	5	0	1	1	10	1	35	0	0	3	.000	1-3	5	95	.672	2.83	3.31
2022 Sea	AL	57	1	9	53.2	206	39	11	10	3	2	0	1	10	1	70	1	3	2	.600	3-5	14	94	.535	1.74	1.68
4 ML YEARS		126	11	23	154.2	632	134	82	71	28	2	3	6	34	3	166	4	4	12	.250	6-11	21	94	.702	3.27	4.13

Matt Swarmer

Pitches: R **Bats:** R **Pos:** RP-6; SP-5   **Ht:** 6'5" **Wt:** 195 **Born:** 9/25/1993 **Age:** 29

		HOW MUCH PITCHED					WHAT HE GAVE UP										THE RESULTS						
Year Team	Lg	G	GS	GF	IP	BFP	H	R	ER	HR	SH	SF	HB	TBB	IBB	SO	WP	W	L	Pct	Sv-Op	Hld	Vel	OPS	ERC	ERA
2022 Iowa	AAA	21	15	1	81.1	345	70	39	35	9	0	3	1	33	1	86	4	3	3	.500	0- -	-	-	.672	3.40	3.87
2022 ChC	NL	11	5	2	34.0	153	33	26	19	12	0	1	0	20	1	36	1	2	3	.400	0-0	0	91	.930	6.48	5.03

Noah Syndergaard

Pitches: R **Bats:** L **Pos:** SP-24; RP-1   sin-DER-gard   **Ht:** 6'6" **Wt:** 242 **Born:** 8/29/1992 **Age:** 30

		HOW MUCH PITCHED					WHAT HE GAVE UP										THE RESULTS						
Year Team	Lg	G	GS	GF	IP	BFP	H	R	ER	HR	SH	SF	HB	TBB	IBB	SO	WP	W	L	Pct	Sv-Op	Hld	Vel	OPS	ERC	ERA
2015 NYM	NL	24	24	0	150.0	603	126	60	54	19	5	3	3	31	2	166	6	9	7	.563	0-0	0	97	.645	2.70	3.24
2016 NYM	NL	31	30	0	183.2	744	168	61	53	11	3	4	2	43	2	218	10	14	9	.609	0-0	1	98	.639	2.79	2.60
2017 NYM	NL	7	7	0	30.1	124	29	14	10	0	1	1	1	3	1	34	3	1	2	.333	0-0	0	98	.573	2.13	2.97
2018 NYM	NL	25	25	0	154.1	644	148	55	52	9	3	3	7	39	2	155	2	13	4	.765	0-0	0	97	.651	3.16	3.03
2019 NYM	NL	32	32	0	197.2	825	194	101	94	24	3	8	6	50	2	202	4	10	8	.556	0-0	0	98	.714	3.66	4.28
2021 NYM	NL	2	2	0	2.0	8	3	2	2	1	0	0	0	0	0	2	0	1	0	1.000	0-0	0	95	1.250	9.22	9.00
2022 2 Tms		25	24	0	134.2	565	138	62	59	14	2	3	4	31	0	95	1	10	10	.500	0-0	0	94	.715	3.70	3.94
22 LAA	AL	15	15	0	80.0	338	75	36	34	9	1	3	4	22	0	64	0	5	8	.385	0-0	0	94	.683	3.48	3.83
22 Phi	NL	10	9	0	54.2	227	63	26	25	5	1	0	0	9	0	31	1	5	2	.714	0-0	0	93	.761	4.02	4.12
Postseason		5	4	0	26.0	103	17	7	7	0	1	0	0	11	1	36	1	2	1	.667	0-0	1	98	.505	1.75	2.42
7 ML YEARS		146	144	0	852.2	3513	806	355	324	78	17	22	23	197	9	872	26	57	41	.582	0-0	1	97	.671	3.17	3.42

Thomas Szapucki

Pitches: L **Bats:** R **Pos:** RP-10; SP-1   sah-POO-kee   **Ht:** 6'2" **Wt:** 210 **Born:** 6/12/1996 **Age:** 27

		HOW MUCH PITCHED					WHAT HE GAVE UP										THE RESULTS						
Year Team	Lg	G	GS	GF	IP	BFP	H	R	ER	HR	SH	SF	HB	TBB	IBB	SO	WP	W	L	Pct	Sv-Op	Hld	Vel	OPS	ERC	ERA
2022 Syrcse	AAA	18	16	0	64.0	269	54	25	24	5	0	0	5	29	0	87	5	2	6	.250	0- -	-	-	.676	3.65	3.38
2022 Scrmto	AAA	7	0	0	8.1	34	7	3	1	0	0	0	0	3	0	15	0	0	0		0- -	-	-	.552	2.46	1.08
2021 NYM	NL	1	0	0	3.2	20	7	6	6	2	0	0	0	3	0	4	0	0	0		0-0	0	91	1.382	17.09	14.73
2022 2 Tms	NL	11	1	2	15.0	67	19	12	12	6	0	0	0	7	0	18	1	0	1	.000	0-0	1	95	1.138	8.71	7.20
22 NYM	NL	1	1	0	1.1	13	7	9	9	4	0	0	0	3	0	2	0	0	1	.000	0-0	0	95	2.969	99.50	60.75
22 SF	NL	10	0	2	13.2	54	12	3	3	2	0	0	0	4	0	16	1	0	0		0-0	1	95	.756	3.45	1.98
2 ML YEARS		12	1	2	18.2	87	26	18	18	8	0	0	0	10	0	22	1	0	1	.000	0-0	1	94	1.193	10.25	8.68

Jameson Taillon

Pitches: R **Bats:** R **Pos:** SP-32   TIE-yohn   **Ht:** 6'5" **Wt:** 230 **Born:** 11/18/1991 **Age:** 31

		HOW MUCH PITCHED					WHAT HE GAVE UP										THE RESULTS						
Year Team	Lg	G	GS	GF	IP	BFP	H	R	ER	HR	SH	SF	HB	TBB	IBB	SO	WP	W	L	Pct	Sv-Op	Hld	Vel	OPS	ERC	ERA
2016 Pit	NL	18	18	0	104.0	418	99	40	39	13	4	1	3	17	1	85	1	5	4	.556	0-0	0	94	.702	3.21	3.38
2017 Pit	NL	25	25	0	133.2	587	152	69	66	11	8	4	4	46	3	125	7	8	7	.533	0-0	0	95	.789	4.61	4.44
2018 Pit	NL	32	32	0	191.0	785	179	69	68	20	4	2	6	46	4	179	2	14	10	.583	0-0	0	95	.681	3.26	3.20
2019 Pit	NL	7	7	0	37.1	158	34	24	17	4	0	1	2	8	1	30	1	2	3	.400	0-0	0	95	.680	2.98	4.10
2021 NYY	AL	29	29	0	144.1	603	130	73	69	24	1	5	6	44	1	140	4	8	6	.571	0-0	0	94	.721	3.74	4.30
2022 NYY	AL	32	32	0	177.1	728	168	78	77	26	2	4	5	32	0	151	3	14	5	.737	0-0	0	94	.713	3.33	3.91
6 ML YEARS		143	143	0	787.2	3279	762	353	336	98	19	17	26	193	10	710	18	51	35	.593	0-0	0	95	.717	3.57	3.84

Domingo Tapia

Pitches: R Bats: R Pos: RP-11   Ht: 6'3" Wt: 263 Born: 8/4/1991 Age: 31

			HOW MUCH PITCHED					WHAT HE GAVE UP											THE RESULTS						
Year Team	Lg	G	GS	GF	IP	BFP	H	R	ER	HR	SH	SF	HB	TBB	IBB	SO	WP	W	L	Pct	Sv-Op Hld	Vel	OPS	ERC	ERA
2022 Omha	AAA	5	0	0	5.0	19	3	2	2	0	0	0	0	3	0	2	0	0	0	-	0- - -	-	.628	2.30	3.60
2022 LsVgs	AAA	27	0	12	30.2	132	25	12	6	1	0	2	3	12	0	29	1	0	0	-	4- - -	-	.604	2.89	1.76
2020 Bos	AL	5	0	0	4.1	19	4	1	1	1	0	0	0	2	0	4	0	0	0	-	0-0 0	99	.786	4.71	2.08
2021 2 Tms	AL	34	0	1	33.2	135	25	10	10	1	0	0	0	15	2	26	2	4	1	.800	0-3 7	97	.571	2.42	2.67
2022 Oak	AL	11	0	4	17.0	90	25	16	16	1	0	1	1	14	1	12	3	0	0	-	0-0 0	98	.971	8.43	8.47
21 Sea		2	0	1	2.0	11	4	0	0	0	0	0	0	1	0	1	0	0	0	-	0-0 0	98	.855	9.72	0.00
21 KC		32	0	0	31.2	124	21	10	10	1	0	0	0	14	2	25	2	4	1	.800	0-3 7	97	.546	2.06	2.84
3 ML YEARS		50	0	5	55.0	244	54	27	27	3	0	1	1	31	3	42	5	4	1	.800	0-3 7	98	.732	4.28	4.42

Raimel Tapia

Bats: L Throws: L Pos: LF-64;CF-38;RF-32;PH-12;PR-2;DH-1   rye-MELL   Ht: 6'3" Wt: 175 Born: 2/4/1994 Age: 29

							BATTING												RUNNING			AVERAGES			
Year Team	Lg	G	AB	H	2B	3B	HR	(Hm	Rd)	TB	R	RBI	RC	TBB	IBB	SO	HBP	SH	SF	SB	CS	GDP	Avg	OBP	Slg	OPS
2016 Col	NL	22	38	10	0	0	0	(0	0)	10	4	3	5	2	0	11	0	0	1	3	0	0	.263	.293	.263	.556
2017 Col	NL	70	160	46	12	2	2	(1	1)	68	27	16	20	8	1	36	2	1	0	5	2	3	.288	.329	.425	.754
2018 Col	NL	25	25	5	2	1	1	(0	1)	12	6	6	5	2	0	7	0	0	0	0	0	0	.200	.259	.480	.739
2019 Col	NL	138	426	117	23	5	9	(6	3)	177	54	44	54	21	0	100	0	0	0	9	3	2	.275	.309	.415	.724
2020 Col	NL	51	184	59	8	2	1	(0	1)	74	26	17	33	14	0	38	2	1	3	8	2	3	.321	.369	.402	.772
2021 Col	NL	133	487	133	26	2	6	(6	0)	181	69	50	67	40	2	70	1	1	4	20	6	8	.273	.327	.372	.699
2022 Tor	AL	128	411	109	20	3	7	(1	6)	156	47	52	45	16	0	81	0	3	1	8	2	12	.265	.292	.380	.672
Postseason		1	1	1	0	0	0	(0	0)	1	0	0	1	0	0	0	0	0	0	0	0	0	1.000	1.000	1.000	2.000
7 ML YEARS		567	1731	479	91	15	26	(14	12)	678	233	188	229	103	3	343	5	6	9	53	15	28	.277	.318	.392	.709

Freddy Tarnok

Pitches: R Bats: R Pos: RP-1   Ht: 6'3" Wt: 185 Born: 11/24/1998 Age: 24

			HOW MUCH PITCHED					WHAT HE GAVE UP											THE RESULTS						
Year Team	Lg	G	GS	GF	IP	BFP	H	R	ER	HR	SH	SF	HB	TBB	IBB	SO	WP	W	L	Pct	Sv-Op Hld	Vel	OPS	ERC	ERA
2022 Missi	AA	15	15	0	62.2	270	54	32	30	8	0	3	3	27	0	75	6	2	2	.500	0- - -	-	.682	3.76	4.31
2022 Gwnntt	AAA	10	8	0	44.0	186	38	18	18	7	0	0	2	17	0	49	2	2	1	.667	0- - -	-	.714	3.84	3.68
2022 Atl	NL	1	0	1	0.2	3	1	0	0	0	0	0	0	0	0	1	0	0	0	-	0-0 0	96	1.000	4.47	0.00

Dillon Tate

Pitches: R Bats: R Pos: RP-67   Ht: 6'2" Wt: 195 Born: 5/1/1994 Age: 29

			HOW MUCH PITCHED					WHAT HE GAVE UP											THE RESULTS						
Year Team	Lg	G	GS	GF	IP	BFP	H	R	ER	HR	SH	SF	HB	TBB	IBB	SO	WP	W	L	Pct	Sv-Op Hld	Vel	OPS	ERC	ERA
2019 Bal	AL	16	0	5	21.0	93	18	15	15	3	0	1	5	9	0	20	2	0	2	.000	0-0 1	94	.729	4.64	6.43
2020 Bal	AL	12	0	1	16.2	64	9	7	6	1	0	2	2	5	0	14	1	1	1	.500	0-0 2	94	.486	1.66	3.24
2021 Bal	AL	62	0	19	67.2	287	61	35	33	7	2	6	7	23	0	49	7	0	6	.000	3-5 7	96	.713	3.74	4.39
2022 Bal	AL	67	0	13	73.2	292	57	29	25	6	0	2	7	16	2	60	3	4	4	.500	5-6 16	94	.615	2.46	3.05
4 ML YEARS		157	0	38	179.0	736	145	86	79	17	2	11	21	53	2	143	13	5	13	.278	8-11 26	95	.656	3.09	3.97

Fernando Tatis Jr.

Bats: R Throws: R Pos: SS   Ht: 6'3" Wt: 217 Born: 1/2/1999 Age: 24

							BATTING												RUNNING			AVERAGES			
Year Team	Lg	G	AB	H	2B	3B	HR	(Hm	Rd)	TB	R	RBI	RC	TBB	IBB	SO	HBP	SH	SF	SB	CS	GDP	Avg	OBP	Slg	OPS
2019 SD	NL	84	334	106	13	6	22	(10	12)	197	61	53	73	30	1	110	5	0	3	16	6	4	.317	.379	.590	.969
2020 SD	NL	59	224	62	11	2	17	(8	9)	128	50	45	48	27	1	61	5	0	1	11	3	6	.277	.366	.571	.937
2021 SD	NL	130	478	135	31	0	42	(18	24)	292	99	97	110	62	6	153	2	0	4	25	4	5	.282	.364	.611	.975
Postseason		6	22	7	2	0	2	(2	0)	15	5	5	5	5	1	7	0	0	0	1	1	0	.318	.444	.682	1.126
3 ML YEARS		273	1036	303	55	8	81	(36	45)	617	210	195	231	119	8	324	12	0	8	52	13	15	.292	.369	.596	.965

Leody Taveras

Bats: B Throws: R Pos: CF-93;PR-6;PH-3;DH-2   lay-OH-dee   Ht: 6'2" Wt: 195 Born: 9/8/1998 Age: 24

							BATTING												RUNNING			AVERAGES			
Year Team	Lg	G	AB	H	2B	3B	HR	(Hm	Rd)	TB	R	RBI	RC	TBB	IBB	SO	HBP	SH	SF	SB	CS	GDP	Avg	OBP	Slg	OPS
2022 RdRck	AAA	49	204	60	12	3	7	(-	-)	99	34	29	32	14	0	48	0	0	3	7	4	5	.294	.335	.485	.820
2020 Tex	AL	33	119	27	6	1	4	(2	2)	47	20	6	15	14	0	43	0	1	0	8	0	0	.227	.308	.395	.703
2021 Tex	AL	49	174	28	6	2	3	(2	1)	47	14	9	12	9	0	60	1	1	0	10	1	3	.161	.207	.270	.477
2022 Tex	AL	99	314	82	14	2	5	(3	2)	115	39	34	35	21	0	88	2	1	3	11	5	2	.261	.309	.366	.675
3 ML YEARS		181	607	137	26	5	12	(7	5)	209	73	49	56	44	0	191	3	3	3	29	6	5	.226	.280	.344	.624

Blake Taylor

Pitches: L Bats: L Pos: RP-19   Ht: 6'3" Wt: 220 Born: 8/17/1995 Age: 27

			HOW MUCH PITCHED					WHAT HE GAVE UP											THE RESULTS						
Year Team	Lg	G	GS	GF	IP	BFP	H	R	ER	HR	SH	SF	HB	TBB	IBB	SO	WP	W	L	Pct	Sv-Op Hld	Vel	OPS	ERC	ERA
2022 SgrLnd	AAA	11	1	0	10.2	44	6	6	6	1	0	1	2	7	0	7	1	2	0	1.000	0- - -	-	.635	3.52	5.06
2020 Hou	AL	22	0	5	20.2	87	13	7	5	2	0	0	0	12	1	17	1	2	1	.667	1-2 5	94	.567	2.64	2.18
2021 Hou	AL	51	0	10	42.2	188	38	19	15	6	1	2	0	22	2	41	5	4	4	.500	0-5 5	93	.720	4.04	3.16
2022 Hou	AL	19	0	4	16.0	75	15	7	7	1	0	0	1	10	0	9	2	1	1	.500	0-0 4	93	.659	4.38	3.94
Postseason		12	0	1	9.0	41	9	2	2	1	0	1	1	4	0	9	0	1	0	1.000	0-0 0	94	.741	4.66	2.00
3 ML YEARS		92	0	19	79.1	350	66	33	27	9	1	2	1	44	3	67	8	7	6	.538	1-7 14	93	.669	3.73	3.06

Chris Taylor

Bats: R **Throws:** R **Pos:** LF-80;2B-22;CF-10;RF-10;PH-7;DH-5;3B-3;SS-1   **Ht:** 6'1" **Wt:** 196 **Born:** 8/29/1990 **Age:** 32

Year	Team	Lg	G	AB	H	2B	3B	HR	(Hm	Rd)	TB	R	RBI	RC	TBB	IBB	SO	HBP	SH	SF	SB	CS	GDP	Avg	OBP	Slg	OPS
2014	Sea	AL	47	136	39	8	0	0	(0	0)	47	16	9	18	11	0	39	2	1	1	5	2	3	.287	.347	.346	.692
2015	Sea	AL	37	94	16	3	1	0	(0	0)	21	9	1	1	6	0	31	0	2	0	3	2	0	.170	.220	.223	.443
2016	2 Tms		36	61	13	2	2	1	(0	1)	22	8	7	5	4	1	15	0	0	0	0	0	3	.213	.262	.361	.622
2017	LAD	NL	140	514	148	34	5	21	(7	14)	255	85	72	88	50	0	142	3	0	1	17	4	2	.288	.354	.496	.850
2018	LAD	NL	155	536	136	35	8	17	(10	7)	238	85	63	75	55	0	**178**	9	0	4	9	6	5	.254	.331	.444	.775
2019	LAD	NL	124	366	96	29	4	12	(8	4)	169	52	52	60	37	3	115	4	2	5	8	0	6	.262	.333	.462	.794
2020	LAD	NL	56	185	50	10	2	8	(5	3)	88	30	32	36	26	0	55	2	1	0	3	2	3	.270	.366	.476	.842
2021	LAD	NL	148	507	129	25	4	20	(13	7)	222	92	73	84	63	2	167	8	1	3	13	1	5	.254	.344	.438	.782
2022	LAD	NL	118	402	89	25	3	10	(6	4)	150	45	43	42	44	2	160	5	0	3	10	1	4	.221	.304	.373	.677
16	Sea	AL	2	3	1	0	0	0	(0	0)	1	0	0	0	0	0	2	0	0	0	0	0	0	.333	.333	.333	.667
16	LAD	NL	34	58	12	2	2	1	(0	1)	21	8	7	5	4	1	13	0	0	0	0	0	0	.207	.258	.362	.620
	Postseason		62	201	52	13	2	9	(7	2)	96	36	25	34	33	0	60	1	0	1	4	1	0	.259	.364	.478	.842
	9 ML YEARS		861	2801	716	171	29	89	(49	40)	1212	422	352	409	296	8	902	33	7	17	68	18	31	.256	.332	.433	.765

Michael A. Taylor

Bats: R **Throws:** R **Pos:** CF-123;PH-6;PR-2;DH-1   **Ht:** 6'4" **Wt:** 215 **Born:** 3/26/1991 **Age:** 32

Year	Team	Lg	G	AB	H	2B	3B	HR	(Hm	Rd)	TB	R	RBI	RC	TBB	IBB	SO	HBP	SH	SF	SB	CS	GDP	Avg	OBP	Slg	OPS
2014	Was	NL	17	39	8	3	0	1	(0	1)	14	5	5	3	3	0	17	1	0	0	3	0	2	.205	.279	.359	.638
2015	Was	NL	138	472	108	15	2	14	(6	8)	169	49	63	60	35	9	158	1	1	2	16	3	5	.229	.282	.358	.640
2016	Was	NL	76	221	51	11	0	7	(1	6)	83	28	16	20	14	0	77	1	0	1	14	3	2	.231	.278	.376	.654
2017	Was	NL	118	399	108	23	3	19	(11	8)	194	55	53	57	29	3	137	1	1	2	17	7	3	.271	.320	.486	.806
2018	Was	NL	134	353	80	22	3	6	(2	4)	126	46	28	33	29	2	116	1	2	0	24	6	9	.227	.287	.357	.644
2019	Was	NL	53	88	22	7	0	1	(1	0)	32	10	3	7	7	0	34	0	2	0	6	0	0	.250	.305	.364	.669
2020	Was	NL	38	92	18	6	0	5	(2	3)	39	11	16	9	6	0	27	1	0	0	5	0	2	.196	.253	.424	.676
2021	KC	AL	142	483	118	16	1	12	(7	5)	172	58	54	50	33	0	144	5	2	5	14	7	9	.244	.297	.356	.653
2022	KC	AL	124	414	105	10	3	9	(6	3)	148	49	43	44	35	0	109	2	2	3	4	2	6	.254	.313	.357	.670
	Postseason		16	38	12	0	0	4	(1	3)	24	7	10	11	4	0	13	1	0	0	0	0	0	.316	.395	.632	1.027
	9 ML YEARS		840	2561	618	113	12	74	(36	38)	977	311	281	283	191	14	819	13	10	13	95	30	37	.241	.296	.381	.677

Tyrone Taylor

Bats: R **Throws:** R **Pos:** CF-84;RF-23;LF-20;PH-9;DH-1;PR-1   **Ht:** 6'0" **Wt:** 194 **Born:** 1/22/1994 **Age:** 29

Year	Team	Lg	G	AB	H	2B	3B	HR	(Hm	Rd)	TB	R	RBI	RC	TBB	IBB	SO	HBP	SH	SF	SB	CS	GDP	Avg	OBP	Slg	OPS
2019	Mil	NL	15	10	4	2	0	0	(0	0)	6	1	1	3	1	0	1	1	0	0	0	0	0	.400	.500	.600	1.100
2020	Mil	NL	22	38	9	4	0	2	(0	2)	19	6	6	5	2	0	8	1	0	0	0	0	1	.237	.293	.500	.793
2021	Mil	NL	93	243	60	9	3	12	(9	3)	111	33	43	36	20	1	59	7	0	1	6	1	6	.247	.321	.457	.778
2022	Mil	NL	120	373	87	21	3	17	(11	6)	165	49	51	52	22	0	102	7	0	3	3	2	11	.233	.286	.442	.729
	Postseason		4	7	0	0	0	0	(0	0)	0	0	0	0	0	0	4	0	0	0	0	0	0	.000	.000	.000	.000
	4 ML YEARS		250	664	160	36	6	31	(20	11)	301	89	101	96	45	1	170	16	0	4	9	3	18	.241	.303	.453	.756

Rowdy Tellez

Bats: L **Throws:** L **Pos:** 1B-139;PH-15;DH-9   **Ht:** 6'4" **Wt:** 255 **Born:** 3/16/1995 **Age:** 28

Year	Team	Lg	G	AB	H	2B	3B	HR	(Hm	Rd)	TB	R	RBI	RC	TBB	IBB	SO	HBP	SH	SF	SB	CS	GDP	Avg	OBP	Slg	OPS
2018	Tor	AL	23	70	22	9	0	4	(3	1)	43	10	14	17	2	0	21	0	0	1	0	0	0	.314	.329	.614	.943
2019	Tor	AL	111	370	84	19	0	21	(12	9)	166	49	54	47	29	3	116	7	0	3	1	1	9	.227	.293	.449	.742
2020	Tor	AL	35	113	32	5	0	8	(5	3)	61	20	23	22	11	1	20	1	0	2	0	1	1	.283	.346	.540	.886
2021	2 Tms		106	297	72	14	2	11	(4	7)	123	34	36	33	23	4	65	4	0	1	0	0	6	.242	.305	.414	.719
2022	Tor	NL	153	529	116	23	0	35	(22	13)	244	67	89	83	62	9	121	5	0	3	2	1	20	.219	.306	.461	.767
21	Tor	AL	50	139	29	4	1	4	(1	3)	47	12	8	7	9	1	33	3	0	0	0	0	3	.209	.272	.338	.610
21	Mil	NL	56	158	43	10	1	7	(3	4)	76	22	28	26	14	3	32	1	0	1	0	0	3	.272	.333	.481	.814
	Postseason		5	11	3	0	0	2	(1	1)	9	3	4	3	0	0	4	0	0	0	0	0	0	.273	.273	.818	1.091
	5 ML YEARS		428	1379	326	70	2	79	(46	33)	637	180	216	202	127	17	343	17	0	10	3	3	36	.236	.307	.462	.769

Ryan Tepera

Pitches: R **Bats:** R **Pos:** RP-59   tuh-PAIR-uh   **Ht:** 6'1" **Wt:** 195 **Born:** 11/3/1987 **Age:** 35

			HOW MUCH PITCHED					WHAT HE GAVE UP												THE RESULTS							
Year	Team	Lg	G	GS	GF	IP	BFP	H	R	ER	HR	SH	SF	HB	TBB	IBB	SO	WP	W	L	Pct	Sv-Op	Hld	Vel	OPS	ERC	ERA
2015	Tor	AL	32	0	12	33.0	128	23	14	12	8	0	0	3	6	0	22	2	0	2	.000	1-1	0	95	.670	2.87	3.27
2016	Tor	AL	20	0	13	18.1	85	17	8	6	1	1	0	3	8	1	18	3	0	1	.000	0-0	0	95	.635	3.81	2.95
2017	Tor	AL	73	0	12	77.2	319	57	35	31	7	1	1	8	31	4	81	5	7	1	.875	2-4	17	95	.633	2.94	3.59
2018	Tor	AL	68	0	19	64.2	263	55	27	26	9	0	3	4	24	1	68	5	5	5	.500	7-15	19	95	.738	3.77	3.62
2019	Tor	AL	23	1	7	21.2	91	20	12	12	5	1	2	0	8	2	14	2	0	2	.000	0-0	2	94	.684	4.29	4.98
2020	ChC	NL	21	0	1	20.2	89	17	9	9	2	0	1	1	12	0	31	1	0	1	.000	0-1	0	94	.684	4.01	3.92
2021	2 Tms		65	0	7	61.1	240	35	19	19	4	0	4	4	19	1	74	4	0	2	.000	2-5	21	93	.514	1.63	2.79
2022	LAA	AL	59	0	12	57.1	232	42	27	23	7	1	1	2	20	3	47	5	5	4	.556	6-11	17	93	.618	2.67	3.61
21	ChC	NL	43	0	3	43.1	165	22	14	14	3	0	3	3	12	0	50	1	0	0	.000	1-3	15	94	.469	1.41	2.91
21	CWS	AL	22	0	4	18.0	75	13	5	5	1	0	1	1	7	1	24	3	0	0	-	1-2	6	93	.613	2.36	2.50
	Postseason		6	0	1	7.2	32	7	5	5	0	1	3	0	3	0	5	2	0	0	-	0-0	0	93	.643	2.92	5.87
	8 ML YEARS		361	1	83	354.2	1447	266	151	138	43	4	12	25	128	12	355	27	17	18	.486	18-37	78	94	.649	2.98	3.50

Jackson Tetreault

Pitches: R Bats: R Pos: SP-4 TAY-troe Ht: 6'5" Wt: 189 Born: 6/3/1996 Age: 27

		HOW MUCH PITCHED					WHAT HE GAVE UP											THE RESULTS								
Year	Team	Lg	G	GS	GF	IP	BFP	H	R	ER	HR	SH	SF	HB	TBB	IBB	SO	WP	W	L	Pct	Sv-Op	Hld	Vel	OPS	ERC	ERA
2022	Roch	AAA	12	12	0	58.0	249	51	30	27	10	0	2	2	24	0	52	1	5	3	.625	0--	-	-	.721	4.04	4.19
2022	Was	NL	4	4	0	21.0	96	23	15	12	4	0	2	0	10	0	9	0	2	2	.500	0-0	0	95	.832	5.49	5.14

Matt Thaiss

Bats: L Throws: R Pos: C-14;1B-11;PH-6;3B-3 THICE Ht: 6'0" Wt: 215 Born: 5/6/1995 Age: 28

			BATTING																RUNNING			AVERAGES			
Year	Team	Lg	G	AB	H	2B	3B	HR	(Hm | Rd)	TB	R	RBI	RC	TBB	IBB	SO	HBP	SH	SF	SB	CS	GDP	Avg	OBP	Slg	OPS
2022	Salt Lk	AAA	77	284	76	16	3	10	(- | -)	128	46	48	48	43	1	61	2	0	3	7	0	7	.268	.364	.451	.815
2019	LAA	AL	53	147	31	7	0	8	(8 | 0)	62	17	23	20	17	0	52	0	0	0	0	0	4	.211	.293	.422	.714
2020	LAA	AL	8	21	3	0	0	1	(0 | 1)	6	3	1	0	4	0	8	0	0	0	0	0	1	.143	.280	.286	.566
2021	LAA	AL	3	7	1	0	0	0	(0 | 0)	1	1	0	0	1	0	1	0	0	0	0	0	0	.143	.250	.143	.393
2022	LAA	AL	29	69	15	1	0	2	(1 | 1)	22	9	8	7	11	1	24	0	0	1	1	0	2	.217	.321	.319	.640
	4 ML YEARS		93	244	50	8	0	11	(9 | 2)	91	30	32	27	33	1	85	0	0	1	1	0	7	.205	.299	.373	.672

Caleb Thielbar

Pitches: L Bats: R Pos: RP-67 THEEL-bar Ht: 6'0" Wt: 205 Born: 1/31/1987 Age: 36

			HOW MUCH PITCHED					WHAT HE GAVE UP											THE RESULTS								
Year	Team	Lg	G	GS	GF	IP	BFP	H	R	ER	HR	SH	SF	HB	TBB	IBB	SO	WP	W	L	Pct	Sv-Op	Hld	Vel	OPS	ERC	ERA
2013	Min	AL	49	0	16	46.0	171	24	11	9	4	0	1	0	14	4	39	1	3	2	.600	0-0	1	90	.530	1.38	1.76
2014	Min	AL	54	0	7	47.2	206	51	19	18	3	1	6	1	16	1	35	0	2	1	.667	0-1	7	89	.738	4.01	3.40
2015	Min	AL	6	0	1	5.0	20	5	3	3	0	1	0	0	0	0	5	1	0	0		0-0	1	90	.579	1.95	5.40
2020	Min	AL	17	0	3	20.0	82	14	6	5	0	0	0	0	9	0	22	2	2	1	.667	0-0	1	90	.500	2.05	2.25
2021	Min	AL	59	0	14	64.0	266	55	24	23	8	3	3	3	20	1	77	3	7	0	1.000	0-0	12	91	.697	3.29	3.23
2022	Min	AL	67	0	10	59.1	245	51	26	23	5	0	1	0	18	1	80	1	4	3	.571	1-2	18	93	.613	2.80	3.49
	Postseason		1	0	1	0.1	2	1	0	0	0	0	0	0	0	0	0	0	0	0		0-0	0	91	1.000	14.52	0.00
	6 ML YEARS		252	0	51	242.0	990	200	89	81	20	5	11	4	77	7	258	8	18	7	.720	1-3	40	91	.637	2.75	3.01

Alek Thomas

Bats: L Throws: L Pos: CF-112;PH-3 Ht: 5'11" Wt: 175 Born: 4/28/2000 Age: 23

			BATTING																RUNNING			AVERAGES			
Year	Team	Lg	G	AB	H	2B	3B	HR	(Hm | Rd)	TB	R	RBI	RC	TBB	IBB	SO	HBP	SH	SF	SB	CS	GDP	Avg	OBP	Slg	OPS
2018	2 Tms	Low	56	246	82	14	6	2	(- | -)	114	50	27	46	24	0	37	1	0	0	12	5	4	.333	.395	.463	.858
2019	2 Tms	Low	114	447	134	23	7	10	(- | -)	201	76	55	81	52	2	105	6	0	1	15	11	7	.300	.379	.450	.829
2021	Amrillo	AA	72	286	81	18	8	10	(- | -)	145	54	41	54	37	0	65	5	0	1	8	6	3	.283	.374	.507	.881
2021	Reno	AAA	33	144	54	11	4	8	(- | -)	97	32	18	38	15	0	33	2	0	5	5	5	1	.375	.441	.674	1.115
2022	Reno	AAA	27	115	37	11	1	4	(- | -)	62	25	19	24	14	0	18	1	0	1	5	2	3	.322	.397	.539	.936
2022	Ari	NL	113	381	88	17	1	8	(1 | 7)	131	45	39	31	22	0	74	3	0	5	4	3	6	.231	.275	.344	.619

Cody Thomas

Bats: L Throws: R Pos: LF-10 Ht: 6'4" Wt: 211 Born: 10/8/1994 Age: 28

			BATTING																RUNNING			AVERAGES			
Year	Team	Lg	G	AB	H	2B	3B	HR	(Hm | Rd)	TB	R	RBI	RC	TBB	IBB	SO	HBP	SH	SF	SB	CS	GDP	Avg	OBP	Slg	OPS
2022	LsVgs	AAA	10	35	7	3	0	1	(- | -)	13	3	8	3	2	0	13	1	0	1	0	0	0	.200	.256	.371	.628
2022	Oak	AL	10	30	8	0	0	0	(0 | 0)	8	1	0	2	2	0	12	0	0	0	0	0	0	.267	.313	.267	.579

Dillon Thomas

Bats: L Throws: L Pos: LF-5;RF-5;PH-1;PR-1 Ht: 6'1" Wt: 215 Born: 12/10/1992 Age: 30

			BATTING																RUNNING			AVERAGES			
Year	Team	Lg	G	AB	H	2B	3B	HR	(Hm | Rd)	TB	R	RBI	RC	TBB	IBB	SO	HBP	SH	SF	SB	CS	GDP	Avg	OBP	Slg	OPS
2022	Salt Lk	AAA	108	399	108	22	2	17	(- | -)	185	72	77	73	55	0	123	17	0	4	6	4	6	.271	.379	.464	.843
2021	Sea	AL	4	9	1	0	0	0	(0 | 0)	1	2	2	1	0	0	7	0	0	0	0	0	0	.111	.111	.111	.222
2022	LAA	AL	8	11	1	0	0	0	(0 | 0)	1	1	0	0	2	0	6	1	0	0	0	0	0	.091	.286	.091	.377
	2 ML YEARS		12	20	2	0	0	0	(0 | 0)	2	3	2	1	2	0	13	1	0	0	0	0	0	.100	.217	.100	.317

Lane Thomas

Bats: R Throws: R Pos: LF-73;CF-56;RF-43;PH-9;DH-1;PR-1 Ht: 6'0" Wt: 191 Born: 8/23/1995 Age: 27

			BATTING																RUNNING			AVERAGES			
Year	Team	Lg	G	AB	H	2B	3B	HR	(Hm | Rd)	TB	R	RBI	RC	TBB	IBB	SO	HBP	SH	SF	SB	CS	GDP	Avg	OBP	Slg	OPS
2019	StL	NL	34	38	12	0	1	4	(3 | 1)	26	6	12	12	4	0	8	2	0	0	1	1	1	.316	.409	.684	1.093
2020	StL	NL	18	36	4	2	0	1	(1 | 0)	9	5	2	1	4	0	13	0	0	0	0	0	1	.111	.200	.250	.450
2021	2 Tms	NL	77	226	53	15	2	7	(4 | 3)	93	35	28	33	37	1	63	0	0	1	6	3	6	.235	.341	.412	.752
2022	Was	NL	146	498	120	26	2	17	(7 | 10)	201	62	52	55	41	0	132	4	0	5	8	4	5	.241	.301	.404	.705
21	StL	NL	32	48	5	1	0	0	(0 | 0)	6	2	1	1	10	1	17	0	0	0	2	1	1	.104	.259	.125	.384
21	Was	NL	45	178	48	14	2	7	(4 | 3)	87	33	27	32	27	0	46	0	0	1	4	2	5	.270	.364	.489	.853
	4 ML YEARS		275	798	189	43	5	29	(15 | 14)	329	108	94	101	86	1	216	6	0	6	15	8	16	.237	.314	.412	.726

Bubba Thompson

Bats: R **Throws:** R **Pos:** LF-35;RF-10;CF-9;PR-4;DH-1   **Ht:** 6'2" **Wt:** 197 **Born:** 6/9/1998 **Age:** 25

					BATTING														RUNNING			AVERAGES			
Year	Team	Lg	G	AB	H	2B	3B	HR	(Hm | Rd)	TB	R	RBI	RC	TBB	IBB	SO	HBP	SH	SF	SB	CS	GDP	Avg	OBP	Slg	OPS
2022	RdRck	AAA	80	346	105	12	4	13	(- | -)	164	77	48	64	22	1	95	6	0	1	49	3	1	.303	.355	.474	.829
2022	Tex	AL	55	170	45	5	0	1	(1 | 0)	53	18	9	13	7	0	56	2	2	0	18	3	2	.265	.302	.312	.613

Keegan Thompson

Pitches: R **Bats:** R **Pos:** SP-17; RP-12   **Ht:** 6'1" **Wt:** 210 **Born:** 3/13/1995 **Age:** 28

			HOW MUCH PITCHED					WHAT HE GAVE UP										THE RESULTS						
Year	Team	Lg	G	GS	GF	IP	BFP	H	R	ER	HR	SH	SF	HB	TBB	IBB	SO	WP	W	L	Pct	Sv-Op	Hld	Vel	OPS	ERC	ERA
2021	ChC	NL	32	6	5	53.1	243	48	22	20	9	2	1	2	31	1	55	4	3	3	.500	1-2	1	94	.745	4.70	3.38
2022	ChC	NL	29	17	4	115.0	485	103	54	48	16	1	1	9	43	0	108	5	10	5	.667	1-2	0	93	.731	4.02	3.76
	2 ML YEARS		61	23	9	168.1	728	151	76	68	25	3	2	11	74	1	163	9	13	8	.619	2-4	1	94	.736	4.24	3.64

Mason Thompson

Pitches: R **Bats:** R **Pos:** RP-24   **Ht:** 6'6" **Wt:** 236 **Born:** 2/20/1998 **Age:** 25

			HOW MUCH PITCHED					WHAT HE GAVE UP										THE RESULTS						
Year	Team	Lg	G	GS	GF	IP	BFP	H	R	ER	HR	SH	SF	HB	TBB	IBB	SO	WP	W	L	Pct	Sv-Op	Hld	Vel	OPS	ERC	ERA
2022	Roch	AAA	11	1	4	15.1	67	15	9	6	0	0	2	1	5	1	19	2	0	4	.000	0- -	-	-	.635	3.04	3.52
2021	2 Tms	NL	31	0	5	24.2	121	32	15	11	4	2	0	1	15	1	23	3	1	3	.250	0-3	6	96	.879	7.24	4.01
2022	Was	NL	24	0	8	24.2	101	19	8	8	2	1	0	1	9	0	15	1	1	1	.500	1-2	0	96	.612	2.76	2.92
21	SD	NL	4	0	1	3.0	13	4	1	1	0	0	0	0	1	0	2	2	0	0	-	0-0	1	98	.801	5.24	3.00
21	Was	NL	27	0	4	21.2	108	28	14	10	4	2	0	1	14	1	21	1	1	3	.250	0-3	5	96	.889	7.53	4.15
	2 ML YEARS		55	0	13	49.1	222	51	23	19	6	3	0	2	24	1	38	4	2	4	.333	1-5	6	96	.756	4.86	3.47

Ryan Thompson

Pitches: R **Bats:** R **Pos:** RP-47   **Ht:** 6'5" **Wt:** 210 **Born:** 6/26/1992 **Age:** 31

			HOW MUCH PITCHED					WHAT HE GAVE UP										THE RESULTS						
Year	Team	Lg	G	GS	GF	IP	BFP	H	R	ER	HR	SH	SF	HB	TBB	IBB	SO	WP	W	L	Pct	Sv-Op	Hld	Vel	OPS	ERC	ERA
2020	TB	AL	25	1	3	26.1	114	29	15	13	4	0	0	0	8	0	23	0	1	2	.333	1-1	4	91	.749	4.61	4.44
2021	TB	AL	36	0	2	34.0	134	26	11	9	3	0	0	2	9	2	37	1	3	2	.600	0-4	11	91	.642	2.47	2.38
2022	TB	AL	47	0	7	42.2	181	39	24	18	4	1	0	2	11	2	39	1	3	3	.500	3-8	10	90	.648	3.05	3.80
	Postseason		9	1	1	9.1	38	7	2	2	1	0	1	1	4	0	10	0	0	1	.000	0-0	3	92	.628	3.42	1.93
	3 ML YEARS		108	1	12	103.0	429	94	50	40	11	1	0	4	28	4	99	2	7	7	.500	4-13	25	91	.673	3.23	3.50

Trayce Thompson

Bats: R **Throws:** R **Pos:** LF-36;RF-29;CF-18;PH-13;DH-4;PR-2   **Ht:** 6'3" **Wt:** 225 **Born:** 3/15/1991 **Age:** 32

					BATTING														RUNNING			AVERAGES			
Year	Team	Lg	G	AB	H	2B	3B	HR	(Hm	Rd)	TB	R	RBI	RC	TBB	IBB	SO	HBP	SH	SF	SB	CS	GDP	Avg	OBP	Slg	OPS
2022	Roch	AAA	16	57	18	4	0	9	(-	-)	49	16	17	20	7	1	18	0	0	1	1	0	2	.316	.385	.860	1.244
2022	Toledo	AAA	25	97	29	7	1	8	(-	-)	62	17	19	22	7	1	30	1	0	0	1	1	2	.299	.352	.639	.992
2015	CWS	AL	44	122	36	8	3	5	(3	2)	65	17	16	20	13	0	26	0	0	3	1	0	3	.295	.363	.533	.896
2016	LAD	NL	80	236	53	11	0	13	(9	4)	103	31	32	26	26	0	66	0	0	0	5	1	3	.225	.302	.436	.738
2017	LAD	NL	27	49	6	2	1	1	(0	1)	13	6	2	1	6	1	23	0	0	0	0	0	0	.122	.218	.265	.483
2018	2 Tms	AL	51	128	15	3	0	3	(2	1)	27	15	9	0	7	1	50	0	1	1	3	1	0	.117	.162	.211	.373
2021	ChC	NL	15	28	7	1	0	4	(1	3)	20	6	9	8	7	0	11	0	0	0	2	0	2	.250	.400	.714	1.114
2022	2 Tms	NL	80	219	56	14	1	13	(6	7)	111	36	41	43	32	0	93	2	0	2	4	1	2	.256	.353	.507	.860
18	Oak	AL	3	7	1	0	0	0	(0	0)	1	1	0	0	0	0	4	0	0	0	0	0	0	.143	.143	.143	.286
18	CWS	AL	48	121	14	3	0	3	(2	1)	26	14	9	0	7	1	46	0	1	1	3	1	0	.116	.163	.215	.378
22	SD	NL	6	14	1	0	0	0	(0	0)	1	1	2	0	2	0	7	0	0	0	0	1	0	.071	.188	.071	.259
22	LAD	NL	74	205	55	14	1	13	(6	7)	110	35	39	43	30	0	86	2	0	2	4	0	2	.268	.364	.537	.901
	6 ML YEARS		297	782	173	39	5	39	(21	18)	339	111	109	98	91	2	269	2	1	3	15	3	10	.221	.303	.434	.736

Zach Thompson

Pitches: R **Bats:** R **Pos:** SP-22; RP-7   **Ht:** 6'7" **Wt:** 250 **Born:** 10/23/1993 **Age:** 29

			HOW MUCH PITCHED					WHAT HE GAVE UP										THE RESULTS						
Year	Team	Lg	G	GS	GF	IP	BFP	H	R	ER	HR	SH	SF	HB	TBB	IBB	SO	WP	W	L	Pct	Sv-Op	Hld	Vel	OPS	ERC	ERA
2021	ElPaso	NL	26	14	2	75.0	315	63	35	27	6	3	3	3	28	1	66	5	3	7	.300	0-0	0	92	.675	3.09	3.24
2022	Pit	NL	29	22	1	121.2	543	138	76	70	19	0	1	3	46	0	90	5	3	10	.231	0-0	0	92	.791	5.25	5.18
	2 ML YEARS		55	36	3	196.2	858	201	111	97	25	3	4	6	74	1	156	10	6	17	.261	0-0	0	92	.749	4.38	4.44

Zack Thompson

Pitches: L **Bats:** L **Pos:** RP-21; SP-1   **Ht:** 6'2" **Wt:** 215 **Born:** 10/28/1997 **Age:** 25

			HOW MUCH PITCHED					WHAT HE GAVE UP										THE RESULTS						
Year	Team	Lg	G	GS	GF	IP	BFP	H	R	ER	HR	SH	SF	HB	TBB	IBB	SO	WP	W	L	Pct	Sv-Op	Hld	Vel	OPS	ERC	ERA
2022	Memp	AAA	19	10	0	53.1	228	44	32	28	6	0	2	4	21	0	67	3	2	3	.400	0- -	-	-	.681	3.41	4.73
2022	StL	NL	22	1	4	34.2	136	20	9	8	3	0	0	0	14	0	27	1	1	1	.500	1-1	0	95	.512	1.87	2.08

Tyler Thornburg

Pitches: R **Bats:** R **Pos:** RP-14   **Ht:** 5'11" **Wt:** 190 **Born:** 9/29/1988 **Age:** 34

Year	Team	Lg	G	GS	GF	IP	BFP	H	R	ER	HR	SH	SF	HB	TBB	IBB	SO	WP	W	L	Pct	Sv-Op	Hld	Vel	OPS	ERC	ERA
2022	StPaul	AAA	13	0	0	14.1	68	17	12	9	1	0	0	3	6	0	15	2	1	0	1.000	0- -	-		.806	5.80	5.65
2012	Mil	NL	8	3	3	22.0	95	24	11	11	8	1	0	1	7	0	20	1	0	0	-	0-0	0	93	.922	6.44	4.50
2013	Mil	NL	18	7	4	66.2	270	53	17	15	1	4	1	3	26	2	48	2	3	1	.750	0-0	0	92	.575	2.59	2.03
2014	Mil	NL	27	0	4	29.2	131	24	14	14	1	1	1	0	21	0	28	4	3	1	.750	0-0	5	94	.670	3.71	4.25
2015	Mil	NL	24	0	9	34.1	151	31	22	14	7	0	2	3	12	1	34	3	0	2	.000	0-0	1	92	.723	4.20	3.67
2016	Mil	NL	67	0	23	67.0	263	38	19	16	6	0	1	2	25	1	90	4	8	5	.615	13-21	20	94	.541	1.82	2.15
2018	Bos	AL	25	0	9	24.0	107	28	15	15	6	0	1	1	10	0	21	2	2	0	1.000	0-0	3	93	.901	6.56	5.63
2019	Bos	AL	16	0	4	18.2	86	21	16	16	4	0	0	1	10	0	22	1	0	0	-	0-0	0	94	.972	6.51	7.71
2020	Cin	NL	7	0	2	7.0	32	6	3	3	0	0	0	0	5	0	10	1	0	0	-	0-0	1	93	.603	3.64	3.86
2022	2 Tms		14	0	9	19.0	87	16	10	7	1	0	1	1	11	0	14	0	0	1	.000	0-1	0	94	.619	3.56	3.32
22	Atl	NL	9	0	6	9.1	47	12	6	4	0	0	1	0	5	0	10	0	0	0	-	0-0	0	94	.728	5.09	3.86
22	Min	AL	5	0	3	9.2	40	4	4	3	1	0	0	1	6	0	4	0	0	1	.000	0-1	0	94	.487	2.21	2.79
9 ML YEARS			206	10	67	288.1	1222	241	127	111	34	6	7	12	127	4	287	18	16	10	.615	13-22	30	93	.684	3.59	3.46

Trent Thornton

Pitches: R **Bats:** R **Pos:** RP-32   **Ht:** 6'0" **Wt:** 190 **Born:** 9/30/1993 **Age:** 29

Year	Team	Lg	G	GS	GF	IP	BFP	H	R	ER	HR	SH	SF	HB	TBB	IBB	SO	WP	W	L	Pct	Sv-Op	Hld	Vel	OPS	ERC	ERA
2022	Buffalo	AAA	21	0	7	28.0	122	26	11	9	1	1	1	1	12	0	30	1	2	2	.500	3- -	-		.649	3.42	2.89
2019	Tor	AL	32	29	0	154.1	677	156	87	83	24	1	7	5	61	0	149	5	6	9	.400	0-0	0	93	.768	4.60	4.84
2020	Tor	AL	3	3	0	5.2	33	15	7	7	0	0	1	0	3	0	6	0	0	0	-	0-0	0	92	1.166	15.41	11.12
2021	Tor	AL	37	3	4	49.0	216	54	33	26	12	1	1	4	16	1	52	3	1	3	.250	0-0	0	94	.880	5.75	4.78
2022	Tor	AL	32	0	6	46.0	189	40	21	21	7	0	2	1	17	0	37	1	0	2	.000	0-1	3	94	.703	3.75	4.11
4 ML YEARS			104	35	10	255.0	1115	265	148	137	43	2	11	10	97	1	244	9	7	14	.333	0-1	3	93	.791	4.86	4.84

Jesus Tinoco

Pitches: R **Bats:** R **Pos:** RP-15; SP-2   hay-SOOS tih-NO-ko   **Ht:** 6'4" **Wt:** 258 **Born:** 4/30/1995 **Age:** 28

Year	Team	Lg	G	GS	GF	IP	BFP	H	R	ER	HR	SH	SF	HB	TBB	IBB	SO	WP	W	L	Pct	Sv-Op	Hld	Vel	OPS	ERC	ERA
2022	RdRck	AAA	35	0	24	44.0	179	33	16	16	3	0	1	0	17	0	51	4	1	2	.333	13- -	-		.571	2.51	3.27
2019	Col	NL	24	0	3	36.0	161	36	23	19	12	0	1	1	22	1	28	1	0	3	.000	1-1	2	94	.965	6.94	4.75
2020	2 Tms	NL	6	0	3	8.2	32	3	1	1	0	0	0	0	7	0	6	2	0	0	-	0-0	0	94	.433	1.80	1.04
2021	Col	NL	1	0	0	1.1	10	5	5	5	3	0	0	1	1	0	0	0	0	0	-	0-0	0	93	2.450	65.75	33.75
2022	Tex	NL	17	2	2	20.2	84	12	5	5	2	0	1	1	10	0	18	0	0	0	-	0-0	4	96	.552	2.36	2.18
20	Mia	NL	3	0	1	5.0	15	0	0	0	0	0	0	0	3	0	3	0	0	0	-	0-0	0	94	.200	0.45	0.00
20	Col	NL	3	0	2	3.2	17	3	1	1	0	0	0	0	4	0	3	2	0	0	-	0-0	0	94	.643	5.09	2.45
4 ML YEARS			48	2	8	66.2	287	56	34	30	17	0	2	3	40	1	52	3	0	3	.000	1-1	6	94	.837	5.38	4.05

Michael Toglia

Bats: B **Throws:** L **Pos:** RF-17;1B-15;PH-1   **Ht:** 6'5" **Wt:** 226 **Born:** 8/16/1998 **Age:** 24

Year	Team	Lg	G	AB	H	2B	3B	HR	(Hm	Rd)	TB	R	RBI	RC	TBB	IBB	SO	HBP	SH	SF	SB	CS	GDP	Avg	OBP	Slg	OPS
2022	Hrtfrd	AA	97	363	85	13	1	23	(-	-)	169	63	66	66	51	0	127	2	0	4	8	1	1	.234	.329	.466	.794
2022	Albq	AAA	17	66	22	7	0	7	(-	-)	50	11	17	21	9	0	22	0	0	0	0	0	0	.333	.413	.758	1.171
2022	Col	NL	31	111	24	8	2	2	(1	1)	42	10	12	14	9	0	44	0	0	0	1	1	2	.216	.275	.378	.653

Ka'ai Tom

Bats: L **Throws:** R **Pos:** RF-1;PH-1   kuh-EYE   **Ht:** 5'9" **Wt:** 185 **Born:** 5/29/1994 **Age:** 29

Year	Team	Lg	G	AB	H	2B	3B	HR	(Hm	Rd)	TB	R	RBI	RC	TBB	IBB	SO	HBP	SH	SF	SB	CS	GDP	Avg	OBP	Slg	OPS
2022	Scrmto	AAA	78	268	64	17	0	10	(-	-)	111	40	47	39	35	0	80	6	1	1	6	3	5	.239	.339	.414	.753
2021	2 Tms		48	108	15	2	1	2	(1	1)	25	10	12	9	17	1	36	5	0	3	1	0	1	.139	.278	.231	.510
2022	SF	NL	1	1	0	0	0	0	(0	0)	0	0	0	0	0	0	0	0	0	0	0	0	0	.000	.000	.000	.000
21	Oak	AL	9	16	1	0	0	0	(0	0)	1	1	1	0	0	0	6	0	0	0	0	0	0	.063	.063	.063	.125
21	Pit	NL	39	92	14	2	1	2	(1	1)	24	9	11	9	17	1	30	5	0	3	1	0	1	.152	.308	.261	.569
2 ML YEARS			49	109	15	2	1	2	(1	1)	25	10	12	9	17	1	36	5	0	3	1	0	1	.138	.276	.229	.505

Justin Topa

Pitches: R **Bats:** R **Pos:** RP-7   **Ht:** 6'4" **Wt:** 200 **Born:** 3/7/1991 **Age:** 32

Year	Team	Lg	G	GS	GF	IP	BFP	H	R	ER	HR	SH	SF	HB	TBB	IBB	SO	WP	W	L	Pct	Sv-Op	Hld	Vel	OPS	ERC	ERA
2022	Nashv	AAA	17	0	0	18.2	87	23	9	9	0	0	1	3	8	0	17	2	2	0	1.000	0- -	-		.724	5.44	4.34
2020	Mil	NL	6	0	2	7.2	30	7	3	2	1	0	0	0	0	0	12	0	0	1	.000	0-0	0	98	.633	2.25	2.35
2021	Mil	NL	4	0	0	3.1	23	12	11	11	2	0	0	0	1	1	1	0	0	0	-	0-0	0	96	1.520	27.35	29.70
2022	Mil	NL	7	0	1	7.1	35	9	6	4	0	0	0	0	4	1	4	0	0	0	-	0-0	1	96	.694	4.79	4.91
Postseason			1	0	0	2.0	7	1	0	0	0	0	0	0	1	0	0	0	0	0	-	0-0	0	97	.452	1.62	0.00
3 ML YEARS			17	0	3	18.1	88	28	20	17	3	0	0	0	5	2	17	0	0	1	.000	0-0	1	96	.893	6.86	8.35

Spencer Torkelson

Bats: R **Throws:** R **Pos:** 1B-109;PH-4   **Ht:** 6'1" **Wt:** 220 **Born:** 8/26/1999 **Age:** 23

Year	Team	Lg	G	AB	H	2B	3B	HR	(Hm	Rd)	TB	R	RBI	RC	TBB	IBB	SO	HBP	SH	SF	SB	CS	GDP	Avg	OBP	Slg	OPS
2021	Wmich	A+	31	109	34	11	1	5	(-	-)	62	21	28	0	24	0	28	4	0	4	3	2	4	.312	.440	.569	1.009
2021	Erie	AA	50	175	46	10	0	14	(-	-)	98	33	36	37	30	0	50	3	0	4	1	1	4	.263	.373	.560	.933
2021	Toledo	AAA	35	131	31	7	1	10	(-	-)	70	31	25	24	18	1	33	3	0	3	0	0	4	.237	.335	.534	.870
2022	Toledo	AAA	35	131	30	6	0	5	(-	-)	51	18	18	19	23	1	41	1	0	0	1	1	1	.229	.348	.389	.738
2022	Det	AL	110	360	73	16	1	8	(3	5)	115	38	28	31	37	0	99	5	0	2	0	1	12	.203	.285	.319	.604

Abraham Toro

Bats: B **Throws:** R **Pos:** 2B-55;3B-31;DH-22;PH-14;PR-5;1B-1;RF-1   **Ht:** 6'0" **Wt:** 225 **Born:** 12/20/1996 **Age:** 26

Year	Team	Lg	G	AB	H	2B	3B	HR	(Hm	Rd)	TB	R	RBI	RC	TBB	IBB	SO	HBP	SH	SF	SB	CS	GDP	Avg	OBP	Slg	OPS
2022	Tacom	AAA	16	58	14	3	1	2	(-	-)	25	6	12	8	10	0	12	0	0	0	3	0	3	.241	.353	.431	.784
2019	Hou	AL	25	78	17	3	2	2	(1	1)	30	13	9	8	9	0	19	1	0	1	1	1	2	.218	.303	.385	.688
2020	Hou	AL	33	87	13	2	0	3	(1	2)	24	13	9	5	3	0	23	7	0	0	1	1	1	.149	.237	.276	.513
2021	2 Tms	AL	95	335	80	12	0	11	(6	5)	125	45	46	47	31	0	54	7	0	2	6	3	5	.239	.315	.373	.688
2022	Sea	AL	109	324	60	13	1	10	(5	5)	105	36	35	32	22	1	65	2	0	4	2	0	4	.185	.239	.324	.563
21	Hou	AL	35	109	23	1	0	6	(2	4)	42	17	20	15	9	0	21	3	0	1	3	1	1	.211	.287	.385	.672
21	Sea	AL	60	226	57	11	0	5	(4	1)	83	28	26	32	22	0	33	4	0	1	3	2	4	.252	.328	.367	.695
	Postseason		1	0	0	0	0	0	(0	0)	0	0	0	0	1	0	0	0	0	0	0	0	0	-	1.000	-	-
	4 ML YEARS		262	824	170	30	3	26	(13	13)	284	107	99	92	65	1	161	17	0	7	10	5	12	.206	.276	.345	.621

Luis Torrens

Bats: R **Throws:** R **Pos:** C-42;DH-9;PH-8;2B-2   **Ht:** 6'0" **Wt:** 217 **Born:** 5/2/1996 **Age:** 27

Year	Team	Lg	G	AB	H	2B	3B	HR	(Hm	Rd)	TB	R	RBI	RC	TBB	IBB	SO	HBP	SH	SF	SB	CS	GDP	Avg	OBP	Slg	OPS
2022	Tacom	AAA	16	61	17	5	0	3	(-	-)	31	7	15	10	5	0	18	0	0	2	0	0	1	.279	.324	.508	.832
2017	SD	NL	56	123	20	3	1	0	(0	0)	25	7	7	4	12	3	30	1	3	0	0	0	1	.163	.243	.203	.446
2019	SD	NL	7	14	3	1	0	0	(0	0)	4	2	0	1	2	0	6	0	0	0	0	0	1	.214	.313	.286	.598
2020	2 Tms	AL	25	70	18	5	0	1	(1	0)	26	5	6	7	7	0	15	0	0	0	0	0	1	.257	.325	.371	.696
2021	Sea	AL	108	346	84	16	2	15	(7	8)	149	39	47	46	28	1	99	1	0	3	0	0	8	.243	.299	.431	.730
2022	Sea	AL	57	151	34	2	0	3	(2	1)	45	13	15	11	12	0	50	1	0	2	0	0	5	.225	.283	.298	.581
20	SD	NL	7	11	3	1	0	0	(0	0)	4	0	0	1	1	0	2	0	0	0	0	0	0	.273	.333	.364	.697
20	Sea	AL	18	59	15	4	0	1	(1	0)	22	5	6	6	6	0	13	0	0	0	0	0	1	.254	.323	.373	.696
	5 ML YEARS		253	704	159	27	3	19	(10	9)	249	66	75	69	61	4	200	3	4	5	0	0	19	.226	.288	.354	.642

Gleyber Torres

Bats: R **Throws:** R **Pos:** 2B-124;DH-9;PH-9;SS-6   **Ht:** 6'1" **Wt:** 205 **Born:** 12/13/1996 **Age:** 26

Year	Team	Lg	G	AB	H	2B	3B	HR	(Hm	Rd)	TB	R	RBI	RC	TBB	IBB	SO	HBP	SH	SF	SB	CS	GDP	Avg	OBP	Slg	OPS
2018	NYY	AL	123	431	117	16	1	24	(13	11)	207	54	77	78	42	3	122	5	1	5	6	2	8	.271	.340	.480	.820
2019	NYY	AL	144	546	152	26	0	38	(20	18)	292	96	90	101	48	3	129	3	1	6	5	2	10	.278	.337	.535	.871
2020	NYY	AL	42	136	33	8	0	3	(1	2)	50	17	16	18	22	0	28	2	0	1	1	0	5	.243	.356	.368	.724
2021	NYY	AL	127	459	119	22	0	9	(6	3)	168	50	51	59	50	1	104	1	2	4	14	6	12	.259	.331	.366	.697
2022	NYY	AL	140	526	135	28	1	24	(17	7)	237	73	76	71	39	2	129	3	1	3	10	5	12	.257	.310	.451	.761
	Postseason		22	80	26	5	0	5	(2	3)	46	14	15	19	12	0	15	0	0	0	4	0	3	.325	.413	.575	.988
	5 ML YEARS		576	2098	556	100	2	98	(57	41)	954	290	310	327	201	9	512	14	5	18	36	15	47	.265	.331	.455	.785

Touki Toussaint

TOO-key TOO-sahnt

Pitches: R **Bats:** R **Pos:** RP-6; SP-2   **Ht:** 6'3" **Wt:** 215 **Born:** 6/20/1996 **Age:** 27

Year	Team	Lg	G	GS	GF	IP	BFP	H	R	ER	HR	SH	SF	HB	TBB	IBB	SO	WP	W	L	Pct	Sv-Op	Hld	Vel	OPS	ERC	ERA
2022	Gwnntt	AAA	13	8	1	41.2	193	42	30	29	7	0	1	5	25	0	53	3	2	2	.500	0- -	-	-	.836	5.95	6.26
2022	Salt Lk	AAA	9	3	1	13.2	62	26	7	6	3	0	1	1	11	0	9	0	0	1	.000	0- -	-	-	.873	7.03	3.95
2018	Atl	NL	7	5	1	29.0	123	18	13	13	1	1	0	2	21	1	32	1	2	1	.667	0-0	0	93	.619	3.05	4.03
2019	Atl	NL	24	1	3	41.2	198	44	28	26	5	2	0	7	26	2	45	6	4	0	1.000	0-0	2	93	.810	6.05	5.62
2020	Atl	NL	7	5	0	24.1	120	27	28	24	7	1	0	5	16	0	30	2	0	2	.000	0-0	0	94	.954	8.17	8.88
2021	Atl	NL	11	10	1	50.0	216	43	28	25	11	2	2	6	22	1	48	2	3	3	.500	0-0	0	93	.777	4.77	4.50
2022	LAA	AL	8	2	2	25.1	108	15	13	13	2	0	0	4	19	0	26	2	1	1	.500	0-0	0	92	.611	3.76	4.62
	Postseason		2	0	0	3.0	13	1	0	0	0	0	0	0	4	0	2	0	1	0	1.000	0-0	0	95	.607	3.31	0.00
	5 ML YEARS		57	23	7	170.1	765	147	110	101	26	6	2	24	104	4	181	13	10	7	.588	0-0	2	93	.766	5.08	5.34

Ezequiel Tovar

Bats: R **Throws:** R **Pos:** SS-9   **Ht:** 6'0" **Wt:** 162 **Born:** 8/1/2001 **Age:** 21

Year	Team	Lg	G	AB	H	2B	3B	HR	(Hm	Rd)	TB	R	RBI	RC	TBB	IBB	SO	HBP	SH	SF	SB	CS	GDP	Avg	OBP	Slg	OPS
2019	2 Tms	Low	73	289	73	6	4	2	(-	-)	93	34	16	34	26	0	69	3	8	3	17	0	3	.253	.318	.322	.640
2021	2 Tms	Low	104	428	123	30	3	15	(-	-)	204	79	72	71	17	0	56	7	9	4	24	6	7	.287	.322	.477	.799
2022	Hrtfrd	AA	66	264	84	15	3	13	(-	-)	144	39	47	56	25	0	64	5	0	1	17	3	5	.318	.386	.545	.932
2022	Col	NL	9	33	7	1	0	1	(0	1)	11	2	2	2	2	0	9	0	0	0	0	0	0	.212	.257	.333	.590

Taylor Trammell

Bats: L **Throws:** L **Pos:** RF-34;CF-7;LF-3;PH-3;PR-3;DH-2 **Ht:** 6'2" **Wt:** 220 **Born:** 9/13/1997 **Age:** 25

							BATTING														RUNNING			AVERAGES			
Year	Team	Lg	G	AB	H	2B	3B	HR	(Hm	Rd)	TB	R	RBI	RC	TBB	IBB	SO	HBP	SH	SF	SB	CS	GDP	Avg	OBP	Slg	OPS
2022	Tacom	AAA	22	87	29	6	0	5	(-	-)	50	18	12	20	11	0	17	0	0	0	8	1	3	.333	.408	.575	.983
2021	Sea	AL	51	156	25	7	0	8	(3	5)	56	23	18	12	17	0	75	3	2	1	2	3	1	.160	.256	.359	.615
2022	Sea	AL	43	102	20	9	0	4	(2	2)	41	15	10	10	13	0	33	0	1	1	2	1	2	.196	.284	.402	.686
	2 ML YEARS		94	258	45	16	0	12	(5	7)	97	38	28	22	30	0	108	3	3	1	4	4	3	.174	.267	.376	.643

Blake Treinen

Pitches: R **Bats:** R **Pos:** RP-5 TRY-nen **Ht:** 6'5" **Wt:** 225 **Born:** 6/30/1988 **Age:** 35

			HOW MUCH PITCHED					WHAT HE GAVE UP										THE RESULTS							
Year	Team	Lg	G	GS	GF	IP	BFP	H	R	ER	HR	SH	SF	HB	TBB	IBB	SO	WP	W	L	Pct	Sv-Op	Hld	Vel	OPS	ERC	ERA
2022	OkCity	AAA	7	0	0	6.0	30	8	5	3	0	0	1	1	1	1	9	1	0	0	-	0- -	-	-	.704	4.19	4.50
2014	Was	NL	15	7	6	50.2	214	57	17	14	1	0	0	2	13	1	30	1	2	3	.400	0-0	0	95	.678	3.86	2.49
2015	Was	NL	60	0	17	67.2	280	62	32	29	4	1	1	2	32	6	65	4	2	5	.286	0-3	10	96	.692	3.76	3.86
2016	Was	NL	73	0	17	67.0	263	51	19	17	5	2	2	0	31	6	63	1	4	1	.800	1-3	22	95	.648	2.92	2.28
2017	2 Tms		72	0	35	75.2	325	80	35	33	6	0	3	5	25	3	74	4	3	6	.333	16-21	5	97	.736	4.24	3.93
2018	Oak	AL	68	0	58	80.1	315	46	12	7	2	1	0	1	21	3	100	6	9	2	.818	38-43	0	97	.417	1.21	0.78
2019	Oak	AL	57	0	35	58.2	266	58	33	32	9	1	1	1	37	1	59	1	6	5	.545	16-21	3	97	.778	5.39	4.91
2020	LAD	NL	27	0	3	25.2	107	23	15	11	1	0	1	2	8	1	22	2	3	3	.500	1-2	9	97	.621	3.03	3.86
2021	LAD	NL	72	0	10	72.1	286	46	20	16	5	0	1	3	25	1	85	3	6	5	.545	7-11	32	97	.512	1.97	1.99
2022	LAD	NL	5	0	1	5.0	17	1	1	1	1	0	0	0	1	0	6	0	1	1	.500	0-0	1	96	.368	0.65	1.80
17	Was	NL	37	0	11	37.2	169	48	24	24	3	0	3	3	13	1	32	1	0	2	.000	3-5	5	97	.832	5.71	5.73
17	Oak	AL	35	0	24	38.0	156	32	11	9	3	0	0	2	12	2	42	3	3	4	.429	13-16	5	97	.633	2.92	2.13
	Postseason		23	0	2	24.2	98	19	13	13	2	0	1	2	5	0	23	1	2	3	.400	1-1	4	97	.643	2.35	4.74
9 ML YEARS			449	7	182	503.0	2073	424	184	160	34	5	9	16	193	22	504	22	36	31	.537	79-104	87	97	.629	3.05	2.86

Alan Trejo

Bats: R **Throws:** R **Pos:** SS-20;2B-13;3B-2;PH-1 **Ht:** 6'2" **Wt:** 205 **Born:** 5/30/1996 **Age:** 27

							BATTING														RUNNING			AVERAGES			
Year	Team	Lg	G	AB	H	2B	3B	HR	(Hm	Rd)	TB	R	RBI	RC	TBB	IBB	SO	HBP	SH	SF	SB	CS	GDP	Avg	OBP	Slg	OPS
2022	Albq	AAA	67	274	81	20	1	16	(-	-)	151	46	52	52	10	0	64	6	0	3	2	2	4	.296	.331	.551	.882
2021	Col	NL	28	46	10	2	0	1	(1	0)	15	7	3	1	3	1	15	0	0	2	0	0	2	.217	.260	.326	.586
2022	Col	NL	35	118	32	6	0	4	(2	2)	50	15	17	17	5	0	31	2	0	0	1	2	3	.271	.312	.424	.736
	2 ML YEARS		63	164	42	8	0	5	(3	2)	65	22	20	18	8	1	46	2	0	1	1	2	5	.256	.297	.396	.693

Jose Trevino

Bats: R **Throws:** R **Pos:** C-112;PH-7;DH-1;PR-1 treh-VEEN-yo **Ht:** 5'10" **Wt:** 215 **Born:** 11/28/1992 **Age:** 30

							BATTING														RUNNING			AVERAGES			
Year	Team	Lg	G	AB	H	2B	3B	HR	(Hm	Rd)	TB	R	RBI	RC	TBB	IBB	SO	HBP	SH	SF	SB	CS	GDP	Avg	OBP	Slg	OPS
2018	Tex	AL	3	8	2	0	0	0	(0	0)	2	0	3	2	0	0	1	0	0	0	0	0	1	.250	.250	.250	.500
2019	Tex	AL	40	120	31	9	0	2	(1	1)	46	18	13	11	3	0	27	0	1	2	0	0	6	.258	.272	.383	.655
2020	Tex	AL	24	76	19	8	0	2	(0	2)	33	10	9	9	3	0	15	1	1	2	0	0	1	.250	.280	.434	.715
2021	Tex	AL	89	285	68	14	0	5	(3	2)	97	23	30	23	12	1	57	0	2	3	1	1	13	.239	.267	.340	.607
2022	NYY	AL	115	335	83	12	1	11	(7	4)	130	39	43	46	15	0	62	2	0	1	2	1	5	.248	.283	.388	.671
	5 ML YEARS		271	824	203	43	1	20	(11	9)	308	90	98	91	33	1	162	3	4	8	3	2	26	.246	.275	.374	.649

Lou Trivino

Pitches: R **Bats:** R **Pos:** RP-64 **Ht:** 6'5" **Wt:** 235 **Born:** 10/1/1991 **Age:** 31

			HOW MUCH PITCHED					WHAT HE GAVE UP										THE RESULTS							
Year	Team	Lg	G	GS	GF	IP	BFP	H	R	ER	HR	SH	SF	HB	TBB	IBB	SO	WP	W	L	Pct	Sv-Op	Hld	Vel	OPS	ERC	ERA
2018	Oak	AL	69	1	10	74.0	299	53	24	24	8	1	1	2	31	4	82	4	8	3	.727	4-9	23	98	.603	2.76	2.92
2019	Oak	AL	61	0	10	60.0	269	61	40	35	7	2	3	3	31	2	57	7	4	6	.400	0-5	17	97	.782	4.90	5.25
2020	Oak	AL	20	0	9	23.1	93	16	10	10	3	0	0	0	10	0	26	1	0	0	-	0-1	0	96	.605	2.76	3.86
2021	Oak	AL	71	0	44	73.2	310	58	32	26	5	2	1	4	34	2	67	7	7	8	.467	22-26	8	96	.622	3.12	3.18
2022	2 Tms		64	0	30	53.2	250	64	31	27	6	0	0	4	24	2	67	3	2	8	.200	11-14	4	96	.796	5.65	4.53
22	Oak	AL	39	0	23	32.0	157	46	25	23	5	0	0	2	14	2	45	2	1	6	.143	10-12	2	96	.906	7.37	6.47
22	NYY	AL	25	0	7	21.2	93	18	6	4	1	0	0	2	10	0	22	1	1	2	.333	1-2	2	96	.607	3.36	1.66
	Postseason		5	0	1	5.2	22	2	1	1	1	0	0	2	2	0	6	0	0	0	-	0-0	1	97	.551	2.44	1.59
5 ML YEARS			285	1	103	284.2	1221	252	137	122	29	5	5	13	130	10	299	22	21	25	.457	37-55	52	97	.687	3.81	3.86

Chadwick Tromp

Bats: R **Throws:** R **Pos:** C-1 **Ht:** 5'8" **Wt:** 221 **Born:** 3/21/1995 **Age:** 28

							BATTING														RUNNING			AVERAGES			
Year	Team	Lg	G	AB	H	2B	3B	HR	(Hm	Rd)	TB	R	RBI	RC	TBB	IBB	SO	HBP	SH	SF	SB	CS	GDP	Avg	OBP	Slg	OPS
2022	Gwnntt	AAA	70	249	63	11	0	12	(-	-)	110	34	41	32	16	0	55	0	0	1	0	1	11	.253	.297	.442	.739
2020	SF	NL	24	61	13	1	0	4	(2	2)	26	11	10	4	1	0	20	0	0	2	0	0	3	.213	.219	.426	.645
2021	SF	NL	9	18	4	0	0	1	(0	1)	7	1	2	2	0	0	4	0	0	0	0	0	0	.222	.222	.389	.611
2022	Atl	NL	1	4	3	2	0	0	(0	0)	5	0	3	2	0	0	0	0	0	0	0	0	0	.750	.750	1.250	2.000
	3 ML YEARS		34	83	20	3	0	5	(2	3)	38	12	15	8	1	0	24	0	0	2	0	0	4	.241	.244	.458	.702

Mike Trout

Bats: R Throws: R Pos: CF-111;DH-7;PH-2 **Ht: 6'2" Wt: 235 Born: 8/7/1991 Age: 31**

							BATTING													RUNNING			AVERAGES			
Year Team	Lg	G	AB	H	2B	3B	HR	(Hm	Rd)	TB	R	RBI	RC	TBB	IBB	SO	HBP	SH	SF	SB	CS	GDP	Avg	OBP	Slg	OPS
2011 LAA	AL	40	123	27	6	0	5	(-	-)	48	20	16	14	9	0	30	2	0		4	0	2	.220	.281	.390	.672
2012 LAA	AL	139	559	182	27	8	30	(16	14)	315	129	83	127	67	4	139	6	0	7	49	5	7	.326	.399	.564	.963
2013 LAA	AL	157	589	190	39	9	27	(13	14)	328	109	97	141	110	10	136	9	0	8	33	7	8	.323	.432	.557	.988
2014 LAA	AL	157	602	173	39	9	36	(19	17)	338	115	111	131	83	8	184	10	0	10	16	2	6	.287	.377	.561	.939
2015 LAA	AL	159	575	172	32	6	41	(20	21)	339	104	90	131	92	14	158	10	0	5	11	7	11	.299	.402	.590	.991
2016 LAA	AL	159	549	173	32	5	29	(14	15)	302	123	100	137	116	12	137	11	0	5	30	7	5	.315	.441	.550	.991
2017 LAA	AL	114	402	123	25	3	33	(20	13)	253	92	72	110	94	15	90	7	0	4	22	4	8	.306	.442	.629	1.071
2018 LAA	AL	140	471	147	24	4	39	(17	22)	296	101	79	140	122	25	124	10	0	4	24	2	5	.312	.460	.628	1.088
2019 LAA	AL	134	470	137	27	2	45	(21	24)	303	110	104	132	110	14	120	16	0	4	11	2	5	.291	.438	.645	1.083
2020 LAA	AL	53	199	56	9	2	17	(10	7)	120	41	46	49	35	4	56	3	0	4	1	1	1	.281	.390	.603	.993
2021 LAA	AL	36	117	39	8	1	8	(5	3)	73	23	18	36	27	5	41	2	0	0	2	0	0	.333	.466	.624	1.090
2022 LAA	AL	119	438	124	28	2	40	(21	19)	276	85	80	99	54	8	139	6	0	1	1	0	6	.283	.369	.630	.999
Postseason		3	12	1	0	0	0	(0	1)	4	1	1	0	3	0	2	0	0	0	0	0	0	.083	.267	.333	.600
12 ML YEARS		1407	5094	1543	296	51	350	(177	173)	2991	1052	896	1247	919	117	1354	92	0	53	204	37	64	.303	.415	.587	1.002

Yoshi Tsutsugo

Bats: L Throws: R Pos: 1B-35;DH-15;PH-1 tsoo-tsoo-go **Ht: 6'1" Wt: 225 Born: 11/26/1991 Age: 31**

							BATTING													RUNNING			AVERAGES			
Year Team	Lg	G	AB	H	2B	3B	HR	(Hm	Rd)	TB	R	RBI	RC	TBB	IBB	SO	HBP	SH	SF	SB	CS	GDP	Avg	OBP	Slg	OPS
2022 Buffalo	AAA	29	98	26	4	0	5	(-	-)	45	15	18	17	19	0	38	0	0	1	0	1	4	.265	.381	.459	.841
2020 TB	AL	51	157	31	5	1	8	(4	4)	62	27	24	22	26	1	50	1	0	1	0	0	5	.197	.314	.395	.708
2021 3 Tms		81	230	50	12	1	8	(3	5)	88	27	32	32	29	0	72	1	1	1	0	1	3	.217	.307	.383	.689
2022 Pit	NL	50	170	29	4	0	2	(1	1)	39	11	19	19	19	0	50	0	0	4	0	1	3	.171	.249	.229	.478
21 TB	AL	26	78	13	4	0	0	(0	0)	17	5	5	4	8	0	27	0	1	0	0	0	1	.167	.244	.218	.462
21 LAD	NL	12	25	3	0	0	0	(0	0)	3	2	2	2	6	0	12	0	0	0	0	0	0	.120	.290	.120	.410
21 Pit	NL	43	127	34	8	1	8	(3	5)	68	20	25	26	15	0	33	1	0	1	0	1	2	.268	.347	.535	.883
Postseason		8	16	2	0	0	0	(0	0)	2	0	0	0	0	0	3	0	0	0	0	0	1	.125	.125	.125	.250
3 ML YEARS		182	557	110	21	2	18	(8	10)	189	65	75	64	74	1	172	2	1	6	0	1	11	.197	.291	.339	.630

Cole Tucker

Bats: B Throws: R Pos: RF-12;2B-6;SS-3;PH-1;PR-1 **Ht: 6'3" Wt: 200 Born: 7/3/1996 Age: 26**

							BATTING													RUNNING			AVERAGES			
Year Team	Lg	G	AB	H	2B	3B	HR	(Hm	Rd)	TB	R	RBI	RC	TBB	IBB	SO	HBP	SH	SF	SB	CS	GDP	Avg	OBP	Slg	OPS
2022 Indy	AAA	10	37	5	1	0	0	(-	-)	6	5	4	0	5	0	12	0	0	0	1	0	1	.135	.238	.162	.400
2022 Reno	AAA	35	114	27	4	0	2	(-	-)	37	14	13	10	11	0	35	0	0	3	4	2	4	.237	.297	.325	.621
2019 Pit	NL	56	147	31	10	3	2	(1	1)	53	16	13	14	10	1	40	1	1	0	0	0	2	.211	.266	.361	.626
2020 Pit	NL	37	109	24	3	0	1	(0	1)	30	17	8	6	5	0	31	0	1	1	1	0	3	.220	.252	.275	.527
2021 Pit	NL	43	117	26	4	2	2	(1	1)	40	15	12	14	13	0	33	0	1	0	2	2	1	.222	.298	.342	.640
2022 Pit	NL	18	63	11	1	1	0	(0	0)	14	3	2	0	0	0	25	0	0	0	1	0	1	.175	.175	.222	.397
4 ML YEARS		154	436	92	18	6	5	(2	3)	137	51	35	34	28	1	129	1	2	2	4	2	8	.211	.259	.314	.573

Kyle Tucker

Bats: L Throws: R Pos: RF-147;DH-3;PH-2 **Ht: 6'4" Wt: 199 Born: 1/17/1997 Age: 26**

							BATTING													RUNNING			AVERAGES			
Year Team	Lg	G	AB	H	2B	3B	HR	(Hm	Rd)	TB	R	RBI	RC	TBB	IBB	SO	HBP	SH	SF	SB	CS	GDP	Avg	OBP	Slg	OPS
2018 Hou	AL	28	64	9	2	1	0	(0	0)	13	10	4	0	6	0	13	2	0	0	1	1	1	.141	.236	.203	.439
2019 Hou	AL	22	67	18	6	0	4	(1	3)	36	15	11	10	4	1	20	1	0	0	5	0	1	.269	.319	.537	.857
2020 Hou	AL	58	209	56	12	6	9	(4	5)	107	33	42	44	18	2	46	0	0	1	8	1	2	.268	.325	.512	.837
2021 Hou	AL	140	506	149	37	3	30	(15	15)	282	83	92	97	53	5	90	1	0	5	14	2	10	.294	.359	.557	.917
2022 Hou	AL	150	544	140	28	1	30	(12	18)	260	71	107	96	59	4	95	1	0	2	25	4	11	.257	.330	.478	.808
Postseason		38	122	34	4	0	5	(2	3)	53	19	21	24	10	0	27	0	0	1	6	0	2	.279	.331	.434	.765
5 ML YEARS		398	1390	372	85	11	73	(32	41)	698	212	256	247	140	12	264	5	0	8	53	8	25	.268	.335	.502	.837

Tanner Tully

Pitches: L Bats: L Pos: RP-3 **Ht: 6'2" Wt: 205 Born: 11/30/1994 Age: 28**

		HOW MUCH PITCHED					WHAT HE GAVE UP											THE RESULTS							
Year Team	Lg	G	GS	GF	IP	BFP	H	R	ER	HR	SH	SF	HB	TBB	IBB	SO	WP	W	L	Pct	Sv-Op	Hld	Vel	OPS	ERC	ERA
2022 Clmbs	AAA	24	20	1	122.0	531	142	70	64	12	1	5	5	26	0	98	1	8	6	.571	0- -	-	-	.747	4.37	4.72
2022 Cle	AL	3	0	2	6.0	30	8	4	4	1	0	0	0	6	1	2	1	0	0	-	0-0	0	91	1.050	9.37	6.00

Spencer Turnbull

Pitches: R Bats: R Pos: P **Ht: 6'3" Wt: 210 Born: 9/18/1992 Age: 30**

		HOW MUCH PITCHED					WHAT HE GAVE UP											THE RESULTS							
Year Team	Lg	G	GS	GF	IP	BFP	H	R	ER	HR	SH	SF	HB	TBB	IBB	SO	WP	W	L	Pct	Sv-Op	Hld	Vel	OPS	ERC	ERA
2018 Det	AL	4	3	0	16.1	69	17	11	11	1	0	0	0	4	0	15	1	0	2	.000	0-0	1	-	.658	3.41	6.06
2019 Det	AL	30	30	0	148.1	656	154	86	76	14	1	4	16	59	1	146	9	3	17	.150	0-0	0	-	.763	4.69	4.61
2020 Det	AL	11	11	0	56.2	242	47	25	25	2	2	1	2	29	1	51	0	4	4	.500	0-0	0	-	.662	3.24	3.97
2021 Det	AL	9	9	0	50.0	201	37	18	16	2	1	1	5	12	0	44	0	4	2	.667	0-0	0	-	.556	2.14	2.88
4 ML YEARS		54	53	0	271.1	1168	255	140	128	19	4	6	23	104	2	256	10	11	25	.306	0-0	1	-	.700	3.79	4.25

Justin Turner

Bats: R **Throws:** R **Pos:** 3B-66;DH-61;PH-1   **Ht:** 5'11" **Wt:** 202 **Born:** 11/23/1984 **Age:** 38

									BATTING											RUNNING			AVERAGES			
Year	Team	Lg	G	AB	H	2B	3B	HR	(Hm | Rd)	TB	R	RBI	RC	TBB	IBB	SO	HBP	SH	SF	SB	CS	GDP	Avg	OBP	Slg	OPS
2009	Bal	AL	12	18	3	0	0	0	(0 | 0)	3	2	3	1	4	0	3	0	0	0	0	0	1	.167	.318	.167	.485
2010	2 Tms		9	17	1	1	0	0	(0 | 0)	2	1	0	0	1	0	3	0	0	0	0	0	0	.059	.111	.118	.229
2011	NYM	NL	117	435	113	30	0	4	(3 | 1)	155	49	51	59	39	2	59	10	2	1	7	2	9	.260	.334	.356	.690
2012	NYM	NL	94	171	46	13	1	2	(2 | 0)	67	20	19	19	9	0	24	4	0	1	1	1	9	.269	.319	.392	.711
2013	NYM	NL	86	200	56	13	1	2	(0 | 2)	77	12	16	17	11	1	34	1	1	1	0	1	6	.280	.319	.385	.704
2014	LAD	NL	109	288	98	21	1	7	(5 | 2)	142	46	43	55	28	1	58	4	0	2	6	1	6	.340	.404	.493	.897
2015	LAD	NL	126	385	113	26	1	16	(8 | 8)	189	55	60	65	36	1	71	13	1	4	5	2	10	.294	.370	.491	.861
2016	LAD	NL	151	556	153	34	3	27	(11 | 16)	274	79	90	96	48	1	107	10	0	8	4	1	16	.275	.339	.493	.832
2017	LAD	NL	130	457	147	32	0	21	(10 | 11)	242	72	71	95	59	5	56	19	1	7	7	1	12	.322	.415	.530	.945
2018	LAD	NL	103	365	114	31	1	14	(9 | 5)	189	62	52	71	47	3	54	12	0	2	2	1	10	.312	.406	.518	.924
2019	LAD	NL	135	479	139	24	0	27	(14 | 13)	244	80	67	84	51	1	88	14	0	5	2	0	11	.290	.372	.509	.881
2020	LAD	NL	42	150	46	9	1	4	(4 | 0)	69	26	23	32	18	0	26	6	0	1	1	0	2	.307	.400	.460	.860
2021	LAD	NL	151	533	148	22	0	27	(13 | 14)	251	87	87	90	61	0	98	12	0	6	3	0	12	.278	.361	.471	.832
2022	LAD	NL	128	468	130	36	0	13	(11 | 2)	205	61	81	79	50	1	89	6	0	8	3	0	13	.278	.350	.438	.788
	10 Bal	AL	5	9	0	0	0	0	(0 | 0)	0	0	0	0	0	0	3	0	0	0	0	0	0	.000	.000	.000	.000
	10 NYM	NL	4	8	1	1	0	0	(0 | 0)	2	1	0	0	1	0	0	0	0	0	0	0	0	.125	.222	.250	.472
	Postseason		82	302	83	19	1	13	(6 | 7)	143	43	42	56	35	1	56	13	0	2	5	0	6	.275	.372	.474	.846
	14 ML YEARS		1393	4522	1307	292	9	164	(90 | 74)	2109	652	663	763	462	16	770	111	5	46	41	10	117	.289	.366	.466	.832

Trea Turner

Bats: R **Throws:** R **Pos:** SS-160   TRAY   **Ht:** 6'2" **Wt:** 185 **Born:** 6/30/1993 **Age:** 30

									BATTING											RUNNING			AVERAGES			
Year	Team	Lg	G	AB	H	2B	3B	HR	(Hm	Rd)	TB	R	RBI	RC	TBB	IBB	SO	HBP	SH	SF	SB	CS	GDP	Avg	OBP	Slg	OPS
2015	Was	NL	27	40	9	1	0	1	(0	1)	13	5	1	2	4	0	12	0	0	0	2	2	0	.225	.295	.325	.620
2016	Was	NL	73	307	105	14	8	13	(7	6)	174	53	40	62	14	0	59	1	0	2	33	6	1	.342	.370	.567	.937
2017	Was	NL	98	412	117	24	6	11	(6	5)	186	75	45	67	30	0	80	4	0	1	46	8	4	.284	.338	.451	.789
2018	Was	NL	162	664	180	27	6	19	(10	9)	276	103	73	105	69	3	132	5	2	0	43	9	7	.271	.344	.416	.760
2019	Was	NL	122	521	155	37	5	19	(11	8)	259	96	57	87	43	2	113	3	0	2	35	5	10	.298	.353	.497	.850
2020	Was	NL	59	233	78	15	4	12	(5	7)	137	46	41	52	22	0	36	2	0	2	12	4	5	.335	.394	.588	.982
2021	2 Tms		148	595	195	34	3	28	(16	12)	319	107	77	109	41	2	110	6	0	4	32	5	18	.328	.375	.536	.911
2022	LAD	NL	160	652	194	39	4	21	(9	12)	304	101	100	106	45	1	131	3	0	6	27	3	9	.298	.343	.466	.809
	21 Was	NL	96	388	125	17	3	18	(10	8)	202	66	49	66	26	0	77	4	0	2	21	3	13	.322	.369	.521	.890
	21 LAD	NL	52	207	70	17	0	10	(6	4)	117	41	28	43	15	2	33	2	0	2	11	2	5	.338	.385	.565	.950
	Postseason		39	167	38	7	0	1	(1	0)	48	19	6	10	10	1	45	1	0	1	5	0	2	.228	.274	.287	.561
	8 ML YEARS		849	3424	1033	191	36	124	(64	60)	1668	586	434	590	268	8	673	24	2	17	230	42	54	.302	.355	.487	.842

Kyle Tyler

Pitches: R **Bats:** R **Pos:** RP-2   **Ht:** 6'0" **Wt:** 185 **Born:** 12/27/1996 **Age:** 26

			HOW MUCH PITCHED					WHAT HE GAVE UP										THE RESULTS						
Year	Team	Lg	G	GS	GF	IP	BFP	H	R	ER	HR	SH	SF	HB	TBB	IBB	SO	WP	W	L	Pct	Sv-Op	Hld	Vel	OPS	ERC	ERA
2022	ElPaso	AAA	15	2	0	21.2	93	11	12	12	2	0	0	1	19	0	27	2	2	1	.667	0--	-	-	.594	3.37	4.98
2021	LAA	AL	5	0	3	12.1	52	8	4	4	1	0	2	2	6	0	6	0	0	0	-	0-0	0	91	.593	3.00	2.92
2022	SD	NL	2	0	1	4.0	14	2	0	0	0	0	0	0	1	0	2	0	1	0	1.000	0-0	0	90	.368	1.01	0.00
	2 ML YEARS		7	0	4	16.1	66	10	4	4	1	0	2	2	7	0	8	0	1	0	1.000			91	.542	2.40	2.20

Edwin Uceta

Pitches: R **Bats:** R **Pos:** RP-10   **Ht:** 6'0" **Wt:** 155 **Born:** 1/9/1998 **Age:** 25

			HOW MUCH PITCHED					WHAT HE GAVE UP										THE RESULTS						
Year	Team	Lg	G	GS	GF	IP	BFP	H	R	ER	HR	SH	SF	HB	TBB	IBB	SO	WP	W	L	Pct	Sv-Op	Hld	Vel	OPS	ERC	ERA
2022	Reno	AAA	28	5	7	50.0	214	35	29	27	9	0	2	5	30	2	70	2	6	1	.857	0--	-	-	.706	4.12	4.86
2021	LAD	NL	14	1	5	20.1	92	19	18	15	3	2	3	0	12	1	25	1	0	3	.000	0-0	0	93	.758	4.62	6.64
2022	Ari	NL	10	0	5	17.0	73	14	12	11	2	0	0	1	7	0	13	1	0	0	-	0-0	0	94	.671	3.43	5.82
	2 ML YEARS		24	1	10	37.1	165	33	30	26	5	2	3	1	19	1	38	2	0	3	.000			93	.718	4.06	6.27

Erich Uelmen

Pitches: R **Bats:** R **Pos:** RP-25   **Ht:** 6'3" **Wt:** 195 **Born:** 5/19/1996 **Age:** 27

			HOW MUCH PITCHED					WHAT HE GAVE UP										THE RESULTS						
Year	Team	Lg	G	GS	GF	IP	BFP	H	R	ER	HR	SH	SF	HB	TBB	IBB	SO	WP	W	L	Pct	Sv-Op	Hld	Vel	OPS	ERC	ERA
2022	Iowa	AAA	28	0	19	42.0	179	29	19	13	2	4	1	4	23	2	52	1	3	3	.500	6--	-	-	.599	2.88	2.79
2022	ChC	NL	25	0	8	27.0	122	25	15	14	3	0	3	6	12	1	21	1	2	1	.667	1-2	3	94	.739	4.70	4.67

Duane Underwood Jr.

Pitches: R **Bats:** R **Pos:** RP-50; SP-1   **Ht:** 6'2" **Wt:** 225 **Born:** 7/20/1994 **Age:** 28

			HOW MUCH PITCHED					WHAT HE GAVE UP										THE RESULTS						
Year	Team	Lg	G	GS	GF	IP	BFP	H	R	ER	HR	SH	SF	HB	TBB	IBB	SO	WP	W	L	Pct	Sv-Op	Hld	Vel	OPS	ERC	ERA
2018	ChC	NL	1	1	0	4.0	16	2	1	1	1	0	0	0	3	0	3	0	0	1	.000	0-0	0	92	.697	3.91	2.25
2019	ChC	NL	12	0	1	11.2	51	13	7	7	2	0	0	1	3	0	13	1	0	0	-	0-0	0	95	.865	5.01	5.40
2020	ChC	NL	17	0	3	20.2	88	25	13	13	5	0	1	6	1	1	27	2	1	0	1.000	0-0	1	95	.939	6.33	5.66
2021	Pit	NL	43	0	6	72.2	320	77	40	35	9	0	4	4	27	1	65	3	2	3	.400	0-0	2	94	.776	4.66	4.33
2022	Pit	NL	51	1	9	57.1	259	58	35	28	1	0	1	5	25	1	57	5	1	6	.143	1-4	10	96	.660	3.89	4.40
	5 ML YEARS		124	2	19	166.1	734	175	96	84	18	0	6	11	64	3	165	11	4	10	.286	1-4	13	95	.760	4.60	4.55

Justin Upton

Bats: R **Throws:** R **Pos:** DH-11;RF-4;LF-2;PH-2 **Ht:** 6'1" **Wt:** 215 **Born:** 8/25/1987 **Age:** 35

Year	Team	Lg	G	AB	H	2B	3B	HR	(Hm	Rd)	TB	R	RBI	RC	TBB	IBB	SO	HBP	SH	SF	SB	CS	GDP	Avg	OBP	Slg	OPS
2022	Tacom	AAA	12	45	9	2	0	2	(-	-)	17	8	6	5	6	0	18	0	0	1	0	0	0	.200	.288	.378	.666
2007	Ari	NL	43	140	31	8	3	2	(2	0)	51	17	11	13	11	4	37	1	0	0	2	0	3	.221	.283	.364	.647
2008	Ari	NL	108	356	89	19	6	15	(12	3)	165	52	42	47	54	6	121	4	0	3	1	4	3	.250	.353	.463	.816
2009	Ari	NL	138	526	158	30	7	26	(14	12)	280	84	86	94	55	3	137	2	1	4	20	5	10	.300	.366	.532	.899
2010	Ari	NL	133	495	135	27	3	17	(8	9)	219	73	69	73	64	5	152	4	1	7	18	8	20	.273	.356	.442	.799
2011	Ari	NL	159	592	171	39	5	31	(20	11)	313	105	88	103	59	9	126	19	0	4	21	9	8	.289	.369	.529	.898
2012	Ari	NL	150	554	155	24	4	17	(11	6)	238	107	67	82	63	5	121	5	0	6	18	8	7	.280	.355	.430	.785
2013	Atl	NL	149	558	147	27	2	27	(13	14)	259	94	70	84	75	4	161	5	1	4	8	1	12	.263	.354	.464	.818
2014	Atl	NL	154	566	153	34	2	29	(18	11)	278	77	102	84	60	1	171	6	0	8	8	4	10	.270	.342	.491	.833
2015	SD	NL	150	542	136	26	3	26	(15	11)	246	85	81	85	68	5	159	4	0	5	19	5	10	.251	.336	.454	.790
2016	Det	AL	153	570	140	28	2	31	(14	17)	265	81	87	77	50	3	179	4	0	5	9	4	15	.246	.310	.465	.775
2017	2 Tms	AL	152	557	152	44	0	35	(17	18)	301	100	109	109	74	3	180	3	0	1	14	5	9	.273	.361	.540	.901
2018	LAA	AL	145	533	137	18	1	30	(22	8)	247	80	85	79	64	1	176	10	0	6	8	2	12	.257	.344	.463	.808
2019	LAA	AL	63	219	47	8	0	12	(5	7)	91	34	40	30	32	0	78	0	0	1	5	1	5	.215	.309	.416	.724
2020	LAA	AL	42	147	30	5	0	9	(5	4)	62	20	22	17	11	0	43	7	0	1	0	2	6	.204	.289	.422	.711
2021	LAA	AL	89	318	67	12	0	17	(13	4)	130	47	41	37	39	0	107	1	0	3	4	1	11	.211	.296	.409	.705
2022	Sea	AL	17	48	6	1	0	1	(1	0)	10	2	3	2	6	0	23	3	0	0	0	0	0	.125	.263	.208	.471
17	Det	AL	125	459	128	37	0	28	(13	15)	249	81	94	98	57	2	147	3	0	1	10	5	6	.279	.362	.542	.904
17	LAA	AL	27	98	24	7	0	7	(4	3)	52	19	15	11	17	1	33	0	0	0	4	0	3	.245	.357	.531	.887
	Postseason		15	48	11	2	1	2	(0	2)	21	7	4	7	10	0	13	2	0	0	1	0	0	.229	.383	.438	.821
16 ML YEARS			1845	6721	1754	350	38	325	(190	135)	3155	1058	1003	1016	785	49	1971	78	3	59	151	59	142	.261	.342	.469	.812

Jose Urena

Pitches: R **Bats:** R **Pos:** SP-17; RP-4 oo-RAIN-yuh **Ht:** 6'2" **Wt:** 208 **Born:** 9/12/1991 **Age:** 31

Year	Team	Lg	G	GS	GF	IP	BFP	H	R	ER	HR	SH	SF	HB	TBB	IBB	SO	WP	W	L	Pct	Sv-Op	Hld	Vel	OPS	ERC	ERA
2022	Albq	AAA	5	5	0	21.0	101	33	18	17	1	0	0	1	12	0	14	1	0	1	.000	0- -	-	-	.921	8.53	7.29
2015	Mia	NL	20	9	4	61.2	274	73	37	36	5	3	5	3	25	2	28	2	1	5	.167	0-1	0	94	.818	5.27	5.25
2016	Mia	NL	28	12	4	83.2	373	91	59	57	11	3	4	6	29	6	58	0	4	9	.308	1-3	1	95	.800	4.70	6.13
2017	Mia	NL	34	28	2	169.2	724	152	77	72	26	5	3	14	64	4	113	5	14	7	.667	0-0	0	95	.735	4.07	3.82
2018	Mia	NL	31	31	0	174.0	712	155	78	77	19	5	4	12	51	8	130	2	9	12	.429	0-0	0	96	.690	3.40	3.98
2019	Mia	NL	24	13	8	84.2	369	99	53	49	13	1	2	2	26	3	62	2	4	10	.286	3-5	0	96	.818	5.16	5.21
2020	Mia	NL	5	5	0	23.1	104	22	15	14	4	0	0	2	13	0	15	1	0	3	.000	0-0	0	95	.783	5.31	5.40
2021	Det	AL	26	18	1	100.2	456	119	70	65	14	0	2	4	42	0	67	4	4	8	.333	0-0	1	94	.837	5.68	5.81
2022	2 Tms	NL	21	17	1	97.0	432	109	62	54	11	0	6	1	43	0	63	2	3	8	.273	0-0	0	96	.776	5.13	5.01
22	Mil	NL	4	0	1	7.2	36	7	5	3	1	0	2	0	5	0	3	1	0	0	-	0-0	0	96	.713	4.55	3.52
22	Col	NL	17	17	0	89.1	396	102	57	51	10	0	4	1	38	0	60	1	3	8	.273	0-0	0	96	.781	5.19	5.14
8 ML YEARS			189	133	20	794.2	3444	820	451	424	103	17	26	44	293	23	536	18	39	62	.386	4-9	2	95	.768	4.55	4.80

Julio Urias

Pitches: L **Bats:** L **Pos:** SP-31 oo-REE-ahs **Ht:** 6'0" **Wt:** 225 **Born:** 8/12/1996 **Age:** 26

Year	Team	Lg	G	GS	GF	IP	BFP	H	R	ER	HR	SH	SF	HB	TBB	IBB	SO	WP	W	L	Pct	Sv-Op	Hld	Vel	OPS	ERC	ERA
2016	LAD	NL	18	15	1	77.0	336	81	32	29	5	4	1	4	31	0	84	3	5	2	.714	0-0	0	93	.728	4.37	3.39
2017	LAD	NL	5	5	0	23.1	102	23	15	14	1	2	0	1	14	1	11	1	0	2	.000	0-0	0	93	.768	4.61	5.40
2018	LAD	NL	3	0	3	4.0	13	1	0	0	0	0	0	0	0	0	7	0	0	0	-	0-0	0	93	.154	0.14	0.00
2019	LAD	NL	37	8	7	79.2	326	59	28	22	7	0	1	5	27	1	85	2	4	3	.571	4-5	5	95	.603	2.60	2.49
2020	LAD	NL	11	10	0	55.0	224	45	20	20	5	0	1	0	18	0	45	2	3	0	1.000	0-0	0	94	.608	2.78	3.27
2021	LAD	NL	32	32	0	185.2	745	151	67	61	19	7	2	7	38	3	195	2	20	3	.870	0-0	0	93	.614	2.48	2.96
2022	LAD	NL	31	31	0	175.0	689	127	51	42	23	0	4	5	41	0	166	0	17	7	.708	0-0	0	93	.599	2.33	2.16
	Postseason		22	5	4	53.2	213	41	22	21	9	1	3	0	12	1	54	2	7	3	.700	1-2	1	94	.636	2.53	3.52
7 ML YEARS			137	101	11	599.2	2435	487	213	188	60	13	9	22	169	5	593	10	49	17	.742	4-5	5	94	.627	2.76	2.82

Luis Urias

Bats: R **Throws:** R **Pos:** 3B-73;2B-46;SS-24;PH-7 oo-REE-ahs **Ht:** 5'9" **Wt:** 186 **Born:** 6/3/1997 **Age:** 26

Year	Team	Lg	G	AB	H	2B	3B	HR	(Hm	Rd)	TB	R	RBI	RC	TBB	IBB	SO	HBP	SH	SF	SB	CS	GDP	Avg	OBP	Slg	OPS
2018	SD	NL	12	48	10	1	0	2	(1	1)	17	5	5	6	3	0	10	1	0	1	1	0	0	.208	.264	.354	.618
2019	SD	NL	71	215	48	8	1	4	(1	3)	70	27	24	22	25	0	56	9	0	0	0	1	8	.223	.329	.326	.655
2020	Mil	NL	41	109	26	4	1	0	(0	0)	32	11	11	11	10	0	32	1	0	0	2	2	4	.239	.308	.294	.602
2021	Mil	NL	150	490	122	25	1	23	(11	12)	218	77	75	80	63	3	116	10	1	3	5	1	9	.249	.345	.445	.789
2022	Mil	NL	119	406	97	17	1	16	(6	10)	164	54	47	48	50	0	99	11	0	5	1	2	9	.239	.335	.404	.739
	Postseason		4	11	3	0	0	0	(0	0)	3	1	0	1	3	0	0	1	0	0	0	0	0	.273	.467	.273	.739
5 ML YEARS			393	1268	303	55	4	45	(19	26)	501	174	162	167	151	3	313	32	1	9	9	6	30	.239	.333	.395	.728

Ramon Urias

Bats: R **Throws:** R **Pos:** 3B-98;2B-21;SS-8;PH-6;DH-2;PR-1 **Ht:** 6'0" **Wt:** 190 **Born:** 6/3/1994 **Age:** 29

Year	Team	Lg	G	AB	H	2B	3B	HR	(Hm	Rd)	TB	R	RBI	RC	TBB	IBB	SO	HBP	SH	SF	SB	CS	GDP	Avg	OBP	Slg	OPS
2020	Bal	AL	10	25	9	2	0	1	(0	1)	14	3	3	6	2	0	6	0	0	0	0	0	1	.360	.407	.560	.967
2021	Bal	AL	85	262	73	14	0	7	(4	3)	108	33	38	46	28	0	76	6	0	0	1	2	3	.279	.361	.412	.774
2022	Bal	AL	118	403	100	17	1	16	(8	8)	167	50	51	53	30	1	98	5	3	4	1	0	7	.248	.305	.414	.720
3 ML YEARS			213	690	182	33	1	24	(12	12)	289	86	92	105	60	1	180	11	3	4	2	2	11	.264	.331	.419	.750

426

Jose Urquidy

Pitches: R Bats: R Pos: SP-28; RP-1   Ht: 6'0" Wt: 217 Born: 5/1/1995 Age: 28

				HOW MUCH PITCHED					WHAT HE GAVE UP												THE RESULTS							
Year	Team	Lg	G	GS	GF	IP	BFP	H	R	ER	HR	SH	SF	HB	TBB	IBB	SO	WP	W	L	Pct	Sv-Op	Hld	Vel	OPS	ERC	ERA
2019	Hou	AL	9	7	0	41.0	167	38	18	18	6	2	0	0	7	0	40	4	2	1	.667	0-0	0	93	.678	3.05	3.95
2020	Hou	AL	5	5	0	29.2	116	22	9	9	4	0	0	1	8	0	17	0	1	1	.500	0-0	0	93	.594	2.63	2.73
2021	Hou	AL	20	20	0	107.0	423	87	43	43	17	2	1	2	19	0	90	2	8	3	.727	0-0	0	93	.663	2.67	3.62
2022	Hou	AL	29	28	0	164.1	681	154	74	72	29	0	6	7	38	0	134	5	13	8	.619	0-0	0	94	.730	3.73	3.94
	Postseason		11	6	1	33.1	146	33	17	15	7	0	1	1	10	0	32	1	3	2	.600	0-0	0	94	.734	4.33	4.05
	4 ML YEARS		63	60	0	342.0	1387	301	144	142	56	4	7	10	72	0	281	11	24	13	.649	0-0	0	93	.692	3.21	3.74

Gio Urshela

Bats: R Throws: R Pos: 3B-136;DH-4;PH-3;SS-2   urr-SHELL-ah   Ht: 6'0" Wt: 215 Born: 10/11/1991 Age: 31

									BATTING														RUNNING			AVERAGES			
Year	Team	Lg	G	AB	H	2B	3B	HR	(Hm	Rd)	TB	R	RBI	RC	TBB	IBB	SO	HBP	SH	SF	SB	CS	GDP	Avg	OBP	Slg	OPS
2015	Cle	AL	81	267	60	8	1	6	(3	3)	88	25	21	19	18	0	58	2	1	0	0	1	9	.225	.279	.330	.608
2017	Cle	AL	67	156	35	7	0	1	(0	1)	45	14	15	10	8	0	22	0	1	0	0	0	6	.224	.262	.288	.551
2018	Tor	AL	19	43	10	1	0	1	(1	0)	14	7	3	2	2	0	10	1	0	0	0	0	1	.233	.283	.326	.608
2019	NYY	AL	132	442	139	34	0	21	(8	13)	236	73	74	80	25	1	87	5	0	4	1	1	13	.314	.355	.534	.889
2020	NYY	AL	43	151	45	11	0	6	(6	0)	74	24	30	31	18	0	25	1	0	4	1	0	6	.298	.368	.490	.858
2021	NYY	AL	116	420	112	18	2	14	(6	8)	176	42	49	50	20	0	109	1	0	1	1	0	16	.267	.301	.419	.720
2022	Min	AL	144	501	143	27	3	13	(7	6)	215	61	64	63	41	2	96	2	0	7	1	0	21	.285	.338	.429	.767
	Postseason		22	76	16	1	0	3	(0	3)	26	8	8	8	4	0	18	0	1	1	0	0	1	.211	.247	.342	.589
	7 ML YEARS		602	1980	544	106	6	62	(31	31)	848	246	256	255	132	3	407	12	2	16	4	2	72	.275	.321	.428	.750

Cesar Valdez

Pitches: R Bats: R Pos: RP-1   Ht: 6'2" Wt: 225 Born: 3/17/1985 Age: 38

				HOW MUCH PITCHED					WHAT HE GAVE UP												THE RESULTS							
Year	Team	Lg	G	GS	GF	IP	BFP	H	R	ER	HR	SH	SF	HB	TBB	IBB	SO	WP	W	L	Pct	Sv-Op	Hld	Vel	OPS	ERC	ERA
2022	Salt Lk	AAA	23	23	0	146.1	586	138	69	64	14	2	5	2	22	0	123	4	10	5	.667	0- -		-	.686	2.87	3.94
2010	Ari	NL	9	2	3	20.0	97	29	19	17	2	0	0	1	10	2	13	3	1	2	.333	0-0	0	89	.889	7.29	7.65
2017	2 Tms	AL	11	4	5	30.2	140	41	29	26	7	0	0	1	11	1	21	1	1	1	.500	0-0	0	88	.988	7.11	7.63
2020	Bal	AL	9	0	7	14.1	53	7	3	2	0	0	1	0	3	0	12	1	1	1	.500	3-3	0	86	.413	0.84	1.26
2021	Bal	AL	39	0	16	46.0	210	62	32	30	8	0	1	1	14	2	45	2	2	2	.500	8-13	0	85	.892	6.33	5.87
2022	LAA	AL	1	0	1	1.0	5	2	2	1	0	0	0	0	0	0	0	0	0	0		0-0	0	86	7.48	9.00	
17	Oak	AL	4	1	2	9.1	44	14	10	10	4	0	0	0	4	0	5	0	0	0	-	0-0	0	88	1.134	10.35	9.64
17	Tor	AL	7	3	3	21.1	96	27	19	16	3	0	0	1	7	1	16	1	1	1	.500	0-0	0	88	.921	5.81	6.75
	5 ML YEARS		69	6	32	112.0	505	141	85	76	17	0	2	3	38	5	91	7	5	6	.455	11-16	0	87	.867	5.79	6.11

Framber Valdez

Pitches: L Bats: R Pos: SP-31   Ht: 5'11" Wt: 239 Born: 11/19/1993 Age: 29

				HOW MUCH PITCHED					WHAT HE GAVE UP												THE RESULTS							
Year	Team	Lg	G	GS	GF	IP	BFP	H	R	ER	HR	SH	SF	HB	TBB	IBB	SO	WP	W	L	Pct	Sv-Op	Hld	Vel	OPS	ERC	ERA
2018	Hou	AL	8	5	0	37.0	154	22	10	9	3	0	4	2	24	0	34	5	4	1	.800	0-0	0	92	.595	3.20	2.19
2019	Hou	AL	26	8	7	70.2	329	74	51	46	9	0	4	4	44	0	68	4	4	7	.364	0-0	0	93	.790	5.65	5.86
2020	Hou	AL	11	10	0	70.2	288	63	32	28	5	1	3	5	16	0	76	6	5	3	.625	0-0	0	93	.635	2.94	3.57
2021	Hou	AL	22	22	0	134.2	572	110	52	47	12	1	1	11	58	1	125	9	11	6	.647	0-0	0	93	.641	3.42	3.14
2022	Hou	AL	31	31	0	201.1	827	166	71	63	11	2	2	11	67	0	194	11	17	6	.739	0-0	0	94	.600	2.82	2.82
	Postseason		9	8	1	43.2	182	42	23	22	9	0	0	2	18	0	42	0	4	2	.667	0-0	0	94	.797	5.06	4.53
	5 ML YEARS		98	76	7	514.1	2170	435	216	193	40	4	10	35	209	1	497	35	41	23	.641	0-0	0	93	.644	3.38	3.38

Phillips Valdez

Pitches: R Bats: R Pos: RP-13   Ht: 6'2" Wt: 160 Born: 11/16/1991 Age: 31

				HOW MUCH PITCHED					WHAT HE GAVE UP												THE RESULTS							
Year	Team	Lg	G	GS	GF	IP	BFP	H	R	ER	HR	SH	SF	HB	TBB	IBB	SO	WP	W	L	Pct	Sv-Op	Hld	Vel	OPS	ERC	ERA
2022	Wrcstr	AAA	14	0	3	17.2	72	11	6	6	0	0	1	0	14	0	19	1	1	0	1.000	0- -		-	.558	3.00	3.06
2022	Tacom	AAA	18	1	1	21.1	98	26	14	10	3	1	0	5	9	0	16	1	1	1	.500	0- -		-	.894	7.05	4.22
2019	Tex	AL	11	0	2	16.0	75	17	7	7	3	0	1	2	9	0	18	1	0	0		0-0	0	92	.818	6.26	3.94
2020	Bos	AL	24	0	5	30.1	137	33	16	11	3	0	1	3	16	0	30	0	1	1	.500	0-1	4	92	.790	5.61	3.26
2021	Bos	AL	28	0	15	40.0	177	35	29	26	4	1	3	7	19	1	35	5	2	0	1.000	1-1	2	93	.700	4.31	5.85
2022	Bos	AL	13	0	8	16.1	72	12	11	8	0	0	1	6	7	0	13	1	0	1	.000	0-0	0	94	.589	3.40	4.41
	4 ML YEARS		76	0	30	102.2	461	97	63	52	10	1	6	18	51	1	96	7	3	2	.600	1-2	6	93	.730	4.83	4.56

Josh VanMeter

Bats: L Throws: R Pos: 2B-39;1B-21;PH-14;3B-2;DH-2;C-1;RF-1;PR-1   Ht: 5'11" Wt: 194 Born: 3/10/1995 Age: 28

									BATTING														RUNNING			AVERAGES			
Year	Team	Lg	G	AB	H	2B	3B	HR	(Hm	Rd)	TB	R	RBI	RC	TBB	IBB	SO	HBP	SH	SF	SB	CS	GDP	Avg	OBP	Slg	OPS
2019	Cin	NL	95	228	54	13	1	8	(3	5)	93	33	23	28	29	0	56	2	0	1	9	3	5	.237	.327	.408	.735
2020	2 Tms	NL	26	70	9	3	0	2	(2	0)	18	9	6	5	7	0	24	2	0	0	1	0	0	.129	.228	.257	.485
2021	Ari	NL	112	274	58	17	2	6	(5	1)	97	26	36	37	33	0	83	1	0	2	3	2	5	.212	.297	.354	.651
2022	Pit	NL	67	171	32	5	2	3	(2	1)	50	15	14	15	19	0	45	0	0	2	4	0	3	.187	.266	.292	.558
20	Cin	NL	14	34	2	1	0	1	(1	0)	6	3	1	0	3	0	16	1	0	0	1	0	0	.059	.158	.176	.334
20	Ari	NL	12	36	7	2	0	1	(1	0)	12	6	5	5	4	0	8	1	0	0	0	0	0	.194	.293	.333	.626
	4 ML YEARS		300	743	153	38	5	19	(12	7)	258	83	79	85	88	0	208	5	0	5	17	5	13	.206	.293	.347	.640

Ildemaro Vargas

Bats: B Throws: R Pos: 3B-43;SS-15;2B-4;PH-2;PR-1   Ht: 6'0" Wt: 180 Born: 7/16/1991 Age: 31

Year Team	Lg	G	AB	H	2B	3B	HR	(Hm Rd)	TB	R	RBI	RC	TBB	IBB	SO	HBP	SH	SF	SB	CS	GDP	Avg	OBP	Slg	OPS
2022 Iowa	AAA	25	104	29	3	4	1	(- -)	43	16	7	13	7	0	12	0	0	1	1	0	1	.279	.321	.413	.735
2022 Roch	AAA	48	174	39	11	0	2	(- -)	56	21	18	15	20	0	25	0	1	2	2	2	4	.224	.301	.322	.623
2017 Ari	NL	12	13	4	1	0	0	(0 0)	5	4	4	2	0	0	3	0	0	0	0	0	1	.308	.308	.385	.692
2018 Ari	NL	14	19	4	0	0	1	(0 1)	7	2	4	4	1	0	4	0	0	0	1	0	1	.211	.250	.368	.618
2019 Ari	NL	92	201	54	9	1	6	(2 4)	83	25	24	26	9	0	24	0	0	1	1	0	6	.269	.299	.413	.712
2020 3 Tms		24	51	10	1	1	1	(0 1)	16	6	3	2	2	0	10	0	0	1	0	0	2	.196	.222	.314	.536
2021 3 Tms	NL	34	77	12	3	1	0	(0 0)	17	7	7	3	6	1	17	0	0	0	1	0	2	.156	.217	.221	.438
2022 2 Tms	NL	63	209	55	13	1	4	(2 2)	82	19	23	22	8	0	23	3	1	1	3	1	6	.263	.299	.392	.691
20 Ari	NL	8	20	3	0	0	0	(0 0)	3	2	0	0	1	0	5	0	0	0	0	0	1	.150	.190	.150	.340
20 Min	AL	10	22	5	1	1	0	(0 0)	8	3	2	1	1	0	2	0	0	1	0	0	1	.227	.250	.364	.614
20 ChC	NL	6	9	2	0	0	1	(0 1)	5	1	1	1	0	0	3	0	0	0	0	0	0	.222	.222	.556	.778
21 ChC	NL	9	21	3	2	0	0	(0 0)	5	3	2	1	3	0	7	0	0	0	1	0	1	.143	.250	.238	.488
21 Pit	NL	7	13	1	0	0	0	(0 0)	1	0	1	0	0	0	3	0	0	0	0	0	0	.077	.077	.077	.154
21 Ari	NL	18	43	8	1	1	0	(0 0)	11	4	4	2	3	1	7	0	0	0	0	0	1	.186	.239	.256	.495
22 ChC	NL	10	23	3	0	1	1	(1 0)	8	4	4	1	3	0	2	0	0	0	0	0	1	.130	.231	.348	.579
22 Was	NL	53	186	52	13	0	3	(1 2)	74	15	19	21	5	0	21	3	1	1	3	1	5	.280	.308	.398	.706
6 ML YEARS		239	570	139	27	4	12	(4 8)	210	63	65	59	26	1	81	3	1	3	6	1	18	.244	.279	.368	.647

Miguel Vargas

Bats: R Throws: R Pos: 1B-8;LF-7;DH-4;3B-1;PR-1   Ht: 6'3" Wt: 205 Born: 11/17/1999 Age: 23

Year Team	Lg	G	AB	H	2B	3B	HR	(Hm Rd)	TB	R	RBI	RC	TBB	IBB	SO	HBP	SH	SF	SB	CS	GDP	Avg	OBP	Slg	OPS
2022 OkCity	AAA	113	438	133	32	4	17	(- -)	224	100	82	90	71	1	76	6	0	5	16	5	11	.304	.404	.511	.915
2022 LAD	NL	18	47	8	1	0	1	(1 0)	12	4	8	5	2	0	13	0	0	1	1	0	0	.170	.200	.255	.455

Louie Varland

Pitches: R Bats: L Pos: SP-5   Ht: 6'1" Wt: 205 Born: 12/9/1997 Age: 25

Year Team	Lg	G	GS	GF	IP	BFP	H	R	ER	HR	SH	SF	HB	TBB	IBB	SO	WP	W	L	Pct	Sv-Op	Hld	Vel	OPS	ERC	ERA
2022 Wich	AA	20	19	0	105.0	450	102	46	39	14	1	2	2	39	0	119	4	7	4	.636	0- -	-	-	.705	4.10	3.34
2022 Min	AL	5	5	0	26.0	106	26	11	11	4	0	0	1	6	1	21	1	1	2	.333	0-0	0	94	.766	3.98	3.81

Daulton Varsho

Bats: L Throws: R Pos: RF-71;CF-54;C-31;DH-15;PH-9   Ht: 5'10" Wt: 207 Born: 7/2/1996 Age: 26

Year Team	Lg	G	AB	H	2B	3B	HR	(Hm Rd)	TB	R	RBI	RC	TBB	IBB	SO	HBP	SH	SF	SB	CS	GDP	Avg	OBP	Slg	OPS
2020 Ari	NL	37	101	19	5	2	3	(1 2)	37	16	9	8	12	0	33	2	0	3	1	1	1	.188	.287	.366	.653
2021 Ari	NL	95	284	70	17	2	11	(2 9)	124	41	38	41	30	3	67	0	1	0	6	0	4	.246	.318	.437	.755
2022 Ari	NL	151	531	125	23	3	27	(11 16)	235	79	74	86	46	0	145	7	2	5	16	6	8	.235	.302	.443	.745
3 ML YEARS		283	916	214	45	7	41	(14 27)	396	136	121	135	88	3	245	9	3	5	25	7	13	.234	.306	.432	.738

Andrew Vasquez

Pitches: L Bats: L Pos: RP-10   Ht: 6'6" Wt: 235 Born: 9/14/1993 Age: 29

Year Team	Lg	G	GS	GF	IP	BFP	H	R	ER	HR	SH	SF	HB	TBB	IBB	SO	WP	W	L	Pct	Sv-Op	Hld	Vel	OPS	ERC	ERA
2022 Buffalo	AAA	10	0	3	11.0	40	3	3	3	0	0	0	2	2	0	15	0	2	0	1.000	1- -	-	-	.286	0.60	2.45
2022 Scrmto	AAA	14	0	2	16.1	66	13	4	4	1	0	0	2	5	1	23	1	5	0	1.000	1- -	-	-	.608	2.83	2.20
2018 Min	AL	9	0	0	5.0	26	5	4	3	0	0	0	3	2	0	7	0	1	0	1.000	0-0	0	90	.766	5.24	5.40
2019 Min	AL	2	0	0	0.0	3	0	3	3	0	0	0	1	2	0	0	0	0	0	-	0-0	0	85			
2021 LAD	NL	2	0	1	1.2	6	1	1	0	0	0	0	0	0	0	3	0	0	0	-	0-1	0	91	.333	0.75	0.00
2022 2 Tms		10	0	3	8.2	39	6	6	6	1	0	0	3	4	0	10	1	0	0	-	0-0	0	89	.615	3.96	6.23
22 Tor	AL	9	0	3	6.2	32	6	6	6	1	0	0	3	3	0	6	1	0	0	-	0-0	0	89	.721	5.77	8.10
22 SF	NL	1	0	0	2.0	7	0	0	0	0	0	0	0	1	0	4	0	0	0	-	0-0	0	-	.143	0.27	0.00
4 ML YEARS		22	0	4	15.1	74	12	14	12	1	0	0	7	8	0	20	1	1	0	1.000	0-1	0	89	.670	4.63	7.04

Andrew Vaughn

Bats: R Throws: R Pos: RF-45;LF-44;DH-29;1B-23;PH-3;2B-2;PR-1   Ht: 6'0" Wt: 215 Born: 4/3/1998 Age: 25

Year Team	Lg	G	AB	H	2B	3B	HR	(Hm Rd)	TB	R	RBI	RC	TBB	IBB	SO	HBP	SH	SF	SB	CS	GDP	Avg	OBP	Slg	OPS
2021 CWS	AL	127	417	98	22	0	15	(8 7)	165	56	48	45	41	0	101	6	0	5	1	1	14	.235	.309	.396	.705
2022 CWS	AL	134	510	138	28	1	17	(6 11)	219	60	76	75	31	0	96	9	0	5	0	0	13	.271	.321	.429	.750
Postseason		2	5	2	1	0	0	(0 0)	3	1	1	1	0	0	2	0	0	0	0	0	0	.400	.400	.600	1.000
2 ML YEARS		261	927	236	50	1	32	(14 18)	384	116	124	120	72	0	197	15	0	10	1	1	27	.255	.315	.414	.730

Terrin Vavra

Bats: L Throws: R Pos: 2B-15;LF-11;DH-8;PH-7;PR-2;RF-1   Ht: 6'1" Wt: 200 Born: 5/12/1997 Age: 26

Year Team	Lg	G	AB	H	2B	3B	HR	(Hm Rd)	TB	R	RBI	RC	TBB	IBB	SO	HBP	SH	SF	SB	CS	GDP	Avg	OBP	Slg	OPS
2022 Norfolk	AAA	45	173	56	14	1	2	(- -)	78	34	18	32	28	0	36	6	1	0	5	1	3	.324	.435	.451	.886
2022 Bal	AL	40	89	23	2	1	1	(1 0)	30	14	12	13	12	0	19	0	0	2	0	1	2	.258	.340	.337	.677

Christian Vazquez

Bats: R **Throws:** R **Pos:** C-108;PH-11;1B-9;2B-1;DH-1   VAZ-kehz   **Ht:** 5'9" **Wt:** 205 **Born:** 8/21/1990 **Age:** 32

								BATTING														RUNNING			AVERAGES			
Year	Team	Lg	G	AB	H	2B	3B	HR	(Hm	Rd)	TB	R	RBI	RC	TBB	IBB	SO	HBP	SH	SF	SB	CS	GDP	Avg	OBP	Slg	OPS
2014	Bos	AL	55	175	42	9	1	1	(1	0)	54	15	20	19	19	1	33	0	3	4	0	0	4	.240	.308	.309	.617
2016	Bos	AL	57	172	39	9	1	1	(1	0)	53	21	12	11	10	1	39	2	0	0	0	0	3	.227	.277	.308	.585
2017	Bos	AL	99	324	94	18	2	5	(4	1)	131	43	32	41	17	0	64	3	0	1	7	2	14	.290	.330	.404	.735
2018	Bos	AL	80	251	52	10	0	3	(2	1)	71	24	16	13	13	1	41	4	1	0	4	1	5	.207	.257	.283	.540
2019	Bos	AL	138	482	133	26	1	23	(8	15)	230	66	72	69	33	3	101	0	3	3	4	2	17	.276	.320	.477	.798
2020	Bos	AL	47	173	49	9	0	7	(2	5)	79	22	23	25	16	0	43	0	0	0	4	3	6	.283	.344	.457	.801
2021	Bos	AL	138	458	118	23	1	6	(3	3)	161	51	49	47	33	0	84	2	1	4	8	4	15	.258	.308	.352	.659
2022	2 Tms	AL	119	398	109	23	0	9	(7	2)	159	41	52	47	22	0	69	3	0	3	1	4	10	.274	.315	.399	.714
22	Bos	AL	84	294	83	20	0	8	(6	2)	127	33	42	39	18	0	51	3	0	3	1	2	7	.282	.327	.432	.759
22	Hou	AL	35	104	26	3	0	1	(1	0)	32	8	10	8	4	0	18	0	0	0	0	2	3	.250	.278	.308	.585
	Postseason		25	75	19	2	0	2	(1	1)	27	10	8	8	4	0	17	0	1	0	0	0	0	.253	.291	.360	.651
	8 ML YEARS		733	2433	636	127	5	55	(28	27)	938	283	276	272	163	6	474	14	8	15	28	16	74	.261	.310	.386	.695

Vince Velasquez

Pitches: R **Bats:** R **Pos:** RP-18; SP-9   **Ht:** 6'3" **Wt:** 212 **Born:** 6/7/1992 **Age:** 31

			HOW MUCH PITCHED					WHAT HE GAVE UP										THE RESULTS							
Year	Team	Lg	G	GS	GF	IP	BFP	H	R	ER	HR	SH	SF	HB	TBB	IBB	SO	WP	W	L	Pct	Sv-Op	Hld	Vel	OPS	ERC	ERA
2015	Hou	AL	19	7	5	55.2	231	50	28	27	5	0	0	2	21	0	58	3	1	1	.500	0-0	0	95	.720	3.58	4.37
2016	Phi	NL	24	24	0	131.0	551	129	64	60	21	9	5	1	45	1	152	3	8	6	.571	0-0	0	94	.765	4.25	4.12
2017	Phi	NL	15	15	0	72.0	315	74	44	41	15	2	2	3	34	1	68	2	2	7	.222	0-0	0	94	.851	5.58	5.13
2018	Phi	NL	31	30	1	146.2	630	138	83	79	16	7	3	8	59	1	161	9	9	12	.429	0-0	0	94	.747	4.04	4.85
2019	Phi	NL	33	23	2	117.1	516	120	69	64	26	3	3	9	43	2	130	5	7	8	.467	0-0	2	94	.833	5.21	4.91
2020	Phi	NL	9	7	0	34.0	154	36	21	21	5	0	0	3	17	1	46	0	1	1	.500	0-0	0	94	.804	5.51	5.56
2021	2 Tms	NL	25	21	1	94.1	417	91	68	66	23	1	0	4	49	2	101	2	3	9	.250	0-0	1	93	.872	5.58	6.30
2022	CWS	NL	27	9	8	75.1	319	68	42	40	11	1	2	2	25	0	69	1	3	3	.500	0-0	1	93	.721	3.64	4.78
21	Phi	NL	21	17	1	81.2	361	76	55	54	17	1	0	4	45	2	85	2	3	6	.333	0-0	1	93	.842	5.27	5.95
21	SD	NL	4	4	0	12.2	56	15	13	12	6	0	0	0	4	0	16	0	0	3	.000	0-0	0	93	1.051	7.55	8.53
	8 ML YEARS		183	136	17	726.1	3133	706	419	398	122	23	15	32	293	8	785	25	34	47	.420	0-0	3	94	.789	4.59	4.93

Andrew Velazquez

Bats: B **Throws:** R **Pos:** SS-124;PR-5   **Ht:** 5'9" **Wt:** 170 **Born:** 7/14/1994 **Age:** 28

								BATTING														RUNNING			AVERAGES			
Year	Team	Lg	G	AB	H	2B	3B	HR	(Hm	Rd)	TB	R	RBI	RC	TBB	IBB	SO	HBP	SH	SF	SB	CS	GDP	Avg	OBP	Slg	OPS
2018	TB	AL	13	10	3	1	0	0	(0	0)	4	3	0	3	1	0	3	1	0	0	1	0	0	.300	.417	.400	.817
2019	2 Tms	AL	15	23	2	2	0	0	(0	0)	4	3	0	0	1	0	13	0	0	0	1	0	0	.087	.125	.174	.299
2020	Bal	AL	40	63	10	1	1	0	(0	0)	13	11	3	3	10	0	23	0	4	0	4	2	2	.159	.274	.206	.480
2021	NYY	AL	28	67	15	4	1	1	(1	0)	24	11	6	5	1	0	23	0	0	0	4	1	1	.224	.235	.358	.594
2022	LAA	AL	125	322	63	8	0	9	(4	5)	98	37	28	26	15	0	119	3	6	3	17	1	3	.196	.236	.304	.540
19	TB	AL	10	12	1	1	0	0	(0	0)	2	2	0	0	0	0	6	0	0	0	0	0	0	.083	.083	.167	.250
19	Cle	AL	5	11	1	1	0	0	(0	0)	2	1	0	0	1	0	7	0	0	0	1	0	0	.091	.167	.182	.348
	Postseason		1	1	0	0	0	0	(0	0)	0	0	0	0	0	0	0	0	0	0	0	0	0	.000	.000	.000	.000
	5 ML YEARS		221	485	93	16	2	10	(5	5)	143	65	37	37	28	0	181	4	10	3	27	4	6	.192	.240	.295	.535

Nelson Velazquez

Bats: R **Throws:** R **Pos:** CF-32;RF-23;PH-15;LF-14;DH-6;PR-6   **Ht:** 6'0" **Wt:** 190 **Born:** 12/26/1998 **Age:** 24

								BATTING														RUNNING			AVERAGES			
Year	Team	Lg	G	AB	H	2B	3B	HR	(Hm	Rd)	TB	R	RBI	RC	TBB	IBB	SO	HBP	SH	SF	SB	CS	GDP	Avg	OBP	Slg	OPS
2022	Tenn	AA	22	80	23	4	1	9	(-	-)	56	16	17	24	14	1	33	0	0	0	5	2	0	.288	.394	.700	1.094
2022	Iowa	AAA	34	123	26	7	0	6	(-	-)	51	21	15	15	13	0	50	1	0	1	7	2	4	.211	.290	.415	.704
2022	ChC	NL	77	185	38	7	3	6	(1	5)	69	20	26	18	19	0	65	2	0	0	5	2	5	.205	.286	.373	.659

Alex Verdugo

Bats: L **Throws:** L **Pos:** LF-102;RF-52;DH-2;PH-1;PR-1   **Ht:** 6'0" **Wt:** 192 **Born:** 5/15/1996 **Age:** 27

								BATTING														RUNNING			AVERAGES			
Year	Team	Lg	G	AB	H	2B	3B	HR	(Hm	Rd)	TB	R	RBI	RC	TBB	IBB	SO	HBP	SH	SF	SB	CS	GDP	Avg	OBP	Slg	OPS
2017	LAD	NL	15	23	4	0	0	1	(1	0)	7	1	1	0	2	0	4	0	0	1	0	1	4	.174	.240	.304	.544
2018	LAD	NL	37	77	20	6	0	1	(0	1)	29	11	4	6	8	0	14	0	1	0	0	0	4	.260	.329	.377	.706
2019	LAD	NL	106	343	101	22	2	12	(5	7)	163	43	44	51	26	1	49	2	0	6	4	1	8	.294	.342	.475	.817
2020	LAD	NL	53	201	62	16	0	6	(2	4)	96	36	15	31	17	1	45	2	0	1	4	0	4	.308	.367	.478	.844
2021	Bos	AL	146	544	157	32	2	13	(6	7)	232	88	63	85	51	6	96	4	0	5	6	2	11	.289	.351	.426	.777
2022	Bos	AL	152	593	166	39	1	11	(5	6)	240	75	74	70	42	2	86	3	0	6	1	3	14	.280	.328	.405	.732
	Postseason		11	42	13	3	0	1	(0	1)	19	5	6	4	5	0	3	0	0	0	1	1	1	.310	.383	.452	.835
	6 ML YEARS		509	1781	510	115	5	44	(19	25)	767	254	201	243	146	10	294	11	1	18	15	7	42	.286	.341	.431	.772

Drew VerHagen

Pitches: R **Bats:** R **Pos:** RP-19   verr-HAY-gen   **Ht:** 6'6" **Wt:** 230 **Born:** 10/22/1990 **Age:** 32

			HOW MUCH PITCHED					WHAT HE GAVE UP										THE RESULTS							
Year	Team	Lg	G	GS	GF	IP	BFP	H	R	ER	HR	SH	SF	HB	TBB	IBB	SO	WP	W	L	Pct	Sv-Op	Hld	Vel	OPS	ERC	ERA
2014	Det	AL	1	1	0	5.0	20	5	3	3	0	0	0	0	3	0	4	0	0	1	.000	0-0	0	91	.753	4.67	5.40
2015	Det	AL	20	0	2	26.1	106	18	6	6	1	1	0	1	14	2	13	1	2	0	1.000	0-1	3	94	.559	2.61	2.05
2016	Det	AL	19	0	4	19.0	90	28	15	15	3	0	1	1	7	1	10	1	1	0	1.000	0-0	2	94	.968	7.50	7.11
2017	Det	AL	24	2	4	34.1	145	42	22	22	10	0	1	0	9	1	25	4	0	3	.000	0-1	5	94	.967	6.43	5.77

Year Team	Lg	HOW MUCH PITCHED					WHAT HE GAVE UP											THE RESULTS								
		G	GS	GF	IP	BFP	H	R	ER	HR	SH	SF	HB	TBB	IBB	SO	WP	W	L	Pct	Sv-Op	Hld	Vel	OPS	ERC	ERA
2018 Det	AL	41	1	4	56.1	233	46	29	29	6	0	4	3	19	0	53	6	3	3	.500	0-2	3	94	.645	3.09	4.63
2019 Det	AL	22	4	3	58.0	258	70	40	38	9	0	1	4	23	1	51	3	4	3	.571	0-0	1	93	.880	6.13	5.90
2022 StL	NL	19	0	3	21.2	106	27	18	16	5	0	1	1	14	1	18	0	3	1	.750	0-1	2	95	.907	7.70	6.65
7 ML YEARS		146	8	20	220.2	958	236	133	129	34	1	8	10	89	6	174	15	13	11	.542	0-5	16	94	.811	5.13	5.26

Justin Verlander

Pitches: R Bats: R Pos: SP-28   Ht: 6'5" Wt: 235 Born: 2/20/1983 Age: 40

Year Team	Lg	HOW MUCH PITCHED					WHAT HE GAVE UP											THE RESULTS								
		G	GS	GF	IP	BFP	H	R	ER	HR	SH	SF	HB	TBB	IBB	SO	WP	W	L	Pct	Sv-Op	Hld	Vel	OPS	ERC	ERA
2005 Det	AL	2	2	0	11.1	54	15	9	9	1	0	0	1	5	0	7	1	0	2	.000	0-0	0	95	.868	6.41	7.15
2006 Det	AL	30	30	0	186.0	776	187	78	75	21	2	4	6	60	1	124	5	17	9	.654	0-0	0	95	.741	4.12	3.63
2007 Det	AL	32	32	0	201.2	866	181	88	82	20	3	1	19	67	3	183	17	18	6	.750	0-0	0	95	.668	3.53	3.66
2008 Det	AL	33	33	0	201.0	880	195	119	108	18	4	6	14	87	8	163	6	11	17	.393	0-0	0	94	.715	4.17	4.84
2009 Det	AL	35	35	0	240.0	982	219	99	92	20	6	4	6	63	5	269	8	19	9	.679	0-0	0	96	.665	3.06	3.45
2010 Det	AL	33	33	0	224.1	925	190	89	84	14	6	8	6	71	0	219	11	18	9	.667	0-0	0	95	.630	2.79	3.37
2011 Det	AL	34	34	0	251.0	969	174	73	67	24	2	3	3	57	0	250	7	24	5	.828	0-0	0	95	.555	1.92	2.40
2012 Det	AL	33	33	0	238.1	956	192	81	70	19	4	3	5	60	2	239	2	17	8	.680	0-0	0	94	.601	2.45	2.64
2013 Det	AL	34	34	0	218.1	925	212	94	84	19	2	6	4	75	1	217	3	13	12	.520	0-0	0	93	.691	3.68	3.46
2014 Det	AL	32	32	0	206.0	893	223	114	104	18	6	5	5	65	1	159	5	15	12	.556	0-0	0	92	.756	4.19	4.54
2015 Det	AL	20	20	0	133.1	535	113	56	50	13	1	6	3	32	1	113	2	5	8	.385	0-0	0	93	.634	2.75	3.38
2016 Det	AL	34	34	0	227.2	903	171	81	77	30	4	7	8	57	1	254	6	16	9	.640	0-0	0	93	.630	2.54	3.04
2017 2 Tms	AL	33	33	0	206.0	849	170	80	77	27	1	4	4	72	4	219	5	15	8	.652	0-0	0	95	.660	3.19	3.36
2018 Hou	AL	34	34	0	214.0	833	156	63	60	28	2	5	8	37	0	290	5	16	9	.640	0-0	0	95	.602	2.16	2.52
2019 Hou	AL	34	34	0	223.0	847	137	66	64	36	0	2	6	42	0	300	4	21	6	.778	0-0	0	95	.579	1.80	2.58
2020 Hou	AL	1	1	0	6.0	21	3	2	2	2	0	0	0	1	0	7	0	1	0	1.000	0-0	0	95	.640	1.95	3.00
2022 Hou	AL	28	28	0	175.0	666	116	43	34	12	1	5	6	29	0	185	3	18	4	.818	0-0	0	95	.497	1.56	1.75
17 Det	AL	28	28	0	172.0	729	153	76	73	23	1	4	3	67	4	176	5	10	8	.556	0-0	0	95	.693	3.67	3.82
17 Hou	AL	5	5	0	34.0	120	17	4	4	4	0	0	1	5	0	43	0	5	0	1.000	0-0	0	95	.464	1.22	1.06
Postseason		31	30	0	187.2	754	140	74	71	26	2	3	3	60	0	205	8	14	11	.560	0-0	0	95	.629	2.73	3.40
17 ML YEARS		482	482	0	3163.0	12880	2654	1235	1139	322	44	69	104	880	27	3198	90	244	133	.647	0-0	0	94	.644	2.89	3.24

Alex Vesia

Pitches: L Bats: L Pos: RP-63   Ht: 6'1" Wt: 209 Born: 4/11/1996 Age: 27

Year Team	Lg	HOW MUCH PITCHED					WHAT HE GAVE UP											THE RESULTS								
		G	GS	GF	IP	BFP	H	R	ER	HR	SH	SF	HB	TBB	IBB	SO	WP	W	L	Pct	Sv-Op	Hld	Vel	OPS	ERC	ERA
2020 Mia	NL	5	0	5	4.1	27	7	10	9	3	0	0	0	7	0	5	0	0	1	.000	0-0	1	92	1.319	19.97	18.69
2021 LAD	NL	41	0	7	40.0	161	17	17	10	6	0	2	2	22	3	54	0	3	1	.750	1-2	9	94	.551	2.04	2.25
2022 LAD	NL	63	0	6	54.1	227	37	14	13	2	2	1	2	24	1	79	2	5	0	1.000	1-3	16	94	.527	2.21	2.15
Postseason		7	0	0	4.1	20	5	1	1	1	0	0	0	3	0	7	0	0	0	-	0-0	0	95	.871	7.50	2.08
3 ML YEARS		109	0	13	98.2	415	61	41	32	11	2	3	4	53	4	138	2	8	2	.800	2-5	26	94	.583	2.67	2.92

Nick Vespi

Pitches: L Bats: L Pos: RP-25   Ht: 6'3" Wt: 215 Born: 10/10/1995 Age: 27

Year Team	Lg	HOW MUCH PITCHED					WHAT HE GAVE UP											THE RESULTS								
		G	GS	GF	IP	BFP	H	R	ER	HR	SH	SF	HB	TBB	IBB	SO	WP	W	L	Pct	Sv-Op	Hld	Vel	OPS	ERC	ERA
2022 Norfolk	AAA	26	0	17	28.2	102	12	3	0	0	0	1	1	5	0	36	1	2	1	.667	8- -	-	-	.345	0.70	0.00
2022 Bal	AL	25	0	4	26.1	112	29	12	12	5	0	1	1	8	1	28	0	5	0	1.000	1-2	1	89	.849	5.13	4.10

Will Vest

Pitches: R Bats: R Pos: RP-57; SP-2   Ht: 6'0" Wt: 180 Born: 6/6/1995 Age: 28

Year Team	Lg	HOW MUCH PITCHED					WHAT HE GAVE UP											THE RESULTS								
		G	GS	GF	IP	BFP	H	R	ER	HR	SH	SF	HB	TBB	IBB	SO	WP	W	L	Pct	Sv-Op	Hld	Vel	OPS	ERC	ERA
2021 Sea	AL	32	0	4	35.0	156	38	25	24	2	1	2	3	18	0	27	3	1	0	1.000	0-0	6	94	.812	5.19	6.17
2022 Det	AL	59	2	8	63.0	272	62	30	28	6	2	7	3	22	0	63	7	3	3	.500	1-1	4	95	.691	3.91	4.00
2 ML YEARS		91	2	12	98.0	428	100	55	52	8	3	9	6	40	0	90	10	4	3	.571	1-1	10	95	.735	4.36	4.78

Cam Vieaux

Pitches: L Bats: L Pos: RP-8   Ht: 6'3" Wt: 200 Born: 12/5/1993 Age: 29

Year Team	Lg	HOW MUCH PITCHED					WHAT HE GAVE UP											THE RESULTS								
		G	GS	GF	IP	BFP	H	R	ER	HR	SH	SF	HB	TBB	IBB	SO	WP	W	L	Pct	Sv-Op	Hld	Vel	OPS	ERC	ERA
2022 Indy	AAA	35	1	5	50.0	198	37	19	17	7	2	1	1	15	0	47	0	5	1	.833	2- -	-	-	.639	2.69	3.06
2022 Pit	NL	8	0	2	8.2	48	15	11	10	2	0	0	1	5	0	15	0	0	0	-	0-0	1	93	1.032	10.80	10.38

Mark Vientos

Bats: R Throws: R Pos: DH-11;PH-7;3B-2;PR-1   Ht: 6'4" Wt: 185 Born: 12/11/1999 Age: 23

Year Team	Lg	BATTING																		RUNNING			AVERAGES			
		G	AB	H	2B	3B	HR	(Hm	Rd)	TB	R	RBI	RC	TBB	IBB	SO	HBP	SH	SF	SB	CS	GDP	Avg	OBP	Slg	OPS
2022 Syrcse	AAA	101	378	106	16	1	24	(-	-)	196	66	72	71	44	2	122	3	0	2	0	2	15	.280	.358	.519	.877
2022 NYM	NL	16	36	6	1	0	1	(0	1)	10	3	3	2	5	0	12	0	0	0	0	0	1	.167	.268	.278	.546

Matt Vierling

Bats: R Throws: R Pos: CF-61;RF-37;LF-30;PH-12;3B-5;2B-4;PR-3;1B-2;DH-1   Ht: 6'3" Wt: 205 Born: 9/16/1996 Age: 26

						BATTING															RUNNING			AVERAGES			
Year	Team	Lg	G	AB	H	2B	3B	HR	(Hm	Rd)	TB	R	RBI	RC	TBB	IBB	SO	HBP	SH	SF	SB	CS	GDP	Avg	OBP	Slg	OPS
2022	LV	AAA	21	85	23	6	2	2	(-	-)	39	15	9	13	10	0	15	0	0	0	8	2	2	.271	.347	.459	.806
2021	Phi	NL	34	71	23	3	1	2	(1	1)	34	11	6	11	4	1	20	1	0	1	2	0	1	.324	.364	.479	.843
2022	Phi	NL	117	325	80	12	2	6	(2	4)	114	41	32	26	23	0	70	3	0	6	7	4	7	.246	.297	.351	.648
	2 ML YEARS		151	396	103	15	3	8	(3	5)	148	52	38	37	27	1	90	4	0	7	9	4	8	.260	.309	.374	.682

David Villar

Bats: R Throws: R Pos: 3B-27;1B-11;DH-10;2B-6;PH-3   Ht: 6'1" Wt: 215 Born: 1/27/1997 Age: 26

						BATTING															RUNNING			AVERAGES			
Year	Team	Lg	G	AB	H	2B	3B	HR	(Hm	Rd)	TB	R	RBI	RC	TBB	IBB	SO	HBP	SH	SF	SB	CS	GDP	Avg	OBP	Slg	OPS
2022	Scrmto	AAA	84	298	82	19	1	27	(-	-)	184	67	82	79	55	0	93	11	0	2	1	1	7	.275	.404	.617	1.022
2022	SF	NL	52	156	36	6	1	9	(0	9)	71	21	24	23	18	0	58	6	0	1	0	1	4	.231	.331	.455	.787

Jonathan Villar

Bats: B Throws: R Pos: 2B-29;3B-28;PH-3;SS-2;PR-2;DH-1   vee-YARR   Ht: 6'0" Wt: 233 Born: 5/2/1991 Age: 32

						BATTING															RUNNING			AVERAGES			
Year	Team	Lg	G	AB	H	2B	3B	HR	(Hm	Rd)	TB	R	RBI	RC	TBB	IBB	SO	HBP	SH	SF	SB	CS	GDP	Avg	OBP	Slg	OPS
2022	Tacom	AAA	37	145	41	9	2	6	(-	-)	72	20	24	22	10	0	34	0	0	0	10	3	7	.283	.329	.497	.826
2013	Hou	AL	58	210	51	9	2	1	(0	1)	67	26	8	22	24	1	71	0	7	0	18	8	5	.243	.321	.319	.640
2014	Hou	AL	87	263	55	13	2	7	(3	4)	93	31	27	24	19	1	80	2	4	1	17	4	4	.209	.267	.354	.620
2015	Hou	AL	53	116	33	7	1	2	(0	2)	48	18	11	15	10	0	29	0	1	1	7	2	3	.284	.339	.414	.752
2016	Mil	NL	156	589	168	38	3	19	(6	13)	269	92	63	102	79	4	174	2	5	4	62	18	7	.285	.369	.457	.826
2017	Mil	NL	122	403	97	18	1	11	(7	4)	150	49	40	45	30	1	132	0	2	1	23	8	4	.241	.293	.372	.665
2018	2 Tms		141	466	121	14	1	14	(6	8)	179	54	46	67	41	0	138	5	1	2	35	5	13	.260	.325	.384	.709
2019	Bal	AL	162	642	176	33	5	24	(16	8)	291	111	73	100	61	0	176	4	2	4	40	9	8	.274	.339	.453	.792
2020	2 Tms		52	185	43	5	0	2	(1	1)	54	13	15	15	19	1	54	0	1	2	16	5	2	.232	.301	.292	.593
2021	NYM	NL	142	454	113	18	2	18	(9	9)	189	63	42	52	46	2	132	3	2	0	14	7	6	.249	.322	.416	.738
2022	2 Tms		59	202	42	6	2	3	(2	1)	61	25	18	17	15	0	59	0	1	2	7	0	4	.208	.260	.302	.562
18	ChC	NL	87	257	67	10	1	6	(2	4)	97	36	22	29	19	0	80	2	0	1	14	2	9	.261	.315	.377	.693
18	Bal	AL	54	209	54	4	0	8	(4	4)	82	28	24	38	22	0	58	3	1	1	21	3	4	.258	.336	.392	.729
20	Mia	NL	30	116	30	4	0	2	(1	1)	40	10	9	10	9	1	32	0	1	1	9	5	2	.259	.315	.345	.660
20	Tor	AL	22	69	13	1	0	0	(0	0)	14	3	6	6	9	0	22	0	0	1	7	0	0	.188	.278	.203	.481
22	ChC	NL	46	153	34	6	2	2	(2	0)	50	19	15	16	11	0	42	0	0	2	6	0	3	.222	.271	.327	.598
22	LAA	AL	13	49	8	0	0	1	(0	1)	11	6	3	1	4	0	17	0	1	0	1	0	1	.163	.226	.224	.451
	Postseason		2	2	0	0	0	0	(0	0)	0	1	0	0	0	0	1	0	0	0	0	0	0	.000	.000	.000	.000
	10 ML YEARS		1032	3530	899	161	19	101	(50	51)	1401	482	343	459	344	10	1045	16	26	17	239	66	56	.255	.322	.397	.719

Meibrys Viloria

Bats: L Throws: R Pos: C-20;PH-6;DH-3   MAY-breez   Ht: 5'11" Wt: 225 Born: 2/15/1997 Age: 26

						BATTING															RUNNING			AVERAGES			
Year	Team	Lg	G	AB	H	2B	3B	HR	(Hm	Rd)	TB	R	RBI	RC	TBB	IBB	SO	HBP	SH	SF	SB	CS	GDP	Avg	OBP	Slg	OPS
2022	RdRck	AAA	54	175	49	13	0	5	(-	-)	77	38	28	32	40	1	49	3	0	0	2	0	7	.280	.422	.440	.862
2018	KC	AL	10	27	7	2	0	0	(0	0)	9	4	4	3	1	0	9	0	1	0	0	0	1	.259	.286	.333	.619
2019	KC	AL	42	133	28	7	0	1	(0	1)	38	7	15	9	10	0	44	0	1	4	0	1	4	.211	.259	.286	.544
2020	KC	AL	15	21	4	1	0	0	(0	0)	5	1	0	2	2	0	9	1	0	0	0	0	0	.190	.292	.238	.530
2022	Tex	AL	26	63	10	1	0	2	(1	1)	17	10	5	5	11	0	29	0	0	1	0	0	0	.159	.280	.270	.550
	4 ML YEARS		93	244	49	11	0	3	(1	2)	69	22	24	19	24	0	91	1	2	5	0	1	5	.201	.270	.283	.553

Arodys Vizcaino

Pitches: R Bats: R Pos: RP-7   ah-ROH-dis vees-kai-EE-no   Ht: 6'0" Wt: 245 Born: 11/13/1990 Age: 32

				HOW MUCH PITCHED				WHAT HE GAVE UP												THE RESULTS						
Year	Team	Lg	G	GS	GF	IP	BFP	H	R	ER	HR	SH	SF	HB	TBB	IBB	SO	WP	W	L	Pct	Sv-Op	Hld	Vel	OPS	ERC	ERA
2022	Omha	AAA	16	0	13	15.1	64	12	3	3	1	0	0	1	6	0	19	0	0	0	-	7- -	-		.648	2.88	1.76
2011	Atl	NL	17	0	2	17.1	77	16	9	9	1	0	0	1	9	1	17	5	1	1	.500	0-2	5	96	.636	3.89	4.67
2014	ChC	NL	5	0	5	5.0	22	5	3	3	1	0	0	0	3	0	4	0	0	0	-	0-0	0	95	.837	5.79	5.40
2015	Atl	NL	36	0	25	33.2	139	27	7	6	1	2	0	0	13	2	37	7	3	1	.750	9-10	3	98	.615	2.42	1.60
2016	Atl	NL	43	0	24	38.2	182	37	25	19	3	1	0	1	26	3	50	3	1	4	.200	10-14	0	97	.685	4.52	4.42
2017	Atl	NL	62	0	28	57.1	235	42	19	18	7	0	1	2	21	1	64	6	5	3	.625	14-17	17	98	.627	2.75	2.83
2018	Atl	NL	39	0	31	38.1	158	30	9	9	4	0	0	2	15	1	40	4	2	2	.500	16-18	1	98	.652	3.09	2.11
2019	Atl	NL	4	0	4	4.0	17	3	1	1	1	0	0	0	3	0	6	0	1	0	1.000	1-2	0	96	.924	5.38	2.25
2022	KC	AL	7	0	1	5.2	29	4	4	4	1	0	0	0	7	0	3	0	0	0	-	0-0	2	97	.743	5.96	6.35
	Postseason		2	0	2	2.0	8	1	0	0	0	0	0	0	1	0	5	1	0	0	-	1-1	0	97	.393	1.41	0.00
	8 ML YEARS		213	0	120	200.0	859	164	77	69	19	3	1	6	97	8	221	25	13	11	.542	50-63	28	97	.658	3.40	3.11

Daniel Vogelbach

Bats: L Throws: R Pos: DH-116;PH-19;1B-5   VOH-guhl-back   Ht: 6'0" Wt: 270 Born: 12/17/1992 Age: 30

						BATTING															RUNNING			AVERAGES			
Year	Team	Lg	G	AB	H	2B	3B	HR	(Hm	Rd)	TB	R	RBI	RC	TBB	IBB	SO	HBP	SH	SF	SB	CS	GDP	Avg	OBP	Slg	OPS
2016	Sea	AL	8	12	1	0	0	0	(0	0)	1	0	0	0	1	0	6	0	0	0	0	0	0	.083	.154	.083	.237
2017	Sea	AL	16	28	6	1	0	0	(0	0)	7	0	2	2	3	0	9	0	0	0	0	0	2	.214	.290	.250	.540
2018	Sea	AL	37	87	18	2	0	4	(2	2)	32	9	13	11	13	0	26	2	0	0	0	0	4	.207	.324	.368	.691
2019	Sea	AL	144	462	96	17	0	30	(12	18)	203	73	76	72	92	2	149	0	0	2	0	0	0	.208	.341	.439	.780
2020	3 Tms		39	115	24	3	0	6	(4	2)	45	16	16	15	20	1	33	1	0	0	0	0	3	.209	.331	.391	.722

Year	Team	Lg	BATTING																			RUNNING			AVERAGES			
			G	AB	H	2B	3B	HR	(Hm	Rd)	TB	R	RBI	RC	TBB	IBB	SO	HBP	SH	SF	SB	CS	GDP	Avg	OBP	Slg	OPS
2021	Mil	NL	93	215	47	8	0	9	(5	4)	82	30	24	30	43	1	57	0	0	0	0	0	6	.219	.349	.381	.730
2022	2 Tms	NL	130	386	92	19	1	18	(8	10)	167	47	59	66	73	2	114	1	0	1	0	0	11	.238	.360	.433	.793
20	Sea	AL	18	53	5	1	0	2	(1	1)	12	3	4	3	11	1	13	0	0	0	0	0	1	.094	.250	.226	.476
20	Tor	AL	2	4	0	0	0	0	(0	0)	0	0	0	0	1	0	2	0	0	0	0	0	0	.000	.200	.000	.200
20	Mil	NL	19	58	19	2	0	4	(3	1)	33	13	12	12	8	0	18	1	0	0	0	0	0	.328	.418	.569	.987
22	Pit	NL	75	237	54	10	1	12	(5	7)	102	29	34	36	40	1	67	0	0	1	0	0	8	.228	.338	.430	.769
22	NYM	NL	55	149	38	9	0	6	(3	3)	65	18	25	30	33	1	47	1	0	0	0	0	3	.255	.393	.436	.830
	Postseason		5	6	1	1	0	0	(0	0)	2	1	0	0	1	0	2	0	0	0	0	0	0	.167	.286	.333	.619
	7 ML YEARS		467	1305	284	50	1	67	(31	36)	537	175	190	196	245	6	394	6	0	3	0	0	30	.218	.343	.411	.755

Stephen Vogt

Bats: L **Throws:** R **Pos:** DH-26;PH-25;C-19;1B-17   VOTE   **Ht:** 6'0" **Wt:** 216 **Born:** 11/1/1984 **Age:** 38

Year	Team	Lg	BATTING																			RUNNING			AVERAGES			
			G	AB	H	2B	3B	HR	(Hm	Rd)	TB	R	RBI	RC	TBB	IBB	SO	HBP	SH	SF	SB	CS	GDP	Avg	OBP	Slg	OPS
2012	TB	AL	18	25	0	0	0	0	(0	0)	0	0	0	0	2	0	2	0	0	0	0	0	0	.000	.074	.000	.074
2013	Oak	AL	47	135	34	6	1	4	(3	1)	54	18	16	15	9	1	28	0	2	2	0	1	2	.252	.295	.400	.695
2014	Oak	AL	84	269	75	10	2	9	(4	5)	116	26	35	38	16	2	39	1	0	1	1	0	2	.279	.321	.431	.752
2015	Oak	AL	136	445	116	21	3	18	(5	13)	197	58	71	75	56	6	97	2	0	8	0	2	9	.261	.341	.443	.783
2016	Oak	AL	137	490	123	30	2	14	(4	10)	199	54	56	51	35	3	83	4	0	3	0	0	6	.251	.305	.406	.711
2017	2 Tms		99	279	65	15	1	12	(6	6)	118	25	40	33	21	1	56	0	1	2	0	1	2	.233	.285	.423	.708
2019	SF	NL	99	255	67	24	2	10	(3	7)	125	30	40	42	20	1	66	1	0	4	3	1	4	.263	.314	.490	.804
2020	Ari	NL	26	72	12	5	0	1	(0	1)	20	6	7	5	8	0	18	0	0	1	0	0	0	.167	.247	.278	.525
2021	2 Tms	NL	78	210	41	6	1	7	(3	4)	70	24	25	20	26	2	56	0	1	1	0	0	0	.195	.283	.333	.616
2022	Oak	AL	70	168	27	4	1	7	(4	3)	54	18	23	16	17	0	46	2	0	4	1	0	4	.161	.241	.321	.562
17	Oak	AL	54	157	34	8	1	4	(3	1)	56	12	20	19	16	1	31	0	0	1	0	1	1	.217	.287	.357	.644
17	Mil	NL	45	122	31	7	0	8	(5	3)	62	13	20	14	5	0	25	0	1	1	0	0	1	.254	.281	.508	.789
21	Ari	NL	52	132	28	6	1	5	(1	4)	51	17	17	16	18	1	36	0	1	0	0	0	2	.212	.307	.386	.693
21	Atl	NL	26	78	13	0	0	2	(2	0)	19	7	8	4	8	1	20	0	0	1	0	0	0	.167	.241	.244	.485
	Postseason		6	19	3	0	1	0	(0	0)	5	2	1	1	2	0	8	0	0	0	0	0	0	.158	.238	.263	.501
	10 ML YEARS		794	2348	560	121	13	82	(32	50)	953	259	313	295	210	16	491	10	4	26	5	5	29	.239	.301	.406	.707

Luke Voit

Bats: R **Throws:** R **Pos:** DH-96;1B-37;PH-3   **Ht:** 6'3" **Wt:** 255 **Born:** 2/13/1991 **Age:** 32

Year	Team	Lg	BATTING																			RUNNING			AVERAGES			
			G	AB	H	2B	3B	HR	(Hm	Rd)	TB	R	RBI	RC	TBB	IBB	SO	HBP	SH	SF	SB	CS	GDP	Avg	OBP	Slg	OPS
2017	StL	NL	62	114	28	9	0	4	(4	0)	49	18	18	12	7	0	31	3	0	0	0	0	4	.246	.306	.430	.736
2018	2 Tms		47	143	46	5	0	15	(7	8)	96	30	36	40	17	0	43	1	0	0	0	0	3	.322	.398	.671	1.069
2019	NYY	AL	118	429	113	21	1	21	(7	14)	199	72	62	79	71	2	142	9	0	1	0	0	12	.263	.378	.464	.842
2020	NYY	AL	56	213	59	5	0	22	(16	6)	130	41	52	46	17	0	54	3	0	1	0	0	4	.277	.338	.610	.948
2021	NYY	AL	68	213	51	7	1	11	(6	5)	93	26	35	27	21	0	74	7	0	0	0	0	12	.239	.328	.437	.764
2022	2 Tms	NL	135	500	113	22	0	22	(14	8)	201	55	69	63	55	1	179	7	0	6	1	1	9	.226	.308	.402	.710
18	StL	NL	8	11	2	0	0	1	(1	0)	5	2	3	2	2	0	4	0	0	0	0	0	0	.182	.308	.455	.762
18	NYY	AL	39	132	44	5	0	14	(6	8)	91	28	33	38	15	0	39	1	0	0	0	0	3	.333	.405	.689	1.095
22	SD	NL	82	298	67	18	0	13	(8	5)	124	38	48	41	39	1	110	3	0	4	1	1	5	.225	.317	.416	.733
22	Was	NL	53	202	46	4	0	9	(6	3)	77	17	21	22	16	0	69	4	0	2	0	0	4	.228	.295	.381	.676
	Postseason		12	42	9	3	1	1	(1	0)	17	7	6	7	8	0	13	0	0	0	0	0	0	.214	.340	.405	.745
	6 ML YEARS		486	1612	410	69	2	95	(54	41)	768	242	272	267	188	3	523	30	0	8	1	1	44	.254	.342	.476	.818

Anthony Volpe

Bats: R **Throws:** R **Pos:** SS   **Ht:** 5'11" **Wt:** 180 **Born:** 4/28/2001 **Age:** 22

Year	Team	Lg	BATTING																			RUNNING			AVERAGES			
			G	AB	H	2B	3B	HR	(Hm	Rd)	TB	R	RBI	RC	TBB	IBB	SO	HBP	SH	SF	SB	CS	GDP	Avg	OBP	Slg	OPS
2021	2 Tms	Low	109	412	121	35	6	27	(-	-)	249	113	86	0	78	1	101	18	0	5	33	9	5	.294	.423	.604	1.027
2022	Smrst	AA	110	422	106	31	4	18	(-	-)	199	71	60	79	57	0	88	10	0	8	44	5	1	.251	.348	.472	.820
2022	S-WB	AAA	22	89	21	4	1	3	(-	-)	36	15	5	12	8	0	30	2	0	0	6	1	1	.236	.313	.404	.718

Jason Vosler

Bats: L **Throws:** R **Pos:** 3B-29;PH-5;LF-3;1B-2;2B-1;SS-1;RF-1;PR-1   **Ht:** 6'1" **Wt:** 220 **Born:** 9/6/1993 **Age:** 29

Year	Team	Lg	BATTING																			RUNNING			AVERAGES			
			G	AB	H	2B	3B	HR	(Hm	Rd)	TB	R	RBI	RC	TBB	IBB	SO	HBP	SH	SF	SB	CS	GDP	Avg	OBP	Slg	OPS
2022	Scrmto	AAA	94	360	87	13	1	18	(-	-)	156	52	47	53	34	0	100	2	2	0	4	0	8	.242	.311	.433	.744
2021	SF	NL	41	73	13	4	0	3	(1	2)	26	12	9	5	7	1	21	1	0	1	2	0	5	.178	.256	.356	.612
2022	SF	NL	36	98	26	6	1	4	(2	2)	46	14	12	15	10	1	29	2	0	1	1	1	3	.265	.342	.469	.812
	2 ML YEARS		77	171	39	10	1	7	(3	4)	72	26	21	20	17	2	50	3	0	2	3	1	8	.228	.306	.421	.727

Austin Voth

Pitches: R **Bats:** R **Pos:** RP-24; SP-17   **Ht:** 6'2" **Wt:** 215 **Born:** 6/26/1992 **Age:** 31

Year	Team	Lg	HOW MUCH PITCHED					WHAT HE GAVE UP											THE RESULTS							
			G	GS	GF	IP	BFP	H	R	ER	HR	SH	SF	HB	TBB	IBB	SO	WP	W	L	Pct	Sv-Op	Hld	Vel	OPS	ERC	ERA
2018	Was	NL	4	2	0	12.1	55	12	9	9	3	1	1	0	6	0	11	1	1	1	.500	0-0	0	91	.780	5.19	6.57
2019	Was	NL	9	8	0	43.2	174	33	16	16	5	1	2	3	13	2	44	0	2	1	.667	0-0	0	93	.677	2.74	3.30
2020	Was	NL	11	11	0	49.2	225	57	36	35	10	0	0	4	18	2	44	1	2	5	.286	0-0	0	92	.923	6.38	6.34
2021	Was	NL	49	1	8	57.1	248	57	35	34	10	3	2	1	28	5	59	1	4	1	.800	0-5	7	94	.818	4.97	5.34

Year	Team	Lg	G	GS	GF	IP	BFP	H	R	ER	HR	SH	SF	HB	TBB	IBB	SO	WP	W	L	Pct	Sv-Op	Hld	Vel	OPS	ERC	ERA
2022	2 Tms		41	17	1	101.2	442	111	52	49	14	0	4	3	31	0	90	5	5	4	.556	0-0	1	94	.761	4.59	4.34
22	Was	NL	19	0	1	18.2	94	34	22	21	4	0	0	0	6	0	18	2	0	0	-	0-0	1	94	.994	9.93	10.13
22	Bal	AL	22	17	0	83.0	348	77	30	28	10	0	4	3	25	0	72	3	5	4	.556	0-0	0	93	.696	3.57	3.04
	5 ML YEARS		114	39	9	264.2	1144	270	148	143	46	5	9	11	96	9	248	8	14	12	.538	0-5	8	93	.793	4.69	4.86

Joey Votto

Bats: L Throws: R Pos: 1B-76;DH-14;PH-1   VAH-toe   **Ht: 6'2" Wt: 220 Born: 9/10/1983 Age: 39**

Year	Team	Lg	G	AB	H	2B	3B	HR	(Hm	Rd)	TB	R	RBI	RC	TBB	IBB	SO	HBP	SH	SF	SB	CS	GDP	Avg	OBP	Slg	OPS
2007	Cin	NL	24	84	27	7	0	4	(4	0)	46	11	17	17	5	1	15	0	0	0	1	0	0	.321	.360	.548	.907
2008	Cin	NL	151	526	156	32	3	24	(14	10)	266	69	84	91	59	9	102	2	0	2	7	5	5	.297	.368	.506	.874
2009	Cin	NL	131	469	151	38	1	25	(14	11)	266	82	84	99	70	10	106	4	0	1	4	1	8	.322	.414	.567	.981
2010	Cin	NL	150	547	177	36	2	37	(18	19)	328	106	113	132	91	8	125	7	0	3	16	5	11	.324	.424	.600	1.024
2011	Cin	NL	161	599	185	40	3	29	(13	16)	318	101	103	131	110	15	129	6	0	6	8	6	20	.309	.416	.531	.946
2012	Cin	NL	111	374	126	44	0	14	(10	4)	212	59	56	97	94	18	85	5	0	2	5	3	8	.337	.474	.567	1.041
2013	Cin	NL	162	581	177	30	3	24	(11	13)	285	101	73	121	135	19	138	4	0	6	6	3	15	.305	.435	.491	.926
2014	Cin	NL	62	220	56	16	0	6	(6	0)	90	32	23	36	47	2	49	3	0	2	1	1	5	.255	.390	.409	.799
2015	Cin	NL	158	545	171	33	2	29	(14	15)	295	95	80	135	143	15	135	5	0	2	11	3	11	.314	.459	.541	1.000
2016	Cin	NL	158	556	181	34	2	29	(16	13)	306	101	97	130	108	15	120	5	0	8	8	1	16	.326	.434	.550	.985
2017	Cin	NL	162	559	179	34	1	36	(20	16)	323	106	100	139	134	20	83	8	0	5	5	1	16	.320	.454	.578	1.032
2018	Cin	NL	145	503	143	28	2	12	(8	4)	211	67	67	98	108	6	101	9	0	3	2	0	15	.284	.417	.419	.837
2019	Cin	NL	142	525	137	32	1	15	(4	11)	216	79	47	72	76	2	123	4	0	3	5	0	14	.261	.357	.411	.768
2020	Cin	NL	54	186	42	8	0	11	(10	1)	83	32	22	26	37	1	43	0	0	0	0	0	5	.226	.354	.446	.800
2021	Cin	NL	129	448	119	23	1	36	(20	16)	252	73	99	101	77	6	127	4	0	4	1	0	7	.266	.375	.563	.938
2022	Cin	NL	91	322	66	18	1	11	(8	3)	119	31	41	45	44	0	97	10	0	0	0	0	8	.205	.319	.370	.689
	Postseason		11	41	10	0	0	0	(0	0)	10	3	1	3	5	1	12	0	0	1	0	0	1	.244	.319	.244	.563
	16 ML YEARS		1991	7044	2093	453	22	342	(190	152)	3616	1145	1106	1470	1338	147	1578	74	0	48	80	29	166	.297	.412	.513	.926

Michael Wacha

Pitches: R Bats: R Pos: SP-23   WAHK-ah   **Ht: 6'6" Wt: 215 Born: 7/1/1991 Age: 31**

Year	Team	Lg	G	GS	GF	IP	BFP	H	R	ER	HR	SH	SF	HB	TBB	IBB	SO	WP	W	L	Pct	Sv-Op	Hld	Vel	OPS	ERC	ERA
2013	StL	NL	15	9	2	64.2	260	52	20	20	5	1	3	0	19	0	65	3	4	1	.800	0-1	0	93	.603	2.52	2.78
2014	StL	NL	19	19	0	107.0	447	95	41	38	6	1	2	5	33	0	94	2	5	6	.455	0-0	0	93	.636	3.00	3.20
2015	StL	NL	30	30	0	181.1	762	162	74	68	19	8	3	6	58	4	153	4	17	7	.708	0-0	0	94	.672	3.28	3.38
2016	StL	NL	27	24	1	138.0	606	159	86	78	15	4	5	1	45	6	114	6	7	7	.500	0-0	0	94	.800	4.66	5.09
2017	StL	NL	30	30	0	165.2	701	170	82	76	17	3	4	3	55	3	158	5	12	9	.571	0-0	0	95	.735	4.07	4.13
2018	StL	NL	15	15	0	84.1	355	68	36	30	9	4	5	2	36	0	71	2	8	2	.800	0-0	0	94	.646	3.24	3.20
2019	StL	NL	29	24	0	126.2	562	143	71	67	26	6	5	3	55	4	104	2	6	7	.462	0-0	0	94	.865	5.88	4.76
2020	NYM	NL	8	7	0	34.0	156	46	26	25	9	0	0	2	7	0	37	2	1	4	.200	0-0	0	94	.951	6.76	6.62
2021	TB	AL	29	23	1	124.2	528	132	73	70	23	1	4	4	31	0	121	5	3	5	.375	0-0	1	94	.784	4.54	5.05
2022	Bos	AL	23	23	0	127.1	515	111	49	47	18	0	4	4	31	0	104	4	11	2	.846	0-0	0	93	.693	3.20	3.32
	Postseason		8	6	1	38.0	160	33	22	22	8	0	0	1	16	4	42	1	4	3	.571	0-0	0	94	.774	4.15	5.21
	10 ML YEARS		225	204	4	1153.2	4892	1138	558	519	147	28	35	30	370	17	1021	35	74	50	.597	0-1	1	94	.734	3.96	4.05

Tyler Wade

Bats: L Throws: R Pos: 2B-31;SS-19;3B-12;PR-8;LF-7;RF-5;CF-2;PH-2   **Ht: 6'1" Wt: 188 Born: 11/23/1994 Age: 28**

Year	Team	Lg	G	AB	H	2B	3B	HR	(Hm	Rd)	TB	R	RBI	RC	TBB	IBB	SO	HBP	SH	SF	SB	CS	GDP	Avg	OBP	Slg	OPS
2022	S-WB	AAA	42	141	32	6	1	4	(-	-)	52	26	16	21	27	0	35	1	0	1	15	1	2	.227	.353	.369	.722
2017	NYY	AL	30	58	9	4	0	0	(0	0)	13	7	2	1	5	0	19	0	0	0	1	1	0	.155	.222	.224	.446
2018	NYY	AL	36	66	11	4	0	1	(0	1)	18	8	5	4	4	0	23	0	0	0	1	0	1	.167	.214	.273	.487
2019	NYY	AL	43	94	23	3	1	2	(2	0)	34	16	11	12	11	0	28	1	2	1	7	0	0	.245	.330	.362	.692
2020	NYY	AL	52	88	15	3	0	3	(3	0)	27	19	10	10	12	0	22	3	1	1	4	1	1	.170	.288	.307	.595
2021	NYY	AL	103	127	34	5	1	0	(0	0)	41	31	5	17	16	1	37	1	0	0	17	6	3	.268	.354	.323	.677
2022	LAA	AL	67	147	32	5	0	1	(1	0)	40	22	8	8	10	0	33	1	5	0	8	5	3	.218	.272	.272	.544
	Postseason		4	0	0	0	0	0	(0	0)	0	1	0	0	1	0	0	0	0	0	0	0	0	-	1.000		
	6 ML YEARS		331	580	124	24	2	7	(6	1)	173	103	41	52	58	1	162	6	8	1	38	13	10	.214	.291	.298	.590

LaMonte Wade Jr.

Bats: L Throws: L Pos: RF-33;1B-22;LF-19;PH-13;DH-10;CF-1   lah-MONT   **Ht: 6'1" Wt: 205 Born: 1/1/1994 Age: 29**

Year	Team	Lg	G	AB	H	2B	3B	HR	(Hm	Rd)	TB	R	RBI	RC	TBB	IBB	SO	HBP	SH	SF	SB	CS	GDP	Avg	OBP	Slg	OPS
2022	Scrmto	AAA	14	44	11	4	0	2	(-	-)	21	11	11	9	10	2	6	2	0	2	0	0	1	.250	.397	.477	.874
2019	Min	AL	26	56	11	2	1	2	(1	1)	21	10	5	9	11	0	9	2	0	0	0	1	0	.196	.348	.375	.723
2020	Min	AL	16	39	9	3	0	0	(0	0)	12	3	1	5	4	0	9	1	0	0	1	1	0	.231	.318	.308	.626
2021	SF	NL	109	336	85	17	3	18	(12	6)	162	52	56	63	33	1	89	5	4	3	6	1	3	.253	.326	.482	.808
2022	SF	NL	77	217	45	7	1	8	(6	2)	78	29	26	30	26	0	51	5	2	1	1	0	0	.207	.305	.359	.665
	Postseason		5	10	1	0	0	0	(0	0)	1	1	0	0	1	0	4	0	0	0	0	0	0	.100	.182	.100	.282
	4 ML YEARS		228	648	150	29	5	28	(19	9)	273	94	88	107	74	1	158	13	6	4	8	3	3	.231	.321	.421	.742

Adam Wainwright

Pitches: R Bats: R Pos: SP-32   Ht: 6'7" Wt: 230 Born: 8/30/1981 Age: 41

Year	Team	Lg	G	GS	GF	IP	BFP	H	R	ER	HR	SH	SF	HB	TBB	IBB	SO	WP	W	L	Pct	Sv-Op	Hld	Vel	OPS	ERC	ERA
2005	StL	NL	2	0	1	2.0	9	2	3	3	1	0	0	0	1	0	0	0	0	0	-	0-0	0	91	.958	7.30	13.50
2006	StL	NL	61	0	10	75.0	309	64	26	26	6	4	1	4	22	2	72	3	2	1	.667	3-5	17	91	.644	2.92	3.12
2007	StL	NL	32	32	0	202.0	882	212	93	83	13	9	5	9	70	4	136	6	14	12	.538	0-0	0	89	.721	4.01	3.70
2008	StL	NL	20	20	0	132.0	544	122	51	47	12	6	4	3	34	1	91	3	11	3	.786	0-0	0	90	.688	3.14	3.20
2009	StL	NL	34	34	0	233.0	970	216	75	68	17	10	5	3	66	1	212	7	19	8	.704	0-0	0	91	.646	3.08	2.63
2010	StL	NL	33	33	0	230.1	910	186	68	62	15	13	6	4	56	2	213	2	20	11	.645	0-0	0	91	.604	2.36	2.42
2012	StL	NL	32	32	0	198.2	831	196	96	87	15	9	6	6	52	3	184	5	14	13	.519	0-0	0	90	.701	3.41	3.94
2013	StL	NL	34	34	0	241.2	956	223	83	79	15	13	2	6	35	2	219	5	19	9	.679	0-0	0	91	.636	2.60	2.94
2014	StL	NL	32	32	0	227.0	898	184	64	60	10	8	3	7	50	5	179	4	20	9	.690	0-0	0	90	.580	2.20	2.38
2015	StL	NL	7	4	2	28.0	111	25	7	5	0	2	0	0	4	0	20	0	2	1	.667	0-0	0	90	.590	1.97	1.61
2016	StL	NL	33	33	0	198.2	847	220	108	102	22	8	9	5	59	4	161	1	13	9	.591	0-0	0	90	.785	4.50	4.62
2017	StL	NL	24	23	0	123.1	546	140	73	70	14	5	1	5	45	4	96	2	12	5	.706	0-0	0	90	.794	4.93	5.11
2018	StL	NL	8	8	0	40.1	181	41	21	20	5	3	2	2	18	1	40	1	2	4	.333	0-0	0	89	.753	4.60	4.46
2019	StL	NL	31	31	0	171.2	745	181	83	80	22	6	5	8	64	7	153	2	14	10	.583	0-0	0	90	.782	4.64	4.19
2020	StL	NL	10	10	0	65.2	262	54	25	23	9	0	1	2	15	0	54	0	5	3	.625	0-0	0	89	.640	2.85	3.15
2021	StL	NL	32	32	0	206.1	828	168	72	70	21	3	1	9	50	3	174	4	17	7	.708	0-0	0	89	.627	2.67	3.05
2022	StL	NL	32	32	0	191.2	803	192	80	79	16	0	6	7	54	1	143	5	11	12	.478	0-0	0	88	.697	3.69	3.71
	Postseason		29	16	9	114.1	464	105	39	36	11	4	2	2	22	1	123	4	4	5	.444	4-5	0	91	.656	2.88	2.83
	17 ML YEARS		457	390	13	2567.1	10632	2426	1028	964	213	99	57	80	695	40	2147	50	195	117	.625	3-5	17	90	.680	3.28	3.38

Cole Waites

Pitches: R Bats: R Pos: RP-7   Ht: 6'3" Wt: 180 Born: 6/10/1998 Age: 25

Year	Team	Lg	G	GS	GF	IP	BFP	H	R	ER	HR	SH	SF	HB	TBB	IBB	SO	WP	W	L	Pct	Sv-Op	Hld	Vel	OPS	ERC	ERA
2022	Eugene	A+	13	0	5	12.2	52	10	5	5	1	0	0	0	4	0	27	0	1	-	.500	1- -	-	-	.247	3.55
2022	Rchmd	AA	18	0	12	21.0	92	12	7	4	0	1	1	1	15	1	38	3	2	2	.500	4- -	-	-	.497	2.28	1.71
2022	Scrmto	AAA	7	0	1	8.0	28	3	0	0	0	0	0	0	3	0	11	0	1	0	1.000	1- -	-	-	.374	0.91	0.00
2022	SF	NL	7	0	3	5.2	25	6	2	2	1	0	0	0	4	0	4	0	0	0	-	0-0	0	96	1.019	6.67	3.18

Ken Waldichuk

Pitches: L Bats: L Pos: SP-7   Ht: 6'4" Wt: 220 Born: 1/8/1998 Age: 25

Year	Team	Lg	G	GS	GF	IP	BFP	H	R	ER	HR	SH	SF	HB	TBB	IBB	SO	WP	W	L	Pct	Sv-Op	Hld	Vel	OPS	ERC	ERA
2021	HudVal	A+	7	7	0	30.2	113	12	0	0	0	0	0	0	13	0	55	3	2	0	1.000	0- -	-	-	1.01	0.00
2021	Smrst	AA	16	14	0	79.1	340	64	44	37	13	1	1	6	38	0	108	6	4	3	.571	0- -	-	-	.710	4.05	4.20
2022	Smrst	AA	6	6	0	28.2	112	16	6	4	2	0	0	1	10	0	46	1	4	0	1.000	0- -	-	-	.479	1.64	1.26
2022	S-WB	AAA	11	11	0	47.2	206	38	20	19	5	2	0	7	23	0	70	2	2	3	.400	0- -	-	-	.695	3.89	3.59
2022	Oak	AL	7	7	0	34.2	146	32	19	19	5	0	1	4	10	0	33	1	2	2	.500	0-0	0	94	.781	4.00	4.93

Christian Walker

Bats: R Throws: R Pos: 1B-150;DH-11;PH-1   Ht: 6'0" Wt: 208 Born: 3/28/1991 Age: 32

Year	Team	Lg	G	AB	H	2B	3B	HR	(Hm	Rd)	TB	R	RBI	RC	TBB	IBB	SO	HBP	SH	SF	SB	CS	GDP	Avg	OBP	Slg	OPS
2014	Bal	AL	6	18	3	1	0	1	(1	0)	7	1	1	0	1	0	9	0	0	0	0	0	0	.167	.211	.389	.599
2015	Bal	AL	7	9	1	0	0	0	(0	0)	1	0	0	1	3	0	4	0	0	0	0	0	0	.111	.333	.111	.444
2017	Ari	NL	11	12	3	1	0	2	(2	0)	10	2	2	2	1	0	5	2	0	0	0	0	0	.250	.400	.833	1.233
2018	Ari	NL	37	49	8	2	0	3	(2	1)	19	6	6	3	3	0	22	1	0	0	1	0	1	.163	.226	.388	.614
2019	Ari	NL	152	529	137	26	1	29	(16	13)	252	86	73	83	67	6	155	6	0	1	8	1	11	.259	.348	.476	.825
2020	Ari	NL	57	218	59	18	1	7	(5	2)	100	35	34	34	19	0	50	3	0	3	1	1	6	.271	.333	.459	.792
2021	Ari	NL	115	401	98	23	1	10	(3	7)	153	55	46	48	38	1	106	4	0	2	0	0	8	.244	.315	.382	.696
2022	Ari	NL	160	583	141	25	2	36	(15	21)	278	84	94	100	69	2	131	8	0	7	2	2	15	.242	.327	.477	.804
	Postseason		2	1	1	0	0	0	(0 | 0)	1	0	0	1	0	0	0	1	0	0	0	0	0	0	1.000	1.000	1.000	2.000
	8 ML YEARS		545	1819	450	96	5	88	(44	44)	820	269	256	271	201	9	482	24	0	13	12	4	41	.247	.328	.451	.779

Jordan Walker

Bats: R Throws: R Pos: 3B   Ht: 6'5" Wt: 220 Born: 5/22/2002 Age: 21

Year	Team	Lg	G	AB	H	2B	3B	HR	(Hm	Rd)	TB	R	RBI	RC	TBB	IBB	SO	HBP	SH	SF	SB	CS	GDP	Avg	OBP	Slg	OPS
2021	2 Tms	Low	82	325	103	25	4	14	(-	-)	178	63	48	70	33	1	87	6	0	2	14	2	3	.317	.388	.548	.936
2022	Sprgfld	AA	119	461	141	31	3	19	(-	-)	235	100	68	92	58	1	116	9	0	8	22	5	10	.306	.388	.510	.898

Steele Walker

Bats: L Throws: L Pos: LF-4;RF-1;PH-1   Ht: 5'11" Wt: 209 Born: 7/30/1996 Age: 26

Year	Team	Lg	G	AB	H	2B	3B	HR	(Hm	Rd)	TB	R	RBI	RC	TBB	IBB	SO	HBP	SH	SF	SB	CS	GDP	Avg	OBP	Slg	OPS
2022	RdRck	AAA	50	191	53	9	0	7	(-	-)	83	32	26	30	20	0	35	3	0	1	6	3	1	.277	.353	.435	.788
2022	Scrmto	AAA	25	89	22	5	1	2	(-	-)	35	10	14	10	4	0	16	1	0	0	2	0	1	.247	.287	.393	.680
2022	Tex	AL	5	14	1	0	0	1	(0	1)	4	1	1	1	2	0	4	0	0	0	0	0	0	.071	.188	.286	.473

Taijuan Walker

Pitches: R Bats: R Pos: SP-29
TIE-wahn
Ht: 6'4" Wt: 235 Born: 8/13/1992 Age: 30

		HOW MUCH PITCHED					WHAT HE GAVE UP											THE RESULTS						
Year	Team	Lg	G	GS	GF	IP	BFP	H	R	ER	HR	SH	SF	HB	TBB	IBB	SO	WP	W	L	Pct	Sv-Op	Hld	Vel	OPS	ERC	ERA
2013	Sea	AL	3	3	0	15.0	60	11	7	6	0	0	2	0	4	0	12	0	1	0	1.000	0-0	0	95	.546	1.63	3.60
2014	Sea	AL	8	5	2	38.0	160	31	12	11	2	0	0	3	18	1	34	2	2	3	.400	0-0	0	95	.642	3.34	2.61
2015	Sea	AL	29	29	0	169.2	706	163	92	86	25	4	5	9	40	1	157	4	11	8	.579	0-0	0	94	.717	3.74	4.56
2016	Sea	AL	25	25	0	134.1	573	129	75	63	27	3	3	8	37	2	119	4	8	11	.421	0-0	0	94	.767	4.20	4.22
2017	Ari	NL	28	28	0	157.1	684	148	76	61	17	5	8	9	61	7	146	7	9	9	.500	0-0	0	94	.732	3.85	3.49
2018	Ari	NL	3	3	0	13.0	56	15	5	5	1	0	0	0	5	0	9	0	0	0	-	0-0	0	94	.749	4.88	3.46
2019	Ari	NL	1	1	0	1.0	4	1	0	0	0	0	0	0	0	0	1	0	0	0	-	0-0	0	93	.750	1.95	0.00
2020	2 Tms	AL	11	11	0	53.1	225	43	23	16	8	0	1	4	19	0	50	1	4	3	.571	0-0	0	93	.661	3.42	2.70
2021	NYM	NL	30	29	0	159.0	654	133	84	79	26	2	3	4	55	0	146	5	7	11	.389	0-0	0	94	.694	3.51	4.47
2022	NYM	NL	29	29	0	157.1	649	143	63	61	15	0	2	6	45	1	132	0	12	5	.706	0-0	0	94	.663	3.28	3.49
20	Sea	AL	5	5	0	27.0	112	21	13	12	5	0	1	3	8	0	25	0	2	2	.500	0-0	0	93	.676	3.42	4.00
20	Tor	AL	6	6	0	26.1	113	22	10	4	3	0	0	1	11	0	25	1	2	1	.667	0-0	0	93	.647	3.41	1.37
	Postseason		1	1	0	1.0	9	4	4	4	1	0	0	0	2	1	3	0	0	1	.000	0-0	0	93	1.810	44.27	36.00
	10 ML YEARS		167	163	2	898.0	3771	817	437	388	121	14	24	43	284	12	806	23	54	50	.519	0-0	0	94	.705	3.65	3.89

Chad Wallach

Bats: R Throws: R Pos: C-12
Ht: 6'2" Wt: 246 Born: 11/4/1991 Age: 31

								BATTING											RUNNING			AVERAGES			
Year	Team	Lg	G	AB	H	2B	3B	HR	(Hm | Rd)	TB	R	RBI	RC	TBB	IBB	SO	HBP	SH	SF	SB	CS	GDP	Avg	OBP	Slg	OPS
2022	Salt Lk	AAA	89	319	70	16	1	9	(- | -)	115	40	43	34	36	0	95	5	0	5	3	0	12	.219	.304	.361	.665
2017	Cin	NL	6	11	1	0	0	0	(0 | 0)	1	0	0	0	0	0	5	0	0	0	0	0	0	.091	.091	.091	.182
2018	Mia	NL	15	45	8	1	0	1	(1 | 0)	12	4	5	4	4	0	23	2	1	0	0	0	0	.178	.275	.267	.541
2019	Mia	NL	19	48	12	3	0	1	(1 | 0)	18	4	3	5	6	0	12	0	0	0	0	0	0	.250	.333	.375	.708
2020	Mia	NL	15	44	10	3	0	1	(1 | 0)	16	2	6	7	3	0	12	0	1	0	0	0	1	.227	.277	.364	.640
2021	Mia	NL	23	60	12	1	0	1	(0 | 0)	16	4	6	3	3	0	32	1	0	2	0	0	1	.200	.242	.267	.509
2022	LAA	AL	12	35	5	1	0	1	(1 | 0)	9	3	4	3	4	0	9	0	1	0	0	0	1	.143	.231	.257	.488
	Postseason		5	14	1	0	0	0	(0 | 0)	1	1	0	0	0	0	6	0	0	0	0	0	1	.071	.071	.071	.143
	6 ML YEARS		90	243	48	10	1	4	(4 | 0)	72	17	24	22	20	0	93	3	3	2	0	0	3	.198	.265	.296	.561

Matt Wallner

Bats: L Throws: R Pos: RF-16;DH-1;PH-1
Ht: 6'5" Wt: 220 Born: 12/12/1997 Age: 25

								BATTING											RUNNING			AVERAGES			
Year	Team	Lg	G	AB	H	2B	3B	HR	(Hm | Rd)	TB	R	RBI	RC	TBB	IBB	SO	HBP	SH	SF	SB	CS	GDP	Avg	OBP	Slg	OPS
2022	Wich	AA	78	268	80	15	1	21	(- | -)	160	61	64	73	62	5	107	7	0	5	8	5	4	.299	.436	.597	1.033
2022	StPaul	AAA	50	190	47	17	3	6	(- | -)	88	29	31	35	35	1	63	4	0	1	0	1	0	.247	.376	.463	.839
2022	Min	AL	18	57	13	3	0	2	(1 | 1)	22	4	10	10	6	1	25	2	0	0	1	0	0	.228	.323	.386	.709

Taylor Walls

Bats: B Throws: R Pos: SS-92;2B-35;3B-25;PR-7;DH-1;PH-1
Ht: 5'10" Wt: 185 Born: 7/10/1996 Age: 26

								BATTING											RUNNING			AVERAGES			
Year	Team	Lg	G	AB	H	2B	3B	HR	(Hm | Rd)	TB	R	RBI	RC	TBB	IBB	SO	HBP	SH	SF	SB	CS	GDP	Avg	OBP	Slg	OPS
2021	TB	AL	54	152	32	10	0	1	(1 | 0)	45	15	15	17	23	0	49	0	1	0	4	2	3	.211	.314	.296	.610
2022	TB	AL	142	407	70	18	2	8	(7 | 1)	116	53	33	31	52	0	120	2	2	2	10	3	6	.172	.268	.285	.553
	2 ML YEARS		196	559	102	28	2	9	(8 | 1)	161	68	48	48	75	0	169	2	3	2	14	5	9	.182	.281	.288	.569

Jake Walsh

Pitches: R Bats: R Pos: RP-3
Ht: 6'1" Wt: 192 Born: 7/20/1995 Age: 27

			HOW MUCH PITCHED					WHAT HE GAVE UP											THE RESULTS						
Year	Team	Lg	G	GS	GF	IP	BFP	H	R	ER	HR	SH	SF	HB	TBB	IBB	SO	WP	W	L	Pct	Sv-Op	Hld	Vel	OPS	ERC	ERA
2022	Memp	AAA	13	0	9	15.1	63	11	3	2	1	0	0	0	7	1	22	1	1	0	1.000	6- -			.554	2.47	1.17
2022	StL	NL	3	0	1	2.2	15	3	4	4	0	0	0	1	2	0	5	0	0	1	.000	0-0	0	95	.650	6.23	13.50

Jared Walsh

Bats: L Throws: L Pos: 1B-118;PH-10;LF-2
Ht: 6'0" Wt: 210 Born: 7/30/1993 Age: 29

								BATTING											RUNNING			AVERAGES			
Year	Team	Lg	G	AB	H	2B	3B	HR	(Hm | Rd)	TB	R	RBI	RC	TBB	IBB	SO	HBP	SH	SF	SB	CS	GDP	Avg	OBP	Slg	OPS
2019	LAA	AL	34	79	16	5	1	1	(1 | 0)	26	6	5	8	6	1	35	2	0	0	0	0	0	.203	.276	.329	.605
2020	LAA	AL	32	99	29	4	2	9	(4 | 5)	64	19	26	21	5	0	15	1	0	3	0	0	0	.293	.324	.646	.971
2021	LAA	AL	144	530	147	34	1	29	(15 | 14)	270	70	98	97	48	6	152	4	0	3	2	1	7	.277	.340	.509	.850
2022	LAA	AL	118	423	91	18	2	15	(8 | 7)	158	41	44	38	27	4	138	4	0	0	2	1	6	.215	.269	.374	.642
	4 ML YEARS		328	1131	283	61	6	54	(28 | 26)	518	136	173	164	86	11	340	11	0	6	4	2	13	.250	.308	.458	.766

Nash Walters

Pitches: R Bats: R Pos: RP-1
Ht: 6'5" Wt: 210 Born: 5/18/1997 Age: 26

			HOW MUCH PITCHED					WHAT HE GAVE UP											THE RESULTS						
Year	Team	Lg	G	GS	GF	IP	BFP	H	R	ER	HR	SH	SF	HB	TBB	IBB	SO	WP	W	L	Pct	Sv-Op	Hld	Vel	OPS	ERC	ERA
2022	Biloxi	AA	42	0	14	47.0	200	44	26	24	3	0	2	3	15	0	66	2	6	3	.667	1- -		-	.682	3.39	4.60
2022	Salt Lk	AAA	7	0	4	5.1	27	5	5	4	2	0	1	1	4	1	4	1	0	1	.000	1- -		-	.942	7.38	6.75
2022	LAA	AL	1	0	0	0.1	3	1	0	0	0	0	0	0	1	0	0	0	0	0	-	0-0	0	-	1.167	29.63	0.00

Donovan Walton

Bats: L **Throws:** R **Pos:** 2B-14;SS-12;PR-2;3B-1;PH-1   **Ht:** 5'10" **Wt:** 190 **Born:** 5/25/1994 **Age:** 29

Year	Team	Lg	G	AB	H	2B	3B	HR	(Hm	Rd)	TB	R	RBI	RC	TBB	IBB	SO	HBP	SH	SF	SB	CS	GDP	Avg	OBP	Slg	OPS
2022	Tacom	AAA	12	51	15	4	2	1	(-	-)	26	10	5	9	6	0	6	0	0	0	2	1	0	.294	.368	.510	.878
2022	Scrmto	AAA	20	71	16	6	0	1	(-	-)	25	10	7	9	12	0	13	1	4	0	3	0	2	.225	.345	.352	.697
2019	Sea	AL	7	16	3	0	0	0	(0	0)	3	2	2	1	3	0	5	0	0	0	0	1	0	.188	.316	.188	.503
2020	Sea	AL	5	13	2	1	0	0	(0	0)	3	0	3	0	1	0	5	0	0	0	0	1	1	.154	.214	.231	.445
2021	Sea	AL	24	63	13	2	1	2	(1	1)	23	6	7	6	4	0	15	0	2	0	1	0	1	.206	.254	.365	.619
2022	2 Tms		25	76	12	8	0	1	(0	1)	23	9	8	4	1	0	16	1	0	0	0	0	1	.158	.179	.303	.482
22	Sea	AL	1	0	0	0	0	0	(0	0)	0	1	0	0	0	0	0	0	0	0	0	0	0	.-	.-	.-	.-
22	SF	NL	24	76	12	8	0	1	(0	1)	23	8	8	4	1	0	16	1	0	0	0	0	1	.158	.179	.303	.482
	4 ML YEARS		61	168	30	11	1	3	(1	2)	52	17	20	11	9	0	41	1	2	0	1	2	3	.179	.225	.310	.534

Andrew Wantz

Pitches: R **Bats:** R **Pos:** RP-41; SP-1   **Ht:** 6'4" **Wt:** 235 **Born:** 10/13/1995 **Age:** 27

Year	Team	Lg	G	GS	GF	IP	BFP	H	R	ER	HR	SH	SF	HB	TBB	IBB	SO	WP	W	L	Pct	Sv-Op	Hld	Vel	OPS	ERC	ERA
2022	Salt Lk	AAA	10	0	2	15.2	60	11	5	5	3	1	3	0	3	0	17	0	1	1	.500	0- --	-		.634	2.29	2.87
2021	LAA	AL	21	0	3	27.1	120	23	17	15	5	0	0	3	11	0	38	1	1	0	1.000	0-1	0	93	.711	4.03	4.94
2022	LAA	AL	42	1	7	50.1	204	37	19	18	8	0	1	2	21	0	52	2	2	1	.667	0-1	7	94	.661	3.32	3.22
	2 ML YEARS		63	1	10	77.2	324	60	36	33	13	0	1	5	32	0	90	3	3	1	.750	0-2	7	94	.679	3.57	3.82

Taylor Ward

Bats: R **Throws:** R **Pos:** RF-125;CF-7;PH-5;3B-2;LF-2;DH-2   **Ht:** 6'1" **Wt:** 200 **Born:** 12/14/1993 **Age:** 29

Year	Team	Lg	G	AB	H	2B	3B	HR	(Hm	Rd)	TB	R	RBI	RC	TBB	IBB	SO	HBP	SH	SF	SB	CS	GDP	Avg	OBP	Slg	OPS
2018	LAA	AL	40	135	24	3	0	6	(4	2)	45	14	15	14	9	0	45	3	0	0	2	0	0	.178	.245	.333	.578
2019	LAA	AL	20	42	8	3	0	1	(1	0)	14	4	2	2	6	0	23	0	0	1	0	0	1	.190	.292	.333	.625
2020	LAA	AL	34	94	26	6	2	0	(0	0)	36	16	5	14	8	0	28	0	0	0	2	0	1	.277	.333	.383	.716
2021	LAA	AL	65	208	52	15	0	8	(7	1)	91	33	33	35	20	0	55	6	2	1	1	1	4	.250	.332	.438	.769
2022	LAA	AL	135	495	139	22	2	23	(10	13)	234	73	65	85	60	0	120	4	0	5	5	3	5	.281	.360	.473	.833
	5 ML YEARS		294	974	249	49	4	38	(22	16)	420	140	120	150	103	0	271	13	2	6	10	4	11	.256	.333	.431	.764

Art Warren

Pitches: R **Bats:** R **Pos:** RP-39   **Ht:** 6'3" **Wt:** 230 **Born:** 3/23/1993 **Age:** 30

Year	Team	Lg	G	GS	GF	IP	BFP	H	R	ER	HR	SH	SF	HB	TBB	IBB	SO	WP	W	L	Pct	Sv-Op	Hld	Vel	OPS	ERC	ERA
2019	Sea	AL	6	0	2	5.1	21	2	0	0	0	0	0	0	2	0	5	1	1	0	1.000	0-0	1	95	.296	0.81	0.00
2021	Cin	NL	26	0	6	21.0	82	11	3	3	1	1	0	1	8	1	34	0	3	0	1.000	0-0	1	95	.483	1.51	1.29
2022	Cin	NL	39	0	15	36.0	165	37	29	26	6	0	1	2	22	1	40	0	2	3	.400	3-6	4	94	.813	5.80	6.50
	3 ML YEARS		71	0	23	62.1	268	50	32	29	7	1	1	3	32	2	79	1	6	3	.667	3-6	6	94	.669	3.63	4.19

Austin Warren

Pitches: R **Bats:** R **Pos:** RP-14   **Ht:** 6'0" **Wt:** 170 **Born:** 2/5/1996 **Age:** 27

Year	Team	Lg	G	GS	GF	IP	BFP	H	R	ER	HR	SH	SF	HB	TBB	IBB	SO	WP	W	L	Pct	Sv-Op	Hld	Vel	OPS	ERC	ERA
2022	Salt Lk	AAA	29	0	3	34.0	145	23	9	8	2	0	0	4	17	0	30	3	2	0	1.000	1- --	-		.545	2.84	2.12
2021	LAA	AL	16	0	1	20.1	84	16	5	4	0	0	0	1	5	0	20	0	3	0	1.000	1-1	2	94	.544	1.90	1.77
2022	LAA	AL	14	0	2	16.0	70	19	10	10	3	1	2	0	5	2	9	1	2	0	1.000	0-1	0	93	.896	5.27	5.63
	2 ML YEARS		30	0	3	36.1	154	35	15	14	3	1	2	1	10	2	29	1	5	0	1.000	1-2	2	94	.701	3.25	3.47

Drew Waters

Bats: B **Throws:** R **Pos:** RF-17;CF-12;LF-4;PR-2   **Ht:** 6'2" **Wt:** 185 **Born:** 12/30/1998 **Age:** 24

Year	Team	Lg	G	AB	H	2B	3B	HR	(Hm	Rd)	TB	R	RBI	RC	TBB	IBB	SO	HBP	SH	SF	SB	CS	GDP	Avg	OBP	Slg	OPS
2022	Gwnntt	AAA	49	191	47	7	3	5	(-	-)	75	26	16	22	16	0	57	1	0	2	5	1	7	.246	.305	.393	.697
2022	Omha	AAA	31	122	36	5	2	7	(-	-)	66	29	17	29	20	0	41	1	0	0	13	0	0	.295	.399	.541	.940
2022	KC	AL	32	96	23	6	1	5	(2	3)	46	14	18	20	12	0	40	0	0	0	0	0	1	.240	.324	.479	.803

Spenser Watkins

Pitches: R **Bats:** R **Pos:** SP-20; RP-3   **Ht:** 6'2" **Wt:** 185 **Born:** 8/27/1992 **Age:** 30

Year	Team	Lg	G	GS	GF	IP	BFP	H	R	ER	HR	SH	SF	HB	TBB	IBB	SO	WP	W	L	Pct	Sv-Op	Hld	Vel	OPS	ERC	ERA
2021	Bal	AL	16	10	4	54.2	255	74	50	49	14	1	3	2	19	0	35	4	2	7	.222	0-0	0	91	.970	7.33	8.07
2022	Bal	AL	23	20	1	105.1	459	119	59	55	11	0	2	4	30	0	63	3	5	6	.455	0-0	0	91	.757	4.53	4.70
	2 ML YEARS		39	30	5	160.0	714	193	109	104	25	1	5	6	49	0	98	7	7	13	.350	0-0	0	91	.832	5.45	5.85

Ryan Weathers

Pitches: L Bats: R Pos: SP-1   Ht: 6'1" Wt: 230 Born: 12/17/1999 Age: 23

			HOW MUCH PITCHED				WHAT HE GAVE UP										THE RESULTS						
Year	Team	Lg	G	GS	GF	IP	BFP	H	R	ER	HR	SH	SF	HB	TBB	IBB	SO	WP	W	L	Pct	Sv-Op	Hld	Vel	OPS	ERC	ERA
2022	ElPaso	AAA	31	22	1	123.0	564	163	101	92	31	1	4	5	57	0	88	4	7	7	.500	0- -	-	-	.987	7.98	6.73
2021	SD	NL	30	18	1	94.2	401	101	57	56	20	5	1	3	30	1	72	2	4	7	.364	1-1	0	94	.836	5.15	5.32
2022	SD	NL	1	1	0	3.2	21	6	4	4	0	0	0	0	4	0	3	0	0	0	-	0-0	0	94	.888	9.89	9.82
	Postseason		1	0	0	1.1	6	0	0	0	0	0	0	0	2	0	1	0	0	0	-	0-0	0	95	.333	1.96	0.00
	2 ML YEARS		31	19	1	98.1	422	107	61	60	20	5	1	3	34	1	75	2	4	7	.364	1-1	0	94	.839	5.33	5.49

Luke Weaver

Pitches: R Bats: R Pos: RP-25; SP-1   Ht: 6'2" Wt: 183 Born: 8/21/1993 Age: 29

			HOW MUCH PITCHED				WHAT HE GAVE UP										THE RESULTS						
Year	Team	Lg	G	GS	GF	IP	BFP	H	R	ER	HR	SH	SF	HB	TBB	IBB	SO	WP	W	L	Pct	Sv-Op	Hld	Vel	OPS	ERC	ERA
2016	StL	NL	9	8	0	36.1	167	46	29	23	7	2	3	2	12	0	45	1	1	4	.200	0-0	0	92	.870	6.23	5.70
2017	StL	NL	13	10	0	60.1	252	59	27	26	7	1	1	1	17	1	72	0	7	2	.778	0-0	0	93	.699	3.66	3.88
2018	StL	NL	30	25	0	136.1	596	150	83	75	19	9	1	3	54	2	121	3	7	11	.389	0-0	0	94	.786	4.93	4.95
2019	Ari	NL	12	12	0	64.1	260	55	22	21	6	0	1	3	14	1	69	0	4	3	.571	0-0	0	94	.645	2.73	2.94
2020	Ari	NL	12	12	0	52.0	236	63	39	38	10	0	1	1	18	0	55	0	1	9	.100	0-0	0	94	.871	5.78	6.58
2021	Ari	NL	13	13	0	65.2	275	58	34	31	11	3	1	1	20	3	62	0	3	6	.333	0-0	0	94	.761	3.45	4.25
2022	2 Tms		26	1	15	35.2	174	52	29	26	1	0	3	3	13	0	38	2	1	1	.500	0-0	0	95	.842	6.29	6.56
22	Ari	NL	12	1	4	16.1	79	24	14	14	1	0	0	1	5	0	19	0	1	1	.500	0-0	0	95	.818	6.26	7.71
22	KC	AL	14	0	11	19.1	95	28	15	12	0	0	3	2	8	0	19	2	0	0	-	0-0	0	95	.863	6.31	5.59
	7 ML YEARS		115	81	18	450.2	1973	483	263	240	61	15	11	14	148	7	462	6	24	36	.400	0-0	0	94	.775	4.50	4.79

Logan Webb

Pitches: R Bats: R Pos: SP-32   Ht: 6'1" Wt: 220 Born: 11/18/1996 Age: 26

			HOW MUCH PITCHED				WHAT HE GAVE UP										THE RESULTS						
Year	Team	Lg	G	GS	GF	IP	BFP	H	R	ER	HR	SH	SF	HB	TBB	IBB	SO	WP	W	L	Pct	Sv-Op	Hld	Vel	OPS	ERC	ERA
2019	SF	NL	8	8	0	39.2	174	44	25	23	5	0	1	1	14	0	37	4	2	3	.400	0-0	0	93	.795	4.81	5.22
2020	SF	NL	13	11	0	54.1	246	61	38	33	4	0	1	7	24	1	46	3	3	4	.429	0-0	0	93	.806	5.31	5.47
2021	SF	NL	27	26	0	148.1	596	128	53	50	9	3	3	8	36	0	158	2	11	3	.786	0-0	1	93	.622	2.76	3.03
2022	SF	NL	32	32	0	192.1	787	174	76	62	11	2	2	7	49	0	163	6	15	9	.625	0-0	0	92	.639	2.89	2.90
	Postseason		2	2	0	14.2	53	9	1	1	0	0	0	0	1	0	17	0	1	0	1.000	0-0	0	93	.419	0.92	0.61
	4 ML YEARS		80	77	0	434.2	1803	407	192	168	29	5	7	23	123	1	404	15	31	19	.620	0-0	1	93	.670	3.29	3.48

Ryan Weber

Pitches: R Bats: R Pos: RP-5   Ht: 6'1" Wt: 175 Born: 8/12/1990 Age: 32

			HOW MUCH PITCHED				WHAT HE GAVE UP										THE RESULTS						
Year	Team	Lg	G	GS	GF	IP	BFP	H	R	ER	HR	SH	SF	HB	TBB	IBB	SO	WP	W	L	Pct	Sv-Op	Hld	Vel	OPS	ERC	ERA
2022	S-WB	AAA	15	8	2	39.2	164	43	23	17	6	0	0	1	5	0	27	0	3	4	.429	0- -	-	-	.799	3.92	3.86
2015	Atl	NL	5	5	0	28.1	109	25	15	15	3	0	0	2	6	0	19	0	0	3	.000	0-0	0	90	.699	3.26	4.76
2016	Atl	NL	16	2	6	36.1	157	46	22	22	7	1	0	2	5	2	23	1	1	1	.500	0-1	0	91	.877	5.40	5.45
2017	Sea	AL	1	1	0	3.2	14	3	1	1	0	0	0	0	0	0	0	0	0	0	-	0-0	0	90	.500	1.32	2.45
2018	TB	AL	2	0	0	5.1	25	5	5	3	0	0	1	1	2	0	1	0	0	1	.000	0-0	0	89	.701	3.36	5.06
2019	Bos	AL	18	3	8	40.2	181	48	25	23	5	1	0	3	8	0	29	2	2	4	.333	0-0	0	89	.789	4.63	5.09
2020	Bos	AL	17	5	3	43.0	185	44	23	21	8	1	1	3	14	0	27	1	1	3	.250	0-0	5	89	.807	4.84	4.40
2021	3 Tms		4	0	3	9.2	45	15	13	13	5	0	1	0	4	0	8	0	0	0	-	0-0	0	89	1.265	12.59	12.10
2022	NYY	AL	5	0	4	10.2	37	6	1	1	1	0	0	0	1	0	3	0	0	0	-	1-1	0	89	.467	1.16	0.84
21	Bos	AL	1	0	0	5.2	30	13	11	11	4	0	1	0	2	0	7	0	0	0	-	0-0	0	89	1.500	19.62	17.47
21	Mil	NL	1	0	1	1.0	3	1	0	0	0	0	0	0	0	0	0	0	0	0	-	0-0	0	89	.667	2.79	0.00
21	Sea	AL	2	0	2	3.0	12	1	2	2	1	0	0	0	2	0	1	0	0	0	-	0-0	0	89	.778	4.68	6.00
	8 ML YEARS		68	16	24	177.2	753	192	105	99	29	3	3	12	40	2	110	4	4	12	.250	1-2	5	89	.802	4.58	5.02

Jordan Weems

Pitches: R Bats: L Pos: RP-32   Ht: 6'4" Wt: 209 Born: 11/7/1992 Age: 30

			HOW MUCH PITCHED				WHAT HE GAVE UP										THE RESULTS						
Year	Team	Lg	G	GS	GF	IP	BFP	H	R	ER	HR	SH	SF	HB	TBB	IBB	SO	WP	W	L	Pct	Sv-Op	Hld	Vel	OPS	ERC	ERA
2022	Roch	AAA	33	0	25	40.0	157	31	14	12	4	0	0	1	12	0	49	1	3	2	.600	16- -	-	-	.648	2.70	2.70
2020	Oak	AL	9	0	4	14.0	58	10	5	5	1	0	1	0	7	0	18	2	0	0	-	0-0	0	95	.593	2.74	3.21
2021	2 Tms		7	0	3	5.2	30	6	10	10	2	0	0	1	6	1	7	1	0	1	.000	0-1	0	95	1.086	9.73	15.88
2022	Was	NL	32	0	3	39.2	166	35	24	23	7	1	1	0	12	1	41	4	0	1	.000	0-0	0	97	.726	3.45	5.22
21	Oak	AL	5	0	3	4.1	18	2	3	3	1	0	0	0	3	0	4	0	0	0	-	0-0	0	95	.678	3.11	6.23
21	Ari	NL	2	0	0	1.1	12	4	7	7	1	0	0	1	3	1	3	1	0	1	.000	0-1	0	95	1.792	38.10	47.25
	Postseason		1	0	0	0.0	3	2	2	2	0	0	0	0	1	0	0	0	0	0	-	0-0	0	95	2.000	-	-
	3 ML YEARS		48	0	10	59.1	254	51	39	38	10	1	2	1	25	2	66	7	0	2	.000	0-1	0	96	.735	3.80	5.76

Zack Weiss

Pitches: R Bats: R Pos: RP-12   Ht: 6'3" Wt: 210 Born: 6/16/1992 Age: 31

			HOW MUCH PITCHED				WHAT HE GAVE UP										THE RESULTS						
Year	Team	Lg	G	GS	GF	IP	BFP	H	R	ER	HR	SH	SF	HB	TBB	IBB	SO	WP	W	L	Pct	Sv-Op	Hld	Vel	OPS	ERC	ERA
2022	Salt Lk	AAA	43	0	11	50.0	219	44	29	25	6	0	1	2	21	0	65	4	2	3	.400	3- -	-	-	.691	3.66	4.50
2018	Cin	NL	1	0	0	0.0	4	2	4	4	2	0	0	0	2	0	0	0	0	0	-	0-0	0	94	5.000	-	-
2022	LAA	AL	12	0	6	13.1	56	7	6	5	2	1	1	1	7	2	18	2	0	1	.000	0-0	1	95	.577	2.34	3.38
	2 ML YEARS		13	0	6	13.1	60	9	10	9	4	1	1	1	9	2	18	2	0	1	.000	0-0	1	95	.780	4.64	6.08

Greg Weissert

Pitches: R **Bats:** R **Pos:** RP-12 **Ht:** 6'2" **Wt:** 215 **Born:** 2/4/1995 **Age:** 28

Year	Team	Lg	G	GS	GF	IP	BFP	H	R	ER	HR	SH	SF	HB	TBB	IBB	SO	WP	W	L	Pct	Sv-Op	Hld	Vel	OPS	ERC	ERA
2022	S-WB	AAA	42	0	38	48.0	190	24	9	9	3	0	4	5	19	1	70	3	2	1	.667	18- -	-	-	.465	1.67	1.69
2022	NYY	AL	12	0	2	11.1	48	6	7	7	1	0	0	2	5	0	11	0	3	0	1.000	0-0	1	95	.515	2.25	5.56

Alex Wells

Pitches: L **Bats:** L **Pos:** RP-2 **Ht:** 6'1" **Wt:** 195 **Born:** 2/27/1997 **Age:** 26

Year	Team	Lg	G	GS	GF	IP	BFP	H	R	ER	HR	SH	SF	HB	TBB	IBB	SO	WP	W	L	Pct	Sv-Op	Hld	Vel	OPS	ERC	ERA
2021	Bal	AL	11	8	2	42.2	197	53	32	32	10	0	1	3	16	0	26	0	2	3	.400	0-0	0	89	.885	6.71	6.75
2022	Bal	AL	2	0	2	3.2	16	5	2	2	2	0	0	0	0	0	6	0	0	0	-	0-0	0	88	1.063	7.47	4.91
	2 ML YEARS		13	8	4	46.1	213	58	34	34	12	0	1	3	16	0	32	0	2	3	.400	0-0	0	89	.900	6.79	6.60

Tyler Wells

Pitches: R **Bats:** R **Pos:** SP-23 **Ht:** 6'8" **Wt:** 255 **Born:** 8/26/1994 **Age:** 28

Year	Team	Lg	G	GS	GF	IP	BFP	H	R	ER	HR	SH	SF	HB	TBB	IBB	SO	WP	W	L	Pct	Sv-Op	Hld	Vel	OPS	ERC	ERA
2021	Bal	AL	44	0	18	57.0	224	40	27	26	9	1	2	1	12	0	65	1	2	3	.400	4-7	1	95	.603	2.20	4.11
2022	Bal	AL	23	23	0	103.2	423	90	49	49	16	2	2	2	28	0	76	0	7	7	.500	0-0	0	94	.691	3.29	4.25
	2 ML YEARS		67	23	18	160.2	647	130	76	75	25	3	4	3	40	0	141	1	9	10	.474	4-7	1	94	.661	2.89	4.20

J.B. Wendelken

Pitches: R **Bats:** R **Pos:** RP-29 **Ht:** 6'1" **Wt:** 242 **Born:** 3/24/1993 **Age:** 30

Year	Team	Lg	G	GS	GF	IP	BFP	H	R	ER	HR	SH	SF	HB	TBB	IBB	SO	WP	W	L	Pct	Sv-Op	Hld	Vel	OPS	ERC	ERA
2022	Reno	AAA	20	0	14	24.0	94	11	8	7	0	1	1	3	9	1	33	2	5	1	.833	4- -	-	-	.410	1.27	2.63
2016	Oak	AL	8	0	3	12.2	64	18	15	14	3	0	0	0	9	0	12	2	0	0	-	0-0	0	93	.931	9.17	9.95
2018	Oak	AL	13	0	3	16.2	62	8	1	1	1	0	0	0	5	0	14	1	0	0	-	0-0	1	95	.438	1.20	0.54
2019	Oak	AL	27	0	4	32.2	131	21	14	13	2	1	1	2	9	2	34	2	3	1	.750	0-1	1	95	.543	1.69	3.58
2020	Oak	AL	21	0	6	25.0	106	17	8	5	2	0	1	0	11	0	31	2	1	1	.500	0-0	2	95	.546	2.30	1.80
2021	2 Tms		46	0	15	43.2	194	44	24	21	4	0	0	0	22	3	39	4	4	3	.571	2-3	6	94	.712	4.32	4.33
2022	Ari	NL	29	0	6	29.0	122	25	18	17	4	0	0	1	14	0	21	1	2	1	.667	0-0	1	95	.702	4.13	5.28
21	Oak	AL	26	0	6	25.0	117	29	15	12	2	0	0	0	13	2	26	4	2	1	.667	0-1	2	94	.734	5.05	4.32
21	Ari	NL	20	0	9	18.2	77	15	9	9	2	0	0	0	9	1	13	0	2	2	.500	2-2	4	95	.679	3.37	4.34
	Postseason		4	0	0	4.2	21	5	6	2	1	0	0	0	1	0	4	0	0	1	.000	0-1	1	94	.736	4.17	3.86
	6 ML YEARS		144	0	37	159.2	679	133	80	71	16	1	2	3	70	5	151	12	10	6	.625	2-4	11	94	.646	3.30	4.00

Joey Wendle

Bats: L **Throws:** R **Pos:** 3B-43;SS-34;2B-33;PH-11;DH-1;PR-1 **Ht:** 6'1" **Wt:** 195 **Born:** 4/26/1990 **Age:** 33

			BATTING																		RUNNING			AVERAGES			
Year	Team	Lg	G	AB	H	2B	3B	HR	(Hm	Rd)	TB	R	RBI	RC	TBB	IBB	SO	HBP	SH	SF	SB	CS	GDP	Avg	OBP	Slg	OPS
2016	Oak	AL	28	96	25	1	0	1	(0	1)	29	11	11	10	6	0	16	0	0	2	2	0	3	.260	.298	.302	.600
2017	Oak	AL	8	13	4	1	0	1	(0	1)	8	3	5	4	1	1	3	0	0	0	0	0	0	.308	.357	.615	.973
2018	TB	AL	139	487	146	33	6	7	(2	5)	212	62	61	70	37	4	96	9	2	10	16	4	11	.300	.354	.435	.789
2019	TB	AL	75	238	55	13	2	3	(2	1)	81	32	19	23	14	0	47	8	0	3	8	3	4	.231	.293	.340	.633
2020	TB	AL	50	168	48	9	2	4	(1	3)	73	24	17	24	10	1	35	5	0	1	8	2	1	.286	.342	.435	.777
2021	TB	AL	136	460	122	31	4	11	(2	9)	194	73	54	59	28	4	113	10	0	1	8	6	9	.265	.319	.422	.741
2022	Mia	NL	101	347	90	24	1	3	(0	3)	125	27	32	38	15	0	50	5	1	3	12	3	7	.259	.297	.360	.658
	Postseason		27	72	14	4	0	0	(0	0)	18	9	6	3	3	0	23	1	0	1	1	0	0	.194	.234	.250	.484
	7 ML YEARS		537	1809	490	112	15	30	(7	23)	722	232	199	228	111	10	360	37	3	22	54	18	35	.271	.322	.399	.722

Joey Wentz

Pitches: L **Bats:** L **Pos:** SP-7 **Ht:** 6'5" **Wt:** 220 **Born:** 10/6/1997 **Age:** 25

Year	Team	Lg	G	GS	GF	IP	BFP	H	R	ER	HR	SH	SF	HB	TBB	IBB	SO	WP	W	L	Pct	Sv-Op	Hld	Vel	OPS	ERC	ERA
2022	Toledo	AAA	12	11	0	48.1	196	37	17	17	6	0	0	1	20	0	53	3	2	2	.500	0- -	-	-	.639	3.17	3.17
2022	Det	AL	7	7	0	32.2	135	23	13	11	2	0	3	1	13	0	27	2	2	2	.500	0-0	0	92	.613	2.34	3.03

Hayden Wesneski

Pitches: R **Bats:** R **Pos:** SP-4; RP-2 **Ht:** 6'3" **Wt:** 210 **Born:** 12/5/1997 **Age:** 25

Year	Team	Lg	G	GS	GF	IP	BFP	H	R	ER	HR	SH	SF	HB	TBB	IBB	SO	WP	W	L	Pct	Sv-Op	Hld	Vel	OPS	ERC	ERA
2022	S-WB	AAA	19	19	0	89.2	371	75	38	35	9	1	6	4	28	0	83	2	6	7	.462	0- -	-	-	.667	3.02	3.51
2022	Iowa	AAA	5	4	1	20.2	86	17	13	13	1	0	1	2	8	1	23	0	0	2	.000	0- -	-	-	.634	3.06	5.66
2022	ChC	NL	6	4	1	33.0	132	24	9	8	3	0	1	3	7	0	33	0	3	2	.600	0-0	0	93	.580	2.23	2.18

Zack Wheeler

Pitches: R Bats: L Pos: SP-26 Ht: 6'4" Wt: 195 Born: 5/30/1990 Age: 33

			HOW MUCH PITCHED					WHAT HE GAVE UP											THE RESULTS							
Year	Team	Lg	G	GS	GF	IP	BFP	H	R	ER	HR	SH	SF	HB	TBB	IBB	SO	WP	W	L	Pct	Sv-Op	Hld	Vel	OPS	ERC	ERA
2013	NYM	NL	17	17	0	100.0	431	90	42	38	10	3	7	4	46	2	84	6	7	5	.583	0-0	0	94	.696	3.88	3.42
2014	NYM	NL	32	32	0	185.1	794	167	84	73	14	5	3	11	79	3	187	9	11	11	.500	0-0	0	95	.678	3.68	3.54
2017	NYM	NL	17	17	0	86.1	386	97	53	50	15	0	1	3	40	1	81	1	3	7	.300	0-0	0	95	.828	5.81	5.21
2018	NYM	NL	29	29	0	182.1	744	150	69	67	14	8	4	9	55	0	179	2	12	7	.632	0-0	0	96	.611	2.81	3.31
2019	NYM	NL	31	31	0	195.1	828	196	93	86	22	8	7	2	50	4	195	1	11	8	.579	0-0	0	97	.694	3.57	3.96
2020	Phi	NL	11	11	0	71.0	288	67	26	23	3	1	0	7	16	2	53	0	4	2	.667	0-0	0	97	.662	3.16	2.92
2021	Phi	NL	32	32	0	213.1	849	169	72	66	16	7	3	8	46	1	247	6	14	10	.583	0-0	0	97	.586	2.29	2.78
2022	Phi	NL	26	26	0	153.0	607	125	52	48	13	0	1	7	34	1	163	1	12	7	.632	0-0	0	96	.626	2.56	2.82
	8 ML YEARS		195	195	0	1186.2	4927	1061	491	451	107	32	26	51	366	14	1189	30	74	57	.565	0-0	0	96	.660	3.24	3.42

Eli White

Bats: R Throws: R Pos: CF-22;LF-21;PR-7;RF-1;DH-1;PH-1 Ht: 6'3" Wt: 195 Born: 6/26/1994 Age: 29

					BATTING															RUNNING			AVERAGES			
Year	Team	Lg	G	AB	H	2B	3B	HR	(Hm	Rd)	TB	R	RBI	RC	TBB	IBB	SO	HBP	SH	SF	SB	CS	GDP	Avg	OBP	Slg	OPS
2020	Tex	AL	19	48	9	2	0	0	(0	0)	11	5	3	2	3	0	16	0	0	1	1	1	0	.188	.231	.229	.460
2021	Tex	AL	64	198	35	6	1	6	(1	5)	61	26	15	14	18	0	66	4	0	1	4	3	2	.177	.259	.308	.567
2022	Tex	AL	47	105	21	2	0	3	(1	2)	32	16	10	10	11	0	41	0	0	1	12	1	0	.200	.274	.305	.578
	3 ML YEARS		130	351	65	10	1	9	(2	7)	104	47	28	26	32	0	123	4	0	2	17	5	2	.185	.260	.296	.556

Mitch White

Pitches: R Bats: R Pos: SP-18; RP-7 Ht: 6'3" Wt: 210 Born: 12/28/1994 Age: 28

			HOW MUCH PITCHED					WHAT HE GAVE UP											THE RESULTS							
Year	Team	Lg	G	GS	GF	IP	BFP	H	R	ER	HR	SH	SF	HB	TBB	IBB	SO	WP	W	L	Pct	Sv-Op	Hld	Vel	OPS	ERC	ERA
2020	LAD	NL	2	0	2	3.0	11	1	0	0	0	0	0	0	1	0	2	0	1	0	1.000	0-0	0	94	.282	0.69	0.00
2021	LAD	NL	21	4	6	46.2	197	38	28	19	6	1	2	0	17	1	49	3	1	3	.250	0-2	0	95	.637	3.00	3.66
2022	2 Tms		25	18	2	99.0	440	110	62	60	9	0	3	3	35	0	78	5	1	7	.125	0-0	0	94	.760	4.52	5.45
22	LAD	NL	15	10	1	56.0	237	51	25	23	6	0	1	2	19	0	47	4	1	2	.333	0-0	0	94	.676	3.51	3.70
22	Tor	AL	10	8	1	43.0	203	59	37	37	3	0	2	1	16	0	31	1	0	5	.000	0-0	0	94	.858	5.92	7.74
	3 ML YEARS		48	22	10	148.2	648	149	90	79	15	1	5	3	53	1	129	8	3	10	.231	0-2	0	94	.714	3.92	4.78

Aaron Whitefield

Bats: R Throws: R Pos: RF-3;CF-2;LF-1;PH-1 Ht: 6'4" Wt: 210 Born: 9/2/1996 Age: 26

					BATTING															RUNNING			AVERAGES			
Year	Team	Lg	G	AB	H	2B	3B	HR	(Hm	Rd)	TB	R	RBI	RC	TBB	IBB	SO	HBP	SH	SF	SB	CS	GDP	Avg	OBP	Slg	OPS
2022	Rock	AA	79	301	79	18	3	9	(-	-)	130	56	38	45	36	1	93	3	0	4	29	10	6	.262	.343	.432	.775
2020	Min	AL	3	1	0	0	0	0	(0	0)	0	1	0	0	0	0	0	0	0	0	0	0	0	.000	.000	.000	.000
2022	LAA	AL	5	11	0	0	0	0	(0	0)	0	0	0	0	0	0	5	0	0	0	0	0	0	.000	.000	.000	.000
	2 ML YEARS		8	12	0	0	0	0	(0	0)	0	1	0	0	0	0	5	0	0	0	0	0	0	.000	.000	.000	.000

Kodi Whitley

Pitches: R Bats: R Pos: RP-14 Ht: 6'3" Wt: 220 Born: 2/21/1995 Age: 28

			HOW MUCH PITCHED					WHAT HE GAVE UP											THE RESULTS							
Year	Team	Lg	G	GS	GF	IP	BFP	H	R	ER	HR	SH	SF	HB	TBB	IBB	SO	WP	W	L	Pct	Sv-Op	Hld	Vel	OPS	ERC	ERA
2022	Memp	AAA	30	0	17	32.2	147	33	16	14	8	0	1	0	16	0	32	1	1	0	1.000	3--	-	-	.795	5.44	3.86
2020	StL	NL	4	0	1	4.2	17	2	1	1	1	0	0	1	0	5	0	0	0	-	0-0	0	94	.489	1.34	1.93
2021	StL	NL	25	0	6	25.1	101	15	8	7	1	0	2	0	12	0	27	1	0	0	-	0-0	4	94	.497	1.90	2.49
2022	StL	NL	14	0	5	12.2	59	11	8	8	2	0	1	2	9	0	12	0	2	0	1.000	0-1	1	93	.777	5.62	5.68
	Postseason		1	0	1	0.1	2	1	1	1	1	0	0	0	0	0	0	0	0	0	-	0-0	0	94	2.500	47.50	27.00
	3 ML YEARS		43	0	12	42.2	177	28	17	16	4	0	3	2	22	0	44	1	2	0	1.000	0-0	5	94	.587	2.82	3.38

Garrett Whitlock

Pitches: R Bats: R Pos: RP-22; SP-9 Ht: 6'5" Wt: 225 Born: 6/11/1996 Age: 27

			HOW MUCH PITCHED					WHAT HE GAVE UP											THE RESULTS							
Year	Team	Lg	G	GS	GF	IP	BFP	H	R	ER	HR	SH	SF	HB	TBB	IBB	SO	WP	W	L	Pct	Sv-Op	Hld	Vel	OPS	ERC	ERA
2021	Bos	AL	46	0	11	73.1	298	64	22	16	6	0	3	3	17	2	81	3	8	4	.667	2-5	14	96	.631	2.77	1.96
2022	Bos	AL	31	9	10	78.1	311	65	32	30	10	0	2	1	15	0	82	2	4	2	.667	6-8	4	95	.639	2.61	3.45
	Postseason		5	0	2	8.1	30	4	2	2	2	0	0	0	2	1	9	0	1	0	1.000	0-1	0	97	.557	1.61	2.16
	2 ML YEARS		77	9	21	151.2	609	129	54	46	16	0	5	4	32	2	163	5	12	6	.667	8-13	18	96	.635	2.69	2.73

Rowan Wick

Pitches: R Bats: L Pos: RP-64 Ht: 6'3" Wt: 234 Born: 11/9/1992 Age: 30

			HOW MUCH PITCHED					WHAT HE GAVE UP											THE RESULTS							
Year	Team	Lg	G	GS	GF	IP	BFP	H	R	ER	HR	SH	SF	HB	TBB	IBB	SO	WP	W	L	Pct	Sv-Op	Hld	Vel	OPS	ERC	ERA
2018	SD	NL	10	0	3	8.1	38	13	6	6	1	0	0	0	1	0	7	0	0	1	.000	0-0	0	95	.936	6.41	6.48
2019	ChC	NL	31	0	7	33.1	140	22	13	9	0	1	0	3	16	1	35	0	2	0	1.000	2-2	5	95	.528	2.18	2.43
2020	ChC	NL	19	0	6	17.1	74	18	6	6	1	0	0	0	6	1	20	0	0	1	.000	4-4	5	95	.721	3.71	3.12
2021	ChC	NL	22	0	8	23.0	100	17	12	11	1	0	1	1	14	0	29	1	0	1	.000	5-8	2	95	.576	3.18	4.30
2022	ChC	NL	64	0	22	64.0	294	79	37	30	9	1	4	1	29	2	69	3	4	7	.364	9-14	4	95	.847	6.00	4.22
	5 ML YEARS		146	0	46	146.0	646	149	74	62	12	2	5	5	66	4	160	4	6	10	.375	20-28	16	95	.730	4.34	3.82

Taylor Widener

Pitches: R Bats: L Pos: RP-14 Ht: 6'0" Wt: 203 Born: 10/24/1994 Age: 28

Year	Team	Lg	G	GS	GF	IP	BFP	H	R	ER	HR	SH	SF	HB	TBB	IBB	SO	WP	W	L	Pct	Sv-Op	Hld	Vel	OPS	ERC	ERA
2022	Reno	AAA	27	0	1	36.2	159	40	24	22	5	0	1	0	12	2	47	2	2	2	.500	0- -	-	-	.765	4.46	5.40
2020	Ari	NL	12	0	4	20.0	88	14	10	10	5	0	0	3	12	1	22	0	0	1	.000	0-0	1	95	.782	4.73	4.50
2021	Ari	NL	23	13	0	70.1	319	65	38	34	14	3	2	7	37	3	73	1	2	1	.667	0-0	1	93	.800	5.11	4.35
2022	Ari	NL	14	0	4	17.1	82	22	8	7	2	0	0	3	5	1	14	0	0	1	.000	0-1	1	94	.798	5.78	3.63
	3 ML YEARS		49	13	8	107.2	489	101	56	51	21	3	2	13	54	5	109	1	2	3	.400	0-1	3	93	.797	5.15	4.26

Collin Wiles

Pitches: R Bats: R Pos: RP-4 Ht: 6'4" Wt: 222 Born: 5/30/1994 Age: 29

Year	Team	Lg	G	GS	GF	IP	BFP	H	R	ER	HR	SH	SF	HB	TBB	IBB	SO	WP	W	L	Pct	Sv-Op	Hld	Vel	OPS	ERC	ERA
2022	LsVgs	AAA	26	26	0	143.1	623	175	100	86	27	0	3	6	27	0	106	2	9	11	.450	0- -	-	-	.835	5.31	5.40
2022	Oak	AL	4	0	1	9.2	41	11	6	5	1	0	0	1	2	0	9	0	0	0	-	0-0	0	91	.815	4.66	4.66

Devin Williams

Pitches: R Bats: R Pos: RP-65 Ht: 6'2" Wt: 200 Born: 9/21/1994 Age: 28

Year	Team	Lg	G	GS	GF	IP	BFP	H	R	ER	HR	SH	SF	HB	TBB	IBB	SO	WP	W	L	Pct	Sv-Op	Hld	Vel	OPS	ERC	ERA
2019	Mil	NL	13	0	1	13.2	67	18	9	6	2	1	0	2	6	0	14	1	0	0	-	0-0	2	96	.894	6.97	3.95
2020	Mil	NL	22	0	1	27.0	100	8	4	1	1	0	0	1	9	0	53	3	4	1	.800	0-0	9	97	.339	0.76	0.33
2021	Mil	NL	58	0	6	54.0	226	36	17	15	5	1	1	2	28	0	87	2	8	2	.800	3-6	23	95	.587	2.81	2.50
2022	Mil	NL	65	0	21	60.2	240	31	17	13	2	0	2	3	30	1	96	5	6	4	.600	15-17	26	94	.472	1.71	1.93
	4 ML YEARS		158	0	29	155.1	633	93	47	35	10	2	3	8	73	1	250	11	18	7	.720	18-23	60	95	.536	2.20	2.03

Luke Williams

Bats: R Throws: R Pos: 3B-31;LF-26;PR-23;2B-14;PH-3;DH-2;1B-1 Ht: 6'1" Wt: 186 Born: 8/9/1996 Age: 26

Year	Team	Lg	G	AB	H	2B	3B	HR	(Hm	Rd)	TB	R	RBI	RC	TBB	IBB	SO	HBP	SH	SF	SB	CS	GDP	Avg	OBP	Slg	OPS
2022	Scrmto	AAA	10	37	14	4	0	0	(-	-)	18	8	7	6	3	0	13	0	0	1	4	2	0	.378	.415	.486	.901
2021	Phi	NL	58	98	24	4	0	1	(1	0)	31	8	6	10	10	0	23	0	0	0	2	2	1	.245	.315	.316	.631
2022	2 Tms	NL	79	127	30	5	1	1	(0	1)	40	21	6	9	9	1	44	0	0	0	11	4	1	.236	.287	.315	.602
22	SF	NL	8	12	3	1	0	0	(0	0)	4	1	3	2	0	0	4	0	0	0	0	0	0	.250	.250	.333	.583
22	Mia	NL	71	115	27	4	1	1	(0	1)	36	20	3	7	9	1	40	0	0	0	11	4	1	.235	.290	.313	.603
	2 ML YEARS		137	225	54	9	1	2	(1	1)	71	29	12	19	19	1	67	0	0	0	13	6	3	.240	.299	.316	.615

Trevor Williams

Pitches: R Bats: R Pos: RP-21; SP-9 Ht: 6'3" Wt: 235 Born: 4/25/1992 Age: 31

Year	Team	Lg	G	GS	GF	IP	BFP	H	R	ER	HR	SH	SF	HB	TBB	IBB	SO	WP	W	L	Pct	Sv-Op	Hld	Vel	OPS	ERC	ERA
2016	Pit	NL	7	1	1	12.2	61	19	13	11	4	0	0	0	5	0	11	0	1	1	.500	0-1	0	93	1.054	8.89	7.82
2017	Pit	NL	31	25	1	150.1	642	145	73	68	14	8	4	9	52	4	117	2	7	9	.438	0-0	0	92	.715	3.82	4.07
2018	Pit	NL	31	31	0	170.2	701	146	64	59	15	6	4	5	55	3	126	4	14	10	.583	0-0	0	90	.659	3.00	3.11
2019	Pit	NL	26	26	0	145.2	636	162	93	87	27	6	8	7	44	3	113	1	7	9	.438	0-0	0	91	.851	5.11	5.38
2020	Pit	NL	11	11	0	55.1	252	66	42	38	15	1	3	4	21	0	49	1	2	8	.200	0-0	0	91	.905	6.74	6.18
2021	2 Tms	NL	23	15	3	91.0	405	105	51	44	11	3	1	3	31	0	90	0	4	2	.667	0-0	0	91	.808	4.98	4.35
2022	NYM	NL	30	9	5	89.2	372	87	34	32	12	1	0	4	23	1	84	1	3	5	.375	1-2	1	91	.720	3.78	3.21
21	ChC	NL	13	12	0	58.2	264	68	37	33	10	0	1	2	22	0	61	0	4	2	.667	0-0	0	91	.833	5.53	5.06
21	NYM	NL	10	3	3	32.1	141	37	14	11	1	3	0	1	9	0	29	0	0	0	-	0-0	0	91	.762	4.02	3.06
	7 ML YEARS		159	118	10	715.1	3069	730	370	339	98	25	20	31	231	11	590	10	38	44	.463	1-3	1	91	.766	4.30	4.27

Bryse Wilson

Pitches: R Bats: R Pos: SP-20; RP-5 Ht: 6'1" Wt: 250 Born: 12/20/1997 Age: 25

Year	Team	Lg	G	GS	GF	IP	BFP	H	R	ER	HR	SH	SF	HB	TBB	IBB	SO	WP	W	L	Pct	Sv-Op	Hld	Vel	OPS	ERC	ERA
2022	Indy	AAA	6	6	0	36.1	147	32	12	12	6	1	0	1	6	0	34	1	5	0	1.000	0- -	-	-	.670	3.01	2.97
2018	Atl	NL	3	1	2	7.0	33	8	5	5	0	0	1	0	6	2	6	0	1	0	1.000	0-0	0	95	.886	5.54	6.43
2019	Atl	NL	6	4	1	20.0	93	26	18	16	5	2	0	0	10	1	16	1	1	1	.500	0-0	0	95	1.050	7.50	7.20
2020	Atl	NL	6	2	2	15.2	73	18	7	7	2	0	0	1	9	0	15	0	1	0	1.000	1-1	0	94	.828	6.18	4.02
2021	2 Tms	NL	16	16	0	74.0	322	85	45	44	15	2	4	1	22	3	46	2	3	7	.300	0-0	0	93	.843	5.26	5.35
2022	Pit	NL	25	20	0	115.2	509	132	80	71	20	1	6	9	32	1	79	2	3	9	.250	0-0	0	92	.826	5.22	5.52
21	Atl	NL	8	8	0	33.2	153	45	23	22	7	1	2	1	12	2	23	1	2	3	.400	0-0	0	93	.914	6.89	5.88
21	Pit	NL	8	8	0	40.1	169	40	22	22	8	1	2	0	10	1	23	1	1	4	.200	0-0	0	93	.778	4.01	4.91
	Postseason		1	1	0	6.0	20	1	1	0	0	0	0	0	1	0	5	0	1	0	1.000	0-0	0	95	.311	0.46	1.50
	5 ML YEARS		56	43	5	232.1	1030	269	155	143	42	5	11	11	79	7	162	5	9	17	.346	1-1	0	93	.853	5.51	5.54

Justin Wilson

Pitches: L Bats: L Pos: RP-5   Ht: 6'2" Wt: 205 Born: 8/18/1987 Age: 35

		HOW MUCH PITCHED					WHAT HE GAVE UP										THE RESULTS							
Year	Team	Lg	G	GS	GF	IP	BFP	H	R	ER	HR	SH	SF	HB	TBB	IBB	SO	WP	W	L	Pct	Sv-Op	Hld	Vel	OPS	ERC	ERA
2012	Pit	NL	8	0	3	4.2	26	10	1	1	0	1	0	0	3	0	7	1	0	0	-	0-0	0	94	1.111	11.83	1.93
2013	Pit	NL	58	0	8	73.2	295	50	17	17	4	3	1	3	28	1	59	5	6	1	.857	0-3	14	95	.543	2.20	2.08
2014	Pit	NL	70	0	15	60.0	256	49	30	28	4	0	0	3	30	5	61	4	3	4	.429	0-3	16	95	.643	3.29	4.20
2015	NYY	AL	74	0	3	61.0	244	49	21	21	3	2	0	2	20	0	66	4	5	0	1.000	0-2	29	95	.602	2.63	3.10
2016	Det	AL	66	0	10	58.2	251	61	29	27	6	1	0	1	17	2	65	4	4	5	.444	1-6	25	95	.708	3.87	4.14
2017	2 Tms		65	0	30	58.0	248	40	23	22	5	0	1	1	35	1	80	4	4	4	.500	13-16	9	96	.633	3.08	3.41
2018	ChC	NL	71	0	12	54.2	236	45	22	21	5	0	1	0	33	1	69	4	4	5	.444	0-3	16	95	.682	3.81	3.46
2019	NYM	NL	45	0	9	39.0	166	33	12	11	4	0	0	2	19	1	44	4	4	2	.667	4-5	9	95	.670	3.78	2.54
2020	NYM	NL	23	0	2	19.2	86	18	10	8	1	1	0	1	9	1	23	3	2	1	.667	0-0	10	95	.623	3.55	3.66
2021	2 Tms		42	0	13	34.0	149	32	22	20	6	0	0	1	16	0	29	2	1	1	.500	0-1	4	94	.766	4.66	5.29
2022	Cin	NL	5	0	0	3.2	13	3	1	1	0	0	0	0	0	0	7	0	0	1	.000	0-0	0	95	.615	1.42	2.45
17	Det	AL	42	0	26	40.1	157	22	12	12	5	0	1	0	16	0	55	3	3	4	.429	13-15	8	96	.563	1.91	2.68
17	ChC	NL	23	0	4	17.2	91	18	11	10	0	0	0	1	19	1	25	1	1	0	1.000	0-1	1	96	.756	5.98	5.09
21	NYY	AL	21	0	7	18.0	83	18	17	15	5	0	0	1	9	0	15	1	1	1	.500	0-1	2	93	.883	5.84	7.50
21	Cin	NL	21	0	6	16.0	66	14	5	5	1	0	0	0	7	0	14	1	0	0	-	0-0	2	94	.623	3.38	2.81
	Postseason		6	0	1	5.1	21	3	1	1	0	0	0	0	3	0	4	1	0	0	-	0-0	0	96	.452	1.87	1.69
11 ML YEARS			527	0	105	467.0	1970	390	188	177	38	8	3	14	210	12	510	35	33	24	.579	18-39	132	95	.652	3.33	3.41

Marcus Wilson

Bats: R Throws: R Pos: RF-2;CF-1;PH-1;PR-1   Ht: 6'2" Wt: 198 Born: 8/15/1996 Age: 26

				BATTING															RUNNING			AVERAGES			
Year	Team	Lg	G	AB	H	2B	3B	HR	(Hm | Rd)	TB	R	RBI	RC	TBB	IBB	SO	HBP	SH	SF	SB	CS	GDP	Avg	OBP	Slg	OPS
2022	Tacom	AAA	91	293	64	18	3	16	(- | -)	136	50	47	53	53	0	126	5	0	4	14	2	5	.218	.344	.464	.808
2022	Sea	AL	3	5	1	0	0	0	(0 | 0)	1	1	0	0	1	0	4	0	0	0	0	0	0	.200	.333	.200	.533

Steven Wilson

Pitches: R Bats: R Pos: RP-49; SP-1   Ht: 6'3" Wt: 221 Born: 8/24/1994 Age: 28

		HOW MUCH PITCHED					WHAT HE GAVE UP										THE RESULTS							
Year	Team	Lg	G	GS	GF	IP	BFP	H	R	ER	HR	SH	SF	HB	TBB	IBB	SO	WP	W	L	Pct	Sv-Op	Hld	Vel	OPS	ERC	ERA
2022	SD	NL	50	1	8	53.0	214	36	20	18	7	1	2	3	20	0	53	4	4	2	.667	1-3	5	95	.623	2.73	3.06

Josh Winckowski

Pitches: R Bats: R Pos: SP-14; RP-1   win-KOW-skee   Ht: 6'4" Wt: 202 Born: 6/28/1998 Age: 25

		HOW MUCH PITCHED					WHAT HE GAVE UP										THE RESULTS							
Year	Team	Lg	G	GS	GF	IP	BFP	H	R	ER	HR	SH	SF	HB	TBB	IBB	SO	WP	W	L	Pct	Sv-Op	Hld	Vel	OPS	ERC	ERA
2022	Wrcstr	AAA	13	12	0	61.1	255	57	38	26	4	0	2	1	18	0	62	0	2	4	.333	0- -	-	-	.653	3.12	3.82
2022	Bos	AL	15	14	1	70.1	316	85	47	46	10	0	4	2	27	1	44	0	5	7	.417	0-0	0	94	.852	5.67	5.89

Josh Winder

Pitches: R Bats: R Pos: SP-11; RP-4   Ht: 6'5" Wt: 210 Born: 10/11/1996 Age: 26

		HOW MUCH PITCHED					WHAT HE GAVE UP										THE RESULTS							
Year	Team	Lg	G	GS	GF	IP	BFP	H	R	ER	HR	SH	SF	HB	TBB	IBB	SO	WP	W	L	Pct	Sv-Op	Hld	Vel	OPS	ERC	ERA
2018	Elizab	R+	9	9	0	38.2	157	37	17	16	1	0	2	0	6	0	42	2	3	1	.750	0- -	-	-	.643	2.44	3.72
2019	Crpds	A	21	21	0	125.2	494	93	43	37	10	1	4	5	30	0	118	5	7	2	.778	0- -	-	-	.575	2.18	2.65
2021	Wich	AA	10	10	0	54.2	208	41	12	12	5	0	1	0	10	0	65	2	3	0	1.000	0- -	-	-	.560	2.01	1.98
2022	StPaul	AAA	5	5	0	16.0	66	11	7	6	3	0	0	1	6	0	11	0	0	0	-	0- -	-	-	.646	3.05	3.38
2022	Min	AL	15	11	0	67.0	287	69	37	35	11	0	3	5	18	0	47	2	4	6	.400	0-0	0	94	.780	4.47	4.70

Jesse Winker

Bats: L Throws: L Pos: LF-118;DH-17;PH-5   Ht: 6'3" Wt: 215 Born: 8/17/1993 Age: 29

				BATTING															RUNNING			AVERAGES			
Year	Team	Lg	G	AB	H	2B	3B	HR	(Hm | Rd)	TB	R	RBI	RC	TBB	IBB	SO	HBP	SH	SF	SB	CS	GDP	Avg	OBP	Slg	OPS
2017	Cin	NL	47	121	36	7	0	7	(2 | 5)	64	21	15	18	15	0	24	0	1	0	1	1	2	.298	.375	.529	.904
2018	Cin	NL	89	281	84	16	0	7	(6 | 1)	121	38	43	54	49	4	46	2	1	1	0	0	6	.299	.405	.431	.836
2019	Cin	NL	113	338	91	17	2	16	(10 | 6)	160	51	38	48	38	2	60	8	0	0	0	2	10	.269	.357	.473	.830
2020	Cin	NL	54	149	38	7	0	12	(8 | 4)	81	27	23	31	28	0	46	5	0	1	1	0	3	.255	.388	.544	.932
2021	Cin	NL	110	423	129	32	1	24	(13 | 11)	235	77	71	90	53	1	75	9	0	0	1	0	14	.305	.394	.556	.949
2022	Sea	AL	136	456	100	15	0	14	(4 | 10)	157	51	53	57	84	1	103	4	0	3	0	0	8	.219	.344	.344	.688
	Postseason		2	6	1	0	0	0	(0 | 0)	1	0	0	0	1	0	2	1	0	0	0	0	0	.167	.375	.167	.542
6 ML YEARS			549	1768	478	94	3	80	(43 | 37)	818	265	243	298	267	8	354	28	2	5	3	3	43	.270	.374	.463	.836

Patrick Wisdom

Bats: R Throws: R Pos: 3B-105;1B-18;RF-7;LF-5;PH-4;DH-3;CF-2;PR-1   Ht: 6'2" Wt: 220 Born: 8/27/1991 Age: 31

				BATTING															RUNNING			AVERAGES			
Year	Team	Lg	G	AB	H	2B	3B	HR	(Hm | Rd)	TB	R	RBI	RC	TBB	IBB	SO	HBP	SH	SF	SB	CS	GDP	Avg	OBP	Slg	OPS
2018	StL	NL	32	50	13	1	0	4	(3 | 1)	26	11	10	8	6	0	19	2	0	0	2	1	1	.260	.362	.520	.882
2019	Tex	AL	9	26	4	1	0	0	(0 | 0)	5	1	1	1	1	0	15	0	1	0	0	0	0	.154	.185	.192	.377
2020	ChC	NL	2	2	0	0	0	0	(0 | 0)	0	0	0	0	0	0	0	0	0	0	0	0	0	.000	.000	.000	.000
2021	ChC	NL	106	338	78	13	0	28	(13 | 15)	175	54	61	48	32	1	153	4	0	0	4	1	7	.231	.305	.518	.823
2022	ChC	NL	134	469	97	28	0	25	(12 | 13)	200	67	66	72	53	1	183	9	1	2	8	4	8	.207	.298	.426	.725
5 ML YEARS			283	885	192	43	0	57	(28 | 29)	406	133	138	129	92	2	370	15	2	2	14	6	16	.217	.301	.459	.760

Matt Wisler

Pitches: R Bats: R Pos: RP-34; SP-5   WISS-lurr   Ht: 6'3" Wt: 215 Born: 9/12/1992 Age: 30

Year Team	Lg	G	GS	GF	IP	BFP	H	R	ER	HR	SH	SF	HB	TBB	IBB	SO	WP	W	L	Pct	Sv-Op	Hld	Vel	OPS	ERC	ERA
2015 Atl	NL	20	19	0	109.0	478	119	59	57	16	4	5	4	40	4	72	2	8	8	.500	0-0	0	93	.819	4.91	4.71
2016 Atl	NL	27	26	1	156.2	671	159	90	87	26	2	4	4	49	3	115	5	7	13	.350	1-1	0	93	.756	4.32	5.00
2017 Atl	NL	20	1	8	32.1	153	43	31	30	5	2	3	2	13	0	22	0	0	1	.000	0-0	0	93	.971	6.68	8.35
2018 2 Tms		18	3	3	40.0	166	41	20	19	8	1	3	0	7	0	32	1	1	1	.500	0-1	0	92	.781	3.95	4.28
2019 2 Tms		44	8	7	51.1	224	56	34	32	10	1	1	0	16	0	63	3	3	4	.429	0-3	5	93	.813	4.85	5.61
2020 Min	AL	18	4	3	25.1	107	15	3	3	2	0	0	2	14	0	35	1	0	1	.000	1-2	3	92	.564	2.59	1.07
2021 Min		48	0	8	48.2	195	41	24	20	6	0	3	1	11	1	62	1	3	5	.375	1-4	10	92	.672	2.79	3.70
2022 TB	AL	39	5	10	44.0	176	30	18	11	6	2	1	0	14	1	35	1	3	3	.500	1-4	5	90	.618	2.28	2.25
18 Atl	NL	7	3	1	26.2	112	30	16	16	6	0	1	0	5	0	21	1	1	1	.500	0-0	0	93	.850	4.82	5.40
18 Cin	NL	11	0	2	13.1	54	11	4	3	2	1	2	0	2	0	11	0	0	0	-	0-1	0	92	.633	2.41	2.03
19 SD	NL	21	0	5	29.0	129	34	17	17	5	1	1	0	10	0	34	3	2	2	.500	0-2	4	93	.822	5.35	5.28
19 Sea	AL	23	8	2	22.1	95	22	17	15	5	0	0	0	6	0	29	0	1	2	.333	0-1	4	93	.800	4.21	6.04
21 SF	NL	21	0	4	19.1	82	19	13	13	4	0	1	0	6	0	26	0	1	2	.333	0-1	3	92	.798	4.32	6.05
21 TB	AL	27	0	4	29.1	113	22	11	7	2	0	2	1	5	1	36	1	2	3	.400	1-3	7	91	.581	1.89	2.15
Postseason		2	0	0	2.1	9	2	2	2	1	0	0	0	0	0	1	0	0	0	-	0-0	0	91	.778	3.45	7.71
8 ML YEARS		234	66	40	507.1	2170	504	279	259	79	12	19	13	164	9	436	14	25	36	.410	4-15	26	93	.765	4.17	4.59

Bobby Witt Jr.

Bats: R Throws: R Pos: SS-98; 3B-55; DH-2; PH-1; PR-1   Ht: 6'1" Wt: 200 Born: 6/14/2000 Age: 23

Year Team	Lg	G	AB	H	2B	3B	HR	(Hm	Rd)	TB	R	RBI	RC	TBB	IBB	SO	HBP	SH	SF	SB	CS	GDP	Avg	OBP	Slg	OPS
2019 Royals	R	37	164	43	2	5	1	(-	-)	58	30	27	21	13	0	35	1	0	2	9	1	4	.262	.317	.354	.670
2021 NWArk	AA	61	244	72	11	4	16	(-	-)	139	44	51	51	25	0	67	6	0	4	14	7	1	.295	.369	.570	.939
2021 Omha	AAA	59	241	71	24	0	17	(-	-)	146	53	44	53	24	1	60	2	1	2	15	2	0	.295	.361	.606	.966
2022 KC	AL	150	591	150	31	6	20	(8	12)	253	82	80	84	30	2	135	6	0	5	30	7	12	.254	.294	.428	.722

Nick Wittgren

Pitches: R Bats: R Pos: RP-29   Ht: 6'2" Wt: 216 Born: 5/29/1991 Age: 32

Year Team	Lg	G	GS	GF	IP	BFP	H	R	ER	HR	SH	SF	HB	TBB	IBB	SO	WP	W	L	Pct	Sv-Op	Hld	Vel	OPS	ERC	ERA
2016 Mia	NL	48	0	9	51.2	213	50	18	18	6	3	2	1	10	2	42	1	4	3	.571	0-2	6	92	.671	3.21	3.14
2017 Mia	NL	38	0	3	42.1	182	46	22	22	5	0	3	0	13	1	43	2	3	1	.750	0-0	5	92	.800	4.29	4.68
2018 Mia	NL	32	0	6	33.2	148	29	13	11	1	1	1	1	15	3	31	2	2	1	.667	0-0	4	92	.629	2.86	2.94
2019 Cle	AL	55	0	13	57.2	231	47	22	18	10	0	0	0	15	1	60	0	5	1	.833	4-6	12	92	.676	2.99	2.81
2020 Cle	AL	25	0	13	23.2	98	18	9	9	4	1	0	5	6	2	28	0	2	0	1.000	0-1	10	93	.706	3.37	3.42
2021 Cle	AL	60	1	13	62.1	258	61	38	35	13	2	3	2	17	5	61	2	2	9	.182	1-1	9	92	.800	4.26	5.05
2022 Mia	NL	29	0	9	29.0	134	35	19	19	1	1	2	4	10	0	17	3	1	0	1.000	1-1	4	91	.787	5.04	5.90
Postseason		1	0	0	1.1	6	0	0	0	0	0	0	0	2	0	3	0	0	0	-	0-0	0	94	.333	1.96	0.00
7 ML YEARS		287	1	59	300.1	1264	286	141	132	40	8	11	13	86	14	282	10	19	15	.559	6-11	50	92	.727	3.68	3.96

Tony Wolters

Bats: L Throws: R Pos: C-1; 2B-1; DH-1; PH-1   WAHL-ters   Ht: 5'10" Wt: 195 Born: 6/9/1992 Age: 31

Year Team	Lg	G	AB	H	2B	3B	HR	(Hm	Rd)	TB	R	RBI	RC	TBB	IBB	SO	HBP	SH	SF	SB	CS	GDP	Avg	OBP	Slg	OPS
2022 OkCity	AAA	61	204	47	9	1	0	(-	-)	58	21	29	17	26	0	58	2	0	2	0	0	3	.230	.321	.284	.605
2016 Col	NL	71	205	53	15	2	3	(2	1)	81	27	30	30	21	2	53	0	4	0	4	1	1	.259	.327	.395	.723
2017 Col	NL	83	229	55	8	1	0	(0	0)	65	30	16	25	33	9	55	2	2	0	0	1	9	.240	.341	.284	.625
2018 Col	NL	74	182	31	4	4	3	(1	2)	52	19	27	18	26	2	33	6	4	0	2	0	6	.170	.292	.286	.577
2019 Col	NL	121	359	94	17	2	1	(0	1)	118	42	42	42	36	5	68	8	2	6	0	1	9	.262	.337	.329	.666
2020 Col	NL	42	100	23	4	0	0	(0	0)	27	10	8	11	6	0	30	1	2	0	0	1	1	.230	.280	.270	.550
2021 ChC	NL	14	24	3	0	0	0	(0	0)	3	3	0	1	5	0	12	0	1	0	0	1	1	.125	.276	.125	.401
2022 LAD	NL	2	4	0	0	0	0	(0	0)	0	0	0	0	0	0	3	0	0	0	0	0	0	.000	.000	.000	.000
Postseason		3	3	2	0	0	0	(0	0)	2	0	1	0	0	0	0	0	0	0	0	0	0	.667	.667	.667	1.333
7 ML YEARS		407	1103	259	48	9	7	(3	4)	346	131	123	127	127	18	254	17	11	8	6	4	27	.235	.321	.314	.635

Connor Wong

Bats: R Throws: R Pos: C-20; PH-3; PR-3; 2B-2; 3B-1; DH-1   Ht: 6'1" Wt: 181 Born: 5/19/1996 Age: 27

Year Team	Lg	G	AB	H	2B	3B	HR	(Hm	Rd)	TB	R	RBI	RC	TBB	IBB	SO	HBP	SH	SF	SB	CS	GDP	Avg	OBP	Slg	OPS
2022 Wrcstr	AAA	81	323	93	20	0	15	(-	-)	158	47	44	57	27	0	80	4	0	1	7	3	5	.288	.349	.489	.838
2021 Bos	AL	6	13	4	1	1	0	(0	0)	7	3	1	2	1	0	7	0	0	0	0	0	0	.308	.357	.538	.896
2022 Bos	AL	27	48	9	3	0	1	(1	0)	15	8	7	6	5	0	16	1	1	1	0	0	0	.188	.273	.313	.585
2 ML YEARS		33	61	13	4	1	1	(1	0)	22	11	8	8	6	0	23	1	1	1	0	0	0	.213	.290	.361	.651

Kolten Wong

Bats: L Throws: R Pos: 2B-131; PH-16; SS-1; DH-1   COLT-enn   Ht: 5'7" Wt: 185 Born: 10/10/1990 Age: 32

Year Team	Lg	G	AB	H	2B	3B	HR	(Hm	Rd)	TB	R	RBI	RC	TBB	IBB	SO	HBP	SH	SF	SB	CS	GDP	Avg	OBP	Slg	OPS
2013 StL	NL	32	59	9	1	0	0	(0	0)	10	6	0	0	3	0	12	0	0	0	3	0	2	.153	.194	.169	.363
2014 StL	NL	113	402	100	14	3	12	(10	2)	156	52	42	41	21	3	71	4	5	1	20	4	12	.249	.292	.388	.680
2015 StL	NL	150	557	146	28	4	11	(5	6)	215	71	61	67	36	2	95	15	0	5	15	8	10	.262	.321	.386	.707
2016 StL	NL	121	313	75	7	7	5	(3	2)	111	39	23	36	34	2	52	9	0	3	7	0	3	.240	.327	.355	.682

						BATTING															RUNNING			AVERAGES			
Year	Team	Lg	G	AB	H	2B	3B	HR	(Hm	Rd)	TB	R	RBI	RC	TBB	IBB	SO	HBP	SH	SF	SB	CS	GDP	Avg	OBP	Slg	OPS
2017	StL	NL	108	354	101	27	3	4	(3	1)	146	55	42	56	41	11	60	12	1	3	8	2	4	.285	.376	.412	.788
2018	StL	NL	127	353	88	18	2	9	(6	3)	137	41	38	46	31	3	60	14	6	3	6	5	6	.249	.332	.388	.720
2019	StL	NL	148	478	136	25	4	11	(1	10)	202	61	59	81	47	5	83	13	6	5	24	4	2	.285	.361	.423	.784
2020	StL	NL	53	181	48	4	2	1	(0	1)	59	26	16	30	20	1	30	4	2	1	5	2	1	.265	.350	.326	.675
2021	Mil	NL	116	445	121	32	2	14	(8	6)	199	70	50	73	31	1	83	13	0	3	12	5	2	.272	.335	.447	.783
2022	Mil	NL	134	430	108	24	4	15	(8	7)	185	65	47	59	46	2	88	14	2	5	17	6	5	.251	.339	.430	.770
Postseason			35	112	21	8	1	5	(3	2)	46	10	15	11	6	2	22	1	1	1	4	0	3	.188	.233	.411	.644
10 ML YEARS			1102	3572	932	180	31	82	(44	38)	1420	486	378	489	310	30	634	98	22	31	117	36	47	.261	.334	.398	.732

Alex Wood

Pitches: L Bats: R Pos: SP-26

Ht: 6'4" Wt: 215 Born: 1/12/1991 Age: 32

			HOW MUCH PITCHED					WHAT HE GAVE UP										THE RESULTS						
Year	Team	Lg	G	GS	GF	IP	BFP	H	R	ER	HR	SH	SF	HB	TBB	IBB	SO	WP	W	L	Pct	Sv-Op	Hld	Vel	OPS	ERC	ERA
2013	Atl	NL	31	11	9	77.2	327	76	29	27	3	6	4	1	27	1	77	4	3	3	.500	0-0	1	92	.670	3.40	3.13
2014	Atl	NL	35	24	2	171.2	694	151	58	53	16	7	3	6	45	1	170	5	11	11	.500	0-0	2	90	.651	3.04	2.78
2015	2 Tms	NL	32	32	0	189.2	801	198	86	81	15	15	3	4	59	4	139	6	12	12	.500	0-0	0	89	.724	3.94	3.84
2016	LAD	NL	14	10	0	60.1	255	56	30	25	5	0	2	3	20	0	66	4	1	4	.200	0-0	1	91	.660	3.49	3.73
2017	LAD	NL	27	25	0	152.1	614	123	50	46	15	4	0	6	38	6	151	2	16	3	.842	0-0	1	92	.620	2.58	2.72
2018	LAD	NL	33	27	0	151.2	637	143	70	62	14	3	7	8	40	5	135	2	9	7	.563	0-0	1	90	.664	3.32	3.68
2019	Cin	NL	7	7	0	35.2	153	41	25	23	11	2	0	1	9	0	30	0	1	3	.250	0-0	0	92	.926	6.02	5.80
2020	LAD	NL	9	2	0	12.2	65	17	11	9	2	0	0	3	6	1	15	1	0	1	.000	0-0	1	91	.918	7.50	6.39
2021	SF	NL	26	26	0	138.2	585	125	63	59	14	0	1	16	39	1	152	7	10	4	.714	0-0	0	92	.680	3.52	3.83
2022	SF	NL	26	26	0	130.2	555	132	78	74	17	2	7	12	30	1	131	4	8	12	.400	0-0	0	92	.721	4.02	5.10
15	Atl	NL	20	20	0	119.1	509	132	50	47	8	11	1	2	36	2	90	5	7	6	.538	0-0	1	89	.729	4.15	3.54
15	LAD	NL	12	12	0	70.1	292	66	36	34	7	4	2	2	23	2	49	1	5	6	.455	0-0	0	88	.714	3.58	4.35
Postseason			21	3	4	37.2	157	29	17	13	9	1	0	3	13	5	40	1	1	2	.333	0-0	6	91	.732	3.59	3.11
10 ML YEARS			240	190	13	1121.0	4686	1062	500	459	112	39	27	60	313	20	1066	35	71	60	.542	0-0	6	91	.688	3.52	3.69

Jake Woodford

Pitches: R Bats: R Pos: RP-26; SP-1

Ht: 6'4" Wt: 215 Born: 10/28/1996 Age: 26

			HOW MUCH PITCHED					WHAT HE GAVE UP										THE RESULTS						
Year	Team	Lg	G	GS	GF	IP	BFP	H	R	ER	HR	SH	SF	HB	TBB	IBB	SO	WP	W	L	Pct	Sv-Op	Hld	Vel	OPS	ERC	ERA
2022	Memp	AAA	11	10	0	43.0	183	39	17	15	2	0	2	2	19	0	39	1	2	3	.400	0--	-	-	.634	3.57	3.14
2020	StL	NL	12	1	4	21.0	85	20	13	13	7	0	1	0	5	0	16	1	1	0	1.000	0-0	0	93	.826	4.76	5.57
2021	StL	NL	26	8	4	67.2	293	66	32	30	7	0	7	8	25	0	50	2	3	4	.429	0-0	0	92	.741	4.35	3.99
2022	StL	NL	27	1	16	48.1	188	43	13	12	1	0	3	1	11	1	24	3	4	0	1.000	0-0	0	92	.610	2.53	2.23
3 ML YEARS			65	10	24	137.0	566	129	58	55	15	0	11	9	41	1	90	6	8	4	.667	0-0	0	92	.710	3.76	3.61

Brandon Woodruff

Pitches: R Bats: L Pos: SP-27

Ht: 6'4" Wt: 243 Born: 2/10/1993 Age: 30

			HOW MUCH PITCHED					WHAT HE GAVE UP										THE RESULTS						
Year	Team	Lg	G	GS	GF	IP	BFP	H	R	ER	HR	SH	SF	HB	TBB	IBB	SO	WP	W	L	Pct	Sv-Op	Hld	Vel	OPS	ERC	ERA
2017	Mil	NL	8	8	0	43.0	184	43	23	23	5	1	0	3	14	1	32	0	2	3	.400	0-0	0	94	.719	4.16	4.81
2018	Mil	NL	19	4	4	42.1	176	36	18	17	4	0	1	2	14	0	47	1	3	0	1.000	1-1	2	95	.641	3.14	3.61
2019	Mil	NL	22	22	0	121.2	493	109	49	49	12	2	2	5	30	0	143	1	11	3	.786	0-0	0	96	.650	3.13	3.62
2020	Mil	NL	13	13	0	73.2	293	55	26	25	9	0	1	4	18	0	91	1	3	5	.375	0-0	0	97	.604	2.51	3.05
2021	Mil	NL	30	30	0	179.1	708	130	54	51	18	4	4	7	43	0	211	2	9	10	.474	0-0	0	96	.573	2.21	2.56
2022	Mil	NL	27	27	0	153.1	620	122	56	52	18	1	2	5	42	0	190	2	13	4	.765	0-0	0	96	.640	2.74	3.05
Postseason			8	4	1	28.1	108	20	10	10	2	1	0	2	4	1	40	1	1	3	.250	0-0	0	96	.540	1.74	3.18
6 ML YEARS			119	104	4	613.1	2474	495	226	217	66	8	10	26	161	1	714	7	41	25	.621	1-1	2	96	.624	2.75	3.18

William Woods

Pitches: R Bats: R Pos: RP-2

Ht: 6'3" Wt: 190 Born: 12/29/1998 Age: 24

			HOW MUCH PITCHED					WHAT HE GAVE UP										THE RESULTS						
Year	Team	Lg	G	GS	GF	IP	BFP	H	R	ER	HR	SH	SF	HB	TBB	IBB	SO	WP	W	L	Pct	Sv-Op	Hld	Vel	OPS	ERC	ERA
2022	Gwnntt	AAA	18	0	5	17.1	76	13	14	10	3	0	1	0	9	0	16	2	1	1	.500	0--	-	-	.709	3.48	5.19
2022	Atl	NL	2	0	1	2.0	8	2	0	0	0	0	0	0	1	0	2	0	0	0	-	0-0	0	95	.661	4.15	0.00

Simeon Woods Richardson

Pitches: R Bats: R Pos: SP-1

Ht: 6'3" Wt: 210 Born: 9/27/2000 Age: 22

			HOW MUCH PITCHED					WHAT HE GAVE UP										THE RESULTS						
Year	Team	Lg	G	GS	GF	IP	BFP	H	R	ER	HR	SH	SF	HB	TBB	IBB	SO	WP	W	L	Pct	Sv-Op	Hld	Vel	OPS	ERC	ERA
2022	Wich	AA	16	16	0	70.2	287	56	25	24	4	0	0	3	26	0	77	5	3	3	.500	0--	-	-	.595	2.78	3.06
2022	StPaul	AAA	7	7	0	36.2	139	21	10	9	2	0	2	0	10	0	38	1	2	0	1.000	0--	-	-	.483	1.39	2.21
2022	Min	AL	1	1	0	5.0	20	3	3	2	1	0	0	0	2	0	3	1	0	1	.000	0-0	0	91	.583	2.55	3.60

Kyle Wright

Pitches: R Bats: R Pos: SP-30   Ht: 6'4" Wt: 215 Born: 10/2/1995 Age: 27

Year Team	Lg	HOW MUCH PITCHED					WHAT HE GAVE UP											THE RESULTS							
		G	GS	GF	IP	BFP	H	R	ER	HR	SH	SF	HB	TBB	IBB	SO	WP	W	L	Pct	Sv-Op	Hld	Vel	OPS	ERC	ERA
2018 Atl	NL	4	0	1	6.0	28	4	3	3	2	0	0	0	6	0	5	0	0	0	-	0-0	0	94	.812	6.25	4.50
2019 Atl	NL	7	4	2	19.2	93	24	19	19	4	0	0	1	13	1	18	2	0	3	.000	0-0	0	95	.966	7.64	8.69
2020 Atl	NL	8	8	0	38.0	168	35	23	22	7	0	0	0	24	1	30	1	2	4	.333	0-0	0	94	.782	5.19	5.21
2021 Atl	NL	2	2	0	6.1	35	7	7	7	2	1	1	4	5	0	6	1	0	1	.000	0-0	0	93	1.096	10.97	9.95
2022 Atl	NL	30	30	0	180.1	738	156	67	64	19	0	3	9	53	0	174	7	21	5	.808	0-0	0	95	.647	3.20	3.19
Postseason		4	2	1	12.1	58	13	8	8	3	0	0	1	7	2	13	0	1	1	.500	0-0	0	94	.842	6.10	5.84
5 ML YEARS		51	44	3	250.1	1062	226	119	115	34	1	4	14	101	2	233	11	23	13	.639	0-0	0	95	.712	4.04	4.13

Austin Wynns

Bats: R Throws: R Pos: C-57;DH-5;PH-3;PR-1   Ht: 6'0" Wt: 190 Born: 12/10/1990 Age: 32

Year Team	Lg	BATTING																			RUNNING			AVERAGES			
		G	AB	H	2B	3B	HR	(Hm	Rd)	TB	R	RBI	RC	TBB	IBB	SO	HBP	SH	SF	SB	CS	GDP	Avg	OBP	Slg	OPS
2022 LV	AAA	33	104	38	5	0	3	(-	-)	52	21	20	27	28	0	18	1	0	0	0	1	0	.365	.504	.500	1.004
2018 Bal	AL	42	110	28	2	0	4	(1	3)	42	16	11	9	5	0	25	0	3	0	0	0	7	.255	.287	.382	.669
2019 Bal	AL	28	70	15	1	0	1	(0	1)	19	8	5	4	3	0	14	0	1	0	0	0	2	.214	.247	.271	.518
2021 Bal	AL	45	130	24	4	0	4	(1	3)	40	14	14	9	8	0	31	0	1	0	0	0	6	.185	.232	.308	.540
2022 SF	NL	66	162	42	7	0	3	(1	2)	58	14	21	16	10	0	38	3	1	1	0	0	9	.259	.313	.358	.671
4 ML YEARS		181	472	109	14	0	12	(3	9)	159	52	51	38	26	0	108	3	6	1	1	0	24	.231	.275	.337	.612

Jimmy Yacabonis

Pitches: R Bats: R Pos: RP-13; SP-1   YAH-cah-bone-iss   Ht: 6'3" Wt: 225 Born: 3/21/1992 Age: 31

Year Team	Lg	HOW MUCH PITCHED					WHAT HE GAVE UP											THE RESULTS							
		G	GS	GF	IP	BFP	H	R	ER	HR	SH	SF	HB	TBB	IBB	SO	WP	W	L	Pct	Sv-Op	Hld	Vel	OPS	ERC	ERA
2022 Jaxnvl	AAA	18	0	13	23.2	100	19	10	9	1	0	0	2	11	1	35	1	4	3	.571	2- -	-		.688	3.14	3.42
2022 Drham	AAA	8	0	3	9.0	33	5	3	3	0	0	0	0	3	0	8	1	2	1	.667	0- -	-		.409	1.32	3.00
2017 Bal	AL	14	0	7	20.2	90	18	10	10	2	0	3	0	14	1	8	1	2	0	1.000	0-0	0	95	.725	4.44	4.35
2018 Bal	AL	12	7	0	40.0	177	40	25	24	8	1	0	5	18	1	33	4	0	2	.000	0-0	0	93	.829	5.57	5.40
2019 Bal	AL	29	4	6	41.0	193	51	32	31	9	0	1	2	24	0	33	4	1	2	.333	0-0	3	94	.953	7.63	6.80
2020 Sea	AL	2	1	1	2.1	13	2	1	1	0	0	0	1	3	0	1	0	1	0	1.000	0-0	0	93	.684	7.40	3.86
2022 2 Tms		14	1	5	14.0	73	20	15	13	4	0	0	2	10	0	21	1	1	1	.500	0-0	0	94	1.061	10.38	8.36
22 Mia	NL	9	0	3	9.1	45	12	8	7	3	0	0	0	5	0	15	1	1	1	.500	0-0	0	94	.978	8.01	6.75
22 TB	AL	5	1	2	4.2	28	8	7	6	1	0	0	2	5	0	6	0	0	0	-	0-0	0	94	1.202	15.25	11.57
5 ML YEARS		71	13	19	118.0	546	131	83	79	23	1	4	10	69	2	96	10	4	6	.400	0-0	3	94	.885	6.65	6.03

Miguel Yajure

Pitches: R Bats: R Pos: RP-11; SP-1   yuh-HOO-ray   Ht: 6'1" Wt: 215 Born: 5/1/1998 Age: 25

Year Team	Lg	HOW MUCH PITCHED					WHAT HE GAVE UP											THE RESULTS							
		G	GS	GF	IP	BFP	H	R	ER	HR	SH	SF	HB	TBB	IBB	SO	WP	W	L	Pct	Sv-Op	Hld	Vel	OPS	ERC	ERA
2022 Indy	AAA	16	14	0	54.2	245	59	38	37	7	0	3	2	23	0	53	4	4	4	.500	0- -	-		.771	4.92	6.09
2020 NYY	AL	3	0	3	7.0	29	3	1	1	1	0	0	1	5	0	8	1	0	0	-	0-0	0	92	.571	3.09	1.29
2021 Pit	NL	4	3	0	15.0	68	17	14	14	6	0	0	1	7	0	11	0	0	2	.000	0-0	0	91	1.034	7.85	8.40
2022 Pit	NL	12	1	4	24.1	119	31	26	24	3	0	0	2	16	1	16	4	1	1	.500	1-1	0	93	.907	7.28	8.88
3 ML YEARS		19	4	7	46.1	216	51	41	39	10	0	0	4	28	1	35	5	1	3	.250	1-1	0	92	.906	6.81	7.58

Ryan Yarbrough

Pitches: L Bats: R Pos: RP-11; SP-9   Ht: 6'5" Wt: 205 Born: 12/31/1991 Age: 31

Year Team	Lg	HOW MUCH PITCHED					WHAT HE GAVE UP											THE RESULTS							
		G	GS	GF	IP	BFP	H	R	ER	HR	SH	SF	HB	TBB	IBB	SO	WP	W	L	Pct	Sv-Op	Hld	Vel	OPS	ERC	ERA
2022 Drham	AAA	7	7	0	27.2	128	32	18	14	3	0	1	3	12	0	26	0	2	2	.500	0- -	-		.814	5.59	4.55
2018 TB	AL	38	6	3	147.1	628	140	70	64	18	1	1	8	50	6	128	1	16	6	.727	0-0	0	89	.730	3.86	3.91
2019 TB	AL	28	14	1	141.2	563	121	69	65	15	0	3	9	20	2	117	0	11	6	.647	0-0	0	88	.650	2.60	4.13
2020 TB	AL	11	9	0	55.2	234	54	22	22	5	2	2	7	12	1	44	2	1	4	.200	0-0	0	87	.689	3.61	3.56
2021 TB	AL	30	21	0	155.0	653	163	96	88	25	4	3	9	27	2	117	1	9	7	.563	0-0	0	86	.764	4.08	5.11
2022 TB	AL	20	9	2	80.0	355	88	44	40	12	1	2	11	22	0	61	3	3	8	.273	0-0	0	87	.790	5.04	4.50
Postseason		8	2	1	17.2	74	18	6	6	5	0	0	1	5	0	8	0	2	0	1.000	0-0	0	88	.854	5.34	3.06
5 ML YEARS		127	59	6	579.2	2433	566	301	279	75	8	11	44	131	11	467	7	40	31	.563	0-0	0	88	.725	3.73	4.33

Mike Yastrzemski

Bats: L Throws: L Pos: RF-104;CF-93;PH-16;DH-1;PR-1   yuh-STREM-skee   Ht: 5'10" Wt: 178 Born: 8/23/1990 Age: 32

Year Team	Lg	BATTING																			RUNNING			AVERAGES			
		G	AB	H	2B	3B	HR	(Hm	Rd)	TB	R	RBI	RC	TBB	IBB	SO	HBP	SH	SF	SB	CS	GDP	Avg	OBP	Slg	OPS
2019 SF	NL	107	371	101	22	3	21	(8	13)	192	64	55	61	32	1	107	4	1	3	2	4	4	.272	.334	.518	.852
2020 SF	NL	54	192	57	14	4	10	(6	4)	109	39	35	43	30	2	55	3	0	0	2	1	2	.297	.400	.568	.968
2021 SF	NL	139	468	105	28	3	25	(8	17)	214	75	71	67	51	4	131	9	1	3	4	0	3	.224	.311	.457	.768
2022 SF	NL	148	485	104	31	2	17	(8	9)	190	73	57	61	61	0	141	5	1	6	5	1	3	.214	.305	.392	.697
Postseason		5	13	0	0	0	0	(0	0)	0	0	0	0	0	0	4	0	0	0	0	0	0	.000	.000	.000	.000
4 ML YEARS		448	1516	367	95	12	73	(30	43)	705	251	218	232	174	7	434	21	3	12	13	6	12	.242	.326	.465	.791

Kirby Yates

Pitches: R Bats: L Pos: RP-9 Ht: 5'10" Wt: 205 Born: 3/25/1987 Age: 36

		HOW MUCH PITCHED					WHAT HE GAVE UP											THE RESULTS								
Year Team	Lg	G	GS	GF	IP	BFP	H	R	ER	HR	SH	SF	HB	TBB	IBB	SO	WP	W	L	Pct	Sv-Op	Hld	Vel	OPS	ERC	ERA
2022 Gwnntt	AAA	5	0	0	5.1	21	2	1	1	0	0	0	1	2	0	4	0	0	0	-	0--	-		.349	1.18	1.69
2014 TB	AL	37	0	12	36.0	156	33	16	15	4	0	1	3	15	3	42	2	0	2	.000	1-2	0	92	.699	3.94	3.75
2015 TB	AL	20	0	10	20.1	92	23	18	18	10	0	0	1	7	0	21	0	1	0	1.000	0-0	0	92	1.004	7.58	7.97
2016 NYY	AL	41	0	11	41.1	184	41	24	24	5	1	1	4	19	1	50	1	2	1	.667	0-2	2	93	.746	4.77	5.23
2017 2 Tms		62	0	12	56.2	231	44	28	25	12	0	1	2	19	2	88	0	4	5	.444	1-4	20	94	.698	3.42	3.97
2018 SD	NL	65	0	28	63.0	250	41	15	15	6	0	3	4	17	0	90	2	5	3	.625	12-13	16	94	.527	2.00	2.14
2019 SD	NL	60	0	51	60.2	243	41	14	8	2	1	1	7	13	1	101	2	0	5	.000	41-44	0	94	.515	1.72	1.19
2020 SD	NL	6	0	3	4.1	25	7	6	6	1	0	1	0	4	0	8	2	0	1	.000	2-2	1	94	.940	10.86	12.46
2022 Atl	NL	9	0	3	7.0	33	6	4	4	2	0	1	0	5	0	6	2	0	0	-	0-0	2	93	.889	5.61	5.14
17 LAA	AL	1	0	0	1.0	5	2	2	2	2	0	0	0	0	1	1	0	0	0	-	0-0	1		2.000	25.07	18.00
17 SD	NL	61	0	12	55.2	226	42	26	23	10	0	1	2	19	2	87	0	4	5	.444	1-4	20	94	.666	3.13	3.72
8 ML YEARS		300	0	130	289.1	1214	236	125	115	42	2	9	21	99	7	406	11	12	17	.414	57-67	41	93	.666	3.36	3.58

Christian Yelich

Bats: L Throws: R Pos: LF-115;DH-36;PH-4;PR-1 YELL-itch Ht: 6'3" Wt: 195 Born: 12/5/1991 Age: 31

		BATTING																	RUNNING			AVERAGES			
Year Team	Lg	G	AB	H	2B	3B	HR	(Hm Rd)	TB	R	RBI	RC	TBB	IBB	SO	HBP	SH	SF	SB	CS	GDP	Avg	OBP	Slg	OPS
2013 Mia	NL	62	240	69	12	1	4	(0 4)	95	34	16	35	31	1	66	1	0	1	10	0	4	.288	.370	.396	.766
2014 Mia	NL	144	582	165	30	6	9	(2 7)	234	94	54	87	70	3	137	3	3	2	21	7	9	.284	.362	.402	.764
2015 Mia	NL	126	476	143	30	2	7	(1 6)	198	63	44	64	47	2	101	2	0	0	16	5	13	.300	.366	.416	.782
2016 Mia	NL	155	578	172	38	3	21	(8 13)	279	78	98	89	72	4	138	4	0	5	9	4	20	.298	.376	.483	.859
2017 Mia	NL	156	602	170	36	2	18	(7 11)	264	100	81	99	80	4	137	6	0	6	16	2	13	.282	.369	.439	.807
2018 Mil	NL	147	574	187	34	7	36	(22 14)	343	118	110	128	68	2	135	7	0	2	22	4	14	.326	.402	.598	1.000
2019 Mil	NL	130	489	161	29	3	44	(27 17)	328	100	97	126	80	16	118	8	0	3	30	2	8	.329	.429	.671	1.100
2020 Mil	NL	58	200	41	7	1	12	(6 6)	86	39	22	28	46	2	76	1	0	0	4	2	4	.205	.356	.430	.786
2021 Mil	NL	117	399	99	19	2	9	(6 3)	149	70	51	67	70	5	113	3	0	3	9	3	5	.248	.362	.373	.736
2022 Mil	NL	154	575	145	25	4	14	(9 5)	220	99	57	77	88	5	162	5	1	2	19	3	9	.252	.355	.383	.738
Postseason		16	60	12	2	0	2	(2 0)	20	8	3	4	13	1	19	0	0	0	3	0	3	.200	.342	.333	.676
10 ML YEARS		1249	4715	1352	260	31	174	(88 86)	2196	795	630	800	652	44	1183	40	4	24	156	32	99	.287	.376	.466	.842

Juan Yepez

Bats: R Throws: R Pos: LF-23;DH-18;RF-17;1B-15;3B-6;PH-5 Ht: 6'1" Wt: 200 Born: 2/19/1998 Age: 25

		BATTING																	RUNNING			AVERAGES			
Year Team	Lg	G	AB	H	2B	3B	HR	(Hm Rd)	TB	R	RBI	RC	TBB	IBB	SO	HBP	SH	SF	SB	CS	GDP	Avg	OBP	Slg	OPS
2022 Memp	AAA	50	188	52	9	0	16	(- -)	109	34	53	41	17	0	46	2	0	1	0	0	4	.277	.341	.580	.921
2022 StL	NL	76	253	64	13	0	12	(6 6)	113	27	30	31	16	0	61	1	0	4	0	0	6	.253	.296	.447	.742

Huascar Ynoa

Pitches: R Bats: R Pos: SP-2 WAH-scar ee-NOH-ah Ht: 6'2" Wt: 220 Born: 5/28/1998 Age: 25

		HOW MUCH PITCHED					WHAT HE GAVE UP											THE RESULTS								
Year Team	Lg	G	GS	GF	IP	BFP	H	R	ER	HR	SH	SF	HB	TBB	IBB	SO	WP	W	L	Pct	Sv-Op	Hld	Vel	OPS	ERC	ERA
2022 Gwnntt	AAA	18	17	0	77.2	337	73	51	49	14	0	4	1	35	0	87	3	5	6	.455	0--	-	-	.771	4.53	5.68
2019 Atl	NL	2	0	1	3.0	16	6	6	6	1	0	0	0	1	0	3	0	0	0	-	0-0	0	94	1.171	12.18	18.00
2020 Atl	NL	9	5	1	21.2	100	23	14	14	2	0	2	2	13	1	17	2	0	0	-	0-0	0	95	.802	5.50	5.82
2021 Atl	NL	18	17	0	91.0	372	76	42	41	14	1	2	4	25	1	100	4	4	6	.400	0-0	0	97	.701	3.20	4.05
2022 Atl	NL	2	2	0	6.2	37	11	10	10	2	0	0	0	6	0	8	1	0	2	.000	0-0	0	97	1.072	12.18	13.50
Postseason		2	0	0	5.0	24	3	2	2	1	0	0	1	5	0	6	0	0	0	-	0-0	0	97	.708	5.62	3.60
4 ML YEARS		31	24	2	122.1	525	116	72	71	19	1	4	6	45	2	128	7	4	8	.333	0-0	0	96	.760	4.20	5.22

Alex Young

Pitches: L Bats: L Pos: RP-24; SP-1 Ht: 6'3" Wt: 220 Born: 9/9/1993 Age: 29

		HOW MUCH PITCHED					WHAT HE GAVE UP											THE RESULTS								
Year Team	Lg	G	GS	GF	IP	BFP	H	R	ER	HR	SH	SF	HB	TBB	IBB	SO	WP	W	L	Pct	Sv-Op	Hld	Vel	OPS	ERC	ERA
2022 Clmbs	AAA	30	0	10	32.0	132	30	14	13	5	0	0	1	7	1	47	0	3	0	1.000	1--	-	-	.691	3.46	3.66
2019 Ari	NL	17	15	0	83.1	349	72	40	33	14	3	0	4	27	4	71	2	7	5	.583	0-0	0	89	.710	3.58	3.56
2020 Ari	NL	15	7	0	46.1	204	51	30	28	11	0	5	1	14	0	39	1	2	4	.333	0-0	1	91	.872	5.24	5.44
2021 2 Tms		40	2	12	52.0	246	65	43	38	12	2	2	3	27	4	43	3	2	6	.250	0-2	4	90	.927	7.23	6.58
2022 2 Tms		25	1	2	26.2	116	29	11	7	0	0	1	1	11	0	21	3	1	1	.500	0-1	5	91	.732	4.11	2.36
21 Ari	NL	30	2	7	41.2	193	50	34	29	11	2	2	1	20	3	38	2	2	6	.250	0-2	3	91	.913	6.81	6.26
21 Cle	AL	10	0	5	10.1	53	15	9	9	1	0	0	2	7	1	5	1	0	0	-	0-0	1	91	.976	8.78	7.84
22 Cle	AL	1	0	1	0.1	2	1	0	0	0	0	0	0	0	0	1	0	0	0	-	0-0	0	90	1.500	14.52	0.00
22 SF	NL	24	1	1	26.1	114	28	11	7	0	0	1	1	11	0	20	3	1	1	.500	0-1	5	91	.717	4.00	2.39
4 ML YEARS		97	25	14	208.1	915	217	124	106	37	5	8	9	79	8	174	9	12	16	.429	0-3	10	90	.807	4.88	4.58

Danny Young

Pitches: L Bats: L Pos: RP-3 Ht: 6'3" Wt: 200 Born: 5/27/1994 Age: 29

		HOW MUCH PITCHED					WHAT HE GAVE UP											THE RESULTS								
Year Team	Lg	G	GS	GF	IP	BFP	H	R	ER	HR	SH	SF	HB	TBB	IBB	SO	WP	W	L	Pct	Sv-Op	Hld	Vel	OPS	ERC	ERA
2022 Tacom	AAA	29	0	7	28.0	118	20	13	12	0	0	0	6	9	0	40	1	1	1	.500	2--	-	-	.554	2.37	3.86

Year	Team	Lg	G	GS	GF	IP	BFP	H	R	ER	HR	SH	SF	HB	TBB	IBB	SO	WP	W	L	Pct	Sv-Op	Hld	Vel	OPS	ERC	ERA
2022	Gwnntt	AAA	11	0	1	8.1	35	5	3	3	0	0	0	2	4	0	17	1	0	1	.000	0- -	-		.556	2.48	3.24
2022	2 Tms		3	0	3	6.1	32	11	3	3	1	0	0	0	2	0	6	0	0	0	-	0-0	0	89	.940	8.59	4.26
22	Sea	AL	2	0	2	3.2	20	7	3	3	1	0	0	0	2	0	5	0	0	0	-	0-0	0	89	1.006	12.01	7.36
22	Atl	NL	1	0	1	2.2	12	4	0	0	0	0	0	0	0	0	1	0	0	0	-	0-0	0	89	.833	4.47	0.00

Jared Young

Bats: L **Throws:** R **Pos:** DH-3;1B-2;RF-1;PH-1   **Ht:** 6'2" **Wt:** 185 **Born:** 7/9/1995 **Age:** 27

Year	Team	Lg	G	AB	H	2B	3B	HR	(Hm	Rd)	TB	R	RBI	RC	TBB	IBB	SO	HBP	SH	SF	SB	CS	GDP	Avg	OBP	Slg	OPS
2022	Iowa	AAA	109	400	92	21	2	17	(-	-)	168	61	59	56	40	2	110	9	2	4	3	2	6	.230	.311	.420	.731
2022	ChC	NL	6	19	5	2	0	0	(0	0)	7	2	0	2	3	0	7	0	0	0	1	0	0	.263	.364	.368	.732

Aneurys Zabala

Pitches: R **Bats:** R **Pos:** RP-2   ah-NOO-riss zah-BAH-lah   **Ht:** 6'3" **Wt:** 259 **Born:** 12/21/1996 **Age:** 26

Year	Team	Lg	G	GS	GF	IP	BFP	H	R	ER	HR	SH	SF	HB	TBB	IBB	SO	WP	W	L	Pct	Sv-Op	Hld	Vel	OPS	ERC	ERA
2022	Jaxnvl	AAA	17	1	4	23.2	119	23	25	25	3	0	1	2	28	0	30	5	0	0	-	0- -	-		.866	7.88	9.51
2022	Mia	NL	2	0	2	2.2	11	3	0	0	0	0	1	0	1	0	2	0	0	0	-	0-0	0	99	.808	4.24	0.00

Rob Zastryzny

Pitches: L **Bats:** R **Pos:** RP-6   za-STRIZ-nee   **Ht:** 6'3" **Wt:** 205 **Born:** 3/26/1992 **Age:** 31

Year	Team	Lg	G	GS	GF	IP	BFP	H	R	ER	HR	SH	SF	HB	TBB	IBB	SO	WP	W	L	Pct	Sv-Op	Hld	Vel	OPS	ERC	ERA
2022	Syrcse	AAA	26	6	2	47.1	208	48	26	19	6	1	1	3	19	0	59	3	1	5	.167	1- -	-		.773	4.60	3.61
2022	Salt Lk	AAA	8	0	2	8.0	33	8	2	2	0	0	1	0	1	0	9	0	0	0	-	0- -	-		.563	2.35	2.25
2016	ChC	NL	8	1	1	16.0	66	12	3	2	0	0	2	1	5	0	17	0	1	0	1.000	0-0	0	90	.497	2.01	1.13
2017	ChC	NL	4	0	0	13.0	62	19	13	12	2	0	0	1	7	0	11	0	0	0	-	0-0	0	90	.973	8.66	8.31
2018	ChC	NL	6	0	2	5.2	26	6	3	3	0	0	0	1	4	0	3	0	1	0	1.000	0-0	0	89	.804	5.82	4.76
2022	2 Tms		6	0	1	4.0	16	3	4	3	0	0	0	0	1	0	3	1	0	0	-	0-0	0	92	.650	1.65	6.75
22	NYM	NL	1	0	0	1.0	4	1	1	1	0	0	0	0	0	0	1	0	0	0	-	0-0	0	93	1.000	1.95	9.00
22	LAA	AL	5	0	1	3.0	12	2	3	2	0	0	0	0	1	0	2	1	0	0	-	0-0	0	92	.523	1.57	6.00
4 ML YEARS			24	1	4	38.2	170	40	23	20	2	0	2	3	17	0	34	1	2	0	1.000	0-0	0	90	.731	4.43	4.66

Seby Zavala

Bats: R **Throws:** R **Pos:** C-58;PH-6;1B-2;DH-2   **Ht:** 5'11" **Wt:** 205 **Born:** 8/28/1993 **Age:** 29

Year	Team	Lg	G	AB	H	2B	3B	HR	(Hm	Rd)	TB	R	RBI	RC	TBB	IBB	SO	HBP	SH	SF	SB	CS	GDP	Avg	OBP	Slg	OPS
2022	Charllt	AAA	41	142	40	12	0	8	(-	-)	76	26	16	30	26	1	60	1	0	0	0	0	4	.282	.396	.535	.932
2019	CWS	AL	5	12	1	0	0	0	(0	0)	1	1	0	0	0	0	9	0	0	0	0	0	0	.083	.083	.083	.167
2021	CWS	AL	37	93	17	3	0	5	(4	1)	35	15	15	10	6	0	41	1	4	0	0	0	0	.183	.240	.376	.616
2022	CWS	AL	61	178	48	14	0	2	(0	2)	68	22	21	26	19	0	64	3	3	2	0	0	1	.270	.347	.382	.729
3 ML YEARS			103	283	66	17	0	7	(4	3)	104	38	36	36	25	0	114	4	7	2	0	0	2	.233	.303	.367	.670

Angel Zerpa

Pitches: L **Bats:** L **Pos:** SP-2; RP-1   **Ht:** 6'0" **Wt:** 220 **Born:** 9/27/1999 **Age:** 23

Year	Team	Lg	G	GS	GF	IP	BFP	H	R	ER	HR	SH	SF	HB	TBB	IBB	SO	WP	W	L	Pct	Sv-Op	Hld	Vel	OPS	ERC	ERA
2022	NWArk	AA	13	13	0	64.0	278	70	34	31	7	0	0	3	21	0	69	4	2	5	.286	0- -	-		.795	4.61	4.36
2022	Omha	AAA	6	6	0	7.2	28	2	1	1	0	0	0	0	4	0	0	0	0	0	-	0- -	-		.339	0.84	1.17
2021	KC	AL	1	1	0	5.0	20	3	2	0	0	1	1	0	1	0	4	0	0	1	.000	0-0	0	94	.446	1.06	0.00
2022	KC	AL	3	2	0	11.0	44	9	3	2	2	0	0	0	3	0	3	1	2	1	.667	0-0	0	94	.639	3.15	1.64
2 ML YEARS			4	3	0	16.0	64	12	5	2	2	1	1	0	4	0	7	1	2	2	.500	0-0	0	94	.582	2.33	1.13

T.J. Zeuch

Pitches: R **Bats:** R **Pos:** SP-3   ZOYK   **Ht:** 6'7" **Wt:** 245 **Born:** 8/1/1995 **Age:** 27

Year	Team	Lg	G	GS	GF	IP	BFP	H	R	ER	HR	SH	SF	HB	TBB	IBB	SO	WP	W	L	Pct	Sv-Op	Hld	Vel	OPS	ERC	ERA
2022	Memp	AAA	5	5	0	19.1	100	39	26	25	6	0	1	1	11	0	20	0	0	4	.000	0- -	-		1.246	14.86	11.64
2022	Lsvlle	AAA	5	5	0	22.1	92	18	10	9	2	0	0	0	10	0	26	0	0	1	.000	0- -	-		.646	3.19	3.63
2019	Tor	AL	5	3	0	22.2	99	22	13	12	2	0	0	0	11	0	20	2	1	2	.333	0-0	0	92	.731	4.15	4.76
2020	Tor	AL	3	1	1	11.1	47	9	2	2	1	0	0	0	4	0	3	0	1	0	1.000	0-0	0	92	.625	2.68	1.59
2021	Tor	AL	5	3	0	15.0	74	21	16	11	6	0	0	0	9	0	8	0	0	2	.000	0-0	0	94	1.082	9.94	6.60
2022	Cin	NL	3	3	0	10.2	64	24	18	18	5	0	1	3	7	0	5	0	0	3	.000	0-0	0	92	1.286	19.44	15.19
4 ML YEARS			16	10	1	59.2	284	76	49	43	14	0	1	3	31	0	36	2	2	7	.222	0-0	0	92	.925	7.51	6.49

Bradley Zimmer

Bats: L **Throws:** R **Pos:** CF-97;PR-18;PH-8;RF-2;DH-1   **Ht:** 6'4" **Wt:** 185 **Born:** 11/27/1992 **Age:** 30

								BATTING												RUNNING			AVERAGES			
Year Team	Lg	G	AB	H	2B	3B	HR	(Hm Rd)	TB	R	RBI	RC	TBB	IBB	SO	HBP	SH	SF	SB	CS	GDP	Avg	OBP	Slg	OPS
2017 Cle	AL	101	299	72	15	2	8	(5 3)	115	41	39	37	26	1	99	4	0	3	18	1	5	.241	.307	.385	.692
2018 Cle	AL	34	106	24	5	0	2	(1 1)	35	14	9	9	7	0	44	1	0	0	4	1	1	.226	.281	.330	.611
2019 Cle	AL	9	13	0	0	0	0	(0 0)	0	1	0	0	1	0	7	0	0	0	0	0	0	.000	.071	.000	.071
2020 Cle	AL	20	37	6	0	0	1	(1 0)	9	3	3	3	7	0	14	5	0	1	2	1	2	.162	.360	.243	.603
2021 Cle	AL	99	299	68	9	1	8	(4 4)	103	44	35	38	30	0	122	15	0	4	15	3	3	.227	.325	.344	.669
2022 2 Tms		109	105	13	5	0	2	(1 1)	24	18	5	3	5	0	45	6	1	0	3	2	0	.124	.207	.229	.435
22 Tor	AL	100	89	9	4	0	2	(1 1)	19	14	5	2	5	0	41	6	1	0	3	2	0	.101	.200	.213	.413
22 Phi	NL	9	16	4	1	0	0	(0 0)	5	4	0	1	0	0	4	0	0	0	0	0	0	.250	.250	.313	.563
6 ML YEARS		372	859	183	34	3	21	(12 9)	286	121	91	90	76	1	331	31	1	8	42	8	11	.213	.298	.333	.631

Bruce Zimmermann

Pitches: L **Bats:** L **Pos:** SP-13; RP-2   **Ht:** 6'1" **Wt:** 215 **Born:** 2/9/1995 **Age:** 28

		HOW MUCH PITCHED					WHAT HE GAVE UP											THE RESULTS							
Year Team	Lg	G	GS	GF	IP	BFP	H	R	ER	HR	SH	SF	HB	TBB	IBB	SO	WP	W	L	Pct	Sv-Op	Hld	Vel	OPS	ERC	ERA
2022 Norfolk	AAA	14	12	0	76.1	329	83	35	32	6	1	0	3	18	0	74	5	5	2	.714	0--	-	-	.711	3.88	3.77
2020 Bal	AL	2	1	1	7.0	31	6	6	6	2	0	0	2	2	0	7	2	0	0	-	0-0	0	91	.767	5.18	7.71
2021 Bal	AL	14	13	0	64.1	285	75	37	36	14	1	2	2	22	0	56	0	4	5	.444	0-0	0	91	.841	5.83	5.04
2022 Bal	AL	15	13	1	73.2	320	97	52	49	21	1	3	2	12	0	49	1	2	5	.286	0-0	1	91	.961	6.54	5.99
3 ML YEARS		31	27	2	145.0	636	178	95	91	37	2	5	6	36	0	112	3	6	10	.375	0-0	1	91	.899	6.15	5.65

Tyler Zuber

Pitches: R **Bats:** R **Pos:** P   **Ht:** 5'11" **Wt:** 195 **Born:** 6/16/1995 **Age:** 28

		HOW MUCH PITCHED					WHAT HE GAVE UP											THE RESULTS							
Year Team	Lg	G	GS	GF	IP	BFP	H	R	ER	HR	SH	SF	HB	TBB	IBB	SO	WP	W	L	Pct	Sv-Op	Hld	Vel	OPS	ERC	ERA
2020 KC	AL	23	0	8	22.0	99	15	11	10	4	1	1	1	20	1	30	1	1	2	.333	0-0	0	-	.736	5.05	4.09
2021 KC	AL	31	0	6	27.1	123	26	20	19	6	0	1	1	17	1	25	2	0	3	.000	0-0	4	-	.819	5.71	6.26
2 ML YEARS		54	0	14	49.1	222	41	31	29	10	1	2	2	37	2	55	3	1	5	.167	0-0	4	-	.784	5.42	5.29

Mike Zunino

Bats: R **Throws:** R **Pos:** C-35;PH-2   zoo-NEE-no   **Ht:** 6'2" **Wt:** 235 **Born:** 3/25/1991 **Age:** 32

								BATTING												RUNNING			AVERAGES			
Year Team	Lg	G	AB	H	2B	3B	HR	(Hm Rd)	TB	R	RBI	RC	TBB	IBB	SO	HBP	SH	SF	SB	CS	GDP	Avg	OBP	Slg	OPS
2013 Sea	AL	52	173	37	5	0	5	(3 2)	57	22	14	13	16	0	49	3	0	1	1	0	5	.214	.290	.329	.620
2014 Sea	AL	131	438	87	20	2	22	(10 12)	177	51	60	39	17	1	158	17	0	4	0	3	12	.199	.254	.404	.658
2015 Sea	AL	112	350	61	11	0	11	(6 5)	105	28	28	14	21	0	132	5	8	2	0	1	6	.174	.230	.300	.530
2016 Sea	AL	55	164	34	7	0	12	(9 3)	77	16	31	28	21	0	65	6	0	1	0	0	0	.207	.318	.470	.787
2017 Sea	AL	124	387	97	25	0	25	(14 11)	197	52	64	55	39	0	160	8	0	1	1	0	8	.251	.331	.509	.840
2018 Sea	AL	113	373	75	18	0	20	(5 15)	153	37	44	29	24	0	150	6	0	2	0	0	7	.201	.259	.410	.669
2019 TB	AL	90	266	44	10	1	9	(5 4)	83	30	32	18	20	0	98	3	0	0	0	0	4	.165	.232	.312	.544
2020 TB	AL	28	75	11	4	0	3	(1 3)	27	8	10	7	6	0	37	3	0	0	0	0	0	.147	.238	.360	.598
2021 TB	AL	109	333	72	11	2	33	(14 19)	186	64	62	55	34	0	132	7	0	1	0	0	7	.216	.301	.559	.860
2022 TB	AL	36	115	17	3	0	5	(2 3)	35	7	16	12	6	0	46	1	0	1	0	0	2	.148	.195	.304	.499
Postseason		23	68	11	1	0	4	(4 0)	24	5	8	4	1	0	33	1	0	1	0	0	1	.162	.183	.353	.536
10 ML YEARS		850	2674	535	114	5	146	(69 77)	1097	315	361	270	204	1	1027	59	8	13	2	4	51	.200	.271	.410	.681

The Manager's Record

Bill James

Mark Kotsay, rookie manager of the Oakland A's, issued 37 Intentional Walks last year. There would have been a time when this was not a remarkable number, or, if it was remarkable, it would have been remarkably low. Frank Robinson, managing Washington in 2006, ordered 93 intentional walks, of which 23 bombed on him. Going back further in history, the numbers were even higher. In 1974 John McNamara (Padres, although he managed everywhere).. . .in 1974 the Padres issued 116 intentional walks. In the late 1960s, 1970s and early 1980s, it was not terribly uncommon for a team to issue 100+ intentional walks in a season. In the 1940s, as much as we can trust the unofficial data, the strategy appears to have been even more common. Ted Lyons, managing the Chicago White Sox in 1947, apparently ordered 121 intentional walks.

Over time, and in particular in the last twenty years, the intentional walk has become dramatically less common. This section of this book may (or may not) have played some role in that change. We say that an intentional walk has bombed on the manager if MULTIPLE runs score in the inning after the intentional walk. In 2008 Ron Washington of Texas issued 44 Intentional walks, of which 20 bombed on him, the 20 bombs being the most of any major league manager that year. When an intentional walk bombs on you, you have almost no chance to win the game. When you intentionally walk a hitter and the next guy hits a two-run double, that's an "L", not 100% of the time, but pretty close to it.

The next year Washington issued only 14 intentional walks, of which only 3 bombed on him. He got the message.

The Intentional Walk has never REALLY made a lot of sense, to be honest; not saying that there are NO appropriate circumstances to intentionally walk a hitter, but there aren't a lot. Managers and coaches in all sports overuse strategies which give them control of the flow of the action. Football coaches punt the ball away when they should go for it, because punting gives them control of the action, whereas going for it on 4th-and-a-foot is a gamble. Basketball coaches call time out in end-game situations in which all they're really doing by calling time out is giving the other team a chance to set up their defense. Managers like to have the reins in their hands. It's human nature; it happens in all offices, in all businesses. Managers over-manage because letting events take their own course feels risky.

Anyway, over time the Intentional Walk has become dramatically less common, so that in 2022 Mark Kotsay's 37 intentional walks was more than twice the average per team, and 13 more than any other major league manager. Ten of the 37 bombed on him, blew up in his face. No other manager gave up more than 4 bombs. Brian Snitker was the most successful at choosing his moments for an IBB, giving up 21 of the suckers, of which 18 got the result that Snitker was looking for, which would be getting out of the inning without any more runs being scored. Dave Roberts, on the other hand, got the result he wanted out of an intentional pass only 4 times in 13 tries. The major league average is 63, 64% success, somewhere in there. For his career, Roberts is at 64%, Snitker at 72%, Buck Showalter at 58%.

The idea of creating a manager's record first came to me in the 1970s, when I looked up some manager in The *Sporting News Baseball Register*, and it told me that he had hit .238 for Elmira in 1937. Don't check on the details; it might have been .237, and it might have been Altoona, rather than Elmira, and it might have been 1939, rather than 1937. The point is that this struck me as spectacularly unhelpful information. It didn't tell me ANYTHING about how he managed.

A related thought was that discussions about managers almost always devolved into debates about where the manager fell along the genius-to-idiot spectrum. Arguing about how GOOD a manager is isn't really helpful unless you have some kind of concrete information about how one manager is different from another.

Years later I was in position to create a "record" for each manager, so I created this form that we have here, asking the question "What information can we get to that describes how he manages his team, what choices he makes?" I can't say, honestly, that this has been a tremendous success. "A tremendous success" would mean that the information is commonly referenced, commonly used, widely understood. We've been doing this every year for about 20 years now, actually started the process in the late 1990s, and I can't say that any of that has been accomplished. Maybe it will be eventually; it hasn't been yet.

To the extent that this has failed, there are three reasons why it has failed. First, this book does not have a large enough circulation that it can drive the discussion to the degree that the books I wrote earlier in my career did.

Second, the game has evolved so rapidly in the last twenty years, with much, much more change in the style of play in the last twenty years than in the previous fifty years. . .the game has evolved so rapidly that no standards have become apparent for managerial normality. For example, when we started doing this, we created rules for what was a "Quick Hook" of a starting pitcher and what was a "Slow Hook", but within three years, the usage of starting pitchers had changed so much that we had to re-write the rules. Or platoon percentages. In the 1980s some managers would platoon at four or five positions. Baseball isn't like that anymore; teams carry so many relief pitchers now that the benches are not for one-position alternatives, but for players who can play wherever they are needed to play.

The rapid evolution of the game, plus the fact that the rules were different in the American and National Leagues, prevented any kind of standards of normalcy from emerging. Without standards, numbers don't generally make a lot of sense. Maybe that sentence doesn't make a lot of sense, but what I am trying to explain is, sports fans interpret player performances by comparing what the player has done to established standards. For WAR, for example, we know what a 4-Win Player is, and we know what a 2-Win Player is, and we know what a 7-Win Player is. Once a stat is established, we make performance standards, then we interpret new performance by relating them to the previous standards. That process has simply never developed for managerial records.

The third reason why this project has not worked as well as I hoped it might is that the Manager's Record has not grown or developed due to limitations of space. To give you an idea of what I mean, I remember reading in a book that Hall of Fame manager Joe McCarthy did not like to use rookies. It's an astonishingly ignorant statement; McCarthy, I might guess, may have put more rookies into the lineup as fulltime regulars than any other manager in history. A manager's record should ideally be the place where tendencies like that are monitored. Does the manager like to use left-handed starting pitchers? Does he like to keep multiple lefties in the bullpen? Does he emphasize speed in the outfield? Does he tend to pull a starting pitcher out of the rotation after three bad starts in a row, or five bad starts in a row, or seven bad starts in a row?

These are objective questions that have objective answers. If we knew what those answers are, the discussion surrounding managers would be a little bit smarter than it is. I had envisioned a manager's record that would grow and develop, but it hasn't, and it can't, in a place that is published once a year and on paper. That's just not the modern world.

But enough about my failures in life; let's focus a minute on what we CAN learn from this data.

Dusty Baker is one of the managers least inclined to tinker with his lineup, with an average of 119 lineups per 162 games.

Dusty used to be what we could almost call a hyperactive manager, with high numbers in lots of different managerial categories. His numbers of long outings were so high, twenty years ago, that he used to be criticized a lot for that. He used to have high or very high numbers of relievers used on consecutive days, stolen base attempts, runners moving with the pitch, and pitchouts ordered. In 2011 he had 226 runners moving with the pitch; in 2022 he had 116. In 1996 he ordered 96 pitchouts; over the last two seasons, combined, he has ordered two.

He doesn't do much of that stuff anymore, and in part that is because nobody does as much of that stuff as they used to, and in part it is because his team is so good that, well, why risk it? He is still a slow hook with his starting pitching, not as extreme as he used to be, but he's become a fairly conservative manager in his old age. (He's the same age I am, if you are curious.) Dusty has now had eleven seasons of 90 or more wins, and has had 90 or more wins in a season with four different teams. I drew a line there at 90 because you have to draw it somewhere; he has also had two seasons of 89 wins, and one of 88. He's had a LOT of good years with a lot of different teams; not sure any manager in baseball history can match him in all categories. His 2022 team (106-56) was his best team, at least in the regular season.

Rocco Baldelli so far in his managerial career (four seasons) has used the running game (stolen base attempts) significantly less than any other major league manager, with an average of only 58 stolen base attempts per 162 games. Make that MUCH less; I don't see anybody else with an average less than 86. No doubt Byron Buxton's endless injuries have quite a bit to do with that, but he has other players who could run more than they do. Max Kepler. OK, they're kind of slow. You got me. Baldelli also had only 58 runners moving with the pitch in 2022, the second-lowest total in the majors; Scott Servais had only 54. Gabe Kapler had only 60.

Baldelli is one of the quickest hooks in the majors—that is, the most anxious to get his starting pitcher out of the game and bring in his bullpen. In 2022 he had 74 quick hooks, the most in the majors. Some of his starting pitching was not good, obviously, but that doesn't mean it is necessarily your best strategy to get them out of the game before they get knocked around.

David Bell is/was a very slow hook. In 2021 he had only 22 quick hooks vs. 56 slow hooks, an almost absurd ratio, and his career ratio is 32/50. He also led the majors in "Long Outings" in 2022 (and has before), a long outing being defined as any start in which a pitcher throws more than 110 pitches.

But we need to redefine the parameters there. When we started doing this in the late 1990s, we defined a Long Outing by a starting pitcher as any start in which the pitcher threw more than 120 pitches. Outings of more than 120 pitches very quickly disappeared, however, so that in 2002 we redefined a Long Outing as 110 or more pitches.

But over the years, those have basically disappeared, too, so we'll need to re-define them again. Probably should have done that before now. We'll study the data, and adjust the definition for next year. The point of the exercise is to demonstrate how one manager is different from another. If everybody is at zero in a category, then we're not accomplishing that.

Bell from 2019 to 2021 had an outstanding ratio of Intentional walks getting a good outcome to those getting a not-good outcome, 52-15. That's +10 relative to the average in that area, meaning that he either did a good job picking his moments, or else he got lucky. But then last year he was 11 and 10, which is terrible although it is only about -2 or -3. But that's the kind of thing that gets a manager fired.

Bud Black used only 36 pinch hitters in 2022, easily the fewest of any major league team. In 2021, with no DH in the National League, he had used 280 pinch hitters, which was kind of a normal number for an NL team. With the DH, he went from 280 to 36, which honestly kind of suggests that the Rockies haven't figured out how to build a roster with a DH yet. His catchers hit .217 with a .274 on base percentage; you can pinch hit for those guys any time.

Kevin Cash has led the American League in Defensive Substitutes used in each of the last three years, 2020 to 2022. His totals before 2020 were also high, although he didn't lead the league. He is also the quickest hook in the American League, career data. In 2022 he had 61 Quick Hooks, only 19 Slow Hooks, career ratio 55-32.

Craig Counsell is THE major league manager least inclined to use pinch runners. He has never in his career used as many as 20 pinch runners in a season. He is also one of the managers least inclined to tinker with his lineup, with an average of 119 lineups used per 162 games.

But Counsell over the course of what is now a fairly long career has been one of the most aggressive managers in terms of base stealing, with a career average of 144 per 162 games. The only recent manager with more has been Joe Madden, who had/has a career average of 146.

As a point of general information, stolen base totals have not really changed very much within this century. 2022 was the best year for base stealing since 2017, but while many things in this century have gone wildly up and down and outside of historically established norms, stolen base totals have been stable, with a mild uptick in the 2009 to 2014 era.

Earlier in his career Counsell used very large numbers of defensive substitutes, as many as 77 in a season, but he hasn't done that in recent years, so that apparently is a roster-construction issue. I don't know the ins and outs of it as well as a Brewers fan or broadcaster would, but probably he had somebody on the roster in the 2018-2019 era who could be a defensive liability with the game on the line.

Terry Francona in his long career has used 36 pinch runners per 162 games, the highest average of any current manager, although other recent managers have had higher numbers. Ron Gardenhire had a career average of 45, and Rich Renteria was at 53. Anyway, Terry has led the league in pinch runners used several times, other years hasn't used so many.

A lot of that depends on the roster construction, of course. The 2022 Guardians were a very fast team, a lot of guys in the lineup who could run, so you wouldn't normally use pinch runners. In 2018 he used 74 pinch runners, but the 2018 team was fast, too, not as fast as the 2022 team, but they led the league in stolen bases. A big reason for the 74 pinch runners in 2018 was that he had Rajai Davis on the roster. Raj in his prime was a great base stealer, but by 2018 he had lost a half-step, maybe. In 2016, when Rajai was 36 years old, he was 43 for 49 as a base stealer. By 2018, though, he was 38 years old, and didn't really help the team as a pinch runner.

Perhaps Terry's most famous managerial moment was in 2004, when he pinch ran Dave Roberts for Kevin Millar in the 4th game of the AL championship series; Roberts stole second and scored the tying run. I remember having a conversation with him about pinch running for David Ortiz, I think probably the conversation was at the winter meetings in 2004. Sometimes in 2003 and 2004 Terry would pinch run for David Ortiz, but that winter he told me that he had decided he wasn't going to do that anymore, because we needed to keep David's bat in the lineup if at all possible. I strongly endorsed the new policy. David was not fast, of course, but he was SUCH a dominating hitter that the gain from using a pinch runner was not enough to offset the value of his bat in extra innings, even when the chance of his batting again seemed to be remote.

Francona's Indi.. . .Guardians led the American League in Stolen Base Attempts in 2022, with 146. He has always liked to run, with a career average of 130 stolen base attempts per 162 games. He has led the league before, and his numbers have always been fairly high except in the 2005-2006 era with the Red Sox.

Joe Girardi uses or used huge numbers of defensive substitutes, as many as 66 in a season. I believe his career average of 41 per 162 games is the highest of any manager who was active in 2022 except Donnie Baseball.

A.J. Hinch used 161 different lineups in 162 games in 2022, the highest of any major league manager. His career average, 145 lineups per 162 games, is high although some guys are higher.

Gabe Kapler in 2022 used a whopping 256 pinch hitters. This is 108 more pinch hitters used than those used by any other National League team, and 92 more than any other major league team.

Kapler has led the National League in Relievers Used on Consecutive Days in each of the last three seasons, with a career average of 127 times per 162 games. Dave Martinez is the only guy close to that, with 125.

Mark Kotsay, in addition to dominating the Intentional Walk list, used 164 pinch hitters, which is not as many as Kapler, but easily more than any other manager. Apparently it is a Bay Area thing. Not that this is relevant, but one time with the Red Sox we had Mark Kotsay on our roster. We researched it, and discovered that there were only three players in major league history who had the letters "kot" in their names, first name or last name, at any point in the name. The three were Kotsay, Casey Kotchman and George Kottaras, all three of whose last names BEGAN with Kot. And the Red Sox had all three of them on the roster at the same time.

Torey Lovullo likes to let his starting pitcher work as long as he can, with career averages of 34 Quick Hooks per 162 games vs. 46 Slow Hooks.

Don Mattingly used 58 pinch runners in 2022, easily the most of any major league manager. Mattingly also led the NL in pinch runners in 2021, with 36, but his career number is NOT notably high, not really high at all. His numbers of defensive substitutes used, however, have generally been very high, averaging 43 per 162 games. Career high of 69 with the Marlins in 2016.

Mattingly's Marlins led the majors in stolen base attempts in 2022, with 151. Mattingly's numbers have generally been fairly high, but this was the first time since 2014 that he had led his league. In 2014 his Dodgers had 188.

Bob Melvin struck a small blow against the notion that managers don't matter in 2022, leaving the A's to manage the Padres. The Padres improved by 10 games. The A's declined by 26 games. Melvin is, and has always been, a conservative manager with middle-of-the-road, centrist tendencies.

Dave Roberts is the quickest hook in the major leagues, with a career ratio of 65 quick hooks/26 slow hooks per 162 games. The "65" is the highest figure in the majors among current managers; the "26" is the lowest.

David Ross in 2022 had 163 runners moving with the pitch, the highest total of any major league manager. It's not really clear what he was doing with that; his team isn't really fast. I suppose he was trying to stay out of double plays.

Scott Servais has gone from being one of the quickest hooks in the major leagues to one of the slowest. From 2016 to 2018 he always had more Quick Hooks than Slow Hooks, with a 2017 ratio of 55-32. But since 2019 he has always had more Slow Hooks than quick hooks, and he is now perhaps the slowest hook in the majors, with a 2022 ratio of 25-47. This could indicate simply that he has more confidence in the starting pitchers he has now than in those he had years ago, or it could indicate a change in how he thinks about the problem. The accounting is set up so that teams with good pitching have neither more quick hooks than teams with weak pitching, nor less. At least that's the intention of the system; in practice, bad teams may have a few more slow hooks.

Derek Shelton, Pittsburgh, is the major league manager most inclined to vary his lineup, using 153 different lineups per 162 games throughout his major league career, and is also the manager who has the highest platoon percentage, with 69% of the players in his lineup having the platoon advantage at the start of the game, throughout the course of his three-year career.

These two categories tend to go together, at least sometimes. Sometimes managers who are comfortable juggling their lineup may sometimes be juggling it to maximize the left-handed hitters in the lineup against right-handed pitchers, and vice versa. Sometimes a high platoon percentage indicates multiple switch hitters who are regulars. The 2022 Pirates had only one regular who was a switch hitter (Bryan Reynolds), which. . .you know, most everybody has one. Their high platoon percentage indicates a manager who likes to try to maximize that day-to-day.

As an aside, I do not recommend this strategy. Work the numbers with me. A very high platoon percentage for a season is .70; a very low one is .50, although teams do occasionally go outside those boundaries. That means that there is a potential gain of 20% of your players having the platoon advantage, or 1.8 players per game. That's an additional 292 players having the platoon advantage over the course of the season. Assuming they have three plate appearances per game before the starting pitcher is no longer relevant, that would be a gain of 876 hitters per season having the platoon edge. Assuming that the platoon advantage is 27 points, or .027, that's going to be a gain of about 24 hits per season, plus maybe a little bit larger gain than that in terms of power and walks, so let's say 60 singles a season, or about 17 runs in a season.

It's not NOTHING; it's a game and a half a year. It's an advantage, but you can pretty easily lose 17 runs in a season, too, if you're not putting your best players on the field. I think platooning is a good strategy if you have two pretty good players who play the same position—i.e. Mike Zunino and Francisco Mejia. Some players have larger-than-normal platoon differentials, some players focus better and play better with more days off, plus the platoon combination protects the team in the case of injury. But if you're short of talent, I think it is smarter to keep the best players you have in the lineup as much as you can, rather than hunting for small percentage advantages.

Mike Shildt, St. Louis manager fired a year ago for reasons not apparent to the outside world, is one of the managers least inclined to tinker with his lineup, averaging 114 lineups per 162 games.

Buck Showalter, now with the Mets, is also one of the managers least inclined to tinker with his lineup, with a career average of 118 lineups per 162 games.

Brian Snitker, Atlanta, stands out as the manager LEAST inclined to tinker with his lineup, using an average of 109 different lineups per 162 games. In 2022 he used 129 different lineups, which is high for him, but was still the third-lowest total in the majors. Snitker also used only 48 pinch hitters, the second-fewest in the major leagues.

Snitker in 2017 ordered 76 sacrifice bunt attempts. In 2022 he ordered only 2. That is primarily an effect of the DH being used in the National League, of course, but the 2016-2017 data was very high, even for a non-DH league, while the 2022 total was easily the lowest in the major leagues.

Chris Woodward is the major league manager least likely to use a reliever who was used yesterday, with a career average of just 65 such events per 162 games. Other managers who don't do that include Buck Showalter (73), Brandon Hyde (76) and Aaron Boone (77). Tendencies in that area seem to be very pronounced, with a manager's totals apparently stable, and not very much dependent on the makeup of his roster.

Thank you all for reading. I hope that this introduction increases your understanding and enjoyment of the Manager's Records section of the book.

Brad Ausmus

Year	Team	Lg	G	LUp	PL%	PH	PR	DS	Quick	Slow	LO	RCD	LS	Rel	SBA	SacA	RM	PO	#	Good	NG	Bomb	W	L	Pct
2014	Tigers	AL	162	103	.51	79	43	44	28	55	43	99	1	473	147	32	144	13	34	17	17	5	90	72	.556
2015	Tigers	AL	161	122	.47	83	38	50	33	59	30	131	4	505	134	37	161	7	32	18	14	7	74	87	.460
2016	Tigers	AL	161	111	.48	89	31	50	41	37	18	93	4	476	87	21	95	3	25	12	13	4	86	75	.534
2017	Tigers	AL	162	131	.50	103	30	24	28	52	17	97	6	510	99	16	104	3	42	26	16	8	64	98	.395
2019	Angels	AL	162	153	.57	98	27	44	34	29	0	105	5	589	85	4	78	1	11	5	6	4	72	90	.444
	162-Game Average			124	.50	91	34	43	33	47	22	105	4	512	111	22	117	5	29	16	13	6	77	85	.475

Dusty Baker

Year	Team	Lg	G	LUp	PL%	PH	PR	DS	Quick	Slow	LO	RCD	LS	Rel	SBA	SacA	RM	PO	#	Good	NG	Bomb	W	L	Pct
1994	Giants	NL	115	76	.53	177	16	9	29	25	2	86	12	288	154	88		78	40	24	16	8	55	60	.478
1995	Giants	NL	144	97	.41	230	36	13	32	50	8	90	8	381	184	101		77	51	32	19	14	67	77	.465
1996	Giants	NL	162	129	.51	250	17	15	24	58	15	94	8	425	166	103		96	60	37	23	15	68	94	.420
1997	Giants	NL	162	114	.71	212	17	22	46	25	17	132	4	481	170	85		93	57	36	21	12	90	72	.556
1998	Giants	NL	162	130	.62	224	20	12	43	38	8	113	5	433	153	111		41	68	42	26	9	89	74	.546
1999	Giants	NL	162	119	.62	233	16	16	30	51	27	111		450	165	113		40	41	25	16	10	86	76	.531
2000	Giants	NL	162	82	.56	233	26	22	38	50	25	91	3	384	118	86		37	26	17	9	2	97	65	.599
2001	Giants	NL	162	122	.48	261	22	19	40	48	10	114	4	439	99	95		45	49	33	16	6	90	72	.556
2002	Giants	NL	162	118	.42	223	32	38	29	56	53	106	8	417	95	89	42	41	44	28	16	10	95	66	.590
2003	Cubs	NL	162	114	.49	272	25	43	24	58	65	111	3	420	104	93	31	24	36	23	13	4	88	74	.543
2004	Cubs	NL	162	113	.44	254	16	19	37	41	42	129	8	460	94	108	71	62	33	22	11	7	89	73	.549
2005	Cubs	NL	162	121	.59	240	21	29	40	46	36	103	2	457	104	88	107	70	48	27	21	7	79	83	.488
2006	Cubs	NL	162	133	.56	271	9	26	45	39	22	165	2	542	170	108	139	46	44	28	16	11	66	96	.407
2008	Reds	NL	162	119	.58	285	28	27	26	63	39	124	2	507	132	100	101	37	40	28	12	4	74	88	.457
2009	Reds	NL	162	130	.45	252	15	35	30	62	35	115	1	478	136	120	118	23	36	29	7	4	78	84	.481
2010	Reds	NL	162	120	.46	258	19	49	36	41	22	140	0	502	136	91	157	13	32	22	10	9	91	71	.562
2011	Reds	NL	162	142	.42	240	29	42	34	51	20	115	0	501	147	102	226	33	47	26	21	5	79	83	.488
2012	Reds	NL	162	121	.43	201	19	39	33	39	30	78	4	425	114	108	148	19	33	22	11	3	97	65	.599
2013	Reds	NL	162	95	.54	236	20	27	39	40	14	90	3	461	102	110	157	21	28	23	5	3	90	72	.556
2016	Nationals	NL	162	112	.57	220	20	27	35	45	21	119	4	508	160	59	161	3	43	28	15	9	95	67	.586
2017	Nationals	NL	162	124	.59	241	33	26	22	53	27	90	2	487	138	57	113	3	39	29	10	6	97	65	.599
2020	Astros	AL	60	49	.48	28	13	7	14	15	1	24	0	193	33	7	36	3	7	4	3	1	29	31	.483
2021	Astros	AL	162	133	.50	94	27	22	38	45	2	81	4	512	69	14	96	0	12	8	4	1	95	67	.586
2022	Astros	AL	162	131	.45	81	11	32	35	45	3	67	0	480	105	15	116	2	6	3	3	2	106	56	.654
	162-Game Average			119	.52	227	22	27	35	47	24	108	4	463	133	89	118	39	40	26	14	7	87	75	.537

Rocco Baldelli

Year	Team	Lg	G	LUp	PL%	PH	PR	DS	Quick	Slow	LO	RCD	LS	Rel	SBA	SacA	RM	PO	#	Good	NG	Bomb	W	L	Pct
2019	Twins	AL	162	145	.62	84	24	35	42	43	1	94	16	524	49	16	56	4	10	9	1	1	101	61	.623
2020	Twins	AL	60	56	.65	29	19	20	14	11	1	29	0	202	21	3	18	0	0	0	0	0	36	24	.600
2021	Twins	AL	162	149	.61	112	28	27	50	50	0	84	6	529	69	11	70	0	13	7	6	3	73	89	.451
2022	Twins	AL	162	152	.58	121	44	34	74	31	0	68	4	548	55	9	58	0	19	15	4	3	78	84	.481
	162-Game Average			149	.61	103	34	34	53	40	1	82	8	535	58	12	60	1	12	9	3	2	85	77	.525

Rod Barajas

Year	Team	Lg	G	LUp	PL%	PH	PR	DS	Quick	Slow	LO	RCD	LS	Rel	SBA	SacA	RM	PO	#	Good	NG	Bomb	W	L	Pct
2019	Padres	NL	8	8	.69	28	2	1	5	0	0	4	0	34	4	2	8	0	0	0	0	0	1	7	.125
	162-Game Average			162	.69	567	41	20	101	0	0	81	0	689	81	41	162	0	0	0	0	0	20	142	.123

Tony Beasley

Year	Team	Lg	G	LUp	PL%	PH	PR	DS	Quick	Slow	LO	RCD	LS	Rel	SBA	SacA	RM	PO	#	Good	NG	Bomb	W	L	Pct
2022	Rangers	AL	48	38	.63	34	11	4	12	13	0	15	1	148	54	5	50	0	4	1	3	1	17	31	.354
	162-Game Average			128	.63	115	37	14	41	44	0	51	3	500	182	17	169	0	14	3	10	3	57	105	.352

David Bell

Year	Team	Lg	G	LUp	PL%	PH	PR	DS	Quick	Slow	LO	RCD	LS	Rel	SBA	SacA	RM	PO	#	Good	NG	Bomb	W	L	Pct
2019	Reds	NL	162	140	.55	319	28	46	36	43	9	104	10	535	118	44	111	1	31	25	6	5	75	87	.463
2020	Reds	NL	60	54	.68	68	17	16	13	18	5	28	1	168	38	1	32	1	6	4	2	2	31	29	.517
2021	Reds	NL	162	133	.56	303	23	33	22	56	2	111	6	579	60	49	68	0	30	23	7	3	83	79	.512
2022	Reds	NL	162	151	.49	119	25	15	36	51	8	76	5	574	91	16	100	1	21	11	10	4	62	100	.383
	162-Game Average			142	.55	240	28	33	32	50	7	95	7	551	91	33	92	1	26	19	7	4	74	88	.457

Bud Black

Year	Team	Lg	G	LINEUPS		SUBSTITUTION			PITCHER USAGE						TACTICS				INTENTIONAL BB				RESULTS		
				LUp	PL%	PH	PR	DS	Quick	Slow	LO	RCD	LS	Rel	SBA	SacA	RM	PO	#	Good	NG	Bomb	W	L	Pct
2007	Padres	NL	163	115	.62	279	18	13	63	28	13	122	0	485	79	85	73	56	48	28	20	11	89	74	.546
2008	Padres	NL	162	113	.63	286	25	20	55	36	17	109	0	491	53	75	78	31	61	30	31	17	63	99	.389
2009	Padres	NL	162	137	.64	264	8	34	50	37	8	118	5	527	111	99	84	55	58	42	16	6	75	87	.463
2010	Padres	NL	162	135	.61	285	16	45	55	33	10	132	7	499	174	99	135	31	51	35	16	8	90	72	.556
2011	Padres	NL	162	140	.58	288	20	43	40	36	10	110	2	490	214	69	184	41	56	31	25	13	71	91	.438
2012	Padres	NL	162	132	.74	280	26	35	45	49	11	126	5	529	201	89	162	21	48	34	14	7	76	86	.469
2013	Padres	NL	162	145	.66	271	24	37	35	46	4	102	1	488	152	78	122	12	31	20	11	8	76	86	.469
2014	Padres	NL	162	157	.74	313	23	29	49	33	13	104	1	481	125	74	116	15	32	24	8	4	77	85	.475
2015	Padres	NL	65	50	.54	113	6	6	8	25	3	40	0	199	54	24	46	2	15	11	4	0	32	33	.492
2017	Rockies	NL	162	111	.51	261	19	14	44	36	4	100	2	549	93	76	149	4	20	14	6	3	87	75	.537
2018	Rockies	NL	163	126	.56	276	20	19	29	49	5	103	1	518	128	65	137	2	24	16	8	5	91	72	.558
2019	Rockies	NL	162	141	.60	305	8	13	27	58	1	114	3	590	102	71	96	5	33	21	12	3	71	91	.438
2020	Rockies	NL	60	52	.60	51	10	9	5	20	0	31	2	189	51	11	37	2	5	3	2	1	26	34	.433
2021	Rockies	NL	161	143	.55	280	13	13	35	51	0	83	1	543	99	64	92	7	19	12	7	4	74	87	.460
2022	Rockies	NL	162	153	.51	36	35	37	23	59	1	82	3	497	65	14	74	4	12	6	6	3	68	94	.420
	162-Game Average			134	.61	260	20	27	41	43	7	107	2	514	123	72	115	21	37	24	14	7	77	85	.475

Bruce Bochy

Year	Team	Lg	G	LINEUPS		SUBSTITUTION			PITCHER USAGE						TACTICS				INTENTIONAL BB				RESULTS		
				LUp	PL%	PH	PR	DS	Quick	Slow	LO	RCD	LS	Rel	SBA	SacA	RM	PO	#	Good	NG	Bomb	W	L	Pct
1995	Padres	NL	144	96	.59	262	30	23	44	41	17	38	3	337	170	68		38	37	19	18	11	70	74	.486
1996	Padres	NL	162	114	.52	289	29	15	51	33	10	67	12	411	164	73		65	47	29	18	12	91	71	.562
1997	Padres	NL	162	111	.60	291	26	9	45	45	3	81	11	426	200	84		58	37	20	17	11	76	86	.469
1998	Padres	NL	162	108	.65	280	62	44	44	45	9	81	12	369	116	84		27	45	31	14	11	98	64	.605
1999	Padres	NL	162	137	.60	298	51	21	44	36	4	68	5	403	241	60		29	48	29	19	13	74	88	.457
2000	Padres	NL	162	134	.52	285	44	14	41	47	14	105	5	443	184	52		27	50	21	29	11	76	86	.469
2001	Padres	NL	162	116	.60	255	54	27	32	47	6	85	10	422	173	43		23	54	31	23	13	79	83	.488
2002	Padres	NL	162	123	.66	259	44	56	39	40	17	106	4	459	115	63	74	14	61	38	23	14	66	96	.407
2003	Padres	NL	162	134	.58	339	20	29	34	43	16	100	3	473	115	63	41	6	52	33	19	12	64	98	.395
2004	Padres	NL	162	96	.54	261	28	47	47	32	15	76	3	437	77	75	96	14	39	24	15	10	87	75	.537
2005	Padres	NL	162	128	.58	285	31	49	46	36	23	87	1	456	143	89	111	16	45	33	12	8	82	80	.506
2006	Padres	NL	162	111	.60	264	64	48	43	42	24	111	2	475	154	77	110	21	63	43	20	10	88	74	.543
2007	Giants	NL	162	128	.72	264	50	45	26	50	36	132	2	496	152	86	119	10	41	29	12	3	71	91	.438
2008	Giants	NL	162	134	.68	276	32	39	24	59	42	97	6	478	154	77	155	5	59	40	19	8	72	90	.444
2009	Giants	NL	162	134	.65	231	21	52	42	40	32	84	8	457	106	93	118	5	49	32	17	10	88	74	.543
2010	Giants	NL	162	126	.55	224	45	70	29	37	40	118	12	477	87	102	144	12	58	41	17	8	92	70	.568
2011	Giants	NL	162	138	.62	245	49	42	38	38	44	108	3	480	136	79	175	11	46	36	10	6	86	76	.531
2012	Giants	NL	162	112	.75	220	32	55	22	50	31	136	9	526	157	87	176	15	42	30	12	6	94	68	.580
2013	Giants	NL	162	109	.70	263	19	45	33	52	23	143	4	524	93	78	164	7	64	46	18	6	76	86	.469
2014	Giants	NL	162	131	.66	236	29	64	45	41	19	102	1	475	83	53	147	12	35	25	10	9	88	74	.543
2015	Giants	NL	162	124	.63	230	12	21	45	32	11	137	2	557	129	54	173	8	28	20	8	3	84	78	.519
2016	Giants	NL	162	121	.66	268	7	29	31	42	28	148	4	575	115	54	178	6	30	25	5	4	87	75	.537
2017	Giants	NL	162	136	.61	298	22	12	22	59	20	93	2	502	110	51	135	3	42	29	13	11	64	98	.395
2018	Giants	NL	162	140	.59	305	16	30	36	38	6	100	0	549	111	43	139	2	37	25	12	5	73	89	.451
2019	Giants	NL	162	141	.67	362	11	25	34	43	4	94	2	587	75	37	101	4	26	16	10	4	77	85	.475
	162-Game Average			124	.62	273	33	37	38	43	20	100	5	474	135	69	131	18	46	30	16	9	80	82	.494

Aaron Boone

Year	Team	Lg	G	LINEUPS		SUBSTITUTION			PITCHER USAGE						TACTICS				INTENTIONAL BB				RESULTS		
				LUp	PL%	PH	PR	DS	Quick	Slow	LO	RCD	LS	Rel	SBA	SacA	RM	PO	#	Good	NG	Bomb	W	L	Pct
2018	Yankees	AL	162	137	.54	71	14	24	45	32	3	75	5	508	84	17	113	3	9	4	5	3	100	62	.617
2019	Yankees	AL	162	155	.49	57	24	32	43	27	1	80	5	545	77	19	81	2	12	9	3	1	103	59	.636
2020	Yankees	AL	60	57	.48	36	15	20	18	17	3	26	1	174	34	4	39	0	5	5	0	0	33	27	.550
2021	Yankees	AL	162	146	.50	94	45	45	50	31	3	73	3	512	81	11	80	6	10	6	4	2	92	70	.568
2022	Yankees	AL	162	146	.47	93	42	24	40	38	5	82	13	507	135	20	141	1	10	6	4	1	99	63	.611
	162-Game Average			147	.50	80	32	33	45	33	3	77	6	514	94	16	104	3	11	7	4	2	98	64	.605

Mickey Callaway

Year	Team	Lg	G	LINEUPS		SUBSTITUTION			PITCHER USAGE						TACTICS				INTENTIONAL BB				RESULTS		
				LUp	PL%	PH	PR	DS	Quick	Slow	LO	RCD	LS	Rel	SBA	SacA	RM	PO	#	Good	NG	Bomb	W	L	Pct
2018	Mets	NL	162	151	.58	258	17	30	41	43	11	72	10	501	110	39	119	6	32	17	15	9	77	85	.475
2019	Mets	NL	162	132	.50	273	42	65	35	57	16	87	6	502	83	42	102	10	40	27	13	6	86	76	.531
	162-Game Average			142	.54	266	30	48	38	50	14	80	8	502	97	41	111	8	36	22	14	8	82	81	.503

Kevin Cash

Year	Team	Lg	G	LINEUPS		SUBSTITUTION			PITCHER USAGE						TACTICS				INTENTIONAL BB				RESULTS		
				LUp	PL%	PH	PR	DS	Quick	Slow	LO	RCD	LS	Rel	SBA	SacA	RM	PO	#	Good	NG	Bomb	W	L	Pct
2015	Rays	AL	162	137	.62	219	23	38	72	33	10	134	3	530	132	27	173	2	23	17	6	3	80	82	.494
2016	Rays	AL	162	142	.55	103	11	28	42	52	18	100	8	485	97	24	146	12	25	16	9	4	68	94	.420
2017	Rays	AL	162	126	.57	123	21	24	39	47	16	89	9	511	122	24	143	12	37	25	12	8	80	82	.494
2018	Rays	AL	162	151	.58	109	25	33	50	18	5	115	10	553	179	37	190	2	34	20	14	9	90	72	.556
2019	Rays	AL	162	152	.59	131	31	43	50	18	0	136	6	603	131	11	166	3	27	14	13	8	96	66	.593
2020	Rays	AL	60	59	.68	66	14	24	22	9	0	35	3	219	57	1	38	1	4	3	1	0	40	20	.667
2021	Rays	AL	162	158	.67	120	36	55	66	37	2	71	10	531	130	6	142	3	27	16	11	7	100	62	.617
2022	Rays	AL	162	158	.63	115	27	40	61	19	0	117	4	572	132	9	108	2	15	7	8	1	86	76	.531
	162-Game Average			147	.60	134	26	39	55	32	7	108	7	543	133	19	150	5	26	16	10	5	87	75	.537

Alex Cora

Year	Team	Lg	G	LINEUPS		SUBSTITUTION			PITCHER USAGE						TACTICS				INTENTIONAL BB				RESULTS		
				LUp	PL%	PH	PR	DS	Quick	Slow	LO	RCD	LS	Rel	SBA	SacA	RM	PO	#	Good	NG	Bomb	W	L	Pct
2018	Red Sox	AL	162	134	.55	96	22	31	58	44	5	101	4	535	156	8	183	1	8	4	4	1	108	54	.667
2019	Red Sox	AL	162	135	.57	123	29	18	45	52	16	134	3	632	98	26	140	2	22	14	8	6	84	78	.519
2021	Red Sox	AL	162	141	.56	95	23	27	36	44	1	116	8	563	61	15	79	0	31	21	10	6	92	70	.568
2022	Red Sox	AL	162	136	.50	92	19	32	44	37	1	104	9	576	72	13	90	0	17	10	7	2	78	84	.481
	162-Game Average			137	.55	102	23	27	46	44	6	114	6	577	97	16	123	1	20	12	7	4	91	72	.558

Craig Counsell

Year	Team	Lg	G	LINEUPS		SUBSTITUTION			PITCHER USAGE						TACTICS				INTENTIONAL BB				RESULTS		
				LUp	PL%	PH	PR	DS	Quick	Slow	LO	RCD	LS	Rel	SBA	SacA	RM	PO	#	Good	NG	Bomb	W	L	Pct
2015	Brewers	NL	162	106	.54	247	14	30	30	47	3	85	1	424	99	56	106	2	30	26	4	3	61	76	.445
2016	Brewers	NL	162	123	.55	284	4	22	40	41	1	115	3	513	237	71	160	2	33	16	17	8	73	89	.451
2017	Brewers	NL	162	123	.53	285	18	44	58	33	5	124	5	550	169	56	159	0	45	30	15	9	86	76	.531
2018	Brewers	NL	163	137	.54	288	17	77	64	29	0	105	18	559	156	38	148	1	34	22	12	7	96	67	.589
2019	Brewers	NL	162	134	.64	317	14	56	60	26	1	97	17	588	126	29	78	3	28	22	6	2	89	73	.549
2020	Brewers	NL	60	53	.62	65	14	16	15	11	0	18	1	189	26	0	22	0	1	1	0	0	29	31	.483
2021	Brewers	NL	162	138	.62	294	13	39	44	29	2	92	2	533	103	35	66	0	19	13	6	2	95	67	.586
2022	Brewers	NL	162	125	.60	125	14	27	35	49	4	113	3	548	126	14	97	1	12	5	7	1	86	76	.531
	162-Game Average			130	.58	264	15	43	48	37	2	104	7	541	144	41	116	1	28	19	9	4	85	77	.525

Terry Francona

Year	Team	Lg	G	LINEUPS		SUBSTITUTION			PITCHER USAGE						TACTICS				INTENTIONAL BB				RESULTS		
				LUp	PL%	PH	PR	DS	Quick	Slow	LO	RCD	LS	Rel	SBA	SacA	RM	PO	#	Good	NG	Bomb	W	L	Pct
1997	Phillies	NL	162	98	.66	288	19	28	28	54	22	102	9	409	148	91		30	42	23	19	9	68	94	.420
1998	Phillies	NL	162	84	.53	256	20	19	34	57	20	88	7	385	142	85		16	27	10	17	8	75	87	.463
1999	Phillies	NL	162	85	.51	239	13	31	29	41	16	111	7	441	160	81		27	24	14	10	6	77	85	.475
2000	Phillies	NL	162	108	.53	278	17	14	38	43	25	102	5	414	132	89		16	32	22	10	7	65	97	.401
2004	Red Sox	AL	162	141	.65	116	65	36	41	48	32	105	8	437	98	18	91	28	28	22	6	4	98	64	.605
2005	Red Sox	AL	162	104	.67	110	46	37	25	55	30	99	3	442	57	21	79	11	28	18	10	5	95	67	.586
2006	Red Sox	AL	162	116	.59	93	54	49	36	44	13	94	9	454	74	33	98	16	25	11	14	7	86	76	.531
2007	Red Sox	AL	162	109	.60	84	34	23	41	35	32	89	4	451	120	14	90	14	20	14	6	4	96	66	.593
2008	Red Sox	AL	162	131	.65	62	40	40	50	30	20	90	11	466	155	40	87	8	17	10	7	4	95	67	.586
2009	Red Sox	AL	162	113	.58	85	47	28	36	50	30	68	6	463	165	29	68	9	24	15	9	6	95	67	.586
2010	Red Sox	AL	162	143	.62	125	48	34	32	63	49	84	3	443	85	36	125	26	30	17	13	4	89	73	.549
2011	Red Sox	AL	162	123	.67	89	44	11	52	46	27	89	4	444	144	29	163	34	11	6	5	2	90	72	.556
2013	Indians	AL	162	121	.75	78	45	24	47	34	18	122	2	540	153	41	158	5	26	15	11	6	92	70	.568
2014	Indians	AL	162	133	.78	123	16	24	37	37	18	150	7	573	131	58	128	3	51	29	22	13	85	77	.525
2015	Indians	AL	161	127	.75	138	21	13	40	36	23	85	8	476	114	63	87	4	27	20	7	5	81	80	.503
2016	Indians	AL	161	101	.73	114	27	29	47	39	18	103	3	504	165	44	126	2	34	22	12	7	94	67	.584
2017	Indians	AL	162	131	.73	93	43	50	48	31	20	106	4	497	111	35	95	2	15	11	4	3	102	60	.630
2018	Indians	AL	162	105	.73	97	74	42	29	48	23	121	10	508	171	44	152	6	29	19	10	6	91	71	.562
2019	Indians	AL	162	132	.73	101	25	15	30	44	29	89	9	522	138	57	100	2	19	11	8	7	93	69	.574
2020	Indians	AL	60	48	.74	37	18	10	8	18	2	27	2	181	35	14	33	0	8	4	4	1	35	25	.583
2021	Indians	AL	162	141	.63	89	17	19	43	45	5	91	3	535	126	25	98	0	12	7	5	1	80	82	.494
2022	Guardians	AL	162	139	.58	96	33	23	30	55	0	84	1	507	146	26	134	2	14	8	6	1	92	70	.568
	162-Game Average			119	.65	131	36	29	38	45	22	98	6	473	130	47	110	12	25	15	10	5	88	74	.543

Ron Gardenhire

Year	Team	Lg	G	LINEUPS		SUBSTITUTION			PITCHER USAGE						TACTICS				INTENTIONAL BB				RESULTS		
				LUp	PL%	PH	PR	DS	Quick	Slow	LO	RCD	LS	Rel	SBA	SacA	RM	PO	#	Good	NG	Bomb	W	L	Pct
2002	Twins	AL	161	111	.69	141	36	42	54	25	10	84	1	435	141	48	44	11	24	16	8	4	94	67	.584
2003	Twins	AL	162	126	.63	144	50	26	49	33	13	85	2	399	138	59	37	14	35	16	19	6	90	72	.556
2004	Twins	AL	162	131	.59	129	45	29	56	21	20	106	4	435	162	66	121	18	27	15	12	7	92	70	.568
2005	Twins	AL	162	135	.58	104	45	26	50	21	5	87	1	396	146	59	138	16	38	28	10	3	83	79	.512

Year	Team	Lg	G	LUp	PL%	PH	PR	DS	Quick	Slow	LO	RCD	LS	Rel	SBA	Sac	RM	PO	#	Good	NG	Bomb	W	L	Pct
2006	Twins	AL	162	97	.62	93	36	21	60	31	3	82	5	421	143	48	130	11	25	14	11	4	96	66	.593
2007	Twins	AL	162	139	.63	104	42	25	45	30	8	99	4	438	142	45	148	11	33	14	19	9	79	83	.488
2008	Twins	AL	163	103	.64	109	26	12	47	29	5	115	3	485	144	73	143	17	38	25	13	8	88	75	.540
2009	Twins	AL	163	129	.63	83	54	34	43	25	12	115	3	480	117	62	100	21	20	9	11	6	87	76	.534
2010	Twins	AL	162	112	.62	86	55	30	57	28	5	106	1	465	96	47	140	14	19	12	7	4	94	68	.580
2011	Twins	AL	162	150	.58	93	48	21	34	44	17	82	1	457	131	44	170	5	37	21	16	9	63	99	.389
2012	Twins	AL	162	121	.62	64	45	24	42	31	4	82	1	499	172	49	207	10	43	27	16	6	66	96	.407
2013	Twins	AL	162	139	.66	103	42	28	41	43	6	78	1	511	85	37	137	14	31	13	18	7	66	96	.407
2014	Twins	AL	162	132	.64	97	44	23	40	40	2	82	2	491	135	31	149	5	24	11	13	6	70	92	.432
2018	Tigers	AL	162	75	.56	75	60	8	40	39	1	99	3	542	100	25	121	6	20	11	9	7	64	98	.395
2019	Tigers	AL	161	155	.48	68	42	7	45	46	2	87	0	577	77	19	93	7	24	13	11	6	47	114	.292
2020	Tigers	AL	50	44	.55	26	21	7	16	12	0	24	0	191	18	1	18	0	1	0	1	1	21	29	.420
	162-Game Average			129	.61	99	45	24	47	33	7	92	2	472	127	47	124	12	29	16	13	6	78	84	.481

Joe Girardi

Year	Team	Lg	G	LUp	PL%	PH	PR	DS	Quick	Slow	LO	RCD	LS	Rel	SBA	Sac	RM	PO	#	Good	NG	Bomb	W	L	Pct
2006	Marlins	NL	162	117	.50	250	44	66	46	40	28	76	3	438	168	97	108	42	58	37	21	7	78	84	.481
2008	Yankees	AL	162	114	.63	97	37	42	60	37	12	88	10	475	157	38	173	36	37	22	15	8	89	73	.549
2009	Yankees	AL	162	106	.73	97	61	42	36	45	27	88	13	461	139	44	83	33	28	14	14	9	103	59	.636
2010	Yankees	AL	162	114	.72	117	44	31	43	39	33	76	3	430	133	47	152	20	37	26	11	6	95	67	.586
2011	Yankees	AL	162	94	.69	72	41	53	51	36	21	88	2	465	193	50	151	26	43	30	13	4	97	65	.599
2012	Yankees	AL	162	107	.70	149	33	48	37	53	21	115	7	485	120	47	145	10	32	17	15	6	95	67	.586
2013	Yankees	AL	162	141	.59	119	15	29	42	50	23	82	4	428	146	49	131	4	34	20	14	6	85	77	.525
2014	Yankees	AL	162	142	.74	100	27	33	51	28	10	95	7	475	138	44	132	8	23	10	13	9	84	78	.519
2015	Yankees	AL	162	126	.79	118	50	57	48	34	9	80	10	497	88	32	92	6	16	8	8	4	87	75	.537
2016	Yankees	AL	162	143	.72	85	32	48	53	44	8	99	7	483	94	35	89	3	15	9	6	4	84	78	.519
2017	Yankees	AL	162	140	.56	112	22	10	49	29	9	79	7	477	112	28	117	3	18	11	7	4	91	71	.562
2020	Phillies	NL	60	51	.59	46	7	7	9	13	4	27	1	189	43	13	28	0	12	6	6	3	28	32	.467
2021	Phillies	NL	162	135	.59	276	10	44	36	52	9	89	6	525	96	66	87	0	37	27	10	5	82	80	.506
2022	Phillies	NL	51	40	.57	28	7	9	13	14	0	30	2	176	36	5	31	0	9	6	3	1	22	29	.431
	162-Game Average			124	.66	131	34	41	45	41	17	88	6	473	131	47	120	15	31	19	12	6	88	74	.543

Andy Green

Year	Team	Lg	G	LUp	PL%	PH	PR	DS	Quick	Slow	LO	RCD	LS	Rel	SBA	SacA	RM	PO	#	Good	NG	Bomb	W	L	Pct
2016	Padres	NL	162	130	.56	249	29	25	46	53	6	119	4	510	170	48	138	3	44	26	18	9	68	94	.420
2017	Padres	NL	162	138	.55	238	10	38	45	43	5	101	2	517	122	63	119	2	28	18	10	4	71	91	.438
2018	Padres	NL	162	146	.62	264	21	38	45	49	5	84	6	535	131	49	109	0	28	17	11	6	66	96	.407
2019	Padres	NL	154	139	.45	263	11	51	52	31	0	99	5	509	103	42	93	0	19	14	5	3	69	85	.448
	162-Game Average			140	.54	257	18	38	48	45	4	102	4	524	133	51	116	1	30	19	11	6	69	93	.426

A.J. Hinch

Year	Team	Lg	G	LUp	PL%	PH	PR	DS	Quick	Slow	LO	RCD	LS	Rel	SBA	SacA	RM	PO	#	Good	NG	Bomb	W	L	Pct
2009	Diamondbacks	NL	133	115	.63	222	10	13	24	50	24	61	5	392	113	64	41	5	24	12	12	6	58	75	.436
2010	Diamondbacks	NL	79	56	.53	120	7	4	12	40	21	39	1	207	58	19	51	7	19	9	10	9	31	48	.392
2015	Astros	AL	162	151	.63	122	40	37	33	41	19	97	0	482	169	31	128	6	17	11	6	2	86	76	.531
2016	Astros	AL	162	143	.55	118	35	27	42	35	9	87	1	500	146	38	137	5	19	11	8	4	84	78	.519
2017	Astros	AL	162	144	.56	73	29	39	57	35	3	83	8	519	140	21	148	6	17	12	5	3	101	61	.623
2018	Astros	AL	162	144	.54	92	34	39	31	35	10	80	4	510	97	9	154	2	4	3	1	0	103	59	.636
2019	Astros	AL	162	134	.46	81	41	26	38	30	7	92	2	492	94	15	96	0	0	0	0	0	107	55	.660
2021	Tigers	AL	162	153	.71	72	41	18	61	35	1	85	8	577	113	16	92	0	10	4	6	3	77	85	.475
2022	Tigers	AL	162	161	.67	85	32	8	44	44	0	82	1	580	71	12	76	0	9	4	5	3	66	96	.407
	162-Game Average			145	.59	119	32	25	41	42	11	85	4	513	120	27	111	4	14	8	6	4	86	76	.531

Clint Hurdle

Year	Team	Lg	G	LUp	PL%	PH	PR	DS	Quick	Slow	LO	RCD	LS	Rel	SBA	SacA	RM	PO	#	Good	NG	Bomb	W	L	Pct
2002	Rockies	NL	140	100	.52	274	28	41	33	45	17	104	3	437	139	46	50	13	38	22	16	11	67	73	.479
2003	Rockies	NL	162	108	.47	317	17	32	35	40	5	87	4	500	100	82	26	16	51	31	20	13	74	88	.457
2004	Rockies	NL	162	131	.57	289	18	35	36	63	20	74	1	473	77	128	67	12	84	54	30	12	68	94	.420
2005	Rockies	NL	162	135	.60	273	21	40	42	60	17	89	2	459	97	114	119	22	54	28	26	15	67	95	.414
2006	Rockies	NL	162	111	.49	259	17	22	34	52	17	107	2	499	135	156	114	28	81	45	36	23	76	86	.469
2007	Rockies	NL	163	96	.51	283	32	29	45	37	13	112	1	529	131	112	109	26	61	30	31	14	90	73	.552
2008	Rockies	NL	162	131	.49	253	20	31	40	43	16	85	2	485	178	111	116	43	49	31	18	6	74	88	.457
2009	Rockies	NL	46	42	.60	73	8	10	11	14	3	31	0	135	45	26	34	3	11	8	3	1	18	28	.391

Year	Team	Lg	G	LUp	PL%	PH	PR	DS	Quick	Slow	LO	RCD	LS	Rel	SBA	SacA	RM	PO	#	Good	NG	Bomb	W	L	Pct
2011	Pirates	NL	162	134	.60	278	26	63	58	27	1	134	3	549	160	101	173	20	65	39	26	13	72	90	.444
2012	Pirates	NL	162	133	.55	270	26	60	50	33	3	74	2	483	125	82	120	17	30	18	12	3	79	83	.488
2013	Pirates	NL	162	127	.51	289	24	61	61	25	7	76	3	465	136	83	172	20	26	22	4	2	94	68	.580
2014	Pirates	NL	162	123	.50	322	28	38	47	40	7	91	0	452	151	85	187	24	43	26	17	7	88	74	.543
2015	Pirates	NL	162	108	.50	269	48	76	39	40	9	124	1	500	143	81	173	9	38	31	7	3	98	64	.605
2016	Pirates	NL	162	125	.41	293	39	73	57	36	1	119	4	525	155	55	154	9	28	15	13	6	78	83	.484
2017	Pirates	NL	162	138	.51	277	23	37	42	39	6	110	8	502	103	59	124	7	32	17	15	7	75	87	.463
2018	Pirates	NL	161	128	.62	267	14	27	44	36	1	88	6	480	108	45	119	2	43	32	11	5	82	79	.509
2019	Pirates	NL	161	131	.67	281	30	38	40	49	0	85	7	548	93	60	117	16	22	15	7	5	69	92	.429
	162-Game Average			124	.53	283	26	44	44	42	9	99	3	497	129	88	122	18	47	29	18	9	79	83	.488

Brandon Hyde

Year	Team	Lg	G	LUp	PL%	PH	PR	DS	Quick	Slow	LO	RCD	LS	Rel	SBA	SacA	RM	PO	#	Good	NG	Bomb	W	L	Pct
2011	Marlins	NL	1	1	.44	0	0	0	0	0	1	1	0	3	0	0	1	0	1	1	0	0	0	1	.000
2019	Orioles	AL	162	150	.70	126	26	42	30	35	1	73	11	533	114	34	82	0	11	5	6	4	54	108	.333
2020	Orioles	AL	60	58	.56	44	21	14	15	10	0	31	4	207	33	15	32	0	2	1	1	1	25	35	.417
2021	Orioles	AL	162	147	.60	86	32	32	41	45	1	75	6	569	77	19	66	0	12	7	5	3	52	110	.321
2022	Orioles	AL	162	142	.61	96	36	38	51	36	2	75	15	541	126	21	104	0	8	7	1	1	83	79	.512
	162-Game Average			147	.63	104	34	37	41	37	1	76	11	549	104	26	84	0	10	6	4	3	63	99	.389

Gabe Kapler

Year	Team	Lg	G	LUp	PL%	PH	PR	DS	Quick	Slow	LO	RCD	LS	Rel	SBA	SacA	RM	PO	#	Good	NG	Bomb	W	L	Pct
2018	Phillies	NL	162	138	.66	295	22	38	38	38	3	117	11	596	95	46	65	0	35	25	10	5	80	82	.494
2019	Phillies	NL	162	106	.55	312	11	21	28	48	3	121	9	564	96	50	69	0	38	31	7	4	81	81	.500
2020	Giants	NL	60	53	.66	73	13	31	17	20	1	50	1	236	27	3	25	0	2	2	0	0	29	31	.483
2021	Giants	NL	162	148	.66	407	26	48	42	29	1	146	2	599	80	47	80	0	20	11	9	2	107	55	.660
2022	Giants	NL	162	153	.65	256	22	31	30	37	2	120	4	576	80	6	60	0	16	8	8	3	81	81	.500
	162-Game Average			137	.63	307	22	39	35	39	2	127	6	588	86	35	68	0	25	18	8	3	86	76	.531

Mark Kotsay

Year	Team	Lg	G	LUp	PL%	PH	PR	DS	Quick	Slow	LO	RCD	LS	Rel	SBA	SacA	RM	PO	#	Good	NG	Bomb	W	L	Pct
2022	Athletics	AL	162	158	.56	164	18	24	39	50	1	81	4	530	101	23	127	0	37	23	14	10	60	102	.370
	162-Game Average			158	.56	164	18	24	39	50	1	81	4	530	101	23	127	0	37	23	14	10	60	102	.370

Tony LaRussa

Year	Team	Lg	G	LUp	PL%	PH	PR	DS	Quick	Slow	LO	RCD	LS	Rel	SBA	SacA	RM	PO	#	Good	NG	Bomb	W	L	Pct
1994	Athletics	AL	114	97	.62	89	28	14	43	21	5	60	4	308	130	31		32	30	20	10	4	51	63	.447
1995	Athletics	AL	144	120	.54	113	38	24	33	38	19	46	7	358	158	42		42	26	18	8	4	67	77	.465
1996	Cardinals	NL	162	120	.52	246	25	13	32	48	24	90	8	413	207	117		41	43	28	15	7	88	74	.543
1997	Cardinals	NL	162	146	.52	307	17	18	34	42	16	81	2	399	224	77		79	34	26	8	2	73	89	.451
1998	Cardinals	NL	162	146	.52	259	7	18	62	31	13	82	14	429	174	85		34	38	25	13	8	83	79	.512
1999	Cardinals	NL	161	138	.47	264	32	28	50	41	13	96	14	454	182	103		30	38	20	18	11	75	86	.466
2000	Cardinals	NL	162	137	.47	240	35	25	40	31	11	63	18	386	138	107		34	28	21	7	6	95	67	.586
2001	Cardinals	NL	162	117	.47	256	26	13	46	36	7	140	7	485	126	102		25	36	21	15	4	93	69	.574
2002	Cardinals	NL	162	117	.52	340	27	41	58	33	23	110	6	472	128	106	75	13	39	25	14	8	97	65	.599
2003	Cardinals	NL	162	126	.50	352	28	51	38	49	36	113	9	460	114	108	56	9	36	28	8	2	85	77	.525
2004	Cardinals	NL	162	119	.53	275	25	69	30	48	31	120	16	469	158	88	158	9	24	17	7	4	105	57	.648
2005	Cardinals	NL	162	138	.55	270	25	48	40	38	22	88	4	436	119	92	153	9	27	16	11	7	100	62	.617
2006	Cardinals	NL	161	131	.56	272	11	53	50	34	21	95	6	469	91	86	123	13	35	21	14	3	83	78	.516
2007	Cardinals	NL	162	148	.60	317	19	37	46	44	8	102	5	516	89	85	120	23	25	10	15	11	78	84	.481
2008	Cardinals	NL	162	140	.64	275	26	57	52	40	16	101	11	506	105	87	114	18	21	13	8	1	86	76	.531
2009	Cardinals	NL	162	126	.52	289	12	51	55	38	17	102	8	481	106	93	91	17	23	15	8	1	91	71	.562
2010	Cardinals	NL	162	135	.55	292	16	28	52	40	16	80	5	455	120	87	151	22	32	17	15	8	86	76	.531
2011	Cardinals	NL	162	126	.57	262	36	86	47	44	20	94	8	468	96	101	179	17	44	23	21	14	90	72	.556
2021	White Sox	AL	162	153	.61	83	22	41	36	49	8	86	9	512	77	32	104	0	16	10	6	2	93	69	.574
2022	White Sox	AL	162	158	.47	71	49	32	32	53	2	97	2	549	68	22	82	3	15	10	5	3	81	81	.500
	162-Game Average			135	.54	249	26	38	45	41	17	94	8	461	133	84	117	24	31	20	12	6	87	75	.537

Torey Lovullo

Year	Team	Lg	G	LINEUPS		SUBSTITUTION			PITCHER USAGE						TACTICS				INTENTIONAL BB				RESULTS		
				LUp	PL%	PH	PR	DS	Quick	Slow	LO	RCD	LS	Rel	SBA	SacA	RM	PO	#	Good	NG	Bomb	W	L	Pct
2015	Red Sox	AL	48	40	.58	17	17	4	9	16	10	28	0	149	35	10	32	0	5	3	2	1	28	20	.583
2017	Diamondbacks	NL	162	129	.55	254	28	36	34	45	6	116	2	513	133	50	85	3	45	32	13	6	93	69	.574
2018	Diamondbacks	NL	162	144	.66	258	13	32	31	45	2	143	2	573	104	60	92	3	43	29	14	4	82	80	.506
2019	Diamondbacks	NL	162	126	.66	256	21	46	32	38	0	105	9	557	102	49	105	5	38	19	19	8	85	77	.525
2020	Diamondbacks	NL	60	56	.69	27	12	3	11	16	0	31	1	200	30	2	14	0	20	13	7	5	25	35	.417
2021	Diamondbacks	NL	162	157	.74	339	22	17	34	54	0	95	2	565	59	40	67	6	45	30	15	7	52	110	.321
2022	Diamondbacks	NL	162	145	.75	148	17	42	44	44	1	96	0	546	133	40	99	7	18	13	5	2	74	88	.457
	162-Game Average			141	.67	229	23	32	34	46	3	108	3	548	105	44	87	4	38	25	13	6	77	85	.475

Joe Maddon

Year	Team	Lg	G	LINEUPS		SUBSTITUTION			PITCHER USAGE						TACTICS				INTENTIONAL BB				RESULTS		
				LUp	PL%	PH	PR	DS	Quick	Slow	LO	RCD	LS	Rel	SBA	SacA	RM	PO	#	Good	NG	Bomb	W	L	Pct
1996	Angels	AL	22	19	.64	21	5	0	7	6	6	10	3	48	11	20		6	4	3	1	1	8	14	.364
1998	Angels	AL	8	4	.57	2	4	0	1	5	3	5	3	12	2	7		0	1	0	1	0	6	2	.750
1999	Angels	AL	29	19	.58	29	4	1	6	0	4	20	0	85	23	12		7	3	1	2	1	19	10	.655
2006	Devil Rays	AL	162	145	.54	81	26	51	41	39	16	79	10	444	186	51	132	48	39	19	20	13	61	101	.377
2007	Devil Rays	AL	162	122	.53	80	19	16	31	56	19	113	1	483	179	40	118	50	31	18	13	4	66	96	.407
2008	Rays	AL	162	115	.69	133	16	39	48	37	14	112	7	448	192	31	113	26	29	15	14	8	97	65	.599
2009	Rays	AL	162	123	.66	140	21	18	28	51	23	139	3	510	255	29	99	15	22	10	12	7	84	78	.519
2010	Rays	AL	162	129	.67	174	31	18	41	34	26	135	2	491	219	45	166	12	34	28	6	3	96	66	.593
2011	Rays	AL	162	130	.67	137	16	31	34	36	47	112	6	438	217	42	187	4	38	23	15	6	91	71	.562
2012	Rays	AL	162	151	.62	156	37	52	43	38	33	123	3	472	178	40	181	7	35	25	10	6	90	72	.556
2013	Rays	AL	163	147	.64	193	27	56	52	38	16	111	6	485	111	26	117	6	38	21	17	11	92	71	.564
2014	Rays	AL	162	130	.58	171	23	15	44	35	26	110	3	494	90	54	143	2	27	20	7	3	77	85	.475
2015	Cubs	NL	162	119	.60	288	22	32	41	31	14	129	2	552	132	48	180	3	38	22	16	10	97	65	.599
2016	Cubs	NL	162	130	.62	236	19	35	56	29	13	100	3	503	100	54	111	6	24	19	5	3	103	58	.640
2017	Cubs	NL	162	143	.65	296	7	51	47	30	10	85	3	531	93	54	122	1	29	18	11	7	92	70	.568
2018	Cubs	NL	163	152	.61	280	18	48	41	44	5	120	2	600	104	56	130	1	33	25	8	6	95	68	.583
2019	Cubs	NL	162	140	.56	244	15	43	40	41	7	103	4	576	69	46	87	3	16	11	5	3	84	78	.519
2020	Angels	AL	60	52	.53	20	13	15	16	17	1	51	6	228	29	6	37	2	8	6	2	1	26	34	.433
2021	Angels	AL	162	146	.50	74	12	41	46	36	6	80	10	562	105	34	117	11	18	9	9	9	77	85	.475
2022	Angels	AL	56	53	.59	38	6	5	21	10	0	18	1	175	46	12	48	3	7	3	4	1	27	29	.482
	162-Game Average			135	.61	174	21	35	43	38	18	109	5	506	146	44	133	13	29	18	11	6	86	76	.531

Oliver Marmol

Year	Team	Lg	G	LINEUPS		SUBSTITUTION			PITCHER USAGE						TACTICS				INTENTIONAL BB				RESULTS		
				LUp	PL%	PH	PR	DS	Quick	Slow	LO	RCD	LS	Rel	SBA	SacA	RM	PO	#	Good	NG	Bomb	W	L	Pct
2022	Cardinals	NL	162	152	.55	127	33	43	44	43	5	61	8	466	120	7	120	1	11	8	3	1	93	69	.574
	162-Game Average			152	.55	127	33	43	44	43	5	61	8	466	120	7	120	1	11	8	3	1	93	69	.574

Dave Martinez

Year	Team	Lg	G	LINEUPS		SUBSTITUTION			PITCHER USAGE						TACTICS				INTENTIONAL BB				RESULTS		
				LUp	PL%	PH	PR	DS	Quick	Slow	LO	RCD	LS	Rel	SBA	SacA	RM	PO	#	Good	NG	Bomb	W	L	Pct
2018	Nationals	NL	162	125	.61	295	23	26	31	62	22	123	4	562	152	55	91	3	37	24	13	6	82	80	.506
2019	Nationals	NL	162	106	.49	253	15	19	32	41	13	136	8	530	145	77	81	0	41	31	10	6	93	69	.574
2020	Nationals	NL	60	54	.61	31	13	7	8	27	5	47	0	202	45	9	35	0	22	13	9	5	26	34	.433
2021	Nationals	NL	162	128	.56	284	14	21	32	53	1	135	5	569	82	57	93	1	46	27	19	11	65	97	.401
2022	Nationals	NL	162	142	.67	67	26	22	29	54	3	104	5	588	106	35	116	4	12	5	7	3	55	107	.340
	162-Game Average			127	.58	213	21	22	30	54	10	125	5	561	121	53	95	2	36	23	13	7	73	89	.451

Mike Matheny

Year	Team	Lg	G	LINEUPS		SUBSTITUTION			PITCHER USAGE						TACTICS				INTENTIONAL BB				RESULTS		
				LUp	PL%	PH	PR	DS	Quick	Slow	LO	RCD	LS	Rel	SBA	SacA	RM	PO	#	Good	NG	Bomb	W	L	Pct
2012	Cardinals	NL	162	122	.62	286	37	33	53	37	8	118	5	506	128	95	144	16	28	13	15	7	88	74	.543
2013	Cardinals	NL	162	89	.56	237	30	41	42	49	25	114	4	483	67	73	125	6	26	20	6	6	97	65	.599
2014	Cardinals	NL	162	119	.56	258	21	35	53	32	17	119	5	485	89	81	155	10	35	20	15	7	90	72	.556
2015	Cardinals	NL	162	135	.52	274	46	41	51	29	11	142	8	515	107	60	168	15	37	29	8	3	100	62	.617
2016	Cardinals	NL	162	146	.50	284	39	42	42	39	8	95	2	481	61	56	107	21	35	19	16	8	86	76	.531
2017	Cardinals	NL	162	144	.45	295	21	30	45	34	5	106	8	546	112	68	125	8	50	33	17	11	83	79	.512
2018	Cardinals	NL	93	69	.47	140	13	34	20	22	3	61	5	321	55	38	57	1	24	13	11	6	47	46	.505
2020	Royals	AL	60	52	.50	50	15	10	19	15	2	52	2	232	69	16	40	0	7	4	3	3	26	34	.433
2021	Royals	AL	162	133	.56	80	32	33	30	54	3	98	5	556	157	42	139	0	16	9	7	4	74	88	.457
2022	Royals	AL	162	137	.57	91	45	26	31	60	0	114	9	560	138	28	120	0	15	7	8	4	65	97	.401
	162-Game Average			128	.54	223	33	36	43	41	9	114	6	524	110	62	132	9	31	19	12	7	85	77	.525

Don Mattingly

Year	Team	Lg	G	LUp	PL%	PH	PR	DS	Quick	Slow	LO	RCD	LS	Rel	SBA	SacA	RM	PO	#	Good	NG	Bomb	W	L	Pct
				LINEUPS		SUBSTITUTION			PITCHER USAGE						TACTICS				INTENTIONAL BB				RESULTS		
2011	Dodgers	NL	161	140	.57	233	29	44	45	40	30	86	1	461	166	93	181	13	48	27	21	12	82	79	.509
2012	Dodgers	NL	162	127	.59	247	22	43	51	39	20	118	2	506	148	105	153	8	62	38	24	15	86	76	.531
2013	Dodgers	NL	162	145	.57	210	18	47	40	30	18	118	3	504	106	99	131	10	44	28	16	7	92	70	.568
2014	Dodgers	NL	162	124	.51	237	17	62	49	31	15	107	5	496	188	67	168	2	35	20	15	8	94	68	.580
2015	Dodgers	NL	161	136	.70	276	20	45	50	30	13	119	1	508	93	67	136	2	32	18	14	5	91	70	.565
2016	Marlins	NL	161	111	.48	281	28	69	48	35	10	145	1	559	99	63	101	2	62	42	20	14	79	82	.491
2017	Marlins	NL	162	98	.52	271	9	20	43	32	4	120	5	580	121	66	125	2	59	39	20	12	77	85	.475
2018	Marlins	NL	161	137	.46	283	19	53	47	43	2	114	0	546	76	45	121	1	73	40	33	19	63	98	.391
2019	Marlins	NL	162	143	.43	293	24	25	34	48	3	112	1	539	85	49	124	0	52	33	19	9	57	105	.352
2020	Marlins	NL	60	55	.54	37	15	14	20	12	0	40	3	215	65	8	36	0	14	8	6	3	31	29	.517
2021	Marlins	NL	162	147	.50	271	36	22	41	23	2	112	2	595	135	46	143	0	43	22	21	4	67	95	.414
2022	Marlins	NL	162	154	.41	89	58	40	37	43	5	110	3	532	151	8	117	1	19	10	9	3	69	93	.426
	162-Game Average			134	.52	240	26	43	45	36	11	115	2	532	126	63	135	4	48	29	19	10	78	84	.481

Lloyd McClendon

Year	Team	Lg	G	LUp	PL%	PH	PR	DS	Quick	Slow	LO	RCD	LS	Rel	SBA	SacA	RM	PO	#	Good	NG	Bomb	W	L	Pct
				LINEUPS		SUBSTITUTION			PITCHER USAGE						TACTICS				INTENTIONAL BB				RESULTS		
2001	Pirates	NL	162	131	.51	255	17	32	45	38	2	85	5	410	166	83		52	74	44	30	19	62	100	.383
2002	Pirates	NL	161	121	.45	261	38	65	62	30	3	98	2	458	135	93	73	67	93	61	32	22	72	89	.447
2003	Pirates	NL	162	114	.57	315	27	59	46	35	27	114	10	457	123	99	55	73	58	34	24	13	75	87	.463
2004	Pirates	NL	161	114	.50	278	13	58	50	40	26	133	1	464	103	100	91	61	64	37	27	16	72	89	.447
2005	Pirates	NL	136	123	.53	218	8	19	37	34	15	86	5	357	84	62	83	37	60	32	28	16	55	81	.404
2014	Mariners	AL	162	141	.69	93	48	33	61	21	11	87	3	497	138	48	187	30	36	21	15	9	87	75	.537
2015	Mariners	AL	162	140	.63	133	52	50	53	31	10	114	5	509	114	49	148	30	41	23	18	10	76	86	.469
2020	Tigers	AL	8	8	.56	5	4	3	2	3	0	5	0	27	7	0	7	0	1	0	1	0	2	6	.250
	162-Game Average			130	.56	227	30	46	52	34	14	105	5	462	127	78	110	51	62	37	25	15	73	89	.451

Bob Melvin

Year	Team	Lg	G	LUp	PL%	PH	PR	DS	Quick	Slow	LO	RCD	LS	Rel	SBA	SacA	RM	PO	#	Good	NG	Bomb	W	L	Pct
				LINEUPS		SUBSTITUTION			PITCHER USAGE						TACTICS				INTENTIONAL BB				RESULTS		
2003	Mariners	AL	162	111	.62	81	62	33	27	46	43	56	6	366	145	44	37	5	24	14	10	4	93	69	.574
2004	Mariners	AL	162	151	.55	109	66	65	26	63	43	82	5	414	152	56	123	24	32	18	14	8	63	99	.389
2005	Diamondbacks	NL	162	120	.68	310	26	38	26	56	36	123	11	458	93	93	101	30	43	27	16	9	77	85	.475
2006	Diamondbacks	NL	162	114	.72	278	11	35	37	42	15	86	0	461	106	83	61	30	44	28	16	8	76	86	.469
2007	Diamondbacks	NL	162	146	.57	243	11	61	35	42	31	96	2	469	133	74	70	25	38	30	8	4	90	72	.556
2008	Diamondbacks	NL	162	134	.57	263	27	30	41	39	16	102	0	444	81	87	79	28	41	27	14	9	82	80	.506
2009	Diamondbacks	NL	29	29	.62	47	6	8	7	4	3	17	0	91	29	17	13	3	3	1	2	2	12	17	.414
2011	Athletics	AL	99	87	.71	33	13	17	24	23	18	59	2	283	103	34	87	23	9	5	4	3	47	52	.475
2012	Athletics	AL	162	132	.71	111	17	18	63	29	5	93	2	462	154	41	116	30	34	21	13	6	94	68	.580
2013	Athletics	AL	162	133	.77	166	14	35	48	28	7	84	7	447	102	32	74	8	23	18	5	3	96	66	.593
2014	Athletics	AL	162	137	.77	187	38	44	45	30	11	101	2	441	103	28	91	16	28	20	8	5	88	74	.543
2015	Athletics	AL	162	137	.65	161	24	35	53	36	10	100	10	487	107	17	130	20	19	8	11	8	68	94	.420
2016	Athletics	AL	162	141	.64	135	28	39	55	36	7	96	3	492	73	19	79	5	28	14	14	8	69	93	.426
2017	Athletics	AL	162	137	.60	126	19	32	39	46	5	114	4	525	79	16	85	9	17	12	5	4	75	87	.463
2018	Athletics	AL	162	121	.55	138	16	23	49	22	1	115	9	578	56	10	74	8	19	14	5	3	97	65	.599
2019	Athletics	AL	162	138	.53	117	11	34	36	30	4	123	10	547	70	10	72	4	19	12	7	4	97	65	.599
2020	Athletics	AL	60	50	.53	32	17	10	12	9	1	34	4	181	29	2	33	1	6	4	2	1	36	24	.600
2021	Athletics	AL	162	153	.56	158	31	21	21	34	3	93	5	504	108	20	102	0	11	7	4	2	86	76	.531
2022	Padres	NL	162	143	.61	111	28	37	30	51	6	75	6	487	71	24	88	4	6	2	4	2	89	73	.549
	162-Game Average			135	.64	164	27	34	39	39	15	96	5	474	105	41	88	16	26	16	9	5	84	78	.519

Charlie Montoyo

Year	Team	Lg	G	LUp	PL%	PH	PR	DS	Quick	Slow	LO	RCD	LS	Rel	SBA	SacA	RM	PO	#	Good	NG	Bomb	W	L	Pct
				LINEUPS		SUBSTITUTION			PITCHER USAGE						TACTICS				INTENTIONAL BB				RESULTS		
2019	Blue Jays	AL	162	158	.59	79	25	15	47	26	1	87	10	591	71	18	86	6	25	20	5	0	67	95	.414
2020	Blue Jays	AL	60	56	.53	37	14	15	14	15	0	26	4	226	39	9	28	3	7	4	3	0	32	28	.533
2021	Blue Jays	AL	162	133	.42	100	39	42	37	32	5	62	5	536	101	14	118	4	10	6	4	3	91	71	.562
2022	Blue Jays	AL	88	80	.35	55	19	22	25	18	0	53	1	318	49	7	53	1	7	4	3	2	46	42	.523
	162-Game Average			147	.48	93	33	32	42	31	2	78	7	574	89	16	98	5	17	12	5	2	81	81	.500

Phil Nevin

Year	Team	Lg	G	LUp	PL%	PH	PR	DS	Quick	Slow	LO	RCD	LS	Rel	SBA	SacA	RM	PO	#	Good	NG	Bomb	W	L	Pct
				LINEUPS		SUBSTITUTION			PITCHER USAGE						TACTICS				INTENTIONAL BB				RESULTS		
2022	Angels	AL	106	100	.62	82	25	37	23	19	1	27	2	315	58	21	52	6	16	11	5	1	46	60	.434
	162-Game Average			153	.62	125	38	57	35	29	2	41	3	481	89	32	79	9	24	17	8	2	70	92	.432

Tom Prince

Year	Team	Lg	G	LUp	PL%	PH	PR	DS	Quick	Slow	LO	RCD	LS	Rel	SBA	SacA	RM	PO	#	Good	NG	Bomb	W	L	Pct
2019	Pirates	NL	1	1	.25	1	0	0	0	0	0	0	0	2	0	0	0	0	0	0	0	0	0	1	.000
	162-Game Average			162	.25	162	0	0	0	0	0	0	0	324	0	0	0	0	0	0	0	0	0	162	.000

Rick Renteria

Year	Team	Lg	G	LUp	PL%	PH	PR	DS	Quick	Slow	LO	RCD	LS	Rel	SBA	SacA	RM	PO	#	Good	NG	Bomb	W	L	Pct
2014	Cubs	NL	162	137	.63	275	9	20	50	42	12	103	1	537	105	77	106	5	37	23	14	8	73	89	.451
2017	White Sox	AL	162	150	.57	86	26	9	31	58	6	108	2	520	102	47	133	1	36	19	17	9	67	95	.414
2018	White Sox	AL	162	142	.60	90	30	25	18	66	9	99	5	553	139	28	126	10	25	15	10	6	62	100	.383
2019	White Sox	AL	161	143	.66	87	27	27	32	48	7	91	4	536	91	35	103	5	30	16	14	5	72	89	.447
2020	White Sox	AL	60	51	.49	22	24	8	15	17	3	37	3	224	28	2	31	0	6	1	5	2	35	25	.583
	162-Game Average			143	.60	128	27	20	33	53	8	100	3	543	107	43	114	5	31	17	14	7	71	91	.438

Dave Roberts

Year	Team	Lg	G	LUp	PL%	PH	PR	DS	Quick	Slow	LO	RCD	LS	Rel	SBA	SacA	RM	PO	#	Good	NG	Bomb	W	L	Pct
2015	Padres	NL	1	1	.63	3	0	0	0	1	0	2	0	3	1	1	0	0	1	1	0	0	0	1	.000
2016	Dodgers	NL	162	120	.69	325	11	26	60	26	6	143	5	606	71	45	120	2	51	36	15	10	91	71	.562
2017	Dodgers	NL	162	147	.67	345	10	30	82	22	3	104	18	550	105	45	97	3	33	23	10	6	104	58	.642
2018	Dodgers	NL	163	155	.67	362	16	51	64	29	3	112	9	593	99	51	87	0	39	26	13	5	92	71	.564
2019	Dodgers	NL	162	139	.62	309	13	16	57	28	2	108	9	545	67	61	44	3	24	12	12	8	106	56	.654
2020	Dodgers	NL	60	57	.56	41	5	11	24	7	0	37	0	249	37	3	32	0	4	2	2	2	43	17	.717
2021	Dodgers	NL	162	146	.53	280	17	35	56	37	8	136	7	600	82	34	67	0	43	33	10	7	106	56	.654
2022	Dodgers	NL	162	123	.54	83	10	8	69	19	1	98	3	563	116	7	102	0	13	4	9	4	111	51	.685
	162-Game Average			139	.61	274	13	28	65	26	4	116	8	579	91	39	86	1	33	21	11	7	102	60	.630

Ron Roenicke

Year	Team	Lg	G	LUp	PL%	PH	PR	DS	Quick	Slow	LO	RCD	LS	Rel	SBA	SacA	RM	PO	#	Good	NG	Bomb	W	L	Pct
2011	Brewers	NL	162	105	.45	260	31	36	36	43	31	92	1	434	125	104	141	14	16	9	7	4	96	66	.593
2012	Brewers	NL	162	110	.45	322	20	25	36	50	23	149	1	512	197	91	152	8	20	12	8	2	83	79	.512
2013	Brewers	NL	162	125	.47	275	15	34	39	47	7	96	2	501	192	86	157	6	29	22	7	6	74	88	.457
2014	Brewers	NL	162	115	.44	253	19	37	33	48	12	114	1	478	145	92	127	11	20	16	4	4	82	80	.506
2015	Brewers	NL	25	24	.39	48	4	5	3	9	2	15	0	72	14	18	17	2	6	5	1	1	7	18	.280
2020	Red Sox	AL	60	52	.57	22	7	2	22	12	0	26	0	232	40	3	25	1	4	2	2	1	24	36	.400
	162-Game Average			117	.46	261	21	31	37	46	17	109	1	493	158	87	137	9	21	15	6	4	81	81	.500

Luis Rojas

Year	Team	Lg	G	LUp	PL%	PH	PR	DS	Quick	Slow	LO	RCD	LS	Rel	SBA	SacA	RM	PO	#	Good	NG	Bomb	W	L	Pct
2020	Mets	NL	60	53	.60	37	19	19	14	15	2	33	4	197	30	1	35	5	7	2	5	3	26	34	.433
2021	Mets	NL	162	133	.65	292	16	36	63	27	1	107	4	543	80	53	79	1	21	15	6	2	77	85	.475
	162-Game Average			136	.64	240	26	40	56	31	2	102	6	540	80	41	83	4	20	12	8	4	75	87	.463

David Ross

Year	Team	Lg	G	LUp	PL%	PH	PR	DS	Quick	Slow	LO	RCD	LS	Rel	SBA	SacA	RM	PO	#	Good	NG	Bomb	W	L	Pct
2020	Cubs	NL	60	54	.61	51	16	23	12	14	1	27	3	188	34	0	46	0	7	4	3	1	34	26	.567
2021	Cubs	NL	162	138	.59	309	15	23	41	43	0	95	7	599	123	47	103	0	25	15	10	8	71	91	.438
2022	Cubs	NL	162	150	.53	133	24	32	60	29	2	90	9	528	148	31	163	0	19	12	7	3	74	88	.457
	162-Game Average			144	.57	208	23	33	48	36	1	89	8	555	129	33	132	0	22	13	8	5	76	86	.469

John Schneider

Year	Team	Lg	G	LUp	PL%	PH	PR	DS	Quick	Slow	LO	RCD	LS	Rel	SBA	SacA	RM	PO	#	Good	NG	Bomb	W	L	Pct
2022	Blue Jays	AL	74	68	.32	50	17	36	18	17	1	62	7	266	53	2	64	2	8	6	2	1	46	28	.622
	162-Game Average			149	.32	109	37	79	39	37	2	136	15	582	116	4	140	4	18	13	4	2	101	61	.623

Scott Servais

Year	Team	Lg	G	LUp	PL%	PH	PR	DS	Quick	Slow	LO	RCD	LS	Rel	SBA	SacA	RM	PO	#	Good	NG	Bomb	W	L	Pct
				LINEUPS		SUBSTITUTION			PITCHER USAGE						TACTICS				INTENTIONAL BB				RESULTS		
2016	Mariners	AL	162	114	.72	166	33	43	42	38	8	93	7	476	84	36	79	1	30	16	14	6	86	76	.531
2017	Mariners	AL	162	120	.52	93	29	18	55	32	3	98	7	527	124	26	99	4	28	15	13	7	78	84	.481
2018	Mariners	AL	162	124	.54	103	42	28	44	42	3	122	3	537	116	43	91	7	21	15	6	4	89	73	.549
2019	Mariners	AL	162	153	.58	82	33	35	33	37	4	58	3	538	162	17	100	7	25	11	14	7	68	94	.420
2020	Mariners	AL	60	59	.56	26	9	7	7	14	0	12	2	189	66	5	37	0	7	6	1	1	27	33	.450
2021	Mariners	AL	162	132	.60	102	12	26	37	43	1	105	7	584	88	19	80	2	23	16	7	3	90	72	.556
2022	Mariners	AL	162	151	.63	127	38	24	25	47	2	101	3	536	110	10	54	0	24	15	9	2	90	72	.556
	162-Game Average			134	.60	110	31	28	38	40	3	92	5	532	118	24	85	3	25	15	10	5	83	79	.512

Derek Shelton

Year	Team	Lg	G	LUp	PL%	PH	PR	DS	Quick	Slow	LO	RCD	LS	Rel	SBA	SacA	RM	PO	#	Good	NG	Bomb	W	L	Pct
				LINEUPS		SUBSTITUTION			PITCHER USAGE						TACTICS				INTENTIONAL BB				RESULTS		
2020	Pirates	NL	60	57	.65	26	15	5	16	18	2	26	0	209	27	7	31	2	3	1	2	0	19	41	.317
2021	Pirates	NL	162	150	.66	290	4	15	48	47	0	64	1	583	90	48	129	0	26	17	9	4	61	101	.377
2022	Pirates	NL	162	156	.72	130	25	28	59	29	0	58	10	504	121	29	142	2	23	15	8	4	62	100	.383
	162-Game Average			153	.69	188	19	20	52	40	1	62	5	547	100	35	127	2	22	14	8	3	60	102	.370

Mike Shildt

Year	Team	Lg	G	LUp	PL%	PH	PR	DS	Quick	Slow	LO	RCD	LS	Rel	SBA	SacA	RM	PO	#	Good	NG	Bomb	W	L	Pct
				LINEUPS		SUBSTITUTION			PITCHER USAGE						TACTICS				INTENTIONAL BB				RESULTS		
2018	Cardinals	NL	69	58	.49	117	22	30	21	11	1	44	3	244	40	29	82	0	25	16	9	2	41	28	.594
2019	Cardinals	NL	162	97	.48	268	30	44	47	33	9	111	10	542	145	57	154	2	41	29	12	4	91	71	.562
2020	Cardinals	NL	58	54	.60	32	9	11	19	13	1	25	4	176	28	5	36	0	8	6	2	1	30	28	.517
2021	Cardinals	NL	162	107	.47	258	11	32	43	39	2	99	5	556	111	55	95	0	30	22	8	3	90	72	.556
	162-Game Average			114	.49	242	26	42	47	34	5	100	8	545	116	52	132	1	37	26	11	4	91	71	.562

Buck Showalter

Year	Team	Lg	G	LUp	PL%	PH	PR	DS	Quick	Slow	LO	RCD	LS	Rel	SBA	SacA	RM	PO	#	Good	NG	Bomb	W	L	Pct
				LINEUPS		SUBSTITUTION			PITCHER USAGE						TACTICS				INTENTIONAL BB				RESULTS		
1994	Yankees	AL	113	79	.59	95	31	3	24	30	0	38	7	241	95	34		22	24	13	11	4	70	43	.619
1995	Yankees	AL	145	107	.68	124	30	20	29	42	37	57	6	302	80	27		29	21	14	7	1	79	65	.549
1998	Diamondbacks	NL	162	124	.62	252	17	15	34	40	7	43	6	368	111	68		13	32	16	16	9	65	97	.401
1999	Diamondbacks	NL	162	97	.63	220	20	17	37	48	25	74	3	382	176	75		15	48	29	19	8	100	62	.617
2000	Diamondbacks	NL	162	99	.60	250	32	11	46	26	18	74	12	390	141	89		10	53	28	25	16	85	77	.525
2003	Rangers	AL	162	133	.61	88	51	41	35	33	12	93	7	494	90	35	80	12	45	24	21	14	71	91	.438
2004	Rangers	AL	162	120	.64	86	15	24	53	30	12	82	10	468	105	30	88	5	29	19	10	3	89	73	.549
2005	Rangers	AL	162	98	.59	57	22	11	42	39	17	79	8	454	82	11	103	5	31	10	21	16	79	83	.488
2006	Rangers	AL	162	95	.57	39	34	22	41	27	10	85	4	489	77	30	72	8	18	11	7	5	80	82	.494
2010	Orioles	AL	57	42	.74	20	11	13	23	9	10	24	1	144	38	13	31	1	10	9	1	1	34	23	.596
2011	Orioles	AL	162	117	.53	60	39	27	43	40	14	61	2	478	106	32	133	6	42	31	11	5	69	93	.426
2012	Orioles	AL	162	120	.62	78	28	31	37	42	10	88	0	492	87	46	145	6	36	25	11	5	93	69	.574
2013	Orioles	AL	162	100	.65	90	23	21	31	39	19	84	4	473	108	37	104	4	32	11	21	13	85	77	.525
2014	Orioles	AL	162	120	.49	77	29	51	37	34	17	89	2	479	64	50	101	10	25	16	9	4	96	66	.593
2015	Orioles	AL	162	145	.60	89	21	35	35	41	6	76	8	453	69	26	95	10	27	12	15	8	81	81	.500
2016	Orioles	AL	162	125	.53	74	31	33	36	50	16	68	9	443	32	21	55	10	23	13	10	5	89	73	.549
2017	Orioles	AL	162	115	.44	95	31	40	27	57	21	93	3	492	45	19	40	8	21	15	6	5	75	87	.463
2018	Orioles	AL	162	152	.55	98	30	31	27	47	7	58	8	490	103	23	75	2	29	21	8	6	47	115	.290
2022	Mets	NL	162	132	.67	98	42	26	46	35	2	49	7	483	84	27	83	1	13	7	6	4	101	61	.623
	162-Game Average			118	.59	111	30	26	38	40	14	73	6	447	94	39	90	10	31	18	13	7	83	79	.512

Brian Snitker

Year	Team	Lg	G	LUp	PL%	PH	PR	DS	Quick	Slow	LO	RCD	LS	Rel	SBA	SacA	RM	PO	#	Good	NG	Bomb	W	L	Pct
				LINEUPS		SUBSTITUTION			PITCHER USAGE						TACTICS				INTENTIONAL BB				RESULTS		
2016	Braves	NL	124	85	.62	214	8	14	31	36	7	96	1	456	83	64	118	7	40	23	17	10	59	65	.476
2017	Braves	NL	162	108	.58	268	38	16	31	52	8	101	1	530	108	76	139	3	39	27	12	9	72	90	.444
2018	Braves	NL	162	103	.65	254	24	21	50	39	8	92	2	553	126	59	137	7	43	32	11	5	90	72	.556
2019	Braves	NL	162	95	.60	265	20	33	44	35	1	96	6	575	117	34	91	3	33	27	6	3	97	65	.599
2020	Braves	NL	60	51	.48	29	9	10	23	12	0	26	1	228	27	3	46	1	13	8	5	2	35	25	.583
2021	Braves	NL	161	100	.51	273	10	37	31	42	1	106	0	581	78	39	107	0	34	23	11	0	88	73	.547
2022	Braves	NL	162	129	.50	48	13	38	29	36	0	73	2	518	118	2	129	0	21	18	3	2	101	61	.623
	162-Game Average			109	.57	220	20	28	39	41	4	96	2	561	107	45	125	3	36	26	11	5	88	74	.543

Rob Thomson

Year	Team	Lg	G	LINEUPS		SUBSTITUTION			PITCHER USAGE						TACTICS				INTENTIONAL BB				RESULTS		
				LUp	PL%	PH	PR	DS	Quick	Slow	LO	RCD	LS	Rel	SBA	SacA	RM	PO	#	Good	NG	Bomb	W	L	Pct
2022	Phillies	NL	111	95	.55	60	18	11	23	28	0	45	3	340	97	9	74	0	7	5	2	0	65	46	.586
	162-Game Average			139	.55	88	26	16	34	41	0	66	4	496	142	13	108	0	10	7	3	0	95	67	.586

Jayce Tingler

Year	Team	Lg	G	LINEUPS		SUBSTITUTION			PITCHER USAGE						TACTICS				INTENTIONAL BB				RESULTS		
				LUp	PL%	PH	PR	DS	Quick	Slow	LO	RCD	LS	Rel	SBA	SacA	RM	PO	#	Good	NG	Bomb	W	L	Pct
2020	Padres	NL	60	56	.59	44	10	13	23	9	1	27	0	218	68	14	46	0	2	1	1	0	37	23	.617
2021	Padres	NL	162	140	.57	307	13	27	47	36	3	106	4	624	149	42	130	0	33	26	7	2	79	83	.488
	162-Game Average			143	.58	256	17	29	51	33	3	97	3	614	158	41	128	0	26	20	6	1	85	77	.525

Chris Woodward

Year	Team	Lg	G	LINEUPS		SUBSTITUTION			PITCHER USAGE						TACTICS				INTENTIONAL BB				RESULTS		
				LUp	PL%	PH	PR	DS	Quick	Slow	LO	RCD	LS	Rel	SBA	SacA	RM	PO	#	Good	NG	Bomb	W	L	Pct
2019	Rangers	AL	162	150	.62	82	14	19	32	48	24	70	2	499	169	19	115	0	11	4	7	5	78	84	.481
2020	Rangers	AL	60	58	.60	30	10	9	13	29	4	29	1	204	63	5	35	0	3	2	1	1	22	38	.367
2021	Rangers	AL	162	145	.61	89	14	4	38	44	2	50	0	507	135	24	123	1	11	4	7	2	60	102	.370
2022	Rangers	AL	114	109	.66	105	28	12	17	26	0	52	0	384	115	12	96	1	12	5	7	3	51	63	.447
	162-Game Average			150	.63	100	21	14	33	48	10	65	1	519	157	20	120	1	12	5	7	4	69	93	.426

Ned Yost

Year	Team	Lg	G	LINEUPS		SUBSTITUTION			PITCHER USAGE						TACTICS				INTENTIONAL BB				RESULTS		
				LUp	PL%	PH	PR	DS	Quick	Slow	LO	RCD	LS	Rel	SBA	SacA	RM	PO	#	Good	NG	Bomb	W	L	Pct
2003	Brewers	NL	162	97	.44	304	22	39	23	59	18	90	6	460	138	85	40	23	43	28	15	9	68	94	.420
2004	Brewers	NL	161	131	.60	283	25	20	39	41	27	63	2	423	178	79	108	8	27	16	11	8	67	94	.416
2005	Brewers	NL	162	99	.46	259	18	35	26	41	42	71	2	395	113	89	97	50	52	23	29	10	81	81	.500
2006	Brewers	NL	162	106	.48	238	12	14	33	44	18	77	4	427	108	80	82	16	34	14	20	12	75	87	.463
2007	Brewers	NL	162	109	.60	259	11	41	37	42	18	117	7	492	128	74	94	19	37	28	9	9	83	79	.512
2008	Brewers	NL	150	74	.48	217	5	16	37	39	23	69	5	399	141	61	105	31	30	17	13	7	83	67	.553
2010	Royals	AL	127	80	.57	56	25	6	22	39	20	65	0	332	127	40	128	18	25	16	9	5	55	72	.433
2011	Royals	AL	162	87	.58	36	28	16	42	42	21	56	7	420	211	65	203	19	42	27	15	5	71	91	.438
2012	Royals	AL	162	118	.57	60	34	15	48	37	10	108	1	500	170	37	149	25	44	29	15	11	72	90	.444
2013	Royals	AL	162	127	.60	79	48	39	43	44	21	72	2	427	185	48	168	25	21	12	9	5	86	76	.531
2014	Royals	AL	162	101	.52	51	63	46	37	51	26	93	1	451	189	45	159	3	14	7	7	3	89	73	.549
2015	Royals	AL	162	83	.57	40	40	26	51	42	13	90	3	493	138	45	126	5	10	7	3	1	95	67	.586
2016	Royals	AL	162	108	.54	50	38	12	49	44	10	85	2	472	156	55	130	0	8	6	2	2	81	81	.500
2017	Royals	AL	162	86	.53	48	29	25	53	31	2	120	0	538	122	20	110	0	24	14	10	6	80	82	.494
2018	Royals	AL	162	150	.58	48	7	12	32	52	6	75	0	483	155	42	136	1	28	15	13	7	58	104	.358
2019	Royals	AL	162	132	.56	58	25	16	30	52	5	85	3	520	156	32	92	0	25	15	10	5	59	103	.364
	162-Game Average			107	.54	133	27	24	38	45	18	85	3	461	154	57	123	15	30	17	12	7	77	85	.475

Categories of this record are Games Managed (G), Number of Different Lineups Used (LUp), the percentage of players who had the platoon advantage at the start of the game (PL%), Pinch Hitters Used (PH), Pinch Runners Used (PR), Defensive Substitutes Used (DS), Quick Hooks (Quick), Slow Hooks (Slow), Long Outings by Starting Pitchers (LO), Relievers Used on Consecutive Days (RCD), Long Saves (LS), Relievers Used (Rel), Stolen Base Attempts (SBA), Sacrifice Bunt Attempts (SacA), Runners Moving with the Pitch (RM), Pitchouts ordered (PO), Intentional Walks issued (#), Intentional Walks resulting in a Good Outcome (Good), Intentional Walks resulting Not in a Good Outcome (NG), Intentional Walks Blowing Up on the Manager (Bomb), Wins (W), Losses (L), and Winning Percentage (Pct).

2022 American League Managers

Manager	G	LUp	PL%	PH	PR	DS	Quick	Slow	LO	RCD	LS	Rel	SBA	SacA	RM	PO	#	Good	NG	Bomb	W	L	Pct
		LINEUPS		SUBSTITUTION			PITCHER USAGE						TACTICS				INTENTIONAL BB				RESULTS		
Brandon Hyde, Bal	162	142	.61	96	36	38	51	36	2	75	15	541	126	21	104	0	8	7	1	1	83	79	.512
Alex Cora, Bos	162	136	.50	92	19	32	44	37	1	104	9	576	72	13	90	0	17	10	7	2	78	84	.481
Terry Francona, Cle	162	139	.58	96	33	23	30	55	0	84	1	507	146	26	134	2	14	8	6	1	92	70	.568
Tony LaRussa, CWS	162	158	.47	71	49	32	32	53	2	97	2	549	68	22	82	3	15	10	5	3	81	81	.500
A.J. Hinch, Det	162	161	.67	85	32	8	44	44	0	82	1	580	71	12	76	0	9	4	5	3	66	96	.407
Dusty Baker, Hou	162	131	.45	81	11	32	35	45	3	67	0	480	105	15	116	2	6	3	3	2	106	56	.654
Mike Matheny, KC	162	137	.57	91	45	26	31	60	0	114	9	560	138	28	120	0	15	7	8	4	65	97	.401
Rocco Baldelli, Min	162	152	.58	121	44	34	74	31	0	68	4	548	55	9	58	0	19	15	4	3	78	84	.481
Aaron Boone, NYY	162	146	.47	93	42	24	40	38	5	82	13	507	135	20	141	1	10	6	4	1	99	63	.611
Mark Kotsay, Oak	162	158	.56	164	18	24	39	50	1	81	4	530	101	23	127	0	37	23	14	10	60	102	.370
Scott Servais, Sea	162	151	.63	127	38	24	25	47	2	101	3	536	110	10	54	0	24	15	9	2	90	72	.556
Kevin Cash, TB	162	158	.63	115	27	40	61	19	0	117	4	572	132	9	108	2	15	7	8	1	86	76	.531
162-Game Average		149	.54	107	33	32	42	40	1	87	5	540	109	18	106	2	17	10	7	3	82	80	.506

Manager	G	LUp	PL%	PH	PR	DS	Quick	Slow	LO	RCD	LS	Rel	SBA	SacA	RM	PO	#	Good	NG	Bomb	W	L	Pct
		LINEUPS		SUBSTITUTION			PITCHER USAGE						TACTICS				INTENTIONAL BB				RESULTS		
Joe Maddon, LAA	56	53	.59	38	6	5	21	10	0	18	1	175	46	12	48	3	7	3	4	1	27	29	.482
Phil Nevin, LAA	106	100	.62	82	25	37	23	19	1	27	2	315	58	21	52	6	16	11	5	2	46	60	.434
Chris Woodward, Tex	114	109	.66	105	28	12	17	26	0	52	0	384	115	12	96	1	12	5	7	3	51	63	.447
Tony Beasley, Tex	48	38	.63	34	11	4	12	13	0	15	1	148	54	5	50	0	4	1	3	1	17	31	.354
John Schneider, Tor	74	68	.32	50	17	36	18	17	1	62	7	266	53	2	64	2	8	6	2	1	46	28	.622
Charlie Montoyo, Tor	88	80	.35	55	19	22	25	18	0	53	1	318	49	7	53	1	7	4	3	2	46	42	.523

2022 National League Managers

Manager	G	LUp	PL%	PH	PR	DS	Quick	Slow	LO	RCD	LS	Rel	SBA	SacA	RM	PO	#	Good	NG	Bomb	W	L	Pct
		LINEUPS		SUBSTITUTION			PITCHER USAGE						TACTICS				INTENTIONAL BB				RESULTS		
Torey Lovullo, Ari	162	145	.75	148	17	42	44	44	1	96	0	546	133	40	99	7	18	13	5	2	74	88	.457
Brian Snitker, Atl	162	129	.50	48	13	38	29	36	0	73	2	518	118	2	129	0	21	18	3	2	101	61	.623
David Ross, ChC	162	150	.53	133	24	32	60	29	2	90	9	528	148	31	163	0	19	12	7	3	74	88	.457
David Bell, Cin	162	151	.49	119	25	15	36	51	8	76	5	574	91	16	100	1	21	11	10	4	62	100	.383
Bud Black, Col	162	153	.51	36	35	37	23	59	1	82	3	497	65	14	74	4	12	6	6	3	68	94	.420
Dave Roberts, LAD	162	123	.54	83	10	8	69	19	1	98	3	563	116	7	102	0	13	4	9	4	111	51	.685
Don Mattingly, Mia	162	154	.41	89	58	40	37	43	5	110	3	532	151	8	117	1	19	10	9	3	69	93	.426
Craig Counsell, Mil	162	125	.60	125	14	27	35	49	4	113	3	548	126	14	97	1	12	5	7	1	86	76	.531
Buck Showalter, NYM	162	132	.67	98	42	26	46	35	2	49	7	483	84	27	83	1	13	7	6	4	101	61	.623
Derek Shelton, Pit	162	156	.72	130	25	28	59	29	0	58	10	504	121	29	142	2	23	15	8	4	62	100	.383
Bob Melvin, SD	162	143	.61	111	28	37	30	51	6	75	6	487	71	24	88	4	6	2	4	2	89	73	.549
Gabe Kapler, SF	162	153	.65	256	22	31	30	37	2	120	4	576	80	6	60	0	16	8	8	3	81	81	.500
Oliver Marmol, StL	162	152	.55	127	33	43	44	43	5	61	8	466	120	7	120	1	11	8	3	1	93	69	.574
Dave Martinez, Was	162	142	.67	67	26	22	29	54	3	104	5	588	106	35	116	4	12	5	7	3	55	107	.340
162-Game Average		142	.58	109	26	29	40	42	3	85	5	529	112	18	106	2	16	9	7	3	81	81	.500

Manager	G	LUp	PL%	PH	PR	DS	Quick	Slow	LO	RCD	LS	Rel	SBA	SacA	RM	PO	#	Good	NG	Bomb	W	L	Pct
		LINEUPS		SUBSTITUTION			PITCHER USAGE						TACTICS				INTENTIONAL BB				RESULTS		
Joe Girardi, Phi	51	40	.57	28	7	9	13	14	0	30	2	176	36	5	31	0	9	6	3	1	22	29	.431
Rob Thomson, Phi	111	95	.55	60	18	11	23	28	0	45	3	340	97	9	74	0	7	5	2	0	65	46	.586

The Best of Baseball Across the Pacific

Mark Simon

One of the cool things that our company has done the last few years is to become fully immersed in tracking NPB and KBO games. We chart every pitch and plate appearance of every game, just like we track MLB.

You'll see on the accompanying pages that we've followed two of the stars, Munetaka Murakami and Woo-jin An, in extensive detail. These are special players. But we don't want to short-change the rest of the league. You can find the league leaderboards for NPB and KBO immediately following those essays. Some things to check out include:

* Outfielder Go Matsumoto of the Nippon Ham Fighters won the NPB batting title, hitting .347. This was somewhat unexpected in that by doing so, Mastumoto raised his career batting average to .281.

* In his second pro season, 20-year-old Roki Sasaki of the Chiba Lotte Marines struck out hitters at a rate of 12 per 9 innings. In 20 starts, Sasaki pitched to a 2.02 ERA. But it was Yoshinobu Yamamoto of the Orix Buffaloes who won his 2nd straight Eiji Sawamura Award as Japan's top pitcher. He led NPB with a 1.68 ERA.

* Jung Hoo Lee of the Kiwoom Heroes led KBO in the three slash line stats, hitting .349 with a .421 on-base percentage and .575 slugging percentage. Lee also led the league with 113 RBI.

* And once you get past An on the KBO pitching leaderboards, you'll run into some familiar names. Eight of the Top 10 pitchers in ERA in the KBO have MLB experience, with former Cardinals pitcher Kwang-hyun Kim now starring with the SSG Landers. He finished second in the league with a 2.13 ERA.

Munetaka Murakami's Amazing Season

Brandon Tew

Munetaka Murakami, like Aaron Judge, was chasing history as well this season in NPB. The 22-year-old third baseman for the Yakult Swallows is one of the best power hitters in baseball and has been dazzling fans in Japan for a few years now.

Murakami won a Central League MVP in 2021, and he backed that up with another MVP in 2022, with video game numbers during a historic season that mirrored Aaron Judge's in many ways. He won the Triple Crown with a .318 BA, 56 HRs, and 134 RBIs. He became the eighth player in league history to do so, while slashing .318/.458/.711 and capturing the slash line Triple Crown as well.

Murakami debuted in 2018, but his first full season came in 2019 when he slugged 36 homers and slashed a respectable .231/.332/.481 with an .814 OPS. That season, his major flaw was 184 strikeouts, the most strikeouts in an NPB season by a Japanese-born player.

Sporting a K% of 31.0% and a 12.5 BB% in 2019, Murakami caused damage but swung and missed a lot. Not anymore.

Season	K%	BB%
2020	22.3%	16.9%
2021	21.6%	17.2%
2022	20.9%	19.2%

Since that first full season he's cut down on his chases and done more damage on pitches in the strike zone. He's completely revamped his approach at the plate and consistently hits the ball hard and covers all parts of the zone. His 45% hard-hit rate is the best in NPB according to our Synthetic Statcast data.

Pitchers will usually start him with a slow curve or splitter to mess with his timing, then attack inside with fastballs, and righty pitchers will use cutters trying to get the ball up under his hands to limit how much he can extend his arms on his swing.

This is where hitters have to succeed with not only high exit velocities but also optimal launch angles. Murakami does the most damage on down-and-in pitches and creates loft from that part of the zone using his hands and legs in his swing.

He faces high velocity in the upper part of the zone regularly. He takes these pitches with ease, rocking back on his heels and maintaining great balance. He doesn't bail or turn away.

Teams have decided the only spot they can really attack is up near his hands. Murakami has adjusted to the league and is more selective in this area of the zone. You have to get the ball up though because he punishes mistakes that are down just slightly below the chest.

Murakami picked up steam again in July when he began the month by hitting home runs in five consecutive plate appearances, an NPB record. He then carried that momentum through an absurd August.

His Hard Hit Rate dropped in September as he chased home run history. That was understandable—Judge faced similar pressure as he also drew his fair share of walks in September.

Murakami's HR pace slowed, but he surpassed international Home Run King Sadaharu Oh's (868 HRs) record of 55 for a single season, hitting his 56th home run in his final at-bat of the regular season.

How does Murakami hit so many moon shots? His batting stance and swing remind me of Matt Olson. Both use their lower halves and a unique starting position to create downward leverage on the baseball.

With slightly more bent knees to start, his bat position and stance are almost identical to Olson's.

Olson and Murakami both use their hands out in front of their bodies as a timing mechanism and as a way to create tension and energy in the body.

Murakami relies on a medium-high leg kick to get energy stored into his back leg and hip. Olson's load is a toe-tap, but both of them load into the back hip and create a solid backside and foundation for stored energy. The bat is in nearly the same spot and angle in the middle of the load.

The biggest difference is when both batters load. For Olson, his hands end up a bit higher and farther back because of a slight turn in the front shoulder. Olson has great bat speed, which he uses to great success.

The short and compact swing by Murakami allows him to let the ball travel deeper into the zone. Murakami stays inside the ball better and pulls the ball less than Olson.

The leverage created from their attack angle downward to the ball is what helps them both hit towering home runs. Both have exceptional bat speed but also smoothness and looseness that is created by excellent rhythm at the beginning of their swings.

Timing can be an issue, with a slight susceptibility to the splitter.

Murakami also flicks off-speed pitches into the gap by delaying rotation and placing the barrel on the ball. Even though he is out of sync and into his front side on certain pitches, Murakami uses the strength in his arms and hands to lift the baseball into the outfield. This helped him not only hit for power but also a high average.

Murakami is an elite hitter. What separates him from most is how often he hits the ball hard, and his knack for being able to hit well even when his timing is off. Couple this with bat speed and strength and he's a dominating power hitter. The scary part is he's only 22 years old, and there are no signs of him slowing down. The confidence, patience, and talent Murakami displayed produced the best season of baseball NPB has ever seen.

Woo-jin An: The KBO's DeGrom

Ted Baarda

The KBO is not known for producing power pitchers. The top pitchers that the KBO has exported to North America recently can be classified as control pitchers who lack power. Hyun-jin Ryu, Kwang-hyun Kim, Josh Lindblom, and Chris Flexen are not at the top of anyone's list of power arms.

However, one KBO pitcher is breaking that mold by becoming a homegrown Korean power arm. Woo-jin An is the KBO's version of Jacob deGrom, a flamethrower who also has a feel for pitching, and whose starts are must-see events.

An has the build of a traditional starter, though he is a bit lean, listed at 6'4" and 202 lbs. At 23 years old, he could add some muscle to his frame if desired.

His bread and butter are a hard fastball paired with a hard slider. While he uses these pitches frequently, he has incorporated his other pitches (a curveball and changeup) more frequently over the last few years. He threw the fastball and slider a combined 83% of the time in 2020 when pitching out of the bullpen, but is down to 73% this year.

Woo-jin An 2022 Pitch Usage

Pitch Type	Avg. Velocity	Pitch Usage
Fastball	95 MPH	43%
Slider	88 MPH	29%
Curveball	80 MPH	17%
Changeup	83 MPH	10%

He throws the hardest fastball in the KBO, as LG Twins closer Woo-suk Go is the only other pitcher who averages 95 MPH. While his fastball averages 95, An will take some velocity off it in obvious bunt situations to save his arm and get the free out, similar to what Zack Greinke will do in similar situations. When throwing at max effort, An's fastball will sit around 95-97 MPH, with the ability to touch triple digits.

His slider is a great weapon in the KBO, as its average velocity of 88 MPH is right around the league average fastball velocity. Since he throws it so hard, it usually does not get a lot of downward break, and can look more like a cutter at times. Despite looking like a cutter, he does not use it to try to jam left-handed hitters, but when he throws it to lefties he usually tries to use it more as a backfoot slider.

He uses the slider vs. right-handers about as often as he uses his fastball, while it is his least-used pitch to left-handed hitters. The slider is also his go-to strikeout pitch against right-handers. KBO hitters as a whole are whiffing on 38% of their swings vs. his slider, with a 40% whiff rate versus right-handed hitters, and a 32% whiff rate by lefties.

In the last couple of years An has made an effort to improve his curveball and changeup, and those are showing encouraging results. His curveball has a good, downward action on it and, like his fastball, he can vary speeds on it. He has a slower version that he can throw around 75 MPH to try to steal a strike early in an at-bat, but he also can reach back for a harder mid 80s breaker when looking for a strikeout.

Having a strong fastball/slider combo at high velocity helps make his curveball more effective. Batters hit only .162 vs. the curveball this season, and are whiffing on 34% of their swings.

His changeup has been a work in progress, but that work is paying off this year. He has already thrown more changeups this season than he did in the previous two seasons combined, and it is his best swing-and-miss pitch, with hitters whiffing on 45% of swings.

His changeup does not feature a lot of drop, but it will show good fade sometimes. The key to his changeup's success is how slow he can throw it. He averages a 12 MPH velocity differential between his fastball and changeup, and with hitters gearing up to hit high velocity they end up way out in front when he throws a changeup.

He uses the changeup almost exclusively to left-handed hitters, though he has started to use it more against right-handers. He threw just 9 changeups to right-handers before the all-star break (in 17 starts), but has thrown 25 in the 13 starts since the all-star break. Eighteen percent of his pitches to lefties have been changeups, with the usage jumping to 28% with two strikes to a lefty. He has struck out 33 left-handed hitters with the changeup so far, which is far more than the 13 total changeups he threw in the 2020 season.

Woo-jin An looks like a future major league pitcher, and at 23 years old he is still fine-tuning his craft. If you had to drop a current KBO pitcher into a MLB rotation today, the best options would be Kwang-hyun Kim (who spent the last two seasons in St. Louis) or An.

His MLB prospects also look encouraging as his team, the Kiwoom Heroes, have had a tendency to allow their players to be posted. Players such as Ha-seong Kim, Byung-ho Park, and Jung-ho Kang were all Heroes before being posted. Woo-jin An will likely become eligible to be posted after the 2024 season. We're looking forward to it.

All data shown is through the end of the 2022 KBO regular season

Best in the Game

Munetaka Murakami was no doubt the dominant player in NPB this season. He led the league in Total Runs by a huge margin, finishing with 160 to Shugo Maki's 115.

In the KBO, the top player wasn't as clearcut. Jung-hoo Lee and José Pirela finished even in Total Runs with 134.

Pirela, who previously played for the Yankees, Padres, and Phillies, hit .342 with 28 home runs and a .976 OPS that exceeded league average by 253 points. Lee hit .349 with 23 home runs and a .996 OPS.

Total Runs measures Runs Created, Baserunning Runs, Pitching Runs Saved, and Defensive Runs Saved, with an adjustment based on position played.

2022 NPB Batting Leaders

Games		Plate Appearances		Batting Average		On Base Percentage	
				(minimum 443 PA)		(minimum 443 PA)	
Asamura, Hideto	143	Asamura, Hideto	633	Matsumoto, Go	.347	Murakami, Munetaka	.458
Sakakura, Shogo	143	Shimauchi, Hiroaki	613	Yoshida, Masataka	.335	Yoshida, Masataka	.447
Maru, Yoshihiro	143	Murakami, Munetaka	612	Murakami, Munetaka	.318	Matsumoto, Go	.398
Sato, Teruaki	143	Nakano, Takumu	610	Ohshima, Yohei	.314	Ohshima, Yohei	.376
Shimauchi, Hiroaki	142	Takabe, Akito	608	Sano, Keita	.306	Yamakawa, Hotaka	.375
Okabayashi, Yuki	142	Okabayashi, Yuki	608	Miyazaki, Toshiro	.300	Shimauchi, Hiroaki	.373
Murakami, Munetaka	141	Maru, Yoshihiro	607	Shimauchi, Hiroaki	.298	Maru, Yoshihiro	.370
Okamoto, Kazuma	140	Sato, Teruaki	603	Imamiya, Kenta	.296	Miyazaki, Toshiro	.365
Nagaoka, Hideki	139	Sakakura, Shogo	599	Viciedo, Dayan	.294	Asamura, Hideto	.365
3 tied with	138	Nakamura, Shogo	596	Chikamoto, Koji	.293	Sano, Keita	.362

Slugging Average		OPS		Home Runs		RBI	
(minimum 443 PA)		(minimum 443 PA)					
Murakami, Munetaka	.710	Murakami, Munetaka	1.168	Murakami, Munetaka	56	Murakami, Munetaka	134
Yamakawa, Hotaka	.578	Yoshida, Masataka	1.008	Yamakawa, Hotaka	41	Yamakawa, Hotaka	90
Yoshida, Masataka	.561	Yamakawa, Hotaka	.953	Okamoto, Kazuma	30	Yoshida, Masataka	88
Maki, Shugo	.507	Maki, Shugo	.861	Maru, Yoshihiro	27	Maki, Shugo	87
Sano, Keita	.490	Maru, Yoshihiro	.859	Asamura, Hideto	27	Ohyama, Yusuke	87
Maru, Yoshihiro	.490	Sano, Keita	.853	Yanagita, Yuki	24	Asamura, Hideto	86
Yanagita, Yuki	.485	Matsumoto, Go	.836	Polanco, Gregory	24	Sato, Teruaki	84
Miyazaki, Toshiro	.470	Miyazaki, Toshiro	.835	Maki, Shugo	24	Okamoto, Kazuma	82
Sato, Teruaki	.470	Yanagita, Yuki	.829	Nakata, Sho	24	Yanagita, Yuki	79
Ohyama, Yusuke	.469	Ohyama, Yusuke	.827	3 tied with	23	Shimauchi, Hiroaki	77

Stolen Bases		Pitches Per Plate App		Pct Pitches Taken		Swing and Miss %	
		(minimum 443 PA)		(minimum 443 PA)		(minimum 443 PA)	
Takabe, Akito	44	Nishikawa, Haruki	4.40	Kondoh, Kensuke	65.4	Sugimoto, Yutaro	34.5
Chikamoto, Koji	30	Abe, Toshiki	4.30	Yoshida, Masataka	64.3	Walker, Adam	33.6
Okabayashi, Yuki	24	Tonosaki, Shuta	4.26	Nishikawa, Haruki	63.8	Yanagita, Yuki	32.1
Shiomi, Yasutaka	24	Murakami, Munetaka	4.21	Nakamura, Akira	61.7	Yamakawa, Hotaka	32.0
Nakano, Takumu	23	Kiyomiya, Kotaro	4.20	Nakamura, Shogo	61.4	O'Grady, Brian	31.5
Shuto, Ukyo	22	McBroom, Ryan	4.18	Kobukata, Hiroto	60.9	Murakami, Munetaka	31.3
Matsumoto, Go	21	Kobukata, Hiroto	4.18	Miyazaki, Toshiro	60.4	Laird, Brandon	30.8
Kobukata, Hiroto	21	Nakamura, Shogo	4.17	Murakami, Munetaka	60.3	Soto, Neftali	30.1
Shimada, Kairi	21	Yamada, Tetsuto	4.16	Asamura, Hideto	60.3	Yamada, Tetsuto	29.9
Mimori, Masaki	20	Polanco, Gregory	4.13	Ohyama, Yusuke	59.9	Kiyomiya, Kotaro	27.4

Highest Strikeout per PA		Lowest Strikeout per PA		Highest GB/FB Ratio		Lowest GB/FB Ratio	
(minimum 443 PA)		(minimum 443 PA)		(minimum 443 PA)		(minimum 443 PA)	
O'Grady, Brian	.277	Miyazaki, Toshiro	.073	Itohara, Kento	2.54	Yamada, Tetsuto	0.55
Yamada, Tetsuto	.259	Yoshida, Masataka	.081	Ohshima, Yohei	2.51	Okamoto, Kazuma	0.62
Kiyomiya, Kotaro	.245	Kinoshita, Takuya	.082	Takabe, Akito	2.30	Kiyomiya, Kotaro	0.62
Nishikawa, Haruki	.228	Yoshikawa, Naoki	.093	Chikamoto, Koji	2.15	Yamakawa, Hotaka	0.62
Sato, Teruaki	.227	Matsumoto, Go	.094	Fukuda, Shuhei	1.92	Kinoshita, Takuya	0.64
Polanco, Gregory	.225	Itohara, Kento	.097	Nakano, Takumu	1.90	O'Grady, Brian	0.65
Asamura, Hideto	.216	Sano, Keita	.099	Matsumoto, Go	1.86	Sato, Teruaki	0.74
Tatsumi, Ryosuke	.216	Fukuda, Shuhei	.100	Okabayashi, Yuki	1.81	Polanco, Gregory	0.77
Yamakawa, Hotaka	.216	Ohshima, Yohei	.108	Yoshikawa, Naoki	1.80	Asamura, Hideto	0.77
Yanagita, Yuki	.216	Chikamoto, Koji	.109	Sano, Keita	1.73	Nakamura, Shogo	0.84

2022 NPB Pitching Leaders

Games			Games Started			Innings Pitched			Relief Innings	
Ise, Hiromu		71	Morishita, Masato		27	Yamamoto, Yoshinobu		193.0	Kizawa, Naofumi	70.1
Escobar, Edwin		70	Takahashi, Kona		26	Morishita, Masato		178.2	Ise, Hiromu	68.0
Taira, Kaima		61	Yamamoto, Yoshinobu		26	Takahashi, Kona		175.2	Escobar, Edwin	63.1
Nishiguchi, Naoto		61	Ogawa, Yasuhiro		25	Togo, Shosei		171.2	Irie, Taisei	63.0
Mizukami, Yoshinobu		60	Tanaka, Masahiro		25	Tanaka, Masahiro		163.0	Yuasa, Atsuki	58.0
Tojo, Taiki		59	Togo, Shosei		25	Aoyagi, Koyo		162.1	Taira, Kaima	57.2
Takanashi, Yuhei		59	6 tied with		24	Ohno, Yudai		157.0	Ota, Taisei	57.0
Yuasa, Atsuki		59				Itoh, Hiromi		155.2	Tojo, Taiki	56.1
3 tied with		57				Ogawa, Yasuhiro		153.1	Fujii, Kouya	56.1
						Yanagi, Yuya		153.1	Ohnishi, Hiroki	56.1

Earned Run Average (minimum 143 IP)			Quality Starts			Saves			Save Pct (minimum 20 Save Ops)	
Yamamoto, Yoshinobu		1.68	Yamamoto, Yoshinobu		22	Martinez, Raidel		39	Ota, Taisei	97.4
Katoh, Takayuki		2.01	Takahashi, Kona		21	McGough, Scott		38	Martinez, Raidel	95.1
Aoyagi, Koyo		2.05	Togo, Shosei		20	Ota, Taisei		37	Matsui, Yuki	94.1
Takahashi, Kona		2.20	Nishi, Yuki		18	Yamasaki, Yasuaki		37	Yamasaki, Yasuaki	92.5
Ohno, Yudai		2.46	Katoh, Takayuki		18	Matsui, Yuki		32	Masuda, Tatsushi	91.2
Togo, Shosei		2.62	Aoyagi, Koyo		18	Masuda, Tatsushi		31	Kuribayashi, Ryoji	91.2
Ogasawara, Shinnosuke		2.76	Morishita, Masato		17	Kuribayashi, Ryoji		31	McGough, Scott	88.4
Ogawa, Yasuhiro		2.82	5 tied with		16	Iwazaki, Suguru		28	Hirano, Yoshihisa	87.5
Itoh, Hiromi		2.95				Hirano, Yoshihisa		28	Moinelo, Livan	85.7
Sugano, Tomoyuki		3.12				Masuda, Naoya		25	Iwazaki, Suguru	84.8

Pitches Per Start (minimum 20 GS)			Most Pitches in a Game			Pitches Per Batter (minimum 120 IP)			Strikeouts Per 9 IP (minimum 120 IP)	
Togo, Shosei		112.2	Imai, Tatsuya		144	Katoh, Takayuki		3.49	Sasaki, Roki	12.04
Yamamoto, Yoshinobu		111.9	Ojima, Kazuya		139	Itoh, Masashi		3.63	Senga, Koudai	9.75
Imanaga, Shota		108.9	Togo, Shosei		138	Ishikawa, Ayumu		3.68	Yamamoto, Yoshinobu	9.56
Takahashi, Kona		108.6	Sugano, Tomoyuki		135	Sasaki, Roki		3.68	Ogasawara, Shinnosuke	8.71
Uwasawa, Naoyuki		107.4	Yamamoto, Yoshinobu		135	Morishita, Masato		3.71	Imanaga, Shota	8.27
Ogasawara, Shinnosuke		107.1	Ohsera, Daichi		135	Yamaoka, Taisuke		3.73	Togo, Shosei	8.07
Aoyagi, Koyo		106.4	Yanagi, Yuya		135	Ohno, Yudai		3.75	Ohnuki, Shinichi	7.77
Itoh, Hiromi		106.3	Itoh, Hiromi		135	Nishi, Yuki		3.75	Kuri, Aren	7.76
Yanagi, Yuya		105.9	3 tied with		134	Tanaka, Masahiro		3.77	Miyagi, Hiroya	7.71
Morishita, Masato		105.0				Ohsera, Daichi		3.83	Kishi, Takayuki	7.53

Strikeouts / Walks Ratio (minimum 120 IP)			Home Runs Per Nine IP (minimum 120 IP)			Opponent Batting Average (minimum 120 IP)			Opponent OPS (minimum 120 IP)	
Katoh, Takayuki		8.91	Yamamoto, Yoshinobu		0.28	Sasaki, Roki		.177	Sasaki, Roki	.495
Sasaki, Roki		7.52	Itoh, Hiromi		0.29	Yamamoto, Yoshinobu		.198	Yamamoto, Yoshinobu	.517
Yamamoto, Yoshinobu		4.88	Aoyagi, Koyo		0.39	Imanaga, Shota		.204	Aoyagi, Koyo	.553
Imanaga, Shota		4.55	Ohno, Yudai		0.40	Senga, Koudai		.208	Senga, Koudai	.556
Miyagi, Hiroya		4.23	Yamaoka, Taisuke		0.42	Aoyagi, Koyo		.215	Katoh, Takayuki	.568
Kishi, Takayuki		4.21	Senga, Koudai		0.44	Ohno, Yudai		.222	Imanaga, Shota	.577
Tanaka, Masahiro		4.20	Takahashi, Kona		0.46	Matsumoto, Wataru		.223	Ohno, Yudai	.579
Itoh, Masashi		4.18	Nishi, Yuki		0.49	Kishi, Takayuki		.224	Nishi, Yuki	.600
Aoyagi, Koyo		4.13	Sasaki, Roki		0.49	Katoh, Takayuki		.226	Itoh, Hiromi	.607
Sugano, Tomoyuki		4.00	Katoh, Takayuki		0.55	Uwasawa, Naoyuki		.230	Itoh, Masashi	.612

2022 KBO Batting Leaders

Games		Plate Appearances		Batting Average (minimum 446 PA)		On Base Percentage (minimum 446 PA)	
Park, Hae-min	144	Na, Sung-bum	649	Lee, Jung-hoo	.349	Lee, Jung-hoo	.421
Bae, Jung-dae	144	Tauchman, Michael	648	Pirela, Jose	.342	Pirela, Jose	.411
Na, Sung-bum	144	Choi, Ji-hoon	640	Park, Kun-woo	.336	Park, Kun-woo	.408
Choi, Ji-hoon	144	Park, Hae-min	636	Lee, Dae-ho	.331	Na, Sung-bum	.402
Tauchman, Michael	144	Pirela, Jose	630	Na, Sung-bum	.320	Hong, Chang-ki	.390
Song, Sung-mun	142	Lee, Jung-hoo	627	Kim, Hye-seong	.318	Choi, Jeong	.386
Lee, Jung-hoo	142	Son, Ah-seop	617	Moon, Bo-gyeong	.315	Choo, Shin-soo	.382
Oh, Ji-hwan	142	Kim, Hyun-soo	604	Brito, Socrates	.311	Moon, Bo-gyeong	.382
Lee, Dae-ho	142	Song, Sung-mun	601	Fernandez, Jose Miguel	.309	Yang, Eui-ji	.380
3 tied with	141	Jung, Eun-won	601	Cho, Yong-ho	.308	Lee, Dae-ho	.379

Slugging Average (minimum 446 PA)		OPS (minimum 446 PA)		Home Runs		RBI	
Lee, Jung-hoo	.575	Lee, Jung-hoo	.996	Park, Byung-ho	35	Lee, Jung-hoo	113
Pirela, Jose	.565	Pirela, Jose	.976	Pirela, Jose	28	Pirela, Jose	109
Park, Byung-ho	.559	Na, Sung-bum	.910	Choi, Jeong	26	Kim, Hyun-soo	106
Na, Sung-bum	.508	Park, Byung-ho	.909	Oh, Ji-hwan	25	Lee, Dae-ho	101
Choi, Jeong	.505	Choi, Jeong	.891	Lee, Jung-hoo	23	Han, Yoo-seom	100
Lee, Dae-ho	.502	Lee, Dae-ho	.881	Lee, Dae-ho	23	Park, Byung-ho	98
Brito, Socrates	.494	Park, Kun-woo	.867	Kim, Jae-hwan	23	Na, Sung-bum	97
Oh, Jae-il	.491	Yang, Eui-ji	.860	Kim, Hyun-soo	23	Yang, Eui-ji	94
Yang, Eui-ji	.480	Han, Yoo-seom	.851	4 tied with	21	Oh, Jae-il	94
Han, Yoo-seom	.478	Kim, Hyun-soo	.848			Hwang, Dae-in	91

Stolen Bases		Pitches Per Plate App (minimum 446 PA)		Pct Pitches Taken (minimum 446 PA)		Swing and Miss % (minimum 446 PA)	
Park, Chan-ho	42	Jung, Eun-won	4.35	Kim, Jun-wan	66.4	Park, Byung-ho	34.3
Kim, Hye-seong	34	Choi, Hyoung-woo	4.24	Jung, Eun-won	63.3	Kim, Jae-hwan	32.9
Choi, Ji-hoon	31	Kim, Tae-yean	4.13	Choi, Jae-hoon	61.5	Oh, Jae-il	30.2
Kim, Ji-chan	25	Bae, Jung-dae	4.12	Park, Seong-han	61.1	Kim, Whee-jip	29.3
Park, Hae-min	24	Hong, Chang-ki	4.10	An, Chi-hong	61.0	Han, Yoo-seom	28.7
Shim, Woo-jun	23	Choo, Shin-soo	4.09	Heo, Kyoung-min	60.7	Kim, In-hwan	28.5
Jo, Soo-haeng	22	Oh, Ji-hwan	4.09	Hong, Chang-ki	60.5	Ha, Ju-suk	28.3
Park, Min-woo	21	Han, Yoo-seom	4.04	Lee, Jung-hoo	60.1	Park, Dong-won	28.2
Oh, Ji-hwan	20	Park, Seong-han	4.02	Kim, Ji-chan	59.8	Yang, Suk-hwan	27.9
Ha, Ju-suk	20	Park, Hae-min	4.02	Kim, Hyeon-joon	59.7	Choi, Jeong	27.9

Highest Strikeout per PA (minimum 446 PA)		Lowest Strikeout per PA (minimum 446 PA)		Highest GB/FB Ratio (minimum 446 PA)		Lowest GB/FB Ratio (minimum 446 PA)	
Park, Byung-ho	.269	Lee, Jung-hoo	.051	Hong, Chang-ki	2.64	Choi, Jeong	0.55
Ha, Ju-suk	.261	Kim, Sun-bin	.080	Jung, Soo-bin	2.55	Yang, Suk-hwan	0.61
Kim, Jae-hwan	.257	Heo, Kyoung-min	.081	Kim, Hye-seong	2.41	Oh, Jae-il	0.65
Han, Yoo-seom	.251	Fernandez, Jose Miguel	.082	Ha, Ju-suk	2.32	Park, Byung-ho	0.69
Oh, Jae-il	.248	An, Chi-hong	.093	Ryu, Ji-hyuk	2.26	Puig, Yasiel	0.75
No, Jin-hyuk	.233	Yang, Eui-ji	.094	Son, Ah-seop	2.11	Yang, Eui-ji	0.78
Kim, Tae-yean	.228	Lee, Dae-ho	.095	Kim, Sun-bin	2.10	Kim, Jae-hwan	0.95
Yang, Suk-hwan	.226	Kim, Hyun-soo	.103	Park, Seong-han	2.10	Choo, Shin-soo	0.98
Bae, Jung-dae	.219	Song, Sung-mun	.108	Cho, Yong-ho	2.08	Choi, Hyoung-woo	0.99
Na, Sung-bum	.211	Park, Chan-ho	.118	Fernandez, Jose Miguel	1.94	Hwang, Dae-in	0.99

2022 KBO Pitching Leaders

Games	
Kim, Beom-su	78
Kim, Min-su	76
Lee, Jun-young	75
Koo, Seung-min	73
Kim, Young-kyu	72
Kim, Yu-yeong	68
Kim, Myeong-sin	68
Choi, Jun-yong	68
Seo, Jin-yong	68
Won, Jong-hyan	68

Games Started	
Rucinski, Drew	31
Barnes, Charlie	31
Yang, Hyeon-jong	30
An, Woo-jin	30
Choi, Won-joon	30
Jokisch, Eric	30
Suarez, Albert	29
Stock, Robert	29
Despaigne, Odrisamer	29
Kim, Min-woo	29

Innings Pitched	
An, Woo-jin	196.0
Rucinski, Drew	193.2
Barnes, Charlie	186.1
Jokisch, Eric	185.1
Font, Wilmer	184.0
Ko, Young-pyo	182.1
Yang, Hyeon-jong	175.1
Suarez, Albert	173.2
Kim, Kwang-hyun	173.1
So, Hyeong-jun	171.1

Relief Innings	
Kim, Min-su	80.2
Kim, Myeong-sin	79.2
Jeong, Cheol-won	72.2
Choi, Jun-yong	71.0
Seo, Jin-yong	67.1
Kim, Jae-yoon	66.1
Kim, Young-kyu	66.0
Kim, Beom-su	66.0
Choi, Min-jun	65.1
Jang, Si-hwan	63.2

Earned Run Average (minimum 144 IP)	
An, Woo-jin	2.11
Kim, Kwang-hyun	2.13
Plutko, Adam	2.39
Suarez, Albert	2.49
Kelly, Casey	2.54
Jokisch, Eric	2.57
Font, Wilmer	2.69
Rucinski, Drew	2.97
Buchanan, David	3.04
So, Hyeong-jun	3.05

Quality Starts	
An, Woo-jin	24
Rucinski, Drew	22
Jokisch, Eric	22
Buchanan, David	21
Ko, Young-pyo	21
Font, Wilmer	20
Kim, Kwang-hyun	19
Kelly, Casey	19
Suarez, Albert	19
3 tied with	18

Saves	
Go, Woo-suk	42
Kim, Jae-yoon	33
Jung, Hai-young	32
Oh, Seung-hwan	31
Lee, Yong-chan	22
Seo, Jin-yong	21
Hong, Geon-hui	18
Kim, Won-jung	17
Kim, Taek-hyeong	17
2 tied with	14

Save Pct (minimum 20 Save Ops)	
Go, Woo-suk	95.5
Jung, Hai-young	88.9
Kim, Won-jung	85.0
Kim, Jae-yoon	84.6
Lee, Yong-chan	84.6
Seo, Jin-yong	84.0
Hong, Geon-hui	81.8
Oh, Seung-hwan	81.6
Kim, Taek-hyeong	73.9

Pitches Per Start (minimum 20 GS)	
Suarez, Albert	101.0
Buchanan, David	100.2
An, Woo-jin	100.1
Stock, Robert	99.2
Font, Wilmer	98.9
Won, Tae-in	98.9
Despaigne, Odrisamer	97.5
Jokisch, Eric	97.1
Rucinski, Drew	95.9
Plutko, Adam	95.5

Most Pitches in a Game	
Despaigne, Odrisamer	121
Stock, Robert	120
Font, Wilmer	119
Suarez, Albert	119
Buchanan, David	119
Stock, Robert	119
Gwak, Been	119
Lee, Eui-lee	118
Jokisch, Eric	117
3 tied with	116

Pitches Per Batter (minimum 120 IP)	
Ko, Young-pyo	3.45
So, Hyeong-jun	3.55
Baek, Jung-hyun	3.69
Lee, In-bok	3.71
Rucinski, Drew	3.73
Barnes, Charlie	3.74
Im, Gi-yeong	3.75
Buchanan, David	3.77
Kelly, Casey	3.79
Kim, Kwang-hyun	3.80

Strikeouts Per 9 IP (minimum 120 IP)	
An, Woo-jin	10.29
Lee, Eui-lee	9.41
Rucinski, Drew	9.02
Um, Sang-back	8.91
Gwak, Been	8.41
Park, Se-woong	8.35
Font, Wilmer	8.32
Kelly, Casey	8.28
Plutko, Adam	8.28
Suarez, Albert	8.24

Strikeouts / Walks Ratio (minimum 120 IP)	
Ko, Young-pyo	6.78
Rucinski, Drew	5.71
Font, Wilmer	5.00
Jokisch, Eric	4.67
Park, Se-woong	4.56
Nolin, Sean	4.50
Kelly, Casey	4.37
An, Woo-jin	4.07
Plutko, Adam	3.92
Won, Tae-in	3.42

Home Runs Per Nine IP (minimum 120 IP)	
An, Woo-jin	0.18
Ko, Young-pyo	0.35
Suarez, Albert	0.36
Barnes, Charlie	0.39
Jokisch, Eric	0.39
So, Hyeong-jun	0.42
Lee, In-bok	0.43
Park, Se-woong	0.46
Stock, Robert	0.49
Nolin, Sean	0.51

Opponent Batting Average (minimum 120 IP)	
An, Woo-jin	.188
Font, Wilmer	.207
Plutko, Adam	.210
Lee, Eui-lee	.221
Kim, Kwang-hyun	.222
Suarez, Albert	.232
Kelly, Casey	.232
Kim, Min-woo	.237
Um, Sang-back	.239
So, Hyeong-jun	.243

Opponent OPS (minimum 120 IP)	
An, Woo-jin	.518
Plutko, Adam	.570
Font, Wilmer	.577
Kim, Kwang-hyun	.578
Kelly, Casey	.583
Suarez, Albert	.583
Jokisch, Eric	.613
So, Hyeong-jun	.614
Nolin, Sean	.628
Barnes, Charlie	.641

Predicting Injury Risk

Sarah Thompson

One of the most valuable things a good player can do is figure out a way to stay on the field (or exclusively in the batter's box). In addition to his accomplishments from an offensive standpoint, one of Aaron Judge's most valuable attributes this season was staying on the field, playing his first season without a trip to the Injured List since 2017. Not only was playing a full season valuable to the Yankees as a team, but also to Aaron Judge himself as he begins free agency this coming offseason.

Which is all to say—injuries and missed time have a huge impact on the game. It'd be nice if we can try to expect the unexpected, and maybe measures can be taken to prevent injuries if they're more than likely to happen.

In last year's handbook, we projected the pitchers most likely to be injured to be José Alvarado, Ryne Stanek, and Max Scherzer.

Alvarado definitely passed the smell test for me on that one. He throws triple digits regularly and is no stranger to the Injured List. But, like most batters who see his cutter, we whiffed on that one. Alvarado had his first IL-stint-free season since 2018, and in the second half of the season, earned the reputation as one of the most dominant relievers in the game.

Scherzer is a different story. We projected him to have the third highest likelihood of injury among pitchers, and he took two trips to the IL due to an oblique injury. Those injuries are especially troubling because those muscles are tough to rest—it's not as simple as, say, ensuring you don't do anything with your throwing arm for a few weeks—and oblique strength often goes hand-in-hand with a pitcher's ability to generate velocity. That combination usually means long IL stints, in addition to recurrence.

In all, 7 of the 11 pitchers that we projected as most likely to have an injury severe enough to hit the IL ultimately did.

For batters, our top three candidates were Alcides Escobar, Kolten Wong, and Xander Bogaerts. And boy were we wrong about Bogaerts.

Bogaerts played in 150 games, the most since he played 155 in 2019. But he's still an interesting study—he didn't hit the IL this year, but most games missed were due to some sort of injury (rather than scheduled rest). He left at least four games early due to injury (mostly hamstring or back issues) and was taken out of the starting lineup on four other occasions for lingering back or hamstring issues.

And for that reason (among others), he's the most likely position player to sustain an IL-worthy injury next season.

Since 2021, Bogaerts boasts the second highest number of sliding, diving, and jumping plays at 150. Sacrificing the body to make an out is great from a team-player, win-at-all-costs perspective, but not from a health perspective. Given that he's only made outs on 10 of his last 72 diving plays, it may be better for all involved if that particular approach started to taper a bit.

So where are we getting these projections from? The backbone of this process is our comprehensive injury database. We log nearly everything deemed significant to a player's physical health—not only whatever we can glean from media reports, but even something as seemingly inconsequential as a batter fouling a ball off his body or a pitcher being struck by a batted ball.

We take that injury data, factor in a player's workload, position, body type, and playing style to figure a likelihood of injury worthy of an IL stint or missing 10 days of time.

For more info on the model, its inputs, and the kinds of insights we've already gained, scan the QR code below with your phone to check out our presentation from the 2021 SABR Analytics Conference.

Let's dive more into injury candidates for next season.

Pitchers with the Highest Predicted Injury Risk Entering 2023

Rank	Player
1	Hunter Greene
2	Seranthony Dominguez
3	Yu Darvish
4	David Price
T-5	Brusdar Graterol
T-5	Robert Suarez
T-7	Max Scherzer
T-7	Ryan Tepera
T-9	Aroldis Chapman
T-9	Albert Abreu

The pitcher list shouldn't be shocking. As much as we love to see high heat clips on Pitching Ninja, velocity is a reliable predictor of future injury. Hunter Greene threw the second-most pitches of at least 100 MPH among all pitchers in 2022, but threw more than twice as many total pitches as the lone pitcher ahead of him.

Seranthony Dominguez also touches triple digits, but in a relief role, and suffered from some late-season tendonitis in his first season back from Tommy John surgery.

Flamethrower Aroldis Chapman made the top 5 last year, and after sustaining injuries this season, makes the top 10 again.

Hitters with the Highest Predicted Injury Risk Entering 2023

Rank	Player
1	Xander Bogaerts
2	Justin Turner
3	Josh Naylor
4	Harold Ramirez
T-5	Jean Segura
T-5	Gavin Sheets
7	Carlos Santana
T-8	Josh Harrison
T-8	Jonathan Schoop
10	Kolten Wong

Seven of the top 10 likeliest batters to sustain an IL-worthy injury in 2023 spent time on the IL in 2022, which goes to show how big of a role injury history, especially recent injury, plays in predicting future injury.

You'll notice the list is 40% second basemen or shortstops—this is where the position someone plays pokes its head into the projection.

We already discussed Bogaerts, so let's look at #2. Justin Turner doesn't have the riskiest playing style, but he is the oldest player to have at least 50 diving, sliding, or jumping plays in the past 3 seasons. He has 80 of those, and 52 of those are dives, which isn't the most optimal makeup.

Baserunning

Mark Simon

Diamondbacks first baseman Christian Walker was asked for one thing to watch with his team as it played spoiler in the final month of the season.

He could have easily picked Zac Gallen, who was in the middle of an amazing 44⅓ inning scoreless streak. But he didn't. He went in a different direction.

"Josh Rojas and his baseball IQ," Walker said. "It's incredible. The things he sees, the things he thinks about. Not elite speed but he has a lot of stolen bases and a lot of plays that aren't close plays at all."

Rojas finished tied for second in our Net Baserunning Gain stat this season, +39.

Net Gain Leaders 2022 Season

Player	Team	Net Gain
Tommy Edman	Cardinals	+51
Bobby Witt Jr.	Royals	+39
Josh Rojas	Diamondbacks	+39
Marcus Semien	Rangers	+36
Jon Berti	Marlins	+35
Geraldo Perdomo	Diamondbacks	+33
Jake McCarthy	Diamondbacks	+30
Jake Cronenworth	Padres	+29
Steven Kwan	Guardians	+29
Adley Rutschman	Orioles	+27
Jorge Mateo	Orioles	+27
Kyle Tucker	Astros	+27
Nicky Lopez	Royals	+27

Rojas had two things going for him. One was the stolen base numbers that Walker cited (23-of-26). The other was that he scored from second on a single 21 times in 25 opportunities. He was 84% successful in something that normally yields about a 60% success rate from season-to-season.

Rojas wasn't the only one of the Diamondbacks with impressive baserunning numbers. Two of his teammates finished in the top 10 in Net Gain. Geraldo Perdomo was sixth (+33). Jake McCarthy finished seventh (+30).

The Diamondbacks finished 74-88 this season but they were high achievers in our baserunning metrics. They finished with 162 Net Gain, the second-best total by a team since SIS began tracking that stat in 2004. Only the 2010 Rays (+197) finished with a larger Net Gain.

Net Gain Leaders – Teams Since 2004

Team	Net Gain
2010 Rays	+197
2022 Diamondbacks	+162
2012 A's	+144
2010 A's	+144
2015 Rangers	+142
2011 Rangers	+133
2007 Phillies	+132
2019 Diamondbacks	+125

Arizona excelled in all aspects of the running game. The Diamondbacks had the second-highest success rate of having a runner go first to third on a single and were third-best at going second to home on a single. They also ranked No. 1 in MLB with 193 combined bases taken on wild pitches, passed balls, sacrifice flies, and defensive indifference. They also had the fifth-fewest baserunning outs and were fifth in SB Gain.

We don't want to shortchange the overall player leader, Tommy Edman, who finished at +51 Net Gain, with a near even split between stolen bases (+26, second-highest) and baserunning (+25, fourth). Edman's baserunning helped make him one of the most valuable players in MLB this season. He was the only player to finish in the Top 5 in Net Gain in both 2021 and 2022.

2022 Baserunning

Player	1st to 3rd Moved	Chances	2nd to Home Moved	Chances	1st to Home Moved	Chances	Bases Taken	Out Adv	Doubled Off	BR Outs	GDP	GDP Opps	BR Gain	SB Gain	Net Gain
Abrams, CJ	3	10	4	9	3	3	6	0	2	2	5	58	-1	-1	-2
Abreu, Jose	15	46	16	23	4	12	16	1	2	3	19	125	-3	0	-3
Acuna Jr., Ronald	18	27	13	17	5	6	20	4	0	4	8	78	+19	+7	+26
Adames, Willy	8	15	5	11	6	6	8	1	0	1	11	131	+9	+2	+11
Adell, Jo	2	7	2	5	2	3	1	1	0	1	6	61	-4	0	-4
Aguilar, Jesus	3	15	5	9	0	3	8	4	0	4	8	93	-9	+1	-8
Albies, Ozzie	3	10	4	5	1	2	6	0	0	0	0	36	+9	-7	+2
Alcantara, Sergio	1	4	1	3	3	4	8	0	0	0	6	36	+4	-3	+1
Alfaro, Jorge	1	5	5	7	1	3	5	2	1	3	5	54	-5	+1	-4
Allen, Nick	4	12	9	13	1	1	9	1	1	2	5	53	+4	-1	+3
Almora Jr., Albert	8	15	2	5	1	3	4	1	1	2	9	47	-6	-1	-7
Alonso, Pete	11	35	14	23	4	11	17	3	1	4	17	154	-2	+3	+1
Altuve, Jose	12	42	13	21	1	8	21	11	3	15	13	71	-38	+16	-22
Alvarez, Yordan	7	26	11	14	5	10	18	2	0	2	12	113	+9	-1	+8
Anderson, Brian	3	21	7	11	2	8	11	1	1	2	7	79	-1	+1	0
Anderson, Tim	8	19	8	10	5	7	7	2	0	3	10	53	-3	+13	+10
Andrus, Elvis	17	26	10	11	4	6	16	2	2	4	11	85	+11	+10	+21
Aquino, Aristides	2	7	3	5	1	1	6	1	1	2	1	52	+3	-4	-1
Arcia, Orlando	2	9	6	9	3	4	6	4	0	4	7	37	-10	0	-10
Arenado, Nolan	5	20	12	19	5	6	14	1	1	2	15	119	+3	-1	+2
Arozarena, Randy	6	24	14	16	1	3	12	9	1	11	17	135	-26	+8	-18
Arraez, Luis	14	45	13	25	3	7	16	2	2	4	6	93	+1	-4	-3
Arroyo, Christian	3	15	4	10	2	5	5	2	0	2	7	56	-8	+3	-5
Azocar, Jose	7	14	6	11	2	3	6	2	0	2	6	42	-1	-7	-8
Baddoo, Akil	7	10	6	8	4	4	6	0	0	0	2	38	+14	-3	+11
Bader, Harrison	6	13	12	15	1	2	7	1	1	2	4	54	+5	+11	+16
Baez, Javier	9	18	11	12	6	10	13	4	3	7	13	123	-4	+5	+1
Barnes, Austin	4	12	2	6	1	5	6	2	1	3	5	39	-8	0	-8
Barnhart, Tucker	2	20	4	8	0	2	7	1	2	3	7	54	-11	0	-11
Bart, Joey	2	14	3	7	2	3	9	1	1	2	5	44	-2	0	-2
Bell, Josh	11	42	13	23	2	9	18	4	3	7	22	129	-22	-2	-24
Bellinger, Cody	4	12	7	13	5	9	15	1	0	1	7	99	+12	+8	+20
Belt, Brandon	5	8	2	5	1	5	6	0	0	0	9	59	+1	+1	+2
Benintendi, Andrew	11	31	6	13	5	10	20	4	0	4	7	101	+7	+2	+9
Berti, Jon	7	15	6	9	3	5	13	1	2	3	6	60	+4	+31	+35
Bethancourt, Christian	3	11	3	5	2	7	3	0	0	0	6	48	-2	+3	+1
Betts, Mookie	5	29	22	33	5	13	19	1	2	3	8	101	+6	+8	+14
Bichette, Bo	6	38	16	22	2	4	11	2	2	4	21	141	-15	-3	-18
Biggio, Cavan	5	17	5	12	4	5	5	0	0	0	2	57	+6	+2	+8
Blackmon, Charlie	10	32	5	12	5	8	11	1	1	2	10	127	+3	+2	+5
Bleday, J.J.	1	6	3	5	1	1	5	0	0	0	5	46	+3	+2	+5
Bogaerts, Xander	14	30	15	19	9	18	21	2	0	2	14	156	+21	+4	+25
Bohm, Alec	13	50	8	14	3	7	16	1	0	1	18	129	+1	-4	-3
Bradley Jr., Jackie	5	12	4	9	1	6	7	0	0	0	5	72	+5	-4	+1
Brantley, Michael	2	13	4	6	0	5	8	2	0	2	1	49	0	-1	-1
Bregman, Alex	12	38	11	16	3	10	11	3	2	5	18	151	-12	-3	-15
Bride, Jonah	2	9	3	7	0	2	9	0	0	0	4	28	+4	+1	+5
Brosseau, Mike	1	8	2	2	1	3	4	0	0	0	0	24	+4	+2	+6
Brown, Seth	7	13	8	12	3	6	15	1	0	2	7	114	+14	+7	+21
Bryant, Kris	3	8	7	8	2	4	1	1	1	2	7	39	-6	0	-6
Burger, Jake	0	10	5	5	1	3	3	0	0	0	7	42	-2	0	-2
Buxton, Byron	3	19	9	11	3	4	10	1	0	1	0	75	+13	+6	+19
Cabrera, Miguel	0	17	1	4	2	8	6	3	0	3	11	73	-18	+1	-17
Cabrera, Oswaldo	2	7	3	7	0	0	3	1	0	1	1	28	-1	-1	-2
Calhoun, Kole	5	15	5	10	0	2	8	2	0	2	6	74	0	-1	-1
Camargo, Johan	2	7	0	0	1	1	3	1	0	1	1	32	+2	0	+2
Candelario, Jeimer	6	19	8	13	2	8	8	1	2	3	9	82	-6	-2	-8
Canha, Mark	6	33	14	19	3	5	8	2	0	4	3	110	-1	+1	0
Caratini, Victor	2	15	0	4	1	2	9	1	1	2	11	65	-8	0	-8
Carlson, Dylan	10	21	11	12	2	3	15	1	0	1	6	83	+19	+1	+20
Carpenter, Matt	2	5	3	6	0	2	5	1	0	1	2	29	+1	0	+1
Casali, Curt	2	8	3	5	1	2	3	0	0	0	1	29	+3	0	+3
Castellanos, Nick	2	23	8	19	4	13	16	3	1	4	15	95	-15	+5	-10

489

2022 Baserunning

Player	1st to 3rd Moved	Chances	2nd to Home Moved	Chances	1st to Home Moved	Chances	Bases Taken	Out Adv	Doubled Off	BR Outs	GDP	GDP Opps	BR Gain	SB Gain	Net Gain
Castillo, Diego	1	6	4	5	1	2	7	0	1	1	7	52	+1	-1	0
Castro, Harold	8	23	5	9	3	6	8	1	0	1	5	66	+5	-2	+3
Castro, Rodolfo	4	7	4	7	1	1	5	1	0	1	6	50	+2	-1	+1
Castro, Willi	5	14	7	11	6	9	12	1	2	3	4	66	+6	+1	+7
Cave, Jake	2	6	2	3	1	1	3	0	0	0	2	40	+5	+2	+7
Celestino, Gilberto	3	23	4	10	1	3	9	3	2	5	13	65	-22	+2	-20
Chang, Yu	6	8	2	5	1	2	4	0	0	0	5	35	+4	-2	+2
Chapman, Matt	13	31	9	17	3	5	13	0	1	1	7	129	+15	-2	+13
Chavis, Michael	2	16	5	8	1	3	7	0	1	1	4	89	+3	-1	+2
Chirinos, Robinson	1	7	1	4	0	1	0	1	0	1	4	37	-8	+1	-7
Chisholm Jr., Jazz	6	9	6	7	2	4	7	1	0	1	0	40	+12	+2	+14
Choi, Ji-Man	2	17	7	11	2	4	7	4	0	4	3	72	-6	0	-6
Clement, Ernie	3	11	2	4	1	1	3	0	0	0	3	33	+2	-2	0
Contreras, William	3	18	10	13	1	8	9	5	0	5	5	59	-11	+2	-9
Contreras, Willson	6	21	8	15	4	12	18	5	1	6	14	90	-11	0	-11
Cooper, Garrett	3	18	8	10	1	4	8	1	0	1	6	61	0	0	0
Cordero, Franchy	4	14	5	5	1	3	8	0	0	0	1	56	+12	+2	+14
Correa, Carlos	9	34	9	14	1	9	16	3	2	5	18	125	-13	-2	-15
Crawford, Brandon	4	26	13	15	3	8	13	0	1	1	12	99	+4	-1	+3
Crawford, J.P.	12	40	7	17	4	6	18	0	0	0	11	89	+9	-1	+8
Cron, C.J.	4	24	5	17	6	8	17	0	0	0	16	133	+4	0	+4
Cronenworth, Jake	11	43	9	11	10	15	16	0	0	0	2	132	+26	+3	+29
Cruz, Nelson	10	33	10	14	1	6	17	3	0	3	16	108	-1	+4	+3
Cruz, Oneil	8	14	5	6	5	5	10	2	2	4	3	71	+8	+2	+10
Culberson, Charlie	2	5	1	4	2	2	6	0	1	1	5	32	0	-4	-4
d'Arnaud, Travis	8	21	3	9	3	10	8	2	1	4	12	74	-14	0	-14
Dalbec, Bobby	5	14	1	7	1	2	9	1	0	1	5	71	+4	+3	+7
Davis, J.D.	5	23	7	12	0	4	11	0	1	1	13	70	-5	-1	-6
Daza, Yonathan	16	31	10	16	5	11	10	0	0	0	12	79	+9	-6	+3
De La Cruz, Bryan	4	19	4	9	0	0	10	2	0	2	8	56	-4	+4	0
DeJong, Paul	2	8	4	8	0	0	2	1	0	1	2	43	-1	-1	-2
Devers, Rafael	10	37	9	22	1	8	17	1	3	4	14	113	-10	+1	-9
Diaz, Aledmys	2	12	4	11	2	4	4	2	1	3	7	64	-12	-1	-13
Diaz, Elias	4	20	4	11	0	2	9	1	2	3	8	65	-10	-2	-12
Diaz, Yandy	18	43	8	23	6	12	23	9	4	13	10	80	-23	-3	-26
Dickerson, Corey	6	13	3	4	0	2	8	2	1	3	4	54	0	0	0
Donaldson, Josh	3	15	2	9	2	6	11	3	0	3	13	104	-10	-2	-12
Donovan, Brendan	17	35	10	14	5	13	11	3	0	4	8	70	+1	-4	-3
Dozier, Hunter	4	17	6	11	1	5	10	8	1	9	14	92	-28	-2	-30
Drury, Brandon	4	24	14	21	0	6	12	2	0	2	8	122	+2	-4	-2
Dubon, Mauricio	2	5	6	11	4	4	6	1	0	1	7	59	+2	-4	-2
Duffy, Matt	6	14	3	5	0	3	7	1	1	2	6	47	-2	0	-2
Duran, Ezequiel	4	14	6	13	0	0	12	3	0	3	3	48	+1	+2	+3
Duran, Jarren	3	10	3	8	1	2	9	1	0	1	1	32	+5	+5	+10
Duvall, Adam	5	13	10	13	0	4	9	1	0	1	2	61	+10	-4	+6
Edman, Tommy	14	30	14	19	3	4	26	1	1	2	10	109	+25	+26	+51
Engel, Adam	3	13	6	10	1	3	18	1	1	2	2	48	+12	+4	+16
Escobar, Eduardo	8	25	9	15	2	7	8	0	0	0	4	125	+13	-4	+9
Espinal, Santiago	4	21	9	11	4	9	12	1	1	2	12	93	0	-6	-6
Estrada, Thairo	9	31	10	18	5	12	25	1	1	2	10	113	+15	+9	+24
Farmer, Kyle	5	19	12	18	4	10	12	3	1	4	20	104	-14	-2	-16
Fletcher, David	3	12	0	1	1	3	5	1	0	1	6	37	-3	+1	-2
Flores, Wilmer	8	39	4	13	1	6	18	4	1	5	7	117	-6	0	-6
Fortes, Nick	1	7	8	9	2	3	6	2	0	2	5	37	-1	-1	-2
Fraley, Jake	4	12	8	9	2	3	11	2	0	2	1	36	+10	+2	+12
France, Ty	6	26	6	12	2	8	25	0	2	2	18	118	+4	0	+4
Franco, Maikel	1	16	7	12	2	6	7	2	0	2	18	80	-16	+1	-15
Franco, Wander	8	21	6	10	2	3	9	1	2	3	5	82	+3	+8	+11
Frazier, Adam	7	27	11	20	6	11	19	1	0	1	15	118	+8	-1	+7
Freeman, Freddie	15	47	11	19	7	12	22	4	0	4	6	154	+15	+7	+22
Friedl, T.J.	2	5	1	5	3	4	6	2	3	5	3	30	-11	+3	-8
Gallo, Joey	5	20	2	10	1	3	10	3	0	3	0	78	+1	+3	+4
Gamel, Ben	4	17	5	8	3	8	13	4	2	6	5	65	-8	+3	-5
Garcia, Adolis	10	23	15	17	6	11	12	2	2	4	9	125	+8	+13	+21

2022 Baserunning

Player	1st to 3rd Moved	Chances	2nd to Home Moved	Chances	1st to Home Moved	Chances	Bases Taken	Out Adv	Doubled Off	BR Outs	GDP	GDP Opps	BR Gain	SB Gain	Net Gain
Garcia, Avisail	6	18	3	6	3	11	8	0	1	1	12	52	-6	+4	-2
Garcia, Leury	7	19	7	12	4	6	10	1	0	1	6	44	+6	+2	+8
Garcia, Luis	3	13	5	10	1	1	4	1	1	2	5	72	-4	-5	-9
Garver, Mitch	3	11	2	3	2	3	4	0	0	0	3	32	+3	-1	+2
Gimenez, Andres	11	28	10	19	5	5	18	3	0	3	9	100	+10	+14	+24
Goldschmidt, Paul	16	36	16	23	3	14	18	3	2	5	7	139	+9	+7	+16
Gomes, Yan	2	11	2	6	1	3	1	0	0	0	15	69	-12	0	-10
Gonzalez, Luis	12	23	3	6	2	5	8	2	3	5	5	68	-4	+6	+2
Gonzalez, Marwin	0	6	2	5	1	2	3	1	0	1	8	49	-7	+3	-4
Gonzalez, Oscar	4	19	5	10	2	5	8	1	2	3	6	56	-7	-3	-10
Gordon, Nick	7	19	4	5	5	7	12	3	2	5	8	91	-1	-2	-3
Gorman, Nolan	3	13	5	9	1	3	12	2	0	2	2	56	+6	+1	+7
Grandal, Yasmani	2	14	0	7	0	4	11	2	1	3	8	71	-9	+1	-8
Greene, Riley	7	19	4	7	1	6	16	1	0	1	8	70	+8	-7	+1
Gregorius, Didi	2	7	3	5	1	2	4	0	1	1	0	37	+3	+1	+4
Grichuk, Randal	8	25	7	12	4	6	12	5	3	8	12	112	-15	+4	-11
Grisham, Trent	10	25	9	12	7	8	12	1	0	1	3	95	+20	+5	+25
Grissom, Vaughn	4	9	5	6	1	1	3	0	1	1	0	30	+5	+1	+6
Grossman, Robbie	7	21	7	13	4	5	13	2	1	3	3	94	+9	+2	+11
Guerrero Jr., Vladimir	6	29	13	17	7	18	11	4	1	5	26	151	-21	+2	-19
Guillorme, Luis	6	24	7	15	3	6	5	3	1	4	15	66	-21	+1	-20
Gurriel Jr., Lourdes	9	35	10	15	1	5	17	5	1	6	11	96	-8	-5	-13
Gurriel, Yuli	4	20	7	15	2	8	14	1	1	2	13	105	-4	+8	+4
Haase, Eric	7	17	4	10	4	5	8	2	0	2	9	66	-1	0	-1
Haggerty, Sam	6	15	3	6	1	2	5	1	0	1	4	34	+1	+11	+12
Hampson, Garrett	6	10	5	7	2	5	6	2	0	2	3	40	+3	+8	+11
Haniger, Mitch	0	10	4	5	0	1	7	1	0	1	7	46	-2	0	-2
Happ, Ian	9	28	7	14	5	8	10	2	0	3	11	107	-4	+1	-3
Harper, Bryce	7	23	6	9	7	12	12	2	1	3	13	103	-1	+3	+2
Harris II, Michael	8	15	11	15	3	7	13	3	2	5	7	76	+1	+16	+17
Harrison, Josh	5	25	6	18	2	4	19	1	1	2	9	70	+1	0	+1
Hayes, KeBryan'	6	25	7	13	1	7	16	1	2	3	12	101	-3	+10	+7
Hays, Austin	11	31	6	17	2	6	21	0	2	3	11	99	+4	-6	-2
Hedges, Austin	2	18	2	8	1	3	2	0	2	2	12	64	-18	+2	-16
Heim, Jonah	6	18	5	15	4	4	8	3	1	4	10	87	-9	+2	-7
Heineman, Tyler	2	8	1	5	0	3	4	2	0	2	3	30	-7	+1	-6
Hernandez, Cesar	14	30	11	20	3	8	15	2	1	3	9	86	+5	+2	+7
Hernandez, Kike	7	17	10	14	3	6	11	0	0	0	11	66	+8	-4	+4
Hernandez, Teoscar	9	27	6	8	6	10	9	3	2	5	18	113	-13	0	-13
Hernandez, Yadiel	6	21	2	8	2	4	7	4	0	4	9	70	-12	0	-12
Herrera, Odubel	1	2	4	5	1	2	3	1	1	2	3	40	-2	+6	+4
Hicks, Aaron	7	26	10	15	3	6	20	1	0	1	10	92	+13	+4	+17
Higashioka, Kyle	1	6	1	3	1	2	4	0	1	1	5	49	-2	-2	-4
Higgins, P.J.	6	20	2	5	0	3	3	1	1	2	2	45	-4	0	-4
Hilliard, Sam	6	12	2	6	1	1	6	1	0	1	2	41	+5	+3	+8
Hiura, Keston	0	6	1	5	1	2	5	3	0	3	3	58	-7	+1	-6
Hoerner, Nico	3	15	9	15	3	5	9	4	0	4	11	97	-9	+16	+7
Hoskins, Rhys	4	29	10	26	2	10	16	1	2	3	12	109	-11	0	-11
Hosmer, Eric	2	21	7	12	1	7	13	1	0	1	12	77	-4	0	-4
Hummel, Cooper	0	4	2	3	1	2	6	0	1	1	4	31	0	+2	+2
Iglesias, Jose	4	26	10	15	4	6	11	1	0	1	11	92	+1	-4	-3
India, Jonathan	6	28	8	12	4	7	9	2	1	3	5	53	-4	-5	-9
Isbel, Kyle	4	9	8	12	1	3	11	2	0	2	5	44	+4	-3	+1
Jansen, Danny	0	8	6	9	2	5	4	0	1	1	1	38	0	+1	+1
Jeffers, Ryan	4	8	5	5	0	3	4	1	1	2	6	41	-3	0	-3
Jimenez, Eloy	3	17	5	8	0	3	4	0	0	0	8	60	-4	0	-4
Joe, Connor	10	32	11	15	2	7	13	1	1	2	8	68	+3	+2	+5
Judge, Aaron	9	23	13	18	3	9	14	2	2	4	14	163	+2	+10	+12
Kelly, Carson	4	14	4	11	1	4	7	0	0	0	10	73	-2	+2	0
Kemp, Tony	12	26	10	13	4	7	16	4	0	4	5	73	+10	+9	+19
Kepler, Max	12	23	4	8	5	9	12	1	1	2	7	103	+11	-1	+10
Kiermaier, Kevin	3	6	4	4	4	6	6	1	2	3	2	39	+2	+4	+6
Kim, Ha-seong	12	28	8	16	3	6	13	3	1	4	9	119	+2	+8	+10
Kiner-Falefa, Isiah	7	22	12	18	3	6	18	2	0	4	13	99	+1	+14	+15

2022 Baserunning

Player	1st to 3rd Moved	1st to 3rd Chances	2nd to Home Moved	2nd to Home Chances	1st to Home Moved	1st to Home Chances	Bases Taken	Out Adv	Doubled Off	BR Outs	GDP	GDP Opps	BR Gain	SB Gain	Net Gain
Kirk, Alejandro	2	29	5	19	1	10	6	2	1	3	11	90	-26	0	-26
Knizner, Andrew	6	17	5	9	0	5	7	0	1	1	9	54	-3	-2	-5
Kwan, Steven	18	46	16	25	2	7	23	0	1	1	9	118	+21	+9	+30
La Stella, Tommy	2	6	0	4	0	4	6	1	0	1	4	37	-3	0	-3
Larnach, Trevor	5	10	3	4	1	4	6	0	0	0	1	26	+8	0	+8
Laureano, Ramon	5	12	6	8	3	7	12	0	0	0	6	75	+14	-1	+13
Leblanc, Charles	1	6	4	5	1	1	5	0	0	0	0	22	+7	0	+7
LeMahieu, DJ	9	29	7	11	4	11	15	3	0	3	12	90	-2	-2	-4
Lindor, Francisco	8	28	16	21	5	13	22	3	0	3	11	178	+17	+4	+21
Longoria, Evan	4	14	6	9	1	5	6	1	0	1	6	65	+1	0	+1
Lopez, Alejo	2	8	2	2	0	2	6	1	0	1	1	31	+3	+1	+4
Lopez, Nicky	14	27	13	17	7	11	17	1	1	2	8	94	+20	+7	+27
Lowe, Brandon	5	12	3	4	3	8	9	2	0	2	1	47	+6	+1	+7
Lowe, Josh	2	12	5	7	0	0	2	0	1	1	1	40	0	+3	+3
Lowe, Nathaniel	6	36	8	17	3	7	4	2	3	5	10	129	-20	-2	-22
Luplow, Jordan	1	10	4	5	0	2	4	0	0	0	5	45	0	+3	+3
Lux, Gavin	9	23	11	17	8	11	16	6	0	6	3	89	+6	+3	+9
Machado, Manny	13	26	13	19	4	9	19	3	1	5	12	162	+10	+7	+17
Machin, Vimael	2	7	1	7	2	7	6	1	0	1	6	41	-5	-1	-6
Madrigal, Nick	4	8	2	3	1	2	12	1	0	1	6	38	+7	+1	+8
Maile, Luke	3	11	3	8	0	3	5	0	0	0	6	46	-1	0	-1
Maldonado, Martin	0	16	3	12	0	6	5	1	0	1	6	54	-12	0	-12
Mancini, Trey	4	21	9	10	2	9	9	3	3	6	12	103	-16	0	-16
Margot, Manuel	12	17	7	11	3	5	7	1	2	3	7	62	+3	+1	+4
Marsh, Brandon	8	20	3	5	4	6	10	3	2	5	4	82	-1	+2	+1
Marte, Ketel	10	21	12	17	2	8	14	1	1	2	12	98	+6	+3	+9
Marte, Starling	6	21	5	11	7	9	14	2	1	3	18	121	-4	0	-4
Martinez, J.D.	5	25	5	20	4	15	11	0	0	0	20	118	-14	0	-14
Massey, Michael	0	3	3	9	1	3	2	0	0	0	1	38	0	+3	+3
Mateo, Jorge	6	14	9	13	6	6	14	3	0	3	8	96	+10	+17	+27
Mazara, Nomar	1	10	4	5	3	5	4	1	0	1	3	33	0	0	0
McCann, James	0	5	3	5	1	1	4	0	0	0	5	41	+1	+3	+4
McCarthy, Jake	9	20	11	14	2	5	16	2	1	3	3	66	+13	+17	+30
McCormick, Chas	4	20	8	11	3	5	8	1	1	2	5	59	0	-2	-2
McCutchen, Andrew	6	22	6	10	4	8	11	2	0	2	10	96	0	-4	-4
McGuire, Reese	1	17	7	9	2	3	4	1	3	4	6	58	-12	+1	-11
McKenna, Ryan	6	9	4	5	5	6	4	0	0	0	3	27	+9	0	+9
McKinstry, Zach	5	9	3	4	2	2	3	0	0	0	0	26	+8	+7	+15
McMahon, Ryan	6	29	14	19	6	10	7	1	0	1	7	92	+4	+1	+5
McNeil, Jeff	10	36	8	17	6	9	23	2	2	5	6	113	+7	+4	+11
Meadows, Austin	4	12	1	2	0	0	2	1	0	1	2	20	-2	-2	-4
Mejia, Francisco	3	8	3	8	1	4	2	2	1	3	6	58	-11	0	-11
Melendez, MJ	9	25	10	14	4	7	13	4	0	4	2	81	+8	-4	+4
Meneses, Joey	5	16	4	7	1	3	5	1	0	2	13	49	-11	+1	-10
Merrifield, Whit	8	28	9	13	1	7	12	1	1	2	11	90	-1	+6	+5
Meyers, Jake	1	6	0	1	1	2	2	0	0	0	1	24	+1	0	+1
Miller, Brad	0	15	6	10	0	1	2	2	0	2	3	44	-9	0	-9
Miller, Owen	4	21	8	17	2	3	15	1	1	2	8	80	+2	+2	+4
Miranda, Jose	8	27	5	7	4	6	6	3	0	4	19	101	-16	-1	-17
Mitchell, Calvin	2	9	2	2	3	4	4	0	0	0	3	40	+5	+1	+6
Molina, Yadier	0	10	0	4	0	2	4	2	0	2	10	51	-15	+2	-13
Moncada, Yoan	8	22	5	10	1	6	9	1	0	1	5	88	+6	+2	+8
Montero, Elehuris	2	7	2	3	1	3	2	1	0	1	4	43	-2	0	-2
Moore, Dylan	5	15	8	10	4	5	8	0	0	0	5	44	+9	+5	+14
Morel, Christopher	13	24	2	3	2	2	10	0	1	1	6	74	+13	-4	+9
Mountcastle, Ryan	7	22	3	5	3	9	18	0	1	1	12	102	+9	+2	+11
Moustakas, Mike	3	15	3	5	2	5	2	0	1	1	8	63	-6	+2	-4
Mullins II, Cedric	10	26	17	26	4	11	18	4	2	6	4	81	+2	+14	+16
Muncy, Max	5	27	5	9	7	16	12	2	0	3	2	103	+4	+2	+6
Murphy, Sean	10	27	6	14	2	7	17	0	0	0	14	103	+7	+1	+8
Myers, Wil	6	14	3	5	2	4	6	2	0	2	7	62	-1	0	-1
Naquin, Tyler	4	12	5	7	2	2	9	0	0	0	3	63	+13	0	+13
Narvaez, Omar	3	17	5	6	0	3	4	2	0	2	4	57	-4	0	-4
Naylor, Josh	6	25	2	8	0	4	9	0	0	0	13	75	-6	+4	-2

2022 Baserunning

Player	1st to 3rd Moved	Chances	2nd to Home Moved	Chances	1st to Home Moved	Chances	Bases Taken	Out Adv	Doubled Off	BR Outs	GDP	GDP Opps	BR Gain	SB Gain	Net Gain
Neuse, Sheldon	2	9	4	5	2	4	6	0	0	0	5	47	+4	+4	+8
Nevin, Tyler	1	7	2	4	0	2	4	1	0	1	4	23	-4	0	-4
Newman, Kevin	10	16	4	6	3	4	6	4	0	4	6	49	-3	+4	+1
Nido, Tomas	0	15	3	9	0	6	7	3	1	4	14	69	-24	0	-24
Nimmo, Brandon	17	46	7	18	6	14	18	2	0	2	9	88	+5	-1	+4
Nola, Austin	7	24	7	15	1	3	11	1	1	2	5	68	+1	0	+1
Nootbaar, Lars	9	25	12	16	3	7	4	4	1	5	3	57	-7	+2	-5
O'Neill, Tyler	4	13	8	11	3	4	6	1	1	2	9	77	-1	+6	+5
Odor, Rougned	3	16	4	10	3	5	17	2	1	3	9	91	+2	+4	+6
Ohtani, Shohei	6	28	10	18	5	7	12	2	4	6	6	129	-5	-7	-12
Olivares, Edward	5	10	5	5	2	2	5	2	3	5	1	31	-4	-4	-8
Olson, Matt	7	21	6	10	3	9	18	3	1	4	13	125	+1	0	+1
Ortega, Rafael	9	18	7	10	0	1	11	6	1	8	10	69	-15	-2	-17
Ozuna, Marcell	2	19	4	7	2	5	9	1	0	1	12	86	-4	0	-4
Pache, Cristian	4	9	6	8	1	2	4	1	1	2	5	37	-2	-2	-4
Paredes, Isaac	3	11	5	7	1	4	6	0	0	0	12	73	-1	-2	-3
Pasquantino, Vinnie	1	17	3	7	1	4	3	1	0	1	5	49	-9	+1	-8
Pederson, Joc	4	23	3	7	1	4	10	0	2	2	5	78	-1	-1	-2
Pena, Jeremy	10	19	6	16	2	5	18	2	1	3	5	103	+11	+7	+18
Peralta, David	5	14	6	8	0	3	5	1	0	1	8	103	+2	-5	-3
Perdomo, Geraldo	6	17	9	14	5	9	23	0	0	0	3	87	+28	+5	+33
Perez, Salvador	3	14	7	15	0	4	5	0	1	2	9	86	-9	0	-9
Peterson, Jace	9	16	8	13	3	3	8	0	1	1	8	57	+7	+10	+17
Pham, Tommy	10	27	15	21	10	14	28	3	1	4	20	127	+13	+2	+15
Phillips, Brett	4	5	6	7	2	3	16	2	0	2	0	35	+17	+7	+24
Pinder, Chad	3	11	5	8	2	5	6	1	0	1	10	66	-3	+2	-1
Plawecki, Kevin	2	9	2	4	0	4	1	0	0	0	6	33	-6	0	-6
Polanco, Jorge	6	24	8	10	4	9	8	1	0	1	4	105	+9	-3	+6
Pollock, A.J.	12	35	7	18	2	8	12	2	0	2	13	108	-4	+1	-3
Profar, Jurickson	12	27	14	18	5	10	10	5	0	5	12	99	-4	+3	-1
Pujols, Albert	1	15	2	6	0	5	1	1	0	1	13	74	-17	-3	-20
Raleigh, Cal	5	14	4	8	0	3	6	0	0	0	5	71	+5	+1	+6
Ramirez, Harold	6	22	7	13	0	5	12	4	1	5	5	90	-6	-7	-13
Ramirez, Jose	14	22	7	13	4	11	20	2	1	3	5	139	+21	+6	+27
Realmuto, J.T.	10	26	11	17	8	11	9	3	0	3	7	92	+4	+19	+23
Refsnyder, Rob	3	9	2	4	2	3	5	0	0	0	1	35	+7	-1	+6
Rendon, Anthony	4	10	2	4	0	1	5	0	0	0	7	43	+1	+2	+3
Renfroe, Hunter	4	21	5	9	1	5	8	1	1	2	11	89	-7	-1	-8
Rengifo, Luis	9	13	4	4	2	3	9	0	0	0	11	83	+10	+2	+12
Reyes, Franmil	5	17	6	8	0	4	6	3	0	3	12	81	-10	0	-10
Reyes, Victor	5	20	5	6	3	4	10	2	1	3	7	64	0	-2	-2
Reynolds, Bryan	12	33	8	13	3	8	13	4	1	5	13	124	-5	+1	-4
Reynolds, Matt	3	10	6	9	1	3	11	1	1	2	7	60	+2	+5	+7
Riley, Austin	10	30	13	20	2	9	11	2	0	3	13	129	-3	+2	-1
Rivas, Alfonso	3	13	6	8	3	4	2	2	1	3	1	42	-4	+4	0
Rivera, Emmanuel	5	17	6	10	3	7	11	0	3	3	8	66	-2	-3	-5
Rizzo, Anthony	11	35	5	11	3	8	7	5	0	5	13	133	-13	-4	-17
Robert, Luis	5	21	8	11	8	12	11	2	0	2	6	87	+7	+5	+12
Robles, Victor	5	15	8	14	5	7	10	3	3	6	3	52	-6	+7	+1
Rodgers, Brendan	9	32	11	14	2	8	17	2	1	3	25	129	-8	0	-8
Rodriguez, Julio	6	18	10	15	4	7	21	1	4	5	7	88	+6	+11	+17
Rojas, Josh	5	20	21	25	3	5	24	1	1	2	7	91	+22	+17	+39
Rojas, Miguel	10	32	5	11	0	1	15	4	1	5	12	79	-9	+3	-6
Rosario, Amed	18	31	15	19	7	17	22	8	2	10	19	133	-7	+10	+3
Rosario, Eddie	2	8	2	5	3	3	10	1	0	1	3	40	+7	+3	+10
Ruf, Darin	4	21	6	14	2	6	13	0	1	1	11	77	-1	+2	+1
Ruiz, Keibert	4	25	6	13	2	4	7	1	0	1	9	85	-5	+4	-1
Rutschman, Adley	8	20	9	15	5	7	22	0	1	1	4	75	+23	+4	+27
Sanchez, Gary	2	18	5	11	2	3	8	3	0	3	12	105	-10	+2	-8
Sanchez, Jesus	2	15	9	16	0	0	3	4	1	5	7	65	-17	+1	-16
Santana, Carlos	8	18	4	10	2	4	15	2	2	4	9	109	+2	0	+2
Santander, Anthony	7	29	16	21	5	7	22	2	0	2	14	160	+18	-4	+14
Schoop, Jonathan	4	20	9	15	5	8	10	2	0	2	15	92	-5	+5	0
Schwarber, Kyle	5	28	5	16	2	9	10	1	0	1	10	101	-7	+8	+1

2022 Baserunning

Player	1st to 3rd Moved	Chances	2nd to Home Moved	Chances	1st to Home Moved	Chances	Bases Taken	Out Adv	Doubled Off	BR Outs	GDP	GDP Opps	BR Gain	SB Gain	Net Gain
Schwindel, Frank	0	10	4	7	0	1	4	1	0	1	12	52	-11	0	-11
Seager, Corey	9	35	14	20	2	8	24	0	1	1	14	128	+15	+3	+18
Segura, Jean	8	21	8	11	2	9	12	1	2	3	16	80	-7	+1	-6
Semien, Marcus	16	30	10	15	6	8	24	0	2	2	7	106	+27	+9	+36
Senzel, Nick	11	38	7	11	0	2	11	4	1	5	7	75	-8	-2	-10
Serven, Brian	4	12	1	3	0	0	4	0	1	1	7	43	-3	0	-3
Sheets, Gavin	2	17	7	13	1	3	7	1	0	1	9	69	-5	0	-5
Siri, Jose	6	14	9	13	5	10	8	2	1	3	3	61	+4	+10	+14
Slater, Austin	7	17	8	11	3	6	19	1	1	2	9	60	+11	+10	+21
Smith, Josh	5	14	4	6	2	4	7	0	1	1	1	29	+6	-2	+4
Smith, Pavin	3	9	4	7	1	1	11	1	1	2	2	50	+7	+1	+8
Smith, Will	5	27	4	15	0	4	13	2	0	2	11	123	-6	+1	-5
Solano, Donovan	0	13	4	6	2	6	3	2	0	2	5	57	-9	0	-9
Soler, Jorge	7	13	2	3	1	4	3	0	0	0	9	65	+1	-4	-3
Sosa, Edmundo	1	7	5	6	4	5	13	1	0	1	6	38	+8	+4	+12
Soto, Juan	15	42	16	22	6	19	16	3	1	4	12	123	+1	+2	+3
Springer, George	17	38	10	12	6	11	14	2	0	2	7	95	+15	+10	+25
Stallings, Jacob	2	14	1	6	0	6	6	1	0	1	15	72	-15	-2	-17
Stanton, Giancarlo	2	19	2	5	1	6	3	1	0	1	8	86	-8	0	-8
Stassi, Max	4	15	1	3	1	3	4	0	0	0	12	60	-6	0	-6
Stephenson, Tyler	1	9	5	6	1	1	1	0	0	0	4	39	0	+1	+1
Story, Trevor	7	16	7	14	1	5	5	0	1	1	9	80	-2	+13	+11
Stott, Bryson	11	25	8	11	6	8	14	1	1	2	3	91	+18	+4	+22
Straw, Myles	18	43	12	14	4	8	6	3	2	5	4	114	+3	+19	+22
Suarez, Eugenio	4	27	4	12	1	3	18	2	0	2	12	116	0	0	0
Suwinski, Jack	4	14	3	6	3	4	8	2	0	2	5	67	+2	0	+2
Suzuki, Seiya	11	22	9	13	2	4	12	1	2	3	8	76	+5	-1	+4
Swanson, Dansby	19	30	11	17	5	10	14	1	0	1	12	113	+17	+4	+21
Tapia, Raimel	12	22	6	8	7	10	15	2	0	2	12	77	+11	+4	+15
Taveras, Leody	6	19	10	14	1	3	13	3	1	4	2	60	+4	+1	+5
Taylor, Chris	3	12	7	12	5	7	14	1	2	3	4	85	+8	+8	+16
Taylor, Michael A.	8	25	6	9	3	5	8	0	0	0	6	75	+8	0	+8
Taylor, Tyrone	4	12	4	9	9	10	3	0	0	0	11	81	+1	-1	0
Tellez, Rowdy	1	23	3	10	4	11	12	3	0	3	20	113	-19	0	-19
Thomas, Alek	12	21	6	10	2	2	16	1	2	3	6	72	+12	-2	+10
Thomas, Lane	6	27	9	19	3	8	9	1	0	1	8	96	-1	0	-1
Thompson, Bubba	4	11	2	2	1	1	3	0	0	0	2	26	+4	+12	+16
Thompson, Trayce	5	11	4	7	3	4	9	1	1	2	2	54	+7	+2	+9
Torkelson, Spencer	3	18	8	15	2	5	10	2	0	2	12	81	-6	-2	-8
Toro, Abraham	3	11	6	11	0	4	3	2	1	3	4	54	-9	+2	-7
Torres, Gleyber	7	27	7	11	5	5	12	4	0	4	12	119	-2	0	-2
Trevino, Jose	1	13	7	13	1	6	8	1	0	1	5	72	0	0	0
Trout, Mike	5	20	14	16	1	6	6	2	0	2	6	99	+2	+1	+3
Tsutsugo, Yoshi	1	6	1	3	0	2	2	0	0	0	3	33	-1	0	-1
Tucker, Kyle	8	20	11	18	0	2	14	0	1	1	11	122	+10	+17	+27
Turner, Justin	6	21	4	12	2	10	15	4	1	6	13	122	-14	+3	-11
Turner, Trea	9	37	14	22	6	11	25	2	5	7	9	127	+2	+21	+23
Urias, Luis	8	23	5	12	4	7	15	2	0	2	9	86	+5	-3	+2
Urias, Ramon	5	11	9	12	1	5	10	1	1	2	7	88	+5	+1	+6
Urshela, Gio	6	28	3	7	8	14	9	5	0	5	21	108	-22	+1	-21
VanMeter, Josh	2	7	2	3	1	1	4	0	0	0	3	31	+4	+4	+8
Vargas, Ildemaro	4	11	4	6	0	2	6	0	0	0	6	45	+3	+1	+4
Varsho, Daulton	9	23	10	16	3	6	19	3	2	5	8	99	+5	+4	+9
Vaughn, Andrew	5	30	6	15	2	5	13	4	0	4	13	115	-12	0	-12
Vazquez, Christian	3	22	3	13	4	7	6	4	1	5	10	65	-23	-7	-30
Velazquez, Andrew	4	19	4	9	2	4	7	1	0	1	3	61	+2	+15	+17
Velazquez, Nelson	6	10	1	3	1	1	2	0	1	1	5	44	0	+1	+1
Verdugo, Alex	11	39	10	23	6	12	18	2	0	2	14	141	+3	-5	-2
Vierling, Matt	4	15	5	8	1	3	3	0	0	0	7	79	+1	-1	0
Villar, David	3	9	0	1	0	0	8	0	0	0	4	32	+6	-2	+4
Villar, Jonathan	6	12	5	7	0	1	6	0	1	1	4	38	+4	+7	+11
Vogelbach, Daniel	4	24	3	10	3	6	8	1	0	1	11	85	-7	0	-7
Voit, Luke	3	24	3	15	0	5	11	4	2	6	9	100	-22	-1	-23
Votto, Joey	3	21	3	9	1	3	6	3	0	3	8	72	-12	0	-12

2022 Baserunning

Player	1st to 3rd		2nd to Home		1st to Home		Bases Taken	Out Adv	Doubled Off	BR Outs	GDP	GDP Opps	BR Gain	SB Gain	Net Gain
	Moved	Chances	Moved	Chances	Moved	Chances									
Wade Jr., LaMonte	3	11	1	5	2	3	4	0	0	0	0	47	+6	+1	+7
Wade, Tyler	2	4	3	7	0	0	7	1	2	3	3	31	-4	-2	-6
Walker, Christian	13	31	6	11	6	12	23	2	0	2	15	119	+13	-2	+11
Walls, Taylor	8	19	9	13	10	12	10	2	0	3	6	73	+7	+4	+11
Walsh, Jared	5	14	5	10	0	2	4	1	0	1	6	70	-2	0	-2
Ward, Taylor	11	21	5	11	2	6	13	5	1	6	5	87	-3	-1	-4
Wendle, Joey	3	15	6	8	2	4	7	3	2	5	7	67	-11	+6	-5
Williams, Luke	6	12	5	6	0	2	5	2	0	2	1	23	+2	+3	+5
Winker, Jesse	3	25	8	9	2	9	13	4	1	6	8	102	-11	0	-11
Wisdom, Patrick	9	23	9	15	2	3	15	1	0	1	8	103	+14	0	+14
Witt Jr., Bobby	13	25	14	19	5	8	21	2	0	2	12	141	+23	+16	+39
Wong, Kolten	4	15	5	10	3	6	9	0	0	0	5	85	+8	+5	+13
Wynns, Austin	1	6	3	5	0	1	3	1	0	1	9	38	-8	0	-8
Yastrzemski, Mike	5	18	12	17	1	4	21	2	2	4	3	91	+12	+3	+15
Yelich, Christian	9	30	9	16	8	14	14	3	0	3	9	104	+2	+13	+15
Yepez, Juan	3	9	1	3	1	3	3	2	0	2	6	44	-7	0	-7
Zavala, Seby	4	14	2	15	1	2	4	1	0	1	1	52	-3	0	-3

Career Baserunning
Players with 1000 Career Games
(Data goes back to 2002)

Player	1st to 3rd Moved	Chances	2nd to Home Moved	Chances	1st to Home Moved	Chances	Bases Taken	Out Adv	Doubled Off	BR Outs	GDP	GDP Opps	BR Gain	SB Gain	Net Gain
Abreu, Jose	73	271	85	136	32	85	139	27	11	39	167	1146	-78	+1	-77
Altuve, Jose	121	357	146	246	51	97	232	60	16	80	171	1206	-87	+117	+30
Andrus, Elvis	209	409	190	251	74	111	303	34	28	63	186	1453	+178	+113	+291
Arenado, Nolan	94	278	93	144	30	63	127	18	8	26	156	1199	-3	-13	-16
Baez, Javier	68	129	75	95	27	47	125	26	10	36	82	825	+42	+26	+68
Belt, Brandon	75	281	85	147	23	75	139	32	6	38	60	1022	+15	+5	+20
Betts, Mookie	113	281	124	188	50	85	191	15	9	24	56	813	+160	+90	+250
Blackmon, Charlie	99	354	119	188	46	81	187	27	12	40	63	830	+54	+26	+80
Bogaerts, Xander	127	269	112	159	57	104	167	30	5	35	114	1100	+92	+40	+132
Bradley Jr., Jackie	69	175	64	104	26	56	112	9	6	15	61	788	+78	+33	+111
Brantley, Michael	88	331	91	163	42	109	194	17	5	23	128	1174	+52	+59	+111
Cabrera, Miguel	148	701	192	364	52	184	283	56	14	72	353	2345	-218	-2	-220
Cain, Lorenzo	101	238	107	154	41	60	154	16	10	26	109	853	+80	+102	+182
Calhoun, Kole	73	216	78	131	32	73	160	27	7	34	74	821	+48	+2	+50
Cano, Robinson	126	461	199	325	48	120	260	46	23	70	286	2033	-82	-25	-107
Carpenter, Matt	92	324	100	186	28	71	158	35	14	49	38	792	-2	-7	-9
Castellanos, Nick	51	204	65	135	25	71	151	24	17	41	100	1014	-36	-15	-51
Crawford, Brandon	67	283	111	168	27	64	175	22	5	27	116	1212	+54	-24	+30
Cruz, Nelson	79	398	111	190	19	102	197	35	12	47	177	1591	-75	+19	-56
Dickerson, Corey	63	183	55	95	24	44	105	25	9	34	68	641	-15	-18	-33
Donaldson, Josh	82	279	79	137	31	84	175	29	15	44	129	1110	-22	+20	-2
Escobar, Alcides	109	299	140	209	50	71	174	17	14	31	113	1065	+99	+88	+187
Escobar, Eduardo	74	227	61	114	28	59	121	23	5	28	57	957	+47	-13	+34
Flores, Wilmer	39	177	38	80	7	35	85	25	6	32	82	697	-79	-1	-80
Freeman, Freddie	122	404	148	235	54	132	214	31	8	40	133	1520	+65	+12	+77
Garcia, Avisail	65	204	62	106	32	61	97	20	7	27	100	765	-28	-15	-43
Goldschmidt, Paul	124	363	148	229	51	111	220	16	8	24	134	1437	+137	+81	+218
Gonzalez, Marwin	46	191	49	92	20	56	102	24	4	29	91	726	-50	-12	-62
Grandal, Yasmani	43	195	31	93	9	71	84	23	8	33	108	839	-128	-2	-130
Gregorius, Didi	68	211	83	119	32	52	108	15	3	18	50	816	+85	+5	+90
Grichuk, Randal	40	137	57	86	19	37	109	18	8	26	87	741	+1	-7	-6
Grossman, Robbie	72	241	67	111	25	62	116	14	3	17	39	627	+55	+9	+64
Harper, Bryce	107	296	96	173	72	127	164	50	21	71	106	1269	-43	+36	-7
Harrison, Josh	66	192	92	133	32	62	134	22	12	35	66	681	+28	+17	+45
Hernandez, Cesar	77	261	85	135	38	79	145	16	11	27	67	672	+32	+11	+43
Heyward, Jason	128	335	130	198	56	87	186	22	8	30	94	1188	+142	+38	+180
Hosmer, Eric	85	355	127	207	48	95	175	31	16	49	162	1270	-58	+16	-42
Iglesias, Jose	62	201	79	122	35	63	102	26	6	32	87	726	-23	-11	-34
LeMahieu, DJ	77	291	119	194	47	105	192	15	12	28	158	990	-1	-1	-2
Lindor, Francisco	76	206	89	145	27	70	145	26	6	33	85	865	+25	+51	+76
Longoria, Evan	89	358	143	223	39	103	190	20	14	35	198	1603	-5	+20	+15
Lowrie, Jed	56	242	88	146	28	81	147	19	3	22	94	992	+35	+2	+37
Machado, Manny	95	278	106	182	36	71	191	33	11	45	163	1277	-5	+17	+12
Maldonado, Martin	22	130	31	81	11	35	62	18	4	22	71	521	-80	-7	-87
Marte, Starling	95	233	121	169	45	73	158	32	14	46	98	960	+35	+128	+163
Martinez, J.D.	65	272	84	173	29	100	148	18	12	30	167	1216	-79	+3	-76
McCutchen, Andrew	119	459	160	247	58	120	191	22	12	35	118	1382	+54	+37	+91
Miller, Brad	23	139	70	111	7	25	95	14	11	26	39	597	-3	+7	+4
Molina, Yadier	72	411	99	227	20	103	177	35	15	52	287	1656	-251	-3	-254
Moustakas, Mike	41	245	73	134	17	65	114	23	10	33	115	1046	-72	+1	-71
Myers, Wil	59	175	89	139	39	65	119	20	4	25	87	760	+29	+41	+70
Odor, Rougned	55	142	58	90	26	44	112	17	11	29	52	794	+52	-34	+18
Ozuna, Marcell	85	247	64	111	32	63	111	16	4	21	109	933	+14	0	+14
Pederson, Joc	49	151	42	83	16	30	83	10	12	22	47	562	+4	-24	-20
Peralta, David	60	173	64	95	16	49	137	8	9	19	70	727	+62	+3	+65
Perez, Salvador	41	207	72	146	12	61	98	16	4	21	154	1023	-94	+4	-90
Pillar, Kevin	58	162	65	105	28	51	97	9	6	15	70	745	+52	+28	+80
Pollock, A.J.	53	176	73	124	22	42	96	12	4	16	75	751	+25	+66	+91
Pujols, Albert	186	625	221	339	60	168	306	77	23	103	405	2749	-184	+36	-148
Ramirez, Jose	84	197	98	137	38	71	162	22	7	31	61	947	+115	+90	+205
Realmuto, J.T.	86	197	70	114	36	52	107	15	10	26	77	811	+44	+42	+86

Career Baserunning
Players with 1000 Career Games
(Data goes back to 2002)

Player	1st to 3rd Moved	1st to 3rd Chances	2nd to Home Moved	2nd to Home Chances	1st to Home Moved	1st to Home Chances	Bases Taken	Out Adv	Doubled Off	BR Outs	GDP	GDP Opps	BR Gain	SB Gain	Net Gain
Rendon, Anthony	69	243	95	137	35	67	140	11	7	18	84	844	+68	+15	+83
Rizzo, Anthony	92	317	89	167	24	101	167	45	16	61	132	1420	-81	-10	-91
Santana, Carlos	106	386	111	198	43	119	206	37	10	49	159	1428	-31	+12	-19
Schoop, Jonathan	58	173	71	112	23	57	124	17	9	26	121	829	-11	+7	-4
Segura, Jean	99	246	129	176	37	75	189	26	25	52	131	909	+4	+63	+67
Semien, Marcus	75	217	96	133	43	63	148	19	6	25	80	857	+85	+40	+125
Simmons, Andrelton	73	202	86	125	23	62	131	18	7	27	163	927	-32	+24	-8
Springer, George	96	245	68	131	44	72	156	23	14	37	71	678	+34	-2	+32
Stanton, Giancarlo	48	252	78	145	24	74	161	26	4	31	125	829	-11	+12	+1
Strange-Gordon, Dee	68	174	86	118	29	51	134	11	8	20	46	582	+95	+132	+227
Suarez, Eugenio	52	246	52	118	17	44	104	23	5	30	99	941	-64	-6	-70
Suzuki, Kurt	75	299	90	179	31	77	125	19	2	22	148	1202	-28	-2	-30
Trout, Mike	168	357	147	207	48	85	202	20	18	39	64	1187	+192	+130	+322
Turner, Justin	88	279	89	158	23	80	146	26	7	37	117	1112	-23	+21	-2
Upton, Justin	131	373	149	215	66	111	177	26	19	45	142	1550	+76	+33	+109
Villar, Jonathan	71	165	67	102	24	38	107	24	13	39	56	590	-1	+107	+106
Votto, Joey	122	528	136	262	45	150	211	51	24	76	166	1664	-144	+22	-122
Wong, Kolten	77	174	73	109	24	47	121	10	10	20	47	698	+91	+45	+136
Yelich, Christian	100	280	122	174	50	78	147	18	10	28	99	1025	+74	+92	+166

2002-2022 MLB Averages

1st to 3rd	2nd to Home	1st to Home
28%	59%	44%

2022 Team Baserunning

Team	1st to 3rd Moved	1st to 3rd Chances	2nd to Home Moved	2nd to Home Chances	1st to Home Moved	1st to Home Chances	Bases Taken	Out Adv	Doubled Off	BR Outs	GDP	GDP Opps	BR Gain	SB Gain	Net Gain
Arizona D-Backs	91	236	104	157	34	72	193	16	11	27	97	1061	+113	+46	+159
Los Angeles Dodgers	74	273	100	177	52	112	178	28	12	42	85	1200	+31	+62	+93
Cleveland Guardians	115	324	100	172	30	73	155	20	11	31	115	1122	+26	+65	+91
Texas Rangers	83	279	104	170	35	66	147	20	12	32	82	1066	+44	+46	+90
Baltimore Orioles	75	231	97	155	38	81	170	24	10	36	95	1074	+45	+33	+78
San Francisco Giants	82	301	88	160	27	79	186	15	11	27	109	1154	+45	+32	+77
St Louis Cardinals	103	287	118	178	31	80	147	25	8	34	112	1121	+25	+45	+70
Oakland Athletics	74	207	82	132	26	73	142	16	5	22	109	964	+35	+32	+67
Atlanta Braves	100	250	107	158	33	84	152	28	7	37	103	1039	+34	+25	+59
Seattle Mariners	67	265	84	151	28	68	172	15	8	24	120	1096	+27	+29	+56
Philadelphia Phillies	81	286	89	160	41	93	143	16	11	27	116	1135	+6	+49	+55
Kansas City Royals	93	268	104	168	40	83	143	28	12	41	101	1110	+7	+36	+43
San Diego Padres	98	304	102	160	46	95	136	25	7	33	95	1183	+33	+5	+38
Milwaukee Brewers	66	242	64	125	46	83	119	19	4	23	117	1123	-4	+36	+32
Pittsburgh Pirates	78	244	68	113	34	68	135	27	11	38	95	1046	+1	+25	+26
Chicago White Sox	89	341	102	194	36	86	159	20	8	29	127	1168	-12	+38	+26
New York Yankees	74	269	83	155	33	77	146	29	6	37	120	1238	-22	+36	+14
Miami Marlins	69	267	90	143	19	61	128	27	9	36	120	1018	-53	+64	+11
Boston Red Sox	88	297	94	190	40	104	147	17	6	23	131	1212	-3	+12	+9
Detroit Tigers	83	265	92	149	44	83	138	24	11	35	108	1033	+3	-1	+2
Chicago Cubs	102	273	82	144	29	64	134	28	12	42	130	1114	-37	+37	0
Los Angeles Angels	75	229	70	127	23	56	107	24	11	35	95	1048	-28	+23	-5
Colorado Rockies	98	316	100	173	41	80	138	18	12	30	139	1197	-10	+5	-5
Tampa Bay Rays	90	257	106	167	43	85	137	38	14	54	93	1087	-27	+21	-6
New York Mets	87	321	104	188	40	94	147	25	10	38	122	1280	-27	+18	-9
Houston Astros	68	260	95	170	24	72	142	26	13	40	118	1086	-54	+39	-15
Toronto Blue Jays	89	325	111	169	44	94	132	22	11	33	136	1180	-26	-3	-29
Minnesota Twins	93	323	86	139	42	94	133	29	12	42	133	1226	-48	+4	-44
Cincinnati Reds	65	269	91	148	33	72	146	28	10	38	127	1111	-37	-8	-45
Washington Nationals	87	317	101	188	30	79	133	28	12	41	140	1093	-87	+13	-74
MLB Totals	2537	8326	2818	4780	1062	2411	4385	705	297	1027	3390	33585			

Stolen Base Attempt Times

Jackson Lewis

Once again, Mariners outfielder Sam Haggerty topped the league with an average 2nd base stealing time of 3.48 seconds, a hefty 50 milliseconds faster than the runner-up, Yankees outfielder Tim Locastro.

While those stats are impressive, from a base-stealing perspective (specifically 2nd base), this was the season of Marlins infielder Jon Berti, our 14th-fastest base-stealer. After spending his first four eligible seasons no lower than 21st on this list, he finally exploded for 41 stolen bases on 46 attempts. His 46 tries this season obliterated his previous career-high of 20. While this breakout can be somewhat attributed to his increase in playing time, he attempted to steal a base almost three times as often compared to previous seasons (29% of base-stealing opportunities, up from 10% in 2021).

One of the more surprising declines this season was Mets outfielder Starling Marte's. Last year's stolen base leader struggled this season, despite virtually no change in his average attempt time. While 3 of his 9 caught stealings can be attributed to J.T. Realmuto's return to prominence, the reason behind the rest of his downswing is difficult to pinpoint.

In terms of speed, Braves right fielder Ronald Acuña Jr. took a step back this season, averaging 3.69 seconds per attempt after hovering around the 3.6 second mark over the past three seasons. While it wasn't reflected in his attempts (he was two short of matching his career high), it was represented in his success rate, which was just under 71%, the lowest of his career.

Stolen Base Times - 2B Only

Runner	Timed Attempts	Average
Haggerty, Sam	9	3.48
Locastro, Tim	9	3.53
White, Eli	6	3.54
Thompson, Bubba	19	3.55
Mitchell, Garrett	6	3.55
Siri, Jose	13	3.55
McCarthy, Jake	19	3.56
Morel, Christopher	11	3.56
Rodriguez, Julio	29	3.56
Eaton, Nate	11	3.56
Mateo, Jorge	32	3.58
Moore, Dylan	20	3.58
Turner, Trea	23	3.58
Berti, Jon	38	3.58
Phillips, Brett	6	3.58
Duran, Jarren	7	3.59
Azocar, Jose	9	3.59
Gimenez, Andres	22	3.59
Chisholm Jr., Jazz	14	3.59
Abrams, CJ	8	3.60
Velazquez, Andrew	15	3.60
Story, Trevor	9	3.60
Gordon, Nick	6	3.60
ONeill, Tyler'	13	3.60
Castro, Willi	12	3.60
Straw, Myles	19	3.61
Allen, Greg	7	3.61
Davis, Jonathan	6	3.61
Ramirez, Jose	22	3.61
Marte, Starling	21	3.61
Altuve, Jose	9	3.62
Peterson, Jace	11	3.62
Merrifield, Whit	13	3.62
Tapia, Raimel	9	3.62
Anderson, Tim	11	3.62
Benintendi, Andrew	9	3.62
Hilliard, Sam	6	3.62
Hayes, KeBryan'	16	3.62
Hoerner, Nico	15	3.62
Robles, Victor	10	3.62
Senzel, Nick	6	3.62
Taveras, Leody	11	3.63
Gonzalez, Luis	11	3.63
Franco, Wander	6	3.63
Bader, Harrison	17	3.63
Mullins II, Cedric	32	3.63
Betts, Mookie	10	3.63
Engel, Adam	12	3.64
Witt Jr., Bobby	28	3.64
Hampson, Garrett	9	3.64
Swanson, Dansby	17	3.64
Garcia, Adolis	24	3.65
Edman, Tommy	26	3.65
Varsho, Daulton	16	3.65
Kwan, Steven	19	3.65
Walls, Taylor	12	3.65
Kelenic, Jarred	6	3.65
McMahon, Ryan	10	3.65
Rosario, Amed	11	3.65
Kiner-Falefa, Isiah	22	3.65
Slater, Austin	9	3.65
Sosa, Edmundo	6	3.65
Hernandez, Teoscar	7	3.65
Springer, George	10	3.66
Yelich, Christian	16	3.66
McCutchen, Andrew	11	3.66
Laureano, Ramon	10	3.66
Albies, Ozzie	7	3.66
Arozarena, Randy	31	3.66
Tucker, Kyle	23	3.66
Brujan, Vidal	7	3.67

Runner	Timed Attempts	Average
Perdomo, Geraldo	9	3.67
Cruz, Oneil	12	3.67
Kim, Ha-seong	11	3.67
Semien, Marcus	24	3.67
Wisdom, Patrick	8	3.68
Estrada, Thairo	21	3.68
Harris II, Michael	16	3.68
Stott, Bryson	10	3.68
Williams, Luke	10	3.68
Rojas, Josh	16	3.68
Ohtani, Shohei	15	3.68
Robert, Luis	11	3.68
Grisham, Trent	6	3.68
Acuna Jr., Ronald	31	3.69
Marsh, Brandon	13	3.69
Wade, Tyler	11	3.69
Judge, Aaron	11	3.69
Wendle, Joey	11	3.69
Wong, Kolten	14	3.69
Frazier, Adam	13	3.70
Vierling, Matt	9	3.70
Lux, Gavin	7	3.71
Smith, Josh	7	3.71
Suzuki, Seiya	10	3.71
Baddoo, Akil	14	3.71
Margot, Manuel	8	3.71
Bellinger, Cody	14	3.71
Brown, Seth	9	3.71
Realmuto, J.T.	12	3.71
Freeman, Freddie	12	3.72
Pham, Tommy	8	3.72
Ortega, Rafael	10	3.72
Joe, Connor	7	3.72
Pena, Jeremy	11	3.72
Reynolds, Bryan	7	3.73
Bichette, Bo	17	3.74
Segura, Jean	12	3.74
Grossman, Robbie	6	3.75
Rengifo, Luis	7	3.75
Lopez, Nicky	14	3.76
Harper, Bryce	6	3.76
Rojas, Miguel	8	3.76
Lindor, Francisco	11	3.76
Farmer, Kyle	6	3.76
Thomas, Lane	11	3.76
Hicks, Aaron	8	3.77
Espinal, Santiago	10	3.77
Fortes, Nick	6	3.78
Andrus, Elvis	12	3.78
Kemp, Tony	11	3.78
Baez, Javier	6	3.78
Hernandez, Cesar	11	3.79
Isbel, Kyle	11	3.79
Neuse, Sheldon	6	3.80
Polanco, Jorge	6	3.80
Newman, Kevin	6	3.80
Guerrero Jr., Vladimir	7	3.83
Velazquez, Nelson	6	3.85
Grissom, Vaughn	6	3.86
Arraez, Luis	7	3.87
Schwarber, Kyle	6	3.88
Machado, Manny	6	3.88
Ramirez, Harold	6	3.91
Garcia, Luis	6	3.91

Lords of the Flies

Mark Simon

Astros right fielder Kyle Tucker is a very good hitter. That swing has produced 30 home runs for Tucker in each of the last two seasons. And there may be some more untapped power potential in his 6-foot-4 frame.

By our measures, Tucker had five outs on balls hit at least 400 feet this season. That matched Adolis García for the most in the majors.

It's the second straight season that Tucker was prolific at making outs on balls hit that deep. His four outs on balls hit at least 400 feet matched Trevor Story's MLB lead in 2021.

That said, we don't think we'd tell Tucker to change anything. After all, if you google his name and "swing comparison," the player most frequently cited is Ted Williams.

Tucker's numbers were among a few things that jumped out on these pages. Another would be the 41 under Aaron Judge in the 400+ column. That means Judge had more 400-foot home runs than all but one player had *total* home runs in 2022. That's ridiculous. Also impressive, C.J. Cron hit 25 of his 29 homers at least 400 feet. That's the highest proportion of 400-foot home runs for someone who hit at least 20 homers in 2022. If we lower the qualifier to 15 home runs, Ronald Acuña Jr. had the highest (13 of 15, 87%).

In the tables that follow, batted balls are grouped by their estimated distance. Each group includes balls within 10 feet in either direction of the distance listed. The 390 group contains balls hit anywhere between 380 and 399 feet. The 400-foot grouping includes all balls hit at least 400 feet. The Long column includes the total number of long fly ball outs (hit at least 300 feet) and the HR column excludes inside-the-park home runs.

The tables include only players who have hit at least 15 home runs or at least 50 long fly ball outs.

Long Outs and Home Runs

Player	Long Out Distances						Home Run Distances					
	330	350	370	390	400+	Long	330	350	370	390	400+	HR
Judge, Aaron	18	13	8	5	1	63	0	1	8	12	41	62
Schwarber, Kyle	17	7	16	7	0	62	0	1	3	9	33	46
Trout, Mike	10	9	8	3	0	41	0	3	3	5	29	40
Alonso, Pete	20	14	4	5	0	64	0	3	4	8	25	40
Riley, Austin	24	13	8	7	0	66	0	2	3	3	30	38
Alvarez, Yordan	11	9	10	10	0	57	0	5	6	4	22	37
Walker, Christian	17	16	16	10	0	73	0	1	1	8	26	36
Tellez, Rowdy	19	13	10	11	0	63	0	0	3	12	20	35
Goldschmidt, Paul	8	15	11	4	0	53	0	0	6	11	18	35
Betts, Mookie	21	23	18	5	2	89	0	1	7	13	14	35
Ohtani, Shohei	15	11	7	7	1	62	0	1	2	10	21	34
Olson, Matt	17	12	7	7	0	58	0	4	3	7	20	34
Seager, Corey	25	23	12	8	1	90	0	1	3	6	23	33
Santander, Anthony	19	16	18	8	1	78	0	2	7	9	15	33
Guerrero Jr., Vladimir	14	10	12	7	0	58	0	3	4	6	19	32
Machado, Manny	16	14	11	3	0	55	0	3	4	8	17	32
Rizzo, Anthony	12	14	11	8	0	59	1	3	6	7	15	32
Adames, Willy	17	20	13	10	0	73	0	1	2	12	16	31
Suarez, Eugenio	15	12	8	8	1	55	0	1	2	12	16	31
Stanton, Giancarlo	7	4	3	2	1	21	1	3	4	9	14	31
Tucker, Kyle	15	20	15	9	5	79	0	3	8	5	14	30
Hoskins, Rhys	15	14	12	7	0	72	0	3	5	12	10	30
Arenado, Nolan	19	15	12	3	0	71	0	2	10	9	9	30
Cron, C.J.	19	9	5	4	3	61	0	0	2	2	25	29
Renfroe, Hunter	17	11	7	6	0	46	1	0	2	7	19	29
Ramirez, Jose	16	20	15	3	0	72	0	2	6	9	12	29
Buxton, Byron	7	9	2	3	0	28	0	1	6	4	17	28
Rodriguez, Julio	12	15	5	5	0	45	0	4	6	3	15	28
Altuve, Jose	12	6	8	5	1	46	0	4	4	9	11	28
Drury, Brandon	14	7	11	5	0	51	0	3	8	6	11	28
Soto, Juan	14	12	6	6	0	54	0	0	1	7	19	27
Chapman, Matt	15	16	17	4	0	73	0	1	4	5	17	27
Lowe, Nathaniel	15	10	4	8	1	52	0	0	3	8	16	27
Garcia, Adolis	18	9	14	8	5	68	0	3	2	6	16	27
Devers, Rafael	15	13	7	5	1	52	0	2	3	7	15	27
Varsho, Daulton	11	20	15	4	0	63	0	0	3	11	13	27
Raleigh, Cal	8	10	6	7	0	44	0	2	5	8	12	27
Reynolds, Bryan	18	8	10	2	0	47	0	0	4	9	13	26
Semien, Marcus	23	21	20	12	1	98	0	2	4	7	13	26
Lindor, Francisco	22	14	15	7	0	78	0	1	7	9	9	26
Hernandez, Teoscar	17	9	6	5	0	45	0	0	3	5	17	25
Wisdom, Patrick	12	6	10	2	0	42	0	0	5	3	17	25
Swanson, Dansby	20	20	8	6	1	74	0	0	4	6	15	25
Brown, Seth	20	13	7	1	0	55	0	1	4	6	14	25
Springer, George	19	6	5	4	0	47	1	1	7	4	12	25
Pujols, Albert	8	13	7	2	0	38	0	0	5	4	15	24
Smith, Will	21	20	16	11	1	91	0	0	3	8	13	24
Bichette, Bo	15	19	7	6	0	59	1	4	3	5	11	24
Torres, Gleyber	15	14	12	4	1	64	1	3	6	9	5	24
Ozuna, Marcell	13	13	10	3	0	57	0	0	1	3	19	23
Ward, Taylor	17	14	10	8	0	67	0	1	0	7	15	23
Pederson, Joc	12	11	4	7	2	48	0	0	3	5	15	23
Perez, Salvador	19	11	12	6	0	64	0	1	3	6	13	23
Bregman, Alex	23	15	13	11	1	87	0	2	8	9	4	23
Correa, Carlos	23	17	6	4	1	59	0	0	2	6	14	22
Mountcastle, Ryan	14	16	10	6	3	61	0	0	3	5	14	22
Voit, Luke	13	15	10	6	0	59	0	0	4	4	14	22
Pena, Jeremy	15	9	4	7	0	52	0	2	4	4	12	22
Contreras, Willson	7	17	4	4	1	42	0	0	6	7	9	22
Realmuto, J.T.	15	12	6	3	0	51	0	4	4	6	8	22
Turner, Trea	11	18	20	7	2	78	0	1	2	5	13	21
Freeman, Freddie	28	24	23	6	1	100	0	0	3	6	12	21
Muncy, Max	22	27	11	4	1	75	0	1	6	8	6	21
McMahon, Ryan	11	9	10	6	2	55	0	0	0	3	17	20
Witt Jr., Bobby	21	13	6	2	3	66	0	0	0	7	13	20
Contreras, William	6	8	6	2	0	25	0	1	2	4	13	20
France, Ty	15	15	2	3	0	56	1	0	3	6	10	20
Escobar, Eduardo	15	16	12	5	0	61	0	2	3	6	9	20
Naylor, Josh	9	10	5	2	0	35	0	2	4	5	9	20
Paredes, Isaac	11	6	4	2	0	33	0	1	5	7	7	20
Grichuk, Randal	13	10	10	7	1	52	0	0	2	6	11	19
Gallo, Joey	12	8	2	1	1	33	0	0	3	5	11	19
Arozarena, Randy	7	9	6	3	1	32	0	1	2	5	11	19

Long Outs and Home Runs

Player	Long Out Distances						Home Run Distances					
	330	350	370	390	400+	Long	330	350	370	390	400+	HR
Harris II, Michael	4	8	6	1	0	25	0	1	4	4	10	19
Suwinski, Jack	6	9	5	2	0	30	0	1	5	3	10	19
Santana, Carlos	12	12	7	8	1	49	0	0	3	7	9	19
Bellinger, Cody	10	14	9	5	1	62	0	0	5	7	7	19
Flores, Wilmer	19	20	7	3	0	70	0	1	6	10	2	19
Murphy, Sean	17	12	9	7	0	62	0	1	1	2	14	18
Melendez, MJ	11	14	10	6	1	55	0	0	0	5	13	18
Harper, Bryce	15	8	3	5	1	38	1	1	2	3	11	18
d'Arnaud, Travis	9	8	7	2	0	36	0	1	1	6	10	18
Vogelbach, Daniel	8	10	6	5	0	40	0	1	2	5	10	18
Cruz, Oneil	6	5	3	3	0	19	0	0	1	4	12	17
Pham, Tommy	16	12	12	3	0	58	1	0	3	2	11	17
Bell, Josh	17	8	8	5	0	49	0	2	2	2	11	17
Taylor, Tyrone	11	11	11	3	0	44	0	0	2	5	10	17
Gimenez, Andres	11	7	6	4	0	41	0	0	4	4	9	17
Yastrzemski, Mike	14	12	13	3	0	54	0	1	3	4	9	17
Grisham, Trent	13	7	8	3	0	40	0	4	2	2	9	17
Vaughn, Andrew	24	10	9	5	0	63	0	0	1	8	8	17
Thomas, Lane	10	10	10	4	0	48	0	2	2	5	8	17
Cronenworth, Jake	19	20	12	3	0	75	0	2	5	2	8	17
Rengifo, Luis	11	6	8	3	0	47	0	0	2	8	7	17
Andrus, Elvis	13	5	8	2	0	41	0	3	1	6	7	17
McCutchen, Andrew	26	12	9	3	0	73	0	2	3	5	7	17
Happ, Ian	17	12	4	5	0	57	0	1	4	6	6	17
Baez, Javier	13	10	4	4	0	40	0	0	5	7	5	17
Mancini, Trey	28	14	13	4	0	71	0	3	4	5	5	17
Blackmon, Charlie	14	10	13	4	1	57	0	0	2	3	11	16
Jimenez, Eloy	4	15	5	2	0	33	0	2	1	2	11	16
Martinez, J.D.	20	10	11	9	2	70	0	0	1	5	10	16
Aguilar, Jesus	15	13	12	6	0	61	0	0	2	4	10	16
Sanchez, Gary	9	9	10	4	0	41	0	1	2	3	10	16
Marte, Starling	10	6	3	0	0	32	0	1	0	6	9	16
Urias, Ramon	12	8	10	3	0	41	0	0	2	5	9	16
Morel, Christopher	10	9	2	2	0	30	0	0	3	4	9	16
Nimmo, Brandon	10	11	12	5	0	54	0	1	2	4	9	16
Polanco, Jorge	14	10	6	7	1	48	0	1	2	4	9	16
Hays, Austin	12	11	11	6	0	59	0	2	3	2	9	16
Urias, Luis	16	11	9	6	0	50	0	2	2	4	8	16
Story, Trevor	9	3	6	3	1	30	0	1	3	6	6	16
Mullins II, Cedric	17	16	5	7	0	66	1	1	5	3	6	16
Heim, Jonah	17	15	5	3	0	50	0	2	3	8	3	16
Acuna Jr., Ronald	6	11	8	5	2	34	0	0	0	2	13	15
Jansen, Danny	6	6	10	5	1	37	0	1	2	2	10	15
Abreu, Jose	21	11	10	12	0	70	0	0	2	4	9	15
Donaldson, Josh	9	11	10	2	0	45	0	1	2	4	8	15
Maldonado, Martin	13	6	2	1	1	35	0	2	1	4	8	15
Sheets, Gavin	13	9	9	1	0	46	0	1	3	4	7	15
Walsh, Jared	13	13	5	1	0	39	0	3	2	4	6	15
Miranda, Jose	13	14	7	4	0	51	0	2	4	3	6	15
Bogaerts, Xander	9	12	7	3	0	47	1	2	1	6	5	15
Profar, Jurickson	12	16	6	2	1	60	1	1	6	3	4	15
Wong, Kolten	15	16	5	3	0	48	0	2	4	7	2	15
Winker, Jesse	12	13	4	3	1	51	0	0	1	5	8	14
Farmer, Kyle	17	15	12	3	0	64	0	2	3	3	6	14
Kirk, Alejandro	16	13	12	4	0	60	0	3	1	6	4	14
Rodgers, Brendan	8	10	7	4	0	52	0	0	0	2	11	13
Urshela, Gio	21	14	8	6	0	66	0	1	1	5	6	13
Castellanos, Nick	15	12	11	6	2	62	0	1	3	3	6	13
Bohm, Alec	20	14	8	7	0	65	0	1	3	3	6	13
Turner, Justin	17	18	4	5	1	61	0	0	3	5	5	13
Edman, Tommy	8	21	12	3	0	57	0	1	2	6	4	13
Canha, Mark	16	15	7	0	0	54	0	1	0	9	3	13
Peralta, David	12	19	6	7	1	56	0	0	1	2	9	12
Marte, Ketel	15	15	13	7	0	65	0	0	1	3	8	12
Rosario, Amed	25	13	5	6	0	63	0	0	1	3	7	11
Kim, Ha-seong	14	15	9	8	0	64	0	0	2	4	5	11
Verdugo, Alex	21	19	11	1	1	76	0	0	1	4	5	11
Schoop, Jonathan	18	10	7	4	0	54	0	0	2	6	3	11
Merrifield, Whit	15	24	12	2	0	70	0	2	2	4	3	11
Hoerner, Nico	17	10	9	1	0	60	0	1	3	5	1	10
Diaz, Yandy	11	22	6	1	0	55	1	0	0	2	6	9
Taylor, Michael A.	17	8	11	5	2	56	0	1	1	1	6	9
Rojas, Josh	17	15	8	5	0	57	0	0	3	0	6	9
McNeil, Jeff	21	11	7	1	0	71	0	0	1	4	4	9
Carlson, Dylan	22	10	7	3	0	59	0	0	1	2	5	8
Arraez, Luis	16	16	12	2	0	66	0	1	4	1	2	8

Long Outs and Home Runs

Player	Long Out Distances						Home Run Distances					
	330	350	370	390	400+	Long	330	350	370	390	400+	HR
Gurriel, Yuli	19	14	11	3	0	74	0	1	2	5	0	8
Hayes, Ke'Bryan	14	11	4	5	0	51	0	1	1	1	4	7
Ruiz, Keibert	19	14	4	4	0	56	0	0	1	4	2	7
Kemp, Tony	25	15	7	2	0	62	0	0	5	2	0	7
Kwan, Steven	17	12	4	1	0	58	0	0	3	2	1	6
Rojas, Miguel	16	14	8	2	0	57	0	1	1	4	0	6
Gurriel Jr., Lourdes	16	11	7	6	0	56	0	0	1	2	2	5
Benintendi, Andrew	13	16	8	5	1	64	0	0	1	2	2	5
Nola, Austin	18	14	9	2	0	54	0	0	0	3	1	4
Frazier, Adam	22	14	6	4	0	68	1	2	0	0	0	3
Lopez, Nicky	16	10	6	4	0	51	0	0	0	0	0	0
Straw, Myles	16	12	6	3	0	61	0	0	0	0	0	0

Hard Hit Balls

Alex Vigderman

When I first read the table on the next page, I had what I'll describe as a "Jeopardy moment": I phrased a player's name in the form of a question.

Trayce Thompson?

Yes, the leaders in hard-hit rate are Aaron Judge and Yordan Alvarez, the two players to post a slugging percentage above .600 this season. But just behind them, in the same little box of five players at the top, is a guy with 39 home runs in six MLB seasons spread across five teams.

In 255 plate appearances in 2022, Thompson posted an OPS that placed him between Julio Rodríguez and José Ramírez. But his inclusion as an elite hard hitter illustrates the double-edged sword at work here.

Hard hit rate as we show on the next page is hard hit balls per ball in play, meaning we're cutting out non-contact plays. We're after pure, bat-to-ball violence, regardless of the consequences of that approach.

In 2022, Thompson struck out more than 36% of the time. When you strike out that much, you need to tear the cover off the ball to get to an .860 OPS (as he did). In fact, only three players with at least 250 PA had even a .750 OPS while striking out at least a third of the time.

This list can also give you a little of a picture of a player's fortune or misfortune, with some caveats.

Mike Trout slugged .415 on soft-hit balls this year, which was more than double the league average and is probably a fluke. Breakout catcher Alejandro Kirk slugged .778 on hard-hit balls, which might appear like bad luck before I tell you that he hit half his balls on the ground. So make sure to consume hard hit ball data responsibly.

Hard Hit Balls
Highest Percentage of Hard Hit Balls - Players with 250+ PA in 2022

Player	In Play	Hard		Medium		Soft		Overall			
		Count	SLG	Count	SLG	Count	SLG	Hard Pct	Medium Pct	Soft Pct	SLG
Judge, Aaron	400	192	1.691	178	.351	30	.233	48.0%	44.5%	7.5%	.990
Alvarez, Yordan	371	164	1.404	173	.314	34	.265	44.2%	46.6%	9.2%	.791
Jimenez, Eloy	224	98	1.083	100	.357	26	.269	43.8%	44.6%	11.6%	.664
Hernandez, Teoscar	347	152	1.211	160	.331	35	.229	43.8%	46.1%	10.1%	.706
Thompson, Trayce	128	54	1.519	62	.433	12	.250	42.2%	48.4%	9.4%	.881
Buxton, Byron	225	94	1.606	98	.247	33	.121	41.8%	43.6%	14.7%	.799
Contreras, Willson	315	131	1.131	134	.316	50	.100	41.6%	42.5%	15.9%	.620
Sanchez, Gary	288	119	1.051	115	.225	54	.167	41.3%	39.9%	18.8%	.558
Muncy, Max	329	135	1.092	157	.199	37	.135	41.0%	47.7%	11.2%	.551
Tellez, Rowdy	411	166	1.224	173	.181	72	.153	40.4%	42.1%	17.5%	.598
Pujols, Albert	258	104	1.350	104	.284	50	.100	40.3%	40.3%	19.4%	.671
Chapman, Matt	373	150	1.205	162	.298	61	.148	40.2%	43.4%	16.4%	.633
Pederson, Joc	284	114	1.241	132	.369	38	.289	40.1%	46.5%	13.4%	.707
Soler, Jorge	181	72	1.250	80	.215	29	.034	39.8%	44.2%	16.0%	.600
McMahon, Ryan	374	148	1.124	189	.259	37	.189	39.6%	50.5%	9.9%	.590
Riley, Austin	451	178	1.435	217	.290	56	.161	39.5%	48.1%	12.4%	.727
Olson, Matt	450	177	1.294	200	.276	73	.151	39.3%	44.4%	16.2%	.659
Garcia, Adolis	428	168	1.078	191	.412	69	.290	39.3%	44.6%	16.1%	.654
De La Cruz, Bryan	243	95	1.032	128	.320	20	.250	39.1%	52.7%	8.2%	.594
Stanton, Giancarlo	264	103	1.382	124	.320	37	.108	39.0%	47.0%	14.0%	.705
Hiura, Keston	124	48	1.766	62	.274	14	.357	38.7%	50.0%	11.3%	.854
Trout, Mike	300	116	1.819	143	.338	41	.415	38.7%	47.7%	13.7%	.923
Schwarber, Kyle	379	146	1.660	171	.251	62	.145	38.5%	45.1%	16.4%	.772
Ohtani, Shohei	428	164	1.348	226	.327	38	.263	38.3%	52.8%	8.9%	.715
Pham, Tommy	392	150	.893	189	.341	53	.208	38.3%	48.2%	13.5%	.535
Betts, Mookie	472	181	1.250	233	.317	58	.121	38.3%	49.4%	12.3%	.652
Cordero, Franchy	154	59	1.052	71	.426	24	.250	38.3%	46.1%	15.6%	.640
Cruz, Oneil	206	79	1.385	89	.315	38	.342	38.3%	43.2%	18.4%	.727
Guerrero Jr., Vladimir	526	201	1.075	245	.289	80	.263	38.2%	46.6%	15.2%	.586
Machado, Manny	447	170	1.302	204	.374	73	.151	38.0%	45.6%	16.3%	.690
Walker, Christian	459	174	1.202	211	.300	74	.176	37.9%	46.0%	16.1%	.615
Voit, Luke	327	123	1.215	155	.305	49	.163	37.6%	47.4%	15.0%	.626
Gordon, Nick	309	116	.991	168	.352	25	.160	37.5%	54.4%	8.1%	.577
Kirk, Alejandro	416	156	.778	198	.330	62	.177	37.5%	47.6%	14.9%	.473
Seager, Corey	495	184	1.072	259	.245	52	.250	37.2%	52.3%	10.5%	.551
Abreu, Jose	495	184	.895	256	.357	55	.273	37.2%	51.7%	11.1%	.546
Pasquantino, Vinnie	226	84	.881	113	.270	29	.414	37.2%	50.0%	12.8%	.518
Castillo, Diego	191	71	1.044	95	.245	25	.240	37.2%	49.7%	13.1%	.535
Contreras, William	232	86	1.424	107	.340	39	.308	37.1%	46.1%	16.8%	.735
Freeman, Freddie	517	191	.925	263	.441	63	.413	36.9%	50.9%	12.2%	.614
Raleigh, Cal	253	93	1.538	120	.287	40	.125	36.8%	47.4%	15.8%	.730
Morel, Christopher	247	91	1.319	115	.327	41	.195	36.8%	46.6%	16.6%	.678
Reyes, Franmil	284	104	1.000	142	.376	38	.132	36.6%	50.0%	13.4%	.569
Suwinski, Jack	213	78	1.403	94	.213	41	.146	36.6%	44.1%	19.2%	.632
Grichuk, Randal	381	139	1.079	184	.242	58	.362	36.5%	48.3%	15.2%	.567
Davis, J.D.	198	72	1.278	96	.372	30	.200	36.4%	48.5%	15.2%	.679
Wisdom, Patrick	289	105	1.500	130	.289	54	.130	36.3%	45.0%	18.7%	.699
Rivera, Emmanuel	248	90	1.067	128	.291	30	.067	36.3%	51.6%	12.1%	.547
Correa, Carlos	405	146	1.160	191	.328	68	.221	36.0%	47.2%	16.8%	.608
Suarez, Eugenio	352	126	1.435	179	.335	47	.255	35.8%	50.9%	13.4%	.718
Calhoun, Kole	255	91	.944	126	.298	38	.158	35.7%	49.4%	14.9%	.508
Caratini, Victor	207	74	.808	93	.326	40	.100	35.7%	44.9%	19.3%	.454
Devers, Rafael	444	158	1.191	222	.418	64	.156	35.6%	50.0%	14.4%	.655
Ward, Taylor	380	135	1.135	198	.338	47	.362	35.5%	52.1%	12.4%	.624
Diaz, Yandy	414	147	.803	209	.341	58	.190	35.5%	50.5%	14.0%	.484
Tucker, Kyle	451	160	1.139	227	.282	64	.250	35.5%	50.3%	14.2%	.579
Melendez, MJ	336	119	1.104	171	.250	46	.261	35.4%	50.9%	13.7%	.550
Gamel, Ben	274	97	.938	136	.294	41	.171	35.4%	49.6%	15.0%	.502
Nootbaar, Lars	224	79	1.211	109	.327	36	.083	35.3%	48.7%	16.1%	.594
Mountcastle, Ryan	408	144	1.127	212	.295	52	.264	35.3%	52.0%	12.7%	.586
Lowe, Nathaniel	446	157	1.146	220	.400	69	.348	35.2%	49.3%	15.5%	.655
Adames, Willy	401	141	1.331	193	.314	67	.194	35.2%	48.1%	16.7%	.650
Renfroe, Hunter	358	126	1.368	166	.284	66	.242	35.2%	46.4%	18.4%	.660
Harper, Bryce	290	102	1.316	159	.340	29	.276	35.2%	54.8%	10.0%	.671
Drury, Brandon	396	139	1.406	189	.263	68	.176	35.1%	47.7%	17.2%	.651
Santana, Carlos	345	121	.975	162	.242	62	.097	35.1%	47.0%	18.0%	.472
Rodgers, Brendan	431	151	.899	216	.291	64	.297	35.0%	50.1%	14.8%	.505
Gorman, Nolan	180	63	1.254	88	.375	29	.241	35.0%	48.9%	16.1%	.661
Naylor, Josh	374	131	1.046	180	.324	63	.159	35.0%	48.1%	16.8%	.550
Brown, Seth	355	124	1.274	165	.293	66	.242	34.9%	46.5%	18.6%	.627
Bichette, Bo	499	174	1.126	272	.367	53	.208	34.9%	54.5%	10.6%	.616
Hernandez, Yadiel	233	81	1.013	117	.350	35	.114	34.8%	50.2%	15.0%	.541

Hard Hit Balls
Highest Percentage of Hard Hit Balls - Players with 250+ PA in 2022

Player	In Play	Hard		Medium		Soft		Overall			
		Count	SLG	Count	SLG	Count	SLG	Hard Pct	Medium Pct	Soft Pct	SLG
Santander, Anthony	457	159	1.237	201	.291	97	.103	34.8%	44.0%	21.2%	.577
Torres, Gleyber	401	139	1.175	211	.325	51	.157	34.7%	52.6%	12.7%	.597
Walsh, Jared	285	99	1.101	140	.279	46	.217	34.7%	49.1%	16.1%	.554
Miranda, Jose	354	123	1.024	177	.301	54	.185	34.7%	50.0%	15.3%	.535
Bellinger, Cody	360	125	1.148	183	.267	52	.154	34.7%	50.8%	14.4%	.554
Marte, Ketel	396	137	.866	200	.343	59	.271	34.6%	50.5%	14.9%	.512
Acuna Jr., Ronald	344	119	1.042	163	.342	62	.242	34.6%	47.4%	18.0%	.566
Martinez, J.D.	393	136	1.083	212	.410	45	.200	34.6%	53.9%	11.5%	.616
Rodriguez, Julio	367	127	1.413	191	.372	49	.224	34.6%	52.0%	13.4%	.710
Naquin, Tyler	218	75	1.147	109	.333	34	.265	34.4%	50.0%	15.6%	.604
Realmuto, J.T.	390	134	1.256	196	.344	60	.133	34.4%	50.3%	15.4%	.626
Myers, Wil	178	61	1.083	87	.353	30	.300	34.3%	48.9%	16.9%	.594
Perez, Salvador	339	116	1.289	183	.297	40	.150	34.2%	54.0%	11.8%	.616
Harris II, Michael	308	105	1.333	147	.404	56	.250	34.1%	47.7%	18.2%	.694
Vierling, Matt	261	89	.667	133	.380	39	.179	34.1%	51.0%	14.9%	.447
Cooper, Garrett	300	102	1.131	155	.340	43	.186	34.0%	51.7%	14.3%	.583
Urias, Ramon	312	106	1.106	151	.301	55	.145	34.0%	48.4%	17.6%	.548
Swanson, Dansby	462	157	1.218	243	.317	62	.323	34.0%	52.6%	13.4%	.624
Alonso, Pete	478	162	1.406	232	.293	84	.214	33.9%	48.5%	17.6%	.659
Taylor, Tyrone	274	93	1.174	141	.367	40	.150	33.9%	51.5%	14.6%	.609
Yelich, Christian	416	141	.936	217	.364	58	.172	33.9%	52.2%	13.9%	.533
Votto, Joey	225	76	1.145	123	.228	26	.154	33.8%	54.7%	11.6%	.529
Varsho, Daulton	393	133	1.323	185	.276	75	.173	33.8%	47.1%	19.1%	.609
Goldschmidt, Paul	424	143	1.496	217	.437	64	.297	33.7%	51.2%	15.1%	.771
Bart, Joey	149	50	1.400	64	.250	35	.257	33.6%	43.0%	23.5%	.638
Gonzalez, Oscar	289	97	1.115	144	.343	48	.229	33.6%	49.8%	16.6%	.582
Ozuna, Marcell	352	118	1.224	176	.253	58	.138	33.5%	50.0%	16.5%	.557
Peralta, David	331	111	1.036	162	.357	58	.207	33.5%	48.9%	17.5%	.560
Laureano, Ramon	242	81	1.148	125	.280	36	.056	33.5%	51.7%	14.9%	.537
Duvall, Adam	188	63	1.333	93	.286	32	.156	33.5%	49.5%	17.0%	.618
Pollock, A.J.	395	132	.977	196	.273	67	.149	33.4%	49.6%	17.0%	.486
Donaldson, Josh	336	112	1.064	175	.322	49	.143	33.3%	52.1%	14.6%	.542
Urshela, Gio	412	137	.903	220	.370	55	.255	33.3%	53.4%	13.3%	.531
Ruf, Darin	232	77	.987	111	.303	44	.114	33.2%	47.8%	19.0%	.493
Mancini, Trey	389	129	1.016	207	.311	53	.226	33.2%	53.2%	13.6%	.529
Taylor, Chris	245	81	1.177	132	.412	32	.094	33.1%	53.9%	13.1%	.620
Story, Trevor	239	79	1.338	116	.368	44	.227	33.1%	48.5%	18.4%	.660
Polanco, Jorge	284	94	1.011	149	.327	41	.268	33.1%	52.5%	14.4%	.543
Choi, Ji-Man	236	78	.987	134	.440	24	.208	33.1%	56.8%	10.2%	.592
Marsh, Brandon	272	90	.933	154	.466	28	.357	33.1%	56.6%	10.3%	.613
Gurriel Jr., Lourdes	372	123	.683	201	.415	48	.298	33.1%	54.0%	12.9%	.489
Vogelbach, Daniel	273	90	1.326	145	.269	38	.263	33.0%	53.1%	13.9%	.614
Gallo, Joey	188	62	1.672	88	.216	38	.105	33.0%	46.8%	20.2%	.668
Solano, Donovan	219	72	.859	118	.325	29	.276	32.9%	53.9%	13.2%	.493
Smith, Will	416	136	1.110	231	.326	49	.224	32.7%	55.5%	11.8%	.573
Isbel, Kyle	184	60	1.033	91	.250	33	.091	32.6%	49.5%	17.9%	.481
Bethancourt, Christian	239	78	1.026	122	.322	39	.282	32.6%	51.0%	16.3%	.546
Rizzo, Anthony	366	119	1.345	183	.298	64	.141	32.5%	50.0%	17.5%	.613
Albies, Ozzie	204	66	1.015	102	.242	36	.306	32.4%	50.0%	17.6%	.505
Greene, Riley	259	84	.901	132	.409	43	.209	32.4%	51.0%	16.6%	.531
Heim, Jonah	321	104	1.077	168	.241	49	.204	32.4%	52.3%	15.3%	.508
Hoskins, Rhys	424	137	1.338	227	.357	60	.167	32.3%	53.5%	14.2%	.648
Longoria, Evan	186	60	1.288	98	.375	28	.286	32.3%	52.7%	15.1%	.656
Cruz, Nelson	332	107	.838	172	.298	53	.226	32.2%	51.8%	16.0%	.459
Yastrzemski, Mike	351	113	1.243	184	.246	54	.148	32.2%	52.4%	15.4%	.552
Springer, George	418	134	1.328	206	.229	78	.231	32.1%	49.3%	18.7%	.586
Murphy, Sean	418	134	1.130	211	.325	73	.178	32.1%	50.5%	17.5%	.554
Suzuki, Seiya	290	93	1.247	145	.289	52	.288	32.1%	50.0%	17.9%	.599
Brantley, Michael	215	69	.841	118	.345	28	.107	32.1%	54.9%	13.0%	.474
Urias, Luis	312	100	1.152	157	.275	55	.145	32.1%	50.3%	17.6%	.534
Turner, Justin	387	124	1.075	214	.324	49	.163	32.0%	55.3%	12.7%	.541
O'Neill, Tyler	238	76	1.125	129	.341	33	.212	31.9%	54.2%	13.9%	.567
Arenado, Nolan	489	156	1.368	235	.302	98	.153	31.9%	48.1%	20.0%	.612
Moore, Dylan	132	42	1.293	66	.338	24	.167	31.8%	50.0%	18.2%	.608
Nola, Austin	297	94	.652	152	.292	51	.235	31.6%	51.2%	17.2%	.397
Torkelson, Spencer	263	83	.795	144	.289	36	.222	31.6%	54.8%	13.7%	.441
Arozarena, Randy	432	136	1.257	211	.344	85	.212	31.5%	48.8%	19.7%	.607
Arroyo, Christian	235	74	.945	121	.356	40	.125	31.5%	51.5%	17.0%	.502
Bohm, Alec	486	153	.912	255	.316	78	.244	31.5%	52.5%	16.0%	.489
Turner, Trea	527	166	1.012	275	.388	86	.388	31.5%	52.2%	16.3%	.583
d'Arnaud, Travis	306	96	1.323	163	.313	47	.191	31.4%	53.3%	15.4%	.611
McCutchen, Andrew	395	124	.992	216	.297	55	.218	31.4%	54.7%	13.9%	.506
Vaughn, Andrew	419	131	1.016	224	.362	64	.125	31.3%	53.5%	15.3%	.529

Hard Hit Balls
Highest Percentage of Hard Hit Balls - Players with 250+ PA in 2022

Player	In Play	Hard Count	Hard SLG	Medium Count	Medium SLG	Soft Count	Soft SLG	Overall Hard Pct	Medium Pct	Soft Pct	SLG
Diaz, Elias	272	85	.976	139	.321	48	.063	31.3%	51.1%	17.6%	.480
Peterson, Jace	208	65	1.031	116	.330	27	.259	31.3%	55.8%	13.0%	.542
Benintendi, Andrew	390	122	.775	230	.350	38	.316	31.3%	59.0%	9.7%	.479
Taylor, Michael A.	310	97	.862	154	.322	59	.305	31.3%	49.7%	19.0%	.485
Cron, C.J.	416	130	1.449	215	.329	71	.211	31.3%	51.7%	17.1%	.655
Lindor, Francisco	504	157	1.071	251	.412	96	.156	31.2%	49.8%	19.0%	.569
Moustakas, Mike	180	56	.945	79	.377	45	.133	31.1%	43.9%	25.0%	.492
Slater, Austin	190	59	1.068	108	.406	23	.304	31.1%	56.8%	12.1%	.601
Alfaro, Jorge	161	50	1.204	86	.369	25	.320	31.1%	53.4%	15.5%	.620
Bregman, Alex	481	149	1.104	251	.316	81	.150	31.0%	52.2%	16.8%	.529
Moncada, Yoan	285	88	.977	161	.281	36	.278	30.9%	56.5%	12.6%	.495
Happ, Ian	428	132	1.191	235	.328	61	.328	30.8%	54.9%	14.3%	.594
Chavis, Michael	279	86	1.214	116	.325	77	.221	30.8%	41.6%	27.6%	.567
Witt Jr., Bobby	461	142	1.220	245	.256	74	.260	30.8%	53.1%	16.1%	.555
Rutschman, Adley	315	97	1.094	171	.373	47	.191	30.8%	54.3%	14.9%	.567
Anderson, Brian	238	73	1.068	128	.268	37	.135	30.7%	53.8%	15.5%	.494
Schwindel, Frank	215	66	.923	110	.266	39	.205	30.7%	51.2%	18.1%	.455
Hayes, Ke'Bryan	385	118	.754	204	.347	63	.238	30.6%	53.0%	16.4%	.454
Garcia, Luis	281	86	1.000	158	.372	37	.162	30.6%	56.2%	13.2%	.533
Robert, Luis	304	93	1.054	153	.329	58	.241	30.6%	50.3%	19.1%	.535
Verdugo, Alex	513	157	.879	282	.312	74	.216	30.6%	55.0%	14.4%	.473
Bogaerts, Xander	446	136	.977	240	.419	70	.357	30.5%	53.8%	15.7%	.579
Hays, Austin	424	129	1.047	203	.351	92	.185	30.4%	47.9%	21.7%	.525
Farmer, Kyle	435	132	.884	232	.322	71	.225	30.3%	53.3%	16.3%	.475
France, Ty	462	140	1.065	239	.356	83	.108	30.3%	51.7%	18.0%	.525
Grisham, Trent	310	94	1.096	164	.323	52	.019	30.3%	52.9%	16.8%	.512
Altuve, Jose	441	133	1.323	230	.367	78	.269	30.2%	52.2%	17.7%	.639
Nimmo, Brandon	470	141	1.007	242	.380	87	.230	30.0%	51.5%	18.5%	.541
Stassi, Max	223	67	.925	113	.297	43	.140	30.0%	50.7%	19.3%	.457
Taveras, Leody	230	69	.853	128	.400	33	.212	30.0%	55.7%	14.3%	.509
Odor, Rougned	321	96	.947	170	.298	55	.236	29.9%	53.0%	17.1%	.479
Rojas, Josh	355	106	.903	201	.361	48	.208	29.9%	56.6%	13.5%	.501
McCormick, Chas	254	76	1.316	152	.245	26	.346	29.9%	59.8%	10.2%	.577
Kepler, Max	326	97	.928	179	.229	50	.100	29.8%	54.9%	15.3%	.419
Reynolds, Bryan	403	120	1.244	231	.370	52	.327	29.8%	57.3%	12.9%	.623
Flores, Wilmer	429	128	1.106	232	.265	69	.145	29.8%	54.1%	16.1%	.491
Aguilar, Jesus	350	104	1.020	182	.335	64	.188	29.7%	52.0%	18.3%	.510
Bell, Josh	456	135	1.038	243	.343	78	.167	29.6%	53.3%	17.1%	.518
Yepez, Juan	196	58	1.393	94	.304	44	.159	29.6%	48.0%	22.4%	.589
Semien, Marcus	547	162	.963	286	.392	99	.192	29.6%	52.3%	18.1%	.525
Garcia, Avisail	250	74	.890	128	.268	48	.292	29.6%	51.2%	19.2%	.456
Kelly, Carson	250	74	.833	125	.293	51	.196	29.6%	50.0%	20.4%	.431
Andrus, Elvis	443	131	.992	233	.339	79	.089	29.6%	52.6%	17.8%	.488
Profar, Jurickson	478	141	.986	241	.290	96	.208	29.5%	50.4%	20.1%	.477
Edman, Tommy	468	138	.957	257	.353	73	.123	29.5%	54.9%	15.6%	.496
Soto, Juan	428	126	1.389	219	.242	83	.108	29.4%	51.2%	19.4%	.554
Hernandez, Kike	294	86	.774	144	.352	64	.109	29.3%	49.0%	21.8%	.421
Haase, Eric	229	67	1.455	120	.331	42	.190	29.3%	52.4%	18.3%	.633
Reynolds, Matt	167	49	.854	103	.330	15	.400	29.3%	61.7%	9.0%	.488
Sanchez, Jesus	222	65	1.369	122	.273	35	.114	29.3%	55.0%	15.8%	.570
Friedl, T.J.	191	56	1.204	107	.272	28	.179	29.3%	56.0%	14.7%	.530
Ramirez, Jose	528	154	1.257	269	.355	105	.238	29.2%	50.9%	19.9%	.595
Maldonado, Martin	234	68	1.313	131	.206	35	.200	29.1%	56.0%	15.0%	.531
Ramirez, Harold	335	97	.832	176	.391	62	.258	29.0%	52.5%	18.5%	.492
Sheets, Gavin	294	85	1.193	151	.287	58	.224	28.9%	51.4%	19.7%	.533
Hicks, Aaron	278	80	.899	142	.264	56	.214	28.8%	51.1%	20.1%	.436
Blackmon, Charlie	428	123	1.049	240	.321	65	.292	28.7%	56.1%	15.2%	.527
Belt, Brandon	174	50	1.080	96	.316	28	.179	28.7%	55.2%	16.1%	.514
Winker, Jesse	356	102	.971	181	.258	73	.164	28.7%	50.8%	20.5%	.445
Diaz, Aledmys	254	73	.945	132	.346	49	.184	28.7%	52.0%	19.3%	.488
Lowe, Brandon	175	50	1.100	96	.337	29	.103	28.6%	54.9%	16.6%	.517
Lux, Gavin	329	94	.914	178	.392	57	.246	28.6%	54.1%	17.3%	.515
Pena, Jeremy	392	112	1.234	217	.325	63	.254	28.6%	55.4%	16.1%	.575
Dalbec, Bobby	203	58	1.298	115	.321	30	.233	28.6%	56.7%	14.8%	.588
Anderson, Tim	277	79	.734	163	.362	35	.400	28.5%	58.8%	12.6%	.473
Canha, Mark	369	105	1.038	187	.310	77	.273	28.5%	50.7%	20.9%	.510
Franco, Wander	285	81	.797	148	.384	56	.214	28.4%	51.9%	19.6%	.466
Nido, Tomas	222	63	.683	128	.360	31	.258	28.4%	57.7%	14.0%	.442
Franco, Maikel	299	85	.906	145	.268	69	.174	28.4%	48.5%	23.1%	.429
Dozier, Hunter	338	96	.979	180	.391	62	.242	28.4%	53.3%	18.3%	.531
Escobar, Eduardo	372	105	1.202	204	.392	63	.159	28.2%	54.8%	16.9%	.582
Paredes, Isaac	266	75	1.419	148	.259	43	.023	28.2%	55.6%	16.2%	.545
Pinder, Chad	246	69	1.304	131	.336	46	.130	28.0%	53.3%	18.7%	.572

Hard Hit Balls
Highest Percentage of Hard Hit Balls - Players with 250+ PA in 2022

Player	In Play	Hard Count	Hard SLG	Medium Count	Medium SLG	Soft Count	Soft SLG	Hard Pct	Medium Pct	Soft Pct	SLG
Grossman, Robbie	286	80	.886	165	.321	41	.146	28.0%	57.7%	14.3%	.454
Candelario, Jeimer	324	90	1.090	172	.272	62	.194	27.8%	53.1%	19.1%	.484
Carlson, Dylan	342	95	.892	188	.382	59	.169	27.8%	55.0%	17.3%	.485
Tapia, Raimel	334	93	.817	175	.392	66	.197	27.8%	52.4%	19.8%	.473
Castellanos, Nick	396	110	.955	219	.378	67	.254	27.8%	55.3%	16.9%	.518
Arraez, Luis	507	141	.799	314	.351	52	.173	27.8%	61.9%	10.3%	.456
Neuse, Sheldon	191	53	.774	112	.286	26	.192	27.7%	58.6%	13.6%	.408
Ruiz, Keibert	347	96	.768	204	.287	47	.234	27.7%	58.8%	13.5%	.413
Thomas, Lane	371	102	1.180	183	.367	86	.198	27.5%	49.3%	23.2%	.549
Bradley Jr., Jackie	269	74	.878	147	.255	48	.104	27.5%	54.6%	17.8%	.401
Kim, Ha-seong	424	116	.904	224	.361	84	.190	27.4%	52.8%	19.8%	.475
Velazquez, Andrew	212	58	1.034	121	.268	33	.242	27.4%	57.1%	15.6%	.483
Hosmer, Eric	317	87	.884	158	.354	72	.181	27.4%	49.8%	22.7%	.459
Stott, Bryson	340	93	.892	186	.299	61	.246	27.4%	54.7%	17.9%	.453
Gurriel, Yuli	475	129	.756	258	.354	88	.102	27.2%	54.3%	18.5%	.415
Trevino, Jose	274	74	1.081	142	.248	58	.259	27.0%	51.8%	21.2%	.476
Biggio, Cavan	174	47	1.043	106	.298	21	.476	27.0%	60.9%	12.1%	.523
Machin, Vimael	179	48	.660	113	.243	18	.333	26.8%	63.1%	10.1%	.364
Mullins II, Cedric	488	131	1.063	263	.345	94	.213	26.8%	53.9%	19.3%	.508
Baez, Javier	411	110	1.211	241	.318	60	.167	26.8%	58.6%	14.6%	.534
Engel, Adam	169	45	.667	96	.406	28	.250	26.6%	56.8%	16.6%	.450
Knizner, Andrew	199	53	.792	101	.290	45	.156	26.6%	50.8%	22.6%	.394
Segura, Jean	297	79	.835	148	.340	70	.300	26.6%	49.8%	23.6%	.463
Rosario, Eddie	185	49	1.000	110	.252	26	.231	26.5%	59.5%	14.1%	.451
McCarthy, Jake	249	66	.909	141	.482	42	.262	26.5%	56.6%	16.9%	.559
Donovan, Brendan	324	86	.682	188	.403	50	.300	26.5%	58.0%	15.4%	.461
Wong, Kolten	349	92	1.154	198	.349	59	.220	26.4%	56.7%	16.9%	.541
Reyes, Victor	242	64	.698	140	.445	38	.237	26.4%	57.9%	15.7%	.479
Rosario, Amed	530	140	.906	304	.381	86	.198	26.4%	57.4%	16.2%	.489
Berti, Jon	270	71	.761	147	.363	52	.269	26.3%	54.4%	19.3%	.450
Wendle, Joey	301	79	.684	170	.355	52	.231	26.2%	56.5%	17.3%	.421
Mateo, Jorge	352	92	1.253	196	.302	64	.234	26.1%	55.7%	18.2%	.539
Margot, Manuel	269	70	.900	153	.349	46	.217	26.0%	56.9%	17.1%	.470
Joe, Connor	308	80	.900	151	.393	77	.182	26.0%	49.0%	25.0%	.472
Thomas, Alek	312	81	.949	176	.225	55	.309	26.0%	56.4%	17.6%	.427
Smith, Pavin	181	47	1.111	94	.333	40	.225	26.0%	51.9%	22.1%	.506
Hernandez, Cesar	451	117	.774	240	.270	94	.266	25.9%	53.2%	20.8%	.399
Vazquez, Christian	332	86	1.024	194	.332	52	.173	25.9%	58.4%	15.7%	.483
Aquino, Aristides	158	41	1.683	69	.232	48	.188	25.9%	43.7%	30.4%	.595
Crawford, Brandon	313	81	.949	175	.316	57	.193	25.9%	55.9%	18.2%	.453
Walls, Taylor	291	75	.893	173	.249	43	.163	25.8%	59.5%	14.8%	.404
India, Jonathan	292	75	1.093	151	.298	66	.288	25.7%	51.7%	22.6%	.500
Gimenez, Andres	386	99	1.216	217	.439	70	.257	25.6%	56.2%	18.1%	.604
Cronenworth, Jake	464	119	1.231	262	.258	83	.229	25.6%	56.5%	17.9%	.502
Marte, Starling	369	94	1.213	212	.392	63	.333	25.5%	57.5%	17.1%	.591
Schoop, Jonathan	378	96	.839	191	.353	91	.110	25.4%	50.5%	24.1%	.414
Bader, Harrison	232	59	1.000	117	.304	56	.179	25.4%	50.4%	24.1%	.452
Harrison, Josh	319	81	.963	200	.265	38	.342	25.4%	62.7%	11.9%	.454
Pache, Cristian	174	44	.591	94	.242	36	.278	25.3%	54.0%	20.7%	.339
Senzel, Nick	300	76	.711	175	.291	49	.204	25.3%	58.3%	16.3%	.384
Ortega, Rafael	250	63	1.082	146	.286	41	.171	25.2%	58.4%	16.4%	.467
Gomes, Yan	235	59	.914	130	.325	46	.152	25.1%	55.3%	19.6%	.439
Merrifield, Whit	427	107	.902	253	.348	67	.149	25.1%	59.3%	15.7%	.451
Miller, Owen	340	85	.778	183	.358	72	.310	25.0%	53.8%	21.2%	.450
Dubon, Mauricio	221	55	.745	127	.252	39	.128	24.9%	57.5%	17.6%	.357
Espinal, Santiago	385	96	.726	213	.362	76	.276	24.9%	55.3%	19.7%	.436
Gonzalez, Luis	241	60	.810	145	.401	36	.222	24.9%	60.2%	14.9%	.475
Grandal, Yasmani	250	62	.581	141	.302	47	.213	24.8%	56.4%	18.8%	.355
Abrams, CJ	238	59	.638	125	.279	54	.389	24.8%	52.5%	22.7%	.393
Adell, Jo	161	40	1.487	92	.326	29	.414	24.8%	57.1%	18.0%	.625
Straw, Myles	454	112	.473	273	.285	69	.246	24.7%	60.1%	15.2%	.326
Daza, Yonathan	320	79	.789	187	.375	54	.259	24.7%	58.4%	16.9%	.455
McNeil, Jeff	477	118	.879	291	.413	68	.309	24.7%	61.0%	14.3%	.513
Rivas, Alfonso	167	41	.825	97	.411	29	.172	24.6%	58.1%	17.4%	.470
Castro, Rodolfo	180	44	1.500	103	.363	33	.152	24.4%	57.2%	18.3%	.603
Dickerson, Corey	235	57	.930	132	.385	46	.196	24.3%	56.2%	19.6%	.481
Narvaez, Omar	207	50	.780	124	.295	33	.152	24.2%	59.9%	15.9%	.390
Rengifo, Luis	411	99	1.111	238	.338	74	.270	24.1%	57.9%	18.0%	.512
Hoerner, Nico	426	102	.843	257	.384	67	.194	23.9%	60.3%	15.7%	.465
Siri, Jose	194	46	1.196	113	.330	35	.286	23.7%	58.2%	18.0%	.528
Wade Jr., LaMonte	169	40	1.275	91	.216	38	.211	23.7%	53.8%	22.5%	.470
Estrada, Thairo	405	96	1.021	230	.367	79	.203	23.7%	56.8%	19.5%	.489
Castro, Harold	346	82	.889	219	.353	45	.267	23.7%	63.3%	13.0%	.469

Hard Hit Balls

Highest Percentage of Hard Hit Balls - Players with 250+ PA in 2022

Player	In Play	Hard		Medium		Soft		Overall			
		Count	SLG	Count	SLG	Count	SLG	Hard Pct	Medium Pct	Soft Pct	SLG
Cabrera, Miguel	301	70	.857	200	.308	31	.194	23.3%	66.4%	10.3%	.426
Toro, Abraham	263	61	1.117	150	.238	52	.058	23.2%	57.0%	19.8%	.405
Smith, Josh	168	39	.368	99	.354	30	.172	23.2%	58.9%	17.9%	.325
Mejia, Francisco	225	52	.962	135	.358	38	.316	23.1%	60.0%	16.9%	.491
LeMahieu, DJ	399	91	1.022	245	.292	63	.206	22.8%	61.4%	15.8%	.444
Stallings, Jacob	266	60	.644	164	.346	42	.167	22.6%	61.7%	15.8%	.384
Perdomo, Geraldo	342	77	.618	202	.307	63	.127	22.5%	59.1%	18.4%	.345
Crawford, J.P.	445	99	.796	250	.316	96	.198	22.2%	56.2%	21.6%	.397
Molina, Yadier	223	49	.854	123	.260	51	.118	22.0%	55.2%	22.9%	.356
Castro, Willi	287	63	1.000	160	.367	64	.234	22.0%	55.7%	22.3%	.473
Iglesias, Jose	386	85	.774	211	.364	90	.289	22.0%	54.7%	23.3%	.436
Lopez, Nicky	384	84	.476	229	.307	71	.169	21.9%	59.6%	18.5%	.319
Hedges, Austin	229	50	.898	136	.194	43	.116	21.8%	59.4%	18.8%	.338
Guillorme, Luis	253	55	.709	166	.335	32	.219	21.7%	65.6%	12.6%	.402
Robles, Victor	277	59	1.000	160	.299	58	.224	21.3%	57.8%	20.9%	.435
Frazier, Adam	478	100	.691	292	.309	86	.151	20.9%	61.1%	18.0%	.359
Rojas, Miguel	414	86	.647	250	.328	78	.205	20.8%	60.4%	18.8%	.371
Garcia, Leury	240	50	.612	141	.299	49	.184	20.8%	58.8%	20.4%	.340
Newman, Kevin	243	50	.898	150	.392	43	.116	20.6%	61.7%	17.7%	.446
Celestino, Gilberto	236	48	.750	142	.336	46	.239	20.3%	60.2%	19.5%	.402
Kiner-Falefa, Isiah	419	84	.726	258	.320	77	.221	20.0%	61.6%	18.4%	.384
Allen, Nick	242	48	.750	147	.271	47	.277	19.8%	60.7%	19.4%	.370
Kemp, Tony	436	84	.866	279	.308	73	.151	19.3%	64.0%	16.7%	.388
Kwan, Steven	509	96	.823	325	.376	88	.295	18.9%	63.9%	17.3%	.447
Barnhart, Tucker	208	39	.718	128	.307	41	.195	18.8%	61.5%	19.7%	.362
McGuire, Reese	202	35	1.059	132	.403	35	.171	17.3%	65.3%	17.3%	.477
All MLB	124264	37552	1.058	66095	.324	20617	.206	30.2%	53.2%	16.6%	.526

Pinch Hitting

Alex Vigderman

Forget saving the bees; can we save the pinch hitter?

I'm sure you're not shocked to hear that there was a dramatic fall-off in pinch hitting appearances in 2022, given that the designated hitter made its debut in the National League. In sum, there were nearly twice as many pinch appearances in 2021 than in 2022.

Last year's leader in pinch-hit at-bats was Ehire Adrianza, whose 64 represented a smidge more than a third of his season. This year's leaders, Ryan O'Hearn and Austin Slater, led the way with 30 pinch at-bats. (Slater had many more pinch plate appearances, as he pinch walked 11 times.)

The good news is that both of them raked in those opportunities. O'Hearn was the worse of the two with a .973 OPS as a pinch hitter. SIS's own favorite Giants fan, Handbook architect Will Creager, thought Slater's frequent pinch hitting did him a disservice relative to his potential.

Slater also led the league in cold cuts, a very important stat that I just made up. His 75 swings as a pinch hitter were eight more than any other player, but that's unsurprising given his overall lead in plate appearances.

The next-most pinch at-bats by a player with a better OPS than those two was 22 by Albert Pujols, who authored a heartwarming season for the ages. His .948 career OPS as a pinch hitter (mostly in his later years) is one point below his career OPS as a first baseman (mostly in his early years).

This year, Mike Brosseau hit .529 with a laughable 1.755 OPS and a league-leading 12 pinch RBIs (four more than anyone else). He is probably best known for a series-winning pinch-hit homer off Aroldis Chapman in the 2020 playoffs, so he might be carrying the torch into the next era of pinch hitters.

Pinch Hitting

Pinch Hitters with 10+ PAs or 10+ Total Bases in 2022

Batter	B	AB	H	2B	3B	HR	RBI	TBB	IBB	SO	GDP	Avg	OBP	Slg	OPS
Adell, Jo	R	12	0	0	0	0	0	6	0	6	0	.000	.000	.000	.000
Aguilar, Jesus	R	9	1	0	0	0	0	1	0	3	0	.111	.200	.111	.311
Alberto, Hanser	R	17	4	1	0	0	0	0	0	5	0	.235	.235	.294	.529
Alfaro, Jorge	R	10	3	0	0	1	5	0	0	4	0	.300	.300	.600	.900
Arraez, Luis	L	11	2	0	0	0	0	2	1	2	0	.182	.308	.182	.490
Azocar, Jose	R	9	2	1	0	0	0	2	0	3	1	.222	.364	.333	.697
Belt, Brandon	L	7	3	1	0	1	3	2	0	2	0	.429	.600	1.000	1.600
Bethancourt, Christian	R	12	2	1	0	1	3	0	0	5	0	.167	.167	.500	.667
Biggio, Cavan	L	14	1	0	0	0	1	2	0	3	1	.071	.235	.071	.307
Brosseau, Mike	R	17	9	2	0	3	12	1	0	5	0	.529	.579	1.176	1.755
Brown, Seth	L	13	5	3	0	0	3	1	0	3	0	.385	.429	.615	1.044
Calhoun, Kole	L	19	3	0	0	0	3	2	0	6	0	.158	.261	.158	.419
Camargo, Johan	B	7	4	0	0	0	0	2	0	0	0	.571	.667	.571	1.238
Canha, Mark	R	10	0	0	0	0	0	0	0	4	0	.000	.000	.000	.000
Caratini, Victor	B	8	1	0	0	0	0	1	0	3	0	.125	.364	.125	.489
Carlson, Dylan	B	9	3	0	0	0	0	1	0	3	0	.333	.400	.333	.733
Carpenter, Matt	L	8	1	1	0	0	0	4	1	5	0	.125	.417	.250	.667
Castillo, Diego	R	18	2	2	0	0	0	1	0	6	1	.111	.158	.222	.380
Celestino, Gilberto	R	12	2	0	0	0	3	2	0	3	1	.167	.286	.167	.452
Chavis, Michael	R	16	4	2	0	0	3	0	0	4	0	.250	.235	.375	.610
Choi, Ji-Man	L	7	4	2	0	0	4	4	1	3	0	.571	.727	.857	1.584
Cordero, Franchy	L	10	2	0	0	1	1	1	0	5	0	.200	.273	.500	.773
Dalbec, Bobby	R	14	4	1	0	1	1	3	0	9	0	.286	.412	.571	.983
Davis, J.D.	R	23	5	1	0	2	4	5	0	9	1	.217	.357	.522	.879
Dickerson, Corey	L	9	1	1	0	0	4	2	0	3	0	.111	.308	.222	.530
Dubon, Mauricio	R	10	2	0	0	0	2	0	0	0	1	.200	.200	.200	.400
Duffy, Matt	R	14	1	1	0	0	0	1	0	3	0	.071	.133	.143	.276
Espinal, Santiago	R	12	2	2	0	0	1	2	0	5	0	.167	.286	.333	.619
Flores, Wilmer	R	14	6	1	0	1	2	4	0	3	0	.429	.556	.714	1.270
Ford, Mike	L	7	1	0	0	0	0	3	0	2	0	.143	.400	.143	.543
Fraley, Jake	L	8	4	1	0	1	1	3	0	2	0	.500	.667	1.000	1.667
Frazier, Adam	L	13	3	0	0	0	0	1	0	5	1	.231	.286	.231	.516
Friedl, T.J.	L	8	2	1	0	0	2	1	0	1	0	.250	.300	.375	.675
Garlick, Kyle	R	17	4	0	0	0	0	0	0	7	0	.235	.316	.235	.551
Gorman, Nolan	L	10	1	0	0	0	1	2	0	5	0	.100	.250	.100	.350
Grisham, Trent	L	11	3	1	0	0	3	1	0	2	0	.273	.333	.364	.697
Grossman, Robbie	B	6	1	1	0	0	0	4	0	2	0	.167	.500	.333	.833
Haase, Eric	R	21	4	0	0	0	1	2	1	10	0	.190	.261	.190	.451
Heim, Jonah	B	16	4	1	0	0	0	2	0	3	1	.250	.333	.313	.646
Hernandez, Yadiel	L	10	3	1	0	0	2	0	0	2	0	.300	.300	.400	.700
Herrera, Odubel	L	9	2	0	0	0	1	1	0	2	1	.222	.300	.222	.522
Hicks, Aaron	B	7	0	0	0	0	0	3	0	5	0	.000	.300	.000	.300
Hummel, Cooper	B	15	0	0	0	0	0	5	0	7	1	.000	.250	.000	.250
Kemp, Tony	L	11	1	0	0	0	1	4	0	4	0	.091	.333	.091	.424
Kirk, Alejandro	R	15	4	0	0	0	3	1	0	5	1	.267	.313	.267	.579
La Stella, Tommy	L	11	4	1	0	0	1	1	0	2	0	.364	.385	.455	.839
Longoria, Evan	R	17	5	2	0	0	4	2	0	4	0	.294	.368	.412	.780
Lopez, Alejo	B	13	0	0	0	0	1	2	0	3	0	.000	.133	.000	.133
Luplow, Jordan	R	24	4	0	0	2	7	3	0	10	0	.167	.259	.417	.676
Machin, Vimael	L	9	4	1	0	0	1	1	0	2	0	.444	.500	.556	1.056
Matijevic, J.J.	L	15	5	0	0	0	1	0	0	7	0	.333	.375	.333	.708
Mazara, Nomar	L	11	2	0	0	0	1	0	0	5	0	.182	.182	.182	.364
McKenna, Ryan	R	10	2	1	0	0	2	1	1	7	0	.200	.333	.300	.633
Mejia, Francisco	B	12	4	1	0	0	4	0	0	1	0	.333	.308	.417	.724
Miller, Brad	L	19	5	2	0	2	6	1	0	9	0	.263	.300	.684	.984
Miller, Owen	R	11	2	0	0	0	0	1	0	4	0	.182	.250	.182	.432
Moore, Dylan	R	11	2	1	0	0	1	5	1	5	0	.182	.438	.273	.710
Naquin, Tyler	L	10	1	0	0	0	1	2	1	8	0	.100	.250	.100	.350
Nootbaar, Lars	L	8	1	0	0	0	2	3	1	5	0	.125	.333	.125	.458
Odor, Rougned	L	15	4	0	0	0	3	1	0	6	0	.267	.313	.267	.579
O'Hearn, Ryan	L	30	11	3	0	1	6	2	0	6	0	.367	.406	.567	.973
Ortega, Rafael	L	18	1	0	0	1	3	4	0	10	0	.056	.227	.222	.449
Palacios, Richie	L	19	5	3	0	0	6	2	1	5	0	.263	.318	.421	.739
Paredes, Isaac	R	15	0	0	0	0	0	1	0	4	0	.000	.063	.000	.063
Pederson, Joc	L	22	4	1	0	0	2	5	0	9	0	.182	.321	.227	.549
Peralta, David	L	15	3	0	2	0	4	2	0	3	1	.200	.278	.467	.744
Peterson, Jace	L	17	5	2	0	0	4	3	0	5	0	.294	.400	.412	.812
Pinder, Chad	R	19	3	0	0	1	5	1	0	9	1	.158	.200	.316	.516

Pinch Hitting

Pinch Hitters with 10+ PAs or 10+ Total Bases in 2022

Batter	B	AB	H	2B	3B	HR	RBI	TBB	IBB	SO	GDP	Avg	OBP	Slg	OPS
Pujols, Albert	R	22	5	0	0	3	8	3	1	6	2	.227	.357	.636	.994
Raleigh, Cal	B	15	4	1	0	2	4	1	0	9	0	.267	.313	.733	1.046
Ramirez, Harold	R	19	9	0	0	0	7	2	0	3	0	.474	.524	.474	.997
Refsnyder, Rob	R	13	4	2	0	0	2	4	0	6	0	.308	.471	.462	.932
Rivas, Alfonso	L	10	2	1	0	0	2	3	0	4	0	.200	.385	.300	.685
Rosario, Eddie	L	11	3	1	0	0	0	2	0	3	0	.273	.385	.364	.748
Ruf, Darin	R	28	6	1	0	1	6	5	0	9	1	.214	.353	.357	.710
Ruiz, Keibert	B	13	5	1	0	0	1	0	0	2	1	.385	.385	.462	.846
Sanchez, Gary	R	9	1	0	0	0	1	2	0	2	0	.111	.273	.111	.384
Sheets, Gavin	L	16	6	1	0	0	4	0	0	6	0	.375	.353	.438	.790
Slater, Austin	R	30	10	2	0	1	6	11	0	8	1	.333	.545	.500	1.045
Smith, Dominic	L	12	3	1	0	0	2	1	0	5	0	.250	.308	.333	.641
Smith, Josh	L	9	4	1	0	0	1	2	0	1	0	.444	.545	.556	1.101
Sosa, Edmundo	R	12	2	0	1	0	1	1	0	5	0	.167	.231	.333	.564
Tapia, Raimel	L	12	2	0	0	0	1	0	0	2	0	.167	.167	.167	.333
Tellez, Rowdy	L	13	1	0	0	1	1	1	0	5	2	.077	.200	.308	.508
Thompson, Trayce	R	13	3	2	0	1	3	0	0	6	1	.231	.231	.615	.846
Toro, Abraham	B	12	4	0	0	0	2	2	0	2	1	.333	.429	.333	.762
VanMeter, Josh	L	13	2	0	0	0	0	1	0	4	0	.154	.214	.154	.368
Vazquez, Christian	R	10	4	0	0	0	1	1	0	1	0	.400	.455	.400	.855
Velazquez, Nelson	R	13	3	0	0	1	3	2	0	6	0	.231	.333	.462	.795
Vierling, Matt	R	11	3	1	0	1	1	1	0	4	0	.273	.333	.636	.970
Vogelbach, Daniel	L	14	3	0	0	2	2	5	0	7	1	.214	.421	.643	1.064
Vogt, Stephen	L	23	4	0	0	1	5	0	0	6	1	.174	.167	.304	.471
Wade Jr., LaMonte	L	8	1	0	0	0	0	4	0	1	0	.125	.462	.125	.587
Walsh, Jared	L	8	2	0	0	1	2	2	1	2	1	.250	.400	.625	1.025
Wendle, Joey	L	10	2	0	0	0	0	0	0	1	0	.200	.273	.200	.473
Wong, Kolten	L	14	3	1	0	0	0	0	0	6	0	.214	.313	.286	.598
Yastrzemski, Mike	L	12	0	0	0	0	2	2	0	5	0	.000	.125	.000	.125

Career Pinch Hitting
Active Pinch Hitters with 100+ PAs in their careers

Batter	B	AB	H	2B	3B	HR	RBI	TBB	IBB	SO	GDP	Avg	OBP	Slg	OPS
								Pinch Hitting							
Adrianza, Ehire	B	153	35	12	1	3	19	12	0	32	1	.229	.289	.379	.668
Aguilar, Jesus	R	144	31	7	0	5	21	17	0	51	6	.215	.297	.368	.665
Almora Jr., Albert	R	117	19	3	0	1	14	3	1	23	6	.162	.187	.214	.401
Barnes, Austin	R	103	23	5	0	2	14	10	0	36	4	.223	.310	.330	.640
Belt, Brandon	L	91	20	4	2	7	23	12	1	37	2	.220	.317	.538	.856
Carpenter, Matt	L	133	26	11	0	5	31	30	1	53	2	.195	.343	.391	.734
Culberson, Charlie	R	153	37	6	3	7	31	7	0	44	7	.242	.276	.458	.734
Dickerson, Alex	L	86	22	3	0	6	17	14	2	24	6	.256	.369	.500	.869
Dickerson, Corey	L	122	27	9	1	0	16	9	4	36	2	.221	.276	.311	.588
Difo, Wilmer	B	126	27	2	2	3	15	17	0	31	0	.214	.306	.333	.639
Flores, Wilmer	R	137	35	8	0	8	28	19	1	33	1	.255	.352	.489	.841
Frazier, Adam	L	101	25	5	0	1	7	15	0	15	3	.248	.361	.327	.688
Gamel, Ben	L	95	15	5	0	1	9	8	0	36	1	.158	.229	.242	.471
Gosselin, Phil	R	189	45	8	0	1	13	13	2	62	2	.238	.284	.296	.581
Grandal, Yasmani	B	91	19	3	0	4	19	20	0	40	3	.209	.351	.374	.725
Happ, Ian	B	84	21	4	1	5	17	13	0	29	2	.250	.360	.500	.860
Harrison, Josh	R	125	22	3	1	3	14	4	0	24	2	.176	.206	.288	.494
Hernandez, Kike	R	163	33	8	0	6	20	17	3	53	1	.202	.275	.362	.637
Kemp, Tony	L	84	19	5	1	2	14	16	0	26	0	.226	.356	.381	.737
La Stella, Tommy	L	198	55	15	0	1	26	27	1	32	5	.278	.374	.369	.743
Miller, Brad	L	155	34	9	1	5	19	12	1	58	3	.219	.280	.387	.667
Pederson, Joc	L	143	27	8	1	4	17	27	2	46	2	.189	.318	.343	.661
Peterson, Jace	L	100	22	4	2	2	11	13	0	27	0	.220	.310	.360	.670
Pinder, Chad	R	96	22	2	0	6	24	8	0	36	3	.229	.292	.438	.730
Pujols, Albert	R	89	27	0	0	7	28	16	5	23	4	.303	.409	.539	.948
Ruf, Darin	R	153	23	2	0	6	21	15	1	61	4	.150	.244	.281	.525
Slater, Austin	R	104	31	7	1	6	29	28	1	37	2	.298	.468	.558	1.025
Smith, Dominic	L	84	24	10	0	3	19	13	0	24	3	.286	.390	.512	.902
Solano, Donovan	R	139	34	3	3	2	13	7	0	33	2	.245	.309	.353	.662
Tapia, Raimel	L	110	26	3	3	5	22	9	1	30	7	.236	.300	.455	.755
Turner, Justin	R	183	48	12	0	7	41	16	1	36	8	.262	.325	.443	.768
Vogt, Stephen	L	135	25	7	1	3	18	20	3	40	1	.185	.285	.319	.603
Wong, Kolten	L	87	24	5	1	2	8	9	1	22	1	.276	.370	.425	.795

Manufactured Runs, Productive Outs, & Unproductive Outs

Sarah Thompson

The Cleveland Guardians finished the regular season scoring 698 runs, 15th in MLB and just 4 runs above league average. They also finished the regular season hitting the second-fewest home runs (127) ahead of only the Detroit Tigers (110), who scored the fewest runs in baseball (557).

In this current baseball climate, those facts don't usually add up. So where did all of the Guardians runs come from? They manufactured them.

The Guardians co-led MLB in Manufactured Runs with 170. The Guardians also employed one of the biggest Manufactured Run contributors, Steven Kwan. Kwan had the second-most Manufactured Run Contributions in MLB with 28, just behind Cedric Mullins II (29).

What exactly comprises a Manufactured Run is a little complicated—you can check the glossary for more information, but know that sacrifice bunts, steals, hit and run plays, bunt hits, and infield hits are important.

What also helped the Guardians is their amount of productive outs. They led MLB with 258. José Ramírez led the team with 32 Productive Outs, ranking 5th among all batters. Nearly one-fourth of their outs advanced a runner in some capacity, and that rate is the fourth-most efficient in baseball this season.

Good things happen when you put the ball in play, they say. The Guardians struck out at the lowest clip in MLB (18%). Kwan (9%) and Ramírez (12%) boasted some of the lowest strikeout rates among qualified batters this season, ranking second and ninth, respectively. Their ability to put the ball in play, make productive outs, and manufacture runs led them to defy low expectations of success and win their division playing a style of baseball that many argue is all but dead.

Manufactured Run Contributions, Productive Outs, & Unproductive Outs Produced by Team

Team	Manufactured Run Contributions	Productive Outs	Unproductive Outs
Arizona Diamondbacks	170	250	667
Atlanta Braves	127	184	736
Baltimore Orioles	150	201	747
Boston Red Sox	130	251	790
Chicago White Sox	126	194	765
Chicago Cubs	126	231	712
Cincinnati Reds	114	188	694
Cleveland Guardians	170	258	797
Colorado Rockies	122	223	753
Detroit Tigers	125	200	686
Houston Astros	102	181	735
Kansas City Royals	147	217	729
Los Angeles Dodgers	137	217	763
Los Angeles Angels	111	207	703
Miami Marlins	127	206	674
Milwaukee Brewers	104	202	746
Minnesota Twins	105	212	764
New York Yankees	145	205	741
New York Mets	134	231	795
Oakland Athletics	111	189	682
Philadelphia Phillies	121	203	708
Pittsburgh Pirates	126	218	671
San Diego Padres	126	224	749
San Francisco Giants	118	203	749
Seattle Mariners	108	167	691
St Louis Cardinals	131	201	715
Tampa Bay Rays	156	219	771
Texas Rangers	158	209	699
Toronto Blue Jays	123	225	723
Washington Nationals	140	215	688

Manufactured Run Contributions, Productive Outs, & Unproductive Outs Allowed by Team

Team	Manufactured Run Contributions	Productive Outs	Unproductive Outs
Arizona Diamondbacks	123	209	700
Atlanta Braves	125	212	701
Baltimore Orioles	131	240	716
Boston Red Sox	146	202	747
Chicago White Sox	141	205	725
Chicago Cubs	130	185	755
Cincinnati Reds	139	213	771
Cleveland Guardians	115	194	681
Colorado Rockies	168	236	752
Detroit Tigers	160	206	739
Houston Astros	104	190	717
Kansas City Royals	178	251	767
Los Angeles Dodgers	105	183	707
Los Angeles Angels	131	198	748
Miami Marlins	101	192	738
Milwaukee Brewers	131	216	704
Minnesota Twins	115	201	722
New York Yankees	91	176	745
New York Mets	95	188	665
Oakland Athletics	142	194	773
Philadelphia Phillies	120	206	725
Pittsburgh Pirates	132	246	729
San Diego Padres	129	208	680
San Francisco Giants	150	235	761
Seattle Mariners	100	206	720
St Louis Cardinals	122	238	683
Tampa Bay Rays	113	203	702
Texas Rangers	163	247	788
Toronto Blue Jays	141	228	729
Washington Nationals	149	223	753

Players with the most Manufactured Run Contributions, Productive Outs, & Unproductive Outs

Manufactured Run Contributions		Productive Outs		Unproductive Outs	
Mullins II, Cedric	29	Verdugo, Alex	42	Santander, Anthony	113
Kwan, Steven	28	Lindor, Francisco	40	Witt Jr., Bobby	107
Rojas, Josh	26	Blackmon, Charlie	38	Lindor, Francisco	104
Rosario, Amed	25	Turner, Trea	34	Adames, Willy	98
Edman, Tommy	24	Ramirez, Jose	32	Alonso, Pete	98
Witt Jr., Bobby	24	Perdomo, Geraldo	32	Bregman, Alex	96
Varsho, Daulton	23	Rosario, Amed	31	Bogaerts, Xander	96
Semien, Marcus	23	Semien, Marcus	31	Chapman, Matt	93
Hernandez, Cesar	22	Yelich, Christian	31	Machado, Manny	92
Nimmo, Brandon	22	Arozarena, Randy	30	Escobar, Eduardo	92
Straw, Myles	22	Guerrero Jr., Vladimir	30	Ramirez, Jose	92
Mateo, Jorge	22	Bichette, Bo	29	Baez, Javier	92
Freeman, Freddie	21	Freeman, Freddie	29	Judge, Aaron	91
Garcia, Adolis	21	Martinez, J.D.	29	Riley, Austin	89
Lopez, Nicky	20	Seager, Corey	29	Wisdom, Patrick	88
Gimenez, Andres	20	Olson, Matt	29	Olson, Matt	85
Rutschman, Adley	20	Santander, Anthony	28	Turner, Trea	85
Springer, George	20	Grisham, Trent	27	Straw, Myles	85
Swanson, Dansby	20	Benintendi, Andrew	27	Arozarena, Randy	85
Turner, Trea	20	Ohtani, Shohei	27	Rodgers, Brendan	84
Diaz, Yandy	19	Lopez, Nicky	27	Rosario, Amed	84
Bader, Harrison	19	Bohm, Alec	26	Cron, C.J.	83
Yelich, Christian	19	Lowe, Nathaniel	26	Goldschmidt, Paul	82
Altuve, Jose	19	Alonso, Pete	26	Swanson, Dansby	82
Pham, Tommy	19	Walker, Christian	26	Freeman, Freddie	81
McCarthy, Jake	19	Ramirez, Harold	26	Garcia, Adolis	81
Rodriguez, Julio	18	Grossman, Robbie	25	Tucker, Kyle	81
Berti, Jon	18	Mancini, Trey	25	Bohm, Alec	80
Machado, Manny	18	Lux, Gavin	25	Martinez, J.D.	80
Marte, Starling	18	Vaughn, Andrew	24	Pham, Tommy	80
Andrus, Elvis	17	Reynolds, Bryan	24	Cronenworth, Jake	80
Goldschmidt, Paul	17	Devers, Rafael	24	Seager, Corey	79
Bogaerts, Xander	17	Straw, Myles	24	Soto, Juan	79
Kiner-Falefa, Isiah	17	Estrada, Thairo	24	Marte, Starling	78
Hayes, KeBryan'	17	Flores, Wilmer	24	Bellinger, Cody	78
Abreu, Jose	17	Bell, Josh	24	Verdugo, Alex	77
Bellinger, Cody	17	Harper, Bryce	24	Reynolds, Bryan	77
Daza, Yonathan	17	Canha, Mark	23	Gimenez, Andres	76
Arozarena, Randy	17	Crawford, J.P.	23	Guerrero Jr., Vladimir	76
Reynolds, Bryan	16	Bradley Jr., Jackie	23	Bichette, Bo	76
Kemp, Tony	16	Cron, C.J.	23	Kim, Ha-seong	76
Judge, Aaron	16	Profar, Jurickson	23	Lowe, Nathaniel	76
Acuna Jr., Ronald	16	Cruz, Nelson	23	Abreu, Jose	76
Robles, Victor	16	Nola, Austin	23	Ozuna, Marcell	76
Merrifield, Whit	16	Gordon, Nick	23	Rizzo, Anthony	75
Lindor, Francisco	16	Kiner-Falefa, Isiah	23	Correa, Carlos	75
Betts, Mookie	16	Edman, Tommy	23	Tellez, Rowdy	75
Baez, Javier	16	Hays, Austin	23	Mateo, Jorge	75
Segura, Jean	16	Garcia, Adolis	23	Gurriel, Yuli	74
		Kirk, Alejandro	23	Mancini, Trey	73
		Kwan, Steven	23	Brown, Seth	73
		Witt Jr., Bobby	23	Murphy, Sean	73
				Voit, Luke	73
				Grichuk, Randal	73

Lefty/Righty Statistics

Mark Simon

I've always been highly impressed by left-handed pitchers who could neutralize right-handed hitters. Lefties typically face three times as many right-handed hitters as they do left-handed hitters. And for good reason.

There was a 90-point difference in opponents' OPS this season for when a left-handed pitcher faced a right-handed batter (.737 opponents' OPS) compared to when they faced a left-handed batter (.647). To be a good left-handed starting pitcher, you have to be able to get righties out.

I want to cite two who were particularly good this season. One is Nestor Cortes of the Yankees. Cortes employed a mix of different deliveries to keep hitters off balance.

Right-handed batters hit an MLB-low .164 against his 4-seam fastball and .199 against a pitch he added this season, a cutter. The Yankees, who ranked No. 1 in MLB in Defensive Runs Saved, did their job behind Cortes as well. Right-handed hitters had just a .241 BABIP against him.

The other was someone who came on strong at the end of the season and who might be a good sleeper pick for Cy Young in 2023, Marlins southpaw starter Jesus Luzardo.

Right-handed batters hit .189 against Luzardo this season, third-lowest for *any* pitcher and the lowest opponents' batting average vs any left-handed starter.

Luzardo neutralizes right-handed batters with a nasty slider (.167 opp BA) and changeup (.171), the latter of which he throws for a strike more than two-thirds of the time. Control has been Luzardo's biggest issue, but he walked only five batters in his last four starts of the season.

Conversely, I always like to look for left-handed batters who can hit left-handed pitchers because there are so few who do it well.

Case in point, Andrés Giménez of the Guardians, Nathaniel Lowe of the Rangers, and Yordan Alvarez of the Astros had special seasons because they were such ferocious hitters against lefties.

They ranked 3-4-5 in batting average vs left-handed pitching by *any* hitter (Giménez .336, Lowe .330, Alvarez .321). Lowe and Alvarez each hit 10 home runs vs left-handed pitchers in the regular season. Only Lowe's teammate, Corey Seager (14), and Alvarez's teammate, Kyle Tucker (13), had more as a left-handed batter.

Other lefties that you wouldn't shy away from using versus a left-handed pitcher include Jeff McNeil (.312 batting average), Charlie Blackmon (.304), and Freddie Freeman (.294). One name to watch in the future is Tigers rookie outfielder Riley Greene, who hit .303 in 109 left-on-left at-bats.

The following pages include platoon splits for all hitters with at least 100 plate appearances and pitchers with at least 100 batters faced in 2022. The lists are alphabetical by last name.

At the end of each set are MLB season numbers for context. If you're looking for split leaderboards, they can be found in the Leaderboards section.

Content Management

If you like our work, there are plenty of other outlets at which you can find more of it.

The SIS Baseball Podcast features interviews with notable MLB players (Byron Buxton, Steven Kwan, Jeremy Peña), and notable people who cover baseball (José Mota, Tyler Kepner) and provides insight into different baseball work being done at our company. It can be found wherever you get your podcasts.

Our company website (SportsInfoSolutions.com) features articles and research written by our R&D team and our Baseball Operations department.

You can also follow us on Twitter at @sportsinfo_SIS and @sis_baseball.

Batters vs. Left-Handed and Right-Handed Pitchers

Batter	vs	Avg	AB	H	2B	3B	HR	RBI	BB	SO	OBP	Slg
Abrams, CJ	L	.157	89	14	2	1	0	6	0	21	.185	.202
Bats Left	R	.287	195	56	10	1	2	15	5	29	.322	.379
Abreu, Jose	L	.294	119	35	9	0	4	17	17	29	.387	.471
Bats Right	R	.307	482	148	31	0	11	58	45	81	.376	.440
Acuna Jr., Ronald	L	.234	107	25	5	0	3	7	18	27	.349	.364
Bats Right	R	.275	360	99	19	0	12	43	35	99	.351	.428
Adames, Willy	L	.224	152	34	12	0	5	20	16	50	.298	.401
Bats Right	R	.243	411	100	19	0	26	78	33	116	.298	.479
Adams, Riley	L	.138	65	9	1	0	1	4	5	17	.200	.200
Bats Right	R	.208	77	16	3	0	4	6	7	29	.282	.403
Adell, Jo	L	.204	103	21	5	1	2	9	4	38	.239	.330
Bats Right	R	.236	165	39	7	1	6	18	7	69	.280	.400
Aguilar, Jesus	L	.196	112	22	3	0	3	9	8	35	.254	.304
Bats Right	R	.247	352	87	16	0	13	42	20	84	.290	.403
Alberto, Hanser	L	.279	104	29	7	1	1	11	1	17	.286	.394
Bats Right	R	.173	52	9	2	1	1	4	2	8	.204	.308
Albies, Ozzie	L	.250	84	21	8	0	3	13	1	11	.261	.452
Bats Both	R	.245	163	40	8	0	5	22	15	36	.309	.387
Alcantara, Sergio	L	.214	56	12	2	0	2	7	4	16	.267	.357
Bats Both	R	.221	149	33	6	1	4	22	8	41	.259	.356
Alfaro, Jorge	L	.269	67	18	1	0	4	10	4	30	.310	.463
Bats Right	R	.238	189	45	13	0	3	30	7	68	.276	.354
Allen, Greg	L	.182	55	10	2	0	1	4	2	19	.220	.273
Bats Both	R	.190	63	12	2	0	1	4	8	23	.292	.270
Allen, Nick	L	.276	87	24	6	0	3	9	5	10	.315	.448
Bats Right	R	.179	212	38	7	0	1	10	14	54	.232	.226
Almora Jr., Albert	L	.224	67	15	4	0	2	9	6	12	.288	.373
Bats Right	R	.223	148	33	6	1	3	20	11	34	.280	.338
Alonso, Pete	L	.247	146	36	6	0	9	25	26	35	.364	.473
Bats Right	R	.279	451	126	21	0	31	106	41	93	.348	.532
Altuve, Jose	L	.340	141	48	15	0	10	21	20	23	.426	.660
Bats Right	R	.285	386	110	24	0	18	36	46	64	.373	.487
Alvarez, Yordan	L	.321	162	52	13	0	10	33	25	37	.411	.586
Bats Left	R	.299	308	92	16	2	27	64	53	69	.404	.627
Anderson, Brian	L	.247	73	18	4	0	3	6	6	29	.321	.425
Bats Right	R	.215	265	57	12	1	5	22	31	72	.308	.325
Anderson, Tim	L	.397	58	23	2	0	2	5	3	8	.426	.534
Bats Right	R	.281	274	77	11	0	4	20	11	47	.321	.365
Andrus, Elvis	L	.283	145	41	9	0	7	21	12	24	.338	.490
Bats Right	R	.236	390	92	23	0	10	37	27	68	.290	.372
Aquino, Aristides	L	.170	100	17	6	0	1	9	8	42	.231	.260
Bats Right	R	.214	159	34	7	0	9	21	9	59	.256	.428
Arcia, Orlando	L	.213	61	13	3	0	1	5	7	14	.290	.311
Bats Right	R	.257	148	38	6	0	8	25	14	37	.327	.459
Arenado, Nolan	L	.250	112	28	6	1	11	25	11	12	.323	.616
Bats Right	R	.303	445	135	36	0	19	78	41	60	.367	.512
Arozarena, Randy	L	.317	120	38	9	1	6	21	9	25	.364	.558
Bats Right	R	.249	466	116	32	2	14	68	37	131	.318	.416
Arraez, Luis	L	.265	113	30	2	1	2	7	10	9	.331	.354
Bats Left	R	.329	434	143	29	0	6	42	40	34	.386	.438
Arroyo, Christian	L	.295	88	26	5	1	2	12	5	21	.333	.443
Bats Right	R	.281	192	54	11	0	4	24	8	28	.317	.401
Azocar, Jose	L	.243	107	26	7	2	0	5	4	22	.268	.346
Bats Right	R	.274	95	26	2	1	0	5	8	22	.330	.316
Baddoo, Akil	L	.231	39	9	1	0	0	4	3	15	.286	.256
Bats Left	R	.198	162	32	2	2	2	5	21	49	.290	.272
Bader, Harrison	L	.212	52	11	1	1	0	5	5	13	.293	.269
Bats Right	R	.258	240	62	9	2	5	25	10	49	.294	.375
Baez, Javier	L	.301	136	41	9	2	5	24	6	30	.326	.507
Bats Right	R	.217	419	91	18	2	12	43	20	117	.262	.356
Barnes, Austin	L	.182	66	12	3	0	3	10	13	15	.325	.364
Bats Right	R	.230	113	26	3	0	5	16	14	22	.323	.389
Barnhart, Tucker	L	.238	63	15	1	0	0	2	6	17	.304	.254
Bats Both	R	.216	218	47	9	0	1	14	19	57	.282	.271
Barrero, Jose	L	.146	41	6	0	0	2	4	3	19	.205	.293
Bats Right	R	.153	124	19	3	0	0	6	6	57	.192	.177
Bart, Joey	L	.182	88	16	1	0	6	13	7	40	.250	.398
Bats Right	R	.231	173	40	5	0	5	12	19	72	.318	.347
Beer, Seth	L	.250	20	5	2	0	0	2	1	5	.286	.350
Bats Left	R	.176	91	16	1	0	1	7	10	26	.276	.220
Bell, Josh	L	.276	181	50	8	2	7	32	24	30	.357	.459
Bats Both	R	.261	371	97	21	1	10	39	57	72	.364	.404
Bellinger, Cody	L	.213	150	32	10	1	2	20	8	44	.250	.333
Bats Left	R	.209	354	74	17	2	17	48	30	106	.272	.412
Belt, Brandon	L	.182	66	12	2	0	1	7	14	22	.341	.258
Bats Left	R	.223	188	42	7	1	7	16	23	59	.319	.383

Batter	vs	Avg	AB	H	2B	3B	HR	RBI	BB	SO	OBP	Slg
Benintendi, Andrew	L	.269	134	36	3	1	1	8	15	19	.347	.328
Bats Left	R	.318	327	104	20	2	4	43	37	58	.384	.428
Berti, Jon	L	.232	82	19	7	0	2	8	8	26	.300	.390
Bats Right	R	.243	276	67	10	3	2	20	34	63	.331	.322
Bethancourt, Christian	L	.252	119	30	5	0	3	13	9	29	.315	.370
Bats Right	R	.251	199	50	12	0	8	21	3	51	.262	.432
Betts, Mookie	L	.308	156	48	12	1	11	29	17	27	.374	.609
Bats Right	R	.255	416	106	28	2	24	53	38	77	.327	.505
Bichette, Bo	L	.262	107	28	5	1	5	16	9	25	.322	.467
Bats Right	R	.295	545	161	38	0	19	77	32	130	.335	.470
Biggio, Cavan	L	.150	40	6	2	0	1	6	5	20	.271	.275
Bats Left	R	.212	217	46	16	1	5	18	33	65	.327	.364
Blackmon, Charlie	L	.304	158	48	7	3	1	31	7	24	.351	.405
Bats Left	R	.247	372	92	15	3	15	47	25	85	.299	.425
Bleday, J.J.	L	.163	43	7	2	0	1	1	0	13	.163	.279
Bats Left	R	.168	161	27	8	2	4	15	30	54	.303	.317
Bogaerts, Xander	L	.382	123	47	11	0	4	21	20	23	.469	.569
Bats Right	R	.286	434	124	27	0	11	52	37	95	.350	.424
Bohm, Alec	L	.352	159	56	17	2	3	19	13	27	.394	.541
Bats Right	R	.253	427	108	7	1	10	53	18	83	.285	.344
Bolt, Skye	L	.188	32	6	2	0	1	5	0	8	.182	.344
Bats Both	R	.203	74	15	0	0	3	8	7	22	.289	.324
Bote, David	L	.182	33	6	4	0	0	1	3	20	.263	.303
Bats Right	R	.289	83	24	4	0	4	11	3	25	.337	.482
Bradley Jr., Jackie	L	.164	73	12	4	0	2	15	7	15	.238	.301
Bats Left	R	.214	271	58	19	1	2	23	17	62	.260	.314
Brantley, Michael	L	.295	78	23	3	0	1	4	7	11	.360	.372
Bats Left	R	.285	165	47	11	1	4	22	24	19	.374	.436
Bregman, Alex	L	.225	187	42	13	0	4	20	32	23	.345	.358
Bats Right	R	.277	361	100	25	0	19	73	55	54	.377	.504
Bride, Jonah	L	.185	54	10	0	0	0	1	5	10	.262	.185
Bats Right	R	.213	108	23	4	0	1	5	14	22	.320	.278
Brosseau, Mike	L	.274	95	26	5	0	3	13	7	32	.343	.421
Bats Right	R	.217	46	10	0	0	3	10	7	16	.345	.413
Brown, Seth	L	.174	92	16	4	0	3	12	6	30	.232	.315
Bats Left	R	.243	408	99	22	3	22	61	45	116	.320	.473
Brujan, Vidal	L	.220	50	11	3	0	2	8	7	11	.316	.400
Bats Both	R	.134	97	13	2	0	1	8	5	26	.181	.186
Bryant, Kris	L	.333	66	22	8	0	3	7	5	9	.389	.591
Bats Right	R	.287	94	27	4	0	2	7	12	18	.367	.394
Burger, Jake	L	.326	43	14	5	0	3	12	5	16	.388	.651
Bats Right	R	.224	125	28	4	1	5	14	5	40	.271	.392
Buxton, Byron	L	.252	103	26	5	0	10	15	10	36	.325	.592
Bats Right	R	.211	237	50	8	3	18	36	24	80	.299	.498
Cabrera, Miguel	L	.289	97	28	1	0	1	14	12	23	.360	.330
Bats Right	R	.243	300	73	9	0	4	29	16	78	.286	.313
Cabrera, Oswaldo	L	.286	28	8	1	1	0	2	3	8	.344	.393
Bats Both	R	.238	126	30	7	0	6	17	12	36	.304	.437
Cain, Lorenzo	L	.068	44	3	2	0	0	2	5	9	.163	.114
Bats Right	R	.228	101	23	3	0	1	7	3	27	.262	.287
Calhoun, Kole	L	.208	77	16	3	0	3	11	6	26	.282	.364
Bats Left	R	.193	311	60	11	1	9	38	21	110	.251	.322
Call, Alex	L	.208	53	11	1	1	1	3	6	14	.288	.321
Bats Right	R	.262	61	16	2	0	4	10	9	16	.375	.492
Camargo, Johan	L	.182	66	12	1	0	2	6	6	19	.250	.288
Bats Both	R	.279	86	24	2	0	1	9	7	18	.333	.337
Candelario, Jeimer	L	.235	115	27	3	0	6	24	5	24	.262	.417
Bats Both	R	.210	314	66	16	2	7	26	23	85	.275	.341
Canha, Mark	L	.241	166	40	8	0	6	23	19	34	.335	.398
Bats Right	R	.280	296	83	16	0	7	38	29	63	.385	.405
Caratini, Victor	L	.168	107	18	4	0	3	8	9	30	.276	.290
Bats Both	R	.218	165	36	8	0	6	26	22	37	.316	.376
Carlson, Dylan	L	.305	128	39	11	1	3	15	11	31	.369	.477
Bats Both	R	.207	304	63	19	3	5	27	34	63	.294	.339
Carpenter, Kerry	L	.217	23	5	0	0	1	1	0	5	.250	.348
Bats Left	R	.263	80	21	4	1	5	9	6	27	.326	.525
Carpenter, Matt	L	.333	33	11	2	0	5	16	4	11	.421	.848
Bats Left	R	.295	95	28	7	0	10	21	15	24	.409	.684
Carroll, Corbin	L	.179	28	5	3	1	0	3	1	7	.233	.357
Bats Left	R	.289	76	22	6	1	4	11	7	24	.365	.553
Casali, Curt	L	.218	55	12	3	0	4	11	11	20	.353	.491
Bats Right	R	.194	93	18	1	0	1	6	13	30	.296	.237
Castellanos, Nick	L	.295	122	36	4	0	2	8	7	25	.331	.377
Bats Right	R	.254	402	102	23	0	11	54	22	105	.297	.393
Castillo, Diego	L	.239	142	34	11	0	9	21	7	40	.281	.507
Bats Right	R	.167	120	20	2	0	2	8	7	35	.215	.233

Batters vs. Left-Handed and Right-Handed Pitchers

Batter	vs	Avg	AB	H	2B	3B	HR	RBI	BB	SO	OBP	Slg
Castro, Harold	L	.303	66	20	4	1	0	11	3	13	.333	.394
Bats Left	R	.266	354	94	17	1	7	36	14	66	.294	.379
Castro, Rodolfo	L	.263	80	21	3	3	6	13	4	17	.306	.600
Bats Both	R	.220	173	38	5	1	5	14	18	57	.295	.347
Castro, Willi	L	.250	120	30	7	1	3	13	1	20	.260	.400
Bats Both	R	.237	245	58	11	1	5	18	14	62	.295	.351
Cave, Jake	L	.273	33	9	2	1	0	4	0	12	.273	.394
Bats Left	R	.198	131	26	5	2	5	16	11	37	.257	.382
Celestino, Gilberto	L	.213	108	23	5	0	1	11	10	29	.292	.287
Bats Right	R	.251	203	51	7	1	1	13	22	48	.324	.310
Chapman, Matt	L	.245	106	26	7	0	4	12	10	30	.322	.425
Bats Right	R	.225	432	97	20	1	23	64	58	140	.324	.435
Chavis, Michael	L	.240	171	41	6	1	8	24	9	61	.276	.427
Bats Right	R	.222	230	51	10	2	6	25	10	65	.257	.361
Chirinos, Robinson	L	.213	89	19	5	0	2	11	8	31	.276	.337
Bats Right	R	.151	106	16	4	0	2	11	11	36	.256	.245
Chisholm Jr., Jazz	L	.143	35	5	3	0	1	5	1	11	.205	.314
Bats Left	R	.275	178	49	7	4	13	40	20	55	.348	.579
Choi, Ji-Man	L	.294	51	15	4	0	0	9	3	19	.351	.373
Bats Left	R	.223	305	68	18	0	11	43	55	104	.340	.390
Clemens, Kody	L	.273	22	6	2	0	2	7	0	6	.273	.636
Bats Left	R	.116	95	11	2	0	3	10	8	27	.181	.232
Clement, Ernie	L	.192	78	15	2	0	0	2	2	12	.232	.218
Bats Right	R	.176	85	15	2	0	0	4	9	14	.253	.200
Contreras, William	L	.354	99	35	7	1	5	15	16	26	.440	.596
Bats Right	R	.247	235	58	7	0	15	30	23	78	.315	.468
Contreras, Willson	L	.219	105	23	7	1	8	14	10	24	.325	.533
Bats Right	R	.251	311	78	16	1	14	41	35	79	.357	.444
Cooper, Garrett	L	.228	92	21	7	0	1	11	8	28	.287	.337
Bats Right	R	.270	322	87	26	2	8	39	32	91	.351	.438
Cordero, Franchy	L	.162	37	6	0	0	2	5	5	17	.279	.324
Bats Left	R	.229	205	47	17	1	6	24	23	75	.304	.410
Correa, Carlos	L	.299	134	40	13	1	6	18	24	28	.400	.545
Bats Right	R	.289	388	112	11	0	16	46	37	93	.353	.441
Crawford, Brandon	L	.241	108	26	4	0	3	16	6	24	.305	.361
Bats Left	R	.227	299	68	11	2	6	36	33	74	.309	.338
Crawford, J.P.	L	.221	154	34	5	3	3	19	21	28	.311	.351
Bats Left	R	.253	364	92	19	0	3	23	47	52	.352	.330
Cron, C.J.	L	.208	178	37	4	2	10	37	16	56	.274	.421
Bats Right	R	.280	397	111	24	1	19	65	27	108	.334	.489
Cronenworth, Jake	L	.232	181	42	8	1	6	26	19	48	.327	.387
Bats Left	R	.241	406	98	22	3	11	62	51	83	.334	.392
Cruz, Nelson	L	.248	149	37	5	0	5	27	19	30	.345	.383
Bats Right	R	.227	299	68	11	0	5	37	30	89	.297	.314
Cruz, Oneil	L	.158	101	16	2	2	3	11	8	59	.225	.307
Bats Left	R	.265	230	61	11	2	14	43	20	67	.324	.513
Culberson, Charlie	L	.275	80	22	6	0	0	8	2	20	.293	.350
Bats Right	R	.200	35	7	0	0	2	4	3	11	.263	.371
Dalbec, Bobby	L	.240	96	23	1	0	5	13	14	36	.348	.406
Bats Right	R	.204	221	45	8	2	7	26	15	82	.253	.353
d'Arnaud, Travis	L	.341	91	31	6	0	5	17	3	15	.375	.571
Bats Right	R	.246	305	75	19	1	13	43	16	75	.303	.443
Davis, J.D.	L	.245	159	39	7	1	6	17	22	62	.344	.415
Bats Right	R	.252	159	40	9	0	6	18	17	60	.335	.421
Daza, Yonathan	L	.341	132	45	9	2	0	12	6	14	.362	.439
Bats Right	R	.279	240	67	12	0	2	22	20	44	.342	.354
De La Cruz, Bryan	L	.184	87	16	0	0	2	8	8	31	.253	.253
Bats Right	R	.277	242	67	20	0	11	35	11	59	.309	.496
DeJong, Paul	L	.151	53	8	5	0	0	2	7	24	.262	.245
Bats Right	R	.159	157	25	4	0	6	23	14	55	.239	.299
Delay, Jason	L	.242	66	16	3	0	1	5	4	18	.286	.333
Bats Right	R	.191	89	17	3	0	0	6	5	32	.250	.225
Devers, Rafael	L	.272	151	41	11	0	4	26	7	42	.315	.424
Bats Left	R	.304	404	123	31	1	23	62	43	72	.374	.557
Diaz, Aledmys	L	.267	90	24	3	0	4	10	9	14	.333	.433
Bats Right	R	.233	215	50	10	0	8	28	9	39	.268	.391
Diaz, Elias	L	.278	133	37	7	1	4	16	6	26	.314	.436
Bats Right	R	.197	218	43	11	1	5	35	19	56	.261	.326
Diaz, Lewin	L	.071	14	1	1	0	0	0	0	5	.133	.143
Bats Left	R	.178	146	26	3	0	5	11	11	49	.233	.301
Diaz, Yandy	L	.310	126	39	14	0	3	16	19	8	.400	.492
Bats Right	R	.291	347	101	19	0	6	41	59	52	.402	.398
Dickerson, Corey	L	.077	26	2	1	0	0	0	1	8	.143	.115
Bats Left	R	.286	255	73	16	1	6	36	11	40	.316	.427
Donaldson, Josh	L	.217	106	23	7	0	4	14	14	24	.311	.396
Bats Right	R	.223	372	83	21	0	11	48	40	124	.307	.368
Donovan, Brendan	L	.279	61	17	3	0	0	8	14	7	.421	.328
Bats Left	R	.282	330	93	18	1	5	37	46	63	.389	.388
Dozier, Hunter	L	.252	127	32	8	3	2	10	13	39	.331	.409
Bats Right	R	.230	335	77	18	1	10	31	21	86	.277	.379
Drury, Brandon	L	.299	147	44	12	0	12	26	6	43	.329	.626
Bats Right	R	.248	371	92	19	2	16	61	32	83	.317	.439
Dubon, Mauricio	L	.267	86	23	4	0	4	15	5	10	.312	.453
Bats Right	R	.185	157	29	5	0	1	9	8	20	.219	.236
Duffy, Matt	L	.239	92	22	5	0	2	9	8	16	.307	.359
Bats Right	R	.257	136	35	3	0	0	7	9	34	.308	.279
Duran, Ezequiel	L	.224	49	11	3	1	2	12	3	16	.269	.449
Bats Right	R	.239	159	38	7	0	3	13	9	38	.280	.340
Duran, Jarren	L	.184	38	7	1	0	0	5	3	13	.238	.211
Bats Left	R	.229	166	38	13	3	3	12	11	50	.293	.398
Duvall, Adam	L	.233	73	17	6	0	6	12	5	23	.282	.562
Bats Right	R	.206	214	44	10	1	6	24	16	78	.274	.346
Eaton, Nate	L	.300	30	9	2	1	1	8	2	8	.353	.533
Bats Right	R	.250	76	19	2	2	0	4	8	22	.322	.329
Edman, Tommy	L	.276	152	42	11	1	5	18	9	27	.321	.461
Bats Both	R	.261	425	111	20	3	8	39	37	84	.325	.379
Engel, Adam	L	.141	71	10	4	0	1	5	5	23	.208	.239
Bats Right	R	.259	174	45	9	1	1	12	6	53	.295	.339
Escobar, Alcides	L	.209	43	9	0	1	0	3	2	12	.244	.256
Bats Right	R	.222	81	18	4	1	0	5	3	20	.267	.296
Escobar, Eduardo	L	.259	162	42	11	2	9	31	9	41	.299	.519
Bats Both	R	.231	333	77	15	2	11	38	31	88	.293	.387
Espinal, Santiago	L	.301	113	34	8	0	3	15	14	13	.375	.451
Bats Right	R	.256	336	86	17	0	4	36	22	55	.304	.342
Estrada, Thairo	L	.283	152	43	8	1	7	23	13	28	.347	.487
Bats Right	R	.250	336	84	14	1	7	39	20	61	.311	.360
Farmer, Kyle	L	.309	139	43	10	1	8	35	13	26	.380	.568
Bats Right	R	.235	387	91	15	0	6	43	20	73	.291	.320
Fletcher, David	L	.250	72	18	1	0	1	5	3	2	.289	.306
Bats Right	R	.257	144	37	8	1	1	12	4	14	.287	.347
Flores, Wilmer	L	.223	175	39	10	0	6	20	21	35	.324	.383
Bats Right	R	.231	350	81	18	1	13	51	38	68	.311	.400
Fortes, Nick	L	.213	61	13	0	0	3	5	5	7	.294	.361
Bats Right	R	.237	156	37	6	1	6	19	13	38	.308	.404
Fraley, Jake	L	.143	28	4	0	0	1	3	2	8	.226	.250
Bats Left	R	.277	188	52	9	0	11	25	24	46	.361	.500
France, Ty	L	.273	154	42	9	0	3	23	9	33	.345	.390
Bats Right	R	.275	397	109	18	1	17	60	26	61	.336	.453
Franco, Maikel	L	.241	108	26	5	0	1	10	7	28	.291	.315
Bats Right	R	.224	263	59	10	0	8	29	5	47	.240	.354
Franco, Wander	L	.304	69	21	3	1	2	9	2	8	.324	.464
Bats Both	R	.269	245	66	17	2	4	24	24	25	.330	.404
Frazier, Adam	L	.210	138	29	8	0	1	11	11	19	.286	.290
Bats Left	R	.248	403	100	14	4	2	31	35	54	.306	.318
Freeman, Freddie	L	.294	180	53	13	1	5	24	17	43	.363	.461
Bats Left	R	.338	432	146	34	1	16	76	67	59	.424	.532
Friedl, T.J.	L	.333	18	6	1	1	1	5	3	2	.455	.667
Bats Left	R	.232	207	48	9	4	7	20	17	38	.301	.415
Gallo, Joey	L	.110	73	8	2	0	2	7	10	40	.217	.219
Bats Left	R	.173	277	48	6	2	17	40	46	123	.297	.394
Gamel, Ben	L	.175	97	17	5	0	1	7	10	28	.273	.258
Bats Left	R	.252	274	69	15	2	8	39	38	70	.342	.409
Garcia, Adolis	L	.235	187	44	12	1	8	29	18	53	.301	.439
Bats Right	R	.256	418	107	22	4	19	72	22	130	.299	.464
Garcia, Aramis	L	.385	26	10	0	0	0	2	1	7	.407	.385
Bats Right	R	.159	82	13	2	0	1	2	2	27	.198	.220
Garcia, Avisail	L	.219	64	14	0	0	2	5	4	24	.265	.313
Bats Right	R	.225	293	66	9	0	6	30	13	85	.266	.317
Garcia, Dermis	L	.167	36	6	3	0	1	8	1	15	.189	.333
Bats Right	R	.225	80	18	3	0	4	12	7	40	.295	.413
Garcia, Leury	L	.188	64	12	2	0	0	1	2	13	.212	.219
Bats Both	R	.216	236	51	6	0	3	19	5	52	.239	.280
Garcia, Luis	L	.235	98	23	6	0	1	8	2	28	.250	.327
Bats Left	R	.290	262	76	17	2	6	37	9	56	.312	.439
Garlick, Kyle	L	.243	74	18	1	0	6	12	4	26	.305	.500
Bats Right	R	.224	76	17	2	0	3	6	4	22	.263	.368
Garver, Mitch	L	.269	52	14	1	0	6	11	10	10	.391	.635
Bats Right	R	.184	136	25	6	0	4	13	13	43	.258	.316
Gimenez, Andres	L	.336	113	38	5	0	4	14	7	21	.400	.487
Bats Left	R	.286	378	108	21	3	13	55	27	91	.362	.460
Goldschmidt, Paul	L	.411	112	46	12	0	11	29	23	25	.515	.813
Bats Right	R	.294	449	132	29	0	24	86	56	116	.374	.519

Batters vs. Left-Handed and Right-Handed Pitchers

Batter	vs	Avg	AB	H	2B	3B	HR	RBI	BB	SO	OBP	Slg
Gomes, Yan	L	.241	83	20	2	0	4	11	3	12	.261	.410
Bats Right	R	.232	194	45	10	0	4	20	5	35	.260	.345
Gonzalez, Luis	L	.214	98	21	2	0	1	7	7	28	.271	.265
Bats Left	R	.272	213	58	15	2	3	29	23	47	.346	.404
Gonzalez, Marwin	L	.207	58	12	4	0	1	5	6	22	.281	.328
Bats Both	R	.175	126	22	3	0	5	13	8	32	.243	.317
Gonzalez, Oscar	L	.266	109	29	4	0	5	12	4	27	.304	.440
Bats Right	R	.308	253	78	23	0	6	31	11	48	.337	.470
Gonzalez, Romy	L	.314	35	11	3	0	1	5	1	13	.324	.486
Bats Right	R	.200	70	14	1	1	1	6	1	26	.222	.286
Gordon, Nick	L	.200	80	16	3	0	1	8	5	20	.267	.275
Bats Left	R	.289	325	94	25	4	8	42	14	85	.329	.465
Gorman, Nolan	L	.211	19	4	2	0	0	2	4	8	.348	.316
Bats Left	R	.227	264	60	11	0	14	33	24	95	.297	.428
Grandal, Yasmani	L	.257	74	19	5	0	1	6	18	15	.409	.365
Bats Both	R	.186	253	47	2	0	4	21	27	64	.265	.241
Greene, Riley	L	.303	109	33	8	1	0	11	8	33	.353	.394
Bats Left	R	.232	267	62	10	3	5	31	28	87	.308	.348
Gregorius, Didi	L	.164	55	9	2	0	0	6	2	9	.230	.200
Bats Left	R	.226	159	36	7	4	1	13	11	27	.275	.340
Grichuk, Randal	L	.308	172	53	12	2	11	37	7	41	.333	.593
Bats Right	R	.234	334	78	9	1	8	36	17	86	.282	.338
Grisham, Trent	L	.203	118	24	4	0	5	13	9	35	.269	.364
Bats Left	R	.177	333	59	12	2	12	40	48	115	.289	.333
Grissom, Vaughn	L	.333	42	14	2	0	2	7	5	7	.417	.524
Bats Right	R	.273	99	27	4	0	3	11	6	27	.324	.404
Grossman, Robbie	L	.320	122	39	12	0	1	18	25	36	.436	.443
Bats Both	R	.163	289	47	7	1	6	27	31	93	.253	.256
Guerrero Jr., Vladimir	L	.245	110	27	4	0	4	12	12	12	.320	.391
Bats Right	R	.280	528	148	31	0	28	85	46	104	.342	.498
Guillorme, Luis	L	.214	84	18	4	0	0	5	11	13	.313	.262
Bats Left	R	.296	213	63	8	1	2	12	23	33	.367	.371
Gurriel, Yuli	L	.265	170	45	18	0	4	20	9	15	.298	.441
Bats Right	R	.232	375	87	22	0	4	33	21	58	.283	.323
Gurriel Jr., Lourdes	L	.278	90	25	8	0	0	8	4	19	.309	.367
Bats Right	R	.295	363	107	24	1	5	44	27	64	.352	.408
Haase, Eric	L	.281	114	32	7	0	4	13	9	36	.331	.447
Bats Right	R	.239	209	50	10	1	10	31	15	61	.291	.440
Haggerty, Sam	L	.364	66	24	5	1	4	12	10	19	.449	.652
Bats Both	R	.191	110	21	4	0	1	11	8	34	.262	.255
Hall, Darick	L	.083	12	1	0	0	0	0	0	7	.083	.083
Bats Left	R	.266	124	33	8	1	9	16	5	37	.300	.565
Hampson, Garrett	L	.296	71	21	5	3	0	7	11	21	.386	.451
Bats Right	R	.164	128	21	2	0	2	8	10	42	.229	.227
Haniger, Mitch	L	.246	61	15	2	0	3	7	8	13	.338	.426
Bats Right	R	.245	163	40	6	0	8	27	12	52	.295	.429
Happ, Ian	L	.305	128	39	9	1	2	16	7	39	.350	.438
Bats Both	R	.261	445	116	33	1	15	56	51	110	.339	.440
Harper, Bryce	L	.256	117	30	11	0	3	17	15	35	.348	.427
Bats Left	R	.300	253	76	17	1	15	48	31	52	.371	.553
Harris II, Michael	L	.238	126	30	8	1	2	17	7	41	.284	.365
Bats Left	R	.323	288	93	19	2	17	47	14	66	.363	.580
Harrison, Josh	L	.250	88	22	3	1	1	5	7	15	.327	.341
Bats Right	R	.258	298	77	16	1	6	22	14	56	.314	.379
Hayes, Ke'Bryan	L	.270	152	41	8	1	4	11	16	21	.343	.414
Bats Right	R	.232	353	82	16	2	3	30	32	101	.302	.314
Hays, Austin	L	.247	146	36	7	1	4	6	11	33	.313	.390
Bats Right	R	.252	389	98	28	1	12	54	23	81	.303	.422
Hedges, Austin	L	.147	68	10	1	0	2	11	10	18	.259	.250
Bats Right	R	.168	226	38	3	0	5	19	15	60	.235	.248
Heim, Jonah	L	.267	120	32	8	1	6	20	11	18	.333	.500
Bats Both	R	.210	286	60	12	0	10	28	30	69	.283	.357
Heineman, Tyler	L	.226	62	14	2	0	0	2	2	6	.250	.258
Bats Both	R	.211	95	20	6	0	0	7	6	11	.292	.274
Henderson, Gunnar	L	.130	23	3	2	0	0	2	3	7	.231	.217
Bats Left	R	.290	93	27	5	1	4	16	13	27	.377	.495
Hernandez, Cesar	L	.282	177	50	10	1	0	13	15	38	.340	.350
Bats Both	R	.232	383	89	18	3	1	21	30	76	.298	.303
Hernandez, Kike	L	.224	85	19	6	0	4	9	14	23	.340	.435
Bats Right	R	.221	276	61	18	0	2	36	20	48	.275	.308
Hernandez, Teoscar	L	.286	91	26	9	0	8	20	6	27	.330	.648
Bats Right	R	.262	408	107	26	1	17	57	28	125	.313	.456
Hernandez, Yadiel	L	.264	53	14	3	0	0	7	2	12	.291	.321
Bats Left	R	.270	252	68	13	0	9	34	17	62	.316	.429
Herrera, Jose	L	.286	21	6	0	0	0	0	1	6	.318	.286
Bats Both	R	.167	90	15	2	0	0	5	8	28	.235	.189

Batter	vs	Avg	AB	H	2B	3B	HR	RBI	BB	SO	OBP	Slg
Herrera, Odubel	L	.300	40	12	3	0	0	4	4	6	.364	.375
Bats Left	R	.221	145	32	6	1	5	17	7	36	.255	.379
Heyward, Jason	L	.217	23	5	0	0	0	0	0	6	.217	.217
Bats Left	R	.202	114	23	5	1	1	10	11	26	.289	.289
Hicks, Aaron	L	.234	107	25	3	0	2	13	12	34	.320	.318
Bats Both	R	.209	277	58	6	2	6	27	50	75	.333	.310
Higashioka, Kyle	L	.254	67	17	2	0	4	13	3	16	.296	.463
Bats Right	R	.216	162	35	5	0	6	18	9	36	.251	.358
Higgins, P.J.	L	.219	73	16	6	0	1	14	4	20	.260	.342
Bats Right	R	.234	128	30	5	1	5	16	18	38	.336	.406
Hilliard, Sam	L	.107	28	3	0	0	1	3	1	9	.161	.214
Bats Left	R	.199	146	29	6	1	1	11	22	48	.302	.274
Hiura, Keston	L	.188	96	18	4	1	3	11	9	49	.275	.344
Bats Right	R	.254	138	35	4	0	11	21	14	62	.344	.522
Hoerner, Nico	L	.294	126	37	7	2	2	16	5	14	.326	.429
Bats Right	R	.276	355	98	15	3	8	39	23	43	.327	.403
Hoskins, Rhys	L	.286	147	42	12	2	8	20	22	41	.387	.558
Bats Right	R	.233	442	103	21	0	22	59	50	128	.313	.430
Hosmer, Eric	L	.324	111	36	4	0	2	9	6	20	.359	.414
Bats Left	R	.245	269	66	15	0	6	35	31	44	.325	.368
Huff, Sam	L	.229	48	11	3	0	2	2	6	15	.315	.417
Bats Right	R	.247	73	18	1	0	2	8	5	27	.295	.342
Hummel, Cooper	L	.149	74	11	0	3	1	5	8	23	.238	.270
Bats Both	R	.196	102	20	8	0	2	12	15	41	.299	.333
Ibanez, Andy	L	.214	42	9	2	0	0	3	2	5	.250	.262
Bats Right	R	.221	77	17	2	0	1	6	7	16	.286	.286
Iglesias, Jose	L	.295	149	44	14	0	2	18	4	21	.323	.430
Bats Right	R	.290	290	84	16	0	1	29	13	35	.330	.355
India, Jonathan	L	.260	104	27	5	1	1	10	10	23	.353	.356
Bats Right	R	.245	282	69	11	1	9	31	21	71	.317	.387
Isbel, Kyle	L	.204	49	10	1	0	0	6	4	15	.278	.224
Bats Left	R	.213	207	44	9	4	5	22	12	60	.260	.367
Jansen, Danny	L	.226	53	12	3	0	3	7	12	7	.373	.453
Bats Right	R	.272	162	44	7	0	12	37	13	37	.326	.537
Jeffers, Ryan	L	.306	62	19	3	1	3	13	7	15	.377	.532
Bats Right	R	.167	150	25	7	0	4	14	16	47	.247	.293
Jimenez, Eloy	L	.300	70	21	3	0	3	11	8	15	.370	.471
Bats Right	R	.293	222	65	9	0	13	43	20	57	.354	.509
Joe, Connor	L	.259	147	38	10	2	2	15	19	32	.349	.395
Bats Right	R	.226	257	58	10	2	5	13	36	65	.332	.339
Judge, Aaron	L	.274	135	37	5	0	14	35	26	50	.388	.622
Bats Right	R	.322	435	140	23	0	48	96	85	125	.436	.706
Kelenic, Jarred	L	.130	54	7	2	0	1	3	4	21	.203	.222
Bats Left	R	.147	109	16	3	1	6	14	12	40	.230	.358
Kelly, Carson	L	.197	122	24	11	0	2	16	9	29	.261	.336
Bats Right	R	.221	195	43	7	0	5	19	20	42	.295	.333
Kemp, Tony	L	.219	73	16	2	0	1	8	8	19	.310	.288
Bats Left	R	.238	424	101	22	2	6	38	37	50	.307	.342
Kepler, Max	L	.243	103	25	8	0	1	10	13	14	.328	.350
Bats Left	R	.221	285	63	10	1	8	33	36	52	.315	.347
Kiermaier, Kevin	L	.256	43	11	3	0	0	3	2	13	.304	.326
Bats Left	R	.221	163	36	5	0	7	19	12	48	.274	.380
Kim, Ha-seong	L	.270	159	43	10	2	2	18	24	19	.369	.396
Bats Right	R	.243	358	87	19	1	9	41	27	81	.304	.377
Kiner-Falefa, Isiah	L	.264	106	28	7	0	0	11	13	14	.352	.330
Bats Right	R	.260	377	98	13	0	4	37	22	58	.303	.326
Kirilloff, Alex	L	.167	24	4	0	0	0	0	3	6	.333	.167
Bats Left	R	.267	120	32	7	0	3	21	2	30	.280	.400
Kirk, Alejandro	L	.276	98	27	3	0	3	9	10	15	.349	.398
Bats Right	R	.288	372	107	16	0	11	54	53	43	.377	.419
Knizner, Andrew	L	.138	58	8	2	0	2	8	6	15	.231	.276
Bats Right	R	.238	202	48	8	0	2	17	20	47	.322	.307
Kwan, Steven	L	.285	130	37	4	0	0	11	6	21	.324	.315
Bats Left	R	.303	433	131	21	7	6	41	56	39	.386	.425
La Stella, Tommy	L	.190	21	4	1	0	0	3	2	1	.261	.238
Bats Left	R	.245	159	39	13	0	2	11	9	29	.285	.365
Langeliers, Shea	L	.276	29	8	2	0	1	4	4	10	.353	.448
Bats Right	R	.204	113	23	8	1	5	18	5	43	.235	.425
Larnach, Trevor	L	.277	47	13	5	0	0	3	4	13	.333	.383
Bats Left	R	.212	113	24	8	0	5	15	14	44	.295	.416
Laureano, Ramon	L	.210	81	17	6	0	2	7	10	24	.333	.358
Bats Right	R	.211	265	56	12	0	11	27	15	80	.272	.381
Leblanc, Charles	L	.239	46	11	3	0	1	4	3	16	.300	.370
Bats Right	R	.273	110	30	7	0	3	7	9	37	.328	.418
LeMahieu, DJ	L	.285	123	35	4	0	4	11	18	19	.385	.415
Bats Right	R	.253	344	87	14	0	8	35	49	52	.348	.363

Batters vs. Left-Handed and Right-Handed Pitchers

Batter	vs	Avg	AB	H	2B	3B	HR	RBI	BB	SO	OBP	Slg
Lindor, Francisco	L	.271	188	51	8	0	9	30	14	35	.327	.457
Bats Both	R	.269	442	119	17	5	17	77	45	98	.343	.446
Longoria, Evan	L	.282	117	33	5	0	6	22	10	33	.333	.479
Bats Right	R	.215	149	32	8	0	8	20	17	50	.302	.430
Lopez, Alejo	L	.256	39	10	2	0	0	0	3	4	.341	.308
Bats Both	R	.264	106	28	3	1	1	10	6	17	.304	.340
Lopez, Nicky	L	.207	111	23	0	1	0	6	6	15	.264	.225
Bats Left	R	.234	325	76	12	3	0	14	23	48	.287	.289
Lowe, Brandon	L	.261	46	12	1	1	3	9	1	13	.271	.522
Bats Left	R	.212	189	40	9	1	5	16	26	48	.317	.349
Lowe, Josh	L	.095	42	4	0	0	0	1	4	19	.174	.095
Bats Left	R	.259	139	36	12	2	2	12	11	47	.318	.417
Lowe, Nathaniel	L	.330	194	64	8	1	10	29	14	41	.384	.536
Bats Left	R	.288	399	115	18	2	17	47	34	106	.346	.471
Lowrie, Jed	L	.184	49	9	2	0	0	5	2	12	.216	.224
Bats Both	R	.178	118	21	3	0	3	11	13	27	.256	.280
Luplow, Jordan	L	.171	111	19	2	0	8	18	15	33	.268	.405
Bats Right	R	.181	94	17	3	0	3	10	10	27	.280	.309
Lux, Gavin	L	.263	99	26	4	1	1	11	10	26	.330	.354
Bats Left	R	.280	322	90	16	6	5	31	37	69	.351	.413
Machado, Manny	L	.259	162	42	5	0	12	22	21	33	.342	.512
Bats Right	R	.313	416	130	32	1	20	80	42	100	.376	.538
Machin, Vimael	L	.154	13	2	0	0	0	1	2	3	.250	.154
Bats Left	R	.224	210	47	12	0	1	12	23	44	.304	.295
Madrigal, Nick	L	.256	78	20	1	0	0	1	2	6	.275	.269
Bats Right	R	.244	131	32	6	0	0	6	12	21	.322	.290
Madris, Bligh	L	.190	21	4	2	0	0	3	0	9	.190	.286
Bats Left	R	.174	92	16	5	0	1	4	10	22	.255	.261
Maile, Luke	L	.300	40	12	3	0	0	8	3	9	.326	.375
Bats Right	R	.199	141	28	7	0	3	9	16	45	.294	.312
Maldonado, Martin	L	.212	99	21	3	0	8	21	8	29	.278	.485
Bats Right	R	.176	245	43	9	0	7	24	14	87	.236	.298
Mancini, Trey	L	.234	171	40	6	1	4	14	14	37	.299	.351
Bats Right	R	.241	348	84	17	0	14	49	39	98	.328	.411
Marcano, Tucupita	L	.239	46	11	1	0	1	6	3	10	.300	.326
Bats Left	R	.193	114	22	5	2	1	7	7	34	.238	.298
Margot, Manuel	L	.346	78	27	4	1	1	13	8	6	.414	.462
Bats Right	R	.252	258	65	14	1	3	34	16	62	.297	.349
Marsh, Brandon	L	.188	96	18	1	0	2	7	5	44	.225	.260
Bats Left	R	.262	328	86	17	4	9	45	23	114	.315	.421
Marte, Ketel	L	.276	134	37	14	0	4	20	11	23	.342	.470
Bats Both	R	.226	358	81	28	2	8	32	44	78	.313	.383
Marte, Starling	L	.302	139	42	8	0	7	18	12	35	.366	.511
Bats Right	R	.287	327	94	16	5	9	45	14	62	.338	.450
Martinez, J.D.	L	.319	119	38	16	1	5	19	17	31	.401	.597
Bats Right	R	.261	414	108	27	0	11	43	35	114	.323	.406
Massey, Michael	L	.200	35	7	1	1	1	6	1	9	.275	.371
Bats Left	R	.254	138	35	8	0	3	11	8	37	.316	.377
Mateo, Jorge	L	.203	148	30	3	3	5	14	7	48	.253	.365
Bats Right	R	.228	346	79	22	4	8	36	20	99	.273	.384
Mazara, Nomar	L	.333	24	8	2	0	0	5	1	7	.360	.417
Bats Left	R	.252	135	34	6	0	2	13	9	33	.308	.341
McCann, James	L	.092	65	6	2	0	1	5	3	17	.155	.169
Bats Right	R	.257	109	28	4	0	2	13	8	29	.317	.349
McCarthy, Jake	L	.281	96	27	5	0	3	12	6	22	.337	.427
Bats Left	R	.284	225	64	11	3	5	31	17	54	.344	.427
McCormick, Chas	L	.340	103	35	6	1	5	14	12	23	.409	.563
Bats Right	R	.207	256	53	6	1	9	30	34	83	.301	.344
McCutchen, Andrew	L	.221	145	32	10	0	7	19	17	39	.303	.434
Bats Right	R	.243	370	90	15	0	10	50	40	85	.320	.365
McGuire, Reese	L	.262	42	11	2	0	0	4	2	12	.295	.310
Bats Left	R	.271	207	56	12	1	3	18	10	44	.309	.382
McKenna, Ryan	L	.270	63	17	6	0	2	6	5	17	.333	.460
Bats Right	R	.215	93	20	4	0	0	5	6	38	.267	.258
McKinstry, Zach	L	.188	16	3	0	0	0	1	2	5	.278	.188
Bats Left	R	.200	150	30	6	3	5	13	14	47	.273	.380
McMahon, Ryan	L	.228	149	34	3	1	3	18	19	42	.320	.322
Bats Left	R	.253	380	96	20	2	17	49	41	116	.329	.450
McNeil, Jeff	L	.312	157	49	8	0	1	9	12	19	.376	.382
Bats Left	R	.332	376	125	31	1	8	53	28	42	.385	.484
Meadows, Austin	L	.229	35	8	1	0	0	6	3	8	.308	.257
Bats Left	R	.258	93	24	5	2	0	5	13	9	.361	.355
Mejia, Francisco	L	.337	86	29	10	0	1	15	1	9	.345	.488
Bats Both	R	.202	203	41	12	0	5	16	6	56	.231	.335
Melendez, MJ	L	.295	112	33	7	1	4	14	11	22	.357	.482
Bats Left	R	.193	348	67	14	2	14	48	55	109	.299	.365

Batter	vs	Avg	AB	H	2B	3B	HR	RBI	BB	SO	OBP	Slg
Meneses, Joey	L	.366	71	26	7	0	5	11	4	16	.408	.676
Bats Right	R	.305	151	46	7	0	8	23	11	36	.348	.510
Mercado, Oscar	L	.200	55	11	4	0	0	2	2	13	.228	.273
Bats Right	R	.212	66	14	2	1	4	14	3	16	.254	.455
Merrifield, Whit	L	.238	143	34	11	0	5	19	12	20	.291	.420
Bats Right	R	.255	361	92	17	1	6	39	26	65	.301	.357
Meyers, Jake	L	.250	52	13	1	1	0	6	1	18	.264	.308
Bats Right	R	.214	98	21	5	1	1	9	6	36	.271	.316
Miller, Brad	L	.158	19	3	0	0	1	3	1	9	.200	.316
Bats Left	R	.217	203	44	3	0	6	29	17	61	.276	.320
Miller, Owen	L	.212	137	29	7	0	3	15	13	35	.290	.328
Bats Right	R	.258	287	74	19	1	3	36	19	58	.306	.362
Miranda, Jose	L	.275	131	36	4	0	9	25	7	24	.309	.511
Bats Right	R	.265	313	83	21	0	6	41	21	67	.331	.390
Mitchell, Calvin	L	.245	53	13	4	0	2	5	1	15	.255	.434
Bats Left	R	.220	159	35	7	0	3	12	17	37	.295	.321
Molina, Yadier	L	.254	63	16	1	0	1	8	2	10	.288	.317
Bats Right	R	.201	199	40	7	0	4	16	3	30	.216	.296
Moncada, Yoan	L	.241	83	20	4	1	4	13	11	22	.330	.458
Bats Both	R	.204	314	64	14	0	8	38	21	92	.257	.325
Montero, Elehuris	L	.261	69	18	8	0	3	10	4	21	.301	.507
Bats Right	R	.215	107	23	7	1	3	10	4	39	.250	.383
Moore, Dylan	L	.247	97	24	4	1	3	11	19	36	.393	.402
Bats Right	R	.204	108	22	7	1	3	13	15	39	.344	.370
Moran, Colin	L	.273	22	6	1	0	1	1	1	6	.304	.455
Bats Left	R	.195	87	17	2	0	4	22	15	24	.305	.356
Morel, Christopher	L	.190	100	19	5	0	3	12	14	34	.297	.330
Bats Right	R	.251	279	70	14	4	13	35	24	103	.313	.470
Mountcastle, Ryan	L	.239	142	34	7	0	5	15	11	41	.299	.394
Bats Right	R	.254	413	105	21	1	17	70	32	113	.308	.433
Moustakas, Mike	L	.207	58	12	3	0	0	3	6	16	.303	.259
Bats Left	R	.216	194	42	9	0	7	22	18	59	.292	.371
Mullins II, Cedric	L	.209	182	38	5	1	4	15	11	48	.265	.313
Bats Left	R	.279	426	119	27	3	12	49	36	78	.340	.441
Muncy, Max	L	.178	118	21	4	0	6	22	22	29	.315	.364
Bats Left	R	.202	346	70	18	1	15	47	68	112	.334	.390
Murphy, Sean	L	.242	132	32	8	1	7	21	24	30	.370	.477
Bats Right	R	.252	405	102	29	1	11	45	32	94	.318	.410
Myers, Wil	L	.264	91	24	3	0	6	22	8	30	.320	.495
Bats Right	R	.259	170	44	12	0	1	19	13	56	.312	.347
Naquin, Tyler	L	.180	61	11	3	0	2	6	1	12	.206	.328
Bats Left	R	.241	249	60	16	4	9	40	18	81	.300	.446
Narvaez, Omar	L	.212	33	7	1	0	0	4	5	7	.333	.242
Bats Left	R	.205	229	47	11	1	4	19	24	50	.285	.314
Naylor, Josh	L	.173	110	19	4	0	1	11	14	34	.276	.236
Bats Left	R	.283	339	96	24	0	19	68	24	46	.334	.522
Neuse, Sheldon	L	.181	105	19	2	1	0	6	4	27	.211	.219
Bats Right	R	.235	166	39	2	1	4	20	16	53	.310	.331
Nevin, Tyler	L	.231	65	15	2	0	2	6	8	21	.324	.354
Bats Right	R	.174	92	16	2	0	0	10	12	25	.282	.196
Newman, Kevin	L	.361	97	35	7	0	0	8	5	11	.404	.433
Bats Right	R	.230	191	44	11	2	2	16	11	37	.271	.340
Nido, Tomas	L	.259	112	29	6	0	2	12	7	28	.303	.366
Bats Right	R	.227	172	39	9	0	1	16	7	48	.258	.297
Nimmo, Brandon	L	.264	201	53	12	3	5	26	24	47	.358	.428
Bats Left	R	.280	379	106	18	4	11	38	47	69	.372	.435
Nola, Austin	L	.285	130	37	6	0	3	17	9	17	.333	.400
Bats Right	R	.230	217	50	9	0	1	23	25	43	.313	.286
Nootbaar, Lars	L	.273	55	15	5	1	1	9	13	13	.400	.455
Bats Left	R	.217	235	51	11	2	13	31	38	58	.325	.447
Odor, Rougned	L	.190	84	16	1	1	2	10	6	25	.284	.298
Bats Left	R	.211	342	72	18	2	11	43	26	84	.273	.371
O'Hearn, Ryan	L	.200	15	3	1	0	0	2	1	2	.250	.267
Bats Left	R	.244	119	29	5	1	1	14	7	33	.295	.328
Ohtani, Shohei	L	.263	205	54	9	2	9	27	19	60	.329	.459
Bats Left	R	.278	381	106	21	4	25	68	53	101	.370	.551
Olivares, Edward	L	.283	46	13	4	0	3	7	3	12	.340	.565
Bats Right	R	.287	115	33	4	0	1	8	7	24	.331	.348
Olson, Matt	L	.235	183	43	12	0	7	36	26	46	.333	.415
Bats Left	R	.242	433	105	32	0	27	67	49	124	.321	.503
O'Neill, Tyler	L	.256	78	20	2	0	4	13	10	19	.352	.436
Bats Right	R	.219	256	56	9	1	10	45	28	84	.295	.379
Ortega, Rafael	L	.211	19	4	0	0	0	0	3	2	.318	.211
Bats Left	R	.242	297	72	14	1	7	35	41	72	.331	.367
Ozuna, Marcell	L	.200	135	27	2	0	1	8	10	35	.260	.237
Bats Right	R	.236	335	79	17	0	22	48	21	87	.280	.484

Batters vs. Left-Handed and Right-Handed Pitchers

Batter	vs	Avg	AB	H	2B	3B	HR	RBI	BB	SO	OBP	Slg
Pache, Cristian	L	.220	82	18	3	1	1	9	7	14	.281	.317
Bats Right	R	.138	159	22	2	1	2	9	8	56	.185	.201
Palacios, Richie	L	.000	2	0	0	0	0	0	3	2	.667	.000
Bats Left	R	.236	110	26	6	0	0	10	6	18	.274	.291
Paredes, Isaac	L	.231	91	21	5	0	7	14	12	16	.324	.516
Bats Right	R	.196	240	47	11	0	13	31	32	51	.297	.404
Pasquantino, Vinnie	L	.352	54	19	3	0	0	4	10	6	.446	.407
Bats Left	R	.279	204	57	7	0	10	22	25	28	.365	.461
Pederson, Joc	L	.245	49	12	2	0	2	11	7	19	.333	.408
Bats Left	R	.278	331	92	17	3	21	59	35	81	.356	.538
Pena, Jeremy	L	.286	140	40	8	0	7	19	8	34	.329	.493
Bats Right	R	.241	381	92	12	2	15	44	14	101	.274	.402
Peralta, David	L	.154	65	10	1	0	1	5	7	20	.247	.215
Bats Left	R	.267	374	100	29	3	11	54	34	94	.329	.449
Perdomo, Geraldo	L	.237	131	31	3	0	0	6	13	21	.306	.260
Bats Both	R	.177	300	53	7	2	5	34	37	82	.276	.263
Perez, Michael	L	.115	26	3	0	0	2	3	2	9	.179	.346
Bats Left	R	.158	95	15	0	0	4	11	8	23	.223	.284
Perez, Salvador	L	.278	108	30	10	0	5	18	8	30	.336	.509
Bats Right	R	.246	337	83	13	1	18	58	10	79	.277	.451
Peterson, Jace	L	.281	32	9	1	1	0	5	2	10	.343	.375
Bats Left	R	.230	256	59	13	1	8	29	31	75	.313	.383
Pham, Tommy	L	.273	139	38	6	0	6	21	14	37	.338	.446
Bats Right	R	.224	415	93	17	1	11	42	42	130	.303	.349
Phillips, Brett	L	.000	34	0	0	0	0	0	1	18	.056	.000
Bats Left	R	.174	167	29	6	0	5	15	15	76	.249	.299
Pinder, Chad	L	.260	150	39	7	0	7	23	5	45	.280	.447
Bats Right	R	.218	211	46	11	0	5	19	9	73	.250	.341
Piscotty, Stephen	L	.190	42	8	1	0	0	2	7	15	.300	.214
Bats Right	R	.190	84	16	3	0	5	12	2	33	.225	.405
Plawecki, Kevin	L	.133	45	6	1	0	0	1	3	10	.204	.156
Bats Right	R	.252	123	31	7	0	1	12	11	22	.316	.333
Polanco, Jorge	L	.226	133	30	5	0	2	14	13	28	.293	.308
Bats Both	R	.240	242	58	11	0	14	42	51	67	.373	.459
Pollock, A.J.	L	.286	126	36	9	0	11	25	5	23	.316	.619
Bats Right	R	.231	363	84	17	1	3	31	27	75	.284	.309
Pratto, Nick	L	.222	36	8	5	0	0	8	5	19	.302	.361
Bats Left	R	.172	122	21	4	1	7	12	14	47	.261	.393
Profar, Jurickson	L	.259	170	44	10	1	3	19	24	22	.352	.382
Bats Both	R	.237	405	96	26	1	12	39	49	81	.322	.395
Pujols, Albert	L	.351	114	40	6	0	13	30	9	19	.400	.746
Bats Right	R	.223	193	43	8	0	11	38	19	36	.312	.435
Raleigh, Cal	L	.212	85	18	7	1	3	14	13	30	.310	.424
Bats Both	R	.211	285	60	13	0	24	49	25	92	.276	.509
Ramirez, Harold	L	.360	111	40	5	0	2	17	9	16	.413	.459
Bats Right	R	.277	292	81	19	0	4	41	10	56	.315	.384
Ramirez, Jose	L	.236	157	37	8	1	6	28	16	25	.315	.414
Bats Both	R	.295	444	131	36	4	23	98	53	57	.369	.550
Realmuto, J.T.	L	.262	141	37	6	3	5	22	14	41	.350	.454
Bats Right	R	.281	363	102	20	2	17	62	27	78	.338	.488
Refsnyder, Rob	L	.359	64	23	6	0	3	8	6	18	.411	.594
Bats Right	R	.270	89	24	5	0	3	13	9	28	.365	.427
Rendon, Anthony	L	.239	46	11	0	0	4	9	10	12	.373	.500
Bats Right	R	.225	120	27	10	0	1	15	13	23	.306	.333
Renfroe, Hunter	L	.258	120	31	4	0	8	16	16	32	.350	.492
Bats Right	R	.254	354	90	19	1	21	56	23	89	.303	.492
Rengifo, Luis	L	.315	165	52	7	1	11	22	5	18	.339	.570
Bats Both	R	.238	324	77	15	3	6	30	12	61	.271	.358
Reyes, Franmil	L	.214	98	21	4	1	3	9	8	33	.271	.367
Bats Right	R	.224	340	76	13	1	11	38	22	124	.273	.365
Reyes, Victor	L	.238	84	20	7	0	0	10	5	19	.283	.321
Bats Both	R	.260	231	60	12	3	3	24	8	58	.291	.377
Reynolds, Bryan	L	.273	154	42	5	0	7	18	15	38	.345	.442
Bats Both	R	.258	388	100	14	4	20	44	41	103	.345	.469
Reynolds, Matt	L	.205	73	15	4	0	1	6	13	25	.326	.301
Bats Right	R	.263	171	45	6	1	2	17	13	53	.317	.345
Riley, Austin	L	.329	149	49	14	2	11	25	20	42	.413	.671
Bats Right	R	.255	466	119	25	0	27	68	37	126	.328	.483
Rivas, Alfonso	L	.069	29	2	0	0	0	1	2	18	.125	.069
Bats Left	R	.257	222	57	5	2	3	24	27	69	.346	.338
Rivera, Emmanuel	L	.264	110	29	6	2	4	15	8	22	.325	.464
Bats Right	R	.218	220	48	10	1	8	25	15	61	.276	.382
Rizzo, Anthony	L	.233	120	28	8	0	10	21	14	22	.343	.550
Bats Left	R	.220	345	76	13	1	22	54	44	79	.336	.455
Robert, Luis	L	.354	79	28	3	0	3	14	7	15	.402	.506
Bats Right	R	.266	301	80	15	0	9	42	10	62	.296	.405

Batter	vs	Avg	AB	H	2B	3B	HR	RBI	BB	SO	OBP	Slg
Robles, Victor	L	.294	126	37	5	2	2	14	8	32	.338	.413
Bats Right	R	.188	240	45	5	0	4	19	9	72	.238	.258
Rodgers, Brendan	L	.317	180	57	9	1	8	28	19	33	.388	.511
Bats Right	R	.239	347	83	21	2	5	35	27	68	.292	.354
Rodriguez, Julio	L	.275	120	33	3	0	7	18	15	40	.356	.475
Bats Right	R	.286	391	112	22	3	21	57	25	105	.341	.519
Rojas, Josh	L	.243	111	27	4	0	2	12	14	35	.333	.333
Bats Left	R	.277	332	92	21	1	7	44	41	63	.354	.410
Rojas, Miguel	L	.215	121	26	6	0	1	5	7	14	.275	.289
Bats Right	R	.243	350	85	13	2	5	31	19	47	.285	.334
Rosario, Amed	L	.295	149	44	11	1	4	16	8	30	.333	.463
Bats Right	R	.279	488	136	15	8	7	55	17	81	.305	.385
Rosario, Eddie	L	.143	28	4	0	1	0	1	5	5	.273	.214
Bats Left	R	.221	222	49	12	0	5	23	12	63	.257	.342
Ruf, Darin	L	.222	158	35	6	0	9	27	20	47	.322	.430
Bats Right	R	.188	176	33	6	0	2	18	25	58	.293	.256
Ruiz, Keibert	L	.237	93	22	4	0	0	10	8	10	.305	.280
Bats Both	R	.256	301	77	18	0	7	26	22	40	.315	.385
Rutschman, Adley	L	.173	98	17	6	0	1	5	16	26	.287	.265
Bats Both	R	.280	300	84	29	1	12	37	49	60	.386	.503
Sanchez, Gary	L	.165	109	18	4	0	3	13	15	37	.270	.284
Bats Right	R	.219	310	68	20	0	13	48	25	99	.287	.410
Sanchez, Jesus	L	.145	55	8	1	0	0	3	0	24	.145	.164
Bats Left	R	.229	258	59	13	3	13	33	26	68	.306	.453
Santana, Carlos	L	.265	117	31	7	0	3	21	22	15	.387	.402
Bats Both	R	.178	314	56	11	0	16	39	49	73	.288	.366
Santander, Anthony	L	.293	157	46	7	0	11	27	18	43	.365	.548
Bats Both	R	.221	417	92	17	0	22	62	37	79	.301	.420
Schoop, Jonathan	L	.186	113	21	5	0	2	10	5	26	.221	.283
Bats Right	R	.207	368	76	18	1	9	28	14	81	.245	.334
Schwarber, Kyle	L	.193	197	38	6	1	10	30	30	70	.301	.386
Bats Left	R	.232	380	88	15	2	36	64	56	130	.334	.566
Schwindel, Frank	L	.211	76	16	2	0	3	8	4	17	.250	.355
Bats Right	R	.236	195	46	9	0	5	28	15	41	.288	.359
Seager, Corey	L	.225	200	45	8	0	14	32	16	36	.286	.475
Bats Left	R	.254	393	100	16	1	19	51	42	67	.332	.445
Segura, Jean	L	.301	103	31	5	0	5	11	9	15	.360	.495
Bats Right	R	.267	251	67	4	0	5	22	16	43	.326	.343
Semien, Marcus	L	.250	180	45	9	2	6	19	22	35	.335	.422
Bats Right	R	.247	477	118	22	3	20	64	31	85	.292	.432
Senzel, Nick	L	.241	112	27	4	0	1	10	6	21	.292	.304
Bats Right	R	.226	261	59	9	0	4	15	24	55	.298	.307
Serven, Brian	L	.227	44	10	2	0	1	3	4	10	.292	.341
Bats Right	R	.196	143	28	2	1	5	13	9	34	.252	.329
Sheets, Gavin	L	.171	41	7	2	0	0	6	4	13	.244	.220
Bats Left	R	.250	336	84	17	0	15	47	23	73	.301	.435
Siri, Jose	L	.156	77	12	4	0	1	8	7	37	.224	.247
Bats Right	R	.232	224	52	9	2	6	16	13	71	.283	.371
Slater, Austin	L	.277	155	43	10	2	4	18	21	46	.379	.445
Bats Right	R	.246	122	30	5	0	3	16	19	43	.350	.361
Smith, Dominic	L	.176	17	3	1	0	0	5	2	6	.318	.235
Bats Left	R	.197	117	23	9	1	0	12	10	31	.269	.291
Smith, Josh	L	.118	34	4	0	0	1	4	4	5	.262	.206
Bats Left	R	.212	179	38	5	0	1	12	24	45	.316	.257
Smith, Kevin	L	.260	50	13	7	0	1	9	3	13	.296	.460
Bats Right	R	.135	89	12	2	1	1	4	4	29	.170	.213
Smith, Pavin	L	.226	62	14	3	0	1	4	2	20	.258	.323
Bats Left	R	.219	183	40	6	0	8	29	26	47	.313	.383
Smith, Will	L	.300	120	36	6	1	6	16	16	19	.391	.517
Bats Right	R	.247	388	96	20	2	18	71	40	77	.327	.448
Solano, Donovan	L	.301	83	25	7	0	1	11	4	15	.348	.422
Bats Right	R	.277	195	54	9	0	3	13	15	46	.335	.369
Soler, Jorge	L	.203	59	12	1	0	6	13	7	19	.294	.525
Bats Right	R	.209	211	44	12	0	7	21	24	71	.295	.365
Sosa, Edmundo	L	.232	82	19	5	3	2	15	2	28	.276	.439
Bats Right	R	.223	94	21	6	1	0	6	3	22	.275	.309
Soto, Juan	L	.210	195	41	5	1	7	23	38	40	.347	.354
Bats Left	R	.261	329	86	20	1	20	39	97	56	.431	.511
Springer, George	L	.252	115	29	3	1	6	18	14	23	.336	.452
Bats Right	R	.271	398	108	19	3	19	58	40	77	.344	.477
Stallings, Jacob	L	.210	62	13	2	0	0	4	9	15	.315	.242
Bats Right	R	.225	284	64	10	0	4	30	20	68	.287	.303
Stanton, Giancarlo	L	.184	103	19	2	0	6	21	13	33	.274	.379
Bats Right	R	.220	295	65	5	0	25	57	37	104	.305	.492
Stassi, Max	L	.162	117	19	4	0	1	7	10	30	.234	.222
Bats Right	R	.190	216	41	8	1	8	23	28	82	.285	.347

Batters vs. Left-Handed and Right-Handed Pitchers

Batter	vs	Avg	AB	H	2B	3B	HR	RBI	BB	SO	OBP	Slg
Stephenson, Tyler	L	.346	52	18	2	0	1	11	6	13	.410	.442
Bats Right	R	.307	114	35	7	0	5	24	6	34	.352	.500
Story, Trevor	L	.253	87	22	5	0	6	22	9	33	.330	.517
Bats Right	R	.233	270	63	17	0	10	44	23	89	.294	.407
Stott, Bryson	L	.263	99	26	7	1	2	14	11	30	.336	.414
Bats Left	R	.226	328	74	12	1	8	35	25	59	.282	.341
Straw, Myles	L	.264	129	34	8	0	0	8	12	25	.324	.326
Bats Right	R	.207	406	84	14	3	0	24	42	62	.281	.256
Stubbs, Garrett	L	.333	24	8	1	0	3	9	4	6	.429	.750
Bats Left	R	.244	82	20	3	1	2	7	10	24	.326	.378
Suarez, Eugenio	L	.269	130	35	9	1	8	23	21	42	.373	.538
Bats Right	R	.225	413	93	15	1	23	64	52	154	.319	.433
Suwinski, Jack	L	.122	98	12	1	0	5	8	11	36	.225	.286
Bats Left	R	.237	228	54	10	0	14	30	30	78	.330	.465
Suzuki, Kurt	L	.088	34	3	0	0	1	2	8	5	.262	.176
Bats Right	R	.210	105	22	4	0	3	13	7	24	.267	.333
Suzuki, Seiya	L	.269	104	28	6	2	4	11	16	18	.367	.481
Bats Right	R	.259	293	76	16	0	10	35	26	92	.325	.416
Swanson, Dansby	L	.297	158	47	10	0	6	14	17	43	.369	.475
Bats Right	R	.270	482	130	22	1	19	82	32	139	.315	.438
Tapia, Raimel	L	.262	65	17	3	0	1	11	2	22	.279	.354
Bats Left	R	.266	346	92	17	3	6	41	14	59	.294	.384
Taveras, Leody	L	.264	91	24	3	0	1	9	7	28	.313	.330
Bats Both	R	.260	223	58	11	2	4	25	14	60	.307	.381
Taylor, Chris	L	.193	119	23	7	1	2	9	16	51	.289	.319
Bats Right	R	.233	283	66	18	2	8	34	28	109	.310	.396
Taylor, Michael A.	L	.238	122	29	2	1	4	13	12	33	.306	.369
Bats Right	R	.260	292	76	8	2	5	30	23	76	.316	.353
Taylor, Tyrone	L	.225	120	27	7	1	5	14	9	34	.295	.425
Bats Right	R	.237	253	60	14	2	12	37	13	68	.282	.451
Tellez, Rowdy	L	.209	115	24	2	0	4	11	17	34	.313	.330
Bats Left	R	.222	414	92	21	0	31	78	45	87	.303	.498
Thomas, Alek	L	.198	91	18	1	0	1	6	4	17	.229	.242
Bats Left	R	.241	290	70	16	1	7	33	18	57	.289	.376
Thomas, Lane	L	.253	186	47	9	1	8	22	14	40	.302	.441
Bats Right	R	.234	312	73	17	1	9	30	27	92	.301	.381
Thompson, Bubba	L	.189	53	10	1	0	1	3	4	21	.259	.264
Bats Right	R	.299	117	35	4	0	0	6	3	35	.322	.333
Thompson, Trayce	L	.174	86	15	7	0	3	11	9	41	.260	.360
Bats Right	R	.308	133	41	7	1	10	30	23	52	.409	.602
Toglia, Michael	L	.200	35	7	3	0	1	5	1	14	.222	.371
Bats Both	R	.224	76	17	5	2	1	7	8	30	.298	.382
Torkelson, Spencer	L	.216	97	21	6	1	2	6	9	21	.290	.361
Bats Right	R	.198	263	52	10	0	6	22	28	78	.283	.304
Toro, Abraham	L	.200	105	21	4	0	1	6	9	19	.265	.267
Bats Both	R	.178	219	39	9	1	9	29	13	46	.226	.352
Torrens, Luis	L	.203	69	14	1	0	3	7	5	21	.263	.348
Bats Right	R	.244	82	20	1	0	8	7	9	29	.300	.256
Torres, Gleyber	L	.255	137	35	6	1	10	22	8	31	.297	.533
Bats Right	R	.257	389	100	22	0	14	54	31	98	.315	.422
Trammell, Taylor	L	.100	20	2	1	0	0	3	2	7	.174	.150
Bats Left	R	.220	82	18	8	0	4	7	11	26	.312	.463
Trejo, Alan	L	.167	24	4	1	0	1	4	3	9	.259	.333
Bats Right	R	.298	94	28	5	0	3	13	2	22	.327	.447
Trevino, Jose	L	.304	69	21	3	0	4	9	5	14	.360	.522
Bats Right	R	.233	266	62	9	1	7	34	10	54	.263	.353
Trout, Mike	L	.310	116	36	11	0	9	19	21	31	.420	.638
Bats Right	R	.273	322	88	17	2	31	61	33	108	.349	.627
Tsutsugo, Yoshi	L	.175	57	10	1	0	1	8	5	24	.234	.246
Bats Left	R	.168	113	19	3	0	1	11	14	26	.256	.221
Tucker, Kyle	L	.228	206	47	8	0	13	47	15	32	.279	.456
Bats Left	R	.275	338	93	21	1	17	60	44	63	.359	.491
Turner, Justin	L	.275	131	36	6	0	3	21	13	28	.345	.389
Bats Right	R	.279	337	94	30	0	10	60	37	61	.352	.457
Turner, Trea	L	.298	168	50	9	1	10	29	11	38	.344	.542
Bats Right	R	.298	484	144	30	3	11	71	34	93	.342	.440
Urias, Luis	L	.269	119	32	7	0	3	10	11	28	.348	.403
Bats Right	R	.226	287	65	10	1	13	37	39	71	.329	.404
Urias, Ramon	L	.222	117	26	7	0	4	15	9	27	.281	.385
Bats Right	R	.259	286	74	10	1	12	36	21	71	.315	.427
Urshela, Gio	L	.291	148	43	12	2	2	13	11	29	.335	.439
Bats Right	R	.283	353	100	15	1	11	51	30	67	.338	.425
VanMeter, Josh	L	.069	29	2	1	0	0	1	4	10	.182	.103
Bats Left	R	.211	142	30	4	2	3	13	15	35	.283	.331
Vargas, Ildemaro	L	.253	79	20	9	0	2	10	1	13	.272	.443
Bats Both	R	.269	130	35	4	1	2	13	7	10	.314	.362

Batter	vs	Avg	AB	H	2B	3B	HR	RBI	BB	SO	OBP	Slg
Varsho, Daulton	L	.221	122	27	5	1	1	13	3	36	.250	.303
Bats Left	R	.240	409	98	18	2	26	61	43	109	.317	.484
Vaughn, Andrew	L	.307	114	35	5	0	1	13	10	14	.363	.377
Bats Right	R	.260	396	103	23	1	16	63	21	82	.309	.444
Vazquez, Christian	L	.304	102	31	9	0	3	13	6	16	.343	.480
Bats Right	R	.264	296	78	14	0	6	39	16	53	.305	.372
Velazquez, Andrew	L	.224	98	22	4	0	1	7	4	27	.252	.296
Bats Both	R	.183	224	41	4	0	8	21	11	92	.229	.308
Velazquez, Nelson	L	.197	71	14	2	2	4	9	10	27	.305	.451
Bats Right	R	.211	114	24	5	1	2	17	9	38	.274	.325
Verdugo, Alex	L	.266	154	41	10	1	1	20	14	24	.329	.364
Bats Left	R	.285	439	125	29	0	10	54	28	62	.327	.419
Vierling, Matt	L	.295	122	36	8	1	2	13	8	23	.333	.426
Bats Right	R	.217	203	44	4	1	4	19	15	47	.275	.305
Villar, David	L	.292	65	19	3	1	5	13	8	24	.378	.600
Bats Right	R	.187	91	17	3	0	4	11	10	34	.299	.352
Villar, Jonathan	L	.188	48	9	2	1	1	4	5	14	.259	.333
Bats Both	R	.214	154	33	4	1	2	14	10	45	.261	.292
Vogelbach, Daniel	L	.139	72	10	1	0	0	7	11	21	.262	.153
Bats Left	R	.261	314	82	18	1	18	52	62	93	.382	.497
Vogt, Stephen	L	.000	9	0	0	0	0	0	1	1	.091	.000
Bats Left	R	.170	159	27	4	1	7	22	16	45	.250	.340
Voit, Luke	L	.174	144	25	8	0	2	15	22	61	.298	.271
Bats Right	R	.247	356	88	14	0	20	54	33	118	.312	.455
Votto, Joey	L	.214	98	21	6	0	2	11	17	41	.364	.337
Bats Left	R	.201	224	45	12	1	9	30	27	56	.298	.384
Wade, Tyler	L	.227	22	5	0	0	0	1	2	7	.292	.227
Bats Left	R	.216	125	27	5	0	1	7	8	26	.269	.280
Wade Jr., LaMonte	L	.100	30	3	0	0	0	4	2	7	.152	.100
Bats Left	R	.225	187	42	7	1	8	22	24	44	.329	.401
Walker, Christian	L	.261	138	36	9	1	9	30	18	30	.352	.493
Bats Right	R	.236	445	105	16	1	29	76	50	101	.319	.472
Wallis, Taylor	L	.164	116	19	6	0	1	9	20	31	.292	.241
Bats Both	R	.175	291	51	12	2	7	24	32	89	.258	.302
Walsh, Jared	L	.200	110	22	4	1	3	11	7	34	.254	.336
Bats Left	R	.220	313	69	14	1	12	33	20	104	.274	.431
Ward, Taylor	L	.268	142	38	5	1	4	14	20	31	.354	.401
Bats Right	R	.286	353	101	17	1	19	51	40	89	.363	.501
Wendle, Joey	L	.230	61	14	4	0	0	12	6	13	.300	.295
Bats Left	R	.266	286	76	20	1	3	20	9	37	.297	.374
White, Eli	L	.204	49	10	2	0	1	2	6	18	.291	.306
Bats Right	R	.196	56	11	0	0	2	8	5	23	.258	.304
Williams, Luke	L	.244	45	11	4	0	0	4	2	17	.277	.333
Bats Right	R	.232	82	19	1	1	1	2	7	27	.292	.305
Winker, Jesse	L	.244	119	29	5	0	6	20	20	25	.357	.437
Bats Left	R	.211	337	71	10	0	8	33	64	78	.339	.312
Wisdom, Patrick	L	.250	124	31	8	0	10	20	12	50	.336	.556
Bats Right	R	.191	345	66	20	0	15	46	41	133	.285	.380
Witt Jr., Bobby	L	.234	141	33	7	3	6	24	5	34	.264	.454
Bats Right	R	.260	450	117	24	3	14	56	25	101	.304	.420
Wong, Kolten	L	.138	80	11	0	0	1	3	11	15	.266	.175
Bats Left	R	.277	350	97	24	4	14	44	35	73	.357	.489
Wynns, Austin	L	.234	64	15	0	0	1	7	3	18	.290	.281
Bats Right	R	.276	98	27	7	0	2	14	7	20	.327	.408
Yastrzemski, Mike	L	.179	123	22	4	1	4	12	10	41	.250	.325
Bats Left	R	.227	362	82	27	1	13	45	51	100	.323	.414
Yelich, Christian	L	.258	182	47	2	1	5	13	18	50	.332	.363
Bats Left	R	.249	393	98	23	3	9	44	70	112	.365	.392
Yepez, Juan	L	.255	55	14	2	0	2	4	14	29	.295	.400
Bats Right	R	.253	198	50	11	0	10	23	12	47	.296	.460
Zavala, Seby	L	.216	37	8	3	0	0	1	6	13	.356	.297
Bats Right	R	.284	141	40	11	0	2	20	13	51	.344	.404
Zunino, Mike	L	.135	37	5	0	0	2	5	3	12	.200	.297
Bats Right	R	.154	78	12	3	0	3	11	3	34	.193	.308
AL	L	.246	-	-	-	-	-	-	-	-	.315	.399
	R	.241	-	-	-	-	-	-	-	-	.307	.398
NL	L	.244	-	-	-	-	-	-	-	-	.315	.398
	R	.243	-	-	-	-	-	-	-	-	.313	.398
MLB	L	.245	-	-	-	-	-	-	-	-	.315	.399
	R	.242	-	-	-	-	-	-	-	-	.310	.393

Pitchers vs. Left-Handed and Right-Handed Batters

Pitcher	vs	Avg	AB	H	2B	3B	HR	RBI	BB	SO	OBP	Slg
Abbott, Cory	L	.268	97	26	7	0	7	13	12	27	.366	.557
Throws Right	R	.207	87	18	5	0	5	12	13	18	.317	.437
Abreu, Albert	L	.191	47	9	0	0	2	7	9	15	.316	.319
Throws Right	R	.268	97	26	5	0	3	12	13	23	.368	.412
Abreu, Bryan	L	.189	106	20	2	0	0	11	12	42	.287	.208
Throws Right	R	.225	111	25	5	0	2	14	14	46	.317	.324
Acevedo, Domingo	L	.215	79	17	3	1	4	12	10	15	.303	.430
Throws Right	R	.201	164	33	8	0	5	19	7	43	.246	.341
Adam, Jason	L	.136	81	11	1	1	2	3	5	25	.186	.247
Throws Right	R	.154	130	20	2	0	3	11	12	50	.253	.238
Adon, Joan	L	.264	121	32	7	3	5	20	22	29	.375	.496
Throws Right	R	.312	141	44	11	1	3	29	17	26	.406	.468
Akin, Keegan	L	.185	119	22	4	0	0	11	7	31	.227	.218
Throws Left	R	.254	185	47	11	0	10	25	13	46	.307	.476
Alcantara, Sandy	L	.196	443	87	21	2	8	37	29	98	.244	.307
Throws Right	R	.231	377	87	11	4	8	27	21	109	.286	.345
Alexander, Jason	L	.331	124	41	6	2	9	27	14	23	.395	.629
Throws Right	R	.297	158	47	9	1	3	14	14	23	.356	.424
Alexander, Tyler	L	.260	100	26	5	0	4	17	3	19	.276	.430
Throws Left	R	.280	293	82	15	2	14	44	22	42	.328	.488
Almonte, Yency	L	.071	42	3	1	0	0	1	3	6	.133	.095
Throws Right	R	.192	78	15	3	0	2	5	7	27	.289	.308
Alvarado, Jose	L	.237	59	14	2	0	1	5	6	19	.308	.322
Throws Left	R	.188	128	24	6	1	1	14	18	62	.291	.273
Anderson, Chase	L	.184	38	7	3	0	1	6	8	11	.333	.342
Throws Right	R	.222	45	10	1	0	2	8	7	12	.345	.378
Anderson, Ian	L	.211	209	44	12	0	2	15	31	49	.313	.297
Throws Right	R	.313	227	71	13	1	10	33	23	48	.375	.511
Anderson, Tyler	L	.234	124	29	4	1	3	14	4	27	.271	.355
Throws Left	R	.218	533	116	27	5	11	36	30	111	.266	.349
Arano, Victor	L	.333	69	23	2	0	4	20	3	16	.356	.536
Throws Right	R	.240	100	24	5	0	1	16	9	28	.327	.320
Archer, Chris	L	.190	153	29	10	0	4	11	25	45	.309	.333
Throws Right	R	.254	228	58	16	0	8	36	23	39	.322	.430
Arihara, Kohei	L	.348	46	16	4	0	2	8	4	7	.412	.565
Throws Right	R	.426	47	20	8	0	2	11	7	7	.518	.723
Armstrong, Shawn	L	.293	82	24	9	0	2	9	8	26	.370	.476
Throws Right	R	.263	160	42	8	0	5	29	9	40	.301	.406
Ashby, Aaron	L	.250	84	21	5	0	2	11	10	30	.351	.381
Throws Left	R	.254	334	85	14	2	13	44	37	96	.332	.425
Ashcraft, Graham	L	.232	194	45	3	0	1	9	14	36	.292	.263
Throws Right	R	.323	229	74	16	0	10	42	16	35	.377	.524
Assad, Javier	L	.290	62	18	3	1	2	5	11	12	.397	.468
Throws Right	R	.202	84	17	2	0	2	7	9	18	.280	.298
Baker, Bryan	L	.225	89	20	5	1	1	7	8	23	.293	.337
Throws Right	R	.233	172	40	3	1	2	20	18	53	.313	.297
Banks, Tanner	L	.246	61	15	2	0	3	6	6	17	.313	.426
Throws Left	R	.199	136	27	3	0	2	17	12	32	.267	.265
Banuelos, Manny	L	.207	58	12	1	0	0	8	10	18	.329	.224
Throws Left	R	.220	91	20	6	1	2	17	11	24	.317	.374
Bard, Daniel	L	.174	121	21	6	0	2	5	16	39	.270	.273
Throws Right	R	.147	95	14	3	0	1	10	9	30	.241	.211
Barlow, Joe	L	.182	55	10	2	0	2	9	8	10	.308	.327
Throws Right	R	.236	72	17	2	1	3	9	5	18	.296	.417
Barlow, Scott	L	.211	123	26	3	1	3	14	8	39	.274	.325
Throws Right	R	.187	139	26	1	0	6	18	14	38	.258	.324
Barnes, Matt	L	.217	60	13	4	1	1	8	9	17	.319	.367
Throws Right	R	.256	90	23	2	0	1	8	12	17	.358	.311
Barria, Jaime	L	.225	120	27	5	1	8	20	12	22	.293	.483
Throws Right	R	.212	170	36	7	2	3	15	7	32	.256	.329
Bass, Anthony	L	.268	97	26	3	0	4	9	6	25	.308	.423
Throws Right	R	.159	157	25	5	1	2	11	14	48	.228	.242
Bassitt, Chris	L	.247	300	74	13	1	11	36	30	84	.328	.407
Throws Right	R	.224	380	85	13	0	8	27	19	83	.271	.321
Baumann, Mike	L	.275	51	14	3	0	1	6	4	12	.345	.392
Throws Right	R	.337	86	29	6	0	2	12	5	11	.374	.477
Bautista, Felix	L	.149	74	11	3	0	3	7	6	31	.213	.311
Throws Right	R	.176	153	27	4	0	4	14	17	57	.260	.281
Baz, Shane	L	.175	40	7	1	0	2	6	5	13	.267	.350
Throws Right	R	.299	67	20	3	1	3	7	4	17	.347	.507
Bednar, David	L	.188	80	15	4	0	1	3	9	30	.270	.275
Throws Right	R	.239	113	27	7	0	3	16	7	39	.289	.381
Beede, Tyler	L	.267	120	32	6	0	4	17	13	22	.336	.417
Throws Right	R	.300	130	39	10	1	3	18	16	17	.397	.462
Beeks, Jalen	L	.219	64	14	4	1	3	8	8	26	.301	.453
Throws Left	R	.219	160	35	9	0	4	13	14	44	.290	.350

Pitcher	vs	Avg	AB	H	2B	3B	HR	RBI	BB	SO	OBP	Slg
Bellatti, Andrew	L	.278	72	20	7	0	3	12	10	26	.366	.500
Throws Right	R	.209	129	27	8	0	2	18	15	52	.291	.318
Bello, Brayan	L	.295	95	28	5	1	1	13	12	19	.370	.400
Throws Right	R	.329	143	47	12	1	0	11	15	36	.400	.427
Berrios, Jose	L	.298	362	108	16	1	20	49	24	68	.351	.514
Throws Right	R	.276	330	91	18	0	9	37	21	81	.327	.412
Bickford, Phil	L	.247	77	19	6	0	3	8	5	20	.310	.442
Throws Right	R	.227	150	34	7	0	9	25	9	47	.264	.453
Bieber, Shane	L	.221	335	74	13	0	9	27	14	100	.252	.340
Throws Right	R	.238	412	98	16	2	9	36	22	98	.278	.352
Bird, Jake	L	.244	86	21	3	2	3	14	15	18	.363	.430
Throws Right	R	.253	95	24	3	0	4	19	8	24	.324	.411
Blach, Ty	L	.179	67	12	3	0	2	11	4	11	.240	.313
Throws Left	R	.361	108	39	11	2	2	22	7	18	.393	.556
Blackburn, Paul	L	.260	223	58	21	0	7	26	16	49	.315	.448
Throws Right	R	.250	208	52	10	2	8	23	14	40	.307	.433
Bleier, Richard	L	.256	90	23	9	0	1	14	4	15	.287	.389
Throws Left	R	.336	119	40	15	0	2	17	6	17	.370	.513
Boxberger, Brad	L	.248	105	26	3	1	2	14	12	26	.325	.352
Throws Right	R	.203	128	26	3	1	4	18	15	42	.291	.336
Bradish, Kyle	L	.235	153	36	5	0	4	12	19	39	.326	.346
Throws Right	R	.280	296	83	13	0	13	44	27	72	.347	.456
Brash, Matt	L	.234	77	18	3	0	1	9	16	25	.372	.312
Throws Right	R	.257	109	28	3	0	2	12	17	37	.362	.339
Brasier, Ryan	L	.306	72	22	9	0	3	20	6	18	.350	.556
Throws Right	R	.269	171	46	13	0	6	28	7	46	.295	.450
Brazoban, Huascar	L	.256	39	10	2	0	2	6	11	9	.420	.462
Throws Right	R	.205	78	16	4	0	1	10	10	31	.311	.295
Brebbia, John	L	.278	97	27	7	2	2	8	8	24	.330	.454
Throws Right	R	.262	168	44	13	1	3	21	10	30	.306	.405
Brieske, Beau	L	.206	136	28	1	1	4	12	13	26	.275	.316
Throws Right	R	.260	173	45	9	0	10	25	12	28	.307	.486
Brigham, Jeff	L	.229	35	8	3	0	1	5	5	11	.325	.400
Throws Right	R	.255	55	14	3	0	2	2	5	17	.317	.418
Brogdon, Connor	L	.241	79	19	3	1	1	8	4	16	.286	.342
Throws Right	R	.263	95	25	5	0	5	16	7	34	.311	.474
Brubaker, JT	L	.269	268	72	23	2	10	36	26	71	.339	.481
Throws Right	R	.272	312	85	16	0	7	42	28	76	.342	.391
Bruihl, Justin	L	.234	47	11	1	1	0	4	2	8	.265	.298
Throws Left	R	.275	40	11	1	0	4	6	4	5	.375	.600
Bubic, Kris	L	.372	113	42	7	1	6	19	17	18	.459	.611
Throws Left	R	.287	397	114	23	0	12	56	46	92	.358	.436
Buehler, Walker	L	.271	144	39	7	1	4	15	10	31	.327	.417
Throws Right	R	.252	111	28	5	0	4	14	7	27	.297	.405
Bumgarner, Madison	L	.263	137	36	9	0	3	22	14	24	.340	.394
Throws Left	R	.286	500	143	41	3	22	68	35	88	.340	.512
Bummer, Aaron	L	.231	39	9	1	0	0	6	7	12	.340	.256
Throws Left	R	.323	65	21	2	0	2	10	3	18	.371	.446
Bundy, Dylan	L	.254	248	63	14	0	7	31	9	28	.286	.395
Throws Right	R	.284	310	88	15	2	17	41	19	66	.321	.510
Burke, Brock	L	.192	78	15	4	0	3	8	8	24	.276	.359
Throws Left	R	.218	220	48	10	1	6	16	16	66	.274	.355
Burnes, Corbin	L	.203	374	76	11	6	10	33	28	124	.265	.345
Throws Right	R	.190	357	68	13	0	13	32	23	119	.256	.336
Bush, Matt	L	.200	80	16	1	0	5	12	11	28	.301	.400
Throws Right	R	.194	139	27	3	0	6	11	7	46	.242	.345
Cabrera, Edward	L	.168	125	21	3	0	2	7	10	32	.241	.240
Throws Right	R	.185	124	23	4	0	8	12	23	43	.344	.411
Cabrera, Genesis	L	.214	56	12	1	0	2	6	9	11	.343	.339
Throws Left	R	.239	113	27	7	0	6	22	11	21	.315	.460
Carrasco, Carlos	L	.250	260	65	15	1	9	32	20	68	.307	.419
Throws Right	R	.288	333	96	23	0	8	27	21	84	.341	.429
Castano, Daniel	L	.267	45	12	3	1	3	5	4	8	.353	.578
Throws Left	R	.303	99	30	9	1	2	14	5	12	.337	.475
Castellanos, Humberto	L	.256	78	20	5	1	4	12	6	12	.302	.500
Throws Right	R	.316	95	30	5	0	3	14	6	20	.374	.463
Castillo, Diego	L	.243	70	17	3	0	2	6	11	14	.346	.371
Throws Right	R	.181	127	23	1	0	3	21	11	39	.255	.260
Castillo, Luis	L	.206	267	55	14	0	8	29	25	77	.287	.348
Throws Right	R	.217	290	63	14	0	5	23	20	90	.272	.317
Castro, Miguel	L	.243	37	9	4	0	0	1	4	7	.317	.351
Throws Right	R	.243	74	18	6	0	2	13	11	24	.371	.405
Cease, Dylan	L	.219	320	70	12	2	6	18	44	98	.319	.325
Throws Right	R	.163	343	56	13	0	10	28	34	129	.238	.289
Cessa, Luis	L	.247	146	36	6	1	4	18	14	27	.313	.384
Throws Right	R	.253	158	40	5	1	10	29	14	32	.318	.487

Pitchers vs. Left-Handed and Right-Handed Batters

Pitcher	vs	Avg	AB	H	2B	3B	HR	RBI	BB	SO	OBP	Slg
Chacin, Jhoulys	L	.250	88	22	6	1	3	16	12	14	.347	.443
Throws Right	R	.308	107	33	12	0	4	25	9	23	.364	.533
Chafin, Andrew	L	.233	90	21	4	0	2	10	10	30	.320	.344
Throws Left	R	.214	126	27	2	1	3	12	9	37	.268	.317
Chapman, Aroldis	L	.162	37	6	1	0	0	1	6	11	.295	.189
Throws Left	R	.198	91	18	4	0	4	15	22	32	.348	.374
Chavez, Jesse	L	.271	118	32	8	2	2	19	10	25	.328	.424
Throws Right	R	.258	151	39	5	2	6	24	10	49	.307	.437
Cimber, Adam	L	.214	103	22	4	1	3	13	6	28	.284	.359
Throws Right	R	.270	163	44	6	1	3	20	7	30	.312	.374
Cishek, Steve	L	.280	82	23	1	1	6	17	14	26	.398	.537
Throws Right	R	.194	160	31	2	0	5	24	13	48	.290	.300
Cisnero, Jose	L	.161	31	5	1	0	0	2	12	9	.395	.194
Throws Right	R	.185	54	10	2	0	0	3	7	14	.290	.222
Civale, Aaron	L	.240	167	40	10	0	7	23	13	52	.293	.425
Throws Right	R	.257	206	53	13	0	7	23	9	46	.305	.422
Clarke, Taylor	L	.250	76	19	4	1	3	12	4	17	.293	.447
Throws Right	R	.267	116	31	6	1	3	21	4	31	.289	.414
Clase, Emmanuel	L	.179	112	20	0	0	2	8	4	35	.207	.232
Throws Right	R	.158	146	23	6	0	1	10	6	42	.195	.219
Clevinger, Mike	L	.211	227	48	4	1	13	27	23	56	.289	.410
Throws Right	R	.257	210	54	12	0	7	22	12	35	.320	.414
Cobb, Alex	L	.269	275	74	12	0	3	33	24	68	.328	.345
Throws Right	R	.256	305	78	12	0	6	31	19	83	.303	.354
Cole, Gerrit	L	.182	324	59	9	1	17	37	30	129	.251	.373
Throws Right	R	.229	414	95	22	1	16	41	20	128	.268	.403
Coleman, Dylan	L	.230	100	23	2	0	2	12	13	30	.336	.310
Throws Right	R	.169	142	24	10	0	3	14	24	41	.293	.303
Colome, Alex	L	.275	80	22	5	2	1	12	10	19	.352	.425
Throws Right	R	.318	110	35	11	0	4	19	12	13	.382	.527
Contreras, Roansy	L	.204	147	30	9	0	6	23	16	30	.287	.388
Throws Right	R	.239	218	52	19	1	7	19	23	56	.311	.431
Corbin, Patrick	L	.321	140	45	7	2	3	29	11	25	.375	.464
Throws Left	R	.320	515	165	28	3	24	77	38	103	.373	.526
Cortes, Nestor	L	.110	82	9	1	0	1	2	7	33	.180	.159
Throws Left	R	.202	490	99	22	0	15	37	31	130	.251	.339
Cotton, Jharel	L	.239	67	16	5	0	3	9	10	20	.346	.448
Throws Right	R	.202	89	18	3	0	4	12	10	19	.282	.371
Crawford, Kutter	L	.275	120	33	12	0	9	23	16	37	.367	.600
Throws Right	R	.265	181	48	9	0	3	17	13	40	.313	.365
Crismatt, Nabil	L	.208	101	21	5	0	2	12	14	16	.299	.317
Throws Right	R	.238	151	36	14	0	3	18	8	49	.282	.391
Crowe, Wil	L	.198	116	23	4	0	2	8	15	30	.288	.284
Throws Right	R	.260	173	45	5	1	6	29	23	38	.357	.405
Cuas, Jose	L	.350	40	14	5	0	1	7	12	10	.519	.550
Throws Right	R	.231	108	25	5	0	1	15	12	24	.328	.306
Cueto, Johnny	L	.277	271	75	20	1	6	30	19	41	.328	.424
Throws Right	R	.258	333	86	17	1	9	31	14	61	.291	.396
Danish, Tyler	L	.275	51	14	3	1	2	9	6	7	.351	.490
Throws Right	R	.245	106	26	3	0	5	13	6	25	.310	.415
Darvish, Yu	L	.185	389	72	16	0	10	27	22	120	.235	.303
Throws Right	R	.233	326	76	7	0	12	32	15	77	.280	.365
Davidson, Tucker	L	.267	45	12	4	0	3	11	12	4	.424	.556
Throws Left	R	.266	158	42	10	1	4	23	23	29	.364	.418
Davies, Zach	L	.222	221	49	9	2	7	21	29	34	.310	.376
Throws Right	R	.255	286	73	11	0	14	39	23	68	.309	.441
Davis, Austin	L	.198	81	16	3	0	1	11	8	22	.283	.272
Throws Left	R	.293	140	41	6	2	4	29	25	42	.406	.450
De Jong, Chase	L	.209	110	23	9	0	4	13	11	27	.302	.400
Throws Right	R	.200	145	29	6	0	6	13	19	32	.297	.366
De Los Santos, Enyel	L	.209	67	14	3	0	1	8	12	15	.333	.299
Throws Right	R	.208	125	26	9	1	2	16	5	46	.239	.344
De Los Santos, Yerry	L	.214	42	9	3	0	2	10	7	10	.327	.429
Throws Right	R	.232	56	13	2	0	1	9	4	16	.295	.321
deGrom, Jacob	L	.165	115	19	2	0	5	9	4	51	.193	.313
Throws Right	R	.184	114	21	5	0	4	12	4	51	.210	.333
Detmers, Reid	L	.209	110	23	2	1	3	9	8	25	.269	.327
Throws Left	R	.237	367	87	25	1	10	40	38	97	.315	.392
Detwiler, Ross	L	.275	51	14	2	0	1	7	4	10	.339	.373
Throws Left	R	.298	57	17	5	0	4	11	6	18	.379	.596
Diaz, Alexis	L	.158	101	16	3	0	3	11	18	30	.301	.277
Throws Right	R	.107	112	12	0	0	2	6	15	53	.221	.161
Diaz, Edwin	L	.101	89	9	1	0	3	7	9	53	.182	.213
Throws Right	R	.202	124	25	2	0	0	4	9	65	.265	.218
Diekman, Jake	L	.250	88	22	4	0	2	13	13	28	.359	.364
Throws Left	R	.234	128	30	7	0	7	29	29	51	.392	.453

Pitcher	vs	Avg	AB	H	2B	3B	HR	RBI	BB	SO	OBP	Slg
Dominguez, Seranthony	L	.209	67	14	5	0	1	7	7	17	.280	.328
Throws Right	R	.190	116	22	4	0	3	13	15	44	.288	.302
Doval, Camilo	L	.261	111	29	4	1	3	14	19	33	.371	.396
Throws Right	R	.182	137	25	7	0	1	16	11	47	.248	.255
Duffey, Tyler	L	.271	70	19	6	0	4	10	7	15	.346	.529
Throws Right	R	.265	98	26	4	0	4	17	8	24	.318	.429
Dunn, Justin	L	.322	59	19	5	0	5	9	13	9	.452	.661
Throws Right	R	.228	57	13	3	0	6	12	4	12	.297	.596
Dunning, Dane	L	.271	291	79	23	2	8	31	35	60	.354	.447
Throws Right	R	.265	298	79	16	0	12	38	27	77	.335	.440
Duran, Jhoan	L	.204	108	22	1	0	3	6	12	34	.295	.296
Throws Right	R	.209	134	28	3	1	3	10	4	55	.239	.313
Edwards Jr., Carl	L	.241	108	26	1	0	2	9	13	22	.322	.306
Throws Right	R	.208	120	25	4	0	6	13	12	34	.281	.392
Effross, Scott	L	.127	71	9	0	0	2	5	9	25	.225	.211
Throws Right	R	.259	139	36	6	1	1	16	6	37	.293	.338
Eflin, Zach	L	.277	137	38	10	2	4	19	9	29	.333	.467
Throws Right	R	.209	153	32	6	0	4	16	6	36	.245	.327
Elder, Bryce	L	.231	91	21	7	0	3	7	9	15	.304	.407
Throws Right	R	.215	107	23	3	0	1	11	14	32	.315	.271
Eovaldi, Nathan	L	.232	164	38	10	0	9	21	9	46	.274	.457
Throws Right	R	.284	271	77	11	0	12	30	11	57	.311	.458
Espino, Paolo	L	.306	209	64	9	1	9	21	13	36	.344	.488
Throws Right	R	.271	247	67	11	0	15	36	11	56	.304	.498
Estevez, Carlos	L	.216	111	24	4	1	6	17	11	24	.287	.432
Throws Right	R	.204	98	20	5	1	1	10	12	30	.292	.306
Faedo, Alex	L	.283	113	32	10	0	5	15	13	18	.352	.504
Throws Right	R	.304	102	31	6	0	2	13	12	26	.379	.422
Falter, Bailey	L	.229	70	16	4	0	3	8	2	18	.257	.414
Throws Left	R	.273	253	69	13	2	13	30	15	56	.324	.494
Familia, Jeurys	L	.309	68	21	1	0	1	8	14	16	.434	.368
Throws Right	R	.330	112	37	9	1	6	26	8	25	.380	.589
Farmer, Buck	L	.226	62	14	4	0	0	8	17	17	.392	.290
Throws Right	R	.202	109	22	5	0	2	18	8	37	.261	.303
Faucher, Calvin	L	.419	31	13	0	0	3	10	3	8	.471	.710
Throws Right	R	.220	59	13	2	0	1	5	7	13	.313	.305
Fedde, Erick	L	.272	246	67	15	0	8	36	27	40	.337	.431
Throws Right	R	.313	262	82	12	0	13	39	31	54	.386	.508
Feltner, Ryan	L	.250	192	48	11	1	8	28	19	41	.321	.443
Throws Right	R	.283	191	54	7	3	8	32	16	43	.344	.476
Ferguson, Caleb	L	.243	37	9	3	0	0	3	6	9	.364	.324
Throws Left	R	.163	86	14	5	0	1	4	11	28	.265	.256
Festa, Matthew	L	.211	76	16	2	0	7	12	8	20	.302	.513
Throws Right	R	.223	121	27	5	2	3	15	10	44	.282	.372
Finnegan, Kyle	L	.163	104	17	6	0	2	13	12	31	.248	.279
Throws Right	R	.264	140	37	4	1	7	21	10	39	.311	.457
Flaherty, Jack	L	.268	82	22	4	2	3	10	10	20	.368	.476
Throws Right	R	.246	57	14	3	0	1	6	12	13	.394	.351
Fleming, Josh	L	.278	54	15	4	0	0	8	1	15	.291	.352
Throws Left	R	.386	101	39	11	0	5	21	11	14	.447	.644
Flexen, Chris	L	.221	249	55	11	2	4	13	31	51	.306	.329
Throws Right	R	.275	280	77	16	1	13	39	20	44	.324	.479
Floro, Dylan	L	.293	75	22	6	0	1	9	8	17	.357	.413
Throws Right	R	.202	129	26	1	1	3	13	7	31	.243	.295
Foley, Jason	L	.349	86	30	2	1	1	16	7	10	.411	.430
Throws Right	R	.269	156	42	6	0	1	20	4	33	.288	.327
Foster, Matt	L	.279	68	19	5	0	2	12	6	13	.338	.441
Throws Right	R	.226	106	24	2	0	4	13	11	29	.297	.358
Freeland, Kyle	L	.315	149	47	8	3	7	26	11	32	.382	.550
Throws Left	R	.271	538	146	39	5	12	60	42	99	.331	.429
Fried, Max	L	.206	155	32	4	0	2	13	8	42	.250	.271
Throws Left	R	.231	537	124	21	2	10	34	24	128	.265	.333
Fulmer, Michael	L	.337	95	32	10	1	2	13	10	23	.404	.526
Throws Right	R	.188	144	27	4	0	2	13	18	38	.287	.257
Gallegos, Giovanny	L	.226	93	21	8	0	4	14	8	24	.282	.441
Throws Right	R	.175	120	21	2	1	2	10	10	49	.237	.258
Gallen, Zac	L	.146	308	45	12	0	7	17	26	97	.220	.253
Throws Right	R	.222	343	76	20	1	8	30	21	95	.282	.356
Garcia, Jarlin	L	.192	99	19	3	1	4	17	7	23	.245	.364
Throws Left	R	.275	149	41	8	0	6	24	11	33	.327	.450
Garcia, Luis	L	.247	93	23	2	0	2	11	10	24	.346	.333
Throws Right	R	.239	142	34	5	0	1	17	7	44	.278	.296
Garcia, Luis	L	.234	274	64	14	4	12	34	18	68	.278	.445
Throws Right	R	.213	315	67	13	0	11	28	29	89	.280	.359
Garcia, Rony	L	.183	93	17	6	0	3	12	5	26	.245	.344
Throws Right	R	.242	95	23	3	1	6	12	8	22	.308	.484

Pitchers vs. Left-Handed and Right-Handed Batters

Pitcher	vs	Avg	AB	H	2B	3B	HR	RBI	BB	SO	OBP	Slg
Garcia, Yimi	L	.222	90	20	7	0	3	7	11	19	.308	.400
Throws Right	R	.211	133	28	4	0	3	17	5	39	.252	.308
Garrett, Amir	L	.106	66	7	2	0	0	7	12	20	.253	.136
Throws Left	R	.228	92	21	4	2	0	13	20	29	.385	.315
Garrett, Braxton	L	.173	81	14	2	0	1	7	6	26	.247	.235
Throws Left	R	.280	257	72	15	3	8	28	18	64	.346	.455
Garza, Ralph	L	.362	58	21	2	1	3	9	6	10	.422	.586
Throws Right	R	.224	76	17	3	0	1	6	10	7	.330	.303
Gausman, Kevin	L	.244	283	69	14	2	4	20	6	76	.258	.350
Throws Right	R	.292	407	119	21	2	11	46	22	129	.328	.435
German, Domingo	L	.230	135	31	8	0	5	12	12	22	.297	.400
Throws Right	R	.243	140	34	9	0	6	18	7	36	.293	.436
Gibaut, Ian	L	.290	62	18	3	0	1	10	9	21	.389	.387
Throws Right	R	.266	79	21	7	2	2	10	9	27	.341	.481
Gibson, Kyle	L	.260	288	75	15	2	10	39	27	54	.333	.431
Throws Right	R	.274	368	101	18	0	14	49	21	90	.318	.438
Gilbert, Logan	L	.201	314	63	16	2	5	22	29	94	.267	.312
Throws Right	R	.276	388	107	25	1	14	44	20	80	.319	.454
Gilbert, Tyler	L	.212	33	7	2	0	1	4	2	7	.250	.364
Throws Left	R	.263	99	26	3	0	7	15	8	13	.324	.505
Gilbreath, Lucas	L	.186	59	11	2	0	0	8	12	25	.329	.220
Throws Left	R	.277	94	26	4	0	2	22	14	24	.381	.383
Ginkel, Kevin	L	.200	35	7	2	0	0	2	5	10	.300	.257
Throws Right	R	.263	76	20	5	0	1	11	6	20	.321	.368
Giolito, Lucas	L	.217	263	57	8	1	7	28	28	87	.295	.335
Throws Right	R	.312	365	114	29	2	17	55	33	90	.370	.542
Givens, Mychal	L	.273	77	21	2	0	4	5	12	23	.371	.455
Throws Right	R	.233	150	35	8	0	4	22	13	48	.310	.367
Gomber, Austin	L	.221	136	30	7	0	3	20	9	26	.274	.338
Throws Left	R	.304	352	107	20	5	17	59	25	69	.348	.534
Gonsolin, Tony	L	.163	246	40	10	3	4	13	19	65	.225	.276
Throws Right	R	.184	212	39	9	0	7	18	16	54	.251	.325
Gonzales, Marco	L	.280	150	42	6	0	7	20	14	27	.351	.460
Throws Left	R	.268	567	152	38	0	23	69	36	76	.314	.457
Gore, MacKenzie	L	.193	57	11	1	2	0	3	13	15	.338	.281
Throws Left	R	.263	209	55	8	0	7	27	24	57	.349	.402
Gott, Trevor	L	.212	66	14	3	0	5	10	8	14	.307	.485
Throws Right	R	.200	105	21	5	0	3	12	4	30	.243	.333
Graterol, Brusdar	L	.292	72	21	5	1	1	10	5	16	.329	.431
Throws Right	R	.165	109	18	3	0	2	15	5	27	.220	.248
Graveman, Kendall	L	.260	123	32	4	2	3	16	13	26	.331	.398
Throws Right	R	.254	130	33	4	0	2	12	13	40	.329	.331
Gray, Jon	L	.248	218	54	13	1	6	26	24	55	.332	.399
Throws Right	R	.201	254	51	4	1	11	30	15	79	.247	.354
Gray, Josiah	L	.265	234	62	8	2	22	36	44	65	.382	.598
Throws Right	R	.221	335	74	12	2	16	44	22	89	.280	.412
Gray, Sonny	L	.202	203	41	4	3	4	17	11	58	.243	.310
Throws Right	R	.244	238	58	12	0	7	23	25	59	.327	.382
Greene, Hunter	L	.205	239	49	11	0	11	30	27	96	.299	.389
Throws Right	R	.239	230	55	10	0	13	24	21	68	.311	.452
Greinke, Zack	L	.286	224	64	12	0	4	21	13	21	.325	.393
Throws Right	R	.286	325	93	18	0	10	38	14	52	.317	.434
Grove, Michael	L	.275	69	19	5	0	4	10	6	15	.333	.522
Throws Right	R	.241	54	13	0	1	2	9	4	9	.293	.389
Gustave, Jandel	L	.207	29	6	0	0	2	3	3	8	.281	.414
Throws Right	R	.247	77	19	1	0	2	12	8	19	.330	.338
Gutierrez, Vladimir	L	.364	77	28	10	2	5	18	17	17	.474	.740
Throws Right	R	.257	70	18	4	1	3	10	7	12	.369	.471
Hader, Josh	L	.209	43	9	3	0	1	9	5	23	.286	.349
Throws Left	R	.230	148	34	5	1	7	20	16	58	.318	.419
Hand, Brad	L	.217	60	13	4	1	1	16	10	16	.319	.367
Throws Left	R	.226	106	24	4	0	1	8	13	22	.344	.292
Harvey, Hunter	L	.179	67	12	4	1	0	4	9	22	.273	.269
Throws Right	R	.284	74	21	5	0	1	12	3	23	.300	.392
Head, Louis	L	.282	39	11	4	0	1	10	5	8	.391	.462
Throws Right	R	.269	78	21	9	0	3	13	10	18	.374	.500
Heaney, Andrew	L	.230	61	14	3	1	1	4	6	21	.309	.361
Throws Left	R	.210	219	46	13	0	13	25	13	89	.278	.447
Hearn, Taylor	L	.270	89	24	4	0	2	16	10	28	.356	.382
Throws Left	R	.267	311	83	25	1	9	34	33	69	.337	.441
Heasley, Jon	L	.269	208	56	11	3	12	34	31	36	.366	.524
Throws Right	R	.265	196	52	11	0	7	28	16	34	.324	.429
Helsley, Ryan	L	.141	92	13	3	0	2	5	8	32	.210	.239
Throws Right	R	.118	127	15	3	0	4	9	12	62	.194	.236
Hendricks, Kyle	L	.291	172	50	10	2	12	29	16	37	.358	.581
Throws Right	R	.226	155	35	8	1	3	14	8	29	.268	.348

Pitcher	vs	Avg	AB	H	2B	3B	HR	RBI	BB	SO	OBP	Slg
Hendriks, Liam	L	.219	96	21	1	1	4	16	5	42	.257	.375
Throws Right	R	.202	114	23	4	1	3	10	11	43	.276	.333
Henry, Tommy	L	.371	35	13	0	0	3	5	1	7	.421	.629
Throws Left	R	.236	144	34	8	0	7	19	20	29	.331	.438
Hentges, Sam	L	.143	91	13	3	0	0	3	3	34	.194	.176
Throws Left	R	.215	130	28	4	0	3	14	16	38	.301	.315
Herget, Jimmy	L	.227	97	22	7	1	2	15	9	23	.303	.381
Throws Right	R	.174	149	26	8	0	2	12	6	41	.212	.268
Hernandez, Carlos	L	.214	98	21	6	1	3	11	14	21	.310	.388
Throws Right	R	.389	131	51	10	0	4	30	17	14	.451	.557
Hernandez, Elieser	L	.273	128	35	9	1	12	26	17	29	.361	.641
Throws Right	R	.264	121	32	9	1	7	23	5	31	.305	.529
Hernandez, Jonathan	L	.255	47	12	4	0	1	7	4	11	.327	.404
Throws Right	R	.215	65	14	1	0	1	4	13	16	.346	.277
Hicks, Jordan	L	.232	82	19	5	1	2	12	17	23	.385	.390
Throws Right	R	.197	137	27	3	0	3	12	18	40	.302	.285
Hill, Garrett	L	.178	90	16	0	0	4	10	20	20	.330	.311
Throws Right	R	.266	139	37	10	0	4	20	9	20	.325	.424
Hill, Rich	L	.277	65	18	3	0	1	9	6	17	.347	.369
Throws Left	R	.255	419	107	24	6	14	50	31	92	.311	.442
Hill, Tim	L	.208	72	15	2	0	0	9	8	12	.301	.236
Throws Left	R	.280	107	30	4	1	1	12	6	13	.328	.364
Hjelle, Sean	L	.205	39	8	2	0	0	2	0	12	.205	.256
Throws Right	R	.373	67	25	1	0	3	11	8	16	.447	.522
Hoffman, Jeff	L	.242	66	16	3	3	0	10	11	19	.363	.379
Throws Right	R	.231	104	24	5	0	5	18	12	26	.316	.423
Holmes, Clay	L	.250	92	23	5	0	1	12	12	20	.355	.337
Throws Right	R	.159	138	22	4	0	1	12	8	45	.237	.210
Houck, Tanner	L	.259	85	22	3	0	3	10	14	21	.376	.400
Throws Right	R	.205	132	27	3	0	0	9	8	35	.269	.227
Houser, Adrian	L	.307	179	55	13	2	5	27	22	34	.379	.486
Throws Right	R	.217	221	48	11	0	3	33	25	35	.298	.308
Howard, Spencer	L	.261	69	18	8	1	2	10	10	12	.354	.493
Throws Right	R	.344	93	32	4	0	10	22	5	20	.380	.710
Hudson, Dakota	L	.263	236	62	13	1	2	20	35	36	.366	.352
Throws Right	R	.281	281	79	11	0	7	40	26	42	.347	.395
Hughes, Brandon	L	.226	84	19	2	1	1	9	7	28	.301	.310
Throws Left	R	.183	126	23	4	0	10	18	14	40	.281	.452
Hutchison, Drew	L	.301	186	56	8	1	11	28	20	37	.369	.532
Throws Right	R	.251	231	58	9	1	4	21	22	31	.319	.351
Iglesias, Raisel	L	.200	100	20	3	0	4	16	5	32	.243	.350
Throws Right	R	.206	126	26	7	0	1	10	9	46	.270	.286
Irvin, Cole	L	.229	144	33	3	0	5	16	8	20	.284	.354
Throws Left	R	.257	549	141	30	3	20	62	28	108	.296	.432
Jackson, Zach	L	.143	63	9	2	0	1	2	15	26	.325	.222
Throws Right	R	.188	101	19	5	0	0	12	18	41	.308	.238
Jansen, Kenley	L	.213	108	23	2	2	5	14	12	39	.289	.407
Throws Right	R	.175	126	22	4	1	3	13	10	46	.245	.294
Javier, Cristian	L	.189	286	54	11	1	8	25	31	90	.274	.318
Throws Right	R	.147	238	35	7	0	9	18	21	104	.225	.290
Jax, Griffin	L	.189	90	17	2	0	3	12	9	23	.284	.311
Throws Right	R	.224	174	39	5	2	4	23	11	55	.267	.345
Jefferies, Daulton	L	.243	74	18	3	0	1	6	5	17	.300	.324
Throws Right	R	.322	87	28	10	0	3	18	3	11	.348	.540
Jimenez, Dany	L	.178	45	8	2	0	1	4	12	13	.351	.289
Throws Right	R	.185	81	15	1	0	1	9	6	21	.239	.235
Jimenez, Joe	L	.253	91	23	6	0	2	12	6	32	.299	.385
Throws Right	R	.206	126	26	3	2	2	13	7	45	.246	.310
Junis, Jakob	L	.307	212	65	17	2	7	25	11	44	.345	.505
Throws Right	R	.235	234	55	16	1	6	25	14	54	.284	.389
Kaprielian, James	L	.237	266	63	13	4	7	26	23	43	.302	.395
Throws Right	R	.241	241	58	14	3	9	30	36	55	.342	.436
Karinchak, James	L	.129	70	9	1	1	1	5	10	29	.247	.214
Throws Right	R	.194	67	13	2	0	1	4	11	33	.304	.269
Keller, Brad	L	.255	255	65	8	2	9	35	28	47	.330	.408
Throws Right	R	.295	298	88	16	2	8	43	29	55	.356	.443
Keller, Mitch	L	.276	290	80	16	1	5	18	34	55	.359	.390
Throws Right	R	.257	319	82	12	1	9	50	26	83	.326	.386
Kelley, Trevor	L	.257	35	9	1	0	4	7	4	10	.350	.629
Throws Right	R	.262	61	16	2	1	3	9	5	13	.328	.475
Kelly, Joe	L	.239	67	16	4	0	1	11	10	27	.342	.343
Throws Right	R	.263	76	20	5	0	1	10	13	26	.385	.368
Kelly, Merrill	L	.229	332	76	22	1	12	33	38	71	.310	.410
Throws Right	R	.224	407	91	18	1	9	36	23	106	.266	.339
Kennedy, Ian	L	.253	75	19	4	0	4	13	10	19	.337	.467
Throws Right	R	.292	130	38	7	1	7	20	12	25	.352	.523

Pitchers vs. Left-Handed and Right-Handed Batters

Pitcher	vs	Avg	AB	H	2B	3B	HR	RBI	BB	SO	OBP	Slg
Kershaw, Clayton	L	.254	71	18	2	0	0	3	8	20	.333	.282
Throws Left	R	.198	394	78	14	1	10	29	15	117	.229	.315
Keuchel, Dallas	L	.353	51	18	6	0	0	5	9	6	.450	.471
Throws Left	R	.349	218	76	15	3	11	61	22	39	.403	.596
Kikuchi, Yusei	L	.198	86	17	3	2	2	9	9	25	.286	.349
Throws Left	R	.256	297	76	18	1	21	51	49	99	.372	.535
Kimbrel, Craig	L	.261	111	29	7	1	3	16	11	29	.354	.423
Throws Right	R	.193	114	22	7	0	1	10	17	43	.295	.281
King, John	L	.254	59	15	0	0	2	10	2	9	.274	.356
Throws Left	R	.315	146	46	6	1	3	18	12	21	.371	.432
King, Michael	L	.179	67	12	2	1	2	8	4	24	.225	.328
Throws Right	R	.200	115	23	5	0	1	7	12	42	.273	.270
Kinley, Tyler	L	.119	42	5	1	0	0	3	3	11	.178	.143
Throws Right	R	.314	51	16	2	1	0	2	3	16	.364	.392
Kirby, George	L	.210	267	56	11	1	4	24	14	77	.250	.303
Throws Right	R	.324	244	79	12	1	9	26	8	56	.354	.492
Kluber, Corey	L	.279	287	80	18	2	8	35	11	64	.313	.439
Throws Right	R	.270	363	98	14	1	12	45	10	75	.297	.413
Knebel, Corey	L	.163	80	13	4	1	1	10	12	17	.277	.275
Throws Right	R	.241	83	20	4	0	3	13	16	24	.370	.398
Koenig, Jared	L	.303	33	10	3	1	1	6	5	3	.410	.545
Throws Left	R	.248	121	30	7	0	3	17	10	19	.321	.380
Kopech, Michael	L	.214	182	39	12	1	5	15	30	62	.326	.374
Throws Right	R	.186	247	46	5	0	10	29	27	43	.269	.328
Krehbiel, Joey	L	.238	80	19	6	0	3	7	9	15	.319	.425
Throws Right	R	.245	139	34	9	0	6	24	9	30	.294	.439
Kremer, Dean	L	.271	170	46	6	0	4	16	16	38	.337	.376
Throws Right	R	.258	299	77	21	0	7	23	18	49	.307	.398
Kuhl, Chad	L	.264	288	76	18	3	14	44	41	65	.355	.493
Throws Right	R	.306	258	79	13	3	11	41	17	45	.355	.508
Kuhnel, Joel	L	.270	89	24	4	0	4	16	4	17	.295	.449
Throws Right	R	.305	141	43	12	0	4	25	10	39	.367	.475
Lambert, Jimmy	L	.225	89	20	5	1	2	14	7	23	.283	.371
Throws Right	R	.230	87	20	3	0	2	10	17	22	.356	.333
Lange, Alex	L	.189	95	18	2	2	3	14	13	36	.284	.347
Throws Right	R	.213	136	29	4	0	2	19	18	46	.325	.287
Lauer, Eric	L	.216	97	21	2	0	3	11	11	23	.296	.330
Throws Left	R	.230	495	114	19	3	24	58	48	134	.299	.426
Lawrence, Justin	L	.316	79	25	6	1	2	21	9	20	.385	.494
Throws Right	R	.218	87	19	3	0	1	9	13	28	.320	.287
Leclerc, Jose	L	.173	81	14	7	0	3	11	15	26	.296	.370
Throws Right	R	.209	91	19	3	0	2	12	6	28	.280	.308
Lee, Dylan	L	.158	76	12	2	0	1	3	1	25	.169	.224
Throws Left	R	.248	113	28	4	0	4	23	9	34	.298	.389
Leiter Jr., Mark	L	.176	131	23	3	1	5	12	11	43	.243	.328
Throws Right	R	.248	117	29	4	1	5	20	14	30	.355	.427
Leone, Dominic	L	.333	75	25	12	0	5	13	12	19	.425	.693
Throws Right	R	.248	121	30	4	1	1	13	12	33	.313	.322
Liberatore, Matthew	L	.235	34	8	1	0	0	3	5	9	.350	.265
Throws Left	R	.327	104	34	11	2	5	14	13	19	.395	.615
Littell, Zack	L	.220	50	11	3	0	2	9	7	12	.322	.400
Throws Right	R	.298	124	37	7	1	6	19	6	27	.328	.516
Loaisiga, Jonathan	L	.243	70	17	2	0	1	10	7	19	.312	.314
Throws Right	R	.228	114	26	0	0	2	10	12	18	.302	.281
Lodolo, Nick	L	.109	46	5	1	0	0	2	4	21	.226	.130
Throws Left	R	.252	337	85	14	3	13	39	35	110	.351	.427
Logue, Zach	L	.235	51	12	3	1	2	6	2	11	.278	.451
Throws Left	R	.309	181	56	15	2	11	37	18	31	.373	.597
Long, Sammy	L	.423	52	22	6	2	3	15	5	10	.483	.788
Throws Left	R	.152	112	17	4	0	5	10	9	23	.213	.321
Lopez, Jorge	L	.218	101	22	4	3	1	14	17	27	.336	.347
Throws Right	R	.199	156	31	2	0	3	11	14	45	.286	.269
Lopez, Pablo	L	.249	354	88	19	4	12	36	35	72	.320	.427
Throws Right	R	.218	317	69	20	2	9	31	18	102	.269	.379
Lopez, Reynaldo	L	.239	92	22	7	1	1	12	6	25	.277	.370
Throws Right	R	.204	142	29	6	2	0	12	5	38	.235	.275
Lorenzen, Michael	L	.233	159	37	10	0	6	17	27	39	.348	.409
Throws Right	R	.217	203	44	8	0	5	24	17	46	.286	.330
Loup, Aaron	L	.238	80	19	2	0	1	8	9	20	.337	.300
Throws Left	R	.233	150	35	12	0	3	19	13	32	.315	.373
Luetge, Lucas	L	.269	78	21	2	0	1	9	8	22	.359	.333
Throws Left	R	.280	150	42	9	1	3	18	9	38	.321	.413
Lugo, Seth	L	.167	102	17	3	0	3	15	8	33	.230	.284
Throws Right	R	.279	147	41	6	0	6	16	10	36	.333	.442
Luzardo, Jesus	L	.203	64	13	1	0	2	7	6	24	.271	.313
Throws Left	R	.189	297	56	17	2	8	25	29	96	.264	.340

Pitcher	vs	Avg	AB	H	2B	3B	HR	RBI	BB	SO	OBP	Slg
Lyles, Jordan	L	.278	306	85	21	1	15	39	32	68	.347	.500
Throws Right	R	.275	404	111	25	0	11	42	20	76	.318	.418
Lynch, Daniel	L	.308	65	20	4	0	2	9	9	13	.400	.462
Throws Left	R	.287	470	135	20	1	19	66	43	109	.348	.455
Lynn, Lance	L	.249	273	68	11	0	12	34	8	60	.287	.421
Throws Right	R	.245	208	51	9	0	7	21	11	64	.291	.389
Machado, Andres	L	.305	105	32	8	0	4	19	10	22	.350	.495
Throws Right	R	.187	123	23	8	0	3	13	16	24	.291	.325
Mahle, Tyler	L	.192	224	43	9	3	5	23	27	67	.276	.326
Throws Right	R	.268	228	61	12	0	11	29	16	59	.319	.465
Manaea, Sean	L	.187	139	26	5	1	4	11	14	30	.276	.324
Throws Left	R	.273	472	129	21	4	25	72	36	126	.322	.494
Manning, Matt	L	.226	115	26	3	0	4	12	12	21	.300	.357
Throws Right	R	.236	123	29	4	0	2	12	7	27	.271	.317
Manoah, Alek	L	.237	392	93	16	1	11	29	40	83	.313	.367
Throws Right	R	.159	321	51	14	0	5	20	11	97	.211	.249
Mantiply, Joe	L	.247	85	21	0	0	1	8	4	28	.297	.282
Throws Left	R	.260	146	38	6	0	5	24	2	33	.272	.404
Marinaccio, Ron	L	.146	82	12	2	1	1	7	10	29	.247	.232
Throws Right	R	.152	66	10	3	0	1	10	14	27	.333	.242
Marquez, German	L	.279	373	104	23	3	17	62	42	82	.350	.493
Throws Right	R	.245	331	81	21	2	13	38	21	68	.293	.438
Marte, Yunior	L	.257	70	18	5	1	0	8	10	16	.354	.357
Throws Right	R	.254	114	29	3	0	5	22	12	28	.348	.412
Martin, Brett	L	.194	62	12	3	0	1	12	4	8	.242	.290
Throws Left	R	.292	130	38	11	0	3	24	14	32	.359	.446
Martin, Chris	L	.232	99	23	5	2	2	9	5	30	.267	.384
Throws Right	R	.229	118	27	4	0	4	12	0	44	.233	.364
Martin, Corbin	L	.294	34	10	3	0	1	3	7	7	.415	.471
Throws Right	R	.288	52	15	1	1	2	7	5	14	.339	.462
Martin, Davis	L	.273	128	35	8	1	4	15	9	25	.319	.445
Throws Right	R	.243	115	28	7	0	4	17	10	23	.320	.409
Martinez, Adrian	L	.297	111	33	5	0	6	16	9	26	.350	.505
Throws Right	R	.293	123	36	3	1	7	19	10	27	.353	.504
Martinez, Nick	L	.225	187	42	6	0	9	25	24	54	.316	.401
Throws Right	R	.251	215	54	13	0	6	25	17	41	.314	.395
Martinez, Seth	L	.280	50	14	1	0	2	6	6	10	.357	.420
Throws Right	R	.135	89	12	1	0	1	4	8	28	.214	.180
Maton, Phil	L	.242	120	29	8	0	5	13	13	26	.328	.433
Throws Right	R	.232	125	29	2	1	5	16	11	47	.315	.384
Matz, Steven	L	.279	43	12	3	0	1	4	3	14	.340	.419
Throws Left	R	.250	152	38	7	0	7	23	7	40	.288	.434
Matzek, Tyler	L	.212	52	11	1	0	2	6	12	9	.348	.346
Throws Left	R	.153	98	15	6	0	1	12	17	27	.288	.245
May, Dustin	L	.148	54	8	1	0	1	6	9	17	.303	.222
Throws Right	R	.241	54	13	1	0	2	8	5	12	.328	.370
May, Trevor	L	.283	46	13	3	0	1	3	3	16	.327	.413
Throws Right	R	.250	56	14	2	0	3	10	6	14	.323	.446
Mayers, Mike	L	.242	91	22	4	0	8	13	11	21	.330	.549
Throws Right	R	.273	110	30	3	0	7	23	7	24	.317	.491
Mayza, Tim	L	.162	74	12	2	1	2	7	4	19	.205	.297
Throws Left	R	.291	103	30	4	0	5	16	8	25	.342	.476
McCarty, Kirk	L	.129	31	4	1	0	1	4	2	5	.194	.258
Throws Left	R	.295	112	33	3	0	10	18	11	21	.358	.589
McClanahan, Shane	L	.204	93	19	3	0	3	7	6	26	.267	.333
Throws Left	R	.192	504	97	13	0	16	37	32	168	.242	.313
McCullers Jr., Lance	L	.165	79	13	4	0	1	3	16	27	.302	.253
Throws Right	R	.258	93	24	5	0	3	9	6	23	.303	.409
McFarland, T.J.	L	.354	48	17	1	1	2	13	1	8	.380	.542
Throws Left	R	.305	82	25	4	0	3	17	10	8	.383	.463
McHugh, Collin	L	.182	110	20	3	0	2	9	6	36	.237	.264
Throws Right	R	.220	141	31	6	0	3	17	8	39	.273	.326
McKenzie, Triston	L	.194	284	55	9	0	10	23	22	87	.258	.331
Throws Right	R	.205	404	83	20	2	15	42	22	103	.249	.376
Medina, Adonis	L	.286	35	10	3	0	0	5	1	4	.342	.371
Throws Right	R	.317	63	20	4	0	2	11	5	13	.386	.476
Megill, Trevor	L	.250	76	19	3	0	1	12	7	29	.321	.329
Throws Right	R	.307	101	31	6	0	3	16	10	20	.366	.455
Megill, Tylor	L	.293	99	29	5	0	5	14	7	20	.343	.495
Throws Right	R	.205	83	17	4	0	2	7	6	31	.256	.325
Melancon, Mark	L	.278	97	27	5	0	3	15	13	17	.369	.423
Throws Right	R	.283	127	36	5	0	2	16	8	18	.326	.370
Merryweather, Julian	L	.268	41	11	3	0	2	11	3	9	.326	.488
Throws Right	R	.308	65	20	6	0	2	15	4	14	.352	.492
Mikolas, Miles	L	.207	358	74	17	2	11	39	18	76	.247	.358
Throws Right	R	.244	393	96	14	0	14	37	21	77	.286	.387

Pitchers vs. Left-Handed and Right-Handed Batters

Pitcher	vs	Avg	AB	H	2B	3B	HR	RBI	BB	SO	OBP	Slg
Miley, Wade	L	.147	34	5	0	0	0	2	1	7	.194	.147
Throws Left	R	.241	108	26	5	1	3	15	13	21	.325	.389
Milner, Hoby	L	.253	91	23	6	0	1	10	6	27	.303	.352
Throws Left	R	.248	153	38	10	0	4	16	9	37	.312	.392
Minor, Mike	L	.232	95	22	3	0	4	12	4	19	.263	.389
Throws Left	R	.316	310	98	22	0	20	59	36	57	.396	.581
Minter, A.J.	L	.132	68	9	3	0	1	9	5	31	.197	.221
Throws Left	R	.222	180	40	9	0	4	16	10	63	.269	.339
Moll, Sam	L	.169	77	13	1	0	3	11	4	22	.220	.299
Throws Left	R	.238	84	20	5	0	2	14	18	24	.381	.369
Montas, Frankie	L	.254	256	65	11	0	11	32	28	65	.330	.426
Throws Right	R	.245	294	72	17	1	7	32	15	77	.288	.381
Montero, Rafael	L	.157	115	18	4	0	2	9	15	34	.260	.243
Throws Right	R	.227	128	29	3	1	1	12	8	39	.275	.289
Montgomery, Jordan	L	.198	106	21	4	0	1	9	1	38	.213	.264
Throws Left	R	.242	571	138	30	2	20	59	35	120	.293	.406
Moore, Matt	L	.243	74	18	4	1	0	5	8	16	.310	.324
Throws Left	R	.165	188	31	4	2	3	20	30	67	.282	.255
Moran, Jovani	L	.229	48	11	2	0	0	3	4	17	.283	.271
Throws Left	R	.144	97	14	6	0	0	9	14	37	.252	.206
Morejon, Adrian	L	.227	44	10	1	0	0	1	2	11	.261	.250
Throws Left	R	.244	86	21	3	0	4	10	7	17	.305	.419
Moreta, Dauri	L	.224	58	13	1	1	6	13	6	12	.324	.586
Throws Right	R	.229	83	19	5	0	4	10	7	27	.293	.434
Morgan, Eli	L	.196	107	21	4	0	6	17	3	24	.218	.402
Throws Right	R	.189	132	25	9	1	4	15	10	48	.253	.364
Morris, Cody	L	.256	39	10	1	0	3	4	6	10	.348	.513
Throws Right	R	.229	48	11	2	0	0	3	6	13	.315	.271
Morton, Charlie	L	.229	314	72	11	2	18	41	33	99	.322	.449
Throws Right	R	.236	326	77	15	0	10	38	30	106	.310	.374
Munoz, Andres	L	.157	115	18	2	0	2	11	8	52	.214	.226
Throws Right	R	.223	112	25	2	0	3	9	7	44	.287	.321
Murfee, Penn	L	.233	90	21	2	1	1	11	5	29	.281	.311
Throws Right	R	.169	160	27	7	0	6	16	13	47	.233	.325
Musgrove, Joe	L	.203	364	74	20	1	10	29	29	106	.275	.346
Throws Right	R	.254	315	80	16	1	12	32	13	78	.295	.425
Nance, Tommy	L	.184	76	14	3	1	2	9	7	30	.262	.329
Throws Right	R	.330	94	31	6	0	3	20	14	27	.432	.489
Naughton, Packy	L	.163	49	8	2	0	1	8	2	16	.212	.265
Throws Left	R	.373	83	31	8	0	2	10	5	15	.409	.542
Nelson, Kyle	L	.194	62	12	5	0	0	9	4	14	.254	.274
Throws Left	R	.194	72	14	6	0	1	5	10	16	.310	.319
Nelson, Nick	L	.256	129	33	8	1	0	19	13	33	.327	.333
Throws Right	R	.258	128	33	9	1	1	17	23	36	.365	.367
Neris, Hector	L	.205	112	23	6	0	1	14	7	38	.252	.286
Throws Right	R	.205	127	26	7	1	2	13	10	41	.294	.323
Newcomb, Sean	L	.311	45	14	3	0	3	10	8	10	.415	.578
Throws Left	R	.271	70	19	2	0	5	19	11	18	.370	.514
Nola, Aaron	L	.200	365	73	14	1	8	34	18	109	.247	.310
Throws Right	R	.237	401	95	25	0	11	35	11	126	.264	.382
Norris, Daniel	L	.176	85	15	4	0	3	14	13	27	.293	.329
Throws Left	R	.233	129	30	8	1	8	20	16	39	.344	.496
Ober, Bailey	L	.258	89	23	6	1	1	7	8	17	.323	.382
Throws Right	R	.205	122	25	4	1	3	15	3	34	.228	.328
Odorizzi, Jake	L	.244	209	51	5	2	8	28	21	45	.318	.402
Throws Right	R	.272	202	55	8	0	6	21	14	41	.320	.401
Ohtani, Shohei	L	.221	290	64	10	2	8	24	24	101	.284	.352
Throws Right	R	.188	320	60	13	0	6	17	20	118	.234	.284
Okert, Steven	L	.239	71	17	4	0	3	9	8	27	.341	.423
Throws Left	R	.152	112	17	3	0	4	10	18	36	.289	.286
Oller, Adam	L	.262	122	32	9	0	8	23	19	21	.366	.533
Throws Right	R	.292	171	50	19	0	9	27	20	25	.366	.561
Ort, Kaleb	L	.200	45	9	3	0	2	10	6	9	.288	.400
Throws Right	R	.366	71	26	3	0	2	15	9	18	.451	.493
Ortega, Oliver	L	.188	48	9	0	0	1	6	4	15	.250	.250
Throws Right	R	.288	80	23	4	0	4	8	14	18	.400	.488
Ottavino, Adam	L	.301	73	22	3	2	2	9	4	21	.358	.479
Throws Right	R	.160	162	26	3	0	4	18	12	58	.226	.253
Otto, Glenn	L	.201	239	48	6	1	8	30	32	51	.295	.335
Throws Right	R	.267	266	71	11	1	13	38	30	56	.365	.462
Overton, Connor	L	.167	54	9	1	0	0	1	7	3	.262	.185
Throws Right	R	.207	58	12	2	0	1	7	4	11	.254	.293
Oviedo, Johan	L	.195	87	17	5	0	0	9	13	18	.307	.253
Throws Right	R	.248	129	32	3	1	5	13	10	36	.312	.403
Pagan, Emilio	L	.213	108	23	4	0	3	7	9	37	.280	.333
Throws Right	R	.270	137	37	10	1	9	27	17	47	.348	.555

Pitcher	vs	Avg	AB	H	2B	3B	HR	RBI	BB	SO	OBP	Slg
Pallante, Andre	L	.246	179	44	7	0	3	15	9	22	.284	.335
Throws Right	R	.295	234	69	11	1	6	28	31	51	.377	.427
Payamps, Joel	L	.188	69	13	2	1	3	9	8	13	.282	.377
Throws Right	R	.311	151	47	7	1	4	20	8	28	.346	.450
Pepiot, Ryan	L	.239	67	16	3	0	3	7	22	23	.440	.418
Throws Right	R	.159	63	10	1	0	3	6	5	19	.232	.317
Peralta, Freddy	L	.145	117	17	3	2	2	5	13	39	.241	.256
Throws Right	R	.222	167	37	7	0	4	24	14	47	.284	.335
Peralta, Wandy	L	.155	71	11	1	0	1	5	4	24	.211	.211
Throws Left	R	.237	131	31	4	0	1	14	13	23	.303	.290
Peralta, Wily	L	.235	51	12	2	0	0	4	7	10	.322	.275
Throws Right	R	.244	90	22	4	0	2	9	17	22	.367	.356
Perez, Cionel	L	.224	76	17	2	0	0	4	6	24	.286	.250
Throws Left	R	.218	133	29	4	0	2	16	15	31	.293	.293
Perez, Martin	L	.219	128	28	7	0	1	9	6	25	.259	.297
Throws Left	R	.246	610	150	30	0	10	54	63	144	.320	.344
Peters, Dillon	L	.160	50	8	2	0	1	7	6	10	.246	.260
Throws Left	R	.284	95	27	5	0	4	11	11	16	.355	.463
Peterson, David	L	.176	85	15	2	0	5	10	9	32	.263	.376
Throws Left	R	.252	309	78	19	1	6	36	39	94	.345	.379
Phelps, David	L	.225	102	23	6	1	0	9	8	19	.301	.304
Throws Right	R	.216	134	29	3	1	2	12	23	45	.335	.299
Phillips, Evan	L	.170	100	17	5	0	0	5	6	32	.229	.220
Throws Right	R	.142	113	16	1	0	2	7	9	45	.210	.204
Pilkington, Konnor	L	.256	39	10	0	1	0	2	6	6	.356	.308
Throws Left	R	.234	184	43	8	0	6	21	26	44	.333	.375
Pineda, Michael	L	.306	98	30	2	1	8	16	7	12	.349	.592
Throws Right	R	.301	93	28	7	1	5	12	1	14	.309	.559
Pivetta, Nick	L	.252	266	67	15	1	12	38	38	66	.347	.451
Throws Right	R	.254	425	108	21	0	15	46	35	109	.314	.409
Plesac, Zach	L	.288	260	75	14	0	11	35	25	44	.356	.469
Throws Right	R	.231	264	61	16	0	8	29	13	56	.272	.383
Poche, Colin	L	.189	53	10	2	1	3	4	8	25	.290	.434
Throws Left	R	.218	165	36	6	0	8	26	14	39	.279	.400
Poppen, Sean	L	.333	30	10	3	0	2	4	7	6	.447	.633
Throws Right	R	.236	72	17	3	1	3	12	5	16	.284	.431
Poteet, Cody	L	.245	53	13	6	0	2	7	6	9	.322	.472
Throws Right	R	.200	50	10	2	0	2	9	5	12	.273	.360
Pressly, Ryan	L	.178	90	16	0	0	3	12	7	41	.235	.278
Throws Right	R	.184	76	14	2	1	1	5	6	24	.244	.276
Price, David	L	.271	59	16	3	0	2	4	2	13	.295	.424
Throws Left	R	.224	98	22	7	0	4	11	7	24	.276	.418
Pruitt, Austin	L	.203	79	16	2	0	6	13	2	13	.220	.456
Throws Right	R	.241	133	32	10	0	5	19	7	25	.282	.429
Puk, A.J.	L	.153	85	13	0	0	3	4	4	29	.250	.259
Throws Left	R	.252	159	40	11	1	4	22	19	47	.343	.409
Quantrill, Cal	L	.228	312	71	12	1	10	33	30	75	.299	.369
Throws Right	R	.274	390	107	18	0	11	38	17	53	.313	.405
Quijada, Jose	L	.115	52	6	1	0	2	5	5	23	.193	.250
Throws Left	R	.204	93	19	10	0	3	12	16	29	.330	.409
Quintana, Jose	L	.219	96	21	5	0	0	7	8	32	.286	.271
Throws Left	R	.251	530	133	30	1	8	45	39	105	.304	.357
Ragans, Cole	L	.222	27	6	2	0	0	2	0	5	.222	.296
Throws Left	R	.282	131	37	5	2	6	20	16	22	.361	.489
Rainey, Tanner	L	.220	50	11	1	0	1	5	6	19	.298	.300
Throws Right	R	.234	64	15	0	1	4	11	7	17	.310	.453
Raley, Brooks	L	.155	71	11	3	0	2	6	3	25	.200	.282
Throws Left	R	.208	125	26	3	1	1	9	12	36	.301	.272
Ramirez, Erasmo	L	.238	126	30	2	1	2	9	5	22	.271	.317
Throws Right	R	.249	197	49	8	1	9	25	9	39	.296	.437
Ramirez, Noe	L	.300	60	18	3	1	1	9	13	12	.432	.433
Throws Right	R	.218	124	27	6	0	8	22	13	39	.300	.460
Ramirez, Yohan	L	.288	52	15	3	0	2	11	10	7	.422	.462
Throws Right	R	.195	87	17	4	0	2	9	10	25	.307	.310
Rasmussen, Drew	L	.207	222	46	6	1	2	9	14	55	.264	.270
Throws Right	R	.232	323	75	17	2	11	31	17	70	.269	.399
Ray, Robbie	L	.212	137	29	6	3	4	10	5	44	.260	.387
Throws Left	R	.236	568	134	23	2	28	69	57	168	.308	.431
Richards, Garrett	L	.243	74	18	3	1	0	3	6	12	.300	.311
Throws Right	R	.277	94	26	9	0	3	19	7	24	.343	.468
Richards, Trevor	L	.237	118	28	5	1	3	20	17	40	.333	.373
Throws Right	R	.238	122	29	4	0	6	23	18	42	.331	.418
Robertson, David	L	.168	113	19	7	0	1	4	18	44	.293	.257
Throws Right	R	.179	112	20	3	0	5	12	17	37	.290	.339
Robles, Hansel	L	.188	32	6	2	0	1	5	6	10	.308	.344
Throws Right	R	.297	64	19	4	0	4	10	8	11	.375	.547

Pitchers vs. Left-Handed and Right-Handed Batters

Pitcher	vs	Avg	AB	H	2B	3B	HR	RBI	BB	SO	OBP	Slg
Rodon, Carlos	L	.179	123	22	4	0	2	5	12	49	.257	.260
Throws Left	R	.207	526	109	27	1	10	49	40	188	.264	.319
Rodriguez, Eduardo	L	.299	67	20	5	0	3	14	11	15	.400	.507
Throws Left	R	.235	285	67	12	1	9	29	23	57	.294	.379
Rodriguez, Elvin	L	.327	49	16	2	0	6	16	6	12	.400	.735
Throws Right	R	.333	78	26	5	1	6	16	9	13	.409	.654
Rodriguez, Joely	L	.233	86	20	5	0	1	6	11	32	.320	.326
Throws Left	R	.220	100	22	2	0	2	10	15	25	.325	.300
Rogers, Josh	L	.079	38	3	0	0	1	2	5	6	.186	.158
Throws Left	R	.333	63	21	3	0	5	15	6	6	.391	.619
Rogers, Taylor	L	.167	60	10	1	2	0	9	6	26	.261	.250
Throws Left	R	.263	179	47	12	1	7	33	13	58	.338	.458
Rogers, Trevor	L	.194	98	19	5	1	1	10	13	33	.288	.296
Throws Left	R	.298	325	97	30	0	14	51	32	73	.366	.520
Rogers, Tyler	L	.317	120	38	8	3	2	15	5	14	.362	.483
Throws Right	R	.208	168	35	9	0	1	22	18	35	.287	.280
Romano, Jordan	L	.202	109	22	2	0	2	10	10	38	.269	.275
Throws Right	R	.179	123	22	3	0	2	10	11	35	.268	.252
Rucker, Michael	L	.259	81	21	3	1	3	9	6	9	.307	.432
Throws Right	R	.230	126	29	3	0	5	17	14	41	.305	.373
Ruiz, Jose	L	.225	89	20	4	0	3	14	11	26	.301	.371
Throws Right	R	.236	140	33	8	1	6	24	22	42	.340	.436
Ryan, Joe	L	.202	267	54	11	2	8	17	27	56	.288	.348
Throws Right	R	.219	279	61	17	0	12	41	20	95	.283	.409
Ryu, Hyun-Jin	L	.222	18	4	2	0	0	1	1	3	.263	.333
Throws Left	R	.308	91	28	10	0	5	14	3	13	.330	.582
Sampson, Adrian	L	.230	200	46	9	1	3	13	15	32	.284	.330
Throws Right	R	.276	199	55	9	1	7	20	12	41	.324	.437
Sanchez, Aaron	L	.265	98	26	6	0	1	9	4	18	.308	.357
Throws Right	R	.364	143	52	10	0	7	30	11	23	.414	.580
Sanchez, Anibal	L	.198	111	22	7	1	4	12	11	22	.268	.387
Throws Right	R	.232	142	33	2	0	9	16	22	26	.351	.437
Sanchez, Cristopher	L	.277	47	13	4	0	0	9	3	13	.358	.362
Throws Left	R	.229	109	25	5	0	5	17	14	22	.323	.413
Sandlin, Nick	L	.231	52	12	2	0	0	6	10	7	.365	.269
Throws Right	R	.149	101	15	3	0	2	13	14	34	.265	.238
Sandoval, Patrick	L	.151	119	18	2	0	0	7	8	32	.217	.168
Throws Left	R	.271	446	121	17	3	8	44	52	119	.349	.377
Sands, Cole	L	.218	55	12	2	0	1	8	8	16	.338	.309
Throws Right	R	.319	72	23	7	0	3	12	5	12	.388	.542
Sanmartin, Reiver	L	.247	89	22	4	0	3	14	10	27	.323	.393
Throws Left	R	.324	136	44	9	2	5	22	19	20	.404	.529
Santana, Dennis	L	.208	77	16	4	0	1	9	12	18	.312	.299
Throws Right	R	.239	142	34	9	0	1	27	16	36	.327	.324
Sawamura, Hirokazu	L	.188	69	13	3	0	2	15	12	17	.301	.319
Throws Right	R	.267	120	32	4	0	2	18	15	23	.341	.350
Sborz, Josh	L	.294	34	10	2	0	1	3	4	10	.368	.441
Throws Right	R	.278	54	15	4	0	3	13	7	22	.355	.519
Scherzer, Max	L	.196	230	45	5	0	10	22	17	76	.273	.348
Throws Right	R	.215	293	63	15	0	3	13	7	97	.239	.297
Schmidt, Clarke	L	.268	82	22	5	0	3	13	11	20	.358	.439
Throws Right	R	.192	125	24	5	0	2	9	12	36	.268	.280
Schreiber, John	L	.198	81	16	6	1	2	16	11	19	.305	.370
Throws Right	R	.193	150	29	8	1	1	16	8	55	.242	.280
Scott, Tanner	L	.231	65	15	1	1	2	8	17	26	.393	.369
Throws Left	R	.238	168	40	6	1	3	23	29	64	.351	.339
Sears, JP	L	.265	49	13	3	0	0	2	6	11	.357	.327
Throws Left	R	.254	213	54	8	1	8	25	17	40	.310	.413
Senzatela, Antonio	L	.332	205	68	13	1	4	25	17	32	.384	.463
Throws Right	R	.369	176	65	15	1	5	22	6	22	.392	.551
Severino, Luis	L	.196	163	32	7	0	8	16	10	34	.243	.387
Throws Right	R	.195	205	40	9	0	6	14	20	78	.278	.327
Sewald, Paul	L	.167	96	16	2	0	5	13	10	37	.245	.344
Throws Right	R	.130	123	16	2	0	5	13	7	35	.200	.268
Shaw, Bryan	L	.271	96	26	5	0	1	12	12	26	.364	.354
Throws Right	R	.239	134	32	6	0	8	22	14	26	.318	.463
Shreve, Chasen	L	.296	54	16	1	0	4	17	3	16	.328	.537
Throws Left	R	.224	49	11	1	0	2	7	7	13	.321	.367
Silseth, Chase	L	.353	51	18	2	0	5	9	7	10	.431	.686
Throws Right	R	.234	64	15	6	0	2	9	5	14	.300	.422
Singer, Brady	L	.233	279	65	11	1	12	25	24	89	.309	.409
Throws Right	R	.259	290	75	8	0	6	26	11	61	.294	.348
Skubal, Tarik	L	.250	100	25	8	0	1	11	1	18	.262	.360
Throws Left	R	.234	338	79	20	2	8	38	31	99	.296	.376
Smeltzer, Devin	L	.308	52	16	1	1	3	6	4	7	.368	.538
Throws Left	R	.239	213	51	10	0	10	22	15	33	.288	.427

Pitcher	vs	Avg	AB	H	2B	3B	HR	RBI	BB	SO	OBP	Slg
Smith, Caleb	L	.170	94	16	1	1	0	1	11	21	.257	.202
Throws Left	R	.246	167	41	10	0	14	35	28	44	.357	.557
Smith, Drew	L	.268	56	15	1	0	3	9	6	12	.339	.446
Throws Right	R	.200	115	23	3	0	6	16	9	41	.256	.383
Smith, Joe	L	.303	33	10	1	0	3	7	5	7	.410	.606
Throws Right	R	.295	78	23	3	1	4	10	4	10	.325	.513
Smith, Will	L	.230	100	23	8	0	2	11	5	30	.267	.370
Throws Left	R	.267	131	35	6	1	7	25	20	35	.365	.489
Smyly, Drew	L	.191	89	17	6	0	2	6	8	13	.277	.326
Throws Left	R	.258	326	84	18	1	14	30	18	78	.301	.448
Snead, Kirby	L	.319	69	22	5	0	2	14	8	11	.392	.478
Throws Left	R	.301	113	34	11	0	3	19	14	24	.377	.478
Snell, Blake	L	.233	86	20	5	0	1	10	9	28	.309	.326
Throws Left	R	.213	390	83	18	2	10	34	42	143	.288	.346
Snider, Collin	L	.302	43	13	3	0	3	13	7	11	.423	.581
Throws Right	R	.300	90	27	5	1	0	11	8	11	.357	.378
Soto, Gregory	L	.245	53	13	4	0	1	3	7	18	.365	.377
Throws Left	R	.218	165	36	8	1	1	24	27	42	.337	.297
Springs, Jeffrey	L	.248	117	29	5	2	5	11	7	26	.291	.453
Throws Left	R	.215	396	85	14	1	9	31	24	118	.260	.323
Stammen, Craig	L	.290	62	18	1	0	3	10	4	11	.348	.452
Throws Right	R	.273	99	27	3	0	6	18	6	24	.308	.485
Stanek, Ryne	L	.175	80	14	2	0	1	8	10	24	.264	.238
Throws Right	R	.198	111	22	5	0	1	9	21	38	.323	.270
Staumont, Josh	L	.277	65	18	9	1	1	8	15	21	.407	.492
Throws Right	R	.247	77	19	1	1	2	9	14	22	.362	.364
Steele, Justin	L	.232	99	23	2	0	1	10	14	34	.330	.283
Throws Left	R	.248	355	88	15	1	7	36	36	92	.318	.355
Stephan, Trevor	L	.280	100	28	4	0	2	9	10	37	.348	.380
Throws Right	R	.207	140	29	9	0	1	13	8	45	.263	.293
Stephens, Jackson	L	.283	92	26	5	0	1	9	14	17	.383	.370
Throws Right	R	.202	114	23	4	0	2	22	9	30	.270	.289
Stephenson, Robert	L	.260	104	27	9	1	4	18	7	25	.301	.481
Throws Right	R	.288	125	36	9	1	6	17	7	30	.331	.520
Strahm, Matt	L	.229	48	11	3	0	1	5	4	13	.333	.354
Throws Left	R	.221	122	27	4	0	4	16	13	39	.301	.352
Stratton, Chris	L	.333	90	30	8	0	2	19	12	18	.408	.489
Throws Right	R	.268	157	42	6	1	2	22	13	42	.326	.357
Strickland, Hunter	L	.282	110	31	7	0	5	17	12	35	.355	.482
Throws Right	R	.229	131	30	11	1	3	20	21	25	.356	.397
Strider, Spencer	L	.202	253	51	8	1	3	16	20	91	.264	.277
Throws Right	R	.156	225	35	9	0	4	16	25	111	.243	.249
Stripling, Ross	L	.215	228	49	11	0	4	20	9	54	.246	.316
Throws Right	R	.240	283	68	17	0	8	26	11	57	.270	.385
Stroman, Marcus	L	.257	268	69	13	1	9	28	15	66	.296	.414
Throws Right	R	.210	257	54	12	0	7	26	21	53	.278	.339
Strzelecki, Peter	L	.222	45	10	3	0	1	5	7	13	.321	.356
Throws Right	R	.220	82	18	5	0	1	11	8	27	.290	.317
Suarez, Jose	L	.202	99	20	4	1	3	9	6	21	.255	.354
Throws Left	R	.256	324	83	20	0	11	36	27	82	.318	.420
Suarez, Ranger	L	.197	122	24	7	0	2	12	5	24	.234	.303
Throws Left	R	.263	476	125	32	2	13	47	53	105	.336	.420
Suarez, Robert	L	.181	72	13	5	0	0	4	12	25	.314	.250
Throws Right	R	.172	93	16	1	0	4	7	9	36	.260	.312
Sulser, Cole	L	.207	58	12	2	0	0	3	3	15	.246	.241
Throws Right	R	.365	74	27	6	0	6	17	13	23	.460	.689
Suter, Brent	L	.200	70	14	3	0	4	15	6	11	.291	.414
Throws Left	R	.250	176	44	10	1	5	21	16	42	.313	.403
Swanson, Erik	L	.200	105	21	7	0	1	7	3	43	.222	.295
Throws Right	R	.205	88	18	1	0	2	5	7	27	.271	.284
Swarmer, Matt	L	.250	64	16	4	0	5	11	13	19	.372	.547
Throws Right	R	.250	68	17	2	1	7	11	7	17	.320	.618
Syndergaard, Noah	L	.272	224	61	11	4	5	24	15	30	.324	.424
Throws Right	R	.256	301	77	13	1	9	33	16	65	.295	.395
Taillon, Jameson	L	.235	293	69	17	2	11	27	22	65	.292	.420
Throws Right	R	.253	391	99	25	1	15	44	10	86	.276	.437
Tate, Dillon	L	.265	83	22	5	0	4	4	9	14	.344	.470
Throws Right	R	.190	184	35	11	0	2	13	7	46	.241	.283
Tepera, Ryan	L	.195	82	16	5	0	3	8	8	19	.267	.366
Throws Right	R	.208	125	26	3	0	4	19	12	27	.286	.328
Thielbar, Caleb	L	.225	80	18	1	0	1	8	9	25	.300	.275
Throws Left	R	.226	146	33	6	1	4	14	9	55	.271	.363
Thompson, Keegan	L	.237	194	46	8	3	4	17	23	52	.327	.371
Throws Right	R	.241	237	57	12	0	12	35	20	56	.314	.443
Thompson, Mason	L	.250	44	11	2	1	0	3	7	8	.353	.341
Throws Right	R	.174	46	8	0	0	2	4	2	7	.224	.304

Pitchers vs. Left-Handed and Right-Handed Batters

Pitcher	vs	Avg	AB	H	2B	3B	HR	RBI	BB	SO	OBP	Slg
Thompson, Ryan	L	.196	51	10	2	0	1	10	3	11	.255	.294
Throws Right	R	.250	116	29	5	1	3	16	8	28	.304	.388
Thompson, Zach	L	.256	227	58	13	1	10	35	25	47	.336	.454
Throws Right	R	.301	266	80	10	0	9	31	21	43	.352	.440
Thompson, Zack	L	.146	48	7	0	0	0	1	5	11	.226	.146
Throws Right	R	.176	74	13	3	0	3	10	9	16	.265	.338
Thornton, Trent	L	.246	61	15	2	0	1	5	10	13	.361	.328
Throws Right	R	.231	108	25	4	0	6	14	7	24	.274	.435
Toussaint, Touki	L	.233	30	7	0	0	1	7	13	4	.477	.333
Throws Right	R	.145	55	8	1	0	1	7	6	22	.266	.218
Trivino, Lou	L	.356	73	26	4	0	3	13	12	15	.453	.534
Throws Right	R	.255	149	38	7	1	3	22	12	52	.323	.376
Uelmen, Erich	L	.308	39	12	2	0	1	7	7	5	.412	.436
Throws Right	R	.210	62	13	3	0	2	10	5	16	.310	.355
Underwood Jr., Duane	L	.298	94	28	6	0	0	18	7	20	.356	.362
Throws Right	R	.224	134	30	6	0	1	14	18	37	.329	.291
Urena, Jose	L	.329	207	68	9	1	5	21	28	34	.407	.454
Throws Right	R	.234	175	41	8	0	6	31	15	29	.291	.383
Urias, Julio	L	.178	129	23	4	0	6	12	3	35	.204	.349
Throws Left	R	.204	510	104	16	3	17	35	38	131	.263	.347
Urquidy, Jose	L	.226	292	66	21	1	10	27	15	63	.272	.408
Throws Right	R	.260	338	88	12	0	19	45	23	71	.310	.464
Valdez, Framber	L	.192	130	25	2	0	1	11	14	36	.274	.231
Throws Right	R	.229	615	141	22	2	10	51	53	158	.300	.320
Varland, Louie	L	.262	42	11	3	0	1	2	2	9	.295	.405
Throws Right	R	.263	57	15	2	1	3	8	4	12	.323	.491
Velasquez, Vince	L	.222	126	28	9	0	3	16	12	36	.293	.365
Throws Right	R	.245	163	40	12	0	8	29	13	33	.303	.466
VerHagen, Drew	L	.353	34	12	1	0	1	6	6	5	.450	.471
Throws Right	R	.268	56	15	3	0	4	10	8	13	.364	.536
Verlander, Justin	L	.163	312	51	6	1	4	14	17	103	.214	.228
Throws Right	R	.208	313	65	9	0	8	26	12	82	.240	.313
Vesia, Alex	L	.130	69	9	0	0	0	4	8	32	.218	.130
Throws Left	R	.217	129	28	6	0	2	11	16	47	.313	.310
Vespi, Nick	L	.362	47	17	2	0	3	8	4	14	.404	.596
Throws Left	R	.218	55	12	4	1	2	6	4	14	.283	.436
Vest, Will	L	.255	98	25	3	0	2	15	15	29	.342	.347
Throws Right	R	.266	139	37	4	0	4	19	7	34	.309	.381
Voth, Austin	L	.283	180	51	12	0	5	12	10	37	.325	.433
Throws Right	R	.269	223	60	9	0	9	32	21	53	.332	.430
Wacha, Michael	L	.188	197	37	5	1	8	13	15	50	.252	.345
Throws Right	R	.265	279	74	17	3	10	33	16	54	.306	.455
Wainwright, Adam	L	.256	336	86	18	2	5	31	38	61	.335	.366
Throws Right	R	.265	400	106	17	1	11	41	16	82	.297	.395
Waldichuk, Ken	L	.138	29	4	1	0	0	3	1	6	.194	.172
Throws Left	R	.275	102	28	11	1	5	16	9	27	.348	.549
Walker, Taijuan	L	.242	236	57	12	1	7	25	23	57	.316	.390
Throws Right	R	.239	360	86	15	0	8	32	22	75	.288	.347
Wantz, Andrew	L	.246	69	17	2	0	2	6	12	22	.366	.362
Throws Right	R	.180	111	20	3	0	6	13	9	30	.246	.369
Warren, Art	L	.197	66	13	2	2	0	10	7	18	.284	.288
Throws Right	R	.324	74	24	1	0	6	21	15	22	.440	.581
Watkins, Spenser	L	.297	185	55	12	0	4	22	13	29	.342	.427
Throws Right	R	.269	238	64	13	1	7	30	17	34	.327	.420
Webb, Logan	L	.263	361	95	27	3	6	40	31	76	.326	.404
Throws Right	R	.216	365	79	11	0	5	22	18	87	.260	.288
Weems, Jordan	L	.182	66	12	2	1	3	11	6	23	.247	.379
Throws Right	R	.267	86	23	5	1	4	18	6	18	.315	.488
Wells, Tyler	L	.193	176	34	6	1	6	12	6	41	.214	.341
Throws Right	R	.263	213	56	12	0	10	31	22	35	.332	.460
Wendelken, J.B.	L	.184	38	7	1	0	0	2	6	5	.295	.211
Throws Right	R	.261	69	18	2	0	4	16	8	16	.346	.464
Wentz, Joey	L	.167	30	5	1	0	1	3	3	5	.229	.300
Throws Left	R	.205	88	18	6	2	1	9	10	22	.290	.352
Wesneski, Hayden	L	.159	44	7	2	0	0	2	1	11	.191	.205
Throws Right	R	.221	77	17	4	0	3	6	6	22	.294	.390
Wheeler, Zack	L	.201	269	54	9	4	7	27	23	83	.269	.342
Throws Right	R	.240	296	71	14	2	6	21	11	80	.278	.361
White, Mitch	L	.246	187	46	11	3	5	27	20	31	.319	.417
Throws Right	R	.302	212	64	15	0	4	28	15	47	.352	.429
Whitlock, Garrett	L	.192	125	24	10	0	3	11	4	28	.215	.344
Throws Right	R	.244	168	41	4	1	7	19	11	54	.329	.405
Wick, Rowan	L	.341	123	42	8	1	3	18	17	35	.418	.496
Throws Right	R	.272	136	37	5	1	6	19	12	34	.329	.456
Williams, Devin	L	.207	87	18	3	0	2	9	10	31	.307	.310
Throws Right	R	.110	118	13	2	0	0	8	20	65	.237	.127
Williams, Trevor	L	.319	138	44	5	2	6	18	9	13	.361	.514
Throws Right	R	.209	206	43	10	0	6	23	14	71	.272	.345
Wilson, Bryse	L	.299	214	64	14	1	11	33	20	40	.365	.528
Throws Right	R	.276	246	68	15	0	9	38	12	39	.320	.447
Wilson, Steven	L	.221	68	15	2	0	0	8	9	18	.308	.250
Throws Right	R	.175	120	21	6	0	7	21	11	35	.259	.400
Winckowski, Josh	L	.285	137	39	4	3	6	20	16	21	.361	.489
Throws Right	R	.315	146	46	10	2	4	23	11	23	.360	.493
Winder, Josh	L	.238	105	25	6	0	4	13	9	19	.305	.410
Throws Right	R	.282	156	44	12	0	7	23	9	28	.331	.494
Wisler, Matt	L	.186	70	13	6	0	1	5	5	20	.240	.314
Throws Right	R	.191	89	17	2	1	5	13	9	15	.263	.404
Wittgren, Nick	L	.311	45	14	2	1	0	9	4	7	.365	.400
Throws Right	R	.292	72	21	5	1	1	8	6	10	.370	.431
Wood, Alex	L	.193	119	23	2	0	1	10	5	36	.228	.235
Throws Left	R	.283	385	109	18	1	16	57	25	95	.340	.460
Woodford, Jake	L	.292	48	14	2	0	0	5	5	6	.364	.333
Throws Right	R	.232	125	29	5	1	1	9	6	18	.263	.312
Woodruff, Brandon	L	.190	269	51	16	2	5	20	21	102	.250	.320
Throws Right	R	.237	299	71	12	0	13	26	21	88	.295	.408
Wright, Kyle	L	.234	355	83	15	1	13	31	34	96	.306	.392
Throws Right	R	.230	317	73	6	0	6	25	19	78	.284	.306
Yajure, Miguel	L	.386	44	17	5	0	0	10	8	4	.491	.500
Throws Right	R	.246	57	14	5	0	3	11	8	12	.348	.491
Yarbrough, Ryan	L	.159	69	11	1	0	2	4	5	20	.253	.261
Throws Left	R	.308	250	77	18	0	10	31	17	41	.367	.500
Young, Alex	L	.340	47	16	3	1	0	8	6	12	.426	.447
Throws Left	R	.232	56	13	5	0	0	7	5	9	.290	.321
Zimmermann, Bruce	L	.352	54	19	6	0	5	12	1	16	.364	.741
Throws Left	R	.315	248	78	15	2	16	37	11	33	.345	.585
AL	L	.234	-	-	-	-	-	-	-	-	.307	.381
	R	.246	-	-	-	-	-	-	-	-	.310	.397
NL	L	.239	-	-	-	-	-	-	-	-	.316	.390
	R	.248	-	-	-	-	-	-	-	-	.313	.404
MLB	L	.236	-	-	-	-	-	-	-	-	.311	.386
	R	.247	-	-	-	-	-	-	-	-	.312	.401

2022 Leaderboards

Alex Vigderman

If you're a Twitter user like I am, you see leaderboards a lot. Regardless of your online-ness, know that I empathize with you if you feel a bit daunted by the 484 leaderboards you're about to face.

So, in the interest of providing a more digestible experience, here is my leaderboard of the best leaderboards in this section (in order of appearance, to make them easier to find).

AL Home Runs (Aaron Judge's season in its most distilled form)

AL OPS Batting Right vs. RHP (Judge wins by nearly 300 points)

AL Lowest First Swing % (Steven Kwan is a statue out there)

NL OPS Second Half (Joey Meneses, replacing Juan Soto, is MVP level)

NL Under Age 26: OPS (Four Braves in the top ten; they're pretty good)

AL Stolen Bases Allowed (Syndergaard leads by 6; he left the AL in July)

NL Rel Opp BA vs LHB / RHB (The Díaz siblings top each list! So cool)

AL Top Game Scores (Angels starting pitching was its best in a while)

NL Power / Speed Number (Two guys who play catcher make this list)

AL Top Batter Game Scores (Four different Yankees with great games)

And, of course:
474 tied for 11th

2022 American League Batting Leaders

Batting Average (minimum 502 PA)		On Base Percentage (minimum 502 PA)		Slugging Average (minimum 502 PA)		Home Runs	
Arraez, Luis	.316	Judge, Aaron	.425	Judge, Aaron	.686	Judge, Aaron	62
Judge, Aaron	.311	Alvarez, Yordan	.406	Alvarez, Yordan	.613	Trout, Mike	40
Bogaerts, Xander	.307	Diaz, Yandy	.401	Altuve, Jose	.533	Alvarez, Yordan	37
Alvarez, Yordan	.306	Altuve, Jose	.387	Devers, Rafael	.521	Ohtani, Shohei	34
Abreu, Jose	.304	Abreu, Jose	.378	Ohtani, Shohei	.519	Santander, Anthony	33
Benintendi, Andrew	.304	Bogaerts, Xander	.377	Ramirez, Jose	.514	Seager, Corey	33
Lowe, Nathaniel	.302	Arraez, Luis	.375	Rodriguez, Julio	.509	Guerrero Jr., Vladimir	32
Altuve, Jose	.300	Benintendi, Andrew	.373	Lowe, Nathaniel	.492	Rizzo, Anthony	32
Kwan, Steven	.298	Kwan, Steven	.373	Hernandez, Teoscar	.491	Stanton, Giancarlo	31
Gimenez, Andres	.297	Kirk, Alejandro	.372	Guerrero Jr., Vladimir	.480	Suarez, Eugenio	31

Games		Plate Appearances		At Bats		Hits	
Semien, Marcus	161	Semien, Marcus	724	Semien, Marcus	657	Bichette, Bo	189
Guerrero Jr., Vladimir	160	Guerrero Jr., Vladimir	706	Bichette, Bo	652	Abreu, Jose	183
Bichette, Bo	159	Bichette, Bo	697	Guerrero Jr., Vladimir	638	Rosario, Amed	180
Abreu, Jose	157	Judge, Aaron	696	Rosario, Amed	637	Lowe, Nathaniel	179
Judge, Aaron	157	Ramirez, Jose	685	Mullins II, Cedric	608	Judge, Aaron	177
Lowe, Nathaniel	157	Abreu, Jose	679	Garcia, Adolis	605	Guerrero Jr., Vladimir	175
Ohtani, Shohei	157	Mullins II, Cedric	672	Abreu, Jose	601	Arraez, Luis	173
Ramirez, Jose	157	Rosario, Amed	670	Ramirez, Jose	601	Bogaerts, Xander	171
3 tied with	156	Ohtani, Shohei	666	3 tied with	593	Kwan, Steven	168
		Seager, Corey	663			Ramirez, Jose	168

Singles		Doubles		Triples		Total Bases	
Rosario, Amed	134	Ramirez, Jose	44	Rosario, Amed	9	Judge, Aaron	391
Arraez, Luis	133	Bichette, Bo	43	Kwan, Steven	7	Ramirez, Jose	309
Kwan, Steven	130	Martinez, J.D.	43	Mateo, Jorge	7	Bichette, Bo	306
Abreu, Jose	128	Devers, Rafael	42	Ohtani, Shohei	6	Guerrero Jr., Vladimir	306
Lowe, Nathaniel	123	Arozarena, Randy	41	Witt Jr., Bobby	6	Ohtani, Shohei	304
Bichette, Bo	121	Abreu, Jose	40	Garcia, Adolis	5	Lowe, Nathaniel	292
Bogaerts, Xander	118	Gurriel, Yuli	40	Ramirez, Jose	5	Devers, Rafael	289
Verdugo, Alex	115	Altuve, Jose	39	Semien, Marcus	5	Alvarez, Yordan	288
Benintendi, Andrew	109	Verdugo, Alex	39	10 tied with	4	Semien, Marcus	282
Guerrero Jr., Vladimir	108	2 tied with	38			Altuve, Jose	281

Runs Scored		RBI		Walks		Strikeouts	
Judge, Aaron	133	Judge, Aaron	131	Judge, Aaron	111	Suarez, Eugenio	196
Altuve, Jose	103	Ramirez, Jose	126	Bregman, Alex	87	Garcia, Adolis	183
Semien, Marcus	101	Tucker, Kyle	107	Winker, Jesse	84	Judge, Aaron	175
Alvarez, Yordan	95	Garcia, Adolis	101	Alvarez, Yordan	78	Chapman, Matt	170
Bregman, Alex	93	Alvarez, Yordan	97	Diaz, Yandy	78	Ohtani, Shohei	161
Bichette, Bo	91	Guerrero Jr., Vladimir	97	Suarez, Eugenio	73	Arozarena, Randy	156
Seager, Corey	91	Ohtani, Shohei	95	Ohtani, Shohei	72	Bichette, Bo	155
Guerrero Jr., Vladimir	90	Bichette, Bo	93	Santana, Carlos	71	Mountcastle, Ryan	154
Ohtani, Shohei	90	Bregman, Alex	93	Ramirez, Jose	69	Hernandez, Teoscar	152
Ramirez, Jose	90	2 tied with	89	2 tied with	68	Donaldson, Josh	148

2022 American League Batting Leaders

Intentional Walks

Ramirez, Jose	20
Judge, Aaron	19
Ohtani, Shohei	14
Devers, Rafael	11
Alvarez, Yordan	9
Trout, Mike	8
Seager, Corey	7
Guerrero Jr., Vladimir	6
Rizzo, Anthony	6
6 tied with	4

BA Bases Loaded
(minimum 10 PA)

Castro, Harold	.667
Kiner-Falefa, Isiah	.583
Vaughn, Andrew	.583
Tapia, Raimel	.571
Devers, Rafael	.500
Tucker, Kyle	.471
Springer, George	.462
Kwan, Steven	.455
Stanton, Giancarlo	.455
2 tied with	.444

Sacrifice Hits

Hedges, Austin	10
Lopez, Nicky	10
Allen, Nick	6
McGuire, Reese	6
Velazquez, Andrew	6
Kemp, Tony	5
Wade, Tyler	5
5 tied with	4

Sacrifice Flies

Bregman, Alex	10
Semien, Marcus	10
Miller, Owen	9
Ramirez, Jose	9
Merrifield, Whit	8
Alvarez, Yordan	7
Bogaerts, Xander	7
Melendez, MJ	7
Mountcastle, Ryan	7
Urshela, Gio	7

BA Close & Late
(minimum 50 PA)

Pollock, A.J.	.403
Reyes, Victor	.370
Kwan, Steven	.362
Gurriel Jr., Lourdes	.352
Benintendi, Andrew	.341
Alvarez, Yordan	.333
Guerrero Jr., Vladimir	.333
Naylor, Josh	.329
Perez, Salvador	.327
Urshela, Gio	.320

Batting Average w/ RISP
(minimum 100 PA)

Arraez, Luis	.366
Trevino, Jose	.355
Judge, Aaron	.346
Vaughn, Andrew	.339
Perez, Salvador	.337
Gimenez, Andres	.333
Ramirez, Jose	.331
Kiner-Falefa, Isiah	.327
Witt Jr., Bobby	.323
Choi, Ji-Man	.323

SLG vs. LHP
(minimum 125 PA)

Altuve, Jose	.660
Trout, Mike	.638
Judge, Aaron	.622
Pollock, A.J.	.619
Martinez, J.D.	.597
Alvarez, Yordan	.586
Rengifo, Luis	.570
Bogaerts, Xander	.569
Arozarena, Randy	.558
Rizzo, Anthony	.550

SLG vs. RHP
(minimum 377 PA)

Judge, Aaron	.706
Devers, Rafael	.557
Ohtani, Shohei	.551
Ramirez, Jose	.550
Rodriguez, Julio	.519
Bregman, Alex	.504
Ward, Taylor	.501
Guerrero Jr., Vladimir	.498
Tucker, Kyle	.491
Altuve, Jose	.487

Leadoff Hitters OBP
(minimum 150 PA)

Judge, Aaron	.481
Diaz, Yandy	.407
Altuve, Jose	.390
Kwan, Steven	.379
Rodriguez, Julio	.362
LeMahieu, DJ	.358
Ward, Taylor	.357
Arraez, Luis	.349
Springer, George	.342
Anderson, Tim	.339

Cleanup Hitters SLG
(minimum 150 PA)

Alvarez, Yordan	.655
Bregman, Alex	.511
Ward, Taylor	.506
Pasquantino, Vinnie	.503
Brown, Seth	.481
Stanton, Giancarlo	.476
Abreu, Jose	.475
Naylor, Josh	.456
Bogaerts, Xander	.453
Santana, Carlos	.439

BA vs. LHP
(minimum 125 PA)

Bogaerts, Xander	.382
Altuve, Jose	.340
Gimenez, Andres	.336
Lowe, Nathaniel	.330
Alvarez, Yordan	.321
Martinez, J.D.	.319
Arozarena, Randy	.317
Rengifo, Luis	.315
Trout, Mike	.310
Diaz, Yandy	.310

BA vs. RHP
(minimum 377 PA)

Arraez, Luis	.329
Judge, Aaron	.322
Abreu, Jose	.307
Devers, Rafael	.304
Kwan, Steven	.303
Bichette, Bo	.295
Ramirez, Jose	.295
Gurriel Jr., Lourdes	.295
Diaz, Yandy	.291
Correa, Carlos	.289

Home BA
(minimum 251 PA)

Altuve, Jose	.328
Arraez, Luis	.327
Devers, Rafael	.323
Bogaerts, Xander	.317
Ohtani, Shohei	.314
Correa, Carlos	.310
Urshela, Gio	.310
Judge, Aaron	.308
Bregman, Alex	.305
Rengifo, Luis	.304

Away BA
(minimum 251 PA)

Abreu, Jose	.334
Diaz, Yandy	.332
Lowe, Nathaniel	.322
Alvarez, Yordan	.318
Judge, Aaron	.313
Kirk, Alejandro	.313
Vaughn, Andrew	.307
Gimenez, Andres	.307
Arraez, Luis	.305
Kwan, Steven	.301

OBP vs. LHP
(minimum 125 PA)

Bogaerts, Xander	.469
Altuve, Jose	.426
Trout, Mike	.420
Alvarez, Yordan	.411
Martinez, J.D.	.401
Correa, Carlos	.400
Diaz, Yandy	.400
Gimenez, Andres	.400
Judge, Aaron	.388
Santana, Carlos	.387

OBP vs. RHP
(minimum 377 PA)

Judge, Aaron	.436
Diaz, Yandy	.402
Kwan, Steven	.386
Arraez, Luis	.386
Kirk, Alejandro	.377
Bregman, Alex	.377
Abreu, Jose	.376
Devers, Rafael	.374
Altuve, Jose	.373
Ohtani, Shohei	.370

2022 American League Batting Leaders

Stolen Bases

Mateo, Jorge	35
Mullins II, Cedric	34
Arozarena, Randy	32
Witt Jr., Bobby	30
Garcia, Adolis	25
Rodriguez, Julio	25
Semien, Marcus	25
Tucker, Kyle	25
Kiner-Falefa, Isiah	22
2 tied with	21

Caught Stealing

Arozarena, Randy	12
Mullins II, Cedric	10
Mateo, Jorge	9
Ohtani, Shohei	9
Bichette, Bo	8
Moore, Dylan	8
Semien, Marcus	8
Ramirez, Jose	7
Rodriguez, Julio	7
Witt Jr., Bobby	7

Highest SB Success Pct
(minimum 15 SBA)

Straw, Myles	95.5
Altuve, Jose	94.7
Velazquez, Andrew	94.4
Siri, Jose	87.5
Springer, George	87.5
Gimenez, Andres	87.0
Tucker, Kyle	86.2
Thompson, Bubba	85.7
Kiner-Falefa, Isiah	84.6
Judge, Aaron	84.2

Lowest SB Success Pct
(minimum 15 SBA)

Ohtani, Shohei	55.0
Baddoo, Akil	60.0
Isbel, Kyle	60.0
Bichette, Bo	61.9
Frazier, Adam	64.7
Laureano, Ramon	64.7
Torres, Gleyber	66.7
Taveras, Leody	68.8
Moore, Dylan	72.4
Arozarena, Randy	72.7

Steals of Third

Andrus, Elvis	6
Mateo, Jorge	6
Arozarena, Randy	5
Bogaerts, Xander	5
Mullins II, Cedric	5
Torres, Gleyber	5
Altuve, Jose	4
Haggerty, Sam	4
Semien, Marcus	4
10 tied with	3

Grounded Into DP

Guerrero Jr., Vladimir	26
Bichette, Bo	21
Urshela, Gio	21
Martinez, J.D.	20
Abreu, Jose	19
Miranda, Jose	19
Rosario, Amed	19
4 tied with	18

Grounded Into DP Pct
(minimum 50 GIDP Ops)

Buxton, Byron	0.00
Gallo, Joey	0.00
Cordero, Franchy	1.79
Zavala, Seby	1.92
Melendez, MJ	2.47
Taveras, Leody	3.33
Biggio, Cavan	3.51
Straw, Myles	3.51
Ramirez, Jose	3.60
Grossman, Robbie	3.64

Hit By Pitch

Gimenez, Andres	25
Rizzo, Anthony	23
France, Ty	21
Harrison, Josh	14
Moore, Dylan	13
Murphy, Sean	13
Santander, Anthony	13
Abreu, Jose	12
Laureano, Ramon	12
2 tied with	11

Pitches Seen

Judge, Aaron	2906
Semien, Marcus	2776
Ramirez, Jose	2742
Abreu, Jose	2730
Kwan, Steven	2643
Chapman, Matt	2637
Santander, Anthony	2618
Suarez, Eugenio	2617
Guerrero Jr., Vladimir	2596
Ohtani, Shohei	2546

At Bats Per Home Run
(minimum 502 PA)

Judge, Aaron	9.2
Alvarez, Yordan	12.7
Rizzo, Anthony	14.5
Ohtani, Shohei	17.2
Santander, Anthony	17.4
Suarez, Eugenio	17.5
Seager, Corey	18.0
Tucker, Kyle	18.1
Rodriguez, Julio	18.3
Altuve, Jose	18.8

Highest GB/FB Ratio
(minimum 502 PA)

Kiner-Falefa, Isiah	2.26
Rosario, Amed	1.92
LeMahieu, DJ	1.88
Guerrero Jr., Vladimir	1.70
Kirk, Alejandro	1.63
Bichette, Bo	1.58
Lowe, Nathaniel	1.57
Diaz, Yandy	1.57
France, Ty	1.56
Arozarena, Randy	1.54

Lowest GB/FB Ratio
(minimum 502 PA)

Santander, Anthony	0.63
Ramirez, Jose	0.64
Rizzo, Anthony	0.67
Bregman, Alex	0.70
Chapman, Matt	0.70
Semien, Marcus	0.72
Tucker, Kyle	0.73
Suarez, Eugenio	0.75
Torres, Gleyber	0.78
Witt Jr., Bobby	0.78

Pitches Per Plate App
(minimum 502 PA)

Chapman, Matt	4.25
Judge, Aaron	4.18
Suarez, Eugenio	4.16
Kwan, Steven	4.14
Melendez, MJ	4.11
Crawford, J.P.	4.11
Correa, Carlos	4.10
Santana, Carlos	4.08
Winker, Jesse	4.08
Ward, Taylor	4.07

Pct Pitches Taken
(minimum 1500 Pitches)

Kwan, Steven	61.9
LeMahieu, DJ	60.5
Grandal, Yasmani	60.3
Paredes, Isaac	60.2
Bregman, Alex	59.7
Straw, Myles	59.5
Rutschman, Adley	59.5
Kirk, Alejandro	59.0
Hicks, Aaron	59.0
Crawford, J.P.	58.7

Best BPS on OutZ
(minimum 502 PA)

Devers, Rafael	.764
Altuve, Jose	.685
Urshela, Gio	.683
Rosario, Amed	.642
Alvarez, Yordan	.631
Arraez, Luis	.599
Witt Jr., Bobby	.573
Ramirez, Jose	.544
Bogaerts, Xander	.530
Suarez, Eugenio	.527

Worst BPS on OutZ
(minimum 502 PA)

Brown, Seth	.261
Winker, Jesse	.262
Hernandez, Teoscar	.322
Donaldson, Josh	.322
Melendez, MJ	.331
Verdugo, Alex	.343
Judge, Aaron	.344
Mateo, Jorge	.344
Schoop, Jonathan	.358
Martinez, J.D.	.365

2022 American League Batting Leaders

Best OPS vs Fastballs
(minimum 251 PA)

Judge, Aaron	1.165
Altuve, Jose	1.046
Alvarez, Yordan	1.006
Trout, Mike	.953
Diaz, Yandy	.919
Torres, Gleyber	.905
Devers, Rafael	.891
Arraez, Luis	.888
Ohtani, Shohei	.872
2 tied with	.869

Best OPS vs Curveballs
(minimum 50 PA)

Ohtani, Shohei	1.312
Semien, Marcus	1.111
Arozarena, Randy	1.027
Mountcastle, Ryan	1.027
France, Ty	1.025
Altuve, Jose	1.007
Ramirez, Jose	.997
Bichette, Bo	.976
Rengifo, Luis	.918
Mullins II, Cedric	.894

Best OPS vs Changeups
(minimum 50 PA)

Alvarez, Yordan	1.395
Gimenez, Andres	1.176
Lowe, Nathaniel	1.043
Hernandez, Teoscar	1.029
Altuve, Jose	1.005
Naylor, Josh	.958
Ward, Taylor	.948
Rosario, Amed	.932
Bichette, Bo	.925
Kepler, Max	.923

Best OPS vs Sliders
(minimum 32 PA)

Refsnyder, Rob	1.240
Judge, Aaron	1.171
Alvarez, Yordan	1.052
Brantley, Michael	1.047
Lowe, Nathaniel	1.040
Naylor, Josh	1.004
Trout, Mike	.994
Buxton, Byron	.987
Pasquantino, Vinnie	.954
Bregman, Alex	.931

OPS
(minimum 502 PA)

Judge, Aaron	1.111
Alvarez, Yordan	1.019
Altuve, Jose	.921
Devers, Rafael	.879
Ohtani, Shohei	.875
Ramirez, Jose	.869
Rodriguez, Julio	.853
Lowe, Nathaniel	.851
Gimenez, Andres	.837
Correa, Carlos	.834

OPS First Half
(minimum 260 PA)

Alvarez, Yordan	1.058
Judge, Aaron	.983
Devers, Rafael	.980
Trout, Mike	.967
Ramirez, Jose	.944
Altuve, Jose	.886
Kirk, Alejandro	.882
Ward, Taylor	.872
Abreu, Jose	.857
Arraez, Luis	.856

OPS Second Half
(minimum 201 PA)

Judge, Aaron	1.286
Alvarez, Yordan	.968
Lowe, Nathaniel	.964
Altuve, Jose	.960
Jimenez, Eloy	.948
Ohtani, Shohei	.927
Bichette, Bo	.921
Pasquantino, Vinnie	.899
Bregman, Alex	.894
Correa, Carlos	.866

OPS by Catchers
(minimum 251 PA)

Kirk, Alejandro	.827
Haase, Eric	.811
Murphy, Sean	.805
Rutschman, Adley	.793
Perez, Salvador	.753
Raleigh, Cal	.748
Melendez, MJ	.733
Heim, Jonah	.699
Vazquez, Christian	.695
Trevino, Jose	.656

OPS by First Basemen
(minimum 251 PA)

Lowe, Nathaniel	.846
Naylor, Josh	.833
Guerrero Jr., Vladimir	.832
Rizzo, Anthony	.814
Arraez, Luis	.810
Abreu, Jose	.809
France, Ty	.785
Mountcastle, Ryan	.753
Miranda, Jose	.709
Choi, Ji-Man	.697

OPS by Second Basemen
(minimum 251 PA)

Altuve, Jose	.935
Gimenez, Andres	.869
Torres, Gleyber	.809
Polanco, Jorge	.780
Story, Trevor	.737
Merrifield, Whit	.729
Semien, Marcus	.728
Espinal, Santiago	.721
Harrison, Josh	.689
Rengifo, Luis	.662

OPS by Third Basemen
(minimum 251 PA)

Ramirez, Jose	.903
Devers, Rafael	.890
Diaz, Yandy	.846
Bregman, Alex	.822
Suarez, Eugenio	.817
Urshela, Gio	.777
Chapman, Matt	.755
Urias, Ramon	.731
Donaldson, Josh	.706
Moncada, Yoan	.632

OPS by Shortstops
(minimum 251 PA)

Bogaerts, Xander	.844
Correa, Carlos	.836
Bichette, Bo	.803
Franco, Wander	.801
Seager, Corey	.774
Witt Jr., Bobby	.759
Anderson, Tim	.734
Andrus, Elvis	.718
Pena, Jeremy	.718
Rosario, Amed	.718

OPS by Left Fielders
(minimum 251 PA)

Kwan, Steven	.822
Arozarena, Randy	.813
Benintendi, Andrew	.768
Gurriel Jr., Lourdes	.740
Hays, Austin	.715
Winker, Jesse	.692
Pollock, A.J.	.681
Verdugo, Alex	.677
Marsh, Brandon	.618

OPS by Center Fielders
(minimum 251 PA)

Judge, Aaron	1.157
Trout, Mike	1.021
Rodriguez, Julio	.848
Springer, George	.838
Robert, Luis	.748
Mullins II, Cedric	.727
Taveras, Leody	.686
Greene, Riley	.682
Taylor, Michael A.	.673
Hernandez, Kike	.647

OPS by Right Fielders
(minimum 251 PA)

Ward, Taylor	.856
Hernandez, Teoscar	.827
Tucker, Kyle	.802
Gonzalez, Oscar	.794
Sheets, Gavin	.765
Santander, Anthony	.738
Garcia, Adolis	.714
Kepler, Max	.651
Bradley Jr., Jackie	.597

OPS by Designated Hitters
(minimum 125 PA)

Alvarez, Yordan	1.003
Ohtani, Shohei	.896
Abreu, Jose	.890
Jimenez, Eloy	.843
Vaughn, Andrew	.836
Buxton, Byron	.829
Arraez, Luis	.808
Martinez, J.D.	.790
Springer, George	.778
Guerrero Jr., Vladimir	.770

2022 American League Batting Leaders

OPS Batting Left vs. LHP (minimum 125 PA)	
Alvarez, Yordan	.998
Lowe, Nathaniel	.920
Rizzo, Anthony	.893
Gimenez, Andres	.887
Melendez, MJ	.839
Winker, Jesse	.794
Ohtani, Shohei	.787
Seager, Corey	.761
Devers, Rafael	.739
Tucker, Kyle	.736

OPS Batting Left vs. RHP (minimum 377 PA)	
Devers, Rafael	.931
Ohtani, Shohei	.921
Ramirez, Jose	.918
Tucker, Kyle	.850
Arraez, Luis	.824
Gimenez, Andres	.822
Lowe, Nathaniel	.817
Kwan, Steven	.811
Brown, Seth	.793
Rizzo, Anthony	.791

OPS Batting Right vs. LHP (minimum 125 PA)	
Altuve, Jose	1.086
Trout, Mike	1.058
Bogaerts, Xander	1.038
Judge, Aaron	1.010
Martinez, J.D.	.998
Correa, Carlos	.945
Pollock, A.J.	.935
Arozarena, Randy	.923
Santander, Anthony	.913
Suarez, Eugenio	.911

OPS Batting Right vs. RHP (minimum 377 PA)	
Judge, Aaron	1.142
Bregman, Alex	.881
Ward, Taylor	.864
Rodriguez, Julio	.860
Altuve, Jose	.860
Guerrero Jr., Vladimir	.841
Springer, George	.821
Abreu, Jose	.816
Bichette, Bo	.805
Diaz, Yandy	.800

OPS vs. LHP (minimum 125 PA)	
Altuve, Jose	1.086
Trout, Mike	1.058
Bogaerts, Xander	1.038
Judge, Aaron	1.010
Alvarez, Yordan	.998
Martinez, J.D.	.998
Correa, Carlos	.945
Pollock, A.J.	.935
Arozarena, Randy	.923
Lowe, Nathaniel	.920

OPS vs. RHP (minimum 377 PA)	
Judge, Aaron	1.142
Devers, Rafael	.931
Ohtani, Shohei	.921
Ramirez, Jose	.918
Bregman, Alex	.881
Ward, Taylor	.864
Altuve, Jose	.860
Rodriguez, Julio	.860
Tucker, Kyle	.850
Guerrero Jr., Vladimir	.841

RC Per 27 Outs vs. LHP (minimum 125 PA)	
Judge, Aaron	10.3
Altuve, Jose	9.9
Trout, Mike	9.7
Bogaerts, Xander	9.3
Martinez, J.D.	8.5
Suarez, Eugenio	8.3
Arozarena, Randy	8.0
Gimenez, Andres	7.7
Lowe, Nathaniel	7.6
2 tied with	7.5

RC Per 27 Outs vs. RHP (minimum 377 PA)	
Judge, Aaron	11.3
Ramirez, Jose	8.2
Devers, Rafael	7.5
Ohtani, Shohei	7.5
Bregman, Alex	7.3
Ward, Taylor	6.8
Gimenez, Andres	6.7
Tucker, Kyle	6.6
Arraez, Luis	6.2
Lowe, Nathaniel	6.2

Highest RBI % (minimum 502 PA)	
Judge, Aaron	48.02
Ramirez, Jose	44.57
Ohtani, Shohei	43.03
Alvarez, Yordan	40.89
Tucker, Kyle	40.00
Vaughn, Andrew	39.26
Rodriguez, Julio	38.86
Devers, Rafael	38.55
Garcia, Adolis	38.37
Springer, George	37.91

Lowest RBI % (minimum 502 PA)	
Straw, Myles	19.16
Schoop, Jonathan	21.23
Frazier, Adam	22.11
Crawford, J.P.	23.50
Gurriel, Yuli	25.04
Mateo, Jorge	25.35
Martinez, J.D.	26.07
Kwan, Steven	27.87
Rengifo, Luis	28.23
Kiner-Falefa, Isiah	29.04

Highest Strikeout per PA (minimum 502 PA)	
Suarez, Eugenio	.312
Hernandez, Teoscar	.284
Garcia, Adolis	.279
Mateo, Jorge	.276
Chapman, Matt	.274
Donaldson, Josh	.271
Brown, Seth	.263
Rodriguez, Julio	.259
Mountcastle, Ryan	.253
Judge, Aaron	.251

Lowest Strikeout per PA (minimum 502 PA)	
Arraez, Luis	.071
Kwan, Steven	.094
Kirk, Alejandro	.107
Diaz, Yandy	.108
Bregman, Alex	.117
Ramirez, Jose	.120
Frazier, Adam	.121
Kemp, Tony	.124
Gurriel, Yuli	.125
LeMahieu, DJ	.131

Home Runs At Home	
Judge, Aaron	30
Seager, Corey	22
Ohtani, Shohei	21
Trout, Mike	21
Alvarez, Yordan	20
Chapman, Matt	19
Guerrero Jr., Vladimir	19
Rizzo, Anthony	19
Stanton, Giancarlo	18
Torres, Gleyber	17

Home Runs Away	
Judge, Aaron	32
Trout, Mike	19
Raleigh, Cal	18
Ramirez, Jose	18
Santander, Anthony	18
Tucker, Kyle	18
Alvarez, Yordan	17
Brown, Seth	17
Lowe, Nathaniel	17
3 tied with	16

Longest Avg Home Run (min 10 over the wall)	
Witt Jr., Bobby	416
Murphy, Sean	415
Sanchez, Gary	412
Melendez, MJ	412
Judge, Aaron	411
Robert, Luis	410
Correa, Carlos	410
Jimenez, Eloy	410
Buxton, Byron	409
Hernandez, Teoscar	409

Shortest Avg Home Run (min 10 over the wall)	
LeMahieu, DJ	377
Bregman, Alex	381
McCormick, Chas	382
Torres, Gleyber	383
Merrifield, Whit	383
Carpenter, Matt	384
Heim, Jonah	384
Diaz, Aledmys	386
Choi, Ji-Man	386
Walsh, Jared	387

2022 American League Batting Leaders

Under Age 26: AB Per HR		Under Age 26: OPS		Under Age 26: RC/27 Outs		Longest Home Run	
(minimum 300 PA)		(minimum 300 PA)		(minimum 300 PA)			
Alvarez, Yordan	12.7	Alvarez, Yordan	1.019	Alvarez, Yordan	8.1	Trout, Mike, 10/5	490
Raleigh, Cal	13.7	Devers, Rafael	.879	Jimenez, Eloy	7.0	Sanchez, Gary, 9/5	473
Paredes, Isaac	16.6	Jimenez, Eloy	.858	Gimenez, Andres	6.9	Trout, Mike, 4/14	472
Tucker, Kyle	18.1	Rodriguez, Julio	.853	Devers, Rafael	6.6	Alvarez, Yordan, 5/30	469
Jimenez, Eloy	18.3	Gimenez, Andres	.837	Rodriguez, Julio	6.4	Buxton, Byron, 4/24	469
Rodriguez, Julio	18.3	Guerrero Jr., Vladimir	.818	Tucker, Kyle	6.1	Garcia, Dermis, 8/31	467
Guerrero Jr., Vladimir	19.9	Tucker, Kyle	.808	Arraez, Luis	5.8	Guerrero Jr., Vladimir, 4/10	467
Devers, Rafael	20.6	Rutschman, Adley	.806	Naylor, Josh	5.7	Judge, Aaron, 7/22	465
Torres, Gleyber	21.9	Bichette, Bo	.802	Rutschman, Adley	5.7	3 tied with	464
Naylor, Josh	22.5	Arraez, Luis	.795	Kirk, Alejandro	5.5		

Swing and Miss %		Highest First Swing %		Lowest First Swing %	
(minimum 1500 Pitches Seen)		(minimum 502 PA)		(minimum 502 PA)	
Calhoun, Kole	35.9	Seager, Corey	49.9	Kwan, Steven	7.4
Stanton, Giancarlo	35.4	Tucker, Kyle	45.5	Arraez, Luis	16.8
Baez, Javier	34.8	Bichette, Bo	44.7	Ramirez, Jose	17.1
Hernandez, Teoscar	33.9	Pena, Jeremy	44.7	Crawford, J.P.	17.6
Buxton, Byron	33.0	Mountcastle, Ryan	43.6	LeMahieu, DJ	18.0
Garcia, Adolis	32.7	Baez, Javier	40.2	Verdugo, Alex	20.6
Donaldson, Josh	32.6	Ohtani, Shohei	40.2	Kirk, Alejandro	20.9
Suarez, Eugenio	31.9	Lowe, Nathaniel	39.2	Kiner-Falefa, Isiah	21.6
Choi, Ji-Man	31.6	Rengifo, Luis	38.5	Diaz, Yandy	21.8
McCormick, Chas	31.4	Torres, Gleyber	38.2	Vaughn, Andrew	21.8

Home RC Per 27 Outs		Road RC Per 27 Outs		Lead Changing RBI	
(minimum 251 PA)		(minimum 251 PA)			
Judge, Aaron	10.2	Judge, Aaron	12.1	Judge, Aaron	35
Ohtani, Shohei	8.7	Alvarez, Yordan	9.1	Ramirez, Jose	35
Bregman, Alex	7.8	Lowe, Nathaniel	8.7	Bichette, Bo	34
Altuve, Jose	7.7	Gimenez, Andres	8.5	Alvarez, Yordan	33
Ramirez, Jose	7.5	Diaz, Yandy	7.7	Garcia, Adolis	32
Alvarez, Yordan	7.2	Ramirez, Jose	7.7	Suarez, Eugenio	32
Devers, Rafael	7.0	Vaughn, Andrew	7.4	Guerrero Jr., Vladimir	29
Bogaerts, Xander	6.8	Tucker, Kyle	7.1	Naylor, Josh	29
Rodriguez, Julio	6.8	Abreu, Jose	6.7	Rizzo, Anthony	29
Seager, Corey	6.7	Trout, Mike	6.7	Santander, Anthony	29

2022 National League Batting Leaders

Batting Average
(minimum 502 PA)

McNeil, Jeff	.326
Freeman, Freddie	.325
Goldschmidt, Paul	.317
Machado, Manny	.298
Turner, Trea	.298
Arenado, Nolan	.293
Marte, Starling	.292
Hoerner, Nico	.281
Bohm, Alec	.280
Turner, Justin	.278

On Base Percentage
(minimum 502 PA)

Freeman, Freddie	.407
Goldschmidt, Paul	.404
Soto, Juan	.401
McNeil, Jeff	.382
Nimmo, Brandon	.367
Canha, Mark	.367
Machado, Manny	.366
Bell, Josh	.362
Arenado, Nolan	.358
Yelich, Christian	.355

Slugging Average
(minimum 502 PA)

Goldschmidt, Paul	.578
Betts, Mookie	.533
Arenado, Nolan	.533
Machado, Manny	.531
Riley, Austin	.528
Alonso, Pete	.518
Freeman, Freddie	.511
Schwarber, Kyle	.504
Drury, Brandon	.492
Renfroe, Hunter	.492

Home Runs

Schwarber, Kyle	46
Alonso, Pete	40
Riley, Austin	38
Walker, Christian	36
Betts, Mookie	35
Goldschmidt, Paul	35
Tellez, Rowdy	35
Olson, Matt	34
Machado, Manny	32
Adames, Willy	31

Games

Olson, Matt	162
Swanson, Dansby	162
Lindor, Francisco	161
Alonso, Pete	160
Turner, Trea	160
Walker, Christian	160
Freeman, Freddie	159
Riley, Austin	159
Cronenworth, Jake	158
Happ, Ian	158

Plate Appearances

Freeman, Freddie	708
Turner, Trea	708
Lindor, Francisco	706
Olson, Matt	699
Swanson, Dansby	696
Riley, Austin	693
Alonso, Pete	685
Cronenworth, Jake	684
Nimmo, Brandon	673
Hoskins, Rhys	672

At Bats

Turner, Trea	652
Swanson, Dansby	640
Lindor, Francisco	630
Olson, Matt	616
Riley, Austin	615
Freeman, Freddie	612
Alonso, Pete	597
Hoskins, Rhys	589
Cronenworth, Jake	587
Bohm, Alec	586

Hits

Freeman, Freddie	199
Turner, Trea	194
Goldschmidt, Paul	178
Swanson, Dansby	177
McNeil, Jeff	174
Machado, Manny	172
Lindor, Francisco	170
Riley, Austin	168
Bohm, Alec	164
Arenado, Nolan	163

Singles

Turner, Trea	130
Freeman, Freddie	129
McNeil, Jeff	125
Bohm, Alec	124
Swanson, Dansby	119
Lindor, Francisco	114
Hernandez, Cesar	106
Nimmo, Brandon	106
Edman, Tommy	105
3 tied with	102

Doubles

Freeman, Freddie	47
Olson, Matt	44
Arenado, Nolan	42
Happ, Ian	42
Marte, Ketel	42
Goldschmidt, Paul	41
Betts, Mookie	40
McNeil, Jeff	39
Riley, Austin	39
Turner, Trea	39

Triples

Lux, Gavin	7
Nimmo, Brandon	7
Blackmon, Charlie	6
Friedl, T.J.	5
Hoerner, Nico	5
Lindor, Francisco	5
Marte, Starling	5
Realmuto, J.T.	5
17 tied with	4

Total Bases

Riley, Austin	325
Goldschmidt, Paul	324
Freeman, Freddie	313
Alonso, Pete	309
Machado, Manny	307
Betts, Mookie	305
Turner, Trea	304
Arenado, Nolan	297
Olson, Matt	294
Schwarber, Kyle	291

Runs Scored

Betts, Mookie	117
Freeman, Freddie	117
Goldschmidt, Paul	106
Nimmo, Brandon	102
Turner, Trea	101
Machado, Manny	100
Schwarber, Kyle	100
Swanson, Dansby	99
Yelich, Christian	99
Lindor, Francisco	98

RBI

Alonso, Pete	131
Goldschmidt, Paul	115
Lindor, Francisco	107
Arenado, Nolan	103
Olson, Matt	103
Cron, C.J.	102
Machado, Manny	102
Freeman, Freddie	100
Turner, Trea	100
Adames, Willy	98

Walks

Soto, Juan	135
Muncy, Max	90
Yelich, Christian	88
Schwarber, Kyle	86
Freeman, Freddie	84
Bell, Josh	81
Goldschmidt, Paul	79
Olson, Matt	75
Profar, Jurickson	73
Vogelbach, Daniel	73

Strikeouts

Schwarber, Kyle	200
Wisdom, Patrick	183
Swanson, Dansby	182
Voit, Luke	179
Olson, Matt	170
Hoskins, Rhys	169
Riley, Austin	168
Adames, Willy	166
Cron, C.J.	164
Yelich, Christian	162

2022 National League Batting Leaders

Intentional Walks	
Alonso, Pete	16
Freeman, Freddie	12
Machado, Manny	10
Harper, Bryce	9
Tellez, Rowdy	9
Cron, C.J.	6
Olson, Matt	6
Reynolds, Bryan	6
Soto, Juan	6
2 tied with	5

BA Bases Loaded (minimum 10 PA)	
Pederson, Joc	.750
Marte, Starling	.714
Cronenworth, Jake	.636
Swanson, Dansby	.600
Alfaro, Jorge	.556
Yelich, Christian	.556
Smith, Will	.545
Naquin, Tyler	.455
Slater, Austin	.455
Lindor, Francisco	.444

Sacrifice Hits	
Nido, Tomas	12
Perdomo, Geraldo	12
Robles, Victor	11
Grisham, Trent	7
Marcano, Tucupita	5
Rojas, Josh	5
Blackmon, Charlie	4
Herrera, Jose	4
11 tied with	3

Sacrifice Flies	
Bohm, Alec	10
Alonso, Pete	9
Nola, Austin	9
Cronenworth, Jake	8
Turner, Justin	8
7 tied with	7

BA Close & Late (minimum 50 PA)	
Turner, Trea	.418
Harris II, Michael	.406
Estrada, Thairo	.395
Gonzalez, Luis	.370
McCarthy, Jake	.340
Blackmon, Charlie	.338
Rojas, Josh	.333
Slater, Austin	.333
Turner, Justin	.333
2 tied with	.320

Batting Average w/ RISP (minimum 100 PA)	
Freeman, Freddie	.391
Pederson, Joc	.388
Harris II, Michael	.383
Harper, Bryce	.354
Iglesias, Jose	.354
Turner, Justin	.339
McNeil, Jeff	.336
Blackmon, Charlie	.331
Edman, Tommy	.324
Swanson, Dansby	.321

SLG vs. LHP (minimum 125 PA)	
Goldschmidt, Paul	.813
Pujols, Albert	.746
Riley, Austin	.671
Drury, Brandon	.626
Betts, Mookie	.609
Grichuk, Randal	.593
Farmer, Kyle	.568
Hoskins, Rhys	.558
Wisdom, Patrick	.556
Turner, Trea	.542

SLG vs. RHP (minimum 377 PA)	
Schwarber, Kyle	.566
Machado, Manny	.538
Freeman, Freddie	.532
Alonso, Pete	.532
Goldschmidt, Paul	.519
Arenado, Nolan	.512
Soto, Juan	.511
Betts, Mookie	.505
Olson, Matt	.503
Tellez, Rowdy	.498

Leadoff Hitters OBP (minimum 150 PA)	
Yelich, Christian	.378
Nimmo, Brandon	.368
Joe, Connor	.352
Slater, Austin	.349
Acuna Jr., Ronald	.347
Betts, Mookie	.340
Profar, Jurickson	.333
Rojas, Josh	.332
India, Jonathan	.320
Edman, Tommy	.318

Cleanup Hitters SLG (minimum 150 PA)	
Riley, Austin	.667
Realmuto, J.T.	.587
Arenado, Nolan	.557
Pederson, Joc	.550
Alonso, Pete	.527
Cron, C.J.	.523
Renfroe, Hunter	.514
Walker, Christian	.478
Suzuki, Seiya	.440
McCutchen, Andrew	.434

BA vs. LHP (minimum 125 PA)	
Goldschmidt, Paul	.411
Bohm, Alec	.352
Pujols, Albert	.351
Daza, Yonathan	.341
Riley, Austin	.329
Rodgers, Brendan	.317
McNeil, Jeff	.312
Farmer, Kyle	.309
Grichuk, Randal	.308
Betts, Mookie	.308

BA vs. RHP (minimum 377 PA)	
Freeman, Freddie	.338
McNeil, Jeff	.332
Machado, Manny	.313
Arenado, Nolan	.303
Turner, Trea	.298
Goldschmidt, Paul	.294
Donovan, Brendan	.282
Realmuto, J.T.	.281
Nimmo, Brandon	.280
Cron, C.J.	.280

Home BA (minimum 251 PA)	
Goldschmidt, Paul	.347
Hoerner, Nico	.318
Realmuto, J.T.	.314
Rodgers, Brendan	.313
Freeman, Freddie	.308
Happ, Ian	.308
Grichuk, Randal	.307
Marte, Starling	.305
Swanson, Dansby	.304
Cron, C.J.	.302

Away BA (minimum 251 PA)	
McNeil, Jeff	.356
Freeman, Freddie	.341
Machado, Manny	.312
Nimmo, Brandon	.309
Arenado, Nolan	.303
Turner, Trea	.303
Thomas, Lane	.293
Goldschmidt, Paul	.290
Canha, Mark	.282
Lindor, Francisco	.280

OBP vs. LHP (minimum 125 PA)	
Goldschmidt, Paul	.515
Riley, Austin	.413
Pujols, Albert	.400
Bohm, Alec	.394
Smith, Will	.391
Rodgers, Brendan	.388
Hoskins, Rhys	.387
Farmer, Kyle	.380
Slater, Austin	.379
McNeil, Jeff	.376

OBP vs. RHP (minimum 377 PA)	
Soto, Juan	.431
Freeman, Freddie	.424
Donovan, Brendan	.389
McNeil, Jeff	.385
Vogelbach, Daniel	.382
Machado, Manny	.376
Goldschmidt, Paul	.374
Nimmo, Brandon	.372
Arenado, Nolan	.367
Yelich, Christian	.365

2022 National League Batting Leaders

Stolen Bases			Caught Stealing			Highest SB Success Pct			Lowest SB Success Pct	
						(minimum 15 SBA)			(minimum 15 SBA)	
Berti, Jon	41		Acuna Jr., Ronald	11		Realmuto, J.T.	95.5		Morel, Christopher	58.8
Edman, Tommy	32		Marte, Starling	9		Edman, Tommy	91.4		Ortega, Rafael	63.2
Acuna Jr., Ronald	29		Morel, Christopher	7		Harris II, Michael	90.9		Marte, Starling	66.7
Turner, Trea	27		Ortega, Rafael	7		Hoerner, Nico	90.9		Segura, Jean	68.4
McCarthy, Jake	23		Swanson, Dansby	7		Turner, Trea	90.0		Chisholm Jr., Jazz	70.6
Rojas, Josh	23		7 tied with	6		Berti, Jon	89.1		Swanson, Dansby	72.0
Estrada, Thairo	21					McCarthy, Jake	88.5		Acuna Jr., Ronald	72.5
Realmuto, J.T.	21					Rojas, Josh	88.5		Lindor, Francisco	72.7
3 tied with	20					Bader, Harrison	88.2		Varsho, Daulton	72.7
						Yelich, Christian	86.4		2 tied with	73.3

Steals of Third			Grounded Into DP			Grounded Into DP Pct			Hit By Pitch	
						(minimum 50 GIDP Ops)				
Hayes, Ke'Bryan	7		Rodgers, Brendan	25		Cronenworth, Jake	1.52		Canha, Mark	28
Berti, Jon	4		Bell, Josh	22		Aquino, Aristides	1.92		Contreras, Willson	24
Hamilton, Billy	4		Farmer, Kyle	20		Muncy, Max	1.94		Riley, Austin	17
Harris II, Michael	4		Tellez, Rowdy	20		Canha, Mark	2.73		Cronenworth, Jake	16
Hoerner, Nico	4		Bohm, Alec	18		Grisham, Trent	3.16		Farmer, Kyle	16
Lindor, Francisco	4		Franco, Maikel	18		Escobar, Eduardo	3.20		Nimmo, Brandon	16
McCarthy, Jake	4		Marte, Starling	18		Duvall, Adam	3.28		5 tied with	14
Segura, Jean	4		Alonso, Pete	17		Stott, Bryson	3.30			
Swanson, Dansby	4		3 tied with	16		Yastrzemski, Mike	3.30			
Williams, Luke	4					Lux, Gavin	3.37			

Pitches Seen			At Bats Per Home Run			Highest GB/FB Ratio			Lowest GB/FB Ratio	
			(minimum 502 PA)			(minimum 502 PA)			(minimum 502 PA)	
Hoskins, Rhys	2897		Schwarber, Kyle	12.5		Yelich, Christian	2.55		Arenado, Nolan	0.59
Olson, Matt	2893		Alonso, Pete	14.9		Rodgers, Brendan	1.96		Escobar, Eduardo	0.63
Schwarber, Kyle	2878		Tellez, Rowdy	15.1		Cruz, Nelson	1.85		Muncy, Max	0.64
Lindor, Francisco	2829		Goldschmidt, Paul	16.0		Hayes, Ke'Bryan	1.71		Schwarber, Kyle	0.65
Profar, Jurickson	2790		Riley, Austin	16.2		Estrada, Thairo	1.71		Smith, Will	0.67
Nimmo, Brandon	2781		Walker, Christian	16.2		Marte, Starling	1.70		Wisdom, Patrick	0.70
Soto, Juan	2765		Betts, Mookie	16.3		Bell, Josh	1.63		Betts, Mookie	0.71
Freeman, Freddie	2755		Renfroe, Hunter	16.3		Edman, Tommy	1.60		Flores, Wilmer	0.74
Swanson, Dansby	2751		Machado, Manny	18.1		Nimmo, Brandon	1.59		Turner, Justin	0.74
Yelich, Christian	2747		Olson, Matt	18.1		Hernandez, Cesar	1.51		Cronenworth, Jake	0.74

Pitches Per Plate App			Pct Pitches Taken			Best BPS on OutZ			Worst BPS on OutZ	
(minimum 502 PA)			(minimum 1500 Pitches)			(minimum 502 PA)			(minimum 502 PA)	
Muncy, Max	4.31		Vogelbach, Daniel	67.8		Goldschmidt, Paul	.732		Voit, Luke	.305
Hoskins, Rhys	4.31		Soto, Juan	64.5		McNeil, Jeff	.681		Yelich, Christian	.306
Schwarber, Kyle	4.30		Donovan, Brendan	61.9		Freeman, Freddie	.668		Walker, Christian	.312
McMahon, Ryan	4.29		Muncy, Max	61.4		Turner, Trea	.594		Yastrzemski, Mike	.323
Profar, Jurickson	4.24		Grisham, Trent	61.2		Realmuto, J.T.	.565		Riley, Austin	.327
Grisham, Trent	4.24		Suzuki, Seiya	61.0		Machado, Manny	.559		Wisdom, Patrick	.332
Yastrzemski, Mike	4.21		Ruf, Darin	59.7		Drury, Brandon	.558		Ozuna, Marcell	.338
Bellinger, Cody	4.18		Joe, Connor	59.6		Rojas, Miguel	.554		Muncy, Max	.340
Wisdom, Patrick	4.18		Schwarber, Kyle	59.4		Bohm, Alec	.550		Profar, Jurickson	.359
Soto, Juan	4.16		Rojas, Josh	59.0		Blackmon, Charlie	.542		Rodgers, Brendan	.361

2022 National League Batting Leaders

Best OPS vs Fastballs	
(minimum 251 PA)	
Goldschmidt, Paul	.952
Soto, Juan	.943
Freeman, Freddie	.910
Arenado, Nolan	.907
Smith, Will	.907
Turner, Trea	.901
Realmuto, J.T.	.892
Reynolds, Bryan	.890
Swanson, Dansby	.866
2 tied with	.858

Best OPS vs Curveballs	
(minimum 50 PA)	
Riley, Austin	1.284
Machado, Manny	1.109
Arenado, Nolan	1.040
Bell, Josh	.943
Tellez, Rowdy	.921
Walker, Christian	.901
Nimmo, Brandon	.880
Rodgers, Brendan	.874
Goldschmidt, Paul	.871
Turner, Trea	.867

Best OPS vs Changeups	
(minimum 50 PA)	
Goldschmidt, Paul	1.263
Machado, Manny	1.107
Hoskins, Rhys	1.095
Alonso, Pete	1.089
Cron, C.J.	1.066
Drury, Brandon	1.057
Riley, Austin	.977
Muncy, Max	.934
Cronenworth, Jake	.927
Schwarber, Kyle	.926

Best OPS vs Sliders	
(minimum 32 PA)	
Chisholm Jr., Jazz	1.287
Gorman, Nolan	1.178
Castro, Rodolfo	1.030
Stephenson, Tyler	.999
Bote, David	.990
Harper, Bryce	.988
Hoerner, Nico	.959
Machado, Manny	.955
Peralta, David	.946
Thomas, Alek	.926

OPS	
(minimum 502 PA)	
Goldschmidt, Paul	.981
Freeman, Freddie	.918
Machado, Manny	.898
Arenado, Nolan	.891
Riley, Austin	.878
Betts, Mookie	.873
Alonso, Pete	.869
Soto, Juan	.853
McNeil, Jeff	.836
Schwarber, Kyle	.827

OPS First Half	
(minimum 260 PA)	
Goldschmidt, Paul	1.004
Harper, Bryce	.985
Freeman, Freddie	.926
Riley, Austin	.922
Cron, C.J.	.902
Soto, Juan	.901
Bell, Josh	.895
Machado, Manny	.890
Arenado, Nolan	.885
2 tied with	.864

OPS Second Half	
(minimum 201 PA)	
Realmuto, J.T.	.949
Goldschmidt, Paul	.947
Meneses, Joey	.930
Freeman, Freddie	.907
Machado, Manny	.907
Arenado, Nolan	.900
McNeil, Jeff	.898
Alonso, Pete	.887
Betts, Mookie	.883
Harris II, Michael	.880

OPS by Catchers	
(minimum 251 PA)	
Contreras, Willson	.858
Realmuto, J.T.	.829
d'Arnaud, Travis	.805
Smith, Will	.725
Gomes, Yan	.703
Bart, Joey	.677
Ruiz, Keibert	.674
Diaz, Elias	.657
Nola, Austin	.642
Caratini, Victor	.631

OPS by First Basemen	
(minimum 251 PA)	
Goldschmidt, Paul	.995
Freeman, Freddie	.918
Alonso, Pete	.877
Bell, Josh	.814
Cron, C.J.	.811
Olson, Matt	.802
Walker, Christian	.796
Tellez, Rowdy	.782
Hoskins, Rhys	.773
Hosmer, Eric	.720

OPS by Second Basemen	
(minimum 251 PA)	
McNeil, Jeff	.852
Edman, Tommy	.779
Wong, Kolten	.777
Lux, Gavin	.763
Gorman, Nolan	.746
Cronenworth, Jake	.739
Rodgers, Brendan	.728
Estrada, Thairo	.725
Segura, Jean	.713
Albies, Ozzie	.705

OPS by Third Basemen	
(minimum 251 PA)	
Machado, Manny	.888
Arenado, Nolan	.885
Riley, Austin	.885
Turner, Justin	.837
Drury, Brandon	.808
Muncy, Max	.753
Wisdom, Patrick	.750
McMahon, Ryan	.737
Escobar, Eduardo	.731
Rojas, Josh	.719

OPS by Shortstops	
(minimum 251 PA)	
Turner, Trea	.809
Lindor, Francisco	.782
Swanson, Dansby	.776
Cruz, Oneil	.774
Adames, Willy	.760
Hoerner, Nico	.739
Kim, Ha-seong	.707
Iglesias, Jose	.702
Stott, Bryson	.690
Farmer, Kyle	.681

OPS by Left Fielders	
(minimum 251 PA)	
Pederson, Joc	.916
Schwarber, Kyle	.846
Canha, Mark	.776
Happ, Ian	.775
Peralta, David	.773
Yelich, Christian	.763
Hernandez, Yadiel	.750
Profar, Jurickson	.730
O'Neill, Tyler	.717
Taylor, Chris	.694

OPS by Center Fielders	
(minimum 251 PA)	
Harris II, Michael	.853
Nimmo, Brandon	.800
Reynolds, Bryan	.786
Carlson, Dylan	.752
Taylor, Tyrone	.737
Yastrzemski, Mike	.691
Daza, Yonathan	.687
Bader, Harrison	.673
Bellinger, Cody	.657
Sanchez, Jesus	.648

OPS by Right Fielders	
(minimum 251 PA)	
Betts, Mookie	.865
Soto, Juan	.849
Nootbaar, Lars	.849
Renfroe, Hunter	.816
Marte, Starling	.809
Suzuki, Seiya	.768
Acuna Jr., Ronald	.754
Grichuk, Randal	.753
Yastrzemski, Mike	.724
Varsho, Daulton	.714

OPS by Designated Hitters	
(minimum 125 PA)	
Harper, Bryce	.890
Pujols, Albert	.808
Marte, Ketel	.808
Cooper, Garrett	.782
Vogelbach, Daniel	.781
Davis, J.D.	.777
Acuna Jr., Ronald	.774
Contreras, Willson	.749
Blackmon, Charlie	.746
Turner, Justin	.719

2022 National League Batting Leaders

OPS Batting Left vs. LHP (minimum 125 PA)	
Freeman, Freddie	.824
Nimmo, Brandon	.786
Harper, Bryce	.775
McNeil, Jeff	.758
Blackmon, Charlie	.756
Olson, Matt	.749
Cronenworth, Jake	.714
Soto, Juan	.701
Yelich, Christian	.694
Schwarber, Kyle	.687

OPS Batting Left vs. RHP (minimum 377 PA)	
Freeman, Freddie	.956
Soto, Juan	.942
Schwarber, Kyle	.900
Vogelbach, Daniel	.879
McNeil, Jeff	.869
Wong, Kolten	.845
Olson, Matt	.824
Reynolds, Bryan	.814
Nimmo, Brandon	.808
Varsho, Daulton	.801

OPS Batting Right vs. LHP (minimum 125 PA)	
Goldschmidt, Paul	1.327
Pujols, Albert	1.146
Riley, Austin	1.084
Betts, Mookie	.983
Drury, Brandon	.955
Farmer, Kyle	.948
Hoskins, Rhys	.945
Bohm, Alec	.935
Grichuk, Randal	.926
Smith, Will	.908

OPS Batting Right vs. RHP (minimum 377 PA)	
Machado, Manny	.915
Goldschmidt, Paul	.893
Alonso, Pete	.880
Arenado, Nolan	.879
Betts, Mookie	.832
Realmuto, J.T.	.826
Cron, C.J.	.823
Riley, Austin	.811
Turner, Justin	.809
Renfroe, Hunter	.794

OPS vs. LHP (minimum 125 PA)	
Goldschmidt, Paul	1.327
Pujols, Albert	1.146
Riley, Austin	1.084
Betts, Mookie	.983
Drury, Brandon	.955
Farmer, Kyle	.948
Hoskins, Rhys	.945
Bohm, Alec	.935
Grichuk, Randal	.926
Smith, Will	.908

OPS vs. RHP (minimum 377 PA)	
Freeman, Freddie	.956
Soto, Juan	.942
Machado, Manny	.915
Schwarber, Kyle	.900
Goldschmidt, Paul	.893
Alonso, Pete	.880
Arenado, Nolan	.879
Vogelbach, Daniel	.879
McNeil, Jeff	.869
Wong, Kolten	.845

RC Per 27 Outs vs. LHP (minimum 125 PA)	
Goldschmidt, Paul	15.7
Betts, Mookie	9.8
Riley, Austin	9.1
Grichuk, Randal	8.7
Pujols, Albert	8.4
Drury, Brandon	7.8
Farmer, Kyle	7.7
Rodgers, Brendan	7.5
Wisdom, Patrick	7.3
Longoria, Evan	7.0

RC Per 27 Outs vs. RHP (minimum 377 PA)	
Freeman, Freddie	8.7
Machado, Manny	8.4
Soto, Juan	7.7
Alonso, Pete	7.6
Goldschmidt, Paul	7.4
Schwarber, Kyle	7.3
Arenado, Nolan	7.2
Vogelbach, Daniel	6.8
McNeil, Jeff	6.5
Cron, C.J.	6.4

Highest RBI % (minimum 502 PA)	
Goldschmidt, Paul	46.98
Alonso, Pete	42.52
Freeman, Freddie	41.68
Machado, Manny	39.47
Realmuto, J.T.	39.31
Schwarber, Kyle	38.59
Swanson, Dansby	38.46
Adames, Willy	38.40
Arenado, Nolan	38.40
Blackmon, Charlie	38.40

Lowest RBI % (minimum 502 PA)	
Hernandez, Cesar	20.90
Hayes, Ke'Bryan	24.33
Rojas, Miguel	24.71
Thomas, Lane	26.96
Marte, Ketel	27.79
Ozuna, Marcell	28.08
Yastrzemski, Mike	28.19
Profar, Jurickson	28.54
Escobar, Eduardo	29.05
Rodgers, Brendan	29.48

Highest Strikeout per PA (minimum 502 PA)	
Wisdom, Patrick	.343
Voit, Luke	.315
Schwarber, Kyle	.299
Grisham, Trent	.286
Bellinger, Cody	.273
Adames, Willy	.269
McMahon, Ryan	.265
Swanson, Dansby	.261
Cron, C.J.	.259
Yastrzemski, Mike	.253

Lowest Strikeout per PA (minimum 502 PA)	
McNeil, Jeff	.104
Hoerner, Nico	.110
Arenado, Nolan	.116
Rojas, Miguel	.120
Freeman, Freddie	.144
Soto, Juan	.145
Profar, Jurickson	.157
Bell, Josh	.158
Betts, Mookie	.163
Estrada, Thairo	.165

Home Runs At Home	
Riley, Austin	24
Cron, C.J.	22
Goldschmidt, Paul	22
Tellez, Rowdy	22
Schwarber, Kyle	21
Adames, Willy	18
Hoskins, Rhys	18
Alonso, Pete	17
Machado, Manny	17
3 tied with	16

Home Runs Away	
Schwarber, Kyle	25
Alonso, Pete	23
Walker, Christian	21
Betts, Mookie	19
Olson, Matt	18
Renfroe, Hunter	18
Reynolds, Bryan	17
Arenado, Nolan	16
Varsho, Daulton	16
2 tied with	15

Longest Avg Home Run (min 10 over the wall)	
McMahon, Ryan	428
Cron, C.J.	426
Acuna Jr., Ronald	426
Rodgers, Brendan	423
Yelich, Christian	419
Soler, Jorge	416
Cruz, Oneil	414
Walker, Christian	414
Hiura, Keston	414
Ozuna, Marcell	414

Shortest Avg Home Run (min 10 over the wall)	
Profar, Jurickson	379
Wong, Kolten	383
Flores, Wilmer	384
Votto, Joey	387
Arenado, Nolan	387
Cronenworth, Jake	388
Farmer, Kyle	389
Realmuto, J.T.	390
Hoskins, Rhys	390
Muncy, Max	391

2022 National League Batting Leaders

Under Age 26: AB Per HR
(minimum 300 PA)

Riley, Austin	16.2
Contreras, William	16.7
Suwinski, Jack	17.2
Soto, Juan	19.4
Cruz, Oneil	19.5
Gorman, Nolan	20.2
Nootbaar, Lars	20.7
Harris II, Michael	21.8
Morel, Christopher	23.7
Sanchez, Jesus	24.1

Under Age 26: OPS
(minimum 300 PA)

Riley, Austin	.878
Contreras, William	.860
Harris II, Michael	.853
Soto, Juan	.853
Nootbaar, Lars	.788
Donovan, Brendan	.773
McCarthy, Jake	.769
Acuna Jr., Ronald	.764
Lux, Gavin	.745
Cruz, Oneil	.744

Under Age 26: RC/27 Outs
(minimum 300 PA)

Harris II, Michael	6.9
McCarthy, Jake	6.6
Soto, Juan	6.3
Riley, Austin	6.2
Contreras, William	6.0
Cruz, Oneil	5.8
Nootbaar, Lars	5.7
Donovan, Brendan	5.2
Acuna Jr., Ronald	4.9
Hoerner, Nico	4.8

Longest Home Run

Cron, C.J., 9/9	504
Yelich, Christian, 9/6	499
Sanchez, Jesus, 5/30	496
McMahon, Ryan, 8/9	495
Cron, C.J., 6/17	486
Drury, Brandon, 9/16	468
Schwarber, Kyle, 4/20	468
Soler, Jorge, 4/29	468
Walker, Christian, 4/24	467
Cron, C.J., 4/16	466

Swing and Miss %
(minimum 1500 Pitches Seen)

Taylor, Chris	39.1
Morel, Christopher	38.1
Voit, Luke	36.9
Wisdom, Patrick	35.2
Contreras, William	33.1
Crawford, Brandon	31.0
Castellanos, Nick	31.0
Cruz, Nelson	30.6
Contreras, Willson	30.0
Swanson, Dansby	29.8

Highest First Swing %
(minimum 502 PA)

Voit, Luke	49.0
Castellanos, Nick	45.4
Reynolds, Bryan	41.0
Machado, Manny	40.4
Swanson, Dansby	39.3
McNeil, Jeff	38.7
Bohm, Alec	37.8
Rodgers, Brendan	36.9
Wisdom, Patrick	36.8
Acuna Jr., Ronald	36.6

Lowest First Swing %
(minimum 502 PA)

Grisham, Trent	18.8
Tellez, Rowdy	19.9
Yelich, Christian	20.8
Thomas, Lane	20.9
Smith, Will	21.5
Yastrzemski, Mike	21.7
Canha, Mark	21.8
Hayes, Ke'Bryan	21.8
Hoskins, Rhys	21.9
Soto, Juan	21.9

Home RC Per 27 Outs
(minimum 251 PA)

Goldschmidt, Paul	11.1
Cron, C.J.	9.5
Alonso, Pete	8.0
Realmuto, J.T.	7.5
Riley, Austin	7.1
Contreras, Willson	7.0
Rodgers, Brendan	6.8
Arenado, Nolan	6.7
Drury, Brandon	6.7
Hoskins, Rhys	6.7

Road RC Per 27 Outs
(minimum 251 PA)

Freeman, Freddie	9.5
Machado, Manny	8.3
Nimmo, Brandon	7.5
Goldschmidt, Paul	6.8
McNeil, Jeff	6.8
Arenado, Nolan	6.8
Betts, Mookie	6.6
Schwarber, Kyle	6.6
Alonso, Pete	6.5
Soto, Juan	6.4

Lead Changing RBI

Alonso, Pete	38
Machado, Manny	34
Walker, Christian	33
Arenado, Nolan	31
Lindor, Francisco	31
Riley, Austin	31
Tellez, Rowdy	31
Adames, Willy	30
Blackmon, Charlie	30
Goldschmidt, Paul	30

2022 American League Pitching Leaders

Earned Run Average
(minimum 162 IP)

Verlander, Justin	1.75
Cease, Dylan	2.20
Manoah, Alek	2.24
Ohtani, Shohei	2.33
McClanahan, Shane	2.54
Valdez, Framber	2.82
Bieber, Shane	2.88
Perez, Martin	2.89
McKenzie, Triston	2.96
Gilbert, Logan	3.20

Winning Percentage
(minimum 15 Decisions)

Verlander, Justin	.818
Cortes, Nestor	.750
Quantrill, Cal	.750
Valdez, Framber	.739
Taillon, Jameson	.737
Manoah, Alek	.696
Gilbert, Logan	.684
Singer, Brady	.667
Garcia, Luis	.652
Cease, Dylan	.636

Opponent Batting Average
(minimum 120 IP)

Javier, Cristian	.170
Verlander, Justin	.186
Cortes, Nestor	.189
Cease, Dylan	.190
McClanahan, Shane	.194
McKenzie, Triston	.201
Manoah, Alek	.202
Ohtani, Shohei	.203
Cole, Gerrit	.209
Ryan, Joe	.211

Baserunners Per 9 IP
(minimum 120 IP)

Verlander, Justin	7.77
Cortes, Nestor	8.41
McClanahan, Shane	8.50
McKenzie, Triston	8.80
Javier, Cristian	8.90
Ohtani, Shohei	9.22
Cole, Gerrit	9.24
Stripling, Ross	9.31
Bieber, Shane	9.45
Rasmussen, Drew	9.56

Games

Cimber, Adam	77
Clase, Emmanuel	77
Lange, Alex	71
Montero, Rafael	71
Acevedo, Domingo	70
Diekman, Jake	70
Neris, Hector	70
Barlow, Scott	69
Brasier, Ryan	68
Coleman, Dylan	68

Games Started

Cole, Gerrit	33
Pivetta, Nick	33
9 tied with	32

Complete Games

Valdez, Framber	3
Eovaldi, Nathan	2
12 tied with	1

Shutouts

Cease, Dylan	1
Cortes, Nestor	1
Detmers, Reid	1
Eovaldi, Nathan	1
Kremer, Dean	1
Perez, Martin	1
Sandoval, Patrick	1
Valdez, Framber	1
Wacha, Michael	1

Wins

Verlander, Justin	18
Valdez, Framber	17
Manoah, Alek	16
Garcia, Luis	15
Ohtani, Shohei	15
Quantrill, Cal	15
Cease, Dylan	14
Taillon, Jameson	14
5 tied with	13

Losses

Gonzales, Marco	15
Keller, Brad	14
Bubic, Kris	13
Irvin, Cole	13
Lynch, Daniel	13
Montas, Frankie	12
Pivetta, Nick	12
Plesac, Zach	12
Ray, Robbie	12
4 tied with	11

No Decisions

Dunning, Dane	17
Archer, Chris	15
Montgomery, Jordan	15
Berrios, Jose	13
Bundy, Dylan	13
Gilbert, Logan	13
Greinke, Zack	13
Taillon, Jameson	13
10 tied with	12

Wild Pitches

Lange, Alex	15
Ohtani, Shohei	14
Keller, Brad	11
Valdez, Framber	11
Pivetta, Nick	10
Rasmussen, Drew	10
Heasley, Jon	9
Jackson, Zach	9
McClanahan, Shane	9
5 tied with	8

Strikeouts

Cole, Gerrit	257
Cease, Dylan	227
Ohtani, Shohei	219
Ray, Robbie	212
Gausman, Kevin	205
Bieber, Shane	198
Javier, Cristian	194
McClanahan, Shane	194
Valdez, Framber	194
McKenzie, Triston	190

Walks Allowed

Cease, Dylan	78
Pivetta, Nick	73
Perez, Martin	69
Valdez, Framber	67
Bubic, Kris	63
Dunning, Dane	62
Otto, Glenn	62
Ray, Robbie	62
Giolito, Lucas	61
Sandoval, Patrick	60

Intentional Walks Allowed

Fulmer, Michael	6
Moll, Sam	6
Lopez, Jorge	5
Acevedo, Domingo	4
Castillo, Diego	4
Jimenez, Dany	4
Quijada, Jose	4
Romano, Jordan	4
Sewald, Paul	4
20 tied with	3

Hit Batters

Manoah, Alek	15
Otto, Glenn	13
Berrios, Jose	11
Dunning, Dane	11
Singer, Brady	11
Valdez, Framber	11
Yarbrough, Ryan	11
5 tied with	10

2022 American League Pitching Leaders

Runs Allowed		Hits Allowed		Doubles Allowed		Home Runs Allowed	
Berrios, Jose	103	Berrios, Jose	199	Lyles, Jordan	46	Cole, Gerrit	33
Gonzales, Marco	97	Lyles, Jordan	196	Gonzales, Marco	44	Ray, Robbie	32
Lyles, Jordan	94	Gonzales, Marco	194	Taillon, Jameson	42	Gonzales, Marco	30
Giolito, Lucas	92	Gausman, Kevin	188	Gilbert, Logan	41	Berrios, Jose	29
Pivetta, Nick	91	Kluber, Corey	178	Dunning, Dane	39	Urquidy, Jose	29
Bubic, Kris	87	Perez, Martin	178	Cueto, Johnny	37	Pivetta, Nick	27
Irvin, Cole	87	Quantrill, Cal	178	Giolito, Lucas	37	Lyles, Jordan	26
Keller, Brad	86	Pivetta, Nick	175	Perez, Martin	37	Taillon, Jameson	26
Kluber, Corey	82	Irvin, Cole	174	Pivetta, Nick	36	Irvin, Cole	25
Cole, Gerrit	81	Bieber, Shane	172	Gausman, Kevin	35	McKenzie, Triston	25

Run Support Per Nine IP		% Pitches In Strike Zone		Pitches Per Start		Pitches Per Batter	
(minimum 120 IP)		(minimum 120 IP)		(minimum 20 GS)		(minimum 120 IP)	
Quantrill, Cal	6.33	Valdez, Framber	43.7	Cole, Gerrit	99.2	Irvin, Cole	3.52
Urquidy, Jose	6.24	Irvin, Cole	43.2	Cease, Dylan	97.5	Kluber, Corey	3.56
Taillon, Jameson	6.24	Gilbert, Logan	43.1	Valdez, Framber	97.4	Berrios, Jose	3.61
Berrios, Jose	5.86	McKenzie, Triston	43.0	Lynn, Lance	96.3	Gonzales, Marco	3.63
Valdez, Framber	5.81	Ohtani, Shohei	42.7	Cueto, Johnny	95.6	Perez, Martin	3.63
Gausman, Kevin	5.72	Pivetta, Nick	42.6	Ray, Robbie	95.2	Bieber, Shane	3.64
Cole, Gerrit	5.65	Urquidy, Jose	42.6	Manoah, Alek	95.1	Cueto, Johnny	3.64
Pivetta, Nick	5.41	Bieber, Shane	41.4	Singer, Brady	94.7	Valdez, Framber	3.65
Gilbert, Logan	5.04	Kluber, Corey	41.4	Gilbert, Logan	94.2	Bundy, Dylan	3.66
Cease, Dylan	5.04	McClanahan, Shane	41.2	Ohtani, Shohei	93.9	Keller, Brad	3.69

Quality Starts		Batters Faced		Innings Pitched		Most Pitches in a Game	
Valdez, Framber	26	Valdez, Framber	827	Valdez, Framber	201.1	Cole, Gerrit	118
Manoah, Alek	25	Perez, Martin	821	Cole, Gerrit	200.2	Cueto, Johnny	118
Bieber, Shane	23	Cole, Gerrit	793	Bieber, Shane	200.0	Lyles, Jordan	117
Perez, Martin	23	Bieber, Shane	791	Manoah, Alek	196.2	Castillo, Luis	115
Cole, Gerrit	21	Manoah, Alek	786	Perez, Martin	196.1	Javier, Cristian	115
Verlander, Justin	21	Gonzales, Marco	783	McKenzie, Triston	191.1	Ray, Robbie	115
5 tied with	18	Ray, Robbie	775	Ray, Robbie	189.0	Cole, Gerrit	114
		Lyles, Jordan	774	Quantrill, Cal	186.1	Valdez, Framber	114
		Pivetta, Nick	773	Gilbert, Logan	185.2	3 tied with	113
		Quantrill, Cal	770	Cease, Dylan	184.0		

Stolen Bases Allowed		Caught Stealing Off		Stolen Base Pct Allowed		Pickoffs	
				(minimum 162 IP)			
Syndergaard, Noah	25	Ray, Robbie	9	Irvin, Cole	0.0	Ray, Robbie	6
Pivetta, Nick	19	Pivetta, Nick	6	Kluber, Corey	50.0	Chapman, Aroldis	4
Gausman, Kevin	18	12 tied with	5	Berrios, Jose	54.5	Berrios, Jose	3
Ray, Robbie	17			Gilbert, Logan	54.5	Oller, Adam	3
Otto, Glenn	16			McKenzie, Triston	54.5	Singer, Brady	3
Quantrill, Cal	16			Manoah, Alek	61.5	Skubal, Tarik	3
Gray, Jon	15			Ray, Robbie	65.4	Springs, Jeffrey	3
Kopech, Michael	15			Cease, Dylan	66.7	16 tied with	2
Blackburn, Paul	13			Cole, Gerrit	68.8		
Detmers, Reid	13			Bieber, Shane	69.2		

2022 American League Pitching Leaders

Strikeouts Per 9 IP
(minimum 120 IP)

Ohtani, Shohei	11.87
Javier, Cristian	11.74
Cole, Gerrit	11.53
Cease, Dylan	11.10
Gausman, Kevin	10.56
McClanahan, Shane	10.50
Ray, Robbie	10.10
Giolito, Lucas	9.85
Springs, Jeffrey	9.58
Verlander, Justin	9.51

Opp On-Base Percentage
(minimum 120 IP)

Verlander, Justin	.227
Cortes, Nestor	.241
McClanahan, Shane	.246
Javier, Cristian	.252
McKenzie, Triston	.253
Ohtani, Shohei	.258
Stripling, Ross	.259
Cole, Gerrit	.260
Bieber, Shane	.266
Rasmussen, Drew	.267

Opp Slugging Average
(minimum 120 IP)

Verlander, Justin	.270
Valdez, Framber	.305
Javier, Cristian	.305
Cease, Dylan	.306
Cortes, Nestor	.313
Manoah, Alek	.314
Ohtani, Shohei	.316
McClanahan, Shane	.317
Sandoval, Patrick	.333
Perez, Martin	.336

Opponent OPS
(minimum 120 IP)

Verlander, Justin	.497
Cortes, Nestor	.554
Javier, Cristian	.557
McClanahan, Shane	.562
Ohtani, Shohei	.574
Manoah, Alek	.582
Cease, Dylan	.584
Valdez, Framber	.600
McKenzie, Triston	.611
Bieber, Shane	.613

Home Runs Per Nine IP
(minimum 120 IP)

Sandoval, Patrick	0.48
Valdez, Framber	0.49
Perez, Martin	0.50
Verlander, Justin	0.62
Manoah, Alek	0.73
Ohtani, Shohei	0.76
Gausman, Kevin	0.77
Cease, Dylan	0.78
Kremer, Dean	0.79
Rasmussen, Drew	0.80

Batting Average vs. LHB
(minimum 125 BF)

Sandoval, Patrick	.151
Montero, Rafael	.157
Munoz, Andres	.157
Verlander, Justin	.163
Cole, Gerrit	.182
Akin, Keegan	.185
Wacha, Michael	.188
Javier, Cristian	.189
Archer, Chris	.190
Whitlock, Garrett	.192

Batting Average vs. RHB
(minimum 225 BF)

Javier, Cristian	.147
Manoah, Alek	.159
Cease, Dylan	.163
Kopech, Michael	.186
Ohtani, Shohei	.188
McClanahan, Shane	.192
Severino, Luis	.195
Gray, Jon	.201
Cortes, Nestor	.202
McKenzie, Triston	.205

Opp BA w/ RISP
(minimum 125 BF)

Manoah, Alek	.148
Cease, Dylan	.163
Garcia, Luis	.164
Taillon, Jameson	.184
Flexen, Chris	.191
Perez, Martin	.214
Lyles, Jordan	.219
Sandoval, Patrick	.220
Montas, Frankie	.220
Urquidy, Jose	.220

OBP vs. Leadoff Hitter
(minimum 120 BF)

Cortes, Nestor	.195
Javier, Cristian	.196
Verlander, Justin	.210
Kopech, Michael	.214
Kluber, Corey	.234
Manoah, Alek	.234
Stripling, Ross	.237
Springs, Jeffrey	.241
Cole, Gerrit	.242
Lynn, Lance	.244

Strikeouts / Walks Ratio
(minimum 120 IP)

Gausman, Kevin	7.32
Kluber, Corey	6.62
Lynn, Lance	6.53
Verlander, Justin	6.38
Kirby, George	6.05
Stripling, Ross	5.55
Bieber, Shane	5.50
Cole, Gerrit	5.14
McClanahan, Shane	5.11
Ohtani, Shohei	4.98

Highest GB/FB Ratio
(minimum 120 IP)

Valdez, Framber	4.16
Perez, Martin	1.73
McClanahan, Shane	1.67
Bieber, Shane	1.53
Quantrill, Cal	1.11
Ohtani, Shohei	1.09
Gausman, Kevin	1.09
Gonzales, Marco	1.07
Cole, Gerrit	1.05
Taillon, Jameson	1.02

Lowest GB/FB Ratio
(minimum 120 IP)

McKenzie, Triston	0.67
Urquidy, Jose	0.80
Kluber, Corey	0.86
Verlander, Justin	0.87
Cease, Dylan	0.88
Manoah, Alek	0.89
Irvin, Cole	0.89
Pivetta, Nick	0.92
Ray, Robbie	0.94
Gilbert, Logan	0.94

Sacrifice Flies Allowed

Bubic, Kris	9
Dunning, Dane	8
Heasley, Jon	8
Cueto, Johnny	7
Detmers, Reid	7
Quantrill, Cal	7
Vest, Will	7
7 tied with	6

Sacrifice Hits Allowed

Burke, Brock	4
Cimber, Adam	4
Gilbert, Logan	4
Perez, Martin	4
Quantrill, Cal	4
Singer, Brady	4
10 tied with	3

GIDP Induced

Valdez, Framber	25
Cueto, Johnny	20
Perez, Martin	20
Bubic, Kris	19
Giolito, Lucas	18
Lyles, Jordan	18
Bieber, Shane	17
Gonzales, Marco	17
Singer, Brady	17
3 tied with	16

GIDP Per Nine IP
(minimum 120 IP)

Bubic, Kris	1.33
Cueto, Johnny	1.14
Valdez, Framber	1.12
Kremer, Dean	1.01
Giolito, Lucas	1.00
Singer, Brady	1.00
Perez, Martin	0.92
Lyles, Jordan	0.91
Montas, Frankie	0.87
2 tied with	0.85

2022 American League Pitching Leaders

Saves		Blown Saves		Save Pct		Save Opportunities	
				(minimum 20 Save Ops)			
Clase, Emmanuel	42	Pagan, Emilio	7	Clase, Emmanuel	91.3	Clase, Emmanuel	46
Hendriks, Liam	37	Graveman, Kendall	6	Soto, Gregory	90.9	Romano, Jordan	42
Romano, Jordan	36	Jax, Griffin	6	Hendriks, Liam	90.2	Hendriks, Liam	41
Pressly, Ryan	33	Lopez, Jorge	6	Pressly, Ryan	89.2	Pressly, Ryan	37
Soto, Gregory	30	Poche, Colin	6	Barlow, Scott	85.7	Soto, Gregory	33
Barlow, Scott	24	Robles, Hansel	6	Romano, Jordan	85.7	Lopez, Jorge	29
Lopez, Jorge	23	Romano, Jordan	6	Holmes, Clay	80.0	Barlow, Scott	28
Holmes, Clay	20	12 tied with	5	Sewald, Paul	80.0	Holmes, Clay	25
Sewald, Paul	20			Lopez, Jorge	79.3	Sewald, Paul	25
Iglesias, Raisel	16					Iglesias, Raisel	19

Easy Saves		Regular Saves		Tough Saves		Holds Adjusted Saves %	
						(minimum 20 Save Ops + Holds)	
Clase, Emmanuel	25	Romano, Jordan	18	Bautista, Felix	5	Duran, Jhoan	100.0
Hendriks, Liam	24	Clase, Emmanuel	17	Lopez, Jorge	5	Perez, Cionel	100.0
Pressly, Ryan	21	Hendriks, Liam	13	Barlow, Scott	4	Chafin, Andrew	95.7
Soto, Gregory	18	Pressly, Ryan	12	Romano, Jordan	4	Tate, Dillon	95.5
Iglesias, Raisel	15	Soto, Gregory	11	Puk, A.J.	2	Moore, Matt	95.0
Romano, Jordan	14	Sewald, Paul	10	Schreiber, John	2	Thielbar, Caleb	95.0
Lopez, Jorge	13	Barlow, Scott	9	Tate, Dillon	2	Montero, Rafael	94.9
Barlow, Joe	12	Holmes, Clay	8	30 tied with	1	Schreiber, John	93.8
Holmes, Clay	12	Bautista, Felix	6			Bautista, Felix	93.3
2 tied with	11	Pagan, Emilio	6			Stephan, Trevor	91.7

Relief Wins		Relief Losses		Relief Games		Holds	
Cimber, Adam	10	Soto, Gregory	11	Cimber, Adam	77	Graveman, Kendall	27
Mayza, Tim	8	Trivino, Lou	8	Clase, Emmanuel	77	Jackson, Zach	26
Barlow, Scott	7	Lopez, Jorge	7	Lange, Alex	71	Fulmer, Michael	25
Burke, Brock	7	Martin, Brett	7	Montero, Rafael	71	Neris, Hector	25
Castillo, Diego	7	Santana, Dennis	7	Acevedo, Domingo	70	Perez, Cionel	24
Holmes, Clay	7	Cimber, Adam	6	Diekman, Jake	70	Montero, Rafael	23
Jax, Griffin	7	Fulmer, Michael	6	Neris, Hector	70	Poche, Colin	23
Lange, Alex	7	Iglesias, Raisel	6	Barlow, Scott	69	4 tied with	22
Perez, Cionel	7	Pagan, Emilio	6	Brasier, Ryan	68		
5 tied with	6	Payamps, Joel	6	Coleman, Dylan	68		

Relief Innings		Inherited Runners Scrd %		Relief Opp On Base Pct		Relief Opp Slugging Avg	
		(minimum 25 IR)		(minimum 50 IP)		(minimum 50 IP)	
Burke, Brock	82.1	Adam, Jason	9.7	Clase, Emmanuel	.200	Clase, Emmanuel	.225
Akin, Keegan	79.1	Chafin, Andrew	13.9	Sewald, Paul	.220	Adam, Jason	.242
Barria, Jaime	74.2	Quijada, Jose	14.3	Adam, Jason	.229	Stanek, Ryne	.257
Barlow, Scott	74.1	Murfee, Penn	14.8	Morgan, Eli	.238	Hentges, Sam	.258
Moore, Matt	74.0	Munoz, Andres	16.0	Bautista, Felix	.245	Holmes, Clay	.261
Tate, Dillon	73.2	Garrett, Amir	16.7	Munoz, Andres	.250	Peralta, Wandy	.262
Clase, Emmanuel	72.2	Thielbar, Caleb	18.6	Murfee, Penn	.250	Romano, Jordan	.263
Jax, Griffin	72.1	Trivino, Lou	18.8	Swanson, Erik	.253	Abreu, Bryan	.267
Lopez, Jorge	71.0	Snider, Collin	19.4	Lopez, Reynaldo	.255	Montero, Rafael	.267
Cimber, Adam	70.2	Bautista, Felix	19.4	Herget, Jimmy	.256	Munoz, Andres	.273

2022 American League Pitching Leaders

Relief Opp BA Vs LHB (minimum 50 AB)		Relief Opp BA Vs RHB (minimum 50 AB)		Relief Opp Batting Average (minimum 50 IP)		Relief Earned Run Average (minimum 50 IP)	
Garrett, Amir	.106	Sewald, Paul	.130	Sewald, Paul	.146	Stanek, Ryne	1.15
Quijada, Jose	.115	Martinez, Seth	.135	Adam, Jason	.147	Clase, Emmanuel	1.36
Karinchak, James	.129	Moran, Jovani	.144	Clase, Emmanuel	.167	Perez, Cionel	1.41
Adam, Jason	.136	Sandlin, Nick	.149	Bautista, Felix	.167	Adam, Jason	1.56
Hentges, Sam	.143	Marinaccio, Ron	.152	Hentges, Sam	.186	Swanson, Erik	1.74
Jackson, Zach	.143	Adam, Jason	.154	Moore, Matt	.187	Duran, Jhoan	1.86
Marinaccio, Ron	.146	Clase, Emmanuel	.158	Stanek, Ryne	.188	Abreu, Bryan	1.94
Bautista, Felix	.149	Holmes, Clay	.159	Raley, Brooks	.189	Moore, Matt	1.95
Puk, A.J.	.153	Cotton, Jharel	.162	Munoz, Andres	.189	Burke, Brock	1.97
2 tied with	.155	Moore, Matt	.165	Romano, Jordan	.190	Romano, Jordan	2.11

Rel OBP 1st Batter Faced (minimum 40 BF)		Rel Opp BA w/ Runners On (minimum 50 IP)		Relief Opp BA w/ RISP (minimum 50 IP)		Fastest Avg Fastball-Relief (minimum 50 IP)	
Sewald, Paul	.172	Adam, Jason	.120	Bautista, Felix	.100	Duran, Jhoan	100.9
Morgan, Eli	.184	Bautista, Felix	.125	Tate, Dillon	.109	Munoz, Andres	100.2
Pagan, Emilio	.190	Tate, Dillon	.142	Adam, Jason	.148	Clase, Emmanuel	99.6
Bautista, Felix	.200	Burke, Brock	.143	Romano, Jordan	.162	Bautista, Felix	99.2
De Los Santos, Enyel	.200	Coleman, Dylan	.169	Duran, Jhoan	.169	Soto, Gregory	98.4
Neris, Hector	.200	Moore, Matt	.172	Hentges, Sam	.172	Stanek, Ryne	98.4
Barlow, Scott	.203	Hentges, Sam	.182	Burke, Brock	.177	Lopez, Jorge	97.7
Barnes, Matt	.205	Duran, Jhoan	.188	Coleman, Dylan	.181	Hendriks, Liam	97.6
Tate, Dillon	.209	Barlow, Scott	.190	Phelps, David	.183	Coleman, Dylan	97.6
Clarke, Taylor	.213	Chafin, Andrew	.198	King, Michael	.185	Abreu, Bryan	97.2

Fastest Average Fastball (minimum 120 IP)		Slowest Average Fastball (minimum 120 IP)		Pitches 100+ Velocity		Pitches 95+ Velocity	
Cole, Gerrit	97.8	Gonzales, Marco	88.5	Duran, Jhoan	451	Cole, Gerrit	1695
Ohtani, Shohei	97.3	Kluber, Corey	88.9	Clase, Emmanuel	298	Gilbert, Logan	1538
Cease, Dylan	96.8	Irvin, Cole	90.6	Bautista, Felix	281	Castillo, Luis	1379
McClanahan, Shane	96.8	Bieber, Shane	91.3	Munoz, Andres	262	Cease, Dylan	1253
Gilbert, Logan	96.2	Lyles, Jordan	91.5	Abreu, Albert	243	Montas, Frankie	1068
Verlander, Justin	95.1	McKenzie, Triston	92.5	Soto, Gregory	147	Gray, Jon	959
Gausman, Kevin	95.0	Perez, Martin	92.7	Cole, Gerrit	116	Verlander, Justin	914
Taillon, Jameson	94.2	Ray, Robbie	93.4	Chapman, Aroldis	83	Kirby, George	905
Valdez, Framber	94.0	Pivetta, Nick	93.5	Ohtani, Shohei	74	Gausman, Kevin	889
Berrios, Jose	94.0	Urquidy, Jose	93.6	Stanek, Ryne	68	Soto, Gregory	852

Pitches Less Than 80 MPH		Lowest % Fastballs (minimum 120 IP)		Highest % Fastballs (minimum 120 IP)		Highest % Curveballs (minimum 120 IP)	
Hill, Rich	944	Kluber, Corey	28.3	Manoah, Alek	62.0	Berrios, Jose	30.9
Gonzales, Marco	836	Ohtani, Shohei	31.3	Ray, Robbie	60.3	Valdez, Framber	27.8
Pivetta, Nick	791	Bieber, Shane	34.5	Irvin, Cole	59.0	Pivetta, Nick	27.1
Yarbrough, Ryan	650	McClanahan, Shane	35.6	McKenzie, Triston	56.1	Kluber, Corey	26.8
Bundy, Dylan	576	Gonzales, Marco	36.7	Gilbert, Logan	55.3	McClanahan, Shane	23.5
Keuchel, Dallas	552	Cease, Dylan	40.7	Berrios, Jose	53.7	McKenzie, Triston	21.9
Voth, Austin	542	Perez, Martin	43.4	Valdez, Framber	52.8	Verlander, Justin	18.8
Valdez, Framber	493	Taillon, Jameson	46.8	Urquidy, Jose	52.7	Bieber, Shane	17.9
Dunning, Dane	483	Quantrill, Cal	47.9	Cole, Gerrit	51.9	Taillon, Jameson	14.8
Javier, Cristian	472	Gausman, Kevin	48.8	Pivetta, Nick	51.0	Urquidy, Jose	14.0

2022 American League Pitching Leaders

Highest % Changeups
(minimum 120 IP)

Gonzales, Marco	30.5
Perez, Martin	27.7
Irvin, Cole	18.2
Berrios, Jose	15.4
Urquidy, Jose	14.9
Quantrill, Cal	11.9
Manoah, Alek	10.9
Lyles, Jordan	10.8
Kluber, Corey	10.2
Valdez, Framber	8.8

Highest % Sliders
(minimum 120 IP)

Cease, Dylan	42.9
Ohtani, Shohei	39.0
Ray, Robbie	37.2
Quantrill, Cal	36.1
Verlander, Justin	28.3
Bieber, Shane	27.9
Manoah, Alek	27.1
Gilbert, Logan	24.2
Lyles, Jordan	23.9
Cole, Gerrit	22.8

Balks

Cole, Gerrit	2
Gausman, Kevin	2
Gray, Jon	2
Hill, Rich	2
Kopech, Michael	2
Lopez, Jorge	2
Lynch, Daniel	2
Perez, Martin	2
Robles, Hansel	2
Thielbar, Caleb	2

Strikeout/Hit Ratio
(minimum 50 IP)

Adam, Jason	2.42
Bautista, Felix	2.32
Sewald, Paul	2.25
Munoz, Andres	2.23
Javier, Cristian	2.18
Abreu, Bryan	1.96
Hendriks, Liam	1.93
King, Michael	1.89
Cease, Dylan	1.80
2 tied with	1.79

Opp OPS vs Fastballs
(minimum 251 BF)

Verlander, Justin	.459
Cortes, Nestor	.468
Ryan, Joe	.545
Javier, Cristian	.559
McKenzie, Triston	.569
Manoah, Alek	.570
Kirby, George	.614
Kopech, Michael	.619
Valdez, Framber	.629
Cease, Dylan	.636

Opp OPS vs Curveballs
(minimum 100 BF)

McClanahan, Shane	.443
Verlander, Justin	.471
McKenzie, Triston	.488
Gray, Sonny	.515
Moore, Matt	.581
Lange, Alex	.596
Greinke, Zack	.599
Bieber, Shane	.611
Valdez, Framber	.614
Voth, Austin	.616

Opp OPS vs Changeups
(minimum 100 BF)

Peralta, Wandy	.542
Richards, Trevor	.583
Beeks, Jalen	.600
Irvin, Cole	.606
Quantrill, Cal	.620
Springs, Jeffrey	.630
Perez, Martin	.641
Wacha, Michael	.647
Stripling, Ross	.662
Cueto, Johnny	.693

Opp OPS vs Sliders
(minimum 64 BF)

Herget, Jimmy	.326
Adam, Jason	.351
Clase, Emmanuel	.351
Munoz, Andres	.363
Cease, Dylan	.445
Abreu, Bryan	.462
Ohtani, Shohei	.472
Javier, Cristian	.475
Stephan, Trevor	.476
Jimenez, Joe	.477

Earned Runs

Berrios, Jose	100
Pivetta, Nick	91
Giolito, Lucas	88
Lyles, Jordan	88
Gonzales, Marco	84
Bubic, Kris	80
Irvin, Cole	80
Keller, Brad	79
Kluber, Corey	79
2 tied with	78

Hits Per Nine Innings
(minimum 120 IP)

Javier, Cristian	5.39
Verlander, Justin	5.97
Cortes, Nestor	6.14
Cease, Dylan	6.16
McClanahan, Shane	6.28
McKenzie, Triston	6.49
Manoah, Alek	6.59
Ohtani, Shohei	6.72
Cole, Gerrit	6.91
Ryan, Joe	7.04

2022 National League Pitching Leaders

Earned Run Average (minimum 162 IP)		Winning Percentage (minimum 15 Decisions)		Opponent Batting Average (minimum 120 IP)		Baserunners Per 9 IP (minimum 120 IP)	
Urias, Julio	2.16	Gonsolin, Tony	.941	Gonsolin, Tony	.172	Gonsolin, Tony	8.15
Alcantara, Sandy	2.28	Wright, Kyle	.808	Strider, Spencer	.180	Kershaw, Clayton	8.62
Fried, Max	2.48	Kershaw, Clayton	.800	Gallen, Zac	.186	Gallen, Zac	8.80
Gallen, Zac	2.54	Woodruff, Brandon	.765	Burnes, Corbin	.197	Scherzer, Max	8.86
Anderson, Tyler	2.57	Anderson, Tyler	.750	Urias, Julio	.199	Urias, Julio	8.90
Rodon, Carlos	2.88	Gallen, Zac	.750	Rodon, Carlos	.202	Nola, Aaron	9.04
Webb, Logan	2.90	Urias, Julio	.708	Kershaw, Clayton	.206	Darvish, Yu	9.11
Quintana, Jose	2.93	Walker, Taijuan	.706	Scherzer, Max	.207	Strider, Spencer	9.16
Musgrove, Joe	2.93	Scherzer, Max	.688	Darvish, Yu	.207	Alcantara, Sandy	9.17
Burnes, Corbin	2.94	Strider, Spencer	.688	Alcantara, Sandy	.212	Burnes, Corbin	9.27

Games		Games Started		Complete Games		Shutouts	
Brebbia, John	76	Burnes, Corbin	33	Alcantara, Sandy	6	Alcantara, Sandy	1
Minter, A.J.	75	Kelly, Merrill	33	Nola, Aaron	2	Buehler, Walker	1
Boxberger, Brad	70	Alcantara, Sandy	32	11 tied with	1	Elder, Bryce	1
Cishek, Steve	69	Lopez, Pablo	32			Greene, Hunter	1
Mantiply, Joe	69	Mikolas, Miles	32			Kuhl, Chad	1
Doval, Camilo	68	Nola, Aaron	32			Montgomery, Jordan	1
Rogers, Tyler	68	Quintana, Jose	32			Nola, Aaron	1
Milner, Hoby	67	Wainwright, Adam	32				
Scott, Tanner	67	Webb, Logan	32				
4 tied with	66	8 tied with	31				

Wins		Losses		No Decisions		Wild Pitches	
Wright, Kyle	21	Corbin, Patrick	19	Davies, Zach	20	Nelson, Nick	13
Urias, Julio	17	Bumgarner, Madison	15	Quintana, Jose	19	Contreras, Roansy	11
Darvish, Yu	16	Fedde, Erick	13	Morton, Charlie	16	Burnes, Corbin	10
Gonsolin, Tony	16	Greene, Hunter	13	Gallen, Zac	15	Rodon, Carlos	10
Anderson, Tyler	15	Marquez, German	13	7 tied with	13	Ashcraft, Graham	9
Bassitt, Chris	15	Mikolas, Miles	13			Fried, Max	9
Carrasco, Carlos	15	Nola, Aaron	13			Marquez, German	8
Webb, Logan	15	6 tied with	12			Moronta, Reyes	8
3 tied with	14					11 tied with	7

Strikeouts		Walks Allowed		Intentional Walks Allowed		Hit Batters	
Burnes, Corbin	243	Gray, Josiah	66	Leone, Dominic	5	Lodolo, Nick	19
Rodon, Carlos	237	Marquez, German	63	Alvarado, Jose	4	Morton, Charlie	18
Nola, Aaron	235	Morton, Charlie	63	Givens, Mychal	4	Freeland, Kyle	16
Alcantara, Sandy	207	Hudson, Dakota	61	Minor, Mike	4	Musgrove, Joe	14
Morton, Charlie	205	Kelly, Merrill	61	Stephens, Jackson	4	Bassitt, Chris	13
Strider, Spencer	202	Keller, Mitch	60	13 tied with	3	Burnes, Corbin	13
Darvish, Yu	197	Lauer, Eric	59			Cishek, Steve	13
Gallen, Zac	192	Fedde, Erick	58			4 tied with	12
Woodruff, Brandon	190	Kuhl, Chad	58				
Musgrove, Joe	184	Suarez, Ranger	58				

2022 National League Pitching Leaders

Runs Allowed

Corbin, Patrick	119
Marquez, German	109
Gibson, Kyle	98
Bumgarner, Madison	97
Freeland, Kyle	96
Manaea, Sean	95
Kuhl, Chad	91
Brubaker, JT	85
Morton, Charlie	85
2 tied with	84

Hits Allowed

Corbin, Patrick	210
Freeland, Kyle	193
Wainwright, Adam	192
Marquez, German	185
Bumgarner, Madison	179
Gibson, Kyle	176
Alcantara, Sandy	174
Webb, Logan	174
Mikolas, Miles	170
Nola, Aaron	168

Doubles Allowed

Bumgarner, Madison	50
Freeland, Kyle	47
Marquez, German	44
Kelly, Merrill	40
Brubaker, JT	39
Lopez, Pablo	39
Nola, Aaron	39
Suarez, Ranger	39
Carrasco, Carlos	38
Webb, Logan	38

Home Runs Allowed

Gray, Josiah	38
Marquez, German	30
Manaea, Sean	29
Morton, Charlie	28
Corbin, Patrick	27
Lauer, Eric	27
Bumgarner, Madison	25
Kuhl, Chad	25
Mikolas, Miles	25
4 tied with	24

Run Support Per Nine IP
(minimum 120 IP)

Wright, Kyle	6.29
Wainwright, Adam	5.64
Urias, Julio	5.40
Gibson, Kyle	5.37
Bassitt, Chris	5.35
Webb, Logan	5.33
Morton, Charlie	5.18
Anderson, Tyler	5.14
Kelly, Merrill	5.08
Freeland, Kyle	4.95

% Pitches In Strike Zone
(minimum 120 IP)

Darvish, Yu	46.2
Bassitt, Chris	44.1
Mikolas, Miles	43.8
Wright, Kyle	43.3
Marquez, German	43.2
Urias, Julio	43.2
Rodon, Carlos	41.8
Anderson, Tyler	41.3
Nola, Aaron	41.1
Alcantara, Sandy	40.9

Pitches Per Start
(minimum 20 GS)

Alcantara, Sandy	101.5
Burnes, Corbin	99.2
Darvish, Yu	99.0
Wainwright, Adam	97.9
Snell, Blake	97.5
Mikolas, Miles	97.3
Rodon, Carlos	96.3
Bassitt, Chris	96.2
Nola, Aaron	95.0
Gallen, Zac	94.7

Pitches Per Batter
(minimum 120 IP)

Anderson, Tyler	3.64
Marquez, German	3.64
Wright, Kyle	3.65
Alcantara, Sandy	3.67
Corbin, Patrick	3.68
Brubaker, JT	3.69
Manaea, Sean	3.70
Freeland, Kyle	3.71
Kershaw, Clayton	3.74
Carrasco, Carlos	3.74

Quality Starts

Darvish, Yu	25
Alcantara, Sandy	24
Mikolas, Miles	22
Burnes, Corbin	21
Fried, Max	21
Musgrove, Joe	21
5 tied with	19

Batters Faced

Alcantara, Sandy	886
Nola, Aaron	807
Mikolas, Miles	805
Kelly, Merrill	804
Wainwright, Adam	803
Burnes, Corbin	797
Webb, Logan	787
Marquez, German	779
Darvish, Yu	771
Freeland, Kyle	766

Innings Pitched

Alcantara, Sandy	228.2
Nola, Aaron	205.0
Mikolas, Miles	202.1
Burnes, Corbin	202.0
Kelly, Merrill	200.1
Darvish, Yu	194.2
Webb, Logan	192.1
Wainwright, Adam	191.2
Fried, Max	185.1
Gallen, Zac	184.0

Most Pitches in a Game

Mikolas, Miles	129
Anderson, Tyler	123
Castillo, Luis	123
Mahle, Tyler	119
Greene, Hunter	118
Alcantara, Sandy	117
Gray, Josiah	117
Snell, Blake	117
Hendricks, Kyle	116
5 tied with	115

Stolen Bases Allowed

Alcantara, Sandy	24
Ottavino, Adam	19
Rodon, Carlos	18
Fedde, Erick	17
Keller, Mitch	17
Minor, Mike	16
Bumgarner, Madison	15
Cobb, Alex	15
Freeland, Kyle	15
Kelly, Merrill	15

Caught Stealing Off

Nola, Aaron	8
Freeland, Kyle	6
Wainwright, Adam	6
8 tied with	5

Stolen Base Pct Allowed
(minimum 162 IP)

Fried, Max	42.9
Gibson, Kyle	50.0
Mikolas, Miles	50.0
Burnes, Corbin	55.6
Urias, Julio	55.6
Wainwright, Adam	57.1
Nola, Aaron	57.9
Quintana, Jose	60.0
Wright, Kyle	60.0
Gallen, Zac	66.7

Pickoffs

Walker, Taijuan	5
Kelly, Merrill	4
Alcantara, Sandy	3
Corbin, Patrick	3
Davies, Zach	3
Fried, Max	3
Minter, A.J.	3
Morton, Charlie	3
Peterson, David	3
Snell, Blake	3

2022 National League Pitching Leaders

Strikeouts Per 9 IP		Opp On-Base Percentage		Opp Slugging Average		Opponent OPS	
(minimum 120 IP)		(minimum 120 IP)		(minimum 120 IP)		(minimum 120 IP)	
Strider, Spencer	13.81	Gonsolin, Tony	.237	Strider, Spencer	.264	Strider, Spencer	.517
Snell, Blake	12.02	Kershaw, Clayton	.246	Gonsolin, Tony	.299	Gonsolin, Tony	.536
Rodon, Carlos	11.98	Urias, Julio	.251	Gallen, Zac	.307	Kershaw, Clayton	.556
Greene, Hunter	11.75	Gallen, Zac	.252	Rodon, Carlos	.308	Gallen, Zac	.560
Woodruff, Brandon	11.15	Strider, Spencer	.254	Kershaw, Clayton	.310	Rodon, Carlos	.571
Burnes, Corbin	10.83	Scherzer, Max	.254	Scherzer, Max	.319	Scherzer, Max	.574
Morton, Charlie	10.73	Darvish, Yu	.256	Fried, Max	.319	Fried, Max	.581
Scherzer, Max	10.71	Nola, Aaron	.256	Alcantara, Sandy	.324	Darvish, Yu	.587
Nola, Aaron	10.32	Burnes, Corbin	.261	Darvish, Yu	.331	Alcantara, Sandy	.588
Kershaw, Clayton	9.76	Fried, Max	.262	Burnes, Corbin	.341	Urias, Julio	.599

Home Runs Per Nine IP		Batting Average vs. LHB		Batting Average vs. RHB		Opp BA w/ RISP	
(minimum 120 IP)		(minimum 125 BF)		(minimum 225 BF)		(minimum 125 BF)	
Quintana, Jose	0.43	Peralta, Freddy	.145	Strider, Spencer	.156	Gray, Josiah	.165
Strider, Spencer	0.48	Gallen, Zac	.146	Gonsolin, Tony	.184	Fried, Max	.167
Webb, Logan	0.51	Gonsolin, Tony	.163	Luzardo, Jesus	.189	Musgrove, Joe	.189
Cobb, Alex	0.54	Cabrera, Edward	.168	Burnes, Corbin	.190	Suarez, Ranger	.194
Hudson, Dakota	0.58	Robertson, David	.168	Kershaw, Clayton	.198	Walker, Taijuan	.217
Fried, Max	0.58	Bard, Daniel	.174	Urias, Julio	.204	Rodon, Carlos	.218
Rodon, Carlos	0.61	Leiter Jr., Mark	.176	Rodon, Carlos	.207	Wright, Kyle	.221
Alcantara, Sandy	0.63	Urias, Julio	.178	Heaney, Andrew	.210	Kelly, Merrill	.221
Anderson, Tyler	0.71	Rodon, Carlos	.179	Stroman, Marcus	.210	Bassitt, Chris	.224
Kershaw, Clayton	0.71	Darvish, Yu	.185	Snell, Blake	.213	Burnes, Corbin	.227

OBP vs. Leadoff Hitter		Strikeouts / Walks Ratio		Highest GB/FB Ratio		Lowest GB/FB Ratio	
(minimum 120 BF)		(minimum 120 IP)		(minimum 120 IP)		(minimum 120 IP)	
Strider, Spencer	.200	Nola, Aaron	8.10	Webb, Logan	2.38	Rodon, Carlos	0.77
Burnes, Corbin	.203	Scherzer, Max	7.21	Wright, Kyle	2.10	Darvish, Yu	0.84
Alcantara, Sandy	.207	Kershaw, Clayton	5.96	Alcantara, Sandy	1.74	Urias, Julio	0.88
Gallen, Zac	.213	Darvish, Yu	5.32	Fried, Max	1.73	Anderson, Tyler	0.95
Scherzer, Max	.216	Fried, Max	5.31	Marquez, German	1.49	Morton, Charlie	1.03
Lauer, Eric	.221	Wheeler, Zack	4.79	Quintana, Jose	1.49	Kelly, Merrill	1.13
Mikolas, Miles	.233	Burnes, Corbin	4.77	Bassitt, Chris	1.44	Freeland, Kyle	1.18
Stroman, Marcus	.239	Rodon, Carlos	4.56	Burnes, Corbin	1.40	Nola, Aaron	1.19
Woodruff, Brandon	.245	Woodruff, Brandon	4.52	Lopez, Pablo	1.39	Musgrove, Joe	1.23
Darvish, Yu	.246	Strider, Spencer	4.49	Gibson, Kyle	1.36	Gallen, Zac	1.27

Sacrifice Flies Allowed		Sacrifice Hits Allowed		GIDP Induced		GIDP Per Nine IP	
						(minimum 120 IP)	
Freeland, Kyle	9	Okert, Steven	4	Hudson, Dakota	25	Hudson, Dakota	1.61
Nelson, Nick	9	Anderson, Tyler	3	Wright, Kyle	25	Keller, Mitch	1.25
Davies, Zach	8	Boxberger, Brad	3	Quintana, Jose	23	Quintana, Jose	1.25
Mikolas, Miles	8	Bruihl, Justin	3	Bassitt, Chris	22	Wright, Kyle	1.25
Alexander, Jason	7	Hudson, Dakota	3	Keller, Mitch	22	Bassitt, Chris	1.09
Marquez, German	7	Kuhl, Chad	3	Webb, Logan	22	Carrasco, Carlos	1.07
Wood, Alex	7	Milner, Hoby	3	Alcantara, Sandy	21	Marquez, German	1.04
10 tied with	6	Nola, Aaron	3	Marquez, German	21	Webb, Logan	1.03
		Scherzer, Max	3	Freeland, Kyle	19	Freeland, Kyle	0.98
		Senzatela, Antonio	3	2 tied with	18	Thompson, Zach	0.96

2022 National League Pitching Leaders

Saves			Blown Saves			Save Pct			Save Opportunities	
						(minimum 20 Save Ops)				
Jansen, Kenley	41		Rogers, Taylor	10		Bard, Daniel	91.9		Jansen, Kenley	48
Hader, Josh	36		Robertson, David	8		Diaz, Edwin	91.4		Rogers, Taylor	41
Bard, Daniel	34		Boxberger, Brad	7		Doval, Camilo	90.0		Hader, Josh	40
Diaz, Edwin	32		Jansen, Kenley	7		Hader, Josh	90.0		Bard, Daniel	37
Rogers, Taylor	31		Scott, Tanner	7		Melancon, Mark	85.7		Diaz, Edwin	35
Doval, Camilo	27		Crowe, Wil	6		Jansen, Kenley	85.4		Doval, Camilo	30
Kimbrel, Craig	22		Gallegos, Giovanny	6		Bednar, David	82.6		Robertson, David	28
Robertson, David	20		Kennedy, Ian	6		Helsley, Ryan	82.6		Kimbrel, Craig	27
Scott, Tanner	20		Mantiply, Joe	6		Kimbrel, Craig	81.5		Scott, Tanner	27
2 tied with	19		4 tied with	5		Rogers, Taylor	75.6		2 tied with	23

Easy Saves			Regular Saves			Tough Saves			Holds Adjusted Saves %	
									(minimum 20 Save Ops + Holds)	
Jansen, Kenley	34		Bard, Daniel	14		Doval, Camilo	3		Garcia, Luis	95.7
Hader, Josh	24		Diaz, Edwin	14		Diaz, Alexis	2		Williams, Devin	95.3
Kimbrel, Craig	21		Hader, Josh	12		Finnegan, Kyle	2		Alvarado, Jose	92.3
Rogers, Taylor	21		Robertson, David	12		Hughes, Brandon	2		Diaz, Edwin	92.3
Bard, Daniel	19		Bednar, David	9		Santillan, Tony	2		Dominguez, Seranthony	92.3
Diaz, Edwin	18		Rogers, Taylor	9		26 tied with	1		Bard, Daniel	91.9
Doval, Camilo	18		Helsley, Ryan	8					Phillips, Evan	91.3
Scott, Tanner	15		4 tied with	7					Minter, A.J.	90.7
Melancon, Mark	11								Doval, Camilo	90.3
Helsley, Ryan	10								2 tied with	90.0

Relief Wins			Relief Losses			Relief Games			Holds	
Stratton, Chris	10		Crowe, Wil	10		Minter, A.J.	75		Minter, A.J.	34
Helsley, Ryan	9		Melancon, Mark	10		Boxberger, Brad	70		Boxberger, Brad	29
Diaz, Alexis	7		Rogers, Taylor	8		Cishek, Steve	69		Williams, Devin	26
Givens, Mychal	7		Colome, Alex	7		Mantiply, Joe	69		Alvarado, Jose	22
Phillips, Evan	7		Kennedy, Ian	7		Doval, Camilo	68		Mantiply, Joe	22
11 tied with	6		Kimbrel, Craig	7		Rogers, Tyler	68		Garcia, Luis	19
			Wick, Rowan	7		Milner, Hoby	67		Okert, Steven	19
			Doval, Camilo	6		Scott, Tanner	67		Phillips, Evan	19
			Gallegos, Giovanny	6		4 tied with	66		Brebbia, John	18
			Garcia, Luis	6					Ottavino, Adam	18

Relief Innings			Inherited Runners Scrd %			Relief Opp On Base Pct			Relief Opp Slugging Avg	
			(minimum 25 IR)			(minimum 50 IP)			(minimum 50 IP)	
Ramirez, Erasmo	80.1		Milner, Hoby	13.5		Helsley, Ryan	.201		Williams, Devin	.205
Rogers, Tyler	75.2		Effross, Scott	14.3		Phillips, Evan	.219		Phillips, Evan	.211
Crowe, Wil	74.0		Diaz, Alexis	14.8		Diaz, Edwin	.230		Diaz, Alexis	.216
De Jong, Chase	71.2		Hughes, Brandon	17.2		Lee, Dylan	.249		Diaz, Edwin	.216
Minter, A.J.	70.0		Martin, Chris	18.5		Martin, Chris	.249		Helsley, Ryan	.237
McHugh, Collin	69.1		Chacin, Jhoulys	23.5		Minter, A.J.	.249		Bard, Daniel	.245
Smith, Caleb	69.0		Lawrence, Justin	25.0		Gallegos, Giovanny	.256		Vesia, Alex	.247
Doval, Camilo	67.2		Vesia, Alex	25.9		Bard, Daniel	.257		Alvarado, Jose	.289
Finnegan, Kyle	66.2		McHugh, Collin	26.3		McHugh, Collin	.257		Robertson, David	.298
Suter, Brent	66.2		Ramirez, Erasmo	27.3		Diaz, Alexis	.260		McHugh, Collin	.299

2022 National League Pitching Leaders

Relief Opp BA Vs LHB (minimum 50 AB)	
Diaz, Edwin	.101
Vesia, Alex	.130
Minter, A.J.	.132
Effross, Scott	.137
Helsley, Ryan	.141
Lee, Dylan	.158
Diaz, Alexis	.158
Knebel, Corey	.163
Finnegan, Kyle	.163
2 tied with	.167

Relief Opp BA Vs RHB (minimum 50 AB)	
Diaz, Alexis	.107
Williams, Devin	.110
Helsley, Ryan	.118
Thompson, Zack	.121
Long, Sammy	.122
Phillips, Evan	.142
Bard, Daniel	.147
Okert, Steven	.152
Matzek, Tyler	.153
Bass, Anthony	.155

Relief Opp Batting Average (minimum 50 IP)	
Helsley, Ryan	.128
Diaz, Alexis	.131
Williams, Devin	.151
Phillips, Evan	.155
Diaz, Edwin	.160
Bard, Daniel	.162
Robertson, David	.173
Okert, Steven	.186
Vesia, Alex	.187
Leiter Jr., Mark	.192

Relief Earned Run Average (minimum 50 IP)	
Phillips, Evan	1.14
Helsley, Ryan	1.25
Diaz, Edwin	1.31
Bard, Daniel	1.79
Diaz, Alexis	1.84
Williams, Devin	1.93
Ottavino, Adam	2.06
Minter, A.J.	2.06
Lee, Dylan	2.13
Vesia, Alex	2.15

Rel OBP 1st Batter Faced (minimum 40 BF)	
Estevez, Carlos	.161
Effross, Scott	.178
Jansen, Kenley	.185
Dominguez, Seranthony	.185
Lee, Dylan	.196
Bass, Anthony	.200
Gott, Trevor	.200
Minter, A.J.	.200
Diaz, Alexis	.220
Garcia, Luis	.222

Rel Opp BA w/ Runners On (minimum 50 IP)	
Helsley, Ryan	.104
Diaz, Edwin	.133
Bard, Daniel	.152
Okert, Steven	.159
Williams, Devin	.163
Diaz, Alexis	.163
Robertson, David	.170
Phillips, Evan	.176
Vesia, Alex	.179
Hughes, Brandon	.184

Relief Opp BA w/ RISP (minimum 50 IP)	
Diaz, Edwin	.093
Robertson, David	.102
Hughes, Brandon	.136
Bard, Daniel	.148
De Jong, Chase	.153
McHugh, Collin	.161
Diaz, Alexis	.162
Helsley, Ryan	.163
Phillips, Evan	.163
Machado, Andres	.172

Fastest Avg Fastball-Relief (minimum 50 IP)	
Helsley, Ryan	99.7
Alvarado, Jose	99.6
Diaz, Edwin	99.1
Doval, Camilo	99.0
Garcia, Luis	98.7
Bard, Daniel	98.0
Dominguez, Seranthony	98.0
Estevez, Carlos	97.6
Hader, Josh	97.5
Finnegan, Kyle	97.1

Fastest Average Fastball (minimum 120 IP)	
Alcantara, Sandy	97.9
Burnes, Corbin	96.3
Rodon, Carlos	95.6
Marquez, German	95.4
Darvish, Yu	95.0
Morton, Charlie	94.9
Wright, Kyle	94.7
Gallen, Zac	94.2
Fried, Max	93.9
Lopez, Pablo	93.6

Slowest Average Fastball (minimum 120 IP)	
Wainwright, Adam	88.5
Freeland, Kyle	90.0
Anderson, Tyler	90.5
Quintana, Jose	91.3
Gibson, Kyle	91.8
Webb, Logan	91.9
Nola, Aaron	92.6
Kelly, Merrill	92.7
Musgrove, Joe	92.9
Bassitt, Chris	92.9

Pitches 100+ Velocity	
Greene, Hunter	482
Hicks, Jordan	346
Helsley, Ryan	303
Alvarado, Jose	281
Doval, Camilo	244
Strider, Spencer	218
Graterol, Brusdar	217
Diaz, Edwin	165
deGrom, Jacob	145
Garcia, Luis	143

Pitches 95+ Velocity	
Alcantara, Sandy	1632
Strider, Spencer	1522
Burnes, Corbin	1505
Woodruff, Brandon	1416
Castillo, Luis	1379
Rodon, Carlos	1374
Wheeler, Zack	1234
Ashcraft, Graham	1230
Greene, Hunter	1175
Snell, Blake	1169

Pitches Less Than 80 MPH	
Quintana, Jose	1382
Wainwright, Adam	1006
Espino, Paolo	856
Mikolas, Miles	686
Nola, Aaron	675
Bassitt, Chris	649
Fried, Max	606
Anderson, Tyler	567
Smyly, Drew	544
Voth, Austin	542

Lowest % Fastballs (minimum 120 IP)	
Burnes, Corbin	7.1
Musgrove, Joe	31.3
Darvish, Yu	34.0
Webb, Logan	36.3
Wainwright, Adam	37.0
Gibson, Kyle	40.4
Wright, Kyle	43.5
Morton, Charlie	44.1
Anderson, Tyler	45.1
Freeland, Kyle	45.4

Highest % Fastballs (minimum 120 IP)	
Rodon, Carlos	61.2
Marquez, German	54.1
Quintana, Jose	52.4
Nola, Aaron	52.4
Alcantara, Sandy	50.0
Mikolas, Miles	49.6
Urias, Julio	49.2
Gallen, Zac	48.1
Bassitt, Chris	46.6
Lopez, Pablo	46.6

Highest % Curveballs (minimum 120 IP)	
Morton, Charlie	38.0
Wright, Kyle	34.1
Urias, Julio	33.3
Wainwright, Adam	31.9
Nola, Aaron	26.5
Marquez, German	23.1
Quintana, Jose	22.4
Gallen, Zac	22.0
Fried, Max	21.6
Mikolas, Miles	21.1

2022 National League Pitching Leaders

Highest % Changeups
(minimum 120 IP)

Lopez, Pablo	35.3
Anderson, Tyler	31.6
Webb, Logan	31.0
Alcantara, Sandy	27.7
Kelly, Merrill	21.3
Quintana, Jose	19.5
Urias, Julio	17.5
Wright, Kyle	15.4
Nola, Aaron	14.6
Gallen, Zac	14.3

Highest % Sliders
(minimum 120 IP)

Webb, Logan	32.7
Rodon, Carlos	31.0
Mikolas, Miles	25.3
Musgrove, Joe	24.4
Freeland, Kyle	22.6
Alcantara, Sandy	22.1
Gibson, Kyle	20.8
Marquez, German	20.0
Fried, Max	18.5
Darvish, Yu	15.8

Balks

Bleier, Richard	3
Brubaker, JT	2
Crismatt, Nabil	2
Lauer, Eric	2
Marquez, German	2
Sanmartin, Reiver	2
Smith, Will	2
Stroman, Marcus	2
Suarez, Ranger	2
36 tied with	1

Strikeout/Hit Ratio
(minimum 50 IP)

Diaz, Edwin	3.47
Helsley, Ryan	3.36
Williams, Devin	3.10
Diaz, Alexis	2.96
deGrom, Jacob	2.55
Strider, Spencer	2.35
Phillips, Evan	2.33
Vesia, Alex	2.14
Alvarado, Jose	2.13
Robertson, David	2.08

Opp OPS vs Fastballs
(minimum 251 BF)

Gallen, Zac	.528
Nola, Aaron	.534
Strider, Spencer	.534
Scherzer, Max	.550
Wheeler, Zack	.575
Rodon, Carlos	.591
Urias, Julio	.593
Fried, Max	.611
Mikolas, Miles	.611
Kelly, Merrill	.629

Opp OPS vs Curveballs
(minimum 100 BF)

Fried, Max	.471
Gallen, Zac	.536
Burnes, Corbin	.551
Quintana, Jose	.553
Brubaker, JT	.579
Mikolas, Miles	.595
Urias, Julio	.600
Marquez, German	.609
Wright, Kyle	.617
Nola, Aaron	.640

Opp OPS vs Changeups
(minimum 100 BF)

Alcantara, Sandy	.416
Williams, Devin	.499
Cabrera, Edward	.513
Anderson, Tyler	.530
Martinez, Nick	.547
Wright, Kyle	.555
Webb, Logan	.589
Davies, Zach	.604
Gallen, Zac	.609
2 tied with	.610

Opp OPS vs Sliders
(minimum 64 BF)

Diaz, Edwin	.339
Gonsolin, Tony	.425
Scherzer, Max	.461
Alvarado, Jose	.463
Darvish, Yu	.473
Strider, Spencer	.473
McHugh, Collin	.497
Doval, Camilo	.501
Castillo, Luis	.502
deGrom, Jacob	.502

Earned Runs

Corbin, Patrick	107
Marquez, German	100
Gibson, Kyle	94
Freeland, Kyle	88
Kuhl, Chad	87
Manaea, Sean	87
Bumgarner, Madison	86
Gray, Josiah	83
Morton, Charlie	83
Fedde, Erick	82

Hits Per Nine Innings
(minimum 120 IP)

Gonsolin, Tony	5.46
Strider, Spencer	5.88
Gallen, Zac	5.92
Burnes, Corbin	6.42
Urias, Julio	6.53
Rodon, Carlos	6.62
Scherzer, Max	6.69
Darvish, Yu	6.84
Kershaw, Clayton	6.84
Alcantara, Sandy	6.85

2022 American League Fielding Leaders

2B Pivot %
(minimum 98 G)

Schoop, Jonathan	0.833
Rengifo, Luis	0.714
Frazier, Adam	0.694
Odor, Rougned	0.658
Altuve, Jose	0.600
Gimenez, Andres	0.595
Torres, Gleyber	0.582
Espinal, Santiago	0.561
Semien, Marcus	0.509

SS Pivot %
(minimum 98 G)

Mateo, Jorge	0.710
Correa, Carlos	0.605
Pena, Jeremy	0.585
Seager, Corey	0.578
Bogaerts, Xander	0.577
Andrus, Elvis	0.577
Velazquez, Andrew	0.563
Witt Jr., Bobby	0.542
Crawford, J.P.	0.532
Kiner-Falefa, Isiah	0.523

Highest Pct CS by Catchers
(minimum 500 INN or 50 SBA)

Higashioka, Kyle	32.1
Perez, Salvador	32.1
Rutschman, Adley	30.6
McGuire, Reese	30.4
Haase, Eric	28.9
Chirinos, Robinson	26.7
Maldonado, Martin	25.8
Kirk, Alejandro	25.5
Maile, Luke	25.0
Sanchez, Gary	25.0

Lowest Pct CS by Catchers
(minimum 500 INN or 50 SBA)

Grandal, Yasmani	13.2
Hedges, Austin	16.1
Heim, Jonah	17.4
Mejia, Francisco	18.2
Stassi, Max	18.5
Murphy, Sean	19.2
Jansen, Danny	23.1
Trevino, Jose	23.1
Raleigh, Cal	23.2
Melendez, MJ	23.7

2B Double Play %
(minimum 98 G)

Rengifo, Luis	0.681
Schoop, Jonathan	0.658
Frazier, Adam	0.636
Odor, Rougned	0.593
Gimenez, Andres	0.545
Altuve, Jose	0.538
Semien, Marcus	0.474
Espinal, Santiago	0.462
Torres, Gleyber	0.443

3B Double Play %
(minimum 98 G)

Urias, Ramon	0.590
Bregman, Alex	0.565
Chapman, Matt	0.493
Urshela, Gio	0.490
Ramirez, Jose	0.481
Diaz, Yandy	0.472
Moncada, Yoan	0.410
Devers, Rafael	0.373
Suarez, Eugenio	0.357
Candelario, Jeimer	0.356

SS Double Play %
(minimum 98 G)

Mateo, Jorge	0.652
Bogaerts, Xander	0.597
Baez, Javier	0.595
Crawford, J.P.	0.587
Correa, Carlos	0.578
Pena, Jeremy	0.569
Kiner-Falefa, Isiah	0.566
Velazquez, Andrew	0.551
Andrus, Elvis	0.548
Rosario, Amed	0.539

Errors

Baez, Javier	26
Bichette, Bo	23
Pena, Jeremy	19
Witt Jr., Bobby	19
Mateo, Jorge	17
Seager, Corey	17
Kiner-Falefa, Isiah	16
Odor, Rougned	16
Rengifo, Luis	15
5 tied with	14

Fielding Errors

Witt Jr., Bobby	12
Bichette, Bo	11
Abreu, Jose	10
Harrison, Josh	10
Mateo, Jorge	10
Neuse, Sheldon	10
Pena, Jeremy	10
Seager, Corey	10
5 tied with	9

Throwing Errors

Baez, Javier	17
Bichette, Bo	12
Walls, Taylor	11
Rengifo, Luis	10
Rosario, Amed	10
Devers, Rafael	9
Pena, Jeremy	9
Donaldson, Josh	8
Odor, Rougned	8
8 tied with	7

Range Factor for 2B
(minimum 98 games)

Gimenez, Andres	4.55
Rengifo, Luis	4.53
Semien, Marcus	4.52
Odor, Rougned	4.46
Schoop, Jonathan	4.23
Frazier, Adam	3.89
Espinal, Santiago	3.84
Torres, Gleyber	3.84
Altuve, Jose	3.35

Range Factor for 3B
(minimum 98 games)

Donaldson, Josh	2.97
Urias, Ramon	2.94
Devers, Rafael	2.88
Chapman, Matt	2.86
Bregman, Alex	2.69
Suarez, Eugenio	2.66
Urshela, Gio	2.65
Ramirez, Jose	2.64
Moncada, Yoan	2.56
Candelario, Jeimer	2.51

Range Factor for SS
(minimum 98 games)

Baez, Javier	4.34
Mateo, Jorge	4.28
Seager, Corey	4.17
Bogaerts, Xander	4.12
Witt Jr., Bobby	4.05
Andrus, Elvis	3.97
Pena, Jeremy	3.81
Correa, Carlos	3.75
Velazquez, Andrew	3.75
Rosario, Amed	3.68

2022 National League Fielding Leaders

2B Pivot %		SS Pivot %		Highest Pct CS by Catchers		Lowest Pct CS by Catchers	
(minimum 98 G)		(minimum 98 G)		(minimum 500 INN or 50 SBA)		(minimum 500 INN or 50 SBA)	
Cronenworth, Jake	0.759	Lindor, Francisco	0.688	Realmuto, J.T.	41.5	Nola, Austin	8.2
Lux, Gavin	0.640	Farmer, Kyle	0.641	Molina, Yadier	31.0	Contreras, William	10.0
Rodgers, Brendan	0.636	Hoerner, Nico	0.625	Gomes, Yan	30.2	Alfaro, Jorge	10.7
Estrada, Thairo	0.614	Iglesias, Jose	0.609	Contreras, Willson	27.3	Smith, Will	11.5
McNeil, Jeff	0.609	Adames, Willy	0.561	Ruiz, Keibert	26.1	Stallings, Jacob	14.1
Hernandez, Cesar	0.605	Rojas, Miguel	0.558	Caratini, Victor	23.1	Bart, Joey	16.4
Wong, Kolten	0.538	Swanson, Dansby	0.527	Knizner, Andrew	22.2	d'Arnaud, Travis	18.5
		Perdomo, Geraldo	0.526	Narvaez, Omar	20.5	Kelly, Carson	18.6
		Crawford, Brandon	0.479	Diaz, Elias	20.0	Nido, Tomas	19.4
		Turner, Trea	0.434	Serven, Brian	19.6	Serven, Brian	19.6

2B Double Play %		3B Double Play %		SS Double Play %	
(minimum 98 G)		(minimum 98 G)		(minimum 98 G)	
Rodgers, Brendan	0.625	Wisdom, Patrick	0.551	Farmer, Kyle	0.634
Cronenworth, Jake	0.610	Arenado, Nolan	0.500	Lindor, Francisco	0.606
McNeil, Jeff	0.560	Machado, Manny	0.500	Perdomo, Geraldo	0.600
Lux, Gavin	0.554	McMahon, Ryan	0.452	Iglesias, Jose	0.590
Estrada, Thairo	0.533	Hayes, Ke'Bryan	0.444	Rojas, Miguel	0.578
Hernandez, Cesar	0.524	Escobar, Eduardo	0.391	Adames, Willy	0.569
Wong, Kolten	0.500	Bohm, Alec	0.344	Hoerner, Nico	0.559
		Franco, Maikel	0.302	Kim, Ha-seong	0.538
		Riley, Austin	0.250	Swanson, Dansby	0.525
				Crawford, Brandon	0.508

Errors		Fielding Errors		Throwing Errors	
Cruz, Oneil	17	Riley, Austin	11	Garcia, Luis	13
McMahon, Ryan	17	Wong, Kolten	10	Adames, Willy	11
Wong, Kolten	17	McMahon, Ryan	9	Crawford, Brandon	11
Crawford, Brandon	16	Hayes, Ke'Bryan	8	Cruz, Oneil	10
Garcia, Luis	16	Hoskins, Rhys	8	Rojas, Josh	10
Riley, Austin	16	Olson, Matt	8	Abrams, CJ	9
Rojas, Josh	16	6 tied with	7	Diaz, Elias	9
Turner, Trea	16			Turner, Trea	9
Abrams, CJ	15			4 tied with	8
4 tied with	14				

Range Factor for 2B		Range Factor for 3B		Range Factor for SS	
(minimum 98 games)		(minimum 98 games)		(minimum 98 games)	
Rodgers, Brendan	4.85	Hayes, Ke'Bryan	3.40	Rojas, Miguel	4.23
Estrada, Thairo	4.22	Arenado, Nolan	2.95	Crawford, Brandon	4.14
McNeil, Jeff	4.08	Franco, Maikel	2.77	Hoerner, Nico	3.91
Hernandez, Cesar	3.96	McMahon, Ryan	2.64	Iglesias, Jose	3.88
Wong, Kolten	3.82	Bohm, Alec	2.61	Perdomo, Geraldo	3.86
Cronenworth, Jake	3.72	Wisdom, Patrick	2.52	Adames, Willy	3.84
Lux, Gavin	3.60	Machado, Manny	2.45	Lindor, Francisco	3.81
		Riley, Austin	2.43	Kim, Ha-seong	3.68
		Escobar, Eduardo	2.23	Swanson, Dansby	3.67
				Farmer, Kyle	3.42

2022 Active Career Batting Leaders

Batting Average (minimum 1000 PA)		On Base Percentage (minimum 1000 PA)		Slugging Average (minimum 1000 PA)		Home Runs	
Arraez, Luis	.314	Soto, Juan	.424	Alvarez, Yordan	.590	Pujols, Albert	703
Cabrera, Miguel	.308	Trout, Mike	.415	Trout, Mike	.587	Cabrera, Miguel	507
McNeil, Jeff	.307	Votto, Joey	.412	Judge, Aaron	.583	Cruz, Nelson	459
Altuve, Jose	.307	Judge, Aaron	.394	Pujols, Albert	.544	Stanton, Giancarlo	378
Trout, Mike	.303	Goldschmidt, Paul	.391	Stanton, Giancarlo	.537	Trout, Mike	350
Turner, Trea	.302	Harper, Bryce	.390	Alonso, Pete	.535	Votto, Joey	342
Cano, Robinson	.301	Freeman, Freddie	.386	Arenado, Nolan	.535	Cano, Robinson	335
Freeman, Freddie	.298	Nimmo, Brandon	.385	Ohtani, Shohei	.532	Longoria, Evan	331
Brantley, Michael	.298	Cabrera, Miguel	.384	Goldschmidt, Paul	.527	Upton, Justin	325
Votto, Joey	.297	Alvarez, Yordan	.384	Soto, Juan	.526	Goldschmidt, Paul	315

Games		At Bats		Hits		Total Bases	
Pujols, Albert	3080	Pujols, Albert	11421	Pujols, Albert	3384	Pujols, Albert	6211
Cabrera, Miguel	2699	Cabrera, Miguel	10022	Cabrera, Miguel	3088	Cabrera, Miguel	5250
Cano, Robinson	2267	Cano, Robinson	8773	Cano, Robinson	2639	Cano, Robinson	4282
Molina, Yadier	2226	Molina, Yadier	7817	Molina, Yadier	2168	Cruz, Nelson	3790
Cruz, Nelson	2006	Andrus, Elvis	7398	Votto, Joey	2093	Votto, Joey	3616
Votto, Joey	1991	Cruz, Nelson	7358	Cruz, Nelson	2018	Longoria, Evan	3350
Andrus, Elvis	1947	Longoria, Evan	7095	Andrus, Elvis	1997	McCutchen, Andrew	3299
Longoria, Evan	1912	Votto, Joey	7044	McCutchen, Andrew	1948	Freeman, Freddie	3247
McCutchen, Andrew	1895	McCutchen, Andrew	7035	Altuve, Jose	1935	Upton, Justin	3155
Upton, Justin	1845	Upton, Justin	6721	Freeman, Freddie	1903	Goldschmidt, Paul	3121

Doubles		Triples		Runs Scored		RBI	
Pujols, Albert	686	Blackmon, Charlie	58	Pujols, Albert	1914	Pujols, Albert	2218
Cabrera, Miguel	607	Escobar, Alcides	58	Cabrera, Miguel	1530	Cabrera, Miguel	1847
Cano, Robinson	572	Strange-Gordon, Dee	55	Cano, Robinson	1262	Cano, Robinson	1306
Votto, Joey	453	Kiermaier, Kevin	51	Votto, Joey	1145	Cruz, Nelson	1302
Longoria, Evan	422	Marte, Starling	51	McCutchen, Andrew	1118	Longoria, Evan	1131
Freeman, Freddie	414	Trout, Mike	51	Freeman, Freddie	1086	Votto, Joey	1106
Molina, Yadier	408	Andrus, Elvis	50	Cruz, Nelson	1081	Goldschmidt, Paul	1042
McCutchen, Andrew	392	McCutchen, Andrew	49	Upton, Justin	1058	Freeman, Freddie	1041
Goldschmidt, Paul	382	Peralta, David	47	Trout, Mike	1052	Molina, Yadier	1022
Altuve, Jose	379	Segura, Jean	45	Goldschmidt, Paul	1045	Upton, Justin	1003

Walks		Intentional Walks		Hit By Pitch		Strikeouts	
Pujols, Albert	1373	Pujols, Albert	316	Rizzo, Anthony	201	Cabrera, Miguel	2031
Votto, Joey	1338	Cabrera, Miguel	238	Marte, Starling	146	Upton, Justin	1971
Cabrera, Miguel	1227	Votto, Joey	147	Pujols, Albert	123	Cruz, Nelson	1870
Santana, Carlos	1148	Trout, Mike	117	Suzuki, Kurt	119	Stanton, Giancarlo	1696
McCutchen, Andrew	983	Freeman, Freddie	114	Abreu, Jose	117	Longoria, Evan	1623
Trout, Mike	919	Cano, Robinson	112	Turner, Justin	111	Votto, Joey	1578
Goldschmidt, Paul	916	Harper, Bryce	112	Canha, Mark	108	Goldschmidt, Paul	1545
Harper, Bryce	879	Goldschmidt, Paul	108	Wong, Kolten	98	McCutchen, Andrew	1542
Freeman, Freddie	860	Longoria, Evan	87	Blackmon, Charlie	93	Martinez, J.D.	1424
Upton, Justin	785	Stanton, Giancarlo	83	2 tied with	92	Freeman, Freddie	1414

2022 Active Career Batting Leaders

Sacrifice Hits		Sacrifice Flies		Stolen Bases		Seasons Played	
Kershaw, Clayton	110	Pujols, Albert	123	Strange-Gordon, Dee	336	Pujols, Albert	22
Andrus, Elvis	103	Cabrera, Miguel	100	Andrus, Elvis	335	Cabrera, Miguel	20
Cueto, Johnny	90	Longoria, Evan	94	Hamilton, Billy	324	Perez, Oliver	20
Escobar, Alcides	87	Molina, Yadier	75	Marte, Starling	314	Greinke, Zack	19
Wainwright, Adam	74	Suzuki, Kurt	67	Altuve, Jose	279	Molina, Yadier	19
Strasburg, Stephen	56	McCutchen, Andrew	66	Villar, Jonathan	239	Cruz, Nelson	18
Scherzer, Max	49	Cano, Robinson	62	Turner, Trea	230	Hill, Rich	18
Greinke, Zack	47	Arenado, Nolan	61	McCutchen, Andrew	205	Cano, Robinson	17
Hamilton, Billy	44	Cruz, Nelson	59	Segura, Jean	205	Verlander, Justin	17
Morton, Charlie	44	Upton, Justin	59	Trout, Mike	204	Wainwright, Adam	17

At Bats Per Home Run (minimum 1000 AB)		Grounded Into DP		Highest SB Success Pct (minimum 100 SBA)		Lowest SB Success Pct (minimum 100 SBA)	
Judge, Aaron	12.0	Pujols, Albert	426	Trout, Mike	84.6	Odor, Rougned	57.1
Gallo, Joey	13.4	Cabrera, Miguel	353	Turner, Trea	84.6	Rizzo, Anthony	63.7
Alonso, Pete	13.4	Molina, Yadier	287	Mondesi, Adalberto	83.6	Molina, Yadier	65.7
Alvarez, Yordan	13.6	Cano, Robinson	286	Yelich, Christian	83.0	Springer, George	66.0
Stanton, Giancarlo	13.9	Longoria, Evan	198	Betts, Mookie	82.3	LeMahieu, DJ	66.4
Schwarber, Kyle	14.0	Andrus, Elvis	186	Hamilton, Billy	81.8	Hernandez, Cesar	69.5
Trout, Mike	14.6	Cruz, Nelson	177	Goldschmidt, Paul	81.7	Margot, Manuel	69.5
Olson, Matt	15.1	Altuve, Jose	171	Pollock, A.J.	81.3	McCutchen, Andrew	70.9
Sanchez, Gary	15.3	Abreu, Jose	167	Cain, Lorenzo	81.2	Harrison, Josh	71.1
Sano, Miguel	15.4	Martinez, J.D.	167	Anderson, Tim	80.6	Blackmon, Charlie	71.1

Strikeouts / Walks Ratio (minimum 1000 AB)		At Bats Per GIDP (minimum 1000 AB)		OPS (minimum 1000 PA)		Secondary Average (minimum 1000 PA)	
Soto, Juan	.882	Gallo, Joey	197.0	Trout, Mike	1.002	Trout, Mike	.505
Arraez, Luis	.956	Buxton, Byron	195.5	Judge, Aaron	.977	Soto, Juan	.495
Pujols, Albert	1.023	Mullins II, Cedric	176.0	Alvarez, Yordan	.973	Judge, Aaron	.493
Bregman, Alex	1.075	Kingery, Scott	173.7	Soto, Juan	.950	Gallo, Joey	.459
Santana, Carlos	1.085	Hamilton, Billy	157.2	Votto, Joey	.926	Harper, Bryce	.447
Diaz, Yandy	1.169	Lowe, Brandon	154.2	Pujols, Albert	.918	Alvarez, Yordan	.431
Votto, Joey	1.179	Meadows, Austin	148.6	Goldschmidt, Paul	.917	Ohtani, Shohei	.429
Ramirez, Jose	1.211	Moncada, Yoan	142.6	Harper, Bryce	.913	Muncy, Max	.429
La Stella, Tommy	1.250	Albies, Ozzie	138.3	Cabrera, Miguel	.908	Acuna Jr., Ronald	.426
Winker, Jesse	1.326	Biggio, Cavan	135.1	Freeman, Freddie	.895	Schwarber, Kyle	.423

Highest Strikeout per PA (minimum 1000 PA)		Lowest Strikeout per PA (minimum 1000 PA)		Plate Appearances		At Bats Per RBI (minimum 1000 AB)	
Gallo, Joey	.373	Arraez, Luis	.083	Pujols, Albert	13041	Alvarez, Yordan	4.7
Sano, Miguel	.364	Fletcher, David	.096	Cabrera, Miguel	11426	Pujols, Albert	5.1
Hiura, Keston	.360	Simmons, Andrelton	.096	Cano, Robinson	9550	Alonso, Pete	5.2
Zunino, Mike	.347	Brantley, Michael	.108	Molina, Yadier	8554	Smith, Will	5.2
Davidson, Matt	.343	Molina, Yadier	.108	Votto, Joey	8504	Judge, Aaron	5.3
Alfaro, Jorge	.341	Pujols, Albert	.108	Cruz, Nelson	8244	Stanton, Giancarlo	5.4
Cave, Jake	.323	La Stella, Tommy	.111	Andrus, Elvis	8197	Cabrera, Miguel	5.4
Chavis, Michael	.317	Gurriel, Yuli	.112	McCutchen, Andrew	8168	Tucker, Kyle	5.4
Souza Jr., Steven	.317	Newman, Kevin	.117	Longoria, Evan	7969	Arenado, Nolan	5.4
Goodrum, Niko	.313	McNeil, Jeff	.119	Upton, Justin	7649	Olson, Matt	5.6

2022 Active Career Pitching Leaders

Earned Run Average
(minimum 750 IP)

Jansen, Kenley	2.46
Kershaw, Clayton	2.48
deGrom, Jacob	2.53
Sale, Chris	3.03
Scherzer, Max	3.11
Smith, Joe	3.14
Clippard, Tyler	3.16
Cole, Gerrit	3.24
Verlander, Justin	3.24
Strasburg, Stephen	3.25

Winning Percentage
(minimum 100 Decisions)

Kershaw, Clayton	.694
Scherzer, Max	.663
Price, David	.657
Verlander, Justin	.647
Cole, Gerrit	.647
Strasburg, Stephen	.646
Ryu, Hyun-Jin	.625
Wainwright, Adam	.625
Kluber, Corey	.614
Greinke, Zack	.613

Opponent Batting Average
(minimum 750 IP)

Jansen, Kenley	.179
Clippard, Tyler	.199
Kershaw, Clayton	.209
deGrom, Jacob	.211
Darvish, Yu	.217
Sale, Chris	.219
Scherzer, Max	.220
Snell, Blake	.221
Strasburg, Stephen	.223
Verlander, Justin	.225

Baserunners Per 9 IP
(minimum 750 IP)

Jansen, Kenley	8.77
deGrom, Jacob	9.13
Kershaw, Clayton	9.15
Sale, Chris	9.93
Scherzer, Max	10.03
Cole, Gerrit	10.16
Strasburg, Stephen	10.19
Clippard, Tyler	10.33
Verlander, Justin	10.35
Kluber, Corey	10.35

Games

Smith, Joe	866
Romo, Sergio	821
Clippard, Tyler	807
Jansen, Kenley	766
Shaw, Bryan	753
Cishek, Steve	737
Melancon, Mark	732
Robertson, David	731
Kimbrel, Craig	709
Perez, Oliver	702

Games Started

Greinke, Zack	514
Verlander, Justin	482
Scherzer, Max	421
Kershaw, Clayton	398
Wainwright, Adam	390
Cueto, Johnny	353
Bumgarner, Madison	351
Sanchez, Anibal	341
Morton, Charlie	322
Price, David	322

Complete Games

Wainwright, Adam	28
Verlander, Justin	26
Kershaw, Clayton	25
Cueto, Johnny	18
Kluber, Corey	18
Greinke, Zack	17
Price, David	17
Bumgarner, Madison	16
Sale, Chris	16
2 tied with	12

Shutouts

Kershaw, Clayton	15
Wainwright, Adam	11
Verlander, Justin	9
Cueto, Johnny	8
Kluber, Corey	8
Bumgarner, Madison	7
Sanchez, Anibal	7
Greinke, Zack	5
Miller, Shelby	5
Scherzer, Max	5

Wins

Verlander, Justin	244
Greinke, Zack	223
Scherzer, Max	201
Kershaw, Clayton	197
Wainwright, Adam	195
Price, David	157
Cueto, Johnny	143
Bumgarner, Madison	134
Cole, Gerrit	130
Lynn, Lance	123

Losses

Greinke, Zack	141
Verlander, Justin	133
Bumgarner, Madison	121
Sanchez, Anibal	119
Wainwright, Adam	117
Kennedy, Ian	113
Cueto, Johnny	107
Corbin, Patrick	103
Scherzer, Max	102
Morton, Charlie	101

Innings Pitched

Greinke, Zack	3247.0
Verlander, Justin	3163.0
Scherzer, Max	2682.0
Kershaw, Clayton	2581.0
Wainwright, Adam	2567.1
Bumgarner, Madison	2192.2
Cueto, Johnny	2192.2
Price, David	2143.2
Sanchez, Anibal	2017.2
Kennedy, Ian	1888.0

Batters Faced

Greinke, Zack	13284
Verlander, Justin	12880
Scherzer, Max	10831
Wainwright, Adam	10632
Kershaw, Clayton	10160
Cueto, Johnny	9105
Bumgarner, Madison	9008
Price, David	8807
Sanchez, Anibal	8607
Kennedy, Ian	8025

Strikeouts

Verlander, Justin	3198
Scherzer, Max	3193
Greinke, Zack	2882
Kershaw, Clayton	2807
Wainwright, Adam	2147
Price, David	2076
Sale, Chris	2064
Bumgarner, Madison	2060
Cole, Gerrit	1930
Cueto, Johnny	1812

Walks Allowed

Verlander, Justin	880
Perez, Oliver	762
Greinke, Zack	739
Scherzer, Max	701
Wainwright, Adam	695
Sanchez, Anibal	686
Kennedy, Ian	640
Morton, Charlie	639
Kershaw, Clayton	629
Cueto, Johnny	619

Hit Batters

Morton, Charlie	156
Cueto, Johnny	117
Scherzer, Max	107
Verlander, Justin	104
Sale, Chris	103
Bumgarner, Madison	88
Perez, Oliver	88
Kennedy, Ian	82
Wainwright, Adam	80
Lynn, Lance	76

Wild Pitches

Greinke, Zack	99
Kershaw, Clayton	95
Gray, Sonny	91
Verlander, Justin	90
Richards, Garrett	87
Kennedy, Ian	79
Darvish, Yu	76
Scherzer, Max	74
Archer, Chris	72
Chapman, Aroldis	68

2022 Active Career Pitching Leaders

Saves		Save Pct		Home Runs Allowed		Strikeouts Per 9 IP	
		(minimum 50 Save Ops)				(minimum 750 IP)	
Kimbrel, Craig	394	Soto, Gregory	89.3	Greinke, Zack	342	Jansen, Kenley	12.96
Jansen, Kenley	391	Chapman, Aroldis	89.2	Verlander, Justin	322	Sale, Chris	11.07
Chapman, Aroldis	315	Kimbrel, Craig	89.1	Scherzer, Max	300	Ray, Robbie	11.04
Melancon, Mark	262	Britton, Zack	88.5	Kennedy, Ian	276	Snell, Blake	10.95
Holland, Greg	220	Giles, Ken	88.5	Bumgarner, Madison	254	deGrom, Jacob	10.91
Diaz, Edwin	205	Romano, Jordan	88.4	Sanchez, Anibal	238	Darvish, Yu	10.82
Colome, Alex	159	Jansen, Kenley	88.3	Cueto, Johnny	232	Scherzer, Max	10.72
Iglesias, Raisel	157	Clase, Emmanuel	88.2	Price, David	221	Strasburg, Stephen	10.55
Robertson, David	157	Holland, Greg	87.3	Wainwright, Adam	213	Cole, Gerrit	10.53
Britton, Zack	154	Diaz, Edwin	86.9	Kershaw, Clayton	206	Nola, Aaron	10.11

Opp On-Base Percentage		Opp Slugging Average		Hits Per Nine Innings		Home Runs Per Nine IP	
(minimum 750 IP)		(minimum 750 IP)		(minimum 750 IP)		(minimum 750 IP)	
Jansen, Kenley	.247	Jansen, Kenley	.296	Jansen, Kenley	5.79	Kershaw, Clayton	0.72
deGrom, Jacob	.259	Kershaw, Clayton	.321	Clippard, Tyler	6.45	Wainwright, Adam	0.75
Kershaw, Clayton	.261	deGrom, Jacob	.327	Kershaw, Clayton	6.82	Kelly, Joe	0.77
Sale, Chris	.275	Smith, Joe	.348	deGrom, Jacob	6.93	Smith, Joe	0.78
Scherzer, Max	.277	Sale, Chris	.353	Darvish, Yu	7.23	deGrom, Jacob	0.79
Strasburg, Stephen	.281	Strasburg, Stephen	.355	Sale, Chris	7.31	Wheeler, Zack	0.81
Cole, Gerrit	.282	Clippard, Tyler	.356	Snell, Blake	7.31	Syndergaard, Noah	0.82
Clippard, Tyler	.282	Wheeler, Zack	.358	Scherzer, Max	7.32	Jansen, Kenley	0.83
Verlander, Justin	.283	Gray, Sonny	.359	Strasburg, Stephen	7.45	Morton, Charlie	0.83
Kluber, Corey	.285	Verlander, Justin	.360	Verlander, Justin	7.55	Richards, Garrett	0.85

Strikeouts / Walks Ratio		Stolen Base Pct Allowed		GIDP Induced		GIDP Per Nine IP	
(minimum 750 IP)		(minimum 750 IP)				(minimum 750 IP)	
Sale, Chris	5.33	Cueto, Johnny	45.6	Greinke, Zack	253	Perez, Martin	1.21
deGrom, Jacob	5.30	Miley, Wade	47.2	Wainwright, Adam	243	Freeland, Kyle	1.11
Jansen, Kenley	4.90	Rodriguez, Eduardo	51.5	Keuchel, Dallas	193	Keuchel, Dallas	1.09
Kluber, Corey	4.85	Kershaw, Clayton	52.7	Gibson, Kyle	181	Gibson, Kyle	1.08
Cole, Gerrit	4.56	Ryu, Hyun-Jin	53.3	Kershaw, Clayton	178	Peralta, Wily	1.05
Scherzer, Max	4.56	Greinke, Zack	53.4	Morton, Charlie	176	Detwiler, Ross	0.99
Kershaw, Clayton	4.46	Wood, Alex	54.9	Perez, Martin	175	Urena, Jose	0.97
Syndergaard, Noah	4.43	Davies, Zach	55.6	Cueto, Johnny	174	Stroman, Marcus	0.96
Strasburg, Stephen	4.37	Wainwright, Adam	57.3	Verlander, Justin	168	Hunter, Tommy	0.92
Pineda, Michael	4.37	Boyd, Matthew	58.2	Price, David	155	Ryu, Hyun-Jin	0.90

Complete Game %		Quality Start Pct		Walks Per 9 IP		Games Finished	
(minimum 100 GS)		(minimum 100 GS)		(minimum 750 IP)			
Alcantara, Sandy	0.08	deGrom, Jacob	73.7	Kluber, Corey	1.97	Jansen, Kenley	573
Wainwright, Adam	0.07	Kershaw, Clayton	71.1	Pineda, Michael	1.97	Kimbrel, Craig	567
Kluber, Corey	0.07	Bieber, Shane	68.5	Ryu, Hyun-Jin	1.99	Chapman, Aroldis	484
Sale, Chris	0.07	Verlander, Justin	67.8	Hendricks, Kyle	2.02	Melancon, Mark	454
Kershaw, Clayton	0.06	Sale, Chris	67.1	Hunter, Tommy	2.04	Holland, Greg	355
Verlander, Justin	0.05	Cole, Gerrit	66.7	Greinke, Zack	2.05	Cishek, Steve	312
Price, David	0.05	Scherzer, Max	65.1	deGrom, Jacob	2.06	Robertson, David	310
Cueto, Johnny	0.05	Alcantara, Sandy	63.6	Sale, Chris	2.08	Diaz, Edwin	307
Keuchel, Dallas	0.05	Price, David	63.0	Syndergaard, Noah	2.08	Iglesias, Raisel	300
Carrasco, Carlos	0.05	Wainwright, Adam	62.1	Milone, Tommy	2.16	Romo, Sergio	300

2022 American League Bill James Leaders

Top Game Scores

Pitcher	Date	Opp	IP	H	R	ER	BB	SO	GS
Bradish, Kyle, Bal	9/22	Hou	8.2	2	0	0	0	10	90
Cease, Dylan, CWS	9/3	Min	9.0	1	0	0	2	7	90
Ohtani, Shohei, LAA	6/22	KC	8.0	2	0	0	1	13	90
Gausman, Kevin, Tor	8/2	TB	8.0	1	0	0	1	10	89
Javier, Cristian, Hou	6/25	NYY	7.0	0	0	0	1	13	89
Detmers, Reid, LAA	5/10	TB	9.0	0	0	0	1	2	88
Sandoval, Patrick, LAA	8/19	Det	9.0	4	0	0	0	9	88
Ohtani, Shohei, LAA	9/29	Oak	8.0	2	0	0	1	10	87
Pivetta, Nick, Bos	5/18	Hou	9.0	2	1	1	0	8	87
Cease, Dylan, CWS	5/2	LAA	7.0	1	0	0	0	11	86
Cortes, Nestor, NYY	10/1	Bal	7.1	1	0	0	2	12	86
Wacha, Michael, Bos	6/6	LAA	9.0	3	0	0	1	6	86

Worst Game Scores

Pitcher	Date	Opp	IP	H	R	ER	BB	SO	GS
Arihara, Kohei, Tex	9/10	Tor	3.0	12	11	11	5	1	-13
Keuchel, Dallas, CWS	4/20	Cle	1.0	10	10	7	1	0	-2
Hatch, Thomas, Tor	7/2	TB	4.2	12	10	10	2	4	2
Rodriguez, Elvin, Det	6/3	NYY	4.1	11	10	10	2	4	3
Bundy, Dylan, Min	5/4	Bal	3.2	11	9	9	2	3	4
Martin, Davis, CWS	10/5	Min	1.2	7	9	9	2	1	4
Patino, Luis, TB	9/11	NYY	1.1	5	9	9	4	0	4
Crawford, Kutter, Bos	8/19	Bal	3.2	11	9	9	0	2	5
Blackburn, Paul, Oak	7/24	Tex	4.1	10	10	10	2	5	6
Martinez, Adrian, Oak	9/10	CWS	3.2	14	7	7	1	2	6

Runs Created

Judge, Aaron	173
Ramirez, Jose	129
Ohtani, Shohei	113
Lowe, Nathaniel	107
Alvarez, Yordan	105
Devers, Rafael	102
Altuve, Jose	101
Guerrero Jr., Vladimir	101
Suarez, Eugenio	99
Trout, Mike	99

Runs Created Per 27 Outs

Judge, Aaron	11.1
Alvarez, Yordan	8.1
Ramirez, Jose	7.6
Altuve, Jose	7.0
Gimenez, Andres	6.9
Ohtani, Shohei	6.8
Lowe, Nathaniel	6.7
Devers, Rafael	6.6
Rodriguez, Julio	6.4
Ward, Taylor	6.1

Offensive Winning %

Judge, Aaron	.857
Alvarez, Yordan	.768
Ramirez, Jose	.749
Altuve, Jose	.740
Gimenez, Andres	.736
Arraez, Luis	.714
Diaz, Yandy	.707
Lowe, Nathaniel	.704
Rodriguez, Julio	.702
Ohtani, Shohei	.700

Secondary Average
(minimum 502 PA)

Judge, Aaron	.598
Alvarez, Yordan	.474
Rizzo, Anthony	.394
Altuve, Jose	.393
Ohtani, Shohei	.387
Ramirez, Jose	.383
Tucker, Kyle	.375
Suarez, Eugenio	.357
Bregman, Alex	.356
Rodriguez, Julio	.352

Isolated Power
(minimum 502 PA)

Judge, Aaron	.375
Alvarez, Yordan	.306
Rizzo, Anthony	.256
Ohtani, Shohei	.246
Ramirez, Jose	.235
Altuve, Jose	.233
Devers, Rafael	.225
Rodriguez, Julio	.225
Hernandez, Teoscar	.224
Suarez, Eugenio	.223

Power / Speed Number
(minimum 502 PA)

Tucker, Kyle	27.3
Rodriguez, Julio	26.4
Garcia, Adolis	26.0
Semien, Marcus	25.5
Judge, Aaron	25.4
Arozarena, Randy	24.6
Witt Jr., Bobby	24.0
Ramirez, Jose	23.7
Altuve, Jose	21.9
Mullins II, Cedric	21.8

Speed Scores

Mullins II, Cedric	8.08
Straw, Myles	7.86
Merrifield, Whit	7.46
Lopez, Nicky	7.15
Anderson, Tim	7.12
Rosario, Amed	7.10
Semien, Marcus	7.02
Ramirez, Jose	6.98
Springer, George	6.86
Garcia, Adolis	6.81

Cheap Wins

Garcia, Luis	6
Gilbert, Logan	4
Gonzales, Marco	4
Kluber, Corey	3
Quantrill, Cal	3
Taillon, Jameson	3
Urquidy, Jose	3
12 tied with	2

Tough Losses

McKenzie, Triston	7
Bieber, Shane	5
Cole, Gerrit	5
Gausman, Kevin	5
Gilbert, Logan	5
Gonzales, Marco	5
Montas, Frankie	5
Syndergaard, Noah	5
7 tied with	4

2022 National League Bill James Leaders

Top Game Scores

Pitcher	Date	Opp	IP	H	R	ER	BB	SO	GS
Strider, Spencer, Atl	9/1	Col	8.0	2	0	0	0	16	94
Mahle, Tyler, Cin	6/14	Ari	9.0	3	0	0	0	12	93
Montgomery, Jordan, StL	8/22	ChC	9.0	1	0	0	0	7	92
Buehler, Walker, LAD	4/25	Ari	9.0	3	0	0	0	10	91
Kershaw, Clayton, LAD	4/13	Min	7.0	0	0	0	0	13	90
Alcantara, Sandy, Mia	7/5	LAA	8.0	2	0	0	0	10	88
Nola, Aaron, Phi	8/25	Cin	9.0	5	0	0	0	11	88
Gallen, Zac, Ari	9/22	LAD	8.0	2	1	1	0	13	87
Rodon, Carlos, SF	7/9	SD	9.0	3	1	1	2	12	87
Burnes, Corbin, Mil	9/8	SF	8.0	3	1	1	0	14	86
Kershaw, Clayton, LAD	7/15	LAA	8.0	1	0	0	0	6	86
Kuhl, Chad, Col	6/27	LAD	9.0	3	0	0	0	5	86

Worst Game Scores

Pitcher	Date	Opp	IP	H	R	ER	BB	SO	GS
Mikolas, Miles, StL	8/9	Col	2.2	14	10	10	0	2	-8
Urena, Jose, Col	8/24	Tex	1.1	9	9	9	3	1	-2
Fedde, Erick, Was	10/5	NYM	2.1	9	9	9	2	1	2
Darvish, Yu, SD	4/12	SF	1.2	8	9	9	2	2	3
Szapucki, Thomas, NYM	5/25	SF	1.1	7	9	9	3	2	3
Eickhoff, Jerad, Pit	6/22	ChC	4.1	10	10	10	1	4	6
Gomber, Austin, Col	5/28	Was	1.1	7	8	8	3	1	6
Megill, Tylor, NYM	5/11	Was	1.1	8	8	8	1	1	6
Walker, Taijuan, NYM	8/5	Atl	1.0	7	8	8	0	0	7
Lopez, Pablo, Mia	9/10	NYM	3.2	10	8	8	3	2	8
Sanmartin, Reiver, Cin	4/26	SD	3.0	8	9	9	1	2	8
Urena, Jose, Col	7/28	LAD	3.0	8	10	7	3	2	8

Runs Created

Goldschmidt, Paul	132
Freeman, Freddie	129
Alonso, Pete	125
Machado, Manny	118
Riley, Austin	108
Schwarber, Kyle	108
Arenado, Nolan	106
Betts, Mookie	106
Turner, Trea	106
Olson, Matt	103

Runs Created Per 27 Outs

Goldschmidt, Paul	8.9
Freeman, Freddie	8.0
Machado, Manny	7.4
Alonso, Pete	7.2
Arenado, Nolan	6.8
Betts, Mookie	6.5
McNeil, Jeff	6.3
Soto, Juan	6.3
Drury, Brandon	6.2
2 tied with	6.2

Offensive Winning %

Goldschmidt, Paul	.799
Freeman, Freddie	.768
Machado, Manny	.751
McNeil, Jeff	.721
Alonso, Pete	.709
Arenado, Nolan	.700
Nimmo, Brandon	.684
Soto, Juan	.675
Riley, Austin	.663
Canha, Mark	.657

Secondary Average
(minimum 502 PA)

Soto, Juan	.479
Schwarber, Kyle	.452
Goldschmidt, Paul	.414
Muncy, Max	.386
Betts, Mookie	.381
Alonso, Pete	.367
Tellez, Rowdy	.363
Olson, Matt	.359
Machado, Manny	.358
Walker, Christian	.357

Isolated Power
(minimum 502 PA)

Schwarber, Kyle	.286
Betts, Mookie	.264
Goldschmidt, Paul	.260
Riley, Austin	.255
Alonso, Pete	.246
Tellez, Rowdy	.242
Arenado, Nolan	.241
Olson, Matt	.237
Renfroe, Hunter	.236
Walker, Christian	.235

Power / Speed Number
(minimum 502 PA)

Turner, Trea	23.6
Realmuto, J.T.	21.5
Swanson, Dansby	20.9
Varsho, Daulton	20.1
Lindor, Francisco	19.8
Acuna Jr., Ronald	19.8
Edman, Tommy	18.5
Betts, Mookie	17.9
Marte, Starling	16.9
Estrada, Thairo	16.8

Speed Scores

Edman, Tommy	8.03
Albies, Ozzie	7.38
Bellinger, Cody	7.19
Taylor, Chris	7.09
Betts, Mookie	6.93
Yastrzemski, Mike	6.93
Turner, Trea	6.89
Wong, Kolten	6.79
Realmuto, J.T.	6.71
Varsho, Daulton	6.61

Cheap Wins

Suarez, Ranger	5
Walker, Taijuan	4
Corbin, Patrick	3
Lauer, Eric	3
Minor, Mike	3
Morton, Charlie	3
Sanchez, Aaron	3
10 tied with	2

Tough Losses

Nola, Aaron	7
Keller, Mitch	6
Mikolas, Miles	6
Bassitt, Chris	5
Greene, Hunter	5
Alcantara, Sandy	4
Burnes, Corbin	4
Cobb, Alex	4
Rodon, Carlos	4
Snell, Blake	4

Additional Bill James Leaders

Top AL Batter Game Scores

Batter	Date	Opp	AB	R	H	HR	RBI	RC	GS
Story, Trevor, Bos	5/19	Sea	4	5	4	3	7	6.54	140
Rizzo, Anthony, NYY	4/26	Bal	4	4	3	3	6	5.28	118
Bregman, Alex, Hou	8/18	CWS	6	4	4	2	6	5.15	117
Guerrero Jr., Vladimir, Tor	4/13	NYY	4	3	4	3	4	6.15	111
Moncada, Yoan, CWS	9/8	Oak	6	3	5	2	5	5.54	110
Carpenter, Matt, NYY	6/12	ChC	4	3	3	2	7	4.54	110
Naylor, Josh, Cle	5/9	CWS	5	2	3	2	8	4.29	108
Paredes, Isaac, TB	6/21	NYY	3	3	3	3	4	5.51	105
Judge, Aaron, NYY	9/18	Mil	5	3	4	2	4	5.28	103
Alvarez, Yordan, Hou	9/16	Oak	4	3	4	3	3	5.77	103
Jansen, Danny, Tor	7/22	Bos	6	4	3	2	6	3.77	103
Torres, Gleyber, NYY	9/21	Pit	4	4	3	2	5	4.18	102

Worst AL Batter Game Scores

Batter	Date	Opp	AB	R	H	SO	DP	RC	GS
Crawford, J.P., Sea	6/21	Oak	5	0	0	2	2	-1.17	3
Judge, Aaron, NYY	5/24	Bal	5	0	0	2	2	-1.17	3
Espinal, Santiago, Tor	6/24	Mil	5	0	0	1	2	-1.15	3
Robert, Luis, CWS	8/25	Bal	5	0	0	1	2	-1.15	3
Stanton, Giancarlo, NYY	7/2	Cle	5	0	0	1	2	-1.15	3
Mancini, Trey, Hou	10/5	Phi	4	0	0	2	2	-1.10	4
Haniger, Mitch, Sea	9/23	KC	4	0	0	2	2	-1.10	4
Perez, Salvador, KC	5/16	CWS	4	0	0	2	2	-1.10	4
Gurriel, Yuli, Hou	4/17	Sea	4	0	0	1	2	-1.08	4
Hicks, Aaron, NYY	8/2	Sea	4	0	0	1	2	-1.08	4
Odor, Rougned, Bal	5/28	Bos	4	0	0	1	2	-1.08	4
Miranda, Jose, Min	9/15	KC	4	0	0	1	2	-1.08	4

Top NL Batter Game Scores

Batter	Date	Opp	AB	R	H	HR	RBI	RC	GS
Pederson, Joc, SF	5/24	NYM	6	3	4	3	8	5.31	123
Perez, Michael, Pit	6/30	Mil	4	3	4	3	5	5.77	113
Tellez, Rowdy, Mil	5/4	Cin	6	2	4	2	8	4.57	111
Adames, Willy, Mil	4/26	Pit	5	2	4	2	7	4.80	108
Diaz, Elias, Col	9/9	Ari	5	2	4	2	7	4.80	108
Goldschmidt, Paul, StL	6/14	Pit	4	3	4	2	5	5.11	106
Reynolds, Bryan, Pit	6/29	Was	5	3	3	3	6	4.53	105
Rodgers, Brendan, Col	6/1	Mia	5	4	3	3	4	5.03	105
Escobar, Eduardo, NYM	6/6	SD	5	3	4	1	6	4.43	104
Hoskins, Rhys, Phi	6/14	Mia	5	2	4	2	6	4.80	103
Wong, Kolten, Mil	9/22	Cin	4	3	3	3	5	4.77	103
Farmer, Kyle, Cin	5/26	ChC	4	3	4	2	5	4.58	101

Worst NL Batter Game Scores

Batter	Date	Opp	AB	R	H	SO	DP	RC	GS
Hernandez, Cesar, Was	7/9	Atl	5	0	0	2	2	-1.17	3
Contreras, Willson, ChC	4/16	Col	5	0	0	1	2	-1.15	3
Suzuki, Seiya, ChC	4/26	Atl	4	0	0	2	2	-1.10	4
Marte, Starling, NYM	8/16	Atl	4	0	0	2	2	-1.10	4
Reyes, Franmil, ChC	9/12	NYM	4	0	0	2	2	-1.10	4
Belt, Brandon, SF	4/27	Oak	4	0	0	1	2	-1.08	4
Anderson, Brian, Mia	7/5	LAA	4	0	0	1	2	-1.08	4
Pham, Tommy, Cin	4/23	StL	4	0	0	1	2	-1.08	4
Aguilar, Jesus, Mia	6/28	StL	4	0	0	1	2	-1.08	4
Voit, Luke, Was	9/26	Atl	4	0	0	1	2	-1.08	4
Alberto, Hanser, LAD	9/10	SD	4	0	0	1	2	-1.08	4
Rodgers, Brendan, Col	8/6	Ari	4	0	0	1	2	-1.08	4

AL Batters Win Shares

Judge, Aaron	45
Ramirez, Jose	34
Altuve, Jose	29
Gimenez, Andres	29
Bogaerts, Xander	28
Bregman, Alex	26
Rodriguez, Julio	26
Alvarez, Yordan	25
Devers, Rafael	25
Suarez, Eugenio	25

NL Batters Win Shares

Freeman, Freddie	34
Goldschmidt, Paul	34
Machado, Manny	32
Lindor, Francisco	31
McNeil, Jeff	30
Swanson, Dansby	30
Alonso, Pete	29
Cronenworth, Jake	28
Nimmo, Brandon	28
4 tied with	27

AL Pitchers Win Shares

Verlander, Justin	20
Cease, Dylan	19
Manoah, Alek	18
Clase, Emmanuel	17
Ohtani, Shohei	17
Valdez, Framber	16
Bieber, Shane	15
Cortes, Nestor	14
McKenzie, Triston	14
3 tied with	13

NL Pitchers Win Shares

Alcantara, Sandy	22
Fried, Max	17
Urias, Julio	17
Bard, Daniel	16
Gallen, Zac	16
Helsley, Ryan	16
8 tied with	15

Career Batters Win Shares

Pujols, Albert	506
Cabrera, Miguel	428
Cano, Robinson	349
Trout, Mike	341
Votto, Joey	340
McCutchen, Andrew	311
Freeman, Freddie	304
Molina, Yadier	301
Goldschmidt, Paul	285
Cruz, Nelson	266

Career Pitchers Win Shares

Verlander, Justin	258
Greinke, Zack	242
Kershaw, Clayton	227
Scherzer, Max	219
Wainwright, Adam	182
Price, David	152
Jansen, Kenley	151
Sale, Chris	148
Cueto, Johnny	144
Kimbrel, Craig	143

AL Component ERA
(minimum 162 IP)

Verlander, Justin	1.56
McClanahan, Shane	2.07
Ohtani, Shohei	2.21
McKenzie, Triston	2.32
Manoah, Alek	2.34
Cease, Dylan	2.48
Bieber, Shane	2.51
Cole, Gerrit	2.72
Valdez, Framber	2.82
Perez, Martin	3.22

NL Component ERA
(minimum 162 IP)

Gallen, Zac	1.97
Rodon, Carlos	2.17
Alcantara, Sandy	2.19
Fried, Max	2.27
Nola, Aaron	2.30
Urias, Julio	2.33
Darvish, Yu	2.35
Burnes, Corbin	2.38
Anderson, Tyler	2.39
Mikolas, Miles	2.72

Win Shares

Mark Simon

First things first, we must salute the remarkable season by Aaron Judge. His 45 Win Shares were the most by any player in a season since Barry Bonds had 48 for the Giants in 2004.

Judge's 45 Win Shares were triple that of the next-closest player on the Yankees. Anthony Rizzo and Gleyber Torres each had 15.

Contrast that with the team across town. The Mets' leader was Francisco Lindor with 31, good for seventh-most in the majors. But they also had Jeff McNeil (30 Win Shares, tied for 8th), Pete Alonso (29, tied for 10th), and Brandon Nimmo (28, tied for 13th). The Mets were the only team with four players in the Top 15 among position players. The Guardians had two (José Ramírez and Andrés Giménez) and the Padres had two (Manny Machado and Jake Cronenworth).

The Mets also had six position players ranked higher than the Yankees second-ranked players, once we factor in Mark Canha (19) and Starling Marte (17).

That was largely indicative of how things went both for the Yankees and Mets this season. The Yankees excelled when Judge carried them. The Mets took more of a group approach.

If you've forgotten what Win Shares are, that's understandable because it's not a stat that is often publicly shared in 2022. Check page 636 in the Glossary for a brief overview and page 568 for the leaderboards. In short, think of it as a way to measure overall contribution to a team, based on how many wins a team actually earns.

Cronenworth is probably the most surprising highly-ranked position player, but keep in mind that he was pretty good for a second baseman. And he was not easily replaceable. When Cronenworth played second base, he hit

.250 with 16 home runs. All the other Padres who played second base in 2022 hit a combined .145 (11-for-76) with 1 home run.

Shohei Ohtani is unique when it comes to Win Shares, given that he accrues them as both a position player/batter and a pitcher. He had 38 in 2022 (21 as a position player and 17 as a pitcher), matching the total he had in 2021. Judge and Ohtani are tied for the most Win Shares since the start of the 2021 season with 76.

Looking at things a little more long-term, Ramírez is the Win Shares leader over the last five seasons. His 120 edge out Judge (115) and Mike Trout (114). Ramírez is a legitimate star and stands out not just for his ability at the plate but his day-to-day availability. He's played in 90% of his team's games in six of the last seven seasons.

I'd like to close with my favorite Win Shares stat. Trout is MLB's overall leader in Win Shares dating back to 2004. His 341 are one more than Joey Votto's 340.

Trout didn't debut until 2011.

Winning Effort

The A's may have finished with one of the worst records in MLB, but no one sacrificed his body more to try to help his team win than their utility man, Tony Kemp.

Kemp made 46 plays by either diving, sliding, or jumping, easily the most in MLB. Dansby Swanson and Ian Happ tied for second with 34 such plays.

Guardians second baseman Andrés Giménez led the majors in diving, sliding, and jumping attempts this season with 87.

WIN SHARES BY YEAR

Player	<13	13	14	15	16	17	18	19	20	21	22	Career
Abreu, Jose			29	27	20	24	17	20	10	19	21	187
Acuna Jr., Ronald							19	28	9	14	16	86
Adam, Jason							0	3	1	0	10	14
Adames, Willy							8	15	9	22	22	76
Adrianza, Ehire		0	1	3	1	6	7	7	1	5	0	31
Aguilar, Jesus			0	1	0	9	19	7	8	15	8	67
Ahmed, Nick			1	8	3	4	15	17	6	7	1	62
Alberto, Hanser					1	1	0	12	4	5	2	25
Albies, Ozzie						8	18	29	5	25	7	92
Alcantara, Sandy						0	2	12	2	12	22	50
Alfaro, Jorge					0	5	12	10	4	5	6	42
Almora Jr., Albert					5	11	13	3	1	0	3	36
Alonso, Pete								24	5	20	29	78
Altuve, Jose	19	11	30	27	36	35	23	17	2	25	29	254
Alvarez, Jose		0	0	5	3	3	7	6	1	6	1	32
Alvarez, Yordan								14	0	18	25	57
Anderson, Brian						2	27	13	12	8	5	67
Anderson, Chase			6	5	6	14	8	7	0	0	0	46
Anderson, Tim					10	7	13	19	7	23	11	90
Anderson, Tyler						8	5	8	3	7	15	46
Andrus, Elvis	78	15	13	21	26	25	7	17	1	9	18	230
Andujar, Miguel						1	21	0	0	1	2	25
Archer, Chris		0	10	11	14	8	10	6	3	1	2	65
Arcia, Orlando					4	18	5	12	5	2	8	54
Arenado, Nolan		9	12	26	26	26	28	24	2	23	26	202
Arozarena, Randy								1	4	21	19	45
Arraez, Luis								14	7	15	23	59
Arroyo, Christian						1	3	1	2	6	9	22
Bader, Harrison						2	13	9	4	15	10	53
Baez, Javier			2	1	14	15	24	19	3	20	18	116
Baez, Pedro			2	4	6	4	8	2	0			32
Bard, Daniel	23	0							4	7	16	50
Barlow, Scott							1	5	2	14	13	35
Barnes, Austin				1	1	13	3	3	3	4	4	32
Barnes, Matt			0	1	5	7	7	7	2	10	3	42
Barnhart, Tucker			1	4	12	14	9	9	5	11	5	70
Bass, Anthony	6	0	0	3	0		1	5	4	3	9	31
Bassitt, Chris			2	4	0		3	9	6	13	12	49
Bautista, Felix											11	11
Beckham, Tim		0			5	5	20	6	9	0		45
Bednar, David								0	0	9	10	19
Bell, Josh					3	16	15	24	2	12	16	88
Bellinger, Cody						23	19	31	9	3	12	97
Belt, Brandon	22	24	5	20	24	12	14	15	7	17	4	164
Benintendi, Andrew					4	19	24	15	0	16	19	97
Berrios, Jose					0	10	12	13	4	13	4	56
Berti, Jon							0	7	6	3	9	25
Bethancourt, Christian			0	1	1	2	0				10	14
Betts, Mookie			8	23	29	26	36	25	13	18	27	205
Bichette, Bo								6	6	24	21	57
Bieber, Shane							7	19	11	8	15	60
Biggio, Cavan								14	10	5	8	37
Blackmon, Charlie	2	7	16	20	22	33	25	21	7	16	12	181
Bleier, Richard					3	6	3	3	1	6	3	25
Bogaerts, Xander		1	7	22	19	16	27	25	6	25	28	176
Bohm, Alec									8	7	14	29
Bote, David							6	9	5	3	4	27
Boxberger, Brad	2	1	8	8	1	3	6	1	1	8	6	45
Boyd, Matthew				0	5	4	8	10	0	4	2	33
Bradley, Archie				0	6	12	7	9	4	5	1	44
Bradley Jr., Jackie		1	5	10	19	14	16	10	5	5	4	89
Brantley, Michael	37	21	31	21	1	10	16	21	9	13	10	190
Bregman, Alex					10	23	36	31	6	11	26	143
Britton, Zack	9	1	17	15	19	6	5	9	4	0	0	85
Brown, Seth								3	0	6	17	26
Bryant, Kris				30	32	26	15	23	3	19	2	150
Buehler, Walker						0	10	13	2	18	4	47
Bumgarner, Madison	32	12	16	17	19	8	9	11	0	5	3	132
Bundy, Dylan	0				7	11	3	6	5	1	3	36
Burnes, Corbin							5	0	7	16	15	43
Buxton, Byron				2	5	14	1	11	5	14	11	63
Cabrera, Miguel	265	37	28	26	25	7	5	9	9	9	8	428
Cain, Lorenzo	13	12	19	27	13	24	25	11	1	9	1	155
Calhoun, Kole	0	8	20	21	19	17	8	14	7	1	5	120
Camargo, Johan						7	16	5	1	0	4	33
Candelario, Jeimer					0	4	11	4	9	22	9	59
Canha, Mark				12	0	1	12	19	11	20	19	94
Cano, Robinson	178	35	34	21	28	23	18	7	5		0	349
Caratini, Victor						1	2	7	4	6	7	27
Carlson, Dylan									2	20	11	33
Carpenter, Matt	9	35	27	30	21	20	28	11	3	4	11	199
Carrasco, Carlos	8	0	12	14	12	18	15	3	6	0	8	96
Casali, Curt			2	4	2	1	4	6	4	6	5	34
Castellanos, Nick		0	13	13	15	18	26	16	3	20	11	135
Castillo, Diego							5	7	4	8	5	29
Castillo, Luis					6	6	16	6	11	11		56
Castro, Harold							0	6	2	8	13	29
Castro, Jason	12	18	10	7	9	12	1	7	3	6	1	86
Castro, Rodolfo										1	8	9
Cease, Dylan								2	3	11	19	35
Chacin, Jhoulys	26	15	2	2	5	10	12	0	0	6	0	78
Chafin, Andrew			1	8	0	5	4	4	0	10	5	37
Chapman, Aroldis	27	12	13	13	15	9	12	12	10	0	3	126
Chapman, Matt						11	25	25	5	14	20	100
Chavez, Jesse	4	3	7	6	3	3	12	5	0	4	5	52
Chirinos, Robinson	1	0	11	4	6	10	13	11	0	3	5	64
Chisholm Jr., Jazz									1	13	13	27
Choi, Ji-Man					0	1	6	14	4	11	16	52
Cimber, Adam							5	5	1	7	8	26
Cishek, Steve	17	14	10	3	11	6	10	8	1	5	3	88
Clase, Emmanuel									3	15	17	35
Claudio, Alex			1	1	5	12	5	4	1	1	0	30
Clevinger, Mike					2	11	17	14	4		5	53
Clippard, Tyler	40	10	10	9	7	3	7	6	3	2	0	97
Cobb, Alex	9	13	13		0	12	3	0	2	7	8	67
Cole, Gerrit		8	7	18	6	10	16	22	6	16	12	121
Colome, Alex		1	2	6	12	12	9	12	5	5	2	66
Contreras, William									0	3	13	16
Contreras, Willson					9	17	14	13	9	14	18	94
Cooper, Garrett						1	1	9	6	8	12	37
Corbin, Patrick	4	13		5	5	11	15	16	2	1	0	72
Correa, Carlos				18	26	26	12	13	6	23	24	148
Cortes, Nestor							0	1	0	8	14	23
Crawford, Brandon	18	11	22	20	21	13	18	13	6	31	11	184
Crawford, J.P.						2	5	10	8	26	16	67
Cron, C.J.			8	9	14	10	12	12	2	18	16	101
Cronenworth, Jake									7	22	28	57
Cruz, Nelson	82	16	22	26	21	24	22	22	8	16	7	266
Cruz, Oneil										1	13	14
Cueto, Johnny	58	5	22	12	19	6	4	0	2	5	11	144
d'Arnaud, Travis		1	8	11	3	10	1	15	6	3	16	74
Darvish, Yu	14	18	10		8	12	1	9	9	6	15	102
Davies, Zach				2	8	13	1	11	6	2	5	48
Davis, J.D.						1	1	14	4	8	8	36
Daza, Yonathan								1		6	10	17
deGrom, Jacob			11	15	11	11	20	21	6	13	5	113
DeJong, Paul						13	16	20	6	9	4	68
DeSclafani, Anthony			0	7	7		3	10	0	12	0	39
Detmers, Reid										0	8	8
Devenski, Chris					11	10	3	3	0	0	0	27
Devers, Rafael						7	9	24	6	25	25	96
Diaz, Aledmys					18	4	12	7	1	8	8	58
Diaz, Alexis											12	12
Diaz, Edwin					8	10	18	3	4	10	15	68
Diaz, Elias				0	0	2	11	5	1	7	6	32
Diaz, Yandy						3	3	7	5	17	23	58
Dickerson, Alex						0	8	6	5	8	0	27
Dickerson, Corey			4	15	8	18	16	10	3	5	7	95
Diekman, Jake	1	3	4	4	7	2	4	3	4	5	3	40
Difo, Wilmer				0	2	8	6	3	0	6	0	25
Dominguez, Seranthony							12	2		0	8	22
Donaldson, Josh	8	32	27	32	28	25	7	25	3	17	12	216
Donovan, Brendan											18	18
Doolittle, Sean	5	8	11	2	4	11	12	9	0	3	1	66
Doval, Camilo										4	11	15
Dozier, Hunter					0	1	16	3	6	5		31

WIN SHARES BY YEAR

Player	<13	13	14	15	16	17	18	19	20	21	22	Career
Drury, Brandon				0	9	12	0	4	0	2	17	44
Duffey, Tyler				5	0	3	0	6	4	6	1	25
Duffy, Matt			2	22	5		18	4		9	5	65
Duran, Jhoan											10	10
Duvall, Adam			0	2	16	12	5	4	4	19	7	69
Edman, Tommy								12	5	20	23	60
Eflin, Zach					0	0	6	9	3	5	4	27
Eovaldi, Nathan	5	5	4	9	6		5	1	3	14	6	58
Escobar, Alcides	38	10	20	15	13	14	4			11	3	128
Escobar, Eduardo	2	2	13	14	7	14	20	22	2	17	12	125
Espinal, Santiago									2	7	12	21
Estevez, Carlos					5	2		7	0	6	7	27
Estrada, Thairo								3	1	5	17	26
Familia, Jeurys	0	0	9	15	16	2	9	1	2	4	0	58
Farmer, Kyle						0	2	4	2	12	13	33
Flaherty, Jack						0	9	17	2	6	1	35
Fletcher, David							8	18	7	17	5	55
Flores, Wilmer		2	7	16	9	8	11	8	5	12	18	96
Floro, Dylan					0	0	7	3	3	10	6	29
France, Ty								5	7	28	21	61
Franco, Maikel			1	13	17	6	13	7	8	1	3	69
Franco, Wander										15	13	28
Frazier, Adam					5	13	12	15	3	21	12	81
Freeland, Kyle						11	21	0	5	8	11	56
Freeman, Freddie	37	35	28	22	28	22	26	28	17	27	34	304
Fried, Max						1	2	12	5	15	17	52
Fulmer, Michael					14	10	4		0	9	5	42
Gallegos, Giovanny						0	1	9	3	13	8	34
Gallen, Zac								7	7	4	16	34
Gallo, Joey				2	0	16	13	11	6	19	7	74
Gamel, Ben					1	13	9	7	2	8	12	52
Garcia, Adolis							0		0	13	19	32
Garcia, Avisail	1	5	4	10	11	22	6	13	3	17	2	94
Garcia, Leury		2	1	1	1	8	9	8	2	13	3	48
Garcia, Luis		2	0	4	0	8	1	3	0	4	5	27
Garcia, Luis									1	11	9	21
Garcia, Luis									3	3	9	15
Garver, Mitch						1	11	18	1	9	3	43
Gausman, Kevin		1	6	5	12	9	9	1	4	16	11	74
Gibson, Kyle		0	8	12	4	7	13	7	2	11	5	69
Gilbert, Logan										5	12	17
Giles, Ken			7	11	6	12	5	11	0		1	53
Gimenez, Andres									3	6	29	38
Giolito, Lucas					0	4	1	15	5	13	6	44
Givens, Mychal				4	7	10	5	5	1	7	4	43
Glasnow, Tyler					1	1	4	8	4	7	1	26
Goldschmidt, Paul	23	36	20	35	25	29	25	21	9	28	34	285
Gomes, Yan	2	14	18	5	4	12	9	8	2	9	4	87
Gonsolin, Tony								4	4	4	14	26
Gonzales, Marco			2	0		1	10	11	5	9	6	44
Gonzalez, Luis									0	0	10	10
Gonzalez, Marwin	2	2	6	8	7	26	13	12	4	4	1	85
Gonzalez, Oscar											11	11
Goodrum, Niko						0	13	7	2	7	0	29
Gordon, Nick										5	12	17
Gorman, Nolan											8	8
Grandal, Yasmani	11	4	12	15	19	12	17	24	7	16	4	141
Graveman, Kendall			0	5	9	6	0		1	11	7	39
Gray, Jon				1	9	10	7	12	1	8	5	53
Gray, Sonny		5	13	16	0	10	6	17	5	8	9	89
Green, Chad					2	9	9	4	3	11	1	39
Greene, Riley											12	12
Greene, Shane			4	0	3	9	5	11	3	0	0	35
Gregorius, Didi		0	10	9	17	16	18	21	11	9	5	121
Greinke, Zack	100	17	15	26	10	18	17	21	3	9	6	242
Grichuk, Randal			1	12	13	7	13	8	8	10	11	83
Grisham, Trent								3	7	14	12	36
Grossman, Robbie		7	10	0	10	10	13	11	7	22	11	101
Guerrero Jr., Vladimir								11	5	28	21	65
Guillorme, Luis							1	1	3	4	8	17
Gurriel, Yuli					2	18	19	20	2	19	9	89
Gurriel Jr., Lourdes							8	9	9	16	12	54
Haase, Eric							0	0	0	11	12	23

WIN SHARES BY YEAR

Player	<13	13	14	15	16	17	18	19	20	21	22	Career
Hader, Josh						6	14	16	4	16	5	61
Hamilton, Billy		2	15	5	9	10	8	3	1	1	0	54
Hand, Brad	1	1	3	1	8	14	12	11	6	7	5	69
Haniger, Mitch					3	12	28	7		27	8	85
Happ, Ian						12	12	7	9	16	19	75
Harper, Bryce	21	19	9	38	20	22	23	27	9	31	15	234
Harris II, Michael											23	23
Harrison, Josh	9	3	25	12	15	15	9	1	2	14	9	114
Hayes, Ke'Bryan									5	11	14	30
Hays, Austin						0		4	2	13	14	33
Heaney, Andrew				0	8	0	8	4	3	4	4	31
Hedges, Austin				2	0	8	5	4	1	5	5	30
Heim, Jonah									2	4	9	15
Helsley, Ryan								3	1	3	16	23
Hendricks, Kyle			7	8	17	11	13	12	7	7	2	84
Hendriks, Liam	0	0	0	5	3	5	1	17	6	16	11	64
Heredia, Guillermo					3	6	7	3	1	7	1	28
Herget, Jimmy								0	2	1	10	13
Hernandez, Cesar		3	1	12	24	18	22	16	8	16	11	131
Hernandez, Kike			5	9	2	9	13	12	4	17	8	79
Hernandez, Teoscar					2	3	11	12	7	22	16	73
Herrera, Odubel				16	25	10	14	2		11	3	81
Heyward, Jason	56	14	23	21	12	14	9	9	4	1		183
Hicks, Aaron		4	4	11	4	11	22	7	7	1	9	80
Hill, Rich	24	0	1	4	12	11	7	5	3	7	6	80
Hiura, Keston								12	4	2	7	25
Hoerner, Nico								3	3	7	20	33
Holland, Greg	20	18	15	7		12	5	4	5	4	0	90
Holmes, Clay							0	1	0	6	11	18
Hoskins, Rhys						10	22	18	6	13	19	88
Hosmer, Eric	23	18	14	22	17	30	16	17	6	13	9	185
Hudson, Dakota							3	12	4	1	5	25
Hudson, Daniel	26	0	4	4	3	2	11	1	5	4		60
Hunter, Tommy	25	10	8	4	3	8	6	1	2	2	2	71
Iglesias, Jose	1	13		12	13	11	15	12	8	10	11	106
Iglesias, Raisel				4	7	14	11	9	6	15	10	76
Inciarte, Ender			10	15	14	22	17	7	1	2	0	88
India, Jonathan										22	9	31
Irvin, Cole								1	0	7	8	16
Jansen, Danny							3	9	3	6	13	34
Jansen, Kenley	27	16	11	12	17	19	10	10	4	14	11	151
Javier, Cristian									3	7	13	23
Jimenez, Eloy								12	9	4	12	37
Judge, Aaron					0	29	19	16	4	31	45	144
Junis, Jakob						6	8	6	0	1	5	26
Keller, Brad							12	9	5	4	3	33
Keller, Mitch								0	2	0	9	11
Kelly, Carson					0	1	0	11	3	8	7	30
Kelly, Joe	5	9	5	6	2	7	5	3	1	5	0	48
Kelly, Merrill								8	3	5	14	30
Kemp, Tony					1	1	9	5	3	18	15	52
Kennedy, Ian	44	2	9	4	14	3	4	10	0	9	1	100
Kepler, Max				0	8	12	13	19	6	11	7	76
Kershaw, Clayton	74	22	22	21	16	19	12	15	6	8	12	227
Keuchel, Dallas	0	3	16	22	6	13	11	7	7	4	0	89
Kiermaier, Kevin		0	9	19	13	13	7	11	6	10	7	95
Kim, Ha-seong										5	22	27
Kimbrel, Craig	39	17	16	11	9	19	14	0	1	10	7	143
Kiner-Falefa, Isiah							5	2	5	16	13	41
Kirk, Alejandro									1	5	22	28
Kluber, Corey	1	9	21	14	20	23	20	1	0	5	5	119
Knebel, Corey			0	4	2	17	8		0	4	5	40
Kremer, Dean									1	0	8	9
Kwan, Steven											24	24
La Stella, Tommy			9	3	4	5	2	8	7	7	2	47
Lagares, Juan		7	15	13	2	2	3	2	0	4	0	48
Lamb, Jake			1	9	16	17	4	4	3	2	0	56
Lauer, Eric							4	6	0	9	9	28
Laureano, Ramon							9	17	7	11	7	51
Leclerc, Jose						1	4	12	8	0	4	29
LeMahieu, DJ	6	8	9	14	22	20	19	33	12	20	14	177
Leon, Sandy	0	0	1	3	12	9	6	3	1	3	1	39
Lindor, Francisco				14	21	27	30	19	6	20	31	168

Player	<13	13	14	15	16	17	18	19	20	21	22	Career
Longoria, Evan	110	24	21	18	20	18	7	14	1	9	9	251
Lopez, Jorge				0		0	2	1	0	2	10	15
Lopez, Nicky								6	3	21	4	34
Lopez, Pablo							2	4	3	7	11	27
Lopez, Reynaldo					1	2	10	6	0	4	7	30
Lorenzen, Michael				2	4	6	7	12	3	3	5	42
Lowe, Brandon							6	14	11	30	8	69
Lowe, Nathaniel								3	1	19	24	47
Lowrie, Jed	32	23	11	6	8	22	29	0		16	0	147
Lugo, Seth					6	3	8	12	2	4	5	40
Lux, Gavin								2	2	12	14	30
Lyles, Jordan	1	2	6	1	2	1	4	8	0	6	7	38
Lynn, Lance	13	7	16	12		11	6	18	7	15	6	111
Machado, Manny	7	20	12	27	28	19	28	18	11	27	32	229
Mahle, Tyler						1	3	2	4	13	7	30
Maldonado, Martin	7	3	4	5	7	11	11	6	7	7	8	76
Manaea, Sean					7	8	9	4	2	11	3	44
Mancini, Trey				1	19	6	17			10	14	67
Manoah, Alek										9	18	27
Margot, Manuel					1	13	10	9	4	13	10	60
Marisnick, Jake		2	5	9	3	6	5	7	1	4	1	43
Marquez, German					1	11	16	13	6	13	10	70
Marsh, Brandon										5	10	15
Marte, Ketel				9	7	6	16	29	5	14	12	98
Marte, Starling	5	20	17	20	17	10	21	21	6	21	17	175
Martinez, J.D.	13	3	19	25	17	20	33	22	2	19	10	183
Mateo, Jorge									0	4	12	16
Matz, Steven				4	9	0	4	8	0	11	1	37
May, Trevor			0	7	2		4	7	2	6	1	29
Mazara, Nomar					16	16	10	10	3	3	6	64
McCann, James			0	10	9	10	6	16	5	9	4	69
McCarthy, Jake										1	16	17
McClanahan, Shane										8	12	20
McCormick, Chas										10	13	23
McCullers Jr., Lance				8	6	5	7		2	13	5	46
McCutchen, Andrew	108	34	33	35	17	22	20	8	6	16	12	311
McGee, Jake	10	5	15	7	4	7	0	2	3	12	0	65
McHugh, Collin	0	0	13	13	8	4	9	4		8	7	66
McKenzie, Triston									3	4	14	21
McMahon, Ryan						0	4	11	4	14	11	44
McNeil, Jeff							11	24	6	6	30	77
Meadows, Austin							5	23	2	22	4	56
Mejia, Francisco						0	1	5	1	11	8	26
Melancon, Mark	13	15	15	17	16	3	3	8	3	12	3	108
Melendez, MJ											16	16
Meneses, Joey											8	8
Merrifield, Whit					8	21	22	21	9	21	12	114
Mikolas, Miles		2	0	0			17	8		1	12	40
Miley, Wade	16	10	7	9	3	4	7	11	0	14	2	83
Miller, Brad		10	11	15	15	6	5	6	5	11	4	88
Miller, Owen										1	9	10
Minor, Mike	10	13	3			11	11	18	0	6	1	73
Minter, A.J.						1	9	0	3	4	11	28
Miranda, Jose											11	11
Molina, Yadier	139	29	19	16	21	19	18	16	4	16	4	301
Moncada, Yoan					0	6	13	23	6	22	9	79
Mondesi, Adalberto					2	1	8	12	5	3	1	32
Montas, Frankie				0		0	3	8	0	13	6	30
Montero, Rafael			1	0	0	2		4	2	1	12	22
Montgomery, Jordan						9	2	0	1	9	11	32
Moore, Dylan								5	5	10	9	29
Moore, Matt	9	13	1	1	10	1	0	1		0	8	44
Moran, Colin					0	1	13	14	2	7	3	40
Morel, Christopher											10	10
Morton, Charlie	12	6	4	2	1	10	13	18	2	13	7	88
Mountcastle, Ryan									5	13	14	32
Moustakas, Mike	18	5	9	21	1	15	19	19	5	2	3	117
Mullins II, Cedric							2	1	3	22	23	51
Muncy, Max				1	2		21	22	5	27	16	94
Munoz, Andres									2	0	8	10
Murphy, Sean								2	5	14	21	42
Musgrove, Joe					3	4	5	7	2	12	13	46
Myers, Wil		14	6	9	19	19	10	10	10	13	8	118

Player	<13	13	14	15	16	17	18	19	20	21	22	Career
Naquin, Tyler					13	0	5	8	2	12	6	46
Narvaez, Omar					3	7	10	14	4	15	6	59
Naylor, Josh								7	0	4	16	27
Neris, Hector			0	2	11	11	3	13	2	8	6	56
Newman, Kevin							1	16	2	6	8	33
Nimmo, Brandon					2	6	22	8	6	15	28	87
Nola, Aaron				4	3	12	22	14	4	8	15	82
Nola, Austin								7	8	8	9	32
Nootbaar, Lars										4	12	16
O'Day, Darren	30	8	10	12	3	6	1	1	2	1	1	75
Odor, Rougned			11	16	18	8	13	13	3	9	11	102
Odorizzi, Jake	0	1	7	11	11	7	7	12	0	5	4	65
Ohtani, Shohei							20	12	1	38	38	109
Olson, Matt					0	9	19	21	8	26	22	105
O'Neill, Tyler							6	3	3	22	10	44
Ortega, Rafael	1			3			1	1		14	6	26
Ottavino, Adam	5	7	6	4	5	3	14	8	1	8	9	70
Owings, Chris		2	8	6	11	9	3	2	1	3	1	46
Ozuna, Marcell		8	19	10	15	29	19	14	13	4	5	136
Pagan, Emilio						4	3	15	2	3	3	30
Paredes, Isaac									1	1	8	10
Pasquantino, Vinnie											10	10
Pederson, Joc			0	15	19	7	11	17	3	11	20	103
Pena, Jeremy											20	20
Peralta, David			7	20	2	16	23	13	6	11	15	113
Peralta, Freddy							4	3	2	12	5	26
Perdomo, Geraldo										1	12	13
Perez, Cionel							1	0	0	0	9	10
Perez, Martin	1	8	2	3	9	9	1	6	3	5	13	60
Perez, Roberto			2	7	5	8	2	18	3	3	2	50
Perez, Salvador	17	23	17	18	18	16	13		7	28	18	175
Peterson, Jace			1	14	9	3	4	2	2	9	8	52
Pham, Tommy			0	7	4	21	17	17	2	9	9	86
Phelps, David	7	3	4	3	12	4		3	2	2	5	45
Phillips, Evan							0	0	0	1	10	11
Pillar, Kevin		1	1	15	15	9	11	16	5	8	0	81
Pina, Manny	0				2	12	8	5	2	7	0	36
Pinder, Chad					1	7	8	8	2	5	6	37
Pineda, Michael	10	8	7	6	5		9	2	7	0		54
Piscotty, Stephen				11	22	7	21	7	4	4	3	79
Pivetta, Nick						1	5	2	1	9	8	26
Plawecki, Kevin				7	3	4	5	4	4	5	3	35
Polanco, Jorge			1	1	8	14	11	26	6	29	15	111
Pollock, A.J.	2	14	10	27	1	15	13	10	5	18	8	123
Pressly, Ryan		4	2	3	6	3	8	9	2	13	10	60
Price, David	56	12	16	19	14	7	14	6		4	4	152
Profar, Jurickson	0	5			6	1	16	10	6	5	19	68
Pujols, Albert	398	10	19	18	17	7	8	10	1	6	12	506
Quantrill, Cal								3	3	12	12	30
Quintana, Jose	9	13	12	15	15	10	9	6	0	1	13	103
Raleigh, Cal										1	16	17
Ramirez, Erasmo	2	2	0	10	6	0	0		2	0	5	33
Ramirez, Harold								9	0	10	13	32
Ramirez, Jose		1	7	4	22	28	29	17	11	29	34	182
Rasmussen, Drew									1	6	10	17
Ray, Robbie			0	6	7	17	7	8	1	17	10	73
Realmuto, J.T.			1	10	19	19	25	22	6	22	27	151
Rendon, Anthony		12	26	9	22	29	22	31	7	4	5	167
Renfroe, Hunter					2	9	12	11	2	15	17	68
Rengifo, Luis								8	1	1	11	21
Reyes, Franmil							8	13	4	13	4	42
Reynolds, Bryan								19	3	28	20	70
Richards, Garrett	1	6	13	14	2	2	4	0	3	6	1	52
Riley, Austin								6	4	23	27	60
Rivas, Alfonso											8	8
Rizzo, Anthony	12	14	28	32	29	25	22	25	5	15	15	222
Robert, Luis									7	13	12	32
Robertson, David	27	12	12	13	10	13	9	0		0	10	106
Robles, Hansel					3	6	3	15	0	6	0	36
Robles, Victor						1	2	15	3	4	4	29
Rodgers, Brendan								1	0	12	14	27
Rodon, Carlos				9	8	3	6	1	0	14	15	56
Rodriguez, Eduardo					8	4	8	10	15	9	4	58

Player	<13	13	14	15	16	17	18	19	20	21	22	Career
Rodriguez, Julio											26	26
Rogers, Taylor					4	7	8	13	2	5	6	45
Rojas, Josh								2	0	11	18	31
Rojas, Miguel			1	4	3	8	13	12	10	14	13	78
Romano, Jordan								0	3	14	12	29
Romine, Austin	0	2	1	0	5	2	7	7	2	0	2	28
Romo, Sergio	36	9	8	5	4	4	7	11	3	3	0	90
Rosario, Amed						2	14	19	1	20	20	76
Rosario, Eddie				12	5	14	16	17	9	11	2	86
Ruf, Darin	1	8	1	7	0			4	11	8		40
Ruiz, Keibert									0	2	10	12
Rutschman, Adley											20	20
Ryan, Joe										2	10	12
Ryu, Hyun-Jin		13	9		0	7	7	18	5	10	1	70
Sale, Chris	35	15	17	15	17	20	18	7		4	0	148
Sanchez, Aaron			6	6	17	1	4	2		2	0	38
Sanchez, Anibal	47	17	8	5	1	1	10	11	0		3	103
Sanchez, Gary				0	11	16	8	15	2	11	10	73
Sanchez, Yolmer			1	7	3	14	15	15	1		1	57
Sandoval, Patrick								1	1	6	11	19
Sano, Miguel				16	11	14	4	17	4	9	0	75
Santana, Carlos	50	26	22	13	19	17	19	24	6	8	12	216
Santander, Anthony						0	1	9	6	3	18	37
Scherzer, Max	50	20	18	18	20	21	22	16	4	16	14	219
Schoop, Jonathan		0	6	9	18	26	8	9	6	19	5	106
Schreiber, John								1	0	0	10	11
Schwarber, Kyle				10	0	10	15	18	6	19	20	98
Seager, Corey				6	29	31	4	20	9	21	20	140
Segura, Jean	4	21	13	12	23	16	24	15	6	20	10	164
Semien, Marcus		2	7	10	21	11	21	36	8	24	23	163
Senzatela, Antonio						9	5	2	7	8	4	35
Severino, Luis				5	1	16	16	1		1	7	47
Severino, Pedro				0	2	0	4	6	4	13	1	30
Sewald, Paul						2	0	1	0	11	12	26
Shaw, Bryan	7	7	8	7	7	7	0	5	0	6	1	55
Shaw, Travis				7	12	22	21	3	3	4	0	72
Sheets, Gavin										6	8	14
Simmons, Andrelton	8	19	13	14	14	24	22	6	2	7	1	130
Singer, Brady									3	4	11	18
Slater, Austin						3	4	7	4	8	10	36
Smith, Dominic						3	1	5	7	8	2	26
Smith, Joe	28	9	14	8	4	6	4	3		2	0	78
Smith, Will	2	3	4	7	3		10	14	1	11	2	57
Smith, Will								10	7	18	20	55
Smyly, Drew	6	10	10	5	4			3	2	6	6	52
Snell, Blake					5	6	22	6	4	6	8	57
Solano, Donovan	8	9	10	1	1			10	7	10	7	63
Soler, Jorge			4	10	7	0	6	18	4	10	5	64
Soto, Juan							15	24	14	31	24	108
Souza Jr., Steven		0	7	10	19	5			0	0	0	41
Spangenberg, Cory			2	10	1	16	6	2			0	37
Springer, George			10	13	23	24	19	25	10	11	20	155
Springs, Jeffrey							2	1	0	4	10	17
Stallings, Jacob					1	1	1	4	4	13	8	32
Stammen, Craig	17	7	4	1		7	10	9	1	7	1	64
Stanek, Ryne						0	5	4	5	5	8	22
Stanton, Giancarlo	51	15	31	14	12	29	18	3	2	20	12	207
Stassi, Max		0	1	1	0	0	9	1	4	8	3	27
Stephenson, Tyler									1	12	9	22
Story, Trevor					13	13	26	22	7	16	13	110
Stott, Bryson											12	12
Strange-Gordon, Dee	9	2	22	26	7	18	11	10	0		1	106
Strasburg, Stephen	21	11	13	8	11	17	7	19	0	1	0	108
Stratton, Chris					1	4	3	3	2	9	5	27
Straw, Myles							1	4	1	17	11	34
Strickland, Hunter			2	5	7	7	4	1	0	5	4	35
Strider, Spencer										0	12	12
Stripling, Ross					4	5	8	6	0	4	10	37
Stroman, Marcus			9	3	10	16	2	14		12	7	73
Suarez, Eugenio			9	10	16	16	21	21	6	8	25	132
Suarez, Ranger							0	6	0	16	9	31
Suter, Brent					2	6	4	4	3	7	4	30
Suzuki, Kurt	69	6	14	8	7	12	10	11	2	3	1	143

Player	<13	13	14	15	16	17	18	19	20	21	22	Career
Suzuki, Seiya											13	13
Swanson, Dansby					4	10	15	15	10	17	30	101
Syndergaard, Noah				9	18	2	11	9		0	7	56
Taillon, Jameson					6	6	14	1		8	10	45
Tapia, Raimel					1	3	1	7	6	10	9	37
Taveras, Leody									3	2	8	13
Taylor, Chris			5	1	1	23	17	13	9	20	9	98
Taylor, Michael A.			1	14	4	14	5	0	1	9	9	57
Taylor, Tyrone								1	1	8	13	23
Tellez, Rowdy							5	6	5	5	15	36
Tepera, Ryan				2	1	8	7	1	1	7	6	33
Thomas, Lane								3	0	7	9	19
Thompson, Trayce				5	5	0	1			2	11	24
Torres, Gleyber							19	28	3	14	15	79
Treinen, Blake			4	3	8	7	19	4	2	12	1	60
Trevino, Jose						0	1	2	3	14		20
Trout, Mike	41	40	40	42	35	29	39	33	10	10	22	341
Tucker, Kyle						0	2	11	22	24		59
Turner, Justin	19	3	18	18	25	24	19	20	8	21	19	194
Turner, Trea				0	17	17	25	19	13	26	27	144
Upton, Justin	84	21	21	21	14	22	17	4	2	5	0	211
Urias, Julio					5	0	0	9	4	16	17	51
Urias, Luis							1	4	2	19	11	37
Urias, Ramon									1	9	13	23
Urquidy, Jose								3	2	7	9	21
Urshela, Gio				3		1	0	21	8	13	16	62
Valdez, Framber							4	1	4	10	16	35
Varsho, Daulton									1	7	18	26
Vaughn, Andrew										6	15	21
Vazquez, Christian			4		3	11	4	15	5	9	12	63
Velasquez, Vince				2	7	2	5	6	1	0	3	26
Verdugo, Alex					0	1	11	5	16	14		47
Verlander, Justin	127	14	8	8	20	17	20	23	1		20	258
Villar, Jonathan		3	5	4	24	8	15	19	2	12	4	96
Vizcaino, Arodys	1		0	6	2	10	7	1			0	27
Vogelbach, Daniel					0	0	2	12	3	5	13	35
Vogt, Stephen	0	4	8	18	9	6		11	1	3	2	62
Voit, Luke						2	10	17	9	5	10	53
Votto, Joey	139	30	8	33	33	33	22	11	3	21	7	340
Wacha, Michael		4	7	14	2	8	6	4	0	2	10	57
Wainwright, Adam	83	16	23	3	10	6	1	9	5	16	10	182
Walker, Christian			0	0		0	0	16	5	7	19	47
Walker, Taijuan	1	3	6	5	11	1	0	4	5	10		46
Walls, Taylor										5	8	13
Walsh, Jared								1	4	22	4	31
Ward, Taylor							2	0	2	7	20	31
Webb, Logan								1	1	12	15	29
Wendle, Joey					2	1	19	5	7	14	10	58
Wheeler, Zack		5	8			1	11	12	5	19	13	74
Williams, Devin							0	5	8	13		26
Williams, Trevor					0	7	13	4	0	4	6	34
Wilson, Justin	0	8	1	7	5	10	4	6	2	2	0	46
Winker, Jesse						3	12	8	5	18	13	59
Wisdom, Patrick							2	0	0	10	15	27
Witt Jr., Bobby											19	19
Wolters, Tony					5	5	3	10	2	0	0	25
Wong, Kolten		1	10	18	9	14	12	24	8	18	15	129
Wood, Alex		4	13	8	2	15	6	0	0	8	3	59
Woodruff, Brandon						2	3	11	6	15	12	49
Wright, Kyle							0	0	1	0	15	16
Yarbrough, Ryan							9	9	3	3	1	25
Yastrzemski, Mike								14	10	16	12	52
Yates, Kirby			2	0	1	4	12	14	0		0	33
Yelich, Christian		8	22	15	21	23	34	33	4	15	19	194
Zavala, Seby								0		2	8	10
Zunino, Mike		2	11	5	8	14	7	5	2	14	2	70

Instant Replay

Ted Baarda

When MLB gave teams the ability to challenge calls nine years ago, rules were put in place to ensure they could not grind the game to a halt by challenging every close play. Teams lose their ability to challenge a call if they have an unsuccessful challenge, but starting in the 8th inning teams who have lost their challenge may request a crew chief review.

Based on those rules, it makes sense that teams would want to have a high degree of certainty that calls will be overturned if they use their challenge early in a game, but are more willing to risk losing their challenge on a close play later in the game. The following bears that out:

Inning	1	2	3	4	5	6	7	8	9	Extras
Challenge Success Rate	64%	64%	61%	65%	51%	54%	43%	39%	30%	29%

Different teams will naturally have different strategies, with some being more aggressive with early-game challenges. Five teams challenged fewer than 10 times in the first four innings in 2022: the White Sox (6), Red Sox (7), Rockies (8), Pirates (8) and Mariners (9). The Rockies went 7 for 8 in those challenges, being the only team to lose their challenge only once in the first four innings. The Pirates had the worst success rate of this group, losing three early challenges while the others lost two in the first four innings.

On the flip side, four teams challenged 20 or more calls in the first four innings: the Giants (20), Orioles (21), Rays (22) and Phillies (22). All of these teams paid for their aggressiveness by losing the ability to challenge for multiple innings. The Phillies were the worst offender, challenging unsuccessfully 12 times, while the others were unsuccessful 8 times. The Dodgers, while not using an early challenge as frequently, deserve an honorable mention for being successful on only 5 of 16 challenges in the first four innings.

In addition to weighing when in a game to challenge, managers also have to take into account *what* they are challenging. This season, the home plate collision rule provided an interesting study. In 2021, only 2 of 21 home plate collision rule challenges were overturned, and previous years had similar totals. In 2022, the league decided to crack down on catchers blocking the plate after the All-Star break, which created some interesting data.

Before the All-Star break, the home plate collision rule was challenged 15 times, with only 2 calls being overturned. Coming out of the All-Star break, 6 of the first 10 challenges of home plate collisions were overturned from July 22 through August 16. After seeing the change in how the rule was enforced, teams became more aggressive challenging this rule. From August 20 to the end of the season, home plate collisions were challenged 19 times but were only overturned twice.

An example of a call that was beneficial to challenge is catcher's interference, particularly on check swings. Overall, catcher's interference calls were overturned by replay 76% of the time, the highest overturn rate of any replay type.

Since catcher's interference calls require the umpire to listen as much as see, awkward plays can lead to missed calls. Of the 25 catcher's interference challenges, 10 were on check swings where catcher's interference was not initially called. All 10 were overturned, as the umpires likely could not hear the sound of bat hitting glove since the batter did not take a full swing.

2022 Instant Replay Summary

Replay Type	Total Replays	Overturned	Percent
Force Play	546	324	59.3
Tag Play	492	211	42.9
Hit By Pitch	110	54	49.1
Fair or Foul	65	10	15.4
Home Plate Collision	44	10	22.7
Boundary Call (Home Run)	38	9	23.7
Trap or Catch	34	17	50.0
Catcher's Interference	25	19	76.0
Fan Interference	21	4	19.0
Slide Interference	14	2	14.3
Missed Base	13	3	23.1
Stadium Boundary	8	2	25.0
Rules Check	6	2	33.3
Tag-Up Play	5	2	40.0
Record Keeping	4	2	50.0
Runner Placement	3	1	33.3
Timing Play	2	0	0.0

2022 Challenges

Team	Challenges	Overturned	Pct	Opponent Challenges	Overturned	Pct	Net
Minnesota Twins	57	28	49.1	40	16	40.0	12
Philadelphia Phillies	59	26	44.1	35	15	42.9	11
St Louis Cardinals	39	25	64.1	34	14	41.2	11
Texas Rangers	56	22	39.3	39	14	35.9	8
Baltimore Orioles	48	26	54.2	38	18	47.4	8
Detroit Tigers	48	27	56.3	35	21	60.0	6
New York Mets	38	30	78.9	46	25	54.3	5
Miami Marlins	44	22	50.0	47	17	36.2	5
Arizona Diamondbacks	54	24	44.4	41	20	48.8	4
Atlanta Braves	39	22	56.4	39	20	51.3	2
Cincinnati Reds	47	25	53.2	42	24	57.1	1
Houston Astros	33	17	51.5	36	16	44.4	1
Milwaukee Brewers	38	20	52.6	43	19	44.2	1
Cleveland Guardians	41	25	61.0	51	25	49.0	0
Tampa Bay Rays	49	22	44.9	46	23	50.0	-1
Seattle Mariners	26	15	57.7	43	16	37.2	-1
Toronto Blue Jays	50	24	48.0	48	25	52.1	-1
Kansas City Royals	46	25	54.3	46	27	58.7	-2
San Francisco Giants	43	20	46.5	51	23	45.1	-3
Washington Nationals	37	16	43.2	40	20	50.0	-4
New York Yankees	38	22	57.9	41	26	63.4	-4
Colorado Rockies	31	15	48.4	37	19	51.4	-4
Chicago Cubs	53	22	41.5	45	27	60.0	-5
Chicago White Sox	26	12	46.2	37	18	48.6	-6
Boston Red Sox	22	12	54.5	35	18	51.4	-6
Pittsburgh Pirates	38	18	47.4	47	24	51.1	-6
San Diego Padres	41	23	56.1	47	30	63.8	-7
Oakland Athletics	40	15	37.5	46	22	47.8	-7
Los Angeles Angels	47	18	38.3	49	27	55.1	-9
Los Angeles Dodgers	39	15	38.5	43	24	55.8	-9

2022 Projections Review

Mark Simon

My father, a Mets fan back to the 1960s, ran out of patience with Eduardo Escobar right around the All-Star Break. He texted me multiple times to vent, understandable given that Escobar spent most of the summer hitting in the .210s and the .220s with an OPS in the mid-.600s.

My reply was succinct: "He'll be fine."

I wasn't basing that on anything other than gut feeling, remembering the times that I worked on ESPN's *Baseball Tonight* and how whenever anyone was slumping, now Braves coach Eric Young Sr. would say two words: "Track record."

In September, Escobar got back on track and was more than fine. After an 0-for-3 to start the month dropped him to a .216 batting average and .648 OPS, Escobar got on a run that won him NL Player of the Month honors. By season's end, he was at .240 with a .726 OPS.

And that was right in line with what we projected for him last November.

Eduardo Escobar

Label	Similarity	G	AB	R	H	D	T	HR	RBI	BB	SO	SB	Avg	Slg
Actual	977	136	495	58	119	26	4	20	69	40	129	0	.240	.430
Projected	977	136	481	63	117	24	4	23	72	41	110	1	.243	.453

The path through a season to an accurate projection is not always a straight line. Our system doesn't know how you're going to run the race. It just makes its best estimate and waits for you at the end point (at which time it makes another set of projections for next year). Both the human and the projection system say they trust the track record. Emotions sometimes get the better of people (like my father) but the projection system is unswayed by them.

The Escobar projection was our fifth-best when we compare actual and projected results using Bill James Similarity Scores, which for those unfamiliar is a point system based on the idea that an exact statistical match would score 1,000. Escobar's scored a 977.

We consider any projection that scored 950 or better to be a "Great" Projection, anything 900 or better to be a "Good" Projection and anything below 800 to be a "Bad" projection.

Here's how the projections have graded out in the last four 162-game seasons.

	Great	Great or Good	Bad
2018 Hitters	17%	62%	6%
2019 Hitters	15%	58%	6%
2021 Hitters	19%	58%	6%
2022 Hitters	19%	59%	5%
2018 Pitchers	16%	49%	9%
2019 Pitchers	12%	49%	10%
2021 Pitchers	9%	47%	10%
2022 Pitchers	13%	50%	6%

Of course, it's hard to know which projections we're going to hit on and which we're going to miss on.

The two hitter projections that scored best were Josh Harrison and Matt Chapman.

Josh Harrison

Label	Similarity	G	AB	R	H	D	T	HR	RBI	BB	SO	SB	Avg	Slg
Actual	980	119	386	50	99	19	2	7	27	21	71	2	.256	.370
Projected	980	117	367	41	96	20	2	7	40	22	62	5	.262	.384

Matt Chapman

Label	Similarity	G	AB	R	H	D	T	HR	RBI	BB	SO	SB	Avg	Slg
Actual	980	155	538	83	123	27	1	27	76	68	170	2	.229	.433
Projected	980	152	554	85	121	28	3	29	78	71	196	2	.218	.437

We correctly forecast that though Austin Riley would lose about 30 points of batting average from his 2021 season, he'd otherwise be on-track for MVP-caliber numbers.

Austin Riley

Label	Similarity	G	AB	R	H	D	T	HR	RBI	BB	SO	SB	Avg	Slg
Actual	972	159	615	90	168	39	2	38	93	57	168	2	.273	.528
Projected	972	158	595	90	163	33	1	35	107	52	177	0	.274	.509

A few years ago, our system had grand expectations for Vladimir Guerrero Jr.'s rookie season, a .310 batting average and 34 home runs. He didn't come close to those, not finding his full potential until 2021. This year, we set the bar similarly high for Julio Rodríguez and he exceeded it. This projection made the list of "Great" ones, scoring a 955.

Julio Rodríguez

Label	Similarity	G	AB	R	H	D	T	HR	RBI	BB	SO	SB	Avg	Slg
Actual	955	132	511	84	145	25	3	28	75	40	145	25	.284	.509
Projected	955	140	502	89	137	25	0	26	87	64	126	16	.273	.478

We also did well by Rodríguez's teammate, Eugenio Suárez. Suárez hit .202 and .198 in 2020 and 2021, respectively. We projected a .235 batting average and 28 home runs. He hit .236 with 31 home runs, albeit in 105 more at-bats than we expected.

Eugenio Suárez

Label	Similarity	G	AB	R	H	D	T	HR	RBI	BB	SO	SB	Avg	Slg
Actual	950	150	543	76	128	24	2	31	87	73	196	0	.236	.459
Projected	950	130	425	62	100	19	1	28	70	52	140	1	.235	.482

Most of our bad hitting projections were injury driven. One exception would be the player who came with Suárez to the Mariners from the Reds in a trade, Jesse Winker. Our process was good here. Look at his track record. The projection was reasonable. There wasn't a way to see this cratering coming.

Jesse Winker

Label	Similarity	G	AB	R	H	D	T	HR	RBI	BB	SO	SB	Avg	Slg
Actual	811	136	456	51	100	15	0	14	53	84	103	0	.219	.344
Projected	811	138	470	70	133	30	1	23	69	64	93	1	.283	.498

Going back to Rodríguez for a second, our worst projection among those in which playing time and projected playing time were comparable was another rookie. Why did Rodríguez exceed his projection and Torkelson clunk his? Wish we knew. The Tigers probably do too.

Spencer Torkelson

Label	Similarity	G	AB	R	H	D	T	HR	RBI	BB	SO	SB	Avg	Slg
Actual	712	110	360	38	73	16	1	8	28	37	99	0	.203	.319
Projected	712	141	501	90	131	27	1	34	98	65	153	2	.261	.523

With pitchers, most of our best projections this year were middle relievers, pitchers like Trevor Megill of the Twins.

Trevor Megill

Label	Similarity	G	GS	IP	H	HR	BB	SO	HB	W	L	Pct	Sv	BR/9	ERA
Actual	982	39	0	45.0	50	4	17	49	1	4	3	0.571	0	13.6	4.80
Projected	982	42	0	40.0	44	6	17	51	2	2	3	0.400	0	14.2	4.51

But we hit on some closers too. For example, the system felt that Kenley Jansen still had something left.

Kenley Jansen

Label	Similarity	G	GS	IP	H	HR	BB	SO	HB	W	L	Pct	Sv	BR/9	ERA
Actual	972	65	0	64.0	45	8	22	85	2	5	2	0.714	41	9.7	3.38
Projected	972	68	0	68.0	48	9	29	82	3	5	2	0.714	35	10.6	3.47

And though we missed on Corbin Burnes' win-loss record, the system sensed that his ace-caliber work was repeatable. We also were on-track with Kevin Gausman having a drop-off, but also being ace-worthy, and with Gerrit Cole and Shane Bieber continuing to pitch well. Trust the track record. These projections all scored 950 or better.

Corbin Burnes

Label	Similarity	G	GS	IP	H	HR	BB	SO	HB	W	L	Pct	Sv	BR/9	ERA
Actual	969	33	33	202.0	144	23	51	243	13	12	8	0.600	0	9.3	2.94
Projected	969	28	28	175.0	140	18	48	237	7	12	7	0.632	0	10.0	3.01

Kevin Gausman

Label	Similarity	G	GS	IP	H	HR	BB	SO	HB	W	L	Pct	Sv	BR/9	ERA
Actual	963	31	31	174.7	188	15	28	205	1	12	10	0.545	0	11.2	3.35
Projected	963	33	33	194.0	174	25	54	218	5	12	10	0.545	0	10.8	3.56

Gerrit Cole

Label	Similarity	G	GS	IP	H	HR	BB	SO	HB	W	L	Pct	Sv	BR/9	ERA
Actual	957	33	33	200.7	154	33	50	257	2	13	8	0.619	0	9.2	3.50
Projected	957	32	32	190.0	148	25	47	249	4	14	7	0.667	0	9.4	3.05

Shane Bieber

Label	Similarity	G	GS	IP	H	HR	BB	SO	HB	W	L	Pct	Sv	BR/9	ERA
Actual	954	31	31	200.0	172	18	36	198	2	13	8	0.619	0	9.5	2.88
Projected	954	29	29	183.0	151	22	47	239	5	12	8	0.600	0	10.0	3.14

But sometimes you have to remember what the track record is.

Robbie Ray pitched to a 2.84 ERA in 2021. Our system wasn't as optimistic that he could duplicate that based on his past performance. We had his ERA jumping a point. And it nearly did.

Robbie Ray

Label	Similarity	G	GS	IP	H	HR	BB	SO	HB	W	L	Pct	Sv	BR/9	ERA
Actual	947	32	32	189.0	163	32	62	212	7	12	12	0.500	0	11.0	3.71
Projected	947	32	32	195.0	169	36	72	244	5	12	9	0.571	0	11.4	3.85

There's a new set of projections waiting for you on the ensuing pages. If you can figure out which players are going to meet them, then I'd like you running my fantasy team.

And while you're at it, could you text my dad and let him know which players he doesn't have to worry about next season? I appreciate it.

2023 Hitter Projections

Hitter	Team	Age	G	AB	H	2B	3B	HR	R	RBI	RC	RC27	BB	SO	SB	CS	SB%	Avg	OBP	Slg	OPS
Abrams, CJ	Was	22	131	406	100	19	2	7	54	41	39	3.3	16	85	13	6	.68	.246	.292	.355	.646
Abreu, Jose	CWS	36	159	615	171	36	1	24	89	98	95	5.6	55	133	1	0	1.00	.278	.351	.457	.808
Acuna Jr., Ronald	Atl	25	129	487	135	28	2	25	90	68	88	6.4	64	139	26	9	.74	.277	.373	.497	.869
Adames, Willy	Mil	27	149	559	138	29	2	29	81	84	81	5.0	57	171	7	4	.64	.247	.319	.462	.780
Adams, Riley	Was	27	49	94	18	4	0	3	10	9	8	2.8	9	38	0	0	.00	.191	.283	.330	.613
Adell, Jo	LAA	24	80	276	56	14	1	11	32	35	26	3.1	18	109	3	2	.60	.203	.262	.380	.642
Aguilar, Jesus	Bal	32	91	303	79	14	0	13	34	49	43	5.0	28	75	1	0	1.00	.261	.329	.436	.765
Ahmed, Nick	Ari	33	90	262	62	15	2	7	32	32	30	3.8	21	63	3	2	.60	.237	.296	.389	.685
Alberto, Hanser	LAD	30	80	203	53	11	1	4	22	20	22	3.7	5	28	1	1	.50	.261	.286	.384	.670
Albies, Ozzie	Atl	26	144	571	153	37	5	23	90	81	85	5.3	41	116	11	4	.73	.268	.321	.471	.793
Alcantara, Sergio	Ari	26	68	122	27	4	1	2	15	11	12	3.2	12	36	1	0	1.00	.221	.296	.320	.616
Alfaro, Jorge	SD	30	97	288	68	12	1	8	28	37	28	3.3	13	108	2	1	.67	.236	.283	.368	.651
Allen, Nick	Oak	24	131	437	97	20	1	6	46	32	39	2.9	37	105	8	4	.67	.222	.287	.314	.601
Alonso, Pete	NYM	28	158	588	150	28	1	40	89	115	100	5.9	68	140	4	1	.80	.255	.346	.510	.856
Altuve, Jose	Hou	33	144	548	153	32	2	24	99	68	92	6.0	60	93	11	3	.79	.279	.358	.476	.834
Alvarez, Francisco	NYM	21	109	335	74	16	0	17	45	48	43	4.3	41	116	0	0	.00	.221	.315	.421	.736
Alvarez, Yordan	Hou	26	135	504	144	33	1	38	93	111	110	8.0	72	126	1	0	1.00	.286	.381	.581	.963
Anderson, Brian	Mia	30	110	369	86	19	1	11	47	43	43	3.9	38	110	2	1	.67	.233	.320	.379	.699
Anderson, Tim	CWS	30	126	525	159	26	2	14	82	54	77	5.4	22	114	15	4	.79	.303	.336	.440	.776
Andrus, Elvis	CWS	34	136	456	117	23	2	12	58	48	55	4.2	31	80	12	4	.75	.257	.308	.395	.703
Andujar, Miguel	Pit	28	50	112	30	6	0	4	14	16	15	4.7	6	19	2	0	1.00	.268	.311	.429	.739
Aquino, Aristides	Cin	29	81	214	43	9	1	11	26	28	23	3.4	18	85	2	1	.67	.201	.269	.407	.676
Arcia, Orlando	Atl	28	74	226	55	11	0	8	27	26	27	4.1	20	51	1	1	.50	.243	.308	.398	.706
Arenado, Nolan	StL	32	152	588	162	36	2	33	78	101	103	6.4	56	88	4	2	.67	.280	.349	.521	.870
Arozarena, Randy	TB	28	142	513	135	34	3	18	74	69	75	5.0	47	146	22	8	.73	.263	.340	.446	.786
Arraez, Luis	Min	26	142	495	153	28	3	6	73	48	76	5.7	48	47	3	2	.60	.309	.372	.414	.787
Arroyo, Christian	Bos	28	103	344	91	20	1	9	41	48	43	4.4	20	73	5	1	.83	.265	.316	.407	.723
Baddoo, Akil	Det	24	121	361	83	17	5	7	50	37	41	3.7	45	106	15	8	.65	.230	.317	.363	.680
Bader, Harrison	NYY	29	112	322	76	15	2	11	47	37	39	4.0	27	83	12	3	.80	.236	.309	.398	.707
Bae, Ji Hwan	Pit	23	88	284	69	12	3	5	44	28	32	3.2	25	70	12	4	.75	.243	.311	.359	.670
Baez, Javier	Det	30	146	530	137	28	4	22	74	78	71	4.7	28	157	9	3	.75	.258	.304	.451	.755
Barnes, Austin	LAD	33	94	277	62	12	0	10	42	35	33	3.9	37	68	2	1	.67	.224	.328	.375	.704
Barnhart, Tucker	Det	32	99	265	62	13	1	4	23	27	27	3.5	27	69	0	0	.00	.234	.310	.336	.645
Barrero, Jose	Cin	25	68	221	41	8	1	6	23	21	16	2.3	13	93	4	2	.67	.186	.241	.312	.553
Bart, Joey	SF	26	81	222	48	8	1	8	28	26	23	3.4	19	89	1	0	1.00	.216	.290	.369	.659
Bell, Josh	SD	30	144	481	119	25	2	18	68	69	69	4.9	68	101	0	0	.00	.247	.344	.420	.764
Bellinger, Cody	LAD	27	142	512	118	27	3	27	79	77	73	4.8	58	146	13	3	.81	.230	.311	.453	.764
Belt, Brandon	SF	35	96	268	63	14	1	12	39	33	39	4.9	40	82	1	0	1.00	.235	.343	.429	.772
Benintendi, Andrew	NYY	28	136	482	127	27	3	12	62	62	67	4.8	55	95	7	3	.70	.263	.343	.407	.749
Berti, Jon	Mia	33	102	292	67	12	2	4	42	25	32	3.6	35	79	22	5	.81	.229	.320	.325	.646
Bethancourt, Christian	TB	31	58	131	30	6	0	4	15	14	13	3.3	7	35	2	1	.67	.229	.273	.366	.640
Betts, Mookie	LAD	30	147	580	164	41	3	35	116	84	115	7.2	72	107	12	3	.80	.283	.370	.545	.915
Bichette, Bo	Tor	25	152	617	179	38	2	23	96	89	98	5.7	42	145	14	5	.74	.290	.338	.470	.808
Biggio, Cavan	Tor	28	108	331	71	17	1	10	50	39	40	4.0	56	110	5	1	.83	.215	.335	.363	.698
Blackmon, Charlie	Col	36	127	421	119	22	4	16	63	58	66	5.6	33	87	3	2	.60	.283	.345	.468	.813
Bleday, J.J.	Mia	25	91	267	54	12	1	11	31	31	30	3.7	37	92	2	1	.67	.202	.306	.378	.684
Bogaerts, Xander	Bos	30	154	576	164	41	1	18	92	86	94	5.9	64	124	7	2	.78	.285	.363	.453	.816
Bohm, Alec	Phi	26	143	481	133	23	1	12	63	61	63	4.7	34	103	3	2	.60	.277	.329	.403	.733
Bote, David	ChC	30	81	206	45	9	1	6	23	25	21	3.3	18	66	2	1	.67	.218	.294	.359	.653
Bradley Jr., Jackie	Tor	33	92	214	48	11	1	5	24	23	22	3.4	18	58	2	1	.67	.224	.294	.355	.649
Brantley, Michael	Hou	36	117	432	127	27	2	10	59	52	67	5.7	40	56	2	1	.67	.294	.358	.435	.793
Bregman, Alex	Hou	29	141	527	143	36	1	23	89	87	93	6.3	84	80	1	0	1.00	.271	.381	.474	.855
Bride, Jonah	Oak	27	83	248	58	12	1	6	31	27	29	4.0	33	56	1	0	1.00	.234	.340	.363	.703
Brosseau, Mike	Mil	29	66	173	39	8	1	7	22	24	21	4.0	16	56	2	0	1.00	.225	.309	.405	.714
Brown, Seth	Oak	30	146	526	117	28	3	22	64	77	62	4.0	46	165	9	2	.82	.222	.289	.413	.701
Bryant, Kris	Col	31	134	501	143	34	2	23	92	71	91	6.5	61	123	4	2	.67	.285	.375	.499	.874
Burdick, Peyton	Mia	26	83	241	46	9	2	10	35	29	25	3.3	28	95	3	1	.75	.191	.288	.369	.658
Buxton, Byron	Min	29	78	286	70	17	2	19	49	43	45	5.4	23	91	5	1	.83	.245	.312	.517	.830
Cabrera, Miguel	Det	40	104	370	91	13	0	8	33	44	39	3.7	32	96	1	0	1.00	.246	.311	.346	.657
Cabrera, Oswaldo	NYY	24	110	364	84	21	2	15	46	50	44	4.1	30	121	9	4	.69	.231	.293	.423	.716
Calhoun, Kole	Tex	35	86	226	50	10	1	9	29	28	26	3.8	22	72	1	0	1.00	.221	.299	.394	.693
Call, Alex	Was	28	77	161	37	8	1	6	23	20	20	4.2	19	41	3	1	.75	.230	.322	.404	.726
Candelario, Jeimer	Det	29	127	415	102	25	2	14	53	52	55	4.5	42	108	0	0	.00	.246	.323	.417	.739
Canha, Mark	NYM	34	143	477	112	24	2	15	77	60	60	4.2	60	116	4	1	.80	.235	.349	.388	.737
Caratini, Victor	Mil	29	106	282	66	13	0	8	30	36	32	3.9	31	71	0	1	.00	.234	.323	.365	.688
Carlson, Dylan	StL	24	132	431	110	27	4	12	59	49	60	4.8	46	105	4	1	.80	.255	.337	.420	.757
Carpenter, Matt	NYY	37	102	272	59	15	1	14	43	39	39	4.7	45	86	1	0	1.00	.217	.341	.434	.774
Carroll, Corbin	Ari	22	147	524	115	27	8	19	72	58	65	4.1	59	179	19	5	.79	.219	.313	.410	.723
Casali, Curt	Sea	34	84	219	45	9	0	7	24	26	22	3.3	27	75	0	0	.00	.205	.301	.342	.644
Casas, Triston	Bos	23	136	495	113	22	3	19	70	65	66	4.5	77	143	3	1	.75	.228	.337	.400	.737
Castellanos, Nick	Phi	31	136	476	130	32	2	19	66	66	71	5.3	33	119	4	2	.67	.273	.326	.468	.794
Castro, Harold	Det	29	118	346	94	15	2	5	33	36	38	3.9	14	72	1	1	.50	.272	.302	.370	.672
Castro, Jason	Hou	36	50	119	23	6	0	4	15	12	12	3.3	16	50	1	0	1.00	.193	.299	.345	.644
Castro, Rodolfo	Pit	24	117	379	80	14	2	15	42	45	38	3.3	31	125	5	3	.63	.211	.280	.377	.657
Castro, Willi	Det	26	116	351	87	17	3	8	46	36	39	3.8	19	89	8	3	.73	.248	.300	.382	.682
Cave, Jake	Bal	30	56	104	25	5	1	3	14	13	13	4.1	9	35	1	0	1.00	.240	.313	.394	.707
Celestino, Gilberto	Min	24	83	186	41	8	0	2	19	15	17	3.0	20	50	2	0	1.00	.220	.303	.296	.599
Chang, Yu	Bos	27	72	145	32	7	1	5	18	20	16	3.7	13	50	0	0	.00	.221	.294	.386	.680
Chapman, Matt	Tor	30	144	496	112	25	2	26	70	70	68	4.6	61	164	2	2	.50	.226	.319	.442	.761

2023 Hitter Projections

Hitter	Team	Age	G	AB	H	2B	3B	HR	R	RBI	RC	RC27	BB	SO	SB	CS	SB%	Avg	OBP	Slg	OPS
Chirinos, Robinson	Bal	39	64	144	29	6	0	5	16	19	14	3.2	16	52	0	0	.00	.201	.299	.347	.646
Chisholm Jr., Jazz	Mia	25	143	489	113	20	6	27	75	76	66	4.5	44	159	22	9	.71	.231	.302	.462	.765
Choi, Ji-Man	TB	32	124	368	82	22	1	13	43	54	48	4.3	58	124	0	0	.00	.223	.333	.394	.727
Clement, Ernie	Oak	27	71	176	40	7	1	2	19	13	15	2.9	11	28	1	0	1.00	.227	.280	.313	.593
Contreras, William	Atl	25	97	352	85	15	1	17	46	48	48	4.7	36	107	1	0	1.00	.241	.315	.435	.750
Contreras, Willson	ChC	31	133	473	115	25	1	24	70	69	68	4.9	54	132	4	3	.57	.243	.346	.452	.798
Cooper, Garrett	Mia	32	114	372	97	23	1	10	42	48	50	4.7	38	109	0	0	.00	.261	.341	.409	.749
Cordero, Franchy	Bos	28	66	138	33	8	1	5	20	19	18	4.4	14	53	2	1	.67	.239	.314	.420	.734
Correa, Carlos	Min	28	151	566	156	33	1	24	86	89	94	5.9	71	131	0	0	.00	.276	.360	.465	.825
Crawford, Brandon	SF	36	138	472	114	25	2	14	62	64	57	4.1	47	114	3	2	.60	.242	.318	.392	.710
Crawford, J.P.	Sea	28	155	590	146	30	3	9	75	59	69	4.0	72	108	4	3	.57	.247	.338	.354	.693
Cron, C.J.	Col	33	136	466	123	25	1	27	64	85	74	5.6	40	129	0	0	.00	.264	.335	.496	.831
Cronenworth, Jake	SD	29	157	575	142	32	4	16	87	74	74	4.4	62	119	3	1	.75	.247	.333	.400	.733
Cruz, Nelson	Was	42	113	347	85	14	0	15	47	53	46	4.6	37	94	2	0	1.00	.245	.326	.415	.741
Cruz, Oneil	Pit	24	131	469	105	18	5	22	69	71	57	4.0	44	162	13	6	.68	.224	.295	.424	.719
Culberson, Charlie	Tex	34	69	121	28	6	1	2	14	12	11	3.2	7	33	2	1	.67	.231	.279	.347	.626
Dalbec, Bobby	Bos	28	97	249	53	9	1	12	30	37	28	3.7	22	95	2	0	1.00	.213	.287	.402	.689
d'Arnaud, Travis	Atl	34	109	389	97	21	1	16	51	62	50	4.4	26	95	0	0	.00	.249	.308	.432	.740
Davis, Brennen	ChC	23	127	411	77	20	0	12	47	38	35	2.7	45	173	1	2	.33	.187	.289	.324	.613
Davis, J.D.	SF	30	112	319	80	18	1	12	43	42	45	4.9	38	112	1	0	1.00	.251	.342	.426	.768
Daza, Yonathan	Col	29	105	304	87	16	2	3	38	27	38	4.5	20	54	1	1	.50	.286	.334	.382	.716
De La Cruz, Bryan	Mia	26	133	442	118	24	2	17	55	58	62	5.0	30	122	4	1	.80	.267	.316	.446	.762
DeJong, Paul	StL	29	83	241	52	11	0	12	31	35	28	3.8	22	77	2	1	.67	.216	.292	.411	.703
Delay, Jason	Pit	28	73	204	39	8	0	2	18	17	13	2.0	12	67	0	0	.00	.191	.243	.260	.503
Devers, Rafael	Bos	26	154	605	167	40	4	31	97	104	102	6.0	56	136	4	3	.57	.276	.343	.502	.846
Diaz, Aledmys	Hou	32	78	207	50	11	0	7	23	26	23	3.8	13	39	1	1	.50	.242	.296	.396	.692
Diaz, Elias	Col	32	108	330	82	17	1	11	37	44	40	4.2	25	72	0	0	.00	.248	.305	.406	.711
Diaz, Lewin	Mia	26	67	106	24	5	0	5	13	14	12	3.9	8	30	0	0	.00	.226	.287	.415	.702
Diaz, Yandy	TB	31	141	505	135	28	1	10	71	58	71	5.0	79	83	3	3	.50	.267	.371	.386	.757
Dickerson, Corey	StL	34	103	302	79	17	2	8	36	34	37	4.3	17	59	1	1	.50	.262	.305	.411	.716
Donaldson, Josh	NYY	37	125	400	90	21	0	18	58	54	53	4.4	58	120	1	1	.50	.225	.330	.413	.743
Donovan, Brendan	StL	26	126	423	111	24	1	7	67	50	55	4.6	59	84	3	3	.50	.262	.370	.374	.743
Dozier, Hunter	KC	31	112	361	84	20	3	11	43	38	42	3.9	33	107	3	2	.60	.233	.302	.396	.698
Drury, Brandon	SD	30	136	493	117	28	1	20	60	66	60	4.1	37	129	1	1	.50	.237	.299	.420	.718
Dubon, Mauricio	Hou	28	98	238	59	11	1	6	28	24	26	3.7	15	42	3	2	.60	.248	.298	.378	.676
Duffy, Matt	LAA	32	69	156	40	6	0	2	17	14	16	3.7	13	35	1	0	1.00	.256	.322	.333	.655
Duran, Ezequiel	Tex	24	97	356	83	24	1	11	41	44	38	3.5	19	99	7	5	.58	.233	.274	.399	.673
Duran, Jarren	Bos	26	59	146	33	6	2	4	19	14	16	3.6	11	46	5	1	.83	.226	.289	.377	.666
Duvall, Adam	Atl	34	122	397	85	18	1	22	55	65	46	3.8	31	135	1	1	.50	.214	.281	.431	.712
Eaton, Nate	KC	26	50	138	32	5	2	3	17	15	15	3.7	11	39	6	1	.86	.232	.303	.362	.665
Edman, Tommy	StL	28	155	590	155	33	4	14	86	58	77	4.6	43	112	26	4	.87	.263	.319	.403	.723
Encarnacion, Jerar	Mia	25	61	178	37	6	0	7	21	22	17	3.1	14	72	1	1	.50	.208	.269	.360	.629
Engel, Adam	CWS	31	91	205	44	10	1	4	25	18	18	2.8	12	64	8	3	.73	.215	.275	.332	.606
Escobar, Eduardo	NYM	34	134	462	110	24	3	19	57	64	58	4.3	39	116	1	1	.50	.238	.300	.426	.727
Espinal, Santiago	Tor	28	138	479	127	26	1	7	55	53	56	4.1	40	79	7	4	.64	.265	.324	.367	.692
Estrada, Thairo	SF	27	113	326	86	16	1	10	46	42	42	4.5	22	64	10	3	.77	.264	.326	.411	.737
Fairchild, Stuart	Cin	27	74	196	42	8	1	9	26	19	22	3.7	18	70	2	1	.67	.214	.303	.403	.706
Farmer, Kyle	Cin	32	145	486	129	25	1	14	54	64	60	4.4	29	98	3	2	.60	.265	.325	.407	.733
Fletcher, David	LAA	29	98	327	88	16	1	3	38	26	36	3.9	19	36	4	1	.80	.269	.313	.352	.665
Flores, Wilmer	SF	31	151	517	132	29	1	20	70	71	72	4.9	51	95	1	0	1.00	.255	.332	.431	.763
Fortes, Nick	Mia	26	82	211	50	8	1	7	28	24	24	3.8	18	43	3	2	.60	.237	.312	.384	.696
Fraley, Jake	Cin	28	98	307	77	14	1	16	45	54	48	5.5	40	92	7	1	.88	.251	.345	.459	.804
France, Ty	Sea	28	144	519	139	28	1	19	68	76	72	4.9	37	100	0	0	.00	.268	.341	.435	.777
Franco, Wander	TB	22	144	539	155	33	7	12	87	71	84	5.6	48	65	11	3	.79	.288	.348	.445	.793
Frazier, Adam	Sea	31	140	464	119	24	3	5	58	41	51	3.8	39	67	7	5	.58	.256	.322	.353	.676
Freeman, Freddie	LAD	33	161	607	184	40	2	27	112	98	121	7.4	85	112	9	3	.75	.303	.395	.509	.904
Friedl, T.J.	Cin	27	99	311	71	12	4	9	41	31	35	3.7	30	70	7	3	.70	.228	.312	.379	.692
Gallo, Joey	LAD	29	108	287	56	11	1	19	46	43	40	4.5	51	127	3	1	.75	.195	.323	.439	.762
Gamel, Ben	Pit	31	104	272	68	15	2	6	36	30	35	4.4	34	75	3	2	.60	.250	.340	.386	.726
Garcia, Adolis	Tex	30	143	552	129	28	3	25	75	84	66	4.0	32	178	16	5	.76	.234	.283	.431	.714
Garcia, Avisail	Mia	32	129	371	92	16	1	12	44	49	43	4.0	25	108	5	2	.71	.248	.306	.394	.700
Garcia, Dermis	Oak	25	90	241	41	8	0	9	28	30	18	2.4	23	117	2	1	.67	.170	.248	.315	.563
Garcia, Leury	CWS	32	121	349	87	14	2	6	46	34	35	3.5	18	82	3	1	.75	.249	.294	.352	.646
Garcia, Luis	Was	23	118	434	112	22	3	12	51	49	51	4.1	21	96	3	2	.60	.258	.294	.406	.699
Garcia, Maikel	KC	23	115	355	82	20	1	6	52	33	36	3.4	30	92	14	4	.78	.231	.293	.344	.636
Garlick, Kyle	Min	31	56	103	22	4	0	5	13	13	11	3.5	7	38	0	0	.00	.214	.270	.398	.668
Garver, Mitch	Tex	32	64	219	51	12	0	12	31	31	31	4.8	28	69	1	1	.50	.233	.328	.452	.780
Gimenez, Andres	Cle	24	145	479	122	25	3	15	62	59	61	4.4	31	119	16	2	.89	.255	.326	.413	.740
Goldschmidt, Paul	StL	35	158	583	162	33	1	32	99	98	107	6.6	78	149	6	1	.86	.278	.368	.503	.870
Gomes, Yan	ChC	35	84	288	71	14	1	10	32	38	34	4.0	16	62	1	0	1.00	.247	.295	.406	.702
Gonzalez, Luis	SF	27	52	96	21	4	0	3	11	10	9	3.2	10	26	3	1	.75	.219	.299	.323	.622
Gonzalez, Marwin	NYY	34	78	206	46	10	0	7	24	26	22	3.5	18	57	2	1	.67	.223	.298	.374	.672
Gonzalez, Oscar	Cle	25	128	402	104	22	2	15	44	53	50	4.3	16	91	1	2	.33	.259	.292	.435	.727
Gordon, Nick	Min	27	130	386	94	21	3	9	43	43	42	3.8	22	103	7	2	.78	.244	.296	.383	.680
Gorman, Nolan	StL	23	118	393	86	15	0	21	54	49	46	3.9	31	145	3	0	1.00	.219	.279	.417	.697
Grandal, Yasmani	CWS	34	108	340	80	14	0	15	44	46	49	4.9	62	92	1	0	1.00	.235	.358	.409	.767
Greene, Riley	Det	22	144	503	123	24	5	11	70	62	59	4.0	50	163	5	3	.63	.245	.319	.378	.697
Grichuk, Randal	Col	31	133	448	115	23	2	22	60	70	61	4.8	25	113	2	1	.67	.257	.302	.464	.766
Grisham, Trent	SD	26	132	412	89	18	3	17	57	52	51	4.1	54	125	8	2	.80	.216	.314	.398	.712
Grissom, Vaughn	Atl	22	121	424	111	14	2	15	59	54	54	4.4	26	92	14	4	.78	.262	.320	.410	.730
Grossman, Robbie	Atl	33	128	394	87	20	2	9	52	43	45	3.8	59	116	7	2	.78	.221	.330	.350	.680

585

2023 Hitter Projections

Hitter	Team	Age	G	AB	H	2B	3B	HR	R	RBI	RC	RC27	BB	SO	SB	CS	SB%	Avg	OBP	Slg	OPS
Guerrero Jr., Vladimir	Tor	24	160	609	174	34	1	36	96	103	113	6.7	67	110	7	3	.70	.286	.362	.522	.884
Guillorme, Luis	NYM	28	114	320	83	13	1	3	35	25	37	4.0	40	54	1	0	1.00	.259	.345	.334	.680
Gurriel Jr., Lourdes	Tor	29	140	501	140	31	1	15	61	72	70	5.0	32	103	3	3	.50	.279	.329	.435	.764
Gurriel, Yuli	Hou	39	140	518	135	32	1	12	64	66	63	4.3	35	72	5	1	.83	.261	.314	.396	.709
Haase, Eric	Det	30	103	318	72	13	2	15	40	47	38	4.1	26	111	1	0	1.00	.226	.289	.421	.710
Haggerty, Sam	Sea	66	139	32	7	1	3	20	15	16	3.9	14	43	8	1	.89	.230	.314	.360	.674
Hampson, Garrett	Col	28	102	259	62	12	3	6	36	20	30	4.0	23	75	12	3	.80	.239	.304	.378	.682
Haniger, Mitch	Sea	32	121	459	114	21	2	23	73	68	67	5.0	48	128	1	0	1.00	.248	.329	.453	.782
Happ, Ian	ChC	151	511	122	27	2	20	69	71	69	4.6	64	152	8	3	.73	.239	.329	.417	.746
Harper, Bryce	Phi	30	149	538	152	37	1	33	101	99	114	7.6	96	140	14	5	.74	.283	.396	.539	.935
Harris II, Michael	Atl	22	114	409	107	27	3	17	71	66	60	5.1	24	105	16	2	.89	.262	.311	.467	.777
Harrison, Josh	CWS	35	134	445	113	22	2	9	54	43	49	3.8	27	81	3	2	.60	.254	.318	.373	.691
Hayes, Ke'Bryan	Pit	26	132	521	128	30	3	10	66	50	62	4.1	50	128	17	4	.81	.246	.318	.372	.690
Hays, Austin	Bal	27	136	487	120	27	2	18	65	62	59	4.2	30	110	2	2	.50	.246	.301	.421	.722
Hedges, Austin	Cle	98	273	48	8	0	8	27	30	19	2.2	21	80	1	0	1.00	.176	.245	.293	.538
Heim, Jonah	Tex	28	128	427	99	21	1	15	46	52	50	3.9	39	92	2	0	1.00	.232	.299	.391	.690
Heineman, Tyler	Pit	32	67	174	41	8	0	2	17	13	16	3.1	13	32	1	1	.50	.236	.300	.316	.616
Henderson, Gunnar	Bal	141	518	123	24	7	18	83	73	72	4.7	71	168	13	3	.81	.237	.337	.415	.752
Hernandez, Cesar	Was	33	139	498	125	24	2	8	65	42	56	3.9	48	109	6	2	.75	.251	.323	.355	.678
Hernandez, Kike	Bos	31	134	514	127	34	2	16	77	68	68	4.5	54	113	1	1	.50	.247	.326	.414	.740
Hernandez, Teoscar	Tor	30	146	564	146	32	2	30	84	92	85	5.2	43	174	7	3	.70	.259	.316	.482	.798
Hernandez, Yadiel	Was	35	121	351	90	15	1	12	41	46	45	4.4	29	90	2	1	.67	.256	.315	.407	.722
Heyward, Jason	ChC	33	74	176	42	8	1	5	23	20	21	4.0	19	38	2	1	.67	.239	.320	.381	.700
Hicks, Aaron	NYY	33	96	258	57	10	1	9	40	33	32	4.1	43	71	5	2	.71	.221	.337	.372	.709
Higashioka, Kyle	NYY	33	85	232	54	10	0	12	26	34	28	4.1	15	60	0	0	.00	.233	.282	.431	.713
Higgins, P.J.	ChC	30	70	168	39	8	1	3	17	21	18	3.5	17	48	0	0	.00	.232	.310	.345	.655
Hilliard, Sam	Col	29	59	113	23	4	1	5	15	13	13	3.6	12	43	2	0	1.00	.204	.286	.389	.675
Hiura, Keston	Mil	26	83	229	50	11	1	14	30	32	30	4.3	22	97	3	2	.60	.218	.306	.459	.765
Hoerner, Nico	ChC	26	122	381	104	19	3	8	47	44	50	4.7	26	52	13	2	.87	.273	.329	.402	.731
Hoskins, Rhys	Phi	30	151	547	132	33	2	30	84	87	87	5.5	79	157	2	1	.67	.241	.345	.473	.819
Hosmer, Eric	Bos	33	113	359	99	19	1	11	44	54	51	5.1	32	69	1	1	.50	.276	.338	.426	.765
Huff, Sam	Tex	25	45	96	20	2	0	5	11	12	10	3.4	8	40	0	0	.00	.208	.276	.385	.662
Ibanez, Andy	Tex	30	52	112	28	6	0	3	13	11	13	4.1	9	22	1	0	1.00	.250	.311	.384	.695
Iglesias, Jose	Col	33	121	459	135	29	1	6	57	55	59	4.7	19	64	2	1	.67	.294	.332	.401	.733
India, Jonathan	Cin	26	113	374	96	19	1	13	57	45	51	4.8	41	95	4	2	.67	.257	.353	.417	.771
Isbel, Kyle	KC	26	97	234	52	11	3	6	32	27	24	3.4	19	66	7	4	.64	.223	.293	.373	.666
Jansen, Danny	Tor	28	103	324	79	17	1	18	46	51	49	5.2	37	73	1	0	1.00	.244	.332	.469	.802
Jeffers, Ryan	Min	26	88	244	53	10	1	11	28	33	28	3.9	26	77	1	1	.50	.217	.298	.402	.699
Jimenez, Eloy	CWS	129	447	120	21	1	25	57	75	70	5.6	35	115	0	0	.00	.268	.326	.488	.813
Joe, Connor	Col	30	83	226	57	12	1	6	31	25	30	4.6	30	58	2	1	.67	.252	.350	.394	.744
Judge, Aaron	NYY	31	149	559	159	27	1	50	112	112	133	8.6	99	177	11	3	.79	.284	.397	.605	1.001
Jung, Josh	Tex	141	484	117	29	2	25	60	80	61	4.1	29	179	5	1	.83	.230	.283	.443	.725
Kelenic, Jarred	Sea	23	82	253	56	15	1	11	33	35	30	3.9	23	74	5	3	.63	.221	.294	.419	.713
Kelly, Carson	Ari	28	108	323	78	17	0	12	40	43	42	4.5	38	73	1	0	1.00	.241	.329	.406	.734
Kemp, Tony	Oak	134	360	94	18	3	6	50	36	46	4.4	38	54	7	2	.78	.261	.342	.378	.719
Kepler, Max	Min	30	125	401	95	22	2	15	59	50	53	4.5	49	79	4	2	.67	.237	.327	.414	.740
Kiermaier, Kevin	TB	33	102	283	64	12	3	7	39	31	30	3.5	23	81	7	2	.78	.226	.291	.364	.655
Kim, Ha-seong	SD	142	507	124	27	2	14	56	61	63	4.2	51	107	10	2	.83	.245	.322	.389	.711
Kiner-Falefa, Isiah	NYY	28	152	561	145	25	2	6	67	49	60	3.7	37	89	19	5	.79	.258	.314	.342	.656
Kirilloff, Alex	Min	25	71	203	53	9	0	8	25	30	27	4.7	15	50	1	0	1.00	.261	.324	.424	.748
Kirk, Alejandro	Tor	24	139	484	136	25	0	16	61	70	77	5.7	65	64	0	0	.00	.281	.372	.432	.804
Knizner, Andrew	StL	28	88	233	52	10	0	5	25	22	22	3.2	22	55	0	0	.00	.223	.304	.330	.634
Kwan, Steven	Cle	25	147	542	157	24	6	8	88	55	79	5.3	59	64	16	5	.76	.290	.367	.400	.767
La Stella, Tommy	SF	34	66	162	41	9	0	4	21	18	20	4.2	15	25	0	0	.00	.253	.320	.383	.703
Langeliers, Shea	Oak	25	82	288	62	13	1	12	34	34	31	3.6	25	99	2	1	.67	.215	.283	.392	.675
Larnach, Trevor	Min	26	86	243	50	11	0	8	29	27	24	3.3	27	93	0	0	.00	.206	.296	.350	.645
Laureano, Ramon	Oak	28	91	272	63	15	1	10	38	31	32	3.9	23	83	7	3	.70	.232	.310	.404	.715
Leblanc, Charles	Mia	27	47	99	21	4	0	3	11	10	9	3.1	8	38	1	0	1.00	.212	.278	.343	.621
LeMahieu, DJ	NYY	34	141	529	146	24	1	12	82	57	72	4.9	60	85	4	3	.57	.276	.354	.393	.747
Lewis, Kyle	Sea	82	275	60	10	0	14	37	38	33	4.0	31	97	1	0	1.00	.218	.302	.407	.709
Lewis, Royce	Min	24	89	271	66	20	1	8	40	25	35	4.4	23	70	10	2	.83	.244	.312	.413	.725
Lindor, Francisco	NYM	29	154	597	153	31	3	25	92	82	87	5.0	61	122	13	4	.76	.256	.333	.444	.777
Longoria, Evan	SF	37	119	403	98	21	1	16	51	55	51	4.4	36	112	1	1	.50	.243	.312	.419	.731
Lopez, Alejo	Cin	27	59	127	33	6	0	2	15	11	14	3.9	11	18	2	1	.67	.260	.329	.354	.683
Lopez, Nicky	KC	28	120	332	85	13	3	2	41	24	35	3.7	28	51	9	2	.82	.256	.320	.331	.651
Lowe, Brandon	TB	28	124	428	105	23	2	23	66	69	65	5.2	49	126	3	1	.75	.245	.333	.470	.802
Lowe, Josh	TB	25	53	123	28	7	1	4	16	16	15	4.2	13	47	4	0	1.00	.228	.307	.398	.705
Lowe, Nathaniel	Tex	27	141	484	131	23	2	21	65	68	76	5.6	55	129	3	1	.75	.271	.349	.457	.805
Luplow, Jordan	Ari	74	161	37	8	1	9	23	24	23	4.8	20	46	2	1	.67	.230	.322	.460	.782
Lux, Gavin	LAD	25	135	482	126	22	5	12	75	56	66	4.8	54	117	7	2	.78	.261	.337	.402	.740
Machado, Manny	SD	30	157	596	162	33	2	31	93	100	101	6.0	66	128	9	3	.75	.272	.346	.490	.836
Machin, Vimael	Oak	75	249	58	12	1	3	26	23	25	3.5	26	50	1	0	1.00	.235	.313	.328	.641
Madrigal, Nick	ChC	26	84	265	72	12	2	1	32	20	29	3.9	17	31	3	1	.75	.272	.325	.343	.669
Maile, Luke	Cle	32	63	143	30	8	0	3	16	15	14	3.1	16	46	0	0	.00	.210	.298	.329	.627
Maldonado, Martin	Hou	36	102	266	53	10	0	9	30	29	24	2.9	23	89	0	0	.00	.199	.276	.338	.614
Mancini, Trey	Hou	31	139	483	115	26	2	18	61	58	61	4.3	46	130	0	0	.00	.238	.315	.412	.727
Marcano, Tucupita	Pit	23	45	124	28	5	1	2	16	10	12	3.1	13	30	1	2	.33	.226	.299	.331	.630
Margot, Manuel	TB	28	104	311	78	16	2	6	37	35	36	4.0	26	61	7	3	.70	.251	.311	.373	.684
Marsh, Brandon	Phi	25	139	445	105	21	4	10	54	48	49	3.7	36	163	11	3	.79	.236	.298	.369	.666
Marte, Ketel	Ari	29	136	523	143	37	5	17	73	63	83	5.6	53	100	5	1	.83	.273	.346	.461	.807
Marte, Starling	NYM	34	129	501	141	25	3	15	81	61	72	5.1	33	107	19	6	.76	.281	.343	.433	.776

586

2023 Hitter Projections

Hitter	Team	Age	G	AB	H	2B	3B	HR	R	RBI	RC	RC27	BB	SO	SB	CS	SB%	Avg	OBP	Slg	OPS
Martinez, J.D.	Bos	35	135	481	130	33	2	22	74	76	79	5.9	50	133	0	0	.00	.270	.344	.484	.828
Massey, Michael	KC	25	99	321	76	19	1	10	35	44	36	3.8	21	98	5	1	.83	.237	.296	.396	.692
Mateo, Jorge	Bal	28	134	412	91	19	5	10	48	41	40	3.2	23	127	23	6	.79	.221	.269	.364	.633
McCann, James	NYM	33	82	213	48	9	0	6	22	24	21	3.3	16	66	2	1	.67	.225	.289	.352	.641
McCarthy, Jake	Ari	25	112	381	93	17	4	10	57	47	46	4.1	33	102	20	5	.80	.244	.316	.388	.704
McCormick, Chas	Hou	28	115	387	90	13	2	13	53	51	46	4.0	46	116	5	2	.71	.233	.319	.377	.696
McCutchen, Andrew	Mil	36	127	460	109	22	1	17	67	61	60	4.4	62	117	6	3	.67	.237	.333	.400	.733
McGuire, Reese	Bos	28	108	387	97	22	1	7	41	37	43	3.8	27	90	1	0	1.00	.251	.306	.367	.673
McKinstry, Zach	ChC	28	73	184	44	8	2	5	24	20	22	4.0	17	50	3	1	.75	.239	.310	.386	.696
McMahon, Ryan	Col	28	149	505	127	28	2	23	66	73	75	5.1	56	152	6	2	.75	.251	.331	.451	.782
McNeil, Jeff	NYM	31	146	515	148	33	2	12	70	60	75	5.3	40	70	3	1	.75	.287	.353	.429	.782
Mead, Curtis	TB	22	139	504	123	38	0	17	57	65	65	4.4	47	128	5	2	.71	.244	.322	.421	.743
Meadows, Austin	Det	28	115	419	107	24	4	15	59	65	60	5.0	45	90	3	2	.60	.255	.335	.439	.774
Mejia, Francisco	TB	27	90	246	58	15	1	6	28	28	25	3.5	12	56	0	0	.00	.236	.282	.378	.660
Melendez, MJ	KC	24	128	417	92	19	2	21	56	60	56	4.4	59	123	3	3	.50	.221	.319	.427	.746
Meneses, Joey	Was	31	121	381	95	18	1	16	44	52	49	4.4	26	103	1	0	1.00	.249	.301	.428	.729
Mercado, Oscar	Cle	28	58	108	25	5	1	3	14	12	12	3.7	9	25	3	1	.75	.231	.303	.380	.682
Merrifield, Whit	Tor	34	139	508	137	31	3	12	70	55	67	4.6	34	89	16	5	.76	.270	.319	.413	.733
Mervis, Matt	ChC	25	112	361	91	23	2	19	47	58	54	5.2	29	90	1	0	1.00	.252	.318	.485	.803
Meyers, Jake	Hou	27	70	182	46	8	1	6	24	23	23	4.4	16	56	2	1	.67	.253	.320	.407	.727
Miller, Brad	Tex	33	94	218	48	7	1	10	28	31	27	4.0	26	73	3	1	.75	.220	.306	.399	.705
Miller, Owen	Cle	26	92	285	67	15	1	5	31	31	29	3.4	21	69	1	0	1.00	.235	.297	.347	.644
Miranda, Jose	Min	25	125	381	104	23	0	14	45	55	53	4.9	25	75	1	2	.33	.273	.329	.444	.773
Mitchell, Calvin	Pit	24	64	137	35	7	0	4	13	17	16	4.1	9	31	2	1	.67	.255	.311	.394	.705
Mitchell, Garrett	Mil	24	82	215	44	8	1	4	28	22	19	2.9	19	83	10	0	1.00	.205	.278	.307	.585
Moncada, Yoan	CWS	28	139	471	115	25	3	17	62	61	64	4.6	54	146	3	1	.75	.244	.327	.418	.745
Mondesi, Adalberto	KC	27	42	142	33	6	2	4	19	16	16	3.8	4	48	13	2	.87	.232	.273	.387	.661
Moniak, Mickey	LAA	25	61	156	31	6	2	6	17	19	14	3.0	10	54	2	1	.67	.199	.251	.378	.630
Montero, Elehuris	Col	24	120	403	87	17	1	16	43	50	41	3.4	30	130	2	2	.50	.216	.282	.382	.664
Moore, Dylan	Sea	30	108	277	55	13	2	8	39	30	27	3.1	32	93	16	7	.70	.199	.302	.347	.648
Morel, Christopher	ChC	24	139	466	99	21	4	19	63	60	50	3.5	42	175	9	6	.60	.212	.283	.397	.680
Moreno, Gabriel	Tor	23	125	408	109	19	1	7	54	49	48	4.2	31	83	5	2	.71	.267	.328	.370	.698
Mountcastle, Ryan	Bal	26	139	517	133	26	1	25	65	80	72	4.9	37	147	3	1	.75	.257	.312	.456	.768
Moustakas, Mike	Cin	34	72	223	52	12	0	11	28	31	29	4.4	21	57	1	0	1.00	.233	.308	.435	.743
Mullins II, Cedric	Bal	28	155	565	141	29	4	17	79	54	72	4.3	47	122	26	7	.79	.250	.315	.405	.720
Muncy, Max	LAD	32	135	441	102	21	1	26	74	70	71	5.4	80	131	2	1	.67	.231	.358	.460	.818
Murphy, Sean	Oak	28	138	476	110	30	1	17	61	61	59	4.2	52	120	1	0	1.00	.231	.321	.405	.726
Myers, Wil	SD	32	117	369	89	21	1	15	46	51	49	4.5	38	121	4	2	.67	.241	.314	.425	.739
Naquin, Tyler	NYM	32	111	322	75	17	2	10	39	43	35	3.7	22	94	3	2	.60	.233	.288	.391	.679
Narvaez, Omar	Mil	31	99	274	66	13	0	7	31	29	32	4.0	32	62	0	0	.00	.241	.327	.365	.692
Naylor, Bo	Cle	23	102	211	41	9	1	7	26	25	21	3.2	26	78	5	1	.83	.194	.292	.346	.638
Naylor, Josh	Cle	26	126	456	115	27	1	16	54	65	61	4.6	41	83	5	1	.83	.252	.321	.421	.742
Neuse, Sheldon	Oak	28	99	289	67	11	1	6	30	32	28	3.2	19	92	4	1	.80	.232	.284	.339	.623
Newman, Kevin	Pit	29	107	340	89	17	2	4	37	29	37	3.8	20	48	6	2	.75	.262	.307	.359	.665
Nido, Tomas	NYM	29	79	203	45	10	0	3	20	21	17	2.7	10	54	0	0	.00	.222	.262	.315	.577
Nimmo, Brandon	NYM	30	143	530	136	27	5	15	87	58	77	5.0	79	122	3	2	.60	.257	.369	.411	.780
Nola, Austin	SD	33	110	359	92	19	1	7	41	45	43	4.2	36	67	2	1	.67	.256	.336	.373	.709
Nootbaar, Lars	StL	25	89	216	52	10	1	10	35	29	32	5.1	33	57	3	1	.75	.241	.344	.435	.779
Odor, Rougned	Bal	29	106	303	65	13	1	10	39	42	30	3.2	25	84	3	2	.60	.215	.287	.363	.650
O'Hearn, Ryan	KC	29	59	108	25	5	0	4	12	14	12	3.9	10	32	0	0	.00	.231	.303	.389	.691
Ohtani, Shohei	LAA	28	145	487	125	26	5	32	99	84	89	6.3	67	146	11	5	.69	.257	.351	.528	.879
Olivares, Edward	KC	27	97	272	67	12	1	8	37	28	31	3.9	19	62	4	2	.67	.246	.305	.386	.691
Olson, Matt	Atl	29	157	545	134	31	0	35	84	98	90	5.7	72	147	1	0	1.00	.246	.341	.495	.837
O'Neill, Tyler	StL	28	124	448	111	20	1	25	73	74	66	5.0	42	150	13	3	.81	.248	.322	.464	.786
Ortega, Rafael	ChC	32	103	275	68	13	2	8	35	28	36	4.4	33	64	8	4	.67	.247	.330	.396	.726
Ozuna, Marcell	Atl	32	130	396	101	18	1	21	53	63	59	5.1	37	101	2	1	.67	.255	.322	.465	.786
Pache, Cristian	Oak	24	109	218	44	9	1	4	20	19	16	2.4	14	70	2	2	.50	.202	.253	.307	.561
Paredes, Isaac	TB	24	101	321	77	14	1	14	38	41	44	4.7	41	66	0	0	.00	.240	.333	.421	.754
Pasquantino, Vinnie	KC	25	131	466	124	27	1	23	57	71	77	5.8	58	75	2	1	.67	.266	.353	.476	.830
Pederson, Joc	SF	31	128	364	88	18	2	20	55	57	53	5.0	40	97	2	2	.50	.242	.330	.467	.797
Pena, Jeremy	Hou	25	136	501	126	21	3	22	69	63	63	4.3	23	133	10	2	.83	.251	.294	.437	.731
Peralta, David	TB	35	131	419	101	24	3	12	45	52	51	4.1	38	102	1	1	.50	.241	.309	.399	.707
Peraza, Oswald	NYY	23	109	349	81	14	1	12	44	36	39	3.7	25	103	15	4	.79	.232	.293	.381	.674
Perdomo, Geraldo	Ari	23	133	428	87	12	4	5	54	39	36	2.7	52	112	7	3	.70	.203	.298	.285	.583
Perez, Salvador	KC	33	134	529	141	26	1	31	64	91	78	5.2	22	136	0	0	.00	.267	.307	.495	.802
Peterson, Jace	Mil	33	110	281	63	14	2	8	39	36	34	4.1	37	82	9	1	.90	.224	.319	.374	.692
Pham, Tommy	Bos	35	109	314	80	15	2	10	52	38	44	4.8	39	90	5	2	.71	.255	.345	.411	.755
Pinder, Chad	Oak	31	106	339	78	19	1	11	41	41	36	3.6	20	108	2	1	.67	.230	.277	.389	.666
Piscotty, Stephen	Cin	32	48	98	22	5	0	4	11	13	11	3.8	8	30	1	0	1.00	.224	.290	.398	.688
Plawecki, Kevin	Tex	32	56	129	31	7	0	2	13	14	13	3.5	11	26	0	0	.00	.240	.315	.341	.656
Polanco, Jorge	Min	29	139	519	135	31	2	22	76	76	79	5.3	59	115	5	3	.63	.260	.340	.455	.795
Pollock, A.J.	CWS	35	124	396	106	23	2	17	55	54	59	5.2	29	85	3	1	.75	.268	.324	.465	.789
Pratto, Nick	KC	24	45	115	22	5	1	6	17	16	14	3.9	16	49	1	0	1.00	.191	.301	.409	.709
Profar, Jurickson	SD	30	144	544	129	31	2	14	74	59	66	4.1	66	100	6	2	.75	.237	.327	.379	.706
Raleigh, Cal	Sea	26	119	394	89	26	1	25	46	64	55	4.7	35	123	1	1	.50	.226	.294	.487	.781
Ramirez, Harold	TB	28	121	385	101	22	1	7	40	47	43	3.9	19	74	2	2	.50	.262	.309	.379	.688
Ramirez, Jose	Cle	30	158	600	166	43	4	32	103	111	113	6.7	75	91	20	6	.77	.277	.363	.522	.884
Realmuto, J.T.	Phi	32	139	517	136	24	4	20	76	80	77	5.2	45	128	15	2	.88	.263	.335	.451	.786
Refsnyder, Rob	Bos	32	79	205	53	13	0	7	30	24	29	5.0	24	63	2	1	.67	.259	.348	.424	.772
Rendon, Anthony	LAA	33	106	357	100	25	1	16	53	63	65	6.6	51	68	2	0	1.00	.280	.378	.490	.868
Renfroe, Hunter	Mil	31	133	444	107	23	1	27	63	70	65	5.0	39	120	1	0	1.00	.241	.307	.480	.786

2023 Hitter Projections

Hitter	Team	Age	G	AB	H	2B	3B	HR	R	RBI	RC	RC27	BB	SO	SB	CS	SB%	Avg	OBP	Slg	OPS
Rengifo, Luis	LAA	26	104	315	77	13	2	10	38	33	36	3.9	22	63	4	2	.67	.244	.300	.394	.694
Reyes, Franmil	ChC	27	121	401	93	17	1	20	50	60	50	4.2	36	139	2	2	.50	.232	.298	.429	.727
Reyes, Victor	Det	28	104	318	85	17	3	6	38	34	38	4.2	16	75	4	2	.67	.267	.307	.396	.703
Reynolds, Bryan	Pit	28	148	511	138	27	4	22	75	68	82	5.7	58	130	5	2	.71	.270	.355	.468	.822
Reynolds, Matt	Cin	32	77	202	45	11	1	3	24	17	20	3.4	23	66	3	1	.75	.223	.308	.332	.640
Riley, Austin	Atl	26	156	579	156	34	1	36	86	99	99	6.1	53	165	1	0	1.00	.269	.344	.518	.862
Rivas, Alfonso	ChC	26	82	202	46	7	1	2	21	20	19	3.1	23	67	3	1	.75	.228	.316	.302	.618
Rivera, Emmanuel	Ari	27	108	353	80	16	2	12	45	39	38	3.6	25	91	2	1	.67	.227	.285	.385	.671
Rizzo, Anthony	NYY	33	137	464	117	23	2	27	70	74	75	5.6	58	93	4	2	.67	.252	.361	.485	.846
Robert, Luis	CWS	25	122	467	131	26	2	20	70	71	72	5.5	26	110	13	2	.87	.281	.327	.473	.800
Robles, Victor	Was	26	139	345	79	18	2	7	45	32	34	3.3	24	96	11	4	.73	.229	.302	.354	.655
Rodgers, Brendan	Col	26	137	506	137	29	2	16	64	62	70	4.9	38	106	0	0	.00	.271	.329	.431	.760
Rodriguez, Endy	Pit	23	142	507	134	35	3	26	74	94	83	5.8	46	112	2	0	1.00	.264	.329	.499	.828
Rodriguez, Julio	Sea	22	132	488	131	24	2	27	82	75	80	5.7	43	133	23	6	.79	.268	.338	.492	.829
Rojas, Josh	Ari	28	124	413	110	25	2	10	60	47	60	5.1	51	101	15	3	.83	.266	.350	.409	.759
Rojas, Miguel	Mia	34	134	445	114	22	2	6	46	42	48	3.8	30	64	8	3	.73	.256	.312	.355	.667
Romine, Austin	Cin	34	46	112	23	4	0	2	11	12	8	2.4	6	37	0	0	.00	.205	.252	.295	.547
Rosario, Amed	Cle	27	150	566	159	26	6	12	76	64	74	4.7	28	111	14	4	.78	.281	.319	.412	.731
Rosario, Eddie	Atl	31	86	239	58	12	1	9	31	34	29	4.1	16	54	3	1	.75	.243	.290	.414	.704
Ruf, Darin	NYM	36	104	232	51	10	1	9	33	32	29	4.1	33	76	1	0	1.00	.220	.325	.388	.713
Ruiz, Keibert	Was	24	120	422	106	21	0	12	43	46	50	4.1	33	56	5	1	.83	.251	.315	.386	.701
Rutschman, Adley	Bal	25	137	511	125	32	2	18	79	59	74	5.0	76	116	4	1	.80	.245	.350	.421	.771
Sanchez, Gary	Min	30	121	376	81	17	0	19	49	57	46	4.0	41	122	1	0	1.00	.215	.303	.412	.715
Sanchez, Jesus	Mia	25	101	294	70	12	2	13	36	41	37	4.3	26	87	2	1	.67	.238	.307	.425	.732
Sano, Miguel	Min	30	97	309	66	15	0	19	45	49	42	4.4	39	130	2	1	.67	.214	.306	.447	.752
Santana, Carlos	Sea	37	121	408	97	17	1	17	54	51	58	4.8	67	84	1	0	1.00	.238	.348	.409	.757
Santander, Anthony	Bal	28	140	516	129	29	1	28	68	77	74	5.0	41	115	1	1	.50	.250	.315	.473	.788
Schoop, Jonathan	Det	31	123	411	103	20	1	14	51	49	48	4.1	21	94	3	0	1.00	.251	.297	.406	.703
Schwarber, Kyle	Phi	30	143	487	110	21	2	36	81	78	80	5.5	74	167	6	2	.75	.226	.334	.499	.833
Seager, Corey	Tex	29	143	564	162	34	2	32	88	92	106	6.9	62	104	2	0	1.00	.287	.365	.525	.890
Segura, Jean	Phi	33	135	510	139	24	2	12	71	53	66	4.5	37	85	12	5	.71	.273	.332	.398	.730
Semien, Marcus	Tex	32	158	621	158	34	3	27	98	82	91	5.0	63	126	18	6	.75	.254	.326	.449	.775
Senzel, Nick	Cin	28	70	168	42	9	1	4	22	15	20	4.0	14	36	3	2	.60	.250	.315	.387	.702
Sheets, Gavin	CWS	27	113	279	64	14	0	12	29	43	33	3.9	22	68	0	0	.00	.229	.290	.409	.699
Siri, Jose	TB	27	75	183	40	8	1	7	28	23	20	3.5	12	71	7	1	.88	.219	.274	.388	.662
Slater, Austin	SF	30	136	388	99	22	2	10	58	47	54	4.8	49	123	13	2	.87	.255	.351	.399	.750
Smith, Dominic	NYM	28	76	183	44	10	0	5	21	23	21	3.9	15	46	1	0	1.00	.240	.308	.377	.686
Smith, Josh	Tex	25	78	271	62	11	2	5	32	30	29	3.5	34	71	5	4	.56	.229	.332	.339	.672
Smith, Kevin	Oak	26	88	239	46	11	1	7	23	26	20	2.7	18	91	4	1	.80	.192	.255	.335	.590
Smith, Pavin	Ari	27	98	288	69	14	2	9	35	35	35	4.2	28	68	1	0	1.00	.240	.309	.396	.705
Smith, Will	LAD	28	135	478	124	25	2	30	71	87	83	6.1	59	106	1	0	1.00	.259	.355	.508	.864
Solano, Donovan	Cin	35	107	335	94	20	0	6	34	35	43	4.6	21	72	0	0	.00	.281	.334	.394	.728
Soler, Jorge	Mia	31	119	376	85	19	0	21	49	53	52	4.7	47	121	0	0	.00	.226	.320	.444	.764
Sosa, Edmundo	Phi	27	95	242	58	11	3	5	32	26	24	3.4	11	64	4	2	.67	.240	.300	.372	.672
Soto, Juan	SD	24	154	540	145	30	2	33	104	90	117	7.7	140	106	8	3	.73	.269	.422	.515	.936
Springer, George	Tor	33	134	516	139	25	2	27	94	80	86	5.9	59	111	10	3	.77	.269	.352	.483	.835
Stallings, Jacob	Mia	33	111	329	79	17	0	7	33	39	36	3.7	31	80	0	0	.00	.240	.313	.356	.669
Stanton, Giancarlo	NYY	33	128	463	109	17	0	33	66	86	72	5.3	59	156	0	0	.00	.235	.326	.486	.812
Stassi, Max	LAA	32	96	276	56	10	0	9	34	30	26	3.1	31	94	0	0	.00	.203	.293	.337	.630
Steer, Spencer	Cin	25	86	287	62	14	1	11	37	34	31	3.6	26	81	1	1	.50	.216	.292	.387	.679
Stephenson, Tyler	Cin	26	102	402	107	21	0	12	58	57	54	4.8	38	108	1	0	1.00	.266	.342	.408	.749
Story, Trevor	Bos	30	137	532	135	35	4	27	82	81	84	5.4	51	167	17	4	.81	.254	.326	.487	.813
Stott, Bryson	Phi	25	141	484	118	24	3	14	63	54	59	4.1	43	119	12	4	.75	.244	.307	.393	.699
Straw, Myles	Cle	28	142	441	110	20	2	1	63	32	47	3.7	49	85	19	2	.90	.249	.326	.311	.637
Stubbs, Garrett	Phi	30	64	137	30	7	1	3	20	15	15	3.6	17	37	2	0	1.00	.219	.310	.350	.660
Suarez, Eugenio	Sea	31	146	498	112	22	1	29	69	77	69	4.7	63	172	1	1	.50	.225	.322	.448	.769
Suwinski, Jack	Pit	24	88	287	59	12	1	15	40	38	34	3.8	34	113	3	2	.60	.206	.296	.411	.707
Suzuki, Seiya	ChC	28	141	499	120	28	2	18	67	61	65	4.4	55	142	10	5	.67	.240	.322	.413	.735
Swanson, Dansby	Atl	29	152	590	152	33	2	23	85	84	82	4.8	53	167	13	5	.72	.258	.323	.437	.760
Tapia, Raimel	Tor	29	114	349	91	18	2	5	41	35	39	3.9	20	68	8	2	.80	.261	.303	.367	.669
Tatis Jr., Fernando	SD	24	116	472	129	26	3	36	94	84	96	7.1	56	149	21	5	.81	.273	.358	.570	.928
Taveras, Leody	Tex	24	119	392	89	18	3	9	47	40	40	3.4	31	117	12	5	.71	.227	.287	.357	.644
Taylor, Chris	LAD	32	124	386	91	23	3	14	57	49	51	4.5	44	138	8	2	.80	.236	.322	.420	.742
Taylor, Michael A.	KC	32	117	332	81	15	2	9	40	37	38	3.9	26	97	4	1	.80	.244	.303	.383	.685
Taylor, Tyrone	Mil	29	121	358	83	18	2	16	45	50	43	4.0	24	95	3	1	.75	.232	.293	.427	.720
Tellez, Rowdy	Mil	28	138	454	110	24	1	27	56	71	68	5.1	47	109	1	1	.50	.242	.320	.478	.798
Thomas, Alek	Ari	23	102	351	83	19	3	8	43	36	38	3.6	27	78	5	4	.56	.236	.297	.376	.673
Thomas, Lane	Was	27	137	417	94	21	2	15	54	52	48	3.9	41	120	7	3	.70	.225	.301	.393	.694
Thompson, Bubba	Tex	25	125	423	96	16	4	9	57	37	41	3.2	21	143	31	5	.86	.227	.272	.348	.619
Thompson, Trayce	LAD	32	66	150	30	6	1	8	20	21	17	3.7	16	62	2	1	.67	.200	.281	.413	.695
Toglia, Michael	Col	24	131	472	91	20	2	19	52	59	46	3.1	48	182	4	2	.67	.193	.270	.364	.635
Torkelson, Spencer	Det	23	122	397	85	18	1	14	51	43	43	3.6	47	117	1	2	.33	.214	.307	.370	.677
Toro, Abraham	Sea	26	91	232	54	12	1	8	29	31	27	4.0	21	48	3	1	.75	.233	.307	.397	.704
Torrens, Luis	Sea	27	91	261	57	12	1	8	25	33	27	3.4	22	81	0	0	.00	.218	.282	.364	.646
Torres, Gleyber	NYY	26	143	525	136	27	1	23	70	78	76	5.0	51	127	11	5	.69	.259	.329	.446	.775
Tovar, Ezequiel	Col	21	138	493	119	19	3	18	51	60	59	4.1	35	138	14	3	.82	.241	.300	.402	.701
Trammell, Taylor	Sea	25	53	110	23	5	0	4	14	12	12	3.4	12	37	3	1	.75	.209	.293	.364	.656
Trejo, Alan	Col	27	59	142	31	8	0	5	15	17	14	3.2	6	42	0	0	.00	.218	.260	.380	.640
Trevino, Jose	NYY	30	106	319	75	14	0	8	32	35	30	3.2	14	63	1	1	.50	.235	.269	.354	.624
Trout, Mike	LAA	31	122	459	130	29	2	38	92	84	109	8.6	83	141	3	1	.75	.283	.403	.603	1.006
Tsutsugo, Yoshi	Tor	31	55	116	24	5	0	4	13	12	12	3.4	15	37	0	0	.00	.207	.298	.353	.651

2023 Hitter Projections

Hitter	Team	Age	G	AB	H	2B	3B	HR	R	RBI	RC	RC27	BB	SO	SB	CS	SB%	Avg	OBP	Slg	OPS
Tucker, Kyle	Hou	26	153	569	153	33	4	34	85	109	103	6.4	60	112	22	3	.88	.269	.342	.520	.862
Turang, Brice	Mil	23	103	278	66	12	1	6	35	32	31	3.8	27	70	10	2	.83	.237	.305	.353	.657
Turner, Justin	LAD	38	145	534	150	32	1	21	79	78	88	5.9	59	102	3	0	1.00	.281	.365	.463	.828
Turner, Trea	LAD	29	158	633	186	39	4	25	105	84	109	6.2	49	128	25	5	.83	.294	.348	.487	.835
Urias, Luis	Mil	26	125	376	90	18	2	14	52	44	50	4.5	46	94	2	1	.67	.239	.336	.410	.746
Urias, Ramon	Bal	29	88	264	66	14	0	9	32	33	33	4.3	23	70	1	1	.50	.250	.320	.405	.725
Urshela, Gio	Min	31	140	501	133	28	2	13	60	64	64	4.5	36	105	1	0	1.00	.265	.319	.407	.726
Varsho, Daulton	Ari	26	142	521	122	26	4	29	79	73	73	4.7	48	138	13	3	.81	.234	.306	.466	.772
Vaughn, Andrew	CWS	25	134	464	120	26	1	18	59	67	63	4.8	36	95	0	0	.00	.259	.323	.435	.758
Vavra, Terrin	Bal	26	111	336	80	18	2	4	48	33	37	3.7	43	89	4	2	.67	.238	.337	.339	.676
Vazquez, Christian	Hou	32	132	463	116	23	1	10	50	52	50	3.7	31	90	3	3	.50	.251	.302	.369	.671
Velazquez, Andrew	LAA	28	90	187	39	8	1	5	24	19	18	3.1	13	69	9	1	.90	.209	.264	.342	.606
Velazquez, Nelson	ChC	24	65	171	34	8	1	7	20	23	18	3.3	17	71	5	2	.71	.199	.279	.380	.659
Verdugo, Alex	Bos	27	146	529	151	34	2	13	73	64	78	5.3	45	86	3	2	.60	.285	.345	.431	.776
Vierling, Matt	Phi	26	78	178	44	7	1	4	22	18	20	3.8	15	41	5	2	.71	.247	.313	.365	.678
Villar, David	SF	26	52	178	39	9	0	11	26	30	24	4.6	21	66	0	0	.00	.219	.322	.455	.777
Villar, Jonathan	Sea	32	73	221	50	9	1	6	27	21	23	3.5	19	66	8	2	.80	.226	.290	.357	.648
Vogelbach, Daniel	NYM	30	122	357	81	15	0	16	45	50	50	4.7	67	105	0	0	.00	.227	.351	.403	.754
Voit, Luke	Was	32	141	463	109	22	1	23	61	70	63	4.6	51	162	1	1	.50	.235	.322	.436	.758
Volpe, Anthony	NYY	22	127	438	97	27	4	13	55	42	51	3.8	41	121	21	4	.84	.221	.300	.390	.690
Votto, Joey	Cin	39	124	451	109	23	1	19	62	60	67	5.1	75	126	1	0	1.00	.242	.358	.424	.782
Wade Jr., LaMonte	SF	29	86	219	50	9	1	8	30	26	27	4.1	28	52	2	1	.67	.228	.327	.388	.715
Walker, Christian	Ari	32	152	560	141	29	2	30	79	83	86	5.3	60	140	2	1	.67	.252	.332	.471	.803
Walker, Jordan	StL	21	82	265	59	15	1	6	36	25	27	3.3	22	83	6	2	.75	.223	.292	.355	.647
Walls, Taylor	TB	26	85	199	40	10	1	5	27	19	20	3.2	27	61	5	2	.71	.201	.300	.337	.636
Walsh, Jared	LAA	29	106	314	75	16	1	15	39	47	41	4.5	26	100	1	0	1.00	.239	.305	.439	.745
Ward, Taylor	LAA	29	125	428	113	24	1	19	63	55	68	5.6	53	112	4	1	.80	.264	.352	.458	.810
Waters, Drew	KC	24	88	255	55	12	2	8	35	25	28	3.6	24	101	7	1	.88	.216	.288	.373	.661
Wendle, Joey	Mia	33	135	456	119	28	3	7	56	49	52	4.0	25	88	11	4	.73	.261	.312	.382	.694
Winker, Jesse	Sea	29	123	373	95	20	1	14	50	48	56	5.3	58	81	0	0	.00	.255	.362	.426	.789
Wisdom, Patrick	ChC	31	121	367	75	17	0	21	52	55	44	3.8	39	150	5	2	.71	.204	.291	.422	.714
Witt Jr., Bobby	KC	23	150	561	142	33	4	24	83	83	77	4.7	36	140	24	7	.77	.253	.305	.455	.760
Wong, Connor	Bos	27	79	234	54	12	0	8	26	27	25	3.6	15	74	2	1	.67	.231	.283	.385	.667
Wong, Kolten	Mil	32	142	505	129	29	4	15	73	58	68	4.7	50	101	15	6	.71	.255	.342	.418	.759
Wynns, Austin	SF	32	70	179	43	6	0	4	20	20	19	3.6	18	43	0	0	.00	.240	.317	.341	.657
Yastrzemski, Mike	SF	32	133	420	97	25	3	18	65	57	57	4.5	49	124	4	2	.67	.231	.319	.433	.752
Yelich, Christian	Mil	31	132	435	110	22	3	15	77	56	67	5.3	69	124	12	2	.86	.253	.360	.421	.781
Yepez, Juan	StL	25	98	298	71	17	0	18	38	49	42	4.8	24	80	0	0	.00	.238	.302	.477	.778
Zavala, Seby	CWS	29	71	153	29	8	0	4	18	16	13	2.7	15	67	0	0	.00	.190	.271	.320	.591
Zimmer, Bradley	Tor	30	73	109	22	4	0	3	15	10	9	2.8	9	45	3	1	.75	.202	.293	.321	.614
Zunino, Mike	TB	32	64	150	31	6	0	9	19	22	17	3.7	12	60	0	0	.00	.207	.279	.427	.705

589

2023 Pitcher Projections

Pitcher	Team	Age	G	GS	IP	H	HR	BB	SO	HB	W	L	Pct	Sv	BR/9	ERA
	PLAYER		HOW MUCH			WHAT HE WILL GIVE UP					THE RESULTS					
Abbott, Cory	Was	27	26	16	90	89	19	47	96	5	3	7	.300	0	14.1	4.85
Abreu, Albert	NYY	27	27	0	32	30	5	18	34	2	2	2	.500	0	14.1	4.50
Abreu, Bryan	Hou	26	61	0	65	50	5	33	88	5	5	3	.625	0	12.2	3.36
Acevedo, Domingo	Oak	29	67	0	64	53	11	16	60	2	3	4	.429	26	10.0	3.63
Adam, Jason	TB	31	65	0	65	39	6	21	76	6	5	3	.625	11	9.1	2.89
Akin, Keegan	Bal	28	47	0	78	78	11	28	74	2	4	5	.444	0	12.5	4.10
Alcantara, Sandy	Mia	27	31	31	207	169	20	54	188	9	12	11	.522	0	10.1	3.37
Alexander, Jason	Mil	30	21	11	75	87	10	26	54	5	3	5	.375	0	14.2	4.80
Alexander, Scott	SF	33	41	8	42	35	4	12	29	1	2	2	.500	0	10.3	3.69
Alexander, Tyler	Det	28	32	18	107	120	20	26	77	5	4	8	.333	0	12.7	4.67
Alvarado, Jose	Phi	28	60	0	57	43	5	35	81	3	4	2	.667	6	12.8	3.46
Anderson, Ian	Atl	25	23	23	125	120	14	61	120	2	7	7	.500	0	13.2	4.10
Anderson, Tyler	LAD	33	30	30	181	167	26	41	139	7	12	8	.600	0	10.7	3.85
Antone, Tejay	Cin	29	34	0	47	42	5	20	52	3	2	3	.400	0	12.4	3.78
Arano, Victor	Was	28	42	0	43	40	5	14	48	4	2	3	.400	0	12.1	3.80
Archer, Chris	Min	34	23	23	101	97	18	45	86	3	5	6	.455	0	12.9	4.50
Armstrong, Shawn	TB	32	54	0	76	75	11	25	84	4	4	4	.500	6	12.3	3.91
Ashby, Aaron	Mil	25	33	21	129	118	16	59	158	6	7	7	.500	0	12.8	3.81
Ashcraft, Graham	Cin	25	22	22	114	126	9	39	92	7	5	7	.417	0	13.6	4.26
Assad, Javier	ChC	25	20	20	99	102	12	39	92	6	4	7	.364	0	13.4	4.27
Baker, Bryan	Bal	28	68	0	74	56	4	32	80	3	5	3	.625	5	11.1	3.22
Banks, Tanner	CWS	31	28	0	46	50	6	13	45	1	3	3	.500	0	12.5	4.11
Banuelos, Manny	Pit	32	50	0	59	54	6	30	56	4	3	4	.429	0	13.4	4.20
Bard, Daniel	Col	38	55	0	62	54	6	29	68	5	4	3	.571	33	12.8	3.82
Barlow, Joe	Tex	27	34	0	32	23	3	14	30	2	2	2	.500	12	11.0	3.53
Barlow, Scott	KC	30	69	0	77	66	8	27	84	3	4	4	.500	27	11.2	3.50
Barnes, Matt	Bos	33	56	0	53	49	6	26	60	4	3	3	.500	11	13.4	4.00
Barria, Jaime	LAA	26	40	0	82	86	16	21	58	3	4	5	.444	0	12.1	4.50
Bass, Anthony	Tor	35	75	0	73	61	9	23	69	1	5	3	.625	0	10.5	3.52
Bassitt, Chris	NYM	34	30	30	190	164	23	54	176	14	11	10	.524	0	11.0	3.66
Baumann, Mike	Bal	27	14	7	50	45	5	20	50	1	3	3	.500	0	11.9	3.68
Bautista, Felix	Bal	28	60	0	66	39	6	26	88	2	5	3	.625	28	9.1	2.72
Bednar, David	Pit	28	56	0	56	46	6	18	72	1	4	3	.571	24	10.4	3.05
Beeks, Jalen	TB	29	49	6	59	54	7	21	64	3	3	3	.500	0	11.9	3.65
Bellatti, Andrew	Phi	31	58	0	57	50	7	25	75	3	4	3	.571	0	12.3	3.60
Bello, Brayan	Bos	24	28	28	151	142	10	61	180	4	10	7	.588	0	12.3	3.47
Berrios, Jose	Tor	29	31	31	172	177	25	44	157	11	10	9	.526	0	12.1	4.06
Bieber, Shane	Cle	28	32	32	196	168	23	42	212	4	13	9	.591	0	9.8	3.19
Bird, Jake	Col	27	47	0	67	60	8	29	66	7	4	4	.500	0	12.9	4.05
Blach, Ty	Col	32	20	0	32	43	5	9	19	1	1	2	.333	0	14.9	5.35
Blackburn, Paul	Oak	29	20	20	106	117	14	29	84	4	4	8	.333	0	12.7	4.29
Bleier, Richard	Mia	36	57	0	55	60	4	10	37	0	3	3	.500	5	11.8	3.90
Boxberger, Brad	Mil	35	75	0	69	57	9	31	75	4	4	4	.500	0	12.0	3.78
Bradish, Kyle	Bal	26	28	28	158	148	19	59	163	6	9	9	.500	0	12.1	3.83
Bradley, Archie	LAA	30	36	0	36	37	3	14	29	1	2	2	.500	0	13.0	4.13
Bradley, Taj	TB	22	18	18	96	75	10	23	98	4	6	4	.600	0	9.6	3.15
Brash, Matt	Sea	25	47	0	51	40	5	29	68	1	3	2	.600	0	12.4	3.43
Brasier, Ryan	Bos	35	71	0	67	71	10	18	67	2	4	4	.500	0	12.2	4.03
Brebbia, John	SF	33	75	16	66	68	8	19	59	2	4	4	.500	0	12.1	3.96
Brieske, Beau	Det	25	13	13	68	67	10	20	51	2	3	4	.429	0	11.8	4.13
Brigham, Jeff	Mia	31	26	0	39	32	6	18	52	1	2	2	.500	0	11.8	3.62
Brogdon, Connor	Phi	28	56	0	55	47	7	18	63	1	4	2	.667	6	10.8	3.39
Brown, Hunter	Hou	24	38	9	112	83	8	47	137	2	8	4	.667	0	10.6	3.04
Brubaker, JT	Pit	29	25	25	131	139	21	47	131	9	6	9	.400	0	13.4	4.43
Bubic, Kris	KC	25	29	29	146	164	23	66	130	6	6	10	.375	0	14.5	4.90
Bumgarner, Madison	Ari	33	27	27	151	167	29	44	113	10	6	10	.375	0	13.2	4.80
Bummer, Aaron	CWS	29	51	0	43	36	3	18	49	3	3	2	.600	0	11.9	3.46
Bundy, Dylan	Min	30	29	29	146	154	27	39	111	6	7	9	.438	0	12.3	4.47
Burke, Brock	Tex	26	51	0	84	77	12	28	93	5	5	5	.500	0	11.6	3.69
Burnes, Corbin	Mil	28	34	34	204	159	24	54	253	11	14	9	.609	0	9.9	3.07
Bush, Matt	Mil	37	67	0	64	45	12	21	76	4	4	3	.571	0	9.8	3.39
Cabrera, Edward	Mia	25	22	22	119	88	18	57	138	9	6	7	.462	0	11.6	3.74
Cabrera, Genesis	StL	26	30	0	34	31	5	16	32	3	2	2	.500	0	13.2	4.37
Canning, Griffin	LAA	27	17	17	86	82	15	35	87	4	5	5	.500	0	12.7	4.30
Carrasco, Carlos	NYM	36	27	27	136	140	21	41	135	6	7	8	.467	0	12.4	4.11
Castillo, Diego	Sea	29	57	0	53	40	6	19	56	3	3	3	.500	6	10.5	3.39
Castillo, Luis	Sea	30	28	28	173	147	18	59	186	7	11	9	.550	0	11.1	3.45
Castillo, Max	KC	24	12	12	51	50	7	20	50	2	2	3	.400	0	12.7	4.15
Cease, Dylan	CWS	27	31	31	193	154	25	82	235	7	12	9	.571	0	11.3	3.48
Cessa, Luis	Cin	31	43	17	114	112	18	40	86	2	5	7	.417	0	12.2	4.31
Chafin, Andrew	Det	33	70	0	66	56	7	21	71	3	4	4	.500	9	10.9	3.40
Chapman, Aroldis	NYY	35	42	0	37	25	5	23	51	1	2	2	.500	14	11.9	3.51
Chargois, JT	TB	32	43	0	46	40	6	18	40	5	2	3	.400	0	12.3	4.05
Chavez, Jesse	Atl	39	66	0	72	70	9	23	73	2	5	3	.625	0	11.9	3.78
Cimber, Adam	Tor	32	82	0	75	72	6	16	57	7	5	4	.556	0	11.4	3.76
Cishek, Steve	Was	37	69	0	66	58	9	31	67	10	3	4	.429	0	13.5	4.30
Cisnero, Jose	Det	34	46	0	43	36	4	23	42	3	2	3	.400	0	13.0	4.01
Civale, Aaron	Cle	28	21	21	113	104	17	28	108	6	6	6	.500	0	11.0	3.74

590

2023 Pitcher Projections

Pitcher	Team	Age	G	GS	IP	H	HR	BB	SO	HB	W	L	Pct	Sv	BR/9	ERA
Clarke, Taylor	KC	30	45	0	45	48	8	13	41	1	2	3	.400	6	12.4	4.30
Clase, Emmanuel	Cle	25	74	0	71	51	4	13	75	1	5	3	.625	33	8.2	2.64
Cleavinger, Garrett	TB	29	27	0	39	27	4	20	58	3	3	2	.600	0	11.5	3.13
Clevinger, Mike	SD	32	28	28	148	137	23	47	128	9	9	8	.529	0	11.7	4.05
Cobb, Alex	SF	35	30	30	176	180	16	55	171	5	10	10	.500	0	12.3	3.77
Cole, Gerrit	NYY	32	33	33	213	164	33	52	268	3	15	8	.652	0	9.3	3.04
Coleman, Dylan	KC	26	69	0	73	54	6	35	85	5	4	4	.500	0	11.6	3.40
Colome, Alex	Col	34	42	0	35	40	4	14	26	1	2	2	.500	0	14.1	4.63
Contreras, Roansy	Pit	23	23	23	121	104	16	44	128	3	7	7	.500	0	11.2	3.65
Corbin, Patrick	Was	33	29	29	147	183	27	50	124	3	5	11	.313	0	14.5	5.12
Cortes, Nestor	NYY	28	26	26	156	121	23	41	161	3	10	7	.588	0	9.5	3.34
Crawford, Kutter	Bos	27	18	18	83	88	14	27	87	2	5	5	.500	0	12.7	4.23
Crismatt, Nabil	SD	28	44	0	64	61	9	19	62	3	4	3	.571	0	11.7	3.85
Crochet, Garrett	CWS	24	48	0	49	39	3	22	59	1	3	2	.600	0	11.4	3.19
Crowe, Wil	Pit	28	55	0	68	72	11	32	62	3	3	5	.375	6	14.2	4.77
Cuas, Jose	KC	29	51	0	41	39	2	18	36	5	2	2	.500	0	13.6	3.99
Cueto, Johnny	CWS	37	28	28	162	178	24	40	114	6	8	10	.444	0	12.4	4.39
Curry, Xzavion	Cle	24	8	8	38	34	6	13	38	1	2	2	.500	0	11.4	3.85
Danish, Tyler	Bos	28	24	0	33	37	6	11	31	2	2	2	.500	0	13.6	4.77
Darvish, Yu	SD	36	30	30	193	161	28	45	202	11	13	8	.619	0	10.1	3.43
Davidson, Tucker	LAA	27	17	17	81	86	12	37	76	3	4	5	.444	0	14.0	4.61
Davies, Zach	Ari	30	30	30	148	154	24	60	111	3	7	10	.412	0	13.2	4.62
De Jong, Chase	Pit	29	50	0	90	87	19	41	82	6	4	6	.400	0	13.4	4.75
De Los Santos, Enyel	Cle	27	53	0	57	47	9	21	68	3	3	3	.500	0	11.2	3.62
deGrom, Jacob	NYM	35	21	21	128	90	14	24	185	2	10	4	.714	0	8.2	2.53
DeSclafani, Anthony	SF	33	23	23	127	135	20	37	112	3	6	8	.429	0	12.4	4.25
Detmers, Reid	LAA	23	25	25	135	124	19	46	148	8	9	6	.600	0	11.9	3.80
Diaz, Alexis	Cin	26	60	0	68	41	6	35	91	6	4	3	.571	23	10.9	3.10
Diaz, Edwin	NYM	29	57	0	61	39	6	21	104	4	5	2	.714	31	9.4	2.51
Diekman, Jake	CWS	36	71	0	57	47	8	37	75	7	3	3	.500	0	14.4	4.27
Dominguez, Seranthony	Phi	28	53	0	53	44	7	26	62	2	3	3	.500	15	12.2	3.71
Doolittle, Sean	Was	36	31	0	30	30	5	11	31	1	1	2	.333	0	12.6	4.05
Doval, Camilo	SF	25	67	0	70	57	6	34	85	4	4	4	.500	29	12.2	3.56
Duffy, Danny	LAD	34	11	11	58	49	10	21	61	2	4	3	.571	0	11.2	3.86
Dunn, Justin	Cin	27	8	8	41	43	8	23	36	4	1	3	.250	0	15.4	5.38
Dunning, Dane	Tex	28	27	27	146	149	19	56	132	10	7	9	.438	0	13.3	4.32
Duran, Jhoan	Min	25	60	0	66	53	5	20	86	4	5	3	.625	14	10.5	2.97
Edwards Jr., Carl	Was	31	63	0	68	53	9	27	66	1	4	4	.500	0	10.7	3.63
Eflin, Zach	Phi	29	17	17	89	91	14	20	80	4	5	5	.500	0	11.6	4.00
Elder, Bryce	Atl	24	13	13	79	69	10	30	73	4	5	4	.556	0	11.7	3.88
Eovaldi, Nathan	Bos	33	29	29	164	174	25	36	160	6	10	8	.556	0	11.9	3.95
Espino, Paolo	Was	36	39	23	126	143	25	29	102	3	5	9	.357	0	12.5	4.58
Estevez, Carlos	Col	30	61	0	62	67	11	23	60	2	3	4	.429	0	13.4	4.58
Fairbanks, Pete	TB	29	39	0	40	32	4	14	56	1	3	2	.600	23	10.6	2.98
Falter, Bailey	Phi	26	22	22	109	103	17	22	105	5	7	5	.583	0	10.7	3.67
Farmer, Buck	Cin	32	57	0	62	57	9	30	69	3	3	4	.429	6	13.1	4.14
Fedde, Erick	Was	30	24	24	115	131	20	49	90	2	4	9	.308	0	14.2	5.01
Feltner, Ryan	Col	26	23	23	119	120	17	42	115	5	6	7	.462	0	12.6	4.16
Ferguson, Caleb	LAD	26	42	0	42	33	5	20	51	3	3	2	.600	0	12.0	3.61
Festa, Matthew	Sea	30	58	0	64	49	10	21	77	3	4	3	.571	0	10.3	3.37
Feyereisen, J.P.	TB	30	48	0	50	32	6	22	50	0	3	2	.600	0	9.7	3.36
Finnegan, Kyle	Was	31	66	0	71	63	8	29	73	1	4	4	.500	23	11.8	3.69
Flaherty, Jack	StL	27	19	19	104	85	14	38	112	6	7	5	.583	0	11.2	3.61
Fleming, Josh	TB	27	7	0	30	35	4	8	22	1	1	2	.333	0	13.2	4.50
Flexen, Chris	Sea	28	34	13	108	112	14	34	77	2	5	7	.417	0	12.3	4.25
Floro, Dylan	Mia	32	64	0	64	59	4	21	57	0	4	4	.500	21	11.3	3.51
Foley, Jason	Det	27	63	0	62	69	6	17	49	4	3	4	.429	0	13.1	4.21
Foster, Matt	CWS	28	31	0	31	28	5	10	32	1	2	2	.500	0	11.3	3.69
Freeland, Kyle	Col	30	30	30	177	206	31	58	134	11	8	12	.400	0	14.0	4.99
Fried, Max	Atl	29	29	29	184	166	17	42	168	6	13	8	.619	0	10.5	3.40
Fulmer, Michael	Min	30	71	0	68	69	8	27	66	5	4	4	.500	0	13.4	4.24
Gallegos, Giovanny	StL	31	56	0	59	41	7	17	70	2	4	2	.667	4	9.2	2.96
Gallen, Zac	Ari	27	31	31	183	140	23	56	194	9	11	9	.550	0	10.1	3.34
Garcia, Bryan	Det	28	6	6	35	35	6	16	28	2	1	3	.250	0	13.6	4.76
Garcia, Jarlin	SF	30	61	0	77	68	10	23	67	2	4	4	.500	3	10.9	3.73
Garcia, Luis	Hou	26	28	28	165	137	22	50	167	2	11	7	.611	0	10.3	3.46
Garcia, Luis	SD	36	65	0	63	58	7	21	67	4	4	3	.571	0	11.9	3.70
Garcia, Yimi	Tor	32	65	0	69	56	10	18	66	4	5	3	.625	0	10.2	3.53
Garrett, Amir	KC	31	66	0	51	43	5	31	55	3	3	3	.500	0	13.6	3.99
Garrett, Braxton	Mia	25	18	18	97	93	12	34	93	7	5	6	.455	0	12.4	3.96
Gausman, Kevin	Tor	32	32	32	193	187	23	39	217	3	13	8	.619	0	10.7	3.34
German, Domingo	NYY	30	26	26	139	122	24	36	120	6	8	7	.533	0	10.6	3.87
Gibaut, Ian	Cin	29	51	0	56	61	6	29	65	2	2	4	.333	0	14.8	4.42
Gibson, Kyle	Phi	35	30	30	173	184	24	57	147	9	9	10	.474	0	13.0	4.35
Gilbert, Logan	Sea	26	31	31	186	172	21	48	180	7	11	10	.524	0	11.0	3.56
Gilbreath, Lucas	Col	27	37	0	33	30	3	19	36	2	2	2	.500	0	13.9	4.09
Ginkel, Kevin	Ari	29	57	0	58	52	7	25	70	1	3	3	.500	0	12.1	3.63
Giolito, Lucas	CWS	28	31	31	178	163	26	61	198	4	11	9	.550	0	11.5	3.71
Givens, Mychal	NYM	33	56	0	61	51	10	28	70	4	3	3	.500	0	12.2	3.93
Glasnow, Tyler	TB	29	22	22	118	76	14	39	169	0	9	4	.692	0	8.8	2.58
Gomber, Austin	Col	29	34	9	107	115	18	34	88	2	5	7	.417	0	12.7	4.46

2023 Pitcher Projections

PLAYER			HOW MUCH			WHAT HE WILL GIVE UP						THE RESULTS					
Pitcher	Team	Age	G	GS	IP	H	HR	BB	SO	HB	W	L	Pct	Sv	BR/9	ERA
Gonsolin, Tony	LAD	29	26	26	146	105	16	49	137	4	11	5	.688	0	9.7	3.34
Gonzales, Marco	Sea	31	32	32	196	199	32	53	123	8	9	13	.409	0	11.9	4.39
Gore, MacKenzie	Was	24	21	21	111	115	15	55	113	6	5	8	.385	0	14.3	4.54
Gott, Trevor	Mil	30	37	0	41	35	7	14	42	2	2	2	.500	0	11.2	3.79
Graterol, Brusdar	LAD	24	35	0	38	30	3	11	34	3	3	1	.750	6	10.4	3.38
Graveman, Kendall	CWS	32	61	0	63	58	5	25	62	5	4	3	.571	0	12.6	3.77
Gray, Jon	Tex	31	20	20	101	94	16	35	102	5	5	6	.455	0	11.9	3.98
Gray, Josiah	Was	25	29	29	163	144	35	71	171	8	7	11	.389	0	12.3	4.34
Gray, Sonny	Min	33	24	24	128	113	14	45	129	7	8	6	.571	0	11.6	3.67
Green, Chad	NYY	32	32	0	36	28	5	9	41	1	2	2	.500	0	9.5	3.19
Greene, Hunter	Cin	23	23	23	121	106	22	46	161	10	6	7	.462	0	12.0	3.80
Greinke, Zack	KC	39	25	25	142	162	18	27	86	3	7	9	.438	0	12.2	4.28
Grove, Michael	LAD	26	14	14	70	67	14	28	75	1	4	3	.571	0	12.3	4.24
Hader, Josh	SD	29	54	0	49	33	8	20	79	3	4	2	.667	32	10.3	2.99
Hand, Brad	Phi	33	48	0	42	39	4	18	39	5	2	2	.500	0	13.3	4.18
Harvey, Hunter	Was	28	56	0	62	63	11	22	66	2	3	4	.429	0	12.6	4.21
Heaney, Andrew	LAD	32	25	25	122	106	24	34	158	10	9	5	.643	0	11.1	3.62
Hearn, Taylor	Tex	28	47	6	119	118	18	51	118	4	6	8	.429	0	13.1	4.28
Heasley, Jon	KC	26	23	23	124	127	24	46	106	7	5	8	.385	0	13.1	4.68
Helsley, Ryan	StL	28	55	0	65	41	7	26	83	0	5	2	.714	30	9.3	2.87
Hendricks, Kyle	ChC	33	17	17	91	98	15	22	68	5	4	6	.400	0	12.4	4.40
Hendriks, Liam	CWS	34	61	0	61	44	7	13	88	2	5	2	.714	36	8.7	2.53
Henry, Tommy	Ari	25	17	17	94	92	15	41	87	3	4	6	.400	0	13.0	4.36
Hentges, Sam	Cle	26	57	0	68	70	8	29	74	2	4	4	.500	9	13.4	4.11
Herget, Jimmy	LAA	29	58	0	83	68	10	27	79	4	5	4	.556	21	10.7	3.59
Hernandez, Carlos	KC	26	40	0	61	62	9	27	48	2	3	4	.429	0	13.4	4.57
Hernandez, Elieser	Mia	28	18	0	45	41	9	14	48	3	2	3	.400	0	11.6	4.00
Hernandez, Jonathan	Tex	26	48	0	53	51	6	30	52	2	2	3	.400	0	14.1	4.34
Hicks, Jordan	StL	26	41	0	62	47	5	38	64	6	4	3	.571	0	13.2	3.91
Hill, Rich	Bos	43	28	28	142	145	20	46	122	8	8	8	.500	0	12.6	4.22
Hill, Tim	SD	33	57	0	51	47	5	17	36	5	3	3	.500	0	12.2	4.03
Hjelle, Sean	SF	26	11	0	41	48	5	16	35	3	2	3	.400	0	14.7	4.83
Hoffman, Jeff	Cin	30	37	0	46	48	10	23	47	3	2	3	.400	0	14.5	5.09
Holmes, Clay	NYY	30	54	0	58	44	4	23	59	6	4	3	.571	29	11.3	3.41
Houck, Tanner	Bos	27	58	0	65	61	5	25	68	7	4	3	.571	26	12.9	3.78
Houser, Adrian	Mil	30	20	20	90	89	10	41	66	4	4	6	.400	0	13.4	4.45
Hudson, Dakota	StL	28	24	24	127	123	12	56	80	7	7	7	.500	0	13.2	4.40
Hughes, Brandon	ChC	27	71	0	72	53	10	25	86	6	4	4	.500	17	10.5	3.33
Iglesias, Raisel	Atl	33	72	0	70	55	9	16	90	3	5	2	.714	0	9.5	2.95
Irvin, Cole	Oak	29	31	31	181	196	27	39	127	8	7	13	.350	0	12.1	4.28
Jackson, Zach	Oak	28	39	0	35	23	3	21	48	1	2	2	.500	7	11.6	3.23
Jameson, Drey	Ari	25	21	21	117	123	17	41	120	7	6	7	.462	0	13.2	4.27
Jansen, Kenley	Atl	35	69	0	69	49	9	28	87	3	5	3	.625	40	10.4	3.23
Javier, Cristian	Hou	26	30	30	164	100	21	65	210	8	12	6	.667	0	9.5	2.99
Jax, Griffin	Min	28	71	0	73	67	10	23	69	3	4	4	.500	0	11.5	3.82
Jimenez, Dany	Oak	29	28	0	31	23	4	17	37	0	1	2	.333	0	11.6	3.58
Jimenez, Joe	Det	28	58	0	54	46	9	20	70	4	3	3	.500	7	11.7	3.63
Junis, Jakob	SF	30	27	19	136	155	25	39	121	6	6	9	.400	0	13.2	4.67
Kaprielian, James	Oak	29	27	27	148	143	21	60	119	6	5	11	.313	0	12.7	4.29
Karinchak, James	Cle	27	60	0	62	40	6	37	95	1	4	3	.571	8	11.3	3.06
Keller, Brad	KC	27	40	14	117	127	14	48	90	4	5	8	.385	0	13.8	4.58
Keller, Mitch	Pit	27	30	30	166	178	17	69	151	11	7	11	.389	0	14.0	4.39
Kelly, Joe	CWS	35	48	0	42	34	4	21	52	4	3	2	.600	0	12.6	3.61
Kelly, Merrill	Ari	34	32	32	196	188	29	59	166	3	10	11	.476	0	11.3	3.97
Kennedy, Ian	Ari	38	57	0	52	57	10	20	48	1	2	4	.333	7	13.5	4.68
Kershaw, Clayton	LAD	35	22	22	130	106	18	25	139	2	10	4	.714	0	9.2	3.13
Kikuchi, Yusei	Tor	32	37	14	96	96	18	43	101	5	5	6	.455	0	13.5	4.55
Kilian, Caleb	ChC	26	14	14	68	67	5	35	73	2	3	4	.429	0	13.8	3.97
Kimbrel, Craig	LAD	35	66	0	66	50	10	31	86	5	5	3	.625	23	11.7	3.56
King, John	Tex	28	33	0	55	59	7	16	40	3	3	4	.429	0	12.8	4.34
King, Michael	NYY	28	51	0	75	63	9	24	87	4	5	3	.625	0	10.9	3.41
Kirby, George	Sea	25	27	27	149	141	15	29	157	7	9	7	.563	0	10.7	3.35
Kluber, Corey	TB	37	30	30	170	178	21	37	145	12	9	10	.474	0	12.0	3.98
Koenig, Jared	Oak	29	12	0	40	40	5	13	33	2	1	3	.250	0	12.4	4.17
Kopech, Michael	CWS	27	22	22	106	84	14	46	104	2	6	5	.545	0	11.2	3.75
Krehbiel, Joey	Bal	30	56	0	57	57	11	21	48	3	3	4	.429	0	12.8	4.58
Kremer, Dean	Bal	27	28	28	146	151	22	47	122	6	7	9	.438	0	12.6	4.32
Kuhl, Chad	Col	30	24	24	127	137	25	59	106	7	5	9	.357	0	14.4	5.11
Kuhnel, Joel	Cin	28	44	0	49	49	7	12	44	3	2	3	.400	0	11.8	3.97
Lambert, Jimmy	CWS	28	55	0	56	55	13	27	57	2	3	4	.429	0	13.5	4.82
Lamet, Dinelson	Col	30	42	0	46	44	6	19	58	3	3	2	.600	0	12.9	3.82
Lange, Alex	Det	27	73	0	66	59	7	34	80	5	3	4	.429	0	13.4	3.89
Lauer, Eric	Mil	28	28	28	158	142	26	59	156	3	9	9	.500	0	11.6	3.96
Law, Derek	Cin	32	31	0	37	39	4	15	36	1	2	2	.500	0	13.4	4.14
Lawrence, Justin	Col	28	50	0	58	55	5	32	70	3	3	3	.500	6	14.0	3.96
Leclerc, Jose	Tex	29	55	0	67	54	7	32	77	5	4	4	.500	17	12.2	3.64
Lee, Dylan	Atl	28	57	0	60	50	8	13	70	1	4	2	.667	0	9.6	3.17
Leiter Jr., Mark	ChC	32	45	0	73	64	12	24	82	7	4	4	.500	0	11.7	3.80
Liberatore, Matthew	StL	23	12	12	58	61	9	21	56	4	3	3	.500	0	13.3	4.43
Littell, Zack	SF	27	37	0	43	43	7	15	40	1	2	3	.400	0	12.3	4.19
Loaisiga, Jonathan	NYY	28	60	0	62	54	6	20	54	2	4	3	.571	0	11.0	3.61

2023 Pitcher Projections

PLAYER			HOW MUCH			WHAT HE WILL GIVE UP					THE RESULTS				
Pitcher	Team	Age	G	GS	IP	H	HR	BB	SO	HB	W	L	Pct	Sv	BR/9	ERA
Lodolo, Nick	Cin	25	23	23	131	116	14	45	171	21	7	7	.500	0	12.5	3.58
Logue, Zach	Oak	27	15	5	53	63	12	19	44	4	1	4	.200	0	14.6	5.43
Lopez, Jorge	Min	30	65	0	69	68	11	29	66	6	3	4	.429	28	13.4	4.44
Lopez, Pablo	Mia	27	31	31	182	162	22	53	178	10	10	10	.500	0	11.1	3.63
Lopez, Reynaldo	CWS	29	64	0	67	67	11	20	65	2	4	4	.500	0	12.0	4.03
Lorenzen, Michael	LAA	31	15	15	88	81	10	37	76	3	5	4	.556	0	12.4	4.02
Loup, Aaron	LAA	35	64	0	62	55	4	20	55	7	4	3	.571	5	11.9	3.66
Luetge, Lucas	NYY	36	47	0	59	58	5	16	60	4	4	3	.571	0	11.9	3.65
Lugo, Seth	NYM	33	63	0	70	65	10	22	76	3	4	4	.500	0	11.6	3.72
Luzardo, Jesus	Mia	25	26	26	157	134	20	62	174	7	8	9	.471	0	11.6	3.66
Lyles, Jordan	Bal	32	31	31	180	201	34	56	142	7	7	13	.350	0	13.2	4.78
Lynch, Daniel	KC	26	30	30	156	190	26	61	146	7	6	11	.353	0	14.9	5.05
Lynn, Lance	CWS	36	27	27	156	148	24	36	159	8	9	8	.529	0	11.1	3.72
Machado, Andres	Was	30	50	0	61	63	8	26	52	4	2	4	.333	0	13.7	4.50
Maeda, Kenta	Min	35	23	23	121	107	19	35	128	5	7	6	.538	0	10.9	3.68
Mahle, Tyler	Min	28	23	23	121	110	18	41	128	5	7	6	.538	0	11.6	3.80
Manaea, Sean	SD	31	29	29	157	150	26	45	156	6	10	8	.556	0	11.5	3.92
Manning, Matt	Det	25	28	28	143	147	17	51	122	3	7	9	.438	0	12.7	4.12
Manoah, Alek	Tor	25	30	30	183	137	17	51	178	18	13	8	.619	0	10.1	3.31
Mantiply, Joe	Ari	32	72	0	62	64	7	13	61	3	4	3	.571	13	11.6	3.68
Marinaccio, Ron	NYY	27	48	0	52	30	5	25	75	5	4	2	.667	0	10.4	2.91
Marquez, German	Col	28	30	30	189	199	30	63	165	4	10	11	.476	0	12.7	4.34
Marte, Yunior	SF	28	44	0	54	48	6	22	56	3	3	3	.500	0	12.2	3.79
Martin, Brett	Tex	28	49	0	49	51	5	15	38	0	3	3	.500	0	12.1	4.06
Martin, Chris	LAD	37	66	0	65	57	8	8	74	2	5	2	.714	6	9.3	2.96
Martinez, Adrian	Oak	26	17	17	86	87	15	29	86	5	3	6	.333	0	12.7	4.29
Martinez, Nick	SD	32	58	0	76	69	12	30	66	3	4	4	.500	8	12.1	4.16
Martinez, Seth	Hou	28	27	0	33	23	3	12	35	1	2	1	.667	0	9.8	3.10
Maton, Phil	Hou	30	67	0	68	64	9	26	78	7	4	3	.571	0	12.8	3.97
Matz, Steven	StL	32	24	24	128	135	21	38	129	6	7	7	.500	0	12.6	4.19
May, Dustin	LAD	25	22	22	118	93	13	39	135	10	9	4	.692	0	10.8	3.35
May, Trevor	NYM	33	38	0	37	33	6	14	45	0	2	2	.500	0	11.4	3.70
Mayza, Tim	Tor	31	66	0	49	44	7	14	45	2	3	2	.600	8	11.0	3.76
McCarty, Kirk	Cle	27	17	0	46	44	10	16	36	1	2	3	.400	0	11.9	4.50
McClanahan, Shane	TB	26	25	25	149	123	18	37	172	3	10	7	.588	0	9.8	3.13
McCullers Jr., Lance	Hou	29	21	21	117	93	10	52	126	6	8	5	.615	0	11.6	3.54
McHugh, Collin	Atl	36	61	0	72	59	7	17	77	4	5	3	.625	0	10.0	3.18
McKenzie, Triston	Cle	25	32	32	187	138	29	56	192	5	12	9	.571	0	9.6	3.40
Means, John	Bal	30	18	18	93	85	19	20	82	3	5	6	.455	0	10.5	3.93
Megill, Trevor	Min	29	49	0	56	63	7	21	65	2	3	3	.500	0	13.8	4.26
Melancon, Mark	Ari	38	61	0	59	65	5	22	41	1	3	4	.429	7	13.4	4.35
Mikolas, Miles	StL	34	33	33	206	198	31	43	152	8	12	11	.522	0	10.9	3.94
Miley, Wade	ChC	36	18	18	101	103	11	35	76	3	5	7	.417	0	12.6	4.19
Milner, Hoby	Mil	32	68	0	70	67	11	15	75	6	4	4	.500	0	11.3	3.77
Minor, Mike	Cin	35	22	22	119	128	26	40	105	6	5	9	.357	0	13.2	4.81
Minter, A.J.	Atl	29	74	0	72	55	6	22	89	2	6	2	.750	5	9.9	2.90
Misiewicz, Anthony	KC	28	37	0	37	38	5	11	35	1	2	2	.500	0	12.2	3.91
Moll, Sam	Oak	31	45	0	37	31	3	19	39	3	2	3	.400	0	12.9	3.82
Montas, Frankie	NYY	30	24	24	131	119	17	40	134	5	8	7	.533	0	11.3	3.68
Montero, Rafael	Hou	32	74	0	73	62	6	24	73	4	5	3	.625	11	11.1	3.46
Montgomery, Jordan	StL	30	31	31	184	179	22	44	166	7	12	9	.571	0	11.3	3.72
Moore, Matt	Tex	34	69	0	75	63	10	37	77	2	4	4	.500	5	12.2	3.94
Moran, Jovani	Min	26	32	0	47	32	4	25	69	2	3	2	.600	0	11.3	3.04
Moreta, Dauri	Cin	27	24	0	31	27	6	10	31	2	2	2	.500	0	11.3	3.95
Morgan, Eli	Cle	27	51	0	67	60	12	18	67	3	4	4	.500	0	10.9	3.76
Moronta, Reyes	Ari	30	52	0	49	42	6	31	53	2	2	3	.400	6	13.8	4.22
Morton, Charlie	Atl	39	30	30	169	150	20	58	189	16	11	8	.579	0	11.9	3.68
Munoz, Andres	Sea	24	65	0	69	44	7	19	102	5	5	2	.714	6	8.9	2.54
Murfee, Penn	Sea	29	64	0	70	57	10	24	77	4	4	4	.500	0	10.9	3.57
Musgrove, Joe	SD	30	31	31	189	163	24	50	194	15	12	9	.571	0	10.9	3.56
Nance, Tommy	Mia	32	43	0	49	43	6	21	57	4	2	3	.400	0	12.5	3.79
Nelson, Nick	Phi	27	53	0	65	65	5	38	69	4	4	4	.500	0	14.8	4.30
Nelson, Ryne	Ari	25	21	21	112	106	20	39	109	3	6	7	.462	0	11.9	4.10
Neris, Hector	Hou	34	70	0	67	53	8	23	80	5	5	3	.625	0	10.9	3.36
Nola, Aaron	Phi	30	31	31	196	175	25	42	224	9	14	8	.636	0	10.4	3.31
Norris, Daniel	Det	30	40	0	72	68	12	29	72	4	3	5	.375	0	12.6	4.19
Ober, Bailey	Min	27	19	19	94	85	13	19	95	3	6	4	.600	0	10.2	3.47
Odorizzi, Jake	Atl	33	25	25	122	120	16	40	106	4	7	6	.538	0	12.1	4.01
Ohtani, Shohei	LAA	28	29	29	183	138	18	54	232	6	14	6	.700	0	9.7	2.91
Okert, Steven	Mia	31	55	0	48	36	8	21	57	5	2	3	.400	0	11.6	3.81
Oller, Adam	Oak	28	19	19	102	95	13	48	85	5	4	8	.333	0	13.1	4.33
Ort, Kaleb	Bos	31	35	0	42	41	3	21	47	3	2	2	.500	0	13.9	3.97
Ottavino, Adam	NYM	37	69	0	72	56	7	29	84	6	5	3	.625	6	11.4	3.44
Otto, Glenn	Tex	27	30	30	163	151	21	64	152	12	8	10	.444	0	12.5	4.07
Oviedo, Johan	Pit	25	20	20	86	85	13	44	84	7	4	6	.400	0	14.2	4.66
Pagan, Emilio	Min	32	58	0	72	62	14	25	87	2	4	4	.500	0	11.1	3.74
Pallante, Andre	StL	24	43	7	87	89	7	34	64	2	5	5	.500	0	12.9	4.15
Payamps, Joel	Oak	29	41	0	55	55	6	16	44	2	2	4	.333	0	11.9	3.96
Pepiot, Ryan	LAD	25	25	25	127	89	19	62	153	11	9	5	.643	0	11.5	3.64
Peralta, Freddy	Mil	27	23	23	98	70	12	37	120	5	6	4	.600	0	10.3	3.20
Peralta, Wandy	NYY	31	54	0	55	48	7	19	45	2	3	3	.500	0	11.3	3.85

2023 Pitcher Projections

Pitcher	Team	Age	G	GS	IP	H	HR	BB	SO	HB	W	L	Pct	Sv	BR/9	ERA
	PLAYER		HOW MUCH			WHAT HE WILL GIVE UP					THE RESULTS					
Perdomo, Luis	Mil	30	16	0	31	28	4	6	25	1	2	2	.500	0	10.2	3.62
Perez, Cionel	Bal	27	66	0	61	57	6	28	60	1	3	4	.429	0	12.7	3.93
Perez, Martin	Tex	32	32	32	194	196	23	69	161	8	10	12	.455	0	12.7	4.13
Peterson, David	NYM	27	29	17	100	95	11	44	113	6	6	6	.500	0	13.1	3.92
Pfaadt, Brandon	Ari	24	19	19	98	86	17	19	125	8	6	5	.545	0	10.4	3.40
Phelps, David	Tor	36	63	0	66	59	8	30	67	4	4	3	.571	0	12.7	3.98
Phillips, Evan	LAD	28	65	0	66	49	6	24	79	4	5	2	.714	0	10.5	3.18
Pilkington, Konnor	Cle	25	14	14	68	58	9	32	68	3	4	4	.500	0	12.3	3.94
Pivetta, Nick	Bos	30	33	33	181	179	29	74	180	6	10	10	.500	0	12.9	4.26
Plesac, Zach	Cle	28	23	23	127	120	19	33	98	5	7	7	.500	0	11.2	3.99
Poche, Colin	TB	29	63	0	59	48	10	22	68	2	3	3	.500	0	11.0	3.67
Pomeranz, Drew	SD	34	33	0	30	26	5	14	37	1	2	2	.500	0	12.3	3.92
Pop, Zach	Tor	26	41	0	48	51	2	14	38	4	3	2	.600	0	12.9	3.88
Pressly, Ryan	Hou	34	48	0	48	35	4	12	60	0	4	1	.800	28	8.8	2.61
Pruitt, Austin	Oak	33	47	0	67	68	11	12	50	3	3	5	.375	0	11.1	4.06
Puk, A.J.	Oak	28	63	0	67	65	10	23	76	7	3	5	.375	9	12.8	4.03
Quantrill, Cal	Cle	28	34	34	186	177	24	50	136	10	10	11	.476	0	11.5	4.00
Quijada, Jose	LAA	27	52	0	52	39	8	27	66	3	3	2	.600	0	11.9	3.71
Quintana, Jose	StL	34	32	32	167	173	17	53	146	3	10	9	.526	0	12.3	3.95
Ragans, Cole	Tex	25	12	12	59	54	8	22	59	2	3	3	.500	0	11.9	3.86
Raley, Brooks	TB	35	62	0	58	47	6	17	67	6	4	3	.571	0	10.9	3.31
Ramirez, Erasmo	Was	33	63	0	91	87	14	21	69	5	4	6	.400	0	11.2	4.01
Ramirez, Yohan	Pit	28	46	0	59	45	7	38	61	9	3	4	.429	6	14.0	4.27
Rasmussen, Drew	TB	27	29	29	168	148	16	45	153	4	10	9	.526	0	10.6	3.46
Ray, Robbie	Sea	31	31	31	194	167	36	68	223	6	11	11	.500	0	11.2	3.78
Richards, Trevor	Tor	30	63	7	69	61	12	30	80	1	4	3	.571	0	12.0	3.92
Robertson, David	Phi	38	59	0	66	50	8	35	80	3	4	3	.571	28	12.0	3.62
Rodon, Carlos	SF	30	29	29	171	132	14	52	223	6	12	7	.632	0	10.0	2.86
Rodriguez, Eduardo	Det	30	31	31	171	169	19	57	169	4	9	10	.474	0	12.1	3.80
Rodriguez, Grayson	Bal	23	23	23	129	93	11	41	171	3	8	6	.571	0	9.6	3.14
Rodriguez, Joely	NYM	31	57	0	59	53	4	28	64	1	4	3	.571	0	12.5	3.65
Rodriguez, Manuel	ChC	26	47	0	43	42	6	26	45	4	2	3	.400	10	15.1	4.71
Rogers, Taylor	Mil	32	66	0	66	58	8	17	85	8	4	3	.571	12	11.3	3.36
Rogers, Trevor	Mia	25	24	24	117	113	13	45	128	5	6	7	.462	0	12.5	3.79
Rogers, Tyler	SF	32	66	0	80	79	6	23	54	6	4	5	.444	0	12.2	3.95
Rolison, Ryan	Col	25	16	16	84	85	12	28	87	6	4	5	.444	0	12.4	4.13
Romano, Jordan	Tor	30	65	0	70	54	10	25	83	4	5	3	.625	33	10.7	3.46
Rucker, Michael	ChC	29	57	0	65	70	11	25	63	2	3	5	.375	0	13.4	4.50
Ruiz, Jose	CWS	28	60	0	61	55	9	29	64	1	3	3	.500	0	12.5	3.99
Ruiz, Norge	Oak	29	27	0	38	45	7	14	34	2	1	3	.250	0	14.4	5.09
Ryan, Joe	Min	27	31	31	169	128	25	48	180	9	11	8	.579	0	9.9	3.39
Ryu, Hyun-Jin	Tor	36	13	13	64	67	9	12	52	1	4	3	.571	0	11.3	3.92
Sampson, Adrian	ChC	31	27	27	143	154	28	43	100	10	5	10	.333	0	13.0	4.85
Sanchez, Aaron	Min	30	18	8	73	81	10	26	51	7	3	5	.375	0	14.1	4.81
Sanchez, Anibal	Was	39	22	22	115	120	20	51	83	5	4	9	.308	0	13.8	4.93
Sanchez, Sixto	Mia	24	21	21	121	121	11	31	108	5	6	7	.462	0	11.7	3.71
Sandlin, Nick	Cle	26	49	0	49	33	4	27	51	4	3	3	.500	0	11.8	3.63
Sandoval, Patrick	LAA	26	27	27	162	154	18	66	166	6	10	8	.556	0	12.6	3.88
Sanmartin, Reiver	Cin	27	55	0	61	67	7	23	60	1	3	4	.429	0	13.4	4.28
Santana, Dennis	Tex	27	57	0	59	58	7	30	56	4	3	4	.429	0	14.0	4.43
Santos, Gregory	SF	23	37	0	44	42	6	26	43	5	2	3	.400	0	14.9	4.71
Scherzer, Max	NYM	38	25	25	167	130	20	35	201	10	12	7	.632	0	9.4	2.98
Schreiber, John	Bos	29	68	0	71	61	6	24	77	3	5	3	.625	9	11.2	3.42
Scott, Tanner	Mia	28	64	0	61	50	5	41	83	5	3	4	.429	19	14.2	3.84
Sears, JP	Oak	27	22	22	107	96	13	30	106	3	5	7	.417	0	10.9	3.55
Senzatela, Antonio	Col	28	24	24	131	167	18	35	78	6	6	9	.400	0	14.3	5.02
Severino, Luis	NYY	29	27	27	148	108	20	42	161	6	10	6	.625	0	9.5	3.23
Sewald, Paul	Sea	33	66	0	67	51	11	20	81	3	4	3	.571	25	9.9	3.31
Shaw, Bryan	Cle	35	56	0	59	58	9	27	51	3	3	4	.429	0	13.4	4.50
Sims, Lucas	Cin	29	44	0	48	38	7	23	62	4	3	3	.500	6	12.2	3.69
Singer, Brady	KC	26	31	31	179	178	23	52	173	12	9	11	.450	0	12.2	3.93
Skubal, Tarik	Det	26	11	11	61	56	10	18	64	2	3	4	.429	0	11.2	3.81
Small, Ethan	Mil	26	10	10	51	42	4	32	55	2	3	3	.500	0	13.4	3.92
Smith, Caleb	Ari	31	40	0	67	58	14	34	65	3	3	4	.429	0	12.8	4.50
Smith, Chad	Col	28	24	0	31	24	4	16	36	1	2	2	.500	0	11.9	3.69
Smith, Drew	NYM	29	31	0	30	23	5	11	33	0	2	1	.667	0	10.2	3.58
Smith, Will	Hou	33	66	0	62	54	12	25	70	2	4	3	.571	0	11.8	3.93
Smyly, Drew	ChC	34	23	23	124	131	25	39	110	4	5	9	.357	0	12.6	4.54
Snead, Kirby	Oak	28	52	0	55	52	5	22	56	3	2	4	.333	0	12.6	3.79
Snell, Blake	SD	30	28	28	164	133	20	71	212	3	11	7	.611	0	11.4	3.39
Snider, Collin	KC	27	42	0	37	41	4	18	27	5	1	3	.250	0	15.1	4.87
Soto, Gregory	Det	28	71	0	69	60	8	39	71	5	3	4	.429	31	13.6	4.17
Springs, Jeffrey	TB	30	25	25	129	117	18	34	140	1	8	7	.533	0	10.6	3.49
Stammen, Craig	SD	39	24	0	32	34	5	6	28	1	2	2	.500	0	11.5	3.95
Stanek, Ryne	Hou	31	57	0	54	39	7	29	60	1	4	2	.667	0	11.5	3.69
Staumont, Josh	KC	29	39	0	39	33	4	24	45	2	2	2	.500	0	13.6	3.93
Steele, Justin	ChC	27	18	18	101	92	10	45	105	4	5	6	.455	0	12.6	3.79
Stephan, Trevor	Cle	27	71	0	68	60	8	26	84	4	4	3	.571	0	11.9	3.56
Stephens, Jackson	Atl	29	40	0	56	58	4	23	50	3	3	3	.500	0	13.5	4.02
Stephenson, Robert	Pit	30	58	0	62	62	11	20	62	2	3	4	.429	0	12.2	4.14
Stiever, Jonathan	CWS	26	8	8	37	40	8	13	37	2	2	2	.500	0	13.4	4.75

2023 Pitcher Projections

Pitcher	Team	Age	G	GS	IP	H	HR	BB	SO	HB	W	L	Pct	Sv	BR/9	ERA
Stout, Eric	Pit	30	32	0	36	34	7	27	44	3	1	3	.250	0	16.0	5.25
Strahm, Matt	Bos	31	48	0	47	47	8	13	49	4	3	3	.500	0	12.3	4.12
Stratton, Chris	StL	32	57	0	65	67	8	26	63	1	4	4	.500	0	13.0	4.16
Strickland, Hunter	Cin	34	61	0	60	59	11	29	56	5	2	4	.333	0	14.0	4.73
Strider, Spencer	Atl	24	31	31	171	119	14	64	258	7	14	5	.737	0	10.0	2.66
Stripling, Ross	Tor	33	28	28	144	138	22	30	119	3	9	7	.563	0	10.7	3.80
Stroman, Marcus	ChC	32	29	29	175	171	19	48	147	5	9	10	.474	0	11.5	3.82
Strzelecki, Peter	Mil	28	47	0	53	42	7	21	69	3	3	3	.500	0	11.2	3.41
Suarez, Jose	LAA	25	25	25	142	138	22	49	131	8	8	7	.533	0	12.4	4.15
Suarez, Ranger	Phi	27	29	29	168	161	17	60	145	5	10	8	.556	0	12.1	3.90
Sulser, Cole	Mia	33	37	0	33	31	4	14	37	0	2	2	.500	0	12.3	3.85
Suter, Brent	Mil	33	59	0	72	67	10	22	61	2	4	4	.500	0	11.4	3.88
Swanson, Erik	Sea	29	63	0	60	51	10	14	70	2	4	3	.571	0	10.1	3.35
Syndergaard, Noah	Phi	30	24	24	132	143	16	32	98	4	8	7	.533	0	12.2	4.13
Taillon, Jameson	NYY	31	32	32	173	163	28	38	148	6	10	9	.526	0	10.8	3.87
Tate, Dillon	Bal	29	65	0	74	64	8	20	58	7	4	4	.500	7	11.1	3.82
Tepera, Ryan	LAA	35	57	0	57	46	7	20	53	2	4	3	.571	21	10.7	3.60
Thielbar, Caleb	Min	36	71	0	65	56	7	19	80	1	4	3	.571	0	10.5	3.18
Thompson, Keegan	ChC	28	25	14	97	84	14	40	93	6	5	6	.455	0	12.1	3.98
Thompson, Mason	Was	25	36	0	40	40	4	16	34	2	2	3	.400	8	13.1	4.17
Thompson, Ryan	TB	31	32	0	31	30	3	9	29	1	2	2	.500	0	11.6	3.69
Thompson, Zach	Pit	29	29	17	121	141	21	45	95	4	5	9	.357	0	14.1	4.95
Thornton, Trent	Tor	29	24	0	36	38	6	14	33	1	2	2	.500	0	13.3	4.50
Tinoco, Jhon	Tex	28	25	0	32	28	5	15	32	1	2	2	.500	0	12.4	4.09
Toussaint, Touki	LAA	27	14	0	37	36	7	24	40	5	2	2	.500	0	15.8	5.23
Trivino, Lou	NYY	31	67	0	59	52	6	27	64	4	4	3	.571	0	12.7	3.78
Turnbull, Spencer	Det	30	18	18	96	90	8	35	87	9	5	6	.455	0	12.6	3.89
Uelmen, Erich	ChC	27	43	0	46	42	7	24	45	8	2	3	.400	0	14.5	4.70
Underwood Jr., Duane	Pit	28	65	1	71	77	8	30	70	4	3	5	.375	0	14.1	4.38
Urena, Jose	Col	31	25	25	142	176	21	62	92	4	6	10	.375	0	15.3	5.33
Urias, Julio	LAD	26	30	30	185	144	23	45	180	6	14	6	.700	0	9.5	3.28
Urquidy, Jose	Hou	28	28	28	167	152	29	36	140	5	10	8	.556	0	10.4	3.83
Valdez, Framber	Hou	29	30	30	195	168	15	70	185	12	13	9	.591	0	11.5	3.58
Velasquez, Vince	CWS	31	31	8	80	81	17	33	78	4	4	5	.444	0	13.3	4.67
Verlander, Justin	Hou	40	26	26	164	118	19	29	169	5	13	6	.684	0	8.3	2.92
Vesia, Alex	LAD	27	63	0	60	37	6	28	86	3	5	2	.714	0	10.2	2.90
Vest, Will	Det	28	64	0	67	71	8	25	63	3	3	4	.429	0	13.3	4.23
Voth, Austin	Bal	31	25	25	106	116	17	35	94	4	5	7	.417	0	13.2	4.50
Wacha, Michael	Bos	31	25	25	149	162	29	41	127	5	8	9	.471	0	12.6	4.53
Wainwright, Adam	StL	41	32	32	187	189	22	55	141	8	11	10	.524	0	12.1	4.09
Waldichuk, Ken	Oak	25	21	21	104	87	16	42	131	10	5	7	.417	0	12.0	3.71
Walker, Taijuan	NYM	30	29	29	159	143	21	51	136	6	9	9	.500	0	11.3	3.84
Wantz, Andrew	LAA	27	49	0	58	50	12	21	61	3	3	3	.500	0	11.5	4.05
Watkins, Spenser	Bal	30	25	25	123	150	25	38	82	4	5	9	.357	0	14.0	5.23
Weaver, Luke	KC	29	32	0	46	54	7	15	45	2	2	3	.400	0	13.9	4.60
Webb, Logan	SF	26	31	31	189	181	14	52	170	9	11	10	.524	0	11.5	3.60
Weems, Jordan	Was	30	34	0	48	46	7	20	52	1	2	3	.400	0	12.6	4.04
Wells, Tyler	Bal	28	26	26	117	101	19	30	94	2	6	7	.462	0	10.2	3.80
Wentz, Joey	Det	25	16	16	79	70	13	38	78	2	4	5	.444	0	12.5	4.22
Wesneski, Hayden	ChC	25	21	21	114	104	14	38	112	7	6	7	.462	0	11.8	3.81
Wheeler, Zack	Phi	33	28	28	172	154	16	41	178	7	12	7	.632	0	10.6	3.31
White, Mitch	Tor	28	26	26	114	120	14	38	98	3	6	6	.500	0	12.7	4.15
Whitley, Forrest	Hou	25	14	5	66	67	10	48	71	4	3	4	.429	0	16.2	5.12
Whitlock, Garrett	Bos	27	43	0	90	86	9	19	93	2	6	4	.600	0	10.7	3.37
Wick, Rowan	ChC	30	62	0	63	67	6	29	69	2	3	4	.429	9	14.0	4.22
Williams, Devin	Mil	28	63	0	61	36	5	31	95	3	4	2	.667	35	10.3	2.73
Williams, Trevor	NYM	31	30	5	91	91	15	28	82	5	5	5	.500	0	12.3	4.20
Williamson, Brandon	Cin	25	12	12	62	62	6	36	65	4	3	4	.429	0	14.8	4.50
Wilson, Bryse	Pit	25	24	24	122	140	20	35	91	6	5	9	.357	0	13.4	4.72
Wilson, Steven	SD	28	53	0	59	39	9	23	66	3	4	2	.667	0	9.9	3.38
Winckowski, Josh	Bos	25	15	15	73	77	8	24	59	2	4	4	.500	0	12.7	4.13
Winder, Josh	Min	26	13	13	59	55	9	15	47	3	3	3	.500	0	11.1	3.95
Winn, Cole	Tex	23	19	19	95	81	10	56	98	5	5	6	.455	0	13.5	4.08
Wood, Alex	SF	32	21	21	110	114	15	29	109	11	6	6	.500	0	12.6	4.05
Woodford, Jake	StL	26	36	0	51	49	6	20	37	3	3	3	.500	0	12.7	4.33
Woodruff, Brandon	Mil	30	30	30	176	142	21	48	211	7	12	8	.600	0	10.1	3.15
Wright, Kyle	Atl	27	28	28	176	167	22	62	169	11	11	9	.550	0	12.3	3.96
Yarbrough, Ryan	TB	31	22	5	86	91	12	20	67	8	4	5	.444	0	12.5	4.24
Young, Alex	SF	29	46	0	52	56	9	20	52	2	2	3	.400	0	13.5	4.50
Zimmermann, Bruce	Bal	28	8	8	45	51	8	12	37	1	2	3	.400	0	12.8	4.60

Career Targets

Mark Simon

Freddie Freeman turned 33 in September. He has 1,903 career hits. He's totaled 191, 176, 180, and 199 in the last four 162-game seasons. He's missed 10 games in the last five years.

By my measures, he's got a very good shot to reach 3,000 career hits. The three players whose careers through their age-32 season are the best comparison by Bill James Similarity Scores—Eddie Murray, Rafael Palmeiro and Carl Yastrzemski—all did.

Without looking, I would have guessed Freeman was close to a 50-50 shot by the Bill James statistical tool, The Favorite Toy. I'm a little off, though not a lot.

Freeman has the best chance of any active player to reach 3,000, 38%, which isn't quite 50-50, but is still pretty good. Freeman's biggest challenge to reaching this hallowed milestone isn't reflected in his current quality of play. It's in whether he stays healthy and minimizes his decline phase as he ages.

Freeman needs 1,097 hits. That's still a lot. If he gets 183 hits a year for the next six years, he's there. Barely. That requires him to be pretty productive deep into his 30s OR to have a couple seasons that exceed that among his next few OR to be in good enough shape such that he's still able to DH regularly, as Murray, Palmeiro, and Yastrzemski did to extend their careers.

Freeman's not the only one with a credible chance for a milestone number. Scour the lists on the next page to see what we think about Giancarlo Stanton's chance for 500 home runs and much more.

Career Targets

762 Home Runs		2,298 RBI	2,296 Runs Scored		4,257 Hits
% chance to break record		% chance to break record	% chance to break record		% chance to break record
Guerrero Jr., Vladimir	< 1%		Soto, Juan	1%	
			Betts, Mookie	< 1%	

900 Home Runs		2,000 RBI		6,857 Total Bases		4,000 Hits
% chance to reach milestone		% chance to reach milestone		% chance to break record		% chance to reach milestone
		Machado, Manny	10%	Guerrero Jr., Vladimir	2%	
		Cabrera, Miguel	10%			
		Ramirez, Jose	7%			
		Guerrero Jr., Vladimir	7%			
		Devers, Rafael	5%			
		Arenado, Nolan	3%			
		Alonso, Pete	3%			
		Freeman, Freddie	2%			
		Tucker, Kyle	< 1%			

800 Home Runs		600 Home Runs		793 Doubles		3,000 Hits	
% chance to reach milestone		% chance to reach milestone		% chance to break record		% chance to reach milestone	
		Judge, Aaron	21%	Devers, Rafael	7%	Cabrera, Miguel	done
		Trout, Mike	16%	Freeman, Freddie	4%	Freeman, Freddie	38%
		Guerrero Jr., Vladimir	11%	Ramirez, Jose	1%	Machado, Manny	26%
		Alonso, Pete	11%			Altuve, Jose	23%
		Machado, Manny	11%			Bogaerts, Xander	17%
		Stanton, Giancarlo	10%			Turner, Trea	15%
		Schwarber, Kyle	8%			Devers, Rafael	11%
		Olson, Matt	6%			Guerrero Jr., Vladimir	11%
		Soto, Juan	4%			Bichette, Bo	10%
						Arenado, Nolan	7%

700 Home Runs		500 Home Runs		1,000 Stolen Bases	Most Likely No-Hitter	
% chance to reach milestone		% chance to reach milestone		% chance to reach milestone	% chance to reach milestone	
Judge, Aaron	6%	Cabrera, Miguel	done		Strider, Spencer	53%
Guerrero Jr., Vladimir	5%	Stanton, Giancarlo	51%		Rodon, Carlos	39%
		Trout, Mike	44%		Javier, Cristian	37%
		Judge, Aaron	40%		Ohtani, Shohei	35%
		Machado, Manny	33%		Cease, Dylan	34%
		Schwarber, Kyle	28%		Cole, Gerrit	33%
		Arenado, Nolan	25%		Burnes, Corbin	32%
		Alonso, Pete	23%		Greene, Hunter	31%
		Harper, Bryce	23%		Snell, Blake	28%
					deGrom, Jacob	26%

598

The 300-Win Candidates

Sarah Thompson

In last year's Handbook, we (and the algorithm) wrote off Justin Verlander's chance at 300 wins. Not to skirt blame, but if we had proposed Justin Verlander would be touching 99 and sitting 95 in his age-39, post-Tommy-John season, we wouldn't be allowed to publish anymore.

Of course, he came back to the game and led AL pitchers in wins at 18. He earned 21 wins in 2019—but prior to that, he hadn't had as many as 18 since 2011 (24). So, the proposed pace of "17 wins a year until he's 43" seemed a little ridiculous—but no longer. We won't count him out just yet, and after this season, Verlander has the highest likelihood among active pitchers to hit 300 wins, albeit only 29%. He can get there if he keeps a 14-per-season pace for the next 4 seasons. This is unlikely but not impossible.

Max Scherzer is behind him at 5%, down 6 percentage points from last year's projection. The two IL stints this season due to oblique injuries didn't help him in this endeavor.

We also welcome Gerrit Cole back to the list, who hasn't been here since 2019 when we projected a 6% chance for him. He has relative youth in his favor and a competitive offense behind him, but if he wants to hit 300, he needs a 17-a-year pace for the next 10 years.

Kershaw's chances have fluctuated wildly over the years, which isn't unexpected—but he actually went up in likelihood since last year by 2 percentage points. He peaked at 31% in 2014 and 2015 and hit his low last year. Adam Wainwright is listed as a possibility, but the model doesn't know he's likely to retire this year, if not next. Johnny Cueto returns to the list for the first time since 2016, in which he had an 18-win season. But he's still worse than a 100-to-1 shot.

So, have we already seen the last 300-win pitcher? Maybe, but we'll be paying very close attention to Justin Verlander's starts next year.

Pitchers on Course For 300 Wins

Name	2022 Age	R/L	W	L	EWL	Momentum	Chance
Verlander, Justin	39	R	244	133	13.8	.737	29%
Scherzer, Max	37	R	201	102	11.7	.702	5%
Cole, Gerrit	31	R	130	71	15.3	.749	4%
Kershaw, Clayton	34	L	197	87	11.2	.675	3%
Wainwright, Adam	40	R	195	117	11.6	.678	3%
Greinke, Zack	38	R	223	141	6.5	.658	1%
Cueto, Johnny	36	R	143	107	6.8	.615	<1%

EWL: Established Win Level

Ballparks and Park Indices

Ted Baarda

In 2022 home run records dominated the storylines in baseball. While Aaron Judge's career year was analyzed with a fine-tooth comb, another home run record had an impact on the 2022 season as well.

The Baltimore Orioles allowed 305 home runs in 2019, shattering the previous record of 258. While the pitching staff was not good, Camden Yards also had a reputation as a hitter's park and, more specifically, as a park prone to home runs. With the Orioles struggling to develop pitchers or attract free agent pitchers, the organization decided to move the left field wall back by as much as 30 feet, while also increasing the wall height.

The changes produced the desired results, as the Orioles went from allowing 155 home runs in 81 games at Camden Yards in 2021, to 72 home runs allowed in 80 games in 2022. The offense suffered to a lesser degree, with Oriole hitters dropping from 122 to 79 home runs from 2021 to 2022.

In terms of Park Factors, the change at Camden Yards was dramatic. From 2019-2021 Camden Yards was the easiest park in baseball to hit a home run in with a Home Run Index of 133, meaning that batters hit home runs 33% more frequently at Camden Yards compared to other parks. If we look at the less stable one-year park factor, in 2021 Camden Yards also led MLB with a 153 Home Run Index.

It is obviously too early to compare three-year park factors, but the one-year stats show a significant reversal. In 2022 Camden Yards dropped to a Home Run Index of 79, or batters hitting 21% fewer home runs at Camden Yards compared to other parks.

Even though the dimension changes were only made in left field, both left and right handed batters were affected by the changes. The left-handed batter Home Run Index dropped from 186 in 2021 to 76 in 2022, while the right-handed batter Home Run Index dropped from 141 to 82.

Arizona Diamondbacks - Chase Field Surface: FieldTurf
LF: 330   CF: 407   RF:334

| | 2022 Season | | | | | | | 2020-2022 | | | | | | |
| | Home Games | | | Away Games | | | | Home Games | | | Away Games | | | |
	D'Backs	Opp	Total	D'Backs	Opp	Total	Index	D'Backs	Opp	Total	D'Backs	Opp	Total	Index
G	81	81	162	81	81	162		192	192	384	192	192	384	
Avg	.232	.248	.240	.229	.246	.237	101	.245	.255	.250	.225	.257	.241	104
AB	2601	2799	5400	2750	2646	5396	100	6316	6725	13041	6521	6269	12790	102
R	353	360	713	349	380	729	98	878	944	1822	772	984	1756	104
H	603	693	1296	629	652	1281	101	1545	1718	3263	1466	1613	3079	106
2B	133	157	290	129	133	262	111	356	396	752	315	339	654	113
3B	10	12	22	14	10	24	92	40	38	78	27	40	67	114
HR	71	79	150	102	112	214	70	169	224	393	206	292	498	77
BB	267	250	517	264	254	518	100	640	626	1266	609	668	1277	97
SO	625	633	1258	716	583	1299	97	1518	1570	3088	1749	1408	3157	96
Foul Outs	70	60	130	55	69	124	105	146	145	291	139	160	299	95
E	42	44	86	44	55	99	87	110	101	211	111	124	235	90
E-Infield	15	20	35	20	14	34	103	44	38	82	47	49	96	85
LHB-Avg	.230	.222	.227	.236	.232	.234	97	.246	.241	.244	.228	.252	.237	103
LHB-HR	36	20	56	61	32	93	61	99	84	183	118	100	218	83
RHB-Avg	.235	.263	.253	.216	.255	.240	105	.243	.265	.257	.220	.261	.244	105
RHB-HR	35	59	94	41	80	121	77	70	140	210	88	192	280	73

Atlanta Braves - Truist Park
LF: 335   CF: 400   RF:325

| | 2022 Season | | | | | | | 2020-2022 | | | | | | |
| | Home Games | | | Away Games | | | | Home Games | | | Away Games | | | |
	Braves	Opp	Total	Braves	Opp	Total	Index	Braves	Opp	Total	Braves	Opp	Total	Index
G	81	81	162	81	81	162		191	191	382	192	192	384	
Avg	.256	.225	.240	.250	.227	.239	100	.256	.231	.243	.247	.235	.241	101
AB	2656	2771	5427	2853	2642	5495	99	6282	6489	12771	6664	6203	12867	100
R	395	282	677	394	327	721	94	988	774	1762	939	779	1718	103
H	680	624	1304	714	600	1314	99	1609	1500	3109	1648	1455	3103	101
2B	137	108	245	161	110	271	92	341	270	611	356	285	641	96
3B	5	6	11	6	10	16	70	16	21	37	18	26	44	85
HR	125	65	190	118	83	201	96	293	193	486	292	207	499	98
BB	244	238	482	226	262	488	100	647	598	1245	611	638	1249	100
SO	754	834	1588	744	720	1464	110	1758	1824	3582	1766	1653	3419	106
Foul Outs	54	45	99	55	63	118	85	118	110	228	130	123	253	91
E	38	44	82	39	36	75	109	99	104	203	83	84	167	122
E-Infield	17	12	29	16	13	29	100	38	33	71	25	34	59	121
LHB-Avg	.233	.228	.230	.251	.207	.226	102	.248	.233	.239	.249	.223	.235	106
LHB-HR	30	29	59	38	38	76	80	82	79	161	94	80	174	97
RHB-Avg	.265	.224	.246	.250	.243	.247	100	.260	.230	.246	.246	.243	.245	100
RHB-HR	95	36	131	80	45	125	105	211	114	325	198	127	325	99

Baltimore Orioles - Oriole Park at Camden Yards
LF: 333   CF: 410   RF:318

| | 2022 Season | | | | | | | 2019-2021 | | | | | | |
| | Home Games | | | Away Games | | | | Home Games | | | Away Games | | | |
	Orioles	Opp	Total	Orioles	Opp	Total	Index	Orioles	Opp	Total	Orioles	Opp	Total	Index
G	80	80	160	82	82	164		195	195	390	189	189	378	
Avg	.238	.260	.249	.234	.252	.243	103	.249	.272	.261	.242	.264	.253	103
AB	2633	2815	5448	2796	2675	5471	102	6488	6916	13404	6554	6334	12888	101
R	338	332	670	336	356	692	99	862	1197	2059	800	1034	1834	109
H	627	732	1359	654	674	1328	105	1615	1879	3494	1583	1672	3255	104
2B	125	135	260	150	154	304	86	309	356	665	311	339	650	98
3B	9	6	15	16	8	24	63	27	26	53	20	39	59	86
HR	79	72	151	92	99	191	79	281	373	654	204	269	473	133
BB	232	228	460	244	215	459	101	552	653	1205	525	663	1188	98
SO	659	609	1268	731	605	1336	95	1632	1549	3181	1771	1420	3191	96
Foul Outs	67	51	118	83	66	149	80	141	153	294	156	153	309	91
E	42	53	95	49	50	99	98	106	114	220	119	111	230	93
E-Infield	16	22	38	23	18	41	95	39	42	81	41	42	83	95
LHB-Avg	.235	.255	.245	.240	.252	.246	100	.241	.261	.251	.227	.251	.239	105
LHB-HR	34	25	59	39	34	73	76	105	127	232	79	91	170	135
RHB-Avg	.240	.264	.252	.230	.252	.241	105	.254	.278	.266	.250	.272	.261	102
RHB-HR	45	47	92	53	65	118	82	176	246	422	125	178	303	132

Boston Red Sox - Fenway Park
LF: 310   CF: 420   RF:302

	2022 Season							2020-2022						
	Home Games			Away Games				Home Games			Away Games			
	Red Sox	Opp	Total	Red Sox	Opp	Total	Index	Red Sox	Opp	Total	Red Sox	Opp	Total	Index
G	81	81	162	81	81	162		193	193	386	191	191	382	
Avg	.272	.262	.267	.244	.250	.247	108	.277	.271	.274	.244	.249	.247	111
AB	2747	2845	5592	2792	2672	5464	102	6543	6813	13356	6574	6265	12839	103
R	392	411	803	343	376	719	112	1022	1018	2040	834	869	1703	119
H	747	744	1491	680	667	1347	111	1810	1845	3655	1603	1562	3165	114
2B	190	147	337	162	145	307	107	457	395	852	343	321	664	123
3B	9	20	29	3	7	10	283	27	33	60	15	21	36	160
HR	86	97	183	69	88	157	114	232	240	472	223	219	442	103
BB	227	263	490	251	263	514	93	591	660	1251	586	664	1250	96
SO	675	669	1344	698	677	1375	96	1584	1717	3301	1720	1693	3413	93
Foul Outs	45	57	102	51	50	101	99	114	116	230	134	118	252	88
E	41	45	86	44	35	79	109	120	120	240	118	94	212	112
E-Infield	15	18	33	13	15	28	118	46	48	94	46	38	84	111
LHB-Avg	.272	.241	.257	.241	.231	.236	109	.274	.251	.263	.241	.232	.237	111
LHB-HR	30	37	67	31	34	65	100	77	76	153	89	75	164	91
RHB-Avg	.272	.273	.273	.245	.260	.253	108	.278	.282	.280	.246	.259	.252	111
RHB-HR	56	60	116	38	54	92	123	155	164	319	134	144	278	110

Chicago Cubs - Wrigley Field
LF: 355   CF: 400   RF:353

	2022 Season							2020-2022						
	Home Games			Away Games				Home Games			Away Games			
	Cubs	Opp	Total	Cubs	Opp	Total	Index	Cubs	Opp	Total	Cubs	Opp	Total	Index
G	81	81	162	81	81	162		195	195	390	189	189	378	
Avg	.248	.236	.242	.229	.252	.240	101	.239	.242	.241	.231	.252	.241	100
AB	2660	2775	5435	2765	2731	5496	99	6245	6641	12886	6404	6235	12639	99
R	324	343	667	333	388	721	93	807	893	1700	820	917	1737	95
H	661	655	1316	632	687	1319	100	1491	1610	3101	1479	1569	3048	99
2B	129	122	251	136	135	271	94	273	305	578	299	325	624	91
3B	19	15	34	12	14	26	132	41	25	66	24	24	48	135
HR	73	91	164	86	116	202	82	214	261	475	229	255	484	96
BB	258	263	521	249	277	526	100	650	629	1279	588	689	1277	98
SO	688	722	1410	760	661	1421	100	1784	1719	3503	1828	1545	3373	102
Foul Outs	40	48	88	56	55	111	80	88	82	170	118	110	228	73
E	45	48	93	51	46	97	96	100	113	213	113	112	225	92
E-Infield	10	23	33	17	17	34	97	39	52	91	44	47	91	97
LHB-Avg	.243	.266	.257	.233	.230	.231	111	.241	.250	.246	.232	.241	.237	104
LHB-HR	13	37	50	19	41	60	84	72	114	186	76	106	182	100
RHB-Avg	.251	.214	.234	.227	.266	.245	96	.238	.237	.237	.230	.259	.244	97
RHB-HR	60	54	114	67	75	142	81	142	147	289	153	149	302	94

Chicago White Sox - Guaranteed Rate Field
LF: 330   CF: 400   RF:334

	2022 Season							2020-2022						
	Home Games			Away Games				Home Games			Away Games			
	White Sox	Opp	Total	White Sox	Opp	Total	Index	White Sox	Opp	Total	White Sox	Opp	Total	Index
G	81	81	162	81	81	162		191	191	382	193	193	386	
Avg	.250	.246	.248	.261	.237	.250	99	.257	.229	.243	.257	.239	.248	98
AB	2728	2843	5571	2883	2655	5538	101	6264	6444	12708	6751	6294	13045	98
R	331	416	747	355	301	656	114	892	841	1733	896	758	1654	106
H	683	700	1383	752	630	1382	100	1607	1477	3084	1735	1506	3241	96
2B	122	139	261	150	125	275	94	284	270	554	357	276	633	90
3B	4	7	11	5	11	16	68	16	17	33	21	30	51	66
HR	77	98	175	72	68	140	124	235	240	475	200	179	379	129
BB	206	273	479	182	260	442	108	597	617	1214	556	618	1174	106
SO	588	739	1327	681	711	1392	95	1502	1808	3310	1727	1753	3480	98
Foul Outs	64	65	129	53	60	113	113	136	153	289	129	135	264	112
E	52	42	94	50	40	90	104	115	118	233	123	113	236	100
E-Infield	24	16	40	23	15	38	105	56	53	109	52	47	99	111
LHB-Avg	.203	.256	.238	.225	.236	.232	102	.223	.226	.225	.228	.241	.235	96
LHB-HR	19	37	56	11	30	41	146	74	87	161	39	74	113	145
RHB-Avg	.265	.239	.253	.273	.238	.259	98	.271	.232	.253	.270	.238	.256	99
RHB-HR	58	61	119	61	38	99	115	161	153	314	161	105	266	122

Cincinnati Reds - Great American Ballpark
LF: 328   CF: 404   RF:325

| | 2022 Season | | | | | | | 2020-2022 | | | | | | |
| | Home Games | | | Away Games | | | | Home Games | | | Away Games | | | |
	Reds	Opp	Total	Reds	Opp	Total	Index	Reds	Opp	Total	Reds	Opp	Total	Index
G	80	80	160	82	82	164		190	190	380	194	194	388	
Avg	.246	.256	.251	.224	.246	.235	107	.250	.248	.249	.226	.237	.232	108
AB	2623	2797	5420	2757	2642	5399	103	6192	6554	12746	6453	6192	12645	103
R	365	416	781	283	399	682	117	948	959	1907	729	859	1588	123
H	646	715	1361	618	651	1269	110	1547	1628	3175	1459	1469	2928	111
2B	119	146	265	116	138	254	104	307	328	635	299	294	593	106
3B	7	10	17	11	13	24	71	15	22	37	19	41	60	61
HR	89	128	217	67	85	152	142	273	299	572	195	187	382	149
BB	249	293	542	203	319	522	103	680	700	1380	564	742	1306	105
SO	706	738	1444	724	676	1400	103	1698	1869	3567	1691	1684	3375	105
Foul Outs	53	79	132	60	54	114	115	114	147	261	108	107	215	120
E	36	40	76	45	46	91	86	90	100	190	109	90	199	97
E-Infield	10	16	26	15	10	25	107	34	46	80	39	31	70	117
LHB-Avg	.232	.235	.234	.221	.232	.227	103	.249	.235	.241	.230	.223	.226	107
LHB-HR	27	50	77	25	26	51	148	116	129	245	76	74	150	163
RHB-Avg	.252	.271	.261	.226	.257	.239	109	.250	.259	.254	.224	.249	.235	108
RHB-HR	62	78	140	42	59	101	139	157	170	327	119	113	232	139

Cleveland Guardians - Progressive Field
LF: 325   CF: 405   RF:325

| | 2022 Season | | | | | | | 2020-2022 | | | | | | |
| | Home Games | | | Away Games | | | | Home Games | | | Away Games | | | |
	Guardians	Opp	Total	Guardians	Opp	Total	Index	Guardians	Opp	Total	Guardians	Opp	Total	Index
G	81	81	162	81	81	162		191	191	382	193	193	386	
Avg	.252	.225	.238	.255	.235	.245	97	.244	.234	.239	.243	.232	.238	100
AB	2695	2770	5465	2863	2677	5540	99	6189	6475	12664	6660	6280	12940	99
R	325	322	647	373	312	685	94	784	801	1585	879	769	1648	97
H	680	623	1303	730	629	1359	96	1508	1513	3021	1617	1460	3077	99
2B	129	118	247	144	128	272	92	292	300	592	325	295	620	98
3B	13	2	15	18	8	26	58	27	13	40	31	22	53	77
HR	50	98	148	77	74	151	99	176	245	421	213	211	424	101
BB	238	228	466	212	207	419	113	575	559	1134	567	555	1122	103
SO	533	716	1249	589	674	1263	100	1455	1733	3188	1571	1669	3240	101
Foul Outs	71	62	133	76	61	137	98	148	119	267	162	154	316	86
E	49	51	100	48	52	100	100	120	111	231	93	124	217	108
E-Infield	20	18	38	12	15	27	141	60	45	105	31	45	76	140
LHB-Avg	.264	.237	.250	.294	.221	.258	97	.248	.236	.242	.255	.220	.237	102
LHB-HR	27	47	74	42	24	66	111	86	101	187	96	80	176	109
RHB-Avg	.244	.216	.230	.229	.245	.236	97	.240	.232	.236	.234	.243	.238	99
RHB-HR	23	51	74	35	50	85	90	90	144	234	117	131	248	96

Colorado Rockies - Coors Field
LF: 347   CF: 415   RF:350

| | 2022 Season | | | | | | | 2020-2022 | | | | | | |
| | Home Games | | | Away Games | | | | Home Games | | | Away Games | | | |
	Rockies	Opp	Total	Rockies	Opp	Total	Index	Rockies	Opp	Total	Rockies	Opp	Total	Index
G	81	81	162	81	81	162		192	192	384	191	191	382	
Avg	.283	.283	.283	.225	.261	.242	117	.281	.275	.278	.223	.261	.242	115
AB	2794	2932	5726	2746	2637	5383	106	6561	6823	13384	6410	6190	12600	106
R	456	476	932	242	397	639	146	1065	1096	2161	647	926	1573	137
H	790	829	1619	618	687	1305	124	1844	1875	3719	1430	1617	3047	121
2B	151	194	345	129	132	261	124	359	411	770	280	325	605	120
3B	22	26	48	12	20	32	141	59	57	116	25	39	64	171
HR	98	102	200	51	82	133	141	237	243	480	157	220	377	120
BB	251	245	496	202	294	496	94	553	598	1151	552	685	1237	88
SO	600	581	1181	730	606	1336	83	1448	1411	2859	1781	1438	3219	84
Foul Outs	43	56	99	54	57	111	84	115	125	240	115	130	245	92
E	54	46	100	46	45	91	110	113	116	229	103	103	206	111
E-Infield	15	20	35	19	18	37	95	44	48	92	37	42	79	116
LHB-Avg	.262	.276	.271	.217	.252	.240	113	.267	.271	.269	.223	.260	.244	110
LHB-HR	25	42	67	14	40	54	114	78	107	185	52	102	154	111
RHB-Avg	.290	.288	.289	.227	.268	.244	119	.289	.278	.284	.223	.263	.240	118
RHB-HR	73	60	133	37	42	79	160	159	136	295	105	118	223	126

Detroit Tigers - Comerica Park
LF: 345   CF: 420   RF:330

	2022 Season							2020-2022						
	Home Games			Away Games				Home Games			Away Games			
	Tigers	Opp	Total	Tigers	Opp	Total	Index	Tigers	Opp	Total	Tigers	Opp	Total	Index
G	82	82	164	80	80	160		190	190	380	192	192	384	
Avg	.233	.245	.239	.228	.250	.239	100	.239	.244	.242	.236	.259	.248	98
AB	2669	2828	5497	2709	2577	5286	101	6125	6500	12625	6522	6279	12801	100
R	285	357	642	272	356	628	100	731	842	1573	772	945	1717	93
H	623	692	1315	617	644	1261	102	1461	1589	3050	1541	1628	3169	97
2B	106	137	243	129	100	229	102	251	333	584	298	260	558	106
3B	18	16	34	9	10	19	172	53	41	94	23	20	43	222
HR	52	71	123	58	96	154	77	160	182	342	191	275	466	74
BB	199	266	465	181	245	426	105	517	646	1163	500	628	1128	105
SO	679	607	1286	734	588	1322	94	1639	1441	3080	1855	1457	3312	94
Foul Outs	55	63	118	57	48	105	108	136	166	302	131	127	258	119
E	50	44	94	44	33	77	119	101	92	193	105	90	195	100
E-Infield	19	23	42	18	13	31	132	46	42	88	47	39	86	103
LHB-Avg	.236	.235	.236	.222	.255	.236	100	.235	.225	.230	.233	.264	.247	93
LHB-HR	18	27	45	24	46	70	63	58	53	111	69	112	181	61
RHB-Avg	.231	.250	.242	.233	.247	.240	101	.241	.256	.249	.239	.256	.248	101
RHB-HR	34	44	78	34	50	84	88	102	129	231	122	163	285	83

Houston Astros - Minute Maid Park
LF: 315   CF: 409   RF:326

	2022 Season							2020-2022						
	Home Games			Away Games				Home Games			Away Games			
	Astros	Opp	Total	Astros	Opp	Total	Index	Astros	Opp	Total	Astros	Opp	Total	Index
G	81	81	162	81	81	162		190	190	380	194	194	388	
Avg	.257	.205	.231	.239	.218	.229	101	.259	.212	.235	.252	.234	.243	97
AB	2611	2660	5271	2798	2635	5433	97	6224	6348	12572	6770	6308	13078	98
R	368	253	621	369	265	634	98	927	671	1598	952	780	1732	94
H	672	546	1218	669	575	1244	98	1611	1347	2958	1704	1477	3181	95
2B	138	98	236	146	106	252	97	330	254	584	356	282	638	95
3B	7	9	16	6	7	13	127	25	22	47	14	20	34	144
HR	116	68	184	98	66	164	116	250	190	440	254	201	455	101
BB	266	217	483	262	241	503	99	661	583	1244	628	641	1269	102
SO	551	834	1385	628	690	1318	108	1331	1872	3203	1510	1634	3144	106
Foul Outs	49	61	110	68	85	153	74	119	127	246	151	162	313	82
E	39	29	68	33	35	68	100	87	89	176	74	90	164	110
E-Infield	15	12	27	12	19	31	87	32	38	70	24	42	66	108
LHB-Avg	.268	.200	.226	.263	.204	.227	100	.271	.209	.234	.263	.224	.240	97
LHB-HR	36	31	67	39	22	61	110	84	79	163	99	69	168	97
RHB-Avg	.253	.210	.234	.231	.230	.230	102	.253	.215	.236	.247	.242	.245	96
RHB-HR	80	37	117	59	44	103	119	166	111	277	155	132	287	103

Kansas City Royals - Kauffman Stadium
LF: 330   CF: 410   RF:330

	2022 Season							2020-2022						
	Home Games			Away Games				Home Games			Away Games			
	Royals	Opp	Total	Royals	Opp	Total	Index	Royals	Opp	Total	Royals	Opp	Total	Index
G	81	81	162	81	81	162		192	192	384	192	192	384	
Avg	.259	.269	.264	.230	.274	.252	105	.259	.266	.263	.233	.256	.244	108
AB	2671	2818	5489	2766	2687	5453	101	6352	6663	13015	6500	6227	12727	102
R	335	399	734	305	411	716	103	843	950	1793	731	920	1651	109
H	691	757	1448	636	736	1372	106	1648	1773	3421	1513	1595	3108	110
2B	136	146	282	111	127	238	118	321	337	658	274	275	549	117
3B	21	15	36	17	11	28	128	43	28	71	31	27	58	120
HR	65	75	140	73	98	171	81	174	193	367	195	245	440	82
BB	219	297	516	241	292	533	96	535	651	1186	518	740	1258	92
SO	566	585	1151	721	606	1327	86	1424	1485	2909	1648	1567	3215	88
Foul Outs	52	50	102	51	60	111	91	128	116	244	121	142	263	91
E	46	34	80	36	45	81	99	109	117	226	88	103	191	118
E-Infield	18	16	34	16	19	35	97	44	53	97	37	45	82	118
LHB-Avg	.249	.262	.255	.231	.263	.245	104	.247	.258	.252	.232	.249	.240	105
LHB-HR	30	32	62	24	45	69	87	52	82	134	61	105	166	77
RHB-Avg	.267	.273	.270	.229	.280	.256	106	.268	.271	.270	.233	.260	.247	109
RHB-HR	35	43	78	49	53	102	77	122	111	233	134	140	274	84

Los Angeles Angels - Angel Stadium of Anaheim
LF: 330   CF: 400   RF:330

| | 2022 Season | | | | | | | 2020-2022 | | | | | | |
| | Home Games | | | Away Games | | | | Home Games | | | Away Games | | | |
	Angels	Opp	Total	Angels	Opp	Total	Index	Angels	Opp	Total	Angels	Opp	Total	Index
G	81	81	162	81	81	162		194	194	388	190	190	380	
Avg	.244	.226	.235	.222	.235	.229	103	.252	.238	.245	.229	.245	.237	103
AB	2676	2768	5444	2747	2618	5365	101	6397	6685	13082	6483	6187	12670	101
R	330	339	669	293	329	622	108	896	915	1811	744	878	1622	109
H	654	625	1279	611	616	1227	104	1611	1589	3200	1486	1517	3003	104
2B	107	135	242	112	129	241	99	291	320	611	290	333	623	95
3B	18	8	26	13	7	20	128	33	19	52	29	19	48	105
HR	106	89	195	84	79	163	118	261	243	504	204	195	399	122
BB	229	261	490	220	279	499	97	606	683	1289	546	648	1194	105
SO	748	745	1493	791	638	1429	103	1682	1768	3450	1741	1591	3332	100
Foul Outs	47	44	91	59	53	112	80	120	101	221	150	132	282	76
E	43	39	82	41	46	87	94	112	81	193	96	116	212	89
E-Infield	17	13	30	11	14	25	120	48	33	81	30	48	78	102
LHB-Avg	.243	.215	.231	.210	.234	.220	105	.246	.234	.240	.222	.243	.232	104
LHB-HR	53	38	91	28	34	62	142	115	113	228	85	80	165	132
RHB-Avg	.246	.232	.238	.232	.236	.234	101	.255	.240	.247	.234	.247	.240	103
RHB-HR	53	51	104	56	45	101	103	146	130	276	119	115	234	115

Los Angeles Dodgers - Dodger Stadium
LF: 330   CF: 395   RF:330

| | 2022 Season | | | | | | | 2020-2022 | | | | | | |
| | Home Games | | | Away Games | | | | Home Games | | | Away Games | | | |
	Dodgers	Opp	Total	Dodgers	Opp	Total	Index	Dodgers	Opp	Total	Dodgers	Opp	Total	Index
G	81	81	162	81	81	162		192	192	384	192	192	384	
Avg	.262	.210	.236	.252	.207	.231	102	.256	.209	.232	.247	.209	.229	101
AB	2673	2701	5374	2853	2635	5488	98	6248	6400	12648	6765	6259	13024	97
R	422	278	700	425	235	660	106	1007	644	1651	1019	643	1662	99
H	699	568	1267	719	546	1265	100	1598	1337	2935	1673	1308	2981	98
2B	164	110	274	161	113	274	102	338	252	590	331	267	598	102
3B	17	9	26	14	13	27	98	28	16	44	33	22	55	82
HR	106	90	196	106	62	168	119	310	216	526	257	163	420	129
BB	280	209	489	327	198	525	95	685	491	1176	763	547	1310	92
SO	665	775	1440	709	690	1399	105	1549	1882	3431	1704	1699	3403	104
Foul Outs	50	76	126	62	71	133	97	121	158	279	142	135	277	104
E	40	45	85	43	38	81	105	98	108	206	114	109	223	92
E-Infield	12	13	25	19	14	33	76	34	35	69	47	44	91	76
LHB-Avg	.254	.220	.238	.244	.207	.228	104	.240	.204	.222	.238	.209	.225	99
LHB-HR	43	26	69	42	20	62	114	120	74	194	113	68	181	109
RHB-Avg	.267	.205	.234	.258	.207	.232	101	.267	.213	.239	.254	.209	.232	103
RHB-HR	63	64	127	64	42	106	122	190	142	332	144	95	239	144

Miami Marlins - Marlins Park Surface: FieldTurf
LF: 344   CF: 400   RF:335

| | 2022 Season | | | | | | | 2020-2022 | | | | | | |
| | Home Games | | | Away Games | | | | Home Games | | | Away Games | | | |
	Marlins	Opp	Total	Marlins	Opp	Total	Index	Marlins	Opp	Total	Marlins	Opp	Total	Index
G	81	81	162	81	81	162		188	188	376	196	196	392	
Avg	.236	.248	.242	.225	.235	.230	105	.237	.240	.239	.229	.248	.239	100
AB	2653	2811	5464	2742	2612	5354	102	6095	6416	12511	6583	6278	12861	101
R	296	347	643	290	329	619	104	718	789	1507	754	892	1646	95
H	625	698	1323	616	613	1229	108	1447	1541	2988	1510	1558	3068	102
2B	132	167	299	116	147	263	111	271	370	641	285	366	651	99
3B	15	13	28	5	15	20	137	32	30	62	16	36	52	123
HR	71	90	161	73	83	156	101	164	200	364	198	217	415	90
BB	221	253	474	215	258	473	98	519	608	1127	558	658	1216	95
SO	678	739	1417	751	698	1449	96	1650	1691	3341	1869	1578	3447	100
Foul Outs	55	43	98	39	48	87	110	123	102	225	109	114	223	104
E	33	46	79	36	54	90	88	110	112	222	121	116	237	98
E-Infield	8	15	23	12	21	33	70	42	44	86	47	55	102	88
LHB-Avg	.225	.243	.237	.215	.221	.219	108	.218	.250	.237	.220	.251	.238	100
LHB-HR	15	40	55	25	23	48	112	42	90	132	62	85	147	93
RHB-Avg	.238	.252	.244	.228	.244	.235	104	.246	.233	.240	.233	.246	.239	100
RHB-HR	56	50	106	48	60	108	96	122	110	232	136	132	268	89

Milwaukee Brewers - American Family Field
LF: 344   CF: 400   RF:345

| | 2022 Season | | | | | | | 2020-2022 | | | | | | |
| | Home Games | | | Away Games | | | | Home Games | | | Away Games | | | |
	Brewers	Opp	Total	Brewers	Opp	Total	Index	Brewers	Opp	Total	Brewers	Opp	Total	Index
G	81	81	162	81	81	162		191	191	382	193	193	386	
Avg	.235	.217	.226	.234	.241	.238	95	.228	.223	.225	.237	.226	.231	97
AB	2647	2750	5397	2770	2656	5426	99	6119	6464	12583	6580	6191	12771	100
R	362	322	684	363	366	729	94	833	797	1630	877	778	1655	100
H	622	598	1220	649	640	1289	95	1393	1443	2836	1558	1397	2955	97
2B	127	123	250	124	117	241	104	280	251	531	309	272	581	93
3B	6	14	20	11	12	23	87	16	31	47	24	23	47	101
HR	110	105	215	109	85	194	111	244	230	474	244	195	439	110
BB	319	238	557	258	283	541	104	737	618	1355	647	629	1276	108
SO	743	824	1567	721	706	1427	110	1742	1964	3706	1769	1798	3567	105
Foul Outs	51	42	93	45	53	98	95	132	118	250	111	104	215	118
E	45	33	78	46	43	89	88	109	92	201	111	116	227	89
E-Infield	15	11	26	20	18	38	68	40	30	70	44	46	90	79
LHB-Avg	.227	.218	.223	.246	.241	.244	91	.224	.221	.222	.235	.230	.233	96
LHB-HR	44	44	88	40	27	67	132	96	88	184	93	75	168	112
RHB-Avg	.241	.217	.228	.226	.241	.233	98	.231	.225	.228	.238	.223	.230	99
RHB-HR	66	61	127	69	58	127	101	148	142	290	151	120	271	108

Minnesota Twins - Target Field
LF: 339   CF: 411   RF:328

| | 2022 Season | | | | | | | 2020-2022 | | | | | | |
| | Home Games | | | Away Games | | | | Home Games | | | Away Games | | | |
	Twins	Opp	Total	Twins	Opp	Total	Index	Twins	Opp	Total	Twins	Opp	Total	Index
G	81	81	162	81	81	162		193	193	386	191	191	382	
Avg	.255	.234	.244	.240	.250	.245	100	.246	.239	.242	.242	.254	.248	98
AB	2693	2787	5480	2783	2671	5454	100	6315	6608	12923	6529	6237	12766	100
R	343	316	659	353	368	721	91	848	824	1672	846	909	1755	94
H	687	652	1339	669	668	1337	100	1555	1577	3132	1580	1583	3163	98
2B	139	132	271	130	138	268	101	310	334	644	311	310	621	102
3B	9	5	14	9	15	24	58	20	16	36	18	31	49	73
HR	89	80	169	89	104	193	87	244	227	471	253	258	511	91
BB	265	252	517	253	216	469	110	636	571	1207	593	551	1144	104
SO	656	726	1382	697	610	1307	105	1608	1674	3282	1678	1514	3192	102
Foul Outs	60	63	123	52	61	113	108	162	126	288	125	141	266	107
E	33	44	77	50	41	91	85	103	100	203	107	95	202	99
E-Infield	7	18	25	16	17	33	76	39	36	75	43	44	87	85
LHB-Avg	.262	.226	.244	.247	.240	.243	100	.252	.244	.248	.242	.249	.245	101
LHB-HR	37	27	64	21	33	54	114	91	86	177	72	91	163	109
RHB-Avg	.250	.239	.244	.236	.257	.246	99	.242	.235	.238	.242	.257	.250	96
RHB-HR	52	53	105	68	71	139	77	153	141	294	181	167	348	83

New York Mets - Citi Field
LF: 335   CF: 408   RF:330

| | 2022 Season | | | | | | | 2020-2022 | | | | | | |
| | Home Games | | | Away Games | | | | Home Games | | | Away Games | | | |
	Mets	Opp	Total	Mets	Opp	Total	Index	Mets	Opp	Total	Mets	Opp	Total	Index
G	81	81	162	81	81	162		191	191	382	193	193	386	
Avg	.253	.224	.238	.265	.248	.256	93	.250	.226	.238	.255	.252	.254	94
AB	2636	2732	5368	2853	2676	5529	97	6069	6295	12364	6653	6290	12943	97
R	376	266	642	396	340	736	87	806	707	1513	888	875	1763	87
H	667	611	1278	755	663	1418	90	1518	1420	2938	1698	1586	3284	90
2B	115	107	222	157	125	282	81	274	267	541	332	318	650	87
3B	13	4	17	14	8	22	80	24	10	34	28	26	54	66
HR	81	68	149	90	101	191	80	199	210	409	234	230	464	92
BB	267	221	488	243	207	450	112	601	583	1184	601	539	1140	109
SO	589	828	1417	628	737	1365	107	1483	1901	3384	1624	1691	3315	107
Foul Outs	52	44	96	51	57	108	92	123	92	215	132	131	263	86
E	39	47	86	28	42	70	123	90	101	191	104	107	211	91
E-Infield	16	17	33	12	15	27	122	39	35	74	36	42	78	96
LHB-Avg	.251	.230	.242	.270	.247	.260	93	.260	.222	.243	.259	.248	.255	95
LHB-HR	31	39	70	41	49	90	84	89	94	183	106	102	208	94
RHB-Avg	.255	.219	.235	.259	.248	.253	93	.240	.228	.233	.251	.255	.253	92
RHB-HR	50	29	79	49	52	101	77	110	116	226	128	128	256	90

New York Yankees - Yankee Stadium
LF: 318 CF: 408 RF:314

| | 2022 Season | | | | | | | 2020-2022 | | | | | | |
| | Home Games | | | Away Games | | | | Home Games | | | Away Games | | | |
	Yankees	Opp	Total	Yankees	Opp	Total	Index	Yankees	Opp	Total	Yankees	Opp	Total	Index
G	81	81	162	81	81	162		193	193	386	191	191	382	
Avg	.240	.211	.226	.242	.226	.234	96	.241	.220	.230	.240	.234	.237	97
AB	2625	2743	5368	2797	2637	5434	99	6186	6491	12677	6482	6202	12684	99
R	419	265	684	388	302	690	99	963	712	1675	870	794	1664	100
H	631	580	1211	677	597	1274	95	1492	1425	2917	1555	1450	3005	96
2B	108	128	236	117	119	236	101	255	271	526	270	303	573	92
3B	3	6	9	5	2	7	130	12	13	25	15	16	31	81
HR	136	71	207	118	86	204	103	309	224	533	261	212	473	113
BB	310	216	526	310	228	538	99	769	556	1325	723	548	1271	104
SO	687	775	1462	704	684	1388	107	1650	1880	3530	1703	1676	3379	105
Foul Outs	67	68	135	61	59	120	114	123	142	265	128	135	263	101
E	31	54	85	43	44	87	98	104	99	203	116	109	225	89
E-Infield	20	20	40	20	18	38	105	53	35	88	55	44	99	88
LHB-Avg	.190	.200	.196	.238	.216	.226	87	.201	.206	.204	.218	.222	.220	93
LHB-HR	40	28	68	37	31	68	100	77	89	166	67	70	137	119
RHB-Avg	.261	.218	.240	.243	.232	.238	101	.257	.227	.242	.248	.240	.245	99
RHB-HR	96	43	139	81	55	136	104	232	135	367	194	142	336	110

Oakland Athletics - RingCentral Coliseum
LF: 330 CF: 400 RF:330

| | 2022 Season | | | | | | | 2020-2022 | | | | | | |
| | Home Games | | | Away Games | | | | Home Games | | | Away Games | | | |
	Athletics	Opp	Total	Athletics	Opp	Total	Index	Athletics	Opp	Total	Athletics	Opp	Total	Index
G	80	80	160	82	82	164		193	193	386	191	191	382	
Avg	.209	.252	.232	.222	.256	.239	97	.220	.244	.233	.233	.254	.243	96
AB	2557	2810	5367	2757	2681	5438	101	6144	6715	12859	6473	6248	12721	100
R	251	396	647	317	374	691	96	721	838	1559	864	851	1715	90
H	534	709	1243	613	685	1298	98	1354	1641	2995	1507	1586	3093	96
2B	127	163	290	122	150	272	108	300	335	635	311	310	621	101
3B	8	14	22	7	14	21	106	23	22	45	22	27	49	91
HR	53	84	137	84	111	195	71	176	200	376	231	255	486	77
BB	219	257	476	214	246	460	105	625	534	1159	591	573	1164	99
SO	637	610	1247	752	593	1345	94	1572	1566	3138	1690	1475	3165	98
Foul Outs	70	77	147	64	59	123	121	177	208	385	149	143	292	130
E	49	37	86	43	45	88	100	101	94	195	89	109	198	97
E-Infield	21	10	31	18	17	35	91	45	25	70	39	45	84	82
LHB-Avg	.214	.243	.229	.217	.249	.234	98	.233	.242	.238	.226	.248	.238	100
LHB-HR	21	32	53	29	41	70	79	76	78	154	91	97	188	83
RHB-Avg	.206	.257	.233	.225	.260	.241	97	.214	.246	.230	.236	.257	.246	93
RHB-HR	32	52	84	55	70	125	67	100	122	222	140	158	298	72

Philadelphia Phillies - Citizens Bank Park
LF: 329 CF: 401 RF:330

| | 2022 Season | | | | | | | 2020-2022 | | | | | | |
| | Home Games | | | Away Games | | | | Home Games | | | Away Games | | | |
	Phillies	Opp	Total	Phillies	Opp	Total	Index	Phillies	Opp	Total	Phillies	Opp	Total	Index
G	81	81	162	81	81	162		194	194	388	190	190	380	
Avg	.260	.238	.249	.247	.253	.250	100	.253	.244	.248	.243	.256	.250	100
AB	2689	2773	5462	2807	2657	5464	100	6329	6612	12941	6481	6207	12688	100
R	396	336	732	351	349	700	105	933	853	1786	854	888	1742	100
H	699	659	1358	693	671	1364	100	1604	1611	3215	1576	1590	3166	99
2B	131	140	271	124	146	270	100	303	325	628	304	343	647	95
3B	17	13	30	12	15	27	111	42	29	71	21	35	56	124
HR	107	81	188	98	69	167	113	250	234	484	235	196	431	110
BB	245	223	468	233	240	473	99	665	569	1234	606	588	1194	101
SO	668	716	1384	695	707	1402	99	1596	1786	3382	1649	1649	3298	101
Foul Outs	78	61	139	54	48	102	136	161	150	311	122	115	237	129
E	38	50	88	31	32	63	140	100	117	217	99	107	206	103
E-Infield	13	27	40	8	9	17	235	37	61	98	41	40	81	118
LHB-Avg	.240	.220	.230	.242	.255	.248	93	.244	.237	.241	.241	.249	.245	98
LHB-HR	53	27	80	50	24	74	107	117	91	208	111	78	189	107
RHB-Avg	.276	.249	.262	.250	.251	.251	104	.261	.248	.254	.245	.261	.253	101
RHB-HR	54	54	108	48	45	93	117	133	143	276	124	118	242	112

Pittsburgh Pirates - PNC Park
LF: 325   CF: 399   RF:320

	2022 Season							2020-2022						
	Home Games			Away Games				Home Games			Away Games			
	Pirates	Opp	Total	Pirates	Opp	Total	Index	Pirates	Opp	Total	Pirates	Opp	Total	Index
G	81	81	162	81	81	162		194	194	388	190	190	380	
Avg	.229	.258	.244	.216	.259	.237	103	.236	.251	.244	.220	.261	.240	102
AB	2627	2871	5498	2704	2668	5372	102	6276	6702	12978	6323	6134	12457	102
R	313	413	726	278	404	682	106	772	963	1735	647	985	1632	104
H	601	742	1343	585	690	1275	105	1484	1685	3169	1388	1598	2986	104
2B	114	152	266	107	172	279	93	291	368	659	246	354	600	105
3B	15	8	23	14	6	20	112	40	25	65	30	24	54	116
HR	74	86	160	84	78	162	97	161	215	376	180	242	422	86
BB	261	284	545	215	302	517	103	635	732	1367	537	709	1246	105
SO	685	627	1312	812	623	1435	89	1582	1585	3167	1764	1513	3277	93
Foul Outs	41	40	81	46	49	95	83	96	110	206	116	116	232	85
E	52	46	98	69	36	105	93	117	107	224	121	85	206	106
E-Infield	24	17	41	34	11	45	91	49	34	83	56	32	88	92
LHB-Avg	.226	.264	.242	.198	.252	.221	110	.235	.251	.242	.212	.260	.233	104
LHB-HR	58	39	97	46	29	75	119	115	92	207	111	104	215	91
RHB-Avg	.233	.254	.247	.239	.264	.253	97	.238	.252	.246	.228	.261	.246	100
RHB-HR	16	47	63	38	49	87	75	46	123	169	69	138	207	80

San Diego Padres - PETCO Park
LF: 336   CF: 396   RF:322

	2022 Season							2020-2022						
	Home Games			Away Games				Home Games			Away Games			
	Padres	Opp	Total	Padres	Opp	Total	Index	Padres	Opp	Total	Padres	Opp	Total	Index
G	81	81	162	81	81	162		194	194	388	190	190	380	
Avg	.230	.218	.224	.251	.247	.249	90	.238	.220	.229	.249	.250	.249	92
AB	2628	2731	5359	2840	2702	5542	97	6266	6539	12805	6558	6226	12784	98
R	301	301	602	404	359	763	79	822	743	1565	937	866	1803	85
H	605	596	1201	712	667	1379	87	1494	1441	2935	1634	1555	3189	90
2B	105	104	209	170	130	300	72	297	276	573	354	312	666	86
3B	7	5	12	11	12	23	54	20	12	32	31	32	63	51
HR	77	86	163	76	87	163	103	218	220	438	210	228	438	100
BB	269	230	499	305	238	543	95	715	556	1271	649	598	1247	102
SO	666	734	1400	661	717	1378	105	1592	1889	3481	1538	1644	3182	109
Foul Outs	61	54	115	68	54	122	97	140	113	253	157	112	269	94
E	39	43	82	37	48	85	96	104	98	202	87	110	197	100
E-Infield	11	17	28	18	19	37	76	41	40	81	31	50	81	98
LHB-Avg	.225	.197	.212	.225	.226	.225	94	.240	.202	.221	.236	.238	.237	93
LHB-HR	36	31	67	30	27	57	124	85	83	168	73	81	154	110
RHB-Avg	.234	.232	.233	.273	.260	.266	87	.237	.234	.235	.260	.258	.259	91
RHB-HR	41	55	96	46	60	106	92	133	137	270	137	147	284	94

San Francisco Giants - Oracle Park
LF: 339   CF: 391   RF:309

	2022 Season							2020-2022						
	Home Games			Away Games				Home Games			Away Games			
	Giants	Opp	Total	Giants	Opp	Total	Index	Giants	Opp	Total	Giants	Opp	Total	Index
G	81	81	162	81	81	162		195	195	390	189	189	378	
Avg	.238	.253	.246	.229	.253	.241	102	.251	.240	.245	.239	.243	.241	102
AB	2629	2830	5459	2763	2687	5450	100	6367	6712	13079	6506	6225	12731	100
R	363	332	695	353	365	718	97	924	799	1723	895	789	1684	99
H	627	717	1344	634	680	1314	102	1597	1612	3209	1556	1513	3069	101
2B	128	161	289	127	140	267	108	341	342	683	292	295	587	113
3B	10	17	27	8	11	19	142	33	42	75	24	29	53	138
HR	86	46	132	97	86	183	72	241	147	388	264	205	469	81
BB	297	220	517	274	221	495	104	742	531	1273	626	536	1162	107
SO	712	716	1428	750	654	1404	102	1673	1756	3429	1749	1527	3276	102
Foul Outs	44	36	80	70	43	113	71	100	108	208	142	134	276	73
E	59	42	101	41	31	72	140	123	92	215	99	82	181	115
E-Infield	20	12	32	15	11	26	123	55	31	86	45	39	84	99
LHB-Avg	.226	.264	.244	.234	.267	.249	98	.244	.241	.243	.241	.245	.243	100
LHB-HR	37	16	53	40	32	72	75	118	54	172	128	76	204	85
RHB-Avg	.249	.247	.248	.226	.244	.235	105	.256	.240	.247	.237	.242	.240	103
RHB-HR	49	30	79	57	54	111	70	123	93	216	136	129	265	77

Seattle Mariners - T-Mobile Park
LF: 331 CF: 405 RF:326

	2022 Season							2020-2022						
	Home Games			Away Games				Home Games			Away Games			
	Mariners	Opp	Total	Mariners	Opp	Total	Index	Mariners	Opp	Total	Mariners	Opp	Total	Index
G	81	81	162	81	81	162		186	186	372	198	198	396	
Avg	.223	.224	.223	.236	.247	.242	92	.218	.226	.222	.236	.257	.246	90
AB	2600	2771	5371	2775	2658	5433	99	5928	6341	12269	6731	6544	13275	98
R	318	299	617	372	324	696	89	744	744	1488	897	930	1827	87
H	580	620	1200	656	657	1313	91	1294	1435	2729	1586	1680	3266	89
2B	101	120	221	128	120	248	90	237	282	519	313	343	656	86
3B	8	3	11	11	16	27	41	16	10	26	19	45	64	44
HR	97	96	193	100	90	190	103	214	228	442	242	234	476	100
BB	284	191	475	312	256	568	85	634	496	1130	704	666	1370	89
SO	696	735	1431	701	656	1357	107	1649	1639	3288	1785	1549	3334	107
Foul Outs	81	88	169	64	47	111	154	169	182	351	144	137	281	135
E	35	38	73	34	43	77	95	79	93	172	92	87	179	102
E-Infield	11	19	30	11	20	31	97	31	40	71	38	39	77	98
LHB-Avg	.196	.203	.199	.226	.230	.228	87	.196	.218	.206	.228	.237	.232	89
LHB-HR	35	25	60	47	32	79	83	83	79	162	116	80	196	94
RHB-Avg	.249	.236	.241	.246	.259	.253	95	.240	.231	.235	.243	.269	.257	91
RHB-HR	62	71	133	53	58	111	114	131	149	280	126	154	280	104

St Louis Cardinals - Busch Stadium
LF: 336 CF: 400 RF:335

	2022 Season							2020-2022						
	Home Games			Away Games				Home Games			Away Games			
	Cardinals	Opp	Total	Cardinals	Opp	Total	Index	Cardinals	Opp	Total	Cardinals	Opp	Total	Index
G	81	81	162	81	81	162		189	189	378	193	193	386	
Avg	.251	.240	.245	.253	.254	.254	97	.246	.231	.238	.246	.243	.245	97
AB	2632	2742	5374	2864	2667	5531	97	6043	6304	12347	6556	6125	12681	99
R	392	283	675	380	354	734	92	817	698	1515	901	840	1741	89
H	661	657	1318	725	678	1403	94	1484	1457	2941	1615	1488	3103	97
2B	139	124	263	151	125	276	98	299	271	570	325	300	625	94
3B	8	11	19	13	10	23	85	22	19	41	28	23	51	83
HR	98	68	166	99	78	177	97	200	171	371	246	196	442	86
BB	270	220	490	267	269	536	94	612	578	1190	608	723	1331	92
SO	543	612	1155	683	565	1248	95	1384	1434	2818	1660	1432	3092	94
Foul Outs	82	54	136	59	46	105	133	163	127	290	133	101	234	127
E	29	48	77	37	37	74	104	81	102	183	102	97	199	94
E-Infield	7	14	21	17	11	28	75	20	32	52	41	33	74	72
LHB-Avg	.237	.225	.231	.254	.245	.249	93	.234	.221	.227	.235	.238	.236	94
LHB-HR	22	18	40	32	29	61	68	41	61	102	66	78	144	71
RHB-Avg	.260	.248	.254	.252	.261	.256	99	.252	.238	.245	.252	.247	.250	98
RHB-HR	76	50	126	67	49	116	112	159	110	269	180	118	298	94

Tampa Bay Rays - Tropicana Field Surface: FieldTurf
LF: 315 CF: 404 RF:322

	2022 Season							2020-2022						
	Home Games			Away Games				Home Games			Away Games			
	Rays	Opp	Total	Rays	Opp	Total	Index	Rays	Opp	Total	Rays	Opp	Total	Index
G	81	81	162	81	81	162		191	191	382	193	193	386	
Avg	.242	.216	.229	.237	.249	.243	94	.239	.217	.228	.241	.249	.245	93
AB	2612	2739	5351	2800	2685	5485	98	6157	6420	12577	6737	6453	13190	96
R	336	279	615	330	335	665	92	871	641	1512	941	853	1794	85
H	631	592	1223	663	668	1331	92	1474	1395	2869	1626	1604	3230	90
2B	150	114	264	146	125	271	100	338	269	607	351	297	648	98
3B	8	10	18	9	11	20	92	34	18	52	31	32	63	87
HR	71	84	155	68	88	156	102	199	190	389	242	236	478	85
BB	244	191	435	256	193	449	99	680	483	1163	648	505	1153	106
SO	667	746	1413	728	638	1366	106	1722	1814	3536	1823	1600	3423	108
Foul Outs	47	95	142	61	56	117	124	140	178	318	141	122	263	127
E	46	40	86	38	42	80	108	109	109	218	88	128	216	102
E-Infield	19	14	33	19	12	31	106	45	49	94	35	46	81	117
LHB-Avg	.215	.204	.210	.213	.248	.228	92	.222	.210	.217	.235	.239	.237	92
LHB-HR	29	28	57	24	26	50	117	91	59	150	115	69	184	85
RHB-Avg	.262	.222	.240	.255	.249	.252	95	.257	.221	.236	.247	.253	.251	94
RHB-HR	42	56	98	44	62	106	95	108	131	239	127	167	294	86

Texas Rangers - Globe Life Field Surface: FieldTurf
LF: 329   CF: 407   RF:326

| | 2022 Season | | | | | | | 2020-2022 | | | | | | |
| | Home Games | | | Away Games | | | | Home Games | | | Away Games | | | |
	Rangers	Opp	Total	Rangers	Opp	Total	Index	Rangers	Opp	Total	Rangers	Opp	Total	Index
G	81	81	162	81	81	162		192	192	384	192	192	384	
Avg	.241	.244	.243	.236	.250	.243	100	.238	.244	.241	.228	.257	.242	100
AB	2676	2807	5483	2802	2645	5447	101	6262	6638	12900	6557	6263	12820	101
R	342	396	738	365	347	712	104	785	929	1714	771	941	1712	100
H	646	685	1331	662	660	1322	101	1490	1619	3109	1492	1607	3099	100
2B	110	148	258	114	131	245	105	257	315	572	272	296	568	100
3B	10	10	20	10	8	18	110	23	26	49	30	24	54	90
HR	101	97	198	97	72	169	116	219	239	458	208	243	451	101
BB	235	300	535	221	281	502	106	540	679	1219	516	651	1167	104
SO	683	703	1386	763	611	1374	100	1590	1613	3203	1785	1429	3214	99
Foul Outs	72	48	120	68	80	148	81	151	138	289	153	164	317	91
E	49	40	89	47	45	92	97	109	95	204	110	99	209	98
E-Infield	19	14	33	23	17	40	83	45	38	83	47	38	85	98
LHB-Avg	.238	.249	.243	.234	.221	.229	106	.230	.247	.238	.222	.235	.228	105
LHB-HR	55	27	82	44	22	66	119	112	84	196	98	78	176	104
RHB-Avg	.244	.241	.243	.238	.264	.252	96	.244	.242	.243	.232	.268	.251	97
RHB-HR	46	70	116	53	50	103	115	107	155	262	110	165	275	99

Toronto Blue Jays - Rogers Centre Surface: FieldTurf
LF: 328   CF: 400   RF:328

| | 2022 Season | | | | | | | 2020-2022 | | | | | | |
| | Home Games | | | Away Games | | | | Home Games | | | Away Games | | | |
	Blue Jays	Opp	Total	Blue Jays	Opp	Total	Index	Blue Jays	Opp	Total	Blue Jays	Opp	Total	Index
G	81	81	162	81	81	162		116	116	232	268	268	536	
Avg	.261	.248	.254	.266	.245	.256	99	.263	.240	.251	.263	.245	.254	99
AB	2670	2802	5472	2885	2691	5576	98	3826	3988	7814	9228	8869	18097	100
R	359	355	714	416	324	740	96	546	485	1031	1377	1169	2546	94
H	696	696	1392	768	660	1428	97	1006	959	1965	2429	2171	4600	99
2B	150	136	286	157	124	281	104	220	185	405	476	428	904	104
3B	4	7	11	8	12	20	56	8	8	16	21	39	60	62
HR	102	102	204	98	78	176	118	158	142	300	392	328	720	96
BB	233	206	439	267	218	485	92	327	279	606	872	868	1740	81
SO	589	708	1297	653	682	1335	99	806	1040	1846	2162	2337	4499	95
Foul Outs	64	61	125	60	74	134	95	93	100	193	159	218	377	119
E	36	34	70	46	52	98	71	49	46	95	162	170	332	66
E-Infield	13	18	31	14	18	32	97	16	24	40	62	70	132	70
LHB-Avg	.211	.255	.243	.229	.228	.228	107	.224	.243	.237	.230	.230	.230	103
LHB-HR	4	39	43	16	31	47	97	7	48	55	58	118	176	82
RHB-Avg	.270	.243	.259	.274	.260	.268	97	.270	.239	.257	.273	.254	.265	97
RHB-HR	98	63	161	82	47	129	125	151	94	245	334	210	544	99

Washington Nationals - Nationals Park
LF: 336   CF: 403   RF:335

| | 2022 Season | | | | | | | 2020-2022 | | | | | | |
| | Home Games | | | Away Games | | | | Home Games | | | Away Games | | | |
	Nationals	Opp	Total	Nationals	Opp	Total	Index	Nationals	Opp	Total	Nationals	Opp	Total	Index
G	81	81	162	81	81	162		195	195	390	189	189	378	
Avg	.239	.255	.247	.258	.278	.268	92	.250	.254	.252	.259	.271	.265	95
AB	2652	2850	5502	2782	2672	5454	101	6287	6692	12979	6500	6216	12716	99
R	297	430	727	306	425	731	99	791	977	1768	829	999	1828	94
H	633	727	1360	718	742	1460	93	1572	1697	3269	1686	1684	3370	94
2B	123	136	259	129	109	238	108	316	312	628	320	285	605	102
3B	8	14	22	12	12	24	91	22	24	46	30	27	57	79
HR	76	124	200	60	120	180	110	201	292	493	183	293	476	101
BB	218	283	501	224	275	499	100	599	655	1254	608	667	1275	96
SO	593	651	1244	628	569	1197	103	1446	1610	3056	1529	1464	2993	100
Foul Outs	64	56	120	45	63	108	110	128	150	278	92	138	230	118
E	54	42	96	50	48	98	98	130	119	249	109	118	227	106
E-Infield	14	20	34	14	13	27	126	50	51	101	45	45	90	109
LHB-Avg	.263	.260	.261	.257	.255	.256	102	.259	.253	.256	.259	.253	.256	100
LHB-HR	28	47	75	27	45	72	103	88	108	196	94	106	200	93
RHB-Avg	.220	.252	.237	.259	.293	.276	86	.243	.254	.249	.260	.283	.271	92
RHB-HR	48	77	125	33	75	108	115	113	184	297	89	187	276	108

2022 American League Ballpark Index Rankings

Home Park	Avg	AB	R	H	2B	3B	HR	BB	SO	FO	E	E-Inf	LHB Avg	LHB HR	RHB Avg	RHB HR
White Sox (Guaranteed Rate Field)	99	101	114	100	94	68	124	108	95	113	104	105	102	146	98	115
Red Sox (Fenway Park)	108	102	112	111	107	283	114	93	96	99	109	118	109	100	108	123
Angels (Angel Stadium of Anaheim)	103	101	108	104	99	128	118	97	103	80	94	120	105	142	101	103
Rangers (Globe Life Field)	100	101	104	101	105	110	116	106	100	81	97	83	106	119	96	115
Royals (Kauffman Stadium)	105	101	103	106	118	128	81	96	86	91	99	97	104	87	106	77
Tigers (Comerica Park)	100	101	100	102	102	172	77	105	94	108	119	132	100	63	101	88
Orioles (Oriole Park at Camden Yards)	103	102	99	105	86	63	79	101	95	80	98	95	100	76	105	82
Yankees (Yankee Stadium)	96	99	99	95	101	130	103	99	107	114	98	105	87	100	101	104
Astros (Minute Maid Park)	101	97	98	98	97	127	116	99	108	74	100	87	100	110	102	119
Blue Jays (Rogers Centre)	99	98	96	97	104	56	118	92	99	95	71	97	107	97	97	125
Athletics (RingCentral Coliseum)	97	101	96	98	108	106	71	105	94	121	100	91	98	79	97	67
Guardians (Progressive Field)	97	99	94	96	92	58	99	113	100	98	100	141	97	111	97	90
Rays (Tropicana Field)	94	98	92	92	100	92	102	99	106	124	108	106	92	117	95	95
Twins (Target Field)	100	100	91	100	101	58	87	110	105	108	85	76	100	114	99	77
Mariners (T-Mobile Park)	92	99	89	91	90	41	103	85	107	154	95	97	87	83	95	114

2022 National League Ballpark Index Rankings

Home Park	Avg	AB	R	H	2B	3B	HR	BB	SO	FO	E	E-Inf	LHB Avg	LHB HR	RHB Avg	RHB HR
Rockies (Coors Field)	117	106	146	124	124	141	141	94	83	84	110	95	113	114	119	160
Reds (Great American Ballpark)	107	103	117	110	104	71	142	103	103	115	86	107	103	148	109	139
Pirates (PNC Park)	103	102	106	105	93	112	97	103	89	83	93	91	110	119	97	75
Dodgers (Dodger Stadium)	102	98	106	100	102	98	119	95	105	97	105	76	104	114	101	122
Phillies (Citizens Bank Park)	100	100	105	100	100	111	113	99	99	136	140	235	93	107	104	117
Marlins (Marlins Park)	105	102	104	108	111	137	101	98	96	110	88	70	108	112	104	96
Nationals (Nationals Park)	92	101	99	93	108	91	110	100	103	110	98	126	102	103	86	115
Diamondbacks (Chase Field)	101	100	98	101	111	92	70	100	97	105	87	103	97	61	105	77
Giants (Oracle Park)	102	100	97	102	108	142	72	104	102	71	140	123	98	75	105	70
Braves (Truist Park)	100	99	94	99	92	70	96	100	110	85	109	100	102	80	100	105
Brewers (American Family Field)	95	99	94	95	104	87	111	104	110	95	88	68	91	132	98	101
Cubs (Wrigley Field)	101	99	93	100	94	132	82	100	100	80	96	97	111	84	96	81
Cardinals (Busch Stadium)	97	97	92	94	98	85	97	94	95	133	104	75	93	68	99	112
Mets (Citi Field)	93	97	87	90	81	80	80	112	107	92	123	122	93	84	93	77
Padres (PETCO Park)	90	97	79	87	72	54	103	95	105	97	96	76	94	124	87	92

2022 AL Home Runs

Home Park	Index
White Sox	124
Blue Jays	118
Angels	118
Rangers	116
Astros	116
Red Sox	114
Mariners	103
Yankees	103
Rays	102
Guardians	99
Twins	87
Royals	81
Orioles	79
Tigers	77
Athletics	71

2022 AL LHB Home Runs

Home Park	Index
White Sox	146
Angels	142
Rangers	119
Rays	117
Twins	114
Guardians	111
Astros	110
Red Sox	100
Yankees	100
Blue Jays	97
Royals	87
Mariners	83
Athletics	79
Orioles	76
Tigers	63

2022 AL RHB Home Runs

Home Park	Index
Blue Jays	125
Red Sox	123
Astros	119
Rangers	115
White Sox	115
Mariners	114
Yankees	104
Angels	103
Rays	95
Guardians	90
Tigers	88
Orioles	82
Royals	77
Twins	77
Athletics	67

2022 NL Home Runs

Home Park	Index
Reds	142
Rockies	141
Dodgers	119
Phillies	113
Brewers	111
Nationals	110
Padres	103
Marlins	101
Cardinals	97
Pirates	97
Braves	96
Cubs	82
Mets	80
Giants	72
Diamondbacks	70

2022 NL LHB Home Runs

Home Park	Index
Reds	148
Brewers	132
Padres	124
Pirates	119
Rockies	114
Dodgers	114
Marlins	112
Phillies	107
Nationals	103
Mets	84
Cubs	84
Braves	80
Giants	75
Cardinals	68
Diamondbacks	61

2022 NL RHB Home Runs

Home Park	Index
Rockies	160
Reds	139
Dodgers	122
Phillies	117
Nationals	115
Cardinals	112
Braves	105
Brewers	101
Marlins	96
Padres	92
Cubs	81
Mets	77
Diamondbacks	77
Pirates	75
Giants	70

2022 AL Avg	
Home Park	Index
Red Sox	108
Royals	105
Orioles	103
Angels	103
Astros	101
Tigers	100
Rangers	100
Twins	100
White Sox	99
Blue Jays	99
Guardians	97
Athletics	97
Yankees	96
Rays	94
Mariners	92

2022 AL LHB Avg	
Home Park	Index
Red Sox	109
Blue Jays	107
Rangers	106
Angels	105
Royals	104
White Sox	102
Twins	100
Tigers	100
Orioles	100
Astros	100
Athletics	98
Guardians	97
Rays	92
Mariners	87
Yankees	87

2022 AL RHB Avg	
Home Park	Index
Red Sox	108
Royals	106
Orioles	105
Astros	102
Angels	101
Tigers	101
Yankees	101
Twins	99
White Sox	98
Guardians	97
Athletics	97
Blue Jays	97
Rangers	96
Mariners	95
Rays	95

2022 NL Avg	
Home Park	Index
Rockies	117
Reds	107
Marlins	105
Pirates	103
Dodgers	102
Giants	102
Diamondbacks	101
Cubs	101
Braves	100
Phillies	100
Cardinals	97
Brewers	95
Mets	93
Nationals	92
Padres	90

2022 NL LHB Avg	
Home Park	Index
Rockies	113
Cubs	111
Pirates	110
Marlins	108
Dodgers	104
Reds	103
Nationals	102
Braves	102
Giants	98
Diamondbacks	97
Padres	94
Mets	93
Phillies	93
Cardinals	93
Brewers	91

2022 NL RHB Avg	
Home Park	Index
Rockies	119
Reds	109
Diamondbacks	105
Giants	105
Phillies	104
Marlins	104
Dodgers	101
Braves	100
Cardinals	99
Brewers	98
Pirates	97
Cubs	96
Mets	93
Padres	87
Nationals	86

2022 AL Doubles	
Home Park	Index
Royals	118
Athletics	108
Red Sox	107
Rangers	105
Blue Jays	104
Tigers	102
Yankees	101
Twins	101
Rays	100
Angels	99
Astros	97
White Sox	94
Guardians	92
Mariners	90
Orioles	86

2022 AL Triples	
Home Park	Index
Red Sox	283
Tigers	172
Yankees	130
Angels	128
Royals	128
Astros	127
Rangers	110
Athletics	106
Rays	92
White Sox	68
Orioles	63
Guardians	58
Twins	58
Blue Jays	56
Mariners	41

2022 AL Errors	
Home Park	Index
Tigers	119
Red Sox	109
Rays	108
White Sox	104
Athletics	100
Guardians	100
Astros	100
Royals	99
Orioles	98
Yankees	98
Rangers	97
Mariners	95
Angels	94
Twins	85
Blue Jays	71

2022 NL Doubles	
Home Park	Index
Rockies	124
Marlins	111
Diamondbacks	111
Giants	108
Nationals	108
Brewers	104
Reds	104
Dodgers	102
Phillies	100
Cardinals	98
Cubs	94
Pirates	93
Braves	92
Mets	81
Padres	72

2022 NL Triples	
Home Park	Index
Giants	142
Rockies	141
Marlins	137
Cubs	132
Pirates	112
Phillies	111
Dodgers	98
Diamondbacks	92
Nationals	91
Brewers	87
Cardinals	85
Mets	80
Reds	71
Braves	70
Padres	54

2022 NL Errors	
Home Park	Index
Giants	140
Phillies	140
Mets	123
Rockies	110
Braves	109
Dodgers	105
Cardinals	104
Nationals	98
Padres	96
Cubs	96
Pirates	93
Marlins	88
Brewers	88
Diamondbacks	87
Reds	86

2020-2022 American League Ballpark Index Rankings

Home Park	TOTALS Avg	AB	R	H	2B	3B	HR	BB	SO	FO	E	E-Inf	LHB Avg	HR	RHB Avg	HR
Red Sox (Fenway Park)	111	103	119	114	123	160	103	96	93	88	112	111	111	91	111	110
Royals (Kauffman Stadium)	108	102	109	110	117	120	82	92	88	91	118	118	105	77	109	84
Angels (Angel Stadium of Anaheim)	103	101	109	104	95	105	122	105	100	76	89	102	104	132	103	115
Orioles (Oriole Park at Camden Yards)[1]	103	102	99	105	86	63	79	101	95	80	98	95	100	76	105	82
Guardians (Progressive Field)	100	99	97	99	98	77	101	103	101	86	108	140	102	109	99	96
Rangers (Globe Life Field)	100	101	100	100	100	90	101	104	99	91	98	98	105	104	97	99
Blue Jays (Rogers Centre)	99	100	94	99	104	62	96	81	95	119	66	70	103	82	97	99
Twins (Target Field)	98	100	94	98	102	73	91	104	102	107	99	85	101	109	96	83
White Sox (Guaranteed Rate Field)	98	98	106	96	90	66	129	106	98	112	100	111	96	145	99	122
Tigers (Comerica Park)	98	100	93	97	106	222	74	105	94	119	100	103	93	61	101	83
Yankees (Yankee Stadium)	97	99	100	96	92	81	113	104	105	101	89	88	93	119	99	110
Astros (Minute Maid Park)	97	98	94	95	94	144	101	101	106	82	110	108	97	97	96	103
Athletics (RingCentral Coliseum)	96	100	90	96	101	91	77	99	98	130	97	82	100	83	93	72
Rays (Tropicana Field)	93	96	85	90	98	87	85	106	108	127	102	117	92	85	94	86
Mariners (T-Mobile Park)	90	98	87	89	86	44	100	89	107	135	102	98	89	94	91	104

2020-2022 National League Ballpark Index Rankings

Home Park	TOTALS Avg	AB	R	H	2B	3B	HR	BB	SO	FO	E	E-Inf	LHB Avg	HR	RHB Avg	HR
Rockies (Coors Field)	115	106	137	121	120	171	120	88	84	92	111	116	110	111	118	126
Reds (Great American Ballpark)	108	103	123	111	106	61	149	105	105	120	97	117	107	163	108	139
Diamondbacks (Chase Field)	104	102	104	106	113	114	77	97	96	95	90	85	103	83	105	73
Pirates (PNC Park)	102	102	104	104	105	116	86	105	93	85	106	92	104	91	100	80
Giants (Oracle Park)	102	100	99	101	113	138	81	107	102	73	115	99	100	85	103	77
Dodgers (Dodger Stadium)	101	97	99	98	102	82	129	92	104	104	92	76	99	109	103	144
Braves (Truist Park)	101	100	103	101	96	85	98	100	106	91	122	121	102	97	100	99
Marlins (Marlins Park)	100	101	95	102	101	123	90	95	100	104	98	88	100	93	100	89
Cubs (Wrigley Field)	100	99	95	99	91	135	96	98	102	73	92	97	104	100	97	94
Phillies (Citizens Bank Park)	100	100	100	99	95	124	110	101	101	129	103	118	98	107	101	112
Brewers (American Family Field)	97	100	96	97	93	101	101	108	105	118	89	79	96	112	99	108
Cardinals (Busch Stadium)	97	99	89	97	94	83	86	92	94	127	94	72	96	71	98	94
Nationals (Nationals Park)	95	99	94	94	102	79	101	96	100	118	106	109	100	93	92	108
Mets (Citi Field)	94	97	87	90	87	66	92	109	107	86	91	96	95	94	92	90
Padres (PETCO Park)	92	98	85	90	86	51	100	102	109	94	100	98	93	110	91	94

2020-2022 AL Home Runs		2020-2022 AL LHB Home Runs		2020-2022 AL RHB Home Runs	
Home Park	Index	Home Park	Index	Home Park	Index
White Sox	129	White Sox	145	White Sox	122
Angels	122	Angels	132	Angels	115
Yankees	113	Yankees	119	Yankees	110
Red Sox	103	Guardians	109	Red Sox	110
Guardians	101	Twins	109	Mariners	104
Rangers	101	Rangers	104	Astros	103
Astros	101	Astros	97	Blue Jays	99
Mariners	100	Mariners	94	Rangers	99
Blue Jays	96	Red Sox	91	Guardians	96
Twins	91	Rays	85	Rays	86
Rays	85	Athletics	83	Royals	84
Royals	82	Blue Jays	82	Tigers	83
Orioles[1]	79	Royals	77	Twins	83
Athletics	77	Orioles[1]	76	Orioles[1]	82
Tigers	74	Tigers	61	Athletics	72

2020-2022 NL Home Runs		2020-2022 NL LHB Home Runs		2020-2022 NL RHB Home Runs	
Home Park	Index	Home Park	Index	Home Park	Index
Reds	149	Reds	163	Dodgers	144
Dodgers	129	Brewers	112	Reds	139
Rockies	120	Rockies	111	Rockies	126
Phillies	110	Padres	110	Phillies	112
Brewers	110	Dodgers	109	Brewers	108
Nationals	101	Phillies	107	Nationals	108
Padres	100	Cubs	100	Braves	99
Braves	98	Braves	97	Padres	94
Cubs	96	Mets	94	Cubs	94
Mets	92	Nationals	93	Cardinals	94
Marlins	90	Marlins	93	Mets	90
Cardinals	86	Pirates	91	Marlins	89
Pirates	86	Giants	85	Pirates	80
Giants	81	Diamondbacks	83	Giants	77
Diamondbacks	77	Cardinals	71	Diamondbacks	73

1. 2022 only

2020-2022 AL Avg	
Home Park	Index
Red Sox	111
Royals	108
Angels	103
Orioles[1]	103
Guardians	100
Rangers	100
Blue Jays	99
Twins	98
White Sox	98
Tigers	98
Yankees	97
Astros	97
Athletics	96
Rays	93
Mariners	90

2020-2022 AL LHB Avg	
Home Park	Index
Red Sox	111
Royals	105
Rangers	105
Angels	104
Blue Jays	103
Guardians	102
Twins	101
Athletics	100
Orioles[1]	100
Astros	97
White Sox	96
Tigers	93
Yankees	93
Rays	92
Mariners	89

2020-2022 AL RHB Avg	
Home Park	Index
Red Sox	111
Royals	109
Orioles[1]	105
Angels	103
Tigers	101
Yankees	99
Guardians	99
White Sox	99
Blue Jays	97
Rangers	97
Astros	96
Twins	96
Rays	94
Athletics	93
Mariners	91

2020-2022 NL Avg	
Home Park	Index
Rockies	115
Reds	108
Diamondbacks	104
Pirates	102
Giants	102
Dodgers	101
Braves	101
Marlins	100
Cubs	100
Phillies	100
Brewers	97
Cardinals	97
Nationals	95
Mets	94
Padres	92

2020-2022 NL LHB Avg	
Home Park	Index
Rockies	110
Reds	107
Pirates	104
Cubs	104
Diamondbacks	103
Braves	102
Nationals	100
Giants	100
Marlins	100
Dodgers	99
Phillies	98
Cardinals	96
Brewers	96
Mets	95
Padres	93

2020-2022 NL RHB Avg	
Home Park	Index
Rockies	118
Reds	108
Diamondbacks	105
Giants	103
Dodgers	103
Phillies	101
Braves	100
Marlins	100
Pirates	100
Brewers	99
Cardinals	98
Cubs	97
Mets	92
Nationals	92
Padres	91

2020-2022 AL Doubles	
Home Park	Index
Red Sox	123
Royals	117
Tigers	106
Blue Jays	104
Twins	102
Athletics	101
Rangers	100
Rays	98
Guardians	98
Astros	95
Angels	95
Yankees	92
White Sox	90
Orioles[1]	86
Mariners	86

2020-2022 AL Triples	
Home Park	Index
Tigers	222
Red Sox	160
Astros	144
Royals	120
Angels	105
Athletics	91
Rangers	90
Rays	87
Yankees	81
Guardians	77
Twins	73
White Sox	66
Orioles[1]	63
Blue Jays	62
Mariners	44

2020-2022 AL Errors	
Home Park	Index
Royals	118
Red Sox	112
Astros	110
Guardians	108
Mariners	102
Rays	102
Tigers	100
White Sox	100
Twins	99
Orioles[1]	98
Rangers	98
Athletics	97
Yankees	89
Angels	89
Blue Jays	66

2020-2022 NL Doubles	
Home Park	Index
Rockies	120
Giants	113
Diamondbacks	113
Reds	106
Pirates	105
Nationals	102
Dodgers	102
Marlins	101
Braves	96
Phillies	95
Cardinals	94
Brewers	93
Cubs	91
Mets	87
Padres	86

2020-2022 NL Triples	
Home Park	Index
Rockies	171
Giants	138
Cubs	135
Phillies	124
Marlins	123
Pirates	116
Diamondbacks	114
Brewers	101
Braves	85
Cardinals	83
Dodgers	82
Nationals	79
Mets	66
Reds	61
Padres	51

2020-2022 NL Errors	
Home Park	Index
Braves	122
Giants	115
Rockies	111
Pirates	106
Nationals	106
Phillies	103
Padres	100
Marlins	98
Reds	97
Cardinals	94
Dodgers	92
Cubs	92
Mets	91
Diamondbacks	90
Brewers	89

Minor League Abbreviation Key

Abbreviation	Team	Level	League	MLB Affiliate	First Year	Last Year
Abrdn	Aberdeen IronBirds	A-	New York-Penn League	Baltimore Orioles	2019	2019
Abrdn	Aberdeen IronBirds	A+	South Atlantic League	Baltimore Orioles	2021	2022
Akron	Akron RubberDucks	AA	Eastern League	Cleveland Guardians	2019	2022
Albq	Albuquerque Isotopes	AAA	Pacific Coast League	Colorado Rockies	2022	2022
Altna	Altoona Curve	AA	Eastern League	Pittsburgh Pirates	2019	2022
Amrillo	Amarillo Sod Poodles	AA	Texas League	San Diego Padres	2019	2019
Amrillo	Amarillo Sod Poodles	AA	Texas League	Arizona Diamondbacks	2021	2022
Angels	AZL Angels	R	Arizona League	Los Angeles Angels	2022	2022
Ark	Arkansas Travelers	AA	Texas League	Seattle Mariners	2021	2022
AsGold	AZL Athletics Gold	R	Arizona League	Oakland Athletics	2022	2022
Astros	GCL Astros	R	Gulf Coast League	Houston Astros	2021	2021
B Jays	GCL Blue Jays	R	Gulf Coast League	Toronto Blue Jays	2018	2018
Beloit	Beloit Snappers	A+	Midwest League	Miami Marlins	2021	2021
BG	Bowling Green Hot Rods	A	Midwest League	Tampa Bay Rays	2018	2019
Biloxi	Biloxi Shuckers	AA	Southern League	Milwaukee Brewers	2022	2022
Bklyn	Brooklyn Cyclones	A-	New York-Penn League	New York Mets	2019	2019
Bklyn	Brooklyn Cyclones	A+	South Atlantic League	New York Mets	2021	2022
Bluefld	Bluefield Blue Jays	R+	Appalachian League	Toronto Blue Jays	2018	2018
Bnghtn	Binghamton Rumble Ponies	AA	Eastern League	New York Mets	2021	2022
Boise	Boise Hawks	A-	Northwest League	Colorado Rockies	2019	2019
Bowie	Bowie Baysox	AA	Eastern League	Baltimore Orioles	2021	2022
Bradtn	Bradenton Marauders	A+	Florida State League	Pittsburgh Pirates	2019	2019
Bradtn	Bradenton Marauders	A	Florida State League	Pittsburgh Pirates	2022	2022
Braves	GCL Braves	R	Gulf Coast League	Atlanta Braves	2019	2019
BrewersB	AZL Brewers Blue	R	Arizona League	Milwaukee Brewers	2022	2022
BrewrsGold	AZL Brewers Gold	R	Arizona League	Milwaukee Brewers	2022	2022
Brham	Birmingham Barons	AA	Southern League	Chicago White Sox	2022	2022
Brstol	Bristol Pirates	R+	Appalachian League	Pittsburgh Pirates	2018	2018
Buffalo	Buffalo Bisons	AAA	International League	Toronto Blue Jays	2021	2022
Cards	GCL Cardinals	R	Gulf Coast League	St Louis Cardinals	2018	2018
Carlina	Carolina Mudcats	A+	Carolina League	Milwaukee Brewers	2019	2019
Carlina	Carolina Mudcats	A	Carolina League	Milwaukee Brewers	2022	2022
Charllt	Charlotte NC Knights	AAA	International League	Chicago White Sox	2022	2022
Charltt	Charlotte FL Stone Crabs	A+	Florida State League	Tampa Bay Rays	2018	2019
Chatt	Chattanooga Lookouts	AA	Southern League	Cincinnati Reds	2021	2022
Clmbs	Columbus Clippers	AAA	International League	Cleveland Guardians	2021	2022
Clrwtr	Clearwater Threshers	A	Florida State League	Philadelphia Phillies	2021	2022
Conn	Connecticut Tigers	A-	New York-Penn League	Detroit Tigers	2019	2019
CpChr	Corpus Christi Hooks	AA	Texas League	Houston Astros	2021	2022
Crpds	Cedar Rapids Kernels	A	Midwest League	Minnesota Twins	2018	2019
Crpds	Cedar Rapids Kernels	A+	Midwest League	Minnesota Twins	2022	2022
CtnSC	Charleston RiverDogs	A	South Atlantic League	New York Yankees	2018	2019
CtnSC	Charleston RiverDogs	A	Carolina League	Tampa Bay Rays	2022	2022
Cubs Blue	AZL Cubs Blue	R	Arizona League	Chicago Cubs	2022	2022
Cubs2	AZL Cubs2	R	Arizona League	Chicago Cubs	2018	2018
Dayton	Dayton Dragons	A	Midwest League	Cincinnati Reds	2018	2019
Dayton	Dayton Dragons	A+	Midwest League	Cincinnati Reds	2022	2022
Dbcks	AZL D-backs	R	Arizona League	Arizona Diamondbacks	2018	2022
Ddgrs	AZL Dodgers 1	R	Arizona League	Los Angeles Dodgers	2022	2022
Dlmrva	Delmarva Shorebirds	A	South Atlantic League	Baltimore Orioles	2018	2019
Dlmrva	Delmarva Shorebirds	A	Carolina League	Baltimore Orioles	2021	2022
Dnedin	Dunedin Blue Jays	A	Florida State League	Toronto Blue Jays	2022	2022
Drham	Durham Bulls	AAA	International League	Tampa Bay Rays	2021	2022
Elizab	Elizabethton Twins	R+	Appalachian League	Minnesota Twins	2018	2018
ElPaso	El Paso Chihuahuas	AAA	Pacific Coast League	San Diego Padres	2021	2022
Erie	Erie SeaWolves	AA	Eastern League	Detroit Tigers	2021	2022
Eugene	Eugene Emeralds	A+	Northwest League	San Francisco Giants	2021	2022
Everett	Everett AquaSox	A-	Northwest League	Seattle Mariners	2019	2019
Everett	Everett AquaSox	A+	Northwest League	Seattle Mariners	2021	2022
Faytvll	Fayetteville Woodpeckers	A+	Carolina League	Houston Astros	2019	2019
Frdrck	Frederick Keys	A+	Carolina League	Baltimore Orioles	2019	2019
Fred	Fredericksburg Nationals	A	Carolina League	Washington Nationals	2022	2022

Minor League Abbreviation Key

Abbreviation	Team	Level	League	MLB Affiliate	First Year	Last Year
Fresno	Fresno Grizzlies	A	California League	Colorado Rockies	2021	2021
Frisco	Frisco RoughRiders	AA	Texas League	Texas Rangers	2021	2022
FtMyrs	Fort Myers Miracle	A+	Florida State League	Minnesota Twins	2018	2019
FtMyrs	Fort Myers Mighty Mussels	A	Florida State League	Minnesota Twins	2022	2022
FtWyn	Fort Wayne TinCaps	A	Midwest League	San Diego Padres	2018	2019
FtWyn	Fort Wayne TinCaps	A+	Midwest League	San Diego Padres	2021	2022
Guardians	AZL Guardians Blue	R	Arizona League	Cleveland Guardians	2018	2022
GdJunc	Grand Junction Rockies	R+	Pioneer League	Colorado Rockies	2019	2019
Giants Blk	AZL Giants Black	R	Arizona League	San Francisco Giants	2022	2022
Giants Orng	AZL Giants Orange	R	Arizona League	San Francisco Giants	2019	2022
Grnsbr	Greensboro Grasshoppers	A	South Atlantic League	Miami Marlins	2018	2018
Grnsbr	Greensboro Grasshoppers	A+	South Atlantic League	Pittsburgh Pirates	2021	2022
Grnvlle	Greenville Drive	A	South Atlantic League	Boston Red Sox	2019	2019
Grnvlle	Greenville Drive	A+	South Atlantic League	Boston Red Sox	2021	2022
Gwnntt	Gwinnett Stripers	AAA	International League	Atlanta Braves	2021	2022
Helena	Helena Brewers	R+	Pioneer League	Milwaukee Brewers	2018	2019
Hkry	Hickory Crawdads	A	South Atlantic League	Texas Rangers	2019	2019
Hkry	Hickory Crawdads	A+	South Atlantic League	Texas Rangers	2021	2021
Hlsbro	Hillsboro Hops	A-	Northwest League	Arizona Diamondbacks	2018	2019
Hlsbro	Hillsboro Hops	A+	Northwest League	Arizona Diamondbacks	2021	2021
Hrsbrg	Harrisburg Senators	AA	Eastern League	Washington Nationals	2021	2022
Hrtfrd	Hartford Yard Goats	AA	Eastern League	Colorado Rockies	2022	2022
HudVal	Hudson Valley Renegades	A+	South Atlantic League	New York Yankees	2021	2021
IndiansR	AZL Indians Red	R	Arizona League	Cleveland Guardians	2018	2019
Indy	Indianapolis Indians	AAA	International League	Pittsburgh Pirates	2021	2022
InldEm	Inland Empire 66ers	A	California League	Los Angeles Angels	2022	2022
Iowa	Iowa Cubs	AAA	International League	Chicago Cubs	2021	2022
Jaxnvl	Jacksonville Jumbo Shrimp	AA	Southern League	Miami Marlins	2019	2019
Jaxnvl	Jacksonville Jumbo Shrimp	AAA	International League	Miami Marlins	2021	2022
Jhscty	Johnson City Cardinals	R+	Appalachian League	St Louis Cardinals	2018	2018
JrsyShr	Jersey Shore BlueClaws	A+	South Atlantic League	Philadelphia Phillies	2021	2022
Jupiter	Jupiter Hammerheads	A+	Florida State League	Miami Marlins	2019	2019
Jupiter	Jupiter Hammerheads	A	Florida State League	Miami Marlins	2021	2022
Kane	Kane County Cougars	A	Midwest League	Arizona Diamondbacks	2019	2019
Lk Cty	Lake County Captains	A	Midwest League	Cleveland Guardians	2018	2019
Lk Cty	Lake County Captains	A+	Midwest League	Cleveland Guardians	2021	2021
Lk Els	Lake Elsinore Storm	A+	California League	San Diego Padres	2019	2019
Lk Els	Lake Elsinore Storm	A	California League	San Diego Padres	2022	2022
Lkland	Lakeland Flying Tigers	A	Florida State League	Detroit Tigers	2022	2022
Lnsng	Lansing Lugnuts	A	Midwest League	Toronto Blue Jays	2019	2019
LsVgs	Las Vegas Aviators	AAA	Pacific Coast League	Oakland Athletics	2022	2022
Lsvlle	Louisville Bats	AAA	International League	Cincinnati Reds	2021	2022
LV	Lehigh Valley IronPigs	AAA	International League	Philadelphia Phillies	2021	2022
Lxngtn	Lexington Legends	A	South Atlantic League	Kansas City Royals	2018	2018
Lynbrg	Lynchburg Hillcats	A+	Carolina League	Cleveland Guardians	2018	2019
Lynbrg	Lynchburg Hillcats	A	Carolina League	Cleveland Guardians	2021	2021
Mdest	Modesto Nuts	A+	California League	Seattle Mariners	2019	2019
Mdest	Modesto Nuts	A	California League	Seattle Mariners	2021	2021
Mdlnd	Midland RockHounds	AA	Texas League	Oakland Athletics	2022	2022
Memp	Memphis Redbirds	AAA	International League	St Louis Cardinals	2021	2022
Mets	GCL Mets	R	Gulf Coast League	New York Mets	2019	2019
MhVlly	Mahoning Valley Scrappers	A-	New York-Penn League	Cleveland Guardians	2018	2019
Missi	Mississippi Braves	AA	Southern League	Atlanta Braves	2021	2022
Mont	Montgomery Biscuits	AA	Southern League	Tampa Bay Rays	2019	2021
Msoula	Missoula Osprey	R+	Pioneer League	Arizona Diamondbacks	2018	2018
Nashv	Nashville Sounds	AAA	International League	Milwaukee Brewers	2021	2022
Nham	New Hampshire Fisher Cats	AA	Eastern League	Toronto Blue Jays	2021	2022
Norfolk	Norfolk Tides	AAA	International League	Baltimore Orioles	2021	2022
NWArk	NW Arkansas Naturals	AA	Texas League	Kansas City Royals	2021	2022
OkCity	Oklahoma City Dodgers	AAA	Pacific Coast League	Los Angeles Dodgers	2022	2022
Omha	Omaha Storm Chasers	AAA	International League	Kansas City Royals	2021	2022
Orioles	GCL Orioles	R	Gulf Coast League	Baltimore Orioles	2018	2019
Padres	AZL Padres	R	Arizona League	San Diego Padres	2019	2022
Peoria	Peoria Chiefs	A	Midwest League	St Louis Cardinals	2018	2019

Minor League Abbreviation Key

Abbreviation	Team	Level	League	MLB Affiliate	First Year	Last Year
Peoria	Peoria Chiefs	A+	Midwest League	St Louis Cardinals	2021	2022
Phillies	GCL Phillies	R	Gulf Coast League	Philadelphia Phillies	2019	2019
PhilliesW	GCL Phillies West	R	Gulf Coast League	Philadelphia Phillies	2018	2018
Pirates	GCL Pirates	R	Gulf Coast League	Pittsburgh Pirates	2019	2021
PlmBh	Palm Beach Cardinals	A+	Florida State League	St Louis Cardinals	2019	2019
PlmBh	Palm Beach Cardinals	A	Florida State League	St Louis Cardinals	2021	2021
Pnscla	Pensacola Blue Wahoos	AA	Southern League	Minnesota Twins	2019	2019
Pnscla	Pensacola Blue Wahoos	AA	Southern League	Miami Marlins	2021	2022
Portlnd	Portland ME Sea Dogs	AA	Eastern League	Boston Red Sox	2021	2022
Prnctn	Princeton Rays	R+	Appalachian League	Tampa Bay Rays	2018	2018
Pulski	Pulaski Yankees	R+	Appalachian League	New York Yankees	2018	2018
QuadC	Quad Cities River Bandits	A	Midwest League	Houston Astros	2019	2019
QuadC	Quad Cities River Bandits	A+	Midwest League	Kansas City Royals	2021	2021
Rays	GCL Rays	R	Gulf Coast League	Tampa Bay Rays	2018	2018
Rchmd	Richmond Flying Squirrels	AA	Eastern League	San Francisco Giants	2022	2022
Rcuca	Rancho Cucamonga Quakes	A	California League	Los Angeles Dodgers	2022	2022
Rdng	Reading Fightin Phils	AA	Eastern League	Philadelphia Phillies	2021	2022
RdRck	Round Rock Express	AAA	Pacific Coast League	Texas Rangers	2021	2022
Reds	AZL Reds	R	Arizona League	Cincinnati Reds	2022	2022
RedSx	GCL Red Sox	R	Gulf Coast League	Boston Red Sox	2018	2021
Reno	Reno Aces	AAA	Pacific Coast League	Arizona Diamondbacks	2021	2022
Rngrs	AZL Rangers	R	Arizona League	Texas Rangers	2019	2022
Roch	Rochester Red Wings	AAA	International League	Washington Nationals	2021	2022
Rock	Rocket City Trash Pandas	AA	Southern League	Los Angeles Angels	2021	2022
Rome	Rome Braves	A	South Atlantic League	Atlanta Braves	2019	2019
Rome	Rome Braves	A+	South Atlantic League	Atlanta Braves	2021	2022
Royals	AZL Royals	R	Arizona League	Kansas City Royals	2019	2019
Salem	Salem Red Sox	A+	Carolina League	Boston Red Sox	2019	2019
Salem	Salem Red Sox	A	Carolina League	Boston Red Sox	2022	2022
Salt Lk	Salt Lake Bees	AAA	Pacific Coast League	Los Angeles Angels	2021	2022
Sbend	South Bend Cubs	A	Midwest League	Chicago Cubs	2019	2019
Sbend	South Bend Cubs	A+	Midwest League	Chicago Cubs	2021	2022
Scrmto	Sacramento River Cats	AAA	Pacific Coast League	San Francisco Giants	2022	2022
SgrLnd	Sugar Land Space Cowboys	AAA	Pacific Coast League	Houston Astros	2021	2022
SlKzr	Salem-Keizer Volcanoes	A-	Northwest League	San Francisco Giants	2019	2019
Smrst	Somerset Patriots	AA	Eastern League	New York Yankees	2021	2022
SnAnt	San Antonio Missions	AA	Texas League	San Diego Padres	2021	2022
SnJos	San Jose Giants	A	California League	San Francisco Giants	2021	2022
Spkane	Spokane Indians	A+	Northwest League	Colorado Rockies	2021	2021
Sprgfld	Springfield Cardinals	AA	Texas League	St Louis Cardinals	2018	2022
Stcktn	Stockton Ports	A	California League	Oakland Athletics	2022	2022
Stluci	St. Lucie Mets	A	Florida State League	New York Mets	2021	2022
Stnlld	Staten Island Yankees	A-	New York-Penn League	New York Yankees	2018	2019
StPaul	St. Paul Saints	AAA	International League	Minnesota Twins	2021	2022
S-WB	Scranton WB RailRiders	AAA	International League	New York Yankees	2021	2022
Syrcse	Syracuse Mets	AAA	International League	New York Mets	2022	2022
Tacom	Tacoma Rainiers	AAA	Pacific Coast League	Seattle Mariners	2022	2022
Tampa	Tampa Tarpons	A	Florida State League	New York Yankees	2021	2022
Tenn	Tennessee Smokies	AA	Southern League	Chicago Cubs	2021	2022
TigersW	GCL Tigers West	R	Gulf Coast League	Detroit Tigers	2019	2019
Toledo	Toledo Mud Hens	AAA	International League	Detroit Tigers	2021	2022
TriCity	Tri-City NY ValleyCats	A-	New York-Penn League	Houston Astros	2018	2019
Tulsa	Tulsa Drillers	AA	Texas League	Los Angeles Dodgers	2022	2022
Visalia	Visalia Rawhide	A+	California League	Arizona Diamondbacks	2019	2019
Wich	Wichita Wind Surge	AA	Texas League	Minnesota Twins	2021	2022
Wilmg	Wilmington Blue Rocks	A+	Carolina League	Kansas City Royals	2019	2019
Wilmg	Wilmington Blue Rocks	A+	South Atlantic League	Washington Nationals	2021	2022
Wisc	Wisconsin Timber Rattlers	A	Midwest League	Milwaukee Brewers	2018	2019
Wisc	Wisconsin Timber Rattlers	A+	Midwest League	Milwaukee Brewers	2022	2022
Wmich	West Michigan Whitecaps	A	Midwest League	Detroit Tigers	2019	2019
Wmich	West Michigan Whitecaps	A+	Midwest League	Detroit Tigers	2021	2022
Wmspt	Williamsport Crosscutters	A-	New York-Penn League	Philadelphia Phillies	2019	2019
Wrcstr	Worcester Red Sox	AAA	International League	Boston Red Sox	2021	2022
Wsox	AZL White Sox	R	Arizona League	Chicago White Sox	2022	2022

Minor League Abbreviation Key

Abbreviation	Team	Level	League	MLB Affiliate	First Year	Last Year
WV	West Virginia Power	A	South Atlantic League	Pittsburgh Pirates	2018	2018
WV	West Virginia Power	A	South Atlantic League	Seattle Mariners	2019	2019

Baseball Glossary

% Inherited Scored
The percentage of inherited baserunners a relief pitcher allows to score.

% Pitches Taken
The percentage of pitches that a batter does not swing at out of the total number of pitches thrown to him.

1st Batter Average
The Batting Average that a relief pitcher allows to the first batter he faces when he enters a game.

1st Batter OBP
The On-Base Percentage that a relief pitcher allows to the first batter he faces when he enters a game.

1st to 3rd (Baserunning)
"Moved" is the number of times a runner goes from 1st base to 3rd base on a SINGLE. "Chances" are the number of times a runner is on 1st base and a batter is credited with a SINGLE.

1st to Home (Baserunning)
"Moved" is the number of times a runner goes from 1st base to home on a DOUBLE. "Chances" are the number of times a runner is on 1st base and a batter is credited with a DOUBLE.

2nd to Home (Baserunning)
"Moved" is the number of times a runner goes from 2nd base to home on a SINGLE. "Chances" are the number of times a runner is on 2nd base and a batter is credited with a SINGLE.

Active Career Batting Leaders
A list of batting leaders among active (appearing in the most recent season) players. An active player is eligible when he meets the minimum requirements for the following categories:

> 1,000 At Bats—Batting Average, On-Base Percentage, Slugging Average, At
> Bats Per HR, At Bats Per GDP, At Bats Per RBI, Strikeout-to-Walk Ratio
> 100 Stolen Base Attempts—Stolen Base Success Percentage

Active Career Pitching Leaders
A list of pitching leaders among active (appearing in the most recent season) players. An active player is eligible when he meets the minimum requirements for the following categories:

> 750 Innings Pitched—Earned Run Average, Opponent Batting Average, all "Per
> 9 Innings" categories, Strikeout-to-Walk Ratio
> 250 Games Started—Complete Game Frequency
> 100 Decisions—Win-Loss Percentage

ART
See PART System

BA w/ RISP
The Batting Average allowed by a pitcher while pitching with runners in scoring position.

Base Taken
A player is credited with a Base Taken whenever he moves up a base on a Wild Pitch, Passed Ball, Balk, Sacrifice Fly, or Defensive Indifference.

Batting Average
Hits divided by at bats.

Batting Average on Balls in Play (BABIP)
Hits in play divided by balls in play. Home runs are not counted as balls in play.

Batting Average Plus Slugging (BPS)
Batting Average plus Slugging Average. Used in Leaderboards on out-of-zone pitches (OutZ).

Blown Save
When a relief pitcher enters a game in a Save Situation (see definition for Save Situation) and allows the other team to score the tying or go-ahead run.

Bomb (Intentional Walk)
An Intentional Walk is counted as a "Bomb" if
1. The next batter, after the IBB, does not ground into a double play, and
2. Multiple runs are scored in the inning, after the intentional walk.

BR Gain (Baserunning)
BR Gain (or Loss if a negative number) is the total of all the types of extra baserunning advances minus the (triple) penalty for all the BR Outs compared with what would be expected based on the MLB averages.

BR Outs (Baserunning)
BR Outs include the sum of Outs Advancing, Doubled Offs, and when a runner is tagged out on the bases when another runner moves up on a Wild Pitch, Passed Ball, or scores on a Sacrifice Fly.

BS Win
A Blown Save Win is a "win" credited to a reliever who has blown a save opportunity.

Career Targets
This method, also called the Favorite Toy, is a way to estimate the probability that a player will achieve a specific career goal. In this example, 3,000 hits will be used. The four components of the formula are:

1. Needed Hits. This is the number of Hits (or any statistic) that a player needs to reach a desired goal.

2. Years Remaining. This is the estimated number of years remaining in the player's career. It is determined using the player's age (on June 30th of the previous year; after a given season ends, use the season when making the calculation). The formula is (42 - age) divided by two. This means a player who is 20 years old will have 11 remaining seasons, a player who is 25 years old will have 8.5 remaining seasons and a player who is 35 years old will have 3.5 remaining seasons. If the player is a catcher, then multiply his remaining seasons by .7. The only stipulation is that years remaining must always be greater than or equal to 1.5.

3. Established Hit Level. The Established Hit Level is a weighted average of the player's hits over the past three seasons. To calculate the Established Hit Level after a given season is complete, add (Hits from two years ago), (Hits from last year multiplied by two), and (Hits from this year multiplied by three), then divide by six. If the Established Hit Level is less than 75% of the most recent performance, then the Established Hit Level is equal to .75 times the most recent performance.

4. Projected Remaining Hits. This is calculated by multiplying Years Remaining by the Established Hit Level.

The probability of achieving the specified goal is found by dividing Projected Remaining Hits by Needed Hits, then subtracting .5. The maximum that any player has of achieving a goal is .85 raised to the power of (Need Hits / Established Hit Level). This prevents the possibility of a player reaching a goal from being higher than 100 percent, which is impossible.

Catcher Pickoffs (CPO, CPkof)
The number of baserunners thrown out when a catcher throws to a base with a leading baserunner, and the runner is tagged out attempting to return to the base. Catcher pickoffs are not an official statistic and are not counted toward Caught Stealing totals.

Catcher's ERA
The ERA for a catcher is equal to the ERA of pitchers pitching while the catcher is playing behind the plate. It is calculated exactly like ERA for pitchers. Take the number of earned runs allowed while the catcher is playing, multiply it by 9 and then divide it by the total number of defensive innings that the catcher was behind the plate.

Cheap Win
A starting pitcher who wins the game with a game score under 50 gets credit for a cheap win. See Game Score.

Clean Outing
A Clean Outing is a game in which the reliever is not charged with a run (earned or otherwise) AND does not allow an inherited runner to score.

Cleanup Slugging Average
The Slugging Average of a batter when he bats in the cleanup spot, or fourth, in the batting order.

Close and Late
A situation in a game that is very similar to a Save Situation. The following requirements are necessary for a Close and Late game:
1. The game is in the seventh inning or later AND
2. The batting team is either leading by one run or tied OR
3. The tying run is on base, at bat, or on deck.

Component ERA (ERC)
A statistic that estimates what a pitcher's ERA should have been, based on his pitching performance. The ERC formula is calculated as follows:

1. Subtract the pitcher's Home Runs Allowed from his Hits Allowed.

2. Multiply Step 1 by 1.255.
3. Multiply his Home Runs Allowed by four.
4. Add Steps 2 and 3 together.
5. Multiply Step 4 by .89.
6. Add his Walks and Hit Batsmen.
7. Multiply Step 6 by .475.
8. Add Steps 5 and 7 together.

This yields the pitcher's total base estimate (PTB), which is:

$$PTB = 0.89 \times (1.255 \times (H - HR) + 4 \times HR) + 0.475 \times (BB + HB)$$

For those pitchers for whom there is intentional walk data, use this formula instead:

$$PTB = 0.89 \times (1.255 \times (H - HR) + 4 \times HR) + 0.56 \times (BB + HB - IBB)$$

9. Add Hits and Walks and Hit Batsmen.
10. Multiply Step 9 by PTB.
11. Divide Step 10 by Batters Facing Pitcher. If BFP data is unavailable, approximate it by multiplying Innings Pitched by 2.9, then adding Step 9.
12. Multiply Step 11 by 9.
13. Divide Step 12 by Innings Pitched.
14. Subtract .56 from Step 13.

This is the pitcher's ERC, which is:

$$\frac{(H + BB + HB) \times PTB}{BFP \times IP} \times 9 - 0.56$$

If the result after Step 13 is less than 2.24, adjust the formula as follows:

$$\frac{(H + BB + HB) \times PTB}{BFP \times IP} \times 9 \times 0.75$$

Consecutive Days
A count of how many times the pitcher was used after having pitched on the previous day or (in a few cases) in an earlier game on the same day.

Defensive Misplay
Any play which is not an error (or a passed ball) on which the fielder surrenders a base advance or the opportunity to make an out when a better play or a different play would have or might have gotten the out or prevented the advancement.

Defensive Runs Saved
Defensive Runs Saved (Runs Saved, for short) is the innovative metric introduced by John Dewan in *The Fielding Bible—Volume II* and modified in each subsequent volume. The Runs Saved value indicates how many runs a player saved or cost his team in the field compared to the average player at his position. A player of zero Runs Saved is about average; a positive number of runs saved indicates above-average

defense, below-average fielders post negative Runs Saved totals. There are eight components of Runs Saved:

PART Runs Saved (all positions; outfielders or players prior to 2013 use the Range and Positioning System)
Range and Positioning Runs Saved (non-catchers prior to 2013 and outfielders from 2013 forward.)
Adjusted Earned Runs Saved (Catchers)
Strike Zone Runs Saved (Catchers)
Stolen Base Runs Saved (Catchers, Pitchers)
Bunt Runs Saved (Corner Infielders, Pitchers, Catchers)
Double Play Runs Saved (Infielders)
Outfield Arm Runs Saved (Outfielders)
Good Play/Misplay Runs Saved (All Positions)

Double Play %
Successful Double Plays divided by the number of Double Play opportunities. This statistic includes both the fielder who started the play and the pivot man.

Double Play Opportunity
A fielder is considered to have a double play opportunity when a ground ball is hit with a runner on first base and less than 2 outs and that fielder is involved in the play. This is used to calculate Double Play % and Pivot %.

Doubled Off
A runner is Doubled Off when he is out for failing to get back to his base before he, or the base, is tagged after a ball hit in the air is caught.

Early Entry
A count of the number of times the reliever entered the game in the sixth inning or earlier.

Earned Run Average
The number of earned runs that a pitcher surrenders per nine innings that he pitches. It is calculated by multiplying the total earned runs allowed by nine and dividing by the total number of innings pitched.

Easy Save
This label is used to separate Saves by difficulty level (Easy or Tough). A Save is considered Easy if the relief pitcher enters the game, pitches one inning or less, and the first batter he faces does not at least represent the tying run.

Fielding Percentage
The percentage of plays a player makes in the field without making an error out of his total opportunities. Calculated by dividing (Putouts plus Assists) by (Putouts plus Assists plus Errors).

Games Finished
The relief pitcher who is in the game for each team when the game ends is credited with a Game Finished.

Game Score (Hitters)
To determine a hitter's Game Score:
Start with 15.
Add 10 times his Runs Created in the game (Runs Created for a single game is described in this Glossary).
Add 5 times his Runs Scored.
Add 5 times his RBI.

Game Score (Pitchers)
To determine the starting pitcher's Game Score:
Start with 50.
Add 1 point for each out recorded by the starting pitcher.
Add 2 points for each inning the pitcher completes after the fourth inning.
Add 1 point for each strikeout.
Subtract 2 points for each hit allowed.
Subtract 4 points for each earned run allowed.
Subtract 2 points for an unearned run.
Subtract 1 point for each walk.

GDP
Grounded into Double Play.

GDP Opportunity
This is a situation where the batter has a chance to ground into a double play. It occurs with at least a runner on first base and less than two outs.

Good Fielding Play (GFP)
A Good Fielding Play is a play that is made when it is not clear whether or not the play can be made. It is a play that is made when, had the play not been made, no one would have faulted the fielder for not making it.

Ground / Fly Ratio (Grd/Fly, GB/FB)
Calculated for both batters and pitchers. For batters, it is the number of groundballs hit divided by the number of flyballs hit. For pitchers, it is exactly the same but uses the number of groundballs and flyballs allowed. Every fair batted ball is included except for bunts and line drives.

Hall of Fame Monitor
Updated in the 2018 Handbook, the Hall of Fame Monitor was invented by Bill James as a quantitative measure of a player's likelihood of induction into the Hall of Fame. Accomplishments like career statistical benchmarks, championship seasons, and awards are all assigned point values, and each player is put on a scale where anyone from 70-130 is a plausible Hall of Famer, and over 130 is a sure-fire candidate.

Hall of Fame Value (HOF-V)
Introduced by Bill James in the 2019 Handbook, a player's Hall of Fame Value is determined by taking his Wins Above Replacement (according to Baseball Reference), multiplying it by four, and adding it to his Win Shares. Catchers receive a multiplier bonus according to how much they caught in their career: 20% for a full career, 10% for half a career, and so on. A score of 500 indicates that the player is worthy of Hall of Fame candidacy (independent of his likelihood of being selected).

Hold

A relief pitcher is given a Hold anytime he enters the game in a Save Situation (see definition for Save Situation), records one out or more, and exits the game without giving up the lead. If the pitcher finishes the game, then he will only earn credit for a Save. He cannot receive credit for both a Hold and a Save.

Holds Adjusted Save Percentage (same as Save/Hold Percentage)

Holds plus Saves divided by Holds plus Saves Opportunities.

Inherited Runner

Any runner who was on base at the time a relief pitcher enters the game.

Isolated Power

Slugging Average minus Batting Average.

K/BB Ratio

Strikeouts divided by Walks.

Leadoff On-Base Percentage

The On-Base Percentage of a batter when he bats leadoff, or first, in the batting order.

Leverage Index

Leverage is the amount of swing in the possible change in win probability, compared to the average swing in all situations. The average swing value, by definition, is indexed to 1.00.

If the score of the game is 12-0 or 14-1 the possible changes in win probability will be very close to negligible. Whether the pitcher gives up a home run or gets a double play ball doesn't really change the outcome of the game. There won't be much swing in either direction for the probability of the win. But in the late innings of a close game, the change in win probability among the various events will have rather wild swings. With a runner on first, two outs, down by one, and in the bottom of the ninth, the game can hinge on one swing of the bat. A home run and an out will both end the game, but with different outcomes for the teams involved. The Leverage Index we use (LI) was developed at the website Tangotiger.net, and compiled at the website FanGraphs.com.

Long Outing

A Long Outing is one in which a starting pitcher throws more than 110 pitches or a relief pitcher throws more than 25 pitches. Prior to 2002, we used 120 pitches as the cutoff for starters in the Manager's Record section.

Long Save

A Long Save is when the pitcher credited with a save pitches more than one inning.

Manufactured Runs

1. A run that scores without a hit, or a run on which the only hit(s) is/are infield hits, is always scored as a Manufactured Run.
2. A run which is driven in by a home run is never scored a Manufactured Run, under any circumstance.
3. A run which is driven in by a double or a triple is scored as a Manufactured Run only if *two* of the four bases result from advancing on one of these four acts: a sacrifice bunt, a stolen base, a hit and run, or a bunt single.

4. Otherwise, a run is considered to be a Manufactured Run if two of the four bases do not result from the runner being forced along by a walk, a hit batsman, or a safe hit reaching the outfield.

5. A forceout or fielder's choice which does not improve the position of the base runners should not be counted as contributing toward a Manufactured Run. Advancing on a forceout or a fielder's choice DOES count toward a manufactured run, if the play is one which improves the position of the baserunners.

6. A base "gained" on a double play does not count as a contribution to a Manufactured Run. A run scored on a double play is a Manufactured Run only if two of the OTHER bases are not attributable to forced advancement.

Net Gain
Net Gain is a statistic that measures baserunning production that includes all baserunning advancements on both hits and outs (BR Gain) and stolen bases (SB Gain).

Not Good Outcome (Intentional Walk)
A Not Good Outcome (NG) for an Intentional Walk occurs when one run scored in the inning after the intentional walk (and the next batter after the intentional walk did not ground into a double play).

Offensive Winning Percentage (OWP)
A player's Offensive Winning Percentage is the winning percentage of a hypothetical team which has an offense consisting of nine of that player, and pitching and defense which is average for the player's league. It is calculated by taking the square of RC/27 (see the definition for Runs Created per 27 Outs), dividing it by the sum of the square of RC/27 and the square of the average runs scored per game in the league.

On-Base Percentage
(Hits plus Walks plus Hit by Pitcher) divided by (At Bats plus Walks plus Hit by Pitcher plus Sacrifice Flies).

$$\frac{H + BB + HBP}{AB + BB + HBP + SF}$$

On-Base Plus Slugging (OPS)
On-Base Percentage plus Slugging Average

$$\frac{H + BB + HBP}{AB + BB + HBP + SF} + \frac{TB}{AB}$$

Opponent Batting Average
Hits Allowed divided by at-bats against a pitcher.

Opposition OPS
The OPS of the hitters facing the pitcher.

Out Advancing
A runner is out advancing when he is tagged out attempting to score from 2nd base on a single or from 1st base on a double, or attempting to go from 1st base to 3rd base on a single.

OutZ
Pitches outside the strike zone

Park Index

To calculate the park index for home runs in a given ballpark, we take the total home runs of both the home team and its opponents at the ballpark and compare it to the total home runs of the home team and its opponents in other games. We then divide each of those totals by the at-bats in the equivalent situations, so that if there are more at-bats in either situation, the index is not skewed. The result is then multiplied by 100 to yield the familiar form.

The park indices for doubles, triples, walks, strikeouts and home runs by lefties and righties are determined like home runs above—relative to at-bats. Indices of at-bats, runs, hits, errors and infield fielding errors (E-Infield) are calculated relative to games. The three batting average indices are calculated as is, since these are already relative to at-bats.

PART System (Positioning, Airballs, Range, and Throwing)

The PART System, introduced in *The Bill James Handbook 2020* and formalized in *The Fielding Bible–Volume V*, is a method for evaluating defensive play on batted balls, and is used in Defensive Runs Saved for infielders from 2013 forward.

The core of the system is similar to the Range and Positioning System, which is still used for DRS prior to 2013 and for outfielders from 2013 forward, in that it evaluates players through a system of credits and debits compared to the average fielder against similar batted balls.

The PART System evaluates players' positioning, range, and throwing based on how frequently they make plays compared to the average player as measured from different points in the play: before considering positioning, after considering positioning, and after the ball was fielded. Positioning Runs Saved, while measured in PART Runs Saved, is considered to be the team's responsibility, and is only included for the purposes of team totals. Individual infielder DRS consists of Air, Range and Throwing Runs Saved, along with the other components of DRS.

PCS (Pitchers' Caught Stealing)

The number of runners officially scored as Caught Stealing where the pitcher initiated the play. PCS plays are often referred to as pickoffs, but differ when the runner breaks towards the next base instead of returning to the base he was on. Pickoffs, which aren't an official statistic, involve the pitcher throwing to the base the runner was leading from, and the runner is out trying to return there.

Pitcher Pickoffs (PPO, PPkof)

The number of baserunners thrown out when a pitcher throws to a base with a leading baserunner, and the runner is tagged out attempting to return to the base. PPO is not an official statistic and does not count toward Caught Stealing totals.

Pivot %

Successful Double Plays turned by pivot man divided by the number of Double Play opportunities with that pivot man involved.

Plate Appearances

At Bats plus Total Walks plus Hit By Pitches plus Sacrifice Hits plus Sacrifice Flies plus Times Reached on Defensive Interference.

Platoon Advantage %

Platoon Advantage % is the percentage of players in the starting lineup who have the platoon advantage (i.e. bats right against a left-handed pitcher or bats left against a right-hander) against the starting pitcher; e.g. if the opposing starting pitcher is right handed and the batting team has six left-handed batters in its lineup, the platoon advantage for that game would be 67%.

PMI (Pitch Mix Index)

A measure of how much a pitcher mixes up his pitches. It is calculated by summing the squares of the pitch usage percentage for each pitch a pitcher throws, then squaring the result.

If a pitcher throws 40% fastballs, 30% sliders, 20% changeups, and 10% curveballs, you would take the square root of .4 (.632456) and add that to the square root of .3 (.547723), the square root of .2 (.447214) and the square root of .1 (.316228). Those sum to 1.944. You square 1.944 to get 3.78. His pitch mix number is 3.78. The higher the number, the more a pitcher mixes his pitches.

Power/Speed Number

A single number that reflects a combination of power and speed. To calculate the Power/Speed Number, multiply Home Runs by Stolen Bases by two, and divide by the sum of Home Runs and Stolen Bases.

$$\frac{2 \times HR \times SB}{HR + SB}$$

Productive Out

An out made by the batter which advances at least one runner. See also Unproductive Out.

Quality Start

A game where the starting pitcher pitches for at least six innings and allows no more than three earned runs.

Quality Start Percentage

Quality Starts divided by Games Started (see the definition for Quality Start).

Quick Hooks

Used in the Manager's Record. For Quick Hooks and Slow Hooks, a score is calculated for each game that is the sum of the number of Pitches plus 10 times the number of Runs Allowed. The bottom 25% of scores in the league are considered to be Quick Hooks.

Range and Positioning System

Formerly called the Plus/Minus System, the Range and Positioning System is a method for evaluating defensive play on batted balls, and is used in Defensive Runs Saved for non-catchers prior to 2013 and outfielders from 2013 forward.

It is made possible by a game scoring system in which each batted ball is rated for type (line drive, grounder, etc.), velocity within its type (based on hang time for flyballs and time to the infielder or through the infield on groundballs), and location on the field.

A player gets credit (a "plus" number) if he makes a play that at least one other player at his position missed during the season and he loses credit (a "minus" number") if he misses a play that at least one player made. The size of the credits are proportional to the percentage of times all players make the play.

All plays for each player at his position are summed to get his total Plays Saved for the season. A total of zero would be average and any other number would approximate how many plays more or less the player made than the average player at the position for the number of chances the player had to field batted balls.

Range Factor
The number of Successful Chances (Putouts plus Assists) times nine divided by the number of Defensive Innings Played.

RBI %
The percentage of all potential runs driven in by a certain hitter. Simply put, it's RBIs divided by RBI Opportunities. RBI Opportunities are defined as RBI plus a weighted total of baserunners who the hitter failed to drive in. Any plays where the batter reached safely and no outs were recorded aren't counted as missed opportunities. They are defined like so:

> 1.00 for each runner on third base with less than 2 outs, plus
>
> .70 for each runner on third base with 2 outs, plus
>
> .70 for each runner on second base, plus
>
> .40 for each runner on first base, plus
>
> .10 for each bases-empty plate appearance.

Regular Saves
Any save which does not meet the definition either of an Easy Save or a Tough Save is a "Regular" Save.

R/P
See Range and Positioning System

Run Support Per 9 IP
The total number of runs scored by a pitcher's team while he is in the game multiplied by nine and divided by total Innings Pitched.

Runs Created
"Runs Created" is an estimate of the number of a team's runs which are created by each individual hitter. There are many different formulas for estimating runs created. . .did you want the one that involves swinging a dead cat in the cemetery under a full moon? Yeah, I don't blame you. . .worm-eaten persimmons are so hard to find in the modern world.

This is the one we use now; it is complicated enough. First, there is an "A" Factor in the formula, a "B" Factor, and a "C" factor. The "A" Factor, which represents the number of times the hitter is on base, is Hits, Plus Walks, Plus Hit Batsmen, Plus Reaching Base on Catcher's Interference, Minus Caught Stealing—all of that times 0.9—Minus Grounded Into Double Play. The "B" Factor, which represents the hitter's ability to advance other runners, is Total Bases, plus .4 times Sacrifice Hits, Sacrifice Flies and Stolen Bases, plus .25 times his Walks minus Intentional Walks, plus 1.71 times Home Runs. The "C" Factor, which represents opportunities, is Plate Appearances minus Sacrifice Hits.

Having made these initial calculations of the A, B and C factors, we then change the "A" factor to "A plus 2.4 times C".

We change the "B" factor to "B plus 3 times C".

We change the "C" factor to "9 times C".

Multiply A times B, divide by the new C ("9 times C"), and subtract .90 times by the original C.

This is our first, temporary estimate of the player's runs created. What we have done here is to ask these questions:

1. How many runs would a team probably score that consisted of eight "ordinary" type of hitters, plus this particular hitter?
2. How many of those runs would be created by the eight ordinary type of hitters?
3. What is the difference and thus, how many runs did our player create?

To estimate this, we have placed our player in the context of eight hitters with a .300 on base percentage (2.4 divided by 8) and a .375 advancement percentage (3 divided by 8). For each trip through the batting order, the eight ordinary-type hitters would produce 9/10 of a run (2.4 times 3, divided by 8). The "9" in the denominator is eight ordinary hitters plus our man. The "-.9" being subtracted at the end is the runs created by the "ordinary" hitters. In essence, we have placed the hitter in a neutral solution, measured the neutral solution without our hitter, measured it with our hitter, and then estimated the contribution of this hitter as being the difference between the two.

We're not quite done. After that, we adjust the player's runs created estimate for his performance in two "run-sensitive" situations. Suppose that a player whose overall batting average is .250, has batted 100 times with runners in scoring position, and has gone 30-for-100. That's five hits better than expected, 30 hits where we would have expected 25. His team will score an extra five runs because he has done that, and so we increase the player's runs created estimate by five runs. If the player has hit poorly with runners in scoring position, we decrease it by the shortfall in the same way.

Suppose that a player has batted 250 times with runners on base, 250 times with the bases empty, and that he has hit 20 home runs overall. We would expect him to have hit 10 with men on base, 10 with the bases empty, right?

Suppose that he didn't. Suppose that he hit 12 with the bases empty, 8 with men on base. His team would score two runs less than expected because he did this, and we would thus penalize him two runs for the shortfall.

This is our second runs created estimate: the player's runs created, adjusted for his batting performance in run sensitive situations.

Suppose, however, that we figure the runs created for all of the individuals on a team, and we add them up, and it doesn't match the runs actually scored by the team? What if the formulas say that the team should have scored 800 runs, but they actually scored 820?

Then obviously, the formulas missed. We're trying to measure the runs ACTUALLY created by each hitter as best we can, in the real world, not the theoretical impact of some combination of singles, doubles, triples and walks. If the actual number is different than the estimates, we have to adjust the estimates to fit the facts. In this case—820 runs scored with only 800 runs created— we would multiply each runs created estimate by 820/800, or 1.025. Then we round it off to an integer, and that's the player's estimated runs created.

Let go of that cat, Arthur. Heck, the moon isn't full for three weeks, anyway.

Runs Created (Single Game)
The single-game Runs Created Formula, like all Runs Created formulas, has an A Factor, a B Factor, and a C Factor.

The A factor, which is basically "Times On Base", is
H + BB + HBP - (IBB/3) - GDP - CS

In other words, intentional walks count as times on base, but they only count as 2/3 of a time on base, because the intentional walk generally occurs late in the inning. Nobody intentionally walks the leadoff hitter.

The B Factor, which is basically "Potential advancement of other runners", is:
TB + (BB + HBP - IBB) * .3 + (SH + SF + 1.6 * SB) * .4 - SO * .07

And the C factor, which is basically "Context", is just plate appearances:
AB + BB + HBP + SH + SF

But these are not put together simply as A * B / C, as some runs created formulas are, but rather are placed in a neutral context before they are evaluated. The formula is:
(11.035 + A Factor) * (13 + B Factor) / (36 + C Factor) - 4 + (.0015 * (C Factor = 0))

So let us say that a player goes 1 for 4 with the one hit being a single, but also has a strikeout in the game. Then his A factor would be 1.00, his B factor would be .93, and his C Factor would be 4. So his Runs Created in the game would be
(12.035 * 13.93) / 40 - 4 + (0)

Which is .191. Basically, we expect his team to score 4 runs in every game, PLUS however many he creates. The +.0015 if the C factor is zero is just a little nuisance thing. .0015 is 1 over 667; for some reason the formula is just that much off of zero if a player has no plate appearance (and no stolen base or caught stealing), which you don't need to worry about unless he has no plate appearances, in which case it looks weird to say that he created .0015 runs.

Or, to take a complicated one, let us suppose that a player in a game goes two-for-four, both singles, but let us suppose that in that game he also has two walks, one of them intentional and the other not, and that in that game he also has a stolen base, a caught stealing, and grounds into a double play. (That would be Paul Molitor on June 8, 1985).   Then in runs created for the game would be:
A Factor = 1.67 (2 + 2 - .333 - 1 - 1)
B Factor = 2.94 (2 + .3 + (.16 * .4))
C Factor = 6

Runs Created = (12.705 * 15.94) / 42 - 4
Which works out to .821.

Add up the Runs Created in each game and it should match a player's season-level Runs Created as nearly as possible.

Runs Created per 27 Outs (RC/27)

This statistic estimates the number of runs per game that a team made up of nine of the same player would score. To calculate RC/27, multiply Runs Created by league outs per team game, divide the result by outs made by the player (the sum of at bats plus sacrifice hits plus sacrifice flies plus caught stealing plus grounded into double plays, minus hits). The formula written out is:

$$\frac{\dfrac{RC \times 3 \times LgIP}{2 \times LgG}}{AB - H + SH + SF + CS + GDP}$$

Runs Saved

See Defensive Runs Saved.

Save Opportunities

The sum of Saves and Blown Saves (see Save Situation).

Save/Hold Percentage (same as Holds Adjusted Saves Percentage)

The sum of Saves and Holds, divided by the sum of Saves, Holds, and Blown Saves.

For several years we figured "Save Percentage", which is simply Saves divided by Save Opportunities, and this stat had some currency in the game. But the Save Percentage severely discriminates against middle relievers, who have no real chance to be credited with the Save, since they will be taken out of the game and replaced by the Closer even if they throw 110 miles an hour and strike out everybody they see. Middle relievers typically have Save Percentages of zero, even if they pitch well. The Save/Hold Percentage is a much more realistic evaluation of a pitcher's success in Save situations.

Save Percentage

A pitcher's Saves divided by the total number of Save Situations he faces (see definition for Save Situation).

Save Situation

A relief pitcher is in a Save Situation when he enters the game with his team in the lead, has the opportunity to finish the game, is not the winning pitcher of record at the time, and meets any one of the three following conditions:

1.The pitcher's team is leading by no more than three runs and the pitcher has the chance to pitch for at least one inning,

OR

2.The pitcher enters the game with the potential tying run on base, at bat, or on deck,

OR

3. The pitcher pitches three or more effective innings regardless of the lead. The determination of a save in this situation is made by the official scorer.

It is not possible to have more than one save credited to a single team in a game.

SB Gain (Baserunning)

Stolen Base attempts must be successful greater than about two-thirds of the time to have a positive result on the number of runs scored. SB gain is therefore the number of bases stolen minus two times the number of caught stealing (SB Gain = SB - 2CS). For example, a runner steals 30 bases and is caught stealing 7 times. His SB Gain would be 30 - 2 * 7 = +16. Another runner steals 10 bases and is caught stealing 6 times. His SB Gain (actually a loss) would be 10 - 2 * 6 = -2.

SB Success Percentage

Stolen Bases divided by the number of Stolen Base attempts (Stolen Bases plus Caught Stealing).

$$\frac{SB}{SB + CS}$$

Secondary Average

A number meant to reflect everything else except for batting average. A player will have a high Secondary Average if he hits for power, takes walks and steals bases. It is calculated with the following formula:

$$\frac{TB - H + BB + SB}{AB}$$

Similarity Score

A number which reflects the similarity between two different statistical lines, either for a player or for a team. A score of 1,000 means that the statistical lines are identical.

Slow Hooks

Used in the Manager's Record. For Quick Hooks and Slow Hooks, a score is calculated for each game that is the sum of the number of Pitches plus 10 times the number of Runs Allowed. The top 25% of scores in the league are considered to be Slow Hooks.

Slugging Average

Total Bases divided by At Bats.

Slugging Average on Balls in Play (SlgBIP)

Total bases gained on balls in play divided by balls in play. Home runs are not counted as balls in play.

Speed Score

Speed score is an estimate of a player's running speed, based on six indicators of running speed found in his batting and fielding records. Those six indicators are stolen base success rate, the frequency of stolen base attempts, triples, grounding into double plays, runs scored as a percentage of times on base, and defensive position and range.

The full process of estimating Speed Scores is long and complex, and can be found on Bill James Online or by contacting Sports Info Solutions.

Stk Sav

The number of strikes a catcher records above or below what would have been expected from an average catcher given the pitches he received and based on factors such as pitch location, count, batter handedness, and how close the pitch was to the catcher's target.

Total Bases (TB)

Hits plus Doubles plus (2 times Triples) plus (3 times Home Runs).

$$H + 2B + (2 \times 3B) + (3 \times HR)$$

Tough Loss

A starting pitcher who loses the game with a game score (see definition for Game Score) over 50 gets credit for a tough loss.

Tough Save

This label is used to separate Saves by difficulty level (Easy or Tough). A Save is considered Tough if the relief pitcher enters the game with the tying run on base.

Total Chances (TC)

The number of plays in which a defensive player participated, determined as Assists + Putouts + Errors.

Unproductive Out

An out made by the batter with runners on base that fails to advance any baserunner or results in a weaker baserunner configuration than before. Excludes the third out of an inning. See also Productive Out.

Win Probability

The probability of a team winning the game determined at any time during the game based on the score, inning, outs and base situation.

Win Shares

Win Shares are a system devised by Bill James for valuing a player's overall contribution to his team over a season. This allows us to more effectively compare players across positions, even between pitchers and position players. The use of the word "shares" is important, because they are split up among players based on how many wins a team actually earns. For each win, a team has three Win Shares to allocate among its players. Those shares are then allocated according to how much each player contributed to the team's run scoring and prevention.

Winning Percentage

Wins divided by (Wins plus Losses).

About Sports Info Solutions (SIS)

Since the company's founding, analytics' place in sports has changed a lot, but Sports Info Solutions (SIS) has remained true to its objective. The company's mission is commitment to enriching and optimizing the decision-making process for sports teams, sportsbooks, and sports fans. SIS is thrilled to work with the majority of Major League Baseball teams as a part of that goal. The company originally operated as Baseball Info Solutions, before expanding its industry footprint delivering NFL and NCAA FBS advanced data to broadcasters, NFL teams and directly to the public, as well as advanced NBA event data and draft prospect data to NBA teams. Even greater diversity in sports covered is planned for 2023 and beyond!

The data is also instrumental in the sports betting and fantasy arenas, providing unique insights and a competitive edge to subscribers and it all begins with the data collection operation. Specifically, SIS's staff of baseball operations analysts does excellent work in organizing the ever-expanding crew of highly trained video scouts, and together they record data from every Major League Baseball, Nippon Professional Baseball, and Korean Baseball Organization game, as well as many minor league games. The products cover everything from basic box score data to pitch locations, types, and velocities to batted ball hang times, defensive shifts, and immensely more. SIS collects unique data points that cannot be found any place else. SIS video scouts log many hours on every game capturing the most in-depth information possible.

SIS's Research and Development department creates analytics and undertakes research projects with the data to help it reach its full potential utility. Its most well-known endeavor is the Defensive Runs Saved statistic, which estimates how many runs fielders save their teams because of a variety of skills such as range, throwing, prevention of stolen bases, pitch framing, and many other factors.

Boston-based Audeo Capital is the majority shareholder of the company. Prior to that, John Dewan co-founded SIS in 2002, having already spent a couple of decades in the industry at the forefront of the sabermetric movement. He got his start in the field as the Executive Director of Project Scoresheet, which was a Bill James–led effort to comprehensively collect baseball data. This led to the incorporation and development of STATS Inc. and ultimate sale to News Corp in 2000. Without those efforts, many of the statistics and analytics that we all take for granted may not even be available at all.

Acknowledgments

This is the 34th edition of *The Bill James Handbook*, and the 2nd edition officially under the Sports Info Solutions (SIS) name after 18 consecutive seasons of Baseball Info Solutions' perfect deliveries. Same great company that has delivered for 20-straight seasons with amazing new ventures to keep the growing audience satiated. And that means that the number of people who contribute to this publication continues to grow as well, and an extra special thank you goes out to each one of them.

As always, at the top of the list of people to thank is Bill James, without whom none of what we all get to do for a living would be possible. He has inspired all of us, and we are grateful for the opportunity to work with him and to continue to be enriched by his insight.

John Dewan has worked very closely with Bill for many years and started the company in 2002 along with Steve Moyer, who has since passed but whose contributions live on. John, along with his wife Sue, has transitioned away from the SIS Board of Directors as they move forward with The Dewan Foundation, a non-profit that provides grants to people in poverty by supporting U.S. based charitable organizations that assist the poorest of the poor to help themselves. John remains part-owner and a consultant to the company.

Replacing John as Chairman of the Board is Bob Forman from Audeo Capital. Bob leads the investor group that is fueling the amazing growth and evolution of the organization. Along with Ryan McConnell, Bob ensures that we are driving the engine toward success.

Dan Hannigan-Daley is the CEO of the company and leads the charge blazing our strategic vision and establishing the environment necessary to take things to the next level.

The President of Sports Info Solutions, Rob Dougherty, carefully orchestrates the day-to-day activities and business operations of the company as it continues to grow. In terms of the book process, Rob oversees things from an executive level and, along with Joe Rosales, works with our publisher to handle the business of the book.

Rosales continues to do a truly extraordinary job as the point person for the production of *The Bill James Handbook*. If there were a statistic for book production that could take into account context akin to the way that DRS adjusts for play difficulty, it would show that Joe had an October that would make Reggie Jackson blush. Mark Simon continues to be an annual All-Star in our production line-up.

Along with Rosales and Simon, there are a few individuals who went above-and-beyond to make this book possible. Jon Vrecsics leads the quality control process on every statistic in the book, a massive undertaking. On the technical side, Will Creager has the unenviable task of coordinating the technical aspects of the book's production. It would be more efficient to list the aspects of the book that Brian Reiff isn't involved in than to list his contributions. On the R&D side, Sarah Thompson was constantly fulfilling requests to keep the book on course.

Our Operations department is responsible for gathering the data that is at the very core of what we do. They deserve great thanks for both their incredible attention to detail and their ability to continually readjust to all the challenges placed in front of us. We welcomed ex-MLB player Bobby Scales this season as our new VP, Baseball. Scales brings a vast wealth of experience and insight into our company. The aforementioned Vrecsics is our Director of Operations, leading a team that includes: Dan Casey, Todd Radcliffe, Nathan Phares, Michael Churchward, Josh Hofer, Ted Baarda, Justin Stine, Evan Butler, Nick Rabasco, Ken Gaffney and Stephen Marciello.

Operations Assistants are full-time employees who contribute to multiple operations within the company. They include: Theo Fornaciari, Jacob Halleen, Trey Lake, Joey Mahon, Chad Tedder, Dan Wallie, Brandon Tew, Danny Worth, Max Nuscher, Shawn Larner, Brett Barnes, Kevin Kistner and Conner Hrabal.

Lead Research Analyst Joe Rosales heads the Baseball R&D team, which includes the key staff responsible for the bulk of the content and analytics that you find in the book. Mark Simon, Sarah Thompson, and Jackson Lewis round out the team, and we'd also like to thank Lindsay Zeck for all of her contributions.

Matt Manocherian has been instrumental in the success of the expansion as Vice President of Football and Research. Dan Foehrenbach quarterbacks the football operations group. They are joined by: Nathan Cooper, Segev Goldberg, Jeff Dean, Jordan Edwards, Jeremy Percy, Michael Morgan, and Jonathan Micklos. John Verros leads the injury operation along with James Rodriguez.

The Football R&D team is spearheaded by Lead Research Analyst Alex Vigderman. He is joined by fellow researchers Bryce Rossler and James Weaver.

Vice President of Basketball and New Initiatives Jake Loos applies his groundbreaking vision in NBA Draft and NBA analytics for our basketball department. Their team is led by Ian McKiernan on the research side, Sergio Santamaria on the business development side, and Max Carlin on strategy and operations. Their department includes: Brooks Bellman, Spencer Pearlman, Baxter Price, Becca MaWhinney, Blake Bejamin, Connor Ayubi, Connor Williamson, David Knopp, Evan Zaucha, Ian Riaf, Jack Klein, Matt Bolanos, Noah Thro, Richard Stockton, Stewart Zahn, Tyson West, and Zachary Smith.

VP Product and Engineering Will Hester, has a dedicated team of engineers that include: Carmen Fortino, Kyle Bennett, Tim Paul, Zach Smith, Ruben Agosto, and Ronan Potts. They work tirelessly to develop new applications for internal and external use. On the product side are Cassie Sosnovich, Noah Gatsik, and Elliott Boswell.

The Information and Security Operations Department is the silent engine that enables all of this data collection and research to make it to our team clients and the public. Director of ISO Patrick Coyle leads an incredibly talented team featuring: Will Creager, Brian Reiff, Brandyn Bechtel, Daniel Stonehouse, Ryne Rogers, and Austin Appel. They service the myriad needs of our clients in all sports.

Michael Montpetit continues to serve as our Director of Sales and Business Development where he spearheads our sales processes and interactions. The company welcomed Nima Billou and Sam Dugdale as new members of the BD team. Nima is our top business analyst, while Sam and Kyle Rodemann excel at making our customers happy and educating our audience on the value of our products and services. The company also welcomed Kelsea Benoit who is leading our marketing initiatives. And we would be remiss not to give a huge thank you to Corey March, who recently moved on to another opportunity, but played a major role in driving SIS's BD efforts for five years.

Jason Trifilo, Our Director of Accounting, makes sure that the finances are in order and Lauren Backsa is also there to provide the assist. Brett Joseph is our legal intern extraordinaire.

On the Human Resources side, Sue Dewan handed off the director responsibilities to Matt Bergey. As Director of People & Talent, Bergey makes sure that we balance our sports enthusiasm with diversity, equity and inclusion. Richard Lively assists us in various areas and Carol Olsen, our office manager, coordinates the various social events that help us to share great memories amongst our coworkers.

We are especially grateful to our outstanding team of scouts. Their dedication and attention to detail provide the foundation of our business. Our Video Scout Associates have spent multiple seasons with us, and they include: Alexander Arcidiacono, Spencer Bayes, Maddisen Bieber, Mark Bricker, Jason Carroll, Matthew Evans, Ben Jaffy, John Keuler, Yen Lai, John Michael Morris, Jake Pennel, Kyle Price, Dominick Ricotta, Dylan Rudolph, Anthony Sagrestano, William Schiff, Bennett Spector, and Jack Yerxa.

Our Video Scouts are made up of: Michael Albee, Britton Barthold, Nicholas Beetel, Zackary Blasé, Dominic Brigante, Aaron Brush, Nathan Carreiro, Cooper Caviness, William Cegelka, Rosario Cerrito, Robert Coghlan, Jordan Coleman, David Cox, James Cullen, Jacob DiCesare, Jonathan Drillings, Alexander Eisert, Michael Factor, Noah Farrell, Benjamin Favela, Shannon Finegan, Manuel Folsom, Dylan Foreaker, Anthony

Garza, Ryan Giglio, Ozney Guillen, Jack Halperin, Collin Haupt, Kevin Herget, Dwayne Hernandez, Bobby Hinker, John Hughes, Kevin Johns, Derek Joyce, Lindsay Kahrs, Brady Kas, Parker Kent, Cade Kronemyer, Andrew Kuhn, Brian Lanyon, James Lewis, Vincent Maltese, Nate Marko, Ryan McDaniel, Austen McMurchy, Brendan Molnar, Robert Molnar, Carlos Munoz, Brady Petree, Clayton Piper, Billy Pleasants, Noah Rachell, Zachary Reifschneider, Ethan Richards, Dylan Riggs, Bryn Romero, Jackson Royal, Owen Ruddock, Colin Sanders, Manuel Santamaria, Vince Santoria, Samuel Schneider, Riley Sonz, Jake Swearingen, Sebastian Szot, Jacob Taylor, Jacob Toepfer, Kyle Vander Meulen, Cole Watts, Robert Yoka, and Jacob Zak.

We also thank our Video Editors: Joona Collier, David Cox, Tyler Deel, Raya Ellsbury, Lou Gabello, Luke Guilbeau, Trevor Henry, Missy Hernandez, Lucas Klein, and Jude Sweeney.

Our partners at ACTA Publications include publisher Greg Pierce, cover designer Tom Wright, Fielding Bible logo designer Patricia Lynch, and customer service and fulfillment team Mary Rickey, Kathy Pierce, and Isz.

Thank you to our friends in the baseball industry who have helped us over the years. They include: Andy Andres, David Appelman, Emma Baccellieri, Scott Bush, Jim Callis, Dave Cameron, Benjie Cherniak, Chris Dial, Rylan Edwards, Tony Farwell, Alyson Footer, Sean Forman, Dave Flemming, Peter Gammons, Vince Genarro, Kirk Gibson, Doug Glanville, Jason Grey, Ben Jedlovec, Christina Kahrl, Brian Kenny, Zach Kram, Peter Kreutzer, Michael Lehrer, Ben Lindbergh, Rob Mains, Moses Massena, Gene McCaffrey, Tim McSweeney, Bob Meyerhoff, Jon Miller, Mike Murphy, Rob Neyer, Alex Patton, Eduardo Pérez, Mike Phillips, David Pinto, Joe Posnanski, Pat Quinn, Adam Richman, Hal Richman, Meg Rowley, Travis Sawchik, Brett Sayre, Peter Schoenke, Ron Shandler, Joe Sheehan, John Sickels, Chris Singleton, Dave Studenmund, Tom Tango, Rick Wilton, Don Zminda, and Pete Zundel. We would also like to thank Steve Ruskowski for his assistance in stat-checking.

There are too many people to thank for making this book possible to fit them all in this section, but you know who you are, and we extend our sincerest gratitude for your help.

Most importantly, thank you to all of our readers. You inspire us and empower us to continue to dive deeper, and we're thrilled that you keep coming back to learn more about the game that we all love. Thank you for your continued support, and we're already excited to share what we learn with you next year.